Current Law

Year Book

2005
VOLUME TWO

THOMSON

SWEET & MAXWELL

AUSTRALIA
LBC Information Services
Sydney

CANADA & USA
Carswell
Toronto

NEW ZEALAND
Brooker's
Auckland

SINGAPORE and MALAYSIA
Sweet & Maxwell Asia
Singapore and Kuala Lumpur

Current Law

Year Book

2005

Being a Comprehensive Statement of the Law of 2005

PRINCIPAL EDITOR
Philip Dye

SWEET & MAXWELL EDITORIAL TEAM

James Aidoo-Baidoe   Jonathan Langtry-Langton
Catherine Aylward   Hetha Duffy   Nina Taylor
Shahnaila Aziz   Lisa Fergusson   Lisa Fergusson
Catherine Berry   Heidi Fletcher   Jane Hodgson
Chris Blagg   Jon Hilton   Emma Whitworth
Ellis Chapman   Alexa Hopwood   Jennifer Young

SWEET & MAXWELL TECHNOLOGY SUPPORT
Roger Greenwood

Editors

English and Commonwealth Law
MICHAEL BLACK, LL.B., *Solicitor*
PATRICK CLARKE, *Barrister*
CRAIG DUNFORD, *Barrister*SHAUN FERRIS, B.A., *Barrister*
STEPHEN GARNER, LL.B., *Barrister*
Dr. ALASTAIR HUDSON, LL.B., LL.M., *Barrister*
CHARLES H JOSEPH, B.A., *Barrister, FCI Arb*
EILEEN O'GRADY, LL.B. (Hons), *Barrister*
PETER OSBORNE, PhD, *Solicitor (Ireland and N Ireland)*
JESSICA PENROSE, LL.B., *Solicitor*
WILLIAM VANDYCK, B.A., *Barrister*
GORDON WIGNALL, M.A., *Barrister*

Scotland
MALCOLM THOMSON, Q.C., LL.B.

Damages Awards
PETER MANTLE, *Barrister*

The Mode of Citation
of the Current Law Year Book is
[2005] C.L.Y. 1282
The 2005 Year Book is published in two volumes.

Published in 2006 by
Sweet & Maxwell Limited of
100 Avenue Road, Swiss Cottage, London NW3 3PF
Typeset by Sweet & Maxwell Limited,
Mytholmroyd, Hebden Bridge
Printed in England by Bath Press Ltd

**A CIP catalogue record for this book is available
from the British Library**

ISBN-10 0-421-93570-7
ISBN-13 978-0-421-93570-9

No forests were destroyed to make this product;
farmed timber was used and then replanted.

PREFACE

The Current Law Year Book 2005 supersedes the issues of *Current Law Monthly Digest* for 2005 and covers the law from January 1 to December 31 of that year.

Jurisdiction

The text of the 2005 Current Law Year Book is divided into three sections respectively: UK, England and Wales and EU, Northern Ireland and Scotland. The European material comprises: cases appearing before the Court of First Instance and European Court of Justice which are published in the reports series and newspapers, and a selection of books.

Cases

The 2005 Current Law Year Book includes digests of cases published in over 90 reports series, journals, *The Times* and *Independent* newspapers, transcripts and ex relatione contributions from barristers and solicitors. A number of reports concerning damages awards in personal injury cases in England and Wales appears under the subject heading PERSONAL INJURY and is collated in tabular form together with Scottish personal injuries cases at the beginning of Vol. 1.

The editor thanks those barristers and solicitors who have submitted case reports, many of which demonstrate developments in county court litigation. Whilst all reasonable care is taken in the preparation of the digests it is not possible to guarantee the accuracy of each digest, particularly those cases ex relatione which are not taken from an authorised judgment.

An alphabetical Table of Cases digested in the 2005 Year Book appears at the beginning of Volume 1. For more details please refer to the Current Law Case Citator series for the years 1947-76, 1977-1997, 1998-2001, 2002-2004 and 2005.

Legislation

All public and private Acts of Parliament published in 2005 are abstracted and indexed. All Statutory Instruments, Scottish Statutory Instruments and Statutory Rules of Northern Ireland are abstracted. Cumulative tables of Statutory Instruments, arranged alphabetically, numerically and by subject are published in Vol. 1. Cumulative tables of Statutory Rules of Northern Ireland arranged alphabeticially, numerically and by subject are also published in Vol. 1.

The Current Law Legislation Citator 2005 appears as a separate bound volume and form part of the series of bound volumes for the years 1989-1995, 1996-1999 and 2000-2001, 2002-2004 and 2005.

Books

The full title, reference and author of books of interest to the legal profession published in 2005 are arranged by subject heading. A separate list, arranged by author is included in Volume 2.

Index

The subject-matter index is closely associated with the Sweet and Maxwell Legal Taxonomy. The 30-year Index from 1947-76 may be found in the 1976 *Current Law Year Book*. The Scottish Index for the years 1972-86 may be found in the Scottish 1986 *Year Book*. Scottish material prior to 1972 can be found in the *Scottish Current Law Year Book Master Volumes*, published in 1956, 1961, 1966 and 1971.

May 2006

CONTENTS

VOLUME 1

THE LAW OF 2005 DIGESTED UNDER TITLES:
Note: Italicised entries refer to Scotland only.

Accountancy, §1
Administration of Justice, §10,
  4440, *4930*
Administrative Law, §57, 4446,
  4957
Agency, §89, *4973*
Agriculture, §93, 4456, *4974*
Animals, §168, 4497, *5012*
Arbitration, §194, 4504
Armed Forces, §215
Arts and Culture, §240
Aviation, §243

Banking and Finance, §255, *5021*

Charities, §280, *5022*
Civil Evidence, §287, *5024*
Civil Procedure, §306, 4505,
  5025
Commercial Law, §499, *5060*
Company Law, §502, 4506
Competition Law, §541, *5061*
Conflict of Laws, §599
Constitutional Law, §630, 4513,
  5062
Construction Law, §641, 4518,
  5067
Consumer Law, §670, 4520, *5074*
Contracts, §695, *5076*

CONTENTS

CONTENTS

DIGEST HEADINGS IN USE

Accountancy
Administration of Justice
Administrative Law
Agency
Agriculture
Animals
Arbitration
Armed Forces
Arts and Culture
Aviation
Banking and Finance
Charities
Civil Evidence
Civil Procedure
Commercial Law
Company Law
Competition Law
Conflict of Laws
Constitutional Law
Construction Law
Consumer Law
Contracts
Criminal Evidence
Criminal Law
Criminal Procedure
Customs
Damages
Defamation
Dispute Resolution
Ecclesiastical Law
Economics
Education
Electoral Process
Employment
Energy
Environment
Environmental Health
Equity
European Union
Extradition
Family Law
Financial Regulation
Fisheries
Food
Forestry
Government Administration
Health and Safety at Work
Health
Heritable Property and Conveyancing (Scotland)
Highways
Hospitality and Leisure
Housing
Human Rights

Immigration
Industry
Information Technology
Insolvency
Insurance
Intellectual Property
International Law
International Trade
Jurisprudence
Landlord and Tenant
Legal Advice and Funding
Legal Methodology
Legal Profession
Legal Systems
Legislation
Licensing
Local Government
Media and Entertainment
Mental Health
Mining
Negligence
Nuisance
Partnerships
Penology and Criminology
Pensions
Personal Injury
Personal Property
Planning
Police
Postal Services
Prescription (Scotland)
Professions
Public Procurement
Rates
Real Property
Reparation (Scotland)
Restitution
Sale of Goods
Science
Sentencing
Shipping
Social Security
Social Welfare
Sport
Succession
Tax
Telecommunications
Torts
Transport
Trusts
Utilities
Vat
Water Law

CURRENT LAW

YEAR BOOK 2005

UK, ENGLAND & WALES & EU

(continued)

INTERNATIONAL LAW

2592. Chemical weapons–Overseas territories

CHEMICAL WEAPONS (OVERSEAS TERRITORIES) ORDER 2005, SI 2005 854; made under the Chemical Weapons Act 1996 s.39; and the Anti-terrorism, Crime and Security Act 2001 s.57. In force: April 22, 2005; £5.50.

This Order extends provisions of the Chemical Weapons Act 1996 and the Anti-terrorism, Crime and Security Act 2001, with exceptions, adaptations and modifications, to the territories listed in Sch.3.

2593. Child abduction–Custody–Parties to Hague and Luxembourg Conventions

CHILD ABDUCTION AND CUSTODY (PARTIES TO CONVENTIONS) (AMENDMENT) ORDER 2005, SI 2005 1260; made under the Child Abduction and Custody Act 1985 s.2, s.13. In force: May 7, 2005; £3.00.

This Order, which revokes the Child Abduction and Custody (Parties to Conventions) (Amendment) Order 2004 (SI 2004 3040), amends the Child Abduction and Custody (Parties to Conventions) Order 1986 (SI 1986 1159) to add Bulgaria, Estonia, Hungary, Macedonia, Moldova, Romania, Serbia and Montenegro and Slovakia to the list of Contracting States to the European Convention on Recognition and Enforcement of Decisions concerning Custody of Children and on Restoration of Custody of Children, signed at Luxembourg on May 20, 1980. It also amends the date of entry into force of that Convention as between the UK and Lithuania, as well as the dates of entry into force of the Convention on the Civil Aspects of International Child Abduction, done at The Hague on October 25, 1980, as between the UK and Belarus; Bosnia and Herzegovina; Burkina Faso; Ecuador; Estonia; Fiji; Latvia; Mexico; New Zealand; Peru; Serbia and Montenegro; Turkey; Turkmenistan; Uruguay; and Uzbekistan. These amendments bring the relevant entry into force dates into line with the dates recorded by the depositories for the two Conventions.

2594. Commonwealth—Immunities and privileges

COMMONWEALTH COUNTRIES AND IRELAND (IMMUNITIES AND PRIVILEGES) (AMENDMENT) ORDER 2005, SI 2005 246; made under the Consular Relations Act 1968 s.12. In force: April 1, 2005; £3.00.

This Order, which amends the Commonwealth Countries and Republic of Ireland (Immunities and Privileges) Order 1985 (SI 1985 1983), affords partial relief from general rates to the offices and residences of the Gibraltar Government Representative in London and the British Virgin Islands Government Representative in London. Similar relief is already granted to the offices and residences of the Falkland Islands Government Representative in London and the Cayman Islands Government Representative in London. These offices perform functions broadly in line with those of a consular post of a foreign country. The Order also deletes references to Hong Kong, which is no longer part of the Commonwealth. Privileges and immunities have been afforded to the Hong Kong Economic and Trade Office under the Hong Kong Economic and Trade Office Act 1996.

2595. Consulates—Fees

CONSULAR FEES ORDER 2005, SI 2005 1465; made under the Consular Fees Act 1980 s.1. In force: July 1, 2005; £3.00.

This Order, which revokes the Consular Fees Order (No.2) 1999 (SI 1999 3132), sets out fees to be charged for consular services. The overall effect is to continue full recovery of costs for fee-bearing consular services by revising charges levied for these services.

2596. Consulates—Fees—Civil partnerships

CONSULAR FEES (CIVIL PARTNERSHIP) ORDER 2005, SI 2005 2762; made under the Consular Fees Act 1980 s.1. In force: December 5, 2005; £3.00.

This Order amends the Consular Fees Order 2005 (SI 2005 1465) to take account of the introduction of consular services in respect of civil partnerships under the Civil Partnership (Registration Abroad and Certificates) Order 2005 (SI 2005 2761). The overall effect is to continue full recovery of costs for fee-bearing consular services. Civil partnership services will be charged at the same rates as the analogous services for marriages.

2597. Consulates—Fees—Determination of fees

CONSULAR FEES ACT 1980 (FEES) ORDER 2005, SI 2005 2112; made under the Finance (No.2) Act 1987 s.102. In force: July 27, 2005; £3.00.

This Order provides that the costs of exercising certain passport related consular services, which the Secretary of State for Foreign and Commonwealth Affairs estimates will be incurred in the financial years 2005/2006 and 2006/2007, are to be taken into account in fixing the fees for those services.

2598. Consulates—Fees—Determination of fees

CONSULAR FEES ACT 1980 (FEES) (NO.2) ORDER 2005, SI 2005 3198; made under the Finance (No.2) Act 1987 s.102. In force: November 4, 2005; £3.00.

This Order provides that the costs of performing certain passport functions are to be taken into account in fixing the fees for the performance of the passport functions specified in the Schedules to the Order. It also provides that, in relation to any functions the costs of which fall to be taken into account in exercising the power to fix fees in relation to the services listed in the Schedules to this Order, the costs which the Secretary of State for Foreign and Commonwealth Affairs estimates will be incurred in the financial years 2005/2006 and 2006/2007 on those functions, are to be taken into account in fixing the fees for those services.

2599. Export controls–Sanctions–Democratic Republic of Congo–Restrictive measures

DEMOCRATIC REPUBLIC OF THE CONGO (RESTRICTIVE MEASURES) (OVERSEAS TERRITORIES) (AMENDMENT) ORDER 2005, SI 2005 1988; made under the Saint Helena Act 1833 s.112; the British Settlements Act 1887; and the British Settlements Act 1945. In force: July 21, 2005; £3.00.

This Order amends the Democratic Republic of the Congo (Restrictive Measures) (Overseas Territories) Order 2003 (SI 2003 2627) to prohibit the exportation of restricted goods to enable their seizure and forfeiture. It also gives effect to the precise wording of the arms embargo wording in Common Position 2005/440 adopted by the Council of the European Union on June 13, 2005 to integrate the arms embargo imposed by Common Position 2002/829 with new measures imposed following the adoption of Resolution 1596 by the Security Council of the United Nations on April 18, 2005. The Order makes it clear that it is prohibited to provide assistance, advice or training related to the provision, manufacture, maintenance and use of arms and related materiel and that the prohibition also applies where advice, assistance or training is provided to any person, entity or body in, or for use in, the Democratic Republic of the Congo.

2600. Export controls–Sanctions–Ivory Coast–Restrictive measures

IVORY COAST (RESTRICTIVE MEASURES) (OVERSEAS TERRITORIES) ORDER 2005, SI 2005 242; made under the Saint Helena Act 1833 s.112; the British Settlements Act 1887; and the British Settlements Act 1945. In force: February 11, 2005; £3.50.

This Order, which applies to each of the territories specified in Sch.1, gives effect to certain measures in Resolution 1572 adopted by the Security Council of the UN on November 15, 2004, as implemented in the EU. The Resolution amongst other things imposes an arms embargo, with certain exemptions, on Ivory Coast with immediate effect; and provided for an assets freeze and travel ban against certain persons to come into effect on December 15, 2004. The targeted persons will be those designated by the Sanctions Committee as constituting a threat to the peace and national reconciliation process in Ivory Coast.

2601. Export controls–Sanctions–Zimbabwe–Restrictive measures

OVERSEAS TERRITORIES (ZIMBABWE) (RESTRICTIVE MEASURES) (AMENDMENT) ORDER 2005, SI 2005 3183; made under the Saint Helena Act 1833 s.112; the British Settlements Act 1887; and the British Settlements Act 1945. In force: November 17, 2005; £3.00.

This Order amends the Overseas Territories (Zimbabwe) (Restrictive Measures) Order 2002 (SI 2002 1077) to replace the list of persons in Sch.4 to the Order with a reference to the list set out in the Annex to Council Common Position 2004/161 ([2004] OJ L50/66). As a result of the new definition of "listed person" future modifications to the list by the Council of the European Union will take effect immediately without requiring amendment of the Order.

2602. International organisations–Immunities and privileges–G8 Gleneagles

G8 GLENEAGLES (IMMUNITIES AND PRIVILEGES) ORDER 2005, SI 2005 1456; made under the International Organisations Act 1968 s.6. In force: July 1, 2005; £3.00.

This Order confers privileges and immunities upon the representatives of the sovereign Powers (other than the UK) at the G8 Gleneagles conference, which is to be held in the UK beginning July 6, 2005.

2603. **International organisations–Immunities and privileges–International Tribunal for the Law of the Sea**

INTERNATIONAL TRIBUNAL FOR THE LAW OF THE SEA (IMMUNITIES AND PRIVILEGES) ORDER 2005, SI 2005 2047; made under the International Organisations Act 1968 s.1, s.5, s.8. In force: in accordance with art 1; £3.00.

This Order which revokes the International Tribunal for the Law of the Sea (Immunities and Privileges) Order 1996 (SI 1996 272), confers the legal capacities of a body corporate and privileges and immunities upon the International Tribunal for the Law of the Sea; and confers privileges and immunities on members of the Tribunal, the Registrar and other officials of the Tribunal, experts appointed under art.289 of the United Nations Convention on the Law of the Sea, agents, counsel and advocates before the Tribunal, witnesses, experts and persons performing missions by order of the Tribunal.

2604. **International Organisations Act 2005 (c.20)**

This Act makes provision about privileges, immunities and facilities in connection with certain international organisations.

This Act received Royal Assent on April 7, 2005.

2605. **International Organisations Act 2005 (c.20)–Commencement Order**

INTERNATIONAL ORGANISATIONS ACT 2005 (COMMENCEMENT) ORDER 2005, SI 2005 1870 (C.80); made under the International Organisations Act 2005 s.11. Commencement details: bringing into force various provisions of the 2005 Act on July 11, 2005 and April 6, 2006; £3.00.

This Order brings into force provisions of the International Organisations Act 2005 which relate to the Commonwealth Secretariat.

2606. **International trade–Legal capacities–European Forest Institute**

EUROPEAN FOREST INSTITUTE (LEGAL CAPACITIES) ORDER 2005, SI 2005 3426; made under the International Organisations Act 1968 s.1. In force: in accordance with Art.1; £3.00.

This Order confers the legal capacities of a body corporate on the European Forest Institute. This legal capacity is conferred in accordance with the Convention on the European Forest Institute. The Order will enable Her Majesty's Government to give effect to Art.12 of that Convention, and will come into force on the date on which the Convention enters into force in respect of the UK.

2607. **Offences–International criminal law–Former Yugoslavia**

INTERNATIONAL CRIMINAL TRIBUNAL FOR THE FORMER YUGOSLAVIA (FINANCIAL SANCTIONS AGAINST INDICTEES) REGULATIONS 2005, SI 2005 1527; made under the European Communities Act 1972 s.2. In force: June 29, 2005; £3.00.

These Regulations, which revoke the International Criminal Tribunal for the Former Yugoslavia (Freezing of Funds and Economic Resources of Indictees) Regulations 2004 (SI 2004 2690) and the International Criminal Tribunal for the Former Yugoslavia (Freezing of Funds and Economic Resources of Indictees) (Amendment) Regulations 2004 (SI 2004 3099), provide that breaches of certain provisions of Council Regulation 1763/2004 ([2004] OJ L315/14) imposing certain restrictive measures in support of effective implementation of the mandate of the International Criminal Tribunal for the former Yugoslavia, relating to financial sanctions, are criminal offences.

2608. Offences–International criminal law–Myanmar

BURMA (FINANCIAL SANCTIONS) REGULATIONS 2005, SI 2005 1526; made under the European Communities Act 1972 s.2. In force: June 29, 2005; £3.00.

These Regulations, which revoke the Burma (Freezing of Funds and Economic Resources) Regulations 2004 (SI 2004 1257) and the Burma (Prohibition on Financing) Regulations 2004 (SI 2004 3100), provide that breaches of certain provisions of Council Regulation 798/2004 ([2004] OJ L125/4) relating to financial sanctions are criminal offences.

2609. United Nations–Sanctions–Democratic Republic of Congo

DEMOCRATIC REPUBLIC OF THE CONGO (UNITED NATIONS MEASURES) ORDER 2005, SI 2005 1517; made under the United Nations Act 1946 s.1. In force: June 9, 2005; £3.00.

This Order gives effect in part to Resolution 1596, adopted by the Security Council of the UN on April 18, 2005. Other instruments will give effect to Resolution 1596 in the overseas territories. Amongst other things, the effect of Resolution 1596 is to require States to prohibit the making available of funds to individuals and entities designated by the relevant Sanctions Committee of the Security Council.

2610. United Nations–Sanctions–Democratic Republic of Congo–Channel Islands

DEMOCRATIC REPUBLIC OF THE CONGO (UNITED NATIONS SANCTIONS) (CHANNEL ISLANDS) ORDER 2005, SI 2005 1468; made under the United Nations Act 1946 s.1. In force: June 9, 2005; £3.00.

This Order applies to the Channel Islands and gives effect, in part, to Resolution 1596 (2005) adopted by the Security Council of the UN on April 18, 2005 which amongst other things imposes financial sanctions against persons designated as acting in violation of the arms embargo by the Sanctions Committee established by Resolution 1533 (2004).

2611. United Nations–Sanctions–Democratic Republic of Congo–Isle of Man

DEMOCRATIC REPUBLIC OF THE CONGO (UNITED NATIONS SANCTIONS) (ISLE OF MAN) ORDER 2005, SI 2005 1469; made under the United Nations 1946 s.1. In force: June 9, 2005; £3.00.

This Order applies to the Isle of Man and gives effect, in part, to Resolution 1596 (2005) adopted by the Security Council of the UN on April 18, 2005 which imposes financial sanctions against persons designated as acting in violation of the arms embargo by the Sanctions Committee established by Resolution 1533 (2004).

2612. United Nations–Sanctions–Democratic Republic of Congo–Overseas territories

DEMOCRATIC REPUBLIC OF THE CONGO (UNITED NATIONS SANCTIONS) (OVERSEAS TERRITORIES) ORDER 2005, SI 2005 1461; made under the United Nations Act 1946 s.1. In force: June 9, 2005; £3.00.

This Order applies to Anguilla, Bermuda, British Antarctic Territory, British Indian Ocean Territory, the Cayman Islands, the Falkland Islands, Montserrat, Pitcairn, Henderson, Ducie and Oeno Islands, St. Helena and Dependencies, South Georgia and the South Sandwich Islands, the Sovereign Base Areas of Akrotiri and Dhekelia in the Island of Cyprus, the Turks and Caicos Islands, and the Virgin Islands. The instrument gives effect in part to Resolution 1596 (2005) adopted by the Security Council of the UN on April 18, 2005 which imposes financial sanctions against persons designated as acting in violation of the arms embargo by the Sanctions Committee established by Resolution 1533 (2004).

2613. United Nations–Sanctions–Ivory Coast

IVORY COAST (UNITED NATIONS SANCTIONS) ORDER 2005, SI 2005 253; made under the United Nations Act 1946 s.1. In force: February 11, 2005; £3.00.

This Order gives effect in part to Resolution 1572, adopted by the Security Council of the United Nations on November 15, 2004. Amongst other things, the effect of Resolution 1572 is to require States to prohibit the making available of funds to individuals and entities designated by the Security Council.

2614. United Nations–Sanctions–Sudan–Channel Islands

SUDAN (UNITED NATIONS MEASURES) (CHANNEL ISLANDS) ORDER 2005, SI 2005 1462; made under the United Nations Act 1946 s.1. In force: June 9, 2005; £3.00.

This Order implements, in part, in the Channel Islands, Resolution 1591 (2005) adopted by the Security Council of the UN on March 29, 2005 which imposes financial sanctions against persons designated by the Sanctions Committee as impeding the peace process, as constituting a threat to stability in Darfur and the region, as committing violations of international humanitarian or human rights law or other atrocities, as violating the arms embargo or as being responsible for certain prohibited military flights.

2615. United Nations–Sanctions–Sudan–Isle of Man

SUDAN (UNITED NATIONS MEASURES) (ISLE OF MAN) ORDER 2005, SI 2005 1463; made under the United Nations Act 1946 s.1. In force: June 9, 2005; £3.00.

This Order implements in part, in the Isle of Man, Resolution 1591 (2005) adopted by the Security Council of the UN on March 29, 2005 which imposes financial sanctions against persons designated by the Sanctions Committee as impeding the peace process, as constituting a threat to stability in Darfur and the region, as committing violations of international humanitarian or human rights law or other atrocities, as violating the arms embargo or as being responsible for certain prohibited military flights.

2616. United Nations–Sanctions–Sudan–Overseas territories

SUDAN (UNITED NATIONS MEASURES) (OVERSEAS TERRITORIES) ORDER 2005, SI 2005 1258; made under the United Nations Act 1946 s.1. In force: May 12, 2005; £3.00.

This Order applies to Anguilla, Bermuda, British Antarctic Territory, British Indian Ocean Territory, Cayman Islands, Falkland Islands, Montserrat, Pitcairn, Henderson, Ducie and Oeno Islands, St. Helena and Dependencies, South Georgia and the South Sandwich Islands, The Sovereign Base Areas of Akrotiri and Dhekelia in the Island of Cyprus, Turks and Caicos Islands, Virgin Islands. It gives effect in part to Resolution 1591 (2005) adopted by the Security Council of the United Nations on March 29, 2005 which, amongst other things, imposes financial sanctions against persons designated by the Sanctions Committee as impeding the peace process, as constituting a threat to stability in Darfur and the region, as committing violations of international humanitarian or human rights law or other atrocities, as violating the arms embargo or as being responsible for certain prohibited military flights.

2617. United Nations–Sudan–Sanctions

SUDAN (UNITED NATIONS MEASURES) ORDER 2005, SI 2005 1259; made under the United Nations Act 1946 s.1. In force: May 12, 2005; £3.00.

This Order gives effect in part to Resolution 1591, adopted by the Security Council of the UN on March 29, 2005. Other instruments will give effect to Resolution 1591 in the overseas territories. Amongst other things, the effect of Resolution 1591 is to require States to prohibit the making available of funds to individuals and entities designated by the relevant Sanctions Committee of the Security Council.

2618. United Nations–Terrorism

TERRORISM (UNITED NATIONS MEASURES) ORDER 2001 (AMENDMENT) REGULATIONS 2005, SI 2005 1525; made under the European Communities Act 1972 s.2. In force: June 29, 2005; £3.00.

These Regulations, which revoke theTerrorism (United Nations Measures) Order 2001 (Amendment) Regulations 2004 (SI 2004 2309), amend the definition of "Council Decision" in the Terrorism (United Nations Measures) Order 2001 (SI 2001 3365) so as to refer to Council Decision 2005/221 ([2005] OJ L69/64) implementing Article 2(3) of Regulation 2580/2001 on specific restrictive measures directed against certain persons and entities with a view to combating terrorism and repealing Decision 2004/306.

2619. United Nations–Terrorism–Lebanon and Syria

LEBANON AND SYRIA (UNITED NATIONS MEASURES) ORDER 2005, SI 2005 3432; made under the United Nations Act 1946 s.1. In force: December 16, 2005; £3.00.

The Security Council has decided that all States are to take certain measures against individuals suspected of an involvement in the terrorist bombing in Beirut, Lebanon on February 14, 2005. This Order, which gives effect to Resolution 1636 (2005) adopted by the Security Council of the United Nations on October 31, 2005, prohibits any dealing with funds, financial assets and economic resources of designated persons, and makes it a criminal offence to contravene this prohibition. It also prohibits making funds, financial assets and economic resources available to designated persons, and makes it a criminal offence to contravene this prohibition; and makes it a criminal offence to circumvent the prohibitions or to facilitate the commission of an offence relating to a prohibition.

2620. Books

Alvarez, Jose E.–International Organisations As Law-makers. Oxford Monographs in International Law. Hardback: £65.00. ISBN 0 19 876562 2. Oxford University Press.

Anglade, Lelia;Tackaberry, John–International Dispute Resolution:Vol1. Materials. Hardback: £89.00. ISBN 0 421 88700 1. Sweet & Maxwell.

Aust, Anthony–Handbook of International Law. Hardback: £55.00. ISBN 0 521 82349 8. Paperback: £24.99. ISBN 0 521 53034 2. Cambridge University Press.

Austin, Greg; Berry, Ken–New Grand Bargain for Peace:Towards a Reformation in International Security Law. Pamphlet/leaflet (stapled/folded): £4.95. ISBN 1 903558 61 1. Foreign Policy Centre.

Bennett, Angela–Geneva Convention. Hardback: £20.00. ISBN 0 7509 4147 2. Sutton Publishing.

Berman, Paul Schiff–The Globalization of International Law. International Library of Essays on Globalization & Law. Hardback: £125.00. ISBN 0 7546 2412 9. Ashgate.

Blokker, Niels M.; Schrijver, N.J.–NetherlandsYearbook of International Law:V. 34. Netherlands Yearbook of International Law Series. Hardback: £70.00. ISBN 90 6704 188 2. Asser Press.

Bossche, Peter van den–Law and Policy of the World Trade Organization: Text, Cases and Materials. Paperback: £45.00. ISBN 0 521 52981 6. Cambridge University Press.

Burchill, Richard–Democracy and International Law. Library of Essays in International Law. Hardback: £130.00. ISBN 0 7546 2422 6. Dartmouth.

Caldwell, Zarrin–International Law: Justice Between Nations? Paperback: £4.95. ISBN 0 85233 008 1. Understanding Global Issues.

Campbell, Dennis–International Protection of Foreign Investment-Volume II. Paperback: £62.20. ISBN 1 4116 5025 5. Lulu Press Incorporated.

Clark, Ian–Legitimacy in International Society. Hardback: £30.00. ISBN 0 19 925842 2. Oxford University Press.

Conrad, Christian–Improving International Competition Order: An Institutional Approach. Hardback: £55.00. ISBN 1 4039 4790 2. Palgrave Macmillan.

Crawford, James R.–Creation of States in International Law. Hardback: £80.00. ISBN 0 19 826002 4. Oxford University Press.

Crawford, James; Lowe, Vaughan–British Year Book of International Law: V. 75. Hardback: £130.00. ISBN 0 19 928493 8. Oxford University Press.

Cryer, Robert–Prosecution of International Crimes: Integration and Selectivity in International Criminal Law. Cambridge Studies in International & Comparative Law. Hardback: £60.00. ISBN 0 521 82474 5. Cambridge University Press.

Cryer, Robert; Bekou, Olympia–International Criminal Court. Library of Essays in International Law. Hardback: £135.00. ISBN 0 7546 2409 9. Ashgate.

Curtin, D.M.; Nollkaemper, P.A.; Barnhoorn, L.A.N.M.–Netherlands Yearbook of International Law: V. 35. Hardback: £70.00. ISBN 90 6704 199 8. Asser Press.

Deplege, Joanna–Organization of Global Negotiations: Constructing the Climate Change Regime. Hardback: £55.00. ISBN 1 84407 046 8. Earthscan.

Doswald-Beck, Louise; Henckaerts, Jean-Marie–Customary International Humanitarian Law: V. 2. Hardback: £280.00. ISBN 0 521 83937 8. Cambridge University Press.

Duffy, Helen–"War on Terror" and the Framework of International Law. Hardback: £55.00. ISBN 0 521 83850 9. Paperback: £27.00. ISBN 0 521 54735 0. Cambridge University Press.

Evans, Malcolm D.–International Law Documents. Blackstone's Statute Books. Paperback: £16.99. ISBN 0 19 928312 5. Oxford University Press.

Fiona Beveridge–Globalization and International Investment. International Library of Essays on Globalization & Law. Hardback: £125.00. ISBN 0 7546 2415 3. Ashgate.

Forsyth, Christopher–Private International Law. Butterworths Common Law S. Hardback: £200.00. ISBN 0 406 96032 1. Butterworths Law.

Gallagher, Peter; Low, Patrick; Stoler, Andrew L.–Managing the Challenges of WTO Participation: 45 Case Studies. Hardback: £60.00. ISBN 0 521 86014 8. Paperback: £29.99. ISBN 0 521 67754 8. Cambridge University Press.

Gazzini, Tarcisio–Changing Rules on the Use of Force in International Law. Melland Schill Studies in International Law. Hardback: £60.00. ISBN 0 7190 7324 3. Manchester University Press.

Glasius, Marlies–International Criminal Court. Routledge Advances in International Relations & Global Politics, V. 39. Hardback: £55.00. ISBN 0 415 33395 4. Routledge, an imprint of Taylor & Francis Books Ltd.

Head, J. W.–Future of the Global Economic Organizations: An Evaluation of Criticisms Leveled At the IMF, the Multilateral Development Banks, and the WTO. Hardback: £92.99. ISBN 1 57105 299 2. Transnational Publishers, Inc.

Henckaerts, Jean-Marie; Doswald-Beck, Louise–Customary International Humanitarian Law. Hardback: £300.00. ISBN 0 521 53925 0. Cambridge University Press.

Jeong, Ho-Won–Peacebuilding in Postconflict Societies: Strategy and Process. Paperback: £16.95. ISBN 1 58826 311 8. Lynne Rienner Publishers.

Johnston, William; Werlen, Thomas–Set-Off Law and Practice: An International Handbook. Hardback: £135.00. ISBN 0 19 929077 6. Oxford University Press.

Kaczorowska, Alina–Public International Law. Paperback: £15.95. ISBN 1 85836 607 0. Old Bailey Press.

Klabbers, Jan–International Organizations. Library of Essays in International Law. Hardback: £125.00. ISBN 0 7546 2447 1. Ashgate.

Koutrakos, Panos–EU International Relations Law. Paperback: £37.50. ISBN 1 84113 311 6. Hart Publishing.

Leane, Geoff–International Law in the South Pacific: Policies and Practices. Hardback: £60.00. ISBN 0 7546 4419 7. Ashgate.

Lee, R.S.–Giving Effect to the International Criminal Court: Methods and Techniques For Handling Issues of Criminal Law, Constitution and

Sovereignty. Hardback: £100.99. ISBN 1 57105 155 4. Transnational Publishers, Inc.

Maslen, Stuart—Commentaries on Arms Control Treaties Volume 1. Hardback: £100.00. ISBN 0 19 929679 0. Oxford University Press.

Maslen, Stuart—Commentaries on Arms Control Treaties: V. 1. Convention on the Prohibition of the Use, Stockpiling, Production, and Transfer of Anti-personnel Mines and on Their Destruction. Oxford Commentaries on International Law S. Paperback: £30.00. ISBN 0 19 928702 3. Oxford University Press.

Mavroidis, Petros C.—Commentaries on the GATT/WTO Agreements: V. 1. General Agreement on Tariffs and Trade. Oxford Commentaries on International Law S. Hardback: £75.00. ISBN 0 19 927813 X. Oxford University Press.

Merrills, J.G.—International Dispute Settlement. Hardback: £65.00. ISBN 0 521 85250 1. Paperback: £33.00. ISBN 0 521 61782 0. Cambridge University Press.

Nabulsi, Karma—Traditions of War: Occupation, Resistance, and the Law. Paperback: £18.99. ISBN 0 19 927947 0. Oxford University Press.

Narlikar, Amrita—World Trade Organization: A Very Short Introduction. Very Short Introduction S. Paperback: £6.99. ISBN 0 19 280608 4. Paperback: £6.99. ISBN 0 19 280608 4. Oxford University Press.

Rao, Palle Krishna—WTO: Text and Cases. Paperback: £17.50. ISBN 81 7446 430 1. Excel Books.

Rosen, Gary—Right War?: The Conservative Debate on Iraq. Hardback: £35.00. ISBN 0 521 85681 7. Paperback: £12.99. ISBN 0 521 67318 6. Cambridge University Press.

Tackaberry, John; Anglade, Lelia; Bui, Victoria—International Dispute Resolution: Vol 2. International Dispute Resolution: Cases and Materials. Hardback: £89.00. ISBN 0 421 88720 6. Sweet & Maxwell.

Tams, Christian J.—Enforcing Obligations Erga Omnes in International Law. Cambridge Studies in International & Comparative Law, No. 43. Hardback: £55.00. ISBN 0 521 85667 1. Cambridge University Press.

UK Ministry of Defence—Manual of the Law of Armed Conflict. Paperback: £30.00. ISBN 0 19 928728 7. Oxford University Press.

Weiler, Todd—International Law and Arbitration: Leading Cases from the ICSID, NAFTA, Bilateral Treaties and Customary International Law. Hardback: £125.00. ISBN 1 905017 07 3. Cameron May.

World Trade Organization—Dispute Settlement Reports: V. 6. World Trade Organization Dispute Settlement Reports. Hardback: £90.00. ISBN 0 521 85996 4. Cambridge University Press.

World Trade Organization—Dispute Settlement Reports: V. 7. World Trade Organization Dispute Settlement Reports. Hardback: £90.00. ISBN 0 521 85997 2. Cambridge University Press.

World Trade Organization—Dispute Settlement Reports: V. 8. World Trade Organization Dispute Settlement Reports. Hardback: £90.00. ISBN 0 521 85998 0. Cambridge University Press.

World Trade Organization—Dispute Settlement Reports: V. 9. World Trade Organization Dispute Settlement Reports. Hardback: £90.00. ISBN 0 521 85999 9. Cambridge University Press.

INTERNATIONAL TRADE

2621. Chemicals—Imports and exports

EXPORT AND IMPORT OF DANGEROUS CHEMICALS REGULATIONS 2005, SI 2005 928; made under the European Communities Act 1972 s.2. In force: April 22, 2005; £3.00.

These Regulations, which revoke the Export of Dangerous Chemicals Regulations 1992 (SI 1992 2415), amend the Notification of New Substances Regulations 1993 (SI 1993 3050) and the Chemicals (Hazard Information and Packaging for Supply) Regulations 2002 (SI 2002 1689). They make provisions which are necessary for the operation in Great Britain of European Parliament and

Council Regulation 304/2003 ([2003] OJ L63/1) concerning the export and import of dangerous chemicals. The Regulations also implement within the European Community the Rotterdam Convention on the prior informed consent (PIC) procedure for certain hazardous chemicals and pesticides in international trade signed by the Community on September 11, 1998, to establish a similar procedure for chemicals which qualify for PIC status, and to maintain in force a common export notification procedure for chemicals either banned for use or whose use is severely restricted within the Community.

2622. Customs and Excise–Statistics of trade

STATISTICS OF TRADE (CUSTOMS AND EXCISE) (AMENDMENT) REGULATIONS 2005, SI 2005 3371; made under the European Communities Act 1972 s.2. In force: January 1, 2006; £3.00.

Intrastat is the system for the production of Community statistics relating to the trading of goods between Member States. These Regulations amend the Statistics of Trade (Customs and Excise) Regulations 1992 (SI 1992 2790) to increase from £221,000 to £225,000 the threshold, expressed in terms of annual value of intra-Community trade, above which a business is required to provide a supplementary declaration for Intrastat. The threshold applies separately for goods dispatched and goods received. They make amendments following the annual review of the threshold in the UK.

2623. Customs officers–Commissioners of Customs and Excise–Functions

CRIME (INTERNATIONAL CO-OPERATION) ACT 2003 (EXERCISE OF FUNCTIONS) ORDER 2005, SI 2005 425; made under the Crime (International Co-operation) Act 2003 s.27. In force: March 23, 2005; £3.00.

This Order enables the Commissioners of Customs and Excise and customs officers to exercise certain functions under the Crime (International Co-operation) Act 2003.

2624. Export controls–Arrest of persons

EXPORT OF GOODS, TRANSFER OF TECHNOLOGY AND PROVISION OF TECHNICAL ASSISTANCE (CONTROL) (AMENDMENT) ORDER 2005, SI 2005 468; made under the Export Control Act 2002 s.1, s.2, s.3, s.5, s.7. In force: March 28, 2005; £3.00.

This Order, which amends the Export of Goods, Transfer of Technology and Provision of Technical Assistance (Control) Order 2003 (SI 2003 2764), provides that the provisions relating to arrest of persons contained in the Customs and Excise Management Act 1979 s.138, allowing the arrest by any customs officer or a member of Her Majesty's armed forces or coastguard, shall apply to certain offences related to transfers of technology or the provision of technical assistance contained in the 2003 Order. The Order also provides that the provisions relating to customs officers' information gathering powers contained in the 1979 Act s.77A apply to persons concerned in an activity requiring a licence under the 2003 Order for the transfer of software or technology and the provision of technical assistance.

2625. Export controls–Arrest of persons

TRADE IN GOODS (CONTROL) (AMENDMENT) ORDER 2005, SI 2005 443; made under the Export Control Act 2002 s.4, s.5, s.7. In force: March 28, 2005; £3.00.

This Order, which amends the Trade in Goods (Control) Order 2003 (SI 2003 2765), provides that the provisions relating to arrest of persons contained in the Customs and Excise Management Act 1979 s.138 allowing the arrest by any customs officer or a member of Her Majesty's armed forces or coastguard apply to any person who has committed, or whom there are reasonable grounds to suspect of having committed an offence. The Order also provides that the provisions relating to customs officers' information gathering powers contained in the 1979 Act s.77A apply to persons concerned in any activity requiring a licence under the 2003 Order.

2626. Export controls–Criminal offences–Democratic Republic of Congo

EXPORT CONTROL (DEMOCRATIC REPUBLIC OF CONGO) ORDER 2005, SI 2005 1677; made under the Export Control Act 2002 s.3, s.4, s.5, s.7. In force: June 27, 2005; £3.00.

This Order, which revokes the Democratic Republic of Congo (Financing and Financial Assistance and Technical Advice, Assistance and Training) Penalties and Licences Regulations 2004 (SI 2004 221), makes provision in respect of the Democratic Republic of Congo in consequence of Council Regulation 889/2005 ([2005] OJ L152/1) imposing certain restrictive measures in respect of the Democratic Republic of Congo and repealing Regulation 1727/2003. The Order also provides that breaches of certain provisions are to be criminal offences; creates offences in respect of the provisions of the Regulation; provides for the licensing of specified transactions; and provide penalties in respect of criminal offences created by the Order and for their enforcement.

2627. Export controls–Criminal offences–Uzbekistan

EXPORT CONTROL (UZBEKISTAN) ORDER 2005, SI 2005 3257; made under the Export Control Act 2002 s.1, s.2, s.3, s.4, s.5, s.7. In force: November 26, 2005; £3.00.

This Order, which amends the Transfer of Technology and Provision of Technical Assistance (Control) Order 2003 (SI 2003 2764) and the Trade in Controlled Goods (Embargoed Destinations) Order 2004 (SI 2004 318), makes provision in respect of Uzbekistan in consequence of Council Regulation 1859/2005 ([2005] OJ L299/23) imposing certain restrictive measures in respect of Uzbekistan and the Council Common Position 2005/792 ([2005] OJ L299/72) concerning restrictive measures against Uzbekistan. The Order provides that breaches of certain provisions of the Regulation are to be criminal offences.

2628. Export controls–Embargoed destinations–Arrest of persons

TRADE IN CONTROLLED GOODS (EMBARGOED DESTINATIONS) (AMENDMENT) ORDER 2005, SI 2005 445; made under the Export Control Act 2002 s.4, s.5, s.7. In force: March 28, 2005; £3.00.

This Order, which amends the Trade in Controlled Goods (Embargoed Destinations) Order 2004 (SI 2004 318), provides that the provisions relating to arrest of persons contained in the Customs and Excise Management Act 1979 s.138 allowing the arrest by any customs officer or a member of Her Majesty's armed forces or coastguard apply to any person who has committed, or whom there are reasonable grounds to suspect of having committed an offence. The Order also provides that the provisions relating to customs officers' information gathering powers contained in the 1979 Act s.77A apply to persons concerned in any activity requiring a licence under the 2004 Order.

2629. Export controls–Iraq and Ivory Coast

EXPORT CONTROL (IRAQ AND IVORY COAST) ORDER 2005, SI 2005 232; made under the Export Control Act 2002 s.1, s.2, s.3, s.4, s.5, s.7. In force: February 9, 2005; £3.00.

This Order, which amends the Export of Goods, Transfer of Technology and Provision of Technical Assistance (Control) Order 2003 (SI 2003 2764) and the Trade in Controlled Goods (Embargoed Destinations) Order 2004 (SI 2004 318), makes provision in respect of Ivory Coast in consequence of Council Regulation 174/2005 ([2005] OJ L29/5) imposing restrictions on the supply of assistance related to military activities to Cote d'Ivoire and the EU Common Position 2004/852 adopted on December 13, 2004, and taking effect on that date. It also makes provision in respect of Iraq as a consequence of the ending of all sanctions, except those related to the sale or supply to Iraq of arms or related material.

2630. Import controls–Potatoes–Netherlands–Wales

POTATOES ORIGINATING IN THE NETHERLANDS (NOTIFICATION) (WALES) ORDER 2005, SI 2005 1162 (W.77); made under the Plant Health Act 1967 s.2, s.3, s.4. In force: April 15, 2005; £3.00.

This Order places certain notification requirements upon persons importing into Wales potatoes originating from the Netherlands which have been grown during 2004 or later. Any person importing relevant potatoes into Wales in the course of business, must give at least two days' notice of such importation, in writing, to an authorised inspector of the National Assembly for Wales. The Order also provides authorised inspectors with powers for the purpose of enforcing this Order and also ensuring compliance with the Plant Health (Great Britain) Order 1993 (SI 1993 1320).

2631. Import controls–Potatoes–Netherlands–Wales

POTATOES ORIGINATING IN THE NETHERLANDS (REVOCATION) (ENGLAND) REGULATIONS 2005, SI 2005 278; made under the European Communities Act 1972 s.2. In force: March 7, 2005; £3.00.

These Regulations revoke the Potatoes Originating in the Netherlands Regulations 1997 (SI 1997 2441) and the Potatoes Originating in the Netherlands (Amendment) Regulations 1998 (SI 1998 3168) insofar as they apply to England.

2632. Import controls–Potatoes–Netherlands–Wales

POTATOES ORIGINATING IN THE NETHERLANDS (REVOCATION) (WALES) REGULATIONS 2005, SI 2005 1161 (W.76); made under the European Communities Act 1972 s.2. In force: April 15, 2005; £3.00.

These Regulations revoke the Potatoes Originating in the Netherlands Regulations 1997 (SI 1997 2441) and the Potatoes Originating in the Netherlands (Amendment) Regulations 1998 (SI 1998 3168) insofar as they apply in relation to Wales. The 1997 Regulations required any person intending to import potatoes originating in the Netherlands (and grown in 1997) to give notification of that intention to a plant health inspector together with related information concerning the importation. The 1997 Regulations also provided plant health inspectors with certain powers of enforcement and prescribed the payment of a fee (payable by those required to provide notifications) where a sample of seed potatoes is taken by an inspector for the purpose of ascertaining whether they are infected with "Pseudomonas solanacearum (Smith) Smith". The 1998 Regulations amended the 1997 Regulations so as to apply the latter to potatoes grown in 1998. They also amended the fee payable in respect of the sampling of seed potatoes. Both Regulations are no longer of practical effect as potatoes originating in the Netherlands and grown in 1997 and 1998 are no longer in existence.

2633. Import controls–Potatoes–Notice–Netherlands

DUTCH POTATOES (NOTIFICATION) (ENGLAND) ORDER 2005, SI 2005 279; made under the Plant Health Act 1967 s.2, s.3, s.4. In force: March 7, 2005; £3.00.

This Order places certain notification requirements upon persons importing potatoes from the Netherlands which have been grown during 2004 or later.

2634. Books

Andenas, Mads; Ortino, Federico–WTO Law and Process. Paperback: £80.00. ISBN 0 903067 68 4. British Institute of International and Comparative.

Bhala, Raj–Modern GATT Law. Hardback: £174.00. ISBN 0 421 79300 7. Sweet & Maxwell.

Bourgeois, Jacques–Trade Law Experienced: Pottering About in the GATT and WTO. Hardback: £125.00. ISBN 1 905017 03 0. Cameron May.

Chuah, Jason–Law of International Trade. Paperback: £28.95. ISBN 0 421 90110 1. Sweet & Maxwell.

Cracknell, D.G.–Law of International Trade. Cracknell's Statutes S. Paperback: £11.95. ISBN 1 85836 582 1. Old Bailey Press.

Dromgoole, Sarah–International Trade Law. Paperback: £26.99. ISBN 0 273 61112 7. FT Prentice Hall.

International Trade and Business Law Review: V.4. Paperback: £41.00. ISBN 1 876905 23 9. Cavendish Publishing Ltd.

Lee, Yong-Shik–Reclaiming Development in the World Trading System. Hardback: £35.00. ISBN 0 521 85296 X. Cambridge University Press.

Mitchell, Andrew–Challenges and Prospects for the WTO. Paperback: £85.00. ISBN 1 905017 04 9. Cameron May.

Nelson, Douglas R.; Vandenbussche, Hylke–WTO and Anti-Dumping. Global Perspectives on the Global Trading System and the WTO S. Hardback: £295.00. ISBN 1 84376 602 7. Edward Elgar.

Schnitzer, Simone–Understanding International Trade Law. Understanding S. Paperback: £20.00. ISBN 1 84641 002 9. Law Matters Publishing.

Vermulst, Edwin–WTO Anti-Dumping Agreement: A Commentary. Oxford Commentaries on International Law S. Hardback: £75.00. ISBN 0 19 927707 9. Oxford University Press.

World Bank–Doing Business in 2006: Services for Business-Creating Jobs. Hardback: £21.50. ISBN 0 8213 5749 2. World Bank.

JURISPRUDENCE

2635. Books

Anderson, Matthew; Sarat, Austin–Studies in Law, Politics and Society. Studies in Law, Politics & Society. Hardback: £59.99. ISBN 0 7623 1189 4. JAI Press.

As-Sadr, Muhammad Baqir–Lessons in Islamic Jurisprudence. Paperback: £16.99. ISBN 1 85168 393 3. Oneworld Publications.

Bassiouni, M.Cherif–Statute of the International Criminal Court and Related Instruments: Legislative History, 1994-2000. Hardback: £282.50. ISBN 1 57105 156 2. Transnational Publishers, Inc.

Bearman, Peri; Peters, Rudolph; Vogel, Frank E.–Islamic School of Law: Evolution, Devolution, and Progress. Hardback: £25.95. ISBN 0 674 01784 6. Harvard University Press.

Berman, Greg–Good Courts: The Case for Problem-Solving Justice. Hardback: £16.99. ISBN 1 56584 973 6. The New Press.

Bernasconi-Osterwalder, Nathalie; Magraw, Daniel; Olivia, Maria Julia; Orellana, Marcus; Tuerk, Elisabeth–Environment and Trade: A Guide to WTO Jurisprudence. Hardback: £79.95. ISBN 1 84407 298 3. Earthscan Publications Ltd.

Bronckers, Marco C. E. J.; Horlick, Gary N.–WTO Jurisprudence and Policy: Practitioners' Perspectives. Hardback: £125.00. ISBN 1 905017 06 5. Cameron May.

Campbell, Joseph Keim; O'Rourke, Michael; Shier, David–Law and Social Justice. Topics in Contemporary Philosophy S., V. 3. Hardback: £45.95. ISBN 0 262 03340 2. Bradford Book.

Cappalli, Richard B.–Advanced Case Law Methods: A Practical Course. Hardback: £44.50. ISBN 1 57105 345 X. Transnational Publishers, Inc.

Carmen, Del; Trulson, Darrel A.–Juvenile Justice Law. Hardback: £34.00. ISBN 0 534 52158 4. Wadsworth.

Charles Sampford; Fredrik Galtung–Measuring Corruption. Law Ethics & Governance. Hardback: £50.00. ISBN 0 7546 2405 6. Avebury Technical.

Coyle, Sean; Pavlakos, George–Jurisprudence or Legal Science? Hardback: £35.00. ISBN 1 84113 504 6. Hart Publishing.

Doherty, Michael–Jurisprudence: The Philosophy of Law. Paperback: £15.95. ISBN 1 85836 601 1. Old Bailey Press.

Donovan, James M.; Anderson III, H. Edwin–Anthropology and Law. Anthropology &....S. Paperback: £13.50. ISBN 1 57181 424 8. Berghahn Books.

Douzinas, Costas; Gearey, Adam–Critical Jurisprudence: A Textbook. Paperback: £22.00. ISBN 1 84113 452 X. Hart Publishing.

Elgar Companion to Law and Economics. Hardback: £180.00. ISBN 1 84542 032 2. Edward Elgar.

Encyclopaedia of Forms and Precedents: V 8. Pt1. Hardback: £201.00. ISBN 0 406 97613 9. Butterworths Law.

Ghose, K.–Beyond the Courtroom: A Lawyer's Guide to Campaigning. Paperback: £20.00. ISBN 1 903307 35 X. The Legal Action Group.

Gordley, James–Foundations of Private Law: Property, Tort, Contract, Unjust Enrichment. Hardback: £50.00. ISBN 0 19 929167 5. Oxford University Press.

Greenfield, Steven; Osborn, Guy–Readings in Law and Popular Culture. Routledge Studies in Law, Society and Popular Culture S., V. 3. Hardback: £85.00. ISBN 0 415 37647 5. Routledge, an imprint of Taylor & Francis Books Ltd.

Greve, Michael S.–Harm-less Lawsuits?: What's Wrong with Consumer Class Actions. Paperback: £10.95. ISBN 0 8447 4215 5. The AEI Press.

Halstead, Peter–Jurisprudence. Key Facts S. Paperback: £5.99. ISBN 0 340 88695 1. Hodder Arnold H&S.

Harries, Jill–Cicero and the Jurists. Hardback: £45.00. ISBN 0 7156 3432 1. Gerald Duckworth & Co. Ltd.

Holm, Soren; Gunning, Jennifer–Ethics Law and Society:Volume 1. Hardback: £60.00. ISBN 0 7546 4583 5. Ashgate.

Hunter, Rosemary; Keyes, Mary–Changing Law: Rights, Regulation, and Reconciliation. Law, Justice & Power S. Hardback: £55.00. ISBN 0 7546 2552 4. Ashgate.

Illes, Judy–Neuroethics in the 21st Century: Defining the Issues in Theory, Practice and Policy. Hardback: £75.00. ISBN 0 19 856720 0. Oxford University Press.

Inns of Court School of Law–Test Yourself in Evidence, Civil Procedure, Criminal Procedure and Sentencing. Blackstone Bar Manual S. Paperback: £17.99. ISBN 0 19 928487 3. Oxford University Press.

Jackson, Frank; Smith, Michael–Oxford Handbook of Contemporary Philosophy. Oxford Handbooks S. Hardback: £55.00. ISBN 0 19 924295 X. Oxford University Press.

John-Salakov, Andre–Journal of Civil and Criminal Justice Systems. Hardback: £25.99. ISBN 1 873156 79 0. Centre For Community Studies.

Jurisprudence Lawcards. Lawcards S. Looseleaf/ring bound: £6.95. ISBN 1 84568 025 1. Cavendish Publishing Ltd.

Kelsen, Hans–General Theory of Law and State. Paperback: £31.50. ISBN 1 4128 0494 9. Transaction Publishers.

Kostal, Rande W.–Jurisprudence of Power: Victorian Empire and the Rule of Law. Oxford Studies in Modern Legal History. Hardback: £50.00. ISBN 0 19 826076 8. Oxford University Press.

LaFollette, Hugh–Oxford Handbook of Practical Ethics. Oxford Handbooks in Philosophy S. Paperback: £27.50. ISBN 0 19 928423 7. Oxford University Press.

MacKinnon, Catharine A.–Women's Lives, Men's Laws. Hardback: £25.95. ISBN 0 674 01540 1. The Belknap Press.

Marmor, Andrei–Interpretation and Legal Theory. Paperback: £30.00. ISBN 1 84113 424 4. Hart Publishing.

McFayden, Norman–Offences Against Justice. Paperback: £40.00. ISBN 1 84592 052 X. Tottel Publishing.

McLeod, Ian–Legal Theory. Palgrave Law Masters S. Paperback: £13.99. ISBN 1 4039 4871 2. Palgrave Macmillan.

Miller, William Ian–Eye for an Eye. Hardback: £16.99. ISBN 0 521 85680 9. Cambridge University Press.

Morley, Iain–Devil's Advocate. Paperback: £12.95. ISBN 0 421 91480 7. Sweet & Maxwell.

Murphy, James Bernard–Philosophy of Positive Law: Foundations of Jurisprudence. Hardback: £25.00. ISBN 0 300 10788 9. Yale University Press.
Murphy, Mark–Natural Law in Jurisprudence and Politics. Hardback: £45.00. ISBN 0 521 85930 1. Cambridge University Press.
Ogowewo, Tunde–Jurisprudence of the Takeover Panel. Hardback: £40.00. ISBN 1 901362 77 9. Hart Publishing.
Oldham, Edwin W.–Freedom To Invent. Hardback: £23.00. ISBN 1 4134 5572 7. Paperback: £14.00. ISBN 1 4134 5571 9. Xlibris Corporation.
Paul, Ellen Frankel; Miller, Fred D.; Paul, Jeffrey–Personal Identity: V. 22. Social Philosophy & Policy S., No. 22. Paperback: £17.99. ISBN 0 521 61767 7. Cambridge University Press.
Pelton, Leroy H.–Frames of Justice: Implications for Social Policy. Hardback: £35.50. ISBN 0 7658 0296 1. Transaction Publishers.
Pierceson, Jason–Courts, Liberalism, and Rights. Hardback: £52.00. ISBN 1 59213 400 9. Temple University Press.
Psychology and Law of Criminal Justice Processes. Hardback: £71.99. ISBN 1 59454 312 7. Nova Science Publishers, Inc.
Reiff, Mark R.–Theory of Enforceability: Punishment, Compensation, and Law. Cambridge Studies in Philosophy & Law. Hardback: £45.00. ISBN 0 521 84669 2. Cambridge University Press.
Riley, Leon; Turner, Chris; Donaldson, Angela; Huxley-Binns, Rebecca–Unlocking Legal Learning. Paperback: £18.99. ISBN 0 340 88761 3. Hodder Arnold H&S.
Rose, F.D.–Statutes on Contract, Tort and Restitution. Blackstone's Statute Book S. Paperback: £14.99. ISBN 0 19 928320 6. Oxford University Press.
Russomanno, Joseph–Defending the First: Commentary on First Amendment Issues and Cases. LEA's Communication Series. Hardback: £52.95. ISBN 0 8058 4925 4. Lawrence Erlbaum Associates, Inc.
Sampford, Charles–Retrospectivity and the Rule of Law. Hardback: £60.00. ISBN 0 19 825298 6. Oxford University Press.
Schmidtz, David–Elements of Justice. Hardback: £40.00. ISBN 0 521 83164 4. Cambridge University Press.
Scott, Sionaidh Douglas–Law After Modernity. Legal Theory Today S. Hardback: £26.00. ISBN 1 84113 562 3. Hart Publishing.
Semple, Piggot Mike–Jurisprudence. Law in a Box S. CD-ROM: £19.95. ISBN 1 904783 85 6. Semple Piggot Rochez (Legal Education Ltd).
Shapiro, Hal–Fast Track: A Legal, Historical and Political Analysis. Hardback: £100.99. ISBN 1 57105 178 3. Transnational Publishers, Inc.
Sherwin, Richard K.–Popular Culture and Law. International Library of Essays in Law & Society S. Hardback: £115.00. ISBN 0 7546 2470 6. Ashgate.
Tan, Alan Khee-Jin–Vessel-source Marine Pollution: The Law and Politics of International Regulation. Cambridge Studies in International & Comparative Law, No. 45. Hardback: £50.00. ISBN 0 521 85342 7. Cambridge University Press.
Tebbit–Philosophy of Law Intro Ed2-2nd Ed. Paperback (B format): £15.99. ISBN 0 415 33441 1. Routledge, an imprint of Taylor & Francis Books Ltd.
Tebbit, Mark–Philosophy of Law: An Introduction. Hardback: £65.00. ISBN 0 415 33440 3. Routledge, an imprint of Taylor & Francis Books Ltd.
Weinreb, Lloyd L.–Legal Reason: The Use of Analogy in Legal Argument. Hardback: £30.00. ISBN 0 521 84967 5. Cambridge University Press.
Williams; Brewer–Psychology and Law: An Empirical Perspective. Hardback: £45.00. ISBN 1 59385 122 7. Guilford Press.
Wintgens, Luc J.–Theory and Practice of Legislation: Essays in Legisprudence. Applied Legal Philosophy S. Hardback: £60.00. ISBN 0 7546 2461 7. Ashgate.
Wolcher, Louis–Beyond Transcendence in Law and Philosophy. Hardback: £60.00. ISBN 1 85941 988 7. Birkbeck Law Press.

LANDLORD AND TENANT

2636. Agricultural holdings–Notices to quit–Notice to quit scheme in Agricultural Holdings Act 1986–Compatibility with tenant's human rights

[Agricultural Holdings Act 1986 Sch.3 Part I Case D; Human Rights Act 1998 s.4(2), s.6(2)(b), s.7, Sch.1 Part I Art.14; European Convention on Human Rights 1950.]

The appellant tenant (T) appealed against an order for possession ([2004] EWHC 776, [2005] 1 P. & C.R. 2) made in respect of his agricultural holding. The respondent local authority was T's landlord and owner of the land. T's tenancy required him to use the holding for agricultural purposes only but the local authority discovered that he was carrying on business there processing, bottling and distributing milk and fruit juices that had not been produced on the holding. The local authority required T to remedy the alleged breaches and then served notice to quit under the Agricultural Holdings Act 1986 Sch.3 Part I Case D based on T's failure to comply with the notice to remedy the breaches. T applied for statutory arbitration under the 1986 Act. The arbitrator determined that the notice to quit was valid and effective and T unsuccessfully challenged his award in court. After the coming into force of the Human Rights Act 1998, T complained that the notice to quit scheme under the 1986 Act was incompatible with the European Convention on Human Rights 1950 because it discriminated contrary to Art.14 between an agricultural tenant facing eviction for failure to maintain a holding and one facing eviction for failure to improve it, since the former could apply for arbitration before a notice to quit had been served whereas the latter could not refer any dispute to arbitration until he had been served with notice to quit. T sought a declaration pursuant to s.4(2) of the 1998 Act that the relevant provisions of the 1986 Act were incompatible with the Convention. The secretary of state, intervening, submitted that T was not entitled to the relief sought since he faced eviction for breach of a user covenant and was therefore not in either class relied on and could not benefit by rectification of the alleged incompatibility. The local authority submitted that, even if the legislation was incompatible with the Convention, by virtue of s.6(2)(b) of the 1998 Act it would not be acting unlawfully if it evicted T.

Held, dismissing the appeal, that (1) it was not the intention of the 1998 Act or the Convention that members of the public should use the provisions to change legislation if they were not adversely affected by it. T could not be regarded as a victim for the purposes of s.7 of the 1998 Act or the Convention. The breach of covenant that he was alleged to have committed had nothing to do with the alleged discrimination on which he relied. Even if the 1986 Act discriminated against T, there was no realistic possibility that if, in consequence, a declaration of incompatibility was granted, any remedial action which could be taken would benefit him in any way. The grant of a declaration of incompatibility was discretionary and the court would not exercise its discretion in favour of T since he could not be affected by the breach of the Convention on which he was attempting to rely. (2) The differential treatment of tenants under the 1986 Act did not depend on their property or status within Art.14 but solely on the content of the covenant alleged to have been breached. In any event, there was a rational objective justification for the different routes available to agricultural tenants facing allegations of breach of covenant because it was not hard to see how the covenant to maintain could become an engine of oppression. (3) A large part of the parliamentary material put forward by the secretary of state to justify the provisions of the 1986 Act was not properly admissible.

LANCASHIRE CC v. TAYLOR; *sub nom.* TAYLOR v. LANCASHIRE CC, [2005] EWCA Civ 284, [2005] 1 W.L.R. 2668, Lord Woolf of Barnes, L.C.J, CA (Civ Div).

2637. Agricultural holdings–Notices to quit–Parallel proceedings–Tenant serving counter notice at same time as notice referring matter to arbitration

[Agricultural Holdings Act 1986 s.28, Sch.3 Part I Case D.]

The applicant landlord (W) applied for a direction that the Agricultural Lands Tribunal state a case in relation to its decision not to consent to a notice to quit served by W on its tenant (P). W had previously served P with a notice to repair which was referred to arbitration and as a result P was given 12 months to remove gorse from a field boundary. W contended that the works had not been completed in time and subsequently served the notice to quit in accordance with the Agricultural Holdings Act 1986 Sch.3 Part I Case D. P served a counter notice and a tenant's notice referring the matter to arbitration under s.28 of the Act. W was confused as to which avenue P wished to take so pursued the matter in the tribunal. W argued that the legislation did not allow P to pursue both arbitration and tribunal proceedings, and as a tenant's notice had been served under s.28(4)(a) the counter notice was ineffective, so that the tribunal had no jurisdiction. The tribunal rejected this on the basis that the counter notice had been served at the same time as the tenant's notice and it refused to consent to the notice to quit and refused to state a case to the High Court.

Held, refusing application that the tribunal could only be directed to state a case where there was an arguable point of law. Neither a counter notice nor a tenant's notice initiated proceedings and the counter notice was not invalid because it was given at the same time as the tenant's notice. It was for W to initiate proceedings before the tribunal and for either W or P to obtain the appointment of an arbitrator.

WILLIAM SMITH (WAKEFIELD) LTD v. PARISRIDE LTD, [2005] EWHC 462, [2005] 2 E.G.L.R. 22, Leveson, J., QBD (Admin Ct).

2638. Agricultural holdings–Repairs notices–Validity of service on landlord–Service on landlord's agent–Trustees as landlord–Effect of death of trustees on legal estate and on agency

[Agricultural Holdings Act 1986 s.93(3), s.96(1); Agriculture (Maintenance, Repair and Insurance of Fixed Equipment) Regulations 1973 (SI 1973 1473).]

The appellant (T) appealed against a judgment that a notice to remedy, issued pursuant to the Agriculture (Maintenance, Repair and Insurance of Fixed Equipment) Regulations 1973 in respect of an agricultural holding, had been validly served by the respondent tenant (L). Three trustees had held the legal estate of the agricultural holding as joint tenants, and as such were the landlord. The trustees had been reduced to two by the death of one of the trustees, and then (KC), one of the two remaining trustees, had died. The only surviving trustee (D) was therefore the landlord. During KC's lifetime, the tenant had paid the rent to her or to her husband (FC). After KC's death, L paid the rent to FC. L purported to serve the notice to remedy by addressing it to KC's executors. However, having died intestate, KC had no executors and the letter was opened by FC. T was FC and KC's daughter and a beneficiary under the trust. The issue for determination was whether the notice was validly served on the landlord.

Held, allowing the appeal, that the notice to remedy had not been sufficiently addressed and served. It was inappropriate to serve a notice addressed to KC's executors because the land remained in trust and automatically vested in D, the surviving trustee. D alone was the person entitled to the rents and profits, *Egerton v. Rutter* [1951] 1 K.B. 472 distinguished. KC as a deceased trustee fell out of the picture. The definition of landlord in the Agricultural Holdings Act 1986 s.96(1), by reference to entitlement to receive the rents and profits, referred to entitlement as between landlord and tenant. Where land was held on trust, the entitlement of a beneficiary to the rents and profits as against a trustee was not relevant. If service on an agent was to suffice as service on a principal, s.93(3) required that there should be a present agency. Any agency which FC had had for KC, his wife, must have ceased on her death and therefore he could not have been the landlord's agent after his wife's death.

LODGEPOWER LTD v. TAYLOR, [2004] EWCA Civ 1367, [2005] 1 E.G.L.R. 1, Peter Gibson, L.J., CA (Civ Div).

2639. Assignment-Breach of covenant-Covenant to convert roof space "as expeditiously as possible"-Reasonableness of landlord's refusal

The appellant (C), reversionary lessee of the roof space of a block of flats, appealed against a decision ([2003] EWHC 2713, [2004] L. & T.R. 16) that it had unreasonably refused its consent to the assignment of the lease by the mortgagee, and dismissing its claim against the mortgagee (F) and the assignee of the lease (A) and a number of underlessees seeking to establish its entitlement to forfeit the lease for breach of covenant. The issues for determination were whether a breach of the covenant to develop the roof space "as expeditiously as possible" was a once and for all breach, or whether the obligation was continuing in the sense that it was broken each day the tenant was in breach, and whether the judge had erred in applying the principle that a landlord could not refuse consent to assignment on grounds unrelated to the landlord and tenant relationship. C had refused its consent because the proposed assignee (T) had refused to assume the obligations under a preliminary agreement relating to the development project.

Held, dismissing the appeal, that (1) a covenant to do something by a specified date could only be breached once. The obligations in the lease were to be construed in the context of the preliminary agreement, which required the proposed development to be completed by a specified date. Therefore the covenant could only be breached once, *Farimani v. Gates* (1984) 271 E.G. 887, [1984] C.L.Y. 1900 considered. (2) There was an insufficient connection between the refusal of consent and the landlord and tenant relationship since the only parties with a direct financial interest in the late completion of the project under the preliminary agreement were A and F, *Ashworth Frazer Ltd v. Gloucester City Council* [2001] UKHL 59, [2001] 1 W.L.R. 2180, [2001] C.L.Y. 4185 considered.

FIRST PENTHOUSE LTD v. CHANNEL HOTELS & PROPERTIES (UK) LTD; CHANNEL HOTELS & PROPERTIES (UK) LTD v. TAMIMI, [2004] EWCA Civ 1072, [2004] L. & T.R. 27, Peter Gibson, L.J., CA (Civ Div).

2640. Assured tenancies-Possession claims-Anti social behaviour by tenant's partner-Reasonableness of possession order

[Housing Act 1988 s.9A.]

The appellant (R) appealed against a final order made in favour of the respondent housing trust (L) for possession of a residence. R had occupied the residence as a tenant of L. R's partner had, in breach of R's tenancy agreement, run a car repair business from the residence. In addition he had intimidated a number of R's neighbours. L brought proceedings for possession of the residence based on R's partner's behaviour and breaches of the tenancy agreement. L subsequently obtained an anti social behaviour order against R's partner and he was added as a defendant to L's possession claim against R. The trial judge, having considered the Housing Act 1988 s.9A, the needs of R and her children and the needs of her neighbours, made a final possession order in favour of L. R submitted that the judge should on the evidence before him have suspended the possession order.

Held, dismissing the appeal, that a final possession order was appropriate. Whilst the judge's reasons could have been clearer, he had directed himself to the relevant matters and to the correct law. On the facts of the instant case, the behaviour exhibited towards R's neighbours had been very bad and there was a limit to which the court could tolerate such behaviour for the sake of the needs of R and her children.

LONDON & QUADRANT HOUSING TRUST v. ROOT; *sub nom.* LONDON QUADRANT HOUSING TRUST v. ROOT, [2005] EWCA Civ 43, [2005] H.L.R. 28, Brooke, L.J., CA (Civ Div).

2641. Assured tenancies–Succession–Position of homosexual partner

[Housing Act 1988 s.17, s.17(4).]

The appellant (N) appealed against a decision allowing the claim of the respondent landlord (S) for possession of a flat, the recorder having found that N was not entitled under the Housing Act 1988 s.17 to succeed to the tenancy. N had been the partner, in a homosexual relationship, of the tenant (R) for two years before R's death. R had occupied the flat under an assured tenancy. On R's death, N applied to succeed to the tenancy. The judge decided that N was not R's spouse for the purposes of s.17(4), primarily because of the apparent lack of permanence in the relationship between N and R. N argued that the judge's emphasis on the apparent lack of permanence in the relationship was too restrictive and was inconsistent with authority.

Held, dismissing the appeal, that the construction of s.17 was governed by the principles in *Ghaidan v. Godin-Mendoza* [2004] UKHL 30, [2004] 2 A.C. 557, [2004] 9 C.L. 334. However, the passage in the judgment of Lord Millett relied on by N was, strictly, not only part of a dissent but also *obiter* to his conclusion. Further, it contrasted with the emphasis of Lord Rodger on the test being applied to "long term homosexual relationships" and with passages in the speech of Baroness Hale. Without a lifetime commitment, at least at some point in the relationship, there was no sufficient similarity to marriage. The test prescribed by the recorder of whether the relationship was an emotional one of mutual lifetime commitment rather than simply one of convenience, friendship, companionship or the living together of lovers, subject to the qualification that the relationship had to be openly and unequivocally displayed to the outside world, was an entirely adequate test and one that was consistent with the authorities, *Ghaidan* applied, and *Helby v. Rafferty* [1979] 1 W.L.R. 13, [1979] C.L.Y. 1630 and *Chios Investment Property Co v. Lopez* (1988) 20 H.L.R. 120, [1988] C.L.Y. 2086 considered. On the findings of fact made by the recorder, he had been entitled to conclude that N had failed to show that his relationship with R displayed a sufficient commitment to permanence to meet the test.

NUTTING v. SOUTHERN HOUSING GROUP LTD, [2004] EWHC 2982, [2005] 1 F.L.R. 1066, Evans-Lombe, J., Ch D.

2642. Assured tenancies–Suspended possession orders–Order granted against tenant's son–Anti social behaviour

[Housing Act 1988 Sch.2 Ground 14.]

N appealed against a court order granting it possession of one of its housing estate properties but suspending the order for a year subject to the tenant, A, showing her capacity to control her 17-year-old son, D. D had been the subject of a number of anti social behaviour orders and, at the time of the judgment, had served one month of a six month prison sentence. A's children and her partner lived in the property. The order was subject to a condition that there would be no further breaches of the Housing Act 1988 Sch.2 Ground 14 during the period of suspension. N argued that there was no evidence that D's behaviour would improve by reason of allowing the 12 month suspension period, and that it would in any event be difficult to prove a breach of Ground 14 given that N's witnesses had all left the estate because of D's behaviour towards them.

Held, allowing the appeal, that N would be granted possession in six weeks. The judge had been correct to hold, applying Ground 14, that the nuisance caused by D was no barrier to a possession order against A. However, the judge had not correctly exercised his discretion in that (i) his own observations indicated that he assumed that D was likely to continue his behaviour once released; (ii) there was no sound basis on which he could have given A the benefit of the doubt or granted her the opportunity to change D's behaviour; and (iii) he had only paid lip service to and largely ignored the interests of the neighbours and the difficulties of proving future breaches of the suspended order, *Canterbury City Council v. Lowe* (2001) 33 H.L.R. 53, [2001] C.L.Y. 3440 followed. There was no real prospect that the family would change its ways in terms of anti social behaviour and indeed, A had given no indication that she was prepared to curb D's behaviour on his release from detention, *West Kent*

Housing Association Ltd v. Davies (1999) 31 H.L.R. 415, [1999] C.L.Y. 3708 followed.

NEW CHARTER HOUSING (NORTH) LTD v. ASHCROFT, [2004] EWCA Civ 310, [2004] H.L.R. 36, Potter, L.J., CA.

2643. Authorised guarantee agreements–Leases–Relief from forfeiture–Assignment–Administrative receivers' personal liability

[Landlord and Tenant (Covenants) Act 1995 s.16.]

The appellant landlord (S) appealed against the decision refusing to strike out a claim for relief from forfeiture brought by the claimant tenant (L). L was the original tenant of a lease of shop premises in Kingston under an underlease. S was the landlord by assignment. L had gone into administrative receivership. The lease thereupon became liable to be forfeited. S had physically reentered the premises and forfeited the lease. L had brought proceedings for relief against forfeiture so that it could assign the benefit of the term to another tenant. By clause 4.9.1 of the lease, prior to assigning the lease L had to execute and deliver to S an authorised guarantee agreement (AGA). The AGA was defined by clause 4.7.1.2 as being both an AGA within the meaning of the Landlord and Tenant (Covenants) Act 1995 s.16 and one in a form which the landlord reasonably required. S had sought an AGA from L in relation to the proposed assignee. S had been offered a guarantee not only from L but also from a third party whose financial standing was not questioned, and a rent deposit. S argued that it was entitled to insist that the relevant guarantee was given not only by L but by the administrative receivers personally. L argued that S was seeking to force the receivers to give a personal guarantee when they were unlikely to do so in order to leave S free to re let the premises to a new tenant.

Held, dismissing the appeal, that if L had not gone into administrative receivership, the AGA it was willing to execute and deliver would fall within clause 4.9.1 and would also be an AGA within the meaning of s.16 of the 1995 Act. If S could object at all, it could only be to the form of the agreement and, even then, only if such objection was reasonable. It followed that, in such circumstances, had S forfeited the lease, L would have an arguable claim for relief against forfeiture. The administrative receivership did not alter that. The AGA, without personal guarantee from the administrative receivers, was still an AGA within the meaning of s.16 of the 1995 Act. It therefore fell within the definition in clause 4.7.1.2 of the lease and met the requirements of clause 4.9.1. The only objection which could be taken to it was that it was not in "such form as the landlord reasonably required". Whether S's insistence on the provision of personal guarantees could be considered reasonable was a question of fact to be decided by the trial judge, *Ashworth Frazer Ltd v. Gloucester City Council* [2001] UKHL 59, [2001] 1 W.L.R. 2180, [2001] C.L.Y. 4185 applied. The trial judge might conclude that, in the context of the lease, the considerations which S could take into account in determining whether the form of the AGA was one which he reasonably required did not include the possibility of requiring the administrative receivers to offer personal guarantees. The lease required guarantees from the outgoing tenant and also on behalf of the incoming new tenant. It did not require any guarantees from the administrative receivers or any other third party. It was at least possible that the trial judge would consider that S's rejection of the AGA was not reasonable. In the circumstances it was not appropriate to strike out L's claim for relief from forfeiture.

LEGENDS SURF SHOPS PLC (IN ADMINISTRATIVE RECEIVERSHIP) v. SUN LIFE ASSURANCE SOCIETY PLC, [2005] EWHC 1438, [2005] B.P.I.R. 1145, Laddie, J., Ch D.

2644. Breach of covenant–Quiet enjoyment–Roadworks blocking business entrance–Liability of local authority landlord exercising statutory powers

The claimant local authority brought an action, as landlord of commercial premises, for rent arrears against the defendant tenant (D) who carried on the business of motor vehicle repairs and sales at the commercial premises. D counterclaimed for breach of the covenant of quiet enjoyment and loss of business caused by drainage works. The lease had contained an express covenant by the local authority for quiet enjoyment. In addition, clause 8 of the lease had stated that "The lease is entered into by the Council as proprietor of the Property and nothing herein shall affect or prejudice the Council's direction powers or obligations as the Local Authority". The local authority had been approached by the lessee of adjoining premises to undertake works to a collapsed private sewer which was located under the public footpath. That footpath was directly in front of D's vehicular access into his garage. In pursuance of statutory powers which enabled it to do so, the local authority had agreed to do the drainage works for which they charged a fee. It had been envisaged that the works would take no more than three days and in May 2001, the local authority contractors had begun digging up the public footpath. It was subsequently discovered that the private sewer might in fact be a public sewer for which the water authority would be responsible and whilst the dispute over ownership of the sewer was ongoing, part of the street on which the demised premises was situated was closed to traffic by the local authority. D had been unable to drive cars into or out of the demised premises for six days as a result of the works, after which time a steel plate was placed over the trench in front of the garage to enable access. The works were finally completed after 66 days. D admitted the arrears and at trial the only issue remaining was whether the local authority as landlord had been in breach of the covenant of quiet enjoyment as a result of the works it had undertaken as contractor.

Held, giving judgment for the local authority, that the local authority had been acting within its statutory capacity in relation to the drainage works. Further, that the covenant of quiet enjoyment in the lease was a qualified covenant and that it was overridden by clause 8 of the lease. In addition, it would be contrary to common sense if D were to succeed in his claim, because a local authority would always be in breach of the covenant when carrying out such works, *Manchester, Sheffield and Lincolnshire Railway Co v. Anderson* [1898] 2 Ch. 394 and *Crown Lands Commissioners v. Page* [1960] 2 Q.B. 274, [1960] C.L.Y. 1719 considered.

SOUTHWARK LBC v. ADELEKUN, November 11, 2004, District Judge Fine, CC (Central London). [*Ex rel.* Samuel Waritay, Barrister, Arden Chambers, 2 John Street, London, WC1N 2ES].

2645. Business tenancies–Break clauses–Tenant's intention to vacate–Continued presence of security measures and non delivery of keys

J, the tenant of commercial premises owned by A, sought a declaration that it had validly terminated the lease of the premises under the terms of a break clause. A counterclaimed for a declaration that the retention of barriers and security personnel on the site, along with the non delivery of the keys, meant that J had not "yielded up" the site as required under the break clause.

Held, giving judgment for J, that there was no prescribed method of yielding up premises following the expiry of the notice period stipulated in a break clause. J's actions in emptying the premises were sufficient to show A that it regarded the lease as terminated. Security measures had been retained on site to deter vandals and travellers, and J's continued possession of the keys was not a continuing assertion of its right to occupy the premises.

JOHN LAING CONSTRUCTION LTD v. AMBER PASS LTD [2005] L. & T.R. 12, Robert Hildyard Q.C., Ch D.

2646. Business tenancies–Break clauses–Tenant's notice to operate break– Mistake in notice as to effective date of break–Understanding of reasonable landlord–Validity of notice

The appellant landlord (P) appealed against the dismissal of its application for summary judgment against the respondent business tenant fix to (C). Under the provisions of a break option clause in the underlease C could determine the lease at the end of the third year of the tenancy by giving at least six months' prior notice of its wish to do so. C had given notice by letter to exercise the break option, but had mistakenly specified that the break would take effect on a date some months prior to the end of the third term. P considered that the notice was invalid by virtue of the mistake as it claimed that the reasonable recipient of the notice would not know on which date C wanted to exercise the break. The lower court concluded that C had given effective notice to activate the break clause despite the mistake. In the instant appeal, C submitted that the question was whether a reasonable recipient, knowing the terms of the lease, could have thought that C meant to effect a termination on the earlier mistaken date. C argued that the court should not accept an unrealistic suggestion as to what P might have been expected to have understood from the notice.

Held, dismissing the appeal, that a reasonable landlord, with knowledge of the break clause provisions in the underlease, would have understood that C's letter was intended to operate those provisions in order to break the lease at the date for which the break clause provided and that the effective date specified in C's letter was a mistake. P's suggestions as to how it might have interpreted the notice were unrealistic, *Garston v. Scottish Widows Fund & Life Assurance Society* [1998] 1 W.L.R. 1583, [1998] C.L.Y. 3614 applied. The contractual provisions did not require the giver of a notice to give specific information as to the precise date upon which it intended its notice to take effect in breaking the lease, *Mannai Investment Co Ltd v. Eagle Star Life Assurance Co Ltd* [1997] A.C. 749, [1997] C.L.Y. 3256 applied.

PEER FREEHOLDS LTD v. CLEAN WASH INTERNATIONAL LTD, [2005] EWHC 179, [2005] 1 E.G.L.R. 47, Evans-Lombe, J., Ch D.

2647. Business tenancies–Covenants–Validity of notice–Construction of reinstatement clauses–Inconsistencies between clause to make good and clause to fit out afresh

The appellant tenant (C) appealed against a determination of preliminary issues as to the true construction of its lease of premises from the respondent landlord (F). Shortly before the expiry of the term, F sent C a letter of notice requiring C to reinstate the premises in accordance with a clause of the lease. In due course F issued proceedings against C claiming damages for breach of that clause. C responded by raising preliminary issues as to the validity of the reinstatement notice on the basis that it purported to invoke alternative, and mutually exclusive, covenants, namely clauses 2 (8) B (i) and (ii). The first required the tenant to remove all its furnishings fixtures and fittings and make good (the make good clause); the second to fit out the premises in accordance with a specification scheduled to the lease (the fit out clause). The judge found that the obligations imposed by those clauses were not alternatives in that F was entitled to require C to comply with either or both; and that the letter of notice had validly imposed obligations on C under the clauses, thereby requiring C to discharge the obligations imposed under them, save to the extent that the obligations in the make good clause were inconsistent with and/or rendered unnecessary by the discharge of the obligations in the fit out clause. C submitted that (1) the two clauses were mutually exclusive clauses as they envisaged the premises being yielded up in completely different states, there was nothing in the lease to inform the tenant how to reconcile inconsistencies between the works required by each clause, and the roles of the landlord and his surveyor were completely different in respect of the two clauses; (2) the notice was void for uncertainty.

Held, dismissing the appeal, that (1) it was true that the two clauses envisaged the premises being yielded up in different states, but that did not make them mutually exclusive. The landlord might choose to require only a small number of items to be removed under the make good clause. There was no reason in principle why the landlord should not be able to give notice under the fit out clause and at the same time require the tenant to remove specific fixtures or fittings, insisting on the restoration of those items to their original condition. There might also be fixtures and fittings that would not need to be removed in the event that the fit out clause was invoked. Although there was no machinery to resolve the inconsistency between the clauses, it was obvious that the fit out clause would take precedence. There was nothing in either clause to indicate that the parties intended that they could not be invoked simultaneously. In both clauses the surveyor was concerned with the "finished product". Although the landlord was entitled to approve the finishes under the fit out clause that was not a reason for saying that the two clauses were mutually exclusive. The judge had been right to hold that the two clauses were not mutually exclusive. (2) It was implicit in the lease that the precise scope of work required under clause 2(8) might not be defined at the end of the term or when notice was given by F and that this would only become clear when the details of the work required to be carried out in accordance with the schedules to the lease were finalised. The notice was not therefore void for uncertainty.

FAIRGATE INTERNATIONAL LTD v. CITIBANK INTERNATIONAL PLC, [2005] EWCA Civ 569, [2006] 1 P. & C.R. 2, Buxton, L.J., CA (Civ Div).

2648. Business tenancies–Enfranchisement–Occupation–Leasehold property divided into self contained flats–Company held leasehold title to property and let flats out

[Landlord and Tenant Act 1954 Part II; Leasehold Reform Act 1967; Commonhold and Leasehold Reform Act 2002.]

The claimant landlords (S) sought declaratory relief against the defendant tenant (T). S owned the freehold reversion of a property. T, a company, had held the leasehold title to the property under a 52 year lease. The lease had recently ended by effluxion of time. The property was divided into six self contained residential flats and the property also contained an office from which T ran its business of letting the flats. For this purpose T used another company (C) as its agent and a representative of C manned the office and arranged the lettings. Some of the lettings were for a period of just a few weeks and for short lettings a short form of agreement was used which was silent as to rent and length of letting. The essential contract of letting, including rent and length of occupation, was oral for the short lettings. Even though T was a company it sought to acquire the freehold under the Leasehold Reform Act 1967, pursuant to recent changes in the law effected by the Commonhold and Leasehold Reform Act 2002. S opposed T's claim and sought a declaration that T's tenancy was a business tenancy to which the Landlord and Tenant Act 1954 Part II applied to prevent enfranchisement because a company could not satisfy the residence condition. A determination was required as to whether T occupied the property.

Held, refusing the declaration, that T was not a tenant within the 1954 Act as there was no occupation by it of the property. The lettings of the flats involved exclusive possession and so the lettings were tenancies, *Street v. Mountford* [1985] A.C. 809, [1985] C.L.Y. 1893 considered. There was no rule of law that a tenancy had to be for any particular period. Therefore the issue was whether T could also be in occupation of the property as well as its tenants. The high degree of on site management, involving C, did not require or involve a degree of occupation or control of the flats. T's right of entry into the self contained flats was a right upon reasonable notice and was not unrestricted. There was no unrestricted right to enter to perform necessary services. Therefore there was no occupation by T, *Graysim Holdings Ltd v. P&O Property Holdings Ltd* [1996] A.C. 329, [1995] C.L.Y. 2969 applied and *Lee-Verhulst (Investments) Ltd v. Harwood Trust* [1973] Q.B. 204, [1972] C.L.Y. 1981 considered.

SMITH v. TITANATE LTD [2005] 2 E.G.L.R. 63, Judge Roger Cooke, CC (Central London).

2649. Business tenancies–Improvements–Tenant not compelled to accept work carried out by landlord in return for rent increase

[Landlord and Tenant Act 1927 s.3.]

N sought a declaration that its landlord, C, who had made a counter offer under the proviso to the Landlord and Tenant Act 1927 s.3(1) to do certain improvements in return for a rent increase, was not entitled to carry out the improvements unilaterally. N's 65-year lease of a hotel contained a covenant prohibiting exterior alterations. N gave notice under s.3(1) that it intended to install air conditioning. C then issued a counter notice under the proviso to s.3(1) that it would carry out the work in return for a rent increase. N preferred to do the work itself and the parties were unable to agree on the amount of the rent increase. N sought to assign the lease, but C's draft licence to assign included a clause requiring any potential assignee to agree to the works being done by C and the rent increase. N withdrew its improvements notice and brought proceedings seeking a declaration.

Held, granting the declaration, that s.3(1) allowed a court to refuse to a certificate authorising the work, and without the certificate, s.3(4) precluded N from carrying out the work. There was no policy reason to compel N to accept the improvement carried out by C if N no longer wanted to continue with the improvement and this was not affected by the fact that C had expended costs in making the offer under the proviso in s.3(1).

NORFOLK CAPITAL GROUP LTD v. CADOGAN ESTATES LTD, [2004] EWHC 384, [2004] 1 W.L.R. 1458, Etherton, J., Ch D.

2650. **Business tenancies–Security of tenure–Contracting out–Change in identity of tenant from order to grant of lease**

[Landlord and Tenant Act 1954 s.24, s.25, s.26, s.27, s.28, s.38(4)(a).]

B appealed against a county court decision that a 1995 lease of business premises had not excluded the Landlord and Tenant Act 1954 s.24 to s.28. B had entered into negotiations with C, two brothers, for their company, G, to lease premises in a leisure centre. The parties agreed to exclude the security of tenure provisions in the Act. An application for a contracting out order was allowed in G's name with C as sureties, but the lease was ultimately entered into by C.

Held, allowing the appeal, that s.38(4)(a) was not to be given an overly complex interpretation, *Metropolitan Police District Receiver v. Palacegate Properties Ltd* [2001] Ch. 131, [2000] C.L.Y. 3893 followed. There was no reason why an application to exclude security of tenure could not include all parties to the lease negotiations. C had been parties to the application and understood that they were giving up security of tenure protection, and there was substantial similarity between the draft and final leases, with the change in tenant being made for tax purposes, *Palacegate* applied.

BRIGHTON AND HOVE CITY COUNCIL v. COLLINSON, [2004] EWCA Civ 678, [2004] L. & T.R. 24, Brooke, L.J., CA.

2651. **Business tenancies–Service charges–Reasonableness–Management fees included as part of service charge–Jurisdiction of leasehold valuation tribunal to construe lease**

[Landlord and Tenant Act 1985 s.18, s.19.]

The appellant landlord (L) appealed against part of a decision of the leasehold valuation tribunal determining that the management fees, payable as a service charge under the lease of a flat, were unreasonable to the extent that they exceeded £1,000. L had demanded payment of £2,087 in accordance with a clause in the lease as management fees. The tribunal maintained that management charges did not fall within the meaning of service charges for the purposes of the Landlord and Tenant Act 1985 s.18. L argued that the tribunal had no jurisdiction to determine the construction of the lease and in any event had construed it wrongly. Even if the tribunal did have jurisdiction, L argued, it was excluded by s.19(2C) of the 1985 Act in that the tenant (M) had agreed, by entering into the lease, to pay the managing agent's charge of 15 per cent of the total service charges.

Held, dismissing the appeal, that the management costs fell within the definition of service charges for the purposes of s.19 of the 1985 Act. The lease provided for an amount to be payable for services, repairs, maintenance or insurance or the landlord's costs of maintenance. That amount was expressed in the lease to vary, at least in part, according to the "'relevant costs'...in connection with the matters for which the service charge is payable.' On a true interpretation of s.18(1)(b), it was sufficient if part of the amount varied according to relevant costs. It was correct to say that the management charges did vary according to the cost incurred in connection with management. A leasehold valuation tribunal did have jurisdiction to construe a lease if it was necessary to do so in order to determine a matter that the tribunal had to decide. If no alternative provision had been made for construction of the lease, the tribunal was under a duty to construe the lease to the extent that was necessary either for determination of an application under s.19 or to consider how it should exercise any such jurisdiction. In the instant case, although M had agreed under the lease to pay 15 per cent of the management fees, that provision was void by reason of s.19(3).

LONGMINT LTD v. MARCUS [2004] 3 E.G.L.R. 171, Judge Rich Q.C., LandsTr.

2652. Collective enfranchisement–Counter notices–Validity of landlord's counter notice

[Leasehold Reform, Housing and Urban Development Act1993 s.21; Leasehold Reform (Collective Enfranchisement) (Counter-notices) (England) Regulations 2002 (SI 2002 3208) Reg.4.]

The appellant landlord (P) appealed against an order that its counter-notice served in response to a notice of collective enfranchisement was invalid and the respondent (R), as the tenants' nominee purchaser, was entitled to acquire the freehold and leasehold interests in the premises. P owned the freehold of premises. The tenants served a notice of collective enfranchisement. P served a counter-notice under the Leasehold Reform, Housing and Urban Development Act 1993 s.21. The notice did not state, as required by the Leasehold Reform (Collective Enfranchisement) (Counter-notices) (England) Regulations 2002 reg.4, whether the premises were in the area of a scheme approved as an estate management scheme. The premises were not in such an area and the counter-notice should therefore have included a negative statement. The judge found that the requirement in para.4 was mandatory and the counter-notice was therefore invalid. P submitted that the requirement in para.4 was directory and therefore failure to comply with it did not invalidate the notice.

Held, allowing the appeal, that para.4 of the Regulations was not to be treated as if it formed part of the requirements of s.21(3) of the Act. It was a self standing requirement. Neither the Regulations nor the Act expressly stated that a notice was not valid unless it complied with the Act or Regulations. The position was left to the courts to determine as a matter of interpretation. The effect of non compliance with a particular statutory requirement depended on the particular statutory scheme, *Burman v. Mount Cook Land Ltd* [2001] EWCA Civ 1712, [2002] Ch. 256, [2001] C.L.Y. 4174 applied. The substance of the statutory requirement and the reasons for it had to be considered, *Petch v. Gurney (Inspector of Taxes)* [1994] 3 All E.R. 731, [1994] C.L.Y. 2529 applied. The Regulations clearly did not contain essential machinery. Paragraph 4 contained two mutually exclusive separate requirements: in certain circumstances it required a negative statement and in other circumstances it required a positive statement. A mere negative statement could not have been intended to be mandatory. There could be no possible prejudice to the tenants or their nominee purchaser if that information was excluded. Further, there was no suggestion in the discussion paper preceding the Regulations that there could be any benefit to tenants in requiring a negative statement where the premises were not subject to an estate management scheme. Therefore, the requirement in para.4 for a negative statement was not mandatory.

7 STRATHRAY GARDENS LTD v. POINTSTAR SHIPPING & FINANCE LTD; *sub nom.* POINTSTAR SHIPPING & FINANCE LTD v. 7 STRATHRAY GARDENS LTD, [2004] EWCA Civ 1669, [2005] H.L.R. 20, Ward, L.J., CA (Civ Div).

2653. Commonhold and Leasehold Reform Act 2002 (c.15)–Commencement No.3, Saving and Transitional Provisions Order–Wales

COMMONHOLD AND LEASEHOLD REFORM ACT 2002 (COMMENCEMENT NO.3 AND SAVING AND TRANSITIONAL PROVISION) (WALES) ORDER 2005, SI

2005 1353 (W.101; C.59); made under the Commonhold and Leasehold Reform Act 2002 s.181. Commencement details: bringing into force various provisions of the 2002 Act on May 31, 2005; £3.00.

This Order brings into force further provisions of the Commonhold and Leasehold Reform Act 2002 Part 2 including provisions amending the Leasehold Reform, Housing and Urban Development Act 1993; new provisions under which, in certain circumstances, long leaseholders may insure their houses otherwise than with an insurer nominated or approved by the landlord; new provisions requiring landlords to notify long leaseholders that rent is due; new provisions preventing the landlord of a long leaseholder from exercising a right of re-entry or forfeiture on account of the leaseholder's failure to pay rent, service or administration charges where the unpaid amount and the period for which any part of it has been payable do not exceed the amount and period prescribed by regulations; new provisions preventing the landlord of a long leaseholder from serving a forfeiture notice in respect of a breach of covenant or condition in the lease unless the leaseholder admits the breach, or a court or arbitral tribunal has finally determined that the breach has occurred; and changes to the conditions that must be satisfied before the landlord of a long leaseholder can exercise a right of re-entry or forfeiture for failure to pay service charges.

2654. **Demoted tenancies–Review of decisions–Wales**

DEMOTED TENANCIES (REVIEW OF DECISIONS) (WALES) REGULATIONS 2005, SI 2005 1228 (W.86); made under the Housing Act 1996 s.143F. In force: April 30, 2005; £3.00.

The Anti-social Behaviour Act 2003 amended the Housing Act 1985 to allow a secure tenancy of a local housing authority, a housing action trust or a registered social landlord to be brought to an end and replaced with a less secure demoted tenancy by a demotion order made by a county court. The 2003 Act inserted further provisions regarding demoted tenancies. If a landlord wishes to end a demoted tenancy it must serve the tenant with a notice stating that the landlord has decided to apply to the court for an order for possession, setting out the reasons for that decision and informing the tenant of the tenant's right to request a review of the decision. These Regulations make provision about the procedure to be followed in such a review; and provide that a review must be undertaken by a person who was not involved in the original decision. If the original decision was made by an officer then any review of that decision by another officer may only be carried out by an officer occupying a more senior position within the landlord's organisation than the officer who made the original decision. The Regulations also require the landlord to give the tenant notice of the date of the review; enable the tenant to obtain an oral hearing in certain circumstances and explains how that right may be exercised; and set out the details of the review procedure.

2655. **Enfranchisement–Leaseholds–Leasehold valuation tribunal–Adjournment of hearing–Dismissal of application as abuse of process**

[Housing Act 1980 Sch.22 para.2; Leasehold Reform, Housing and Urban Development Act 1993 s.42; Rent Assessment Committee (England and Wales) (Leasehold Valuation Tribunal) Regulations (SI 1993 2408) Reg.4B.]

The appellants (D), who were tenants under long leases, appealed against a refusal by the leasehold valuation tribunal to reinstate a matter which had been dismissed as an abuse of process. D had served notices on the respondent (T), their landlord, under the Leasehold Reform, Housing and Urban Development Act 1993 s.42, exercising their right to acquire new leases on their respective flats. T admitted the rights but disputed the suggested premiums and other terms. D applied to the leasehold valuation tribunal for determination of the disputed matters. D and T agreed on the premium just prior to the first hearing and sought an adjournment since other matters were still in dispute. In November 2003 the leasehold valuation tribunal issued a date by which the parties should confirm their agreement and stated that non compliance would result in the application being dismissed as an abuse of process. The parties were still in dispute by the stipulated date and the leasehold valuation tribunal dismissed the application, purporting to exercise its powers under the Rent Assessment Committee (England and Wales) (Leasehold Valuation Tribunal) Regulations (SI 1993 2408) Reg.4B. D applied to have the matter reinstated, but the leasehold valuation tribunal refused. On appeal, D argued that the leasehold valuation tribunal had no jurisdiction to dismiss the application and that their application had been dismissed by the leasehold valuation tribunal without their having appeared before it to be heard.

Held, allowing the appeal, that (1) while the leasehold valuation tribunal did have power to enforce its rules of process and strike out applications as an abuse of process, it had departed from the requirements of justice in the instant case. The leasehold valuation tribunal's letter of November 2003 fell short of the requirement to give specific notice of its intention to exercise its power under Reg.4B of the 1993 Regulations in the absence of cause being shown to the contrary, and in the absence of opportunity to show cause being given. The sanction applied by the leasehold valuation tribunal was disproportionate to D's fault. (2) The leasehold valuation tribunal's decision in the matter was regulated by the Housing Act 1980 Sch.22 para.2, which provided that a person dissatisfied with a decision of the leasehold valuation tribunal was able to appeal to the Lands tribunal if that person had appeared before the leasehold valuation tribunal. In the instant case, D had "appeared" before the leasehold valuation tribunal when they were granted an adjournment. Accordingly, the dismissal of their application constituted a decision in respect of which D had "appeared" before the leasehold valuation tribunal for the purposes of Sch.22 para.2 and it followed that they were entitled to appeal.

DE CAMPOMAR v. PETTIWARD'S ESTATE TRUSTEES [2005] 1 E.G.L.R. 83, Judge Rich Q.C., Lands Tr.

2656. Enfranchisement – Restrictive covenants – Sub underlease permitting use as "live/work unit" – Concurrent residential and business use

[Leasehold Reform, Housing and Urban Development Act 1993 s.42, s.45, s.46.]

B sought a declaration under the Leasehold Reform, Housing and Urban Development Act 1993 s.46 that C, a sub-underlessee, was not entitled to a new extended lease of a flat, termed a "live/work unit". C used the majority of the flat for living accommodation with only a small part for his work. Although "live/work" use was permitted by a variation to the headlease and in the sub-underlease, the underlease stipulated that the premises were only for factory or office use. C applied by way of a notice under s.42 and B responded with a counter-notice issued under s.45, arguing that the commercial nature of the underlease prevented C from obtaining an extended lease and also that the premises did not amount to separate living and working accommodation.

Held, refusing the application, that C's sub-underlease allowed him to live and work in the unit and he had not breached the restrictions on use in either the headlease or the sub-underlease. "Live/work" amounted to concurrent user and did not require C to use the unit for business purposes. Accordingly, the failure to do so would not breach the covenant.

BISHOPSGATE FOUNDATION v. CURTIS [2004] 3 E.G.L.R. 57, Judge Roger Cooke, CC (Central London).

2657. Forfeiture – Registration – Right to forfeit lease of registered land between execution of transfer of reversion and registration

[Law of Property Act 1925 s.141 (2).]

The appellant (S) appealed against a decision that it was sufficient, for the purposes of a valid forfeiture of a lease by the third respondent (B), that the transfer of the freehold reversion to B had been executed and notice given to the lessee, notwithstanding that the transfer had not been registered. S had leased two floors of business premises from the first respondents (R) who were registered as the freehold proprietors of the premises. S later assigned the lease to the fourth respondents (C). R assigned its reversionary interest in the freehold to the third respondent (B) pursuant to the terms of a transfer document. On the same day, B gave notice to C of the assignment and required C to pay the rent to it. B re entered the premises on the grounds of arrears of rent notwithstanding that the transfer had not been registered at the Land Registry. The issue was whether it was sufficient that the transfer of the reversion had been executed and notice given to the lessee.

Held, dismissing the appeal, that B was the 'person entitled to income' for the purposes of the Law of Property Act 1925 s.141 (2) and was entitled to the right to enforce the lease. The word "entitled" did not of itself import a distinction between legal and equitable interests. It connoted simply an enforceable right to the relevant income. An equitable assignee of the right to rent had such an enforceable right as against the assignor and, at least following notice, against the lessee. It did not matter if in theory that resulted in B having the right to income concurrently with the legal owner. The forfeiture was therefore valid, *Turner v. Walsh* [1909] 2 K.B. 484, *Schalit v. Joseph Nadler Ltd* [1933] 2 K.B. 79 and *John Lewis Properties Plc v. Inland Revenue Commissioners* [2002] 1 W.L.R. 35, [2001] C.L.Y. 5205 considered.

SCRIBES WEST LTD v. RELSA ANSTALT (NO.3); *sub nom.* SCRIBES WEST LTD v. ANSTALT (NO.3), [2004] EWCA Civ 1744, [2005] 1 W.L.R. 1847, Mummery, L.J., CA (Civ Div).

2658. Forfeiture—Rights of re-entry—Prescribed sum and period—Wales

RIGHTS OF RE-ENTRY AND FORFEITURE (PRESCRIBED SUM AND PERIOD) (WALES) REGULATIONS 2005, SI 2005 1352 (W.100); made under the Commonhold and Leasehold Reform Act 2002 s.167, s.179. In force: May 31, 2005; £3.00.

The Commonhold and Leasehold Reform Act 2002 prevents a landlord under a long lease of a dwelling from exercising a right of re-entry or forfeiture for failure by a tenant to pay an amount consisting of rent, service charges or administration charges (or a combination of them) unless the unpaid amount exceeds the prescribed sum or consists of, or includes, an amount which has been payable for more than a prescribed period. These Regulations, which apply only in relation to dwellings in Wales, prescribes the sum of £350 and a period of three years.

2659. Ground rent—Form of notice—Wales

LANDLORD AND TENANT (NOTICE OF RENT) (WALES) REGULATIONS 2005, SI 2005 1355 (W.103); made under the Commonhold and Leasehold Reform Act 2002 s.166. In force: May 31, 2005; £3.00.

These Regulations relate to the form and content of notices requiring the payment of ground rent.

2660. Hostels—Homelessness—Shared and temporary accommodation provided by local authority—Protection from eviction

[Protection from Eviction Act 1977 s.3, s.3A; Housing Act 1985 s.622; Housing Act 1996 s.188.]

The appellant (R) appealed against an order which dismissed his claim that he and his partner (P) had been unlawfully evicted. Their accommodation, consisting of two bedrooms, kitchen and bathroom, had been provided by the respondent local authority under a licence agreement pursuant to the Housing Act 1996 s.188 pending its decision as to whether it had a duty to house them. It was an express term of the licence that R could be required to move from one unit to another and share with a stranger. The local authority later informed R and P that it did have a duty to house them and that they would be offered other accommodation when available. Subsequently R and P were served with a notice to quit for breaching licence rules and evicted without a court order. R had argued that he had been entitled to four weeks' notice followed by an order for possession under the Protection from Eviction Act 1977 s.3(1). The judge held that the accommodation was temporary and had not been occupied as a dwelling for the purposes of s.3 of the 1977 Act. Furthermore, since it was not a "separate and self contained set of premises", it was a hostel within the meaning of the Housing Act 1985 s.622 and did not attract s.3 protection by virtue of being classified as an "excluded tenancy" under s.3A of the 1977 Act. On appeal, R argued that the judge had erred in law by holding that the premises had been occupied (1) as a hostel; (2) not under licence as a dwelling for the purposes of the 1977 Act, since although the accommodation was not originally described as a dwelling and was occupied by R and P pending the local authority's decision concerning their housing rights, the position altered as soon as that decision had been made, the accommodation no longer being occupied for a limited purpose.

Held, dismissing the appeal, that (1) the accommodation was not separate and self contained as R and P were potentially compelled to share it with a stranger and the second bedroom did not constitute separate residential accommodation, *Uratemp Ventures Ltd v. Collins* [2001] UKHL 43, [2002] 1 A.C. 301, [2001] C.L.Y. 4148 and *Brennan v. Lambeth LBC* (1998) 30 H.L.R. 481, [1998] C.L.Y. 3028 applied. (2) The fact that the original intention was for the accommodation to be temporarily occupied did not determine the nature of the residence, which might change over time because of the ongoing relationship between the licensor and licensee. The time to judge whether the accommodation had become the licensee's dwelling was upon the service of the notice to quit. The judge had been wrong to concentrate on the original purpose for which the accommodation had been provided. Following the local authority's recognition of its duty to house, R and P had been allowed to occupy the premises on a basis which could no longer be regarded as transient; therefore the accommodation could then be properly regarded as their dwelling, *Mohamed v. Manek* (1995) 27 H.L.R. 439, [1995] C.L.Y. 2531 distinguished and *Uratemp* applied. However, the appeal failed on the first ground.

ROGERSON v. WIGAN MBC, [2004] EWHC 1677, [2005] 2 All E.R. 1000, Elias, J., QBD.

2661. Lands Tribunal–Jurisdiction–Judicial review–Refusal of permission to appeal against leasehold valuation tribunal decision

[Lands Tribunal Act 1949 s.3(4).]

S, a landlord, sought judicial review of a Lands Tribunal decision refusing permission to appeal against a leasehold valuation tribunal decision disallowing S's service charge expenditure.

Held, refusing the application, that the Lands Tribunal Act 1949 s.3(4) provided that a decision of the Lands Tribunal was final in nature and appeals could only be made on a point of law. S was seeking to reargue the points taken before the leasehold valuation tribunal and the issues of fact, law and valuation involved were those that Parliament had intended the tribunal to determine. Although S had couched its application in terms of a challenge on *Wednesbury* grounds, judicial review would only be granted in exceptional circumstances, *R. (on the application of Sivasubramaniam) v. Wandsworth County Court* [2002] EWCA Civ 1738, [2003] 1 W.L.R. 475, [2003] C.L.Y. 66 applied.

R. (ON THE APPLICATION OF SINCLAIR GARDENS INVESTMENTS (KENSINGTON) LTD) v. LANDS TRIBUNAL; *sub nom.* SINCLAIR GARDENS INVESTMENTS (KENSINGTON) LTD v. LANDS TRIBUNAL, [2004] EWHC 1910, [2004] 3 E.G.L.R. 15, Sullivan, J., QBD (Admin Ct).

2662. Leaseholds–Insurance policies–Notice of cover

LEASEHOLD HOUSES (NOTICE OF INSURANCE COVER) (ENGLAND) (AMENDMENT) REGULATIONS 2005, SI 2005 177; made under the Commonhold and Leasehold Reform Act 2002 s.164. In force: February 28, 2005; £3.00.

Where a long lease of a house requires the tenant to insure it with an insurer nominated or approved by the landlord, a tenant may avoid that requirement if the provisions of the Commonhold and Leasehold Reform Act 2002 are satisfied and he gives a notice of cover to the landlord within the period specified. A notice of cover must specify the name of the insurer, the risks covered by the policy, the amount and period of the cover and the further information prescribed by the Leasehold Houses (Notice of Insurance Cover) (England) Regulations 2004 (SI 2004 3097). These Regulations amend the 2004 Regulations to correct an error.

2663. Leaseholds–Insurance policies–Notice of cover–Wales

LEASEHOLD HOUSES (NOTICE OF INSURANCE COVER) (WALES) REGULATIONS 2005, SI 2005 1354 (W.102); made under the Commonhold and Leasehold Reform Act 2002 s.164. In force: May 31, 2005; £3.00.

Where a long lease of a house requires the tenant to insure it with an insurer nominated or approved by the landlord, a tenant may avoid that requirement if the provisions of the Commonhold and Leasehold Reform Act 2002 relating to the insurer, the interests and risks covered and the amount of the cover, are satisfied and the tenant gives a notice of cover to the landlord within the period specified. A notice of cover must specify the name of the insurer, the risks covered by the policy, the amount and period of the cover and such further information as may be prescribed. These Regulations prescribe the further information that is to be included in a notice of cover.

2664. Leaseholds–Service charges–Consultation requirements–Wales

SERVICE CHARGES (CONSULTATION REQUIREMENTS) (AMENDMENT) (WALES) REGULATIONS 2005, SI 2005 1357 (W.105); made under the Landlord and Tenant Act 1985 s.20, s.20ZA. In force: May 31, 2005; £3.00.

These Regulations, which amend the Service Charges (Consultation Requirements) (Wales) Regulations 2004 (SI 2004 684 (W.72)), provide for the application of the Landlord and Tenant Act 1985 s.20 to certain agreements entered into, by or on behalf of a landlord or superior landlord, for a term of more than twelve months, where relevant costs incurred under the agreement in any accounting period exceed an amount which results in the relevant contribution of any tenant, in respect of that period, being more than £100. The amendments affect any landlord who intends to enter into a qualifying long term agreement on or after May 31, 2005 but only if that person has not previously made up service charge accounts referable to a qualifying long term agreement in respect of the dwellings to which the intended agreement is to relate.

2665. Leases–Assignment–Clauses limiting liability on landlord's covenants–Attempted avoidance of statutory release procedures

[Landlord and Tenant (Covenants) Act 1995 s.3(6)(a), s.8, s.25(1), s.28(1).]

The appellant former lessee of a headlease (P) appealed against an order that it pay damages to the respondent sublesees (M) for breach of the landlord's covenant contained in the subleases to pay rent to the head lessor (H). Clause 6 of the sublease purported to limit P's liability on the covenant if P disposed of its interest in the property. P had assigned the headlease to a third party (D). D then defaulted on the rent and H took action. M joined the action to avoid forfeiture. H and M came to an agreement that M would pay the arrears and H's costs. The trial judge then ordered P to pay indemnifying damages to M. M submitted that the clause purporting to limit P's liability was void under the Landlord and Tenant (Covenants) Act 1995 s.25(1); M further argued that P had not taken the necessary steps outlined in s.8 of the Act to obtain release from its obligations under the lease on assignment of it and was therefore still liable on the covenant. P submitted that the wording of Clause 6 created a personal covenant which was not a covenant "falling to be complied with by the landlord of premises demised by the tenancy" under s.28(1); as such it was exempted from the release procedures under s.3(6)(a) of the Act.

Held, dismissing the appeal, that the covenant was binding on P's successors in title and was therefore a landlord's covenant, *BHP Petroleum Great Britain Ltd v. Chesterfield Properties Ltd* [2001] EWCA Civ 1797, [2002] Ch.

194, [2002] C.L.Y. 3033 applied. The clause purporting to limit P's liability on disposal was void under s.25(1) of the Act as it was a clear attempt to obtain release in advance and was intended to frustrate the provisions of the Act. P was still liable as it had not followed the procedure under s.8 for obtaining release from the covenant.

AVONRIDGE PROPERTY CO LTD v. MASHRU; *sub nom.* LONDON DIOCESAN FUND v. PHITHWA; MASHRU v. AVONRIDGE PROPERTY CO LTD; AVONRIDGE PROPERTY CO LTD v. LONDON DIOCESAN FUND; LONDON DIOCESAN FUND v. AVONRIDGE PROPERTY CO LTD, [2004] EWCA Civ 1306, [2005] 1 W.L.R. 236, Pill, L.J., CA (Civ Div).

2666. Leases–Flats–Grant of long leases for 29 flats sought by tenant–Meaning of "qualifying tenant"–Apportionment of rent

[Leasehold Reform, Housing and Urban Development Act 1993 s.5, s.39, s.56(1)(a).]

The applicant landlord (M) applied for declaratory relief under the Leasehold Reform, Housing and Urban Development Act 1993. M held the freehold of a block of 28 flats of which the respondent H was the tenant. H had served notices under the Act requiring a new grant of long leases for the flats. M refused on the basis that H was not a qualifying tenant because there were no provisions in the Act to amend the lease to apportion the consideration of the rent. If new leases were granted there would be a different lease in force for the parts of the building not included in the flats. Finally, the Act required the surrender and regrant of the leases.

Held, giving judgment for H was a qualifying tenant under s.5(1) and s.39. The new lease would replace the existing lease to the extent of the premises covered by the new lease under s.56(1)(a). Rent could be apportioned under the common law principle of apportionment.

MAURICE v. HOLLOW-WARE PRODUCTS LTD; *sub nom.* MAURICE v. HOLLOWARE PRODUCTS, [2005] EWHC 815, [2005] 2 E.G.L.R. 71, David Donaldson Q.C., Ch D.

2667. Leases–Rent reviews–Tenant's right to review yearly rent

The claimant tenant (H) sought judgment in its dispute with the defendant landlord (C) as to the construction of a rent review clause in a lease governing the commercial tenancy. Under the lease, the "yearly rent" became payable quarterly and in advance from June 24, 1982. The yearly rent was defined as meaning the "appropriate percentage" to the expiration of the term reserved out of the demised premises, namely 60 per cent of the open market rack rental value. Clause 5(3)(i) provided that the landlord had the right to review the yearly rent at specified dates in intervals of seven years. It was common ground that because of the defined meaning of "the appropriate percentage" and Clause 5(3)(ii), the yearly rent for the period from June 24, 1982 could never be less than 60 per cent of the open market value. H wanted a rent review to take place, but C was content with the passing rent of £375,000 per annum and did not wish to initiate a review. C contended that the right contained in clause 5(3) to review the yearly rent was exercisable by the landlords alone. H contended that if no rent review was initiated, then the definition of "the appropriate percentage" had the effect of reducing the passing rent to 60 per cent of the open market rack rental value of the premises on June 24, 1982. H further contended C's interpretation would run contrary to the purpose of a rent review clause and would allow H to convert what was in terms an open review clause into an upward only rent review.

Held, giving judgment for C, that (1) the definition of "the appropriate percentage" expressly contemplated that the 1982 rental value could be increased by review, in which case it was that figure that became the appropriate percentage and in consequence the yearly rent. The problem with C's argument was that it failed to give sufficient weight to the provisions of clause 5(3)(ii) of the deed and, in light of that clause, if no further reviews took place, the yearly rent would remain £375,000 until the end of the term.

Accordingly, the construction of clause 5(3)(i) was to be approached on the basis that if the right to review the rent was exclusive to the landlords, they would be able to avoid a downwards review of the rent simply by refusing to implement the review machinery. H would therefore be held to a rent that could, throughout the remainder of the term, exceed the open market rental value of the premises as defined in accordance with clause 5(3). (2) There was no presumption that a rent review clause, even one incorporating an open review, ought to be exercisable by both parties to the lease, *United Scientific Holdings Ltd v. Burnley BC* [1978] A.C. 904, [1977] C.L.Y. 1758 considered, *Basingstoke and Deane BC v. Host Group* [1988] 1 W.L.R. 348, [1988] C.L.Y. 2069 explained, *Royal Bank of Scotland Plc v. Jennings* (1995) 70 P. & C.R. 459, [1996] C.L.Y. 3805 and *Addin Investments Ltd v. Secretary of State for the Environment* [1997] 1 E.G.L.R. 99, [1997] C.L.Y. 3322 distinguished, *Australian Mutual Provident Society v. National Mutual Life Association of Australasia Ltd* [1995] 1 N.Z.L.R. 581 and *Board of Trustees of the National Provident Fund v. Shortland Securities Ltd* [1996] 1 N.Z.L.R. 45 followed. Everything depended on the form of review that the parties had chosen to incorporate. When, as in the instant case, the lease provided in clear terms for the right to review the rent to be exercisable by the landlord alone, the absence of an upwards only review formula was not sufficient to require or permit the court to construe the clause as requiring either a mandatory review or one that was exercisable by both landlord and tenant. The opening words of clause 5(3)(i) had a clear meaning that had to be given effect to. The reference to a review date of June 24, 1982 was not sufficient to alter that conclusion.

HEMINGWAY REALTY LTD v. CLOTHWORKERS CO; *sub nom.* HEMINGWAY REALTY LTD v. MASTER WARDENS AND COMMONALTY OF FREEMAN OF THE ART OR MYSTERY OF CLOTHWORKERS OF THE CITY OF LONDON, [2005] EWHC 299, [2005] L.& T.R. 21, Patten, J., Ch D.

2668. Leases–Restrictive covenants–Construction of user clause

The claimant lessee (J) sought the determination of whether the grant of a sublease of certain premises would breach a user clause of a lease under which it held the premises. The first defendant freeholder (M) was the successor in title to the original lessor. The lease contained a user clause prohibiting use of the premises, without previous written consent, for the trades of "victuallers, vintners, tavern keepers, restaurateurs and coffeehouse keepers". J proposed allowing a subtenant to occupy the premises as a retail outlet that sold preprepared sandwiches and beverages for consumption mainly off the premises. J sought a declaration (i) that use of the premises as a shop for the sale of preprepared sandwiches and hot and cold drinks for consumption off the premises did not constitute a breach of the user clause or (ii) that use of the premises for the sale of such goods off the premises with ancillary consumption on the premises was not a breach of the clause. M sought a declaration that use of the premises as a shop for the sale of preprepared sandwiches breached the user clause

Held, giving judgment for J in part, that the court had to construe the covenant to ascertain whether the intended use was within the scope of the forbidden activities and how the expressions "victualler" and "coffeehouse keeper" were understood at the time the lease was entered into, being the 1950s. The ordinary and common understanding of "victualler" in the 1950s was no more than that of a publican. The meaning of "coffeehouse keeper" extended to a snack bar where food was consumed on the premises and accordingly the first declaration sought by J was granted with the inclusion of the word "exclusively", *Mortimer Investments Ltd v. Mount Eden Land Ltd* (Unreported, March 26, 1997) considered.

JOINT LONDON HOLDINGS LTD v. MOUNT COOK LAND LTD; *sub nom.* MOUNT COOK LAND LTD v. JOINT LONDON HOLDINGS LTD, [2005] EWHC 507, *The Times*, May 12, 2005, Blackburne, J., Ch D.

2669. Leases-Surrender-Need for unequivocal conduct

The appellant landlord (B) appealed against a decision that it had accepted a surrender of the tenancy by the respondent tenant (T).The tenancy had been taken byT in August 2000, but she had not paid any rent under the terms of the tenancy and had vacated the property soon after its commencement. T wrote to B's management agent stating that she no longer wished to deal with either the agent or B. B was aware that the property had been vacated, but informed the local authority that T had been liable for business rates as the tenant of the property. During the relevant period B had not made any demands upon T for rent arrears or service charges. In November 2001 B forfeited the tenancy for non payment of rent and sought all the arrears. The judge found that B had accepted T's surrender of the tenancy by its failure to demand the service charges and by failing to make any demands for rent arrears. B argued that the judge had been wrong to find that it had accepted T's surrender of the tenancy since any acceptance had to be expressed by deed or by operation of law. It argued that its mere failure to act by not making demands for the outstanding payments could not amount to unequivocal conduct sufficient for acceptance of the purported surrender.

Held, allowing the appeal, that for there to have been an acceptance at law by a landlord of a tenant's surrender of a tenancy, there had to be unequivocal conduct by the parties that was inconsistent with the tenancy. All that happened in the instant case was that the landlord had not demanded rent arrears or service charges from the tenant. A mere omission to do something was not unequivocal conduct. Accordingly, in the instant case, there were no acts by B amounting to unequivocal conduct capable of constituting acceptance of the purported surrender..

BELLCOURT ESTATES LTD v. ADESINA, [2005] EWCA Civ 208, [2005] 2 E.G.L.R. 33, Peter Gibson, L.J., CA (Civ Div).

2670. Licences-Agreements-Erection of advertising stations-No tenancy created

[Landlord and Tenant Act 1954 Part II, s.23.]

The applicant company (C) sought a declaration that it held tenancies of 13 advertising sites belonging to the respondent landlord (M). M counterclaimed for a declaration that C occupied those and a 14th site as licensee. M had agreed that C could erect advertising stations on 13 sites in return for an agreement that C would pay rent, calculated as a percentage of profit. M gave C licence to enter the land and C erected concrete bases to which advertising hoardings were bolted. Draft written agreements were prepared but never executed. At the end of the period covered by the agreement, M purported to terminate C's rights of occupation, but C claimed that it had a tenancy protected by the Landlord and Tenant Act 1954 Part II. C argued that (1) it had enjoyed exclusive possession of the area occupied by the concrete bases and it had factual possession of the sites; (2) it was an annual tenant of the 14th site.

Held, refusing the application, that (1) whether the nature of C's use of the sites was referable to a tenancy or a licence did not depend on the labels used by the parties but on the substantive rights and obligations conferred and imposed on C, *Street v. Mountford* [1985] A.C. 809, [1985] C.L.Y. 1893 applied. On the facts, the sites were not the concrete bases but larger undefined areas of land owned by M. Only general addresses were referred to in the draft documentation, not specific locations. Further, the draft documentation did not contain an express grant of a right of way to and from the sites, which was a surprising omission if the demise was limited to the concrete bases. The terms of the agreement made far better sense as licences than tenancies. As the sites were undefined areas of land owned by M, it was clear that there had been no intention to grant exclusive possession to C. (2) The draft documents in relation to the 14th site showed an intention to grant a lease over the area occupied by the advertising station. It was much larger than the other structures and would be much more difficult to remove. The inclusion of a prohibition against assignment, subletting or parting with possession clearly showed an intention to grant a tenancy. C occupied the 14th site as a periodic annual tenant. C's acts of use, maintenance and control of the site for the purposes of its business amounted to occupation for the purposes of s.23 of the Act, having regard to the purpose of the provisions of Part II of the Act, the nature of the site and the use to which it might reasonably be put, *Graysim Holdings Ltd v. P&O Property Holdings Ltd* [1996] A.C. 329, [1995] C.L.Y. 2969 applied.

CLEAR CHANNEL UK LTD v. MANCHESTER CITY COUNCIL, [2004] EWHC 2873, [2005] 2 P. & C.R. 2, Etherton, J., Ch D.

2671. New business tenancies—Break clauses—Fresh evidence as to intentions of developer—Admissibility—Correct approach to determining terms of break clause

[Landlord and Tenant Act 1954 s.35.]

The appellant landlord (C) appealed against a decision that a new unopposed tenancy for a term of 14 years requested by the respondent lessee (D) of business premises should include a redevelopment break clause operable after five years on a notice period of 11 months. The effect of the judge's order was that the tenancy could not be terminated earlier than February 2010. C had originally intended to sell the property to a developer who planned to redevelop that building and several others in the vicinity as an island site. Prior to the appeal hearing, C successfully applied to have new evidence admitted to the effect that the property had been sold to another developer (S) who intended to redevelop the property as a stand alone project. The new evidence showed that S contemplated a development of the property which was radically different from the scheme which had been put before the judge. C argued that (1) having found that the property was "ripe for redevelopment", the judge had applied the wrong test in determining the terms of the break clause, and (2) in the light of the new evidence, the judge's order should be set aside and a break clause exercisable on six months' notice at any time after September 2005 inserted.

Held, allowing the appeal in part, that (1) The judge correctly balanced the redevelopment aspirations of the landlords against the business interests of the tenant without allowing the latter to frustrate the former. The only scheme of development which had been presented to the judge was the original island site scheme. He had had regard to the nature and timing of that scheme in determining the nature of the break clause. In selecting the five year period, the judge might have been at the borders of the discretion given in the Landlord and Tenant Act 1954 s.35, but he had not exceeded it, *Adams v. Green* [1978] 2 E.G.L.R. 46, [1979] C.L.Y. 1576, *JH Edwards & Sons v. Central London Commercial Estates* [1984] 2 E.G.L.R. 103, [1984] C.L.Y. 1878 considered. (2) It was clear that the assertion that S intended to develop the property as a stand alone site was false. In fact, S planned to assemble the island site as part of a joint venture. There was an argument for dismissing the appeal on that ground alone but, once the decision to admit the fresh evidence had been taken, it would be unjust for the appeal court not to take it into account, *Hertfordshire Investments Ltd v. Bubb* [2000] 1 W.L.R. 2318, [2000] C.L.Y. 562 and *Bwllfa and Merthyr Dare Steam Collieries (1891) Ltd v. Pontypridd Waterworks Co* [1903] A.C. 426 considered. A fixed term of the length ordered by the judge below would impede S's fall back strategy of selling the property to a developer within two to four years. Thus, in all the circumstances, the judge's order would be varied to permit the landlord to terminate the tenancy on or after June 1, 2008. However, in the absence of additional evidence as to the length of notice required, the notice period specified in the judge's order would remain unchanged.

DAVY'S OF LONDON (WINE MERCHANTS) LTD v. CITY OF LONDON CORP; DAVY'S OF LONDON (WINE MERCHANTS) LTD v. SAXON LAND BV, [2004] EWHC 2224, [2004] 3 E.G.L.R. 39, Lewison, J., Ch D.

2672. Options–Leases–Assignment–Interpretation of option agreement concerning reassignment of lease

The appellants (C) appealed and the respondent (L) cross appealed against the judge's interpretation ([2004] EWHC 496, [2004] 12 E.G.C.S. 171) of a lease and an option agreement between the parties. L had granted C a lease on a property. The parties had also entered into a separate option agreement under which C could reassign the lease back to L for no consideration. The option was exercisable in 2004 and in 2010. In due course, C assigned the lease. In March 2003, C gave notice under the option agreement. L contended that C could only give effective notice if they were, and had remained since the date of the assignment, the registered proprietors of the lease. Accordingly, C assigned the lease back to themselves. Thereafter C again gave notice under the option agreement. A dispute then arose between the parties as to the interpretation of the lease and the option agreement. The judge held that the exercise of the option in March 2003 had been invalid because the lease had not then been vested in C. However, there was nothing to stop C from exercising the option after they had reassigned the lease back to themselves, in spite of the fact that the lease had not been vested in C throughout. C appealed in respect of the former decision, whilst L appealed against the latter. L argued that the option ceased to be exercisable once C had assigned the lease.

Held, dismissing the appeal and cross appeal, that (1) the option holder under the agreement was the "purchaser". The option agreement defined the purchaser as C and did not allow any change to the identity of the purchaser. Thus the judge had been correct to hold that the option could not be exercised if C were not the registered proprietors of the lease. The option agreement showed that the parties were prohibited from any assignment of the agreement. It also showed that the character of the person exercising the option was material. Accordingly, it followed that "purchaser" as defined in the option agreement had to be the registered proprietors of the lease. As C had not been the registered proprietors of the lease in March 2003, it followed that their attempt to exercise the option had been invalid. (2) The option holder was described as the "purchaser" and not by another expression, which restricted capacity to that of a tenant under a lease. The option agreement was not personal to the purchaser in the sense that the purchaser had to retain exactly the same interest in the lease throughout the duration of the option agreement. The judge had therefore been correct to hold that the option became exercisable again when the lease had been revested in C.

BP OIL UK LTD v. LLOYDS TSB BANK PLC; MOBIL EXPLORATION & PRODUCTION UK LTD v. LLOYDS TSB BANK LTD, [2004] EWCA Civ 1710, [2005] 1 E.G.L.R. 61, Kennedy, L.J., CA (Civ Div).

2673. Options–Surrender of rent free life tenancy–Undue influence

D, the holder of a rent free life tenancy, appealed against a decision that an option agreement was not affected by undue influence. Under the agreement, D had contracted to give up his tenancy if he failed to build a bungalow on the property within a certain time. D had lived all his life on land that he owned. His bungalow was demolished after being condemned by the local council and he obtained planning permission to build a replacement. In the meantime, D lived in a caravan. He sold the land to M in return for the life tenancy. One month before the planning permission expired, M laid foundations and entered into the option agreement with D, which provided that he would surrender his life tenancy for a premium of £5,000 if the bungalow was not completed within three years. At the end of the three years, M sought to enforce the option after D had failed to commence building.

Held, allowing the appeal, that D had shown a dependency on M, who was in a much stronger position and able to dictate disadvantageous terms to D, *Royal Bank of Scotland Plc v. Etridge (No.2)* [2001] UKHL 44, [2002] 2 A.C. 773, [2001] C.L.Y. 4880 applied. The judge below had failed to consider whether the option agreement required an explanation as to why D had given M the right to acquire the rent free life tenancy for a mere £5,000 and there was no basis for finding that D had obtained any benefit from the agreement.

MacKLIN v. DOWSETT, [2004] EWCA Civ 904, [2004] 2 E.G.L.R. 75, Auld, L.J., CA.

2674. Possession claims–Adjournment–Power to order adjournment to enable tenant to defeat claim

[Housing Act 1988 s.9(6), Sch.2 Part I Ground 8.]

The appellant tenant (M) appealed against the district judge's refusal to adjourn an application for possession brought by the respondent housing association (N). M was an assured tenant of residential property belonging to N. N had begun possession proceedings on the basis of M's arrears of rent. At least eight weeks' rent was unpaid at the date of the hearing before the district judge. On the face of it the district judge was, on that basis, obliged to order possession under the Housing Act 1988 Sch.2 Part I Ground 8. M was entitled to housing benefit and had asserted that her inability to pay the rent had been caused by the unjustified failure of the housing benefit authority to pay housing benefit to her. M had applied to adjourn the possession proceedings in order to give herself time to obtain money either to meet the arrears, or at least to bring her below the eight-week threshold at which the court was obliged to order possession. M argued that it was in the interests of justice to adjourn the hearing of the claim in order to afford her a defence which she did not have at the date of the first hearing.

Held, dismissing the appeals, that in principle, it was not legitimate for the court, before it was satisfied that the landlord was entitled to possession, to order an adjournment designed to achieve a result which the law current at the date of the hearing would not permit, *R. v. Walsall Justices, ex p. W* [1990] 1 Q.B. 253, [1990] C.L.Y. 774 applied. The power to adjourn a hearing date for the purpose of enabling a tenant to reduce the arrears below the threshold in Sch. 2 Part I Ground 8 of the Act could only be exercised in exceptional circumstances. The power was not to be exercised so as to defeat the policy of the Act or the rights which it conferred on landlords, *Bristol City Council v. Lovell* [1998] 1 W.L.R. 446, [1998] C.L.Y. 3055 considered. The fact that arrears were attributable to maladministration on the part of the housing benefit authority was not an exceptional circumstance, and the non receipt of housing benefit could not, of itself, amount to an exceptional circumstance which would justify the exercise of the power to adjourn so as to enable the tenant to defeat the claim. Once the court had expressed the conclusion that the landlord was entitled to possession then, by virtue of s.9(6) of the Act, there was no power to grant an adjournment in any circumstances.

NORTH BRITISH HOUSING ASSOCIATION LTD v. MATTHEWS; NORTH BRITISH HOUSING ASSOCIATION LTD v. SNAITH; NORTH BRITISH HOUSING ASSOCIATION LTD v. MASOOD; LONDON AND QUADRANT HOUSING LTD v. MORGAN, [2004] EWCA Civ 1736, [2005] 1 W.L.R. 3133, Brooke, L.J., CA (Civ Div).

2675. Possession orders–Stay of execution–Anti social behaviour orders–Relevant considerations

The applicant tenants (H), who were awaiting the hearing of their appeal against a possession order, applied for a stay of execution of the order pending the hearing. Following complaints from neighbouring tenants, the landlord (M) had originally obtained an injunction requiring H to leave the area immediately. At that time H had been a tenant of M for three years and there had been no previous complaints against them. M had given no warning to H that such a measure was about to be taken. A partial stay of the injunction had been granted, but M had then obtained the possession order and also an anti social behaviour order, due to come into immediate effect, which banned H from entering an exclusion zone which included the area in which they lived. Permission to appeal against that order had also been granted. H had four children and the orders had been applied for without consultation with social services or the education authorities family. In the circumstances, undertakings from H as to their behaviour and the control of their children, with the possible sanction of imprisonment for any significant breach of the undertakings, would be sufficient to protect the interests of neighbouring tenants. M could apply for the stay to be lifted were there further complaints against H.

MOAT HOUSING GROUP-SOUTH LTD v. HARRIS (APPLICATION FOR STAY OF EXECUTION), [2004] EWCA Civ 1852, *The Times*, January 13, 2005, Brooke, L.J., CA (Civ Div).

2676. Protected tenancies–Joint tenancies–Transitional provisions–Continuity of protected tenant status–Scope of s.34(1)(b) Housing Act 1988

[Housing Act 1988 s.34(1)(b).]

The appellant landlord (S) appealed against a decision that the first respondent (T) was entitled to protected tenancy status by virtue of the Housing Act 1988 s.34(1)(b). T had been a tenant in S's property under a succession of annual tenancy agreements, with a variety of other tenants, which had begun after the 1988 Act came into effect. T's first tenancy was as a joint tenant along with two other tenants, one of whom had immediately previously been a joint tenant in the same property with a tenant who had been a protected tenant. S sought possession of the property. T submitted that the protected tenancy status could be passed on to new joint tenants, as long as any of the immediately previous tenants, alone or jointly with others, took a new tenancy.

Held, allowing the appeal, that there was nothing to indicate that s.34(1)(b) was intended to extend its protection to parties who became tenants of the landlord for the first time after the commencement of the new assured tenancy regime in the 1988 Act. The function of the transitional provision was to protect the original protected tenant who, alone or jointly with others, made a new tenancy after the commencement of the 1988 Act on January 15, 1989. The whole premise of the transitional protection afforded by s.34(1)(b) was that the protected tenant was a protected tenant on the commencement of the Act. Such a requirement was inherent in the subsection. Therefore T was not a tenant within the protection of s.34(1)(b).

SECRETARIAL & NOMINEE CO LTD v. THOMAS, [2005] EWCA Civ 1008, [2006] H.L.R. 5, Auld, L.J., CA (Civ Div).

2677. Protected tenancies–Possession claims–Landlord relying on availability of alternative accommodation owned by tenant

[Rent Act 1977 s.98(1)(a).]

The appellant landlord (L) appealed against a decision refusing to grant its application for possession of a residential property let to the respondent (S). The property had been let to S in 1978, and accordingly the provisions of the Rent Act 1977 applied. L had sought possession on the ground, inter alia, that suitable alternative accommodation owned by S would be available to S when a possession order took effect. That alternative accommodation was one of many residential properties owned by S and rented out as investment properties. It had been held on an assured shorthold tenancy by one of S's tenants, but that tenancy on the likely impact of the orders on the children. It was common ground that the events which had resulted in the application for the original injunction had been triggered by the much more serious conduct of Hs former neighbours. M submitted that the judge's findings of fact at the hearing that resulted in the orders described an appalling history of anti social behaviour on the part of H and their children and, unless and until those findings were overturned, the presumption must be that the other residents in the locality should be given the fullest attention.

Held, granting the application, that in deciding whether to grant a stay, consideration had to be given to the possible prejudice to the parties in respect of the outcome of the appeal. Consideration also had to be given to the impact upon the children of enforcing the order and its implications for their education. The court took into account that the proceedings had been brought without

LANDLORD AND TENANT

comment upon.

Held, allowing the application, that the award gave the appearance that the arbitrator had made his calculations on a basis that was contrary to the agreed assumptions of the parties and confused the valuation methods used by their experts. Therefore a substantial injustice had been caused to S and the award was remitted to the arbitrator, *Warborough Investments Ltd v. S Robinson & Sons (Holdings) Ltd* [2003] EWCA Civ 751, [2004] 2 P. & C.R. 6, [2003] C.L.Y. 2778, *Checkpoint Ltd v. Strathclyde Pension Fund* [2003] EWCA Civ 84, [2003] L. & T.R. 22, [2003] C.L.Y. 190 and *Zermalt Holdings SA v. Nu-Life Upholstery Repairs Ltd* [1985] 2 E.G.L.R. 14, [1985] C.L.Y. 95 considered.

ST GEORGE'S INVESTMENT CO v. GEMINI CONSULTING LTD, [2004] EWHC 2353, [2005] 1 E.G.L.R. 5, John Jarvis Q.C., Ch D.

2679. Rent reviews-Delay-Validity of rent review

The appellant tenant (D) appealed against a decision in relation to a rent review clause. D had been granted a 12 year lease from February 5, 1997 at a rent. The lease contained provisions for rent review at the end of every four years. On February 19, 2002, 54 weeks after the first review date, the respondent landlords (L) gave D notice that the basic rent from the review date of February 5, 2001 was £30,000 per annum. D replied by letter that the notice was invalid as the terms of the lease required one year notice of any rent review. L asserted that the rent review provisions in the lease had been properly implemented because the rent review clause contained no time limit by which a trigger notice had to be served. Thereafter a review was conducted by an independent surveyor which fixed the rent at £28,000. Two issues were raised before the judge: (i) whether L had lost the right to review the rent as a consequence of failing to serve a trigger notice on or before February 5, 2001; (ii) if not, whether D's letter had operated as a valid counter notice. The judge found against D on both issues such that D was fixed with the rent specified in the trigger notice. The judge found that it was open to L to serve the trigger notice after the rent review date specified in the lease because time was not of the essence of that date and that D's letter was not a valid counter notice as it challenged L's right to review the rent, not the amount proposed. D argued that time was of the essence of the time limit in the rent review clause.

Held, allowing the appeal in part, (Brooke, L.J. dissenting on the issue of counter notice) that (1) the judge had reached the correct conclusion on the first issue in holding that, though the trigger notice was late, it was nonetheless valid because time was not of the essence of the time limit in the rent review clause relating to trigger notices. There was by contrast the express provision that time was of the essence in respect of the counter notice. The fact that the parties had described the rent review as an "option" for the landlord did not mean that it was to be treated as an option in the legal sense, with the consequence that time was of the essence of any stipulation as to its implementation, *United Scientific Holdings Ltd v. Burnley BC* [1978] A.C. 904, [1977] C.L.Y. 1758 applied. L was accordingly entitled to implement the rent review with effect from February 5, 2001. (2) As to whether D's letter constituted a valid counter notice under the lease, the counter notice had to be in terms which were sufficiently clear to L, *Nunes v. Davies Laing & Dick Ltd* (1986) 51 P. & C.R. 310, [1986] C.L.Y. 1923 applied. However that test should not be approached in a legalistic way but with a sensible degree of common sense. The question was simply whether the letter informed the landlord that the tenant did not accept the proposed annual amount. The landlord's actual reaction to the counter notice played no part in the legal test to be applied, *Patel v. Earlspring Properties Ltd* [1991] 2 E.G.L.R. 131, [1992] C.L.Y. 2742 considered. It was clear from his letter that D was not accepting L's proposed rent. The purpose of the letter, which was headed "Rent Increase" was to dispute the rent increase. Accordingly, D had served a valid counter notice and therefore the rent under the lease with effect from February 5, 2001 was £28,000 per annum. D's appeal on the second issue succeeded.

LANCECREST LTD v. ASIWAJU, [2005] EWCA Civ 117, [2005] L.&T.R. 22, Brooke, L.J., CA (Civ Div).

2680. **Rent reviews – Expert – Procedure for appointment of independent chartered surveyor – Jersey**

The appellant landlord (E) appealed against the dismissal of its application challenging the appointment of a surveyor in a rent review dispute with the respondent tenant (B). B operated a clothing and household retail store from the demised premises in Jersey. The lease allowed for an independent surveyor to be appointed by the President of the Royal Institute of Chartered Surveyors as an expert to decide the rent review issue. The surveyor had to have relevant experience of assessing "broadly similar" properties in Jersey unless no such properties existed, in which case experience of properties in the UK was acceptable. B applied for a surveyor to be appointed, and the President decided that there were no surveyors with the relevant experience in Jersey and appointed a London-based surveyor. E challenged the appointment, but its application was dismissed by the Royal Court, which held that the appointment had been properly made. In the instant appeal, E argued that (1) the premises had been wrongly identified as a "variety store" with the result that no surveyors with relevant experience were available in Jersey; (2) the President's decision had been unreasonable in the *Wednesbury* sense because he had taken account of irrelevant information in requiring that the surveyor appointed be a member of his own panel of experts.

Held, dismissing the appeal, that (1) the President had adopted the correct approach, in accordance with industry practice, of first deciding what retail category the premises fell in to. The evidence of B's expert pointed clearly towards it being within the "variety store" category and that evidence was to be preferred. As there were no similar variety stores on Jersey, it was right that an outside expert be appointed. (2) The President had followed the required procedure and had taken into account the relevant factors for the appointment of the surveyor; his decision could not be impugned by the fact that he had then used his discretion to add the additional "good sense" factor of trying to choose a member of his own panel.

EPOCH PROPERTIES LTD v. BRITISH HOME STORES (JERSEY) LTD [2004] 3 E.G.L.R. 34, Michael Beloff Q.C., CA (Jer).

2681. **Rent reviews – Rental value – Supermarkets – Failure to disregard potential for petrol station despite restrictive covenant**

[Arbitration Act 1996 s.69.]

The applicant (S) applied under the Arbitration Act 1996 s.69 for permission to appeal against an arbitrator's rent determination in respect of leased premises comprising a retail store and a petrol filling station. The lease provided for five yearly rent reviews. The rent initially payable was split as between the retail store on the one hand and the filling station on the other. The lease stated that any effect on rental value attributable to the existence and carrying on of the business of the petrol filling station was to be disregarded when ascertaining the open market rental value of the store for the purposes of a rent review. The arbitrator had disregarded the petrol filling station when ascertaining the comparative open market value, but took into account the fact that there was the potential for a petrol filling station. S argued that (1) the arbitrator's treatment of the filling station was obviously wrong as a matter of law as he had overlooked the extent of the hypothetical demise and the restricted use covenant in the hypothetical lease which did not permit use as a filling station, and (2) the arbitrator's error substantially affected the rights of the parties pursuant to s.69(3) of the Act giving rise to a right of appeal.

Held, refusing the application, that (1) it was clear from the lease that the subject matter of the hypothetical lease was the retail store alone. Accordingly the arbitrator was wrong in concluding that the site had the capacity for a petrol filling station. (2) The arbitrator did not assume that the hypothetical demise had a petrol filling station, merely that there was potential for a petrol filling station. Any adjustments which he made to comparables in relation to the potential for a filling station must have been less than seven and a half per cent. Of the comparables identified, two had no filling station and another had a filling station but it was to be disregarded on rent review. Accordingly the parties' rights were not substantially affected and thus the right of appeal under s.69(3) did not arise.

SAFEWAY STORES v. LEGAL AND GENERAL ASSURANCE SOCIETY LTD, [2004] EWHC 415, [2005] 1 P. & C.R. 9, Lewison, J., Ch D.

2682. **Repair covenants – Breach – Value of reversionary interest**

D brought a Part 20 claim for damages for breach of covenants in a lease of an office building of which S was the tenant. The lease had run for 25 years from October 1976. Prior to its termination in October 2001, S had carried out a number of repairs. D alleged that despite the works, S had not adequately performed the obligations in the repairing and decorating covenants in the lease, and in the current application he sought damages in the region of £200,000. S contended that even if there had been breaches of the covenants D had suffered no loss as he had sold the property in March 2002 for over £2.6 million and there had therefore been no diminution in the property's value.

Held, giving judgment for S, that D had not suffered a loss given the price at which he had been able to dispose of the property. Although S had been in breach of the covenants to the value of approximately £70,000, D had "achieved an extremely advantageous sale" that was far higher than could have been anticipated and did not reflect the state of the premises. There had thus been no diminution in value of D's reversionary interest and he was not entitled to damages.

SIMMONS v. DRESDEN, [2004] EWHC 993, 97 Con. L.R. 81, Judge Richard Seymour Q.C., QBD (T&CC).

2683. Repair covenants–Breach of covenant–Implied repairing covenant under Landlord and Tenant Act 1985 s.11–Measure of damages

[Landlord and Tenant Act 1985 s.11.]

The appellant landlord (E) appealed against an order in favour of the respondent (S), a secure tenant of one of E's flats, in an action based on E's breach of its repairing covenant. S had complained for years about the condition of his flat. After inspection, E had concluded that S needed to move out while substantial repairs were undertaken. S had refused and instead sought compensation for stress and anxiety caused by the disrepair, which E treated as a claim for damages for breach of the implied repairing covenant in the Landlord and Tenant Act 1985 s.11. After two years of various offers of alternative accommodation, expert reports, orders, appeals and failures to attend court, S had finally moved out. The judge had awarded S general damages of £19,000 plus costs. E argued that (1) the judge had failed to follow the guidance set out in *Wallace v. Manchester City Council* (1998) 30 H.L.R. 1111, [1998] C.L.Y. 3678 by not cross checking the award against the average annual rent of £2,600 and should have reduced the award to reflect S's refusal to vacate; (2) he had failed to award E its costs of hearings at which costs had been reserved or allow its awarded High Court costs to be set off against the damages award.

Held, allowing the appeal, that when assessing general damages for discomfort and inconvenience arising from a landlord's breach of the repairing covenant implied by s.11 of the Act, a court should not award damages in excess of the rent payable during the breach without giving clear reasons for departing from the guidance in *Wallace*. The judge's award was manifestly excessive, and he had not explained how he had reached it. S had wrongly failed to mitigate his damage by not accepting offers of alternative accommodation, in breach of his own undertakings and court orders. Accordingly, there was nothing which appeared to warrant departure from the basic rule that damages should not exceed the rental value of the premises, and a substantial discount was required to reflect S's conduct. The appropriate award was £8,000, *Wallace* applied. (2) The judge's behaviour in refusing to reconsider the reserved costs or to deal with E's application for set off had been unacceptable. E was entitled to its costs of the interlocutory hearings, and as the High Court order for costs was effectively an order made in the proceedings, there was no reason why the costs could not be set off against the damages payable to the plainly impecunious S.

ENGLISH CHURCHES HOUSING GROUP v. SHINE; *sub nom*. SHINE v. ENGLISH CHURCHES HOUSING GROUP; ENGLISH CHURCHES HOUSING GROUP v. SHRINE, [2004] EWCA Civ 434, [2004] H.L.R. 42, Keene, L.J., CA.

2684. Repair covenants–Dilapidations–Adequacy of repair as opposed to replacement

The applicant landlord (R) sought damages against the respondent former tenant (B) for alleged breach of repairing covenants within the lease. The covenants obliged B to repair the rented property, and to yield it up "in good and substantial repair" at the end of the lease. R alleged that when B surrendered the lease, the roof of the property was in a dilapidated condition and required replacement. R replaced it and sought the cost from B. B maintained that repair work which it had carried out immediately before leaving had been sufficient to comply with the covenant.

Held, granting the application, that where a landlord and tenant disputed whether part of the demised premises needed replacement or repair, replacement would only be required if repair were not reasonably possible, *Ultraworth Ltd v. General Accident Fire & Life Assurance Corp Plc* [2000] L. &

T.R. 495, [2001] C.L.Y. 4191 and *Dame Margaret Hungerford Charity Trustees v. Beazeley* (1994) 26 H.L.R. 269, [1993] C.L.Y. 2544 considered. A repair covenant of the type in the instant case did not require the property to be put into perfect repair or pristine condition. (1) The experts' reports and advice obtained by B showed that the roof was capable of being repaired to the covenanted standard and therefore replacement had been unnecessary. (2) On the evidence, the actual repair work carried out by B was sufficiently good to render the roof in substantial repair.

RIVERSIDE PROPERTY INVESTMENTS LTD v. BLACKHAWK AUTOMOTIVE, [2004] EWHC 3052, [2005] 1 E.G.L.R. 114, Judge Peter Coulson Q.C., QBD (TCC).

2685. Secure tenancies–Grounds for possession–Meaning of "induced" under Sch.2 Ground 5 Housing Act 1985–False statement inducing grant of tenancy–Withdrawal of housing benefit creating arrears situation

[Housing Act 1985 Sch.2.]

The appellant local authority appealed against a recorder's decision that it had failed to establish a ground for possession of the subject property, which had been let to the respondent (R) and her son on a secure tenancy. R applied for and was granted housing benefit in relation to the subject property. Prior to being housed, R stated that she did not own any property or receive rental income from any property. In fact R jointly owned a property with her son and received rental income from it. The local authority sought to recover overpaid housing benefit from R and served a notice seeking possession, relying on the Housing Act 1985 Sch.2 Ground 1 and Ground 5. The local authority argued that the recorder had erred in law in his approach to the evidence, and that had the correct approach been applied, then he would have concluded that R's false statement had induced the grant of the tenancy. The local authority contended that the recorder had further erred in law in concluding that it had wrongfully created a situation in which R was in arrears of rent by withdrawing her housing benefit payments.

Held, allowing the appeal, that the local authority had made out Ground 1 and Ground 5 as grounds for possession. The issue of whether it was reasonable to make an order for possession was therefore remitted. In relation to Ground 5 the issue was what had to be proved to establish inducement. The 1985 Act did not define "induced". Account therefore had to be taken of all the evidence. The recorder had chosen to disregard evidence from the local authority's housing manager that the tenancy would not have been granted had the local authority been aware of R's joint ownership of another property. Furthermore, the recorder had not considered the materiality of R's false statement. In relation to Ground 1 there had been no challenge by way of judicial review to the determination that R was not entitled to housing benefit. It was not apparent, therefore, how the recorder was able to conclude that the local authority had behaved wrongfully in creating a situation in which R was in arrears. In the circumstances, the recorder's conclusions could not stand, *Pyx Granite Co Ltd v. Ministry of Housing and Local Government* [1960] A.C. 260, [1959] C.L.Y. 3260 considered.

WALTHAM FOREST LBC v. ROBERTS, [2004] EWCA Civ 940, [2005] H.L.R. 2, Peter Gibson, L.J., CA (Civ Div).

2686. Secure tenancies–Notice requirements–Wales

SECURE TENANCIES (NOTICES) (AMENDMENT) (WALES) REGULATIONS 2005, SI 2005 1226 (W.84); made under the Housing Act 1985 s.83. In force: April 30, 2005; £3.00.

These Regulations amend the Secure Tenancies (Notices) Regulations 1987 (SI 1987 755) as they apply in Wales to prescribe the form of notice which should be served on a secure tenant before a landlord begins proceedings for a demotion order. The Anti-social Behaviour Act 2003 amended the Housing Act 1985 to allow a secure tenancy to be brought to an end and replaced with a less secure demoted tenancy by a demotion order made by a county court. The Housing Act

1985 also provides that a court may not entertain proceedings for a demotion order unless either a notice in the prescribed form and containing certain specified information has been served on the secure tenant, or the court considers it just and equitable to dispense with such a notice.

2687. Secure tenancies–Possession claims–Correct approach to application for possession based on tenant's anti social behaviour

[Housing Act 1985 s.85, Sch.2.]

The appellant housing authority appealed against a decision dismissing its possession proceedings brought against the respondent tenant (F). The claim for possession had been brought on the grounds that F's conduct was causing nuisance or annoyance to, and constituted harassment of, her neighbours. The judge found that the Housing Act 1985 Sch.2 Ground 1 and Ground 2 had been made out on the evidence. At the stage of deciding whether it was reasonable to make a possession order, he found that a suspended possession order would be pointless. He chose not to make an outright order for possession on the ground that to do so would put F at risk of losing the right to buy, or actually losing her home altogether. The judge accordingly dismissed the claim but went on to grant a post judgment application on behalf of the local authority for injunctive relief. The local authority argued that the judge had been wrong to refuse an order for possession on the ground that such an order suspended on conditions would provide no basis for the control of F's anti social behaviour in circumstances in which it was, nevertheless, thought appropriate to seek to control that behaviour by an injunction.

Held, allowing the appeal, that the judge had erred in the exercise of his discretionary duty. Whilst he had been right to ask himself whether the instant case was one in which, if a possession order was made, it could be postponed, stayed or suspended, he had been wrong, at the stage of deciding whether it was reasonable to make a possession order, to rule out the possibility that the court could meet the circumstances of the case by postponing the date for possession and imposing conditions. The judge had been wrong to assume, without examining the terms upon which an order for possession might be suspended, that a suspended order would have been pointless. He had overlooked the possibility that, by postponing the date for possession upon appropriate conditions, the situation could have been controlled by the court, and he overlooked the possibility that, by imposing the condition that the date for possession should be postponed until after a further application to the court by the local authority, the court could ensure that the tenancy was not brought to an end without further consideration of the circumstances. In those circumstances, the court had the power to exercise its own discretion. This was a reasonably clear case for a possession order and was a case in which the court had to take steps to bring the current state of affairs to an end. An injunction was not an appropriate response. Parliament clearly had in mind that where there had been unacceptable behaviour over a consistent period of time, the court should seek to balance the legitimate interests of the landlord, and of the tenant's neighbours, in securing compliance with the terms of the tenancy agreement, with the interests of the tenant in remaining in her home, by the use of powers conferred by s.85(2) and s.85(3) of the Act. In the circumstances, an order for possession was made but postponed. The case was remitted to the county court for determination of the terms to be imposed upon postponement.

NORWICH CITY COUNCIL v. FAMUYIWA, [2004] EWCA Civ 1770, *The Times*, January 24, 2005, Chadwick, L.J., CA (Civ Div).

2688. Secure tenancies–Right to buy–Local authority employee required to live in accommodation–Transfer of undertakings

[Housing Act 1985 Sch.1 para.2.]

The appellant (G) appealed against the dismissal of his claim for a secure tenancy of a property he occupied as a condition of his employment at a special residential school. At first instance, the local authority had relied on the Housing Act 1985 Sch.1 para.2, which provided that a tenancy was not a secure tenancy giving rise to a right to buy if the tenant was a local authority employee whose employment contract required occupation of a property for the better performance of employment duties. However, an issue arose as to whether consensual variations to G's contract on a transfer of undertakings when a private trust took over the school meant that the requirement to live in the accommodation was removed entirely or merely substituted for another property.

Held, dismissing the appeal, that (1) the judge had been entitled to find that G's occupation of the property remained referable to his employment but that it was the local authority's intention to end its role as G's landlord, *South Glamorgan CC v. Griffiths* (1992) 24 H.L.R. 334, [1992] C.L.Y. 2329 and *Elvidge v. Coventry City Council* [1994] Q.B. 241, [1993] C.L.Y. 2107 considered. (2) (Obiter) The local authority had not adduced sufficient evidence to prove on the balance of probabilities that it had ceased to be G's landlord after the trust took over the running of the school.

GODSMARK v. GREENWICH LBC, [2004] EWHC 1286, [2004] H.L.R. 53, Hart, J., Ch D.

2689. Subtenancies — Consent — Reasonableness of refusal and time taken to reach decision

[Landlord and Tenant Act 1954; Landlord and Tenant Act 1988 s.1 (3).]

The appellant landlord (R) appealed against the decision that it had unreasonably withheld its consent to a proposed underletting. The claimant (N) was the tenant of business premises in London. The lease was for a term of 25 years from 1984. Any underletting had to be at the best rent obtainable in the open market or the existing rent if greater and required the landlord's consent which was not to be unreasonably withheld. N proposed an underletting at a time when the market rent was less than the rent payable so that N would have to pay the new tenant a substantial reverse premium equating to most of the contractual rent over the remainder of the term. N asked R for consent to sublet and provided financial information about the proposed tenant. R refused consent on the grounds of the covenant strength of the proposed undertenant combined with the unsatisfactory position with regard to the financial terms of the proposed underletting. In proceedings by N the judge declared that R was in breach of the Landlord and Tenant Act 1988 s.1 (3), both in failing to make a decision within a reasonable time and in refusing consent on grounds which were not reasonable.

Held, allowing the appeal, that (1) the judge was wrong to hold that the decision to refuse consent was not made within a reasonable time. This was not an uncomplicated transaction capable of summary treatment. Whatever earlier discussions there had been, R was entitled to adequate time following receipt of the completed application to consider the serious financial and legal implications of a refusal with its advisers, and if necessary to report to the relevant board. In the absence of special exceptional circumstances, the period of three weeks actually taken could not be categorised as inherently unreasonable for that process. (2) The judge was entitled to hold that the unusual terms of the lease were not on the evidence a reasonable ground of refusal. R was unable to show at trial that there was any foundation for its concerns about the unusual characteristics of the arrangement. The arrangement would not adversely affect the forthcoming rent review, since the market rent was likely to remain well below the current lease rent. Similarly, although R's bankers' consent would have needed to be obtained, R failed to adduce any evidence to show that that would have been a practical obstacle. (3) The judge was not entitled to regard the strength of the prospective tenant's covenant as wholly irrelevant because of the continuing liability of N as head lessee. He was entitled to give great weight to the security provided by N's covenant during the remainder of the lease, but a reasonable lessor could be expected also to take account of the position at the end of the lease when the subtenant, if still in occupation, would have a right to seek a new tenancy under the Landlord and Tenant Act 1954. The expert evidence was that there was a material difference in the value attributable to the prospect of a single new letting, albeit at the market value, and the possibility of smaller leases of a vacant building. Therefore R's concern about the weakness of the subtenant's covenant had been reasonable and it was not suggested that it had not been genuine. R's refusal to consent to the underletting was reasonable.

NCR LTD v. RIVERLAND PORTFOLIO NO.1 LTD (NO.2), [2005] EWCA Civ 312, [2005] 2 P. & C.R. 27, Ward, L.J., CA (Civ Div).

2690. **Tenancies at will–Termination–Position of tenant**

[Housing Act 1985 s.79, s.80, s.81, s.86, Part IV, Sch.1 para.1.]

The appellant local authority appealed against a decision dismissing its Part 20 claim for possession of a dwelling house occupied by the respondent (B). B had originally held the property under a long lease, the reversion to which was vested in the local authority. When the lease expired, B remained in occupation but did not pay any rent. The local authority gave notice of its intention to recover possession. The judge below concluded that after termination of the long lease B remained in occupation as a tenant at will, which the judge found was a secure tenancy under the Housing Act 1985 Part IV. On that basis he refused the local authority an order for possession. The local authority contended that the judge had erred in failing to understand that s.86 of the Act provided that a secure tenancy could not arise simply because a tenant continued to occupy a property after his fixed term tenancy ended in a case where the fixed term was for more than 21 years. B submitted that s.86 was intended to create a system by which secure fixed term tenancies became secure periodic tenancies upon termination of the contractual term. B argued that s.86 did not have the effect of preventing a secure tenancy from coming into existence under s.79 of the Act if it would otherwise do so.

Held, allowing the appeal, that following the termination of B's fixed term tenancy, he had remained in possession as a tenant at will. Section 86 of the Act did not apply because the fixed term tenancy that B had previously held was not itself a secure tenancy. It was a "long tenancy", which, by virtue of Sch.1 para.1 of the Act, could not be a secure tenancy. No periodic tenancy had arisen when the fixed term tenancy ended. The judge had erred in concluding that a tenancy that fulfilled the conditions in s.80 and s.81 was a secure tenancy for the purposes of Part IV. Security of tenure was dependent on there being a tenancy that the landlord could not bring to an end without obtaining an order for possession, *Harrison v. Hammersmith and Fulham BC* [1981] 1 W.L.R. 650, [1982] C.L.Y. 1479 considered. A tenancy at will could be brought to an end without a court order. Part IV gave no security of tenure where the tenancy at will was brought to an end before the court determined whether to make an order for possession. A tenancy at will would always be brought to an end before that time because the issuing of possession proceedings would in itself bring it to an end. (Obiter) It was doubtful whether Parliament intended that a tenancy at will could be a secure tenancy for the purposes of Part IV, even where the conditions in s.80 and s.81 were satisfied. It was difficult to see how the provisions in Part IV could have effect against the landlord's wishes where the landlord had an unrestricted right to bring to an end the tenancy at will.

BANJO v. BRENT LBC, [2005] EWCA Civ 292, [2005] 1 W.L.R. 2520, Thorpe, L.J., CA (Civ Div).

2691. **Tenants rights–Local authority granting licence to housing association– Housing association granting tenancy to appellant–Appellant's rights as against local authority**

The appellant occupier (O) appealed against a decision that he had no defence in law to possession proceedings brought by the respondent local authority freeholder (C). C had granted a licence to a housing association, under which the association, as licensee, was entitled to provide temporary housing accommodation at the property. The licence could be terminated on notice by either the licensee or licensor, upon which the association was to give vacant possession. The first defendant had occupied the property temporarily, but occupation was taken over by O when C served the association with written notice to terminate the licence. In possession proceedings brought by C, O put up a defence that the termination of the licence had not terminated his inferior interest in the property. That defence was found to be unsustainable, and on that basis the possession order was granted and upheld on appeal. O argued that the contract that had given rise to his tenancy from the association had been authorised by C in the licence, and that C had held the association out to have authority to grant a tenancy over the property. Further, O argued that, as a principle of law, where a fee simple owner had given consent to a third party to create a tenancy, the freehold owner was bound by the tenancy as a matter of property even though there was no privity of contract between him and the tenant.

Held, dismissing the appeal, that the foundation of O's defence was that in entering into the tenancy, the association was acting as C's agent within the scope of its authority under the licence. However, it did not follow that because the licence envisaged that the association would grant rights to third persons, in doing so it was acting for C. The important question to be considered was to determine what C, as the freeholder and licensor, had consented to in the licence. If the freeholder was not consenting to an arrangement that affected his freehold estate, then O's defence failed. The source of the supposed consent was said by O to be the licence, but the licence had not authorised the creation of a tenancy that was binding on C; rather, it had made it clear that upon termination the association was to give up vacant possession. C's intention under the licence was not to create a tenancy binding upon its own interest in the property. Accordingly, the association had no authority or estate from which to grant an estate to O, but even if it had, any tenancy granted to O was terminated by the termination of the licence under the principle that when a headlease ended, whether through expiry of time, forfeiture or notice, any subtenancy that had derived under it also ended, except where the headlease was ended by surrender. In those circumstances, O had not established that he had a sustainable defence to the possession proceedings.

ISLINGTON LBC v. GREEN; ISLINGTON LBC v. O'SHEA, [2005] EWCA Civ 56, [2005] H.L.R. 35, Peter Gibson, L.J., CA (Civ Div).

2692. Turnover rents–VAT–Turnover for purposes of calculating additional rent under lease–Gross amount of total sales including VAT

The appellant landlord (S) appealed against the decision ([2004] EWHC 2940, [2005] S.T.C.171) that VAT was not to be included in the tenant's turnover figures for the purpose of calculating turnover rent. The respondent (D) was the tenant of S of department store premises in Swindon. The rent payable was made up of a fixed annual amount and an additional rent calculated as a proportion of turnover, meaning the gross amount of total sales. The lease had been granted for a term of 99 years less 10 days from October 1, 1965. For many years D had paid rent on the basis that for the purposes of calculating the additional rent the turnover included VAT. D had applied to the court to determine whether that was so.

Held, allowing the appeal, that the words did not have a single plain and unambiguous meaning. The words were to be construed in their commercial context. The lease had to be construed as of 1965. In 1965 VAT did not exist and it could not have formed part of the thinking of either party. What did exist, however, was purchase tax which was imposed only on wholesalers of goods. What would have mattered to the businessmen negotiating the lease was money. Form would have been a secondary consideration. Purchase tax would have had a significant effect on what was actually paid by way of rent since it was an inbuilt cost to D. In the real world purchase tax affected ultimate prices, just like VAT. On that basis the parties would not have regarded a substitute for purchase tax which also affected ultimate prices as excluded by the words "gross amount of the total sales including services from trade". As a commercial matter, VAT was included just as purchase tax had been included originally. The fact that purchase tax would not appear in the company accounts was a secondary consideration to the actual money involved. In substance purchase tax did appear, as part of the price of goods, in the turnover figures, *Lynn v.*

Nathanson (1931) 2 D.L.R. 457 and *Yates v. Yates* (1913) 33 N.Z.L.R. 281 distinguished.
DEBENHAMS RETAIL PLC v. SUN ALLIANCE & LONDON ASSURANCE CO LTD; *sub nom.* DEBENHAMS RETAIL PLC v. SUN ALLIANCE & LONDON INSURANCE CO LTD, [2005] EWCA Civ 868, [2005] S.T.C. 1443, Judge, L.J., CA (Civ Div).

2693. Underleases–Covenants–Prohibitions on underletting–Mandatory conditions in commercial leases–Wrongful interference with contract

[Landlord and Tenant Act 1988 s.1.]
The claimant landlords (L) sought an injunction ordering the surrender of an underlease by the second defendant underlessee (M) to the first defendant lessee (T) of commercial premises, and damages from both. T counterclaimed for declarations that L had unreasonably withheld consent to the underlease. L had granted a lease of the premises to T subject to a covenant restricting the grant of an underlease. T was required to insure in the joint names of L and itself. Although T insured against physical damage, it deliberately omitted to make it a joint policy and persistently delayed disclosure of that fact. For want of confirmation of the joint policy, L kept its own insurance on risk and served a notice to repair on T as the premiums had increased following squatter damage. T applied to sublet to M. L refused to grant the licence to sublet until the insurance position had been settled, but T sublet without complying. L submitted that (1) T had granted the underlease to M in breach of covenant because L did not consent to it, and the underlease was on different terms from the lease; (2) by accepting the underlease, M had unlawfully interfered with the contractual relations between L and T.
Held, giving judgment for L, that (1) the issue was whether T was entitled to require L to consider its application for consent to grant of the underlease and not unreasonably to withhold consent. At all times T remained subject to an absolute obligation not to underlet; L were under no obligation to consider an application to do so, and the Landlord and Tenant Act 1988 s.1 had no application. On a proper construction of the lease, the circumstances were limited in which an absolute prohibition on underletting was qualified to give a tenant the right to request consent. There were mandatory conditions that had to be satisfied, which were common in commercial leases and were recognised as intended to control the terms of any underlease, *Allied Dunbar Assurance Plc v. Homebase Ltd* [2002] EWCA Civ 666, [2003] 1 P. & C.R. 6, [2002] C.L.Y. 3048 applied. The underlease was granted subject to covenants that were "like", in other words the same in substance, if not in form, as those in the lease, and the dissimilarity of the repairing covenants in the underlease was of substance. The lease was designed to ensure that T had like rights and protection against an underlessee to those that L had against T, and the absence of such a repairing covenant in the underlease meant that the condition precedent to any obligation on the part of L to consider T's application for consent to the grant of the underlease to M was never satisfied. Accordingly, T's counterclaim was dismissed. (2) M committed the tort against L of wrongful interference with contract by agreeing to the grant of the underlease, and was liable in damages. In principle, L had the remedy of an order against T and M for surrender of the lease. On the evidence, M had had the necessary knowledge that T was committing a breach of contract, and M intended by accepting the underlease to procure such breach. (3) Compensatory damages could be awarded on the basis of the sum that L could reasonably have demanded at the date of the breach for relaxing the covenant against underletting for the period that no injunction was in force, and could take into account any possible arrangement available to T and M that might affect the sum agreed, *Amec Developments Ltd v. Jury's Hotel Management (UK) Ltd* [2002] T.C.L.R. 13, [2001] C.L.Y. 1549 applied. An inquiry as to damages would be directed, *Robinson v. Bird* [2003] EWCA Civ 1820, [2004] W.T.L.R. 257 applied.
CRESTFORT LTD v. TESCO STORES LTD, [2005] EWHC 805, [2005] L. & T.R. 20, Lightman, J., Ch D.

2694. **Underleases–Premiums–Covenant   prohibiting   underletting   below contractual rent–Reverse premium to subtenant–Construction of lease**

The claimant (N) sought a declaration that a proposed underlease of premises was authorised by the head lease. The preliminary issue to be decided was whether clause 3.11 of the head lease prohibited the payment of a premium in consideration of reservation of rent payable at the rate required by the head lease. N was the tenant of office premises let by the defendant (R). Under the lease, an annual rent of £338,000 was reserved to be reviewed every five years on an upwards only basis. The annual rent since 1990 had been £710,000. By clause 3.11 of the head lease N covenanted: "...not to underlet the whole of the demised premises or permit any underlease of the whole of the demised premises to be derived directly or indirectly...out of this lease unless (i) the underlease is granted at the best rent obtainable in the open market without the grantor taking any premium or other capital consideration or, if greater, the rent then payable thereunder...". N proposed to underlease the premises to T. T was willing, in compliance with clause 3.11, to pay an annual rent of £710,000 but, as the rent was in excess of the market rent, T required from N a premium of £3 million in consideration for entering into the underlease. R refused to consent to the underlease, arguing that taking into account the premium, the proposed rent was less than the market rent. R submitted that the premium was disguised rent which, when split between the residue of the term and the reduced rent, meant that the true rent payable under the proposed underlease would be approximately £210,000 per annum, which was half the open market rent and one third of the rent payable under the lease.

Held, granting the declaration, that the reverse premium did not infringe the terms of the head lease. The decision in *Allied Dunbar Assurance Plc v. Homebase Ltd* [2002] EWCA Civ 666, [2003] 1 P. & C.R. 6, [2002] C.L.Y. 3048 turned on the construction of particular documents before the court at the time, from which it was dangerous, particularly in landlord and tenant matters, to derive general principles of law, *Allied Dunbar* distinguished. A major and significant difference between the instant case and *Allied Dunbar* was that in that case the figures in the underlease were based on an entirely fictional calculation. In the instant case, absent any claim that the premium was not genuine and was a sham, there was no justification for treating it as being anything other than a premium. Without any challenge to the documentation, it was not permissible for the court to rewrite an underlease and change a premium into a figure and incorporate it as rent. On the facts, the obligations contained in the underlease were substantially in excess of what would be the open market value of a new lease. A genuine reverse premium could not be a breach of clause 3.11 and N was entitled to the declaratory relief sought.

NCR LTD v. RIVERLAND PORTFOLIO NO.1 LTD (NO.1), [2004] EWHC 921, [2005] 1 P. & C.R. 3, Peter Smith, J., Ch D.

2695. **Books**

Brennan, Gabriel–Landlord and Tenant Law. Law Society of Ireland Manuals S. Paperback: £39.99. ISBN 0 19 928025 8. Oxford University Press.

Lamont, Camilla; Stacey, Myriam; Seifert, Anne–Lease Renewal. Case in Point S., No. 6. Paperback: £24.99. ISBN 1 84219 226 4. RICS.

Male, John; Jefferies, Tom–Rent Review. Case in Point S. Paperback: £24.95. ISBN 1 84219 225 6. RICS.

Redman, John E.–Law of Landlord and Tenant: Issue 48. Looseleaf/ring bound: £145.00. ISBN 0 406 97248 6. Butterworths Law.

Reynolds, Kirk; Clark, Wayne–Renewal of Business Tenancies. Hardback: £274.00. ISBN 0 421 82980 X. Sweet & Maxwell.

Rosenthal, Adam; Dray, Martin; Groves, Christopher–Barnsley's Land Options. Hardback: £160.00. ISBN 0 421 85610 6. Sweet & Maxwell.

Shaw, Edward–Dilapidations-Letters, Forms and Schedules. CD-ROM: £47.00. ISBN 1 84219 184 5. RICS.

Shepperson, Tessa–Residential Lettings. Paperback: £11.99. ISBN 1 904053 90 4. Law Pack Publishing.

Sproston, Roger–Straightforward Guide to Your Rights As a Private Tenant. Paperback: £8.99. ISBN 1 903909 59 7. Straightforward Publishing.
Stewart, Moira–Landlord's Guide to Letting: How to Buy and Let Residential Property for Profit. Paperback: £9.99. ISBN 1 85703 750 2. How To Books.

LEGAL ADVICE AND FUNDING

2696. Access to justice–Membership organisations–Approved bodies

ACCESS TO JUSTICE (MEMBERSHIP ORGANISATION) REGULATIONS 2005, SI 2005 2306; made under the Access to Justice Act 1999 s.30. In force: November 1, 2005; £3.00.

These Regulations revoke the Access to Justice (Membership Organisation) Regulations 2000 (SI 2000 693), in respect of arrangements entered into after November 1, 2005, and make new, simplified client-care provisions for the purposes of arrangements entered into on or after that date. Section 30 of the Access to Justice Act 1999 applies where a body of a description to be specified in regulations undertakes (in accordance with arrangements satisfying conditions to be so specified) to meet liabilities which members of the body or other persons who are parties to proceedings may incur to pay the costs of other parties. These Regulations specify bodies which are for the time being approved by the Secretary of State for this purpose and the conditions which the arrangements must satisfy. Under s.30(2) of the 1999 Act an additional amount may be included in costs payable to a member of such a body or other person to cover insurance or other provision made by the body against the risk of having to meet those liabilities of the member or other person. Under s.30(3) of the 1999 Act that additional amount must not exceed a sum determined in a way specified by regulations. These Regulations specify that sum as the likely cost to the member or other person of the premium of an insurance policy against the risk in question.

2697. CDS funding–Conferences–Travel expenses to attend conference with assisted person

[Criminal Defence Service (Funding) Order 2001 Sch.4 Para.19(1A).]

Counsel for the appellant (P) appealed against the disallowance of his claim for payment for time spent and expenses arising in travelling to a conference with an assisted person. Under the Criminal Defence Service (Funding) Order 2001 Sch.4, only one conference was allowed where the trial, as in this case, was not to exceed ten days. P's counsel had two conferences, and whilst he did not claim payment for the second conference, he did claim for his travelling time and expenses on the basis that the 2001 Order was silent as to these items.

Held, dismissing the appeal, that whilst the 2001 Order did not specifically exclude remuneration for travelling time and expenses, it was the clear intention of Sch.4 Para.19(1A) to restrict the number of conferences for which payment would be made out of public funds. To allow recoupment of travelling time and expenses in such circumstances would be to undermine the intention of placing a cap on the number of conferences that might be held under the terms of the 2001 Order.

R. v. PICKETT (COSTS) [2004] 3 Costs L.R. 529, Deputy Costs Judge Pollard, Supreme Court Costs Office.

2698. CDS funding–Counsels fees–Fees determined on ex post facto basis rather than under graduated fees scheme where trial estimated to last three weeks

[Criminal Defence Service (Funding) Order 2001 Sch.4.]

Counsel of the appellant (F) appealed against a finding of the determining officer that his fees for F's representation fell to be claimed under the graduated fee scheme (GFS) and were not to be determined ex post facto. F had been granted a representation order in August 2001 in respect of an indictment containing a number of counts of sexual offences. His counsel had attended on numerous pre trial hearings and a six day public interest immunity hearing. The trial commenced in October 2002 but was adjourned to the following March after F's counsel failed to secure a dismissal of the case for abuse of process. A jury was then sworn and directed by the trial judge to acquit F. The determining officer, in dealing with the fees claim, found that the trial had not been estimated to last more than ten days, and that counsel's fees therefore fell to be determined under the GFS. On appeal, F's counsel argued that the case fell outside the Criminal Defence Service (Funding) Order 2001 Sch.4 as the trial had only failed to exceed ten days because it had been terminated without the jury being required to consider its verdict, and as such it should be dealt with on an ex post facto basis.

Held, allowing the appeal, that the court log showed that the case had been estimated to last for three weeks, and that therefore the determining officer had been wrong to find that it had never been estimated to last more than ten days. This accordingly took the case outside Sch.4 of the 2001 Order, as did the fact that the combined length of the trial itself and the abuse of process hearings exceeded ten days. It followed that F's counsel's fees were to be determined ex post facto and not under the GFS.

R. v. FOOT (COSTS) [2004] 3 Costs L.R. 525, Costs Judge Campbell, Supreme Court Costs Office.

2699. CLS funding—Funding—Third parties—Entitlement to costs where assisted litigant in receipt of private funding

[Civil Legal Aid (General) Regulations 1989 (SI 1989) Reg.64.]

The appellant (S) appealed against a refusal to make a costs order in his favour in respect of the hearing of a preliminary issue decided in S's favour. S had had the benefit of a civil legal aid certificate but had received private funds from a third party (M) to fund the proceedings on the preliminary issue, as he believed the legal aid certificate did not cover those proceedings. The judge had found that the legal aid certificate did cover the proceedings; thus the receipt of private funds was contrary to the Civil Legal Aid (General) Regulations 1989 Reg.64. The judge then refused to make a costs order in S's favour because any costs ordered to be paid by the respondent (P) would in turn be paid out to M since the Legal Services Commission had incurred no liability to S's solicitors. S contended that the fact that a third party had agreed to fund a litigant's costs was irrelevant to any question of costs provided that the successful litigant remained liable to pay those costs.

Held, allowing the appeal, that the judge had been wrong to decide that any costs which P was ordered to pay would be paid to M. The finding that the legal aid certificate covered the proceedings led inevitably to a conclusion that S's solicitors would have to pay any costs they received from P to the Legal Aid Board. Furthermore, a breach of Reg.64 did not automatically preclude S from being awarded his costs. Although the appeal court should be slow to interfere with the exercise of a discretion not to award costs, where that exercise had been erroneously conducted the decision could not stand. Given the fact that the breach of Reg.64 was not conscious or deliberate, the refusal to award S costs was neither just nor proportionate.

STACY v. PLAYER; *sub nom.* STACEY v. PLAYER, [2004] EWCA Civ 241, [2004] 4 Costs L.R. 585, Lord Phillips of Worth Matravers, M.R., CA.

2700. Conditional fee agreements—Revocation

CONDITIONAL FEE AGREEMENTS (REVOCATION) REGULATIONS 2005, SI 2005 2305; made under the Courts and Legal Services Act 1990 s.58, s.58A, s.119, s.120. In force: November 1, 2005; £3.00.

These Regulations revoke the Conditional Fee Agreements Regulations 2000 (SI 2000 692), the Collective Conditional Fee Agreements Regulations 2000 (SI 2000 2988), the Conditional Fee Agreements (Miscellaneous Amendments) Regulations 2003 (SI 2003 1240) and the Conditional Fee Agreements (Miscellaneous Amendments) (No. 2) Regulations 2003 (SI 2003 3344) in respect of conditional fee agreements and collective conditional fee agreements entered into on or after November 1, 2005.

2701. Conditional fee agreements–Solicitors powers and duties–Duty to enquire about legal expenses insurance

[Conditional Fee Agreements Regulations 2000 (SI 2000 692) Reg.4(2)(C).]

The appellant (S) appealed against a decision of the principal costs officer, on a detailed assessment, disallowing all his costs. S was a taxi driver. He had made a modest personal injury claim arising from a road traffic accident. He had signed an agreement with a claims management company, which involved taking out an after the event insurance policy for a premium of £798. The claims management company referred the matter to solicitors on the basis that S did not have any pre existing legal expenses insurance cover. That was confirmed by S's insurance broker. S recovered damages of £1,814. The costs officer disallowed S's costs on the basis that it had not been shown that, before after the event insurance had been taken out and a conditional fee agreement entered into, proper enquiries had been made by S's legal representatives into whether S's liability for costs was covered by any pre existing insurance. He decided that there had accordingly been a breach of the Conditional Fee Agreements Regulations 2000 Reg.4(2)(C), that the conditional fee agreement was therefore unenforceable and that no costs were recoverable. S argued that since there was no evidence indicating that anything was amiss, there was no valid basis on which the court could go behind the documentation which he had signed. The respondent (L) argued that the solicitors had not conducted their own enquiry into whether S's liability for costs was covered by pre existing insurance and that there had accordingly been a material breach of the Regulations.

Held, dismissing the appeal, that (1) the premium sought for the after the event insurance policy was, on the face of it, disproportionate in a straightforward case involving minimal damages. That demanded investigation. It was therefore appropriate to go behind the solicitor's signature on the bill. (2) The solicitor did not carry out any independent enquiry as to legal expenses insurance. He did not consider whether S's risk of incurring liability for costs was insured against, but relied entirely on the enquiries made by the claims management company. The solicitor did not make any or any sufficient enquiries of S as to the existence of legal expenses insurance. If there had in fact been delegation by the solicitor to the claims management company, the enquiries made by the latter were inadequate and insufficient to comply with the Regulations. S was never asked about any policy but his motor policy. (3) The failure properly to consider whether S's risk of incurring a liability for costs in respect of the proceedings to which the conditional fee agreement related was insured against under an existing contract of insurance had a materially adverse effect on the protection afforded to S, since he had entered into a conditional fee agreement, a loan agreement and an after the event insurance policy costing £798. Since S's damages were never going to exceed £2,000, the premium was disproportionate. If it was appropriate for S to have agreed to take out a policy with a premium of that size, the solicitor was clearly under a duty to carry out a careful investigation as to alternative sources of insurance. If solicitors were permitted to skimp on the proper investigation of legal expenses insurance, the administration of justice would be badly served. In the circumstances, there had been a material breach of Reg.4(2)(C) and the conditional fee agreement was unenforceable.

SAMONINI v. LONDON GENERAL TRANSPORT SERVICES LTD [2005] P.I.Q.R. P20, Master Hurst (Senior Costs Judge), Sup Ct Costs Office.

2702. **Conditional fee agreements–Success fees–Agreement entered into before April 1, 2000–Application of restrictions in Access to Justice Act 1999 (Transitional Provision) Order 1999**

[Access to Justice Act 1999; Access to Justice Act 1999 (Transitional Provisions) Order 1999.]

The appellant (C) appealed against the disallowance of his recovery from the respondent (M) of a success fee £42,537 out of a total bill of £170,000. C had brought proceedings in 1996 against M in respect of personal injuries. He had made a conditional fee arrangement (CFA) with his solicitors in 1996. He had then changed solicitors and in early 2000 he instructed a third firm with whom he entered into two CFAs, in October 2000 and January 2001. C's claim to recover the success fee from M was made on foot of the provisions of the Access to Justice Act 1999. At first instance, the district judge refused recovery on the basis that no sufficient notice had been given of the CFA. On appeal, M argued that C's recovery of the success fee was barred by the provisions of the Access to Justice Act 1999 (Transitional Provisions) Order 1999.

Held, dismissing the appeal, that the fact that C had entered into a CFA in the same proceedings before April 1, 2000, being the date on which the 1999 Order came into force, was conclusive and it was not relevant whether the CFA was still effective as at that date. Although the 1999 Order did not specifically deal with the situation where a CFA had been entered into prior to April 1, 2000 but had ceased to exist by that date, on a purposive construction it operated to bar recovery of a success fee under the 1999 Act from a defendant where a claimant had had the benefit of a CFA in relation to those proceedings prior to 1 April 2000.

C v. MERSEYSIDE REGIONAL AMBULANCE SERVICE NHS TRUST, [2003] EWHC 250, [2004] 3 Costs L.R. 363, Sumner, J., Fam Div.

2703. **Conditional fee agreements–Success fees–Appropriate level of success fee determined on assessment of prospect of success**

The appellant (S) appealed against a decision as to the appropriate level of a success fee under a conditional fee arrangement (CFA). The widow of the respondent (E) had entered into a CFA for a claim against S for damages for E's mesothelioma arising from asbestos exposure. S had paid £165,000 into court at an advanced stage in the action and E's solicitors had advised refusal of the payment in. The action was compromised on the first day of the trial, with an award of agreed damages of £180,000 and costs to be assessed in default of agreement. Liability had already been admitted shortly before trial. Under the CFA, E's solicitors sought recovery of an uplift of 87 per cent. The costs judge upheld the uplift on the basis of the facts and circumstances reasonably known to E's solicitors when the CFA was entered into. On appeal, it was recognised that this had not been a straightforward case and that the only reported authority available related to straightforward cases.

Held, dismissing the appeal, that E's solicitors had, in their success fee calculation undertaken at the outset of the case, assessed the chances of success at 53 per cent, and that this had translated into a success fee of 87 per cent by reference to a Law Society ready reckoner. The use of this reckoner was usual and simple, and success fees derived from it were not unfairly high. At the time of the CFA, it was possible to be optimistic that E would succeed on liability, but such success was not certain. The remaining factors in the case all went to quantum, and advising on quantum in the instant case had been far from straightforward. In the circumstances, the costs judge had been entitled to hold that the success fee of 87 per cent was reasonable, *Callery v. Gray (No.1)* [2002] UKHL 28, [2002] 1 W.L.R. 2000, [2002] C.L.Y. 360 considered.

SMITHS DOCK LTD v. EDWARDS, [2004] EWHC 1116, [2004] 3 Costs L.R. 440, Crane, J., QBD.

2704. **Conditional fee agreements–Success fees–Personal injury claims arising from road traffic accidents–Reasonableness of success fees**

[Civil Procedure Rules 1998 (SI 1998 3132) Part 45.]

The appellants in conjoined appeals (X and H) appealed against decisions as to the appropriate level of success fee for solicitors acting on conditional fee agreements (CFAs) in connection with personal injury claims arising out of road traffic accidents. In each case the CFA had been entered into during the regime which had been in place before the introduction of the arrangements in the Civil Procedure Rules 1998 Part 45 governing CFAs in road traffic accident cases. In the first case, X had sustained injuries when he lost control of his motorcycle on a roundabout because of the negligent driving of the respondent (L). The claim was settled; however, at the costs hearing, the judge found that the level of risk had not been substantially higher than in any other road traffic accident occurring on a roundabout and reduced the success fee from 100 per cent to 50 per cent. X appealed unsuccessfully. In the second case, the respondent (E) had suffered injuries when H reversed his vehicle into her while she was walking in a car park. E brought proceedings under a CFA with a success fee of 60 per cent, but the case was settled after the defence had been filed. The judge below held that E was reasonably entitled to 30 per cent by way of a success fee. H contended that the claim was modest and straightforward and that a success fee of 20 per cent was appropriate.

Held, allowing the appeals in part, that (1) the reasonableness of the success fee was to be assessed by reference to what was, or should have been, known to the solicitor at the time the CFA was entered into, *Callery v. Gray (No.1)* [2002] UKHL 28, [2002] 1 W.L.R. 2000, [2002] C.L.Y. 360 and *Halloran v. Delaney* [2002] EWCA Civ 1258, [2003] 1 W.L.R. 28, [2003] C.L.Y. 330 applied. In X's case, the judge had been right to consider the matter from the standpoint of a reasonably careful solicitor assessing the risk on the basis of what was known to him at the time, and his figure of 50 per cent was well within the range reasonably available to him. X's appeal was dismissed. (2) The guidance given in *Callery* could be applied by analogy to H's case even though H's case had been allocated to the multi track and had settled for a sum exceeding £15,000. There were no factors which could legitimately have taken the success fee over 20 per cent. The fact that there was uncertainty about the identity of the driver could have been resolved by E's solicitor making a single telephone call to the police before entering into the CFA. The only significant risk related to the possibility of E not beating a payment into court, which was refused on her solicitor's advice, and that risk justified a success fee of 20 per cent. H's appeal was allowed. (3) Under the old regime, it was permissible and desirable for a CFA to include a two stage success fee. It was not permissible, when assessing the reasonableness of a success fee in a road traffic accident case, simply to adopt the new fixed rates for success fees introduced by the 1998 Rules where the CFA was not governed by the new rules.

ATACK v. LEE; ELLERTON v. HARRIS, [2004] EWCA Civ 1712, [2005] 1 W.L.R. 2643, Brooke, L.J., CA (Civ Div).

2705. **Conditional fee agreements–Validity–Proportion of success fee unclear–Breach of Conditional Fee Agreements Regulations 2000 Reg.3(1)(b)**

[Courts and Legal Services Act 1990 s.58(1); Conditional Fee Arrangements Regulations 2000 (SI 2000 692) Reg.3(1)(b).]

The appellant (S) appealed against a finding that the conditional fee arrangement (CFA) he had entered into with his solicitor was unenforceable. S had brought a personal injury claim against W, and that action had been compromised with an order for costs in S's favour. The CFA S had entered into with his solicitors provided for a 75 per cent success fee, but it was not clear as to what part, if any, of that success fee related to the costs to S's solicitors of the postponement of payment of their costs and outlays. The district judge held that the omission amounted to a breach of the Conditional Fee Arrangements Regulations 2000 Reg.3(1)(b) and assessed Part 2 of S's solicitors' bill at nil on the basis that this breach was material for the purposes of the Courts and Legal Services Act 1990 s.58(1), which obliged him to disallow the claim to recovery of the success fee in such circumstances. On appeal, S argued that the court was empowered, and ought, to apply the provisions of s.58(1) in a proportionate manner, depending on the seriousness of the breach, and that it was not obliged simply to disallow all costs where such a breach had occurred.

Held, dismissing the appeal, that s.58(1) of the 1990 Act did not bear the interpretation for which S had argued. Where, as in the instant case, there had been a material breach of the 2000 Regulations, then the wording of the 1990 Act made it quite clear that the court was obliged to disallow the costs in their entirety. There was no room for the graduated approach for which S had argued, *Hollins v. Russell* [2003] EWCA Civ 718, [2003] 1 W.L.R. 2487, [2003] C.L.Y. 334 applied.

SPENCER v. WOOD (T/A GORDON'S TYRES), [2004] EWCA Civ 352, [2004] 3 Costs L.R. 372, Brooke, L.J., CA.

2706. Criminal Defence Service–Funding

CRIMINAL DEFENCE SERVICE (FUNDING) (AMENDMENT) ORDER 2005, SI 2005 2621; made under the Access to Justice Act 1999 s.14. In force: October 3, 2005; £3.00.

The amendments made by this Order to the Criminal Defence Service (Funding) Order 2001 (SI 2001 855) include: an appeal to the High Court against a costs judge's decision will be governed by Part 52 of the Civil Procedure Rules 1998 (SI 1998 3132 (L.17)) instead of Part 8 of those rules; the power to grant an uplift of solicitors' fees is restricted to certain types of work in respect of certain offences and to a maximum of 100 per cent in all cases; Schedule 4 to the 2001 Order which concerns fees for advocacy in the Crown Court is amended so that it covers all guilty pleas and cracked trials; new scales of graduated fees for trials in the Crown Court are substituted; a new payment scheme for guilty pleas and cracked trials is introduced by the substitution of new scales in the table; the proportions of the fees payable to advocates other than Queen's Counsel where two trial advocates are instructed to represent the same person are altered; and the rates of pay in very high cost cases for preparation, advocacy and preliminary hearings are altered by the substitution of new tables.

2707. Criminal Defence Service–Recovery of costs

CRIMINAL DEFENCE SERVICE (RECOVERY OF DEFENCE COSTS ORDERS) (AMENDMENT) REGULATIONS 2005, SI 2005 2783; made under the Access to Justice Act 1999 s.17, s.26. In force: October 31, 2005; £3.00.

These Regulations amend the Criminal Defence Service (Recovery of Defence Costs Orders) Regulations 2001 (SI 2001 856) in order to increase the level of income a funded defendant must have before his income is taken into account for the purpose of calculating his financial resources.

2708. Legal aid–Civil legal aid–Enforcement of charges–Deferment

CIVIL LEGAL AID (GENERAL) (AMENDMENT NO.2) REGULATIONS 2005, SI 2005 1802; made under the Legal Aid Act 1988 s.16, s.34, s.43. In force: July 25, 2005; £3.00.

These Regulations amend the Civil Legal Aid (General) Regulations 1989 (SI 1989 339). They amend the provisions about deferment of enforcement of the charge created by the Legal Aid Act 1988 s.16(6) to provide for the circumstances in which enforcement of the charge will not be deferred and decisions to defer enforcement of the charge will be reviewed.

2709. Legal aid–Civil legal aid–Fixed interest rates

CIVIL LEGAL AID (GENERAL) (AMENDMENT) REGULATIONS 2005, SI 2005 591; made under the Legal Aid Act 1988 s.16, s.34. In force: April 1, 2005; £3.00.

These Regulations amend the Civil Legal Aid (General) Regulations 1989 (SI 1989 339) to prescribe the rate of interest payable by a client where the Commission postpones the enforcement of a statutory charge in its favour, to prescribe a fixed interest rate of 5 per cent per annum (which has been the applicable rate since April 1, 1994) for the period April 1, 2005 to September 30, 2005, and thereafter a fixed interest rate of 8 per cent per annum from October 1, 2005.

2710. Legal aid–Legal representation–Road traffic offence–Foreign national with limited English seeking legal aid

[Road Traffic Act 1988 s.7; Human Rights Act 1998 Sch.1 Part I Art.6; Access to Justice Act 1999 Sch.3 para.5(2).]

The claimant (M) applied for judicial review of a decision of the defendant magistrates' court refusing to grant him legal aid for legal representation at his criminal trial. M had been arrested and cautioned for failing to provide an evidential specimen contrary to the Road Traffic Act 1988 s.7. M's case was that, owing to his poor language skills, he did not understand what was required of him in relation to the breath tests, and therefore he had a reasonable excuse amounting to a defence for not providing the samples as charged. M entered a plea of not guilty and the trial date was set. He subsequently applied for legal aid. His application and renewed application were refused on the basis that it was not in the interests of justice. In particular, the court found that the case was not complex and did not involve a substantial question of law. A further application was also refused on the grounds, inter alia, that there was no risk of serious damage to M's reputation and that an interpreter would be provided because of M's limited knowledge of the English language. M submitted that the court's refusal to grant legal aid was unreasonable as his case met at least three relevant criteria under the Access to Justice Act 1999 Sch.3 para.5(2), namely that he was likely to lose his liberty or livelihood, that the case might involve consideration of a substantial question of law and that he might be unable to understand the proceedings or state his own case. M further submitted that the grant of an interpreter did not negate the need for legal representation.

Held, granting the application, that the requirement that the proceedings be in a language that a defendant understood was merely one aspect of the requirement that a person had to be able to effectively participate in criminal proceedings against him pursuant to the guarantee of a fair trial under the Human Rights Act 1998 Sch.1 Part I Art.6, and did not of itself negate the need for legal representation. Even if all the criteria were not made out, at least one of the criteria was met, which made the refusal of legal aid unreasonable to a degree which entitled the instant court to intervene. It was important not to lose sight of the fact that the test was a test of "the interests of justice", and it was in the interests of justice that M should be granted legal aid. The availability of an interpreter did not meet the point that it was M's case that he was unable to understand what was being said at the time of his arrest. That was a point which lay at the heart of his defence. It went to his ability to state his own case and the overall fairness of the trial. The case should be remitted for reconsideration.

R. (ON THE APPLICATION OF MATARA) v. BRENT MAGISTRATES COURT, [2005] EWHC 1829, (2005) 169 J.P. 576, Smith, L.J., QBD (Admin).

2711. Legal aid–Serious fraud cases–200 per cent uplift on basic legal aid rates

The solicitors acting on behalf of the appellant (S) appealed against the refusal of the determining officer to allow more than 100 per cent costs enhancement on their preparation of S's case. S had been jointly charged with three others with offences of theft and forgery, involving the theft of a cheque for some £250,000 and a series of transfers of the proceeds of the cheque at different times into accounts held by the various defendants. After a trial, S's three codefendants were convicted but S was acquitted. The determining officer had refused S's solicitors' application for enhancement on the basis that the case was not one of serious or complex fraud.

Held, allowing the appeal in part, that the question of whether serious or complex fraud was present was an issue of fact in each case. The Serious Fraud Office took as a rough guide the figure of £1 million as being lost or at risk because of fraud as an indicator of serious fraud, although it was recognised that this figure was not a determining factor. The Inland Revenue regarded as serious frauds those involving substantial amounts of at least £50,000, use of false documents, material non disclosure during an investigation, involvement of a professional person in the suspected fraud and conspiracy between two or more persons to defraud the Crown. In the instant case, the facts amounted to a case of serious and complex fraud and S's solicitors were therefore entitled to an enhancement of 200 per cent rather than the 100 per cent claimed. No enhancement was allowed for attending counsel at court, however, and there was no enhancement other than on 50 per cent of S's solicitors' telephone calls and letters, *Murria v. Lord Chancellor* [2000] 2 All E.R. 941, [2000] C.L.Y. 3973 applied and *R. v. Alwan (Hisham)* [2000] 2 Costs L.R. 326, [2001] C.L.Y. 1114 considered.

R. v. SOOD (ANURAG) (COSTS) [2004] 3 Costs L.R. 520, Costs Judge Rogers, Supreme Court Costs Office.

2712. Legal services–Asylum and immigration appeals–Appellants costs

COMMUNITY LEGAL SERVICE (ASYLUM AND IMMIGRATION APPEALS) REGULATIONS 2005, SI 2005 966; made under the Nationality, Immigration and Asylum Act 2002 s.103D. In force: April 4, 2005; £3.00.

These Regulations make provision about the exercise of powers in the Nationality, Immigration and Asylum Act 2002 s.103D(1)(3) for the High Court or the Asylum and Immigration Tribunal to order payment of an appellant's costs out of the Community Legal Service Fund. These Regulations give effect to a special legal aid scheme for applications under s.103A of the 2002 Act by an appellant for a review of the Tribunal's decision on an asylum or immigration appeal, and proceedings for the reconsideration by the Tribunal of its decision following an order made on such an application, under which the High Court or the Tribunal decides when it determines an application or reconsiders an appeal whether to order the payment out of the Fund of costs incurred by the appellant's legal representative.

2713. Legal services–Community Legal Service–Assessment of financial resources

COMMUNITY LEGAL SERVICE (FINANCIAL) (AMENDMENT) REGULATIONS 2005, SI 2005 589; made under the Access to Justice Act 1999 s.7, s.10. In force: in accordance with Reg.1; £3.00.

These Regulations amend the Community Legal Service (Financial) Regulations 2000 (SI 2000 516), which govern the financial aspects of the provision of services funded by the Legal Services Commission in civil matters as part of the Community Legal Service. They amend the financial eligibility limits and thresholds for payment of contributions for various levels of service, and in particular align the financial eligibility limits for Legal Help, Help at Court and Family Mediation with those for Legal Representation; give the Legal Services Commission power to waive the upper disposable income limit for eligibility for Legal Representation in proceedings where a client is seeking an order for protection from harm to the person, or committal of a person for breach of such an order; provide for allowance from income of childcare costs for those who are self employed, when determining eligibility for services; and amend provisions about the calculation of a client's disposable capital.

2714. Legal services–Community Legal Service–Enforcement of order for costs

COMMUNITY LEGAL SERVICE (COST PROTECTION) (AMENDMENT) REGULATIONS 2005, SI 2005 2006; made under the Access to Justice Act 1999 s.11, s.26. In force: July 25, 2005; £3.00.

These Regulations amend the Community Legal Service (Cost Protection) Regulations 2000 (SI 2000 824) consequential upon changes to the Funding Code criteria which abolish Support Funding. They also make amendments to the 2000 Regulations which provide for enforcement of a costs order so that its provisions only apply where cost protection applies.

2715. Legal services–Community Legal Service–Funding

COMMUNITY LEGAL SERVICE (FINANCIAL) (AMENDMENT NO.3) REGULATIONS 2005, SI 2005 1793; made under the Access to Justice Act 1999 s.7, s.10, s.26. In force: July 25, 2005; £3.00.

These Regulations amend the Community Legal Service (Financial) Regulations 2000 (SI 2000 516), which govern financial aspects of the provisions of services funded by the Legal Services Commission in civil matters as part of the Community Legal Service. They provide for amendments to Reg.3 of the 2000 Regulations, which sets out the areas in which funded services are available irrespective of the financial resources of the client; permit waiver of the eligibility limit where any legal services, and not only advocacy, are provided and permit waiver of contributions where the client is ineligible financially for legal aid as well as where he is eligible; and provide for the circumstances in which enforcement of the charge will not be postponed, and decisions to postpone enforcement of the charge will be reviewed.

2716. Legal services–Community Legal Service–Funding

COMMUNITY LEGAL SERVICE (SCOPE) REGULATIONS 2005, SI 2005 2008; made under the Access to Justice Act 1999 s.6, s.26. In force: July 25, 2005; £3.00.

These Regulations amend the Access to Justice Act 1999 Sch.2 so as to exclude from the scope of the Community Legal Service help in relation to any allegations of personal injury or death (before this amendment, only help in relation to allegations of negligently caused injury or death was excluded) in relation to applications for funded services made on or after July 25, 2005; and to include within the scope of the Community Legal Service advocacy in the Crown Court in an application for a restraint order under the Proceeds of Crime Act 2002 Part 2.

2717. Legal services–Community Legal Service–Funding–Counsel in family proceedings

COMMUNITY LEGAL SERVICE (FUNDING) (COUNSEL IN FAMILY PROCEEDINGS) (AMENDMENT) ORDER 2005, SI 2005 184; made under the Access to Justice Act 1999 s.6. In force: February 28, 2005; £3.00.

This Order amends the system for the payment of graduated fees for counsel for work in family proceedings as set out in the Community Legal Service (Funding) (Counsel in Family Proceedings) Order 2001 (SI 2001 1077). It clarifies specified definitions; provides that the 2001 Order does not apply where the use of counsel has not been authorised in advance by the Legal Services Commission, or where the use of counsel is not considered to have been necessary on a costs assessment; makes an amendment to provide that in mixed or multiple claims, payment of the base fee under functions F1 and F4 may be claimed up to two times in a category; creates three new Special Issue Payments which may arise and be claimed, where applicable; provides for new increased rates for financial dispute resolution hearing payments; provides for new increased rates for care proceedings payments; inserts a new payment for enforcement procedures and contested injunction hearings; and clarifies that where an early settlement supplement is payable it is calculated on the single base fee or hearing unit fee, whether or not multiple fees have been claimed in respect of a single set of proceedings. It also reduces the time limit for a claim for payment to be submitted to two months following the conclusion of the main hearing for the purposes of function F5, and for all other functions to two months following the discharge or revocation of a certificate.

2718. Legal services–Community Legal Service–Persons subject to control orders

COMMUNITY LEGAL SERVICE (FINANCIAL) (AMENDMENT NO.2) REGULATIONS 2005, SI 2005 1097; made under the Access to Justice Act 1999 s.7. In force: in accordance with Reg.1; £3.00.

These Regulations amend the Community Legal Service (Financial) Regulations 2000 (SI 2000 516) to make legal help and representation under the Community Legal Service available to a person subject to a control order under the Prevention of Terrorism Act 2005 without reference to the person's financial resources.

2719. Legal services–Community Legal Service–Remuneration rates

COMMUNITY LEGAL SERVICE (FUNDING) (AMENDMENT) ORDER 2005, SI 2005 571; made under the Access to Justice Act 1999 s.6. In force: April 4, 2005; £3.00.

This Order amends the Community Legal Service (Funding) Order 2000 (SI 2000 627) in consequence of the establishment of the Asylum and Immigration Tribunal, which replaces immigration adjudicators and the Immigration Appeal Tribunal. It makes amendments so that the maximum rates of remuneration under contracts specified in that article do not apply in relation to Legal Representation before the Asylum and Immigration Tribunal or the High Court in applications under the Nationality, Immigration and Asylum Act 2002 s.103A, or before the Asylum and Immigration Tribunal in proceedings for the reconsideration of an appeal pursuant to an order under s.103A.

2720. Solicitors remuneration–Liens–Solicitors' charge on clients' property– Agreement that solicitors be paid out of settlement monies

[Solicitors Act 1974 s.73; Supreme Court Act 1981 s.35A; Civil Procedure Rules 1998 (SI 1998 3132) Part 8.]

The claimant firm of solicitors (C) applied under the Civil Procedure Rules 1998 Part 8 for a charge under the Solicitors Act 1974 s.73 for their costs and disbursements in acting for the defendants (S) in previous litigation, the charge being claimed over settlement monies received by S in that litigation. S operated an interior design and refurbishment business. C acted for S in relation to a dispute they had with D. Under C's terms of business, payment was due within 28 days of C sending S the final bill and interest was payable for late payment at the rate of 15 per cent. Halfway through the trial S gave a second charge to C over their house, stipulating a rate of 8 per cent interest for monies due. D and S settled their dispute on the basis that D would continue to pursue one of the other defendants and that S would be paid 50 per cent of D's net recoveries up to a maximum of £500,000. C informed S that they intended to look to any recoveries made under the settlement by way of payment for their services. D succeeded in their claim against the other defendant and paid the agreed sum over to S's new solicitors, who had replaced C. C applied for an injunction preventing S from demanding, receiving, disposing or dealing with any of the settlement monies, which was granted on a temporary basis. S argued that (1) the taking of any alternative security of substance and value without an express reservation of C's existing rights was sufficient to operate as a waiver of those rights; (2) C's entitlement under the security to interest on their fees was inconsistent with C's s.73 right as, notwithstanding the fact that C's terms of business provided for interest at 15 per cent, that provision was unenforceable in the light of the fact that C did not specifically draw it to the attention of S or give any advice about it. C argued that nevertheless their right to security revived in view of their informing S that they intended to look to any recoveries under the settlement. C also argued that there was an agreement between the parties, amounting to an equitable charge in favour of C, that settlement monies would first be used to discharge C's costs.

Held, giving judgment for C, that (1) the taking of any alternative security by a solicitor would not necessarily waive his lien. A solicitor only waived his lien if he took a security that was inconsistent with the lien. (2) A solicitor could not enforce a stipulation for interest markedly higher than would ever be allowed by the court under the Supreme Court Act 1981 s.35A against a client unless he established that he had informed the client that the law would not otherwise enable him to claim interest at such a rate, *Lyddon v. Moss* (1859) 4 De G. & J. 104 applied. A solicitor who took security conferring a right to interest that he did not otherwise possess waived his right to a lien unless he expressly reserved it. The same principle applied to C and their s.73 right, which they had therefore waived by taking the charge. (3) Once the rights were waived, it was necessary for there to be a fresh agreement between solicitor and client that the rights were to be exercisable after all. C were therefore not able to revive their s.73 rights simply by making it clear to S that they expected to look to any recoveries under the settlement. However, if S were able to have the security avoided then C's s.73 rights would revive as they would be entitled to be put back in the same position they would have been in had the security never been granted. (4) On the facts, S had agreed to the settlement monies being used to pay disbursements and costs. Although there was no formal agreement, C had in the discussions leading up to the settlement made their position abundantly clear and S had not dissented from this. This was sufficient to have created an equitable charge over the settlement monies in favour of C.

CLIFFORD HARRIS & CO v. SOLLAND INTERNATIONAL LTD (NO.2), [2005] EWHC 141, [2005] 2 All E.R. 334, Christopher Nugee Q.C., Ch D.

2721. Books

Biggs, Ak—Lawyers Costs and Fees: Probate. Paperback: £13.95. ISBN 0 7545 2939 8. Tolley Publishing.

Biggs, Keith—Lawyers Costs and Fees: Fees and Fixed Costs in Civil Actions. Paperback: £14.95. ISBN 1 84592 216 6. Tottel Publishing.

Timms, Judith—Children's Representation. Paperback: £60.00. ISBN 0 421 62630 5. Sweet & Maxwell.

Wignall, Gordon; Napier, Michael—Conditional Fees: A Guide to Funding Litigation. Paperback: £39.95. ISBN 1 85328 992 2. Law Society Publications.

LEGAL METHODOLOGY

2722. Books

Backhouse, Constance; Backhouse, Nancy L.—HeiressVs. the Establishment: Mrs. Campbell's Campaign for Legal Justice. Law & Society S. Paperback: £19.95. ISBN 0 7748 1053 X. University of British Columbia Press.

Bonsignore, John J.; Katsh, Ethan; D'Errico, Peter; Pipkin, Ronald M.; Arons, Stephen; Rifkin, Janet—Before the Law: An Introduction to the Legal Process. Hardback: £23.95. ISBN 0 618 50345 5. Houghton Mifflin Co.

Cranston, Ross—How Law Works: The Machinery and Impact of Civil Justice. Hardback: £50.00. ISBN 0 19 929207 8. Oxford University Press.

Current Law Case Citator 2002-2004. Hardback: £120.00. ISBN 0 421 91680 X. Sweet & Maxwell.

Current LawYearbook 2004 S/O Service. Hardback: £230.00. ISBN 0 421 91640 0. Sweet & Maxwell.

Ekern,Yvonne; Hames, Joanne Banker—Legal Research, Analysis, andWriting: An Integrated Approach. Paperback: £53.99. ISBN 0 13 118888 7. Prentice Hall.

Ekern,Yvonne; Hames, Joanne Banker—Introduction to Law. Paperback: £57.99. ISBN 0 13 118381 8. Prentice Hall.

Encyclopaedia of Forms and Precedents 22: Part 2 OB. Hardback: £201.00. ISBN 1 4057 0124 2. Butterworths Law.

Encyclopaedia of Forms and Precedents Consolidated Index. Paperback: £245.00. ISBN 1 4057 0826 3. Butterworths Law.

Encyclopaedia of Forms and Precedents Form Finder. Paperback: £245.00. ISBN 1 4057 0824 7. Butterworths Law.

Encyclopaedia of Forms and Precedents Volume 16 (2): V. 16. Hardback: £245.00. ISBN 1 4057 0128 5. Butterworths Law.

Encyclopaedia of Forms and Precedents: Vol.35. Hardback: £201.00. ISBN 0 406 97478 0. Butterworths Law.

Hare–Documentary Credits: Law and Practice. Hardback: £195.00. ISBN 1 84311 428 3. Informa Business Publishing.

Himma, Kenneth Einar; Bix, Brian–Law and Morality. International Library of Essays in Law & Legal Theory: Second Series. Hardback: £130.00. ISBN 0 7546 2577 X. Ashgate.

Holder, Jane–Current Legal Problems. Current Legal Problems, V. 58. Hardback: £80.00. ISBN 0 19 928539 X. Oxford University Press.

Inns of Court School of Law–Drafting. Blackstone Bar Manual S. Paperback: £26.99. ISBN 0 19 928152 1. Oxford University Press.

Jones, Stephen–Criminology. Paperback: £21.99. ISBN 0 19 928238 2. Oxford University Press.

Law Reports Set. Other printed material: £504.00. ISBN 1 4057 0623 6. Butterworths Law.

Loyita Worley–Bial Handbook of Legal Information Management. Hardback: £70.00. ISBN 0 7546 4182 1. Ashgate.

McAdams, Tony–Law, Business, and Society. Hardback: £96.99. ISBN 0 07 304810 0. Higher Education.

McLeod, Ian–Legal Method. Palgrave Law Masters S. Paperback: £14.99. ISBN 1 4039 4870 4. Palgrave Macmillan.

Milner, Alan–Jersey Law Reports: Pt. 1. Paperback: £35.00. ISBN 1 902907 74 4. Law Reports International.

Rose, Francis–General Average: Law and Practice. Hardback: £160.00. ISBN 1 84311 418 6. Informa Business Publishing.

Taylor, William–Geography of Law: Landscape, Identity and Regulation. Onati International Series in Law & Society. Hardback: £35.00. ISBN 1 84113 556 9. Hart Publishing.

"Times" Law Reports Bound. Other printed material: £149.00. ISBN 1 4057 0888 3. Butterworths Law.

Wilman, John–Brown: GCSE Law. Paperback: £13.95. ISBN 0 421 89790 2. Sweet & Maxwell.

LEGAL PROFESSION

2723. **Foreign lawyers–Registration–Law Society's power to impose conditions after initial entry made in register**

[Solicitors Act 1974; Courts and Legal Services Act 1990 Sch.14 para.2(3), Sch.14 para.12(2), Sch.14 para.13, Sch.14 para.14(1)(d).]

The Law Society applied to judicially review a decision that, under the Courts and Legal Services Act 1990 Sch.14 para.2(3) it could only impose conditions on a foreign lawyer on the initial making of an entry in the register of foreign lawyers. The Law Society had imposed conditions under Sch.14 para.2(3) on the registration of the interested party, who was a foreign lawyer, even though he had been registered for some years. On appeal to the Master of the Rolls, it was accepted that the word "registration" in Sch.14 para.2(3) was ambiguous and could mean either (i) that the initial making of an entry in the register could be subject to such conditions as the Law Society saw fit, or (ii) that the entry that had been made in the register could be subject to such conditions that the Law Society saw fit at any time to impose. The Master of the Rolls held that the first meaning applied so that the Law Society had no general power to impose conditions after the initial making of an entry on the register. The Law Society argued that the second meaning was, as a matter of language, the more natural interpretation. It contended that it was necessary to give the provision a purposive construction because if there was no general power to impose conditions after the initial making of the entry, there could be a lacuna where subsequent concerns about the conduct of a registered foreign lawyer arose. Given that the power to impose conditions after initial entry in respect of solicitors under the Solicitors Act 1974 was almost unrestricted, the Law Society argued that the power in relation to registered foreign lawyers should be similar.

Held, refusing the application, that both the language and broader context and purpose of the scheme of registration showed that under Sch.14 para.2(3), the Law Society only had the power to impose conditions on the initial making of the entry in the register. Schedule 14 para.12(2) and Sch.14 para.13 gave the Law Society the express power to impose conditions when suspension was terminated or when a registration was revived. If there had been a general power to impose conditions at any time, there would have been no need for such express powers. There would also have been no need in Sch.14 para.14(1)(d) to specify that there was a right of appeal to the Master of the Rolls against the imposition of conditions under Sch.14 para.12(2) and Sch.14 para.13. Further, the fact that such appeals had to be brought within one month of the date on which the Law Society notified the applicant of its decision on his application suggested that the grounds of appeal were dependent on an application by the registered foreign lawyer. That was consistent with Sch.14 para.2(3) referring to the initial making of an entry. In the wider context of the regulation of solicitors and registered foreign lawyers, Parliament had properly circumscribed the power in relation to solicitors and it could not be inferred from those powers that there was a similar unrestricted power over registered foreign lawyers after the initial registration. The lacuna created was not very significant because the primary body responsible for a foreign lawyer was the regulatory body within the jurisdiction in which the lawyer was admitted and if the subsequent conduct of a lawyer gave the Law Society cause for concern, it could report the matter to that regulatory body.

R. (ON THE APPLICATION OF THE LAW SOCIETY) v. MASTER OF THE ROLLS; *sub nom.* LAW SOCIETY v. MASTER OF THE ROLLS, [2005] EWHC 146, [2005] 1 W.L.R. 2033, Thomas, L.J., QBD (Admin).

2724. Law firms–Conflict of interest–Confidentiality of former client– Representation of consortium in takeover bid for former client's company

The applicant (F), a firm of solicitors, applied for permission to appeal against a decision (*The Times*, June 18, 2004) granting an injunction in favour of the respondent supermarket (M). The injunction restrained F from acting for a client consortium (R) which wished to take over M. F had acted for M in previous commercial transactions, including negotiating a major contract with a clothing designer (D). F submitted that (1) there was no inherent conflict of interest as the transaction with R was separate from those where it had acted for M and the principle established in *Bolkiah v. KPMG* [1999] 2 A.C. 222, [1999] C.L.Y. 1 was limited to "same transaction" cases; (2) there was no real risk of conflict of interest because (i) an undertaking had been offered by F and R that information about the contract with D would be neither sought nor shared; (ii) the takeover would not necessarily be hostile; (3) a broader approach should be adopted in takeover cases and the concept of confidentiality should be given more limited operation. Chinese wall arrangements could be put in place to protect M's confidentiality.

Held, refusing the application, that (1) there was an inherent conflict where transactions between a present and former client had some degree of relationship. The principle in *Bolkiah* was not confined to "same transaction" cases, *Bolkiah* applied. In the instant case there was a real or serious risk of a conflict of interest. (2) (i) The undertaking did not detract from a conflict of interest existing and that conflict would not be avoided by such an undertaking;

(ii) there was potential for hostility to arise in a takeover situation and a solicitor could not assume that it would not, nor adopt a wait and see position before deciding whether it was appropriate to act. (3) The systems which F had in place had not been sufficient to prevent a conflict of interest arising and the judge had been right to come to the conclusion that Chinese walls would be insufficient to protect M's confidentiality. The fact that F had advised in a substantial way in D's arrangements would have alerted F to the possibility of conflict.

MARKS & SPENCER PLC v. FRESHFIELDS BRUCKHAUS DERINGER, [2004] EWCA Civ 741, [2005] P.N.L.R. 4, Pill, L.J., CA.

2725. Legal profession–Law Society–Intervention in solicitor's practice–Remedies available

[Solicitors Act 1974 Sch.1 para.6(4); Human Rights Act 1998 Sch.1 Part II Art.1.]

The appellant solicitor (K) appealed against an order dismissing his application for withdrawal of an intervention notice served by the respondent Law Society on the grounds of suspected dishonesty. There had been a substantial cash shortage in K's firm's client account which had arisen due to transfers of sums from the client account to the office account over a long period of time. K's practising certificate had been suspended. On an application by K, the judge refused to direct the withdrawal of the intervention notices, refused to restore K's practising certificate, refused to direct that K be given access to the files and refused to discharge a freezing injunction in respect of K's assets. The judge found that the choice of remedy was limited to allowing the intervention to continue or wholly reversing it and that the balance lay in favour of allowing it to continue. However he expressed regret that there was not a remedy which more satisfactorily addressed the problem. There was no challenge to the judge's finding that there were reasons to suspect K of dishonesty but K submitted that the judge should not have allowed the intervention to continue as the Law Society and the court's powers under the Solicitors Act 1974 Sch.1 were not so circumscribed.

Held, dismissing the appeal, that the judge had been correct to find that the choice was between the intervention continuing or being wholly reversed. Some form of supervision and control was required and, if that could not be provided by the exercise of powers short of full intervention, there was no alternative to the intervention continuing. The statutory regime under which powers of intervention were conferred on the Law Society was not of itself inconsistent with the Human Rights Act 1998 Sch.1 Part II Art.1 and the Law Society was not to be criticised for taking the view that it should act in accordance with the statutory regime, rather than seek to adopt some alternative procedure, *Holder v. Law Society* [2003] EWCA Civ 39, [2003] 1 W.L.R. 1059, [2003] C.L.Y. 2824 applied. When deciding whether to dismiss an application under Sch.1 para.6(4) of the 1974 Act, in circumstances where the Law Society's decision to exercise its statutory powers of intervention was not flawed, a court was not required to ask itself whether it should fashion an alternative remedy. Parliament had prescribed the form that intervention should take and it was not for the Law Society to seek some other remedy from the court and it was not for the court to substitute a remedy of its own. The judge was right to allow the intervention to continue. K's appeals against the judge's further orders were also dismissed.

SRITHARAN v. LAW SOCIETY; *sub nom.* LAW SOCIETY v. SRITHARAN, [2005] EWCA Civ 476, [2005] 1 W.L.R. 2708, Chadwick, L.J., CA (Civ Div).

2726. Legal representation–Institute of Trade Mark Attorneys–Designation

INSTITUTE OF TRADE MARK ATTORNEYS ORDER 2005, SI 2005 240; made under the Courts and Legal Services Act 1990 s.29, Sch.4 Part I. In force: April 1, 2005; £3.00.

This Order designates the Institute of Trade Mark Attorneys as an authorised body for the purposes of the Courts and Legal Services Act 1990 s.27 and s.28, under which authorised bodies may grant, respectively, rights of audience and rights to conduct litigation.

2727. **Professional conduct–Solicitors–Standard of proof applied in disciplinary proceedings**

The appellant lawyer (C) appealed against the decision of the Court of Appeal of Trinidad and Tobago that a disciplinary committee had been right to find that a complaint of professional misconduct against him had been substantiated. The complaint had been made in 1987 by the person (S) now represented by the respondent executrix (H). The essence of the complaint was that S had given C a sum to purchase land that S understood C to own, but that C had neither conveyed the land nor returned the purchase price. The substantive hearing took place a year after the complaint was made, but it was not until 1996 that the committee produced its findings and orders. The Court of Appeal dismissed C's appeal, which had been made on grounds not advanced before the Board. Before the Board, C argued that (1) the committee should have applied the criminal standard of proof in their determination of the complaint, but had in fact applied a lesser standard; (2) the eight year delay in the delivery of the committee's judgment was intrinsically unfair and adversely affected the quality of the judgment.

Held, dismissing the appeal, that (1) the criminal standard of proof was the correct standard to be applied in all disciplinary proceedings concerning the legal profession. If and in so far as the Privy Council in *Bhandari v. Advocates Committee* [1956] 1 W.L.R. 1442, [1956] C.L.Y. 6608 might be thought to have approved some lesser standard, that decision ought no longer to be followed, *Bhandari* and *Solicitor, Re* [1993] Q.B. 69, [1992] C.L.Y. 4089 considered. There was nothing in the committee's determination to suggest that it applied a lower, let alone materially lower, standard of proof than that of beyond reasonable doubt. The expressions used by the Court of Appeal as relied on by C related to how a number of factual sub issues fell to be resolved, not to the critical final issue of whether the allegation of professional misconduct had been made out. To find the complaint proved it was not necessary for the committee or the Court of Appeal to find each and every sub issue proved beyond reasonable doubt. In any event, the evidence against C had been overwhelming. (2) For the committee to have delayed eight years in giving judgment was highly reprehensible. However, it did not follow that C had a sustainable ground of appeal on that basis. C had made no attempt to encourage the committee to accelerate its deliberations and judgment. Moreover, the delay had been to his own benefit, the only injustice being to S. The delay had not adversely affected the committee's determination, *Goose v. Wilson Sandford & Co (No.1)* Times, February 19, 1998, [1998] C.L.Y. 50 distinguished.

CAMPBELL v. HAMLET (EXECUTRIX OF SIMON ALEXANDER), [2005] UKPC 19, [2005] 3 All E.R. 1116, Lord Hope of Craighead, PC (Trin).

2728. **Solicitors–Disciplinary procedures–Solicitor challenging intervention in High Court–Summary judgment following outcome of disciplinary proceedings but before appeal**

The appellant solicitor (S) appealed against a decision ([2004] EWHC 1706) granting summary judgment and costs on an indemnity basis to the respondent Law Society. The Law Society brought intervention proceedings against S. S challenged the intervention in the High Court. Following the commencement of disciplinary proceedings, it was agreed by a consent order that the High Court proceedings should await the "final conclusion" of the disciplinary proceedings. The outcome of the disciplinary proceedings was a decision upholding most of the charges. S appealed to the Divisional Court. Before the appeal was heard, the Law Society was granted summary judgment in the High Court proceedings and S was ordered to pay costs on an indemnity basis on the ground that S must have realised all along that the Law Society was justified at least in suspecting that he had been conducting part of his practice dishonestly. S was ordered to make an interim payment towards costs of £150,000. The Divisional Court upheld the tribunal's decision. S argued that (1) the judge should have awaited the final conclusion of the disciplinary proceedings; (2) the judge's decision on costs was unjustified; (3) the interim payment was wrong as the judge had been given no detailed breakdown of the costs in question and was therefore not in any position to form a proper view as to the likely level of costs following taxation.

Held, allowing the appeal in part, that (1) the expression "final conclusion" in the consent order did not in terms deprive either party of the right to apply for any form of relief for which a case could be made at an earlier stage. Indeed, the order specifically gave each party "liberty to apply" without qualification. Thus there was nothing in the order which, in itself, precluded the Law Society's application. After two judgments in the Law Society's favour, it was difficult realistically to envisage any outcome which would lead to the conclusion that it did not have "reason to suspect" dishonesty, and that was enough to justify intervention. Furthermore, once the disciplinary proceedings had begun, the practical value of the High Court proceedings disappeared. (2) When considering an application for the award of costs on an indemnity basis, the court was concerned with the losing party's conduct of the case, rather than with the substantive merits of his position, *Kiam v. MGN Ltd (Costs)* [2002] EWCA Civ 66, [2002] 1 W.L.R. 2810, [2002] C.L.Y. 347 applied. The court was normally reluctant to interfere with a judge's exercise of discretion as to the basis on which costs were awarded. This, however, was a very marginal case for an award on an indemnity basis. S's position throughout had been consistent. Furthermore, contrary to the judge's assumption, one of the effects of an order for costs on the indemnity basis was to displace the issues of proportionality, which were expressly provided for on the standard basis. That limitation on the scope of the arguments in the assessment was an important additional factor which tipped the balance in favour of an award on the standard basis. In view of the judge's error, that part of the appeal was allowed and an order for costs on the standard basis substituted. (3) Even if S's arguments about proportionality were accepted, the judge was entitled to take the view that the costs were unlikely to reduce to a figure below £150,000. In the unlikely event that the figure proved excessive, there was no doubt about S's ability to repay the excess or that it could be set against the other liabilities in the disciplinary proceedings. Thus in the special circumstances of the case it was impossible to conclude that the judge was not entitled as a matter of discretion to order the interim payment that he did.

SIMMS v. LAW SOCIETY, [2005] EWCA Civ 849, *The Independent*, July 14, 2005, Auld, L.J., CA (Civ Div).

2729. Solicitors–Inadequate professional services–Compensation

SOLICITORS (COMPENSATION FOR INADEQUATE PROFESSIONAL SERVICES) ORDER 2005, SI 2005 2749; made under the Solicitors Act 1974 Sch.1A para.3. In force: January 1, 2006; £3.00.

This Order increases from £5,000 to £15,000 the maximum compensation that the Council of the Law Society may direct a solicitor to pay his client for inadequate professional services.

2730. Solicitors–Intervention–Withdrawal of intervention–Existence of evidence to support suspicion of dishonesty

The applicant solicitor (S) applied under the Solicitors Act 1974 Sch.1 para.6(4) and Sch.1 para.9(8) to have the intervention by the defendant Law Society in her practice withdrawn. Without giving its reasons, the Adjudication Panel of the Law Society, pursuant to s.35 of the Act, had intervened in S's sole practice. The Law Society submitted that it had been justified in intervening because (1) it had reason to suspect S of dishonesty under Sch.1 para.1(1)(a); (2) it was satisfied as required by Sch.1 para.1 (1) (c) that S had failed to comply with the Solicitors'Accounts Rules made under s.32 of the Act.

Held, granting the application, that (1) the court was not limited to considering the materials that had been before the panel, *Giles v. Law Society* (1996) 8 Admin. L.R. 105, [1996] C.L.Y. 3917 applied. Further evidence from S led to the conclusion that there was no reason to suspect dishonesty in any way that could justify the drastic step of intervention. (2) There had been some breaches of the Rules, but they were not serious enough to merit the drastic and, in the case of a sole practitioner, effectively terminal step of intervention. Where there were breaches and no dishonesty then an intervention should be unusual as the Law Society had other suitable avenues by which to improve compliance, such as the Solicitors' Disciplinary Tribunal. Besides, S had since undertaken to improve her compliance. (3) There were legitimate grounds for concern by the Law Society regarding other aspects of the firm's practice, but they were not remotely as bad or unacceptable as claimed, and it was very doubtful that matters other than those bearing on the issues of dishonesty or breach of the Rules could play a part in the court's decision as to whether or not the intervention should be withdrawn. This was so even though the court was not limited to considering the materials that had been before the panel. A general opinion by the panel that a practice was unsatisfactory was an insufficient foundation for intervention under the Act, and it was similarly doubtful that it should carry any substantial weight when the issue of withdrawal was being decided. (4) It seemed that Parliament had imagined that applications under Sch.1 para.6(4) and para.9(8) could and would be brought to court and dealt with quickly, because by that time the solicitor would know what was alleged against him or her. In most cases that would be true because, once the solicitor had seen the material that had been before the Panel, the reasons for the intervention would be obvious. However, in S's case, although S and her advisers did have the materials that the Panel had had, they did not make it at all clear what the alleged dishonesty was or what the grounds for suspecting it were. The Panel had given absolutely no particulars of its reason to suspect dishonesty or of the alleged breaches of the Rules; this absence had caused considerable difficulty. S, her legal advisers and the court itself could only speculate as to the case that S had to meet. Even the Law Society's own legal advisers were in the same position. This difficulty had greatly increased the length of the trial and judgment, in circumstances where all delay was potentially damaging to S's practice.

SHEIKH v. LAW SOCIETY, [2005] EWHC 1409, [2005] 4 All E.R. 717, Park, J., Ch D.

2731. Solicitors–Professional conduct–Extent to which solicitor's behaviour amounted to dishonesty–Action comprising utilisation of client's funds

The appellant solicitor (D) appealed against a decision of the Solicitors Disciplinary Tribunal to strike him off the roll of solicitors for, amongst other things, breaching the terms of a professional undertaking; acting in his professional capacity towards a third party in a deceitful or misleading way and utilising client's funds for his own benefit. D's client (C) had approached an American company (H) to take part in an investment transaction relating to United States treasury bonds. H had agreed to make an advance payment to cover C's disbursements in the acquisition of those bonds on the understanding that the funds would be held in D's client account and on D's undertaking that he would not make any payments from the account without H's express instructions. However, D knowingly gave H the bank co-ordinates of C's personal account into which funds were transferred. No mention was made of the account holder. The bond transaction subsequently fell through and H demanded return of the funds which C did not repay. In another transaction involving C and a company (M), D was granted a power of attorney by M to receive funds. Instead those funds were paid into the client account of C's US attorney. D, in accordance with C's instructions, instructed money to be disbursed from the US attorney's account. It transpired that, although the exact path of the funds was unknown, a proportion of the disbursed funds had been utilised for D's personal use. D accepted that money in the US attorney's account belonging to M had, as a result of C's instructions, been wrongly appropriated. D submitted that (1) the allegation of dishonesty had not been established; (2) the allegation that he had utilised client finds had not been proved.

Held, dismissing the appeal, that (1) the tribunal had correctly applied the test set out in *Twinsectra Ltd v. Yardley* [2002] UKHL 12, [2002] 2 A.C. 164, [2002] C.L.Y. 249, *Twinsectra* applied. Therefore, the tribunal had been entitled to reach the conclusion that D had been dishonest by failing to inform H that the bank details provided were in fact for C's personal bank account, and he could only have done so in order to obscure the actual destination of the funds. (2) The tribunal had failed to deal clearly with the precise route by which D had received money originating from the account of the US attorney. However the main thrust of the complaint was that D had been party to instructions given by C as to the disbursement of M's funds when D knew that those funds should not have been disbursed on C's instructions. Accordingly the tribunal'ns finding that D had used client money for his own benefit was correct.

DUTTON v. LAW SOCIETY, [2005] EWHC 125, *The Times*, January 31, 2005, Latham, L.J., QBD (Admin).

2732. **Solicitors–Professional conduct–Improper transfer of client ledger balances–Propriety of solicitor's striking off**

The Law Society appealed against a decision ([2004] EWHC 1370) to reduce the penalty imposed on a solicitor (B) guilty of dishonesty from striking off to suspension from practice for two years. B cross appealed against the finding of dishonesty. B had practised as the sole equity partner together with a salaried partner. An investigation by the Office for the Supervision of Solicitors (OSS) detected a shortfall of clients' funds, much of which related to relatively small client ledger credit balances which had been improperly transferred to the office bank account. The firm's reporting accountant had declined to sign the accountant's report on the firm's accounts in 1999 unless a number of old credit balances on client account were removed. In the time available it was not possible to deal properly with the credit balances and a system was devised of creating false debit notes, on the basis of which B signed a cheque transferring a composite sum of client balances to the office account. The nature of the dishonesty alleged against B in disciplinary proceedings was transferring clients' funds to the office account without knowing or caring whether or not the firm was entitled to be paid those funds, even if there was an intention to repay those funds if it was subsequently found that the firm was not in fact entitled to the sums transferred. The position was not regularised before the OSS investigation. The Solicitors' Disciplinary Tribunal found B guilty of dishonesty and ordered his name to be struck off the roll of solicitors. The Divisional Court found that B had been dishonest even if he had intended to carry out an analysis of the individual client ledgers at a later time, but substituted for striking off the penalty of a suspension from practice for two years. B submitted that he was not dishonest because he had not intended permanently to deprive anyone of anything and that what had been done was done to satisfy the requirements of the reporting accountant and was not done by B personally but by others. The Law Society submitted that dishonesty by a solicitor in connection with the operation of a client account should lead all but automatically to an order for striking off.

Held, allowing the appeal and dismissing the cross appeal, that (1) proof of dishonesty in the context of the instant case did not depend on proving an intention permanently to deprive. B signed a cheque transferring client funds to his office account without any supporting documentation and thus, it had to be inferred, without knowing or caring whether his firm was entitled to be paid those funds. That satisfied the relevant test for dishonesty, *Twinsectra Ltd v. Yardley* [2002] UKHL 12, [2002] 2 A.C. 164, [2002] C.L.Y. 249 applied. When B became aware of the debit notes, it must have been clear that those bogus documents had been used to clear the credit balances, but he did nothing. He was guilty of conscious impropriety amounting to dishonesty in endorsing what had been done. That was not a momentary error of judgment but a clear case of dishonesty of a serious kind. (2) Although B did not devise the scheme and the scheme did not jeopardise clients as much as it would have done if the office account were not in credit and there was no paper trail, there was serious dishonesty. There was no compelling reason for B to do what he did and the sum of money involved was significant. False documents were created and continued to exist and there was no clear cut evidence of restitution. On the facts and authorities B had to be struck off. If leniency were to be extended in the instant case, it would lower the tariff and make it difficult to strike off anyone guilty of dishonesty not amounting to theft.

BULTITUDE v. LAW SOCIETY, [2004] EWCA Civ 1853, *The Times*, January 14, 2005, Kennedy, L.J., CA (Civ Div).

2733. **Solicitors–Professional indemnity insurance–Premium for cover under assured risks pool**

[Competition Act 1998; Solicitors Indemnity Insurance Rules 2000.]

The claimant (Q) and the Law Society (L) applied to strike out a defence to a claim for £56,847.73. A solicitor (R), being unable to obtain professional indemnity insurance on the open market, had obtain cover from Q, which ran the Assured Risks Pool, a scheme set up by L for those in the same situation as R. R refused to pay the premium on the grounds that the Solicitors Indemnity Insurance Rules 2000 and the ARP created by the Rules breached the Competition Act 1998 as they amounted to an agreement that restricted competition and abused a dominant position by charging excessive premiums.

Held, giving judgment for Q, that the scheme was not a separate market from the wider one, it was not exclusive and there was no suggestion that insurers outside the scheme refused coverage so as to force those seeking it inside the scheme. Q held no dominant position, and its premiums, though they could be higher than the open market, were not always so, and so were not excessive. Q was not anti competitive, as solicitors were encouraged to insure themselves on the open market.

QUALIFYING INSURERS SUBSCRIBING TO THE ARP v. ROSS & CO, [2004] EWHC 1181, [2004] U.K.C.L.R. 1483, Sir Andrew Morritt V.C., Ch D.

2734. **Solicitors–Professional negligence–Hearings–Right to fair trial–Disciplinary penalties and alleged breach of solicitor's human rights**

[Human Rights Act 1998 Sch.1 Part I Art.6, Part II Art.1.]

T, a solicitor, sought judicial review of the Law Society's disciplinary sanctions imposed on him following two unrelated complaints to the Office for the Supervision of Solicitors. T was found to have provided inadequate professional services and was ordered to refund his costs and pay compensation. He was also referred to the Solicitors Disciplinary Tribunal (SDT) and it was ordered that a discretion should vest in the renewal of his practising certificate. In the second case T's application to the adjudication panel for an oral hearing was dismissed on the basis that the matter was not of sufficient complexity to warrant an oral hearing and because the written material was sufficiently detailed to allow the panel to arrive at a fair conclusion on it alone. T argued that (1) in each case he ought to have been afforded an opportunity to make oral representations; (2) the failure to provide such opportunities infringed his rights at common law as well as his right to fair trial under the Human Rights Act 1998 Sch.1 Part I Art.6; (3) the requirement that he refund his accrued costs infringed his right to peaceful enjoyment of possessions under Sch.1 Part II Art.1 of the 1998 Act.

Held, refusing the application, that T's failure to request an oral hearing on the first case was fatal to his claim at common law and the complaints could in any case be determined on the written evidence. With regard to the second case, the panel had applied the correct test when dismissing the application, namely whether the disputed issues might fairly be resolved without an oral hearing, and there was no disputed question of fact which could not fairly be resolved without oral evidence. In neither case was the decision not to grant an oral hearing unfair at common law, *R. (on the application of Smith) v. Parole Board* [2003] EWCA Civ 1269, [2004] 1 W.L.R. 421, [2003] C.L.Y. 2144 applied. Only where a solicitor's right to practise was taken away could there be any determination of civil rights to which Art.6 might apply and a mere reprimand could not trigger any Art.6 issue, *Le Compte v. Belgium (A/43)* [1982] E.C.C. 240 applied. The direction to pay compensation would only have legal effect when the SDT had determined that it be enforced; therefore T's civil rights were not engaged. Although an accrued right to costs was indeed a possession for the purposes of Sch.1 Part II Art.1, there had been no breach of Art.6 and thus no breach of T's Convention rights.

R. (ON THE APPLICATION OF THOMPSON) v. LAW SOCIETY, [2004] EWCA Civ 167, [2004] 1 W.L.R. 2522, Kennedy, L.J., CA.

2735. Solicitors–Suspension–Power of Solicitors Disciplinary Tribunal to impose conditions on practising certificates

[Solicitors Act 1974 s.47.]

C, a solicitor, appealed against the tribunal's decision to suspend him indefinitely. At a previous hearing the period of suspension had been reduced to 18 months subject to certain practising conditions. On the instant appeal, the Law Society, L argued that, for reasons of policing and enforcement and also to allow L to exercise its discretion over the issuing of practising certificates on the basis of facts available at the time of application for a new certificate, the tribunal ought not to impose conditions but should instead continue its existing practice of imposing a suspension for either a finite or an indefinite period, leaving L to decide and implement any conditions. L further submitted that, in the case of an indefinite suspension with conditions attached and permission to apply to the court to vary those conditions, the tribunal ought never to exercise its power to vary because of the adverse resource implications that might have for L, which would be required to keep files open for an indefinite period. C submitted that the conditions should be imposed for a finite period. It was common ground that the tribunal itself had the power to impose conditions on practising certificates pursuant to the Solicitors Act 1974 s.47.

Held, allowing the appeal, that in each case in which the tribunal considered that restrictions were necessary, it was under a duty to consider imposing such restrictions itself. L was not bound to follow any recommendation made by the tribunal in the exercise of its disciplinary function and neither the court nor the tribunal could be certain that the penalty imposed would be the one that would be most in the public interest. The tribunal was therefore under a duty in each case to consider whether the public interest could be best be served by imposing (1) a penalty that it was certain would be implemented, or (2) leaving the matter entirely to L. Only for exceptional reasons should the tribunal refrain from itself imposing the conditions that it considered most appropriate. In the instant case the appropriate course was for the court to impose the conditions necessary for the protection of the public and a failure to do so would be an abdication of its responsibility. Although there was no reason why the tribunal might not impose conditions for an indefinite period, with permission to apply to it to have them reviewed, since such an approach would have no significant resource implications, in the instant case the conditions would be imposed for a fixed period only.

CAMACHO v. LAW SOCIETY (NO.2); *sub nom.* R. (ON THE APPLICATION OF CAMACHO) v. LAW SOCIETY (NO.2), [2004] EWHC 1675, [2004] 1 W.L.R. 3037, Thomas, L.J., QBD (Admin Ct).

2736. Books

Adler, Mark–Effective Legal Writing. Paperback: £24.95. ISBN 1 85328 985 X. Law Society Publications.

Allen, Robert–Crazy Laws and Lawsuits. Paperback: £6.99. ISBN 1 86105 843 8. Robson Books.

Asher, J.–Client Connection. Paperback: £25.99. ISBN 1 58852 123 0. ALM Publishing.

Askey, Simon; McLeod, Ian–Studying Law. Palgrave Study Guides. Paperback: £11.99. ISBN 1 4039 9926 0. Palgrave Macmillan.

Bailey, David–Teaching Legal Skills. Hardback: £39.50. ISBN 1 85521 648 5. Paperback: £15.00. ISBN 1 85521 654 X. Ashgate.

Bar Directory. Hardback: £99.00. ISBN 0 421 92160 9. Sweet & Maxwell.

Bellomo, Michael–LSAT Exam Cram. Paperback: £17.99. ISBN 0 7897 3414 1. Que.

Bobrow, Jerry–Pass Key to the LSAT. Paperback: £5.99. ISBN 0 7641 2414 5. Barron's Educational Series.

Boyle, Fiona; Capps, Deveral; Plowden, Philip; Sandford, Clare–Practical Guide to Lawyering Skills. Paperback: £25.95. ISBN 1 85941 975 5. Cavendish Publishing Ltd.

Burnett, Justina–Getting Into Law. Getting Into Course Guides. Paperback: £11.99. ISBN 1 84455 067 2. Trotman.

Calabrese, Marianne; Calabrese, Susanne–So You Want to Be a Lawyer? Paperback: £12.95. ISBN 0 88391 136 1. Frederick Fell Publishers.

Cane, Peter; Tushnet, Mark–Oxford Handbook of Legal Studies. Paperback: £30.00. ISBN 0 19 924817 6. Oxford University Press.

Cheeseman, Henry R.–Student Study Guide. Paperback: £13.99. ISBN 0 13 144051 9. Prentice Hall.

Cheyne, Ann–Legal Secretary's Guide. Paperback: £27.99. ISBN 0 19 926840 1. Oxford University Press.

Elkington–Skills for Lawyers. Paperback: £25.95. ISBN 0 905835 85 9. The College of Law.

Estrin, Chere B.–Paralegal Career Guide. Paperback: £24.99. ISBN 0 13 118533 0. Prentice Hall.

Fallen: Confessions of a Disbarred Lawyer. Paperback: £14.98. ISBN 1 4116 0055 X. Lulu Press Incorporated.

Felstiner, Bill–Reorganization and Resistance: Legal Professions Confront a Changing World. Paperback: £35.00. ISBN 1 84113 246 2. Hart Publishing.

Fins, Alice–Opportunities in Paralegal Careers. Opportunities In... S. Paperback: £8.99. ISBN 0 07 143844 0. Higher Education.

Fitch–Introduction Law Paralegal. Hardback: £32.99. ISBN 0 13 863861 6. Pearson US Imports & PHIPEs.

Fullerton, Karen; Macgregor, Megan–Legal Research Skills. Paperback: £22.00. ISBN 0 414 01589 4. W.Green & Son.

Greens Solicitors Professional Handbook. Paperback: £29.00. ISBN 0 414 01615 7. W.Green & Son.

Gupta, Udayan–Entrepreneurial Lawyer: How Testa, Hurwitz, Thibeault Shaped a High-tech Culture. Hardback: £19.99. ISBN 1 896209 95 5. Bayeux Arts Incorporated.

Heward, Edmund–Lives of the Judges: Jessel, Cairns, Sowen and Bramwell. Hardback: £22.00. ISBN 1 902681 32 0. Barry Rose Law Publications.

Hodgart, Alan; Mayson, Stephen W.–Legal Business Guide to Law Firm Management. Paperback: £125.00. ISBN 1 903927 62 5. Legalease.

Holder, Jane–Current Legal Problems: V. 57. Current Legal Problems. Hardback: £75.00. ISBN 0 19 927468 1. Oxford University Press.

Hutton, Rosalie; Hutton, Glenn–Passing the National Admissions Test for Law (LNAT). Guides. Paperback: £12.00. ISBN 1 84641 001 0. Law Matters Publishing.

Inns of Court School of Law–Case Preparation. Blackstone Bar Manual S. Paperback: £26.99. ISBN 0 19 928148 3. Oxford University Press.

Inns of Court School of Law–Conference Skills. Blackstone Bar Manual S. Paperback: £26.99. ISBN 0 19 928150 5. Oxford University Press.

Inns of Court School of Law–Drafting. Blackstone Bar Manual S. Paperback: £26.99. ISBN 0 19 928152 1. Oxford University Press.

Inns of Court School of Law–Evidence. Blackstone Bar Manual S. Paperback: £26.99. ISBN 0 19 928153 X. Oxford University Press.

Inns of Court School of Law–Opinion Writing. Blackstone Bar Manual S. Paperback: £26.99. ISBN 0 19 928155 6. Oxford University Press.

Inns of Court School of Law–Professional Conduct. Blackstone Bar Manual S. Paperback: £26.99. ISBN 0 19 928156 4. Paperback: £26.99. ISBN 0 19 928156 4. Oxford University Press.

Inns of Court School of Law–Remedies. Blackstone Bar Manual S. Paperback: £26.99. ISBN 0 19 928157 2. Paperback: £26.99. ISBN 0 19 928157 2. Oxford University Press.

Kay, Dale; Baker, Janet–Solicitors' Accounts: A Practical Guide. Legal Practice Course Guides. Paperback: £26.99. ISBN 0 19 928137 8. Oxford University Press.

Keppel-Palmer, Marcus; Maughan, Caroline; Maughan, Mike; Webb, Julian; Boon, Andy–Lawyers' Skills. Blackstone Legal Practice Course Guide S. Paperback: £26.99. ISBN 0 19 928138 6. Oxford University Press.

Law Society–Directory of Solicitors and Barristers. Hardback: £94.95. ISBN 1 85328 963 9. Law Society Publications.

Markovits, D.–Adversary Lawyer. Hardback: £17.95. ISBN 0 691 12162 1. Princeton University Press.

Martin, Jacqueline–GCSE Law. Paperback: £14.99. ISBN 0 340 88939 X. Hodder Arnold H&S.

McMaster, Jodi–Interviewing and Investigating for Paralegals. Paperback: £41.99. ISBN 0 13 111891 9. Prentice Hall.

Miles, George; Laidlaw, Pauline; Ollerenshaw, Zoe; Deneyer, Paulene; Smart, Elizabeth; Clout, Imogen; Firth, Clare; Cutts, Rachel–Foundations for the LPC. Blackstone Legal Practice Course Guide S. Paperback: £26.99. ISBN 0 19 928139 4. Oxford University Press.

Montagu, Gerald; Weston, Mark–Legal Practice Companion. Companions. Paperback: £29.95. ISBN 1 84641 013 4. Law Matters Publishing.

Moore, Matthew; Verry, John–Risk and Quality Management in Legal Practice. Paperback: £39.95. ISBN 1 85328 947 7. Law Society Publications.

Orlik, Deborah–Ethics: Top Ten Rules for Paralegals. Paperback: £19.99. ISBN 0 13 119321 X. Prentice Hall.

Paterson, Alex K.–My Life At the Bar and Beyond. Hardback: £29.95. ISBN 0 7735 2988 8. McGill-Queen's University Press.

Paterson, A.A.; Ritchie, Bruce–Solicitors Practice, Conduct and Discipline. Paperback: £40.00. ISBN 0 414 01439 1. W.Green & Son.

Pervasive and Core Topics. Paperback: £25.95. ISBN 0 905835 87 5. The College of Law.

Powell, Vincent–Legal Companion. A Think Book S. Hardback: £9.99. ISBN 1 86105 838 1. Robson Books.

Putman, William–Legal Research. Paperback: £26.99. ISBN 1 4018 7958 6. Delmar.

Rhode, Deborah L.–Public Service and the Professions: Pro Bono in Principle and in Practice. Stanford Law & Politics. Hardback: £31.50. ISBN 0 8047 5106 4. Paperback: £12.95. ISBN 0 8047 5107 2. Stanford University Press.

Sandon, Teresa–Lex 100: A Student Guide to the UK's Premier Law Firms 2005 / 06. Paperback: £9.99. ISBN 1 903927 53 6. Legalease.

Sarat, Austin–Law in the Liberal Arts. Paperback: £12.50. ISBN 0 8014 8905 9. Cornell University Press.

Shuttleworth, Colin; Julyan, Alan J.–Checklists for Solicitors. Paperback/Floppy disk: £55.00. ISBN 0 7520 0509 X. Sweet & Maxwell.

Statsky–Essentials of Paralegalism 4e. Book (details unknown): £58.00. ISBN 1 4018 6193 8. Delmar.

Stefancic, Jean; Delgado, Richard–How Lawyers Lose Their Way: A Profession Fails Its Creative Minds. Hardback: £52.00. ISBN 0 8223 3454 2. Paperback: £12.95. ISBN 0 8223 3563 8. Duke University Press.

Steyn, Johan–Democracy Through Law: Selected Speeches and Judgments. Collected Essays in Law S. Hardback: £60.00. ISBN 0 7546 2404 8. Ashgate.

Strong, S.I.–How to Write Law Essays and Exams. Paperback: £15.99. ISBN 0 19 928755 4. Oxford University Press.

Toulson, Roger; Phipps, Charles–Confidentiality. Hardback: £135.00. ISBN 0 421 87630 1. Sweet & Maxwell.

Ventura, John–Law for Dummies. Paperback: £14.99. ISBN 0 7645 5830 7. Hungry Minds Inc.

Wagner, Andrea–How to LandYour First ParalegalJob. Paperback: £17.99. ISBN 0 13 118382 6. Prentice Hall.

Welsh, Tom; Greenwood, Walter; Banks, David–McNae's Essential Law for Journalists. Paperback: £16.99. ISBN 0 19 928418 0. Oxford University Press.

LEGAL SERVICES

2737. Books

Butterworths Law Directory. Hardback: £69.00. ISBN 1 4057 0985 5. Butterworths Law.

Current LawYearbook 2004. Hardback: £365.00. ISBN 0 421 91720 2. Sweet & Maxwell.

Lipton, Jacqueline–Information Law and Policy: Legal and Commercial Aspects ofValuable Information. Hardback: £45.00. ISBN 1 84113 332 9. Hart Publishing.

LEGAL SYSTEMS

2738. Books

Ahdar, Rex; Leigh, Ian–Religious Freedom in the Liberal State. Hardback: £50.00. ISBN 0 19 925362 5. Oxford University Press.

Anderson, Matthew; Sarat, Austin–Studies in Law, Politics and Society. Studies in Law, Politics & Society. Hardback: £70.49. ISBN 0 7623 1179 7. JAI Press.

Bell, John; Bell, John–Comparative Legal Cultures. International Library of Essays in Law & LegalTheory: Second Series -. Hardback: £120.00. ISBN 0 7546 2093 X. Dartmouth.

Benacchio, Gian Antonio; Pasa, Barbara–Common Law For Europe. Hardback: £25.95. ISBN 963 7326 33 2. Central European University Press.

Blanco, E.Merino–Spanish Legislation System. Paperback: £22.95. ISBN 0 421 90230 2. Sweet & Maxwell.

Brown–LegalTerminology. Book (details unknown): £28.99. ISBN 1 4018 2012 3. Delmar.

CambridgeYearbook of European Legal Studies: V. 7. Hardback: £85.00. ISBN 1 84113 561 5. Hart Publishing.

Cracknell, D G–English Legal System. Paperback: £11.95. ISBN 1 85836 588 0. Old Bailey Press.

Dadamo, C.–French Law & Legal System. Book (details unknown): £26.95. ISBN 0 421 74090 6. Sweet & Maxwell.

Darbyshire, Penny–Darbyshire on the English Legal System. Paperback: £15.95. ISBN 0 421 90150 0. Sweet & Maxwell.

Delacroix, Sylvie–Legal Norms and Normativity: A Genealogical Enquiry. Hardback: £32.00. ISBN 1 84113 455 4. Hart Publishing.

Doherty, Michael–English and European Legal Systems. Paperback: £15.95. ISBN 1 85836 597 X. Old Bailey Press.

Doyle, Francis R.–Searching the Law. Paperback: £100.99. ISBN 1 57105 349 2. Transnational Publishers, Inc.

Elliott, Catherine–English Legal System. Paperback: £23.99. ISBN 1 4058 1165 X. Longman.

English Legal System Lawcard. Lawcards S. Looseleaf/ring bound: £6.95. ISBN 1 84568 040 5. Cavendish Publishing Ltd.

Ethnographics of Law and Social Control. Sociology of Crime, Law & Deviance,V. 6. Hardback: £59.99. ISBN 0 7623 1128 2. JAI Press.

Finkelstein, Claire–Hobbes on Law. Philosophers & Law. Hardback: £110.00. ISBN 0 7546 2178 2. Ashgate.

French Civil Code. University of Texas At Austin Studies in Foreign & Transnational Law S. Hardback: £65.00. ISBN 1 84472 132 9. Paperback: £25.00. ISBN 1 84472 131 0. UCL Press.

Geoghegan, Thomas–Law in Shambles. Paperback: £7.00. ISBN 0 9728196 9 X. Prickly Paradigm Press.

Glenn, H.Patrick–On Common Laws. Hardback: £50.00. ISBN 0 19 928754 6. Oxford University Press.

Gubby, Helen–English Legal Terminology: Legal Concepts in Language. Paperback: £17.95. ISBN 90 5454 499 6. Boom Juridische Uitgevers.

Hassan, Abdullah Alwi Haji–Contracts in Islamic Law. Hardback: £37.50. ISBN 1 85043 929 X. I.B. Tauris.

Hutchinson, Allan C.–Evolution and the Common Law. Hardback: £45.00. ISBN 0 521 84968 3. Paperback: £19.99. ISBN 0 521 61491 0. Cambridge University Press.

Kennedy, Helena–Just Law. Paperback: £8.99. ISBN 0 09 945833 0. Vintage.

king-Devoreaux, Kelsee–Stunts Court = (Family/Children's Court-The Legal System). Hardback: £23.00. ISBN 1 4134 8047 0. Xlibris Corporation.

Letwin, Shirley Robin–On the History of the Idea of Law. Hardback: £48.00. ISBN 0 521 85423 7. Cambridge University Press.

Malleson, Kate–Legal System. Core Texts S. Paperback: £16.99. ISBN 0 19 928241 2. Paperback: £16.99. ISBN 0 19 928241 2. Oxford University Press.

Martin, Jacqueline–English Legal System. Paperback: £14.99. ISBN 0 340 89991 3. Hodder Arnold H&S.

Martin, Jacqueline–Key Facts: The English Legal System. Key Facts. Paperback: £5.99. ISBN 0 340 91335 5. Hodder Arnold H&S.

Maughan, Caroline; Webb, Julian–Lawyering Skills and the Legal Process. Law in Context S. Paperback: £24.99. ISBN 0 521 61950 5. Cambridge University Press.

Parisi, Francesco; Rowley, Charles K.–Origins of Law and Economics: Essays by the Founding Fathers. Locke Institute S. Hardback: £95.00. ISBN 1 84064 9631. Edward Elgar.

Pasa, Barbara; Benacchio, Gian Antonio–Harmonization Of Civil And Commercial Law In Europe. Hardback: £28.95. ISBN 963 7326 35 9. Central European University Press.

Piggot, Mike Semple–English Legal System. Law in a Box S., No. 3. CD-ROM: £23.44. ISBN 1 904783 59 7. Semple Piggot Rochez (Legal Education Ltd).

Pocket Guide to Legal Writing. Paperback: £10.99. ISBN 1 4018 6597 6. Delmar.

Simply Legal: A Guide for Development Workers on the Legal Forms and Organisational Types for Community-based Organisations Across the Social Economy Sector. Paperback: £15.00. ISBN 0 9549677 0 4. Co-operatives UK.

Slapper, Gary; Kelly, D.–English Legal System Q&A. Q & A S. Paperback: £11.95. ISBN 1 84568 001 4. Cavendish Publishing Ltd.

Summers, Robert S.–Form and Function in a Legal System: A General Study. Hardback: £45.00. ISBN 0 521 85765 1. Cambridge University Press.

Unlocking the English Legal System. Paperback: £18.99. ISBN 0 340 88693 5. Hodder Arnold H&S.

Wade, Peter–You and Your Legal Rights. Emerald Home Lawyers S. Paperback: £9.99. ISBN 1 903909 61 9. Straightforward Publishing.

Wellman, Christopher; Simmons, John–Is There a Duty to Obey the Law? For & Against S. Hardback: £30.00. ISBN 0 521 83097 4. Paperback: £12.99. ISBN 0 521 53784 3. Cambridge University Press.

Wheeler, John–Essentials of the English Legal System. Frameworks S. Paperback: £19.99. ISBN 1 4058 1167 6. Longman.

You and the Law in Spain. Paperback: £19.95. ISBN 84 89954 41 0. Santana Books (Santana, Ediciones, S.L.).

LEGISLATION

2739. Consolidated Fund Act 2005 (c.23)

This Act authorises the use of resources for the service of the years ending with March 31, 2006 and March 31, 2007 and applies certain sums out of the Consolidated Fund to the service of the years ending with March 31, 2006 and March 31, 2007.

This Act received Royal Assent on December 19, 2005.

2740. Public health–Tobacco products–Restrictions on advertising–Interference with right to free expression–Proportionality

[Human Rights Act 1998 Sch.1 Part I Art.10; Tobacco Advertising and Promotions Act 2002 s.4(3); Tobacco Advertising and Promotion (Point of Sale) Regulations 2004 (SI 2004 765); Treaty of Rome 1957 Art.28.]

The applicants (B), manufacturers and suppliers of tobacco products, challenged the lawfulness of the Tobacco Advertising and Promotion (Point of Sale) Regulations 2004 made pursuant to the Tobacco Advertising and Promotions Act 2002 s.4(3). B submitted that the limited exception to tobacco advertising contained in the Regulations was disproportionately restrictive of advertising at the point of sale, having regard to the legitimate aims that the Regulations were designed to pursue. In particular, B submitted that (1) the Regulations were so restrictive as to impair the very essence of commercial free speech in contravention of the Human Rights Act 1998 Sch.1 Part I Art.10; (2) the Regulations failed to distinguish between different types of retail outlet and went beyond what was necessary for their express purpose of protecting children; (3) they infringed the Treaty of Rome 1957 Art.28; (4) there was no evidence to suggest that the secretary of state had considered less stringent regulations.

Held, refusing the application, that (1) freedom of commercial expression was traditionally of less significance than freedom of political or artistic expression and the Regulations were directed at the very important goal of protecting public health (and not just children's health). The question was whether the Regulations went further than was necessary to attain their legitimate objective. The enormous health risks and economic costs to society caused by smoking meant that the Regulations were a proportionate and responsible approach. The Secretary of State had to be afforded a considerable discretion in drawing the line between the competing interests of protecting free speech and public health. (2) The failure to draw a distinction between different types of retail outlet was not a disproportionate response either. (3) It was not necessary to resolve the argument about Art.28 since the test of objective justification of a restriction engaging Art.28 was similar to that which applied under Art.10. (4) The Secretary of State had consulted and produced the Regulations, drawing the line where he saw fit to achieve their objective. The proportionality of his decision was not to be impugned simply because he addressed grievances in more detail in subsequent litigation than when the policy decision was taken.

R. (ON THE APPLICATION OF BRITISH AMERICAN TOBACCO UK LTD) v. SECRETARY OF STATE FOR HEALTH, [2004] EWHC 2493, *The Times*, November 11, 2004, McCombe, J., QBD (Admin).

2741. Regulatory reform orders–Execution of deeds and documents

REGULATORY REFORM (EXECUTION OF DEEDS AND DOCUMENTS) ORDER 2005, SI 2005 1906; made under the Regulatory Reform Act 2001 s.1. In force: in accordance with Art.1 (1); £3.00.

This Order amends the Law of Property Act 1925, the Powers of Attorney Act 1971, the Companies Act 1985, the Law of Property (Miscellaneous Provisions) Act 1989, the Companies Act 1989 and the Land Registration Act 2002. It reforms the legislation governing the execution of deeds and documents in order to standardise the formal requirements for companies, corporations and individuals.

2742. Statutory interpretation–Penal acts–Effect of commencement order– Application of s.132(1) Serious Organised Crime and Police Act 2005 to continuing demonstrations

[Serious Organised Crime and Police Act 2005 s.132, s.133, s.134, s.135, s.136, s.137, s.138, s.178(10); Serious Organised Crime and Police Act 2005 (Commencement No. 1, Transitional and Transitory Provisions) Order 2005 (SI 2005 1521) Art.3, Art.4(2).]

The claimant demonstrator (H) applied for judicial review of the refusal of the second defendant commissioner of police to confirm that the notice and authorisation regime set out in the Serious Organised Crime and Police Act 2005 s.132, s.133, s.134, s.135, s.136, s.137 and s.138 did not apply to him. H had maintained a permanent political demonstration in an area close to the Houses of Parliament. That area was for the purposes of s.132(1) a designated area in which it was a criminal offence for a person to demonstrate if, when the demonstration started, authorisation for the demonstration had not been given by the commissioner. Section 178(10) of the Act conferred on the first defendant secretary of state power to make such provision as he considered appropriate for "transitory, transitional or saving purposes in connection with the coming into force of any provision" of the Act. By the Serious Organised Crime and Police Act 2005 (Commencement No. 1, Transitional and Transitory Provisions) Order 2005 Art.3 and Art.4(2), the secretary of state purported that continuing demonstrations that had commenced before s.132(1) of the Act came into force required notice to, and authorisation from, the commissioner. H wrote to the defendants for confirmation that the notice and authorisation regime set out in s.132, s.133, s.134, s.135, s.136, s.137 and s.138 of the Act did not apply to him but both refused to give the confirmation sought. H contended that those parts of the Order that required authorisation for a continuing demonstration that had commenced before the Act came into force were ultra vires the Act as they amounted to an amendment for which there was no power under s.178(10) of the Act. The secretary of state contended that the court should apply a modern purposive approach to the interpretation of the Act.

Held, granting the application, that (1) (Simon J dissenting) the Act as enacted did not apply to a continuing demonstration that had commenced before s.132(1) of the Act came into force. The Order extended the application of s.132(1) so as to criminalise conduct that was not so under the Act. As such the alteration made by the Order was in fact an amendment and ultra vires s.178(10) of the Act. Accordingly, Art.3(1)(p), Art.3(5) and Art.4(2) of the Order would be quashed, *Utah Construction & Engineering Pty v. Pataky* [1966] A.C. 629, [1965] C.L.Y. 376 and *R. v. Secretary of State for Social Services, ex p. Britnell* [1991] 1 W.L.R. 198, [1991] C.L.Y. 3366 considered. (2) It could not be said that Parliament intended the Act to catch continuing demonstrations. There was no room for a modern purposive approach as the words of the Act were clear and could be given effect. In addition penal statutes should be given a statutory construction that was in favour of the liberty of the individual, *Pepper (Inspector of Taxes) v. Hart* [1993] A.C. 593 and *Inco Europe Ltd v. First Choice Distribution* [2000] 1 W.L.R. 586, [2000] C.L.Y. 220 considered.

R. (ON THE APPLICATION OF HAW) v. SECRETARY OF STATE FOR THE HOME DEPARTMENT, [2005] EWHC 2061, [2006] 2 W.L.R. 50, Smith, L.J., QBD (Admin).

2743. Books

Bennion, F.A.R.–Statutory Interpretation. Paperback: £55.00. ISBN 0 406 96648 6. Butterworths Law.

Current Law Statutes. Hardback: £455.00. ISBN 0 421 91980 9. Sweet & Maxwell.

Current Law Statutes: V. 1. Hardback: £167.00. ISBN 0 421 91430 0. Sweet & Maxwell.

Current Law Statutes: V. 2. Hardback: £167.00. ISBN 0 421 91450 5. Sweet & Maxwell.

Current Law Statutes: V. 3. Hardback: £167.00. ISBN 0 421 91470 X. Sweet & Maxwell.

Greenberg, Daniel; Goodman, Michael J–Craies on Legislation: A Practitioner's Guide to the Nature, Process, Effect and Interpretation of Legislation, Edition 8 Plus Supplement. Hardback: £235.00. ISBN 0 421 93780 7. Sweet & Maxwell.

Greenberg, Daniel; Goodman, Michael J–Craies on Legislation: A Practitioner's Guide to the Nature, Process, Effect and Interpretation of Legislation, 1st Supplement. Paperback: £40.00. ISBN 0 421 92740 2. Sweet & Maxwell.

Halsbury's Statutes Consolidated Index. Paperback: £170.00. ISBN 0 406 97194 3. Butterworths Law.

Halsbury's Statutes: Citator. Paperback: £187.00. ISBN 1 4057 0059 9. Butterworths Law.

Halsbury's Statutes: Consolidated Index. Hardback: £187.00. ISBN1 4057 0454 3. Butterworths Law.

Halsbury's Statutes: Cumulative Supplement 2005. Hardback: £282.00. ISBN 1 4057 0064 5. Butterworths Law.

Halsbury's Statutes: Table of Cases 2005. Hardback: £187.00. ISBN 1 4057 0060 2. Butterworths Law.

Halsbury's Statutes: V. 42. Looseleaf/ring bound: £226.00. ISBN 1 4057 0955 3. Butterworths Law.

Halsbury's Statutory Instruments: Consolidated Index and Alphabetical List of Statutory Instruments. Paperback: £108.00. ISBN 1 4057 0206 0. Butterworths Law.

Halsbury's Statutory Instruments: EC Legislation Implementator. Paperback: £78.00. ISBN 1 4057 0112 9. Butterworths Law.

Is It in Force? Paperback: £187.00. ISBN 1 4057 0061 0. Butterworths Law.

Stewart, Andrew F.–Session Cases: Incorporating Issue 6. Hardback: £265.00. ISBN 0 414 01622 X. W.Green & Son.

Tomes, Jonathan P.–Sevicemember's Legal Guide. Paperback: £10.99. ISBN 0 8117 3232 0. Stackpole Books.

Woodley, M.; Bone, Sheila–Osborn's Concise Law Dictionary. Paperback: £9.95. ISBN 0 421 90050 4. Sweet & Maxwell.

LIBRARIES

2744. Public lending right–Scheme variations

PUBLIC LENDING RIGHT SCHEME 1982 (COMMENCEMENT OF VARIATION) (NO.2) ORDER 2005, SI 2005 3351; made under the Public Lending Right Act 1979 s.3. In force: December 29, 2005; £3.00.

This Order varies the Public Lending Right Scheme 1982 (SI 1982 719) to increase the rate per loan as set out in the Scheme from 5.26 pence to 5.57 pence. The rate per loan is the sum attributable to each qualifying loan for the purpose of calculating the amount payable in respect of loans of a particular book by public libraries.

LICENSING

2745. Airports–Sale of intoxicating liquor–Licensed premises

AIRPORTS LICENSING (LIQUOR) ORDER 2005, SI 2005 1733; made under the Licensing Act 1964 s.87. In force: July 20, 2005; £3.00.

The Licensing Act 1964, s.87 provides that, at an international airport where that section is in operation, s.59 of that Act (which prohibits the sale of intoxicating liquor except during permitted hours) shall not apply to licensed premises which are within the examination station approved for the airport under the Customs and Excise Management Act 1979 s.22. This Order, which revokes the Airports Licensing (Liquor) Order 1983 (SI 1983 1217); the Airports Licensing (Liquor) Order 1985 (SI 1985 653); the Airports Licensing (Liquor) (No.2) Order 1985 (SI 1985 1730); the Southend Airport Licensing (Liquor) Order 1986 (SI 1986 525); the Exeter Airport Licensing (Liquor) Order 1986 (SI 1986 971); London City Airport Licensing (Liquor) Order 1987 (SI 1987 1982); the Manston Airport Licensing (Liquor) Order 1990 (SI 1990 1043); and the Sheffield City Airport Licensing (Liquor) Order 1998 (SI 1998 1769), consolidates existing orders and brings s.87 of the 1964 Act into operation at Coventry Airport.

2746. Airports–Sale of intoxicating liquor–Licensed premises–Blackpool Airport

BLACKPOOL AIRPORT LICENSING (LIQUOR) ORDER 2005, SI 2005 3119; made under the Licensing Act 1964 s.87. In force: November 16, 2005; £3.00.

The Licensing Act 1964 s.87 provides that, at an international airport where that section is in operation, s.59 of that Act (which prohibits the sale of intoxicating liquor except during permitted hours) shall not apply to licensed premises which are within the examination station approved for the airport under the Customs and Excise Management Act 1979 s.22. This Order brings the Licensing Act 1964 s.87 into operation at Blackpool Airport.

2747. Alcohol–Certificates–Second appointed day

LICENSING ACT 2003 (SECOND APPOINTED DAY) ORDER 2005, SI 2005 2091; made under the Licensing Act 2003 Sch.8 para.1, Sch.8 para.13. In force: November 24, 2005; £3.00.

This Order appoints November 24, 2005 as the second appointed day for the purposes of the taking effect of the new licence and new certificate, as defined in the Licensing Act 2003.

2748. Fees–Premises licenses

LICENSING ACT 2003 (TRANSITIONAL CONVERSIONS FEES) ORDER 2005, SI 2005 80; made under the Licensing Act 2003 Sch.8 para.2, Sch.8 para.14. In force: February 7, 2005; £3.00.

This Order makes provision for the determination of the fees to be paid in respect of premises for the conversion of existing licences and registered certificates to new premises licences and club premises certificates under the Licensing Act 2003.

2749. Licences–Applications–Relevant offences

LICENSING ACT 2003 (PERSONAL LICENCE: RELEVANT OFFENCES) (AMENDMENT) ORDER 2005, SI 2005 2366; made under the Licensing Act 2003 s.113. In force: September 16, 2005; £3.00.

This Order amends the list of offences that are treated as relevant offences for the purposes of an application for a personal licence under the Licensing Act 2003 Part 6.

2750. Licences-Consequential amendments

LICENSING ACT 2003 (CONSEQUENTIAL AMENDMENTS) ORDER 2005, SI 2005 3048; made under the Licensing Act 2003 s.198. In force: November 24, 2005; £3.00.

This Order amends the Visiting Forces and International Headquarters (Application of Law) Order 1999 (SI 1999 1736), the Criminal Justice and Police Act 2001, the Local Authorities (Alcohol Consumption in Designated Public Places) Regulations 2001 (SI 2001 2831) and the Penalties for Disorderly Behaviour (Amount of Penalty) Order 2002 (SI 2002 1837). It also revokes the Licensing Act 1964 (Amendment) Regulations 1979 (SI 1979 1476), the Deregulation (Employment in Bars) Order 1997 (SI 1997 957), the Deregulation (Licence Transfers) Order 1998 (SI 1998 114), the Deregulation (Millennium Licensing) Order 1999 (SI 1999 2137), the Regulatory Reform (Special Occasions Licensing) Order 2001 (SI 2001 3937), the Deregulation (Sunday Licensing) Order 2001 (SI 2001 920), the Deregulation (Restaurant Licensing Hours) Order 2002 (SI 2002 493), the Regulatory Reform (Golden Jubilee Licensing) Order 2002 (SI 2002 1062) and the Regulatory Reform (Special Occasions Licensing) Order 2002 (SI 2002 3205). It makes consequential amendments in connection with the commencement of provisions of the Licensing Act 2003.

2751. Licences-Gaming machine permits-Transfer

LICENSING ACT 2003 (AMENDMENT OF THE GAMING ACT 1968) (TRANSFER OF GAMING MACHINE PERMITS) ORDER 2005, SI 2005 3027; made under the Licensing Act 2003 s.198. In force: November 24, 2005; £3.00.

By virtue of the Gaming Act 1968, a s.34 permit (authorising the provision of gaming machines) is not transferable, and, in the case of alcohol licensed premises, ceases to have effect if the holder of the permit ceases to be the holder of the relevant alcohol licence. This Order amends Sch.9 to disapply the effect of para.20(1) in the particular circumstance of a conversion under Sch.8 to the Licensing Act 2003 of a justices' licence to a premises licence under that Act, where the person holding the licence is different in each case. Under the amendments any associated s.34 permit in force at the time when the premises licence takes effect is transferred to the holder of that licence.

2752. Licences-Local authorities powers and duties-Licensing authority's statement of licensing policy-Imposition of licence conditions beyond those specified under Licensing Act 2003

[Licensing Act 2003 s.4(3), s.5, s.17, s.18, s.19, s.20, s.21; Licensing Act 2003 (Premises licences and club premises certificates) Regulations 2005 (SI 2005 42).]

The claimants (C) challenged a statement of licensing policy published by the defendant local licensing authority under the Licensing Act 2003 s.5. The Act had created a new licensing regime, introducing a single integrated scheme for licensing premises which sold alcohol or provided regulated entertainment or late night refreshment. The concerns underlying the instant challenge related to situations where relevant representations were made and they were not made by responsible authorities or interested parties in response to applications made pursuant to s.17 of the Act. The effect of s.17 and s.18 appeared to be that where no representations were made, the local authority had to grant the licence in accordance with the application, subject only to such conditions as were consistent with the operating schedule referred to in s.17(4) and conditions which were mandatory by virtue of s.19, s.20 and s.21. Where relevant representations were made, the Act generally required a hearing, and a discretionary decision had to be made by the local authority. The two situations were considered in the guidance issued by the secretary of state pursuant to s.4(3) of the Act. In reaction to the judicial review challenge, the local authority proposed to adopt an addendum to the policy that it published under the Act. C submitted in essence that the local authority's published policy was overly prescriptive with regard to the contents of an application for a licence and stated or implied that the local authority had greater power than it did to assess applications and to impose conditions, and that the addendum did not overcome the objections that it had to the main text of the policy. C further submitted that certain passages of the policy, which referred to assessment of applications without indicating that such assessment would arise only if relevant representations were made by responsible authorities or interested parties, misrepresented the statutory scheme. C argued that the correct position was that applications would be considered "on their merits" only if relevant representations were made in respect of them, and that, in the absence of representations, the application had to be granted, subject to conditions consistent with the operating schedule and the relevant mandatory conditions.

Held, giving judgment accordingly, that (1) the scheme of the Act was to leave it to applicants to determine what to include in their applications, subject to the requirements of s.17 and the Licensing Act 2003 (Premises licences and club premises certificates) Regulations 2005 as to the prescribed form and the inclusion of a statement of specified matters in the operating schedule. An applicant who made the right judgment, so that the application gave rise to no relevant representations, was entitled to the grant of a licence without the imposition of conditions beyond those consistent with the content of the operating schedule and any mandatory conditions. The local authority had no power at all to lay down the contents of an application and had no power to assess an application, or to exercise substantive discretionary powers in relation to it, unless there were relevant representations and the decision making function under s.18(3) was engaged. If a policy created a different impression, and in particular if it misled an applicant into believing that he had to meet certain requirements in relation to his application and that he lacked the freedom accorded to him by the Act and Regulations, the policy was contrary to the legislative scheme and was unlawful, *Padfield v. Minister of Agriculture, Fisheries and Food* [1968] A.C. 997, [1968] C.L.Y. 1667 applied. (2) The local authority's policy should be read as a whole, against the background of the legislation and guidance issued by the secretary of state. The meaning and effect of individual passages had to be judged in a common sense way, *R. (on the application of Chorion Plc) v. Westminster City Council (No.1)* [2001] EWHC Admin 754 considered. The policy in its unamended form was overly prescriptive in a number of places, suggesting the existence of requirements that could not lawfully be imposed on applicants. The policy failed to observe the distinction between the different stages in the procedure. It failed in particular to make clear that it was for applicants to determine the contents of their applications, subject to compliance with the Act and Regulations, and that the additional requirements, expectations and powers of assessment applied only if, and in so far as was relevant, representations were made and the local authority's decision making powers under s.18(3) were engaged. Accordingly, the policy in its unamended form was unlawful. (3) The proposed addendum, on the other hand, represented a substantial improvement in the policy. It set out clearly the different stages in the procedure and explained at what point the matters covered in the policy could bite on applications. If the rest of the document was read in the light of the addendum, a careful reader might understand that the prescriptive language of later passages was not to be taken at face value. Although the policy was unlawful, there was a sufficiently strong assurance that the proposed addendum would be adopted as to make it unnecessary and inappropriate to grant any relief, namely that the court should order the deletion of the offending passages. The addendum would mitigate the problems but would not remedy them completely. Nevertheless, the policy as amended by the inclusion of the addendum was unlikely to mislead applicants. There was no evidence that any had been misled, even by the policy in its unamended form. However, the addendum would not remedy the problems completely. The local authority would be obliged to carry out a further review of the policy. Pending the completion of that review, the policy as amended by the addendum would remain in force.

BRITISH BEER & PUB ASSOCIATION v. CANTERBURY CITY COUNCIL, [2005] EWHC 1318, (2005) 169 J.P. 521, Richards, J., QBD (Admin).

2753. Licences–Premises–Transfer

LICENSING ACT 2003 (AMENDMENT OF THE LOTTERIES AND AMUSEMENTS ACT 1976) (TRANSFER OF AMUSEMENTS WITH PRIZES PERMITS) ORDER 2005, SI 2005 3028; made under the Licensing Act 2003 s.198. In force: November 24, 2005; £3.00.

By virtue of the Lotteries and Amusements Act 1976, a s.16 permit (authorising the provision of commercial amusements with prizes) is not transferable, and, in the case of certain alcohol licensed premises, ceases to have effect if the holder of the permit ceases to be the holder of the relevant alcohol licence. This Order amends Sch.3 to disapply the effect of para.17(1) in the particular circumstance of a conversion under the Licensing Act 2003 Sch.8 of a justices' licence to a premises licence under that Act, where the person holding the licence is different in each case. Under the amendments any associated s.16 permit in force at the time when the premises licence takes effect is transferred to the holder of that licence.

2754. Licences–Taxis–Local authorities powers and duties–Policy requiring information as to driving standard

[Local Government (Miscellaneous Provisions) Act 1976 s.57(1), s.59(1)(a).]

The appellant local authority appealed by way of case stated against a decision of a magistrates' court. The court had allowed the appeal of the respondent (K) against the local authority's refusal to renew his hackney carriage driver's licence. The local authority had altered its policy on the renewal of all such licences by requiring applicants to pass, on one occasion only, the Driving Standards Agency taxi test and to supply a pass certificate with their applications. K had refused to take the test. The questions asked by the court were (i) whether the requirement to pass the test had been a request for information as envisaged by the Local Government (Miscellaneous Provisions) Act 1976 s.57(1) or a condition which had to be fulfilled before the local authority would consider whether to grant a hackney carriage driver's licence, and (ii) whether information as to whether K had passed the test had been reasonably required and necessary to establish if he was a fit and proper person to hold a licence pursuant to s.59(1)(a).

Held, allowing the appeal, that (1) when considering K's application for renewal, the only question for the local authority was whether it was satisfied that he was a fit and proper person to hold a licence pursuant to s.59(1)(a). It had been entitled to adopt a policy that it would not regard a person as a fit and proper person to hold a licence unless he had passed the Driving Standards Agency taxi test. The requirement to pass the test was not a condition precedent to the grant of a licence, *Wathan v. Neath and Port Talbot CBC* [2002] EWHC 1634 distinguished. (2) Given its policy, the local authority had been entitled to consider it reasonably necessary to require information as to whether K had passed the test. The request for information fell within s.57(1). (3) The magistrates had rightly considered K's appeal by way of a rehearing but had erred in law by failing to accept and apply the local authority's policy when considering whether K was a fit and proper person to hold a licence, *Sagnata Investments Ltd v. Norwich Corp* [1971] 2 Q.B. 614, [1971] C.L.Y. 5081 applied, *R. (on the application of Westminster City Council) v. Middlesex Crown Court* [2002] EWHC 1104 followed. The matter would be remitted for rehearing by a differently constituted court.

DARLINGTON BC v. KAYE, [2004] EWHC 2836, [2005] R.T.R. 14, Wilkie, J., QBD (Admin).

2755. Licences–Temporary events–Notices

LICENSING ACT 2003 (PERMITTED TEMPORARY ACTIVITIES) (NOTICES) REGULATIONS 2005, SI 2005 2918; made under the Licensing Act 2003 s.100, s.102, s.107. In force: November 10, 2005; £3.00.

These Regulations prescribe the forms to be used for temporary event notices given by premises users under the Licensing Act 2003, and the prescribed matters and information to be contained in such notices.

2756. Licensed premises–Occasional licences–Quashing of hotel's licence by special removal–Lawfulness of magistrates thereupon granting occasional licences to hotel

[Licensing Act 1964 s.15(1), s.180.]

R sought the quashing of three occasional licences granted by magistrates under the Licensing Act 1964 s.180 to U, its commercial rival, in respect of a hotel it owned. The magistrates' decision came immediately after the Court of Appeal upheld the High Court's quashing of the hotel's licence by special removal which licensing justices had earlier granted U. That licence was quashed because the requirements of s.15(1) had not been met, in that U's premises from which it wanted to remove the licence, in order to transfer it to the hotel, were not about to be pulled down at the time of the licence application. R contended that it was an abuse of process for U to bring proceedings by way of an application to the magistrates in order to obtain a remedy for which it had deliberately not applied in the earlier proceedings before the Court of Appeal, to which it could have applied for a stay of the quashing order.

Held, refusing the application, that it was not an abuse of process for U to apply for occasional licences after a licence by special removal for the same hotel had been quashed, nor did the magistrates' granting of the occasional licences render the preceding Court of Appeal judgment nugatory. Once the special licence was quashed it was perfectly legitimate for U to look for ways of enabling trading to continue lawfully at the hotel. One way would have been to apply to the Court of Appeal for a stay of the quashing order. But another way was to apply for occasional licences until a fresh application for a special removal could be considered. The application for occasional licences was plainly not a matter for the Court of Appeal and could only be dealt with by the magistrates.

RINDBERG HOLDING CO LTD v. NEWCASTLE UPON TYNE JUSTICES, [2004] EWHC 1903, (2005) 169 J.P. 20, Richards, J., QBD (Admin Ct).

2757. Licensing Act 2003 (c.17)–Commencement No.6 Order

LICENSING ACT 2003 (COMMENCEMENT NO.6) ORDER 2005, SI 2005 2090 (C.91); made under the Licensing Act 2003 s.201. Commencement details: bringing into force various provisions of the 2003 Act on August 7, 2005; £3.00.

This Order brings into force provisions of the Licensing Act 2003 in respect of the variation of premises licences; the transfer of premises licences; the variation of club premises certificates; and related appeals.

2758. Licensing Act 2003 (c.17)–Commencement No.7 and Transitional Provisions Order

LICENSING ACT 2003 (COMMENCEMENT NO.7 AND TRANSITIONAL PROVISIONS) ORDER 2005, SI 2005 3056 (C.131); made under the Licensing Act 2003 s.197, s.201. Commencement details: bringing into force various provisions of the 2003 Act on November 10, 2005 and November 24, 2005; £3.00.

This Order brings into force those provisions of the Licensing Act 2003 which have not already been brought into force.

2759. Licensing authorities-Fees

LICENSING ACT 2003 (FEES) REGULATIONS 2005, SI 2005 79; made under the Licensing Act 2003 s.55, s.92, s.100, s.110, s.133, s.178. In force: February 7, 2005; £3.00.

These Regulations provide for the determination of the fees to accompany the making of applications and the giving of notices under the Licensing Act 2003 and the payment of those fees. They also make provision for the payment of annual fees in respect of premises licences and club premises certificates granted under the Act.

2760. Licensing authorities-Fees

LICENSING ACT 2003 (FEES) (AMENDMENT) REGULATIONS 2005, SI 2005 357; made under the Licensing Act 2003 s.55. In force: February 23, 2005; £3.00.

These Regulations amend the Licensing Act 2003 (Fees) Regulations 2005 (SI 2005 79) to correct errors concerning the fees payable where an application is made for the conversion of an existing licence during the transitional period and an application to vary is made at the same time.

2761. Licensing authorities-Hearings

LICENSING ACT 2003 (HEARINGS) REGULATIONS 2005, SI 2005 44; made under the Licensing Act 2003 s.9, s.183. In force: February 7, 2005; £3.00.

These Regulations make provision for the holding of hearings required to be held by licensing authorities under the Licensing Act 2003. In particular, the Regulations provide for the timing of hearings and the notification requirements to parties to a hearing of the date, time and place of a hearing and information to accompany that notification. In addition, provision is made for a party to a hearing to provide information to the licensing authority about attendance at a hearing, representations, the seeking of permission for another person to attend to assist the authority and whether the party believes a hearing to be necessary. The Regulations provide for a range of procedural issues to govern the way in which preparations are made for a hearing, for the procedures to be followed, the rights of parties at a hearing, and various administrative matters, for example, the keeping of a record of the hearing and the manner of giving notices. The Regulations also make provision for the timing of the licensing authority's determination following a hearing.

2762. Licensing authorities-Hearings

LICENSING ACT 2003 (HEARINGS) (AMENDMENT) REGULATIONS 2005, SI 2005 78; made under the Licensing Act 2003 s.183. In force: February 7, 2005; £3.00.

These Regulations amend the Licensing Act 2003 (Hearings) Regulations 2005 (SI 2005 44) to correct an omission concerning the provision of a timescale within which a licensing authority must give notice of a hearing to specified persons. These Regulations add a new regulation requiring a licensing authority to give notice of a hearing in cases other than those specified within 10 working days before the day, or the first day, of the hearing.

2763. Licensing authorities-Premises

LICENSING ACT 2003 (PREMISES LICENCES AND CLUB PREMISES CERTIFICATES) REGULATIONS 2005, SI 2005 42; made under the Licensing Act 2003 s.13, s.17, s.24, s.29, s.30, s.34, s.37, s.47, s.51, s.54, s.69, s.71, s.78, s.84, s.87, s.91, s.167, s.178, s.197. In force: February 7, 2005; £12.00.

The Licensing Act 2003 provides for the licensing of premises for the sale by retail of alcohol, the supply of alcohol by or on behalf of a club to, or to the order of a member of the club, the provision of regulated entertainment and the provision of late night refreshment. These Regulations set out the detailed requirements relating to applications, notices and representations given or made under Part 3 and Part 4 of the Act and reviews made under those Parts and Part 8 of the Act.

2764. Licensing authorities–Premises

LICENSING ACT 2003 (TRANSITIONAL PROVISIONS) ORDER 2005, SI 2005 40; made under the Licensing Act 2003 Sch.8 para.2, Sch.8 para.6, Sch.8 para.11, Sch.8 para.12, Sch.8 para.14, Sch.8 para.18, Sch.8 para.23. In force: February 7, 2005; £6.50.

This Order makes provision for the detailed requirements to be fulfilled by applicants to convert existing authorisations to use premises for the sale and supply of alcohol, the provision of regulated entertainment and the provision of late night refreshment to new premises licences under the Licensing Act 2003 Sch.8. Also, it makes provision for the detailed requirements to be fulfilled by a registered club under the Licensing Act 1964 to convert authorisations under its existing registration certificate to a new club premises certificate under Sch.8 to the Act. In both cases the Order prescribes the application form to be used by the applicant or club, the information to be supplied and the plan to accompany the application. Further it prescribes the form to be used in relation to a simultaneous application to vary any existing authorisations. The Order requires the relevant licensing authority to provide application forms etc. for applicants and clubs on request and provides a discretion to provide these on its website.

2765. Licensing authorities–Registers–Information

LICENSING ACT 2003 (LICENSING AUTHORITY'S REGISTER) (OTHER INFORMATION) REGULATIONS 2005, SI 2005 43; made under the Licensing Act 2003 s.8. In force: February 7, 2005; £3.00.

These Regulations prescribe the further information each licensing authority is required to record in the register it is required to keep under the Licensing Act 2003. In addition to the records identified, each licensing authority must record in its register operating schedules and club operating schedules, or revisions of these, and plans of premises which accompany applications for premises licences or club premises certificates, or variations of these and Schedules of works and plans of the work being or about to be done which accompany applications for provisional statements. Further, each licensing authority must record in its register the ground or grounds for reviews set out in applications for a review of a premises licence or club premises certificate and the determination of the magistrates' court on its consideration of a closure order. Finally, a record must be kept of the existing licensable activities and existing qualifying club activities and plans of the premises which accompany applications (for conversion of existing licences and existing club certificates).

2766. National Lottery–Distributing bodies–New Opportunities Fund

NEW OPPORTUNITIES FUND (SPECIFICATION OF INITIATIVES) (NO.2) ORDER 2005, SI 2005 3235; made under the National Lottery etc. Act 1993 s.43B, s.43C, s.60. In force: November 17, 2005; £3.00.

This Order, which revokes the New Opportunities Fund (Specification of Initiatives) Order 1998 (SI 1998 1598), the New Opportunities Fund (Specification of Initiatives) Order 1999 (SI 1999 966), the New Opportunities Fund (Specification of Initiatives) Order 2001 (SI 2001 1404) and the New Opportunities Fund (Specification of Initiative) Order 2004 (SI 2004 143), specifies initiatives concerned or connected with health, education or the environment and accordingly allows the New Opportunities Fund to make grants, or make or enter into arrangements, under the National Lottery etc. Act 1993 s.43B which are designed to give effect to those initiatives.

2767. Operators licences–Private hire vehicles–Operation of licensed hackney carriage as private hire vehicle–Statutory interpretation

[Town Police Clauses Act 1847; Local Government (Miscellaneous Provisions) Act 1976 s.46(1)(d), s.55, s.80.]

The prosecutor appealed against the district judge's acquittal of the defendant (G) of knowingly operating a vehicle as a private hire vehicle in a controlled district without having an operator's licence. Both the vehicle and G were properly licensed as a hackney carriage and a hackney carriage driver respectively. The district judge posed a question for the opinion of the High Court: whether it was necessary to hold a licence under the Local Government (Miscellaneous Provisions) Act 1976 s.55, in an area where that Act was in force, to operate a hackney carriage, duly licensed as such under the Town Police Clauses Act 1847, as a private hire vehicle.

Held, dismissing the appeal, that it was not necessary to hold a licence under s.55 to operate a hackney carriage, duly licensed as such, as a private hire vehicle. Section 46(1)(d) of the 1976 Act was not breached where a licensed hackney carriage and a licensed hackney carriage driver were provided for the relevant conveyance of a passenger, albeit that they were provided through an operator. In those circumstances, an operator's licence under s.55 was not appropriate, since that section did not cover hackney carriages. It was apparent that s.80 of the 1976 Act excluded hackney carriages from s.46(1)(d).

BRENTWOOD BC v. GLADEN, [2004] EWHC 2500, [2005] R.T.R. 12, Collins, J., QBD (Admin Ct).

2768. Personal licences–Requirements

LICENSING ACT 2003 (PERSONAL LICENCES) REGULATIONS 2005, SI 2005 41; made under the Licensing Act 2003 s.120, s.125, s.133. In force: February 7, 2005; £3.00.

These Regulations make provision for the detailed requirements to be fulfilled by applicants for personal licences under the Licensing Act 2003 Part VI.

2769. Books

Barker, K.–Licensing: The New Law. Paperback: £39.00. ISBN 0 85308 989 2. Jordans.

Chambers, David; Butterfield, Roger–Alcohol & Entertainment Licensing: A Practical Guide. Paperback: £21.95. ISBN 0 7219 1690 2. Shaw & Sons.

Hewitson, Russell; Moss, Tom–Licensing Law Handbook: A Practical Guide to Liquor and Entertainment Licensing. Paperback: £49.95. ISBN 1 85328 954 X. Law Society Publications.

Jones, K.V. Prichard; Adams, John N.–Franchising. Hardback: £135.00. ISBN 0 406 97734 8. Butterworths Law.

Kolvin, Philip–Licensed Premises: Law and Practice, with Updating Supplement. Hardback: £85.00. ISBN 1 84592 291 3. Tottel Publishing.

Kolvin, Philip–Licensed Premises: Law and Practice Supplement. Paperback: £20.00. ISBN 1 84592 289 1. Tottel Publishing.

Mehigan, Simon; Saunders, John; Philips, Jeremy–Paterson's Licensing Acts 2006. Hardback: £234.00. ISBN 1 4057 0634 1. Butterworths Law.

Mehigan, Simon; Saunders, John; Phillips, Jeremy–Paterson's Licensing Acts 2005. Hardback: £225.00. ISBN 0 406 97987 1. Butterworths Law.

Musgrove, Nigel–Licensing Handbook: A Guide to Obtaining a Licence and Running Licensed Premises. Fitzwarren Handbooks. Paperback: £11.95. ISBN 0 9545934 1 3. Fitzwarren Publishing.

Philips, Jeremy; Mehigan, Simon; Saunders, John–Patersons Licensing Acts. Paperback: £39.00. ISBN 1 4057 0799 2. Butterworths Law.

LOCAL GOVERNMENT

2770. Anti-social Behaviour Act 2003 (c.38)–Commencement No.5 Order–England

ANTI-SOCIAL BEHAVIOUR ACT 2003 (COMMENCEMENT NO.5) (ENGLAND) ORDER 2005, SI 2005 710 (C.31); made under the Anti-social Behaviour Act 2003 s.93. Commencement details: bringing into force various provisions of the 2003 Act on June 1, 2005; £3.00.

This Order brings into force provisions of the Anti-social Behaviour Act 2003 which give local authorities the power to deal with complaints about high hedges which are having an adverse effect on a neighbour's enjoyment of his or her domestic property (other than complaints about the effect of the roots of a high hedge).

2771. Anti social behaviour–Hedgerows–Appeals

HIGH HEDGES (APPEALS) (ENGLAND) REGULATIONS 2005, SI 2005 711; made under the Anti-social Behaviour Act 2003 s.72, s.94. In force: June 1, 2005; £3.00.

The Anti-social Behaviour Act 2003 Part 8 gives local authorities power to deal with complaints about high hedges which are having an adverse effect on a neighbour's enjoyment of his or her domestic property. A complaint may be made by the owner or occupier of a domestic property on the grounds that his or her reasonable enjoyment of the property is being adversely affected by the height of the hedge situated on land owned or occupied by another person. A complaint must be made to the local authority in whose area the land on which the hedge is situated lies and the complaint must be accompanied by such fee, if any, as is determined by the local authority. The Act sets out the rights of appeal against a local authority's decisions under s.68 (procedure for dealing with complaints) and s.70 (withdrawal, waiver or relaxation of remedial notices) of the Act and against any remedial notices issued by the local authority under s.69. Any appeals in relation to hedges in England must be made to the Secretary of State. The Secretary of State may appoint under s.72 a person to hear and determine the appeal on his behalf. This appointment may also be revoked. These Regulations deal with the procedure for appeals under s.71 of the Act; set out grounds of appeal against the issue of a remedial notice; set out the grounds of appeal against the withdrawal, waiver or relaxation of a remedial notice; set out the grounds of appeal against decisions by the local authority under s.68(3) of the Act that are unfavourable to the complainant; and set out the procedure for making an appeal and for the conduct of the appeal.

2772. Best value–Local authorities–Performance indicators–Wales

LOCAL GOVERNMENT (BEST VALUE PERFORMANCE INDICATORS) (WALES) ORDER 2005, SI 2005 665 (W.55); made under the Local Government Act 1999 s.4, s.29. In force: April 1, 2005; £3.00.

This Order specifies, for Wales, performance indicators by reference to which the performance of county councils and county borough councils, in exercising their functions, will be measured from April 1, 2005.

2773. Best value–Local authorities–Performance indicators–Wales

LOCAL GOVERNMENT (BEST VALUE PERFORMANCE INDICATORS) (WALES) (REVOCATION) ORDER 2005, SI 2005 664 (W.54); made under the Local Government Act 1999 s.4, s.29. In force: April 1, 2005; £3.00.

This Order revokes the Local Government (Best Value Performance Indicators) (Wales) Order 2002 (SI 2002 757 (W.80)) which specifies, for Wales, performance indicators by reference to which the performance of county councils, county borough councils and national park authorities (as best value authorities), in exercising their functions, were to be measured from the April 1, 2002. This order will come into force on April 1, 2005.

2774. Best value—Local authorities powers and duties—Performance indicators and standards

LOCAL GOVERNMENT (BEST VALUE) PERFORMANCE INDICATORS AND PERFORMANCE STANDARDS (ENGLAND) ORDER 2005, SI 2005 598; made under the Local Government Act 1999 s.4, s.28. In force: April 1, 2005; £4.50.

This Order, which amends the Police Authorities (Best Value) Performance Indicators Order 2004 (SI 2004 644) and the Fire and Rescue Services Act 2004 (Consequential Amendments) (England) Order 2004 (SI 2004 3168), revokes the Local Government (Best Value) Performance Indicators and Performance Standards Order 2003 (SI 2003 530), the Local Government (Best Value) Performance Indicators and Performance Standards (Amendment) (England) Order 2003 (SI 2003 864), the Local Government (Best Value) Performance Indicators and Performance Standards (Amendment) Order 2004 (SI 2004 589) and the Local Government (Best Value) Performance Indicators and Performance Standards (Amendment) (No.2) Order 2004 (SI 2004 1176). The Local Government Act 1999 (Best Value) places requirements on local authorities and other authorities relating to economy, efficiency and effectiveness in the exercise of their functions. That Act provides the Secretary of State with a power to specify by Order best value performance indicators and standards. This Order specifies performance indicators by reference to which a best value authority's performance in exercising functions can be measured. The Order also specifies standards in respect of particular functions and particular best value authorities.

2775. Civil Contingencies Act 2004 (c.36)—Commencement No.2 Order

CIVIL CONTINGENCIES ACT 2004 (COMMENCEMENT NO.2) ORDER 2005, SI 2005 772 (C.33); made under the Civil Contingencies Act 2004 s.34. Commencement details: bringing into force various provisions of the 2004 Act on April 1, 2005; £3.00.

This Order brings into force the provisions of the Civil Contingencies Act 2004 which repeal s.3, s.3A and s.3B of the Civil Defence Act 1948 in so far as those provisions relate to a financial year beginning on or after April 1, 2005. This Order also brings into force the provision of the Act which alters the name by which metropolitan county fire and civil defence authorities are to be known by.

2776. Civil Contingencies Act 2004 (c.36)—Commencement No.3 Order

CIVIL CONTINGENCIES ACT 2004 (COMMENCEMENT NO.3) ORDER 2005, SI 2005 2040 (C.89); made under the Civil Contingencies Act 2004 s.34. Commencement details: bringing into force various provisions of the 2004 Act on July 22, 2005, November 14, 2005 and May 15, 2006; £3.00.

This Order brings into force the provisions of the Civil Contingencies Act 2004 Part 1, except in so far as that Part confers functions on the Scottish Ministers. It also commences sections which enable the Minister for the Cabinet Office to make and lay regulations to come into force on November 14, 2005; and which permit local authorities to provide advice and assistance to the public in relation to business continuity.

2777. Clean Neighbourhoods and Environment Act 2005 (c.16)—Commencement No.1 Order

CLEAN NEIGHBOURHOODS AND ENVIRONMENT ACT 2005 (COMMENCEMENT NO.1) ORDER 2005, SI 2005 1675 (C.69); made under the Clean Neighbourhoods and Environment Act 2005 s.108. Commencement details: bringing into force various provisions of the 2005 Act on July 1, 2005; £3.00.

This Order brings into force the Clean Neighbourhoods and Environment Act 2005 s.32.

2778. Council tax—Alteration of lists—Wales

COUNCIL TAX (ALTERATION OF LISTS AND APPEALS) (AMENDMENT) (WALES) REGULATIONS 2005, SI 2005 181 (W.14); made under the Local Government Finance Act 1992 s.24, s.113. In force: February 2, 2005; £3.00.

These Regulations, which amend the Council Tax (Alteration of Lists and Appeals) Regulations 1993, provide that subject to four exceptions, no proposal for the alteration of a valuation list compiled under the Local Government Finance Act 1992 may be made later than December 31, 2005; and provide that, subject to specified provisions in the 1993 Regulations, where in relation to a dwelling shown in a s.22B valuation list on the day on which that list is compiled, a billing authority or an interested person is of the opinion that the list is inaccurate by reason of the listing officer having determined an incorrect valuation band, any proposal for the alteration of the list as regards that matter must be made not later than September 30, 2006.

2779. Council tax—Billing authorities—Civil partnerships

COUNCIL TAX (CIVIL PARTNERS) (ENGLAND) REGULATIONS 2005, SI 2005 2866; made under the Local Government Finance Act 1992 s.11A, s.18, s.116, Sch.1 para.11, Sch.4 para.1, Sch.4 para.5. In force: December 10, 2005; £3.00.

These Regulations amend the Council Tax (Additional Provisions for Discount Disregards) Regulations 1992 (SI 1992 552), the Council Tax (Administration and Enforcement) Regulations 1992 (SI 1992 613) and the Council Tax (Prescribed Classes of Dwellings) (England) Regulations 2003 (SI 2003 3011) in relation to financial years commencing on or after April 1, 2006, in the light of the Civil Partnership Act 2004. The Civil Partnership Act 2004 provides that two people of the same sex may form a civil partnership and will then be given many of the same rights and responsibilities as those that accompany marriage. These Regulations apply in relation to billing authorities in England.

2780. Council tax—Exempt classes of dwellings

COUNCIL TAX (EXEMPT DWELLINGS) (AMENDMENT) (ENGLAND) ORDER 2005, SI 2005 2865; made under the Local Government Finance Act 1992 s.4. In force: December 10, 2005; £3.00.

This Order amends the Council Tax (Exempt Dwellings) Order 1992 (SI 1992 558) as it applies to billing authorities in England. That Order exempts certain classes of dwellings so that they are not liable for council tax. Most of the amendments are consequential changes in the light of the Civil Partnership Act 2004. That Act provides that two people of the same sex may form a civil partnership and will then be given many of the same rights and responsibilities as those that accompany marriage. It also inserts a definition of "civil partnership" into the Interpretation Act 1978.

2781. Council tax—Job-related dwellings—Discounts

COUNCIL TAX (PRESCRIBED CLASSES OF DWELLINGS) (AMENDMENT) (ENGLAND) REGULATIONS 2005, SI 2005 416; made under the Local Government Finance Act 1992 s.11A. In force: April 1, 2005; £3.00.

These Regulations amend the Council Tax (Prescribed Classes of Dwellings) (England) Regulations 2003 (SI 2003 3011), to provide, that where a council tax payer has a job-related dwelling and another home, a council tax discount of 50 per cent is retained on the second home in England when his or her main home is in England, Wales or Scotland, (regardless of whether it is the main dwelling or the second home which is job-related). Previously, the Regulations only prevented the billing authority for the area within which the second home was situated from reducing the discount on that dwelling from 50 per cent if the main home was also in England. The effect of the amendments is also to preserve the second home council tax discount of 50 per cent where a member of service personnel or a minister of religion has a second home in England but lives in a job-related dwelling in England, Wales or Scotland.

2782. Council tax–Local authorities–Budget requirements–Maximum amounts

COUNCIL TAX LIMITATION (ENGLAND) (MAXIMUM AMOUNTS) ORDER 2005, SI 2005 2032; made under the Local Government Finance Act 1992 s.52F. In force: July 21, 2005; £3.00.

This Order, which applies to Aylesbury Vale, Daventry, Hambleton, Huntingdonshire, Mid Bedfordshire, North Dorset, and South Cambridgeshire district councils and Runnymede borough council, states the amount which the amount calculated by each of those authorities as its budget requirement for the financial year beginning in 2005 is not to exceed.

2783. Council tax–Valuation bands–Wales

COUNCIL TAX (REDUCTIONS FOR DISABILITIES AND TRANSITIONAL ARRANGEMENTS) (WALES) (AMENDMENT) REGULATIONS 2005, SI 2005 702 (W.61); made under the Local Government Finance Act 1992 s.13, s.13B. In force: March 16, 2005; £3.00.

These Regulations amend the Council Tax (Reductions for Disabilities) Regulations 1992 (SI 1992 554) and the Council Tax (Transitional Arrangements) (Wales) Regulations 2004 (SI 2004 3142 (W.270)), to take account of the effect of the Council Tax (Valuation Bands) (Wales) Order 2003 which introduced valuation band I in Wales and amends typographical errors in the 2004 Regulations.

2784. Council tax–Valuation lists–Wales

COUNCIL TAX (SITUATION AND VALUATION OF DWELLINGS) (WALES) (AMENDMENT) REGULATIONS 2005, SI 2005 701 (W.60); made under the Local Government Finance Act 1992 s.21, s.116. In force: March 16, 2005; £3.00.

The Local Government Finance Act 1992 provides that the Commissioners of Inland Revenue shall carry out such valuations of dwellings in England and Wales and furnish listing officers for billing authorities with such information obtained in carrying out valuations as they consider necessary for the purpose of facilitating the compilation and maintenance by listing officers of valuation lists. These Regulations amend the Council Tax (Situation and Valuation of Dwellings) Regulations 1992 (SI 1992 550) to require the listing officer for a billing authority to compile and then maintain new valuation lists in accordance with the 1992 Act.

2785. Councillors–Codes of conduct–Compliance with code of conduct of parish council–Personal and prejudicial conduct

[Local Government Act 2000 s.79(15).]

The appellant councillor (S) appealed under the Local Government Act 2000 s.79(15) against findings made against him by the case tribunal of the Adjudication Panel for England that he had failed on one occasion to declare a prejudicial interest and on another a personal interest, and accordingly had failed to comply with the code of conduct of a parish council. The issue was whether, in determining whether a councillor had failed to comply with the requirements of the code as regards personal and prejudicial interests, the proper test to be applied by a case tribunal was (i) whether the councillor, on the information available to him on the occasion in question, could rationally have taken the view he did as to whether he had a personal or prejudicial interest, or (ii) whether, viewed objectively, the councillor had a personal or a prejudicial interest in the matter. The tribunal held that the test was entirely objective. S's main submission was that a councillor did not fail to comply with the code if he reasonably but mistakenly concluded that he did not have a personal or prejudicial interest.

Held, dismissing the appeal, that none of the provisions of the code suggested a subjective test for their application or for compliance. A subjective test would confer considerable latitude on the conduct of a member. It would seriously detract from the express object of the Act and the purpose of the code, namely the promotion and maintenance of high standards of conduct by members. Whether a member had a personal or a prejudicial interest was a question to be determined objectively, *R. (on the application of Richardson) v. North Yorkshire CC* [2003] EWCA Civ 1860, [2004] 1 W.L.R. 1920, [2004] C.L.Y.3092 explained. The mistaken but reasonable view of the member that he had no such interest was irrelevant. The test for a failure to comply with the code was similarly objective. The fact that a member made an error of judgment and reasonably considered that he did not have a relevant interest would be highly material to the question of penalty.

SCRIVENS v. ETHICAL STANDARDS OFFICER, [2005] EWHC 529, [2005] B.L.G.R. 641, Stanley Burnton, J., QBD (Admin).

2786.   Councillors–Conduct–Certainty of local authority's code of conduct

[Human Rights Act 1998 Sch.1 Part I Art.10; Local Government Act 2000 s.79(15).]

The appellant former councillor (S) appealed pursuant to the Local Government Act 2000 s.79(15) against the decision of a case tribunal disqualifying him from being a councillor for two years on the ground that he had failed to comply with the local authority's code of conduct by not treating others with respect and by conduct which could reasonably be regarded as bringing his office or authority into disrepute. S had been a councillor and leader of Peterborough City Council. Carrickfergus Borough Council had passed a resolution recording its serious concern at the unexplained death of a soldier with the Royal Irish Regiment at barracks in Holywood. The resolution requested the chief executive to seek the support of other local authorities in the United Kingdom. The chief executive of Carrickfergus sent a letter to the chief executives of all UK local authorities asking them to bring the letter to members' attention. The chief executive of Peterborough City Council passed the letter to S to deal with as leader. S's unreflective response to the letter created a media storm. The respondent ethical standards officer investigated and reported on the matter and concluded that S had failed to comply with the local authority's code of conduct in respect of the way he had responded to the approach of Carrickfergus and in his subsequent comments to the media. The case tribunal accepted that view. S submitted that (1) the code of conduct was too uncertain to enable a person to know when he might be in breach of it; (2) the case tribunal erred in failing to have regard to the fact that the instant case involved his rights under the Human Rights Act 1998 Sch.1 Part I Art.10.

Held, allowing the appeal in part, that (1) the code of conduct was sufficiently precise to comply with the requirement of Art.10(2) that any restriction on freedom of speech was "prescribed by law". The terms of the code were specific in describing the nature of the conduct or its consequence. Failure to treat others with respect was a concept which was perfectly capable of being applied by a reasonable person, and conduct which could reasonably be regarded as bringing his office or authority into disrepute was also a well known concept. (2) Article 10 was engaged and the case tribunal erred in failing to consider it. The case tribunal was fully entitled to conclude that S's conduct was in breach of the code of conduct. S's statements did not attract the high degree of protection to which the expression of political opinion was entitled, because they were not an expression of political views at all but expressions of personal anger and abuse. The finding of the case tribunal that S had breached the code of conduct and its notification of that finding to his local authority constituted an interference with S's freedom of expression but one which was lawful under Art.10(2). (3) The case tribunal was not referred to the relevant guidance on disqualification, suspension and partial suspension. S's conduct did not call for disqualification. The relevant guidance indicated that the case tribunal would not usually take into account the electoral cycle of the particular body, but in this case the electoral cycle was of great importance since S had been re elected as an independent after being removed as council leader and expelled from his political party as a result of the events which had happened. In the light of S's re election to the council after the events complained of, the case tribunal was wrong to disqualify him. An appropriate and proportionate sanction was to suspend S for one year from the role of leader in which the breaches of the code of conduct had occurred.

SANDERS v. KINGSTON (NO.1), [2005] EWHC 1145, [2005] B.L.G.R. 719, Wilkie, J., QBD (Admin).

2787. Crown Estate–Parks–Regulation

ROYAL PARKS (REGULATION OF SPECIFIED PARKS) ORDER 2005, SI 2005 1522; made under the Serious Organised Crime and Police Act 2005 s.162. In force: July 1, 2005; £3.00.

This Order specifies the parks, gardens, recreation grounds, open spaces or other land in the metropolitan police district to which the Parks Regulation Act 1872 will cease to apply when the Royal Parks Constabulary is abolished under the Serious Organised Crime and Police Act 2005 s.161. The Parks Regulation (Amendment) Act 1926 s.2 will continue to apply to the specified parks in the same way as it applies to other parks to which the 1872 Act applies.

2788. Crown Estate–Parks–Termination of employment and transfer

ROYAL PARKS (ESTABLISHMENT OF ELIGIBILITY FOR TRANSFER AND TERMINATION OF EMPLOYMENT) REGULATIONS 2005, SI 2005 2868; made under the Serious Organised Crime and Police Act 2005 Sch.13 para.2, Sch.13 para.8. In force: November 10, 2005; £3.00.

These Regulations impose requirements on persons serving as Royal Parks constables for the purposes of establishing whether they are eligible to be employed by the Metropolitan Police Authority or to serve as Metropolitan Police constables when the Royal Parks Constabulary is abolished under the Serious Organised Crime and Police Act 2005 s.161. The Secretary of State has power to terminate the Crown employment of any Royal Parks constables who fail to comply with any of these requirements, and the Regulations provide that constables shall not be eligible for compensation for early retirement or severance under the Civil Service Compensation Scheme if their Crown employment is terminated in this way. The Regulations also provide that constables who are eligible to serve as Metropolitan Police constables who do not wish to transfer to the Metropolitan Police shall not be eligible for compensation if their Crown employment is terminated by a transfer scheme.

2789. Elections–Mayors–Children's services–Lead member

LOCAL AUTHORITIES (ELECTED MAYORS) (ENGLAND) REGULATIONS 2005, SI 2005 2121; made under the Local Government Act 2000 s.39, s.105. In force: in accordance with Reg.1 (1); £3.00.

The Local Government Act 2000 provides for the Secretary of State to make regulations specifying, for the purposes of certain enactments, that an elected mayor of a local authority is to be treated as a member or councillor of that authority. The Regulations specify that an elected mayor is to be treated as a member for the purposes of the Children Act 2004 s.19, which provides that a children's services authority in England must designate one of their members as the "lead member for children's services". The effect of the Regulations is to allow a local authority to designate an elected mayor as the lead member for children's services, and the Regulations will come into force at the same time as s.19 of the 2004 Act.

2790. Emergency powers–Contingency planning

CIVIL CONTINGENCIES ACT 2004 (CONTINGENCY PLANNING) REGULATIONS 2005, SI 2005 2042; made under the Civil Contingencies Act 2004 s.2, s.4, s.6, s.12, s.15, s.17. In force: November 14, 2005; £5.50.

These Regulations relate to the extent of the duties imposed on certain persons and bodies listed in the Civil Contingencies Act 2004 under s.2 and s.4 of that Act (duties to assess, and plan for emergencies and duties to provide advice and assistance to business) and the manner in which those duties are to be performed.

2791. Fire services–Consequential amendments–Wales

FIRE AND RESCUE SERVICES ACT 2004 (CONSEQUENTIAL AMENDMENTS) (WALES) ORDER 2005, SI 2005 2929 (W.214); made under the Fire and Rescue Services Act 2004 s.53, s.60, s.62. In force: October 25, 2005; £4.50.

This Order, which amends the Local Government Act 2003, makes consequential amendments predominantly to secondary legislation in relation to Wales, in particular by updating existing references to "fire authorities", "fire brigades" and "the Fire Services Act 1947".

2792. Fire services–National framework–Wales

FIRE AND RESCUE SERVICES (NATIONAL FRAMEWORK) (WALES) ORDER 2005, SI 2005 760 (W.64); made under the Fire and Rescue Services Act 2004 s.21, s.60, s.62. In force: March 17, 2005; £3.00.

The Fire and Rescue Services Act 2004 s.21 requires the National Assembly for Wales to prepare a Fire and Rescue National Framework, which must set out priorities and objectives for fire and rescue authorities and may provide guidance. Fire and rescue authorities must have regard to the Framework in carrying out their functions This Order gives effect to the Fire and Rescue National Framework (Wales) 2005.

2793. Health authorities–List of responders

CIVIL CONTINGENCIES ACT 2004 (AMENDMENT OF LIST OF RESPONDERS) ORDER 2005, SI 2005 2043; made under the Civil Contingencies Act 2004 s.13. In force: November 14, 2005; £3.00.

This Order, which amends the Civil Contingencies Act 2004, provides that the Health Protection Agency is a Category 1 responder only in so far as its functions relate to Great Britain. It also amends Schedule 1 so as to provide that Strategic Health Authorities are Category 2 responders.

2794. Inland waterways–Norfolk and Suffolk Broads–Constitution

NORFOLK AND SUFFOLK BROADS ACT 1988 (ALTERATION OF CONSTITUTION OF THE BROADS AUTHORITY) ORDER 2005, SI 2005 1067; made under the Norfolk and Suffolk Broads Act 1988 s.7, s.24. In force: June 1, 2005; £3.00.

This Order amends the Norfolk and Suffolk Broads Act 1988 so as to reduce the membership of the Broads Authority from 35 to 21 members, and to make some consequential changes.

2795. Local authorities–Armorial bearings–Ystradgynlais Town Council–Wales

LOCAL AUTHORITIES (ARMORIAL BEARINGS) (WALES) ORDER 2005, SI 2005 1960; made under the Local Government Act 1972 s.247. In force: July 20, 2005; £3.00.

This Order authorises Ystradgynlais Town Council to bear and use the armorial bearings of the former Ystradgynlais Rural District Council.

2796. **Local authorities–Audit Commission–Categorising performance of local authorities–Lawfulness of categorisation**

[Local Government Act 2003 s.99.]

The appellant Audit Commission appealed against a decision ([2005] EWHC 195, Times, March 2, 2005) that it had acted unlawfully in categorising the performance of the respondent local authority as poor, and the local authority cross appealed. The Audit Commission was required under the Local Government Act 2003 s.99 to categorise the performance of local authorities. The Audit Commission used a system called comprehensive performance assessment which contained rules limiting a local authority's overall category if its score fell below a certain level on education, social care or financial standing. The respondent local authority would have been categorised as good by virtue of its scores on core service performance and council ability but because it had received a zero rating from the Commission for Social Care Inspection in respect of its social services performance it could not be categorised as better overall than weak. The local authority sought judicial review of that decision on the ground that the Audit Commission had acted unlawfully by adopting a rule which automatically downgraded a local authority; by so acting, the Audit Commission failed to apply its own mind to the reasons for the zero rating and whether those reasons warranted downgrading the local authority's category. The Audit Commission submitted that there was nothing unlawful about having a rule which made use of the ratings of other specialist inspectorates so long as the rule was a rational one, that the Audit Commission's task was to devise an overall system of categorisation and that a system which required the Audit Commission to reconsider how the underlying ratings had been arrived at would be unworkable. The local authority submitted that the rule clearly subordinated the Audit Commission's decision to the previous Commission for Social Care Inspection decision and was therefore unlawful.

Held, allowing the appeal and dismissing the cross appeal, that the Audit Commission had not unlawfully delegated its s.99 decision to the Commission for Social Care Inspection. The latter's ratings followed automatically from the underlying scores, which the local authority did not challenge. The Audit Commission had in effect adopted as its own a series of weightings, produced by the Commission for Social Care Inspection, which resulted in a rating in an entirely predictable way. It was entitled to do that. It was not delegating its decision in any individual case to the Commission for Social Care Inspection since the Commission for Social Care Inspection did not make any such individual decision once it had arrived at the underlying scores. It was simply that the Audit Commission had itself decided to adopt certain principles for achieving its categorisation, *H Lavender & Son Ltd v. Minister of Housing and Local Government* [1970] 1 W.L.R. 1231, [1970] C.L.Y. 2757 distinguished. That conclusion did not result in any real prejudice to the local authority, which could have sought to challenge the Commission for Social Care Inspection's decisions about the individual scores and ratings, but had chosen not to do so.

R. (ON THE APPLICATION OF EALING LBC) v. AUDIT COMMISSION; *sub nom.* EALING LBC v. AUDIT COMMISSION; AUDIT COMMISSION FOR ENGLAND AND WALES v. EALING LBC, [2005] EWCA Civ 556, (2005) 8 C.C.L. Rep. 317, Lord Phillips of Worth Matravers, M.R., CA (Civ Div).

2797. **Local authorities–Contracting out–Billing authorities–Business levy**

LOCAL AUTHORITIES (CONTRACTING OUT OF BID LEVY BILLING, COLLECTION AND ENFORCEMENT FUNCTIONS) ORDER 2005, SI 2005 215; made under the Deregulation and Contracting Out Act 1994 s.70, s.77, Sch.16 para.3. In force: February 4, 2005; £3.00.

This Order makes provision to enable a billing authority in England and Wales in relation to the Business Improvement Districts (BID) levy to authorise another person, or that person's employees, to exercise functions relating to the administration and enforcement of the BID levy.

2798. Local authorities-Executives-Functions

LOCAL AUTHORITIES (FUNCTIONS AND RESPONSIBILITIES) (AMENDMENT) (NO.2) (ENGLAND) REGULATIONS 2005, SI 2005 929; made under the Local Government Act 2000 s.13, s.105. In force: April 22, 2005; £3.00.

These Regulations amend the Local Authorities (Functions and Responsibilities) (England) Regulations 2000 (SI 2000 2853) to specify as functions that are not to be the sole responsibility of the authority's executive certain functions conferred on authorities under the Planning and Compulsory Purchase Act 2004 Part 2 and under the Town and Country Planning Act 1990 s.171E. They also make amendments so that functions relating to development plan documents and joint committees established under the 2004 Act are the shared responsibility of the authority and any executive of the authority.

2799. Local authorities-Functions-Hedgerow complaints

LOCAL AUTHORITIES (FUNCTIONS AND RESPONSIBILITIES) (AMENDMENT) (ENGLAND) REGULATIONS 2005, SI 2005 714; made under the Local Government Act 2000 s.13, s.105. In force: June 1, 2005; £3.00.

The Local Government Act 2000 provides for the discharge of a local authority's functions by an executive of the authority unless those functions are specified as functions that are not to be the responsibility of the authority's executive. These Regulations amend the Local Authorities (Functions and Responsibilities) (England) Regulations 2000 (SI 2000 2853) which set out functions of a local authority which are not to be the responsibility of an executive of the authority. The Regulations make amendments by inserting a new item (item 47A) in respect of functions relating to complaints about high hedges under the Anti-social Behaviour Act 2003 Part 8.

2800. Local authorities-Performance-Categorisation

LOCAL AUTHORITIES (CATEGORISATION) (ENGLAND) ORDER 2005, SI 2005 694; made under the Local Government Act 2003 s.99. In force: April 11, 2005; £3.00.

This Order, which revokes the Local Authorities (Categorisation) (England) (No.2) Order 2004 (SI 2004 3211), categorises local authorities in England into five categories according to performance.

2801. Local authorities-Performance-Categorisation

LOCAL AUTHORITIES (CATEGORISATION) (ENGLAND) (NO.2) ORDER 2005, SI 2005 2416; made under the Local Government Act 2003 s.99. In force: September 28, 2005; £3.00.

This Order revokes the Local Authorities (Categorisation) (England) Order 2005 (SI 2005 694) and categorises local authorities in England into five categories according to performance.

2802. Local authorities-Plans and strategies-Obligations-Disapplication

LOCAL AUTHORITIES' PLANS AND STRATEGIES (DISAPPLICATION) (ENGLAND) ORDER 2005, SI 2005 157; made under the Local Government Act 2000 s.6, s.105; and the Local Government Act 2003 s.100. In force: February 1, 2005; £3.00.

This Order amends the Transport Act 1985, the Home Energy Conservation Act 1995, the Environment Act 1995, the Crime and Disorder Act 1998, the Countryside and Rights of Way Act 2000, the Transport Act 2000 and the Homelessness Act 2002. The Local Government Act 2000 provides for the Secretary of State by order to amend, repeal, revoke or disapply any enactment which requires a local authority to prepare, produce or publish any plan or strategy relating to any particular matter, if he considers that it is not appropriate for such an enactment to apply to the authority, or that such an enactment should be amended so that it operates more effectively in relation to the authority. This power may be exercised in relation to particular descriptions of local authority. This Order disapplies seven separate obligations to prepare, produce or (as the case may be) publish particular plans and strategies. It makes consequential modifications to the primary legislation in which certain of those obligations are enshrined.

2803. **Local authorities powers and duties–Childrens services–Assessment of age–Clarity of reasons for rejecting evidence**

[Children Act 1989.]

The claimant (C) applied for judicial review of a decision by the defendant local authority that she was aged 18 or over and was not entitled to support under the Children Act 1989. C had travelled to the United Kingdom using false documentation. She claimed asylum and provided copies of her alleged birth certificate, which showed that she was 17 years old. C was refused support by the local authority on the basis that it believed that she was in fact 18 years old or over. That assessment remained unchanged despite expert evidence obtained by C that estimated her age as being 17 years, plus or minus 2 years, on the basis of her physical characteristics and the social, schooling and narrative history provided by her. C argued that the local authority had failed (1) to have adequate regard to her birth certificate; (2) to properly assess the expert opinion.

Held, granting the application, that (1) there was no doubt that the local authority had considered the copy of the birth certificate and it had given reasons why it did not find it cogent or convincing in support of C's assertion about her age. (2) On the face of the decision letter, the local authority had not explained why it did not agree with the expert's opinion. It was wrong to impose too legalistic a role on local authorities in such a context, but it was incumbent on local authorities to express in a clear and concise way why a claimant's case was being rejected. There was no doubt that the entirety of the assessments and internal documentation had amply laid the groundwork for departing from the expert's opinion. However, the central feature of C's case was the expert's opinion and it was necessary for the local authority in the circumstances to explain, albeit briefly, why it did not accept that opinion. The decision letter was flawed and the decision was quashed.

R. (ON THE APPLICATION OF C) v. MERTON LBC, [2005] EWHC 1753, [2005] 3 F.C.R. 42, Davis, J., QBD (Admin).

2804. **Local authorities powers and duties–Declaratory orders–Local government–Declaration made in conjunction with an injunction under s.222 Local Government Act 1972**

The appellant (H) appealed against the grant of an injunction to the respondent local authority, by virtue of the Local Government Act 1972 s.222, that restrained her from keeping any more than three dogs of the same gender at her property at any one time, and a declaration which imposed instructions on H as to the delivery up to other persons of dogs removed from H and in the possession of the local authority. H had kept dogs on her land for some 30 years. She had, during that time, been convicted of a number of offences of cruelty to dogs and of unlawfully keeping a breeding establishment for dogs. In 1996 H was disqualified for seven years from having custody of dogs and was ordered to deliver up to the local authority the dogs in her custody at that time. During 2001, pursuant to a further order, 26 more dogs were removed from her custody. The local authority had sought an injunction preventing the return of the dogs to H upon the expiry of the disqualification order and a declaration that it was entitled to sell or dispose of the dogs in its possession. On appeal the issues for consideration were the rights and duties of the local authority when the bailment created by the orders came to an end, the principles applicable to the granting of injunctions under s.222 of the 1972 Act, and whether the court had the power to grant the declaration. The local authority appealed against the decision not to award it damages relating to the expense of caring for the dogs while in its custody.

Held, allowing the appeals in part (Sir Martin Nourse dissenting in part) that (1) the local authority had no statutory or common law right, nor the benefit of a court order, enabling it to retain possession of the dogs when the bailment created by the order came to an end. It was obliged to return the dogs to H unless it was able to show that redelivering them to H would be aiding and abetting a criminal offence, *Worcestershire CC v. Tongue* Times, October 1, 2003 applied. If the dogs had been returned to H they would have been at serious risk of unnecessary suffering and there was a serious possibility that H would have again committed the offence which had caused the disqualification. (2) Section 222 of the 1972 Act gave a local authority the power to institute and maintain proceedings to enforce obedience to the criminal law within its district, *Stoke on Trent City Council v. B&Q (Retail) Ltd* [1984] A.C. 754, [1984] C.L.Y. 3231 and *City of London Corp v. Bovis Construction Ltd* [1992] 3 All E.R. 697, [1989] C.L.Y. 3133 followed. It was not necessary for a local authority to establish that there had been a deliberate and flagrant flouting of the criminal law. The question to be asked was whether, in the circumstances, criminal proceedings were likely to prove ineffective in achieving the public interest purposes for which the legislation in question had been enacted, *Portsmouth City Council v. Richards* [1989] 1 C.M.L.R. 673, [1990] C.L.Y. 3704 and *Wychavon DC v. Midland Enterprises (Special Event) Ltd* [1988] 1 C.M.L.R. 397, [1988] C.L.Y. 3271 applied. The instant case was exceptional; there was something more than the risk of a mere infringement of the criminal law. The grant of the injunction was upheld. (3) The declaration granted by the judge could not stand. The court had sought to grant relief, not in aid of the criminal law by preventing unlawful breeding and cruelty to the dogs, but to make good a gap in the law, *Chief Constable of Leicestershire v. M* [1989] 1 W.L.R. 20, [1988] C.L.Y. 2877 applied. (4) Whilst the court could sympathise with the local authority's claim for damages to cover the expenses of caring for the dogs whilst they had been in its custody, there was no legal basis upon which the local authority was entitled to damages.

GUILDFORD BC v. HEIN, [2005] EWCA Civ 979, [2005] B.L.G.R. 797, Waller, L.J., CA (Civ Div).

2805. Local authorities powers and duties – Street trading – Power to levy charges on street traders – Extent of charges

[City of Westminster Act 1999 s.22(2), s.22(5).]

The claimant (W) applied for judicial review of a decision of the defendant local authority to implement changes in relation to charges for street trading. W was an unincorporated association representing approximately 100 street traders, the majority of which operated from isolated licensed pitches rather than street markets. The local authority had the power pursuant to the City of Westminster Act 1999 s.22(2) to recover from licence holders charges to cover its reasonable costs of collection, removal and disposal of refuse and other services rendered by them to such licence holders. Many of W's members had benefited from an exemption from refuse collection charges on the basis that they declared that their business did not require such a service. The local authority's proposal envisaged a reduction in charges for market stalls, but an increase for traders from isolated pitches, particularly those who had not previously paid for refuse collection. The Major Licensing Applications Committee decided to implement the proposed charges subject to a subsequent review of refuse provision. W contended that the local authority had misconstrued its charging powers in determining that it was obliged to recoup its costs in their entirety and that it was entitled to charge all licence holders for refuse collection services whether such a service was desired or necessary.

Held, refusing the application, that the local authority had embarked upon a full recovery of its costs in accordance with the principles formulated in *R. v. Tower Hamlets LBC, ex p. Tower Hamlets Combined Traders Association* [1994] C.O.D. 325, [1995] C.L.Y. 89, *Tower Hamlets LBC* applied. On a true construction of the legislation, s.22(2) of the Act identified certain services that the local authority was bound to supply to street traders such as waste disposal and enforcement which enured for their benefit. Section 22(5) allowed the local authority to provide other services that by majority vote could be imposed on one market or area of traders, with the cost then being met by all the members of that market or area. In s.22(2) the word "reasonable" qualified the valuation of the service provided to the group, and not to the individual trader. The local authority had been entitled to decide that it was unfair to those who paid for refuse collection that others, who chose not use the service, caused the cost to those who did use it to increase. The local authority had prepared a consultation paper that proposed bringing refuse provision for isolated pitches into line with pitches at market locations on the basis that market locations paid for cleansing regardless of the amount of refuse generated. The local authority's approach to refuse collection was neither unlawful nor irrational.

R. (ON THE APPLICATION OF WEST END STREET TRADERS ASSOCIATION) v. WESTMINSTER CITY COUNCIL, [2004] EWHC 1167, [2005] B.L.G.R. 143, Leveson, J., QBD (Admin Ct).

2806. Local government finance–Allocation of grants–Council tax calculations

GREATER LONDON AUTHORITY (ALLOCATION OF GRANTS FOR PRECEPT CALCULATIONS) REGULATIONS 2005, SI 2005 221; made under the Greater London Authority Act 1999 s.88, s.89. In force: February 9, 2005; £3.00.

The Greater London Authority Act 1999 s.88 and s.89 set out how the Greater London Authority is to calculate the amounts of its council tax for the City of London and the remainder of Greater London. Separate calculations are necessary for these two parts of Greater London because the Metropolitan Police Authority is not responsible for the provision of police services in the City of London. These Regulations which apply for the financial year beginning on April 1, 2005, prescribe the amounts of redistributed non-domestic rates and specified grants, which the First Secretary of State considers relate to the police and non-police expenditure of the Greater London Authority and functional bodies, which the Greater London Authority must take into account when carrying out the calculations of the amounts of council tax for the two parts of Greater London.

2807. Local government finance–Budget requirements–Amendment to calculations

LOCAL AUTHORITIES (ALTERATION OF REQUISITE CALCULATIONS) (ENGLAND) REGULATIONS 2005, SI 2005 190; made under the Local Government Finance Act 1992 s.32, s.33, s.43, s.44, s.113; and the Greater London Authority Act 1999 s.86, s.88, s.89, s.420. In force: February 5, 2005; £3.00.

The Local Government Finance Act 1992 sets out how a billing authority and a major precepting authority other than the Greater London Authority (GLA) are to calculate their budget requirements for a financial year, and sets out how a billing authority and such a major precepting authority are to calculate the basic amount of their council tax. This Order amends the 1992 Act to exclude expenditure to be charged to a business improvement district (BID) Revenue Account from the expenditure that the authority must aggregate but to include expenditure incurred by the authority in paying a BID levy for which it is liable or in making a financial contribution or taking action under the Local Government Act 2003.

2808. Local government finance–Public expenditure–Limits

LOCAL AUTHORITIES (DISCRETIONARY EXPENDITURE LIMITS) (ENGLAND) ORDER 2005, SI 2005 419; made under the Local Government Act 1972 Sch.12B para.4. In force: March 29, 2005; £3.00.

The Local Government Act 1972 s.137 enables local authorities in England to incur expenditure for certain purposes not otherwise authorised. This expenditure must not exceed the amount produced by multiplying a specified sum by the relevant population of the authority's area. The relevant population is currently the number of electors resident in the authority's area. In the case of a parish council in England, the specified sum is £5 or other such sum as by Order be specified. This Order increases to £5.30 the sum specified.

2809. Recreational services–Revocation of parish council byelaws

RECREATION GROUNDS (REVOCATION OF PARISH COUNCIL BYELAWS) ORDER 2005, SI 2005 867; made under the Local Government Act 1972 s.262. In force: April 12, 2005; £3.00.

This Order revokes specified byelaws which were made in exercise of the powers conferred on parish councils by the Local Government Act 1894 s.8(1)(d). The byelaws are revoked as being substantially superseded by byelaws made under other enactments.

2810. Urban regeneration–Business improvement districts–Proposals–Wales

BUSINESS IMPROVEMENT DISTRICTS (WALES) REGULATIONS 2005, SI 2005 1312 (W.94); made under the Local Government Act 2003 s.47, s.48, s.49, s.51, s.52, s.54, s.55, s.56, s.58, s.123. In force: May 13, 2005; £7.50.

These Regulations, which make provision in relation to business improvement districts (BID), provide for the billing authority to supply information from its non-domestic rates records to persons developing BID proposals. They specify the persons who may draw up BID proposals and specify the procedures to be followed in connection with drawing up of BID proposals. The Regulations also provide that the returning officer for local elections in the billing authority area is to be the ballot holder for any ballot in respect of BIDs required; provide for who is entitled to vote in a ballot; confer a power on the National Assembly to declare a ballot void in cases of material irregularity and procedures connected therewith; enable a billing authority to recover the costs of a BID ballot or a renewal ballot from the BID proposer or BID body in the prescribed circumstances; provide for the billing authority to supply information from its non-domestic rates records for the purpose of canvassing in relation to a ballot; and prescribe the circumstances in which a billing authority may veto BID proposals.

2811. Books

Sharland, John–Practical Approach to Local Government Law. Paperback: £39.95. ISBN 0 19 928347 8. Oxford University Press.

MEDIA AND ENTERTAINMENT

2812. Breach of confidence–Economic torts–Unauthorised publication of photographs of wedding reception

[Human Rights Act 1998 Sch.1 Part I Art.10(2).]

The appellant magazine publisher (H) appealed against decisions on liability ([2003] EWHC 786, [2003] 3 All E.R. 996) and quantum ([2003] EWHC 2629, [2004] E.M.L.R. 2) in the respondents' claims for damages for breach of confidence, and the respondents cross appealed. The first and second respondents (D) were film stars who had entered into an agreement with the third respondent magazine publisher (N) for N to publish in N's popular magazine an article and exclusive photographs of D's wedding. D had made efforts to prevent unauthorised photographs from being taken at their wedding. Unauthorised photographs had been taken and had been published by H in its rival magazine. In proceedings by D and N against H, the judge had held that D were entitled to damages for breach of confidence on the grounds that the wedding reception was a private event and that N was entitled to damages for breach of confidence but not for deliberate interference with N's business or conspiracy to injure. The judge awarded D damages of £14,750 for distress and inconvenience. He awarded N damages of just over £1 million, representing N's loss of profit resulting from lost sales attributable to the publication of the unauthorised photographs. H appealed against the award in favour of D in respect of liability only and against the award in favour of N in respect of liability and quantum. H argued that D had no cause of action against H, whether in terms of confidence or privacy, as a result of the publication of the unauthorised photographs and that N did not have a cause of action based on confidence as a result of the publication of the unauthorised photographs; and that the judge had erred when assessing the effect of publication of the unauthorised photographs on N's profits. N argued that if H was not liable to N in confidence, it was nonetheless liable to it on the basis of one or more of the economic torts. D argued that the damages awarded to them should be equivalent to the licence fee which they would have negotiated with H for the publication of the unauthorised photographs.

Held, giving judgment accordingly, that (1) the unauthorised photographs of D's wedding reception plainly portrayed aspects of their private life and fell within the protection of the law of confidentiality, as extended to cover private or personal information, *Campbell v. Mirror Group Newspapers Ltd* [2004] UKHL 22, [2004] 2 A.C. 457, [2004] C.L.Y. 2673 applied. (2) A claim for breach of confidence was to be categorised not as a tort but as a restitutionary claim for unjust enrichment, and the proper law was the law of the country where the enrichment occurred. (3) The law of New York did not have any direct application on the facts of the instant case. The cause of action was based on the publication in the UK and the complaint was that private information was conveyed to readers in the UK. The test of whether the information was private so as to attract the protection of English law was governed by English law. That test was whether H knew or ought to have known that D had a reasonable expectation that the information would remain private, *Campbell* applied. The law of New York clearly entitled D to arrange for their wedding to take place in circumstances designed to ensure that events at the wedding remained private, at least so far as photographs were concerned. (4) The agreement that authorised photographs could be published did not provide a defence to a claim, brought under the law of confidence, for the publication of unauthorised photographs. The effect of entering into the contract with N was not to preclude D from contending that their wedding was a private occasion and, as such, protected by the law of confidence. (5) There were no grounds for interfering with the judge's award of £3,750 to each of D in respect of the distress caused by the unauthorised photographs. (6) The judge had been entitled to award D £7,000 as compensation for the interference with the commercial exploitation of their wedding. Where an individual had at his disposal information which he had created or which was private or personal and to which he could properly deny access to third parties, and he reasonably intended to profit commercially by using or publishing that information, then a third party who was or ought to be aware of those matters and who had knowingly obtained the information without authority would be in breach of duty if he used or published the information to the detriment of the owner, *Prince Albert v. Strange* (1849) 18 L.J. Ch. 120, *Gilbert v. Star Newspaper Co Ltd* (1894) 51 T.L.R. 4, *Saltman Engineering Co v. Campbell Engineering Co (1948)* [1963] 3 All E.R. 413 (Note), *Mustad v. Dosen* [1964] 1 W.L.R. 109 (Note), [1963] C.L.Y. 3338, *Shelley Films Ltd v. Rex Features Ltd* [1994] E.M.L.R. 134 and *Creation Records Ltd v. News Group Newspapers Ltd* [1997] E.M.L.R. 444, [1997] C.L.Y. 1041 considered. However, that confidential or private information, which was capable of commercial exploitation but which was only protected by the law of confidence, did not fall to be treated as property that could be owned and transferred. (7) The appeal against the judgment against D was therefore dismissed. (8) The interest of D in the private information about events at the wedding did not amount to a right of intellectual property. Their right to protection of that interest did not arise because they had some form of proprietary interest in it, *Boardman v. Phipps* [1967] 2 A.C. 46, [1966] C.L.Y. 11052 applied. The grant to N of the right to use the approved photographs was no more than a licence, albeit an exclusive licence, to exploit commercially those photographs for a nine month period. A mere exclusive licence to use authorised photographs of an event did not (in the absence of a statutory provision) carry with it the right to sue a third party for infringement of a right vested in the licensor to object to the publishing of other photographs of that event. The unauthorised photographs invaded the area of privacy which D had chosen to retain and D, not N, had the right to protect that area of privacy or confidentiality. Therefore the judge was wrong to hold that N had a right of commercial confidence in relation to the photographs published by H, and H's appeal was to that extent allowed. (9) If it was wrong that N had no right of commercial confidence in the unauthorised photographs, then the judge was right that N's action in bringing forward the publication of the authorised photographs, so that it was approximately simultaneous with publication by H of the unauthorised photographs, did not have the effect of destroying such rights of confidentiality as N had. (10) When H decided to publish the photographs, it was reasonably foreseeable that the development of English law might result in H being held to have infringed D's rights of privacy or confidence and therefore the court rejected the argument that upholding the claims against H imposed a restriction on H's right to freedom of expression that was not at the time prescribed by law of sufficient certainty within the Human Rights Act 1998 Sch.1 Part I Art.10(2). (11) The judge found and was entitled to find that H had not aimed, directed or targeted its conduct at N and that H had no specific object to cause economic harm to N. The highest that it could be put was that H knew that its conduct might cause economic harm to N and was recklessly indifferent to that risk. In all cases of alleged unlawful interference with economic interests and unlawful means conspiracy where liability had been established, the necessary object or purpose of causing the claimant economic harm would not be made out unless the conduct could be shown to have been aimed or directed at the claimant, *Lonrho Ltd v. Shell Petroleum Co Ltd (No.2)* [1982] A.C. 173, [1981] C.L.Y. 2649 and *Lonrho Plc v. Al-Fayed (No.1)* [1992] 1 A.C. 448, [1992] C.L.Y. 4130 applied. The subjective recklessness demonstrated in the instant case did not suffice as the mental element of the torts of economic loss, and the economic tort claims and N's cross appeal failed. If the test of intention had been made out, the test of use of unlawful means would have been satisfied. (12) The judge's assessment of N's damages in respect of lost profits on the basis that the unauthorised photographs had been used in other newspapers was not erroneous. (13) D were not entitled to damages on a notional licence fee basis.

DOUGLAS v. HELLO! LTD (NO.6); *sub nom.* DOUGLAS v. HELLO! LTD (TRIAL ACTION: BREACH OF CONFIDENCE) (NO.3), [2005] EWCA Civ 595, [2006] Q.B. 125, Lord Phillips of Worth Matravers, M.R., CA (Civ Div).

2813. **Broadcasting–Television–Interim injunction to restrain broadcast unless advance disclosure of material for exercise of right of reply–Public interest and owner of information's right of reply**

[Human Rights Act 1998 s.12(3).]

The claimant (T) applied for an interim injunction to restrain the broadcast of a television programme unless certain conditions were met. T's case was based on confidentiality. T was a company involved in the provision of frozen meals to NHS hospitals. The first defendant (C) was a broadcasting company and the second defendant (S) was a film production company. The programme in question was a piece of investigative journalism into alleged bad practice involving an undercover journalist who had obtained employment at T's factory. T sought advance sight of the material which related to the principal allegations. T claimed that it had a right of response. T argued that broadcast should be restrained until the material was provided. T submitted that the journalist's activities amounted to a breach of trust and confidence and that the film that he took amounted to confidential information. As such, T contended, publication without a proper right to reply was not in the public interest.

Held, refusing the application, that the Human Rights Act 1998 s.12(3) applied. T would clearly fail at trial because the ingredients of the cause of action were not present. In any claim for misuse of confidential information, a claimant had to establish that there was information of the relevant quality of confidentiality. Public interest in disclosure was not qualified by a need to give the owner of the information a right to respond or reply. As there was no right of reply available to T, there was no ancillary right to see material allegedly necessary for a worthwhile right of reply.

TILLERY VALLEY FOODS v. CHANNEL FOUR TELEVISION CORP, [2004] EWHC 1075, *The Times*, May 21, 2004, Mann, J., Ch D.

2814. **Films–Cinematic co production agreements–Additional countries–Armenia**

EUROPEAN CONVENTION ON CINEMATOGRAPHIC CO-PRODUCTION (AMENDMENT) ORDER 2005, SI 2005 247; made under the Films Act 1985 Sch.1 para.4. In force: April 1, 2005; £3.00.

The European Convention on Cinematographic Co-production Order 1994 (SI 1994 1065) provides that films made in accordance with the European Convention on Cinematographic Co-production are to be treated as British films for the purposes of the Films Act 1985. For the Convention to apply where there are only two co-producers one must be established in the UK and the other in one of the countries set out in the 1994 Order. For the Convention to apply where there are three or more co-producers one must be established in the UK and at least two others in different countries set out in the 1994 Order. This Order amends 1994 Order by adding Armenia to the countries set out in it. Certain tax benefits may accrue in respect of a film which is a British film.

2815. **Films–Cinematic co production agreements–Additional countries–Turkey**

EUROPEAN CONVENTION ON CINEMATOGRAPHIC CO-PRODUCTION (AMENDMENT) (NO.2) ORDER 2005, SI 2005 1464; made under the Films Act 1985 Sch.1 para.4. In force: July 1, 2005; £3.00.

The European Convention on Cinematographic Co-production Order 1994 (SI 1994 1065) provides that films made in accordance with the European Convention on Cinematographic Co-production are to be treated as British films for the purposes of the Films Act 1985 Sch.1. For the Convention to apply where there are only two co-producers one must be established in the UK and the other in one of the countries set out in the Schedule to the 1994 Order. For the Convention to apply where there are three or more co-producers one must be established in the UK and at least two others in different countries set out in the Schedule to the 1994 Order. This Order amends the Schedule to the 1994 Order by adding Turkey to the countries set out in it.

2816. **Books**

Article 19–Model Public Service Broadcasting Law: International Standards Theory. Paperback: £10.00. ISBN 1 902598 71 7. Article 19.

Calvert, Clay; Pember, Don R.–Mass Media Law. Paperback: £68.99. ISBN 0 07 312685 3. McGraw Hill Higher Education.

Carey, P.; Verow, R.–Media and Entertainment Law. Paperback: £24.95. ISBN 0 905835 84 0. The College of Law.

Epstein, Adam–Entertainment Law. Hardback: £40.99. ISBN 0 13 114743 9. Prentice Hall.

McTernan, Sean–Introduction to Media Law. Medialex Guidebook Series. Paperback: £25.00. ISBN 1 905394 00 4. MEDIALEX PUBLICATIONS.

Parker, Nigel–Music Business Infrastructure, Practice and Law. Paperback: £52.00. ISBN 0 421 89930 1. Sweet & Maxwell.

Pember, Don R.–Mass Media Law. Paperback: £36.99. ISBN 0 07 110721 5. Higher Education.

Sadler, Roger L.–Electronic Media Law. Paperback: £45.00. ISBN 1 4129 0588 5. Sage Publications Ltd.

Schulenberg, Richard–Legal Aspects of the Music Industry. Hardback: £22.50. ISBN 0 8230 8364 0. Billboard Books.

MENTAL HEALTH

2817. **Absolute discharge–Mental health review tribunals–Tribunal's reliance on patient's other mental disorders–Compatibility with Sch.1 Part I Human Rights Act 1998**

[Mental Health Act 1983 s.37, s.41, s.73(2), s.75; Human Rights Act 1998 Sch.1 Part I Art.6, Art.8.]

The claimant (C) applied for judicial review of the decision of the defendant tribunal refusing his application for an absolute discharge in respect of his detention under the Mental Health Act 1983. C had been convicted before a Crown Court, which later made a hospital order under s.37 of the Act. It also made a restriction order that C should be subject to the special restrictions in s.41 indefinitely. C was conditionally discharged by the tribunal under s.73(2). C applied to the tribunal under s.75(2) for a direction under s.75(3)(b) that the restriction order cease to have effect. The defendant secretary of state opposed C's absolute discharge. In refusing C's application, the tribunal took into account evidence from previous psychiatric assessments that diagnosed "psychopathic personality", whereas the only form of mental disorder specified by the Crown Court in imposing the restriction order was "mental illness". C submitted that (1) the tribunal's reliance upon the evidence from previous diagnoses of "psychopathic personality" was reliance on an irrelevant matter; (2) s.75(3) of the Act was incompatible with his rights under the Human Rights Act 1998 Sch.1 Part I Art.6 and Art.8 since it provided no criteria for the exercise of a tribunal's discretion on an application under s.75(2).

Held, refusing the application, that (1) there was nothing in *R. (on the application of B) v. Ashworth Hospital Authority* [2003] EWCA Civ 547, [2003] 1 W.L.R. 1886, [2003] C.L.Y. 2949 to compel the result for which C contended, *Ashworth* distinguished, *R. (on the application of Secretary of State for the Home Department) v. Mental Health Review Tribunal* [2004] EWHC 1029 followed and *R. (on the application of AL) v. Secretary of State for the Home Department* [2004] EWHC 1025 applied. It followed from both the case law and the language of s.73 that there was no necessary link between the disorder from which a restricted patient was previously classified as suffering and the grounds for conditional discharge in accordance with s.73. There was no reason to import any such link when the tribunal, as in the instant case, was considering the exercise of its powers under s.75. It was lawful for a tribunal, in deciding whether to exercise its power under s.75(3)(b), to bear in mind disorders other than that from which the patient was classified as suffering, whether by the Crown Court in accordance with s.37, or subsequently by the tribunal in accordance with s.72(5). (2) The 1998 Act did not preclude the exercise of a broad discretion by authorities acting in a judicial capacity. Even if the discretion conferred by s.75(3) was broad and on the face of it unfettered, the statute itself contained a number of powerful indications as to the kind of factors that the tribunal was likely to have to consider, particularly bearing in mind s.37, s.41 and s.73. One of the key questions that a tribunal would need to consider was whether it was satisfied that it was not appropriate for the patient to remain liable to be recalled to hospital for further treatment. At each stage of the process in relation to an application under s.75(2) important safeguards of the patient's rights were available either in the tribunal and/or by way of judicial review. Those safeguards adequately protected the patient from all risk of arbitrariness. The instant case was one in which the availability of appropriate mechanisms of judicial control or judicial review of discretionary decision making could, when taken in conjunction with all other circumstances, satisfy the requirements of the Convention. Section 75(3) was not incompatible with the Convention. The relevant law was so formulated as to be both sufficiently foreseeable and adequate to protect a patient in C's position from all risk of arbitrariness.

R. (ON THE APPLICATION OF C) v. MENTAL HEALTH REVIEW TRIBUNAL; *sub nom.* R. (ON THE APPLICATION OF SC) v. MENTAL HEALTH REVIEW

TRIBUNAL, [2005] EWHC 17, *The Times*, January 24, 2005, Munby, J., QBD (Admin).

2818. Detention–Mental patients rights–Compatibility of the Mental Health Act 1983 s.2 and s.29(4) with Human Rights Act 1998 Sch.1 Part I Art.5(4)

[Mental Health Act 1983 s.2, s.23, s.25, s.29, s.29(4); Human Rights Act 1998 Sch.1 Part I Art.5, Art.5(4).]

The appellant (M), who suffered from Down's Syndrome, appealed against a decision ([2004] EWHC 56) that her detention under the Mental Health Act 1983 was compatible with the Human Rights Act 1998 Sch.1 Part I Art.5. M had been detained under s.2 of the 1983 Act. M's nearest relative had sought a discharge under s.23 but had been barred under s.25 of the 1983 Act. Prior to the expiration of M's s.2 order, an application had been made under s.29 of the 1983 Act to displace M's nearest relative, and M had remained subject to detention under the s.2 order significantly beyond the normal period of 28 days. M complained that her disability was sufficiently serious for her to have been unable either to make an application to a mental health review tribunal herself against the s.2 order or to authorise others to make an application on her behalf. M argued that to accommodate her difficulty a generous reading was required of Sch.1 Part I Art.5(4) of the 1998 Act and objected to the statutory scheme under the 1983 Act on the grounds that (1) a competent s.2 patient had access to the tribunal, whereas an incompetent patient such as M did not; (2) s.29(4) might extend a s.2 detention for many months after the expiry of its statutory term, and neither the competent nor the incompetent patient had any recourse to the tribunal in respect of that extension.

Held, allowing the appeal, that (1) the state was obliged to place the incompetent patient in the same position as the competent patient with regard to access to the tribunal. Section 2 of the 1983 Act was incompatible with Sch.1 Part 1 Art.5(4) of the 1998 Act as it was not attended by adequate provision for the reference to a court of a patient detained pursuant to s.2 in circumstances in which she had a right to make an application to the tribunal but was incapable of exercising that right on her own initiative. The absence of any mechanism enabling an incompetent patient to apply to a tribunal within the 28-day period provided for by s.2 rendered it inconsistent with Sch.1 Part I Art.5(4), and the court accordingly made a declaration of incompatibility. The tribunal was a specialist court designed to make an assessment of a person's medical condition and judicial review could not be a substitute for a review on the merits of a case as required by Sch.1 Part I Art.5(4), *R. (on the application of N) v. M* [2002] EWCA Civ 1789, [2003] 1 W.L.R. 562, [2003] C.L.Y. 2958 considered. (2) M should have had the right to return to the tribunal to obtain a judicial decision on her continued detention. Section 29(4) of the 1983 Act was incompatible with Sch.1 Part I Art.5(4) in that it was not attended by provision for the reference to a court of the case of a patient detained pursuant to s.2 whose period of detention was extended by operation of s.29(4), and the court made an appropriate declaration of incompatibility.

R. (ON THE APPLICATION OF H) v. SECRETARY OF STATE FOR HEALTH; *sub nom*. R. (ON THE APPLICATION OF MH) v. SECRETARY OF STATE FOR HEALTH, [2004] EWCA Civ 1609, [2005] 1 W.L.R. 1209, Buxton, L.J., CA (Civ Div).

2819. Guardianship orders–Mental patients rights–Displacement orders–Nearest relative–Judge's exercise of discretion

[Mental Health Act 1983 s.7(2), s.29; Human Rights Act 1998 Sch.1 Part I Art.6, Art.8; Civil Procedure Rules 1998 (SI 1998 3132) Sch.2 Ord.49 r.12(3)(b).]

The appellant (L) appealed against a decision confirming an interim order which displaced her as nearest relative to her daughter (M). M had Down's syndrome. Concerns as to M's welfare arose and a case conference was convened to consider whether the local authority should intervene. The medical opinion of M's psychiatrist was sought. Evidence suggested that there had been a significant deterioration in M's well being and conduct and it became clear that L was exhausted by the burden of caring for M and that, without active intervention, there could be a tragic outcome. A warrant was issued and M was admitted to a mental hospital. A review carried out by the mental health review tribunal dismissed the application for M's discharge and L's challenge to the decision by way of judicial review was also dismissed. The local authority successfully applied under the Mental Health Act 1983 s.29 to displace L as nearest relative and to assume guardianship. Further guardianship renewals were intermittently made. L submitted that (1) the judge had erred in preferring the evidence of M's psychiatrist to that of an expert consultant in social work; (2) the relevant date for the determination of whether or not the criteria for applications of guardianship were satisfied was the date of the hearing; (3) the judge had erred in the exercise of his discretion to reject the submission that the local authority should apply for a best interests declaration on the ground that the conclusion was plainly wrong, and in the alternative the judge's ruling was flawed since he had omitted rights under the Human Rights Act 1998 Sch.1 Part I Art.8 from the balancing exercise.

Held, dismissing the appeal, that (1) having regard to all the material evidence, the judge was entitled to prefer the evidence of M's psychiatrist. (2) In order to succeed on an application under s.29, an applicant had to demonstrate that the statutory criteria were made out. However, the language of s.29(3)(c) made it clear that the relevant date for establishing the court's jurisdiction to deal with an application was the date of the application. Moreover, the judge had to be satisfied that the grounds under s.29(3)(c) existed at the date of the final hearing. In the instant case, jurisdiction having been established under s.29(3)(c) at the date of issue of the originating application, the judge was right to hear evidence about M's condition as at the date of the hearing. Further, the judge was fully entitled to conclude that M continued to satisfy the criteria under s.7(2). (3) Once the local authority had established its entitlement to the order sought under the Act, the suggestion that the judge should in the exercise of his discretion refuse the relief and send the local authority to another court to seek a best interests declaration was unlikely to succeed. Parliament had conferred a discretion on the judge by its use of the word "may" in the opening phrase of s.29. The judge had exercised his discretion in a manner that was not open to criticism. The Official Solicitor's proposal for the implementation of the amended Civil Procedure Rules 1998 Sch.2 Ord.49 r.12(3)(b) to ensure compliance with a patient's human rights should be endorsed. Although the new rule did not require it, the patient had to be served with the proceedings and notified of the right to be joined. In addition, the county court judge should at the earliest stage enquire whether the patient had been so served and ensure that appropriate steps were taken to secure the patient's rights under Sch.1 Part I Art.6 and Art.8 of the 1998 Act. Furthermore, enquiry should be made into the patient's capacity in order to establish that a person willing to act as a litigation friend had been identified and served.

LEWIS v. GIBSON, [2005] EWCA Civ 587, [2005] 2 F.C.R. 241, Thorpe, L.J., CA (Civ Div).

2820. Hospital orders—Mental patients rights—Classification of mental disorder— Treatment without consent

[Mental Health Act 1983 s.63.]

The appellant hospital (X) appealed against the decision of the Court of Appeal ([2003] EWCA Civ 547, [2003] 1 W.L.R. 1886) upholding judicial review proceedings brought by a compulsorily detained psychiatric patient (B) against his transfer to, and treatment in a ward designed to treat personality disorders. B had been convicted of manslaughter and detained under a hospital order with a restriction order of indefinite duration under the Mental Health Act 1983. B was classified as suffering from mental illness, namely schizophrenia, and admitted into the hospital. Eventually, having concluded that B's mental illness was being successfully controlled by medication, and following tests, X transferred B to a ward particularly designed to address traits of personality disorder. He was not however reclassified to show both mental illness and psychopathic disorder. The new regime was less agreeable to B than the one he had previously enjoyed. B argued that he should not have been transferred to a ward for patients with psychopathic disorder. Judicial review proceedings were commenced seeking an order to quash the decision to place B on the ward, a declaration that the placement was unlawful, and a declaration that his treatment for personality disorder was unlawful. The main issue was whether a patient detained for treatment under the Act could be treated under s.63 of the Act against his will for any mental disorder from which he was suffering or only for the particular form or mental disorder from which he was classified as suffering for the purpose of the order or application authorising his detention.

Held, allowing the appeal, that the Act's definition of mental disorder encompassed not only each of the four specific forms of disorder which might be relevant under the Act but the broader concepts of "arrested or incomplete development of mind" and "any other disorder or disability of the mind". Thus the natural and ordinary meaning of the words of s.63 was that the patient might be treated without consent for any mental disorder from which he was suffering and any treatment ancillary to that. If it had been intended to limit s.63 to treatment for the specific form of mental disorder under which the patient was detained, then the section would have read "for the form of mental disorder from which he is suffering". The fact that a restricted patient could only be reclassified after a Mental Health Review Tribunal hearing reinforced the conclusion that classification had no bearing on treatment. The time taken to gather the necessary reports and evidence and to arrange a hearing could be considerable and it was unlikely that Parliament intended that the patient could not be treated without his consent in the meantime, particularly as the patient might find ways of delaying the tribunal hearing. Furthermore, it was not easy to disentangle which features of a patient's presentation stemmed from a disease of the mind and which stemmed from his underlying personality traits. The psychiatrist's aim was to treat the whole patient. B's mental illness having been stabilised on medication, the aim was to address the underlying features of his personality which were getting in the way of his transfer back to a less restrictive setting. Once the state had taken away a person's liberty and detained him in a hospital with the view to medical treatment, the state should be able to provide him with the treatment he needed. Accordingly, s.63 did authorise a patient to be treated for any mental disorder from which he was suffering, irrespective of whether this fell within the form of disorder from which he was classified as suffering in the application, order or direction justifying his detention.

R. (ON THE APPLICATION OF B) v. ASHWORTH HOSPITAL AUTHORITY, [2005] UKHL 20, [2005] 2 A.C. 278, Lord Bingham of Cornhill, HL.

2821. Mental Capacity Act 2005 (c.9)

This Act makes new provision relating to persons who lack capacity; establishes a superior court of record called the Court of Protection in place of the office of the Supreme Court called by that name; and makes provision in connection with the Convention on the International Protection of Adults signed at the Hague on January 13, 2000.

This Act received Royal Assent on April 7, 2005.

2822. Mental health review tribunals–Hearings–Determination to hold public hearing–Powers to control publicity–Reasons–Exercise of discretion

[Mental Health Review Tribunal Rules 1983 (SI 1983 942) r.21.]

The claimant NHS trust applied for judicial review of the decision of the defendant tribunal to hold the statutory review hearing of a restricted patient (B) in public following a request from B. B was an interested party in the instant proceedings. The Mental Health Review Tribunal Rules 1983 r.21 created a presumption that hearings before mental health review tribunals were in private. The NHS trust's view, supported by the evidence of the responsible medical officer (RMO), was that a public hearing would be contrary to B's interests. The NHS trust contended that the tribunal had erred as to its powers to control publicity and it had failed to give adequate reasons for its decision. The NHS trust argued that the tribunal had failed to have regard to material considerations. B submitted that the tribunal was only required to consider the interests of the patient.

Held, granting the application, that the tribunal had erred as to its powers to prevent or restrict the publication of evidence and information disclosed at a public hearing. This error affected its assessment of whether holding such a hearing would be contrary to B's interests. Although r.21 (5) covered both public and private hearings, a tribunal's powers if a hearing was in public were substantially more limited because the protection afforded by the strict liability contempt rule was for only a limited period and there was difficulty in determining in advance what kind of public comment about proceedings would create a substantial risk that the course of justice would be prejudiced or seriously impeded, *Pickering v. Liverpool Daily Post and Echo* [1991] 2 A.C. 370, [1991] C.L.Y. 2456 considered. The tribunal's reasons did not comply with the principles derived from *R. (on the application of H) v. Ashworth Hospital Authority* [2002] EWCA Civ 923, [2003] 1 W.L.R. 127, [2002] C.L.Y. 3230, *Ashworth* applied. Particular weight should have been given to the RMO's views in light of his long involvement with B's treatment. There was a particular need for reasons to be given where his views were rejected. It was not apparent from the decision that the tribunal had considered concerns about B's safety at a public hearing and the impact on his condition of the extra security required. As a tribunal was not necessarily required to sit in public where the two prerequisites contained in r.21 (1) were met, it followed that a tribunal had a discretion. In the exercise of the discretion, a tribunal had to take account of relevant matters raised.

R. (ON THE APPLICATION OF MERSEY CARE NHS TRUST) v. MENTAL HEALTH REVIEW TRIBUNAL, [2004] EWHC 1749, [2005] 1 W.L.R. 2469, Beatson, J., QBD (Admin Ct).

2823. Mental illness–Medical treatment–Refusal to consent to treatment–Therapeutic or medical necessity for treatment–Breaches of human rights

[Mental Health Act 1983; Human Rights Act 1998 Sch.1 Part I Art.3, Art.8(1), Art.8(2).]

The claimant (B) sought judicial review of a decision to give him treatment to which he refused to consent. B was detained under the Mental Health Act 1983. The first and second defendants (S and G) wished to treat him with anti-psychotic drugs. B refused consent. S and G considered that B did not have capacity to make the decision. Accordingly, they sought and authorised compulsory treatment under s.58(3) of the Act. B argued that (1) he had the capacity to refuse medical treatment; (2) the compulsory treatment proposed engaged the Human Rights Act 1998 Sch.1 Part I Art.3 and therefore could only be justified if it met the test in *Herczegfalvy v. Austria (A/242-B)* (1993) 15 E.H.R.R. 437, [1993] C.L.Y. 2154, namely that it had been convincingly shown that there was a therapeutic or medical necessity for it, which was not indicated by the evidence; (3) the proposed treatment interfered with his rights under Art.8 and was not permitted under Art.8(2). The test in *Herczegfalvy* applied to Art.8 as it did to Art.3 such that a therapeutic or medical necessity was required to be convincingly shown.

Held, refusing the application, that (1) B did not have capacity to refuse medical treatment. B was able to comprehend and retain information concerning his proposed treatment. However, B did not believe that he was or might be mentally ill. The fact of his illness was a cornerstone of the factors to be taken into account in considering the information about his proposed treatment. It followed that B was not able to use and weigh in the balance the relevant information concerning that treatment in reaching a decision as to whether or not to accept it. (2) Art.3 was not engaged. It was not the case that the mere fact that compulsory treatment was capable of reaching the Art.3 threshold meant that it could only be justified if it met the test in *Herczegfalvy*, *Herczegfalvy* considered. Strictly, it was only when what was proposed reached the appropriate degree of severity to engage Art.3 that the question of medical or therapeutic necessity arose. The determination of that question was for the court itself and in so doing it was quite proper for the court to place particular weight on the evidence of the responsible medical officer and the second appointed doctor. The relevance of their day to day experience as to the nature and extent of any relevant medical dispute was an important consideration in deciding between competing arguments. In the instant case it was unlikely that B would physically resist treatment and it was unclear whether his continued objection to it would cause him marked distress. It was hoped that the proposed treatment would enable B to reach capacitated decisions which could include a continued refusal of treatment. In those circumstances, it was unlikely that compulsory administration of an anti psychotic drug would result in intense physical or mental suffering sufficient to engage Art.3. (3) The test in the case of *Herczegfalvy* did not apply to Art.8 and a therapeutic or medical necessity was not required to be convincingly shown. The European Court of Human Rights did not state that that was the case and there was no other authority to support that proposition. The justification for an interference with rights under Art.8(1) by reason of medical treatment turned on the application of the orthodox three stage test in Art.8(2). However, the parties had proceeded on the basis that if the court was satisfied that it had been convincingly shown that that the proposed treatment was a therapeutic or medical necessity all the elements of Art.8(2) would be satisfied. The evidence indicated that there were sound and compelling reasons to believe that the treatment would achieve many or all of its purposes to a significant degree. In all the circumstances the proposed treatment was a therapeutic or medical necessity.

R. (ON THE APPLICATION OF B) v. S (RESPONSIBLE MEDICAL OFFICER, BROADMOOR HOSPITAL), [2005] EWHC 1936, [2005] H.R.L.R. 40, Charles, J., QBD (Admin).

2824. Mental patients—Conditional discharge—Accommodation—Duty of authorities before discharge—Practical requirement of prior consideration of proposed discharge

[Mental Health Act 1983 s.37, s.41, s.117; National Health Service and Community Care Act 1990 s.47; Human Rights Act 1998 s.6, s.8, Sch.1 Part I Art.5, Sch.1 Part I Art.8.]

The claimant mental patient (B) sought damages against the first defendant local authority and the second defendant mental health trust (together, C) for alleged infringements of his rights under the European Convention on Human Rights 1950. B had been convicted of grievous bodily harm and unlawful wounding, and detained under the Mental Health Act 1983 s.37 and s.41. C were authorities in relation to after care for B under s.117 of the Act. B's initial detention had been outside Camden, as an exclusion zone order was in place to protect B's victims, and while he was there he was conditionally discharged and in need of immediate hostel accommodation. A suitable place was found, but the move was delayed for eight and a half months after the discharge while disputes about jurisdiction and funding took place. C submitted that (1) they owed no duty to B under s.117 of the Act until he was discharged from detention; (2) they had not delayed unduly thereafter.

Held, refusing the application, that (1) C were under no duty to take any steps in consequence of B's conditional discharge until they were informed of it almost two months later. They accepted that they were thereafter under the duty. It was owed only when a person left detention. However, practicality required s.117 authorities to be under a duty before discharge, at least where a tribunal had provisionally decided that a discharge was appropriate, as one had in respect of B, *R. (on the application of W) v. Doncaster MBC* [2004] EWCA Civ 378, [2004] B.L.G.R. 743 and *R. (on the application of K) v. Camden and Islington HA* [2001] EWCA Civ 240, [2002] Q.B. 198, [2001] C.L.Y. 4430 applied. It was inconsistent with the lack of an express duty that a s.117 authority should have to monitor the condition of a patient before discharge with a view to deciding whether to exercise its discretion to arrange for services should he be discharged. It could be expected that a hospital, or a patient's lawyer, would inform the s.117 authorities of any tribunal decision. Department of Health concessions did not go beyond what was accepted in .K. v. Camden. Neither was there a duty under the National Health Service and Community Care Act 1990 s.47 for a s.117 authority to monitor a detained patient in case he should later be in need. (2) On the evidence there was a lack of effective action on the parts of C, but not until more than seven months after B's conditional discharge. There were other bodies involved in the arrangements and B had not shown that C's delay had led to any delay in his discharge from detention. (3) (Obiter) Even if B had been entitled to damages the court would have followed the obiter decision in W v. Doncaster, and would have held that a detaining body could not have been in breach of the Human Rights Act 1998 Sch.1 Part I, as it could not have acted differently, and that it was not logical that a third party could nevertheless be in breach of Art.5 or liable for damages under the Human Rights Act 1998 s.6 and s.8. If it was only a detaining body that could potentially be liable for a breach of Art.5, no different rule should apply to Art.8, the vaguest Convention right.

R. (ON THE APPLICATION OF B) v. CAMDEN LBC, [2005] EWHC 1366, [2006] B.L.G.R. 19, Stanley Burnton, J., QBD (Admin).

2825. Mental patients–Discharge–Mental health review tribunals–Assessing criteria for satisfaction under Mental Health Act 1983 s.72–Requirement to apply civil standard of proof

[Mental Health Act 1983 s.72, s.73 (1) (b).]

The claimant mental health patients (D) sought judicial review of the decisions of two mental health review tribunals not to discharge them from hospital. The central issue was whether the tribunals had erred in applying the civil standard of proof of a balance of probabilities when determining whether they were satisfied of the criteria for detention under the Mental Health Act 1983 s.72 and s.73. D argued that (1) the standard of proof that the detaining authority had to meet if seeking to prove the criteria for detention was the criminal standard of beyond reasonable doubt; (2) alternatively, the applicable standard was the "clear and convincing evidence" standard applied by the United States Supreme Court in *Addington v. Texas* (1979) 441 US 418; (3) the discharge of all the criteria under Mental Health Act 1983 s.72 and s.73 was susceptible to a standard of proof and the default position under both sections had to be, as a minimum, the ordinary civil standard of proof.

Held, refusing the applications, that (1) there was no support for the proposition that either the criminal standard of proof or some heightened standard of proof, which was indistinguishable from the criminal standard, had any application to anything that a tribunal was called upon to do. The application of such a standard would be utterly impracticable having regard to the nature of the issues before the tribunal, *JJB Sports Plc v. Office of Fair Trading* [2004] CAT 17, [2005] Comp. A.R. 29 and *Addington* considered. (2 The applicable standard was the ordinary civil standard of proof *R v. Secretary of State for Scotland* [1999] 2 A.C. 512, [1999] C.L.Y. 6363 and *R. (on the application of H) v. Mental Health Review Tribunal for North and East London Region* [2001] EWCA Civ 415, [2002] Q.B. 1, [2001] C.L.Y. 4432 followed. That view was confirmed by a purposive construction of the Act and a consideration of the statutory context in which the tribunal operated. To raise the standard of proof above the ordinary civil standard of proof would be to subvert the obvious purpose of the Act, which sought to protect the interests of the patient whose ability to act in his own best interest had been impaired, and to enable a proportionate balance to be struck between individual and public interests. The standard to be applied under both s.72 and s.73 was the ordinary civil standard of proof as explained in *H (Minors) (Sexual Abuse: Standard of Proof), Re* [1996] A.C. 563 and *Secretary of State for the Home Department v. Rehman* [2001] UKHL 47, [2003] 1 A.C. 153, [2001] C.L.Y. 3662, *Re H* and *Rehman* followed. (3) Under both s.72 and s.73, with the exception of the question of whether the patient was suffering from a disorder under s.72(1)(b)(i), the discharge of the remaining criteria did not involve a standard of proof but an exercise of judgment or evaluation. The exception in s.72(1)(b)(i) fell to be determined by reference to the civil standard of proof. The fact that there was an onus or persuasive burden on the detaining authority did not necessarily carry with it some corresponding standard of proof and that proposition was contrary to authority. The mere fact that a statute required the court to be "satisfied" of something before it made an order did not mean that it had to be satisfied to the civil standard of proof. The default position under s.72 was that if the tribunal was not satisfied of the matters referred to in either s.72(1)(b)(i) or (ii), then it had to direct the discharge of the patient. In any other case, it might direct his discharge. Under s.73 the default position was that if the tribunal was not satisfied of any of the matters referred to in s.72(1)(b)(i) or (ii) or in s.73(1)(b), then it must direct the conditional discharge of the patient. In any other case, the tribunal would not direct discharge of the patient. (4) (Obiter) The tribunal had to have regard to the particular dangers involved in relying upon hearsay evidence and had to bear in mind the need for proof to the civil standard in relation to past events which were important to the decision it had to take. It had to bear in mind the potential difficulties of relying upon hearsay, and if the incident was really fundamental to its decision, fairness might require that the patient to be given the opportunity to cross examine the witnesses if their evidence was to be relied on.

R. (ON THE APPLICATION OF AN) v. MENTAL HEALTH REVIEW TRIBUNAL (NORTHERN REGION); R. (ON THE APPLICATION OF DJ) v. MENTAL HEALTH REVIEW TRIBUNAL, [2005] EWHC 587, *The Times*, April 18, 2005, Munby, J., QBD (Admin).

2826. Mental patients–Proceedings–Permission to issue–Proceedings commenced without leave of High Court

[Mental Health Act 1983 s.136, s.139(2).]

The appellant (S) appealed against a decision that part of his claim for damages against the respondent chief constable was properly struck out because he had failed to obtain permission for the proceedings from the court under the Mental Health Act 1983 s.139(2). S had been unable to park his car at his mother's house because other vehicles were in the way and the police had been called. S had been arrested inside the house for breach of the peace. S claimed that there had been no lawful grounds for arresting him. The police had then decided to remove S to a place of safety under s.136 of the 1983 Act. He had been detained for some days under the 1983 Act. At the very end of the limitation period S had brought proceedings against the police for damages. The district judge struck out the whole claim on the ground that the proceedings were a nullity because S had failed to obtain the necessary permission for them from the High Court under s.139(2) of the Act. On appeal the county court judge reinstated that part of the claim that did not relate to the police's purported exercise of power under s.136. S submitted that the judge should have reinstated his whole claim including the part relating to the police's action under s.136 which should have been stayed until S had obtained the necessary permission under s.139(2); that there was a line of authority which suggested that the failure to obtain leave to commence proceedings did not automatically render the proceedings a nullity and that the modern approach in civil proceedings was to treat provisions such as s.139(2) as directory rather than mandatory where it was possible to do so.

Held, dismissing the appeal, that looking at the natural meaning of the words "no proceedings shall be brought" in the section, in the light of the history of the mental health legislation, the conclusion was that proceedings brought without permission were a nullity. The intention of the legislature was that the consequence of failure to obtain the necessary consent should be the same for both criminal and civil proceedings and it appeared that the failure to obtain consent for criminal proceedings would render them a nullity, *R. v. Angel (Robert Charles)* [1968] 1 W.L.R. 669, [1968] C.L.Y. 892 and *Pountney v. Griffiths* [1976] A.C. 314, [1975] C.L.Y. 2128 considered. There was no doubt that the courts would strive anxiously to interpret procedural provisions flexibly where that furthered the interests of justice, *Rendall v. Blair* (1890) L.R. 45 Ch. D. 139, *Saunders (A Bankrupt), Re* [1997] Ch. 60, [1996] C.L.Y. 3444, *R. v. Secretary of State for the Home Department, ex p. Jeyeanthan* [2000] 1 W.L.R. 354, [1999] C.L.Y. 3162 and *R. v. Sekhon (Daljit Singh)* [2002] EWCA Crim 2954, [2003] 1 W.L.R. 1655, [2003] C.L.Y. 840 considered. A great deal turned on the wording and purpose of the particular statute under consideration. Where Parliament had made it absolutely clear what the consequences were of the failure to take a particular step it was not for the courts to import a discretion or flexibility that was not there. The wording of s.139(2) was very clear and the failure to obtain the necessary consent before the proceedings were begun rendered the proceedings a nullity.

SEAL v. CHIEF CONSTABLE OF SOUTH WALES, [2005] EWCA Civ 586, [2005] 1 W.L.R. 3183, Clarke, L.J., CA (Civ Div).

2827. Mental patients–Receivers–Allegation of impropriety–Justification for ordering account

[Mental Health Act 1983; Court of Protection Rules 2001 (SI 2001 824) r.61.]

The applicant (B), who had been appointed under the Mental Health Act 1983 as a receiver in respect of a patient (M), sought, inter alia, an order against the respondent (W) that the accounts that W delivered in his capacity as receiver of M for the year ending April 1994 and thereafter annually until the year ending April 2002 be reopened or set aside. M was involved in a road traffic accident and suffered severe injuries. Personal injury proceedings were brought on his behalf and were later settled. About eight months later, W was appointed as M's receiver. However, by a court order, W was removed as receiver and B was appointed in his place. At the hearing, it was alleged that W had taken advantage of M financially over the last nine years. In particular, it was alleged that the actual expenditure for M's care and maintenance was far less than that obtained by W from the funds held on his behalf. The court gave B authority to appoint an expert to calculate the quantum of the apparent profit made by W from his role of receiver. B submitted that W's conduct was fraudulent, or alternatively a negligent misstatement, or pure negligence in relation to the accounts which he had produced year on year for approval from the Court of Protection, and that there were substantial diversions of money which was supposed to be spent on M for the benefit of W and his wife.

Held, refusing the application, that (1) the relationship of a receiver with a patient was that of a fiduciary and like all fiduciaries he was not entitled to benefit from that relationship. However, he was entitled to recover general expenses where they related to the property or welfare of the patient. The expert report produced by B, which showed a figure far less than the amount W had applied in respect of the value of the services provided, was not accurate. In particular, the maker of the report had no access to W and his wife to determine how they would value their services and what they did in order to attend to M's needs. W's account had followed the same form as the approved accounts of previous receivers. Although the payments total sum was substantially in excess of the monthly payments previously paid, that was attributable entirely to capital projects, all of which were agreed in advance with the Court of Protection. None of the accounts ever attracted a query from the court over the nine years of the receivership, and nothing was hidden. Therefore, it could not be said that the accounts were fraudulent or misleading. B had not made out a sufficiently clear case for it to be said that there was material which justified the ordering of an account. The evidence provided was speculative and not founded on any clear basis. (2) Further, where a fixed sum had been ordered in respect of the maintenance of a patient, the court would not require an account, save in the case of fraud or misrepresentation or where the services had not actually been provided or the patient was not being properly maintained, *Jodrell v. Jodrell* (1851) 14 Beau 397 applied. However, where the payments were not a fixed sum but a general permission to spend such sums as were necessary for the maintenance of the patient, then the receiver would have to account under the Court of Protection Rules 2001 r.61. That accorded with a general Court of Protection practice that the payments were to be a fixed sum payable for maintenance. In the accounts for all the receivers, the payments were identified as such. There was no fraud or mistake and no question of a failure to provide maintenance.

BUNTING v.W, [2005] EWHC 1274, (2005) 86 B.M.L.R. 39, Peter Smith, J., CP.

2828. **Mental patients-Removal-Magistrate's power to impose conditions in warrant to search for and remove patients-Legality of warrant or its execution**

[Mental Deficiency Act 1913 s.15(2); Mental Health Act 1959; Mental Health Act 1983 s.135, s.135(1); Police and Criminal Evidence Act 1984.]

The appellant NHS Trust appealed against a decision ([2003] EWCA Civ 1152, [2003] 1 W.L.R. 2413) that an execution of a warrant under the Mental Health Act 1983 s.135 against the respondent and her removal to and detention in the Trust's hospital was unlawful because conditions imposed in the warrant by the magistrate had not been complied with. The warrant directed that the constable executing it should be accompanied by a particular named consultant psychiatrist, a named approved social worker and a named medical practitioner. At the time of the execution, the medical practitioner named in the warrant was not present. The issue was whether the magistrate, when issuing the warrant, was entitled to impose additional conditions in the warrant other than those expressly provided for under s.135, and in particular to insist that only named professionals should be involved in its execution.

Held, allowing the appeal, that there were several factors that pointed strongly to the conclusion that on its true construction s.135 contained no power enabling the magistrate to identify named professionals who were to accompany the constable in the execution of the warrant. The statutory history indicated a progressive relaxation of the requirement to name names in the warrant. The origin of s.135 was to be found in the Mental Deficiency Act 1913 s.15(2) which required that the constable executing the warrant and the doctor accompanying be named. However, following enactment of the Mental Health Act 1959 there was no requirement to name the doctor and the Police and Criminal Evidence Act 1984 removed the requirement to name the constable. Nothing in s.135 itself, or elsewhere in the 1983 Act, gave the magistrate power to impose conditions in the warrant or to name the professionals to be involved in its execution. The main purpose of s.135(1) was to enable access to be gained in order to make proper arrangements for the treatment and care of someone who was believed to be suffering from mental disorder, and the object was to protect them from harm. That purpose was more likely to be achieved if the powers under the warrant were not limited by insisting that named people be present, or by allowing the magistrate to impose other limitations. Although the presence of a doctor and social worker was required at least in part so that a person was not removed when they judged that the basis upon which the warrant was granted was not made out, it was not necessary for the proper functioning of s.135. Accordingly, the names in the warrant were surplus to requirements and therefore had no effect on the legality of the warrant or of its execution. Further for the purpose of deciding the instant case, it was not necessary to consider whether the power to impose other conditions, in particular a time limit, could be implied. However, unlike an application for compulsory admission to hospital, s.135 contained no express time limit within which a warrant had to be executed.

WARD v. COMMISSIONER OF POLICE OF THE METROPOLIS, [2005] UKHL 32, [2006] 1 A.C. 23, Lord Steyn, HL.

2829. Mental patients—Seclusion—Departure from code of practice—Lawfulness of hospital policy—Compatibility of policy with patients human rights

[Mental Health Act 1983 s.118(1); Human Rights Act 1998 Sch.1 Part I Art.3, Art.5, Art.8.]

The appellant NHS trust appealed against the decision ([2003] EWCA Civ 1036, [2004] Q.B. 395) that its policy governing the seclusion of psychiatric patients detained at its high security mental hospital departed from the code of practice issued by the secretary of state pursuant to the Mental Health Act 1983 s.118(1) and was unlawful. The respondent (M) was a patient, detained under the 1983 Act, at the trust's hospital. He had been placed in seclusion for periods in excess of four days. The aim of the code was to contain severely disturbed behaviour that was likely to cause harm to others. The code provided, inter alia, that hospitals should have clear guidelines on the use of seclusion, including the frequency of reviews of the need to continue the procedure. The central issues were (i) whether the trust's policy was unlawful under domestic law, and (ii) whether the policy had failed to comply with the Human Rights Act 1998 Sch.1 Part I Art.3, Art.5 and Art.8. M contended that the policy was unlawful under domestic law as it provided for less frequent medical review of seclusion, particularly after day seven, than was laid down in the code.

Held, allowing the appeal (Lords Steyn and Brown dissenting), that (1) the code provided guidance and not instruction. However, it was guidance that any hospital had to consider with great care, and from which it should depart only if it had cogent reasons for doing so. On the evidence, the code had been very carefully considered by the trust and large parts had been reproduced in the policy. Although the policy had departed from the code in providing for less frequent medical review after day seven, the trust had explained the justification for the policy in very considerable detail. The trust had been entitled to take account of three matters: (i) the code had been directed to the generality of mental hospitals and had not addressed the special problems of high security hospitals; (ii) the code had not recognised the special position of patients whom it was necessary to seclude for longer than a very few days; (iii) the statutory scheme, whilst providing for the secretary of state to give guidance, had deliberately left the power and responsibility of the final decision to those who had the legal and practical responsibility for detaining, treating, nursing and caring for the patients. Accordingly, the trust had shown good reasons for adopting the policy it had adopted. (2) The policy, properly operated, would be sufficient to prevent any possible breach of the Art.3 rights of a patient secluded for more than seven days, and there was no evidence that the frequency of medical review provided in the policy risked any breach of those rights. As regards Art.5, the policy, properly applied, did not permit a patient to be deprived of any residual liberty to which he was properly entitled. It was difficult to see why the policy would be incompatible with Art.8, as its purpose was to define standards to be followed and to prevent abuse and arbitrariness. In any event, the policy was justified under Art.8(2): it was necessary for the prevention of disorder or crime, for the protection of health or morals, or for the protection of the rights and freedoms of others. The policy satisfied the requirements of precision and accessibility and was in accordance with the law. In the circumstances, the Court of Appeal had given the code a stronger effect than was permissible.

R. (ON THE APPLICATION OF MUNJAZ) v. MERSEY CARE NHS TRUST; R. (ON THE APPLICATION OF S) v. AIREDALE NHS TRUST (APPEAL); *sub nom*. R. (ON THE APPLICATION OF MUNJAZ) v. ASHWORTH HOSPITAL AUTHORITY (NOW MERSEY CARE NHS TRUST); R. (ON THE APPLICATION OF COLONEL M) v. ASHWORTH HOSPITAL AUTHORITY (NOW MERSEY CARE NHS TRUST); MUNJAZ v. MERSEY CARE NHS TRUST; S v. AIREDALE NHS TRUST, [2005] UKHL 58, [2005] 3 W.L.R. 793, Lord Bingham of Cornhill, HL.

2830. Mental patients' rights–Consent–Administration of necessary medication without consent–Capacity to refuse consent to treatment

[Mental Health Act 1983; Mental Health Act 1983 s.58.]

The claimant mental patient (B) applied for judicial review of decisions by the defendants (H, R and W) to authorise the administration of, and to administer, medication without his consent. B had been detained under a hospital order with a restriction order without limitation of time under the Mental Health Act 1983. H, B's responsible medical officer, had considered that B required treatment with anti psychotic medication. R had issued a certificate authorising such treatment and B had received treatment in the form of the forcible administration of an anti psychotic drug. Following the lodging of B's claim, H had undertaken not to administer the medication without B's consent. However, he later concluded that treatment was still necessary and W had granted a further certificate authorising treatment, though restricting the type and amount of medication. Reports from a psychiatrist and a psychologist maintained that B was not suffering from any mental disorder but that his problems were the result of long standing emotional difficulties. The issues were whether (i) B was suffering from mental disorder; (ii) he had capacity to refuse consent to the proposed treatment; (iii) the proposed treatment was necessary and would be effective. B submitted that the administration of the medication without his consent was a breach of his human rights.

Held, refusing the application, that (1) having regard to the history of B's behaviour, the opinions of the psychiatrist and the psychologist had to be rejected. B was suffering from a mental disorder. Further, it was not necessary to classify the type of disorder from which he was suffering. Provided that the proposed treatment was convincingly needed to alleviate whatever mental disorder afflicted him, it was immaterial what classification applied, *R. (on the application of B) v. Ashworth Hospital Authority* [2003] EWCA Civ 547, [2003] 1 W.L.R. 1886 followed. (2) There was a presumption in favour of capacity, and the fact that a patient was suffering from a mental disorder could not of itself mean that he lacked capacity. However, B lacked capacity within the terms of s.58 of the Act. The conclusion of the doctor, instructed on H's behalf to give an independent view, was correct; B's arguments about drug treatment were fallacious and there was psychopathology about body image and bodily integrity which distorted B's thinking to the extent that he could not weigh in the balance of arguments for and against drug treatment. (3) In considering the need for the treatment, the only question was whether the patient's treatment had been convincingly shown to be medically necessary, *R. (on the application of Wilkinson) v. Broadmoor Hospital* [2001] EWCA Civ 1545, [2002] 1 W.L.R. 419, [2001] C.L.Y. 4431, *R. (on the application of N) v. M* [2002] EWCA Civ 1789, [2003] 1 W.L.R. 562, [2003] C.L.Y. 2958 applied. It was obvious that that test would not be met unless the patient's responsible medical officer and the registered medical practitioner were convinced that the treatment would alleviate his condition. After considering all the evidence, they had at least to be persuaded that the patient was suffering from a mental disorder for which the treatment was required. It was, therefore, important to see whether there were indications that the proposed treatment would alleviate B's condition. On the evidence, the anti psychotic medication had in the past resulted in an alleviation of B's condition and, accordingly, there was good reason to believe it was likely to do so again. The decision reached by the defendants was not open to challenge.

R. (ON THE APPLICATION OF B) v. HADDOCK, [2005] EWHC 921, (2005) 85 B.M.L.R. 57, Collins, J., QBD (Admin).

2831. Restricted patients–Recall to hospital–Secretary of state's power to recall patient conditionally discharged

[Criminal Procedure (Insanity) Act 1964 s.5(1); Mental Health Act 1983 s.37, s.41, s.42(3, s.75(1) (a).]

The appellant (L) appealed against a decision ([2004] EWHC1023) refusing to grant judicial review of the respondent secretary of state's decision to recall and detain L under the Mental Health Act 1983 s.42(3). In 1991, L killed his 17 year old girlfriend. A jury found him not guilty of murder by reason of insanity and he was admitted to hospital under the Criminal Procedure (Insanity) Act 1964 s.5(1). Following the coming into force of the 1983 Act L was treated "as if he had been...admitted" in pursuance of a hospital order under s.37 of the 1983 Act, together with a s.41 restriction order without limitation of time. L periodically made applications to the Mental Health Review Tribunal but his detention was continued on the grounds that he still suffered from a sufficiently serious mental illness. Some time later L was conditionally discharged. Subsequently it emerged that L had formed a relationship with a vulnerable 17 year old girl, and that a pattern of behaviour was developing that mirrored the circumstances at the time he had killed his girlfriend. The secretary of state issued a warrant for the recall of L under s.42(3) of the 1983 Act. A medical report was prepared which stated that L was not suffering from a mental illness but that he had a psychopathic disorder. L argued that, as with hospital orders made under s.37 of the 1983 Act, the secretary of state's power to recall and detain a restricted patient could only be used where the patient was found to be suffering from the same form of mental disorder that was the foundation of his original detention in hospital.

Held, dismissing the appeal, that (1) where a patient had been detained in hospital as the result of an order made under s.5(1)(a) of the 1964 Act, after a jury had returned a special verdict of "not guilty by reason of insanity", there was no process of identifying the particular form of mental disorder that existed, unlike the situation where a s.37 hospital order was made. Neither the jury's verdict nor the court's order contained any "classification" of the particular form of mental disorder. The 1983 Act gave no power to doctors in mental hospitals to make "classifications" of the importance contended by L. Therefore L's argument, based on the classification of a particular form of mental disorder, could not succeed. (2) (Obiter) A restricted patient may, before being conditionally discharged, have gone through several classifications or reclassifications of his mental disorder as a result of tribunal decisions. While in the community, following his conditional discharged, the patient might suffer a recurrence not of the form most recently diagnosed but of an earlier classified form of mental disorder. There was no reason why the secretary of state's powers of recall could not operate in such circumstances. There was a significant safeguard of the patient's rights in the requirement that the secretary of state had to refer the case to a tribunal within one month under s.75(1)(a).

R. (ON THE APPLICATION OF L) v. SECRETARY OF STATE FOR THE HOME DEPARTMENT; *sub nom.* R. (ON THE APPLICATION OF AL) v. SECRETARY OF STATE FOR THE HOME DEPARTMENT, [2005] EWCA Civ 2, [2006] 1 W.L.R. 88, Brooke, L.J., CA (Civ Div).

2832. Books

Bartlett, Peter–Blackstone's Guide to the Mental Capacity Act. Blackstone's Guide S. Paperback: £29.95. ISBN 0 19 928903 4. Paperback: £29.95. ISBN 0 19 928903 4. Oxford University Press.

Brown, Rob; McKee, Heather; Treasaden, Ian; Puri, Basant–Mental Health Law. Paperback: £19.99. ISBN 0 340 88503 3. Hodder Arnold H&S.

Cantor, N.L.–Making Medical Decisions for the Profoundly Mentally Disabled. Hardback: £22.95. ISBN 0 262 03331 3. The MIT Press.

Edis, Anne–Mental Capacity Law and Practice. Paperback: £45.00. ISBN 1 903927 64 1. Legalease.

Greaney, Nicola; Morris, Fennella; Taylor, Beverley–Mental Capacity: A Guide to the New Law. Paperback: £39.95. ISBN 1 85328 903 5. Law Society Publications.

Jones, Richard—Mental Health Act Manual: 1st Supplement. Paperback: £29.00. ISBN 0 421 91840 3. Sweet & Maxwell.

Jones, Richard—Mental Health Capacity Act Manual. Paperback: £35.00. ISBN 0 421 91820 9. Sweet & Maxwell.

Kaczmarek, Peggy; Levine, Elaine S.; Segal, Anne F.—Law and Mental Health Professionals: New Mexico. Hardback: £78.50. ISBN 1 59147 284 9. American Psychological Association.

Mental Capacity: The New Law. Paperback: £40.00. ISBN 0 85308 976 0. Jordans.

Patrick, Hilary—Mental Health. Paperback: £45.00. ISBN 1 84592 062 7. Tottel Publishing.

Prashad, B.K.—Encyclopaedic Survey of the Handicapped. Hardback: £125.00. ISBN 81 261 1967 5. Anmol Publications Pvt Ltd.

Ward, Adrian—Adults with Incapacity Legislation. Paperback: £38.00. ISBN 0 414 01580 0. W.Green & Son.

NEGLIGENCE

2833.   Causation—Contribution—Non causative loss—Assessment of contribution

[Civil Liability (Contribution) Act 1978 s.2.]

The appellant architectural practice (H) appealed against a decision that acts and omissions that were not causative of loss could be taken into account in assessing the level of contribution it should pay pursuant to the Civil Liability (Contribution) Act 1978 s.2 to the respondent mechanical and engineering consultants (W). H and W had been involved in the development of a site which incorporated retail, leisure and restaurant facilities. Due to the arrangement of the doors and the design of the facade, cold draughts entered the building and adversely affected the internal climate. Remedial work undertaken by W was unsuccessful. The owner of the site commenced proceedings against W seeking damages for negligence and breach of contract and the cost of further remedial work. W made a Part 20 claim for contribution or indemnity against H. W and the owner settled their claim. The judge found that H had been in breach of duty as alleged by W in relation to specific aspects of its consultation but that such breaches had not been causative of any loss. However, the judge concluded that acts and omissions that were not causative of loss could be taken into account for the purpose of assessing what, if any, contribution should be ordered pursuant to s.2 of the 1978. H contended that the judge, in reaching his conclusion in respect of the non causative loss, had incorrectly applied the law.

Held, dismissing the appeal, that for the purposes of s.2(1) of the 1978 Act, if the non causative factor also involved a breach of duty relied on in the action, it was more likely to be a relevant factor in determining the level of contribution. It was established law that the court could have regard to both the causative potency of the fault of a party and also the blameworthiness of a party; both elements were included in the concept of responsibility for the purposes of s.2(1), *Madden v. Quirk* [1989] 1 W.L.R. 702, [1989] C.L.Y. 2555 applied. Relevant material for the purposes of s.2 was not limited to causative material although causative responsibility was likely to be the most important factor in the assessment of contribution, *Re Source America International Ltd v. Platt Site Services Ltd* [2004] EWCA Civ 665, 95 Con. L.R. 1, [2005] 2 C.L. 74 followed. However, the court should not place unrestricted weight on non causative material. In the manner in which s.2(1) was expressed, Parliament had particularly directed the courts when exercising their powers under that section to have regard to the extent of the defendant's responsibility for the damage in question. Section 2(1) was a semi structured discretion which directed the court to attach most weight to the defendant's responsibility for the damage in question. If the defendant's action did not cause the damage, it could not, as such, form part of the responsibility for the damage. It might, quite separately, be relevant to the court's evaluation of the blameworthiness component of responsibility. If non causative material was brought into account it could only play a limited role. It must be given less weight than the material showing the defendant's responsibility for the act in question. Additionally, if non causative material was brought into account, the resulting order for contribution had to be just and equitable within s.2(1). There had to be sufficient relationship between the non causative material and the damage in question. Although in the instant case the judge did not state precisely how he had used the non causative material, he had formed the view that W should bear the greater share of liability before taking the non causative material into account. He could have done no more than treat the material as showing the seriousness of H's conduct. Alternatively, he must have treated the material as constituting additional factors on which to make his determination as to contribution. Either way, the judge had been entitled to take that course.

BRIAN WARWICKER PARTNERSHIP PLC v. HOK INTERNATIONAL LTD; *sub nom.* BURFORD NW3 LTD v. BRIAN WARWICKER PARTNERSHIP PLC, [2005] EWCA Civ 962, 103 Con. L.R. 112, Sir Andrew Morritt V.C., CA (Civ Div).

2834. Causation–Secondary victims–Post traumatic stress disorder–Death of daughter in hospital as result of clinical negligence

The claimant (W) sought to recover damages from the defendant NHS trust (the trust) for psychiatric injury following the death of her daughter caused by the trust's admitted negligence. W's daughter had failed to regain consciousness after an operation for the removal of her wisdom teeth. W contended that the time spent at the hospital prior to her daughter's death and seeing her daughter in the mortuary had resulted in her suffering post traumatic stress disorder. The trust argued that W's illness was an adjustment disorder with anxiety and depression and that such a reaction had been inevitable; therefore there was no causal link between its negligence and W's condition.

Held, giving judgment for the trust, that the diagnostic criteria for a finding of post traumatic stress disorder required a shocking event of a particularly horrific nature and the death of a loved one in hospital did not meet that description unless also accompanied by circumstances that were wholly exceptional in some way so as to shock or horrify. In the instant case, no causal link between the death of W's daughter and her psychiatric condition could be established. The death of W's daughter was not outside the range of human experience and there was no evidence that the surrounding events at the hospital had caused the post traumatic stress disorder, *Alcock v. Chief Constable of South Yorkshire* [1992] 1 A.C. 310, [1992] C.L.Y. 3250 and *McLoughlin v. O'Brian* [1983] 1 A.C. 410, [1982] C.L.Y. 2153 considered.

WARD v. LEEDS TEACHING HOSPITALS NHS TRUST, [2004] EWHC 2106, [2004] Lloyd's Rep. Med. 530, Judge Hawkesworth Q.C., QBD.

2835. Clinical negligence–Anaesthesia–Timing of bronchospasm–Conflict of expert evidence as to its cause

The appellant anaesthetist (E) appealed against a decision that he was liable in negligence in respect of his treatment of the respondent patient (W). In 1995 E put W under a general anaesthetic for an operation using atracurium, a muscle relaxant. It was common ground that W suffered a bronchospasm, which prevented air from entering her lungs at some point before she was taken into theatre, but that the spasm was eased by the injection of a bronchodilator drug and the subsequent operation was successful. Four years later, W underwent another operation, not attended by E, and suffered an adverse reaction that subsequent investigation revealed was an allergic reaction to a muscle relaxant associated with atracurium. W alleged that after the 1995 operation E had negligently failed to refer her for investigation in respect of the cause of the spasm or warn her of the possibility of an adverse drug reaction in the future. The judge found that the 1995 spasm occurred shortly before W was intubated, as argued in W's primary case, and as a result there was a reasonable suspicion that an adverse drug reaction was the cause of the spasm. Accordingly, she held that the obligation to investigate and warn arose, so that it was negligent of E not to have done so. The judge also found the alternative case proved that, whether the spasm occurred before or after intubation, E should have suspected an adverse drug reaction. In doing so, she accepted the evidence of W's medical expert. E argued that (1) there was no evidential basis for the judge's primary finding of fact or it was against the weight of evidence; (2) the judge's reasoning was fatally affected by her recording that it was common ground between the experts that the adverse reaction was likely to take two to three minutes from the time the drug was injected.

Held, dismissing the appeal, that (1) given the difficulties that E had in recalling the incident, there was no direct evidence on which the judge could rely in considering W's primary case. However, there was evidence of the opinions of the experts, and it was simply wrong to assert that there was no evidence to support the judge's primary finding. (2) It did not make a significant difference to the judge's thinking that she mistakenly thought that it was agreed that the adverse reaction was likely to take two to three minutes from the time the drug was injected. (3) The real question was whether the judge should have acted on the evidence that she accepted. In the light of the conflicting expert evidence as to the time for a drug induced reaction to occur, it was open to the judge to accept that W's spasm manifested itself shortly before intubation, as suggested by the evidence of W's expert. If the judge accepted the evidence of W's expert that the bronchodilator drug administered by E could be effective in treating an anaphylactoid reaction, then she was entitled to make the finding that she did as to the timing of the spasm. Although it was not clear from the judgment how the judge dealt with certain arguments in relation to the significance of the intensity of the spasm, and it was impossible for the court to say that they may not have helped tip the balance in W's favour, the judge was not plainly wrong. (4) The judge was entitled to prefer the approach of W's expert in finding W's alternative case proved, bearing in mind that the experts had agreed that the duty to report and investigate arose if there was suspicion of an adverse drug reaction.

EASTWOOD v. WRIGHT, [2005] EWCA Civ 564, (2005) 84 B.M.L.R. 51, Ward, L.J., CA (Civ Div).

2836. **Clinical negligence—Birth defects—Failure to identify sign of serious condition in foetus—Standard of reasonable care and skill**

The claimant (P) sought damages from the defendant NHS trust (the trust) following the birth of her son, who had a serious and complex congenital bladder and bowel deformity. A routine ultrasound scan during pregnancy had revealed the existence of a possible abnormality and P was referred to a specialist unit for further investigations. Following the specialist ultrasound examination, P was informed that her baby son would be born with a relatively minor condition which could be rectified surgically. P contended that (1) if the specialist scans had been conducted with reasonable care and skill, they would have shown that her son was suffering from a more serious condition; (2) she would have terminated her pregnancy had she been aware of the true extent of the abnormality. The trust argued that (1) any erroneous visualisation did not amount to a failure to exercise due care and skill; (2) P needed to show that a correct diagnosis would have made her choose a termination

Held, giving judgment for P, that (1) the mistaken identification of a bladder during a routine anomaly scan would not necessarily amount to negligence. However, P had been referred by another hospital and the standard of care and skill required in relation to the specific issue of whether the foetus lacked a bladder was a high one. The trust's failure to carry out further checks on the object misidentified as the bladder fell below that high standard. (2) On a balance of probabilities it was likely that P would have opted for a termination if she had been given the correct diagnosis.

P v. LEEDS TEACHING HOSPITALS NHS TRUST; *sub nom.* P v. LEEDS TEACHING HOSPITAL NHS TRUST, [2004] EWHC 1392, [2004] Lloyd's Rep. Med. 537, Holland, J., QBD.

2837. Clinical negligence–Causation–Delay in diagnosis of cancer–Reduced chance of survival–Doctor's liability

The appellant (G) appealed against a decision ([2002] EWCA Civ 1471, [2003] Lloyd's Rep. Med. 105) that his medical negligence claim against the defendant doctor (S) failed. G had visited S because he had a lump under his arm. S negligently misdiagnosed G's condition as benign. A year later another general practitioner referred G to hospital for an examination and it was discovered that G had cancer of a lymph gland. By that time the tumour had spread to G's chest. G suffered pain and had to undergo a course of chemotherapy. He was left with poor prospects of survival. G sued S, alleging that S should have referred him to hospital and that if S had done so his condition would have been diagnosed earlier and there would have been a high likelihood of a cure. The judge held that on the expert evidence the delay in diagnosis had reduced G's chances of surviving for more than 10 years from 42 per cent to 25 per cent. He therefore dismissed G's action because the delay had not deprived G of the prospect of a cure, meaning surviving more than 10 years, because, at the time of his misdiagnosis, G had less than a 50 per cent chance of surviving more than 10 years anyway. The Court of Appeal dismissed G's appeal. G submitted that (1) the delay in diagnosis and treatment had caused physical injury, in the shape of the spread of the cancer before his therapy began, and the losses he had suffered were consequential on that physical damage; (2) apart from any other injury, the reduction in his chances of survival was itself a compensatable head of damage.

Held, dismissing the appeal (Lord Nicholls and Lord Hope dissenting), that (1) even if the quantification of future losses was conventionally decided on the evaluation of risks and chances, G had to show that the loss was consequential on injury caused by S's negligence. Causation had to be shown on the balance of probabilities. On the judge's findings it had not been shown that on the balance of probabilities the delay in commencing G's treatment that was attributable to S's negligence had affected the course of his illness or his prospects of survival, which had never been as good as even. (2) Liability for the loss of a chance of a more favourable outcome should not be introduced into personal injury claims. (3) (Per Lord Nicholls and Lord Hope) The significant reduction in the prospects of a successful outcome for G which S's negligence caused was a loss for which G was entitled to be compensated. The fact that G was already suffering from illness at the date of S's negligence, from which G had at that date significant prospects of recovery, provided him with a cause of action for the reduction in those prospects that resulted from the negligence. What had to be valued was what G had lost, and the principle on which that loss had to be calculated was the same, irrespective of whether the prospects were better or less than 50 per cent.

GREGG v. SCOTT, [2005] UKHL 2, [2005] 2 A.C. 176, Lord Nicholls of Birkenhead, HL.

2838. Clinical negligence–Causation–Propriety of judge's approach to expert evidence

[Civil Procedure Rules 1998 (SI 1998 3132) Part 52 r.52.11 (3) (b).]

The appellant (B) appealed against the decision of a county court judge that the respondent general practitioner (S) was not liable to pay damages in respect of the death of B's partner (L). The judge held that S had negligently examined L. However, he held that B had failed to establish, on the balance of probabilities, that L's sudden cardiac death would have been avoided if S had acted with reasonable skill and care. In so finding, the judge preferred the evidence of S's cardiologist, stating that it was "compellingly supported...by recent literature". The judge had never been provided with copies of either of the relevant medical papers cited by S's expert and took on trust what that expert said were the contents of the papers. B submitted that, in assessing which expert's evidence to accept on the issue of causation, the judge had placed more weight on the "literature" than he should have done. She contended that she had had no proper opportunity to demonstrate that the papers were at least neutral as between the experts and at best supported the evidence of B's expert over that of S's expert. S argued that B was attempting to introduce fresh evidence that was not admissible and that she should have obtained both papers before trial and/or judgment.

Held, allowing the appeal, that the issue was not whether fresh evidence was to be admitted but rather, under the Civil Procedure Rules 1998 Part 52 r.52.11 (3) (b), whether the judge's decision upon the matter under appeal was unjust because of a serious procedural or other irregularity in the proceedings. Neither of the papers was produced on behalf of S. Their contents, as relayed by S's expert in his evidence, were unwittingly portrayed to the judge inaccurately and/or incompletely. The judge placed more weight on the "literature" than he should have done in the unusual circumstances of the case. B was deprived of the opportunity to show the judge that neither paper supported the evidence of S's expert, which B arguably would have done. Accordingly, it would be unjust to leave the matter as it was and it should be remitted for retrial.

BREEZE v. AHMAD, [2005] EWCA Civ 223, [2005] C.P. Rep. 29, Sedley, L.J., CA (Civ Div).

2839. **Clinical negligence–Consultants–Advice to operate on penis–Advice accordance with body of reasonable medical opinion**

E brought a claim in negligence for damages against a consultant urologist, C, and another consultant urologist, D. E had gone to see C in 1990 complaining of a lump on the glans of his penis and that the glans was softer than the shaft when the penis was erect. C told him that the lump was benign and offered to carry out surgery to remove it and to improve E's erectile function generally through ligation of the veins. E agreed and also asked to be circumcised at the same time. Following the surgery E had some concerns. He was reexamined and further ligation surgery was carried out. E was still not satisfied and in 1991 obtained a second opinion from D, who also carried out surgery. E claimed that he had been wrongly advised by C, that the surgery was unnecessary and that it had been negligently carried out by both C and D.

Held, giving judgment for C and D, that neither of them had been negligent. Given the time that had passed since the surgery, there were evidential difficulties and generally the evidence of C and D was to be preferred. In the early 1990s veinous surgery was widely used to enhance erectile function, and it was not until the middle of that decade that it was discredited as providing only short term benefits. C had therefore been "acting in accordance with a body of reasonable medical opinion" at that time and had not been negligent in offering the surgery, *Bolam v. Friern Hospital Management Committee* [1957] 1 W.L.R. 582, [1957] C.L.Y. 2431 applied. C had properly advised E of the risks and had carried out the surgery adequately. Although the surgery carried out by D might have been ill advised with hindsight, it was not, on the balance of probabilities, "indefensible" and therefore not negligent.

E v. CASTRO, [2003] EWHC 2066, (2004) 80 B.M.L.R. 14, Judge Holman, QBD.

2840. **Clinical negligence–Medical treatment–Adequacy of pre surgical advice given by operating surgeon**

The claimant patient (M) claimed damages in respect of alleged negligence in the treatment she had received from the defendant health authority. M had sustained a compound fracture of a lumbar vertebra in an unrelated accident and after three weeks in hospital the surgeon (C) concluded that an operation was appropriate. C had a discussion with M about the surgery, at which, M asked for a second opinion and also had reservations about having the operation. C claimed that he had told M that the fracture was unstable; that she should have an operation which had advantages and disadvantages; and that he had listed the possible complications of non surgical treatment. Despite her previous reservations M consented to the operation the following day. Six hours after the operation M suffered from a failure of the blood supply to her spinal cord and for a time lost the use of her legs. M submitted that her right to choose whether to have the surgery had been "usurped or overborne" by a failure of the surgeon to give an adequate explanation of the advantages and the disadvantages of not having the operation. It was also argued that the risks of the conservative course of treatment had been exaggerated and overstated to her and she had not been given sufficient indication that a non surgical course of treatment was viable.

Held, giving judgment for the trust, that (1) a patient should be given sufficient information about the advantages and disadvantages of the course of action proposed by a surgeon to enable her to validly decide whether to accept the advice. This advice should involve some fair mention of the alternative to surgery and the patient should also be given a clear view of what the surgeon thought was the correct course of action. How and in what language this was done was a matter for the individual surgeon. However, there had to be scope for considerable discretion depending on the surgeon's views and the attitude of the patient. In the instant case, C had formed a very firm view of the desirability of surgery and believed that it was the right course of action. It had not been negligent of C to express his view as firmly as it appeared he had done. Accordingly, on a balance of probabilities, C had given M a sufficient indication that although he was strongly in favour of operating, she could, if she wished, reasonably decide not to have the operation and elect to be treated conservatively. (2) (Obiter) Medical evidence had indicated that the cause of the lesion to M's spine was unknown and therefore, it was hard to find on the balance of probability that the lesion had been caused by a properly carried out operation. M had failed to establish the necessary causative link between the operation and her injury.

MARKOSE v. EPSOM & ST HELIER NHS TRUST, [2004] EWHC 3130, [2005] Lloyd's Rep. Med. 334, Judge Charles Harris Q.C., QBD.

2841. Clinical negligence–Surgical procedures–Failure to warn patient of small inherent risk of surgery

The appellant (X), a consultant neurosurgeon, appealed against a finding ([2002] EWCA Civ 724, [2003] Q.B. 356) that he was liable in damages for his failure to warn the respondent (C) of a risk inherent in surgery that he had performed on her. C suffered repeated episodes of low back pain and had been referred for surgery to X, who was experienced in disc surgery. C underwent the surgery and suffered a rare complication known as cauda equina syndrome, a risk in respect of which X had failed to warn her in advance. The judge had not found that X had been negligent in the actual performance of the surgery. However, he had found that X had failed to warn C of the small risk that the operation could adversely affect her, and that had she been warned of the risk, she would not have undergone the surgery at the time she did.

Held, dismissing the appeal (Lords Bingham and Hoffmann dissenting), that a judgment in C's favour could not be based on conventional causation principles. The "but for" test was satisfied since C would not have had the operation when she did if the warning had been given. But the risk of which she should have been warned was not created by the failure to warn. It was already there, as an inevitable risk of the operative procedure itself, however skillfully and carefully it was carried out. The risk was not increased, nor were the chances of avoiding it lessened, by what X had failed to say about it. However, the duty of a surgeon to warn of the dangers inherent in an operation was intended to help minimise the risk to the patient and was also intended to enable the patient to make an informed choice whether to undergo the treatment recommended and, if so, at whose hands and when. X had violated C's right to choose for herself, even if he had not increased the risk to her. The function of the law was to enable rights to be vindicated and to provide remedies when duties had been breached. Unless that was done, the duty to warn would be a hollow one. On policy grounds the test of causation was satisfied in the instant case. The risk was within the scope of the duty to warn so that the injury could be regarded as having been caused, in the legal sense, by the breach of that duty, *Chappel v. Hart* [1999] Lloyd's Rep. Med. 223 and *Fairchild v. Glenhaven*

Funeral Services Ltd (t/a GH Dovener & Son) [2002] UKHL 22, [2003] 1 A.C. 32 considered.

CHESTER v. AFSHAR, [2004] UKHL 41, [2005] 1 A.C. 134, Lord Bingham of Cornhill, HL.

2842. Contributory negligence—Accidents—Bicycles—Requirement for wearing cycle helmet

The claimant (C) brought an action against the defendant dog walking company (D) for damages for personal injury sustained when a dog being walked by D's representative ran into the path of C knocking him off his bicycle. C had been cycling along the outer carriage drive of Battersea Park in London when the collision happened. D admitted liability, but alleged contributory negligence for C's failure to wear a cycle helmet. D claimed that C should have worn a helmet as advised by the Highway Code and that his reason for not doing so, namely that he would have felt silly, was not a good one, *Froom v. Butcher* [1976] Q.B. 286, [1975] C.L.Y. 2295 cited. C argued that contributory negligence was inappropriate on the facts. Alternatively, that any reduction should be small as it was less blameworthy not to wear a cycle helmet as compared to a seat belt given that it was not a legal requirement.

Held, granting judgment for the C, that there was no contributory negligence on C's part in not wearing a cycle helmet. Whilst it was recommended by the Highway Code, it was not a legal requirement. The public campaign for the wearing of cycle helmets had not reached a level comparable to that for the wearing of seat belts at the time that *Froom* was decided, *Froom* distinguished. There was no plan to make cycle helmets compulsory. C was an experienced cyclist who for several years had been cycling in the confined and sanitised environment of Battersea Park, away from the traffic. To wear a cycle helmet would have been over cautious, although it might have been different had the accident taken place on the road. Alternatively, as contributory negligence would only affect that part of the general damages relating to the head injury, agreed to be only a few hundred pounds at most, any deduction for contributory negligence of 10 or 15 per cent would have reduced the damages by only £20 or £30. As that was a de minimis reduction, the court would have refused to make it in any event.

SWINTON v. ANNABEL'S (BERKELEY SQUARE) LTD, July 8, 2004, Judge Cox, CC (Lambeth). [*Ex rel.* Tim Petts, Barrister, 12 King's Bench Walk, London].

2843. Contributory negligence—Road traffic accidents—Third party insurance—Statutory duty to insure for third party risk

[Road Traffic Act 1988 s.143(1)(a), s.145(3)(a).]

The appellant (B) appealed against a decision that she was liable for damages for breach of the duty under the Road Traffic Act 1988 s.143(1)(a) not to use a motor vehicle without insurance for third party risks. B had been a passenger in a car driven by her fiance (P) who was killed in a collision with a van driven by the defendant (H). P had purchased the car but it was registered and insured in B's name. P had been driving the car without insurance and was impecunious. The judge determined that P had been 25 per cent liable for the injuries sustained by B in the accident and that H had been 75 per cent liable. The judge found that B had an interest in the car and that she was a "user" of it because she had sufficient control over its use at the time of the accident. On that basis he allowed H's counterclaim for damages for breach of B's duty under s.143(1)(a), in that as a result of her breach H was unable to recover from P's impecunious estate in respect of his liability to contribute 25 per cent of the damages due to B. B submitted on appeal that (1) P's driving had not contributed to the accident; (2) she had not been a "user" of the car; (3) the judge was wrong to allow the counterclaim because the Act was only concerned with third party injury to person or property and H was not entitled to recover for pure economic loss.

Held, allowing the appeal, that (1) The judge had been correct to conclude that the speed at which P had been driving had played a material part in the causation of the accident and in the severity of its consequences. (2) The evidence was consistent with an intention that the car was to belong to B, or at least be joint property and the judge's finding that B had an interest in the car could not be said to be wrong. It followed that his conclusion as to user was correct. (3) The obligation in the Act to insure for third party risk was limited by s.145(3)(a) to liability for death or bodily injury or damage to property, *Norman v. Ali (Limitation Period)* [2000] R.T.R. 107, [2000] C.L.Y. 3548 considered. The only personal injury claim in the instant case was from B, but hers was not a third party loss. H had not claimed for personal injury, his claim was for contribution from P in respect of his own liability to B, which was pure economic loss. B's duty to insure her use of the car was owed to the public as a whole, but not to herself. A user was not bound to insure against the liability of one tortfeasor to contribute with another tortfeasor in respect of their joint liability to the user, *Monk v. Warbey* [1935] 1 K.B. 75 considered.

BRETTON v. HANCOCK, [2005] EWCA Civ 404, [2005] R.T.R. 22, Ward, L.J., CA (Civ Div).

2844. Duty of care–Auctioneers–Duty of care in catalogue description

The appellant auctioneers (C) appealed against a decision ([2004] EWHC 1101, [2004] P.N.L.R. 42) that they were in breach of duty and liable in damages to the respondent (T) in respect of certain urns or vases sold to her at auction, and T cross appealed. The urns had been consigned for sale by the third defendant. They had no provenance before 1921. They had been described in C's auction catalogue as a pair of Louis XV porphyry and gilt bronze two handled vases. T bought the vases. T later claimed against C on the ground that the vases were made in the 19th century and were therefore worth much less than she had paid. The judge held that the vases were probably made in the 18th century so that C had not been negligent in cataloguing them as Louis XV. However, because T was a "special client" of C, they owed her a more exacting duty to give her a full picture of any doubts or queries about the dating of the vases. C submitted that the judge, having correctly found that they were not negligent in their cataloguing, was wrong and inconsistent to find them in breach of any duty to T and that the judge was wrong in his finding as to the measure of damages. T submitted that the judge was wrong not to find that the vases were made in the 19th century or that C should have qualified their catalogue entry.

Held, allowing the appeal and dismissing the cross appeal, that (1) on the evidence the judge was entitled to hold on the balance of probabilities that the vases were made in the 18th century. (2) C owed a single duty of care in describing the vases in the catalogue and to T. If C were entitled at the relevant time to describe the vases as Louis XV in the catalogue, there was no need to inform T of any doubts of which they were aware. (3) The judge was entitled to conclude that C's dating of the urns as Louis XV without qualification in the catalogue was an opinion which an auctioneer of their standing could reasonably reach and that there was no breach of duty in that regard. Although there were reasons for caution, there were no real rather than fanciful doubts pointing to a later date. Since C at the time of the sale held, and were reasonably entitled to hold, the certain and definite opinion that the vases were 18th century and to be described without qualification as "Louis XV", they were not obliged to express any different opinion to T. The judge's contrary conclusion was inconsistent with his own findings and erroneous. Since C were not in breach of duty to T, her claim for misrepresentation also failed. (4) The measure of damages would have been the difference between what T paid for the vases and their value at auction if C had described them as "probably Louis XV", *Lynall v. Inland Revenue Commissioners* [1972] A.C. 680, [1971] C.L.Y. 3309 applied.

THOMSON v. CHRISTIE MANSON & WOODS LTD, [2005] EWCA Civ 555, [2005] P.N.L.R. 38, May, L.J., CA (Civ Div).

2845. Duty of care–Banks–Bank's duty to comply with freezing injunction

The appellant (Customs) appealed against an order ([2004] EWHC122, [2004] 1 W.L.R. 2027) that the respondent bank (B) did not owe a duty of care to Customs in relation to a freezing injunction obtained by Customs over a customer's bank account. Customs obtained the freezing injunctions in respect of outstanding VAT against two companies, who subsequently effected transfers of substantial sums from the accounts. B failed to stop the transfers and Customs brought a claim in negligence against B. B successfully argued that it did not owe Customs a duty of care to prevent the transfers. On appeal, Customs argued that B did owe a duty of care because, inter alia, (1) the loss it had suffered was foreseeable; (2) there was a proximate relationship between the parties once B had been served with the freezing orders; (3) the judge had been wrong to conclude that, in order for B to have assumed responsibility, there must have been express representations between B and Customs.

Held, allowing the appeal, that (1) B was not a party to the litigation and was not in an adverse position to Customs; therefore its situation was not analogous with opposing parties in litigation for the purposes of determining whether there was sufficient proximity to establish an express assumption of responsibility. The judge had wrongly imputed the requirement of such an assumption into the definition of proximity, *Al-Kandari v. JR Brown & Co* [1988] Q.B. 665, [1988] C.L.Y. 3376 doubted. (2) Applying the threefold approach of foreseeability, proximity and fairness, (i) it was foreseeable that Customs would suffer loss from B's failure to prevent the transfers; (ii) the fact that B were aware of Customs' interest in the accounts meant that their relationship was a proximate one; (iii) it was fair that B, having received notice of the freezing order, should be required to comply with it, *Caparo Industries Plc v. Dickman* [1990] 2 A.C. 605, [1990] C.L.Y. 3266 applied. (3) Although there had been no express assumption of responsibility by B such as to give rise to a duty of care, it was sufficient that there was an assumption imposed by law, *Phelps v. Hillingdon LBC* [2001] 2 A.C. 619, [2000] C.L.Y. 1947 applied. Further, applying an incremental approach, the imposition of a duty of care on B was no greater liability than that to which banks were accustomed to assume at the hands of their customers.

CUSTOMS AND EXCISE COMMISSIONERS v. BARCLAYS BANK PLC, [2004] EWCA Civ 1555, [2005] 1 W.L.R. 2082, Peter Gibson, L.J., CA (Civ Div).

2846. Duty of care–Contractors–Fitting of open fireplace not in accordance with manufacturer's instructions–Liability for damage by fire–South Africa

G appealed against a finding of negligence. G, a building company, was contracted to build a hotel for C. The building was severely damaged by a fire that started in an open fireplace in the lobby. G had fitted the fireplace without properly following the manufacturer's instructions, resulting in combustible materials being placed too close to the heat source. The judge below found that G had been negligent and awarded damages to C. On appeal, G argued that it could not be liable as it had only been carrying out the design of the architect.

Held, dismissing the appeal, that G was liable in negligence. Even though it had followed the architect's design, G owed a separate duty to C to carry out the work properly and with due awareness of relevant safety matters, which meant not building something that was obviously unsafe. The co-existing duty owed by the architect did not negate that owed by G.

SM GOLDSTEIN & CO (PTY) LTD v. CATHKIN PARK HOTEL (PTY) LTD [2004] B.L.R. 369, Smallberger, J.A.,] (Sup Ct (SA)) Supreme Court, Appellate Division (South Africa).

2847. Duty of care–Defective premises–Economic loss–Extent of duty owed by design engineer to subsequent owner of premises

The appellant (W) appealed against the Australian Court of Appeal's decision that its purported claim against the respondent (C), a firm of consulting engineers, disclosed no cause of action. C had designed the foundations for a warehouse and offices built on land which was owned by a property trust. The building was subsequently sold to W, with no contractual warranty that it was free from defect. Neither was there any assignment of rights that the seller may have had against third parties in respect of any such defects. It was discovered that the foundations were defective and W alleged that C owed it a duty of care in designing the building. C denied any duty of care and contended that it had advised W's predecessor in title to conduct certain tests, but that it had been ordered to proceed without them. The issue for the Court of Appeal was whether the amended statement of claim disclosed a cause of action in negligence against C, and the court ruled that it did not. On appeal, W argued that a subsequent purchaser of premises was not absolutely precluded from recovering damages for pure economic loss from a professional who was negligent in the design of those premises and that economic loss in those circumstances was a foreseeable consequence of that negligence.

Held, dismissing the appeal, that the statement of claim did not disclose any cause of action in negligence, *Bryan v. Maloney* 74 B.L.R. 35, [1996] C.L.Y. 4436 disapproved. On the facts, C owed no duty to W to take reasonable care to avoid causing it economic loss. Indeed, it could not be said that C owed W's predecessor in title a duty to take reasonable care, given the fact that the original owner had ignored advice to conduct a geotechnical test and had proceeded without it. Further, it was not certain that the defects could not have been discovered by W prior to purchase if it had conducted the appropriate investigations.

WOOLCOCK STREET INVESTMENTS PTY LTD v. CDG PTY LTD (FORMERLY CARDNO & DAVIES AUSTRALIA PTY LTD) [2005] B.L.R. 92, Gleeson, C.J., HC (Aus).

2848. **Duty of care–Doctors–Persons to whom doctors owed duty of care in child abuse cases**

The appellant parents (P) appealed against the decision ([2003] EWCA Civ 1151, [2004] Q.B. 558) that their claims for damages for psychiatric injury brought against doctors or social workers who had wrongly determined that P had abused or harmed their children had to be dismissed on public policy grounds. P's claims were based on allegations that their children's illness or injuries had been negligently misdiagnosed as having a non accidental origin and that as a result of that misdiagnosis P had suffered a recognised form of psychiatric injury and in some cases financial loss. P submitted that the health care professionals' duty to exercise due skill and care in the investigation of suspected abuse extended to the child's parents as primary carers as well as to the child.

Held, dismissing the appeals (Lord Bingham dissenting), that (1) health professionals responsible for investigating suspected child abuse did not owe the person suspected of having committed the abuse a duty sounding in damages if they carried out that investigation in good faith but carelessly. At common law alleged interference with family life did not justify according a suspected parent a higher level of protection than other suspected perpetrators. That was because there was a conflict between the interests of the parents and the child where the parent was the suspected abuser. Health professionals, acting in good faith in what they believed were the best interests of the child, should not be subject to potentially conflicting duties when deciding whether a child might have been abused, or whether their doubts should be communicated to others, or what further investigatory or protective steps should be taken, *Sullivan v. Moody* 207 C.L.R. 562 considered. The appropriate level of protection for a parent suspected of abusing his child was that clinical and other investigations must be conducted in good faith. That afforded suspected parents a similar level of protection to that afforded generally to persons suspected of committing crimes. (2) The respondents did not owe substantially the same duty of care to P as to the children since P were not in sufficient proximity to give rise to a duty of care. As the Court of Appeal held, there were cogent reasons of public policy for holding that no common law duty of care should be owed to P and that it was accordingly not fair, just and reasonable to impose such a duty, *Caparo Industries Plc v. Dickman* [1990] 2 A.C. 605, [1990] C.L.Y. 3266 applied.

JD v. EAST BERKSHIRE COMMUNITY HEALTH NHS TRUST; K v. DEWSBURY HEALTHCARE NHS TRUST; RK v. OLDHAM NHS TRUST; *sub nom.* MAK v. DEWSBURY HEALTHCARE NHS TRUST; D v. EAST BERKSHIRE COMMUNITY NHS TRUST, [2005] UKHL 23, [2005] 2 A.C. 373, Lord Bingham of Cornhill, HL.

2849. **Duty of care–Hearing impairment–Exposure to noise–Duty to provide practicable precautions**

[Noise at Work Regulations 1989 (SI 1989 1790) Reg.11.]

The appellant train driver (H) appealed against a decision dismissing his claim for damages for hearing loss sustained whilst employed by the second respondent (E). E cross appealed against a decision that H had been exposed to noise above a certain level regularly and over a significant period. H was a train driver for 25 years. During that period he was exposed to the noise of various types of locomotive. The judge found that although E was liable in principle to H for exposure to noise above 85 decibels, it was not liable in common law because it had conscientiously considered the possibility of taking precautions and had reasonably rejected that course. The judge rejected H's statutory claim brought under the Noise at Work Regulations 1989 on the basis that the proposed precautions in the form of ear protection that had been advanced on H's behalf were not practicable. Despite dismissing H's claim, the judge assessed that if H had been successful, damages in the sum of £10,000 would have been awarded. E submitted that the threshold for the purposes of assessing risk was 90 decibels and not 85 decibels.

Held, allowing the appeal and dismissing the cross appeal, that (1) on the factual and expert evidence available, the judge had been entitled to reach the conclusion that H had been exposed to sound above 85 decibels, and that the exposure had been regular and over a significant period, namely 16 years, and involved a particular measurable risk of noise induced deafness. (2) In the light of the evidence, the judge had been entitled to reach the decision that a duty of care was owed by E to H in relation to exposure to sound at a level above 85 decibels. On the facts of the instant case, the judge was entitled to conclude that a lower than normal threshold level of noise, namely 85 decibels, was the appropriate level upon which to assess H's exposure. (3) The judge had incorrectly reached a decision that E had not breached its common law duty of care to H in failing at least to provide H with the opportunity to wear ear protection when driving noisier trains. E should have provided ear protection to H. The evidence suggested that E had considered that provision in some detail and either wholly overlooked the need or desirability of actually doing anything about it or took the view that it would be easier for it to do nothing about it. It was clear to E that it had knowingly exposed people to a situation which would make them deaf. (4) E had breached its statutory obligations to H under Reg.11 of the Regulations, as it had failed to provide him with any information in connection with possible risk of damage to hearing, steps for him to take to minimise exposure, and steps that he had to take to obtain ear protectors. If H had been given that advice, he would have requested ear protectors. However, H was unable to request ear protectors. The judge had been incorrect to conclude that the provision of ear protection was not practicable. (5) Damages were awarded in the sum of £10,000.

HARRIS v. BRB (RESIDUARY) LTD, [2005] EWCA Civ 900, [2005] I.C.R.1680, Rix, L.J., CA (Civ Div).

2850. **Duty of care–Highway authorities–Safety of bollard system in bus gate**

The claimant motorist (F) brought a claim in negligence against the defendant local authority. F had been following a bus along a road at the mouth of which was a bus gate. At that point, the road narrowed and was blocked by a bollard. Buses and other permitted vehicles were fitted with a transponder which sent an electronic signal as they passed a gate in the road. The signal lowered the bollard to ground level and after the permitted vehicle had passed through, the bollard would rise back into place. Despite the presence of signs reading "except permit holders", F followed the bus through the narrowed road, at which point the bollard rose up and came into contact with the underside of her vehicle, triggering the vehicle's airbags and causing injury to her. F argued, inter alia, that the local authority had been negligent in the design of the bollard system.

Held, giving judgment for the local authority, that the bollard system did not create a trap or danger. The interval between the passing of a permitted vehicle and the rising of the bollard accorded with Department of Transport guidance and was reasonable. Road users were not entitled to suppose that their journeys would be free from hazard or that the need for care would generally be highlighted so as to protect them from their own negligence, *Gorringe v. Calderdale MBC* [2004] UKHL 15, [2004] 1 W.L.R. 1057, [2004] C.L.Y. 2752 applied. F had been wholly the author of her own misfortune.

FOYLE v. BRACKNELL FOREST BC, January 21, 2005, Judge Horowitz, CC (Slough). [*Ex rel.* David White, Barrister, 12 King's Bench Walk, Temple, London].

2851. **Duty of care–Independent financial advisers–Failure to recognise high risk nature of investment in overseas fund**

[Financial Services Act 1986 s.62(1), s.62A, s.76, s.207; Financial Services (Promotion of Unregulated Collective Investment Schemes) Regulations 1991.]

The claimant (S) sought damages from the first defendant financial adviser (O) and the second defendant finance company (Z) in respect of allegedly negligent financial advice. O sought an indemnity from Z based on its alleged negligence in recommending a particular investment fund as appropriate for S. S had sold his farm and sought to invest the proceeds. S had consulted O for investment advice, requiring a short term, low risk investment where his money could be easily realised and readily accessible. O consulted Z about potential investment products for S and was introduced to an offshore fund run by a company in the Bahamas which guaranteed a high return. Z indicated that the fund was low risk and that the company managing it had been checked out. A memorandum was circulated by Z just before the cancellation period had expired which raised concerns about the safety of the fund. Z did not pass the information on to O and S went ahead and invested in the fund. The fund management company soon went into liquidation and S lost all of his investment. O submitted that she should be judged by the standards of competence of a high street financial adviser, not by the more stringent standards applicable to a larger firm and that she had been entitled to rely on the information provided by Z about the fund. O also maintained that if she were found liable, Z should indemnify her for its negligent representations regarding the fund. S submitted that he had a statutory cause of action under the Financial Services Act 1986 s.62(1) in respect of any contravention of the Adopted FIMBRA Rules by O that had caused him loss and that O had been in breach of s.62(1) of the Act in advising S to participate in an unregulated collective investment scheme contrary to s.76 of the Act. S also argued that Z had also been in breach of s.62(1) in causing an advertisement to be issued, in the form of a fund prospectus, inviting participation in that unregulated scheme and that Z owed a duty of care to S in respect of the information and advice it had given to O.

Held, giving judgment accordingly, that (1) in cases of professional negligence the standard to be applied was that of a reasonably competent professional, that standard varying according to whether the professional has specialist expertise. That distinction did not assist O because she had sufficient expertise to recognise that an offshore unregulated fund involving investment in shares with fluctuating value that was unprotected by a statutory compensation scheme was high risk. O should also have realised that the scheme was unsuitable as money from the fund was not easily realisable or accessible, notice of redemption being required and the funds having to be repatriated from abroad. Z was no more than a product provider, it was not Z's function to tell O what to advise S. (2) By recommending an unsuitable investment and not fully explaining the risks involved, O had failed to comply with the Adopted FIMBRA Rules and had breached her statutory duty under s.62(1) of the 1986 Act. She had also breached s.62(1) by recommending a collective investment scheme and failing to comply with the Financial Services (Promotion of Unregulated Collective Investment Schemes) Regulations 1991. (3) Z was under a duty to pass on the contents of the warning memorandum to O as failure to do so had meant that S continued to maintain his investment in the fund relying on O's belief that it continued to be a safe investment. Z was therefore liable to indemnify O for a proportion of the overall liability. (4) It was not a valid interpretation of s.76(1)(a) and s.207 of the Act to describe Z giving a fund prospectus to O as being a further issuing of the prospectus by Z or as an instance of Z causing it to be issued. (5) Under s. 76(1)(b) if Z gave advice it was to O and not to S nor had Z procured S to invest in the fund. Z had merely supplied O with information that she used to procure S. The criteria for establishing a duty of care between Z and S had not been met, *Caparo Industries Plc v. Dickman* [1990] 2 A.C. 605, [1990] C.L.Y. 3266 applied. Z did not assume responsibility for the advice given to S and the relationship between S and Z was not sufficiently close. The relevant provisions of the Adopted FIMBRA Rules placed responsibility for recommendations given on the professional whose clients were relying on that advice. S was O's client and that structure would be avoided if a direct duty was imposed on Z. S's claim against O was partially successful, S's claim against Z was dismissed, O's Part 20 claim against Z succeeded to the extent of two-thirds of her liability to S.

SEYMOUR v. CAROLINE OCKWELL & CO; *sub nom.* SEYMOUR v. OCKWELL, [2005] EWHC 1137, [2005] P.N.L.R. 39, Judge Havelock-Allan Q.C., QBD (Merc Ct).

2852. **Duty of care–Local authorities–Hostels–Establishing allegations of negligence at common law–Prospect of success**

The appellant (B) appealed against a decision dismissing her appeal against the striking out of her claim against the first respondent local authority for negligence. B also applied to amend her particulars of claim. B had sustained serious injuries after jumping from a third floor window to escape an attack by three non residents of the hostel premises in which a social worker from the local authority had helped her find accommodation. Although B's mother and father had parental responsibility, the local authority had undertaken to advise and befriend B. B's claim against the local authority for negligence at common law was struck out on the basis that, particularly with regard to breach and causation, it was not remotely sustainable. The local authority submitted that (1) there was no real prospect of B establishing the requisite knowledge for breach of duty by the local authority's social worker and there was insufficient evidence to substantiate her claim; (2) B should not be allowed to make such a late amendment of her particulars of claim.

Held, allowing the appeal, that (1) in light of the inadequacy of the particulars of claim as currently pleaded, the Court of Appeal could and should look at the facts before it to see whether they revealed a viable and pleadable claim. There was little difficulty in seeing that B relied on the social worker in the matter of accommodation and that the social worker assumed a responsibility to B in that respect. More importantly, B's case required that her social worker knew or ought to have known that the hostel was an establishment at which a young woman, such as B, was at significant risk of serious physical attack. In the instant appeal, not all substantial facts relevant to the allegations of negligence, which were reasonably capable of being before the court, were before the court. There were the bones of a possible case that the hostel was known to be one that was materially insecure and at risk of dangerously violent incursion by intruders. Although B's claim against the local authority had its obvious problems, the court should not, at the instant stage, say that it was bound to fail. On the contrary, B had a pleadable case against the local authority that had some real prospect of success, *S v. Gloucestershire CC* [2001] Fam. 313, [2000] C.L.Y. 4212 considered. (2) There were extenuating circumstances explaining the lateness of the application to amend. In principle permission would be granted to amend to enable B to plead particulars of duty, breach of duty and the consequent loss within the framework indicated in the instant judgment.

BLUETT v. SUFFOLK CC, [2004] EWCA Civ 1707, [2005] 1 F.C.R. 89, May, L.J., CA (Civ Div).

2853. Duty of care—Local authority housing—Mother's request for safety locks on windows—Refusal by local authority on fire safety grounds—Duty to locate and provide unrequested safety catches

The appellant local authority appealed against a decision that it was liable in negligence for an accident suffered by the respondent infant (S) in falling out of the window of his local authority house. S had sued through his mother and litigation friend (M). M, who had been concerned about the possibility of one of her children falling out of the window, had asked the local authority to fit window safety locks. M's request was refused on the basis of the local authority's policy that window locks should not be fitted for reasons of fire safety. The judge below had found that the policy on window locks was justifiable. The issue for determination was whether the local authority was under a duty to act and take exceptional measures for the protection of this particular family and therefore locate and install a special form of safety catch to the windows in response to M's requests.

Held, allowing the appeal, that no breach of any pre existing duty by the local authority had been established. The case against the local authority did not involve any breach of the local authority's duties as a landlord. There was no duty of care to provide special child proof safety catches to M's windows. The request that had been made by M was for window locks, not safety catches, and there was no emergency or external threat which called for local authority action. The local authority had based its refusal of locks on its safety policy, which was reasonably based upon experience of past tragedies in fires, *Stockley v. Knowsley MBC* [1986] 2 E.G.L.R. 141, [1986] C.L.Y. 2249 not applied.

STEVENS v. BLAENAU GWENT CBC, [2004] EWCA Civ 715, [2004] H.L.R. 54, Potter, L.J., CA.

2854. Duty of care—Local education authorities—Pupil suffering from dyslexia—Suitability of mainstream school

The claimant (H) brought a claim in negligence against the defendant local authority, alleging that it was vicariously liable for the acts of individuals involved in his education. It was common ground that H had experienced primary educational and behavioural difficulties, specific learning difficulties/dyslexia and secondary emotional and behavioural difficulties arising from his learning difficulties. H argued that (1) the educational psychologist who had assessed him when he was aged eight and at primary school had failed to diagnose his specific learning difficulties and to prescribe the appropriate remedial teaching; (2) the county's principal educational psychologist had been negligent in advising that he should attend a mainstream secondary school as opposed to a small special school that could have addressed his learning difficulties as well as his emotional and behavioural difficulties.

Held, giving judgment for the local authority, that (1) the evidence showed that H had not shown any significant symptoms or signs of dyslexia when he was tested at the age of eight. In any event, there had at the relevant time been a body of educational psychologists, including the educational psychologist who had assessed H, who did not subscribe to the concept of dyslexia/specific learning difficulties, *Bolam v. Friern Hospital Management Committee* [1957] 1 W.L.R. 582, [1957] C.L.Y. 2431 applied. (2) The decision to place H in a mainstream school had been within the range of reasonable responses of the local authority and of the principal educational psychologist. The mainstream school that H had attended had had an integrated special needs unit. Further, the only small special school that would have been able to accommodate H had been one that would not have been acceptable to his parents. (3) Even if an actionable breach of duty been established, H would not have recovered damages as the outcome would not have been any different had he been sent to a dyslexic school. (4) (Obiter) Had H succeeded in his claim, he would have been awarded general damages of £10,000, *DN v. Greenwich LBC* [2004] EWCA Civ 1659, [2005] 1 F.C.R. 112, [2005] 2 C.L. 126 considered.

HARDIE v. DEVON CC, January 14, 2005, Judge Overend, CC (Plymouth). [*Ex rel.* Veitch Penny Solicitors, 1 Manor Court, Dix's Field, Exeter].

2855. Duty of care–Local education authorities–Supply teacher alleging delay in carrying out of background check

The claimant teacher (B) brought a claim in negligence against the defendant local authority (S). B had applied in the summer of 2002 to be placed on the county supply teaching register. The procedure involved, among other things, the carrying out of a background check aimed at ensuring that applicants were suitable to work with children. Before March 2002, the procedure involved checking the national List 99, a central list held by the Department of Education and Skills (DES) of all teachers who had been banned from working with children. The check also included a police check with the local force. In March 2002, the DES introduced a new system whereby schools would refer to the Criminal Records Bureau (CRB), which would carry out the necessary checks. The CRB struggled to deal with the volume of enquiries received, with the result that on September 5, 2002 the DES issued amended guidance to the effect that local education authorities should temporarily revert to the former procedure. B's application was referred to the CRB on September 11 notwithstanding the amended guidance and she was not authorised to work as a supply teacher until November 13. B sought to recover the supply teaching income that she claimed she should have received between September and November 2002. She argued that S owed her a duty of care to process her application as speedily as possible and that it had breached that duty by referring her application to the CRB when the DES had made it clear that it was entitled to use the old List 99 procedure.

Held, giving judgment for S, that merely because an unsolicited application had been received, it could not be said that there was a duty of care to process that application speedily or at all. In any event, this was a claim for pure economic loss and was therefore bound to fail. Further, B had failed to show that any loss had been caused by any putative breach. Had S owed a duty to B, there would have been no breach of that duty. Any delay had been caused by the CRB. Moreover, the amended guidance issued by the DES was no more than guidance, and it remained at S's discretion to use whichever method it chose to ensure B's suitability. B had been told in advance that her application would be subject to a CRB check and S had owed her no obligation to use the List 99 procedure.

BOUGHY v. SOMERSET CC, February 3, 2005, District Judge Smith, CC (Yeovil). [*Ex rel.* Veitch Penny Solicitors, 1 Manor court, Dix's Field, Exeter, Devon].

2856. Duty of care–Proximity–No direct contractual relationship–Pure economic loss

The appellants (MBS and MBUK) appealed against a decision of the Singapore court in favour of the respondent shipowner (B) concerning an oil tanker which a shipbuilder (MSE) had agreed to build. It was clearly contemplated in the contract that MSE would obtain the engine from a third party. MSE sourced the engine from MBS, a supplier which sold and serviced engines manufactured by MBUK, its parent company. The engine gave trouble within a few weeks of delivery and subsequently broke down completely, whereupon B brought proceedings against MBS and MBUK in negligence, claiming that they were in breach of a duty of care owed to B. B sought damages for the cost of the engine and loss of business, namely pure economic loss. The judge below concluded that there was sufficient proximity between B and MBUK to give rise to a duty of care on the part of MBUK to exercise due diligence in the design and manufacture of the engine so that it would be fit for the operation of the ship. With regard to MBS, the judge concluded that its assertions as to the engine's reliability and the fact that it had actively marketed the engine was sufficient to establish a duty of care towards B.

Held, allowing the appeals, that it would not be just or reasonable in the circumstances to impose a duty of care on MBS or MBUK, *Dutton v. Bognor Regis Urban DC* [1972] 1 Q.B. 373, [1972] C.L.Y. 2352 applied. The landmark case of *RSP Architects Planners and Engineers v. Ocean Front Pte Ltd* (1998) 14 Const. L.J. 139, [1998] C.L.Y. 3924, decided by the Singapore Court of Appeal, found that a property developer was liable in tort for losses suffered by the management corporation of the development and in reaching that decision, the two stage test set out in *Anns v. Merton LBC* [1978] A.C. 728, [1977] C.L.Y. 2030 was followed, *Ocean Front* and *Anns v. Merton* considered. The general application of *Ocean Front* was, however, limited by its particular set of facts. In the instant case, the contractual arrangements between B and MSE were such that MSE's obligation was limited to repairing defects and it was B's choice not to enter into a direct contractual relationship with MBS or MBUK. Accordingly, B was limited to seeking redress from MSE alone and was precluded from asserting any reliance on promises by MBS or MBUK to deliver a satisfactory engine. There was, therefore, insufficient proximity between B and MBS or MBUK to give rise to a duty of care. Neither was there any justification for extending the law to offer a remedy to B, who had had the opportunity to modify the limitation of liability clauses in the contract with MSE and had chosen not to do so.

MAN B&W DIESEL SE ASIA PTE LTD v. PT BUMI INTERNATIONAL TANKERS (2005) 21 Const. L.J. 126, Yong Pung Hon, C.J., CA (Sing).

2857. **Duty of care—Reasonableness—No liability between public authorities for care expenses of negligently injured third party**

The appellant local authority appealed against a decision ([2004] EWHC 1754) dismissing its action in negligence against the respondent hospital trust on the basis that the trust did not owe a duty of care to the local authority. A third party (J) had been injured through the negligence of the trust and as a result required residential care, which was provided by the local authority. The local authority was unable to recover the cost of care from J due to her impecuniosity and therefore J made no claim for those costs against the trust. The local authority was precluded by legislation from recovering the cost of care from the structured settlement agreed between J and the trust. Accordingly, the local authority sought to recover the cost of care from the trust in an action in negligence. The local authority contended that a duty of care was owed to it because it was reasonably foreseeable that a breach of the duty of care to J, through causing her injury and her consequent need for care, would thereby cause it loss. The local authority argued that it was unreasonable and unfair that the trust should escape its liability for part of the results of its negligence because of the double accident that J was being cared for by a public body and that J was unable to pay for that care.

Held, dismissing the appeal, that the judge had set too high a standard in determining what was foreseeable. The precise manner in which the injury occurred did not have to be foreseeable. In the instant case the trust did not have to know that J would require local authority care and would not be able to pay for it. It only needed to have institutional knowledge, which it did, that some patients with J's disability would fall into that category. It was reasonably foreseeable that J would suffer an injury as a result of the trust's negligence that required care at public expense. The question of whether there was a sufficient relationship of proximity between the parties was closely related to the question of whether it would be fair, just and reasonable to impose a duty of care on the trust. Fair, just and reasonable was not to be read literally, nor was it to be read solely in the context of the relationship between the instant parties. There were important and overriding considerations why the court should not extend the law of negligence. It was impossible for the court to know, within the confines of a particular case and with the benefit of only a sparse amount of evidence and its own commonsense, the wider implications of extending the law. In addition, although the local authority and the trust were both public authorities they were public authorities of different sorts with different sources of funding. Any solution was a matter for Parliament rather than for the courts. Also, if a private tortfeasor passed the test of foreseeability, that would raise a different set of issues as to the economic implications of extending liability to a private tortfeasor for costs that were viewed as a public liability. It was also difficult to rationalise the existence of a direct action by the local authority against the tortfeasor in a context where neither a private provider of care nor the NHS enjoyed such a right. In the circumstances it would not be fair just and reasonable to impose a duty of care on the trust.

ISLINGTON LBC v. UNIVERSITY COLLEGE LONDON HOSPITAL NHS TRUST, [2005] EWCA Civ 596, [2006] B.L.G.R. 50, Buxton, L.J., CA (Civ Div).

2858. **Duty of care—Report on Bangladeshi ground water chemistry—Lack of proximity or causation to found duty of care toward persons poisoned by drinking water**

N appealed against a decision refusing to strike out a claim in negligence brought by 700 Bangladeshi nationals. S claimed that N owed him a duty of care for failing to test for arsenic in drinking water in Bangladesh. N had been funded by the Overseas Development Agency, ODA, to provide research services for an irrigation project in Bangladesh. With surplus funding and approval from the agency, N also carried out a short pilot study of ground water chemistry in certain aquifers, an ancillary purpose of which was to test potability of the water. The study did not test for arsenic. The concluding report was produced for ODA and circulated amongst Bangladesh water authorities, which did not have the means to check potability. The class action was brought on behalf of Bangladesh claimants after they suffered serious health problems from drinking water contaminated by arsenic.

Held, allowing the appeal (Clarke L.J. dissenting), that the claims must be struck out because allowing a claim based on the pilot project's findings would render the concept of proximity virtually meaningless. In the instant case there was no nexus between N and those who drank the water and policy considerations militated against the imposition of a duty of care. N had been financed by ODA, to whom it submitted the report. N had not created the hazard and did not owe a duty to those affected by drinking the water as it was not under a duty to provide potable water. The report's primary purpose was not to express a view on potability and N had not assumed any responsibility towards those who read the report or who could be affected by drinking the water, *Perrett v. Collins* [1998] 2 Lloyd's Rep. 255, [1998] C.L.Y. 3923 and *Watson v. British Boxing Board of Control Ltd* [2001] Q.B. 1134, [2001] C.L.Y. 4468 applied, and *X (Minors) v. Bedfordshire CC* [1995] 2 A.C. 633, [1995] C.L.Y. 3452 distinguished. Furthermore, the duty to strike out claims where liability could not be proved increased in proportion to the likely expense and length of the litigation.

SUTRADHAR v. NATURAL ENVIRONMENT RESEARCH COUNCIL, [2004] EWCA Civ 175, [2004] P.N.L.R. 30, Kennedy, L.J., CA.

2859. **Duty of care—Schools—Pupil sexually abused by teacher**

[Limitation Act 1980 s.2, s.11.]

The appellant (C) appealed against the dismissal of his claim for negligence and vicarious liability against the respondent local authority. As a child C had been placed in a school run by the local authority and had remained there until 1988. Shortly before he left the school, he complained to a social worker that he had been sexually abused by a teacher. In 2002, C claimed damages for the psychiatric and consequential damage. His claim was based on an alleged failure by the local authority to make an appropriate assessment of his needs and a failure to provide proper supervision, in particular to provide supervision by a social worker sooner than it had. C also claimed vicarious liability on the basis that the local authority was liable for the actions of the teacher. To this end, he maintained that there was ample evidence that ought to have raised suspicions as to the teacher's behaviour towards children at the school. Despite the fact that the claim for negligence was out of time, the judge allowed it to proceed. In due course he held that, notwithstanding a breach of duty by the local authority, there was no harm caused to C. As to the vicarious liability claim, the judge held that it was actually a claim for trespass to the person and was therefore caught by the non extendable time limit in the Limitation Act 1980 s.2. Accordingly, he dismissed both claims. C argued that (1) the judge had failed to deal with the allegation that the local authority ought to have assigned him a social worker sooner. Had it done so, the abuse might have been identified earlier. Further, the judge had been wrong to conclude that C had suffered no harm; (2) the judge had erred in holding that the evidence was insufficient to give rise to the suspicion that the teacher was an abuser other than in retrospect; (3) the judge had erred in holding that the claim for vicarious liability fell within s.2 and was therefore statute barred.

Held, dismissing the appeal, that (1) there had been no expert evidence before the judge as to proper social work practice, which made it difficult to sustain the argument that the local authority's failure to provide C with a social worker sooner than it had could amount to a breach of duty. As to the judge's conclusions on causation, there was ample evidence to support his view that C had suffered no resultant harm. (2) Although the school knew about visits by boys to the teacher's room, the teacher had always provided innocent explanations. If the visits had been capable of giving rise to concern as to abuse, the school would have taken action. The fact that the teacher had also visited C at his home only assumed significance in hindsight. At the material time, the school did not view the matter as a cause for concern, as the teacher also visited other children's homes when he was passing. There was also evidence of the teacher giving presents to the children. However, that evidence only came to the fore at trial. In the light of those facts, the judge had been entitled to hold that the school had made reasonable investigations and that the evidence only showed the teacher to be an abuser in hindsight. (3) It was clear that where an action for which an employer was held vicariously liable consisted of deliberate abuse, the cause of action fell within the limitation period specified in s.2, not s.11 of the Act, *Stubbings v. Webb* [1993] A.C. 498, [1993] C.L.Y. 2608 and *KR v. Bryn Alyn Community (Holdings) Ltd (In Liquidation)* [2003] EWCA Civ 85, [2003] 3 W.L.R. 107, [2003] C.L.Y. 432 applied.

C v. MIDDLESBROUGH BC, [2004] EWCA Civ 1746, [2005] 1 F.C.R. 76, Chadwick, L.J., CA (Civ Div).

2860. Duty of care-Ships-Passenger going overboard

[Civil Procedure Rules 1998 (SI 1998 3132) Part 35.]

The claimant (D) brought a claim against the defendant ferry company (S) in respect of the death by drowning of her husband (X). X had gone overboard unobserved during a ferry crossing in rough seas on a vessel owned by S. Following a passenger sighting of a man in the sea, the crew carried out S's operational procedures for man overboard but no preparations were made to retrieve X from the sea when he was found. The weather conditions were too bad for the ferry's rescue boat to be launched but another vessel had sighted X in good condition in the water and had a fast rescue boat that was ready and able to launch. However, the ferry captain decided to try and recover X by manoeuvring close to him, throwing him a line and pulling him to a door in the side of the ferry. During the manoeuvres X was seen to be dead in the water. At the start of the trial S submitted that D's expert evidence should be excluded because most of the work carried out by the experts had been on a contingency fee basis.

Held, giving judgment for D, that (1) although most of the work of the experts had been carried out under contingency fee arrangements contrary to the Code of Guidance on Expert Evidence annexed to the Civil Procedure Rules 1998 Part 35 PD 35, prior to the signing of the reports the arrangements had been changed to a deferred payment basis. The delay and wasted costs that would have occurred if the expert evidence was excluded at the start of the trial would have conflicted with the overriding objective and been wholly disproportionate. Any risk of bias could be explored in cross examination. (2) S had been aware of the near impossibility of rescuing a man overboard to a high sided vessel like the ferry but had failed to carry out any appropriate risk assessment or training of the captain and crew. Given the industry wide awareness of the problem and the likelihood of such an emergency happening on the particular route, those were serious and negligent failures by S. The failure of the captain to prepare a careful and detailed rescue plan or to have a rescue plan available was negligent. The captain's rescue plan was so hopeless and risky both to X and to the safety of the ferry and its crew that it had been negligent to attempt it. There was a strong possibility that X would have been recovered alive if the other vessel had been asked to launch its fast rescue boat, and the captain had been negligent in failing to make such a request. Appropriate advice and training would have provided the captain with the clear guidance that he should have considered other available options for recovering a man overboard where the ferry's own rescue boat could not be launched. The captain's manoeuvres had fallen significantly short of what was expected of a reasonably competent and prudent master mariner and X had drowned as a direct consequence of the change in sea conditions caused by the ferry movement around him.

DAVIS v. STENA LINE LTD, [2005] EWHC 420, [2005] 2 Lloyd's Rep. 13, Forbes, J., QBD.

2861. Duty of care–Special educational needs–Duty of care owed by education officer to child with special educational needs

[Education Act 1981.]

The appellant (C) appealed against a decision that the respondent local authority had not breached its duty of care towards him in that over a substantial period of his schooling it had failed to provide him with suitable education. C's development in primary school had been slow. An education officer (M) employed by the local authority believed, on the basis of assessments under the Education Act 1981, that C had learning and language difficulties as well as emotional and behavioural problems. C moved to a junior school (N) where the placement broke down and consideration was given to a transfer to another school. In the meantime, a statement of special educational needs was prepared. C was placed at a school (B) which catered for children with emotional and behavioural difficulties. There were indications of progress, but as time went on, it was clear that C was struggling. The local authority's psychologist recommended a transfer to "a more appropriate setting". A number of shortcomings in the performance of the school itself also began to emerge. The local authority experienced considerable practical difficulties in securing alternative education. C remained at the school for over a year before transferring to a school for children with dyslexia. The judge below had found that the local authority had approached C's case in a manner which would be regarded as acceptable by a body of educational opinion. C contended that the local authority was vicariously liable for M's negligence in failing to reassess his educational needs following the breakdown of his placement at N, and that the judge had erred in not finding the local authority vicariously liable for M's negligence in allowing C to remain at B without reassessment.

Held, dismissing the appeal, that (1) there were only two areas of potential enquiry where the issue arose whether a public authority was liable for negligence in the exercise of its statutory functions. The first was whether the decision was justiciable at all. The second was the application of the three stage test in *Caparo Industries Plc v. Dickman* [1990] 2 A.C. 605: foreseeability of damage, proximity, and whether it was just and reasonable that the law should impose a duty of care, *Caparo* applied. (2) The question whether an education officer owed a duty of care to children with special needs could not be answered by the assertion that there was no duty where there was no private law right to claim damages for breach of statutory duty. Where an education officer, in the performance of his or her statutory functions, entered into relationships with or assumed responsibilities towards a child, then he or she might be found to owe a duty of care to that child. Whether such a duty was in fact owed would depend on an application of the *Caparo* test. It was not necessary to ask whether the officer's decision was so unreasonable as to fall outside the ambit of his discretion altogether. Accordingly, an education officer did not enjoy blanket immunity for the performance of his statutory functions under the 1981 Act, *Phelps v. Hillingdon LBC* [2001] 2 A.C. 619, [2000] C.L.Y. 1947 applied. (3) The decision to transfer C to B school had been taken after a careful assessment of his needs and with the benefit of expert advice obtained from relevant professionals. The judge's conclusion that the decision was not negligent was unassailable. (4) The judge had made the critical finding that, whilst it had been right to seek a more appropriate setting for C, B school had not been an inappropriate setting. Having regard to the delicate decisions that education officers had to make, he had been right to find that the decision to keep C at B school for a limited period was not negligent.

CARTY v. CROYDON LBC, [2005] EWCA Civ 19, [2005] 1 W.L.R. 2312, Dame Elizabeth Butler-Sloss (President), CA (Civ Div).

2862. Duty of care–Stress–Employee alleging lack of support by employer

The appellant employee (V) appealed against a decision ([2004] EWHC 2102, [2005] P.I.Q.R. P9) dismissing her claim against the respondent employer (F) for damages for negligence and breach of contract. V had claimed that F had caused her to suffer severe clinical depression. V had been employed by F as a reception class teacher and assistant head until her dismissal for ill health. V claimed that, owing to a government scheme resulting in changes to the school's teaching methods, she had suffered stress, and that F had failed to provide her with sufficient support in order for her to return to work after a period of absence. Her claim was dismissed on the basis that the evidence showed that her mental condition had collapsed under the strain arising from her attempts, albeit with reasonable support, to make fundamental changes to her teaching methods, with which she had been unable to cope. The judge concluded that it followed that her instances of severe depressive illness were not caused by any breach of duty on the part of F. V argued that the judge had been wrong to dismiss the claim since there was evidence to show that F had failed to support her adequately. Among other things, F should have sent her home.

Held, dismissing the appeal, that (1) there was evidence to support the judge's findings that V's mental condition had collapsed under the strain arising from her attempts to make fundamental changes to her teaching methods, with which she had been unable to cope. The evidence showed that F had put into place support mechanisms. The staff at the school were anxious for her to return to work, and it was difficult to see what more could have been done without F being intrusive or unsupportive. There was no merit in V's submission that F should have sent her home; such an action would be bound to have been seen as a hostile act since it would have indicated a lack of confidence in V and been just the sort of conduct that might have brought on a relapse. The judge had therefore been fully entitled to dismiss the claim. (2) (Obiter) As the courts had settled many of the principles in stress at work cases, litigants really should mediate cases such as this one. It was a great pity that mediation had not taken place.

VAHIDI v. FAIRSTEAD HOUSE SCHOOL TRUST LTD; *sub nom*. VALIDI v. FAIRSTEAD HOUSE SCHOOL TRUST LTD, [2005] EWCA Civ 765, [2005] E.L.R. 607, Ward, L.J., CA (Civ Div).

2863. Financial advice–Investment funds–Applicable principles of causation– Measure of damages

The appellant (B) appealed against the decision ([2004] EWHC 1608) dismissing his claim for damages for negligent financial advice by an employee (J) of the respondent independent financial advisers in respect of methods of dealing with his pension fund. In light of B's intention to retire, J had advised B to transfer his share of assets in his self administered pension scheme into a broker managed fund and to take a cash free lump sum and a yearly drawdown income on his retirement. Relying on that advice, B withdrew a tax free lump sum from the scheme and the balance remained subject to a drawdown plan invested in the broker managed fund. It was admitted that, in breach of the duty owed to B, J failed to advise him as to alternative methods of dealing with his pension fund, in particular, the possibility of using the money to buy an immediate annuity. However, the judge held that B would not have purchased an immediate annuity if J had explained the possibility but not advised him to do so, with the result that causation was not established. B submitted that (1) the case in relation to the annuity as in fact presented to the judge was that J was negligent in recommending the particular fund that he recommended; (2) having found that B would have accepted and acted on J's advice unquestioningly, the judge should have asked himself (i) what advice J would have given as a matter of fact on the balance of probabilities, if he had not been negligent, and (ii) if, as a matter of fact, J would still have advised the drawdown arrangement as opposed to an immediate annuity, whether that advice would have been negligent; (3) in the alternative, even if the judge was right to find that B had not proved that he would have purchased an annuity if he had been properly advised, he ought nevertheless to have found that B was entitled to recover the loss incurred as a result of investing in the fund on the basis of the reasoning in *Chester v. Afshar* [2004] UKHL 41, [2005] 1 A.C. 134, [2005] 1 C.L. 297.

Held, dismissing the appeal, that (1) the whole emphasis at trial was on the relative merits of drawdown contracts and annuity contracts for someone in B's position. The case being advanced by B was that it was negligent to recommend a drawdown contract rather than an annuity contract and that, if he had been properly advised, he would have purchased an annuity. In those circumstances the judge could not be criticised for not dealing with a case based on an allegation of negligence in recommending investment in the particular fund that was recommended. (2) In the instant case, there was no scope for the application of the principle in *Bolitho v. City and Hackney Health Authority* [1997] 3 W.L.R. 1151, *Bolitho* distinguished. The negligence lay in failing to advise on the possibility of an annuity, advice which the judge found would not have led B to reject the recommendation of the fund. In such a case, it was meaningless to ask what J would have done if he had not been negligent. If he had not been negligent, what J should have done and what he would have done were one and the same, namely advise on the possible option of buying an annuity. (3) The only issue for the judge on the annuity claim was whether, if the option of buying an annuity had been drawn to his attention, B would have adopted that option. On the facts, there was no reason for not applying the conventional approach to causation as the judge did, *Chester* distinguished. In any event, the principle in Chester should not be applied generally in claims for negligent financial advice. (4) Permission to appeal on three further grounds was refused.

BEARY v. PALL MALL INVESTMENTS, [2005] EWCA Civ 415, [2005] P.N.L.R. 35, Keene, L.J., CA (Civ Div).

2864. Foreseeability—Asbestos—Wife exposed to asbestos from husband's clothing—Liability for mesothelioma caused by exposure

The appellant companies (H) appealed against a decision ([2004] EWHC 577) that they were liable for personal injuries suffered by the respondent (M) on the basis that the risk of serious injury to her health had been obvious at the relevant time. M had been exposed to asbestos dust brought home by her husband on his work clothes whilst he had been employed by H between 1961 and 1965 as a boilermaker at H's shipyard. As a result M had contracted mesothelioma. H admitted that it had been in breach of its common law duty to M's husband by exposing him to asbestos dust. The judge below had concluded that, given the state of actual or imputed knowledge before 1965, H ought reasonably to have foreseen that M was at risk of pulmonary injury from her secondary exposure. H submitted that the judge had not been entitled to conclude that the risk of injury to M was reasonably foreseeable at any time before her husband stopped working for H in early 1965 and that H was not in breach of any duty to M since it was not reasonably foreseeable that its failure to take proper precautions would injure anyone except M's husband.

Held, allowing the appeal (Mance, L.J .dissenting), that the fact that H should have appreciated the risk of harm to M's husband as its employee, and taken precautions for his safety, did not mean that it should have appreciated the familial risk to M arising from secondary exposure. Before 1965 there had been no suggestion from the industry generally; those responsible for health and safety; the factory inspectorate or the medical profession that it was necessary or even prudent for risks arising from familial exposure to be addressed by the industry. It was not reasonably foreseeable between 1960 and 1965 that a wife washing the clothes of a husband who had been exposed to asbestos to a negligent degree would herself be likely to suffer risk of personal injury. The submission that before 1965, and ahead of contemporary understanding, H should have appreciated that M was at risk of pulmonary or other asbestos related injury was rejected and H's failure to appreciate that risk and to take appropriate precautions for her safety was not negligent, *Gunn v. Wallsend Slipway and Engineering Co* Times, January 23, 1989, *Owen v. IMI Yorkshire Copper Tube* (Unreported, June 15, 1995) and *Shell Tankers UK Ltd v. Jeromson* [2001] EWCA Civ 101, [2001] I.C.R. 1223, [2001] C.L.Y. 4492 considered. (*Per* Mance, L.J.) H had allowed M's husband to become excessively contaminated and had behaved in disregard of any responsible and recommended practices in relation to its employees and had clearly expanded the risks of asbestos contamination to an extent that might include third parties outside its premises. H should be held liable for the more remote consequences which it should reasonably have foreseen might occur, even if only in the most unusual case, as a result of its serious disregard of proper procedures for reducing asbestos dust as far as practicable. It might not be easy to foresee precisely all the consequences of H's irresponsible behaviour, but injury to others like M was sufficiently foreseeable for H to be liable to her.

MAGUIRE v. HARLAND & WOLFF PLC, [2005] EWCA Civ 1, [2005] P.I.Q.R. P21, Judge, L.J., CA (Civ Div).

2865. **Limitations – Professional negligence claim against former solicitor – Failure to advise on extent of claim against bank**

[Civil Procedure Rules 1998 (SI 3132) Part 3 r.3.4(2).]

P, a former partner in a firm of solicitors, A, appealed against a decision refusing his application to strike out Es particulars of claim and an alternative claim for summary judgment against E. E had instructed A to act for him in a claim in negligence against a bank, B. In July 1989, B advised E to take a larger loan than he had intended to finance the construction of a bungalow. E contended that B then advised him in November 1989 to increase the amount borrowed still further to improve his chances of selling the property. E failed to sell the bungalow in 1990 and the bank sold it as mortgagee at an alleged undervalue for £180,500 in 1992. E instructed A in 1995, but, in spite of assurances from A's senior partner, no progress was made with the claim before A's practice was terminated in June 1998. P's application to strike out E's claim under the Civil Procedure Rules 1998 Part 3 r.3.4(2) was refused and the judge allowed E to amend the particulars of claim by alleging that A failed to advise him to sue the bank in negligence in respect of the increased loan and for breach of contract in selling the property at an undervalue.

Held, allowing the appeal in part, that the claim arising from the loan in July 1989 was struck out as it was statute barred by the time E instructed A in 1995, *Forster v. Outred & Co* [1982] 1 W.L.R. 86, [1982] C.L.Y. 1849 followed. The claim alleging the sale at an undervalue could proceed as it was still in time when A was instructed and A's negligence had contributed to E's loss. Further, it was at least arguable that A's duty toward E survived in some form after the termination of his instructions in June 1998, *MacPherson & Kelley v. Kevin J Prunty & Associates* [1983] V.R. 573, [1983] C.L.Y. 3610 considered. However, the amendments to the particulars of claim could not stand as the claims against A became statute barred in February 1998 and could not now be revived by way of an amendment.

ENSOR v. ARCHER, [2004] EWHC 1541, [2005] P.N.L.R. 5, Keith, J., QBD.

2866. **Measure of damages–Professional negligence–Solicitors–Conveyancing– Failure to discover defects in title–Measure of damages–Diminution in value or cost of extrication**

The claimant (G), a property development company, brought an action against the defendant (C), a firm of solicitors, claiming damages for negligence arising out of C's handling of a property purchase. The property had been bought by G in 1993 for £240,000 with a view to converting it into flats. C admitted that it had negligently failed to perform an adequate check on the title adduced by the vendor when it came to light that the property was subject to three outstanding charges. In 1996, the vendor's solicitors paid to remedy the defect in title. In 2000, under pressure from its bankers, G was forced to sell the property for £129,000. G sought damages from C on a cost of extrication basis, representing the sums spent on acquiring, repairing and improving the property less the sum received when it came to be sold. C argued that (1) G had failed to prove that it would not have completed the purchase if it had been advised of the want of good title; (2) the proper measure of damages was diminution in value.

Held, assessing damages, that (1) on the balance of probabilities, G would not have completed the purchase but for C's negligence. No reasonable property developer would have completed without a good marketable title. (2) The diminution in value approach was the only basis of assessment which could do justice in the case. G had not paid the cost of remedying the defect in title, the direct expenses incurred in maintaining the property until the defect was lifted must have been modest and the financial loss caused by the title not being perfected until 1996 was not quantified and had to be highly speculative. Moreover, G had retained the property, and the cost of maintaining it until 2000 could not be regarded as a cost of extrication, *County Personnel (Employment Agency) Ltd v. Alan R Pulver & Co* [1987] 1 W.L.R. 916, [1987] C.L.Y. 3551 and *Hayes v. James & Charles Dodd (A Firm)* [1990] 2 All E.R. 815, [1990] C.L.Y. 1524 distinguished, *Carter (t/a New Chapel Developments) v. TG Baynes & Sons* [1998] E.G.C.S. 109 doubted. With good title, the property would have been worth £130,000 in 1993. With defects in title that would have taken three years to clear, it would have been worth £85,000. Hence, G would be awarded damages of £45,000.

GREYMALKIN LTD v. COPLEYS, [2004] EWCA Civ 1155, [2004] P.N.L.R. 44, Lawrence Collins, J., Ch D.

2867. **Professional negligence–Accountants–Negligent advice–Interpretation of exclusion clause**

The appellant (P), a firm of accountants, appealed against a decision ([2003] EWHC 1595, [2004] P.N.L.R. 8, [2004] 2 C.L. 381) that it was liable for negligently advising the respondent university in connection with the implementation of a profit related pay scheme and that the university was entitled to damages for loss of anticipated savings under the scheme. The case revolved around the interpretation of a clause in P's terms of engagement. The first limb stated that, subject to a limit on liability which was equal to twice the anticipated savings, P accepted "liability to pay damages in respect of loss or damage suffered by the university as a direct result of our providing the Services". The second limb stated: "All other liability is expressly excluded, in particular consequential loss, failure to realise anticipated savings or benefits and a failure to obtain registration of the scheme". The judge had held that the two limbs were self contradictory and that primacy should be given to the first. P argued that the judge had erred in failing to find a meaning for the second limb. P contended that the second limb clearly represented losses which the parties had agreed to exclude and clearly covered a failure to achieve anticipated savings and benefits.

Held, dismissing the appeal, that the first and second limbs were to be read as a whole and the court should endeavour to give meaning to both limbs, *Pagnan SpA v. Tradax Ocean Transportation SA* [1987] 3 All E.R. 565, [1988] C.L.Y. 3174 followed. The first limb was a positive statement of that for which P accepted liability. The use of the word "other" in the opening words of the second limb told the reader that the first limb had precedence over the second. Considering the opening words of the first limb and the imposition of a cap which limited liability to twice the anticipated savings under the scheme, it was clear that the phrase "all other liability" in the second limb included losses within the first limb which exceeded the cap on liability. Thus, loss and damage were excluded by the second limb only if they represented loss not covered by the first. The two limbs were not self contradictory, nor was the second limb in any relevant respect unclear. The judge had reached the right conclusion in finding that the loss claimed was not excluded by the clause.

UNIVERSITY OF KEELE v. PRICE WATERHOUSE, [2004] EWCA Civ 583, [2004] P.N.L.R. 43, Buxton, L.J., CA.

2868. **Professional negligence–Actuaries–Duty of care–Reliance on actuarial valuation report**

The appellant (P) appealed against the dismissal of its claim against the respondent actuaries (M) for damages for professional negligence. M cross appealed on the finding that P had relied on its actuarial valuation report. M had prepared the report for one of the pension funds of a company (S). The report described the position in S's pension scheme as at a certain date and showed a deficit of £1.35 million. In fact the calculations in the report were negligently prepared and the deficit should have been £4.5 million. P, in purported reliance on the figures in the report, made an offer for shares in S and, through its parent company, entered into a confidentiality agreement with S purporting to exclude liability for the negligence of S's agents in relation to any information supplied to P. The judge concluded that M owed P no duty of care with respect to the preparation of the report, that M was entitled to rely on the exclusion clause in the agreement and that P was contributorily negligent in failing to instruct its own independent actuary as initially advised by its solicitors. M accepted that the report had been prepared without the standard of care to be expected of professional actuaries. P contended that (1) M owed P a duty of care in that P was an entity whom M expressly recognised might rely on the report and that the provision of the report to P pursuant to their due diligence enquiry was implicit agreement to P relying on the report. M did not have to know precisely how the information was to be used, it only needed to know the general nature of the purpose; (2) the information was not confidential information because pension scheme beneficiaries had statutory rights to obtain the report; (3) it should be immune from a finding of contributory negligence because the error was not one against which the taking of actuarial advice was intended to protect it. M argued that contrary to the judge's findings, P could not possibly have relied on the report.

Held, dismissing the appeal and the cross appeal, that (1) M agreed only to P having the information and could not therefore be taken to have agreed to their relying on the information for a particular purpose because they did not know what type of transaction was envisaged. Without a clearer idea of P's purpose M could not be said to have agreed to it. The purpose in the instant case was to see whether, when M provided the report, it did so in circumstances which, viewed objectively, meant that it was responsible to the ultimate recipient if the information was negligently prepared, *Hedley Byrne & Co Ltd v. Heller & Partners Ltd* [1964] A.C. 465, [1963] C.L.Y. 2416 and *Caparo Industries Plc v. Dickman* [1990] 2 A.C. 605, [1990] C.L.Y. 3266 applied. The precise limits of the concept of assumption of responsibility were still in a state of development and there was no comprehensive list of guiding principles to help the court determine when an assumption of responsibility could be said to arise. The courts therefore had to look at all the relevant circumstances and determine whether they fell within the situations in which an assumption of liability had previously been held to exist or whether the circumstances were closely analogous to and consistent with the situations in which liability had been imposed in previous cases. The exclusion clause in the agreement did not help M. The question of the assumption of responsibility could not depend on the terms of a private transaction such as the agreement between P and S which formed no part of the matrix of fact said to give rise to an assumption of responsibility, *Williams v. Natural Life Health Foods Ltd* [1998] 1 W.L.R. 830, [1998] C.L.Y. 920 applied. M and P had no existing relationship. M had provided historic information, which could just as easily have been provided by the trustee of the pension scheme. If S had provided the information rather than M, there would have been no assumption of responsibility by M. P did not communicate with M directly or inform M why the information was requested. In all the circumstances M could not be taken to have assumed responsibility to P. It would not be fair, just or reasonable to impose liability on M in those circumstances. (2) Information which was available to a limited number of third parties was not "generally available". (3) There were good reasons why P did not take separate actuarial advice but its decision not to do so disregarded the legal advice and P should not be immune from the finding of contributory negligence. (4) The judge had been entitled to reach his conclusion on P's reliance.

PRECIS (521) PLC v. WILLIAM M MERCER LTD, [2005] EWCA Civ 114, [2005] P.N.L.R. 28, Kennedy, L.J., CA (Civ Div).

2869. **Professional negligence–Barristers–Advice based on assessment of prospects of success–Construction of s.1(5) Civil Liability (Contribution) Act 1978**

[Civil Liability (Contribution) Act 1978 s.1 (5).]

The appellant counsel (C) appealed against a decision ([2002] EWCA Civ 875, [2002] C.P.L.R. 619) that although her assessment of the prospects of success of the application was not negligent, she had been negligent in failing to give the respondent (M) sufficiently detailed advice in deciding whether to accept a payment into court or to proceed with his claim. C had given advice to C on his prospects of beating a payment in during the course of medical negligence litigation in which a firm of solicitors (P) had acted for C. The advice was complicated by the fact that C was applying for the introduction of necessary evidence on C's behalf and the outcome of C's claim depended to an extent on whether or not that evidence was admitted. C had framed her advice to C on the basis that she was hopeful the evidence would be admitted and C decided to proceed. In the event the application to adduce further evidence failed and C consequently accepted a reduced offer. M brought a claim for negligence against P, and C was joined as a Part 20 defendant and codefendant. The trial judge held that C was not negligent and made an award solely against P. P appealed to the Court of Appeal which allowed their appeal and held C to have been negligent and liable for a proportion of the agreed damages payable to C. C submitted that (1) the approach of the Court of Appeal was incorrect and that if C's assessment of the risk was not negligent, it was difficult to see how the advice based on it could be negligent; (2) the judgment given by the trial judge in C's favour was, by the provision in the Civil Liability (Contribution) Act 1978 s.1 (5), made conclusive so that it could not be challenged by P either in subsequent proceedings for contribution or by appeal in the action in which the judgment was given.

Held, allowing the appeal, that (1) public interest did not require advocates to be held immune from suit for the consequences of their negligence but that interest did require that the application of the principle should not stifle advocates' independence of mind and action in the manner in which they conducted litigation and advised their clients, *Arthur JS Hall & Co v. Simons* [2002] 1 A.C. 615, [2000] C.L.Y. 4269 applied. The Court of Appeal had judged C's actions too harshly when account was taken of all the circumstances. The instant court agreed with the trial judge that C's advice fell within the range of that to be expected of reasonably competent counsel of C's seniority and purported experience. It was possible that in hindsight C's advice to C to proceed was a wrong decision, but the court was not convinced that it was as mistaken a decision in all the circumstances as had been represented. C had had much to gain if the application to adduce evidence had succeeded and the action would then have been fairly straightforward. Above all there was a strong case to be made that it would have been artificial and unjust, despite all the errors of omission, to deprive C of the opportunity to adduce evidence that would have made such a profound difference to the value of his claim. It was not incumbent on C to spell out all her reasoning, so she was not in breach of her duty of care to C in the advice she gave. (2) Section 1 (5) of the 1978 Act should be construed so as not to bar an appeal in a case such as the instant one and P's right of appeal was not barred by its operation.

MOY v. PETTMAN SMITH (A FIRM), [2005] UKHL 7, [2005] 1 W.L.R. 581, Lord Nicholls of Birkenhead, HL.

2870. Professional negligence–Barristers–Duty of care–Advising client to accept settlement as claim "almost certain" to be struck out

L brought a professional negligence action against his former solicitors, W, and a barrister, A, whom W had instructed. In 1995 L instructed a firm of solicitors, K, to commence proceedings for malicious falsehood and defamation against his former employers, the MoD, in which he claimed damages amounting to £240,000 in respect of loss of earnings and pension rights owing to his forced resignation from the army following his involvement in whistleblowing. K did not instruct a barrister, A, until 1999, at which point she advised that there was a strong chance that the claim would be struck out by reason of the delay. L then instructed new solicitors, W, who also sought advice from A, who at that point stated that L's action would almost certainly be struck out. On A's advice, L accepted the MoD's offer of settlement in the sum of £10,000. L contended that A and W had been negligent in advising acceptance of the settlement and had expressed too pessimistic a view with regard to the chances of the action not being struck out.

Held, giving judgment for W and A, that W had been under a duty to exercise the skill and care of a reasonably skilful and careful litigation solicitor and in advising L, A had been under a duty to exercise the skill and care of a reasonably skilful and careful barrister specialising in defamation and malicious falsehood matters, *Saif Ali v. Sydney Mitchell & Co* [1980] A.C. 198, [1978] C.L.Y. 2323 applied. The fact that an exercise of judgment was necessary was in no way an abrogation of the requirement that reasonable skill and care must be exercised, *G (A Child) v. Kingsmill (No.2)* [2001] EWCA Civ 934 applied. The MoD had had, if settlement was not achieved, every incentive to apply for a strike out order, in order to avoid a lengthy trial at the suit of a legally aided claimant and A had been entitled to conclude that it would be remarkable if the MoD did not make such an application. This was an exercise of judgment in a specialist field and the circumstances had given rise to strong grounds for belief that the action would indeed be struck out on the basis of the substantial unexplained delay in prosecuting the case. A's strong assertion that the action would almost inevitably be struck out had therefore been justified.

LUKE v. WANSBROUGHS (A FIRM), [2003] EWHC 3151, [2005] P.N.L.R. 2, Davis, J., QBD.

2871. Professional negligence–Psychologists–Special educational needs–Failure to diagnose special educational needs–Causative link

The applicant local authority appealed against a decision that it was liable for the negligence of an educational psychologist in relation to the assessment of and provision for the special educational needs of the respondent dyslexic (C), and the subsequent costs order. The judge held that, but for the psychologist's failure to diagnose C's special educational needs and failure to recommend C's placement in a special school, C would have attended a special school for a period of three years. He further held that the breach of duty had caused damage to C in that he had been deprived of a specialist education by specialist teachers who would have helped him to overcome his difficulties with reading and writing. C was awarded £25,000 in special damages for loss of earnings. The local authority was ordered to pay all of C's costs, although some of his claims were dropped or rejected at trial. The local authority contended that (1) the correct test was whether attendance at the special school would have made "a measurable difference" and the evidence failed to establish that was the case; (2) the award for loss of earnings was speculative and had been wrongly allowed by the judge without giving a sufficient explanation; (3) C was entitled to only a proportion of his costs as he had failed to prove all but one of his allegations.

Held, allowing the appeal in part, that (1) there was sufficient evidence for the judge to find a causative link between the psychologist's negligence and C's loss of remedial teaching to ameliorate the adverse effects of his dyslexia. The judge was entitled to find for C on the basis of clear evidence which showed that the majority of pupils with similar problems who attended the special school derived some benefit. There was no need to find that attendance would have "a measurable difference" as that expression had not been used by the House of Lords in *Phelps v. Hillingdon LBC* [2001] 2 A.C. 619, [2000] C.L.Y. 1947. It was more accurate to say that the remedial teaching would probably have made "a real difference". (2) The evidence given to the judge was sufficient to entitle him to make an award for loss of employment and earnings. The method of awarding a lump sum was the correct approach and, in the instant case, the size of the award was not outside the permissible range, *Phelps* followed. (3) It was wrong to characterise all educational negligence cases as being single claims for a failed education over a period of time as if special rules applied to them. The jurisdiction to award damages in such cases was not to be seen as a charter for claimants to make allegations against all the professionals who had been involved in a child's education secure in the knowledge that, provided they succeed in one allegation against one professional, they would recover all their costs from the local education authority. The interests of professionals needed to be considered as well as the right of a child to claim damages in negligence. The allegations in the instant case could not be regarded as a single claim as they did not relate to a single episode or incident but related to different periods in C's life. The judge had erred in not reflecting in his costs order C's very considerable measure of failure in relation to wholly discrete issues. C should have been awarded 70 per cent of his costs, rather than 100 per cent.

CLARK v. DEVON CC; *sub nom.* DEVON CC v. CLARKE, [2005] EWCA Civ 266, [2005] C.P. Rep. 42, Mummery, L.J., CA (Civ Div).

2872. Professional negligence–Research and development–Tax relief–Negligent failure to provide tax relief advice

[Income and Corporation Taxes Act 1988 s.837A; Finance Act 2000.]

The claimant company (B) claimed damages for losses arising from breach of a retainer and negligence by the defendant accountants (S). B specialised in computer software and had retained S to provide taxation and accounting services. Following the Finance Act 2000, a new provision, s.837A, was inserted into the Income and Corporation Taxes Act 1988 clarifying the extent and meaning of "research and development" for the purposes of the 1988 Act and defining expenditure qualifying for research and development relief. S did not inform B of the new provisions and B did not become aware of the provisions until two years later when application was made for the consequent payment by the Revenue. In that two year period there had been a steady decline in software business and B had 'mothballed' its business. B had not kept records of the nature of the work that its staff had been engaged in from day to day and in particular whether such work qualified for the relief. S accepted that the failure to notify B of the possible availability of the relief constituted a breach of their retainer and negligence. B claimed that if it been told of the availability of the relief in good time it would have retained a skeleton staff and carried on its business to exploit its existing stock, complete development work and undertake any fresh work which was offered. B submitted that the absence of records proving its entitlement to the relief flowed directly from S's breach of duty in not informing B of the existence of the relief until after its business was mothballed. S argued that the Revenue had made payment on B's claims for the relief in error because B had never qualified for the relief, or if it had, only in respect of sums much smaller than it had actually received. Consequently, B having received payment of their claim for the relief, albeit late, had suffered no loss resulting from S's admitted breach.

Held, giving judgment for S, that the burden of proof rested on B to prove that it had suffered damage as a result of S's breach of duty and it was a necessary part of that burden that B had to satisfy the court that it had originally been entitled to receive the relief. In order to do so B had to show that, at any relevant time, it had been engaged in a qualifying project and if so, which employees were so engaged and for what proportion of their working time. No evidence had been produced that B had been engaged in qualifying research and development work. S could not be blamed for the absence of records of work done by B on potentially qualifying projects. Had the Revenue inquired into B's operations and received no further information than had been provided in evidence, B's claims for the relief would have been rejected. That was sufficient to dispose of B's claim. Even if B had been entitled to the relief, in the prevailing market conditions it would not have realised sufficient net revenue to cover the costs of maintaining itself even in a partially mothballed state, and there had been no real prospect of raising fresh capital to carry it forward until the market recovered. B would not have survived but would have been compelled later to carry out the further cost reductions. B's position would have been no different had S informed it of the potential for the relief and B had therefore not suffered loss as a result of S's breach.

BE STUDIOS LTD v. SMITH & WILLIAMSON LTD, [2005] EWHC 1506, [2005] B.T.C. 361, Evans-Lombe, J., Ch D.

2873. **Professional negligence–Solicitors–Consequences of solicitors giving incorrect advice**

The appellant (W) appealed against a decision that the respondents (P), his former solicitors, were entitled to their costs of acting for him and dismissing W's counterclaim for damages for negligence. A housing association had served on W a notice seeking possession of the property in which he resided and a notice to quit. W retained P to act for him in the subsequent possession proceedings, in which W counterclaimed seeking to exercise the right to buy. The association applied to amend its claim. The amendment was permitted on the grounds that the association pay W's costs up to that date. W was then advised that he had no defence to the possession proceedings. W nevertheless appealed unsuccessfully. The association obtained possession. W appealed but later withdrew the appeal. W changed his solicitors and P began proceedings for their unpaid fees. W counterclaimed for damages for negligence on the grounds that P should have advised him that the effect of the notice to quit was to terminate the tenancy and that the failure to give proper advice caused W to take a course which was bound to fail. The judge gave judgment for P and dismissed the counterclaim. W argued that (1) the case was one of incorrect advice on which he had relied and not of failure to advise, that he had relied on the advice and had suffered loss as a consequence; (2) he should not have to pay for P's work which turned out to be useless.

Held, dismissing the appeal, that (1) assuming that P had been negligent in failing to investigate the facts fully and to advise on the effect of the notice to quit, W had failed to show any loss flowing from that negligence. If it was necessary to categorise the alleged breach in the instant case it was a case of failing to give proper advice rather than giving incorrect advice, *Bristol and West Building Society v. Mothew (t/a Stapley & Co)* [1998] Ch. 1, [1996] C.L.Y. 4503 considered. W could not show that he had suffered loss by reason of P's failure to advise on the effect of the notice to quit because, on the judge's findings, he would not have acted differently if he had had that advice. He could not meet that point by showing that he had relied on other advice which P gave. That advice was not the real cause of his loss. (2) The work performed by P had not been useless. There was no total failure of consideration. P had put in a defence and counterclaim which had kept W's claim alive. That allowed him to remain in occupation and assert a right to buy. Some lack of skill along the way, which would not have affected how the case had been conducted, was not sufficient to deprive P of its fees.

WHITE v. PAUL DAVIDSON & TAYLOR, [2004] EWCA Civ 1511, [2005] P.N.L.R. 15, Ward, L.J., CA (Civ Div).

2874. Professional negligence–Solicitors–Deeds of variation–Speculation as to approval of deed of variation

[Mental Health Act 1983 s.95(1).]

The appellant trust company (J) appealed against the decision ([2004] EWHC 703, [2004] W.T.L.R. 533, [2005] 3.C.L. 393) dismissing its claim in one action and the respondent solicitors (K) cross appealed against the finding that they had been negligent in a second action brought by J. K had been retained by the executors and trustees of a will and J claimed to be interested, as trustee of a Jersey trust, in the property comprised in the deceased's estate. By the will the deceased devised certain land to his trustees on trust to permit his wife to occupy a dwelling house during her life and to pay the remaining income to her during her lifetime with power to pay capital to her or for her benefit. Subject to that he left the land to his nephew. The wife was at that time incapable of managing her own affairs and her brother was appointed by the Court of Protection to act as her receiver. With a view to reducing the inheritance tax potentially payable on the wife's death, the trustees applied to the Court of Protection for approval to vary the will to effect a surrender of the wife's life interest in exchange for a capital sum. A deed of variation was executed accordingly and £750,000 was paid to the wife. The nephew assigned his interest in the land to a Jersey settlement of which J was the trustee. J brought two sets of proceedings: The first action (the deed of variation action) a claim for damages allegedly suffered by reason of the negligence of K in connection with the application to the Court of Protection for approval on behalf of the wife of the deed of variation on the basis that the sum of £750,000 was substantially in excess of what should properly have been paid and that unnecessary costs had been incurred. The judge dismissed the claim holding that although K had been negligent it was purely speculative whether, even if there had been no negligence, the wife's receiver and the Court of Protection would have approved a deed of variation which provided for payment of less than £750,000. In the second action (the capital gains tax action) J claimed damages arising from negligent advice said to have been given by K in relation to capital gains tax matters. The judge found negligence on the part of K in disregarding counsel's advice and failing to advise the executors against vesting the land in themselves as trustees in 1997 before the death of the wife which gave rise to a deemed disposal of the land for capital gains tax purposes on that death. He directed an enquiry whether any, and if so what, loss had been caused by that negligence.

Held, dismissing the appeal and allowing the cross appeal, that (1) the judge had been correct to dismiss the deed of variation action on the basis that it was "purely speculative" whether the wife's receiver would have been willing to agree the variation at a lower price. There was nothing before the judge to indicate why the receiver was persuaded to withdraw his opposition to the Court of Protection application, and it was therefore impossible to hold that he could have been persuaded to withdraw earlier if the price had been right. Also the claim was bound to fail because there was nothing to show how the judge was able to come to the view on the material before the Court of Protection that a case for the exercise of its powers under the Mental Health Act 1983 s.95(1) had been made out. There was nothing to suggest that he, or another judge in the Court of Protection, would have come to that view if he had been asked to approve a variation which provided for a price of less than £750,000. So although K were negligent in their handling of the application, there was nothing to suggest that there was ever any real chance that the variation would be approved by the Court of Protection at a price less than £750,000. (2) Counsel had advised in 1996 that there would be a capital gains tax charge on the wife's death if the executors had assented to the vesting of the land in themselves as trustees before the wife's death, but his advice also assumed that there would be such an assent. The judge erred in finding that counsel had not advised that the executors should assent. Even if counsel did not advise that an assent should be made it was reasonable for K to advise the executors to proceed in that way despite the capital gains tax disadvantage because that liability was likely to be modest compared with the inheritance tax saving which it was thought might be achieved.

JEMMA TRUST CO LTD v. KIPPAX BEAUMONT LEWIS, [2005] EWCA Civ 248, [2005] W.T.L.R. 683, Chadwick, L.J., CA (Civ Div).

2875. Professional negligence–Solicitors–Draft will prepared but not executed–Failure to send out reminder

The appellant (JA) appealed against the dismissal of her professional negligence claim against the defendant solicitors (D). JA's father (W) had originally made a valid will leaving the whole of his estate to her. W realised that the will had been invalidated when he remarried and he contacted D and gave instructions to a partner (K) that he wanted to make a new will which would give his wife a life interest in his house and the beneficial interest in the estate to JA. A draft will was prepared and sent to W for his approval. There was no further communication between D and W, save for a circular letter which was sent out some two years later informing clients that K had moved to another firm and asking whether title deeds and wills should be transferred to K's new firm. W returned the enclosed form and made a note on the letter that the will had been transferred to K's new firm. W subsequently died intestate and the whole of his estate passed to his widow; upon her death, the estate passed to her daughter by a previous marriage. It was discovered that W had signed the copy of the draft will that had been sent out to him. At first instance it was held that K had not been under a duty to chase the matter up and that the evidence did not support the contention that W would have behaved differently had a reminder been sent out to him. On appeal, JA maintained that (1) K had been negligent in failing to send out a reminder and circumstances had not arisen in which termination of K's retainer could be justified; (2) the fact that W had signed the draft will and that he had made the note relating to the transfer of the will on the letter sent out by D demonstrated that W would have proceeded with the execution of the draft will had he been sent a reminder.

Held, dismissing the appeal, that (1) JA's reliance upon the retainer rules was misplaced. A solicitor who had prepared a draft will was under no invariable and inevitable duty to follow the matter up. It was not uncommon for clients to change their minds in such situations. It was the responsibility of clients to pursue the matter. The judge had been entitled to conclude that the failure to send out a reminder did not amount to a negligent failure to uphold the standards expected of a competent solicitor. (2) Neither the note W had written on the letter nor his signature on the draft will demonstrated that W would have executed the draft will had K sent out a reminder. The evidence showed that W had been fully aware of the consequences of a failure to execute a new will; a reminder from K would have made no difference to W's actions.

ATKINS v. DUNN & BAKER (A FIRM), [2004] EWCA Civ 263, [2004] W.T.L.R. 477, Pill, L.J., CA.

2876. Professional negligence–Solicitors–Duty of care–Counterclaim in arbitration proceedings–Failure to advise on professional indemnity cover

The appellant construction company (J) appealed against a decision ([2003] EWHC 2894) dismissing its claim in negligence against the respondent firm of solicitors (N). J had brought the action as assignees of N's former client (C), a company in liquidation. J had employed C as subcontractors on a large scale construction project. The contract required C to maintain professional indemnity insurance. C had instructed N to recover debts allegedly owed by J, and N had instituted arbitration proceedings. J threatened to bring a large contingent claim against C, but C failed to notify its insurers when renewing its cover. J subsequently served its defence and counterclaim. The arbitrator rejected C's claim but awarded J damages and costs of over £one million. C's insurers declined to meet J's claim on the ground of non disclosure or misrepresentation. J maintained that N's retainer had been extended to cover every aspect of J's counterclaim, including an obligation to ask whether C was insured against such a claim and to advise C to notify the claim to its insurers.

Held, dismissing the appeal, that N had not been retained to advise on insurance. C had been perfectly capable of dealing with such matters. The judge had correctly held that, faced with what was thought to be a tactical counterclaim, a reasonably competent solicitor would not have immediately asked about insurance and advised notification. That conclusion was supported by the fact that such questions had not occurred at the time to other experienced solicitors. With regard to causation, the judge had been entitled to conclude that C would not have followed any advice on insurance and notification that N might have given.

JOHN MOWLEM CONSTRUCTION PLC v. NEIL F JONES & CO SOLICITORS, [2004] EWCA Civ 768, [2004] B.L.R. 387, Judge, L.J., CA.

2877. **Professional negligence–Solicitors–Failure to advise client of means of securing share of project's profits–Loss of opportunity–Breach of fiduciary duty**

The claimant (B) brought proceedings against the defendant firm of solicitors (D) for professional negligence and breach of fiduciary duty. B had helped to create the Eden Project along with his co founder (S). B and S had instructed D in connection with the formation of the project. D advised that a charitable trust should be created as a vehicle for carrying the project forward and applying for funding from the Millennium Commission and other sources. B maintained that he had made it clear to D that he expected to share in the financial success of the project, but in the event, B obtained no financial benefit apart from his expenses. B argued that (1) D had negligently failed to protect his interests by setting up the trust without advising of the need to enter into a bidding agreement with the trustees to secure his right to a share in the project's profits; (2) D had been in breach of fiduciary duty by acting for the trustees in an action brought by B in the Chancery Division in an attempt to receive recognition of his asserted rights.

Held, giving judgment for B, that (1) the creation of the trust without any legal protection for B adversely affected his position. D's failure to warn B of this potential adverse effect and advise him of the need to seek a preliminary agreement with the trustees was negligent. B would have accepted such advice. Moreover, there was a real and substantial chance that S would have accepted such advice, that the trustees would have accepted a bidding agreement allowing for a fair and reasonable payment to B and that the Millennium Commission would have agreed to a reward for the founders by way of equity and/or royalties in view of the project's unusual nature. Taking account of the risk of failure, B was entitled to damages of £1,809,285 for loss of the chance of achieving a better financial outcome, *Allied Maples Group Ltd v. Simmons & Simmons* [1995] 1 W.L.R. 1602, [1996] C.L.Y. 4489 followed. (2) In acting for the trustees in the Chancery action, D had acted against B's interests whilst in the possession of confidential information as to his negotiating position and had thus been in breach of fiduciary duty. However, no damages would be awarded as B had already been fully compensated for the loss he had suffered.

BALL v. DRUCES & ATTLEE (A FIRM) (NO.2), [2004] EWHC 1402, [2004] P.N.L.R. 39, Nelson, J., QBD.

2878. Professional negligence–Solicitors–Implications of leading counsel's advice–Law firm's failure to explain implications

[Consumer Credit Act 1974.]

The claimant company (X) alleged that the defendant law firm (H) had been negligent in not explaining to its managing director (E) the implications of advice obtained from leading counsel as to the recoverability of hire charges under a credit hire agreement operated by X. X arranged the credit hire of vehicles to drivers whose own vehicles had been damaged in road traffic accidents and who could expect to recover the cost of such hire from the third party insurers of the other motorist involved in the accident. E had retained H and leading counsel in respect of a separate matter. In his advice, leading counsel pointed out that the credit hire agreement used by X was regulated by the Consumer Credit Act 1974 but was unenforceable against drivers because it did not comply with the Act, with the result that third party insurers might be able to resist claims for hire charges. He advised that the problem might be resolved by exempting the credit hire agreement from the Act by inserting a term requiring payment within 12 months. In subsequent advice, leading counsel reiterated his view. X was later the subject of an acquisition. Following the acquisition, leading counsel was once again retained in respect of another matter. He alerted E to recent county court decisions where third party insurers had resisted claims for hire charges where hire agreements were unenforceable for failing to comply with various provisions as required by the Act. E then left X's employment and X amended its credit hire agreement to incorporate the 12 month exemption. Thereafter, the Court of Appeal confirmed the views of the county court, with the result that X found itself unable to recover for hire charges in respect of the period before the credit hire agreement had been amended. X argued that H had failed to explain to E the implications of leading counsel's advice and that had E understood that the agreement ran the risk of being totally unenforceable, with the result that third party insurers would be able to resist claims for hire charges, he would have caused X to amend the credit hire agreement to incorporate the 12 month exemption earlier.

Held, giving judgment for H, that E was one of the most experienced operators in the field of credit hire in the United Kingdom and would not have initiated inquiries of both H and leading counsel as to whether the credit hire agreement was compliant with the Act if he had not understood the possible implications of compliance and exemption, so far as enforceability and recoverability were concerned. That was supported by correspondence with H in which he referred to the problem of recoverability. It was not surprising that E had not acted with any urgency before the acquisition as X had not experienced any problems with recoverability since its inception. Amendments to the credit hire agreement at the time would have required marketing changes and would also have alerted X's purchaser to a potential vulnerability in the business. Also, the prevailing view at the time was that the courts were unlikely to find for third party insurers on the basis of such a technicality. If E had not initially appreciated the full impact of leading counsel's advice, the same could not be said after leading counsel's post acquisition advice that drew the county court decisions to E's attention. In sum, E had fully appreciated the implications of leading counsel's advice. Even if that were not so, the court was not satisfied that H should have appreciated that E did not understand the implications and therefore H was not liable for failing to explain the implications to him.

ACCIDENT ASSISTANCE LTD v. HAMMONDS SUDDARDS EDGE (A FIRM), [2005] EWHC 202, [2005] P.N.L.R. 29, Hart, J., Ch D.

2879. Professional negligence–Solicitors–Incorrect advice–Acquisition of lease in company name rather than as personal lease–Potential consequences on resale

P sought damages from W, her solicitors. P alleged that W had given her incorrect advice. P had acquired a leasehold investment property using a company nominated by her. Therefore, instead of being acquired personally, the lease was acquired as a company lease. The motivation for that arrangement was to save tax on a resale of the property by avoiding capital gains tax and instead incurring a smaller liability to corporation tax on any profit made. However, the company lease could only be assigned to another company on resale. When P resold the property, it was on the market for more than a year and she had to lower the asking price significantly before she eventually achieved a sale. P contended that she had sought advice from W before the acquisition of the lease as to the potential consequences on a resale of the lease if it was acquired by a company nominated by her, rather than by her personally. P submitted that W was in breach of duty in relation to the advice given.

Held, giving judgment for P, that there was a breach of duty by W. It was foreseeable that if W gave incorrect advice to P on the implications of taking the lease in the name of a company, then the consequences could include a much more limited market for the property, consisting of just corporate, not individual, potential purchasers with resulting delay and other related losses on resale of the property. If P had been given the correct advice she would have decided that the risks associated with the company lease outweighed her desire to reduce the tax liability upon any profit or gain. P would have taken the lease in her own name.

POWELL v. WHITMAN BREED ABBOT & MORGAN (A FIRM), [2003] EWHC 1169, [2005] P.N.L.R. 1, Tugendhat, J, QBD.

2880. **Professional negligence—Solicitors—Settlement refused as result of legal advice—Discount to reflect chance other party could have refused settlement on particular terms**

The appellant (C), a firm of solicitors, appealed against an award of damages made against them in a professional negligence action brought by the respondent (M), a former client. M had instructed C in an adverse possession claim brought by W against him following the purchase of land. M had obtained £100,000 from G, the solicitors who had acted for him in the purchase of the land, in settlement of a separate professional negligence claim relating to G's alleged failure to discover W's pending application for registration of title to part of the land by adverse possession. W offered to abandon his claim against M for £25,000, inclusive of costs, in 1996. M having made payments into court totalling £12,000 between 1994 and 1996, C advised him not to settle as he would not be liable for any costs incurred after the payments in if W recovered less than £12,000 in damages. M therefore refused W's offer and W's estate, acting by his executrix, went on to claim possession of the land, £2,914 in damages and costs. M contended that he would have settled W's claim but for C's negligent advice, and the deputy judge awarded him £17,500 in damages, representing the difference between the value of W's land and the amount, namely £20,000, that M would, in the deputy judge's opinion, have paid in settlement, along with the costs that he had incurred since 1996. C argued that the deputy judge had erred by failing to take into account the £100,000 that M had obtained from G and by not allowing a discount to reflect the possibility that W might not have agreed to settle.

Held, allowing the appeal in part, that the loss caused by C arose after M's claim against G and should have been treated as a separate matter, so that no allowance could be made for the £100,000 that M had obtained from G. The two claims were unrelated, C's advice being a fresh act of negligence. The judge had incorrectly refused to discount the damages, since W might have refused to settle for £20,000, and the damages were reduced by 20 per cent to reflect that possibility, *Allied Maples Group Ltd v. Simmons & Simmons* [1995] 1 W.L.R. 1602, [1996] C.L.Y. 4489 applied.

MADEN v. CLIFFORD COPPOCK & CARTER, [2004] EWCA Civ 1037, [2005] 2 All E.R. 43, Sedley, L.J., CA (Civ Div).

2881. Professional negligence–Solicitors–Solicitors having two irreconcilable duties

The appellant (H) appealed against a decision ([2002] EWCA Civ 723, [2002] Lloyd's Rep. P.N. 500) dismissing his claim for damages against the respondent solicitors (B) for breach of their contractual duty. H had instructed B to act as his solicitors in respect of his property development business. He had agreed to purchase a development site, build flats on it and sell the developed property to another client of B. B did not disclose to H that they had a conflict of interest because they were lending their client the deposit for the purchase, nor did they disclose to H their knowledge that their client had been declared bankrupt and was a convicted fraudster. B's client failed to complete the transaction and the property was sold by the bank as mortgagee. H's business collapsed. In proceedings by H against B, the judge found that if H had been informed of B's client's antecedents, he would not have become involved in the transaction. The judge held that B were in breach of duty but that the breach had caused no loss. The Court of Appeal dismissed H's appeal on the basis that B's retainer and duty of disclosure to H were subject to an implied exclusion of information which B were obliged to treat as confidential.

Held, allowing the appeal, that (1) B could not properly act on both sides of the transaction in question and had been under a duty to inform H that they could not act for him and that he should seek legal advice from other solicitors. (2) The notion of confidentiality, as generally understood by lawyers, was not really relevant to the issues in the instant case. It was a solicitor's duty to act in his client's best interests and not do anything likely to damage his client's interests, so far as that was consistent with the solicitor's professional duty. To disclose discreditable facts about a client, and to do so without the client's informed consent, was likely to be a breach of duty, even if the facts were in the public domain. Disclosure by B of their client's past would have been a breach of their duty to him. (3) The Court of Appeal had been wrong to hold that the retainer of B by H contained an implied exclusion from the duty of disclosure. Such an implied term would not satisfy the well known tests for implied terms and would have amounted to H's agreeing that, because his solicitors had failed in their duty to tell him to take separate advice and had instead proceeded to act for him as well as for their client, in a matter in which they had a financial interest, their duty to him had to be curtailed in order to accommodate their first breach of duty. The notion that one breach of duty by B should exonerate B in respect of a subsequent and more serious breach of duty was contrary to common sense and justice. If a solicitor put himself in a position of having two irreconcilable duties, it was his own fault. If he had a personal interest which conflicted with his duty, he was even more obviously at fault, *Moody v. Cox* [1917] 2 Ch. 71 applied. B were not exonerated from liability by the fact that they could not satisfy their duty both to H and to their client. The quantum of damages due to H should be assessed by a judge if it could not be agreed.

HILTON v. BARKER BOOTH & EASTWOOD; *sub nom.* HILTON v. BAKER BOOTH & EASTWOOD; HILTON v. BARIKER BOOTH & EASTWOOD, [2005] UKHL 8, [2005] 1 W.L.R. 567, Lord Hoffmann, HL.

2882. Professional negligence–Valuers–Negligent valuation of rugby club ground–Failure to consider planning prospects–Measure of damages

The claimants (W), trustees of a rugby club, brought a claim against the defendant company (L), surveyors and valuers, for breach of contract and negligence arising out of a valuation of W's ground. In 1996, L valued the ground at £832,500, whereupon it was transferred to W's company in exchange for 100 per cent of the shares in that company at that valuation. A few months later, those shares were exchanged for shares in another company (LR) which had, unknown to W, received a valuation of the ground from another valuer at £5.7 million. The ground was eventually sold with outline planning permission for residential development for £11.9 million in 1999. W argued that L had been negligent in failing to make planning enquiries prior to valuing the land in 1996 and that its correct value at that time was £3.42 million. L admitted negligence in carrying out the valuation but argued that in 1996 there had been little prospect of obtaining planning permission. It contended that a correct valuation as at that date would have been £1.534 million to £1.64 million.

Held, giving judgment for W, that a proper valuation would have shown that the planning prospects at the relevant time were more than 50 per cent, and on that basis the correct valuation would have been £3.25 million. On the evidence, it was unlikely that W would have included the ground in an alternative transaction at that time because of the level of speculation and risk involved and would not have pursued the planning opportunities available. There was, therefore, no basis for W pursuing the same outcome as that ultimately achieved by LR in 1999. However, with a proper valuation W would have realised that value, namely £3.25 million, for the benefit of the club by the end of 1996. It followed that a fair assessment of the loss suffered by W was the difference between the valuation of £832,500 and the proper valuation of £3.25 million, amounting to £2,417,500.

MONTLAKE v. LAMBERT SMITH HAMPTON GROUP LTD, [2004] EWHC 938, [2004] 3 E.G.L.R. 149, Langley, J., QBD (Comm Ct).

2883. **Psychiatric harm–Employers liabilities–Damages for psychiatric injury arising from stress at work–Application of general principles to different factual situations**

The court gave judgment in six appeal cases involving claims for damages for psychiatric injury arising out of stress at work. (1) The employment of the respondent (H) as a nursing auxiliary in a centre for children with learning difficulties had been terminated as a result of her ill health from depression and anxiety. The judge accepted evidence that, but for pressures at work, her condition would not have become chronic or lasted so long. He found that H was in a high risk occupation that imposed on employers a higher than normal standard of alertness in respect of the risk of psychiatric injury and that the employer had failed to protect her from foreseeable harm as it was aware of her pre existing vulnerability and there had been complaints about staff shortages. (2) The respondent (B) had retired through ill health from his job as a senior lecturer following a breakdown. The judge concluded that the university knew of the excessive work burden on B and had enough information to realise that he was at a real and immediate risk of a breakdown. (3) The respondent (W) had given up her job as a customer services representative for a bank as a result, so the judge found, of a moderate depressive episode with panic attacks. The judge found that the bank had been aware through their occupational health department of impending harm to W but had failed to discuss it with her. (4) The respondent (G) had retired through ill health from his job as chief sub editor following a breakdown. He had written a memorandum complaining about his workload but the judge found that his employer could not have foreseen that his inability to cope was more than occupational stress. (5) The respondent (M) had retired through ill health caused by a colleague's sustained bullying for which his employer was held liable. The employer appealed on the ground that the damages for loss of earnings should have been apportioned to take account of non negligent stressors. (6) The respondent (X), a prison health care officer, retired with a stress related illness after dealing with an inmate's suicide. The foreseeability of his illness was tried as a preliminary issue and decided in his favour. His employer appealed, arguing that the judge had erred in finding them liable for X's stress related injury because he had identified a risk of harm to a group of workers rather than considering whether X had shown signs of impending injury.

Held, giving judgment accordingly, that the general principles to be applied in claims for psychiatric injury arising out of stress at work had been set out by the Court of Appeal, although care was required in their application to the particular facts of each case, *Barber v. Somerset CC* [2002] EWCA Civ 76, [2002] 2 All E.R. 1, [2002] C.L.Y. 3264 applied. Nothing said by the House of Lords on appeal had been intended to alter the practical guidance given by the Court of Appeal, *Barber v. Somerset CC* [2004] UKHL 13, [2004] 1 W.L.R. 1089,

[2004] C.L.Y. 2713 considered. It was foreseeable injury flowing from the employer's breach of duty that gave rise to liability for injury caused by stress at work. (1) There was no basis for concluding that caring for children with learning difficulties imposed on H's employer a higher standard of alertness to the risk that its employees would sustain psychiatric injury. The fact that H might be vulnerable had been confidential information and her employer could not be fixed with knowledge of it. Despite general complaints of staff shortages, in the absence of signs that she was particularly vulnerable there had been nothing to indicate that H could not cope with her work. It was not reasonably foreseeable to her employer that H would suffer psychiatric injury, so it was not in breach of duty to her. (2) The finding that B's breakdown was reasonably foreseeable was vitiated by errors of fact by the judge and was contrary to the weight of the evidence. There were no sufficient indications of harm to B's health arising from stress at work. The outcome of B's claim did not depend on his failure to use the university's counselling service but it was a factor that the judge should have given credit for when considering whether the university was in breach if its duty of care. (3) It would only be in exceptional circumstances that a person working part time would be able to succeed in a claim for injury caused by stress at work. The bank had breached its duty to W by failing to act on its own advice and to take steps to reduce the stress on her and the judge had been entitled to find on the medical evidence that this breach of duty had caused her to suffer an identifiable psychiatric injury. (4) The judge had been justified in concluding that the employer's response to G's memo had been reasonable. (5) Once the work related stress had been shown to be the cause of M's loss of earnings it was for his employer to show that there were other potential causes as well in order for damages to be apportioned. It had failed to do this, and the only non negligent stressors identified related to M's work. (6) X's employer had foreseen the risk of injury for the type of work but in X's case it had failed to implement a system that it had designed to deal with that risk. The mere fact that an employer offered an occupational health service should not lead to the conclusion that the employer had foreseen risk of psychiatric injury to any individual or class of employee due to stress at work.

HARTMAN v. SOUTH ESSEX MENTAL HEALTH AND COMMUNITY CARE NHS TRUST; BEST v. STAFFORDSHIRE UNIVERSITY; WHEELDON v. HSBC BANK LTD; GREEN v. GRIMSBY AND SCUNTHORPE NEWSPAPERS LTD; MOORE v. WELWYN COMPONENTS LTD; MELVILLE v. HOME OFFICE, [2005] EWCA Civ 6, [2005] I.C.R. 782, Lord Phillips of Worth Matravers, M.R., CA (Civ Div).

2884. **Psychiatric harm–Remoteness–Police officers–Involvement in fatal shooting–Foreseeability of harm arising from subsequent criminal and disciplinary proceedings**

The applicant local authority (S) applied to strike out three paragraphs of the claimant's (F) particulars of claim of the respondent. F was a police officer who had been involved in an investigation that had resulted in the fatal shooting of a suspect. Following the shooting an independent police force had carried out an inquiry pursuant to which criminal charges were brought against F. Although F was acquitted he was later subjected to internal disciplinary proceedings. F claimed that S had failed to maintain a safe system of work, which had led to the fatal shooting with the foreseeable consequences that F would be blamed, charged and disciplined; that it had failed to properly manage the post acquittal process, and that it ought to have foreseen, but had not, that such failings would cause him stress and psychiatric harm. S submitted that the damage claimed was too remote.

Held, granting that application, that F had no real prospect of successfully claiming that he had suffered damage as a result of any corporate failure on the part of S that had resulted in the fatal shooting. F was neither a primary nor a secondary victim and the damage claimed was too remote, *White v. Chief Constable of South Yorkshire* [1999] 2 A.C. 455, [1999] C.L.Y. 4059 applied. Furthermore, there was no real prospect of F successfully arguing that psychiatric injury had been caused by undue stress at work. There were no signs that F was particularly vulnerable to stress and at risk of personal injury even after the shooting, *Barber v. Somerset CC* [2004] UKHL 13, [2004] 1 W.L.R 1089, [2004] C.L.Y. 2713 applied. There was no common law duty of care owed by an investigating officer in respect of delay in the conduct of an investigation, *Calveley v. Chief Constable of Merseyside* [1989] A.C. 1228, [1989] C.L.Y. 2863 applied. Accordingly, there was no real prospect of success in the claim arising out of the decision to institute and thereafter to proceed with the internal disciplinary process after F's acquittal.

FRENCH v. SUSSEX CC, [2004] EWHC 3217, [2005] P.I.Q.R. P18, Wilkie, J., QBD.

2885. Solicitors–Date of knowledge–Damage attributable to loss of break clause in lease

See CIVIL PROCEDURE: 3M United Kingdom Plc v. Linklaters & Paines (A Firm). §433

2886. Standard of care–Landlords–Tenant injured in fall from front path with low wall into basement stairwell–Liability of landlord for tenant's injury–Tenant's contributory negligence

The claimant (L) sought damages for personal injury allegedly caused by the negligence of his landlord (O). L had sustained paraplegia when he fell nine feet into a concrete stairwell next to his front door, the path to which was bounded by a low wall. There were no eyewitnesses to the accident which occurred around 5 or 6 pm. L, who admitted to being an alcoholic, stated that he had spent most of that day travelling on public transport, and had consumed alcohol during the journey. He was carrying a heavy electrician's bag weighing about 30 kilograms. L contended that as he stood at the front door with the bag over one shoulder searching for his keys in his pocket, the weight of the bag caused him to overbalance and fall over the wall. L argued that O had breached his duty of care to make reasonably sure that users of the path were reasonably safe.

Held, giving judgment for L, that a professional landlord had a duty to take such care as was reasonable in all circumstances to ensure that people he anticipated using the path to the front door were reasonably safe to do so, and the standard of care was higher than that for a mere householder. O had to cater for all types of tenant and could readily have foreseen that any of them might return home in a state of inebriation. This was especially so in the case of L, who was O's longest serving tenant and whom he had seen drunk on many occasions. O's omission to act by putting a rail on the wall was negligent, but because L had encumbered himself with a very heavy bag and had been drinking, his contributory negligence amounted to two thirds.

LIPS v. OLDER, [2004] EWHC 1686, [2005] P.I.Q.R. P14, Mackay, J., QBD.

2887. Standard of care–Medical examinations–Failure to diagnose child's meningococcal infection

The claimant (M), suing by his mother and litigation friend (C), brought an action in negligence against the defendant general practitioner (H). H had been called out to see M when M suffered from a high temperature and repeated sickness during the course of an afternoon. On first examination, H concluded that M might have gastroenteritis. She also advised C to look out for any sensitivity to light and the presence of a rash. In the evening, H was again called out to see M. On second examination, H took M's temperature, examined M's rash and considered whether M was sensitive to the light. She concluded that M did not have meningitis. Later that night, C took M to hospital where he was diagnosed with meningococcal septicaemia and treated with antibiotics. As a result of the septicaemia M's right leg had to be amputated and he lost a number of digits on both hands. C maintained that, on H's first visit, she had informed H of symptoms indicative of meningitis, notably that M did not like bright lights. Consequently, M maintained that H fell below the standard required of a reasonably competent general practitioner in not referring him to hospital on the first occasion when she attended to treat him.

Held, giving judgment for the claimant, that (1) H's first examination of M did not fall below the standard expected of a reasonably competent general practitioner. H's assessment of the possibility of gastroenteritis was reasonable at that time and it was good practice for H to advise the monitoring of the situation with particular aims in mind. On the evidence, M had not expressed a dislike of, or shown a sensitivity to, electric lights by the time of H's first visit. C must have been mistaken in her recollection; if M had already developed sensitivity to the lights by the time of the first visit, it made no sense for H to have advised C, as it was agreed she had, to observe whether M became sensitive to the lights. (2) H's second examination was deficient and too cursory in a number of respects. H had failed to examine M's ears, limbs, neck and movement. Her examination of M's back and chest were deficient. H should have done more to check for stiffness, irritability, sensitivity to light and the existence of a rash. There were important deficiencies in the history that H took from M's family. H had failed to allow suspicion of meningococcal infection to exist during her examination when greater suspicion and enquiry was called for. The facts as they must have presented themselves to H could not reasonably lead to the conclusion H came to, namely that M's condition was better than at the first examination. If H had carried out a proper second examination, she would have referred M to hospital and M would have received treatment approximately three to four hours earlier. (3) The proper standard of care required of general practitioners should not be seen as requiring them, whenever they see a child with a high temperature, to refer the child to hospital. However, referral to hospitals in cases of suspected meningococcal infection should be made without waiting for the illness to develop to the point where specific signs and symptoms had developed. There was a requirement that general practitioners should assess the aggregate set of symptoms and signs that existed, even if those symptoms and signs could be individually capable of being assessed as non indicative of meningococcal infection. A doctor should consider whether, by reason of their aggregate presence or their totality, when taken with the general condition of the child, a decision not to refer to hospital would involve a calculable risk of harm to the child.

McDONNELL v. HOLWERDA, [2005] EWHC 1081, [2005] Lloyd's Rep. Med. 423, Newman, J., QBD.

2888. Tripping and slipping – Highway maintenance – Tripping accident on pedestrian crossing – Extent of statutory duty

[Highways Act 1980 s.41, s.58.]

The applicant (C) claimed damages from the defendant local authority (D) for personal injuries he sustained after tripping on a pothole in a road between two pedestrian crossing points. At the time of the accident it was dark and raining. D operated a policy that defects in the pavement or the carriageway were not recorded and noted for repair unless they were 25mm deep or 40mm deep respectively. C argued that (1) the defect had existed at the time of the accident, and since it had measured some 25mm or more deep, it had posed a real danger to pedestrians in breach of the Highways Act 1980 s.41; (2) since the defect had been between designated crossing pedestrian points, the pavement standard was applicable. A pedestrian would primarily look for vehicles on the road, not where his feet were falling; (3) the test for repair was not whether the defect was 25mm on the pavement or 40mm on the carriageway, but whether or not the defect posed a real risk to highway users; (4) on the balance of probability the defect had been present at the time of D's regular six monthly inspection, some six months after the accident, and it had either been missed or not recorded as being 40mm deep. A defence pursuant to s.58 of the 1980 Act was therefore not applicable.

Held, giving judgment for C, that there had been a breach of D's statutory duty. D was responsible for maintenance of the highway and the pothole had caused C's trip. The pothole had been on a pedestrian crossing at a busy road junction in a poorly lit area where there were shops, churches and schools. A person crossing the road would have had to look for vehicles potentially coming from three different directions. The pothole had posed a real danger to pedestrians in circumstances where the surface should have been as good as or better than the pavement, *Mills v. Barnsley MBC* [1992] P.I.Q.R. P291, [1993] C.L.Y. 2967 applied. A defence pursuant to s.58 was not applicable. This was a part of the carriageway where pedestrians were encouraged to cross and therefore, although six monthly inspections were adequate, D should have applied the pavement standard to that area of the carriageway. Had that been the case the defect would have been recorded and action would have been taken. D's policy had been defective and it could not be said that D had taken such care as in all the circumstances was reasonably required to secure that part of the highway.

IDOWU v. ENFIELD LBC, April 29, 2004, District Judge Bowles, CC (Romford). [*Ex rel.* Richard Nall-Cain, Barrister, 2-4 St Peters Street, St Albans].

2889. Vicarious liability–Control–Control exercised over door stewards

[Third Parties (Rights against Insurers) Act 1930 s.1 (1).]

The claimant (C) sought damages in negligence arising from an assault on him outside an entertainment venue owned by the first defendant (L) carried out by an employee (W) of the second defendant (S). The instant judgment was on liability only. S provided security services, including door stewards, to L. S had a contract for "combined liability insurance for the security industry" with the third defendant (F) covering both employers' liability and public liability. W was a door steward provided by S to L. In the course of his employment W had assaulted C. C alleged that L and S were each liable for the acts of W on the basis of their respective negligence. He sought to enforce the indemnity for public liability in respect of "accidental bodily injury". Default judgment had been entered against S after it failed to file a defence. C submitted that W was a temporary deemed employee of L so as to fix L with vicarious liability for W's tortious act against C and that the liability attaching to S was to be regarded as a liability for accidental bodily injury within the meaning of the insurance policy held by S with F. L submitted that assuming the level of control that L had over S's employees was such as to give rise to a situation in which the stewards would normally be deemed to be temporary employees of L, then, if those facts constituted the normal arrangements between club operators and security service providers, the requirement for "exceptional circumstances" referred to in the case law would require something in addition to that requisite level of control in order for vicarious liability to pass from S to L. F contended that the bodily injury had to be accidental from the perspective of the perpetrator and C's injury was not accidental from that perspective

Held, giving judgment accordingly, that (1) the paramount test for whether L could be held vicariously liable was that of the nature and extent of control that L had over the door stewards supplied by S, *Mersey Docks and Harbour Board v. Coggins & Griffith (Liverpool) Ltd* [1947] A.C. 1 applied. It was not relevant that in the contract between S and L there was a specific provision that all stewards provided by S would be employees of S and that nothing in the agreement should be deemed to render any of them employees of L. Having regard to both the contractual documentation, the regulatory documentation and the written and oral evidence as to what happened in practice, it was plain that L sought to have and did exercise detailed control, not only over what the door stewards were to do in supplying services, but how they were to do it. The control that L had over S's employees was such as to make them temporary deemed employees of L for the purposes of vicarious liability. Therefore L was vicariously liable for the conduct of W and was liable to C for the injuries caused by W's unlawful conduct towards him. (2) The core issue between the parties in respect of F's liability to indemnify S was from whose perspective the bodily injury had been "accidental". The use of the word "accidental" in the policy was not rendered otiose if viewed from the perspective of the assured. Furthermore, the natural way of construing an insurance contract was to construe it from the point of view of the assured and it would take an exceptional set of circumstances to make it correct to view a core provision, such as the instant one, from the point of view of a third party rather than the assured. F correctly conceded that, if viewed from S's perspective, C's bodily injury was accidental. In light of that fact, such liability for C's injuries as S had under the default judgment fell, within the cover provided under the policy, in the first instance to S. C was entitled to the benefit of that indemnity under the Third Parties (Rights against Insurers) Act 1930 s.1 (1).

HAWLEY v. LUMINAR LEISURE PLC, [2005] EWHC 5, [2005] Lloyd's Rep. I.R. 275, Wilkie, J., QBD.

2890. **Vicarious liability–Employers liabilities–Dual vicarious liability–Two separate employers vicariously liable for negligence of single employee**

[Civil Liability (Contribution) Act 1978.]

The appellant (D3) appealed against the decision that it was vicariously liable for the negligence of a fitter's mate who had caused a flood at a factory. The claimant (C) had engaged the first defendant (D1) to install air conditioning in C's factory. D1 had subcontracted ducting work to the second defendant (D2) and D2 had contracted with D3 to provide fitters and fitters' mates on a labour only basis. A fitter's mate supplied by D3, who was working with a fitter supplied by D3, both under the supervision of a fitter contracted to D2, negligently caused a flood. The judge determined that D3 and not D2 was vicariously liable for the negligence of the fitter's mate. The issue on appeal was whether both D2 and D3, rather than only one of them, could be vicariously liable for the negligence of the fitter's mate. D3 submitted that dual vicarious liability was not a legal possibility and that D2 alone should be liable. D2 submitted that D3 alone should be liable but that dual vicarious liability was a legal possibility.

Held, allowing the appeal, that (1) correctly formulated, the question to determine vicarious liability was who was entitled to exercise control over the relevant act or operation of the fitter's mate. To look for a transfer of a contract of employment was distracting and misleading. The fitter's mate's employment was not transferred. The inquiry should concentrate on the relevant negligent act and then ask whose responsibility it was to prevent it: who was entitled and obliged to give orders as to how the work should or should not be done. Entire and absolute control was not a necessary precondition of vicarious liability, *Mersey Docks and Harbour Board v. Coggins & Griffith (Liverpool) Ltd* [1947] A.C. 1 and *Denham v. Midland Employers Mutual Assurance* [1955] 2 Q.B. 437 considered. (2) On the facts of the instant case both D2's fitter and D3's fitter had been entitled, and if they had had the opportunity obliged, to prevent the mate's negligence. (3) It had been assumed since the early 19th century to be the law that where an employee who was lent by one employer to work for another was negligent, liability had to rest on one employer or the other, but not both. But the foundation on which that rested was a slender one and the contrary had never been properly argued. There was no authority binding the court to hold that dual vicarious liability was legally impossible, *Donovan v. Laing Wharton and Down Construction Syndicate Ltd* [1893] 1 Q.B. 629, [1994] C.L.Y. 6118 and *Esso Petroleum Co Ltd v. Hall Russell & Co Ltd (The Esso Bernicia)* [1989] A.C. 643, [1989] C.L.Y. 3392 considered. (4) Dual vicarious liability was legally possible and both D2 and D3 were vicariously liable for the mate's negligence. (5) If the relevant relationships led to the conclusion of dual control over the employee, it was likely that the measure of control was equal. That was so in the instant case and, applying the Civil Liability (Contribution) Act 1978, the just and equitable division of responsibility between D2 and D3 was equal. D2 and D3 should contribute 50 per cent of their several liabilities to C.

VIASYSTEMS (TYNESIDE) LTD v. THERMAL TRANSFER (NORTHERN) LTD, [2005] EWCA Civ 1151, [2006] 2 W.L.R. 428, May, L.J., CA (Civ Div).

2891. Vicarious liability–Health authorities–General practitioner indecently assaulting patients–Extent of statutory duty and common law duty of care

[National Health Service Act 1977 s.29.]

The defendant health authority (K) applied to strike out a claim for damages brought against it by the claimant (G). G were all former patients of a general practitioner who had indecently assaulted or negligently treated them. The GP had subsequently been struck off, convicted of indecent assault and sentenced to four years' imprisonment. G argued that K (1) had breached its common law duty of care towards them, that duty arising under the National Health Service Act 1977 s.29; (2) was liable to them for damages under the ordinary common law principle of vicarious liability.

Held, granting the application in part, that (1) under the provisions of the 1977 Act medical practitioners rather than health authorities were responsible for providing health services, *Gorringe v. Calderdale MBC* [2004] UKHL 15, [2004] 1 W.L.R. 1057, [2004] 5 C.L. 405 and *Stovin v. Wise* [1996] A.C. 923, [1996] C.L.Y. 4058 applied. Therefore K did not owe G a duty of care under the Act and that part of G's claim was struck out. (2) However, there was nothing in the Act that excluded the existence of a common law duty of care owed by K's employees to act on information received concerning the risk posed by the GP. It was arguable that K was vicariously liable for any breach of that duty, *Phelps v. Hillingdon LBC* [2001] 2 A.C. 619, [2000] C.L.Y. 1947 and *Caparo Industries Plc v. Dickman* [1990] 2 A.C. 605, [1990] C.L.Y. 3266 considered. There was a possibility that such a claim would succeed and it should not be struck out.

GODDEN v. KENT AND MEDWAY STRATEGIC HA, [2004] EWHC 1629, [2004] Lloyd's Rep. Med. 521, Gray, J., QBD.

2892. Books

Booth, Cherie; Squires, Daniel–Negligence Liability of Public Authorities. Hardback: £125.00. ISBN 0 19 926541 0. Oxford University Press.

Buckley, R.A.–Law of Negligence. Hardback: £195.00. ISBN 0 406 95941 2. Butterworths Law.

Flenley, William; Leech, Tom–Solicitors' Negligence. Paperback: £68.00. ISBN 1 84592 060 0. Tottel Publishing.

Powell, John; Stewart, Roger; Jackson–Jackson and Powell on Professional Negligence, 4th Supplement. Paperback: £49.00. ISBN 0 421 91460 2. Sweet & Maxwell.

Walston-Dunham, Beth–Medical Malpractice Law. Hardback: £29.99. ISBN 1 4018 5246 7. Delmar.

Walton, Christopher; Cooper, Roger; Wood, Simon E; Percy, R a–Charlesworth and Percy on Negligence, 4th Supplement. Paperback: £49.00. ISBN 0 421 90630 8. Sweet & Maxwell.

NUISANCE

2893. Floods–Foreseeability–Application of common enemy rule–Right to respect for private and family life–Protection of property

[Human Rights Act 1998 Sch.1 Part I Art.6, Art.8, Part II Art.I.]

The appellants (Y) appealed against a decision dismissing their claims in nuisance against the first and second respondents (C and M) for damage to their property caused by flooding. M owned a large recreation area known as Grove Fields, which was susceptible to flooding. In 1972 C agreed with M to deposit coal waste from an adjacent tip onto Grove Fields in order to raise the level to create a playing area. In October 1998 a river overflowed and caused damage to Y's properties. C and M accepted that the raised level of Grove Fields was a material cause to the damage. However, the judge dismissed the claims, primarily relying on the doctrine of common enemy and holding that it had not been reasonably foreseeable, at the time the work was carried out, that the infilling of Grove Fields might cause flood damage to Y's properties. Y contended that (1) the common enemy rule had no application on the facts because Y's properties were inland of the river and Y could not have been expected to take protective measures against the flooding; (2) the common enemy rule, if potentially applicable, should be more narrowly confined in the light of the court's obligation to protect Y's rights under the Human Rights Act 1998 Sch.1 Part I Art.6 and Sch.1 Part II Art.1; (3) it had been reasonably foreseeable that the infilling of Grove Fields might cause flood damage to Y's properties.

Held, dismissing the appeal, that (1) it was a necessary premise of Y's case that the flooding of their properties was reasonably foreseeable and therefore the waters of the river were a common enemy. Accordingly the common enemy rule applied. The fact that Y's properties were some distance from the riverbank had no legal significance. (2) The arguments relating to rights acquired by Y under the 1998 Act were irrelevant to the dispute between the parties as the Act was not in force at the material time. Nevertheless, the application of the common enemy rule was, in principle, inoffensive to Art.8 and Sch.1 Part II Art.1. The rule struck a balance between the right of the occupier to do what he liked with his own land and the right of his neighbour not to be interfered with. Furthermore, the rule balanced the interests of persons whose homes and property were affected and the interests of the general public, *Marcic v. Thames Water Utilities Ltd* [2003] UKHL 66, [2004] 2 A.C. 42, [2004] 3 C.L. 364 applied. The common enemy rule also satisfied the fair balance principle in *Sporrong & Lonnroth v. Sweden (A/52)* (1983) 5 E.H.R.R. 35, *Sporrong* considered. (3) None of the responsible agencies had thought that the infilling would have given rise to a flood risk to Y's properties. Indeed, it had taken a great deal of expert analysis and up to the minute technology to even establish that the infilling was "probably" causative of the damage for the purposes of the instant action. Thus, the judge had been entitled to conclude that it had not been reasonably foreseeable, at the time the work was carried out, that the infilling might cause flood damage to Y's properties.

ARSCOTT v. COAL AUTHORITY, [2004] EWCA Civ 892, [2005] Env. L.R. 6, Tuckey, L.J., CA.

2894. **Statutory nuisance–Noise–Evidence of two environmental health officers–Failure to justify rejection of evidence**

[Human Rights Act 1998 Sch.1 Part I Art.7.]

The local authority, W, appealed against a decision dismissing an information laid by it against M, a busker, alleging breach of an abatement notice. The district judge had, of her own motion, determined that there was no *prima facie* case to answer because (1) there was no evidence from any witness who worked in the affected premises; (2) there was no scientific acoustic evidence, and (3) the evidence from the environmental health enforcement officers was limited to observations from premises for no more than 10 minutes. M contended that, in relation to the Human Rights Act 1998 Sch.1 Part I Art.7, it was necessary for there to be certainty in order for an offence to be validly charged and pursued.

Held, allowing the appeal, that (1) in establishing that noise amounting to a nuisance had occurred in contravention of the requirement of a statutory notice, it was not necessary to prove that a particular occupier of property had actually suffered interference with his reasonable enjoyment of his property, *Cooke v. Adatia* (1989) 153 J.P. 129, [1989] C.L.Y. 2784 applied; (2) neither was the production of acoustic measurement evidence a precondition for conviction, *Lewisham LBC v. Hall* [2002] EWHC 960, [2003] Env. L.R. 4, [2003] C.L.Y. 3036 applied; (3) it had not been suggested that the time spent by the officers was so limited as to prevent them from properly assessing the volume and impact of the noise emanating from M. The mere fact that their observations were relatively short and from one location was not a proper basis for not accepting what they had to say. Accordingly, there was a clear prima facie case on the evidence that was called and the district judge had put forward no valid reasons for rejecting the evidence of two experienced environmental health officers. It was too early to seek to determine the issue in relation to Art.7, *Godfrey v. Conwy CBC* [2001] Env. L.R. 38, [2001] C.L.Y. 4550 considered.

WESTMINSTER CITY COUNCIL v. McDONALD, [2003] EWHC 2698, [2005] Env. L.R. 1, Royce, J., QBD (Admin Ct).

PARTNERSHIPS

2895. Contributions—Restrictions

PARTNERSHIPS (RESTRICTIONS ON CONTRIBUTIONS TO A TRADE) REGULATIONS 2005, SI 2005 2017; made under the Income and Corporation Taxes Act 1988 s.118ZN; and the Finance Act 2004 s.122A. In force: July 22, 2005; £3.00.

The Income and Corporation Taxes Act 1988 contain restrictions on the extent to which limited partners, members of a limited liability partnership and non-active partners can set off their share of a partnership's trading losses against their other income or gains. The restrictions are (broadly) that losses are restricted to the individual's capital contribution to the relevant trade. The Finance Act 2004 imposes a charge to income tax where an individual has claimed film related losses in excess of his capital contribution to the trade. The Finance Act 2005 supplement these provisions by giving the Commissioners of Inland Revenue a regulatory power to exclude amounts of any description specified in the regulations when computing the individual's capital contribution to the trade. These Regulations exclude amounts in two situations. The first is where the individual takes out a loan to finance a contribution to a trade, and the loan is on limited or non-recourse terms, or in the event, the cost of repaying the loan is borne, assumed or released by someone else. There is a backup test whether the individual's loan repayment costs over any period of five years are less than they would be on arm's length commercial terms. The second is where arrangements are made so that the financial cost to the individual of making a contribution to a trade can be reimbursed by someone else.

2896. Limited liability partnerships—Administration orders

LIMITED LIABILITY PARTNERSHIPS (AMENDMENT) REGULATIONS 2005, SI 2005 1989; made under the Limited Liability Partnerships Act 2000 s.14, s.15, s.17. In force: October 1, 2005; £3.00.

These Regulations amend the Limited Liability Partnerships Regulations 2001 (SI 2001 1090) which apply certain provisions of the Companies Act 1985 and the Insolvency Act 1986 to limited liability partnerships. The Regulations amend the modifications to the 1986 Act as set out in Sch.3 to the 2001 Regulations and make transitional provision for cases where a petition for an administration order has been presented before the commencement of these Regulations. In such a case the amendments made by these Regulations shall not apply.

2897. Partners—Solicitors—Solicitor holding himself out as partner in firm—Client's reliance on solicitor's representation

[Partnership Act 1890 s.14.]

The court was asked to determine a preliminary issue as to whether or not the second defendant (H) was liable in negligence proceedings on the basis that he was either a partner in the defendant firm (B) at the relevant time or that he was held out as such. The claimant (S) had been the victim of a scam engineered by a mortgage broker (W), who persuaded S to lend him money that he failed to repay. W arranged for B to act as solicitors for S and himself. S commenced proceeding against the two defendant partners of B alleging that they had negligently failed to protect her interests. An agreement entitled "partnership agreement" between the first defendant and H described the first defendant as "principal" and H as "partner" and provided that H was entitled to a percentage of fees payable to B in respect of one particular client. H's name was put on B's letterheads. During the relevant time, H was a partner in another firm and never had any personal involvement with B. It was common ground that the agreement did not create any partnership in law and that H had not taken a share in B's profits. S contended that H was estopped from denying that he was a partner in B at the material time and relied on the Partnership Act 1890 s.14. H accepted that he had held himself out as a partner but argued that S had not relied on any such representations.

Held, granting a declaration in favour of S, that the evidence showed that W had induced S to retain B as her solicitors on the basis that it was a two partner firm rather than a sole practitioner. H was estopped from denying that he was at all times material to the claim a partner in B.

SANGSTER v. BIDDULPHS (A FIRM); *sub nom*. SANGSTER v. BIDDULPH, [2005] EWHC 658, [2005] P.N.L.R. 33, Etherton, J., Ch D.

2898. **Partnership agreements–Dissolution–Transfer of partnership assets to limited company**

The appellants (D) appealed against a decision that a partnership between them and the respondent (C) had continued for a period of 18 years, notwithstanding that the partnership business and assets were transferred to a limited company which then operated the business. D acquired a freehold property together with the goodwill of a leisure caravan site business. C contributed towards the purchase price. An adjoining piece of land was subsequently acquired by way of a purchase of the shares by D in the vendor company. Shortly after, the freehold property was transferred back to the company, and the business was conducted by the company. Thereafter, the whole of the property was sold. After the sale, a dispute arose between C and D as to C's entitlement to a proportion of the sale price obtained. C commenced proceedings seeking a declaration that there had been a partnership between them and that it ought to be dissolved. At a trial of preliminary issues, it was determined that there had been a partnership between the parties and that it had not come to an end because of the transfer of the business to the limited company. D argued that as a matter of law, a partnership would normally be dissolved when all the assets and operational functions of the partnership were transferred to a limited company whose shares were issued to the partners.

Held, dismissing the appeal, that the judge had been correct to conclude that on the unusual facts, the transfer to the limited company of the business, previously owned and run by the partnership, and of the land, being the asset of the partnership, did not operate to dissolve the partnership, *National Westminster Bank Plc v. Jones* [2001] 1 B.C.L.C. 98, [2000] C.L.Y. 3471 applied. The facts of the case were such that they justified a departure from the natural inference that the partnership had been dissolved on the transfer to the limited company. There had been no allocation of shares to C in the company to which the business and assets of the partnership had been transferred. Additionally, C had not been involved in the decision to transfer the land and business from the partnership to the limited company. Where one of the partners had not been involved in the relevant actions at all, and had only been peripherally involved in those discussions, it would be difficult to establish that there had been an agreement between D and C that the partnership would be dissolved. Further, authority to carry on business on behalf of the partnership, even if extended to acquiring new assets, did not carry a right to agree to put an end to a partnership.

CHAHAL v. MAHAL, [2005] EWCA Civ 898, [2005] 2 B.C.L.C. 655, Arden, L.J., CA (Civ Div).

2899. Partnership assets–Dissolution–Meaning of "share of the partnership assets" in s.42 Partnership Act 1890

[Partnership Act 1890 s.42, s.44.]

The appellant (S) appealed against a decision of a master regarding the entitlement of the respondent (G) to a share of partnership profits after dissolution. S and G were partners at will in the purchase and running of a residential care home. S was manager, with net profits applied to his salary and then divided equally, and partnership assets belonging equally. They contributed equally to the capital of the partnership, although S borrowed part from G pending the sale of other properties, whose rent went to G in lieu of interest. G excluded S from the care home and ran it profitably on his own account. On dissolution, the assets sufficed to pay debts to non partners and advances from the partners, which were greater for G, but not to repay their capital in full. It was common ground that S owed G in respect of the repayment of the loan. The full proceeds of sale fell to be applied in accordance with the Partnership Act 1890 s.44. The master decided that S was entitled to a half share of the revenue profits between dissolution and winding up, subject to payment to G for his services. The issue between the parties focused on the meaning of the words "share of the partnership assets" in s.42 of the Act. S submitted that "share of the partnership assets" in s.42 meant "share of the proprietary ownership of everything belonging to the partnership at the date of dissolution having money value"; that the profits were attributable in part to the services of G, and for the rest, to the use of partnership assets; and that subject to payment to G for his services, the balance should be divided equally between them. G relied on *Taylor v. Grier (No.3)* (Unreported, May 12, 2003) and contended that the value of S's share of net partnership assets was nil or considerably less than half.

Held, dismissing the appeal, that under the partnership deed, S and G had equal proprietary interests in the assets of the partnership. In s.42, the words "share of the partnership assets" meant the outgoing partner's share in the proprietary ownership of assets belonging to the partnership, *Manley v. Sartori* [1927] 1 Ch. 157 considered, and *Pathirana v. Pathirana* [1967] 1 A.C. 233, [1966] C.L.Y. 8954 and *Popat v. Shonchhatra* [1997] 1 W.L.R. 1367, [1997] C.L.Y. 3874 cited. That construction was confirmed by the fact that, where in the Act reference was intended to be made to a partner's interest in "net assets" or the surplus of the partnership assets after satisfying the partnership liabilities, that was expressly stated. The only authority to the contrary cited was *Taylor*. However, the judge's reasoning in that case was flawed and was inconsistent with *Manley*, as well as with the obiter observations of Nourse, L.J. in *Popat*, *Taylor* not followed. The decision of the master was plainly correct as to S's entitlement to a half share of profits.

SANDHU v. GILL; *sub nom.* GILL v. SANDHU, [2005] EWHC 43, [2005] 1 W.L.R. 1979, Lightman, J., Ch D.

2900. Partnership property–Survivorship–Presumption that partnership property held in common–Evidence of agreement to contrary

The appellant (S) appealed against a decision that he had not become beneficial owner of the whole of a partnership property on dissolution of the partnership. S and the respondent (B) had been in partnership in the business of selling darts equipment. There was no written partnership agreement and profits were divided equally. S and B had purchased a property using partnership funds as an investment and for storing partnership stock. The transfer stated that they held the property on trust for themselves as joint tenants. After B's death a dispute arose as to whether the right of survivorship applied to the beneficial interests in the property. It was S's case that the property had ultimately been purchased outside the partnership for tax reasons and that they had specifically agreed to a right of survivorship in respect of the business as a whole and the property in particular. The judge below concluded that there was no express agreement between S and B that they would purchase the property outside the partnership and that consequently there was no right of survivorship.

Held, allowing the appeal, that (1) the judge had erred in viewing the issue solely in terms of whether the property was an asset of the partnership and had not considered whether S and B had agreed to vary the normal rule that property bought with partnership money was deemed to have been bought for the partnership. (2) S bore the burden of proving that a decision had been made to take the property outside the partnership. There was no support for such an argument and all the circumstantial evidence pointed to the property being bought for the partnership. (3) There was no inconsistency between a beneficial joint tenancy and partnership property; the only inconsistency was between the rule of survivorship and the presumption that partnership property was held in common. However, the presumption that partnership property was held in common could be overturned by evidence of an agreement to the contrary. There was clear evidence that S and B had agreed to take the property as beneficial joint tenants in full knowledge of what that would mean, *Barton v. Morris* [1985] 1 W.L.R. 1257, [1985] C.L.Y. 2944 distinguished.

BATHURST v. SCARBOROW; *sub nom.* BATHURST v. SCARBOROUGH, [2004] EWCA Civ 411, [2005] 1 P. & C.R. 4, Rix, L.J., CA.

2901. Books

Gray, Nichola; Brazil, Dominic–Blackstone's Guide to the Civil Partnerships Act 2004. Paperback: £34.95. ISBN 0 19 928570 5. Oxford University Press.
I'anson Banks, Roderick–Lindley and Banks on Partnership, 1st Supplement. Paperback: £59.00. ISBN 0 421 91500 5. Sweet & Maxwell.

PENOLOGY AND CRIMINOLOGY

2902. Crime prevention–Highways–Designated areas

CRIME PREVENTION (DESIGNATED AREAS) ORDER 2005, SI 2005 829; made under the Highways Act 1980 s.118B. In force: April 21, 2005; £3.00.

The Highways Act 1980 enables a council (which is a highway authority), for the purposes of crime prevention, to make orders for the stopping up or diversion of certain highways within areas designated by the Secretary of State. This Order designates areas within the cities of Nottingham and Wolverhampton, and the district of North East Lincolnshire Council.

2903. Crime prevention–Highways–Designated areas

CRIME PREVENTION (DESIGNATED AREAS) (NO.2) ORDER 2005, SI 2005 914; made under the Highways Act 1980 s.118B. In force: April 20, 2005; £3.00.

The Highways Act 1980 enables a council (which is a highway authority), for the purposes of crime prevention, to make orders for the stopping up or diversion of certain highways within areas designated by the Secretary of State. This Order designates areas within the Metropolitan Borough of Stockport and the Metropolitan Borough of Wigan.

2904. Crime prevention–Partnerships–South Somerset

CRIME AND DISORDER ACT 1998 (RESPONSIBLE AUTHORITIES) (NO.2) ORDER 2005, SI 2005 3343; made under the Crime and Disorder Act 1998 s.5. In force: January 1, 2006; £3.00.

This Order provides that two crime and disorder partnerships in South Somerset are to be combined to form a single partnership covering the area. The combined area will comprise the local government areas of Mendip District Council and South Somerset District Council.

2905. Crime prevention–Partnerships–South Worcestershire

CRIME AND DISORDER ACT 1998 (RESPONSIBLE AUTHORITIES) ORDER 2005, SI 2005 1789; made under the Crime and Disorder Act 1998 s.5. In force: August 1, 2005; £3.00.

This Order provides that the three crime and disorder partnerships in South Worcestershire are to be combined to form a single partnership covering the area. The combined area will comprise the local government areas of Worcester City Council, Malvern Hills District Council and Wychavon District Council.

2906. Domestic Violence, Crime and Victims Act 2004 (c.28)–Commencement No.1 Order

DOMESTIC VIOLENCE, CRIME AND VICTIMS ACT 2004 (COMMENCEMENT NO.1) ORDER 2005, SI 2005 579 (C.26); made under the Domestic Violence, Crime and Victims Act 2004 s.60, s.61. Commencement details: bringing into force various provisions of the 2004 Act on March 21, 2005 and March 31, 2005; £3.00.

This Order brings into force specified provisions of the Domestic Violence, Crime and Victims Act 2004.

2907. Parole–Release on licence–Return to custody–Reliance by board on prosecution for new offence

The claimant (C) sought judicial review of the decision of the defendant board to refuse to release him on licence and a mandatory order requiring the Parole Board to recommend his release on licence. C had been sentenced to 12 years' imprisonment for robbery and had been released early on licence. He had then been arrested whilst driving a van which contained 40 kilograms of cannabis and had been charged with conspiracy to supply a controlled drug. The Home Secretary then ordered C's recall to prison because of the arrest and charge. C was then granted conditional bail by the Crown Court in the trial proceedings. The prosecution in objecting to bail did not contend that there was a risk of reoffending. The grant of bail was ineffective because of the revocation of C's licence. The board reviewed C's release on licence five months before the date fixed for trial. The board decided that C was not suitable for release because of the original serious offence of robbery and its connection with drugs, his previous convictions and his recent arrest and charge. C submitted that the board had before it only the facts of the charge which he denied. He argued that the board did not have any of the evidence before it on which those charges were based and in those circumstances there was no material upon which the Parole Board could rationally conclude that the charge and his pending trial were evidence of the risk of reoffending. He also argued that the board should have taken account of the grant of bail and the fact that the prosecution in the trial proceedings had not suggested that there was a risk of reoffending.

Held, refusing the application, that the fact of a charge and a pending prosecution alone could not without more justify a conclusion that there was a risk of reoffending. The board, however, was entitled to consider the undisputed facts that C was driving the van and that a large and valuable quantity of cannabis was hidden in the van. It was also entitled to have regard to C's past association with drug dealers. The board was entitled to have regard to a judicial decision to grant bail but the board had to make its own decision under a different jurisdiction on what might be different information and facts. The fact that the prosecution did not rely on the risk of reoffending was of little, if any, weight. The board may, therefore, have proceeded upon an incorrect basis in considering that it was sufficient that C had been charged and that a trial was pending when deciding that there was a risk of reoffending. However, having regard to the imminent board proceedings to reconsider the matter and the imminent criminal trial, it was inappropriate to grant any relief in respect of the previous board decision and the claim for judicial review was refused, *R. (on the application of Smith) v. board* [2005] UKHL 1, [2005] 1 W.L.R. 350, [2005] 6

C.L. 396 and *R. (on the application of Brooks) v. board* [2004] EWCA Civ 80, (2004) 148 S.J.L.B. 233 considered.

R. (ON THE APPLICATION OF BROADBENT) v. PAROLE BOARD OF ENGLAND AND WALES; *sub nom.* BROADBENT v. BOARD OF ENGLAND AND WALES, [2005] EWHC 1207, *The Times*, June 22, 2005, Stanley Burnton, J., QBD (Admin).

2908. Prison discipline–Bias–Deputy prison governor ruling on lawfulness of search order–Presence at time order was confirmed

The appellants (C) appealed against the decision ([2001] EWCA Civ 1224, [2002] 1 W.L.R. 545) that disciplinary proceedings against them had been conducted fairly. C were prisoners who had refused to squat following a general order for a squat search of prisoners. In subsequent disciplinary proceedings, the deputy governor of the prison (D) ruled that in both cases the order to squat was lawful and he accordingly found each of the appellants guilty of an offence against discipline. D had been present when the general order for a squat search had been approved by the prison's governor. C submitted that D could not bring the necessary degree of independence and impartiality to the task of deciding whether the order was lawful, given that he was present when the general order for a squat search had been approved by the prison's governor. The respondent secretary of state contended that there was no real possibility of bias because D had not been exercising "any legislative, executive or advisory function" in respect of the squat order.

Held, allowing the appeals, that there could be no doubt that D undertook the adjudications in the best of good faith. However, by the very fact of his presence when the search order was confirmed, D gave it his tacit assent and endorsement. When thereafter, the order was disobeyed and D had to rule upon its lawfulness, a fair minded observer could all too easily think him predisposed to find it lawful, *Porter v. Magill* [2001] UKHL 67, [2002] 2 A.C. 357, [2002] C.L.Y. 3185 and *Lawal v. Northern Spirit Ltd* [2003] UKHL 35, [2004] 1 All E.R. 187, [2003] C.L.Y. 1251 applied, *Davidson v. Scottish Ministers (No.2)* [2004] UKHL 34, 2004 S.L.T. 895 considered. For D to have decided otherwise would have been to acknowledge that the governor ought not to have confirmed the order and that he himself had been wrong to acquiesce in it. To have avoided the appearance of bias, D would either have had to make plain at the adjudications that he had been present when the order was confirmed and sought the parties' consent to his hearing the charges, or stood down. Once proceedings had been successfully impugned for want of independence and impartiality on the part of the tribunal, the decision itself had to be regarded as tainted by unfairness. Accordingly, the findings of guilt had to be quashed.

R. (ON THE APPLICATION OF CARROLL) v. SECRETARY OF STATE FOR THE HOME DEPARTMENT; R. (ON THE APPLICATION OF GREENFIELD) v. SECRETARY OF STATE FOR THE HOME DEPARTMENT; R. (ON THE APPLICATION OF AL-HASAN) v. SECRETARY OF STATE FOR THE HOME DEPARTMENT; *sub nom.* R. v. SECRETARY OF STATE FOR THE HOME DEPARTMENT, *ex p.* CARROLL, [2005] UKHL 13, [2005] 1 W.L.R. 688, Lord Bingham of Cornhill, HL.

2909. Prison discipline–Life prisoners–Right to fair and public hearing–Additional days–Right of life prisoners tried by independent adjudicator

[Human Rights Act 1998 s.7, Sch.1 Part I Art.6; Prison Rules 1999 (SI 1999 728) r.51 (1), r.51 (20), r.53A.]

The appellant prisoner (T) appealed against the rejection of his challenge to the lawfulness of two decisions made by the first respondent prison governor that T was guilty of two offences contrary to the Prison Rules 1999 r.51 (1) and r.51 (20). T was a life prisoner who had been charged, whilst in prison, with the two offences and ordered to serve seven days' cellular confinement for each offence. The second respondent secretary of state found that the decisions should be set aside because there were material errors of fact and accordingly the findings of guilt were quashed. T argued that he was nevertheless a victim within the Human Rights Act 1998 s.7 because he remained at risk of a similar situation occurring in the future. Rule 53A of the 1999 Rules provided for a reference to an independent adjudicator where it became apparent to the prison governor that additional days should be awarded. No express reference was made in r.53A to life prisoners but it had been interpreted by the secretary of state and the prison service as excluding life prisoners, save where a determinate sentence prisoner was charged with an offence arising out of the same incident and his case was referred to an adjudicator. T submitted that he should have been tried by an independent adjudicator rather than by the prison governor and that (1) trial by the prison governor amounted to a breach of the Human Rights Act 1998 Sch.1 Part I Art.6; (2) there had been a breach of his right to a fair hearing at common law. T argued that it was irrelevant that he could not have additional days added to his sentence, as the outcome still had a potentially serious impact on his future liberty in that it would be taken into account by the parole board when it reviewed his case.

Held, dismissing the appeal, that (1) when considering the boundary between criminal and disciplinary proceedings in a prison context the question was at what point Art.6 was engaged so as to require adjudication by an independent adjudicator. *Engel v. Netherlands (A/22)* (1979-80) 1 E.H.R.R. 647 identified three main criteria as to whether proceedings were to be considered disciplinary or criminal under Art.6: (i) the classification of the offence in domestic law; (ii) the nature of the offence; and (iii) the severity and nature of the punishment, *Engel* applied. Those three criteria had to be considered in the context of the prison system, *Campbell v. United Kingdom (A/80)* (1985) 7 E.H.R.R. 165 applied. *Ezeh v. United Kingdom (39665/98)* (2004) 39 E.H.R.R. 1, [2003] C.L.Y. 2141 had emphasised that the first of the three criteria identified in *Engel* was no more than a starting point, *Ezeh* applied. Of much more significance were the second and third criteria. The three criteria were both separate and cumulative. It was difficult to envisage circumstances in which the third criteria in *Engel* would be met in the case of a life prisoner, although the possibility could not be ruled out. Article 6 was not engaged on the facts of the instant case. T, as a life prisoner, was never vulnerable to the punishment of additional days and there were no consequences sufficiently serious to trigger the third of the *Engel* criteria, even in combination with the other two. The penalty of which T complained was that his eventual release might be prejudiced. That did not trigger the third criteria because (a) that penalty was not imposed by the decision of the decision maker on the adjudication; and (b) any decision by the parole board not to release was a decision based on risk to the public rather than punishment to the prisoner. The decision to release or not was made by the parole board. (2) T's argument that there was a breach of his right to a fair hearing at common law sought to extract from the common law a principle of fairness that would impose a higher standard than that imposed by Art.6, which was, as already held, inapplicable on the facts of the instant case. There was no such common law principle. If T could not succeed under Art.6, he could not succeed at common law.

TANGNEY v. GOVERNOR OF ELMLEY PRISON; *sub nom.* R. (ON THE APPLICATION OF TANGNEY) v. SECRETARY OF STATE FOR THE HOME DEPARTMENT, [2005] EWCA Civ 1009, [2005] H.R.L.R. 36, Sir Mark Potter (President), CA (Civ Div).

2910. Prison discipline–Prison governors–Records pursuant to the Prison Discipline Manual 1995 para.4.23–Obligations on adjudicating officers

[Prison Rules 1999 (SI 1999 728) r.51 (20A).]

The claimant (G), a prisoner, sought judicial review of a decision of the defendant Secretary of State for the Home Department upholding a finding of guilt made against G by the adjudicating prison governor in disciplinary proceedings. G had been found guilty of using threatening, abusive or insulting racist words or behaviour, contrary to the Prison Rules 1999 r.51 (20A), towards the complainant prison employee. At the disciplinary hearing the governor had not allowed G to question the complainant directly, insisting that all questions were asked through her. The governor had failed to comply with the Prison Discipline Manual 1995 para.4.23 to record on form F256 the reasons she rejected G's defence. G contended that the governor had erred in (1) failing to consider adequately his defence; (2) requiring G's questions to the complainant to be directed through her, contrary to the Discipline Manual para.5.17. Further, form F256 was incomplete as there was no reference to the governor's requirement.

Held, refusing the application, that (1) the governor's evidence established that she had adequately considered G's defence, although she had not recorded this on form F256, and there was nothing to suggest that the reasons that she gave in her statement might have been composed after the event to support her decision. There was no statutory duty on the governor to give reasons and the adequacy of reasons was not, of itself, a condition of the legality of the decision. However, it was important that governors comply fully with para.4.23 of the Discipline Manual and that the prisoner, the secretary of state and the parole board were provided with a full and reliable record of the course of the adjudication and the reasons for rejecting a prisoner's defence, *R. (on the application of Nash) v. Chelsea College of Art and Design* [2001] EWHC Admin 538, Times, July 25, 2001, [2001] C.L.Y. 95 considered. (2) G's submissions regarding the requirement for G to ask questions of the complainant through the governor were completely untenable, as G had already made those submissions, but had not advanced them, in earlier proceedings. There was no reason why a claimant, having abandoned grounds of challenge, should be allowed to raise them again at a later stage. G had known at all times that he had been required to ask questions of the complainant indirectly and that the requirement was not on the record.

R. (ON THE APPLICATION OF GLEAVES) v. SECRETARY OF STATE FOR THE HOME DEPARTMENT, [2004] EWHC 2522, *The Times*, November 15, 2004, Lightman, J., QBD (Admin).

2911. Prison officers—Industrial action

REGULATORY REFORM (PRISON OFFICERS) (INDUSTRIAL ACTION) ORDER 2005, SI 2005 908; made under the Regulatory Reform Act 2001 s.1. In force: March 22, 2005; £3.00.

The Criminal Justice and Public Order Act 1994 enables the Secretary of State (or, in Scotland, the Scottish Ministers) to bring an action against any person who causes loss or damage by inducing a prison officer to withhold his services as such an officer or to commit a breach of discipline. The effect of the amendments made by this Order is that s.127 will no longer apply in relation to such an inducement in respect of a prison officer in England and Wales, or in Scotland, although it will continue to apply in respect of such a prison officer in Northern Ireland as well as in respect of a custody officer and a prisoner custody officer as defined in s.127(4)(c) of the 1994 Act.

2912. Prisoners—Release on licence—Transfer to mental hospital—Recall to prison following breach of condition—Power of recall

[Mental Health Act 1983 s.47, s.50, s.74.]

The applicant (M), a prisoner, challenged the lawfulness of the secretary of state's decision to recall him to prison after he had breached his licence conditions following his transfer to a mental hospital pursuant to the Mental Health Act 1983 s.47. M had been transferred two days before he was due to be released on licence and he was notionally on licence when an incident at the hospital occurred. M submitted that the secretary of state had no power to recall him to prison, and he was therefore in prison unlawfully. Since the transfer had taken place so close to M's release date the secretary of state had not imposed a restriction direction. M contended that the power to recall contained in s.50 and s.74 of the 1983 Act was confined to cases where a restriction direction had been ordered and therefore there was no power of recall in the instant case.

Held, refusing the application, that the sentence, and accordingly the power to impose licence conditions, continued to run, notwithstanding that there had been a transfer to hospital and notwithstanding the absence of a restriction direction, *R. v. Secretary of State for the Home Department, ex p. H (No.1)* [1995] Q.B. 43, [1995] C.L.Y. 4256 considered. The policy underlying the actions of the secretary of state was consistent with the approach that transfer did not affect sentence.

R. (ON THE APPLICATION OF MIAH) v. SECRETARY OF STATE FOR THE HOME DEPARTMENT, [2004] EWHC 2569, *The Times*, September 10, 2004, Collins, J., QBD (Admin Ct).

2913. Prisoners–Right to respect for correspondence–Restrictions on correspondence with NHS consultant–Proportionality

[Human Rights Act 1998 Sch.1 Part I Art.8.]

The appellants, the prison governor and the secretary of state, appealed against a decision that restrictions placed on the correspondence of the respondent (S) with his NHS consultant were unlawful. S was a Category B prisoner in a high security prison. He suffered from a life threatening condition. The governor initially granted his request to correspond in confidence with his consultant neuroradiologist. Under Prison Service Order 1000 Ch.36.21 that correspondence would be read as a matter of routine. The governor's decision was overruled by headquarters and S's medical correspondence was opened and checked for authenticity by the prison medical officer. The judge held that the restrictions placed on S's correspondence interfered disproportionately with his rights under the Human Rights Act 1998 Sch.1 Part I Art.8. The appellants contended that the judge's reasoning was flawed and that the matter should be approached deferentially by giving the secretary of state, as rule maker and author of the corrective direction to the governor, a wide margin of discretion.

Held, allowing the appeal, that the reading of a prisoner's correspondence was directed to the prevention of crime and the protection of the rights and freedoms of others. The requirement that S's correspondence with his neuroradiologist be read by the prison medical officer was a proportionate interference with his Art.8 rights. It answered the legitimate and pressing policy objectives tabulated in Ch.36.1 of the Prison Service Order. Short of withdrawing all scrutiny, there was no less invasive measure available to the prison service. Reading by the prison medical officer was not excessive. The process by which the measure was decided upon was not arbitrary, nor did the restriction deny the essence of S's Art.8 rights. The inescapable risk of abuse arising from the reading of S's medical correspondence, which had been minimised by confining surveillance to the prison medical officer, was outweighed by the foregoing factors. It was possible that in another case Art.8 would make it disproportionate to refuse to waive Ch.36.21 in relation to medical correspondence. However, in the instant case the appellants had established that the limited interference with S's Art.8(1) rights fell within the justification afforded by Art.8(2).

R. (ON THE APPLICATION OF SZULUK) v. GOVERNOR OF FULL SUTTON PRISON, [2004] EWCA Civ 1426, *The Independent*, November 4, 2004, Lord Phillips of Worth Matravers, M.R., CA (Civ Div).

2914. Prisoners rights–Freedom of expression–Right to work on autobiography prior to intended publication–Proportionality

[Prison Act 1952; Human Rights Act 1998 Sch.1 Part I Art.10.]

The appellant (N), a prisoner serving a life sentence for murder, appealed against the refusal of his application for judicial review ([2003] EWHC 3160, [2004] E.M.L.R. 9) of the respondent governor's decision to stop him receiving from his solicitor a typescript of his autobiography. N wanted its return so that he could finish working on it prior to publication. The governor relied on a standing order provision that provided that, subject to certain exceptions, a prisoner's general correspondence could not contain material that was intended for publication or that was likely to be published which contained details of an inmate's crimes. N contended that (1) the restrictions contained in the relevant provision of the standing order fell outside the powers conferred on the Secretary of State by the Prison Act 1952. N argued that the Act was concerned with the administration of prisons and did not confer power on the Secretary of State to prohibit publication of a prisoner's autobiography describing his offences, and (2) the provision relied on was an infringement of his right to free expression under the Human Rights Act 1998 Sch.1 Part I Art.10, and its application in the instant case was disproportionate.

Held, dismissing the appeal, that (1) the powers of the Secretary of State under the Prison Act 1952 included the power to have regard, when considering what a prisoner could or could not do, to the natural incidents of penal imprisonment. Whilst it was not easy to define what were the natural incidents of penal imprisonment, regard could be had to the expectations of right thinking members of the democracy whose laws had deprived the prisoner of his liberty. The wording of the relevant provision of the standing order struck the appropriate balance between what was and was not acceptable conduct on the part of the prisoner, *Raymond v. Honey* [1983] 1 A.C. 1, [1982] C.L.Y. 2613 and *R. v. Secretary of State for the Home Department, ex p. Simms* [2000] 2 A.C. 115, [1999] C.L.Y. 4105 distinguished, *R. (on the application of Mellor) v. Secretary of State for the Home Department* [2001] EWCA Civ 472, [2002] Q.B. 13, [2001] C.L.Y. 4579 applied. (2) The application of the provision in the standing order was not a disproportionate interference with N's Art.10 right. It was not disproportionate if imprisonment carried with it some restrictions on freedom of expression nor for those restrictions to have regard to the effect of the exercise of that freedom outside the prison. There was no evidence that N intended to use the work to make serious representations about the safety of his conviction or the penal system. In the circumstances the Secretary of State's decision was entirely lawful.

R. (ON THE APPLICATION OF NILSEN) v. FULL SUTTON PRISON GOVERNOR; *sub nom.* NILSEN v. FULL SUTTON PRISON GOVERNOR, [2004] EWCA Civ 1540, [2005] 1 W.L.R. 1028, Lord Phillips of Worth Matravers, M.R., CA (Civ Div).

2915. Prisoners rights—Mental hospitals—Prison Service believing prisoner ought to be transferred—Secretary of state's duties

[Mental Health Act 1983 s.47; Human Rights Act 1998 Sch.1 Part I Art.8.]

The claimant (D) sought declarations that the first defendant secretary of state and the second defendant National Assembly for Wales (W) had delayed in transferring him from prison to an appropriate hospital and thereby had infringed his rights to private and family life under the Human Rights Act 1998 Sch.1 Part I Art.8. While detained at a young offender institution in Wales, D had engaged in self harm and showed symptoms of mental disorder. Psychiatrists discussed transfer to a secure hospital over an eight month period. Following the commencement of the instant proceedings, a place in a secure hospital was allocated to D for a date 10 days after his release. By a consent order, the Prison Service undertook to get the two medical recommendations necessary for his interim transfer under the Mental Health Act 1983 s.47, and the Mental Health Unit of the Home Office undertook to speed up the matter. The secretary of state was unable to locate an interim placement but, under pressure of a court order to facilitate the matter, the secure hospital admitted D immediately on his release. It was common ground that D improved after transfer. D submitted that the defendants were responsible for the delay in transferring him to a suitable secure hospital for psychiatric treatment, thereby infringing his rights under Art.8. The secretary of state argued that the duty only arose in appropriate circumstances, according to the provisions of the Code of Practice s.118, unless there was good reason otherwise. W submitted that its duty was limited to planning, purchase or monitoring of the delivery of specialised child and adolescent mental health services, and that the duty was to fund D's treatment, not to identify a suitable placement.

Held, refusing the application, that once the Prison Service had reasonable grounds to believe that a prisoner required treatment in a mental hospital, the secretary of state was under a duty expeditiously to take reasonable steps to obtain appropriate medical advice and, if transfer was advised, to take reasonable steps to effect a transfer. The steps that were reasonable would depend on the circumstances, including the apparent risk to the health of the prisoner if no transfer was effected. On the facts, D's suffering in the institution was not the result of any breach by the secretary of state or W of D's Convention rights. The delay arose from the difficulties in satisfying the conditions for the exercise of the power under s.47 of the Act, and especially from the lack of agreement as to diagnosis and treatment and the lack of appropriate places in institutions caring for young persons with mental disorders generally, and for those with D's disorder in particular. (Obiter) The establishment of a secure database of suitable hospitals would have expedited the matter and if a claim such as D's were to be made in future, on the basis that the lack of such a database caused an infringement of Convention rights, the finding of the court might be different. Complex claims like the instant one should be treated procedurally as professional negligence claims, and the parties should have clear notice of specific allegations.

D v. SECRETARY OF STATE FOR THE HOME DEPARTMENT; *sub nom.* R. (ON THE APPLICATION OF D) v. SECRETARY OF STATE FOR THE HOME DEPARTMENT, [2004] EWHC 2857, *The Times*, December 27, 2004, Stanley Burnton, J., QBD (Admin).

2916.   Prisoners rights–Parole Board–Lawfulness of special advocate procedure

[Criminal Justice Act 1991 Sch.5 para.1 (2); Crime (Sentences) Act 1997 s.28; Criminal Justice Act 2003.]

The appellant (R) appealed against a decision ([2004] EWCA Civ 1031, [2005] Q.B. 410, [2004] C.L.Y. 2779) to dismiss his appeal in respect of the procedure used in the appointment of a special advocate in a "closed" parole hearing. In 1966 R had received a mandatory sentence of life imprisonment, with a tariff of 30 years, for the murder of three police officers. Following an initial Parole Board review R had been transferred in 2000 to an open prison. After allegations that R had been involved in drug dealing and other unlawful behaviour, he was returned to a closed prison in 2001 pending completion of his ongoing review by the board. During the review, the secretary of state put before the board material that had been withheld from R and his solicitor relating to R's removal back to the closed prison. After balancing the interests of the public, R's interests and those of the source of the sensitive material, the board ruled that the material should only be disclosed to a specially appointed advocate and not to R or his legal representatives. R applied for judicial review, and the judge conducted a two stage hearing; in the first stage R's counsel was present and in the second, which took place in the absence of R's counsel, the withheld material was heard. R's application was refused and he applied to the Court of Appeal to challenge the lawfulness of the proposed procedure in principle. His appeal was dismissed. R submitted, inter alia, that as a question of vires, the board had no power to create and apply, to the detriment of a life sentence prisoner's legal right to an adversarial hearing, a special advocate procedure absent of express legal authority.

Held, dismissing the appeal (Lords Bingham and Steyn dissenting), that (1) there was an express authorisation to withhold any information contained in the Parole Board Rules 2004 r.6(3) but, if that was wrong, the authorisation was to be implied from the duty of the board to conduct hearings which would enable it to reconcile the interests of the prisoner, the public and the informant. The authorisation to appoint a special advocate was implied from the implicit duty of the board under the Crime (Sentences) Act 1997 s.28 to conduct its decision making process in a manner which was practical and appropriate in the circumstances to ensure that the prisoner was fairly treated. Provided the appointment of a special advocate was not used as an excuse to lower the standards of fairness, the presence of the special advocate could only mitigate the disadvantage to which the prisoner would otherwise be subject, and the legislation and rules should not be interpreted as preventing the use of a special advocate. In the instant case, there was no reason why a special advocate should not have been appointed. Courts should be slow to restrict the implied power of an administrative body to enhance the fairness available to a person who would be otherwise adversely affected. (2) The board had an implied power under domestic administrative law to control its own procedure so as to deal with a person in the position of R as fairly as the circumstances permitted. A special advocate was able to advance R's contentions and the board was able to evaluate his arguments, taking into account the "closed facts", and give a "closed judgment" on those facts. The result may have been adverse to R but the fact that the process could be taken showed its value. (3) The appointment of a special advocate was not detrimental to any legal right of the prisoner. The appointment of a special advocate should not be used as a justification for reducing the rights that the prisoner would otherwise have but should be used as a way of mitigating the disadvantage that he would otherwise suffer. Any complaint of R should not have been directed at the use of the special advocate but at the non disclosure. If there was no right by the secretary of state of non disclosure to R, then the special advocate could not correct the failure to make disclosure. It was only if the secretary of state had a right of non disclosure that the special advocate could have a role. That the special advocate procedure had a role in appropriate circumstances was inherent in the flexible nature of the requirement that R was treated with fairness. (4) Although there was a minimum entitlement for any life prisoner to be able to test evidence bearing on the legality of his detention, there was an issue as to what was the minimum and the instant case was being approached as a matter of principle. The instant case could not be approached on the facts as the facts were unknown. The nature of the panel who made the decision provided the greatest protection for the prisoner owing to the need to balance carefully the conflicting interests before deciding whether non disclosure was justified. (5) (Per Lords Bingham and Steyn) There was nothing in the Criminal Justice Act 1991 or the Criminal Justice Act 2003 which expressly authorised the board to hold an oral hearing which did not accord with the principles of natural justice. Existing situations in which specially appointed advocates were appointed had been authorised by primary legislation under rules approved in Parliament. Schedule 5 para.1 (2) of the 1991 Act, empowering the board to do such things and enter into such transactions as were incidental or conducive to its statutory functions, could not be taken to imply an intention by Parliament to authorise a procedure which interfered with the exercise of fundamental rights. The appointment of the special advocate was ultra vires.

R. (ON THE APPLICATION OF ROBERTS) v. PAROLE BOARD; *sub nom.* ROBERTS v. PAROLE BOARD, [2005] UKHL 45, [2005] 2 A.C. 738, Lord Bingham of Cornhill, HL.

2917. Prisoners rights–Young offender institutions–Opportunity to make representations before making of segregation order

[Children Act 1989.]

The appellant secretary of state appealed against a decision in judicial review proceedings that a prison governor's decision to segregate the respondent (S) had been unfair because S had not been given the opportunity to make representations before the segregation order was made. S, who was aged 17 and on remand awaiting sentence on a charge of robbery which had involved violence, had been placed in a segregation unit pursuant to the institution's rules in order to maintain good order and discipline. The reason for the segregation, which was given in writing to S at the time of her removal to the segregation unit, was that it was necessary for the safety of others following her disclosure that she had felt like putting razor blades in a piece of soap to harm someone. She was not asked to comment on the reason for her removal. The secretary of state submitted that the post decision safeguards in relation to segregation were such that fairness did not require that S be given an opportunity to comment prior to the making of the decision. S submitted that if she had been given the opportunity to respond to the allegation made against her, she would have explained that what she had said was in response to having been bullied by another inmate and had said it in anger, without meaning what she had said.

Held, dismissing the appeal, that the judge had been right in his conclusion that given the importance of the governor's initial decision, fairness in this context did require that S should have been given the opportunity to make representations before a segregation order was made. He was also correct to conclude that he was not bound by *R. v. Deputy Governor of Parkhurst Prison, ex p. Hague* [1992] 1 A.C. 58, [1992] C.L.Y. 3651, since the claimant in the instant case was a child, *Hague* distinguished. This conclusion applied to inmates who were under the age of 18 and who faced removal to a segregation unit for reasons of good order and discipline, but did not extend beyond an opportunity to comment on the "tentative" reasons for the segregation. It did not provide an inmate with the rights available when disciplinary charges were brought. Any decision to remove to a segregation unit was made on a factual basis and the best way of checking the facts was by asking for a prisoner's comments before a decision was made, after which time it would be difficult to persuade the decision maker that his decision had been wrong, *R. v. Secretary of State for the Home Department, ex p. Hickey (No.2)* [1995] 1 W.L.R. 734, [1995] C.L.Y. 960 applied. The contemporary standards of fairness and the principles in the Prison Service Order 4950 required the secretary of state to give S an opportunity to make representations before the order was made. There was a substantial difference between the regime for a 17 year old prisoner in her own unit and in the segregation regime. Although not a formal punishment, in reality removal to the segregation unit was the most severe punishment that could be awarded following disciplinary charges for an inmate of a young offender institution. If S had been given the opportunity to respond, that might have influenced the initial decision and steps taken to prevent further bullying, thus fulfilling Prison Service Order requirements to deal with inmates "fairly and openly". Fairness also played a part in helping to prevent unnecessary grievances within the closed prison service, *R. (on the application of Daly) v. Secretary of State for the Home Department* [2001] UKHL 26, [2001] 2 A.C. 532, [2001] C.L.Y. 4578 applied. Further, obtaining the child inmate's views about the tentative reasons for removing her from her unit and friends was consistent with the paramountcy principle of safeguarding a child's welfare pursuant to the Children Act 1989.

R. (ON THE APPLICATION OF P) v. SECRETARY OF STATE FOR THE HOME DEPARTMENT; *sub nom.* SECRETARY OF STATE FOR THE HOME DEPARTMENT v. SP; R. (ON THE APPLICATION OF SP) v. SECRETARY OF STATE FOR THE HOME DEPARTMENT, [2004] EWCA Civ 1750, *The Times*, January 21, 2005, Ward, L.J., CA (Civ Div).

2918. Prisons—Health care

PRISON (AMENDMENT) (NO.2) RULES 2005, SI 2005 3437; made under the Prison Act 1952 s.47. In force: January 3, 2006; £3.00.

These Rules amend the Prison Rules 1999 (SI 1999 728) to include a definition of "fixed-term prisoner", "health care professional" and "the 2003 Act". They enable registered medical practitioners, registered nurses and other health care professionals to work with medical officers in providing health care for prisoners; enable the relevant registered medical practitioner to report to the governor on a prisoner's health; enable any person deemed by the governor to be competent to inspect and report on food deficiencies; provide that medical officers or practitioners are no longer to prescribe intoxicating liquor to prisoners; remove the requirement in r.29 for every prisoner to be medically assessed prior to undergoing physical activity; enable the relevant medical practitioner or registered nurse to provide a note excusing a prisoner from work; provide that the decision to remove a prisoner from association rests with the Secretary of State, and to require the governor to consider any recommendation of a registered medical practitioner when considering whether to return the prisoner to association; and remove the role of boards of visitors in authorising temporary confinement of a prisoner.

2919. Prisons-Rules

PRISON (AMENDMENT) RULES 2005, SI 2005 869; made under the Prison Act 1952 s.47. In force: April 18, 2005; £3.00.

These Rules amend the Prison Rules 1999 (SI 1999 728) to provide that references to an "adjudicator" mean a District Judge (Magistrates' Courts) or a Deputy District Judge (Magistrates' Courts) approved by the Lord Chancellor; to prohibit a copy of any personal record being given to a person not authorised to receive it; to establish the procedure which is to apply where an officer requires a prisoner to provide a sample under the Prison Act 1952 s.16B; to change the way in which certain offences under the Prison Rules apply; and to provide a defence to the disciplinary offences of being intoxicated or having consumed alcohol. They also provide for a reviewer to review a punishment imposed by an adjudicator and sets out the procedure to be followed when a prisoner requests such a review; provide that the Secretary of State may not under that rule consider adjudications referred to an adjudicator, although a governor may do so on grounds of good behaviour; and provide that those visiting prisons in whatever capacity may be photographed, fingerprinted or required to submit to other physical measurement.

2920. Release on licence-Return to custody-Requirement for Parole Board to hold oral hearing-Compatibility with Sch.1 Part I Art.5 and Sch.1 Part I Art.6 Human Rights Act 1998

[Human Rights Act 1998 Sch.1 Part I Art.5, Art.6.]

The appellants (S and W), formerly prisoners serving determinate sentences, appealed against decisions ([2003] EWCA Civ 1269, [2004] 1 W.L.R. 421 and [2002] EWCA Civ 1641, [2003] 1 W.L.R. 705) upholding the refusal of the Parole Board to hold oral hearings in respect of their opposition to the revocation of their licences. W had been sentenced to three years' imprisonment for affray. He was released on licence after serving half the sentence. W's licence had been revoked and he had been recalled to prison following allegations that he had breached the terms of his licence by visiting his former partner, staying other than at his approved address and failing to keep an appointment with his probation officer. W's solicitors had made written representations on his behalf and requested an oral hearing because W wanted to explore the facts which the probation officer alleged justified the recall. The board rejected W's version of the facts and declined to hold a hearing. W served the remaining eight months of the licence period before being released. S had been sentenced to eight years' imprisonment for rape and making threats to kill. He was released on licence but recalled because although he had otherwise complied with his licence conditions, he had tested positive on two occasions for class A drugs. S's solicitors made lengthy written representations to the board, although they did not request an oral hearing. S's application for release was refused by the board and he served the remaining 22 months of his sentence. S and W argued that where a prisoner sought to resist the revocation of his licence, the board should offer an oral hearing at which the prisoner could present his arguments. The failure to offer that opportunity was procedurally unfair and contravened the Human Rights Act 1998 Sch.1 Part I Art.5 and both the civil and criminal limbs of Sch.1 Part I Art.6.

Held, allowing the appeals, that while the common law duty of procedural fairness did not require the board to hold an oral hearing in every case where a determinate sentence prisoner released on licence resisted his recall to prison, the board's duty was not as constricted as had hitherto been held and assumed. Even if important facts were not in dispute, they might be open to explanation or mitigation, or might lose some of their significance in the light of other new facts. While the board's task was certainly to assess risk, it might well be greatly assisted in discharging that task by exposure to the prisoner or the questioning of those who had dealt with him. It could often be very difficult to address effective representations without knowing the points which were troubling the decision maker. The prisoner should have the benefit of a procedure which fairly reflected, on the facts of his case, the importance of what was at stake for him and for society. In the instant case, S and W should have been offered an oral hearing. (2) It was plain that in cases such as the instant case, the sentence of the trial court satisfied Art.5(1) not only in relation to the initial term served by the prisoner but also in relation to revocation and recall, since conditional release subject to the possibility of recall formed an integral component of the composite sentence passed by the court. Further, the board's review of a recall would satisfy the requirements of Art.5(4) provided that it was conducted in a manner which met the requirement of procedural fairness. (3) As to Art.6, while a challenge to the revocation of a licence could lead to detention imposed to protect the public, it could not lead to punishment; it could not therefore be said that a revocation hearing involved the determination of a criminal charge. The question whether the civil right under Art.6(1) was engaged had to be decided in the light of the proceedings that were in issue and the nature of the dispute. The Art.6 civil right was not infringed by proceedings of the kind that were in issue in the instant case, so long as the individual had access to the domestic courts to assert his right to liberty. The proceedings of the board did not deprive S or W of that right of access.

R. (ON THE APPLICATION OF SMITH) v. PAROLE BOARD; R. (ON THE APPLICATION OF WEST) v. PAROLE BOARD; *sub nom.* SMITH v. PAROLE BOARD, [2005] UKHL 1, [2005] 1 W.L.R. 350, Lord Bingham of Cornhill, HL.

2921. **Return to custody–Life prisoners–Importance of giving full and prompt reasons–Delay–Measure of damages for delay**

[Crime (Sentences) Act 1997 s.32(1); Human Rights Act 1998 Sch.1 Part I Art.5.]

The claimant (H), a life prisoner who had been released on licence, sought judicial review of several aspects of his recall to prison. Having been released on life licence after almost 25 years in prison, H had displayed a number of serious behavioural difficulties, resulting in verbal and written warnings, a notice of eviction from his probation hostel and a police warning. About two months after his release, H had been recalled to prison under the Crime (Sentences) Act 1997 s.32(1). Upon arrest, he had been told simply that he was being recalled. The secretary of state aimed to provide a recalled lifer with a dossier of reasons for recall within three days, but in the instant case, it was delayed. No further information was provided until at least eight days after detention. The dossier was not ready until 10 days after detention and then went astray within the internal post, causing a further delay of 14 days. H submitted that (1) an executive decision to recall and to detain was unlawful because, properly construed, the words in the Human Rights Act 1998 Sch.1 Part I Art.5(1)(c) "when it is reasonably considered necessary to prevent his committing an offence" caused Art.5(3) to become applicable, so that a judicial hearing was required promptly after detention; (2) his right under Art.5(2) to prompt reasons for his delivery to custody had not been met.

Held, granting the application, that (1) the scheme under s.32 of the 1997 Act was compatible in principle with Sch.1 Part I Art.5 of the 1998 Act, since Art.5(1)(c) and Art.5(3) had to be read together. The latter referred to a forthcoming trial, which did not appear to include a hearing such as that before the parole board, and the former was not designed to cater for the circumstances of the instant case. (2) Eight days for the giving of reasons could not possibly be described as prompt and it was not established that the reasons were, in any event, adequate. Accordingly, there had been a breach of Art.5(2). Reasons for a recall to custody had to be given, even when they were obvious. Reliance on alleged past knowledge of misbehaviour was a dubious basis for dispensing with the giving of adequate reasons, *Fox v. United Kingdom (A/182)* (1991) 13 E.H.R.R. 157, [1990] C.L.Y. 2526 distinguished. (3) The word "speedily" in Art.5(4) had no fixed definition and was to be determined on a case by case basis, *E v. Norway (A/181-A)* (1994) 17 E.H.R.R. 30, [1994] C.L.Y. 2381, *R. (on the application of Noorkoiv) v. Secretary of State for the Home Department (No.2)* [2002] EWCA Civ 770, [2002] 1 W.L.R. 3284, [2002] C.L.Y. 3339 and *R. (on the application of C) v. Mental Health Review Tribunal* [2001] EWCA Civ 1110, [2002] 1 W.L.R. 176, [2001] C.L.Y. 4424 considered. In the instant case, there was a breach of Art.5(4) to the limited extent that there had been a failure to proceed speedily with the early part of the process by which H could obtain a decision as to whether his recall was justified. A period of 14 days was the fair period that could be regarded as breaching Art.5(4). (4) With regard to the assessment of damages, a finding that there had been a breach of Art.5(2) was, on the facts, adequate recompense. In relation to the breach of Art.5(4), H's claim amounted to the distress of being ignorant to some extent of the reasons for his return to custody and to a release date of around two weeks later than it would otherwise have been. On the authorities, a modest award of £1,500 was appropriate.

R. (ON THE APPLICATION OF HIRST) v. SECRETARY OF STATE FOR THE HOME DEPARTMENT, [2005] EWHC 1480, *The Times*, July 4, 2005, Crane, J., QBD.

2922. Young offender institutions—Rules

YOUNG OFFENDER INSTITUTION (AMENDMENT) RULES 2005, SI 2005 897; made under the Prison Act 1952 s.47. In force: April 18, 2005; £3.00.

These Rules amend the Young Offender Institution Rules 2000 (SI 2000 3371) to provide that references to an "adjudicator" mean a District Judge (Magistrates' Courts) or Deputy District Judge (Magistrates' Courts) approved by the Lord Chancellor; to prohibit a copy of any personal record being given to a person not authorised to receive it; establish the procedure which is to apply where an officer requires an inmate to provide a sample under the Prison Act 1952 s.16B; to change the way in which certain offences under the Young Offender Institution Rules apply; provide a defence to the disciplinary offences of being intoxicated or having consumed alcohol; provide for a reviewer to review a punishment imposed by an adjudicator and sets out the procedure to be followed when an inmate requests such a review; and provide that the Secretary of State may not under that rule consider adjudications referred to an adjudicator although a governor may do so on grounds of good behaviour. They also provide that those visiting young offender institutions in whatever capacity may be photographed, fingerprinted or required to submit to other physical measurement.

2923. Young offenders—Life prisoners—Periodic reviews—Requirement of continuing review of minimum term—Duty of secretary of state to review minimum term of young persons detained at Her Majesty's pleasure

[Children and Young Persons Act 1933 s.53; Human Rights Act 1998 Sch.1 Part I Art.6; Criminal Justice and Court Services Act 2000 s.60; Powers of Criminal Courts (Sentencing) Act 2000 s.82A.]

The appellant secretary of state appealed against a decision ([2004] EWCA Civ 99, [2004] Q.B. 1341) that a sentence of detention during Her Majesty's pleasure under the Children and Young Persons Act 1933 s.53(1) imposed before November 30, 2000 on conviction of a child or young person for murder imported a requirement that the minimum term to be served by that person be subject to periodic review, even though the length of that term had been fixed by the Lord Chief Justice. The respondent (S) had been convicted of murder and detained at Her Majesty's pleasure (HMP). At the time of the murder S was 17 years old. After considering the recommendations from the Lord Chief Justice, the secretary of state set the tariff at 15 years. Following the decision in *R. v. Secretary of State for the Home Department, ex p. Venables* [1998] A.C. 407, [1997] C.L.Y. 1595, the secretary of state reviewed S's tariff and reduced it to 13 years. Thereafter, in light of the decision in *T v. United Kingdom (24724/94)* [2000] 2 All E.R. 1024 (Note), [2000] C.L.Y. 3198, the secretary of state adopted a legislative scheme to govern new cases in the Criminal Justice and Court Services Act 2000 s.60, which came into force on November 30, 2000. The secretary of state adopted an informal procedure to govern cases of detainees sentenced prior to the date when the legislation came into force. Pursuant to the secretary of state's policy in respect of the transitional cases, the Lord Chief Justice reviewed S's tariff, but found no grounds for reducing it further. The secretary of state declined to order further review of S's minimum term. The secretary of state disagreed with the Court of Appeal's conclusion and submitted that (1) the case of *Venables* applied only to cases where the minimum term was set by the secretary of state and had no application where it had been set judicially; (2) there was no inherent requirement of continuing review where the detainee was no longer a child or young person, and that S was an adult when the Lord Chief Justice had set her minimum term; (2) the court should be slow to re impose a duty on the secretary of state to review sentences of HMP detention or refer them to the court, in light of the decision in *T v. United Kingdom*; (3) a continuing duty to review the progress of pre November 30, 2000 HMP detainees would be anomalous, since no such duty was imposed in the case of HMP detainees covered by the Powers of Criminal Courts (Sentencing) Act 2000 s.82A, nor in the case of those detained under s.53(2) of the 1933 Act, and it would be anomalous both to impose a duty on the secretary of state and to impose it in relation to a detainee who had come of age.

Held, dismissing the appeal, that (1) the majority opinions of the House of Lords in *Venables* would have upheld a requirement of continuing review even if the minimum term had been set judicially, because that was an intrinsic feature of the sentence, *Venables* considered. Protection of the interest of the young offender called for continuing review. (2) The requirement to impose a sentence of HMP detention was based not on the age of the offender when sentenced but on the age of the offender when the murder was committed, and it reflected the humane principle that an offender deemed by statute to be not fully mature when committing his crime should not be punished as if he were. It would in many cases subvert the object of that unique sentence if the duty of continuing review were held to terminate when the child or young person became legally of age. (3) The authorities on the Human Rights Act 1998 Sch.1 Part I Art.6 had considered the application of Art.6 only in relation to the initial setting of the minimum term. Whilst it would be wrong for that term to be subsequently increased by executive decision, it did not follow that the same considerations necessarily applied to a reduction, even if pursuant to a review mandated by domestic law. A reduction in the sentence imposed by a court was a well recognised exercise of executive clemency. If the secretary of state should prefer the decisions on whether to reduce the minimum sentence to be taken by the judiciary, it was open to him to adopt the same informal procedure for seeking the advice of the Lord Chief Justice as he had done for the purpose of reconsidering the original minimum terms. It would in any case be impracticable for him to expect the judiciary to perform the task of reviewing and monitoring the progress of the detainee in custody. That was a task that only those for whom the secretary of state was answerable could perform. (4) It was true that no continuing duty of review applied to other sentences imposed on young offenders, because other sentences did not have the special features of HMP detention: that was anomalous only if it was thought that they should have those features. There was nothing anomalous in according a monitoring role to the secretary of state. Nor was it anomalous to continue to treat a person who committed a crime as a child or young person differently from one who committed a crime as an adult. In referring to detention during Her Majesty's pleasure, the 1933 Act indicated that a crime committed by a person who was under age did not cease to be such because he later became an adult. Accordingly, the progress of those sentenced to HMP detention before November 30, 2000, whose minimum terms had been set by the Lord Chief Justice and had not expired, should remain subject to continuing review for reconsideration of the minimum term imposed if clear evidence of exceptional and unforeseen progress was reasonably judged to require it, *T v. United Kingdom* considered.

R. (ON THE APPLICATION OF SMITH) v. SECRETARY OF STATE FOR THE HOME DEPARTMENT; R. (ON THE APPLICATION OF DUDSON) v. SECRETARY OF STATE FOR THE HOME DEPARTMENT; *sub nom.* SECRETARY OF STATE FOR THE HOME DEPARTMENT v. SMITH; DUDSON v. SECRETARY OF STATE, [2005] UKHL 51, [2006] 1 A.C. 159, Lord Bingham of Cornhill, HL.

2924. **Books**

Abadinsky, Howard–Probation and Parole: Theory and Practice. Hardback: £50.99. ISBN 0 13 118894 1. Prentice Hall.

Aertsen, Ivo; Daems, Tom; Robert, Luc–Institutionalising Restorative Justice. Paperback: £27.50. ISBN 1 84392 158 8. Willan Publishing.

Johnstone, Gerry; Van Ness, Daniel–Handbook of Restorative Justice. Hardback: £65.00. ISBN 1 84392 151 0. Paperback: £29.50. ISBN 1 84392 150 2. Willan Publishing.

Leech, Mark–Prisons Handbook: The Definitive 800-page Annual Guide to the Penal System of England and Wales. Paperback: £65.00. ISBN 0 9544829 2 1. MLA Press Ltd.

Leo Zaibert–Punishment and Retribution. Law, Justice & Power. Hardback: £50.00. ISBN 0 7546 2389 0. Avebury Technical.

Liebling, Alison–Prisons and Their Moral Performance: A Study of Values, Quality, and Prison Life. Clarendon Studies in Criminology. Paperback: £19.99. ISBN 0 19 929148 9. Oxford University Press.

Pavlich, George–Governing Paradoxes of Restorative Justice. Criminology S. Paperback: £25.00. ISBN 1 904385 19 2. The Glasshouse Press.

Tewksbury, Richard–Behind Bars: Readings on Prison Culture. Paperback: £29.99. ISBN 0 13 119072 5. Prentice Hall.

PENSIONS

2925. **Appeals–Pensions Appeal Tribunal**

PENSIONS APPEAL TRIBUNALS (ENGLAND AND WALES) (AMENDMENT) RULES 2005, SI 2005 709 (L.17); made under the Pensions Appeal Tribunals Act 1943 Sch.para.5. In force: April 6, 2005; £3.00.

These Rules amend the Pensions Appeal Tribunals (England and Wales) Rules 1980 (SI 1980 1120) to provide for a new route of appeal from the Pensions Appeal Tribunal to the Social Security Commissioners, who for these purposes are to be known as Pensions Appeal Commissioners.

2926. **Armed forces–Compensation–Appeals**

ARMED FORCES (PENSIONS AND COMPENSATION) ACT 2004 (TRANSITIONAL PROVISION) ORDER 2005, SI 2005 660; made under the Armed Forces (Pensions and Compensation) Act 2004 s.10. In force: April 6, 2005; £3.00.

This Order contains transitional provision in relation to the commencement of provisions of the Armed Forces (Pensions and Compensation) Act 2004 which amend the Pensions Appeal Tribunals Act 1943. Under the 1943 Act a Pensions Appeal Tribunal hears appeals on certain decisions made in relation to claims for war pensions and compensation. The 1943 Act also provides for appeals from those decisions. The amendments to the 1943 Act change the route of appeal against decisions of a Tribunal. After the commencement of provisions of the 2004 Act, the 1943 Act will provide that the right of appeal is to a Social Security Commissioner (with a further right of appeal to the Court of Appeal or Court of Session) rather than to the High Court. This Order provides that, in any case where a Tribunal has made a decision before April 6, 2005, the amendments to the 1943 shall not have effect. The right of appeal to the High Court is therefore preserved in such a case.

2927. **Armed forces–Disablement or death in service**

NAVAL, MILITARY AND AIR FORCES ETC. (DISABLEMENT AND DEATH) SERVICE PENSIONS (AMENDMENT) ORDER 2005, SI 2005 851; made under the Naval and Marine Pay and Pensions Act 1865 s.3; the Pensions and Yeomanry Pay Act 1884 s.2; the Air Force (Constitution) Act 1917 s.2; and the

Social Security (Miscellaneous Provisions) Act 1977 s.12, s.24. In force: in accordance with Art.1 (1); £3.00.

This Order amends the Naval, Military and Air Forces Etc. (Disablement and Death) Service Pensions Order 1983 (SI 1983 883) which makes provision for pensions and other awards in respect of disablement or death due to service in the naval, military and air forces. The Order restricts awards to circumstances where a death or disablement is due to service before April 6, 2005; provides that only service before April 6, 2005 will be relevant for decisions on eligibility for pensions for disablement or death assessment of disablement or rate of pension or gratuity; provides that only service before April 6 will be relevant for the purpose of decisions on defraying medical or funeral expenses; provides that awards to widows, widowers or unmarried dependants living as spouses of former members who died or whose service terminated on or before the March 31, 1973 shall not cease in the event of the widow, widower or unmarried dependant living as a spouse marrying or living with another person as the spouse of that person, provided that such marriage or living with another commences on or after the April 6, 2005; increases the amount of a widow's or widower's pension payable; and varies the rates of retired pay, pensions, gratuities and allowances in respect of disablement or death due to service in the armed forces.

2928. Armed forces–Disablement or death in service

NAVAL, MILITARY AND AIR FORCES ETC. (DISABLEMENT AND DEATH) SERVICE PENSIONS (AMENDMENT) (NO.2) ORDER 2005, SI 2005 1471; made under the Naval and Marine Pay and Pensions Act 1865 s.3; the Pensions and Yeomanry Pay Act 1884 s.2; the Air Force (Constitution) Act 1917 s.2; and the Social Security (Miscellaneous Provisions) Act 1977 s.12, s.24. In force: July 15, 2005; £3.00.

This Order amends the Naval, Military and Air Forces Etc. (Disablement and Death) Service Pensions Order 1983 (SI 1983 883) which makes provision for pensions and other awards in respect of disablement or death due to service in the naval, military and air forces. It increases the amount of supplementary widow or widower's pension payable to £64.68 per week from April 6, 2005 and £66.62 per week from April 11, 2005.

2929. Armed forces–Disablement or death in service

NAVAL, MILITARY AND AIR FORCES ETC. (DISABLEMENT AND DEATH) SERVICE PENSIONS (AMENDMENT) (NO.3) ORDER 2005, SI 2005 3187; made under the Naval and Marine Pay and Pensions Act 1865 s.3; the Pensions and Yeomanry Pay Act 1884 s.2; the Air Force (Constitution) Act 1917 s.2; and the Social Security (Miscellaneous Provisions) Act 1977 s.21, s.24. In force: December 5, 2005; £3.00.

These Regulations, which amend the Service Pensions Order 1983 (SI 1983 883), clarify that injuries or deaths giving rise to benefits under the Armed Forces (Pensions and Compensation) Scheme 2005 shall not be accepted as due to service for the purposes of the 1983 Order. They also remove marriage-related eligibility requirements in the definition of an adult dependant for the purposes of the Order. All other paragraphs provide that marriage related benefits are paid equally to civil partners in consequence of the introduction of civil partnerships by the Civil Partnership Act 2004.

2930. Armed forces–Early departure payments scheme

ARMED FORCES EARLY DEPARTURE PAYMENTS SCHEME ORDER 2005, SI 2005 437; made under the Armed Forces (Pensions and Compensation) Act 2004 s.1, s.10. In force: April 6, 2005; £3.00.

This Order establishes the Armed Forces Early Departure Payments Scheme which is a new scheme for making payments to members of the armed forces leaving service before they are entitled to retirement pensions or other benefits from the Armed Forces Pension Scheme 2005. The Scheme replaces existing arrangements for such payments for persons joining the armed forces on or after April 6, 2005 or in service immediately before that date and transferring to the Armed Forces Pension Scheme 2005.

2931. Armed forces–Pension schemes

ARMED FORCES PENSION SCHEME ORDER 2005, SI 2005 438; made under the Armed Forces (Pensions and Compensation) Act 2004 s.1, s.3, s.10. In force: April 6, 2005; £7.50.

This Order, which amends the Occupational Pension Schemes (Assignment, Forfeiture, Bankruptcy etc.) Regulations 1997 (SI 1997 785), establishes a new pension scheme for the armed forces for persons joining the armed forces on or after April 6, 2005 or in service immediately before that date and wishing to join the scheme.

2932. Armed forces–Ulster Defence Regiment–Civil partnerships

ULSTER DEFENCE REGIMENT (AMENDMENT) ORDER 2005, SI 2005 3189; made under the Social Security (Miscellaneous Provisions) Act 1977 s.12. In force: December 5, 2005; £3.00.

This Order amends the Order by Her Majesty dated January 4, 1971 in consequence of the introduction of civil partnerships by the Civil Partnership Act 2004.

2933. Armed forces–War pensions–Appeals

PENSIONS APPEAL TRIBUNALS (ARMED FORCES AND RESERVE FORCES COMPENSATION SCHEME) (RIGHTS OF APPEAL) REGULATIONS 2005, SI 2005 1029; made under the Pensions Appeal Tribunals Act 1943 s.5A. In force: April 6, 2005; £3.00.

The Pensions Appeal Tribunals Act 1943 allows a claimant to appeal to the Pensions Appeal Tribunal against certain decisions of the Secretary of State relating to war pensions, including "specified decisions", which are decisions specified by regulations made under the 1943 Act s.5A. The 1943 Act was amended by the Armed Forces (Pensions and Compensation) Act 2004 to permit the Secretary of State to include, under the category of specified decisions, decisions relating to compensation schemes for the armed and reserve. These Regulations extend the category of "specified decisions" (and hence rights of appeal to the Pensions Appeal Tribunal) to decisions which relate to entitlement to benefit, and the amount of benefit payable, under schemes under the 2004 Act.

2934. Armed Forces (Pensions and Compensation) Act 2004 (c.32)– Commencement No.2 Order

ARMED FORCES (PENSIONS AND COMPENSATION) ACT 2004 (COMMENCEMENT NO.2) ORDER 2005, SI 2005 356 (C.13); made under the Armed Forces (Pensions and Compensation) Act 2004 s.8. Commencement details: bringing into force various provisions of the 2004 Act on February 22, 2005 and April 6, 2005; £3.00.

This Order brings into force provisions of the Armed Forces (Pensions and Compensation) Act 2004.

2935. Auditors–Registered pension schemes

REGISTERED PENSION SCHEMES (AUDITED ACCOUNTS) (SPECIFIED PERSONS) REGULATIONS 2005, SI 2005 3456; made under the Finance Act 2004 s.250. In force: April 6, 2006; £3.00.

These Regulations prescribe the persons who may be the auditors of the accounts of a registered pension scheme under the Finance Act 2004 s.250(6). They prescribe persons who may be the auditors of a registered pension scheme, subject to the exceptions in reg.3, which prevent a person who has a personal interest in a scheme either a member, an employer, an employee of the scheme administrator or a person precluded under company law from auditing the accounts of an employer in relation to the scheme.

2936. Civil service–Pension schemes–Injury benefits–Increase

PENSIONS INCREASE (CIVIL SERVICE INJURY BENEFITS SCHEME) REGULATIONS 2005, SI 2005 698; made under the Pensions (Increase) Act 1971 s.5. In force: April 8, 2005; £3.00.

These Regulations, which revoke the Pensions Increase (Civil Service Injury Benefits Scheme) Regulations 2004 (SI 2004 1711), apply the provisions of the Pensions (Increase) Act 1971 to any pension payable under the Civil Service Injury Benefits Scheme. The rate of any such pension is thereby increased annually in accordance with the Retail Prices Index.

2937. Contribution notices–Restoration orders–Appropriate persons

PENSIONS REGULATOR (CONTRIBUTION NOTICES AND RESTORATION ORDERS) REGULATIONS 2005, SI 2005 931; made under the Pensions Act 2004 s.38, s.52, s.315, s.318. In force: April 6, 2005; £3.00.

These Regulations make provision relating to the "moral hazard" provisions in the Pensions Act 2004 s.38 and s.52 which provide for two of the powers of the Pensions Regulator known as the "moral hazard" provisions, that is, the Regulator's power to issue contribution notices and to make restoration orders. They prescribe "appropriate persons" who may be involved in a transaction involving scheme assets which is at an undervalue.

2938. Early retirement–Retained benefits–Actuarial reductions–Definition of normal pension age

[Pension Schemes Act 1993 s.71, s.72, s.74, s.180(1).]

U sought directions as to whether its method of calculating the retirement benefits of deferred pensioners complied with the Pension Schemes Act 1993 s.71, s.72, s.74 and s.180. U was a large pension scheme covering staff employed in universities and colleges. Its members could move from one institution to another and still remain in membership, although they might have different retirement ages in their individual contracts of employment. In calculating benefits, U treated all members as having a "normal pension age" of 65, irrespective of the actual contractual retirement age, and then made an actuarial reduction for pensions taken before the member reached 65. S was a member who was entitled to retire at 60. He complained that he would be unfairly treated if he chose to leave pensionable service early, as any pension he received between the ages of 60 and 65 would be actuarially reduced.

Held, giving directions, that the method used meant that short service benefits were not computed on the same basis as long service benefits, contrary to s.74. Section 71 and s.180(1) required that "normal retirement age" was to be determined by reference to the individual member's terms of service, so that the imposition of an all inclusive notional retirement age was incorrect.

UNIVERSITIES SUPERANNUATION SCHEME LTD v. SIMPSON; UNIVERSITIES SUPERANNUATION SCHEME LTD v. McADOO; UNIVERSITIES SUPERANNUATION SCHEME LTD v. UNIVERSITY OF LONDON; *sub nom.* UNIVERSITIES SUPERANNUATION SCHEME LTD, *Re*, [2004] EWHC 935, [2004] I.C.R. 1426, Lloyd, J., Ch D.

2939. Employers—Pension protection

TRANSFER OF EMPLOYMENT (PENSION PROTECTION) REGULATIONS 2005, SI 2005 649; made under the Pensions Act 2004 s.258, s.315, s.318. In force: April 6, 2005; £3.00.

These Regulations concern the obligations of an employer under the Pensions Act 2004 s.258 towards a person in relation to whom s.257 of that Act applies. Section 258(2)(c) provides that a scheme in relation to which the transferee is the employer, if it is not a money purchase scheme, must satisfy a standard provided for in the Pension Schemes Act 1993, or, if regulations so provide, comply with prescribed requirements. For the purposes of this provision, these Regulations require that either the value of the benefits provided for by the transferee's scheme must be at least 6 per cent of pensionable pay for each year of employment in addition to any contributions made by him or that the scheme must provide for the employer to make relevant contributions on behalf of his employees. Section 258(7) provides for "relevant contributions" to be defined in regulations. These Regulations provide that such contributions must be made in respect of each period for which the employee contributes to the pension scheme, and that the amount contributed must equal the employee's contribution subject to an upper limit of 6 per cent of basic pay.

2940. Employers contributions—Tax relief—Restrictions

REGISTERED PENSION SCHEMES (RESTRICTION OF EMPLOYERS' RELIEF) REGULATIONS 2005, SI 2005 3458; made under the Finance Act 2004 s.196A. In force: April 6, 2006; £3.00.

The Finance Act 2004 s.196A provided that Regulations could be made restricting the extent to which contributions paid by an employer under a registered pension scheme in respect of an individual are subject to tax relief in two circumstances. The first is where payment of benefits to or in respect of that individual under the scheme are payable only if benefits are not so paid under an employer financed retirement benefits scheme. The second is where, because benefits are or may be payable to or in respect of that individual under an employer-financed retirement benefits scheme, the value of a transfer out of a registered pension scheme will or may be reduced. These Regulations restrict employers' tax relief in those two circumstances. They provide the amount of the restriction, the method of which is based on the calculation of a member's pension input amount for a scheme (for the purposes of the Annual Allowance Charge) set out in the Finance Act 2004 s.230 to s.237, with the modifications set out in the Regulations. The aggregate pension input amount is excluded from tax relief.

2941. Financial assistance—Reviewable determinations—Internal review

FINANCIAL ASSISTANCE SCHEME (INTERNAL REVIEW) REGULATIONS 2005, SI 2005 1994; made under the Pensions Act 2004 s.286, s.315, s.318. In force: July 20, 2005; £3.00.

These Regulations make provision for the internal review of reviewable determinations made under the Financial Assistance Scheme which was established to allow payments to be made to, or in respect of, certain members of certain occupational pension schemes where the liabilities of those schemes to those members are unlikely to be satisfied in full.

2942. Financial provision—Dissolution—Civil partnerships

DISSOLUTION ETC (PENSIONS) REGULATIONS 2005, SI 2005 2920; made under the Civil Partnership Act 2004 Sch.5 para.19, Sch.5 para.27, Sch.5 para.28, Sch.5 para.57, Sch.7 para.14. In force: December 5, 2005; £3.00.

These Regulations make provision relating to orders made under the Civil Partnership Act 2004, including those made after proceedings overseas, for ancillary relief in proceedings for dissolution, separation or nullity of civil partnership which relate to the pension rights of a party to the civil partnership. The Regulations provide in particular for: the valuation of pension rights by the court; notices of change of circumstances to be provided by the person responsible for the pension arrangement to the civil partner without pension rights, or by that civil partner to the person responsible to the pension arrangement; and the stay period during which pension sharing orders cannot take effect.

2943. Fire services–Firefighters–Pension scheme

FIREFIGHTERS' PENSION SCHEME (AMENDMENT) (ENGLAND) ORDER 2005, SI 2005 2980; made under the Fire Services Act 1947 s.26; and the Superannuation Act 1972 s.12. In force: November 21, 2005; £3.50.

This Order amends the Firefighters' Pension Scheme, as set out in the Firemens' Pension Scheme Order 1992 (SI 1992 129), as it has effect in England. Many of the amendments are consequential on the revocation of the Fire Services Act 1947 and its replacement by the Fire and Rescue Services Act 2004. For example, references to fire authorities (unless retained for transitional purposes) are amended to references to fire and rescue authorities, and references to brigades are amended to references to fire and rescue services or, depending on the particular context, to fire and rescue authorities.

2944. Industry wide schemes–Employers contributions–Interpretation of "participating employers"

The applicant (M) sought a determination as to the types of employer constituting "participating employers" within the current rules of the pension scheme of which it was trustee. The scheme was an industry wide exempt approved occupational pension scheme. In 1978 the scheme was split into two sections, the pre 1978 section and the post 1978 section. M executed a deed of amendment in 2000 which varied the definition of "participating employers" and introduced a new rule on contributions by participating employers in order to remedy a funding deficiency in relation to the post 1978 part of the scheme. The respondents represented three classes of employers participating in the scheme, including the employers who employed no active members in the scheme as at the date the deed was executed, as represented by the first respondent (R) and employers who continued to employ active members of the scheme as at that date. The main dispute was whether the former could be made liable to fund the deficiency. R submitted that M's ability to pass the liability for additional contributions to the first and second respondents depended on whether they agreed to submit themselves to that exercise of M's powers by signing the accession agreement and "participating employers" as used in the accession agreement should be limited to the type of employer who was still had active members as employees at the relevant times. M submitted that it would be inconsistent with the separation of assets and liabilities effected by the 1978 division of the scheme for employers who only participated in the pre 1978 period of the scheme to be asked to contribute to a post 1978 deficiency in liabilities.

Held, giving judgment accordingly, that (1) R was correct that what mattered in the first instance was to identify the obligations that the employers undertook by executing the accession agreement. The draftsman of that agreement obviously realised that it was necessary to bind the incoming employer not only to the existing trust deed and rules, but also to any subsequent variation in them and accordingly the first respondent's submissions about the construction of "participating employers" when used in the agreement had to be rejected. By the agreement, the obligations assumed by the employer were those under the trust deed and rules "or under any subsequent variation that may be made therein". That was clearly a reference to a subsequent variation in the trust deed and rules and not in the obligation referred to. R's construction of the agreement was inconsistent with the express provisions of the clause empowering M to vary the trust deed or rules and also with the structure of the scheme in general. The variation clause provided for a general power of amendment and had to be interpreted as such. Against an accepted background of a widely-drawn power to cater for deficiencies by amending scheme liabilities it was difficult to identify any particular contextual considerations that required "participating employers" to be given anything but its usual defined meaning when used in the accession agreements, *Stevens v. Bell* [2002] EWCA Civ 672, [2002] O.P.L.R. 207, [2002] C.L.Y. 3390 applied. (2) Although the 1978 deed created what might be regarded as two separate funds, it preserved the rules about dealing with deficiencies and the power to amend as general powers exercisable by reference to the "scheme" rather than to the individual sections within it. Employers who ceased to have active members as employees prior to the 1978 division of the scheme were included in the class of participating employers from whom M could seek additional contributions in accordance with the new rule introduced by the 2000 deed of amendment.

MNOPF TRUSTEES LTD v. FT EVERARD & SONS LTD; *sub nom.* MERCHANT NAVY OFFICERS PENSION FUND TRUSTEES LTD v. FT EVERARD & SONS LTD, [2005] EWHC 446, [2005] Pens. L.R. 225, Patten, J., Ch D.

2945. Judicial office holders–Civil partnerships

CIVIL PARTNERSHIP (JUDICIAL PENSIONS AND CHURCH PENSIONS, ETC.) ORDER 2005, SI 2005 3325; made under the Civil Partnership Act 2004 s.255, s.259. In force: in accordance with Art.1; £6.50.

This Order makes amendments to 6 Acts, 7 Church Measures, 1 SR and 19 SIs to provide that a civil partner of a judicial office holder will be entitled to the payment of a surviving civil partner's pension should the judicial office holder die in service or in retirement; to provide that eligible children will be entitled to the payment of a children's pension; and to provide that a judicial office holder, who is a member of the scheme before December 5, 2005 and subsequently forms a civil partnership whilst in judicial office, may choose whether any period of service before the date this Order comes into force is to be considered for the purposes of calculating a civil partner's pension. The Order sets out the arrangements for making payment from the office holder's lump sum benefits (except in respect of members of a scheme constituted under the 1993 Act) or by way of making periodic contributions in respect of a surviving civil partner's pension, and for making additional periodical payments to reflect a judicial office holder's choice that service before December 5, 2005 is to be counted for the purposes of calculating any resultant surviving civil partner's pension benefit; where a person ceased to hold judicial office before December 5, 2005 and they subsequently form a civil partnership there shall only be entitlement to a surviving civil partner's guaranteed minimum pension calculated in accordance with the Pension Schemes Act 1993 or the Pensions Schemes (Northern Ireland) Act 1993.

2946. Local government–Investment of funds

LOCAL GOVERNMENT PENSION SCHEME AND MANAGEMENT AND INVESTMENT OF FUNDS (AMENDMENT) REGULATIONS 2005, SI 2005 2004; made under the Superannuation Act 1972 s.7, s.12. In force: August 17, 2005; £3.00.

These Regulations amend the Local Government Pension Scheme Regulations 1997 (SI 1997 1612) and the Local Government Pension Scheme (Management and Investment of Funds) Regulations 1998 (SI 1998 1831). They update references made by the Fire and Rescue Services Act 2004; update the definition of "qualified in occupational health medicine"; insert a provision to be addressed by administering authorities prior to making a decision to increase the limit on their investments in securities transferred by the authority under stock lending arrangements; make a consequential amendment where, following a review, an administering authority has decided to continue to use the increased limit on their investments in securities transferred under stock lending arrangements; and allow administering authorities to increase the limit on their investments in securities transferred by the authority under stock lending arrangements from 25 per cent to 35 per cent of the total of their pension fund investments.

2947. Local government-Pension schemes-Civil partnerships

LOCAL GOVERNMENT PENSION SCHEME (CIVIL PARTNERSHIP) (AMENDMENT) (ENGLAND AND WALES) REGULATIONS 2005, SI 2005 3069; made under the Superannuation Act 1972 s.7, s.12, s.24. In force: December 5, 2005; £3.00.

These Regulations amend the Local Government (Discretionary Payments) Regulations 1996 (SI 1996 1680), the Local Government Pension Scheme Regulations 1997 (SI 1997 1612), the Local Government Pension Scheme (Transitional Provisions) Regulations 1997 (SI 1997 1613) and the Local Government (Early Termination of Employment) (Discretionary Compensation) (England and Wales) Regulations 2000 (SI 2000 1410). They provide survivor benefits for same sex partners of Local Government Pension Scheme members or eligible persons where the same sex partners have registered a civil partnership under the terms of the Civil Partnership Act 2004.

2948. Local government-Pension schemes-Policy statements

LOCAL GOVERNMENT PENSION SCHEME (AMENDMENT) (NO.2) REGULATIONS 2005, SI 2005 3199; made under the Superannuation Act 1972 s.7, s.12, s.24. In force: December 14, 2005; £3.00.

These Regulations amend the Local Government Pension Scheme Regulations 1997 (SI 1997 1612) to require each administering authority to prepare, maintain and publish a governance policy statement as to whether they delegate their function or part of their function in relation to maintaining a pension fund to a committee, sub-committee or an officer. The Regulations also require each administering authority to prepare, maintain and publish a statement concerning their policy on communicating with members, members' representatives, prospective members and employing authorities.

2949. Occupational pension schemes-Audited accounts

OCCUPATIONAL PENSION SCHEMES (ADMINISTRATION AND AUDITED ACCOUNTS) (AMENDMENT) REGULATIONS 2005, SI 2005 2426; made under the Pension Schemes Act 1993 s.113, s.181, s.182; and the Pensions Act 1995 s.41, s.47, s.49, s.87, s.88, s.124, s.174. In force: in accordance with Reg.1; £3.00.

These Regulations, which amend the Occupational Pension Schemes (Scheme Administration) Regulations 1996 (SI 1996 1715), the Occupational Pension Schemes (Requirement to obtain Audited Accounts and a Statement from the Auditor) Regulations 1996 (SI 1996 1975) and the Personal Pension Schemes (Payments by Employers) Regulations 2000 (SI 2000 2692), implement European Parliament and Council Directive 2003/41 ([2003] OJ L235/10) on the activities and supervision of Institutions for Occupational Retirement Provision. They are consequential on the coming into force of the Finance Act 2004 and the Pensions Act 2004.

2950. Occupational pension schemes-Deficiency in assets

[Pensions Act 1995 s.75; Occupational Pension Schemes (Deficiency on Winding Up etc.) Regulations 1996 (SI 1996 3128).]

The applicants (C) applied for summary judgment. C was a trustee of a multi employer final salary occupational pension scheme. The respondent (N) was an employer in relation to the scheme until it ceased to employ anybody who was a member of the scheme. At the time of N's withdrawal the scheme's liabilities exceeded its assets as per the Pensions Act 1995 s.75. The deficit was valued and certified, in the manner specified in the Occupational Pension Schemes (Deficiency on Winding Up etc.) Regulations 1996, and over 16 per cent of the deficit was apportioned to N. C contended that the deficit had been correctly calculated and certified and that N owed that sum as a debt to it. C contended that the certificate and apportionment was binding on N and could not be challenged except in limited circumstances that did not exist in the instant case.

S challenged the certificate, alleging the actuary had failed to carry out his calculations as provided for by the Act and the Regulations.

Held, granting the application, that in principle the parties were bound by the certificate and opinion of the actuary in calculating the amount of debt. The language of s.75 of the Act was emphatic in entrusting the deficiency calculation to the relevant person with the method of calculation being prescribed by the regulations. It was reasonable to infer that Parliament intended the parties to be bound by the actuary's calculation. The apportionment calculation was more analogous to a contractual position and could be open to attack, *Pitmans Trustees Ltd v. Telecommunications Group Plc* [2004] EWHC 181, [2004] Pens. L.R. 213, [2004] C.L.Y. 2818 considered. There were no grounds upon which either the certificate or the apportionment could be attacked and C was entitled to summary judgment.

CORNWELL v. NEWHAVEN PORT & PROPERTIES LTD, [2005] EWHC 1469, [2005] Pens. L.R. 329, Lewison, J., Ch D.

2951. Occupational pension schemes—Exemptions

OCCUPATIONAL PENSION SCHEMES (TRUST AND RETIREMENT BENEFITS EXEMPTION) REGULATIONS 2005, SI 2005 2360; made under the Pensions Act 2004 s.252, s.255, s.315, s.318. In force: September 22, 2005; £3.00.

These Regulations prescribe the description of schemes which are exempt from the requirement in the Pensions Act 2004 that trustees or managers of an occupational pension scheme with its main administration in the UK must not accept funding payments unless the scheme is established under irrevocable trust. The Regulations also prescribe the description of a scheme which is exempt from the requirement in the Act, that an occupational pension scheme with its main administration in the UK must be limited to retirement-benefit activities.

2952. Occupational pension schemes—Indexation and disclosure of information

PERSONAL AND OCCUPATIONAL PENSION SCHEMES (INDEXATION AND DISCLOSURE OF INFORMATION) (MISCELLANEOUS AMENDMENTS) REGULATIONS 2005, SI 2005 704; made under the Pension Schemes Act 1993 s.12C, s.19, s.28, s.28A, s.113, s.168, s.181, s.182; the Pensions Act 1995 s.51, s.124, s.125, s.174; and the Welfare Reform and Pensions Act 1999 s.40, s.83. In force: April 6, 2005; £3.00.

These Regulations reflect amendments made in the Pensions Act 2004 to provisions that require increases in the indexation of certain pensions. They amend the Pensions Act 1995, the Personal and Occupational Pension Schemes (Protected Rights) Regulations 1996 (SI 1996 1537), the Occupational Pension Schemes (Disclosure of Information) Regulations 1996 (SI 1996 1655), the Occupational Pension Schemes (Indexation) Regulations 1996 (SI 1996 1679), the Occupational Pension Schemes (Discharge of Liability) Regulations 1997 (SI 1997 784), the Personal and Occupational Pension Schemes (Miscellaneous Amendments) Regulations 1997 (SI 1997 786) and the Pension Sharing (Pension Credit Benefit) Regulations 2000 (SI 2000 1054).

2953. Occupational pensions—Benefits—Revaluation percentages

OCCUPATIONAL PENSIONS (REVALUATION) ORDER 2005, SI 2005 3156; made under the Pension Schemes Act 1993 Sch.3 para.2. In force: January 1, 2006; £3.00.

This Order specifies revaluation percentages for the purpose of the revaluation on or after January 1, 2006 of benefits under occupational pension schemes, as required by the Pension Schemes Act 1993 s.84 and Sch.3.

2954. Occupational pensions–Civil service–Entitlement to injury benefits– Construction of Principal Civil Service Pension Scheme r.11.3(i)

The appellant minister appealed against a decision of the Pensions Ombudsman in relation to entitlement to injury benefits pursuant to the Principal Civil Service Pension Scheme r.11.3(i). The case before the Ombudsman concerned the entitlement of the respondent labourer (O) to benefits for a depressive illness caused by incidents at work which were incidental to his duties. The instant appeal was concerned with the construction of r.11.3(i). The rule dealt with a person's eligibility for benefits and read as follows: "who suffers an injury in the course of official duty, provided that such injury is solely attributable to the nature of the duty or arises from an activity reasonably incidental to the duty...". The Ombudsman concluded that the word "solely" did not qualify "...arises from an activity reasonably incidental to the duty...". The minister disagreed and argued that the rule should be construed so that effectively the word "solely" was written in a second time.

Held, allowing the appeal, that the matter was remitted to the Ombudsman to reconsider the case on the basis that the word "solely" was to be introduced into the latter part of the rule to qualify it so that it read "...or solely arises from an activity reasonably incidental to the duty...". The logical intendment argument was preferred to the linguistic argument. In looking for a reasonable legislative purpose, it was not possible to justify the presence of the word in the first part but not in the second part of the rule. It was not clear why the test for the benefits should be more relaxed the less the connection between the nature of the duty and the injury. It appeared that the Ombudsman had failed to get to grips with the logical intendment argument. As it was a test case, despite being successful, the minister was ordered to pay O's costs.

MINISTER FOR THE CIVIL SERVICE v. OAKES, [2003] EWHC 3314, [2004] O.P.L.R. 235, Lindsay, J., Ch D.

2955. Occupational pensions–Contracted out schemes–Transfer of payments

PROTECTED RIGHTS (TRANSFER PAYMENT) (AMENDMENT) REGULATIONS 2005, SI 2005 2906; made under the Pension Schemes Act 1993 s.28, s.181, s.182. In force: November 28, 2005; £3.00.

These Regulations amend the Protected Rights (Transfer Payment) Regulations 1996 (SI 1996 1461) to include among the schemes that may give effect to a member's protected rights by making a transfer payment to an appropriate personal pension scheme or an occupational pension scheme, the money purchase part of a mixed benefit contracted-out scheme and a scheme which has ceased to be the money purchase part of a mixed benefit contracted-out scheme. The Regulations also provide for transfer payments to be made to a money purchase contracted-out scheme or the money purchase part of a mixed benefit contracted-out scheme.

2956. Occupational pensions–Contracting out–Restoration of state scheme rights

OCCUPATIONAL PENSION SCHEMES (CONTRACTING-OUT) (AMOUNT REQUIRED FOR RESTORING STATE SCHEME RIGHTS) AMENDMENT REGULATIONS 2005, SI 2005 891; made under the Pension Schemes Act 1993 s.181, s.182, Sch.2 para.5; and the Pension Schemes (Northern Ireland) Act 1993 s.176, Sch.1 para.5. In force: April 21, 2005; £3.00.

These Regulations amend the Occupational Pension Schemes (Contracting-out) (Amount Required for Restoring State Scheme Rights and Miscellaneous Amendment) Regulations 1998 (SI 1998 1397) and the Occupational Pension Schemes (Contracting-out) (Amount Required for Restoring State Scheme Rights and Miscellaneous Amendment) Regulations (Northern Ireland) 1998 (SR 1998 208). The 1998 Regulations deal with the calculation of the amount required for restoring certain rights under the State retirement pension scheme of members of occupational pension schemes that are wound up underfunded. They amend the definition of "relevant weekly amount" so that the calculation covers relevant employment after April 5, 2002; in the case of members within 10 years of pensionable age, they change the percentage to be used as the numerator in calculating the market level indicator from 3.5 per cent to 3 per cent; and set out new actuarial factors to be used for the purposes of the calculation.

2957. Occupational pensions–Contributions–Notice to terminate pension scheme–Demanding buy out shortfall as contribution–Effect of provisions of pension scheme before expiration of termination notice

The appellant firm of solicitors (P) appealed against an order ([2004] EWHC 2874, [2005] Pens. L.R. 251) that, under the rules of a company's occupational pension scheme, the former trustees of the scheme had power, before the effective date of a termination notice in respect of the scheme, to require the company to pay contributions to the scheme in an amount equal to any shortfall in the scheme's funds. The respondent (C), the present trustee of the scheme, had claimed damages against P for professional negligence in failing to advise the former trustees that they could demand that the company pay a "buy out" contribution to the scheme. Rule L.1.1 of the scheme provided for contributions to the scheme by the company as determined by the trustees. The company gave notice to terminate its liability to contribute to the scheme. The trustees subsequently made a decision to administer the scheme under r.J.2 as a closed scheme. Thereafter, an actuarial valuation of the scheme estimated that there was a buy out deficit. The trustees later resolved to wind up the scheme under r.J.4. The judge held that, although the trustees had power to demand contributions before the expiration of the termination notice, they had no such power after its effective date. P submitted, inter alia, that there was no express requirement that the company should give reasonable notice or any notice of its intention to terminate the scheme and its liability to make contributions to it, and that it was impracticable to compute the exact amount of the buy out deficit before the winding up of the scheme had commenced, its assets were realised, the costs met and the benefits of the members ascertained. P further submitted that there was no requirement for further funding once the scheme had been terminated and was being wound up, and that, although such funding might be required to build up the pension fund while the scheme was ongoing so that it was sufficient to meet the liability to pay the members' accruing benefits, a buy out deficit was not such a liability and the company was not liable to make a contribution for it.

Held, dismissing the appeal, that the ambit of r.L.1.1 should be determined by reference to its language, read in the context of the whole scheme and its practical purpose. According to the plain meaning of the rule, it was for the trustees to determine what contribution was "appropriate" to enable the benefits under the scheme, which were a form of deferred pay, to be funded in practice. That power of the trustees to make an appropriate demand for a contribution by the company was not subject to any express restriction. It continued to be exercisable during the notice period. Only after the termination date did the company cease to be liable to make contributions. The word "appropriate" meant "sufficient to fund the benefits stated in the scheme in the circumstances of the case". On the one hand, the rule would not entitle the trustees to demand a contribution for the purposes of building up a surplus, and, on the other hand, if the trustees were advised that there would be a shortfall, they could decide that it was appropriate to require the company to pay a lump sum to make good the shortfall. The judge's construction of r.L.1.1 made good commercial sense. It effected the object sought, which was to enable the trustees to ensure that the benefits promised to members were funded on a winding up. It gave effect to the plain and unrestricted meaning of the words that the trustees should have power to decide that it was appropriate for the company to make a contribution to the scheme to enable the benefits to its members to be funded in practice. The liability of the company to make an "appropriate" contribution did not terminate until the end of the period of notice given by it. During the notice period, the rules remained in full force and effect, and the trustees were entitled, in the light of the notice given by the company, to invoke the powers and discretions in the deeds while it was still current.

PINSENT CURTIS v. CAPITAL CRANFIELD TRUSTEES LTD; *sub nom.* CAPITAL CRANFIELD TRUSTEES LTD v. PINSENT CURTIS (A FIRM); CAPITAL CRANFIELD TRUSTEES LTD v. WALSH; K&J HOLDINGS LTD, *Re*, [2005] EWCA Civ 860, [2005] 4 All E.R. 449, Mummery, L.J., CA (Civ Div).

2958. Occupational pensions–Cross border activities

OCCUPATIONAL PENSION SCHEMES (CROSS-BORDER ACTIVITIES) REGULATIONS 2005, SI 2005 3381; made under the Pensions Act 2004 s.287, s.288, s.289, s.291 s.292, s.293, s.315, s.318. In force: December 30, 2005; £3.50.

These Regulations, which amend the Occupational Pension Schemes (Trust and Retirement Benefits Exemption) Regulations 2005 (SI 2005 2360), make provision relating to the carrying out by the Pensions Regulator of its functions in relation to cross-border activity within the European Union by occupational pension schemes and their trustees or managers, or by European pensions institutions.

2959. Occupational pensions–Early leavers–Consent required for drawing of pension before normal retirement date–Chairman's agreement to early pension–Apparent authority

G, a trustee of company E's pension scheme, appealed against the Pensions Ombudsman's determination that, in refusing to provide N, who was a member of the scheme and an executive director of E, with an early retirement pension, the trustees were guilty of maladministration and causing injustice to N. Under the rules of the scheme, a member who retired early had a basic entitlement to a deferred pension commencing from the normal retirement date, but could draw a reduced pension earlier with the consent of the trustees. The Ombudsman agreed with N's contention that W, who was E's chairman and a trustee of the pension scheme, had consented to N taking his pension early as part of his severance package.

Held, allowing the appeal, that W did not have ostensible authority to grant N an early pension, there being no evidence that the trustees had made any express or implied representation that W had authority to act on their behalf and give consent, as required by the scheme's rules, *Armagas Ltd v. Mundogas SA (The Ocean Frost)* [1986] A.C. 717, [1986] C.L.Y. 37 applied.

GREENWOOD v. NEWMAN, [2004] EWHC 484, [2004] O.P.L.R. 283, Etherton, J., Ch D.

2960. Occupational pensions–Employer debt

OCCUPATIONAL PENSION SCHEMES (EMPLOYER DEBT) REGULATIONS 2005, SI 2005 678; made under the Pensions Act 1995 s.40, s.49, s.57, s.60, s.68, s.75, s.75A, s.89, s.118, s.119, s.124, s.125, s.174. In force: April 6, 2005; £3.00.

These Regulations, which revoke the Occupational Pension Schemes (Deficiency on Winding Up etc.) Regulations 1996 (SI 1996 3128), amend the Occupational Pension Schemes (Minimum Funding Requirement and Actuarial Valuations) Regulations 1996 (SI 1996 1536), the Occupational Pension Schemes (Winding Up) Regulations 1996 (SI 1996 3126) and the Occupational Pension Schemes (Investment) Regulations 1996 (SI 1996 3127). The Regulations are made as a consequence of provisions in the Pensions Act 2004 relating to occupational pension schemes. They identify the two Actuarial Guidance Notes that will be used in connection with the calculation of debts; provide for all liabilities in respect of pensions or other benefits to be valued on the basis that the trustees or managers will provide for them by buying annuities, but, apart from that, for similar principles to apply as apply for the purpose of minimum funding valuations and for the valuation certificate; apply to multi-employer schemes; provide that a debt only arises under the Pensions Act 1995 s.75(2) while a multi-employer scheme is being wound up if a deficit in the scheme assets occurs before a relevant event has occurred in relation to all the employers, and all the employers are then responsible for a share of the debt; and provide that sectionalised schemes covering UK and foreign employment are to be treated as separate schemes.

2961. Occupational pensions–Employer debt

OCCUPATIONAL PENSION SCHEMES (EMPLOYER DEBT ETC.) (AMENDMENT) REGULATIONS 2005, SI 2005 2224; made under the Pensions Act 1995 s.10, s.56, s.75, s.75A, s.89, s.118, s.119, s.124, s.125, s.174; and the Pensions Act 2004 s.93, s.135, s.315, s.318, Sch.1 para.21. In force: September 2, 2005; £3.00.

These Regulations amend the Occupational Pension Schemes (Minimum Funding Requirement and Actuarial Valuations) Regulations 1996 (SI 1996 1536), the Pension Protection Fund (Entry Rules) Regulations 2005 (SI 2005 590), the Occupational Pension Schemes (Employer Debt) Regulations 2005 (SI 2005 678) and the Pensions Regulator (Financial Support Directions etc.) Regulations 2005 (SI 2005 2188). They make amendments so that where a debt has arisen under the Pensions Act 1995 s.75 on the leaving of an employer and an approved withdrawal arrangement has applied, valuations for events happening later are to ignore the debts that arose when the employer left; provide that where a debt arises under s.75 because of an employer ceasing to employ people in employments covered by an occupational pension scheme where there was more than one such employer, and an arrangement is approved by the Pensions Regulator under which parties to the arrangement are bound to make payments to the scheme if certain events occur, the debt becomes partly payable by the leaving employer, and partly by the guarantors at a later time; and provide for the part payable by the leaving employer to be calculated on the same basis as is used for minimum funding valuations under s.56 of the 1995 Act, except that a deduction is made where liabilities attributable to employment with the employer have been transferred out before the withdrawal arrangement was approved; and make provision about the exercise of functions of the Pensions Regulator.

2962. Occupational pensions–Equal treatment

OCCUPATIONAL PENSION SCHEMES (EQUAL TREATMENT) (AMENDMENT) REGULATIONS 2005, SI 2005 1923; made under the European Communities Act 1972 s.2; and the Pensions Act 1995 s.63, s.66, s.124, s.174. In force: August 10, 2005; £3.00.

These Regulations amend the Equal Pay Act 1970, the Pensions Act 1995 and the Occupational Pension Schemes (Equal Treatment) Regulations 1995 (SI 1995 3183) to reflect requirements of European Community law, as applied in a number of cases before the European Court of Justice and the domestic courts. They apply to occupational pension schemes generally; introduce new provisions applying only to armed forces occupational pension schemes; modify the time limits that apply to proceedings about failure to comply with the equal treatment rule; modify the time limits that apply to proceedings about failure to comply with the equal treatment rule; extend the time limits on the backdating of a declaration of a person's right to be admitted to a pension scheme; and remove the obligation on the employer to contribute funds where rights to be admitted to the scheme are backdated.

2963. Occupational pensions–Financial assistance scheme

FINANCIAL ASSISTANCE SCHEME REGULATIONS 2005, SI 2005 1986; made under the Pensions Act 2004 s.286, s.315, s.318. In force: in accordance with Reg.1; £4.50.

These Regulations establish a financial assistance scheme, allowing for payments to be made to, or in respect of, certain members or former members of certain occupational pension schemes where the liabilities of the scheme to those members are unlikely to be satisfied in full.

2964. Occupational pensions–Financial assistance scheme–Appeals

FINANCIAL ASSISTANCE SCHEME (APPEALS) REGULATIONS 2005, SI 2005 3273; made under the Pensions Act 2004 s.213, s.286, s.315, s.318. In force: November 29, 2005; £4.00.

The Financial Assistance Scheme (FAS) is established by the Financial Assistance Scheme Regulations 2005 (SI 2005 1986) to allow payments to be made to, or in respect of, certain members of certain occupational pension schemes where the liabilities of those schemes to, or in respect of, those members are unlikely to be satisfied in full. These Regulations make provision for the Ombudsman for the Board of the Pension Protection Fund, or a Deputy PPF Ombudsman, to investigate and determine appeals against review decisions made by the scheme manager of FAS.

2965. Occupational pensions–Financial assistance scheme–Miscellaneous amendments

FINANCIAL ASSISTANCE SCHEME (MODIFICATIONS AND MISCELLANEOUS AMENDMENTS) REGULATIONS 2005, SI 2005 3256; made under the Pensions Act 2004 s.168, s.190, s.203, s.286, s.315, s.318. In force: November 24, 2005; £3.00.

These Regulations amend the Pensions Act 2004, the Financial Assistance Scheme Regulations 2005 (SI 2005 1986), the Financial Assistance Scheme (Internal Review) Regulations 2005 (SI 2005 1994) and the Financial Assistance Scheme (Provision of Information and Administration of Payments) Regulations 2005 (SI 2005 2189). They make provision to confer information gathering functions on the Ombudsman; for regulations to be made in relation to Financial Assistance Scheme (FAS) appeals to make provision for the costs or expenses of prescribed persons; for the Ombudsman to refer any question of law arising on the investigation of matters arising on a FAS appeal to the High Court (in England and Wales, or in Northern Ireland) or the Court of Session; and for the publication of any matter by the Ombudsman in connection with a FAS appeal to be absolutely privileged.

2966. Occupational pensions–Financial assistance scheme–Provision of information

FINANCIAL ASSISTANCE SCHEME (PROVISION OF INFORMATION AND ADMINISTRATION OF PAYMENTS) REGULATIONS 2005, SI 2005 2189; made under the Pensions Act 2004 s.168, s.190, s.203, s.315, s.318. In force: in accordance with Reg.1 (1); £3.00.

These Regulations make provision relating to the information to be provided by, or to, the scheme manager of the financial assistance scheme. Such information is required to be provided both by trustees, managers and other persons acting in relation to occupational pension schemes in respect of which members may qualify for assistance from the financial assistance scheme, and by or on behalf of persons who may be entitled to payments from the financial assistance scheme. They make provision as to the information to be provided by appropriate persons in relation to schemes to the scheme manager and vice versa, and as to the information to be provided by appropriate persons to members of schemes; make provision as to the information to be provided by beneficiaries or potential beneficiaries to the scheme manager; make provision as to the method of providing information and as to certain details to be included whenever information is provided by beneficiaries or potential beneficiaries to the scheme manager; provides that the scheme manager may refuse to make a determination if he has no, insufficient or unsuitable information and requires him to notify the person who provided, or should have provided, the information accordingly; and make provision for recovery of overpayments where payments have been made in excess of entitlement under the FAS Regulations.

2967. Occupational pensions–Fraud compensation payments

OCCUPATIONAL PENSION SCHEMES (FRAUD COMPENSATION PAYMENTS AND MISCELLANEOUS AMENDMENTS) REGULATIONS 2005, SI 2005 2184; made under the Pensions Act 2004 s.182, s.183, s.185, s.186, s.190, s.203, s.206, s.207, s.307, s.315, s.318; and the Welfare Reform and Pension Act 1999 Sch.1 para.1. In force: September 1, 2005; £5.50.

These Regulations make provision in relation to the payment by the Board of the Pension Protection Fund of fraud compensation under the Pensions Act 2004. Fraud compensation is payable from September 1, 2005 where an employer in relation to an occupational pension scheme is insolvent, or unlikely to continue as a going concern, and the scheme has suffered a loss as a result of an act or omission which qualifies as an offence prescribed under these Regulations. The Regulations amend the Pension Protection Fund (Reviewable Matters) Regulations 2005 (SI 2005 600), the Pension Protection Fund (Review and Reconsideration of Reviewable Matters) Regulations 2005 (SI 2005 669) and the Pension Protection Fund (Provision of Information) Regulations 2005 (SI 2005 674). They specify the schemes and types of schemes which cannot apply for fraud compensation payments; provide that the prescribed offence is any offence involving dishonesty; provide for the conditions which must be satisfied by an employer, who is an employer in relation to a scheme which is not an eligible scheme, and is unlikely to continue as a going concern; specify who may make an application for fraud compensation and what information an application must contain; specify what must be contained in a notice confirming that a scheme status notice has become binding; set out how the Board will calculate amounts paid as fraud compensation; and set out the liabilities in respect of which interim fraud compensation payments can be made. It also makes other provision with regard to the making of interim payments.

2968. Occupational pensions–Guaranteed minimum pensions–Increase

GUARANTEED MINIMUM PENSIONS INCREASE ORDER 2005, SI 2005 521; made under the Pension Schemes Act 1993 s.109. In force: April 6, 2005; £3.00.

This Order is made in consequence of a review under the Pension Schemes Act 1993. It specifies 3 per cent as the percentage by which that part of any guaranteed minimum pension attributable to earnings factors for the tax years 1988-89 to 1996-97 and payable by contracted-out, defined benefit occupational pension schemes is to be increased.

2969. Occupational pensions–Ill health–Company withholding consent to ill health benefit–Correct test under pension rules

The appellant company (M) appealed against judgment for the respondent (K) on her pension fund claim with damages to be assessed. K had been employed by M as a survey plotter. She was subsequently diagnosed with tenosynovitis. She was seen by several doctors over a five year period as her symptoms altered. There were conflicting opinions from the doctors, some finding no physical signs of her injury that would prevent her from returning to work and others diagnosing her with chronic tenosynovitis. After two years' absence from work as a result of her condition, her employment was terminated by M on medical grounds. Accordingly K applied for an ill health retirement pension. M asserted that the pension fund rules required it to consent to the award of such a pension prior to the matter being considered by the pension trustees but that they felt unable to do so and such consent was therefore withheld. K argued that M owed a duty not to refuse consent arbitrarily. The judge rejected any evidence that K was malingering and found that the dismissal was arbitrary in that it prevented the trustees from fulfilling their duty under the rules of determining whether K qualified for an ill health pension. The judge awarded 50 per cent as the appropriate value of the chance that K would have been awarded a pension in full. M submitted that the judge had failed to take all relevant considerations into account.

Held, dismissing the appeal, that (1) M had misdirected itself on the approach to be taken to K's pension entitlement. However, the judge had wrongly approached the issues in the case. The pension fund rules actually required that M was not the primary decision maker but the filter before the trustees' decision. The correct test that M should have applied was to consider whether there was a real prospect of the trustees deciding that K was entitled to an ill health pension. M had applied the wrong test. (2) Therefore the question arose as to what M would have decided had it applied the correct test. M's attitude at the time it terminated K's employment had to be judged in the light of the material available to it at that time. On such evidence, if M had applied the correct test it would, as a matter of probability, have decided that there was a real prospect that the pension trustees would on investigation conclude that she was suffering from some physical or mental incapacity of a permanent nature that prevented her from performing her normal job even though not so serious as to prevent her from obtaining less well remunerated employment elsewhere. It would have been arbitrary to have reached any other conclusion. (3) The lack of express reasoning by the judge on the assessment of K's loss of chance lessened confidence that he had taken all relevant considerations into account. Justifiable criticisms of him went beyond lack of express reasoning and accordingly the appropriateness of his assessment had to be reconsidered having regard to his rejection of any suggestion of malingering. Taking into account all the medical material, K had a worthwhile prospect of having her claim to an ill health pension accepted by the trustees. However, the absence of objective symptoms after the early period of her complaints, and the inability of several doctors to identify any substantial problem preventing her return to work, threw substantial doubt on her prospects. The correct percentage had been 50 per cent and the damages would be assessed accordingly.

KELLY v. MERSEY DOCKS & HARBOUR CO, [2004] EWCA Civ 1676, [2005] Pens. L.R. 133, Waller, L.J., CA (Civ Div).

2970. Occupational pensions—Ill health—Suspension of ill health pension on determination that pensioner fit to return to work—Pensions Ombudsman—Findings of fact on inadequate evidence

The appellant (B) appealed against a determination of the Pensions Ombudsman not to uphold B's challenge against the withdrawal of his ill health pension paid by his former employer (L). The first respondent (T) was the trustee of L's pension scheme. B had worked as a bus driver from 1975 until his dismissal for ill health in 1992 and was subsequently paid an ill health pension. Annual medical reports were submitted to T and in 1994 to 1996 the reports stated that B was fit to return to work, but not as a bus driver. In 1997 the pension was withdrawn. Following B's complaint under T's internal dispute resolution procedure, a specialist report was obtained and this stated that B was capable of driving professionally. On appeal, B argued that the Ombudsman had accepted evidence for which there was no proper basis and that he had been assured by T's representative (M) before the termination of his employment that there was no possibility of the pension being stopped in the future as long as he did not return to work for L. On the strength of this representation, B maintained that he had accepted his dismissal on grounds of ill health but would not have done so otherwise. T argued that this alleged misrepresentation had not previously been brought up before the Ombudsman and could not be raised for the first time on appeal.

Held, allowing the appeal, that on the evidence the alleged misrepresentation by M had been raised as part of B's complaint to the Ombudsman. Further, there had been a serious procedural flaw, namely that no reasons had been given for advice in a letter to B in 1992 that his pension would be paid as long as he remained unfit for employment, or that if he recovered sufficiently it could be suspended until he reached 62. That appeared to be a finding of fact, but no explanation was given as to the basis of reasoning behind it. On the evidence, the Ombudsman's investigation had not been full and fair and was set aside accordingly.

BRENNAN v. LRT PENSION FUND TRUSTEE CO LTD, [2003] EWHC 3301, [2004] O.P.L.R. 195, Etherton, J., Ch D.

2971. Occupational pensions—Independent trustees

OCCUPATIONAL PENSION SCHEMES (INDEPENDENT TRUSTEE) REGULATIONS 2005, SI 2005 703; made under the Pension Schemes Act 1993 s.113, s.168, s.181, s.182; the Pensions Act 1995 s.22, s.23, s.118, s.124, s.125, s.174; and the Pensions Act 2004 s.10, s.93, s.97, s.315, s.318, Sch.1 para.21. In force: April 11, 2005; £3.00.

These Regulations, which revoke the Occupational Pension Schemes (Independent Trustee) Regulations 1997 (SI 1997 252), make provision about the trustee register to be compiled and maintained by the Pensions Regulator, and further provision about independent trustees. They amend the Pensions Act 1995 and the Pensions Act 2004 and partially revoke the Personal and Occupational Pension Schemes (Miscellaneous Amendments) (No.2) Regulations 1997 (SI 1997 3038) and the Occupational Pension Schemes (Winding up Notices and Reports etc.) Regulations 2002 (SI 2002 459).

2972. Occupational pensions—Internal controls

OCCUPATIONAL PENSION SCHEMES (INTERNAL CONTROLS) REGULATIONS 2005, SI 2005 3379; made under the European Communities Act 1972 s.2; and the Pensions Act 2004 s.90, s.318. In force: December 30, 2005; £3.00.

These Regulations amend the Pensions Act 2004 to implement the requirement in the European Parliament and Council Directive 2003/41 ([2003] OJ L235/10) Art.14(1), on the activities and supervision of institutions for occupational retirement provision that the trustees or managers of an occupational pension scheme must have adequate internal control mechanisms.

2973. Occupational pensions—Judiciary—Qualifying offices

ENTERPRISE ACT 2002 (JUDICIAL PENSIONS AND RETIREMENT ACT 1993) (CONSEQUENTIAL AMENDMENT) ORDER 2005, SI 2005 53; made under the Enterprise Act 2002 s.277. In force: February 9, 2005; £3.00.

This Order amends the Judicial Pensions and Retirement Act 1993 by adding the office of President of the Competition Appeal Tribunal to the list of offices which may be judicial offices for the purposes of the arrangements in respect of judicial pensions contained in Part 1 of that Act. Service in this office since its creation is to be treated as service in a qualifying judicial office.

2974. Occupational pensions—Levies

OCCUPATIONAL PENSION SCHEMES (LEVIES) REGULATIONS 2005, SI 2005 842; made under the Pensions Act 2004 s.117, s.126, s.174, s.181, s.189, s.209, s.315, s.318. In force: April 1, 2005; £3.00.

These Regulations impose the administration levy, the initial levy and the PPF Ombudsman levy provided for in the Pensions Act 2004.

2975. Occupational pensions—Local government pension scheme—85 year rule

LOCAL GOVERNMENT PENSION SCHEME (AMENDMENT) REGULATIONS 2005, SI 2005 1903; made under the Superannuation Act 1972 s.7, s.12. In force: August 3, 2005; £3.00.

These Regulations, which revoke the Local Government Pension Scheme (Amendment) (No.2) Regulations 2004 (SI 2004 3372), amend the Local Government Pension Scheme Regulations 1997 (SI 1997 1623) to restore to the Local Government Pension Scheme the so-called "85-year rule".

2976. Occupational pensions–Maladministration–Agreement to admit employee to pension scheme–Appropriate remedy

[Pension Schemes Act 1993 s.151 (2).]

The appellant (H) appealed against a determination of the Pensions Ombudsman that H was entitled to membership of his former employer's pension scheme instead of a remedy in damages. H had commenced employment with the respondent (S) in 1989 and maintained that S had agreed some three years later that he would be immediately admitted into the firm's pension scheme with retrospective effect to 1989. This was never done and in 1996 H left S's employment. H subsequently complained to the Ombudsman, whose decision was unclear on whether S were in breach of contract. The Ombudsman did, however, find that there had been maladministration on the part of S, resulting in injustice to H. On appeal, S argued that the Ombudsman's change in wording in a draft conclusion from "contract" to "agreement" must have been intended to distinguish between a legally binding contract and an agreement which fell short of that when making his findings as to the agreement to grant H entry into the pension scheme. H argued that if S were in breach of contract, the only remedy open to the Ombudsman to order was a payment of damages.

Held, giving judgment accordingly, that on balance the correct interpretation of the Ombudsman's conclusion was that he had found a binding agreement between H and S that H would be admitted into the pension scheme, and that S were in breach of that agreement. It was even more likely, on the evidence, that what the Ombudsman had meant was that although S were probably in breach of contract, it was more to the point that they were certainly guilty of maladministration and H's remedy was awarded accordingly, in terms of entitlement to pension rights rather than damages. Even if the Ombudsman had been uncertain about his decision on the issue of breach of contract, for the avoidance of doubt it was clear that there was a binding contract and S were in breach of it. The Ombudsman had jurisdiction under the Pension Schemes Act 1993 s.151 (2) to award a remedy to H to rectify S's failure to perform their contractual obligation, *Wakelin v. Read* [2000] O.P.L.R. 277, [2000] C.L.Y. 4393 applied. Although the remedy he awarded appeared to have been based on maladministration, he had a measure of discretion in deciding what award to make and in general the court ought not to interfere with that. It followed that the Ombudsman had not erred in applying the remedy he deemed most appropriate to address the subject matter of the complaint.

HENDERSON v. STEPHENSON HARWOOD, [2005] EWHC 24, [2005] O.P.L.R. 21, Park, J., Ch D.

2977. Occupational pensions–Members of the European Parliament–UK representatives

EUROPEAN PARLIAMENT (UNITED KINGDOM REPRESENTATIVES) PENSIONS (AMENDMENT) ORDER 2005, SI 2005 1924; made under the European Parliament (Pay and Pensions) Act 1979 s.4. In force: August 12, 2005; £3.00.

This Order amends the European Parliamentary (United Kingdom Representatives) Pensions (Consolidation and Amendment) Order 1994 (SI 1994 1662) to increase the contribution rate for participants with a 1/40th accrual rate from 9 per cent to 10 per cent with effect from April 1, 2004. It amends the early retirement provisions; introduces provisions for surviving civil partners and surviving partners who were neither married nor a civil partner; make pensions to adult survivors payable for life; and introduces provisions that reduce the adult survivor's pension where the adult survivor is more than 12 years younger than the participant.

2978. Occupational pensions–Miscellaneous amendments

OCCUPATIONAL PENSION SCHEMES (MISCELLANEOUS AMENDMENTS) REGULATIONS 2005, SI 2005 2113; made under the Pensions Act 2004 s.10, s.69, s.206, s.207, s.307, s.315, s.318, Sch.7 para.23. In force: in accordance with Reg.1; £6.00.

These Regulations make various miscellaneous amendments to the Pensions Act 2004, the Pension Protection Fund (Compensation) Regulations 2005 (SI 2005 670), the Pension Protection Fund (Entry Rules) Regulations 2005 (SI 2005 590), the Pension Protection Fund (Multi-employer Schemes) (Modification) Regulations 2005 (SI 2005 441), the Pensions Regulator (Notifiable Events) Regulations 2005 (SI 2005 900), the Pension Protection Fund (Provision of Information) Regulations 2005 (SI 2005 674), the Pension Protection Fund (Review and Reconsideration of Reviewable Matters) Regulations 2005 (SI 2005 669) and the Pension Protection Fund (Valuation) Regulations 2005 (SI 2005 672).

2979. Occupational pensions–National Health Service–Injury benefits

NATIONAL HEALTH SERVICE (PENSION SCHEME AND INJURY BENEFITS) AMENDMENT REGULATIONS 2005, SI 2005 661; made under the Superannuation Act 1972 s.10, s.12, Sch.3. In force: April 5, 2005; £4.00.

These Regulations amend the National Health Service Pension Scheme Regulations 1995 (SI 1995 300) and the National Health Service (Injury Benefits) Regulations 1995 (SI 1995 866). They insert various definitions relating to the types of medical services provided, and the persons or bodies who provide them; deal with the date from which a company which satisfies the conditions to be an OOH provider, is to be approved as an "employing authority"; enable an employee of an OOH provider that has retrospectively been approved as an employing authority for the purposes of the scheme to opt-out, join or rejoin the scheme during that retrospective period; and provide that where an employing authority has failed to deduct contributions, the Secretary of State may recover the amount of those contributions by deduction from benefits payable to, or in respect of the member if that would be to the member's advantage and the member agrees to the deduction.

2980. Occupational pensions–National Health Service–Injury benefits–Civil partnerships

NATIONAL HEALTH SERVICE (PENSION SCHEME, INJURY BENEFITS, ADDITIONAL VOLUNTARY CONTRIBUTIONS AND COMPENSATION FOR PREMATURE RETIREMENT) (CIVIL PARTNERSHIP) AMENDMENT REGULATIONS 2005, SI 2005 3074; made under the Superannuation Act 1972 s.10, s.12, s.24, Sch.3. In force: December 5, 2005; £3.00.

These Regulations make amendments to the National Health Service Pension Scheme Regulations 1995 (SI 1995 300), the National Health Service (Injury Benefits) Regulations 1995 (SI 1995 866), the National Health Service Pension Scheme (Additional Voluntary Contributions) Regulations 2000 (SI 2000 619) and the National Health Service (Compensation for Premature Retirement) Regulations 2002 (SI 2002 1311). The amendments extend provisions to civil partners, their dependants and surviving civil partners to enable them to receive benefits under the relevant legislation following the introduction of civil partnership when the Civil Partnership Act 2004 comes into force.

2981. Occupational pensions–Notifiable events

PENSIONS REGULATOR (NOTIFIABLE EVENTS) REGULATIONS 2005, SI 2005 900; made under the Pensions Act 2004 s.69, s.315, s.318. In force: April 6, 2005; £3.00.

These Regulations prescribe those events the occurrence of which there is a duty upon the appropriate person to notify the Pensions Regulator. In relation to events in respect of certain occupational pension schemes the duty falls on the trustees or managers of the scheme; in relation to events in respect of employers in relation to eligible pension schemes, the duty falls on the employers.

2982. Occupational pensions–Parliamentary pensions

PARLIAMENTARY PENSIONS (AMENDMENT) REGULATIONS 2005, SI 2005 887; made under the Parliamentary and other Pensions Act 1987 s.2. In force: April 14, 2005; £3.00.

These Regulations amend the Parliamentary Pensions (Consolidation and Amendment) Regulations 1993 (SI 1993 3253) to introduce provisions for surviving civil partners and surviving partners who were neither married nor a civil partner and to make pensions to adult survivors payable for life. They also increase the contribution rate for participants with a 1/40th accrual rate from 9 per cent to 10 per cent with effect from April 1, 2004; amend the early retirement provisions; and introduce provisions that reduce the adult survivor's pension where the adult survivor is more than 12 years younger than the participant.

2983. Occupational pensions–Part time employment–Police officers

POLICE PENSIONS (PART-TIME SERVICE) REGULATIONS 2005, SI 2005 1439; made under the Police Pensions Act 1976 s.1. In force: June 22, 2005; £3.00.

These Regulations amend the Police Pensions Regulations 1987 (SI 1982 257) and the Police Pensions (Purchase of Increased Benefits) Regulations 1987 (SI 1987 2215) to make provision for part-time police officers' pension benefits to be calculated as if they had been full-time officers, and then pro-rated for periods of part-time service. This replaces the previous basis of calculation under which part-time working counted as pensionable service on the basis of the actual hours served.

2984. Occupational pensions–Pension protection

OCCUPATIONAL PENSION SCHEMES (MODIFICATION OF PENSION PROTECTION PROVISIONS) REGULATIONS 2005, SI 2005 705; made under the Pensions Act 2004 s.167, s.315, s.318. In force: April 6, 2005; £3.00.

These Regulations amend the Pensions Act 2004 to provide pensions or other benefits to or in respect of any member or members under an occupational pension scheme that is an eligible scheme is discharged during an assessment period or on the day when that period will begin; that the actuarial valuations that are used to determine if the Board of the Pension Protection Fund is to assume responsibility for a scheme under s.127, s.128 or s.158 of the Act must take into account the effect of a relevant discharge that occurs before the valuation is approved by the Board; and provides that where a relevant discharge occurs the compensation payable under that Schedule is determined on the basis that the discharge occurred immediately before the assessment period began, and the scheme rules provided for it to occur, and hence for the rights corresponding to the discharged liabilities to cease.

2985. Occupational pensions–Personal pension schemes–General levy

OCCUPATIONAL AND PERSONAL PENSION SCHEMES (GENERAL LEVY) REGULATIONS 2005, SI 2005 626; made under the Pension Schemes Act 1993 s.168, s.175, s.181, s.182. In force: April 1, 2005; £3.00.

These Regulations, which revoke the Occupational and Personal Pension Schemes (Levy) Regulations 1997 (SI 1997 666), make provision for the imposition and payment of a levy for the purpose of meeting the cost of the Pensions Ombudsman, the Regulatory Authority (including its establishment under the Pensions Act 2004), grants made by the Regulatory Authority to advisory bodies, and the scheme established under s.106 of that Act for legal assistance in connection with proceedings before the Pensions Regulator Tribunal. They also make provision as to how the amount of the levy is to be determined, the times at which it is to be paid, and the circumstances in which it may be waived.

2986. Occupational pensions–Personal pension schemes–Payments

OCCUPATIONAL AND PERSONAL PENSION SCHEMES (PENSION LIBERATION) REGULATIONS 2005, SI 2005 992; made under the Pensions Act 2004 s.19, s.21, s.315, s.318. In force: April 27, 2005; £3.00.

These Regulations make provision in relation to payments made into an occupational or personal pension scheme by reason of a restitution order made by a court under the Pensions Act 2004 s.19 or of a repatriation order made by the Pensions Regulator. The Regulations modify certain references in the Pension Schemes Act 1993 to "a transfer payment" and to "transfer credits" so that those terms apply appropriately to payments made to schemes under orders made under the 2004 Act. They also modify the statutory discharges given to trustees or managers of schemes in the 1993 Act, then the trustees or managers shall have the benefit of those discharges if they have met the duty specified.

2987. Occupational pensions–Personal pension schemes–Reviewable matters–Reconsideration

OCCUPATIONAL PENSION SCHEMES AND PENSION PROTECTION FUND (AMENDMENT) REGULATIONS 2005, SI 2005 993; made under the Pensions Act 1995 s.60, s.124, s.174; and the Pensions Act 2004 s.38, s.52, s.122, s.126, s.129, s.135, s.139, s.140, s.141, s.143, s.146, s.150, s.151, s.207, s.307, s.315, s.318, Sch.7 para.23. In force: April 1, 2005; £3.00.

These Regulations amend the Pension Protection Fund (Multi-employer Schemes) (Modification) Regulations 2005 (SI 2005 441), the Pension Protection Fund (Entry Rules) Regulations 2005 (SI 2005 590), the Pension Protection Fund (Reviewable Ill Health Pensions) Regulations 2005 (SI 2005 652), the Pension Protection Fund (Review and Reconsideration of Reviewable Matters) Regulations 2005 (SI 2005 669), the Pension Protection Fund (Compensation) Regulations 2005 (SI 2005 670), the Pension Protection Fund (Valuation) Regulations 2005 (SI 2005 672), the Occupational Pension Schemes (Employer Debt) Regulations 2005 (SI 2005 678) and the Pensions Regulator (Contribution Notices and Restoration Orders) Regulations 2005 (SI 2005 931). They provide that the Reconsideration Committee must notify the Board of the Pension Protection Fund as well as any interested persons when it decides to reconsider a reviewable matter otherwise than on an application; and correct defective cross references.

2988. Occupational pensions–Personal pensions–Registers

REGISTER OF OCCUPATIONAL AND PERSONAL PENSION SCHEMES REGULATIONS 2005, SI 2005 597; made under the Pensions Act 2004 s.59, s.60, s.61, s.307, s.315, s.318. In force: in accordance with Reg.1; £3.00.

These Regulations, which revoke the Register of Occupational and Personal Pension Schemes Regulations 1997 (SI 1997 371) and the Register of Occupational and Personal Pension Schemes (Amendment) Regulations 1997 (SI 1997 1405), amend the Personal and Occupational Pension Schemes (Miscellaneous Amendments) (No.2) Regulations 1997 (SI 1997 3038), the Occupational and Personal Pension Schemes (Levy and Register) (Amendments) Regulations 1998 (SI 1998 600), the Occupational and Personal Pension Schemes (Penalties) Regulations 2000 (SI 2000 833), the Pension Sharing (Consequential and Miscellaneous Amendments) Regulations 2000 (SI 2000 2691) and the Occupational Pension Schemes (Republic of Ireland Schemes Exemption) Regulations 2000 (SI 2000 3198). The Regulations make provision about the register of occupational and personal pension schemes to be compiled and maintained under the Pensions Act 2004.

2989. Occupational pensions–Polish Forces–Civil partnerships

PENSIONS (POLISH FORCES) SCHEME (AMENDMENT) ORDER 2005, SI 2005 3040; made under the Polish Resettlement Act 1947 s.1. In force: December 5, 2005; £3.00.

This Order amends the Pensions (Polish Forces) Scheme 1964 (SI 1964 2007) in consequence of the introduction of civil partnerships by the Civil Partnership Act 2004.

2990. Occupational pensions–Rectification–Amendments not reflecting parties' intentions

[Social Security Pensions Act 1975.]

The claimant (G) sought a declaration and/or rectification in respect of a new rule on pension increases introduced into three occupational pension schemes under which G was the principal employer and of which the first defendant (X) was trustee. Following the coming into force of the Social Security Pensions Act 1975, the schemes became contracted out of the State Earnings Related Pensions Scheme (SERPS) and, accordingly, were required to pay a guaranteed minimum pension (GMP) to all members in respect of the members' pensionable service. The GMP element of the pension was, in effect, increased by the state through increases to the SERPS element of the state pension. From 1980, G began considering options for providing pension increases. There was discussion on the idea of ignoring that part of the company pension equal to the GMP when granting increases each year in order to avoid duplication of increases. In 1987 a new rule 7A was introduced into the schemes via deeds of amendment. Rule 7A provided for "pensions in payment from the [f] und" to be increased every year for 10 years at a rate, known as "2 per cent limited price indexation", equal to the lower of 2 per cent or the increase in the retail prices index. G argued that (1) properly interpreted, the words "pensions in payment from the fund" in rule 7A meant pensions in payment in excess of the GMP; (2) in the alternative, rectification of the 1987 deeds was necessary on the ground that the common intention of G and the trustee of the schemes at the time was that the increases under the new rule 7A would not apply to the GMP element of the pensions.

Held, giving judgment accordingly, that (1) the deeds had to be interpreted objectively, in their context and against their factual background. Their meaning could not be coloured by the subsequent conduct of the parties. The words were perfectly clear and bore their natural and ordinary meaning and not the meaning for which G contended. There was no reason why the court should reject as obviously wrong the conclusion, consistent with the clear and unambiguous language of rule 7A, that G and the trustee of the schemes intended that for a limited 10 year period there should be a guaranteed minimum increase of 2 per cent limited price indexation on the whole pension in payment, rather than simply a discretionary annual increase, usually in excess of that amount, but limited to the excess over the GMP. (2) The court could, in appropriate circumstances, make an order for rectification to bring an amendment to a pension scheme into line with the true intentions of the parties to the deed of amendment. Rectification was in principle available where the claimant could show convincingly a continuing common intention by the principal employer and the trustee which, by mistake, was not given effect to by the deed of amendment, and objective manifestation or outward expression of the continuing common intention was not a separate requirement, *AMP (UK) Plc v. Barker* [2001] O.P.L.R. 197, [2001] C.L.Y. 4595 followed. It was permissible in claims for rectification to have regard to events after the transaction as evidence of the parties' intentions at the time of the transaction and (where required) as objectively manifesting that intention. A decision in principle had been taken in late 1980 within the company that annual discretionary increases in pensions in payment should be restricted to the part of pension in excess of the GMP. That policy was consistently implemented each year thereafter. G was entitled to an order for rectification of the 1987 deeds.

GALLAHER LTD v. GALLAHER PENSIONS LTD, [2005] EWHC 42, [2005] O.P.L.R. 57, Etherton, J., Ch D.

2991. Occupational pensions–Redundancy–Retirement at employer's request–Entitlement to enhanced pension rights

The applicants (T), the trustees of an occupational pension scheme, sought determination as to whether certain members of the scheme whose employment had been terminated by redundancy were entitled to an enhancement of their pensions on the grounds of early retirement. The defendants (K) instituted a final salary scheme which provided for an enhanced pension where a member retired from service either at K's request or where K agreed to a member's request for retirement, subject to age and service criteria. K also set up a redundancy programme whereby requests were made for volunteers for redundancy. Following this, further employees were chosen for compulsory redundancy. The court was asked to determine whether those employees who had taken voluntary redundancy or been selected for compulsory redundancy were entitled to an enhanced pension under the rules of K's pension scheme.

Held, granting a declaration, that the word "retire" should be given its ordinary English meaning and involved an employee's decision to terminate his employment on grounds of increasing age or incapacity. The concept of retirement at the employer's request was a potential extension of that interpretation, but must still involve the employee's agreement in order to be regarded as retirement. Voluntary redundancy therefore fell within the definition of "retires at the employer's request" under the scheme. By contrast, the dismissal of an employee for any reason, including compulsory redundancy, did not involve consent by the employee and was at odds with the definition of retirement. It was noted that a number of employees had entered into redundancy agreements which expressly reserved their pension rights. In the absence of any such express reservation, however, it was unlikely that a term could be implied excluding the right to an enhanced pension.

AKESTER v. KINGSTON COMMUNICATIONS (HULL) PLC [2005] Pens. L.R. 153, Judge Hegarty Q.C., Ch D.

2992. Occupational pensions–Regulatory own funds

OCCUPATIONAL PENSION SCHEMES (REGULATORY OWN FUNDS) REGULATIONS 2005, SI 2005 3380; made under the European Communities Act 1972 s.2; and the Pensions Act 2004 s.60, s.223, s.232, s.315, s.318. In force: December 30, 2005; £3.00.

These Regulations, which amend the Pensions Act 2004 and the Occupational Pension Schemes (Scheme Funding) Regulations 2005 (SI 2005 3377), implement the European Parliament and Council Directive 2003/41 ([2003] OJ L235/10) Art.17, on the activities and supervision of institutions for occupational retirement provision. They require that where an occupational pension scheme itself, rather than an employer, covers any liability for risks linked to death, disability or longevity, guarantees any investment performance, or guarantees to provide defined benefits, the scheme must have additional assets above its technical provisions, which are no less than the minimum required. The additional assets must be free of foreseeable liabilities and must absorb discrepancies between anticipated and actual expenses and profits under the scheme. They also provide that penalties under the Pensions Act 1995 apply to a trustee or manager who has failed to take all reasonable steps to ensure compliance with the requirements in that regulation.

2993. Occupational pensions–Retirement–Scheme funding

OCCUPATIONAL PENSION SCHEMES (SCHEME FUNDING) REGULATIONS 2005, SI 2005 3377; made under the Pension Schemes (Northern Ireland) Act 1993 s.68, s.124, s.174; and the Pensions Act 2004 s.69, s.221, s.222, s.223, s.224, s.226, s.227, s.228, s.229, s.230, s.231, s.232, s.315, s.318. In force: December 30, 2005; £6.50.

These Regulations, which revoke Occupational Pension Schemes (Minimum Funding Requirement and Actuarial Valuations) Regulations 1996 (SI 1996 1536), and the Occupational Pension Schemes (Minimum Funding Requirement and Actuarial Valuations) Amendment Regulations 2004 (SI 2004 3031), amend the Occupational Pension Schemes (Contracting Out) Regulations 1996 (SI 1996 1172) Occupational Pension Schemes (Disclosure of Information) Regulations 1996 (SI 1996 1655), the Occupational Pension Schemes (Scheme Administration) Regulations 1996 (SI 1996 1715), the Occupational Pension Schemes (Transfer Values) Regulations 1996 (SI 1996 1847), the Personal and Occupational Pension Schemes (Pensions Ombudsman) Regulations 1996 (SI 1996 2475), the Occupational Pension Schemes (Deficiency on Winding Up etc.) Regulations 1996 (SI 1996 3126), the Occupational Pension Schemes (Investment) Regulations 1996 (SI 1996 3127), the Occupational Pension Schemes (Contracting-out) Regulations (Northern Ireland) 1996 (SR 1996 493), the Personal and Occupational Pension Schemes (Miscellaneous Amendments) (No.2) Regulations 1997 (SI 1997 786), the Personal and Occupational Pension Schemes (Miscellaneous Amendments) (No.2) Regulations 1997 (SI 1997 3038), the Personal and Occupational Pension Schemes (Miscellaneous Amendments) Regulations 1999 (SI 1999 3198), the Occupational Pension Schemes (Miscellaneous Amendments) Regulations 2000 (SI 2000 679), the Pension Sharing (Valuation) Regulations 2000 (SI 2000 1052), the Pension Sharing (Implementation and Discharge of Liability) Regulations 2000 (SI 2000 1053), the Pension Sharing (Pension Credit Benefit) Regulations 2000 (SI 2000 1054), the Stakeholder Pension Schemes Regulations 2000 (SI 2000 1403), the Pension Sharing (Consequential and Miscellaneous Amendments) Regulations 2000 (SI 2000 2691), the Occupational Pension Schemes (Republic of Ireland Schemes Exemption) Regulations 2000 (SI 2000 3198), the Occupational Pension Schemes (Minimum Funding Requirement and Miscellaneous Amendments) Regulations 2002 (SI 2002 380), the Occupational Pension Schemes (Employer Debt) Regulations 2005 (SI 2005 678), the Occupational Pension Schemes (Winding up etc.) Regulations 2005 (SI 2005 706), the Occupational Pension Schemes (Employer Debt etc.) (Amendment) Regulations 2005 (SI 2005 2224), and the Occupational Pension Schemes (Administration and Audited Accounts) (Amendment) Regulations 2005 (SI 2005 2426). They implement European Union Directive 2003/41 ([2003] OJ L235/10) Art.15 and Art.16, on the activities and supervision of institutions for occupational retirement provision.

2994. Occupational pensions–Teachers

TEACHERS' PENSIONS (AMENDMENT) REGULATIONS 2005, SI 2005 2198; made under the Superannuation Act 1972 s.9, s.12, s.24, Sch.3. In force: Reg.1: September 1, 2005; Reg.8: September 1, 2005; Reg.9: September 1, 2005; Reg.31: September 1, 2005; remainder: December 5, 2005; £3.00.

These Regulations amend the Teachers' Superannuation (Additional Voluntary Contributions) Regulations 1994 (SI 1994 2924), the Teachers (Compensation for Redundancy and Premature Retirement) Regulations 1997 (SI 1997 311) and the Teachers' Pensions Regulations 1997 (SI 1997 3001). Most of the amendments made by this instrument make provision following the creation of the status of civil partner by the Civil Partnership Act 2004. They also make amendments so that "dependant" includes a surviving civil partner; provide for the period for which short-and long-term compensation is payable to the surviving civil partner of a teacher who was credited with a period of service on termination of employment; enable a Scheme member to allocate his pension to provide an alternative benefit for his civil partner; and clarify the circumstances in which a survivor's pension is payable to both a widower and a beneficiary on the death of certain women members of the Scheme.

2995. Occupational pensions-Trustees-Investments

OCCUPATIONAL PENSION SCHEMES (INVESTMENT) REGULATIONS 2005, SI 2005 3378; made under the Pensions Act 1995 s.35, s.36, s.36A, s.40 s.118, s.123, s.124, s.125, s.174. In force: December 30, 2005; £3.00.

These Regulations, which revoke the Occupational Pension Schemes (Investment) Regulations 1996 (SI 1996 3127), amend the Personal and Occupational Pension Schemes (Miscellaneous Amendments) Regulations 1997 (SI 1997 786), the Occupational Pension Schemes (Reference Scheme and Miscellaneous Amendments) Regulations 1997 (SI 1997 819), the Occupational Pension Schemes (Investment, Assignment, Forfeiture, Bankruptcy etc.) (Amendment) Regulations 1999 (SI 1999 1849), the Stakeholder Pension Schemes Regulations 2000 (SI 2000 1403), the Occupational Pension Schemes (Republic of Ireland Schemes Exemption) Regulations 2000 (SI 2000 3198), the Financial Services and Markets Act 2000 (Consequential Amendments and Repeals) Order 2001 (SI 2001 3649), the Occupational and Personal Pension Schemes (Contracting-out) (Miscellaneous Amendments) Regulations 2002 (SI 2002 681) and the Occupational Pension Schemes (Employer Debt) Regulations 2005 (SI 2005 678). The Regulations supplement changes made to the Pensions Act 1995 by the Pensions Act 2004. They include provisions to implement certain requirements of the European Parliament and Council Directive 2003/41 ([2003] OJ L235/10) on the activities and supervision of institutions for occupational retirement provision. The Regulations impose requirements on trustees of occupational pension schemes in relation to the statement of investment principles required under s.35 of the 1995 Act and in relation to the choosing of investments. They impose restrictions on borrowing and the giving of guarantees by trustees and in respect of employer-related investments.

2996. Occupational pensions-Trustees powers and duties-Effect on pension scheme of US insolvency proceedings-Direction sought that trustees' proposed exercise of discretion was permissible

[Bankruptcy Code (United States) Ch.11.]

The instant application was made by the claimant trustees (A) of a retirement benefit scheme, which was a defined benefit occupational pension scheme. The third defendant (TNL) had been the principal employer involved in the scheme. A applied for a direction that they were permitted to vote against a plan, or at least not to support the plan, for the rearrangement of the assets and liabilities of a group of companies (F), of which TNL was the principal English subsidiary. The plan had been promulgated as part of proceedings under the Bankruptcy Code (United States) Ch.11 occasioned by the scale of claims made against F for asbestos related conditions alleged to have been caused by the products which TNL and some of its subsidiaries or associated companies had manufactured or used. A sought to obtain confirmation from the court that in exercising the discretion vested in them under the scheme to oppose the plan, they would be acting properly and permissibly.

Held, granting the application, that A were permitted not to accept or support the plan and the court directed that they should be given a wide discretion as to the manner in which they gave effect to that. A decision not to support the plan and to seek to recover outside it was one which A were reasonably entitled to make on the material before them. It was not the function of the court to determine whether the proposed exercise of the discretion was one which the court would itself perform in that particular way. The court's task was to satisfy itself that in reaching a decision about whether or not to support the plan, A had taken all relevant matters into account, not had regard to anything irrelevant or impermissible and had reached a conclusion which a reasonable body of trustees, faced with the same decision, could reasonably come to. Subject to satisfying the court on those matters, it was for A to make the decision. It was difficult to see how the court was ever likely to be in a better position than trustees to determine what was in the best interests of the beneficiaries they served.

ALEXANDER FORBES TRUSTEE SERVICES LTD v. JACKSON; *sub nom.* T&N RETIREMENT BENEFITS SCHEME (1989), *Re*, [2004] EWHC 2448, [2004] O.P.L.R. 391, Patten, J., Ch D.

2997. Occupational pensions–Trustees powers and duties–Validity of resolutions apportioning employer's pension debt deficit

[Insolvency Act 1986 s.124(1); Pensions Act 1995 s.68(2), s.75(2)(b), s.75A; Pensions Act 2004; Occupational Pension Schemes (Employer Debt) Regulations 2005 (SI 2005 678) Reg.5, Reg.6(2)(a), Reg.16, Sch.1; Pension Protection Fund (Multi-employer Schemes) (Modification) Regulations 2005 (SI 2005 441).]

The applicant employer (P) sought injunctive relief to restrain the respondent (T), the sole trustee of a pension scheme, from either presenting a petition to wind up P or applying for an administration order in its respect. P maintained that debts allegedly due by it to T of £400 million and £25 million were both bona fide disputed on substantial grounds. The scheme was a multi employer scheme under the Pension Protection Fund (Multi-employer Schemes) (Modification) Regulations 2005. T had wound up the scheme and the deficit then attributable to P, under the Pensions Act 1995 s.75(2)(b) and s.75A, and the Occupational Pension Schemes (Employer Debt) Regulations 2005, had been about £200,000. T had also purported to make an amendment deed to the scheme under either r.5 of the scheme or s.68(2) of the 1995 Act so as to assume power of absolute discretion in apportioning the deficit amongst the employers. Nine days later, P told T of its inability to pay about £15 million, which T had indicated it would seek from P under those powers. T had then that day passed a resolution that all participating scheme employers were to be jointly and severally liable for the whole deficit of about £400 million. Six days after the resolution, P went into creditors' voluntary winding up and was the fifth of the six employers to sustain an insolvency event. T passed a second resolution, 14 days after the first one, apportioning £25 million as the share of the £400 million deficit which was to be attributable to P whilst reserving a right to apportion a further part of the deficit to P. The issues were: firstly, whether the deed had been authorised by either power on which T had relied, and, if so, secondly, whether the first resolution had been authorised by r.35.1 of the deed, and, if so, whether it had been properly exercised; if not, then thirdly, whether the second resolution had similarly been authorised and properly exercised; fourthly, whether T had locus standi to petition for P to be wound up and, if so, for what debt and on what terms. P submitted that (1) T was bound to have regard to P's interests when exercising its power to amend the scheme in r.5, and the limitation as to apportionment that might be made under Reg.16 of the Employer Debt Regulations was to be imported into any apportionments made pursuant to r.5 amendments; (2) the first resolution had been ineffective because no debt had arisen to be apportioned and the imposition of a joint and several liability could not constitute an apportionment; (3) the second resolution was void because no debt had arisen to be apportioned.

Held, granting the application, that (1) when exercising its power, granted under the deed's amendment of the scheme, of absolute discretion in apportioning the debt, T was bound under r.5 of the scheme to have regard to P's interests, but there was no indication that it had not done so. Regulation 16 of the Employer Debt Regulations did not apply, as r.5 of the scheme had authorised the amending deed. (2) The first resolution had not been a valid exercise of the deed's power of apportionment. No debt had arisen under s.75A of the 1995 Act as the debt could only arise after the commencement of the winding up of the scheme when the actuary had made the prescribed calculations and a deficit emerged and was certified by him in accordance with Reg.5 of and Sch.1 to the Employer Debt Regulations. Moreover, the purported creation of a joint and several liability for the whole debt could not be an apportionment in shares of it amongst a class of six employers. (3) The second resolution was invalid as no debt had arisen under s.75A of the 1995 Act. (4) P's share of the debt deficit of about £200,000 under Reg.6(2)(a) of the

Employer Debt Regulations was a contingent or prospective liability such as to entitle T under the Insolvency Act 1986 s.124(1) to present a petition for P's winding up, *Mann v. Goldstein* [1968] 1 W.L.R. 1091, [1968] C.L.Y. 456 and *Stonegate Securities Ltd v. Gregory* [1980] Ch. 576, [1980] C.L.Y. 294 applied. P would be given the option to secure the relevant sum. (5) Although it was not necessary to consider them, three serious issues could have demonstrated the existence of a bona fide dispute on substantial grounds, namely: firstly, whether both resolutions had been vitiated by any intention and purpose of T to have P wound up so as to oblige the Pensions Protection Fund under the Pensions Act 2004 to accept the scheme, *Vatcher v. Paull* [1915] A.C. 372 considered; secondly, whether an exercise of the power to apportion might be set aside for mistake if such obligation of the Pensions Protection Fund had been misunderstood, *Hastings-Bass (Deceased), Re* [1975] Ch. 25, [1974] C.L.Y. 993 considered; thirdly, whether T had properly considered all appropriate factors when exercising its discretion in the passing of the second resolution.

PHOENIX VENTURE HOLDINGS LTD v. INDEPENDENT TRUSTEE SERVICES LTD, [2005] EWHC 1379, [2005] Pens. L.R. 379, Sir Andrew Morritt V.C., Ch D (Companies Ct).

2998. Occupational pensions—Winding up

OCCUPATIONAL PENSION SCHEMES (WINDING UP ETC.) REGULATIONS 2005, SI 2005 706; made under the Pension Schemes Act 1993 s.9, s.25, s.97, s.101I, s.101L, s.113, s.181, s.183; the Pensions Act 1995 s.49, s.56, s.57, s.68, s.73, s.73A, s.73B, s.74, s.76, s.91, s.118, s.119, s.124, s.174; and the Welfare Reform and Pensions Act 1999 s.30, s.83, Sch.5 para.8. In force: in accordance with Reg.1 (2); £4.50.

These Regulations amend the Pensions Act 1995, the Occupational Pension Schemes (Contracting-out) Regulations 1996 (SI 1996 1172), the Occupational Pension Schemes (Minimum Funding Requirement and Actuarial Valuations) Regulations 1996 (SI 1996 1536), the Occupational Pension Schemes (Disclosure of Information) Regulations 1996 (SI 1996 1655), the Occupational Pension Schemes (Transfer Values) Regulations 1996 (SI 1996 1847), the Occupational Pension Schemes (Payments to Employers) Regulations 1996 (SI 1996 2156), the Occupational Pension Schemes (Winding Up) Regulations 1996 (SI 1996 3126), the Occupational Pension Schemes (Assignment, Forfeiture, Bankruptcy etc.) Regulations 1997 (SI 1997 785), the Pension Sharing (Valuation) Regulations 2000 (SI 2000 1052), the Pension Sharing (Implementation and Discharge of Liability) Regulations 2000 (SI 2000 1053) and the Pension Sharing (Pension Credit Benefit) Regulations 2000 (SI 2000 1054). The Regulations are made as a consequence of provisions in the Pensions Act 2004 and relate to the winding up of occupational pension schemes. They modify provisions relating to pension compensation so that when they apply for determining the corresponding PPF liability by reference to which the liabilities within the 1995 Act s.73(4)(b) are capped, they apply differently from the way in which they apply for determining compensation from the Pension Protection Fund; provide that where a person's pensionable service ceases when the scheme begins to be wound up, he is treated as having opted for a contribution refund; prescribe when trustees or managers of schemes are required to adjust entitlements to discretionary awards and to survivors' benefits when schemes are winding up; and contain provisions about the calculation of the value or amount of scheme assets and liabilities.

2999. Occupational pensions—Winding up—Multi employer schemes

OCCUPATIONAL PENSION SCHEMES (WINDING UP) (MODIFICATION FOR MULTI-EMPLOYER SCHEMES AND MISCELLANEOUS AMENDMENTS) REGULATIONS 2005, SI 2005 2159; made under the Pensions Act 1995 s.56, s.73, s.73B, s.118, s.124, s.174. In force: August 31, 2005; £3.00.

These Regulations amend the Occupational Pension Schemes (Minimum Funding Requirement and Actuarial Valuations) Regulations 1996 (SI 1996

1536) and the Occupational Pension Schemes (Winding up etc.) Regulations 2005 (SI 2005 706). They modify the position under the Pensions Act 1995 where an occupational pension scheme that has more than one employer or has had more than one employer at any time since April 6, 2005 and whose rules do not provide for the partial winding up of the scheme if it is being wound up. They provide for cases where an insolvency event has occurred in relation to one of the persons who is an employer in relation to an occupational pension scheme since April 6, 2005 and the trustees or managers of the scheme have determined in the last 3 months that it is probable that the scheme will enter an assessment period in the next 12 months (that is, a period when the Board of the Pension Protection Fund determine whether to assume responsibility for the scheme for the purposes of pension protection).

3000. Occupational pensions–Winding up–Surplus–Trustee's discretion to augment payments to existing members

The claimant (L), the trustee of a pension scheme established by a company M, sought directions from the court on two issues which arose from the winding up of the scheme following M's voluntary liquidation. The scheme had been wound up in accordance with the scheme's rules and had a large surplus. L sought determination of whether, under the rules, it could (1) apply the surplus to augment the pensions of those members who were already receiving payments at the time of the liquidation; (2) allocate funds in a way that would neutralise the discrimination against male members, whose guaranteed minimum pension was less valuable than that of females because the men's normal retirement age was 65, whereas the women's was 60.

Held, giving directions, that (1) the scheme's rules relating to winding up conferred no discretionary powers on L to augment payments to existing pensioners. The rules only provided for L to secure the pensions and other benefits to which existing pensioners were entitled, *Thrells Ltd v. Lomas* [1993] 1 W.L.R. 456, [1993] C.L.Y. 3064 applied. L did have the discretionary power to increase payments to prospective pensioners, being those who were not receiving payments at the time of the liquidation. (2) Accordingly, L had a discretion to augment payments to prospective male members, in order to neutralise discrimination. This would be entirely proper in view of the fact that such discrimination could conflict with Community law, *Barber v. Guardian Royal Exchange Assurance Group (C262/88)* [1991] 1 Q.B. 344, [1990] C.L.Y. 1915 applied. This discretion did not however extend to existing members.

LEADENHALL INDEPENDENT TRUSTEES LTD v. WELHAM, [2004] EWHC 740, [2004] O.P.L.R. 115, Park, J., Ch D.

3001. Occupational pensions–Winding up–Transfer value

OCCUPATIONAL PENSION SCHEMES (WINDING UP, DEFICIENCY ON WINDING UP AND TRANSFER VALUES) (AMENDMENT) REGULATIONS 2005, SI 2005 72; made under the Pension Schemes Act 1993 s.113, s.181, s.182; and the Pensions Act 1995 s.73, s.75, s.124, s.174. In force: February 15, 2005; £3.00.

These Regulations amend the Occupational Pension Schemes (Transfer Values) Regulations 1996 (SI 1996 1847), the Occupational Pension Schemes (Winding Up) Regulations 1996 (SI 1996 3126) and the Occupational Pension Schemes (Deficiency on Winding Up etc.) Regulations 1996 (SI 1996 3128). The changes provide for the calculation of liabilities in the case of any occupational pension scheme. The Regulations also make amendments to require the scheme's liabilities to be calculated and valued on a basis which assumes that any accrued rights to a pension or other benefit under the scheme for members with more than two years of pensionable service, as well as any entitlement to the payment of a pension that has arisen under the scheme (including any increase in a pension), will be discharged by the purchase of annuities; and to require trustees who receive a request for a statement of entitlement to a guaranteed cash equivalent to inform the member, where the scheme is being wound up, that the value of the member's guaranteed cash equivalent may be affected by the scheme winding up, that a decision to take a guaranteed cash equivalent should be given careful consideration, and that the member should consider taking independent financial advice before deciding whether to take the guaranteed cash equivalent.

3002. Pension attachment–Calculation of attachable part of pension–Income tax payable in Member State of residence not taken into account–Freedom of movement–European Community

[EC Treaty Art.18.]

The Finnish Supreme Court sought a preliminary ruling on the interpretation of the EC Treaty Art.18. Upon his retirement, a Finnish national (P) had settled in Spain. He received an invalidity pension in Finland which was paid into a Finnish bank account. An attachment on P's pension was authorised, pursuant to national laws on enforcement, for the purpose of recovering a debt. P was subject to income tax in Spain under the provisions of a double taxation convention and therefore was not subject to any deduction at source in Finland. According to the national legislation, the attachable part of his pension was calculated on the basis of his gross pension without taking account of the tax payable in Spain. P was left with a monthly disposable sum which was less than he would have received if he had continued to reside in Finland. The national court asked the European Court of Justice to rule on whether such legislation was precluded by Art.18 of the Treaty.

Held, giving a preliminary ruling, that (1) in principle, the requirements of Art.18 of the Treaty precluded national legislation under which the attachable part of a pension paid at regular intervals in that Member State to a debtor was calculated by deducting the income tax prepayment levied in that State, while the tax which the holder of such a pension would have to pay on it in his Member State of residence was not taken into account for the purpose of calculating the attachable portion of that pension. (2) Community law did not preclude such national legislation if it provided for tax to be taken into account on condition that the debtor prove the level of his income tax liability in his State of residence. However, that was only the case to the extent that (a) the right of the debtor to have tax taken into account was clear from the legislation; (b) the rules for taking tax into account were such as to guarantee to the interested party the right to obtain annual adjustment of the attachable portion of his pension to the same extent as if the tax had been deducted at source in the Member State in which the legislation had been enacted; (c) the rules did not have the effect of making it impossible or excessively difficult to exercise that right.

PUSA v. OSUUSPANKKIEN KESKINAINEN VAKUUTUSYHTIO (C224/02) [2004] All E.R. (EC) 797, Judge Jann (President), ECJ.

3003. Pension benefits peaceful enjoyment of possessions–Objective justification for discriminatory provision

See SOCIAL SECURITY: R. (on the application of Carson) v. Secretary of State for Work and Pensions. §3835

3004. Pension protection–Board of the Pension Protection Fund–Appointment of members–Procedure

PENSION PROTECTION FUND (APPOINTMENT OF ORDINARY MEMBERS) REGULATIONS 2005, SI 2005 616; made under the Pensions Act 2004 s.315, s.318, Sch.5 para.2. In force: April 6, 2005; £3.00.

These Regulations set out the procedure which the Board of the Pension Protection Fund must follow in making any appointment of ordinary members to the Board.

3005. Pension protection–Board of the Pension Protection Fund–Review and reconsideration

PENSION PROTECTION FUND (REVIEW AND RECONSIDERATION OF REVIEWABLE MATTERS) REGULATIONS 2005, SI 2005 669; made under the Pensions Act 2004 s.207, s.315, s.318. In force: April 6, 2005; £3.00.

These Regulations provide for the review and reconsideration by the Pension Protection Fund Board of the reviewable matters specified in the Pensions Act 2004 Sch.9.

3006. Pension protection–Compensation

PENSION PROTECTION FUND (COMPENSATION) REGULATIONS 2005, SI 2005 670; made under the Pensions Act 2004 s.315, s.318, Sch.7 para.4, Sch.7 para.6, Sch.7 para.9, Sch.7 para.12, Sch.7 para.13, Sch.7 para.16, Sch.7 para.17, Sch.7 para.18, Sch.7 para.20, Sch.7 para.23, Sch.7 para.24, Sch.7 para.25, Sch.7 para.26, Sch.7 para.28, Sch.7 para.31, Sch.7 para.33. In force: April 6, 2005; £3.50.

The Board of the Pension Protection Fund is established to provide compensation for members of certain occupational pension schemes in the event of the insolvency of the scheme's sponsoring employer and where the pension scheme is under-funded at a certain level. Provisions in these Regulations: set out the conditions under which a person can receive early payment of compensation from the Board before he attains normal pension age; prescribe the circumstances in which a widow or widower will not be entitled to receive periodic compensation following the death of his spouse; prescribe the circumstances in which a relevant partner or a surviving dependant will be entitled to receive periodic compensation following the death of his partner (in the case of a relevant partner) or his parent (in the case of a surviving dependant); and prescribe the amount of periodic compensation that can be paid to surviving dependants who qualify for periodic compensation.

3007. Pension protection–Compensation–Provision of information

PENSION PROTECTION FUND (PROVISION OF INFORMATION) REGULATIONS 2005, SI 2005 674; made under the Pensions Act 2004 s.190, s.203, s.315, s.318. In force: April 6, 2005; £3.00.

These Regulations make provision relating to the information which the Board of the Pension Protection Fund, the members and beneficiaries of certain occupational pension schemes, the trustees and managers of such schemes and certain insolvency practitioners are required to provide where compensation is, or may become, payable by the Board.

3008. Pension protection–Eligible schemes

PENSION PROTECTION FUND (ENTRY RULES) REGULATIONS 2005, SI 2005 590; made under the Pensions Act 2004 s.120, s.121, s.122, s.123, s.126, s.129, s.130, s.133, s.134, s.135, s.138, s.139, s.146, s.147, s.148, s.150, s.151, s.315, s.318. In force: in accordance with Reg.1 (2); £5.50.

These Regulations make provision relating to various requirements under the Pensions Act 2004 Part 2 which include setting out those schemes which are not "eligible schemes".

3009. Pension protection–Eligible schemes–Assessment of assets and liabilities

PENSION PROTECTION FUND (VALUATION) REGULATIONS 2005, SI 2005 672; made under the Pensions Act 2004 s.143, s.145, s.179, s.190, s.315, s.318. In force: April 6, 2005; £3.00.

These Regulations provide for the assessment of the assets and liabilities of eligible schemes in accordance with the Pensions Act 2004 s.143 and s.179.

3010. **Pension protection – Hybrid schemes**

PENSION PROTECTION FUND (HYBRID SCHEMES) (MODIFICATION) REGULATIONS 2005, SI 2005 449; made under the Pensions Act 2004 s.135, s.307, s.315, s.318. In force: April 6, 2005; £3.00.

These Regulations modify how the provisions of Part 2 of the Pensions Act 2004 operate in relation to hybrid schemes. They prescribe the circumstances in which, and the conditions subject to which, the prohibition in s.135(4) on transferring, or making transfer payments in respect of, any member's rights and discharging any liability to, or in respect of, a member, does not apply. They also provide for the Board to give directions to a relevant person regarding the exercise of his powers during an assessment period in respect of discharging liabilities of the scheme which relate to money purchase benefits.

3011. **Pension protection – Ill health pensions – Reviews**

PENSION PROTECTION FUND (REVIEWABLE ILL HEALTH PENSIONS) REGULATIONS 2005, SI 2005 652; made under the Pensions Act 2004 s.140, s.141, s.315, s.318, Sch.7 para.37. In force: April 6, 2005; £3.00.

These Regulations provide for the review of reviewable ill health pensions by the Board of the Pension Protection Fund, the procedure to be followed in relation to a review and the determination of compensation payable in respect of an ill health pension where the conditions set out in the Pensions Act 2004 s.141(3) are satisfied.

3012. **Pension protection – Insolvent partnerships – Insolvency events**

PENSION PROTECTION FUND (INSOLVENT PARTNERSHIPS) (AMENDMENT OF INSOLVENCY EVENTS) ORDER 2005, SI 2005 2893; made under the Pensions Act 2004 s.121. In force: November 10, 2005; £3.00.

This Order amends the Pensions Act 2004 as a consequence of the Insolvent Partnerships (Amendment) Order 2005 (SI 2005 1516).

3013. **Pension protection – Investigations – Maladministration**

PENSION PROTECTION FUND (MALADMINISTRATION) REGULATIONS 2005, SI 2005 650; made under the Pensions Act 2004 s.208, s.315, s.318. In force: April 6, 2005; £3.00.

These Regulations provide for the investigation by the Board of the Pension Protection Fund of allegations of maladministration under the Pensions Act 2004 s.208. They provide that the Board must investigate certain complaints; provide that an application must generally be made within 28 days of the day on which the complainant became aware of the act or omission by the Board; provide for the form that the complaint must take; set out the matters to be considered by the Board in giving a decision; provide for the time by which a decision must be given and makes further provision for an interim reply; provide that the Board may pay compensation to the complainant; set out the matters to be included in a decision; provide that the Board must send a copy of the decision to the complainant and a summary of the decision to other persons if it considers that they may have suffered injustice, unless the Board considers that any injustice is likely to have been trivial; provide that after the Board has given a decision a complainant may apply to a committee of the Board for further investigation of the complaint and a further decision; provide that an application must be sent to the committee of the Board within 28 days of the day on which the Board sent the complainant a copy of the decision; and make further provision for the Board to give a decision where an application is made outside this time limit in certain circumstances. The Regulations also provide for the form that an application must take; set out the matters to be considered by the committee of the Board in giving a decision; provide for the time by which a decision must be given by the committee of the Board and make further provision for an interim reply; provide for the powers of the committee of the Board in making a review decision, including the power to pay compensation to the complainant; provide for matters to be included in a decision by the committee of the Board; provide that the committee of the Board must send a copy of the decision to the complainant and a summary of the decision to other persons if it considers that they may have suffered injustice, unless the Board considers that any injustice is likely to have been trivial. They further provide that a person concerned with an act or omission by the Board that gives rise to a complaint of maladministration must not participate in the investigation or a decision in respect of a relevant complaint; provide that an application for investigation and a decision in respect of a relevant complaint may be made by a person on behalf of the complainant; and provide for representation where the complainant dies or is incapable of acting.

3014. Pension protection—Investment costs—Payments

PENSION PROTECTION FUND (PAYMENTS TO MEET INVESTMENT COSTS) REGULATIONS 2005, SI 2005 1610; made under the Pensions Act 2004 s.173, s.315, s.318. In force: July 7, 2005; £3.00.

These Regulations make provision for the Board of the Pension Protection Fund to make payments from the Pension Protection Fund to fund managers or custodians in relation to contractual liabilities relating to the investment of the Fund. The contracts entered into must be necessary for the prudent management of the Fund. The Board is required to appoint a minimum of two fund managers. As these Regulations are made before the expiry of the period of six months beginning with the coming into force of the provisions of the Act by virtue of which they are made, the requirement for the Secretary of State to consult such persons as he considers appropriate does not apply.

3015. Pension protection—Levies consultation

PENSION PROTECTION FUND (PENSION PROTECTION LEVIES CONSULTATION) REGULATIONS 2005, SI 2005 1440; made under the Pensions Act 2004 s.176, s.315, s.318. In force: June 20, 2005; £3.00.

These Regulations prescribe the manner and publication requirements for the consultation required under s.176 of the Pensions Act 2004. Section 176(1), which provides that the Board of the Pension Protection Fund must consult such persons as it considers appropriate before determining matters relating to the pension protection levies specified in s.175(5) of the Act. They prescribe the manner of the consultation and provide that the Board shall include details of how it proposes to determine the matters relating to s.175(5) of the Act in the consultation document, that the Board shall publish the consultation document on its website and in paper format if so requested, and that the Board shall publish a summary of non-confidential responses it receives to the consultation in the same way. They also prescribe the manner of publication of details of any determination under s.175 of the Act. That regulation provides that those details shall be published on the Board's website and in a paper format to any person upon request. As these Regulations are made before the expiry of the period of six months beginning with the coming into force of the provisions of the Act by virtue of which they are made, the requirement for the Secretary of State to consult such persons as he considers appropriate does not apply.

3016. Pension protection—Limit on borrowing

PENSION PROTECTION FUND (LIMIT ON BORROWING) ORDER 2005, SI 2005 339; made under the Pensions Act 2004 s.115. In force: March 9, 2005; £3.00.

The Board of the Pension Protection Fund is established under the Pensions Act 2004 which enables the Board to borrow such sums as it may require for exercising any of its functions. The Act also provides that the Board may not borrow if to do so would take the aggregate amount outstanding of the principal sums borrowed by it over its borrowing limit or increase the amount by which the outstanding aggregate amount exceeds that limit. It also defines "borrowing limit" as such limit which may be specified by order. This Order specifies that limit as £25 million.

3017. Pension protection–Multi-employer schemes

PENSION PROTECTION FUND (MULTI-EMPLOYER SCHEMES) (MODIFICATION) REGULATIONS 2005, SI 2005 441; made under the Pensions Act 2004 s.307, s.315, s.318. In force: in accordance with Reg.1; £7.50.

These Regulations amend the Pensions Act 2004 as it applies in relation to a section of a segregated multi-employer scheme with only one employer in relation to that section so that Part 2 of the Act can apply in relation to such a section as if it were separate scheme; as it applies in relation to a section of a segregated multi-employer scheme with at least two employers in relation to that section; and as it applies in relation to a non-segregated multi-employer section of a segregated multi-employer scheme. They also make amendments as the Act applies in relation to a non-segregated multi-employer scheme the rules of which contain a provision for the partial winding up of the scheme in certain specified circumstances; as it applies in relation to a non-segregated multi-employer scheme the rules of which do not contain a provision for the partial winding up of the section in certain specified circumstances; and as it applies in relation to a multi-employer section of a segregated scheme the rules of which contain an option for the trustees or managers of the scheme to segregate such part of the assets of the section which are attributable to the liabilities of the section to provide pensions or other benefits to or in respect of the pensionable service of members by reference to an employer in relation to the section in specified circumstances.

3018. Pension protection–Ombudsman–Functions

PENSION PROTECTION FUND (PPF OMBUDSMAN) ORDER 2005, SI 2005 824; made under the Pensions Act 2004 s.209, s.210, s.315. In force: April 6, 2005; £3.00.

This Order makes provision in respect of the PPF Ombudsman and the Deputy PPF (Pension Protection Fund). It provides that the Secretary of State may make payments to the PPF Ombudsman, or a Deputy PPF Ombudsman, by way of remuneration, compensation, pension and allowances. It makes provision for the reimbursement of expenses in respect of the same persons; provides for the appointment of staff by the PPF Ombudsman; provides that the Secretary of State may make available additional staff and facilities to the PPF Ombudsman; provides that the PPF Ombudsman may (with certain exceptions) delegate any functions to a member of his staff or (subject to authorisation by him) an additional member of staff made available by the Secretary of State; and makes provision about restrictions on the disclosure of information held by the PPF Ombudsman.

3019. Pension protection–Overseas schemes–Transfer of payments

CONTRACTING-OUT, PROTECTED RIGHTS AND SAFEGUARDED RIGHTS (TRANSFER PAYMENT) AMENDMENT REGULATIONS 2005, SI 2005 555; made under the Pension Schemes Act 1993 s.12C, s.20, s.28, s.68D, s.181, s.182. In force: April 6, 2005; £3.00.

These Regulations amend the Contracting-out (Transfer and Transfer Payment) Regulations 1996 (SI 1996 1462), the Protected Rights (Transfer Payment) Regulations 1996 (SI 1996 1461) and the Pension Sharing (Pension Credit Benefit) Regulations 2000 (SI 2000 1054). They make amendments so the Regulations apply in respect of transfer payments made to an overseas arrangement; to remove the permanent emigration requirement in relation to transfer payments to overseas schemes or arrangements in respect of guaranteed minimum pensions; to insert a definition of "overseas arrangement"; to remove the permanent emigration requirement in relation to transfer payments to overseas schemes or arrangements in respect of protected rights.

3020. Pension protection–Partially guaranteed schemes

PENSION PROTECTION FUND (PARTIALLY GUARANTEED SCHEMES) (MODIFICATION) REGULATIONS 2005, SI 2005 277; made under the Pensions Act 2004 s.307, s.315, s.318. In force: in accordance with Reg.1 (1); £3.00.

These Regulations are made under the Pensions Act 2004 which contains a power to modify the provisions of Part 2 of the Act in relation to partially guaranteed schemes. The Regulations modify Part 2 of the Act in respect of partially guaranteed schemes. The modifications operate so that the Board only takes into account the assets and liabilities of the unsecured part of a partially guaranteed scheme and can only assume responsibility for that part. As these Regulations are made before the expiry of the period of six months beginning with the coming into force of the provisions of the Act by virtue of which they are made, the requirement of the Secretary of State to consult such persons as he considers appropriate does not apply.

3021. Pension protection–Pensions regulator–Financial support directions

PENSIONS REGULATOR (FINANCIAL SUPPORT DIRECTIONS ETC.) REGULATIONS 2005, SI 2005 2188; made under the Pensions Act 2004 s.43, s.44, s.45, s.307, s.315, s.318. In force: September 1, 2005; £3.00.

These Regulations make further provision about s.43 and related sections of the Pensions Act 2004, known as one of the anti-avoidance provisions, that is, the Regulator's power to issue financial support directions. They also, in relation to all the anti-avoidance provisions (that is, contribution notices, financial support directions and restoration orders) extend the meaning of employer to include former employers in specified circumstances and modify those provisions of the Act in their application to multi-employer schemes.

3022. Pension protection–Reviewable matters

PENSION PROTECTION FUND (REVIEWABLE MATTERS) REGULATIONS 2005, SI 2005 600; made under the Pensions Act 2004 s.206, s.307, s.315, s.318. In force: April 6, 2005; £3.00.

These Regulations make provision in respect of certain reviewable matters specified in the Pensions Act 2004 Sch.9.

3023. Pension protection–Statement of investment principles

PENSION PROTECTION FUND (STATEMENT OF INVESTMENT PRINCIPLES) REGULATIONS 2005, SI 2005 675; made under the Pensions Act 2004 s.114, s.315, s.318. In force: April 6, 2005; £3.00.

These Regulations make provision relating to a statement of investment principles which the Board of the Pension Protection Fund is required to prepare, review and if necessary revise in accordance with the Pensions Act 2004 s.114.

3024. Pension protection fund–Compensation cap

PENSION PROTECTION FUND (PENSION COMPENSATION CAP) ORDER 2005, SI 2005 825; made under the Pensions Act 2004 Sch.7 para.26. In force: April 6, 2005; £3.00.

This Order specifies the amount of the compensation cap for the purposes of the Pensions Act 2004. The compensation cap is an amount used by the Board of the Pension Protection Fund to determine the amount of compensation payable to a person who is under normal pension age on the assessment date and whose compensation is not derived from a pension payable on the grounds of ill health or a survivor's pension.

3025. Pension protection fund–Ombudsman–Investigation of complaints

PENSION PROTECTION FUND (INVESTIGATION BY PPF OMBUDSMAN OF COMPLAINTS OF MALADMINISTRATION) REGULATIONS 2005, SI 2005 2025; made under the Pensions Act 2004 s.214, s.315, s.318. In force: July 21, 2005; £3.00.

These Regulations provide for matters to be referred to, and investigated and determined by, the PPF Ombudsman if they have been the subject of a complaint of maladministration about which there has either been an investigation and decision by both the Board of the Pension Protection Fund and a committee of the Board under the Pension Protection Fund (Maladministration) Regulations 2005 (SI 2005 650) or such an investigation and decision by the Board and an application for an investigation and decision by such a committee without a decision having been given by the committee within the required time.

3026. Pension protection fund–Ombudsman–Investigations–Disclosure of information

PENSION PROTECTION FUND (PPF OMBUDSMAN) AMENDMENT ORDER 2005, SI 2005 2023; made under the Pensions Act 2004 s.316. In force: July 21, 2005; £3.00.

This Order amends the Pension Protection Fund (PPF Ombudsman) Order 2005 (SI 2005 824) which makes provision in respect of the Ombudsman for the Board of the Pension Protection Fund and the Deputy PPF Ombudsman. It provides that the PPF Ombudsman may, during the course of his investigation of a reviewable matter referred to him by virtue of Regulations made under the Pensions Act 2004 or of a complaint of maladministration referred to him by virtue of Regulations made under the Act, disclose to specified persons information obtained during the course of the investigation.

3027. Pension protection fund–Ombudsman–Reviewable matters

PENSION PROTECTION FUND (REFERENCE OF REVIEWABLE MATTERS TO THE PPF OMBUDSMAN) REGULATIONS 2005, SI 2005 2024; made under the Pensions Act 2004 s.213, s.315, s.318. In force: July 21, 2005; £3.00.

These Regulations provide for a reviewable matter to be referred to, and investigated and determined by, the Ombudsman for the Board of the Pension Protection Fund following a reconsideration decision given by the Reconsideration Committee of the Board of the Pension Protection Fund under the Pension Protection Fund (Review and Reconsideration of Reviewable Matters) Regulations 2005 (SI 2005 669).

3028. Pension protection fund–Tax

PENSION PROTECTION FUND (TAX) (2005-06) REGULATIONS 2005, SI 2005 1907; made under the Finance Act 2005 s.102. In force: August 3, 2005; £3.00.

The Pensions Act 2004, Part 2 establishes the Board of the Pension Protection Fund. The Board is a body corporate and has two main functions: it administers the Pension Protection Fund, from which compensation will be paid to members of certain pension schemes which are underfunded and no longer have a solvent sponsoring employer; and it is to administer the Fraud Compensation Fund, from which compensation will be paid to certain pension schemes which no longer have a solvent sponsoring employer in cases of fraud and misappropriation of scheme assets. The Finance Act 2004 made new provision relating to pension schemes but this provision does not take effect until April 6, 2006. These Regulations make provision for the application of income tax, corporation tax and capital gains tax in relation to the Board, the Pension Protection Fund and the Fraud Compensation Fund during the period beginning on April 6, 2005 and ending on April 6, 2006.

3029. Pension protection scheme—Companies—Winding up

PENSION PROTECTION FUND (ENTRY RULES) AMENDMENT REGULATIONS 2005, SI 2005 2153; made under the Pensions Act 2004 s.121, s.125, s.126, s.129, s.315, s.318. In force: August 24, 2005; £3.00.

These Regulations amend the Pension Protection Fund (Entry Rules) Regulations 2005 (SI 2005 590) to insert a definition of the Pension Protection Fund (Multi-employer Schemes) (Modification) Regulations 2005 (SI 2005 441); to correct cross references to the Pensions Act 1995 s.75; to add further insolvency events where a company or partnership in administration commences winding up or where a proposal for a voluntary arrangement is made; and provide that where the employer is a trade union in relation to which it is not possible for an insolvency event to occur, the trustees or managers of an eligible scheme must apply to the Board of the Pension Protection Fund for it to assume responsibility for that scheme under the Pensions Act 2004 s.128 where the condition in s.129(1)(a) of the Act is satisfied.

3030. Pension schemes—Accounting and assessment

REGISTERED PENSION SCHEMES (ACCOUNTING AND ASSESSMENT) REGULATIONS 2005, SI 2005 3454; made under the Finance Act 2004 s.254, s.255. In force: April 6, 2006; £3.00.

These Regulations, which modify the Finance Act 1998, make provisions in relation to the making of assessments and related matters in connection with charges to tax under the Finance Act 2004 Pt 4 in respect of pension schemes which are or have been registered under that Part of that Act.

3031. Pension schemes—Categories

PENSION SCHEMES (CATEGORIES) REGULATIONS 2005, SI 2005 2401; made under the Pension Schemes Act 1993 s.1, s.181, s.182; and the Welfare Reform and Pensions Act 1999 s.8, s.83. In force: in accordance with Reg.1; £3.00.

These Regulations provide for certain pension schemes to fall within the definition of "occupational pension scheme" in the Pension Schemes Act 1993. They also provide that certain stakeholder pension schemes which are occupational pension schemes are to be treated as personal pension schemes.

3032. Pension schemes—Discharge of liabilities

REGISTERED PENSION SCHEMES (DISCHARGE OF LIABILITIES UNDER SECTIONS 267 AND 268 OF THE FINANCE ACT 2004) REGULATIONS 2005, SI 2005 3452; made under the Finance Act 2004 s.267, s.268. In force: April 6, 2006; £3.00.

These Regulations make provision supplementing s.267 and s.268 of the Finance Act 2004 in connection with the making of applications by scheme administrators of registered pension schemes and other persons for relief from the lifetime allowance charges under s.267 and the unauthorised payments surcharge, and the scheme sanction charge under s.268. They provide for the form and content of a s.267 application or s 268 application; provide for s.267 applications and s.268 applications to be made on behalf of persons who are incapacitated, within the meaning of the Taxes Management Act 1970 s.118, by those managing their affairs; and provide for the making of supplementary applications where the applicant discovers that the original application contained a mistake or error.

3033. Pension schemes—Early retirement—Employee's right to incapacity pension— Approach of pensions ombudsman

[Pension Schemes Act 1993 s.151.]

The appellant trustees (S) appealed against a decision of a Pensions Ombudsman requiring them to pay the respondent (C) incapacity pension. S were the trustees of a pension scheme of the company for which C had worked as a process operator. As a result of a fall at work C had suffered a back injury which required surgery. However due to his obesity C was unable to have the operation and it became increasingly unrealistic for C to do the physical work that was required of his job. Thereafter C left employment and applied for incapacity pension under the pension scheme. Under the rules of the scheme, C was entitled to the pension if S were satisfied that C had left employment by reason of a permanent incapacity arising from ill health which was likely to incapacitate him permanently or for an indefinite period from doing his ordinary work. S refused C's application. S argued that (1) the ombudsman ought to have held that the phrase "ordinary work" included work of a similar grade, status and salary as the job C was doing, including supervisory or clerical work; (2) the ombudsman was wrong in law in his approach to the question of whether C's injury was likely to incapacitate him "permanently or for an indefinite period"; (3) the ombudsman had no power to grant the pension but should have remitted the matter back to S for reconsideration.

Held, dismissing the appeal, that (1) the rule referred not just to "ordinary work" but to "his ordinary work". The expression meant work of the same general nature as that which C had done before he became incapacitated from doing it. It did not include work of a wholly different nature, even if the grades, statuses and salaries of the two kinds of work were similar. As the benefit under the rules was not a discretionary benefit S were under an obligation to pay it to C if he met the conditions for it. (2) In general, a court (and thus the Pensions Ombudsman) should not interfere with decisions which trustees take in relation to claims for benefits under the rules of their particular scheme. However, if the trustees decide a question in a way which the court considered perverse the court would intervene, *Harris v. Lord Shuttleworth (Trustees of the National & Provincial Building Society Pension Fund)* [1994] I.C.R. 991, [1995] C.L.Y. 3837 considered. Although there was medical evidence which made several references to C's obesity, it did not do so in the context of saying that he could cure it himself and thereby take a critical step towards ending his incapacity to do what had been his ordinary work. The ombudsman was therefore right to conclude that S had come to a perverse decision unsubstantiated by the evidence. (3) In view of his determination that S had acted perversely, the ombudsman had acted within his powers in deciding to grant the pension rather than remitting the matter back to S. The ombudsman had the statutory power under Pension Schemes Act 1993 s.151 to direct any person responsible for the management of the scheme to take such steps as he might specify in the written statement of his determination.

SAFFIL PENSION SCHEME TRUSTEES v. CURZON, [2005] EWHC 293, [2005] O.P.L.R. 113, Park, J., Ch D.

3034. Pension schemes–Employer loans–Interest rates

REGISTERED PENSION SCHEMES (PRESCRIBED INTEREST RATES FOR AUTHORISED EMPLOYER LOANS) REGULATIONS 2005, SI 2005 3449; made under the Finance Act 2004 s.179. In force: April 6, 2006; £3.00.

The Finance Act 2004 s.179 prescribes conditions which must be met before a loan made by a registered pension scheme to a sponsoring employer is an authorised employer loan. One of the conditions is that the rate of interest payable on the loan is not less than the rate prescribed by regulations. These Regulations prescribe that rate for a period beginning on the sixth working day of one month and ending on the day preceding the sixth working day of the next month, as one per cent more than the relevant interest rate found on the reference date preceding the start of the period.

3035. Pension schemes–Firefighters–Survivor benefits–Civil partnerships

FIREFIGHTERS' PENSION SCHEME (CIVIL PARTNERSHIP AMENDMENTS) (ENGLAND AND SCOTLAND) ORDER 2005, SI 2005 3228; made under the Civil Partnership Act 2004 s.259. In force: December 5, 2005; £3.00.

This Order makes amendments to the Firemen's Pension Scheme Order 1992 (SI 1992 129) consequential on the Civil Partnership Act 2004 and enables civil partners to qualify for survivor benefits under the Scheme on a similar basis to spouses. The main difference is that the calculation of benefits for a civil partner is based on the firefighter's service from April 6, 1988.

3036. Pension schemes–Freezing orders–Time limits

PENSIONS REGULATOR (FREEZING ORDERS AND CONSEQUENTIAL AMENDMENTS) REGULATIONS 2005, SI 2005 686; made under the Pension Schemes Act 2003 s.93A, s.99, s.181, s.182; and the Pensions Act 2004 s.23, s.24, s.30, s.315, s.318. In force: April 6, 2005; £3.00.

Trustees or managers of pension schemes are required to abide by specified time limits in taking certain actions in relation to members' entitlements, such as issuing a statement of entitlement to a member of a salary related occupational pension scheme, or carrying out what the member requires in response to an application received from the member to take his cash equivalent. If, however, the scheme in question is the subject of a freezing order which contains certain directions, it may be impossible for the trustees or managers to abide by the time limits set out in the Pensions Schemes Act 1993 or regulations made under it. These Regulations, which amend the Pension Schemes Act 1993 and the Occupational Pension Schemes (Transfer Values) Regulations 1996 (SI 1996 1847), prescribe the qualifications necessary for a person to be brought within the meaning of "the actuary"; take account of the fact that it may be impossible to abide by time limits, and extends the time limits where appropriate if a freezing order containing a relevant direction is or has been in effect; and prescribe the period within which trustees or managers must give notice to the Regulator and to the member of failure to pay a contribution, where they were required to do so by the Regulator.

3037. Pension schemes–Legal assistance schemes

PENSIONS REGULATOR TRIBUNAL (LEGAL ASSISTANCE SCHEME) REGULATIONS 2005, SI 2005 781; made under the Pensions Act 2004 s.106. In force: April 15, 2005; £3.00.

These Regulations govern the provision of legal assistance in respect of matters which are referred to the Pensions Regulator Tribunal under the Pensions Act 2004 or the Pensions (Northern Ireland) Order 2005 (SI 2005 255 (NI.1)). In particular, the Regulations provide for the manner in which applications for legal assistance are to be made; the circumstances in which an individual may receive legal assistance, including with regard to his financial eligibility; the assessment of his financial resources, including the calculation of his disposable income and disposable capital; the determination of any contribution payable; the assignment and change of representatives; the withdrawal of legal assistance and duty to report abuse; and the constitution of the Tribunal.

3038. Pension schemes–Legal assistance schemes–Costs

PENSIONS REGULATOR TRIBUNAL (LEGAL ASSISTANCE SCHEME -COSTS) REGULATIONS 2005, SI 2005 782; made under the Pensions Act 2004 s.106. In force: April 15, 2005; £3.00.

These Regulations make provision for the remuneration of work done under a legal assistance order in respect of cases which are before the Pensions Regulator Tribunal established under the Pensions Act 2004 s.102. The Regulations include provisions dealing with disbursements; interim payments and staged payments in long cases; hardship payments; how claims are to be made, determined and paid; and the redetermination of costs by an appropriate officer, appeals from the appropriate officer to a costs judge, and appeals from the costs judge to the High Court.

3039. Pension schemes–Minimum contributions

REGISTERED PENSION SCHEMES (MINIMUM CONTRIBUTIONS) REGULATIONS 2005, SI 2005 3450; made under the Finance Act 2004 s.202. In force: April 6, 2006; £3.00.

These Regulations make provision supplementing the provisions of the Finance Act 2004 s.202. They provide for the application of provisions of the Taxes Management Act 1970 as if a sum representing basic rate tax payable on the amount of minimum contributions paid by Commissioners for Her Majesty's Revenue and Customs were a repayment of tax to which the recipient was not entitled.

3040. Pension schemes–Pensionable age and occupations

REGISTERED PENSION SCHEMES (PRESCRIBED SCHEMES AND OCCUPATIONS) REGULATIONS 2005, SI 2005 3451; made under the Finance Act 2004 Sch.36 para.19, Sch.36 para.23. In force: April 6, 2006; £3.00.

The Finance Act 2004 Sch.36 para.19 provides that members of registered pension schemes which are prescribed by regulations can preserve their full entitlement to benefits under those schemes in the event that they take such benefits before they reach normal minimum pension age. These Regulations prescribes the pension schemes for the purposes of Sch.36 para.19, members of which may take their pensions before normal minimum pension age without a reduction in the lifetime allowance; and prescribe the occupations for the purposes of Sch.36 para.23, members of which may take their pension at the time which is the member's protected pension age rather than normal minimum pension age.

3041. Pension schemes–Provision of information–Description of persons

REGISTERED PENSION SCHEMES AND EMPLOYER-FINANCED RETIREMENT BENEFITS SCHEMES (INFORMATION) (PRESCRIBED DESCRIPTIONS OF PERSONS) REGULATIONS 2005, SI 2005 3455; made under the Finance Act 2004 s.252. In force: April 6, 2006; £3.00.

These Regulations prescribe the descriptions of persons to whom the Inland Revenue may give a notice requiring the production of documents and the provision of information in connection with the matters mentioned in the Finance Act 2004 s.252(3). Section 252(3) relates, among other things, to information about pension schemes which are or have been registered under Pt 4 of that Act, or which are the subject of an application for registration and annuities purchased with sums or assets held for the purposes of a registered pension scheme.

3042. Pension schemes–Trustees powers and duties–Money purchase schemes–Scope of trustee's powers to reduce deficit

[Pension Schemes Act 1993 s.181 (1); Pensions Act 1995 s.56, s.67, s.124(5).]

The first defendant (K), the principal employer in a contracted in occupational pension scheme, appealed against determinations made on questions arising in the administration of the scheme ([2004] EWHC 1844, [2005] 1 W.L.R. 995). The second defendant cross appealed against part of the decision finding that cl.8.5 of the scheme empowered the trustee to reduce pensions already in payment. The scheme had run into substantial deficit. A danger had arisen that the scheme would run out of money unless K was obliged to make good the deficit or the trustee had the power to reduce pensions already in payment. The trustee sought clarification as to whether it had such a power and to find out what obligation, if any, K had to fund the deficit. Subject to restrictions, cl.8.4 of the scheme gave the trustee power to reduce contributions or increase benefits by declaring bonuses when the scheme was in surplus. Clause 8.5, also subject to restrictions, gave the trustee power to make "adjustments and amendments to the benefits secured or thereafter accruing" when the scheme was in deficit. Rule 7 set out the method of calculating a pension commencing at the normal retirement date. The judge below had found that: (i) the scheme was not a "money purchase scheme" within the meaning of the Pension Schemes Act 1993 and the Pensions Act 1995. As a result, s.56 of the 1995 Act applied to the scheme imposing a "minimum funding requirement" which had the effect of requiring K to make good the scheme's deficit; (ii) cl.8.5 of the scheme empowered the trustee to reduce pensions already in payment; (iii) cl.8.5 was a power to "modify" the scheme within the meaning of s.67 of the 1995 Act and was, therefore, subject to the restrictions imposed by s.67(2) of the 1995 Act. The issues for determination by the court were (1) whether the scheme was a "money purchase scheme" within the meaning of the 1993 Act and the 1995 Act; (2) whether cl.8.5 of the scheme empowered the trustee to reduce pensions already in payment; (3) whether cl.8.5 was a power to "modify" the scheme within the meaning of s.67 of the 1995 Act.

Held, dismissing the appeal and allowing the cross appeal, that (1) a "money purchase scheme" was defined by s.124(5) of the 1995 Act and s.181(1) of the 1993 Act as a pension scheme in which all the benefits provided were "money purchase benefits." Neither of the two components of the pension benefit prescribed by rule 7, the standard pension and any benefits declared under cl.8.4, were "money purchase benefits." Therefore, the scheme was not a "money purchase scheme". (2) On the true construction of the scheme the calculation of a pension was a once and for all calculation, carried out as at the date when the pension first came into payment. Therefore, a power to reduce pensions already in payment would require the clearest words. Clause 8.5 did not clearly confer such a power. The power was expressed to adjust or amend "the benefits secured or thereafter accruing" and that indicated that what was envisaged was a situation in which a member was still accruing pension rights, year on year. The clause, therefore, did not empower the trustee to reduce pensions already in payment. (3) The power to reduce benefits in cl.8.5 was a power to "modify" the scheme within the meaning of s.67 of the 1995 Act and was, therefore, subject to the restrictions imposed by s.67(2) of the 1995 Act.

AON TRUST CORP LTD v. KPMG, [2005] EWCA Civ 1004, [2006] 1 W.L.R. 97, Mummery, L.J., CA (Civ Div).

3043. Pension schemes—Trustees powers and duties in dealing with surplus—Rights of existing pensioners

The appellant pensioner (B) appealed against the dismissal of his maladministration complaint to the Pensions Ombudsman (P). B was receiving a pension from the Commonwealth War Graves Commission Superannuation Scheme. In 1992 the fund was found to be in surplus. Rule 6(A) of the scheme required the trustees (T) to deal with any surplus by reducing contributions or increasing benefits to scheme members, who were defined as members of the scheme still employed by the commission. T decided to use its discretionary power under r.15 of the scheme to alter the scheme rules to provide increased benefits to future retirees. B, as an existing retiree, contended that the decision was an abuse and discriminatory as it only benefited future pensioners and made no improvement to his pension. P dismissed the claim on the ground that T had a duty to treat all members equitably, which did not mean treating them all the same. On appeal, B argued that P's decision was wrong.

Held, dismissing the appeal, that there had been no error of law in P's decision. T had used its discretionary power appropriately in order to carry out the requirements of r.6(A). The rules did not allow surplus to be paid to those who had already retired since they were no longer "members" within the definition of the rules. In any event, T could not properly carry out its function of acting in the best interest of the scheme as a whole if it were always required to make any improvements across the board.

BALYAN v. PENSIONS OMBUDSMAN, [2003] EWHC 1826, [2003] O.P.L.R. 387, Patten, J., Ch D.

3044. Pensions Act 2004 (c.35)–Appointed Day Order–S.126(2)

PENSION PROTECTION FUND (ELIGIBLE SCHEMES) APPOINTED DAY ORDER 2005, SI 2005 599 (C.28); made under the Pensions Act 2004 s.126. Commencement details: bringing into force various provisions of the 2004 Act on April 6, 2005; £3.00.

This Order appoints the day for the purposes of the Pensions Act 2004 s.126(2) as April 6, 2005.

3045. Pensions Act 2004 (c.35)–Commencement No.2, Transitional Provisions and Consequential Amendments

PENSIONS ACT 2004 (COMMENCEMENT NO.2, TRANSITIONAL PROVISIONS AND CONSEQUENTIAL AMENDMENTS) ORDER 2005, SI 2005 275 (C.10); made under the Pensions Act 2004 s.315, s.322. Commencement details: bringing into force various provisions of the 2004 Act in accordance with Art.2; £3.00.

This Order, which transitionally modifies the Pension Schemes Act 1993 and amends the Paternity and Adoption Leave Regulations 2002 (SI 2002 2788), provides for specified provisions to come into force on specified dates.

3046. Pensions Act 2004 (c.35)–Commencement No.3, Transitional Provisions and Amendment Order

PENSIONS ACT 2004 (COMMENCEMENT NO.3, TRANSITIONAL PROVISIONS AND AMENDMENT) ORDER 2005, SI 2005 695 (C.29); made under the Pensions Act 2004 s.300, s.315, s.322. Commencement details: bringing into force various provisions of the 2004 Act in accordance with Art.2; £3.00.

This Order makes further provision for the coming into force of the Pensions Act 2004. In particular, it makes provision in connection with the coming into force of the Pensions Act 2004 s.300(1) which provides for the dissolution of the Occupational Pensions Regulatory Authority and under s.300(2) of the Act for the transfer of property, rights and liabilities of the Authority to the Pensions Regulator. The Order also transitionally modifies the Pension Schemes Act 1993, the Pensions Act 1995, the Pensions Act 2004 and amends the Pensions Act 2004 (Commencement No.2, Transitional Provisions and Consequential Amendments) Order 2005 (SI 2005 275 (C.10)).

3047. Pensions Act 2004 (c.35)–Commencement No.4 and Amendment Order

PENSIONS ACT 2004 (COMMENCEMENT NO.4 AND AMENDMENT) ORDER 2005, SI 2005 1108 (C.46); made under the Pensions Act 2004 s.91, s.315, s.322. Commencement details: bringing into force various provisions of the 2004 Act on April 6, 2005; £3.00.

This Order appoints the day for the coming into effect of the Pensions Regulator Code of Practice No.1: Reporting breaches of the law as April 6, 2005. It also amends the Pensions Act 2004 (Commencement No.3, Transitional Provisions and Amendment) Order 2005 (SI 2005 695 (C.29)) so as to make a transitional saving in respect of the repeals of the Pensions Act 1995 s.74.

3048. Pensions Act 2004 (c.35)–Commencement No.5 Order

PENSIONS ACT 2004 (COMMENCEMENT NO.5) ORDER 2005, SI 2005 1436 (C.63); made under the Pensions Act 2004 s.315, s.322. Commencement details: bringing into force various provisions of the 2004 Act in accordance with Art.2; £3.00.

This Order makes further provision for the coming into force of provisions of the Pensions Act 2004.

3049. Pensions Act 2004 (c.35)–Commencement No.6,Transitional Provisions and Savings Order

PENSIONS ACT 2004 (COMMENCEMENT NO.6,TRANSITIONAL PROVISIONS AND SAVINGS) ORDER 2005, SI 2005 1720 (C.73); made under the Pensions Act 2004 s.91, s.302, s.315, s.322. In force: June 28, 2005; £3.00.

This Order makes further provision for the coming into force of provisions of the Pensions Act 2004.

3050. Pensions Act 2004 (c.35)–Commencement No.7 Order

PENSIONS ACT 2004 (COMMENCEMENT NO.7) ORDER 2005, SI 2005 2447 (C.102); made under the Pensions Act 2004 s.315, s.322. Commencement details: bringing into force various provisions of the 2004 Act on September 1, 2005; September 22, 2005; November 1, 2005; November 14, 2005 and April 6, 2006; £3.00.

This Order makes further provision for the coming into force of provisions of the Pensions Act 2004.

3051. Pensions Act 2004 (c.35)–Commencement No.8 Order

PENSIONS ACT 2004 (COMMENCEMENT NO.8) ORDER 2005, SI 2005 3331 (C.141); made under the Pensions Act 2004 s.315, s.322. Commencement details: bringing into force various provisions of the 2004 Act in accordance with Art.2 and Art.3; £3.00.

This Order makes further provision for the coming into force of provisions of the Pensions Act 2004.

3052. Pensions Appeal Tribunals–Posthumous appeals

PENSIONS APPEAL TRIBUNALS (POSTHUMOUS APPEALS) (AMENDMENT) ORDER 2005, SI 2005 245; made under the Social Security Act 1980 s.16. In force: in accordance with Art.1 (1); £3.00.

This Order amends the Pensions Appeal Tribunals (Posthumous Appeals) Order 1980 (SI 1980 1082) to reflect changes made to the route of onward appeal from the Pensions Appeal Tribunal.

3053. Pensions ombudsman–Disclosure of information–Specified persons

PENSIONS OMBUDSMAN (DISCLOSURE OF INFORMATION) (AMENDMENT OF SPECIFIED PERSON) ORDER 2005, SI 2005 2743; made under the Pension Schemes Act 1993 s.149. In force: November 1, 2005; £3.00.

This Order amends the Pensions Schemes Act 1993 by adding to the list of persons to whom the Pensions Ombudsman may disclose any information which he obtains for the purposes of an investigation, if he considers that the disclosure would enable or assist that person to discharge any of his functions. The persons added to the list are the body corporate which operates the Financial Ombudsman Service, and any ombudsman of that service.

3054. Pensions Ombudsman–Maladministration–Pension based on initial assessment of level of disability–Relevance of later medical evidence

The appellant local authority appealed against a decision relating to the pension payable to the respondent (W), a former fireman. W had taken early retirement on ill health grounds. He had been assessed as being 25 per cent disabled with a hearing impairment. He did not appeal against that decision. Seven years later, he was examined by a different doctor as part of a regular review procedure. The second doctor assessed him as being 60 per cent disabled but expressed the view that his hearing impairment was largely unchanged since his retirement. W complained to the Pensions Ombudsman, who concluded that the first doctor had been wrong, made a finding of maladministration and back dated the second doctor's assessment to W's retirement. The local authority argued that the Pensions

Ombudsman had erred in his approach to the complaint and had not been entitled to make a finding of maladministration based on the decision of the first doctor rather than on the basis of an act by the local authority, which was the body responsible for the pension scheme's administration.

Held, allowing the appeal, that the Pensions Ombudsman had erred in law and his decision could not stand. The first doctor was not herself responsible for administering the pension scheme and it was impossible to see how the local authority could be found liable for her acts and accordingly guilty of an act of maladministration in relation to the pension awarded to W on his retirement, *R. (on the application of Britannic Asset Management Ltd) v. Pensions Ombudsman* [2002] EWCA Civ 1405, [2002] 4 All E.R. 860, [2002] C.L.Y. 3400 applied. The required causal connection was not present, nor was the complaint concerned with the manner in which the local authority carried out its duties rather than what it did, *R. v. Local Commissioner for Administration for England, ex p. Eastleigh BC* [1988] Q.B. 855, [1988] C.L.Y. 2200 applied. The Pensions Ombudsman had failed to ask himself the right question, namely how the acts complained of could amount to maladministration, where all the local authority had done was to act upon the undisputed opinion of an independent doctor. Further, it had been perverse to conclude that the first doctor had been wrong just because a second doctor had taken a different view.

SUFFOLK CC v. WALLIS, [2004] EWHC 788, [2004] O.P.L.R. 301, Peter Smith, J., Ch D.

3055. Pensions   Ombudsman–Maladministration–Teachers–Maladministration not causative of loss

The second appellant (the local authority), as administrators of the Teachers' Pension Scheme, appealed against a determination made by the Pensions Ombudsman in favour of the respondent executors (F) of the estate of a deceased teacher (D). D had retired in 1978 and died in 1997 without ever having claimed her pension under the scheme. F were paid the arrears of benefits under the scheme together with interest from 1996, the date from which an entitlement to interest arose under the terms of the scheme. F claimed interest for the whole of the period and complained that the local authority should have informed D of her right to claim a pension. On F's complaint to the Ombudsman it was found that the local authority had been guilty of maladministration in failing to send D a form notifying her of her pension entitlement and that there had been further maladministration in failing to take steps to find D to inform her of her benefits. The Ombudsman awarded interest on the gross sum from 1978.

Held, allowing the appeal, that an appeal against a determination of the Ombudsman could only be made on a point of law. The finding made that no letter had been sent out to D was a finding of fact that could not be challenged. However, the finding that the absence of one letter had caused D to fail to claim her pension was flawed and could be challenged. As the maladministration had not caused the loss the Ombudsman's determination was set aside. Further, the finding that there had been maladministration in failing to take steps to locate D was wrong in law as there was no statutory or common law duty to advise members on their rights under the scheme. By awarding interest on the gross sum without any deduction for tax the Ombudsman had awarded the executors more than the amount that D would have received.

SECRETARY OF STATE FOR EDUCATION AND SKILLS v. FARLEY, [2004] EWHC 1768, [2004] O.P.L.R. 353, Peter Smith, J., Ch D.

3056. Public services–Increase in rates

PENSIONS INCREASE (REVIEW) ORDER 2005, SI 2005 858; made under the Social Security Pensions Act 1975 s.59. In force: April 11, 2005; £3.00.

Under the Social Security Pensions Act 1975, the Treasury (in whom the functions conferred by those provisions are now vested) are required to provide by order for the increase in the rates of public service pensions. This Order specifies the increases for pensions which became payable on or after April 12, 2004 and before April 11, 2005.

3057. Registered pension schemes–Relief at source

REGISTERED PENSION SCHEMES (RELIEF AT SOURCE) REGULATIONS 2005, SI 2005 3448; made under the Finance Act 2004 s.192. In force: April 6, 2006; £3.00.

These Regulations make provision for relief from tax on payments made to scheme administrators of registered pension schemes under the Finance Act 2004 Pt 4. They prescribe conditions which are to be satisfied in order for relief to be given at source in respect of payments of contributions to registered pension schemes; deal with persons under a legal disability and those who have physical difficulties in signing documents; make provision for electronic documents; make provision about claims to relief; deal with the recovery of relief in circumstances where it should not have been allowed; deal with information which is required to be given to HM Revenue and Customs for inspection by them of records maintained by the scheme administrator; and contain a transitional provision continuing the effectiveness of information delivered, and declarations made, under the Personal Pension Schemes (Relief at Source) Regulations 1988 (SI 1988 1013).

3058. Retirement pensions–Deferment

SOCIAL SECURITY (DEFERRAL OF RETIREMENT PENSIONS, SHARED ADDITIONAL PENSION AND GRADUATED RETIREMENT BENEFIT) (MISCELLANEOUS PROVISIONS) REGULATIONS 2005, SI 2005 2677; made under the Social Security Contributions and Benefits Act 1992 s.62, s.122, s.136, s.137, s.175, Sch.5 para.A1, Sch.5 para.3C, Sch.5A para.1; the Social Security Administration Act 1992 s.5, s.189; the Social Security Act 1998 s.9, s.10, s.11, s.18, s.79, s.84; the Child Support, Pensions and Social Security Act 2000 Sch.7 para.3, Sch.7 para.4, Sch.7 para.20, Sch.7 para.23; the State Pension Credit Act 2002 s.15, s.17; and the Pensions Act 2004 Sch.11 para.27. In force: April 6, 2006; £3.00.

These Regulations amend Social Security (Claims and Payments) Regulations 1987 (SI 1987 1968), the Housing Benefit (General) Regulations 1987 (SI 1987 1971), the Council Tax Benefit (General) Regulations 1992 (SI 1992 1814), the Social Security and Child Support (Decisions and Appeals) Regulations 1999 (SI 1999 991), the Housing Benefit and Council Tax Benefit (Decisions and Appeals) Regulations 2001 (SI 2001 1002), the State Pension Credit Regulations 2002 (SI 2002 1792), the Social Security (Graduated Retirement Benefit) Regulations 2005 (SI 2005 454) and the Social Security (Retirement Pensions etc.) (Transitional Provisions) Regulations 2005 (SI 2005 469). The Regulations make provision relating to changes to the regime for deferring entitlement to state pension made by the Pensions Act 2004 which provide for a choice between increments and a lump sum for those who have deferred their entitlement to retirement pension, shared additional pension or graduated retirement benefit, for 12 months or more.

3059. Retirement pensions–Deferment

SOCIAL SECURITY (RETIREMENT PENSIONS ETC.) (TRANSITIONAL PROVISIONS) REGULATIONS 2005, SI 2005 469; made under the Pensions Act 2004 Sch.11 para.27. In force: April 6, 2005; £3.00.

These Regulations modify the provisions relating to the deferral of entitlement to retirement pension that are inserted in the Social Security Contributions and Benefits Act 1992 by the Pensions Act 2004. They also modify the new Sch.5A relating to the deferral of entitlement to shared additional pension.

3060. Stakeholder pensions—Members rights

STAKEHOLDER PENSION SCHEMES (AMENDMENT) REGULATIONS 2005, SI 2005 577; made under the Welfare Reform and Pensions Act 1999 s.1, s.8, s.83. In force: April 6, 2005; £3.00.

These Regulations amend the Stakeholder Pension Schemes Regulations 2000 (SI 2000 1403) by inserting provisions for the rights of a member of a stakeholder pension scheme who has made no choice as to how his contributions should be invested to be subject to "lifestyling", from at least five years before his retirement date.

3061. State pension credit—Age related payments—Lump sum

AGE-RELATED PAYMENTS REGULATIONS 2005, SI 2005 1983; made under the Age-Related Payments Act 2004 s.7. In force: September 1, 2005; £3.00.

These Regulations make provision for the payment of a one-off lump sum of £200 or £100 to households with occupants who have attained the age of 65, and £50 to households with occupants who have attained the age of 70 (if they are also in receipt of state pension credit guarantee credit), no later than the end of the week commencing Monday September 19, 2005 and who are ordinarily resident in Great Britain on any day in that week.

3062. Superannuation—Civil service pension scheme—Additional employments

SUPERANNUATION (ADMISSION TO SCHEDULE 1 TO THE SUPERANNUATION ACT 1972) ORDER 2005, SI 2005 3171; made under the Superannuation Act 1972 s.1. In force: December 15, 2005; £3.00.

This Order amends the Superannuation Act 1972 which permits the Minister for the Civil Service to make schemes which make provision for pensions and other benefits in respect of civil servants and persons serving in an employment or office listed in Sch.1 to the Act. The Order adds employment by Architecture and Design Scotland, the China-Britain Business Council, the NHS Confederation (Employers) Company Ltd, the Health Protection Agency (Yr Asiantaeth Diogelu Iechyd), the Nuclear Decommissioning Authority, Partnerships for Schools Ltd, Culture Northwest Ltd, Culture North East Ltd, Culture South West Ltd, Yorkshire Culture Ltd, Culture East Midlands Ltd, Living East Ltd, West Midlands Life Ltd, Culture South East Ltd, the Wine Standards Board, the Commissioner for Public Appointments in Scotland, the Risk Management Authority, the Joint Nature Conservation Committee and the Health and Social Care Information Centre and the JNCC Support Co to those listed.

3063. Tribunals—Pensions Regulator Tribunal—Rules

PENSIONS REGULATOR TRIBUNAL RULES 2005, SI 2005 690; made under the Pensions Act 2004 s.102, s.104, Sch.4 para.9; and the Pensions (Northern Ireland) Order 2005 (SI 2005 255 (NI.1)) Art.98. In force: April 6, 2005; £3.50.

These Rules regulate the procedure for references to the Pensions Regulator Tribunal established under the Pensions Act 2004 s.102. These Rules in particular provide for the making of a reference by the applicant filing a reference notice with the Tribunal; the filing, by the Pensions Regulator, of a statement of case; the filing, by the applicant, of a reply; direction-making powers for the Tribunal; power to summon witnesses; hearings by the Tribunal; the publication of the Tribunal's decision; the awarding of costs; and appeals from the Tribunal's decision.

3064. Trustees liability—Maladministration—Pensions Ombudsman's change of view after preliminary conclusions—Procedural fairness of later hearing

P, a former pension scheme trustee, appealed against a Pensions Ombudsman's decision that he was liable for serious breaches of trust amounting to maladministration. P and his fellow trustees had made an unsecured loan to the scheme's principal employer. The employer went into liquidation and the loan proved irrecoverable. The Ombudsman's preliminary conclusions were that the trustees had been guilty of maladministration, but in the absence of sufficient evidence of a lack of good faith or any suggestion of conscious misconduct, they were entitled to rely on an exoneration clause in the pension plan. The complainant challenged the Ombudsman's interpretation of the clause, contending that recklessness should be enough to deprive the trustees of its protection. Following an oral hearing which P did not attend, the Ombudsman proceeded to his final determination, concluding that P had been guilty of wilful misconduct amounting to dishonesty and was not entitled to rely on the exoneration clause. P contended that the Ombudsman's determination was procedurally flawed.

Held, allowing the appeal, that it was procedurally unfair that P be given no prior warning or chance to address the Ombudsman's dramatic change of view. The change was unexpected in that the finding of dishonesty was not based on any new evidence, but on the same submissions and evidence that led to the Ombudsman's preliminary conclusions. The change was also unexpected because it was not made in response to the complainant's representations.

PAYNE v. PENSIONS OMBUDSMAN, [2003] EWHC 3218, [2004] O.P.L.R.185, Etherton, J., Ch D.

3065. War pensions-Civil partnerships

WAR PENSIONS COMMITTEES (AMENDMENT) REGULATIONS 2005, SI 2005 3032; made under the Social Security Act 1989 s.25, s.29; and the Social Security Contributions and Benefits Act 1992 s.175. In force: December 5, 2005; £3.00.

These Regulations amend the War Pensions Committees Regulations 2000 (SI 2000 3180) in consequence of the introduction of civil partnerships by the Civil Partnership Act 2004.

3066. War pensions-Mercantile marine-Civil partnerships

WAR PENSIONS (MERCANTILE MARINE) (AMENDMENT) SCHEME 2005, SI 2005 3033; made under the Pensions (Navy, Army, Air Force and Mercantile Marine) Act 1939 s.3, s.4, s.7. In force: December 5, 2005; £3.00.

This Scheme amends the War Pensions (Mercantile Marine) Scheme 1964 (SI 1964 2058) in consequence of the introduction of civil partnerships by the Civil Partnership Act 2004.

3067. Books

Ellison, Robin-Pension Trustee's Handbook. Hardback: £20.00. ISBN 1 85418 360 5. Thorogood.

Ellison, Robin; Jones, Grant-Dealing with Pensions: The Practical Impact of the Pensions Act 2004 on Mergers, Acquisitions and Insolvencies. Paperback: £95.00. ISBN 1 904905 06 4. Spiramus Press.

Marshall, Jane-Pensions Act 2004: Guide to the New Law. Paperback: £49.95. ISBN 1 85328 923 X. Law Society Publications.

Pollard, Dave-Guide to the Pensions Act 2004. Paperback: £44.95. ISBN 0 7545 2730 1. Tolley Publishing.

Poore, Martin; Jenkins, Martin-Blackstone's Guide to the Pensions Act 2004. Paperback: £39.95. ISBN 0 19 928190 4. Oxford University Press.

Self, Roger-Tottel's Pension Fund Trustee Handbook. Paperback: £36.95. ISBN 1 84592 175 5. Tottel Publishing.

Seres, Jonathan; Mitchell, Feargus-Pensions Risk and Strategy. Paperback: £59.00. ISBN 1 898830 75 4. City and Financial Publishing.

PERSONAL INJURY

3068. Damages–Periodical payments–Variation

DAMAGES (VARIATION OF PERIODICAL PAYMENTS) ORDER 2005, SI 2005 841; made under the Damages Act 1996 s.2B. In force: April 1, 2005; £3.00.

This Order enables courts to vary orders and agreements in personal injury cases under which all or part of the damages take the form of periodical payments. It restricts the circumstances in which variation is permissible to those where there is a chance that the claimant will develop some serious disease or suffer some serious deterioration, or enjoy some significant improvement, in his physical or mental condition, and the court has ordered, or the parties have agreed, that the order or agreement is to be capable of variation. The decision that an order may be varied in the future may be made on the application of a party, or with the consent of the parties or of the court's own initiative. The person applying for permission to apply to vary an order or agreement is required to show that the specified disease, deterioration or improvement has occurred and that it has caused or is likely to cause an increase or decrease in the claimant's financial loss.

3069. Funeral expenses–Payments to civilians

PERSONAL INJURIES (CIVILIANS) (AMENDMENT) (NO.2) SCHEME 2005, SI 2005 1639; made under the Personal Injuries (Emergency Provisions) Act 1939 s.1, s.2. In force: July 15, 2005; £3.00.

This Scheme further amends the Personal Injuries (Civilians) Scheme 1983 (SI 1983 686) which makes provision for the payment of pensions and allowances to or in respect of civilians who were killed or injured during the 1939-45 World War by increasing the amount of allowance paid under the principal Scheme to £64.68 per week from April 6, 2005 and £66.62 per week from April 11, 2005.

3070. Human Tissue Act 2004 (c.30)–Commencement No.1 Order

HUMAN TISSUE ACT 2004 (COMMENCEMENT NO.1) ORDER 2005, SI 2005 919 (C.40); made under the Human Tissue Act 2004 s.58, s.60. Commencement details: bringing into force various provisions of the 2004 Act on April 1, 2005; £3.00.

This Order provides for the coming into force of provisions of the Human Tissue Act 2004 which enable the Human Tissue Authority to be established, confer certain functions upon it and deal with certain consequential amendments.

3071. Measure of damages–Periodical payments

[Damages Act 1996 s.2(1)(a); Civil Procedure Rules 1998 Part 41 PD 41B.]

The claimant (G) claimed damages for personal injury and the court was asked to assess the major elements of future recurring costs and losses, namely future lost earnings and the costs of care and accommodation, transport and the cost of the receiver appointed by the Court of Protection. While using a pedestrian crossing, G had been struck and seriously injured by a motor car driven by the first defendant. Liability was not in dispute. G had sustained serious head and orthopaedic injuries for which general damages for pain, suffering and loss of amenity had been agreed at £110,000. G had developed epilepsy as a result of the head injury. He required round the clock supervision and was totally incapable of work. Before the accident G had had limited mental capacity. He had worked as a road sweeper and had worked long hours of overtime. Since leaving his parents' home G had lived for over 20 years with his elder sister and her husband. The defendants submitted that (1) the figure for future loss of earnings overstated the multiplicand because it assumed wrongly that G would have continued to work overtime at the same rate until he retired; (2) the local authority was bound to accept that G was in critical need and would meet that need by the provision of accommodation in a care home for him after he ceased to reside with his sister.

Held, assessing the damages, that (1) G had been dedicated to his job and that was evidenced by the long hours he had worked. He did not appear to have any pressing need for the extra pay. There was no evidence of ill health which would have prevented him from continuing to work at the same rate, or of a fall in demand for his work by his employers. Accordingly G's pre accident earnings were representative of what he would have achieved but for the accident, and damages for loss of future earnings were calculated accordingly. (2) Despite the shortcomings in his present circumstances, G would not wish to leave his current home unless compelled to do so. The cost of care was calculated on the basis that he would continue to live there for four and a half years. No allowance should be made for the possibility that VAT would be charged on the case manager's fee, *Mitchell v. Alasia* [2005] EWHC 11 not followed. As a matter of law the fees were VAT exempt. The costs of transport and of the receiver were allowed as claimed. After four and a half years, residence in a care home would be the appropriate long term option. The defendants failed to discharge the burden which was on them of showing that the option of a privately funded care home was unreasonable, *Sowden v. Lodge* [2004] EWCA Civ 1370, [2005] 1 All E.R. 581 applied. (3) Damages for future lost earnings were awarded as a lump sum but a periodical payments order under the Damages Act 1996 s.2(1)(a) was made for recurring care and related costs. A periodical payments order for recurring costs best met G's needs having regard to the factors set out in the Civil Procedure Rules 1998 Part 41 PD 41B. It would eliminate uncertainty, and so the risk of unfairness either to G or to the defendants, as to G's life expectancy. It also made it easier to match expense to income because the income stream was secure and not dependent on investment returns.

GODBOLD v. MAHMOOD, [2005] EWHC 1002, [2006] P.I.Q.R. Q5, Mitting, J., QBD.

3072. Measure of damages—Residential care—Severe brain damage—Cost of reasonable accommodation—Local authority or private provision

[National Assistance Act 1948 s.21.]

The appellant (S) appealed on the issue of the use of the "best interests" test for determining the measure of damages necessary to meet her care costs, and whether it had been correctly applied in her case. S had sustained severe brain damage in a road traffic accident and had lived in a home with other disabled people for four years. It was not clear where S wanted to live and she had no contact with her family. S contended that a private arrangement would be most suitable, but the judge below, applying the "best interests" test, ruled that her best interests would be served by residing in a local authority home, provided under National Assistance Act 1948 s.21, with other disabled people, but the judge also awarded an extra amount of damages to cover the additional care S would require for long periods of each day.

Held, allowing the appeal in part, that the correct test was to determine what was the most reasonable accommodation for S. In the absence of evidence as to the practicality of the extra sum, S should have the opportunity of establishing that private, as opposed to local authority, provision was more practical, with the respondent being liable for the difference in cost between local authority and private provision. The test used by the judge was incorrect, although he had been entitled to treat arrangements that were in S's best interests as reasonable, *Rialas v. Mitchell* (1984) 128 S.J. 704, [1984] C.L.Y. 1013 and *Wells v. Wells* [1999] 1 A.C. 345, [1998] C.L.Y. 1446 applied

SOWDEN v. LODGE; CROOKDAKE v. DRURY, [2004] EWCA Civ 1370, [2005] 1 W.L.R. 2129, Pill, L.J., CA (Civ Div).

3073. **Medical records–Disclosure orders–Entitlement to disclosure order of claimant's medical records**

The applicant public house owner (Y) applied for an order that the claimant (C) provide copies of his medical records to Y's solicitors. C had brought an action against Y seeking damages for personal injuries sustained after falling down a trap door leading to a cellar at Y's premises. The accident had occurred in January 2001. C, aged 55 at the time of the accident, had received no medical treatment, but had taken one week off work. Y had admitted liability. In December 2003, C had been examined by a medical expert instructed by his solicitors. Y had not objected to the expert, but he was not jointly instructed. The report had stated that C had serious persisting symptoms in his neck, lower back and left knee and ongoing headaches. A firm prognosis was not given but the expert had suggested that the symptoms might be permanent. The expert had read C's medical records and noted that he had received treatment following a fall in August 1997 and that X rays taken of C's spine shortly after the instant accident had revealed marked degenerative changes which the radiologist had suggested were not attributable to the instant accident. The expert had not commented on the extent to which C's ongoing symptoms were attributable to the instant accident. C's claim included the costs of future medical treatment and care. After being served with the expert's report, Y's solicitors requested that C grant authority for Y's solicitors to obtain copies of C's medical records. C refused. Y's solicitors therefore applied for an order compelling C to grant authority on the ground that the records were relevant to the issue of to what extent C's injuries were attributable to the instant accident. C's solicitors opposed the application claiming that medical records should only be disclosed in exceptional circumstances and as Y had not yet instructed its own medical expert, there could be no purpose for which it required the medical records, *Bennett v. Compass Group UK & Ireland Ltd* [2002] EWCA Civ 642, [2002] C.P. Rep. 58, [2003] C.L.Y. 402 cited.

Held, granting the application, that the issue of whether a claimant's medical records should be disclosed was placed at the discretion of the judge at first instance, *Bennett* applied, but it required the judge to think long and hard before ordering such disclosure. Given the extent of C's symptoms in relation to an accident that was on the face of it minor, requiring little time off work, and the possibility of degenerative conditions affecting a man of C's age, Y's solicitors were put on inquiry that the full extent of C's symptoms might not be attributable to the instant accident. The extent of C's claim for future medical and care expenses was also a factor in favour of Y's application. The fact that Y's solicitors had not yet instructed a medical expert did not mean that medical records should not be disclosed. Y was not entitled to its own medical expert as a matter of course: it was required to ask questions of C's experts before applying for its own expert, *D (A Child) v. Walker* [2000] 1 W.L.R. 1382, [2000] C.L.Y. 321 applied. Y's solicitors may have needed to see the records before formulating the questions to be asked of C's expert. C was ordered to disclose all medical records in relation to any physical injury or disability.

CATCHPOLE v. YOUNG & CO'S BREWERY PLC, August 16, 2004, District Judge Bennett, CC (St Helens). [*Ex rel.* Chris Middleton, Barrister, Oriel Chambers, 14 Water Street, Liverpool].

3074. **Payments to civilians–Civil partnerships**

PERSONAL INJURIES (CIVILIANS) (AMENDMENT) (NO.3) SCHEME 2005, SI 2005 3031; made under the Personal Injuries (Emergency Provisions) Act 1939 s.1, s.2. In force: December 5, 2005; £3.00.

This Scheme amends the Personal Injuries (Civilians) Scheme 1983 (SI 1983 686) in consequence of the introduction of civil partnerships by the Civil Partnership Act 2004.

3075. Permanent injuries—Pension benefits—NHS Pension Agency—Computation of permanent injury benefits

[National Health Service (Injury Benefits) Regulations 1974 (SI 1974 1547) Reg.4(2); National Health Service (Injury Benefits) Regulations 1995 (SI 1995 866) Reg.4(2), Reg.3(1), Reg.2(1)(b), Reg.2(1)(b)(iii).]

The claimant (M) applied for judicial review of a determination made by the respondent secretary of state as to the quantification of his permanent injury benefit. M had practised as a dentist. In January 1987, he suffered an injury. In December 1990 he was medically retired. Subsequently, M applied for permanent injury benefits under the National Health Service (Injury Benefits) Regulations 1974 Reg.4(2). A dispute arose between the parties as to whether the 1974 Regulations applied or whether the National Health Service (Injury Benefits) Regulations 1995 Reg.4(2) was applicable. In addition, the parties were unable to agree whether the benefits ran from January 1987 or December 1990. In due course, the secretary of state assessed M's permanent injury benefit under the 1995 Regulations as starting in December 1990. The issues for determination were (1) whether the 1974 Regulations applied or whether the 1995 Regulations applied; (2) the date from which the permanent injury benefits ran; (3) the computation of the permanent injury benefits.

Held, refusing the application, that (1) As M had never formally served notice on the secretary of state opting for the 1974 Regulations, it followed that M's claim fell under Reg.4(2) of the 1995 Regulations. (2) The permanent injury benefits ran from December 1990, that being the date when M ceased to be employed pursuant to Reg.3(1) of the 1995 Regulations. (3) Given that M was a practitioner, his average remuneration fell to be assessed by reference to Reg.2(1)(b) of the 1995 Regulations, namely the uprated yearly average of M's remuneration from the date he commenced work with the NHS. His claim under Reg.4(2) then fell to be calculated by reference to Reg.2(1)(b)(iii).

R. (ON THE APPLICATION OF MALEKOUT) v. SECRETARY OF STATE FOR HEALTH, [2004] EWHC 2879, *The Times*, January 4, 2005, Wilkie, J., QBD (Admin).

3076. War pensions—Payments to civilians

PERSONAL INJURIES (CIVILIANS) (AMENDMENT) SCHEME 2005, SI 2005 655; made under the Personal Injuries (Emergency Provisions) Act 1939 s.1, s.2. In force: in accordance with Art.1(1); £3.00.

This Scheme further amends the Personal Injuries (Civilians) Scheme 1983 (SI 1983 686) which makes provision for the payment of pensions and allowances to or in respect of civilians who were killed or injured during the 1939-45 World War by increasing the amounts of allowances, pensions and awards payable under the principal Scheme and the amounts of income to be disregarded for the purposes of certain parts of the Scheme. It amends the 1983 Order by substituting a new heading and by providing that awards to widows, widowers or unmarried dependants living as spouses of former members shall not cease in the event of the widow, widower or unmarried dependant living as a spouse marrying or living with another person as the spouse of that person, provided that such marriage or living with another commences on or after April 6, 2005. It also substitutes new tables, thereby varying the rates of pension and allowances payable in respect of disablement and also earning or income thresholds; varying the rates of pensions and allowances payable in respect of death; and varying the amounts to be deducted under Art.64.

Personal Injuries or Death—Quantum

Details have been received of the following cases in which damages for personal injuries or death were awarded. The classification and sequence of the classified awards follows that adopted in Kemp and Kemp. *The Quantum of Damages*, Vol.2. Unless there is some statement to the contrary, the age of the applicant is his age at the time of the court hearing. Unless specified the damages are stated on the basis of full liability, *ie.* ignoring any deduction made for contributory negligence. The sum is the total amount of the damages awarded unless otherwise stated. For a cumulative guide to *quantum* of damages cases reported in Current Law during 2003, see the *Quantum* of Damages table. We must stress that we are entirely dependent on the contributor of an unreported case for the accuracy of his or her report; it is impracticable for us independently to check the facts stated to us. We welcome contributions and are most grateful for all the reports received. We would appreciate reports of any alterations to awards noted here, either in, or in anticipation of, appeal.

Multiple injuries

3077.   B, male, a graphic designer, aged 25 at the date of the accident and 30 at trial, suffered multiple injuries after being thrown to a concrete floor from a cherry picker mobile elevating platform when the platform collapsed. B sustained a fractured skull with prolonged post traumatic amnesia lasting for one to two days. The wound to the back of the head was sutured, which left a permanent scar within the hairline, although that was not ordinarily visible. For the first eight months after the accident, B suffered daily migrainous headaches, lasting three or four hours. Thereafter, the headaches occurred about three times each week and were expected to cease after a further two to three years following specific treatment by his GP. B suffered a complete loss of his sense of smell (anosmia) and almost entirely lost his sense of taste, save for a residual ability slightly to taste spicy curries and malt whisky. B suffered a 15dB bilateral hearing loss at 1, 2 and 3 kHz, which manifested itself as obscure auditory dysfunction and slight tinnitus, which occurred for about an hour every month. B also suffered bilateral fractures of the lower jaw, the left side being comminuted, which were reduced and plated and a laceration to the underside of the left chin, which was sutured and left an oblique faded 1.5cm scar. The inferior aveolar nerve on the left was traumatised with resultant numbness and tingling over the left chin and lip regions, with associated dribbling of fluids and intermittent clicking in the left jaw joint. In addition, there was a slight but noticeable alteration in the dental occlusion, with a gap between the lower right canine and first premolar teeth together with palpable plating and uncomfortable surgical scarring within the mouth with associated sensitivity of the lower anterior teeth. Neurological examination revealed a significant risk of post traumatic epilepsy, in the region of eight per cent, which would reduce to six per cent from four years after the accident until year nine and to 0.5 per cent in year 10. Damages were awarded on a provisional basis, disregarding the risk of post traumatic epilepsy, until the end of year 10. *General Damages*: (Provisional) £38,000.
    BLOWER v. MERCADEL PLANT & MACHINERY LTD, June 16, 2004, Judge Heath, CC (Lincoln). [*Ex rel.* Andrew Maguire, Barrister, St Philips Chambers, 55 Temple Row, Birmingham].

Multiple injuries

3078.   S, male, a roofer, aged 41 at the date of the accident and 46 at trial, sustained serious multiple injuries when he fell through a roof. He suffered a compound comminuted fracture to the tibia, fibula, and talar head of his left ankle which required to be pinned; bilateral wrist fractures of the distal radii which required fixation by a plate and "K" wires to the left and right respectively; a burst type fracture to the L4 vertebrae which was fused surgically; and fractures to two right ribs which united with conservative treatment. S was an in patient for two months. His mobility was severely restricted for six months and only achieved by the use of elbow crutches indoors and a wheelchair outdoors. He suffered constant aching at all fracture sites with intermittent pain. There was virtually no movement in the lower back although he was able to compensate for this to some extent by bending at the thoracic spine and at the hips. Mobility continued to be restricted to the date of the trial and although S was able to walk a limited distance he struggled to walk uphill and up stairs and limped. There was a shortening of the left leg by 1.5cm. C was left with a significant loss of mobility, an inability to lift and carry anything over and above very light items, and a difficulty in standing for long periods. At trial no further recovery was expected. It was likely that S would develop osteoarthritis starting between the age of 55 to 60 in both wrists, left ankle and lower back. S had not worked since the accident and would never carry out even moderately heavy manual work again. At trial C stated that his injuries significantly interfered with his ability to play with his grandchildren. An occupational physician confirmed that S was capable of some limited forms of supported employment. *General Damages*: £35,000. Future loss of earnings: £: 90,090. Total award (including interest): £171,330.

STRICKLAND v. FOGG, June 22, 2004, Judge Armitage Q.C., CC (Manchester). [*Ex rel.* Christopher Taft, Barrister, St James' Chambers, 68 Quay Street, Manchester].

Multiple injuries

3079.   C, female, a chef, aged 29 at the date of the road traffic accident and 33 at the disposal hearing, sustained a fractured sternum and soft tissue injuries to the neck, both knees and the right shoulder. As a result of her injuries, C was absent from work immediately after the accident for a period of six weeks. C was right hand dominant. She was unable to tend for herself at all during that period and her mother effectively moved in and cared for all of her domestic needs, including personal grooming, housework, gardening and shopping. On her return to work, C was forced to reduce her shifts because she could not remain on her feet for the same periods as she had before, owing to ongoing pain across the front of her knees and also because she could not raise her right arm above shoulder height or hold pots and pans for significant periods. The fractured sternum caused C continuous pain for a period of six weeks before settling. C's neck, right shoulder and knee pain was particularly intense for the first few months after the accident, before gradually settling. At the hearing, three years and nine months after the accident, C still suffered ongoing pain in her neck, right shoulder and both knees. The judge considered the pain in all limbs to be just above nuisance level and assessed general damages on the basis that C would continue to suffer permanent ongoing symptoms. The judge also made an award for handicap on the open labour market because it was clear that if C were to lose her job, she would have difficulty obtaining another, particularly as she had worked in catering all her working life and had no other formal qualifications. *General Damages*: £10,000. Smith v. Manchester Award: £5,000.

CEMM v. BRYANT (QUANTUM), December 2, 2004, Recorder Evans Q.C., CC (Stourbridge). [*Ex rel.* Stephen Garner, Barrister, 8 Fountain Court, Birmingham].

Brain damage: very severe

3080.   D, male, unemployed, aged 42 at the date of the assault and 54 at trial, suffered serious head injuries when he was attacked by two men with a hammer. He sustained multiple skull fractures, widespread bruising and damage to the left part of the brain. He required neurosurgery to clean the wound and remove skull fragments. He also sustained a puncture to his left lung and fractures to his left hand. He regained consciousness slowly but was left permanently paralysed down the right side of his body. Apart from an expletive or a made up word he was unable to communicate verbally. His condition was permanent and would not get any better. He was hospitalised for seven months, and then spent four months in a rehabilitation centre and one month in a residential care centre. He was discharged into the care of his mother and moved into an adapted housing association property with her. However, accommodation did not form part of the claim as D's experts believed that the housing association property was suitable for his needs and was held under a secure tenancy by his receiver. His mother looked after D until her death 10 years later. Thereafter D was cared for by other relatives, friends and neighbours. D attended a day centre on a daily basis. The panel allowed a claim for past care and accepted that the claim for past care did not cease with the death of D's late mother. The panel accepted that D would survive until aged 70 and allowed a multiplier of 11.4. Claims for the cost of D's professional receiver and case manager were reduced due to an overlap in their roles. The panel acknowledged a need for a statutory will and allowed a contribution towards its cost. *General Damages*: £115,000. Past care award: £75,000. Future case management costs: £47,600. Future professional receiver costs: £33,488. Contribution towards Court of Protection and statutory will costs: £1,000. Total award: £325,060.

D (CICB: QUANTUM: 2004: BRAIN INJURY), *Re*, May 6, 2004, Williams (Chairman), CICA (London). [*Ex rel.* Russell-Cooke, Solicitors, 2 Putney Hill, Putney, London].

Brain damage: moderately severe

3081.   T, a girl, aged three months at the date of the non accidental injury caused to her by her father and 20 years at the date of the hearing, was found to have a bilateral subdural haematoma and haemorrhages into the retina of the left eye on admission to hospital. Following T's emergency transfer to a specialist unit, haemorrhages in the left fundus were confirmed and there was evidence of bilateral pyramidal signs particularly in the lower limbs. Increasing respiratory difficulty had necessitated T being placed on a ventilator on the day of the injury and thereafter for the next three days. Accumulating blood necessitated daily subdural aspirations. T had CT scans on the day of the injury and four days later and T's consultant paediatric neurologist concluded that T had suffered extensive brain injury which involved bleeding over the surface of the brain in the first instance and subsequent bleeding into the substance of the brain together with severe swelling to both sides of the brain, right more than the left. There had been a probable fracture of the right occipital bone associated with scalp bruising. After discharge from the specialist unit a month after the date of the injury, T remained a hospital in patient for six weeks. T was left with considerable residual damage. There was a left hemiplegia. T's intellectual impairment was delayed. She was epileptic and required regular administration of Sodium Valproate. T's assessment by a consultant neurologist, 30 months after the date of the injury, included cognitive delay. The left hemiplegia was accompanied by undergrowth to the left side of the body and her left leg was 1cm shorter than the right. She had speech delay and some hearing loss. She had a left hemiplegia which left her with problems with placing the left foot on the ground. She had an achilles lengthening procedure eight years after sustaining the injury and splinting thereafter to help her with walking difficulties. Her tibialis posterior was also surgically lengthened. She had a further series of left foot operations eight years later, including a tendon operation to release the left foot. Although her walking improved following these operations her left foot suffered from being swollen. She had to wear an ankle foot orthosis during the day and night for a number of months. Seventeen years after the date of the injury T's consultant orthopaedic surgeon reported that T had little function in the left arm but was able to walk in a slow fashion. He suspected that T should be classified as 80 per cent disabled and that there was no likelihood of any improvement. Two years later T's GP advised that she had to have special shoes because of the swelling in the ankle and T had lymphoedema treatment. There was obvious swelling of the left foot and ankles. Six months later a consultant child neurologist, on behalf of the panel, confirmed that T was very severely handicapped. She was at times wheelchair dependent and he believed that she would always remain so. T would continue indefinitely to be highly dependent on carers on a daily basis in order to cope with daily living activities, such as washing and cleaning herself after using the toilet, and would never be able to live independently or be economically productive or economically independent. T had a slight but noticeable speech impediment, difficulty hearing when there was background noise and impaired vision to the left side. The panel's consultant child neurologist also advised, and the panel accepted, that T's life expectancy should be assumed to be the same as for the remainder of the population but reduced by a decade. Past loss of earnings were assessed on the basis T would have earned £12,000 gross per annum on leaving school at 18. For T's future losses a full life multiplier advanced on behalf of T of 29.05 was accepted. With regard to future loss of earnings, the panel accepted the claim advanced on the basis of national average earnings and allowed the claim advanced in full. *General Damages*: £145,000. Past loss of earnings: £27,443. Future loss of earnings: £288,450. Future care: £1,147,790. Total award: £1,991,885.

T (A CHILD) (CICAP: QUANTUM: 2004: SEVERE BRAIN DAMAGE), *Re*, July 13, 2004, Diana Cotton (Chairwoman), CICAP. [*Ex rel.* Colin Mendoza, Barrister, Devereux Chambers, Devereux Court, London].

Brain damage: minor

3082.   S, a boy, aged 4 at the date of the accident and 12 at the child settlement approval hearing, sustained an injury to the head when he fell 6ft from where he was playing. On admission to hospital later that day he was found to have sustained a linear skull fracture and was detained overnight before discharge. Following the accident he complained of frequent headaches, especially when exposed to bright light. He developed a "lazy" right eye, which was corrected with glasses. He experienced an unpleasant tingling on the left side of the head which caused problems when he washed his hair or went to the barbers. On examination four years after the accident a palmomental reflex was elicited which was indicative of a subtle frontal lobe injury. An MRI scan revealed no major damage. There was no cognitive impairment or personality change. Since S had had a neonatal convulsion in the past he was considered to be at risk of developing epilepsy in the future. He would have a tendency to suffer migraines as a result of the accident. He was originally prescribed Calpol for his headaches. However, as he got older he preferred not to take medication and to lie down in a darkened room. He also used eye shades. He had the occasional day off school when his headaches were bad. No other drugs were prescribed because of his age. Provisional damages were awarded on the basis that he would not develop epilepsy, but leave was given to apply for further damages in the event of his developing epilepsy in the course of his lifetime. *General Damages* (Provisional) (approved and agreed): £9,000.

S (A CHILD) v. ISLINGTON LBC, June 25, 2004, Deputy District Judge Bury, CC (Clerkenwell). [*Ex rel.* J David Cook, Barrister, Chambers of Ami Feder, Lamb Building, Temple, London].

General psychiatric disorders

3083.   G, a girl, aged 9 at the date of the accident and 15 at the child settlement approval hearing, was injured when she fell heavily from her wheelchair onto a concrete floor. G had been severely handicapped since birth, having been born with a lumbo sacral myelo meningocele, whereby the lower part of the nervous system at the lumbar spine was exposed without a proper skin covering. That was repaired shortly after birth. G also suffered with spina bifida and had been diagnosed with having a chiari base ii malformation, in that the base of her brain was situated at the top of the neck. She had limited use of her left side, speech difficulties and obstructive sleep apnoea, and she was therefore dependent upon constant care and assistance. Immediately after the accident G underwent a head X ray which revealed no skull fracture and she was discharged from hospital. She was off school for two weeks after the accident, returning for two weeks before the summer holidays began. On examination by a consultant neurologist 21 months after the accident G was diagnosed as having suffered a relatively mild physical injury which had upset the fragile balance of her nervous system. The medical opinion was that G's condition was already deteriorating as a result of her constitutional condition. Although it had been difficult to measure any physical deterioration in the light of G's pre existing difficulties, the opinion was that G had recovered from the upset of balance in her nervous symptoms within one year after the accident. However G also suffered psychological symptoms as a result of the accident. On examination by a consultant psychologist 33 months after the accident, it was found that G was prone to panic attacks, became tearful, and was also fearful in circumstances that previously had not troubled her, such as when she was transferred to and from her wheelchair, or when in the shower. Since the accident G had not liked to be handled by people she did not know and that presented practical difficulties in the light of her disability. Her enthusiasm for life had been eroded through a considerable loss of confidence. She became more withdrawn from her friends and her personal relationships suffered. G was diagnosed as having sustained an adjustment disorder as a direct result of the accident and it was recommended that she undergo cognitive behavioural therapy. G subsequently had 44 sessions of cognitive behavioural therapy over a period of 18 months. Following the treatment medical opinion was that G had made a remarkable recovery in overcoming her fears and anxiety problems, although she would never make a complete recovery. G was still more anxious in some situations which, before the accident, had posed no problems whatsoever. The prognosis was that G would remain vulnerable to psychological reactions in the future as a direct consequence of the accident and a provision for future cognitive behavioural therapy was made in case of a relapse. At the hearing it was agreed that G's claim fell within the JSB Guidelines for psychiatric damage category 3(A)(b), and that consideration had to be given to the impact on G's already limited functions. *General Damages*: £14,900.

G (A CHILD) v. ESSEX CC, June 10, 2004, District Judge Hallett. [*Ex rel.* Hodgkinsons, Solicitors, The Old Manse, 14 Lumley Avenue, Skegness, Lincs].

General psychiatric disorders

3084.   H, male, a schoolboy aged seven at the date of the road traffic accident and 12 at the child settlement approval hearing was involved in a head on collision. Immediately after the accident, H started to develop pain in his neck. He was also shocked and tearful. He was taken to hospital where a diagnosis of a whiplash injury was made. H's mother gave him Calpol to contain the neck pain for the first two days after the accident. H's neck pain was constant for one week after the accident, especially when he awoke first thing in the morning. He also suffered from constant headaches for the first two to three days before they eased. H also suffered nightmares after the accident. They occurred once a week. He suffered from flashbacks of the accident for one to two weeks and was more clingy towards his mother over the same time frame. H also experienced travel anxiety as a passenger. He was nervous, hypervigilant, sweated and shook whilst travelling. He constantly looked in the car mirrors to check for approaching traffic. Those psychological symptoms were diagnosed as a specific phobia. On examination three months after the accident, H still awoke with neck pain about once a week. The pain and stiffness lasted between one to two hours. He also still suffered from occipital headaches which occurred once or twice a week and lasted about two hours. H also continued to suffer from nightmares and specific travel phobia. The prognosis was for the neck symptoms and the headaches to settle within four and a half months of the accident and the psychological symptoms, including the specific phobia, to settle within four years of the accident. H confirmed at the hearing that both his physical and psychological symptoms had settled in accordance with the prognosis. H was absent from school for one day on account of his injuries. *General Damages* (agreed and approved): £4,500.

H (A CHILD) v. PULISCIANO, September 22, 2004, Deputy District Judge Maughan, CC (Birmingham). [*Ex rel.* Stephen Garner, Barrister, 8 Fountain Court, Birmingham].

Post-traumatic stress disorder

3085.   K, female, a registered mental health nurse, aged 30 at the date of the assault and 38 at the hearing, sustained psychiatric damage when she was attacked at work by a patient who rendered her unconscious when he tried to strangle her. From the date of the assault she suffered significant disabling psychological symptoms of post traumatic stress disorder and depression. She returned to work five months after the assault on a part time basis on a different unit. After eight months she went on sick leave due to the deterioration of her self confidence, and her employment was terminated 22 months later. K received numerous different forms of treatment for her psychiatric and psychological symptoms, including regular counselling and cognitive behavioural therapy. At the hearing date she was still under psychiatric review, on high dose anti-depressants, and receiving counselling on a fortnightly basis. Further cognitive behavioural therapy had been recommended. Medical evidence supported diagnoses of post traumatic stress disorder, depressive disorder, and dysthymia. K's marriage had broken down as a result of her symptoms. She rarely left her home and avoided meeting people from the hospital where she had worked. She could no longer cook and her sleep pattern was affected. She either suffered from insomnia or could sleep excessively and yet remain tired during the day. She experienced panic attacks approximately every two weeks. The carrying out of household tasks and shopping were difficult for her to perform and complete, and took up a disproportionate part of her time. K had started to help at a centre for women, which involved small tasks such as making cups of tea, but this made her exhausted after three sessions a week. She stopped these sessions following discussions with her GP and counsellor. The prognosis was that she would continue to be severely disabled by her psychiatric syndrome but that in three to four years' time would probably be able to do some form of work. It was accepted that she would never return to nursing and that any work that she obtained was likely to be part time and at a lower salary than she had earned previously. Her attempt to retrain in beauty therapy and sports therapy had failed after the initial training due to her symptoms that prevented her from being able to work due to her fear of strangers, especially men. *General Damages* were awarded for a "permanently disabling mental disorder confirmed by diagnosis". The panel used their discretion not to be bound by the multipliers set out at Note 3 of the Scheme and referred to the Ogden tables. They agreed that the appropriate tables were tables 19 to 36. Future loss of earnings: £344,240. *General Damages*: £20,000.
     K (CICA: QUANTUM:2004: POST TRAUMATIC STRESS DISORDER), *Re*, July 5, 2004, P Anderson (Chairman), CICAP. [*Ex rel.* Karen Johnson, Barrister, Guildford Chambers, Stoke House, Leapale Lane, Guildford].

Post-traumatic stress disorder

3086.   B, female, a housewife and mother, aged 24 at the date of the accident and 29 at trial, sustained injury when she slipped and became impaled on a loose strand of wire fencing. B's physical injury, a puncture wound 5mm long and of unknown depth to the breast, was not serious. She was treated at hospital and the pain reduced after five to six weeks. Her main injury was psychological. She already had long standing psychological problems which predated the accident. As a result of the accident she had suffered from moderately severe post traumatic stress disorder which restricted her from taking care of herself and gave her feelings of inadequacy and guilt, flashbacks, nightmares, anger and irritability. On examination three years after the accident she was found to have suffered from co morbid clinical depression within the moderate to severe range. The court found that she was unusually vulnerable to traumatic stress, and her underlying difficulties formed a significant contributory link. B had almost recovered by trial but some minor symptoms such as anxiety, avoidance of the scene of the accident, and occasional nightmares would persist indefinitely without professional help. The prognosis with professional help was for a full recovery within a short period of time. The court held that B's post traumatic stress disorder fell into the "moderately severe" category of the JSB Guidelines. *General Damages*: £18,500 (apportioned £17,500 for the post traumatic stress disorder and £1,250 for the physical injury).

BUCHANAN v. BROADLEIGH DEVELOPMENTS LTD, July 8, 2004, Judge Swanson, CC (Sheffield). [*Ex rel.* Pankaj Madan, Barrister, Zenith Chambers, 10 Park Square, Leeds].

Post-traumatic stress disorder–Neck: whiplash injury: no previous condition

3087.   S, male, bus driver, aged 42 at the date of the accident and 43 at trial, suffered injuries as a result of a road traffic accident. S sustained a soft tissue whiplash injury to his neck. He was absent from work for two weeks as a result of his injury, during which period he rested at home. He then returned to work until about five months after the accident, taking odd days off work because of neck pain. S found that driving buses aggravated his neck pain. The neck symptoms gradually settled over a few months, and had largely resolved by about eight months after the accident. By 10 months after the accident S was only getting an occasional ache after long shifts at work. There was some slight tenderness over his right trapezius muscle and neck movements were slightly reduced. The prognosis was that residual symptoms would have resolved by 16 months after the accident. S also suffered psychological injury. S met the DSM IV criteria for full post traumatic stress disorder (PTSD) for a period of five months, and beyond that point he continued to suffer from a number of PTSD symptoms. S suffered from distressing dreams of the accident for up to eight months, from flashbacks for nine months, from physiological reactivity and distress upon exposure to situations resembling the circumstances before the accident for seven months, avoidance of thoughts and feelings relating to the accident for 12 months, emotional numbness, irritability and outbursts of anger for 10 months. His marital relationship was put under significant strain by his condition. As part of S's PTSD he developed anxiety relating to bus driving. That caused him to be absent from work for a period of about five months, beginning at five months after the accident. Upon his return to work he managed to cope with bus driving by driving very carefully and slowly. S was not anxious when driving, or travelling as a passenger in, a car. S also suffered from some depressed moods as part of his PTSD and that was treated with anti depressant medication by his GP. The depression persisted to some extent until S returned to work at about nine months after the accident. However, some symptoms of depression lingered beyond that time. Damages were assessed on the basis of the prognosis that S's residual PTSD symptoms would resolve with the passage of time, full recovery occurring between 21 and 24 months after the accident. S was expected to remain vulnerable to a disproportionately bad reaction to any further road traffic accident or traumatic event occurring within a period of three to four years of the accident. *General Damages*: £6,000 (apportioned £3,000 for the neck injury and £3,000 for the psychological injury).

SPENCER v. FIRST WEST YORKSHIRE LTD, December 9, 2004, District Judge Taylor, CC (Leeds). [*Ex rel.* Tom Nossiter, Barrister, Park Lane Chambers, 19, Westgate, Leeds].

Post-traumatic stress disorder–Reproductive organs: male

3088.   S, male, a track welder, aged 30 the date of the accident and 34 at trial, suffered injuries when the vehicle in which he was travelling as a passenger overturned and came to a halt on the opposite carriageway in the path of oncoming traffic. As a result of the accident S sustained a fractured rib, a whiplash injury to his neck, and psychiatric injuries. He was off work for five weeks and then on light duties for a further four weeks. He was still in pain on his return to work, had post traumatic headaches for eight weeks, neck pain for three to six months and pain from the fractured rib for six months after the accident. He made a complete recovery from the orthopaedic injuries. He began to suffer from symptoms of post traumatic stress disorder (PTSD) within a few days of the accident, experiencing flashbacks, intrusive thoughts, stress, nightmares, heightened startle response, irritability, a phobia about travelling by car and avoidance of the location of the accident. His condition was described by a medical expert as of some severity. S was treated with anti-depressants and had about 20 counselling sessions. Some two and a half years after the accident his symptoms had largely subsided. S's only remaining problem was impotence. Soon after the accident S realised that his sex drive had been affected by the accident and his GP prescribed viagra. The medical expert stated that S's problems with sexual function were to be seen as part of his PTSD and were largely psychological rather than physical. However, as the PTSD resolved, his impotence did not. S received treatment in a specialist clinic but to no effect. He was not totally impotent as he could obtain an erection if he took medication, and indeed his wife gave birth to their fourth child nearly four years after the accident. However, it had to be quite strong medication, viagra at 100mg, as viagra at 50mg had no effect. There was no further treatment which he could have and the experts could not say whether he would ever return to spontaneous sexual function. It was a matter of "'wait and see".There was a lack of guidance in the JSB Guidelines in terms of less than total impotence, where the prognosis was uncertain, and for a young man. There was no bracket for partial impotence. *General Damages*: £20,000 (apportioned £4,000 for the orthopaedic injuries, £6,000 for the PTSD and £10,000 for the impotence).

S v. BALFOUR BEATTY RAIL MAINTENANCE, May 17, 2004, District Judge Powell, CC (Newcastle). [*Ex rel.* Bruce Silvester, Barrister, Devereux Chambers, Devereux Court, London].

Head

3089.   B, female, aged 81 at the date of the accident and 82 at trial, suffered injuries when a bus collided with the bus shelter in which she was standing. She was hit on the head and left shoulder by a piece of the shelter, and was knocked unconscious. She was upset and shaken by the accident and attended hospital. B had sustained a head injury, with scalp haematoma and a lump developed on the left side of her head. Those injuries resolved uneventfully leaving no scars or marks. B suffered a soft tissue injury to her neck and left shoulder. She had bruising down her left upper arm. She underwent a course of physiotherapy for seven months. She used paracetamol for seven months and thereafter stronger anti inflammatories. On examination five months after the accident, B had continuing daily neck and left shoulder symptoms. There was moderate limitation of neck movements. The prognosis was that B's symptoms would continue for up to two years after the accident, but there was a possibility that B would thereafter continue to suffer some episodic neck discomfort and stiffness. At the hearing, one year after the accident, B continued to suffer from daily neck and left shoulder pain. B also experienced headaches affecting the area at the back of the neck up to the top of her head. They were ongoing at five months after the accident, being intermittent, but tending to come on when the neck discomfort developed. The medical opinion was that they were fairly typical cervical migraine type headaches, and they were expected to resolve within two years of the accident. Medical opinion was that B had suffered some slight impairment, between 10 and 15 per cent, of her recent memory as a result of the accident. The effect of the injury was to accelerate the effects on the memory of the normal ageing process by one to two years. B also suffered nightmares about the accident which occurred on a nightly basis during the first weeks after the accident. Five months after the accident the nightmares were less frequent, although still occurring. At trial the nightmares were still occurring occasionally. B developed a phobia about bus travel and about being anywhere near the bus shelter. The phobia was expected to improve with time, and by one year after the accident, although she was still anxious, B had returned to travelling on buses. Medical opinion was that the accident had removed the confidence and independence that B, a previously fit and sprightly lady, had enjoyed. Prior to the accident B had been doing very well for a lady of her age, but the accident had disturbed her way of life and as a result she felt less able to do the independent activities, such as decorating DIY and gardening, which she had done before. B was still able to attend to her own day to day living requirements. *General Damages*: £6,000.

BRAITHWAITE v. FIRST WEST YORKSHIRE LTD, July 23, 2004, Recorder Michael Smith, CC (Leeds). [*Ex rel.* Tom Nossiter, Barrister, Park Lane Chambers, 19, Westgate, Leeds].

Head

3090.   H, a boy, aged two at the date of the accident and nearly three at the child settlement approval hearing, suffered injuries as a result of a road traffic accident. H was taken to hospital after the accident where he was noted to have a bruise to his right cheek and he was discharged with a head injury leaflet. H was examined by his GP the day after the accident when his injuries were confirmed. All H's symptoms had resolved by two weeks following the accident. H had also suffered acute distress. *General Damages* (agreed and approved): £1,000.

HUNT v. POOLE, April 7, 2005, Deputy District Judge Day, CC (Bromley). [*Ex rel.* Nicholas Preston, Barrister, 53, Curzon Road, London].

Head

3091.   R, female, a sales assistant, aged 39 at the date of the accident and 43 at trial, suffered injury in a shopping centre when she walked into a glass shelf which was invisible to her. R banged her head on the corner of the shelf and sustained a cut to the corner of her left eye which bled profusely. She fainted momentarily and was taken to hospital where it was noted that she had a small laceration under her eye, which was dressed accordingly. R suffered from headaches around the peri orbital area for two to three weeks after the accident, along with a black eye, which took a fortnight to resolve. The swelling subsided within a week. The small cut over the corner of her eye healed completely within 10 days of the accident without leaving any residual scarring. R took a week off work and suffered no consequential loss except that she felt that her surprise 40th birthday party, four days after the accident, was ruined because of her black eye. *General Damages*: £750.

ROBERTS v. WREXHAM CITY COUNCIL, April 4, 2005, District Judge Reeves, CC (Wrexham). [*Ex rel.* Karim Sabry, Barrister, 8 King Street Chambers, 8 King Street, Third Floor, Manchester].

Head–Neck: whiplash injury: no previous condition

3092.   P, male, a plumbing and heating engineer, aged 30 at the date of the accident and 36 at trial, sustained head and whiplash injuries when he was involved in a road traffic accident whilst riding his bicycle. He collided with a vehicle and upon landing struck his head on the pavement or kerb. P suffered a head injury with concussion, a whiplash injury to the neck, and bruising and grazes to his right knee. He was taken to hospital for accident and emergency treatment and was subsequently seen by his GP on numerous occasions. He was confined to bed for six weeks after the accident. P initially suffered principally from episodes of dizziness. He later developed a range of symptoms, including impaired concentration and memory, loss of confidence, anxiety, low mood, disturbed sleep, fatigue and headaches. He was diagnosed by a neuropsychologist as having sustained a concussive head injury of moderate severity but with no evidence of any organic brain damage. The psychological symptoms suffered after the accident represented a post-concussional syndrome and had arisen as a direct result of the head injury. Such symptoms were likely to result in a significant decrease in an individual's ability to maintain the same level of performance as before the accident. Four years after the accident, a course of psychological treatment had markedly improved P's symptoms. However, he continued to suffer an ongoing vulnerability to symptoms of fatigue, impaired memory and concentration, and dizzy spells. The prognosis was that although P would not suffer from these symptoms constantly he would have a permanent vulnerability to them, especially when he was under physiological or psychological stress. An orthopaedic expert concluded that the physical aspects of the neck injury had resolved by three years after the accident and that any pain after then was possibly related to a psychological overlay. Before the accident P worked on a self employed basis on short and medium contracts, including heavy pipe work. He returned to work on lighter duties within six weeks after the accident but had to stop approximately two years later due to ongoing symptoms. At the time of trial he had not returned to work but was intending to resume work shortly doing domestic work, part time at first, which offered greater flexibility. He considered that he would no longer be able to do heavy lifting or other heavy manual work or work at heights because of his tendency to dizziness. *General Damages*: £16,500. Smith v. Manchester award: £6,500.

PARKER v. ALLSOP, June 24, 2004, Recorder Price, CC (Derby). [*Ex rel.* Jonathan Hand, Barrister, Outer Temple Chambers, Outer Temple, 222 The Strand, London].

Head–Neck: whiplash injury: no previous condition

3093.   M, male, a general warehouseman, aged 57 at the date of the accident and 61 at trial, sustained a head and neck injury at work when an insecure load fell on him. He was taken to hospital and kept under observation for a few hours before being discharged. On the evening following the accident M suffered a severe headache and pain in the neck and shoulders which subsided after one week and allowed him to return to work in his usual capacity, although with an increased amount of lighter work as a forklift truck driver. Thereafter, the headaches continued to recur approximately three times a week, reducing to twice monthly by 19 months after the accident and continuing at the date of the trial, four years after the accident when M was still taking Ibuprofen. Eight months after the accident M described himself as being 85 per cent recovered. After a further 11 months the recovery was estimated to be 95 per cent with a slightly reduced range of movement in all planes, and the prognosis at that stage was that M would be expected to continue to improve. However, at trial, M's continuing symptoms showed that the condition had stabilised with continuing discomfort amounting to more than nuisance level. M's wife assisted him in his daily routine, household chores, DIY, gardening, and shopping immediately after the accident until two years later for an average of four hours a week, and for a further year for two hours a week, and from the third anniversary of the accident continued to help him one hour a week. The judge found that the injury fell at the bottom of the moderate band of the JSB Guidelines (6th Edition) Chapter 6 bracket (A) (b) (i). *General Damages*: £7,500.

MAIDMENT v. SOUTHAMPTON CITY COUNCIL, August 31, 2004, District Judge Ainsworth, CC (Southampton). [*Ex rel.* Stuart McGhee, Barrister, College Chambers, 19 Carlton Crescent, Southampton].

Head–Facial scarring

3094.   C, male, aged four at the date of the accident and 10 at the child settlement approval hearing, sustained injuries when he tripped over the edge of a raised drain cover and fell to the ground, suffering a blow to the head. C sustained abrasions and a laceration near his eyebrow. He experienced significant headaches for three weeks, during which period he was absent from school. At the medical examination four years and three months after the accident, C complained of ongoing occasional headaches. The examination revealed a horizontal scar measuring 1cm and a vertical scar measuring 1.5cm on the right side of the forehead. Both scars were grey in colour and visible, but not tender. The scars were also prone to swelling in cold weather but C did not appear to be embarrassed by them. The scars were permanent. The scars were noticeable but not disfiguring. Any ongoing symptoms were expected to resolve over the next two years, being within six years and three months after the accident. *General Damages* (agreed and approved): £4,300.

C (A CHILD) v. WALTHAM FOREST LBC, April 22, 2005, District Judge Vokes, CC (Bow). [*Ex rel.* Adam Walker, Barrister, Lamb Chambers, Lamb Building, Elm Court, Temple, London].

Face

3095.   Y, female, a part time medical secretary, aged 43 at the date of the road traffic accident and 47 at the hearing, suffered neck pain and an initial, but transient, exacerbation of her back pain. Y had a long history of neck and back problems including degenerative changes. The neck pain radiated into the arm for the first month and gave persisting mild to moderate pain for several months before becoming intermittent. The specialist limited the neck exacerbation to three months, with arm and shoulder discomfort for one month. Y was also diagnosed with a facial discomfort as a result of the injury. Two weeks after the accident, Y developed numbness in the top back teeth, outer rim of the ear, the right occiput and the right cheek, which could be more pronounced when she had headaches. The prognosis was for a full recovery in five years. Y reported feelings of very bad pins and needles in the face and the numbness had a great effect on her daily lifestyle, being sensitive to touch and troublesome when brushing her hair or teeth, which she found unbearable. She had problems applying makeup and lipstick and lost confidence. When eating Y had problems from lack of sensation in the mouth and she adapted by taking only very small mouthfuls and needed someone to check whether foodstuffs had remained lodged in her teeth. She felt as if she had had a stroke and despite reassurance from her husband that there was no objective sign, she perceived she was disfigured. At night she would place a cushion on her right side to prevent herself rolling over on the numb side to avoid pressure which exacerbated the symptoms. Medication had been prescribed, Gabapentin, which because of side effects from the maximum dosage, was changed. The first two years were the worst before improvement began. *General Damages*: £5,000.

YATES v. HAWTHORNE, November 16, 2004, District Judge Peake, CC (Birkenhead). [*Ex rel.* Michael J Pickavance, Barrister, 7 Harrington St, Liverpool].

Face

3096.   H, a boy aged three years at the date of the accident and eight at the hearing, was injured when he fell from a slide in a play area. He landed on his face striking his forehead and mouth causing pain and swelling and lacerations to his lips and gums. His upper incisor milk teeth were loosened. There was no loss of consciousness. Medical treatment was not sought immediately. Some hours later he began to vomit and was miserable and drowsy. H was admitted to hospital for observation on account of the head injury, for two nights. Forty eight hours after the incident, H was no longer complaining of forehead discomfort. There were no marks of injury such as bruising. H was noticeably clingy for two to three weeks. *General Damages*: £1,500.

H (A CHILD) v. IKEA LTD, September 15, 2004, District Judge Rogers, CC (Crewe). [*Ex rel.* Richard Mullan, Barrister, Sedan House, Stanley Place, Chester].

Ear–Non-facial scarring

3097.   W, a girl, aged 5 at the date of the accident and 11 at the child settlement approval hearing, sustained injuries when she slipped in a supermarket. She suffered a blow to the side of her head and laceration of her right ear. Her head injury consisted of minor bruising to the scalp over the right tempero parietal region. The injury to the ear consisted of a full thickness laceration of the skin of the posterior aspect of the ear, the underlying cartilage of the ear protruding to produce a puncture wound over the anterior aspect of the wound. She immediately experienced pain in both the right side of her head and in her right ear, which was bleeding. She was taken to hospital, where an antiseptic dressing was applied to her ear and antibiotics were prescribed. The following day, the wound to her ear was surgically repaired under anaesthetic. W found this process distressing. Her ear was moderately painful for one week the pain becoming relatively minor, although constant, for three weeks thereafter. W's ear was extremely tender during this time, to the extent that she was unable to wear her glasses or wash her hair. She missed three days of school, did not attend physical education for one week and was unable to swim for two to three weeks. The wound progressed well and after five months it had healed with minimal scarring. After about six months, a small haematoma in the scar discharged as a blister, after which the residual symptoms resolved. The vertical linear scar was about 7mm by 1mm on the posterior aspect of the upper part of the ear. The prognosis was that the scar would be permanent and would increase in size, although it would not become any more visible. At the hearing, over five years after the accident, the scar did not trouble W and was deemed to be barely visible. *General Damages* (agreed and approved): £1,800.

W (A CHILD) v. TESCO STORES LTD, October 18, 2004, District Judge Field, CC (St Albans). [*Ex rel.* Gurion Taussig, Barrister, 199 Strand, London].

Sight

3098.   P, a girl, aged five at the date of the accident and nine at the child settlement approval hearing, suffered a full thickness corneal laceration of the right eye together with a traumatic cataract after falling from her bicycle onto a thorn bush. An emergency primary repair of the laceration was undertaken, followed by cataract extraction and lens implantation. P suffered a significant decrease in vision of the right eye to 6/12, and the left eye to 6/8. She was advised to have occlusion therapy to the left eye two hours per day to address the problem of amblyopia. The lens implant was a permanent feature for life. P was at an increased risk, due to the perforated eye injury, of glaucoma, uveitis, and retinal detachment, assessed at 5 per cent. Her level of vision had been improved by laser treatment, together with the wearing of spectacles, to 6/9-2 in the right eye and 6/6-3 in the left eye. The initial injury, the cataract, the cataract surgery and the permanent lens implantation had all given rise to a permanent decrease in the vision in her right eye. S would also suffer permanent myopia. General damages were awarded on a provisional basis in the event that there was a likely deterioration in P's vision throughout adolescence and adult life, with a "cut off" point where P might return for a further assessment of damages in 2014 when P would be almost 21 years of age. Medical evidence stated that if P's eyesight was to deterioate, this would occur in very early adulthood. *General Damages* (provisional): £8,500.

P (A CHILD) v. HALLAM HOUSING SOCIETY LTD, June 21, 2004, Deputy District Judge Bellamy, CC (Doncaster). [*Ex rel.* Frank Allen Pennington Solicitors, 5-7 Regent Terrace, South Parade, Doncaster].

Sight

3099.   R, a girl, aged 15 at the date of the road traffic accident and 16 at the child settlement approval hearing, suffered injuries when a side window of the vehicle in which she was travelling was smashed in a road traffic accident and a fragment of glass entered R's left eye. The affected area was intensely painful and the eye closed up and watered profusely. R's sister removed the glass at the scene of the accident, but R was still in a lot of pain. R was taken home and her mother, who was a nurse, washed the eye out. R was taken to hospital and was transferred from there to a specialist ophthalmic casualty unit at another hospital where an X ray of the eye was taken. The X ray revealed no foreign objects in the eye, but two scratches on the surface. R was given eye drops and discharged. R's eye was sore and painful for 10 days with gradual improvement. R suffered throughout that period from watering, sensitivity to light and blurred vision. She could only use one eye comfortably and, although she did not take any time off school, she was in pain and discomfort and had to move to the front of the class because of difficulties with her vision. After two weeks R had made a complete recovery. *General Damages* (agreed and approved): £1,350.

R (A CHILD) v. FULLER, February 22, 2005, Deputy District Judge Brooks, CC (Dartford). [*Ex rel.* Joanna Kerr, Barrister, Lamb Chambers, Lamb Building, Temple, London].

Neck: whiplash injury: no previous condition

3100. B, male, aged 29 at the date of the accident and 31 at the date of the hearing, sustained a whiplash injury to his cervical spine and a laceration to his left forearm as a result of a road traffic accident. The pain in his neck was severe for the first six to seven months after the accident. He continued to suffer intermittent pain on exertion until 22 months after the accident. The laceration to the left forearm resulted in a noticeable red, raised scar which was embarrassing to B. It would be permanent. The judge rejected P's argument that the scar was worth less simply because B had a pre existing scar on his forearm. The current scar was more noticeable than the earlier scar. As a result of the accident, B also suffered from minor Post Traumatic Stress Disorder and acute stress which made him irritable and frustrated. A course of cognitive behavioural therapy (CBT), was recommended and the prognosis was that symptoms would resolve within six months of the commencement of such therapy. Damages were assessed on the basis that the symptoms would completely resolve two years and six months after the accident following the course of CBT. *General Damages*: £8,000 (apportioned £3,250 whiplash, £2,000 scar, £3,250 PTSD discounted to reflect an overlap in awards.)

BELL v. PATTERSON, February 26, 2004, District Judge Henthorn, CC (Southport). [*Ex rel.* Claire Hill, Pupil Barrister, St James's Chambers, 68 Quay Street, Manchester].

Neck: whiplash injury: no previous condition

3101. G, female, a district nurse, aged 35 at the date of the accident and 39 at the date of trial, suffered a whiplash injury when she was involved in a vehicle rear end shunt. Following the accident, she suffered immediate discomfort in the neck, shoulders and arms. The accident had happened on a Thursday and the pain worsened over the weekend to include pain in her back and leg. G took Ibuprofen and attended her GP, who prescribed Voltarol. The neck pain kept G awake for one to two weeks after the accident. Her back and leg pain resolved within a week. G suffered a lot of pain in her neck for two to three months after the accident and was unable to do her principal hobbies of gardening and needlework for some three to four months. Although G did not initially take any time off work, the court considered this remarkable, describing her as a stoic individual. Following a flare up of her remaining symptoms three months after the accident, G was off work for four days. She was prescribed Diclofenac tablets and referred for physiotherapy. She had five sessions of physiotherapy during the following six weeks which were helpful but did not settle the pain completely. Upon seeing an orthopaedic expert six months after the accident she complained of neck pain which came on after a long day's work. Her occupation involved a lot of driving and she had to wear a collar frequently in the evening due to the neck discomfort. She had difficulty with some surgical procedures. Examination revealed mild tenderness of the trapezius muscles in the distal on both sides. Following this examination G's condition then became fairly static, with morning stiffness and discomfort at the end of the day, and with intermittent periods of exacerbation. She had intermittent days off work due to her symptoms. Further examinations, 25 and 40 months after the accident, revealed a 15 per cent reduction in the neck movement in all directions on the first examination, and tenderness and a 10 per cent reduction of such movement on the second, by which time she was taking six painkillers a week. She had reduced this medication, taking painkillers only as needed from time to time, but she still wore a cervical collar on occasions at the trial date. Her gardening, needlework, housework and aerobics were still affected. There were no signs of degenerative changes but her symptoms were likely to be permanent with intermittent exacerbations. The court found that G's case came at the top end of bracket 6 (A) (b) (ii) of the JSB Guidelines (6th Ed). The court refused to make an award of Smith and Manchester damages because, as a nurse, there was no real risk of losing her employment, *Fryers v. Hirst* [2000] C.L.Y. 1568 considered. *General Damages*: £6,750.

GREGORY v. BUNCHER & HASELER LTD, April 7, 2004, Judge Darroch, CC (Norwich). [*Ex rel.* Cameron Brown, Barrister, 4 King's Bench Walk, Temple, London].

Neck: whiplash injury: no previous condition

3102.   S, female, a personal assistant, aged 26 at the date of the accident and 29 at trial, suffered soft tissue injuries to the cervical and lumbar spine together with a head injury and associated headaches as a result of a head on collision with P's motor vehicle. S was shocked and dazed and was taken to hospital. No X rays were taken although she was experiencing pain in her head, neck and back. She was diagnosed with a muscular neck injury and a minor head injury and was discharged. S sought medical attention from her GP and was referred for physiotherapy treatment. She had two weeks off work. Her headaches/head injury and back pain resolved after a few days. Her neck pain continued but had greatly improved after two months although she was left with intrusive symptoms. S still found it difficult to do any housework, decorate and play squash. She was, however, able to drive without any discomfort and could swim despite it causing slight stiffness. She managed to continue with her work and had no further time off although she sometimes had to leave work early on account of neck pain brought on by computing and proof reading. S continued with her physiotherapy treatment. Starting two months after the accident she had seven sessions of physiotherapy over a two month period, and five months later had a further 18 sessions over the next 12 months. Thereafter she continued to have physiotherapy approximately every two months. Nearly 24 months after the accident S was 80 per cent recovered from the neck injury and the prognosis was that whilst there was the possibility of further improvement S would be left with permanent residual problems which would not deteriorate. By trial S confirmed that the symptoms were of nuisance value only. *General Damages*: £6,500.

SYKES v. PATEL, May 4, 2004, Deputy District Judge Matthews, CC (Southampton). [*Ex rel.* Levenes Solicitors, 35 Dale End, Birmingham].

Neck: whiplash injury: no previous condition

3103.   P, female, a nurse, aged 37 at the date of the accident and 41 at trial sustained personal injuries in a road traffic accident. P suffered a whiplash injury to her neck. She suffered from pain in the left side of her neck and shoulder, her left elbow and the interior part of her chest. She suffered from pins and needles in the left arm radiating to her hand. She required a course of physiotherapy, undergoing weekly sessions for three months. She was absent from work for five months. P had difficulty with heavy lifting, decorating, gardening and shopping. Symptoms attributable to the accident persisted for two years. Thereafter, remaining symptoms were constitutional. In the immediate aftermath of the accident, P also developed an acute stress reaction which lasted a matter of days. P developed a phobic travel anxiety disorder with significant symptoms for six months, including panic attacks and anxiety when travelling. Her symptoms gradually resolved over a period of four years from the date of the accident and were finally resolved by the date of the trial. *General Damages*: £6,300. (Apportioned £4,000 for the whiplash injury and £3,000 for the phobic travel anxiety disorder reduced by 10 per cent to represent an overlap in pain and suffering).

PRIESTLEY v. DEMAINE, March 4, 2004, Deputy District Judge Smythe, CC (Sheffield). [*Ex rel.* Andrew Hogan, Barrister, 24, The Ropewalk, Nottingham].

Neck: whiplash injury: no previous condition

3104.   B, male, a bricklayer, aged 49 at the date of the accident and 53 at trial, suffered a whiplash injury to his neck when the vehicle in which he was a passenger was hit from behind by another vehicle. At the time of the accident B was not working due to an ankle injury and B had not returned to work by the date of trial. B's neck symptoms were at their worst for the first month after the accident, when they were constant and unremitting. The symptoms gradually improved thereafter, becoming intermittent, although aggravated by neck rotation and heavy lifting. B had also suffered some minor initial lumbar discomfort which had fully resolved by a few months after the accident. During the collision B had also knocked out the bridge which replaced his upper left central incisor and as a result suffered some transient discomfort. The bridge was replaced soon afterwards. On examination 10 months after the accident, when B was no longer taking any painkilling medication, his neck continued to be stiff and intermittently painful. He experienced occasional sleep disturbance. At that date B suffered no restriction in his daily activities but he had been unable to return to playing football. Driving, especially for long journeys, provoked discomfort. There was a 30 per cent restriction of neck movements. The injury was considered to be minor but physiotherapy was recommended. B received physiotherapy which concentrated on back and sciatic symptoms. Sciatic symptoms had only recently developed and the judge found that they were constitutional in origin and not caused by the accident. On examination at 39 months after the accident there had been some further improvement, although B was still having intermittent neck pain which radiated to the right shoulder. He had not returned to playing football and driving still provoked pain. The medical evidence was to the effect that the neck injury would prevent B from playing football; however, his constitutional back and sciatic symptoms would have prevented this in any case. B felt that he could not return to work as a bricklayer. This would provoke his neck pain, but it was also the case that his constitutional back symptoms would prevent him from returning to any work involving lifting or heavy tasks even without the neck symptoms. His neck movements remained limited by 30 per cent. The prognosis was that B's neck symptoms would not improve further. Damages were assessed on the basis that although the neck symptoms were persisting there had been significant improvement since the accident. *General Damages*: £5,500.

BRAZIL v. RICKELL, August 13, 2004, District Judge Rodgers, CC (Doncaster). [*Ex rel.* Tom Nossiter, Barrister, Park Lane Chambers, Leeds].

Neck: whiplash injury: no previous condition

3105.   C, female, a part time garage attendant, aged 49 at the date of the accident and 52 at trial, suffered injuries as a result of a road traffic accident. C was taken to hospital by ambulance where she was given a neck collar and was prescribed analgesic medication. She was also told to rest for a few days. Following the accident C was unable to carry out her pre accident housework, had difficulty reversing her car and was no longer able to go to the gym. On examination five months after the accident C was suffering tenderness and pain at the end range of movement in her cervical spine. C required constant non prescription pain relief for 24 months after the accident. She had six sessions of physiotherapy and eight sessions of osteopathy. Damages were awarded on the finding that C had suffered minor soft tissue whiplash symptoms which resolved 24 months after the accident. *General Damages*: £4,250.

ALARAKHIA v. BAYLEY, January 17, 2005, District Judge Cohen, CC (Willesden). [*Ex rel.* Sadie Crapper, Pupil Barrister, 3, Paper Buildings, Temple, London].

Neck: whiplash injury: no previous condition

3106. H, female, an office worker, aged 30 at the date of the accident and 33 at trial, sustained a whiplash injury when she was involved in a car accident. The injury affected her neck and shoulders. Initially, H had no time off work. However, due to her continuing symptoms, she consulted her GP about six weeks after the accident when it was noted that her symptoms were "intermittent" and had "almost settled". She was still suffering some symptoms when she was involved in a second, more minor, car accident five months after the first. According to medical opinion, the injury H had sustained in the second accident aggravated the pre existing symptoms in her cervical spine caused by the first accident for a further six months. Before the second accident, it had been expected that H would have made a full recovery from the first accident within 18 months of it happening. At trial, three and a half years after the first accident, H stated that she still suffered symptoms in her neck if she kept her head in the same place for a lengthy period. As a consequence, she avoided doing so by taking breaks from computer work by standing up and walking around, or doing some different kind of work for a period, but she did not have any time off work. She also had to take breaks from driving by stopping more frequently than she would have done before the accident to stretch or have a walk. The medical evidence suggested that there was a possibility of permanent minor symptoms. The judge found that because H's recovery was not complete his would indicate an award in category 6(A)(b)(ii) of the JSB Guidelines (6th Ed) but reduced the amount of general damages to take into account the consequences of the second accident. *General Damages*: £4,000.

HOUGH v. EAST, May 26, 2004, Judge Shawcross, CC (Portsmouth). [*Ex rel.* Andrew Stafford, Barrister, 4 King's Bench Walk, Temple, London].

Neck: whiplash injury: no previous condition

3107. N, female, a costume designer, aged 29 at the date of the road traffic accident and 32 at trial, sustained a whiplash injury to her neck. After the initial shock, pain developed within 24 hours which radiated to her back and arms. Within 48 hours her neck movements became poor, with severe muscle spasm in the left side. N experienced spasms in her arms for about two weeks. Pain localised in the neck and upper back and was constant. N was unable to perform any household chores for a week, and found them difficult for three weeks thereafter. She was off work for three weeks, and was still in pain when she returned. For two months the pain was moderate to severe. For a further six months N suffered intermittent moderate symptoms, and then a further 15 months of intermittent mild to moderate discomfort. She undertook 15 sessions of osteopathy, which improved her symptoms. Although the medical report stated that a full recovery had been made after 23 months, at trial, over three years after the accident, N still complained of occasional twinges in the back of the neck, particularly after a long day at work. N also suffered travel anxiety, and at trial, was still apprehensive when she approached the roundabout where the accident had occurred. N's injuries had disturbed her sleep and occasionally continued to do so. *General Damages*: £4,000.

NETHERCOAT v. PMI CONSTRUCTION LTD, October 4, 2004, Recorder Levy, CC (Barnet). [*Ex rel.* Gurion Taussig, Barrister, 199 The Strand, Temple, London].

Neck: whiplash injury: no previous condition

3108.   B, a girl, aged 11 at the date of the first accident, 12 at the date of the second accident and 14 at the child settlement approval hearing, sustained injury when the vehicle in which she had been a rear seat passenger was hit from behind by another vehicle. B suffered injury to the cervical spine. B was immediately distressed by the crash. Symptoms in the cervical spine developed and were still present when B was examined four months after the accident. She did not take any time off school. A prognosis for full recovery within eight months of the accident from all neck pain and symptoms had been given. B had also suffered sleep disturbance for three weeks after the accident and over the same period she felt unable to get into cars. The travel anxiety settled over time and it had been expected that the minor continuing sense of caution felt when travelling as a passenger in a car at four months after the accident would subside within a year of the accident. Unfortunately B was involved in a second accident five months after the first. She had been a front seat passenger in a stationary car when it was hit by another vehicle from behind. Following the impact she was upset and shaken, and felt pain in her neck. When she got home she took paracetamol and rested. The next morning she woke after a restless night with further pain and stiffness. B's movements were uncomfortable and she experienced difficulty in getting dressed. She also had episodes of dizziness. The second accident had happened over a weekend and by Monday she was able to go to school. When examined six months after the second accident B was still suffering symptoms in her neck and taking paracetamol. Since the second accident she had been suffering anxiety as a passenger. A prognosis for full recovery within nine months of the second accident was given. At the hearing it was confirmed that B had recovered fully. *General Damages* (agreed and approved): £3,750 (apportioned £2,000 for the first accident and £1,750 for the second accident).

B (A CHILD) v. NAIK, June 23, 2004, District Judge Hasan, CC (Central London). [*Ex rel.* Joanna Kerr, Barrister, Lamb Chambers, Lamb Building, Temple, London].

Neck: whiplash injury: no previous condition

3109.   R, female, an office worker, aged 55 at the date of the accident and 56 at trial, was injured in a side impact road traffic accident. R was immediately aware of pain in her neck, and was taken by ambulance to hospital. X rays showed no bony injury and she was diagnosed with a whiplash injury. The next morning R awoke with a very stiff and painful neck and back. She also felt pain in her left elbow, right wrist, and in both hips. the neck and back symptoms were most intrusive during the first four days of the accident, during which R remained off work. She also had trouble sleeping during this period. There was a gradual improvement of all symptoms. The left elbow injury resolved two weeks after the accident, and the left hip was pain free one month after the accident. R had four sessions of chiropractic treatment. Upon examination some three months after the accident the expert noted a full range of movements with some tenderness in the right trapezius and the L4 and L5 vertabrae. Pain was noted in the cervical, thoracic and lumbar spine, right hip and right wrist. R also reported anxiety and nervousness when driving past side roads. The medical expert advised that all symptoms would resolve within six months of the accident. No further medical opinion was obtained. At trial, one year and four months after the accident, the judge accepted R's evidence that although her injuries were almost completely corrected she still felt a weakness in her neck and back after sitting for more than three quarters of an hour, and she was still experiencing nervousness when she drove past the site of the accident. *General Damages*: £3,250.

ROLLERSON v. CLARK, February 5, 2004, District Judge Pelly, CC (Cambridge). [*Ex rel.* Joanna Kerr, Barrister, Lamb Chambers, Lamb Building, Temple].

Neck: whiplash injury: no previous condition

3110. C, male, a health and safety manager, aged 46 at the date of the accident and 49 at trial, suffered injuries as a result of a road traffic accident. He attended hospital the day after the accident when he was noted to have pins and needles in his right hand and discomfort in his right shoulder. C was examined by his GP six weeks after the accident, having developed torticollis, when tenderness of the neck was noted, but with a good range of movement. He was advised to take Ibuprofen and to stretch. C was not absent from work as a result of his injuries, although his work included some "hands on involvement" and some driving. He had continued to exercise at the gym, although he modified his regime and played racket ball rather than squash. At no time after the accident had his domestic activities been affected. On examination 10 and a half months after the accident C had a full range of neck movement, save for lateral flexion and rotation to the right, which were restricted by 10 per cent. At the time of that medical examination C complained of a constant dull ache which had persisted since the accident, and that his sleep was disturbed roughly twice a month, requiring Ibuprofen to get back to sleep. The medical evidence suggested that degenerative changes would be responsible for all symptoms from the point of 12 months after the examination onwards, i.e. from 22 months after the accident. C had also suffered from flashbacks for a few months after the accident. *General Damages*: £2,750.

ANDERSON v. WALL, January 10, 2005, Recorder Darbyshire, CC (Birmingham). [*Ex rel.* Matthew Brunning, Barrister, No. 5 Chambers, Steelhouse Lane, Birmingham].

Neck: whiplash injury: no previous condition

3111. F, female, a teacher aged 36 at the date of the accident and 37 at trial, suffered injury as a result of a road traffic accident. F was three months pregnant at the date of the accident. Although F was initially unaware of the injury, she developed neck pain, radiating towards her right shoulder, over the 24 hours following the accident. F was examined by her GP twice during the first two months after the accident. She suffered acute symptoms during the first four weeks after the accident, requiring assistance with domestic tasks and avoiding driving during that time. After the first four weeks K's injuries settled and she was having only occasional symptoms when she was medically examined approximately nine months after the accident. The judge accepted medical evidence that K's residual symptoms would resolve within six months of the hearing, about 27 months after the accident. *General Damages*: £2,500.

FALSHAW v. SENJACK, January 6, 2005, District Judge Crispin, CC (Romford). [*Ex rel.* Justyn Turner, Barrister, 4 King's Bench Walk, Temple, London].

Neck: whiplash injury: no previous condition

3112. W, female, a telecommunications officer, aged 28 at the date of the accident and 30 at trial, sustained a whiplash injury when B's vehicle rolled forward and collided with the rear of the stationary car in which she was sitting in a queue of traffic. W felt a violent jolt on impact and immediate pain. She sought hospital treatment on the day of the accident, was diagnosed as having a whiplash injury, and given analgesics. Since the pain persisted she visited her GP two weeks later and was referred for physiotherapy. The pain was constant for a further two weeks but physiotherapy assisted and improvement began one month after the accident. For six months after the accident W was anxious when driving and although she was pain free most of the time after this period she still suffered symptoms in her neck in the mornings and after driving for over two hours. She took no time of work due to the accident. The prognosis was that all neck symptoms would settle within 18 months of the accident. W's claim for recovery of the cost of her gym membership for a period of one month, to compensate her for being unable to use the gym during this period due to her injury, was disallowed on the basis that it represented a loss of amenity for which she was properly compensated for in general damages. *General Damages*: £2,500.

WHIBBERLEY v. BARTLETT, June 4, 2004, Judge McIntyre, CC (Reading). [*Ex rel.* Joanna Kerr, Barrister, Lamb Chambers, Lamb Building, Temple, London].

Neck: whiplash injury: no previous condition

3113. W, male, steel erector, aged 31 at the date of the accident and 35 at trial, suffered injuries as a result of a road traffic accident. W began to develop pain in his neck, especially on the right side, immediately after the accident. W's neck and upper back gradually seized up over a period of a few hours. W attended hospital and was diagnosed as having suffered a soft tissue whiplash injury to the neck with associated symptoms in the upper back. The symptoms were acute for a period of two weeks before steadily settling down. W was free of symptoms within three months of the accident. However, W's most significant injuries were psychological. The accident was extremely frightening, and W had genuinely thought that he was going to die in the accident. W was so frightened that he did not drive for two months after the accident and the experience had affected his confidence as a driver. He began to drive again reluctantly and because he had to do so for work purposes. He was especially worried about driving at night and he was a more wary, anxious and hesitant driver. W also became a terrible passenger as a result of the accident, always telling the driver to slow down and pressing imaginary brakes. W was diagnosed as having suffered from focused post traumatic anxiety associated with phobic anxiety. The psychological symptoms resolved two years after the accident. W was absent from work for two weeks after the accident and was unable to carry out any domestic tasks for four weeks. *General Damages*: £2,300 (apportioned as to £1,250 for the whiplash injury and £1,250 for the psychological injury with a reduction for overlap).

WATSON v. FARMER, February 18, 2005, District Judge Waterworth, CC (Nuneaton). [*Ex rel.* Stephen Garner, Barrister, 8 Chambers, Fountain Court, Steelhouse Lane, Birmingham].

Neck: whiplash injury: no previous condition

3114. B, male a steel fitter aged 26 at the date of the road traffic accident and 28 at trial, awoke the morning after the accident with pain in his neck. The pain worsened over the course of the next 48 hours, staying at that level for approximately one week, at which point his symptoms began to gradually improve. He made a full functional recovery within four to six weeks of the accident. On examination, eight months after the accident he reported symptoms occurring approximately once a week, which lasted a couple of hours at a time. At trial, B described them as twinges. On examination, the medical expert found minimal tenderness over the trapezius muscle. B did not seek medical attention. He had suffered whiplash following previous accidents and did not feel that medical attention would assist him on the instant occasion. B took one day off work. He worked with two other fitters and left the heavier duties to them, although he was able to do assembly work involving a hammer. B was a keen bodybuilder, attending the gym five times a week before the accident. He did not return to the gym while his symptoms lasted as he was concerned that the gym exercises might aggravate them. The judge found that B had recovered from his injuries in line with the medical expert's prognosis being within 12 months of the accident. Further, that the injuries fell within bracket 6(A)(c)(ii) of the Judicial Studies Board Guidelines, seventh edition. Whilst he accepted that the duration of the injury and the loss of amenity with regard to B's hobby of bodybuilding pushed the claim towards the top of the bracket, he found that owing to the relatively minor symptomology, an award at the top of the bracket was not justified. *General Damages*: £2,250.

BROTHERTON v. YOUNG, November 19, 2004, District Judge Hovington, CC (Salford). [*Ex rel.* Chris Middleton, Oriel Chambers, 14 Water Street, Liverpool].

Neck: whiplash injury: no previous condition

3115. D, a girl, aged 15 at the date of the accident and 16 at the child settlement approval hearing, had been a front passenger in a car travelling on the M1 driven by her mother when the car was hit on its offside by another car and pushed into the side reservation and then into the central reservation. D's head hit her mother's head and then the passenger door window. Police and paramedics attended the scene and it was found that D had sustained soft tissue injuries to her left shoulder, the left side of the neck and head. She took two days of school and missed PE for a month because of her injuries. D was also unable to partake in her hobby of Indian dancing for three months. She suffered from headaches for two months after the accident, and upon examination three months after the accident was found to have some restricted movement of the neck and left shoulder. D had also suffered shock at the scene of the accident and for several days after the accident had flashbacks to the event. Three months after the accident she was still frightened of travelling in cars especially on long journeys. A prognosis was made for a full recovery from all physical and psychological injuries within six months of the accident and at the hearing it was confirmed that the prognosis had been correct. *General Damages* (agreed and approved): £2,000.

D (A CHILD) v. NOOR, June 3, 2004, District Judge Sturdy, CC (Kingston upon Thames). [*Ex rel.* Joanna Kerr, Barrister, Lamb Chambers, Lamb Building, Temple, London].

Neck: whiplash injury: no previous condition

3116. E, female, a trainee hairdresser, aged 17 at the date of the accident and 17 at the date of the child settlement approval hearing, was involved in a rear end shunt road traffic accident. Immediately after the accident E was shaken and aware of an aching sensation in the back of her neck. The day after the accident E was physically sick and so attended her GP. A diagnosis of whiplash was made. Her GP gave E a sick note for two weeks absence from work and prescribed painkillers. E experienced constant and severe pain in her neck for the first 10 days following the accident and then noted a gradual improvement. On examination three months after the accident, E still experienced occasional pain in the neck approximately once every two weeks, especially in cold weather. The pain lasted for about five minutes or so, and consisted of an ache and was of a minor nature. E also suffered symptoms of travel anxiety. She was apprehensive as a passenger and found herself checking her mirrors more readily. E's neck symptoms and travel anxiety symptoms resolved completely within nine months of the accident, *B (A Child) v. Evans* [2003] C.L.Y. 3296 (Unreported, June 28, 200), [2003] C.L.Y. 3296 considered. *General Damages*: £1,800.

E (A CHILD) v. WALTON, February 10, 2004, Deputy District Judge Robins, CC (Wolverhampton). [*Ex rel.* Stephen Garner, Barrister, No. 8 Chambers, Steelhouse Lane, Birmingham].

Neck: whiplash injury: no previous condition

3117. B, female, a student, aged 15 at the date of the road traffic accident and 17 at the child settlement approval hearing, began to develop pain in the right side of her neck immediately after the accident. She was also shocked and tearful. She later felt dizzy and nauseous for 24 hours. B attended her GP two days after the accident. She was diagnosed as having suffered a whiplash injury to her neck. She was prescribed analgesia, which she took for two weeks. B's neck symptoms began to ease gradually after a few days. She also developed headaches. They were frequent at first with each lasting for about an hour. The headaches resolved after two months. B also developed passenger specific travel anxiety, especially when she approached roundabouts or the accident scene. On examination four months after the accident, B still suffered pain in her neck once a week. The pain consisted of a sharp pain in the right side of her neck if she turned her head quickly to the right. The pain eased off after a few minutes. She was also still anxious as a passenger in a car. B was absent from school for two days on account of her injuries. She was unable to do PE for two to three weeks. The prognosis was for the whiplash injury to the neck to settle within seven to eight months of the accident and the remaining psychological travel anxiety symptoms to settle within eight to 10 months. B confirmed at the hearing that her symptoms had settled in accordance with the expert's prognosis. *General Damages* (agreed and approved): £1,800.

B (A CHILD) v. MUNDA, September 8, 2004, Deputy District Judge Robins, CC (Birmingham). [*Ex rel.* Stephen Garner, Barrister, 8 Fountain Court, Steelhouse Lane, Birmingham].

Neck: whiplash injury: no previous condition

3118.　P, a boy, aged 11 at the date of the accident and 12 at the child settlement approval hearing, sustained a whiplash injury to the neck when involved in a road traffic accident. He began to feel pain during the morning following the accident, mainly in the back of his neck. He took analgesic medication for two days. P did not miss any school but was unable to play football or rugby for five days and found sitting at his desk uncomfortable for a week. His sleep was disturbed for a few days following the accident. After a week P's neck was no longer stiff and painful. Five months after the accident he still experienced intermittent discomfort in the back and left side of his neck. His symptoms fully resolved eight to nine months after the accident. *General Damages* (agreed and approved): £1,750.

P (A CHILD) v. COGGINS, April 8, 2004, District Judge Caddick, CC (Medway). [*Ex rel.* Gurion Taussig, Barrister, 199 The Strand, London].

Neck: whiplash injury: no previous condition

3119.　M, a boy, aged seven at the date of the accident and nine at the child settlement approval hearing, was injured when the car in which he was travelling was hit from behind. He felt pain in his neck and developed headaches. M attended hospital on the day of the accident and was given paracetamol for pain relief. His neck pain was acute for two days, as were his headaches, and during that period he was in shock and felt dizzy. His neck pain was diagnosed as a mild hyperextension and flexion injury and resolved fully within seven months after the accident. M suffered from nightmares and a fear of car horns for approximately two months after the accident. During that time he also wanted to sleep with his parents. At the hearing M's injury had completely resolved. M was not absent from school or PE lessons as a result of his injury. *General Damages* (agreed and approved): £1,750.

M (A CHILD) v. SMITH, August 27, 2004, Deputy District Judge Paul, CC (Croydon). [*Ex rel.* Thomas Wood, Barrister, 199 Strand Chambers, London].

Neck: whiplash injury: no previous condition

3120.　P, a girl, aged four at the date of the accident and five at the child settlement hearing, suffered injuries as a result of a road traffic accident. P felt shocked immediately after the accident and had a severe pain in her neck and a headache. She was taken home and given analgesics. The day after the accident the headache had gone but the neck pain was worse. P was examined at hospital and given analgesics. P continued to suffer headaches occasionally and visited her GP 11 days after the accident when she was advised to take paracetamol. P was not absent from nursery school but was unable to participate in swimming, ballet and tennis activities for three weeks after the accident. On examination two months after the accident P no longer suffered from headaches and the neck pain had largely resolved, although there was some tenderness to the region of her cervical spine. P was diagnosed with a whiplash injury from which she was expected to recover within six to eight months of the accident. On examination eight months after the accident it was established that post accident headaches had resolved, but it was discovered that P had previously been suffering from travel anxiety. Both the neck symptoms and the travel anxiety had completely resolved within six months of the accident. *General Damages* (agreed and approved): £1,750.

P (A CHILD) v. KUMAR, February 15, 2005, District Judge Chrispin, CC (Romford). [*Ex rel.* Joanna Kerr, Barrister, Lamb Chambers, Lamb Building, Temple, London].

Neck: whiplash injury: no previous condition

3121.   T1 and T2, girls, aged nine and four respectively at the date of the road traffic accident and 11 and six at the child settlement approval hearing, were both rear seat passengers when the car in which they were travelling was involved in a rear end shunt. Both girls were wearing seatbelts and both experienced head and neck movements upon impact, first forwards and then backwards. T1 suffered significant neck pain for the first two weeks after the accident and was taken to attend her GP one week after the accident, when painkillers were prescribed. She was unable to do gym for four months after the accident. The neck pain lessened and eventually disappeared six months after the accident. Upon examination by a medical expert, it was confirmed that T1's physical injury was a whiplash injury to the cervical spine. T1 also suffered psychological symptoms, experiencing nightmares and flashbacks relating to the accident, for approximately six months. As a result of the accident, T2 experienced headaches which persisted for two months after the accident. She was also taken to see her GP one week after the accident, but received no specific treatment. In addition to her headaches, which were completely resolved after two months, T2 was generally more nervous and apprehensive for six months after the accident. *General Damages* (agreed and approved): £1,750 (for T1) and £1,500 (for T2).

T (CHILDREN) v. MEGICKS, September 10, 2004, Deputy District Judge Spon-Smith, CC (Edmonton). [*Ex rel.* Joanna Kerr, Barrister, Lamb chambers, Lamb Building, Temple, London].

Neck: whiplash injury: no previous condition

3122.   M, a schoolgirl aged 11 at the date of the accident and 12 at the child settlement approval hearing, was a passenger in a vehicle involved in a rear end shunt. M suffered a whiplash injury to her neck. She was immediately shaken and soon after began to experience aching in the small of her back. She was shocked for the rest of the day. The next morning, she felt very stiff. Paracetamol was prescribed and taken. M continued to experience stiffness in her arms especially when lifting her school bag. This also caused discomfort in her back. She was attending physiotherapy for pre existing rheumatoid arthritis and on advice, was also treated by the physiotherapist for the whiplash injury. At four months after the accident, M continued to be nervous when in a car which was being followed by another vehicle. M made a full recovery within six months of the accident. *General Damages*: £1,650.

M (A CHILD) v. BRITISH SCHOOL OF MOTORING LTD, September 16, 2004, Deputy District Judge Haddow, CC (Aldershot & Farnham). [*Ex rel.* Gurion Taussig, Barrister, 199 Strand, London].

Neck: whiplash injury: no previous condition

3123.   C, female, a housewife, aged 34 at the date of the road traffic accident and 36 at trial, suffered a soft tissue whiplash injury to her neck. She had immediate pain in her left shoulder and neck. C attended hospital and was given anti inflammatory medication and painkillers. The next day her neck was very stiff and painful and she found it difficult to care for her children, one of whom was aged 16 months. C was very restricted in the housework she could do. The heavier tasks were very difficult, and she required assistance from family and friends in that respect for about four weeks. When C saw her GP one week after the accident she was prescribed further anti-inflammatory medication and painkillers. She had headaches and aching at the back of the head for about two months after the accident. C had significant neck symptoms for three to four months and thereafter had intermittent attacks of short lived shooting pains running up the back of her neck to her head. Five months after the accident she had no physical symptoms attributable to the accident. She had also suffered seat belt bruising across the chest which had been red, bruised and sore for about a week. She had difficulty sleeping and flashbacks to the accident for about four weeks after the accident. C also had psychological sequelae in the form of a reluctance to travel by car for at least five months. C remained nervous and a "back seat driver" at the date of trial, 25 months after the accident. *General Damages*: £1,600.

CLARKE v. HYNES, November 4, 2004, District Judge Rodgers, CC (Doncaster). [*Ex rel.* Tom Nossiter, Barrister, Park Lane Chambers, 19 Westgate, Leeds].

Neck: whiplash injury: no previous condition

3124.   W, a girl, aged eight at the date of the accident and nine at the child settlement approval hearing, suffered injuries as a result of a road traffic accident. W sustained a soft tissue strain of the cervical spine and adjoining right shoulder of mild to moderate severity. Pain had developed within a few minutes of the accident and by the following morning W's neck and right shoulder were stiff. On examination by her GP three days after the accident, she was prescribed Ibuprofen and paracetamol. W took painkillers for approximately four weeks after the accident. She missed two days of school and two dance lessons. The majority of her symptoms improved within six to eight weeks of the accident. On examination five and a half months after the accident W still had slight discomfort at the end of range of left lateral flexion movement and slight tenderness over the mid cervical region posteriorly. W's symptoms fully resolved in line with the prognosis, eight and a half to nine months after the accident. W also suffered from mild travel anxiety which had resolved within 12 months of the accident. *General Damages* (agreed and approved): £1,519.

W (A CHILD) v. HOPCRAFT, July 1, 2004, District Judge Lacey, CC (Wellingborough). [*Ex rel.* Gurion Taussig, Barrister, 199, Strand, London].

Neck: whiplash injury: no previous condition

3125.   G, a boy, aged 12 at the date of the accident and 13 at the child settlement approval hearing, had been one of three rear seat passengers in a vehicle that had been hit from behind behind by another vehicle. Upon impact he was emotionally shaken and distressed, and immediately felt pain in his neck. He was taken to hospital, where he was reassured and prescribed analgesics. No physiotherapy was recommended. G took two days off school. He returned to his GP once within the first three months after the accident and his enjoyment of his hobby of horse riding was affected during that period of time. When G was examined three months after the accident the medical expert diagnosed a whiplash injury to the cervical spine. G indicated that he had felt 90 per cent better at that point, although residual symptoms were still present occasionally which were irritating rather than debilitating. A prognosis for a full recovery within a further three months, or by six months after the accident, was made. At the hearing it was confirmed that this prognosis had had been correct. *General Damages* (agreed and approved): £1,500.

G (A CHILD) v. RUSSELL, June 24, 2004, District Judge Blomfield, CC (Bedford). [*Ex rel.* Joanna Kerr, Barrister, Lamb Chambers, Lamb Building, Temple, London].

Neck: whiplash injury: no previous condition

3126.   P, a boy, aged 16 at the date of the accident and at the child settlement approval hearing, sustained injuries in a road traffic accident in which he was a front seat passenger. Immediately after the accident he felt anxious and was physically shaking. These symptoms lasted acutely for about two days, during which time he also felt sick. He developed a bruise on the back of his head as a result of striking it on the head restraint. Pain started immediately after the accident and lasted for three to four days before resolving. The most serious injury was to his neck, which sustained a mild flexion/extension injury. Pain and stiffness developed immediately after the accident and lasted three to four days before settling. P did not attend hospital but was seen by his GP. After three and a half months he was still suffering occasional neck stiffness and twinges of pain in class, especially when bending forwards. These symptoms occurred two or three times per week. The neck pain resolved by about six months after the accident. *General Damages* (agreed and assessed): £1,500.

P (A CHILD) v. PEMBERTON, October 14, 2004, District Judge Taylor, CC (Horsham). [*Ex rel.* Gurion Taussig, Barrister, 199 Strand, London].

Neck: whiplash injury: no previous condition

3127.   J, male, aged three years at the date of the road traffic accident and four at the child settlement approval hearing, was strapped into a child booster seat in the rear of a stationary car which was hit from behind. J was shocked and upset after the accident and was taken to hospital by ambulance where he was diagnosed with a whiplash injury to his neck and was discharged. J was quieter than usual and tearful for three to four days after the accident. J's mother took J to his GP the day following the accident due to the severity of the discomfort he was reporting. J was prescribed paracetamol which he took for two weeks. By two to three weeks after the accident, the majority of the discomfort had settled and the whiplash injury resolved within two months of the accident. J also struck his forehead in the accident. A surface bruise developed over his left eye which resolved within two weeks of the accident. He also had intermittent headaches during this period. J had nightmares about the accident once or twice a month and had to sleep with his mother each night for just over three months after the accident. J also had some minor travel anxiety, initially refusing to enter a vehicle. However this also resolved within this period. At the medical examination three and a half months after the accident, all J's physical and psychological symptoms had resolved and the position was the same at the hearing, 10 months after the accident. *General Damages* (agreed and approved): £1,450.

J (A CHILD) v. ROSSITER, September 7, 2004, District Judge Burgess, CC (Ashford). [*Ex rel.* Mathew Gullick, Barrister, 3 Paper Buildings, Temple, London].

Neck: whiplash injury: no previous condition

3128.   L, a girl, aged 11 at the date of the accident and 11 at the child settlement approval hearing, and M, a boy, aged four at the date of the accident and five at the hearing, sustained injuries when the stationary vehicle in which they were sitting was hit from the rear by another vehicle. L suffered a whiplash injury to her neck, which resolved approximately three months after the accident, together with psychological symptoms of shock and travel anxiety for three to four months after the accident. M suffered headaches for a few days after the accident and psychological symptoms of shock and travel anxiety for approximately three to four months after the accident. No treatment was received by either claimant. *General Damages* (agreed and approved): L £1,250. M £700.

L (CHILDREN) v. BOWER, August 16, 2004, District Judge Murphy, CC (Liverpool). [*Ex rel.* Heather Belbin, Barrister, Oriel Chambers, 14 Water Street, Liverpool].

Neck: whiplash injury: no previous condition

3129.   L, male, a sheet metal worker, aged 22 at the date of the road traffic accident and 24 at the date of trial, suffered a whiplash injury to his neck when his stationary vehicle was hit from behind. L attended hospital on the day of the accident complaining of pain and stiffness in his neck, and he attended his GP on one occasion two weeks after the accident with similar symptoms. L had half a day off work. For a period of around two weeks the symptoms caused him particular pain when going fishing, and interfered with the time he could spend on this hobby. L suffered from pain and stiffness in his neck for around six weeks in total. *General Damages*: £1,075.

LONG v. WILTSHIRE, January 19, 2004, District Judge Toombs, CC (Lincoln). [*Ex rel.* Mark Henley, Barrister, Zenith Chambers, 10 Park Square, Leeds].

Neck: whiplash injury: no previous condition

3130.   W, a boy, aged 12 at the date of the accident and 13 at the child settlement approval hearing, suffered injuries as a result of a road traffic accident. W was wearing a seatbelt. He was jerked forwards and backwards, but did not strike any part of his body on the car. W immediately experienced discomfort in his neck. He was examined by his GP on the day of the accident and advised appropriately. W's neck discomfort had largely resolved within a period of two weeks of the accident, but he continued to experience intermittent discomfort thereafter. W was taken to a chiropractor for treatment and his condition improved after a single session. His symptoms had totally resolved by six weeks after the accident. In addition to the neck symptoms W experienced difficulty sleeping, as a result of the discomfort, for a period of two weeks. He was initially a nervous passenger, but that had resolved by the date of his examination by the medical expert three months after the accident. *General Damages* (agreed and approved): £1,000.

W (A CHILD) v. HUSSEIN, April 4, 2005, District Judge Gerlis, CC (Barnet). [*Ex rel.* Adam Walker, Barrister, Lamb Chambers, Elm Court, Temple, London].

Neck: whiplash injury: no previous condition

3131.   B, male, a schoolboy, aged 11 at the date of the accident and 15 at the child settlement approval hearing, was involved in a rear end shunt road traffic accident. Immediately after the accident B was shaken up but did not experience any symptoms of pain and discomfort. The next day however B began to suffer symptoms of severe pain in his lumbar spine and in his neck. The pain became constant and was aggravated by bending and twisting movements. B attended his GP and a diagnosis of whiplash injury was confirmed. B was prescribed Calpol and an anti inflammatory gel for pain relief. Both neck and back pain were at their most severe during the first month before gradually improving. B was totally symptom free after two months. Although he did not take any time off school on account of his injuries he was unable to participate in PE for one month after the event, *S (A Child) v. Gurnani* [2002] 6 Q.R. 17, [2002] C.L.Y. 3598 considered. *General Damages*: £1,000.

B (A CHILD) v. BARNICKLE, February 9, 2004, District Judge Ridgeway, CC (Coventry). [*Ex rel.* Stephen Garner, Barrister, Fountain Court, Steelhouse Lane, Birmingham].

Neck: whiplash injury: no previous condition

3132.   K, a girl, aged seven at the date of the accident and 12 at the child settlement approval hearing, suffered injuries as a result of a road traffic accident. The vehicle in which she was travelling was hit from the rear causing K to be jolted violently forwards and backwards. She had no immediate discomfort, but became aware of pain in her neck and the lower part of her back upon her return home. K attended her GP the day after the accident and whiplash injury was diagnosed. Tenderness over the right side muscles of the torso and neck pains were recorded. She was prescribed painkillers. The pains subsided and there was full recovery within three months. K was not absent from school as a result of the accident. *General Damages* (agreed and approved): £1,000.

K (A CHILD) v. HARRIS, January 17, 2005, District Judge Swindley, CC (Bolton). [*Ex rel.* Tony Thorndike, Barrister, Central Chambers, 89 Princess Street, Manchester].

Neck: whiplash injury: no previous condition

3133. C, a girl, aged 10 at the date of the accident and 12 at the child settlement approval hearing, sustained injuries as a result of a road traffic accident when the vehicle in which she was travelling was struck from the rear. C suffered a soft tissue injury to her neck and attended her GP who diagnosed a mild whiplash injury with associated headaches. The symptoms in the neck settled within a few weeks, with intermittent headaches settling approximately eight weeks after the accident. C also suffered disturbed sleep patterns for about a week after the accident. All C's symptoms resolved completely. *General Damages* (agreed and approved): £1,000.

C (A CHILD) v. SAMUDA, July 23, 2004, District Judge Allen, CC (Brentford). [*Ex rel.* David McHugh, Barrister, 1, Essex Court Chambers, 1st Floor, Temple, London].

Neck: whiplash injury: no previous condition

3134. H, a boy, aged 14 at the date of the accident and 16 at the child settlement approval hearing, had been a rear seat passenger in a vehicle which was hit whilst stationary by another vehicle from behind. The force of the impact jolted him forwards and backwards in his seat. H immediately felt pain in the right side of his neck, and when he arrived home took paracetemol. Next morning he awoke after a restless night with worsening pain and stiffness in his neck. Slight movements were uncomfortable and made dressing difficult. Four days later he visited his GP and was advised to rest and to take analgesics. H took three days off school and although he did not miss any PE lessons upon his return to school he participated in them with care. For two weeks he refrained from playing football with his friends. The neck symptoms resolved within three to four weeks of the accident, and when examined 11 weeks after the accident a full recovery was reported. He had been nervous when travelling as a passenger for the first few weeks after the accident. *General Damages* (agreed and approved): £1,000.

H (A CHILD) v. SHADRACK, June 2, 2004, District Judge Butcher, CC (Chelmsford). [*Ex rel.* Joanna Kerr, Barrister, Lamb Chambers, Lamb Building, Temple, London].

Neck: whiplash injury: no previous condition

3135. B, male, teacher, aged 24 at the date of the accident and 25 at trial, suffered injuries as a result of a road traffic accident. Immediately after the accident B experienced mild pain along the left side of his cervical spine. His neck pain gradually worsened throughout the day of the accident. B attended hospital on the evening following the accident, where he was examined, advised to take painkillers, given written instructions for the management of his neck injury, and discharged. The following morning his neck pain was worse and his neck felt stiff. A few days after the accident the pain had radiated to his left shoulder. B's neck was quite painful for the first week after the accident, during which time he took regular doses of Ibuprofen and paracetamol. His sleep was interrupted for the first few nights after the accident. Two weeks after the accident his neck pain had improved. He continued to feel occasional pain at the back of his neck, but was pain free five to six weeks after the accident. B continued to go to school but did not do any teaching during that period. He could not write as he was left hand dominant. Having considered the Preface to the JSB Guidelines (7th Edition), the Judge held that a period of five to six weeks was more than a few weeks and awarded damages accordingly. *General Damages*: £1,000.

BAGLEY v. PHILLIPS, October 29, 2004, Deputy District Judge Grosscurth, CC (Birkenhead). [*Ex rel.* Justin Valentine, Barrister, Atlantic Chambers, 4-6 Cook Street, Liverpool].

Neck: whiplash injury: no previous condition

3136.   R, a girl, aged 11 at the date of the accident and 15 at the child settlement approval hearing, sustained injuries in road traffic accident. The vehicle in which she was travelling, as a front seat passenger wearing a seat belt, was struck from the rear. C suffered soft tissue injuries to her neck and her thighs. She took paracetamol for pain relief during the first few days after the accident. As a result of her injuries she was unable to participate fully in sports for approximately two weeks after the accident. The symptoms in her neck and thighs had fully settled within two to three weeks after the accident. *General Damages* (agreed and approved): £600.

R (A CHILD) v. PATEL, July 27, 2004, District Judge Beattie, CC (Bow). [*Ex rel.* David McHugh, Barrister, 1, Essex Court Chambers, 1st Floor, Temple, London].

Neck: whiplash injury: no previous condition

3137.   M, a girl, aged eight at the date for the accident and nine at the child settlement approval hearing, suffered injuries as a result of a road traffic accident. Upon impact M was shocked and shaken and was taken to hospital, where she was reported as having a stiff neck, and was discharged with analgesics. M took the analgesics for one week and did not seek any other medical attention. During that first week M's neck symptoms were a significant nuisance, and she tended to have to rub her neck and complained of stiffness when watching the television over the Christmas holidays. After the first week the physical symptoms improved quickly, resolving completely within two weeks of the accident. After two weeks the only remaining symptoms were psychological. M was anxious when travelling by car and felt more car sick than she had before the accident. Upon examination three and a half months after the accident the prognosis was for full recovery from her travel anxiety within six months of the accident. At the hearing it was confirmed that M had made a full recovery in accordance with the prognosis. Her social activities and schooling were unaffected by the accident. *General Damages*: £500.

M (A CHILD) v. YATES, April 1, 2005, District Judge Plaskow, CC (Brentford). [*Ex rel.* Joanna Kerr, Barrister, Lamb Chambers, Lamb Building, Temple, London].

Neck: whiplash injury: no previous condition

3138.   R, a girl aged seven years at the date of the road traffic accident and 10 at the child settlement approval hearing, was injured when the car in which she was a passenger was hit from behind. Two days after the accident, she felt pain in her neck and was taken to see her GP who prescribed pain relief. She was also shocked and had impaired concentration for seven days after the accident. R's neck pain resolved seven days after the accident. At the hearing, two years and three months after the accident, R's injury had completely resolved. R was not absent from school, but missed PE lessons for four days. *General Damages* (agreed and approved): £500.

R (A CHILD) v. POPAT, August 31, 2004, Deputy District Judge Brar, CC (Watford). [*Ex rel.* Thomas Wood, Barrister, 199 Strand Chambers, London].

Neck: whiplash injury: no previous condition–Ankle

3139.   D, male, a mechanic, aged 22 at the date of the accident and 23 at trial, suffered multiple personal injuries as a result of a road traffic accident. During the impact, D's car struck two trees and the footwell was forced some distance into the car crushing D's ankles. On emerging from the car, D collapsed from the pain in his ankles. As well as soft tissue injuries to both ankles, D sustained a soft tissue whiplash injury to the neck, soft tissue seatbelt bruising to the chest, and soft tissue seatbelt bruising to the pelvis. D attended hospital immediately after the accident, where he was diagnosed as having suffered multiple soft tissue injuries. He was absent from work for a period of one week as a result of the accident. The seatbelt bruising to the chest and pelvis resolved after a period of one month. D's most serious injuries were to his neck and ankles. D suffered acute pain in the neck and constant stiffness in the ankles for three months after the accident. For the first week after the accident D could hardly walk due to the persistent pain in his ankles. During that week he required considerable help with daily tasks from his girlfriend. During the second week after the accident, by which time D had returned to work as a mechanic, D had to mobilise with the aid of crutches. His ability to do his work was affected by ongoing neck and ankle pain. The prognosis had been for D's ongoing neck pain and the stiffness in the ankles to settle six months after the accident. At trial D confirmed that his symptoms had settled in accordance with the prognosis. The judge assessed general damages on the basis that D had suffered six months of symptoms in his neck and ankles. *General Damages*: £2,200.

   DREW v. McHALE, January 4, 2005, District Judge Daniels, CC (Bristol). [*Ex rel.* Stephen Garner, Barrister, 8, Fountain Court, Steelhouse Lane, Birmingham].

Neck: whiplash injury: no previous condition–Excretory organs: bowels

3140.   H, female, a housewife, aged 36 at the date of the accident and 38 at trial, suffered injuries as a result of a rear end shunt road traffic accident. H sustained a whiplash injury to her neck, shoulder and lower back, and a flare up of her pre existing ulcerative colitis. H suffered symptoms of pain, stiffness and limitation of movement in her neck, all of which resolved within two years of the accident. She suffered pain, limitation of movement and stiffness in her lower back, such symptoms resolving within one year of the accident. Prior to the accident H had suffered for many years with bouts of ulcerative colitis. That condition had been relatively asymptomatic for some time prior to the accident. However, H suffered a flare up of her ulcerative colitis as a result of the anti-inflammatory medication she was prescribed by her GP. The symptoms she experienced as a result of the flare up were persistent abdominal pain, frequent use of the toilet, disturbed sleep and interference with social activities. Those symptoms resolved within approximately nine months of the accident. The flare up of H's ulcerative colitis was attributed to the accident. The court held that if H's only injury had been a flare up of the ulcerative colitis, the award for general damages would have been in the region of £1,000. However, the court took the view that there was significant overlay in pain, suffering and loss of amenity between the neck and back injury and to a lesser extent between those injuries and the flare up of H's ulcerative colitis. *General Damages*: £4,275.

   HARRIS v. SAUNDERS, May 13, 2004, District Judge Smedley, CC (Liverpool). [*Ex rel.* Heather Belbin, Barrister, Oriel Chambers, 14, Water Street, Liverpool].

Neck: whiplash injury: making a previously asymptomatic condition symptomatic

3141.   R, female, a school dinner lady, aged 53 at the date of the accident and 58 at trial, sustained a whiplash injury when the vehicle she was driving was hit from behind by another vehicle. That evening, R began to suffer neck pain and stiffness with referred pain into the arms, with pins and needles. She also suffered from associated occipital headaches and developed mid and upper thoracic pain. She was diagnosed with a whiplash injury and advised to take Ibuprofen medication by her GP. Two months after the accident, the GP referred her for a course of chiropractic treatment which completely relieved the occipital pain. The neck, thoracic, and referred pain into the arms with pins and needles persisted. X rays confirmed that R had significant pre existing wear and tear in three of her lower cervical discs. Any neck pain which had persisted beyond two years after the accident was attributable to degeneration and not to the accident although R had been asymptomatic before the accident. Therefore damages were assessed on the basis of a two-year period. *General Damages*: £5,000.

ARNOLD v. ZAKO, May 12, 2004, Judge Harris Q.C., CC (Birmingham). [*Ex rel.* Stephen Garner, Barrister, No 8 Chambers, Fountain Court, Steelhouse Lane, Birmingham].

Neck: whiplash injury: making a previously asymptomatic condition symptomatic

3142.　　J, male, a retired company director, aged 72 at the date of the road traffic accident and 74 at trial, was injured when his car was struck from behind by another vehicle when he was stationary in traffic. J suffered a whiplash injury to the neck, with pain across the neck and shoulders accompanied by loss of neck movement. He attended hospital on the evening of the accident, where he was given a soft collar and advised to take analgesia. He assessed his pain level immediately after the accident as "7 to 9 out of ten" and for six weeks after the accident as "6 to 9 out of 10". For the first few weeks after the accident J found that the pain was aggravated by turning his head. During this time J's symptoms slowed him down in his daily activities and made strenuous tasks like cleaning and heavy lifting difficult. He found this stressful and frustrating. His symptoms continued to interfere with working on the computer, his social life and his role as Welfare Officer for the Royal Artillery Association. The pain declined to "4 to 7 out of 10" for a further six months before decreasing to "2 to 4 out of 10". J suffered from headaches and from pins and needles in the left hand. His sleep continued to be disturbed 8 months after the accident. On examination eight months after the accident, J reported residual right sided neck discomfort. Extension and lateral flexion and rotation in both directions were restricted to a marked degree and accompanied by stiffness and discomfort, but there was no muscular tenderness or neurological deficit. A deep seated soft tissue/musculo ligamentous injury was diagnosed. At this time J was able to carry out all his daily activities, but was aware of discomfort while doing so. In 1996 J had been diagnosed as suffering from a degenerative spinal condition which affected his neck and had been reactivated by the accident, having been asymptomatic prior to the accident. The prognosis was that J's symptoms would resolve gradually and would cease completely within 19 months of the accident if he undertook eight to ten sessions of physiotherapy and adjusted his daily activities. J in fact recovered better than expected. He did not undertake physiotherapy and at trial it was found that J's symptoms had effectively resolved within 12 months of the accident, after which point there were only infrequent and minor recurrences. *General Damages*: £2,750.

JACKSON v. FARMER, March 15, 2005, Judge Sleman, CC (Guilford). [*Ex rel.* Chris Middleton, Barrister, Oriel Chambers, 14 Water Street, Liverpool].

Neck: whiplash injury: acceleration or exacerbation of pre-existing symptomatic condition

3143.　　F, male, a car mechanic, aged 47 at the date of the road traffic accident and 49 at trial, sustained a whiplash type injury involving a sprain of the cervical spine and scapular muscles. Almost immediately after the accident, F experienced pain in the back of his neck and scapular muscles. He was taken to hospital where he was given a sling and a soft collar which he wore for 10 days. Acute pain and stiffness improved after three to four weeks. Three months after the accident, the pain and stiffness had reduced by 40 per cent at which point, F underwent a course of physiotherapy sessions. His condition continued gradually to improve. He was off work for three weeks. After three months, he was carrying out about 80 per cent of the strenuous work he was doing prior to the accident. He resumed full duties after one year. F was also unable to participate in his leisure activities of air rifle and clay pigeon shooting for one year. At home his sleep was disturbed for three to four weeks. He was unable to carry out any household chores for one month and resumed all chores after one year. F was suffering from a pre existing, albeit mildly symptomatic cervical spondylosis. Symptoms relating to the accident were present for two years, neck pain after this time being attributable to the cervical spondylosis. F also suffered minor psychological injury. He experienced flashbacks for the first few weeks after the accident and was anxious when travelling by road for about one month. *General Damages*: £3,450.

FLITNEY v. COLUMBIA MARKETING LTD, August 31, 2004, District Judge Marin, CC (Barnet). [*Ex rel.* Gurion Taussig, Barrister, 199 Strand, London].

Neck: whiplash injury: acceleration or exacerbation of pre-existing symptomatic condition

3144. T, female, police officer, aged 35 at the date of the accident and 36 at trial, suffered injuries in a side impact road traffic accident. T sustained a whiplash injury to her neck and cervical spine. The neck pain began to develop immediately after the accident. Over the following few days T suffered increasing symptoms of pain and stiffness in the rear of her neck, radiating to the right shoulder as each day progressed. T did not seek medical advice after the accident. She had sustained a whiplash injury as a result of an accident five years earlier and was still suffering ongoing neck symptoms at the date of the instant accident. T knew that she had to self medicate, and that was what she did. The medical expert diagnosed T as having sustained an exacerbation of her previous whiplash symptoms over a period of two months. Damages were assessed on the basis that T had suffered a two month whiplash injury. T was not absent from work on account of her injury. *General Damages*: £1,250.

TONGUE v. DUGGER, October 11, 2004, District Judge Knifton, CC (Birmingham). [*Ex rel.* Stephen Garner, Barrister, 8, Fountain Court, Steelhouse Lane, Birmingham].

Neck: non-whiplash injuries–Shoulder

3145. K, male, bus driver, aged 52 at the date of the accident and 54 at trial, suffered injuries when he tripped over an obstruction on his bus, grabbing a handrail as he fell. As a result he wrenched his shoulder and neck, sustaining a left trapezius muscle strain. Pain developed in the left side of his neck and the upper border of his left shoulder within hours of the accident. K attended hospital and was advised to use analgesia, which he did for approximately four weeks. He was absent from work for five days. On his return to work K worked in intrusive discomfort for four weeks. He had sleep disturbance for two to three weeks because of pain in his left shoulder. He could not do housework to his usual levels for about four weeks. On examination nine months after the accident K felt that he was 80 per cent recovered. Improvement was ongoing. He found he could have five to six days symptom free, but then the left shoulder symptoms might be precipitated by reaching for something or by unusual exertion. K avoided carrying heavy shopping with his left arm in order to avoid precipitating the symptoms. Medical opinion was that K was still recovering, and that his symptoms, which were assessed to be of low grade nuisance value, would settle within 12 to 15 months of the accident. At trial, 20 months after the accident, K gave evidence that he was still suffering from some shoulder pain during the night if he lay on his left side. During the daytime he had the occasional twinge if he drove over a pothole in the bus. He felt that he was still improving. Damages were assessed on the basis that the residual symptoms had been slower to recover than the medical expert had expected, but would resolve within a short period after trial. *General Damages*: £2,750.

KEEDY v. FIRST WEST YORKSHIRE LTD, December 20, 2004, Recorder Miller, CC (Leeds). [*Ex rel.* Tom Nossiter, Barrister, Park Lane Chambers, 19, Westgate, Leeds].

Back and spine: no previous condition

3146.   C, male, a computer operator, aged 24 at the date of the accident and 28 at trial, suffered injuries as a result of an accident at work when lifting heavy rolls of UPVC. C suffered a low back disc protusion with associated nerve root problems. He was prescribed painkillers by his GP and underwent extensive but only partially relieving physiotherapy and osteopathic treatment. At the time of the trial C was continuing to experience pain on the right side of his lumbosacral spine and right sided sciatica extending to the right foot. The pain was almost constant and was aggravated by twisting, bending or lifting, to the extent that he could not even lift a full kettle of water without pain. When aggravated the increased pain lasted for up to two days. The pain woke him early in the mornings. He could not sit still for long, preferring to kneel rather than sit, and was unable to stand still or to run. He found driving difficult, although he could ride a motor cycle. He also suffered from unrelated but much less severe neck pain and shoulder problems. The experts agreed that there was an increased likelihood of degenerative disease at the lumbosacral level. They also agreed that he was now permanently unfit for strenuous exercise and heavy manual work, such as that required in his pre accident work. He could manage only semi sedentary work and at the time of trial was employed as a ticket salesman for a ferry company. The recorder took account of the fact that a preplanned trip around the world was made less enjoyable by his injuries. The award reflected the possibility that, but for the accident, C might have been able to fulfil an ambition to become a firefighter in the near future; it also took into account medical evidence that there was a chance that he would have developed similar back symptoms in any event. *General Damages*: £15,000. Smith v. Manchester award: £13,500.

ARGYLE v. PHOTOBITION LTD, May 13, 2004, Recorder David Blunt Q.C., CC (Southampton). [*Ex rel.* James Counsell, Barrister, Outer Temple Chambers, Outer Temple, 222 Strand, London].

Back and spine: no previous condition

3147.   C, female, a hospital theatre sister, aged 41 at the date of the accident and 44 at trial, suffered injury during the course of her employment. While reassembling a theatre table C felt a sharp stabbing pain in her lower back. By 7 to 10 days after the incident C's condition had deteriorated gradually and she attended hospital. Arrangements were made for her to have physiotherapy for a 10 month period, which she found helpful. C also attended her GP several times during that period, and she was seen by a spinal assessment clinical nurse. Two months after the accident C was referred to a consultant orthopaedic surgeon and a scan was taken of the lower lumbar spine. It was revealed that C had suffered an annuler tear. She was absent from work for a period of six months following the accident, and returned to work working four hours per day on three days per week. C's working hours were restricted for the first year after her return to work, but she returned to normal working thereafter. However, she had to sit down during long operations and no longer helped to turn over patients on the operating table. She had difficulty using a lead apron because of the weight and she relied heavily upon her colleagues for assistance. C remained unable to do any decorating or DIY as she had done prior to the accident and had great difficulty with any gardening activities. She had difficulty with ironing and bed making and had stopped going to the gym because of the pain in her back. C was able to drive for short distances but found difficulty with longer journeys because of back ache. Her social activities with friends and her children had been limited as a result of the accident. C continued to suffer from a residual feeling of tightness in the lower back and the symptoms were worse when sitting, standing, driving and during physical activity. The symptoms tended to last as long as the physical activity she was doing. C still swam three or four times a week. Medical evidence obtained from a consultant neurologist stated that C had sustained a 7 to 10 year acceleration to symptomatic lumbar degenerative disease and that she would be vulnerable on the open labour market. It was not expected that C would become completely symptomatic in the future. *General Damages*: £12,000. Smith v. Manchester award: £3,000.

QUANTRILL v. SOUTH TYNESIDE HEALTH CARE NHS TRUST, September 27, 2004, Judge Moir, CC (Newcastle). [*Ex rel.* Thompsons, Solicitors, St. Nicholas Building, St. Nicholas Street, Newcastle].

Back and spine: no previous condition

3148. S, aged 18 at the date of the accident and 21 at trial, suffered injury to his lower back when he lifted a fire surround unassisted during the course of his employment. The accident caused an initially undetected fracture of the pars interarticularis at S1. He suffered a sudden severe pain in his back, which persisted so that he had to leave work early. Pain also started to spread into his right leg. He attended his GP the following day and was referred for physiotherapy, which had not helped after one month. After three months of continuing symptoms he was placed in a plaster cast around the trunk and put on a waiting list for surgery. For the first four weeks in plaster S was much better, but deteriorated during the last two weeks. When examined five and a half months after the accident he was still experiencing pain in the L3/4 region of the lower back, which radiated down into the right buttock, back of the right thigh and back of the right knee. He was taking regular painkillers and was woken every couple of hours at night by pain. Sitting and lying down were painful. His walking distance was reduced to 300 yards. He was unable to get into or out of the bath without help. He had to stop his hobbies of football and long walks with his dog. Two injections into the back each provided some temporary relief. Fourteen months after the accident S underwent an operation on the lower spine, during which it was confirmed that the accident had caused a fracture of the pars interarticularis at S1. A pseud arthrosis was removed and hypertrophic bone in the area was refreshed. Screws were inserted to stabilise the bone and a graft was taken from the left side of the back of the pelvis. On examination, nine weeks after the operation, S had already made good progress. His back pain had decreased considerably and there was little leg pain. The wound and graft site had healed well. Movements were still stiff and painful, but he was able to walk again and travel for an hour in a car without discomfort. Six months after the first operation S underwent a further operation on his back to remove the screws. When the operative wound had healed a course of physiotherapy was arranged to reduce stiffness. He was examined for a medico legal report 22 months after the accident, at which time there was mild stiffness in the lower back, which was worse in the mornings but eased on activity. He still avoided exerting his back too much and took painkillers to manage occasional discomfort. He was able to undertake domestic activities and had returned to walking normally. On examination 27 months after the accident S had improved further. He had returned to work and had resumed playing badminton and cycling. He experienced a little stiffness in his back towards the end of the day, but no pain in the back or leg. He had recovered an almost full range of back movement. His overall recovery was expected to be completed without future problems. The district judge concluded that the injury came within the "moderate" bracket of the JSB Guidelines on back injuries. *General Damages*: £8,500.

SUGDEN v. B&Q PLC, January 14, 2004, District Judge Harvey, CC (Exeter). [*Ex rel.* Adrian Posta, Barrister, Albion Chambers, Broad Street, Bristol].

Back and spine: no previous condition

3149.   S, a girl, aged 16 at the date of the accident and 17 at the child settlement approval hearing, had been riding her moped when she was hit from behind by a car whilst stationary at traffic lights. She was shunted forward and thrown upwards off her moped, landing on the ground. S immediately felt pain in the back of the neck and was taken to hospital by ambulance. X-rays revealed no bony injury and she was advised to take painkilling medication and to rest. Pain also developed in the lower back, and she took two weeks off from college and her part time job. Symptoms in the neck resolved within three weeks, but constant pain in the lower back continued. S had two courses of physiotherapy for her back, and took analgesics regularly. Pain also radiated down the back of her thighs sometimes as far as the knees, and caused S particular difficulties when sitting for a time. The symptoms in the lower back resolved within 16 months of the accident, by which point she had made a complete recovery. *General Damages* (agreed and approved): £3,000.

S (A CHILD) v. LEWIS, June 3, 2004, Judge not specified, CC (Kingston Upon Thames). [*Ex rel.* Joanna Kerr, Barrister, Lamb Chambers, Lamb Building, Temple, London].

Back and spine: no previous condition

3150.   B, male, a bus driver, aged 29 at the date of the accident and 30 at the date of trial, suffered a soft tissue injury to his lower back as a result of a road traffic accident. B was aware of a niggle in his back immediately after the accident, and he awoke the following morning with pain in his lower back. B was off work for two weeks. B saw his GP, who prescribed Ibuprofen, and he used painkillers for six months. When he returned to work he found that prolonged periods of driving a bus aggravated his symptoms. B was unable to use the gym for eight weeks after the accident. When examined six months after the accident B was still suffering from pain at the centre of his lumbar spine, which was aggravated by his job. He found the pain to be relieved by rest, walking, swimming, and going to the gym, where he did lighter activity than he had done before the accident. He found the pain to be aggravated by certain other activities, such as his hobby of DIY. Medical examination showed marked spasm in the erector spinae muscles, although there was a full range of lumbar movements. At trial, 16 months after the accident, B indicated that he was still suffering from symptoms approximately twice each week, which lasted two to three hours. He had given up the gym, finding that it had started to aggravate his symptoms. His DIY was still limited. However, he had changed to a desk based job 12 months after the accident, which had helped to alleviate his symptoms, and overall he felt his symptoms were improving. Damages were assessed on the basis that a full recovery would be achieved within 18 months of the accident. *General Damages*: £3,000.

BURTON v. M&S THOMPSON PLANT HIRE LTD, May 13, 2004, Recorder Dobbin, CC (York). [*Ex rel.* Tom Nossiter, Barrister, Park Lane Chambers, 19, Westgate, Leeds].

Back and spine: no previous condition

3151.   M, a girl, aged 10 at the date of the accident and 11 at the child settlement approval hearing, suffered injuries as a result of a road traffic accident. M had been sitting in the front passenger seat and sustained a hyper extension/flexion injury to the cervical spine. Symptoms of pain in the posterior part of her neck at the C6/7 level radiating out towards both shoulders and her scapular regions, and down to the upper thoracic spine, developed two days after the accident. On the third day M attended her GP who advised the administration of analgesics. M had to take one day off school from school. The pain was at its peak for the first month after the accident, during which time M was unable to do PE at school and could not attend Girl Guides, as her symptoms were aggravated by limited physical activity.

Thereafter M's symptoms began to reduce. However, on examination four months after the accident M was still experiencing neck pain radiating to both scapular regions. The pain was intermittent, occurring on 2 or 3 days a week, but led M to take painkillers. At that stage the prognosis was that M would recover within six months of the accident. A full recovery did not take place in that timescale, and on examination one year after the accident, although her symptoms had reduced in severity and frequency, M was still experiencing pain once or twice each week. The revised prognosis was then that M would fully recover within 18 months of the accident. Physiotherapy was recommended. M underwent five or six physiotherapy sessions and at the hearing, approximately two years after the accident, M indicated that she had made a virtually complete recovery. She had stated that she experienced occasional twinges but said that she could not remember the last time she had felt one. On that basis the judge was prepared to approve the award. *General Damages* (agreed and approved): £2,650.

M (A CHILD) v. LEMON, January 10, 2005, Deputy District Judge Trigg, CC (Staines). [*Ex rel.* Joanna Kerr, Barrister, Lamb Chambers, Lamb Building, Temple, London].

Back and spine: no previous condition

3152.   V, a girl, aged 11 at the date of the accident and 13 at the child settlement approval hearing, suffered injury in a road traffic accident. V sustained a hyper extension/flexion injury to the cervical spine. Neck pain and stiffness began immediately after the accident, and on the day of the accident V attended hospital where she was examined and x rays were taken. No bony injury was found. V was provided with a soft collar, which she wore for two weeks, during which time she stayed away from school as a result of her injuries. V also took painkillers. The neck pain and stiffness continued for three weeks after the accident before resolving completely. The accident also caused V to suffer psychological symptoms of anxiety. At the time of the accident V was screaming hysterically and was clearly very shaken. For one month after the accident she had difficulty sleeping because of intrusive thoughts, and was generally more anxious about being driven. On examination three months after the accident V was still anxious, frequently gripping the interior furniture of the car and criticising reasonable driving manoeuvres. The prognosis was that she would recover from these symptoms within six months of the accident. At the hearing the litigation friend confirmed that the anxiety had resolved in accordance with the prognosis. *General Damages* (agreed and approved): £1,000.

V (A CHILD) v. TRUJILLO, January 11, 2005, District Judge Pearl, CC (Watford). [*Ex rel.* Joanna Kerr, Barrister, Lamb Chambers, Lamb Building, Temple, London].

Back and spine: no previous condition

3153.   G, a girl, aged nine at the date of the accident and 10 at the child settlement approval hearing, suffered an injury to her mid thoracic spine as a result of a road traffic accident. Pain developed approximately two days after the accident, was treated with Nurofen and had resolved within a week of the accident. G suffered one episode of back pain three months after the accident, but the pain was shortlived and did not recur. G was upset and tearful at the time of the accident, but did not suffer any long term psychological effects. There was no effect on G's social activities. *General Damages* (agreed and approved): £500.

G (A CHILD) v. MAKOWSKI, June 15, 2004, District Judge Eynon, CC (Hertford). [*Ex rel.* Gurion Taussig, Barrister, 199 Strand, London].

Back and spine: making a previously asymptomatic condition symptomatic

3154.   P, male aged 34 at the date of the accident and 37 at trial, sustained multidirectional cervical soft tissue injury, low back injury and a three month ankle injury after being knocked from his bicycle and over the bonnet of a car. P felt immediate pain in his back which intensified. P attended his GP and was prescribed painkillers. P was also referred and underwent a course of physiotherapy and ultrasound and carried out recommended exercises with limited success. Almost four years after the accident, the back movement was still restricted to two thirds the normal range and P experienced pain every two weeks, which lasted between five and six days. During that period, P would take painkillers and he would be woken with the pain at night. Standing, lifting and bending brought on the symptoms. P continued to experience less intrusive but similar symptoms in the neck: crepitus and some pain lasting for three days, occurring every two weeks or so. The agreed medical evidence was that the symptoms in the back, but not the neck, were an acceleration of a symptomless degeneration in the lumbar spine at L4. The period of acceleration was estimated to be 11 years. P continued to run his own retail hydroponics gardening shop. Although he was able to manage at work, he found lifting and carrying deliveries difficult and often asked others for help. Although able to carry out gardening and DIY, except when in pain, driving without a break was limited to a distance of about 50 miles. A father of two, P found playing with his children and tasks such as strapping the baby into the car very difficult. The judge considered that although P's business was reasonably secure, he ought to be entitled to a small award to take account of the fact that there was a risk of his having to look for other work in the context of a previous lengthy period of unemployment and that his injuries would make it more difficult for him to find work. *General Damages*: £12,000. Smith v. Manchester award: £1,500.

PRICE v. THOMSON, June 7, 2004, Recorder Tim Lamb Q.C., CC (Southampton). [*Ex rel.* James Counsell, Barrister, Outer Temple Chambers, Outer Temple, 222 Strand, London].

Back and spine: acceleration or exacerbation of pre-existing symptomatic condition

3155.   S, male, part time university research assistant, aged 48 at the date of the accident and 53 at the trial, sustained injuries as a result of a road traffic accident whilst a passenger on a bus. S suffered soft tissue injuries to his cervical and dorsal spine. The initial prognosis was for a full recovery within two years. However, on examination by an orthopaedic surgeon two years after the accident, S's symptoms had worsened and he had developed chronic pain syndrome. S had constant aching discomfort in his neck. He complained of a blanket of pain over the back of his neck and chest, with electric shock pain radiating into his upper limbs, down his back and into his right thigh and knee. At the time of the accident S had pre existing symptoms in his right upper limb, in the form of complex regional pain syndrome, or reflex sympathetic dystrophy. The accident led to a more widespread chronic pain syndrome than he would have had but for the accident. Damages were assessed on the basis that 60 per cent of S's ongoing symptomology had been caused as a direct result of the accident. S did not take any time off from his employment. He tried extensive physiotherapy, hydrotherapy, electrotherapy, acupuncture and a TENS machine, with little improvement in his condition. He took painkillers on a daily basis and tried numerous different medications and creams to ease his pain. Although he was able to work, he was unable to assist with household duties, gardening, DIY or with his newly born child. This apparent contradiction was explained by the fact that S exerted all his energies at work and was therefore very tired and in pain by the time he arrived home from work. S was compromised before the accident in respect of his ability to undertake heavy household tasks and gardening, although he had played badminton and gone swimming. He ceased those sporting activities after the accident. The accident and the more widespread chronic pain syndrome had led to a quantum decrease in S's function levels and had affected his family and personal life. The prognosis was that S would permanently suffer from pain, which would sometimes be severe, and there was no treatment available for that pain. However, it was recommended that he undertake a 12 month multi disciplinary rehabilitation programme, with the aim of raising his function levels. The course included cognitive behavioural therapy, physiotherapy and orthopaedic input. The judge approached the award on the basis that there was likely to be a 50 per cent improvement in his function levels as a result of the course. S suffered from pre existing anxiety and stress as a result of unconnected life and family events, as well as travel anxiety as a result of the accident, for which a short course of cognitive behavioural therapy was recommended. S was psychologically vulnerable prior to the accident. S's inability to carry out domestic tasks was caused partly by his pre existing stress and anxiety, although it was not possible to be more precise in medical terms. The judge took the view that 40 per cent of the ongoing psychological symptoms were related directly to the accident. At the date of the hearing S was working in a school as a laboratory assistant on a permanent contract. He did not have to undertake any strenuous physical activity. It was accepted that he was handicapped on the open labour market prior to the accident, given his regional right upper limb pain syndrome. That was in relation to manual work, although it was accepted that that was not his likely field of employment given his qualifications. The judge's view was that S should be awarded a sum in damages reflecting the additional disadvantage caused by the accident and, in particular, the additional period of search for work which he would face lose his current employment. *General Damages*: £7,000. Smith v. Manchester award: £3,500.

SAFAR v. BERGIN & WOLSTENHOLME (T/A BELLSURE MOTOR CO), July 12, 2004, Judge Warnock, CC (Manchester). [*Ex rel.* James Hurd, Barrister, St. James' Chambers, 68 Quay Street, Manchester].

Back and spine: acceleration or exacerbation of pre-existing symptomatic condition

3156. M, male aged 65 at the date of the road traffic accident and 69 at trial, sustained injuries to his back. He had a long history of lower back pain and left sided sciatica and had had two operations on his lumbar spine in the 1970s, but he had worked until he was 60 and enjoyed a number of leisure pursuits. M's evidence was that whilst he had had a bad back for 30 years, he knew how to look after it. His level of pain increased substantially following the accident with pain radiating down his leg. He was unable to sit or stand in the same position for long and would have to take breaks every hour when driving. He was prescribed painkillers by his GP, not having been on painkillers before the accident. He was unable to carry on with DIY or gardening or other hobbies as he had before the accident. Osteopathic treatment was recommended, but in fact exacerbated his symptoms for a while. Acupuncture and Chinese herbal treatment did not improve his condition either. The medical evidence was that M would have had some back pain and sciatica even without the accident, but the accident had caused an acceleration in the severity of his symptoms for a period of between three and four years. *General Damages*: £6,000.

MASSARELLA v. PHEE, August 6, 2004, Recorder Pelling Q.C., CC (Maidstone). [*Ex rel.* Tim Petts, Barrister, 12 King's Bench Walk, London].

Back and spine: acceleration or exacerbation of pre-existing symptomatic condition

3157. T, male, a warehouse manager, aged 63 at the date of the accident and 67 at the hearing, suffered injuries as a result of an accident at work, when a six foot tyre fell on him. T sustained a lower back strain, causing significant pain and stiffness. He was absent from work for about three weeks and then returned on light duties.

Shortly afterwards T retired from work. During the first three weeks after the accident he was in considerable pain and unable to do normal household tasks. His sleep was disturbed by pain for about a month after the accident and his hobbies of gardening and fishing were affected for some months. He took painkillers and had three sessions of physiotherapy. His back remained very stiff. T had previously experienced some lower back trouble due to pre existing degenerative changes. The expert medical prognosis was that he would make a complete recovery from the effects of the accident after two years, and that any back problems after that period would be attributable to natural degenerative changes, rather than the accident. At trial, four years after the accident, T still suffered from a very stiff back. *General Damages*: £4,000.

TYE v. KIRKBY (TYRES) LTD, May 25, 2004, District Judge Cardinal, CC (Birmingham). [*Ex rel.* Adam Farrer, Barrister, 5 Fountain Court, Steelhouse Lane, Birmingham].

Back and spine: acceleration or exacerbation of pre-existing symptomatic condition

3158.   J, male, aged 65 at the date of the accident, suffered injuries as a result of a road traffic accident. J had a medical history of chronic lower back pain and pain in his legs. Prior to the accident he had been complaining of moderate central lower back pain but he had not been troubled with any pain in his legs for several months. Due to the accident J complained of an aggravation of his moderate lower back pain to a severe level of discomfort, with pain radiating into the left thigh, left knee and left calf. He was prescribed painkilling medication by his GP. J had fully recovered from his injuries by eight months after the accident. J embarked upon a pre booked holiday to Spain two weeks after the accident and his enjoyment of this holiday was very hampered and limited. He could not walk any significant distance and he could not drink alcohol with the painkillers that he had been prescribed. *General Damages*: £1,750. Award for loss of enjoyment of holiday: £750.

JAMES v. HUNTER, March 23, 2005, Deputy District Judge Munro, CC (Birkenhead). [*Ex rel.* Michael W Halsall, Solicitors, 2 The Parks, Newton le Willows].

Back and spine: acceleration or exacerbation of pre-existing symptomatic condition—Knee

3159.   C, female, aged 38 at the date of the road traffic accident and 41 at trial, sustained soft tissue injury to both knees and a whiplash injury to her neck and lower back together with bruising to her shoulder, chest and hand. C was absent from work for two weeks before returning to her office job. The symptoms in the neck, shoulder, chest and hand all settled within three to four weeks. C had a history of low back pain that had caused her to undergo a spinal fusion at L5/S1 five years prior to the accident. Her back had been pain free but with residual stiffness following the fusion and up to the accident. The injury to the lower back caused by the accident continued to cause minor intermittent symptoms. The prognosis was that those symptoms would continue indefinitely on a minimal/nuisance basis, but that no active treatment would be needed. The major symptoms were in C's knees, particularly the right knee. C felt pain if she tried to kneel or squat. The symptoms in her knees did not interfere with C's work, but did cause her to hire a cleaner for two hours a week. A diagnosis of post traumatic chondromalacia was made at 22 months after the accident, but no active treatment was suggested. On examination 29 months after the accident, a knee specialist suggested that the knee symptoms, described as mild post traumatic anterior knee pain, were amenable to appropriate physiotherapy known as McConnell physiotherapy. C immediately commenced physiotherapy, five months before the trial, but symptoms were still ongoing at trial. The court found that physiotherapy was likely to resolve the symptoms in the knees. The judge found that if he had been assessing the aggravation to the lower back and other symptoms apart from the knees then he would have awarded £4,000 general damages based on the initial symptoms then on a nuisance level from about 18 to 24 months after the accident. With regard to the knee injury, the judge placed it in bracket 6(M)(b)(ii) of the JSB Guidelines, moderate knee injuries, holding that C's knee symptoms were still ongoing requiring continuing treatment but likely to resolve within three years six months of the accident with physiotherapy. *General Damages*: £8,000 (apportioned as to £4,000 for the aggravation to the lower back and other symptoms, apart from the knees, and £4,500 in respect of the injury to the knees, and applying a discount).

CORNISH v. CUNNINGHAM, April 21, 2004, Judge Sleaman, CC (Guildford). [*Ex rel.* David McHugh, Barrister, 8, Bell Yard Chambers, DX: 416 London/ Chancery Lane].

Back and neck: whiplash injury: no previous condition

3160.   M, female, a local authority plans process officer, aged 29 at the date of the road traffic accident and 32 at trial, sustained a whiplash injury to her neck and a strain to the lumbar region of her back when her stationary vehicle was hit from the rear by another vehicle. Her neck was painful and stiff for a few days after the accident, but after a week these symptoms resolved. M's GP recorded that a few days after the accident, the low back pain had been getting worse. Although M did not take time off work, when examined five months after the accident she was experiencing varying degrees of pain in her lower back and was taking painkillers. The consultant orthopaedic surgeon noticed a "marked restriction" in M's spinal movements. There was no significant improvement despite M having attended sessions of physiotherapy. Her back symptoms had been aggravated by sitting and pouring over site plans at work as well as daily household jobs, particularly vacuuming, ironing and shopping. M was unable to walk her large dog unless accompanied, in case the dog needed sudden restraint. Before the accident M had swum three times a week and attended a gym, but she had had to give up these activities. M underwent osteopathic treatment. On examination 18 months after the accident, M's spine remained tender, and although her lumbar spine movements had improved, she remained restricted by about 30 per cent. She reported a moderate improvement in the pain and stiffness but was still suffering on a daily basis and was restricted in a range of normal everyday activities at work and home. The medical expert described the pain and aching as "mild to moderately intrusive" and opined that no further improvement was likely on the balance of probabilities. By that time, M had returned to swimming. At trial, 34 months after the accident, M gave evidence that she suffered symptoms particularly when standing for long periods and took painkillers perhaps once or twice a month. The medical evidence was that the lumbar strain had caused previous asymptomactic degenerative changes in M's back to become symptomatic and thereby accelerated the onset of symptoms of lumbar spondylosis by between 10 to 15 years. The judge considered that the back injury fell within the "moderate" bracket within the JSB Guidelines (6th Edition) Chapter 6 bracket (B)(b)(ii), but noted that the cases at the higher end of that range involved far more pain and discomfort to a claimant than was present in the instant case, even though the period of acceleration might not have been as long, *Garrett v. British Airways Plc* (Unreported, March 12, 1997), [2001] C.L.Y. 16421997] C.L.Y. 1927, *O'Brien v. Royal Society for Mentally Handicapped Children and Adults* [2001] C.L.Y. 16422001] 1 Q.R. 9 and *Ward v. Batten & Stamford Asphalt Co Ltd* (Unreported, June 13, 1997), [1997] C.L.Y. 1935 considered. *General Damages*: £9,000.

MARCHANT v. FIBERNET GROUP PLC, August 25, 2004, District Judge Fuller, CC (Basingstoke). [*Ex rel.* Marcus Pilgerstorfer, Barrister, Old Square Chambers, 1 Verulam Buildings, Gray's Inn, London].

Back and neck: whiplash injury: no previous condition

3161. S, female, aged 30 at the date of the accident and 33 at trial, suffered injuries as a result of a road traffic accident when her vehicle was struck from the rear. She had sustained a whiplash injury in a road traffic accident four years earlier and it was impossible to say whether or not she had made a complete recovery from that injury by the date of the relevant accident. S required seven weeks off work. She attended hospital on the day of the accident and visited her GP on a number of subsequent occasions. She suffered a low back strain and a whiplash injury to her neck. Physiotherapy treatment began five months after the accident and, following treatment, there was a substantial improvement in her symptoms. However, S was continuing to have low grade symptoms, arising mainly from her back, at the date of the medical examination about 18 months after the accident. She continued to suffer from similar symptoms in her back at the date of the hearing. S had made a virtually full recovery from her neck injury within 18 months of the accident, although she still suffered from some minor residual symptoms, of nuisance value only, at the date of the hearing. The judge came to the conclusion that the instant case fell between the moderate and minor brackets for back injuries. S's witness statement set out a number of circumstances in which S noticed discomfort and, on balance, S's back injury was more than nuisance value only. *General Damages*: £6, 250.

SMITH v. JENKINS, March 9, 2004, District Judge Chapman, CC (Salford). [*Ex rel.* Jonathan Thompson, Barrister, King Street Chambers, 8, King Street, Manchester].

Back and neck: whiplash injury: no previous condition

3162. H, female, a nursery nurse, aged 21 at the date of the accident and 24 at trial, sustained injuries when a go kart in which she was travelling at a theme park failed to respond when she applied the brakes. This resulted in a low speed collision. H had not been provided with a helmet and her go kart was not fitted with a seatbelt. H immediately experienced pain in her knees and shins, which sustained a direct blow. She went home that evening and over the course of the following week H developed pain in her neck and back. The week after the accident H consulted her GP, who diagnosed soft tissue injuries to the legs, neck and back. She was advised to take painkillers. H's legs were sore for two weeks and she was absent from work for around four weeks. She began a 12 month course of physiotherapy on her neck and back eight months after the accident, attending intermittently when she could afford it. At the date of the medical examination three years and three months after the accident, H continued to experience stiffness and tightness in her neck and difficulty sleeping as a result of discomfort in her neck. The medical evidence showed that approximately 18 months of the symptoms were due to the accident and any remaining symptoms thereafter were attributable to other accidents in which H had been injured between the date of the index accident and the examination. *General Damages*: £3,000.

HARTLEY v. PLEASURELAND LTD, April 15, 2005, Judge Byrne, CC (Blackpool). [*Ex rel.* Adam Walker, Barrister, Lamb Chambers, Lamb Building, Elm court, Temple, London].

Back and neck: whiplash injury: no previous condition

3163. B, female, a senior special needs assistant, aged 43 at the date of the road traffic accident and 44 at trial, sustained soft tissue injuries to the cervical and lumbar spine. B immediately felt shaken, shocked and tearful and was worried for the safety of her children in the car with her. She attended her GP the day after the accident, complaining of soreness in her neck. Examination revealed tenderness of the neck and the lower lumbar spine and restriction of movement. She was prescribed diazepam and anti inflammatory medication. In addition she took paracetamol. On advice from her GP, B took four days off work. For three weeks after the accident B experienced constant pain from the neck and across the left shoulder. Neck movements were restricted. The pain then began to improve. On examination two months after the accident B was still experiencing a dull ache from the left side of the neck and across the left shoulder, towards the end of her working day. She also suffered pain from the central lower back on getting up in the morning and at the end of the working day. Work appeared to aggravate the symptoms. She took paracetamol when required. There was a full range of movements but with discomfort at some extremes. The symptoms were improving. B had previously attended Pilates but had not done so for two months after the accident and had felt restricted in her pastime of gardening, as she had been unable to lift anything or push the mower. Her physical symptoms had fully resolved some eight months after the accident. B also suffered from travel anxiety following the accident. Initially she did not want to travel in her car and would feel distressed when thinking about the accident. Two months after the accident she still felt anxious when driving or travelling as a passenger and would check her rear view mirror frequently. Her anxiety when travelling as a driver or passenger in a car had been expected to resolve after eight months but was still ongoing at the date of the hearing. *General Damages*: £2,750.

BULL v. THOMAS, October 15, 2004, Deputy District Judge Bard, CC (Northampton). [*Ex rel.* Cogent Solicitors, 3 Bedford Court, Croydon CR9 2ZL].

Back and neck: whiplash injury: no previous condition

3164.   S, a boy aged 11 at the date of the road traffic accident and 13 at the date of the hearing, was a rear seat passenger in a vehicle involved in a collision. He sustained a whiplash type injury. He attended hospital that day with numbness in his right arm and pain over the second and third cervical vertebrae, particularly when rotating his head to the right. Significant pain and discomfort continued in his neck and lower back. He took a week off school and was off games for three to four weeks. At three months, S still suffered from pain and a tight feeling in the neck. At six months, S was 70 per cent recovered. Residual neck and back pain resolved in line with the prognosis by nine months after the accident. S also suffered from associated headaches. The headaches, which represented an exacerbation of pre-existing migraines, started to settle after two months and resolved in four months. *General Damages*: £2,600.

S (A CHILD) v. SANMARTIN, June 22, 2004, District Judge Letts, CC (Epsom). [*Ex rel.* Gurion Taussig, Barrister, 199 Strand, London].

Back and neck: whiplash injury: no previous condition

3165.   L, a boy, aged 11 at the date of the accident and 15 at the child settlement approval hearing, suffered injuries as a result of a road traffic accident. L sustained bruising to his back, and there was a possibility that that injury caused a muscular strain in his neck and along the whole thoraco lumbar paraspinal muscles. Pain developed during the days following the accident and L was examined by his GP. L's sleep was disturbed for a few days and he also suffered from associated headaches. The acute phase of pain, bruising and headaches lasted for two to three weeks. After that date L's back remained relatively stiff for a boy of his age. Although some of the symptoms were a result of physical tightness of the muscles, they were also attributed to a fear of movement linked to the accident. Five months after the accident headaches had become occasional, while L's back ached following strenuous activity or a hard day of work at school. All symptoms had resolved within eight to 11 months after the accident. L was absent from school for two days as a result of the accident. He did not participate in PE lessons for two to three weeks, and for a few months thereafter only participated in each lesson for 15 to 20 minutes. He did not play badminton or participate in athletics for at least five months after the accident. He could not help with shopping and household chores for three weeks after the accident. *General Damages* (agreed and approved): £2,250.

L (A CHILD) v. STEWART, June 15, 2004, District Judge Eynon, CC (Hertford). [*Ex rel.* Gurion Taussig, Barrister, 199 Strand, London].

Back and neck: whiplash injury: no previous condition

3166.   X, male, aged 23 at the date of the accident and 24 at the date of the hearing, sustained personal injury when his stationary vehicle was shunted unexpectedly from behind by another vehicle. He was jolted significantly on impact. He suffered a whiplash type injury to his cervical and lumbar spine. His acute symptoms in his cervical spine lasted four to five weeks and thereafter became intermittent. He had constant background pain in his lumbar spine which was aggravated by lifting and bending activities. His symptoms were worse in cold weather. When his pain was at its worst his leisure and social activities were affected to the extent that he avoided playing football, going to the cinema and bowling. There was no evidence of any absence from work as a result of the injuries. On examination two and a half months after the accident there was a full range of movement, although there was continuing pain in the lower cervical and lumbar areas. A full recovery was expected for the neck within nine to 12 months of the accident and for the lower back within 10 to 12 months of the accident. *General Damages*: £2,000.

ALI v. USMAN, December 18, 2003, District Judge Stevens, CC (Manchester). [*Ex rel.* Claire Hill, Pupil Barrister, St Jame's Chambers, 68 Quay Street, Manchester].

Back and neck: whiplash injury: no previous condition

3167.   C1 and C2, girls aged 10 and 7 at the date of the accident and 11 and 8 respectively at trial, were injured when the car in which they were travelling was shunted sideways, before coming to a sudden stop, in a collision with another vehicle. C1 had been a rear passenger and C2 had been a front seat passenger. An ambulance was called, and both girls were assessed by a paramedic but not taken to hospital. C1 was jolted, dazed and shaken, and almost immediately felt pain in her neck and lower back. The day after the accident she attended her GP. She took three days off school, but pain was constant for 10 days, at which point she attended her GP again. The neck pain then became intermittent but the back pain remained for a further two weeks before becoming intermittent. When examined five months after the accident C1 said that she felt 50 per cent better, although her movements were restricted by 20 per cent. C1's sports activities at school were affected for five months, and she was unable to cycle for approximately six months. She was also very anxious when travelling by car. C2 had been upset and had started to cry immediately after the accident. She had pain and stiffness in her neck and lower back and had shaken all over. She took three days off school, after which the pain became intermittent. C2 attended her GP three weeks after the accident complaining of tenderness. When examined five months after the accident she felt 50 per cent better and her movements were not restricted. C2 also suffered from disturbed sleep and had nightmares most nights for the first month after the accident, during which time she slept with her mother. Five months after the accident she was still having occasional nightmares about the accident, had lost confidence at school and when riding her bicycle. At that stage, she had not participated in school sports activities since the accident but resumed them shortly thereafter. The prognosis was that C1 and C2 would make a full recovery from all symptoms within 12 months of the accident, and at the hearing it was confirmed that they had in fact recovered 10 months after the accident. *General Damages* (agreed and approved): C1 £1,900. C2 £1,900.

C (CHILDREN) v. ZANAGA, June 28, 2004, Deputy District Judge Hayward, Mayor's and City of London. [*Ex rel.* Joanna Kerr, Barrister, Lamb Chambers, Lamb Building, Temple, London].

Back and neck: whiplash injury: no previous condition

3168. H, male, a schoolboy aged seven at the date of the road traffic accident and 12 at the child settlement approval hearing, was involved in a rear end shunt. Immediately after the accident, H started to develop pain in his neck and lower back. He was shocked and screaming hysterically. H was taken to hospital where a diagnosis of a whiplash injury was made. H suffered from a nagging ache and stiffness in his neck which was aggravated by movement for one week after the accident. H's neck pain then settled. Similarly, H had a dull ache in his lower back for one week after the accident which then settled. H also suffered nightmares about once a week after the accident. He suffered from flashbacks for six weeks and was generally more clingy towards his mother and was dependent on her for the same period of time. H also experienced travel anxiety as a passenger. He was anxious at road junctions and zebra crossings, the latter being where the accident had occurred. The prognosis was for H's psychological travel anxiety symptoms to settle within six to nine months of the accident. H confirmed at the hearing that his symptoms had settled in accordance with the prognosis. H was absent from school for one week on account of his injuries. *General Damages* (agreed and approved): £1,750.

H (A CHILD) v. WEST MIDLANDS AMBULANCE NHS TRUST, September 22, 2004, Deputy District Judge Maughan, CC (Birmingham). [*Ex rel.* Stephen Garner, Barrister, 8 Fountain Court, Birmingham].

Back and neck: whiplash injury: no previous condition

3169. K, a girl, aged 10 at the date of the accident and 13 at the date of the child settlement approval hearing, suffered injuries as a result of a road traffic accident. Within two hours of the accident K was suffering from discomfort in her neck and attended the medical room at her school. The following day symptoms were still present. C did not attend school and she was examined at the local hospital where she was diagnosed as having sustained a whiplash injury. K was advised to take analgesics. She also attended her GP who noted discomfort in K's neck and back. K's discomfort was most significant for the first few weeks after the accident, during which time she was unable to participate in games or sports. Her sleep pattern was also affected. On examination four months after the accident K was still experiencing neck and back discomfort, particularly when involved in games or sports. Her sleep was still disturbed from time to time. However, she continued to swim regularly, and examination revealed that her movements were not restricted. The prognosis was that she would recover within five months of the accident. At the hearing K confirmed that she had recovered in accordance with the prognosis. *General Damages* (agreed and approved): £1,600.

K (A CHILD) v. NUGENT, February 10, 2005, District judge Cohen, CC (Edmonton). [*Ex rel.* Joanna Kerr, Barrister, Lamb Chambers, Lamb Building, Temple, London].

Back and neck: whiplash injury: no previous condition

3170. N1 and N2, girls, aged respectively 12 and 8 at the date of the accident and 13 and 9 at trial, sustained personal injury when they were rear seat passengers involved in a road traffic accident. N1 sustained a whiplash injury to her cervical and lumbar spin together with pain, headaches, and a restriction of movement. She was prescribed analgesic medication. The symptoms resolved after about eight weeks. She also suffered a soft tissue injury to both hips and precordium. These symptoms resolved in 10 weeks. N1 missed one day of school and became more anxious, aware and apprehensive when in circumstances similar to that of the accident. Her symptoms of minor anxiety resolved within 12 months after the accident. N2 sustained soft tissue injuries to her left cheek, back of her skull, left knee and left leg, together with pain, discomfort and restriction of general dynamic movement. She was also prescribed analgesic medication. Her symptoms resolved in two weeks. N2 also suffered some superficial grazes to the left side of her skull which resolved after three weeks. *General Damages*: N1 £1,250. N2 £650.

N (A CHILD) v. CHARTERIS, May 28, 2004, District Judge Hickman, CC (Milton Keynes). [*Ex rel.* Gurion Taussig, Barrister, 199 The Strand, London].

Back and neck: whiplash injury: no previous condition

3171.   S, female, aged 43 at the date of the road traffic accident and 44 at trial, sustained injuries when P's car was driven into the rear of her car as she remained stationary in a queue of traffic. S's vehicle was shunted into the van in front as a result of the collision. S sustained a minor whiplash injury to the neck and a musculo ligamentous injury to the lower back. She immediately felt pain to her neck, radiating to both shoulders, and in her lower back. She attended hospital where a whiplash injury to the cervical spine was diagnosed and low back pain was noted. S attended hospital again three days later when a diagnosis of soft tissue injury was made again. S was provided with anti inflammatory medication. Thereafter, she received treatment and advice from her GP. S took no time off her work as a hairdresser, but was unable to perform domestic chores or engage in any activity involving bending for one week after the accident. During that period she required help from family and friends with the cleaning and shopping. As a result of the accident S had difficulty with personal care, especially washing her hair and taking a bath. S was a keen swimmer and enjoyed long country walks, and for one month after the accident she was unable to do either. S's symptoms resolved completely one month after the accident. *General Damages*: £1,200.

SIMPSON v. PRESCOTT THOMAS LTD, February 25, 2005, Judge Levey, CC (Barnet). [*Ex rel.* Joanna Kerr, Barrister, Lamb Chambers, Lamb Building, Temple, London].

Back and neck: whiplash injury: no previous condition–Post-traumatic stress disorder

3172.   C, female, a student, aged 18 at the date of the accident and 20 at trial, suffered a whiplash injury and psychological trauma following a side impact road traffic accident. Immediately after the accident C became aware of a tingling sensation affecting the whole of her right dominant arm from the root of the neck right down to the fingers of the right hand. C attended hospital and was diagnosed as having suffered a soft tissue whiplash type injury to the neck with referred pain down the right arm into the fingers. She was prescribed Ibuprofen for pain relief. Over the next few days, C developed a persistent tingling in the right arm, along with neck pain and low back pain. C was absent from her studies at college on account of her injuries for a period of two weeks. On examination seven months after the accident, C was still troubled by pain in the right arm with associated tingling into the arm and fingers. Her neck and low back were also stiff. C underwent physiotherapy and experienced a gradual tapering off of her ongoing symptoms. She had fully recovered from all physical symptoms within 23 months of the accident. C also experienced psychological trauma after the accident. She was immediately shocked and shaken and started to cry at the scene. She began to suffer repeated nightmares, following which she woke up in a cold sweat feeling very frightened. C also suffered from flashbacks to the accident, intrusive thoughts which frightened her and hyper arousal. She became edgy and irritable with her family and friends. C was diagnosed as having suffered post traumatic stress disorder with a prognosis for full recovery within 12 months of the accident. Thereafter C continued to suffer symptoms of persistent travel anxiety both as a driver and as a passenger. She did not drive for three months after the accident because of her fear and was increasingly wary when she finally recommenced driving at her pre accident level. The travel anxiety resolved within two years of the accident. The general damages were apportioned as to £4,000 for the whiplash injury and as to £3,000 for the psychological injury, then reduced to take account of overlap. *General Damages*: £5,750.

COWEN v.WHITEHEAD, April 29, 2005, District Judge Bennett, CC (St Helens). [*Ex rel.* Stephen Garner, Barrister, No 8 Chambers, Fountain Court, Steelhouse Lane, Birmingham].

Back and neck: whiplash injury: no previous condition—Hearing and speech: tinnitus

3173.   M, female, a solicitor, aged 34 at the date of the road traffic accident and 38 at trial, sustained whiplash type injuries to her neck and back, and developed tinnitus within a few days of the accident. At the time of the accident she had just become pregnant. She had suffered temporary back pain with her two previous pregnancies, but it was more severe on this occasion. Her lower back pain was especially bad when driving long distances or sitting for long periods of time. Both of those activities also exacerbated her neck and shoulder pain and caused pins and needles in her arms and hands. M temporarily stopped yoga and swimming. The neck pain was likely to be permanent. The back pain was expected to resolve, although at the date of trial it had not. The orthopaedic injuries were described as an inconvenience rather than a handicap. M attended her GP and an osteopath but she preferred not to take painkillers. The pain would resolve if she got up and moved about. She required increased assistance from her partner in heavier household and gardening tasks on an ongoing basis. The tinnitus was not too bad when M was in a noisy environment, but very noticeable when it was quiet. The medical expert categorised it as between mild and moderate. There was no attributable hearing loss. The symptoms were increasingly annoying when she was working. Although they did not prevent her from sleeping, if she awoke they could prevent her from returning to sleep. The tinnitus was not expected to improve, and if anything its effects were slightly worse as M found herself working more in a quiet environment. *General Damages*: £15,500 (apportioned as to £8,000 for the orthopaedic injuries and £7,500 for the tinnitus).

MARS v. HALL, June 17, 2004, Recorder Griffith-Jones Q.C., CC (Tunbridge Wells). [*Ex rel.* Andrew Roy, Barrister, 12 Kings Bench Walk, Temple, London].

Back and neck: whiplash injury: no previous condition—Shoulder

3174.   S, male, aged 19 at the date of the accident and 25 at trial, suffered injuries to his neck, back and shoulder, as a result of a road traffic accident. On the day of the accident he was examined at hospital where he was prescribed Ibuprofen. He was absent from work for eight weeks. His GP recommended physiotherapy. S had three separate courses of physiotherapy during the following two and a half years. After an initial acute period S experienced intermittent pain relating to his spinal injuries, especially in the morning or while reading. The neck and back injuries gradually settled. However, S continued to have problems from tendonitis in the shoulder. The shoulder pain was provoked by sudden movement or overhead work and S was unable to lie on his right side. The shoulder pain resolved after a cortisone injection. The judge awarded damages on the basis that symptoms had continued, on a reducing basis, for about two and a half years, and that the level of damages therefore fell at the top end of the JSB Guidelines (7th Edition) category 6 (A) (c) (i). *General Damages*: £4,250.

SENIARAY v. ROSE, October 18, 2004, District Judge Davies, CC (Birmingham). [*Ex rel.* Andrew Granville Stafford, Barrister, 4, King's Bench Walk, Temple, London].

Back and neck: whiplash injury: no previous condition—Knee

3175.   B, female, a pharmacist, aged 36 at the date of the road traffic accident and 40 at trial, suffered various injuries. Immediately after the accident B developed left sided neck pain and lower back pain. She also developed pain and stiffness in the right knee. The day after the accident B's GP diagnosed a whiplash injury to the neck and back and a soft tissue injury to the right knee. B was off work for two weeks on account of her injuries. She was prescribed a course of non steroidal anti inflammatory tablets. When examined eight months after the accident, B was still experiencing a constant dull ache in her lower back, associated with intermittent stiffness, and pain in the neck. She was also still troubled by a painful right knee, which tended to give way and click. The injuries prevented B from playing squash. On examination 27 months after the accident B was still troubled by left sided neck pain and pain in the lower back area, although she considered the symptoms to have improved by 60 per cent. B's right knee injury had resolved. At trial, some three years and 10 months after the accident, B stated that she was still suffering intermittent neck and lower back symptoms after sitting in a car for a long time, after standing for prolonged periods or if she turned her head quickly. Those episodes occurred once every two weeks and the pain was short lived and relieved by pain killing medication. The judge assessed general damages on the basis that B's remaining intermittent neck and low back symptoms would settle within four years and three months to four years and six months of the accident. *General Damages*: £6,000.

BARNES v. TAYLOR, October 14, 2004, District Judge Jenkins, CC (Birmingham). [*Ex rel.* Stephen Garner, Barrister, No 8 Chambers, Fountain Court, Steelhouse Lane, Birmingham].

Back and neck: whiplash injury: making a previously asymptomatic condition symptomatic

3176.   C, male, aged 52 at the date of the accident and 57 at the hearing, sustained personal injuries in a road traffic accident. C was practically stationary at traffic lights as a driver of a small car on the exit slip of a motorway when he was struck from behind by a van. C was wearing a seat belt and the car was fitted with head restraints. The impact from behind was of sufficient force to drive C's car into and partially under a lorry in front. Except for the sound of skidding from behind, there was no real warning of the impending collision. The impact caused C to be thrown forwards and then backwards and on backward movement the driver's seat broke and he came to rest in a horizontal position. C experienced shock but was able to return home. On getting home, he experienced pain in his right leg and a headache and went straight to bed. The following morning he had a very stiff neck and back together with pains in his chest and abdomen. C attended accident and emergency and was prescribed with a support collar and analgesia. C's neck pain was severe (six to seven on scale) for two to three weeks subsiding thereafter to minor discomfort at the time of the medical examination, two years seven months after the accident. C had particularly severe pain in his lower back (eight to nine on scale) and continued at that level for about a year with occasional spasms. C was conscious of back pain (four to five on scale) at the date of the medical examination. C experienced some loss of sleep but limited psychological disturbance. C was a nervous passenger and more wary of other road users. C subsequently attended his GP who prescribed more painkillers and he undertook a course of physiotherapy for approximately five months which resulted in some temporary alleviation of his symptoms. He later underwent chiropractic treatment which was more effective than the physiotherapy in alleviating symptoms. C, who was a self employed recruitment manager, lived in a listed farm house with smallholding including commercial stabling. His injury had a particular impact on renovation work to the farm house and with heavier work in the garden and smallholding. C's immediate symptoms attributable to neck strain settled and were substantially improved by physiotherapy. The injury was expected to settle 18 months to two years after the medical examination. There was possible acceleration of non symptomatic pre existing degenerative disease in the neck by a period of five years. There was significant acceleration of a pre existing asymptomatic degenerative change in C's back with C having reached the limit of conservative treatment at the date of the medical examination. With future pain management therapies drugs and or injections there was a 50 to 75 per cent chance of improving symptoms to the extent of leaving only minor discomfort in the back. Thus there was a finding of acceleration by five to seven years of a pre existing asymptomatic degenerative disease in C's back, with no hope of resolution or cure. The best hope was for the alleviation of symptoms through pain management therapies. C was referred to a consultant in anaesthetics and pain management. Treatment consisted of a series of injections to trigger points of pain in C's lower back together with a recommendation for future treatment by injections in the back. C continued to experience muscle spasms and acute pain in the area treated which lasted for two to three days at a time and recurred fortnightly. He experienced severe discomfort and a sensation of paraesthesia in the left leg. *General Damages*: £12,500.

CAUSTON v. CHAMBERS, March 4, 2004, Recorder Seagroatt Q.C., CC (Oxford). [*Ex rel.* Jude Durr, Barrister, East Anglian Chambers, 53 North Hill, Colchester, Essex].

Back and neck: whiplash injury: acceleration or exacerbation of pre-existing symptomatic condition–Shoulder

3177.   H, female, aged 35 at the date of the road traffic accident and 38 at trial, was injured when her vehicle was involved in a rear end shunt. She suffered whiplash injuries to her neck, left shoulder and low back. She experienced intense pain in her neck immediately after the accident and pain in her shoulder and back shortly afterwards. When examined by a medical expert nine months after the accident, H was experiencing a dull ache in the neck for two to three hours a day, with radiation of the pain to the scapula, and a dull ache in the low back twice weekly for a few hours. H had pre existing back symptoms, the increase in which had been accelerated by 10 to 20 years. At trial H's symptoms had increased and she was experiencing a dull pain in the neck and back all the time, with radiation to the scapula. There was no medical explanation for the deterioration, but it was not suggested that it was not genuine. H was affected in many of her daily activities such as housework, cooking, gardening, walking the dog and other leisure activities. She had difficulty standing or sitting for long periods. The medical evidence indicated that her back symptoms could have been significantly improved if H had embarked upon a rigorous course of physiotherapy and hydrotherapy and then exercises at home, but H had been unwilling to undergo physiotherapy because she said it was too rough. It was accepted that it was unreasonable of H not to have even tried the physiotherapy, although it was unlikely that she would have completed it anyway in view of her domestic circumstances. H had had to give up her job as a home carer to two elderly disabled people but had requalified and obtained part time work as a home care assessor. She found her work as an assessor difficult because it involved a good deal of standing and she was concerned as to whether she would be able to continue in that employment until retirement. A Smith v. Manchester award was made on the basis of net annual earnings of £5,000 for part time work, taking into account the fact that H was currently looking after her daughter, but might be able to work longer hours in the future. *General Damages*: £15,000. Smith v. Manchester award: £7,500. Loss of congenial employment: £3,500.

HANCOCK v. HOLLIDAY, September 22, 2004, Recorder Blunt Q.C., CC (Southampton). [*Ex rel.* James Counsell, Barrister, Outer Temple Chambers, Outer Temple, 222 Strand, London].

Shoulder

3178.   B, female, a senior meal supervisor, aged 60 at the date of the accident and 63 at trial, slipped on some mud and fell to the ground, landing on her right elbow and right shoulder. She grazed her right elbow and injured her right shoulder. She was taken to hospital and X rayed which revealed no bony injury. She was allowed home with a sling and a supply of painkillers. She continued to have pain in her right shoulder. She was advised to do exercise and later on referred for physiotherapy.

PERSONAL INJURY

She was off work for six weeks. She had an injection into her shoulder which did not alleviate her symptoms. Approximately a year and a half after the accident she underwent a right shoulder arthroscopy and subacromial decompression. The diagnosis following this procedure was of an impingement of the superior cuff. She was off work for a further eight weeks after this procedure. On returning to work, she managed reasonably well although she did sometimes feel the shoulder if she jarred it while in a crowded area in the dining room. Some three years after the accident, she continued to experience problems with her right shoulder particularly with activities. The shoulder would ache in bed at night and pain could disturb her sleep. She could not lie on her right side. She found it difficult to get dressed, particularly reaching up behind her back. She managed most activities and was managing to carry on with her work. She had difficulties with housework. Examination three years after the accident revealed tenderness around the subacromial bursa and particularly the acromio clavicular joint. There was slight limitation in movement in the right shoulder with a painful arc of movement from 80 degrees to the end of the range. There was pain on stressing the acromio clavicular joint. Medical expert opinion accepted by the judge was that continuing problems related to the acromio clavicular joint and possibly the rotator cuff tendon. There were degenerative changes in the rotator cuff and the acromio clavicular joint which undoubtedly had pre existed the accident. The accident had exacerbated this pre-existing condition by between 5 and 10 years. She would have experienced her symptoms at any rate even if it had not been for the accident as a result of the natural progression of the underlying condition. There was some possibility that she might benefit from further surgical treatment in the form of excision of her acromio clavicular joint but even following this type of surgery she was likely to experience permanent weakness and discomfort of the right shoulder particularly with strenuous activities. She would be able to participate in the majority of her social activities in the future but may find that she was restricted in particularly strenuous activities. *General Damages*: £10,000.

BROOKS v. CAMDEN LBC, February 12, 2004, District Judge Aarmon-Jones, CC (Clerkenwell). [*Ex rel.* Colin Mendoza, Barrister, Devereux Chambers, Devereux Court, London].

Shoulder

3179.   S, male, aged 72 at the date of the accident and 76 at trial, suffered injuries as a result of a road traffic accident. He sustained bruising to his right hand, which took six to eight weeks to fully disappear. He also suffered injury to his lower back, which exacerbated a pre existing back problem for a period of 12 months, causing him significant pain and difficulty walking. In addition, he sustained a rotator cuff tear to his dominant right shoulder. The medical evidence was that the tear would have developed in any event approximately five years after the accident. S was unable to lift his right arm above shoulder height, which caused him difficulty with many day to day tasks, and he suffered from daily pain and discomfort as a result of the shoulder injury. S was subject to depression and low moods for a period of 12 months after the accident, and experienced travel anxiety, which was expected to persist for about 31 months. He was anxious when driving and tended to avoid driving when he could. Consequently he did not go out as much as he had done prior to the accident. He did not receive any specific treatment. S had not enjoyed the best of health before the accident because of angina and he had a successful triple by-pass operation four months after the accident. The judge found that the case fell into the lower end of the "serious shoulder injury" bracket of the JSB Guidelines. *General Damages*: £7,250.

SMITH v. THOMPSON, April 20, 2004, District Judge Owen, CC (Birmingham). [*Ex rel.* Adam Farrer, Barrister, 5, Fountain Court, Birmingham].

Shoulder

3180.   M, male, a labourer, aged 28 at the date of the accident and 30 at the date of the hearing, sustained an injury to his shoulder. M was unblocking a concrete-crushing machine with a steel pole whilst the impeller blades were still in motion when a dislodged piece of concrete struck the base of the steel pole and was knocked back forcibly into M's shoulder. M suffered a soft tissue injury and was found to have a traumatic capsulitis of the left shoulder. He suffered considerable bruising for some weeks and required physiotherapy treatment. He was unable to return to work for a period of eight weeks after the accident. Thereafter he suffered symptoms of discomfort for a period of about 16 months after activity and during damp weather. There was no lasting disability. *General Damages*: £2,250.
    MILES v. TINGLEY (T/A TINGLEY SKIPS), July 19, 2004, District Judge Robinson, CC (Eastbourne). [*Ex rel.* Nikolas Clarke, Barrister, Lamb Building, Temple, London].

Shoulder

3181.   G, male, a mini cab driver, aged 43 at the date of the accident and 45 at trial, suffered injuries in a road traffic accident. During the evening after the accident G developed pain in his right shoulder, right knee and right thigh. The day after the accident he was examined by his GP who prescribed painkillers. G was absent from work for six days after the accident and worked half days throughout the following week. Two weeks after the accident G's symptoms had reduced such that he was able to return to his usual working capacity, and by 15-20 days after the accident his pains had improved without further treatment. On examination some six months after the accident G's leg pains had resolved completely, but he had a "trigger point" of tenderness in his right trapezius muscle and some pain on movement. At that stage he was also experiencing shoulder pain, after a long day at work, two or three times a week. Osteopathy and massage treatment were recommended, and the prognosis was that, with that treatment G would probably recover within nine months of the accident, and without it probably within 13 months. G gave evidence, at trial, that he had asked his GP for further treatment following that recommendation, but that he had not received a referral for the recommended treatment. The judge found that G had not failed to mitigate his loss, since he had visited his GP in response to the recommendation, but his GP had decided not to give him any further treatment. G was entitled to compensation for the full extent of his injuries up to 13 months after the accident. The judge found that the similarities between JSB Guidelines Chapter 6(A)(c)(i)/(ii) and 6(C)(d)(i)/(ii) meant that comparable neck whiplash injury cases were helpful in determining the appropriate level of compensation for shoulder injury cases. *General Damages*: £2,200.
    GENC v. EIDARUS, January 4, 2005, Deputy District Judge Brar, CC (Shoreditch). [*Ex rel.* Joanna Kerr, Barrister, Lamb Chambers, Lamb Building, Temple, London].

Shoulder–Neck: whiplash injury: no previous condition

3182.   M, male, a school pupil, aged 14 at the date of the accident and 17 at the date of the child assessment approval hearing, suffered injury when he was involved in a rear end shunt road traffic accident. M struck his right shoulder against the side of his seat on impact. He felt the immediate onset of frontal chest pain and felt dizzy and shocked. Shortly after the accident M began to develop increasing pain in the neck and right shoulder. He was diagnosed as having suffered a whiplash injury to the neck and a soft tissue contusion injury to the right shoulder. M was prescribed an anaesthetic gel and anti inflammatory medication. The pain in the neck and right shoulder was initially severe for a period of about three weeks before it began to ease. M was absent from school for one week on account of the accident. He was unable to participate in PE lessons at all for eight weeks after the accident because of ongoing neck and right shoulder pain. M experienced neck and right shoulder symptoms for approximately eight months before the symptoms generally settled. However M continued to suffer some residual pain in the right shoulder until 23 months after the accident, particularly after taking part in sporting activities such as cricket. The episodes of pain in the shoulder lasted for 10 to 20 minutes and resolved when M stopped the activity. *General Damages*: £3,250.

M (A CHILD) v. KHAN, August 12, 2004, District Judge Davies, CC (Birmingham). [*Ex rel.* Stephen Garner, Barrister, No 8 Chambers, Fountain Court, Steelhouse Lane, Birmingham].

Arm: less severe injuries

3183.   H, a boy, aged 13 at the date of the accident and 14 at the child settlement approval hearing, sustained an undisplaced fracture of the lower end of the left radius when he had slipped at school whilst playing hockey on a concrete surface. His arm had been put into a back slab on the day of the accident. However, the back slab had to be changed the following day because of discomfort, and was then exchanged for a full plaster two days later. H remained in plaster for three weeks and had largely recovered from the injury within a further two to three weeks. However he suffered some residual symptoms of stiffness and discomfort for about 12 months after the accident. Thereafter H's injury completely resolved without any risk of the onset of premature degenerative arthritis. *General Damages* (approved and agreed): £4,000.

H (A CHILD) v. REDBRIDGE LBC, July 21, 2004, District Judge Mullis, CC (Romford). [*Ex rel.* Nikolas Clarke, Barrister, The Chambers of Ami Feder, Lamb Building, Temple, London].

Arm: less severe injuries

3184.   B, a girl aged three at the date of the accident and nine at the child settlement approval hearing, was playing on swings at a playground when she slid off the seat of a swing and fell to the concrete surface beneath. As she fell, her right arm went underneath her and although she was able to get up, she could not move her right arm which became painful and swollen. X rays taken at hospital the same day, revealed an undisplaced fracture of the distal radius and a greenstick fracture of the distal right ulna. B also had a super condyle fracture of the distal right humerus bone at the elbow. A plaster of paris support was applied to the right forearm and the fractures were monitored until the plaster was finally removed four weeks after the accident. At that point, some tenderness was evident, but B required no further physiotherapy or other clinical treatment. The injury delayed B's entry into nursery school for three weeks and thereafter she missed out on some activities at nursery school for a further six weeks. All symptoms resulting from the injury resolved within three months of the accident. The judge found that the injury was a relatively straightforward greenstick fracture injury meriting an award within bracket 6(F)(d) of the seventh edition of the JSB Guidelines. *General Damages* (agreed and approved): £3,650.

B (A CHILD) v. BARKING AND DAGENHAM LBC, September 28, 2004, District Judge Crispin, CC (Romford). [*Ex rel.* Joanna Kerr, Barrister, Lamb Chambers, Lamb Building, Temple, London].

Arm: less severe injuries

3185.   P, male, a supermarket assistant, aged 22 at the date of the accident and 24 at trial, was injured in a road traffic accident, as a result of which he was thrown sideways and his right arm struck the door of his car. He began to develop pain in the right upper arm approximately one hour after the accident and was in a state of shock for one day. P's pain was aggravated by lifting but was fully settled after approximately one week. P was not absent from work as a result of his injuries, and there was no adverse effect on his ability to carry out his domestic chores.

The judge accepted that, as P's job involved lifting, P would have suffered discomfort while at work and should be given credit for taking no time off. *General Damages*: £400.

PANCHAL v. MAGUIRE, December 3, 2004, Deputy District Judge Wagner, CC (Edmonton). [*Ex rel.* Nigel Ffitch, Barrister, Phoenix Chambers, Gray's Inn Chambers, Gray's Inn, London].

Elbow

3186. M, male, a construction worker, aged 36 at the date of the accident and 38 at trial, sustained injury when he was struck by a bucket of a JCB digger. He suffered an undisplaced fracture of the left elbow and a soft tissue injury to the superficial musculature of his left shoulder blade. M was given painkillers and a soft cervical collar for support and advised to rest upon his discharge from hospital. The soft tissue injury caused M pain, generalised discomfort and restriction of movement for a two-week period after the accident before he made a full recovery. The elbow required immobilisation in an above elbow plaster cast for six weeks after the accident, during which period M suffered significant and continuous discomfort. Once the plaster cast was removed M undertook 10 sessions of physiotherapy. When M returned to work eight weeks after the accident he was limited to light duties for a number of months but the symptoms in the elbow were almost resolved during the next four weeks. When M was examined nearly 11 months after the accident normal movement had returned to the elbow and no future complications were expected. Although at the date of trial M continued to suffer minor discomfort in the elbow when it was exposed to extremes of low temperature the prognosis in the medical report was for this to resolve. *General Damages*: £4,500.

MAIR v. MATTHEWS PLANT HIRE, June 25, 2004, District Judge Thomas, CC (Truro). [*Ex rel.* Adrian Posta, Barrister, Albion Chambers, Broad Street, Bristol].

Wrist

3187. C, male, machine operator, aged 42 at the date of the accident and 46 at trial, suffered injuries as a result of an accident at work. In the process of unblocking a machine C's dominant right wrist was forcefully pronated. C attended hospital after work on the day of the accident, where it was suspected that he had suffered a hairline fracture. His wrist was put in a plaster cast. C was absent from work on account of his injury for a total of eight weeks. After the accident he was unable to drive for seven weeks, he was unable to attend to his personal hygiene or daily domestic tasks for eight weeks, and he could not mow the lawn or tend the garden for 12 weeks. The plaster cast was removed after four weeks, but C still had intermittent pain in the right wrist, especially after performing repetitive tasks. On examination, two years and seven months after the accident, the medical opinion was that C had not suffered a fracture but had suffered a soft tissue right wrist sprain. C presented on examination with a little tenderness over the tip of the ulnar styloid at the origin of the ulnar collateral ligament. C described his residual right wrist pain as like a toothache, especially in cold weather. The prognosis was that C's residual symptoms would settle over time. At trial C advised that he still had some minor right wrist pain following repeated exertion at work, and particularly in cold, damp weather conditions. The judge accepted that C's ongoing symptoms were slight, but served as an occasional reminder of the accident. *General Damages*: £3,500.

COBURN v. SONORA FOODS, February 17, 2005, District Judge Ridgeway, CC (Nuneaton). [*Ex rel.* Stephen Garner, Barrister, 8 Chambers, Fountain Court, Steelhouse Lane, Birmingham].

Wrist

3188.   J, female, aged 31 at the date of the accident and 33 at trial, suffered injuries when the vehicle she was driving was involved in a road traffic accident. She sustained a soft tissue injury to her right dominant wrist. J's wrist was jarred by the impact and was immediately painful. She experienced constant pain in her wrist for three to four months after the accident. For the first six weeks the pain was moderately to severely painful. For three to four months J found steering when driving and working on computers at work painful. She was unable to use weights in her right hand when at the gym, carry out domestic chores or cut up her food. Three to four months after the accident the pain became intermittent. She experienced momentary pain over the index finger meta carpal consistent with periosteal bruising when carrying shopping or suitcases. J's symptoms had resolved 20 months after the accident. *General Damages*: £2,000.

JEANS v. NELSON, July 20, 2004, District Judge Banks, CC (Uxbridge). [*Ex rel.* Gurion Taussig, Barrister, 199 Strand, London].

Wrist–Non-facial scarring

3189.   P, male, a project manager, aged 32 at the date of the accident and at the disposal hearing, suffered injuries when he was knocked off his bicycle. P sustained a very deep abrasion to his right elbow, which was initially accompanied by some stiffness. Those symptoms settled slowly. P was left with irregular scarring, spread over an area about 4 to 5cm long and 1cm wide. P also sustained a deep abrasion to his right buttock, which, over the course of about one month, settled leaving an irregular scar about 3cm long and 2.5cm wide. There was a reddish discolouration visible within both scars seven months after the accident. Medical opinion was that the scars were likely to be permanent. The judge found that the elbow scar was more serious as it was more likely to be visible to others. However the buttock scar was also of concern to P. P also sprained his right, non dominant, wrist in the accident. Initially he experienced pain whenever he used his wrist or hand, but when medically examined six weeks after the accident, P reported that his wrist was about 90 per cent better, although it still ached on occasions. On examination no tenderness or restriction of movement was found. Medical opinion was that P would recover from his wrist symptoms within three months of the accident. P also suffered minor cuts and bruising to his upper right thigh, left hip, left elbow, upper right arm and the right side of his back. His sleep was disturbed for two weeks after the accident and he was nervous on returning to cycling. He still experienced flashbacks to the accident and nervousness at the scene of the accident seven months after the accident. P did not attend either hospital or his GP in relation to his scarring or his wrist symptoms. He applied dressings to the scars for one week and took painkillers for his wrist and elbow symptoms. P did see a doctor about the pain in his thighs, but the judge found that that was a very minor consequence of the accident. P took three days off work and his hobby of cycling was affected for about two weeks after the accident. *General Damages*: £3,250 (apportioned as to £1,750 in respect of the elbow scar, £500 for the buttock scar and £1,000 in respect of the wrist injury).

POOLE v. SMITH, May 24, 2004, Deputy District Judge Flanagan, CC (Birkenhead). [*Ex rel.* Chris Middleton, Barrister, Oriel Chambers, 14 Water Street, Liverpool].

Finger

3190.   B, aged 46 at the date of the accident and 48 at trial, suffered crush injuries to the fingers of his left (non dominant) hand when the door of his employer's draywagon dropped onto his left hand. He was treated at hospital on the day of the accident. His hand was swollen and bruised and he was in a lot of pain. There were two lacerations over the palmer aspect of the left ring and little fingers. X rays revealed an undisplaced fracture of the proximal phalanx of the little finger. The injuries were treated with neighbour strapping, which B wore for one month, followed by physiotherapy for approximately two months. B was absent from work for eight weeks and then on light duties for a further two weeks. He then resumed his work as a drayman for approximately eight months. He was eventually made redundant for reasons unconnected with the injury and obtained work as a joiner/shopfitter for six months. Both those positions involved relatively heavy work and aggravated B's symptoms. Ultimately, because of his symptoms, he resigned from his job as a shopfitter and he was unemployed at the time of trial. On examination, 14 months after the accident, B complained of a constant ache over the proximal interphalangeal joints of his left ring and little fingers, which was worse in cold weather. He had stiffness and difficulty moving his ring and little fingers when he woke up in the morning and after a hard day's work. He had pins and needles in the middle, ring and little fingers. His power grip in his left hand was weaker and he experienced pain in the little finger when he gripped objects. That caused difficulty in his work as a joiner. As far as his hobbies of golf, archery and clay pigeon shooting were concerned, he had managed to adapt to his injuries but found his restrictions frustrating. The prognosis was for the persistent aching pain in the hand to improve by 26 months after the accident. However, B was expected to suffer symptoms brought on by the cold on a permanent basis. The little finger would always be slightly stiff in the mornings. The pins and needles were expected to resolve by about 26 months after the accident. B's power grip in his left hand was expected to remain weaker on a permanent basis. That was expected to cause him difficulty with using certain narrow tools at work, and with lifting heavy objects. Otherwise he had adapted to his injuries extremely well. At trial, some 26 months after the accident, B gave evidence to the effect that his pins and needles had improved but not resolved. He was still suffering from aching pain in the left little finger. His grip remained weaker. *General Damages*: £4,500.

BANHAM v. SCOTTISH & NEWCASTLE PLC, April 23, 2004, District Judge Giles, CC (Leeds). [*Ex rel.* Tom Nossiter, Barrister, Park Lane Chambers, 19, Westgate, Leeds].

Finger

3191.   H, male, a chartered accountant, aged 62 at the date of the accident and 64 at trial, was injured on board a cruise ship when a sudden gust of wind blew a door shut on his left, non dominant, hand. H sustained a compound fracture of the terminal phalanx of his left middle finger and laceration to the volar/ulna side of his index finger. The ship's surgeon amputated the tip of the terminal phalanx of his middle finger and the laceration was sutured. On returning to the United Kingdom, H underwent a skin graft from his left forearm onto the deficit of the terminal phalanx of the middle finger. Eighteen months after the accident, H's middle finger remained shortened and the nail remained deformed. Scarring remained on the left index finger and where the skin was taken from the left forearm. H continued to be conscious of the scar on his forearm. The terminal phalanx of the middle finger no longer experienced the same sensation as H's other fingers and remained vulnerable to intermittent bleedings. There was no physical pain, but H did suffer from some loss of dexterity. *General Damages*: £4,250 (apportioned £3,500 for the physical injury and £750 for the scarring).

HARRIS v. GLOBE TRAVEL LTD, September 27, 2004, Judge Wulwik, CC (Edmonton). [*Ex rel.* Turner & Debenhams Solicitors, Ivy House, 107 St Peter's Street, St Albans, Herts].

Work-related upper limb disorders

3192.   B, female, aged 40 at the onset of illness and 45 at trial, developed bilateral medial and lateral epicondylitis (golfer's and tennis elbow in both elbows) after six months of manoeuvering pallet trucks loaded with frozen goods weighing about 840 kg and requiring between 40 and 60 kg of force to move them. The four conditions of epicondylitis occurred more or less simultaneously after six months. B had not dealt with such loads before. The judge found that the heavy work had caused the onset of the four conditions and not just aggravated them. B had been injected with steroids in both elbows two and eight months after the conditions occurred. Thereafter B was put under the hospital care of a consultant orthopaedic surgeon. He gave further injections and prescribed physiotherapy. After approximately 20 months B was admitted to hospital for injections and manipulations under anaesthesia. She was absent from work for 12 weeks. The manipulations did not work. B underwent an open left tennis elbow release operation approximately two years and seven months after the conditions occurred and was absent from work for a further 13 weeks. Symptoms were temporarily relieved but crept back. Three years and six months after the conditions occurred B had a further operation on the medial side of the left elbow and she was absent from work for a further 13 weeks. At trial, B continued to complain of bilateral elbow pain, worse on the left side. The pains were described as like constant toothache, aggravated by the use of the arms. B had rejected operative treatment on the right elbow as it had not alleviated symptoms on the left. The operations had left a 7cm longitudinal scar over the lateral side of the left elbow and a 4cm scar along the medial aspect of the left elbow. The latter scar remained reddened and widened and slightly keloid. There was discolouration to either side of the scar and some fat loss caused by the fat necrosis secondary to the steroid injection. B remained permanently unfit to perform heavy manual work, however she remained able to perform lighter work. Smith v. Manchester award: £4,000. *General Damages*: £12,000.

BAGGOTT v. ASDA STORES LTD, February 6, 2004, Recorder Walker, CC (Stourbridge). [*Ex rel.* Alastair Smail, Barrister, St Philips Chambers, 55 Temple Row, Birmingham].

Work-related upper limb disorders

3193.   N, a production line operative, aged 27 at the date of the onset of symptoms and 30 at trial, had developed an unspecified work related upper limb disorder after having undertaken strenuous and repetitive work with both hands in a car door module department. The judge accepted that N had developed the disorder after performing this work for approximately three to four years. N suffered from pain and stiffness in the hands (metacarpo-phalangeal and inter-phalangeal joints) along with generalised swelling and tenderness. He was still able to work, albeit with discomfort during rest breaks and morning stiffness. This had continued for approximately 18 to 24 months before he was forced to take seven weeks off work because of very bad pain in the right and left elbow, forearm and fingers. N had returned to work when the pain had subsided. However he continued to suffer symptoms of pins and needles, stiffness and some pain radiating down his right arm. The symptoms lasted for three years in total. At trial N had been employed by V for six years. General damages were awarded in accordance with the JSB Guidelines (6th Edition) 6(K) between brackets (b) and (c). *General Damages*: £6,000.

O'NEILL v. VAUXHALL LTD, July 12, 2004, Judge Hamilton, CC (Luton). [*Ex rel.* Paul McGrath, Barrister, 1 Temple Gardens, Temple, London].

Vibration white finger syndrome

3194.   M, aged 45 at the date of trial, was continuously employed for 30 years as a gardener using hand held vibrating machinery for about eight months of the year. In 1997 to 1998 he became aware of the onset of vibration white finger symptoms mainly in the index and middle fingers of both hands. He continued to work with hand held machinery until December 2000. At examination in May 2002, he was assessed at Stage I/II on the Taylor Pelmear Scale, and Stage 1/2 on the vascular and sensorineural Stockholm scale on both left and right. He suffered numbness and tingling in the fingers, particularly in cold weather, with episodic blanching. His symptoms improved from 2001. M had continued his employment. He was no longer required to use hand held vibrating machinery; there was likely to be a deterioration in his condition if he did so. No separate award was made under Smith v. Manchester. *General Damages* (agreed and approved): £6,000.

McQUEEN v. GLENDALES LTD, February 12, 2004, Recorder Braslavsky Q.C., CC (Liverpool). [*Ex rel.* David Binns, Barrister, 68 Quay Street, Manchester].

Vibration white finger syndrome

3195.   S, male, aged 34 at trial, was continuously employed for 21 years as a gardener using hand held machinery. In 1999 he became aware of the onset of vibration white finger symptoms. He was assessed at stage ON/T on the Taylor Pelmear Scale, and stage 0 vascular and 1 sensorineural on the Stockholm scale both left and right. S had continued his employment. He was no longer required to operate hand held machinery but was able to do so, if necessary. He suffered from tingling in the fingers in cold weather. The judge concluded that there was no real risk that S would lose his employment and so did not make a Smith v. Manchester award. *General Damages*: £4,500.

SUTTON v. GLENDALES LTD, October 31, 2003, Judge Mackay, CC (Liverpool). [*Ex rel.* David Binns, Barrister, 68 Quay Street, Manchester].

Sacrum, pelvis and hip

3196.   S, female, aged 31 at the date of the accident and 35 at trial, was injured when she tripped and fell over a bicycle tyre that was lying around the base of a lamp post in a pavement. S sustained a posterior fracture dislocation of her right acetabulum and experienced immediate and severe pain. She was taken to hospital where the hip was relocated under general anaesthetic. The fracture was unstable and S underwent an open posterior reduction of the pelvis five days later. She gradually mobilised onto crutches after four months but was heavily dependent on others for care and assistance for several months after her discharge. The surgery was successful but S was left with permanent residual symptoms. She complained of increasing pain and aching in the right groin, radiating into the right buttock. She occasionally limped and felt stiffness in the right hip joint. Although her leg lengths were equal, she favoured the left hip, which caused it to ache. The symptoms were present irrespective of weather conditions, but were particularly noticeable in cold or damp weather. X rays of the right femoral head revealed some degenerative changes. It was anticipated that her symptoms would increase gradually and the likelihood of a hip replacement by the age of 60 was 25 per cent higher than her peer group and 50 per cent higher at the age of 70. S described herself as feeling as if she were aged 60 or 70 on account of her residual disability and symptoms. In addition, S was left with a permanent and cosmetically disfiguring surgical scar measuring 29cm in length, which curved over her right upper thigh and buttock. She was very conscious of the scar and always wore clothes to cover it. There were also two small traction pin scars over the right knee and a small scar over the left ankle caused by a laceration when her foot became tangled in the tyre. S was a single mother. Prior to the accident she had enjoyed flower arranging, travelling and swimming but after the accident became sedentary and something of a recluse. There were no restrictions in her working activities as a result of her injuries, but she was considering moving abroad to warmer weather in order to alleviate her symptoms. S's injuries were such as to place her claim above the mid point of the recommended range of awards in the "moderate" bracket of section 6(D) of the JSB guidelines. *General Damages*: £18,500.

STANFORD v. KINGSTON UPON HULL CITY COUNCIL, February 1, 2005, Recorder Robinson, CC (Kingston upon Hull). [*Ex rel.* Craig Moore, Barrister, Park Lane chambers, 19 Westgate, Leeds].

Sacrum, pelvis and hip

3197.   S, female, aged 77 at the date of the accident and 80 at trial, sustained a fracture to the neck of her right femur when she was knocked over by a large dog. S required operative treatment with plates and screws, staying in hospital for 11 days. S had physiotherapy in hospital but did not receive any outpatient physiotherapy as she made a good recovery. She was discharged on two elbow crutches which she kept for three months. She required full time live in care for six weeks. For a month afterwards she used one elbow crutch. S had to start walking with the aid of a stick, but only at times as she could otherwise walk one mile. S needed painkillers for a few weeks after the injury which gradually reduced over three months. S had difficulty walking up and down stairs without a handrail, and kneeling due to unrelated arthritis in the knee. S had previously been an active member of the local community and enjoyed country walks, all of which she had not abandoned. S suffered considerable loss of confidence which the judge considered amounted to a significant loss of amenity. She was restricted in domestic chores, having to increase the hours worked by her cleaner into the foreseeable future. Two and a half years after the accident S did not suffer any pain in her right hip. *General Damages*: £11,000.

SHAW v. TOFARI, March 17, 2005, Judge Campbell, CC (Reading). [*Ex rel.* Colin Nugent, Barrister, Hardwicke Building, New Square, Lincoln's Inn, London].

Leg: severe leg injuries

3198.   S, male, aged 20 at the date of the road traffic accident and 23 at trial, sustained serious and permanently disabling orthopaedic, psychiatric and neurological injuries when he was involved in a head on collision. S underwent a 10 hour operation which involved the insertion of metal work to the right knee and lower leg and 150 stitches to his face. He remained in hospital for two months. At trial, the principal symptoms affected his right leg and to a lesser extent, his left leg. In his right leg, the knee and ankle swelled and became "puffy". There was restriction in flexion in the knee, constant aching in the ankle and weakness in the right leg as a whole. The pain, swelling and restriction of movement were increased by exercise and even by standing. The knee and ankle swelled over the course of the day. In the left leg, there was tenderness in the left forefoot. S could only kneel with difficulty and he could not kneel on hard surfaces at all, or straighten from a squatting position. S could not walk for more than 200 yards; he limped and could only kneel with difficulty. He had developed degenerative disease in the right knee and ankle, and would require operations for patella resurfacing within three to five years and for ankle arthrodesis at some time in the future. In addition to the leg injuries a number of other complications resulted from the accident. S was less able to halt the progress of symptoms arising from his pre existing osteoporosis by reason of his inactivity after the accident. He had suffered extensive scarring to the face, hands and legs, about which he was extremely self conscious. Further surgery to the eyelid and nose was contemplated. S had had a previous history of depression and the accident had aggravated that condition, leading to intrusive thoughts, increased irritability and tearfulness, panic attacks and anxiety as a car passenger. He had been diagnosed as suffering from post traumatic stress disorder after the accident but had recovered by trial, after extensive therapy. S's head injury had caused post concussional syndrome, resulting in migraine headaches, dizziness, tiredness, reduced memory and concentration and poor balance, from which he would recover over a period of four to five years. There was a minor increased risk of epilepsy. A year before trial S underwent two operations to remove a kidney stone which, according to urological evidence, had been caused by his inactivity after the accident. S had become highly dependent on his mother and hardly went out without her. He had just embarked on a career in hairdressing at the time of the accident, but as a result of the accident his ambition to become a hairdressing lecturer had ceased and he was retraining to become a receptionist. A Smith v. Manchester award was based on two years' net earnings. The award for loss of chance of fulfilling his career ambition was assessed at 33 per cent and a Blamire lump sum award was made. *General Damages*: £40,000. Smith v. Manchester award: £20,000. Award for loss of chance of fulfilling career ambition: £30,000. Loss of congenial employment: £3,000.

STEPTON v. WOLSELEY, January 17, 2005, Recorder Williamson Q.C., CC (Southampton). [*Ex rel.* James Counsell, Barrister, Outer Temple Chambers, 222 Strand, London].

Leg: severe leg injuries

3199. B, male, a farm labourer, aged 31 at the date of the accident and 36 at trial, had sustained a fracture of the left tibia and fibula when he fell off the back of a tractor unit. The injury had been treated by surgery with the insertion of a nail into his leg. He was non weight bearing for about three months after the accident and had to use a stick or crutch for a further three to four months. On review one year after the accident, B was still experiencing a considerable amount of pain and discomfort together with limitation of mobility. Twenty months after the accident he underwent an unsuccessful operation for the removal of the nail, which was eventually removed four months later after a prolonged operation and with some difficulty. When seen for the purposes of a medical report three and a half years after the accident, B was still suffering from significant pain around the anterior aspect of his left knee, the lower third of the tibia and the left ankle. These symptoms were having a significant impact on his employment, hobbies and activities of daily living. However it was considered that the symptoms had plateaued at that time, it being unlikely that there would be any further improvement or deterioration in the future. B had been unable to resume his usual pre accident employment as a farm worker because of his injuries and had been forced to work in a glass fibre factory, which employment necessitated the wearing of a face mask through which air was fed by line to reduce the risk of his breathing in fibres. The judge commented that B's injuries did not fall neatly within the JSB Guidelines (6th Edition) chapter 6 category (L) (c) (i) or (L) (b) (iv) because whilst there were none of the aggravating features of category (L) (b) (iv), nevertheless B was in constant pain. The judge awarded B a sum for the loss of congenial employment to reflect the fact that B's injuries had forced him to give up work in the open air as a farm worker in which capacity he had worked all his working life until the accident. *General Damages*: 17,500. Loss of congenial employment: £5,000. *Smith and Manchester* award: £11,000. Total award (including interest): £52,540.

BATRAM v. CHAPMAN, July 9, 2004, Judge Barham, CC (Norwich). [*Ex rel.* Jackman Smith & Mulley, Solicitors, Oak House, Northgate Street, Ipswich, Suffolk].

Leg: less severe leg injuries

3200. H, male, aged 11 at the date of the accident and 16 at trial, sustained injuries when he was struck by O riding a motorcycle as he attempted to cross the road. Following the accident H was taken to hospital and diagnosed with an open fracture of the tibia and fibula of the right leg. He also sustained a closed fracture to his left clavicle, which healed within four weeks of the accident. H underwent surgery to reduce the leg fracture and an external fixator was applied, which remained in place for three months. After that, H's leg remained in plaster for 15 weeks. He then had a removable cast which he was required to wear for a further four weeks. The tibia was slow in healing and H required ultrasound treatment to it to stimulate the healing process. The tibia had healed 12 months after the accident and H was discharged from the fracture clinic 17 months after the accident. As a result of the leg injury, H was required to take five months off school. Upon examination three years after the accident, H's right leg was found to be 1.5cm shorter than his left but this did not cause any physical or functional problems. He did not limp, nor did he experience any backache. No long term problem was anticipated as a result of the difference in length. H's calf muscle on his right leg was 1cm slimmer than on the left leg. It was anticipated that he would continue to put on muscle bulk as he grew. H was found to have a normal range of movement in the right leg. The power of the leg was clinically normal and a full functional recovery was found to have occurred within two years of the accident. The long term prognosis was good. H was left with scarring to the right leg which measured 8cm at the back of the calf but this was not considered to have a marring effect and was expected to continue to fade with time. *General Damages*: £12,000.

H (A CHILD) v. OLDROYD, April 18, 2005, Deputy District Judge Reed, CC (Wakefield). [*Ex rel.* Hodgkinsons, Solicitors, The old Manse, 14 Lumley Avenue, Skegness, Lincolnshire].

Leg: less severe leg injuries–Non-facial scarring

3201.   C, female, production line worker, aged 50 at the date of the road traffic accident and 51 at trial, sustained bruising to the shin and calf of her right leg and was unable to stand without pain. She was absent from work for two weeks and had to rely on her husband for help with the household tasks. The bruising took three weeks to settle, but at 11 weeks after the accident C was still experiencing intermittent aching. Healing was slightly delayed by the formation of local scar tissue on the anterior point of contact. Although physiotherapy sessions were recommended, C was prevented from attending by another unrelated medical matter. Full recovery took seven and a half months, in line with the medical prognosis. C had a residual depression scar measuring approximately 5 cm by 8 cm. The judge expressed the view that this was tissue necrosis, common in cases of heavy bruising but of minimal cosmetic significance. *General Damages*: £1,400.

CUTTS v. SHARMAN, February 16, 2005, Recorder Hampton, CC (Lincoln). [*Ex rel.* James Earle, Barrister, Regency Chambers, Cathedral Square, Peterborough].

Knee

3202.   B, female, retired, aged 60 at the date of the accident and 63 at trial, suffered injuries as a result of a road traffic accident. Following the accident B was very shaken and was taken to hospital, but was discharged with pain killers. She had sustained a soft tissue injury to her right knee, causing a tear to the anterior lateral meniscus. An MRI scan was performed and 12 months after the accident an arthroscopy was performed on the knee, under general anaesthetic, to repair the tear. Two years after the accident B's knee had returned to about 75 to 80 per cent of its pre accident level. The medical evidence, which was accepted by the judge, was that the accident had accelerated the effects of natural age deterioration of the knee by 10 years, with half of the 20 to 25 per cent loss of functions being due to the acceleration of normal wear of the knee and half due to the direct effects of the accident. Prior to the accident B did not have any knee problems. The effect of B's permanent knee problems was that she could not run, squat, kneel or walk on uneven ground without difficulty, and after activity her knee was stiff and achy. B was a very keen club level golfer, but the accident had largely stopped her playing golf, and gardening, for 18 months. Two pre booked golfing holidays were spoilt in the six months following the accident. At trial, 42 months after the accident, B could play a full round of golf without difficulty. However, she could no longer play golf on successive days due to her knee problems. B also sustained a lower back strain. She suffered moderately severe back pain for three months following the accident. B underwent physiotherapy, which improved her symptoms, resulting in only occasional pain by nine months after the accident and a full recovery after 12 months. B also developed a moderately severe driving specific phobia. She experienced some panic attacks and was generally a very nervous driver, avoiding driving if she could. She did not drive for a period of six weeks following the accident, and at the date of trial only drove short local journeys. Her annual mileage was reduced to less than half her pre accident distance, and she no longer shared the driving with her husband on long journeys. B was also a very anxious hyper vigilant passenger. Cognitive behavioural therapy had been recommended some 12 months before the trial. Medical opinion was that with treatment over a six month period B would make a full recovery. The judge found that B should have had the treatment, and assessed damages on the basis that B should have made a full recovery some three years after the accident. *General Damages*: £11,000 (apportioned £8,000 for the knee injury, £2,250 for the back injury and £2,250 for the psychological injury and discounted to take account of overlap).

BARKER v. JONES, January 19, 2005, Judge Atkins, CC (Luton). [*Ex rel.* Adam Farrer, Barrister, 5, Fountain Court, Steelhouse Lane, Birmingham].

Knee

3203.   M, female, retired, aged 61 at the date of the accident and 64 at trial, suffered a wrenching injury to the muscles and tendons at the back of her left knee when she tripped over a defective paving stone. The knee became swollen and she attended hospital directly after the fall, where it was noted that she had a tender left knee at the lateral meniscal area with marked swelling. A tubigrip bandage was provided. M wore this for 10 days continuously and intermittently for a month thereafter. The knee remained swollen for almost three months and M visited her GP six months after the accident because of continuing weakness in the knee. An elastic knee support was provided. At the date of the medical report a year after the accident, M was able to walk for 30 minutes before developing an ache at the back of her leg to the calf and thigh. The knee support was of some assistance although her overall walking capacity had been reduced significantly. She was unable to wear heels over an inch in height and had difficulty with stairs. Kneeling brought on occasional numbness. The only change in M's lifestyle was that brought about by the restriction in walking. That restriction was expected to persist indefinitely. *General Damages*: £6,000.

MILNER v. LANCASHIRE CC, April 27, 2005, District Judge Heyworth, CC (Burnley). [*Ex rel.* Karim Sabry, Barrister, 8 King Street, Manchester].

Knee

3204.   B, a girl, aged 11 at the date of the accident and 17 at the child settlement approval hearing, suffered injuries when the vehicle in which she was travelling as a rear seat passenger, was involved in a road traffic accident. She felt severe pain in both knees immediately upon impact. Both knees were bruised, and the left knee was put in a tubigrip. B took anti inflamatory painkillers. Nine months after the accident B was suffering a minor degree of anterior knee pain daily, which was aggravated by physical exercise and by climbing stairs. Prior to the accident B suffered from Osgood's Schlatters disease, and the knee pain attributable to the disease was exacerbated by the accident. B did not participate in P.E., swimming or horseriding for at least nine months after the accident. The knee pain attributable to the accident resolved within two to three years of the accident. *General Damages* (agreed and approved): £3,250

B (A CHILD) v. CARTER, July 6, 2004, District Judge Mullis, CC (Romford). [*Ex rel.* Gurion Taussig, Barrister, 199 Strand, London].

Knee–Non-facial scarring

3205.   L, female, an office manager, aged 52 at the date of the accident and 54 at trial, sustained an injury to the knee when she fell on an icy landing stage after an evening river cruise. She sustained a displaced intra articular comminuted fracture of the right kneecap and was detained in hospital for four days. Following open reduction and internal fixation she was given early active mobilisation. She received physiotherapy as an outpatient for eight months after the accident. She had returned to work three weeks after the accident, being transported by car from and to home by her husband. L and her husband had booked a winter holiday which had had to be cancelled. L's operation left an ugly 15cm scar on the front of her knee, but that had faded by the trial date and was not cosmetically distressing. The metalwork was not removed from her knee and was visible through her skin. She recovered movement in the knee gradually, from nil to 115 degrees. Before the accident L was very fit and her principal pleasure was hill walking both in this country and abroad. She had been accustomed to walking over 15 miles a day over rough country, and had purchased a property with her husband for their retirement in a location convenient for hill walking. By the trial date L's condition had improved so that she could, with the assistance of two walking poles, walk up to eight miles with modest gradients, but that caused her considerable pain. She could not run, kneel or squat. She suffered pain through prolonged sitting, when she got up from a chair or got in or out of a motor car, and when she walked up steep stairs or down stairs; no improvement was expected. It was probable that L would, within five to 10 years of the accident, develop osteoarthritis, that she would have severe disability in going up or down stairs, and would not be able to walk down anything more than a slight incline. In addition she would suffer pain after driving her car for more than 20 to 30 minutes, and would have to finish her hill walking activities. *General Damages*: £21,500.

LIGHTLY v. HOWARD, March 19, 2004, District Judge Wildsmith, CC (York). [*Ex rel.* John Collins, Barrister, Zenith Chambers, 10 Park Square, Leeds].

Knee–Non-facial scarring–Post-traumatic stress disorder

3206.   B, female, a shop owner, aged 34 at the date of the accident and 37 at trial, suffered a markedly depressed comminuted fracture through the lateral tibial plateau of the left knee with associated scarring when she was knocked down by a van that mounted the pavement. B also developed post traumatic stress disorder. Immediately after the accident B was taken to hospital. X rays were taken and it was confirmed that she had suffered a significant fracture to the left knee. Because of the complexity and swelling, B was rested to allow the swelling to settle before an open reduction and internal fixation was undertaken. B remained in hospital for a period of 16 days after the operation. The left leg was encased in plaster for four months, during which time B attended the fracture clinic regularly. B also underwent two courses of physiotherapy followed by rehabilitation at the gym. The bone used for the fixation operation was taken from the iliac crest. Following the operation B was left with two large and apparent scars. The scar to the knee measured 14.5cm and was situated on the antero lateral aspect of the upper tibia. It had slightly reduced sensation. The scar to the iliac crest measured 7.5cm. Both scars were permanent and prominent. B was embarrassed about the appearance of the scars and refused to wear short skirts or bikinis, trying to keep the areas covered at all times. B had made a remarkable recovery from the fractured knee within 12 months of the accident. She had regained a relatively full range of movement but would always have some permanent ongoing residual loss of mobility and tenderness over the metalwork, especially in cold and damp weather. B was virtually incapacitated for four months after the accident. She could not attend to any domestic duties or look after her children. She was unable to go horse riding or cycling. She was absent from work for four months because of impaired mobility. B also suffered post traumatic stress disorder. She found the accident very frightening. She had had her two children with her at the time of the accident and had been very anxious about their safety, ruminating that they could have been killed. She suffered repeated nightmares and intrusive thoughts and became very apprehensive whilst walking on pavements or beside busy roads. As a former heroin addict, B was already emotionally vulnerable at the time of the accident. The accident and consequent scarring heightened her insecurities and this was taken into account when assessing general damages. The prognosis was for the post traumatic stress disorder to settle within three years of the accident. *General Damages*: £17,500.

BICE v. BIRMINGHAM MOTOR TYRES, May 3, 2005, Judge MacDuff Q.C., CC (Birmingham). [*Ex rel.* Stephen Garner, Barrister, No 8 Chambers, Fountain Court, Steelhouse Lane, Birmingham].

Knee–Arthritis and osteopathic conditions

3207. W, male, a self employed manager, aged 51 at the date of the accident and 57 at trial, suffered injuries when jogging. He had stumbled on a defect in the pavement, sustaining a twisting injury to his right knee and right foot. The right knee became swollen following the accident. W refrained from running for four weeks after the accident, but then found it painful when he tried to run on a treadmill. He also found it difficult to kneel or squat. W was a very keen road runner who ran 30 or 40 miles each week, was a member of a running club and trained beginners. He had also completed the London Marathon. Two months after the accident he saw his GP who recommended a course of physiotherapy. After six sessions W tried to run on a treadmill but suffered considerable pain and swelling. Thereafter, the consultant to whom he was referred performed an arthroscopy with a partial medial meniscectomy and debridement of articular cartilage in the medial femoral condyle. Following the arthroscopy W was advised to undergo a course of hyaluronic injections and another arthroscopy if the pain continued. W's condition improved after the arthroscopy, although he implemented his own regime of care by a regular course of herbal supplements, nutrients and vitamins supplied by a herbalist, who also provided advice as to how to look after the joint. W also greatly reduced his physical activities. He stopped all running and cycling. W continued to suffer pain, particularly in cold and damp weather, and gave evidence of a constant ache which he had learnt to cope with. Medical opinion was agreed that W had a pre existing asymptomatic osteoarthritic condition. W's expert was of the view that the accident had accelerated osteoarthritic degenerative changes by 10 years; H's expert said five years. This was relevant to general damages and the issue of future medical treatment. In addition there was dispute between the experts as to whether the accident had increased the probability of W requiring a total knee replacement. The judge found that W was stoical and had made no effort to exaggerate his symptoms, and that it was to his credit that he had maintained a regime that had controlled his problems. He had also lost his principal leisure and social activity. The judge found that the acceleration period was closer to the upper scale suggested by W's expert. The judge did not find that W was likely to require a total knee replacement, but declared that the possibility of that would be reflected in the general damages awarded. Furthermore, the judge was willing to award W the future cost of one arthroscopy, one course of hyaluronic injections, and three years of future cost of herbal remedies, nutrients and supplements. *General Damages*: £9,000.

WATSON v. HILLINGDON, October 28, 2004, District Judge Banks, CC (Uxbridge). [*Ex rel.* Pankaj Pathak, Barrister, 2, Paper Buildings, Temple, London].

Foot

3208. S, a schoolboy, aged 13 at the date of the accident and 16 at the date of the child settlement approval hearing, sustained personal injury in a skateboarding accident when his right foot became trapped between the skateboard and a loose slat on the skateboard ramp. S immediately felt extreme pain in his right foot and also in the middle of his back. He was taken to hospital where X rays were taken. The X rays revealed that S had sustained fractures of the base of the second, third and fourth metatarsal bones with associated soft tissue injury to the right foot. He was given a below knee plaster cast and crutches. He was prescribed painkillers. S was also diagnosed as having sustained a twisting injury to his middle back. S experienced symptoms of bruising, swelling and extreme pain in the right foot. He was unable to weight bear and his right foot was numb. The plaster was removed after six weeks. On removal, S had swelling, tenderness and stiffness of the joints in the foot. His right foot symptoms were generally severe before settling six months after the accident. S's back injury settled after a month. Although the accident occurred during the summer vacation, so S did not miss any time from school, S was not able to participate in PE lessons for some weeks after his return in the new school term. S was depressed for two months after the accident as he was not able to go out and skateboard, which ruined his summer holiday. *General Damages*: £4,300.

S (A CHILD) v. WARWICK DC, March 3, 2004, District Judge Jones, CC (Warwick). [*Ex rel.* Stephen Garner, Barrister, No 8 Chambers, Fountain Court, Steelhouse Lane, Birmingham].

Foot

3209.   M, male, a chartered accountant, aged 40 at the date of the road traffic accident and 41 at trial, suffered injuries after being knocked off his motorcycle and catapulted into the roadway. M was very dazed and distressed. An X-ray was taken at hospital which revealed that M had sustained a fracture of the fifth metatarsal bone of the left foot. He was put into a plaster cast for about four weeks. M used crutches during that time and his weight bearing ability was very limited. Once the plaster cast was removed M was quickly back to normal. Initially his chest and left leg were very bruised and painful. The bruising settled two weeks after the accident. M was off work for 10 days. *General Damages*: £3,000.

MITCHELL v. CENTRICA PLC, November 5, 2004, Judge Farnworth, CC (Luton). [*Ex rel.* Stephen Garner, Barrister, No 8 Chambers, Fountain Court, Birmingham].

Facial scarring

3210.   C, female, a university student, aged 20 at the date of the accident and 24 at trial, suffered serious bites to her face when she was bitten by a St. Bernard dog which she had been grooming. She sustained bites around her right eye, as well as lower on her right cheek and on the right side of her neck, together with a small chip off one front tooth. The wounds were sutured under general anaesthetic, but became infected and C had a course of antibiotics. Her face remained painful and swollen for approximately three months, with continuing pain for a further three months. The scars were thereafter well healed and were not obviously visible, apart from one scar which ran from the corner of her right eye down onto her cheek for about 2.5cm and had a grooved appearance. There was a slight loss of sensation in that area. Plastic surgery would not have improved the appearance of the scars. The judge found that the appearance of the scars was not ugly or disfiguring, but that C was acutely conscious of them. C also developed a fear of large animals, which was continuing at the date of trial over four years later and was categorised as an adjustment disorder. C had been between the second and third year of a degree course in animal science at the time of the incident and had always intended to work with agricultural animals. That proved impossible because of her phobia and she was restricted to working with small animals, which she found less satisfying or enjoyable. It was possible that cognitive behavioural therapy might help her, but otherwise she was likely to continue to be fearful in the presence of large animals. C had become much less outgoing and her anxiety on meeting people for the first time had affected her social life. She used cosmetics to hide and soften the appearance of the scars. The judge felt that the claim fell between the JSB Guidelines Chapter 7(B)(a)(iii) and (iv) regarding the facial disfigurement of females. *General Damages*: £9,000.

GRIFFITHS v. GRIFFIN, December 9, 2004, Judge Anthony King, CC (Oxford). [*Ex rel.* Alicia Collinson, Barrister, Harcourt Chambers, 2, Harcourt Buildings, Temple, London].

Facial scarring

3211.   T, male, a roofer, aged 41 at the date of the accident and 43 at trial, was climbing over a wall in the course of his employment when he tripped and fell, cutting his chin. T saw "stars" and was nearly rendered unconscious. He sustained a laceration to his chin. The left side was described as hanging off like a flap. T attended hospital where the laceration required seven sutures. T was able to return home the same day. T's chin was swollen, tender and bruised and he also had lower gum and mouth pain. Because of the pain he was unable to eat solids easily. T had significant pain for one week, during which time he needed to take several painkillers a day. Thereafter there was some improvement. When T was examined, 18 months after the accident, T had an upside down reverse letter 'L' shaped faded scar to the left of the midline of the chin. This would be permanent. T was not embarrassed about his scar. There was also a permanent loss of sensation on the chin which was due to superficial nerve damage. This caused T to feel as though he was slavering, and that something was running down his chin when he was eating. The judge found that the scar fell into the less significant scarring bracket 7 (b) (iv) of the JSB Guidelines. *General Damages*: £4,000.

THIRKELL v. CARILLION HOUSING, September 7, 2004, District Judge Arkless, CC (Middlesbrough). [*Ex rel.* Monica Whyte, Barrister, 22 Old Buildings, Lincoln's Inn, London].

Facial scarring

3212.   W, male, a handyman, aged 50 at the date of the accident and 53 at trial sustained injury as a result of an accident at work. A screwdriver struck and pierced the underside of his chin. The wound bled profusely. W attended hospital, where the wound was cleaned and sutured. The suture was removed by W's GP 11 days later, at which time it was noted that the wound had healed. The chin and jaw were sore and caused W difficulty when shaving. W suffered some headaches. He was left with a slightly depressed 1cm mature linear scar under the chin, which was initially very sensitive and sore in cold weather. The judge described the scar as being "a nasty and unpleasant injury" but concluded that W had "no residual problem save for the scar", which was of "minor effect". *General Damages*: £1,750.

WRIGHTSON v. SOUTHERN CROSS HEALTHCARE LTD, June 17, 2004, District Judge Oldham, CC (Sheffield). [*Ex rel.* Gordon Stables, Barrister, Paradise Chambers, 26 Paradise Square, Sheffield].

Facial scarring–Skull

3213.   G, a girl, aged three at the date of the accident and eight at the child settlement approval hearing, sustained injuries when the car in which she was travelling was involved in a head on collision with another vehicle. G sustained a severe laceration to her forehead which exposed the bone, and was deeply shocked and frightened. At hospital an X ray revealed a depressed fracture to the skull. The facial laceration was sutured. During two days as an inpatient under observation G was easily irritated and suffered repeated bouts of vomiting. She also wet the bed and suffered intense nightmares about the accident. On discharge from hospital G continued to wet the bed and to vomit and her sleep pattern was badly disrupted. She was unable to attend nursery because of her injuries for a period of three months. The laceration to her forehead left a very obvious scar on the hairline. On her return to nursery she was teased by other children about her scar. The scar was still obvious on examination 12 months after the accident. It was irregular and an inverted T shape. The scar was keloid and its longest extent was 6cm long. G tried to hide it by growing a fringe. The prognosis was that the scar would be permanent. The bed wetting and nightmares stopped approximately six months after the accident. A diagnosis of nocturnal enuresis consequent on the accident was made. G also suffered symptoms of travel anxiety consisting of wariness and hypervigilance when travelling by car. On examination 30 months after the accident G continued to suffer from travel anxiety. The prognosis for G's residual psychological travel anxiety was that it would settle within 36 months of the accident. The district judge did not indicate any apportionment between the scarring and the psychological injury. *General Damages* (agreed and approved): £10,000.

G (A CHILD) v. DHILLON, June 23, 2004, Deputy District Judge Bard, CC (Birmingham). [*Ex rel.* Stephen Garner, Barrister, No 8 Chambers, Fountain Court, Steelhouse Lane, Birmingham].

Burns

3214. E, a girl, aged nine at the date of the accident and 13 at the child settlement approval hearing, suffered injuries to both hands when she was scalded by hot tea. The tea had been purchased at a football match in a plastic cup and E sustained injuries when she was jolted. The injuries consisted of burns to the index and middle fingers of the left hand and burns to the index, middle and ring fingers of the dominant right hand. E was unable to attend to her normal daily needs for 10 days after the accident. E required a Calpole Flamizine bag to the right hand and Jelonet dressing to the fingers of the left hand. Blisters were incised and the wounds required redressing. The burns to the left hand healed within two weeks but left marks for up to two months. The burns to the right hand healed within three weeks of the accident but left marks for up to three months. Both of E's hands were tender for six weeks. She was unable to do PE for three weeks, or to play the guitar for six weeks after the accident. E made a full recovery with no scarring. *General Damages* (agreed and approved): £1,000.

E (A CHILD) v. SCUNTHORPE UNITED F.C. LTD., October 4, 2004, District Judge Chesterfield, CC (Scunthorpe). [*Ex rel.* Martin & Haigh, Solicitors, 12-18-Frances Street, Scunthorpe, North Lincolnshire].

Respiratory organs: asbestos-related

3215. O, male, a lagger aged 51 at the onset of symptoms and 52 at the date of death, developed mesothelioma as a result of his exposure to asbestos. He had been exposed to asbestos for the first time when he was about 42 and he had about seven to eight years exposure. O, a non smoker, was admitted to hospital as an emergency case in January 2002 with a history of shortness of breath and feeling unwell for the previous two weeks. He had a fever and accompanied sputum. He was given antibiotics, steroids and bronchodilators and eventually discharged. Three months later he was prescribed steroids by his GP following complaints of shortness of breath, coughing, wheezing, and chest pain. On June 21, 2002 O was suddenly taken ill with chest pain. He was sent home from work and prescribed antibiotics and inflammatories. O kept returning to his GP with complaints of worsening chest pain. At the end of July 2002 O was readmitted to hospital. On September 16, 2002 he was informed that he had a tumour in his chest. On October 3, 2002 a diagnosis of mesothelioma was given. O was in intense pain and was given opiates. He was referred for a cordotomy to sever chest nerves to reduce the pain. O became house bound. He was given radiotherapy to the biopsy site and opiates were rapidly increased. On November 21, 2002 O was admitted to a hospice for pain control and on January 30, 2003 he died aged 52 years. *General Damages*: (agreed between counsel): £51,000. Bereavement Award: £10,000. Total award (agreed, including interest): £303,000.

OVERTON v. CAPE INDUSTRIAL SERVICES LTD, July 16, 2004, Master Whitaker, QBD. [*Ex rel.* Joel Donovan, Barrister, Cloisters, 1 Pump Court, London].

Poisoning: food

3216. D, female, aged 53 at the date of the accident and 57 at trial, suffered an acute gastrointestinal infection which began three days from the end of a package holiday. The acute phase of diarrhoea and stomach cramps lasted three days. While visiting the bathroom she fainted and injured her face and knee. On her return to the United Kingdom D was off work for six weeks and was treated for worms in her stools in addition to a campylobacter bacterium infection. She had existing depression which was worsened as a result of her symptoms. D recovered from her facial injury within three weeks and her knee injury within two months. Her condition developed into post infective irritable bowel syndrome, which showed some improvement, although at the date of trial she was suffering diarrhoea approximately every week, constipation every two to three weeks, swelling of the stomach every two to four weeks, and wind every two to three weeks. Once every three months D suffered acute symptoms of diarrhoea as well as severe stomach cramps. D was careful as to what she ate and her condition could be embarrassing in company. She was unable to plan events as much as before and had to take medication. The prognosis was that she would have symptoms indefinitely but that they would improve with time. *General Damages* (to include loss of enjoyment of the holiday): £15,000.

DOREE v. FIRST CHOICE HOLIDAYS & FLIGHTS LTD, January 12, 2005, Recorder Baker Q.C., CC (Reditch). [*Ex rel.* Ian Miller, Barrister, No.1 Serjeants' Inn, Fleet Street, London].

Minor injuries

3217.   C, female, aged 12 at the date of the accident and 13 at the date of the child settlement approval hearing, was seated in the middle rear passenger seat in her mother's car when it was involved in a head on collision. C could not remember the incident at all and probably lost consciousness for a few seconds. Upon getting out of the vehicle, C was shocked, dizzy and shaking and remained so for three days after the accident. She sustained multiple minor facial injuries including cuts to the right side of her nose and the right side of her forehead. She had swelling to the right side of her lower lip and the day after the accident, she developed a black eye on the right side. C was also aware of a lump on the right side of her head. The cuts did not require suturing and resolved spontaneously as did the other facial injuries: the swelling on the lip after one week, the black eye after two weeks and the rest of the facial injuries within three weeks of the accident. C was aware of a constant pounding headache immediately after the accident which lasted for 24 hours. Thereafter she had intermittent headaches daily for one week and then approximately twice a week for three months after the accident. C also suffered from neck pain associated with stiffness from the day following the accident until eight weeks after the accident. Her hobby of playing netball was affected for three months. Upon examination three months after the accident, C's injuries had resolved, but for the headaches and some tenderness to her right upper trapezius muscle. She was advised to undertake physiotherapy to address the ongoing problems and it was thought that with such treatment the headaches and tenderness would dissipate within nine months of the accident. In fact, C recovered completely after six physiotherapy sessions within six months of the accident. *General Damages* (agreed and approved): £2,000.

A (A CHILD) v. MORRISH, September 23, 2004, District Judge Pearl, CC (Watford). [*Ex rel.* Joanna Kerr, Barrister, Lamb Chambers, Lamb Building, Temple, London].

Minor injuries

3218.   C, a schoolgirl, aged seven at the date of the accident and eight at the child settlement approval hearing, was involved in a front end collision road traffic accident. She was distressed after the event. C was thrown forward by the force of the impact and she struck her left cheek against the seat in front. She suffered bruising and grazing to the left cheek which spread across the left cheek area under the eye and towards the ear. The area was sore and tender. The bruising and grazing healed over a period of three weeks from the date of the accident without any scarring. C also developed pain and bruising over the tops of her thighs towards the hips where she had been restrained by the seat belt. The area was painful and tender and it hurt when C walked. The bruising faded over a four to five week period.

C also suffered sleep disturbance with unpleasant, intrusive dreams after the accident. She was frightened when travelling by car. On examination, C still experienced symptoms of travel anxiety and general apprehension in a car. The prognosis was for the residual travel anxiety symptoms to resolve within six to nine months of the accident. C was off school on account of her injuries for one week and she avoided PE for a further two weeks. At the approval hearing C confirmed that her travel anxiety symptoms had settled in accordance with the prognosis. *General Damages*: £1,500.

C (A CHILD) v. PATEL, February 17, 2004, Deputy District Judge Murdoch, CC (Wolverhampton). [*Ex rel.* Stephen Garner, Barrister, No 8 Chambers, Fountain Court, Steelhouse Lane, Birmingham].

Minor injuries

3219.   B, a girl, aged nine at the date of the accident and 11 at the child settlement approval hearing, had been a front seat passenger in a vehicle which was hit on its rear passenger side by another vehicle on its rear passenger side. Although the force of the impact caused B's vehicle to spin around approximately 45 degrees, no airbags were activated. B bit her tongue during the accident and was shaken and upset. She felt pain in the neck and left upper arm. When B arrived home, an ice pack was applied to the left upper arm and visible bruising had developed. The next morning B awoke after a restless night with further bruising to the arm, and pain and stiffness in the neck. By the following morning, her neck pain had increased such that she was taken to hospital. No X rays were taken, and she was discharged with advice and painkillers. B's tongue was sore for up to a week after the accident, and the bruising to the left upper arm persisted for two months. The pain in B's neck was very uncomfortable, when she moved it, for the first few weeks after the accident. The accident had happened on a Friday, and B had taken that day off school. She returned to school the following Monday after having rested over the weekend. B had been unable to play sports for seven days, and had to take care in rougher games for a further seven days. B was unable to assist with domestic chores, as was her habit, for approximately a week after the accident. B suffered nightmares for a few days after the accident, and had become a much more nervous passenger, preferring her mother's sedate style of driving to that of others. When examined four months after the accident the medical expert found that B had recovered from all physical symptoms within six to eight weeks of the accident, and had given a prognosis for recovery from the symptoms of travel anxiety within seven to nine months of the accident. At the hearing, nine months after the accident, the litigation friend informed the court that B's symptoms of anxiety were ongoing but very mild and lessening with time. *General Damages* (agreed and approved): £1,500.

B (A CHILD) v. OSTERMEYER, July 29, 2004, District Judge Collier, CC (Basildon). [*Ex rel.* Joanna Kerr, Barrister, Lamb Chambers, Lamb Building, Temple, London].

Minor injuries

3220.   C, a boy, aged 16 at the date of the accident and 17 at the date of the child settlement approval hearing, was thrown from his moped when he was struck from the side by P's car. C was thrown over the bonnet of P's vehicle and banged his head on the ground. He was dizzy and shocked immediately after the accident and had difficulty weight bearing on his right leg. P also experienced pain in his head, neck and right shoulder. C was taken home by a passer by, before being taken to the hospital, where a laceration was noticed on his right leg. X-rays revealed no bony injury and the wound was dressed. C slept poorly that night and the following day he experienced increasing stiffness in his neck and right shoulder. He consulted his GP, who noted tenderness on the right side of his neck. C was advised to take anti-inflammatory drugs and to mobilise his neck. One week after the accident C's leg was bruised and his walking had improved. Three weeks after the accident C was able to walk normally and six weeks after the accident C had returned to all normal activities, including running and karate, without any significant pain in the leg or neck. On examination, six months after the accident, C indicated that he suffered from an occasional ache in his leg, although without any precipitating factor, and that he occasionally woke up in the mornings with a stiff neck. The medical evidence noted that at six months the ongoing symptoms were becoming less frequent, and at the date of the hearing had resolved entirely. *General Damages* (agreed and approved): £1,500.

P (A CHILD) v. PENNY, March 26, 2004, District Judge Cooksley, CC (Chelmsford). [*Ex rel.* Adam Walker, Barrister, Lamb Chambers, Lamb Building, Elm Court, Temple, London].

Minor injuries

3221. B, a boy, aged 10 at the date of the accident and 12 at the child settlement approval hearing, suffered injuries as a result of a road traffic accident. B's injuries consisted of an acute neck sprain which resolved within three days, a significant contusion to the anterior chest wall causing significant pain and discomfort for up to two weeks, a contusion to the abdominal wall with a full recovery within two weeks, and a possible concussion injury as evidenced by amnesia relating to the events surrounding the accident. His memory of those events had not returned. B took no pain relief for his injuries. *General Damages* (agreed and approved): £1,500.

B (A CHILD) v. BOTFIELD, October 22, 2004, Deputy District Judge Thorn, CC (Scunthorpe). [*Ex rel.* Martin & Haigh, Solicitors, 12-18 Frances Street, Scunthorpe, North Lincolnshire].

Minor injuries

3222. T, a girl, aged 15 at the date of the accident and 17 at the child settlement approval hearing, suffered injuries as a result of a road traffic accident. At the time of impact T, a rear seat passenger, was leaning forward and her face and knees came into collision with the front seat. She immediately experienced pain in her face and discomfort in her neck. The morning after the accident T awoke with a stiff and painful neck, a headache and visible bruising to her face and knees. She visited her GP that day and was prescribed painkillers. Within four days of the accident the bruising had settled, and one week after the accident the bruising had subsided. The neck symptoms resolved within six weeks of the accident. T took two days off school, and upon her return was unable to participate fully in sports for a further two weeks. T also suffered from nervousness and anxiety when travelling in cars. She was particularly reluctant to travel in cars without rear passenger doors because she felt she could be trapped. Those symptoms had largely resolved within two months of the accident, although some heightened awareness of the movement of traffic was present for up to 15 months after the accident. *General Damages* (agreed and approved): £1,250.

T (A CHILD) v. WACKETT, July 6, 2004, District Judge Burgess, CC (Maidstone). [*Ex rel.* Joanna Kerr, Barrister, Lamb Chambers, Lamb Buildings, Temple, London].

Minor injuries

3223. K, a girl, aged four at the date of the road traffic accident and six at the child settlement approval hearing, sustained injuries when the vehicle in which she was a rear seat passenger suffered a rear end shunt. K sustained soft tissue injuries to both cheeks. She attended hospital and was diagnosed as having suffered concussion. The tenderness of the cheeks subsided after a week. K's most significant injury was psychiatric. When examined seven months after the accident it was found that K had, since the accident, experienced nightmares and general sleep disturbance approximately one night each week. The symptoms were continuing. K was also more cautious, aware and apprehensive of her surroundings when in similar situations to those of the accident. K's ability to enjoy physical activities had been marred by such feelings. Her examining expert considered the symptoms to be minor in nature, not amounting to post traumatic stress disorder and that they would gradually resolve over a 12 month period from the date of the accident, which they did. The judge found that the psychiatric injury fell within the lower part of the JSB Guidelines (7th Edition) category 3(A)(d), although not at the very bottom of that bracket. *General Damages* (approved and agreed): £1,250.

K (A CHILD) v. BOYE-DOE, October 8, 2004, District Judge Silverman, CC (Edmonton). [*Ex rel.* Joanna Kerr, Barrister, Lamb Chambers, Lamb Building, Temple, London].

Minor injuries

3224.   J, male, aged 46 at the date of the accident and 49 at trial, sustained injuries as a result of an accident during the course of his employment as a warehouse operative. He struck his right testicle on an obstruction at work, suffering swelling and bruising to his right testicle and inside the scrotum. J was in significant pain for the first three weeks after the accident and lesser discomfort thereafter until 12 weeks after the accident. The bruising and swelling settled after three weeks. He took pain killers on a daily basis for about eight weeks. He did not take any time off work, but worked on light duties for several weeks. His sleep was disturbed for several weeks by the pain. He made a full recovery from the injury after 12 weeks. *General Damages*: £1,200.

JOHNSON v. STEELITE INTERNATIONAL PLC, April 15, 2004, District Judge Schroder, CC (Stoke on Trent). [*Ex rel.* Adam Farrer, Barrister, 5, Fountain Court, Steelhouse Lane, Birmingham].

Minor injuries

3225.   C, a boy, aged 10 at the date of the road traffic accident and at the child assessment approval hearing, sustained injuries in a collision involving the car in which he was a front seat passenger. After the impact C felt pain in his left non dominant arm and left knee, and developed a headache over his left eye. He was taken to hospital where X rays of the left arm and neck revealed no fractures. C was discharged with advice to take painkillers as necessary, which he took for three days. By the third day following the accident C had no further headache symptoms and after a week his knee pain had resolved. The majority of the left arm pain dissipated within three weeks but when examined eight weeks after the accident some tenderness was detected in the left arm area. This residual mild tenderness resolved completely within three months of the accident, marginally more quickly than expected. *General Damages* (agreed and approved): £1,200.

P (A CHILD) v. PARKER, November 8, 2004, District Judge Nicholson, CC (West London). [*Ex rel.* Joanna Kerr, Barrister, Lamb Chambers, Lamb Building, Temple, London].

Minor injuries

3226.   J, female aged 63 at the date of the road traffic accident and 65 at trial, suffered a whiplash injury of the cervical spine, bruising to her left shoulder and some psychological injury. Neck pain developed by the next morning, stiffness and discomfort resolving by two to three weeks. Shoulder pain began immediately after the accident. A large bruise developed thereafter. Pain and bruising in the shoulder resolved by four to five weeks. As J was going on holiday, she did not see her GP, but did take painkillers intermittently for two to three weeks. Despite being in some discomfort, she was able to carry on with her housework. Psychologically, J was badly shocked and shaken by the accident. She was unable to sleep for two nights. She had vivid recall of the accident for one week. She became nervous when travelling as a passenger in a car. This anxiety lasted a few weeks. *General Damages*: £1,100 (apportioned £800 for the whiplash injury, £150 for the shoulder injury and £150 for the psychological injury).

JONES v. PATNELL, September 20, 2004, District Judge Glasner, CC (Edmonton). [*Ex rel.* Gurion Taussig, Barrister, 199 Strand, London].

Minor injuries

3227.   M, a boy, aged three at the date of the accident and six at the child settlement approval hearing, suffered personal injury in a head on collision road traffic accident. Immediately after the accident M felt shaken and tearful. He reported feeling pain in his thoracic area where the seat belt had tightened on impact and he suffered some minor cuts to his trunk and face. M was taken to hospital where was was diagnosed as having suffered a soft tissue seat belt bruising injury to his thoracic area and superficial cuts to the face and trunk. M's mother was advised to administer Calpol for pain relief. The thoracic injury affected M's ability to reach or carry objects. He also had difficulty when lying on his front at night. The cuts to M's face and trunk settled within two weeks. The thoracic injury settled within one month. M also suffered symptoms of situation specific travel anxiety. He was particularly anxious in situations comparable to the accident. These symptoms settled six months after the accident. *General Damages*: £1,000.

M (A CHILD) v. ALI, June 9, 2004, District Judge Cole, CC (Birmingham). [*Ex rel.* Stephen Garner, Barrister, No 8 Chambers, Fountain Court, Steelhouse Lane, Birmingham].

Minor injuries

3228.   C, a girl, aged eight at the date of the accident and nine at the child settlement approval hearing, suffered injuries in a rear end shunt road traffic accident. Immediately after the accident C was shocked and shaken. She experienced the immediate onset of pain down the back of her neck and across her abdomen, where she had been restrained by a seat belt. A diagnosis of a whiplash injury to the neck and minor seat belt bruising was made at hospital. C's neck pain had fully settled within 24 hours of the accident and so had the bruising to the abdomen caused by the seat belt. The most significant injury suffered by C was her psychological travel anxiety. She became a nervous passenger and did not like travelling at speed of over 40 mph. The symptoms of travel anxiety resolved within seven months of the accident. C was not absent from school on account of her injuries. *General Damages*: £1,000.

A (A CHILD) v. GURU, November 1 2004, Deputy District Judge Harris, CC (Coventry). [*Ex rel.* Stephen Garner, Barrister, No.8 Chambers, Fountain Court, Steelhouse Lane, Birmingham].

Minor injuries

3229.   R, a boy aged 12 at the date of the road traffic accident and 13 at the date of the child settlement approval hearing, sustained injuries when the car in which he was a passenger was involved in a collision. He was shocked and distressed and immediately complained of lower abdominal pain where he had been thrown against the lap strap of his seatbelt. The pain resolved soon afterwards. He also sustained a hyperflexion hyperextension whiplash type injury to the cervical spine. Pain and stiffness developed over the next day of two and during this time his sleep was disturbed and he experienced cervicogenic headaches. Neck pain resolved within two weeks. R also suffered psychological trauma and was nervous as a passenger. The travel anxiety resolved after about a month. *General Damages* (agreed and approved): £800.

R (A CHILD) v. NURSE, August 18, 2004, District Judge Evans, CC (Ipswich). [*Ex rel.* Gurion Taussig, Barrister, 199 Strand, London].

Minor injuries

3230. C, female, aged three at the date of the accident and four at the date of the child settlement approval hearing, was involved in a rear end shunt road traffic accident. Immediately after the accident C was shocked and crying. She was taken to hospital by her parents and whilst in accident and emergency, C, who suffered from Down's Syndrome, began clutching at her chest and signing towards her chest. On examination by a casualty officer, a red, inflamed area of skin was noticed running across C's chest. A diagnosis of seat belt bruising was made. The seat belt bruising settled within two days of the accident. C remained shocked, tearful and off her food for 72 hours after the event. C also suffered from noticeable travel anxiety after the accident. For the first week, she became reluctant to get into the family car. She had to be coaxed into the car by her parents who noted that she appeared nervous and agitated as a passenger. For one to two months after the event, C kept wanting to get out of the car. C's symptoms of travel anxiety completely resolved within three months of the accident. C was absent from nursery on account of her injuries for one week. She also missed several swimming lessons during the same period. *General Damages*: £750.

C (A CHILD) v. FORREST, February 16, 2004, District Judge Marston, CC (Worcester). [*Ex rel.* Stephen Garner, Barrister, No 8 Chambers, Fountain Court, Steelhouse Lane, Birmingham].

Minor injuries

3231. B, a boy, aged three at the date of the road traffic accident and five at the child settlement approval hearing, was shocked and upset immediately after the accident. B saw his GP the following day and was referred to hospital. B was diagnosed as having a soft tissue injury to the right shoulder and mid thoracic region posteriorly. He was discharged without any formal treatment. For the following two weeks B had general aches and pains, which did not disrupt his everyday activities. B was examined by an orthopaedic surgeon six months after the accident when he was judged to have recovered completely from his physical injuries. B also developed mild travel anxiety and was reluctant to travel in a car for one month after the accident. He had intrusive thoughts about the incident for up to two months after the accident and had some minor sleep disturbance. On examination by a psychologist 11 months after the accident it was found that the duration of significant accident related nervous symptoms was between one and two months. *General Damages* (agreed and approved): £750.

B (A CHILD) v. GALWAY, July 5, 2004, Deputy District Judge Liston, CC (Croydon). [*Ex rel.* Mathew Gullick, Barrister, 3, Paper Buildings, Temple, London].

Minor injuries

3232. B, male, aged two at the date of the road traffic accident and five at the assessment of damages hearing, was in the front passenger seat, wearing a seat belt, when the car was involved in a side impact collision. B was shocked and distressed by the accident. He was checked by paramedics at the scene, but did not attend hospital. After the accident, B immediately complained of pain in his left arm and left thigh and he subsequently developed bruising in those areas. This caused him obvious pain for four days after the accident which made him irritable and restless. He was given Calpol during this period to relieve the pain. For four days after the accident, he also had considerable sleep disturbance and nightmares. He had not had any problems sleeping prior to the accident. B attended at his GP surgery five days after the accident and was advised that the bruising would disappear within a few days. All B's symptoms resolved fully by one week after the accident. In her judgment, the District Judge stated that B's physical injuries were at the lower end of the scale and more to the point were the obvious distress and the nightmares suffered by such a young child. *General Damages*: £625.

B (A CHILD) v. B, November 9, 2004, District Judge Burgess, CC (Maidstone). [*Ex rel.* Mathew Gullick, Barrister, 3 Paper Buildings, Temple, London].

Minor injuries

3233.   G, a boy, aged 16 months at the date of the accident and three and a half years at the child settlement approval hearing, suffered soft tissue bruising to both sides of his neck as a result of being restrained by the straps of his child seat during a road traffic accident. The bruising on the neck lasted for about one to two weeks. G was psychologically upset for about two weeks. During that period he became upset when travelling by car and was quiet and withdrawn at home and at nursery. G fully recovered two weeks after the accident. *General Damages* (agreed and approved): £600.

G (A CHILD) v. HYNES, November 4, 2004, District Judge Rodgers, CC Doncaster. [*Ex rel.* Tom Nossiter, Barrister, Park Lane Chambers, Leeds].

Minor injuries

3234.   SJ and SV, a boy and a girl aged nine and 11 respectively at the date of the road traffic accident and 11 and 12 respectively at the child settlement approval hearing, both sustained a minor neck strain, when the car in which he was a rear seat passenger and she was a front seat passenger was involved in a collision. SJ was immediately aware of pain in the posterior part of his neck, between C3 and C7 and SV was immediately aware of pain in the posterior part of her neck radiating into the upper thoracic spine. They both attended hospital on the day of the accident. SJ was given Nurofen for pain relief and made a full recovery within one week of the accident. SV's symptoms settled within three days. *General Damages* (agreed and approved): £250 (for SJ) and £250 (for SV).

S (CHILDREN) v. TURNEY, September 7, 2004, District Judge McCullock, CC (Staines). [*Ex rel.* Gurion Taussig, Barrister, 199 Strand, London].

Minor injuries–Neck: whiplash injury: no previous condition

3235.   N, male, aged 30 at the date of the accident and 31 at trial, sustained a whiplash injury when his stationary vehicle was jolted forward by 2 to 3ft by a rear end shunt despite the hand brake being on. N did not hit his head but his head was jerked forwards and backwards. After the accident N drove home to rest rather than continuing his journey to work. Although N woke up the next morning with an aching, stiff neck he felt able to return to work and did not take any further time off as a result of his injuries. The following day, N's neck was very sore, movement was restricted, and he also began to suffer from paraesthesiae in the hands and arms. On the third day after the accident N attended his GP and was advised to take analgesics. N's neck was stiff and painful for two weeks after the accident before resolving. He also suffered disturbed sleep for about a month after the accident, during which time he was a nervous driver. The paraesthesiae continued persistently for a month after the accident before reducing gradually and becoming limited to his hands. Upon examination four months after the accident these symptoms were only suffered twice daily for 10 minutes before settling spontaneously. The prognosis was for a recovery from the remaining paresthesiae within 7 to 10 months of the accident. *General Damages*: £1,000.

ANDREWS v. HILL, May 21, 2004, Deputy District Judge Glen, CC (Romford). [*Ex rel.* Joanna Kerr, Barrister, Lamb Chambers, Lamb Building, London].

Claims for death of parent

3236. [Fatal Accidents Act 1976.]

K1 and K2, girls, and K3 and K4, boys, aged 14, 11, 10 and 7 respectively at the date of their father's instantaneous death in a road traffic accident, and 17, 14, 13 and 11 respectively at the assessment hearing, sought damages for loss of dependency under the Fatal Accidents Act 1976. A global award of damages for loss of dependency was apportioned as between the widow and each child. Guidance was taken from Kemp and Kemp [Appendix 1 at 23-050], which made it clear that the longer the period to age 18 years the greater the loss to the child. The judge approved the apportionment of the sum of £27,000 (equivalent to 15.4 per cent of the global award) between the children, in the knowledge that all children continued to live with the widow who would use the major part of the award to support the family until the children each attained at least 18 years. *General Damages* (agreed and approved): K1 £3,500. K2 £6,000. K3 £7,500. K4 £10,000.

K (CHILDREN) v. FROST, July 21, 2004, District Judge Mills, CC (Romford). [*Ex rel.* David McHugh, Barrister, 1st Floor, 1 Essex Court Chambers, Temple, London].

Other fatal accident act claims

3237. [Law Reform (Miscellaneous Provisions) Act 1934; Fatal Accidents Act 1976; Human Rights Act 1998 Sch.1 Part I Art.8, Art.14.]

C sought damages under the Law Reform (Miscellaneous Provisions) Act 1934 and the Fatal Accidents Act 1976 after her cohabitant of two years was killed in a road traffic accident. There were three children of the family two of whom (M and L), aged 1 and 2 at the date of the death and 3 and 4 at the hearing, were natural children of the deceased; the eldest child (B), aged seven at the date of death and 10 at the hearing, was not. Because C, aged 33 at the date of the death and 35 at the hearing, had not been married to the deceased, she was neither entitled to an award of bereavement damages under the 1934 Act or the 1976 Act, nor was B entitled to a dependency claim despite having been treated as a child of the family. C pleaded that both Acts contravened the Human Rights Act 1998 Sch.1 Part I Art.8 and Art.14 by discriminating against unmarried couples living as though married and because the 1998 Act provided for the right to respect for family life, not confined to a nuclear family based on marriage. A settlement was reached whereby in principle it appeared that M had accepted, during negotiations, that the award of damages included an amount for both C's bereavement and for B's dependency. It was submitted that there should be no discrimination between the three children as all three were regarded as children of the family and that there should be a parity between the three children despite their differing ages on the basis that B was likely to be dependent upon his parents for longer than M and L since he had mild learning difficulties. Concessions were made in respect of the bereavement claim because it was accepted that the claim by a common law spouse may have been unsuccessful at first instance. C's dependency was agreed as being for life, with the children's being to age 16. All calculations were from the date of trial. The judge approved the settlement and accepted that C had recovered in respect of bereavement damages and that B should be entitled to a proportion of the dependency claim. The dependency claim of C and her children was agreed at £270,000 and property losses, bereavement damages and other ancillary matters were agreed at £70,000, with interest agreed at £10,000. *General Damages* (agreed and approved): £350,000 (apportioned as follows: C: £297,500 and £17,500 each to M, L and B).

CHIVERS v. METCALFE, June 16, 2004, Judge Harrison, QBD. [*Ex rel.* Graham Leigh Pfeffer & Co, Solicitors, Maple House, Haymarket Street, Bury].

3238. Books

Barrie, Peter–Personal Injury Law: Liability, Compensation, Procedure. Paperback: £69.00. ISBN 0 19 927571 8. Oxford University Press.

Butterworths Personal Injury Litigation Service: V. 74. Looseleaf/ring bound: £172.00. ISBN 1 4057 0653 8. Butterworths Law.

Dow, David; Lill, Jeff–Personal Injury and Clinical Negligence Litigation. Paperback: £24.95. ISBN 0 905835 83 2. Paperback: £25.95. ISBN 1 905391 08 0. The College of Law.

Hogarth, Andrew; Awadalla, Katherine–Butterworths Personal Injury Litigation Service. Paperback: £31.50. ISBN 0 406 97588 4. Butterworths Law.

Kemp and Kemp: Personal Injury Law, Practice and Procedure. Looseleaf / ring bound: £175.00. ISBN 0 421 90510 7. Sweet & Maxwell.

Langstaff, Brian; Buchan, Andrew; Latimer-Sayer, William–Personal Injury Schedules: Calculating Damages. Paperback: £82.00. ISBN 1 84592 053 8. Tottel Publishing.

Malleson, Andrew–Whiplash and Other Useful Illnesses. Paperback: £17.95. ISBN 0 7735 2994 2. McGill-Queen's University Press.

Marshall, David; McCarthy, Frances–APIL Personal Injury Law, Practice and Precedents. Hardback: £295.00. ISBN 0 85308 993 0. Jordans.

Nelson-Jones, Rodney–Butterworths Personal Injury Damages Statistics. Paperback: £35.00. ISBN 1 4057 1012 8. Butterworths Law.

Personal Injury Litigation-Issue 70. Looseleaf/ring bound: £162.00. ISBN 0 406 96373 8. Butterworths Law.

Solomon, Nicola; Middleton, Simon–Personal Injury Practice and Procedure. Paperback: £72.00. ISBN 0 421 87550 X. Sweet & Maxwell.

PERSONAL PROPERTY

3239. Reversionary interests–Bailors–Bailor's rights of recovery–Reversioner's entitlement to claim for damage to rolling stock in train derailment

The claimant (H) sought damages from the defendant (N) in respect of payments made by H's insurers for rolling stock damaged in a train derailment. H was the owner of rolling stock which was operated under a leasing agreement by a train operating company (G). N was the owner and operator of the railway track infrastructure, and had allowed G to use the railway network under the terms of a number of agreements. Two coaches were damaged beyond economic repair in the derailment and had subsequently been written off. The remaining coaches had been damaged and subsequently repaired at G's expense. N had admitted liability for negligence in that it had been aware of the dangerous condition of the rail at the accident site, but had failed to take adequate steps to reduce the danger. The joint material damage insurers made payments to G to reimburse them for the cost of repairing the damaged coaches and for the write off value of the two other coaches. The insurers sought to recover the payments from N in the name of H. H argued that (1) although it had only a reversionary interest, it was entitled to recover the repair costs and the write off value of the lost coaches in full, as a bailor with only a reversionary interest could recover in full all loss or damage in like manner to a bailee whether or not there was permanent injury to the reversionary interest; (2) the damage to the rolling stock constituted permanent injury and was thus within the scope of the reversioner's entitlement to claim.

Held, giving judgment for N, that (1) a bailor with no right to possession did not have coextensive rights of recovery to those of a bailee. It was well established that claims founded on a reversionary proprietary interest required proof of actual and permanent injury to the interest, *Mears v. L&SWR Co* (1862) 11 C.B. (N.S.) 1029 considered. (2) The issue of whether the injury was sufficiently permanent to constitute injury to a reversion was a question of fact, *Mayfair Property Co v. Johnston* [1894] 1 Ch. 508 and *Jones v. Llanrwst Urban DC* [1911] 1 Ch. 393 considered. Where the thing complained of would have continued indefinitely unless something was done about it, that would be sufficient to render the subject of complaint as something which was potentially permanent. Whether in consequence there was damage to the reversion involved a further question. If it could not be remedied or removed, it did so. If the subject of the complaint could be remedied, but it was nonetheless clear that no remedy would be forthcoming, the reversion was damaged. However, where the subject of complaint was in fact remedied or removed, as in the instant case, no cause of action accrued, *Candlewood Navigation Corp v. Mitsui Osk Lines (The Mineral Transporter and The Ibaraki Maru)* [1986] A.C. 1, [1985] C.L.Y. 2310 applied.

HSBC RAIL (UK) LTD v. NETWORK RAIL INFRASTRUCTURE LTD (FORMERLY RAILTRACK PLC), [2005] EWHC 403, [2005] 1 All E.R. (Comm) 689, David Steel, J., QBD (Comm).

3240. **Books**

Wood, Roderick J.; Cuming, Ronald C.C.; Walsh, Catherine—Personal Property Security Law. Paperback: £32.00. ISBN 1 55221 110 X. Irwin Law Inc.

PLANNING

3241. **Blight notices—Interests in land—Increase in annual rateable value limit**

TOWN AND COUNTRY PLANNING (BLIGHT PROVISIONS) (ENGLAND) ORDER 2005, SI 2005 406; made under the Town and Country Planning Act 1990 s.149, s.333. In force: April 1, 2005; £3.00.

The blight notice provisions in the Town and Country Planning Act 1990 enable persons holding certain interests in categories of land to require the appropriate authority to acquire their interest in the land. One of the interests in land which qualifies for protection is the interest of an owner-occupier of a hereditament where the annual value of the hereditament does not exceed such amount as may be prescribed by the Secretary of State. This Order, which revokes the Town and Country Planning (Blight Provisions) (England) Order 2000 (SI 2000 539), increases the annual value limit from £24,600 to £29,200 to take account of the rating revaluation in the year 2005.

3242. **Blight notices—Interests in land—Increase in annual rateable value limit— Wales**

TOWN AND COUNTRY PLANNING (BLIGHT PROVISIONS) (WALES) ORDER 2005, SI 2005 367 (W.33); made under the Town and Country Planning Act 1990 s.149, s.333; and the Local Government Finance Act 1988 s.143, s.147. In force: April 1, 2005; £3.00.

The blight notice provisions in the Town and Country Planning Act 1990 enable persons holding certain interests in categories of land to require the appropriate authority to acquire their interest in the land. One of the interests in land which qualifies for protection is an interest of an owner-occupier of a hereditament where the annual value of the hereditament does not exceed such amount as may be prescribed by the Secretary of State. The power to prescribe that amount, so far as exercisable in relation to Wales, is now vested in the National Assembly for Wales and, in the exercise of its powers, the National Assembly for Wales, by this Order, increases the annual value limit from £24,600 to £29,200 to take account of the rating revaluation in the year 2005. The Order also revokes the Town and Country Planning (Blight Provisions) (Wales) Order 2000 (SI 2000 1169 (W.94)).

3243. Building operations–Buildings–Mobile structure for agricultural storage–Meaning of "building" in s.55(1) Town and Country Planning Act 1990

[Town and Country Planning Act 1990 s.55(1).]

The applicant local authority sought an order for the removal of a mobile shed from land owned by the respondent (K). The structure comprised two chassis, each with a pair of wheels, bolted together, to which a towing connection could be made. It was used for the purposes of agricultural storage and housing chickens. The local authority submitted that the setting up of the shed was a "building operation" for the purposes of the Town and Country Planning Act 1990 s.55(1). K denied that the structure was a building.

Held, refusing the application, that the structure was not a building. The definition of "building" incorporated structures that would not ordinarily be considered as buildings, *Barvis v. Secretary of State for the Environment* (1971) 22 P. & C.R. 710, [1971] C.L.Y. 11383 applied. Each case turned on its own facts but the main factor was that the shed was not attached to the land and could be moved freely. Accordingly, the work done on site in assembling the structure was not a building operation.

TEWKESBURY BC v. KEELEY, [2004] EWHC 2594, [2005] J.P.L. 831, Jack, J., QBD.

3244. Canals–Compulsory acquisition of land–Ashby de la Zouch

LEICESTERSHIRE COUNTY COUNCIL (ASHBY DE LA ZOUCH CANAL EXTENSION) ORDER 2005, SI 2005 2786; made under the Transport and Works Act 1992 s.3, s.5, Sch.1 para.1, Sch.1 para.2, Sch.1 para.3, Sch.1 para.4, Sch.1 para.5, Sch.1 para.7, Sch.1 para.8, Sch.1 para.10, Sch.1 para.11, Sch.1 para.12, Sch.1 para.13, Sch.1 para.15, Sch.1 para.16, Sch.1 para.17. In force: October 8, 2005; £4.50.

This Order authorises Leicestershire County Council compulsorily to acquire land and construct works to restore to navigation a disused length of the Ashby de la Zouch Canal. The length to be restored extends from the current terminus of the Ashby Canal near Snarestone to Measham in the District of North West Leicestershire.

3245. Caravan sites–Gypsies–Gypsies in breach of planning control–Propriety of decision to suspend injunction

[Town and Country Planning Act 1990 s.187B.]

The appellant local planning authority appealed against a decision to suspend the operation of an injunction restraining the defendants (B) from using land for residential purposes until the determination of a planning application by B. B had moved caravans and their families on to agricultural land bought by one of them in a green belt area and an area of great landscape value. They did so in breach of planning control and after the local authority had obtained an ex parte injunction to restrain the occupiers of the land, where hard core was being laid down, from causing or permitting entry on to the land of any caravan or mobile home and from using the land for residential purposes. The local authority had sought an injunction under the Town and Country Planning Act 1990 s.187B to restrain the use as an unauthorised caravan site on the basis that it was necessary and expedient in the public interest to do so. B had applied for planning permission to use the land as a gypsy residential site. The local authority submitted that the judge had exercised his discretion incorrectly and that the injunction should only have been suspended for a reasonable period to enable B to move off the land.

Held, allowing the appeal, that the judge's decision to suspend the operation of the injunction pending the determination of the planning application did not take proper account of the vital role of the court in upholding the important principle that the orders of the court were meant to be obeyed and not ignored with impunity. Instead of even attempting to follow the correct procedure for challenging the ex parte injunction, B had pressed on with their plan as if no court order had ever been made in order to steal a march on the local authority and achieve the very state of affairs which the injunction was designed to prevent. The practical effect of suspending the injunction had been to allow B to change the use of the land and to retain the benefit of occupation with caravans for residential purposes in defiance of a court order properly served on them and explained to them. There was a real risk that suspension of the injunction would be perceived as condoning the breach and would send out the wrong signal to those tempted to do the same. It was appropriate to suspend the injunction for four weeks to give B a reasonable time in which to make arrangements to move their caravans and vehicles from the land.

MID-BEDFORDSHIRE DC v. BROWN, [2004] EWCA Civ 1709, [2005] 1 W.L.R. 1460, Lord Phillips of Worth Matravers, M.R., CA (Civ Div).

3246. Change of use—Museums—Flights offered to helicopter museum visitors— Use ancillary to aviation museum

M sought judicial review of decisions by the local authority, NS, not to take enforcement action in respect of helicopter flights carried out by a helicopter museum situated on neighbouring land. The flights had increased since the museum obtained planning permission in 1988 and M had complained to NS about the noise and dust levels they generated. The planning permission did not mention helicopter flights and the museum unsuccessfully applied for a certificate of lawfulness to use the site for that purpose. Reports to NS's planning committee recommended that flights for museum visitors should be permitted but that uncontrolled flights could prejudice developments in the area. NS decided that visitor experience flights and flights bringing people to the site were permissible ancillary uses that should be permitted, subject to future monitoring. M contended that NS had failed to determine whether the flights amounted to a material change of use and that the reports had failed to consider the impact of the flights on the neighbouring area.

Held, refusing the application, that the reports showed that NS had considered whether the two permitted uses were a material change of use. The functionality test, which identified activities that were not capable of being ancillary uses and cleared the way for determining whether the activities in issue amounted to material changes of use, was not wrong in principle, *Harrods Ltd v. Secretary of State for the Environment, Transport and the Regions* [2002] EWCA Civ 412, [2002] J.P.L. 1258 considered. NS's conclusion that the two uses were ancillary was not irrational as they were reasonably incidental to transport and aviation museums. That conclusion was reached on the basis of the current level of activity and was subject to further monitoring to prevent intensification.

R. (ON THE APPLICATION OF I'M YOUR MAN LTD) v. NORTH SOMERSET COUNCIL, [2004] EWHC 342, [2004] 4 P.L.R. 1, Forbes, J., QBD (Admin Ct).

3247. Change of use—Planning permission—Proposed development of crematorium and cemetery on green belt land

The claimant developer (K) applied for judicial review of a decision of a planning inspector, appointed by the first defendant secretary of state, dismissing its appeal against a refusal of planning permission by the second defendant local authority. K wanted to develop a green belt site for use as a cemetery and crematorium. The development would have resulted in part of the site no longer being used as a sports ground and playing fields. The planning application was a full application for the change of use of the site, but in other respects it was an application for outline planning permission only, limited to siting and means of access. The inspector had decided that (i) the development was inappropriate development in the green belt; (ii) it would be injurious to the green belt; (iii) justification for the loss of the playing fields had not been demonstrated; and (iv) there were no very special circumstances that outweighed the presumption against inappropriate development. He stated that crematoria were not appropriate development in the green belt, that the viability of the proposal depended on the provision of a crematorium, and that the secretary of state had earlier dismissed an appeal for a chapel and crematorium on the same site. K submitted that (1) the inspector's reasons for determining that the proposed development was inappropriate were either wrong or irrelevant, and ignored the fact that the crematorium was merely a small element in the proposed development; (2) the inspector had wrongly thought that the only circumstance advanced by K as outweighing the presumption against inappropriate development was the need, locally, for disposal of the dead, and he had failed to consider whether K had robustly assessed the need for the retention of the playing fields; (3) to the extent that Planning Policy Guidance 17 para.10 (PPG 17) required the developer to show that its proposals were widely supported by the local community, that requirement was unlawful.

Held, refusing the application, that (1) the inspector's conclusion that the proposed development was inappropriate development within the green belt was not flawed. The question of whether the proposed development was injurious to the green belt had formed part of his reasoning. It was not right to say that the inspector had not considered whether the use of the land as a crematorium was a use that preserved the openness of the green belt. The relative importance of the crematorium to the success of the proposed development was not a discrete part of his reasoning. His comment on the importance of the provision of a crematorium for the viability of the proposal was only laying the ground for his view that it was the crematorium, rather than the cemetery, that would contribute particularly to the intensity of the use of the site, which was one of the factors that would cause a reduction in the openness of the site and an encroachment into the countryside. The inspector did not have to consider whether the building housing the chapels would be an essential facility for the cemetery if he concluded that the proposed development amounted to a use of the land that did not preserve the openness of the green belt. He had to be regarded as saying merely that the earlier appeal dismissed by the secretary of state lent weight to the proposition that a crematorium, whether accompanied by a cemetery or not, would be inappropriate development within the green belt. It was entirely appropriate for the inspector to approach the earlier appeal in that way. (2) The nature of the assessment required under para.10 of PPG 17 was one that addressed the question of whether the site could be used for a purpose other than playing fields in a way that preserved its essential feature as open space. The comprehensive assessment that K had commissioned on the need for the playing fields to continue to be used as such did not address that question. It followed that the criticism that the inspector had failed to consider whether K had robustly assessed the need for the retention of the playing fields missed the point. It was open to the inspector to conclude that the absence of such an assessment was something to which considerable weight should be attached. The inspector could not be criticised for regarding as significant the fact that the surveys commissioned by K did not seek public opinion on the scheme as an alternative to the playing fields. (3) PPG 17 gave guidance only and it was for the local planning authority, and for the inspector on an appeal, to decide what weight to attach to the absence of local community support, bearing in mind the guidance that a proposal should not be permitted to proceed without it. The guidance in para.10 of PPG 17 that developers should show that their proposals were widely supported by the local community was lawful.

KEMNAL MANOR MEMORIAL GARDENS LTD v. FIRST SECRETARY OF STATE, [2004] EWHC 2638, [2005] 2 P. & C.R. 12, Keith, J., QBD (Admin).

3248.   Compulsory purchase–Compensation–Claim for injurious affection based on breach of restrictive covenant–Calculation of diminution in value

[Compulsory Purchase Act 1965 s.10.]

The claimant (P) sought a determination as to his entitlement to compensation for injurious affection. P had purchased a property in Sidcup with the benefit of a covenant restricting development in the surrounding area. The local authority had initiated a town centre development scheme which included the building of a large supermarket nearby. Parcels of land subject to the covenant were compulsorily acquired and road alterations were carried out in connection with the scheme. P sold the house in 2003 for £260,000. P contended that he was entitled to compensation for a diminution in the value of his property on the basis that he would have achieved a further £20,000 on the sale, had the restrictive covenant not been breached by the local authority.

Held, giving judgment for the local authority, that there had been no diminution in the value of the property capable of giving rise to compensation for injurious affection under the Compulsory Purchase Act 1965 s.10. P had relied on national indices of house prices, which did not provide an accurate guide to local trends. Taking into account the regional analysis, the sale price that P had achieved indicated that the value of his property had not been diminished by the execution of the works.

PUTTOCK v. BEXLEY LBC [2004] R.V.R. 216, PR Francis FRICS, Lands Tr.

3249. **Compulsory purchase–Compensation–Deduction to reflect time owner of failing business could have devoted to other activities–Procedural impropriety**

F appealed against a Lands Tribunal decision determining the amount of compensation payable following the compulsory acquisition of his estate agency premises. F had progressively transferred the business to other premises, but the business had declined and he ceased trading three years before the acquisition. The compensation included additional profits that would have been earned in the absence of the acquisition, subject to a deduction to represent the time F could have spent on other business activities. However, the deduction was made by the tribunal without reference to F.

Held, allowing the appeal, that it was procedurally unfair to make the deduction without giving the F the opportunity to adduce evidence on the matter. The amount deducted was added to the award because the tribunal had failed to consider the reasonableness of its actions by reference to F's working methods or the other activities he could have pursued. Further, the reasoning behind the deduction amounted to a finding that F had failed to mitigate his losses in the declining business but there was no evidence for such a finding.

FARADAY v. CARMARTHENSHIRE CC, [2004] EWCA Civ 649, [2004] 2 E.G.L.R. 5, Peter Gibson, L.J., CA.

3250. **Compulsory purchase–Compensation–Determination of planning assumptions–Site subject to certificate of specified purposes–Residential development, parking and access issues**

Planning assumptions to be used in assessing compensation for the compulsory purchase a 0.67 hectare site comprising part of a larger 1.67 hectare site overlooking the River Tyne fell to be determined as a preliminary issue. Except for a grade II listed building the site had been cleared by the valuation date of May 29, 2000 and was subject to a certificate of specified purposes, which included a residential development and highway improvements. Listed building consent was obtained for the demolition of the building subsequent to the valuation date and the owner (N) argued that a residential development up to eight storeys in height would be appropriate. The local authority asserted that greater parking provision was needed than allowed for by N and that it was unnecessary to adopt the site access road, although this would add to the volume of traffic using a junction leading to the site.

Held, giving judgment, that compensation should be assessed on the assumption that planning permission would have been obtained for the residential development but without an assumption that listed building consent would be granted as retention formed the basis of the certificate of specified purposes and no appeal was envisaged on the valuation date. Although the local authority had stated that additional parking was needed on the basis of one for every three resident spaces, parking would be assumed only on the basis of one 2.5 metre by 5 metre space per resident, based on the central location of the site, the guidance given in draft PPG13 and the unitary development plan. The issues surrounding the access road, which included a strip of land of unknown ownership, were only relevant to valuation and not planning assumptions. Traffic generated by the development would be sufficient to justify a contribution of £40,000 toward junction improvements.

NOMAD DEVELOPMENTS LTD v. GATESHEAD BC [2005] R.V.R. 187, George Bartlett Q.C. (President), Lands Tr.

3251. Compulsory purchase–Compensation–Industrial unit used for car dismantling and spare parts storage–Failure to mitigate loss

[Compulsory Purchase Act 1965 s.20(1).]

The claimant (M) sought compensation for the compulsory purchase of his leasehold interest in an industrial unit used for car dismantling and repairs and for the storage of used vehicle spares. M sought compensation for the costs and losses caused by the enforced relocation to nearby alternative premises, totalling £129,428.43.

Held, giving judgment, that (1) the disputed heads of claim fell to be decided on the basis of causation, remoteness and duty to mitigate, *Director of Buildings and Lands v. Shun Fung Ironworks Ltd* [1995] 2 A.C. 111, [1995] C.L.Y. 664 applied. (2) As at the valuation date of January 30, 1996, the lease could have been determined on June 30, 1996 and M's interest in the premises was to be valued on the basis that the lease would have terminated on that date, *Bishopsgate Space Management Ltd v. London Underground Ltd* [2004] 2 E.G.L.R. 175, [2004] C.L.Y. 3207 and *Greenwoods Tyre Services Ltd v. Manchester Corp* (1972) 23 P. & C.R. 246, [1972] C.L.Y. 410 considered. (3) Although compensation for the market value of the acquired land and compensation for disturbance was to be assessed separately, the two elements combined to give the value of the land to M, *Hughes v. Doncaster MBC* [1991] 1 A.C. 382, [1991] C.L.Y. 453 followed. (4) The evidence showed that the defendant had tried to assist M in relocating his business and that he had failed to mitigate his loss. M could have continued in business on a temporary basis from an alternative site and in the circumstances the compensation payable to him was £26,520.

MYERS v. SOUTH LAKELAND DC [2004] R.V.R. 279, PR Francis FRICS, Lands Tr.

3252. Compulsory purchase–Compensation–Leasehold shop–Total extinguishment of business–Calculation of post possession loss to retail chain business

The applicant (O) sought compensation for the compulsory purchase of a leasehold shop forming part of a retail development in Birmingham city centre. O owned a chain of shops. The compulsory purchase order was made in January 1999 and the local authority (B) took possession in April 2000. The parties agreed the value of O's leasehold interest in the property and that O's consequential loss should be calculated on a total extinguishment basis. However, the loss of profit calculation was disputed, with O claiming that there had been a decline in turnover in the previous year due to building works, the nearby vacant premises and short lets to inferior business. B argued that the scheme had not caused the decline in turnover, except for the last three months of trade. Further, there was a dispute regarding post possession loss of profits. O and B agreed that compensation for disturbance should be assessed on the value to O and O accepted that that should be calculated by the open market value of the business. It was agreed that this loss should be assessed by the earnings multiple approach, disregarding the planned development. O submitted that this loss should be calculated based primarily on estimated annual branch contribution to O's profits. O further argued that it should be calculated on the capitalisation of the estimated post tax contribution made by the branch by price earning multiples of 11.2 to 12.6. B argued that the post possession loss should be calculated using the capitalisation of the estimated maintainable branch contribution without deduction of interest, tax, depreciation and amortisation (EBITDA) method multiplied by 4.9 or 5.9. O agreed that this was a valid basis to assess the loss and also that other factors should be considered, including earnings multiples for similar companies in the same or similar sectors, earning multiples in transactions in the same or similar sectors with a discount applied to multiples for private companies.

Held, giving judgment accordingly, that the compulsory purchase order had not resulted in a decline in trade in the area but was rather a consequence of the area's decline. Whilst the building work was part of the scheme it only began in the last three months of O's trading and it was unlikely that the vacant shops affected trading until those last three months. Therefore the evidence showed a decline in the last three months of trading that was attributable to the scheme and therefore compensation was payable for that period only. The post possession loss was to be calculated on the basis suggested by B. The compensation should place O in the position it would have been in had its premises not being compulsorily purchased, subject to its satisfying the conditions of causation, remoteness and mitigation. The compensation could include future loss of profit but this was to be calculated from the valuation date. There were flaws in O's revised calculation method in that it required assumptions regarding future earnings for which there was inadequate evidence. The calculation breached the principle of equivalence because it allowed no discount to ensure the loss was as at the date of dispossession. O's original approach to capitalisation based on branch contribution with that adjusted was preferred. EBITDA was the most appropriate method as it had a wider comparable base and it was likely that a price/earnings multiple would lead to distortions because it took into account the effects of funding and taxation.

OPTICAL EXPRESS (SOUTHERN) LTD v. BIRMINGHAM CITY COUNCIL [2005] 2 E.G.L.R. 141, PH Clarke, FRICS, LandsTr.

3253. **Compulsory purchase–Compensation–Limitations–Notice of reference received over six years from date possession taken of site**

[Limitation Act 1980 s.9(1).]

The respondent local authority (B) argued that a claim for compensation for the compulsory acquisition of a quarry was statute barred under the Limitation Act 1980 s.9(1). The notice of reference was received from the claimant (W) on January 6, 2004 and B asserted that possession was taken of the site on a date prior to October 9, 1996. The matter fell to be determined as a preliminary issue.

Held, giving judgment for B, that the evidence showed that B took possession at some time prior to October 9, 1996 so that W's claim was made after the expiry of the six year limitation period in an action to recover money. An adjournment sought by W's solicitor was refused as the matter it related was not such that agreement could have been reached between W and B, with the result that B could not have been prevented from advancing its limitation claim.

WOOLHOUSE v. BARNSLEY MBC [2005] R.V.R. 178, George Bartlett Q.C. (President), LandsTr.

3254. **Compulsory purchase–Compensation–Ransom value–Highways improvements**

[Land Compensation Act 1961 s.5(3).]

The applicant company (P) applied for the calculation of compensation for the compulsory purchase of its land. The land, totalling 270 square metres, had been acquired for a road widening scheme. P contended that the land had a ransom value of £1,550,000 as it was required for access to adjoining housing land, and that that value existed independently of the road widening scheme. The local authority argued that the land only had a nominal value in the "no scheme world" and that any additional value was entirely attributable to the scheme and therefore fell to be disregarded.

Held, allowing the application in part, that the compensation payable for the land was £1,139,000. The scheme underlying the acquisition included both the road widening work and the formation of an access road to the adjoining housing site. The scheme came into existence in July 1990 when the local authority passed its first resolution to compulsorily purchase the land. The "no scheme world" was the same as the real world at the valuation date, except that no road widening scheme existed and the local authority did not have compulsory purchase powers over the land. The suitability of the land for the highway works giving access to the housing site could be taken into account in the valuation as no statutory powers were needed for those works; therefore the Land Compensation Act 1961 s.5(3) did not apply. The land did have a ransom value which would have been recognised by potential developers of the housing site.

PERSIMMON HOMES (WALES) LTD v. RHONDDA CYNON TAFF CBC [2005] R.V.R. 59, PH Clarke, FRICS, Lands Tr.

3255. **Compulsory purchase–Compensation–Vacant and derelict block of flats– Evidence of value**

[Lands Tribunal Act 1949 s.3(5).]

The applicant (C) sought compensation in respect of the compulsory purchase of a block of flats. C contended that the flats were worth £110,000. The respondent local authority argued that they were worth nothing due to their location in a run down area and their derelict condition, which meant that the cost of refurbishment outweighed any value the property might accrue. There was no demand locally either to purchase or let the flats. C argued that the tribunal should exercise its discretion under the Lands Tribunal Act 1949 s.3(5) and award costs in his favour on the grounds that it was not unreasonable for him to have pursued the matter and tested the evidence given the nil valuation. C also argued that the local authority had prolonged the proceedings unnecessarily.

Held, giving judgment for the local authority, that the valuation had to take account of the fact that the property was vacant, derelict and seriously vandalised. It was located in the middle of a large council estate suffering from severe social problems and there was no evidence that the site would be of interest to a private development. It was unlikely that the individual flats could be either sold or let. Nominal compensation of £1 was awarded. Costs were awarded to the local authority as the claim had failed and there were no exceptional circumstances to allow a departure from the usual principle.

COHEN v. KNOWSLEY MBC [2005] R.V.R. 40, PR Francis FRICS, Lands Tr.

3256. **Compulsory purchase–Compensation–Valuation of sheltered housing development on basis of single sale–No compensation for loss of profit**

[Land Compensation Act 1961 s.5(6).]

R appealed against a Lands Tribunal decision ([2003] R.V.R. 49, [2003] C.L.Y. 3370), awarding compensation of £2.06 million for the compulsory purchase of the freehold of a sheltered housing development. The development comprised 37 flats and 5 bungalows, which the tribunal held should be valued on the basis of a sale to a single purchaser with no allowance for loss of profits under the Land Compensation Act 1961 s.5(6). R argued that the valuation should have been based on the sale of separate properties, with compensation valued at £2.4 million.

Held, dismissing the appeal, that valuation on the basis of a single sale was correct in the instant case. Although R had been denied the profit of the sale of each property, it had avoided the attendant risk that some properties would have remained unsold. Further, the additional value attributable to separate sales was based on land value and therefore excluded from s.5(6).

RYDE INTERNATIONAL PLC v. LONDON REGIONAL TRANSPORT, [2004] EWCA Civ 232, [2004] 2 E.G.L.R. 1, Sir Andrew Morritt V.C., CA.

3257. **Compulsory purchase–Compensation–Vehicular access to landfill site– Planning permission for extension and additional tipping on original site**

S sought compensation for the compulsory purchase of a piece of land required to improve access to a waste disposal tip operated by the local authority. The tip had planning permission for an extension and for additional tipping on the original site, subject to the access works being carried out. S contended that the development value of the tip was £8.4 million on a residual valuation basis, with an overall ransom value of 50 per cent of that sum. The authority gave a development value of £828,000, based on a comparable sale three years prior to the valuation date, with a ransom value of 30 per cent on the grounds that there were alternative highway routes, that there was competition for tipping and that the number of ransomers reduced the total ransom value.

Held, giving judgment, that S was entitled to compensation of £660,000, representing 60 per cent of the total ransom value of £1,102,338. Hypothetical negotiators would have refused to consider widening the access route in the absence of planning permission for the extension or the viability of the alternative routes. Therefore, the ransom value was determined on the basis that there were no viable alternatives, and the existence of a number of ransomers did not mean that the local authority could expect to pay less than if it only had to negotiate with a single owner.

SNOOK v. SOMERSET CC [2005] 1 E.G.L.R. 147, George Bartlett Q.C. (President), Lands Tr.

3258. **Compulsory purchase–Property comprising commercial and residential accommodation–"house" for purposes of Housing Act 1985 s.17**

[Acquisition of Land Act 1981 s.23, s.24; Housing Act 1985 s.17(1)(b); Human Rights Act 1998 Sch.1 Part II Art.1.]

A challenged a compulsory purchase order made by W, a local authority, and the order's confirmation by the Secretary of State by way of an appeal under the Acquisition of Land Act 1981 s.23 and s.24. A owned a freehold property consisting of a four storey front building and a three storey rear building, separated by a courtyard. The ground floor and basement of the front part was used as a sex shop, the remainder for prostitution. An inspection by W revealed extensive structural problems. Although A asserted that it was planning to renovate the property, no work was undertaken. An inspector recommended that W issue a compulsory purchase order for the property, noting that purchase of the shop, which use could be retained, was only incidental to the overall purpose of increasing residential accommodation in the area. The order was confirmed by the Secretary of State. The four issues before the court were (1) whether compulsory purchase of the shop and its retention for retail use was permitted under the Housing Act 1985 s.17(1)(b); (2) whether the order was made as a last resort; (3) whether the Secretary of State's confirmation was supported by sufficient evidence and adequate reasoning, and (4) whether the order violated the rights of two purported tenants under the Human Rights Act 1998 Sch.1 Part II Art.1.

Held, dismissing the appeal, that (1) acquisition of the commercial part was incidental to the purchase of the residential part. The test was not one of absolute necessity, *Loweth v. Minister of Housing and Local Government* (1971) 22 P. & C.R. 125, [1971] C.L.Y. 1531 followed. The property was a "house" for the purpose of s.17(1)(b), *Butler, Re* [1939] 1 K.B. 570 followed. Once this decision was reached it was then necessary to determine if it was required for residential use, not whether each part of it was required for that purpose; (2) A did not intend to carry out any work on the property, despite detailed evidence of its inadequate condition, and the inspector had correctly concluded that it was necessary to acquire the commercial part to prevent problems occurring with a flying freehold or a repairing covenant; (3) the Secretary of State had given adequate reasons for confirming the order, and (4) it had not been shown that any tenancies existed but the order was in the public interest so that there had been no violation of Sch.1 Part II Art.1.

AINSDALE INVESTMENTS LTD v. FIRST SECRETARY OF STATE, [2004] EWHC 1010, [2004] H.L.R. 50, Owen, J., QBD (Admin Ct).

3259. **Conservation areas–Listed buildings–Compilation of lists**

PLANNING (LISTED BUILDINGS AND CONSERVATION AREAS) (AMENDMENT) (ENGLAND) REGULATIONS 2005, SI 2005 1085; made under the Planning (Listed Buildings and Conservation Areas) Act 1990 s.2, s.93. In force: May 1, 2005; £3.00.

These Regulations amend the Planning (Listed Buildings and Conservation Areas) Regulations 1990 (SI 1990 1519) to reflect the fact that the Secretary of State for Culture, Media and Sport is responsible for the compilation of lists of buildings of special architectural or historic interest under the Planning (Listed Buildings and Conservation Areas) Act 1990 s.1. It also amends the note to the prescribed form notifying the inclusion of a building in one of the lists and inserts a note to the prescribed form notifying the exclusion of a building.

3260. Development–Building operations–Commencement of development within time stipulated in consent–Nature of material operations

[Town and Country Planning Act 1990 s.56(4)(d).]

The appellant company (X) appealed against the decision of a planning inspector appointed by the respondent secretary of state that development pursuant to planning consent had not been commenced within the time stipulated by the consent. X also sought permission to apply for judicial review of the inspector's decision as to costs. Planning consent had been granted to X for the construction of a golf course. The consent stipulated that the permitted development had to be commenced within five years. Within that time X had pegged out an area of the site to establish the position of the boundary and had accurately pegged the eastern boundary of a private access road. The pegs had, however, been removed in order to prevent injury to horses grazing nearby. X had also stripped topsoil from an area of land in the vicinity of the approved access road and car park. X submitted that the inspector had erred in law in finding that neither of these operations amounted to a "material operation" within the meaning of the Town and Country Planning Act 1990 s.56(4)(d) and that development had not, therefore, begun on the site within the stipulated time.

Held, allowing the appeal, that (1) in finding that the pegging out was not a material operation for the purposes of s.56(4)(d) of the Act, the inspector had misdirected himself. Having decided that the main objective of the pegging out was to determine the sufficiency of land within X's ownership, he had failed to take sufficient account of his finding that the eastern boundary of the road had been accurately pegged. Having made that finding of fact he ought to have gone on to consider whether such pegging out was capable of satisfying s.56(4)(d) of the Act. Furthermore, the inspector had erred in law in seeming to be influenced by the view that, as a precondition of the operation being a material one within the meaning of s.56(4)(d), there had to be a degree of permanence in the nature of the pegging out, *Malvern Hills DC v. Secretary of State for the Environment* 81 L.G.R. 13, [1983] C.L.Y. 3722 followed. (2) The inspector had correctly directed himself in law that the stripping of the topsoil had to relate to a recognisable feature of the approved development and that the start of operations had to bear some relationship to the approved development on any objective basis if it were to be considered a material operation. However, he ought to have focused on the similarities as well as the differences between the work undertaken and that authorised, *Commercial Land Ltd v. Secretary of State for Transport, Local Government and the Regions* [2002] EWHC 1264, [2003] J.P.L. 358, [2003] C.L.Y. 3430 followed. Moreover, material consideration had to be given to whether the operations relied on had sustained usability in the context of the permitted development. There was evidence to indicate that the stripping of the topsoil did relate to a recognisable feature of the approved development, namely the access road, and was, in part at least, substantially usable for the proposed development. The inspector had failed to give proper reasons for his conclusion that the topsoil stripping was "haphazard scratching over an undefined random area" and, as such, was not sufficient to amount to a material operation. (3) The question of costs was underpinned by the inspector's decision letter. Since the decision letter could not stand it was appropriate to grant permission for judicial review and to remit the question of costs to the inspector for further consideration.

AER LINK LEISURE LTD (IN LIQUIDATION) v. FIRST SECRETARY OF STATE; *sub nom.* R. (ON THE APPLICATION OF AERLINK LEISURE LTD (IN LIQUIDATION)) v. FIRST SECRETARY OF STATE, [2004] EWHC 3198, [2005] 2 P. & C.R. 15, Davis, J., QBD (Admin).

3261. Development–Enforcement notices–Crown immunity–Public private partnerships–Meaning of "by or on behalf of the Crown" in s.294(1) Town and Country Planning Act 1990

[Town and Country Planning Act 1990 s.294(1), s.299(1), s.299A.]

The appellant local planning authority appealed against a decision ([2004] EWHC 724, [2004] 2 P. & C.R. 27) refusing judicial review of the First Secretary's approval of Home Office proposals for the construction of an accommodation centre for asylum seekers. The instant appeal raised points of general importance in relation to the use of the non statutory procedure introduced by Department of Environment Circular 18/84 (Crown Land and Crown Development) in connection with public/private partnership development projects. The local authority challenged the First Secretary's decision that the instant development would clearly be development by the Crown. The local authority argued that (1) where, as in the instant case, development on Crown land was to be undertaken by a private contractor, occupying the development site by virtue of its own property interest under a lease, the development could not be development "by or on behalf of the Crown" within the meaning of the Town and Country Planning Act s.294(1); (2) as the development was not by or on behalf of the Crown it had not been open to the Home Office to invoke the non statutory planning procedure. A statutory application for planning permission should have been made under s.299(1) of the Act; (3) if a statutory application had been made the developer would have been subject to the statutory enforcement process.

Held, dismissing the appeal, that (1) in the circumstances the only conclusion that the First Secretary could have reached was that the development was to be carried out by or on behalf of the Crown. The accommodation centre was to be constructed and operated for the purposes of the Home Office. The existence of a private interest in land did not prevent it from being Crown land. Whether a development was "by or on behalf of the Crown" was a question of fact and degree, turning on the particular circumstances of each case, *Hillingdon LBC v. Secretary of State for the Environment, Transport and the Regions* [2000] Env. L.R. D11 approved. (2) It had been open to the Home Office to invoke either planning procedure. The statutory application procedure was not mandatory. (3) As the development was on behalf of the Crown, and the land would be Crown land at the time the development was carried out, the developer would be protected from enforcement proceedings by s.294(1) of the Act. This would have been so even if a statutory application for planning permission had been made. Enforcement against the developer would be possible, with the consent of the Home Office, within the terms of the planning obligations agreement entered into by the Home Office pursuant to s.299A of the Act.

R. (ON THE APPLICATION OF CHERWELL DC) v. FIRST SECRETARY OF STATE, [2004] EWCA Civ 1420, [2005] 1 W.L.R. 1128, Chadwick, L.J., CA (Civ Div).

3262. Enforcement notices–Aircraft–Hanger within curtilage of dwelling house– Purpose incidental to enjoyment of dwelling house

The appellant (H) appealed against a planning inspector's decision concerning two enforcement notices issued in relation to an aircraft hanger on H's land. H owned four aircraft. The outbuildings within the curtilage of H's dwelling house included a barn used for housing one of the aircraft and a hanger used for housing the other three aircraft. The inspector found that the provision of the hanger was for a purpose incidental to the enjoyment of the dwelling house. H contended, amongst other things, that the inspector had erred in law by applying the test of whether an activity was one that was reasonably incidental to the enjoyment of dwelling houses generally, rather than whether it was incidental to the enjoyment of his particular dwelling house.

Held, dismissing the appeal, that there had been no error of law. The inspector had had regard to the normal use of a dwelling house and had then gone on to consider whether the hanger accommodating the three aircraft could, as a matter of fact and degree, be for a purpose incidental to the enjoyment by H of his particular dwelling house. This was the correct approach and the inspector had applied an objective test of reasonableness, *Wallington v. Secretary of State for Wales* (1991) 62 P. & C.R. 150, [1992] C.L.Y. 4162 and *Emin v. Secretary of State for the Environment and Mid Sussex CC* (1989) 58 P. & C.R. 416, [1990] C.L.Y. 4357 applied.

HOLDING v. FIRST SECRETARY OF STATE, [2003] EWHC 3138, [2004] J.P.L. 1405, Harrison, J., QBD (Admin Ct).

3263. **Enforcement notices—Change of use—Tenancy for more than 90 days interrupted use as temporary sleeping accommodation**

[Town and Country Planning Act 1990 s.171B(3), s.191(2), s.191(2); Greater London Council (General Powers) Act 1973 s.25.]

The appellant flat owner (F) appealed against a decision ([2004] EWHC 1807, [2005] J.P.L. 369) dismissing F's appeal against an enforcement notice alleging that without planning permission there had been a change of use of the flat from permanent residential accommodation to use for short term letting purposes as temporary sleeping accommodation within the meaning of the Greater London Council (General Powers) Act 1973 s.25. The flat had been used for more than ten years before January 1999 as temporary sleeping accommodation as defined in s.25 of the 1973 Act in breach of planning control. Then in February 1999 a tenant had taken a series of back to back tenancies lasting for a total period of 155 days, thereby exceeding the 90 day period mentioned in s.25 for temporary sleeping accommodation. Thereafter the flat was again let as temporary sleeping accommodation. The local authority issued an enforcement notice and F appealed to the inspector who held that the back to back tenancies for a period of more than 90 days in 1999 caused a break in the claimed period of letting for less than 90 days, and that the resumption of short term lettings thereafter was a fresh change of use within s.25 for which there was no planning permission. Therefore F could not show that there was a ten year period since the breach of planning control which would prevent enforcement action being taken by virtue of the Town and Country Planning Act 1990 s.171B(3), s.191(2). F submitted that the judge's decision was in conflict with the rationale of fairness which underlay the ten-year time limit on enforcement and that the accrued planning use right which arose after the first ten years use as temporary sleeping accommodation could only be lost by abandonment or a material change of use which the inspector did not find.

Held, dismissing the appeal, that (1) by virtue of the first ten years use as temporary sleeping accommodation that became a lawful use by virtue of s.191(2) of the 1990 Act. The inspector did not find that the back to back tenancies for some five months amounted to a material change of use. Therefore that use was not to be treated as development which required planning permission and, but for s.25 of the 1973 Act, the five month interruption of over 14 years of use as temporary sleeping accommodation would ordinarily be insufficient to destroy that accrued right. If s.25 did have that destructive effect it would operate as an exception to the general rule. (2) The interruption of the sequence of short term occupations, represented by the occupation of the flat for a five month period, brought s.25 of the 1973 Act into play and recommencement of use for temporary sleeping accommodation was deemed to be a material change of use. The purpose of s.25 was to give the local authority a greater and easier means of planning control in order to enhance permanent residential accommodation in Greater London and restrict the random spread of temporary sleeping accommodation, *R. v. Kensington and Chelsea RLBC, ex p. Lawrie Plantation Services Ltd* [1999] 1 W.L.R. 1415, [1999]

C.L.Y. 4180 considered. Section 25 operated when an actual use as residential accommodation changed to actual use as temporary sleeping accommodation. The issue was not whether the intervening tenancy itself involved a material change from the previous lawful use. It was enough that the continuity of the sequence of short term occupations was broken. The moment the long term occupation of five months ceased and the pattern of short term occupations resumed there was "use as temporary sleeping accommodation of ... residential premises in Greater London" within s.25. That was deemed to be a material change of use and accordingly there was a breach of planning controls and the local authority was entitled to issue its enforcement notice.

FAIRSTATE LTD v. FIRST SECRETARY OF STATE; *sub nom.* R. (ON THE APPLICATION OF FAIRSTATE LTD) v. FIRST SECRETARY OF STATE, [2005] EWCA Civ 283, [2005] 2 P.L.R. 127, Ward, L.J., CA (Civ Div).

3264. Green belt–Planning permission–Caravan site for single gypsy family–Combination of factors constituting very special circumstances

The applicant local authority applied to quash a decision of the respondent secretary of state to grant retrospective planning permission for change of use of land in the green belt to a gypsy caravan site. The site had been occupied by one gypsy (G) and his family without planning permission. G's children attended local schools, G made his income locally from landscaping work and breeding horses and the family had relatives nearby. Following an enquiry, the secretary of state's inspector concluded that although the change of use was inappropriate to the green belt, this was outweighed by the "very special circumstances" that moving the family on would cause disruption to the children's education and to G's employment. Moreover, the inspector was uncertain whether the family would adapt to local authority housing, particularly as they would no longer be able to keep the horses. The local authority contended that the inspector (1) had been wrong to find that the factors listed amounted to very special circumstances since none of them taken alone could be said to be very special; (2) had failed to deal adequately with the issue of whether the family could live in a house and whether their horses could be put out to graze.

Held, refusing the application, that (1) to suggest that every factor in itself had to be "very special" was artificial. Factors which were otherwise quite ordinary could cumulatively become very special circumstances, *R. (on the application of Chelmsford BC) v. First Secretary of State* [2003] EWHC 2978, [2004] 2 P. & C.R. 34, *Doncaster MBC v. Secretary of State for the Environment, Transport and the Regions* [2002] EWHC 808, [2002] J.P.L. 1509, [2003] C.L.Y. 3391 and *Basildon DC v. Secretary of State for the Environment, Transport and the Regions* [2001] J.P.L. 1184, [2001] C.L.Y. 4708 considered. Only when a single factor was relied on did it have to be shown that it was in itself very special. The inspector had taken the right approach and balanced the circumstances of G's case against the limited harm that would be caused to the green belt. (2) The inspector's reasoning in relation to whether the family could live in a bricks and mortar home was impeccable. The family had never lived in such a home and the inspector had therefore been entitled to be uncertain as to whether they would adapt to such a lifestyle. The issue of the horses was not a major factor in the inspector's decision and she had dealt with it adequately and applied common sense.

R. (ON THE APPLICATION OF BASILDON DC) v. FIRST SECRETARY OF STATE, [2004] EWHC 2759, [2005] J.P.L. 942, Sullivan, J., QBD (Admin).

3265. Inquiries–Fees–Standard daily amount–Wales

TOWN AND COUNTRY PLANNING (COSTS OF INQUIRIES ETC.) (STANDARD DAILY AMOUNT) (WALES) REGULATIONS 2005, SI 2005 371 (W.35); made under the Town and Country Planning Act 1990 s.303A. In force: April 1, 2005; £3.00.

These Regulations apply where the National Assembly for Wales is authorised to recover costs borne by it in connection with inquiries or other hearings relating to unitary development plans, local plans or simplified planning zones which have effect in Wales. The Regulations prescribe a standard daily amount which may be charged for each day the person appointed to hold the inquiry or hearing is engaged in the conduct of it, or is otherwise engaged on work connected with it. The amount prescribed by these Regulations, in relation to an inquiry or other hearing which opens on or after April 1, 2005, is £679. This replaces the amount of £618, which was prescribed for the 2004/2005 year by the Town and Country Planning (Costs of Inquiries etc) (Standard Daily Amount) (Wales) Regulations 2002 (SI 2002 2801) (W.269)), otherwise than in relation to a qualifying inquiry to which those Regulations applied and which opened before, and remains open after, April 1, 2005.

3266. Joint committees–Establishment–North Northamptonshire

NORTH NORTHAMPTONSHIRE JOINT COMMITTEE ORDER 2005, SI 2005 1552; made under the Planning and Compulsory Purchase Act 2004 s.29. In force: July 7, 2005; £3.00.

This Order establishes a joint committee for North Northamptonshire. The constituent authorities are Northamptonshire County Council, Corby Borough Council, East Northamptonshire District Council, Kettering Borough Council and Wellingborough Borough Council.

3267. Listed buildings–Works of architecture–Issue of certificate of immunity from listing–Special architectural importance–Relevance of practical problems with design of school building

[Planning (Listed Buildings and Conservation Areas) Act 1990 s.6.]

The applicant architect (B) sought permission to apply for judicial review of the secretary of state's decision to issue a certificate of immunity from listing for a school building under the Planning (Listed Buildings and Conservation Areas) Act 1990 s.6. B had designed the school in the 1960s and the building had won a national architecture prize. However, the local authority proposed its demolition because of practical problems, including solar gain due to the amount of south facing glass. The proposal prompted an application for the school to be spot listed, but on the advice of English Heritage, the secretary of state refused. Later, English Heritage changed its mind and recommended a Grade II listing, but the secretary of state still declined and eventually issued the immunity from listing certificate. B contended that, when considering the application for the certificate, the secretary of state took into account irrelevant matters by considering the practical problems with the building's design.

Held, refusing the application, that in determining whether a building was of special architectural interest, the secretary of state was entitled to take into consideration its design flaws. In the case of a building designed as a school, it would be quite impracticable as well as misconceived to divorce the aesthetic qualities of the structure from the degree to which its design successfully fulfilled its practical function of providing a school building that worked. The secretary of state would not, however, be entitled to take into account the way in which the building currently failed to fulfil its functions, except to the extent that that reflected on the design of the building. On the facts of the instant case there was sufficient material upon which a secretary of state approaching the matter rationally could have concluded that design flaws made a substantial contribution to the building's practical problems and accordingly she was entitled to take them into consideration as relevant factors. Her decision was neither plainly wrong nor unlawful.

R. (ON THE APPLICATION OF BANCROFT) v. SECRETARY OF STATE FOR CULTURE, MEDIA AND SPORT, [2004] EWHC 1822, [2005] 2 P. & C.R. 10, Gibbs, J., QBD (Admin Ct.)

3268. **Local authorities–Local development plans–Wales**

TOWN AND COUNTRY PLANNING (LOCAL DEVELOPMENT PLAN) (WALES) REGULATIONS 2005, SI 2005 2839 (W.203); made under the Planning and Compulsory Purchase Act 2004 s.62, s.63, s.64, s.69, s.72, s.76, s.77; and the Town and Country Planning Act 1990 Sch.4A para.5. In force: October 15, 2005; £5.50.

The Planning and Compulsory Purchase Act 2004 Part 6 establishes a new system of local development plans in Wales. These Regulations make provision for the operation of that system.

3269. **Local plans–Local authorities powers and duties–Duty to comply with transitional provisions of Planning and Compulsory Purchase Act 2004 Sch.8**

[Town and Country Planning Act 1990; Planning and Compulsory Purchase Act 2004; Planning and Compulsory Purchase Act 2004 Sch.8 para.10.]

The claimant landowner (M) sought to quash a decision of the defendant local authority to abandon the statutory process relating to the local plan, and to commence work on the local development framework (LDF) as required by the Planning and Compulsory Purchase Act 2004. M owned a piece of land and believed that the site was appropriate for a housing development. It had entered into discussions with the local authority about having the area entered into the local plan. The site was included in the first draft of the local plan but was subsequently removed. Work on the local plan under the Town and Country Planning Act 1990 process was then abandoned so that the local authority's resources could be concentrated on developing the LDF. This had the effect that M was deprived of the opportunity to have its case tested by an inspector, who would have considered the merits of the application under the 1990 Act procedure. The local authority submitted that its decision had produced no prejudice to M. It had made economic and practical sense to abandon the existing procedure and concentrate on the LDF.

Held, granting the application, that the 2004 Act dealt with the position where the process of producing a local plan was already underway. Sch.8 Para.10 of the 2004 Act, Sch.8 showed Parliament's conclusion that in such circumstances the procedure of the 1990 Act should continue to public inquiry. The 1990 Act process would be carried out in the knowledge that long term considerations would be given pursuant to the LDF. An inspector's view of the local plan proposals would be likely to be highly relevant for the LDF and the scope for shortening inquiries under the 2004 Act regime would mean that costs would be saved. Although there was no statutory provision which permitted a local authority to abandon or withdraw from an emerging local plan, the power did exist, *R. (on the application of Persimmon Homes (Thames Valley) Ltd) v. North Hertfordshire DC* [2001] EWHC Admin 565, [2001] 1 W.L.R. 2393, [2001] C.L.Y. 4718 considered. However, this power should not be used to override provisions set out by parliament to deal with a particular situation. The transitional arrangements in Sch.8 to the 2004 Act should be followed unless there was a very good reason not to do so, *Pioneer Aggregates (UK) Ltd v. Secretary of State for the Environment* [1985] A.C. 132, [1984] C.L.Y. 3465 applied. In the instant case the local authority's view that it would have been more economical and sensible to abandon work on the local plan had not been a good reason and the claim was allowed.

R. (ON THE APPLICATION OF MARTIN GRANT HOMES LTD) v. WEALDEN DC, [2005] EWHC 453, [2006] 1 P. & C.R. 11, Collins, J., QBD (Admin Ct).

3270. **Outline planning permission–Reserved matters–Need for environmental impact assessment**

The appellant (N) appealed against the decision ([2004] EWHC 2576, [2005] Env. L.R. 25) approving matters reserved on the grant of outline planning permission for a leisure development without requiring an environmental impact assessment (EIA) in respect of those matters. The respondent local planning authority had granted outline planning permission in 1997 for a business park in

Ramsgate. The developer had not provided an EIA with its application and the local authority had not required one. In 2002 the local authority had granted outline permission for a leisure development on part of the business park site. The authority had not required an EIA with the application because it had previously concluded in 2000 that an EIA was not required. In 2004 the developer had sought approval of reserved matters in respect of its proposed leisure development consisting of a detached multiplex cinema with associated car parking, servicing, vehicle access and landscaping. The local authority had conducted a screening exercise and concluded that no EIA was needed before the reserved matters were approved. N argued that the approval of reserved matters should be quashed because the decision that no EIA was needed was based upon a comparison with the grant of the business park outline permission in respect of which there had been no consideration of whether an EIA was necessary, or was based upon a comparison with the leisure park outline permission which was unlawful as a result of the decision not to require an EIA.

Held, dismissing the appeal, that (1) in considering whether an EIA was necessary at the approved matters stage the local authority's essential comparison had been with the leisure outline planning permission, not the business park permission. (2) It was a matter for the planning judgment of a planning authority, challengeable only on a *Wednesbury* basis, whether it had sufficient material before it at the outline planning stage to decide whether a proposed development would be likely to have such significant effects on the environment as to require an EIA, *R. (on the application of Jones) v. Mansfield DC* [2003] EWCA Civ 1408, [2004] Env. L.R. 21, [2003] C.L.Y. 3421 applied. In the instant case there was no basis for a *Wednesbury* challenge to the authority's decision not to require an EIA at the leisure park outline permission stage. The particularity of the proposed development at the outline stage was such as to have enabled the authority to conclude that it did not require an EIA. (3) There was nothing perverse about the local authority conducting a screening exercise at the reserved matters stage even though it had already done so at the permission stage and concluded that an EIA was not necessary. That decision to screen again was eminently rational given the legal uncertainty over the necessity for an EIA at the reserved matters stage. (4) It was clear law, and clear on the facts, that N could not challenge directly or indirectly either of the outline planning permissions or the screening decision in respect of the second of them. The challenge to the decision not to require an EIA at the approval of reserved matters stage was, in the way it had been formulated by N, an impermissible collateral challenge to those decisions. There was no scope for a challenge to the approval, without an EIA, of reserved matters on the basis that it was a later decision adopting an earlier erroneous decision, since the authority had not relied on its 2000 screening decision in respect of the 2002 leisure park outline permission, but simply took that permission into account as a relevant factor. If either of the two outline planning permissions required and were not the subject of a valid screening exercise, there had been a clear domestic remedy by way of judicial review for quashing either of them and the screening opinion at the leisure park outline permission stage. (5) It was not necessary to make a reference to the European Court of Justice.

R. (ON THE APPLICATION OF NOBLE ORGANISATION) v. THANET DC, [2005] EWCA Civ 782, [2006] Env. L.R. 8, Auld, L.J., CA (Civ Div).

3271. **Permitted development–Agricultural buildings–Consideration of proposed development in component parts–Relevance of developer's intended operations**

[Town and Country Planning (General Permitted Development) Order 1995 (SI 1995 418) Sch.2 Part 2 Class A, Part 6 Class A.2(2).]

The claimant (D) sought judicial review of a decision of the defendant local authority that the building of a silage clamp was permitted development for the purposes of the Town and Country Planning (General Permitted Development) Order 1995 and was not subject to prior notification requirements. The farmer of land next to D's home (V) had applied to the local authority for a determination as to whether prior approval was required for a new silage pit. Two months later, V had demolished a barn and laid concrete over the site and adjacent land. V had applied for planning permission for the erection of a silage clamp using the concreted area as its base and two proposed walls as sides. The local authority considered that it was entitled to treat the floor and walls separately because the floor was an existing base, being the base of the demolished barn, and silage was already being stored on it. D contended that (1) the local authority had erred in disassembling the silage clamp into its component parts rather than considering the proposed development as a single scheme; (2) the principal purpose of the walls was to retain the stored silage, as opposed to enclosing an area of land, and their construction constituted the erection of a building within Sch.2 Part 6 Class A.2(2) of the Order rather than the erection of a 'wall or other means of enclosure' within Sch.2 Part 2 Class A.

Held, granting the application, that (1) the question of whether a proposed development constituted a single scheme or more than one scheme was a matter of fact and degree for the local authority to determine, but in doing so, it was required to have regard to all relevant considerations and disregard irrelevant ones. The local authority had failed to have regard to the totality of V's intended operations, as evidenced in his original application, or to the fact that the base of the pit shown therein had been concreted shortly afterward, *Sage v. Secretary of State for the Environment, Transport and the Regions* [2003] UKHL 22, [2003] 1 W.L.R. 983, [2003] C.L.Y. 3386 considered. Furthermore, it had taken an irrelevant consideration into account, namely the inaccurate belief that the floor of the clamp was an existing base to which walls were to be added. (2) Not every wall which could be said to have some enclosing function would necessarily fall within Sch.2 Part 2 Class A. Each case was fact sensitive and would depend on the nature and location of the wall, *Prengate Properties Ltd v. Secretary of State for the Environment* 71 L.G.R. 373, [1973] C.L.Y. 3234 considered. It had been open to the local authority to conclude that the proposed walls, even if viewed in isolation, were part of a building to hold silage and that any enclosing function was purely incidental, so that the construction of the walls fell more naturally within Part 6 Class A.2(2) than Part 2 Class A. The local authority had failed to properly consider the relevant factual issues.

R. (ON THE APPLICATION OF DENNIS) v. SEVENOAKS DC, [2004] EWHC 2758, [2005] 2 P. & C.R. 4, Sullivan, J., QBD (Admin).

3272. Planning and Compulsory Purchase Act 2004 (c.5)–Commencement No.3 Order–Wales

PLANNING AND COMPULSORY PURCHASE ACT 2004 (COMMENCEMENT NO.3 AND CONSEQUENTIAL AND TRANSITIONAL PROVISIONS) (WALES) ORDER 2005, SI 2005 1229 (W.87; C.56); made under the Planning and Compulsory Purchase Act 2004 s.121, s.122. Commencement details: bringing into force various provisions of the 2004 Act on April 30, 2005; £3.00.

This Order brings into force provisions of Part 6 of the Planning and Compulsory Purchase Act 2004 into force, namely s.62, s.63, s.72 and s.73. Part 6 of the Act applies only to Wales and establishes a system of local development plans in place of the unitary development plans required under the Town and Country Planning Act 1990. The effect of the Order will be to enable those local planning authorities which have expressed a wish to commence work on the preparation of their plans to do so.

3273. Planning and Compulsory Purchase Act 2004 (c.5)–Commencement No.4 and Consequential Provisions Order–Wales

PLANNING AND COMPULSORY PURCHASE ACT 2004 (COMMENCEMENT NO.4 AND CONSEQUENTIAL, TRANSITIONAL AND SAVINGS PROVISIONS) (WALES) ORDER 2005, SI 2005 2722 (W.193; C.110); made under the Planning and Compulsory Purchase Act 2004 s.121, s.122. Commencement details: bringing into force various provisions of the 2004 Act on October 5, 2005 and October 15, 2005; £3.00.

This Order brings the remaining provisions of the Planning and Compulsory Purchase Act 2004 Part 6 which applies in relation to Wales and establishes a system of local development plans (LDPs) in place of unitary development plans required under the Town and Country Planning Act 1990. It also makes provision for a Wales Spatial Plan.

3274. Planning and Compulsory Purchase Act 2004 (c.5)–Commencement No.4 and Savings Order–England

PLANNING AND COMPULSORY PURCHASE ACT 2004 (COMMENCEMENT NO.4 AND SAVINGS) ORDER 2005, SI 2005 204 (C.8); made under the Planning and Compulsory Purchase Act 2004 s.121, s.122. Commencement details: bringing into force various provisions of the 2004 Act on March 7, 2005 and April 1, 2005; £3.00.

This Order provides for the coming into force of various provisions of the Planning and Compulsory Purchase Act 2004.

3275. Planning and Compulsory Purchase Act 2004 (c.5)–Commencement No.5 and Savings Order

PLANNING AND COMPULSORY PURCHASE ACT 2004 (COMMENCEMENT NO.5 AND SAVINGS) ORDER 2005, SI 2005 2081 (C.90); made under the Planning and Compulsory Purchase Act 2004 s.121, s.122. Commencement details: bringing into force various provisions of the 2004 Act on August 24, 2005; £3.00.

This Order brings into force provisions of the Planning and Compulsory Purchase Act 2004 relating to the power to decline to determine applications; major infrastructure projects; the duration of permission and consent; and the duty to respond to consultation.

3276. Planning and Compulsory Purchase Act 2004 (c.5)–Commencement No.6, Transitional Provisions and Savings Order–Wales

PLANNING AND COMPULSORY PURCHASE ACT 2004 (COMMENCEMENT NO.6, TRANSITIONAL PROVISIONS AND SAVINGS) ORDER 2005, SI 2005 2847 (C.118); made under the Planning and Compulsory Purchase Act 2004 s.121, s.122. Commencement details: bringing into force various provisions of the 2004 Act on October 15, 2005; £3.00.

This Order brings into operation various provisions of the Planning and Compulsory Purchase Act 2004.

3277. Planning appeals–Expert reports–Interested parties' right to service–Meaning of "statutory party"

[Town and Country Planning (General Development Procedure) Order 1995 (SI 2000 1626) Art.19(1)(b)(i); Town and Country Planning (Hearings Procedure)(England) Rules 2000 (SI 2000 1626) r.2, r.4(2), r.6(6).]

The applicant (H) applied to quash a planning decision made following an appeal hearing held pursuant to the Town and Country Planning (Hearings Procedure) (England) Rules 2000. H's garden abutted the property to which the planning application related. H had made representations to the local planning authority on the original application and had therefore been sent notice of the appeal, by a letter inviting him to contact the authority if he needed further information. However, he was not served with hearing statements or notified of his right pursuant to r.6(6) of the Rules to inspect such statements. H submitted that as a statutory party he should have been served with an acoustic report which had been stated by the planning inspector to underpin her decision. The lack of opportunity to study the report had substantially prejudiced his interests at the appeal hearing.

Held, refusing the application, that H was not a statutory party. Under r.2 of the Rules a statutory party was defined as a person whose representations the secretary of state was required to take into account under the Town and Country Planning (General Development Procedure) Order 1995 Art.19(1)(b)(i) or "such a person" whose representations the local planning authority was required to take into account. The words "such a person" referred to Art.19(1)(b)(i). Art.19(1)(b)(i) of the Order was confined to owners of land to which the application related who had been served with notice of the application or appeal. Nevertheless, natural justice demanded that as an interested party H was entitled to know his opponent's case. On the evidence H had not been prejudiced at the appeal by the lack of opportunity to inspect the report prior to it. However, the secretary of state should consider amending r.4(2) to oblige local planning authorities to give notice to interested parties of the right under r.6(6) to inspect such documents.

HAMSHER v. FIRST SECRETARY OF STATE; *sub nom*. R. (ON THE APPLICATION OF HAMSHER) v. FIRST SECRETARY OF STATE, [2004] EWHC 2299, [2005] J.P.L. 491, Judge Rich Q.C., QBD (Admin).

3278. Planning applications – Bias – Apparent bias or predetermination – Conduct of chairman of planning committee – Chairman's participation in close vote

The applicant (G) applied for judicial review of the defendant local authority's decision to grant planning permission for a major redevelopment of Harlow town centre. G owned commercial premises that would have been affected by the proposed development. G produced as evidence transcripts of telephone conversations between himself and the chairman of the local authority's planning committee. The transcripts revealed that the chairman was close to the developers and knew a lot about the development and its financing. The transcripts also showed that the chairman had been engaged in discussions with G with a view to enabling the development to go ahead. At planning committee meetings the chairman had been asked to vacate the chair and to withdraw but he had not done so. G contended that there was a real possibility that the chairman had been biased in the sense of approaching the planning permission decision with a closed mind and without impartial consideration of all relevant planning issues.

Held, granting the application in part, that there was apparent bias or predetermination in relation to the chairman. The chairman ought to have stood down as he had been requested to do. A fair minded and informed observer would have concluded from the telephone conversations and their context that there was a real possibility that the chairman had made up his mind in favour of the proposed development and that he would approach the decision on the planning application with a closed mind and without impartial consideration of all the relevant planning issues, *Georgiou v. Enfield LBC* [2004] EWHC 779, [2004] B.L.G.R. 497, [2005] 2 C.L. 330 applied. A predisposition did not equate to a predetermination or a closed mind, but the evidence in the instant case was of more than a mere predisposition. As the decision to grant planning permission was arrived at on a close vote of four votes to three, the inappropriateness of the chairman's participation in the decision making process led inevitably to the quashing of the planning permission.

GHADAMI v. HARLOW DC, [2004] EWHC 1883, [2005] B.L.G.R. 24, Richards, J., QBD (Admin Ct).

3279. Planning applications – Bias – Listed building consent – Councillors sitting on both conservation advisory group and planning committee

G sought judicial review of a decision to grant listed building planning consent, arguing that there was the appearance of bias in the decision making process. C, a mental healthcare provider, had lodged applications for building consent and planning permission with E so that it could undertake repairs to a listed building. E's conservation advisory group (CAG) supported both the initial application and later revised versions. E's planning committee subsequently approved the applications by eight votes to seven, with three votes in favour coming from councillors who sat on both the CAG and the planning committee. G claimed that the voting pattern of the dual members was evidence of bias, given the lack of instructions to disregard CAG's decisions and the apparent lack of training for one dual member.

Held, granting the application, that an objective and informed observer would have concluded that there was a real possibility of bias in the decision making process, *Porter v. Magill* [2001] UKHL 67, [2002] 2 A.C. 357, [2002] C.L.Y. 3185 applied. No reference was made at the planning committee meeting to CAG's limited function or the need for dual members to disregard CAG's support for the application. In terms of voting, three dual members had supported the application, one of whom had no planning law experience or training. Further, there had been a failure to communicate transport concerns to the planning committee, *R. v. Selby DC, ex p. Oxton Farms* [1997] E.G.C.S. 60, [1997] C.L.Y. 4114 applied, and the committee had not been provided with up to date information on health and social services issues.

GEORGIOU v. ENFIELD LBC; *sub nom.* R. (ON THE APPLICATION OF GEORGIOU) v. ENFIELD LBC, [2004] EWHC 779, [2004] B.L.G.R. 497, Richards, J., QBD (Admin Ct).

3280. Planning applications–Telecommunications masts–Compulsory purchase powers–Alternative feasible sites

[Telecommunications Act 1984 Sch.2 para.5.]

The appellants (S) appealed against a decision ([2004] EWHC 512, [2004] J.P.L. 1581) refusing to quash the grant of planning permission for a telecommunications mast granted by a planning inspector appointed by the respondent Secretary of State. Following a public inquiry the inspector had allowed an appeal by the telecommunications operator against the local authority's refusal to grant permission for the mast. The inspector had considered the relevant development plan policy and Planning Policy Guidance 8. He had identified possible sites alternative to that proposed by the operator, and, in particular, sites at a police building and in the car park of a railway station. However, for technical and operational reasons the landowners had declined to make those sites available. The inspector had considered the use of the power available to operators under the Telecommunications Act 1984 Sch.2 para.5 to acquire land compulsorily for a base station in circumstances where consent was withheld by the landowner but concluded that the use of the power was likely to be rejected by the county court because of the existence of the appeal site as a feasible alternative. The inspector concluded that the appeal site was acceptable and that decision was upheld. S submitted that, having regard to the qualified duty on the county court in Sch.2 para.5, an owner's objection to the use of a site was not a sufficient reason for excluding that site from consideration. It was argued that the inspector should have considered whether use of the site involved prejudice to the owner, whether any such prejudice was capable of being adequately compensated for by money and whether the prejudice was outweighed by the benefit accruing to users of the system. The Secretary of State submitted that the power to go to the county court was properly to be categorised as a power of last resort to be used typically where there was a single feasible site and the owner would not consent to its use.

Held, dismissing the appeal, that the scope of the power of the county court not to make an order if application was made under Sch.2 was limited and the county court was not permitted to conduct the overall assessment of the benefits and disbenefits of land use which was appropriate to the decision of a planning authority. An applicant for planning permission was not obliged either to go to the county court and fail on an alternative site or to satisfy the planning authority that he would fail if he did so. While a planning authority was entitled to have regard to the existence of the power in Sch.2, it was not obliged to ignore, as a material consideration, the stand taken by occupiers of sites alternative to that advocated in the application. Resort to the county court should not readily or routinely be contemplated. The views of the police and railway station owners, as interested landowners, could properly be taken into account as a consideration so that the inspector was not required in the instant case to make other detailed comparisons between sites or analyse how the county court would have reacted to applications. Since he could take those views into account, the inspector was entitled to conclude that there was no location better than the appeal site on the information before him.

ST LEGER-DAVEY v. FIRST SECRETARY OF STATE, [2004] EWCA Civ 1612, [2005] 2 P. & C.R. 6, Pill, L.J., CA (Civ Div).

3281. Planning authorities–Environmental statements–Information required to gauge environmental effects of development

The claimant (H) brought judicial review proceedings to quash a decision of the defendant local authority (X) to grant planning permission for a waste treatment and recycling facility subject to the supply of further information concerning emissions. The environmental statement provided by the developer had stated that the development would not cause a major increase in pollution. However, the subsequent planning officer's report had recommended conditions relating to air pollution control measures and those conditions had been adopted by the planning authority and incorporated into the planning permission. H maintained that the planning authority could legitimately have made a finding that there were no significant environmental effects, thereby accepting the environmental assessment, but that it never actually made such a finding, its report having made contrary assumptions that there was, in fact, potential for significant environmental effects. H argued that the proper way of dealing with those assumptions was to have required further information prior to granting planning permission, which would have ensured compliance with the requirement to publicly consult. X contended that the conditions could be properly imposed because they were merely to ensure that mitigating measures to keep insignificant emissions under scrutiny were properly and effectively implemented.

Held, granting the application, that (1) The decision whether an activity had significant environmental effects and whether there was sufficient information to enable a judgment to be made was for the planning authority. It had to have sufficient details about the nature of the development, its impact on the environment, and also any mitigating measures, so long as they were available, sufficiently specific and there was no real doubt about their effectiveness. If there was any uncertainty about the environmental effects, the planning authority had to either seek further information from the developer, by way of an environmental statement or a supplement to an existing statement, before reaching a conclusion. It could not seek to regulate future potential difficulties by the imposition of conditions, nor could it dispense with the need for further information on the basis that other enforcement agencies would ensure that steps were taken to prevent improper pollution, *Smith v. Secretary of State for the Environment, Transport and the Regions* [2003] EWCA Civ 262, [2003] Env. L.R. 32 and *Gillespie v. First Secretary of State* [2003] EWCA Civ 400, [2003] Env.L.R. 30, [2003] C.L.Y. 3416 applied. (2) In the instant case, there was no indication that the planning officer had concluded that there were no significant environmental effects resulting from the proposed activity. On such an important matter, he could be expected to be clear about his assessment. Conditions were not to be imposed unless they were necessary and, on the facts, it was difficult to see why it would be necessary to impose a condition merely as a method of monitoring emissions that the officer was satisfied were insubstantial. (3) There was no absolute bar to considering in judicial review proceedings subsequent evidence to resolve a lack of clarity in a report, but the information had to elucidate or explain and not contradict the written reasons for a decision, *R. (on the application of Nash) v. Chelsea College of Art and Design* [2001] EWHC Admin 538, Times, July 25, 2001, [2001] C.L.Y. 95 and *R. v. Westminster City Council, ex p. Ermakov* [1996] 2 All E.R. 302, [1995] C.L.Y.

2568 applied. However, in the instant case, supplementary reasons were inappropriate and the planning permission was quashed.

R. (ON THE APPLICATION OF HEREFORD WASTE WATCHERS LTD) v. HEREFORDSHIRE CC; *sub nom.* HEREFORD WASTE WATCHERS LTD v. HEREFORD COUNCIL, [2005] EWHC 191, [2005] Env. L.R. 29, Elias, J., QBD (Admin).

3282. Planning conditions—Extensions of time—Determination of conditions by mineral planning authorities—Extension of statutory time limit by agreement

[Environment Act 1995 Sch.13 para.9.]

The appellant mineral planning authority appealed against a decision that, pursuant to the Environment Act 1995 Sch.13 para.9(9), the authority should be treated as having determined that the conditions to which two planning permissions were subject were those proposed by the respondent (B) in its application for approval of conditions, because the authority had failed to give its decision on the application in time. B had an interest in a quarry that had the benefit of two planning permissions for the extraction of minerals granted in 1950 and 1959. In accordance with its duty under the 1995 Act, the authority had produced a list of mineral sites which included the quarry and had informed B that the quarry had been added to the list and that an application for determination of conditions had to be made by a particular date. B had delivered a written application for determination of the conditions in accordance with para.9 the day before the period expired. The application did not include an environmental assessment. Over a month later, the authority had requested additional information to enable the application to be considered. The authority had stated that the three month period for determination under para.9 (9) would commence on receipt of that information, but requested B's agreement to extend the period for determination to at least six months. B had replied by sending the additional information but refusing a six month extension on the basis that the three month statutory period would continue to apply. The authority confirmed in reply that a valid application had been made on receipt of the additional information and that the three month period would run from that date. Within three months of receipt of the additional documents, the planning authority determined the conditions to be applied. B appealed against the conditions imposed by the authority and took the point that the authority's determination was out of time, because the three month period ran from the date of the original application, which had complied with the terms of para.9(2). The planning authority submitted that (1) the letter of application did not constitute an application as it did not include the environmental statement required by Community law; (2) it had made a request for further information in accordance with para.9(10); (3) the parties had agreed to an extension of the three month period within which the authority had to make its determination as to the applicable conditions; (4) in any event, in order to comply with Community law in respect of the supply and consideration of an environmental statement, the conditions should be those put forward by the authority, not by B.

Held, allowing the appeal, that (1) the judge rightly concluded that by its letter B had made an application in accordance with the requirements of para.9(2). Accordingly, the time started to run from then. To conclude otherwise would not give effect to para.9(2). It was the authority's own view that the application complied with the requirements of para.9(2) despite the lack of an environmental statement. (2) There was no valid notice seeking further particulars under para.9(10) since the authority's letter requesting further information was outside the one month period allowed. (3) The correspondence embodied an agreement between the parties to extend the time for determination. When construing the relevant correspondence between the parties, the court should take into account the framework in which it was written and the way the parties conducted themselves thereafter. The subsequent conduct of the parties was only consistent with B's acceptance of the statement by the authority that the three months allowed for determination would begin on receipt of the further information requested. It followed that the determination by the authority was in time. (4) The authorities seemed to establish that an individual might enforce a European directive against the state when the state had not implemented the directive. There was also support for the proposition that the courts would not impose obligations derived from a directive on private parties. Those propositions supported B's submission that to disregard the rights given to B under para.9(9) would amount to giving direct effect to the directive against an individual, which was impermissible, but it was not necessary to decide that issue.

WIRRAL BC v. BROCK PLC, [2004] EWCA Civ 1611, [2005] Env. L.R. 26, Potter, L.J., CA (Civ Div).

3283. Planning control-Caravan sites-Local authority's powers of removal-Consideration of gypsies' aversion to traditional housing

[Town and Country Planning Act 1990 s.178, s.187B; Housing Act 1996 s.175; Human Rights Act 1998 Sch.1 Part I Art.6.]

The claimants (L), who were gypsies, sought judicial review of a decision granting an application for an injunction, made by the defendant local authority (N), pursuant to the Town and Country Planning Act 1990 s.178. The injunction enabled N to enter the land upon which L had pitched and to take steps required by an enforcement notice, including the removal of caravans and other items from the land and recovering that cost and the cost of reinstating the land to its original condition from L. L had entered a green belt site and pitched a number of caravans, occupied by families, without having obtained or applied for planning permission to do so. Prior to N's application under s.178 of the Act, N had successfully obtained an injunction under s.187B of the Act. The injunction stipulated that there should be no further breach of planning control, that occupation of the site had to be ended and that the site had to be reinstated by a particular date. N had applied under s.178 due to L's previous non compliance with the injunction and enforcement notice. The lack of permitted gypsy caravan sites in the area meant that removal could render the families homeless under the Housing Act 1996 s.175. Approximately six weeks before the compliance deadline, N wrote to the families offering them temporary accommodation. One week before the planned removal a letter was received by N from L. The letter set out N's obligations to homeless gypsies, which included taking into account their cultural aversion to conventional housing, and sought assurance that N's interim duty to secure culturally appropriate accommodation would be met by allowing continued occupation of the site whilst investigation was made into possible alternative sites. N met the next day and confirmed the decision to go ahead with the removal. L contended that (1) N was not entitled to use s.178 as it had already pursued an action under s.187B. If the matter had gone back to the county court, L could have made submissions and called evidence to show that N had not done all it ought to have done to identify alternative sites, and it was unreasonable of the authority to expect the claimants to accept temporary accommodation in conventional housing. In those circumstances the breach of the injunction could not be regarded as culpable; (2) use of s.178 was in breach of the Human Rights Act 1998 Sch.1 Part I Art.6 as L were not given a hearing before an independent tribunal.

Held, giving judgment, that (1) N was entitled to use s.178 even though it had originally decided to use s.187B. Although no court order was necessary to use s.178, the decision to do so was susceptible to judicial review and the court had considered the same arguments that would have been considered had the case gone back to court under s.187B. However, N had a duty when using s.178 to approach the matter in a reasonable way and have regard to its obligations under the 1996 Act. N had erred in not deferring the planned date of removal in order to make enquiries into L's aversion to traditional accommodation, *South Buckinghamshire DC v. Porter* [2001] EWCA Civ 1549, [2002] 1 W.L.R. 1359, [2001] C.L.Y. 4729 considered. (2) The enforcement action under s.178 followed full consideration before two independent tribunals which included the inspector and the administrative court. Accordingly, the issue as to whether there had been a breach of Art.6 did not and could not apply to the instant case.

R. (ON THE APPLICATION OF LEE) v. NUNEATON AND BEDWORTH BC, [2004] EWHC 950, [2004] J.P.L. 1698, Collins, J., QBD (Admin Ct).

3284. Planning control–Injunctions–Court's power to grant relief against persons unknown–Service of injunction

[Town and Country Planning Act 1990 s.187B; Civil Procedure Rules 1998 (SI 1998 3132) Part 6 r.6.8.]

The appellant local authority appealed against the dismissal of its application for an interim injunction against persons unknown. The local authority had sought to prevent the deposit of hardcore and the stationing of mobile residential accommodation on a site adjacent to a legitimate gypsy caravan site. The judge refused the application on the basis that there was no power to make the injunction in the terms sought against persons unknown.

Held, allowing the appeal, that there was power to make an interim injunction to prevent a breach of planning control in the terms sought against persons unknown under the Town and Country Planning Act 1990 s.187B. Furthermore, the court was completely satisfied on the evidence that it was expedient and necessary to grant relief. By virtue of the Civil Procedure Rules 1998 Part 6 r.6.8, service would be permitted by documents placed in plastic bags nailed to posts in prominent positions on the site.

SOUTH CAMBRIDGESHIRE DC v. PERSONS UNKNOWN, [2004] EWCA Civ 1280, [2004] 4 P.L.R. 88, Brooke, L.J., CA (Civ Div).

3285. Planning control–Injunctions–Use of green belt land as base for travelling show people and fairground operators–Persistent and deliberate breach of planning controls

[Town and Country Planning Act 1990 s.187B; Human Rights Act 1998 Sch.1 Part I Art.8.]

The appellants (D), a group of travelling show people and fairground operators, appealed against a grant of injunctive relief under the Town and Country Planning Act 1990 s.187B to the respondent local planning authority in respect of D's occupation of D's field in breach of planning control. The site was in the green belt and was part of an area designated in the local plan as a special landscape area. D, in deliberate breach of planning control, had brought onto the site their caravans and fairground equipment and developed the site despite enforcement notices, in respect of which time for compliance had long since expired. D argued that enforcement of the order to vacate the site would violate their rights pursuant to the Human Rights Act 1998 Sch.1 Part I Art.8. D submitted that the judge below had wrongly conflated the issue of planning merits, which was exclusively for the planning authorities, and the issue of whether the court should enforce the planning decision by injunction.

Held, dismissing the appeal, that decisions on planning merits were for the planning authorities and decisions on whether to enforce such decisions were for the courts, taking into account all the relevant considerations, including personal hardship to the party against whom injunctive relief was sought. The judge below had shown deference to the planning decisions but had clearly made up his own mind on the issue of whether to grant an injunction against D. The judge had given full consideration to all the relevant considerations. The judge had considered the most weighty factors in favour of the grant of an injunction, namely the serious violations by D of planning controls and the severely detrimental impact on the openness of the green belt; the deliberate nature of the violations with full knowledge of their unlawfulness; and the persistent defiance of the law for three years. The judge was entitled to conclude that those considerations outweighed the hardship to D in having to leave the site, *South Buckinghamshire DC v. Porter (No.2)* [2003] UKHL 26, [2003] 2

A.C. 558, [2003] C.L.Y. 3381 and *Chapman v. United Kingdom (27238/95)* (2001) 33 E.H.R.R. 18, [2001] C.L.Y. 4744 applied.

TONBRIDGE AND MALLING BC v. DAVIS; *sub nom.* DAVIS v. TONBRIDGE AND MALLING BC, [2004] EWCA Civ 194, *The Times*, March 5, 2004, Auld, L.J., CA.

3286. Planning control–Temporary stop notices–Caravans

TOWN AND COUNTRY PLANNING (TEMPORARY STOP NOTICE) (ENGLAND) REGULATIONS 2005, SI 2005 206; made under the Town and Country Planning Act 1990 s.171F. In force: March 7, 2005; £3.00.

The Town and Country Planning Act 1990 enables a local planning authority to issue a temporary stop notice ("TSN") if they think that there has been a breach of planning control and that it is expedient that the activity, or any part of it, which amounts to the breach, is stopped immediately. The Act provides that a TSN does not prohibit the use of a building as a dwelling house and enables the Secretary of State to prescribe descriptions of activities which are not prohibited by a TSN, and circumstances in which the carrying out of an activity is not prohibited by a TSN. These Regulations prescribe the stationing of a caravan on land where the land is used for that purpose immediately before the issue of the TSN, and the caravan is at that time occupied by a person as his main residence unless the local planning authority consider that the risk of harm to a compelling public interest arising from the stationing of the caravan is so serious so as to outweigh any benefit to the occupier of the caravan in the stationing of the caravan for the period for which the temporary stop notice has effect.

3287. Planning control–Use classes

TOWN AND COUNTRY PLANNING (USE CLASSES) (AMENDMENT) (ENGLAND) ORDER 2005, SI 2005 84; made under the Town and Country Planning Act 1990 s.55, s.333. In force: April 21, 2005; £3.00.

This Order amends the Town and Country Planning (Use Classes) Order 1987 (SI 1987 764) which specifies classes for the purposes of the Town and Country Planning Act 1990. The Act provides that a change of use of a building or other land does not involve development for the purposes of the Act if the new use and the former use are both within the same specified class. This Order amends the 1987 Order by excluding from the specified classes use as a retail warehouse club, and use as a nightclub. It also has the effect of including in the shops class (Class A1), use as an internet cafe, and splitting the former A3 use class (food and drink), into three new classes: Class A3, use as a restaurant or cafe; Class A4, use as a public house, wine-bar or other drinking establishment; and Class A5, use as a hot food takeaway.

3288. Planning inspectors–Assessment–Reasonableness–Separation of facing windows in dwelling houses less than standard specified in unitary development plan

The applicant neighbour (P) sought to quash the grant to the third defendant of planning permission for a housing development. The development site was sandwiched between the rears of existing properties on two parallel roads. The distances between the windows of the four new houses and the existing houses specified in the unitary development plan was 21 metres. P contended that (1) each of the proposed houses had a pair of facing windows which were only three metres to four metres apart and that the inspector had dealt with that departure from the 21 metre standard in an inadequate manner when he stated that the feature was acceptable and would be obvious to any incoming resident; (2) the inspector had failed to take into account a fundamental issue raised in the neighbouring residents' statement of planning issues that the local authority's supplementary planning guidance required dwellings to be designed so that habitable rooms overlooked the front entrance and the street; (3) the inspector had not had sufficient evidence to reasonably conclude that there would not be an unacceptable reduction of outlook and open aspect to the neighbouring properties.

Held, refusing the application, that (1) the 21 metre standard in the unitary plan was only concerned with the distance between facing windows in different buildings, not windows in the same dwelling. (2) The point made in the residents' statement had not been a principal issue. It was not something on which the inspector had been required to state a specific conclusion. His failure to make express reference to it did not mean he had not taken it into account. (3) It would take a lot to persuade a court that a planning inspector had reached a *Wednesbury* unreasonable conclusion. Whether a decision maker had enough material to enable him to reach a decision was a matter of judgment for that decision maker. The inspector had a large number of plans, had made a site visit and was an expert in assessing what effect a development would have on neighbouring properties. It could not be said that it was unreasonable for the inspector, armed with all of that information, to make that assessment.

R. (ON THE APPLICATION OF PATERSON) v. FIRST SECRETARY OF STATE, [2004] EWHC 185, [2005] 1 P. & C.R. 21, Richards, J., QBD (Admin Ct).

3289. **Planning obligations—Section 106 agreements—Repudiation claim seeking modification or discharge of planning obligation**

[Town and Country Planning Act 1990 s.106, s.106A.]

The appellant charitable trustees (C) appealed against the decision ([2004] EWHC 763) that they were not entitled to the return of a "highways improvement payment" deposited under an agreement pursuant to the Town and Country Planning Act 1990 s.106. C had purchased the site of a former school from the respondent local authority with a view to developing it as a temple for which planning permission had been obtained. C had later agreed to sell the site to a developer which had obtained planning permission for residential development. A condition of that permission was that C should enter into an agreement pursuant to s.106 of the Act. The agreement provided in clause 5 for a "highways improvement payment". That required C to deposit with the local authority the sum of £550,000 which was to be held in a designated interest bearing account and was to be used to carry out the necessary highway improvements. The unexpended balance in the account was to be returned to C. The residential development had then been carried out but the highway improvements had not. After five years C had asked for the return of the deposit. The local authority then carried out certain highway works which it claimed were covered by the provisions of the clause and returned a small balance of the deposit to C. C submitted that (1) they were entitled to the return of the whole deposit on the ground that the delay in carrying out the works amounted to a repudiation of the agreement, which C had accepted; (2) none or only part of the work carried out was work for which the local authority was entitled to payment out of the deposited sum pursuant to the agreement.

Held, allowing the appeal in part, that (1) C's claim that the local authority was in breach of clause 5 amounted to seeking a modification or discharge of a planning obligation within the meaning of s.106 and the only method by which they could achieve that objective was by using the statutory procedure set out in s.106A. C's argument that its only planning obligation under clause 5 was to deposit the required sum and that payment of that sum discharged their obligations was too simplistic. The planning obligation created by clause 5 was more complex; the deposit created a form of trust and the obligation was not merely to deposit the money but to permit the local authority to use it for the purposes of the trust. It was accordingly an extant planning obligation at all relevant times and s.106A(1) of the 1990 Act precluded C from seeking the discharge of that obligation under the guise of their claim that the local authority had repudiated the agreement. (2) The judge was wrong to conclude that all the work done was work for which the local authority was entitled to draw on the deposited sum. Under the agreement the works had to comprise alterations to a particular junction and "comprising" was a word of limitation. Work which did not relate to that junction would not be within the clause even if there was a highway engineering justification for making that work part of the overall scheme. An inquiry was necessary as to the extent of the work which qualified.

PATEL v. BRENT LBC (NO.3), [2005] EWCA Civ 644, [2006] 1 P. & C.R. 7, Auld, L.J., CA (Civ Div).

3290. Planning permission—Applications and deemed applications—Fees

TOWN AND COUNTRY PLANNING (FEES FOR APPLICATIONS AND DEEMED APPLICATIONS) (AMENDMENT) (ENGLAND) REGULATIONS 2005, SI 2005 843; made under the Town and Country Planning Act 1990 s.303. In force: April 1, 2005; £3.00.

These Regulations amend the Town and Country Planning (Fees for Applications and Deemed Applications) Regulations 1989 which make provision for the payment of fees to local planning authorities in respect of applications made under the Town and Country Planning Act 1990 for planning permission for development or for approval of matters reserved by an outline planning permission, in respect of fees for applications for certificates of lawful use or development, in respect of applications for consent for the display of advertisements and in respect of certain applications made under the Town and Country Planning (General Permitted Development) Order 1995; and for the payment of fees to the Secretary of State in respect of applications for planning permission which are deemed to have been made in connection with an appeal against an enforcement notice. They increase all fees payable under those Regulations and alter the basis of the calculation of the fee payable in some cases.

3291. Planning permission—Building extensions—Obligation to notify third party of informal hearing

[Town and Country Planning Act 1990 s.78, s.288; Town and Country Planning (Hearings Procedure) (England) Rules 2000 (SI 2000 1626).]

The appellant (R) appealed under the Town and Country Planning Act 1990 s.288 against the decision of an inspector allowing an appeal by his neighbour (D) against a refusal of D's application for planning permission. R had objected through an agent to the three planning applications made by D for a two storey extension immediately next to the fence separating R and D's properties. When D appealed to the inspector against the refusal of the applications under s.78 of the Act, R was not informed of the oral hearing and the inspector was unaware of R's objections. R contended that there had been procedural unfairness in that there was a legitimate expectation that he would be informed of the hearing, and the fact that he had not been so informed had prevented him from making representations. He argued that, had he done so, there was a real possibility that the outcome would have been different.

Held, allowing the appeal, that whilst there was no requirement to notify neighbours of informal hearings under the Town and Country Planning (Hearings Procedure) (England) Rules 2000, there was an established practice by which people who had made representations at the application stage should be informed of any appeal. This policy and established practice gave rise to a legitimate expectation that R would be informed of any such developments and removed the need for him to make frequent enquiries regarding the stage of proceedings. He had, therefore, been denied an opportunity to make representations. As the inspector had allowed the applications on wider grounds than their effect on R, was unaware of R's objections and had not visited R's property in the course of his inspection, R had discharged the burden upon him to establish that there was a real prospect that the outcome of the appeal would have been different had he been afforded the opportunity to make representations.

RUBIN v. FIRST SECRETARY OF STATE; *sub nom.* R. (ON THE APPLICATION OF RUBIN) v. FIRST SECRETARY OF STATE, [2004] EWHC 266, [2004] 3 P.L.R. 53, Pitchford, J., QBD (Admin Ct).

3292. Planning permission—Caravan sites—Use of land as private gypsy site—Balancing exercise

[Human Rights Act 1998 Sch.1 Part I Art.8, Art.8(2).]

The secretary of state and the three applicants appealed against a decision to quash the grant of planning permission to the applicants for the use of land as a private gypsy site with mobile homes and associated outbuildings. One of the applicants bought the site in 1999 and subdivided it into three main plots with services. The applicants then moved their mobile homes and caravans onto the site and began to live there without applying for planning permission. The site was in the countryside but quite close to settlements and an A road. It was largely hidden from view by trees and hedges. The site was not within an area subject to any special designation by reference to its landscape qualities and was not within the green belt or other designation of land where the policy was strongly to resist development. Departmental Circular 1/94 required local authorities to make adequate provision for gypsy sites and to have regard to their special needs. The secretary of state's appointed inspector granted planning permission for the site. Considering local plan policy RE22, which permitted the establishment of gypsy sites in rural areas subject to stringent criteria, he held that permission was merited even though the development would cause some planning harm and was arguably in breach of structure plan policy C1 which pre dated Circular 1/94. He further held that the local authority's refusal of planning permission violated the applicants' rights under the Human Rights Act 1998 Sch.1 Part I Art.8 to respect for their private and family life. The local authority successfully appealed against the inspector's decision. The judge held that the inspector had erred in failing to find a material breach of policy C1, had given too much weight to the personal circumstances of one of the applicants and had wrongly concluded that in effect Art.8 imposed a duty on the local authority to exercise its planning powers to provide an adequate number of gypsy sites. The secretary of state and the applicants submitted that the judge's decision should be reversed because the inspector (1) was entitled to approach the structure plan policy as he did; (2) did not err in his consideration of the personal circumstances of one of the applicants; (3) had correctly carried out the balancing exercise under Art.8(2).

Held, allowing the appeal (Auld, L.J. dissenting on the Art.8 issue), that (1) it was the inspector's clear conclusion that policy RE22 itself raised no objection in principle to the use of the site for a gypsy caravan site. That policy reflected not only the relevant policies of the structure plan, including C1, but also the secretary of state's subsequent policy in Circular 1/94. In those circumstances the inspector's finding, that the development was not objectionable in principle under the relevant local plan policy, would not have been affected by a finding that the structure plan policy was breached, whether that breach was technical or material. The inspector's consideration of the policy issues was in accordance with the guidance in the case law, *R. v. Leominster DC, ex p. Pothecary* (1998) 10 Admin. L.R. 484, [1997] C.L.Y. 4116 applied. (2) The inspector adequately explained his approach to the questions of general need and personal circumstances and why both were material considerations that weighed in favour of one of the applicants. (3) The inspector did not err in his application of Art.8 and the judge was wrong to find that he did. The appeal should accordingly be allowed and the decision of the inspector restored. Article 8 was clearly engaged in respect of the caravans which were the applicants' homes, and the question for the inspector was whether or not the interference by way of enforcement action by the local authority was necessary and proportionate under Art.8(2). The inspector was entitled to balance the limited environmental harm caused by the site against the personal circumstances of the applicants and the fact that the local authority had failed to meet the policy objective of providing sites set out in Circular 1/94. The judge was wrong to hold that the inspector considered Art.8 as imposing on the local authority a duty to exercise its planning powers to help achieve the end of providing an adequate number of gypsy sites.

CHICHESTER DC v. FIRST SECRETARY OF STATE; *sub nom.* FIRST SECRETARY OF STATE v. CHICHESTER DC, [2004] EWCA Civ 1248, [2005] 1 W.L.R. 279, Auld, L.J., CA (Civ Div).

3293. Planning permission–Conditions–Restrictions on vehicular access– Construction of outline planning permission–Derogation from grant

The appellant secretary of state appealed against a decision ([2003] EWHC 3094, [2004] J.P.L. 1273) that conditions imposed on detailed planning permission for the construction of access to development land derogated from the original grant of outline planning permission made 50 years previously. The outline permission allowed for three access points, namely 6A, 6B and 6C, to the land from then existing public highways and placed restrictions upon the use of 6B as a delivery and despatch point, the nearest existing highway being unsuitable for heavy traffic. However, no restrictions of the type placed on 6B had been referred to in respect of 6C. The conditions imposed by the secretary of state restricted access to 6C to public service vehicles only. Outline permission had originally been granted subject to a condition, Cond.5, of obtaining detailed approval for the precise location of the access points and detailed construction plans "in order to ensure safe and satisfactory means of access to existing highways and to ensure that these means of access shall conform to any improvements to the existing highways that might be proposed." When outline permission had been granted the public highway adjoining 6C was a general purpose road with no restrictions on the type of traffic which could use it. The secretary of state submitted that Cond.5 should be construed as including as a reserved matter the classes of vehicle which could use the access points, as that was relevant to considerations of ensuring safe and satisfactory access to highways existing at the time of the grant and also to the prevailing conditions when the detailed application was made. Traffic conditions had changed since the original grant, motorways had been built and congestion was now a problem. The restriction imposed in respect of 6B was particular to the existing highway at that point and the absence of an express restriction on 6C did not imply that the permission granted all purpose access.

Held, dismissing the appeal, that to the reasonable reader the natural and ordinary sense of the language of the grant of the outline permission was that access point 6C was for the traffic using the existing public highway at the time the grant was made, namely all purpose traffic. The reserved matters were the precise location of the access points and the detailed construction plans and did not include class of traffic user. The changed traffic conditions since the grant was made might afford ground for revoking or modifying the original permission, but could not justify the construction of Cond.5 argued for by the secretary of state. The noticeable absence of express restrictions in respect of 6C compared with 6B also supported a grant of all purpose access. The conditions imposed on the detailed permission were an impermissible modification of the original grant.

REDROW HOMES LTD v. FIRST SECRETARY OF STATE; *sub nom.* R. (ON THE APPLICATION OF REDROW HOMES LTD) v. FIRST SECRETARY OF STATE, [2004] EWCA Civ 1375, [2005] J.P.L. 502, Mummery, L.J., CA (Civ Div).

3294. Planning permission–Development–Government policy safeguarding land for airport runway–Objectors' opportunities for review

The claimant (P), a house builder and member of a consortium which included a local authority and English Partnerships, sought judicial review of the defendant secretary of state's alleged failure or refusal to institute an appropriate mechanism for the continual and proactive review of a policy relating to air transport adopted in a White Paper which had been presented to Parliament in December 2003. In 1998, P had sought planning permission to develop a large area of land near Gatwick Airport for residential and business use. In 1999, the secretary of state made a direction preventing the local authority from granting planning permission without special authorisation. The White Paper described the Government's support for a new runway at Heathrow Airport and provided that if "stringent environmental limits" could not be met at Heathrow, land near to Gatwick should be safeguarded so that a wide spaced runway could be constructed there. P argued, inter alia, that (1) the opportunity that it had to make written representations to the secretary of state was inadequate, and fairness required that there should be some form of hearing or inquiry so that evidence, such as that relating to its suggestion that a "hybrid" runway at Gatwick be considered, could be tested; (2) fairness also required that the secretary of state should commission work from the British Airports Authority and the Civil Aviation Authority, and within the Department of Transport, relating to the potential of a hybrid runway option; (3) the secretary of state should arrange for the British Airports Authority, the Civil Aviation Authority and the Department of Transport to attend any planning inquiry.

Held, refusing the application, that (1) fairness did not require that the secretary of state should arrange for some form of extra statutory hearing or inquiry. P could present its case at a planning inquiry. The secretary of state's direction merely prevented the local planning authority from granting planning permission; it did not prevent P from appealing against the non determination of the 1998 application, or any new application that the consortium might choose to make. A planning inquiry was not merely an appropriate forum for P's arguments; it was the appropriate forum for such arguments. Even if the opportunity of a planning inquiry was not available to P, it would not be unfair or unreasonable to confine it to making written representations. P had accepted that the secretary of state could lawfully make the policy, after considering written representations in the consultation exercise; it was therefore not the least unfair or unreasonable for the secretary of state to suggest that P should make written representations should it wish to argue that the policy be reviewed. (2) As a matter of principle, it was difficult to see how a duty to commission particular research in respect of a particular policy could exist. The secretary of state's department's technical advisers had concluded that the material produced by P did not materially alter the basis on which the policies in the White Paper had been prepared. It was impossible to say that the secretary of state was not entitled, in the light of that advice, to conclude that he would not commission any further work. There appeared to be no reason why P could not commission further work itself. (3) If an inquiry was arranged, the bodies referred to by P would be able to decide whether, and if so how, they wished to participate. It was, however, quite unrealistic to seek "assurances" at this stage as to their future conduct, even if it was in the secretary of state's power to give such assurances in relation to an inquiry arranged by the planning inspectorate, when the detail of P's case was not known.

R. (ON THE APPLICATION OF PERSIMMON HOMES (SOUTH EAST) LTD) v. SECRETARY OF STATE FOR TRANSPORT, [2005] EWHC 96, [2005] 2 P. & C.R. 24, Sullivan, J., QBD (Admin).

3295. Planning permission–Development plans–Method of interpretation of development plans

[Human Rights Act 1998 Sch.1 Part I Art.8.]

The applicant parish council (C) sought to quash a decision by the respondent secretaries of state to grant planning permission for the construction of an underground gas storage facility. The relevant local authority had refused planning permission. As a result of that decision being appealed, the secretaries of state appointed a planning inspector to conduct an inquiry. Although the planning inspector had recommended a refusal of planning permission, the secretaries of state granted planning permission. Issues arose as to whether the secretaries of state had (1) given proper regard to the pertinent development plan; (2) properly considered alternative sites and the impact of the site in environmental and risk terms; (3) given clear and sufficient reasons; (4) had sufficient regard for C's rights under the Human Rights Act 1998.

Held, refusing the appeal, that (1) the secretaries of state had given proper regard to the pertinent development plan. In considering development plans it was appropriate to adopt an interpretative approach that considered the purpose of the plan rather than an approach that was semantic or too legalistic. There were pragmatic reasons for that approach. Development plans were drafted by planners for planners, were often loosely drafted and were not intended to be legally binding, *Edinburgh City Council v. Secretary of State for Scotland* [1997] 1 W.L.R. 1447, [1997] C.L.Y. 6350 considered, *R. v. Derbyshire CC, ex p. Woods* [1998] Env. L.R. 277, [1997] C.L.Y. 4106 applied. (2) The secretaries of state had properly considered alternative sites and the impact of the site in environmental and risk terms. (3) The secretaries of state had given clear and sufficient reasons. (4) A balance was to be struck between competing rights of individuals and the community as a whole. The secretaries of state had carried out a balancing procedure that had complied with the Human Rights Act 1998 Sch.1 Part I Art.8, *Lough v. First Secretary of State* [2004] EWCA Civ 905, [2004] 1 W.L.R. 2557, [2004] 9 C.L. 391 applied.

CRANAGE PARISH COUNCIL v. FIRST SECRETARY OF STATE, [2004] EWHC 2949, [2005] 2 P. & C.R. 23, Davis, J., QBD (Admin).

3296. **Planning permission–Green belt–Contaminated land–Existence of very special circumstances for setting aside presumption against development–Public interest in removing asbestos–Failure to give reasons**

The appellant (D), the owner of a property in a green belt area, appealed against the planning inspector's refusal to set aside the presumption against inappropriate development in the green belt. D had sought planning permission for residential development of the site which had derelict buildings on it and was contaminated with asbestos. Planning permission had been refused by the local authority on green belt policy grounds and D had appealed to the secretary of state, arguing that removing the asbestos constituted "very special circumstances" and justified the grant of planning permission. Removal and disposal of the asbestos was strongly recommended by Planning Policy Guidance Note 2 on Green Belts, the local environment officer and the fire service. D was unable to fund the removal herself without the monies generated by the development. The Inspector referred to guidance contained in Circular 02/2000 and concluded that whilst it would be in the public interest to remove the asbestos, it did not constitute "very special circumstances" and was not sufficient to set aside the presumption against inappropriate development in the green belt. On appeal, D argued that the inspector had been misinterpreted the policy and had failed to give adequate reasons for rejecting the "very special circumstances" argument.

Held, allowing the appeal in part, that (1) the inspector had not misinterpreted or misapplied the advice in the Circular. It was clear from the wording he had used that he was not applying a general principle that contamination could never amount to "very special circumstances" and on that basis he was entitled to conclude that the risk posed by the contamination in the instant case did not justify the proposed development. (2) The inspector had, however, failed to give adequate reasons for his conclusions and there was, at least, substantial doubt as to whether the necessary balancing exercise had been carried out. Having concluded that the public interest required the risk to be dealt with and that there was no obvious appropriate green belt use that would facilitate the removal of the hazard, he had then failed to address the question of why the contamination did not amount to "very special circumstances" in the instant case. There was no evidence that the inspector had considered the impact of the proposed development in this regard and D had been prejudiced as a result, *South Buckinghamshire DC v. Porter (No.2)* [2004] UKHL 33, [2004] 1 W.L.R. 1953, [2004] C.L.Y. 3087 applied. The inspector's decision was, accordingly, quashed.

DOWMUNT-IWASZKIEWICZ v. FIRST SECRETARY OF STATE, [2004] EWHC 2537, [2005] Env. L.R. 19, Owen, J., QBD (Admin).

3297. Planning permission–Green belt–Gypsies seeking to develop site–Evidence of availability of alternative sites

The applicant gypsy (S) applied to quash a decision of the first respondent secretary of state to uphold an enforcement notice served by the second respondent local authority requiring S to discontinue use of metropolitan green belt land for stationing caravans for residential purposes. It was not in dispute that the use of the land as a private gypsy caravan site constituted development that was inappropriate in the green belt. The material question was whether very special circumstances existed to justify such development. The inspector appointed to deal with the defence to the enforcement notice decided that such circumstances existed because, among other factors, there was a lack of alternative sites available to S. However, the secretary of state, having called in the appeal, concluded that there was "no clear evidence" of any efforts by S to find alternative sites, aside from enquiries in respect of one site, and that the lack of evidence of a search for other sites weighed against S. He decided that there were no very special circumstances sufficient to clearly outweigh the harm to the green belt. S argued that the conclusion reached by the secretary state that there was "no clear evidence" or "a lack of evidence" of any other efforts on his part to find alternative sites was unjustified. The secretary of state argued that there was a specific evidential burden on gypsies to put evidence before an inspector in connection with their searches for alternative sites.

Held, granting the application, that where a gypsy sought to obtain permission to develop a site in the green belt, the decision as to whether there were very special circumstances for permitting the development in the green belt would require consideration to be given to the evidence of the availability of an alternative site in the relevant planning district in which the application had been made. The overall burden was upon an applicant for planning permission for development in the green belt to establish that very special circumstances existed. However, in respect of gypsy cases, it was obvious from the contents of Departmental Circular 1/94 (Gypsy Sites and Planning) and the existence of advice to local planning authorities that invaluable data would not come from the applicant for permission. The best evidence likely to be available in connection with alternative sites in the relevant planning district would be from statistics and information available to the local authority. The purpose of the guidance to local authorities contained in Circular 1/94 was to secure that such evidence was available. It was not the case that where the evidence established that no alternative sites were available, the failure of a gypsy to search was relevant. Conversely, the failure of a gypsy to search could mean a fact finder was unable to conclude that there were no alternative sites. That did not mean evidence as to availability of alternative sites outside the green belt and district in which the application was made would not generally be relevant. The secretary of state's conclusion that there was "no clear evidence" or "a lack of evidence" was not to the point. The inspector had no difficulty in coming to the conclusion that there were no alternative sites available. The secretary of state had ignored material which suggested that there had been searches, as well as S's evidence in connection with alternative sites that had proved too expensive. He regarded Circular 1/94 as a source of an obligation, the non fulfilment of which he held against S, where it was plain that the inspector had concluded that no advice or assistance would have been forthcoming, save that which was in the local plan. Further, the secretary of state had not indicated how he weighed against S the lack of evidence in connection with his searches for other sites. Since, on a true reading of the secretary of state's conclusion, he had rejected the finding of the lack of available sites simply because of the lack of clear evidence of searches by S, he had plainly failed to take account of all the evidence.

SIMMONS v. FIRST SECRETARY OF STATE, [2005] EWHC 287, [2005] 2 P. & C.R. 25, Newman, J., QBD (Admin).

3298. Planning permission—Landfill sites—Environmental impact assessments—Integrated pollution prevention and control—Setting of parameter constraints for separate but overlapping processes

[Town and Country Planning (Environmental Impact Assessment) (England and Wales) Regulations 1999 (SI 1999 293) Sch.4 Part II para.3; Pollution Prevention and Control (England and Wales) Regulations 2000 (SI 2000 1973).]

The applicant (K), a local resident, applied to quash a decision of the respondent Secretary of State to grant planning permission for the use of part of an active rock salt mine for waste disposal purposes. The proposed landfill was subject to control under both the Town and Country Planning (Environmental Impact Assessment) (England and Wales) Regulations 1999 and the Pollution Prevention and Control (England and Wales) Regulations 2000. K contended that (1) the environmental assessment process had been inadequate because the types of waste to be deposited had not been specified with sufficient particularity in the environmental statement for the purposes of Sch.4 Part II para.3 of the 1999 Regulations; (2) the Secretary of State had erred in law in dealing with an environmental effect by way of a planning condition, requiring a scheme for monitoring airborne particulates to be agreed with the county planning authority, instead of dealing with it as part of the environmental statement.

Held, refusing the application, that (1) the description of generic waste types in the environmental statement provided sufficient information for the Secretary of State to be able to identify and assess the main effects of the development on the environment and to set the parameters within which future details could be worked out, *R. (on the application of Jones) v. Mansfield DC* [2003] EWCA Civ 1408, [2004] Env. L.R. 21, [2003] C.L.Y. 3421 applied, *R. (on the application of Blewett) v. Derbyshire CC* [2003] EWHC 2775, [2004] Env. L.R. 29, [2004] 6 C.L. 377 followed. (2) Although there could be some overlap between the two control regimes, they were separate regimes with different functions. A decision maker in the environmental impact assessment process was concerned with the development's impact on the use of land; a decision maker in the pollution prevention and control process was concerned with its potential polluting effect on the environment. The decision maker in the environmental impact assessment process had to set the parameters or constraints within which the likely significant effects of a development were to be determined but was then entitled to rely on the proper operation of further controls, whether by way of planning condition or under the permit system of the 2000 Regulations, *Smith v. Secretary of State for the Environment, Transport and the Regions* [2003] EWCA Civ 262, [2003] Env. L.R. 32, [2003] C.L.Y. 3420 applied.

R. (ON THE APPLICATION OF KENT) v. FIRST SECRETARY OF STATE; *sub nom.* KENT v. FIRST SECRETARY OF STATE, [2004] EWHC 2953, [2005] Env. L.R. 30, Sir Michael Harrison, QBD (Admin).

3299. Planning permission—Major infrastructure projects—Inquiries procedure

TOWN AND COUNTRY PLANNING (MAJOR INFRASTRUCTURE PROJECT INQUIRIES PROCEDURE) (ENGLAND) RULES 2005, SI 2005 2115; made under the Tribunals and Inquiries Act 1992 s.9. In force: August 24, 2005; £3.50.

These Rules, which revoke the Town and Country Planning (Major Infrastructure Project Inquiries Procedure) (England) Rules 2002 (SI 2002 1223), prescribe the procedure to be followed in connection with local inquiries relating to applications for planning permission or for the approval of a local planning authority required under a development order held by the Secretary of State in England, where he thinks that the development to which the application relates is of national or regional importance.

3300. Planning permission–Notices–Planning authorities–Obligation to give reasons for decision–Discretion of court to quash defective notice

[Town and Country Planning (General Development Procedure) Order 1995 (SI 1995 419) Art.22(1)(a); Town and Country Planning (General Development Procedure) (England) (Amendment) Order 2003 (SI 2003 2047) Art.5.]

The claimant (W) sought judicial review of a decision of the local authority (B) to grant planning permission for a block of flats to be built on property adjoining W's garden. The decision notice had included a summary of the relevant policy documents taken into account by B in arriving at the decision but had not set out, as required by the Town and Country Planning (General Development Procedure) Order 1995 Art.22(1)(a) as amended by the Town and Country Planning (General Development Procedure) (England) (Amendment) Order 2003 Art.5, its reasons for concluding that permission should be granted. Following W's commencement of judicial review proceedings B's lawyers had contacted individual councillors to ask for their reasons and had prepared an amended decision notice. Initial responses from two of the councillors had included factual errors in respect of the size of the proposed new building. B submitted that the original decision notice should be replaced by the amended notice. W contended that the notice should be quashed.

Held, granting the application, that it was unlawful for a local authority to issue a grant of planning permission that did not include a summary of the reasons for its decision, and the court should exercise its discretion to quash the defective notice unless there were good reasons not to do so, *R. v. Westminster City Council, ex p. Ermakov* [1996] 2 All E.R. 302, [1995] C.L.Y. 2568 applied, *R. (on the application of Richardson) v. North Yorkshire CC* [2003] EWCA Civ 1860, [2004] 1 W.L.R. 1920, [2004] 2 C.L. 423 and *Younger Homes (Northern) Ltd v. First Secretary of State* [2004] EWCA Civ 1060 distinguished. The legislation was intended to ensure that planning decisions were taken in public and that the public were informed of the reasons for the decision so that they could challenge it if necessary. It was possible that where a decision notice had been issued without a summary of reasons, but a local authority subsequently attempted to rectify the defect by holding a further committee meeting in public session at which the reasons were agreed, the court would exercise its discretion to allow amendment of the notice. However, it was not sufficient, especially since the councillors' recollection of their reasons had been imperfect, for the reasons to be elicited in private correspondence between B's lawyers and the committee members.

R. (ON THE APPLICATION OF WALL) v. BRIGHTON AND HOVE CITY COUNCIL, [2004] EWHC 2582, [2005] 1 P. & C.R. 33, Sullivan, J., QBD (Admin).

3301. Planning permission–Permitted development–Satellites and microwave antenna

TOWN AND COUNTRY PLANNING (GENERAL PERMITTED DEVELOPMENT) (ENGLAND) (AMENDMENT) (NO.2) ORDER 2005, SI 2005 2935; made under the Town and Country Planning Act 1990 s.59, s.60, s.333. In force: November 25, 2005; £3.00.

This Order amends the Town and Country Planning (General Permitted Development) Order 1995 (SI 1995 418) which confers permitted development rights in respect of the erection of satellite and microwave antenna.

3302. Planning permission–Permitted development–Use classes

TOWN AND COUNTRY PLANNING (GENERAL PERMITTED DEVELOPMENT) (AMENDMENT) (ENGLAND) ORDER 2005, SI 2005 85; made under the Town and Country Planning Act 1990 s.59, s.333. In force: April 21, 2005; £3.00.

This Order amends the Town and Country Planning (General Permitted Development) Order 1995 (SI 1995 418) which grants planning permission for certain changes of use by reference to classes of use specified in the Town and Country Planning (Use Classes) Order 1987 (SI 1987 764). That Order is amended by the Town and Country Planning (Use Classes) (Amendment)

(England) Order 2005 (SI 2005 84) which substitutes for the former Class A3 (food and drink), three new use classes: restaurants and cafes (A3), drinking establishments (A4) and hot food takeaways (A5). This Order reflects the three new use classes, which replace the former Class A3 (food and drink). The three new use classes are given permitted development rights to change to shops (A1) uses or financial and professional services (A2) uses specified in the 1987 Order.

3303. Planning permission–Planning conditions–Absence of construction conditions–Implied conditions

The claimant local authority (S) appealed against a decision of the Secretary of State to quash an enforcement notice in respect of the construction of earth bunds on a golf course by the second respondent (P). P had been granted planning permission for the construction of a golf course. It was a condition of the grant that details of the engineering works had to be submitted and approved. The details were subsequently submitted but earth bunds were later constructed on the golf course in a manner that was not in accordance with the details. The Secretary of State considered that in the absence of a construction condition he could not imply into the condition a requirement that any construction had to be in accordance with the details. S argued, in reliance on *Crisp from the Fens Ltd v. Rutland CC* (1950) 114 J.P. 105, that planning consents were not to be construed strictly in the manner of a statute but in a common sense way with their purpose in mind. The Secretary of State contended that the planning permission condition was clear and unambiguous.

Held, dismissing the appeal, that in the absence of a construction condition, a planning inspector could not imply into a condition for details of engineering works a requirement that any construction had to be in accordance with such details. Planning permission was no longer considered by reference to the intention of either the applicant or the local planning authority. A planning permission was a public document and breaches of it could have serious repercussions. Therefore, it was essential that any condition was clearly and expressly imposed. It was not possible for a condition to be implied, nor was it possible for an obligation to be implied into a condition as that amounted to an implied condition. In the instant case the planning permission was clear and unambiguous and the Secretary of State was correct to quash the enforcement notice, *Trustees of Walton on Thames Charities v. Walton and Weybridge Urban DC* 68 L.G.R. 488, [1970] C.L.Y. 2785 and *Carter Commercial Developments Ltd (In Administration) v. Secretary of State for Transport, Local Government and the Regions* [2002] EWCA Civ 1994, [2003] J.P.L. 1048, [2003] 8 C.L. 407 considered, *Crisp* cited.

SEVENOAKS DC v. FIRST SECRETARY OF STATE; *sub nom.* R. (ON THE APPLICATION OF SEVENOAKS DC) v. FIRST SECRETARY OF STATE, [2004] EWHC 771, [2005] 1 P. & C.R. 13, Sullivan, J., QBD (Admin Ct).

3304. Planning permission–Planning conditions–Curtailing rights previously granted

The appellant (M), a company which ran an indoor market, appealed against a planning inspector's decision to uphold an enforcement notice issued by a local authority. The market had been developed in two stages: the original building was constructed pursuant to an outline planning permission and a reserved matters approval granted in 1991, and an extension was constructed pursuant to planning permission granted in 1994. Both the 1991 reserved matters approval and the 1994 permission had restricted the use of the market to Saturdays and Sundays. However, the market had been used on a number of days other than Saturdays and Sundays. To remedy this breach of planning control, the local authority granted planning permission in 1997, of which condition 6 allowed trading on Saturdays and Sundays and 10 other days per year. M had proceeded to hold a market every Wednesday, thereby exceeding the 10 permitted days. The local authority had then issued the enforcement notice. The inspector found that the conditions in the 1991 reserved matters approval which restricted the use of the market to Saturday and Sunday were invalid, therefore from 1991 it had been lawful to hold markets in the original building without any restrictions as to the days of the week. M submitted that (1) the inspector was wrong to conclude that the 1994 permission had effected an alteration to the conditions of use of the original building; (2) following the test of reasonableness of a condition as stated in *Newbury DC v. Secretary of State for the Environment* [1981] A.C. 578, [1980] C.L.Y. 2667 the inspector had erred in law in concluding that the restrictions of the 1994 permission were valid; (3) (i) it was not open to the local authority, by condition 6 of the 1997 permission, to confine the use of the overall building, (ii) if it was, alternatively the 1997 permission had not been implemented, (iii) in any event condition 6 was not a valid condition; (4) the inspector had erred in law by virtue of the lack of reasons he gave in his decision letter.

Held, dismissing the appeal, that (1) the mere fact that the inspector had used the expression "a new chapter in the planning history" when referring to the 1994 permission did not mean that he had found that it swept away previous rights, *South Staffordshire DC v. Secretary of State for the Environment* (1988) 55 P. & C.R. 258, [1988] C.L.Y. 3436 considered. The inspector did not find that the unfettered rights of use were lost by the implementation of the 1994 permission. (2) The conditions in the 1994 permission were valid as they were imposed for a planning purpose and were reasonable considering the tests of *Newbury*. (3) (i) It was open to a local authority to restrict the use of a building, curtailing rights previously given in prior planning permission. In the instant case the local authority was free to impose condition 6 of the 1997 permission, *Jennings Motors Ltd v. Secretary of State for the Environment* [1982] Q.B. 541, [1982] C.L.Y. 3130 followed, (ii) the opening of the market on days other than Saturday and Sunday was unlawful as regards the extension building. The 1997 permission allowed for a relaxation of the restriction on days of use: it followed that because the use of the market on days other than Saturday and Sunday continued after the grant of the 1997 permission, that permission was implemented, (iii) considering that M had written to the local authority to vary the restrictions on days contained in the reserved matters decision relating to the initial market construction and acknowledged it would be happy to accept such a condition, the submission that condition 6 was not valid was completely unfounded. In any event, the court was persuaded that condition 6 satisfied the tests for lawfulness of a condition found in *Newbury*. (4) M had not been substantially prejudiced by any inadequacies of the decision letter, albeit that at least one of the paragraphs of the inspector's decision was questionable, *South Buckinghamshire DC v. Porter (No.2)* [2004] UKHL 33, [2004] 1 W.L.R. 1953 and *Newbury* followed.

MARKETS SOUTH WEST (HOLDINGS) LTD v. FIRST SECRETARY OF STATE, [2004] EWHC 1917, [2005] J.P.L. 684, Blackburne, J., QBD (Admin Ct).

3305. Planning permission–Planning procedures–Court's discretion to quash decision following serious irregularities in application process

[Town and Country Planning Act 1990 s.65(6); Town and Country Planning (General Development Procedure) Order 1995 (SI 1995 419) Art.6(1).]

The claimants (P) sought judicial review of the defendant local authority's decision to grant planning permission for a development on land adjoining P's garden. The planning applicant (D) had submitted an application involving land partly owned by P without serving prior notice upon P as required by the Town and Country Planning (General Development Procedure) Order 1995 Art.6(1). D falsely certified, contrary to the Town and Country Planning Act 1990 s.65(6), that all the relevant land was owned by him, and later falsely certified that the required owners' notice had been served. Although it should have realised that the certificates were false, the local authority proceeded in the mistaken belief that it was under a duty to determine the application within eight weeks of receipt and accordingly, held the planning hearing without allowing P the full statutory notice period. The local authority submitted that, although voidable, the decision should be allowed to stand as it had acted in good faith and P had suffered no prejudice.

Held, granting the application, that the grant of planning permission would be quashed. Although the court had a discretion to uphold permission despite irregularities in the application process, to preserve the benefit of the permission in the light of D's complete disregard of the mandatory requirements of a statutory certificate would come close to undermining the purpose of the legislation, *Main v. Swansea City Council* (1985) 49 P. & C.R. 26, [1985] C.L.Y. 3463 distinguished. Nor could it be accepted that the law as stated in *Main* anticipated saving voidable grants of planning permission where there had been a deliberate failure to comply with mandatory requirements of the legislative scheme to which the local planning authority, acting in good faith, had been party and where, under an error of law, it had unnecessarily gone on to press for a prompt determination. Further, the local authority had not convincingly answered P's complaint that they had had too short a time to consider the application and had failed to realise that they could have raised a point relating to D's proposed turning circle at the hearing.

R. (ON THE APPLICATION OF PRIDMORE) v. SALISBURY DC, [2004] EWHC 2511, [2005] 1 P. & C.R. 32, Newman, J., QBD (Admin).

3306. Planning permission – Quarries – Review of old mineral planning permissions – Challenge to entry on list

[Environment Act 1995 Sch.13 para.2(4), Sch.13 para.9; Civil Procedure Rules 1998 (SI 1998 3132).]

The appellant quarry owner (S) appealed against a decision ([2004] EWHC 1475, [2005] Env. L.R. 4) refusing declarations that a 1952 planning permission remained active and that two quarries could be worked in accordance with that permission. S was the leasehold owner of two quarries which were treated as a single planning unit. The planning status of the quarries depended on the true construction of a 1952 letter by which the minister granted planning permission for the winning and working of stone from those quarries and other quarries. The issue in relation to the letter was whether it granted a single permission in respect of all the quarries or separate planning permissions. Since the relevant planning permission had been granted before 1982 and the site was within a national park, it was a Phase I site under the Environment Act 1995 Sch.13 para.2(4). Schedule 13 to the 1995 Act provided a scheme for the review of old mineral planning permissions and required the mineral planning authority to prepare lists of the mineral sites in its area. The two quarries were entered in the list as a dormant site, but the other quarries covered by the minister's letter were listed as active sites. S challenged that conclusion on the basis that those two quarries were part of an active site with the other quarries covered by the 1952 permission, which constituted all the quarries as a single mineral site, and sought declarations that the 1952 permission remained active and that the two quarries could be worked in accordance with that permission.

Held, dismissing the appeal, that (1) it was impossible to be confident that either construction of the 1952 permission letter was plainly correct or wrong. Therefore the appeal court would not interfere with the judge's conclusion that the letter contained separate permissions for planning purposes. (2) In any event, the court could not make the declarations sought by S because they would purport to permit what Parliament clearly intended to forbid under the provisions of the 1995 Act, whose effect was that whether the two quarries were treated as a separate but dormant site (as they in fact appeared in the list) or as part of a larger composite site, which was not shown as such on the list, the 1952 permission no longer authorised the carrying out of minerals development at that site. The court would have to set aside or go behind the list, which could only be done in judicial review proceedings. There were formidable difficulties in the way of a judicial review application to challenge a decision made in 1996, which had since been acted upon and not challenged in the court below. (3) The judge was right to reject the submission that, by way of an evidential presumption of regularity, the list could be read as if it had been drawn to include the quarries in a single site, *Calder Gravel Ltd v. Kirklees MBC* (1990) 60 P. & C.R. 322, [1991] C.L.Y. 3516 distinguished. (4) A condition in an individual planning permission could be the subject of declaratory relief in private law proceedings since there was no reason to suppose that anyone apart from the landowner would be affected. The position in the instant case was very different. The quarries were no longer in the same ownership. If the scheme under the 1995 Act was to work as intended, a challenge to the list should be made before the dates specified in the list by which applications were to be made and conditions determined under Sch.13 para.9. A judicial review application brought within the time prescribed by the Civil Procedure Rules 1998 would have met that requirement.

STANCLIFFE STONE CO LTD v. PEAK DISTRICT NATIONAL PARK AUTHORITY, [2005] EWCA Civ 747, [2006] Env. L.R. 7, Chadwick, L.J., CA (Civ Div).

3307. Planning permission–Retail development–Effect of planning officer's error concerning extent of restriction on use of premises

[Town and Country Planning Act 1990 s.106.]

The claimant (L) sought to quash two planning permissions granted by the defendant (R) to the interested party (P). L also sought to quash a deed of agreement entered into pursuant to the Town and Country Planning Act 1990 s.106, which was conditional upon the granting and implementation of the second planning permission. The permissions related to a site on which there was a substantial building which had been used as a retail warehouse. A previous owner of the land entered into a planning obligation agreement (the 1993 obligation) pursuant to s.106 which provided that the land should be used solely as a retail warehouse for the storage and distribution of durable goods. P had acquired the site and wished to divide the existing building to comprise six separate units, each to be a retail warehouse, and to build three further units. The first permission covered the works needed for the division of the existing building and the second the erection of the three new units. P also offered R a s.106 agreement which limited the use of the new retail units and the extent of floor space permitted for trading purposes. The planning officer (X) recommended the approval of both applications, in the case of the second application subject to a satisfactory s.106 agreement. By the time of the hearing P had already carried out most of the work for which permission had been granted. L submitted that (1) R had misconstrued the 1993 obligation, and that the restriction in relation to durable goods extended not only to Units 5 and 6 but also to the whole of one and a small part of another of the three units to be constructed pursuant to the second planning application; (2) the 1993 obligation also limited the use of the permission to use "solely as a retail warehouse", and therefore the subdivision was prohibited and only one unit was permitted. R and P accepted that the extent of the limitation to durable goods was misunderstood and X accepted that he had been wrong, but they contended that the error was not one which should lead to the quashing of the permissions since the benefits resulting from the overall development with the restrictions contained in the obligation were such as would have, in any event, produced the same result. R submitted that L's conduct and motives were such as to justify rejection of the claim in that L, as neighbouring landowners, were concerned about traffic generation and wanted improvements to the neighbouring road which would benefit them.

Held, allowing the application that (1) It was plain that X did regard the lack of limitation to durable goods as of some significance and therefore the error could not be said to be trivial. The planning permission would probably have been granted, despite real concerns, but the conditions attached and any benefits which would be contained in a s.106 agreement might well have been more onerous for P. The court could not rule out that possibility and so it could not be said that R would necessarily have reached the same decision. Accordingly the planning permissions should be quashed, *Simplex GE (Holdings) Ltd v. Secretary of State for the Environment* (1989) 57 P. & C.R. 306, [1989] C.L.Y. 3578 applied. (2) The words in the 1993 obligation did not limit the number of units to be permitted on the premises but only limited the use of any such units to retail warehousing. The use of the indefinite article in "solely as a retail warehouse" did not of itself bear an implication of singularity, *Martin v. David Wilson Homes Ltd* [2004] EWCA Civ 1027, [2004] 39 E.G. 134 applied. The second ground therefore failed. (3) Motive was generally speaking irrelevant in judicial reviews of planning permissions and should not lead to the exercise of discretion not to grant relief where an error of law had been established, *R. (on the application of Mount Cook Land Ltd) v. Westminster City Council* [2003] EWCA Civ 1346, [2004] C.P. Rep. 12, [2004] 8 C.L. 47 considered.

R. (ON THE APPLICATION OF LEGAL & GENERAL ASSURANCE SOCIETY LTD) v. RUSHMOOR BC, [2004] EWHC 2094, [2005] 1 P. & C.R. 26, Collins, J., QBD (Admin Ct).

3308. **Planning permission – Screening opinions – Failure to comply with mandatory procedures for issuing opinion – Lawfulness of opinion**

[Town and Country Planning Act 1990 s.106, s.288; Town and Country Planning (Environmental Impact Assessment) (England and Wales) Regulations 1999 (SI 1999 293) Reg.6(4), Reg.8.]

The appellant company (Y) appealed against a judge's refusal ([2003] EWHC 3058) to quash a planning permission which had been granted by the Secretary of State. Developers sought permission for a retail development. Following an inquiry the Secretary of State was minded to grant permission subject to an agreement under the Town and Country Planning Act 1990 s.106. One developer sold its holding to Y. Y wished to develop part of the site for residential use. The Secretary of State refused to reopen the inquiry. He did not make a screening direction under the Town and Country Planning (Environmental Impact Assessment) (England and Wales) Regulations 1999 Reg.6(4) and Reg.8 because there already existed a screening opinion of the local planning authority. The s.106 agreement was signed by the other developers and permission was issued. Y argued that (1) the screening opinion put forward by the Secretary of State did not constitute an opinion lawfully made within the meaning of the Regulations; (2) the Secretary of State had granted permission without undertaking the procedures for ascertaining whether the development applied for was an EIA development; (3) the permission was liable to be quashed under s.288 of the 1990 Act.

Held, dismissing the appeal, that (1) the screening opinion was lawful. Although the opinion was unsigned, had not been placed on the planning register and had not been sent to the applicant for planning permission, those breaches of the Regulations were not capable of taking the document outside the statutory definition of a screening opinion, *R. (on the application of Lebus) v. South Cambridgeshire DC* [2002] EWHC 2009, [2003] Env. L.R. 17, [2003] C.L.Y. 3422 considered. (2) The local authority considered that no environmental statement was required because, in the event of the development being held to be an EIA development, the necessary traffic information would be given in a traffic assessment. That was wrong as a matter of law. However, there had been transparency in the EIA process and any errors were de minimis. (3) Before the court could quash the permission under s.288 of the 1990 Act, Y had to show that its interests had been substantially prejudiced. That had not been demonstrated, *Berkeley v. Secretary of State for the Environment, Transport and the Regions (No.1)* [2001] 2 A.C. 603, [2000] C.L.Y. 4460 considered.

YOUNGER HOMES (NORTHERN) LTD v. FIRST SECRETARY OF STATE, [2004] EWCA Civ 1060, [2005] Env. L.R. 12, Dame Elizabeth Butler-Sloss (President), CA (Civ Div).

3309. Planning permission–Telecommunications masts–Effect of late issue of local authority's notice of refusal of prior approval

[Town and Country Planning Act 1990 s.174(2); Human Rights Act 1998 s.3, Sch.1 Part I Art.6; Town and Country Planning (General Permitted Development) Order 1995 (SI 1995 418); European Convention on Human Rights 1950.]

The claimant (N) applied for judicial review of the decision of a planning inspector, appointed by the defendant secretary of state, that the second interested party (T), a mobile phone company, had planning permission under the Town and Country Planning (General Permitted Development) Order 1995 for the erection of a telecommunications mast. The local authority had issued T with enforcement notices after T, having taken the view that the local authority's notice of refusal of prior approval for the siting and appearance of the mast had been issued out of time, erected the mast. The inspector allowed T's appeal against the enforcement notices on the ground of the Town and Country Planning Act 1990 s.174(2)(c) and found that T were not in breach of planning control and were free to begin development. Accordingly, the inspector did not consider T's ground of appeal under s.174(2)(a) of the Act and did not rule on the merits of the points raised by N and other local residents in relation to the effects of the mast on health and the value of their homes. N submitted that (1) by serving its notice of refusal late, the local authority had prevented its determination from having any effect, thereby giving rise to a breach of her right to a fair trial; (2) the inspector should have held, in relation to s.174(2)(c), that T did not in fact have planning permission; he should have determined the merits under s.174(2)(a); and by virtue of the Human Rights Act 1998 s.3 the words of the 1995 Order and the 1990 Act could be read so as not to deprive N of her right to a fair trial.

Held, refusing the application, that (1) N's rights under Sch.1 Part I Art.6 of the 1998 Act had been infringed. N had been deprived of her right under Art.6 to an effective determination by the local authority in respect of her representations on health issues and the appearance of the mast as it affected local residents and the value of their homes. (2) The scheme under the Order and the legislation could be operated compatibly with the European Convention on Human Rights 1950. To contemplate adding in words that would have the effect of undoing the rights of a third party and forcing it to remove that which it had had a right to erect, because the statute had been operated by the local authority in a way that infringed a Convention right, went beyond what s.3 of the 1998 Act had in contemplation. N's attack on the decision of the inspector was misconceived. On the issue under s.174(2)(c) of whether T actually had planning permission, N's points on the merits of siting and appearance had no relevance and her Art.6 rights were not engaged. N had a complaint of substance in relation to circumstances for which only the local authority had responsibility, namely the failure to make effective the determination that prior approval should be refused and the fact that she was deprived of the right to make her points on the merits in an appeal against the local authority's determination on prior approval. T had done nothing to affect or interfere with N's Art.6 rights. The inspector hearing the appeal against the enforcement notices had no jurisdiction to consider what should flow from the determination of the local authority not being effective. Nor was it the scheme in the Order that prevented the determination of N's rights from being effective.

R. (ON THE APPLICATION OF NUNN) v. FIRST SECRETARY OF STATE, [2005] EWCA Civ 101, [2005] 2 All E.R. 987, Waller, L.J., CA (Civ Div).

3310. Planning permission–Time limits–Site developer's deal to transfer adjacent land to local authority–Legitimate expectation of extension for reserved matters

[Town and Country Planning Act 1990 s.73, s.106, s.288.]

The Secretary of State appealed against the quashing of his planning inspector's decision to uphold a local authority's refusal to grant K, a property developer, more time to obtain approval of its plans for a residential development on a green field site which it owned. In 1998 the original owner of K's site entered into an agreement with the local authority under the Town and Country Planning Act 1990 s.106. It was agreed that, for a nominal sum of £1, the owner would transfer land adjoining the site to the authority for community facilities. A few days later K's predecessor was given outline planning permission for the development, subject to a condition that it applied to the local authority for approval of reserved matters within three years and started work within five years. The adjoining land was transferred, but the owner did not apply for approval of reserved matters within the three years. When K subsequently acquired the site it applied under s.73 for an extension of another two years. The local authority refused because changes in planning policy since 1998 now meant previously developed land should be reused before green field sites were developed. K appealed but the planning inspector upheld the local authority's refusal. K challenged the planning inspector's decision under s.288 of the 1990 Act and the judge held that K should have been granted an extension because (1) as a result of the transfer of adjoining land, K had a legitimate expectation of a substantive benefit, and (2) when the inspector considered the local authority's obligation to K, he should have given more weight to the fact that the landowner had a continuing obligation to the local authority under the s.106 agreement.

Held, allowing the appeal, that (1) the legitimate expectation of a substantive benefit could not be the renewal of planning permission at any date into the future; it meant only that the application for outline planning permission would be granted and that any subsequent s.73 application for a time extension would be dealt with in accordance with established legal principles, which was what the original landowner and K received, and (2) it was not appropriate for the court to construe the inspector's decision letter as showing that he left out of account a matter of which he was clearly aware, *Seddon Properties Ltd v. Secretary of State for the Environment* [1981] 42 P. & C.R. 26, [1981] C.L.Y. 2730 applied. The obligation was more hypothetical than real in that it did not apply until the site was developed and therefore it did not need to be weighed against the planning policy objections.

KEBBELL DEVELOPMENT LTD v. FIRST SECRETARY OF STATE; *sub nom.* KEBBELL DEVELOPMENTS LTD v. SECRETARY OF STATE FOR THE ENVIRONMENT, TRANSPORT AND REGIONS; R. (ON THE APPLICATION OF KEBBELL DEVELOPMENT LTD) v. FIRST SECRETARY OF STATE, [2003] EWCA Civ 1855, [2004] J.P.L. 1710, Keene, L.J., CA.

3311. Planning policy–Exercise of planning functions–Isles of Scilly

TOWN AND COUNTRY PLANNING (ISLES OF SCILLY) ORDER 2005, SI 2005 2085; made under the Town and Country Planning Act 1990 s.319; and the Planning and Compulsory Purchase Act 2004 s.116. In force: August 24, 2005; £3.00.

This Order which revokes with saving the Town and Country Planning (Isles of Scilly) Order 1992 (SI 1992 1620) and revokes the Town and Country Planning (Isles of Scilly) Order 1990 (SI 1990 2233), provides for the exercise of planning functions in the Isles of Scilly by the Council of the Isles of Scilly.

3312. Planning policy–General development procedure

TOWN AND COUNTRY PLANNING (GENERAL DEVELOPMENT PROCEDURE) (AMENDMENT) (ENGLAND) ORDER 2005, SI 2005 2087; made under the Town and Country Planning Act 1990 s.59, s.71, s.76A, s.77, s.78, s.78A, s.79, Sch.1 para.7; and the Planning and Compulsory Purchase Act 2004 s.54. In force: August 24, 2005; £3.00.

This Order amends the Town and Country Planning (General Development Procedure) Order 1995 (SI 1995 419) in consequence of provisions in the Planning and Compulsory Purchase Act 2004. It also makes certain other minor amendments.

3313. **Planning policy guidance–Floods–Assessment of flood risk–Sequential test in guidance–Consideration of existence of flood defences**

The applicant housing developer (B) sought to quash a decision that planning permission should not be granted for B's proposed site because it was at high risk of tidal flooding. The inspector had decided that although the developer was prepared to reinforce existing flood defences, the site would remain at high risk of a 1 in 200 year tidal flood, and as such it should not be developed because there were other housing sites with a lower flood risk. under Planning Policy Guidance 25, development sites fell into one of three zones: little or no risk; low to medium risk; or high risk. The site was within the high risk Zone 3, which was defined as land where the annual probability of tidal and coastal flooding was 0.5 per cent or greater. B contended that the inspector failed to take into account the existence of a flood defence and so (1) did not properly apply the sequential test in the guidance because he did not consider the actual risk of flooding; (2) erred in concluding that the site was at higher risk of tidal flooding than other sites.

Held, granting the application, that (1) under the planning policy guidance relating to flood risk, planning authorities should apply the precautionary principle so that a development would be permitted in a higher risk category only if there were no reasonable options available in a lower risk category. The risk categories were based on flood plain maps and therefore the existence of flood defences did not need to be taken into account at this stage. However, their existence would come into consideration if there was no reasonable option available in a lower risk category. The inspector, therefore, correctly applied the sequential test. (2) The inspector's references to the site's higher flooding risk were derived from the flood plain map and while that was justifiable for the purposes of the sequential test, for other purposes it was necessary to take fully into account the possibility that the site had a level of flood protection that complied with the standard required by the guidance.

R. (ON THE APPLICATION OF THOMAS BATES & SON LTD) v. SECRETARY OF STATE FOR TRANSPORT, LOCAL GOVERNMENT AND THE REGIONS, [2004] EWHC 1818, [2005] 2 P. & C.R. 11, Harrison, J., QBD (Admin Ct).

3314. **Planning policy guidance–Telecommunications masts–Interpretation of Government Planning Policy Guideline 8**

The appellant secretary of state appealed against a decision ([2004] EWHC 1713, Times, July 8, 2004) quashing a planning inspector's refusal to grant planning permission. The respondent developers (T) had applied for planning permission to extend an existing mobile phone transmission station by building a mobile phone mast and headframes. The local planning authority had refused permission and T appealed to the inspector. He had considered the Government Planning Policy Guideline 8 (PPG8), which dealt with planning aspects of telecommunications, and held that although the proposal had met the guidelines issued by the International Commission on Non ionising Radiation Protection (ICNIRP), insufficient reassurances had been given that there could be no material harm, in terms of health concerns, to the living conditions of children in nearby schools. The inspector's decision was quashed on the grounds, inter alia, that T had given sufficient reassurances to all concerned and that the inspector had misunderstood PPG8 by expressing the view that it was open ended. The secretary of state argued that on a proper construction of PPG8, an actual health risk was distinct from a perceived health risk since PPG8 specifically provided that they each amounted to material planning considerations, and that accordingly the inspector had been entitled to take into account perceived health risks notwithstanding that the proposal had met the requirements of ICNIRP.

Held, dismissing the appeal, that the judge had been correct to hold that the inspector had misunderstood PPG8. The inspector had been wrong to find that although the proposal had met the ICNIRP guidelines levels, the policy was open ended. The judge had been correct to hold that the guidance contained in

PPG8 had been perfectly clear and that there was nothing open ended about the policy.

T MOBILE (UK) LTD v. FIRST SECRETARY OF STATE; HUTCHINSON 3G UK LTD v. FIRST SECRETARY OF STATE; ORANGE PERSONAL COMMUNICATIONS SERVICES LTD v. FIRST SECRETARY OF STATE, [2004] EWCA Civ 1763, [2005] Env. L.R. 18, Pill, L.J., CA (Civ Div).

3315. Planning procedures–Decisions–Timetables

TOWN AND COUNTRY PLANNING (TIMETABLE FOR DECISIONS) (ENGLAND) ORDER 2005, SI 2005 205; made under the Planning and Compulsory Purchase Act 2004 Sch.2 para.3. In force: April 1, 2005; £3.00.

The Planning and Compulsory Purchase Act 2004 Sch.2 requires the Secretary of State to make timetables for the purposes of decisions to which that Schedule applies, and enables him by order to specify decisions or descriptions of decisions to which a timetable is not to apply. This Order specifies those descriptions of decision.

3316. Rural areas–Countryside access–Appeals procedures–Wales

COUNTRYSIDE ACCESS (APPEALS PROCEDURES) (WALES) (AMENDMENT) REGULATIONS 2005, SI 2005 1154 (W.71); made under the Countryside and Rights of Way Act 2000 s.32, s.44. In force: April 29, 2005; £3.00.

Under the Countryside and Rights of Way Act 2000, the National Assembly for Wales has the power to make regulations to set out the procedures to be followed in determining appeals brought under Part I of the Act. These Regulations amend the Countryside Access (Appeals Procedures) (Wales) Regulations 2002 (SI 2002 1794) (W.169) by inserting a new Part VA and by making the necessary minor consequential amendments to enable the other provisions of the Appeals Procedures Regulations to apply to an appeal against a decision of a relevant authority not to act in accordance with an application for a direction under s.25(1)(a) of the Act, where appropriate. The new provisions introduce a fast-track procedure for the determination of an appeal brought by a person who applied to the relevant authority (the Countryside Council for Wales or, as the case may be, the relevant National Park authority) for a direction permitting the exclusion or restriction of access to land for the purposes of fire prevention and the relevant authority decided not to give the direction applied for; and enable a hearing to be held once the National Assembly has received the relevant preliminary information from the parties to enable the appeal to proceed.

3317. Tree preservation orders–Compensation–Local authority not responding to request for consent to fell trees subject to order–Deemed refusal of consent

[Town and Country Planning Act 1990.]

The claimant (D) sought the determination of preliminary issues arising in her claim against the defendant local authority for damage caused to her property by trees subject to a tree preservation order. D had notified her insurers (P) when cracks began appearing in her house. On investigation, these were attributed to subsidence caused by the trees' roots. D applied to the local authority for consent to fell the trees. No reply was forthcoming within the two month statutory time limit, and D appealed to the Secretary of State for Transport, Local Government and the Regions on the basis that the local authority's silence amounted to a deemed refusal of consent. Three years later, the secretary of state dismissed the appeal. In the meantime, D had sold the property, having been paid compensation of £50,000 by P for diminution in value. The preliminary issues that arose were (i) the actual date of refusal for the purposes of the claim, and (ii) whether compensation was payable for damage caused prior to that date.

Held, determining the preliminary issues, that (1) the order should be applied on the basis that a failure to determine an application for consent constituted a deemed refusal on which a claim for compensation could be based, and the date of the deemed refusal was two months after the local authority's receipt of the application. The meaning of "refusal" in the order had to be construed without reference to the Town and Country Planning Act 1990, *Bell v. Canterbury City Council* 86 L.G.R. 635, [1988] C.L.Y. 3533 followed. The role of the secretary of state was simply to decide whether to allow or dismiss an appeal. Consent was only capable of being given or refused by the local authority. (2) Only damage caused by the tree roots as a result of the refusal of consent could be the subject of compensation. Damage occurring before the date of refusal was irrelevant except in so far as it could be shown that the refusal had necessitated more costly works than would have been needed if consent had been given. Past damage might also be relevant to any issue of compensation for a loss in market value arising from a refusal of consent.

DUNCAN v. EPPING FOREST DC (PRELIMINARY ISSUES) [2004] R.V.R. 213, George Bartlett Q.C. (President), Lands Tr.

3318. Tree preservation orders—Compensation—Refusal of consent to fell—Diminution in value to property affected by tree roots—Measure of damages

The claimant (D), the refusal by the defendant (E) sought compensation for damage caused to a house she was trying to sell arising from E's refusal to grant consent to cut down two trees adjacent to the property that were subject to tree preservation orders and which D contended had caused a reduction in value. D asserted that she was entitled to the diminution in the market value and professional fees incurred in pursuing the appeal against the deemed refusal of consent. E said that compensation was payable to reflect the amount paid by D's insurers, less the likely cost of additional works necessary to protect the building from future damage if the trees remained.

Held, giving judgment for D, that the measure of D's loss included £50,000 diminution in the value of the house in its damaged state, less the cost of repairs D would have incurred if consent had been given. The expert evidence was that only repairs to the cracks at a cost of £5,500 would have been necessary if consent had been given. It was that amount that fell to be deducted from the diminution in value of the house, giving a figure of £44,500. As to professional fees incurred in pursuit of the appeal, it was reasonable for D to contest E's contention that the tree roots were a relatively minor cause of the damage. There was no dispute as to the reasonableness of the fees, apart from her solicitor's fees relating to advice on compensation. Therefore, subject to a deduction in respect of those fees, D was entitled to £24,639, added to £44,500, giving £69,139 in total.

DUNCAN v. EPPING FOREST DC [2004] R.V.R. 275, George Bartlett Q.C. (President), Lands Tr.

3319. Tree preservation orders—Confirmation—Misleading report to planning committee

[Human Rights Act 1998 Sch.1 Part II Art.1.]

The appellant (G) appealed against a decision to confirm a tree preservation order (TPO) in respect of four trees in his garden. Officers from the local planning authority (R) visited G's property and decided that four trees required protection by way of a TPO. G had made an application for planning permission to demolish the single dwelling on the land and replace it with two new dwellings, but the application stated that the trees would not be affected by the development. G wrote to R objecting to the TPO's confirmation on the basis that it would restrict future owners of the property if they wanted to redesign the garden. A report was provided to the member's of R's planning committee, informing them that they had to decide whether to confirm the order with or without modifications or to refuse to confirm it, thereby allowing the trees to be felled. On appeal, G argued that the report gave the erroneous impression that a failure to confirm the TPO would lead to the trees being felled. He also contended that the committee had failed to consider whether the TPO would interfere with his rights under the Human Rights Act 1998 Sch.1 Part II Art.1.

Held, allowing the appeal, that the report was misleading as there was no suggestion in the planning permission application that the trees would be felled, merely a suggestion that it could happen in the future. It could not be assumed that the committee would have reached the same decision if it had not been misled by the report. The TPO system complied with the 1998 Act. Whilst a TPO could affect both property value and the outcome of planning applications, the possibility of trees being felled was a factor that would always be considered when a planning application was made.

R. (ON THE APPLICATION OF GILMAN) v. RUTLAND CC, [2004] EWHC 2792, [2005] J.P.L. 970, Collins, J., QBD (Admin).

3320. Urban areas—Planning functions—London Thames Gateway Development Corporation

LONDON THAMES GATEWAY DEVELOPMENT CORPORATION (PLANNING FUNCTIONS) ORDER 2005, SI 2005 2721; made under the Local Government, Planning and Land Act 1980 s.149. In force: October 31, 2005; £3.00.

The London Thames Gateway Development Corporation was established by the London Thames Gateway Development Corporation (Area and Constitution) Order 2004 (SI 2004 1642) for the purpose of regenerating the London Thames Gateway urban development area. This Order describes, with the use of maps, the portions of the urban development area in which this Order confers planning functions on the development corporation.

3321. Urban areas—Planning functions—Thurrock Development Corporation

THURROCK DEVELOPMENT CORPORATION (PLANNING FUNCTIONS) ORDER 2005, SI 2005 2572; made under the Local Government, Planning and Land Act 1980 s.149. In force: October 12, 2005; £3.00.

The Thurrock Development Corporation was established by the Thurrock Development Corporation (Area and Constitution) Order 2003 (SI 2003 2896) for the purpose of regenerating the Thurrock urban development area. This Order makes the corporation the local planning authority in the development area in relation to specified kinds of development for the purposes of the Town and Country Planning Act 1990. It also confers on the corporation those functions of the Planning (Listed Buildings and Conservation Areas) Act 1990 which are specified in the Local Government, Planning and Land Act 1980 as are set out in the table in the Schedule to this Order.

3322. Books

Blackhall, J. Cameron—Planning Law and Practice. Paperback: £28.95. ISBN 1 85941 748 5. Cavendish Publishing Ltd.

Changes of Use of Buildings and Land: The Town and Country Planning (Use Classes) Order 1987. Paperback: £7.00. ISBN 0 11 753944 9. The Stationery Office Books.

Lee, Robert; Stokes, Elen—Land Use and Liability. Hardback: £35.00. ISBN 1 84568 041 3. Cavendish Publishing Ltd.

Moore, Victor—A Practical Approach to Planning Law. Practical Approach S. Paperback: £29.95. ISBN 0 19 927279 4. Oxford University Press.

Mynors, Charles—Listed Buildings, Conservation Areas and Monuments. Hardback: £125.00. ISBN 0 421 75830 9. Sweet & Maxwell.

Needham—Property Rights and Land Use Planning. Hardback: £75.00. ISBN 0 415 34373 9. Routledge, an imprint of Taylor & Francis Books Ltd. Paperback (B format): £25.00. ISBN 0 415 34374 7. Routledge, an imprint of Taylor & Francis Books Ltd.

O'Carroll, Maurice—Planning Law Enforcement. Paperback: £40.00. ISBN 1 84592 114 3. Tottel Publishing.

Planning for Town Centres: Planning Policy Statement Office of the Deputy Prime Minister 6. Paperback: £12.00. ISBN 0 11 753945 7. The Stationery Office Books. Telling, A.E.; Duxbury, Robert—Telling and Duxbury's Planning Law and Procedure. Paperback: £26.99. ISBN 0 19 928804 6. Paperback: £26.99. ISBN 0 19 928804 6. Oxford University Press.

POLICE

3323. Criminal record certificates—Fees

POLICE ACT 1997 (CRIMINAL RECORDS) (AMENDMENT) REGULATIONS 2005, SI 2005 347; made under the Police Act 1997 s.113, s.114, s.115, s.116, s.125. In force: Reg.1: March 25, 2005; Reg.2: March 25, 2005; Reg.3: April 1, 2005; £3.00.

These Regulations amend the Police Act 1997 (Criminal Records) Regulations 2002 (SI 2002 233) to insert a new Sch.3 setting out revised fees payable to the police for each request for information. The amendments substitute new fees for applications for criminal record certificates and enhanced criminal record certificates.

3324. Enhanced criminal record certificates—Duty of disclosure—Procedural fairness—Social worker—Indecent exposure allegations

[Police Act 1997 s.115, s.117; Human Rights Act 1998 Sch.1 Part I Art.8(2).]

The appellant Chief Constable (C) appealed against a judgment ([2004] EWHC 61, [2004] 1 W.L.R. 1518) quashing his decision to provide information contained in an enhanced criminal record certificate (the ECRC) and ordering that C should not provide information relating to indecent exposure allegations that had been made against the respondent social worker (X) that had been included in the ECRC. The instant appeal was concerned with the responsibility of chief police officers under the Police Act 1997 s.115. X had applied for the ECRC as it was required for the purposes of a job application. X considered that the ECRC that had been issued had blighted his opportunity to obtain employment in social work. The ECRC had been challenged by X on the basis that the decision to disclose the information by C was procedurally unfair.

Held, allowing the appeal, that the information which was disclosed by the ECRC was information which a responsible employer in this field would want to know before making a decision as to whether to employ X. X was seeking to prevent that information from being available. The making available of that information was in accordance with the law and could not be contrary to the Human Rights Act 1998 Sch.1 Part I Art.8(2). The court was not required, either on the grounds of fairness or because of Art.8(2), to form its own opinion as to what might be the relevance of the disclosed information. Having regard to the language of s.115 of the 1997 Act, a Chief Constable was under a duty to disclose if the information might be relevant, unless there was some good reason for not making such a disclosure. It imposed too heavy an obligation on a Chief Constable to require him to give an opportunity for an applicant for an ECRC to make representations before the Chief Constable performed his statutory duty of disclosure. Under s.117 of the 1997 Act, X was given an opportunity, which he had not taken advantage of, to correct the certificate. In addition, X could have given his version of events to his proposed employer. X's position was no worse than it would have been if the prospective employer had asked the question, in accordance with good employment practice for this class of employment, whether X had ever been charged with any criminal offence.

R. (ON THE APPLICATION OF X) v. CHIEF CONSTABLE OF THE WEST MIDLANDS; *sub nom.* X v. CHIEF CONSTABLE OF THE WEST MIDLANDS, [2004] EWCA Civ 1068, [2005] 1 W.L.R. 65, Lord Woolf of Barnes, L.C.J., CA.

3325. Organised crime-Designated areas

SERIOUS ORGANISED CRIME AND POLICE ACT 2005 (DESIGNATED AREA) ORDER 2005, SI 2005 1537; made under the Serious Organised Crime and Police Act 2005 s.138. In force: July 1, 2005; £3.00.

This Order designates the area for the purposes of the Serious Organised Crime and Police Act 2005 s.132, s.133, s.134, s.135, s.136 and s.137.

3326. Organised crime-Designated sites

SERIOUS ORGANISED CRIME AND POLICE ACT 2005 (DESIGNATED SITES) ORDER 2005, SI 2005 3447; made under the Serious Organised Crime and Police Act 2005 s.128, s.129. In force: April 1, 2006; £3.00.

The Secretary of State has determined that it is in the interests of national security to designate the sites listed in the Schedule. The sites in England are designated under s.128, and the sites in Scotland under the Serious Organised Crime and Police Act 2005 s.129. Under s.128 of the Act, a person commits an offence if he enters, or is on, any designated site in England or Wales as a trespasser. Under s.129 of the Act, a person commits an offence if he enters, or is on, any designated Scottish site without lawful authority. An offence under s.128 is punishable on summary conviction by imprisonment for a term not exceeding 51 weeks, or a fine not exceeding level 5 on the standard scale, or both. An offence under s.129 is punishable on summary conviction by imprisonment for a term not exceeding 12 months, or a fine not exceeding level 5 on the standard scale, or both.

3327. Organised crime-Powers of arrest

SERIOUS ORGANISED CRIME AND POLICE ACT 2005 (POWERS OF ARREST) (CONSEQUENTIAL AMENDMENTS) ORDER 2005, SI 2005 3389; made under the Serious Organised Crime and Police Act 2005 s.173. In force: January 1, 2006; £3.00.

This Order amends the Police and Criminal Evidence Act 1984 (Application to Customs and Excise) Order 1985 (SI 1985 1800), the Serbia and Montenegro (United Nations Sanctions) Order 1992 (SI 1992 1302), the United Nations Arms Embargoes (Liberia, Somalia and the Former Yugoslavia) Order 1993 (SI 1993 1787), the Channel Tunnel (International Arrangements) Order 1993 (SI 1993 1813), the Libya (United Nations Sanctions) Order 1993 (SI 1993 2807), the Channel Tunnel (Security) Order 1994 (SI 1994 570), the Haiti (United Nations Sanctions) Order 1994 (SI 1994 1323), the Conservation (Natural Habitats, etc.) Regulations 1994 (SI 1994 2716), the United Nations (International Tribunal) (Former Yugoslavia) Order 1996 (SI 1996 716), the United Nations (International Tribunal) (Rwanda) Order 1996 (SI 1996 1296), the Police and Criminal Evidence Act 1984 (Application to Armed Forces) Order 1997 (SI 1997 15), the Federal Republic of Yugoslavia (United Nations Sanctions) Order 1998 (SI 1998 1065), the Iraq (United Nations Sanctions) Order 2000 (SI 2000 3241), the Terrorism (United Nations Measures) Order 2001 (SI 2001 3365), the Al-Qa'ida and Taliban (United Nations Measures) Order 2002 (SI 2002 111), the Police and Criminal Evidence Act 1984 (Department of Trade and Industry Investigations) Order 2002 (SI 2002 2326), the Somalia (United Nations Sanctions) Order 2002 (SI 2002 2628), the Iraq (United Nations Sanctions) Order 2003 (SI 2003 1519), the Nationality, Immigration and Asylum (Juxtaposed Controls) Order 2003 (SI 2003 2818), the Extradition Act 2003 (Police Powers) Order 2003 (SI 2003 3106), the Liberia (United Nations Sanctions) Order 2004 (SI 2004 348), the Sudan (Technical Assistance and Financing and Financial Assistance) (Penalties and Licences) Regulations 2004 (SI 2004 373), the Liberia (Technical Assistance and Financing and Financial Assistance) (Penalties and Licences) Regulations 2004 (SI 2004 432), the Zimbabwe (Sale, Supply, Export, Technical Assistance, Financing and Financial Assistance and Shipment of Equipment) (Penalties and Licences) Regulations 2004 (SI 2004 559), the Police (Complaints and Misconduct) Regulations 2004 (SI 2004 643), the Ministry of Defence Police (Conduct) Regulations 2004 (SI 2004 653), the Burma (Sale, Supply, Export, Technical Assistance,

Financing and Financial Assistance and Shipment of Equipment) (Penalties and Licences) Regulations 2004 (SI 2004 1315), the Ivory Coast (United Nations Sanctions) Order 2005 (SI 2005 253), the Sudan (United Nations Measures) Order 2005 (SI 2005 1259) and the Democratic Republic of the Congo (United Nations Measures) Order 2005 (SI 2005 1517). The Serious Organised Crime and Police Act 2005 removes the distinction between criminal offences which are arrestable and those which are not and provides that a constable may, provided certain criteria are met, arrest a person in relation to any criminal offence. The 2005 Act makes a number of consequential amendments to primary legislation and repeal those powers of arrest which are not contained within PACE and which apply to constables. This Order makes equivalent consequential amendments to secondary legislation.

3328. Organised crime—Serious offences

SERIOUS ORGANISED CRIME AND POLICE ACT 2005 (AMENDMENT) ORDER 2005, SI 2005 3496; made under the Serious Organised Crime and Police Act 2005 s.173. In force: January 1, 2006; £3.00.

This Order amends the Serious Organised Crime and Police Act 2005 and provisions in the Police Act 1997 and Police and Criminal Evidence Act 1984 which are prospectively inserted by the Serious Organised Crime and Police Act 2005, correcting minor typographical errors.

3329. Police authorities—Best value—Performance indicators

POLICE AUTHORITIES (BEST VALUE) PERFORMANCE INDICATORS ORDER 2005, SI 2005 470; made under the Local Government Act 1999 s.4. In force: April 1, 2005; £3.00.

The Local Government Act 1999 imposes requirements on police authorities, and other authorities, to secure continuous improvement in the way in which their functions are exercised, having regard to a combination of economy, efficiency and effectiveness. It also confers a power on the Secretary of State to specify by Order best value performance indicators applicable local authorities, police authorities and other authorities. This Order, which revokes the Police Authorities (Best Value) Performance Indicators Order 2004 (SI 2004 644), specifies that the performance indicators set out in the Schedule to this Order are to be the indicators by which a police authority's performance can be measured.

3330. Police authorities—Lay justice members—Appointments—Selection panel

POLICE AUTHORITIES (LAY JUSTICES SELECTION PANEL) REGULATIONS 2005, SI 2005 584; made under the Police Act 1996 Sch.3A para.5. In force: April 1, 2005; £3.00.

Following amendments to the Police Act 1996 by the Courts Act 2003, lay justice members replace magistrate members as the third category of member of a police authority (in addition to councillor members and independent members). Lay justice members are appointed by councillor members and independent members from among candidates included on a short-list prepared by a selection panel in accordance with the 1996 Act. These Regulations provide for the procedures to be followed in relation to the preparation of such a short-list, and the conduct of the proceedings of the selection panel.

3331. Police officers—Appointments

POLICE (AMENDMENT) REGULATIONS 2005, SI 2005 2834; made under the Police Act 1996 s.50; and the Police Act 1997 s.79A. In force: October 17, 2005; £3.00.

These Regulations, which amend the Police Regulations 2003 (SI 2003 527), have the effect that nationals of the 10 States which acceded to the EU on May 1, 2004 may now qualify for appointment to a police force without having indefinite leave to enter or remain in the UK. An ambulatory reference to Member States of the

EU is used to avoid the need for further amendments to the regulation if additional countries accede to the EU. They introduce a power to test for controlled drugs the following categories of person: applicants to police forces, officers who give cause to suspect that they have used such drugs, probationers, officers whose work involves dealing with drugs, and officers in specialist roles. In the latter case, a power to test for alcohol is also introduced. The Secretary of State is given a power to set out in a determination the consequences of testing positive in any of these situations. The Regulations also implement, in part, the Police Negotiating Board for the United Kingdom Circular 04/11 (Advisory) which relates to the merger of the Royal Parks Constabulary with the metropolitan police service; ensure that the personal record of a member of a police force shall contain details of his service (if any) with the Royal Parks Constabulary; enable officers joining or rejoining a police force on or after July 1, 2004 to count service with the Royal Parks Constabulary for the purposes of pay and leave; and provide that where members of the Royal Parks Constabulary in receipt of a housing allowance transfer to a police force on or after July 1, 2004 they are entitled to a replacement allowance.

3332. Police officers—Disabled persons—Injury pensions—Date of assessment of degree of disablement

[Police Pensions Regulations 1987 (SI 1987 257) Reg.H1 (2) (d).]

The appellant police authority (P) appealed against a decision ([2004] EWHC 1617) that for the purposes of the Police Pensions Regulations 1987 Reg.H1 (2) (d) on an appeal to the medical referee, a claimant's degree of disablement was to be determined as at the date of the appeal and not as at the date of the prior decision by the selected medical practitioner. The claimant in the first case (M) and the interested party in the second case (B) had both been disabled as a consequence of their police service. Both officers had appealed decisions of the selected medical practitioner to medical referees. In M's case, the degree of disablement had been determined as at the date of the decision of the selected medical practitioner. In B's case, the degree of disability had been determined as at the date of the appeal before the referee. Both M and, in the second case, P had applied for judicial review at which it was held that, for the purposes of Reg.H1 (2) (d), the degree of disablement was to be determined as at the date of the appeal before the referee and not as at the date of the decision of the selected medical practitioner. P argued, inter alia, that the judge had been wrong as the referee's task had been to decide whether the selected medical practitioner had been correct on the materials before him or her at the time of the selected medical practitioner's decision.

Held, dismissing the appeal, that there were clear indications that the appeal to the referee was a rehearing to be determined on the materials available at that date. The selected medical practitioner had been appointed by P under the Regulations, so the referee was the first independent person to assess the matter. Accordingly it was an appeal from P itself, under which the referee had to look at matters in the round at the date upon which he or she was making his or her decision, *R. (on the application of Caine) v. Cavendish* [2001] EWHC Admin 18, *R. (on the application of Metropolitan Police Authority) v. Medical Referee (No.1)* [2001] EWHC Admin 753, and *City of London Police Authority v. Medical Referee* [2004] EWHC 897 approved.

R. (ON THE APPLICATION OF McGINLEY) v. SCHILLING (MEDICAL REFEREE); R. (ON THE APPLICATION OF METROPOLITAN POLICE SERVICE) v. BECK (MEDICAL REFEREE); *sub nom.* R. (ON THE APPLICATION OF McGINLEY) v. MEDICAL REFEREE, [2005] EWCA Civ 567, [2005] I.C.R. 1282, Pill, L.J., CA (Civ Div).

3333. Police officers–Disciplinary procedures–Discrimination by investigating officer–Application of principles of agency

[Sex Discrimination Act 1975; Police (Discipline) Regulations 1985 (SI 1985 518).]

Y appealed against the dismissal of his claim of sex discrimination. Y was a serving police officer who claimed that he had been discriminated against by a fellow officer appointed to act in disciplinary proceedings. The issue arose as to the proper interpretation of "agent" for the purposes of the Sex Discrimination Act 1975. Y contended that the word should be given its general meaning of "a person who acts on behalf of another person with their authority" and not its common law meaning, with the effect that the discrimination had occurred whilst the officer was acting as agent for Y's Chief Constable.

Held, dismissing the appeal, that an officer appointed to act in disciplinary proceedings was not an agent for the Chief Constable. The word "agent" bore its common law meaning in the Act, by which acts done by the agent with the principal's authority were capable of affecting the relationship between the principal and any third parties. The Act expressly departed from that definition only in so far as making both the principal and agent capable of being found to have carried out discrimination. No other meaning could therefore be imputed into the Act. Under the Police (Discipline) Regulations 1985 a Chief Constable could not act as investigating officer in disciplinary proceedings. An investigating officer appointed under the Regulations could not therefore be the agent of the Chief Constable since an agent could not carry out an act that a principal could not do himself. The investigating officer therefore acted independently and no action could be brought by Y against his Chief Constable.

YEARWOOD v. COMMISSIONER OF POLICE OF THE METROPOLIS; COMMISSIONER OF POLICE OF THE METROPOLIS v. MILLER; CHIEF CONSTABLE OF MERSEYSIDE v. HUSAIN; KOCHAR v. COMMISSIONER OF POLICE OF THE METROPOLIS; JEFFREY v. COMMISSIONER OF POLICE OF THE METROPOLIS [2004] I.C.R. 1660, Judge McMullen Q.C., EAT.

3334. Police officers–Disciplinary procedures–Suspension of police officer–Terminating suspension–Matters of public interest

[Police Act 1996 s.87(1).]

The claimants (C) applied for judicial review and sought a declaration that a decision of the defendant chief constable (D) to terminate the suspension of a chief inspector (K) was unlawful. K had been the senior investigating officer in a murder investigation and bore day to day responsibility for its conduct. C were subsequently charged with that murder. Their indictment was stayed on the grounds of abuse of process and C were discharged. The trial judge found that K had removed relevant evidence from consideration by the parties. K was thereafter suspended from duty for alleged misconduct. However, K was later reinstated and was allowed to retire. C submitted that para.3.18 and 3.20 of the Home Office Guidance on disciplinary procedures of December 12, 2002 was statutory guidance issued pursuant to the Police Act 1996 s.87(1) and therefore imposed a statutory obligation on D to have regard to it.

Held, granting a declaration in favour of the claimants, that the guidance in paragraphs 3.18 and 3.20 was not statutory guidance. The legal effect of the guidance fell to be determined by general principles of administrative law. However, the guidance fell within the category of matters which were so obviously material to the decision whether to remove the suspension of K that anything short of direct consideration of them by the decision maker would not be in accordance with the intention of the statutory scheme, *R. v. Chief Constable of Devon and Cornwall, ex p. Hay* [1996] 2 All E.R. 711, [1996] C.L.Y. 4859 applied. On the evidence, D's decision to lift the suspension was flawed in the Wednesbury sense as he had failed to have regard to a relevant consideration namely, the element of public interest in paragraph 3.18 that public interest might require that an officer should be required to face disciplinary proceedings notwithstanding that the officer might wish to retire from the service. To that extent, D had failed to articulate that he was aware of this aspect of the guidance, that he had regard to it, and his reasons for deciding in a way which was contrary to that potential public interest. Accordingly, D's decision to lift the suspension was unlawful.

R. (ON THE APPLICATION OF COGHLAN) v. CHIEF CONSTABLE OF GREATER MANCHESTER, [2004] EWHC 2801, [2005] 2 All E.R. 890, Wilkie, J., QBD (Admin).

3335. Police officers–Promotion–Qualifying examinations

POLICE (PROMOTION) (AMENDMENT) REGULATIONS 2005, SI 2005 178; made under the Police Act 1996 s.50. In force: March 1, 2005; £3.00.

These Regulations amend the Police (Promotion) Regulations 1996 (SI 1996 1685) and introduce an alternative to Part II of the qualifying examination. Police forces will be able to promote their members either by using the current system of practical assessments, or by using work-based assessments.

3336. Police powers–Codes of practice

POLICE AND CRIMINAL EVIDENCE ACT 1984 (CODES OF PRACTICE) ORDER 2005, SI 2005 3503; made under the Police and Criminal Evidence Act 1984 s.67. In force: January 1, 2006; £3.00.

This Order, which revokes the Police and Criminal Evidence Act 1984 (Codes of Practice) Order 2004 (SI 2004 1887) and the Police and Criminal Evidence Act 1984 (Codes of Practice) (Revisions to Code C) Order 2005 (SI 2005 602), appoints January 1, 2006 as the date on which revised codes of practice will come into operation, superseding codes of practice which have been in operation since August 1, 2004.

3337. Police powers–Codes of practice–Revisions to Code C

POLICE AND CRIMINAL EVIDENCE ACT 1984 (CODES OF PRACTICE) (REVISIONS TO CODE C) ORDER 2005, SI 2005 602; made under the Police and Criminal Evidence Act 1984 s.67. In force: April 1, 2005; £3.00.

This Order amends the Police and Criminal Evidence Act 1984 Code of Practice for the Detention, Treatment and Questioning of Persons by Police Officers (Code C) to include the police areas of Gwent, Northamptonshire and South Wales in the list of police areas in which the power to test adults for specified Class A drugs under the Police and Criminal Evidence Act 1984 s.63B can be exercised.

3338. Police powers–Motor vehicles–Retention and disposal

POLICE (RETENTION AND DISPOSAL OF MOTOR VEHICLES) (AMENDMENT) REGULATIONS 2005, SI 2005 2702; made under the Police Reform Act 2002 s.60. In force: November 1, 2005; £3.00.

These Regulations amend the Police (Retention and Disposal of Motor Vehicles) Regulations 2002 (SI 2002 3049) to provide a definition of the term "working days"; provide that the steps which the authority must take to serve a seizure notice on the person appearing to be the owner of the vehicle must be those which are reasonably practicable; and provide that the date provided in the seizure notice, on or before which the person to whom the notice is directed is required to claim the vehicle, must be a date not less than 7 working days from the day on which the notice was given to that person.

3339. Police powers and duties–Demonstrations–Breach of the peace–Crowd detained within police cordon–Lawfulness of detention

[Public Order Act 1986 s.12(1)(a), s.14; Human Rights Act 1998 Sch.1 Part I Art.5.]

The claimants (X) claimed damages for false imprisonment and breach of their rights under the Human Rights Act 1998 Sch.1 Part I Art.5 against the defendant

Commissioner of Police. In response to a surprise political procession, the police had detained thousands of people in a cordon for several hours, including X, in order to prevent a breakdown in law and order. The police had intended to carry out a controlled release of the detained crowd but that was delayed due to the violent behaviour of other groups that had converged in the area making a group release unsafe. Some individuals were released but X's requests for their individual release were refused. It was accepted that X had not themselves been threatening a breach of the peace but others in the group had been doing so. X submitted that they were deprived of their liberty contrary to Art.5, alternatively that any justification for the initial imposition of the cordon had to be shown to have continued until each claimant was released and the defence of necessity was not available. The commissioner submitted that the detention was lawful pursuant to the common law duty to maintain the peace; was a mere restriction on freedom of movement, which did not engage Art.5(1), alternatively that the exception in Art.5(1)(c) applied; was necessary, pursuant to the legitimate aim of protecting public safety and was proportionate.

Held, giving judgment for the defendant, that (1) necessity could be a factor which, amongst others, might lead to a conclusion that Art.5 did not apply, *Guenat v. Switzerland (No.24722/94)* (1995) 810A D.R. 130 applied. If the detention was prior to arrest, when arrest was not yet decided upon or not yet practicable, a conditional intention to arrest and bring the person concerned before a judge might suffice in principle to fall within the exception under Art.5(1)(c). Necessity could amount to a defence to a claim for false imprisonment. The test for deciding whether a measure short of arrest could be lawfully taken against a given individual was reasonable suspicion that that individual was presenting the relevant threat. The burden of proof was on the claimant to show that the exercise of discretion to detain was unreasonable, *Al-Fayed v. Commissioner of Police of the Metropolis (No.3)* [2004] EWCA Civ 1579, (2004) 148 S.J.L.B. 1405 and *Castorina v. Chief Constable of Surrey* Times, June 15, 1988, [1988] C.L.Y. 578 applied. The court should accord a high degree of respect for the police officer's appreciation of the risks of what members of the crowd might do if not contained. At the same time the court should subject to very close scrutiny the practical effect that derogating measures had on individual human rights, the importance of the rights affected, and the robustness of any safeguards intended to minimise the impact of the derogating measures on individual human rights. (2) On the facts, X's detention was a deprivation of liberty within Art.5(1) but was justified under Art.5(1)(c) as the detention was imposed with the conditional purpose of arresting those whom it would be lawful and practicable to arrest and take before a judge, and to prevent such persons from committing violent offences. It was reasonable for the police to consider that all persons in the cordon, including X, were demonstrators and about to commit a breach of the peace and to continue in that belief after X had requested their individual releases. The police had reasonably believed that the facts necessary to fulfil the Public Order Act 1986 s.12(1)(a) and s.14(1)(a) were present and it was immaterial that none of the officers had those sections in mind at the time. A direction to disperse under s.14 of the Act could include a direction to disperse by a specified route and to stay in a specified place for as long as necessary to enable the dispersal to take place safely and without disorder. X had been falsely imprisoned but it had been necessary for the protection of everyone to detain the crowd until dispersal could be arranged safely. The need to contain the procession had not arisen out of any negligence by the police.

AUSTIN v. COMMISSIONER OF POLICE OF THE METROPOLIS, [2005] EWHC 480, [2005] H.R.L.R. 20, Tugendhat, J., QBD.

3340. Police powers and duties–Demonstrations–Conditions–Necessary contents of direction given under s.14 Public Order Act 1986

[Public Order Act 1986 s.14; Human Rights Act 1998 Sch.1 Part I Art.10, Art.11.]
The applicant (B) applied for judicial review of a decision of the respondent chief constable to give a direction, under the Public Order Act 1986 s.14, imposing

POLICE

conditions prohibiting him and fellow demonstrators from demonstrating outside a shop in a city centre. Demonstrations had taken place outside the same shop every Saturday for several years. Counter demonstrations had also begun occurring within the same area as B's demonstration. The conditions had prohibited the demonstrations from taking place outside the shop on a Saturday for a specific number of weeks over the Christmas season. The chief constable had suggested an alternative site for demonstrating, which was away from the shop. The issues for determination were (1) whether the chief constable had been under a duty to give reasons for imposing conditions under s.14 and had not done so; (2) if reasons had been given, whether the chief constable's belief that the demonstrations might give rise to the consequences outlined in s.14 (1) had been reasonable; (3) whether the conditions imposed were proportionate to the interference with B's rights under the Human Rights Act 1998 Sch.1 Part I Art.10 and Art.11.

Held, refusing the application, that (1) where a direction to demonstrators under s.14(2)(a) was given at the scene of a demonstration by the most senior police officer present it was not necessary for reasons to be given. However, s.14(2)(b), which was applicable in the instant case, required the chief officer of police to identify which subsection of s.14(1) was being relied on. If s.14(1)(a) was relied on, as in the instant case, the chief officer had to identify whether the possible consequence of the demonstration was reasonably believed to be serious public disorder, serious damage to property, serious disruption to the life of the community, or a combination of the three. Although extensive detail was not required, the chief officer had to provide sufficient information on the reasons for his belief for a demonstrator to understand why directions were being given and, if the matter went to court, for the court to assess whether the belief was reasonable. In the instant case the chief officer had clearly given reasons why conditions were to be imposed. (2) Section 14 required a reasonable belief that an intended public assembly might result in the consequences outlined in s.14(1)(a), not that the assembly would result in those consequences. The decision of the chief officer in the instant case had assessed the impact of two demonstrations, the chief constable being entitled to take into account the counter demonstration. His assessment had not been irrational nor unreasonable in the manner outlined in *R. v. Ministry of Defence, ex p. Smith* [1996] Q.B. 517, [1996] C.L.Y. 383, *Smith* applied. (3) Whether a decision was proportional was an assessment to be made on the facts of an individual case. In the instant case the area where the demonstration would have taken place would have been busy over the Christmas period, the restrictions were only applicable on one day a week and an alternative site had been suggested. The chief constable had a legitimate aim in preventing serious disruption in the city centre. The prohibition interfered with B's human rights, but, considering the limited nature of the interference, did not have a disproportionate effect, *R. (on the application of Samaroo) v. Secretary of State for the Home Department* [2001] EWCA Civ 1139, [2001] U.K.H.R.R. 1150, [2001] C.L.Y. 3660 applied.

R. (ON THE APPLICATION OF BREHONY) v. CHIEF CONSTABLE OF GREATER MANCHESTER, [2005] EWHC 640, *The Times*, April 15, 2005, Bean, J., QBD (Admin).

3341. Police powers and duties–Demonstrations–Removal of demonstrators by preventive actions short of arrest or detention

[Human Rights Act 1998 s.6, Sch.1 Part I Art.10, Sch.1 Part I Art.11.]

The appellant Chief Constable appealed against a finding ([2004] EWHC 253, [2004] 2 All E.R. 874) that the decision of a chief superintendent to forcibly return the respondent protestor (L) to London from a protest at an RAF base in Gloucestershire was unlawful. L cross appealed against the finding that the decision to prevent her from proceeding to the protest was lawful. The police had stopped and searched several coaches within the proximity of the protest site, including the one upon which L was travelling. The chief superintendent had ordered the coaches to return directly to London with the passengers aboard, and had provided an escort of police motorcycle outriders. The decision had been based upon the presence on the coaches of hardcore members of a particular group, items found upon the coaches, and police intelligence. L submitted that the court had applied the wrong test in determining whether the preventive action short of arrest or detention was legitimate and had been wrong to conclude that the preventive action taken, which was contrary to the common law and the Human Rights Act 1998 s.6 and Sch.1 Part I Art.10 and Sch.1 Part I Art.11, was justified in the circumstances of the case. The chief constable contended that the decision of the court below made practical policing impossible, because the court had found that the chief superintendent was under a duty to prevent the coaches from proceeding to the protest, but had also decided that he was not entitled to take the only practical measures that would have achieved that result.

Held, dismissing the appeal and cross appeal, that (1) it was reasonable for the police to apprehend a breach of the peace and to decide to prevent L and her fellow passengers from proceeding to the protest. The court below had correctly followed *Moss v. McLachlan* (1985) 149 J.P. 167, [1985] C.L.Y. 647 in determining whether the preventive actions taken by the police in the instant case were legitimate, *Moss* approved. What was sufficiently "imminent" to justify taking action to prevent a breach of the peace was dependent on all the circumstances. Action was not to be taken until it was necessary and reasonable to take the action in the particular circumstances of the case. What preventive action was necessary and proportionate was to be determined by how close in proximity, both in place and time, the location of the apprehended breach of the peace was. The chief superintendent had been correct to take a blanket approach to the possibility of disruption by returning all individuals on the coaches to London. In view of the attitude adopted generally by the passengers on the coaches it would not have been possible to identify those who would not cause a breach of the peace. The need to prevent an apprehended breach of the peace might require action to be taken which risked affecting a wholly innocent individual. There was ample evidence to justify the chief superintendent's assessment of the situation and order the action he did. (2) The action of escorting the vehicles back to London without allowing any stops was disproportionate and not justifiable at common law. Action could have been taken which was more limited in its impact on the passengers' rights to freedom of action.

R. (ON THE APPLICATION OF LAPORTE) v. CHIEF CONSTABLE OF GLOUCESTERSHIRE, [2004] EWCA Civ 1639, [2005] Q.B. 678, Lord Woolf of Barnes, L.C.J., CA (Civ Div).

3342. Police powers and duties–Duty of care–Victim of crime alleging existence of duties

[Race Relations Act 1976 s.20.]

The appellant commissioner of police and individual serving police officers appealed against a decision ([2002] EWCA Civ 407, Daily Telegraph, April 11, 2002) that the respondent (B) could claim damages in negligence and for breaches of the Race Relations Act 1976 s.20 arising from the manner in which B was treated by the police when he was a victim of crime and an eyewitness to murder. B had been the victim of a racist gang attack in which his friend was murdered. B consequently developed post traumatic stress disorder and sought damages from the commissioner on the grounds of negligence, false imprisonment and misfeasance in public office and from the individual officers for breaches of s.20 of the 1976 Act. The appellants submitted that the primary function of the police was to preserve the Queen's peace, and that, in the course of performing their function of investigating crime, the police owed no legal duties to take care that either a victim or a witness as such did not suffer psychiatric harm as a result of police actions or omissions. The appellants relied on *Hill v. Chief Constable of West Yorkshire* [1989] A.C. 53, [1988] C.L.Y. 2435 as authority for that proposition. B did not challenge the decision in *Hill* but contended that it did not stand in the way of his submission that the police owed him a common law duty sounding in damages to: (i) take reasonable steps to assess whether he was a victim of crime and then accord him reasonably appropriate protection, support, assistance and treatment if he was so assessed; (ii) take reasonable steps to afford him the protection, assistance and support commonly afforded to a key eyewitness to a serious crime of violence; and (iii) afford reasonable weight to the account that he gave and act upon it accordingly.

Held, allowing the appeal, that there was no basis for sensibly imposing on the police any of the three legal duties asserted by B, as those duties would cut across the freedom of action the police ought to have when investigating serious crime. The principle in *Hill* had to be judged in the light of legal policy and the bill of rights, *Hill* applied. With hindsight, not every principle in *Hill* could now be supported and a more sceptical approach to the carrying out of all public functions was necessary. However, the core principle of *Hill* had remained unchallenged in domestic jurisprudence and European jurisdiction for many years and it had to stand. The three alleged duties of care were undoubtedly inextricably bound up with the police function of investigating crime, which was covered by the principle in *Hill*. Making full allowance for the facts that the instant proceedings were a strike out application, and that the law regarding the liability of the police in tort was not set in stone, the court was satisfied that the three duties of care put forward were conclusively ruled out by the principle in *Hill*, as restated, and had to be struck out.

BROOKS v. COMMISSIONER OF POLICE OF THE METROPOLIS, [2005] UKHL 24, [2005] 1 W.L.R. 1495, Lord Bingham of Cornhill, HL.

3343. Police powers and duties–Police inquiries–Conduct of prosecuting authorities–Payments by insurance companies to assist police investigations–Abuse of process

[Police Act 1996 s.3, s.4, s.6, s.14, s.101 (1), Sch.1.]

The appellants (H, M and B) appealed against their convictions for conspiracy to defraud. They had been convicted due to their participation in a dishonest scheme involving the acquisition of vehicles that were used in staged road traffic collisions. The damaged vehicles were then the subject of inflated claims made to insurance companies. Towards the end of the Crown's case it was disclosed to the defence that three of the insurance companies that had paid out on claims made by the appellants had paid sums to the investigating police force, at the force's request, to assist in funding the arrest stage of the investigation. The appellants subsequently applied for the proceedings to be stayed as an abuse of process. The judge refused the application. H and M also applied for the discharge of the jury on the ground that two previous convictions of M had been inadvertently disclosed to the jury on the back of a document in the jury bundle. That application was refused and the issue was addressed in the judge's summing up. On appeal, the Crown conceded that in seeking and accepting payments from the insurance companies, the police were acting outside their statutory powers. The appellants submitted that (1) the judge was wrong to conclude that the investigating officer was acting in good faith when obtaining the funds from the insurance companies, and the contributions were so unlawful and contrary to public policy that the court should not have allowed the prosecution to proceed; (2) the failure by the Crown to disclose the funding documents as part of primary disclosure also constituted an abuse of process; (3) the judge was wrong to refuse the application for the jury to be dismissed.

Held, dismissing the appeals, that (1) the Police Act 1996 s.3, s.4, s.6, s.14, s.101 (1) and Sch.1, seen in the context of the Act as a whole, showed that the Crown's concession was correct and the judge's conclusion, that the payments were not prima facie illegal, had been wrong. It was for the defence to prove on the balance of probabilities that the conduct of the prosecuting authorities was so serious that the court, in the exercise of its discretion, should stay the proceedings. The judge had heard all the evidence, including detailed cross examination of the investigating officer, and was entitled to find that the officer had not been acting in bad faith. The soliciting, by the police, of funds from potential victims of fraud was fraught with danger, as well as being ultra vires. It could compromise police independence and objectivity when carrying out a criminal investigation. However, on the facts of the instant case, the conduct of the police fell short of conduct that required the prosecution to be stayed, *R. v. Horseferry Road Magistrates Court, ex p. Bennett (No.1)* [1994] 1 A.C. 42, [1993] C.L.Y. 1867 and *R. v. Mullen (Nicholas Robert) (No.2)* [2000] Q.B. 520, [1999] C.L.Y. 972 considered. (2) The Court of Appeal could not go behind the judge's finding that the material on funding had not been deliberately withheld at the stage of primary disclosure. The judge had been entitled to find that the failure by the prosecution to disclose the material earlier was not a sufficient reason to stay the proceedings. (3) The judge had not wrongly exercised his discretion by refusing to discharge the jury. H had not been prejudiced in any way by the fact that M's convictions came before the jury. Any prejudice there may have been to M was slight, due to the relative triviality of the previous convictions, and had been completely cured by the judge's direction.

R. v. HOUNSHAM (ROBIN EDWARD); R. v. MAYES (RICHARD); R. v. BLAKE (MICHAEL), [2005] EWCA Crim 1366, *The Times*, June 16, 2005, Gage, L.J., CA (Crim Div).

3344. Police records–Recordable offences

NATIONAL POLICE RECORDS (RECORDABLE OFFENCES) (AMENDMENT) REGULATIONS 2005, SI 2005 3106; made under the Police and Criminal Evidence Act 1984 s.27. In force: December 1, 2005; £3.00.

These Regulations amend the National Police Records (Recordable Offences) Regulations 2000 (SI 2000 1139) which list those offences which are recordable but which do not attract the possibility of a custodial sentence. The Regulations adds a number of offences under the Licensing Act 2003 to the list of recordable offences and removes references to offences under the Licensing Act 1964. They also delete references to offences which are repealed by the Licensing Act 2003.

3345. Serious Organised Crime and Police Act 2005 (c.15)–Commencement No.1, Transitional and Transitory Provisions Order

SERIOUS ORGANISED CRIME AND POLICE ACT 2005 (COMMENCEMENT NO.1, TRANSITIONAL AND TRANSITORY PROVISIONS) ORDER 2005, SI 2005 1521 (C.66); made under the Serious Organised Crime and Police Act 2005 s.178. Commencement details: bringing into force various provisions of the 2005 Act on July 1, 2005, August 1, 2005 and April 1, 2006; £3.00.

This Order brings into force provisions of the Serious Organised Crime and Police Act 2005.

3346. Serious Organised Crime and Police Act 2005 (c.15)–Commencement No.2 Order

SERIOUS ORGANISED CRIME AND POLICE ACT 2005 (COMMENCEMENT NO.2) ORDER 2005, SI 2005 2026 (C.86); made under the Serious Organised Crime and Police Act 2005 s.178. Commencement details: bringing into force various provisions of the 2005 Act on August 1, 2005; £3.00.

This Order brings into force specified provisions of the Serious Organised Crime and Police Act 2005.

3347. Serious Organised Crime and Police Act 2005 (c.15)–Commencement No.3 Order

SERIOUS ORGANISED CRIME AND POLICE ACT 2005 (COMMENCEMENT NO.3) ORDER 2005, SI 2005 3136 (C.135); made under the Serious Organised Crime and Police Act 2005 s.178. Commencement details: bringing into force various provisions of the 2005 Act on January 1, 2006; £3.00.

This Order brings into force provisions of the Serious Organised Crime and Police Act 2005.

3348. Books

Bernstein, Jeffrey I.–Prentice Hall's Test Prep Guide to Accompany Police Field Operations. Paperback: £16.99. ISBN 0 13 170128 2. Prentice Hall.

Clayton, Richard; Tomlinson, Hugh–Clayton Civ Act Against Police, 3rd Ed. Paperback: £46.00. ISBN 0 421 92260 5. Sweet & Maxwell.

Connor, Paul–Blackstone's Police Investigators' Q&A. Paperback: £14.99. ISBN 0 19 928757 0. Oxford University Press.

Connor, Paul–Blackstone's Police Sergeants' Mock Examination Paper. Paperback: £14.99. ISBN 0 19 928831 3. Oxford University Press.

Connor, Paul; Pinfield, David; Taylor, Neil; Chapman, Julian–Blackstone's Police Investigator's Workbook. Blackstone's Police Manuals. Paperback: £35.00. ISBN 0 19 928919 0. Oxford University Press.

English, Jack; Card, Richard–Police Law. Paperback: £24.95. ISBN 0 19 928405 9. Oxford University Press.

Fielding, Nigel–Police and Social Conflict. Contemporary Issues in Public Policy. Paperback: £22.00. ISBN 1 904385 23 0. The Glasshouse Press.

Fitzpatrick, Brian–Police Officer's Guide to Going to Court. Paperback: £27.95. ISBN 0 19 928414 8. Oxford University Press.

Fraser, Gary; Giles, Trefor; Crow, David; Form, Amanda–Mastering Policing Skills. Policing Skills S. Paperback: £19.00. ISBN 1 84641 012 6. Law Matters Publishing.

Grzasko, Christina; Gribbin, Michael; Abel, Damian–Police Station Guide. Paperback: £75.00. ISBN 0 9549906 0 9. iLaw Publishing.

Natarajan, Mangai–Women Police. International Library of Criminology, Criminal Justice & Penology 2nd Series. Hardback: £125.00. ISBN 0 7546 2445 5. Ashgate.

Pinfield, David–Blackstone's Police Investigators' Mock Examination Paper. Paperback: £14.99. ISBN 0 19 928832 1. Oxford University Press.

Que Development–Police Officer Exam Practice Questions. Exam Cram 2 S. Paperback/CD-ROM: £13.99. ISBN 0 7897 3273 4. Que.

Roberson, Cliff; Birzer, Michael–Policing Today and Tomorrow. Paperback: £37.99. ISBN 0 13 119068 7. Prentice Hall.

Sampson, Fraser–General Police Duties: V. 4. Blackstone's Police Manuals. Paperback: £14.50. ISBN 0 19 928522 5. Paperback: £14.50. ISBN 0 19 928522 5. Oxford University Press.

Sampson, Fraser; Hutton, Glenn; Johnston, Dave–Blackstone's Police Manuals. Blackstone's Police Manuals. Paperback: £55.80. ISBN 0 19 928523 3. Paperback: £55.80. ISBN 0 19 928523 3. Oxford University Press.

Sampson, Fraser; Hutton, Glenn; Johnston, David–Blackstone's Police Manuals. Blackstone's Police Manuals. CD-ROM: £55.00. ISBN 0 19 928542 X. CD-ROM: £64.62. ISBN 0 19 928542 X. Oxford University Press.

Sampson, Fraser; Hutton, Glenn; Johnston, David–Blackstone's Police Investigator's Manual. Blackstone's Police Manuals. Paperback: £35.00. ISBN 0 19 928759 7. Oxford University Press.

Sampson, Fraser; Hutton, Glenn; Johnston, David–Blackstone's Police Manuals. Blackstone's Police Manuals. Paperback: £84.76; CD-ROM: £55.00. ISBN 0 19 928524 1; CD-ROM: 0 19 928542 X. Paperback: £84.76; CD-ROM: £55.00. ISBN 0 19 928524 1; CD-ROM: 0 19 928542 X. Oxford University Press.

Sampson, Fraser; Hutton, Glenn; Johnston, David; Connor, Paul; Pinfield, Dave; Taylor, Neil; Chapman, Julian–Blackstone's Police Investigator's Manual and Workbook Pack. Blackstone's Police Manuals. Hardback: £65.00. ISBN 0 19 928760 0. Oxford University Press.

Smart, Huw; Watson, John–Evidence and Procedure. Blackstone's Police Q & A S. Paperback: £11.95. ISBN 0 19 928526 8. Oxford University Press.

Smart, Huw; Watson, John–General Police Duties. Blackstone's Police Q&As. Paperback: £11.95. ISBN 0 19 928528 4. Paperback: £11.95. ISBN 0 19 928528 4. Oxford University Press.

Smart, Huw; Watson, John–Roads Policing. Blackstone's Police Q & A S. Paperback: £11.95. ISBN 0 19 928527 6. Oxford University Press.

Smart, Huw; Watson, John – Blackstone's Police Q&As. Blackstone's Police Q & A S. Paperback: £46.00. ISBN 0 19 928529 2. Paperback: £46.00. ISBN 0 19 928529 2. Oxford University Press.

PROFESSIONS

3349. **Dentists – Suspension – Suspension for 12 months following offences involving child pornography – Gravity of offending**

[Protection of Children Act 1978.]

The appellant council appealed against the decision of the first respondent's professional conduct committee to suspend the registration of the second respondent dentist (F) for a period of 12 months. The committee's decision had been made after F was sentenced for offences under the Protection of Children Act 1978 involving downloading child pornography from the internet. Over a thousand of the images downloaded by F were of a Level 4 or 5 degree of seriousness under the scale in *R. v. Oliver (Mark David)* [2002] EWCA Crim 2766, [2003] 1 Cr. App. R. 28, [2003] C.L.Y. 3745. F had pleaded guilty to the charges but claimed that his behaviour had been caused by depression. The judge took into account the fact that F's mother and mother in law were dependent on him and there was no one else to look after them as his wife was ill. He decided that F was not likely to pose a danger to children and sentenced F to a community rehabilitation order for three years. F was ordered to remain on the Sex Offenders Register for five years and was prohibited from having unsupervised access to children under 16 years. Furthermore it was a condition of the order that F participate in a sex offenders' treatment programme.

Held, allowing the appeal, that since F had been sentenced to a community rehabilitation order for a period of three years, if he were merely suspended for 12 months, he would be able to resume his practice before he had satisfied his sentence. The decision to suspend was the more surprising because of the conditions attached to the order, particularly the requirement to participate in a sex offenders' treatment programme. It was clear that the committee had not sufficiently considered the significance of the sentence imposed by the Crown Court. As a general principle, where a practitioner had been convicted of a serious criminal offence or offences he should not be permitted to resume his practice until he had satisfactorily completed his sentence. The protection of the public would not be served by the application of a different standard at erasure from that which was applied when considering an application for registration. Had an application been received from F during the currency of his community rehabilitation order it was inconceivable that it would have been accepted. A man who participated in conduct that corrupted children and caused them harm in order to alleviate his depression caused the same harm as the man who derived pleasure from it. The Act penalised the conduct and not the motive. The decisive factor leading to F not being sent to prison had little or nothing to do with the gravity of his offending and everything to do with the health of his dependants, a consideration that was irrelevant to the committee's deliberations. The committee had lost sight of the true gravity of what F had done because F was not sent to prison. *Oliver* was not merely a guideline case on sentencing, but was also a guide to assessing the gravity of the offending. F's offending was clearly outside and well beyond the category of offending normally meriting a sentence of imprisonment and there were also aggravating features. Furthermore, the committee had not given sufficient weight to the need to maintain the reputation of the profession and to maintain public confidence in the profession, *Bolton v. Law Society* [1994] 1 W.L.R. 512, [1994] C.L.Y. 4220 and *Oliver* applied. The 12 month suspension had been unduly lenient and wrong. Erasure was the only appropriate penalty.

COUNCIL FOR THE REGULATION OF HEALTH CARE PROFESSIONALS v. GENERAL DENTAL COUNCIL, [2005] EWHC 87, *The Times*, February 8, 2005, Newman, J., QBD.

3350. Books

O'Donnell, David–Professional Responsibility. Paperback: £40.00. ISBN 1 84592 054 6. Tottel Publishing.

Sokol, Daniel; Bergson, Gillian; McKimm, Ashley–Medical Ethics and Law: Surviving on the Wards and Passing Exams. Paperback: £14.95. ISBN 0 9547657 1 0. Trauma Publishing.

PUBLIC PROCUREMENT

3351. Competitive tendering–Proceedings–Time limits–Requirement for promptness

[Human Rights Act 1998 Sch.1 Part I Art.6; Utilities Contracts Regulations 1996 (SI 1996 2911), Reg.32(4).]

The claimant (H) sought the determination of a preliminary issue in its action against the defendant utilities company (S). H claimed that in its procurement procedures for a major contract S had breached the Utilities Contracts Regulations 1996. Under Reg.32(4) of the Regulations a complainant was required to inform the utility of an apprehended breach before bringing proceedings and was also required to bring proceedings "promptly" and, except with the court's permission, not more than three months after the breach had occurred. Alleged breaches of the procedures had taken place between May and August 2003. H wrote informing S of its intention to take action in November 2003 and issued proceedings the next day. H submitted that the requirement to bring a case promptly infringed its rights under the Human Rights Act 1998 Sch.1 Part I Art.6.

Held, determining the preliminary issue in favour of S, that the claim was time barred under Reg.32(4) in respect of all except the alleged breaches occurring in August. As these consisted merely of a refusal to extend the time for tendering for the contract, they did not amount to a breach of the Regulations. As to the earlier allegations, even had they amounted to breaches, the court would not have extended time for the claim to be pursued. H had made no effort to pursue the matters promptly and had advanced no good reason for the delay. Regulation 32(4) did not infringe H's rights under Art.6 of the 1998 Act, *Lam v. United Kingdom (Admissibility) (41671/98)* (Unreported, July 5, 2001) applied. There was a public interest in requiring promptness as speedy review of complaints was essential to an effective procurement process.

M HOLLERAN LTD v. SEVERN TRENT WATER LTD, [2004] EWHC 2508, [2005] Eu. L.R. 364, Cooke, J., QBD (Comm).

3352. Invitations to tender–Subcontractors–Lawfulness of restriction on use of subcontractors–Review procedures–Enforcement of review decisions–Admissibility–European Community

[Council Directive 89/655 on the coordination of the laws, regulations and administrative provisions relating to the application of review procedures to the award of public supply and public works contracts Art.2(7); Council Directive 92/50 relating to the coordination of procedures for the award of public service contracts Art.25, Art.32(2) (c).]

The Austrian Federal Procurement Office (B) sought a preliminary ruling on the interpretation of Council Directive 89/655, as amended by Council Directive 92/50. The Central Association of Austrian Social Security Institutions (H) had sought tenders for the award of a public supply and service contract. The invitation to tender included a clause (Point 1.8) which placed a limit on the percentage of the services which might be sub contracted out. H informed three of the consortia that had submitted tenders that the contract was to be awarded to a fourth consortium (E). The unsuccessful consortia initiated a series of review proceedings before B with the aim of preventing the award of the contract to E and obtaining an annulment of H's decision to refuse to cancel the invitation to tender. On April 5,

2001, B granted an application for an interim injunction which prevented H from awarding the contract until April 20, 2001. On that date, B granted the application to have H's decision to refuse to cancel the invitation annulled. Notwithstanding that decision, H decided, on April 23, 2001, to award the contract to E as it took the view that the interim measures had expired and that no legally binding decision had been taken that its own decision to award the contract to E was invalid or ought to have been annulled. One of the unsuccessful consortia (S) brought fresh review proceedings claiming that B's decision of April 20, 2001 had annulled the first contract award procedure and thus H's decision to award the contract was unlawful as it had taken place in the context of a second award procedure, which had not satisfied the requirements pertaining to publicity. Prior to a decision of the Austrian Constitutional Court annulling B's decision of April 20, 2001, B stayed proceedings in S's case and referred questions on (1) how Directive 89/655 applied to situations where national law did not provide for the effective and compulsory enforcement of a review body's decisions against a contracting authority, and (2) whether Art.2(7) of Directive 89/655, read in conjunction with Art.25 and Art.32(2)(c) of Directive 92/50, had to be construed as meaning that a contract concluded at the end of the procedure for the award of a public supply and service contract, the proper conduct of which was affected by the incompatibility with Community law of a provision in the invitation to tender, had to be treated as void where the applicable national law treated illegal contracts as being void.

Held, giving a preliminary ruling, that (1) the fact that the decision of April 20, 2001 was not mandatorily enforceable provided the essential grounds for the request for the preliminary ruling. As that decision had since been annulled, those questions had become hypothetical. The European Court of Justice did not give opinions on general or hypothetical questions. (2) The object and wording of the relevant provisions was to prevent the elimination of a party from the procedure for awarding a public service contract solely on the ground that the party intended to use the resources of third parties in order to carry out the contract, *Holst Italia SpA v. Comune di Cagliari (C176/98)* [1999] E.C.R. I-8607 followed. However, Directive 92/50 did not preclude a restriction on the use of sub contractors in a case where the contracting authority had not been in a position to verify the technical and economic capacities of the sub contractors at the examination stage of the tendering procedure. A tenderer could only be excluded if it failed to demonstrate that it had the relevant technical and economic capacities at its disposal. It was for B to determine whether Point 1.8 of the invitation to tender related to the examination and selection stage of the procedure for the award of the contract or to the performance phase of the contract. If Point 1.8 were found to be contrary to Directive 92/50, the national legal system had to provide for the possibility of relying on that incompatibility in the review procedures referred to in Directive 89/655.

SIEMENS AG OSTERREICH v. HAUPTVERBAND DER OSTERREICHISCHEN SOZIALVERSICHERUNGSTRAGER (C314/01) [2004] 2 C.M.L.R. 27, Judge Skouris (President), ECJ.

3353. **Public supply contracts–Pricing–Framework agreement for supply of drugs to NHS trusts–Variation–Tendering procedure**

[Public Supply Contracts Regulations 1995 (SI 1995 201).]

The claimant drug supplier (D) sought declaratory relief in respect of a circular issued by the defendant agency. The agency had concluded framework agreements with D and other drug suppliers to facilitate the purchase of a particular drug by NHS trusts and contracting authorities. Following a review of pricing under the framework agreements, the agency took the view that D was acting outside the terms of its agreement by offering reduced prices. The agency issued a circular indicating that trusts interested in contracting on reduced prices should enter into a "local tendering exercise" which could be undertaken by advertising in the Official Journal and issuing tender documentation to all potential suppliers. D contended that (1) the parties' exchange of correspondence did not give rise to an agreement precluding it from offering reduced prices under the terms of the framework agreement; (2) the circular had unlawfully required the trusts to enter into a long form tender procedure pursuant to the Public Supply Contracts Regulations 1995 in circumstances where the mini competition procedure was required.

Held, granting the declaration in part, that (1) D remained free to resort to the provisions of the price change clause in the framework agreement. The agency's letter inviting D's price review proposal could not be read as ousting the operation of that clause, and in any event D had not agreed to such an amendment in writing as required by the framework agreement. That requirement was designed to prevent informal or debatable oral assents to amendments and thus had a clear commercial purpose. D's email had submitted revised prices without any express statement of agreement to the terms proposed in the agency's letter. (2) The mini competition procedure set out in Option 2 of the Office of Government Commerce 2002 guidance notes on framework agreements fulfilled the principles of equality of treatment, competition and transparency and was consequently permissible in circumstances where an NHS trust was contemplating accepting a reduced offer made under a framework agreement which had itself been properly concluded in accordance with the Regulations. However, it was up to the NHS trust in those circumstances whether it wished to adopt the long form tendering process or the mini competition process. The circular fell short of a direction to enter the long form process and could not be regarded as unlawful.

DENFLEET INTERNATIONAL LTD v. NHS PURCHASING AND SUPPLY AGENCY, [2005] EWHC 55, [2005] Eu. L.R. 526, Davis, J., QBD (Admin).

3354. **Public works contracts-Tenderers-Persons carrying out preparatory works-Prohibition on participation in tendering procedure-European Community**

[Council Directive 89/665 on the coordination of the laws, regulations and administrative provisions relating to the application of review procedures to the award of public supply and public works contracts; Council Directive 92/50 relating to the coordination of procedures for the award of public service contracts.]

The Belgian court sought a preliminary ruling on the interpretation of Council Directive 92/50 and Council Directive 89/665. Belgian law precluded a person who had been involved in research, experiments, studies or development in connection public works from participating in or submitting a tender for the contract for those works. The European Court of Justice was required to rule as to (1) the lawfulness of national provisions which did not allow an opportunity for such a person to prove that, in the circumstances of the case, the experience he had acquired was not capable of distorting competition; (2) whether the contracting entity was precluded, until the end of the procedure for the examination of tenders, from refusing to allow an undertaking connected with any such a person to participate in the contracting procedure even though, when questioned on the point, the undertaking stated that it had not obtained an unfair advantage capable of distorting competition.

Held, giving a preliminary ruling, that (1) it was at the heart of the public procurement directives that the principle of equal treatment required comparable situations not to be treated differently and different situations not to be treated the same unless such treatment could be objectively justified, *Concordia Bus Finland Oy AB (formerly Stagecoach Finland Oy AB) v. Helsingin Kaupunki (C513/99)* [2004] All E.R. (EC) 87, [2004] C.L.Y. 3162 and *R. (on the application of Swedish Match AB) v. Secretary of State for Health (C210/03)* [2005] 1 C.M.L.R. 26, [2005] 4 C.L. 185 followed. A person who had been involved in preparatory steps in connection with a public works contract was not necessarily in the same situation when tendering for the award of that contract as someone who had not carried out such preparatory work. Indeed such a person might be at an advantage in formulating his tender on account of the information concerning the contract in question which he received when carrying out preparatory work. However, national rules did not afford a person who had carried out preparatory work any opportunity to demonstrate that the experience he had gained was not capable of distorting competition. Such a rule was precluded by the public procurement Directives as it went beyond what was necessary to attain the objective of equal treatment of all tenderers. (2) The possibility that the contracting authority might delay, until the procedure had reached a very advanced stage, taking a decision as to whether an undertaking might participate in the procedure or submit a tender deprived that undertaking of the opportunity to rely on Community rules on the award of public contracts as against the awarding authority for a period which was solely within that authority's discretion and which, where necessary, might be extended until a time when the infringements could no longer be usefully rectified was capable of depriving Council Directive 92/50 and Council Directive 89/665 of all practical effect.

FABRICOM SA v. BELGIUM (C21/03) [2005] 2 C.M.L.R. 25, Judge Timmermans (President), ECJ.

3355. Public works contracts–Time–Failure to publish contract notice–European Community

[Council Directive 93/37 concerning the coordination of procedures for the award of public service contracts, public supply contracts and public works contracts respectively Art.7(3).]

The Commission sought a declaration that the Italian authorities, in authorising public works contracts to ensure flood safety without previously publishing a contract notice, had not complied with Council Directive 93/37, to which the contracts were subject, and particularly with Art.7(3), which laid down the only situations in which a contract notice was not required. The Italian authorities contended that the works fell within Art.7(3)(e) on the basis that they consisted of works done by those companies which had been awarded the original contract and who were doing similar work within three years of the original contract. They argued that the relevant date was the date of completion of the works, not the date on which the contract was awarded. Alternatively, the Italian authorities sought to argue that it had made an excusable error due to misinterpretation of the Italian version of Art.7(3).

Held, granting the declaration, that Italy was in breach of its obligations. The date of the end of the original contract was not the date when the work had been finished, but the date when that original contract was agreed. In the derogation permitted by Art.7(3)(e), the interpretation restricting the provision was to be preferred to that which extended it. Legal certainty was required where public procurement contracts were concerned, therefore it was necessary objectively to define the date on which the period began to run as opposed to the date on which it might be said to end, which was less susceptible to precise determination. In the instant case, it followed that the three year period ran from the date on which the original contracts were entered into and Art.7(3)(e) did not apply. Neither could the concept of excusable error be relied upon to justify a failure to comply with obligations under a directive, *Commission of the European Communities v. Spain (C83/99)* [2001] E.C.R. I-445 applied.

COMMISSION OF THE EUROPEAN COMMUNITIES v. ITALY (C385/02); *sub nom.* FLOOD SAFETY WORKS IN THE RIVER PO, *Re* (C385/02) [2005] 1 C.M.L.R. 52, Judge Timmermans (President), ECJ.

3356. Books

Arrowsmith, Sue–Law of Public and Utilities Procurement. Hardback: £145.00. ISBN 0 421 75850 3. Sweet & Maxwell.

Bovis, Christopher–Public Procurement in the European Union. Hardback: £55.00. ISBN 1 4039 3607 2. Palgrave Macmillan.

Nielsen, Ruth;Treumer, Steen–New EU Public Procurement Directives. Paperback: £16.00. ISBN 87 574 1244 8. DJOF Publishing.

RATES

3357. Courts powers and duties–Magistrates courts–Power to set aside liability orders–Appropriate form of legal challenge–Delay

The local authority applied for judicial review of the magistrates' decision to set aside liability orders made against the interested party (H) requiring him to pay national non domestic rates in respect of a property. The interested party had refused to pay and had failed to comply with a subsequent statutory demand and so the local authority had issued bankruptcy proceedings. H successfully applied to have the liability orders set aside. H maintained that (1) judicial review proceedings were inappropriate to challenge the justices' decision and the proper course was to appeal by way of case stated, and (2) the justices had not acted outside their jurisdiction in setting aside the liability orders.

Held, granting the application, that (1) although the appropriate challenge to the justices' decision was by way of case stated, in the exercise of its discretion, the court would permit the case to proceed by judicial review. An error in the form of proceedings should not cause a good claim to be defeated unless prejudice had been caused to a party or for some other good reason. As neither the justices nor the interested party had filed an acknowledgment of service or challenged the form of proceedings earlier, the objection to judicial review was belated. The justices had not objected to the form of the proceedings and there was no evidence that any prejudice would be caused to H, *R. (on the application of A (A Child)) v. Leeds Magistrates Court* [2004] EWHC 554, Times, March 31, 2004 considered. (2) As a general rule, a magistrates' court should not set aside a liability order unless it was satisfied that there was a genuine and arguable dispute as to the liability for the rates in question, the order was made as a result of a substantial procedural error, defect or mishap and the application to set aside the order had been made promptly. Promptness usually required action within days, or at most a few weeks, rather than months and certainly not as much as a year. In the present case, the justices had not considered those issues properly and had made a decision that was not open to them, *Liverpool City Council v. Plemora Distribution Ltd* [2002] EWHC 2467, [2003] R.A. 34, [2003] C.L.Y. 37 followed.

R. (ON THE APPLICATION OF BRIGHTON AND HOVE CITY COUNCIL) v. BRIGHTON AND HOVE JUSTICES, [2004] EWHC 1800, [2004] R.A. 277, Stanley Burnton, J., QBD (Admin Ct).

3358. Non domestic rates–Alteration of lists–Appeals

NON-DOMESTIC RATING (ALTERATION OF LISTS AND APPEALS) (ENGLAND) REGULATIONS 2005, SI 2005 659; made under the Local Government Finance Act 1988 s.42, s.53, s.55, s.143, Sch.7A para.10, Sch.7A para.11, Sch.7A para.12, Sch.9 para.6, Sch.11 para.1, Sch.11 para.4, Sch.11 para.5, Sch.11 para.6, Sch.11 para.8, Sch.11 para.11, Sch.11 para.12, Sch.11 para.14, Sch.11 para.15, Sch.11 para.16. In force: April 1, 2005; £4.50.

These Regulations revoke the Non-Domestic Rating (Alteration of Lists and Appeals) Regulations 1993 (SI 1993 291), the Non-Domestic Rating (Alteration of Lists and Appeals) (Amendment) Regulations 1994 (SI 1994 1809), the Non-Domestic Rating (Alteration of Lists and Appeals) (Amendment) Regulations 1995 (SI 1995 609), the Local Government Changes for England (Non-Domestic Rating, Alteration of Lists and Appeals) Regulations 1995 (SI 1995 623), the Non-Domestic Rating (Alteration of Lists and Appeals) (Amendment) (England) Regulations 2000 (SI 2000 598), the Non-Domestic Rating (Alteration of Lists and Appeals) (Amendment) (England) Regulations 2001 (SI 2001 1271), the Non-Domestic Rating (Alteration of Lists and Appeals) (Amendment) (England) Regulations 2002 (SI 2002 498), the Non-Domestic Rating (Alteration of Lists and Appeals) (Amendment) (England) Regulations 2003 (SI 2003 1999) and the Non-Domestic Rating (Alteration of Lists and Appeals) (Amendment) (England) Regulations 2004 (SI 2004 3057) (with savings). They also amend the Valuation and Community Charge Tribunals Regulations 1989 (SI 1989 439) and the Non-Domestic Rating (Payment of Interest) Regulations 1990 (SI 1990 1904). The Regulations concern the alteration of local and central non-domestic rating lists. They cover the alteration of non-domestic rating lists by valuation officers, proposals for such alterations from other persons and appeals to valuation tribunals where there is disagreement about a proposal between the valuation officer and another person.

3359. Non domestic rates–Alteration of lists–Appeals–Wales

NON-DOMESTIC RATING (ALTERATION OF LISTS AND APPEALS) (WALES) REGULATIONS 2005, SI 2005 758 (W.63); made under the Local Government Finance Act 1988 s.42, s.53, s.55, s.143, Sch.11 para.1, Sch.11 para.4, Sch.11 para.5, Sch.11 para.6, Sch.11 para.8, Sch.11 para.11, Sch.11 para.12, Sch.11 para.14, Sch.11 para.15, Sch.11 para.16. In force: April 1, 2005; £4.50.

These Regulations amend the Valuation and Community Charge Tribunals Regulations 1989 (SI 1989 439), the Non-Domestic Rating (Payment of Interest) Regulations 1990 (SI 1990 1904), the Non-Domestic Rating (Material Day for List Alterations) Regulations 1992 (SI 1992 556), the Non-Domestic Rating (Alteration of Lists and Appeals) Regulations 1993 (SI 1993 291). They also revoke the Non-Domestic Rating (Alteration of Lists and Appeals) (Amendment) Regulations 1994 (SI 1994 1809) (with savings), the Non-Domestic Rating (Alteration of Lists and Appeals) (Amendment) Regulations 1995 (SI 1995 609) (with savings), the Non-Domestic Rating (Chargeable Amounts) (Wales) Regulations 1999 (SI 1999 3454 (W.51)), the Non-Domestic Rating (Alteration of Lists and Appeals) (Amendment) (Wales) Regulations 2000 (SI 2000 792 (W.29)), the Non-Domestic Rating (Alteration of Lists and Appeals) (Amendment) (Wales) Regulations 2001 (SI 2001 1203 (W.64)) and the Non-Domestic Rating (Alteration of Lists and Appeals) (Amendment) (Wales) Regulations 2002 (SI 2002 1735 (W.165)) (with saving). The Regulations concern the alteration of local and central non-domestic rating lists. They cover the alteration of non-domestic rating lists by valuation officers, proposals for such alterations from other persons and appeals to valuation tribunal where there is disagreement about a proposal between the valuation officer and another person.

3360. Non domestic rates–Alteration of lists–Material day

NON-DOMESTIC RATING (MATERIAL DAY FOR LIST ALTERATIONS) (AMENDMENT) (ENGLAND) REGULATIONS 2005, SI 2005 658; made under the Local Government Finance Act 1988 s.143, Sch.6 para.2. In force: April 1, 2005; £3.00.

The Local Government Finance Act 1988 Sch.6 provides for the valuation of hereditaments. Where an alteration is to be made to the rateable value for a hereditament shown on a rating list, the matters mentioned in para.2(7) of that Schedule are taken to be as they are assumed to be on the material day. The Non-Domestic Rating (Material Day for List Alterations) Regulations 1992 (SI 1992 556) prescribes the rules under which the material day is to be determined. The 1992 Regulations are amended to provide for: an alteration which has effect under the Non-Domestic Rating (Alteration of Lists and Appeals) Regulations 1993 Reg.13(2A) or (8BA), the material day is March 31, 2000; and for alterations to lists compiled on or after April 1, 2005, where the circumstances are not covered by the earlier provisions of Reg.3 of the 1992 Regulations, the material day will be the day the proposal giving rise to the alteration was made, or where there is no proposal, the day the circumstances giving rise to the alteration occurred or, where that date is not reasonably ascertainable, the date the alteration is made.

3361. Non domestic rates–Appurtenances–District heating systems supplying council housing estates–Rateable value

[Local Government Finance Act 1988 s.66(1)(b).]

The appellant valuation officer appealed against the tribunal's decision that several district heating systems which supplied council housing estates were rateable and should be entered onto the non domestic rating list at a nominal value of £1. The heating systems were owned and operated by the respondent local authority, which contended that they were appurtenant to the residences within the meaning of Local Government Finance Act 1988 s.66(1)(b) and ought, therefore, to be classed as domestic property. The valuation officer argued that each heating system consisted entirely of non domestic property and ought to be assessed on the contractor's basis, which would result in rateable values of £5,025 to £70,650.

Held, dismissing the appeal, that the systems were not rateable and should be deleted from the rating list. The heating systems were appurtenances to the residences within the statutory context, particularly since s.66(1)(b) referred to an appurtenance being "enjoyed with" property as distinct from "belonging to" it, which latter description indicated ownership rather than occupation. The systems were part of and served the building, which was entirely residential, and they would pass with the building on sale. The interpretation contended for by the valuation officer would require all the common parts of the building, as well as its gardens and car parks, also to be classed as non domestic property and therefore rateable. (Obiter) If the appeal had been decided in the valuation officer's favour, there was no reason why the contractor's basis of assessment should not be used and the values would be those contended for by the valuation officer.

HEAD (VALUATION OFFICER) v. TOWER HAMLETS LBC [2005] R.A. 177, George Bartlett Q.C. (President), Lands Tr.

3362. Non domestic rates–Calculation of contributions

NON-DOMESTIC RATING CONTRIBUTIONS (AMENDMENT) (ENGLAND) REGULATIONS 2005, SI 2005 3333; made under the Local Government Finance Act 1988 s.143, Sch.8 para.4, Sch.8 para.6. In force: December 31, 2005; £3.00.

These Regulations amend the rules contained in the Non-Domestic Rating Contributions (England) Regulations 1992 (SI 1992 3082) for the calculation of non-domestic rating contributions and the assumptions to be made in calculating the provisional amount of the non-domestic rating contributions for financial years beginning on or after April 1, 2006. They make amendments in relation to the offset for a special authority; the national cost of collection figure; the cost factors; the buoyancy factor; and the losses in collection percentages.

3363. Non domestic rates–Calculation of contributions–Wales

NON-DOMESTIC RATING CONTRIBUTIONS (WALES) (AMENDMENT) REGULATIONS 2005, SI 2005 3345 (W.259); made under the Local Government Finance Act 1988 s.140, s.143, Sch.8 para.4, Sch.8 para.6. In force: December 7, 2005; £3.00.

Under the Local Government Finance Act 1988, billing authorities in Wales are required to pay amounts (called non-domestic rating contributions) to the National Assembly for Wales. Rules for the calculation of those amounts are contained in the Non-Domestic Rating Contributions (Wales) Regulations 1992 (SI 1992 3238). These Regulations amend the 1992 Regulations by substituting a new multiplier and a new Sch.4.

3364. Non domestic rates–Chargeable amounts–Transitional relief scheme

NON-DOMESTIC RATING (CHARGEABLE AMOUNTS) (ENGLAND) (AMENDMENT) REGULATIONS 2005, SI 2005 991; made under the Local Government Finance Act 1988 s.57A, s.140, s.143. In force: March 31, 2005; £3.00.

These Regulations correct errors in the Non-Domestic Rating (Chargeable Amounts) (England) Regulations 2004 (SI 2004 3387) by way of the correction of references to April 1, 2000, which should have been references to April 1, 2005; and the insertion of references to liability for rates for hereditaments shown on the central rating list.

3365. Non domestic rates–Charities–Use of false charity number

[Local Government Finance Act 1988 s.43(6).]

The claimant (T), which claimed to be a charitable organisation under the Local Government Finance Act 1988 s.43(6), applied for judicial review of a liability order for unpaid non domestic rates. For a number of years, T had claimed the benefit of the 80 per cent mandatory relief from non domestic rates as a charity, but the relief was withdrawn after the local authority discovered that the registered charities number which T had been using was false. The justices subsequently made a liability order, which included the amount of the relief claimed. T argued that the local authority had not been entitled to withdraw the mandatory relief. Moreover, the justices had erred in failing to adjourn the hearing of the application for the liability order pending the outcome of its application to the Charity Commissioners for registration.

Held, refusing the application, that there was no question that the local authority had been entitled to withdraw the mandatory relief in the light of the use of a false charity registration number. Furthermore, T had failed to adduce any evidence before the justices to enable them to conclude that it was a charitable organisation entitled to mandatory relief from non domestic rates.

R. (ON THE APPLICATION OF TOWER OF REFUGE MINISTRY) v. HIGHBURY CORNER MAGISTRATES COURT, [2004] EWHC 2372, [2004] R.V.R. 269, Moses, J., QBD (Admin).

3366. Non domestic rates–Demand notices–Wales

NON-DOMESTIC RATING (DEMAND NOTICES) (WALES) (AMENDMENT) REGULATIONS 2005, SI 2005 256 (W.22); made under the Local Government Finance Act 1988 Sch.9 para.1, Sch.9 para.2; and the Welsh Language Act 1993 s.26. In force: February 25, 2005; £3.00.

These Regulations, which amend the Non-Domestic Rating (Demand Notices) (Wales) Regulations 1993 (SI 1993 252), amend explanatory information which must be supplied by billing authorities in Wales so that it refers to changes to the rules surrounding the making of proposals or appeals under the new rateable values; explains that new rateable values will be used to calculate business rates; refers to the introduction of mandatory rate relief for community amateur sport clubs registered with the Inland Revenue; and removes obsolete information relating to "Transitional Arrangements" and "Small Property Relief".

3367. Non domestic rates–Exemptions–Exemption for church halls and chapel halls–Power of tribunal to correct rating list by substituting two hereditaments for one incorrectly identified

[Local Government Finance Act 1988 Sch.5 para.11.]

The appellant ratepayer appealed against the entry in the rating list as a single hereditament of a gift shop and refectory located in a cathedral. The gift shop and refectory were run by a company directed by members of the chapter and congregation so as to comply with the rules of the charity commissioners. The entrances to the shop, the refectory and the cathedral building were all separate. The issues were (1) whether the hereditament was to be treated as exempt as a church hall or similar building under the Local Government Finance Act 1988 Sch.5 para.11; (2) whether the property could correctly be regarded as a single hereditament, and if not, whether two hereditaments could be substituted to correct the rating list.

Held, allowing the appeal, that (1) the hereditament was not exempt since the company, rather than the church, was the rateable occupier. The company had a separate identity and its objectives were distinct from those of the church; furthermore, the company had control of the entrances and the running of the shop and refectory, and the church did not, *Glenwright (Valuation Officer) v. St Nicholas Parochial Church Council* [1988] R.A. 1, [1988] C.L.Y. 3007 considered. The refectory, though sometimes used for church groups, had as its main use a cafe with a very good turnover and permanent features which indicated that its use as a cafe was the most significant. The church use of the shop was not significant, *Attorney General Ex rel Bedfordshire CC v. Howard United Reformed Church Trustees, Bedford* [1975] Q.B. 41, [1974] C.L.Y. 3750 applied. The dual uses should be considered as a matter of valuation rather than exemption. (2) Two separate hereditaments existed since they were run entirely separately, not interchangeably, and were in separate, self contained units, *Green (Valuation Officer) v. Barnet LBC* [1994] R.A. 235, [1995] C.L.Y. 4297 considered. However, there was no power to create two hereditaments in place of the incorrect one since notice had to be given to the parties prior to an alteration being made, and although here the ratepayer was aware of the appeal, this would not always be the case and could lead to a liability being created without the occupier being able to make representations.

ST ALBANS CATHEDRAL (CHAPTER OF THE ABBEY CHURCH) v. BOOTH (VALUATION OFFICER) [2004] R.A. 309, A Bryant (Chairman), Valuation Tribunal.

3368.   Non domestic rates–Light railways

NON-DOMESTIC RATING (COMMUNICATIONS AND LIGHT RAILWAYS) (ENGLAND) REGULATIONS 2005, SI 2005 549; made under the Local Government Finance Act 1988 s.64, s.65, s.143. In force: April 1, 2005; £3.00.

These Regulations provide in relation to England that certain property occupied, or, if unoccupied, owned by Greater Manchester Metro Ltd, South Yorkshire Supertram Ltd or any of the communications operators mentioned in the Schedule which would, apart from these Regulations, be more than one hereditament, shall be treated as one hereditament. The Regulations also specify who shall be treated as occupying each hereditament and the billing authority area in which each hereditament shall be treated as situated.

3369.   Non domestic rates–Valuation–Method of assessing rateable value of opencast coal sites–Market evidence

The rate payer company (B) appealed against the determination of assessments by local valuation tribunals in the 1990 rating list of a number of opencast coal sites. The method of valuation used was a royalty rent per tonne for coal and surface applied to the agreed output, less agreed disability allowances, plus the annual values of buildings and rateable plant and machinery, which was also agreed. The dispute concerned the royalty rents. B argued that there was insufficient market evidence of coal royalties, therefore the royalty rent should be established indirectly by comparing the appeal hereditaments with the British Coal opencast sites, where a royalty rent of £6 per tonne was agreed. This comparison produced royalty rents for the appeal sites of £1.98 to £2.87 per tonne. The respondent valuation officers argued that there existed sufficient evidence of coal royalties to find that the royalty rent for the sites in question was £6 per tonne, and that even if an indirect method were used it would result in the same finding on the basis of a conventional receipts and expenditure valuation.

Held, dismissing the appeals, that on the evidence the correct royalty rent to be applied to the annual output of coal at each site was £6 per tonne. The appropriate method of valuation was by direct comparison with market evidence and there was enough reliable value evidence available to enable a royalty rent to be determined for the appeal hereditaments, by reference to royalties for alienated coal, surface royalties and comparable assessments, *Garton v. Hunter (Valuation Officer) (No.1)* [1969] 2 Q.B. 37, [1969] C.L.Y. 3017 considered. Even if there had been a lack of adequate value evidence, the valuation by B's expert was fundamentally flawed, being contrived to support B's complaint that it had been rated unfairly. The correct approach was to ask whether the assessments for the appeal sites were correct, not whether they were too high in comparison with British Coal assessments, and there was no evidence to support that contention.

HJ BANKS & CO LTD v. SPEIGHT (VALUATION OFFICER); HJ BANKS & CO LTD v. SNOWBALL (VALUATION OFFICER) [2005] R.A. 61, PH Clarke, FRICS, LandsTr.

3370. Rateable value – Golf courses – Course on land subject to commoners' rights – Exclusive possession

The appellant ratepayer (T) appealed against the respondent valuation officer's refusal to alter the rating list for a particular year in relation to T's golf club. T had made two proposals to reduce the rateable value of the golf club, the issue being whether it was in rateable occupation of the golf course as well as the clubhouse and immediate surrounds. The course was on open moorland subject to commoners' rights, and the right to use it as a golf course had been granted by a deed made in 1957 with the freeholders and an agreement with the commoners made in 1982. The land was also subject to national park by laws. The moorland was used for grazing and the course was unfenced so wandering ponies would disturb games, and sometimes non members would play on the course. It was agreed that three of the elements of rateable occupation, as set out in *John Laing & Son v. Kingswood Assessment Committee* [1949] 1 K.B. 344, were present, but T disputed that it was in exclusive possession of the course, stating that the documents provided no exclusive rights, the course being on land which remained subject to the rights of commoners.

Held, dismissing the appeals, that T was both in rateable occupation of the course and in exclusive possession of it. Regard had to be given to deeds and agreements with commoners as well as other elements such as by laws, since no single document was capable of granting exclusive rights of user in respect of land that was subject to commoners' rights, *Laing* applied. The by laws as well as the two documents did effectively grant exclusive occupation of the course for the playing of golf since the 1957 deed prevented the landlords from granting the same rights to construct and maintain a course for that use while the lease ran, which was as much of an exclusive right as the landlords were able to give. The 1982 agreement allowed the construction or erection of, for instance, bunkers, flags and huts to be used only for the purposes of playing golf and this effectively created a duty on T to prevent others from using those things. The existence of public rights over the land did not in itself show that there was not exclusive occupation for the purpose of playing golf. The non members who sometimes played without permission could be discouraged by the enforcement of the by laws that they were almost certainly breaching by their activity. The rateable value was reduced by almost half and reduced further for a period when the course had been closed due to foot and mouth disease.

TAVISTOCK GOLF CLUB v. WEST DEVON VALUATION OFFICER [2004] R.A. 289, Judge not specified, Valuation Tribunal.

3371. Valuation – Central rating lists – Designation of hereditaments

CENTRAL RATING LIST (ENGLAND) REGULATIONS 2005, SI 2005 551; made under the Local Government Finance Act 1988 s.53, s.64, s.65, s.143. In force: in accordance with Reg.1 (1); £3.00.

With a view to securing the central rating en bloc of certain hereditaments, regulations may be made which designate a person and prescribe in relation to that person one or more descriptions of non-domestic hereditament. In relation to the central rating list for England which is to be compiled on April 1, 2005, these Regulations designate the persons and prescribe the descriptions of hereditament against the names of those persons. The descriptions of hereditament prescribed in this way are: railway hereditaments, light rapid transit hereditaments, communications hereditaments, national and regional gas transportation hereditaments, local gas transportation hereditaments, gas meter hereditaments, electricity transmission hereditaments, electricity distribution hereditaments, electricity meter hereditaments, water supply hereditaments, canal hereditaments and long-distance pipe-line hereditaments. The Regulations require the names of the designated persons and the hereditaments situated in England which are within the prescribed descriptions and are occupied (or, if unoccupied, owned) by those persons to be shown in the central non-domestic rating list for England compiled on or after April 1, 2005; and require the list to show certain information about the designated persons and the date from which a rateable value shown in the list has effect. The Regulations, which amend the Central Rating Lists (England) Regulations 2000 (SI 2000 525), revoke the Non-Domestic Rating (Electricity Generators) Regulations 1991 (SI 1991 475), the Non-Domestic Rating (Railways, Telecommunications and Canals) Regulations 1994 (SI 1994 3123) and the Central Rating Lists (England) (Amendment) Regulations 2001 (SI 2001 737).

3372. Valuation–Central rating lists–Designation of hereditaments–Wales

CENTRAL RATING LIST (WALES) REGULATIONS 2005, SI 2005 422 (W.40); made under the Local Government Finance Act 1988 s.53, s.64, s.65, s.143. In force: in accordance with Reg.1 (1); £3.00.

These Regulations revoke with savings in relation to Wales the Non-Domestic Rating (Electricity Generators) Regulations 1991 (SI 1991 475), the Non-Domestic Rating (Railways, Telecommunications and Canals) Regulations 1994 (SI 1994 3123), the Central Rating Lists (Wales) Regulations 1999 (SI 1999 3453), the Central Rating Lists (Wales) (Amendment) Regulations 2001 (SI 2001 2222) and the Central Rating List (Wales) (Amendment) Regulations 2003 (SI 2003 3225). With a view to securing the central rating en bloc of certain hereditaments, regulations may be made under the Local Government Finance Act 1988 which designate a person and prescribe in relation to that person one or more descriptions of non-domestic hereditament. In relation to the central rating list for Wales which is to be compiled on April 1, 2005, these Regulations designate persons and prescribe the descriptions of hereditament against the names of those persons. There are thereby designated: railway hereditaments, communications hereditaments, national and regional gas hereditaments, local gas hereditaments, gas meter hereditaments, electricity transmission hereditaments, electricity distribution hereditaments, electricity meter hereditaments, water supply hereditaments, canal hereditaments and long-distance pipe-line hereditaments.

REAL PROPERTY

3373. Access to the countryside–Appeals–Wales

COUNTRYSIDE ACCESS (MEANS OF ACCESS, APPEALS ETC.) (WALES) REGULATIONS 2005, SI 2005 1270 (W.90); made under the Countryside and Rights of Way Act 2000 s.32, s.38, s.44. In force: May 6, 2005; £3.00.

The Countryside and Rights of Way Act 2000 s.36(3) provides that, if an owner or occupier fails to observe any restriction in an agreement under s.35 of the Act, the access authority may give to the person with whom it has entered into the agreement notice to carry out works to remedy the breach of the restriction. Section 38(1) provides the owner and occupier the right to appeal against a notice under s.36(3) or s.37(1) and these Regulations, which amend Countryside Access (Appeals Procedures) (Wales) Regulations 2002 (SI 2002 1794), make provision for the initial stages of such an appeal.

3374. Access to the countryside–Maps–Corrections

ACCESS TO THE COUNTRYSIDE (CORRECTION OF PROVISIONAL AND CONCLUSIVE MAPS) (ENGLAND) (AMENDMENT) REGULATIONS 2005, SI 2005 2027; made under the Countryside and Rights of Way Act 2000 s.11, s.44, s.45. In force: August 22, 2005; £3.00.

These Regulations amend the Access to the Countryside (Correction of Provisional and Conclusive Maps) (England) Regulations 2003 (SI 2003 1591) which make provision for the Countryside Agency to correct maps issued in provisional and conclusive form under the Countryside and Rights of Way Act 2000. These Regulations prescribe an additional set of circumstances in which a conclusive map may be corrected by the Countryside Agency. There is no longer a time limit for correcting a conclusive map. The time limit for correcting a provisional map under the 2003 Regulations has been relaxed, so that the time limit of three months from the date of issue of the provisional map only applies where the correction consists of the showing of additional land on that map.

3375. Adverse possession–Abandonment–Erection of temporary fence–Interruption of possession

The appellant (C) appealed against a decision that the respondent (G) had acquired title to a strip of land by way of adverse possession. C was the freehold paper owner of the strip which was contained within an industrial estate. G had sought a declaration that it had acquired title by way of adverse possession since it had occupied the strip uninterrupted since 1987. C argued that G had excluded itself from part of the strip thereby defeating its claim in regard to that area. That exclusion had been by way of a temporary fence which G had erected for three months in 1997 in connection with separate proceedings and had been specifically erected by G to exclude itself from the area. The judge found that the erection of the fence had not amounted to an abandonment by G of possession, and accordingly he found that the area was included within the strip of which G had established adverse possession. C argued (1) that the judge had been wrong to find adverse possession had been established in respect of the strip of land; (2) that the judge had been wrong to find that the erection of the fence in order to exclude itself from the area had not amounted to an abandonment of possession by G.

Held, allowing the appeal in part, that (1) on the facts the judge had been entitled to find that G had established adverse possession to the strip of land subject to the determination of the dispute concerning the fenced off area. (2) The unusual act of temporary voluntary self exclusion from land was sufficient to amount to interruption of possession to defeat adverse possession. It was clear that G had intended to exclude itself from the area of land contained within the strip and could not thereafter claim that it was in actual or intended possession for that period of exclusion, and that was not changed by the temporary nature of that exclusion. Accordingly, the judge had been wrong to find that G had established adverse possession in respect of that area of the strip.

GENERAY LTD v. CONTAINERISED STORAGE CO LTD, [2005] EWCA Civ 478, [2005] 2 E.G.L.R. 7, Peter Gibson, L.J., CA (Civ Div).

3376. Adverse possession–Deprivation of possessions–Human rights compatibility of adverse possession law prior to October 2003–Interpretation of statutory provisions to ensure compatibility

[Land Registration Act 1925 s.75; Limitation Act 1980 s.17, s.32(1)(b); Human Rights Act 1998 s.3, Sch.1 Part II Art.1; European Convention on Human Rights 1950.]

The claimant (B) sought an order restraining the defendant (P) from entering or using a field of which B was the registered owner. In 1983 P was granted permission by the then owner to continue his use of the field to graze animals. In October 1986 that owner asked P to vacate the field in anticipation of the completion of its sale. However, as P heard nothing further from the new owners, he continued to use the field for grazing. P subsequently applied to the

Land Registry for first registration of title by adverse possession on the basis that he had had exclusive possession and control of the field at all times after October 1, 1986, having enclosed the field and used it to graze cattle and horses for a period in excess of 12 years. The proceedings before the Land Registry were adjourned pending the outcome of the instant proceedings. B submitted that (1) P's use of the field was not sufficient to found a claim for adverse possession of it as he had made no, or no significant, use of the land from 1988, or at least from 1991 onwards; (2) even if P had exclusive possession of the field from October 1986, time did not begin to run until the end of June 1991 because P had deliberately concealed his trespass and therefore the 12 year period ended in June 2003, so that B could take advantage of the Human Rights Act 1998. In that regard, the effect of the Land Registration Act 1925 s.75, read together with the relevant provisions of the Limitation Act 1980, was to deprive B of its property without compensation, and there was no justification for such provisions, so that they were contrary to the 1998 Act Sch.1 Part II Art.1 and the court was obliged by s.3 of the 1998 Act to read and give effect to the provisions in such a way as to render them compatible with the European Convention on Human Rights 1950 if possible.

Held, giving judgment for P, that (1) P had had exclusive possession of the field since he became a trespasser in October 1986 as a result of providing secure fencing, padlocking the only entrance to the field other than that from his own property, allowing horses to graze on it daily, agreeing to work being done on it by a third party, and giving away a small portion of the land to a neighbour, *JA Pye (Oxford) Ltd v. Graham* [2002] UKHL 30, [2003] 1 A.C. 419, [2002] C.L.Y. 3805 applied. (2) (i) P had deliberately concealed his trespass so that, under s.32(1)(b), the limitation period did not begin to run until the withheld fact became known. However, the trespass was not concealed after June 1991 so that, on the basis of s.75 of the 1925 Act, B had become trustee of the field for P on or about June 27, 2003 as a result of P having had exclusive possession of it for the 12 previous years with the requisite intention to exclude everybody else, including the registered owner. (ii) As beneficial ownership in the field was transferred to P by operation of law after the 1998 Act came into force, the issue arose as to whether English law relating to adverse possession, as it stood before October 2003, was compatible with the Convention and, if not, whether the relevant statutory provisions could be read and given effect to, in accordance with s.3 of the 1998 Act, in such a way as to make them compatible. The practical effect of s.17 of the 1980 Act and s.75 of the 1925 Act in the instant case was that they affected the substantive rights of B as landowner, *Wilson v. First County Trust Ltd (No.2)* [2003] UKHL 40, [2004] 1 A.C. 816, [2004] C.L.Y. 628 applied. The effect of the legislation as a whole was to deprive the landowner of all his rights to it and of any means of recovering possession of it, and thus to transfer the right to possession and title to the trespasser. That was properly to be characterised as a deprivation of possession within Sch.1 Part II Art.1 of the 1998 Act, and not as a bar to access to the court within Sch.1 Part I Art.6 or merely a control over the use of the property. There was nothing in *Wilson* to support the argument that Sch.1 Part II Art.1 was not engaged because the relevant provisions existed when B bought the field. Schedule 1 Part II Art.1 was engaged where a property right was acquired that was subject to a law with the potential for depriving the owner of it, *Pennycook v. Shaws (EAL) Ltd* [2004] EWCA Civ 100, [2004] Ch. 296, [2004] C.L.Y. 2494 applied. Laws affecting purely private transactions engaged Sch.1 Part I Art.1, *Pennycook* applied and *Family Housing Association v. Donnellan* [2002] 1 P. & C.R. 34, [2002] C.L.Y. 3803 doubted. The second rule in Sch.1 Part I Art.1 was engaged. There was no public or general interest justifying the deprivation, *James v. United Kingdom (A/98)* (1986) 8 E.H.R.R. 123, [1986] C.L.Y. 1650 considered. The expropriation of registered land without compensation in circumstances such as the instant case did not advance any of the legitimate aims of the statutory provisions and was disproportionate. Therefore, B's loss of the disputed land in accordance with s.75 of the 1925 Act was incompatible with Sch.1 Part I Art.1. It was not possible to reinterpret the relevant statutory provisions in accordance with s.3 of the 1998 Act so as to give B a right to compensation, *Mount Carmel Investments Ltd v. Thurlow* [1988] 1 W.L.R. 1078,

[1989] C.L.Y. 2278 applied. However, s.75 of the 1925 Act could be interpreted as being applicable to those cases in which the trespasser established "possession" in accordance with the case law in existence at the time of its enactment. Since P's action was not inconsistent with any use or intended use of the land by B, his possession of it was not adverse and his claim to have acquired the field failed as a result.

BEAULANE PROPERTIES LTD v. PALMER, [2005] EWHC 817, [2006] Ch. 79, Nicholas Strauss Q.C., Ch D.

3377. **Adverse possession—Limitation periods—Person claiming through Crown—Right of action first accrued to Crown—Meaning of Sch.1 para.12 Limitation Act 1980**

[Limitation Act 1980 Sch.1 para.12.]

The claimants (C) claimed title to land by adverse possession from the defendant (T) and compensation for the compulsory acquisition of the disputed land. The disputed land comprised the land between and airspace enclosed by 10 arches supporting a road flyover. The former Greater London Council (GLC) had been the registered proprietor of the land. When the GLC was abolished in 1986, the disputed land became Crown land. In July 2000 the disputed land was by order vested in T. C claimed adverse possession by virtue of its occupation of the arches since 1985, when the GLC had sold the land adjacent to the arches. C's case was that, no action to recover possession having been taken by the GLC or its successor in title, the Crown, the paper title became extinguished by adverse possession at the moment the disputed land was vested by the Crown in T in 2000. C submitted that T had no right of action under the Limitation Act 1980 Sch.1 para.12 because the right of action had not "first accrued to the Crown" but to the GLC so that all that was needed to defeat T's title was 12 years of adverse possession prior to 2000 in circumstances in which the right to recover possession first accrued to an owner other than the Crown, the title was then transferred to the Crown, and more than 12 years after the right of action first accrued the Crown's title was transferred to T. T submitted that Sch.1 para.12 was a complete answer to the claim since the word "first" in the phrase "first accrued to the Crown" in para.12 meant "earlier" or "previously" rather than "originally" so that even if the right of action originally accrued to the GLC it accrued to the Crown before T so that time was still running in T's favour.

Held, giving judgment for T, that (1) the meaning of the word "first" in the phrase "first accrued to the Crown" in Sch.1 para.12 was "earlier" or "previously" and not "originally". The Crown enjoyed a 30 year limitation period from the date when the right of action originally accrued, whether that right accrued to the Crown or to its predecessor in title. The primary intention of para.12 was to prescribe the limitation period applicable to a person claiming through the Crown. Paragraph 12 gave the Crown's successor in title the benefit of the 30 year period, under para.12(a), or, under para.12(b), 12 years from when title was acquired from the Crown, whichever expired first. That showed that the feature of paramount importance in the scheme of para.12 was that the claimant in possession was someone claiming through the Crown, which itself had had a right of action. Whether or not the right originally accrued to the Crown or to someone else appeared to be a subtlety lacking a rational basis since in any event the longer 30 year period ran from the date of the original accrual. Paragraph 12 provided a complete code for claims brought by persons claiming through the Crown, whether the right of action accrued originally to the Crown or only so accrued earlier. Therefore C's claim failed, whether or not they could prove that they were in adverse possession of the disputed land from 1985. (2) On the evidence C were in adverse possession from 1987 onwards but they were not in such possession from before the important date in 1986, so that even if the court was wrong in its interpretation of Sch.1 para.12, C's claim failed on the facts.

HILL v. TRANSPORT FOR LONDON, [2005] EWHC 856, [2005] Ch. 379, Rimer, J., Ch D.

3378. Beneficial ownership–Constructive trusts–Need for communication to establish common intention constructive trust

The appellant (L) appealed against a decision ([2004] EWHC 840) dismissing his claim that he had a beneficial half share in a freehold property. In ancillary relief proceedings between the parties, L had agreed to transfer to the respondent (B) his share in the matrimonial home, and that transfer had taken place. However, L continued to make payments towards the capital in and maintenance of the house. Further, the parties went through a period of reconciliation and they agreed to remarry and share everything jointly. L claimed that by virtue of the payments he had made, he held a beneficial half share in the property. The judge found, inter alia, that the mere fact of the payments could not give rise to an equitable interest in the absence of some arrangement or understanding that L should have one. L argued that the judge had been wrong to rely upon *Springette v. Defoe* [1992] 2 F.L.R. 388, [1992] C.L.Y. 2031 since that decision had been overruled by the decision of *Oxley v. Hiscock* [2004] EWCA Civ 546, [2004] 3 W.L.R. 715, [2004] 9 C.L. 409 on the issue of the parties' intention when determining the existence of constructive trusts. L further argued that the judge had failed to consider all the relevant evidence.

Held, dismissing the appeal, that it was clear that the requirement of communication to establish the existence of common intention constructive trusts had not been dispensed with by the decision in *Oxley*. The need for communication was only held to be unnecessary when determining the size of the beneficial interest to be apportioned. It was clear that the judge had not misdirected himself, *Springette* and *Oxley* considered. Further, it was clear that the judge had considered all the relevant evidence, upon which he had been entitled to conclude that no trust existed.

LIGHTFOOT v. LIGHTFOOT-BROWN, [2005] EWCA Civ 201, [2005] 2 P. & C.R. 22, Auld, L.J., CA (Civ Div).

3379. Beneficial ownership–Constructive trusts–Property dispute following breakdown of relationship–Engagement ring–Rebuttable presumption of absolute gift

[Law Reform (Miscellaneous Provisions) Act 1970 s.3(2).]

The female claimant (C) sought judgment against the male defendant (J) in respect of certain items of property. C and J were a formerly engaged couple but the relationship had ended. The instant property dispute ensued. The arguments concerned ownership of the leasehold of a flat registered in J's name, a freehold house registered in J's sole name and the engagement ring. C argued that J had purchased the flat as nominee for her and held it on trust for her absolutely. C contended that although J had provided the funds for the house, it was held on trust for both C and J in equal shares as that was the understanding on which it was purchased. Additionally, C had put a lot of effort into its restoration as an intended home for C and J.

Held, giving judgment accordingly, that (1) it was inequitable for J to hold the flat for himself absolutely; rather he held it on constructive trust for C absolutely; *Banner Homes Holdings Ltd (formerly Banner Homes Group Plc) v. Luff Developments Ltd (No.2)* [2000] Ch. 372, [2000] C.L.Y. 2317 applied. There had been an understanding between J and C that it was purchased for her. Based on that understanding, C had stopped her attempt to find methods of funding for the property. After the purchase, C managed the flat. (2) C was entitled to a 25 per cent beneficial interest in the house. Although there had been an agreement to own the house jointly, that agreement did not provide for the house to be held in equal shares. C had acted to her detriment by spending a substantial amount of time concentrating on the renovation of the house rather than her employment. It was inequitable for J to deny C an equitable interest in the house, *Lloyds Bank Plc v. Rosset* [1991] 1 A.C. 107, [1990] C.L.Y. 706 applied. A determination of the percentage of C's interest in the house, depended upon an assessment of what was fair having regard to the whole course of dealing between C and J in relation to the property, *Oxley v. Hiscock*

[2004] EWCA Civ 546, [2004] 3 W.L.R. 715 applied. J had funded the entirety of the purchase, the works and the mortgage repayments. (3) J failed to rebut the presumption that the engagement ring was an absolute gift as stated in the Law Reform (Miscellaneous Provisions) Act 1970 s.3(2).

COX v. JONES, [2004] EWHC 1486, [2004] 2 F.L.R. 1010, Mann, J., Ch D.

3380. Beneficial ownership–Intention–Tenants in common–Size of beneficial interest under constructive trust–Application of fairness test

[Law of Property Act 1925 s.53(1)(b).]

The appellant wife (H) appealed against a registrar's decision declaring that a property was beneficially owned in equal shares by her and the respondent trustee in bankruptcy (S) of her husband (X). The property had been the couple's matrimonial home. It was accepted that H and X were tenants in common and that, under a constructive trust, they owned beneficial shares in the property, as they had in their previous matrimonial home. The transfer of the property to H and X contained no express declaration as to their beneficial interests. However, they had subsequently made written statements in connection with X's then proposed individual voluntary arrangement (IVA) to the effect that they each had an equal share in the beneficial ownership. X also made other statements to a similar effect in correspondence. The registrar held that the IVA statements constituted written declarations of trust within the Law of Property Act 1925 s.53(1)(b) and, even if they did not, they justified the court inferring a common intention on the part of H and X to hold the property on trust for themselves in equal shares beneficially. H contended that, primarily on the basis of their respective contributions to the purchase of the property and their previous matrimonial home, X's share of the beneficial ownership of the property was no more than 15 per cent. She argued that S could not rely on the IVA statements given that the IVA failed and that the registrar had erred in his assessment of the contributions made by H and X to the purchase price.

Held, dismissing the appeal, that (1) neither H's nor X's statements in connection with the unsuccessful IVA were declarations of trust in relation to property. Neither of them purported to create a trust where either no trust or some different trust had existed before. The registrar had failed to consider it necessary to decide whether H and X shared the common intention expressed in their IVA statements at any earlier time, *Mortgage Corp v. Shaire* [2001] Ch. 743, [2000] C.L.Y. 4659 considered. He had not made a finding as to inferred common intention at the time of the purchase of the property and the court therefore had to consider that question afresh. (2) It could not be inferred that H and X had a common intention as to equal beneficial ownership at the time of purchase of the property. Apart from the substantial lapse of time between the purchase and the IVA statements, it was artificial to attribute to H and X a common intention that the extent of their respective beneficial interests should be fixed as from the time of purchase, *Oxley v. Hiscock* [2004] EWCA Civ 546, [2005] Fam. 211, [2004] C.L.Y. 3196 applied. Accordingly, the size of the respective beneficial interests fell to be determined on the basis of what appeared to be fair by reference to all the parties' conduct at the time of and after the property purchase. The registrar was right to describe the IVA statements as a compelling factor in the assessment of what was fair. It would be very unfair if, having made the statement that she did to X's creditors, H could obtain, in litigation between herself and a trustee for those same creditors, a determination that her beneficial interest exceeded 50 per cent. It was no answer that the IVA failed. Overall, a 50/50 apportionment was fair both to H and X's creditors.

HURST v. SUPPERSTONE; *sub nom.* SUPPERSTONE v. HURST, [2005] EWHC 1309, [2006] 1 F.C.R. 352, Michael Briggs Q.C., Ch D.

3381. Beneficial ownership–Laches–One party to joint venture failing to make payments during property slump

The appellants (C) appealed against a decision ([2004] EWHC 1683) that their claims for beneficial interests in properties had been barred by laches. C had claimed a beneficial interest in a number of properties which were purchased in the names of one or more of the respondents (D). The purchase of the properties was by way of a joint venture and had required the investors in that venture to contribute to any shortfalls that arose in respect of mortgage payments and moneys received. During the property slump in the early 1990s D had continued to make payments towards the properties; however, the investors, including C's predecessor in title, had failed to make any payments towards shortfalls. The judge had found that in all the circumstances, it had been unconscionable for C to assert a beneficial interest in the properties, since throughout the property slump D had taken on the whole burden of keeping the properties afloat and C had only made their presence known once there was a profit to be shared. C argued that the judge had incorrectly applied the principles of laches in that he should not have applied them to a claim to beneficial interests held by a trustee.

Held, dismissing the appeal, that the judge had applied the test that the doctrine of laches was of great importance where persons had agreed to become partners, and one of them had unfairly left the other to do all the work, and then, there being a profit, had come forward and claimed a share of it; in such cases, the claimant's conduct opened him up to the remark that nothing would have been heard of him had the joint venture ended in loss instead of gain; and a court would not aid those who could be shown to have remained quiet in the hope of being able to evade responsibility in case of loss, but of being able to claim a share of gain in case of ultimate success. That principle had been established within the setting of a partnership, and was equally applicable in the instant case of a joint venture. However, there was a more overarching principle which embraced laches and delay and which could be invoked in equitable defences of property rights claims, namely whether, in all the circumstances, it was unconscionable for the claimants to assert a beneficial interest in the properties, *Frawley v. Neill* [2000] C.P. Rep. 20, [1999] C.L.Y. 4369 applied. Accordingly, what had to be determined was whether the conduct of C, as found by the judge, was so unconscionable that it released D from the equitable obligations under the trust. On the basis that this was a collaborative commercial agreement in which all involved were to have worked together to fulfil an aim of trading in property, the venture ceased to be joint when there were no further contributions made and D was left to do everything to keep the venture afloat. The creation of the resulting trust was not the aim of the venture, but was merely a bi product. The judge had been correct to find that C's acts, or lack of them, had been so unconscionable that they released D from the equitable obligations under the trusts.

PATEL v. SHAH, [2005] EWCA Civ 157, [2005] W.T.L.R. 359, Mummery, L.J., CA (Civ Div).

3382. Boundaries–Consent orders–Boundary dispute–Consent order settling dispute not void for uncertainty

The appellant (D) appealed against the decision ([2003] EWHC 1601, [2003] N.P.C. 90) that a consent order compromising a boundary dispute between the parties was void for uncertainty. D had commenced proceedings against her neighbours (S) in order to determine the precise line of the boundary between them. The parties' properties were contiguous over a distance of about 200 metres. In the area of the boundary between the two properties was a track running roughly north/south. A hedgerow ran for most of that distance on a bank to the immediate west of the track, but the hedge did not continue to the northern or southern ends of the properties. The consent order settling those proceedings declared that the boundary was the line shown on a plan annexed to the order running along the western bank of the hedgerow where there was a hedge. The parties' surveyors attempting to settle the boundary on the ground encountered difficulties at the northern and southern ends of the boundary in part because there had not in the past been any physical division between the properties. S then began proceedings to set aside the consent order as void for uncertainty or mistake. The county court judge held that the surveyors' task of locating the agreed boundary provided for by the consent order was practically impossible because the line of the plan and words of the order conflicted and because there was insufficient data to locate with certainty the points at the southern end of the boundary. On appeal the judge upheld the decision that the consent order was void for uncertainty because it was without practical meaning and needed further agreement in order to be implemented.

Held, allowing the appeal, that the judges below had erred in concluding that it was impossible to implement the parties' agreement. The surveyors in fact did so implement it and even if the parties were entitled to dispute the surveyors' solution it was a non sequitur to argue from a disagreement about the meaning and effect of a contract to its legal uncertainty. It was not practically or legally impossible to give the parties' agreement any sensible content even if it was difficult or even very difficult to find the line of the boundary on the ground. The declared boundary was, where the hedge existed, the western bank of the hedgerow, and the plan was to be interpreted accordingly. North and south of the hedge the boundary line was to proceed in a straight line. However that left a telegraph pole on the wrong side of the line. A solution was to step the boundary line back to the centre of the hedge at its northern end. The consent order was not void for uncertainty. The most that could be said was that its implementation threw up a relatively small practical problem of detail which in turn involved a problem of interpretation. It would be a complete injustice to conclude, because of the difficulty about the precise position of the boundary line in relation to the telegraph pole, that the parties had completely failed on grounds of uncertainty to settle their litigation at all when that was what they plainly intended to do and did in fact do with the aid of a detailed consent order and plan. The agreement in the consent order was not an agreement to agree and did not contain terms requiring further agreement.

DICKER v. SCAMMELL; *sub nom.* SCAMMELL v. DICKER, [2005] EWCA Civ 405, [2005] 3 All E.R. 838, Ward, L.J., CA (Civ Div).

3383. Boundaries–Plans–Evidence of contractual agreement–Limits of general boundaries rule

The claimants (C) sought judgment against the defendant development company (G) in relation to a boundary dispute. C had sold to G development land with permission for five houses. C subsequently exercised an option to purchase a plot on completion of the building of that plot. G sold to its owners (H) a plot neighbouring C's plot. A boundary dispute arose as to the ownership of the steep bank of land which separated C's property from that of their neighbour H. C contended that the transfer interpreted in the light of the admissible evidence and the general boundaries rule contained in *Lee v. Barrey* [1957] Ch. 251, [1957] C.L.Y. 1900 would have led a reasonable layman to suppose that the bank had been transferred to C and that there was no boundary agreement to displace that argument. H contended that C was estopped from asserting rights to the land in dispute.

Held, giving judgment for G, that as the transfer was unclear extrinsic evidence was admissible, *Partridge v. Lawrence* [2003] EWCA Civ 1121, [2004] 1 P. & C.R. 14, [2004] 3 C.L. 415 and *Jackson v. Bishop* (1984) 48 P. & C.R. 57, [1984] C.L.Y. 3625 followed. The boundary rules contained in *Barrey* were relevant to the correction of the filed plan and did enable the registrar to alter the transfer plan, which represented the contractual bargain between the parties, *Barrey* distinguished. The replacement of the contract plan by a different plan on the transfer deed indicated that the position between the parties had changed since the contract plan and the transfer had been signed. Two meetings had taken place at which the position of the fence had been agreed and those meetings amounted to a boundary agreement. Further, a supplemental agreement establishing the relocation of the boundary fence had been concluded prior to the completion of the transfer. It was possible to establish estoppel as H had acted to his detriment in the expectation that C would release a right over H's land.

CHADWICK v. ABBOTSWOOD PROPERTIES LTD, [2004] EWHC 1058, [2005] 1 P. & C.R. 10, Lewison, J., Ch D.

3384. Cautions—Equitable remedies—Arbitration by Beth Din under Jewish law—Power to confer proprietary interest in property

[Arbitration Act 1996 s.66(1).]

The appellant (K) appealed against an order made in proceedings brought by him to recover losses he had incurred as a result of an investment induced by fraud. The parties had agreed to arbitration under Jewish law, before the Beth Din, who had permitted K to register a caution at the Land Registry against a property owned by the respondent (J) and had directed that J could not sell the property, to which J agreed. In breach of that order, J sold the property to a third party (S), who had constructive notice of the caution although their solicitor had overlooked it. S were unable to register the property because of the caution. An interim charging order under the Arbitration Act 1996 s.66(1) allowed K to enforce the award in his favour against J's interest in the property, but this was found to have no effect and S were entitled to registration. It was found that the agreement to arbitration under Jewish law allowed the Beth Din to direct the registration of a caution, but that direction did not give K a proprietory interest in the property nor imply that the award should be satisfied out of that or any other frozen asset. The application of Jewish law was limited to determining the dispute, and even were K entitled to a lien on the property under Jewish law, which he was not in these circumstances, S had not agreed to their rights being determined by the Beth Din. On appeal, K argued that J's promise to observe the Beth Din's orders created a proprietary estoppel or constructive trust which was binding on S, since S had had constructive notice of the caution.

Held, dismissing the appeal, that the order of the Beth Din did not give K any proprietary interest in the property and there were no grounds on which to interfere with the judge's decision in this respect. English law could not transform the limited freezing order, even though J had agreed to comply with it, into an equitable remedy for K against a third party. The order operated only in personam against J. Although S had had constructive notice of the order, they had made no promise on which K had relied, *Gillett v. Holt* [2001] Ch. 210 and *PW & Co v. Milton Gate Investments Ltd* [2003] EWHC 1994, [2004] Ch. 142, [2004] C.L.Y. 2539 distinguished. The result would not have been different under English law.

KASTNER v. JASON; SHERMAN v. KASTNER, [2004] EWCA Civ 1599, [2005] 1 Lloyd's Rep. 397, Lord Woolf of Barnes, L.C.J, CA (Civ Div).

3385. Collective enfranchisement—Charitable trusts—Long leases—Meaning of "housing accommodation" in s.5(2)(b) Leasehold Reform, Housing and Urban Development Act 1993

[Housing Act 1985 s.6; Leasehold Reform, Housing and Urban Development Act 1993 s.5, s.94, s.95, s.96.]

The appellant charitable housing trust (R) appealed against declarations that the respondent tenants (B) were entitled to exercise the right to collective enfranchisement under the Leasehold Reform, Housing and Urban Development Act 1993. R owned two blocks of flats in which at least half of the flats were held on long leases, with the remainder being the subject of assured tenancies. B had all acquired long leases. It was common ground that the assured tenancies amounted to housing accommodation provided by R in pursuit of its charitable purposes. R submitted that the judge below had erred in holding that B were qualifying tenants within the meaning of s.5 of the Act and should have held that B were excluded from the right to collective enfranchisement because each flat formed part of the housing accommodation provided by R in the pursuit of its charitable purposes within the meaning of s.5(2)(b).

Held, dismissing the appeal, that the fact that R was a charitable housing trust, and that some flats in the blocks were let by it in the pursuit of its charitable objects, did not disqualify the participating tenants from the right to collective enfranchisement. Having regard to the wording of the Housing Act 1985 s.6, expressly referred to in s.5(2) of the 1993 Act, it was clear that "housing accommodation" provided by a housing trust was the social housing it provided. In the instant case, "housing accommodation" included the flats let on assured tenancies, but not those on long leases, which could not be regarded as provided in the pursuit of charitable objects. To conclude otherwise would mean that when a charitable trust acquired the freehold of a block of flats where the majority were let on long leases and the minority on assured tenancies, the tenants with long leases would lose both their right to collective enfranchisement and their individual right to acquire a new lease under Part I of the 1993 Act, and at the expiration of their long leases would have no capital asset and would become assured tenants. If Parliament had intended to exclude such cases from the right to collective enfranchisement, s.5(2)(b) would have contained provisions relating to charitable housing trusts such as those in s.94, s.95 and s.96, and would have expressly excluded "relevant premises that include accommodation provided by a charitable trust in the pursuit of its charitable purposes".

BRICK FARM MANAGEMENT LTD v. RICHMOND HOUSING PARTNERSHIP LTD; *sub nom.* RICHMOND HOUSING PARTNERSHIP LTD v. BRICK FARM MANAGEMENT LTD, [2005] EWHC 1650, [2005] 1 W.L.R. 3934, Stanley Burnton, J., QBD.

3386. **Collective enfranchisement–Counter notices–Requirement for "realistic" proposed purchase price**

[Leasehold Reform, Housing and Urban Development Act 1993 Part I Chapter 1, s.13, s.21, s.25.]

The appellant tenants (C) appealed against the dismissal of their claim challenging the validity of a counter notice served by the respondent local authority landlord (K). C were tenants of flats in the same building who had sought to exercise their right of collective enfranchisement under the Leasehold Reform, Housing and Urban Development Act 1993 Part I Chapter 1. C had served an initial notice under s.13 on K specifying a proposed purchase price of £210. K served a counter notice proposing a price of £130,000, based on a professional valuation. C challenged the counter notice on the basis that it proposed an unrealistically high price. C sought a declaration that the counter notice was invalid so as to enable them to proceed with the acquisition at their proposed price in default of a counter notice. The judge heard that K's valuer had overvalued the property. The judge held that the requirement from *Viscount Chelsea v. Morris* (1999) 31 H.L.R. 732, [1998] C.L.Y. 3657 of a "realistic" proposal also applied to a landlord's counter notice but that the word "realistic" imposed a subjective test, that it had to be genuine in the sense of more than a nominal figure and that it had to be bona fide. The judge found that K's proposal had been made in good faith and dismissed C's claim. C argued that (1) the *Viscount Chelsea* test applied to a landlord's counter notice; (2) it was not enough for the proposal to be genuine but it also had to be realistic. K submitted that the requirement of a realistic proposal did not apply to a landlord's counter notice or that, if it did, it was satisfied where, as in the instant case, the proposed price was made bona fide and on advice from a professional valuer. K further argued that its counter notice was valid as it raised an issue between the parties as to the price at which C should be entitled to exercise their right of enfranchisement, and that the appropriate price should be determined by a leasehold valuation tribunal.

Held, dismissing the appeal, that (1) the requirement of a "realistic" proposal did not apply to a landlord's counter notice under s.21 of the Act, *Viscount Chelsea* considered. The word "proposed" in the term "proposed purchase price" in s.13(3)(d) did not have the same meaning as the expression "any proposal" in s.21(3)(a)(i). There was an important difference between them due to the effect of s.25 as no default advantage accrued to a landlord if, for any reason, a s.13 or s.21 notice was rendered invalid or ineffective, *Willingale v. Globalgrange Ltd* (2001) 33 H.L.R. 17, [2000] C.L.Y. 3899 and *Sun Life Assurance Plc v. Thales Tracs Ltd (formerly Racal Tracs Ltd)* [2001] EWCA Civ 704, [2001] 1 W.L.R. 1562, [2001] C.L.Y. 4158 considered. (2) The second issue did not therefore arise though it was considered. The county court should be wary of developing what could turn into parallel litigation of attempting to resolve disagreements as to valuation at the notice and counter notice stage by developing a form of "strike out" or default procedure. The judge was correct to find that lack of good faith was the sole necessary precondition for a declaration of the invalidity of a landlord's counter notice under the provisions of the Act.

9 CORNWALL CRESCENT LONDON LTD v. KENSINGTON AND CHELSEA RLBC, [2005] EWCA Civ 324, [2005] 4 All E.R. 1207, Auld, L.J., CA (Civ Div).

3387. Collective enfranchisement–Leaseholds–Vesting orders–Investigations by leasehold valuation tribunal

[Leasehold Reform, Housing and Urban Development Act 1993 s.26, s.27.]

The claimant landlord (F) applied for judicial review of a decision of the leasehold valuation tribunal to vest the entire freehold of a property that he owned to a company owned by his tenants. In 1981 F had purchased a freehold property and divided it into flats. F subsequently sold all the flats as leasehold properties with 99 year leases. In addition to retaining the freehold to the whole property F retained a garage that he had converted into a dwelling house for his own purposes. The garage and the land on which it stood did not appear on any of the leases that he had granted to the tenants of the flats. Over the ensuing years the tenants experienced some difficulty in contacting F. In 2000 the tenants formed a company for the purpose of purchasing the freehold of the property pursuant to the Leasehold Reform, Housing and Urban Development Act 1993. As the tenants had been unable to contact F they applied under s.26 of the Act to the county court for an order vesting the freehold of the property to the special purposes company. The county court made the order sought subject to a payment into court for the value of the freehold. The valuation of the freehold was a matter for the respondent tribunal. The tribunal considered the evidence put forward by the tenants, including a written valuation of the flat that had a lease of the garden. That valuation included the garage as a part of the lease for that flat and valued the garage as a garage rather than a dwelling house. The tenant of that flat gave oral evidence to the effect that the garage had been used as a dwelling house by another party. The tribunal decided that the garage was included in the lease for the relevant flat and subject to collective enfranchisement. When a final notice was attached to the garage door, a relative of F's contacted him and the current proceedings were commenced. F contended that the garage should have been excluded from the enfranchisement process as he had never granted a lease for it and that he had upon occasion occupied it as a dwelling house.

Held, granting the application, that the tribunal had a discretion under s.27 of the 1993 Act to go behind a vesting order so that it was able to say that the whole of a freehold title should not be vested in the person or company appointed under the order. There were obvious limitations as to what could be expected from the tribunal; it was not there to provide representation for a missing landlord. There was no duty on the tribunal to seek out evidence that was not before it or evidence that ought to have been before it. However, if the evidence before the tribunal disclosed a significant doubt then it ought to make further inquiries to ascertain the true position and to ensure that an injustice was not done to a party. In the instant case there was an obvious and apparent conflict between the relevant lease and the freehold for the property. The tribunal ought to have contacted the Land Registry to investigate the matter further and its failure to do so was an error of law. Accordingly the decision was quashed and the matter remitted for reconsideration.

R. (ON THE APPLICATION OF FORD (T/A DAVID SAYERS)) v. LEASEHOLD VALUATION TRIBUNAL, [2005] EWHC 503, [2005] H.L.R. 36, Collins, J., QBD (Admin).

3388. Collective enfranchisement–Residential property–Calculation of area of non residential part of premises–Common areas disregarded

[Leasehold Reform, Housing and Urban Development Act 1993 s.4, s.4(1)(a), s.4(3), s.101 (1).]

The claimant (I) claimed collective enfranchisement as nominee purchaser under the Leasehold Reform, Housing and Urban Development Act 1993 on behalf of residential tenants of flats converted from two adjoining buildings. A dispute arose as to whether the non residential part of the premises exceeded 25 per cent in which case no enfranchisement was possible. The defendant landlord (T) contended that, on the proper construction of s.4 of the 1993 Act, premises were not capable of enfranchisement where the combined area of the non residential parts and the common parts exceeded 25 per cent of the internal floor area of the building as defined by s.4(3). T also disputed the categorisation of certain areas. I maintained that the 1993 Act required the surveyors to compare non residential with residential, disregarding the common parts throughout the calculation.

Held, giving judgment for the claimant, that (1) The object of s.4(1)(a) of the 1993 Act was not to aggregate anything but to identify the "business" area, i.e. that part of a building which was neither residential nor common. The "business" area was then compared with the total internal floor area. However, under s.4(3) the internal floor area for the purposes of the calculation was defined as excluding common parts. The Act required an examination of the ratio that business bore to residential even though it was not expressed in those terms. For that purpose, common parts were treated as irrelevant and left out of both sides of the calculation. Section 101 (1) of the 1993 Act defined common parts in relation to a building or part thereof as including "structure and exterior of that building or part and any common facilities within it". That included party walls. (2) The onus was on T to prove that a building was not within the 1993 Act and to prove the exception in s.4. In the present case, I succeeded on all the disputed areas apart from the conservatory which was not to be regarded as part of the building and the meter cupboard which was part of the common parts. In all the circumstances, I succeeded by less than one per cent in establishing its claim to enfranchise since the non residential area amounted to 24.11126 per cent of the aggregate.

INDIANA INVESTMENTS LTD v. TAYLOR [2004] 3 E.G.L.R. 63, Judge Roger Cooke, CC (Central London).

3389. Commonhold and Leasehold Reform Act 2002 (c.15)–Commencement No.5 and Saving and Transitional Provision Amendment Order–England

COMMONHOLD AND LEASEHOLD REFORM ACT 2002 (COMMENCEMENT NO.5 AND SAVING AND TRANSITIONAL PROVISION) (AMENDMENT) (ENGLAND) ORDER 2005, SI 2005 193 (C.7); made under the Commonhold and Leasehold Reform Act 2002 s.181. In force: February 3, 2005; £3.00.

This Order amends the Commonhold and Leasehold Reform Act 2002 (Commencement No.5 and Saving and Transitional Provision) Order 2004 (SI 2004 3056) which brings into force on February 28, 2005, in relation to England, provisions of the Commonhold and Leasehold Reform Act 2002 relating to the collective enfranchisement by tenants of flats. Among those provisions is s.126 which changes the date at which the price payable on enfranchisement is calculated under the Leasehold Reform, Housing and Urban Development Act 1993. Currently that date is the date on which it is agreed or decided what interests are to be acquired on behalf of the qualifying tenants. When s.126 comes into force, the calculation date will be the date on which the notice under s.13 of the 1993 Act claiming to exercise the right of enfranchisement is given by the tenant. The new saving provision inserted by this Order means that the changes made by s.126 of the 2002 Act will not have effect where notice is given under s.13 of the 1993 Act, or application for a vesting order is made under s.26 of the 1993 Act, before February 28, 2005.

3390. **Compensation–Noise–Alterations to airport–Meaning of "a greater number of aircraft" in Land Compensation Act 1973 s.9(6)(b)**

[Land Compensation Act 1973 s.9(6)(b).]

The appellant property owners (B) appealed against a decision of the Lands Tribunal on a preliminary issue in their claims for compensation in respect of noise from aircraft using the airport of the respondent (S). P owned houses near the northern end of the runway and immediately beneath one of the principal flight paths. B claimed that the value of their houses had been diminished by increased noise from aircraft movements arising from alterations made at the airport between 1993 and 1995. S claimed, and the Lands Tribunal ruled, that the alterations to the taxiways and aprons were not within the Land Compensation Act 1973 s.9(6)(b) since they did not have the effect of increasing the aggregate number of aircraft movements at the airport, although they did facilitate an increase in the movements of larger aircraft at the expense of movements of smaller aircraft. B argued that (1) s.9(6)(b) was satisfied in a case where the aircraft throughput of the aerodrome was not projected to increase as a result of the apron additions but where there was a projected increase in aircraft types; (2) alternatively, s.9(6)(b) was satisfied because the sole or primary intention of S's parent company in carrying out the works was to increase the number of commercial passenger aircraft using the airport, and the fact that there would be an incidental and more than compensating reduction in the number of other categories of aircraft using the airport was irrelevant.

Held, dismissing the appeal (Ward, L.J. dissenting) that (1) the words "a greater number of aircraft" in s.9(6)(b) could mean an increase in types of aircraft but their natural meaning in context was that the "greater number" of aircraft was to be assessed by reference to the total number of aircraft which, over a given period, could be accommodated by the aerodrome in question, in other words its potential throughput. A scheme which gave a right to compensation for an increase in aircraft types would not eliminate anomalies and would be uncertain in effect. (2) It was more consistent with justice, practicality and the scheme of s.9(6) generally to give the word "purpose" in s.9(6)(b) a relatively objective meaning so as to make the objectively likely result of the works significant. P's wholly subjective interpretation was rejected. The intention of the airport operator might be relevant but was not determinative, *R. (on the application of Plymouth City Airport Ltd) v. Secretary of State for the Environment, Transport and the Regions* [2001] EWCA Civ 144, (2001) 82 P. & C.R. 20, [2001] C.L.Y. 4681 considered.

BRUNT v. SOUTHAMPTON INTERNATIONAL AIRPORT LTD, [2005] EWCA Civ 93, [2005] Env. L.R. 28, Ward, L.J., CA (Civ Div).

3391. **Coownership–Beneficial interests–Significance of declaration in transfer deed not understood by parties–Inference in respect of intentions as to beneficial ownership**

The appellant (D) appealed against a decision to grant an order that a property (property C) was held upon trust between herself and the respondent (S) as tenants in common in equal shares. D and S had purchased property C in their joint names. The deposit for the property had been paid from a savings account, which had been in D's name. Upon completion, the balance had been funded from the sale of a property (property P), which had been in D's sole name. The balance had been funded through a mortgage advance, which had been in both D and S's names. At the time of the purchase of property C, D and S had been living together as man and wife and had four children. The transfer deed for property C had included a clause that the survivor of them was entitled to give a valid receipt for capital money arising from a disposition of the property. However, it was unclear whether the parties had discussed how they wished to own the property. D and S eventually separated and S was granted a declaration that property C was held upon trust by him and D as tenants in common in equal shares. He was also granted a payment of £900 per month as recompense for his cost of renting alternative accommodation. S submitted that the court should uphold the order directing payment out of the proceeds of sale to the parties in equal shares on the grounds that the property had been transferred subject to an express trust declared in the transfer deed, that the beneficial interests of the parties under that express trust were as joint tenants and that the beneficial joint tenancy under that express trust had been converted into a beneficial tenancy in common in equal shares by severance.

Held, allowing the appeal, that (1) it was impossible to reach a conclusion that was fair, having regard to the whole course of dealing between the parties in relation to property C, that their beneficial shares should be equal. If the whole of the purchase price for property C, other than the mortgage advance, was provided by D from her own funds, that conclusion would have failed to give proper weight to her financial contribution to the acquisition of the property. The judge had not reached his conclusion on the basis that the whole of the purchase price for property C other than the mortgage advance was provided by D from her own funds. He had treated S as having some beneficial interest in the proceeds of sale from property P and he had treated the savings as joint savings. The judge's approach had failed to address the question "whether there was evidence from which to confer a common intention, communicated by each to the other, that each shall have a beneficial share in the property", *Oxley v. Hiscock* [2004] EWCA Civ 546, [2005] Fam. 211, [2004] C.L.Y. 3196 applied. It was extremely doubtful whether anything less than a direct contribution to the purchase price by a person who did not become the legal owner would justify an inference that it was the common intention that he was to have a beneficial interest. The judge's reasoning had provided no basis for a conclusion that S would have been entitled to any share in the proceeds of the sale from property P. The judge had been wrong to treat S as having any beneficial interest in the proceeds of sale from property P and was therefore wrong to treat the application of those proceeds towards the purchase of property C as representing a contribution by S to that purchase. (2) If it had been established that the parties understood the significance of the declaration in the transfer deed, the inference that they intended to hold the property as beneficial joint tenants would have been irresistible. However, there had been no finding of fact that both parties had understood the significance of the declaration. Therefore, an inference could not be drawn in respect of the parties' intention as to beneficial ownership. If the parties did not understand why the declaration was in the transfer deed, it was impossible to rely upon it for the purpose of drawing an inference as to their intentions; it was only indicative of a common intention that they should be bound by it in respect of the matter for which it actually provided. The judge had erred in holding that the parties were entitled beneficially to equal shares in property C. (3) There was no basis upon which to make an order that D should pay an occupation rent or that it could be assessed at £900 per month. In awarding a payment of £900 per month to S until the sale of property C had been completed, the judge had overlooked the need of the parties' four children to be provided with a home.

STACK v. DOWDEN; *sub nom.* DOWDEN v. STACK, [2005] EWCA Civ 857, [2006] 1 F.L.R. 254, Chadwick, L.J., CA (Civ Div).

3392. **Countryside and Rights of Way Act 2000 (c.37)–Commencement No.6 Order–Wales**

COUNTRYSIDE AND RIGHTS OF WAY ACT 2000 (COMMENCEMENT NO.6) (WALES) ORDER 2005, SI 2005 423 (W.41; C.19); made under the Countryside and Rights of Way Act 2000 s.103. Commencement details: bringing into force various provisions of the 2000 Act on May 28, 2005; £3.00.

This Order brings into force certain provisions of the Countryside and Rights of Way Act 2000 in relation to Wales which introduce a new public right of access to "access land"; relate to the effect of the right of access on the rights and liabilities of owners and occupiers; create an offence of displaying on access land notices deterring public use; and contain general restrictions to be observed by persons exercising their right of access on access land.

3393. **Countryside and Rights of Way Act 2000 (c.37)–Commencement No.7 Order–England**

COUNTRYSIDE AND RIGHTS OF WAY ACT 2000 (COMMENCEMENT NO.7) ORDER 2005, SI 2005 827 (C.34); made under the Countryside and Rights of Way Act 2000 s.103. Commencement details: bringing into force various provisions of the 2000 Act on May 28, 2005; £3.00.

This Order brings into force, in relation to England only, the Countryside and Rights of Way Act 2000 s.2 relating to access land which is shown as open country or registered common land on a map in conclusive form and which lies within an area covered by one of the maps in conclusive form issued by the Countryside Agency; and relating to access land which is dedicated as access land under s.16 of the Countryside and Rights of Way Act 2000, which is not shown as open country or registered common land on a map in conclusive form, but which lies within an area covered by one of the maps in conclusive form.

3394. **Countryside and Rights of Way Act 2000 (c.37)–Commencement No.7 Order–Wales**

COUNTRYSIDE AND RIGHTS OF WAY ACT 2000 (COMMENCEMENT NO.7) (WALES) ORDER 2005, SI 2005 1314 (W.96; C.58); made under the Countryside and Rights of Way Act 2000 s.103. Commencement details: bringing into force various provisions of the 2000 Act on May 31, 2005, July 15, 2005 and November 21, 2005; £3.00.

This Order brings into force certain provisions of the Countryside and Rights of Way Act 2000 Part II in relation to Wales which enable local highway authorities to consolidate their definitive maps where they are fragmented as a result of previous local government reorganisations; enable local highway authorities to close or divert footpaths, bridleways and, in due course, restricted byways, for the purpose of protecting school children and staff by assisting authorities to provide improved security at schools where public paths cross land occupied for the purposes of a school; and require local highway authorities to compile and maintain three new registers relating to public path and modification orders.

3395. **Countryside and Rights of Way Act 2000 (c.37)–Commencement No.8 Order–England**

COUNTRYSIDE AND RIGHTS OF WAY ACT 2000 (COMMENCEMENT NO.8) ORDER 2005, SI 2005 1901 (C.81); made under the Countryside and Rights of Way Act 2000 s.103. Commencement details: bringing into force various provisions of the 2000 Act on August 28, 2005; £3.00.

This Order brings into force the Countryside and Rights of Way Act 2000 s.2 for certain purposes.

3396. **Countryside and Rights of Way Act 2000 (c.37)–Commencement No.9 Order–England**

COUNTRYSIDE AND RIGHTS OF WAY ACT 2000 (COMMENCEMENT NO.9) ORDER 2005, SI 2005 2459 (C.104); made under the Countryside and Rights of Way Act 2000 s.103. Commencement details: bringing into force various provisions of the 2000 Act on September 27, 2005; £3.00.

This Order brings into force provisions of the Countryside and Rights of Way Act 2000.

3397. **Countryside and Rights of Way Act 2000 (c.37)–Commencement No.10 Order–England**

COUNTRYSIDE AND RIGHTS OF WAY ACT 2000 (COMMENCEMENT NO.10) ORDER 2005, SI 2005 2752 (C.112); made under the Countryside and Rights of

Way Act 2000 s.103. Commencement details: bringing into force various provisions of the 2000 Act on October 31, 2005; £3.00.

This Order brings into force certain provisions of the Countryside and Rights of Way Act 2000 which include a new right of access to access land.

3398. **Dispositions of property—Coownership—Property registered to father and daughter jointly—Payment of mortgage by father—Disposition of property on father's death**

The claimant mother (C) brought proceedings asserting that her late husband (K) had been the beneficial owner of a property which had passed to her under the intestacy provisions. K and his family were Greek Cypriots. K had bought a council property in the names of himself and his only daughter (P). P married, and she and her husband provided financial assistance to K when he had difficulties paying the mortgage. When K died, P transferred the property into her sole name although C continued to live there with one of the three sons. P remortgaged the property and gave C notice to quit. C argued that, despite the registration of the property in P's name, she was the sole beneficial owner following K's death and that K had exercised his right to buy with P's assistance as surety or nominee, but it had never been intended that P would have a beneficial interest in it. P argued that the property was intended as a gift or dowry to her and had been purchased for that purpose.

Held, giving judgment for C, that she was entitled to be registered as sole owner of the flat. On the evidence, it had been agreed at a family meeting prior to the purchase that P would enter into the mortgage to enable K to obtain a 100 per cent mortgage and avoid having to pay a deposit and was therefore acting merely as nominee and quasi surety for K. It was either stated or assumed that the surviving parent would divide the house equally between the children. At the time of the purchase, both P and K contemplated that K would pay the mortgage from his own money. K did not intend to give P the flat as a dowry and his representations concerning a dowry had simply been made for the sake of appearances. His purpose was to buy the property as a family home. K was therefore the purchaser and the cash assistance from P and her husband were no more than contributions to K's general finances.

KYRIAKIDES v. PIPPAS, [2004] EWHC 646, [2004] 2 F.C.R. 434, Gabriel Moss Q.C., Ch D.

3399. **Dispositions of property—Leases—Power of Lord Chancellor to effect grant of new leases of magistrates' courts by responsible authorities**

[Courts Act 2003 Sch.2.]

The claimant Lord Chancellor sought a declaration as to his powers under the Courts Act 2003 Sch.2. Immediately before the Act, responsibility for the administration of magistrates' courts was in the hands of local magistrates' courts committees, and the premises of magistrates' courts outside Greater London were provided by local authorities as "responsible authorities". While some magistrates' courts premises were entire buildings, others were parts of buildings, the remainder of which was occupied by the local authority. In the purported exercise of his powers under the Act, the Lord Chancellor made the Transfer of Property (Abolition of Magistrates' Courts Committees) Scheme 2005 for the transfer of property rights in the magistrates' courts estate. The defendant Chief Land Registrar expressed doubt as to whether the Act conferred power on the Lord Chancellor on behalf of the local authority to create new leases of magistrates' courts, and declined to register leases created under the 2003 Act in the absence of a court declaration. A local authority affected by the proposals owned the freehold of a building that was occupied only in part for the purposes of a magistrates' court, and resisted the Lord Chancellor's claim that he had the power to compel the transfer of the entirety of the freehold in the building. The issues for determination were (1) whether the Lord Chancellor had the power under Sch.2 to effect a grant by a local authority of a lease of that part of a building which comprised a magistrates' court in circumstances where the magistrates' court was only part of the building; (2) whether the Lord Chancellor could compel a local authority to transfer the entirety of its freehold or leasehold interest in a building, only part of which was a magistrates' court.

Held, granting a declaration in favour of the Chief Land Registrar, that (1) although Parliament had conferred on the Lord Chancellor the power to transfer property, that was not a power to create leases or to grant them. There was an obvious difference between the transfer of property and the creation or grant of a new property interest. Had Parliament intended that there should be a power to grant leases, then different words were required and would have been used in Sch.2. A transfer of property transferred the bundle of rights and obligations relating to a building whereas the creation of a lease did not transfer any rights or obligations. It merely subjected the lessor's rights to those of the lessee. The Act did not make any provision for the determination of the provisions of a new lease. Although the Lord Chancellor had claimed to be entitled to determine the terms of a new lease unilaterally, nothing in the Act authorised him to do so. Had Parliament intended to grant him this far reaching power, then it would have done so in express terms. Accordingly, the Lord Chancellor had no power under Sch.2 to effect the grant of new leases of magistrates' courts by responsible authorities. (2) The obvious intention of the words "in connection with or otherwise attributable to a magistrates' court" in Sch.2 para.1 (1) (b) was to include premises such as the offices used in connection with the magistrates' court itself, and rights that were ancillary to the magistrates' court accommodation itself. Those words could not drastically enlarge the scope of the power to take property, so as to include the legal estate in accommodation that was not used in connection with and was not in any meaningful sense attributable to the magistrates' court. Accordingly, Sch.2 did not confer on the Lord Chancellor power to effect a transfer by a responsible authority, or a local authority, of an entire building where part only was occupied as a magistrates' court.

R. (ON THE APPLICATION OF THE LORD CHANCELLOR) v. CHIEF LAND REGISTRAR, [2005] EWHC 1706, [2005] 4 All E.R. 643, Stanley Burnton, J., QBD (Admin).

3400. Dispositions of property–Setting aside–Undue influence

The claimant (W) sought to set aside a transfer of half of his property to the defendant (H). W, a property and land owner, had allowed H to store some of his equipment at his property while H had helped W to maintain his house and land. W had decided to leave his property to H and had executed a will accordingly. W then transferred half the property to H to provide H with some security. Their relationship deteriorated and W decided that he no longer wanted to leave the property to H and changed his will. W then sought to set aside the transfer on grounds of undue influence.

Held, giving judgment for W, that the relationship between H and W had been an unusual one that had been potentially susceptible to abuse. The transaction had been a substantial one, for which W had received nothing in return. The evidence was sufficient to raise a presumption of undue influence and there was not sufficient evidence to rebut that presumption. The transfer would be set aside.

WRIGHT v. HODGKINSON, [2004] EWHC 3091, [2005] W.T.L.R. 435, Judge Hegarty Q.C., Ch D.

3401. Dispositions of property–Undue influence–Gift of property by elderly person to family member–Legal advice insufficient to rebut presumption of undue influence

M appealed against a decision voiding a deed of gift of a house to her from her brother on the ground that the deed had been procured by undue influence. M's brother B, aged 70, had been mentally and physically disadvantaged for most of his life. He had lived with his mother in a house that his mother had gifted to him, but after suffering a serious fall, B spent six months in hospital then moved into a nursing home. M looked after his affairs and took care of their mother. While in hospital, after discussions between B, his solicitor, his mother, M and her daughter, B made a will and gave M power of attorney. After the solicitor explained that the value of his house would be taken into account in an assessment of his assets for the purpose of paying nursing home fees, B gifted the house to M. M subsequently sold the house to H and the deed of gift was set aside on the grounds that (i) B had placed trust in M; (ii) there was no satisfactory explanation for the gift, and (iii) the solicitor, who was friendly with M, had not given independent legal advice. On appeal, M argued that she had done nothing wrong, that she had done her best to ensure that B received legal advice and that the burden of proof should not be on her to show that the gift had not been made under undue influence.

Held, dismissing the appeal, that the law of undue influence was not concerned with dishonest or wrongful acts but, as a matter of public policy, with the presumed influence arising from a relationship of trust and confidence which should not disadvantage the victim if the transaction was not satisfactorily explained by ordinary motives, *Allcard v. Skinner* (1887) L.R. 36 Ch. D. 145 applied. It was the nature of the continuing relationship between the parties, rather than any specific act on the part of the recipient, that was relevant when considering undue influence. The participation of a solicitor would not rebut the presumption of undue influence in every case, *Inche Noriah v. Shaik Allie bin Omar* [1929] A.C. 127, [1970] C.L.Y. 1145 considered. B's solicitor's advice was not such as a competent adviser would give, if acting solely in B's interests. The judge had correctly applied the law relating to undue influence and had been entitled to reach his conclusion.

PESTICCIO v. HUET; *sub nom.* NIERSMANS v. PESTICCIO, [2004] EWCA Civ 372, [2004] W.T.L.R. 699, Pill, L.J., CA.

3402. Dispositions of property—Undue influence—Propriety of judge's approach

The appellants (X) appealed against a decision that they held the leasehold of a property on trust for the respondent (T). T had entered into a tenancy agreement with X, his daughter and son in law, to rent a house that X had purchased. T subsequently entered into a deed with X whereby it was agreed that T would pay X a sum of money to clear the mortgage on the house and certain other debts that X had. In return X were to transfer a long leasehold interest in the house to T. T fulfilled his requirements under the deed and subsequently brought proceedings to enforce the deed. X contended that the deed should be set aside on the grounds of presumed undue influence. The judge found that on the facts of the case, although the relationship between the parties had been one of trust and confidence, the transaction had been readily explicable by the relationship between them.

Held, dismissing the appeal, that it was an evidential matter for a court to decide whether presumed undue influence impeded a transaction. The first element to be shown was that the facts raised that presumption and the second element was whether the presumption was rebuttable. On the facts of the instant case, the judge was entitled to find that the transaction was readily explicable by the relationship of the parties and that a presumption of undue influence had not properly arisen, *Royal Bank of Scotland Plc v. Etridge (No.2)* [2001] UKHL 44, [2002] 2 A.C. 773, [2001] C.L.Y. 4880 and *Macklin v. Dowsett* [2004] EWCA Civ 904, [2004] 2 E.G.L.R. 75, [2005] 2 C.L. 265 applied.

TURKEY v. AWADH, [2005] EWCA Civ 382, [2005] 2 F.C.R. 7, Chadwick, L.J., CA (Civ Div).

3403. Easements—Land drainage—Site development leading to loss of easement—Increased burden on servient tenement—Radical change in character of dominant land

The appellant (M), a property developer, appealed against the dismissal of its claim for damages against the respondent (R) for interference with an easement. M had built two houses on a site in place of a bakery, which it had demolished. The bakery had been built by the owner of a cottage on adjoining land and the drain to the bakery ran under the cottage before connecting with the public sewer. At the time of M's acquisition of the site, the bakery had been left derelict for a number of years. R, who owned the cottage, prevented M from using the drain for the two houses it had built. M sought its costs in providing an alternative connection to the public sewer, claiming that R was in breach of its easement of drainage under the rule in *Wheeldon v. Burrows* (1879) L.R. 12 Ch. D. 31.

Held, dismissing the appeal, that although M was entitled to an easement, *Wheeldon* applied, the increased flow of water through the pipe as a result of the redevelopment of the site represented a substantial increase in the burden on the servient land, so that the dominant owner's right to enjoy the easement was lost, *Harvey v. Walters* (1872-73) L.R. 8 C.P. 162 and *Wimbledon and Putney Commons Conservators v. Dixon* (1875-76) L.R. 1 Ch. D. 362 considered. Further, the development of the land constituted a "radical change in character" or a "change in the identity" of the site, *Wimbledon* and *Milner's Safe Co Ltd v. Great Northern and City Railway Co* [1907] 1 Ch. 208 considered. This went beyond a mere change or intensification in the use of the site, *British Railways Board v. Glass* [1965] Ch. 538, [1964] C.L.Y. 1204 and *Cargill v. Gotts* [1981] 1 W.L.R. 441, [1981] C.L.Y. 742 applied. The judge below had applied the correct legal principles and was entitled to reach the conclusion that he had reached.

McADAMS HOMES LTD v. ROBINSON, [2004] EWCA Civ 214, [2005] 1 P. & C.R. 30, Peter Gibson, L.J., CA.

3404. Easements—Vehicular access—Acquisition by prescription or lost modern grant notwithstanding illegal use

[Law of Property Act 1925 (c.20) s.193(4); Vehicular Access Across Common and Other Land (England) Regulations 2002) (SI 2002 1711) Reg.10.]

The applicant (W) sought his costs in relation to proceedings for an easement under the Vehicular Access Across Common and Other Land (England) Regulations 2002 Reg.10. W had brought the proceedings in order to obtain vehicular access over T's land from the public highway to W's farm. Subsequently, the House of Lords gave a judgment in *Bakewell Management Ltd v. Brandwood* [2004] UKHL 14, [2004] 2 A.C. 519, [2004] 5 C.L. 480.

Held, ordering that each party bear its own costs, that the decision in *Bakewell* rendered the 2002 Regulations unnecessary. The Regulations had been necessary to counteract the decision of the Court of Appeal in *Hanning v. Top Deck Travel Group Ltd* (1994) 68 P. & C.R. 14, [1995] C.L.Y. 1858, which prevented the owners of land whose only vehicular access to their land was by crossing over common land or land other than a road from gaining an easement by prescription because the driving was a criminal offence under the Law of Property Act 1925 s.193(4). However, the position had been reversed by the decision in *Bakewell*. Since then, if an easement could be lawfully granted by a landowner it could also be obtained by prescription notwithstanding any criminal use, *Bakewell* followed and *Hanning* considered.

WILLCOX v. TUCKER [2004] R.V.R. 302, George Bartlett Q.C. (President), Lands Tr.

3405. Enfranchisement—Improvements—Valuation of unimproved property—Relevance of development potential

[Leasehold Reform Act 1967 s.9(1A)(d); Lands Tribunal Rules 1996 (SI 1996 1022) r.50(4).]

The appellant tenants (F) appealed against a decision determining the price that they had to pay to acquire from the respondent landlord (J) the freehold of the property in which they lived. The property was originally a four bedroom house with no bathroom or garage. After F carried out extensive works, the property had seven bedrooms and seven bathrooms, a swimming pool complex and two garages. F had served notice to acquire the freehold from J under the Leasehold Reform Act 1967. The Lands Tribunal had determined the price to be paid but, pursuant to the Lands Tribunal Rules 1996 r.50(4), it had further ascertained lower alternative amounts that it would have determined if it had come to a different decision on points of law put forward by F in relation to valuation under s.9 (1A) (d) of the 1967 Act. F submitted that (1) development potential including, in particular, the value of any planning permission was to be left out of account in valuing the property; (2) the value of the property should be assessed by taking its improved value and then deducting the value of tenant's improvements; (3) if the property was valued on the basis that the improvements had never been carried out then the planning permissions that enabled them to be carried out should also be disregarded.

Held, dismissing the appeal, that (1) the assumption in s.9 (1A) (d), that the price was to be diminished by the extent to which the value of the house and premises had been increased by any improvement carried out by the tenant, did not imply that the value of the potential for improvement had to be excluded from the valuation of the unimproved house. Assumption (d) required a calculation of the amount of the increase in value caused by the improvements. That involved a valuation of the property as it would have been on the valuation date if it had not been improved. Any potential for improvement would be included in the achieved sale prices of unimproved properties so that a valuation of an unimproved house and premises would include the value of any such potential. Therefore an increase in value caused by an actual improvement had to be calculated as an excess over the unimproved valuation including the value of the potential for improvement, notwithstanding that the potential was merged in or absorbed by the actual improvement. (2) Section 9 (1A) (d) did not restrict the valuer in his analysis to a "top down" basis of valuation, as F contended, thus preventing him from considering unimproved comparables. Assumption (d) simply required that the price be diminished by the extent stated. It did not impose any requirement that the house and premises should be valued either from the top down or from the bottom up. The method adopted was a matter of valuation, not of law. The method adopted of valuing the property as if it had never been improved at all was the standard method adopted by the Lands Tribunal. (3) Assuming that the issue of the planning permissions was a separate point from the first point, F's submission failed. An improvement was a physical concept, *Shalson v. John Lyon Free Grammar School Governors* [2003] UKHL 32, [2004] 1 A.C. 802, [2003] C.L.Y. 2746 applied. It was the increase in value caused by the physical works that had to be subtracted and the existence or availability of planning permission was not part of those works.

FATTAL v. JOHN LYON FREE GRAMMAR SCHOOL GOVERNORS; *sub nom.* FATTAL v. KEEPERS AND GOVERNORS OF THE POSSESSIONS REVENUES AND GOODS OF THE FREE GRAMMAR SCHOOL OF JOHN LYON, [2004] EWCA Civ 1530, [2005] 1 W.L.R. 803, Buxton, L.J., CA (Civ Div).

3406. Enfranchisement–Reversions–Central London residential property– Unimproved leasehold vacant possession value and percentage deferment rate

[Leasehold Reform Act 1967 s.9 (1C).]

The appellant underlesees (P) appealed and the respondent freeholder (C) cross appealed against a leasehold valuation tribunal decision which determined the price of the freehold of a Central London residential property at £462, 854 under the Leasehold Reform Act 1967 s.9 (1C) with the valuation determined at £489,505. The parties agreed on the unimproved freehold vacant possession value, the capitalised head rent and the equal apportionment of marriage value but there was continued disagreement as to the unimproved leasehold vacant possession value and the rate of reversion deferment.

Held, dismissing the appeal and the cross appeal, that (1) the unimproved leasehold vacant possession value of £1,105,000 was half way between the figures put forward by the parties' valuers and it could not be determined which, if any, had a higher degree of error. (2) The 5.25 per cent deferment rate put forward by C was accepted on the basis that it was not too low. Although the accepted rate for the area was 6 per cent, this did not take into account fluctuations in the Central London residential property market and had only remained in use because of a lack of reliable evidence. The fact that deferment rates of less than 6 per cent had been rejected by the tribunal in other recent cases did not assist P as the evidence before the tribunal supported its finding that it was too high in the instant case.

CADOGAN HOLDINGS LTD v. POCKNEY [2005] R.V.R. 197, NJ Rose, FRICS, Lands Tr.

3407. Equitable interests—Resulting trusts—Contributions to purchase price—Discount pursuant to right to buy

[Land Registration Act 1925 s.56; National Assistance Act 1948.]

K applied for judicial review of the local authority's refusal to apply to vacate a caution registered in respect of a property which she owned in part. The property had been held by K's father under a secure tenancy that had passed to K's mother, M. K lived with her mother, who exercised her right to buy the property. The property was valued at £120,000 but M received a discount of £50,000. The balance was funded by K by way of mortgage. K and M were the joint transferees of the property but there was no indication on the transfer form as to the manner in which the legal and beneficial interests were held. Just prior to the transfer M went into hospital and thereafter to a residential home. Under the National Assistance Act 1948 she paid only nominal fees on the basis of her means. However, after M's death the local authority became aware of her possible interest in the property and registered a caution against it with a view to recovering the cost of her residential care. K argued that the property had always been intended for the sole use of herself and her children and M had never intended to live there; K had paid the entire mortgage and M had made no contribution whatsoever, and accordingly there was no evidence to support the conclusion that M had had any beneficial interest in the property. K argued that the caution was invalid and that it was perverse for the local authority to refuse to apply to vacate it.

Held, refusing the application, that (1) the local authority's refusal to apply to vacate the caution was not perverse. Had K appealed against the refusal under the extant procedure in the Land Registration Act 1925 s.56, evidence could have been put in and tested under cross examination. However, the evidence available to the court on the instant application was insufficient to show that M had no beneficial interest in the property; (2) in the absence of such evidence or any express declaration, K and M held the property on resulting trust for themselves in the proportion to which they had contributed, which contribution could include any discount that had increased the value of the asset, *Springette v. Defoe* [1992] 2 F.L.R. 388, [1992] C.L.Y. 2031 considered, and (3) whilst M had made no contribution towards payment of the mortgage she had received a discount of £50,000 by virtue of the exercise of her right to buy. Accordingly, M had a five twelfths equitable interest in the property and H had lawfully refused to vacate the caution.

R. (ON THE APPLICATION OF KELLY) v. HAMMERSMITH AND FULHAM LBC; *sub nom.* KELLY v. HAMMERSMITH LBC, [2004] EWHC 435, (2004) 7 C.C.L. Rep. 542, Wilson, J., QBD (Admin Ct).

3408. Housing—Home loss payments

HOME LOSS PAYMENTS (PRESCRIBED AMOUNTS) (ENGLAND) REGULATIONS 2005, SI 2005 1635; made under the Land Compensation Act 1973 s.30. In force: September 1, 2005; £3.00.

These Regulations increase the amount of home loss payments payable under the Land Compensation Act 1973 and formerly prescribed in the Home Loss Payments (Prescribed Amounts) (England) Regulations 2004 (SI 2004 1631) which are revoked with savings. A person is entitled to a home loss payment when he is displaced from a dwelling by compulsory purchase or in the other circumstances specified in s.29 of the Act as last amended by the Planning and Compulsory Purchase Act 2004.

3409. Housing – Home loss payments – Wales

HOME LOSS PAYMENTS (PRESCRIBED AMOUNTS) (WALES) REGULATIONS 2005, SI 2005 1808 (W.139); made under the Land Compensation Act 1973 s.30. In force: September 1, 2005; £3.00.

These Regulations, which revoke with a saving the Home Loss Payments (Prescribed Amounts) (Wales) Regulations 2004 (SI 2004 1758 (W.189)), increase the maximum and minimum amounts of home loss payments payable under the Land Compensation Act 1973 to those with an owner's interest in a dwelling. They also increase the amount of home loss payment payable in any other case.

3410. Injunctions – Laches – Covenantee delayed in applying for interim injunction to halt building by neighbour in breach of restrictive covenant – Effect of delay on covenantee's application for final injunction

The appellant (B) appealed against a decision to grant a mandatory injunction to demolish an extension which he had built in breach of a restrictive covenant or to alter it so that it would not affect light to the adjoining house belonging to the respondent (M). After B had decided that he wanted to build an extension, he raised the matter with the covenantee, his neighbour M, who objected to the plan. B decided that M was withholding consent unreasonably and went ahead with building the extension. M's solicitors threatened action and two months later, when the work on the extension was close to completion, M applied for an interim injunction. That application was refused on the *American Cyanamid* principle that damages would be an adequate remedy and because M had delayed too long. Afterwards M sought the mandatory injunction, which was granted because it would not have been oppressive to B where he had chosen to proceed in the full knowledge of the covenant and of M's lack of consent. B contended that M's application for the mandatory injunction should have been refused on the ground of M's delay in applying for the interim injunction. It was submitted that a person who, knowing that he had clearly enforceable rights and the ability to enforce them, stood by whilst a permanent and substantial structure was erected, ought not be granted an injunction to have it pulled down.

Held, dismissing the appeal, that it was doubtful whether a covenantee who had not sought, or timeously sought, an interim injunction when he knew that a building was being erected in breach of covenant would generally be debarred from obtaining a final injunction to pull down the building. His application for the final injunction would be more likely to be granted if he had made clear his intention to object to the breach and to bring proceedings for it, although his failure to seek interlocutory relief could then be a factor taken into account. M had not suggested he would be willing to receive damages in lieu of an injunction, *Gafford v. Graham* (1999) 77 P. & C.R. 73, [1998] C.L.Y. 4341 distinguished. Although M had been slow to seek the mandatory injunction, he had warned B shortly after work had commenced that proceedings would be brought if the construction continued. M could not be said to have acted unconscionably. Accordingly, there was no justification for interfering with the exercise of the judge's discretion to grant the injunction.

MORTIMER v. BAILEY, [2004] EWCA Civ 1514, [2005] B.L.R. 85, Peter Gibson, L.J., CA (Civ Div).

3411. Land charges – Home rights

LAND CHARGES (AMENDMENT) RULES 2005, SI 2005 1981; made under the Land Charges Act 1972 s.16; and the Family Law Act 1996 s.32, Sch.4 para.4. In force: in accordance with r.1; £3.00.

These Rules amend the Land Charges Rules 1974 (SI 1974 1286) to take account of the Family Law Act 1996 and the Civil Partnership Act 2004. They replace outdated references to previous legislation with references to the Family Law Act 1996, and prescribe new forms for applications to register, renew and cancel land charges relating to home rights under that Act, as amended by the Civil Partnership Act 2004.

3412. Land registration–Forms of restriction

LAND REGISTRATION (AMENDMENT) RULES 2005, SI 2005 1766; made under the Land Registration Act 2002 s.14, s.27, s.43, s.66, s.67, s.68, s.69, s.70, s.73, s.75, s.76, s.88, s.126, s.127, s.128, s.134, Sch.10 para.5, Sch.10 para.6, Sch.10 para.8, Sch.12 para 2. In force: October 24, 2005; £3.00.

These rules amend the Land Registration Rules 2003 (SI 2003 1417). They add a new r.91A to the 2003 Rules; provide that a person named in a standard form of restriction set out in Sch.4 to 2003 Rules must provide an address for service where an address is required by that restriction and so must a person named in any other restriction that requires his consent, certificate or the giving of notice to him; provide that the Legal Services Commission shall be regarded as having a sufficient interest in the entry of a restriction in Form JJ in the circumstances specified; allow a qualifying applicant who applies for a search in the index of proprietors' names to apply at the same time, in the Form CIT attached to the Form PN1, for official copies of the registers identified in the results of that search; and widens the definition of "conveyancer" in r.217(1) of the 2003 rules to include a duly certificated notary public.

3413. Land registration–Prescribed clauses lease

LAND REGISTRATION (AMENDMENT) (NO.2) RULES 2005, SI 2005 1982; made under the Land Registration Act 2002 s.1, s.25, s.34, s.70, s.126, s.127, s.128, Sch.10 para.6, Sch.10 para.8; and the Family Law Act 1996 s.32, Sch.4 para.4. In force: in accordance with r.2; £4.00.

These Rules amend the Land Registration Rules 2003 (SI 2003 1417) which prescribe that part of the contents (and its form) which must be contained in all prescribed clauses leases, subject to a new exception. A prescribed clauses lease is a lease for a term of years absolute, granted on or after June 19, 2006 out of a registered estate in land, which is required to be completed by registration, subject to the exceptions contained in the definition. They provide for the entries which the registrar must make in respect of interests contained in a lease created on or after June 19, 2006 which is being completed by registration under the Land Registration Act 2002 s.27(2)(b); provide for circumstances where the registrar need not make an entry; take account of the Civil Partnership Act 2004; and provide, subject to an exception, for forms replaced by these rules to be used for a transitional period.

3414. Land registration–Proper office–Designation–Certificated notary public

LAND REGISTRATION (PROPER OFFICE) (AMENDMENT) ORDER 2005, SI 2005 1765; made under the Land Registration Act 2002 s.100. In force: October 24, 2005; £3.00.

The Land Registration (Proper Office) Order 2003 (SI 2003 2040) designates particular offices of the land registry as the proper office for the receipt of specified descriptions of application under the Land Registration Act 2002. The Order does not apply to, amongst other applications, an application to the registrar delivered in accordance with a written agreement as to delivery made between the registrar and the applicant's conveyancer. This Order amends the definition of "conveyancer" in art.2(2) of the 2003 Order to include a certificated notary public.

3415. Lands Tribunal–Jurisdiction–Dispute over nature of user covenants in lease

[Law of Property Act 1925 s.84.]

The appellant landlord (C) appealed against a decision that the Lands Tribunal had jurisdiction to determine an application by the respondent tenant (B) to modify certain covenants in a lease. The lease had contained covenants specifying that certain parts of a building had to be occupied by a particular organisation together with accommodation for a housekeeper employed by that organisation. The organisation ceased to occupy the property at the end of their sublease. By agreement with C, a deed of variation of those user covenants had been executed to allow for residential occupation of the part formerly occupied by the organisation. B applied to the tribunal for further modification of the user covenants to allow the housekeeper's accommodation to be used for residential occupation. C submitted that the user covenants were positive obligations, not restrictive covenants, and therefore that the tribunal did not have jurisdiction under the Law of Property Act 1925 s.84. B contended that to construe the covenants as containing a positive obligation led to an unreasonable result, namely that at the expiration of the organisation's tenancy, B would be in breach of covenant, which the parties could not have intended.

Held, dismissing the appeal, that each covenant had to be construed in the context of the particular lease. The user covenants had originally been included to ensure that a respectable tenant occupied the property. It was not right to construe the covenants as a positive obligation rendering the tenant liable to find himself in breach of covenant in circumstances which he had no power to prevent. If the parties had intended that result when the user covenants had been created, they would have made it clear. The covenant was restrictive and therefore the tribunal had jurisdiction to deal with B's application.

BLUMENTHAL v. CHURCH COMMISSIONERS FOR ENGLAND, [2004] EWCA Civ 1688, [2005] 2 P. & C.R. 20, Waller, L.J., CA (Civ Div).

3416. Lands Tribunal – Jurisdiction – Lack of consideration – Discharge of restrictive covenant – Conveyance making gift of land for use as village hall

[Law of Property Act 1925 s.84.]

The applicant (R) applied under the Law of Property Act 1925 s.84 to discharge a restrictive covenant on land conveyed by a 1924 indenture, which made a gift of the land for use as a village hall. It fell to be decided as a preliminary issue whether the Lands Tribunal had jurisdiction to determine the application where the land had not been conveyed for any consideration when s.84(7) stated that the section did not apply in the absence of consideration. R contended that a separate clause in the conveyance, which referred to rent, amounted to consideration for the grant.

Held, refusing the application, that R was not entitled to apply for the discharge of the covenant. The clause relied upon dealt with how rent received for use of the hall was to be applied and did not provide consideration for the covenant. In any event, the covenant was personal in nature and had ceased to be enforceable on the death of the last surviving grantor.

ROBINS APPLICATION, *Re* [2005] R.V.R. 217, George Bartlett Q.C. (President), Lands Tr.

3417. Lands Tribunal – Practice directions – Procedure

[Lands Tribunal Rules 1996 (SI 1996 1022); Civil Procedure Rules 1998 (SI 1998 3132).]

The President of the Lands Tribunal issued a practice direction to supersede all previous practice directions relating to the Lands Tribunal Rules 1996 as amended. The practice direction gave procedural guidance on (1) the application of procedure analogous to the overriding objective of the Civil Procedure Rules 1998; (2) case management, including written representation procedure and standard procedure; (3) stay of proceedings pending negotiation or alternative dispute resolution; (4) appeals from leasehold valuation tribunals; (5) statement of case and reply; (6) preliminary issues; (7) extensions of time; (8) arranging the hearing; (9) venue of the hearing; (10) negotiations, settlements and withdrawals; (11) documentation to be lodged prior to the hearing; (12) evidence; (13) expert evidence; (14) representation; (15) procedure at the hearing; (16) site inspections; (17) delivery of decisions; (18) fees; (19) costs; (20) appeals to the Court of Appeal.

PRACTICE DIRECTION (LANDS TR: PROCEDURE) [2005] R.V.R. 9, George Bartlett Q.C. (President), Lands Tr.

3418. Leaseholds–Sale of property–Lessor's covenants–Subject matter of sale–Assignment of benefit

The first defendant property consultant (P) and second defendant company (C) appealed against an order for summary judgment in favour of the claimant property developer (E). E had sold some shops at auction in several lots. A lessor's covenant restricted sale or letting for certain uses and required E to insert a corresponding covenant in any sale or letting agreement. C, via P as agent, bought Lot 11 with the covenant inserted, but it was not inserted for the other lots. Before completion, C and P were refused finance on the ground that the buyer of Lot 11 would become landlord of a tenant who had power to litigate against it if the primary business of one of the other properties sold was in breach of the user covenant. The market value of Lot 11 fell accordingly. C and P alleged that E had acted in breach of its duties as trustee for not inserting an appropriate covenant and so could not enforce the contract of sale. E sought specific performance and obtained summary judgment. (1) P submitted that P was only acting as agent for C and that E was estopped by convention from asserting that P was the buyer or joint buyer; (2) there was no limitation on the duty of the trustee for sale of the property sold. E argued that by virtue of the terms of the auction conditions P was jointly and severally liable with C under the auction contract, and was personally liable to buy at the bid price and indemnify E for any loss. There was no evidence of a common underlying assumption that only C was the buyer; E also argued that it was not obliged to impose the covenant on the other lots sold; its duty did not extend to properties other than those that were the subject of the sale.

Held, dismissing the appeal, that (1) the auctioneer's notices clearly emphasised both the personal liability of an agent, and the joint and several liability of the agent and principal under the contract of sale. There was nothing in the communications between P, C and the auctioneers following the sale that was inconsistent with the auction conditions, and no conduct by E amounting to their waiver or variation. (2) It was not arguable that, in the absence of agreement to the contrary, E had a duty to require the purchasers of the lots sold after Lot 11 to comply with the user covenant. Case law had established that, where the existence of the trust or the identity of the property was not in question, the seller's trust was to preserve the property in its state as at the time of the contract, since equity imposed duties on the seller to protect, pending completion, the buyer's interest acquired under the contract. The seller had to give good title and, subject to the terms of the contract of sale, to avoid any steps that might result in forfeiture, *Dowson v. Solomon* (1859) 1 Drew & Sm 1 considered. However, the covenant in the instant case was a lessor's covenant, and the actions of the seller could not have led to forfeiture of the interest that was the subject matter of the sale. If the benefit of an agreement, vested in the seller, was not part of the property being sold then it did not survive the sale, and if the buyer could not compel the seller to assign the benefit, then he could not complain if the seller chose not to do so, *Heronsgate Enterprises Ltd v. Harman (Chesham) Ltd* (Unreported, January 21, 1993) applied.

ENGLEWOOD PROPERTIES LTD v. PATEL, [2005] EWHC 188, [2005] 1 W.L.R. 1961, Lawrence Collins, J., Ch D.

3419. Legal charges–Professional negligence–Chartered surveyor's failure to enquire about status of planning permission–Bank's duty as mortgagee

The claimant landowner (F) sought a declaration that her property was free of a legal charge in favour of the defendant bank. The Part 20 defendants (K) were surveyors and receivers for the bank. Loans by the bank to F and her husband had been secured by legal charges over a piece of land and F's dwelling house. After F's husband had been made bankrupt, the land was sold with clawback provisions in the event of sale or the grant of planning permission for the site. The buyer approached the bank seeking variation of the clawback provisions, including capping of the sums payable, and the bank instructed K to investigate the offer. Upon K's advice the bank then agreed to the buyer's request for variation of the clawback provisions on moderate terms. Not long afterwards, the site was zoned for development and the buyer sold it at a high profit. Meanwhile, a possession order had been obtained by the bank against F's dwelling house in order to recoup money outstanding under the bank loans. F submitted that, by agreeing to the variation of the clawback provisions, the bank had been in breach of an equitable duty it owed as mortgagee of the site to F as a person interested in the equity of redemption. F suggested that the bank should either have refused the variation or agreed to much more favourable terms, resulting in a profitable sale to the bank and wiping out F's indebtedness under the loans. The bank denied acting in breach of equitable duty to F in as much as it properly instructed K and acted on its advice. The bank alleged that K had been in negligent breach of duty in its advice on the variation, and claimed damages to the extent of what would have been realised by the clawback provisions without the variation.

Held, giving judgment accordingly, that on the evidence, K had been in negligent breach of duty to the bank in not enquiring properly as to future zoning plans affecting the site. The bank had been negligent in carrying out its duty to F as a party interested in the equity of redemption, and was responsible for the negligence of K as its agent, *Raja v. Austin Gray (A Firm)* [2002] EWCA Civ 1965, [2003] B.P.I.R. 725, [2003] C.L.Y. 2993 followed. On the balance of probabilities, without K's negligence the bank would not have agreed to the variation. As a result the bank had lost a real, rather than a purely speculative, two to one chance that the clawback provisions would have come into operation, *Allied Maples Group Ltd v. Simmons & Simmons* [1995] 1 W.L.R. 1602, [1996] C.L.Y. 4489 applied. Consequently, F had lost the benefit of the two to one chance of the bank profiting from their operation and applying her property in satisfaction of her indebtedness.

FRANCIS v. BARCLAYS BANK PLC, [2004] EWHC 2787, [2005] P.N.L.R. 18, Sir Donald Rattee, Ch D.

3420. Mistake–Settlors–Unforeseen effect of transaction–Right to set aside

The applicants (W), who were husband and wife, applied to set aside a reversionary lease granted by them to their two daughters as part of an inheritance tax saving scheme; applied for a declaration as to whether that lease was held on the trusts of a certain settlement; and, so far as necessary, applied for an order setting aside that settlement. The applications were made on the basis that the transactions were voluntary ones of which W had had insufficient understanding or that they laboured under a serious mistake as to their effect. The scheme involved a reversionary lease of their house in favour of their daughters. The scheme documents executed by W were a 1997 lease for a term of 125 years starting in June 2017 at a yearly peppercorn rent (if demanded) and a trust deed which proceeded on the basis that the lease had been transferred to the settlement by W when in fact it had been granted to the daughters. W subsequently came to appreciate that from June 2017 they would have no right to stay in the house and would be at the mercy of their daughters or their successors in title to the lease. If the daughters allowed them to stay on free of charge then the tax implications would be likely to deprive the scheme of its inheritance tax saving features since W would be receiving a benefit. W's application to set aside the lease and, if necessary, the trust deed was not opposed by the trustees or children.

Held, granting the application, that (1) when they entered into the lease W did not know that the effect of it was to deprive them of their right to occupy the property in 2017. They would not have entered into the transaction if its effect on their rights of residence had been pointed out to them. (2) The trust deed was manifestly defective and did not coincide with W's intentions since it gave the daughters interests in income only and W intended them to have access to capital. W would not have entered into a scheme which did not provide for that. (3) W intended to give away an interest to their daughters but there were limits to that gift. It was to take effect in the future and was not to deprive them of the rights of occupation that they had enjoyed hitherto. They had made a significant mistake as to the legal effect of the lease and were entitled to have it set aside, *Gibbon v. Mitchell* [1990] 1 W.L.R. 1304, [1991] C.L.Y. 1724 and

AMP (UK) Plc v. Barker [2001] O.P.L.R. 197, [2001] C.L.Y. 4595 applied. (Obiter) the setting aside of the lease meant that there was no asset in the trust. If necessary the trust deed would have been set aside for the same reason as the lease. In any event there was no real prospect of establishing that the lease was held for the trust as a trust asset.

WOLFF v. WOLFF, [2004] EWHC 2110, [2004] S.T.C. 1633, Mann, J., Ch D.

3421. Mortgages–Securitisation–Title to sue–Interest rates–Implied terms–Extortionate credit bargains

[Law of Property Act 1925 s.114, s.136; Consumer Credit Act 1974 s.138.]

The appellants (P) appealed against the decision ([2003] EWHC 2834) not to set aside a possession order. P had borrowed £75,000 from the respondent lender (C) to renovate the property of which they were the registered proprietors. The loan was secured by a legal charge of which C was the registered proprietor. C's mortgage conditions provided that interest on the loan would be charged at such rate as C from time to time determined. Mortgages including P's mortgage had been sold by C to a special purpose vehicle (SPV) in a process known as securitisation, under which C had retained the legal title to the mortgage and had entered into successive administration agreements with the SPV. P had fallen into arrears and C had taken possession proceedings. A possession order had been made, subject to the proviso that it was not to be enforced without the leave of the court. Thereafter P had made monthly payments but in lesser sums than the amounts due with the result that the arrears increased. C had issued a warrant for possession and P had applied to set aside the possession order. P submitted that (1) C had no title to sue since by virtue of the securitisation process the right to take possession proceedings was vested in the SPV and not in C; (2) P were not in default under the legal charge and it was C which had breached an implied obligation not to vary the rates of interest charged improperly or capriciously; (3) the legal charge was an extortionate credit bargain under the Consumer Credit Act 1974 because C's power to vary the interest rate had been fettered by the successive administration agreements with the SPV and C had failed to disclose that fact to P.

Held, dismissing the appeal, that (1) C had title to sue. As registered proprietor of the legal charge, C retained legal ownership of it and the right to possession of the mortgaged property. The uncompleted agreement to transfer the legal charge to the SPV did not divest C of that right. The SPV as the owner of the charge in equity was not a necessary party to the claim: there was no issue between the SPV and C, and the SPV had by virtue of the administration agreements authorised C to exercise such rights on its behalf. It did not matter that C failed to describe itself as suing as trustee. P's reliance on the Law of Property Act 1925 s.114 was misconceived as that applied only to unregistered land. Reliance on s.136 of the 1925 Act was also misplaced. (2) The power to vary interest rates was subject to an implied term that it would not be exercised improperly or capriciously, *Paragon Finance Plc (formerly National Home Loans Corp) v. Nash* [2001] EWCA Civ 1466, [2002] 1 W.L.R. 685, [2001] C.L.Y. 4874 applied. But that did not mean that a lender could not, for a genuine commercial reason, adopt a policy of raising interest rates to levels at which its borrowers generally, or a particular category of its borrowers, would consider refinancing their borrowings with other commercial lenders. Save as otherwise expressly agreed with its borrowers, a commercial lender was free to conduct its business in what it genuinely believed to be its best commercial interests. In any event there was no evidence that C had embarked on a policy of forcing its borrowers to redeem their mortgages, still less that P had been singled out for special treatment in that respect. If there had been any discrimination between old and new borrowers, that would have been for a good commercial reason. Therefore there was no breach of the implied obligation. (3) There was no evidence that as at the date when the legal charge was granted, securitisation arrangements were in place which had the effect of qualifying C's power to vary interest rates by imposing a minimum rate. Accordingly the allegation of failure to disclose the existence of that qualification at that date was not made out on the facts. In any event such a failure, had it occurred, would not have rendered the bargain an extortionate credit bargain within the meaning of s.138 of the 1974 Act, because there was no evidence C had a policy of operating the power to vary interest rates in a particular way, or of not operating it at all, such that the apparently unqualified terms of that power misrepresented the true position in that respect, with the result that ordinary principles of fair dealing required disclosure of the policy, *Broadwick Financial Services Ltd v. Spencer* [2002] EWCA Civ 35, [2002] 1 All E.R. (Comm) 446, [2002] C.L.Y. 694 considered. The rates of interest actually charged by C did not support the allegation that such rates were grossly exorbitant or that they otherwise grossly contravened ordinary principles of fair dealing.

PARAGON FINANCE PLC (FORMERLY NATIONAL HOME LOANS CORP LTD) v. PENDER, [2005] EWCA Civ 760, [2005] 1 W.L.R. 3412, Ward, L.J., CA (Civ Div).

3422. Possession–Adverse possession–Owner allowed farmer to use land–Same use continued after expiry of agreement–Effect of earlier licence on issue of later possession

The appellant (E), the registered proprietor of a piece of land, appealed against a judgment that the respondent (T) had established adverse possession. Prior to the 12 year period required for adverse possession, T had used the land under grazing agreements. When the agreements expired, T continued to use the land for the same purposes. E argued that, under the grazing agreements, T had only had a licence to carry out certain prescribed activities on the land, not a right to possession; and so, since T had merely continued to use the land in the same way, which would have been consistent with further grazing agreements, that use did not amount to possession.

Held, dismissing the appeal, that a squatter would establish factual possession if he could show that he used land in a way that would have been expected of him if he had been the true owner and in such a way that the owner was excluded, *JA Pye (Oxford) Ltd v. Graham* [2002] UKHL 30, [2003] 1 A.C. 419, [2002] C.L.Y. 3805 applied. Any such use by the squatter that would amount to factual possession could not be diluted by dealings between him and the true owner which related exclusively to an earlier period. So, in the instant case, the earlier grazing agreements could have no impact whatever on the issue of whether T's activities on the disputed land during the relevant period amounted to factual possession.

TOPPLAN ESTATES LTD v. TOWNLEY, [2004] EWCA Civ 1369, [2005] 1 E.G.L.R. 89, Pill, L.J., CA (Civ Div).

3423. Possession–Promissory estoppel–Failure to establish factual basis for defence of promissory estoppel–Reasonable notice to vacate property

The claimant (B) sought possession of a leasehold property and damages for the alleged unlawful occupation and use of the property by the defendant (Y). B was a British citizen. During his divorce proceedings in the United Kingdom, he had visited Pakistan and married Y in a religious ceremony. B alleged that he had been forced into the marriage. Following the marriage, Y had obtained a decree absolute, which dissolved his first marriage. Thereafter, Y had obtained entry clearance on the basis of a sponsorship declaration made by B. The entry type was stated to be visa marriage. She had subsequently joined B in the UK and occupied the property. However, the marriage was not a success. Possession proceedings were commenced to remove Y from the property. It was accepted by Y that B was entitled to possession of the property unless she established a defence of promissory estoppel and alternatively a defence of want of reasonable notice. Y submitted that B had represented to her that he was free to marry and wished to enter into a valid marriage, and that she had acted to her detriment by giving up her unmarried status and accommodation in Pakistan. Y submitted further that B had represented to her that the property was to be their matrimonial home and before their marriage was dissolved under Islamic law B had informed her that she could stay in the property as long as she liked.

Held, giving judgment for the B that (1) Y was not a reliable witness and B's story, which was corroborated by a number of witnesses, was plausible. B's unchallenged evidence suggested that he had been reluctant to enter into the marriage and only did so as a result of pressure from his family. No representations had been made by B or his parents that he was free to marry Y, and in particular that he was divorced. Y's parents were aware of B's marital status, but were keen to take advantage of the opportunity presented by B's impending divorce for their daughter to marry a British husband. Further, Y was aware of the date of the decree absolute and was therefore aware that B was married at the time of the religious marriage ceremony. B had never made any representations to Y about her right to occupy the property other than a representation by conduct that Y had permission to stay there for the time being. Also, Y had never believed that she had any right to occupy the property. In the circumstances, Y had not established the factual basis for her defence of promissory estoppel. The exception was the sponsorship declaration, in which B undertook to the Home Office to maintain, support and accommodate Y during her stay in the UK. However, the sponsorship declaration on its own was not sufficient to establish a defence of promissory estoppel. It also followed that B had not established the factual basis for her counterclaim for deceit. (2) In the absence of any promissory estoppel, Y occupied the property as a bare licensee, and her occupation was terminable upon reasonable notice. The period which had elapsed between the arrival of a letter requiring Y to vacate the property and the commencement of the proceedings was sufficient time for Y to find alternative accommodation.

BABAR v. ANIS, [2005] EWHC 1384, [2005] 3 F.C.R. 216, Richard Arnold Q.C., Ch D.

3424. Possession claims–Gypsies–Right to respect for private and family life–Effect of conflicting authorities

[Human Rights Act 1998 Sch.1 Part I Art.8; European Convention on Human Rights 1950.]

The appellant gypsies (P) appealed against a decision that they were not entitled to argue by way of defence to an action by the respondent local authority for an order for possession of land that such possession would infringe their rights under the Human Rights Act 1998 Sch.1 Part I Art.8. It was not disputed that the local authority had title to the land and that P had entered into and remained in occupation of the land without consent. In deciding that P could not raise the Art.8 defence, the judge held that the decision of the House of Lords in *Qazi v. Harrow LBC* [2003] UKHL 43, [2004] 1 A.C. 983, [2003] C.L.Y. 2786 was not incompatible with the decision of the European Court of Human Rights in *Connors v. United Kingdom (66746/01)* (2005) 40 E.H.R.R. 9, [2004] 12 C.L. 270, and that he was bound to follow *Qazi*. P submitted that (1) *Qazi* was incompatible with *Connors*; (2) the court was bound to follow *Connors* in order to satisfy the obligation to take into account the decisions of the ECtHR. The local authority contended that the decision in *Connors* had no significance because it had been decided on the basis of the government's concession that Art.8 was engaged and all that it demonstrated was that there was one area of English law that was incompatible with the Convention, namely that dealing with a local authority's right to recover possession of land forming part of a gypsy site; the court was bound to follow the decision of the House of Lords in *Qazi*.

Held, dismissing the appeal, that (1) the reasoning of the ECtHR in *Connors* was not founded on the government's concession that Art.8 was engaged, and it was clear that the court considered that the concession had been properly made. The reasoning of the ECtHR in *Connors* could not be confined to gypsies, *Kay v. Lambeth LBC* [2004] EWCA Civ 926, [2004] 3 W.L.R. 1396, [2004] 11 C.L. 240 considered. That reasoning was incompatible with *Qazi*, *Connors* explained. *Connors* could not be treated as simply identifying a discrete exception to the general rule propounded by the majority in *Qazi*. The decision in *Connors* did not exclude the possibility that a particular statutory regime could itself achieve the balance required by Art.8(2) so that, if the judge complied with it, the requirements of Art.8(2) would be satisfied. Equally, however, it did not exclude the possibility that, if a statutory regime was to comply with the European Convention on Human Rights 1950, it had to require a public authority to weigh in the balance the impact of its actions on the individual affected and permit that individual to challenge in the courts the conclusion reached by the public authorities. (2) To accept that the court should follow *Connors* would subvert the principle of legal certainty. The ECtHR did not purport to be making new law in *Connors*. In the instant case, there had been no change in circumstances, but simply a decision of the ECtHR that conflicted with a previous decision of the House of Lords, *JD v. East Berkshire Community Health NHS Trust* [2003] EWCA Civ 1151, [2004] Q.B. 558, [2003] C.L.Y. 3004 distinguished. In those circumstances, the only permissible course was to follow the decision of the House of Lords but to give permission, if sought and not successfully opposed, to appeal to the House of Lords, *Qazi* followed.

LEEDS CITY COUNCIL v. PRICE; *sub nom.* PRICE v. LEEDS CITY COUNCIL, [2005] EWCA Civ 289, [2005] 1 W.L.R. 1825, Lord Phillips of Worth Matravers, M.R., CA (Civ Div).

3425. Public rights of way—Classification—Reclassification of road used as public path—Modification of definitive map to show right of way as byway

[National Parks and Access to the Countryside Act 1949 s.32(4)(b); Countryside Act 1968 Sch.3 Part III para.9, Part III para.10; Wildlife and Countryside Act 1981 s.56.]

The claimant, a motorcycle trail rider (T), applied for judicial review of a decision of an inspector appointed by the defendant secretary of state not to confirm an order modifying a definitive county map and statement. The order showed a right of way as a byway open to all traffic instead of as a bridleway. The sole reason given by the inspector for refusing to confirm the order was that public vehicular rights over the way had been extinguished by an earlier reclassification as a bridleway pursuant to the Countryside Act 1968 Sch.3 Part III para.9 and para.10. The way was shown in the original definitive map and statement, prepared by the local authority under the National Parks and Access to the Countryside Act 1949, as a road used as a public path. The Secretary of State submitted that (1) on a true construction of the legislation the reclassification under para.9 and para.10 of Part III of Sch.3 of the 1968 Act had the effect of extinguishing any public vehicular rights; (2) those public vehicular rights could not be revived or restored by the operation of the Wildlife and Countryside Act 1981.

Held, granting the application, that (1) by reason of the proviso in s.32(4)(b) of the 1949 Act, which remained unaltered by the 1968 Act, when the definitive map and statement showed a bridleway the entry was conclusive evidence that there was a public right of way on foot and by horseback, but, by reason of the proviso, the entry on the map did not exclude the possible existence of a public right of way for vehicular purposes. The proviso could not be construed as amended so as to render it inapplicable to a reclassified bridleway. Further, para.9 and para.10 of Sch.3 could not be construed as providing that any vehicular rights which existed over the way should be extinguished upon reclassification. That position was maintained under s.56 of the 1981 Act. (2) It was not necessary to consider possible revival or restoration of an extinguishment.

R. (ON THE APPLICATION OF KIND) v. SECRETARY OF STATE FOR THE ENVIRONMENT, FOOD AND RURAL AFFAIRS, [2005] EWHC 1324, [2006] Q.B. 113, Lightman, J., QBD (Admin).

3426. Public rights of way—Registration of applications

PUBLIC RIGHTS OF WAY (REGISTER OF APPLICATIONS UNDER SECTION 53(5) OF THE WILDLIFE AND COUNTRYSIDE ACT 1981) (ENGLAND)

REGULATIONS 2005, SI 2005 2461; made under the Wildlife and Countryside Act 1981 s.53B. In force: September 27, 2005; £3.00.

The Wildlife and Countryside Act 1981 enables any person to apply to a surveying authority for an order to modify the definitive map and statement concerning public rights of way. The Act requires every surveying authority to keep a register of applications under s.53(5) of the Act. These Regulations prescribe the information to be contained in that register and the manner in which that register is to be kept by the surveying authority.

3427. Regulation of Financial Services (Land Transactions) Act 2005 (c.24)

This Act enables activities relating to certain arrangements involving the acquisition or disposal of land to be regulated under the Financial Services and Markets Act 2000.

This Act received Royal Assent on December 19, 2005.

3428. Repossession–Mortgagees powers and duties–Sale to connected company–Burden of proving best price obtained

The appellant mortgagor (R) appealed against a decision that he had failed to discharge the burden of proving that the respondent mortgagee (B) had sold mortgaged property at an undervalue. B had issued proceedings seeking to recover the shortfall that had arisen after the sale of the mortgaged property. By his defence and counterclaim R had alleged that the property had been sold at an undervalue. After the hearing of the trial of the matter, but before the judge had given his judgment, R had sought to put before the court fresh evidence that he alleged showed that the sale of the property by B had been to a connected company. R sought to argue that B had failed to take reasonable steps to obtain the best price reasonably obtainable for the property. The judge refused to allow that fresh evidence to be adduced on the basis that R had failed to discharge the burden of proving that the sale had been at an undervalue.

Held, allowing the appeal, that had the judge made himself fully aware of the information that R was seeking to adduce by way of fresh evidence, namely that the sale of the property by B had been, as alleged by R, to a connected company, he should have found that it was for B to satisfy the burden of proof. On a sale of a repossessed property by a mortgagee to a connected company, the evidential burden of proof was on the mortgagee to show that it had taken all reasonable steps to comply with its duty to obtain the best price reasonably obtainable for the property, *Mortgage Express v. Mardner* [2004] EWCA Civ 1859 applied. Accordingly, the judge had erred by upholding B's claim in the action on the basis that R had not satisfied the burden of proof. The matter was remitted for a retrial.

BRADFORD & BINGLEY PLC v. ROSS, [2005] EWCA Civ 394, *The Times*, May 3, 2005, Ward, L.J., CA (Civ Div).

3429. Repossession–Transactions at an undervalue–Farm business tenancy subject to base rent and market rent payments–Commercial reality of grant

[Law of Property Act 1925 s.205(1)(xxiii); Insolvency Act 1986 s.423; Agricultural Tenancies Act 1995 s.9.]

B sought possession of a farm following a default in mortgage payments by H. B asserted that a tenancy agreement concluded between H and a company he controlled was invalid as the rent payable by the company was at an undervalue. H had bought the farm with the benefit of a loan from B. In order to put the freehold beyond B's reach, H entered into a 20-year tenancy agreement with the company. The rent comprised a base rent that increased substantially after five years, and a market rent that was subject to five yearly reviews. A supplemental agreement allowed the tenancy to continue by way of a rent re-evaluation if the consideration was found to be at an undervalue under the Insolvency Act 1986 s.423. The base rent was described as a "repayable loan" from H that represented the surrender value of the tenancy. A rectification agreement stipulated that the open market rent was separate from the base rent for the purposes of the Agricultural Tenancies Act 1995.

Held, granting the claim, that the base rent complied with the definition given under the Law of Property Act 1925 s.205(1)(xxiii) and was paid for use of the land, as opposed to being made for a personal advantage, *Escalus Properties Ltd v. Robinson* [1996] Q.B. 231, [1996] C.L.Y. 3758 applied. In terms of commercial reality, the sums paid by the company were compensation for the value it had obtained, and requiring payment of an additional periodic sum as rent would allow the agreement to displace the statutory formula for rent arbitrators, in breach of s.9 of the 1995 Act. Even if the supplementary agreement was effective, B could not be required to accept the company as its tenant when it had no desire to be a landlord and had no control over future assignments. The tenancy agreement was set aside as the company was H's alter ego and he could not continue to operate the business given the extent of his indebtedness.

BARCLAYS BANK PLC v. BEAN [2005] B.P.I.R. 563, Judge Langan, Ch D.

3430. Residential development–Restrictive covenants–Effect of the word "a" on number of residential buildings envisaged by restrictive covenant

The defendant housing developer, D, appealed against a decision on a preliminary issue arising from the enforcement of a restrictive covenant. A local authority development corporation had sold two plots of land, Plots 2 and 3, each of which was subject to a restrictive covenant designed to prevent the land from being used for any purpose other than as "a private dwellinghouse". A dwellinghouse was built on each plot. D acquired a large part of both Plot 2 and 3, not including the existing dwellinghouses, and began the construction of 24 dwellinghouses. The claimant, M, claimed the benefit of the covenants. At a preliminary hearing the court decided that the indefinite article in the phrase "a private dwellinghouse" meant that no more than one building on each plot could be used as a dwellinghouse.

Held, allowing the appeal, that (1) the presence of the indefinite article "a" in the covenant restricted the manner of use but not the number of buildings; (2) the schedule to the conveyances containing the covenant referred to "any buildings", clearly envisaging the possibility that there might be several; (3) the use of the indefinite article in the phrase "a private dwellinghouse" did not imply singularity; (4) there was nothing in the factual matrix to displace this conclusion, *Crest Nicholson Residential (South) Ltd v. McAllister* [2002] EWHC 2443, [2003] 1 All E.R. 46, [2003] C.L.Y. 3595 considered.

MARTIN v. DAVID WILSON HOMES LTD, [2004] EWCA Civ 1027, [2004] 3 E.G.L.R. 77, Buxton, L.J., CA (Civ Div).

3431. Restrictive covenants–Extinguishment–Unity of seisin of local authority–Dominant and servient tenements held for different statutory purposes

[Law of Property Act 1925 s.78.]

The claimant university (U) sought to sell one of its three campuses free from the restrictive covenants entered into by its predecessor in title (E). The land had formed part of housing estate land which was owned by the defendant local housing authorities (D and R), whose statutory predecessor (L) had conveyed the campus to E, a local education authority. By the conveyances, E and E's "successors and assigns" had entered into covenants with L and L's "successors and assigns" and the covenants were subject to the Law of Property Act 1925 s.78. Two restrictive covenants prohibited (i) use of the campus for purposes other than public educational purposes, and (ii) the erection of any buildings on the campus except in accordance with plans approved by L. A third pre emption covenant prohibited the sale or, save for educational purposes, the parting with possession of the campus without first offering to sell it to L, the appropriate price to be determined by an arbitrator. U wished to sell the campus for housing purposes. D and R claimed that U should pay consideration for release from the covenants. The issues for determination were (1) whether the covenants in the conveyances constituted a single covenant or were separate and distinct; (2) who was entitled to benefit from, and enforce, the covenants; (3) who was intended to be subjected to the covenants; (4) whether the campus should be valued by the arbitrator as subject to, or free from, the covenants; (5) whether the benefit of the covenants had vested in D and R on transfer from their immediate predecessor; (6) the effect of any loss of the right to consent to or approve plans, or the right of pre emption; (7) whether the covenants had been extinguished by unity of seisin.

Held, giving judgment for U in part, that (1) the covenants were separate and distinct, although they complemented each other and were aimed at furthering the same single purpose of protecting the estate. (2) Interpreting the conveyances in their historical context, the intention was expressed that the benefit of the covenants was to be confined to L and any other body to which, by statute, L's statutory housing functions and the estate were transferred, and to which, incidental to that transfer, the contractual rights were also transferred. Accordingly, neither tenants of D and R nor purchasers of properties on the estate from L or its successors were entitled to the benefit of, or to enforce, the restrictive covenants. Further, the area of the estate protected by the restrictive covenants had been at all times subject to reduction by the disposal by way of sale of properties on the estate by L or its successors, including D and R, in the exercise of their statutory powers, *Crest Nicholson Residential (South) Ltd v. McAllister* [2004] EWCA Civ 410, [2004] 1 W.L.R. 2409, [2004] 7 C.L. 403 applied. (3) The burdens of the covenants fell upon the successors in title of E who performed the same statutory functions as it. (4) The terms of the pre emption covenant made it plain that the covenants were not intended to bind a purchaser from E. Accordingly, U was free to sell the campus for its full market value free of the restrictive covenants. By doing so, U would trigger the pre emption clause. If D and R exercised the right of pre emption they would be required to pay the full market price free from the restrictive covenants. (5) Upon the statutory division of the estate between D and R, the pre emption covenant continued to be enforceable by D and R acting together, although neither was individually entitled to enforce it. (6) (*Obiter*) Had the benefit of the covenants not vested in D and R acting together there would no longer have been any person who could consent to change of user, and the user covenant would have become absolute. The approval covenant and the pre emption covenant would have been discharged, *Crest Nicholson* applied. (7) There was no extinguishment of restrictive covenants when dominant and servient properties were held by the same trustee on distinct trusts, *Chambers v. Kingham* (1878-79) L.R. 10 Ch. D. 743 applied. The same principle applied when both properties were held by a public authority for different statutory purposes. A blanket rule requiring such common ownership to operate to extinguish all restrictive covenants would prejudice the performance by the local authority of its statutory duties.

UNIVERSITY OF EAST LONDON HIGHER EDUCATION CORP v. BARKING AND DAGENHAM LBC, [2004] EWHC 2710, [2005] Ch. 354, Lightman, J., Ch D.

3432. Restrictive covenants–Residential development–Covenant restricting use of site to two storey private residence–Use of part of site for access road not permitted

M appealed against declaratory relief in the form of the interpretation of a restrictive covenant contained in a 1964 conveyance. The covenant prevented the construction of anything other than a two storey building on land occupied by a dwelling house and contained the words "use the same as a private residence only". J subsequently purchased the property and wanted to construct a new dwelling on part of the site, along with an access road leading to a further 10 new dwellings.

Held, allowing the appeal, that the words used showed that the land was only to be used for a private residence, which did not include the use of part of the site for an access road. The covenant was intended to bind the original owners and their successor in title, including licensees, and be for the benefit of the neighbouring property, which had been built on land retained by the former owner of the site.

JARVIS HOMES LTD v. MARSHALL, [2004] EWCA Civ 839, [2004] 3 E.G.L.R. 81, Thorpe, L.J., CA.

3433. Restrictive covenants–Rights of way–Modification or discharge of covenant–Corresponding change to right of way

[Law of Property Act 1925 s.84(1).]

H appealed against a declaration in favour of M as to the construction of a grant of a right of way. M was the owner of a property (the house) which had enjoyed the benefit of a right of way along a roadway running over adjoining land owned by H. The grant of the right of way had been contained in a conveyance granted to M's predecessors in title in 1965 (the conveyance). The right of way had been for all purposes in connection with the use of the house as authorised by a restrictive covenant which had restricted the use of the house to be used only for offices and for purposes ancillary thereto (Clause D). M had made an application to the Lands Tribunal under the Law of Property Act 1925 s.84(1) seeking to discharge or modify the restrictive covenant so as to permit the house to be used for holiday lettings and a health and fitness centre. By these proceedings H had sought a declaration that the right of way could only have been exercised for the purposes as originally authorised in the conveyance notwithstanding any modification or discharge of the restrictive covenant that the Lands Tribunal might have made. H argued that the words of Clause D had been imported into the grant of the right of way and had thereby become part of it, and accordingly could not have been affected by any order of the Lands Tribunal. The trial judge made a declaration that M had been entitled to use the right of way for such purposes as were permitted following any modification or discharge of use that may have been made by the Lands Tribunal.

Held, dismissing the appeal, that the language of the conveyance made an express link between the use of the right of way to the house and the use of the house itself. The restriction upon the use of the house contained in the conveyance had always been subject to a modification or discharge under s.84 of the 1925 Act, the jurisdiction of which could not have been ousted. That had been a relevant circumstance when the conveyance had been granted. In those circumstances, it would have been unreasonable to have said that the user of the house would have expected to modify or discharge a restriction upon the use of the house without a corresponding change to the right of way.

HOTCHKIN v. McDONALD, [2004] EWCA Civ 519, [2005] 1 P. & C.R. 7, Thorpe, L.J., CA.

3434. Right to light–Prescription, Grant under s.62 Law of Property Act 1925 of right in process of being acquired

[Prescription Act 1832 s.3, s.4; Law of Property Act 1925 s.62; Town and Country Planning Act 1990 s.237.]

The claimants (M and L), freeholder and leaseholder respectively of a London office building, sought injunctive relief, or damages in lieu, against the defendant owner (C) of a neighbouring development site. C had planning permission for an office complex on the site and M and L alleged that the development would interfere with their right to light, acquired by prescription pursuant to the Prescription Act 1832 s.3 and s.4. M's freehold was subject to leases which had been granted in 1978 and 1993, the former expiring in 2001 and the latter commencing on the former's expiry and extending to 2018. At the time of trial it was conceded that M had acquired a right to light. However, L could only show enjoyment pursuant to the 1993 lease, at which time M was still in the process of acquiring the right. During the trial, therefore, M granted L a right to light in respect of the property and L applied to amend its claim accordingly. L submitted that it should have permission to amend in order to rely on the grant of a right to light by M, but that in any event rights in the course of being acquired under the 1832 Act were capable of passing under the Law of Property Act 1925 s.62 so the right to light in the process of being acquired by M had passed by implication on the occasion of the1993 lease. C submitted that it was entitled to interfere with the claimants' rights to light on the basis of a 1930 conveyance of part of its site which contained a provision intended to prevent the operation of s.3 of the 1832 Act. Moreover, as part of its site had been acquired by the local authority for planning purposes in 1956 as part of the regeneration of London following war damage, C argued that theTown and Country Planning Act1990 s.237 overrode any right to light. C also argued that any loss of natural light was immaterial because a London office building was always lit internally by artificial light.

Held, giving judgment accordingly, that (1) L should have permission to amend so as to allow it to rely on the grant of a right of light by M. However, in any event, the wording of s.62 of the 1925 Act was sufficiently wide to pass on rights in the course of being acquired, even if they were precarious. (2) The clear purpose of the provisions in the 1930 conveyance was to enable the owners of C's site, and their successors, to redevelop the site notwithstanding that that might interfere with the light then or thereafter enjoyed by the owners or occupiers of the neighbouring property. That agreement negatived the effect of s.3 of the 1832 Act. In respect of that land, C could rely on the provisions of the 1930 conveyance to override any rights to light enjoyed by the area of land affected by that conveyance, *Marlborough (West End) Ltd v. Wilks Head & Eve* (Unreported, December 20, 1996) followed. (3) Where land had been appropriated by a local authority for a planning purpose, and the authority, or its successor in title, wished to rely on the power to override under s.237 of the 1990 Act, the proposed development had to be related to the planning purposes for which the land was originally acquired or appropriated. In the instant case, C's proposed development was completely unconnected with the original purpose of the 1956 acquisition. Therefore, C could not rely on s.237, *R. v. City of London Corp, ex p. Mystery of the Barbers of London* (1997) 73 P. & C.R. 59, [1996] C.L.Y. 4750 considered. Thus, with the exception of the land affected by the 1930 conveyance, M and L had established rights of light and C's development of its site would affect those rights. (4) C's development would cause an interference with the M and L's rights to light amounting to a nuisance even if in practical terms no use was made of the natural light to the building because the offices were lit by artificial light. (5) M was only interested in the property from a money making point of view and if the value of the property had been diminished, that could be calculated and compensated. There was probably no present loss because of the existing lease and it seemed that M had in mind redevelopment proposals of its own, which would make the injunction academic. Consequently, M was not entitled to an injunction and was entitled to damages to be assessed for infringement of its right to light, *Jaggard v. Sawyer* [1995] 1 WLR 269 and *Colls v. Home & Colonial Stores Ltd* [1904] A.C. 179 applied. For similar reasons, L was not entitled to an injunction. Its rights, if infringed, would suffer even less damage than those of M. (6) The court directed an inquiry as to damages.

MIDTOWN LTD v. CITY OF LONDON REAL PROPERTY CO LTD; JOSEPH v. CITY OF LONDON REAL PROPERTY CO LTD, [2005] EWHC 33, [2005] 1 E.G.L.R. 65, Peter Smith, J., Ch D.

3435. Rights of water−Easements−Right granted to farmer to take water from reservoir−Construction of conveyance

The appellants (P) appealed against a decision that the right of the respondent (M) to draw water as was reasonably required for farm and domestic purposes from a reservoir situated on P's land was not limited to the residue of water after P had taken water for their residential use. P were the freehold owners of property which adjoined farmland and a farmhouse owned by M. Upon P's property was a concrete reservoir which was filled by a spring from which water was piped down hill to M's property. By a conveyance M had a right to take water from the reservoir via the pipe in common with the vendor and its successors in title. That right was to draw water reasonably required for domestic and farm purposes. In the action P asserted that M's right had been limited to the residue of water in the reservoir after

P had drawn their water for residential use. Accordingly, the issue was whether upon the construction of the conveyance M was entitled to draw an amount of water reasonably required for domestic and farm purposes before or after P had drawn from the reservoir. P argued that where an easement had been granted for the taking of water through a pipe in common, the downhill beneficiary of that easement was only entitled to use it after the uphill neighbour had taken his draw from the water, and that the use of the words "in common with the vendor" meant that the supply was to be shared.

Held, dismissing the appeal, that this was a pure construction case and as such no point of principle arose. Accordingly, the phrase "in common with the vendor" was to be construed in the context of the entirety of the grant, but that phrase did no more than indicate that M's rights were non exclusive. The provision gave M a clear right against P to draw water from the reservoir subject to a requirement to only take what was reasonably required for the stated purposes. Whilst such a right did create practical difficulties for P, that did not justify a departure from the clear meaning of the conveyance as found by the judge.

MITCHELL v. POTTER, [2005] EWCA Civ 88, *The Times*, January 24, 2005, Sedley, L.J., CA (Civ Div).

3436. **Rights of way–Abandonment–Intention to abandon right of way–Creation of wider right of way–Consistency with existing right–Inference of abandonment**

The appellant (F) appealed against a decision that the respondent company (C) retained a right of way over land for the purpose of access to three garages. The right of way had originally been created by an express easement over land in part owned by F and was for the benefit of the owner of the then adjacent hotel. The right to pass and repass over the land had been expressed to be "for all purposes connected with the use and enjoyment of the three garages". However, when the hotel was converted to a different use, the garages were demolished and replaced by two ramps for a car park. C later acquired the former hotel, redeveloped it and reinstated the three garages. The judge held that C's right of way over the land was extant. C had not abandoned the right of way because the demolition of the garages and their replacement with ramps showed an intention to claim a wider "way", albeit unlawfully, for access to parking that would have included the then existing right of way. F argued that C had abandoned the right of way. The demolition of the garages and the fact that the site had been destroyed beyond restoration indicated that at the time of the creation of the ramps it could not have been contemplated that the right of way could have been used for access to three garages again. Further, the creation of a wider right of way was inconsistent with the then existing right of way and was in any event unlawful.

Held, dismissing the appeal, that C had not abandoned the right of way. A dominant owner was required to manifest an intention to abandon a right of way in the sense of making it clear that neither he nor his successor wished to continue the use in question, and such an intention should not be lightly inferred, *Gotobed v. Pridmore* (1971) 115 S.J. 78, [1971] C.L.Y. 3714 considered. Moreover, in relation to any wider right of way, there was doubt that any excessive use could suspend an easement as such use could be restrained, *Graham v. Philcox* [1984] Q.B. 747, [1984] C.L.Y. 1153 considered. In the instant case, substantial as the works had been, they did not justify the inference that the owner had intended to abandon the right of way forever. On the facts and accepting that it was inherently a matter of impression, it was not a case where the burden of showing an inference of abandonment had been discharged.

CDC2020 PLC v. FERREIRA, [2005] EWCA Civ 611, [2005] 3 E.G.L.R. 15, Brooke, L.J., CA (Civ Div).

3437. Rights of way–Overriding interest–Rectification of register to indicate overriding interest

[Law of Property Act 1925 s.2, s.70(3), s.82(3); Land Registration Act 1925; Road Traffic Act 1988 s.34; Land Registration Rules 1925 (SI 1925 1093) r.258.]

The appellants (N) appealed against a decision that the respondents (S) had a vehicular right of way over a part of their land. The first appellant was the owner of a property known as the Old Forge and S were owners of an adjoining property known as the Forge Meadow. S also owned another adjoining property, namely the Northern Field. Vehicular access to the properties was gained from a public highway called Forge Road. The right of access over the yard forming part of the Old Forge had apparently been granted to S's predecessors in title by a transfer in 1988. However, the 1988 conveyance contained no express right of way across the retained land and S failed to register the right of way as a land charge. The main issues were: (i) whether S were entitled to the vehicular access from Forge Road over Old Forge Yard to Forge Meadow as either a way of necessity or a right arising by way of proprietary estoppel; (ii) whether S were entitled to vehicular access from Forge Road over Old Forge Yard as appertaining to the Northern Field; and (iii) whether the judge had been entitled to make the orders for rectification of title that he did in consequence of his conclusions. N submitted that (1) it was not open to the judge to find that the "right enjoyed with" Forge Meadow passed over Old Forge Yard at the point where it joined Old Forge Road; (2) the access over the Old Forge Yard partly passed over a public footpath and therefore the use of it as a vehicular access was contrary to the Road Traffic Act 1988 s.34; (3) equity to which the judge found S to be entitled, requiring a declaration of a right of way, was overreached on the 1988 transfer; (4) even if S were entitled to the right they claim as appurtenant to the Northern Field, they could not exercise it for obtaining access to Forge Meadow; (5) the judge was wrong to rectify the register of the title to Old Forge and Old Forge Yard by placing a note in respect of the overriding interests.

Held, dismissing the appeal, that (1) the vehicular access enjoyed by S's predecessor in title over part of Old Forge came within the Land Registration Rules 1925 r.258 so as to constitute an overriding interest binding on N. (2) It was not established that there was a public footpath over any part of Old Forge Yard. Further there was no evidence that the footpath, if existed over the Old Forge Yard, was subject to any public rights. (3) The Law of Property Act 1925 s.2 could only overreach "any equitable interest or power" affecting the estate transferred. However equity arising from a proprietary estoppel was not an "equitable interest" capable of being overreached, *ER Ives Investment Ltd v. High* [1967] 2 Q.B. 379, [1967] C.L.Y. 2196 and *Birmingham Midshires Mortgage Services Ltd v. Sabherwal (Equitable Interest)* (2000) 80 P.&C.R. 256 applied. Further the Land Registration Act 1925 specifically provided that a registered disposition was effective to transfer the freehold estate in the land transferred subject to the overriding interests affecting it. In the instant case, N took the land subject to S's overriding interest. In the circumstances, S were entitled to the vehicular access from Forge Road over Old Forge Yard to Forge Meadow. (4) The right of way was reputed to appertain to the Northern Field for the purposes of r.258 at the time of registration of the transfer in favour of N. It was not possible to preclude that right of way from being an overriding interest by an entry on the register of title to Old Forge and Old Forge Yard. (5) The restriction on rectifying the register contained in s.82(3) of the Land Registration Act 1925 s.82(3) did not apply to rectification "for the purpose of giving effect to an overriding interest or an order of the court". Moreover s.70(3) of the Land Registration Act showed that there was no prohibition on noting an overriding interest on the register. The title to the Old Forge Yard on first registration contained such a notice and should be restored.

SWEET v. SOMMER; *sub nom.* SOMMER v. SWEET, [2005] EWCA Civ 227, [2005] 2 All E.R. 64 (Note), Sir Andrew Morritt V.C., CA (Civ Div).

3438. Sale of land–Undue influence–Enduring powers of attorney–Attorney breaching statutory and fiduciary duty by procuring transfer manifestly disadvantageous to donee

[Enduring Powers of Attorney Act 1985 s.3, s.3(5).]

The applicant (V), a 78 year old widower, sought to set aside a transaction whereby he transferred his home to the first respondent (J), his great nephew, subject to a mortgage in return for the right to live there rent free. V had entrusted the second respondent (T), J's father, with the task of putting the arrangements into effect under a power of attorney. J had then obtained a building society loan to discharge V's mortgage without disclosing that V was to remain in the property. V's future occupation was never reduced to writing. After the transfer, J and T asked V to vacate the property at which point he registered a caution against the property. V contended that the transaction had been procured by undue influence and that T was in breach of his fiduciary duty by transferring the property to J and had also breached the Enduring Powers of Attorney Act 1985 s.3(4) or s.3(5).

Held, granting the application, that the transfer was manifestly disadvantageous to V and J and T had failed to rebut the presumption of undue influence, with the result that the transaction was voidable, *Royal Bank of Scotland Plc v. Etridge (No.2)* [2001] UKHL 44, [2002] 2 A.C. 773, [2001] C.L.Y. 4880 applied. T had breached his fiduciary duty and s.3(4) or s.3(5) of the Act by assisting J in the transaction in circumstances where J had been aware of his father's breaches of duty.

VALE v. ARMSTRONG, [2004] EWHC 1160, [2004] W.T.L.R. 1471, Evans-Lombe, J., Ch D.

3439. Title to land–Adverse possession–Inference of implied licence to remain

The appellant (H) appealed against a decision allowing a claim made by the respondent (C) for adverse possession of land. The land was part of a site used by C as a car park. H alleged that she had lived with her husband in one of the terraced houses that stood on the site until demolition in 1958. In response to C's claim, H counterclaimed by reference to a paper title to that property. The judge found that H had proved her paper title to part of the site but had lost her title to C by the time of her counterclaim. He found that C had established the necessary intention to possess, and that such possession was adverse and did not depend on an implied licence to remain alleged by H to have arisen from negotiations for the purchase of the land by C. H submitted that the judge was wrong to decline to infer, from the correspondence between the parties as to the purchase of the land by C, an implied licence to remain at least until negotiations for the purchase of the land drew to a close, some time just within 12 years before the counterclaim. C contended that the judge was wrong to find that the paper title had been established and there was no implied licence as alleged.

Held, allowing the appeal, that (1) there was no uncertainty in H's identification in 1990 of the relevant property as her former home. The judge had been correct that H had proved that the house she and her husband had lived in lay within the area now occupied by C's car park. H had proved her paper title to part of the site. (2) In deciding there was no implied licence to remain, the judge had been wrong to find assistance in *JA Pye (Oxford) Ltd v. Graham* [2002] UKHL 30, [2003] 1 A.C. 419, [2002] C.L.Y. 3805, *JA Pye* distinguished. He was also mistaken in characterising the facts of the instant case as in any way demonstrating or dependent on a request to vacate. The essence of the decision in *Bath and North East Somerset DC v. Nicholson* [2002] 10 E.G.C.S. 156 was that it was natural to draw an inference of permission where a person was in possession pending negotiations for the grant of an interest in that land. In the instant case, the implication of the correspondence was that C could remain on H's property only if negotiations proceeded for its sale to them, *Nicholson* applied and *BP Properties Ltd v. Buckler* (1988) 55 P. & C.R. 337, [1988] C.L.Y. 2155 considered. A reasonable person in H's or C's position would conclude that C was being permitted to remain on the land pending completion of the negotiations. Accordingly, C could not establish a full 12 years' adverse possession.

COLIN DAWSON WINDOWS LTD v. KING'S LYNN AND WEST NORFOLK BC; *sub nom.* COLIN DAWSON WINDOWS LTD v. HOWARD, [2005] EWCA Civ 9, [2005] 2 P. & C.R. 19, Rix, L.J., CA (Civ Div).

3440. **Village greens-Land registration-Substantive effect of "Class C" registration**

[Inclosure Act 1857 s.12; Commons Act 1876 s.29; Commons Registration Act 1965 s.1 (2), s.10, s.13, s.22(1) (a).]

The appellant registration authority appealed against the decision of the court ([2004] EWHC 12, [2004] Ch. 253) giving guidance on issues arising from the application by the second respondent (R) under the Commons Registration Act 1965 s.13 for registration of land owned by the first respondent local authority as a town or village green. The land was undeveloped and had been acquired in 1975 by the local authority, which wished to use it for housing development. It had been described as a typical case of institutionally owned land on the urban fringe which was neglected by the landowner because it had long term development plans and which attracted use by local people for informal recreation. Part of the land was inaccessible reed beds which were permanently under water. R applied for registration of the land as a "Class C" green within s.22(1) (a) of the 1965 Act on the basis that by 1990, local residents had used it for lawful pastimes as of right for an unbroken period of 20 years and continued to do so. R later attempted to amend the application by excluding certain parts of the land. After a non statutory inquiry the registration authority applied to the High Court which gave guidance on the interpretation and application of the 1965 Act. The main issues on appeal were (1) the substantive effect of Class C registration; (2) the meaning of the words "continue to do so" in s.22(1) (a) and whether the lawful sports and pastimes had to continue up to the date of the application to register or the date of registration or some other (and if so what) date; (3) whether the application could succeed on the basis stated by R in Part 4 of her application, namely that the land became a green on August 1, 1990, or whether an application which specified in Part 4 a date earlier than the date immediately preceding the date of the application had to fail; (4) whether the registration authority had the power to treat the application as if a different date had been specified in Part 4, to permit the application to be amended so as to refer to some lesser area and to accept the application in respect of, and to register as a green, part only of the land included in the application.

Held, allowing the appeal in part, that (1) registration of land as a Class C green under the 1965 Act did not of itself confer or imply any rights on the part of the local inhabitants to indulge in lawful sports and pastimes on that land, *R. v. Oxfordshire CC, ex p. Sunningwell Parish Council* [2000] 1 A.C. 335, [1999] C.L.Y. 4393 and *R. v. Suffolk CC, ex p. Steed* (1998) 75 P. & C.R. 102, [1996] C.L.Y. 4936 considered. Even if Class C greens had enjoyed customary rights in the past, those rights had been extinguished by s.1 (2) of the 1965 Act. Land registered as a Class C green fell within the scope of the penal restrictions in the Inclosure Act 1857 s.12 and the Commons Act 1876 s.29. (2) The words "continue to do so" in the amended definition of Class C greens meant that the lawful sports and pastimes had to continue up to the date of registration. In the absence of any other indication, the words "continue to do so" could only be taken as referring to the time when the statute required the definition to be applied, namely the date when the register was amended under s.13 of the 1965 Act. (3) All applications for registration of land as a Class C green made on or after January 30, 2001 when s.22 was amended automatically engaged, and engaged only, the amended definition of Class C green. The application had to be considered under the amended 1965 Act because, as from that date, an application could only be made under the 1965 Act so amended. The application could not, as a matter of law, succeed on the basis that the land became a green on August 1, 1990. The 1965 Act created no new legal status, and no new rights or liabilities, other than those resulting from the proper interpretation of s.10, which only took effect on registration. There was therefore no legal basis for treating the land as having acquired village green status by virtue of an earlier period of qualifying use. The mere fact that land would, at some earlier time, have come within the statutory definition was irrelevant if it was not registered as such. (4) The general duty of a registration authority to maintain the register carried with it a duty to ensure that procedures were fair and orderly, and that the register itself was accurate and accessible. The registration authority had a discretion to permit amendment and to determine the application for a lesser area. The registration authority had to deal with an application under the 1965 Act procedurally in a way that was just to the applicant, taking account of the positions of other parties including the public, *Inverclyde DC v. Secretary of State for Scotland* 1982 S.C. (H.L.) 64, [1982] C.L.Y. 3191 applied. The registration authority had power to treat the application as if a different date, namely a date immediately preceding the date of the application, had been specified in Part 4, to permit R's application to be amended to refer to a lesser area as proposed by her and to register as a green part only of the land included in the application.

OXFORDSHIRE CC v. OXFORD CITY COUNCIL, [2005] EWCA Civ 175, [2006] Ch. 43, Peter Gibson, L.J., CA (Civ Div).

3441. Books

Abbey, Robert; Richards, Mark–Practical Approach to Conveyancing. Paperback: £32.99. ISBN 0 19 928135 1. Paperback: £32.99. ISBN 0 19 928135 1. Oxford University Press.

Ahuja, Ajay–Buy-to-let Bible. Paperback: £11.99. ISBN 1 904053 91 2. Law Pack Publishing.

Bell, Cedric D.–Land:The Law of Real Property. Paperback: £15.95. ISBN 1 85836 602 X. Old Bailey Press.

Butt, Paul–Commercial Property. Paperback: £24.95. ISBN 0 905835 80 8. Paperback: £25.95. ISBN 1 905391 04 8. The College of Law.

Butt, Paul–Property Law and Practice. Paperback: £25.95. ISBN 0 905835 89 1. The College of Law.

Callo, Kat–Making Sense of Leasehold Property. Paperback: £11.99. ISBN 1 904053 12 2. Law Pack Publishing.

Cant, Christopher; Wood, Lana–Property Development Handbook: Transaction Structures. Paperback: £75.00. ISBN 1 903927 63 3. Legalease.

Casey, Nuala; Brennan, Gabriel–Conveyancing. Law Society of Ireland Manuals S. Paperback: £49.99. ISBN 0 19 928028 2. Oxford University Press.

Chappelle, Diane–Land Law. Foundation Studies in Law S. Paperback: £29.99. ISBN 1 4058 1223 0. Longman.

Clarke, Alison; Kohler, Paul–Property Law: Commentary and Materials. Law in Context S. Paperback: £34.99. ISBN 0 521 61489 9. Cambridge University Press.

Cooke, Elizabeth–Modern Studies in Property Law:V.3. Hardback: £55.00. ISBN 1 84113 558 5. Hart Publishing.

Cowen, Gary; Driscoll, James; Target, Laurence–Commonhold: A Guide to the New Law. Paperback: £49.95. ISBN 1 85328 867 5. Law Society Publications.

Cracknell, D.G.–Land: The Law of Real Property. Cracknell's Statutes S. Paperback: £11.95. ISBN 1 85836 585 6. Old Bailey Press.

Fergusson, Anne; D'Inverno, Isobel–Macroberts Commercial Property. Hardback: £65.00. ISBN 0 414 01618 1. W. Green & Son.

Francis, Andrew–Restrictive Covenants and Freehold Land. Hardback: £85.00. ISBN 0 85308 936 1. Jordans.

Friedman, Jack P.; Harris, Jack; Diskin, Barry–Real Estate Handbook. Hardback: £25.00. ISBN 0 7641 5777 9. Barron's Educational Series.

Gaunt, Jonathan; Morgan, Paul–Gale on the Law of Easements. Paperback: £40.00. ISBN 0 421 89500 4. Sweet & Maxwell.

Gooddie, Howard–Buying Bargains At Property Auctions. Paperback: £11.99. ISBN 1 904053 89 0. Law Pack Publishing.

Gray, Kevin J.; Gray, Susan Francis–Land Law. Core Texts S. Paperback: £16.99. ISBN 0 19 928445 8. Paperback: £16.99. ISBN 0 19 928445 8. Oxford University Press.

Hayden, Tim; Wilmott, Clarke–Licensing for Conveyancers: A Practical Guide. Paperback: £44.95. ISBN 1 85328 966 3. Law Society Publications.

Hewitson, Russell–Conveyancers' Yearbook. Paperback: £23.50. ISBN 0 7219 1567 1. Shaw & Sons.

Jacobus–Real Estate Law. Hardback: £17.99. ISBN 0 324 20176 1. South Western College Publishing.

James, Frances–Straightforward Guide to the Process of Conveyancing. Paperback: £9.99. ISBN 1 903909 72 4. Straightforward Publishing.

Jessell, C.–Farms and Estates. Paperback: £49.50. ISBN 0 85308 984 1. Jordans.

King, Harry–Knowing the Law in Spain: An Essential Guide for the British Property Owner, Resident or Long-term Visitor to Spain. Paperback: £12.99. ISBN 1 84528 059 8. How To Books.

Levy, Martyn–Leaseholders Handbook. Paperback: £8.99. ISBN 1 900694 28 X. Straightforward Publishing.

Megarry; Wade–Megarry & Wade: the Law of Real Property. Hardback: £165.00. ISBN 0 421 84100 1. Sweet & Maxwell.

Moran, Alan; Luther, Peter–Core Statutes on Property Law. Core Statutes S. Paperback: £10.00. ISBN 1 84641 010 X. Law Matters Publishing.

Nightingale, Paul–Lawyers Costs and Fees: Conveyancing Fees and Duties. Paperback: £17.95. ISBN 1 84592 070 8. Tottel Publishing.

Piggot Semple, Mike–Conveyancing. Law in a Box S. CD-ROM: £19.95. ISBN 1 904783 84 8. Semple Piggot Rochez (Legal Education Ltd).

Piggot, Mike Semple–Land Law. Law in a Box S., No. 7. CD-ROM: £19.95. ISBN 1 904783 63 5. Semple Piggot Rochez (Legal Education Ltd).

Property Transactions: Planning and Environment. Paperback: £79.00. ISBN 0 421 91760 1. Sweet & Maxwell.

Radevsky, Anthony; Greenish, Damian–Hague on Leasehold Enfranchisement: 1st Supplement. Paperback: £48.00. ISBN 0 421 90680 4. Sweet & Maxwell.

Rennie, Robert–Land Tenure and Tenements Legislation. Paperback: £36.00. ISBN 0 414 01613 0. W. Green & Son.

Salvesen, Magda; Cousineau, Diane–Artists' Estates: Reputations in Trust. Hardback: £23.50. ISBN 0 8135 3604 9. Rutgers University Press.

Scamell, Ernest H.–Butterworths Property Law Handbook. Paperback: £70.00. ISBN 1 4057 0207 9. Butterworths Law.

Scott, M.–Conveyancer's Fact Finder. Paperback: £14.99. ISBN 0 85308 965 5. Jordans.

Searl, David–You and Your Property in Spain: Your Essential Guide to Property Ownership and Rental. Paperback: £12.99. ISBN 84 89954 46 1. Santana Books, Spain.

Sherriff, Gerald–Sherriff: Service Charges for Leasehold, Freehold and Commonhold. Paperback: £80.00. ISBN 1 84592 120 8. Tottel Publishing.

Silverman, Frances–Conveyancing Handbook. Hardback: £79.95. ISBN 1 85328 928 0. Law Society Publications.

Smith, Roger J.–Property Law. Longman Law S. Paperback: £31.99. ISBN 1 4058 0114 X. Longman.

Swinton, Ken; Paisley, Roderick–Property. Law Basics S. Paperback: £12.50. ISBN 0 414 01373 5. W. Green & Son.

Thomas, Meryl–Statutes on Property Law. Blackstone's Statute Books. Paperback: £14.99. ISBN 0 19 928317 6. Paperback: £14.99. ISBN 0 19 928317 6. Oxford University Press.

Thomas, Michael–Stamp Duty Land Tax. Paperback: £75.00. ISBN 0 521 60632 2. Cambridge University Press.

Timothy, Patrick; Barker, Alison–Wontner's Guide to Land Registry Practice: Practitioner Series. Hardback: £75.00. ISBN 0 421 90040 7. Sweet & Maxwell.

Wade, Peter–Practical Guide to Residential Conveyancing. Emerald Home Lawyers S. Paperback: £9.99. ISBN 1 903909 60 0. Straightforward Publishing.

Webber, Gary; Dovar, Daniel–Residential Possession Proceedings. Paperback: £85.00. ISBN 0 421 91880 2. Sweet & Maxwell.

RESTITUTION

3442. Dispositions of property—Undue influence—Property transferred into joint name of sole owner and long term partner—Failure to obtain independent legal advice

The appellant (L) appealed against a decision not to restore to L her title in a property that had once been in her sole name. In the context of a long term relationship with the respondent (S), L had agreed to put the property into their joint names in return for S discharging the mortgage outstanding on the property. S paid off the remaining mortgage to the value of £5,000 (a small proportion of the value of the property) and had a deed of consent drawn up by his legal advisers. The deed of consent was sent to L with a letter advising her to obtain independent legal advice before signing the deed. The deed was in fact prejudicial to L's interests, in that inter alia it empowered S to force a sale, and she signed it without obtaining advice. S then sought to enforce the deed by selling the property and taking half of the profits thus depriving L of her property rights and home. L submitted that the reasoning of the district judge had been inadequate and that he had failed to identify and determine the key issue in the case, namely whether the deed of consent in which L gave up half her share in her home should be set aside because of undue influence.

Held, allowing the appeal, that L was in a position where she was putting her trust and confidence in S, *Royal Bank of Scotland Plc v. Etridge (No.2)* [2001] UKHL 44, [2002] 2 A.C. 773, [2001] C.L.Y. 4880 applied. The transaction was manifestly to the disadvantage of L and to the advantage of S. Theirs was a long term relationship and L had allowed S to provide legal advice. There was no doubt that this was the sort of case where on the facts a situation of possible undue influence arose. The test was not whether L knew what she was doing but rather why she was doing it and, on that basis, a presumption of undue influence arose that could not be rebutted. The transaction would be set aside and S's payment viewed as a loan that would be repaid by L to S with interest.

STEVENS v. NEWEY; *sub nom.* STEVENS v. LEEDER; LEEDER v. STEVENS, [2005} EWCA Civ 50, *The Times*, January 14, 2005, Jacob, L.J., CA (Civ Div).

3443. Fiduciary duty—Bribery—Secret commissions paid to employee—Contract price inflated to cover bribes

The claimant (M) and his holding companies (D) sought to hold the fifth defendant (K) accountable as constructive trustee for commission payments made by the first defendant (S) in connection with the procurement of contracts for the refurbishment of M's properties. K had been appointed as a properties and administration manager in M's private office and had been entrusted to deal with the refurbishment of several of M's properties. K negotiated design and refurbishment contracts with S and the second defendant company (B), which had been incorporated in the British Virgin Islands. It was agreed between K, S and B that K would receive a 10 per cent commission on each contract and that the contract price would be inflated so as to cover the commission payment. M had no knowledge of the commission payments made to K and the evidence showed that S had created B specifically to allow for the payment of the secret commissions to K. M argued that K was liable as a constructive trustee because he had been engaged under a contract of employment and the payment of secret commissions had been made in breach of his fiduciary duties; therefore a restitutionary remedy was appropriate so as to allow for the tracing of the proceeds of the bribes in the hands of recipients.

Held, giving judgment for the claimants, that it was clear that K had acted in breach of the fiduciary duties he owed to M and therefore a restitutionary remedy was justified. The contract prices had been increased by an amount equivalent to the monies paid to K. M and D had believed, as a consequence of a fraudulent misrepresentation made by S to which K had been a party, that the sums paid covered the cost of property refurbishment only, *Lister & Co v. Stubbs* (1890) L.R. 45 Ch. D. 1 distinguished and *Attorney General of Hong Kong v. Reid* [1994] 1 A.C. 324, [1994] C.L.Y. 2083 considered. (Obiter) Had the instant case not been distinguishable from *Lister*, the court would have applied the reasoning in *Reid* because there were powerful policy reasons for ensuring that a fiduciary did not retain gains made in breach of his duty, whether or not he was insolvent. *Reid* was a recent decision and it had been made by the Privy Council after hearing full argument on the correctness of *Lister*.

DARAYDAN HOLDINGS LTD v. SOLLAND INTERNATIONAL LTD, [2004] EWHC 622, [2005] Ch. 119, Lawrence Collins, J., Ch D.

3444. Proprietary rights–Bank accounts–Funds in frozen bank account–Application of rule in Clayton's Case [1814-23] All E.R. Rep.1

[Civil Procedure Rules 1998 (SI 1998 3132) Sch.1 Ord.17 r.3.]

The applicant bank (C) brought interpleader proceedings pursuant to the Civil Procedure Rules 1998 Sch.1 Ord.17 r.3 to determine its course of action regarding claims by apparently innocent claimants to funds in frozen accounts. The Financial Investigation Unit of the City of London Police had withdrawn consent for C to obey payment instructions from a Nigerian bank (M) in respect of two correspondent accounts suspected of connection with money laundering, and in particular, from dealing with monies in six transactions with a certain client. Funds in the accounts were mixed, and other, apparently innocent clients, some victims of suspected fraud, sought recovery of their money as interpleader claimants. The issues to be determined where whether each claimant had a proprietary right in the funds and not simply a debt due from M and how the funds were to be distributed as the claims exceeded the available funds.

Held, giving judgment accordingly, that on the balance of probabilities, the claimants had shown they had a proprietary right and not just a debt due from M. Most were entitled to trace monies on the basis of being defrauded, or because M was an actual or constructive trustee of their money. Even if M had not been a party to fraud, its state of knowledge made it unconscionable to retain the benefit of the monies' receipt, *Bank of Credit and Commerce International (Overseas) Ltd v. Akindele* [2001] Ch. 437, [2000] C.L.Y. 2315 applied. It was not clear whether a claimant who had made a payment into the accounts by mistake had a proprietary right, but where a claimant had made double payment at the request of M it would be unconscionable for M to retain the benefit, *Westdeutsche Landesbank Girozentrale v. Islington LBC* [1996] 5 Bank L.R. 341 applied. In instances where money had been paid for a purpose not fulfilled, M held it on trust for the payer. As the amount of the claims far exceeded the sums in the accounts the claimant beneficiaries would be paid pari passu, according to the amount of their contributions. It would be both impractical and unjust to apply the rule in *Clayton's Case* [1814-23] All E.R. Rep.1, *Clayton's Case* not followed. Because of the nature of a correspondent account there had been mixing and payment away of the money held on trust for the claimants but it would be extremely onerous, and perhaps impossible, to determine what sums M had paid away. To adopt the fiction of first in, first out would be to apportion a common misfortune through a test that bore no relation to the justice of the case, and that need only be applied when it was convenient and could do broad justice, *Barlow Clowes International Ltd (In Liquidation) v. Vaughan* [1992] 4 All E.R. 22, [1992] C.L.Y. 2050 applied.

COMMERZBANK AKTIENGESELLSCHAFT v. IMB MORGAN PLC, [2004] EWHC 2771, [2005] 2 All E.R. (Comm) 564, Lawrence Collins, J., Ch D.

3445. Books

Jones, Gareth–Goff and Jones: 1st Supplement: The Law of Restitution. Paperback: £55.00. ISBN 0 421 87390 6. Sweet & Maxwell.

Unjust Enrichment: Lawbasics. Paperback: £9.95. ISBN 0 414 01597 5. W. Green & Son.

ROAD TRAFFIC

3446. Bridges–Erewash Canal

DERBYSHIRE COUNTY COUNCIL (EREWASH CANAL BRIDGE) SCHEME 2003 CONFIRMATION INSTRUMENT 2005, SI 2005 1867; made under the Highways Act 1980 s.106. In force: in accordance with Art.1; £3.00.

This Instrument confirms the Derbyshire County Council (Erewash Canal Bridge) Scheme 2003.

3447. Bridges–Tolls–Severn Bridges

SEVERN BRIDGES TOLLS ORDER 2005, SI 2005 3461; made under the Severn Bridges Act 1992 s.9. In force: January 1, 2006; £3.00.

The Severn Bridges Act 1992 provides for the tolls for the use of the bridges to be fixed by annual orders made in December of each year. This Order revokes the Severn Bridges Tolls Order 2004 (SI 2004 4214) and fixes the tolls payable for use of the two bridges, commonly known as the Severn Bridge and the Second Severn Crossing, during the year 2006.

3448. Buses–Bus lane contraventions–Approved local authorities

BUS LANE CONTRAVENTIONS (APPROVED LOCAL AUTHORITIES) (ENGLAND) ORDER 2005, SI 2005 2755; made under the Transport Act 2000 s.144. In force: November 1, 2005; £3.00.

The Bus Lane Contraventions (Penalty Charges, Adjudication and Enforcement) (England) Regulations 2005 (SI 2005 2757) provide for the enforcement of bus lane restrictions through the imposition, by approved local authorities, of penalty charges in respect of contraventions of such restrictions. This Order specifies the authorities as approved local authorities for the purposes of the Transport Act 2000 s.144.

3449. Buses–Bus lane contraventions–Enforcement

BUS LANE CONTRAVENTIONS (PENALTY CHARGES, ADJUDICATION AND ENFORCEMENT) (ENGLAND) REGULATIONS 2005, SI 2005 2757; made under the Transport Act 2000 s.144, s.160. In force: November 1, 2005; £4.00.

These Regulations make provision for the enforcement of bus lane contraventions, by local authorities which are approved local authorities for the purposes of the Transport Act 2000 s.144. The names of the authorities concerned are set out in the Schedule to the Bus Lane Contraventions (Approved Local Authorities) (England) Order 2005 (SI 2005 2755).

3450. Buses–Bus lane contraventions–Penalty charges–Approved devices

BUS LANES (APPROVED DEVICES) (ENGLAND) ORDER 2005, SI 2005 2756; made under the Transport Act 2000 s.144, s.160. In force: November 1, 2005; £3.00.

The Bus Lane Contraventions (Penalty Charges, Adjudication and Enforcement) (England) Regulations 2005 (SI 2005 2757) provide for the imposition of penalty charges in respect of contraventions of bus lane restrictions in England. Those Regulations permit the imposition of penalty charges only on the basis of a record produced by an "approved device". This Order provides that a device which is of a description specified is an approved device in England. It provides that a specified device must also be type approved by the Secretary of State and used in compliance with any conditions subject to which the approval was given.

3451. Buses–Bus lane contraventions–Tribunals–Bus lane adjudicators

TRIBUNALS AND INQUIRIES (BUS LANE ADJUDICATORS) (ENGLAND) ORDER 2005, SI 2005 2758; made under the Tribunals and Inquiries Act 1992 s.13. In force: November 1, 2005; £3.00.

This Order amends the Tribunals and Inquiries Act 1992 so as to add bus lane adjudicators appointed in relation to England by virtue of regulations made under the Transport Act 2000 s.144 (civil penalties for bus lane contraventions) to the list of tribunals under the direct supervision of the Council on Tribunals.

3452. Congestion charges–Payments–Wrong vehicle registration number supplied–Adjudicator's discretion to cancel penalty charge

[Human Rights Act 1998 Sch.1 Part I Art.6; Greater London (Central Zone) Congestion Charging Order 2001 Art.6; Road User Charging (Enforcement and Adjudication) (London) Regulations 2001 (SI 2001 2313) Reg.13(3)(b), Reg.16.]

The claimant (W) sought judicial review of the defendant adjudicator's decision to dismiss her appeal against two penalty charges imposed following her alleged failure to pay congestion charges pursuant to the Central London Congestion Charge Scheme contained in the Greater London (Central Zone) Congestion Charging Order 2001. W had used her car on two separate days within the charging area of the scheme. She had paid the charge on both days using the internet but made an error in specifying the registration number of her car. W's appeal against the penalty charges, which had taken eight months to be heard, was rejected as was a subsequent review. W submitted that (1) the adjudicator had incorrectly applied the provisions of the scheme: she had paid the congestion charge in respect of both of the dates in question and therefore she should not have been penalised as the licence was payable for and specific to a vehicle, not a registration number; (2) the adjudicator, in the exercise of his discretion under the Road User Charging (Enforcement and Adjudication) (London) Regulations 2001, should have allowed her appeal.

Held, granting the application, that (1) it was difficult to envisage a charging scheme not being registration number specific as only by identifying particular vehicles by their registration mark could a charging authority know when a contravention had occurred. The licence that W had purchased was for a single vehicle having the registration number that she had specified when she had purchased the ticket. The vehicle that she had driven had a different registration mark. Any other interpretation of Art.6 of the 2001 Order would have rendered the scheme unworkable. (2) The Regulations conferred a discretion on the adjudicator in cases such as the instant case. After considering W's representations on the ground set out in Reg.13(3)(b) of the Regulations, the adjudicator was entitled under Reg.16(2) to "give the charging authority...such directions as he [considered] appropriate". Given the mitigating circumstances, he might reasonably have considered it appropriate to direct that the penalty charge notice be cancelled even though the ground had not formally been established. Interpreting Reg.16 so as to confer a discretion on the adjudicator had the effect of reconciling the provisions of the scheme as a whole with its purposes, which were to ensure that charges were paid for cars that entered the zone and that those who failed to pay were penalised. It was not a purpose of the scheme to penalise those who made a genuine error as to their vehicle's registration number. It was open to the adjudicator to direct that the penalty notices served on W should be cancelled. There was good reason to do so and therefore the decision was quashed. (3) There had been a breach of W's rights under the Human Rights Act 1998 Sch.1 Part I Art.6 as the time taken to determine her appeal was unreasonably long. However, W had suffered no significant or discernible loss as a result of the delay in the determination of her appeal. Therefore, she was not entitled to a remedy under Art.6.

R. (ON THE APPLICATION OF WALMSLEY) v. LANE, [2005] EWHC 896, [2005] R.T.R. 28, Stanley Burnton, J., QBD (Admin Ct).

3453. Crime prevention–Highways–Designated areas

CRIME PREVENTION (DESIGNATED AREAS) (NO.3) ORDER 2005, SI 2005 2463; made under the Highways Act 1980 s.118B. In force: September 27, 2005; £3.00.

The Highways Act 1980 enables a council (which is a highway authority), for the purposes of crime prevention, to make orders for the stopping up or diversion of certain highways within areas designated by the Secretary of State under s.118B(1)(a) of the 1980 Act. This Order designates an area within the district of North Lincolnshire Council.

3454. Heavy goods vehicles–Operators licences–Loss of good repute–Burden of proof

[Goods Vehicles (Licensing of Operators) Act 1995 s.13, s.26, s.27; Council Directive 96/26 Art.6.]

The appellant company (M) and two directors (D1, D2) appealed against the decision of the transport tribunal revoking M's operator's licence under the Goods Vehicles (Licensing of Operators) Act 1995 s.26 and s.27 and disqualifying M and D1 and D2 from holding operator's licences for five years. D1 and D2 were mother and daughter. D2 was the owner of M. D2's husband was the transport manager of M. After complaints of fly tipping the traffic commissioner held a public inquiry to consider the revocation of M's licence. D1 and D2 did not attend the inquiry. D2's husband did attend and made representations. The commissioner revoked M's licence because it had failed to demonstrate its financial standing and had lost its good repute, determined that the husband had lost his good repute and disqualified the appellants from holding operator's licences. The transport tribunal dismissed the appellants' appeal. The appellants submitted that the traffic commissioner had erred in (1) not adjourning the hearing to allow M to appear; (2) not permitting D2's husband to represent M; (3) holding that the burden lay on M to satisfy him not to revoke M's licence.

Held, allowing the appeal, that (1) in all the circumstances the commissioner was plainly entitled to proceed in the absence of M on the basis that it had received proper notice and had chosen not to attend or had taken the risk that D2's husband would be permitted to represent it. (2) The commissioner should have permitted D2's husband to represent M but in the circumstances there was no further assistance that M could have provided to the commissioner which would have made any difference to the commissioner's decisions. The commissioner was well aware of the distinction between M and its transport manager. But in the instant case, as the commissioner held, D2's husband was the true controller of the company and the loss of his good repute entailed the loss of the company's good repute. The commissioner had been entitled to conclude either that D1 and D2 were complicit in the husband's activities or that they had abdicated their responsibilities. By finding the facts concerning M's operations and by finding on the balance of probabilities that D2's husband controlled M, the commissioner had met any burden that rested on him to be satisfied as to the loss of good repute of D2's husband and therefore also of M. The loss of good repute meant that M's licence had to be revoked under s.27. M's appeal was dismissed. (3) The applicant for a licence bore the burden under s.13 of the 1995 Act of satisfying the commissioner that it fulfilled the relevant requirements but the language of s.27 was different. The Act implemented Council Directive 96/26 and Art.6 of the Directive provided for revocation of licences if the competent authorities established that the relevant conditions of good repute, financial standing and professional competence were no longer satisfied. Accordingly for revocation to be possible under s.26 or mandatory under s.27 it was the commissioner who had to be satisfied of the ground of revocation and not the licence holder who had to satisfy him to the contrary. (4) The commissioner had failed to carry out a proper balancing exercise before disqualifying D1 and D2 because had they been represented there might have been something which could have been said on their behalf if they had been ignorant of M's activities. The decision to disqualify D1 and D2 was quashed and the matter of their disqualification remitted to the commissioner for reconsideration in the light of any representations which they might wish to make.

MUCK IT LTD v. SECRETARY OF STATE FOR TRANSPORT; *sub nom.* TRAFFIC COMMISSIONER v. MUCK IT LTD, [2005] EWCA Civ 1124, [2006] R.T.R. 919, Tuckey, L.J., CA (Civ Div).

3455. **International carriage by road–Carriers liabilities–Loss of consignment– Effect of restriction in carrier's standard terms**

[Carriage of Goods by Road Act 1965 Sch.1 Art.17.1, Art.17.2, Art.23.]

The claimants (D and B), consignor and consignee, sought damages for breach of contract against the defendant carriers (U). D's distribution agents had arranged for U to carry computer processors from D's warehouse in the United Kingdom to B's agents in Holland. The consignment comprised three packages. Although U's standard terms of contract restricted the value of any consignment to $50,000, it was not disputed that each of the packages contained goods worth considerably more than that sum. The goods were collected by one of U's drivers. D and B claimed that the goods never arrived and alleged that the goods were stolen by U's employees. They asserted that the carriage of the goods was subject to the Convention on the Contract for the International Carriage of Goods by Road, as set out in the Carriage of Goods by Road Act 1965 Sch.1. D and B argued that (1) U's liability under Sch.1 Art.17.1, for the loss of the goods, was not limited by Art.23 as the loss was caused by the "wilful misconduct" on the part of the servants of U acting within the scope of their employment; (2) the parties' conduct of their business and exchanges evinced an intention that the $50,000 restriction should not be incorporated into the contract of carriage. Alternatively, U had waived reliance on the restriction as it was aware that D's consignments included packages valued over the restricted amount. U argued that the loss was caused by D's own wrong because, but for their breach of contract in presenting packages worth more than $50,000, the packages would not have come into U's possession and would not have been lost in transit. U further argued that it was relieved of liability under Art.17.2 as the loss was due to the "wrongful act" of D.

Held, giving judgment for D and B, that (1) on the evidence, the goods were not delivered to B. When applying the provisions of an international convention, the court should not adopt anything other than a properly rigorous approach to such evidence as was available before it made findings of fact on which a determination of wilful misconduct was based, *Laceys (Wholesale) Footwear Ltd v. Bowler International Freight Ltd* [1997] 2 Lloyd's Rep. 369, [1997] C.L.Y. 4287 applied. It was too speculative to hold that the goods were taken by or with the assistance of an employee of U as there was no sufficient evidence to support that theory. Accordingly D and B had not discharged their burden of proving on the balance of probabilities that their loss resulted from theft to which an employee of U was party. (2) The parties' conduct of their business and exchanges did not evince an intention that the $50,000 restriction should not be incorporated into the contract of carriage nor did U waive the restriction by its conduct. However, U's standard terms did not provide that there would be no contract of carriage if a package over the restricted value was presented and accepted. Unless U exercised its right to refuse to carry the packages, which it did not, there was a contract that U would carry the packages. (3) The $50,000 restriction was an express contractual provision with consequences for not complying with it. There was no necessity or requirement to imply such a warranty term in order to give business efficacy to the arrangement between the parties, and it would have been contrary to the intention of the parties expressed in the standard terms for such a warranty to be implied. (4) It was not a "wrongful act" within the meaning of Art.17.2 for D to have consigned packages worth more than $50,000 to U. U's argument did not identify a sufficient causal connection between the loss and D's wrongful act. The loss was not caused by the fact that the packages came into U's possession for carriage by it. The claim therefore succeeded but the damages were limited under Art.23.

DATEC ELECTRONIC HOLDINGS LTD v. UNITED PARCELS SERVICE LTD, [2005] EWHC 221, [2005] 1 Lloyd's Rep. 470, Andrew Smith, J., QBD (Comm).

3456. Motorways—Hard shoulder

M42 (JUNCTIONS 3A TO 7) (ACTIVELY MANAGED HARD SHOULDER AND VARIABLE SPEED LIMITS) REGULATIONS 2005, SI 2005 1671; made under the Road Traffic Regulation Act 1984 s.17. In force: July 27, 2005; £3.00.

These Regulations modify the Motorways Traffic (England and Wales) Regulations 1982 (SI 1982 1163) in respect of the M42 Motorway, Junctions 3A to 7 and the adjoining slip roads. The Regulations introduce variable speed limits and create the concept of an "actively managed hard shoulder", which is a section of hard shoulder which may, in certain circumstances, be driven on.

3457. Motorways—Speed limits—M275 and M27

M275 AND M27 MOTORWAY (SPEED LIMIT) REGULATIONS 2005, SI 2005 1999; made under the Road Traffic Regulation Act 1984 s.17. In force: August 12, 2005; £3.00.

These Regulations impose speed limits of 50 mph and 60 mph on specified lengths of the M275 Motorway and specified slip roads of it and the M27 Motorway at Portsmouth. It replaces the existing 70 mph speed limit imposed by the Motorways Traffic (Speed Limit) Regulations 1974 (SI 1974 502).

3458. Operators licences—Revocation—Transport manager with ineffective control of operations—Proportionality of disqualification

[Goods Vehicles (Licensing of Operators) Act 1995 s.27(1), s.58(1), Sch.3 para.8(2).]

The appellant haulage companies (T) appealed against a decision of the Transport Tribunal to uphold the revocation under the Goods Vehicles (Licensing of Operators) Act 1995 s.27(1) of their standard international operator's licences and against the decision to disqualify the largest company indefinitely. T were controlled by one operator and had the same transport manager. Following an application to increase its vehicle authorisation T were called to a public inquiry. The transport commissioner found the transport manager's control of operations to be ineffective under s.58 of the Act and revoked the licences. The tribunal found that the transport manager had been divested of certain transport management functions and that control of the vehicles and drivers was largely undertaken by the operators. T argued that (1) there was nothing in the Act which required the transport manager to carry out the management of transport operations himself; (2) the definition in s.58(1) allowed the transport manager to discharge his duties either by himself or with others; (3) the findings of the commissioner and the tribunal did not justify the order made and revocation of their licences was disproportionate.

Held, allowing the appeal in part, that (1) Sched.3 para.8(2) of the Act provided that a company had to employ a transport manager with the relevant qualifications. If a company failed to meet that requirement its application for a licence would fail or its licence would be revoked. Given the finding that T had no transport manager, the decision to revoke could not be faulted. (2) By virtue of s.58(1) a transport manager was required to have "continuous and effective responsibility" for the management of the transport operations. Someone who did not have such continuous and effective responsibility was not, for those purposes, a transport manager. A transport manager could use other staff to help him fulfil his duties but he had to be the responsible person within the company. T's transport manager was not responsible for the transport management functions discharged by a superior colleague. As such the finding that T had no transport manager was fully justified. (3) Given that T had failed to meet a core requirement of the Act it was entirely proportionate to revoke their licences. However, where disqualification was contemplated the licence holder had to be able to see that a proper balancing exercise had been carried out by the traffic commissioner, *Crompton (t/a David Crompton Haulage) v. Department of Transport North Western Area* [2003] EWCA Civ 64, [2003] R.T.R. 34, [2003] C.L.Y. 4413 considered and *Bryan Haulage Ltd v. Vehicle Inspectorate (No.1)* Unreported, June 25, 2002 approved. In the instant case, that balancing exercise was not evident.

ANGLOROM TRANS (UK) LTD, *Re; sub nom.* PARAMOUNT KITCHENS LTD, *Re,* [2004] EWCA Civ 998, [2005] R.T.R. 6, Pill, L.J., CA.

3459. Parking–Harbours–Local authority powers–Use of harbour legislation for parking control

[Harbours Act 1964 s.14, s.44(3), Sch.2 para.3(c); Human Rights Act 1998 Sch.1 Part II Art.1.]

The appellant resident (R) appealed against a decision ([2003] EWHC 2532, (2003) 100(40) L.S.G. 32) that the respondent local authority (P) had been entitled to use powers conferred for harbour management purposes in order to control the parking of vehicles nearby. P had passed directions pursuant to 1995 by laws, which had been made pursuant to a 1975 harbour revision order, which in turn had been made pursuant to the Harbours Act 1964 s.14. The issue was whether P had acted lawfully within the powers derived from s.14 and Sch.2 para.3(c) of the Act in adopting the directions controlling parking of vehicles in so far as they had extended to controlling parking at a raised terrace outside R's house, which was near a harbour. R submitted that (1) P had adopted the directions primarily, not for harbour operational purposes, but for the legally improper purposes of alleviating traffic congestion and improving pedestrian safety in the town centre; (2) by adopting the directions in respect of his property, which was not a highway, P had breached his private property rights under the Human Rights Act 1998 Sch.1 Part II Art.1. P contended that fresh evidence would show that the words "town centre" included areas along and inland from the harbour shore.

Held, allowing the appeal, that (1) P's stated reason that the directions had been adopted because of concern about traffic in "the town centre" was too broad to justify the argument that the primary reason for the directions was based on harbour operational considerations. (2) P had failed to give proper consideration to the possibility that the adoption of the directions might invade a property right of R without adequate justification and without compensation. (3) Credible and authoritative evidence was admissible only to explain or resolve any ambiguity in the reasons for a decision to adopt the directions, *Breen v. Amalgamated Engineering Union* [1971] 2 Q.B. 175, [1971] C.L.Y. 11754 and *R. v. Westminster City Council, ex p. Ermakov* [1996] 2 All E.R. 302, [1995] C.L.Y. 2568 applied. It would not be appropriate to admit the fresh evidence relied on by P where the stated reasons for recommending and adopting the directions were ultra vires. (4) For what were ultimately constitutional reasons, it might be said that a preclusive provision such as s.44(3) of the 1964 Act should be read as narrowly as possible. Assuming that it did preclude judicial review of the 1975 harbour revision order, it might not necessarily preclude judicial review of instruments made under that order, *R. v. Secretary of State for the Environment, ex p. Ostler* [1977] Q.B. 122, [1976] C.L.Y. 19 and *R. v. Cornwall CC, ex p. Huntington* [1994] 1 All E.R. 694, [1994] C.L.Y. 65 considered.

R. (ON THE APPLICATION OF RICHARDS) v. PEMBROKESHIRE CC, [2004] EWCA Civ 1000, [2005] B.L.G.R. 105, Dame Elizabeth Butler-Sloss (President), CA (Civ Div).

3460. Parking–Special parking areas–Barnsley

ROAD TRAFFIC (PERMITTED PARKING AREA AND SPECIAL PARKING AREA) (METROPOLITAN BOROUGH OF BARNSLEY) ORDER 2005, SI 2005 1385; made under the Road Traffic Act 1991 Sch.3 para.1, Sch.3 para.2, Sch.3 para.3. In force: July 4, 2005; £3.00.

This Order designates the metropolitan borough of Barnsley, other than the excepted roads, as both a permitted parking area and a special parking area in accordance with the Road Traffic Act 1991. It also applies with modifications various provisions of that Act to the designated area and modifies the Road Traffic Regulation Act 1984 in relation to the designated area.

3461. Parking – Special parking areas – Broxbourne

ROAD TRAFFIC (PERMITTED PARKING AREA AND SPECIAL PARKING AREA) (COUNTY OF HERTFORDSHIRE) (BOROUGH OF BROXBOURNE) ORDER 2005, SI 2005 405; made under the Road Traffic Act 1991 Sch.3 para.1, Sch.3 para.2, Sch.3 para.3. In force: May 9, 2005; £3.00.

This Order applies to the whole of the borough of Broxbourne, except the road specified. It designates the borough of Broxbourne, other than the excepted roads, as both a permitted parking area and a special parking area in accordance with the Road Traffic Act 1991. It also applies with modifications various provisions of that Act to the designated area and modifies the Road Traffic Regulation Act 1984 in relation to the designated area.

3462. Parking – Special parking areas – Chiltern

ROAD TRAFFIC (PERMITTED PARKING AREA AND SPECIAL PARKING AREA) (COUNTY OF BUCKINGHAMSHIRE) (DISTRICT OF CHILTERN) ORDER 2005, SI 2005 2151; made under the Road Traffic Act 1991 Sch.3 para.1, Sch.3 para.2, Sch.3 para.3. In force: September 1, 2005; £3.00.

This Order applies to the whole of the district of Chiltern with the exception of the roads specified. The Order designates the district of Chiltern, other than the excepted roads, as both a permitted parking area and a special parking area in accordance with the Road Traffic Act 1991. It also applies with modifications various provisions of that Act to the designated area and modifies the Road Traffic Regulation Act 1984 in relation to the designated area.

3463. Parking – Special parking areas – Coventry

ROAD TRAFFIC (PERMITTED PARKING AREA AND SPECIAL PARKING AREA) (CITY OF COVENTRY) ORDER 2005, SI 2005 378; made under the Road Traffic Act 1991 Sch.3 para.1, Sch.3 para.2, Sch.3 para.3. In force: April 4, 2005; £3.00.

The Order designates the City of Coventry, other than the excepted roads, as both a permitted parking area and a special parking area in accordance with the Road Traffic Act 1991. It also applies with modifications various provisions of that Act to the designated area and modifies the Road Traffic Regulation Act 1984 in relation to the designated area.

3464. Parking – Special parking areas – Doncaster

ROAD TRAFFIC (PERMITTED PARKING AREA AND SPECIAL PARKING AREA) (METROPOLITAN BOROUGH OF DONCASTER) ORDER 2005, SI 2005 1383; made under the Road Traffic Act 1991 Sch.3 para.1, Sch.3 para.2, Sch.3 para.3. In force: July 4, 2005; £3.00.

This Order designates the metropolitan borough of Doncaster, other than the excepted roads, as both a permitted parking area and a special parking area in accordance with the Road Traffic Act 1991. It also applies with modifications various provisions of that Act to the designated area and modifies the Road Traffic Regulation Act 1984 in relation to the designated area.

3465. Parking – Special parking areas – Elmbridge

ROAD TRAFFIC (PERMITTED PARKING AREA AND SPECIAL PARKING AREA) (COUNTY OF SURREY) (BOROUGH OF ELMBRIDGE) ORDER 2005, SI 2005

3407; made under the Road Traffic Act 1991 Sch.3 para.1, Sch.3 para.2, Sch.3 para.3. In force: January 9, 2006; £3.00.

This Order applies to the whole of the borough of Elmbridge, except the roads specified. The Order designates the borough of Elmbridge, other than the excepted roads, as both a permitted parking area and a special parking area in accordance with Schedule 3 to the Road Traffic Act 1991. It also applies with modifications various provisions of that Act to the designated area and modifies the Road Traffic Regulation Act 1984 in relation to the designated area.

3466. Parking–Special parking areas–Epsom and Ewell

ROAD TRAFFIC (PERMITTED PARKING AREA AND SPECIAL PARKING AREA) (COUNTY OF SURREY) (BOROUGH OF EPSOM AND EWELL) ORDER 2005, SI 2005 388; made under the Road Traffic Act 1991 Sch.3 para.1, Sch.3 para.2, Sch.3 para.3. In force: April 4, 2005; £3.00.

The Order designates the borough of Epsom and Ewell as both a permitted parking area and a special parking area in accordance with the Road Traffic Act 1991. It also applies with modifications various provisions of that Act to the designated area and modifies the Road Traffic Regulation Act 1984 in relation to the designated area.

3467. Parking–Special parking areas–Hartlepool

ROAD TRAFFIC (PERMITTED PARKING AREA AND SPECIAL PARKING AREA) (BOROUGH OF HARTLEPOOL) ORDER 2005, SI 2005 1438; made under the Road Traffic Act 1991 Sch.3 para.1, Sch.3 para.2, Sch.3 para.3. In force: July 4, 2005; £3.00.

This Order designates the metropolitan borough of Hartlepool, other than the excepted roads, as both a permitted parking area and a special parking area in accordance with the Road Traffic Act 1991. It also applies with modifications various provisions of that Act to the designated area and modifies the Road Traffic Regulation Act 1984 in relation to the designated area.

3468. Parking–Special parking areas–Havant

ROAD TRAFFIC (PERMITTED PARKING AREA AND SPECIAL PARKING AREA) (COUNTY OF HAMPSHIRE) (BOROUGH OF HAVANT) ORDER 2005, SI 2005 233; made under the Road Traffic Act 1991 Sch.3 para.1, Sch.3 para.2, Sch.3 para.3. In force: April 4, 2005; £3.00.

The Order designates the borough of Havant, other than the excepted roads, as both a permitted parking area and a special parking area in accordance with Sch.3 to the Road Traffic Act 1991. It also applies with modifications various provisions of Part II of the 1991 Act to the designated area and modifies the Road Traffic Regulation Act 1984 in relation to the designated area.

3469. Parking–Special parking areas–Horsham

ROAD TRAFFIC (PERMITTED PARKING AREA AND SPECIAL PARKING AREA) (COUNTY OF WEST SUSSEX) (DISTRICT OF HORSHAM) ORDER 2005, SI 2005 3492; made under the Road Traffic Act 1991 Sch.3 para.1, Sch.3 para.21, Sch.3 para.3. In force: January 23, 2006; £3.00.

The Order designates the district of Horsham as both a permitted parking area and a special parking area in accordance with sch.3 to the Road Traffic Act 1991. It also applies with modifications various provisions of Part II of that Act to the designated area and modifies the Road Traffic Regulation Act 1984 in relation to the designated area.

3470. Parking–Special parking areas–Ipswich

ROAD TRAFFIC (PERMITTED PARKING AREA AND SPECIAL PARKING AREA) (COUNTY OF SUFFOLK) (BOROUGH OF IPSWICH) ORDER 2005, SI 2005 2362;

made under the Road Traffic Act 1991 Sch.3 para.1, Sch.3 para.2, Sch.3 para.3. In force: October 1, 2005; £3.00.

This Order designates the borough of Ipswich, other than the A14, and other roads to which it applies as both a permitted parking area and a special parking area in accordance with the Road Traffic Act 1991. It also applies with modifications various provisions of that Act to the designated area and modifies the Road Traffic Regulation Act 1984 in relation to the designated area.

3471. Parking–Special parking areas–Leeds

ROAD TRAFFIC (PERMITTED PARKING AREA AND SPECIAL PARKING AREA) (METROPOLITAN DISTRICT OF LEEDS) ORDER 2005, SI 2005 95; made under the Road Traffic Act 1991 Sch.3 para.1, Sch.3 para.2, Sch.3 para.3. In force: March 1, 2005; £3.00.

This Order designates the metropolitan district of Leeds, other than the excepted roads, as both a permitted parking area and a special parking area in accordance with the Road Traffic Act 1991 Sch.3. It also applies with modifications various provisions of Part II of that Act to the designated area and modifies the Road Traffic Regulation Act 1984 in relation to the designated area.

3472. Parking–Special parking areas–Mid Sussex

ROAD TRAFFIC (PERMITTED PARKING AREA AND SPECIAL PARKING AREA) (COUNTY OF WEST SUSSEX) (DISTRICT OF MID SUSSEX) ORDER 2005, SI 2005 3494; made under the Road Traffic Act 1991 Sch.3 para.1, Sch.3 para.2, Sch.3 para.3. In force: January 23, 2006; £3.00.

The Order designates the district of Mid Sussex, other than the excepted roads, as both a permitted parking area and a special parking area in accordance with the Road Traffic Act 1991 Sch.3. It also applies with modifications various provisions of Part II of that Act to the designated area and modifies the Road Traffic Regulation Act 1984 in relation to the designated area.

3473. Parking–Special parking areas–New Forest

ROAD TRAFFIC (PERMITTED PARKING AREA AND SPECIAL PARKING AREA) (COUNTY OF HAMPSHIRE) (DISTRICT OF NEW FOREST) ORDER 2005, SI 2005 3295; made under the Road Traffic Act 1991 Sch.3 para.1, Sch.3 para.2, Sch.3 para.3. In force: January 1, 2006; £3.00.

This Order, which applies to the whole of the District of New Forest, designates the District of New Forest, other than the excepted roads, as both a permitted parking area and a special parking area in accordance with the Road Traffic Act 1991. It also applies with modifications various provisions of Part II of that Act to the designated area and modifies the Road Traffic Regulation Act 1984 in relation to the designated area.

3474. Parking–Special parking areas–Rotherham

ROAD TRAFFIC (PERMITTED PARKING AREA AND SPECIAL PARKING AREA) (METROPOLITAN BOROUGH OF ROTHERHAM) ORDER 2005, SI 2005 1384; made under the Road Traffic Act 1991 Sch.3 para.1, Sch.3 para.2, Sch.3 para.3. In force: July 4, 2005; £3.00.

This Order designates the metropolitan borough of Rotherham, other than the excepted roads, as both a permitted parking area and a special parking area in accordance with the Road Traffic Act 1991. It also applies with modifications various provisions of that Act to the designated area and modifies the Road Traffic Regulation Act 1984 in relation to the designated area.

3475. Parking–Special parking areas–Sheffield

ROAD TRAFFIC (PERMITTED PARKING AREA AND SPECIAL PARKING AREA) (CITY OF SHEFFIELD) ORDER 2005, SI 2005 194; made under the Road Traffic Act 1991 Sch.3 para.1, Sch.3 para.2, Sch.3 para.3. In force: April 4, 2005; £3.00.

The Order designates the city of Sheffield, other than the excepted roads, as both a permitted parking area and a special parking area in accordance with the Road Traffic Act 1991 Sch.3. It also applies with modifications various provisions of Part II of the 1991 Act to the designated area and modifies the Road Traffic Regulation Act 1984 in relation to the designated area.

3476. Parking–Special parking areas–Spelthorne

ROAD TRAFFIC (PERMITTED PARKING AREA AND SPECIAL PARKING AREA) (COUNTY OF SURREY) (BOROUGH OF SPELTHORNE) ORDER 2005, SI 2005 403; made under the Road Traffic Act 1991 Sch.3 para.1, Sch.3 para.2, Sch.3 para.3. In force: April 4, 2005; £3.00.

This Order applies to the whole of the borough of Spelthorne, except the roads specified. It designates the borough of Spelthorne, other than the excepted roads, as both a permitted parking area and a special parking area in accordance with the Road Traffic Act 1991. It also applies with modifications various provisions of Part II of that Act to the designated area and modifies the Road Traffic Regulation Act 1984 in relation to the designated area.

3477. Parking–Special parking areas–Stevenage

ROAD TRAFFIC (PERMITTED PARKING AREA AND SPECIAL PARKING AREA) (COUNTY OF HERTFORDSHIRE) (BOROUGH OF STEVENAGE) ORDER 2005, SI 2005 452; made under the Road Traffic Act 1991 Sch.3 para.1, Sch.3 para.2, Sch.3 para.3. In force: June 1, 2005; £3.00.

The Order designates the borough of Stevenage, as both a permitted parking area and a special parking area in accordance with the Road Traffic Act 1991. It also applies with modifications various provisions of that Act to the designated area and modifies the Road Traffic Regulation Act 1984 in relation to the designated area.

3478. Parking–Special parking areas–Stockport

ROAD TRAFFIC (PERMITTED PARKING AREA AND SPECIAL PARKING AREA) (METROPOLITAN BOROUGH OF STOCKPORT) ORDER 2005, SI 2005 81; made under the Road Traffic Act 1991 Sch.3 para.1, Sch.3 para.2, Sch.3 para.3. In force: April 4, 2005; £3.00.

This Order applies to the whole of the metropolitan borough of Stockport, except the roads specified. The Order designates the metropolitan borough of Stockport, other than the excepted roads, as both a permitted parking area and a special parking area in accordance with the Road Traffic Act 1991. It also applies with modifications various provisions of Part II of that Act to the designated area and modifies the Road Traffic Regulation Act 1984 in relation to the designated area.

3479. Parking–Special parking areas–Thurrock

ROAD TRAFFIC (PERMITTED PARKING AREA AND SPECIAL PARKING AREA) (BOROUGH OF THURROCK) ORDER 2005, SI 2005 370; made under the Road Traffic Act 1991 Sch.3 para.1, Sch.3 para.2, Sch.3 para.3. In force: April 1, 2005; £3.00.

The Order designates the borough of Thurrock, other than the excepted roads and area, as both a permitted parking area and a special parking area in accordance with the Road Traffic Act 1991. It also applies with modifications various provisions of that Act to the designated area and modifies the Road Traffic Regulation Act 1984 in relation to the designated area.

3480. Parking–Special parking areas–Torbay

ROAD TRAFFIC (PERMITTED PARKING AREA AND SPECIAL PARKING AREA) (BOROUGH OF TORBAY) ORDER 2005, SI 2005 387; made under the Road Traffic Act 1991 Sch.3 para.1, Sch.3 para.2, Sch.3 para.3. In force: April 4, 2005; £3.00.

The Order designates the borough of Torbay as both a permitted parking area and a special parking area in accordance with the Road Traffic Act 1991. It also applies with modifications various provisions of that Act to the designated area and modifies the Road Traffic Regulation Act 1984 in relation to the designated area.

3481. Parking–Special parking areas–Welwyn Hatfield

ROAD TRAFFIC (PERMITTED PARKING AREA AND SPECIAL PARKING AREA) (COUNTY OF HERTFORDSHIRE) (DISTRICT OF WELWYN HATFIELD) ORDER 2005, SI 2005 779; made under the Road Traffic Act 1991 Sch.3 para.1, Sch.3 para.2, Sch.3 para.3. In force: June 1, 2005; £3.00.

The Order designates the district of Welwyn Hatfield as both a permitted parking area and a special parking area in accordance with the Road Traffic Act 1991. It also applies with modifications various provisions of that Act to the designated area and modifies the Road Traffic Regulation Act 1984 in relation to the designated area.

3482. Road safety–Traffic signs

TRAFFIC SIGNS (AMENDMENT) REGULATIONS AND GENERAL DIRECTIONS 2005, SI 2005 1670; made under the Road Traffic Regulation Act 1984 s.64, s.65. In force: July 27, 2005; £4.00.

This Instrument amends the Traffic Signs Regulations and General Directions 2002 (SI 2002 3113) so as to enable certain traffic signs to be used to convey information, requirements, prohibitions or restrictions applying to an actively managed hard shoulder of a motorway.

3483. Road traffic regulation–Speed limits–Extent of statutory power to imposed restricted road status

[Road Traffic Regulation Act 1984 s.82(1)(a), s.82(2)(a), s.82(2)(b), s.84(1).]

The appellant DPP appealed by way of case stated against a decision to acquit the respondent (E) of driving on a restricted road in excess of the 30 mph speed limit. The road had speed restriction signs and had purportedly been designated a restricted road by orders made under the Road Traffic Regulation Act 1984 s.82(2)(b). The road did not conform to the definition of a restricted road in s.82(1)(a) in that it did not have the requisite system of street lighting. E argued that such a road could only lawfully be made subject to a 30 mph speed limit by use of the power conferred by s.84(1), the power under s.82(2)(b) being limited to reversing the derestriction of a road under s.82(2)(a).

Held, allowing the appeal, that s.82(2)(b) could be used to impose restricted status and therefore a 30 mph speed limit on a road without a system of lighting as defined in s.82(1)(a). The wording of s.82(2)(b) was clear and unambiguous and, although that subsection and s.84(1)(a) overlapped, there was no inconsistency and no reason to restrict the powers under either subsection. The power under s.82(2)(b) was plainly not restricted to cases where the local authority sought to reverse an earlier decision under s.82(2)(a).

DPP v. EVANS, [2004] EWHC 2785, (2005) 169 J.P. 237, Laws, L.J., QBD (Admin).

3484. Road works–Form of records–Wales

STREET WORKS (RECORDS) (WALES) REGULATIONS 2005, SI 2005 1812 (W.142); made under the New Roads and Street Works Act 1991 s.79, s.104. In force: December 1, 2005; £3.00.

These Regulations prescribe the form of records of apparatus placed in streets to be kept by undertakers. They provide that such records must be in the form of a location or route map or a statement of co-ordinates and may be either on paper or in the form of an electronic record or a combination of both. They also make provisions on the use of electronic records and prescribe exceptions to the duty to keep a record in certain cases.

3485.   Road works–Recovery of costs–Wales

STREET WORKS (RECOVERY OF COSTS) (WALES) REGULATIONS 2005, SI 2005 1810 (W.141); made under the New Roads and Street Works Act 1991 s.96, s.104. In force: July 8, 2005; £3.00.

These Regulations prescribe the basis for calculating the costs or expenses which an authority, body or person may recover under the New Roads and Street Works Act 1991 Part III.

3486.   Road works–Sharing of costs–Wales

STREET WORKS (SHARING OF COSTS OF WORKS) (WALES) REGULATIONS 2005, SI 2005 1721 (W.133); made under the New Roads and Street Works Act 1991 s.85, s.104. In force: July 1, 2005; £3.00.

These Regulations replace and revoke the Street Works (Sharing of Costs of Works) Regulations 1992 (SI 1992 1690) which make provision for the sharing of costs between the highway, bridge or transport authority and the undertaker where the undertaker's apparatus in a street is affected by major highway, bridge or transport works and measures are required to protect that apparatus. The principal change effected by the Regulations is that the undertaker's share of the costs of diversionary works required in the case of certain major transport works is now 7.5 per cent rather than the 18 per cent provided for by the 1992 Regulations.

3487.   Roads–Strategic roads–Designation

TRAFFIC MANAGEMENT (STRATEGIC ROADS IN GREATER LONDON) DESIGNATION ORDER 2005, SI 2005 476; made under the Traffic Management Act 2004 s.60. In force: April 7, 2005; £3.50.

The Traffic Management Act 2004 enables the Secretary of State to designate roads and proposed roads in Greater London, other than roads for which the Secretary of State or Transport for London is the traffic authority, as strategic roads for the purposes specified in that section; namely the purposes of the Highways Act 1980 s.31A and the Road Traffic Regulation Act 1984 s.121B (each of which imposes restrictions on the exercise by London borough councils of powers under the relevant Act so as to affect a GLA road, a strategic road or a road in another London borough other than a GLA road or strategic road). The designated roads are specified in the Order and they will become strategic roads with effect from September 5, 2005.

3488.   Schools–Protection of staff and pupils–Special extinguishment and diversion orders–Wales

HIGHWAYS (SCHOOLS) (SPECIAL EXTINGUISHMENT AND SPECIAL DIVERSION ORDERS) (WALES) REGULATIONS 2005, SI 2005 1809 (W.140); made under the Highways Act 1980 s.28, s.118B, s.119B, Sch.6 para.1, Sch.6 para.3, Sch.6 para.4, Sch.6 para.6. In force: July 15, 2005; £3.50.

Provisions inserted into the Highways Act 1980 by the Countryside and Rights of Way Act 2000 respectively enable orders to be made to stop up (by a "special extinguishment order") and divert (by a "special diversion order") certain highways for the purposes of crime prevention or for the protection of pupils or staff of schools. These Regulations prescribe the forms and notices, and make provision as to the procedure, for special extinguishment orders and special diversion orders which relate to highways crossing land occupied for the purposes of a school and which are required to protect pupils or staff. The application of these types of orders for the purposes of crime prevention will be implemented at a later date.

3489. Trailers–Roadworthiness–Condition of trailer at time of sale

[Road Traffic Act 1988 s.75.]

The appellant local authority (N) appealed by way of case stated against a decision of the magistrates' court on an information laid against the defendants (L). L, who were joint owners of a defective four wheel trailer, had admitted selling the trailer to a purchaser (D). The trailer, which had unserviceable brakes and a corroded chassis, had caused damage to another vehicle while being towed, but since the trailer had been empty and had not been in "use" within the meaning of the Road Traffic Act 1988 s.75(3), the magistrates' court had concluded that it was not unroadworthy within the meaning of s.75(1) and acquitted L. The issue which fell to be decided was whether the magistrates' court had been correct in law, given that L were aware that D intended to pull the trailer behind his vehicle in order to get it back home immediately after its purchase, to find that L had reasonable cause to believe that the trailer would not be used on a road in Great Britain until it had undergone the necessary repairs. N submitted that the magistrates' court had put too much emphasis on the intended use of the trailer rather than its actual condition, and that the trailer had to be roadworthy for every conceivable purpose for which it was to be used.

Held, dismissing the appeal, that the magistrates' court had been entitled to find that the trailer was not unroadworthy within the meaning of s.75(1) of the 1988 Act, despite its unserviceable brakes and corroded chassis. The magistrates had based their finding on their assessment of L's evidence as to what D had represented to them and on whether they were satisfied that L had reasonable cause to believe that the trailer would not be used on a road in Great Britain until it had been put into a condition in which it could be used lawfully. Having examined the facts and having been satisfied that L had been truthful, the magistrates' court had been entitled to consider the statutory defence under s.75(6). Accordingly, the decision reached by the magistrates' court was within its powers as the tribunal of fact.

R. (ON THE APPLICATION OF NEWCASTLE UPON TYNE CITY COUNCIL) v. LE QUELENEC; *sub nom.* NEWCASTLE UPON TYNE CITY COUNCIL v. LE QUELENEC, [2005] EWHC 45, *The Times*, January 17, 2005, Latham, L.J., QBD.

3490. Trunk roads–Classification–A1

A1 TRUNK ROAD (NORTHUMBERLAND AND TYNE AND WEAR, VARIOUS LOCATIONS AND DETRUNKING) ORDER 2005, SI 2005 73; made under the Highways Act 1980 s.10. In force: March 1, 2005; £3.00.

This Order provides a specified length of road to cease to be a trunk road.

3491. Trunk roads–Classification–A2

A2 TRUNK ROAD (PEPPERHILL TO COBHAM AND SLIP ROADS) ORDER 2005, SI 2005 2933; made under the Highways Act 1980 s.10, s.41. In force: October 27, 2005; £3.00.

This Order provides for a specified length of road to be classified as a trunk road.

3492. Trunk roads–Classification–A2

A2 TRUNK ROAD (PEPPERHILL TO COBHAM AND SLIP ROADS) SUPPLEMENTARY ORDER 2005, SI 2005 2928; made under the Highways Act 1980 s.10, s.41. In force: October 27, 2005; £3.00.

This Order provides for a proposed new highway to become a trunk road.

3493. Trunk roads–Classification–A2

A2 (PEPPERHILL TO COBHAM) (DETRUNKING) ORDER 2005, SI 2005 2934; made under the Highways Act 1980 s.10. In force: October 27, 2005; £3.00.

This Order provides a specified length of road to cease to be a trunk road.

3494. Trunk roads–Classification–A7

A7 TRUNK ROAD (CARLISLE CITY BOUNDARY TO THE SCOTTISH BORDER) (DE-TRUNKING) ORDER 2005, SI 2005 60; made under the Highways Act 1980 s.10, s.12. In force: April 1, 2005; £3.00.
This Order provides a specified length of road to cease to be a trunk road.

3495. Trunk roads–Classification–A11

A11 TRUNK ROAD (ATTLEBOROUGH BYPASS IMPROVEMENT) SLIP ROADS ORDER 2005, SI 2005 1266; made under the Highways Act 1980 s.10, s.41. In force: May 19, 2005; £3.00.
This Order provides for a specified length of road to be classified as a trunk road.

3496. Trunk roads–Classification–A21

A21 TRUNK ROAD (LAMBERHURST) (DERESTRICTION) ORDER 2005, SI 2005 1143; made under the Road Traffic Regulation Act 1984 s.82, s.83, s.122. In force: March 23, 2005; £3.00.
This Order provides for a specified length of road to be classified as a trunk road.

3497. Trunk roads–Classification–A21

A21 TRUNK ROAD (LAMBERHURST BYPASS) (24 HOURS CLEARWAY) ORDER 2005, SI 2005 1142; made under the Road Traffic Regulation Act 1984 s.1, s.2, s.4, s.122, Sch.9 para.27. In force: March 23, 2005; £3.00.
This Order provides for a specified length of road to be classified as a trunk road.

3498. Trunk roads–Classification–A21

A21 TRUNK ROAD (SCHOOL HILL AND SPRAY HILL, LAMBERHURST) (RESTRICTED ROAD) ORDER 2005, SI 2005 1300; made under the Road Traffic Regulation Act 1984 s.82, s.83, s.84, Sch.9 para.27. In force: March 23, 2005; £3.00.
This Order provides for specified pieces of road to be restricted roads.

3499. Trunk roads–Classification–A30

A30 TRUNK ROAD (BODMIN TO INDIAN QUEENS IMPROVEMENT AND SLIP ROADS) ORDER 2005, SI 2005 76; made under the Highways Act 1980 s.10, s.41. In force: January 17, 2005; £3.00.
This Order provides for a specified main new road and specified slip roads to become trunk roads.

3500. Trunk roads–Classification–A30

A30 TRUNK ROAD (BODMIN TO INDIAN QUEENS IMPROVEMENT AND SLIP ROADS) (DETRUNKING) ORDER 2005, SI 2005 77; made under the Highways Act 1980 s.10, s.12. In force: January 17, 2005; £3.00.
This Order provides a specified length of road to cease to be a trunk road.

3501. Trunk roads–Classification–A40

A40 TRUNK ROAD (M5 MOTORWAY JUNCTION 11 TO THE GLOUCESTERSHIRE/OXFORDSHIRE COUNTY BOUNDARY) (DETRUNKING) ORDER 2005, SI 2005 1574; made under the Highways Act 1980 s.10, s.12. In force: July 1, 2005; £3.00.
This Order provides a specified length of road to cease to be a trunk road.

3502. Trunk roads–Classification–A40

LONDON-FISHGUARD TRUNK ROAD (A40) (COMBINED FOOTPATH/ CYCLEWAY, WINDYHALL, FISHGUARD) ORDER 2005, SI 2005 3034 (W.222); made under the Highways Act 1980 s.10. In force: November 18, 2005; £3.00.

This Order provides provides for a specified length of road to become a trunk road.

3503. Trunk roads–Classification–A66

A66 TRUNK ROAD (LONG NEWTON GRADE SEPARATED JUNCTION SLIP ROADS) ORDER 2005, SI 2005 211; made under the Highways Act 1980 s.10, s.41. In force: February 17, 2005; £3.00.

This Order provides for specified slip roads and a length of highway to become trunk roads.

3504. Trunk roads–Classification–A120

A120 TRUNK ROAD (STANSTED TO MARKS TEY) ORDER 2005, SI 2005 239; made under the Highways Act 1980 s.10. In force: March 7, 2005; £3.00.

This Order provides for the specified main road, the link road, slip roads and roundabouts and the new link roads to become trunk roads.

3505. Trunk roads–Classification–A419

A419 TRUNK ROAD (COMMONHEAD JUNCTION IMPROVEMENT AND SLIP ROADS) ORDER 2005, SI 2005 2080; made under the Highways Act 1980 s.10, s.41. In force: July 20, 2005; £3.00.

This Order provides for a specified length of road to be classified as a trunk road.

3506. Trunk roads–Classification–A419

A419 TRUNK ROAD (COMMONHEAD JUNCTION IMPROVEMENT AND SLIP ROADS) (DETRUNKING) ORDER 2005, SI 2005 2079; made under the Highways Act 1980 s.10, s.12. In force: July 20, 2005; £3.00.

This Order provides a specified length of road to cease to be a trunk road.

3507. Trunk roads–Classification–A428

A428 TRUNK ROAD (CAMBOURNE TO HARDWICK IMPROVEMENT) (DETRUNKING) ORDER 2005, SI 2005 1152; made under the Highways Act 1980 s.10, s.41. In force: April 11, 2005; £3.00.

This Order provides a specified length of road to cease to be a trunk road.

3508. Trunk roads–Classification–A428

A428 TRUNK ROAD (CAMBOURNE TO HARDWICK IMPROVEMENT AND SLIP ROADS) ORDER 2005, SI 2005 1151; made under the Highways Act 1980 s.10, s.41. In force: April 11, 2005; £3.00.

This Order provides for the specified main road and slip roads to become trunk roads.

3509. Trunk roads–Classification–A428

A428 TRUNK ROAD (CAXTON GIBBET TO CAMBOURNE IMPROVEMENT) ORDER 2005, SI 2005 1149; made under the Highways Act 1980 s.10, s.41. In force: April 11, 2005; £3.00.

This Order provides for a specified length of road to be classified as a trunk road.

3510. Trunk roads–Classification–A428

A428 TRUNK ROAD (CAXTON GIBBET TO CAMBOURNE IMPROVEMENT) (DETRUNKING) ORDER 2005, SI 2005 1150; made under the Highways Act 1980 s.10, s.41. In force: April 11, 2005; £3.00.
This Order provides a specified length of road to cease to be a trunk road.

3511. Trunk roads–Classification–A470–Wales

CARDIFF TO GLAN CONWY TRUNK ROAD (A470) (BLAENAU FFESTINIOG TO CANCOED IMPROVEMENT) ORDER 2005, SI 2005 2291 (W.170); made under the Highways Act 1980 s.10. In force: September 1, 2005; £3.00.
This Order provides for a specified length of road to be classified as a trunk road.

3512. Trunk roads–Classification–A500

A500 TRUNK ROAD IN CHESHIRE (BASFORD-HOUGH-SHAVINGTON BYPASS TO M6 JUNCTION 16) (DETRUNKING) ORDER 2005, SI 2005 2249; made under the Highways Act 1980 s.10, s.12. In force: October 3, 2005; £3.00.
This Order provides a specified length of road to cease to be a trunk road.

3513. Trunk roads–Classification–A6514

A6514 TRUNK ROAD (A52 TO A60) (DETRUNKING) ORDER 2003 (REVOCATION) ORDER 2005, SI 2005 1391; made under the Highways Act 1980 s.10, s.12. In force: July 12, 2005; £3.00.
This Order provides a specified length of road to cease to be a trunk road and revokes the A6514 Trunk Road (A52 to A60) (Detrunking) Order 2003 (SI 2003 1122).

3514. Trunk roads–Classification–M40

M40 MOTORWAY JUNCTION 4 (HANDY CROSS) CONNECTING ROAD SCHEME 2005, SI 2005 1301; made under the Highways Act 1980 s.16, s.17, s.19. In force: May 3, 2005; £3.00.
This Order provides for a specified length of road to be classified as a trunk road.

3515. Books

Sampson, Fraser–Roads Policing: V. 3. Blackstone's Police Manuals. Paperback: £14.50. ISBN 0 19 928521 7. Oxford University Press.
Smart, Huw; Watson, John–Roads Policing. Blackstone's Police Q&As. Paperback: £11.95. ISBN 0 19 928527 6. Oxford University Press.

3516. Books

Stationery Office Books–Well-maintained Highways, Code of Practice for Highway Maintenance Management. Paperback: £25.00. ISBN 0 11 552643 9. The Stationery Office Books.

SALE OF GOODS

3517. Delivery–Apparent authority–Company ordering goods for supply to person later revealed as fraudster–Company's security guard accepting goods–Company's liability

The appellant (ICM) appealed against orders made against it following conjoined proceedings by the respondent suppliers for the price of goods sold and delivered. A fraudster, purportedly acting on behalf of a reputable company, had placed three substantial orders with ICM for electrical goods. ICM acted on the orders and in turn placed orders with the suppliers for the said goods. In accordance with the fraudster's instructions, ICM requested that the suppliers deliver the goods to a named individual at a given business address, subject to ICM's standard conditions. A security guard at the business address signed for the goods, as was his job. His records showed that the goods were later collected by the named individual. In the event, ICM did not receive payment for the orders. Consequently, the suppliers successfully brought proceedings for the price of the goods. On appeal, the sole question was whom ICM had held out to the suppliers as the person authorised to receive the dispatched goods at the given business address.

Held, dismissing the appeal, that the terms of the orders showed that the goods were to be delivered to the named individual. Given that the goods had been collected by the named individual, it followed that the suppliers had delivered the goods in accordance with the terms of the orders placed by ICM. The fact that they had been signed for by the security guard did not affect that conclusion. It was clear that he had authority to receive goods on behalf of persons carrying on business at the business address, *Galbraith & Grant Ltd v. Block* [1922] 2 K.B. 155 applied. There was no reason for the courier to suspect that the named individual and the reputable company were not carrying on business at the business address.

COMPUTER 2000 DISTRIBUTION LTD v. ICM COMPUTER SOLUTIONS PLC; *sub nom.* ICM COMPUTER SOLUTIONS PLC v. COMPUTER 2000 DISTRIBUTION LTD, [2004] EWCA Civ 1634, [2005] Info. T.L.R. 147, Judge, L.J., CA (Civ Div).

3518. Books

Dobson, Paul—Sale of Goods and Consumer Credit. Paperback: £28.00. ISBN 0 421 90130 6. Sweet & Maxwell.

Framework Agreement. Book (details unknown): £18.95. ISBN 0 418 82630 7. Sweet & Maxwell.

Framework Agreement Guide. Book (details unknown): £15.95. ISBN 0 418 82640 4. Sweet & Maxwell.

Framework Agreement Non-Binding. Book (details unknown): £18.95. ISBN 0 418 82650 1. Sweet & Maxwell.

Mills, Stephen—Bills of Lading: A Guide to Good Practice. Paperback: £30.00. ISBN 0 9546537 1 8. North of England P&I Association.

Schlechtriem, Peter; Schwenzer, Ingeborg—Commentary on the UN Convention on the International Sale of Goods (CISG). Hardback: £165.00. ISBN 0 19 927518 1. Oxford University Press.

Treitel, Guenter H.; Reynolds, Francis M.B.—Carver on Bills of Lading. Hardback: £263.00. ISBN 0 421 87700 6. Sweet & Maxwell.

SCIENCE

3519. Books

McLean, Sheila A.M.—Genetics and Gene Therapy. The International Library of Medicine, Ethics & Law. Hardback: £120.00. ISBN 0 7546 2055 7. Ashgate.

SENTENCING

3520. **Abuse of position of trust–Teachers–Defendant exposing himself to nine year old girl**

[Criminal Justice and Court Services Act 2000 s.28; Sexual Offences (Amendment) Act 2000 s.3(1)(b).]

E, a teacher, applied for permission to appeal against a sentence of 15 months' imprisonment, imposed following a contested trial for abuse of a position of trust contrary to the Sexual Offences (Amendment) Act 2000 s.3(1)(b). E was also disqualified from working with children for five years pursuant to the Criminal Justice and Court Services Act 2000 s.28 and placed on the Sex Offenders Register for 10 years. E had exposed himself to a nine-year-old girl in his classroom. E suffered acute anxiety and depression following the allegation. The family left the area and E's partner and five-year-old daughter began to live apart from him. E contended that his sentence was manifestly excessive or wrong in principle. In particular, E contended that the judge had arrived at a sentence of over 12 months for the purpose of ensuring that he would be disqualified from working with children.

Held, refusing the application, that the judge had been entitled to ask counsel what was the minimum sentence which would result in a disqualification from working with children. The real issue was the appropriate term of imprisonment in the circumstances of E's case. The judge had rightly taken account of the potential effect of the conviction on E's family life and his depression following the allegation, but also the gravity of the offence and the effect on the victim, who had suffered the kind of damage typically caused by such serious offences. In the circumstances, there was nothing manifestly excessive or wrong about imposing a sentence of 15 months' imprisonment following a trial, and if anything, the sentence was on the low side, *R. v. MacNicol (Andrew Brian)* [2003] EWCA Crim 3093, [2004] 2 Cr. App. R. (S.) 2, [2004] 7 C.L. 420 distinguished.

R. v. EYRE (CHRISTOPHER PETER), [2004] EWCA Crim 1114, [2005] 1 Cr. App. R. (S.) 4, Scott Baker, L.J., CA (Crim Div).

3521. **Actual bodily harm–Racially aggravated offences–Need for deterrent sentence–Assault on taxi driver accompanied by racial abuse**

The appellant (J) appealed against a sentence of 15 months' imprisonment for racially aggravated assault occasioning actual bodily harm. J was a passenger in a taxi driven by a man of Asian origin. The driver asked J whether he had the fare for the journey. J punched the driver in the face. J got out of the car, went to the driver's side and punched the driver again. J twice asked the driver what he was doing in this country. J then ran off. The driver had to attend hospital for treatment. J was convicted after a trial at which the driver had to give evidence. The judge regarded a sentence of 12 months as commensurate with the seriousness of J's case, had there been no racial aggravation and then added three months to mark the racism displayed in the racial aggravation. J argued that his sentence was excessive given his previous good character, his disqualification from a career in the Army due to his conviction and the interruption to his time as a university student caused by his imprisonment.

Held, dismissing the appeal, that a sentence of 15 months' imprisonment was not excessive. Whilst regard had to be given to J's personal mitigation, J was convicted after a trial. There was a need for a deterrent sentence for assaults occasioning actual bodily harm, even by a person of previous good character in the circumstances of the instant case. The judge was right to mark the racism displayed in the racial aggravation by adding a further three months to J's sentence. The racial aggravation could not be described as minor or incidental abuse. It was questionable whether J's remarks were so out of character as was suggested. J made similar racist comments on the subject evening to police officers and ambulance crew. The offence of racially aggravated assault occasioning actual bodily harm committed against those who were providing a public service merited both custody and deterrence, *R. v. Kelly (Lewis)* [2001] EWCA Crim 170, [2001] 2 Cr. App. R. (S.) 73, [2001] C.L.Y. 1191 followed.

R. v. ALEXANDER (JAMES), [2004] EWCA Crim 3398, [2005] 2 Cr. App. R. (S.) 49, Rose, L.J., CA (Crim Div).

3522. Actual bodily harm–Sentence length–Aggravating circumstances of racism

The appellant (M) appealed against a sentence of three years' imprisonment following his guilty plea to assault occasioning actual bodily harm. M had also been charged with racially aggravated assault, but the prosecution had offered no evidence on that count and, as a result, a not guilty verdict was entered. The victim, a black male, had been involved in an argument with another man. M, who was close by with his dog, shouted "get him" at the dog and said something to the effect that the victim should get back to his own country. He then made a movement with his arm towards the victim and the dog ran over and bit the victim. M later made further derogatory remarks. When sentencing M, who had previous convictions for assault and racially threatening behaviour, the recorder took the view that the assault had been racially aggravated and increased the sentence from two to three years. M contended that it had not been open to the recorder to increase the sentence in those circumstances as the Crown had offered no evidence on the count of racially aggravated assault.

Held, allowing the appeal, that it had not been open to the recorder, irrespective of the view that he had taken of the facts, to sentence M on the basis that he was in fact guilty of a racially aggravated assault when he had been found not guilty on that count. The sentence was otherwise unobjectionable. Accordingly, the sentence passed by the recorder would be replaced by one of two years' imprisonment.

R. v. McGILLIVRAY (ATHOLL), [2005] EWCA Crim 604, [2005] 2 Cr. App. R. (S.) 60, Bodey, J., CA (Crim Div).

3523. Actual bodily harm–Unprovoked attack by young offender

The appellant (B) appealed against a sentence of 18 months' detention imposed following his plea of guilty to an offence of assault occasioning actual bodily harm. B, who was 19 at the time of the offence and had four previous convictions for assault, had pleaded guilty on the basis that he mistakenly believed that the complainant was following him to resume an altercation which had just taken place outside a nearby public house. B punched the complainant, who fell to the ground, sustaining various injuries. B relied, inter alia, on his plea of guilty and argued that although there were previous offences of violence on his record, they had been of an unusual nature. Only one of the incidents had involved a stranger and that was an incident of spitting at a motorist.

Held, allowing the appeal, that the sentence was manifestly excessive in the circumstances. There was substantial personal mitigation available to B, in particular the fact that the sentence imposed was his first custodial sentence. Further, he had been in a very highly emotional and distressed state when the assault had taken place. The sentence was reduced to eight months, *R. v. Blewitt (Kevin Stanley)* (1994) 15 Cr. App. R. (S.) 132 and *R. v. Marples (Christopher)* [1998] 1 Cr. App. R. (S.) 335, [1998] C.L.Y. 1106 considered.

R. v. BOWERS (ARAN), [2004] EWCA Crim 1247, [2005] 1 Cr. App. R. (S.) 28, Clarke, L.J., CA (Crim Div).

3524. Aggravated burglary–Conspiracy to pervert course of justice–Offender on licence at relevant time–Undue leniency

The Attorney General referred to the court as unduly lenient a concurrent sentence of six years' imprisonment imposed on the offender (O) following his plea of guilty to aggravated burglary and conspiracy to pervert the course of justice. O and an accomplice had broken into the victims' house at night while the victims were asleep and had threatened the male victim with a knife and a piece of wood. O demanded money from the victims and the accomplice took the female victim from the bedroom to find money in the house. The male victim suffered injuries and both victims were severely traumatised by the event, resulting in the breakdown of their relationship. Prior to the trial, O had attempted to bribe the male victim to retract his statement. Both offences had been committed while O was on licence for a previous offence. The Attorney General submitted that the sentence failed to reflect the severity of the offences and that the sentencing judge had erred in imposing a concurrent sentence for the offence of conspiracy to pervert the course of justice.

Held, allowing the reference, that the sentencing judge should have ordered O to serve the unexpired portion of the licence in relation to his previous sentence. An appropriate sentence for the aggravated burglary would have been in the region of six or seven years, to run consecutively to the serving of the unexpired portion of the licence. It would have been expected that the sentence for conspiracy would run consecutively to the sentence for aggravated burglary. The original sentence was quashed as unduly lenient and, taking into account the running of the licence to the time of the instant hearing and double jeopardy, a sentence of seven years and six months' imprisonment was imposed, consisting of six years for the aggravated burglary and 18 months consecutively for conspiracy to pervert the course of justice.

ATTORNEY GENERAL'S REFERENCE (NO.92 OF 2004), *Re* [2004] EWCA Crim 2823, Rose, L.J. (Vice President), CA (Crim Div).

3525. **Aggravated burglary–Elderly persons–Series of offences against vulnerable people**

The appellant (H) appealed against a total sentence of 12 years and 6 months' imprisonment following his guilty pleas to offences of burglary and aggravated burglary, and 240 days' imprisonment for breach of licence. H had been released on licence from a five year sentence for burglaries when he committed a further five domestic burglaries over an eight month period together with an offence of aggravated vehicle taking. On two occasions he had broken into the homes of elderly people whilst they were asleep and in one incident he had threatened the victims with a hammer. For those offences he had received concurrent sentences of nine years' imprisonment. The judge took account of H's guilty plea but confirmed he would not be entitled to a full discount as he had been caught by reason of his fingerprints. H had previous convictions for 56 offences of dishonesty including 12 burglaries. H contended that based on the principle of totality the sentence was too long and that insufficient credit had been given for his guilty pleas and efforts to address his addiction to drugs.

Held, allowing the appeal, that for an offender with two or more convictions for previous domestic burglary, the presence of more than one high relevance factor could bring the sentence for an offence of this level significantly above the recognised starting point of four and six months, *R. v. McInerney (William Patrick)* [2002] EWCA Crim 3003, [2003] 1 All E.R. 1089, [2003] C.L.Y. 3636 considered. H had targeted one of the victims on more than one occasion and he had threatened an elderly couple with violence in the presence of an accomplice. Furthermore, he had committed a series of offences, *Attorney General's Reference (No.35 of 2001), Re* [2001] EWCA Crim 1271, [2002] 1 Cr. App. R. (S.) 44, [2002] C.L.Y. 3870 and *R. v. Harrison (Simon)* [2001] EWCA Crim 2117, [2002] 1 Cr. App. R. (S.) 107, [2002] C.L.Y. 3874 considered. The two concurrent nine year sentences were fully justified in the circumstances of the case which the judge had described as appalling. Nevertheless, having regard to the principle of totality, the sentence of 12 years and 6 months was too long. The consecutive sentence of two years which had been imposed on H for the initial burglary after his release should run concurrently, with the effect that the total sentence was reduced to 10 years and 6 months with 240 days which had been imposed for the earlier breach of licence.

R. v. HUNTER (NEIL PETER), [2004] EWCA Crim 3240, [2005] 2 Cr. App. R. (S.) 36, May, L.J., CA (Crim Div).

3526. Anti social behaviour orders–Breach–18 months' imprisonment for second breach of ASBO–Breach committed while released on licence

T appealed against a sentence of 18 months' imprisonment imposed for breaching an anti-social behaviour order and a one month consecutive term for theft. The order prevented T from going into four specified shops and was imposed because he had gone into them while drunk, stolen goods and been abusive and threatening to staff when asked to leave. T had previously breached the ASBO, for which he was sentenced to five months' imprisonment. The breach in the instant appeal occurred eight days after he was released on licence when he again went into one of the specified stores and stole goods. The 18 month term was made consecutive to the 69 days of licence recall.

Held, dismissing the appeal, that the sentence was justified by T's record of persistent offending and his blatant disregard of the ASBO.

R. v. THOMAS (JOHN ANTHONY), [2004] EWCA Crim 1173, [2005] 1 Cr. App. R. (S.) 9, Owen, J., CA (Crim Div).

3527. Anti social behaviour orders–Breach–Nature of breach–Custodial sentence

The appellant (D) appealed against a sentence of 18 months' imprisonment imposed following his guilty plea for breach of an anti social behaviour order. D had been made subject to an anti social behaviour order which prohibited him from, among other things, using abusive language, being drunk, begging or possessing any open vessel containing intoxicating liquor in a public place. He had, subsequently, entered a bookshop and been abusive to, and begged money from, the shopkeeper. Police had later found him drinking from a can of lager in public and in a drunken state. D had an extensive criminal record. D submitted that the sentence was too long and that it failed to reflect the fact that this was the first occasion on which he had breached the order and that the breach itself was relatively minor.

Held, allowing the appeal, that given the circumstances of the breach and the fact that it was the first breach of the order, a sentence of 18 months' imprisonment was too long. Accordingly, a sentence of eight months' imprisonment was substituted.

R. v. DICKINSON (NEVILLE), [2005] EWCA Crim 289, [2005] 2 Cr. App. R. (S.) 78, Davis, J., CA (Crim Div).

3528. Anti social behaviour orders–Breach–Offender excluded from city centre for five years–Repeated breaches

The applicant (B) sought leave to appeal against his sentence of three and a half years' imprisonment for two breaches of an anti social behaviour order. Following a complaint by the local authority, an order had been made prohibiting B from entering a city centre for five years; using threatening language or behaviour; or threatening or engaging in violence or criminal damage. Since the order was made, B had breached it four times. For the first two breaches, he had been previously sentenced to four years' imprisonment, reduced on appeal to two years. Within a few months of his release from prison, B again breached its terms twice more by aggressively begging in the city centre, and for those breaches he received the sentence under appeal. B's previous convictions included nine for using threatening language or behaviour, and nine for offences of violence. B contended that his conduct was at the lower end of the range of anti social behaviour.

Held, refusing the application, that an anti social behaviour order was designed to protect the public from repeated misbehaviour, and to breach its terms was to commit a serious criminal offence. Whilst B might consider his conduct trivial, it had to be treated as serious because of its persistence. He had breached the order four times and the public was entitled to be protected from him.

R. v. BRAXTON (CURTIS) (APPLICATION FOR LEAVE TO APPEAL), [2004] EWCA Crim 1374, [2005] 1 Cr. App. R. (S.) 36, Hooper, L.J., CA (Crim Div).

3529. Anti social behaviour orders–Duration–Indefinite period replaced by five year term–Theft offences committed within district council's area

V appealed against an anti-social behaviour order prohibiting him from entering the area covered by Forest Heath DC in Suffolk for an indefinite period of time, except for the purposes of attending court. The ASBO was imposed following V's conviction for theft from a motor vehicle with 15 similar offences taken into account. V had admitted breaking into vehicles belonging to American service personnel living in the area covered by the district council.

Held, allowing the appeal, that although the order was justified by reference to the facts of the offences, the indefinite duration was replaced by a five-year period, *R. v. P (Shane Tony)* [2004] EWCA Crim 287, [2004] 2 Cr. App. R. (S.) 63, [2004] 3 C.L. 421 considered.

R. v. VITTLES (ANTHONY MALCOLM), [2004] EWCA Crim 1089, [2005] 1 Cr. App. R. (S.) 8, Rose, L.J. (Vice President), CA (Crim Div).

3530. Appeals against sentence–Citation of authorities–Need for caution

The appellant (L) appealed against a sentence of five years' imprisonment following convictions of causing grievous bodily harm with intent and dangerous driving. L had been involved in a road rage incident where he had headbutted the driver of another vehicle.

Held, dismissing the appeal, that (1) when the full court granted leave to appeal, it stated that a sentence of five years was fully justified but that it appeared in *Attorney General's Reference (No.88 of 2000), Re* [2001] EWCA Crim 68, [2001] C.L.Y. 1335 and *R. v. Holmes(Christopher)* (Unreported, May 22, 1997) that a lower tariff had been set, *Attorney General's Reference (No.88 of 2000)* and *Holmes* considered. The instant case gave the court the opportunity to comment on those two authorities and to make some general observations about the citation of authorities in sentencing appeals. Neither *Attorney General's Reference (No.88 of 2000)* nor *Holmes* purported to set a tariff and neither was a guideline case. (2) One or two decisions of the court which were neither guideline cases nor expressed to be of general application were unlikely to be a reliable guide to the appropriate sentencing bracket for a particular offence, because the facts and circumstances of cases varied infinitely. That was why, generally, the court was and would continue to be reluctant, in sentencing appeals, to look at cases which were merely illustrative of the sentence appropriate on particular facts. (3) Particular caution was necessary in relation to judgments given in Attorney General's references, which, unless they expressly contained statements of general application, were unlikely to identify a general sentencing level. That was because, on a reference, in addressing the question of whether a sentence was unduly lenient, the court was likely to focus on the least sentence which could properly have been passed in the court below, and that might not involve identifying a sentencing bracket. (4) L's sentence was appropriate.

R. v. LYON (CLAYTON), [2005] EWCA Crim 1365, *The Times*, May 19, 2005, Rose, L.J., CA (Crim Div).

3531. Appeals against sentence–Hearings–Appellant's right to be present

[Criminal Appeal Act 1968 s.22(1), s.22(3).]

The appellants sought to have their cases reheard following successful renewed applications for leave to appeal sentences when they had not been present. The two unrelated cases raised the same point for consideration, namely, when an applicant on a renewed application to the full court for leave to appeal sentence was, in his absence, granted leave and his sentence was reduced, in what circumstances should the matter be relisted for reconsideration in his presence.

Held, dismissing the appeals, that (1) under the Criminal Appeal Act 1968 s.22(3) the Court of Appeal had the power to pass a sentence on a person not present, however that did not negate an appellant's right to be present at a hearing of an appeal under s.22(1) of the Act. Where an appeal succeeded it was the practice of the court to indicate that, as the appellant was not present and had not waived any right, the sentence would be reduced unless, within seven days, he applied for the matter to be relisted. It was also the practice of the Registrar to write to the appellant a "do better" letter stating inter alia that the decision would not be varied unless there was new material that had a bearing on the hearing. Such a letter fairly reflected an appellant's statutory right to be present but it should only be sent to an unrepresented appellant on a renewed application. Where an appellant was represented, instructions should, where possible, be obtained prior to the hearing to act in his absence if leave was granted. If not possible, instructions should be sought on the day of the hearing or the result should be communicated to the appellant. If, at the appellant's request, the matter was relisted for him to be present there would only be a rehearing if there was new material with an important bearing on the hearing. If there was no new material the appellant would only be invited to comment on the previous decision. The relisting may or may not be before the same constitution which heard the original application and the question of a representation order for counsel would not normally be considered before the hearing and not normally be made unless there was new material. (2) In the present cases there was no new material that had any bearing on the hearings and the sentences substituted by the Court of Appeal on the renewed applications would stand.

R. v. SPRUCE (RONALD ARTHUR); R. v. ANWAR (KAMRAN), [2005] EWCA Crim 1090, [2006] 1 Cr. App. R. (S.) 11, Rose, L.J., CA (Crim Div).

3532. Assault by penetration—Guilty pleas—Reduction of sentence for early plea—Undue leniency

[Sexual Offences Act 2003 s.2.]

The Attorney General referred as unduly lenient a sentence of 15 months' detention imposed upon the offender (H), who had been convicted of assault by penetration contrary to the Sexual Offences Act 2003 s.2. H, whilst under the influence of alcohol and ecstasy, had entered a bedroom where the drunken victim was sleeping, and undressed her. He performed penetrative oral sex on her for approximately one minute, then lay naked on top of her, at which point she awoke and he ended the assault. The Attorney General submitted that the sentence was unduly lenient considering that H had taken advantage of a vulnerable victim, the assault was highly invasive and the victim had suffered greatly. H submitted in mitigation that he had attended the police station of his own volition and had pleaded guilty as soon as he was questioned by the police, that he was of previous good character and that the incident was his first contact with drugs. The offending had had a serious impact upon him and he had shown genuine remorse and empathy for his victim.

Held, refusing the reference, that an appropriate starting point for the offence would have been four years' imprisonment, but as H was a young offender, was of previous good character and the period of penetration was short, the starting point would have been reduced to approximately three years and three months. As H had made an early guilty plea, which was of considerable importance, that sentence would have been reduced by approximately one third; consequently the sentence would have been in the region of two years, *Attorney General's Reference (No.104 of 2004), Re* [2004] EWCA Crim 2672, *The Times*, October 29, 2004 followed. If the instant court altered the sentence there would be a reduction from that two years to allow for double jeopardy. In all the circumstances the sentence of 15 months' detention, although lenient, was not unduly so and would remain.

ATTORNEY GENERAL'S REFERENCE (NO.128 OF 2004), *Re*; *sub nom*. R. v. HOLNESS (PETER PHILLIP), [2004] EWCA Crim 3066, [2005] 2 Cr. App. R. (S.) 17, Kennedy, L.J., CA (Crim Div).

3533. Assault with intent to rob—Innocent victim punched and threatened with knife—Undue leniency

The Attorney General referred as unduly lenient a two year community rehabilitation order imposed on the offender (X) following his guilty pleas to assault of a former female partner, occasioning her actual bodily harm, assault with intent to rob and common assault. X had gone to the home of his former partner, whom he was prohibited from contacting. He forced her over the arm of a settee and his dog bit her a number of times before he seized her jaw, forcing her head back. His plea was on the basis that he had not deliberately set the dog on her. On a separate occasion, X had asked another victim for money and punched him in the face when he refused. X pursued the victim, punched him twice and threatened to stab him with a knife. After he was arrested, X kicked out at the victim, striking him at waist height. The Attorney General contended that, save in wholly exceptional circumstances, immediate custody was the appropriate penalty for offences of robbery committed with violence or threats of violence from a lethal weapon. It was argued that the sentence failed to reflect the gravity of the offences and the aggravating features which were present.

Held, allowing the reference, that the sentence was unduly lenient and an appropriate total sentence would have been four years' imprisonment. Taking account of double jeopardy, X's failure to respond to the sentence which had been imposed and the fact that he was now going into custody, a total sentence of three years was appropriate. That term comprised two and a half years for the assault with intent to rob, a concurrent sentence of six months for the common assault on the same victim, and a consecutive sentence of six months for assault occasioning actual bodily harm.

ATTORNEY GENERAL'S REFERENCE (NO.147 OF 2004), *Re* [2005] EWCA Crim 845, Rose, L.J. (V-P), CA (Crim Div).

3534. Assisting illegal entry—Aggravating features—Facilitating illegal entry as part of professional enterprise

The appellant (S) appealed against a sentence of two years' imprisonment following a guilty plea to a count of facilitating the entry of a single illegal immigrant. S had been stopped at Dover docks with a passenger in his motor car. S claimed to have known the passenger for a year but did not know his name. The immigration officer was not satisfied about the passenger's identity in spite of the production by the passenger of a German identity card and, after further investigation, the passenger was eventually returned to France. Evidence showed that S had been in and out of the country on five separate occasions, accompanied by a passenger who gave a similar name on four of those occasions. S contended that the sentence was manifestly excessive given his early guilty plea and the fact that he had not acted for commercial gain.

Held, dismissing the appeal, that the sentence was not manifestly excessive. The judge had been entitled to conclude that the offence was part of a commercial enterprise, *R. v. Le (Van Binh)* [1999] 1 Cr. App. R. (S.) 422, [1998] C.L.Y. 1245 applied.

R. v. SACKEY (ALEX QUAYSON), [2004] EWCA Crim 566, [2004] 2 Cr. App. R. (S.) 85, Rix, L.J., CA (Crim Div).

3535. Assisting illegal entry—Conspiracy—Group providing complete illegal entry service—Requirement of cruelty, danger or exploitation for maximum sentence

The appellants (S and D), who had pleaded guilty to conspiracy to facilitate the entry into the United Kingdom of persons whom they knew to be illegal immigrants, appealed against their respective sentences of five years' and seven and a half years' imprisonment. Another codefendant (K) was sentenced to four years' imprisonment, while two others received three years and three and a half years each. The codefendants were members of a group which provided a complete illegal entry service and made significant profits. D was the principal organiser, K was his lieutenant, and S was more of a "foot soldier". D argued that his sentence was excessive for an offence which was not of the worst variety since the immigrants were not subjected to cruelty, danger or exploitation. He also complained of his sentence's disparity with the three years' imprisonment that one codefendant received. S argued that he had been unfairly sentenced in comparison to K, who had received significant payment and had been involved in the conspiracy for longer.

Held, dismissing the appeals, that (1) a maximum sentence of 10 years, after trial, did not require the offence to involve actual cruelty, danger or exploitation. If those features were present the offender could be charged with other offences which would attract their own consecutive sentences. The judge had been right to take a starting point at or near the maximum sentence because D had been a prime mover in a conspiracy which contained several aggravating features, *R. v. Le (Van Binh)* [1999] 1 Cr. App. R. (S.) 422, [1998] C.L.Y. 1245 considered. (2) There was no disparity between D's sentence and that of the other codefendant, who had been sentenced on the specific and limited basis of his plea. (3) Whilst K did receive money and S did not, the judge was entitled to find that S's later involvement had been enthusiastic. Furthermore, K had received more credit because his guilty plea had been earlier.

R. v. SAINI (JARNAIL SINGH); R. v. KALYAN (SOHAN LAL); R. v. DEO (SARWAN SINGH); *sub nom.* R. v. SAINI (JARNEIL SINGH), [2004] EWCA Crim 1900, [2005] 1 Cr. App. R. (S.) 62, Maurice Kay, L.J., CA (Crim Div).

3536. **Assisting illegal entry–Women induced to come to UK forced into prostitution–Coercion and corruption–Kidnapping–Undue leniency**

The Attorney General referred to the court as unduly lenient concurrent sentences totalling 10 years' imprisonment imposed on P following a guilty plea to charges of facilitating illegal entry, living on the earnings of prostitution, kidnapping and incitement to rape. P had a leading part in an organisation that approached young women from Romania with offers to arrange their passage to the UK where they would work in a bar. Instead, the women were required to work as prostitutes.

Held, allowing the reference, that the sentence of 10 years' imprisonment was unduly lenient and would be replaced by concurrent sentences totalling 23 years' imprisonment. Since P had commercially exploited illegal immigrants, five years was an appropriate sentence following a guilty plea, *R. v. Le (Van Binh)* [1999] 1 Cr. App. R. (S.) 422, [1998] C.L.Y. 1245 followed. As to living on the earnings of prostitution, there was evidence of coercion and corruption in the case of three of the victims, so that five years was appropriate in the circumstances, *R. v. Powell (Ashna George)* [2001] 1 Cr. App. R. (S.) 76, [2000] C.L.Y. 1385 followed. Two other victims could be treated differently as they had lived with P, but there was still evidence of coercion and corruption that justified three years' imprisonment. For kidnapping, a sentence of 10 years was appropriate where the women had been held against their will, *R. v. Spence (Clinton Everton)* (1983) 5 Cr. App. R. (S.) 413, [1984] C.L.Y. 876 followed. Finally, eight years was appropriate in respect of the single count of incitement to rape, *R. v. Millberry (William Christopher)* [2002] EWCA Crim 2891, [2003] 1 W.L.R. 546, [2003] C.L.Y. 3829 followed.

ATTORNEY GENERAL'S REFERENCE (NO.6 OF 2004), *Re*; *sub nom.* R. v. PLAKICI (LUAN), [2004] EWCA Crim 1275, [2005] 1 Cr. App. R. (S.) 19, Latham, L.J., CA (Crim Div).

3537. **Attorney Generals references–Remand–Power of Court of Appeal to remand defendant in custody pending medical reports**

[Criminal Justice Act 1988 s.36.]

The Attorney General referred as unduly lenient a two year suspended sentence imposed on the offender (S) following his plea of guilty to causing grievous bodily harm with intent. S, who had recently been diagnosed as suffering from Asperger's syndrome, had attacked his estranged partner, striking her several times over the head with the wooden handle of a hammer. Psychiatric reports revealed that S had become convinced that his partner had taken away his son, who had also been diagnosed with Asperger's syndrome. The pre sentence report regarded S as posing a significant risk of reoffending unless he maintained a commitment to addressing his behaviour.

Held, allowing the reference, that the mitigation of S's guilty plea, his Asperger's syndrome and the fact that he had sought help after the attack had to be set against the very serious violence. The attack was sustained and serious, and there was a really serious risk that S would offend again. The sentence passed was unduly lenient and, even allowing for the principle of double jeopardy, a fresh sentence was required. However, before the appropriate sentence could be decided, further medical evidence of S's condition was required to assess the element of danger posed to the public at large and, in particular, to the victim and her son. Upon hearing a reference and quashing a sentence, under the Criminal Justice Act 1988 s.36, the Court of Appeal had the same powers as a sentencing court to remand a defendant in custody pending medical reports.

ATTORNEY GENERAL'S REFERENCE (NO.129 OF 2004), *Re*; *sub nom*. R. v. SSAN (ARCHIT) [2005] EWCA Crim 363, Judge, L.J., CA (Crim Div).

3538. Automatic life imprisonment–Release on licence–Seriousness of offence–Appropriate tariff

[Mental Health Act 1983 s.45A; Powers of Criminal Courts (Sentencing) Act 2000 s.82A(2), s.82A(3), s.82A(4).]

The appellant (M) appealed against an order that early release provisions should not apply to his automatic life sentence following a guilty plea to manslaughter on the grounds of diminished responsibility. The trial judge had declined to make an order under the Powers of Criminal Courts (Sentencing) Act 2000 s.82A(2) and s.82A(3) specifying a minimum term to be served before M was eligible to apply to the Parole Board for release. Instead an order under s.82A(4) of the 2000 Act was made that the early release provisions should not apply together with an order under the Mental Health Act 1983 s.45A. M argued that the trial judge had been obliged to but had failed to consider whether the seriousness of the offence irrespective of risk to the public justified the order under s.82A(4) of the 2000 Act, the effect of which was that there was no way that M could be put before the Parole Board in due course for any assessment of future risk. In fact the offence was not so serious as to justify the order.

Held, allowing the appeal, that having regard to the complex statutory provisions, it was probable that the trial judge had not appreciated the effect of not exercising the power to set a tariff. Whilst the offence was grave, it was not of such seriousness that it was inappropriate to set a tariff at all and in that regard the judge had erred. It was important that in due course there could be an opportunity for M's case to be reviewed and the judge should have considered the appropriate tariff as regards seriousness without any consideration of future risk. In all the circumstances it was appropriate to specify that a period of nine years should elapse before M could be even referred to the Parole Board.

R. v. McMILAN (PAUL); *sub nom*. R. v. McMILLAN, [2005] EWCA Crim 222, [2005] 2 Cr. App. R. (S.) 63, Kennedy, L.J., CA (Crim Div).

3539. Automatic life imprisonment–Risk of reoffending–Public protection–Nature of risk

[Powers of Criminal Courts (Sentencing) Act 2000 s.109.]

The appellant (M), who had a previous conviction for a firearms offence, appealed against the automatic imposition under the Powers of Criminal Courts (Sentencing) Act 2000 s.109 of a life sentence for possessing a firearm with intent to commit an indictable offence. M had pleaded guilty to that offence and also to possession of a Class A drug with intent to supply. M had not been carrying ammunition for the firearm and the basis of his plea was that he had not intended to use the firearm in furtherance of the drugs related offence.

Held, allowing the appeal, that the nature of the exceptional circumstances permitting the imposition of an automatic life sentence to be circumvented arose where the defendant did not pose a future risk of violent or sexual offending, *R. v. Offen (Matthew Barry) (No.2)* [2001] 1 W.L.R. 253, [2000] C.L.Y. 1347, *R. v. Richards (Darrell) (No.1)* [2001] EWCA Crim 2712, [2002] 2 Cr. App. R. (S.) 26, [2002] C.L.Y. 4035, *R. v. Stark (Barry John)* [2002] EWCA Crim 542, [2002] 2 Cr. App. R. (S.) 104, [2002] C.L.Y. 4052, *R. v. Tonks (William)* [2004] EWCA Crim 1392 and *R. v. Smith (Ruben)* [2001] EWCA Crim 1700, [2002] 1 Cr. App. R. (S.) 82, [2002] C.L.Y. 4020 considered. In the instant case, the sentencing judge had imposed M's sentence on the basis of the risk of the commission of future drugs offences. Therefore, the sentence was wrong in principle and four years' imprisonment was appropriate.

R. v. MAGALHAES (ELISIU), [2004] EWCA Crim 2976, [2005] 2 Cr. App. R. (S.) 13, Maurice Kay, L.J., CA (Crim Div).

3540. **Bigamy–Aiding and abetting–Party to bigamous marriage–Intention of defeating immigration laws–Deterrent sentences**

The first appellant (B) appealed against a sentence of two years' imprisonment for aiding and abetting one count of bigamy. The second appellant (K) appealed against a sentence of two years and three months' imprisonment for two counts of bigamy. K's sentence comprised 12 months for one offence of bigamy and 15 months for the second offence. K was legitimately married. K took part in two marriage ceremonies with Bangladeshi nationals. B witnessed one of the marriages. Each ceremony was a sham with the object of defeating immigration laws. K attended a police station and made an admission. The judge said that a deterrent sentence was needed as the subject behaviour was not to be tolerated. B argued that his sentence was manifestly excessive given that he was involved in only one bigamous marriage, he had pleaded guilty and was of good character. K argued that her sentence was manifestly excessive given that she instigated the investigation, made full and frank admissions and was of good character.

Held, allowing B's appeal and dismissing K's appeal, that B was sentenced for aiding and abetting one bigamous marriage, that for which K, the principal, was sentenced to 15 months' imprisonment. Even after the balancing exercise of B's plea against K's early plea, two years seemed too far in excess of 15 months. In relation to K, the judge had properly underlined the evil behind the indicted offences, namely the flouting of immigration provisions. Deterrence was a legitimate aim of judicial disposition and there was nothing impeachable in the sentence imposed on K. A sentence of 18 months' imprisonment was substituted in B's case.

R. v. KHAN (BAJLU ISLAM); R. v. KENNEDY (KAREN MARY), [2004] EWCA Crim 3316, [2005] 2 Cr. App. R. (S.) 45, Judge, L.J., CA (Crim Div).

3541. **Bomb hoaxing–Three false reports to police–Early plea taken into account**

C appealed against a sentence of 30 months' imprisonment imposed following a guilty plea to three offences of communicating a bomb hoax. On each occasion, C had called the police using a mobile phone, stating that bombs had been left at certain locations. On appeal, C contended that the sentence was manifestly excessive.

Held, allowing the appeal, that the offences were serious, both in terms of public distress and waste of police time and resources. However, the general level of sentence indicated by the authorities showed that the sentence was too high in the instant case, taking C's early plea into account, and it was reduced to 21 months' imprisonment, *R. v. Smith (Stuart)* [2002] EWCA Crim 1946, *R. v. Spencer (Paul)* (Unreported, June 29, 1998), *R. v. Enright (Georgina)* [2001]

EWCA Crim 62, *R. v. Walters (Alexander Farrar)* [2002] EWCA Crim 1114 and *R. v. Hall* [2003] EWCA Crim 1714 considered.

R. v. CANN (JACKSON), [2004] EWCA Crim 1075, [2005] 1 Cr. App. R. (S.) 12, Roderick Evans, J., CA (Crim Div).

3542. **Buggery–Life imprisonment–Multiple offences against boys over long period–Undue leniency**

The Attorney General referred as unduly lenient a sentence of life imprisonment with a specified minimum period of six years and two months. The defendant (G) had pleaded guilty to 14 counts of buggery involving boys under the age of 16. The offences had begun in 1965 and had continued for a long period. G had given the boys money and gifts after the incidents and had often threatened them with violence. The judge sentenced G to life imprisonment with a recommendation that he serve a minimum of six years and two months before being considered for parole. The Attorney General contended that the sentence was unduly lenient as the minimum period to be served by G failed to take account of the gravity of the offences and the aggravating features of the case. G argued that he was entitled to a proper allowance for his guilty plea even if it was late.

Held, dismissing the reference, that the court was wholly satisfied that the judge had not erred and had carried out a careful sentencing exercise. G had been sentenced to life imprisonment and the judge had made it clear that he would not be released until the authorities were perfectly satisfied that he no longer posed a threat to anyone, and that in G's case a life sentence might mean life.

ATTORNEY GENERAL'S REFERENCE (NO.131 OF 2004), *Re*; *sub nom*. R. v. GOAD (WILLIAM ALEXANDER) [2005] EWCA Crim 16, Kennedy, L.J., CA (Crim Div).

3543. **Burglary–Conspiracy–Animal rights activist breaking into laboratory–Undue leniency**

The Attorney General referred to the court as unduly lenient a 230 hour community punishment order that had been imposed, after a trial, on the offender (X) for conspiracy to burgle. X, an animal rights activist, had, with two others, broken into a laboratory during the night and removed laboratory records together with 700 mice and their cages. Although virtually all of the mice were recovered after X's arrest, there was substantial disruption to the experiments that were being undertaken at the laboratory. In imposing a non custodial sentence, the judge took into account the fact that X was the sole carer of his partner, who suffered from substantial physical and mental disabilities. The Attorney General relied, inter alia, on the following matters: the offence had been carefully planned and sophisticated; X had caused financial damage to a legitimate business; X had been the prime mover and had recruited others in order to carry out his plan; and X had relevant previous convictions which had been committed against a background of longstanding animal rights activism.

Held, allowing the reference, that the matters relied on by the Attorney General justified the imposition of a custodial sentence. In 1996, X had had a sentence of 14 years' imprisonment reduced on appeal to 11 years, the main reason for the reduction being X's assertion that he no longer intended to pursue his beliefs in animal rights by illegal means. The current offence cast significant doubt on the expressions of intent expressed by X at that time. Further, X's moral justification for his actions did not make them any the less illegal, and the courts had repeatedly stated that unless unlawful action was dealt with appropriately, there would in effect be anarchy. X could have expected to receive a sentence of 18 months to two years' imprisonment. Taking into account double jeopardy and the position of X's partner, a sentence of 12 months' imprisonment was imposed.

ATTORNEY GENERAL'S REFERENCE (NO.54 OF 2005), *Re*; *sub nom*. R. v. MANN (KEITH) [2005] EWCA Crim 1896, Latham, L.J., CA (Crim Div).

3544. Burglary–Drug treatment and testing orders–Adjournment to assess suitability–Fairness of imposition of custodial sentence

[Powers of Criminal Courts (Sentencing) Act 2000 s.111.]

The appellant (G) appealed against a sentence of three years' imprisonment imposed following his guilty plea to two counts of domestic burglary. G had many previous convictions and had just been released from an earlier sentence. He was liable to a minimum sentence of three years' imprisonment under the Powers of Criminal Courts (Sentencing) Act 2000 s.111 unless there were particular circumstances relating to the offences or to G that would make such a sentence unjust. Counsel for G had persuaded the judge to adjourn sentencing to obtain a pre sentence report dealing with G's suitability for a drug treatment and testing order. The judge expressed reservations as to that course but granted an adjournment, making it clear that imprisonment was still a likely option. At subsequent hearings further adjournments were granted and, at one such hearing, the pre sentence report indicated that G was a suitable candidate for a drug treatment and testing order if accommodation could be found. At that stage, accommodation was not available and the judge indicated that, if accommodation could be found she would be compelled to make the order sought. At a subsequent hearing the judge was told that accommodation would soon be available but nevertheless imposed the minimum sentence.

Held, allowing the appeal, that there was clear authority indicating that once a judge had postponed sentence so that an alternative to prison could be examined and that alternative was found to be satisfactory in all respects then the court should adopt that alternative course, *R. v. Gillam (Leslie George)* (1980) 2 Cr. App. R. (S.) 267, [1981] C.L.Y. 525.41 applied. A judge could make it plain that, despite considering the alternative course, prison was still a real option and so the sense of injustice that might arise from a subsequent custodial sentence would be eliminated. In the instant case, the judge had initially given that indication but at the relevant hearing she had clearly indicated that if a residential placement was available then a drug treatment and testing order would be made. G had been led to expect that such an order would be made. It was clear that the judge had then been bound to pass that sentence if a placement became available. The sentence was quashed and a drug treatment and testing order imposed.

R. v. GIBSON (KARL MARK), [2004] EWCA Crim 593, [2004] 2 Cr. App. R. (S.) 84, Laws, L.J., CA (Crim Div).

3545. Burglary–Fixed sentences–Conviction and concurrent sentences not following sequence set out in Powers of Criminal Courts (Sentencing) Act 2000 s.111

[Crime and Disorder Act 1998 s.51; Powers of Criminal Courts (Sentencing) Act 2000 s.111.]

H appealed against an automatic sentence of three years' imprisonment for a dwelling house burglary imposed under the Powers of Criminal Courts (Sentencing) Act 2000 s.111. The judge, believing that the sentence was mandatory, imposed it for the burglary of a flat in count one of the indictment. The judge also imposed concurrent sentences for burglaries of another flat in count two and a food shop in count three. H contended that he only had one prior conviction for dwelling house burglary since the commencement of s.111, and that his conviction on count three did not fall within the sequence set out in s.111. H had a substantial burglary record and a heroin addiction.

Held, dismissing the appeal, that the automatic sentence of three years' imprisonment for count one was unlawful and should be set aside because s.111 did not apply as H only had one conviction in the requisite period, not two; and if the sentence had been automatic, H should have been sent to the Crown Court under the Crime and Disorder Act 1998 s.51 for trial by indictment. A drug treatment and testing order should be made because it was clear from the probation and prison reports that H was unwilling to engage properly in the drug treatment scheme. In the light of H's very bad criminal record and history of non compliance with non custodial sentences, his sentence should have been in the region of four and a half years, *R. v. McInerney (William Patrick)* [2002] EWCA Crim 3003, [2003] 1 All E.R. 1089, [2003] C.L.Y. 3636 considered. However, while the three year sentence was extremely light, it could not be increased.

R. v. HOARE (JAMIE MATTHEW), [2004] EWCA Crim 191, [2004] 2 Cr. App. R. (S.) 50, Mantell, L.J., CA (Crim Div).

3546. Careless driving–Death–Defendant significantly affected by alcohol–Undue leniency

The Attorney General referred as unduly lenient a 240 hour community punishment order and six month curfew order imposed on the defendant (G) following his plea of guilty to causing death by careless driving. G and his friend, the victim, had been drinking. G was persuaded to drive, although he appreciated that he was significantly affected by alcohol. G swerved to the wrong side of the road and hit an oncoming car and the victim was killed. A blood sample showed that G was two and a half times the permitted alcohol limit. The Attorney General contended there were three aggravating features, namely (i) G had made an unnecessary journey at a time when he must have known he was affected by drink; (ii) he was uninsured; and (iii) he was twice the legal alcohol limit. In mitigation were his plea of guilty, the real remorse shown, his relatively young age and his previous good character. The Attorney General argued that the case clearly fell within the intermediate category in *Attorney General's Reference (No.152 of 2002), Re* [2003] EWCA Crim 996, [2003] 3 All E.R. 40 whereby the appropriate sentence was between two and three years, and that the judge was wrong to consider that *Attorney General's Reference (No.77 of 2002), Re* [2002] EWCA Crim 2312, [2003] 1 Cr. App. R. (S.) 111, [2003] C.L.Y. 3645 provided him with the appropriate guidance when sentencing G.

Held, finding the sentence to be unduly lenient but not varying it, that the instant case did not clearly fall within the intermediate category set out in *Attorney General's Reference (No.152 of 2002), Attorney General's Reference (No.152 of 2002)* considered. The proper sentence was one of 18 months' imprisonment and, accordingly, the sentence was unduly lenient. However, there were factors making it difficult to substitute a sentence of imprisonment. G had completed 178 hours of the community punishment order, which, taken together with the fact that any sentence passed now would have to be discounted to take into account double jeopardy, meant that it was not appropriate to interfere with the sentence, *Attorney General's Reference (No.77 of 2002)* distinguished.

ATTORNEY GENERAL'S REFERENCE (NO.157 OF 2004), *Re; sub nom.* R. v. GREEN (RYAN KEITH) [2005] EWCA Crim 537, Latham, L.J., CA (Crim Div).

3547. Causing death by dangerous driving–Aggravating features–Driving through red lights–Pedestrian struck on pelican crossing–Undue leniency

The Attorney General referred to the court as unduly lenient a sentence of three years and six months' imprisonment imposed on the defendant (C) following his plea of guilty to causing death by dangerous driving. C had set off from a petrol station without paying for the petrol. He went along a dual carriageway towards some traffic lights, 50 metres beyond which was a pelican crossing. There were warning signs for both the traffic lights and the pelican crossing and visibility was good. The traffic lights were timed to allow a 10 second delay between the red stop signal for traffic and the green light on the pelican crossing. A crossing patrol warden (B) was on duty at the pelican crossing, wearing reflective clothing and carrying a school crossing patrol board. Travelling at between 40 and 60 miles per hour, C drove through the red traffic lights, through the pelican crossing and struck B and three other pedestrians, including a four year old child. Witnesses gave evidence that C made no attempt to avoid the pedestrians or to slow down. C drove away at speed, swerving in and out of the traffic. One of the pedestrians died, B suffered severe head trauma and the other two pedestrians, including the child, suffered minor injury. C informed the sentencing judge that he was addicted to heroin and that he had been out in his car that day to try to find some drugs. In his current application, the Attorney General contended that the case fell into the highest category of most serious culpability, with a starting point of six years' imprisonment or more on a plea of not guilty, and that the number of aggravating features meant that the sentence failed to mark the true level of C's culpability.

Held, allowing the reference, that the offence clearly fell into the most serious of the four categories of causing death by dangerous driving, that of most serious culpability, *Attorney General's Reference (No.152 of 2002), Re* [2003] EWCA Crim 996, [2003] 3 All E.R. 40, [2004] 2 C.L. 455 applied. C had blatantly ignored all warnings and had driven through lights that had been red for some considerable time. The aggravating features were numerous and serious, including the fact that C was driving uninsured and without a licence, that he had caused injury as well as death, that he had failed to stop when he must have known that he had caused serious injuries and that thereafter he had driven aggressively and dangerously over a considerable distance in the morning rush hour. C's mitigation of an early but inevitable plea of guilty and remorse following his arrest was meagre in the circumstances of the case. The appropriate starting point on a plea of not guilty would have been a sentence of seven years' imprisonment. Having regard to C's plea of guilty and mitigation, that sentence would have been reduced to five years and six months. However, allowing for double jeopardy, the original sentence would be replaced by one of four years and six months' imprisonment.

ATTORNEY GENERAL'S REFERENCE (NO.90 OF 2004), *Re; sub nom.* CHAMBERS (STEPHEN PAUL) [2004] EWCA Crim 3285, Auld, L.J., CA (Crim Div).

3548. **Causing death by dangerous driving–Aggravating features–Excessive speed–Multiple deaths–Length of disqualification period**

The appellant (P) appealed against his sentence of five years' imprisonment and eight years' disqualification from driving following his conviction of causing death by dangerous driving. P had been driving on a single carriageway road with a 60 mile per hour speed limit. He went round a corner at 80 miles per hour, causing his car to spin and collide with an oncoming car, the driver and passenger of which were both killed immediately. P and his passenger were both injured. P was convicted after a trial in which he denied speeding. The sentencing judge based the sentence on the aggravating factors of greatly excessive speed, showing off and multiple deaths. He also considered the mitigating factors of good character and the fact that P had sustained lasting injuries. P contended (1) that less weight should have been attached to the factor of multiple deaths since his culpable dangerousness was the same whether one or two persons had been killed. (2) The disqualification period was excessive given that P had not been shown to present an ongoing risk to other road users.

Held, allowing the appeal in part, that (1) the judge had achieved the right balance between the aggravating and mitigating factors in what was clearly a very serious case. He had been right to view greatly excessive speed as an aggravating factor and had ensured that the weight attached to the multiple deaths remained proportionate to P's culpability. The sentence was therefore appropriate in all the circumstances, *Attorney General's Reference (No.152 of 2002), Re* [2003] EWCA Crim 996, [2003] 3 All E.R. 40, [2004] C.L.Y. 3333 followed. (2) With respect to the disqualification period, the aggravating and mitigating factors brought the case within the middle band of culpability as set out in *Attorney General's Reference (No.152 of 2002)*, which warranted a period of only five years. Thus, the disqualification period of eight years was reduced to five.

R. v. PIELESZ (MARK), [2005] EWCA Crim 230, [2005] 2 Cr. App. R. (S.) 72, Judge, L.J., CA (Crim Div).

3549. Causing death by dangerous driving—Aggravating features—Speeding—Most serious category of culpability

The appellant (R) appealed against his sentence of five years' imprisonment imposed following a late plea to two counts of causing death by dangerous driving. R had driven his fiancee and another young woman in his mother's car at speeds of up to 120 mph on a road with a speed limit of 60 mph. He collided with an oncoming car, and R's fiancee and the other driver were killed. R, who was seriously injured, pleaded guilty at a pre trial review on the bases that he was driving at approximately 100 mph and was not under the influence of drink or drugs. Further, that the oncoming car was beginning to overtake, whereas his car was on the correct side of the road, and his fiancee was not wearing a seatbelt. The sentencing judge stated that R was not entitled to full credit for his guilty pleas as they were late, and he found the following aggravating factors: R drove at a grossly excessive speed and was showing off; he tried to blame the driver he had killed; he had not learnt from a previous speeding disqualification; and two people had died. R contended that there were four categories of culpability in causing death by dangerous driving, and his sentence meant that the judge must have put him in the most serious category, instead of just the higher category.

Held, dismissing the appeal, that the culpability of a motorist who caused death by dangerous driving was most serious when three or more aggravating factors were present, whereas his culpability would only be in the higher category where there were just one or two such factors. In the instant case, there were sufficient aggravating features to render R's culpability most serious: the excessive speed and his showing off; the disregard of his passengers' warning; prolonged very bad driving; aggressive driving; previous convictions for motoring offences; and the deaths of two people. Six or more years' imprisonment was the starting point in contested cases for that degree of culpability, *Attorney General's Reference (No.152 of 2002), Re* [2003] EWCA Crim 996, [2003] 3 All E.R. 40, [2004] 2 C.L. 455 considered. Accordingly, R's five year sentence was appropriate after his late guilty pleas.

R. v. ROBERTS (IAN); *sub nom.* R. v. ROBERTS (JAMES), [2004] EWCA Crim 1445, [2005] 1 Cr. App. R. (S.) 40, Clarke, L.J., CA (Crim Div).

3550. Causing death by dangerous driving—Child killed as result of overtaking manoeuvre

The appellant (M) appealed against a sentence of three years and nine months' imprisonment following a plea of guilty to causing death by dangerous driving. M had a head on collision with another car whilst he was overtaking a coach on a narrow road at a point where his view was restricted. The female driver of the other vehicle was seriously injured and her three year old son, who had been strapped in a car seat, was killed. When first interviewed, M said the coach had been parked and blamed the coach driver for the collision. M argued that the judge misapplied the guidelines and wrongly treated the offence as one of higher culpability.

Held, allowing the appeal, that (1) when sentencing for offences involving death by dangerous driving, several points ought to be borne in mind, namely (i) every case represented a human tragedy, particularly where it was a child's life that was lost, and no term of imprisonment would cure the bereaved of their loss. There could be no comparison between the length of sentence and the life lost; (ii) unlike other cases, there was no intention on the behalf of a defendant to cause harm. There had to be some proportionality between cases of the instant kind and cases where violence was intended; (iii) courts should strive to achieve consistency in following the guidelines. The fact that a sentence passed at Crown Court was lower than expected, or reduced on appeal, whilst disappointing, did not mean that it did not recognise the loss. (2) The judge misapplied the guidelines and placed M in the higher level of culpability. As the offence was not aggravated by, for example, drink or drugs, M did not fall within that category. M carried out a highly dangerous and inappropriate manoeuvre and fell within the intermediate category. The sentence was quashed and one of two years and six months' imprisonment was substituted, *Attorney General's*

Reference (No.152 of 2002), Re [2003] EWCA Crim 996, [2003] 3 All E.R. 40, [2004] C.L.Y. 3333 applied.

R. v. MARTIN (JUSTIN THOMAS), [2005] EWCA Crim 748, [2005] 2 Cr. App. R. (S.) 99, Rose, L.J., CA (Crim Div).

3551. **Causing death by dangerous driving–Drivers racing each other involved in high speed collision–Undue leniency**

The Attorney General referred to the court as unduly lenient sentences of three and a half years and two and a half years' imprisonment that had been imposed on L and M respectively following their convictions for causing death by dangerous driving. L and M had been racing each other on a dual carriageway in open countryside at a speed estimated by an accident investigator to have been roughly 110 mph. Their vehicles collided and M's hit a tree, causing fatal injuries to one of his passengers and serious injuries to himself and to his two other passengers. M pleaded guilty to the offence on the day set down for the start of the trial. Both L and M were of previous good character and had good driving records. The Attorney General argued that the case fell into the "most serious culpability" category of the categories identified in *Attorney General's Reference (No.152 of 2002), Re* [2003] EWCA Crim 996, [2003] 3 All E.R. 40, [2004] C.L.Y. 3333, and that the sentences imposed failed to reflect L and M's culpability.

Held, dismissing the references, that although the sentences were lenient, they were not unduly so. The essence of L and M's culpability was speed accompanied by competitive racing over a relatively short distance; the correct categorisation of the case was at the lower end of the higher rung of culpability, *Attorney General's Reference (No.152 of 2002)* considered. Although this was a bad case of competitive driving at a grossly excessive speed, the competitive driving had not been prolonged and had not taken place in a congested urban area. The correct starting point would have been a sentence of the order of four years. In M's case, regard should be had to his plea of guilty, albeit at a late stage, the fact that he had been seriously injured himself and the serious effects that his imprisonment had had on his wife and children.

ATTORNEY GENERAL'S REFERENCE (NOS.11 AND 12 OF 2005), *Re* [2005] EWCA Crim 450, Dyson, L.J., CA (Crim Div).

3552. **Causing death by dangerous driving–Driving while over the limit–Driving at high speed in crowded street resulting in death of pedestrian**

The appellant (S) appealed against a sentence of six years' imprisonment and disqualification for 15 years for causing death by dangerous driving. S had driven at speed down a busy shopping street whilst intoxicated. He had been driving a badly maintained vehicle. S braked and skidded before colliding with two pedestrians, one of whom died from her injuries. On appeal, S submitted that he had not been given sufficient credit for his guilty plea, the basis of which was that he had not seen the pedestrians.

Held, allowing the appeal, that insufficient credit had been afforded to S for his guilty plea. It appeared that the sentencing judge had categorised the offence as one of high culpability, *Attorney General's Reference (No.152 of 2002), Re* [2003] EWCA Crim 996, [2003] 3 All E.R. 40, [2004] C.L.Y. 3333 considered. Although horrific, the offence was not so serious that it justified a sentence of nine years' imprisonment following a contested trail. Therefore, some reduction in sentence was necessary. S was entitled to full credit for his very early guilty plea and therefore the sentence was reduced to five years' imprisonment. The period of disqualification was excessive and was reduced to seven years.

R. v. SMITH (CRAIG ASHLEY), [2004] EWCA Crim 2867, [2005] 2 Cr. App. R. (S.) 8, Rose, L.J., CA (Crim Div).

3553. Causing death by dangerous driving–Driving while over the limit–Unroadworthy motorcycle–Highly culpable standard of driving

The appellant (O) appealed against his sentence of six and a half years' imprisonment, having pleaded guilty to causing death by dangerous driving. O had consumed at least three and a half pints of lager and had then driven his motorcycle at between 80 and 100 mph on a road with a 60 mph speed limit with his girlfriend riding pillion. While overtaking a car, O clipped its rear and he and his passenger were flung from the motorcycle. His girlfriend died almost immediately from head injuries. O was found to have had 116 milligrams of alcohol in 100 millilitres of blood and had smoked cannabis the previous evening. He did not have a licence and was uninsured. He also knew that the brakes were defective. O had a previous conviction for driving with excess alcohol and was released on licence from a young offender institution with 19 months of a sentence for armed robbery still unexpired. O contended that a starting point of between nine and 10 years' imprisonment was too high.

Held, allowing the appeal, that the seriousness of a particular offence of causing death by dangerous driving depended upon the degree of the driver's culpability. In the instant case, O's driving was of a highly culpable standard. However, the starting point for an offence of that seriousness was eight years' imprisonment, *Attorney General's Reference (No.152 of 2002), Re* [2003] EWCA Crim 996, [2003] 3 All E.R. 40, [2004] 2 C.L. 455 considered. In the light of O's guilty plea and remorse, his sentence should have been five and a half years' imprisonment.

R. v. O'ROURKE (STEPHEN MICHAEL), [2004] EWCA Crim 1808, [2005] 1 Cr. App. R. (S.) 53, Hooper, L.J., CA (Crim Div).

3554. Causing death by dangerous driving–Fatigue–Driving knowingly deprived of sleep–Undue leniency

The Attorney General referred as unduly lenient a sentence of 18 months' imprisonment imposed upon the offender (E) following his conviction of an offence of causing death by dangerous driving. E, a lorry driver, had fallen asleep at the wheel of his vehicle, which had drifted across the carriageway, killing the driver of an oncoming vehicle. E had failed to get an adequate amount of sleep the night before driving. He had been exceeding the speed limit and had used his mobile phone while driving. E had not awakened until his vehicle came to rest after the collision, and had sought to blame the victim for the accident. Although E had pleaded guilty he had challenged the factual basis for the sentence.

Held, allowing the reference, that the aggravating features of the offence, namely that E must have known that he was deprived of adequate sleep and rest, warranted a starting point above the category of intermediate seriousness and into the next category of higher culpability, *Attorney General's Reference (No.152 of 2002), Re* [2003] EWCA Crim 996, [2003] 3 All E.R. 40, [2004] C.L.Y. 3333 applied. The appropriate sentencing bracket was four to five years' imprisonment. Any mitigation afforded by E's guilty plea was reduced by his refusal to admit the full extent of his culpability until close to the hearing. Accordingly, having regard to the principle of double jeopardy, the sentence was quashed and substituted with a sentence of three years' imprisonment.

ATTORNEY GENERAL'S REFERENCE (NO.158 OF 2004), *Re; sub nom.* R. v. ELLIS (RUSSELL JOHN), [2005] EWCA Crim 1588, [2006] 1 Cr. App. R. (S.) 50, Gage, L.J., CA (Crim Div).

3555. Causing death when under the influence–Careless driving–Four year custodial term

The appellant (S) appealed against a sentence of four years' imprisonment imposed after she was convicted of causing death by driving without due care and attention whilst unfit to drive through drink or drugs. S had lost control of her car whilst attempting to negotiate a notoriously hazardous series of bends on a country road. The car left the road and struck a tree. One of S's passenger died as a result of the injuries he sustained. Both S and a second passenger suffered serious injuries. A blood specimen taken at the hospital after the accident revealed that S had between 76 and 136 milligrammes of alcohol in 100 millilitres of her blood. An accident investigator had concluded that the likely cause of the accident was that S had misjudged the bend, being inattentive on the approach, or had been travelling at a marginally excessive speed to negotiate the bend. At trial S had maintained that she had not been the driver of the car although she subsequently accepted the facts of her conviction. In imposing the four year term, the judge below had considered the fact that S had no previous convictions, that she herself had suffered serious injury and that she was a young single mother whose son would be deprived of her care whilst she was in custody.

Held, allowing the appeal, that although the sentencing judge had taken all the relevant factors into account, he had imposed an unnecessarily long sentence. The four year term was quashed and a sentence of three years' imprisonment was substituted.

R. v. SZLUKOVINYI (JUNE ELIZABETH), [2004] EWCA Crim 1788, [2005] 1 Cr. App. R. (S.) 55, Keene, L.J., CA (Crim Div).

3556. **Causing death when under the influence—Mitigation—Meritorious conduct unconnected with offence**

The appellant (W) appealed against a sentence of four years' imprisonment for causing death by careless driving when under the influence of alcohol. W had pleaded guilty upon rearraignment but had previously maintained that his wife had been driving at the material time. Between the date of the accident and sentencing, W had saved the life of a driver whose vehicle had skidded down an embankment, notwithstanding the risk to himself.

Held, allowing the appeal, that there was clear authority for taking into account unconnected and commendable actions of a defendant in mitigation, *R. v. Reid (Ian)* (1982) 4 Cr. App. R. (S.) 280, [1983] C.L.Y. 855, *R. v. Dawn (Andrew Stephen)* (1994) 15 Cr. App. R. (S.) 720, [1995] C.L.Y. 1444 and *R. v. Alexander (Adrian Stephen)* [1997] 2 Cr. App. R. (S.) 74, [1997] C.L.Y. 1576 considered. W's conduct demonstrated that he was both brave and trustworthy and it was appropriate to reduce his sentence to three years' imprisonment.

R. v. WENMAN (FRANK SAMUEL), [2004] EWCA Crim 2995, [2005] 2 Cr. App. R. (S.) 3, Lord Woolf of Barnes, L.C.J., CA (Crim Div).

3557. **Cheating the Revenue—Confiscation orders—Company used for purposes of fraud—Lifting of corporate veil**

The appellant (O) appealed against a confiscation order in the sum of £790,649 payable within 12 months, with a period of three years' imprisonment consecutive in default. O was convicted of an offence of cheating the Public Revenue. O had allowed his company (C) to be used for the purposes of fraud. O's wife owned half the shares in C. A number of properties had been bought out of the profits made by C. The judge lifted the corporate veil and found that a benefit had accrued to O. O argued that the judge was wrong to lift the corporate veil and to treat the benefit as attributable to him rather than to C; that the properties that had been purchased were the property of C, not O, and that the order was unfair because half of the value of C's assets was owned by O's wife as a 50 per cent shareholder.

Held, dismissing the appeal, that the confiscation order made by the judge was well within his discretion. The order was neither unfair nor created a risk of serious injustice. C was used by O for the purposes of fraud. It was O's alter ego, with O running it and making all the decisions, including decisions on the purchase of the properties. The judge was fully entitled to lift the corporate veil and to treat the benefit accruing during the period of C's involvement in the fraud as a benefit of O. Once the corporate veil was lifted the judge was entitled to treat the properties as assets of O, even though they had been purchased with C's money. O's wife's involvement in C was nominal. Although she was a shareholder, all the relevant decisions, including the decisions to purchase the relevant properties, were made by O. As such it was difficult to see on what basis the order could be said to be unfair, *R. v. Benjafield (Karl Robert) (Confiscation Order)* [2002] UKHL 2, [2003] 1 A.C. 1099, [2002] C.L.Y. 3897 considered.

R. v. OMAR (BASSAM), [2004] EWCA Crim 2320, [2005] 1 Cr. App. R. (S.) 86, Scott Baker, L.J., CA (Crim Div).

3558. Child abduction—Assault by penetration—Undue leniency

[Sexual Offences Act 2003.]

The Attorney General referred as unduly lenient, an extended sentence comprising four years' imprisonment and an extended licence period of three years following pleas of guilty by the defendant (Y) to abducting a child and assault of a child under 13 by penetration. Y had approached the victim (V), a five year old child, who had been waiting outside a shop. He took her to his home where he took off her underwear and licked her vagina to the extent of penetration. V's mother was told that she had been seen going into Y's home and she was rescued. Y firstly gave a no comment interview then contended that V had followed him but denied touching her. Forensic evidence matched Y's DNA with saliva found in V's underwear. The Attorney General contended that the aggravating features were the fact that V was only five years old and especially vulnerable, she was abducted by a stranger and she was only released when others intervened. In mitigation were Y's pleas of guilty and his lack of previous convictions for sexual offences. The Attorney General argued that the judge had failed to have regard to the aggravating factor of abduction, which should have been reflected in the sentence for the assault or by imposing a consecutive sentence. Further, that insufficient regard had been had to the Sexual Offences Act 2003 under which the maximum sentence was life imprisonment.

Held, allowing the reference, that the sentence passed was unduly lenient. Given the seriousness of the abduction, a sentence separate from and consecutive to the offence of assault was called for. Where offences were charged separately it was only right to impose consecutive sentences and it was preferable to treating the abduction as an aggravating feature. If the trial had been contested, a sentence of between five to six years for the assault and four to five years for the abduction running consecutively would have been appropriate in the court below. Given the early plea Y was entitled to a significant discount and, at first instance, a custodial sentence of six years minimum would have been appropriate. Taking into account double jeopardy the sentence for the assault was quashed with an extended sentence of three years' imprisonment and extended licence period of three years substituted. The two year sentence for the abduction would remain the same but run consecutively.

ATTORNEY GENERAL'S REFERENCE (NO. 112 OF 2004), Re; sub nom. R. v. YEMM (ANDREW NEIL) [2005] EWCA Crim 961, Kennedy, L.J., CA (Crim Div).

3559. Child abduction—Attempts—Longer than commensurate sentence due to risk of reoffending—Jurisdiction to impose longer sentence for child abduction

[Child Abduction Act 1984; Powers of Criminal Courts (Sentencing) Act 2000 s.80(2)(b), s.161(2).]

B, who was convicted of attempted child abduction, appealed against his sentence of seven years' imprisonment imposed under the Powers of Criminal Courts (Sentencing) Act 2000 s.80(2)(b). B had approached an eight year old boy and asked him if he would like an ice cream. The boy went to ask his father, who called the police. B had a long criminal record which included a conviction for indecent assault on a male child under the age of 14 and another for abducting a child. A pre sentence report indicated a very high risk that B would reoffend and that there was a potential risk of serious harm to the public, in particular to young males. For that reason the judge imposed a longer than commensurate sentence, stating that a commensurate sentence would have been five years' imprisonment. On appeal, B contended that (1) there was no jurisdiction to impose a longer than normal sentence as child abduction did not come within the Act; (2) a commensurate sentence of five years was manifestly excessive given that this was only an attempt.

Held, allowing the appeal, that the judge did not have the power to impose a longer than commensurate sentence, but five years imprisonment was appropriate. (1) A longer than commensurate sentence could only be imposed under s.80 of the Act for a violent or sexual offence, but "sexual offence" as defined in s.161(2) did not include an offence committed under the Child Abduction Act 1984, *R. v. Wrench (Peter)* [1996] 1 Cr. App. R. 340, [1996] C.L.Y. 1566 applied. Accordingly, although the judge assumed the offence was sexual, she did not have jurisdiction to impose such a sentence on B. In the absence of any findings of B having physical contact with the child, it was not possible to view B's offence as violent, *R. v. Newsome (Peter Alan)* [1997] 2 Cr. App. R. (S.) 69, [1977] C.L.Y. 1428 distinguished. (2) Although seven years' imprisonment was the statutory maximum for the substantive offence of child abduction, a sentence of five years was not excessive for an attempt where the judge had found the defendant clearly intended indecency towards the victim. B had an appalling record, including convictions for offences of the same kind, and he had not pleaded guilty or shown remorse.

R. v. BAILEY (WILLIAM), [2004] EWCA Crim 3058, [2005] 2 Cr. App. R. (S.) 16, Maurice Kay, L.J., CA (Crim Div).

3560. **Child abduction–Disqualification from working with children–Unlawful sentences–No power to impose order for offence under Child Abduction Act 1984 s.2**

[Child Abduction Act 1984 s.2; Criminal Justice and Court Services Act 2000 s.28, Sch.4.]

The appellant (P) appealed against a sentence of four years' imprisonment and disqualification from working with children, having pleaded guilty to an offence of abducting a child contrary to the Child Abduction Act 1984 s.2. P had asked a nine year old boy at a fireworks party to go with him to a shop. He had then assaulted the child by hitting him in the face, kicking his leg and scratching his neck before running off. P had a single previous conviction for violent disorder, for which he was sentenced to 18 months' imprisonment. P gave no reason for the assault, a pre sentence report considered that he presented a risk to children. P contended that the sentencing judge (1) had treated the case more seriously than the facts warranted and failed to give sufficient credit for his guilty plea or took too high a starting point; (2) lacked jurisdiction to impose the disqualification.

Held, allowing the appeal, that (1) seven years' imprisonment was the maximum sentence for child abduction under the 1984 Act and a starting point of about six years in the instant case was too high for an unpremeditated offence that lasted under an hour and lacked any sexual touching. Three years' imprisonment was appropriate after a guilty plea. (2) An offender could only be disqualified from working with children under the Criminal Justice and Court Services Act 2000 s.28 for offences set out in Sch.4 to that Act. Therefore the sentencing judge did not have the power to impose a disqualification order under s.28. (3) (Obiter) Concern was expressed at this apparent omission and the need for an urgent amendment was to be brought to the attention of the secretary of state.

R. v. PRIME (ROY VINCENT), [2004] EWCA Crim 2009, [2005] 1 Cr. App. R. (S.) 45, Judge, L.J., CA (Crim Div).

3561. **Child cruelty–Mother allowing boyfriend to hit child with stick–History of domestic violence–Insufficient credit given for early plea**

The appellant (O) appealed against a sentence of two years' imprisonment having pleaded guilty to cruelty to a child. O had allowed her boyfriend to hit her six year old daughter with a stick on a number of occasions. When seen by child protection officers and social services, the child was found to have extensive bruising and a limp. O contended that the sentencing judge did not take fully into account her early plea. O submitted that the child's injuries were not of the gravest nature and that she had not inflicted them. Further, she was of previous good character and had also been the victim of her boyfriend's violence.

Held, allowing the appeal, that although the sentence was correct, O should have been given greater credit for her early plea. A delay of nearly eight months from plea to sentencing was caused by the disappearance of the boyfriend.

R. v. O (TINA DONNA), [2004] EWCA Crim 1750, [2005] 1 Cr. App. R. (S.) 47, Kennedy, L.J., CA (Crim Div).

3562. Child cruelty–Parents–Unreasonable chastisement–Appropriateness of a non custodial sentence–Undue leniency

[Children and Young Persons Act 1933 s.1 (1).]

The Attorney General referred as unduly lenient a two year community rehabilitation order imposed on the offender (V) who had pleaded guilty to three offences of child cruelty contrary to the Children and Young Persons Act 1933 s.1 (1). The offences, committed over a period of 12 months against three of his children aged 8, 10 and 13, had involved V using various ill treatments as means of chastisement. The order imposed on V contained a condition that he cooperate with the Probation Service and local authority to address his offending behaviour. The Attorney General outlined the aggravating features, namely that there were three separate victims; the ill treatment occurred over a significant period of time, and the victims were the offender's own children and were, therefore, particularly vulnerable. In mitigation V submitted that he had pleaded guilty at the first appearance, that the offences had involved excessive horseplay and inappropriate forms of punishment and chastisement; that he had expressed genuine remorse and a desire to improve his parenting skills; that he had no previous offences for any kind of violence.

Held, refusing the reference, that in balancing the mitigating and aggravating features V's sentence was not outside the range of sentences properly available to the judge on the facts of the instant case and was not unduly lenient. The judge had been entitled to find that the need to change V's attitude towards his parenting responsibilities, and the fact that he still had young children, were more important factors than the benefits a short term prison sentence would have had on him and on deterring others. Cases involving ill treatment of a child were always regarded as serious and prison was often appropriate, particularly where there was evidence of bruising or other injuries to the child. An appropriate sentence should also reflect the age of the victim and the motive behind the ill treatment. Chastisement for a child's misbehaviour which went too far was less serious than the infliction of pain gratuitously or from malice, *R. v. Howard (John)* (1992) 13 Cr. App. R. (S.) 720, [1993] C.L.Y. 1010, *R. v. Burrows (Lorraine Shirley)* [1998] 2 Cr. App. R. (S.) 407, [1999] C.L.Y. 1097 and *R. v. AS* (Unreported, February 28, 2000) considered.

ATTORNEY-GENERAL'S REFERENCE (NO.105 OF 2004), Re; sub nom. R. v. H, [2004] EWCA Crim 3295, [2005] 2 Cr. App. R. (S.) 42, Keene, L.J., CA (Crim Div).

3563. Committal for contempt–Suspended committal orders–Custody not appropriate for breach of court order

The appellant father (F) appealed against an order for his committal to prison for seven days suspended for six months on terms. The underlying proceedings had related to the future of the children of F and the respondent mother and in particular their daughter (K). An order had been made that F collect K from school on one occasion and return her to the home of M by no later than 4 pm. M had issued contempt proceedings alleging, inter alia, that F had returned K ten minutes late. That had been denied by F, but at the committal hearing the judge found the allegation proved. In sentencing the judge found that a fine was not appropriate as F had limited means. The judge asked counsel for M for comments upon the appropriate disposal of the application. M stated that she thought prison was appropriate; however, the judge intimated that he considered that custody was not an appropriate sentence for the breach. On that basis the judge made the suspended order for committal on terms. F argued that (1) the judge had been wrong to find that he was in breach of the order, and (2) the sentence was excessive.

Held, allowing the appeal, that (1) the judge was entitled upon the evidence to find that F had breached the order by returning K late. (2) The judge's approach to sentencing was however contrary to principle. He had clearly considered that a fine would have been appropriate but for F's lack of means, and on that basis he resorted to custody, albeit suspended. The court was not entitled to impose a sentence of custody simply because the defendant did not have the means to pay a fine. Further, the court was not entitled to make an order suspending committal to prison unless it was first satisfied that custody was justified. It was also unusual to invite comment from the applicant on an application for committal as to the appropriate penalty to be imposed. That was a matter for the court. However, the exchange that did occur between the judge and M's counsel reinforced the fact that the judge did not consider that custody was appropriate. The judge's sentence was therefore quashed and replaced by one of no order for the breach found.

M (A CHILD) (CONTACT ORDER: COMMITTAL FOR CONTEMPT), *Re*; *sub nom*. M (CHILDREN), *Re*, [2005] EWCA Civ 615, [2005] 2 F.L.R. 1006, Ward, L.J., CA (Civ Div).

3564. **Community punishment and rehabilitation orders–Disparity of sentence–Power to refer offences under s.20 Offences against the Person Act 1861–Undue leniency;**

[Offences against the Person Act 1861 s.20.]

The Attorney General referred, as unduly lenient, a community punishment and rehabilitation order comprising 80 hours' punishment and 12 months' rehabilitation following a plea of guilty to robbery by the defendant (G). G, who had been 17 at the time of the offence, and a co-defendant (T) attacked the 16 year old victim (V) outside his own home believing him to have money and drink belonging to them. T punched V's face and, when he fell to the ground, G kicked him to the face with his steel capped boot and ripped a chain from V's neck. When arrested T admitted assaulting V but denied knowledge of the robbery. G was interviewed on three occasions and denied the offence. Following identification by V, G still denied the offence, but eventually pleaded guilty to robbery. T's plea of guilty to unlawful wounding under the Offences against the Person Act 1861 s.20 was accepted by the Crown and he was sentenced to a community punishment and rehabilitation order. The Attorney General contended that the judge was in error to pass a non-custodial sentence given the aggravating features that: (i) gratuitous and excessive violence was used in a public place; (ii) V was 16 and defenceless; (iii) there had been a motive of retribution and revenge; (iv) the attack was just outside V's home; (v) the offence followed an episode of binge drinking and the courts should make it clear that such offences would be dealt with severely; and (vi) G had several previous convictions. The Attorney General submitted that the sentence fell outside the reasonable discretion of the judge and that the offence should have carried a sentence of three years following conviction and up to two years following a plea.

Held, finding the sentence to be unduly lenient but not varying it, that the sentence was unduly lenient and immediate custodial sentences should have been imposed on both G and T. The steel capped boot with which G kicked V was plainly a weapon. The judge was placed in some difficulty when sentencing by reason of the fact that the Crown accepted T's plea to the s.20 offence when the reality of the case was a joint attack started by T and completed by G. The Attorney General had made no application in relation to T as he had no power to refer in cases involving sentences passed under s.20 of the Act. Section 20 offences carried a maximum five year sentence whereas the maximum penalty for robbery was life imprisonment. The court expressed surprise that the Attorney General had no power to refer sentences under s.20 as there were many cases under that section dealt with across the country and a frequent number of instances where public concern was expressed in relation to leniency. The fact that the Attorney General had no power to refer T's sentence gave rise to real problems of disparity in the instant case. In all the circumstances it was not appropriate to vary G's sentence as, if the sentence were increased, there would be an immediate significant and unjust disparity between G and T. Further, G had made considerable progress since the sentence was passed and had done everything expected of him and it was not in the public interest to terminate the community punishment and rehabilitation order.

ATTORNEY GENERAL'S REFERENCE (NO.44 OF 2005), *Re; sub nom.* R. v. GUIRDHAM (DANIEL) [2005] EWCA Crim 2211, Scott Baker, L.J., CA (Crim Div).

3565. Community punishment and rehabilitation orders–False imprisonment– Judge taking exceptional course–Undue leniency

The Attorney General referred to the court as unduly lenient, a 100 hour community punishment order and a two year rehabilitation order following a plea of guilty to false imprisonment. The defendant (G) assaulted his landlady (V) and was arrested, charged and bailed. Bail conditions prohibited G from contacting V or from returning to the area where she lived. Three days later he returned, bursting into V's house and locking the doors after him. He pulled out the phone wire and pushed V's son and daughter out of the house. G held a knife against V's throat but said he wouldn't hurt her. When interviewed G stated he had drank a large amount of alcohol and had returned to the house to collect his clothes. He admitted holding a knife to V's throat but said he had mental problems and would have killed himself and not her. A psychiatric report stated G was suffering from bereavement reaction and was on anti depressants, and that he did not represent a serious risk of reoffending and was not a risk to the victim or women in general. The judge took into account the 10 weeks G had spent in custody prior to being sentenced and held that G had behaved out of character and that it was an exceptional case. The Attorney General contended the penalty failed to reflect the gravity of the offence and the aggravating features. This had been the second offence against the same victim, it was an invasion of V's family home where V and her children were vulnerable, it took place in breach of bail conditions, a weapon had been used and threats to kill had been made and, at the time, G was the subject of an order of the court in relation to a previous offence. In mitigation were G's early admissions, his expression of remorse, his plea of guilty and his mental condition. The starting point for false imprisonment had to be a substantial term of imprisonment and the judge was not justified in taking this exceptional course. G contended there was an exceptional circumstance, G's mental condition and the judge was anxious to reflect that circumstance in the sentence he passed.

Held, allowing the reference but not varying the sentence, that the sentence was unduly lenient but the public interest would not be served by sending G to prison. The judge had had an extremely difficult sentencing exercise and, no doubt, if there had been no exceptional circumstances in mitigation the sentence would properly have been in the order of three years following a plea of guilty. As had been said on many occasions sentencing was an art and not a science and where a Crown Court judge had a proper basis for imposing a lenient sentence, even an unduly lenient sentence, the Court of Appeal ought not interfere lightly. There was a proper basis for the judge to take the exceptional course he did, namely, G's conduct was entirely out of character and the terms of the psychiatric report which asserted the absence of risk posed to women in general and the victim in particular.

ATTORNEY GENERAL'S REFERENCE (NO.25 OF 2004), *Re; sub nom.* R. v. GAY (ALAN THOMAS), [2004] EWCA Crim 1203, [2005] 1 Cr. App. R. (S.) 15, Rose, L.J. (Vice President), CA (Crim Div).

3566. Community rehabilitation orders—Custodial sentence imposed on default—Account taken of early release under home detention curfew scheme

[Powers of Criminal Courts (Sentencing) Act 2000 Sch.3 Part II para.5(1A).]

D appealed against a six month custodial sentence imposed after he failed to attend community rehabilitation, arguing that his previous remand period equated to a 12 month sentence under the home detention curfew scheme. In a dispute involving their children, D had hit his former partner and drawn a knife. After spending three months on remand, he was sentenced to two years' community rehabilitation. After initially attending meetings with his probation officer, D, who had a significant criminal record, failed to continue. On resentencing for the initial offences, the judge began with a figure of 12 months' imprisonment then settled on a concurrent sentence of six months' imprisonment. D appealed on the ground that applying the provisions of the Powers of Criminal Courts (Sentencing) Act 2000 Sch.3 Part II para.5(1A), which allowed for early release under home detention curfew, he had effectively already been remanded for the equivalent of a 12 month sentence, so that the judge was not entitled to pass a custodial sentence.

Held, dismissing the appeal, that allowing for the three month remand period in resentencing meant that the judge had made the appropriate reduction in sentence to allow for the time spent in custody. The judge had avoided precise calculations for the purposes of the early release on home detention curfew scheme. The scheme was discretionary, with its details changing from time to time, and the consequences of applying the scheme were likely to be more arbitrary than the consequences of ignoring it. In some respects, D was fortunate to receive a concurrent sentence, given the extent of his criminal record.

R. v. DALE (ANDREW PETER), [2004] EWCA Crim 231, [2004] 2 Cr. App. R. (S.) 58, Kay, L.J., CA (Crim Div).

3567. Conditional discharge—Indecent photographs of children—Discharge regarded as conviction—Defendant required to notify police as consequence

[Sex Offenders Act 1997 s.1, s.2; Powers of Criminal Courts (Sentencing) Act 2000 s.14(1).]

The Powers of Criminal Courts (Sentencing) Act 2000 s.14(1) has the effect of preventing an order for conditional discharge made on conviction for an offence other than under the Sex Offenders Act 1997 from being classed as a conviction for the purposes of s.1(1) of the 1997 Act and thus of avoiding the notification requirements for sex offenders under the 1997 Act.

The appellant, (L), who was given concurrent 12 month conditional discharges after pleading guilty to two offences of making an indecent photograph or pseudophotograph of children, appealed against the judge's ruling that the discharges counted as convictions under the Sex Offenders Act 1997 s.1 and so he was required by s.2 to notify certain prescribed information to the police. L contended that under the Powers of Criminal Courts (Sentencing) Act 2000 s.14(1) a conditional discharge was deemed not to be a conviction for any purpose other than the purposes of the proceedings.

Held, dismissing the appeal, that although he received conditional discharges, L would be subject to the notification requirements because under s.14(1) of the 2000 Act a discharge was to be regarded as a conviction for the purposes of the proceedings in which the order was made, and the notification requirements under s.2 of the 1997 Act fell within the ambit of those purposes.

R. v. LONGWORTH (GARY DEAN), [2004] EWCA Crim 2145, [2005] 1 Cr. App. R. (S.) 81, Potter, L.J., CA (Crim Div).

3568. Confiscation orders—Compatibility with human rights

[Criminal Justice Act 1988; Human Rights Act 1998 Sch.1 Part I Art.6, Art.8, Part II Art.1.]

The appellant offender (G) appealed against a confiscation order in the sum of £14,822, which had been made following his conviction for theft. G had misappropriated the sum involved from his former employer (B) and appeared to have spent the money on gambling. The judge making the confiscation order concluded that G's interest in the family home amounted to roughly £39,000 and represented a realisable asset. Before the court on the instant appeal was a letter from B stating that G had agreed to repay the money taken. G argued that (1) the confiscation order interfered with his rights under the Human Rights Act 1998 Sch.1 Part I Art.6, Art.8 and Sch.1 Part II Art.1 together with his wife's rights under Art.8; (2) the court should impose a compensation order rather than a confiscation order as he would be doubly penalised were he to repay the amount involved under his agreement with B and be subject to a confiscation order.

Held, dismissing the appeal, that (1) the authorities clearly showed that the confiscation regime introduced by the Criminal Justice Act 1988 did not infringe Art.6 or Sch.1 Part II Art.1, *Phillips v. United Kingdom (41087/98)* 11 B.H.R.C. 280, [2001] C.L.Y. 3537 and *R. v. Rezvi (Syed)* [2002] UKHL 1, [2003] 1 A.C. 1099, [2002] C.L.Y. 3896 followed. It followed that the regime did not contravene Art.8 either. The terms of Art.8(2) were, in their material respects, just as wide as the qualifying second sentence of Sch.1 Part II Art.1. As to G's wife, her Convention rights would be capable of being said to be infringed if, and only if, the home was to be sold to raise the money needed to pay the amount in question. On the material available, it did not appear that such a sale would prove to be necessary. (2) The arrangement between G and B appeared to be thoroughly nebulous. On the information before the court, G was not suffering a double penalty and, indeed, might never do so. There was therefore no justification for replacing the confiscation order with a compensation order, *R. v. Mitchell (Clive)* [2001] 2 Cr. App. R. (S.) 29, [2001] C.L.Y. 1238 considered.

R. v. GOODENOUGH (ALAN JOHN), [2004] EWCA Crim 2260, [2005] 1 Cr. App. R. (S.) 88, May, L.J., CA (Crim Div).

3569. Confiscation orders–Jurisdiction–Defendant pleaded guilty to number of offences–Charges included one which predated commencement of Proceeds of Crime Act 1995–Jurisdiction to make confiscation order under 1995 Act

[Criminal Justice Act 1988; Proceeds of Crime Act 1995 s.16(5).]

The appellant (M) appealed against a confiscation order made under the Proceeds of Crime Act 1995. M had pleaded guilty to 24 offences of dishonesty and had asked for a further 14 offences to be taken into consideration. The confiscation schedule included one count which predated the commencement of the 1995 Act. Following a challenge by M, the Crown had to abandon reliance on that count. M contended that as the Crown had sought a confiscation order in respect of that count, then, under s.16(5), the confiscation proceedings should not have been brought under the 1995 Act.

Held, dismissing the appeal, that a court had jurisdiction to make a confiscation order under the 1995 Act relating to a number of counts, even though one count predated the Act, if the Crown had expressly abandoned any reliance on that count. It was immaterial that the Crown could have sought an order under the Criminal Justice Act 1988. The court would have lacked jurisdiction only if the Crown was seeking, or could still seek, a confiscation order under the 1988 Act, *R. v. Simpson (Ian McDonald)* [2003] EWCA Crim 1499, [2004] Q.B. 118, [2003] C.L.Y. 900 followed.

R. v. ASLAM (MOHAMMED), [2004] EWCA Crim 2801, [2005] 1 Cr. App. R. (S.) 116, Rose, L.J. (V-P), CA (Crim Div).

3570. Confiscation orders–Proceeds of crime–Benefit obtained by receiving and transferring money paid into dormant bank account

[Criminal Justice Act 1988 s.71 (1A), s.93A(1)(a).]

A appealed against an order confiscating funds that had been placed in his bank account, which he claimed he did not know were the proceeds of criminal activity. A had reactivated a dormant business account to assist an acquaintance in transferring money to the United Kingdom from Nigeria to facilitate the setting up of a business. The sum of £121,570 was placed in A's account through the use of a forged letterhead. On discovering the transfer and surprised at the amount, A became suspicious but later agreed to transfer the money to two third party accounts in other banks. A was convicted of an offence under the Criminal Justice Act 1988 s.93A(1)(a). The total amount transferred to his account was held to be a benefit received by A, who was ordered to pay £67,000, being that part of the total transfer that the bank had been unable to recover from the other accounts. A contended that he had obtained the money innocently and not benefited from any criminal conduct under s.71 (1A).

Held, dismissing the appeal, that by dealing with the money with a guilty mind following instructions from the alleged criminal, A had obtained property in connection with the commission of an offence. A's benefit was the value of the property so obtained because benefit under s.71 did not mean personally enjoying the fruits of the criminal conduct. If A, knowing or suspecting that the funds were criminally sourced, had gone to the police without dealing with the funds, no offence would have been committed under either s.71 or s.93A(1)(a).

R. v. ALAGBALA (MICHAEL); *sub nom.* R. v. ALAGOBOLA (MICHAEL), [2004] EWCA Crim 89, [2004] 2 Cr. App. R. (S.) 48, Latham, L.J., CA (Crim Div).

3571. **Confiscation orders–Realisable assets–Right to respect for private and family life–Discretion of court to exclude matrimonial home from assessment**

[Criminal Justice Act 1988 s.71 (6) (b), s.74; Proceeds of Crime Act 1995; Human Rights Act 1998 Sch.1 Part I Art.8.]

The appellants (M and G) appealed against confiscation orders imposed upon them under the Criminal Justice Act 1988 as amended following their convictions. In each case the judge had assessed the figure which, in accordance with the 1988 Act, was to be taken as the benefit that M and G had obtained from their criminal activity. He had then made the confiscation orders based on his assessment of their respective realisable assets, taking into account in each case the value of M's and G's half share in his matrimonial home. The judge had accepted evidence from the families that the houses would probably have to be sold to meet the confiscation order. The judge accepted that he had a discretion whether or not to include those shares but concluded that there were no exceptional circumstances which justified his excluding them. M and G submitted that (1) the judge was correct in concluding that he had a discretion but he exercised it wrongly in refusing to exclude the value of the share in the matrimonial home; (2) the making of the confiscation order infringed their families' rights under the Human Rights Act 1998 Sch.1 Part I Art.8.

Held, dismissing the appeals, that (1) the judge had wrongly concluded that he had a discretion. Prior to the amendment of 1988 Act the court had a general discretion in relation to the making of a confiscation order, but the Proceeds of Crime Act 1995 made substantial changes to the confiscation provisions of the 1988 Act. A power to make a confiscation order was changed to a duty where the prosecution gave appropriate notice. The court had no discretion as to whether to make an order. As to the amount of the order, the court was required to make an order calculated in accordance with s.71 (6) of the 1988 Act. The words "the amount appearing to the court" in s.71 (6) (b) did not import any discretion and merely referred to the arithmetical exercise under s.74 of computing what was in effect a statutory debt. (2) Since the process of assessing the value of realisable property did not involve any discretion or any assessment of the way in which the debt would ultimately be paid, no questions arose under Art.8 at that stage. Different considerations would arise if the debt was not met and the prosecution determined to take enforcement action. Article 8 rights would be engaged if the court was then asked to order the sale of the matrimonial homes. It would be at that stage that the court would have to consider whether it was proportionate to make such an order.

R. v. AHMED (MUMTAZ); R. v. QURESHI (GHULAM); *sub nom.* R. v. AHMED (MUMTAZ), [2004] EWCA Crim 2599, [2005] 1 W.L.R. 122, Latham, L.J., CA (Crim Div).

3572. Conspiracy–Conversion of firearms–Conversion of weapons for use by criminals

The appellant (H) appealed against his sentence of six years' imprisonment, having pleaded guilty to conspiracy to convert imitation firearms. H and his brother had adapted blank firing guns to allow them to fire live ammunition. It was accepted that the weapons would be used by criminals. The sentencing judge indicated that he was allowing only a minor discount from the maximum sentence of seven years' imprisonment for the guilty plea, because H had already benefited from the Crown's not proceeding with a second count of conspiracy to sell firearms and ammunition. H had 35 previous court appearances for more than 77 offences, including two convictions for firearms offences. He contended that the judge was wrong to use the Crown's decision not to proceed with the more serious count as a reason for reducing the credit for the guilty plea.

Held, dismissing the appeal, that whilst the Crown's decision not to proceed with a more serious count on the indictment was not a reason to discount the credit for a guilty plea, nonetheless H's sentence of six years' imprisonment was appropriate for what was still a very serious offence of conspiracy to convert imitation firearms.

R. v. HAMPSON (ANTHONY); R. v. HAMPSON (DAVID JAMES), [2004] EWCA Crim 2011, [2005] 1 Cr. App. R. (S.) 51, Hallett, J., CA (Crim Div).

3573. Conspiracy–Violent disorder–Football supporters arranging to fight other football supporters at railway station–Violence carefully planned

The appellant football supporters appealed against sentences of four years' imprisonment for conspiracy to cause violent disorder. Spontaneous violence broke out at a match between two professional football clubs. Following the match, one of the appellants posted an entry on a website asking if supporters would be attending the return fixture. Arrangements were made on the website for violence to take place between supporters of both clubs at a railway station near to where the return match was being played. Supporters met at the station as planned and violence broke out. Members of the public were frightened and three participants were knocked unconscious. The appellants were sentenced on the basis that they had organised the violence or taken part in the initial communications. The appellants argued that the judge's starting point of four years was too high, particularly given that only bottles were used as weapons and they were thrown rather than wielded, the fighting was brief and there was no serious injury and the incident was not an attack on the public but an arranged fight.

Held, dismissing the appeals, that although a sentence of four years' imprisonment was only a year short of the maximum for the offence of violent disorder, the judge was right to state four years as the starting point for the appellants. What the appellants planned was violent disorder. That did not just mean violence between rival gangs, but conduct which would make members of the public fearful of injury to themselves. It was obvious from the chosen battleground that the public would be present. The amount of planning involved was considerable and arrangements were made well in advance to bring supporters from different parts of the country not just for a football match but for a fight. Mindless violence at or near football grounds was prevalent and had to be discouraged by deterrent sentences. Even though the violence was brief, the plan was an evil one. For those reasons substantial sentences were called for, *R. v. Najeeb (Parvais)* [2003] EWCA Crim 194, [2003] 2 Cr. App. R. (S.) 69, [2003] C.L.Y. 3837 and *Attorney General's Reference (Nos.148, 149, 150, 151, 152, 153, 154 and 155 of 2001), Re* [2002] EWCA Crim 1313, [2002] C.L.Y. 4079 considered.

R. v. GREENALL (WILLIAM), [2004] EWCA Crim 3430, [2005] 2 Cr. App. R. (S.) 46, Rose, L.J., CA (Crim Div).

3574. Crime (Sentences) Act 1997 (c.43)–Commencement No.4 Order

CRIME (SENTENCES) ACT 1997 (COMMENCEMENT NO.4) ORDER 2005, SI 2005 932 (C.41); made under the Crime (Sentences) Act 1997 s.57. Commencement details: bringing into force various provisions of the 1997 Act on April 4, 2005; £3.00.

This Order brings into force the repeal of the Criminal Justice Act 1967 s.67 (computation of sentences of imprisonment passed in England and Wales) subject to a transitional provision.

3575. Criminal procedure–Electronic monitoring of offenders–Accreditation body

CRIMINAL JUSTICE (SENTENCING) (PROGRAMME AND ELECTRONIC MONITORING REQUIREMENTS) ORDER 2005, SI 2005 963; made under the Criminal Justice Act 2003 s.202, s.215, s.330. In force: April 1, 2005; £3.00.

This Order identifies the accreditation body and electronic monitoring provider for the purposes of the programme requirement and electronic monitoring requirement respectively. It continues the designation in relation to the accreditation body made under the Criminal Justice (Sentencing) (Programme and Electronic Monitoring Requirements) Order 2004 (SI 2004 117) which is revoked, and reflects changes made to the police areas covered by the two electronic monitoring providers.

3576. Criminal procedure–Electronic monitoring of offenders–Police areas

CRIMINAL JUSTICE (SENTENCING) (CURFEW CONDITION) ORDER 2005, SI 2005 986; made under the Criminal Justice Act 2003 s.253, s.330. In force: April 4, 2005; £3.00.

This Order makes provision for the different persons responsible for the electronic monitoring of offenders subject to a curfew condition imposed under the Criminal Justice Act 2003 s.246 (power to release prisoners on licence before required to do so). The areas covered by the monitoring providers are set out in Sch.1 and Sch.2 to the Order.

3577. Criminal procedure–Offences–Licence conditions

CRIMINAL JUSTICE (SENTENCING) (LICENCE CONDITIONS) ORDER 2005, SI 2005 648; made under the Criminal Justice Act 2003 s.250, s.330. In force: April 4, 2005; £3.00.

This Order, which revokes the Criminal Justice (Sentencing) (Licence Conditions) Order 2003 (SI 2003 3337), prescribes the conditions for inclusion in a prisoner's licence when he is released from prison.

3578. Cultivation of cannabis–Effect of reclassification of cannabis as Class C drug

[Misuse of Drugs Act 1971 s.6; Criminal Justice Act 2003 Sch.28.]

The appellant (H) appealed against sentence following his plea of guilty to an offence of cultivating cannabis contrary to the Misuse of Drugs Act 1971 s.6. H's landlord attended his premises to collect rent and saw what he thought was a body and contacted the police. The police found no body but discovered 52 cannabis plants under cultivation. Following H's guilty plea the judge sentenced him to 12 months' imprisonment. H submitted that following the reclassification of cannabis as a Class C drug, the sentence of 12 months' imprisonment was too high. H further submitted that Parliament had intended that simple possession should be regarded less seriously and that should be reflected in sentences for cultivation of cannabis where it was clear that the cannabis was for personal use alone.

Held, allowing the appeal, that s.6 of the Act covered a wide spectrum of criminality from industrial farming for a substantial profit to those who kept a few cannabis plants for personal use. A widening of the gap in sentencing between those cases where supply was an object and those where it was not would reflect what Parliament had sought to achieve through the increased penalties prescribed in the Criminal Justice Act 2003 Sch.28. Where it was clear that the cultivation of cannabis was for personal use and there was a guilty plea, a sentence of between six and nine months' imprisonment was appropriate, *R. v. Davy (Leonard Francis)* [1997] 1 Cr. App. R. (S.) 17, [1997] C.L.Y. 1517, *R. v. Bennett (John)* [1998] 1 Cr. App. R. (S.) 429, [1998] C.L.Y. 1193 and *R. v. Evans (Roger Paul)* [2000] 1 Cr. App. R. (S.) 107, [2000] C.L.Y. 1205 considered. However, no reduction of sentence should be made where an element of supply was involved, *R. v. Donovan (Terrence Mark)* [2004] EWCA Crim 1237, [2005] 1 Cr. App. R. (S.) 16, [2005] 4 C.L. 457 and *R. v. Mitchell (Natalie)* [2004] EWCA Crim 2945 followed. In the circumstances, a sentence of six months' imprisonment was appropriate.

R. v. HERRIDGE (MATTHEW JOHN), [2005] EWCA Crim 1410, [2006] 1 Cr. App. R. (S.) 45, Waller, L.J., CA (Crim Div).

3579. Custody—Remand—Concurrent and consecutive sentences

REMAND IN CUSTODY (EFFECT OF CONCURRENT AND CONSECUTIVE SENTENCES OF IMPRISONMENT) RULES 2005, SI 2005 2054; made under the Criminal Justice Act 2003 s.240. In force: July 23, 2005; £3.00.

These Rules provide for the cases in which a court is not required to direct that the number of days spent by an offender remanded in custody is to count as time served by him as part of his sentence. The Rules provide that no direction should be made if, while on remand, the offender was also serving another sentence of imprisonment and was not released on licence; and that no direction is to be made where a court imposes a sentence to be served consecutively on a sentence to which the Criminal Justice Act 1967 s.67 applies.

3580. Dangerous dogs—Keeping aggravated dogs dangerously out of control—Appropriateness of custodial sentence

[Dangerous Dogs Act 1991 s.3(1).]

C appealed against a nine-month prison sentence imposed following a guilty plea to the offence of keeping aggravated dogs dangerously out of control, contrary to the Dangerous Dogs Act 1991 s.3(1). C's household contained five dogs and other animals. While she was in the bath, the dogs escaped and savaged a boy in a park. He suffered multiple puncture wounds and serious scarring. The pre sentence report showed that C, although of good character, lived in a chaotic home with poor care and control over the dogs. A probation officer suggested that she was negligent to the point of reckless. The judge found that the offence was so serious that only a custodial sentence was justified.

Held, allowing the appeal, that by creating an aggravated form of the offence, Parliament required that the courts consider injury as a seriously aggravating feature. A custodial sentence was an appropriate means of marking the nature and extent of the obligation that dog owners owed to all who could be affected if their dogs roamed free. However, C should only be deprived of her liberty for three months rather than nine because she was of good character and she would normally have ensured that the dogs stayed at home. A short sentence remained useful because it was important to recognise the harm done to the victim and the public interest in requiring dog owners to control their dogs.

R. v. COX (JACQUELINE), [2004] EWCA Crim 282, [2004] 2 Cr. App. R. (S.) 54, Lord Woolf of Barnes, L.C.J., CA (Crim Div).

3581. Dangerous driving—Disqualification—Driving in excess of 100 miles per hour—Previous conviction for similar offence

[Powers of the Criminal Courts (Sentencing) Act 2000 s.1.]

The appellant (U) appealed against the imposition of a three year driving disqualification after he had pleaded guilty to an offence of dangerous driving. The plea of guilty had been entered on rearraignment on the day of the trial. Police officers had observed U driving at high speed on a dual carriageway. U's speed was recorded at 137 miles per hour. U had a previous conviction for driving in excess of 100 miles per hour in respect of which he had been disqualified for a period of 50 days in 1999. U submitted that the three year disqualification period was manifestly excessive as the only aggravating feature in his case was the previous conviction and thus, the level of culpability did not support the imposition of a driving ban which was three times longer than the minimum disqualification period.

Held, dismissing the appeal, that U had driven at grossly excessive speed and the slightest incident could have had very serious consequences. U had driven at an appalling speed which constituted a second speeding offence for driving in excess of 100 miles per hour. In those circumstances, it was impossible to say that the three year disqualification period was in any way excessive, *Attorney General's Reference (No.152 of 2002), Re* [2003] EWCA Crim 996, [2003] 3 All E.R. 40, [2004] C.L.Y. 3333 considered.

R. v. UNDERWOOD (ANTHONY), [2004] EWCA Crim 1816, [2005] 1 Cr. App. R. (S.) 54, Hooper, L.J., CA (Crim Div).

3582. Dangerous driving–Grievous bodily harm–Driving while disqualified– Passenger seriously injured–Appropriateness of consecutive sentences

The appellant (B) appealed against a total sentence of three years and four months' detention in a young offender institution following pleas of guilty to driving whilst disqualified, dangerous driving and causing grievous bodily harm. B had committed a number of driving offences whilst evading the police, and a passenger in his car had been seriously injured when he had crashed. The judge had imposed a sentence of 18 months' detention for dangerous driving, a consecutive sentence of four months' detention for driving whilst disqualified and a further consecutive sentence of 18 months' detention for grievous bodily harm to B's passenger. B argued that it had been inappropriate to charge him with dangerous driving and grievous bodily harm as both offences concerned the same underlying illegality. Moreover, to impose consecutive sentences for those offences meant that effectively he had been sentenced twice for the same offence. B contended that, in those circumstances, the total sentence was manifestly excessive.

Held, allowing the appeal, that there was nothing wrong in principle and there was no abuse involved in charging a driver with dangerous driving and grievous bodily harm. However, it had been wrong to impose consecutive terms of detention for those offences as they had both arisen out of the same incident. Nonetheless, the judge below had had in mind the totality of the sentence. B's passenger had sustained serious injury and, given a possible maximum sentence of five years' imprisonment for the offence of grievous bodily harm alone, a sentence of three years' imprisonment for that offence alone would not have been manifestly excessive. In those circumstances, bearing in mind B's guilty plea and his age of 19 years, a total sentence of two years and 10 months' detention was substituted and the sentences for grievous bodily harm and dangerous driving ordered to run concurrently.

R. v. BAIN (STEVEN WILLIAM), [2005] EWCA Crim 7, [2005] 2 Cr. App. R. (S.) 53, Clarke, L.J., CA (Crim Div).

3583. Deferment of sentence–Attorney General's references–Time limit for application for leave

The Attorney General referred to the court as unduly lenient a sentence comprising a two-year conditional discharge and two years' registration on the Sex Offenders Register imposed on B following his guilty pleas to two offences of unlawful intercourse with a girl under the age of 13. B, who at the time had been 17, had met the 12-year-old victim, E, through an internet chat room. They had consensual, unprotected sexual intercourse on two occasions at E's family home. Following the advice of a friend who was a police constable, B attended a local police station and informed an officer that he had engaged in unprotected sex with E. At that stage no complaint had been received by the police. A psychologist assessed B and concluded that custody or participation in a sex offender programme would be potentially damaging. He recommended a programme of individual therapy under his supervision. Sentence was deferred by the judge in the expectation that, if B attended the therapy, the judge would be able to pass a community sentence. When B returned for sentence, the psychologist was confident that there was no significant risk that B would reoffend. B contended that the court should not give leave to refer as a deferral of sentence was itself a sentence which the Attorney General could seek the leave of the court to consider since the judge was bound to indicate that at the end of the deferral period a non custodial disposal could be made. The Attorney General argued that he should not be barred from seeking leave in the instant case when he had only become aware of the circumstances after the initial period of deferral.

Held, refusing the reference, that (1) an application for leave should have been made within 28 days of the date on which the sentence had been deferred. The effect of the deferral was that the judge had, in effect, tied his hands to a non custodial disposal. The court would be extremely reluctant to grant leave after sentence had been passed at the end of the deferral period. It was possible that the matter had only come to the notice of the Attorney General at the instigation of the public or press, but those were the same vehicles that could be used in relation to every sentence passed. Furthermore, the Crown was represented by the Crown Prosecution Service, which was always in a position to refer a case to the Attorney General if it considered that it was appropriate to do so. (2) (Obiter) The sentence in the instant case was lenient. However, the judge had been provided with a number of reasons why leniency was appropriate: B had no record of any kind, E had taken the initiative and she had not been protected by her family as well as she might have been. Furthermore, B had reported the matter to the police, and the psychologist had confirmed that B was not a sexual predator. Normally, a conditional discharge would not reflect the culpability of an offender who had twice had sexual intercourse with a girl of 12 and the need to deter others. However, in the instant case, deterrence could not be the determining factor. Examination of the circumstances of the offences and the available options showed that the judge had done the right thing for the victim, who appeared to have no desire to punish B, for B himself and ultimately for society.

ATTORNEY-GENERAL'S REFERENCE (NO.118 OF 2004), *Re*; *sub nom*. R. v. BARRETT (MICHAEL), [2004] EWCA Crim 3220, [2005] 2 Cr. App. R. (S.) 18, Kennedy, L.J., CA (Crim Div).

3584. **Disqualification–Driving–Power to disqualify drivers not limited to driving offences**

[Powers of Criminal Courts (Sentencing) Act 2000 s.146.]

The appellant (C) appealed against an order disqualifying him from driving for two years pursuant to the Powers of Criminal Courts (Sentencing) Act 2000 s.146 following his conviction for affray. C, a caretaker of student accommodation, had been drinking. He approached a student (G), who rejected his advances. He then drove a vehicle for a short distance and struck a parked car. He returned to the accommodation and obtained a BB gun from his room. G was unsure whether it was a real gun and locked herself in a room. C fired plastic ball bearings at the door of that room, kicked in the door and then left. He was sentenced to 15 months' imprisonment. C contended that s.146 did not give the judge the power to disqualify him since there was no nexus between the offence and his driving.

Held, allowing the appeal, that s.146 was wide in its ambit. It was not necessary for the offence to be connected with the use of a motor vehicle. Section 146 provided an additional punishment available to the court. That did not mean that a court could impose a period of disqualification arbitrarily; it had to have a sufficient reason for doing so. In the instant case, there were good reasons for the judge to make an order disqualifying C since he had admitted that he had driven a vehicle on the night of the offence whilst influenced by drink or drugs. In those circumstances, the judge had been both entitled and right to exercise his powers under s.146. However, it was not necessary for the period of disqualification to have been so long and it was reduced to nine months.

R. v. CLIFF (OLIVER LEWIS), [2004] EWCA Crim 3139, [2005] 2 Cr. App. R. (S.) 22, Gage, L.J., CA (Crim Div).

3585. Driving while disqualified–Anti social behaviour orders–Maximum sentences–Persistent offenders

The appellant (W) appealed against an anti social behaviour order (ASBO). W had admitted to being in breach of a community rehabilitation order, which had been imposed, along with a disqualification from driving order, following his conviction of driving offences. The judge revoked the rehabilitation order but left the disqualification in place. W had 223 convictions for a multitude of offences, many of which were driving offences. The judge had recognised that the ASBO was unusual but had imposed it in order to reinforce the effect of the disqualification. Following the breach of an ASBO a court was able to impose a sentence of up to five years' imprisonment, whereas the maximum sentence for driving whilst disqualified available in the magistrates' court, and that was the only court in which a hearing for such an offence could take place, was six months. The issue was whether, as a matter of principle, an ASBO was available in the instant case.

Held, allowing the appeal, that the imposition of an ASBO following conviction of a driving offence, with the underlying objective of giving the court higher sentencing powers in the event of future offending, was something which should be done only in exceptional circumstances, *R. v. Kirby (Lee)* [2005] EWCA Crim 1228 followed and *R. v. Hall (Billy Paul)* [2004] EWCA Crim 2671, [2005] 1 Cr. App. R. (S.) 118 considered. Such circumstances did not exist in the instant case, consequently the ASBO was quashed.

R. v. WILLIAMS (THEO YESTIN), [2005] EWCA Crim 1796, [2006] 1 Cr. App. R. (S.) 56, Mance, L.J., CA (Crim Div).

3586. Driving while over the limit–Disqualification–Driver unaware drink strengthened with additional alcohol–Driving ability unimpaired

The DPP appealed by way of case stated against a decision that there were special reasons why the defendant (S) should not be disqualified from driving following her conviction for driving with excess alcohol. S had been stopped by police and a breath test had shown that she had consumed a little over twice the legal limit of alcohol. Before being stopped, S had visited a nightclub with a friend and had consumed two bottles of a drink containing vodka and a mixer. Without S's knowledge, her friend had added a double measure of vodka to each drink. The magistrates had found that had S consumed only the two bottled drinks without the additional vodka, she would not have been over the limit. They also found that S had not experienced any effects of intoxication or displayed any signs of impairment as a result of her alcohol consumption, and that there had been nothing unusual about her manner of driving. The magistrates' findings amounted to a partial rejection of expert evidence which suggested that an average person would have been very conscious of being affected by alcohol at the level at which it was detected in S's breath. The DPP submitted that even on the facts found, the magistrates should not have concluded that special reasons for not disqualifying S had been established. He submitted that it was for the driver whose drink had been laced to establish both that it had been laced and that he did not know or suspect that it had been. It was also for the driver to establish that without the additional alcohol he would not have been over the prescribed limit. Expert evidence would often be required to demonstrate those facts and could well impinge on the credibility of the driver's own evidence.

Held, dismissing the appeal, that even though the magistrates' conclusion that S had been unaware of the additional alcohol and that her ability to drive had been unimpaired might seem surprising, it was one which they had been entitled to reach. There was no evidence that S had driven erratically; both S and the police officers who had stopped her had given evidence that her driving was unimpaired, and she had not been examined by a forensic medical examiner to see whether or not her ability was impaired. The magistrates had had broadly in mind the guidance given in *DPP v. O'Connor* (1992) 95 Cr. App. R. 135, [1992] C.L.Y. 1263, and they had found all the necessary facts, *O'Connor* considered. Though their conclusion was one which not every bench might have reached, it was neither perverse nor wrong in law.

DPP v. SHARMA; *sub nom*. R. (ON THE APPLICATION OF DPP) v. SHARMA, [2005] EWHC 879, [2005] R.T.R. 27, Mitting, J., QBD (Admin).

3587. Drug offences – Community punishment and rehabilitation orders – Failure to impose custodial sentence for possession of Class A drugs – Exceptional character references – Undue leniency

The Attorney General referred to the court as unduly lenient a community punishment order of 100 hours and a three year community rehabilitation order imposed on the offender (C) following his guilty plea to possession and possession with intent to supply heroin. C had been stopped whilst alighting a train and was found to be carrying a large quantity of heroin. Since the commission of the offence C had made positive progress and had been involved in activities with the Prince's Trust, who had provided character references stating that he was highly regarded. The Attorney General identified a number of aggravating features including the quantity, quality and value of the drugs and that C was already the subject of a community punishment and rehabilitation order at the time of the offence. The Attorney General identified as mitigating features C's age, guilty plea, the quality of his character references and the positive progress he had made since the offence. The Attorney General submitted that a non custodial sentence could not be justified in a case involving the carrying and supplying of a significant quantity of Class A drugs as the public harm caused by the carrying and supplying of Class A drugs outweighed the interests of the offender.

Held, dismissing the reference, that there were no grounds for the proposition that a non custodial sentence could never be imposed in circumstances such as those in the instant case. However, it would only be in very exceptional circumstances that a non custodial sentence would be imposed, *R. v. Singh (Satvir)* (1988) 10 Cr. App. R. (S.) 402, [1990] C.L.Y. 1290, *Attorney General's Reference (No.146 of 2002), Re* [2003] EWCA Crim 1010, [2003] 2 Cr. App. R. (S.) 107, [2003] C.L.Y. 3691 and *R. v. Jones (Gail Lesley)* [1996] 2 Cr. App. R. (S.) 134, [1996] C.L.Y. 1852 considered. In the instant case the progress that C had made and the strength of his character references justified the judge's conclusion that such exceptional circumstances existed.

ATTORNEY GENERAL'S REFERENCE (NO.21 OF 2005), *Re; sub nom*. R. v. CORRIETTE (JEAN-YVES), [2005] EWCA Crim 1675, [2006] 1 Cr. App. R. (S.) 51, Clarke, L.J., CA (Crim Div).

3588. Drug offences – Drug trafficking – Travel restriction orders – Repeated offences of importing cannabis – Length of order

[Criminal Justice and Police Act 2001 s.33.]

The appellant (C), a man aged 47, appealed against a sentence of seven years' imprisonment and a 10 year travel restriction order imposed under the Criminal Justice and Police Act 2001 s.33 following his conviction of one count of being knowingly concerned in the fraudulent evasion of the prohibition on the importation of a Class B drug. Upon arrival at Gatwick airport, C had been found in possession of 17 kilograms of cannabis resin, which had a street value of £51,000. He had five previous convictions for drugs offences, which included three for the importation of drugs. C contended that the term of imprisonment was manifestly excessive and that the travel restriction was excessive in length and should not in any event run from the date of sentence as had been ordered.

Held, allowing the appeal, that C had shown that he would continue to import drugs regardless of the sentence imposed by the courts. Having demonstrated that, he could expect to receive a significantly longer sentence than would have been imposed for a single importation, *R. v. Aramah (John Uzu)* (1983) 76 Cr. App. R. 190, [1983] C.L.Y. 764.19 considered. Despite C's previous convictions, the sentence was too long and a term of six years' imprisonment was substituted. With regard to the travel restriction order, it was clear from s.33 that it should run from the date of C's release and not from the date of sentence. The court had to consider the duration of the order in terms of how long it was necessary to protect the public from the risk posed by C. Taking into account factors such as C's age, previous convictions, risk of reoffending and family connections, it was apparent that he posed a real risk of future drug trafficking, *R. v. Mee (Jason David)* [2004] EWCA Crim 629, [2004] 2 Cr. App. R. (S.) 81, [2004] C.L.Y. 3458 considered. In view of C's history of similar offences, an order of five years commencing from his release date was appropriate.

R. v. CAMPBELL (MICHAEL GEORGE), [2004] EWCA Crim 2333, [2005] 1 Cr. App. R. (S.) 92, Rose, L.J., CA (Crim Div).

3589. Drug offences–Foreign nationals–Additional penalties imposed by native jurisdiction–Relevance to sentence length

The appellant (U), a 54 year old Nigerian national who had pleaded guilty to being knowingly concerned in the fraudulent evasion of the prohibition on the importation of a Class A drug, appealed against a sentence of 12 years' imprisonment. When stopped at an airport, having arrived on an international flight, U had admitted carrying heroin, although he was found to be carrying packages of cocaine. At trial, U had initially relied on a defence of duress. However, following an investigation by Customs officers sent to Nigeria, which found that the evidence in support of U's defence was false, he had changed his plea to guilty. U had submitted in mitigation that he was of good character, he was merely a courier of the drugs and he had pleaded guilty. U now submitted that (1) given that he had been found to be in possession of the equivalent of 3.13 kilos of cocaine at 100 per cent purity, the judge had not adopted the correct starting point. Alternatively, he had adopted the correct starting point but had failed to deduct a sufficient discount taking into account the mitigating factors; (2) the sentence should be reduced to take into account the fact that when he was returned to Nigeria U would be liable to further punishment or imprisonment for the offence.

Held, dismissing the appeal, that (1) the sentence of 12 years' imprisonment was not manifestly excessive or wrong in principle. U had been correctly sentenced in between the guideline sentencing thresholds set in *R. v. Aranguren (Jose de Jesus)* (1994) 99 Cr. App. R. 347, [1995] C.L.Y. 1364, *Aranguren* followed. The judge had been correct to limit the sentence discount for U's guilty plea. The plea had been tendered late in the proceedings and had only been made following an attempted defence of duress. U was a trusted courier who had been depended on to deliver valuable drugs, a fact that was reflected in his sentence, *R. v. Akyeah (Christiana)* [2003] EWCA Crim 1988, [2004] 1 Cr. App. R. (S.) 36, [2004] 5 C.L. 496 and *R. v. Van Tattenhove (Frans Willem)* [1996] 1 Cr. App. R. 408 followed. (2) The fact that a citizen of a foreign country convicted of a drugs offence in England or Wales might be liable to a further term of imprisonment in his home country as a result of that conviction was not a relevant consideration when passing sentence, *R. v. Nwoko (Roseline)* (1995) 16 Cr. App. R. (S.) 612 followed. The possibility of the imposition of additional imprisonment of a foreign offender by his native country was a factor for the Secretary of State for the Home Department to take into account when considering deportation, *R. v. Nazari (Fazlollah)* [1980] 1 W.L.R. 1366, [1980] C.L.Y. 581 applied.

R. v. UKOH (CHIBO), [2004] EWCA Crim 3270, [2005] 2 Cr. App. R. (S.) 38, Lord Woolf of Barnes, L.C.J., CA (Crim Div).

3590. Drug offences–Possession with intent to supply–Deferment of sentence for warehousing offence–Undue leniency

The Attorney General referred to the court as unduly lenient an order to defer sentence under the Powers of Criminal Courts (Sentencing) Act 2000 s.1 following the conviction of an offender (P) for possession of a Class A drug with intent to supply, and for supplying a Class A drug. P had stored 253 grammes of cocaine at his house, acting as a warehouseman for a local drug dealer. He had been paid by the drug dealer in cocaine, to which he was addicted. P had confessed to the police at interview and had pleaded guilty. The pre sentence report had indicated that P was clearly intent, if he could, on ridding himself of his drug habit and had concluded that, if that was indeed his intention, there was a low risk of harm to the public. P was of previous good character. The sentencing judge had been prepared to allow P an opportunity to demonstrate whether or not his intention to keep free from drugs was one which he could put into effect, and had deferred sentence. The Attorney General submitted that the order was unduly lenient and that in cases such as the instant one a custodial sentence was almost inevitable.

Held, allowing the reference, that warehousing was an involvement in the supply chain of drugs which almost inevitably carried with it a sentence of immediate imprisonment. A person involved in warehousing was carrying out an important function in the distribution of drugs. Personal mitigation in relation to the offender's background was unlikely in itself to be of great significance because it was often the good character of the warehouseman which was of importance to those in the supply chain, in order to avoid detection. Given the mitigating factors, particularly the fact that P had been paid in drugs and not in money, the sentencing court would have been justified in reducing the inevitable custodial sentence to one of three to four years' imprisonment. However, given that the instant court was dealing with a reference where P had had an indication that had suggested to him that the court was not going to impose a custodial sentence, the element of double jeopardy was of greater significance and the sentence could be mitigated further. In all the circumstances, the deferred sentence was unduly lenient. It was replaced with a sentence of two years' imprisonment, *R. v. Djahit (Turkesh)* [1999] 2 Cr. App. R. (S.) 142, [1999] C.L.Y. 1137 and *Attorney General's Reference (No.80 of 2003), Re* [2004] EWCA Crim 398, [2004] C.L.Y. 3414 considered.

ATTORNEY GENERAL'S REFERENCE (NO.152 OF 2004), *Re; sub nom.* R. v. PACKER (PETER), [2005] EWCA Crim 456, [2005] 2 Cr. App. R. (S.) 90, Latham, L.J., CA (Crim Div).

3591. Drug offences–Possession with intent to supply–Equivalent of 618 grammes of cocaine at 100 per cent purity–Appellant acted as courier– Seven year term

The appellant (S) appealed against a sentence of seven years' imprisonment which had been imposed after he pleaded guilty to possession of a Class A drug with intent to supply. S had been found in possession of the equivalent of 618 grammes of cocaine at 100 per cent purity. S was sentenced on the basis that he had acted as a courier. The sentencing judge took no significant account of the fact that S had been fined for two offences of possessing a controlled drug with intent to supply in 1991. Any credit which was to be given for his plea and his admissions to police had been considered in the light of the fact that he had been caught red handed. S argued that the sentence was excessive when compared with the sentences handed down in *Attorney General's Reference (Nos.64 and 65 of 1997), Re* [1999] 1 Cr. App. R. (S.) 237, [1999] C.L.Y. 1145.

Held, dismissing the appeal, that it appeared that in *Attorney General's Reference (Nos.64 and 65 of 1997)* the Court of Appeal probably had in mind a sentence of something like eight years but for the particular circumstances involved in the re hearing of the matter of sentence. Crown Court judges were right to follow the guidance given in *R. v. Aranguren (Jose de Jesus)* (1994) 99 Cr. App. R. 347, [1995] C.L.Y. 1364 when dealing with offenders who had acted as couriers. The sentence handed down in the instant case was stern, but it was not outside the legitimate range of sentences for the circumstances of the particular case, *Attorney General's Reference (Nos.64 and 65 of 1997)* and *Aranguren* considered.

R. v. SMITHERINGALE (KEITH), [2004] EWCA Crim 1974, [2005] 1 Cr. App. R. (S.) 58, Maurice Kay, L.J., CA (Crim Div).

3592. **Drug offences–Possession with intent to supply–Prisoners–Attempt to supply 12.3 grammes of cannabis resin to inmate–21 months' imprisonment–Deterrence**

The appellant (J) appealed against a sentence of 21 months' imprisonment imposed after he pleaded guilty on rearraignment to an offence of possessing a Class B drug with intent to supply. J had attempted to supply 12.3 grammes of cannabis resin to an inmate whilst on a prison visit. J had previous convictions for drug offences. J argued that the sentence was too long and was out of line with decided cases.

Held, dismissing the appeal, that those caught passing drugs to prisoners or attempting to do so had to expect sentences which were designed to deter others. J's previous conviction for supply was an aggravating feature that distinguished the instant case from *R. v. Freeman (John)* [1997] 2 Cr. App. R. (S.) 224, [1997] C.L.Y. 1518, *Freeman* distinguished. J's sentence was severe but could not be described as manifestly excessive.

R. v. ALGER (JAMES TERRANCE), [2004] EWCA Crim 1868, [2005] 1 Cr. App. R. (S.) 69, Hooper, L.J., CA (Crim Div).

3593. **Drug trafficking–Confiscation orders–Dealer acquired real properties partly with proceeds of crime and partly with bank loans–Assessment of confiscation sum based on equity in properties**

[Drug Trafficking Act 1994 s.4, s.7.]

The applicant (M), who had been convicted of conspiracy to supply a Class A controlled drug, sought permission to appeal against the sum he was required to pay under a confiscation order. The judge found M was a large scale dealer in class A drugs who had acquired a number of real properties partly with cash which had been derived from his drug dealing, and partly with loans from banks and other financial institutions. Those properties had subsequently risen in value and the sums due under the confiscation orders were calculated on the basis of the equity held by M in each of the relevant properties. M contended that the benefit that he had derived from the properties was not the property itself, but a proportion of the property represented by the payment of a deposit which had been derived from drug dealing.

Held, refusing the application, that the Drug Trafficking Act 1994 s.4 and s.7 required that the property, rather than the deposit he placed on it, be valued at the date of the confiscation order, subject to any charges. There was nothing unjust in taking the benefit of M's drug dealing to be the equity he had acquired in the property. It was in the public interest that those who trafficked drugs should be deprived of their benefit from drug trafficking in the largest possible way.

R. v. MOULDON (LESLIE JAMES); *sub nom.* R. v. MOULDEN (LESLIE JAMES), [2004] EWCA Crim 2715, [2005] 1 Cr. App. R. (S.) 121, Clarke, L.J., CA (Crim Div).

3594. **Drug trafficking–Confiscation orders–Value of realisable assets–Expenses incurred in commissioning of offence**

The appellant (V), who had pleaded guilty to importing a Class A drug and was sentenced to eight years' imprisonment, appealed against a confiscation order of £3.2 million. The judge assessed V's proceeds of the drug trafficking to be £3.2 million and concluded that V had realisable assets to that amount. V contended that a deduction should have been made to reflect the expenses which he had incurred in trafficking the drugs.

Held, dismissing the appeal, that a drug trafficker would be able to contest the value of a confiscation order based on the identifiable proceeds of his trafficking if he could show that his realisable assets were less than the proceeds. In the instant case, the judge was entitled to conclude that V had realisable assets to the value of £3.2 million until V proved otherwise, which he had singularly failed to do.

R. v. VERSLUIS (PIETER WILLEM), [2004] EWCA Crim 3168, [2005] 2 Cr. App. R. (S.) 26, Hooper, L.J., CA (Crim Div).

3595. **Drug trafficking–Conspiracy–Fake class A drugs–Confiscation orders– Meaning of "benefits received both in connection with drug trafficking and some other connection"**

[Drug Trafficking Act 1994 s.4(4), s.63(2); Proceeds of Crime Act 2002.]

The appellants (M) had appealed against confiscation orders made against them following conviction for conspiracy to offer for supply Class A drugs. The court had quashed the orders. It now gave reasons and considered the applicability of the Drug Trafficking Act 1994 s.63(2) in circumstances where tablets containing diazepam had been sold as ecstasy. M had been found to have benefited from drug trafficking in the sum of £3.5 million following the large scale manufacture and distribution of tablets which were sold as ecstasy, and looked like ecstasy, but were not ecstasy. Some of the tablets contained diazepam, a Class C drug, and it was only by virtue of that fact that a confiscation order under the 1994 Act had been possible. The trial judge had not been asked to make any findings about the quantity of diazepam supplied. The question for the court was whether the presence of diazepam in some of the tablets justified a finding that M's benefit from drug trafficking was the whole benefit of the indicted conspiracy. The court was particularly concerned with how to interpret, from s.63(2) of the Act, the words "references to anything received in connection with drug trafficking include a reference to anything received both in that connection and in some other connection". The Crown submitted that the supply of a single tablet containing diazepam was enough to trigger s.63(2) and that the £3.5 million, less an unquantified amount in respect of payments received for the supply of diazepam, was received in connection with that supply of diazepam. M contended that s.63(2) was not designed to convert activity that was not drug trafficking into drug trafficking and, that if the Crown's assertions were correct, the safeguards regarding assumptions in s.4(4) of the Act would be bypassed.

Held, allowing the appeals, that s.63(2) was not applicable on the facts of the instant case, *Attorney General's Reference (No.25 of 2001), Re* [2001] EWCA Crim 1770, [2002] 1 W.L.R. 253, [2001] C.L.Y. 1111 considered. It was not necessary or desirable to attempt to list the kind of cases in which the section could be relevant. However, the word "both" limited the scope of the section so that if a person was to receive £100 from a drug addict, £20 of which represented the sale of heroin and £80 of which represented work done in the addict's garden, the section would not apply because the £80 would not have been received in "both" connections. The Crown's argument was unrealistic. The court briefly considered alternative methods of confiscation under the Proceeds of Crime Act 2002.

R. v. METCALFE (CARL JAMES) (APPEAL AGAINST CONFISCATION ORDERS); R. v. METCALFE (VALERIE), [2004] EWCA Crim 3253, [2005] 2 Cr. App. R. (S.) 50, Hooper, L.J., CA (Crim Div).

3596. **Drug trafficking–Controlled drugs–Pregnant woman with dependent children acting as courier**

The appellant (B) appealed against her sentence of 10 years' imprisonment imposed following her conviction of knowingly being concerned in the fraudulent evasion of the prohibition or restriction of a Class A controlled drug. B, a Ghanaian national, had arrived at Heathrow airport on a flight from Ghana.

She had been intercepted by Customs and was found to have a large amount of cocaine in her bag. B had been pregnant at the time of her arrest and she had given birth whilst on remand in prison. B also had two children and a husband who lived in Ghana. B's husband was unable to work and could not afford proper medical treatment for the children, who were seriously ill. As a result of the offence, B's family had received death threats and there had been attempts to kidnap the children. The child that she had given birth to whilst in prison was unable to leave the United Kingdom and had to be looked after by a relative. B had been of previous good character and was an educated woman who had been in employment before the offence had been committed. B submitted that drugs couriers with dependent children who came from underdeveloped countries should be treated more leniently than other offenders domiciled in the United Kingdom.

Held, allowing the appeal, that when a parent committed a serious offence, there was sometimes no alternative to prison. Drug addiction was a blight on society and the courts had no choice but to impose substantial sentences upon those who were willingly involved. However, all cases depended on their own facts and guideline cases only provided guidelines. They did not impose a straitjacket on sentencing judges. A judge would try to do justice to each case by assessing the role of the offender, the extent of his culpability, the harm that his behaviour had caused, his attitude to the offence and his personal circumstances, *R. v. Aramah (John Uzu)* (1983) 76 Cr. App. R. 190, [1983] C.L.Y. 764.19 and *R. v. Whitehead (Patricia Anne)* [1996] 1 Cr. App. R. (S.) 111, [1996] C.L.Y. 1709 considered. The sentence of 10 years was well within the existing guidelines. However, given B's difficulties and the way that she was behaving in the prison system, a modest reduction in the sentence was possible. Therefore, the sentence of 10 years' imprisonment was quashed and replaced with a sentence of eight years' imprisonment.

R. v. ATTUH-BENSON (IRENE CYNTHIA), [2004] EWCA Crim 3032, [2005] 2 Cr. App. R. (S.) 11, Rose, L.J., CA (Crim Div).

3597. Drug trafficking–Importation of heroin–Intention to act as custodian–Reluctance to participate in offence

The appellant (NA) appealed against a sentence of 18 years' imprisonment imposed on a conviction following trial of importing heroin. Sixty kilograms of heroin had been imported in a lorry and delivered to NA, who was arrested while carrying a holdall containing some of the heroin from the lorry to a car. NA owed money to a drug dealer (P) who had previously threatened and then shot NA in the arm for refusing to work for him. NA had unsuccessfully pleaded duress at his trial. NA argued that the sentence was manifestly excessive having regard to the facts that (1) P had received a sentence of 16 years' imprisonment for a similar offence; (2) NA had participated only reluctantly in the offence and had sustained injury as a result of his earlier refusal; (3) the judge had been wrong to take into account NA's past offences when sentencing by referring to the fact that NA had not only arranged the importation but was going to store the drugs and deal with the proceeds, despite the fact that NA had not been charged with any matter other than the importation.

Held, dismissing the appeal, that (1) NA's sentence could not be compared to that of P, who had been convicted of conspiracy to supply half the amount of heroin involved in NA's case and who had a significantly better record than NA. (2) The sentencing judge had assessed NA's defence of duress and had rejected it. There was no further evidence before the court as to NA's reluctance to act as a courier and no basis on which to reach a different conclusion. NA's age, 56, and his state of health were relevant, but only limited account could be taken of personal mitigation in cases such as this involving drug importation, *R. v. Kayar (Sakir)* [1998] 2 Cr. App. R. (S.) 355, [1999] C.L.Y. 1129 considered. (3) The critical factor was the degree and extent of NA's involvement and the nature of the enterprise. NA had been entrusted with a store of valuable drugs and it was accepted that this was his role in the offence, *R. v. Rimmer (Martin)* [1999] 1 Cr. App. R. (S.) 234, [1999] C.L.Y. 1125 considered. The judge's statement was relevant to NA's role in the instant importation and did not indicate that he had taken any previous importation into account when sentencing, *R. v. Kaynak (Hussein)* [1998] 2 Cr. App. R. (S.) 283, [1998] C.L.Y. 1185 distinguished. Couriers played a key part in drug importation and having regard to the amount of heroin involved in the instant case the sentence was not manifestly excessive, *R. v. Aramah (John Uzu)* (1983) 76 Cr. App. R. 190, [1983] C.L.Y. 764.19, *R. v. Serdeiro (Roberto Newton)* [1996] 1 Cr. App. R. (S.) 251, [1996] C.L.Y. 1871 and *R. v. Unlu (Ali)* [2002] EWCA Crim 2220, [2003] 1 Cr. App. R. (S.) 101 considered.

R. v. ANDERSON (NORMAN), [2005] EWCA Crim 75, [2005] 2 Cr. App. R. (S.) 54, Auld, L.J., CA (Crim Div).

3598. Drug trafficking–Involvement akin to role of courier–Knowledge of importation

The appellant (C) appealed against a sentence of 16 years' imprisonment on a guilty plea to being knowingly concerned in the fraudulent evasion of the prohibition on the importation of cocaine. C collected packages sent from the West Indies from two mail boxes which he had set up using a false identity. The police intercepted the last of six deliveries to the boxes. This contained 5.95kg of cocaine, equivalent to 4.27kg at 100 per cent purity. C admitted that he knew that five of the deliveries contained cocaine, but not the amount involved. He claimed he was receiving the parcels for a friend to whom he owed money and who had threatened him and his family with violence if he did not help with the importation. C had several previous convictions, mostly for offences of dishonesty, and had been imprisoned a number of times.

Held, allowing the appeal, that a probable starting point of at least 20 years' imprisonment was too high, given that C's role was not significantly different from that of a courier. When the weight of the drugs at 100 per cent purity was of the order of 5kg or more, sentences of 14 years' imprisonment would be appropriate after a contested trial, *R. v. Aranguren (Jose de Jesus)* (1994) 99 Cr. App. R. 347, [1995] C.L.Y. 1364 considered. In the instant case, the starting point should have been about 16 years' imprisonment, to reflect C's knowledge that the previous four consignments contained cocaine, but also his relatively unimportant role. A discount for C's early plea meant his sentence should have been 11 years' imprisonment, rather than the 16 years imposed.

R. v. CASSIDY (THOMAS JOSEPH), [2004] EWCA Crim 1480, [2005] 1 Cr. App. R. (S.) 44, Hooper, L.J., CA (Crim Div).

3599. Explosives offences–Sentence length–Devices produced in public places on two occasions

The appellant (H) appealed against a total sentence of four years' imprisonment following guilty pleas to placing an article in a place with the intention of inducing a person to believe it would explode and communicating false information with the intention of inducing a person to believe that there was a bomb present. H had placed a mobile telephone taped to a metal timer in a town centre. The town centre was cordoned off. H was charged and released on bail. Whilst on bail and in an Indian restaurant, H produced a box with wires attached and a flashing light. The device bleeped and H said that it would explode. There was conflicting evidence at trial as to his mental state but the trial judge concluded that there was no evidence of any treatable disorder. A pre sentence report stated that H presented at least a medium and possibly a high future risk. H was sentenced to two years' imprisonment on each count to run consecutively. H argued that whilst the offences were serious, they were not so serious as to justify a sentence of four years' imprisonment, and his overall criminality did not justify such a sentence. He further submitted that insufficient weight had been given to his psychiatric history, alcohol problems and guilty pleas.

Held, allowing the appeal, that the offences had been serious. H's actions went far beyond verbal threats, the second offence had been committed whilst he had been on bail and H had caused fear and disruption. H presented at least a medium future risk and the court's first duty was to protect the public.

However, in the light of the authorities, a total sentence of four years' imprisonment was too high, *R. v. Harrison (Christopher Arthur)* [1997] 2 Cr. App. R. (S.) 174, [1997] C.L.Y. 1713 and *R. v. Mason (Auburn)* 2001] EWCA Crim 1138, [2002] 1 Cr. App. R. (S.) 29 considered. Accordingly, his sentence was quashed and a total sentence of three years' imprisonment substituted, comprising 18 months' imprisonment on each count to run consecutively.

R. v. HARRIS (PHILLIP GEOFFREY), [2005] EWCA Crim 775, [2005] 2 Cr. App. R. (S.) 103, Latham, L.J., CA (Crim Div).

3600. **Extended sentences–Sexual offences–Detention and training orders– Indecency with child–Addition of extended period of licence to detention and training orders**

[Criminal Justice Act 1991 s.39(2); Powers of Criminal Courts (Sentencing) Act 2000 s.85, s.85(1)(b), s.85(2), s.101(5).]

The appellant (B) appealed against his extended sentence of two years, which comprised a detention and training order (DTO) for six months and an extended period of licence of 18 months pursuant to the Powers of Criminal Courts (Sentencing) Act 2000 s.85. B's sentence followed his conviction of indecency with a child, which had comprised kissing a seven year old girl in the area of her vagina after they had both removed their clothes at his suggestion. B was 16 years old at the time of the offence. B argued that (1) a custodial sentence was inappropriate as the offence committed was not serious in that there had been no touching, grabbing or penetration of any sort; (2) the judge had erred in imposing an extended sentence with a DTO in the light of the provisions of the Criminal Justice Act 1991 and the 2000 Act. The legislation on DTOs formed a complete and discrete code for those subject to such an order with sanctions for reoffending during the term. It was so different from the regime that applied to those sentenced to imprisonment that it could not have been the intention of Parliament that the extended sentence regime should apply to the DTO scheme.

Held, allowing the appeal in part, that (1) The offence had to be seen in the light of what had happened immediately before and after it occurred. B had suggested to the child that they take their clothes off, and B's penis was erect; it seemed clear therefore that he had committed the offence to arouse himself. The victim was in her own home and B had been entrusted with her well being. The pre sentence report noted that B's continued denial of guilt made it difficult to conduct any constructive work with him and he was at significant risk of reoffending. In those circumstances, there could be no criticism of the six month DTO. (2) The requirement in s.85(1)(b) of the 2000 Act for imposing an extended sentence was not satisfied where the proposed sentence was a DTO and therefore the trial judge did not have the power to impose an extended sentence with the DTO. There were several reasons for this conclusion. First, it was significant that while s.85(2) showed that the extended sentence regime was based on the inadequacy of the licence period in the sentence imposed, an integral part of a DTO was the requirement for supervision during the second half of the period of the DTO after the offender had been released from detention. In other words, a DTO did not have any form of licence period. The difference in terminology, given that the relevant statutory provisions of both extended sentences and DTOs were contained in Part IV of the 2000 Act, indicated that the regimes were meant to be different, *Gibson v. Skibs A/S Marina* [1966] 2 All E.R. 476, [1966] C.L.Y. 8343 considered. Second, there was no provision in the 2000 Act or elsewhere that stated expressly or impliedly that an extended sentence could be added to a DTO. The words "if any" in s.85(2) were not a reference to forms of detention that carried no licence period, such as DTOs; rather, the phrase applied to pre existing licence periods. Third, s.85(2) indicated that an extended sentence was meant to supplement a licence period but DTOs did not have licence periods; only periods of supervision. The supervision started, in the case of an offender subjected (like B) to a six month DTO, when the offender was automatically released from detention after three months and ended when the term of the order ended. That indicated that the DTO regime did not envisage an extended sentence being added to it. Fourth, the fact that under s.85(2) the term of an extended sentence could not exceed the maximum term permitted for an offence did not sit comfortably with the requirement that a DTO could only be for one of a number of specified periods of which the longest was 24 months. Even if a DTO were for any reason to exceed 24 months, it was only effective for 24 months by virtue of s.101(5) of the 2000 Act. Fifth, although s.39(2) of the 1991 Act provided for the recall of offenders released on licence to "prison"; the word prison did not include detention under a DTO. Thus, it was difficult to see to what institution a person detained under a DTO with an extended sentence could be recalled. Sixth, the consequences of an offender subject to a DTO committing another offence during the currency of the DTO were listed in the 2000 Act whereas there were different provisions in the 1991 Act in respect of a prisoner offending while subject to an extended term. Thus, if an offender was sentenced to a DTO with an extended sentence, there would be difficulties in determining what would happen if he committed an offence in the fifth month of his sentence as he would still be subject to both supervision under his DTO and the licence provisions of the extended sentence. Seventh, although there were provisions in the 2000 Act that explained what happened when an offender received both a DTO and a sentence of detention in a Young Offender Institution, there were no similar provisions in respect of a DTO passed with an extended sentence. That omission showed that Parliament had not intended that extended sentences could be imposed with DTOs.

R. v. B, [2005] EWCA Crim 312, [2005] 2 Cr. App. R. (S.) 87, Hooper, L.J., CA (Crim Div).

3601. **Extended sentences–Sexual offences–Making extended sentence consecutive to determinate sentence**

[Powers of Criminal Courts (Sentencing) Act 2000 s.85.]

The appellant (B), a man aged 58, appealed against a total sentence of 17 years' imprisonment, which was subject to an extension of four years under the Powers of Criminal Courts (Sentencing) Act 2000 s.85. The offences, which had been committed during two periods, namely before 1983 and after 1995, involved the serial sexual abuse of B's four stepdaughters, including the repeated rape of one of them and the repeated digital penetration of three of them, and violence towards their mothers and B's one daughter. In respect of the first period, B received 12 years for rape and the following concurrent sentences: 18 months for an assault on his first wife; three years and six months for an attack on his second wife; and 18 months for cruelty towards his daughter and one stepdaughter. As to the second period, B received a custodial sentence of five years and an extended sentence of four years for indecently assaulting three of his stepdaughters. B argued that given his age and his early guilty plea, the sentences were excessive.

Held, allowing the appeal, that while it was not possible to quarrel seriously with the individual component sentences, the overall sentence imposed on a man of B's age was, despite his appalling behaviour, too long. The entering of a plea of guilty, which B had done at an early stage, was always very significant, especially in cases of sexual abuse, where it had the effect of relieving vulnerable witnesses from rehearsing their experiences in public. B's sentence for rape was reduced to 10 years and his sentence for the offences of indecent assault was reduced to four years, making the total sentence one of 14 years. The judge had been justified in imposing an extended sentence on B. Making an extended sentence consecutive to a determinate sentence, which the judge had done, was something that could be done in appropriate cases. Indeed, the occasion for it might well arise in cases of sexual offences, some of which were committed before September 1998 and others after that time, so that only some of them were capable of attracting an extended sentence. The extended licence period to which B was subject was increased to six years.

R. v. B (RAY), [2004] EWCA Crim 3216, *The Times*, December 10, 2004, Kennedy, L.J., CA (Crim Div).

3602. **False descriptions–Trade descriptions–Sale of celebrity photographs bearing forged signatures–Custody threshold**

The appellant (B) appealed against suspended sentences of six months' imprisonment and a £10,000 fine for selling celebrity photographs with false signatures on them. A purchaser (V) had bought a photograph with a false signature in November 1998. V discovered in March 2000 that the signature was forged and complained to trading standards officers. B was not interviewed until April 2001. The judge found that B had passed the custody threshold as he had continued to sell photographs with fake signatures after his attention had been drawn to the forgeries in November 1998. B, who had no previous convictions, had pleaded guilty. He claimed that he had not known the signatures were forgeries and had relied on his stepson, who supplied them. He further argued that only 27 out of 1080 photographs were forged and that he was in substantial financial difficulty as a result of the failure of his business and a prosecution costs order of more than £35,000.

Held, allowing the appeal, that it was not clear, and indeed it seemed unlikely, that V's purchase put B on notice that some of his stock might have contained false signatures. As no complaint or issue arose until March 2000, the underlying reason for suggesting the custody threshold had been passed was probably based on a misunderstanding by the judge. A conditional discharge running for two years was accordingly substituted for the suspended sentences of imprisonment. Due to B's extremely difficult financial circumstances it was not appropriate to replace the sentences of imprisonment with a financial penalty. Further, because B was unable to pay the wholly excessive prosecution costs, the £10,000 fine was reduced to £100.

R. v. BORE (LARRY), [2004] EWCA Crim 1452, (2005) 169 J.P. 245, Aikens, J., CA (Crim Div).

3603. **False imprisonment–Assault–Imprisonment of house vendor after withdrawal from prospective sale**

The appellant (S) appealed against a sentence of three years' imprisonment following trial for falsely imprisoning and assaulting the vendor of a property after a house purchase had fallen through. S had agreed to purchase a property but shortly before exchange of contracts the vendor, who had had the property revalued, withdrew it from the market. S knew that the vendor had had heart surgery. S drove to the property, was abusive to the vendor, threatened to rip his heart out, punched the vendor in the jaw, prevented him from leaving the property and tore the telephone from the wall. After a time the vendor began to feel ill and went to lie down. S refused the vendor's requests to call an ambulance. After two hours S left the property.

Held, dismissing the appeal, that the sentence was not manifestly excessive. The offences merited a prison sentence in years rather than months as S had subjected the vendor to a terrifying ordeal for some time.

R. v. STACEY (LESTER JOHN), [2004] EWCA Crim 564, [2004] 2 Cr. App. R. (S.) 87, Laws, L.J., CA (Crim Div).

3604. **False imprisonment–Offender's girlfriend handcuffed and assaulted–Undue leniency**

The Attorney General referred as unduly lenient a community punishment and rehabilitation order, which required the offender (N) to do 100 hours' community service. N had met a young woman and had a short relationship with her, but when it ended and after an argument at his flat, he slapped and punched her and then handcuffed her, naked, to the bed, committing further assaults on her until he released her six hours later.

Held, allowing the reference, that the offence occurred in the context of the previous relationship and was therefore at the lower end of kidnapping offences. Although a sentence of two to three years' imprisonment would have been appropriate, this would be reduced to 18 months' imprisonment in the instant case as N had already performed 100 hours of community service, *R. v. Spence (Clinton Everton)* (1983) 5 Cr. App. R. (S.) 413, [1984] C.L.Y. 876 considered.

ATTORNEY GENERAL'S REFERENCE (NO.2 OF 2004), *Re; sub nom*. R. v. NEVILLE (DANIEL JOHN), [2004] EWCA Crim 1280, [2005] 1 Cr. App. R. (S.) 14, Latham, L.J., CA (Crim Div).

3605. **False instruments–Forgery–Conspiracy to create and distribute forged passports and identification papers–Undue leniency**

The Attorney General referred to the court as unduly lenient sentences passed on four offenders in relation to offences of conspiracy to have false instruments, conspiracy to make false instruments and transferring criminal proceeds. The second offender (R) had brought 500 forged passports into the United Kingdom from Thailand and had delivered them to the first offender (C). C had then given 170 and 150 of the passports to the third offender (K) and the fourth offender (S) respectively. There had also been discovered at S's address materials which could have been used to add identities to forged passports and identity cards. C had also sent £86,042 in cash to Thailand over a significant period. C pleaded guilty to conspiracy to have false instruments and transferring criminal proceeds and received a sentence of three and a half years' imprisonment. R pleaded guilty to conspiracy to have false instruments and received a sentence of two and a half years' imprisonment. K pleaded not guilty and was convicted of conspiracy to have false instruments and received a sentence of four years' imprisonment. S pleaded guilty to conspiracy to make false instruments and received a sentence of three years' imprisonment. The issue for determination was whether the sentences passed were unduly lenient.

Held, dismissing the references, that the sentences had been imposed after the most meticulous and comprehensive approach by the sentencing judge. It could not be said that he had over emphasised the mitigation or that there was an aspect of his analysis of the aggravating features of the case which he had not properly attended to. The sentences fell at the lower end of the appropriate sentencing bracket but they were not so out of balance that they could be regarded as unduly lenient. Therefore, the sentences could not be interfered with, *R. v. Cheema (Gurmit Singh)* [2002] EWCA Crim 325, [2002] 2 Cr. App. R. (S.) 79, [2002] C.L.Y. 3950, *R. v. Muller (Roland)* [2003] EWCA Crim 2499 and *R. v. Le (Van Binh)* [1999] 1 Cr. App. R. (S.) 422, [1998] C.L.Y. 1245 considered.

ATTORNEY GENERAL'S REFERENCE (NOS.27, 28, 29 AND 30 OF 2005), *Re; sub nom*. R. v. CHELLOUJ (TARIQ); R. v. KAMEL (IZEM); R. v. ROUVIER (DELPHINE); R. v. SMAINE (MOUMEN) [2005] EWCA Crim 2081, Judge, L.J., CA (Crim Div).

3606. **Fines–Mitigation–Trawler owner fined for strict liability offence–Damage caused to offshore installation by collision at sea**

[Petroleum Act 1987 s.23(2).]

A, a trawler owner, appealed against a £40,000 fine imposed following a conviction for entering the safety zone around an offshore gas installation, contrary to the Petroleum Act 1987 s.23(2) and damaging it. A guilty plea was entered since the offence was one of strict liability. The captain was very experienced and had implemented a safety management system. The collision occurred during reduced visibility and when the second mate, then in charge of the bridge, did not slow down as instructed and the ship changed direction and collided with the installation, causing £650,000 of damage.

Held, allowing the appeal, that the fine would be quashed and replaced by a fine of £15,000. A had a good safety record and had used an experienced crew. There had also been full cooperation with the investigation. A had sustained losses as a result of the offence, which, along with its low level of culpability in the matter, should have been taken into account in determining the level of the fine.

R. v. ARMANA LTD, [2004] EWCA Crim 1069, [2005] 1 Cr. App. R. (S.) 7, Kay, L.J., CA (Crim Div).

3607. Firearm offences–Possession of firearms with intent–Threatening to kill–Imitation firearms–Repeated threats to kill police officers–Five year custodial term

The appellant (D) appealed against a total sentence of five years' imprisonment imposed after he pleaded guilty to having a firearm, or imitation firearm, with intent to resist arrest, possessing an imitation firearm with intent to cause fear or violence and making a threat to kill. Police officers had been called to an address in east London after D was reported to have been causing a disturbance. Upon their arrival, D ran into a house and a name search revealed that he was sought on a warrant that was not backed by bail. D produced a black handgun and told an officer that he was going to shoot him. He then pointed the gun at three other officers and threatened to shoot them too. D made further threats to shoot officers after his girlfriend was taken away under arrest. In the event, the siege lasted for eight and a half hours. The sentencing judge accepted that the officers believed that the weapons were imitation, but stressed that belief was not the same as certainty. D argued that (1) the judge erred in considering that little credit should be given for the guilty plea; (2) the five year term was excessive.

Held, dismissing the appeal, that (1) it was well established that the court could withhold discounts for a plea of guilty or substantially reduce the credit where the offender pleaded guilty in the face of overwhelming evidence, *R. v. Costen (Sharon Elizabeth)* (1989) 11 Cr. App. R. (S.) 182, [1991] C.L.Y. 1134 followed. (2) The sentencing judge had quite deliberately passed a sentence which expressed grave disapproval and sent out a deterrent message. In making those remarks, he was indicating that he was handing down a severe sentence. Hours of police time had been wasted and officers had been subjected to a very frightening experience. In the very grave circumstances of the instant case, the sentence was entirely appropriate.

R. v. DUFFY (NICHOLAS THOMAS), [2004] EWCA Crim 2054, [2005] 1 Cr. App. R. (S.) 75, Auld, L.J., CA (Crim Div).

3608. Firearm offences–Prohibited firearms–Sentence length–Specific counts on indictment–Statutory minimum sentence–Undue leniency

[Firearms Act 1968 s.5(1); Criminal Justice Act 2003 s.287.]

The Attorney General applied for leave to refer as unduly lenient a total sentence of three years and six months' imprisonment imposed following pleas of guilty to possession of a firearm with intent to cause another to believe there would be unlawful violence and two counts of possession of a bladed article. The offender (M) had fired a gun into the air outside a nightclub. The weapon was a prohibited firearm under the Firearms Act 1968 s.5(1), however no offence of possession of a prohibited weapon had been included in the indictment. The Attorney General submitted that the sentence was unduly lenient and failed to reflect the gravity of the offence and public concern about firearm offences, due to the following aggravating features: (a) the firearm was a prohibited weapon; (b) M had deliberately armed himself; (c) the weapon had been discharged in a public place; (d) M was assessed as presenting a high risk of causing serious harm; and (e) such offences were prevalent. The Attorney General contended that it was not necessary to incorporate in the indictment a count alleging possession of a prohibited weapon contrary to s.5 of the 1968 Act to trigger the statutory minimum term of five years' imprisonment contained in the Criminal Justice Act 2003 s.287.

Held, refusing the application, that (1) an indictment had to include a count alleging possession of a prohibited weapon under s.5 of the 1968 Act in order to invoke the statutory minimum term contained in the 2003 Act, *R. v. Benfield (Anthony John)* [2003] EWCA Crim 2223, [2004] 1 Cr. App. R. 8, [2003]

C.L.Y. 3778 distinguished. It was not surprising that at the time the judge passed sentence he was unaware that the firearm in question was said to be a prohibited weapon. A separate count should have been added to the indictment. If that course was adopted it would avoid confusion in the Crown Court and make clear to a defendant, and those advising him, that he was at risk of a minimum term of five years' imprisonment. (2) The defendant was of good character which was comparatively unusual in offences concerning firearms. Taking into account all the circumstances, the sentence passed was within the proper ambit.

ATTORNEY GENERAL'S REFERENCE (NO.114 OF 2004), *Re*; *sub nom*. R. v. McDOWELL (STEVEN), [2004] EWCA Crim 2954, [2005] 2 Cr. App. R. (S.) 6, Rose, L.J., CA (Crim Div).

3609. Firearms offences–Concurrent sentences–Chain of criminal conduct charged as conspiracy–Overall seriousness and range of individual counts

The applicant Attorney General referred the sentences of the defendant offenders (H) as unduly lenient. H had pleaded guilty to three conspiracy charges for their part in the conversion of blank firing weapons into fully functional prohibited weapons. The trial judge indicated that he would sentence them concurrently on the three counts as they were "part and parcel of one enterprise". He took nine years as a starting point and, after giving them "full credit" for their pleas of guilty, sentenced each to concurrent sentences of six years' imprisonment on each count. The Attorney General identified the aggravating features of the offences as the vast quantity of weapons involved, the length of the conspiracies and H's intention as part of the conspiracies to equip criminals with fully functioning firearms to put fear into others. He submitted that those aggravating features clearly outweighed the single mitigating factor of the pleas of guilty and that the total sentence of six years' imprisonment in each case failed to mark the gravity of the offences and public concern about such a vast scale of offending with firearms. The Attorney General contended that H should have been sentenced by way of consecutive sentences in order to properly to mark the gravity of the offences.

Held, allowing the references, that the evidence against H embraced the whole chain of criminal conduct from manufacture to sale and to holding possession for future distribution to criminals. In such cases, if the true culpability of an offender could be marked properly by concurrent sentences for what could be regarded as one course of criminal conduct, it was within the sentencer's discretion to adopt that course. But where, as in the instant case, the seriousness and range of the individually indicted components of the criminal conduct charged as a conspiracy, looked at overall, called for a higher sentence than that permitted for any one of them considered on its own, the sentencer should reflect that seriousness by consecutive sentences. Despite the judge having given an early indication that he had concurrent sentences provisionally in mind, he gave no commitment before rearraignment to adopt that approach, and H could have had no legitimate expectation that he would impose concurrent sentences when the time came. The conspiracies in the instant case required sentences of a very high order. The appropriate starting point would have been a total of 15 years' imprisonment in each case, with a reduction to nine years after allowing for the "full discount" promised to H by the judge and a period to allow for the double jeopardy inherent in the instant reference. Consistent with the judge's view that the counts were all part of a single course of conduct and that there was no reason to differentiate between the offenders, the only appropriate way of achieving that outcome was to deal with the matter in each case by way of three consecutive sentences of three years' imprisonment each reduced to that level on account of totality and the element of overlap between the counts. The reference was granted and a total sentence of nine years' imprisonment substituted for the sentence imposed by the judge.

ATTORNEY GENERAL'S REFERENCE (NOS.120 AND 121 OF 2004), *Re*; *sub nom*. R. v. HERBERT (STEPHEN RONALD); R. v. BEARD (GARY COLIN),

[2005] EWCA Crim 890, [2006] 1 Cr. App. R. (S.) 7, Auld, L.J., CA (Crim Div).

3610. Forgery—Passports—Review of sentencing authorities

[Forgery and Counterfeiting Act 1981 s.3, s.5(1), s.5(2).]

The appellant (K) appealed against a total sentence of 16 months' imprisonment following pleas of guilty to two counts of possession of a false instrument with intent contrary to the Forgery and Counterfeiting Act 1981 s.5(1). K had been in possession of a forged Nigerian passport and a stolen British passport. Consecutive sentences of eight months had been passed for each offence. K contended that the sentence was manifestly excessive as it was bad practice to impose consecutive sentences in relation to the two different passports.

Held, dismissing the appeal, that (1) (i) it was apparent that the existing authorities had not always distinguished as clearly as they should have done between the different offences commonly charged in relation to false passports under the 1981 Act, the maximum sentences for which were not all the same. The maximum for using a false instrument contrary to s.3 and for having a false instrument with intent contrary to s.5(1) was 10 years' imprisonment. The maximum for having a false instrument contrary to s.5(2) was two years' imprisonment. (ii) There was a passage in *R. v. Singh (Daljit)* [1999] 1 Cr. App. R. (S.) 490, [1998] C.L.Y. 1227, which had not been expressed as clearly as it might have been and had led to misapprehension by the court in *R. v. Siliavski (Boyan Yossifov)* [2000] 1 Cr. App. R. (S.) 23, [2000] C.L.Y. 1255. The issue which had been addressed in *Singh* was the use of a single passport and the sentence of six months indicated in *Siliavski* was an inadequate reflection of the culpability of someone carrying four false passports. (iii) *Siliavski* had received further criticism in *R. v. Cheema (Gurmit Singh)* [2002] EWCA Crim 325, [2002] 2 Cr. App. R. (S.) 79, [2002] C.L.Y. 3950 and should no longer be regarded as authoritative as to the level of sentence appropriate for couriers of false passports since *Cheema* was the more appropriate guide. (2) In the instant case, the sentence had to reflect the fact that K had been in possession of two false passports. Furthermore, international events in recent years and increasing public concern justified deterrent sentences at a higher level than was appropriate six years previously when *Singh* had been decided. For that reason *R. v. Balasubramaniam (Ravindran)* [2001] EWCA Crim 2680, [2002] 2 Cr. App. R. (S.) 17, [2004] 9 C.L. 427, in which the court had followed *Singh*, could no longer be regarded as authoritative. Where one false passport had been used or held with the intention of use, the appropriate sentence, even on a guilty plea by a person of good character, was 12 to 18 months. Accordingly, K's sentence of 16 months in relation to two passports was not manifestly excessive, *Singh* considered, *Siliavski* doubted, *Cheema* applied and *Balasubramaniam* doubted.

R. v. KOLAWOLE (DAVID OLADOTUN), [2004] EWCA Crim 3047, [2005] 2 Cr. App. R. (S.) 14, Rose, L.J., CA (Crim Div).

3611. Fraud—Conspiracy—Architect adviser and quantity surveyors defrauded trust of £2 million—Undue leniency

The Attorney General referred to the court as unduly lenient a sentence of three years' imprisonment imposed on P and suspended sentences of nine months' imprisonment imposed on G and B after they were each convicted of conspiracy to defraud. P, an architect and the ringleader in the conspiracy, had been appointed as an adviser to a charitable land owning trust. During his involvement over 11 years on building projects for the trust, P defrauded the trust by arranging for the overpayment of monies to a building contractor and the overpayment of fees to himself and the firm of quantity surveyors in which G and B were senior partners. The trust was thereby defrauded of £2 million. The Attorney General maintained that the sentences failed to reflect the gravity of the offence or the full extent of the dishonesty and gross breach of trust.

Held, allowing the references in part, that a sentence of three years' imprisonment imposed on P was far too lenient given that he had set up a major crime of dishonesty at massive personal profit, persisted with the fraud over a long period and involved others in the scheme. Allowing for double jeopardy, P's sentence would be raised to six years' imprisonment, *R. v. Barrick (John)* (1985) 81 Cr. App. R. 78, [1985] C.L.Y. 765 and *R. v. Clark (Trevor)* [1998] 2 Cr. App. R. 137, [1998] C.L.Y. 1392 considered. G and B had received suspended sentences because they were subservient to P and those sentences were thought to be unduly lenient. However, after taking account of the double jeopardy principle, it was possible and right to temper the exercise of justice with mercy. Thus, the sentences imposed in G and B would not be altered.

ATTORNEY GENERAL'S REFERENCE (NO.59 OF 2004), *Re*; ATTORNEY GENERAL'S REFERENCE (NO.60 OF 2004), RE; ATTORNEY GENERAL'S REFERENCE (NO.61 OF 2004), *Re*; *sub nom.* R. v. POUND (GUY); R. v. GREEN (ANTHONY); R. v. BEARD (PETER) [2004] EWCA Crim 2488, Judge, L.J., CA (Crim Div).

3612. Fraud-Conspiracy-Defendant facilitating creation and use of cloned credit and debit cards-Undue leniency

The Attorney General referred as unduly lenient a 220 hour community punishment order following a plea of guilty by the defendant (T) to conspiracy to defraud the central clearing banks. T had facilitated the creation and use of cloned credit and debit cards on a large scale. He derived a significant personal benefit of £2,500; however, he was sentenced on the basis he was not the instigator or principal organiser. The Attorney General contended there were three aggravating features: (i) it was a large scale conspiracy using sophisticated equipment and the character of the offence undermined the integrity of banking and credit card systems nationally; (ii) substantial profits were made with a significant benefit to T; and (iii) the conspiracy continued over two years and would have carried on if there had been no police intervention. In mitigation were T's early guilty plea, the fact he was not the instigator and the absence of previous convictions.

Held, allowing the reference, that the sentence passed was unduly lenient. T's culpability called for a sentence of between two years and six months and three years in the court below. Regard had to be had to the principle of double jeopardy, particularly as a non custodial sentence was initially passed, and to the fact that T had performed 87 hours of his community service. In all those circumstances, a sentence of 15 months' imprisonment would be substituted, *Attorney General's Reference (No.73 of 2003), Re* [2004] EWCA Crim 183, [2004] 2 Cr. App. R. (S.) 62, [2004] 6 C.L. 407 considered.

ATTORNEY GENERAL'S REFERENCE (NO.141 OF 2004), *Re*; *sub nom.* R. v. THOMAS (KENNETH KINCE), [2005] EWCA Crim 653, [2005] 2 Cr. App. R. (S.) 94, Rose, L.J., CA (Crim Div).

3613. Fraud-Conspiracy-Sentence length-Judge's starting point too high-Appropriate reduction-Deterrent element-Cloning of payment cards

The appellant (D) appealed against a sentence of five years' imprisonment for conspiracy to defraud. Over a period of more than two years, D conspired with his five co accused to defraud financial institutions and retail shops by cloning and skimming payment cards. The skimmed or cloned cards were used at premises under the control of the conspirators. Incriminating invoices, credit card slips and sales receipts were found at D's house. The Crown alleged that the loss to banks and other companies was in excess of £241,000 and attempts were made to cause further losses in the amount of £244,000. D pleaded guilty on rearraignment. The judge said there needed to be a deterrent element in the sentence. D argued that the judge's starting point of seven years was too high, particularly when the circumstances of *R. v. Taj (Kamran)* [2003] EWCA Crim 2633 were examined, and there should be an appropriate reduction from a lower starting point.

Held, allowing the appeal, that a sentence of four years' imprisonment was substituted. In the case of *Taj* the defendants were involved in more sophisticated criminal conduct with much greater illicit profit than D and they were sentenced to terms of imprisonment ranging from five and a half years to three years. The judge in D's case took a starting point of seven years. That was too high. The judge specifically said that there was a deterrent element in sentence and he was plainly right to do so. However, that objective could have been achieved by a sentence which, whilst substantial, was at a lower level, *Taj* considered.

R. v. DIN (AMEEN); R. v. DEB (PETER); R. v. ZAHEER (MOHAMMED); R. v. HUSSAIN (SAJID); R. v. DIN (YASIN); R. v. NAJIB (PARVAZ), [2004] EWCA Crim 3364, [2005] 2 Cr. App. R. (S.) 40, Rose, L.J., CA (Crim Div).

3614. Fraud–Conspiracy–Use of cloned debit and credit cards to obtain cash from bank accounts–Deterrent element in sentence to reflect prevalence of such offences

The appellant (C) appealed against a sentence of six years' imprisonment imposed on a conviction for conspiracy to defraud. C had used cloned debit and credit cards to withdraw cash from various bank accounts in a sophisticated operation involving the use of high tech equipment. C, who had pleaded guilty to the charges in the face of overwhelming evidence, argued on appeal that insufficient credit had been given for his guilty plea and previous good character in view of the fact that the maximum possible sentence for the offence was 10 years' imprisonment.

Held, dismissing the appeal, that the fraud in the instant case was of a more sophisticated nature than in the authorities relied on by C, *Attorney General's Reference (No.73 of 2003), Re* [2004] EWCA Crim 183, [2004] 2 Cr. App. R. (S.) 62, [2004] 6 C.L. 407 distinguished. Limited credit was given for the guilty plea because of the weight of the evidence against him. Moreover, a strong deterrent element was justified in view of the prevalence of such offences and the fact that his was the sort of fraud which undermined public confidence in the electronic banking system. It followed that the sentence, although near the top end of the scale, was not manifestly excessive.

R. v. CHIRILA (REMUS TENISTOCLE); R. v. MONTEANU (ADRIAN); R. v. CHIRILA (ADINA RAMOVA), [2004] EWCA Crim 2200, [2005] 1 Cr. App. R. (S.) 93, Latham, L.J., CA (Crim Div).

3615. Fraud–Postal voting–Abuse of voting system

The appellant (H) appealed against a sentence of three years and seven months' imprisonment following a plea of guilty to conspiracy to defraud. The conspiracy had consisted of a widespread abuse of the postal voting system whereby H, an official Labour party candidate, collected uncompleted postal votes from households and completed them in his favour.

Held, dismissing the appeal, that (1) government, both national and local, was usually free from any form of corruption. If the electoral system were contaminated by corruption or fraud, it would be rendered worthless, and the responsibility of the courts, so far as possible, was to protect the electoral system. In June 2001, legislation was enacted with a view to greatly extending postal voting, and the result was an increase in voting, with the disadvantage that the system was easier to corrupt. (2) The sentence passed was appropriate and it was hoped that it would send the message that was intended, namely that conduct undermining the country's system of democracy would not be tolerated. It was important that the punishment passed deterred others. A deterrent sentence had to be proportionate to the offence. However, a deterrent sentence was passed with the primary object of deterring, and the circumstances of the individual, which in H's case included his age of 62 and the fact that he suffered from angina, were significantly less important. H had taken advantage of his own community, many of whom did not understand the English language. Whilst an analogy could be drawn with cases involving interference with the proper administration of justice, a fraud on this scale was more serious.

R. v. HUSSAIN (MOHAMMED), [2005] EWCA Crim 1866, [2006] 1 Cr. App. R. (S.) 62, Lord Woolf of Barnes, L.C.J, CA (Crim Div).

3616. Fraudulent evasion of duty—Confiscation orders—£5,000 paid to offender for knowing assistance in operation—Appropriate amount of confiscation order

[Criminal Justice Act 1988 s.71.]

The appellant (E), who had pleaded guilty to fraudulent evasion of duty, appealed against a confiscation order in the sum of £129,756. E had been involved in importing six million cigarettes, on which the duty should have been £1,120,850. E had been paid £5,000 out of a promised £10,000. He pleaded guilty on the basis that he knowingly assisted in the operation, but was not the overall organiser, financier or end user. A confiscation order was made for £129,756 being the sum of E's realisable assets. E contended that since he did not obtain any benefit from the importation of the cigarettes or from the £1,120,850 pecuniary advantage, the confiscation order should have been based on the £5,000 he actually received.

Held, dismissing the appeal, that when a confiscation order was made under the Criminal Justice Act 1988 s.71, the sum which an offender had to pay was not restricted to what he had received for his part in the offence, but was based on the benefit he obtained through his criminal conduct. Under s.71, 'benefit' did not mean the fruits of criminal conduct which the offender personally enjoyed. If the offender received property, then his benefit would be the value of the property to him when he obtained it. If he derived a pecuniary advantage, his benefit would likewise be the value of the advantage when he obtained it, *R. v. Smith (David Cadman)* [2001] UKHL 68, [2002] 1 W.L.R. 54, [2002] C.L.Y. 3898 applied. In the instant case, E had obtained property and a pecuniary advantage was derived by the avoidance of the payment of duty. He had therefore obtained a benefit in excess of £1m, and so the confiscation order was made in the correct sum.

R. v. ELLINGHAM (PAUL ROBERT), [2004] EWCA Crim 3446, [2005] 2 Cr. App. R. (S.) 32, Pill, L.J., CA (Crim Div).

3617. Grievous bodily harm—Assault on constables—Serious and sustained assault on police officer—Undue leniency

[Offences against the Person Act 1861 s.18.]

The Attorney General referred to the court as unduly lenient a sentence of 30 months' imprisonment imposed on the offender for causing grievous bodily harm with intent to resist or prevent the lawful apprehension or detainer of himself and another, contrary to the Offences against the Person Act 1861 s.18. The offender was convicted for a violent attack on a police officer who had been called to deal with a disturbance at a club. The Attorney General pointed to five aggravating factors: the offender attacked a uniformed police officer on duty; he had continued with the serious and sustained assault while the officer was defenceless; he had used his feet as a weapon; he had contested the matter, and he had previous convictions for violence, including violence against the police. There were three mitigating factors: the offender had since attempted to tackle his alcohol and anger management problems, his wife was mentally unwell and this was his first incarceration.

Held, allowing the reference, that the sentence was unduly lenient and the offence should have attracted a sentence of at least five years' imprisonment at trial, *Attorney General's Reference (No.35 of 1995), Re* [1996] 1 Cr. App. R. (S.) 413, [1996] C.L.Y. 1904, *Attorney General's Reference (No.47 of 1994), Re* (1995) 16 Cr. App. R. (S.) 865, [1996] C.L.Y. 1910 and *Attorney General's Reference (No.76 of 1998), Re* [1999] 2 Cr. App. R. (S.) 361, [1999] C.L.Y. 1175 applied. However, taking into account double jeopardy and the progress that the offender had made in prison, the sentence would only be increased to three years and 11 months.

ATTORNEY GENERAL'S REFERENCE (NO.99 OF 2003), Re, [2004] EWCA Crim 1622, [2005] 1 Cr. App. R. (S.) 33, Rose, L.J., CA (Crim Div).

3618. Grievous bodily harm–HIV–Question of public importance certified

The applicant (D) sought leave to appeal against a conviction for inflicting grievous bodily harm. D, who had been diagnosed as HIV positive, had infected the complainant after having unprotected consensual sexual intercourse with her. D was convicted on a retrial following his successful appeal against conviction. At the retrial the judge held himself bound by the Court of Appeal decision on the issue of consent as a defence. As D's original appeal against conviction had been allowed no application for leave to appeal to the House of Lords had been made. D therefore sought leave to appeal so that the original decision of the Court of Appeal could be reconsidered in the House of Lords.

Held dismissing the appeal, that like the trial judge, the Court of Appeal was also bound by its own decision in the first appeal and also by decisions in *R. v. Barnes (Mark)* [2004] EWCA Crim 3246, [2005] 1 W.L.R. 910, [2005] 2 C.L. 92 and *R. v. Konzani (Feston)* [2005] EWCA Crim 706, [2005] 2 Cr. App. R. 14, [2005] 9 C.L. 98, Barnes and Konzani applied. However if the first appeal against conviction had been dismissed, the Court of Appeal would have certified a question of law of public importance and that importance had not diminished because of the lapse of time. Permission to appeal against conviction would therefore be granted, and a question of public importance would be certified, namely, "in what circumstances, if any, may a defendant who knows or believes he is infected with a serious sexually transmitted infection and recklessly transmits it to another through consensual sexual activity be convicted of an offence of inflicting grievous bodily harm contrary to the Offences against the Person Act 1861 s.20." Leave to appeal to the House of Lords was refused.

R. v. DICA (MOHAMMED), [2005] EWCA Crim 2304, *The Times*, September 7, 2005, Judge, L.J., CA (Crim Div).

3619. Grievous bodily harm–Intention–Car driven at police officer–Intent to cause really serious harm

The appellant (H) appealed against a sentence of nine years' imprisonment following his conviction after trial of one count of attempting to cause grievous bodily harm with intent. H had also pleaded guilty to one count of dangerous driving and one count of assault occasioning actually bodily harm. H had been seen driving away from a service area behind some shops by an officer who believed that H had been drinking alcohol. The officer stepped out into the road and signalled to H to stop the vehicle. H started to comply but then put the car into gear and appeared to drive at the officer, who was struck by the car. The officer ended up on the roof of the car clinging to the sunroof as H drove around the town centre at excessive speed, at one point reaching 60 mph. He drove the wrong way round a roundabout, lurched from side to side and tried to close the sunroof in order to throw the officer off the car. Eventually, H succeeded in throwing the officer into the road, leaving him with a number of injuries. H submitted that the sentence was manifestly excessive due to the relatively superficial nature of the injuries.

Held, dismissing the appeal, that the sentence was appropriate. Although it was accepted that the officer's injuries were much less serious than might have been expected in the circumstances, it was H's intent that was relevant to determining the extent of his criminality and his determined efforts to throw the officer off the car plainly showed his intention to cause really serious harm to the officer, who was acting in the course of his public duty, *R. v. Cooper (Mark Anthony)* [1996] 1 Cr. App. R. (S.) 303, [1996] C.L.Y. 1970, *R. v. Boulter (Andrew Paul)* [1996] 2 Cr. App. R. (S.) 428, *R. v. Hall (Darren David)* [1997] 1 Cr. App. R. (S.) 62, [1997] C.L.Y. 1569 and *Attorney General's Reference (No.78 of 2000), Re* [2001] EWCA Crim 2114, [2002] 1 Cr. App. R. (S.) 116,

[2001] C.L.Y. 1334 considered. H's actions were motivated by a desire to avoid a prison sentence and it was irrelevant to his culpability that the officer's injuries were relatively minor.

R. v. HUNTROYD (SEAN), [2004] EWCA Crim 2182, [2005] 1 Cr. App. R. (S.) 85, May, L.J., CA (Crim Div).

3620. Grievous bodily harm—Multiple injuries—Acid attack injuring number of victims—Undue leniency

The Attorney General referred as unduly lenient a total sentence of four years' imprisonment imposed on the defendant (J) following her guilty pleas to one offence of causing grievous bodily harm with intent, two offences of causing grievous bodily harm and two offences of assault. J had been barred from a public house. She returned only to be ejected once more by the landlady's son (F). She had with her a cosmetics pot containing a corrosive substance used for clearing drains which was made up of 96 per cent sulphuric acid. She threw the contents of the pot at F with the result that he and 27 other people in the premises were injured, some severely. In his current application, the Attorney General stressed that there were several aggravating features, including that J had armed herself with the acid and had inflicted serious injury in an unprovoked attack on a large number of victims. J had previous relevant convictions and the offences had been committed while J was on bail. The mitigating features were the fact that the attack had not been planned, that J had not known the true nature of the liquid and that she herself had been permanently scarred by the liquid. The Attorney General contended that the sentence should have been five and a half to six years.

Held, dismissing the reference, that although the sentence was unduly lenient, it was not one with which the court should interfere. An appropriate starting point would have been five, not six, years' imprisonment, given the lack of premeditation and J's own injuries. Given the principle of double jeopardy and the fact that J had been making good progress in prison towards understanding the offence and seeking ways to change her behaviour in the future, the sentence of four years' imprisonment should stand.

ATTORNEY GENERAL'S REFERENCE (NO.119 OF 2004), *Re*; *sub nom*. R. v. JACKSON (LEANNA), [2005] EWCA Crim 69, [2005] 2 Cr. App. R. (S.) 52, Rose, L.J. (V-P), CA (Crim Div).

3621. Grievous bodily harm—Non custodial sentences—Defenceless victim kicked in head—Failure to reflect gravity of offence—Undue leniency

The Attorney General referred as unduly lenient a community rehabilitation order for a period of two years for causing grievous bodily harm with intent, for affray and for causing criminal damage at a public house. The 19-year-old offender (O) was sentenced concurrently on each of the three counts. O had punched a doorman and kicked a third party in the head. O had a previous conviction for violence. The Attorney General argued that there were aggravating features, including the fact that the kick was administered when the victim was lying defenceless on the floor; the fact that in order to administer the kick O had run up to his victim and kicked him in the head with a shod foot; and O's previous conviction for violence. The Attorney General further contended that a non custodial sentence for the offence failed adequately to reflect the gravity of the offence, that it failed to act as a deterrent and that it failed to protect those employed to preserve public order in public houses.

Held, allowing the reference, that the sentence passed was entirely inappropriate and unduly lenient. A sentence of three years' detention in a young offender institution would have been appropriate. However, a discount needed to be applied by reason of double jeopardy and a further discount would be required if the court were to send to detention someone who had hitherto, in relation to the instant offence, not been deprived of his liberty. A further discount would be called for because O had already completed five months of the curfew which was imposed upon him. A further consideration was that if O were incarcerated he would lose his job. It was inevitable therefore that any sentence of custody would be a comparatively short one. In the circumstances it would not serve the public interest to impose a short sentence on O and therefore the court would not interfere.

ATTORNEY GENERAL'S REFERENCE (NO.77 OF 2004), *Re* [2004] EWCA Crim 2464, Rose, L.J., CA (Crim Div).

3622. Grievous bodily harm—Racially aggravated offences—Attack on Turkish football fans—Undue leniency

[Offences against the Person Act 1861 s.20.]

The Attorney General referred as unduly lenient sentences of two years' imprisonment following pleas of guilty from all the defendants (S, B and M) to racially aggravated grievous bodily harm. Following an international football match between England and Turkey, the two victims, who were Turkish, were attacked by the defendants and others outside a pub. Racial abuse was shouted and one of the victims, who fell to the ground, was kicked four times to the head by M and kicked and stamped on by S and B. The defendants were charged with GBH with intent but on the day of the trial the prosecution accepted pleas of guilty to racially aggravated GBH on the basis that the defendants were so drunk that they were unable to form an intention to cause really serious harm. S also pleaded guilty to a charge of racially aggravated actual bodily harm. S had previous convictions but none for violent offences, B had a number of previous convictions for dishonesty and one for assault and M had no previous convictions but had been cautioned for common assault. S also received a consecutive sentence of 12 months' imprisonment for the racially aggravated ABH. The Attorney General contended that whilst the sentences of two years could not be faulted if passed for a simple Offences Against the Person Act 1861 s.20 offence, the judge did not take account of the racial element, which should have increased the sentences by between 15 and 18 months. The defendants accepted the submission that two years was the appropriate sentence but argued that the uplift sought was too great and that given the pleas of guilty and double jeopardy, it could not be said that the sentences were unduly lenient.

Held, allowing the references, that it was doubtful whether sentences of two years, if passed for simple Offences against the Person Act 1861 s.20 offences, were correct given the nature of the attack. However, in fairness to the defendants, as no increase was sought it was not right for the court to take a higher starting point than the one accepted by the Attorney General. The sentences were unduly lenient and had to be uplifted to reflect the racial element. The appropriate uplift in the court below should have been 18 months. Bearing in mind the element of double jeopardy, the sentences should be increased by 12 months, giving a total sentence of three years' imprisonment for B and M and four years for S.

ATTORNEY GENERAL'S REFERENCE (NOS.86, 87 AND 88 OF 2004), *Re; sub nom.* R. v. SELLARS (DYLAN BRIAN); R. v. BROAD (SIMON RONALD); R. v. MATTHEWS (JAMIE LEE), [2005] EWCA Crim 527, [2005] 2 Cr. App. R. (S.) 91, Tuckey, L.J., CA (Crim Div).

3623. Grievous bodily harm—Wounding with intent—Serious injuries inflicted on victim—Insufficient credit for guilty plea

The appellant (S) appealed against a sentence of 12 years' imprisonment imposed following his guilty plea to causing grievous bodily harm with intent. S had used a knife to stab the victim (Q) in the lower back, causing lacerations to both his kidney and liver. At hospital, Q suffered a cardiac arrest. He also had to have a kidney removed, with the consequence that his life expectancy was reduced. S had previously been the victim of a horrific attack and, at the time of the assault on Q, was under the false assumption that Q had been behind that attack. S submitted that the sentence imposed had been out of line with previous decisions on the appropriate sentence for such cases and that inadequate weight had been given to the guilty plea and the personal mitigation available to him.

Held, allowing the appeal, that this had been a vicious and unprovoked attack, in which life threatening injuries had been inflicted with the consequence of reducing the victim's life expectancy. However, S had been entitled to some credit for his guilty plea. The sentence in the instant case had been manifestly excessive and was replaced with a sentence of 7 years' imprisonment, *Attorney General's Reference (No.4 of 1998), Re* [1998] 2 Cr. App. R. (S.) 388, [1998] C.L.Y. 1407 and *Attorney General's Reference (No.52 of 2001), Re* [2001] EWCA Crim 1906, [2001] C.L.Y. 1501 considered.

R. v. SAMUELS-FURNESS (ANTHONY), [2005] EWCA Crim 265, [2005] 2 Cr. App. R. (S.) 84, Waller, L.J., CA (Crim Div).

3624. Grievous bodily harm—Wounding with intent—Single punch resulting in serious brain injury

The appellant (F) appealed against a sentence of three years and six months' imprisonment for maliciously inflicting grievous bodily harm. The incident had occurred when F pushed past another man while passing him on the street. F had then run back to deliver a single punch after a night club doorman had intervened. The victim had fallen and hit his head on the pavement causing him serious injuries with permanent effects. In the instant appeal, F contended that the sentence was manifestly excessive in the light of his guilty plea, remorse and the impulsive nature of the offence.

Held, allowing the appeal, that although F had pleaded guilty and it was accepted that he had not intended to cause such serious harm, the extent of the injury and F's inflammatory behaviour were serious aggravating features. Such cases, where injury was the consequence of a single blow, were far too common for comfort. It was foreseeable that serious harm could result when the victim fell in a paved street. However, the maximum sentence for an offence of this nature was five years' imprisonment regardless of the severity of the injury caused. Given F's plea, a sentence of two years and six months was appropriate, *R. v. Jeffrey (Wayne Peter)* [2003] EWCA Crim 2098, [2004] 1 Cr. App. R. (S.) 25, [2004] C.L.Y. 3354 considered.

R. v. FOOTE (TERRY ANDREW), [2004] EWCA Crim 2820, [2005] 2 Cr. App. R. (S.) 5, Rix, L.J., CA (Crim Div).

3625. Grievous bodily harm—Wounding with intent—Stabbing of estranged wife

The appellant (F) appealed against a sentence of 10 years' imprisonment for wounding his estranged wife with intent to cause grievous bodily harm. F had also been sentenced to six years' imprisonment concurrent for threatening to kill her. F had returned to the matrimonial home and locked his wife out of the house before dragging her inside. Police were called to the premises but F produced a knife after the police had left. He stabbed his wife several times and threatened to kill her. F had a previous conviction for assaulting his wife. In the instant appeal, F submitted that the starting point taken by the sentencing judge was too high.

Held, allowing the appeal, that notwithstanding the vicious nature of the unprovoked attack, aggravated by the threats to kill, a sentence of 10 years was too high. If guilt had been contested, 15 years would have been appropriate for such a serious attack; however more credit should have been attributed to F for his guilty plea. The sentence for wounding with intent was reduced to six years' imprisonment with three years concurrent for the threats to kill, *R. v. Standing (Colin Frederick)* [2002] EWCA Crim 1547, [2003] 1 Cr. App. R. (S.) 52, [2003] C.L.Y. 3728 and *Attorney General's Reference (No.89 of 2000), Re* [2001] EWCA Crim 137, [2001] 2 Cr. App .R. (S.) 65, [2001] C.L.Y. 1202 considered.

R. v. FLETCHER (RAYMOND), [2004] EWCA Crim 2959, [2005] 2 Cr. App. R. (S.) 4, Clarke, L.J., CA (Crim Div).

3626. Grievous bodily harm–Wounding with intent–Sustained attack involving hammer blows to victim's head–Level of offence most serious of its type

The appellant (H) appealed against a sentence of 12 years imprisonment imposed on his plea of guilty to causing grievous bodily harm with intent on an indictment of attempted murder. H had been drinking alcohol in a public house. He had left and was going to his van when the victim (B), who had also been drinking, asked him for a lift. H agreed. During the journey B had picked up a hammer which was in the van and waved it around. H stopped the van, took the hammer from B and hit him over the head with it. He then pushed him out of the van. As he began to drive off, H saw that B had got up so he drove back and hit him over the head two or three more times, then drove home. H tried to destroy evidence of the attack by disposing of his bloodstained clothing and washing the blood off the hammer. B had sustained multiple head injuries and required major surgery. There was a degree of permanent injury and B would never work again, but the prognosis was uncertain. H submitted that the sentencing judge had taken too high a starting point for an offence of causing grievous bodily harm with intent and that he had received insufficient credit for his guilty plea which, whilst not entered at the first available opportunity, had been entered some weeks before his trial was due to take place.

Held, dismissing the appeal, that whilst the sentence was severe it was justified. The only issue was whether sufficient credit had been given for H's plea of guilty. This offence was at the most serious level for its type. H had left his victim for dead and had tried to destroy evidence of the attack. He had a record of violent offences, and although he frequently lost his temper whilst intoxicated he continued to abuse alcohol. There were further aggravating features in that H was still driving around with a hammer in his van despite his previous conviction and that he had returned to the scene when he saw that B was still alive in order to continue the attack. In all the circumstances, the sentence was not manifestly excessive.

R. v. HORROCKS (TERRENCE ALAN), [2004] EWCA Crim 2129, [2005] 1 Cr. App. R. (S.) 80, May, L.J., CA (Crim Div).

3627. Harassment–Restraining orders–Guidelines on sentencing for breach

The appellant (P) appealed against the imposition of a sentence of two years' imprisonment for breach of a restraining order. An order had been made six months before the offence, requiring P not to contact or harass an individual (D). Whilst drunk, P had met D by chance. He had accosted her and attempted to embrace her. When D rebuffed him and tried to walk away he attempted to force her to return by pretending to have a knife. Terrified, D ran away and called the police. The incident lasted about 10 minutes. P had an extensive criminal record and at the time of the offence was in breach of a community rehabilitation order and a community punishment order imposed for other offences.

Held, allowing the appeal, that when sentencing for breach of a restraining order courts should take into account (i) the nature of the act giving rise to the breach, violence or threat of violence being an aggravating feature, (ii) the effect on the victim, (iii) whether the offence was the first breach or the latest in a series of breaches, (iv) the record of the offender, especially his previous response to community penalties and (v) the need to protect the person named in the order. In the instant case a custodial penalty was called for in the light of the need to protect D, P's previous record, the length of time P persisted in the harassment and the threat that he had a knife. However, the two-year sentence was excessive taking into account the facts that the offence was spontaneous, that it was the first time P had breached the order and that he had abided by the order for six months. Accordingly, a sentence of 18 months' imprisonment was imposed on P in place of the original sentence.

R. v. PACE (DAVID PAUL), [2004] EWCA Crim 2018, [2005] 1 Cr. App. R. (S.) 74, Keene, L.J., CA (Crim Div).

3628. Harassment–Restraining orders–Persistent breaches–Sentence length

[Protection from Harassment Act 1997 s.2, s.4.]

The appellant (D) appealed against a sentence of 30 months' imprisonment following his guilty pleas to an offence of breaching a restraining order imposed in accordance with the Protection from Harassment Act 1997, one count of assault with intent to resist arrest and driving whilst disqualified. D was subject to a restraining order, which prevented him contacting a woman with whom he had had a relationship. He had breached the order on a number of occasions and had received custodial sentences for a number of those breaches. On this occasion he made numerous telephone calls to the victim. She answered only one of them and told him to stop contacting her. He was arrested several months later. D contended that the sentence was manifestly excessive because he had not been afforded credit for his guilty plea, which was on the basis that no threats were made during the telephone call.

Held, allowing the appeal, that this offence was serious because of D's persistent offending and his record of breaching court orders, although it was not an offence under s.4 of the Act and it was necessary to distinguish between s.2 and s.4 offences when sentencing, *R. v. Liddle (Mark) (Appeal against Sentence)* [1999] 3 All E.R. 816, [1999] C.L.Y. 1188 considered. Notwithstanding his guilty plea, D had made remarks while in prison which indicated that he did not appreciate the gravity of the offence. The victim had been frightened and required protection, and there was a high risk that D would reoffend. However, the offence in question had involved a single act of harassment which had not been repeated in the months between the offence and arrest, no threats of violence were made and D had pleaded guilty. Therefore, whilst the offence merited a sentence of more than 15 months' imprisonment, thirty months was manifestly excessive. The sentence was accordingly reduced to one of 20 months' imprisonment.

R. v. DADLEY (ANDREW MARK), [2004] EWCA Crim 2216, [2005] 1 Cr. App. R. (S.) 87, Mance, L.J., CA (Crim Div).

3629. Harassment–Restraining orders–Repeated breaches

[Protection from Harassment Act 1997.]

The appellant (B), who had pleaded guilty to an offence of breach of a restraining order, appealed against a sentence of 18 months' imprisonment. The restraining order had been imposed under the Protection from Harassment Act 1997 following conduct towards his mother amounting to harassment and prohibited him from going to her home, ringing her doorbell or attempting to contact her. B breached the order two days after it was made, and then again less than two months later upon his release from prison. Some months later, B's mother saw him in her garden and he repeatedly rang her doorbell that day. As a consequence, the sentence of 18 months' imprisonment was imposed. B had also persistently failed to keep appointments with the probation service and attend court. A pre sentence report indicated that B did not appreciate the consequences of his actions and therefore posed a high risk of reoffending.

Held, dismissing the appeal, that the sentence was not manifestly excessive given the terms of the pre sentence report. This was a third offence, and although he had not bee violent toward his mother on that occasion, he had nevertheless caused emotional and psychological harm. B's failure to cooperate with the conditions of his bail should also be taken into account. B's conduct was continuous or repeated over a period of time and the judge had been justified in imposing a significant custodial sentence, *R. v. Liddle (Mark) (Appeal against Sentence)* [1999] 3 All E.R. 816, [1999] C.L.Y. 1188 considered.

R. v. BENNETT (ANDREW), [2005] EWCA Crim 603, [2005] 2 Cr. App. R. (S.) 59, Bodey, J., CA (Crim Div).

3630. Health and safety offences–Fines–Culpability of hotel owner in respect of contraventions of fire certificate

[Fire Precautions Act 1971.]

The appellant (E) appealed against fines of £300,000 and £100,000 imposed for two offences of contravening the requirements of a fire certificate, contrary to the Fire Precautions Act 1971. E had operated a hotel in respect of which a fire certificate was in force. The fire certificate required all escape routes to be free of obstacles and combustible materials. A major fire that occurred at the hotel resulted in two human fatalities. A subsequent investigation disclosed that the fire had been started by a porter at the hotel maliciously setting alight beds that were being stored on a hotel corridor (an escape route). The porter had been instructed to remove the beds. The investigation further disclosed that another hotel corridor had had a mattress stored on it and that a risk assessment at the hotel had disclosed that there was a problem with the storage of combustible materials. E pleaded guilty to two offences of contravening the requirements of a fire certificate. The first offence related to the storage of beds on the hotel corridor where the fire started and the second offence related to the mattress stored on a different hotel corridor. The judge imposed a fine of £300,000 for the first offence and £100,000 for the second offence. In imposing the fines, the judge took as an aggravating factor E's failure to heed the earlier risk assessment and as mitigating factors E's guilty plea, the generally good health and safety record at the hotel and the fact that the breaches were not deliberate or made with a view to achieving a profit. In calculating the fines, the judge assessed E's profits on its turnover. E contended that the fines were excessive as (1) they did not reflect E's reduced degree of culpability; (2) E's profits had not been properly assessed as E's gross turnover was not an adequate measure of profits.

Held, allowing the appeal, that (1) it was important in determining the level of penalty for health and safety breaches to take into account the degree of risk, the scope of risk and the degree of culpability. The potential for risk of serious injury in a building where people slept was considerable. In the instant case, had the beds not been in the hotel corridor, the fire would not have occurred. The degree of culpability for the first offence was reduced by the fact that E had taken steps to remove the beds and was greater for the second as no steps had been taken to remove the mattress. The judge had failed to properly take account of the steps taken by E to remove the beds, *R. v. Friskies Petcare (UK) Ltd* [2000] 2 Cr. App. R. (S.) 401, [2001] C.L.Y. 3296, *R. v. Colthrop Board Mills Ltd* [2002] EWCA Crim 520, [2002] 2 Cr. App. R. (S.) 80, [2002] C.L.Y. 3968 and *R. v. Fresha Bakeries Ltd* [2002] EWCA Crim 1451, [2003] 1 Cr. App. R. (S.) 44, [2003] C.L.Y. 1923 considered. (2) In considering the effect a fine would have on a company, it was desirable for the court to have regard to the pre tax profits of a company rather than its turnover. In the instant case, the judge had given inadequate weight to E's financial position, *R. v. F Howe & Son (Engineers) Ltd* [1999] 2 All E.R. 249, [1998] C.L.Y. 2839 considered. Accordingly the appropriate fines were £175,000 for the first offence and £75,000 for the second offence.

R. v. ESB HOTELS LTD, [2005] EWCA Crim 132, [2005] 2 Cr. App. R. (S.) 56, Auld, L.J., CA (Crim Div).

3631. Health and safety offences–Fines–Death of trainee during diving exercise–Breach of Diving at Work Regulations 1997 not causative of death

[Health and Safety at Work etc. Act 1974 s.3(1); Diving at Work Regulations 1997 (SI 1997 2776).]

The appellants (W) appealed against a fine of £3000 imposed on each of them after they pleaded guilty on rearraignment to an offence under the Health and Safety at Work etc. Act 1974 s.3(1). W also appealed against an order that they were to pay prosecution costs of £15,000. W ran training courses for scuba divers. The charges were brought against W after one of their trainees died during the course of a diving exercise. The prosecution alleged that W had had a total and flagrant disregard for the Diving at Work Regulations 1997. The prosecution's expert witness had raised dozens of criticisms of W's diving procedures but, after hearing the report of the expert witness for the defence, the judge only considered three of the allegations made against W. Thus, the judge focused on W's ignorance as to the requirement that they were to operate in accordance with the 1974 Regulations, that they had failed to produce a written diving project plan and that there had been no appointment of a diving contractor or supervisor. W argued that insufficient account had been taken of the fact that the judge had found no causal link between the trainee's death and W's failures on the day in question.

Held, allowing the appeal, that once it was accepted that there had been no causal link between the trainee's death and W's shortcomings, it was necessary to focus on the extent to which the breaches jeopardised the general safety aspects of what was in any event a hazardous occupation. W were both highly qualified and were normally extremely conscientious with regards to safety matters. W's operation could not be described as a cavalier outfit or one that operated in disregard of safety. Far lower fines had been imposed upon persons whose conduct had drawn very strong remarks from the Bench. In all the circumstances the fines were excessive. Accordingly, a fine of £1500 was substituted. With regard to costs, as a great deal of what the prosecution had alleged had failed to pass the winning post the costs payable by W had been placed too high. It was appropriate to reduce the costs payable by W to £8000.

R. v. WILSON (IAN); R. v. MAINPRIZE (CRAIG), [2004] EWCA Crim 2086, [2005] 1 Cr. App. R. (S.) 64, Thomas, L.J., CA (Crim Div).

3632. **Hospital orders–Drug trafficking–Causal connection between mental illness and commission of offence**

[Mental Health Act 1983 s.37, s.47, s.49.]

The appellant (N) appealed against his sentence of 12 years' imprisonment. N had pleaded guilty to an offence of being knowingly concerned in the fraudulent evasion of the prohibition on the importation of a Class A drug, namely 30 kilograms of cocaine with a street value of around £1.8 million. Psychiatric expert witnesses had recommended that a hospital order under the Mental Health Act 1983 s.37 would be appropriate as N was suffering from schizophrenia, although he was responsive to medication and there were ways in which he could be treated within the prison system. N submitted that (1) the judge had been wrong in principle or had erred in the exercise of his discretion by imposing a custodial sentence instead of making a hospital order; (2) the sentence was excessive.

Held, dismissing the appeal, that no real point of principle was involved and the judge had properly exercised his discretion under s.37. There had been no causal connection between the mental illness and the offending, so N had known at the time what he was doing and that it was wrong, *R. v. Howell (Seymour Joseph)* (1985) 7 Cr. App. R. (S.) 360, [1987] C.L.Y. 913, *R. v. Mbatha (Vermet)* (1985) 7 Cr. App. R. (S.) 373, [1987] C.L.Y. 992, *R. v. Fairhurst (David)* (1996) 1 Cr. App. R. (S.) 242, [1996] C.L.Y. 2001 and *R. v. Birch (Beulah)* (1990) 90 Cr. App. R. 78, [1991] C.L.Y. 1136 distinguished. Policy considerations caused the courts in dealing with such offending to focus primarily on the offence itself and the need for effective deterrence whereas N could be medically treated in prison or transferred to a hospital under s.47 or s.49 of the Act. The sentence was not excessive in all the circumstances, taking into account N's guilty plea, the huge quantity of drugs involved and the fact that N had known what he was doing.

R. v. NAFEI (ABDELKHALEK), [2004] EWCA Crim 3238, [2005] 2 Cr. App. R. (S.) 24, Laws, L.J., CA (Crim Div).

3633. **Illegal importation–Offensive weapons–Flick knives and knuckle duster hidden in luggage–Sentence length**

The appellant (P), who had pleaded guilty to two counts of being knowingly concerned in the fraudulent evasion of the restriction on the import of goods, appealed against his sentence of three years' imprisonment. When P returned from holiday, customs officers had found three flick knives and a knuckle duster hidden in his luggage. The flick knives also functioned as cigarette lighters. In interview P stated that he had bought the items as presents for friends. P had numerous previous convictions, including assault and threatening behaviour; all the offences were associated with drink and attendance at football matches. P pointed out that there were no authorities indicating the appropriate level of sentence for his offence and contended that his sentence was manifestly excessive.

Held, dismissing the appeal, that in determining the sentence to be imposed for importing prohibited weapons it was necessary to take account of the need to deter others, the number and nature of the weapons and the risk to the public if they were disseminated, the offender's actual intention, and the likely eventual use of weapons. Whilst P maintained that the weapons were bought as gifts and not intended for criminal use, it was clear that a knuckle duster had only violent uses and the knives were very likely to be used for inflicting violence, bearing in mind P's previous convictions and his having hidden and not declared the items. Even after credit for the guilty pleas, a sentence of three years' imprisonment was well within the correct bracket, if not merciful for someone with P's record.

R. v. PRICE (KEVIN), [2005] EWCA Crim 1757, [2006] 1 Cr. App. R. (S.) 55, Thomas, L.J., CA (Crim Div).

3634. Increase of sentence–Court of Appeal–Procedure to be followed–Trinidad and Tobago

[Supreme Court of Judicature Act 1980 (Trinidad and Tobago) s.44(3), s.49(1).]

The appellant (W) appealed against the decision of the Court of Appeal of Trinidad and Tobago to increase his sentence of imprisonment. W was a police officer who had been convicted of raping a woman whilst on duty at a police station. He was sentenced to 25 years' imprisonment at hard labour. The Court of Appeal refused W leave to appeal against his conviction and sentence. However, pursuant to the Supreme Court of Judicature Act 1980 (Trinidad and Tobago) s.44(3) and s.49(1), it increased W's sentence to 30 years' hard labour to take effect from the date of conviction. W submitted that the Court of Appeal had failed to give leave to appeal against sentence and to quash the trial judge's sentence as required by s.44(3). W further argued that the Court of Appeal should have given his counsel the opportunity to present reasons why the sentence should not be increased or to ask the leave of the court to withdraw the application for leave to appeal against sentence, and should have given reasons why the sentence was wrong and had to be increased.

Held, allowing the appeal, that (1) the normal course for the Court of Appeal, if it intended to vary a sentence under s.44(3), would have been to consider the correctness of the judge's sentence, decide whether it should be varied, give leave to appeal against sentence, quash the judge's sentence, and substitute a varied sentence. The court did not take any of those steps, nor could it be said to have followed that procedure by necessary implication. Nor did it appear that in invoking s.49(1) the Court of Appeal adverted to the question whether there was an appeal before it. Since leave to appeal was not given, there was never an appeal against sentence in being and the power to increase sentence conferred by s.44(3) did not come into operation. Therefore the purported increase of sentence was of no effect. (2) An appellate court that was considering exercising its power to increase a sentence should invariably give the applicant leave to appeal against sentence or give his counsel an indication to that effect and an opportunity to address the court on the increase, or to ask for leave to withdraw the application. Failure to do so would be unfair and a breach of natural justice.

WILLIAMS v. TRINIDAD AND TOBAGO, [2005] UKPC 11, [2005] 1 W.L.R. 1948, Lord Bingham of Cornhill, Privy Council (Trinidad and Tobago).

3635. Increase of sentence–Magistrates courts–Use of power in Magistrates' Courts Act 1980 s.142

[Magistrates' Courts Act 1980 s.142.]

The applicant (H) applied for judicial review to quash a decision of the magistrates' court to reopen his sentence following a conviction for dangerous driving. H had travelled through a built up area at a speed in excess of the 30 mph speed limit. He drove through a red light at a pedestrian crossing and knocked down a pedestrian. H was charged with dangerous driving. There was evidence before the magistrates' court that the pedestrian had suffered serious injuries. The magistrates' court convicted H of dangerous driving and sentenced him to 50 hours' community service, a disqualification from driving for 12 months and a requirement to sit a driving test. A relative of the pedestrian subsequently complained about what she perceived was an unduly lenient sentence given the extent of the pedestrian's injuries. As a result the CPS sought to have the case reopened. The magistrates' court decided to reopen the case on the basis that the original counsel for the prosecution had not addressed the extent of the pedestrian's injuries and that the difference between the sentence imposed and a probable custodial sentence that it would have imposed had it known all the facts offended the principles of natural justice.

Held, granting the application, that in some circumstances a failure of the magistrates' court to be aware of certain material facts meant that it was appropriate for it to invoke its power under the Magistrates' Courts Act 1980 s.142 to reopen a case for sentencing. It would only be in rare circumstances that it would be appropriate for the magistrates' court to resort to its power under s.142 to increase a sentence, in particular to impose a custodial sentence. If the power under s.142 was invoked, the matter had to be dealt with expeditiously. The facts of the instant case did not justify the magistrates' court's use of s.142 and it was not clear that it had been misled, *R. v. Secretary of State for the Home Department, ex p. Pierson* [1998] A.C. 539, [1997] C.L.Y. 1627 and *R. v. Croydon Youth Court, ex p. DPP* [1997] 2 Cr. App. R. 411, [1998] C.L.Y. 1069 considered.

R. (ON THE APPLICATION OF HOLME) v. LIVERPOOL MAGISTRATES COURT; *sub nom.* HOLME v. LIVERPOOL CITY JUSTICES, [2004] EWHC 3131, (2005) 169 J.P. 306, Collins, J., QBD (Admin Ct).

3636. Indecent assault–10 year old girl assaulted by neighbour–Three year conditional discharge–Undue leniency

[Powers of Criminal Courts (Sentencing) Act 2000 s.79(2).]

The Attorney General referred as unduly lenient a three-year conditional discharge imposed on B for indecent assault against a 10-year-old girl. B, a 64-year-old neighbour, had touched the girl's breasts and made sexual references. He had pleaded guilty on the basis that he had intended his behaviour to be a joke rather than sexual, but accepted that it was inappropriate. The judge, on the basis of reports in relation to a sex offender treatment programme and from a probation officer, determined that the conditional discharge was the appropriate choice rather than custody, and also ordered that a compensatory fine of £500 be paid by B to the girl. The Attorney General argued that there was insufficient punishment in the conditional discharge sentence. It was contended that the assault had passed the custody threshold or, at least, that B should be punished with a community rehabilitation order.

Held, refusing the application, that although every indecent assault required punishment, not every indecent assault met the criteria for a custodial sentence under the Powers of Criminal Courts (Sentencing) Act 2000 s.79(2). The judge had failed to examine an intermediate position between the two alternatives that he considered open to him and the correct sentence would have been a community rehabilitation order. However, while the sentence was lenient, it was not unduly lenient. The stigma of conviction and threat of reference hanging over B's head carried sufficient elements of punishment. The compensation order should not have been made because it would be widely misunderstood as being a reflection of the court's view of the gravity of the events, *Attorney General's Reference (No.35 of 1994), Re* (1995) 16 Cr. App. R. (S.) 635, [1996] C.L.Y. 1782 followed and because the impression should not be given that the offender was being allowed to buy his way out of a custodial sentence.

ATTORNEY GENERAL'S REFERENCE (NO.70 OF 2003), *Re; sub nom.* R. v. BATES (ALAN ROY), [2004] EWCA Crim 163, [2004] 2 Cr. App. R. (S.) 49, Latham, L.J., CA (Crim Div).

3637. Indecent assault–Children–Assault by defendant on friend's 15 year old daughter–Entering victim's bedroom whilst asleep–Undue leniency

The Attorney General referred to the court as unduly lenient a sentence of eight months' imprisonment imposed on the offender (S) following his conviction, after a trial, for indecent assault. S was aged 35 and a friend of the victim's father. The victim was aged 15. S had been invited into their house and once inside he had asked if he could use the lavatory. At some point he entered the victim's room whilst she was sleeping and lay on the bed next to her. The victim, aware that someone was laid in bed with her, pretended to be asleep. S then proceeded to place his hand inside her knickers and penetrated her vagina with two fingers. The Attorney General relied on the following aggravating features: the victim had been indecently assaulted in her own home whilst she was sleeping; there had been no contact between the victim and S which could have given him any indication that she wished to have anything to do with him; S was significantly older; and the assault had had a significant effect on the victim. The Attorney General also submitted that if the offence had been committed now, S would not have been charged with indecent assault but with the offence of assault by penetration, which had a maximum sentence of life imprisonment.

Held, allowing the reference, that the appropriate sentencing guidelines were those that applied under the old law of indecent assault. A sentence of two years' imprisonment was the appropriate starting point where, as in the instant case, there had been no plea of guilty, no remorse and no indication from a pre sentence report that the incident had been a one off incident, *R. v. L (Indecent Assault: Sentencing)* [1999] 1 Cr. App. R. 117, [1998] C.L.Y. 1257 considered. There were no special circumstances in the instant case and the lowest sentence which could have been considered appropriate for this offence was one of two years' imprisonment. However, due to the rules on double jeopardy and S being shortly due for release if his current sentence was maintained, the sentence was replaced with a sentence of 18 months' imprisonment.

ATTORNEY GENERAL'S REFERENCE (NO.156 OF 2004), *Re; sub nom.* R v. S (CHRISTOPHER) [2005] EWCA Crim 724, Latham, L.J., CA (Crim Div).

3638. Indecent assault–Children–Assault on sister in law aged between 10 and 14–Undue leniency

The Attorney General referred to the court as unduly lenient a sentence of six months' imprisonment imposed on the offender (N) following his conviction of five counts of indecent assault. N had indecently assaulted his sister in law on a substantial number of occasions during the period from 1976 to 1980. The victim had been aged between 10 and 13 at the time, while N had been aged 19 to 23. The indecent assaults included W's touching her around her vaginal area, penetrating her digitally and exposing himself to her. N had also used force on occasions to facilitate the assaults. The Attorney General relied on the following aggravating features: the age of the victim at the time of the offences; the breach of trust involved; the fact that force had been used on occasions; the fact that the offences were repeated; the profound and long term detrimental effect on the victim; and the fact that N had not pleaded guilty to the offences.

Held, allowing the reference, that a significant sentence of imprisonment was both inevitable and necessary. Even though the offences were old it was not something which the court could take into consideration as a significant feature in mitigation, *R. v. Millberry (William Christopher)* [2002] EWCA Crim 2891, [2003] 1 W.L.R. 546, [2003] C.L.Y. 3829 considered. However, the offences had been committed when N was between the ages of 19 and 23. Nothing had happened since and whatever it was that had motivated him to commit the offences had disappeared. The appropriate sentence would have been three years' imprisonment. However, in all the circumstances the sentence of six months' imprisonment was quashed and replaced with a sentence of two years' imprisonment.

ATTORNEY GENERAL'S REFERENCE (NO.6 OF 2005) (UNDULY LENIENT SENTENCE), *Re; sub nom.* R v. N (JAMES) [2005] EWCA Crim 500, Latham, L.J., CA (Crim Div).

3639. Indecent assault–Children–Victim under 14–Maximum sentence dependent on victim's age as expressed in indictment–Undue leniency

The instant proceedings involved a consideration by the Court of Appeal of the sentences it had earlier imposed on the offender when determining the Attorney General's reference. The sentences were for offences of indecent assault against a child. The case had been relisted before the Court of Appeal after concern was expressed by the trial judge as to the court's sentencing of the offender. The court had determined earlier that a sentence of six months' imprisonment for a series of indecent assaults over a period of years committed against a child who was between the ages of 10 and 13 was unduly lenient and so the sentence was increased to a total sentence of two years' imprisonment. One of the five counts in the indictment, the first count, identified the child's age expressly as being under 13 as it identified her as aged 10. Therefore the maximum sentence available for this count was five years' imprisonment. The trial judge had considered this count to be a comparatively minor assault to be treated leniently. He had considered himself to be mainly constrained by the maximum sentences of two years' imprisonment available for the other counts, which had expressed the victim's age as being "either 11, 12 or 13" and were therefore classified as indecent assaults on a child under 14.

Held, giving judgment accordingly, that the total sentence previously given by the court was upheld. A total sentence of three years' imprisonment would have been appropriate at first instance, but this was reduced to two years having regard to double jeopardy. The trial judge had erred in his approach to sentencing for a course of abuse over a period of years on a child between the ages of 10 and 13. The first count might not have been an offence of the most serious type, but it represented the start of the prolonged abuse. Therefore it was inevitable that that count should carry a significant sentence of imprisonment in itself. The court was aware of the sentencing constraints. However, the court should not previously have expressed itself so as to suggest that the offender was receiving the maximum sentence for each of counts two to five. Therefore so as to clarify the distinction between the maximum sentences available on count one as opposed to the other counts, the court expressed the individual sentences as follows: 12 months' imprisonment was imposed for count one to be served consecutively with concurrent sentences of 12 months' imprisonment for counts two to five.

ATTORNEY GENERAL'S REFERENCE (NO.6 OF 2005), *Re; sub nom.* N (JAMES) [2005] EWCA Crim 844, Latham, L.J., CA (Crim Div).

3640. Indecent assault–Extended sentences–Disqualification from working with children–Meaning of "qualifying sentence" in s.28 of Criminal Justice and Court Services Act 2000 s.28

[Crime and Disorder Act 1998 s.117; Powers of Criminal Courts (Sentencing) Act 2000 s 76, s.85; Criminal Justice and Court Services Act 2000 s.28.]

The appellant (W) appealed against an extended sentence and disqualification order imposed after he had pleaded guilty on the morning of his trial to indecently assaulting a 14 year old girl and to 10 counts of possessing indecent photographs of her. W had made contact with the girl on the internet and arranged to meet her. At their fourth meeting W undressed the girl and indecently assaulted her as well as performing other sexual acts with her. He took indecent photographs of her. The judge sentenced W to six months' imprisonment with an extended term of 18 months under the Powers of Criminal Courts (Sentencing) Act 2000 s.85. W contended that the disqualification order prohibiting him from working with children imposed under the Criminal Justice and Court Services Act 2000 s.28 was unlawful because the extended sentence was not a qualifying sentence within s.28 as it was not a term of imprisonment for 12 months or more.

Held, dismissing the appeal, that a sentence was a "qualifying sentence" for the purposes of s.28 if it was for a term of imprisonment of 12 months or more. Section 85 provided that the court could impose an extended sentence comprising a custodial term and an extension period. "Custodial sentence" was defined by s.76 of the same Act as, among other things, a "term of imprisonment" which included the extension period and it was not confined to the custodial term. That approach was consistent with the modern approach to sentencing and imprisonment where a sentence was not an order for a period of incarceration for a fixed period but an order for a period of restricted freedom which began with incarceration and might include a period of release on licence. The extended sentence merely adjusted that second period. It followed that, for the purposes of s.28, the whole length of the extended sentence had to be taken into account and, on that basis, the sentence passed on W was a qualifying sentence which required the judge to impose a disqualification unless there were grounds to believe that W was not likely to re offend. No such grounds existed. The approach taken was inconsistent with that adopted in *R. v. S (Graham)* [2001] 1 Cr. App. R. 7, [2000] C.L.Y. 1301 but in that case the attention of the court had not been drawn to the provisions of the Crime and Disorder Act 1998 s.117, *R. v. S (Graham)* doubted.

R. v. WILES (ALAN RALPH), [2004] EWCA Crim 836, [2004] 2 Cr. App. R. (S.) 88, Rose, L.J., CA (Crim Div).

3641. **Indecent assault–Father abusing 16 year old daughter with learning difficulties–Undue leniency**

The Attorney General referred to the court as unduly lenient concurrent extended sentences consisting of a custodial term of six months' imprisonment and an extended licence period of two years and nine months imposed on the defendant (K) after he was convicted on two counts of indecent assault on a woman. The victim, K's 16 year old daughter, had learning difficulties and was immature for her age. The Attorney General submitted that the sentence was unduly lenient, given that K had committed a gross breach of trust, the victim was vulnerable, he had penetrated her with his toe, and she suffered, as a result, a complete loss of the support of her family.

Held, allowing the reference, that the custodial term which should have been imposed after a contested hearing was one of 18 months' imprisonment, *Attorney General's Reference (No.43 of 1999), Re* [2000] 1 Cr. App. R. (S.) 398, [2000] C.L.Y. 1287 considered. Allowing for the element of double jeopardy, the length of the concurrent extended sentences of three years and three months would remain the same, but the custodial part would be increased to 12 months' imprisonment.

ATTORNEY GENERAL'S REFERENCE (NO.97 OF 2004), *Re; sub nom.* R v. FK [2004] EWCA Crim 2311, Kennedy, L.J., CA (Crim Div).

3642. **Indecent assault–Indecent photographs of children–Offences committed by doctor against patients–Grave breach of trust–Undue leniency**

The Attorney General referred as unduly lenient an extended sentence of five and a half years, the custodial part of which was three and a half years' imprisonment, imposed as a total sentence for a number of sexual offences committed by a general practitioner. The offender had pleaded guilty to 23 counts, comprised of indecent assaults on females and making and possessing indecent photographs of children. The offender was also disqualified from working with children. The Attorney General drew attention to eight aggravating features, namely that the offences were committed against patients in a gross breach of trust, they were repeated, at least four patients had their medical examinations recorded, some of the indecent assaults involved penetration of the victims, some of the victims were particularly vulnerable by reason of youth or age, an elderly patient had a degree of mental impairment and was subjected to particularly degrading and humiliating treatment, the impact on the victims and the very large number of indecent images of children found.

Held, allowing the reference, that the extended sentence and the custodial term were both unduly lenient. An extended sentence of eight years and, even on a plea of guilty, a custodial term of at least five and a half years' imprisonment would have been appropriate. However, having regard to double jeopardy, an extended sentence of eight years was imposed but with a custodial term of four and a half years' imprisonment. The four matters which had to be taken into account when approaching sentence in cases of this kind were: the degree of harm done to the victims, the level of culpability of the offender, the level of risk which the offender posed and the need for deterrence. In the instant case, particular account was taken of the serious consequences to the victims and the high degree of culpability on the offender's part because of the grave breach of trust which occurred in the doctor and patient relationship. A deterrent element in relation to doctors had to be incorporated into the sentencing process because of the effect on public confidence in the medical profession.

ATTORNEY GENERAL'S REFERENCE (NO.79 OF 2004), *Re*; *sub nom.* R. v. HUSAIN (SYED); R. v. HUSSAIN (SYED), [2004] EWCA Crim 2722, [2005] 1 Cr. App. R. (S.) 112, Rose, L.J., CA (Crim Div).

3643. Indecent assault–Repeated assaults on 10 year old girl–Undue leniency

The Attorney General referred as unduly lenient an extended sentence comprising a two year custodial term and an extended period of two years imposed on the defendant (G) following his conviction on four counts of indecent assault and one count of indecency with a child. Over a period of 18 months G indecently assaulted a 10 year old girl (V), who was a friend of his stepdaughter. V often stayed overnight at G's home and went on holidays with the family. The offences included kissing, touching her vagina, placing his penis on her vagina and masturbating himself. G was sentenced to a consecutive three month sentence for a Bail Act offence committed during the course of the trial. The Attorney General contended there were four aggravating features: (i) G was in a position of responsibility and the offence concerned a betrayal of trust; (ii) V's youth and vulnerability; (iii) repetition of the offences; and (iv) the nature of the conduct in touching the vagina of a 10 year old girl. Mitigation was found in the fact that G had no previous convictions for sexual abuse. The Attorney General argued that the sentence failed to reflect the public concern over cases of this nature and that a deterrent sentence ought to have been passed.

Held, dismissing the reference, that in the circumstances it was not appropriate to interfere with the sentence. A sentence of three years in the court below, following trial, could have been expected. If a three year sentence had been passed, it was unlikely that the consecutive sentence for the Bail Act offence would have been as long as three months. It followed that the sentence was unduly lenient so far as the custodial aspect was concerned. However, it was doubtful that the sentence could properly be characterised as unduly lenient, taking into account the extended period.

ATTORNEY GENERAL'S REFERENCE (NO.142 OF 2004), *Re*; *sub nom.* R. v. G (RICHARD SHANE) [2005] EWCA Crim 654, Rose, L.J. (V-P), CA (Crim Div).

3644. Indecent assault–Sexual activity with children–Circumstances calling for imposition of consecutive sentences–Undue leniency

The Attorney General referred as unduly lenient concurrent sentences of eight months' imprisonment imposed on the 30-year-old offender (B), who had pleaded guilty to a number of sexual offences against a 13-year-old girl. The offences included indecent assault, indecency with a child and unlawful sexual intercourse. The girl had been groomed by B over the internet and had been a willing participant in the activities. Upon their first meeting B had digitally penetrated the girl but he did not have intercourse with her. That incident was the basis of the indecent assault charge. At their subsequent meetings they had performed oral sex on each other and had full sexual intercourse. At the time the offences were committed the maximum sentence for unlawful sexual intercourse with a girl aged 13 to 16 was two years' imprisonment.

Held, finding the sentence unduly lenient but not varying it, that although there were situations in which indecent assault preliminary to unlawful sexual intercourse could properly be regarded as a distinct matter justifying the imposition of a consecutive sentence, such a sentence would usually only be appropriate where it could be shown that the indecent assault had had an additional damaging or corrupting influence on the victim. In the instant case, there was no evidence that the indecent assault had inherently increased the damaging consequences of the full sexual relationship that had developed, *R. v. Cronshaw (Michael George)* [2004] EWCA Crim 2057 applied and *Attorney General's Reference (No.42 of 2003), Re* [2003] EWCA Crim 3068, [2004] 1 Cr. App. R. (S.) 79, [2003] C.L.Y. 3864 considered. It would be wrong in principle to impose a consecutive sentence for the assault in order to circumvent the limitations on the court's sentencing powers for unlawful sexual intercourse when this did not reflect normal sentencing practice. The sentences of eight months' imprisonment had been unduly lenient given the degree of grooming that had taken place. However, as B had already been released from custody, and taking into account double jeopardy, it was not appropriate to increase the sentence.

ATTORNEY GENERAL'S REFERENCE (NO.127 OF 2004), *Re*; sub nom. R. v. BRIGGS (DAVID MICHAEL), [2005] EWCA Crim 257, [2005] 2 Cr. App. R. (S.) 74, Judge, L.J., CA (Crim Div).

3645. Indecent photographs of children—Conspiracy—Facilitating distribution of images—Limited knowledge of content of images—Undue leniency

The Attorney General referred to the court as unduly lenient an extended sentence of 12 months' imprisonment with an extended licence period of four years imposed on the offender (P) following his pleas of guilty to offences of conspiracy to distribute indecent photographs of children, and of making indecent photographs of children. P had been an administrator of a password-protected bulletin board which enabled those interested in paedophilia to communicate with each other and to share information. A search of P's computer and software revealed 174 indecent images of children, most of which fell within levels one and two of the categories defined in *R. v. Oliver (Mark David)* [2002] EWCA Crim 2766, [2003] 1 Cr. App. R. 28, [2003] C.L.Y. 3745. P had pleaded guilty on the basis that there had been no evidence that he had uploaded images; that his own interest was mostly in images at levels one and two; and that as an administrator he had been facilitating the ability of others to distribute. The Crown had opened the case by stating that web addresses on the bulletin board gave an indication, but were not wholly descriptive, of the content of the images, and a person facilitating distribution would not have known the level of the material that was being distributed. Two counts of doing an act tending and intended to pervert the course of justice, in relation to programmes run by P to eradicate material from his computer, were not pursued following pleas of not guilty. The Attorney General contended that the judge's attention should have been drawn to the contents of the bulletin board at the time of P's arrest, and had that been done the judge would have inferred that the material, which P was facilitating, extended to hard core paedophilia up to level five.

Held, refusing the reference, that (1) had the circumstances been such that the sentencing judge ought to have drawn inferences from the bulletin board then the sentence would have been unduly lenient to a significant degree. However, it had not been open to the judge to draw such inferences. The Crown had clearly come to the conclusion that the material on the bulletin board was not sufficiently suggestive of material at higher levels, and it had not challenged

P's assertion that he was in ignorance of the content of the material. That being so, it was not open to the Attorney General to invite the court to sentence on a different basis. The judge had been entitled to find that the Crown had failed to demonstrate that P was knowingly facilitating the distribution of material at levels significantly in excess of level two. A sentence of two years' imprisonment would have been justified had the matter been contested, but if the sentence was any higher it would be difficult to reconcile with sentences suggested for those who, for example, distributed images at level four or five, *Oliver* considered. (2) (*Obiter*) In an appropriate case the use of programmes designed to eradicate material might assist a court to draw the inference that the material erased was illegal and that the reason for erasing it was to thwart a criminal investigation. However, if the Crown included in an indictment counts which related to the use of such programmes but then decided not to proceed with those counts after pleas of not guilty were entered, it was difficult to envisage circumstances in which a sentencing judge could properly infer, without hearing evidence, that the programmes had been used to pervert the course of justice. (3) (*Obiter*) Advocates instructed to appear in the Court of Appeal had an obligation to advise the Criminal Appeal Office if, in their opinion, the time allowed for a hearing was seriously inaccurate. Accurate time estimates were essential if there was to be effective listing, and effective listing was in the interests of everyone.

ATTORNEY GENERAL'S REFERENCE (NO.89 OF 2004), *Re*; *sub nom*. R. v. COX (EARL WEBSTER), [2004] EWCA Crim 3222, *The Times*, January 10, 2005, Kennedy, L.J., CA (Crim Div).

3646. **Indecent photographs of children—Extended sentences—Vast number of images downloaded from internet—Concurrent custodial terms of five and four years**

The appellant (T) appealed against an extended sentence of six years, comprising a custodial term of five years and an extension period of one year, and a concurrent four year custodial term imposed after he pleaded guilty to 15 counts of making an indecent photograph of a child and one count of possessing an indecent photograph of a child respectively. Police seized computer equipment, video tapes and compact discs from T's home and work addresses. T was found to be in possession of almost half a million indecent photographs and video images of children. Using the categories given in *R. v. Oliver (Mark David)* [2002] EWCA Crim 2766, [2003] 1 Cr. App. R. 28, [2003] C.L.Y. 3745, 472,000 were at Level 1; 9,149 were at Level 2; 10,966 were at Level 3, and 336 at Level 5. T had made all the images by downloading them from the internet. The vast majority of the images were stored on computer hard drives and had been categorised under specific headings. The one count of possession of images which attracted the four year term represented the totality of the material seized. There was no evidence that T had distributed the images to any other person. T maintained that given his early plea and previous good character, the sentences were excessive when considered in the light of the guidance given in *Oliver*.

Held, dismissing the appeal, that the instant case was one of exceptional gravity. It had certain of the aggravating features set out in *Oliver* to an exceptional degree, most notably the vast number of images, including the very high number of images at Levels 4 and 5. Moreover, the way in which T had organised his collection of images demonstrated a very high level of interest in the material. There were a significant number of particularly young children who had been abused for the purposes of the original making of the images. The sentencing judge's assessment of the gravity of the case could not be faulted. The sentences imposed were not excessive individually or in their totality, *Oliver* followed.

R. v. TATAM (ANDREW), [2004] EWCA Crim 1856, [2005] 1 Cr. App. R. (S.) 57, Maurice Kay, L.J., CA (Crim Div).

3647. Indecent photographs of children—Video recordings—Application of sentencing guidelines

The appellant (S) appealed against an extended sentence with a custodial term of four years and an extension period of three years for making indecent videotapes and taking indecent photographs of young children. S had pleaded guilty to taking indecent photographs of young children and 22 offences of taking indecent photographs were taken into consideration. Video tapes containing indecent images of three children had also been found at S's home. S admitted to making the images and to downloading similar images from the internet. S contended that the sentence was so out of line with the guidelines given in *R. v. Oliver (Mark David)* [2002] EWCA Crim 2766, [2003] 1 Cr. App. R. 28, [2003] C.L.Y. 3745 that it was wrong in principle or manifestly excessive.

Held, dismissing the appeal that this case fell outside the guidelines laid down in *Oliver*. Guidelines were not to be seen as a straitjacket. *Oliver* was a valuable case for sentencing in cases where images had been downloaded from the internet but the taking of photographs and making of video tapes was a different matter giving rise to serious considerations for sentencing. In the instant case, two of the children had suffered adverse consequences as a result of S's conduct. S had many previous convictions for similar offences and the sentence was thoroughly merited, *Oliver* considered.

R. v. SAUNDERS (RICHARD), [2004] EWCA Crim 777, [2004] 2 Cr. App. R. (S.) 86, Rose, L.J., CA (Crim Div).

3648. Juvenile offenders—Grievous bodily harm with intent—Provocation by victim—Risk of reoffending—No justification for longer than commensurate sentence

CA, aged 18 at the time of the offence and conviction, appealed against a longer than commensurate sentence of 10 years' detention in a young offender institution following his conviction on a guilty plea to causing grievous bodily harm with intent. After an altercation in a nightclub with the victim, P, CA responded to a punch from P by punching back, kicking P four or five times on the floor and then stamping on his head. P suffered serious injuries, including traumatic brain damage and paralysis to one side, he required continuous care and had lost the ability to read and write unaided.

Held, allowing the appeal, that the longer than commensurate sentence was not justified on the facts. Although CA had two previous convictions for inflicting grievous bodily harm and was at risk of reoffending, P was not blameless for the assault and had struck the first blow. The 10-year term was replaced by a seven-year extended custodial sentence and a three year extension period, *R. v. Crow (William John)* (1995) 16 Cr. App. R. (S.) 409 and *R. v. Nelson (Patrick Alan)* [2001] EWCA Crim 2264, [2002] 1 Cr. App. R. (S.) 134, [2001] C.L.Y. 1369 considered.

R. v. ALLEN (CRAIG MICHAEL), [2004] EWCA Crim 1030, [2005] 1 Cr. App. R. (S.) 2, Rose, L.J., CA (Crim Div).

3649. Kidnapping—Sentence length—Kidnapping driver of car containing children

W appealed against a total sentence of six years' imprisonment for three counts of kidnapping. The three counts related to three individuals, a nanny and two children. The victims were about to drive off in their car when W jumped into the front passenger seat. W locked the doors. W had a jacket wrapped around his arm and he thrust it at the nanny. The nanny feared the jacket concealed a firearm. W told the nanny to drive. W searched the nanny's bags for money. The nanny screamed to a passer by for help. W managed to escape. W pleaded guilty on the basis that had he known there were children in the car he would not have got in and that he had not threatened the nanny or the children in any way. W had 33 previous convictions for offences of dishonesty. The judge took a starting point of eight or nine years. W argued that his sentence was excessive and that the judge's starting point for the offence was too high.

Held, allowing the appeal, that the starting point adopted by the judge might have been appropriate for a professionally planned offence for profit or one in which substantial violence had been used, but for a spur of the moment offence committed in panic and on the accepted basis of the plea the sentence was too high. There was an absence of many of the traditional aggravating features. The judge should have taken a starting point of five or six years, reduced by a discount for the guilty plea to a sentence of four years' imprisonment. It was not appropriate to reduce W's sentence further with a view to making him a short rather than a long term prisoner, *R. v. Spence (Clinton Everton)* (1983) 5 Cr. App. R. (S.) 413, [1984] C.L.Y. 876 considered. Accordingly, a total sentence of four years' imprisonment was substituted.

R. v. WINSLOW (TERENCE EDWARD); *sub nom.* R. v. WINSLOW (TERRENCE EDWARD), [2004] EWCA Crim 3417, [2005] 2 Cr. App. R. (S.) 51, Potter, L.J., CA (Crim Div).

3650. Life imprisonment–Automatic life imprisonment–Need for verdict or admission on possession of firearm issue where second serious offence fell within s.109(5)(h) of the Powers of Criminal Courts (Sentencing) Act 2000

[Powers of Criminal Courts (Sentencing) Act 2000 s.109.]

The appellant (H), who had been convicted of robbery, appealed against his sentence of life imprisonment imposed under the Powers of Criminal Courts (Sentencing) Act 2000 s.109 owing to an earlier conviction for robbery and wounding with intent. The earlier offence had involved the use of a firearm. During the instant robbery, H had carried a lump hammer and his accomplice (M) had carried a loaded sawn off shotgun. The victim was threatened with violence in front of his 12 year old son and his Rolex watch was taken. The judge had found that the instant offence had been a joint venture and that both H and M had been in joint possession of the firearm during the robbery; therefore s.109(5)(h) applied. H contended that the sentence should be quashed on the ground that where the second offence specified by s.109 fell within s.109(5)(h), a sentence of life imprisonment could only be imposed where the jury's verdict found the defendant to have been in possession of a firearm, or if the defendant specifically admitted that. H had denied any involvement in the robbery and had not raised any issues as to the facts, other than the second robber's identity. The indictment had not included a count of possession of a firearm. Therefore there was no specific verdict as to possession nor had there been any admissions.

Held, allowing the appeal, that a sentence of automatic life imprisonment could only be imposed under s.109 for a defendant's second serious offence involving possession of a firearm if he admitted possession of a firearm during the offence or if the jury specifically reached that verdict, *R. v. Benfield (Anthony John)* [2003] EWCA Crim 2223, [2004] 1 Cr. App. R. 8, [2003] C.L.Y. 3778, *R. v. Murphy (Brendan William)* [2002] EWCA Crim 1624, [2003] 1 Cr. App. R. (S.) 39, [2003] C.L.Y. 3776 and *R. v. Eubank (Winston)* [2001] EWCA Crim 891, [2002] 1 Cr. App. R. (S.) 4, [2001] C.L.Y. 1140 applied and *R. v. Flamson (Lee Andrew)* [2001] EWCA Crim 3030, [2002] 2 Cr. App. R. (S.) 48, [2003] C.L.Y. 3777 considered. Neither condition was met in the instant case; therefore s.109(5)(h) did not apply. However, this decision was limited to the requirements of s.109(5)(h). H's sentence of life imprisonment would be replaced by the determinate sentence of 14 years' imprisonment which the judge determined he would have applied but for s.109.

R. v. HYLANDS (ROBERT STANFORD), [2004] EWCA Crim 2999, [2005] 2 Cr. App. R. (S.) 25, Rix, L.J., CA (Crim Div).

3651. Life imprisonment–Grievous bodily harm–Racially aggravated offence– Specified minimum period of automatic life sentence

[Powers of Criminal Courts (Sentencing) Act 2000 s.109.]

The appellant (R) appealed against a specified minimum term of imprisonment of four years and three months when he received an automatic life sentence following his guilty plea to one count of causing grievous bodily harm with intent. R and two others had offered to fight the victim, who was of a different ethnic origin. The victim, who was sitting in his car, produced some pliers and told R to go away. R forcibly took the pliers from the victim, struck him repeatedly to the head, pulled him out of the car and then kicked and punched him as he lay on the ground. As a consequence of the attack the victim lost the sight in his right eye. R had previous convictions for similar offences and received an automatic life sentence in accordance with the Powers of Criminal Courts (Sentencing) Act 2000 s.109. The sentencing judge used a starting point of 11 years as the sentence that would have been imposed on a conviction after trial, then added two years to reflect the element of racial aggravation. He applied a three year discount to reflect the guilty plea, achieving a notional determinate sentence of ten years. This was then halved and the time spent by R in custody was deducted to achieve the minimum term. R argued that both the starting point of 11 years and the two year uplift for racial aggravation were excessive.

Held, allowing the appeal, that the starting point was too high and should have been eight years, having regard to the level of violence used, *R. v. Meredith (Christopher)* [2000] 1 Cr. App. R. (S.) 508, [2000] C.L.Y. 1267 considered. The sentencing judge had been correct to add a further two years' imprisonment for the racial aggravation, *R. v. Morrison (Jamie Joe)* [2001] 1 Cr. App. R. (S.) 5, [2001] C.L.Y. 1221 and *R. v. Kelly (Lewis)* [2001] EWCA Crim 170, [2001] 2 Cr. App. R. (S.) 73, [2001] C.L.Y. 1191 considered. R's guilty plea attracted a reduction of two and a half years, producing a notional determinate sentence of seven and a half years. This resulted in a minimum term of three years and nine months' imprisonment, which was reduced by the nine months that R had spent in custody, giving a specified minimum term of three years' imprisonment.

R. v. RIDLEY (JOHN HAMILTON), [2004] EWCA Crim 2275, [2005] 1 Cr. App. R. (S.) 94, Latham, L.J., CA (Crim Div).

3652. Life imprisonment–Minimum term–Changes in sentencing practice–Lack of retrospective effect

The appellant (M), who, 10 years previously, had been convicted of abducting a child, wounding with intent to do grievous bodily harm, false imprisonment, rape and buggery, appealed against a sentence of life imprisonment comprising a determinate sentence of 30 years and a specified minimum term of 18 years. M had abducted the victim, aged 12 at the time of the offence, and taken her to his flat where he had stripped her, bound and gagged her, and struck her twice over the head with a piece of wood before putting her in a suitcase. M had then taken her to another flat where he subjected the victim to the sexual offences outlined. M submitted that the determinate sentence of 30 years' imprisonment was excessive.

Held, allowing the appeal, that the determinate sentence of 30 years' imprisonment was manifestly excessive and had been so at the time it was imposed. It was quashed and replaced with a determinate sentence of 22 years imprisonment. The specified minimum term was reduced to 14 years' imprisonment, based on the ratio of the specified period to the determinate sentence originally set by the trial judge, which had lawfully been between one half and two thirds of the determinate sentence. However, the trial judge had erred in failing to deduct from the specified period the 18 months that M had already served in custody prior to sentencing. Therefore, the specified period was reduced to 12 and a half years' imprisonment. The specified period, if set at the time of the instant hearing, would have been regarded as too lengthy, because current practice was to set it at one half of the determinate sentence except in exceptional circumstances. However, an offender could not rely on changes in the courts' sentencing practice which had occurred since the sentence had been imposed at trial. Changes in sentencing practice and tariff did not apply retrospectively.

R. v. MILLS (BRETT MARK), [2004] EWCA Crim 3506, *The Times*, December 3, 2004, Pill, L.J., CA (Crim Div).

3653. Life imprisonment–Murder–Release on licence–Disapplication of early release provisions–Protection of public

[Criminal Justice Act 2003 s.269(4), Sch.21.]

The appellant (L) appealed against a life sentence with an order under the Criminal Justice Act 2003 s.269(4) that the early release provisions should not apply, following his conviction of murder. L, who had previously been convicted of the manslaughter of his wife on the grounds of diminished responsibility and had subsequently had his hospital order discharged, murdered a prostitute. L suffered from mental illness and had regular anti psychotic injections and took lithium. When sentencing, the judge disapplied the early release provisions to protect the public. L contended that the judge should not have made an order under s.269(4) as the protection of the public was an inappropriate reason for disapplying the provisions.

Held, allowing the appeal, that the judge had been in error in ordering that the early release provisions did not apply and basing his decision on the protection of the public. The public were protected by the life sentence itself and the Parole Board, which considered the protection of the public when the minimum term expired. The judge should only be concerned with the seriousness of the offence. When assessing the seriousness of the offence, Sch.21 of the Act should be considered. The case did not fall within the exceptionally serious category, as specified in Sch.21, which required a full life sentence, as L had been convicted of a previous offence of manslaughter not murder. Taking into account the 2003 Act, the transitional provisions and the relevant Practice Directions, the minimum term should be 22 years with allowance made for any period spent on remand prior to sentence, *R. v. Sullivan (Melvin Terrence)* [2004] EWCA Crim 1762, [2005] 1 Cr. App. R. 3, [2004] C.L.Y. 3401 considered.

R. v. LEIGERS (GEORGE), [2005] EWCA Crim 802, [2005] 2 Cr. App. R. (S.) 104, Dyson, L.J., CA (Crim Div).

3654. Life imprisonment–Wounding with intent–Second serious offence–Public protection–Considerations in setting notional determinate sentence

[Powers of Criminal Courts (Sentencing) Act 2000 s.82A, s.109.]

M appealed against a sentence of life imprisonment with a notional determinate sentence of 14 years and a specified period of 6 years and 20 weeks, which sentence was imposed pursuant to the Powers of Criminal Courts (Sentencing) Act 2000 s.109 on a count of wounding with intent to cause grievous bodily harm. M had inflicted knife wounds on the victim resulting in severe blood loss, which was treated with a massive blood transfusion and subsequent skin grafts. M had a history of violent offending and on passing sentence the judge said that there was no doubt that he posed a risk of causing serious harm to the public. The judge also stated that a determinate sentence would have required a longer than commensurate sentence, and would have been 14 years' imprisonment. On appeal, M argued that it was wrong in principle to set the notional determinate sentence by reference to a longer than commensurate sentence where an automatic life sentence under s.109 applied.

Held, allowing the appeal, that the need to protect the public should be omitted as a factor when determining the notional determinate sentence, since that need was being met in any event by the imposition of a life sentence, *R. v. M (Young Offender: Time in Custody on Remand)* [1999] 1 W.L.R. 485, [1998] C.L.Y. 1269 applied. The judge below had therefore erred in taking into account the need for public protection. The setting of a notional determinate sentence where an automatic life sentence had been imposed was a separate exercise and was part of the process of specifying under s.82A the minimum period an offender must serve before he could be considered for parole. In the instant case, an appropriate notional determinate sentence would have been one of 12 years' imprisonment with a specified period of 5 years and 20 weeks.

R. v. MAGUIRE (THOMAS), [2004] EWCA Crim 2220, [2005] 1 Cr. App. R. (S.) 84, Scott Baker, L.J., CA (Crim Div).

3655. **Living on prostitution–13 year old boy groomed for role as male prostitute–Undue leniency**

The Attorney General referred as unduly lenient sentences of eight and seven years' imprisonment that had been imposed on the offenders (E and H) respectively. E had been sentenced to five years for living on the earnings as a prostitute of the victim (B) and to three years for conspiring with H to live on B's earnings as a male prostitute. He also received a concurrent sentence of two years and six months for inciting a child under 16 to commit an act of gross indecency. H had been sentenced to one year for abducting B, to four years for living wholly or partly on B's earnings as a prostitute, and to two years for living wholly or partly on the prostitution earnings of a girl and three men. He also received a concurrent sentence of three years for conspiring with E to live on B's earnings as a prostitute and a concurrent sentence of two years and six months for inciting B to commit an act of gross indecency. E and H pleaded guilty to the offences at the start of what was to be their trial. E was alleged over a period of time beginning when B was 13 to have groomed and corrupted him for the sole purpose of exploiting him as a prostitute. E incited B to commit acts of indecency with men for money before selling him to H so that he could be used as a prostitute in another part of the country. H, too, incited B to commit acts of indecency with men for money. The services provided by B while working for E and H included anal and oral sex. At the relevant time, H was also living on the earnings of other young prostitutes and was arranging with other men for the prostitution of an under age boy. The Attorney General relied, inter alia, on the severe and lasting effects that E and H's offending had had on B.

Held, allowing the references, that the sentences were unduly lenient. The correct sentence for E's offence of inciting a child under 16 to commit an act of gross indecency was seven years, since that was a specimen count that could be taken as reflecting the grooming of B. His sentence for living on B's earnings as a prostitute should have been one of four years, while the judge had been correct to impose a consecutive sentence of three years for the offence of conspiring with H to live on B's earnings as a prostitute. However, given double jeopardy and the fact that, shortly before the trial, E had been sentenced to five years' imprisonment for offences of theft, it would be appropriate to order that the sentence for conspiring with H to live on B's earnings as a prostitute be served concurrently with the other sentences, making a fresh sentence of 11 years. H should have received the following sentences: three years for conspiring with E to live on B's earnings as a prostitute, a concurrent sentence of three years for living wholly or partly on B's earnings as a prostitute, two years for abduction, four years for inciting B to commit an act of gross indecency and two years for living wholly or partly on the prostitution earnings of the girl and three men. However, to allow for double jeopardy, the last sentence would be served concurrently, so that B would serve nine years.

ATTORNEY GENERAL'S REFERENCE (NO.122 AND 123 OF 2004), *Re*; *sub nom.* R. v. EYRE; R. v. HAWTHORNE [2005] EWCA Crim 1059, Kennedy, L.J., CA (Crim Div).

3656. **Living on prostitution–Good character–Prostitutes offering sex services from sex shop premises–Subsequent offence committed while on bail**

The appellant (M) appealed against a total sentence of 12 months' imprisonment, having pleaded guilty to two counts of living on the earnings of prostitution. M's shop sold lingerie and sex toys. Upstairs he ran a massage parlour where sexual services were performed. He was arrested following an undercover police operation and charged with the first offence. The activities continued after his release on bail, and he was charged again. For the first count he received a nine month sentence, and for the second he received a further three months, to run consecutively. M, who had no relevant previous convictions, contended that, in the light of the authorities, nine months for the first count was excessive.

Held, allowing the appeal, that six months' imprisonment would be an appropriate sentence for a count of living on the earnings of prostitution where the offender was of good character, had pleaded guilty, had not coerced the prostitutes and had not caused offence or disruption to the neighbours, *R. v. Rousseau (Nicholas James)* [2002] EWCA Crim 1252, [2003] 1 Cr. App. R. (S.) 15, [2003] C.L.Y. 3784 considered. However, the three month sentence for the second count was correctly imposed, so M's total term would become nine months' imprisonment.

R. v. MIDDLETON (JOHN DICKETTS), [2004] EWCA Crim 1487, [2005] 1 Cr. App. R. (S.) 42, Tuckey, L.J., CA (Crim Div).

3657. Mandatory life imprisonment–Minimum term–Compatibility of Criminal Justice Act 2003 Sch.22 para.11 (1) with Human Rights Act 1998 Sch.1 Part I Art.6(1)

[Human Rights Act 1998 s.3(1), Sch.1 Part I Art.6(1); Criminal Justice Act 2003 Sch.22 para.6, Sch.22 para.11 (1), Sch.22 para.14.]

The claimant (H), who had been convicted of murder, sought a declaration that the Criminal Justice Act 2003 Sch.22 para.11 (1) should be read in a manner that was compatible with the Human Rights Act 1998 Sch.1 Part I Art.6(1). The tariff term of H's sentence had not been determined by the Secretary of State for the Home Department but had been referred to the High Court under Sch.22 para.6 of the 2003 Act. H had applied unsuccessfully to the High Court for an oral hearing to be convened. H submitted that the procedure under Sch.22 para.11 (1) that prevented an oral hearing in every case was incompatible with Sch.1 Part I Art.6(1) of the 1998 Act and therefore Sch.22 para.11 (1) should be made subject to the implied condition that the High Court could, in its discretion, allow an oral hearing where it was required to satisfy a prisoner's rights under Art.6(1). The Secretary of State contended that Sch.22 para.11 (1) was compatible with Art.6(1) as a case that required oral submissions could be appealed under Sch.22 para.14 to the Court of Appeal, where oral submissions could be heard.

Held, granting a declaration in favour of H, that a court of first instance within the ordinary judicial structure of a state should provide the fundamental guarantees under Art.6(1), *De Cubber v. Belgium (A/86)* (1985) 7 E.H.R.R. 236 followed and *Goc v. Turkey (36590/97)* (Unreported, July 11, 2002) considered. As Sch.22 para.11 (1) prevented an oral hearing from taking place, it was *prima facie* incompatible with Art.6(1). The fact that oral submissions could be made on appeal did not remedy the incompatible effect of Sch.22 para.11 (1). In applying s.3(1) of the 1998 Act, it was possible to interpret Sch.22 para.11 (1) in a manner that was compatible with Art.6(1). A declaration was made to the effect that Sch.22 para.11 (1) should be read as subject to the implied condition that a High Court judge had the discretion to order an oral hearing, where such a hearing was required to comply with the prisoner's rights under Art.6(1). Guidance was given on the procedure to be followed in the rare cases where an oral hearing would be required.

R. (ON THE APPLICATION OF HAMMOND) v. SECRETARY OF STATE FOR THE HOME DEPARTMENT, [2004] EWHC 2753, [2005] 4 All E.R. 1127, Thomas, L.J., QBD (Admin).

3658. Manslaughter–Arson–Intent to endanger life–Fire bombing of occupied dwelling house

The applicant (M) sought permission to appeal against a sentence of imprisonment totalling 18 years for manslaughter in circumstances where eight people were killed when petrol bombs had been thrown into a house causing it to catch fire. H and two other men had manufactured the petrol bombs and had driven to a house into which they then threw the petrol bombs inside. The house caught fire and eight people in the house, including six children, died. H was convicted of eight counts of manslaughter and one of conspiracy to commit arson with intent to endanger life. The sentencing judge approached the case on the basis that H had agreed to take part in the attack knowing that life would be at risk but that H did not originate the plot. H contended that the sentence was manifestly excessive in the light of the authorities.

Held, refusing the application, that the judge was bound to have regard to the number of people killed in the incident and none of the cases relied upon by H had involved multiple deaths. The manslaughter had occurred in horrific circumstances and it could not be said that the sentence was excessive, *Attorney General's Reference (Nos.78, 79 and 85 of 1998), Re* [2000] 1 Cr. App. R. (S.) 371, [2000] C.L.Y. 1132, *R. v. Palma (Aniello)* (1986) 8 Cr. App. R. (S.) 148, [1987] C.L.Y. 1006, *R. v. Archer (Patrick John)* [1998] 2 Cr. App. R. (S.) 76, [1998] C.L.Y. 1304 and *R. v. Nedrick (Ransford Delroy)* [1986] 1 W.L.R. 1025, [1986] C.L.Y. 651 considered, *R. v. Wacker (Perry)* [2002] EWCA Crim 1944, [2003] Q.B. 1207, [2002] C.L.Y. 802 distinguished.

R. v. HUSSAIN (NAZAR), [2004] EWCA Crim 763, [2004] 2 Cr. App. R. (S.) 93, Rose, L.J., CA (Crim Div).

3659. Manslaughter—Babies—Childminder shaking baby out of frustration—Undue leniency

The Attorney General referred to the court as unduly lenient a sentence of 3 years' imprisonment imposed on the offender (W) following her conviction of the manslaughter of a five month old baby. The baby had died of a head injury whilst in the care of W, who was a registered childminder. Expert evidence indicated that the baby had been subjected to an acceleration deceleration injury significantly in excess of injuries that might result from rough handling or accidental trauma. The Crown's case was that W must have shaken the baby out of frustration and stress when he would not settle. The Attorney General identified as aggravating features the fact that W was an experienced and trained childminder, that she had lied to the emergency services in not revealing that she had shaken the baby, and that she had caused further distress to the baby's parents in not pleading guilty. In mitigation, B submitted that she was of previous good character and that as a result of the offence her husband had begun divorce proceedings and she had been permitted only limited and supervised contact with her children.

Held, dismissing the reference, that it was impossible to say that the sentence was unduly lenient. Although the sentencing judge had passed what he recognised was a lenient sentence, it was not outside the range of sentencing options open to him. The appellate court had to remember that it could only increase sentences which it concluded were unduly lenient. It was doubtful whether the fact that W was a registered childminder could properly be characterised as an aggravating feature when most parents of small babies were aware that shaking could cause brain injury. As was not uncommon in cases of this kind, W's conduct had taken place in a short space of time as a result of frustration and exasperation. Moreover, there was no evidence to suggest that the treatment given to the baby would have been any different had W not lied to the emergency services. Finally, a significant mitigating feature was the fact that W had been convicted following a retrial. During the first trial, the jury had been discharged to allow the Crown to consider whether or not to proceed in the light of conflicts in the medical evidence and following the court's judgment in the case of *R. v. Cannings (Angela)* [2004] EWCA Crim 1, [2004] 1 W.L.R. 2607, [2004] C.L.Y. 714, *Cannings* referred to. Although the Crown had concluded that the proceedings should continue, and W had been retried 10 months later, she had in the interim been entitled to entertain at least a hope that the proceedings might be dropped.

ATTORNEY GENERAL'S REFERENCE (NO.16 OF 2005), *Re; sub nom.* R. v. WILSON (REBECCA), [2005] EWCA Crim 1285, [2006] 1 Cr. App. R. (S.) 28, Rose, L.J., CA (Crim Div).

3660. Manslaughter–Carbon monoxide poisoning–Landlords–Installation of gas fire without adequate ventilation

The appellant (R), a landlord who rented properties to tenants in receipt of state benefits, appealed against a sentence of five years' imprisonment for two counts of manslaughter. Following complaints from tenants and problems with the gas system in a converted flat, and despite not being registered as installers of gas or having any relevant experience, R had fitted a used gas fire to the existing system, then later installed another following further problems. Neither was appropriate for the system and carbon monoxide escaped into the flat, killing the two tenants. In the instant appeal, R submitted that the sentence was manifestly excessive given the facts and his guilty plea.

Held, dismissing the appeal, that the sentence was not manifestly excessive. R had been given full credit for his guilty plea even though R had lied initially before expressing remorse. Although R had not intended to cause injury he had been reckless and had undertaken the repairs himself to save money.

R. v. RODGERS (STANLEY JOHN), [2004] EWCA Crim 3115, [2005] 2 Cr. App. R. (S.) 19, Waller, L.J., CA (Crim Div).

3661. Manslaughter–Children–Two year old killed by father–Unexplained injuries

The appellant (K) appealed against a sentence of seven years' imprisonment imposed following his conviction for the manslaughter of his two-year-old son. A pathologist's report revealed that the child had died from a blow to the back of the head and a post mortem report showed that he had suffered bruising consistent with having been shaken. K, a serving soldier, claimed that his son had fallen down the stairs and that he had delayed an hour before calling an ambulance as he was trying to revive the child. K had not acknowledged responsibility for the offence and had chosen to remain silent.

Held, dismissing the appeal, that the sentence was not manifestly excessive given that the offence with which K was charged was at the high end of the appropriate sentencing range. The judge had had the advantage of hearing the evidence at trial and had considered the relevant authorities, *R. v. Bennett (Michael)* [2003] EWCA Crim 2446, [2004] 1 Cr. App. R. (S.) 65, [2004] 9 C.L. 434 and *R. v. Yates (Paul Joseph)* [2001] 1 Cr. App. R. (S.) 124, [2001] C.L.Y. 1416 considered.

R. v. KHAIR (LEE MICHAEL), [2004] EWCA Crim 1296, [2005] 1 Cr. App. R. (S.) 29, Waller, L.J., CA (Crim Div).

3662. Manslaughter–Criminal intent–Death caused by fall to ground following single punch–Lack of intent to cause really serious harm

[Powers of Criminal Courts (Sentencing) Act 2000 s.109(5) (e).]

The appellant (B) appealed against a sentence of two and a half years' imprisonment imposed on a guilty plea to an offence of manslaughter. B and the victim (K) had been drinking in a public house. B had drunk a moderate amount and K was described as being drunk. K offered to fight B outside and both parties went out into the car park. B hit K a single punch and K fell, striking his head on the ground and sustaining a fatal injury. B had a number of previous convictions, mostly more than 20 years old, including one serious offence which meant that B was now eligible for an automatic life sentence under the Powers of Criminal Courts (Sentencing) Act 2000 s.109(5) (e).

Held, allowing the appeal, that there were exceptional circumstances justifying a reduction in sentence. B had only entered into a fight at K's invitation and had only struck one blow with moderate force. B was less affected by drink than K was. He had pleaded guilty on rearraignment and was remorseful. Most of his previous convictions were a long time ago apart from one some six years previously for common assault. Although an offence resulting in loss of life was obviously serious and attracted a custodial sentence, in the circumstances it was appropriate to substitute a sentence of 18 months' imprisonment, *R. v. Coleman (Anthony Neville)* (1992) 95 Cr. App. R. 159,

[1993] C.L.Y. 1224 and *R. v. Edwards (Brynley Maldwin)* [2001] EWCA Crim 862, [2001] 2 Cr. App. R. (S.) 125, [2001] C.L.Y. 1425 considered.

R. v. BINSTEAD (DAVID CHARLES), [2005] EWCA Crim 164, [2005] 2 Cr. App. R. (S.) 62, Gage, L.J., CA (Crim Div).

3663. Manslaughter–Criminal intent–Single punch without provocation– Offender and victim under influence of alcohol

The appellant (L) appealed against a sentence of three years' imprisonment for manslaughter. L had punched a man who had been ejected from a nightclub with enough force to cause him to fall backwards resulting in fatal injuries. The attack was unprovoked and both L and the victim had been drinking. L submitted that the sentence was manifestly excessive given that he had delivered only one blow with moderate force, the lack of pre meditation and the fact that the victim was so intoxicated that he was unable to break his fall.

Held, dismissing the appeal, that the victim had been drunk and unable to defend himself. L had had no reason to interfere and the attack had been unprovoked. L's plea and remorse were mitigating features but the court was entitled to take a serious view of offences of this nature and the sentence could not be considered manifestly excessive, *R. v. Grad (David Karl)* [2004] EWCA Crim 44, [2004] 2 Cr. App. R. (S.) 43 and *R. v. Cheetham (David Edward)* [2004] EWCA Crim 409, [2004] 2 Cr. App. R. (S.) 53 considered.

R. v. LUMSDEN (GEORGE ARTHUR), [2004] EWCA Crim 3187, [2005] 2 Cr. App. R. (S.) 27, Laws, L.J., CA (Crim Div).

3664. Manslaughter–Diminished responsibility–Dispute with neighbour– Stabbing whilst suffering from depression

The appellant (D), a woman aged 54 who had entered a guilty plea to manslaughter by reason of diminished responsibility on an indictment for murder, appealed against a sentence of six years' imprisonment. D had been in dispute with her neighbour about the level of noise emanating from the neighbour's property. One evening D threw stones at the windows of the neighbour's house and was heard to make threats. Upon discovering this, the neighbour went to D's home to remonstrate with her. D went to the door with a knife in her hand and inflicted one single stab wound which entered the neighbour's heart. Pre sentence psychiatric reports stated that at the time of the killing D had been suffering from clinical depression with associated anxiety and insomnia. On appeal, D contended that insufficient credit had been given for her early guilty plea and her good character.

Held, allowing the appeal, that the sentencing judge had stated that full credit would be given for D's early guilty plea. This indicated that he had taken a starting point of nine years' imprisonment. That was plainly excessive in the circumstances. A term of no more than four years was appropriate where there were extenuating factors such as D's mental state and good character, *R. v. Davies* [1996] 1 Cr. App. R. (S.) 28, *R. v. Wright (John Steven)* (1995) 16 Cr. App. R. (S.) 877 and *Attorney General's Reference (No.19 of 1999), Re* [2000] 1 Cr. App. R. (S.) 287, [1999] C.L.Y. 1259 considered. The sentence was quashed and substituted by a term of three years and six months.

R. v. DEREKIS (THERESA ANNE), [2004] EWCA Crim 2729, [2005] 2 Cr. App. R. (S.) 1, Potter, L.J., CA (Crim Div).

3665. Manslaughter–Driving vehicle known to have defective brakes–Undue leniency

The Attorney General referred as unduly lenient a sentence of 12 months' imprisonment following a plea of guilty to manslaughter by the defendant (R). R had been employed as HGV driver. R, who was not responsible for service and maintenance of his vehicle, reported to his employers that his brakes were defective following a minor collision. His employers told him that if it was discovered that the brakes were operating correctly, he would be held responsible for the crash and would lose his job. R continued driving the vehicle and the following week, realising he would not be able to stop at a crossing in time, he took evasive action, mounted the pavement and hit a pedestrian from behind, killing her. It transpired that the vehicles were supposed to be serviced every six weeks by the employers. R was charged with manslaughter, not causing death by dangerous driving, to enable the prosecution to bring charges against the employers.

Held, dismissing the reference, that the sentence was not unduly lenient. R's criminality amounted to driving a vehicle knowing the brakes to be defective. R was responsible, as a driver, to ensure that the vehicle was not on the road in an unroadworthy condition; however, he was not the sole person responsible for the vehicle being on the road. On paper the sentence was lenient; however, the sentencing decision was not based on the papers. The sentencing judge was very experienced and well able to form a view as to the culpability of R and the codefendants and the sentence passed was not one that should be interfered with.

ATTORNEY GENERAL'S REFERENCE (NO.134 OF 2004), *Re*, [2004] EWCA Crim 3286, [2005] 2 Cr. App. R. (S.) 47, Judge, L.J., CA (Crim Div).

3666. **Manslaughter–Extended sentences–Offender killed girlfriend during drunken fight–Further non consensual injuries to victim's anus**

[Powers of Criminal Courts (Sentencing) Act 2000 s.80(2)(b).]

The Attorney General referred as unduly lenient a sentence of six years' imprisonment imposed on the offender (Q) after he pleaded guilty to an offence of manslaughter. Q had killed his girlfriend during a drunken fight in which he punched her to the face before applying considerable pressure to her chest. After hearing evidence at a *Newton* hearing, the judge below found that death had occurred as result of blunt trauma to the chest inflicted by compression injuries. He also found that Q had inflicted non consensual injuries to the victim's anus during the incident. The offence had been committed during the unexpired part of an earlier custodial sentence for an offence of violence. In fact, Q had a total of 27 previous convictions including repeated offences of violence. The Attorney General submitted that (1) the six year term, as a commensurate sentence, was unduly lenient in that it failed to reflect the sexual aspect of the attack and Q's appalling record for committing offences of violence, and (2) the judge should have passed a longer than commensurate sentence under the Powers of Criminal Courts (Sentencing) Act 2000 s.80(2)(b) in order to protect the public from serious harm.

Held, allowing the reference, that (1) approaching this matter as commensurate sentence with a straightforward plea of guilty demonstrating remorse, a term of five years' imprisonment could have been appropriate as a starting point, despite Q's record, *R. v. Silver (Michael)* (1994) 15 Cr. App. R. (S.) 836, [1995] C.L.Y. 1431 and *R. v. Tzambazles (Christos)* [1997] 1 Cr. App. R. (S.) 87, [1997] C.L.Y. 1158 considered. However, the sentence passed failed to reflect the extent of the violence used by Q. Moreover, the forceful penetration of the victim's anus by some object was an aggravating feature that needed to be reflected in the term of imprisonment. In those circumstances, this was a case which, at first instance, called for a sentence as a commensurate sentence of between seven and eight years. (2) All the evidence from Q's previous record indicated that he was a man who could not control his violent instincts, especially when he had been drinking. In order to protect the public, a longer than commensurate sentence of 10 years should have been imposed at first instance under s.80(2)(b). Taking account of the principle of double jeopardy, a sentence of nine years' imprisonment was substituted.

ATTORNEY GENERAL'S REFERENCE (NO.49 OF 2004), *Re*; *sub nom*. R. v. QUINN (KIERAN JAMES), [2004] EWCA Crim 1952, [2005] 1 Cr. App. R. (S.) 72, Keene, L.J., CA (Crim Div).

SENTENCING

3667. Manslaughter–Grievous bodily harm–Unprovoked late night attack by young offenders–Undue leniency

The Attorney General referred as unduly lenient sentences of four months' detention in a young offender institution for the first defendant (C) and 18 months' detention in a young offender institution for the second defendant (L). L had been drinking and became aggressive towards his girlfriend in the street following an incident in a nightclub. The victim (V) remonstrated with him. A fight ensued. V was beaten but L struck him a further blow, which caused him to fall and hit his head on the pavement. C then arrived on the scene and kicked V at least once in the head or in the armpit. V died from the impact of his head on the pavement. L was convicted of manslaughter. C was convicted of attempting to cause grievous bodily harm. Both L and C were 19 at the time of the attack and previously of good character. The Attorney General argued that both sentences were unduly lenient. In L's case the aggravating features were that he had been drinking and he had been the aggressor in an unprovoked attack leading to a blow sufficiently severe to cause V to fall to the ground. In C's case it had been a cowardly attack with serious intent on a helpless victim and it had only been a matter of luck that it had not been causative of serious injury to V.

Held, finding the sentences to be unduly lenient but not varying them, that in L's case, the starting point for manslaughter caused by one blow was 12 months' custody following a guilty plea, *R. v. Coleman (Anthony Neville)* (1992) 95 Cr. App. R. 159, [1993] C.L.Y. 1224 considered. However, that could not be the starting point for L as he had failed to recognise his culpability at the time. Although he had subsequently shown remorse, that could only assist him to a limited extent as, given his not guilty plea, he had never formally admitted the full nature of his responsibility. In those circumstances, L should have received a sentence of two to three years' custody. However, the court had to consider first whether a sentence was unduly lenient and then the effect of double jeopardy. Putting those considerations together, the court did not consider it appropriate to interfere with the sentence imposed by the court below. In C's case, given the intent to cause serious harm, it was difficult to see how a sentence of less than 18 months' custody was appropriate. The sort of behaviour involved gave rise to a serious risk to life and limb, was only too prevalent and could only be met by a significant period of detention. In those circumstances, the sentence was unduly lenient. However, C had already served the sentence imposed, he was employed and his actions had been out of character to the extent that he posed no future risk. In all those circumstances, the court exercised its discretion not to interfere with the sentence.

ATTORNEY GENERAL'S REFERENCE (NOS.3 AND 4 OF 2005), *Re; sub nom.* R. v. CRAWLEY (ALEXANDER STEVEN); R. v. LLEWELLYN (DAVID STEPHEN), [2005] EWCA Crim 574, [2005] 2 Cr. App. R. (S.) 98, Latham, L.J., CA (Crim Div).

3668. Manslaughter–Police officer killed whilst trying to apprehend appellant for TWOC–Consecutive sentence for TWOC

The appellant (P) appealed against a total sentence of 13 years' imprisonment imposed for his criminality. The biggest component of that total sentence was a sentence of 12 years' imprisonment for manslaughter. P had also received a consecutive sentence of 12 months' imprisonment made up of concurrent sentences for theft, driving whilst disqualified, burglary and taking a conveyance. The police had been looking for P in relation to the theft of a car which he had been driving whilst disqualified. In trying to evade the police P had driven off in a taxi, without the taxi driver's consent, and killed a policeman who had attempted to stop P's getaway and was hanging on to the taxi as P accelerated and tried to dislodge him. P had been tried for murder but had only been convicted of manslaughter. P had admitted his guilt of manslaughter at an early stage. P submitted that the sentence for manslaughter was manifestly excessive. P contended that he ought to be sentenced as if he had pleaded guilty throughout to manslaughter, as he would have done if permitted by the prosecution. P also argued that, having regard to the totality of sentence, he ought not to have received a consecutive sentence of 12 months' imprisonment.

Held, dismissing the appeal, that the sentence for manslaughter was within the range that was appropriate bearing in mind the aggravating features. The proper approach was to deal with the sentence as if it had been a plea of guilty to manslaughter throughout since, but for the prosecution wishing the jury to determine whether it was murder, that is what it would have been. However, this was a very serious case. P, who was in breach of his licence having been released from prison, had committed offences and had been approached by a police officer doing his duty. It was therefore a particularly aggravated form of manslaughter. The taxi driver and the police officer were making clear to P that he should stop driving. Common sense would have dictated to anyone that to continue in the circumstances in which he was driving was as dangerous an act as could be imagined, and the danger involved was of very serious injury or death. In general, where a person had committed offences and caused injury to another in his attempt to escape, particularly to a police officer, that should attract a consecutive sentence so that offenders knew that if they aggravated the offences that they had committed by harming others they would get additional penalties.

R. v. PARFITT (DAVID ANDREW), [2004] EWCA Crim 1755, [2005] 1 Cr. App. R. (S.) 50, Kay, L.J., CA (Crim Div).

3669. Manslaughter–Provocation–Two unprovoked assaults by victim–Retaliatory use of knife

The appellant (L) appealed against a sentence of 10 years' imprisonment for manslaughter. L had been the victim of an unprovoked attack by his victim. An hour later the two had met again by chance and L was again attacked. L stabbed his victim four times. It was accepted that L carried a knife with him when he went out at night. L submitted that the sentence was excessive in view of the nature and extent of the provocation that he had suffered; that he had not deliberately gone out armed with a knife; and that regard should be had to his previous good character and the circumstances of the offence.

Held, allowing the appeal, that L had suffered extreme provocation and it was apparent from the circumstances leading up to the offence that he was not a man who carried a knife intending to use it as an offensive weapon. A term of eight years' imprisonment was substituted for the original sentence.

R. v. LAHBIB (HASSAN), [2004] EWCA Crim 1877, [2005] 1 Cr. App. R. (S.) 68, Maurice Kay, L.J., CA (Crim Div).

3670. Manslaughter–Seriousness of offence–Sustained and forceful attack on vulnerable victim–Undue leniency

The Attorney General referred to the court as unduly lenient a sentence of two years and six months' imprisonment which had been imposed on the offender (X) following her guilty plea to the offence of manslaughter. The victim was a 68 year old alcoholic. X had attacked him in his home, repeatedly hitting him with a piece of wood in the area of the abdomen. A post mortem examination revealed that the victim had been subjected to a sustained and forceful assault. The Attorney General contended that the sentence failed to mark the gravity of the offence, the need for punishment, and public concern about the needless loss of life. He identified as aggravating features the sustained, forceful and unprovoked nature of the attack; the use of a weapon; the age and vulnerability of the victim; and the fact that the offender had left the victim without seeking any medical attention. X argued that this was her first custodial sentence and that it had impacted significantly on her and her young family.

Held, allowing the reference, that the sentence imposed was unduly lenient. Taking into account the mitigation and the guilty plea, a sentence of four years and six months' imprisonment would have been appropriate in the court below. However, the principle of double jeopardy and the progress the offender had made in prison had to be taken into account. Nevertheless, the judge had been unduly influenced by the mitigation in relation to X and had paid too little regard to the gravity of the offence. The sentence of two years and six months' imprisonment was quashed and replaced with a sentence of three years and six months' imprisonment, *Attorney General's Reference (Nos.19, 20 and 21 of 2001), Re* [2001] EWCA Crim 1432, [2002] 1 Cr. App. R. (S.) 33, [2002] C.L.Y. 4032 considered.

ATTORNEY GENERAL'S REFERENCE (NO.64 OF 2004), *Re*, [2004] EWCA Crim 2618, [2005] 1 Cr. App. R. (S.) 107, Rose, L.J., CA (Crim Div).

3671. Manslaughter–Unintended death resulting from single blow–Public concern about gratuitous violence–Undue leniency

The Attorney General referred to the court as unduly lenient a sentence of two years' imprisonment imposed on the offender (U) following his conviction of manslaughter. The victim (V), a 66 year old man who had been drinking, had been walking towards his home when U approached and punched him once in the face. The blow had caused V to fall backwards, sustaining a serious fracture of the skull from which he died a week later without regaining consciousness. Several people had witnessed the incident, including two 11 year old girls. U had fled the country when he heard of V's death, but later returned to face arrest. At trial U had claimed self defence, saying that V had made racist comments and had punched him first. The judge had rejected such suggestions as they did not accord with what was known of V's personality. The judge had sentenced U on the basis that he had wielded a single punch and that had V not consumed alcohol he might not have sustained the fatal fall.

Held, allowing the reference, that having had regard to many authorities the court could not treat what was described as "single punch" manslaughter as comprising a single identical set of circumstances. Cases varied widely in their seriousness. In the instant case, U was not of good character, there had been no guilty plea and there had been an attack on V's character which dissipated to a certain extent the mitigating effect of U's return to the country to face arrest. Unnecessary violence in residential areas created increasing public concern. People expected their streets to be safe, particularly for children and the elderly. The instant case had the aggravating feature that two children had witnessed the attack. Having regard to double jeopardy the appropriate sentence was one of three and a half years' imprisonment.

ATTORNEY GENERAL'S REFERENCE (NO.9 OF 2004), *Re; sub nom.* R. v. UDDIN (ALIM); ATTORNEY GENERAL'S REFERENCE (NO.9 OF 2005), *Re*, [2005] EWCA Crim 812, [2005] 2 Cr. App. R. (S.) 105, Judge, L.J., CA (Crim Div).

3672. Manslaughter by gross negligence–Children–18 month old child dying from dehydration after being left alone by mother

The applicant (O) applied for permission to appeal against a sentence of six years' detention imposed following her plea of guilty to the manslaughter of her 18-month-old son. On the day the child died, O, who was then aged 20, had left him alone from 11 am to 6.45 pm. A post mortem had indicated that the most likely cause of the child's death was dehydration.

Held, refusing the application, that in the circumstances of the case the sentence imposed was not excessive. This was a case of gross negligence towards the child for at least a week before his death. A six-year sentence of detention was appropriate and well within the range of the judge's discretion. It was clear from his sentencing remarks that the judge had taken O's personal circumstances, which included her previous good character and evidence that she had previously been a caring and attentive mother, into account.

R. v. ONLEY (HALEY NICOLA), [2004] EWCA Crim 1383, [2005] 1 Cr. App. R. (S.) 26, Rose, L.J. (Vice President), CA (Crim Div).

3673. Money laundering–Conspiracy–Minor role in converting proceeds of unidentified crime

The appellant (Y) appealed against a sentence of six years' imprisonment following guilty pleas to two offences of conspiracy to convert the proceeds of drug trafficking or other criminal conduct. Y was part of an operation to convert the proceeds of crime from sterling into dollars and euros. A codefendant owned hotels where Y would receive money from other codefendants. The money would be exchanged at bureaux de change. Y pleaded guilty on the bases that the money was not from drug trafficking or serious crime, and that he had been laundering it on only some of the occasions observed by Customs and Excise officers, whereas at other times he had been carrying on legitimate business. Y contended that, in the light of the authorities, his sentence was too long.

Held, allowing the appeal, that although significant sums of money were involved, six years' imprisonment was too long given the bases for the guilty pleas. An appropriate sentence would be four years' imprisonment, *R. v. Everson (Louis) (Appeal against Sentence)* [2001] EWCA Crim 2262, [2002] 1 Cr. App. R. (S.) 132 and *R. v. Basra (Ajaib Singh)* [2002] EWCA Crim 541, [2002] 2 Cr. App. R. (S.) 100, [2002] C.L.Y. 4036 considered.

R. v. YOONUS (NAUSHAD), [2004] EWCA Crim 1734, [2005] 1 Cr. App. R. (S.) 46, Kennedy, L.J., CA (Crim Div).

3674. Murder–Aggravating features–Strangulation of young victim–Relevance of age difference between appellant and victim

The appellant (B) appealed against a sentence of 14 years and 357 days' imprisonment imposed following his guilty plea to murder and arson. B, a 31 year old man, had been in a turbulent relationship with the victim, an 18 year old woman. B had been managing a pub and had been told that it was going to be sold and he could not be the licensee. B had burnt down the pub and asked the victim to corroborate his story that she had been working in the pub but she had refused. The following day, B, who was intoxicated, had plied the victim with alcohol and then strangled her. B submitted that the sentence imposed was too high and that the judge should not have added five years on to the starting point of 14 years. B argued that there was only one aggravating feature, namely that he had concealed the victim's body, and that the victim's age was not an aggravating feature as B's personality meant he was not in such an influential position towards her as might be supposed.

Held, allowing the appeal, that there had not been sufficient material for the judge properly to treat the age of the victim as an aggravating feature. B's state of mind at the time of the offence was such as to largely exclude any reliance which might otherwise have been appropriate by the judge on the difference in age between B and the victim. A sentence of 13 years and 174 days' imprisonment was substituted.

R. v. BECKETT (GUY PHILIP), [2005] EWCA Crim 274, [2005] 2 Cr. App. R. (S.) 71, Rose, L.J. (V-P), CA (Crim Div).

3675. Murder–Attempts–Sentence length–Victim shot during car chase

The appellant (D) appealed against a total sentence of 20 years' imprisonment imposed following his conviction of attempted murder, possessing a shotgun with intent to endanger life and driving offences. The applicants (W, L and C) applied for permission to appeal against their sentences of 8, 14 and 14 years' detention respectively, imposed following their convictions, in the cases of W and L, of conspiracy to commit grievous bodily harm, and in the case of C, of unlawful wounding and conspiracy to commit grievous bodily harm. W, L and C had carried out two attacks on the victim (F) in his home. On the first occasion F had been injured with a weapon. On the second occasion W, L, C and another had gone to F's house with a number of weapons including a loaded gun. F had been shot and beaten. In reprisal for the attacks on F, D had later attacked L. D had chased L in his car, rammed L's car and had shot at him at close range with a sawn off shotgun. D had been sentenced to 18 years' imprisonment for the offence of attempted murder,

15 years to run concurrently for possessing a shotgun with intent to endanger life and two years to run consecutively for the driving offences. D submitted that the sentence of 18 years' imprisonment was excessive and that the appropriate sentence after a trial was 14 years. W argued that his sentence was excessive given that the judge had accepted that he did not know that a loaded gun was being carried. C submitted that the judge had had no basis for concluding that he was aware that a loaded gun was being carried, and that his sentence was excessive. L submitted that he ought to have been treated as being effectively of good character.

Held, allowing the appeal and refusing the applications, that (1) the case of *R. v. White (Edward)* (1992) 13 Cr. App. R. (S.) 108, [1992] C.L.Y. 1152 no longer provided appropriate sentencing guidance in relation to offences of attempted murder involving the use of firearms, *White* not followed. The tariff in relation to the carrying and use of firearms had increased since *White* had been decided, *R. v. Avis (Tony)* [1998] 1 Cr. App. R. 420, [1998] C.L.Y. 1214 followed. D had been on licence at the time of the offence and there was increasing concern on the part of the public and the courts about the use of firearms. The offence of attempted murder had been a serious one and the judge had been entitled to impose a deterrent sentence. However, the total sentence of 20 years' imprisonment in relation to D's conduct was excessive. It was not a case where a consecutive sentence ought to have been imposed for the driving offences. The sentence of 18 years' imprisonment was replaced by a term of 16 years and the two year sentence for the driving offences was ordered to run concurrently. (2) W, L and C's sentences were not excessive and permission to appeal was refused. The judge had been entitled to reach the conclusion that both L and C had known that a loaded gun was being carried, although it would have been preferable had he spelt out in the course of his sentencing remarks the evidence supporting that conclusion.

R. v. DOCKING (JASON); R. v. WILD (JAMES MATTHEW); R. v. LEWIS (LEROY MARVIN); R. v. COOK (JORDAN), [2004] EWCA Crim 2675, [2005] 1 Cr. App. R. (S.) 119, Rose, L.J. (Vice President), CA (Crim Div).

3676. Murder – Extreme violence used in sexually motivated attack – Undue leniency

The Attorney General referred as unduly lenient a life sentence with a specified minimum period of 14 years following a guilty plea to murder. The defendant (T) was 18 years old at the time of the offence and 19 when sentenced. He had committed an offence of attempted grievous bodily harm two hours prior to the murder. The attempt had been sexually motivated. The murder, involving the use of a piece of wood found to hand, was also sexually motivated and the victim had suffered 68 external injuries and a torn vulva. The Attorney General argued that in the light of the sexual motivation, the extreme and gratuitous violence, the extent of the injuries and the time proximity of the prior attack the sentence failed adequately to reflect the seriousness of the attack.

Held, allowing the reference, that the appropriate starting point for sentencing in T's case was 20 years. The court took into account T's guilty plea and his young age. However, the deductions for those factors should have been 18 months in respect of the guilty plea and 2 years and 6 months in respect of T's age. Accordingly, the sentence of 14 years was unduly lenient and a sentence of 16 years was substituted.

ATTORNEY GENERAL'S REFERENCE (NO.130 OF 2004), *Re; sub nom.* R. v. THORNHILL (LEIGH JAMES), [2005] EWCA Crim 278, [2005] 2 Cr. App. R. (S.) 75, Rose, L.J., CA (Crim Div).

3677. Murder – Mandatory life imprisonment – Determination of minimum term in transitional cases – Undue leniency

[Criminal Justice Act 2003 Sch.21, Sch.22.]

The Attorney General referred as unduly lenient the minimum term of 13 years specified in relation to a sentence of life imprisonment imposed on the offender (K) for an offence of murder. K was an illegal immigrant, liable to deportation, who had been experiencing difficulties in obtaining access to his 10 month old son (H). On the day of the offence K had followed his ex partner, her mother and H into a bakery and demanded access to H. Upon access being refused K pulled a large kitchen knife from inside his jacket and a struggle ensued during which K took hold of H and deliberately cut his throat, killing him. K's ex partner and her mother were also injured. It was common ground that K had been suffering from a depressive condition at the time of the offence. In fixing the minimum term the sentencing judge, by reference to the Criminal Justice Act 2003 Sch.21 and Sch.22, had identified a starting point of 15 years which, having found none of the aggravating features in Sch.21 para.10, he then reduced to take into account the mitigation of K's depressive illness. The Attorney General contended that there were aggravating features, including the extreme youth and vulnerability of the victim.

Held, allowing the reference, that the judge had erred in concluding there were no statutory aggravating features. Amongst the matters the judge should have referred to when setting the minimum term was the aggravating factor, under para.10(b), of the vulnerability of the victim by reason of his age. Guidance was available, in the form of practice directions, to assist judges in relation to the cap on the minimum term which could be imposed in transitional cases, such as the instant one, where the offence was committed before the 2003 Act came into force, *R. v. Sullivan (Melvin Terrence)* [2004] EWCA Crim 1762, [2005] 1 Cr. App. R. 3, [2004] 10 C.L. 408 applied. Whilst para.19 of *Practice Statement (Crime: Life Sentences)* [2002] 1 W.L.R. 1789, [2002] C.L.Y. 901, which indicated that a term of 20 years or more could be appropriate in respect of the murder of a young child, was not directly applicable to cases considered under Sch.21 it had to be looked at as providing a general indication of the level of sentence. Parliament had not intended Sch.21 to reduce the applicable minimum term. In the instant case, a substantial increase on the starting point of 15 years had been called for before any reduction was made to take into account the mitigation. Given the seriousness of the offence, not least because of its effect on the victim's family and on members of the public who witnessed the violence, the minimum specified term was increased to 16 years. Under the Act no deduction was to be made for the element of double jeopardy.

ATTORNEY GENERAL'S REFERENCE (NO.106 OF 2004), *Re; sub nom.* R. v. KABIR (SHAHAJAN), [2004] EWCA Crim 2751, [2005] 1 Cr. App. R. (S.) 120, Lord Woolf of Barnes, L.C.J., CA (Crim Div).

3678. **Murder – Minimum term – Appellant shooting wife after quarrel – Transitional provisions under Sch.22 Criminal Justice Act 2003 – Length of minimum period**

[Criminal Justice Act 2003 Sch.22.]

The appellant (O), aged 65 at the time of the offence, appealed against a minimum term of 14 years imposed on a mandatory life sentence. O and his wife (W), who had been married for 40 years, had temporarily separated when W had discovered that O had been having an affair and she had indicated that she intended to divorce him. O had shot W in the chest with a shotgun and killed her following an argument during which she had threatened to ruin him financially. O had then telephoned the police and admitted what he had done. At trial, the evidence showed that O had been suffering from a depressive illness resulting from features of his personality and his domestic situation. O argued on appeal that the sentencing judge had adopted too high a starting point and had failed to take into account significant mitigating features.

Held, allowing the appeal, that the case was governed by the transitional provisions in the Criminal Justice Act 2003 Sch.22. The minimum term to be served under a life sentence was to be assessed by (1) establishing the starting point under the 2003 Act; (2) considering the aggravating and mitigating features before arriving at the minimum period under the 2003 Act; (3) establishing the starting point under the *Practice Direction (CA (Crim Div): Criminal Proceedings: Consolidation)* [2002] 1 W.L.R. 2870, [2002] C.L.Y. 899 for offences committed between May 31, 2002 and December 18, 2003; (4)

considering the aggravating and mitigating features before arriving at the appropriate minimum period which would have been notified by the secretary of state; (5) imposing the lower of the resulting two terms. In the instant case, the starting point under (1) was 30 years because the use of a firearm was involved. The aggravating and mitigating features under (2) would not produce a minimum term of less than 14 years. The starting point under (3) was 12 years because the case involved the killing of an adult victim arising from a quarrel between two people who knew each other, *R. v. Sullivan (Melvin Terrence)* [2004] EWCA Crim 1762, [2005] 1 Cr. App. R. 3, [2004] C.L.Y. 3401 applied. The aggravating features under (4) were the use of the gun, which was specifically mentioned in the practice direction. The mitigating features were O's depression, again specifically referred to in the practice direction, and his age. As the sentence stood, O would not be eligible for parole until the age of 80. In the circumstances the secretary of state was likely to have arrived at a minimum period of 12 years, which was less than that which would have been arrived at under the 2003 Act. Under (5), therefore, the minimum period of 14 years was reduced to 12 years.

R. v. WALKER (JOHN OWEN), [2005] EWCA Crim 82, [2005] 2 Cr. App. R. (S.) 55, Hooper, L.J., CA (Crim Div).

3679. Murder–Minimum term–Deliberate shooting of innocent victim– Transitional provisions under Sch.22 Criminal Justice Act 2003–Length of minimum period

[Criminal Justice Act 2003 s.269, s.269(5)(6), Sch.21, Sch.22.]

The appellant (O), a man aged 22 who had been convicted of murder, appealed against a specified minimum period of 23 years, one month and 23 days. O had been struck on the head with an ash tray in a public house by a man (G) who was a member of a family with whom O had animosity. O had left the public house and gone to his friend's house, then returned to the pub armed with a shotgun. He had fired the gun into a car in which G and others were sitting, inflicting fatal injuries on the driver and wounding a passenger in the arm. O had a number of previous convictions, including two for robbery. The sentencing judge, in applying the mandatory life sentence, specified a minimum period of 24 years discounted by the amount of time O had spent on remand. He indicated that if O had had to be sentenced under the Criminal Justice Act 2003 Sch.21 the appropriate starting point would have been 30 years, with a slight reduction to reflect O's age. However, since the offence had been committed before the commencement date of December 18, 2003, the minimum term had to be calculated in accordance with the law applicable at the time of the offence. On that basis, the judge indicated that the appropriate starting point was 12 years under the guidance in *R. v. Sullivan (Melvin Terrence)* [2004] EWCA Crim 1762, [2005] 1 Cr. App. R. 3, [2004] C.L.Y. 3401. O argued that the minimum period of 24 years was manifestly excessive.

Held, allowing the appeal, that the aggravating feature of the case was that O had gone to arm himself and had then returned to commit the offence, having made clear his intention to kill. The sentencing judge had correctly indicated that the appropriate starting point under the previous regime would have been 30 years, but the minimum term had to be calculated in accordance with the law at the time the offence was committed, *Sullivan* applied. Under s.269 of the 2003 Act, the court had to specify the minimum period to be served unless the offence was so serious that it was not appropriate to do so. In the instant case it was appropriate to make an order. In considering the seriousness of the offence, the court had to have regard to the general principles in s.269(5)(b). On that basis, the starting point would have been 30 years because of the firearm involvement. However, O's case was governed by the transitional provisions under Sch.22 to the 2003 Act, under which the court was prohibited from making an order for a minimum term which was greater than the term that could have been imposed at the time the offence was committed. Guidance as to starting points was given in *Practice Statement (Sup Ct: Crime: Life Sentences)* [2002] 1 W.L.R. 1789, [2002] C.L.Y. 901, later incorporated into *Practice*

Direction (Sup Ct: Crime: Mandatory Life Sentences) (No.2) [2004] 1 W.L.R. 2551, [2005] 4 C.L. 458, indicating starting points of 12 years, 15 to 16 years, 20 years and over, and 30 years and over, according to the gravity of the offence, applied. It was clear from *Sullivan* that it was necessary to determine what would have been the appropriate starting point under the practice statement. In the instant case, the aggravating feature justified a higher starting point of 15 to 16 years, although the offence could not be classified as one which was "especially grave" for the purposes of the 20 year and upwards category. On that basis, the specified minimum period of 24 years was manifestly excessive and an appropriate period was 18 years, less the time spent on remand.

R. v. O'BRIEN (MICHAEL), [2005] EWCA Crim 173, [2005] 2 Cr. App. R. (S.) 58, Clarke, L.J., CA (Crim Div).

3680. **Murder–Minimum term–Guidelines on credit for guilty plea when determining minimum term**

[Criminal Justice Act 2003 Sch.21.]

The appellants, who had all pleaded guilty to murder, appealed against their respective minimum terms. The appellants had been involved in four separate murder cases. The issue involved the approach to be adopted by the court in assessing the amount of credit to be given for a guilty plea in respect of determining the minimum term that each appellant had to serve prior to being considered for release on licence by the Parole Board. The terms were considered in the light of the Sentencing Guidelines Council's guidelines on Reduction in Sentence for a Guilty Plea which had come into effect on January 10, 2005,

Held, allowing the appeals in part, that the Reduction in Sentence for a Guilty Plea Guidelines applied to offences committed before the guidelines came into force. The guidelines existed to assist a judge in determining, in the case of murder, the minimum term. The guidelines and the Criminal Justice Act 2003 Sch.21 indicated the matters which the judge had to take into account when he exercised his discretion. Although every court had to consider the guidelines and Sch.21 they did not invariably have to be followed. However, unless a defendant showed that he would be prejudiced by the application of the guidelines it was sensible for them to be adopted. If a court departed from the guidelines or Sch.21 it had to give the reasons underlying that exercise of its discretion. Schedule 21 did not seek to identify all the aggravating and mitigating factors which might be considered by the court; it merely provided relevant examples.

R. v. LAST (EMMA); R. v. HOLBROOK (LEE DAVID); R. v. CRANE (SARA); R. v. QUILLAN (EDWARD STEVEN); R. v. QUILLAN (JAMES ANGUS), [2005] EWCA Crim 106, [2005] 2 Cr. App. R. (S.) 64, Lord Woolf of Barnes, L.C.J., CA (Crim Div).

3681. **Murder–Minimum term–Knives–Aggravating and mitigating features of offence**

The appellant (R) appealed against the imposition of a minimum term of 12 years' imprisonment for murder. R and the victim, who had undergone heart surgery, had been walking their dogs on a golf course when an argument broke out after a fight between the parties' dogs. R had stabbed the victim in the back once, in response to physical blows from the victim. The jury had rejected defences of self defence, provocation and accident. R submitted that too much weight had been attributed to the aggravating features of the offence and too little to the mitigating features.

Held, dismissing the appeal, that the mitigating and aggravating factors were of equal weight. There had been no premeditation, R had not been in the best of health following surgery and there had been some provocation. Weighed against those factors was the serious matter of R's production and use of an illegal knife in an act of revenge. Such factors had to be weighed according to the circumstances of each individual case rather than being given precise measurement across the board since sentencing was not an exact science, *R. v. Sullivan (Melvin Terrence)* [2004] EWCA Crim 1762, [2005] 1 Cr. App. R. 3, [2004] C.L.Y. 3401 considered.

R. v. REID (DAVID WILLIAM), [2004] EWCA Crim 2930, [2005] 2 Cr. App. R. (S.) 12, Rix, L.J., CA (Crim Div).

3682. **Murder–Minimum term–Requirement to take into account aggravating and mitigating factors in Sch.21 Criminal Justice Act 2003**

[Criminal Justice Act 2003 s.269(2), Sch.21 para.10, Sch.21 para.11.]

The appellants (P, R and C), in three unrelated cases, appealed against determinations of the minimum term in relation to mandatory life sentences imposed on them under the Criminal Justice Act 2003 s.269(2) following guilty pleas and conviction of murder. P and R were 19 years of age when they committed murder, and 20 when sentenced to custody for life, and C was 18 when she committed murder and when she was sentenced. The minimum term specified in respect of P was nine years and in respect of R and C was 12 years. Allowance was however made for P and R in respect of the time already spent in custody. P argued that the judge had failed sufficiently to take account of his guilty plea, the absence of an intention to kill, and that neither of the specific aggravating features in Sch.21 para.10 to the Act were present. R submitted that his case should have been treated as a case on the borderline between manslaughter and murder. C submitted that her crime lacked any of the aggravating features specified in Sch.21 para.10.

Held, giving judgment accordingly, that (1) guidelines, whether resulting from case law or produced by the Sentencing Guidelines Council, were guidelines and no more. The circumstances of the offence and the offender might vary, and therefore an individual sentencing decision appropriate for the unique circumstances of each case was required, *R. v. Sullivan (Melvin Terrence)* [2004] EWCA Crim 1762, [2005] 1 Cr. App. R. 3, [2004] 10 C.L. 408 and *R. v. Last (Emma)* [2005] EWCA Crim 106, Times, January 31, 2005, [2005] 3 C.L. 457 applied. The legislative framework, namely Sch.21 to the Act, recognised that even in murder cases an identical level of seriousness could not be attributed to each case. Schedule 21 provided a series of criteria to be taken into account when the court was determining the appropriate minimum term to reflect the "seriousness" of the individual offence. Although Sch.21 identified the starting point for the minimum term, the court must further address any relevant aggravating factors listed in Sch.21 para.10 and mitigating factors listed in Sch.21 para.11. However the court was not rigidly bound by or limited to the specific features in the lists. The true seriousness of the offence, which the minimum term was intended to reflect, inevitably represented a combination and, simultaneously, a balancing of all relevant factors in the case. (2) In respect of P, it was clear from the judge's sentencing remarks that he had the relevant features in mind. It was not necessary for him to set out and identify which of the features found in Sch.21 para.10 were absent, and which of those included in Sch.21 para.11 were present. His reasons for reaching a minimum term of nine years were sufficiently explained. (3) In respect of R, the trial judge took into account all the relevant factors. The judge was right to find that it was not a borderline case. In all the circumstances the minimum term fixed by the trial judge fell within the appropriate range for the offence. (4) As regards C, the 12 year minimum term did not sufficiently reflect her youth, and the emotional immaturity for which she was not responsible. Having regard to C's mitigation and the aggravating factors, the appropriate minimum term should be nine years, which should be further reduced by the time spent on remand.

R. v. PETERS (BENJAMIN); R. v. PALMER (DANIEL ROY); R. v. CAMPBELL (SHANTELLE JAMIE), [2005] EWCA Crim 605, [2005] 2 Cr. App. R. (S.) 101, Judge, L.J., CA (Crim Div).

3683. **Murder–Violence by father culminating in daughter's death–Determination of minimum term**

[Criminal Justice Act 2003 Sch.21 para.6, Sch.22.]

The appellant (Q) appealed against a sentence of life imprisonment with a minimum period of 16 years and 198 days' imprisonment imposed following his conviction of murder. Q had been abusing his two year old daughter for two to three weeks and there had been at least three occasions where he had been violent towards her. Whilst preparing to go to work, and under pressure due to Ramadan, a tooth abscess and his daughter's crying, Q had struck his daughter five times with his fist on her scalp. Each time that his daughter had fallen over he picked her up again, eventually rendering her unconscious. An ambulance was called over an hour later. On arrival at hospital Q's daughter was placed on a ventilator, but was subsequently found to be brain dead and the ventilator was switched off. A post mortem revealed that she had died from her head injuries. At trial Q had pleaded not guilty of murder on the ground that he had not had the necessary intent. When sentencing, the judge considered the aggravating factors that the victim had been vulnerable, the physical suffering previously caused, the abuse of Q's position of trust, the delay in calling an ambulance and Q's previous convictions of assault occasioning actual bodily harm. The judge also considered the mitigating factors that there had been no intention to kill and that the offence had not been premeditated. Under the Criminal Justice Act 2003 Sch.21 para.6 the judge had adopted the starting point of 15 years' imprisonment. However, the aggravating features had outweighed the mitigating features and the sentence to be served for the purposes of retribution was 18 years' imprisonment. However, the offence had occurred before the Act had fully come into force and the transitional provisions under Sch.22 to the Act had to be taken into account. Under the transitional provisions the starting point was a sentence of 14 years' imprisonment with a final recommendation of 17 years' imprisonment. Under the Act the lower sentence had to be taken into account, and the sentence passed by the judge was 17 years' imprisonment less the time spent on remand. Q submitted that (1) under the 2003 Act, the balancing of the aggravating and mitigating factors by the judge, leading to an addition of three years to the relevant starting point under the Act, was in error; (2) under the *Practice Statement (Sup Ct: Crime: Life Sentences)* [2002] 1 W.L.R. 1789, [2002] C.L.Y. 901, further allowance had to be made as the element of aggravation consisting in the murder of a vulnerable child had already been built into the starting point of 15 or 16 years' imprisonment.

Held, allowing the appeal, that (1) there was force in Q's submissions. The aggravating factor of the murder of a child should not have been underestimated and such infants merited the strongest protection that the state could bring. However, on the other side there was the mitigating factor that there had been no intent to kill. The fact that there was no intent to kill but only to cause grievous bodily harm, coupled with the absence of premeditation, was a very important factor. Q also had previous convictions for assault occasioning actual bodily harm and nothing could be said to mitigate those features; nevertheless, the factors as a whole balanced themselves out. Q had also stood trial on the issue of specific intent; however, on the first day of the trial he accepted responsibility for causing the injuries to his daughter and reliance had to be placed on that as mitigation. (2) The aggravating feature of the murder of a child was built into the starting point of a 15 or 16 year sentence. The range of starting points under the practice statement went from 15 to 20 years' imprisonment. In the instant case a starting point significantly above 15 years would have been appropriate for the murder of an infant with intent to kill, such that, taking account of all the other aggravating and mitigating features, and in particular the important mitigating factor of a lack of intent to kill, a sentence of 15 years' imprisonment would have been appropriate. Therefore, the sentence was quashed and replaced with a sentence of 15 years' imprisonment less the time spent by Q on remand.

R. v. QADAR (MOHAMMED), [2004] EWCA Crim 2881, [2005] 2 Cr. App. R. (S.) 7, Rix, L.J., CA (Crim Div).

3684. Obtaining leave by deception—Mitigation—Relevance of genuineness and strength of asylum claim

[Immigration Act 1971 s.24A; Immigration and Asylum Act 1999 s.31.]

The appellant (K) appealed against a nine-month sentence imposed following a plea of guilty to seeking to obtain leave to enter or remain in the UK by deception. K, who was a national of Congo, had entered the UK by using a forged passport and visa. Upon arrival she had been fingerprinted and admitted as a visitor. Subsequently K had claimed asylum and had given false details regarding her entry into the UK. K argued that the sentence was manifestly excessive as the judge had given insufficient weight to her motivation for misleading the authorities and had failed to distinguish between her genuine claim for asylum and bogus claims. K argued that while the defence under the Immigration and Asylum Act 1999 s.31 was not available where, as in the instant case, the offence was charged under the Immigration Act 1971 s.24A, the sentence should, nevertheless, reflect the genuineness of her asylum claim.

Held, dismissing the appeal, that the sentence passed was not manifestly excessive. The genuineness of a claim for asylum was a question for the Home Office and the appellate system thereafter. It was not appropriate for a sentencing court to routinely assess the genuineness and strength of asylum claims unless a defence under s.31 of the 1999 Act was raised. While anomalies arose between cases where a defence under s.31 was available and those where it was not available, it was not for the court to resolve those anomalies. There was a public interest in passport controls, and the judge had not been obliged to assess the circumstances of the case or the strength of K's claim for asylum, or to treat her as a person with a good claim for asylum.

R. v. KISHIENTINE (MICHELINE BULANKAY), [2004] EWCA Crim 3352, [2005] 2 Cr. App. R. (S.) 28, Pill, L.J., CA (Crim Div).

3685. Obtaining property by deception—Multiple offences committed by confidence trickster

The appellant (C), a skilled professional confidence trickster, appealed against a sentence of six years' imprisonment imposed for eight offences of obtaining property by deception committed while he was on early release licence. C would pretend to be connected to a restaurant and would persuade people to part with money for champagne which was never supplied. The total amount obtained by C in respect of the offences and other offences taken into consideration was £26,725. He had 16 previous court appearances for 78 offences, which were predominantly for dishonesty, and had served four custodial sentences previously. A pre sentence report indicated that he had shown little remorse, that he lacked the persistence and determination to treat his admitted gambling addiction successfully, and that he presented a high risk of reoffending. C argued, inter alia, that the sentence did not reflect the guilty pleas which he had entered at the first opportunity.

Held, allowing the appeal, that in all the circumstances the sentence was manifestly excessive. The offences committed by C would not have justified a total term of imprisonment in the region of nine years had he contested the charges, and the total sentence in the circumstances of the case was too long. The sentence was reduced to four years' imprisonment.

R. v. CLUGSTON (JOHN), [2004] EWCA Crim 1324, [2005] 1 Cr. App. R. (S.) 30, Buxton, L.J., CA (Crim Div).

3686. Outraging public decency—Indecent exposure—Three incidents of exposure on public beach in view of children

[Sexual Offences Act 2003.]

The appellant (C) appealed against three consecutive 18 month sentences totalling four and half years' imprisonment for outraging public decency. C had exposed himself on a beach three times in one afternoon in front of families with children. C had previously been charged with at least 13 instances of similar offences over the past 20 years or so and continued to deny the commission of the offences.

Held, allowing the appeal, that it was appropriate to replace the consecutive sentences with concurrent ones, resulting in a total sentence of 18 months' imprisonment, because the offences represented three incidents in a single course of conduct. In view of the lack of reported authority on offences of outraging public decency, guidance was obtained from the fact that the Sexual Offences Act 2003 prescribed a maximum sentence of two years' imprisonment for indecent exposure.

R. v. COSCO (MICHAEL NICOLA), [2005] EWCA Crim 207, [2005] 2 Cr. App. R. (S.) 66, Kennedy, L.J., CA (Crim Div).

3687. Perjury – Custodial sentences – Bigamy committed following false statement to registrar as to marital status – Offender with history of dishonesty

The appellant (M) appealed against a sentence of nine months' imprisonment having pleaded guilty to bigamy and perjury. M was still married when he took part in a marriage ceremony to a second woman. At the register office he signed a notice of marriage, certifying that there was no impediment to his marrying because his marriage had been dissolved nine years earlier and he had not been married since. M had a substantial record for offences of dishonesty, for which he had twice served sentences of imprisonment. M submitted that whilst perjury was a serious offence, his offence of lying to the registrar did not warrant imprisonment.

Held, dismissing the appeal, that perjury required an immediate custodial sentence in the absence of exceptional circumstances. M's record of dishonesty prior to committing perjury in the instant case was such that there were no exceptional circumstances capable of vitiating the need for a custodial sentence.

R. v. MITCHELL (ROY), [2004] EWCA Crim 1516, [2005] 1 Cr. App. R. (S.) 41, Hooper, L.J., CA (Crim Div).

3688. Perverting the course of justice – Making false statements – Boyfriend implicated in murder investigation

C, aged 18 and heavily pregnant at the time of the offence, appealed against a sentence of 18 months' detention in a young offender institution following her conviction for perverting the course of justice by making a false statement. C's boyfriend and another man were suspected of being involved in an incident in which a van owner was run over and killed during the theft of the vehicle. C claimed that she had overheard a conversation implicating both men. They were subsequently charged and detained in custody. She then said she had not overheard the conversation, and the proceedings were discontinued.

Held, allowing the appeal, that a custodial sentence was appropriate in principle because the false statement in a murder case had led to the detention of two people. However, C, who had a history of depression, was in labour when she made the statement and later claimed that she was confused at the time. The sentence was reduced to nine months' detention, taking account of C's early plea and the fact that she had been separated from her young children, *R. v. Evans (Daniel John)* [1998] 2 Cr. App. R. (S.) 72, [1998] C.L.Y. 1325 considered.

R. v. COLLINS (KERRIE JANE), [2004] EWCA Crim 1269, [2005] 1 Cr. App. R. (S.) 22, Scott Baker, L.J., CA (Crim Div).

3689. Perverting the course of justice – Sentence length – Interference with jurors – Degree of interference

H appealed against a sentence of 30 months' imprisonment for perverting the course of justice. Two men were on trial for causing grievous bodily harm. Throughout the victim's evidence H sat in the public gallery. H's presence made the victim apprehensive. H approached a juror and told the juror to find the defendants not guilty. The juror complained. The trial was aborted. H pleaded guilty on the basis that his encounter with the juror was accidental. The judge said jurors had to be able to go about their service without hindrance and considerable public money was wasted when trials were aborted. H argued that his sentence was manifestly excessive because he had not intimidated a juror, there were no aggravating features, the encounter with the juror was not planned and no direct threat was made or money offered and he had pleaded guilty at the earliest opportunity.

Held, allowing the appeal, that a sentence of 21 months' imprisonment was substituted. Jurors were entitled to perform their public service unimpeded by threat or encounter designed to dissuade them from the proper performance of their task. Custody and sometimes substantial periods of custody was inevitable for those who interfered with jurors. That said, regard had to be paid to the nature and degree of interference. The subject juror resisted the implicit threats made to him and reported the matter as soon as practicable. The consequence, namely the aborting of the trial, was a serious matter to which the judge was fully entitled to have regard. But taking all the other circumstances into account, including H's plea of guilty, the sentence of 30 months' imprisonment was too long, *R. v. Williams (Mark)* [1997] 2 Cr. App. R. (S.) 221, [1997] C.L.Y. 1641, *R. v. Baxter (Robert Peter)* [2002] EWCA Crim 1516, [2003] 1 Cr. App. R. (S.) 50, [2003] C.L.Y. 3746 and *R. v. Goult (Raymond Arthur)* (1983) 76 Cr. App. R. 140, [1983] C.L.Y. 582 considered.

R. v. HARDY (GARY), [2004] EWCA Crim 3397, [2005] 2 Cr. App. R. (S.) 48, Rose, L.J., CA (Crim Div).

3690.   **Possession of firearms–Guilty pleas–Minimum term under s.51A Firearms Act 1968**

[Firearms Act 1968 s.5(1)(aba), s.51A; Powers of Criminal Courts (Sentencing) Act 2000 s.152.]

The appellants (J, C and R) appealed against sentences of five years' imprisonment, five years' detention and two years six months' imprisonment respectively following pleas of guilty to possession of a prohibited firearm contrary to the Firearms Act 1968 s.5(1)(aba). In the three unrelated cases the appellants had all been found in possession of prohibited firearms following searches by the police. R was sentenced on the basis that his explanation, that he believed the firearm to be an imitation, was an "exceptional circumstance" which justified a reduction in the specified minimum term of five years' imprisonment under s.51(A) of the 1968 Act. J and C contended that credit should have been given for their guilty pleas as s.51(A) contained no express exclusion preventing the Powers of Criminal Courts (Sentencing) Act 2000 s.152 from applying. R contended that his sentence was manifestly excessive as, once exceptional circumstances had been established, the judge should not have restricted himself by reference to the minimum term and should have had regard to guideline cases and ordinary principles of sentencing.

Held, dismissing the appeals, that (1) the minimum term in respect of J and C was correct and no discount should have been given for pleas of guilty. Section 51(A) was plain and unambiguous and it was clear that Parliament had not intended a reduction in the minimum term for pleas of guilty. The absence in s.51(A) of any reference to s.152 of the 2000 Act was plainly deliberate. The rigour of s.51(A) was mitigated by the possibility of finding exceptional circumstances which justified a reduction. (2) The sentence imposed in relation to R was not manifestly excessive as it was doubtful whether R's explanation amounted to an exceptional circumstance. However, without the intervention of the Attorney General the court had no power to increase the sentence. Cases where exceptional circumstances arose would be rare but where they did arise the sentence was at large. The judge was permitted to take into account a number of factors which included the minimum sentence, guideline cases, and all available mitigation, *R. v. Avis (Tony)* [1998] 1 Cr. App. R. 420, [1998] C.L.Y.

1214 considered. A plea of guilty could be taken into account where an exceptional circumstance was held to exist.

R. v. JORDAN (ANDREW JAMES); R. v. ALLEYNE (CARL ANTHONY); R. v. REDFERN (DAVID CHRISTOPHER), [2004] EWCA Crim 3291, [2005] 2 Cr. App. R. (S.) 44, Rose, L.J., CA (Crim Div).

3691. Possession of firearms–Imitation firearms–Airports–Inadvertent inclusion in luggage

[Aviation Security Act 1982 s.4.]

The appellant (B), who had pleaded guilty to possessing an imitation firearm at an airport contrary to the Aviation Security Act 1982 s.4, appealed against a sentence of four months' imprisonment. B had been found to have a semi automatic ball bearing pistol in his luggage at Stansted airport. B's account, which was accepted by the prosecution and judge, was that he had bought the pistol some six months previously and had put it away in a bag to keep it from his young daughter. He had then inadvertently taken the bag to the airport without checking its contents or being aware of the presence of the pistol. B contended that the sentence was wrong in principle or manifestly excessive.

Held, allowing the appeal, that the facts were at the lowest level of culpability but a prison sentence was still appropriate. The offence itself was serious and the need to ensure security for air travel could not be exaggerated. Careful steps had to be taken by air passengers to ensure that luggage did not contain forbidden articles. Whilst a custodial sentence was appropriate the length was excessive and the term was reduced to 28 days' imprisonment.

R. v. BURROWS (DAVID JOHN), [2004] EWCA Crim 677, [2004] 2 Cr. App. R. (S.) 89, Forbes, J., CA (Crim Div).

3692. Possession of firearms–Imitation firearms–Possession for short period only–No brandishing weapon in public–Sentence length

The appellant (R) appealed against a sentence of 15 months' imprisonment imposed for an offence of having an imitation firearm in a public place. R had encountered two other people known to him including a young girl (F) and 15 year old boy (B) and had asked B to feel his back. B had done so and had felt the handle of a gun. R had then shown B the gun in his waistband. B had asked whether it was a "BB gun" and R had replied ambiguously. B, R and F had then gone into F's house and R had put the gun under a top on the sofa. Later that day, F's brother called the police and armed police officers arrested R as he was leaving the house. They were told immediately that the weapon was an imitation firearm. R's psychiatric report indicated that he had some mental and behavioural disorders from abuse of cannabis and alcohol. He had a number of previous convictions for dishonesty and drug offences.

Held, allowing the appeal, that all offences involving firearms, whether real or imitation, were serious and likely to lead to a sentence of imprisonment. The possession of an imitation firearm was capable of causing a danger by the reaction of others, who might not appreciate that it was imitation. In the instant case, the police had been told at an early stage that the gun was imitation, R had been in possession of it only since the previous day and he had not brandished it in public. R's mental difficulties were also taken into consideration. Having regard to all the circumstances, the sentence was manifestly excessive and was reduced to 10 months' imprisonment, *R. v. Avis (Tony)* [1998] 1 Cr. App. R. 420, [1998] C.L.Y. 1214 and *R. v. Fielding (Ian Thomas)* [2004] EWCA Crim 502 considered.

R. v. RATTIGAN (PHILIP), [2005] EWCA Crim 162, [2005] 2 Cr. App. R. (S.) 61, Gage, L.J., CA (Crim Div).

3693. Possession of firearms—Minimum term—Exceptional circumstances

[Firearms Act 1968 s.5(1)(aba), s.51A(2); Human Rights Act 1998 s.3; European Convention on Human Rights 1950.]

The appellants (R and W) appealed against mandatory minimum sentences of five years' imprisonment imposed under the Firearms Act 1968 s.51A(2) following their convictions for offences committed under s.5(1)(aba) of the Act. R was a collector of models. He pleaded guilty to an offence contrary to s.5(1)(aba). He had purchased, in his own name and with his own credit card, a replica firearm from an internet site. R had stored the firearm under his bed. R cooperated fully with the police when they executed the search warrant. R did not think it was illegal to own the gun and he did not know that it could be converted. R was of previous good character, had a degree and, until he was sentenced, was employed by Customs and Excise. W was also of good character and a collector of weapons. He was the manager of a surveillance company and had carried out important work with Army cadets. W cooperated fully with the police in their investigation. On a search of his house, the majority of the guns were in locked cabinets. However, a shortened shotgun was found in the loft. He was sentenced to five years' imprisonment in respect of nine counts in relation to firearms offences. R and W argued that (1) a wide interpretation of the words "exceptional circumstances" in s.51A was required to ensure that the court did not act in a way that was incompatible with the European Convention on Human Rights 1950; (2) there were exceptional circumstances in both cases relating to the offence or the offender to justify not imposing the minimum term of five years' imprisonment.

Held, allowing the appeals in part, that (1) s.5 of the Act created an absolute offence. The purpose of the provision was to ensure that, absent exceptional circumstances, the courts would always impose deterrent sentences. It was not necessary to read s.51A down, relying on the Human Rights Act 1998 s.3 so as to comply with the Convention. The words were clearly capable of being interpreted as complying with the Convention. Circumstances were exceptional for the purposes of s.51A(2) if it would mean that to impose five years' imprisonment would result in an arbitrary and disproportionate sentence, *R. v. Offen (Matthew Barry) (No.2)* [2001] 1 W.L.R. 253, [2000] C.L.Y. 1347 considered. (2) In respect of R, the judge had been wrong to conclude that there were no exceptional circumstances. R had no knowledge of the unlawfulness of the one weapon that he had in his possession. R had pleaded guilty at the first opportunity, was 24 years old and of previous good character, had cooperated throughout the search and arrest procedure and had been a valued employee. In the light of all the circumstances, the court was not required to impose the minimum term. Although a custodial sentence had been necessary to achieve the deterrent message that Parliament had intended, a period of 12 months' imprisonment would have been sufficient. Accordingly, the sentence of five years' imprisonment was quashed. In relation to W, if the court interfered with the sentence of five years' imprisonment imposed, it would not be properly applying the statutory provision imposed by Parliament. W should have understood that he should not have had the weapon in his possession. He had not checked whether it was lawful to possess it. The fact that W had committed other offences demonstrated that he did not attach sufficient significance to the very strict statutory provisions that applied to the possession of firearms. Although the other offences did not relate to s.51A they showed a carelessness on W's part in relation to the possession of firearms that prevented the court from treating the circumstances as exceptional. Accordingly the sentence of five years' imprisonment would remain.

R. v. REHMAN (ZAKIR); R. v. WOOD (GARY DOMINIC), [2005] EWCA Crim 2056, *The Times*, September 27, 2005, Lord Woolf of Barnes, L.C.J., CA (Crim Div).

3694. **Possession of firearms–Minimum term–Mental disorder–"exceptional circumstances" under s.51A Firearms Act 1968**

[Firearms Act 1968 s.51 (A).]

The appellant (M) appealed against a total sentence of five years' imprisonment imposed following his pleas of guilty to various firearms offences. M had been arrested taking delivery of an imitation firearm. A search of his property led to the discovery of a handgun that had been converted from firing blanks to live ammunition, two CS gas canisters, and email correspondence with companies supplying imitation guns. The statutory minimum sentence of five years' imprisonment had been imposed, under the Firearms Act 1968 s.51A, in relation to the converted handgun. M, a schizophrenic, had given a no comment interview, but later told the sentencing court that he had found the altered weapon when out walking one day. The psychiatric report submitted to the court state that although M suffered from paranoid schizophrenia he had considerable insight into his illness, which was controlled by medication such that he was able to live a normal life. The report had not contained an assertion that M's obtaining and keeping of the handgun was attributable to his schizophrenia, or a recommendation of a hospital order. However it stated that prison would have a detrimental effect on M's mental condition. M submitted, in relation to the sentence imposed under s.51A, that his psychiatric history, which provided the background to the commission of the offences, together with the circumstances of the offence amounted in combination to exceptional circumstances, permitting the court to impose a sentence less than the statutory minimum.

Held, dismissing the appeal, that while, as a matter of law, exceptional circumstances purely relating to an offender might be sufficient, the personal circumstances relied on by M were equivocal as mitigation, because they could increase the danger to the public and they did not provide any explanation for the offence. M clearly had a fixation with guns and, in the light of his psychiatric condition, that obsession plainly had potential for causing great risk of serious injury or even death to others, *R. v. Jordan (Andrew James)* [2004] EWCA Crim 3291, [2005] Crim. App. R.(S) 44 considered.

R. v. McENEANEY (JOHN PAUL), [2005] EWCA Crim 431, [2005] 2 Cr. App. R. (S.) 86, Smith, L.J., CA (Crim Div).

3695. **Possession of firearms–Supply of drugs–Appellant supplying handguns and drugs to undercover police officer–Undue leniency**

The Attorney General referred as unduly lenient a total sentence of five years and six months' imprisonment following pleas of guilty to offering to supply Class A drugs, producing Class B drugs, three counts of possession of a prohibited firearm and possession of ammunition without a certificate by the defendant (G). G had supplied an undercover police officer with two handguns with live ammunition and specially adapted bullets and had also offered to supply two kilos of cocaine. Following his arrest and subsequent search of his properties a substantial cannabis cultivation system and a sawn off shotgun were discovered. Sentences of five years and six months were passed for the firearm offences, two years and six months for the cocaine offence and 18 months for the cannabis offence. The sentences were to run concurrently. The Attorney General contended that where firearm offences were committed in association with other offences, in particular those involving Class A drugs, sentencing principles dictated consecutive sentences, and that the judge should have ordered the sentences for the drug offences to run consecutively between themselves and the firearms offences.

Held, allowing the reference, that the judge ought to have passed consecutive sentences in relation to the cocaine offence and the separate offence of producing cannabis. In the court below a sentence of three years for the cocaine offence with one year consecutive for the cannabis offence would have been appropriate. Taking into account the principle of double jeopardy, in that G was being sentenced for a second time, the sentence of two years for the cocaine offence was appropriate, but a sentence of one year would be substituted for the cannabis offence. All the sentences were to run consecutively, giving a total of nine years' imprisonment.

ATTORNEY GENERAL'S REFERENCE (NO.77 OF 2003), *Re; sub nom.* R. v. GRIERSON (ERNEST ROY) [2004] EWCA Crim 3394, Rose, L.J. (V-P), CA (Crim Div).

3696. Possession of firearms with intent–Conspiracy–Firearm possessed for purpose of blackmail–Undue leniency

The Attorney General referred as unduly lenient sentences imposed on two offenders (D and T). D had been sentenced to nine years' imprisonment for an offence of conspiracy to possess a firearm with intent to endanger life and four years' imprisonment concurrently for an offence of conspiracy to blackmail. T had been sentenced to four years' imprisonment in relation to the possession offence, two years' imprisonment for an offence of possession of a Class A drug with intent to supply and six months' imprisonment for an offence of witness intimidation. D had supplied drugs to an individual (H) who as a result owed him £100,000. A coconspirator had held a business associate of H in a flat threatening that he would not be permitted to leave until he had settled a part of the debt owed by H. The man was permitted to leave after he had paid a small amount of the debt. D decided to attempt to force payment of the debt by means of a drive by shooting at H's home. Shots had been fired into the house, frightening H's relatives inside. In relation to D, the judge considered the possession offence and the conspiracy to blackmail offence as part of the same criminal enterprise and therefore passed concurrent sentences. T was described as a gofer who had obtained the car used in the drive by shooting. T's home had been searched and heroin and cash had been found. The Attorney General submitted that (1) D's sentence for the possession offence did not reflect the seriousness of that offence; (2) there was no justification for D's sentences being concurrent as the drive by shooting offence stood alone and should have attracted a separate sentence; (3) although T was a gofer, the sentence of four years' imprisonment did not adequately reflect the seriousness of the offence. Further, the sentence for witness intimidation was too short and it was wrong for the sentences to be served concurrently.

Held, allowing the references, that (1) a longer term than that imposed was appropriate for D. The offence was particularly serious because it was committed in circumstances that clearly gave rise to a significant risk of injury or death, and nine years failed to reflect the gravity of the offence, *R. v. Cioffo (Antonio)* [1996] 1 Cr. App. R. (S.) 427, [1996] C.L.Y. 1730 and *R. v. Avis (Tony)* [1998] 1 Cr. App. R. 420, [1998] C.L.Y. 1214 considered. D was also not a man of good character. The appropriate sentence was one of 14 to 15 years. Bearing in mind double jeopardy, a sentence of 13 years' imprisonment was imposed. (2) Ordinarily, firearms offences, when connected to other criminal activity, were properly dealt with by way of consecutive sentences. However, given the length of D's amended sentence for the possession offence and double jeopardy, the sentence would remain concurrent. (3) The sentences imposed on T were lenient. The judge had also been wrong in principle not to have imposed consecutive sentences. Because of double jeopardy, the individual sentences were not increased, but they would now be served consecutively, making the total sentence one of six and a half years' imprisonment.

ATTORNEY GENERAL'S REFERENCE (NO.311 OF 2004), *Re; sub nom.* R. v. DAD (ARIF MAHMOOD); R. v. TEALE (JOSEPH MICHAEL), [2005] EWCA Crim 1837, [2006] 1 Cr. App. R. (S.) 57, Latham, L.J., CA (Crim Div).

3697. Possession of firearms with intent–Youth carrying disguised firearm loaded with live bullets–Undue leniency

The Attorney General referred as unduly lenient a total sentence of four years' detention in a young offender institution following pleas of guilty by the defendant (O) to possession of a firearm with intent to endanger life, possession of a disguised firearm, possession of ammunition with no certificate and various driving offences. O, who had been aged 19 at the time of the offences and on bail awaiting sentencing for various driving offences, had been observed riding a bicycle in a residential area. He was arrested when he abandoned the bicycle and attempted to dispose of a small metal item resembling a key fob. The item was a firearm which had been adapted for use and loaded with two live bullets. O was wearing ballistic body armour and thick gloves. O pleaded guilty on the first day of trial. When sentencing, the judge found that there were exceptional circumstances for not passing the statutory minimum five year term for the offence of possession of a disguised firearm. The Attorney General argued that the sentence for the disguised firearm failed to reflect the statutory minimum or the aggravating features that: (i) the firearm was disguised and adapted with no other purpose but to cause injury; (ii) the firearm was loaded with live ammunition and carried with intent to endanger life; (iii) O had been wearing body armour and gloves at the time; (iv) the gun was carried in the evening in a residential area; (v) the offences were committed whilst on bail. The Attorney General submitted that given the prevalence of the carrying and using of guns, a deterrent sentence was called for. In mitigation were O's guilty plea, the fact that the gun had not been used, O's relative youth and his lack of relevant previous convictions.

Held, allowing the reference, that it appeared that the sole basis for the judge finding an exceptional circumstance for not passing the statutory minimum sentence was the pre sentence report assessing O as presenting a low risk of reoffending. As a matter of law, that was not, and could not be, an exceptional circumstance. The offences were serious and there was no reason why the statutory minimum term should not have been passed. Despite O's comparative youth, a sentence of at least seven years could have been expected in the court below given his late pleas of guilty. Taking into account double jeopardy, the sentence of four years was quashed and six years' detention in a young offender institution was substituted.

ATTORNEY GENERAL'S REFERENCE (NO.5 OF 2005), *Re*; *sub nom.* R. v. ORR (ROBERT HORATIO) [2005] EWCA Crim 880, Rose, L.J. (V-P), CA (Crim Div).

3698. Possession of offensive weapons–Airports–Cosh, lock knife and CS gas canister found in appellant's bag

The appellant (C) appealed against a total sentence of two months' imprisonment imposed after he was convicted on counts of possessing a prohibited weapon, possessing an offensive weapon and possessing a bladed article. C had arrived at Stansted airport intending to board a flight to Ireland. However, he was stopped as he passed through an X ray machine and a cosh and a lock knife were found in his luggage. Upon a further search of his bag, police officers found a CS gas canister. The sentencing judge had accepted C's assertion that he had packed his bag in haste and had forgotten that the items were there. She also took account of C's good character and his contrition. C maintained that the imposition of custodial term was manifestly excessive given the nature of the offences and the quality of the mitigation. C placed particular emphasis on the fact that he had not known that he was carrying the weapons and that, on the evidence as accepted at trial, there had been no sinister intent.

Held, dismissing the appeal, that the possession of such weapons at an airport or airport check in was to be viewed with considerable gravity. Notwithstanding the considerable mitigation available in C's case, the combination of weapons in C's bag and the importance of security in the air meant that a short custodial sentence of the length passed by the recorder could not be described as either wrong in principle or manifestly excessive, *R. v. Poulton (Sarah Jane)* [2002] EWCA Crim 2487, [2003] 4 All E.R. 869, [2002] C.L.Y. 4042 applied. Moreover, C could not claim the credit which would have been available had he pleaded guilty.

R. v. CHARLES (ANTHONY ROGER), [2004] EWCA Crim 1977, [2005] 1 Cr. App. R. (S.) 56, Henriques, J., CA (Crim Div).

3699. Possession with intent to supply–Basis of plea–Limited involvement in handling substantial quantities of drugs–Undue leniency

The Attorney General referred to the court as unduly lenient sentences of two years' imprisonment imposed on the offenders (H) and (C) following their guilty pleas to possession of cannabis with intent to supply. H had been driving a van followed by C in his car. The van was stopped by police and found to contain 120kg of cannabis worth over £500,000. H and C entered guilty pleas on the grounds that they had been asked to transport a van containing cannabis for £400 each, and that the single delivery had been the full extent of their involvement and, as a result, they were unaware of the exact quantity or value of the drugs.

Held, dismissing the reference, that by reference to sentencing standards for the amount of cannabis involved the sentences were unduly lenient. However, having regard to the principle of double jeopardy and the agreed basis of plea, it was not appropriate to increase them. H and C had handled substantial quantities of cannabis, but their involvement had been very limited and their profit from the venture was minuscule. That basis of plea was troubling given the surrounding circumstances of the offence, but it had to be assumed that counsel had been justified in reaching the agreement and that there had been powerful evidence to support it. If not, it would be surprising that H and C had not had any contact with the drugs before the morning of the offence and, in effect, had no knowledge of anything except that they had been asked to transport the van containing cannabis. That proposition was not realistic. It was noted that counsel and judges examining written bases of pleas ought to scrutinise the entire process carefully, *R. v. Underwood (Kevin)* [2004] EWCA Crim 2256, [2005] 1 Cr. App. R. 13 considered.

ATTORNEY GENERAL'S REFERENCE (NOS.115 AND 116 OF 2004), *Re; sub nom.* R. v. HISCOCK (CHRISTOPHER); R. v. COOMBES (JEFFREY IAN) [2004] EWCA Crim 3487, Judge, L.J., CA (Crim Div).

3700. Possession with intent to supply–Commercial dealing–Undue leniency

The Attorney General referred, as unduly lenient, a 12 month drug treatment and testing order imposed following conviction of the defendant (C) on three counts of possessing Class A drugs, namely heroin, cocaine and ecstasy, with intent to supply, and possession of a Class A drug, namely heroin. Following a search of C's car and home quantities of drugs and drug paraphernalia were discovered. C's fingerprints were found on a wrap of cocaine but in interview C denied all knowledge of the drugs. Following conviction C disclosed that he had a serious addiction to drugs. The Attorney-General contended that C was a commercial street level dealer of drugs and the drug treatment and testing order failed to reflect the gravity of the offences, the menace of Class A drugs in society and the need for deterrence.

Held, allowing the reference, that a drug treatment and testing order was unduly lenient and a custodial sentence was required, *Attorney General's Reference (No.66 of 2003), Re* [2003] EWCA Crim 3514, [2004] 2 Cr. App. R. (S.) 22, [2004] C.L.Y. 3344, applied. The proper sentence in the court below was one of six years' imprisonment however, taking into account the principle of double jeopardy, the drug treatment and testing order would be quashed and four years and six months' imprisonment substituted, *R. v. Afonso (Americo Practicio)* [2004] EWCA Crim 2342, [2005] 1 Cr. App. R. (S.) 99, [2004] C.L.Y. 3454 and *R. v. Twisse (Michael James)* [2001] 2 Cr. App. R. (S.) 9, [2001] C.L.Y. 1282 considered.

ATTORNEY GENERAL'S REFERENCE (NO.42 OF 2005), *Re; sub nom.* R. v. CAMERON (DAVID) [2005] EWCA Crim 1722, Pill, L.J., CA (Crim Div).

3701. Possession with intent to supply–Controlled drugs–Classification of dried magic mushroom as Class A drug

The appellant (T) appealed against a sentence of two years' imprisonment following conviction for possession of Class A drugs with intent to supply. H had been found with 73 bags of magic mushrooms in a dried condition in his possession. He admitted that he had intended to sell some and the rest were for his own personal use. T contended that the sentence was manifestly excessive as the offence did not pass the custody threshold. Alternatively, that the judge had erred in equating magic mushrooms with other Class A drugs and had given insufficient credit for his previous good character.

Held, dismissing the appeal, that the sentence was neither wrong in principle nor manifestly excessive and reflected the mitigation of T's previous good character. T's admission of an intent to sell could be equated with small scale retail selling. No distinction should be drawn between magic mushrooms and other Class A drugs. Magic mushrooms had a powerful hallucinogenic effect similar, but milder, to LSD, even in low doses. Taking them could prove lethal and once a trip was started it could not be controlled or stopped.

R. v. THOMAS (STEPHEN FRANCIS), [2004] EWCA Crim 3092, [2005] 2 Cr. App. R. (S.) 10, Rose, L.J., CA (Crim Div).

3702. Possession with intent to supply—Fourth drug trafficking conviction—Mandatory minimum sentence of seven years' imprisonment

[Powers of Criminal Courts (Sentencing) Act 2000 s.110.]

The appellant (P) appealed against a sentence of seven years' imprisonment following her conviction for possessing a Class A drug with intent to supply. The mandatory sentence had been imposed under the Powers of Criminal Courts (Sentencing) Act 2000 s.110. P had a number of previous convictions and since August 1998 had been imprisoned three times for drug offences, which included both supplying and possessing with intent to supply Class A drugs. P contended that in the circumstances of the case it was unjust for the judge to have imposed the mandatory sentence of seven years. It was argued that P had intended to pass the drugs on to her partner and there was no suggestion of commercial supply.

Held, dismissing the appeal, that the judge had correctly concluded that he had no option but to impose the minimum term of seven years pursuant to s.110, *R. v. McInerney (William Patrick)* [2002] EWCA Crim 3003, [2003] 1 All E.R. 1089, [2003] C.L.Y. 3636 and *R. v. Harvey (Winston George)* [2000] 1 Cr. App. R. (S.) 368, [2000] C.L.Y. 1228 applied. The basis on which the judge had sentenced P for the instant offence could be capable of amounting to circumstances which would make it unjust to apply the full impact of s.110. However, that offence had resulted in P's fourth conviction for drug trafficking and since she had somehow escaped a seven year sentence for the third conviction, she must have been well aware of the consequences of committing yet another such offence.

R. v. PEARCE (LISA JAYNE), [2004] EWCA Crim 2029, [2005] 1 Cr. App. R. (S.) 73, Thomas, L.J., CA (Crim Div).

3703. Possession with intent to supply—Heroin valued at £250,000 found in taxi—Trusted position in supply chain—Undue leniency

The Attorney General referred as unduly lenient a sentence of five years' imprisonment imposed following conviction for possessing heroin with intent to supply. MA's taxi was stopped by the police and a 4.1kg bag, containing the equivalent of 1kg pure heroin was found inside. MA gave "no comment" replies when interviewed but told the officers that the bag had been left in the taxi by a passenger.

Held, allowing the reference, that the sentence was unduly lenient and would be increased to eight years' imprisonment. The offence was aggravated by the quantity of pure heroin, which had a value of £250,000, indicating that MA held a trusted position in the supply chain.

ATTORNEY GENERAL'S REFERENCE (NO.81 OF 2003), *Re; sub nom.* R. v. ATTIQ (MOHAMMED), [2004] EWCA Crim 994, [2005] 1 Cr. App. R. (S.) 3, Keene, L.J., CA (Crim Div).

3704. Possession with intent to supply–No evidence of significant dealing–12 months' imprisonment too long for guilty plea

D appealed against a sentence of 12 months' imprisonment for possessing cannabis with intent to supply. D admitted possessing 5.61 grammes of cannabis when his car was stopped by the police. A further 218.2g was found at his flat, along with a bag containing 409.9g of cannabis wrapped in cling film packets. D was originally charged with possession with intent to supply in relation to all three amounts. He pleaded not guilty, but accepted that he was guilty of possession. He was found guilty of possessing the two smaller amounts and of possession with intent to supply in respect of the larger amount. D was sentenced to one year's imprisonment on the count of possession with intent to supply and ordered to pay £363.50 towards prosecution costs.

Held, allowing the appeal, that there was no evidence that D had supplied significant amounts of cannabis and he had maintained throughout that it was for his personal use for pain relief purposes. The sentence was therefore too long and would be reduced to six months' imprisonment to reflect the fact that the judge had treated all three counts as guilty pleas. Although cannabis had been reclassified as a Class C drug, the maximum penalty for supplying Class C drugs had been increased to 14 years and possession with intent to supply invariably attracted a custodial sentence, *R. v. Doyle (Kevin)* [1996] 1 Cr. App. R. (S.) 449, [1996] C.L.Y. 1857 considered.

R. v. DONOVAN (TERRENCE MARK); *sub nom.* R. v. DONOVAN (TERENCE MARK), [2004] EWCA Crim 1237, [2005] 1 Cr. App. R. (S.) 16, Rose, L.J., CA (Crim Div).

3705. Possession with intent to supply–Possession of drugs–Fraudulent evasion of duty–Offences committed while defendant on bail–Undue leniency

The Attorney General referred, as unduly lenient, a sentence deferred for six months following a plea of guilty by the defendant (W) to possession of Class A drugs (cocaine) with intent to supply, possession of Class C drugs (cannabis) and being knowingly concerned in the fraudulent evasion of duty on tobacco. Police officers executed a search warrant at W's home and found 6.5 grams of cocaine and items associated with drug dealing. 2.4 kilograms of hand rolling tobacco was also discovered along with £4,000 in cash. W was released on bail and, some weeks later, was stopped by police and found in possession of 3 grams of cannabis, contraband tobacco and £4,300 in cash. W pleaded guilty on the basis that he supplied small amounts of cocaine to friends but took no money from them; his own drug use was subsidised by the sale of tobacco. The cash found came from tobacco sales and a loan repayment. The prosecution did not accept the basis of plea. The judge indicated that he did not believe W's account but later contradicted himself and accepted that W might be telling the truth that the cash came from tobacco sales. The Attorney General contended that a deferred sentence was unduly lenient and failed to mark the gravity of the offence, the need for deterrence, public concern and the aggravating features of (i) the degree of stock held and repeated supply, (ii) the fact that more than one offence had been committed whilst on bail, and (iii) the fact that the supplies made, albeit to a limited extent, had been commercial. In mitigation were W's pleas of guilty, his cooperation with the probation services, the comparatively small amount of drugs involved and the fact that he had become drug free since arrest. W contended that he was entitled to believe that he was being sentenced on the basis of the admissions made, despite the judge's approach to the sentencing process. The offence was not a conspiracy or the supply of drugs over a long period of time. The interests of W and of the public would be best served if he remained at liberty, especially as he was a considered a low risk of reoffending, he was working and had suffered financial loss as his money and car had been seized.

Held, allowing the reference, that the judge's sentencing comments were ambiguous. Having regard to the potential importance of knowing the precise basis on which a sentence was passed, it was unfortunate that no Newton hearing was ordered. In the circumstances of the case, particularly the commission of offences whilst on bail and the involvement in illicit tobacco, even on a plea, a sentence of at least three years was to be expected in the court below, together with a possible consecutive sentence for the tobacco offences. It followed that deferment of the sentence was unduly lenient and was quashed. A sentence of two years' imprisonment was substituted; however, taking into account double jeopardy and the financial penalty imposed on W, it was not appropriate to impose a consecutive sentence for the tobacco offences.

ATTORNEY GENERAL'S REFERENCE (NO.139 OF 2004), *Re; sub nom.* R. v. WORTH (DUNCAN) [2005] EWCA Crim 749, Rose, L.J. (V-P), CA (Crim Div).

3706. Possession with intent to supply—Prison officers—Heroin smuggled into prison—Cooperation by naming supplier and intended recipient

The appellant (M) appealed against a sentence of seven years' imprisonment following a guilty plea to possessing a Class A controlled drug, heroin, with intent to supply. M, a prison officer, was found in possession during a search at work. He admitted smuggling it into prison for the use of a named inmate. M also named the person who had given him the drugs, who became his codefendant, and admitted that he had smuggled in a package two weeks earlier. M offered to give evidence for the prosecution against his codefendant.

Held, allowing the appeal, that six years' imprisonment was appropriate for a prison officer who had smuggled heroin into prison for the use of an inmate, but who had cooperated fully with the authorities by naming both the supplier and intended recipient, and offering to give evidence against the supplier, *R. v. Prince (James Peter)* [1996] 1 Cr. App. R. (S.) 335, [1996] C.L.Y. 1853 and *R. v. Whenman (Andrew Henry)* [2001] EWCA Crim 328, [2001] 2 Cr. App. R. (S.) 87, [2001] C.L.Y. 1281 considered.

R. v. MILLS (GARY), [2004] EWCA Crim 1466, [2005] 1 Cr. App. R. (S.) 38, Hooper, L.J., CA (Crim Div).

3707. Possession with intent to supply—Sentence length—Supply to non users—Commercial supply—Young offenders—Ecstasy

The 19 year old appellant (M) appealed against a sentence of four years' detention in a young offender's institution for possession of a Class A drug with intent to supply. Plain clothes officers saw M and his co defendant (C) approach people in the street and offer to sell them Ecstasy. M and C were arrested. ecstasy was found concealed upon M and C. M pleaded guilty. M had previous convictions for criminal damage and resisting a police officer. The recorder said that M was engaged in the intended commercial supply of Class A drugs and it was an aggravating feature that M and C were seeking to draw in non users. M argued that (1) his sentence was excessive and would make him a long term prisoner for his first offence involving drugs; (2) the recorder placed too great an emphasis on deterrence; (3) insufficient account had been taken of the fact that no money was found upon him, indeed rather than being involved in commercial supply, he had been involved in an unsophisticated act of drunken stupidity.

Held, allowing the appeal, that (1) having regard to M's age and the impact on a young man of being made a long term prisoner, to do so on M's first custodial sentence was excessive. (2) The recorder had been entitled to regard as an aggravating feature that M was not offering to supply other drug users, but was offering to supply passing members of the public in the street. (3) The way the drugs were concealed upon M and his codefendant suggested something other than mere drunken stupidity, however there was no evidence that the subject incident was anything other than a single occasion of supply, *R. v. Weeks (David Alexander)* [1999] 2 Cr. App. R. (S.) 16, [1999] C.L.Y. 1148 and *R. v. Djahit (Turkesh)* [1999] 2 Cr. App. R. (S.) 142, [1999] C.L.Y. 1137 and *R. v. Twisse (Michael James)* [2001] 2 Cr. App. R. (S.) 9, [2001] C.L.Y. 1282 considered. Accordingly a sentence of three and a half years' detention in a young offender's institution was substituted.

R. v. McCOURT (RICHARD JOSEPH), [2004] EWCA Crim 3294, [2005] 2 Cr. App. R. (S.) 41, May, L.J., CA (Crim Div).

3708. Practice directions–Custodial sentences–Release on licence

The Lord Chief Justice has handed a down a practice direction amending *Practice Direction (Criminal Proceedings: Consolidation)* [2002] 1 W.L.R. 2870, [2002] C.L.Y. 899. An additional section was added to Part I of the 2002 consolidated criminal practice direction and amendments were made to Annex C. The Secretary of State had a power to direct that a prisoner might be released early on home detention curfew. Notwithstanding the exercise of that power, the purpose of the amendments was to make clear that *Practice Direction (CA (Crim Div): Custodial Sentences: Explanations)* [1998] 1 W.L.R. 278, [1998] C.L.Y. 1333 continued to have effect subject to the amendments.

PRACTICE DIRECTION (SUP CT: CUSTODIAL SENTENCES: EXPLANATIONS); *sub nom.* CONSOLIDATED CRIMINAL PRACTICE DIRECTION (AMENDMENT NO.7) (EXPLANATIONS FOR THE IMPOSITION OF CUSTODIAL SENTENCES) [2004] 1 W.L.R. 1878, Lord Woolf of Barnes, L.C.J., Sup Ct.

3709. Practice directions–Mandatory life imprisonment–Procedure under Criminal Justice Act 2003 s.269 and Sch.21–Transitional arrangements under s.267 and Sch.22–Practice of Secretary of State prior to December 2002

[Criminal Justice Act 2003 s.267, s.269, Sch.21, Sch.22.]

The Lord Chief Justice issued a practice direction which replaced *Practice Direction (Sup Ct: Crime: Mandatory Life Sentences) (No.1)* [2004] 1 W.L.R. 1874, [2005] 3 C.L. 459. Its purpose was to give practical guidance as to the procedure for passing a mandatory life sentence under the Criminal Justice Act 2003 s.269 and Sch.21. The direction also gave guidance as to the transitional arrangements under s.267 of and Sch.22 to the Act. It clarified the correct approach to the examination of the practice of the Secretary of State prior to December, 2002 for the purposes of Sch.22 to the Act in the light of the judgment in *R. v. Sullivan (Melvin Terrence)* [2004] EWCA Crim 1762, [2005] 1 Cr. App. R. 3, [2004] 10 C.L. 408.

PRACTICE DIRECTION (SUP CT: CRIME: MANDATORY LIFE SENTENCES) (NO.2) [2004] 1 W.L.R. 2551, Lord Woolf of Barnes, L.C.J., Sup Ct.

3710. Practice directions–Mandatory life imprisonment–Release on licence

The Lord Chief Justice handed down a practice direction amending *Practice Direction (Criminal Proceedings: Consolidation)* [2002] 1 W.L.R. 2870, [2002] C.L.Y. 899. The revised direction contained, amongst other things, a paragraph dealing with mandatory life sentences and a paragraph and amended annex dealing with explanations for the imposition of custodial sentences. The purpose of the amendments was to make it clear that *Practice Direction (CA (Crim Div): Custodial Sentences: Explanations)* [1998] 1 W.L.R. 278, [1998] C.L.Y. 1333 continued to have effect subject to the amendments the 2002 direction.

PRACTICE DIRECTION (SUP CT: CRIME: MANDATORY LIFE SENTENCES) (NO.1); *sub nom.* PRACTICE DIRECTION (CRIMINAL PROCEEDINGS: CONSOLIDATION (AMENDMENT)); CONSOLIDATED CRIMINAL PRACTICE DIRECTION (AMENDMENT NO.6) (MANDATORY LIFE SENTENCES) [2004] 1 W.L.R. 1874, Lord Woolf of Barnes, L.C.J., Sup Ct.

3711. Prison mutiny—Custodial sentences—Four year starting point for serious offence by serving prisoners not manifestly excessive

[Prison Security Act 1992 s.1.]

W and other offenders appealed against sentences of four years or more for participating in a mutiny at a young offenders' institution. The offenders had, at various levels of involvement, manufactured weapons, assaulted prison officers, kidnapped and assaulted a prison officer, lit fires and ransacked offices. The riot, which lasted nine hours, caused damage worth £250,000. The sentencing judge formed the view that a minimum four-year sentence was appropriate for all offenders, then, depending on each offender's level of involvement, imposed either the minimum or longer sentences. The offenders argued that the judge's overall starting level was manifestly excessive and that the lesser involvement of some offenders put them at a much lower level.

Held, dismissing the appeals, that the judge had rightly concluded that anyone who participated with the intention of overthrowing lawful prison authority was committing the serious offence of mutiny under the Prison Security Act 1992 s.1. The exact degree of involvement did not need to be taken into account under s.1, because the more who joined in, however limited their involvement, the worse the situation became. The judge had correctly determined that four years was the overall starting level because it was a serious offence, with substantial damage and violence to an officer, even if some offenders had not committed any aggravating aspects. The judge had given significant credit to the one offender who had offered a guilty plea at the earliest opportunity. The judge was right not to reduce the sentences on the basis that the totality of the offenders' mutiny sentences and their existing sentences was very long because the mutiny related offences were very serious, *R. v. Ali (Idris)* [1998] 2 Cr. App. R. (S.) 123, [1998] C.L.Y. 1237 followed.

R. v. WHITEMAN (MARK); R. v. BROWN (BILLY); R. v. SPOKES (PAUL GEORGE); R. v. DRAPER (JAMES THOMAS); R. v. BRIGHT (BARRY JAMES), [2004] EWCA Crim 569, [2004] 2 Cr. App. R. (S.) 59, Kay, L.J., CA (Crim Div).

3712. Public nuisance—Improper use of telecommunications—Hoax calls to emergency services—Sentence reflecting need for public protection

The appellant (L) appealed against a sentence of eight years' imprisonment imposed following his guilty plea to 12 counts of public nuisance. L had made a series of hoax phone calls to the emergency services claiming, inter alia, that he was reporting a fire or that he required an ambulance. L had numerous previous convictions for similar offences and had only been recently released from prison following a term of five years' imprisonment for public nuisance. Psychiatric reports indicated that L was suffering from a severe personality disorder which was not likely to respond to treatment and was at a high risk of reoffending. L submitted that the sentencing judge's starting point was too high.

Held, dismissing the appeal, that whilst this was a lengthy sentence there was no reason to believe that L would alter his behaviour upon release from prison. He had shown no signs of changing his behaviour after previous sentences despite strenuous efforts to help him deal with his problems and he had no real insight into his condition. His behaviour was having a significant impact upon public safety and there was a real risk that his offending would adversely affect someone in real danger due to emergency resources being engaged on his hoax call.

R. v. LOWRIE (ROBIN JASON), [2004] EWCA Crim 2325, [2005] 1 Cr. App. R. (S.) 95, Latham, L.J., CA (Crim Div).

3713. Public nuisance—Telephones—Threatening telephone calls—Animal rights campaigners

[Protection from Harassment Act 1997 s.2, s.4, s.5.]

The appellants (H) and (L), animal rights campaigners, appealed against sentences of 18 months' imprisonment and five years' imprisonment respectively for causing a public nuisance. Both appellants had pleaded guilty. The context of the offences was that there had been a letter bomb campaign. Neither appellant had anything to do with the sending of such bombs. However, some of those targeted in that campaign thereafter received malicious telephone calls. The appellants were particularly involved in telephoning people connected with Huntingdon Life Sciences. Some of the calls made by L were threatening, with some of the threats referring to the fact that letter bombs had been sent. L only pleaded guilty at the last moment. H made over 1,000 nuisance calls, but none of the calls contained any reference to letter bombs or any threat in relation to them. L submitted that in arriving at his sentence the judge must have taken a figure of about seven years as a starting point. L submitted that that was too high. L submitted that the sentencing judge had failed to give proper weight to the fact that the phone calls were not repeated to any particular victim, no actual violence was offered to anyone and no property was damaged.

Held, allowing the appeals, that the sentencing judge should have considered that had the prosecution brought proceedings against H under the Protection from Harassment Act 1997 s.2 there would only have been available a maximum sentence of six months' imprisonment. In appropriate cases that form of prosecution rather than prosecution for public nuisance was commended as there was power to make a restraining order to protect any victim from further conduct pursuant to s.5. The appropriate sentence for H was nine months' imprisonment. With respect to L, a starting point of seven years was manifestly excessive. L was a man of good character and was not in a conspiracy with the bomber. Although it was a serious crime, there was no actual violence or criminal damage sustained. The facts were less grave than in *R. v. Schilling (Rae)* [2002] EWCA Crim 3198, *Schilling* considered. It was borne in mind that under s.4 the maximum sentence would have been five years. The appropriate sentence for L was 30 months' imprisonment.

R. v. HOLLIDAY (PAUL); R. v. LEBOUTILLIER (PAUL), [2004] EWCA Crim 1847, [2005] 1 Cr. App. R. (S.) 70, Clarke, L.J., CA (Crim Div).

3714. Rape–Aggravating features–Victim detained in hotel room–Multiple anal and vaginal rape–Forced oral sex

S appealed against a sentence of 12 years' imprisonment following his conviction on four counts of rape. S had broken into the victim's hotel room, threatened to kill her, raped her twice anally and vaginally and made her perform oral sex. He also ejaculated in her vagina. S used force to detain the victim in the room for two hours and ripped the telephone from the wall.

Held, dismissing the appeal, that the sentence was severe but not excessive. The offence was aggravated by the use of force, the mental effect on the victim, including the fear that she might have contracted the HIV virus, and the fact she had been forced to perform oral sex, *R. v. Millberry (William Christopher)* [2002] EWCA Crim 2891, [2003] 1 W.L.R. 546, [2003] C.L.Y. 3829 considered.

R. v. STEWARD (WILLIAM), [2004] EWCA Crim 1093, [2005] 1 Cr. App. R. (S.) 5, Rose, L.J. (Vice President), CA (Crim Div).

3715. Rape–Attempts–Indecent assault–Offender abusing granddaughter over many years–Undue leniency

The Attorney General referred as unduly lenient a total sentence of three years' imprisonment for attempted rape, gross indecency with a child and indecent assault. The defendant (W) was 70 years of age at the time of trial and had committed the offences over a period of eight years prior to the year 2000. The victim (V) was W's granddaughter and had been between six and 13 at the time of the offences. The Attorney General argued that the offences comprised a deliberate and escalating course of conduct over a number of years that had only recently ceased. V had been forced to give evidence at trial and W had shown no remorse. Whilst account was to be taken of W's age, his ill health and the need for him to look after his sick wife, the sentence imposed failed to adequately reflect the gravity of the offences and their impact upon V. The appropriate sentence was eight years' imprisonment.

Held, allowing the reference, that taking into account the course of conduct over a number of years, the gravity of the offences and W's not guilty plea, the sentence was unduly lenient. In those circumstances, the sentence was quashed and a sentence of four years and six months' imprisonment was substituted.

ATTORNEY GENERAL'S REFERENCE (NO.125 OF 2004), *Re* [2005] EWCA Crim 259, Rose, L.J. (V-P), CA (Crim Div).

3716. Rape–Children–Sexual abuse of daughter aged between 14 and 27–Undue leniency

The Attorney General referred to the court as unduly lenient a total sentence of five years' imprisonment imposed on the offender (X), following his pleas of guilty to two specimen counts of indecent assault, four counts of rape and eleven counts of incest, in respect of his daughter (V). X had pleaded guilty on the day fixed for trial. He had been sentenced to 12 months' imprisonment on each count of indecent assault, committed when V had been aged upwards of 14; five years' imprisonment for each count of rape, committed when she had been 15 or 16; and two years' imprisonment for each count of incest, committed when she had been between 17 and 27. The sentences were to run concurrently. X's abuse of his daughter had progressed from touching her breasts over her clothes, to digital penetration of her vagina, and to rape. Thereafter, he had regularly had sexual intercourse with her, as a result of which she had twice conceived. The Attorney General relied on the following aggravating features: a gross breach of trust was involved; the offences had started when V was aged 14; pregnancies had resulted; the offences were planned, repeated and represented a course of conduct with a background of fear and violence; V had suffered a profound and long term detrimental effect, particularly impeding her ability to form normal relationships, and her children had been taken into care. The mitigation relied on included X's guilty plea, the argument that his conduct could not be categorised as a campaign of rape when there were only four specific occasions when the offence of rape had been committed, and the fact that he did not present a risk to the public at large.

Held, allowing the reference, that the sentence was unduly lenient. Irrespective of whether the four offences of rape should properly be characterised as a campaign, X had over many years sexually abused his daughter. That abuse had been of increasing gravity and had culminated in the offences of rape. Having regard to the very late plea of guilty, which could only attract a very modest discount, concurrent sentences of 12 years' imprisonment for the offences of rape would have been appropriate. Therefore, the sentences of five years' imprisonment for each offence of rape were lenient to a very significant degree. Taking into account the element of double jeopardy, sentences of ten years' imprisonment were imposed in respect of each offence of rape, to run concurrently with each other and with the sentences imposed below for the offences of indecent assault and incest.

ATTORNEY GENERAL'S REFERENCE (NO.8 OF 2005), *Re* [2005] EWCA Crim 1002, Rose, L.J. (V-P), CA (Crim Div).

3717. Rape–Discretionary life imprisonment–Notional determinate sentence incorporating element reflecting danger to public–Double punishment

The appellant (W) appealed against a specified minimum sentence of eight years' imprisonment imposed on a discretionary life sentence following his conviction of two counts of rape. On both occasions he had attacked strangers at night in the street, overpowering his victim and then raping her. His second victim was 14 years old. A psychiatric report stated that W was at grave and unpredictable risk of committing further sexual offences. W contended that (1) it was wrong to base the specified period on the 15 year plus category specified in *R. v. Millberry (William Christopher)* [2002] EWCA Crim 2891, [2003] 1 W.L.R. 546, [2003] C.L.Y. 3829 because that category included an extension to the sentence due to the dangerousness of a person convicted of more than one offence. Thus, an element of double sentencing was involved as the necessity of protecting the public from the danger posed by W was satisfied by the imposition of the life sentence; (2) the sentencing judge had failed to follow the approach set out in *R. v. M (Young Offender: Time in Custody on Remand)* [1999] 1 W.L.R. 485, [1998] C.L.Y. 1269 in that he had not deducted the number of days spent on remand, which did not count towards the specified minimum period.

Held, allowing the appeal, that (1) when fixing the determinate term, the sentencing judge should have discounted from it the element reflecting the need to protect the public from the danger posed by W, because that was already reflected in the imposition of a discretionary life sentence. However, these were particularly serious offences and when their circumstances were considered, together with the fact that W had been convicted after trial, a sentence of 16 years' imprisonment was appropriate. This consisted of five years for the first offence and 11 years for the second, *Millberry* considered. The fixing of a notional determinative sentence was not a precise calculation but required a balancing exercise to take account of the risk of double punishment and ensure that the public risk element was not included. However, it was appropriate to reflect an element of of deterrence as necessary, *R. v. M* considered. W's sentence should have been reduced to reflect the time he had spent on remand, therefore the minimum term was amended to eight years less 304 days.

R. v. WHEATON (DAVID GEORGE), [2004] EWCA Crim 2270, [2005] 1 Cr. App. R. (S.) 82, Rose, L.J., CA (Crim Div).

3718. Rape–Indecent assault–Prolonged campaign–Length of minimum term

The appellant (S) appealed against a sentence of life imprisonment with a specified period of eight years and four and a half months which was derived from a notional determinate sentence of 19 years for rape, attempted rape and indecent assault. S had been convicted of three counts of rape, four counts of indecent assault and one count of attempted rape having earlier pleaded guilty to one count of rape and one of indecent assault. The rapes had been committed over a short period of time on different women. Each offence had involved violence and degrading acts. On at least one occasion S had produced a handgun. One of the rapes had been committed in the company of another man. S appealed against the specified period, contending that the notional determinate sentence was excessive because it allowed for the protection of the public which was not necessary as his release would be on licence.

Held, dismissing the appeal, that the notional determinate sentence was appropriate. The submission that the notional determinate sentence had taken account of the need to protect the public was wrong. The judge had decided on the notional determinate sentence in accordance with guidance given in other cases which was the correct approach. The question of the protection of the public was a matter for the Parole Board and had not influenced the judge's decision. It was difficult to think of a worse example of a campaign of rape, *R. v. O'Connor (Michael Joseph)* (1994) 15 Cr. App. R. (S.) 473, *R. v. M (Young Offender: Time in Custody on Remand)* [1999] 1 W.L.R. 485, [1998] C.L.Y. 1269, *R. v. Billam (Keith)* [1986] 1 W.L.R. 349, [1986] C.L.Y. 868, *R. v. Millberry (William Christopher)* [2002] EWCA Crim 2891, [2003] 1 W.L.R. 546, [2003] C.L.Y. 3829 and *R. v. Henry (Errol George)* (1988) 10 Cr. App. R. (S.) 327, [1989] C.L.Y. 1070 applied.

R. v. SMITH (DAVID), [2004] EWCA Crim 1040, [2004] 2 Cr. App. R. (S.) 92, Potter, L.J., CA (Crim Div).

3719. Rape–Kidnapping–16 year old offender abducted victim at knife point

The appellant (M) appealed against a sentence of three years' detention for kidnapping and a concurrent sentence of six years' detention for rape. M was aged 16 at the time of the offences. M had abducted the victim at knife point before forcing her to perform oral sex and then raping her twice. M was traced through DNA samples left at the scene. M initially denied all allegations but eventually pleaded guilty on rearraignment. M had a number of previous convictions and had not responded to community punishments. M was in custody for other matters at the time of his trial. M argued that (1) the judge had taken too high a starting point when sentencing him; (2) the judge had given insufficient credit for his plea and his age; (3) he had shown remorse and had made substantial efforts to improve himself whilst in custody.

Held, dismissing the appeal, that there was nothing whatever wrong with the sentence passed by the judge. M had a bad record, even at his young age. He had had the chance of responding to community punishments, but had chosen not to. The rape in the instant case plainly attracted the higher starting point of eight years, *R. v. Millberry (William Christopher)* [2002] EWCA Crim 2891, [2003] 1 W.L.R. 546, [2003] C.L.Y. 3829 considered. The complainant was abducted and was raped twice. Moreover, there were significant aggravating features, namely the forced oral sex and the use of a knife. The instant case was a grave and deeply disturbing one. The discount given by the judge for age and plea, bearing in mind that the plea came after M had been traced through DNA, was both ample and substantial. In a case of the instant nature, progress in custody, whilst welcome, would not persuade the court to reduce M's sentence further.

R. v. M (PATRICK), [2004] EWCA Crim 1679, [2005] 1 Cr. App. R. (S.) 49, Kennedy, L.J., CA (Crim Div).

3720. Rape–Trapping victim in car to carry out offence–Undue leniency

The Attorney General referred to the court as unduly lenient a sentence of four years' imprisonment imposed on the offender (H) following his conviction, after a trial, of rape. H and two other men had accosted two women as they left a nightclub. The victim had been trapped in the front of a car, where H touched her breasts, digitally penetrated her and raped her for a very short period of time, which was thought to be about 10 seconds. Whilst this was going on, a second person began to fondle her breasts. The victim then tried to escape from the car but was prevented from doing so. The Attorney General relied on the following aggravating features: the assault had taken place whilst the victim had been detained in the car; the victim had been indecently assaulted by another man; and the offence should have attracted a sentence in excess of the five year guideline for a rape without any aggravating or mitigating features.

Held, dismissing the reference, that there were no features which justified the conclusion that a sentence of less than five years' imprisonment was appropriate in the case. However, the rape had involved the use of minimal violence and had lasted for a relatively short period of time. There were no circumstances in which the appropriate sentence could have been raised above the basic five years' imprisonment. A sentence of four years' imprisonment was lenient. However, taking into account the rules on double jeopardy, it was not unduly lenient so as to justify the interference of the court.

ATTORNEY GENERAL'S REFERENCE (NO.143 OF 2004), *Re; sub nom*. R. v. HASAN (MIRIWAN ALI) [2005] EWCA Crim 506, Latham, L.J., CA (Crim Div).

3721. Rape–Violence–18 year old offender absconding from bail for 22 years–Undue leniency

The appellant (M) appealed against consecutive sentences of six years' imprisonment to rape and 10 months' imprisonment for absconding from bail. M had committed the rape when aged 18 and had used violence over and above that needed to commit the offence. He had met the victim (V) in a nightclub and afterwards a group of five people, including M and V, had gone to the house of V's friend. V had left to get a taxi in the early hours of the morning and M had followed her outside, then pulled her into a passageway and raped her. She had then escaped, whereupon M had chased after her and hit her several times. M had been arrested and released on bail. He absconded from bail and was only apprehended 22 years later. He had not been convicted of any further offences during that time. The rape had a devastating effect on V, who had been admitted to a psychiatric hospital for a period of time, had a drink problem and had made a number of suicide attempts. M argued that the sentence for the offence of rape was excessive in the light of the authorities and at the time of the offence. In relation to the sentence for the bail offence, M argued that it amounted to double jeopardy in that he was being sentenced again for the anguish caused to V over a 22 year period.

Held, allowing the appeal, that although the sentence was not manifestly excessive a reduction in the rape sentence was justified. The judge had been correct to sentence in accordance with current sentencing guidance despite the fact that the offence had been committed more than 20 years before when sentences for rape were lower, *R. v. Millberry (William Christopher)* [2002] EWCA Crim 2891, [2003] 1 W.L.R. 546, [2003] C.L.Y. 3829 applied. There were two aggravating features, namely the fact that M had used excessive violence and the severe consequences for V in terms of serious and long term psychological trauma. M's age at the time of the commission of the offence was a relevant mitigating factor, *R. v. Matthews (Paul)* [1998] 1 Cr. App. R. (S.) 220, [1998] C.L.Y. 1339 and *Attorney General's Reference (No.54 of 1998), Re* [2000] 1 Cr. App. R. (S.) 219, [1999] C.L.Y. 1315 considered. In view of M's age and guilty plea, the sentence of six years' imprisonment for the offence of rape was reduced to one of five years' imprisonment. The sentence for breach of bail had been imposed because of the length of time for which M had absconded. He had left the jurisdiction and changed his name, and had failed to surrender to justice in later years when he was more mature. The judge had accordingly been entitled to impose a sentence towards the upper end of the 12 month maximum for this offence.

R. v. McKENDRICK (GARY GORDON), [2005] EWCA Crim 180, [2005] 2 Cr. App. R. (S.) 68, Clarke, L.J., CA (Crim Div).

3722. Restraining orders – Breach – Repeated breach

[Mental Health Act 1983; Protection from Harassment Act 1997 s.4.]

The appellant (T) appealed against a total sentence of four years and two months' imprisonment comprising 10 months for breach of licence and a consecutive term of three years and four months' imprisonment for breach of a restraining order. T had been sentenced twice previously for breaching the restraining order. The order had been imposed following T's harassment of an elderly lady contrary to the Protection from Harassment Act 1997 s.4. The most recent breach had occurred when T approached the victim's door and rang her doorbell, causing her severe distress; T had also been drinking, contrary to his licence conditions. A psychiatric report stated that T was dependent on alcohol and suffered from a paranoid psychotic disorder caused by alcohol abuse. T submitted that whilst his behaviour had caused distress to the victim, it was not violent and he did not pose a risk of violence. T argued that the judge had failed to take account of his early guilty plea and had not acknowledged his mental state.

Held, dismissing the appeal, that the totality of T's sentence in the circumstances was not too long and the sentencing judge had been entitled to make him a long term prisoner. T had a history of disobedience of court orders, had been convicted of the more serious of the offences under the Act and had caused the victim great fear hence the sentence was rightly towards the top end of the scale of sentencing powers available to the judge, *R. v. Liddle (Mark) (Appeal against Sentence)* [1999] 3 All E.R. 816, [1999] C.L.Y. 1188 considered. The credit given to T for his guilty plea had been limited due to him not making that plea until he had been confronted with closed circuit television footage of the offence. It was acknowledged that T had problems with his mental condition, however those problems were not sufficient to enable a hospital order or guardianship order to be made under the Mental Health Act 1983. T remained unwilling to address his offending behaviour and as a consequence he represented a great risk of reoffending.

R. v. TETLEY (JOHN), [2004] EWCA Crim 3228, [2005] 2 Cr. App. R. (S.) 35, May, L.J., CA (Crim Div).

3723. Restraining orders–Repeals–Validity of restraining order following repeal of s.5A Sex Offenders Act 1997

[Criminal Appeal Act 1968 s.11 (3) (b); Interpretation Act 1978 s.17(2) (b); Sex Offenders Act 1997 s.5A; Powers of Criminal Courts (Sentencing) Act 2000 s.155; Sexual Offences Act 2003.]

The appellant (M) appealed against the imposition of a restraining order erroneously made under the Sex Offenders Act 1997 s.5A after its repeal by the Sexual Offences Act 2003. On April 23, 2004, M had pleaded guilty to making indecent photographs of a child and was sentenced. Owing to an oversight, no application was made for a restraining order under s.5A of the 1997 Act. Thereafter, the case was relisted in order for a restraining order to be added to the sentence. On May 1, the 1997 Act was repealed and replaced by the 2003 Act. When the case came before a judge on May 14, the fact that the law had changed was overlooked by all the parties. A restraining order was made under s.5A of the 1997 Act for a period of three years, from the date of the hearing rather than from the date of sentence. The judge subsequently became aware of the error and concluded that the restraining order was unlawful and ineffective. The Crown argued that (1) the order was valid and effective; (2) as a result of the Interpretation Act 1978 s.17(2) (b), the restraining order had effect as if it had been made under the 2003 Act; (3) the court should exercise its discretion under the Criminal Appeal Act 1968 s.11 (3) (b) to replace the restraining order made under the 1997 Act with a sexual offences prevention order pursuant to the 2003 Act.

Held, allowing the appeal, that (1) the Powers of Criminal Courts (Sentencing) Act 2000 s.155(2) enabled the Crown Court to vary or rescind an order within 28 days of the date on which the sentence was originally imposed. In the instant case, although the matter had gone back to the court within 28 days, the default position in s.155(5) did not apply as the judge had specifically directed that the restraining order take effect from May 14 and not from April 23, when sentence was originally passed and before the repeal of the 1997 Act. (2) Arguments based on s.17(2) of the 1978 Act were flawed in that they assumed that the 2003 Act reenacted with modifications the provisions of the 1997 Act. Even if that were accepted, the Crown's argument assumed that what was done on May 14 was a "thing done" under the 1997 Act, although by that date it had been repealed. It thus assumed the very matter at issue, namely the validity or effectiveness of what had been done on May 14. In the instant case, the application for a restraining order had been made after the 1997 Act had been repealed. It therefore followed that what was done on May 14 was not done "under" the 1997 Act. (3) Under the 2003 Act, a sexual offences order had to be made for a period of not less than five years or until further order whereas orders under the 1997 Act could be for a shorter period. In the instant case, the judge indicated that he was not prepared to make an order for longer than three years. The instant court was required by s.11 (3) (b) of the 1968 Act not to exercise its discretion so that, taking the case as a whole, an appellant was dealt with more severely on appeal than he was by the trial judge. Accordingly, the instant court felt unable to impose a sexual offences prevention order. The restraining order was invalid, of no effect and was accordingly set aside.

R. v. MONUMENT (ANDREW), [2005] EWCA Crim 30, [2005] 2 Cr. App. R. (S.) 57, May, L.J., CA (Crim Div).

3724. Robbery–Elderly victim's car and purse stolen–Undue leniency

The Attorney General referred as unduly lenient sentences of 30 months' imprisonment and 30 months' detention in a young offender institution following guilty pleas to robbery. The defendants (J and M) had tricked their way into the elderly victim's home. They had stated falsely that they had a gun and had proceeded to steal the victim's car keys and her purse. They subsequently used her car keys to steal her car to commit a further offence. J was 18 years old and M was 27. J, who was on bail at the date of the offence, was sentenced to a further consecutive sentence of 15 months' detention in a young offender institution in respect of five other offences, bringing his total sentence to three years and nine months. J also asked for 66 other offences to be taken into account. The Attorney General argued that given that the robbery had taken place in the house of an elderly victim, that the value of the goods taken had been high and that J and M had claimed to have a gun, the sentence did not reflect the seriousness of the offence.

Held, allowing the reference, that taking account of the aggravating features, sentences of 30 months' imprisonment and 30 months' detention were quite plainly unduly lenient. The sentences that could be expected were five years' imprisonment and five years' detention. The sentences would be quashed and, taking into account double jeopardy, they would be replaced with sentences of four years. Bearing in mind the totality of J's sentence, the 15 months' detention for the other offences was ordered to run concurrently.

ATTORNEY GENERAL'S REFERENCE (NOS.144 AND 145 OF 2004), *Re; sub nom.* R. v. JOHNSTON (GEORGE); R. v. McSHEFFERTY (JASON), [2005] EWCA Crim 280, [2005] 2 Cr. App. R. (S.) 77, Rose, L.J., CA (Crim Div).

3725. Robbery–Gang attack on middle aged couple in home at night

The Attorney General referred as unduly lenient concurrent sentences imposed on the offender (W) of five years' imprisonment for robbery, 12 months for attempted theft and 18 months for assault occasioning actual bodily harm. Two further counts of burglary and wounding with intent were left to remain on the file. W, who had pleaded guilty to the offences, had with two associates committed a burglary of a remote property owned by the victims, an elderly couple. W had confronted the female victim (F), who was asleep in her bedroom. The associates confronted her husband. W dragged F, who suffered from Crohn's disease, from her bed by her hair. She was attacked with a bottle and kicked as demands for money were made. She was forced to hand over her rings following threats of death. F's husband was struck on the head with an ashtray and in the face with a cup. Money, a mobile phone and computer equipment were stolen in addition to the jewellery. There had also been an attempt to steal F's husband's car. The Attorney General relied on the night time and group nature of the offence, the fact that F was a vulnerable victim and the fact that the sustained violence was in excess of that required to commit an offence of robbery.

Held, dismissing the reference, that attacks on vulnerable victims in their own homes were particularly despicable and would merit very severe punishment with a likely sentence in double figures, *Attorney General's Reference (Nos.32 and 33 of 1995), Re* [1996] 2 Cr. App. R. (S.) 346, [1997] C.L.Y. 1421 considered. Nine years' imprisonment was an appropriate starting point because despite the appalling nature of the events, the group had not gone armed with a weapon and did not use a knife, although an ashtray and a bottle were used. It followed that a sentence within the bracket of four to seven years' imprisonment would be appropriate where there was a single offence and a guilty plea was made, *Attorney General's Reference (No.48 of 2000), Re* [2001] 1 Cr. App. R. (S.) 123, [2000] C.L.Y. 1413 considered. A sentence of six years' imprisonment would have been appropriate allowing for the standard reduction of a third for a guilty plea. Accordingly, having regard to the principle of double jeopardy, it was wrong in principle to interfere with the sentence. The sentence of five years for robbery, although lenient, was not unduly so. There had been no error of principle in the sentence so that public confidence would not be damaged if the sentence was not altered, *Attorney General's References (Nos.31, 45, 43, 42, 50 and 51 of 2003), Re* [2004] EWCA Crim 1934, [2005] 1 Cr. App. R. (S.) 76, [2004] C.L.Y. 3304 considered.

ATTORNEY GENERAL'S REFERENCE (NO.38 OF 2005), *Re* [2005] EWCA Crim 1678, Clarke, L.J., CA (Crim Div).

3726. Robbery–Mitigation–Level of violence–Appropriate reduction–Undue leniency

The Attorney General referred as unduly lenient a concurrent sentence of three years' imprisonment imposed on the defendant (G) who had pleaded guilty to robbery, assault occasioning actual bodily harm and unlawfully inflicting grievous bodily harm. G and another offender had attacked a group of three strangers. G had attacked two of the victims, punching one in the face and beating the other with a weapon, causing serious and permanent injury. G had threatened the victims saying that he had a firearm, and he had stolen a mobile phone, cash and an item of jewellery from the second victim. The Attorney General submitted that the sentence was unduly lenient because it failed to acknowledge the gravity of the offences, and to take into account the need for deterrence, the level of public concern regarding the prevalence of robberies at night in public places, and the aggravating features of the instant case.

Held, allowing the reference, that the sentence was unduly lenient. The appropriate sentence was five years' imprisonment to reflect G's previous convictions for similar offences and the degree of violence used with a weapon. However, the mitigating factors, including pleas of guilty, expressions of remorse and G's young age, meant that the sentencing judge had been correct in not making G a long term prisoner by imposing a sentence of four years' imprisonment. Accordingly, and taking into account the principle of double jeopardy, the sentence of three years' imprisonment for robbery was quashed and a sentence of three years and nine months' imprisonment was substituted, *Attorney General's Reference (Nos.4 and 7 of 2002), Re* [2002] EWCA Crim 127, [2002] 2 Cr. App. R. (S.) 77, [2002] C.L.Y. 4066 and *Attorney General's Reference (Nos.150 and 151 of 2002), Re* [2003] EWCA Crim 1165, [2003] 2 Cr. App. R. (S.) 111 considered. In cases where the correct starting point had been recognised and the real dispute was whether the sentence had been appropriately reduced to reflect any mitigating factors, the reference of cases should not be encouraged unless there was an obvious and substantial departure from good sentencing practice, some peculiar feature of local outrage, or some other special consideration that made it appropriate for the Attorney General to seek leave.

ATTORNEY GENERAL'S REFERENCE (NO.96 OF 2004), *Re; sub nom*. R. v. KEENAN (MARTIN THOMAS) [2004] EWCA Crim 2853, Potter, L.J., CA (Crim Div).

3727. **Robbery–Possession of offensive weapons–Excessive violence used in robbery of snooker hall–Undue leniency**

The Attorney General referred sentences of four years' detention and five years and six months' detention as unduly lenient, following pleas of guilty from two defendants (D and S) and the conviction of one defendant (K) of robbery and possession of an offensive weapon. All three defendants had at young ages come separately to the United Kingdom from Kosovo without any other members of their families. In the early morning the defendants, aged 20, 21 and 19 years' old, armed with a stun gun and cosh, had carried out a carefully planned robbery on a snooker hall. They subjected the owner to a brutal attack with D pressing the stun gun into him and repeatedly firing it and S hitting him over the head with the kosh four or five times. Fearing for his life the owner collapsed and pretended to be dead and D continued to fire the stun gun into him. All three defendants had previous convictions for various offences. The Attorney General contended that the sentences failed to reflect the gravity and the aggravating features: that the robbery was carefully planned, the premises were deliberately targeted and were particularly vulnerable, the defendants were armed, the robbery was committed at night by three men, the victim was subjected to gratuitous and excessive violence, and the victim suffered physical and psychological harm. In mitigation were the defendants' ages, their troubled background and S and D's pleas of guilty. D contended that the sentence was clearly lenient but was passed by a highly experienced judge. S accepted the case had aggravating features but argued that he was only 20, had pleaded guilty, albeit late, and in his own country he was a victim of ethnic cleansing and the judge was right to reduce the sentence. K contended that he had a difficult background and had deep seated emotional difficulties.

Held, allowing the reference, that the sentences were unduly lenient. No distinction should be drawn between the premises robbed and other premises such as a corner shop; both were likely to be equally vulnerable. Further, there was no special feature in the difficult background of the defendants because of their troubled past in Kosovo. Defendants with a violent criminal background often came before the courts and whilst that background might explain why the crimes were committed it did not mitigate the sentence appropriate for the conduct of the defendant. Taking into account all the circumstances, including the age of the defendants, a sentence of at least 10 years' following trial could have been expected in the court below and, if there had been prompt pleas of guilty, sentences of seven years could have been expected. Having regard to the very late pleas, the appropriate sentence for D and S in the court below was nine years' detention. The appropriate sentence for K was 10 years. Taking into account double jeopardy, S and D's sentence was increased to seven years' detention and K's to eight years' detention, *Attorney General's Reference (No.29 of 1995), Re* [1996] 2 Cr. App. R. (S.) 60, [1996] C.L.Y. 2074 and *R. v. Evans (Glenn Clifford)* [2000] 1 Cr. App. R. (S.) 454, [2000] C.L.Y. 1424 considered.

ATTORNEY GENERAL'S REFERENCE (NOS.135, 136 AND 137), *Re*; R. v. SEJDIAL; R. v. KALEMI; *sub nom*. R. v. DERVISHI [2005] EWCA Crim 468, Rose, L.J. (V-P), CA (Crim Div).

3728. Robbery—Unlawful wounding—Night time knife attack on taxi driver—Offence committed during currency of suspended sentence—Undue leniency

The Attorney General referred to the court as unduly lenient concurrent sentences of two years' imprisonment imposed on the offender (P) following his guilty pleas to offences of robbery and unlawful wounding. P had robbed a taxi driver at knife point during the night with the victim sustaining a deep wound to his hand. After asking the taxi driver to stop so that he could obtain money to pay the fare, P had obtained the knife from his home and returned to commit the offence. Although P claimed to have no memory of the incident, evidence found at his home left little doubt as to his guilt. At the time of the offence, P was not allowed to work and found it difficult to be without means. A psychiatric report concluded that he was likely to have been suffering from depression. P had a previous conviction for attempted robbery and theft for which he had received a sentence of two years' imprisonment suspended for a period of two years. The instant offence was committed during the currency of that period of suspension. The Attorney General contended that the robbery had been at night time against a lone taxi driver; P had deliberately armed himself with a large knife; the knife had been used not only to threaten, but to wound the taxi driver; P had been involved in a previous offence where a knife had been used, and because of that offence he had been in breach of a suspended sentence.

Held, allowing the reference, that the sentence was unduly lenient. If the matter had been contested the minimum sentence would have been at least five years' imprisonment, *Attorney General's Reference (No.38 of 1995), Re* [1996] 2 Cr. App. R. (S.) 103, [1996] C.L.Y. 2069 and *R. v. Shaw (Carl William)* [1998] 2 Cr. App. R. (S.) 233, [1998] C.L.Y. 1377 considered. There was no reason why the judge should not have brought into effect in full the suspended sentence, *R. v. Chuni (Narinder)* [2000] 2 Cr. App. R. (S.) 64, [2000] C.L.Y. 1191 applied. That would have led to a total sentence in excess of seven years. Having regard to the plea of guilty, the appropriate sentence would have been three and a half years' imprisonment, with the suspended sentence being implemented in full, making a total of five and a half years' imprisonment. However, taking account of double jeopardy, it was appropriate to set aside the sentence of two years' imprisonment in respect of the robbery and to replace it with a sentence of two and a half years' imprisonment. The sentence in respect of the unlawful wounding would remain concurrent, but the suspended sentence of two years' imprisonment would take effect consecutively, making a total of four and a half years' imprisonment in all.

ATTORNEY GENERAL'S REFERENCE (NO.126 OF 2004), *Re*; *sub nom*. R. v. PORTILLO (JOSE), [2004] EWCA Crim 3218, [2005] 2 Cr. App. R. (S.) 20, Kennedy, L.J., CA (Crim Div).

3729. Robbery—Violence—Robberies of small businesses—Undue leniency

The Attorney General referred to the court as unduly lenient a total sentence of four and a half years' imprisonment imposed on the offender (H) following his guilty plea to four counts of robbery and two counts of burglary. H had burgled two residential properties while the owners were away. He then committed three robberies of businesses where the victims were put in a position of fear. On two occasions he had used a weapon. Whilst leaving the scene of one of the robberies, he stole a vehicle from an 85 year old man. The judge was provided with a letter from the offender in which he set out his remorse and his determination to rid himself of his drug habit. The Attorney General argued that the sentence did not adequately reflect the seriousness of the offences.

Held, allowing the reference, that despite the mitigation which was present, the minimum appropriate sentence in the instant case would have been one of eight years' imprisonment, *Attorney General's Reference (No.9 of 1989), Re* (1990-91) 12 Cr. App. R. (S.) 7, [1991] C.L.Y. 1214 followed. Taking into account double jeopardy and the mitigation which had influenced the judge, an appropriate sentence was one of six years' imprisonment for the robbery offences.

ATTORNEY GENERAL'S REFERENCE (NO.154 OF 2004), *Re; sub nom.* R. HENRY (ANDREW JOHN) [2005] EWCA Crim 455, Latham, L.J., CA (Crim Div).

3730. Robbery—Violence—Series of armed raids on sub post offices—Victims subjected to violence and threats

The appellants (X and S) appealed against their respective sentences of 25 and 19 years' imprisonment for conspiracy to rob. X contested the case, but S pleaded guilty on the first day of the trial. They had been the leaders in arranging a series of armed robberies of sub post offices. There were nine robberies and two attempted robberies, resulting in a total of £424,000 being stolen, but X and S had not participated in all of them. Violence was used on the victims, who were also threatened with guns and knives. X contended that, in view of the authorities, his sentence was manifestly excessive. S contended that he had not been given full credit for his guilty plea.

Held, allowing the appeals, that in cases of multiple armed robberies, a sentence of 25 years' imprisonment was at the top of the range and should be reserved for the gravest offences, *R. v. Turner (Bryan James)* (1975) 61 Cr. App. R. 67, *R. v. Schultz (Karl)* [1996] 1 Cr. App. R. (S.) 451 and *R. v. Adams (David Anthony)* [2000] 2 Cr. App. R. (S.) 274 considered. In the instant case there had been no actual physical injury caused to the victims, and on the facts X's sentence was reduced to 22 years' imprisonment. The discount given to S for his guilty plea was insufficient and his sentence was accordingly reduced to one of 15 years' imprisonment.

R. v. ATKINSON (GLYNN); R. v. SMITH (PAUL); *sub nom.* R. v. ATKINSON (GLYN), [2004] EWCA Crim 3223, [2005] 2 Cr. App. R. (S.) 34, Pill, L.J., CA (Crim Div).

3731. Robbery—Violence—Violent attack on elderly couple in own home—Undue leniency

The Attorney General referred to the court as unduly lenient a total sentence of five years' imprisonment imposed on the offender (F) following his pleas of guilty to robbery, supplying Class C drugs and possession of a bladed article. F had robbed an elderly couple in their own home. He had hit the male victim on the head three times with a claw hammer and had robbed the female victim, who had been suffering from asthma and emphysema, of her handbag. At the time of his arrest, F had been in possession of a lock knife, and in interview had admitted taking valium as well as supplying it to two friends. The Attorney General contended that there were several aggravating features: the victims were a vulnerable elderly couple robbed in their own home; excessive violence had been used; the injuries suffered were significant; the victims had suffered psychologically; and F had a number of previous convictions, including convictions of burglary and assault, and had previously robbed an elderly victim in the street.

Held, finding the sentence unduly lenient but declining to vary it, that following a contested trial, and taking into account the offending as a whole, a sentence of eight or nine years' imprisonment would have been appropriate. However, the case had not been contested and that sentence had to be discounted to an appropriate level in order to allow for F's plea of guilty. That would bring the appropriate sentence down to one of six years' imprisonment. The sentence of five years' imprisonment was therefore lenient but, having regard to the plea of guilty and the element of double jeopardy, there was no reason to interfere with it.

ATTORNEY GENERAL'S REFERENCE (NO.113 OF 2004), *Re; sub nom.* R. v. FOLLOWS (DEAN JOHN) [2004] EWCA Crim 3209, Kennedy, L.J., CA (Crim Div).

3732. Robbery—Violence used in robbery of petrol station shop—Undue leniency

The Attorney General referred to the court as unduly lenient a sentence of six months' imprisonment that had been imposed on the offender (G) following his plea of guilty to robbery. G, who at the time was 19, had entered the shop of a petrol station and struck a male shop assistant on the head with a credit card chip and pin machine before throwing some chocolate bars at him and making off with a display which held lotto scratch cards. The offence took place at 8pm. When he was interviewed, G stated that he had been drinking since lunchtime and that he could not recall the incident. He had a number of previous convictions, two of which were for offences of minor violence. The Attorney General relied on three aggravating features: firstly, the victim had been injured, having sustained a laceration to his forehead, although the injury had no lasting consequences; secondly, as a shop assistant working at night, the victim was vulnerable; thirdly, G had plainly been binge drinking before the incident. In mitigation were G's age, the fact that he had pleaded guilty at the earliest opportunity and his expressions of remorse.

Held, allowing the reference, that while the instant offence was less serious than a typical robbery of vulnerable premises, it was nevertheless a serious offence, and G had previous convictions. The sentence was unduly lenient. The appropriate sentence at first instance should have been at least two years. Having regard to all the circumstances, including double jeopardy, a sentence of 15 months' imprisonment would be imposed, *Attorney General's Reference (Nos.60 and 61 of 1995), Re* [1996] 2 Cr. App. R. (S.) 243, [1997] C.L.Y. 1696, *Attorney General's Reference (No.18 of 1997), Re* [1998] 1 Cr. App. R. (S.) 151, [1997] C.L.Y. 1694, *Attorney General's Reference (No.68 of 1999), Re* [2000] 2 Cr. App. R. (S.) 50, [2000] C.L.Y. 1423 and *R. v. Rees (Louis)* [2005] EWCA Crim 1857, Times, July 22, 2005, [2005] 9 C.L. 464 considered.

ATTORNEY GENERAL'S REFERENCE (NO.66 OF 2005), *Re* [2005] EWCA Crim 2445, Gage, J., CA (Crim Div).

3733. Robbery—Weapons, victims threatened and bound

The appellants (M and H) appealed against sentences of 15 years and 8 years' imprisonment respectively imposed following guilty pleas. M had been convicted on two counts of robbery and two counts of possession of imitation firearms; the sentence for each robbery was made concurrent with that imposed for the linked firearms offence and those sentences, of seven years and eight years' imprisonment, were ordered to be served consecutively. H's sentence was imposed in respect of a robbery committed with M, for which he received the same sentence as M. M had taken an imitation handgun to each of the robberies with which he had threatened the victims. H had armed himself with a metal truncheon. On both occasions the victims had been tied up. Following his arrest H had cooperated with the police, naming M and giving evidence against him. M submitted that his sentence failed to reflect credit for his guilty pleas or to have regard to the totality principle. H submitted that the sentencing judge had erred in giving insufficient credit for his cooperation with the police and in failing to draw a meaningful distinction between H and M as regards their respective roles and their behaviour following arrest.

Held, allowing the appeals, that on conviction of robbery sentences of considerable length were inevitable where offenders had armed themselves with guns, whether real or imitation, or other weapons capable of inflicting serious injury, particularly where the terror experienced by the victims was exacerbated by their being tied up in confined spaces. However, when sentencing for more than one offence the courts should take care to ensure that the overall sentence was such as to impose a punishment that appropriately reflected the total criminality of the offender. Moreover, where offenders had engaged in a joint enterprise the court should ensure that the sentences imposed on the individual offenders reflected the differences in role and subsequent behaviour of those offenders. In cases such as that of M, where an offender had been convicted of two similar offences it was inappropriate to set the overall sentence by adding together sentences imposed for each offence as that would result in an excessive sentence. The correct approach in such cases was to decide the sentence for one offence and add to that an additional term of years to reflect the additional offending, *R. v. Turner (Bryan James)* (1975) 61 Cr. App. R. 67, [1975] C.L.Y. 559 applied, *R. v. McCarthy (Denis Lewis)* [2002] EWCA Crim 2579, [2003] 1 Cr. App. R. (S.) 119 and *R. v. Davies (Craig Darren)* [2003] EWCA Crim 850, [2003] 2 Cr. App. R. (S.) 104, [2003] C.L.Y. 3854 considered. In M's case that approach led to a starting point of 16 years' imprisonment for the overall sentence which was then reduced to 12 years to reflect M's guilty pleas. An offender, such as H, who had demonstrated contrition by a willingness to assist the authorities was entitled to have that reflected in his sentence, especially where he had indicated a willingness to give evidence against an offender jointly charged, even where that offer had not been taken up. Consequently, H's sentence was reduced to seven years' imprisonment.

R. v. MILLER (STEPHEN); R. v. HENRY (CARL ANTHONY), [2004] EWCA Crim 3323, [2005] 2 Cr. App. R. (S.) 43, Keene, L.J., CA (Crim Div).

3734. **Sentencing guidelines–Child sex offences–Factors to be taken into consideration**

[Sexual Offences Act 2003 s.5, s.6, s.7, s.9, s.10, s.11.]

The court heard together four unrelated cases, each of which, at least in part, involved consideration of a sentence passed in relation to one or more of the new offences created by the Sexual Offences Act 2003. The court took advantage of the opportunity offered to give further, preliminary, non prescriptive guidance to sentencers. The offences in respect of which guidance was provided were: rape of a child under 13, contrary to s.5; assault of a child under 13 by penetration, contrary to s.6; sexual assault of a child under 13, contrary to s.7; causing or inciting a child under 13 to engage in sexual activity, contrary to s.8; sexual activity with a child, contrary to s.9; causing or inciting a child to engage in sexual activity, contrary to s.10; engaging in sexual activity in the presence of a child, contrary to s.11 and causing a child to watch a sexual act, contrary to s.12.

Held, giving judgment accordingly, that (1) the appropriate sentence for an offence under s.5 fell within a wide bracket and was dependent on all the circumstances. There would be very few cases where an immediate custodial sentence would not be called for, even in the case of young offenders. Where there was lack of consent together with significant aggravating features, as identified in *R. v. Millberry (William Christopher)* [2002] EWCA Crim 2891, [2003] 1 W.L.R 546, a long determinate sentence, or a life sentence, would be called for, *Millberry* applied. Consent by the victim would be material, particularly in relation to young offenders. In the case of young offenders their age, of itself and when compared with the age of the victim, was an important factor. A very short period of custody or, in exceptional cases, a non custodial sentence might be appropriate for a young offender where the other party consented. However, if the offender was much older that the victim a substantial term of imprisonment would usually be called for. Other factors included the nature of the relationship between the parties and their respective characters and maturity; the number of occasions, and the circumstances, in which penetration occurred, including whether contraception was used; the physical and emotional consequences for the victim; the degree of remorse shown by the offender and the likelihood of repetition. A reasonable belief that the victim was 16 would be a mitigating factor, particularly for a young offender. A plea of guilty would also be pertinent. (2) The factors to be taken into consideration when sentencing in relation to penetrative sexual activity under s.9 and s.10 were the same as those relevant in relation to s.5, save that, where the victim was 13 or over, reasonable belief that he or she was 16 would afford a defence, irrespective of the offender's age, rather than merely mitigation. Offences under s.9 and s.10 would attract lighter sentences than an offence under s.5, even where the victim was under 13, and the sentence would be likely to be even less where the victim was under 16 rather than under 13. (3) Factors relevant to sentencing for s.7 and s.8 offences included the nature of the assault and the period of time it lasted, together with all the factor relevant to s.5, other than the age of the offender and consent by the victim, appropriately adjusted in the case of s.7 offences to take account of the fact that the offence did not involve penetration. The custody threshold would not always be passed in relation to s.7 offences. (4) Sentences under s.11 and s.12 would usually be less than those under s.5, s.7, s.8, s.9, or s.10. Factors relevant in sentencing were the age and character of the offender; the age of the child; the nature and duration of the sexual activity engaged in or depicted; the number of occasions when sexual activity was observed; the impact on the child; the degree of remorse shown by the offender and the likelihood of repetition. (5) Digital penetration of the anus of a child under 13, contrary to s.6, was a very serious offence that could justify a life sentence.

R. v. CORRAN (BEN); R. v. CUTLER (JASON); R. v. HEARD (KEVIN PHILLIP); R. v. WILLIAMS (ANTHONY MICHAEL), [2005] EWCA Crim 192, [2005] 2 Cr. App. R. (S.) 73, Rose, L.J., CA (Crim Div).

3735. **Sentencing guidelines–Effect of being caught red handed in case of guilty plea–Need for evidence where prevalence of crime in particular area relied on**

[Powers of Criminal Courts (Sentencing) Act 2000 s.155(1); Criminal Justice Act 2003 s.172, s.240(3).]

The appellant (O) appealed against a sentence of two years' detention imposed following his plea of guilty to robbery. The judge had expressed a wish that the period spent by O in custody on remand should count towards his sentence, although the judge had not been aware of the period. O had committed a premeditated robbery of a handbag from a woman in the middle of the day in the centre of Guildford; he had been caught by a nearby off duty police officer. O had not previously received a custodial sentence and two other offences had been taken into consideration when sentence had been imposed, namely the theft of a mobile telephone from a friend and the obtaining of property by deception, being goods from his employer, with the use of a stolen credit card. The judge had decided that the sentence should be deterrent owing to the prevalence of robbery of handbags from women on the streets of Guildford and that O's entitlement to a discounted sentence should be reduced as he had been caught red handed. O submitted that the judge had erred in (1) making the starting point of the custodial term too high as the appropriate upper limit for street robbery where no weapon was used was three years. Additionally, the statutory changes to the length of licence periods would result in his being vulnerable to a longer period of recall; (2) imposing a deterrent sentence, as there had been no evidence with reference to the prevalence of street crime in Guildford; (3) reducing the discount for his plea of guilty because he had been caught red handed.

Held, dismissing the appeal, that (1) the starting point of three years for sentencing for the two rather unpleasant offences as well as the robbery had not been too high, *Attorney General's Reference (Nos.4 and 7 of 2002), Re* [2002] EWCA Crim 127, [2002] 2 Cr. App. R. (S.) 77, [2002] C.L.Y. 4066 considered.

There was no criticism to be made of the sentence on consideration of the Sentencing Guidelines Council's Guideline on New Sentences: Criminal Justice Act 2003 December 2004 para.2.1.9. (2) In the absence of statistics or other evidence identifying the particular prevalence of a crime in a particular area, even a judge with experience of that area should not assume that prevalence was more marked in that area than nationally, *R. v. Stockdale (Rae)* [2005] EWCA Crim 1582 doubted. Judges had to have regard under the Criminal Justice Act 2003 s.172 to guidelines without necessarily following them, *R. v. Last (Emma)* [2005] EWCA Crim 106, [2005] 2 Cr. App. R. (S.) 64, [2005] 3 C.L. 457 and *R. v. Peters (Benjamin)* [2005] EWCA Crim 605, Times, March 29, 2005, [2005] 5 C.L. 485 applied. (3) A reduction in sentence for a guilty plea should not be withheld or reduced simply because an offender was caught red handed, *R. v. Greenland (Jason)* [2002] EWCA Crim 1748, [2003] 1 Cr. App. R. (S.) 74, [2003] C.L.Y. 3852 not applied. (4) An omission by a sentencing judge to give a direction under s.240(3) of the 2003 Act was not of itself a ground for an appeal against sentence; a variation of the sentence should have been sought under the Powers of Criminal Courts (Sentencing) Act 2000 s.155(1). A direction was given under s.240(3) that the time spent by O on remand in custody was to count as time served as part of the sentence.

R. v. OOSTHUIZEN (LEE), [2005] EWCA Crim 1978, *The Times*, September 5, 2005, Rose, L.J., CA (Crim Div).

3736. Sentencing powers–Delay–Unmeritorious application for leave to appeal– Loss of time orders

[Criminal Appeal Act 1968 s.29; European Convention on Human Rights 1950.]

The applicant (K) renewed his applications for an extension of time for leave to appeal against conviction. The single judge had refused K's original application as no sufficient grounds had been put forward to explain a delay of 20 months. The court considered whether, given the lack of merit in K's applications, it was appropriate to make a loss of time order.

Held, refusing the application, that under the Criminal Appeal Act 1968 s.29 the court had the power to order that time spent in custody would not count towards an applicant's sentence where an application without merit was made if, in its discretion, it was right to do so. The notice and grounds of appeal form, which applicants had to sign, made that clear. Moreover, loss of time orders had been held to be compatible with the European Convention on Human Rights 1950 by the European Court of Human Rights, *Monnell v. United Kingdom (A/ 115)* (1988) 10 E.H.R.R. 205, [1988] C.L.Y. 1803 considered. Unmeritorious applications caused real problems in delaying the hearing of meritorious appeals and the court took the opportunity of reminding applicants and practitioners to take notice of its discretionary powers to make loss of time orders. Accordingly, K would lose 14 days in consequence.

R. v. K (HERBERT), [2005] EWCA Crim 955, *The Times*, May 17, 2005, Lord Woolf, L.C.J, CA (Crim Div).

3737. Sentencing powers–Racially aggravated offences–Validity of uplift on sentence where racial aggravation not raised during trial

The appellant (O) appealed against a sentence of 18 months' imprisonment imposed for an offence of actual bodily harm. In an unprovoked attack, O had struck the victim, an Asian youth, in the face with a bag containing video tapes. He had punched him about the head and had fallen on top of him. The victim had sustained abrasions to his face, and had fractured his ankle in the fall. The judge had rejected O's account that the victim had threatened to head butt him. He concluded that O's actions were racially motivated and made it clear that the sentence passed comprised a basic sentence of 15 months' imprisonment for the assault with an uplift of three months' imprisonment for the element of racial aggravation. O argued that (1) it was wrong in principle for the judge to have proceeded as he did. There was no material on which he could properly have concluded that the attack had been racially aggravated, race had not been an evidential issue during the trial, the jury had not been invited to consider the issue of racial aggravation and O had been given no opportunity to challenge the judge's decision; (2) the judge had failed to take account of O's medical history, his age and the accidental nature of H's injury.

Held, allowing the appeal in part, that (1) a judge was entitled to interpret the verdict of the jury, and there could be no objection to him sentencing on the basis of evidence disclosing aggravating features which could have resulted in a more serious charge. However, he could not sentence on the basis that a more serious offence had been committed, *R. v. Clark (Raymond Dennis)* [1996] 2 Cr. App. R. 282, [1996] C.L.Y. 1944 applied. The question of racial aggravation could have been legitimately dealt with as part of the sentencing process, even though it had not arisen during the trial. A Newton hearing should have been held to establish the existence of any aggravating features in the case. Alternatively, the judge should have given notice of his intention to consider sentencing on an enhanced or aggravated basis. In the absence of any of those things, the three month uplift was wrong in principle and was removed, reducing the sentence to 15 months. (2) The sentence imposed for the basic element of the offence was not manifestly excessive. The offence had been serious and unprovoked, and there was no benefit available for a plea of guilty. The injury sustained was serious and the fact that it had not been deliberately inflicted did not cast doubt on the judge's treatment of the fact of the injury as constituting an aggravating feature. Any sympathy for O was plainly outweighed by the need to pass robust sentences for unprovoked offences of violence.

R. v. O'CALLAGHAN (PATRICK), [2005] EWCA Crim 317, [2005] 2 Cr. App. R. (S.) 83, Grigson, J., CA (Crim Div).

3738. Sex offenders–Sex Offenders Register–Failure to comply with notification requirements–Sentence length

[Sex Offenders Act 1997; Sexual Offences Act 2003 s.91 (1) (a).]

The appellant (B), a 51 year old man, appealed against a sentence of six months' imprisonment imposed on his conviction following a guilty plea of failing to comply with the notification requirements of the Sexual Offences Act 2003 s.91 (1) (a). B had previously been sentenced to five years' imprisonment for an offence of attempted rape but had been released on licence after three years. He had also been ordered to register under the Sex Offenders Act 1997 for an indefinite period. B had failed to notify the police of his name and address within three days of his release on licence. He had left a hostel where he was required to live as a condition of his licence and was arrested some weeks later.

Held, allowing the appeal, that although B had a long criminal record, the offence of attempted rape was the first one of a sexual nature. His other offences involved dishonesty and other offences against the person. The provisions of the 1997 Act, re enacted in the 2003 Act, were vital for the protection of the public and potentially the offender. The fact that there was a maximum sentence of five years' imprisonment for failure to comply with the notification requirements was an indication of their importance. Although a custodial sentence was justified in the instant case, six months was excessive in the circumstances and a sentence of three months' imprisonment was substituted accordingly.

R. v. B (DAVID), [2005] EWCA Crim 158, [2005] 2 Cr. App. R. (S.) 65, Auld, L.J., CA (Crim Div).

3739. Sexual abuse–Children–Stepdaughters–Offending resumed 20 years later with abuse of step granddaughter–Undue leniency

The Attorney General referred as unduly lenient a sentence of four years' imprisonment imposed on B upon his conviction on 12 counts of indecent assault, one count of attempted rape and one count of assault occasioning actual bodily harm. B had sexually abused two stepdaughters more than 20 years earlier and, more recently, had also abused a step granddaughter. In each case the girls were between 11 and 15 years old. The judge took into account B's age of 62, his lack of previous convictions and the delay which had occurred since the earlier offences. The Attorney General submitted that the offences were aggravated by a number of factors: there were three young victims; the offending restarted after a lapse of 20 years; the repeated offences involved threats, violence and attempted rape, and B had grossly abused his position of trust and responsibility.

Held, allowing the reference, that in light of the aggravating features, the shortest total sentence which could have been imposed on B following a trial was one of eight years' imprisonment, *R. v. Millberry (William Christopher)* [2002] EWCA Crim 2891, [2003] 1 W.L.R. 546, [2003] C.L.Y. 3829 and *Attorney General's Reference (No.3 of 1995), Re* [1996] 1 Cr. App. R. (S.) 26, [1996] C.L.Y. 1775 considered. Taking account of double jeopardy, the total sentence should be one of seven years' imprisonment, which included an increased term of five years for the attempted rape.

ATTORNEY GENERAL'S REFERENCE (NO.150 OF 2004), *Re* [2005] EWCA Crim 680, Tuckey, L.J., CA (Crim Div).

3740. **Sexual activity with children–Indecent assault–Number of offences committed against young female victims–Undue leniency**

The Attorney General referred to the court as unduly lenient an overall extended sentence of five years, with a custodial element of two years' imprisonment, imposed on B following his guilty pleas to two offences of sexual intercourse with a girl under 16 years of age, one offence of indecency with a child, and four offences of indecent assault on a female. The Attorney General submitted that there were aggravating features: the seven offences over a two week period had concerned six young female victims, one as young as 11; one indecent assault involved digital penetration of a 14 year old in front of others; there was no use of condoms or other protective devices during the acts of sexual intercourse; there was an element of planning, with B targeting young girls by offering them cigarettes, alcohol and other items; at the time B was subject to a community rehabilitation order for an unrelated offence of harassment; and the offences had a considerable impact upon the victims. B submitted there were mitigating factors: his early guilty plea; his lack of previous convictions for sexual offences; there was no extraneous force; his depression, alcohol dependence and hyperthyroidism; and he was sought out by the victims, who, broadly speaking, consented.

Held, allowing the reference, that it was clear from the pre sentence report that B presented a considerable risk to girls of the age of the victims in the instant case, and that was a matter to which the judge had rightly had regard. The total sentence was unduly lenient, *Attorney General's Reference (Nos.120, 91 and 119 of 2002), Re* [2003] EWCA Crim 5, [2003] 2 All E.R. 955, [2003] C.L.Y. 3866 considered. The custodial element of the total sentence should have been in the region of four to four and a half years, even allowing for the guilty plea. But allowing for the element of double jeopardy, the appropriate custodial sentence would be three and a half years. Furthermore, there would be no challenge to the judge's conclusion that the case called for an extended sentence in relation to certain of the offences.

ATTORNEY GENERAL'S REFERENCE (NO.76 OF 2004), *Re*; *sub nom*. R. v. B (COLIN) [2004] EWCA Crim 2310, Kennedy, L.J., CA (Crim Div).

3741. **Sexual offences–Battery–Battery with intent to commit sexual offence– Sentencing guidelines**

[Sexual Offences Act 2003 s.62.]

The appellant (W) appealed against a total sentence of seven years' imprisonment which had been imposed on him following his pleas of guilty to two offences of battery with intent to commit sexual offences contrary to the Sexual Offences Act 2003 s.62. W had grabbed the first victim from the street late at night and had lifted her over a wall. She had managed to escape and had sustained cuts and bruises. Later the same week, in a similar attack, a second victim had been dragged into church grounds and pushed to the floor. W had said "you and me sex" and had lain on top of her. A passer by had scared W away. The second victim subsequently identified W in an identity parade. Consecutive sentences of two years for the first offence and five years for the second offence had been passed. W argued that the starting point in relation to both offences had been too high and that both sentences failed properly to reflect the guilty pleas.

Held, allowing the appeal, that there was substance in each submission. Battery with intent to commit sexual offences was one of several new offences created by the 2003 Act. However, conduct giving rise to the new offences was not new and authorities decided before the Act continued to give guidance to sentencers. In relation to battery with intent, account should be taken of (a) the method and degree of force used; (b) the nature and extent of the indecency perpetrated or intended; (c) the degree of harm to the victim; (d) the nature and general circumstances of the attack, including the time, the place and the level of risk posed by the offender; (e) good character, which afforded only limited mitigation. The maximum sentence set by Parliament was 10 years' imprisonment compared with life imprisonment for rape and attempted rape. Save where a great deal of violence was used, the appropriate sentence for battery with intent was generally lower than that for rape or attempted rape committed in similar circumstances. W had committed both offences late at night on a lone victim; however, no weapon was used and the indecency that actually occurred was limited in nature. The fact that the second victim had to identify W, prolonging her ordeal, was an aggravating feature, and a substantial discount for the early pleas of guilty could have been greater if W had admitted the offences in interview. The sentence for the first offence was reduced to 18 months' imprisonment and the sentence for the second offence to three years and six months, giving a total sentence of five years, *R. v. Millberry (William Christopher)* [2002] EWCA Crim 2891, [2003] 1 W.L.R. 546, [2003] C.L.Y. 3829, *Attorney General's Reference (Nos.120, 91 and 119 of 2002), Re* [2003] EWCA Crim 5, [2003] 2 All E.R. 955, *Attorney General's Reference (Nos. 37, 38, 44, 54, 51, 53, 35, 40, 43, 45, 41 and 42 of 2003), Re* [2003] EWCA Crim 2973, [2004] 1 Cr. App. R. (S.) 84, [2004] 6 C.L. 409 and *R. v. Nelson (Patrick Alan)* [2001] EWCA Crim 2264, [2002] 1 Cr. App. R. (S.) 134, [2001] C.L.Y. 1369 considered.

R. v. WISNIEWSKI (MARIUZS); *sub nom.* R. v. WISNIEWSKI (MARIUSZ), [2004] EWCA Crim 3361, [2005] 2 Cr. App. R. (S.) 39, Rose, L.J., CA (Crim Div).

3742. **Sexual offences–Racially aggravated offences–Criminal damage–Specimen charges–Multiple offending**

The appellants (S and T) appealed against the length of their sentences on the ground that they were manifestly excessive. S had been convicted of three offences of sexual assault; on counts 1 and 4 to three years' imprisonment on each, and on count 2 to five years' imprisonment. His sentences were concurrent so his sentence was a total of five years' imprisonment. The judge had sentenced S on count 2 on the basis that it was a sample count of repeated indecent assaults over a substantial period of years. T had been convicted of two counts of racially aggravated criminal damage (counts 10 and 11) and pleaded guilty to nine counts relating to the possession of weapons, ammunition and explosives (counts 1 to 9). Although T had faced, and been convicted on, two counts only of racially aggravated criminal damage, the judge had sentenced on the basis that the two counts were in reality "specimen counts", comprising simply two incidents out of a total of 17 similar offences, for which no charges had been included in the indictment and T had made no admission. T was sentenced to a total of 11 years' imprisonment, comprising eight years for counts 1 to 9 and three years for counts 10 and 11 to run concurrently. S submitted that as a matter of law the judge was not entitled when sentencing S to treat count 2 as a sample count. T submitted that the sentence of eight years' imprisonment, in respect of counts 1 to 9, was manifestly excessive in light of the fact that the arsenal was never used, he had pleaded guilty, and he was of previous good character. T also submitted that it was wrong in principle for the judge to treat counts 10 and 11 as specimen counts. T further contended that, on the basis that counts 10 and 11 were no more than two individual counts of racially aggravated criminal damage, the sentence of three years' imprisonment, consecutive, was manifestly excessive.

Held, giving judgment accordingly, that (1) in passing S's sentences the judge was being entirely consistent with the evidence. However, it was clear that in so doing he had acted inconsistently with the indictment as drafted and with the principles set out in *R. v. Clark (Raymond Dennis)* [1996] 2 Cr. App. R. 282, [1996] C.L.Y. 1944 and *R. v. Kidd (Philip Richard)* [1998] 1 W.L.R. 604, [1997] C.L.Y. 1492, *Clark* and *Kidd* applied, *Barton v. DPP* [2001] EWHC Admin 223, (2001) 165 J.P. 779, [2002] C.L.Y. 866 considered. The judge was put in that position by the inadequacy of the indictment. It was not practical to have a count to represent every occasion of offending but it would have been preferable if there had been three counts for each year over the period of the offending. S's sentence could not be upheld as it represented three isolated incidents. The sentence of five years' imprisonment on count 2 was quashed and a sentence of three years concurrent was substituted. (2) No proper criticism was to be made of the judge's sentence on counts 1 to 9. Possession of an arsenal including high grade explosives and a machine gun amply warranted the sentence passed. On no view was it manifestly excessive. (3) The judge's treatment of counts 10 and 11 as specimen or sample counts was unsustainable having regard to the terms of the indictment. (4) However, it did not follow that those sentences should be reduced and it was appropriate to have regard to the context. There was evidence to show that T was racist and the context included the possession of the arsenal forming the subject of counts 1 to 9. Taking counts 10 and 11 alone it was permissible to infer that T's motive was to excite intercommunal tension and hostility. Accordingly those counts had wider impact than the damage done in such cases as *R. v. O'Brien (Ronan Stephen)* [2003] EWCA Crim 302, [2003] 2 Cr. App. R. (S.) 66, [2003] C.L.Y. 3673, *O'Brien* considered. The sentence of three years' imprisonment concurrent for counts 10 and 11, but consecutive to the sentence passed in respect of counts 1 to 9, was justified and not manifestly excessive. T's appeal was dismissed.

R. v. TOVEY (DAVID); R. v. SMITH (PETER JOHN), [2005] EWCA Crim 530, [2005] 2 Cr. App. R. (S.) 100, Lord Woolf of Barnes, L.C.J, CA (Crim Div).

3743. Sexual offences–Violent offences–Guidance on imposition of extended sentences

[Powers of Criminal Courts (Sentencing) Act 2000 s.80, s.85, s.155; Criminal Justice Act 2003 s.224, s.225, s.226, s.227, s.228, s.229, s.230, s.231, s.232, s.233, s.234, s.235, s.236.]

The appellants, in unrelated cases heard together, appealed against the imposition of extended sentences under the Powers of Criminal Courts (Sentencing) Act 2000 s.85. It was common ground that in each case it had been inappropriate to impose an extended sentence and the instant court heard the cases together in order to illustrate some of the traps into which a sentencer might fall when seeking to impose such a sentence, particularly if unassisted by counsel.

Held, allowing the appeals, that (1) the five appeals did not provide the basis for the court to give further general guidance and *R. v. Nelson (Patrick Alan)* [2001] EWCA Crim 2264, [2002] 1 Cr. App. R. (S.) 134, [2001] C.L.Y. 1369 should continue to be the sentencer's first port of call when grappling with the legislation, however, certain observations could be made, *Nelson* applied. It should be borne in mind, in relation to offences committed on or after April 4, 2005, that the provisions of s.85 of the 2000 Act would be replaced by the Criminal Justice Act 2003 s.224 to s.236, providing a new regime of public protection sentences for specified violent or sexual offences committed by dangerous offenders of any age. (2) When imposing sentences for several offences the sentencer should always identify to which offence the extended sentence was intended to relate. That would assist in focusing on whether the sentence complied with the statutorily imposed criteria, considering particularly (i) whether the offence was committed before or after September 30, 1998; (ii) the need not to exceed the maximum sentence for the offence; (iii) the fact that different restrictions applied to sexual and violent offences. For sexual offences the extended sentence must not exceed ten years and for violent offences the custodial sentence must be at least four years and the extended period not more than five years. (3) The purpose of an extended sentence under s.85(1)(b) of the 2000 Act was to prevent the commission of further offences and to secure the rehabilitation of the offender. It was not to protect the public from harm. That was the role of a longer than commensurate sentence under s.80 of the 2000 Act. (4) A judge who was minded to impose an extended sentence should always invite submissions from counsel which should help to avoid errors. Counsel should be reminded of their duty in two respects (i) prosecution counsel should always be ready to draw the court's attention to relevant legislation and authorities; (ii) if an error was made when sentencing, particularly in relation to a judge's powers, counsel, whether prosecution or defence, should be alive to the possibility of rectifying the sentence using the slip rule under s.155 of the 2000 Act. (5) Attention was drawn to the Attorney General's guidelines on the acceptance of pleas and the prosecution's role in the sentencing exercise which would hopefully be produced within the next six months, *R. v. Evans (Alan Roy)* [2004] EWCA Crim 632, Times, March 22, 2004, [2004] C.L.Y. 838 and *Attorney General's Reference (No.52 of 2003), Re* [2003] EWCA Crim 3731, Times, December 12, 2003, [2004] C.L.Y. 3443 considered.

R. v. PEPPER (JEREMY PAUL); R. v. BARBER (KENNETH LESLIE); R. v. LAMONT (MARTIN); R. v. G; R. v. MURRAY (RICHARD ALEXANDER), [2005] EWCA Crim 1181, [2006] 1 Cr. App. R. (S.) 20, Rose, L.J., CA (Crim Div).

3744. **Sexual offences–Voyeurism–Appropriateness of custodial sentence**

[Sex Offenders Act 1997; Powers of Criminal Courts (Sentencing) Act 2000 Sch.2; Sexual Offences Act 2003 s.67.]

The appellant (P) appealed against two concurrent sentences of eight months' imprisonment imposed after pleas of guilty to offences under the Sexual Offences Act 2003 s.67(1) and s.67(4). P had installed a video camera in the bathroom of his home so that he could view his 24 year old stepdaughter in the shower. P had connected the camera to a screen in a bedroom, and had watched and recorded the images. P submitted that he was of previous good character and had made a guilty plea at the first opportunity.

Held, allowing the appeal, that, considering the mitigating factors and the fact that P was in need of therapy, custodial sentences were inappropriate. The initial sentences were quashed, and two concurrent sentences of one year community rehabilitation orders were imposed with a condition that under the Powers of Criminal Courts (Sentencing) Act 2000 Sch.2 P participate in a community sex offender group work programme throughout the period of that order. The requirement for P to notify for registration under the Sex Offenders Act 1997 was reduced to a period of five years.

R. v. IP, [2004] EWCA Crim 2646, [2005] 1 Cr. App. R. (S.) 102, Rose, L.J. (Vice President), CA (Crim Div).

3745. **Sexual offences against mentally disordered persons–Learning difficulties–No position of trust–Early guilty plea**

The appellant (Y) appealed against a sentence of 15 months' imprisonment following a guilty plea to an offence of sexual intercourse with a defective. Although Y was not in a position of trust in relation to the victim he was aware of her learning difficulties. Y submitted that the sentence was manifestly excessive in view of his early guilty plea, previous good character and remorse.

Held, allowing the appeal, that in view of Y's previous good record, remorse, early guilty plea and the absence of any position of trust in respect of the victim, the sentence imposed was excessive, *R. v. Adcock (Deric James)* [2000] 1 Cr.

App. R. (S.) 563, [2000] C.L.Y. 1302 applied. A term of nine months' imprisonment was substituted for the original term.

R. v. YOUNG (ROBERT), [2004] EWCA Crim 1183, [2005] 1 Cr. App. R. (S.) 11, Owen, J., CA (Crim Div).

3746. Shoplifting–Sentencing guidelines

The defendants applied for leave to appeal against their sentences. The court took the opportunity to give guidelines on sentence levels for offences of shoplifting.

Held, giving judgment accordingly, that when dealing with adult shoplifters, sentencers should bear in mind the following principles (1) it was a classic offence for which custody should be the last resort; custody would almost never be appropriate for a first offence. Where the offence had been aggravated by the use of a child, immediate custody had been and was still merited. A community penalty might in some cases be appropriate on a guilty plea by a first time offender, even where other adults were involved and the offence was organised; (2) where offences were attributable to drug addiction, a drug treatment and testing order would often be appropriate; (3) a short custodial term of not more than one month might be appropriate for a defendant who persistently offended on a minor scale. Where that persistence also involved preparation of equipment by the defendant to facilitate the offence, two months might be called for; (4) even where a defendant had to be sentenced for a large number of such offences, or where he had a history of persistent similar offending on a significant scale, the comparative lack of seriousness of the offence and the need for proportionality between the sentence and the particular offence would, on a plea of guilty, rarely require a total sentence of more than two years and would often merit no more than 12 to 18 months; (5) young offenders would usually be dealt with appropriately by a non custodial penalty, where there was no evidence that they were being used by adults; (6) nothing in the guidelines was intended to affect the level of sentence appropriate for shoplifting by organised gangs. When that occurred repeatedly or on a large scale, sentences of the order of four years might well be appropriate, even on a plea of guilty. If violence was used to a shopkeeper and a charge of robbery was inapt, a sentence in excess of four years was likely to be appropriate. However, shoplifting by isolated individuals, not accompanied by threats or violence, although it was a nuisance, particularly to shopkeepers, was generally not dangerous or frightening and did not damage public confidence. Victims were not usually particularly vulnerable by reason of age or youth, *R. v. Roth (Alfred)* (1980) 2 Cr. App. R. (S.) 65, [1981] C.L.Y. 525.183, *R. v. MacLeod (Donald Gerrard)* (1981) 3 Cr. App. R. (S.) 247, [1982] C.L.Y. 684.76, *R. v. Keogh (Brian)* (1994) 15 Cr. App. R. (S.) 279, [1994] C.L.Y. 1318 and *R. v. Reeves (Audrey Doris)* (1980) 2 Cr. App. R. (S.) 35, [1980] C.L.Y. 571.72 disapproved, *R. v. Moss (Linda)* (1986) 8 Cr. App. R. (S.) 276, [1987] C.L.Y. 1059, *R. v. Goldrick (Valerie May)* (1988) 10 Cr. App. R. (S.) 346, [1990] C.L.Y. 1430 and *R. v. Mariconda (Liana)* (1988) 10 Cr. App. R. (S.) 356, [1990] C.L.Y. 1428 considered, and *Attorney General's Reference (No.64 of 2003), Re* [2003] EWCA Crim 3948, [2004] 2 Cr. App. R. (S.) 38, [2004] 7 C.L. 415 approved.

R. v. PAGE (CYRIL EDWARD); R. v. MAHER (GERRARD MARTIN); R. v. STEWART (DAVID IAN), [2004] EWCA Crim 3358, [2005] 2 Cr. App. R. (S.) 37, Rose, L.J., CA (Crim Div).

3747. Supply of drugs–18 year old supplying crack cocaine to undercover police officers–Imposition of non custodial sentence–Undue leniency

The Attorney General referred to the court as unduly lenient a sentence comprising a two year community rehabilitation order and 100 hours' community punishment that had been imposed on the offender (M) following his plea of guilty to seven offences of supplying a Class A controlled drug. M, who was 18, had on seven occasions provided undercover police officers with crack cocaine. On five occasions, the amount involved was in the region of 200 to 250 milligrammes. On the other two occasions, double that amount was supplied. In imposing a non custodial sentence, the judge took into account, inter alia, M's age, the fact that he had no criminal record and the contents of the pre sentence report, which commented, inter alia, that M had been somewhat naive about drugs, that he had learnt his lesson from his arrest and that he was unlikely to reoffend.

Held, dismissing the reference, that the general principle was clear: those who dealt in drugs would, for the purposes of deterring others and the protection of the public, face significant custodial sentences. There had, however, been sufficient material before the judge to justify his taking the exceptional course of imposing a non custodial sentence on M. Although the sentence was clearly lenient, it would not be appropriate to interfere with it.

ATTORNEY GENERAL'S REFERENCE (NO.20 OF 2005), *Re*; *sub nom*. R. v. MAY (MICHAEL ANTHONY) [2005] EWCA Crim 1861, Latham, L.J., CA (Crim Div).

3748. Supply of drugs–Aggravating features–Runners between cocaine suppliers and undercover police–Late guilty plea–Undue leniency

The Attorney General referred as unduly lenient sentences of three and a half years' imprisonment and three years' imprisonment imposed on the offenders S and H respectively following guilty pleas for the offences of conspiracy to supply and being concerned in the supply of cocaine. The offenders had acted as runners between drug suppliers and undercover police officers. The Attorney General contended that there were a number of aggravating features: the supplies of cocaine were repeated and continued over a two month period in relation to S and a 12 month period in relation to H; the supply was on a large and escalating scale; the role played by each offender was vital to the distribution of cocaine, and S had a previous conviction for possession of cocaine; The Attorney General submitted that the sentences imposed failed to properly reflect the gravity of the offences, the aggravating features, the need for deterrence and public concern about the supply of cocaine and its social consequences.

Held, allowing the references in part, that the sentence passed upon S was unduly lenient. In the circumstances of his late plea on the day of trial, a sentence of six years or possibly more would have been appropriate. However, taking into account double jeopardy, the sentence was increased to five years' imprisonment. The sentence given to H was plainly lenient, and might have been unduly lenient. However, having regard to double jeopardy and the important factor that he had already been released from prison, the sentence was not altered. With respect to the roles played by runners in the supply of drugs, what was significant was the amount of drug supplied and the period over which it was supplied. The proximity of a runner to the major source of supply was also a factor to be considered, *R. v. Twisse (Michael James)* [2001] 2 Cr. App. R. (S.) 9, [2001] C.L.Y. 1282, *R. v. Djahit (Turkesh)* [1999] 2 Cr. App. R. (S.) 142, [1999] C.L.Y. 1137 and *R. v. Afonso (Americo Practicio)* [2004] EWCA Crim 2342, [2005] Crim. L.R. 73, [2004] C.L.Y. 3454 considered.

ATTORNEY GENERAL'S REFERENCE (NOS.74 AND 75 OF 2004), *Re*; *sub nom*. R. v. SCOTT (MARK RAYMOND); R. v. HOLMES (ANTHONY JAMES) [2005] EWCA Crim 262, Rose, L.J. (V-P), CA (Crim Div).

3749. Supply of drugs–Confiscation orders–Judge ignoring Crown concession of no prior involvement in drug trafficking

[Drug Trafficking Act 1994 s.4.]

The defendant (L) appealed against a confiscation order under the Drug Trafficking Act 1994 following his plea of guilty to conspiring to supply drugs. The Crown had accepted that L had no prior involvement in drug trafficking. However, the judge relied on the statutory presumptions in s.4(3) of the Act on the basis that there was no serious risk of injustice under s.4(4) in doing so, but he failed to give any reasons why he had chosen to ignore the Crown's concession. The Crown contended that a defendant could be sentenced on the basis that he had not previously been involved in drug trafficking but still have a confiscation order made against him relating to previous drug trafficking.

Held, allowing the appeal, that where the Crown had made a concession that a defendant had no previous involvement in drug trafficking, unless that concession was withdrawn, there would be an apparent injustice if it were ignored. A fully reasoned explanation was required if the court concluded that the statutory assumptions should still apply. The appropriate course where a concession had been wrongly made was for the Crown to withdraw it, thereby giving the defendant the opportunity to prove that he was a first time offender, or of satisfying the court that there was a serious risk of injustice for some other reason if the statutory assumptions were applied, *R. v. Benjafield (Karl Robert) (Confiscation Order)* [2002] UKHL 2, [2003] 1 A.C. 1099, [2002] C.L.Y. 3897 followed. In the instant case the failure to give reasons for the application of the statutory presumption meant that it was impossible to conclude that the judge had applied his mind to the Crown's concession.

R. v. LUNNON (HENRY JOSEPH), [2004] EWCA Crim 1125, [2005] 1 Cr. App. R. (S.) 24, Kay, L.J., CA (Crim Div).

3750. **Supply of drugs–Conspiracy–Wholesale distribution of cocaine–Comparison with sentences imposed on importers–Undue leniency**

The Attorney General referred as unduly lenient various sentences imposed on the offenders (W, N, L and C) after they pleaded guilty to offences of conspiracy to supply drugs. W, N, L and C had been involved in a lengthy operation distributing cocaine at the wholesale level. W had also pleaded guilty to conspiracy to supply large quantities of cannabis. Records seized by the police indicated that over 400kg of cocaine had been distributed by the group over an 18 month period and that their turnover had been in the region of £7.6 million. W had acted as the ringleader of the operation. The other defendants played lesser but still significant roles in the distribution operation. W, N, L and C were sentenced to terms of imprisonment of 12, 7, 9 and 8 years respectively. The Attorney General argued that (1) there was no material distinction between the sentences that should be imposed upon those playing a major role in the importation of class A drugs and those playing a role in the distribution of such drugs within the United Kingdom; (2) in relation to W, he had been the ringleader of a highly organised high value commercial operation over a period of 18 months and, given a starting point for sentencing of 20 years, the sentence imposed had failed to reflect the gravity of the offence, and (3) in relation to N, although he had only been involved in a single consignment of drugs, the sentence failed to address the need for deterrence and public concern. In contrast, L had been a member of the group for a long time and had made a significant contribution to its operation and C had also made a significant contribution to the operation.

Held, giving judgment accordingly, that (1) generally speaking those responsible for organising the importation of drugs into the United Kingdom should receive somewhat higher sentences than those responsible for distribution within the United Kingdom, *R. v. Lowe (Paul)* [2003] EWCA Crim 3182 and *R. v. Soares (Ronald)* [2003] EWCA Crim 2488 considered. (2) If W had been tried, a sentence of 20 years' imprisonment would have been at the bottom of the appropriate bracket. W was a major organiser in the wholesale distribution of drugs, albeit he was not at the top of the chain. The sentence imposed was conspicuously over generous. Given the lateness of W's plea, a sentence of between 15 and 16 years would have been appropriate. In those circumstances the sentence was unduly lenient. However, taking account of double jeopardy, the sentence imposed was not one with which the court would interfere. (3) In relation to N, L and C, the court would have expected each of their sentences to have been somewhat higher. However, without analysing whether their sentences were unduly lenient, it was apparent that when double jeopardy was taken into account the sentences passed were not sentences with which the court could properly interfere.

ATTORNEY GENERAL'S REFERENCE (NOS. 99, 100, 101 AND 102 OF 2004), *Re*; R. v. NADARAJAH; R. v. LONG; R. v. CONNELL; *sub nom.* R. v. WHITEWAY,

[2005] EWCA Crim 294, [2005] 2 Cr. App. R. (S.) 82, Rose, L.J., CA (Crim Div).

3751. Supply of drugs–Drug addict supplying small quantities of heroin and cocaine on behalf of dealer–Sentence length

The appellant (W) appealed against a total sentence of six years' imprisonment imposed for offences of possessing with intent and supplying heroin and cocaine. W had been observed supplying a woman with a quantity of drugs. When the police approached, he was seen to swallow something and he later passed two packages containing the drugs. W was heavily addicted to heroin and funded his addiction by selling drugs on behalf of a dealer, in return for which he would receive a free supply for his own use and a small amount of cash. W pleaded guilty, his basis of plea being that he had no proprietary interest in the drugs in his possession but was carrying out the transactions at another's direction. His dealer had offered to discharge W's debt to him if W agreed to act on his behalf in this way. There was evidence that since his arrest, W had made efforts to overcome his addiction. On appeal, W argued that in the light of the authorities the sentencing judge had taken too high a starting point, and that the sentence did not reflect the basis of plea.

Held, allowing the appeal, that a sentence of six years' imprisonment following a guilty plea was too high, *R. v. Singh (Satvir)* (1988) 10 Cr. App. R. (S.) 402, [1990] C.L.Y. 1290, *R. v. Aramah (John Uzu)* (1983) 76 Cr. App. R. 190, [1983] C.L.Y. 764.19, *R. v. Djahit (Turkesh)* [1999] 2 Cr. App. R. (S.) 142, [1999] C.L.Y. 1137 and *R. v. Afonso (Americo Practicio)* [2004] EWCA Crim 2342, [2005] 1 Cr. App. R. (S.) 99, [2004] C.L.Y. 3454 considered. In *Djahit* it was said that an appropriate sentence following a trial for a low level retailer with no previous convictions selling to other addicts mainly to fund his own habit was six years' imprisonment. However, in *Afonso* the court reviewed its decision in *Djahit* and concluded that for offenders who were addicts motivated solely by the desire to fund their own addiction, held no stock of drugs and had made few retail supplies to undercover police officers only, the appropriate sentence was in the region of two and a half years. In the instant case, W was supplying two different types of Class A drug to numerous different customers. The effect of *Afonso* was to encourage more leniency for drug dealers who acted solely or mainly out of a desire to fund their own habit and were not commercial operators as such. On that basis, and having regard to the early guilty plea and the other mitigating features, the sentence of six years' imprisonment was reduced to one of three and a half years.

R. v. WADE (SCOTT PATRICK), [2005] EWCA Crim 183, [2005] 2 Cr. App. R. (S.) 69, Clarke, L.J., CA (Crim Div).

3752. Supply of drugs–Drugs sold to fund recreational drug use and studying–Undue leniency

The Attorney General referred as unduly lenient an 80 hour community punishment order and an 18 month community rehabilitation order imposed on the offender (W) following his pleas of guilty to five counts of supplying Class A drugs, four counts of being knowingly concerned in the supply of Class A drugs and two counts of offering to supply Class A drugs. Over a 15 day period W had supplied, or arranged to supply, small amounts of crack cocaine and heroin to undercover police officers. A pre sentence report stated that W had come to the United Kingdom from Jamaica to study in 2003 but had faced financial difficulties. He used crack cocaine to relieve stress and sold the drugs to fund his drug use and college course. W was held to be unsuitable for a drug treatment and testing order as he was only a recreational user of drugs. The Attorney General contended that there were three aggravating features: (i) the offences occurred over a 15 day period; (ii) W was prepared to use others to sell drugs on his behalf; (iii) two types of Class A drugs were involved. Further, the sentence was unduly lenient as there were no exceptional features which justified a non custodial term, and a sentence of between two years and two years and six months was appropriate. In mitigation were W's early plea of guilty, his previous good character and the remorse that he had shown. W contended that it was not a case where he had a stock of drugs and that he had been contacted by the undercover officer.

Held, allowing the reference, that a sentence of between two years and two years and six months in the court below would have been favourable to W; however, it would be wrong in principle to impose such a sentence as W had already performed more than half of the community punishment order, and the principle of double jeopardy had to be taken into account. The sentences would be quashed and sentences of 12 months substituted for each count to run concurrently, *R. v. Afonso (Americo Practicio)* [2004] EWCA Crim 2342, [2005] 1 Cr. App. R. (S.) 99, [2004] C.L.Y. 3454 distinguished.

ATTORNEY GENERAL'S REFERENCE (NO.35 OF 2005), *Re; sub nom.* R. v. WHYTE (LINCOLN) [2005] EWCA Crim 1750, Clarke, L.J., CA (Crim Div).

3753. Supply of drugs–Possession with intent to supply–Class A drugs–Undue leniency

The Attorney General referred as unduly lenient a two year community rehabilitation order imposed on an offender (S) following guilty pleas to four drug offences arising from the commercial supply of Class A drugs. S, a taxi driver, had been sentenced to concurrent two year community rehabilitation orders for possession of cocaine with intent to supply, supply of cocaine, possession of ecstasy and possession of diazepam. S had made admissions in interview, had pleaded guilty at the first opportunity and had shown remorse. The Attorney General considered that the aggravating factors were the repeated, systematic and commercial retail supply of Class A drugs to members of the public and the fact that S was in a position of employment serving the public. The Attorney General submitted that S's sentence failed to reflect serious public concern about such offences and the need to deter others. The Attorney General argued that a custodial sentence should have been imposed.

Held, allowing the reference, that the total sentence was unduly lenient and was replaced with one of three years' imprisonment. The fact that S was a taxi driver was not a significant aggravating feature. However, S had been involved in the commercial supply of Class A drugs over two and a half months to several friends and customers, and deterrent sentences were required for the supply of Class A drugs. Although a sentencing judge had to exercise a degree of discretion, it was wrong for him to step outside the normal framework of sentencing guidelines unless there were very exceptional circumstances. S's case was not exceptional, and a community sentence for such offending was clearly unduly lenient, even allowing for the important mitigating factors in S's case. At first instance, a sentence of four years' imprisonment would have been appropriate but a lesser sentence was warranted, having regard to the element of double jeopardy and the fact that S had been led to believe that he could serve his sentence in the community. It would be appropriate to impose concurrent sentences of three years' imprisonment for possession with intent to supply and supply of cocaine, together with a 12 month concurrent sentence for possession of ecstasy. No separate penalty was imposed for the possession of diazepam, *R. v. Djahit (Turkesh)* [1999] 2 Cr. App. R. (S.) 142, [1999] C.L.Y. 1137 considered.

ATTORNEY GENERAL'S REFERENCE (NO.46 OF 2005), *Re; sub nom.* R. v. STEPHENSON (MATTHEW JOHN) [2005] EWCA Crim 2146, Keene, L.J., CA (Crim Div).

3754. Supply of drugs–Possession with intent to supply–Drugs partially disposed of before police raid–Basis for calculating missing amount–Undue leniency

The Attorney General referred to the court as unduly lenient a sentence of four years' imprisonment imposed on the offender (G), who had pleaded guilty to four counts of possessing a controlled drug of Class A with intent to supply, and a sentence of three years' imprisonment imposed on offender (Z) for being concerned in supplying a controlled drug of Class A. The police had kept G under surveillance, and he was alleged to have paid £24,000 to a supplier (B) for 1.3 kg of cocaine. Z was alleged to have driven B when the cocaine was delivered. The police raided G's home and discovered G's partner had washed some of the cocaine down a sink. G pleaded guilty on the first day of his trial, whilst Z was convicted. They submitted that they should be sentenced on the basis of the amount of cocaine actually seized because any calculation as to the amount that had been washed away was purely speculative. The Attorney General argued that it was possible to calculate the total amount based on the £24,000 that had been paid for it. On that basis and since G was not a low level retailer of cocaine, the Attorney General argued, his sentence was unduly lenient. G argued that the level of the sentences imposed could have been due to the judge's possessing confidential mitigation on behalf of one of the defendants and that where that was the case any other defendants were entitled to the benefit of its effect.

Held, allowing the references in part, that (1) the offenders should be sentenced on the basis of the total amount of drugs that had been involved before the partial disposal. The cash seized could give an indication of the weight of drugs there had been. It would be wrong to allow the act of washing away some of the cocaine to affect the gravity of the case. (2) Given the amount of cash seized, G was not a low level retailer. (3) It would be extraordinary if the offenders were entitled to the benefit arising from confidential mitigation on behalf of one of them. (4) The proper sentence for a high level retailer such as G would be about 10 years' imprisonment, reduced by about one year for the late guilty plea, *Attorney General's Reference (Nos.13, 14, 15, 16, 17 and 18 of 2004), Re* [2004] EWCA Crim 1885, [2005] 1 Cr. App. R. (S.) 66, [2004] C.L.Y. 3450 and *R. v. Aranguren (Jose de Jesus)* (1994) 99 Cr. App. R. 347, [1995] C.L.Y. 1364 considered. Taking into account double jeopardy and the delay in the proceedings, the appropriate sentence for G would be six years' imprisonment. (5) Z could have properly expected a sentence in the region of eight years' imprisonment. But as a result of the delay it would not be fair to increase Z's sentence more than a year after it had been passed and four to five months after his release from prison. So although his sentence had been unduly lenient, it would not be varied.

ATTORNEY GENERAL'S REFERENCE (NOS.83 AND 85 OF 2004), *Re; sub nom.* R. v. GARDNER; R. v. AFZAL [2005] EWCA Crim 1537, Hooper, L.J., CA (Crim Div).

3755. Supply of drugs – Release on licence – Need to inform court of early release where reference pending – Undue leniency

The Attorney General referred to the court as unduly lenient total sentences of two years' imprisonment and two years and six months' imprisonment imposed on the offenders (B and H) respectively following guilty pleas to two counts of conspiracy to supply class A drugs. During a surveillance operation B and H had been observed supplying heroin and crack cocaine. At the time of the offences B was subject to a 12 month community rehabilitation order. H, a Jamaican citizen and the mother to two young children, was of previous good character. When sentencing the judge took into account the fact that once her sentence had been served H would be removed to Jamaica. By the time the reference came to be considered by the court H, had been released on home detention curfew.

Held, finding the sentence unduly lenient but not varying it, that (1) even allowing for the mitigating factors and the principles of double jeopardy the sentences were unduly lenient. However, H was the mother of two small children, whose father had been returned to Jamaica, and the interests of those children had to be taken into account. As an act of mercy to the children and to do justice between the defendants the sentences would not be increased. However, an order would be made recommending the deportation of H. (2) Where a defendant was to be released before the statutory earliest release date as a matter of practice the Court of Appeal should be informed, in writing and in advance, of any application by the Attorney General. Whilst it would not be right to hold up release simply because the Attorney General had a reference pending, if proper notice was given by the prison service of an intention to release a defendant, before the statutory earliest release date, the Attorney

General could let the court know and the date of the hearing could be brought forward to a date before release.

ATTORNEY GENERAL'S REFERENCE (NOS.132 AND 133 OF 2004), *Re*; *sub nom*. R. v. BURDEN (SARAH); R. v. HILL (DEBRA), [2005] EWCA Crim 354, *The Times*, March 21, 2005, Judge, L.J., CA (Crim Div).

3756. Threatening to kill–Sentence length–Threats of revenge made while intoxicated and in police custody

The appellant (L) appealed against a sentence of 16 months' imprisonment following a plea of guilty for an offence of threatening to take revenge. L and his father had had an argument regarding money which resulted in L punching his father and then taking some money from him. His father had made a complaint to the police. L discovered this and threatened to kill his father. he also threatened to inform local people that his father was a paedophile. L had a long record of previous offences and there was evidence that he had difficulty controlling his anger. The sentencing judge stated that he considered the starting point was two years' imprisonment and then gave an appropriate reduction for the plea of guilty.

Held, allowing the appeal, that although any threats to kill were a serious offence, the starting point in the instant case had been too high. Whilst L had a criminal record including offences of threatening behaviour and violence, the threats in the instant case had been made while he was intoxicated. Further, when some of the threats were made he had been in police custody and plainly unable to carry them out. An appropriate starting point in the instant case was accordingly 12 months' imprisonment, discounted to eight months for the guilty plea.

R. v. LAWRENCE (DANIEL KENT), [2004] EWCA Crim 2219, [2005] 1 Cr. App. R. (S.) 83, Mance, L.J., CA (Crim Div).

3757. Totality of sentence–Consecutive sentences–False imprisonment–Conspiracy to commit gross indecency with child–Multiple drug offences–Undue leniency

The Attorney General referred as unduly lenient a total sentence of five years' imprisonment imposed on an offender (W) following guilty pleas to 10 offences. The total sentence was made up of the following concurrent sentences: five years' imprisonment for supplying heroin and cocaine; three years' imprisonment for the supply of amphetamine; five years' imprisonment for possession of heroin with intent to supply; three years' imprisonment for possession with intent to supply amphetamine; 18 months' imprisonment for possession of crack cocaine for personal use; 15 months' imprisonment for possession of cannabis resin for personal use; 15 months' imprisonment for conspiracy to commit an act of gross indecency with a boy; 18 months' imprisonment for false imprisonment of a man; and two years' imprisonment for the supply of crack cocaine. The Attorney General submitted that the following aggravating features were present: the drug dealing was over an extended period; and the child victim of the sexual offence and the victim of the false imprisonment had been humiliated by the filming of the offences.

Held, allowing the reference, that the total sentence was unduly lenient. There was no justification for imposing the concurrent sentences in respect of the false imprisonment and the gross indecency. The false imprisonment was a severe offence which was additional to the supply of drugs. It called for a significant additional sentence. The minimum sentence which should have been imposed at first instance was a consecutive sentence of two and a half years' imprisonment. Furthermore, the offending in relation to the boy was grave. The incident was deliberate and humiliating, with the offence being filmed, and it appeared that the victim was being groomed. The minimum sentence which should have been imposed was a consecutive sentence of three years' imprisonment. Although the sentences for the drugs offences were lenient they were not varied as, having regard to totality of the sentence, it was justifiable to limit the term of imprisonment to five years. At first instance, therefore, a total sentence of ten and a half years' imprisonment would have been appropriate. However, having regard to double jeopardy, the sentence in respect of false imprisonment was ordered to be served concurrently so that the total sentence imposed was eight years' imprisonment.

ATTORNEY GENERAL'S REFERENCE (NO.138 OF 2004), *Re; sub nom.* R. v. WHITE (SHANE) [2005] EWCA Crim 198, Kennedy, L.J., CA (Crim Div).

3758. Totality of sentence–Robbery–Manslaughter–Elderly victims targeted– Overall criminality

The appellants (Z and L) appealed against sentences of nine years six months and ten years respectively following pleas of guilty to various counts of robbery, handling stolen goods and manslaughter. All the offences involved street robberies of elderly vulnerable victims who had been specifically targeted. The offence of manslaughter involved the robbery of an 83 year old woman (S). Z had grabbed her bag and she had fallen to the ground suffering fatal head injuries. Z ran off and escaped in a car driven by L. When sentencing the judge had treated the offences as ones of joint enterprise and had only allowed a six month difference between sentences to reflect the fact that Z had been aged 21 whilst L had been aged over 30 years old. The appellants contended that the judge had given insufficient credit for their guilty pleas and for their relatively modest criminal records.

Held, dismissing the appeals, that the judge had had to form an overall view on the criminality of each appellant, and the sentences passed reflected the various submissions made on behalf of each appellant and could not be described as manifestly excessive, *Attorney-General's Reference (Nos.19, 20 and 21 of 2001), Re* [2001] EWCA Crim 1432, [2002] 1 Cr. App. R. (S.) 33 applied. The appellants had repeatedly gone out and targeted elderly people in the street. Neither Z nor L had checked to see if S was all right before they fled, leaving her lying on the ground. The offences were committed to fund drug addiction. The growing threat of street robberies was a matter of grave public concern and the need for deterrence had to be reflected in the sentences passed by the courts. In the instant case, given the numerous offences, other than the one that led to a death, consecutive sentences could have been passed. However, it was good practice not to pass consecutive sentences and for the totality of the sentence to reflect the fact that there had been a number of offences over a number of days, some involving violence.

R. v. ALI (ZUBER MAKBUL); R. v. LOTAY (ANADEEP), [2004] EWCA Crim 2735, [2005] 2 Cr. App. R. (S.) 2, Potter, L.J., CA (Crim Div).

3759. Unlawful wounding–Imitation firearms–Forced entry into home at night– Community rehabilitation orders–Undue leniency

[Offences Against the Person Act 1861 s.20; Firearms Act 1968 s.16A.]

The Attorney General referred as unduly lenient a sentence of a three year community rehabilitation order with a condition that the offender (M) attend a "Think First" course and be under curfew for four months following a guilty plea to offences of unlawful wounding contrary to the Offences Against the Person Act 1861 s.20 and possession of an imitation firearm contrary to the Firearms Act 1968 s.16A. M had, with her two coaccused, forcefully entered the house of a family with whom they had been quarrelling at 23.30. The three of them rushed at the wife and attacked her with a knife. M then threatened the husband with an imitation handgun. The Attorney General contended that the sentence failed to take account of a number of aggravating features including that the offence took place at night, in a private home, after forced entry; that children were present; that the offences were pre planned and that the firearm offence took place after an attack with a knife that was motivated by a desire for revenge.

Held, allowing the reference, that in view of the aggravating features of the offence a sentence of two and a half years' to three years imprisonment would have been the appropriate sentence, *R. v. Avis (Tony)* [1998] 1 Cr. App. R. 420, [1998] C.L.Y. 1214, *Attorney General's Reference (No.49 of 1999), Re* [2000] 1 Cr. App. R. (S.) 436, [2000] C.L.Y. 1244 and *Attorney General's Reference*

(No.71 of 2001), Re [2001] EWCA Crim 2838, [2002] 2 Cr. App. R. (S.) 23, [2002] C.L.Y. 3942 considered. There were several mitigating factors, in particular M's remorse and her attempts to address her pattern of behaviour. Taking into account double jeopardy and that a custodial sentence was to be imposed for the first time, a sentence of 15 months' imprisonment was appropriate.

ATTORNEY GENERAL'S REFERENCE (NO.155 OF 2004), *Re* [2005] EWCA Crim 968, Rose, L.J., CA (Crim Div).

3760. **Unlawful wounding—Racially aggravated offences—Victim racially abused and slashed with knife—Undue leniency**

The Attorney General referred as unduly lenient a sentence of three years' imprisonment imposed on C for racially aggravated unlawful wounding. The sentence had been increased from 10 months by the sentencing judge, as the probation service were of the view that the drug treatment and testing order that he had reimposed was inappropriate to the nature of the offence. However, the judge had previously told C's counsel that he would not impose a custodial sentence beyond the six months C had already served if C pleaded guilty as this would allow him to benefit further from the drug treatment order. The judge reiterated his view when prosecuting counsel expressed his disapproval of the case being dealt with on the basis of a simple unlawful wounding. C, who had several previous convictions and was, at the time of the offence, subject to a drug treatment and testing order, racially abused the victim when he approached C's girlfriend, with whom the victim had been at school. Then, C took out a knife and slashed the victim's neck.

Held, finding the sentence unduly lenient but declining to vary it, that the Attorney General was entitled to seek a review, even though the judge's view as to the sentence had caused C to change his plea. Since the prosecution had allowed the judge's proposed course of action on sentencing to continue, C's counsel submitted that the Attorney General should not be allowed to ask for the sentence to be changed. This was correct, but here it was not the case that prosecution counsel had given C an expectation of a particular sentence, since the prosecution, in meetings with the judge and defence counsel, had indicated only that the prosecution would not be prepared to deal with the case as one of simple unlawful wounding and, when the judge confirmed his own view of the matter, accepted the situation as inevitable. As to the sentence, it depended on the wound's seriousness and by how much the racial element had affected the seriousness of the offence. C had caused a significant wound which could have led to worse consequences, so that the appropriate sentence on a guilty plea would be at least two and a half years, and the racial aggravation would increase it by one and a half years, *R. v. Saunders (Joseph Brian)* [2000] 1 Cr. App. R. 458, [2000] C.L.Y. 1388 and *R. v. Kelly (Lewis)* [2001] EWCA Crim 170, [2001] 2 Cr. App. R. (S.) 73, [2001] C.L.Y. 1191 followed. Taking account of the double jeopardy element, three years was the correct sentence.

ATTORNEY GENERAL'S REFERENCE (NO.19 OF 2004), *Re*; *sub nom.* R. v. CHARLTON (BRETT), [2004] EWCA Crim 1239, [2005] 1 Cr. App. R. (S.) 18, Latham, L.J., CA (Crim Div).

3761. **Violent disorder—Young offenders—Deterrent sentences**

The appellants (R, M, C, K and B) appealed against custodial sentences of 34 months, four years and six months, 27 months, 30 months and 27 months respectively following pleas of guilty to violent disorder. In incidents following two football matches, large groups of England supporters aged between 16 and 25 years old, including the appellants, who had all been drinking heavily, went on rampages in the streets causing widespread damage to property and injury to police officers. K was involved in both the incidents and was sentenced to consecutive custodial terms of 30 months and two years. With the exception of M, who had previous convictions for disorderly behaviour and racially threatening behaviour, the appellants were all of good character. M, C and B were all young offenders aged 18 and 19 years old.

Held, allowing the appeals in part, that (1) offences of violent disorder could take various forms, from the extremely serious to those amounting to little more than affray, and it was important that the courts pitched sentences to give effect to the level of seriousness. The nature of violent disorder often involved young men who had otherwise been of exemplary good character. Whilst the courts had to have regard to the personal characteristics of defendants, regard also had to be had to the effect of the violent disorder on the public. Violent disorder could cause real anxiety and distress to the public. It was not just the individual conduct of one defendant but the nature of the offence as a whole. When it was the habit of the young to drink excessively and then behave out of character it was important that the courts sent the message of the very great dangers of embarking on binge drinking. While courts wished to be sympathetic they had to consider the effect of the offence as a whole on the public. (2) With the exception of K's sentence, none of the sentences was manifestly excessive. Whilst the sentences were severe they were necessary to deter others and to protect the public. Credit was given for the guilty pleas and where the pleas of guilty had been entered late that credit was reduced. In its totality the sentence imposed on K was manifestly excessive. The sentence of 30 months would be quashed and substituted with one year nine months, giving a total sentence of three years nine months' imprisonment, *R. v. Chapman (Andrew Edward)* [2002] EWCA Crim 2346, (2002) 146 S.J.L.B. 242 considered.

R. v. REES (LOUIS); R. v. McELROY (SEAN JAMES); R. v. CARROLL (MATTHEW); R. v. KILLICK (BILL GEORGE); R. v. MORRIS-BROOKS (STUART), [2005] EWCA Crim 1857, *The Times*, July 22, 2005, Lord Woolf, L.C.J, CA (Crim Div).

3762. Wounding with intent – Sentence length – Undue leniency

The Attorney General referred to the court as unduly lenient a total sentence of two years eight months' imprisonment imposed on the offender (K), who had pleaded guilty to wounding with intent and destroying property. K, who had been drinking heavily, went to his former partner's home, kicked down the door and attacked her new partner, whose ear and nose were partly bitten off. The incident was witnessed by K's young twin daughters. The Attorney General submitted that there were several aggravating features. K had been drunk, had broken into the property at night and, in the presence of his young children, had attacked his victim, who suffered severe trauma and was left permanently disfigured. K had previously been bound over to keep the peace after making threats to kill his former partner, and he had several previous convictions including a conviction for wounding. The Attorney General contended that the judge's starting point of four years after a trial was too low.

Held, finding the sentence unduly lenient but not varying it, that the starting point on conviction was at least five years, *Attorney General's Reference (No.59 of 2003), Re* [2003] EWCA Crim 3010 considered. That sentence had to be reduced by one third to reflect the plea. The principle of double jeopardy had to be taken into account and, whilst not determinative of the decision, the court gave weight to letters from K's former partner and the victim asking for the sentence not to be increased because of the effect on K's daughters. Whilst the sentence was lenient, it was not one with which the court should interfere.

ATTORNEY GENERAL'S REFERENCE (NO.31 OF 2005), *Re*; *sub nom.* R. v. KEANE (MICHAEL) [2005] EWCA Crim 1589, Gage, L.J., CA (Crim Div).

3763. Wounding with intent – Seriousness of offence – Unprovoked violent attack – Undue leniency

The Attorney General referred as unduly lenient a sentence of five years' imprisonment imposed on the offender for wounding with intent. The Attorney General pointed to the following aggravating features: the offender had instigated the attack and had enlisted the assistance of two others; a steering lock and knife had been used as weapons and the victim was unarmed; the attack was unprovoked and was planned; and the injuries to the victim were extremely severe and permanent. The Attorney General submitted that the sentence passed was inadequate to mark the gravity of the offence and its aggravating features, to deter others and to take account of public concern over the gratuitous use of violence.

Held, allowing the reference, that the offence was very grave and the sentence imposed was unduly lenient. A sentence of at least 12 years' imprisonment would have been appropriate. However, having regard to double jeopardy and personal mitigation, the sentence was increased to nine years' imprisonment.

ATTORNEY GENERAL'S REFERENCE (NO.20 OF 2004), *Re*; *sub nom.* R. v. BARKER (DANIEL), [2004] EWCA Crim 2723, [2005] 1 Cr. App. R. (S.) 111, Rose, L.J., CA (Crim Div).

3764. Young offenders–Burglary–Extreme vulnerability of victim–Undue leniency

[Powers of Criminal Courts (Sentencing) Act 2000 s.91.]

The Attorney General referred as unduly lenient sentences of 12 months' detention, 14 months' detention and an eight month detention and training order imposed on the offenders (D, S and W) following pleas of guilty to burglary, attempted burglary, attempted robbery and conspiracy to rob. The victim (V) of all the offences was an 85 year old partially sighted man. D's parents carried out domestic duties for V and his wife and had the keys to his house. When V's wife was taken into hospital D kept watch on V's home until V left and then burgled the house, using the keys entrusted to his parents, and stole purses containing in excess of £1,000. V's wife died and while V was visiting the chapel of rest S and W tried to kick down his door in order to carry out a burglary, but were disturbed by neighbours. A few days later S and W forced their way into V's home, S pinned him to the floor and, when he tried to get up, forced his head down. V's screams were heard by neighbours and S and W left empty handed. All three offenders had been overheard discussing and arranging the robbery a few days prior to the offence. D and S were 18 and W was 17 at the time of sentence. The Attorney General contended that there were five aggravating features: (i) V was highly vulnerable given his age and partial sight, and he was recently bereaved; (ii) V was deliberately targeted; (iii) a large amount of cash was taken; (iv) D acted in breach of trust by using the keys and in further breach by passing information to S and W; and (v) S and W tried to rob V in his own home and the offence was only prevented because of the intervention of neighbours. In mitigation were the pleas of guilty, with S and W pleading guilty at the earliest opportunity; D was of previous good character, S had two cautions and W one caution; all the offenders had expressed remorse; and the ages of the offenders, in particular S who was of low intelligence with a mental age of 10 and a half. The Attorney General submitted that the sentences were unduly lenient, failed to reflect the gravity of the offences and held no deterrent element.

Held, allowing the references, that the sentences passed were not only unduly lenient but were derisory. Each offender was guilty of repeatedly targeting the home of V who could scarcely have been more vulnerable. The financial loss to V was very great, and physical injuries at his age were deeply distressing, but those factors paled into insignificance given the immense distress caused by the offenders who knowingly and deliberately targeted him knowing firstly that his wife was ill and then that she had died. On any view each offender had behaved with persistence and in circumstances of great cruelty in relation to V, for which their youth and, in the case of S, low intelligence provided no explanation and only modest mitigation. Even a 10 year old would recognise the vulnerability of V and the wickedness he was subjecting him to. In the court below, sentences of four years' detention for D, four years and six months' detention for S, and four years' detention under the Powers of Criminal Courts (Sentencing) Act 2000 s.91 for W would have been expected. Accordingly, the sentences were quashed and respective sentences of three years' detention, three years and six months' detention and three years' detention, under s.91 of the Act, would be substituted.

ATTORNEY GENERAL'S REFERENCE (NOS.39, 40 AND 41 OF 2005); *sub nom.* R.V DALE (ADAM); R. v. SHEARMAN, PETER; R. v. W [2005] EWCA Crim 1961, Rose, L.J. (V-P), CA (Crim Div).

3765. Young offenders–Burglary–Systematic dwelling house burglaries with view to vehicle theft

The appellant (P) appealed against a sentence of three years' detention for his part in a campaign of domestic burglary. P and his co accused had pleaded guilty to various offences of burglary, attempted burglary and handling stolen goods. They had been involved in a series of systematic burglaries whereby households with expensive or valuable motor cars were targeted and burgled so that the keys to the cars could be taken and the vehicles stolen. In most cases entry was forced and the houses ransacked. A total of 35 burglaries had taken place and 22 cars had been stolen, of which 18 were recovered. P had been serving a three year term for burglary at the date of sentencing for the index offences and he argued that he had effectively been given a six year sentence.

Held, dismissing P's appeal, that the sentence for the index offence had been imposed to run concurrently with the earlier term and it was not excessive given the gravity of the offences. P's co accused (W) had been 17 at the dates of the offences and 18 when sentenced. The five year sentence imposed on him was substantial given his age and early guilty plea. However, W had played a major part in the crimes and had many earlier convictions; therefore the sentence was justified. Another codefendant who had been 16 or 17 at the dates of the offences would have been liable to a maximum sentence of a two year drug treatment and testing order had he been sentenced at 17. He had played a more minor role and had pleaded guilty. His sentence was reduced from two years to 18 months' detention, *R. v. Ghafoor (Imran Hussain)* [2002] EWCA Crim 1857, [2003] 1 Cr. App. R. (S.) 84, [2002] C.L.Y. 4047, *R. v. LM* [2002] EWCA Crim 3047, [2003] 2 Cr. App. R. (S.) 26, [2003] C.L.Y. 3751 and *R. v. Storey (Stephen David)* (1984) 6 Cr. App. R. (S.) 104, [1985] C.L.Y. 810 considered.

R. v. PALMER (JUSTIN ANTHONY); R. v. O'LEARY (DANIEL CHRISTOPHER); R. v. WOODEN (JAMES RAY), [2004] EWCA Crim 1039, [2004] 2 Cr. App. R. (S.) 97, Rose, L.J., CA (Crim Div).

3766. Young offenders–Causing death by dangerous driving–Two passengers killed as result of high speed driving

The appellant (K) appealed against a sentence of four years' detention in a young offender institution and 10 years' disqualification from driving, with the requirement that he then pass an extended driving test at the end of that period. K, who was 17 years old at the time of the offence, had pleaded guilty to two counts of causing death by dangerous driving. He had bought a car but then failed his driving test. Nevertheless, he drove the car until his mother put a lock on the gate to the drive to prevent him. K and a 17 year old friend sawed through the lock and took the car, later picking up a 14 year old boy. A witness described K as driving at more than 100 mph on a road with a 60 mph speed limit before he lost control and hit a tree. The 14 year old died at the scene and the other friend died three days later in hospital. The judge found that K's culpability was in the "higher" category because two people died as a result of his driving deliberately badly at high speed and without a licence or insurance. However, there were mitigating factors: K had no previous convictions; he was a good student; he had pleaded guilty; and he felt genuine remorse. K contended that since the starting point for the "higher culpability" category was four to five years' imprisonment, the judge must have either given insufficient weight to the mitigating factors or used too high a starting point.

Held, allowing the appeal in part, that four years' detention was a severe sentence for a young man who had caused the death of his two passengers by dangerous driving, but the judge's weighing of the aggravating and mitigating features was not to be criticised and he had not used too high a starting point,

Attorney General's Reference (No.152 of 2002), Re [2003] EWCA Crim 996, [2003] 3 All E.R. 40, [2004] 2 C.L. 455 and *Attorney General's Reference (Nos.14 and 24 of 1993), Re* [1994] 1 W.L.R. 530, [1994] C.L.Y. 1193 considered. However, the 10 years' disqualification from driving was too long and would be reduced to five years. A driving ban was designed to protect road users in the future, and there was a strong likelihood that K had learnt his lesson and would no longer be a threat to the public.

R. v. KELLY (JAMES STEPHEN), [2004] EWCA Crim 1629, [2005] 1 Cr. App. R. (S.) 39, Hooper, L.J., CA (Crim Div).

3767. Young offenders–Criminal damage–Graffiti on underground trains– Deterrent effect of custodial sentence

The appellant (V) appealed against a sentence of two years' detention in a young offender institution, having pleaded guilty to nine counts of criminal damage. V, aged 17 and 18 at the time of the offences, had sprayed graffiti on underground trains. He submitted that a custodial sentence was not justified, given that the offences were anti social and economic in nature and did not embody the threat of violence or physical injury.

Held, allowing the appeal, that a deterrent sentence was necessary to stamp out the widespread activity of spraying graffiti on public transport. However, V's sentence of two years' detention was unnecessarily long and would be reduced to 18 months.

R. v. VERDI (CHARAN), [2004] EWCA Crim 1485, [2005] 1 Cr. App. R. (S.) 43, Tuckey, L.J., CA (Crim Div).

3768. Young offenders–Immigration offences–Entering the United Kingdom without passport contrary to Asylum and Immigration (Treatment of Claimants, etc) Act 2004–Possession of passport for short period of time prior to entry

[Asylum and Immigration (Treatment of Claimants, etc.) Act 2004 s.2(1).]

The appellant asylum seeker (B) appealed against a sentence of 10 months' detention imposed following her guilty plea to entering the United Kingdom without a passport contrary to the Asylum and Immigration (Treatment of Claimants, etc.) Act 2004 s.2(1). B, who was Chinese, had arrived at an airport without either a passport or a ticket. For the previous six months she had been travelling through various countries, accompanied by an agent. The agent had kept both her passport and her ticket and she had only been given the travel documents for the purpose of showing them to the travel authorities to check. The agent had kept the documents at all other times. B submitted that (1) she had not intentionally disposed of her passport in order to deceive the authorities as to her identity and she had only been in possession of the passport for a few brief moments; (2) the judge had wrongly exercised his discretion when he had recommended that the appellant should be deported.

Held, allowing the appeal, that (1) in normal circumstances a custodial sentence was inevitable when offences of this type had been committed as they had the potential to undermine the whole system of immigration control. Although credit should be accorded for guilty pleas and personal mitigation, because the offences were so prevalent the dominant consideration when imposing sentence should be the public interest requirement of its deterrent effect on others. Judges should be alert to hold *Newton* hearings to avoid false mitigation being advanced. In the instant case the judge had insufficiently addressed in his sentencing remarks all the issues raised by counsel. However, B had fallen to be sentenced on the basis that she had had possession of her passport for a very short time and not on the basis that she had destroyed her immigration documents, which was the particular vice at which the provision was directed. B had pleaded guilty and also had an extant asylum claim. A significantly shorter sentence would have reflected her criminality. Therefore, the sentence was quashed and replaced with a sentence of two months' detention. (2) The proper approach of the courts when deciding whether to recommend that an accused should be deported was to assess whether the accused's presence in the UK was to its detriment and a minor offence would not merit a recommendation of that kind, *R. v. Nazari (Fazlollah)* [1980] 1 W.L.R. 1366, [1980] C.L.Y. 581 considered. The question of whether to make the recommendation should have been addressed independently of B's immigration position and it was B's history and her criminal record that was of importance, *R. v. Kandhari* (Unreported, April 24, 1979) considered. In the instant case B was a young woman of good character and the commission of this sole criminal offence had not provided a sustainable basis for the judge to conclude that her continued presence in the UK was to its detriment. There had been no proper basis for recommending her deportation.

R. v. WANG (BEI BEI), [2005] EWCA Crim 293, [2005] 2 Cr. App. R. (S.) 79, Davis, J., CA (Crim Div).

3769. Young offenders–Indecent assault–Digital penetration of victims' vaginas–Undue leniency

The Attorney General referred as unduly lenient the absolute discharge of the defendant (L) following convictions for indecent assault. The offences had occurred in the late 1970s when L was between 9 and 16 years old. The offences had involved digital penetration of the victims' vaginas. At the time of the trial L had a mental age of between six and nine years of age and was unlikely to have had a higher mental age at the time of the offences. He had committed no other offence since 1977. The Attorney General argued that the aggravating features were that L had committed a course of conduct over three years, his victims were as young as six years old and the assaults had had enduring consequences for them. The absolute discharge had failed sufficiently to take into account the interests of his victims.

Held, allowing the reference, that the sentence was unduly lenient. Whilst there was nothing to show a risk of reoffending, there was no doubt that L had acted criminally towards his victims. That behaviour required acknowledgement of his guilt by a criminal court and punishment. Moreover, there was force in the submission that the interests of the victims had not been sufficiently taken into account. The victims were entitled to see the process of the law carried through, but the outcome in the instant case had been inappropriate. There was no possibility of any future risk to the victims or any other young person, but L's behaviour at the time of the offences crossed the custody threshold. However, that was not an appropriate disposal in all the circumstances. There would be no purpose in sending L to prison as he posed no risk and, equally, it would have no deterrent effect. In those circumstances, a community rehabilitation order for a period of three years was imposed with limited conditions.

ATTORNEY GENERAL'S REFERENCE (NO.146 OF 2004), *Re* [2005] EWCA Crim 246, Kennedy, L.J., CA (Crim Div).

3770. Young offenders–Manslaughter–Act of reckless arson resulting in death–Belief that door could be opened and victim released

[Powers of Criminal Courts (Sentencing) Act 2000 s.91.]

The appellant (K), a boy aged 15, appealed against a sentence of four years' detention imposed under the Powers of Criminal Courts (Sentencing) Act 2000 s.91 following his conviction after trial of manslaughter by an unlawful act, namely arson, being reckless as to whether life would be endangered. K and two other boys had been playing on bicycles at the back of a retail park. After some time one of the boys had placed the victim's bicycle in a waste container which contained wood and paper. The victim went into the container and was locked in by the other two. K then lit a piece of paper and dropped it into the container through a narrow gap. A fire started. Unbeknown to the boys, the door was jammed and the victim could not escape. K and the other boy made strenuous efforts to release the victim but by the time he was rescued by the fire brigade he was badly burned and died soon after. A pre sentence report indicated that K's behaviour in detention was exceptionally good and that, given his family support and circumstances, he was unlikely to reoffend. K, who was of previous good character, submitted that the sentence was manifestly excessive and failed to take into account all the mitigating factors, especially his belief that the door could be opened and his low risk of reoffending.

Held, allowing the appeal, that the appropriate sentence was one of three years' detention. K had the benefit of substantial mitigation but had persisted in his not guilty plea. This was a serious offence which had involved K acting recklessly as to whether life would be endangered when he threw the lit paper into the container, and his act had resulted in the death of the victim. A substantial custodial sentence was justified as a consequence, but taking into account all the mitigating factors, the reduction from four years to three was appropriate.

R v. KC, [2004] EWCA Crim 2361, [2005] 1 Cr. App. R. (S.) 97, Hooper, L.J., CA (Crim Div).

3771. Young offenders–Manslaughter–Consecutive sentences–Risk that facts of dangerous driving and theft offences taken into account when sentencing for manslaughter

F, aged 18 at the time of the offence, renewed his application for leave to appeal against his conviction for manslaughter and his sentence of 10 years' detention in a young offender institution, imposed consecutively to a nine month term for dangerous driving and three months for theft. F, who had spent the day drinking and taking cocaine with three others, stole a mobile phone from a person in a pub and left in a stolen car, driven by F. One of F's associates, W, was detained by the phone's owner and F returned in the car to rescue him. F then chased one of the men who had detained W. He swerved into the man, who later died of his injuries. F surrendered to the police on learning of the death but denied that he had deliberately swerved in order to kill or do grievous bodily harm to the victim.

Held, granting the application and allowing the appeal against the sentence, that the crime was of a serious nature as F had used the car as a weapon and to escape from the scene of the theft. He had also consumed alcohol and drugs. However, F only had some minor previous convictions and the consecutive sentences carried the risk that the facts of the other offences had been taken into account when sentencing him for manslaughter. The sentences for dangerous driving and theft were made concurrent to the manslaughter term, giving an overall sentence of 10 years' detention, *R. v. Gault (Michael Paul)* (1995) 16 Cr. App. R. (S.) 1013, *R. v. Ripley (Samuel)* [1997] 1 Cr. App. R. (S.) 19 and *Attorney General's Reference (No.64 of 2001), Re* [2001] EWCA Crim 2028, [2002] 1 Cr. App. R. (S.) 94, [2001] C.L.Y. 1426 considered.

R. v. FRANKS (JAMIE JOHN), [2004] EWCA Crim 1241, [2005] 1 Cr. App. R. (S.) 13, Rose, L.J., CA (Crim Div).

3772. Young offenders–Manslaughter by gross negligence–Intoxicated driver– Prolonged course of dangerous driving

[Criminal Appeal Act 1995 s.13.]

The appellant (B) appealed against a sentence of 11 years' detention following a conviction of gross negligence manslaughter on a reference by the Criminal Cases Review Commission. B, who had been 17 years old at the time of the offence, had driven in an erratic and dangerous manner; he had repeatedly mounted the pavement, driving at groups of pedestrians; made hand brake turns and had driven at speed. Eventually, B had swerved towards the middle of the road hitting the victim, who had died a short time later. When breathalysed, B had been three times over the legal limit. B contended that the sentence was manifestly excessive and that the authorities indicated a sentencing bracket which was below 10 years.

Held, dismissing the appeal, that (1) the sentence, whilst severe and at the top end of the bracket, was not manifestly excessive. B had put numerous people at grave risk and it was the victim's misfortune that he had paid the price for B's total disregard for the safety of many. The matter had been prosecuted as gross negligence manslaughter, and not as causing death by dangerous or careless driving, in order to make available to the court greater sentencing powers. The authorities cited by B, involving cases of gross negligence manslaughter, were not as serious as the instant case and no authority concerned such a long course of dangerous driving which exposed so many to risk. (2) It had been a misjudgement on the part of the commission to refer the instant case to the court. The commission had failed to identify any point of law or information not raised in previous proceedings. Reference had been made to numerous authorities, none of which were considered to be "information" within the meaning of the Criminal Appeal Act 1995 s.13.

R. v. BALLARD (RUSS FRANCOIS), [2004] EWCA Crim 3305, [2005] 2 Cr. App. R. (S.) 31, Maurice Kay, L.J., CA (Crim Div).

3773. Young offenders–Manslaughter by gross negligence–Setting fire to mattress on which intoxicated man slept–Length of detention

The appellant (W), aged 18 at the time of sentence, appealed against a sentence of six years' detention in a young offender institution following his guilty plea to one count of manslaughter by gross negligence and one count of assault occasioning actual bodily harm for which he received a concurrent sentence of 15 months' detention. W was of very low intelligence and tended to abuse alcohol. He was in a pattern of offending that was based on low self esteem, prompting him to resort to violence. The victim (O) was an alcoholic who was vulnerable to being abused when intoxicated. Whilst intoxicated he went with W to an outbuilding where he would sometimes sleep on a mattress. During horseplay a lighted item of clothing landed on the mattress and it caught fire. W fled but did not obtain assistance and O subsequently died from extensive burns. W submitted that the sentence was manifestly excessive and failed to reflect adequate credit for his early guilty plea, his youth and his psychological background.

Held, dismissing the appeal, that this was an appropriate sentence for the offence. W's actions had led to the death of an innocent man who, over a considerable period of time, had suffered violence when intoxicated. W's actions during the horseplay were dangerous. He had made no attempt to rescue O or to extinguish the fire, but had effectively abandoned him to his fate.

R. v. WALTERS (DANIEL), [2004] EWCA Crim 2587, [2005] 1 Cr. App. R. (S.) 100, Scott Baker, L.J., CA (Crim Div).

3774. Young offenders–Manslaughter;driving away in stolen vehicle–Owner thrown into road and killed

The appellant (D), an 18 year old woman who had entered a guilty plea to one count of theft of a motor vehicle and one count of manslaughter, appealed against a sentence of seven years' detention for manslaughter. D had stolen the car from the victim, with whom she was acquainted, and had driven off while the victim hung on to the bonnet. After the victim had fallen into the road, D drove through a red light and away without stopping, selling the car later the same day. D had pleaded guilty on the basis that she had not realised that the victim had fallen from the bonnet and that she did not drive to shake him off, but this contradicted D's previous prepared statement. D contended that the starting point taken by the sentencing judge was too high.

Held, allowing the appeal, that D had previous convictions and there were serious aggravating factors in relation to the instant offence. Driving with a person clinging to the bonnet of a vehicle was extremely dangerous and D's driving had been careless and, arguably, reckless. The maximum sentence for manslaughter was life but causing death by dangerous driving carried a maximum of 10 years' imprisonment. Where sentence was being passed for manslaughter the approach of the court should be different from the approach taken where statutory offences had been committed, *R. v. Gault (Michael Paul)* (1995) 16 Cr. App. R. (S.) 1013 considered. If D's guilt had been contested the sentence would have been 10 years' detention but, taking into account her plea, remorse and troubled history the appropriate sentence was five years' detention.

R. v. DWYER (MONIQUE ZOE), [2004] EWCA Crim 2982, [2005] 2 Cr. App. R. (S.) 9, Clarke, L.J., CA (Civ Div).

3775. **Young offenders–Murder–Review of minimum term of detention in transitional cases–Extent of right to fair and public hearing**

[Human Rights Act 1998 Sch.1 Part I Art.6(1).]

The appellant (D) appealed against a decision ([2004] EWCA Civ 99, [2004] Q.B. 1341) that the respondent secretary of state had acted properly in reviewing his minimum term of imprisonment and setting his tariff at 16 years. D, who was 16 years old at the time of his offence, had been detained for a minimum term of 18 years following his conviction of murder. Following a decision of the European Court of Human Rights that the setting of a tariff in the case of a young person detained at Her Majesty's pleasure was a sentencing exercise that engaged the Human Rights Act 1998 Sch.1 Part I Art.6(1) and should not be conducted by ministers, the Lord Chief Justice had reviewed D's tariff in accordance with the procedure set out in *Practice Statement (CA (Crim Div): Juveniles: Murder Tariff)* [2000] 1 W.L.R. 1655, [2000] C.L.Y. 1095. Although providing for written representations from both the detainee's legal advisers and the Director of Public Prosecutions, the procedure made no provision for the making of oral submissions. Having considered written representations, the Lord Chief Justice had recommended that D's tariff be reduced to 16 years. That recommendation had been accepted by the secretary of state and the tariff set. D submitted that he had a right under Art.6(1) to an oral hearing before the Lord Chief Justice before his tariff was set.

Held, dismissing the appeal, that Art.6(1) required that there be a fair and public hearing but it did not say that there had to be an oral hearing at every stage in the proceedings for that requirement to be satisfied. It was not disputed that D had had a fair and public hearing at his trial. None of the cases considered by the court was directly comparable with the process of review undertaken by the Lord Chief Justice in D's case. However, a number of principles could be extracted. What was at issue was a general right to a fair and public hearing, and there was no absolute right to a public hearing at every stage in the proceedings at which the applicant was heard orally. The application of Art.6 to proceedings other than those at first instance depended on the special features of the proceedings in question, and account had to be taken of the proceedings in their entirety; the role of the person conducting them; the nature of the system in which they were being conducted; and the scope of the powers being exercised, *Fejde v. Sweden (A/212-C)* (1994) 17 E.H.R.R. 14, [1994] C.L.Y. 2411 applied, *Goc v. Turkey (36590/97)* (Unreported, July 11, 2002) considered. The overriding question was whether the issue to be dealt with could properly, as a matter of fair trial, be determined without hearing the applicant orally. The absence of an oral hearing in D's case did not violate Art.6(1). All the signs were that an oral hearing in his case would merely have been a formality. Most of the relevant issues had been determined on the basis of evidence led in public at the trial. What the Lord Chief Justice had been required to do was merely to make an assessment of the extent to which adjustment of the tariff was necessary in the light of D's behaviour after conviction and on the basis of the written representations. It was of particular importance that D had not suggested that an oral hearing was required so he could give evidence in person, but had requested an oral hearing solely on the ground that it was an ordinary part of the sentencing exercise. D's legal advisers had had ample opportunity to make written representations and it was unlikely that any information they could have provided at an oral hearing would have added anything. Moreover, in reviewing cases such as D's, the Lord Chief Justice had taken on a substantial task. He had to have regard to the public interest as well as the interests of each detainee, and to his obligation under Art.6(1) to carry out the exercise within a reasonable time. To provide for oral hearings in each case would have caused much delay and it had not been shown that any good purpose would have been served by adopting such a procedure generally.

R. (ON THE APPLICATION OF DUDSON) v. SECRETARY OF STATE FOR THE HOME DEPARTMENT, [2005] UKHL 52, [2005] 3 W.L.R. 422, Lord Bingham of Cornhill, HL.

3776. Young offenders—Rape—Appropriate starting point

[Sexual Offences Act 2003 s.1 (1), s.3.]

The appellant (D) appealed against a total sentence of six years' detention in a young offender institution following pleas of guilty to rape contrary to the Sexual Offences Act 2003 s.1 (1) and sexual assault under s.3 of the Act. The victim of the offence, a 16 year old virgin, was sexually assaulted by D who put his hands inside her clothing and touched her vagina. He then forced her to suck his penis and ejaculated in her mouth, threatening to stab her if she refused. During the attack D slapped and punched the victim. The victim managed to dial the emergency services on her mobile phone and the whole incident, which lasted 12 minutes, was recorded. D was later traced through DNA after a mass screening programme and at first he denied the assault saying the victim had consented. D subsequently pleaded guilty at the plea and directions hearing. No victim impact statement or pre sentence report was ordered. D submitted that the sentence was manifestly excessive given the plea of guilty and his age. Looking at the description of relevant starting points in *R. v. Millberry (William Christopher)* [2002] EWCA Crim 2891, [2003] 1 W.L.R. 546, [2003] C.L.Y. 3829 the five year starting point was more applicable to D than the eight year starting point.

Held, dismissing the appeal, that (1) the sentence was one that could appropriately be passed by the judge. Section 1 of the Act extended the definition of rape to include penetration of the anus or mouth and when considering sentence no distinction should be made between the categories of rape. Even taking into account guidance in previous cases it should be emphasised that it was very difficult to produce a starting point, particularly in cases involving rape, that covered all the appropriate circumstances. A sentence for a young offender would be appreciably shorter than that for an adult. At 18 years of age, D was at the top end of the category of defendants entitled to that benefit. Approached in a purely mechanical way there was significant argument in favour of D, however, guidelines were only guidelines and it was the court that had to decide the appropriate sentence, *Millberry* considered, *R. v. Corran (Ben)* [2005] EWCA Crim 192, Times, March 8, 2005 approved. (2) A victim impact statement should be routine in cases of this nature and was absolutely essential in the present case given the young age of the victim. It was also regrettable, given the appellant's young age, that a pre sentence report was not prepared.

R. v. ISMAIL (ABOKAR AHMED); *sub nom.* R. v. ISMAIL (ABOKOR AHMED), [2005] EWCA Crim 397, [2005] 2 Cr. App. R. (S.) 88, Lord Woolf of Barnes, L.C.J., CA (Crim Div).

3777. Young offenders—Robbery—Actual bodily harm—Gratuitous violence used in group attack on lone individual at night—Undue leniency

The Attorney General referred to the court as unduly lenient a sentence of 30 months' detention that had been imposed on the offender (M) following his plea of guilty to robbery. M had also pleaded guilty to assault occasioning actual bodily harm, for which he received a concurrent sentence of 12 months' detention. M, who was 17 at the time of the offences, had, together with three other youths, attacked a man who had been waiting for a taxi at night. The victim was punched, knocked to the ground and kicked in his head, shoulder and back. As he lay on the ground, cash, a mobile phone and a number of cigarette lighters were taken from him. After walking off, M returned to the scene and kicked and stamped on the victim, who sustained deep bruising to the head, back and shoulders as a result of the attack. The Attorney General relied on five aggravating features: the robbery had been committed by a group of four on a single individual; it had taken place at night;

shod feet had been used as weapons; the violence exceeded what was necessary for the robbery; finally, further and wholly gratuitous violence had been used after the robbery had been committed.

Held, allowing the reference, that having regard to the aggravating features relied on and to the mitigation to be found in M's pleas of guilty and his age, the sentence was unduly lenient. A sentence of at least five years' detention would have been appropriate. Bearing in mind double jeopardy, a sentence of four years' detention would be imposed for the robbery. The sentence of 12 months' detention for the assault offence would stand, *R. v. Gordon (Neil)* [2001] 1 Cr. App. R. (S.) 58, [2001] C.L.Y. 1207 and *Attorney General's Reference (Nos.4 and 7 of 2002), Re* [2002] EWCA Crim 127, [2002] 2 Cr. App. R. (S.) 77, [2002] C.L.Y. 4066 considered.

ATTORNEY GENERAL'S REFERENCE (NO.98 OF 2004), *Re*; *sub nom.* R. v. MEAKIN (JOEL), [2004] EWCA Crim 2769, [2005] 1 Cr. App. R. (S.) 125, Rose, L.J., CA (Crim Div).

3778. Young offenders–Robbery–Attempts–Train passenger threatened

The appellant (W) appealed against a sentence of five years' detention in a young offender institution following a conviction for attempted robbery. W had been one of a number of youths involved in an attack on passengers on a London Underground train. The group had surrounded the first victim and W had repeatedly punched him. W then threatened and demanded the wallet of the second victim. The second victim managed to escape to an adjacent carriage. In the first trial W was found guilty of certain offences in relation to the first victim but the jury could not agree as to the attempted robbery in relation to the second victim. Accordingly, a retrial followed and W was then convicted of that offence. W argued that insufficient regard had been paid to the absence of aggravating features. In particular there had been no violence or physical harm to the victim and no weapon had been used. Moreover, the trial judge had appeared to indicate that W had been responsible for the retrial, with the consequence of greater distress to the victim whereas the cause was clearly the inability of the jury to agree.

Held, allowing the appeal, there had been no physical injury to the victim, who had managed to escape to the next carriage of the train and nothing had been taken from him. Moreover, the remarks at sentencing held W responsible for the retrial whereas the real cause was the inability of the jury to agree. Those factors led the court to conclude that the sentence of five years' detention was manifestly excessive in all the circumstances and a sentence of four years' detention was substituted.

R. v. ALLEN (WESLEY), [2005] EWCA Crim 667, [2005] 2 Cr. App. R. (S.) 95, Rose, L.J., CA (Crim Div).

3779. Young offenders–Robbery–Burglary of occupied house followed by robbery of betting shop with imitation firearm–Undue leniency

The Attorney General referred to the court as unduly lenient a sentence of 30 months' detention imposed on the offender, who pleaded guilty to offences of robbery, possession of an imitation firearm at the time of committing an offence, and burglary. In the first incident, the offender and two or three other men had broken into a house at night and the occupants had to barricade themselves into a bedroom. In the second incident the offender, who was with two accomplices, pointed an imitation handgun at a cashier as they robbed a betting shop. The aggravating features were that the burglary and the robbery were a few days apart, frightening, planned and carried out with others. The burglary was committed at night when the victims, including a young child, were on the premises; and the robbery victims believed the firearm to be genuine. The mitigating factors were the offender's guilty plea, youth, immaturity, few minor convictions, remorse and susceptibility to peer pressure.

Held, allowing the reference, that it was necessary for courts to make clear that robbery of vulnerable premises such as betting shops would result in condign punishment of the offender, *Attorney General's Reference (Nos.3, 4, 8,*

9, 10, 11, 14 and 16 of 1990), Re (1991) 92 Cr. App. R. 166, [1991] C.L.Y. 1213 considered. Sentencers should not permit the youth of an offender to outweigh the need in an appropriate case for condign punishment when there were repeated attacks on vulnerable victims. In the instant case, an appropriate sentence would have been one of five years and six months' detention; but in order to allow for the element of double jeopardy, a sentence of four years and six months' detention would be imposed, consisting of three years for the robbery, 18 months consecutive for the burglary, and 18 months concurrent for the firearm offence.

ATTORNEY GENERAL'S REFERENCE (NO.26 OF 2005), *Re* [2005] EWCA Crim 1973, Rose, L.J., CA (Crim Div).

3780. Young offenders–Robbery–Two robberies carried out by offenders acting in concert on same victim in short period of time–Appropriate sentencing bracket

The applicant (D), who had pleaded guilty to an offence of robbery, applied for leave to appeal against a sentence of three and a half years' detention in a young offender institution. D, accompanied by another offender (H), had approached the victim, who was walking home in the early hours of the morning. H then headbutted the victim, who fell to the floor. H and D then kicked and punched the victim and stole a leather jacket and two CDs. The victim got up and continued on his way home only to come across H and D, who attacked him again and stole his mobile telephone. The victim suffered several injuries. D had a criminal record, which included theft, affray and assault. D submitted that the sentence was excessive given that the victim was not particularly vulnerable, no weapons had been used, the offence had not been planned and he had not been the instigator of the attack. It was argued that the judge should have taken a lower starting point when sentencing.

Held, refusing the application, that (1) although there were absent from the instant case some of the aggravating features often found in cases of this kind, there were several aggravating features for consideration. H and D had acted in concert; there had been two separate attacks; the victim had received a beating which went beyond that which was required to effect the theft of the property taken; and D had a poor criminal record, which included offences of violence but not robbery. Consequently the sentence, although severe when imposed upon a young man, was within the range of sentences available to the judge and it was not excessive, *Attorney General's Reference (Nos.4 and 7 of 2002), Re* [2002] EWCA Crim 127, [2002] 2 Cr. App. R. (S.) 77, [2002] C.L.Y. 4066 considered. (2) It would not, in general, be appropriate for the advice of the Sentencing Advisory Panel to be cited to the Court of Appeal. Only the full guidance given by the Sentencing Guidelines Council was to be applied by the courts.

R. v. DOIDGE (CARL), [2005] EWCA Crim 273, *The Times*, March 10, 2005, Rose, L.J., CA (Crim Div).

3781. Young offenders–Wounding with intent–Unprovoked attack with bottle–Undue leniency

[Powers of Criminal Courts (Sentencing) Act 2000 s.91.]

The Attorney General referred to the court as unduly lenient an 18 month detention and training order imposed on the offender (M) for wounding with intent to cause grievous bodily harm. M, aged 17 at the time of the offence, pleaded guilty to repeatedly striking his victim (T) in the face with a broken bottle. In the early hours, M and another youth had approached and exchanged words with three people outside a town centre night club. T, who was one of the three people, tried to calm the situation, but M hit him on the head with a bottle, which broke, and then pushed the broken bottle into his face six or seven times. T required 20 stitches and was referred for plastic surgery. M, who had been brought up by an aunt, had a substantial criminal record: in six years he had appeared before the courts 15 times for more than 30 offences. The Attorney General submitted that the sentence did not act as a deterrent to others or reflect the public's concern over the prevalence of such offences.

Held, allowing the reference, that a young offender with a substantial record who repeatedly struck an entirely innocent victim in the face with a broken bottle, at night and in the street, should have been sentenced to four years' detention, even after pleading guilty. M's sentence failed to reflect the gravity of his conduct and too much weight had been given to his personal circumstances. Taking into account the element of double jeopardy, the new sentence would be three years' detention under the Powers of Criminal Courts (Sentencing) Act 2000 s.91, *Attorney General's Reference (Nos.59, 60 and 63 of 1998), Re* [1999] 2 Cr. App. R. (S.) 128, [1999] C.L.Y. 1371 and *Attorney General's Reference (No.121 of 2002), Re* [2003] EWCA Crim 684, (2003) 147 S.J.L.B. 267, [2003] C.L.Y. 3768 considered.

ATTORNEY GENERAL'S REFERENCE (NO.28 OF 2004), *Re; sub nom.* R. v. McCLUSKIE (GEORGE), [2004] EWCA Crim 1440, [2005] 1 Cr. App. R. (S.) 35, Rose, L.J., CA (Crim Div).

3782. Young offenders–Wounding with intent–Victim struck in face with broken bottle–Separate offence of affray–Undue leniency

[Criminal Justice Act 1988 s.35, s.36, s.116.]

The Attorney General referred to the court as unduly lenient a total sentence of two years' detention imposed on the offender (O) after he pleaded guilty to offences of wounding with intent and affray. In the wounding incident, O had joined a group of youths who were attacking some passers by and he had deliberately broken a beer bottle and then struck the victim in the front of the neck with it. In the affray incident, committed when O was on bail in relation to the first offence, he had smashed the windows of the victim's car with a seven foot pole. O had three previous convictions for common assault, criminal damage and unlawful wounding. He had been released from a 30 month sentence for the latter offence just a month before the wounding offence and both of the more recent offences were committed while he was still on licence. O contended, by reference to the terms of the Criminal Justice Act 1988 s.35 and s.36, that (1) the offence of affray was not triable solely on indictment and thus the Court of Appeal could not interfere with the sentence for that offence; (2) since the trial judge had not exercised his powers under s.116 of the 1988 Act, the Court of Appeal did not have the power to order that any part of the unexpired portion of the sentence for the earlier unlawful wounding offence should be served.

Held, allowing the reference, that (1) when the Attorney General referred a case to the Court of Appeal to review the sentence passed, the court had, by virtue of s.36(1), the power to quash any sentence passed on the offender in the proceedings and to pass such sentence as it thought appropriate, so long as the imposition of the new sentence would have been in the power of the court below when dealing with the offender. (2) The fact that the judge did not exercise his power under s.116 did not preclude the Court of Appeal from exercising that power to order an offender to serve any part of the unexpired portion of a sentence for an earlier offence. The sentence for the wounding with intent was unduly lenient and should have been at least three and a half years' detention. Furthermore, a significant consecutive sentence should have been imposed for the affray and the offender should have been ordered to serve substantially the whole of the unexpired portion of his earlier sentence. Taking into account the element of double jeopardy and the requirement for the offender to have to return to custody, the appropriate sentences would be two years' detention in a young offender institution for the wounding and a consecutive term of 12 months' detention for the affray. In addition, O would be required to serve nine months in relation to the unexpired portion of the earlier sentence, thus making a total sentence of three years and nine months.

ATTORNEY GENERAL'S REFERENCE (NO.32 OF 2004), *Re* [2004] EWCA Crim 2644, Rose, L.J., CA (Crim Div).

3783. Books

Ashworth, Andrew–Sentencing and Criminal Justice. Law in Context S. Paperback: £21.99. ISBN 0 521 67405 0. Cambridge University Press.

Easton, Susan; Piper, Christine–Sentencing and Punishment: The Quest for Punishment. Paperback: £22.99. ISBN 0 19 927087 2. Oxford University Press.

Hirsch, Andrew von; Ashworth, Andrew–Proportionate Sentencing: Exploring the Principles. Oxford Monographs on Criminal Law & Justice. Hardback: £50.00. ISBN 0 19 927260 3. Oxford University Press.

Inns of Court School of Law–Criminal Litigation and Sentencing. Blackstone Bar Manual S. Paperback: £26.99. ISBN 0 19 928151 3. Oxford University Press.

SHIPPING

3784. Berths–Demurrage–Equipment leasing–Pipelines–Meaning of "breakdown of equipment"–Additional costs arising from shifting operations

The claimant shipowners (P) appealed against a judgment ([2003] EWHC 1904, [2004] 1 All E.R. (Comm) 269) allowing the charterers (V) to recover $455,851.44 by way of demurrage. The vessel was to carry fuel oil from two ports in the US Gulf to various destinations, including Dakar. The Dakar discharge was to be in three stages. One parcel of oil was destined for the M'bao sealine with two further discharges at the Societe Africaine De Raffinage (SAR) terminal. However, as the M'bao discharge was taking place a serious leak occurred. Divers discovered its cause to be a gap in the pipeline, leading to a significant leakage of oil, necessitating repairs and slowing down the rate of discharge. P claimed (1) demurrage in the sum of $455,851.44; (2) additional agency fees and expenses incurred by reason of the additional shifting operations necessitated by the leak. V relied on limitation clauses in the charter that purported to restrict what would constitute used laytime or demurrage. Contesting the claim for additional agency fees, V argued that the instructions to shift came mainly from SAR. It was held at first instance that the leak was not due to any "breakdown of equipment in or about the plant of the consignee of the cargo"as provided for by clause 8 of the charter and that V was entitled to recover the additional costs incurred by way of the shifting operations. On appeal, P relied on clause 8 in support of its contention that laytime or demurrage ran at only half time and disputed the finding in relation to clause 9, namely that V was entitled to recover the additional costs incurred by way of the shifting operations.

Held, allowing the appeal, that (1) the pipeline clearly qualified as "equipment in or about the plant of the consignee of the cargo" within the meaning of clause 8. (2) The breakdown in the discharge pipe occurred when it ceased to function as a pipeline and a breakdown occurred every time there was a malfunction resulting in excessive leakage, *Olbena SA v. Psara Maritime Inc (The Thanassis A)* (Unreported, March 22, 1982) applied. (3) The full period of the delay was caused by the breakdown and there had been no break in the chain of causation. (4) M was entitled to half demurrage only in respect of the whole period in dispute. (5) Clause 9 contained express terms concerned only with V's right to shift the vessel "from one safe birth to another" and the language of clause 8 did not confer any right on V to order the vessel off the berth for the purpose of repairs to be carried out to the berth. Neither did it contain any promise on V's part to pay the costs arising. Accordingly, the order to move the vessel from berth was not given pursuant to clause 9 but rather was simply a response to the breakdown of the equipment. It followed that V was not liable for the additional expenses.

PORTOLANA COMPANIA NAVIERA LTD v. VITOL SA INC (THE AFRAPEARL); AFRAPEARL, THE, [2004] EWCA Civ 864, [2004] 1 W.L.R. 3111, Ward, L.J., CA.

3785. Carriage by sea–Bills of lading–Bill of lading made out to named consignee

[Carriage of Goods by Sea Act 1971 s.1; Hague-Visby Rules Art.I(b), Art.IV r.5.]

The appellant carrier (M) appealed against the decision ([2003] EWCA Civ 556, [2004] Q.B. 702, [2003] C.L.Y. 3885) that a "straight" bill of lading was "a bill of lading or any similar document of title" within the Hague Visby Rules Art.I(b). M had issued a set of three documents, described as bills of lading, in relation to the carriage of goods by sea. Subject to the fact that it could not be transferred by endorsement, the bill of lading contained the usual terms to be found in a bill of lading. The goods were damaged and the respondent buyer's case was that the contract for the carriage of the goods was covered by "a bill of lading or any similar document of title" within the meaning of the Carriage of Goods by Sea Act 1971 s.1(4) and Art.I(b) of the Rules, which were given the force of law in the UK by s.1(2) of the 1971 Act, so that the claim was governed by the more generous package limits prescribed in Art.IV r.5 of the Rules. The issue was whether a "straight" bill of lading, meaning a bill of lading providing for delivery of goods to a named consignee and not to order or assigns or bearer, and so not transferable by endorsement, was "a bill of lading or any similar document of title" within the Rules.

Held, dismissing the appeal, that an expansive interpretation of the expression "a bill of lading or any similar document of title" in the Hague Visby Rules Art.I(b) was appropriate and was apt to cover the document issued in the instant case. There was no reason why it should have been intended to exclude straight bills from the scope of the Rules. The document was also a document of title given that on its express terms it had to be presented to obtain delivery of the goods.

JI MacWILLIAM CO INC v. MEDITERRANEAN SHIPPING CO SA (THE RAFAELA S); RAFAELA S, THE, [2005] UKHL 11, [2005] 2 A.C. 423, Lord Bingham of Cornhill, HL.

3786. Carriage by sea–Carrier's liabilities–Enumeration of units–Application of Hague Visby Rules 1968 Art.IV r.5(c)–Relevant value calculated by reference to port of discharge

[Hague Visby Rules 1968 Art.IV r.5(b), r.5(c).]

The appellants (E) appealed against the amount of damages awarded in respect of damage beyond any possibility of salvage found to have been caused to a cargo of posters and prints being carried by sea from Australia to Greece. The respondent (M) cross appealed from the court's decision that all the posters and prints in the container constituted one "unit" for purposes of limitation of liability in the amended Hague Visby Rules 1968 Art.IV r.5(c). The goods had been made up into about 2000 packages which had then been packed into a single container. The bill of lading stated that the container was said to contain 200,945 pieces. However, the column headed "No. of Pkgs" simply contained the number "1". Clause 21 of the bill included a provision whereby it was said to have been expressly agreed that each container should constitute one package for the purposes of applying limitations to M's liability. The judge had found that the damage to the goods was caused by sea water during the voyage and that M was liable for that damage. As a consequence of the perceived inadequacy of the evidence as to the value of the goods in Greece, the judge assessed the value of the goods by reference to the value of the goods in Australia as opposed to the port of discharge. On the cross appeal, M argued that the judge erred in concluding that the words and numbers "200945 pieces posters and prints" amounted to an enumeration of units for the purposes of Art.IV r.5(c). With regard to the appeal, E argued that the judge erred in deciding that the calculation of value by reference to the port of discharge given in Art.IV r.5(b) was only a prima facie measure and that she was entitled to use other measures for calculating the value of the goods if the circumstances so required.

Held, dismissing the appeal and allowing the cross appeal (Beaumont, J. dissenting), that (1) The evident purpose of Art.IV r.5(c) was to make the enumeration in the bill effective. The enumeration would generally be on the face of the bill. There was no reason to read into the word "enumeration" in r.5(c) a requirement, beyond its ordinary meaning of identifying the number, that the enumeration had to be contractually agreed to be binding. Enumeration meant the setting out of numbers on the face of the bill and if the carrier issued a bill which contained an enumeration, Art.IV r.5(c) was satisfied. The enumeration had to stand for limitation purposes so it could be used as the basis for freight and insurance. Thus, where a bill enumerated packages or units, a provision such as Clause 21 in the instant bill of lading would not be effective to gainsay the existence of enumeration. (2) Article IV r.5(c) provided for the number of packages or units enumerated in the bill as packed in the container, viewing the container as the article of transport and so as part of the ship. In that sense "units" meant shipping units and it was not what was in fact within the container but what was stated on the bill which was relevant, *Owners of Cargo Lately Laden on Board the River Gurara v. Nigerian National Shipping Line Ltd* [1996] 2 Lloyd's Rep. 53, [1996] C.L.Y. 5306 followed. (3) On the facts of the present case, there was no enumeration in the sea carriage document for the purposes of Art.IV r.5(c) of the amended Rules and M was entitled to limit its liability. Consequently, the E's appeal necessarily failed. (4) Giving primacy to the words of Art.IV r.5(b) of the amended Rules, the total amount recoverable was to be calculated by reference to the value of goods at the place and time at which the goods were discharged from the ship in accordance with the contract, or as they should have been so discharged.

EL GRECO (AUSTRALIA) PTY LTD v. MEDITERRANEAN SHIPPING CO SA [2004] 2 Lloyd's Rep. 537, Black, C.J., Fed Ct (Aus) (Full Ct).

3787. Carriage by sea – Carriers liabilities – Charterparty transferring risk of damage to cargo from shipowners to charterers – Effect of Hague Visby Rules

[Hague Visby Rules Art.III r.2, r.8.]

The appellant shippers and cargo owners (J) appealed against a decision ([2003] EWCA Civ 144, [2003] 1 All E.R. (Comm) 747, [2003] C.L.Y. 3887) that the respondent shipowners (S) were not liable for damage to the cargo allegedly caused by defective loading, stowage or discharge. J's cargo had been carried in S's vessel and had been shipped under two bills of lading on the Cogenbill form which incorporated the terms and conditions of the voyage charterparty. The Hague Visby Rules were applicable to the shipment. Under the charterparty, the shippers, charterers or receivers were to put the cargo on board, stow it, lash it, secure it, dunnage it and discharge it. J submitted that Art.III r.2 of the Rules imposed upon the shipowners, as carrier of the goods, the duty to properly and carefully perform those functions, and that in so far as it purported to transfer that duty from the shipowners to the shippers, charterers and consignees, the charterparty was invalidated by Art.III r.8 of the Rules.

Held, dismissing the appeal, that the duty to load, stow and discharge the cargo could be transferred by agreement from the shipowners to the cargo interests, and the effect of Art.III r.2 of the Rules was not to override the freedom of contract to reallocate responsibility for the functions described in that rule, *Pyrene Co Ltd v. Scindia Steam Navigation Co Ltd* [1954] 2 Q.B. 402, [1954] C.L.Y. 3197 considered. An agreement transferring responsibility for the loading, stowage and discharge of cargo from the shipowners to the shippers, charterers and consignees was not invalidated by Art.III r.8 of the Rules, *GH Renton & Co Ltd v. Palmyra Trading Corp of Panama (The Caspiana)* [1957] A.C. 149, [1957] C.L.Y. 3300 followed. There was no justification for departing from the decision in *Renton*. J had not shown that the decision worked unsatisfactorily and produced unjust results, *R. v. G* [2003] UKHL 50, [2004] 1 A.C. 1034, [2003] C.L.Y. 775 applied. The rule had been consistently applied for 50 years and certainty in all mercantile transactions was important. The common thread and ratio of the majority in *Renton* was a purposive rather than a literal reading of Art.III r.2 and represented a principled and reasonable approach to the rule's interpretation. The case against departing from *Renton* was overwhelming. It had been applied in many international cases and had not suffered any criticism in subsequent legislation or academic thought.

JINDAL IRON & STEEL CO LTD v. ISLAMIC SOLIDARITY SHIPPING CO JORDAN INC; JORDAN II, THE; TCI TRANS COMMODITIES AG v. ISLAMIC SOLIDARITY SHIPPING CO JORDAN INC, [2004] UKHL 49, [2005] 1 W.L.R. 1363, Lord Bingham of Cornhill, HL.

3788. Carriers liabilities–Exclusion clauses–Interpretation of carrier's exclusion clause

The claimant (M) made a claim for damage to perishable goods shipped by the defendant carriers (E) and as a preliminary issue the court had to determine the application of a carrier's exemption clause in the bills of lading. By its claim, M alleged that some of the frozen goods that E had shipped for it were damaged as a result of E's negligence or the unseaworthiness or uncargoworthiness of E's vessel. E relied on the exemption clause as exempting them from liability for any damage caused by reason of the vessel's refrigeration system not working properly. That clause provided that the carrier was not responsible for any loss or damage to or in connection with the goods, however caused. M submitted that the exemption clause was unenforceable because it was incompatible with the commercial purpose of the contracts of carriage contained in or evidenced by the bills of lading. It argued that the exemption clause purported to exclude entirely what would otherwise be E's secondary obligations under each contract, and without those obligations the contracts were illusory because there was no sanction for any breach of E's primary obligations.

Held, determining the preliminary issue, that whether and to what extent E could rely on the exemption clause fell to be determined as a matter of common law. The wide and somewhat repetitious language of the exemption clause was plainly intended to relieve the carrier of liability for loss of, or damage to, the goods shipped caused by, amongst other things, the unseaworthiness or uncargoworthiness of the vessel, or the negligence of the carrier, its servant or agents. When considered in their context as parts of contracts for the carriage of goods from one port to another, it was plain that the words "however caused", "or otherwise howsoever" and "arising or resulting from...any other cause whatsoever" did not operate to relieve the carrier of liability for any and every breach of contract. The exemption clause did not operate to relieve the carrier of all secondary obligations under the contracts. There was no reason to reject the exemption clause as part of each of the contracts contained in or evidenced by the bills of lading and it protected E where damage to the goods shipped resulted from negligence or the unseaworthiness or uncargoworthiness of E's vessel.

MITSUBISHI CORP v. EASTWIND TRANSPORT LTD (THE IRBENSKIY PROLIV); IRBENSKIY PROLIV, THE, [2004] EWHC 2924, [2005] 1 All E.R. (Comm) 328, Ian Glick Q.C., QBD (Comm).

3789. Charterparties–Deductions–Withholding of hire payment instalment for anticipated dry docking–Validity of ship owners' notice of withdrawal

The claimant charterers (W) brought proceedings against the defendant ship owners (L) claiming damages for wrongful withdrawal of a vessel and repudiation of a charterparty. W had entered into a charterparty with L in respect of a bulk carrier. Hire payment was due in advance and L's option to withdraw the vessel if W was in default was subject to a provision that 72 hours' notice would be given to W before exercising the option. W made deductions from a hire payment in respect of an anticipated seven days of dry docking and a $500 bunker cancellation fee already paid by them. W also made a pro rated payment of $600 for cables and victualling. L served notice of withdrawal on W. Not wishing to give L the opportunity to withdraw, W remitted the amount previously withheld for dry docking. W did not however pay over the $500 bunker cancellation fee as they claimed they did not think that payment of that sum was a precondition of L not withdrawing the vessel. L withdrew the vessel because of the $500 deduction. W argued that (1) far from underpaying the hire instalment they had actually overpaid it as they were entitled to deduct the anticipated dry docking, as well as the $500 bunker cancellation fee and the $600 payment for cables and victualling which was payable in arrears and not in advance; (2) by the time they had made the payment for dry docking the vessel had actually been dry docked for three days resulting in an overpayment; (3) long standing practice had created an estoppel that L would not seek to withdraw the vessel for non payment of small deductions; (4) the notice sent by L was defective as it failed to give a clear and unambiguous ultimatum to W.

Held, giving judgment for W, that (1) in the absence of a provision to the contrary, W were not entitled to make a deduction for anticipated off hire, however certain it was that the vessel would be off hire, *Tonnelier v. Smith* (1897) 2 Com. Cas. 258 applied. With respect to the $500, there was no evidence that W actually suffered any loss or prejudice in their use of the vessel. The loss of the $500 cancellation fee did not impeach L's right to hire as it was altogether too remote. As for the pro rata payment of $600, there had been a long and invariable practice between the parties that payment for the cables and victualling was paid 15 days in advance even though the charterparty was silent on the topic. If W wished to depart from this practice they should have given notice to L. W could not redesignate this sum ex post facto. (2) As and when hire paid in advance proved to have been overpaid because the vessel was off hire, W was entitled to recover that hire as money overpaid for consideration that had wholly failed, *CA Stewart & Co v. PHS Van Ommeren (London) Ltd* [1918] 2 K.B. 560 applied. However that did not mean that the hire was not payable in full on the payment date, *Pan Ocean Shipping Co v. Creditcorp (The Trident Beauty)* [1994] 1 W.L.R. 161, [1994] C.L.Y. 529 applied. The right to repayment did not start to accrue until after the hire was due and payable. (3) L never said that they would not seek to withdraw the vessel for small deductions which were improperly made. Furthermore L had made threats from time to time that they would protect their position in the face of small deductions. (4) The notice had to be formal, in writing and had to put L on notice that unless they rectified their failure to pay hire within 72 hours the vessel would be withdrawn. Although it was not ordinarily necessary for W to spell out in the notice exactly what sum had to be paid, it was important that there was no ambiguity. In this respect the notice was defective and created confusion. W were in breach of the charterparty in withdrawing the vessel.

WESTERN BULK CARRIERS K/S v. LI HAI MARITIME INC; LI HAI, THE, [2005] EWHC 735, [2005] 2 Lloyd's Rep. 389, Jonathan Hirst Q.C., QBD (Comm).

3790. Charterparties–Demurrage–Time limits for claim

[Hague-Visby Rules 1971 Art.III r.6.]

The applicant shipowners (O) applied for summary judgment against the respondent charterers (C) in respect of a cancelled charterparty. O had chartered a vessel to C for the carriage of cargo. Subsequently, C repudiated the charterparty due to continued problems with purchase of the cargo. O accepted the repudiation and claimed a cancelling fee comprising the lost freight and demurrage less saved port costs and bunkers and mitigation by way of a substitute voyage. C submitted that O's claim was "any other claim by Charterers for any and all other amounts which are alleged to be for Charterer's account" and was therefore subject to the time limits for presentation of a claim imposed by clause 20 of the charterparty. They argued that where the cargo was not discharged, a term should be implied that the start date for the time limits should be the date on which the goods should have been discharged. C also contended that O could not claim demurrage as part of damages.

Held, refusing the application, that (1) the words of clause 20 did not clearly include claims against charterers for damages for breach of their obligations under the charter. Time bar clauses were to be construed strictly. Objectively construed, clause 20 was not intended to include claims for damages. The fact that clause 20 only made provision for time limits to run from the date that the cargo was discharged suggested that the clause was intended to have a limited application. In addition, the charterparty had expressly incorporated the significantly longer time limit in the Hague Visby Rules 1971 Art.III r.6 for presentation of claims where no cargo had been discharged. In the light of those facts, it followed that where no cargo had been discharged through no fault of the shipowner, there were no time limits for claims against the charterer within the meaning of clause 20. It therefore followed that C had no real prospect of successfully defending the claim. (2) In the instant case, there was a failure to provide cargo, which ultimately led to the termination of the charterparty, but there was also a failure to load within the laydays, in respect of which C were liable to pay demurrage. Although the vessel had been restored to O sooner than if the contract had been performed, it was not possible to say that C's breach before termination had caused no loss because damages for such breach were liquidated by the demurrage clause, *SIB International Srl v. Metallgesellschaft Corp (The Noel Bay)* [1989] 1 Lloyd's Rep. 361, [1990] C.L.Y. 4121 distinguished. O were entitled to claim demurrage that had accrued before repudiation together with a further sum of demurrage by way of damages in respect of the time that it would have taken to load and discharge the cargo.

ODFJELL SEACHEM A/S v. CONTINENTALE DES PETROLES ET D'INVESTISSEMENTS; *sub nom.* ODFJFELL SEACHEM A/S v. CONTINENTALE DES PETROLES ET D'INVESTISSEMENTS, [2004] EWHC 2929, [2005] 1 All E.R. (Comm) 421, Nigel Teare Q.C., QBD (Comm).

3791. Charterparties–Indemnities–Right of third party to enforce contractual term–Terms of letters of indemnity for benefit of shipowner

[Contracts (Rights of Third Parties) Act 1999 s.1 (1) (b).]

The appellant (R) appealed against a decision ([2004] EWHC 2738, [2005] 1 Lloyd's Rep. 632) that the respondent shipowner (S) was entitled to enforce against it the terms of its letter of indemnity by reason of the terms of the Contracts (Rights of Third Parties) Act 1999. R was the receiver of cargo shipped on board S's vessel pursuant to a charterparty. Pursuant to a clause of the charterparty and on a request by the charterer (C), R faxed a letter of indemnity instructing the master to allow the vessel to commence discharge and deliver the cargo to R without production of the original bills of lading. By providing its letter of indemnity to C, R sought to obtain delivery through the agency of S. S complied with C's instructions to deliver the cargo to R. After discharge was completed, the vessel was arrested by the bank with which R had opened a letter of credit. The bank alleged that it held the original bills of lading and asserted a claim for the value of the cargo. S was granted a declaration that it was entitled to enforce R's letter of indemnity against R and that S was entitled to an order that both C and R provide the bail or other security required to secure the release of the vessel from arrest. On R's appeal the issues were (1) whether, on the true construction of R's letter of indemnity, S was C's agent in delivering the cargo to R without insisting upon receiving the original bills of lading; (2) whether the judge was right to hold that R had failed to discharge the burden of showing that the parties did not intend the terms of R's letter of indemnity to be enforceable by a third party. R submitted that the judge had reached the wrong conclusion on both issues.

Held, dismissing the appeal, that (1) S was the agent of C for the purpose of complying with R's request in its letter of indemnity that the cargo be delivered to R and had to be the primary party intended to be covered by the reference to the "agents" whom R promised to indemnify in its letter of indemnity. The judge was right that the terms of R's letter of indemnity relied upon by S purported to confer a direct benefit on S within the meaning of s.1 (1) (b) of the Act. It followed that S was entitled to enforce the letter of indemnity in its own name subject to the second issue concerning the parties' intention as to enforceability. (2) Everything depended on the construction of R's letter of indemnity. The reasoning behind the conclusions on the first issue pointed to the correct resolution of the second issue. If it was correct that certain terms of R's letter of indemnity were intended for the benefit of S, it made no sense to hold that it was nevertheless intended that R's liability should not be directly to S. There was nothing in R's letter of indemnity which led to the conclusion that the parties did not intend the relevant terms to be enforceable by S. The whole purpose of R's letter of indemnity was to ensure that R received the cargo from the vessel without production of the original bills of lading and to ensure that S was fully protected from the consequences of arrest that might be taken by the holders of the original bills of lading. The judge had been correct on both issues.

LAEMTHONG INTERNATIONAL LINES CO LTD v. ARTIS (THE LAEMTHONG GLORY) (NO.2); LAEMTHONG GLORY, THE (NO.2); *sub nom.* LAEMTHONG INTERNATIONAL LINES CO LTD v. ABDULLAH MOHAMMED FAHEM & CO, [2005] EWCA Civ 519, [2005] 2 All E.R. (Comm) 167, Sir Andrew Morritt V.C., CA (Civ Div).

3792. **Charterparty by demise–Arbitration clauses–Commencement of court proceedings–Application for stay pending arbitration**

[Arbitration Act 1996 s.9.]

The applcant ship owner (H) applied under the Arbitration Act 1996 s.9 to stay proceedings commenced against it by the respondent charterers (N) pending arbitration. H had agreed to charter two vessels to N by two bareboat charterparties on the Barecon 89 Form. Under the terms of the charterparties the courts of England had jurisdiction to settle any disputes. In addition, H had the option of referring any dispute to arbitration. A dispute had arisen between the parties and N issued proceedings. H purported to exercise its right to refer the dispute to arbitration and appointed an arbitrator. N argued that its action should not be stayed because when it commenced proceedings it had not been acting in breach of any covenant in the contract and under the terms of the charterparties its only forum of choice was England. H submitted that the option to refer disputes to arbitration did not prevent it from bringing proceedings.

Held, granting the application, that once H had exercised its option the parties had agreed that the disputes should be arbitrated. By refusing a stay the court would not be according H its autonomy. Under the charterparties N's right to litigate against H was limited to bringing proceedings in the English court. Normally where a dispute arose the parties would seek to resolve whether that dispute was to be arbitrated or litigated, but with a reservation of a right to H to decide to have that dispute referred to arbitration. Thus it would have been in the contemplation of the parties that the issue of arbitration would be decided before proceedings were commenced in the courts by N. However, N had not initiated any such discussion and no letter before action had been sent. In the circumstances N was bound to start an action in the English courts. However, H's option of bringing disputes to arbitration remained and the charterparties gave H the right to stop or stay a court action brought against it.

NB THREE SHIPPING LTD v. HAREBELL SHIPPING LTD, [2004] EWHC 2001, [2005] 1 All E.R. (Comm) 200, Morison, J., QBD (Comm).

3793. **Charterparty by demise–Default–Vessel for sale by hire purchase agreement–Withdrawal for failure to make payments–Discretion to grant relief from forfeiture**

The claimant shipowner (M) and the defendant bareboat charterer (D) brought cross applications for summary judgment. M bareboat chartered its vessel (J) to D under an amended Barecon 89 Form, including a hire purchase agreement which allowed title to pass to D on payment of deposits, monthly payments and certain lump sums during the currency of the 48 month charter term. However, following three late payments and a dispute as to underpayment of lump sums due, M gave notice that it was withdrawing J. D argued (1) that the conditional sale meant that time was not of the essence for payment; (2) M had waived its right to withdraw J for non payment as it had not done so in a reasonable time period; (3) alternatively, that D should be granted relief from forfeiture by virtue of the demise charter.

Held, giving judgment for M, that (1) there was no requirement to make time of the essence as the charter itself stipulated the consequences of non or late payment. M retained the right to withdraw J from service by giving notice or otherwise informing D that the charterparty was terminated. (2) M had not waived its right to withdraw as it had sought payment in full for three months before withdrawing J. (3) Although there was a discretion to grant relief from forfeiture on the basis of the rights granted to D during the term of the charterparty it would not be exercised as D and M had negotiated the terms of the hire purchase agreement and D had accepted the risk of wasted payments and the loss of its chance to purchase J if it failed to make payments specified under the charterparty, *Scandinavian Trading Tanker Co AB v. Flota Petrolera Ecuatoriana (The Scaptrade)* [1983] 2 A.C. 694, [1983] C.L.Y. 3405, *On Demand Information Plc (In Administrative Receivership) v. Michael Gerson (Finance) Plc* [2001] 1 W.L.R. 155, [2000] C.L.Y. 2326 and *Shiloh Spinners Ltd v. Harding (No.1)* [1973] A.C. 691, [1973] C.L.Y. 1867 considered.

MORE OG ROMSDAL FYLKESBATAR AS v. DEMISE CHARTERERS OF THE JOTUNHEIM; JOTUNHEIM, THE, [2004] EWHC 671, [2005] 1 Lloyd's Rep. 181, Cooke, J., QBD (Comm Ct).

3794. Collisions at sea – Apportionment – Responsibility for collision – Causative fault

The owners of the Global Mariner (GM) claimed against the owners of the Atlantic Crusader (AC) on the ground that the collision between those two vessels was the fault of the latter. The collision had taken place in the River Orinoco off the port of Matanzas, Venezuela. AC had been anchored in the navigable channel. There was a strong current and AC had had to be re anchored several times because she had been dragging her anchor. GM had been berthed port side to alongside a berth on an upriver heading. A vessel was anchored abeam of GM distant some three cables off the berth. AC was some five cables astern of that vessel. The collision occurred when GM undertook a 180 degree starboard turn to commence her downriver passage. GM submitted that AC was solely to blame, alternatively should bear the preponderance of blame, because she had been anchored in an unsafe anchorage and had failed to take any or adequate steps to control her yaw, drag and sway; the duty to control yaw, drag and sway was acute, given that AC had anchored in a narrow channel in close proximity to busy berths; control could have been achieved by the adoption of an open moor (anchoring with two anchors, to an angle of about 60 degrees), together with use of helm and engines; had such measures been taken, AC would have been more to the north of the channel and a collision would probably have been avoided or its nature would have been less serious. AC submitted that GM was solely to blame for the collision or was preponderantly to blame since GM, underway, had struck a vessel at anchor; AC's yawing was not unusual for a vessel at anchor in a river with a fast flowing current; her anchorage was not unsafe; she was not dragging or any dragging was minimal and immaterial; the fault lay with the failure of those on board GM to make any appreciation prior to unberthing or to maintain a proper lookout before or after departure from the berth; GM's manoeuvring was such that any failure on the part of AC to control her yaw and sway was not causative of the collision.

Held, giving judgment for AC, that (1) AC's anchorage position was not as such unsafe. Ships were accustomed to anchor in the channel. (2) Having anchored in a narrow channel in close proximity to busy berths AC was under a duty to control her yawing and swaying as a matter of good seamanship. AC was in breach of that duty because the master could and should have given instructions to control yaw and sway, anchored to an open moor and used the helm to control yaw and sway. (3) GM was at fault in terms of appreciation and lookout. A prudent seaman would have carried out a radar plot of the position of the AC since an accurate assessment of the position of vessels in the vicinity of the berth was part of the formulation of a prudent unberthing plan. GM failed to form an accurate appraisal of the AC's position. A proper lookout on GM would have detected the yawing of AC. Those on GM were at fault in failing to observe the yawing and to plan their passage accordingly. The failure of appreciation and lookout on the part of GM prior to conducting the turn was causative of the collision. (4) GM was at fault in respect of the unberthing manoeuvre. There was a failure to plan the manoeuvre. There was a comprehensive failure in the execution of the turn: the vessel proceeded too far to the north, came too close to the vessel anchored abeam of the berth, came too far downstream and came out of the turn too quickly. All of those matters flowed both from the prior failure of appreciation and lookout and from the unusual decision to use the engines, for a sustained period, half ahead and, thereafter, full ahead, in the course of the turn. There had been no or no satisfactory explanation of the decision to use the engines in that way and there was no need to conduct the turn in such a manner. As a result GM rapidly encountered a close quarters situation with AC for which those on board GM were unprepared. The conduct of the turn was a major cause of the collision. (5) There was sufficient water for GM, differently manoeuvred, to have passed AC safely, even at the extremity of her yaw; accordingly, the faults of GM, in respect of appreciation, lookout and the manner in which her unberthing manoeuvre was conducted, were causative of the collision. AC was at fault in failing to control her yaw but that failure was not causative because the collision would have occurred even if she had controlled her yaw. Therefore GM was solely to blame. (6) If AC's fault had been causative, liability would have been apportioned 90 per cent to GM and 10 per cent to AC. (7) The Admiralty Court set out the proper practice in collision cases for dealing with the answers of the nautical assessors to questions posed by the judge, *Owners of the Bow Spring v. Owners of the Manzanillo II* [2004] EWCA Civ 1007, [2005] 1 W.L.R. 144, [2004] C.L.Y. 3495 considered.

OWNERS OF THE GLOBAL MARINER v. OWNERS OF THE ATLANTIC CRUSADER; GLOBAL MARINER, THE; ATLANTIC CRUSADER, THE, [2005] EWHC 380, [2005] 2 All E.R. (Comm) 389, Gross, J., QBD (Admlty).

3795. Demurrage–Laytime–Acceptance of notice of readiness–Charterers' implied representations

[Arbitration Act 1996 s.68, s.69.]

The applicant shipowners (X) applied under the Arbitration Act 1996 s.68 to remit an award made by arbitrators in respect of X's claim for demurrage against the respondent charterers (R) on the basis that there had been a serious irregularity in the arbitration process. X also applied for leave to appeal under s.69 of the Act submitting that the arbitrators had made a serious error of law. The charterparty had contained express clauses requiring the holds of the vessel R chartered from X to be clean (Clause 23(b)) and requiring X to bear any expenses caused by time lost at loading ports due to crew failure (Clause 25). Following the ship's arrival at port, R summarily inspected the holds and certified them clean. R then accepted a notice of readiness from X and commenced loading. The loading process was interrupted by the discovery of contaminants in the holds and could not be recommenced until several days later. When calculating the demurrage due to X, the days lost to cleaning were deducted from the final amount by R on the ground that this was a crew failure under Clause 25. Alternatively, that this was to offset the damages that would be due to them from breach of Clause 23(b). X contended that (1) the arbitrators had erred in not considering the argument that R was estopped from asserting the breaches by reason of its acceptance of the notice of readiness which X had relied on in permitting commencement of loading. The fact that cargo was in the holds had made the subsequent cleaning operation more time consuming and difficult; (2) the removal of the ship from its berth for cleaning had permitted the earlier loading of another ship by the same charterers resulting in savings in demurrage on that charterparty. In calculating damages due for breach of Clause 23(b) this benefit to R should be taken into account. The arbitrators had erred in not ordering disclosure by R of documents relating to that charterparty.

Held, refusing the applications, that (1) the representation implied by R by acceptance of the notice of readiness was that on the basis of the inspection conducted the holds appeared clean. It was not a representation that there had been no breach of Clause 23(b) or Clause 25. R was not estopped from asserting a right to deduct time lost as a result of crew failure as this was not resiling from a previously held position. (2) There had been no evidence submitted by X to counter R's evidence of loss and X had made no formal application for disclosure. The arbitrators had been entitled to quantify the award on the basis that all the evidence which was mutually agreed by the parties to be material was before them. Further, even if there had been a serious irregularity in quantifying damages under Clause 23(b) it could not have caused substantial injustice to X as R's rights under Clause 25 operated regardless of set off for breach of charterparty.

ALPHAPOINT SHIPPING LTD v. ROTEM AMFERT NEGEV LTD (THE AGIOS DIMITRIOS); AGIOS DIMITRIOS, THE, [2004] EWHC 2232, [2005] 1 Lloyd's Rep. 23, Colman, J., QBD (Comm Ct).

3796. Docks–Dockyard port–Portsmouth

DOCKYARD PORT OF PORTSMOUTH ORDER 2005, SI 2005 1470; made under the Dockyard Ports Regulation Act 1865 s.3, s.5, s.6, s.7. In force: June 10, 2005; £3.00.

This Order, which revokes the Dockyard Port of Portsmouth Order 1978 (SI 1978 1881), is made under the Dockyard Ports Regulation Act 1865, which provides for defining the limits of a dockyard port, the appointment of a Queen's harbour master for the port and the making of rules concerning the lights or signals to be carried or used and the steps for avoiding collisions by vessels navigating the waters of the port. The Order makes provision for an increase in the maximum penalty for offences from £50 to level 3 on the standard scale; controls on jet-skiing, parascending and windsurfing; and movement of small boats; and changes to rules on anchoring and mooring; fishing; swimming and diving; water-skiing; speed limits; reserved and recreational areas; firearms, weapons and explosives; port radio communication; shipping movement control; restriction of movement in poor visibility; and temporary restrictions on movement within the Dockyard Port.

3797. Harbours–Revision–Constitution–Cattewater

CATTEWATER HARBOUR REVISION (CONSTITUTION) ORDER 2005, SI 2005 2932; made under the Harbours Act 1964 s.14. In force: October 24, 2005; £3.00.

This Order, which revokes in part the Cattewater Harbour Order 1915, the Cattewater Harbour Order 1925, the Cattewater Harbour Order 1950 and the Harbour Authorities (Constitution) Order 1985 (SI 1985 1504) and revokes the Cattewater Harbour Revision Order 1986 (SI 1986 137), re-constitutes the Cattewater Harbour Commissioners and increases the borrowing powers of the Commissioners from £1 million to £5 million.

3798. Harbours–Revision–Great Yarmouth

GREAT YARMOUTH OUTER HARBOUR REVISION ORDER 2005, SI 2005 2601; made under the Harbours Act 1964 s.14. In force: October 6, 2005; £3.00.

This Order amends the Great Yarmouth Outer Harbour Act 1986 to provide that development authorised by the Act and begun before November 8, 2010 is permitted development. It empowers the Authority to stop up permanently and extinguish public rights of way over a portion of the esplanade detailed, being so much of the esplanade as is situated within the limits of deviation for the works already authorised by the Act, when it is ready to commence so much of those works as requires the closure of the esplanade. It also contains protective provisions for Great Yarmouth Borough Council and Waveney District Council, the Environment Agency and Associated British Ports.

3799. Harbours–Revision–Great Yarmouth

GREAT YARMOUTH OUTER HARBOUR (NO.2) REVISION ORDER 2005, SI 2005 2602; made under the Harbours Act 1964 s.14. In force: October 6, 2005; £3.00.

This Order provides for the repeal of the Great Yarmouth Outer Harbour Act 1986 which prohibits the use of ship passenger and goods dues from the existing harbour for the purposes of the construction and operation of the Outer Harbour.

3800. Harbours–Revision–Pilotage–Langstone

LANGSTONE (PILOTAGE) HARBOUR REVISION ORDER 2005, SI 2005 1141; made under the Harbours Act 1964 s.14. In force: April 1, 2005; £3.00.

This Order extends the limits of jurisdiction of the Langstone Harbour Board for pilotage purposes under the Pilotage Act 1987 so as to include an area outside the port in respect of which the authority considers that pilotage should be compulsory.

3801. Limitation claims–Anti suit injunctions–Limitation action in absence of claim subject to limitation–Anti suit injunction only to restrain unconscionable proceedings

[Supreme Court Act 1981 s.20; Merchant Shipping Act 1995 Sch.7; Civil Procedure Rules 1998 (SI 1998 3132) Part 61 r.61.11; Convention on Limitation of Liability for Maritime Claims 1976 Art.10, Art.11.]

The appellant (T) appealed against a decision ([2005] EWHC 460, [2005] 2 All E.R. (Comm) 51) that the respondent shipowners (S) were entitled to a limitation decree under the Merchant Shipping Act 1995, and S appealed against the refusal of an injunction to restrain T proceeding against S for damages in Texas. S's seismic survey vessel had been towing streamers in the North Sea when the streamers collided with a marker buoy positioned at a well head in T's oilfield. It was alleged that as a result the buoy had been dragged from its position and the well head installation damaged. S had admitted liability for negligence and had obtained from the English court a decree limiting their liability. The claim form for the limitation decree had been served on T in England, since T was an English registered company. T submitted that the English court had no subject matter jurisdiction over it because a shipowner in the position of S could only launch limitation proceedings when underlying legal or arbitration proceedings had been commenced within the jurisdiction; that conclusion was to be inferred from the provisions of the Convention on Limitation of Liability for Maritime Claims 1976 as set out in Sch.7 to the 1995 Act. S submitted that by continuing with the liability proceedings in Texas T was flouting the English court and its judgment, and that the English court should grant an injunction to ensure that its judgment was not undermined.

Held, dismissing the appeal, that (1) there was no general jurisdiction provision in the Convention stating where the right of limitation was to be invoked. It therefore appeared that in principle the Convention permitted a party to seek to limit its liability in any contracting state which had personal jurisdiction over the defendant. Since there was no express restriction, any such restriction would have to be implied and there was nothing in the Convention to lead to the implication of any such restriction on the invocation of the right to limit. Neither Art.10 nor Art.11 contained such a restriction, either expressly or by necessary implication. The second sentence of Art.10.1 had not been included in Sch.7 because the United Kingdom had not introduced a provision of the kind for which it provided, namely that limitation could only be invoked where a fund had been constituted in a jurisdiction where a claim had been made. That was entirely consistent with the express provision in the first sentence that limitation could be invoked without the constitution of a fund and with the conclusion that a limitation action could be brought in such a case in the absence of an action to enforce a claim subject to limitation. Article 11 simply conferred a right on a person invoking limitation to constitute a limitation fund if he so wished. It did not require him to do so. The right to invoke limitation where no fund had been constituted was expressly conferred by Art.10.1 without any limitation or restriction, and by Art.10.3 questions of procedure were to be decided under the law of the forum. The Supreme Court Act 1981 s.20 and the Civil Procedure Rules 1998 Part 61 r.61.11 permitted such a limitation action to be brought and served on a person within the jurisdiction, *Vessel SA v. CP Ships (UK) Ltd* [2004] EWHC 3305, [2005] 2 All E.R. (Comm) 47 approved. (2) The essential touchstone for the grant of an anti suit injunction was whether there had been unconscionable conduct or the threat of unconscionable conduct,

Royal Bank of Canada v. Cooperatieve Centrale Raiffeisen-Boerenleenbank BA [2004] EWCA Civ 7, [2004] 2 All E.R. (Comm) 847, [2004] C.L.Y. 573 considered. In the instant case T's Texan proceedings had not been brought in breach of contract. T was not acting unconscionably. As a matter of comity it was for the Texan court to consider what steps to take in the light of the decree and whether it should be recognised or enforced. The limitation decree did not qualify T's right to bring liability proceedings in Texas so that it was not unconscionable for T to proceed in Texas. That remained so even on the assumption that T could not enforce in England a judgment for a larger amount obtained in Texas. S's admission of liability together with the limitation decree did not make the proceedings in Texas unconscionable.

SEISMIC SHIPPING INC v. TOTAL E&P UK PLC (THE WESTERN REGENT); WESTERN REGENT, THE; *sub nom.* OWNERS OF THE WESTERN REGENT v. CHARTERERS OF THE WESTERN REGENT, [2005] EWCA Civ 985, [2005] 2 All E.R. (Comm) 515, Clarke, L.J., CA (Civ Div).

3802. Merchant shipping—Fees

MERCHANT SHIPPING (FEES) (AMENDMENT) REGULATIONS 2005, SI 2005 580; made under the Merchant Shipping Act 1995 s.302. In force: April 1, 2005; £3.00.

The Regulations amend the Merchant Shipping (Fees) Regulations 1996 (SI 1996 3243) by increasing the hourly rate for fees for the issue of certificates pursuant to the Radio Rules. In the case of certificates issued pursuant to the Radio Rules, where a survey was performed abroad by a locally appointed surveyor, the hourly rates applicable to work involving the issue of a certificate are increased from £32 to £36. The Regulations make increases in the hourly rates charged for services in relation to the Radio Rules by increasing the hourly survey rates of £32 to £36. They also increase the flat rate charged for administration and other work from £50 to £75.

3803. Pollution control—Oil pollution

MERCHANT SHIPPING (PREVENTION OF OIL POLLUTION) (AMENDMENT) REGULATIONS 2005, SI 2005 1916; made under the European Communities Act 1972 s.2; the Merchant Shipping (Prevention of Oil Pollution) Order 1983 (SI 1983 1106) Art.3; the Merchant Shipping Act 1995 s.85, s.86; and the Merchant Shipping (Prevention of Pollution) (Law of the Sea Convention) Order 1996 (SI 1996 282) Art.2. In force: August 4, 2005; £3.00.

These Regulations, which amend the Merchant Shipping (Prevention of Oil Pollution) Regulations 1996 (SI 1996 2154), implement European Parliament and Council Regulation 1726/2003 ([2003] OJ L249/1) amending Regulation 417/2002 on the accelerated phasing in of double-hull or equivalent design requirements for single-hull oil tankers and Commission Regulation 2172/2004 ([2004] OJ L371/26) amending Regulation 417/2002 of the European Parliament and of the Council on the accelerated phasing-in of double-hull or equivalent design requirements for single-hull oil tankers. The Regulations make amendments in order to provide that a ship may be detained where it is suspected of contravening specified requirements.

3804. Pollution control—Oil pollution—Drilling rigs and platforms

MERCHANT SHIPPING (PREVENTION OF POLLUTION) (DRILLING RIGS AND OTHER PLATFORMS) ORDER 2005, SI 2005 74; made under the Railways and Transport Safety Act 2003 s.112. In force: March 1, 2005; £3.00.

This Order applies to drilling rigs and other platforms which are used, navigated or situated wholly or partly in or on water. It provides for the Merchant Shipping Act 1995 s.128(1)(e) to apply in relation to such rigs and other platforms. Section 128(1)(e) is a provision by which Her Majesty may by Order in Council give effect to international agreements relating to pollution from ships and which have been ratified by the UK.

3805. Ports-Security

SHIP AND PORT FACILITY (SECURITY) (AMENDMENT) REGULATIONS 2005, SI 2005 1434; made under the European Communities Act 1972 s.2. In force: July 1, 2005; £3.00.

These Regulations amend the Ship and Port Facility (Security) Regulations 2004 (SI 2004 1495) to correct defects.

3806. Safety at sea-Accidents-Investigations

MERCHANT SHIPPING (ACCIDENT REPORTING AND INVESTIGATION) REGULATIONS 2005, SI 2005 881; made under the Merchant Shipping Act 1995 s.267. In force: April 18, 2005; £3.00.

These Regulations revoke the Merchant Shipping (Accident Reporting and Investigation) Regulations 1999 (SI 1999 2567) to reflect the current working practices of the Marine Accident Investigation Branch of the Department for Transport and to align them, where possible, with practices applicable to the investigation of accidents in other transport modes.

3807. Safety at sea-Reporting requirements-Exemptions

MERCHANT SHIPPING (AMENDMENTS TO REPORTING REQUIREMENTS) REGULATIONS 2005, SI 2005 1092; made under the European Communities Act 1972 s.2; the Merchant Shipping (Prevention and Control of Pollution) Order 1987 (SI 1987 470) Art.3; the Merchant Shipping (Dangerous Goods and Marine Pollutants) Regulations 1990 (SI 1990 2595) Art.3; the Merchant Shipping (Prevention of Pollution) (Law of the Sea Convention) Order 1996 (SI 1996 282) Art.2; and the Merchant Shipping Act 1995 s.85, s.86. In force: April 27, 2005; £3.00.

These Regulations amend the Merchant Shipping (Reporting Requirements for Ships Carrying Dangerous or Polluting Goods) Regulations 1995 (SI 1995 2498) and the Merchant Shipping (Vessel Traffic Monitoring and Reporting Requirements) Regulations 2004 (SI 2004 2110) to remove reporting requirements from fishing vessels, traditional ships, recreational craft having a length of less than 45 metres and bunkers of less than 5000 tonnes for use on board ships.

3808. Safety at sea-Seamen-Medical fitness certificates

MERCHANT SHIPPING (MEDICAL EXAMINATION) (AMENDMENT) REGULATIONS 2005, SI 2005 1919; made under the Merchant Shipping Act 1995 s.85, s.86. In force: August 9, 2005; £3.00.

These Regulations amend the Merchant Shipping (Medical Examination) Regulations 2002 (SI 2002 2055) to correct a defect so that it refers to Merchant Shipping Notice No. MSN 1788(M) which is a new separate Merchant Shipping Notice which lists the non UK countries whose national seafarer medical certificates are deemed to be equivalent to a medical fitness certificate issued under the 2002 Regulations. They also make amendments so that a seafarer employed on a non UK ship may hold a medical fitness certificate as defined in the 2002 Regulations or an ILO compliant certificate.

3809. Safety at sea-Small passenger ships-Bridge visibility

MERCHANT SHIPPING (BRIDGE VISIBILITY) (SMALL PASSENGER SHIPS) REGULATIONS 2005, SI 2005 2286; made under the Merchant Shipping Act 1995 s.85, s.86. In force: September 6, 2005; £3.00.

These Regulations apply to passenger ships under 45 metres in length which are engaged in voyages as specified. The Regulations implement the recommendations of the Marine Accident Investigation Branch on bridge visibility on passenger ships set out in their Report into the loss of "the Marchioness". The provision contained in these Regulations was previously contained in the Merchant Shipping (Passenger Ships of Classes IV, V, VI and

VI (A) (Bridge Visibility) Regulations 1992 (SI 1992 2357), which were repealed by the Merchant Shipping (Safety of Navigation) Regulations 2002 (SI 2002 1473). The 2002 Regulations make provision for bridge visibility for ships of 45 metres in length and above in accordance with the requirements of the SOLAS Convention, but do not make provision for ships below that length. These Regulations require ships to be so constructed that the helmsman has good visibility over an arc of 360 degrees of the horizontal plane.

3810. **Salvage–Towage–Tug and tow in breach of duty to take care– Apportionment of responsibility**

[Arbitration Act 1996 s.69(3)(c); International Convention on Salvage 1989 Art.13.]

The claimants (M) appealed against an appeal arbitrator's decision to reduce an award granted to M for salvaging the oil rig of the defendant (K). M agreed to move K's oil rig a distance of 38 miles across the eastern Mediterranean using three tugs. Originally the operation was expected to take 17 hours but when the tow ran into terrible weather conditions M had to deploy a much larger tug, the rig's tanks were beached and the whole operation ended up taking approximately 11 days. An arbitrator held that the rig came into danger to an extent to justify a claim of salvage and that the services rendered by M constituted salvage services for which they were entitled to an award under the International Convention on Salvage 1989 Art.13. The arbitrator awarded a notional base award of $3 million less $1.2 million to reflect the extent to which he found that M had contributed to the danger. The appeal arbitrator, pursuant to the Arbitration Act 1996 s.69(3)(c), reduced the notional award to $2 million less $1 million in respect to M's contribution to the danger. M argued that as K, as the tow, had overall responsibility and command for the move, and M, as the tug, merely had a duty to obey such commands together with a duty to warn if any of those commands were believed to be flawed, K was more to blame for giving flawed commands than M was for failing to warn of those flaws.

Held, dismissing the appeal, that where both those on board the rig and those on board the tugs had failed in their respective duties, the one by failing to order that the tugs heave to and the other by failing to advise that the order given was flawed, the assessment of relative responsibility under Art.18 of the Convention was not made by reference to the fact that those on board the rig were in overall charge of the tow. It was necessary to assess the causative potency and blameworthiness of the salvor's faults relative to the causative potency and blameworthiness of the rig's faults. There was nothing in the case law to support M's proposition that overall command of a towage convoy imported with it an enhanced degree of fault in circumstances where both tug and tow had fallen short of their mutual duty to take care. The appeal arbitrator was therefore entitled to conclude as he did that those on board the rig and those on board the tugs were equally at fault.

OWNERS OF THE MARIDIVE VII, MARIDIVE XIII, MARIDIVE 85 AND MARIDIVE 94 v. OWNERS AND DEMISE CHARTERERS OF THE KEY SINGAPORE; MARIDIVE VII, THE; KEY SINGAPORE, THE, [2004] EWHC 2227, [2005] 1 All E.R. (Comm) 99, David Steel, J., QBD (Comm).

3811. **Ships–Arrest–Letters of undertaking–Discharge of liabilities**

The claimant time charterer (C) claimed payment under a letter of undertaking issued by the defendant protection and indemnity club (U) on behalf of the owners of the chartered vessel in respect of an agreement for the vessel's release from arrest. C had subchartered the vessel under a voyage charterparty to a company (X) for the shipping of a cargo of wheat. A dispute arose as a result of damage to the cargo during the voyage. Following arbitration proceedings X was awarded damages against C, for which the owners were ordered to indemnify C. Due to non payment by the owners C arrested the vessel. As a result of negotiations to release the vessel, U provided a letter of undertaking to pay on demand such sum as was due from the owners to C "in respect of your said claim and legal costs against owners". In accordance with the terms of a side letter U sent the amount of the arbitration award directly to X. X refused to accept that sum in payment of the arbitration award on the terms on which it was sent, and retained the monies to the order of U. C then demanded payment of the amount of the arbitration award under the letter of undertaking. U submitted that (1) on its proper construction, the letter of undertaking did not cover the arbitration award, but only covered certain costs; (2) C was estopped from demanding payment of the arbitration award under the letter of undertaking because other correspondence between U and C indicated an understanding that payment of the arbitration award to X would extinguish liability for that sum; (3) the letter of undertaking only covered sums actually "due to" C from the owners and no such sums were actually due because of the remittance by U to X.

Held, giving judgment for the claimant, that (1) the letter of undertaking, construed in its commercial context, clearly covered payment of the arbitration award itself and the legal costs incurred in connection with the arbitration proceedings. There was nothing in the factual matrix that required the court to give the words in the letter of undertaking anything other than their natural and ordinary meaning. There was no obvious mistake that would enable the court to read in terms that were not in the letter. (2) A proper analysis of the correspondence established that there had been no representation, agreed course of dealing or convention, or agreement not to demand payment of the arbitration award under the letter of undertaking as alleged by U. It was impossible to regard the evidence as showing that both parties had laboured under that common assumption. There was no evidential basis to support the argument that the letter of undertaking and the side letter did not reflect the common intentions of the parties. (3) A creditor accepted payment either by expressly declaring its unconditional assent to the payment, or by acceptance or by treating the money as its own. X had clearly not accepted the payment made by U. Therefore, no payment sufficient to discharge the owner's liability under the arbitration award had been made by U. Accordingly, it could not be said that no sum was owing to C from the owner because C was still liable to pay the arbitration award to X.

CANMER INTERNATIONAL INC v. UK MUTUAL STEAMSHIP ASSURANCE ASSOCIATION (BERMUDA) LTD (THE RAYS); RAYS, THE, [2005] EWHC 1694, [2005] 2 Lloyd's Rep 479, Gloster, J., QBD (Comm).

3812. **Ships–Detention–Vessel detained awaiting inspection by US Coast Guard– Implied indemnities**

The claimant charterers (H) sought a declaration that the correct interpretation of the off hire clause in a single trip time charter on an amended NYPE form was that the vessel was off hire while awaiting inspection by the United States Coast Guard as a "high interest vessel". The vessel had been hired from the defendant owners (F) for a "one time charter trip via safe anchorage(s), safe berth(s), safe ports always afloat, always Institute Warranty Limits from US Gulf to South Korea with bulk grain, duration of about 65-75 days without guarantee". The vessel had been built in 2001 and since this was her first trip to a US port the vessel's agents in New Orleans anticipated that the vessel would be designated a "high interest vessel", with the result that she would be prevented from entering port until such time as the US Coast Guard had conducted a security boarding. Before the vessel arrived at New Orleans the US Coast Guard prohibited the vessel from entering the lower Mississippi river and directed her to await inspection by a Coast Guard boarding team. H submitted that the vessel was "detained" within the meaning of the off hire clause in the charterparty while awaiting inspection by the US Coast Guard. F submitted that (1) the vessel was not detained because she was not in US territorial waters when the order to await inspection was received; (2) even if the vessel was detained within the meaning of the off hire clause, the proviso to that clause applied, because the detention was caused by H's order to proceed to and load cargo at New Orleans and was thus "occasioned by [a] calling port of trading" under the charter; (3) if the vessel was off hire during the period in question, F could recover the hire lost by way of the indemnity to be implied in the time charter against any losses or expenses incurred by F in complying with the directions of H.

Held, granting a declaration in favour of H, that (1) in the context of a charterparty, a vessel was detained when, as a result of some geographical or physical constraint upon her movement, she was prevented from proceeding as directed under the charterparty, and if there was some such constraint on a vessel's movement which prevented her from proceeding on the course directed by charterers, the fact that she was not prevented from proceeding elsewhere did not negate "detention", *Nippon Yusen Kaisha Ltd v. Scindia Steam Navigation Co Ltd (The Jalagouri)* [2000] 1 All E.R. (Comm) 700, [2000] C.L.Y. 4703 applied. The vessel was kept from proceeding to her loading port; she was sent to wait at a specific location; she was kept waiting there for about six days; she was stopped. That amounted to a constraint upon her movements in relation to her service under the charter. Accordingly the vessel was detained. The clause was a period off hire clause under which once the detention had been established the vessel remained off hire as long as it lasted. It did not require an enquiry into the progress the vessel would have made or delays she would have encountered but for the detention. (2) The scope for application of the "calling port of trading" proviso was more limited in a single trip time charter than in a time charter for an extended period. The vessel's proceeding to a US Gulf port for loading was not the result of the exercise of some trading discretion reserved to H but was the subject of mutual agreement recorded in the charterparty. The evidence led to the conclusion that the risk of boarding and inspection by the US Coast Guard under laws enacted after the World Trade Centre attack was a risk general to any vessel calling at any US Gulf port, particularly if she was calling at a US port for the first time. That risk did not flow from an act or omission of H or from their nomination of New Orleans as a US Gulf port. It was a risk inherent in the voyage agreed in the single trip time charter. (3) By agreeing to carry cargo from the US Gulf, F agreed to run the risk of being stopped for inspection under whatever laws applied generally to US Gulf ports. Such a risk was an ordinary incident of trading at the range of ports in question. The implied indemnity on which F relied could not apply so as to reverse an allocation of risk agreed expressly in the charterparty.

HYUNDAI MERCHANT MARINE CO LTD v. FURNESS WITHY (AUSTRALIA) PTY (THE DORIC PRIDE); DORIC PRIDE, THE, [2005] EWHC 945, [2005] 2 Lloyd's Rep. 470, Michael Crane Q.C., QBD (Comm).

3813. Time charterparties–Accidents–Chief officer falling into hold–Shipowner and charterers holding each other responsible

The appellant shipowner (C) appealed against the decision that an injury to the chief officer of its vessel caused by the negligence of stevedores was its responsibility. C chartered its vessel to charterers (S) under a time charter on the Baltime 1939 form, which provided by clause 4 in its standard terms that S was to arrange and pay for all cargo operations. The hatch cover to the vessel's hold consisted of 11 interlocking pontoons that could be removed and replaced by a hatch gantry crane that moved on rails running either side of the hold. In certain circumstances the configuration of containers stowed on deck meant that it was more convenient to use a shore crane instead of the gantry crane to remove and replace pontoons. Such operations were carried out by S's stevedores. While a shore crane was being used to replace a pontoon, the vessel's chief officer fell into the hold and was injured. The judge concluded that the accident was caused by the negligence of the stevedores' signalman or crane driver, but that the stevedores were performing C's work at the time in replacing the pontoon, so that C's claim against S for the cost of settling the chief officer's claim failed. S submitted that the opening and closing of hatches was part of C's exclusive responsibility, even when the hatch pontoons were being handled by agreement by S's stevedores. C submitted that the relevant hatch operations should be regarded as part of loading and discharging, for which S was responsible under the charter.

Held, allowing the appeal, that (1) C bore primary responsibility for hatch handling under the charter. The hatch was part of the vessel's equipment. (2) The charter placed primary responsibility for cargo operations on S. It was for the master to decide how to load and discharge, but it was for S and its stevedores to execute the cargo operations without negligence. (3) The hatch handling occurred within the time and space of the overall cargo operation and was conducted by S's stevedores as an integral part of that operation without extra payment and pursuant to an accord or agreement between the parties. Therefore the hatch closing operation in which the chief officer was injured was to be treated as part of the overall cargo operation for which S was responsible, *SG Embiricos Ltd v. Tradax Internacional SA (The Azuero)* [1967] 1 Lloyd's Rep. 464, [1967] C.L.Y. 3622 applied. (4) The judge was right to find that the effective cause of the chief officer's accident was S's stevedores' negligence. (5) C was entitled to the cost of settling the chief officer's claim from S as damages for breach of contract.

CV SCHEEPVAARTONDERNEMING FLINTERMAR v. SEA MALTA CO LTD (THE FLINTERMAR); FLINTERMAR, THE, [2005] EWCA Civ 17, [2005] 1 All E.R. (Comm) 497, Waller, L.J., CA (Civ Div).

3814. Time charterparties–Implied indemnities–Amended NYPE form–Cost of defouling vessel's hull off hire

The appellant shipowners (S) appealed against an arbitration award on two points of law. S time chartered its bulk carrier to charterers (B) on an amended NYPE form. The trading limits under the charterparty were "always within Institute Warranty Limits" (line 15), subject to the exclusion of the countries and other areas set out in clause 88 of the charterparty. B subchartered the vessel to subcharterers on an amended NYPE form in terms identical to those of the charterparty apart from the provisions relating to the period of the charter and the hire. The subcharterers then sub subchartered the vessel, also on an amended NYPE form, for a time charter trip for the carriage of coal from South Korea to Visak in India. Discharge of the cargo at Visak was delayed and the vessel remained there for over three weeks. S claimed that, whilst at Visak, the vessel's hull became seriously fouled by barnacles and S claimed the cost of defouling the vessel (approximately £180,000) from B under an implied indemnity in the charterparty. S also claimed that B had wrongfully put the vessel off-hire while the de-fouling work was being done and claimed unpaid hire of £47,811 for that period. Arbitrators held that the cost of de fouling was not within the scope of the implied indemnity in the charterparty and that the vessel was off hire while the de fouling work was carried out. S submitted that (1) the arbitrators had wrongly concluded that, because the particular employment which led to the fouling at Visak was within the Institute Warranty Limits, and hence permitted under the charterparty, S had agreed to accept the risks (falling short of danger) ordinarily incident at the ports of the subcontinent, including fouling of the hull and the costs of removing it; (2) time spent removing marine growth which had attached itself to the hull of the vessel in the course of service under the charterparty did not amount to time lost within the meaning of clause 15 of the charterparty. B submitted that (1) the arbitrators had not erred in law in concluding that the vessel remained at Visak not because of anything the charterers did or failed to do but because of operational considerations at the port, and that the risk of fouling as a result of that employment was a risk that S could be taken to have accepted; (2) the arbitrators founded their off hire decision on clause 54 of the charterparty (deviation for owners' matters) and not clause 15.

Held, dismissing the appeal, that (1) the arbitrators were entitled to conclude that the risk of the vessel suffering hull fouling, by being inactive at a warm water port for 22 days as a result of a legitimate order of B as to the employment of the vessel, was something that was foreseeable and foreseen by both sides at the time the charterparty was made, and that the risks that the vessel's performance would suffer as a result of hull fouling and S subsequently having to clean her hull as soon as they could were also foreseeable and foreseen by both parties at the time the charterparty was concluded. The arbitrators were further entitled to conclude that that type of risk was one that S agreed to accept and was not therefore within the scope of the implied indemnity, *Triad Shipping Co v. Stellar Chartering and Brokerage Inc (The Island Archon)* [1995] 1 All E.R. 595, [1994] C.L.Y. 4059 applied. The arbitrators found that the expenses of cleaning the hull fouling were ordinary expenses of trading under the charterparty and that the parties (at the time the charterparty was made) would have so regarded that type of expense, and that de fouling had to be carried out by S because of their obligation to keep the vessel in a thoroughly efficient state throughout her service. If a loss by shipowners was a consequence of a lawful order of the charterers, if the loss (or expense) had arisen from a risk that the shipowner had agreed to run, then there was no right to an indemnity. (2) The arbitrators made a finding that the vessel was off hire within the terms of clause 54 of the charterparty. They concluded that the stop for de fouling was for "owners' purposes", reflecting the wording in clause 54. If the arbitrators had intended to refer to clause 15 then they would have been expected to make a finding of fact as to the loss of time actually suffered as a result of the de fouling stop but they did not do so. Further, if the arbitrators had intended to refer to clause 15 then their ruling would have been contrary to authority which they must have been aware of and did not mention.

ACTION NAVIGATION INC v. BOTTIGLIERI DI NAVIGATIONE SpA (THE KITSA); KITSA, THE; *sub nom.* ACTION NAVIGATION INC v. BOTTIGLIERE NAVIGATION SPA, [2005] EWHC 177, [2005] 1 Lloyd's Rep. 432, Aikens, J., QBD (Comm).

3815. **Time charterparties–Maritime arbitration–Interpretation–Rejection of goods–Clausing**

The appellant shipowner (S) appealed against a final declaratory award granted in favour of the respondent head charterer (M) in arbitration proceedings concerning a dispute as to the correct interpretation of clause 52 in a time charterparty. The master of S's vessel had refused to accept for carriage a cargo of steel pipes because they were in a damaged condition. A letter of indemnity was issued and the cargo was allowed. The ship proceeded to the next port where the master refused to allow a cargo of steel coils on board as they were in damaged condition. The parties entered into a without prejudice agreement and the cargo was loaded. The master stated that he had refused both shipments in accordance with clause 52 which provided that he had the right and obligation to reject any cargo subject to clausing. There was no dispute as to the actual condition of the goods tendered for shipment. The issues to be determined were whether (i) under clause 52 of the charterparty, the master was entitled and obliged to reject cargo which would probably be the subject of a reservation in the bill of lading as to the apparent good order and condition of the cargo or the packing; or whether the master was entitled and obliged to reject cargo, only if, once loaded, it would be properly described in the bill of lading in a way which would qualify the statement of the apparent order and condition of the cargo ultimately proposed to be stated in the bill of lading by the shipper, and (ii) depending on the answer, whether the master was entitled and obliged to reject the cargo presented for shipment.

Held, dismissing the appeal, that on a proper construction of clause 52, the master did not have the right to reject the cargo. The arbitrators had correctly interpreted clause 52. Clause 52 contemplated that the master would inspect cargo before loading otherwise he could not reject it. The construction was consistent with the practice, at the time of the presentation of cargo and the presentation of the draft bills of lading. It was also consistent with the implied requirement that the parties would act reasonably to make the contract work. When clause 52 was agreed, the parties had contemplated that there would be room for negotiation as to the description of the cargo in the bills of lading before the goods were loaded. It was only if the shippers continued to insist on their description and the master concluded that that the cargo would be described in the bill of lading in a way which was inconsistent with a statement as to the cargo's apparent order and condition, that the master had the right and duty to reject that cargo. That did not mean that he had the right to finally reject cargo as first described in a draft bill of lading.

SEA SUCCESS MARITIME INC v. AFRICAN MARITIME CARRIERS LTD, [2005] EWHC 1542, [2005] 2 All E.R. (Comm) 445, Aikens, J., QBD (Comm).

3816. Time charterparties—Time limits—Meaning of clause in Shelltime 4 form

[Hague Rules; Hague Visby Rules Art. III r.6.]

The claimant charterers (B) made claims for breach of a charterparty and a preliminary issue was tried as to whether the claims were time barred. B had chartered a product tanker from the respondent owners (P) on a time charter on the Shelltime 4 form. Clause 27 (c) (ii) provided that claims arising out of any loss of or damage to or in connection with cargo would be subject to the Hague Visby Rules or the Hague Rules. The tanker carried a cargo of palm oil and was then subchartered on the Asbatankvoy form for a voyage from Rotterdam to West Africa. After discharge of the cargo of palm oil, the vessel's tanks were cleaned but the subcharterer cancelled the subcharter because of the poor condition of the vessel's tanks, which were not suitable to load the nominated cargo of gasoline. B claimed against P for breach of a number of terms of the charterparty. The loss claimed was the subcharter freight, wasted bunkers and the balance of account on the final hire statement. P claimed that the claims for freight and bunkers were time barred because suit had not been commenced within one year as required by Art. III r.6 of the Hague Visby Rules. P submitted that a claim would be time barred if it arose in connection with cargo which could be identified, whether shipped or not, and that in the instant case the claim was based on the vessel not being clean enough to receive a particular cargo, as a result of which that particular cargo was lost, for which was claimed the loss of freight to be earned on that particular cargo, and that therefore the claim arose in connection with cargo and was time barred. B submitted that its claims were not claims "arising out of any loss of or damage to or in connection with cargo" within the meaning of clause 27 (c) (ii) of the Shelltime 4 form nor were they claims "in respect of the goods" within Art. III r.6 of the Hague Visby Rules; rather its claims were for breaches of charter obligations independent of the Hague Visby Rules and clause 27 (c) (ii) of the Shelltime 4 form did not apply to such claims.

Held, determining the preliminary issue in favour of B, that clause 27 (c) (ii) of Shelltime 4 was concerned with what would be regarded in the marine market as "cargo claims". It referred only to claims sufficiently connected with cargo, namely claims (whether original or derivative) of the sort which were normally brought by cargo interests (bill of lading holders), claiming loss or damage arising in relation to the cargo and measured by reference to the cargo. Included in that category were claims for physical loss of cargo and claims for physical damage to cargo. Also included were claims for financial loss such as a fall in the value of a particular cargo or the costs of storing/transshipping a particular cargo, *Navigazione Alta Italia SpA v. Concordia Maritime Chartering AB (The Stena Pacifica)* [1990] 2 Lloyd's Rep. 234, [1991] C.L.Y. 182 followed and *Noranda Inc v. Barton (Time Charter) Ltd (The Marinor)* [1996] 1 Lloyd's Rep. 301 distinguished. In the instant case, no claim was made for (a) loss of cargo, (b) damage to cargo, (c) loss in connection with cargo (in the sense contemplated by clause 27 (c) (ii) or (d) damage in connection with cargo (in that sense). The claim was not a cargo claim in the sense understood in the marine market. B claimed damages for loss of use of the vessel. Accordingly, B's claims were not time barred.

BORGSHIP TANKERS INC v. PRODUCT TRANSPORT CORP LTD (THE CASCO); CASCO, THE, [2005] EWHC 273, [2005] 1 Lloyd's Rep. 565, Cresswell, J., QBD (Comm).

3817. Voyage charterparties—Demurrage—Construction of strike clause

The appellant charterer of a vessel (F) appealed against an arbitration award upholding a claim by the respondent owners of the vessel (S) for demurrage. S chartered the vessel to F for a voyage. The vessel arrived at the discharge port on December 12, 2001 and discharge of cargo commenced the following day, but the discharge was not completed until January 17, 2002 because of a strike by the employees of the consignees of the cargo. Clause 9 of the charterparty provided that the cargo was to be discharged free of risk and expense to the vessel at the average rate of 10,000 metric ton per weather working day of 24 consecutive hours, and that the consignee was to pay for the demurrage if the vessel was detained longer. The clause further provided that in case of strikes, lockouts, civil commotions, or any other causes beyond the control of the consignee which delayed the discharging, such time would not count. It was accepted by F that clause 26 had the effect of making it liable for demurrage at the discharge port. The arbitrators found that, although F could not have avoided the strike, it was not outside the control of the consignee, and accordingly upheld the claim by S for demurrage and awarded a sum in respect of it. F argued that the natural reading of clause 9 of the charterparty was that in the event of a strike delaying discharge, the laytime clock would stop and in the event of some different cause, the laytime clock would stop, but only if that other cause was beyond the control of the consignee. Further, the words "any other cause beyond the control of the consignee" were intended to enlarge the protection conferred by the clause.

Held, dismissing the appeal, that the arbitrator's construction of clause 9 was correct. The clause provided for both specified and unspecified events to interrupt the running of laytime. The natural construction of the clause, which stated that the "consignee" was to pay demurrage, was that the words "beyond the control of the consignee" applied not only to "any other causes or accidents" but also to the specified events of strikes, lockouts and civil commotions. The operation of exceptions from laytime depended on the events or causes being beyond the control of the consignees and not the charterers. If the parties had intended to focus on the role of the charterer at the discharge port, they could have amended clause 9 to do so. Where the consignee's own workforce was on strike, it would be a question of fact whether the strike was beyond the control of the consignee and, in order to show that the strike delayed the discharge, a detailed factual investigation might be necessary into events of which F had no knowledge.

FRONTIER INTERNATIONAL SHIPPING CORP v. SWISSMARINE CORP INC (THE CAPE EQUINOX); CAPE EQUINOX, THE, [2005] EWHC 8, [2005] 1 All E.R. (Comm) 528, Nigel Teare Q.C., QBD (Comm).

3818. Wrecks–Protection–Restricted area designation

PROTECTION OF WRECKS (DESIGNATION) (ENGLAND) ORDER 2005, SI 2005 1974; made under the Protection of Wrecks Act 1973 s.1. In force: July 20, 2005; £3.00.

This Order designates as a restricted area for the purposes of the Protection of Wrecks Act 1973 an area in the West Bay in Lyme Bay, Dorset. This area is thought to be the wreck site of a vessel which the Secretary of State is satisfied ought to be protected, as a matter of immediate urgency, from authorised interference on account of its historical, archaeological or artistic importance.

3819. Books

Bills Gaskell–Bills of Lading: Law and Practice. Hardback: £250.00. ISBN 1 84311 398 8. Informa Business Publishing.

Blanco, Luis Ortiz–Shipping Conferences Under EC Antitrust Law: Criticism of a Legal Paradox. Hardback: £125.00. ISBN 1 84113 527 5. Hart Publishing.

Bools, Lord and Aikens–Bills of Lading. Lloyd's Shipping Law Library. Hardback: £260.00. ISBN 1 84311 438 0. Informa Business Publishing.

Davis, Mark–Bareboat Charters. Lloyd's Shipping Law Library. Hardback: £240.00. ISBN 1 84311 423 2. Informa Business Publishing.

Grime, R.–Shipping Law. Paperback: £28.00. ISBN 0 421 60670 3. Sweet & Maxwell.

Hassan, Daud–Protecting the Marine Environment from Land-Based Sources of Pollution. Hardback: £50.00. ISBN 0 7546 4601 7. Ashgate.

Jackson, David–Enforcement of Maritime Claims. Hardback: £250.00. ISBN 1 84311 424 0. Informa Business Publishing.

Mandaraka-Sheppard, Alexandra–Modern Admiralty Law. Paperback: £80.00. ISBN 1 85941 895 3. Cavendish Publishing Ltd.

SOCIAL SECURITY

3820. Benefits–Child tax credit

SOCIAL SECURITY (TAX CREDITS) AMENDMENT REGULATIONS 2005, SI 2005 2294; made under the Social Security Contributions and Benefits Act 1992 s.123, s.124, s.135, s.136, s.137, s.175; and the Jobseekers Act 1995 s.4, s.12, s.13, s.35, s.36. In force: September 8, 2005; £3.00.

These Regulations amend the Social Security (Working Tax Credit and Child Tax Credit) (Consequential Amendments) Regulations 2003 (SI 2003 455). They make provision in connection with the abolition of the special amounts and premia in income support and jobseeker's allowance for those with responsibility for children and young persons. Such amounts and premia are replaced by child tax credit under that Act. The amendments ensure that, during the transitional period, no new awards of such amounts and premia are made except to existing claimants who already have an amount in respect of a child or young person included in their applicable amount.

3821. Benefits–Claims and payments

SOCIAL SECURITY (CLAIMS AND PAYMENTS AND PAYMENTS ON ACCOUNT, OVERPAYMENTS AND RECOVERY) AMENDMENT REGULATIONS 2005, SI 2005 34; made under the Social Security Administration Act 1992 s.5, s.71, s.189, s.191. In force: May 2, 2005; £3.00.

These Regulations amend the Social Security (Claims and Payments) Regulations 1987 (SI 1987 1968) and the Social Security (Payments on account, Overpayments and Recovery) Regulations 1988 (SI 1988 664). They enable a person to make a claim for graduated retirement benefit and retirement pension by telephone unless the Secretary of State directs that the claim must be made in writing; enable a person who has made such a claim to amend it by telephone; and provide for the date of a claim for graduated retirement benefit or retirement pension made by telephone. The Regulations enable the Secretary of State to give notice of the effect Reg.11 of the 1988 Regulations would have, in the event of an overpayment, to a person who makes a claim for retirement pension and graduated retirement benefit by telephone, either orally or in writing.

3822. Benefits–Claims and payments

SOCIAL SECURITY (PAYMENTS ON ACCOUNT, OVERPAYMENTS AND RECOVERY) AMENDMENT REGULATIONS 2005, SI 2005 3476; made under the Social Security Administration Act 1992 s.74, s.189, s.191. In force: January 19, 2006; £3.00.

These Regulations amend the Social Security (Payments on account, Overpayments and Recovery) Regulations 1988 (SI 1988 664) to include payments made under the Financial Assistance Scheme Regulations 2005.

3823. Benefits–Claims and payments–Time limits

SOCIAL SECURITY (CLAIMS AND PAYMENTS) AMENDMENT (NO.2) REGULATIONS 2005, SI 2005 777; made under the Abolition of Domestic Rates Etc. (Scotland) Act 1987 Sch.2 para.7A; the Local Government Finance Act 1988 Sch.4 para.6; the Criminal Justice Act 1991 s.24, s.30; the Social

Security Administration Act 1992 s.5, s.189, s.191; and the Local Government Finance Act 1992 s.14, s.113, s.116, Sch.4 para.1, Sch.4 para.6. In force: April 11, 2005; £3.00.

These Regulations amend the Social Security (Claims and Payments) Regulations 1987 (SI 1987 1968) in respect of the time for claiming benefit and deductions from benefit for payment to other persons.

3824. Benefits–Electronic communications

SOCIAL SECURITY (ELECTRONIC COMMUNICATIONS) (MISCELLANEOUS BENEFITS) ORDER 2005, SI 2005 3321; made under the Electronic Communications Act 2000 s.8, s.9. In force: January 30, 2006; £3.00.

This Order amends the Social Security (Claims and Payments) Regulations 1987 (SI 1987 1968) to enable a claim to be made by electronic communication for attendance allowance, disability living allowance, graduated retirement benefit, retirement pension and shared additional pension.

3825. Benefits–Entitlement–Reciprocal agreements

SOCIAL SECURITY (RECIPROCAL AGREEMENTS) ORDER 2005, SI 2005 2765; made under the Social Security Administration Act 1992 s.179. In force: December 5, 2005; £3.00.

This Order amends the Social Security Administration Act 1992, the Social Security Contributions and Benefits Act 1992 and 32 SIs. It provides for social security legislation to be modified, to reflect changes made to the benefit entitlement of spouses and civil partners by the Welfare Reform and Pensions Act 1999 and the Civil Partnership Act 2004, in relation to the Orders in Council listed in Schedule 2 which give effect to agreements made between the Governments of the UK and other countries providing for reciprocity in certain social security matters.

3826. Benefits–Hospital in-patients

SOCIAL SECURITY (HOSPITAL IN-PATIENTS) REGULATIONS 2005, SI 2005 3360; made under the Social Security Contributions and Benefits Act 1992 s.113, s.123, s.124, s.130, s.131, s.135, s.136, s.137, s.138, s.175; the Social Security Administration Act 1992 s.5, s.73, s.189; the Jobseekers Act 1995 s.4, s.36; and the State Pension Credit Act 2002 s.2, s.3, s.17, s.19. In force: in accordance with Reg.1; £3.00.

These Regulations amend the Social Security (General Benefit) Regulations 1982 (SI 1982 1408), the Social Security (Abolition of Injury Benefit) (Consequential) Regulations 1983 (SI 1983 186), the Social Security (Severe Disablement Allowance) Regulations 1984 (SI 1984 1303), the Social Security (Dependency, Claims and Payments and Hospital In-Patients) Amendment Regulations 1984 (SI 1984 1699), the Social Security (Claims and Payments, Hospital In-Patients and Maternity Benefit) Amendment Regulations 1986 (SI 1986 903), the Income Support (General) Regulations 1987 (SI 1987 1967), the Housing Benefit (General) Regulations 1987 (SI 1987 1971), the Income Support (General) Amendment No.4 Regulations 1988 (SI 1988 1445), the Income Support (General) Amendment Regulations 1990 (SI 1990 547), the Council Tax Benefit (General) Regulations 1992 (SI 1992 1814), the Social Security (Miscellaneous Provisions) Amendment (No.2) Regulations 1992 (SI 1992 2595), the Jobseeker's Allowance Regulations 1996 (SI 1996 207), the Child Benefit, Child Support and Social Security (Miscellaneous Amendments) Regulations 1996 (SI 1996 1803), the Social Security (Miscellaneous Amendments) Regulations 1998 (SI 1998 563), the Social Security (Hospital In-Patients, Attendance Allowance and Disability Living Allowance) (Amendment) Regulations 1999 (SI 1999 1326), the Social Fund Winter Fuel Payment Regulations 2000 (SI 2000 729), the Social Security (Benefits for Widows and Widowers) (Consequential Amendments) Regulations 2000 (SI 2000 1483), the State Pension Credit Regulations 2002 (SI 2002 1792), the

State Pension Credit (Consequential, Transitional and Miscellaneous Provisions) Regulations 2002 (SI 2002 3019), the State Pension Credit (Consequential, Transitional and Miscellaneous Provisions) (No.2) Regulations 2002 (SI 2002 3197), the Social Security (Working Tax Credit and Child Tax Credit) (Consequential Amendments) Regulations 2003 (SI 2003 455), the Social Security (Hospital In-Patients and Miscellaneous Amendments) Regulations 2003 (SI 2003 1195), the Social Security (Third Party Deductions and Miscellaneous Amendments) Regulations 2003 (SI 2003 2325), the Social Security (Miscellaneous Amendments) Regulations 2004 (SI 2004 565) and the Civil Partnership (Pensions, Social Security and Child Support) (Consequential, etc. Provisions) Order 2005 (SI 2005 2877). They also revoke the Social Security (Hospital In-Patients) Regulations 1975 (SI 1975 555), the Social Security (Hospital In-Patients) Amendment Regulations 1977 (SI 1977 1693), the Social Security (Hospital In-Patients) Amendment Regulations 1979 (SI 1979 223), the Social Security (Hospital In-Patients) Amendment Regulations 1987 (SI 1987 31), the Social Security (Hospital In Patients) Amendment (No.2) Regulations 1987 (SI 1987 1683) and the Social Security (Hospital In-Patients) Amendment Regulations 2004 (SI 2004 101). The Regulations make amendments so that, except in specified cases, a person's benefit is no longer adjusted when the person has been receiving free medical treatment as a hospital in-patient for 52 weeks.

3827. **Benefits–Income support–Income support dependent child allowance– Discrimination based on nationality**

[Income Support (General) Regulations 1987 (SI 1987 1967) Reg.16(5); Council Regulation 1612/68 Art.7(2); Council Regulation 1408/71.]

The appellant secretary of state appealed against a decision of the social security commissioner that the respondent (B) was entitled to argue that he had been discriminated against on the ground of his nationality under Council Regulation 1612/68 Art.7(2) in respect of a claim for income support dependent child allowance, and B cross appealed against the commissioner's finding that discrimination was not obviously there. B was a Portuguese national who had arrived in the United Kingdom as a "worker". He became permanently incapable of work and thereafter received disablement allowance and income support dependent child allowance in respect of his step daughter. The secretary of state sought to recover overpaid allowance on the basis that the step daughter had spent periods in Portugal. An appeal tribunal revised that decision but ordered B to submit a list of dates his step daughter was in Portugal. On appeal the commissioner found that B had been discriminated against in the application of the Income Support (General) Regulations 1987 Reg.16(5) on the ground of his nationality under Art.7(2) of the 1968 Regulation. The matter was remitted to the tribunal to consider whether B could establish discrimination. In the instant appeal, B conceded that if the case went back to the tribunal for the discrimination question he would not rely on Art.7 of the 1968 Regulation. Both parties had agreed that the issue of discrimination was to be decided under Council Regulation 1408/71. Accordingly the only remaining issue to be decided was in relation to the cross appeal. In his cross appeal, B contended that the provision in Reg.16(5) indirectly discriminated against him on grounds of nationality and that it was an impossible task for him to produce statistical evidence to prove that there was in fact discrimination against him as a migrant worker, and in any event he was not required to undertake such a task.

Held, allowing the appeal and allowing the cross appeal, that it was enough in cases of discrimination based on nationality that the effect of the provision was intrinsically liable to be discriminatory, *O'Flynn v. Adjudication Officer (C237/94)* [1996] All E.R. (EC) 541, [1996] C.L.Y. 5517 and *Biehl v. Administration des Contributions du Grand-Duche de Luxembourg (C175/88)* [1991] S.T.C. 575 considered. In those cases the court had not insisted on statistical evidence. The court was entitled to take a broad approach and to find that indirect discrimination was liable to affect a significant number of migrant workers on the ground of nationality without statistical proof being available.

The proper approach was to compare the children of migrant workers with British children whose families were normally resident in the UK. It was intrinsically likely that significantly more of the former than the latter would be prejudiced by Reg.16(5) of the 1987 Regulations. The cross appeal succeeded and the appeal tribunal was required to decide whether the discrimination could be justified by the secretary of state.

SECRETARY OF STATE FOR WORK AND PENSIONS v. BOBEZES, [2005] EWCA Civ 111, [2005] 3 All E.R. 497, Pill, L.J., CA (Civ Div).

3828. **Benefits–Industrial diseases–Entitlement**

SOCIAL SECURITY (INDUSTRIAL INJURIES) (PRESCRIBED DISEASES) AMENDMENT REGULATIONS 2005, SI 2005 324; made under the Social Security Contributions and Benefits Act 1992 s.108, s.122, s.175; and the Social Security Administration Act 1992 s.5. In force: March 14, 2005; £3.00.

These Regulations amend the Social Security (Industrial Injuries) (Prescribed Diseases) Regulations 1985 (SI 1985 967) which prescribe diseases for which industrial injuries benefit is payable. They make an amendment in respect of concurrent employment in two or more occupations in relation to occupational deafness and deletes, with consequential changes, obsolete exceptions which relate to claims in respect of occupational deafness made before October 3, 1984. They also add osteoarthritis of the hip, Lyme disease and anaphylaxis to the list of prescribed diseases and add to the description of allergic rhinitis and asthma. The Regulations also makes changes to the description of the occupations in relation to which anthrax, ankylostomiasis and hepatitis are prescribed diseases.

3829. **Benefits–Jobseekers   allowance–Employment   programmes–Intensive activity period**

SOCIAL SECURITY (INTENSIVE ACTIVITY PERIOD 50 TO 59 PILOT) REGULATIONS 2005, SI 2005 636; made under the Jobseekers Act 1995 s.19, s.29, s.35, s.36. In force: April 4, 2005; £3.00.

These Regulations, which amend the Jobseeker's Allowance Regulations 1996 (SI 1996 207), replace the pilot scheme established by the Social Security (Intensive Activity Period 50 to 59 Pilot) (No.2) Regulations 2004 (SI 2004 869), which related to persons who claimed a jobseeker's allowance and who fulfilled the specified criteria as to age, period over which they had been receiving benefit and the location of the appropriate offices at which they were claiming benefit, as identified in the Schedule to those Regulations. These Regulations provide for an extended Pilot Scheme which is to last for one year from January 9, 2006 to January 8, 2007, unless revoked with effect from an earlier date.

3830. **Benefits–Jobseekers   allowance–Employment   programmes–Intensive activity period**

SOCIAL SECURITY (INTENSIVE ACTIVITY PERIOD 50 TO 59 PILOT) (NO.2) REGULATIONS 2005, SI 2005 637; made under the Jobseekers Act 1995 s.19, s.29, s.35, s.36. In force: January 9, 2006; £3.00.

These Regulations replace the pilot scheme established by the Social Security (Intensive Activity Period 50 to 59 Pilot) (No.2) Regulations 2004 (SI 2004 869) which related to persons who claimed a jobseeker's allowance and who fulfilled the criteria specified in Reg.3 of those regulations as to age, period over which they had been receiving benefit and the location of the appropriate offices at which they were claiming benefit, as identified in the Schedule to those Regulations. The Regulations, which amend the Jobseeker's Allowance Regulations (SI 1996 207), provide for an extended Pilot Scheme which is to last for one year from January 9, 2006 to January 8, 2007, unless revoked with effect from an earlier date.

3831. Benefits–Miscellaneous amendments

SOCIAL SECURITY (MISCELLANEOUS AMENDMENTS) REGULATIONS 2005, SI 2005 574; made under the Social Security Contributions and Benefits Act 1992 s.123, s.136, s.136A, s.137, s.175; the Jobseekers Act 1995 s.12, s.35, s.36; and the State Pension Credit Act 2002 s.15, s.17. In force: April 4, 2005; £3.00.

These Regulations amend the Income Support (General) Regulations 1987 (SI 1987 1967), the Housing Benefit (General) Regulations 1987 (SI 1987 1971), the Council Tax Benefit (General) Regulations 1992 (SI 1992 1814), the Jobseeker's Allowance Regulations 1996 (SI 1996 207) and the State Pension Credit Regulations 2002 (SI 2002 1792). They amend the interpretation provisions of the Income-related Benefits Regulations and the State Pension Credit Regulations in relation to the introduction of the Armed Forces and Reserve Forces Compensation Scheme; add certain payments made under the new scheme to the descriptions of income which are prescribed for the purposes of the State Pension Credit Act 2002 s.15(1)(j); include within the notional income and notional capital rules, payments made under the new scheme; provide a £10 weekly income disregard for guaranteed income payments made under the new scheme; and remove references to "rates", "eligible rates" and "rateable unit".

3832. Benefits–Miscellaneous amendments

SOCIAL SECURITY (MISCELLANEOUS AMENDMENTS) (NO.2) REGULATIONS 2005, SI 2005 2465; made under the Social Security Contributions and Benefits Act 1992 s.123, s.134, s.136, s.137, s.175; the Jobseekers Act 1995 s.12, s.13, s.35, s.36; and the State Pension Credit Act 2002 s.15, s.17. In force: in accordance with Reg.1; £3.00.

These Regulations amend the Income Support (General) Regulations 1987 (SI 1987 1967), the Housing Benefit (General) Regulations 1987 (SI 1987 1971), the Council Tax Benefit (General) Regulations 1992 (SI 1992 1814), the Jobseeker's Allowance Regulations 1996 (SI 1996 207) and the State Pension Credit Regulations 2002 (SI 2002 1792). The Regulations make amendments to increase the lower capital limit of £3,000 to £6,000; remove some of the provisions that provide different capital limits in special circumstances and to update references to capital limits in the regulations that deal with tariff income; provide that a person aged under 60, who opts not to take an occupational pension available to him or her under early release, is not treated as possessing the amount of any income or capital deferred; ensure that where money is paid to a third party on behalf of a claimant and is subsequently used by the third party to provide benefits in kind to the claimant, the money will not be disregarded; change references in the Regulations to adopters in the income and capital disregards of financial support in order to take account of the commencement of the Adoption and Children Act 2002. The Regulations also provide that a person aged 60 or over, who opts not to take an occupational pension available to him or her, shall be treated as possessing the amount of any income foregone from the date on which it could be expected to be acquired were an application to be made; and to make it clear, in the case of a claimant aged 60 or over, that income which could be obtained from money purchase benefits under an occupational pension scheme is treated in the same way as such income under a personal pension scheme.

3833. Benefits–Mortgage interest payments–Administration fees

SOCIAL SECURITY (CLAIMS AND PAYMENTS) AMENDMENT (NO.3) REGULATIONS 2005, SI 2005 2154; made under the Social Security Administration Act 1992 s.15A, s.189, s.191. In force: September 1, 2005; £3.00.

These Regulations amend the Social Security (Claims and Payments) Regulations 1987 (SI 1987 1968) by reducing from £0.78 to £0.31 the fee which qualifying lenders pay for the purpose of defraying administrative expenses incurred by the Secretary of State in making payments in respect of mortgage interest direct to qualifying lenders.

3834. Benefits–Overpayments–Claimant's duty to disclose change in circumstances

[Social Security Administration Act 1992 s.71 (1); Social Security (Claims and Payments) Regulations 1987 (SI 1987 1968) Reg.32(1).]

The appellant Secretary of State appealed against the dismissal ([2003] EWCA Civ 138, [2003] 1 W.L.R. 2018) of his claim to recoup an overpayment of serious disability premium from the respondent (H). H had been overpaid for a period of two years following the cessation of her entitlement to a serious disability premium, which had been added to her disability living allowance for a period of five years. Because of administrative inefficiencies at the social security office, the premium continued to be added to her allowance after the expiration of the five-year period. The Secretary of State sought to recover the overpayment under the Social Security Administration Act 1992 s.71 (1). The Secretary of State claimed that the requirements of the section were satisfied as H had failed to disclose the material fact that she had been overpaid. H appealed. The tribunal found that it was reasonable to expect H to have followed the simple instructions on her order book to inform the relevant social security office if there was a change in her circumstances. The Court of Appeal overturned that finding on the basis that there had been no failure to disclose as there had been no duty on H to inform the social security office because the disability allowance department knew that the premium was not renewed and a reasonable Secretary of State would have put in place a system to enable the two offices to provide each other with knowledge of material facts. The Court of Appeal held that disclosure to, or knowledge of, the decision makers in the disability allowance office was sufficient.

Held, allowing the appeal, that the Court of Appeal had been wrong to overturn the decisions of the commissioners. The principles that they had devised to give effect to the legislative scheme dealing with overpayments were entitled to great respect. The legislative policy was that the primary onus of keeping the appropriate office informed rested with the claimant. The one person who could usually be depended on to know all the benefits that a claimant was receiving was the claimant himself. The commissioners had rejected submissions that disclosure had to be made to the Secretary of State but had concentrated on what H had done to convey the information to the official who made the actual decision about the amount of benefit. H was not concerned with making or entitled to make assumptions about the internal administrative arrangements of the department. Her duty was to comply with the instruction in the order book to inform the social security office of any change in her circumstances. The duty of the claimant was the duty imposed by the Social Security (Claims and Payments) Regulations 1987 Reg.32(1) or implied by s.71 of the 1992 Act to make disclosure to the person or office identified to the claimant as the decision maker. The latter was not deemed to know anything which he did not actually know. The decision of the commissioners was restored.

HINCHY v. SECRETARY OF STATE FOR WORK AND PENSIONS, [2005] UKHL 16, [2005] 1 W.L.R. 967, Lord Hoffmann, HL.

3835. Benefits–Peaceful enjoyment of possessions–Objective justification for discriminatory provision

[Human Rights Act 1998 Sch.1 Part I Art.14, Part II Art.1.]

The appellants (C and R) appealed against the decision ([2003] EWCA Civ 797, [2003] 3 All E.R. 577) that their claims of discrimination in relation to the payment of pension and social security benefits failed. C had moved to South Africa and received her UK state pension there. Because there was no reciprocal treaty between the UK and South Africa under which cost of living increases were payable, C's UK pension would not be increased in line with increases paid to pensioners in the UK. She complained of unfair discrimination contrary to the Human Rights Act 1998 Sch.1 Part I Art.14 on the basis that she had paid the same National Insurance contributions as a UK resident and should receive the same pension. R was under the age of 25 and for that reason received a lower rate of jobseeker's allowance and income support than if she had been over the age of 25. She claimed that Art.14 entitled her to be treated equally with people over the age of 25.

Held, dismissing the appeals (Lord Carswell dissenting in part), that (1) it was common ground that contributory social security benefits were a possession within the Human Rights Act 1998 Sch.1 Part II Art.1 and the court was prepared to assume that non-contributory rights were also a possession. (2) C's foreign residence and R's age were "personal characteristics" for the purposes of Art.14, *R. (on the application of S) v. Chief Constable of South Yorkshire* [2004] UKHL 39, [2004] 1 W.L.R. 2196, [2004] C.L.Y. 710 applied, but the discrimination in issue was a question of general social policy and did not concern the right of the individual to equal respect. (3) C had failed to show that she had been discriminated against because she could not properly compare herself with a pensioner resident in the UK or in a country which had the benefit of a bilateral agreement. For the purposes of the Strasbourg jurisprudence she was not in a sufficiently "analogous situation" to that of her chosen comparators. In any event any difference in the treatment of C could be justified. The amount paid to pensioners resident abroad was a matter for Parliament. (4) In Art.14 cases it was not always necessary to follow the sequential analysis set out in *Wandsworth LBC v. Michalak* [2002] EWCA Civ 271, [2003] 1 W.L.R. 617, [2003] C.L.Y. 2789, *Michalak* considered. (5) R could be considered to be in an analogous situation to a person aged 25 but there was an objective justification for such discrimination, namely the need for legal certainty and a workable rule. The demarcation at age 25 was not manifestly without reasonable foundation. The precise point at which the line should be drawn was a matter for Parliament. (6) (per Lord Carswell) C's situation was analogous to that of other contributing pensioners resident in the UK and in countries where a reciprocal updating agreement existed. The failure to pay C uprated payments was discriminatory and contravened her rights under Art.14 of the Act taken together with Art.1 of Sch.1 Part II.

R. (ON THE APPLICATION OF CARSON) v. SECRETARY OF STATE FOR WORK AND PENSIONS; R. (ON THE APPLICATION OF REYNOLDS) v. SECRETARY OF STATE FOR WORK AND PENSIONS; *sub nom.* CARSON v. SECRETARY OF STATE FOR WORK AND PENSIONS, [2005] UKHL 37, [2005] 2 W.L.R. 1369, Lord Nicholls of Birkenhead, HL.

3836. Benefits—Social fund—Maternity and funeral expenses

SOCIAL FUND MATERNITY AND FUNERAL EXPENSES (GENERAL) REGULATIONS 2005, SI 2005 3061; made under the Social Security Contributions and Benefits Act 1992 s.138, s.175. In force: December 5, 2005; £3.00.

These Regulations amend the Social Fund (Miscellaneous Amendments) Regulations 1990 (SI 1990 580), the Social Security (Social Fund and Claims and Payments) (Miscellaneous Amendments) Regulations 1997 (SI 1997 792), the Social Security and Child Support (Tax Credits) Consequential Amendments Regulations 1999 (SI 1999 2566), the Social Security Amendment (Capital Disregards and Recovery of Benefits) Regulations 2001 (SI 2001 1118), the Social Fund (Miscellaneous Amendments) Regulations 2002 (SI 2002 2323), the State Pension Credit (Consequential, Transitional and Miscellaneous Provisions) Regulations 2002 (SI 2002 3019), the Social Security (Working Tax Credit and Child Tax Credit) (Consequential Amendments) Regulations 2003 (SI 2003 455), the Social Security (Working Tax Credit and Child Tax Credit) (Consequential Amendments) (No.3) Regulations 2003 (SI 2003 1731), the Social Security (Miscellaneous Amendments) (No.2) Regulations 2004 (SI 2004 1141) and the Social Security (Care Homes and Independent Hospitals) Regulations 2005 (SI 2005 2687). They revoke the Social Fund Maternity and Funeral Expenses (General) Regulations 1987 (SI 1987 481), the Social Fund Maternity and Funeral Expenses (General) Amendment Regulations 1988 (SI 1988 36), the Social Fund Maternity and Funeral Expenses (General) Amendment Regulations 1989 (SI 1989 379), the Social Fund Maternity and

Funeral Expenses (General) Amendment Regulations 1992 (SI 1992 2149), the Social Fund Maternity and Funeral Expenses (General) Amendment Regulations 1994 (SI 1994 506), the Social Fund Maternity and Funeral Expenses (General) Amendment Regulations 1995 (SI 1995 1229), the Social Fund Maternity and Funeral Expenses (General) Amendment Regulations 1996 (SI 1996 1443), the Social Fund Maternity and Funeral Expenses (General) Amendment Regulations 1997 (SI 1997 2538), the Social Fund Maternity and Funeral Expenses (General) Amendment Regulations 1999 (SI 1999 3266), the Social Fund Maternity and Funeral Expenses (General) Amendment Regulations 2000 (SI 2000 528), the Social Fund Maternity and Funeral Expenses (General) Amendment Regulations 2001 (SI 2001 3023), the Social Fund Maternity and Funeral Expenses (General) Amendment Regulations 2002 (SI 2002 79), the Social Fund Maternity and Funeral Expenses (General) Amendment (No.2) Regulations 2002 (SI 2002 470), the Social Fund Maternity and Funeral Expenses (General) Amendment Regulations 2003 (SI 2003 471), the Social Fund Maternity and Funeral Expenses (General) Amendment (No.2) Regulations 2003 (SI 2003 1570) and the Social Fund Maternity and Funeral Expenses (General) Amendment Regulations 2004 (SI 2004 2536). The Regulations make provision for payments to be made out of the social fund to meet maternity expenses and funeral expenses.

3837. Benefits–Up rating

SOCIAL SECURITY BENEFITS UP-RATING ORDER 2005, SI 2005 522; made under the Social Security Administration Act 1992 s.150, s.151, s.189. In force: in accordance with Art.1; £7.50.

This Order, which revokes the Social Security Benefits Up-rating Order 2004 (SI 2004 552), amends the National Insurance Act 1965, the Social Security (Graduated Retirement Benefit) (No.2) Regulations 1978 (SI 1978 393), Statutory Maternity Pay (General) Regulations 1986 (SI 1986 1960), the Support (General) Regulations 1987 (SI 1987 1967), the Housing Benefit (General) Regulations 1987 (SI 1987 1971), the Social Security (Disability Living Allowance) Regulations 1991 (SI 1991 2890), the Council Tax Benefit (General) Regulations 1992 (SI 1992 1814), the Social Security Administration Act 1992, the Pension Schemes Act 1993, the Social Security (Incapacity Benefit) Regulations 1994 (SI 1994 2946), the Social Security (Incapacity Benefit) (Transitional) Regulations 1995 (SI 1995 310), the Jobseeker's Allowance Regulations 1996 (SI 1996 207), the State Pension Credit Regulations 2002 (SI 2002 1792), the Statutory Paternity Pay and Statutory Adoption Pay (Weekly Rates) Regulations 2002 (SI 2002 2818) and the Housing Benefit and Council Tax Benefit (State Pension Credit) Regulations 2003 (SI 2003 325). The Order is made as a consequence of a review under the Social Security Administration Act 1992 and includes details of the sums mentioned in s.150. It relates to social security benefits and pensions; increases the rates and amounts of certain pensions and allowances; increases the rates of certain workmen's compensation and industrial injuries benefits in respect of employment before July 5, 1948; and specifies earnings limits for child dependency increases. The Order also increases the weekly rate of statutory sick pay; specifies the weekly rate of statutory maternity pay; specifies the weekly rates of statutory paternity pay and statutory adoption pay; increases the rate of graduated retirement benefit; increases the rates of disability living allowance; increases the weekly rates of age addition to long-term incapacity benefit; and relates to income support, housing benefit and council tax benefit.

3838. Benefits–Up rating

SOCIAL SECURITY BENEFITS UP-RATING REGULATIONS 2005, SI 2005 632; made under the Social Security Contributions and Benefits Act 1992 s.90, s.113, s.122, s.175; and the Social Security Administration Act 1992 s.155, s.189, s.191. In force: April 11, 2005; £3.00.

These Regulations, which amend the Social Security Benefit (Dependency) Regulations 1977 (SI 1977 343), revoke the Social Security Benefits Up-rating

Regulations 2004 (SI 2004 583). They provide that where a question has arisen about the effect of the Social Security Benefits Up-rating Order 2005 (SI 2005 522) on a benefit already in payment, the altered rates will not apply until that question is determined by the Secretary of State, an appeal tribunal or a Commissioner. They raise from £165 to £170 and from £21 to £22 the earnings limits for child dependency increases payable with a carer's allowance. These increases were abolished by the Tax Credits Act 2002 but are saved for transitional cases by virtue of the Tax Credits Act 2002 (Commencement No.3 and Transitional Provisions and Savings) Order 2003 (SI 2003 938).

3839. Benefits–Work focused interviews

SOCIAL SECURITY (INCAPACITY BENEFIT WORK-FOCUSED INTERVIEWS) AMENDMENT REGULATIONS 2005, SI 2005 3; made under the Social Security Administration Act 1992 s.2A, s.189, s.191. In force: February 7, 2005; £3.00.

These Regulations amend the Social Security (Incapacity Benefit Work-focused Interviews) Regulations 2003 (SI 2003 2439) to extend the numbers of persons that can be required to attend work-focused interviews as a condition of their continued entitlement to full benefit.

3840. Benefits–Work focused interviews

SOCIAL SECURITY (INCAPACITY BENEFIT WORK-FOCUSED INTERVIEWS) AMENDMENT (NO.2) REGULATIONS 2005, SI 2005 2604; made under the Social Security Administration Act 1992 s.2A, s.189, s.191. In force: October 31, 2005; £3.00.

These Regulations amend the Social Security (Incapacity Benefit Work-focused Interviews) Regulations 2003 (SI 2003 2439) to increase the numbers of persons that can be required to attend work-focused interviews as a condition of their continued entitlement to full benefit. The Regulations and the 2003 Regulations apply to certain persons who claim incapacity benefit, severe disablement allowance, income support on the grounds of incapacity or income support whilst they are appealing against a decision which embodies a determination that they are not incapable of work.

3841. Benefits–Work focused interviews

SOCIAL SECURITY (WORK-FOCUSED INTERVIEWS) AMENDMENT REGULATIONS 2005, SI 2005 2727; made under the Social Security Administration Act 1992 s.2A, s.189, s.191. In force: October 31, 2005; £3.00.

These Regulations amend the Social Security (Work-focused Interviews) Regulations 2000 (SI 2000 897), the Social Security (Work-focused Interviews for Lone Parents) Miscellaneous Amendments Regulations 2000 (SI 2000 1926), the Social Security (Jobcentre Plus Interviews) Regulations 2001 (SI 2001 3210), the Social Security (Jobcentre Plus Interviews) Regulations 2002 (SI 2002 1703) and the Social Security (Quarterly Work-focused Interviews for Certain Lone Parents) Regulations 2004 (SI 2004 2244). The Regulations make amendments to require claimants taking part in most work-focused interviews to create and discuss an action plan for employment; to introduce into the Lone Parents Regulations a requirement for lone parents who have been in receipt of income support (other than income support on the grounds of incapacity or income support whilst appealing against a decision which embodies a determination that they are not incapable of work) for 12 months and who are responsible for a youngest child aged 14 to take part in a work-focused interview every 13 weeks; and to provide that a claimant in receipt of only Carer's Allowance or Bereavement Benefit is no longer required to take part in a work-focused interview. They also change the date on which a first work-focused interview is to take place for claimants of incapacity benefit, severe disablement allowance, income support on the grounds of incapacity and income support whilst appealing against a decision which embodies a determination that they are not incapable of work; and change the circumstances in which a claimant is classed as disabled.

3842. Child benefit–Guardians allowance–Miscellaneous amendments

CHILD BENEFIT AND GUARDIAN'S ALLOWANCE (MISCELLANEOUS AMENDMENTS) REGULATIONS 2005, SI 2005 343; made under the Social Security Administration Act 1992 s.5, s.13; the Social Security Administration (Northern Ireland) Act 1992 s.5, s.11; the Social Security Act 1998 s.9, s.10, s.12; and the Social Security (Northern Ireland) Order 1998 (SI 1998 1506) Art.10, Art.11, Art.13. In force: March 18, 2005; £3.00.

These Regulations amend the Child Benefit and Guardian's Allowance (Administration) Regulations 2003 (SI 2003 492) and the Child Benefit and Guardian's Allowance (Decisions and Appeals) Regulations 2003 (SI 2003 916) so that an advance award of child benefit or guardian's allowance can be superseded where there is a change of circumstances between the date when the award was made, and when it was due to take effect. The Regulations also specify the date from which a decision by the Board shall take effect in circumstances where there has been an appeal against that decision, the result of which is to reverse the Board's decision in whole or in part; provide that the Board shall provide a written statement of reasons within 14 days of receipt of the request or as soon as practicable thereafter; provide for an interim payment where it is impractical to satisfy national insurance number requirements; and make further provision for the extinguishment of the right to payment of benefit. They also make further provision in respect of the handling of a claim where the claimant has died.

3843. Child benefit–Guardians allowance–Rates

GUARDIAN'S ALLOWANCE UP-RATING REGULATIONS 2005, SI 2005 719; made under the Social Security Contributions and Benefits Act 1992 s.113, s.122, s.175; the Social Security Administration Act 1992 s.155, s.189, s.191; the Social Security Contributions and Benefits (Northern Ireland) Act 1992 s.113, s.121, s.171; and the Social Security Administration (Northern Ireland) Act 1992 s.135, s.165, s.167. In force: April 11, 2005; £3.00.

These Regulations provide that where a question has arisen about the effect of the Child Benefit and Guardian's Allowance Up-rating Order 2005 (SI 2005 682) or the Child Benefit or Guardian's Allowance Up-rating (Northern Ireland) Order (SI 2005 683) on a guardian's allowance already in payment, the altered rates will not apply until that question is determined by the Inland Revenue, an appeal tribunal or a Commissioner. They apply provisions of the Social Security Benefit (Persons Abroad) Regulations 1975 (SI 1975 563) and the Social Security Benefit (Persons Abroad) Regulations (Northern Ireland) 1978 (SR 1978 114) so as to restrict the application of the increases specified in the Up-rating Orders in cases where the beneficiary lives abroad.

3844. Child benefit–Guardians allowance–Weekly rates–Increase

CHILD BENEFIT AND GUARDIAN'S ALLOWANCE UP-RATING ORDER 2005, SI 2005 682; made under the Social Security Administration Act 1992 s.150, s.189. In force: April 11, 2005; £3.00.

This Order increases the weekly rates of child benefit prescribed in the Child Benefit and Social Security (Fixing and Adjustment of Rates) Regulations 1976 (SI 1976 1267) from £16.50 to £17.00 and from £11.05 to £11.40 respectively. It also increases the weekly rate of guardian's allowance prescribed in the Social Security Contributions and Benefits Act 1992 from £11.85 to £12.20.

3845. Child Benefit Act 2005 (c.6)

This Act makes provision for and in connection with altering the descriptions of persons in respect of whom a person may be entitled to child benefit.

This Act received Royal Assent on March 24, 2005.

3846. Child support–Appeals

SOCIAL SECURITY AND CHILD SUPPORT COMMISSIONERS (PROCEDURE) (AMENDMENT) REGULATIONS 2005, SI 2005 207; made under the Social Security Act 1998 s.14, s.15, s.16, s.79, s.84, Sch.5 para.1, Sch.5 para.3, Sch.5 para.4, Sch.5 para.5; the Child Support Act 1991 s.22, s.24, s.25; the Child Support, Pensions and Social Security Act 2000 Sch.7 para.8, Sch.7 para.9, Sch.7 para.10, Sch.7 para.20, Sch.7 para.23; and the Forfeiture Act 1982 s.4. In force: February 28, 2005; £3.00.

These Regulations amend the Social Security Commissioners (Procedure) Regulations 1999 (SI 1999 1495), the Child Support Commissioners (Procedure) Regulations 1999 (SI 1999 1305) and the Social Security Commissioners (Procedure) (Tax Credits Appeals) Regulations 2002 (SI 2002 3237) to: provide for service of documents by email; provide for notice to be given where a party receives funding of legal services; provide for people, organisations or their representatives to be present at a hearing by means of a live television link; provide that where a refusal to set aside a decision is due to the application to set aside being out of time, the time during which an appeal must be made is not affected.

3847. Children–Trust funds–Appeals

CHILD TRUST FUNDS (APPEALS) REGULATIONS 2005, SI 2005 990; made under the Social Security Act 1998 s.7, s.12, s.14, s.16, s.28, s.79, s.84, Sch.1 para.7, Sch.1 para.11, Sch.1 para.12, Sch.5 para.1, Sch.5 para.2, Sch.5 para.3, Sch.5 para.4, Sch.5 para.5, Sch.5 para.6. In force: March 25, 2005; £3.00.

These Regulations are made in consequence of the Child Trust Funds Act 2004 which provides that people who appeal under s.22 of the Act may appeal to an appeal tribunal constituted under provisions in the Social Security Act 1998 as applied and modified by the Child Trust Funds (Non-tax Appeals) Regulations 2005 (SI 2005 191) made by the Treasury. These Regulations provide for the procedure for such child trust funds appeals. The procedure is almost the same as that prescribed for other appeals to such appeal tribunals.

3848. Children–Trust funds–Qualifying investments

CHILD TRUST FUNDS (AMENDMENT NO.3) REGULATIONS 2005, SI 2005 3349; made under the Child Trust Funds Act 2004 s.3, s.6, s.13, s.28. In force: December 27, 2005; £3.00.

These Regulations amend the Child Trust Funds Regulations 2004 (SI 2004 1450) to provide that shares or units in non-UCITS retail schemes (a new type of collective investment scheme recognised by the Financial Services Authority) are qualifying investments for Child Trust Funds (CTFs), provided that the shares or units can be redeemed at least twice monthly; to allow CTF providers to choose which stakeholder product to use when opening Revenue allocated accounts; and to provide for Alternative Financial Arrangements (described in the Finance Act 2005 and which include Shari'a contracts) to be qualifying investments for CTFs.

3849. Civil partnerships–Categorisation of earners–Equal treatment

SOCIAL SECURITY (CATEGORISATION OF EARNERS) (AMENDMENT) REGULATIONS 2005, SI 2005 3133; made under the Social Security Contributions and Benefits Act 1992 s.2. In force: December 5, 2005; £3.00.

These Regulations amend the Social Security (Categorisation of Earners) Regulations 1978 (SI 1978 1689) in consequence of the coming into force of the main provisions of the Civil Partnership Act 2004. They amend references to spouses in the 1978 Regulations so as to secure equality of treatment between civil partners and spouses in the application of the categorisation rules for the purposes of National Insurance Contributions.

3850. Civil partnerships—Consequential amendments

SOCIAL SECURITY (CIVIL PARTNERSHIP) (CONSEQUENTIAL AMENDMENTS) REGULATIONS 2005, SI 2005 2878; made under the Social Security Contributions and Benefits Act 1992 s.48, s.113, s.122, s.123, s.134, s.135, s.136, s.137, s.175, Sch.5 para.2, Sch.5 para.3B, Sch.5 para.7B; the Security Administration Act 1992 s.5, s.189, s.191; the Social Security Act 1998 s.9, s.10, s.79, s.84; and the Child Support, Pensions and Social Security Act 2000 Sch.7 para.20. In force: December 5, 2005; £3.00.

These Regulations amend the Social Security (Widow's Benefit and Retirement Pensions) Regulations 1979 (SI 1979 642), the Social Security (General Benefit) Regulations 1982 (SI 1982 1408), the Income Support (General) Regulations 1987 (SI 1987 1967), the Social Security (Claims and Payments) Regulations 1987 (SI 1987 1968), the Housing Benefit (General) Regulations 1987 (SI 1987 1971), the Social Security and Child Support (Decisions and Appeals) Regulations 1999 (SI 1999 991), the Housing Benefit and Council Tax Benefit (Decisions and Appeals) Regulations 2001 (SI 2001 1002) and the Social Security (Deferral of Retirement Pensions) Regulations 2005 (SI 2005 453). The Regulations make minor amendments to a number of statutory instruments dealing with social security to reflect the new status of civil partnership. The amendments are consequential upon the Civil Partnership Act 2004.

3851. Contributions—Amounts to be disregarded

SOCIAL SECURITY (CONTRIBUTIONS) (AMENDMENT NO.4) REGULATIONS 2005, SI 2005 1086; made under the Social Security Contributions and Benefits Act 1992 s.3, s.175; and the Social Security Contributions and Benefits (Northern Ireland) Act 1992 s.3, s.171. In force: April 5, 2005; £3.00.

These Regulations amend the Social Security (Contributions) (Amendment No.3) Regulations 2005 (SI 2005 778) to correct errors making it clear that the total amount that can be disregarded, in respect of the period beginning with April 6, 2005 and ending on October 5, 2005, is £1,300.

3852. Contributions—Calculation of earnings

SOCIAL SECURITY (CONTRIBUTIONS) (AMENDMENT NO.5) REGULATIONS 2005, SI 2005 2422; made under the Social Security Contributions and Benefits (Northern Ireland) Act 1992 s.3. In force: October 3, 2005; £3.00.

These Regulations, which amend the Social Security (Contributions) Regulations 2001 (SI 2001 1004), specify which of the later provisions concerning the disregard, in the calculation of earnings for contributions purposes, of certain sums which relate to training or similar courses do not extend to Northern Ireland. Part 7 para.9 of the 2001 Regulations did not originally extend to Northern Ireland, because the payments to which it related could not be made there. However, with effect from October 3, 2005 payments under a return to work credit scheme can be made in Northern Ireland under a pilot scheme. The Employment Act 1973 does not extend to Northern Ireland but the Contributions Regulations provide a rule of construction so that, in the application of the Regulations to Northern Ireland, references to enactments applying in Great Britain are to be construed as including a reference to the corresponding enactment in Northern Ireland. The corresponding enactment in this case is the Employment and Training Act (Northern Ireland) 1950 s.1 (1).

3853. Contributions—Earnings limits and tax thresholds

SOCIAL SECURITY (CONTRIBUTIONS) (AMENDMENT) REGULATIONS 2005, SI 2005 166; made under the Social Security Contributions and Benefits Act 1992 s.5, s.122, s.175; and the Social Security Contributions and Benefits (Northern Ireland) Act 1992 s.5, s.121, s.171. In force: April 6, 2005; £3.00.

These Regulations amend the Social Security (Contributions) Regulations 2001 (SI 2001 1004) to specify the levels of the lower and upper earnings limits for primary Class 1 contributions and the primary and secondary thresholds for primary and secondary Class 1 contributions for the tax year beginning April 6, 2005. The Regulations also provide for the equivalents of the primary and secondary thresholds where the earnings period is a month or a year.

3854. Contributions—Gender recognition

SOCIAL SECURITY (CONTRIBUTIONS) (AMENDMENT NO.3) REGULATIONS 2005, SI 2005 778; made under the Social Security Contributions and Benefits Act 1992 s.3, s.10, s.13, s.14, s.175; and the Social Security Contributions and Benefits (Northern Ireland) Act 1992 s.3, s.10, s.13, s.14, s.171. In force: April 6, 2005; £3.00.

These Regulations amend the Social Security (Contributions) Regulations 2001 (SI 2001 1004) and the Social Security (Contributions, Categorisation of Earners and Intermediaries) (Amendment) Regulations 2004 (SI 2004 770).They insert new definitions of "the acquired gender" and "full gender recognition certificate"; and make provision for the earnings periods of a person who was born a woman, is a company director, and is aged between 60 and 64 when a full gender recognition certificate is issued recognising the person's gender as male.

3855. Council tax benefit—Housing benefit—Miscellaneous amendments

HOUSING BENEFIT AND COUNCIL TAX BENEFIT (MISCELLANEOUS AMENDMENTS) (NO.2) REGULATIONS 2005, SI 2005 573; made under the Social Security Contributions and Benefits Act 1992 s.123, s.131, s.135, s.136, s.136A, s.137, s.175; the Social Security Administration Act 1992 s.6, s.189, s.191; and the Child Support, Pensions and Social Security Act 2000 Sch.7 para.4, Sch.7 para.20, Sch.7 para.23. In force: in accordance with Reg.1 (1); £3.00.

These Regulations make various miscellaneous amendments to the Housing Benefit (General) Regulations 1987 (SI 1987 1971) and the Council Tax Benefit (General) Regulations 1992 (SI 1992 1814) which include: a new provision which deals with the treatment of prisoners on temporary release and by making other minor, technical amendments; new provisions which provide for the treatment of temporary absences from a person's dwelling; provide that certain specified categories of retirement pension income will not be treated as notional income; remove a provision excluding the award of an Enhanced Disability Premium in respect of a child whose capital exceeds a specified amount; and provide for certain income from capital to be disregarded when calculating a claimant's income.

3856. Discrimination—Foreign nationals—Residence—Right of host Member State to deny state assistance to citizen of another Member State—European Community

[EC Treaty Art.12, Art.18, Art.39, Art.43, Art.49; Council Directive 90/364 on the right of residence Art.1.]

The Tribunal du Travail de Bruxelles applied to the European Court of Justice (ECJ) for a preliminary ruling to ascertain whether a homeless person (T), a French national resident in a Salvation Army hostel in Belgium, was entitled to claim social security assistance. T had lived in Belgium for two years without registering. He lived at the hostel and performed a variety of duties for up to 30 hours a week in return for board and lodging plus pocket money. In the instant application the ECJ was asked to rule (1) whether T could claim a right of residence in Belgium as a worker, a self employed person or a provider or recipient of services within the meaning of the EC Treaty 1957 Art.39, Art.43 or Art.49; (2) if not, whether a person in T's circumstances might, simply on the basis of being an EU citizen, be entitled to enjoy a right of residence in the host Member State by direct application of the EC Treaty 1957 Art.18.

Held, giving a preliminary ruling, that (1) the meaning of a "worker" under Art.39 was independent of national laws and should not be interpreted narrowly. Anyone pursuing real and genuine activities, other than those on such a small scale as to be marginal and ancillary, was a worker, *Lawrie-Blum v. Land Baden-*

Wurttemberg (66/85) [1986] E.C.R. 2121, [1987] C.L.Y. 1569 and *Collins v. Secretary of State for Work and Pensions (C138/02)* [2005] Q.B. 145, [2004] C.L.Y. 3597 applied. In the instant case, the national court had established that the benefits in kind paid to T amounted to consideration for the services he performed under the direction of the hostel, and that this established the constituent elements of an employment relationship. However, for T to be properly regarded as a worker, the national court had to establish that the duties were real, genuine and part of the normal labour market, *Ninni-Orasche v. Bundesminister fur Wissenschaft, Verkehr und Kunst (C413/01)* [2004] All E.R. (EC) 765, [2004] C.L.Y. 1263 and *Bettray v. Staatssecretaris van Justitie (344/87)* [1989] E.C.R. 1621, [1991] C.L.Y. 4000 considered. The rights of freedom of establishment and freedom to provide services under Art.43 and Art. 49 did not include the right to take up paid employment and did not protect activities carried out on a permanent basis, *Pfeiffer Grosshandel GmbH v. Lowa Warenhandel GmbH (C255/97)* [1999] E.C.R. I-2835, [2000] C.L.Y. 3799 and *Payroll Data Services (Italy) Srl, Re (C79/01)* [2002] E.C.R. I-8923 applied. (2) Whilst it was true that citizens of one Member State had the right to reside in another by operation of EC Treaty 1957 Art.18, this right was subject to the limitations imposed both by the Treaty and by Council Directive 90/364 Art.1 which enabled host Member States to require citizens of other Member States wishing to exercise their right of residence to have sufficient resources to avoid becoming a burden to the social security system. Applying the test of proportionality to the instant case, it was clear that Belgium's failure to recognise T's Art.18 right of residence was within its discretion under Council Directive 90/364, *Baumbast v. Secretary of State for the Home Department (C413/99)* [2002] E.C.R. I-7091, [2002] C.L.Y. 2628 distinguished. The fact that Belgium's national legislation barred social assistance to other Member States' citizens was in breach of the prohibition of discrimination on grounds of nationality contrary to EC Treaty Art.12, but it was nevertheless entitled to take steps, within the limits set by EC law, to remove T on the basis that his recourse to state assistance put him in breach of his right of residence, *Grzelczyk v. Centre Public d'Aide Sociale d'Ottignies Louvain la Neuve (C184/99)* [2003] All E.R. (EC) 385, [2001] C.L.Y. 2496 applied.

TROJANI v. CENTRE PUBLIC D'AIDE SOCIALE DE BRUXELLES (CPAS) (C456/02) [2004] All E.R. (EC) 1065, Judge Skouris (President), ECJ.

3857. Energy conservation – Grants

HOME ENERGY EFFICIENCY SCHEME (ENGLAND) REGULATIONS 2005, SI 2005 1530; made under the Social Security Act 1990 s.15. In force: July 1, 2005; £3.00.

These Regulations revoke the Home Energy Efficiency Scheme (England) (Amendment) Regulations 2002 (SI 2002 115), the Home Energy Efficiency Scheme (England) (Amendment) Regulations 2003 (SI 2003 1017), the Home Energy Efficiency Scheme (England) (Amendment) (No.2) Regulations 2003 (SI 2003 2263) and the Home Energy Efficiency Scheme (England) (Amendment) Regulations 2004 (SI 2004 2430) (with saving). The Regulations enable the Secretary of State to make or arrange for the making of grant for the improvement of energy efficiency in dwellings occupied by persons on low incomes with children, elderly persons on low incomes or persons in receipt of benefit relating to ill health.

3858. Food – Milk – Entitlement

WELFARE FOOD (AMENDMENT) REGULATIONS 2005, SI 2005 688; made under the Social Security Act 1988 s.13; and the Social Security Contributions and Benefits Act 1992 s.175. In force: April 6, 2005; £3.00.

These Regulations, which amend the Welfare Food Regulations 1996 (SI 1996 1434), revoke the Welfare Food (Amendment) Regulations 2004 (SI 2004 723) and the Welfare Food (Amendment No.2) Regulations 2004 (SI 2004 2311). They raise to £13,910 the figure for the income level that determines whether a person receiving child tax credit but not working tax credit and who meets other conditions is entitled to benefit under the scheme.

3859. **Free movement of persons–Ancillary insurance benefits payable to carer of disabled child in receipt of German care benefits–Child and carer resident in another Member State–European Community**

[EC Treaty Art.39; Council Regulation 1408/71 on the application of social security schemes to employed persons and their families moving within the Community Art.4(1)(a), Art.19(1)(b).]

The German Social Court sought a preliminary ruling on the interpretation of Council Regulation 1408/71. G was a German citizen, married to a French citizen and living in France. The couple both worked in Germany and had a disabled child, C, who required their care. C received care insurance benefits under German law, which were paid by way of a monthly care allowance. G had taken out old age insurance, and requested C's insurers, K, to pay the contributions, on the ground that C was reliant on G as his carer. K refused, arguing that it had no responsibility to pay as G was not resident in Germany. G brought a claim against K and questions were referred for a preliminary ruling as to whether the payments constituted a sickness benefits, as defined in Art.4(1)(a) of the Regulation. Further, whether K was discriminating against G in breach of the EC Treaty Art.39 because she had chosen to live in another Member State.

Held, giving a preliminary ruling, that G's old age insurance premium payments were "sickness benefits" for C, because he indirectly benefited from them, *Molenaar v. Allgemeine Ortskrankenkasse Baden-Wurttemberg (C160/96)* [1998] E.C.R. I-843 applied. The payments were also a sickness insurance cash benefit because they were ancillary to care insurance proper and thus came within Art.19(1)(b) of the Regulation, which required that such benefits should be paid to recipients living in other Member States, unless similar benefits were paid by that Member State. France did not provide such benefits, and therefore the payments fell to be made by K in accordance with German domestic legislation. Denying the payments on the basis of residence meant that comparable situations would be treated differently by reference to a factor that was not objectively justifiable and therefore was in breach of Art.39 EC.

GAUMAIN-CERRI v. KAUFMANNISCHE KRANKENKASSE-PFLEGEKASSE (C502/01) [2004] 3 C.M.L.R. 27, Judge Timmermans (President), ECJ (2nd Chamber).

3860. **Frontier workers–Unemployment benefits–Interim assistance payable under collective agreement–Effect of German wage tax deduction–European Community**

[EC Treaty Art.39; Council Regulation 1612/68 on freedom of movement for workers within the Community Art.7(4).]

The German Federal Labour Court sought a preliminary ruling as to whether the German wage tax charged on the interim assistance payable to a former frontier worker was compatible with the EC Treaty Art.39 and Council Regulation 1612/68 Art.7(4). M, a French resident, had formerly been a civilian employee of the French forces stationed in Germany. Under the terms of a bilateral agreement between France and Germany, M's remuneration was taxable in France, after the deduction of German social security contributions. Following his redundancy, M received interim assistance for one year under a Franco German collective social security agreement. However, the German authorities deducted both German social security contributions and German wage tax from M's interim assistance payment. M challenged the tax deduction on the ground that the benefit was only liable to be taxed in France and the German court stayed proceedings pending the preliminary ruling.

Held, giving a preliminary ruling, that Art.39 of the EC Treaty and Art.7(4) of the Regulation precluded provisions in a collective agreement that discriminated against frontier workers, including benefits payable on dismissal, *Schoning-Kougebetopoulou v. Freie und Hansestadt Hamburg (C15/96)* [1998] All E.R.

(EC) 97, [1998] C.L.Y. 2155 and *Commission of the European Communities v. France (C35/97)* [1998] E.C.R. I-5325 followed. In the instant case, the deduction of German wage tax placed M at a disadvantage when compared with former workers resident in Germany, whose interim assistance would have corresponded to the net salary they would have received if they had remained in employment.

MERIDA v. GERMANY (C400/02) [2004] 3 C.M.L.R. 52, JudgeTimmermans (President), ECJ.

3861. Graduated retirement benefit – Claims

SOCIAL SECURITY (CLAIMS AND PAYMENTS) AMENDMENT REGULATIONS 2005, SI 2005 455; made under the Social Security Administration Act 1992 s.5, s.189, s.191. In force: in accordance with Reg.1 (1); £3.00.

These Regulations amend the Social Security (Claims and Payments) Regulations 1987 (SI 1987 1968) in respect of claims for retirement pension or graduated retirement benefit. They provide for claims for a Category A or B retirement pension or graduated retirement benefit to be made in advance of the date on which a period of deferment ends; provide that the time for claiming retirement pension or graduated retirement benefit for any day on which the claimant is entitled to the pension or benefit is the period of 12 months immediately following that day, instead of the period of 3 months beginning with that day; introduce the 12 month period gradually as a transitional measure; and make further provision for claims for a Category A or B retirement pension and graduated retirement benefit made on behalf of a person who has died.

3862. Graduated retirement benefit – Deferment

SOCIAL SECURITY (GRADUATED RETIREMENT BENEFIT) REGULATIONS 2005, SI 2005 454; made under the Social Security Contribution and Benefits Act 1992 s.62, s.175. In force: April 6, 2005; £3.00.

These Regulations, which amend the National Insurance Act 1965 and the Social Security (Graduated Retirement Benefit) (No.2) Regulations 1978 (SI 1978 393), make provision relating to the deferment of graduated retirement benefit arising from changes in the rules relating to the deferment of retirement pension made by the Pensions Act 1995 and Pensions Act 2004. The Regulations repeal and re-enact the existing rules relating to increments of graduated retirement benefit where entitlement to either retirement pension or to graduated retirement benefit alone is deferred, so that they correspond with the rules for deferment of entitlement to retirement pension enacted in the Social Security Contributions and Benefits Act 1992 Sch.5.

3863. Graduated retirement benefit – Deferment

SOCIAL SECURITY (GRADUATED RETIREMENT BENEFIT) (AMENDMENT) REGULATIONS 2005, SI 2005 846; made under the Social Security Contribution and Benefits Act 1992 s.62. In force: April 5, 2005; £3.00.

These Regulations amend the Social Security (Graduated Retirement Benefit) Regulations 2005 (SI 2005 454) to correct an erroneous cross-reference in those Regulations relating to when certain provisions come into effect.

3864. Housing benefit – Council tax benefit – Miscellaneous amendments

HOUSING BENEFIT AND COUNCIL TAX BENEFIT (GENERAL) AMENDMENT REGULATIONS 2005, SI 2005 2904; made under the Social Security Administration Act 1992 s.75, s.76, s.189, s.191. In force: April 10, 2006; £3.00.

These Regulations amend the Housing Benefit (General) Regulations 1987 (SI 1987 1971) and the Council Tax Benefit (General) Regulations 1992 (SI 1992 1814) to change the meaning of "overpayment" and "excess benefit". The Regulations insert an additional condition in the list of prescribed circumstances that must be satisfied for an overpayment not to be recovered from the person to whom it was paid; amend the terminology used in respect of an authority administering housing benefit; insert an additional method of recovery in the case of a claimant who changes his address; ensure a claimant's change of address is not treated as being a change of circumstances when calculating housing benefit payable in respect of the overpayment period; and provide for recovery of overpaid housing benefit from benefits paid by Switzerland following the Agreement between the European Community and its Member States and the Swiss Confederation on the free movement of persons, signed at Brussels on June 21, 1999.

3865. Housing benefit–Council tax benefit–Miscellaneous amendments

HOUSING BENEFIT AND COUNCIL TAX BENEFIT (MISCELLANEOUS AMENDMENTS) REGULATIONS 2005, SI 2005 273; made under the Social Security Contributions and Benefits Act 1992 s.123, s.136, s.136A, s.137, s.175. In force: in accordance with Reg.1 (2)-(4); £3.00.

These Regulations make various amendments to the Housing Benefit (General) Regulations 1987 (SI 1987 1971) and the Council Tax Benefit (General) Regulations 1992 (SI 1992 1814).

3866. Housing benefit–Council tax benefit–Miscellaneous amendments

HOUSING BENEFIT AND COUNCIL TAX BENEFIT (MISCELLANEOUS AMENDMENTS) (NO.3) REGULATIONS 2005, SI 2005 2502; made under the Social Security Contributions and Benefits Act 1992 s.123, s.130, s.131, s.135, s.136, s.136A, s.137, s.175; the Social Security Administration Act 1992 s.5, s.6, s.189; and the Social Security Act 1998 s.34, s.79, s.84. In force: in accordance with Reg.1 (1); £3.00.

These Regulations make various amendments to the Housing Benefit (General) Regulations 1987 (SI 1987 1971) and the Council Tax Benefit (General) Regulations 1992 (SI 1992 1814) which include: the removal of provisions which provide for the reduction of a claimant's applicable amount where he or his partner are a long term patient; the removal of the requirement that arrears of working tax credit or child tax credit must be paid as a result of a change of circumstances in order to be disregarded in a claimant's assessment of capital; the addition of discretionary housing payments and working tax credit to the list of benefits which may be disregarded as capital in the assessment of a claimant's capital; and the removal of the requirement to refer in a decision notice to the amount of any child tax credit or child benefit where a person on state pension credit is entitled only to savings credit.

3867. Housing benefit–Council tax benefit–Miscellaneous amendments

HOUSING BENEFIT AND COUNCIL TAX BENEFIT (MISCELLANEOUS AMENDMENTS) (NO.4) REGULATIONS 2005, SI 2005 2894; made under the Social Security Administration Act 1992 s.5, s.6, s.7A, s.189, s.191; the Social Security Act 1998 s.79; the Security Contributions and Benefits Act 1992 s.130, s.135, s.136, s.136A, s.137, s.175; and the Child Support, Pensions and Social Security Act 2000 Sch.7 para.1, Sch.7 para.13, Sch.7 para.14, Sch.7 para.15, Sch.7 para.20, Sch.7 para.23. In force: November 10, 2005; £3.00.

These Regulations make amendments to the Housing Benefit (General) Regulations 1987 (SI 1987 1971), the Council Tax Benefit (General) Regulations 1992 (SI 1992 1814) and the Housing Benefit and Council Tax Benefit (Decisions and Appeals) Regulations 2001 (SI 2001 1002). They provide that a person is considered to be disabled for the purpose of determining child care charge deductions if they cease to be registered as blind within the period that begins 28 weeks before the first Monday in September following their fifteenth birthday and ends on the day preceding the first Monday in September following the person's sixteenth birthday; provide that the tax rates to be used to determine the amount of tax and contributions that should be deducted to find the net amount of profit or earnings shall be the rate applicable to the assessment period; introduce two new rules for determining the date of claim; and shorten the time before a relevant authority can terminate an award of housing benefit or council tax benefit following suspension of payment.

3868. Housing benefit–Council tax benefit–Miscellaneous amendments

HOUSING BENEFIT AND COUNCIL TAX BENEFIT (MISCELLANEOUS AMENDMENTS) (NO.5) REGULATIONS 2005, SI 2005 3294; made under the Social Security Contributions and Benefits Act 1992 s.123, s.136, s.136A, s.137, s.175. In force: December 30, 2005; £3.00.

These Regulations amend the Housing Benefit (General) Regulations 1987 (SI 1987 1971), the Council Tax Benefit (General) Regulations 1992 (SI 1992 1814) and the Housing Benefit and Council Tax Benefit (Miscellaneous Amendments) (No.3) Regulations 2005 (SI 2005 2502). They provide that children placed for adoption in accordance with the Adoption and Children Act 2002 shall not be considered to be a member of the claimant's household for housing benefit purposes. It also updates the reference to the Scottish regulations.

3869. Housing benefit–Council tax benefit–Offence of making false statements–Applicant completing forms with help of third party

[Social Security Administration Act 1992 s.112(1)(a).]

The appellant local authority appealed against the acquittal by justices of the respondent (J) on six informations alleging that she had made statements on housing benefit/council tax benefit application forms which she knew to be false, contrary to the Social Security Administration Act 1992 s.112(1)(a). J had asserted that she was not good at reading or writing and that the acquaintance who had helped her to complete the forms had told her that she only needed to mention one of the two jobs that she had. The justices accepted her evidence and took the view that J did not know that her statements were false when she completed the forms.

Held, dismissing the appeal, that dishonesty was not an element of the offence created by s.112, although a person making a statement which he knew to be false would invariably be regarded as having acted dishonestly. Further, if he was to be convicted of an offence under s.112, a defendant had to know that the statement that he was making was material to his application for benefit, *Harrison v. Department of Social Security* [1997] C.O.D. 220, [1997] C.L.Y. 4659 considered. Accordingly, in the instant case, it had to be proved that J had known that the statement that she was making was false when she completed the application forms. On the evidence, it could not be said that the decision reached by the justices was not one which was reasonably open to them, even though a different bench might have come to a different conclusion.

HASTINGS BC v. JONES; *sub nom.* R. (ON THE APPLICATION OF HASTINGS BC) v. JONES, [2004] EWHC 2414, [2004] R.V.R. 270, Keith, J., QBD (Admin).

3870. Housing benefit–Discretionary payments–Non audit claims

DISCRETIONARY HOUSING PAYMENTS (GRANTS) AMENDMENT ORDER 2005, SI 2005 2052; made under the Social Security Administration Act 1992 s.140B, s.140C, s.189. In force: September 1, 2005; £3.00.

This Order amends the Discretionary Housing Payments (Grants) Order 2001 (SI 2001 2340) which sets out the procedure by which the Secretary of State will make payments to local authorities towards the cost of discretionary housing payments in accordance with the Child Support, Pensions and Social Security Act 2000 s.70. It amends the 2001 Order to provide that a claim by any authority in England, Wales or Scotland in respect of a total amount of less than £50,000 for any year need not be audited by the authority's auditor; and substitutes a new date by which an authority needs to submit a claim showing the amount of discretionary housing payments they have made over the relevant year.

3871. **Housing benefit-Income-Calculation of income other than earnings for housing benefit purposes-Inferences regarding intention and use of payments**

[Council Tax Benefit (General) Regulations 1992 (SI 1992 1814) Sch.4 para.13(2).]

The appellant secretary of state appealed against a social security commissioner's decision that although monthly sums of money which the respondent pensioner (P) received from his son formed part of his income, they should be disregarded for the purposes of assessing his entitlement to housing benefit. The commissioner had found that P's two pensions were sufficient to pay for food, household fuel, rent, clothing and footwear. He had concluded that P's son's gifts were not intended or used for those basic essentials and that under the Council Tax Benefit (General) Regulations 1992 Sch.4 para.13(2), they were voluntary payments which did not affect P's entitlement to benefit payable to meet those basic essentials and housing costs. The secretary of state contended that the commissioner's finding that the gifts were not intended or used for those basic essentials had not been based on sufficient findings of fact.

Held, dismissing the appeal, that in order to determine whether voluntary payments to a recipient of housing benefit were income which affected the donee's entitlement to that benefit, it was necessary to decide whether the money was intended or used for any of the basic essentials specified in Sch.4 para.13(2). In order to do that, a tribunal should not make any presumptions but, having considered all the evidence, it was entitled to draw inferences from the facts. In the instant case, although the commissioner used terms such as "presumed" and "assumption", it appeared that he had based his conclusion on inferences from the facts.

SECRETARY OF STATE FOR WORK AND PENSIONS v. PERKINS, [2004] EWCA Civ 1671, [2005] H.L.R. 19, Ward, L.J., CA (Civ Div).

3872. **Housing benefit-Overpayment of benefits-Extent of social security commissioner's powers on appeal**

The appellant local authority appealed against a decision that housing benefit paid in respect of a tenant of the respondent landlord (T) was not recoverable as an overpayment. The tenant had obtained housing benefit from the local authority on the basis that he was renting a room from T, who occupied the other bedroom. Thereafter, T and his tenant informed the local authority that T had moved out of the property and the tenant continued to claim housing benefit on the basis of sole occupancy. The local authority subsequently discovered that T had never ceased to occupy the flat. T and his tenant were convicted of conspiracy to defraud and the local authority demanded repayment of housing benefit overpaid. A social security appeal tribunal, having regard to the conviction, found in favour of the local authority, but on a subsequent appeal a social security commissioner decided that the purpose of the scam had been to obtain relief from council tax and that no extra housing benefit had been obtained. The local authority submitted that the commissioner had exceeded his powers by allowing the appeal of T for reasons of fact and not on grounds of law.

Held, allowing the appeal, that a social security commissioner was only entitled to interfere with a tribunal's decision on a question of law and was not entitled to substitute his views of the facts simply because it appeared to him that the tribunal was wrong in its conclusions. A finding of fact only became an error of law if no reasonable tribunal could have reached that decision. In the instant case, the commissioner had interfered with the fact finding task of the tribunal without justification in law, *R. v. Hillingdon LBC, ex p. Puhlhofer* [1986] A.C. 484, [1986] C.L.Y. 1619 applied. There was overwhelming evidence from the criminal trial in support of the tribunal's decision that the local authority had suffered prejudice in respect of the overpayment of housing benefit. Where there was a conflict of apparently credible but conflicting evidence, it was a matter of judgment for the tribunal as to what was the correct interpretation of the true facts. The commissioner might disagree with the tribunal's choice but he had erred in holding that its decision was erroneous in law.

BRAINTREE DC v. THOMPSON; sub nom. THOMPSON v. BRAINTREE DC, [2005] EWCA Civ 178, [2005] H.L.R. 37, Ward, L.J., CA (Civ Div).

3873.   Housing benefit-Registered owners-Meaning of "owner" in Housing Benefit (General) Regulations 1987 Reg.2(1)(a)

[Land Registration Act 1925 s.20(1); Social Security Contributions and Benefits Act 1992 s.130; Housing Benefit (General) Regulations 1987 (SI 1987 1971) Reg.2(1)(a); Housing Benefit (General) Regulations 1987 Reg.10(2)(c).]

The appellant (B) appealed against a social security commissioner's decision that he was not entitled to housing benefit. B had made an application under the Social Security Contributions and Benefits Act 1992 s.130 for housing benefit in relation to a property of which he was registered as the sole proprietor with title absolute and for which he was the sole mortgagor. A deed executed at the time the property was purchased recorded that B's mother had contributed to the purchase of the property, and it created a trust, declaring that B and his mother were joint tenants in common and trustees for sale of the property, which they held as trustees of the trust. B subsequently retired as a trustee and that was evidenced by a further deed executed before B submitted his application for housing benefit. However, the transfer of the freehold of the property to the trustees and the registration of that transfer did not take place until after B had submitted his application. B had argued that when he made his application he was a tenant of the trust and contractually liable to pay rent to the trust on a commercial basis. The commissioner's decision was that B was not entitled to receive housing benefit on the basis that he was the owner of the property for the purposes of the Housing Benefit (General) Regulations 1987 Reg.2(1)(a). B contended that he did not come within the definition of "owner" in Reg.2(1)(a) as he had had no beneficial interest in the property and he had not been entitled to dispose of the fee simple as such a disposal would have been in breach of trust.

Held, dismissing the appeal, that until the register was amended and no longer showed B as the sole owner with title absolute, B remained the "owner" of the property within the meaning of Reg.2(1)(a), and that entitled him to dispose of the fee simple, irrespective of the status conferred on him by the various deeds. At any time before B transferred the legal estate in the property to the trust, he could have conveyed the fee simple to a third party, who would have taken the property free of any interest by the trust under the Land Registration Act 1925 s.20(1). The term "owner" was not restricted to beneficial ownership of a property, Fairbank v. Lambeth Magistrates Court [2002] EWHC 785, [2003] H.L.R. 7 approved and R. v. Sheffield Housing Benefit Review Board, ex p. Smith (1996) 28 H.L.R. 36, [1995] C.L.Y. 2597 considered. The payments that he was making to the trust were therefore "payments by an owner" under Reg.10(2)(c) of the Regulations, and B was disqualified from receiving housing benefit.

BURTON v. NEW FOREST DC, [2004] EWCA Civ 1510, The Independent, November 18, 2004, Wall, L.J., CA (Civ Div).

3874.   Housing benefit-Rent officers-Functions

RENT OFFICERS (HOUSING BENEFIT FUNCTIONS) (LOCAL HOUSING ALLOWANCE) AMENDMENT ORDER 2005, SI 2005 236; made under the Housing Act 1996 s.122. In force: in accordance with Art.1(2)(3); £3.00.

This Order amends the Rent Officers (Housing Benefit Functions) Order 1997 (SI 1997 1984) and the Rent Officers (Housing Benefit Functions) (Scotland) Order 1997 (SI 1997 1995) which confer functions on rent officers in connection with housing benefit and rent allowance subsidy. The amendments provide that the new arrangements for rent officer determinations introduced by the Rent Officers (Housing Benefit Functions) (Local Housing Allowance) Amendment Order 2003 (SI 2003 2398) for the areas of specified local authorities will apply in the areas of nine additional local authorities which will become pathfinder authorities.

3875. Housing benefit–Statutory reviews, official errors

[Housing Benefit (General) Regulations 1987 (SI 1987 1971) Reg.79 (now repealed), Reg.79(1)(b) (now repealed); Housing Benefit and Council Tax Benefit (Decisions and Appeals) (Transitional and Savings) Regulations 2001 (SI 2001 1264); Housing Benefit and Council Tax Benefit (Decisions and Appeals) (Transitional and Savings) Regulations 2001 (SI 2001 1264) Reg.4(2).]

The appellant (B) appealed against a decision that his case be remitted to the appeal tribunal to make factual findings before the respondent local authority could be required to revise a decision to refuse a claim for housing benefit. B had applied to the local authority for a review of its decision to refuse housing benefit. A housing benefit review board confirmed the local authority's refusal to grant the benefit. B requested a review of the review board's decision under the Housing Benefit (General) Regulations 1987 Reg.79. That application was refused by the local authority on the ground that Reg.79(1)(b) had been repealed. B appealed and the appeal tribunal ordered the local authority to consider B's application as one for revision or supersession pursuant to the Housing Benefit and Council Tax Benefit (Decisions and Appeals) (Transitional and Savings) Regulations 2001. The social security commissioner upheld that decision but remitted the matter to the appeal tribunal to determine whether any written representations had been made within the period required by Reg.79. B argued that Reg.4(2) of the 2001 Regulations provided a route whereby the council could revise its original decision on the ground that it arose from an official error.

Held, dismissing the appeal, that the difficulty with B's appeal was that even if his request to the local authority could have been interpreted as a request that it should revise its original decision on the ground of an official error, the local authority had refused to entertain his request and no appeal had been brought against that refusal.

BELTEKIAN v. WESTMINSTER CITY COUNCIL, [2004] EWCA Civ 1784, *The Times*, December 15, 2004, Brooke, L.J., CA (Civ Div).

3876. Housing benefit–Subsidies–Recovery of overpaid housing benefit subsidy from local authority

[Social Security Administration Act 1992 s.137(6), s.140C(3); Housing Benefit and Community Charge Benefit (Subsidy) Order 1992 (SI 1992 739).]

The claimant local authority sought judicial review of a decision of the defendant secretary of state to resume recovery of overpaid housing benefit subsidy. The local authority had failed to refer rents to rent officers as required by the Housing Benefit and Community Charge Benefit (Subsidy) Order 1992. The secretary of state made payments to the local authority on the basis that references were being duly made. Consequently sums were paid that were substantially in excess of the subsidy due. The secretary of state, who had power of adjustment under the Social Security Administration Act 1992 s.137(6) and power of recovery under s.140C(3) of that Act, made a decision (the 1998 decision) to recover the overpaid subsidy but with repayments spread over a period of 10 years. The local authority accepted that decision, and deductions were duly made from subsequent payments of subsidy. Thereafter, the secretary of state postponed further deductions pending his decision on the local authority's request to abandon recovery of the outstanding overpayment on the ground of its financial circumstances. However, the secretary of state decided to continue recovering the outstanding sum in accordance with its policy set out in Circular HB/CTB S1/2002. The local authority submitted that (1) it was perverse and disproportionate to continue to recover the outstanding sum, given that recovery had already been made of sums that far exceeded the loss to the public purse; (2) the secretary of state acted irrationally in treating the local authority as on a par with other authorities that had completed repayment of their overpayments in accordance with decisions taken under the original policy of full recovery; (3) the secretary of state's concern that for him to accede to the local authority's request would lead to other local authorities making claims was flawed; (4) the secretary of state erred in considering that the discretion conferred by the s.137(6) differed from that conferred by s.140C.

Held, refusing the application, that (1) the relevant terms of the Order did not suggest any concern for the calculation of loss to the public purse or even for the concept of such loss. They dealt specifically with the calculation of subsidy to which local authorities were entitled. Any payment of subsidy in excess of that to which a local authority was entitled involved a loss to the purse of central government. Recovery of an overpayment of subsidy did not involve the imposition of a penalty in any legal sense. It was simply the recovery of an overpayment, *R. (on the application of Isle of Anglesey CC) v. Secretary of State for Work and Pensions* [2003] EWHC 2518, [2004] B.L.G.R. 614, [2004] C.L.Y. 3581 applied. Section 137(6) provided no more than machinery for recovery of overpayments of subsidy. That subsection did not expressly confer a discretion on the secretary of state and did not expressly exclude recovery at common law. In the circumstances, it was neither perverse nor disproportionate for the secretary of state to continue to make recovery under s.137(6), which continued in force in relation to the local authority's outstanding debt. (2) There was no irrationality in treating the local authority as on a par with other local authorities that had completed repayment of their overpayments. To treat the local authority differently would confer on it an uncovenanted advantage from the deferment of its liability made in the 1998 decision. It would be to treat a more serious default in complying with the requirements for subsidy more leniently than a less serious default. Those were lawful and weighty considerations that the secretary of state was entitled to take into account. (3) Given that the decision to resume recovery of the overpaid subsidy was made on a claim by the local authority for both repayment of sums already recovered from it and for the cessation of any further recovery, the secretary of state was entitled to take into account the effect of his decision on other local authorities who had overpaid subsidy, and to be concerned that a decision to accede to the local authority's request might lead to requests from other authorities for repayment that could be sensibly be the subject of a different decision. (4) It did not matter whether the scope of the discretion under s.137(6) differed from that under s.140C. The difference, if any, between the two statutory regimes was not the basis of, or a reason for, the decision to resume recovery. That decision was to maintain the 1998 decision. The secretary of state was not required by s.140C or his published policy contained in Circular HB/CTB S1/2002 to reconsider the 1998 decision and exercise his discretion afresh.

R. (ON THE APPLICATION OF LAMBETH LBC) v. SECRETARY OF STATE FOR WORK AND PENSIONS, [2005] EWHC 637, [2005] B.L.G.R. 764, Stanley Burnton, J., QBD (Admin).

3877. **Housing benefit–Tenancies–Rent free periods–Assistance scheme**

HOUSING BENEFIT (GENERAL) (AMENDMENT) REGULATIONS 2005, SI 2005 1719; made under the Social Security Contributions and Benefits Act 1992 s.123, s.136A, s.137, s.175. In force: August 1, 2005; £3.00.

These Regulations further amend the Housing Benefit (General) Regulations 1987 (SI 1987 1971) to preserve the policy that housing benefit, for those whose tenancy has a rent free period, assists with the full rent only in the weeks in which the rent is actually due.

3878. **Incapacity benefit–Allowances**

SOCIAL SECURITY (INCAPACITY) (MISCELLANEOUS AMENDMENTS) REGULATIONS 2005, SI 2005 2446; made under the Social Security Contributions and Benefits Act 1992 s.30E, s.122, s.171D, s.171G, s.175, Sch.7 para.2. In force: October 1, 2005; £3.00.

These Regulations amend the Social Security (General Benefit) Regulations 1982 (SI 1982 1408), the Social Security (Incapacity Benefit) Regulations 1994 (SI 1994 2946) and the Social Security (Incapacity for Work) (General) Regulations 1995 (SI 1995 311). They increase from £4,056 to £4,212 the amount which can be earned in a year before a person is disqualified from receiving unemployability supplement to disablement pension; increase the weekly earnings limit for councillor's allowance from £78.00 to £81.00; and increase from £78.00 to £81.00 the weekly limit for earnings from work which may be undertaken by a person without his being treated as being capable of work.

3879. Income related benefits–Grants

INCOME-RELATED BENEFITS (AMENDMENT) (NO.2) REGULATIONS 2005, SI 2005 3391; made under the Social Security Contributions and Benefits Act 1992 s.123, s.136, s.136A, s.137, s.138, s.175; the Jobseekers Act 1995 s.12, s.35, s.36; the Social Security (Recovery of Benefits) Act 1997 s.29, Sch.1 para.8; and the State Pension Credit Act 2002 s.15, s.17. In force: December 12, 2005; £3.00.

These Regulations amend the Income Support (General) Regulations 1987 (SI 1987 1967), the Housing Benefit (General) Regulations 1987 (SI 1987 1971), the Council Tax Benefit (General) Regulations 1992 (SI 1992 1814), the Jobseeker's Allowance Regulations 1996 (SI 1996 207), the Social Security (Recovery of Benefits) Regulations 1997 (SI 1997 2205), the State Pension Credit Regulations 2002 (SI 2002 1792) and the Social Fund Maternity and Funeral Expenses (General) Regulations 2005 (SI 2005 3061). They make provision for grants paid by the London Bombings Relief Charitable Fund, and certain payments derived from these grants, to be disregarded when calculating that person's capital or income for the purpose of an award of benefit.

3880. Income related benefits–Subsidy to authorities

INCOME-RELATED BENEFITS (SUBSIDY TO AUTHORITIES) AMENDMENT ORDER 2005, SI 2005 369; made under the Social Security Administration Act 1992 s.140B, s.140C, s.140F, s.189. In force: March 20, 2005; £3.00.

This Order amends the Income-related Benefits (Subsidy to Authorities) Order 1998 (SI 1998 562) which provides for subsidy to be payable to authorities administering housing benefit and council tax benefit. It makes amendments concerned with the calculation of subsidy.

3881. Income related benefits–Subsidy to authorities

INCOME-RELATED BENEFITS (SUBSIDY TO AUTHORITIES) AMENDMENT (NO.2) ORDER 2005, SI 2005 535; made under the Social Security Administration Act 1992 s.140B, s.140F, s.189. In force: April 1, 2005; £3.00.

This Order amends the Income-related Benefits (Subsidy to Authorities) Order 1998 (SI 1998 562) which provides for the calculation and payment of housing benefit subsidy to local authorities in England and Wales, in respect of rent rebates for dwellings within the authorities' Housing Revenue Accounts. It substitutes the GDP deflator, the annual factor and the weekly rent limit for the purposes of determining whether or not an authority is liable to a deduction from subsidy payable for 2005-06; substitutes a rebate proportion for that year for the purpose of calculating the amount of the deduction; substitute the specified amount "O" and the guideline rent increase for the purposes of determining whether or not an authority is liable to a deduction from subsidy payable for 2005-06; and substitutes a rebate proportion for that year for the purpose of calculating the amount of the deduction.

3882. Income support–Asylum seekers–Person temporarily admitted to United Kingdom–Meaning of "lawfully present"

[Immigration Act 1971 s.11 (1), Sch.2 para.21; Social Security (Immigration and Asylum) Consequential Amendments Regulations 2000 (SI 2000 636) Sch.1 para.4.]

The appellant (S) appealed against a decision ([2003] EWCA Civ 1131, Times, August 22, 2003, [2003] C.L.Y. 3944) that he was not "lawfully present in the United Kingdom" within the meaning of the Social Security (Immigration and

Asylum) Consequential Amendments Regulations 2000 Sch.1 para.4 and was therefore not entitled to income support. S, a Polish national, had been temporarily admitted to the United Kingdom under the written authority of an immigration officer pursuant to the Immigration Act 1971 Sch.2 para.21. He was granted indefinite leave to remain but was refused asylum. His claim for income support was also refused. The issue for determination was whether a person temporarily admitted to the United Kingdom under Sch.2 para.21 of the 1971 Act was "lawfully present in the United Kingdom" within the meaning of Sch.1 para.4 of the 2000 Regulations. The respondent secretary of state argued that lawful presence was only gained by having lawfully entered the United Kingdom with leave to enter, and that S was not to be regarded as "present" by virtue of s.11 (1) of the 1971 Act.

Held, allowing the appeal, that the purpose of s.11 (1) was not to safeguard the person admitted from prosecution for unlawful entry, but rather to exclude him from the rights given to those granted leave to enter. Even if s.11 would otherwise be capable of affecting the construction of the 2000 Regulations, it would be wrong to carry that fiction beyond its originally intended purpose and deem a person who was in fact lawfully in the country not to be here at all, *Bugdaycay v. Secretary of State for the Home Department* [1987] A.C. 514, [1987] C.L.Y. 1989 and *Kaya v. Haringey LBC* [2001] EWCA Civ 677, [2002] H.L.R. 1, [2001] C.L.Y. 3421 considered. There was no possible reason why Sch.1 para.4 should be construed as requiring more by way of any positive legal authorisation for someone's presence in the United Kingdom other than that they were at large here pursuant to the express written authority of an immigration officer provided for by statute. S was therefore lawfully present in the United Kingdom within the meaning of Sch.1 para.4 and the decision to award him income support was reinstated.

SZOMA v. SECRETARY OF STATE FOR WORK AND PENSIONS, [2005] UKHL 64, [2005] 3 W.L.R. 955, Lord Bingham of Cornhill, HL.

3883. **Income support–Housing benefit–Abandonment–Separation from husband through husband's imprisonment–Meaning of "abandoned" in Sch.3 para.8(3)(b) Income Support (General) Regulations 1987**

[Income Support (General) Regulations 1987 (SI 1987 1967) Sch.3 para.8(3)(b).]

The appellant secretary of state appealed against a decision of a social security commissioner that the respondent (W) had been "abandoned" by her husband under the Income Support (General) Regulations 1987 Sch.3 para.8(3)(b) for the purposes of a housing costs claim. W had made a claim to have her housing costs included in her applicable amount for the purpose of calculating her entitlement to income support. In her application she stated that her husband was expecting a custodial sentence. Thereafter, her husband was imprisoned for sexual offences and she later obtained a divorce. W's claim was refused on the basis that a woman separated from her husband through the latter's imprisonment was not "abandoned" under Sch.3 para.8(3)(b). On appeal, the commissioner held that the nature of the offences committed by W's husband had made it impossible for him to live with her and the children and made it extremely likely that she would find it intolerable to live with him again. As a result, W's husband had caused their separation and was guilty of constructive desertion. The secretary of state accepted that "abandonment" had the same meaning as "desertion" in matrimonial law but argued that if what was relied on by W was constructive abandonment, then she had to show unreasonable behaviour by her husband and an intention on her part to treat the relationship as at an end at the date when she made her claim. The secretary of state contended that the commissioner had failed to adopt the correct approach towards causation.

Held, dismissing the appeal, that (1) desertion required both physical separation and an intention on the part of the deserting party to desert the other party. Physical separation could be achieved by imprisonment or other forms of compulsory separation, although in such cases there had to be an intention to desert, *Beeken v. Beeken* [1948] P. 302 and *Ingram v. Ingram* [1956] P. 390,

[1956] C.L.Y. 2546 considered. It was clear from the authorities that there could only be desertion from the time when that intention was formed or could be inferred. Imprisonment alone was not enough. An intention on the part of the offender to abandon his partner was sufficient. It was the intention on the part of the deserting party which was relevant. If a man persisted in doing things which he knew his wife would probably not tolerate, and which no ordinary woman would tolerate, and she left, he had deserted her whatever his desire or intention may have been. In such a case, the "intention" to bring the relationship to an end was attributed to him; and such conduct amounted to constructive desertion, *Lang (Eric) v. Lang (Jean Wauchope)* [1955] A.C. 402, [1954] C.L.Y. 964 applied. The party alleging abandonment did not have to show that she regarded the relationship had come to an end; their mental state was not relevant. What was important was either direct evidence of an intention on the part of the abandoning party to end the relationship or evidence from which that intention could be inferred. In the instant case, the commissioner correctly had regard to the nature of the offences committed by W's husband. They were offences which no ordinary woman would tolerate and which entitled an inference that he could not have intended the relationship to continue. The reality was that W's husband could not be allowed back into the matrimonial home given the nature of the offences. Neither W nor the local authority would have let that happen given the threat to the children. By the time W had submitted her claim, her husband had acknowledged his guilt and was expecting a prison sentence, physical separation existed, and the situation was such that her husband's intention to end the relationship could be inferred. (2) Tribunals approaching the issue of causation should not draw too fine a distinction, in cases such as the instant case, about what caused a claim for income support to be made, *Special Commissioner's Decision (CIS/2790/1998), Re* considered. They should adopt a robust, common sense approach which did not seek too readily to distinguish between the abandonment of the innocent party and the conduct of the other party which formed the basis of the abandonment. Those claiming income support were unlikely to regard such a distinction as a real one and tribunals would also find it a difficult and complex exercise.

SECRETARY OF STATE FOR WORK AND PENSIONS v. W, [2005] EWCA Civ 570, *The Times*, June 10, 2005, Keene, L.J., CA (Civ Div).

3884. Industrial injuries–Compensation–Adjustments to lower rate of incapacity benefit

WORKMEN'S COMPENSATION (SUPPLEMENTATION) (AMENDMENT) SCHEME 2005, SI 2005 832; made under the Social Security Contributions and Benefits Act 1992 Sch.8 para.2; and the Social Security Administration Act 1992 Sch.9 para.1. In force: April 13, 2005; £3.00.

This Scheme amends the Workmen's Compensation (Supplementation) Scheme 1982 (SI 1982 1489) by making adjustments to the rate of lesser incapacity allowance, such adjustments being consequential upon the increase in the maximum rate of that allowance made by the Social Security Benefits Up-rating Order 2005 (SI 2005 522).

3885. Industrial injuries–Dependants–Permitted earnings limits

SOCIAL SECURITY (INDUSTRIAL INJURIES) (DEPENDENCY) (PERMITTED EARNINGS LIMITS) ORDER 2005, SI 2005 633; made under the Social Security Contributions and Benefits Act 1992 Sch.7 para.4. In force: April 13, 2005; £3.00.

Where a disablement pension with unemployability supplement is increased in respect of a child or children and the beneficiary is one of two persons who are spouses residing together or an unmarried couple, the Social Security Contributions and Benefits Act 1992 provides that the increase shall not be payable in respect of the first child if the other person's earnings are £165 a week or more and in respect of a further child for each complete £21 by which the earnings exceed £165. This Order increases the amounts of £165 to £170 and the amount of £21 to £22.

3886. Jobseekers allowance–Equal treatment–Discriminatory effect of Jobseeker's Allowance Regulations 1996 Reg.77

[Jobseeker's Allowance Regulations 1996 (SI 1996 207) Reg.77; Council Directive 79/7 on equal treatment for men and women in matters of social security Art.4.]

The appellant (H) appealed against the decision of a social security commissioner that although the Jobseeker's Allowance Regulations 1996 Reg.77 had a disparately adverse impact on men and could not be objectively justified in so far as it linked entitlement to child premium to receipt of child benefit, it was not indirectly discriminatory or was objectively justifiable in so far as it provided that only one person could be eligible for the premium in respect of any child in any week and that in the absence of a claim for child benefit the person entitled to the premium should be the person with whom the child usually lived. The secretary of state cross appealed. H was the father of two children and had separated from his wife. A joint residence order had been made dividing the children's care roughly equally between H and his wife. H was unemployed and applied for jobseeker's allowance. The adjudication officer decided that H was entitled to income based jobseeker's allowance but without any additional amount in respect of the children, because H was not in receipt of child benefit, which was being paid to the mother, and was therefore not to be treated as responsible for them, applying the provisions of Reg.77. H submitted that the 1996 Regulations, which linked the supplement payable for children to the receipt of child benefit, was discriminatory contrary to the equal treatment provisions of Council Directive 79/7.

Held, allowing the appeal and dismissing the cross appeal, that the challenged measure had to be both suitable and necessary to achieve a legitimate policy aim, *Nolte v. Landesversicherungsanstalt Hannover (C-317/93)* [1995] E.C.R. I-4625 and *R. v. Secretary of State for Employment, ex p. Seymour-Smith (C167/97)* [1999] E.C.R. I-623 applied. The link between the additional child supplement and the receipt of child benefit could not be objectively justified. Regulation 77(5) prevented appropriate subsistence from being paid to one parent in shared care cases. Because that parent was usually the father, the provision was discriminatory. The discriminatory provisions of Reg.77 had not been justified. The court should not apply Reg.77 in so far as it breached H's directly effective rights under Art.4 of the Directive. On that basis the appropriate remedy was that H should receive jobseeker's allowance with additional payments for the children.

HOCKENJOS v. SECRETARY OF STATE FOR SOCIAL SECURITY, [2004] EWCA Civ 1749, [2005] Eu. L.R. 385, Ward, L.J., CA (Civ Div).

3887. Jobseekers allowance–Pilot schemes–Mandatory activity

JOBSEEKER'S ALLOWANCE (JOBSEEKER MANDATORY ACTIVITY) PILOT REGULATIONS 2005, SI 2005 3466; made under the Jobseekers Act 1995 s.19, s.29, s.35, s.36. In force: April 3, 2006; £3.00.

These Regulations, which amend the Jobseeker's Allowance Regulations 1996 (SI 1996 207), introduce the Jobseeker Mandatory Activity Pilot made under the pilot-making power in s.29 of the Jobseekers Act 1995. The Regulations provide that any person who fails to take part in or attend any part of the pilot may be sanctioned for one week for each failure to attend and provide that a person ceases to be required to attend the programme if he changes address and is required to attend an office of the Department for Work and Pensions which is not in the pilot areas.

3888. Migrant workers – Benefits – Indirect discrimination – Early receipt of pension due to unemployment – Condition of prior receipt of unemployment benefit – European Community

[EEC-Turkey Association Agreement Art.9; Decision 3/80 on the application of the social security schemes of the Member States to Turkish workers and members of their families Art.3(1).]

The Austrian Supreme Court referred to the European Court of Justice (ECJ) the question of whether the Austrian law regarding retirement pensions was compatible with the EEC-Turkey Association Agreement Art.9. Under Decision 3/80 Art.3(1), persons to whom the decision applied who were resident in a Member State were entitled to the same benefits as nationals of that state. O, who was Turkish, lived in Germany but had previously worked in both Austria and Germany. He had received unemployment benefit in Germany and was granted a German retirement pension. However, the Austrian authorities precluded him from receiving the Austrian pension on the ground that O had been unemployed for 15 months prior to the qualifying date and had not received unemployment benefit in Austria. The question for the ECJ was whether Austria's failure to take into account O's receipt of unemployment benefit in Germany for the purpose of granting retirement pension amounted to indirect discrimination.

Held, giving a preliminary ruling, that O was entitled to rely upon Art.3(1) as a person who was or had been subject to the legislation of one or more Member States and could claim retirement pension notwithstanding the fact that he was now resident in Germany. Whilst the Austrian legislation applied regardless of nationality, the requirement of receiving unemployment benefit for a certain period was more easily fulfilled by Austrian citizens and therefore amounted to indirect discrimination. Furthermore, the difference in treatment could not be objectively justified as a legitimate social measure. Whilst it could be argued that the early retirement pension was awarded because a worker was unlikely to reintegrate into the work force due to his age, it nevertheless remained an old age pension which was calculated on the basis of contributions to the Member State's pension scheme. It followed that Art.3(1) was to be interpreted as precluding the application of legislation of a Member State which made entitlement to an early retirement pension in the event of unemployment conditional on the applicant having received unemployment benefit from that Member State alone for a period prior to his application.

OZTURK v. PENSIONSVERSICHERUNGSANSTALT DER ARBEITER (C373/02) [2004] 2 C.M.L.R. 47, Judge Skouris (President), ECJ.

3889. Migrant workers – Pension benefits – Determination of applicant's date of birth – European Community

[EEC-Turkish Association Agreement Art.9; Decision 3/80 on the application of the social security schemes of the Member States to Turkish workers and members of their families Art.3(1).]

The German Federal Social Security Court referred to the European Court of Justice the question of whether the German law regarding pension entitlement was compatible with the non discrimination and equal treatment requirements of the EEC-Turkish Association Agreement. K, who was Turkish, had worked in Germany and was affiliated to the German social security scheme, decided to take early retirement. He applied to O for his retirement pension. According to the German Code of Social Law, for the purposes of receiving an age related benefit, the applicant's date of birth was the first declaration that had been made to the social security institution unless there was a clerical error, or unless a document issued before that declaration was made gave a different date. K's date of birth was recorded as October 20, 1933 but in 1985 the Turkish courts declared his date of birth to be 1926. K's application for a pension was refused as O decided that the Turkish courts' decision could not be considered.

Held, giving a preliminary ruling, that under Art.9 of the Association Agreement there was a principle of non discrimination on the ground of nationality. This applied to all direct and indirect acts of discrimination. However, in the circumstances of the instant case there was no discrimination as the same provisions applied irrespective of nationality and Turkish documents were not considered to be of lower probative value than German ones, *Dafeki v. Landesversicherungsanstalt Wurttemberg (C336/94)* [1998] All E.R. (EC) 452, [1998] C.L.Y. 4520 distinguished. Indeed, Turkish law imposed similar provisions. There were differences between the German and Turkish approaches to recording civil status, but it was not permissible to require that the German scheme considered circumstances that arose under Turkish legislation on civil status. Turkish nationals who, like K, had been subject to the legislation of a Member State, were covered by Decision 3/80 Art.3(1), which was to be interpreted as not precluding a Member State from taking the first given date of birth as conclusive in the absence of a prior document.

KOCAK v. LANDESVERSICHERUNGSANSTALT OBERFRANKEN UND MITTELFRANKEN (C102/98); ORS v. BUNDESKNAPPSCHAFT (C211/98) [2004] 2 C.M.L.R. 46, Judge Rodriguez Iglesias (President), ECJ.

3890. National insurance contributions

SOCIAL SECURITY (CONTRIBUTIONS) (RE-RATING AND NATIONAL INSURANCE FUNDS PAYMENTS) ORDER 2005, SI 2005 878; made under the Social Security Administration Act 1992 s.141, s.142, s.143, s.144; the Social Security Administration (Northern Ireland) Act 1992 s.129, s.165; the Social Security Act 1993 s.2; and the Social Security (Northern Ireland) Order 1993 (SI 1993 592 (NI.2)) Art.4. In force: April 6, 2005; £3.00.

This Order increases the rates of Class 2 and Class 3 contributions specified in the Social Security Contributions and Benefits Act 1992 from £2.05 to £2.10 and from £7.15 to £7.35 respectively. It increases the amount of earnings specified in the Act, below which an earner may be excepted from liability for Class 2 contributions from £4,215 to £4,345. The Order also increases, from £4,745 to £4,895 and from £31,720 to £32,760 respectively, the lower and upper limits of profits or gains specified in those sections, between which Class 4 contributions are payable at the main Class 4 percentage rate. The Order also makes provision for Northern Ireland by making amendments to the Social Security Contributions and Benefits (Northern Ireland) Act 1992.

3891. National insurance contributions–Civil partnerships

SOCIAL SECURITY (CONTRIBUTIONS) (AMENDMENT NO.6) REGULATIONS 2005, SI 2005 3130; made under the Social Security Contributions and Benefits Act 1992 s.3; and the Social Security Contributions and Benefits (Northern Ireland) Act 1992 s.3. In force: December 5, 2005; £3.00.

These Regulations amend the Social Security (Contributions) Regulations 2001 (SI 2001 1004) in consequence of the coming into force of the Civil Partnership Act 2004. They make amendments to secure equality of treatment between civil partners and spouses in the application of the National Insurance Contributions regime.

3892. National insurance contributions–Directors–Employment in more than one company–Aggregation of earnings–Carrying on of business in association

[Social Security (Contributions) Regulations 1979 (SI 1979 591) Reg.12(1)(a).]

An insurance broking company (S) appealed against decisions of the Inland Revenue that the earnings of its director, who was also director of various other companies owned by S, should be aggregated as a single payment of earnings from one employment for the purposes of national insurance contributions. Staff at the other companies were employed by S, which provided administration services. The first issue was whether S and the companies it had bought carried on business in association with each other under the Social Security (Contributions) Regulations 1979 Reg.12(1)(a), with S's director arguing that a directorship was not an employment and related only to a particular company. The second issue was whether it was "reasonably practicable" under Reg.12(1) to aggregate the earnings. The Inland Revenue claimed that it took 15 minutes to aggregate the payments for each year under appeal.

Held, dismissing the appeal, that S's director's earnings should be aggregated. The phrase "carry on business in association" in Reg.12(1)(a) was an ordinary expression without any technical meaning. The companies carried on business in association because all the businesses related to insurance broking, S provided the administration services and employed all employees of the group and the director was a director of all the companies, which were under common ownership. It was not relevant that the director's duties related to each company separately. The phrase "reasonably practicable" should similarly be defined by its ordinary meaning. There was nothing impracticable in making the aggregation, which was a simple calculation.

SAMUELS & SAMUELS LTD v. RICHARDSON (INSPECTOR OF TAXES) [2005] S.T.C. (S.C.D.) 1, John F Avery Jones, Sp Comm.

3893. National insurance contributions—Due diligence—Requirement to make enquiries

[Social Security (Crediting and Treatment of Contributions, and National Insurance Numbers) Regulations 2001 (SI 2001 769) Reg.6; Social Security (Contributions) Regulations 2001 (SI 2001 1004) Reg.50.]

The appellant (X), who had not paid national insurance contributions for a number of years, appealed against the Revenue's decision that whilst her failure to pay was attributable to her ignorance or error she had not exercised due care and diligence and as such was not permitted to make late payments under the Social Security (Contributions) Regulations 2001 Reg.50 and the Social Security (Crediting and Treatment of Contributions, and National Insurance Numbers) Regulations 2001 Reg.6. X contended that it was not possible to exercise due care and diligence over something of which she was ignorant.

Held, dismissing the appeal, that exercising due diligence involved the positive step of making enquiries which X had failed to do. X's argument would only have had force if she had never heard of national insurance, for then she could not have been expected to have made enquiries. However, X was aware of the national insurance scheme and must have known that benefits were linked to contributions. Accordingly, X's failure to make enquiries constituted a failure to exercise due care and diligence, *Walsh v. Secretary of State for Social Security* (Unreported, March 28, 1994) followed.

ADOJUTELEGAN v. CLARK [2004] S.T.C. (S.C.D.) 524, John F Avery Jones, Sp Comm.

3894. National insurance contributions—Employee training

SOCIAL SECURITY (CONTRIBUTIONS) (AMENDMENT NO.2) REGULATIONS 2005, SI 2005 728; made under the Social Security Contributions and Benefits Act 1992 s.3, s.10; and the Social Security Contributions and Benefits (Northern Ireland) Act 1992 s.3, s.10. In force: April 6, 2005; £3.00.

These Regulations amend the Social Security (Contributions) Regulations 2001 (SI 2001 1004) to secure parity of treatment, for income tax and national insurance purposes, of payments made by employers secondary contributors to employees in respect of the employees' attendance for long-term training at recognised educational establishments. Such payments are not subjected to income tax by virtue of Inland Revenue Statement of Practice 4/86, a revised version which was published on March 16, 2005.

3895. National insurance contributions—Exemptions—School fees—Company's payment of school fees on behalf of directors

[Social Security (Contributions) Regulations 1979 (SI 1979 591) Reg.19(1)(d).]

The appellant company (F) appealed against a decision that it was liable to pay further Class 1 national insurance contributions in relation to the three year period beginning in April 1997. F had been wholly owned during the relevant period by its two directors (X), a married couple. X had a son (B) who started attending a preparatory school in 1997. X had initially paid the fees but towards the end of that year, the school agreed to invoice F instead. F paid the fees and treated them as a benefit in kind forming part of X's remuneration package. The arrangement continued until F was sold and X resumed paying the fees themselves. F contended that its payment of the school fees constituted the provision of "services or other facilities" to X and fell to be disregarded for the purposes of calculating national insurance liability in accordance with the Social Security (Contributions) Regulations 1979 Reg.19(1)(d).

Held, dismissing the appeal, that by applying to the school, X had undertaken to be responsible for B's fees so long as he remained at the school. It could not be doubted that B's acceptance by the school had been on the basis of that undertaking. There was no evidence that the school had approached X for a similar undertaking. The arrangement between the school and F, in which F was directly billed for the fees, was made for X's convenience and did not alter their continuing contractual liability for the fees. F was merely discharging a direct liability of X, and therefore the disregard did not apply, *Ableway Ltd v. Inland Revenue Commissioners* [2002] S.T.C. (S.C.D.) 1, [2002] C.L.Y. 4229 followed.

FROST SKIP HIRE (NEWCASTLE) LTD v. WOOD (INSPECTOR OF TAXES) [2004] S.T.C. (S.C.D.) 387, MS Johnson (Chairman), Sp Comm.

3896. **National insurance contributions–Intermediaries**

SOCIAL SECURITY CONTRIBUTIONS (INTERMEDIARIES) (AMENDMENT) REGULATIONS 2005, SI 2005 3131; made under the Social Security Contributions and Benefits Act 1992 s.4A, s.122, s.175. In force: in accordance with Reg.1 (2)(3); £3.00.

These Regulations amend the Social Security Contributions (Intermediaries) Regulations 2000 (SI 2000 727) to take account of changes made to legislation. As a result of the bringing into force of the Commissioners for Revenue and Customs Act 2005, the functions of the Commissioners of Inland Regulation have been transferred to the Commissioners for Her Majesty's Revenue and Customs. The definition of "the Commissioners" has accordingly been amended. As a result of the bringing into force of the Pensions Act 2004, it is necessary to amend the 2000 Regulations to deal with payments made under the levies for which that Act provides. The Regulations accordingly make the necessary amendments. As a result of the bringing into force of the Civil Partnership Act 2004, it is necessary to amend the 2000 Regulations to take account of the existence of civil partnerships. The Regulations accordingly makes transitional provision for the tax year 2005-06 in the case of a person to whom the 2000 Regulations would not apply but for an amendment coming into force during the tax year rather than at the beginning of a tax year. They also deal with the changes made to the tax provisions relating to pensions by the Finance Act 2004.

3897. **National insurance contributions–Share fishermen**

SOCIAL SECURITY (CONTRIBUTIONS) (RE-RATING) CONSEQUENTIAL AMENDMENT REGULATIONS 2005, SI 2005 915; made under the Social Security Contributions and Benefits Act 1992 s.117, s.175; and the Social Security Contributions and Benefits (Northern Ireland) Act 1992 s.117, s.171. In force: April 6, 2005; £3.00.

These Regulations, which amend the Social Security (Contributions) Regulations 2001 (SI 2001 1004), are made in consequence of the annual up-rating order and alter the special rate of any Class 2 contributions payable by share fishermen from £2.70 to £2.75.

3898. Pensions–Earnings factors–Calculation of additional pension

SOCIAL SECURITY REVALUATION OF EARNINGS FACTORS ORDER 2005, SI 2005 216; made under the Social Security Administration Act 1992 s.148, s.189. In force: April 6, 2004; £3.00.

This Order directs that the earnings factors relevant to the calculation of the additional pension in the rate of any long term benefit or of any guaranteed minimum pension, or to any other calculation required under the Pension Schemes Act 1993 Part III, are to be increased for the tax years specified in the Schedule to the Order by the percentage of their amount specified in that Schedule. This Order also provides for the rounding of fractional amounts for earnings factors relevant to the calculation of the additional pension in the rate of any long term benefit.

3899. Pensions–State pension credit–Assessed income

STATE PENSION CREDIT (AMENDMENT) REGULATIONS 2005, SI 2005 3205; made under the Social Security Contributions and Benefits Act 1992 s.175; and the State Pension Credit Act 2002 s.7, s.16, s.17. In force: December 18, 2005; £3.00.

These Regulations amend the State Pension Credit Regulations 2002 (SI 2002 1792) by removing the references to the claimant's retirement pension scheme or annuity contract. The effect of this is that where the arrangements under which the assessed amount is paid contain no provision for periodic increases in the amount payable, the claimant's assessed amount is deemed not to change during their assessed income period. The Regulations also make amendments by removing the same references from the definition of "increased payment date"; and add financial assistance scheme payments to the descriptions of income listed as retirement pension income in the State Pension Credit Act 2002 s.16(1).

3900. Prisoners–Payment of advance maintenance by state–Transfer of father serving prison sentence in one state to state of origin–Applicable law– European Community

[Council Regulation 1408/71 on the application of social security schemes to employed persons and their families moving within the Community Art.3, Art.13(2).]

A question was referred to the European Court of Justice as to the correct interpretation of Council Regulation 1408/71 on the application of social security schemes to employed persons and their families moving within the Community. The applicant Austrian minor (E) was awarded monthly advances on maintenance payments by Austria after his German father (F) was imprisoned in Austria in 2000. F was transferred to a German prison in 2001 to serve the remainder of his prison sentence there. He undertook paid work as part of his sentence and was released in April 2003. In 2002, Austria terminated the payments to E on the ground that it was no longer required under domestic legislation to make them, since F was no longer in prison in Austria. E brought proceedings in the domestic court challenging that decision and a question was referred to the court as to whether Art.3 of the Regulation precluded a national rule that discriminated against a Community citizen in receipt of advances on maintenance payments, where the father liable for maintaining that citizen was serving a criminal sentence in his Member State of origin.

Held, giving a preliminary ruling, that under Art.13(2) of the Regulation, where a prisoner had been transferred to his state of origin the legislation of that state applied to any benefits payable to his family. Taken on its own, Art.13(2)(a) had the effect that an employed person temporarily moving to another state where he did not work remained bound by the legislation of the state in which he last worked. However, the insertion of Art.13(2)(f), following the landmark case of *Ten Holder v. Nieuwe Algemene Bedrijfsvereniging (302/84)* [1986] E.C.R. 1821, now meant that Art.13(2)(a) did not apply where the person had ceased all occupational activity in the state he had left, whether temporarily or definitively, *Ten Holder* followed. Thus, in the instant case, the fact that F had left Austria and ceased all occupational activity there meant that the law of Austria no longer applied to matters covered by the Regulation, such as family benefits. It followed that the Regulation was not to be interpreted so as to preclude the legislation of a Member State from granting family benefits to the members of a family of a person who had ceased to carry on an occupation there, subject to the condition that that person maintained his residence there.

EFFING, *Re* (C302/02) [2005] 1 C.M.L.R. 43, Judge Jann (President), ECJ.

3901. Recovery of benefits–Confiscation orders–Deduction in respect of notional entitlement to sum under working families tax credit scheme

[Criminal Justice Act 1988 s.71; Civil Procedure Rules 1998 (SI 1998 3132) Part 7, Part 8.]

The appellant (R) appealed against a confiscation order. R had pleaded guilty to specimen charges of making a false statement or representation so as to obtain benefit. He had dishonestly received income support for a period of over three years after failing to inform the respondent government department of changes to his personal circumstances. The total sum involved was derived from the department's overpayment decision. The department indicated that it would not be taking civil action. It was common ground that, but for the payments induced by his misrepresentation, R was notionally entitled to a sum under the Working Families Tax Credit scheme. The judge ruled that that notional tax credit should not be taken into account for the purpose of the confiscation proceedings so as to reduce the outstanding sum. R submitted that (1) the judge had to make an inquiry into the extent to which an offender had in fact benefited, which justified the deduction of the tax credit because it would have been an entitlement in the absence of fraudulent conduct and such entitlement derived from the state when viewed as one entity; (2) alternatively, the department could be taken to have instituted or intended to institute civil proceedings and accordingly its discretionary powers were invoked.

Held, dismissing the appeal, that (1) the Criminal Justice Act 1988 s.71(4) pertained to the moment when the property was obtained or the pecuniary advantage was derived, *R. v. May (Raymond George)* [2005] EWCA Crim 97, Times, February 15, 2005 applied. It followed that no allowance could be made for notional financial returns that might have been recovered from the victim in the absence of dishonest conduct, any more than the value of costs that might have been avoided or legitimate profits that might have been made as a consequence of acting honestly. A tax credit as such gave rise to no entitlement or debt irrespective of the facts of the instant case, *Larusai v. Secretary of State for Work and Pensions* [2003] EWHC 371 considered. In light of the clear meaning and policy behind s.71, R could not net off whatever the state as a whole might have saved, *R. v. Smith (David Cadman)* [2001] UKHL 68, [2002] 1 W.L.R. 54, [2002] C.L.Y. 3898 applied. Section 71(1B) afforded no discretion, whatever the impact on the offender might be. (2) Civil proceedings meant proceedings whereby the civil jurisdiction of the court was invoked by the issue and service of the claim form under the Civil Procedure Rules 1998 Part 7 or Part 8. If any proceedings were contemplated by the department they were expressly criminal. Further, the existence of a statutory recovery scheme could not be perceived as coming under the umbrella of civil proceedings.

R. v. RICHARDS (MICHAEL); *sub nom.* DEPARTMENT FOR WORK AND PENSIONS v. RICHARDS, [2005] EWCA Crim 491, [2005] 2 Cr. App. R. (S.) 97, Rose, L.J., CA (Crim Div).

3902. Residential accommodation–Assessment of resources–Civil partnerships

NATIONAL ASSISTANCE (ASSESSMENT OF RESOURCES) (AMENDMENT) (ENGLAND) REGULATIONS 2005, SI 2005 3277; made under the National Assistance Act 1948 s.22. In force: Reg.1: December 5, 2005; Reg.2: December 5, 2005; Reg.3(a): December 5, 2005; Reg.3(b): December 30, 2005; Reg.4: December 30, 2005; £3.00.

These Regulations amend the National Assistance (Assessment of Resources) Regulations 1992 (SI 1992 2977) which concern the assessment of the ability of a person to pay for accommodation arranged by local authorities under the National Assistance Act 1948 Part 3. They make amendments in the light of the Civil Partnership Act 2004 which provides that two people of the same sex may form a civil partnership and makes provision for civil partners to be treated in the same or similar way as spouses in relation to certain benefits and obligations.

3903. Residential accommodation–Assessment of resources–Wales

NATIONAL ASSISTANCE (ASSESSMENT OF RESOURCES) (AMENDMENT) (WALES) REGULATIONS 2005, SI 2005 662 (W.52); made under the National Assistance Act 1948 s.22. In force: April 11, 2005; £3.00.

These Regulations make amendments to the National Assistance (Assessment of Resources) Regulations 1992 (SI 1992 2977) which determine the way that local authorities assess the ability of a person to pay for the accommodation which local authorities arrange under the National Assistance Act 1948 Part 3. The Regulations increase the capital limits. The upper capital limit sets the amount of capital above which a resident is not eligible for local authority support. The lower capital limit sets the amount below which a resident is not required to contribute to his or her accommodation from capital. They also raise the levels of savings credit disregard from £4.75 to £4.85 in the case of a single person and from £6.95 to £7.20 in the case of a resident with a partner. There is a new disregard for payments made under the arrangements to support "special guardians" under the Children Act 1989 s.14F. They also provide that payments made to "special guardians" are also disregarded as capital.

3904. Residential accommodation–Assessment of resources–Wales

NATIONAL ASSISTANCE (ASSESSMENT OF RESOURCES) (AMENDMENT NO.2) (WALES) REGULATIONS 2005, SI 2005 3288 (W.251); made under the National Assistance Act 1948 s.22. In force: December 6, 2005; £3.00.

These Regulations make amendments to the National Assistance (Assessment of Resources) Regulations 1992 (SI 1992 2977) to determine the way that local authorities assess the ability of a person to pay for the accommodation which local authorities arrange under the National Assistance Act 1948 Part III. They allow for certain age-related payments made under the Age-Related Payments Act 2004 s.7 to be disregarded as capital by local authorities.

3905. Residential accommodation–Sums for personal requirements

NATIONAL ASSISTANCE (SUMS FOR PERSONAL REQUIREMENTS AND ASSESSMENT OF RESOURCES) (AMENDMENT) (ENGLAND) REGULATIONS 2005, SI 2005 708; made under the National Assistance Act 1948 s.22. In force: April 11, 2005; £3.00.

These Regulations, which revoke the National Assistance (Sums for Personal Requirements and Assessment of Resources) (Amendment) (England) Regulations 2004 (SI 2004 760) and the National Assistance (Assessment of Resources) (Amendment) (No.2) (England) Regulations 2004 (SI 2004 2328), amend the National Assistance (Assessment of Resources) Regulations 1992 (SI 1992 2977) and the National Assistance (Sums for Personal Requirements) (England) Regulations 2003 (SI 2003 628). The Regulations make amendments so that the weekly sum which local authorities in England are to assume, in the absence of special requirements, that residents in accommodation arranged under the National Assistance Act 1948 Part 3 will need for their personal requirements is £18.80; so that the capital limit becomes £20,500; so that the capital limits become £12,500 and £20,500; and provides for an increase of up to £4.85 in the amount of any savings credit to be disregarded where a resident has qualifying income not exceeding the standard minimum guarantee, and for an increase to £4.85 in the amount to be disregarded if a resident has qualifying income that exceeds the standard minimum guarantee.

3906. Residential accommodation—Sums for personal requirements—Wales

NATIONAL ASSISTANCE (SUMS FOR PERSONAL REQUIREMENTS) (WALES) REGULATIONS 2005, SI 2005 663 (W.53); made under the National Assistance Act 1948 s.22. In force: April 11, 2005; £3.00.

These Regulations, which revoke the National Assistance (Sums for Personal Requirements) (Wales) Regulations 2004 (SI 2004 1024 (W.121)), set out the weekly sum which local authorities in Wales are to assume, in the absence of special circumstances, that residents in accommodation arranged under the National Assistance Act 1948 Part III, will need for their personal requirements. From April 11, 2005 all such residents will be assumed to need £19.10 per week for their personal requirements.

3907. Retirement pensions—Deferment

SOCIAL SECURITY (DEFERRAL OF RETIREMENT PENSIONS) REGULATIONS 2005, SI 2005 453; made under the Social Security Contributions and Benefits Act 1992 s.54, s.122, s.175, Sch.5 para.2, Sch.5 para.3, Sch.5 para.3B, Sch.5 para.7B. In force: April 6, 2005; £3.00.

These Regulations, which amend the Social Security (Widow's Benefit and Retirement Pensions) Regulations 1979 (SI 1979 642), make provision relating to changes to the regime for deferring entitlement to state pension made and brought forward by the Pensions Act 2004 which provide, in particular, for an increased incremental rate for those deferring their state pension and for a choice between increments and a lump sum for those who have deferred their entitlement for 12 months or more. They make amendments in consequence of changes to the Social Security Contributions and Benefits Act 1992 made originally by the Pensions Act 1995 and which were due to come into force in 2010 but are now to come into force in 2005, to allow for both elections and consents to elections to be treated as not entitled to a retirement pension to be made by telephone and to make further provision in relation to the calculation of days of increment for those who start deferring their state pension on or after April 6, 2005.

3908. Retirement pensions—Harmonisation

SOCIAL SECURITY (SHARED ADDITIONAL PENSION) (MISCELLANEOUS AMENDMENTS) REGULATIONS 2005, SI 2005 1551; made under the Social Security Contributions and Benefits Act 1992 s.54, s.113, s.122, s.175, Sch.5A para.1, Sch.5A para.3, Sch.5A para.5; and the Social Security Administration Act 1992 s.1 s.5, s.7, s.71, s.73, s.189, s.191. In force: in accordance with Reg.1 (1); £3.00.

These Regulations amend the Social Security Benefit (Persons Abroad) Regulations 1975 (SI 1975 563), the Social Security (Overlapping Benefits) Regulations 1979 (SI 1979 597), the Social Security (Widow's Benefit and Retirement Pensions) Regulations 1979 (SI 1979 642), the Social Security (General Benefit) Regulations 1982 (SI 1982 1408), the Social Security (Claims and Payments) Regulations 1987 (SI 1987 1968), the Social Security (Payments on account, Overpayments and Recovery) Regulations 1988 (SI 1988 664) and the Social Security (Deferral of Retirement Pensions) Regulations 2005 (SI 2005 453). The Regulations make provision for the harmonisation of the rules for claiming and paying Shared Additional Pension with those relating to Retirement Pension and Graduated Retirement Benefit.

3909. Retirement pensions—Widowers—Civil partnerships

SOCIAL SECURITY (RETIREMENT PENSIONS AND GRADUATED RETIREMENT BENEFIT) (WIDOWERS AND CIVIL PARTNERSHIP) REGULATIONS 2005, SI 2005 3078; made under the Social Security Contribution and Benefits Act 1992 s.62, s.122, s.175; the Pensions Act 2004

Sch.11 para.27; and the Social Security Administration Act 1992 s.5, s.189. In force: in accordance with Reg.1 (1); £3.00.

These Regulations, which amend the Social Security (Graduated Retirement Benefit) (No.2) Regulations 1978 (SI 1978 393), the Social Security (Claims and Payments) Regulations 1987 (SI 1987 1968) and the Social Security (Graduated Retirement Benefit) Regulations 2005 (SI 2005 454), make provision relating to widowers, civil partners and surviving civil partners. They extend to civil partners the same inheritance rights as apply to widowers in respect of a deceased person's graduated retirement benefit, including any increments or lump sum in a case where the deceased had deferred his or her entitlement. The Regulations also enable a claim for a Category A or B retirement pension or graduated retirement benefit to be made where a widower is under pension age at the time of his wife's death.

3910. SERPS – State pension – Civil partnerships

SOCIAL SECURITY (INHERITED SERPS) (AMENDMENTS RELATING TO CIVIL PARTNERSHIP) REGULATIONS 2005, SI 2005 3030; made under the Welfare Reform and Pensions Act 1999 s.52, s.83. In force: December 5, 2005; £3.00.

These Regulations extend the provisions of the Social Security (Inherited SERPS) Regulations 2001 (SI 2001 1085) to surviving civil partners. They make provision for surviving civil partners whose civil partner dies on or after December 5, 2005 to receive an increase in the rate of the additional (earnings related) pension under the State Earnings Related Pensions Scheme (SERPS) in the same way as a surviving spouse. They also allow for the proportion of the additional pension used in the calculation of the surviving civil partner's inheritable increments or lump sum to be increased in line with the provisions set out in those Regulations relating to the calculation of the additional pension for surviving civil partners.

3911. SERPS – State pension – Deferment

SOCIAL SECURITY (INHERITED SERPS) (AMENDMENT) REGULATIONS 2005, SI 2005 811; made under the Welfare Reform and Pensions Act 1999 s.52, s.83. In force: April 6, 2005; £3.00.

These Regulations make provision relating to changes to the regime for deferring entitlement to state pension made by the Pensions Act 2004 which provide, in particular, for a choice between increments and a lump sum for those who have deferred their entitlement for 12 months or more. In particular, they amend the Social Security (Inherited SERPS) Regulations 2001 (SI 2001 1085) to allow for the proportion of the additional pension used in the calculation of the widowed person's lump sum to be increased in line with the provisions set out in those Regulations relating to the calculation of additional pension for widowed persons.

3912. Social fund – Cold weather payments

SOCIAL FUND COLD WEATHER PAYMENTS (GENERAL) AMENDMENT REGULATIONS 2005, SI 2005 2724; made under the Security Contributions and Benefits Act 1992 s.138, s.175. In force: November 1, 2005; £3.00.

These Regulations amend the Social Fund Cold Weather Payments (General) Regulations 1988 (SI 1988 1724) principally by substituting new Schedules to those Regulations in relation to the lists of weather stations and applicable postcode districts in Schedule 1, and alternative weather stations in Schedule 2, but also by amending the interpretation provisions. The Regulations delete from the interpretation provisions of the 1988 Regulations a number of definitions for terms which are no longer used in the Regulations. They also amend the definition of "claimant" by adding references to "state pension credit" and "income-based jobseeker's allowance" and adds a definition of "state pension credit".

3913. Social security administration–Care homes–Independent hospitals

SOCIAL SECURITY (CARE HOMES AND INDEPENDENT HOSPITALS) REGULATIONS 2005, SI 2005 2687; made under the Social Security Contributions and Benefits Act 1992 s.67, s.72, s.123, s.130, s.135, s.136, s.136A, s.137, s.138, s.175; the Social Security Administration Act 1992 s.1, s.5, s.189; the Jobseekers Act 1995 s.4, s.12, s.20, s.20B, s.35, s.36, Sch.1 para.1, Sch.1 para.8, Sch.1 para.8A, Sch.1 para.10, Sch.1 para.12; the Housing Act 1996 s.122; the Child Support, Pensions and Social Security Act 2000 s.62, s.63, s.65; the Social Security Fraud Act 2001 s.7, s.8, s.11; and the State Pension Credit Act 2002 s.2, s.6, s.15, s.17. In force: October 24, 2005; £3.50.

These Regulations, which revoke the Income Support and Jobseeker's Allowance (Amounts for Persons in Residential Care and Nursing Homes) Regulations 2001 (SI 2001 1785), amend the Social Fund Maternity and Funeral Expenses (General) Regulations 1987 (SI 1987 481), the Income Support (General) Regulations 1987 (SI 1987 1967), the Social Security (Claims and Payments) Regulations 1987 (SI 1987 1968), the Housing Benefit (General) Regulations 1987 (SI 1987 1971), the Social Fund Cold Weather Payments (General) Regulations 1988 (SI 1988 1724), the Social Security (Attendance Allowance) Regulations 1991 (SI 1991 2740), the Social Security (Disability Living Allowance) Regulations 1991 (SI 1991 2890), the Council Tax Benefit (General) Regulations 1992 (SI 1992 1814), the Jobseeker's Allowance Regulations 1996 (SI 1996 207), the Social Fund Winter Fuel Payment Regulations 2000 (SI 2000 729), the Social Security (Breach of Community Order) Regulations 2001 (SI 2001 1395), the Social Security (Loss of Benefit) Regulations 2001 (SI 2001 4022) and the State Pension Credit Regulations 2002 (SI 2002 1792). The Regulations make amendments to social security legislation that are consequential upon the introduction of a new regulatory system in England and Wales of "care homes" and "independent hospitals" by the Care Standards Act 2000 and, in Scotland, of "care home services" and "independent health care services" by the Regulation of Care (Scotland) Act 2001. This has replaced the previous system of regulation of residential care homes and nursing homes, as provided for by the Registered Homes Act 1984 in England and Wales, and, in Scotland by the Nursing Homes Registration (Scotland) Act 1938 and the Social Work (Scotland) Act 1968. The new systems also require the registration of care homes provided by local authorities, which were previously unregulated.

3914. Social security administration–Statutory maternity and sick pay– Production of documentation by employers

STATUTORY MATERNITY PAY (GENERAL) AND STATUTORY SICK PAY (GENERAL) (AMENDMENT) REGULATIONS 2005, SI 2005 989; made under the Social Security Administration Act 1992 s.113, s.130, s.132, s.189. In force: in accordance with Reg.1 (2); £3.00.

These Regulations amend the Statutory Sick Pay (General) Regulations 1982 (SI 1982 894) and the Statutory Maternity Pay (General) Regulations 1986 (SI 1986 1960) to require employers to produce records relating to statutory maternity pay to an authorised officer of the Inland Revenue within 30 days of a notice being issued to that effect; and to specify the types of documents that must be produced, where production must take place and that production does not affect any lien over the records.

3915. Social security commissioners–Appeals–Procedure

SOCIAL SECURITY COMMISSIONERS (PROCEDURE) (AMENDMENT) REGULATIONS 2005, SI 2005 870; made under the Pensions Appeal Tribunals Act 1943 s.6A, s.6C, s.6D, s.11A; the Social Security Act 1998 s.14, s.15, s.16, s.28, s.79, s.84, Sch.4, Sch.5; the Child Support, Pensions and Social Security Act 2000 Sch.7 para.8, Sch.7 para.9, Sch.7 para.10, Sch.7 para.19, Sch.7

para.20, Sch.7 para.23; and the Forfeiture Act 1982 s.4. In force: April 6, 2005; £3.00.

The Pensions Appeal Tribunal Act 1943, as amended by the Armed Forces (Pension and Compensation) Act 2004, provides for an onward right of appeal from the Pensions Appeal Tribunal to the Social Security Commissioners constituted under the Social Security Act 1998. These Regulations amend the Social Security Commissioners (Procedure) Regulations 1999 (SI 1999 1495) to provide procedure for the Social Security Commissioners to deal with applications for leave to appeal and appeals from the Pensions Appeal Tribunal in the same way as they deal with applications and appeals from the appeal tribunal constituted under the Social Security Act 1998.

3916. Social security commissioners–Appeals and applications–Procedure

SOCIAL SECURITY COMMISSIONERS (PROCEDURE) (CHILD TRUST FUNDS) REGULATIONS 2005, SI 2005 1031; made under the Social Security Act 1998 s.14, s.15, s.16, s.28, s.79, s.84, Sch.4, Sch.5. In force: March 25, 2005; £3.00.

These Regulations regulate the procedure of the Social Security Commissioners in determining appeals and applications arising from decisions of appeal tribunals in relation to child trust funds.

3917. Social security offences–Housing benefit–Offence of failing to notify change in circumstances–Meaning of Sch.2 para.13 Tax Credits Act 1999

[Social Security Administration Act 1992 s.112, s.116(2)(b), s.116(3)(b); Tax Credits Act 1999 Sch.2 para.13.]

The appellant (E) appealed by way of case stated against her convictions in the magistrates' court for offences under the Social Security Administration Act 1992. E had been convicted of two separate offences of failing to promptly notify the respondent local authority of a relevant change in her circumstances, when she knew that the change would affect her entitlement to housing benefit, contrary to s.112(1A) of the 1992 Act. The change of circumstances relied upon by the local authority in the magistrates' court was an increase in E's entitlement to working families tax credit. Before the magistrates' court E argued that the provisions of the Tax Credits Act 1999 Sch.2 para.13 precluded the local authority from bringing a prosecution under s.112(1A) of the 1992 Act. E also argued that the information laid against her was outside the time limit specified in s.116(2)(b) of the 1992 Act. The magistrates' court found that Sch.2 para.13 of the 1999 Act provided no defence to E. The court further found that the delay in instituting proceedings against E had been satisfactorily explained by her failure to attend for interview on three occasions. On appeal issues arose as to whether in the instant case (1) Sch.2 para.13 of the 1999 Act prevented a prosecution relating to the obtaining of housing benefit under s.112(1A) of the 1992 Act; (2) the information laid against E had been laid outside the time limit specified in s.116(2)(b) of the 1992 Act.

Held, allowing the appeal, that (1) Sch.2 para.13 of the 1999 Act did not prevent a prosecution relating to the obtaining of housing benefit under s.112(1A) of the 1992 Act. In applying Sch.2 para.13, the question to be determined was whether a benefit or failure to notify referred to a tax credit or not. In the instant case, the benefit was plainly a housing benefit and did not relate to a tax credit. Although the change in circumstances had related to E's tax credit, it had affected her entitlement to housing benefit, so that her failure to promptly notify the local authority amounted to an offence under s.112(1A) of the 1992 Act. (2) The information laid against E had been laid outside the time limit specified in s.116(2)(b) of the 1992 Act. The statutory test in s.116(2)(b) focused on the date on which sufficient evidence was available to justify a prosecution and not on justifications for delaying a prosecution. In the circumstances of the instant case, it had not been open to the magistrates' court to rely upon the certificate of sufficient evidence, as issued under s.116(3)(b) of the 1992 Act. In addition, the information relied on had been available without there being a need to interview E. Accordingly, the magistrates' court had erred in finding that delaying instituting proceedings against E had been satisfactorily explained by her failure to attend for interview on three occasions.

EYESON v. MILTON KEYNES COUNCIL, [2005] EWHC 1160, [2005] H.L.R. 38, Maurice Kay, L.J., QBD (Admin Ct).

3918. State pension credit−Interim assistance grant

INCOME-RELATED BENEFITS (AMENDMENT) REGULATIONS 2005, SI 2005 2183; made under the Social Security Contributions and Benefits Act 1992 s.123, s.136, s.137, s.175; the Jobseekers Act 1995 s.12, s.35, s.36; and the State Pension Credit Act 2002 s.15, s.17. In force: August 5, 2005; £3.00.

These Regulations amend the Income Support (General) Regulations 1987 (SI 1987 1967), the Housing Benefit (General) Regulations 1987 (SI 1987 1971), the Council Tax Benefit (General) Regulations 1992 (SI 1992 1814), the Jobseeker's Allowance Regulations 1996 (SI 1996 207) and the State Pension Credit Regulations 2002 (SI 2002 1792). The Regulations make provision for an interim assistance grant paid by the London Bombings Relief Charitable Fund to a person who was injured, or was a partner or close relative of someone killed, in or as a result of the terrorist attacks carried out in London on July 7, 2005, to be disregarded when calculating that person's capital for the purpose of an award of benefit where the grant is paid during the award. The disregard will last for the remainder of that award. They also provide for an interim assistance grant paid by that Fund to a person who was a partner or close relative of someone killed in, or as a result of, those attacks to be disregarded when calculating that person's income from capital for the purpose of an award of state pension credit where the grant is paid during the award. Again, the disregard will last for the remainder of that award.

3919. State retirement pension−Home responsibilities

SOCIAL SECURITY PENSIONS (HOME RESPONSIBILITIES) (AMENDMENT) REGULATIONS 2005, SI 2005 48; made under the Social Security Contributions and Benefits Act 1992 s.122, s.175, Sch.3 para.5. In force: February 9, 2005; £3.00.

These Regulations amend the Social Security Pensions (Home Responsibilities) Regulations 1994 (SI 1994 704) by the insertion of a new paragraph which applies to tax years from 2004-2005 onwards where child benefit entitlement is transferred to a person in respect of a child in the first three months of a tax year and child benefit would have been payable to that person for the part of that year falling before that transfer but for the provisions of the Child Benefit (General) Regulations 2003 (SI 2003 493). Where it applies, the new paragraph provides that such a person shall be treated as if he were entitled to child benefit and as if child benefit had been payable to him for that part of that year, in order to be treated for the purpose of the 1994 Regulations as precluded from regular employment in that year due to responsibilities at home.

3920. State retirement pension−Low earnings threshold

SOCIAL SECURITY PENSIONS (LOW EARNINGS THRESHOLD) ORDER 2005, SI 2005 217; made under the Social Security Administration Act 1992 s.148A. In force: April 6, 2005; £3.00.

This Order directs that the low earnings threshold for the tax years following 2004-2005 shall be £12,100.

3921. Statutory maternity pay−Entitlement

STATUTORY MATERNITY PAY (GENERAL) (AMENDMENT) REGULATIONS 2005, SI 2005 729; made under the Social Security Contributions and Benefits Act 1992 s.164, s.171, s.175. In force: April 6, 2005; £3.00.

These Regulations amend the Statutory Maternity Pay (General) Regulations 1986 (SI 1986 1960) by inserting a definition of statutory maternity leave. They also make amendments to include in normal weekly earnings for the purpose of calculating entitlement to statutory maternity pay any pay increase which applies to the whole or any part of the period between the beginning of the period when pay is calculated to determine entitlement to statutory maternity pay and the end of the period of statutory maternity leave; and to provide that where a woman is entitled to statutory maternity pay in consequence of a pay increase, the employer shall only make payments of statutory maternity pay in any week if, and to the extent by which, her statutory maternity pay exceeds any maternity allowance received by her.

3922. Students-Discrimination-Eligibility of national of another Member State for student loan-Rights of residence-European Community

[EC Treaty Art.12, Art.18, Art.149(1).]

A question was referred to the European Court of Justice for a preliminary ruling as to whether the EC Treaty Art.12 prohibiting discrimination on grounds of nationality applied to the allocation of student loans and grants. The claimant (B), a French national, had lived in the United Kingdom for three years and had completed his secondary education there. He commenced a university course and was given assistance with his tuition fees, but was told that he was not eligible for a student loan as he was not settled in the United Kingdom, a status that students could not obtain. B brought proceedings in the United Kingdom against the respondent local authority, claiming he was being discriminated against contrary to Art.12. The English court referred questions as to (1) whether maintenance assistance to students fell outside the scope of Art.12; (2) what criteria could be applied to the granting of assistance in order to ensure it was done objectively and not on grounds of nationality.

Held, giving a preliminary ruling, that (1) all nationals of Member States were guaranteed citizenship of the EU and this status was not lost by those, including students, who moved to other Member States. A person such as B, who had completed his secondary education in another Member State without recourse to public funds, had a right to residence under Art.18 of the Treaty, *D'Hoop v. Office National de l'Emploi (C224/98)* [2003] All E.R. (EC) 527, [2003] C.L.Y. 1445 applied. Since the introduction of Art.149(1) to the Treaty, cooperation between Member States in respect of education was to be encouraged, and in particular the free movement of students and teachers. Thus, maintenance assistance to such students, lawfully resident in another Member State, did come within Art.12, *Martinez Sala v. Freistaat Bayern (C85/96)* [1998] E.C.R. I-2691 and *Grzelczyk v. Centre Public d'Aide Sociale d'Ottignies Louvain la Neuve (C184/99)* [2003] All E.R. (EC) 385, [2001] C.L.Y. 2496 applied. (2) Member States were entitled to limit maintenance assistance to those showing a sufficient degree of integration into the society of the State, for example through being resident there for a specific period. However, the UK blanket prohibition on students obtaining settled status meant that no such student could ever qualify for assistance no matter how integrated they were. Thus such measures did not meet the requirement of objectivity and were precluded by Art.12.

R. (ON THE APPLICATION OF BIDAR) v. EALING LBC (C209/03) [2005] Q.B. 812, Judge Skouris (President), ECJ.

3923. Students-Income related benefits

SOCIAL SECURITY (STUDENTS AND INCOME-RELATED BENEFITS) AMENDMENT REGULATIONS 2005, SI 2005 1807; made under the Social Security Contributions and Benefits Act 1992 s.123, s.136, s.137, s.175; and the Jobseekers Act 1995, s.12, s.35, s.36. In force: in accordance with Reg.1; £3.00.

These Regulations further amend the Council Tax Benefit (General) Regulations 1992 (SI 1992 1814), the Housing Benefit (General) Regulations 1987 (SI 1987 1971), the Income Support (General) Regulations 1987 (SI 1987 1967), the Jobseeker's Allowance Regulations 1996 (SI 1996 207) and the Social Security (Working Tax Credit and Child Tax Credit) (Consequential Amendments) Regulations 2003 (SI 2003 455) in so far as they relate to students and sums to be disregarded in the calculation of their entitlement to benefit under the Income-related Benefits Regulations.

3924. Tax credits–Child support–Miscellaneous amendments

SOCIAL SECURITY, CHILD SUPPORT AND TAX CREDITS (MISCELLANEOUS AMENDMENTS) REGULATIONS 2005, SI 2005 337; made under the Vaccine Damage Payments Act 1979 s.4; the Child Support Act 1991 s.20; the Social Security Contributions and Benefits Act 1992 s.124, s.137, s.175; the Social Security Administration Act 1992 s.5, s.6, s.7A, s.71, s.73, s.74, s.189, s.191; the Social Security (Recovery of Benefits) Act 1997 s.11; the Social Security Act 1998 s.6, s.9, s.10, s.12, s.14, s.16, s.17, s.28, s.79, s.84, Sch.5 para.1, Sch.5 para.3, Sch.5 para.4, Sch.5 para.6; and the Child Support, Pensions and Social Security Act 2000 s.68, Sch.7 para.3, Sch.7 para.6, Sch.7 para.10, Sch.7 para.20, Sch.7 para.23. In force: March 18, 2005; £3.00.

These Regulations amend the Social Security (Overlapping Benefits) Regulations 1979 (SI 1979 597), the Social Security (Industrial Injuries) (Prescribed Diseases) Regulations 1985 (SI 1985 967), the Income Support (General) Regulations 1987 (SI 1987 1967), the Social Security (Claims and Payments) Regulations 1987 (SI 1987 1968), the Housing Benefit (General) Regulations 1987 (SI 1987 1971), the Social Security (Payments on account, Overpayments and Recovery) Regulations 1988 (SI 1988 664), the Council Tax Benefit (General) Regulations 1992 (SI 1992 1814), the Social Security and Child Support (Decisions and Appeals) Regulations 1999 (SI 1999 991), the Housing Benefit and Council Tax Benefit (Decisions and Appeals) Regulations 2001 (SI 2001 1002) and the Tax Credits (Appeals) (No.2) Regulations 2002 (SI 2002 3196). They make amendments to add further circumstances in which a social security benefit decision may be revised; add further circumstances in which a benefit decision may be superseded; make further provision for making appeals; remove the need for the appellant's consent to the use of a live television link at an appeal hearing; clarify the procedure and time for applying for leave to appeal to a Commissioner; provide for the finality of a specified determination necessary to a benefit decision; and make further provision in respect of specified benefit claims made to a designated office or an authorised local authority. The Regulations also make further provision in respect of those appointed to act for a benefit claimant; provide for an interim payment where it is impractical to satisfy national insurance number requirements; provide for the recovery of duplicate payments of benefit from payments of contribution-based jobseeker's allowance; and clarify a limitation on the right to deduct a recoverable overpayment from prescribed benefits.

3925. Tax credits–Civil partnerships

CIVIL PARTNERSHIP ACT 2004 (TAX CREDITS, ETC.) (CONSEQUENTIAL AMENDMENTS) ORDER 2005, SI 2005 2919; made under the Civil Partnership Act 2004 s.254, s.259. In force: December 5, 2005; £3.00.

The Civil Partnership Act 2004 introduced the concept of "civil partnership" for couples of the same sex. As a result of that Act this Order makes consequential amendments to the Child Benefit and Social Security (Fixing and Adjustment of Rates) Regulations 1976 (SI 1976 1267), the Child Benefit and Social Security (Fixing and Adjustment of Rates) (Northern Ireland) Regulations 1976 (SR 1976 223), the Social Security Benefit (Computation of Earnings) Regulations 1996 (SI 1996 2745), the Social Security Benefit (Computation of Earnings) Regulations (Northern Ireland) 1996 (SR 1996 520), the Working Tax Credit (Entitlement and Maximum Rate) Regulations 2002 (SI 2002 2005), the Tax Credits (Definition and Calculation of Income) Regulations 2002 (SI 2002 2006), the Child Tax Credit Regulations 2002 (SI 2002 2007), the Tax Credits (Claims and Notifications) Regulations 2002 (SI 2002 2014), the Tax Credits (Payments by the Commissioners) Regulations 2002 (SI 2002 2173), the Tax Credits (Immigration) Regulations 2003 (SI 2003 653), the Tax Credits (Residence) Regulations 2003 (SI 2003 654), the Tax Credits (Provision of Information)

(Functions Relating to Health) Regulations 2003 (SI 2003 731), the Child Benefit (General) Regulations 2003 (SI 2003 493), the Guardian's Allowance (General) Regulations 2003 (SI 2003 495), the Child Benefit and Guardian's Allowance (Administration) Regulations 2003 (SI 2003 492) and the Child Trust Funds Regulations 2004 (SI 2004 1450). The amendments relate to terminology and in particular introduce new definitions of "partner" and "couple".

3926. **Widows benefits–Sex discrimination–Widow's pension–Infringement of Convention rights**

[Social Security Contributions and Benefits Act 1992 s.36, s.37, s.38; Human Rights Act 1998 s.6, s.7(1)(a), Sch.1 Part I Art.8, Sch.1 Part I Art.14, Sch.1 Part II Art.1; Welfare Reform and Pensions Act 1999.]

The appellant secretary of state appealed against the decision ([2003] EWCA Civ 813, [2003] 1 W.L.R. 2623) in relation to claims by the respondent widowers (W) to social security and pension payments to which they would have been entitled had they been widows, and W cross appealed. W had claimed that after the death of their wives the non payment to them of amounts equivalent to widow's payment under the Social Security Contributions and Benefits Act 1992 s.36, widowed mother's allowance under s.37 of that Act and widow's pension under s.38, was contrary to their rights under the Human Rights Act 1998 Sch.1 Part I Art.14 read with Sch.1 Part II Art.1 and Sch.1 Part I Art.8. The Welfare Reform and Pensions Act 1999 abolished widow's benefits for widows whose husbands died on or after April 9, 2001. W brought proceedings on the basis that after the coming into force of the 1998 Act the secretary of state had acted incompatibly with their Convention rights and therefore contrary to s.6(1) of the 1998 Act in denying them the benefits that a widow would have received, and that they were victims of the secretary of state's unlawful acts or omissions and therefore entitled to bring proceedings under s.7(1)(a) of the 1998 Act. The secretary of state submitted that (1) discrimination between men and women in the payment of widow's pension was objectively justified; (2) although discrimination in the payment of widow's payment and widowed mother's allowance infringed the Convention rights of widowers, it was not unlawful under s.6(1) because the application of that subsection was excluded by s.6(2) of the 1998 Act.

Held, allowing the appeal and dismissing the cross appeal, that (1) the preservation of widow's pension for widows bereaved before April 9, 2001 was objectively justified on grounds that older widows as a class were likely to be needier than older widowers as a class or younger widows as a class, and involved no breach of Convention rights. (2) The secretary of state was entitled to rely on the s.6(2) defence, either under s.6(2)(b), on the basis that in deciding not to make matching payments the secretary of state "was acting so as to give effect to" s.36 and s.37 of the 1992 Act, which mandated payment of the benefits to widows only, or under s.6(2)(a), on the basis that, "as a result of" s.36 and s.37, the secretary of state "could not have acted differently" because he had to pay the widows and could not lawfully have made matching payments to widowers. (3) (Obiter) W would have been victims for the purposes of bringing an action under s.7(1)(a) because they had done enough in the circumstances to demonstrate that they would have made a claim for the relevant benefits if that had been possible. (4) (Obiter) If the secretary of state had not been protected by s.6(2), he would not have been able to resist liability on the grounds that a period for changing the law ought to have been taken into account, *Walden v. Liechtenstein (Admissibility) (33916/96)* (Unreported, March 16, 2000) considered. (5) (Obiter) The government's refusal to make extra statutory payments to W in the same way as it had to widowers who had petitioned the European Court of Human Rights before the 1998 Act came into force was not itself discrimination contrary to Art.14

R. (ON THE APPLICATION OF HOOPER) v. SECRETARY OF STATE FOR WORK AND PENSIONS; R. (ON THE APPLICATION OF WITHEY) v. SECRETARY OF STATE FOR WORK AND PENSIONS; R. (ON THE APPLICATION OF NAYLOR) v. SECRETARY OF STATE FOR WORK AND PENSIONS; R. (ON THE APPLICATION OF MARTIN) v. SECRETARY OF STATE FOR WORK AND PENSIONS; *sub nom.*

HOOPER v. SECRETARY OF STATE FOR WORK AND PENSIONS, [2005] UKHL 29, [2005] 1 W.L.R. 1681, Lord Nicholls of Birkenhead, HL.

3927. Books

Arrowsmith, Peter; Golding, Jon—Tolley's National Insurance Contributions: Main Annual. Paperback: £86.00. ISBN 0 7545 2765 4. Tolley Publishing.

Arrowsmith, Peter; Golding, Jon—Tolley's National Insurance Contributions: Main Annual Plus Supplement. Paperback: £99.95. ISBN 0 7545 2866 9. Tolley Publishing.

Bonner, David; Hooker, Ian; White, Robin—Social Security Legislation: Vol 1. Non Means Tested Benefits, 2004/2005 Supplement (Supplement to Vols I, II, III and IV). Paperback: £42.00. ISBN 0 421 90560 3. Sweet & Maxwell.

Bonner, David; Hooker, Ian; White, Robin—Social Security Legislation: V. 1. Non Means Tested Benefits. Paperback: £77.00. ISBN 0 421 92030 0. Sweet & Maxwell.

Browne, Kevin; Pothecary, Judith—Welfare Benefits and Immigration Law. Paperback: £24.95. ISBN 0 905835 78 6. Paperback: £25.95. ISBN 1 905391 11 0. The College of Law.

Buck, Trevor—Social Fund: Law and Practice. Paperback: £72.00. ISBN 0 421 88120 8. Sweet & Maxwell.

Buck, Trevor; Bonner, David; Sainsbury, Roy—Making Social Security Law: The Role and Work of the Social Security and Child Support Commissioners. Hardback: £50.00. ISBN 0 7546 4381 6. Ashgate.

Burca, Grainne de—EU Law and the Welfare State: In Search of Solidarity. Collected Courses of the Academy of European Law. Paperback: £22.50. ISBN 0 19 928741 4. Oxford University Press.

Enalls, Simon—Social Security Benefits: A Practical Guide. Paperback: £49.95. ISBN 1 84592 197 6. Tottel Publishing.

Findlay, Lorna; Wright, Stewart; George, Carolyn; Poynter, Richard—CPAG's Housing Benefit and Council Tax Benefit Legislation. Paperback: £71.00. ISBN 1 901698 82 3. CPAG.

McDowell, Jacqui—Child Support Handbook. Paperback: £21.50. ISBN 1 901698 80 7. CPAG.

Pestieau, Pierre—Welfare State in the European Union: Economic and Social Perspectives. Hardback: £45.00. ISBN 0 19 926101 6. Paperback: £20.00. ISBN 0 19 926102 4. Oxford University Press.

Rowland, Mark; White, Robin—Social Security: Vol 3. Administration, Adjudication and the European Dimension: Legislation 2005. Paperback: £77.00. ISBN 0 421 92070 X. Sweet & Maxwell.

Seddon, Duran; Fitzpatrick, Pamela—Migration and Social Security Handbook. Paperback: £21.00. ISBN 1 901698 77 7. CPAG.

Stagg, Paul—Supplement: CPAG's Housing Benefit and Council Tax Benefit Legislation. Paperback: £20.00. ISBN 1 901698 70 X. CPAG.

Wikeley, Nick; Williams, David—Social Security: V. 4. Tax Credits: Legislation 2005. Paperback: £77.00. ISBN 0 421 92090 4. Sweet & Maxwell.

Wood, Penny; Wikeley, Nick; Poynter, Richard; Bonner, David—Social Security: Vol 2. Income Related Benefits: Legislation 2005. Paperback: £77.00. ISBN 0 421 92050 5. Sweet & Maxwell.

SOCIAL WELFARE

3928. Care—Children—Severely disabled children—Local authority's entitlement to have regard to parents' resources

[Chronically Sick and Disabled Persons Act 1970 s.2; Children Act 1989 s.17, s.29.]

The appellant children (S) appealed, by their mother as litigation friend, against the decision ([2004] EWHC 2314) that the respondent local authority was entitled to have regard to the resources of S's parents in deciding whether it was necessary to provide assistance to S as disabled children under the Chronically Sick and Disabled Persons Act 1970 s.2. S were two severely disabled boys. Their parents looked after them at home with the help of carers. The home needed alterations in order to enable the boys to be cared for safely. The parents contended that the local authority was under a statutory duty to provide and pay for the alterations. The local authority contended that whether it owed such a duty depended on whether the parents could reasonably be expected to pay for the alterations themselves. In order to reach a decision on that question the local authority asked the parents to provide details of their means. The parents declined to do so and commenced judicial review proceedings to determine whether the local authority was entitled to take their means into account when deciding whether or not to pay for the alterations. The judge held that the local authority could do so. The local authority submitted that if it paid for the alterations it would have a statutory right to recover from the parents all or part of the costs incurred.

Held, dismissing the appeal, that (1) where a local authority provided services in accordance with obligations imposed by s.2 of the 1970 Act by exercising functions under the Children Act 1989 s.17 the provision of those services was subject to such rights to charge as were conferred by s.29 of the 1989 Act. In the instant case that right to charge could only arise in respect of the brother who was under the age of 16. (2) As a general proposition a local authority could reasonably expect that parents who could afford the expense would make any alterations to their home that were necessary for the care of their disabled children, if there was no alternative source of providing them. It was also reasonable to anticipate that some parents with means would not do so if they believed that that would result in the local authority making the alterations for them. Having regard to those considerations the judge was right to hold that a local authority could, in circumstances such as those in the instant case, properly decline to be satisfied that it was necessary to provide services to meet the needs of disabled children until it had been demonstrated that, having regard to their means, it was not reasonable to expect their parents to provide them, *R. v. Gloucestershire CC, ex p. Barry* [1997] A.C. 584, [1997] C.L.Y. 4714 applied.

R. (ON THE APPLICATION OF SPINK) v. WANDSWORTH LBC, [2005] EWCA Civ 302, [2005] 1 W.L.R. 2884, Lord Phillips of Worth Matravers, M.R., CA (Civ Div).

3929. Care homes—Managers—Burden of proof on registration requirements

[Registered Homes Act 1984; Care Standards Act 2000 Part II; Care Homes Regulations 2001 (SI 2001 3965) Reg.9.]

The appellant (J) appealed against a decision ([2004] EWHC 918) upholding the refusal of the National Care Standards Commission to grant him registration under the Care Standards Act 2000 Part II as manager of a care home. The commission had refused J's application to be registered as manager of a care home under the registration process set out under the 2000 Act and the Care Homes Regulations 2001 Reg.9. J had deliberately concealed disciplinary proceedings pending against him when he completed his registration form, and had failed to impress the commission's representatives about his knowledge of the law and theoretical management of care homes during the course of the registration process. J appealed to the Care Standards Tribunal, which decided the appeal in J's favour, stating that the burden was upon the commission to prove J's lack of fitness on the balance of probabilities, and made a finding that the balance favoured J. On appeal from the tribunal, the burden of proof question was left undecided. The court allowed the commission's appeal on other grounds.

Held, dismissing the appeal, that the provisions of Reg.9 represented an attempt to codify the effect of former case law, with the significant difference that under the old scheme, as laid down under the repealed Registered Homes Act 1984, the registration authority had to be satisfied that the person concerned was not a fit person for the purpose before it could refuse registration, while under the new scheme of the 2000 Act and the 2001 Regulations, the registration authority had to be satisfied that a person was so fit before it could grant his application. Therefore an applicant had to demonstrate to the commission, and if there was an appeal, to the tribunal, that he was a fit person before he could qualify for registration. The tribunal had therefore erred in stating that the burden was upon the commission to prove J's unfitness. The 2001 Regulations clearly set out the conditions which an applicant had to satisfy before he could be registered as a manager of a care home under the 2000 Act. He had to be a person of integrity and good character; he needed to have the requisite qualifications, skills and experience necessary for managing the care home and he needed to be both physically and mentally fit. The court, having stated the legal principles which ought to underscore a tribunal's approach, remitted the case to a differently constituted tribunal for determination.

JONES v. COMMISSION FOR SOCIAL CARE INSPECTION; *sub nom.* R. (ON THE APPLICATION OF NATIONAL CARE STANDARDS COMMISSION) v. JONES, [2004] EWCA Civ 1713, [2005] 1 W.L.R. 2461, Brooke, L.J., CA (Civ Div).

3930. Care plans–Childrens welfare–Appointment of child's personal adviser– Completion of pathway plan

[Children (Leaving Care) Act 2000; Children (Leaving Care) (Wales) Regulations 2001 (SI 2001 2189) Reg.12.]

The applicant (J) sought declarations and mandatory orders requiring the respondent local authority to produce a lawful assessment and pathway plan for him, and to provide suitable accommodation for him. The local authority had been granted a full care order in September 2002 in respect of J, who was 17 years old. J was a "looked after" child for the purposes of the Children (Leaving Care) Act 2000. J had a long criminal record and had been in detention. J had not cooperated with the local authority in its attempts to help him. A personal adviser (S) had been appointed by the local authority for J but no pathway plan was completed for him. J sent a letter before claim in November 2004 and the local authority responded that a needs assessment and pathway plan had been completed but that the documents had not been shared with J. The documents were in fact incomplete, unsigned and undated. Following the commencement of proceedings, the local authority produced revised pathway plans completed by S. J was released from a young offender's institution in January 2005. J submitted that (1) it was wrong in principle to appoint S to act as J's personal adviser as he was a member of the local authority's own staff, and that S had misunderstood his role; (2) the process by which the assessments and pathway plans were produced was deficient; (3) the content of the assessments and pathway plans was inadequate; and (4) the local authority had failed to provide him with suitable accommodation on his release and accordingly had neglected its parental responsibilities towards J. The local authority submitted that it had taken extensive steps to try to find accommodation for J but that J's electronic tag was an obstacle for private landlords.

Held, granting the application in part, that (1) there was nothing in the case law or relevant legislation which made it unlawful or undesirable to appoint an employee of the local authority as a child's personal adviser. However, it was important that both the adviser and the local authority recognised that the adviser was acting in the role of adviser to the child and not in some other conflicting role. It was in breach of the Children (Leaving Care) (Wales) Regulations 2001 Reg.12 for S to have prepared J's pathway plans. J was entitled to a mandatory order for the local authority to appoint a more suitable personal adviser. (2) The deficiencies in the process were obvious. The local authority had embarked on the process too late. The pathway plan should have been completed by September 2003. The steps taken to involve J in the process were also inadequate. (3) The pathway plans were hopelessly inadequate and contained little more than aspirations. The local authority used standard pro forma pathway plans which failed to address financial support and would have been better advised to have used the Department of Health's pro forma prepared in 2002. The original pathway plan, as well as the revised plans, failed to meet the requirements of the Regulations. A pathway plan had to clearly identify the child's needs, and what was to be done about them, by whom and by when. J was entitled to declarations that the pathway plans failed to comply with the Regulations and mandatory orders requiring the local authority to produce a lawful assessment and pathway plan. (4) J would not be granted relief for the failure to find suitable accommodation as the court was not in a position to make findings of fact which entitled it to reject the local authority's clear evidence that all its extensive efforts had proved unsuccessful. (5) The fact that a child was uncooperative was no reason for a local authority not to carry out its obligations under the Act and the Regulations; the local authority had to do its best. Any hindrance due to a child's lack of engagement had to be clearly documented in the assessment and pathway plan.

R. (ON THE APPLICATION OF J) v. CAERPHILLY CBC, [2005] EWHC 586, [2005] 2 F.L.R. 860, Munby, J., QBD (Admin).

3931. **Care plans–Disabled persons–Assessment of health needs–Requirement to comply with Circular LAC (2002) 13: Fair Access to Care Services**

[National Assistance Act 1948 s.29; Chronically Sick and Disabled Persons Act 1970 s.2; Local Authority Social Services Act 1970 s.7(1); National Health Service and Community Care Act 1990 s.47.]

The applicant (H) sought judicial review of the assessment of his health needs undertaken by the local authority pursuant to its obligations under the National Health Service and Community Care Act 1990 s.47. H, a man aged nearly 47, was severely handicapped, being almost completely blind and suffering from Still's disease. The local authority was obliged to provide him with care under the National Assistance Act 1948 s.29 and the Chronically Sick and Disabled Persons Act 1970 s.2. The local authority's care plan indicated that H required 24 and a half hours of care a week but H claimed his condition urgently required care at levels of 27 to 30 hours a week. He argued that S's method of assessment of his needs had failed to follow the Fair Access to Care Services (FACS) guidelines issued by the Department of Health under the Local Authority Social Services Act 1970 s.7(1) in Circular LAC (2002), and that on a correct application of those guidelines, S's assessment was perverse.

Held, granting the application, that in assessing a person's eligibility for care, an authority was required to assess the presenting person's needs and the risks to the person's independence. The FACS guidance identified four bands within the eligibility framework: critical, substantial, moderate and low. The FACS guidance required a risk evaluation exercise to be undertaken, and in carrying out that exercise the local authority had been required to treat risks attending significant health problems as bringing the case within the critical band. It had in fact wrongly treated those risks pertaining to H's health as falling with the substantial band. The care plan was accordingly remitted to the local authority for reconsideration on this basis, although on the evidence the court was not able to say that the allocation of 24 and a half hours was perverse.

R. (ON THE APPLICATION OF HEFFERNAN) v. SHEFFIELD CITY COUNCIL, [2004] EWHC 1377, (2004) 7 C.C.L. Rep. 350, Collins, J., QBD (Admin Ct).

3932. **Care plans–Disabled persons–Local authority's failure to provide pathway plan in accordance with statutory obligations**

[Children Act 1989 Sch.2 para.19B(4); Children (Leaving Care) (England) Regulations 2001 (SI 2001 2874).]

The applicant (P), a severely disabled boy aged 17, made an application for judicial review of the local authority's failure properly to assess his future needs once he attained the age of 18 and ceased to be a child looked after by the local authority. Under the Children Act 1989 Sch.2 para.19B(4), the local authority was required to assess P's needs in order to determine the assistance he would require at that time, and prepare a pathway plan. P's grandmother had unsuccessfully attempted to obtain that information and commenced proceedings on his behalf. The local authority maintained that there was a transitional plan in place whereby P would be transferred to adult services at the age of 19.

Held, granting the application, that whilst the local authority had made appropriate arrangements for P, it had failed to comply with the 1989 Act or with the Children (Leaving Care) (England) Regulations 2001 in that it had failed to prepare a satisfactory pathway plan.

R. (ON THE APPLICATION OF P) v. NEWHAM LBC, [2004] EWHC 2210, [2005] 2 F.C.R. 171, Ouseley, J., QBD (Admin).

3933. Care standards–Adoption support agencies–Registration

CARE STANDARDS ACT 2000 (COMMENCEMENT NO.9 (ENGLAND) AND TRANSITIONAL AND SAVINGS PROVISIONS) (AMENDMENT) 2005, SI 2005 3397; made under the Care Standards Act 2000 s.118, s.122. In force: December 8, 2005; £3.00.

This Order amends the Care Standards Act 2000 (Commencement No.9 (England) and Transitional and Savings Provisions) Order 2001 (SI 2001 3852) to make transitional provision in relation to the registration of adoption support agencies.

3934. Care standards–Social workers–Registers

CARE STANDARDS ACT 2000 (RELEVANT REGISTERS OF SOCIAL WORKERS) REGULATIONS 2005, SI 2005 491; made under the Care Standards Act 2000 s.61, s.118. In force: April 1, 2005; £3.00.

These Regulations prescribe the registers of social workers maintained under provisions of Scottish and Northern Irish legislation which correspond to the registers maintained by the General Social Care Council and the Care Council for Wales respectively under the Care Standards Act 2000. The purpose of prescribing these registers is to ensure that an individual registered in either of them will not be guilty of an offence if he takes or uses the title "social worker" while working in such a capacity in either England or Wales.

3935. Care Standards Act 2000 (c.14)–Commencement No.21 Order–Wales

CARE STANDARDS ACT 2000 (COMMENCEMENT NO.21) ORDER 2005, SI 2005 375 (W.36; C.17); made under the Care Standards Act 2000 s.118, s.122. Commencement details: bringing into force various provisions of the 2000 Act on March 1, 2005 and April 1, 2005; £3.00.

This Order brings into force the Care Standards Act 2000 s.61 (2) (b), in so far as it is not already in force, for the purpose of making regulations which will prescribe the registers of social workers maintained in Scotland and Northern Ireland which correspond to the registers maintained by the General Social Care Council and the Care Council for Wales; and s.61, in so far as it is not already in force, which provides for the protection of the title "social worker" by the creation of an offence, punishable by a fine of up to level 5 on the standard scale, for a person who is not registered as a social worker to use that title or hold himself out as a registered social worker with an intention to deceive. An individual will not be guilty of an offence if they are registered with an equivalent regulatory body in another part of the UK.

3936. Carers–Equal opportunities–Scilly Isles

CARERS (EQUAL OPPORTUNITIES) ACT 2004 (ISLES OF SCILLY) ORDER 2005, SI 2005 1096; made under the Carers (Equal Opportunities) Act 2004 s.6. In force: April 28, 2005; £3.00.

This Order provides that in its application to the Isles of Scilly the Carers (Equal Opportunities) Act 2004 s.3 shall have effect with the modification that any reference to a local authority shall, in relation to the Isles of Scilly, be construed as a reference to the Council of the Isles of Scilly. This does not apply to the reference in subsection (5)(a) which, in relation to a request made by the Council, shall have effect as if the word "other" is omitted, but the Order adds the Council of the Isles of Scilly to the list of authorities mentioned in s.3(5) of the Act in relation to a request made by a local authority.

3937. **Carers–Expenses–Local authority recovery of home care costs–Care provided by family member–Application of local authority policy**

The appellant (S) appealed against the dismissal of her application for judicial review ([2004] EWHC 2228, [2005] 1 F.C.R.165) of a decision by the respondent local authority that payments made for care provided by S's daughter were to be disregarded when calculating how much S should pay towards the cost of home care provided by the local authority. The judge decided that the local authority's policy that no allowance should be made for care provided by a family member was not irrational.

Held, allowing the appeal, that the judge had correctly concluded that the family member policy was not irrational but he had not considered whether the policy was applied properly. The policy depended on the propositions that the family member would normally perform the service voluntarily and that the recipient of the services would not expect to pay, or be expected to pay, for them. Neither proposition applied in the instant case because S had only been willing to allow her daughter to give up work in order to provide care for her on the basis that S compensated her for doing so. It was not necessary to consider such an arrangement in contractual terms or to import into it an intention between S and her daughter to create legal relations in order to advance the proposition that these were services related to S's disability for which she was paying, and in relation to which it was not certain that they would have been either instituted or continued voluntarily if S had not insisted that they be paid for. Those highly unusual circumstances made it necessary for the local authority to consider carefully whether the case constituted an exception to the family member policy, and it had failed to do so. The local authority had treated the policy as a rule and had failed to exercise the discretion implicit in the policy.

R. (ON THE APPLICATION OF STEPHENSON) v. STOCKTON ON TEES BC, [2005] EWCA Civ 960, [2005] 3 F.C.R. 248, Sedley, L.J., CA (Civ Div).

3938. **Carers (Equal Opportunities) Act 2004 (c.15)–Commencement Order–England**

CARERS (EQUAL OPPORTUNITIES) ACT 2004 (COMMENCEMENT) (ENGLAND) ORDER 2005, SI 2005 876 (C.37); made under the Carers (Equal Opportunities) Act 2004 s.6. Commencement details: bringing into force various provisions of the 2004 Act on April 1, 2005; £3.00.

This Order provides for the coming into force on April 1, 2005, in relation to England, of the Carers (Equal Opportunities) Act 2004.

3939. **Carers (Equal Opportunities) Act 2004 (c.15)–Commencement Order–Wales**

CARERS (EQUAL OPPORTUNITIES) ACT 2004 (COMMENCEMENT) (WALES) ORDER 2005, SI 2005 1153 (W.70; C.53); made under the Carers (Equal Opportunities) Act 2004 s.6. Commencement details: bringing into force various provisions of the 2004 Act on April 18, 2005; £3.00.

This Order brings the Carers (Equal Opportunities) Act 2004 into force in relation to Wales.

3940. Childrens services–Children and young people's plans–Publication and review

CHILDREN AND YOUNG PEOPLE'S PLAN (ENGLAND) REGULATIONS 2005, SI 2005 2149; made under the Children Act 2004 s.17, s.66. In force: September 1, 2005; £3.00.

These Regulations provide for children's services authorities to prepare, consult upon, publish and review a children and young people's plan. They set out the matters which must be dealt with in the plan; provide that the first plan is to be published by April 1, 2006 and thereafter each plan must be published no later than six weeks after the end of the last plan period; provide for the way in which the plan shall be published; provide for consultation during the preparation of the plan; and provide for the authority to review the plan in each year in which a new plan is not required to be published with provision made for further limited consultation. They also make provision for exemption from the requirements for authorities categorised, by order made by the Secretary of State, as excellent under the Comprehensive Performance Assessment conducted annually by the Audit Commission.

3941. Childrens services–Children and young persons–List of services

CHILDREN ACT 2004 (CHILDREN'S SERVICES) REGULATIONS 2005, SI 2005 1972; made under the Children Act 2004 s.23, s.66. In force: September 1, 2005; £3.00.

The Children Act 2004 is concerned with the inspection of children's services; defines children's services; provides for the review of children's services in the area of a children's services authority in England; provides for there to be a Framework for Inspection of Children's Services containing principles to be applied when a person or body conducts a review, or any other type of assessment of children's services; and requires persons or bodies with a function of conducting an assessment of children's services to co-operate with each other, and permits delegation of their assessment functions to another such body. These Regulations specify and prescribe as children's services a list of services, done for or in relation to children and relevant young persons; and specify and prescribe as children's services a list of services done for or in relation to children and relevant young persons in so far as they relate to children.

3942. Childrens services–Reviews

CHILDREN ACT 2004 (JOINT AREA REVIEWS) REGULATIONS 2005, SI 2005 1973; made under the Children Act 2004 s.20, s.66. In force: September 1, 2005; £3.00.

The Children Act 2004 provides for the review of children's services in the area of a children's services authority in England. These Regulations make provision for the purposes of such reviews.

3943. Executive agencies–Commission for Social Care Inspection–Fees

COMMISSION FOR SOCIAL CARE INSPECTION (FEES AND FREQUENCY OF INSPECTIONS) (AMENDMENT) REGULATIONS 2005, SI 2005 575; made under the Care Standards Act 2000 s.12, s.15, s.16, s.118; and the Children Act 1989 s.87D. In force: April 1, 2005; £3.00.

These Regulations amend the Commission for Social Care Inspection (Fees and Frequency of Inspections) Regulations 2004 (SI 2004 662) in order to increase the amount of the fees that are to be paid to the Commission for Social Care Inspection by establishments and agencies (other than voluntary adoption agencies, independent hospitals, independent clinics, independent medical agencies and local authority fostering services) under the Care Standards Act 2000.

3944. Food–Welfare food scheme

HEALTHY START SCHEME AND WELFARE FOOD (AMENDMENT) REGULATIONS 2005, SI 2005 3262; made under the Social Security Act 1988 s.13; and the Social Security Contributions and Benefits Act 1992 s.175. In force: November 28, 2005; £3.00.

These Regulations, which amend the Welfare Food Regulations 1996 (SI 1996 1434), establish a scheme in the area in the West of England encompassed within postcode districts commencing with "L", "TR", "TQ" and "EX" to provide benefits for pregnant women, mothers and children.

3945. Funding–Local authorities–Welfare services–Loan offered by local authority to fund adaptations to disabled child's home–Legality of conditions attached to loan

[Chronically Sick and Disabled Persons Act 1970 s.2(1), s.28A.]

The claimant (B) applied for judicial review to challenge the legality of certain conditions attached to a loan offered to him by the defendant local authority in compliance with the Chronically Sick and Disabled Persons Act 1970 s.2(1) and s.28A. The loan, secured by way of a legal charge, had been offered by the local authority in order to meet a shortfall in funding for adaptations to B's home necessitated by his severe physical and mental disabilities. The offer stated that the legal charge would be discharged after a period of 20 years without any requirement for repayment. However, the offer was subject to conditions, inter alia, that the local authority would not seek repayment unless B ceased to reside at the property during those 20 years and that any amount repayable was subject to interest. The main issue was whether the conditions of the loan offered by the local authority in the exercise of its discretion were lawful. B argued, inter alia, that (1) a condition that the loan was repayable if within 20 years B died or no longer permanently resided at the property was unreasonable; (2) the 20 year period of the loan was unreasonably long and out of all proportion to the local authority's need to protect its funds; (3) it was unreasonable to require payment of interest on the loan on the occurrence of an event triggering liability to repay the loan itself; (4) the local authority had adopted a blanket policy and had given insufficient consideration to his particular needs; (5) the local authority had not given proper regard to the means of his parents when setting the conditions of the loan.

Held, refusing the application, that (1) the conditions were reasonably related to the purpose for which financial assistance was provided, namely to enable B to reside at home on a long term basis. In those circumstances, it was reasonable for the local authority to make provision for repayment, especially in view of its limited financial resources and overall responsibilities. If the loan could be recovered when it was no longer achieving its purpose, the money could then be used to assist others in need. (2) The period of 20 years was long but not unreasonably long in the particular circumstances of the case. It was a reasonable reflection of the long term purpose for which the adaptations were to be carried out. (3) There could be no objection in principle to requiring that interest be paid, as it ensured that monies repayable retained their value in real terms. Moreover, the local authority had indicated that, if an event triggered the liability to repay, it would have regard to the family's personal and financial circumstances and would not act unreasonably by insisting on repayment immediately or on terms that would result in financial hardship. That founded a legitimate expectation as to the local authority's future conduct. In the circumstances, the liability to pay interest was reasonable. (4) The local authority had been fully aware of the need to consider the individual circumstances of each case and to avoid the application of an inflexible rule. It had considered whether the circumstances had justified an exception to the terms normally applied, but had reasonably concluded that they had not. (5) There was abundant evidence to show that the local authority had had full regard to the means of B's parents when setting the conditions of the loan and that it would have regard to their future means.

R. (ON THE APPLICATION OF B) v. MEDWAY COUNCIL; *sub nom.* R. (ON THE APPLICATION OF BG) v. MEDWAY COUNCIL, [2005] EWHC 1932, [2005] 3 F.C.R. 199, Richards, J., QBD (Admin).

3946. **Local authorities powers and duties—Vulnerable adults—Extent of duties where adult's welfare threatened by criminal act**

[National Assistance Act 1948 s.29; Suicide Act 1961 s.1, s.2; Local Authority Social Services Act 1970 s.7; Local Government Act 1972 s.222; National Health Service Act 1977; National Health Service and Community Care Act 1990; Human Rights Act 1998 Sch.1 Part I Art.2.]

The claimant local authority sought an injunction preventing a husband (H) from removing his wife from England for the purpose of travelling to Switzerland for an assisted suicide. The wife had cerebella ataxia, a condition which attacked the part of the brain that controlled the body's motor functions. She had become increasingly disabled by the condition, which was incurable and irreversible. Although she continued to live at home, she required extensive support from the local authority, and her needs had grown as her condition had deteriorated. She had attempted suicide and wished H to arrange an assisted suicide in Switzerland. H so informed the local authority, which concluded that the wife was a vulnerable person living in its area and obtained an interim injunction from the High Court.

Held, giving judgment accordingly, that the expert evidence was that the wife was legally competent to make her own decisions. The local authority owed duties to her under the National Assistance Act 1948 s.29, the National Health Service Act 1977 and the National Health Service and Community Care Act 1990. The local authority was obliged to treat the wife as a vulnerable adult under the Department of Health guidance issued under the Local Authority Social Services Act 1970 s.7. The court had no basis in law for exercising the jurisdiction so as to prohibit the wife from taking her own life. The right and responsibility for such a decision belonged to her alone. Suicide was not punishable as a criminal act under the Suicide Act 1961 s.1, but aiding, abetting, counselling or procuring suicide or attempted suicide was an offence under s.2 of the Act. Although assisted suicide was not criminal under the law of Switzerland, H would contravene s.2 by making arrangements and taking steps in the UK to assist his wife to travel to Switzerland for that purpose. In order for the wife to implement her decision, it would require criminal conduct on the part of H. A jurisdiction to restrain criminal acts was available to the High Court, and, in appropriate circumstances, a local authority could apply for that jurisdiction to be exercised under the Local Government Act 1972 s.222. In the context of a person of full capacity, the right to life under the Human Rights Act 1998 Sch.1 Part I Art.2 was engaged, but it did not assume primacy over the rights of autonomy and self determination. In a case such as this, a local authority had duties to: investigate the position of a vulnerable adult; consider whether she was legally competent; consider whether she was being influenced; consider whether to invoke the inherent jurisdiction of the High Court so that the question of competence could be judicially investigated and determined; if the adult was not competent, provide such assistance as might reasonably be required to determine and give effect to her best interests; if the adult was competent, allow her in any lawful way to give effect to her decision; where there were reasonable grounds for suspecting that the commission of a criminal offence might be involved, draw that to the attention of the police; and, very exceptionally, invoke the court's jurisdiction under s.222 of the 1972 Act, *Airedale NHS Trust v. Bland* Times, December 10, 1992, [1992] C.L.Y. 2957 applied. The local authority had no duty to seek the continuation of the injunction, and the court would not do so of its own motion where no one with the necessary standing sought any such order, where the criminal justice agencies had the necessary powers to prosecute any breach of the criminal law and where the effect of the injunction was to deny a seriously disabled but competent person a right that could not be exercised by reason of the disability.

Z (LOCAL AUTHORITY: DUTY), *Re; sub nom.* A LOCAL AUTHORITY v. Z; Z (AN ADULT: CAPACITY), *Re,* [2004] EWHC 2817, [2005] 1 W.L.R. 959, Hedley, J., Fam Div.

3947. **Residential accommodation–Disabled persons–Local authorities powers and duties–Duty to provide suitable accommodation**

[National Assistance Act 1948 s.21 (1) (a); Housing Act 1996 s.189(1), s.193(2); Human Rights Act 1998 Sch.1 Part I Art.8.]

The claimant (H) sought judicial review of the way the defendant local authority had carried out the statutory duties it owed to him. H also sought damages for the authority's breach of his right to respect for his private and family life. H had suffered from severe mental and physical disabilities since birth and lived with his mother, who was his principal carer. The authority had assessed H's accommodation and welfare needs after he became 18 in April 2003 and acknowledged that the house in which he lived had for some time been totally unsuitable in respect of the access and facilities which he needed. It was envisaged that suitable adapted accommodation would not become available until August 2005 at the earliest. The authority submitted that, contrary to H's claim, it had no duties under either the National Assistance Act 1948 s.21 (1) (a) or the Local Authority Circular 93/10 App.1 para.2(1) in respect of his accommodation needs. Any duty to provide accommodation for him would be owed under the Housing Act 1996 s.193(2).

Held, granting the application in part, that (1) H had a priority need for accommodation under s.189(1) of the 1996 Act, but under s.193(2) the authority could only meet his ordinary housing needs, *R. (on the application of Wahid) v. Tower Hamlets LBC* [2002] EWCA Civ 287, [2003] H.L.R. 2, [2003] C.L.Y. 2046 considered. The authority had breached its duty under s.21 (1) (a) of the 1948 Act and under the Local Authority Circular 93/10 App.1 para.2(1) to provide H with accommodation adapted for the additional needs of his disabilities, *R. v. Sefton MBC, ex p. Help the Aged* [1997] 4 All E.R. 532, [1997] C.L.Y. 4721 applied. (2) Although the protection of H's dignity and personal integrity would be improved by the provision of suitable accommodation, the limitations imposed upon his enjoyment of private and family life arose from his own condition. The authority's shortcomings in fulfilling its statutory duties to H had not breached his right to respect for his private and family life under the Human Rights Act 1998 Sch.1 Part I Art.8 as the impact of those shortcomings had been reduced by his mother's efforts. In any event, it could not be said that the high threshold required under Art.8 had been crossed, *Anufrijeva v. Southwark LBC* [2003] EWCA Civ 1406, [2004] Q.B. 1124, [2004] 1 C.L. 186 applied. Weekend respite care was to be provided and a reassessment made of H's welfare needs within 28 days.

R. (ON THE APPLICATION OF HUGHES) v. LIVERPOOL CITY COUNCIL, [2005] EWHC 428, [2005] B.L.G.R. 531, Mitting, J., QBD (Admin).

3948. **Residential accommodation–Residential care–Local authority's decision to move elderly resident from care home to nursing home–Propriety of decision making process**

The appellant (G), an elderly woman in residential care accommodation whom the local authority decided should be moved to a nursing home, appealed against the refusal of her application to have that decision quashed. The local authority made its decision after G was admitted to hospital following a fall in the care home. G's daughter (L) challenged its conclusion and the local authority referred the case to the Local Continuing Care Panel, a joint health and social services panel, for its consideration. L was not allowed to attend the panel's meeting as it claimed to be only considering "clinical evidence". The panel recommended G be moved to a nursing home. After that meeting a social work team manager of the local authority undertook an assessment which concluded that G was well enough to stay at her care home. The local authority instructed a doctor, who confirmed, without seeing her, that G needed nursing care. L was not informed of the reference to a doctor or involved in his decision making. The local authority then gave its decision to L. A few weeks later a meeting was convened involving L, the doctor and the local authority, which confirmed its decision. G contended that the local authority's decision making process was defective and there was a failure to apply own policy.

Held, allowing the appeal, that when deciding whether a resident in its care needed to be placed in a nursing home, a local authority was under a duty to take a rounded decision, which took into account all relevant factors, rather than treat a doctor's views on the resident's nursing needs as determinative. In the instant case, the local authority's decision making process was sufficiently defective to vitiate its decision. It had based its decision that G should be put in a nursing home on the assessment of a panel to which it had referred the case and the apparent confirmation of that assessment by a doctor which it had later instructed. But the panel's recommendation was flawed because, in breach of the local guidance, it kept no written record of its discussions or conclusions; it made its decision without having before it the community care assessment, which was carried out afterwards and contradicted its view; and it should have allowed L to attend the meeting, at which not just "clinical" issues were discussed. The local authority had therefore received defective advice. And it was not cured by subsequent events, because the manner in which the doctor was instructed was unacceptable: he was not being asked to provide an independent second opinion, but was being asked to confirm the panel's decision. The doctor undertook a very limited role of reviewing the panel's assessment and the doctor's decision could only be one factor in, and not determinative of, the local authority's decision. The local authority's decision was therefore based on its perception of the panel's assessment being confirmed by the doctor and there was no evidence that it took into account other relevant considerations.

R. (ON THE APPLICATION OF GOLDSMITH) v. WANDSWORTH LBC, [2004] EWCA Civ 1170, (2004) 7 C.C.L. Rep. 472, Brooke, L.J., CA (Civ Div).

3949. Residential care–Children–Choice of placements–Local authority's duty to consider child's preference

[Children Act 1989 s.20(6)(b).]

The claimant (T), a 17 year old girl requiring special care and education owing to a mental condition, claimed that the local authority's failure to provide her with a residential placement was in breach of its duties under the Children Act 1989 s.20. T wanted to be placed at a particular residential care home and refused to go to another care home which the local authority had concluded would be more suitable.

Held, giving judgment for the local authority, that the local authority's refusal to provide T with the residential placement of her choice was not a breach of its duties. Under s.20(6)(b) the local authority had a duty to give due consideration to T's wishes, but it was not bound to comply with them. If the child was capable of making a sensible choice, then under s.20(6)(b) her wishes would be determinative in the event of the establishments being equally suitable. In the event of both establishments being suitable, albeit not equally so, and the child's refusing to go to the preferred establishment, the local authority would not be absolved from complying with its s.20 duties. However, in T's case, the local authority's view that it might be possible to persuade her to overcome her objection did not put it in breach of s.20(6)(b).

R. (ON THE APPLICATION OF T) v. CALDERDALE MBC, [2004] EWHC 1998, (2005) 8 C.C.L. Rep. 101, Stanley Burnton, J., QBD (Admin Ct).

3950. Residential care–Disabled persons–Assessment of needs of claimant suffering from Asperger's syndrome–Provision of supported housing instead of residential accommodation

The claimant (R), a 35 year old man who suffered from Asperger's syndrome, sought judicial review of S's decision that his needs should be met by the provision of supported housing and 28 hours a week of one to one support instead of the 55 hours a week he had been receiving. R's mother wanted R to go into residential accommodation at a particular location. R's solicitors obtained a report from a leading authority in autistic spectrum disorder, which concluded that the risks of R's condition worsening were such as to warrant his placement in residential accommodation. S obtained a clinical psychiatrist's report before making a final decision. S considered this report, but did not invite R's solicitors to participate in that meeting before recommending that R be given supported living accommodation with 24 hour staff availability.

Held, refusing the application, that S had not acted irrationally in opting for supported housing instead of residential care, and in so doing, preferring the evidence of one medical expert over another. Nor was the decision in respect of the amount of weekly care irrational, since 24 hour support was on hand, and there was the possibility of an upwards review if warranted. The requirements of fairness did not oblige S to allow R to be represented at the meeting which considered the contents of R's medical expert. Such representation would not, in any event, have affected the outcome of the meeting. This was not a dispute that either S's own complaints procedure or a form of alternative dispute resolution would have been likely to resolve.

R. (ON THE APPLICATION OF RODRIGUEZ-BANNISTER) v. SOMERSET PARTNERSHIP NHS AND SOCIAL CARE TRUST; *sub nom.* RODRIGUEZ-BANNISTER v. SOMERSET PARTNERSHIP NHS AND SOCIAL CARE TRUST, [2003] EWHC 2184, (2004) 7 C.C.L. Rep. 385, Hooper, J., QBD (Admin Ct).

3951. **Residential care–Gifts–Transfer of house by deed of gift to avoid residential care charges**

[Insolvency Act 1986 s.423; Human Rights Act 1998 Sch.1 Part I Art.6.]

The first appellant (S) and the second appellant, the estate of S's father (K), appealed against the decision allowing the claims of the respondents under the Insolvency Act 1986 s.423 against them. Prior to being discharged from a hospital into a nursing home, K had transferred his house, by deed of gift, to his children. The first respondent local authority thereafter assumed responsibility for payment of part of K's nursing home charges. Later the local authority and the second respondent sought to recover sums in respect of those charges. Parts of S's defence and counterclaim were struck out and S was debarred from playing any further part in the proceedings until he complied with an interlocutory order for costs, which he never did. When the matter came to trial the judge allowed S to present his own defence and that of K's estate, but he refused S's application for an adjournment. The judge gave judgment against both S and K's estate in relation to the charges and made orders under the Act effectively requiring the house to be retransferred to K's estate. S argued that (1) his right and the right of K's estate to a fair trial had been breached because he had not been allowed to present their cases properly; (2) the judge had been wrong in law in concluding that to determine the liability of K's estate he was not entitled to look at the legality of the local authority revisiting its decision to enter into the original placement agreement; (3) in his conclusions of fact the judge had entered into the realms of speculation and his findings were not securely based upon the evidence.

Held, allowing the appeal in part, that (1) the procedural history indicated that the court had provided proper case management in terms of ensuring that the proceedings were focused on what was relevant, and gave effect to the new rules of court. The orders were made in pursuit of a legitimate aim, namely to ensure proper process in the interests of justice as between litigants. The disadvantage visited upon S was a disadvantage that was effectively self inflicted. In those circumstances there could not be any breach of the Human Rights Act 1998 Sch.1 Part I Art.6. (2) As a matter of law, a litigant was entitled to raise as a defence an issue of public law that undermined the basis of a claim, *Wandsworth LBC v. Winder (No.1)* [1985] A.C. 461, [1985] C.L.Y. 9 applied. Therefore the matter had to be remitted to the judge for him to consider the extent to which the matters raised by S were matters that undermined the local authority's entitlement to the sums claimed. (3) The conclusion that the judge reached on the application of s.423 was not merely open to him on the facts but any other conclusion could well have been perverse.

DERBYSHIRE CC v. AKRILL, [2005] EWCA Civ 308, (2005) 8 C.C.L. Rep. 173, Brooke, L.J., CA (Civ Div).

3952. Residential care–Learning disabled persons–Registration of care homes– Provision of accommodation under assured tenancy

[Care Standards Act 2000 s.3, s.15(1)(b); Care Homes Regulations 2001 (SI 2001 3965).]

The appellants (M), residents of registered care homes, appealed against a decision ([2004] EWHC 2481, [2005] B.L.G.R. 179, [2004] 5 C.L. 523) that the provision of accommodation by way of an assured tenancy did not exclude, either expressly or by implication, an establishment from being a care home for the purpose of the Care Standards Act 2000 s.3. M had severe learning disabilities which necessitated the receipt of nursing and personal care in homes. The homes had originally been run by a charity (F) which provided both housing and personal services. A second charity (H) was established to facilitate the move towards supported and assisted living. The freehold of the homes had been transferred to H, with F providing the care. H had then granted an assured tenancy to each resident. F contended that as the accommodation element was provided by an assured tenancy the establishment ceased to be a care home as defined by s.3, and accordingly sought to deregister the homes under s.15(1)(b) of the 2000 Act. Deregistration was refused. M argued that neither H nor F provided accommodation for the purposes of s.3. M maintained that the buildings were occupied by them not as residential institutions, but as separate dwellings. Further, that the intention of the legislature as expressed in the 2000 Act and in the Care Homes Regulations 2001 was to offer a range of different models for living and to impose different schemes of regulation upon registered care homes, domiciliary care agencies and other agencies and establishments.

Held, dismissing the appeal, that the judge had been correct. Although the intention of the legislature was to include a range of models of care facilities within the 2000 Act, there was no reason why an establishment could not provide accommodation within the meaning of that word in s.3 of the Act, whether or not the accommodation was provided by lease or licence. The crucial consideration was whether the establishment provided accommodation together with nursing or personal care. That was a question of fact which did not arise in the instant case as M had accepted for the purpose of the appeal that H and F, together with each house, were an establishment. The fact that a relationship was one of lessor and lessee could be an indication of a situation where an establishment did not provide both accommodation and care, but was not determinative.

R. (ON THE APPLICATION OF MOORE) v. CARE STANDARDS TRIBUNAL; *sub nom.* MOORE v. CARE STANDARDS TRIBUNAL, [2005] EWCA Civ 627, [2005] 1 W.L.R. 2979, Waller, L.J., CA (Civ Div).

3953. Residential care–Special educational needs–Decision of local authority based on cost alone–Fettered discretion

[National Health Service and Community Care Act 1990 s.47.]

The claimant (C) applied for judicial review of the decision of the defendant local authority to place him in particular residential accommodation (R). C was a 19 year old male who suffered from severe autism and learning difficulties. C required a permanent placement after his time at boarding school had ended and his parents wanted him to go to an establishment (H) that was part of the same group as his former school. The local authority carried out an assessment of C's needs in accordance with their duty under the National Health Service and Community Care Act 1990 s.47 and recommended that C should be placed at H, but no such placement was made. Subsequently, an annual review was held and it was noted that changes had occurred in C's behaviour and development. Consequently, placement at R was recommended. C contended that the local authority, in failing to secure his placement at H, had made a decision based on cost and was in breach of s.47(1).

Held, granting the application, that the local authority had erred in its decision making. It was clear that H had been ruled out as a placement for C on grounds of cost before any viable alternatives had been found; therefore there had been no fair comparison made of different placement options and the local authority had unlawfully fettered its discretion. The decision to accept a placement at R was quashed. However, it was inappropriate to order that the placement at H be accepted because it was a matter for the local authority, and not the court, to make a new decision. Although it was not necessary to carry out a new assessment under s.47, the local authority was obliged to take account of up to date information including, but not limited to, the assessment already carried out.

R. (ON THE APPLICATION OF ALLOWAY) v. BROMLEY LBC, [2004] EWHC 2108, (2005) 8 C.C.L. Rep. 61, Crane, J., QBD (Admin Ct).

3954. Social services–Complaints procedure–Wales

SOCIAL SERVICES COMPLAINTS PROCEDURE (WALES) REGULATIONS 2005, SI 2005 3366 (W.263); made under the Children Act 1989 s.26A, s.26ZB; and the Health and Social Care (Community Health and Standards) Act 2003 s.114, s.115. In force: April 1, 2006; £4.00.

These Regulations make provision for complaints to local authorities about the exercise of their social services functions, with the exception of functions capable of being considered as representations under the Children Act 1989.

3955. Special guardianship orders–Support services

SPECIAL GUARDIANSHIP REGULATIONS 2005, SI 2005 1109; made under the Children Act 1989 s.14A, s.14F, s.24, s.104. In force: December 30, 2005; £3.00.

These Regulations make provision in relation to special guardianship orders. They deal with the provision of services; financial support; assessment of a person's needs for special guardianship support services, plans for provision of services and notifications of proposals and decisions in relation to the provision of services; and reviews of special guardianship support services.

3956. Welsh Assembly–Social services explanations

NATIONAL ASSEMBLY FOR WALES (SOCIAL SERVICES EXPLANATIONS) REGULATIONS 2005, SI 2005 1510 (W.114); made under the Health and Social Care (Community Health and Standards) Act 2003 s.101, s.195. In force: July 1, 2005; £3.00.

These Regulations permit the National Assembly for Wales to require any person listed to provide an explanation to the Assembly of anything listed in Reg.2(1), for example a document removed from premises by an authorised Assembly inspector under the Health and Social Care (Community Health and Standards) Act 2003 s.99.

3957. Books

Albert, Raymond; Skolnik, Louise–Social Welfare Programs: Narratives from Hard Times. Paperback: £21.00. ISBN 0 534 35918 3. Wadsworth.

Brayne, Hugh; Carr, Helen–Law for Social Workers. Paperback: £24.99. ISBN 0 19 927551 3. Oxford University Press.

Ferrera, Maurizio–Boundaries of Welfare: European Integration and the New Spatial Politics of Social Solidarity. Hardback: £50.00. ISBN 0 19 928466 0. Hardback: £50.00. ISBN 0 19 928466 0. Oxford University Press.

Freeman, Michael–Child Welfare and the Law. Paperback: £26.95. ISBN 0 421 33990 X. Sweet & Maxwell.

Johns, Robert–Using the Law in Social Work. Transforming Social Work Practice S. Paperback: £14.00. ISBN 1 84445 030 9. Learning Matters.

MacLean, Iain—Social Care and the Law. Spiral/comb bound: £10.00. ISBN 1 903575 34 6. Kirwin Maclean Associates.

MacLean, Iain; Maclean, Siobhan—Social Care and the Law: An NVQ Related Reference Guide for Direct Care Staff. Spiral/comb bound: £10.00. ISBN 1 903575 30 3. Kirwin Maclean Associates.

Mandelstam, Michael—Community Care Practice and the Law. Paperback: £39.95. ISBN 1 84310 233 1. Jessica Kingsley Publishers.

Pearl, David—Care Standards Legislation Handbook. Paperback: £35.00. ISBN 0 85308 964 7. Jordans.

Simmons, David; Winfield, Helen—Paying for Care Handbook: A Guide to Services, Charges and Welfare Benefits for Adults in Need of Care in the Community or in Care Homes. Paperback: £18.50. ISBN 1 901698 81 5. CPAG.

SPORT

3958. Football—Football grounds—Seating

FOOTBALL SPECTATORS (SEATING) ORDER 2005, SI 2005 1751; made under the Football Spectators Act 1989 s.11. In force: August 1, 2005; £3.00.

This Order directs the Football Licensing Authority to include in any licence to admit spectators to the football grounds specified in Sch.1 a condition imposing the requirements specified in Sch.2 as respects the seating of spectators at designated football matches. "Designated football matches" are those association football matches designated by the Secretary of State under the powers conferred by the Football Spectators Act 1989 s.1 (2) and they include all association football matches played at the premises specified in Sch.1 of this Order.

3959. Horse racing—Disqualification—Jockey breaking rules of racing—Deprivation of right to work

The appellant jockey (B) appealed against a decision ([2004] EWHC 2164) dismissing his claim for an injunction and damages against the respondent Jockey Club (J). B had been a successful steeplechase jockey until 1999 when, following his retirement, he became a blood stock agent. In 2001 a jockey friend of B's was tried for conspiracy to import cocaine and B was called to give evidence about payments of money and presents made to the jockey from a professional gambling organisation. In cross examination, B confirmed that he had also received money and presents in return for sensitive information about horses, which the stables would not have wished to be divulged. An inquiry was held by the disciplinary body, which held that B had breached several of the Rules of Racing. He was disqualified for eight years and as a result he was prevented from working as a blood stock agent. Following an appeal, the appeal board reduced the disqualification to five years. Proceedings were issued claiming breach of contract and an injunction. The claim was dismissed and it was held that the courts had a supervisory jurisdiction similar to that of judicial review. B contended that the sanction imposed was disproportionate as the disqualification order excessively interfered with his right to work and it was the duty of the High Court to protect that right.

Held, dismissing the appeal, that the judge had reached the correct decision. Professional and trade disciplinary bodies were better placed to oversee breaches of rules of trade to which they related. Where an individual took up a profession that critically depended on the observation of rules, and then broke those rules, it could not be contended that he had a vested right to work within that profession. Disciplinary boards and courts had to have regard to the circumstances that required disqualification where that penalty deprived a person of his right to work.

BRADLEY v. JOCKEY CLUB, [2005] EWCA Civ 1056, *The Times*, July 14, 2005, Lord Phillips of Worth Matravers, M.R., CA (Civ Div).

3960. Olympic games—London

OLYMPIC LOTTERIES (DECLARATION THAT LONDON IS TO HOST THE 2012 OLYMPIC GAMES) ORDER 2005, SI 2005 1830; made under the Horserace Betting and Olympic Lottery Act 2004 s.22. In force: July 7, 2005; £3.00.

This Order declares that London has been elected as the host city for the 2012 Olympic Games. This declaration enables Olympic Lottery games to be promoted if licensed in accordance with the National Lottery etc. Act 1993 s.6 and the Horserace Betting and Olympic Lottery Act 2004 s.21.

3961. Recreational services—Sports grounds—Designation for criminal law purposes

SPORTS GROUNDS AND SPORTING EVENTS (DESIGNATION) ORDER 2005, SI 2005 3204; made under the Sporting Events (Control of Alcohol etc.) Act 1985 s.9. In force: December 14, 2005; £3.00.

This Order, which amends the Sports Grounds and Football (Amendment of Various Orders) Order 1992 (SI 1992 1554), revokes the Sports Grounds and Sporting Events (Designation) Order 1985 (SI 1985 1151) and the Sports Grounds and Sporting Events (Designation) (Amendment) Order 1987 (SI 1987 1520). This Order designates any sports ground and classes of sporting events taking place at those grounds or outside England and Wales for the purposes of the Sporting Events (Control of Alcohol etc.) Act 1985. The Act does not apply to any sporting event in which all competitors are to take part otherwise than for reward and to which all spectators are to be admitted free of charge.

3962. Sports—Sports grounds—Safety certificates

SAFETY OF SPORTS GROUNDS (DESIGNATION) ORDER 2005, SI 2005 1748; made under the Safety of Sports Grounds Act 1975 s.1. In force: July 23, 2005; £3.00.

This Order designates the Ricoh Arena in Coventry and The New Stadium in Swansea as sports grounds requiring safety certificates under the Safety of Sports Grounds Act 1975.

3963. Sportspersons—Drug testing—Freedom to provide services—Non economic nature of anti doping legislation—European Community

[EC Treaty Art.49, Art.81, Art.82.]

The applicant (M), a professional swimmer, sought the annulment of a Commission decision that the anti doping legislation enacted by the International Olympic Committee (IOC), subsequently adopted by the International Swimming Federation (FINA), did not breach the EC Treaty Art.81 and Art.82. M had tested positive for nandrolone, for which he was suspended from competitions by FINA for four years. This was reduced to two years on appeal to the Council of Arbitration for Sport. Although a further appeal lay to the Swiss Federal Court, M complained to the Commission that the anti doping regime breached Art.81 or Art.82.

Held, refusing the application, that high level sport only fell to be considered under the EC Treaty Art.49, Art.81 or Art.82 to the extent that it included an economic activity. However, the IOC's anti doping legislation was intended to preserve the unique nature of sporting activity and was not economic in nature, with the result that Art.49, Art.81 or Art.82 were not engaged, *Wouters v. Algemene Raad van de Nederlandse Orde van Advocaten (C309/99)* [2002] All E.R. (EC) 193 distinguished.

MECA-MEDINA v. COMMISSION OF THE EUROPEAN COMMUNITIES (T313/02) [2004] 3 C.M.L.R. 60, Judge Legal (President), CFI.

SPORT AND LEISURE

3964. Books

Blackshaw, Ian S.; Seikmann, Robert C.R.–Sports Image Rights in Europe. Hardback: £65.00. ISBN 90 6704 195 5. Asser Press.

Day, Frederick J.–Sports and Courts: An Introduction to Principles of Law and Legal Theory Using Cases from Professional Sports. Paperback: £10.41. ISBN 0 595 34315 5. iUniverse.com.

SUCCESSION

3965. Administration of estates–Domicile of choice–Assessment of intention of permanent or indefinite residence

[Inheritance (Provision for Family and Dependants) Act 1975.]

The claimant (C), the long term girlfriend of the deceased (N), issued a claim under the Inheritance (Provision for Family and Dependants) Act 1975 against the defendants (D), the family of N and the executors under the will. The question whether N had died domiciled in England and Wales was tried as a preliminary issue. N had died leaving an estate of over £6m. Under the terms of his will N left a substantial legacy to C, further legacies to family members, and his residuary estate to his daughter and granddaughter. N's domicile of origin was Cyprus, his country of birth. N had left Cyprus in 1958 to avoid marriage and the anger of his fiancee's family. N stayed in England for the next 14 years, buying property in London and abroad. He returned to Cyprus in 1972. Following the Turkish invasion of Cyprus in 1974, N relocated to London, which he regarded as a convenient place to live and work until the situation in Cyprus was resolved. For the last 30 years of his life N resided in England, developing a successful hotel business, as Cyprus had remained under Turkish control. Throughout that period N continued to visit Cyprus, and moved large sums of money there which totalled £1.3m at his death. N retained a strong sense of Cypriot identity while living in London, immersing himself within the Cypriot community. N lived for 15 years as man and wife with a Mrs Johnson in London and they had a daughter together. The couple had not married as N had seemingly feared such a commitment. Mrs Johnson had left N for a more settled existence, fearing his intention was to return to Cyprus. N then developed a long term and sustained relationship with C, whom he had initially employed as a hotel cleaner. There was a dispute over N's intentions concerning his relationship with C.

Held, determining the preliminary issue in favour of C, that as N's domicile of origin was Cyprus, the issue to be decided was whether his domicile had changed by a combination of residence and intention of permanent or indefinite residence. A mere intention by N to return to Cyprus on a doubtful contingency would not prevent residence in England from putting an end to his domicile of origin, *Inland Revenue Commissioners v. Bullock* [1976] 1 W.L.R. 1178, [1976] C.L.Y. 1414 applied. It was a difficult task to identify the intentions of N, a man who kept his intentions to himself and whose statements about his intentions were often not reliable. N held money in Cyprus and had in mind that this would enable him to buy, build or alter property there. This would be consistent with an intention to retire in Cyprus; it was also consistent with N positioning himself for a later retirement to Cyprus if that were later decided upon, while at the same time having no definite plan to do so. N's main assets were in England, as were his work, his cash generation, his life and the person closest to him. N was 63 years old, and it was consistent with his relationship with C, its duration and stability, and with C's undoubted wish, that N was willing at last to marry after 10 years. N had a very strong tie to his blood relations in Cyprus. However, his own life revolved around his world in London. For 30 years he had chosen to live in England rather than in Cyprus, where his parents lived. N had mental independence from his family, so that although he valued his family ties, he valued his independence and ability to lead his own life. When it came to it, leading his life as he wished took precedence over family ties. N formed a successful relationship with C, with whom he lived as man and wife, and they would have become man and wife. At some point between 1995 and 1999, N had crossed the line where he intended to reside in England and Wales "permanently or indefinitely". N had died domiciled in England and Wales.

CYGANIK v. AGULIAN; *sub nom.* AGULIAN v. CYGANIK, [2005] EWHC 444, [2005] W.T.L.R. 1049, Nicholas Davidson Q.C., Ch D.

3966. Administration of estates–Injunctions–Funerals–Application without notice–Failure to make full disclosure

M applied to discharge an injunction obtained without notice by A. M was the estranged wife of G, a prominent Nigerian citizen, who died in the UK on September 23, 2003. A was named as a trustee under G's will. M made arrangements for G to be buried in London on October 18, but A sought to make different arrangements for a state funeral in Nigeria. A's Nigerian solicitor wrote to M on October 14, stating that A wanted to arrange the funeral. The letter was sent to M's Nigerian address, but she was by that time already in the UK. On October 15, A obtained the injunction restraining M from burying G, as he asserted that M was planning to hold the funeral on October 17; that repeated unsuccessful requests had been made to her not to do so; and that A was the executor of G's estate. In the instant application, M argued that the injunction should be discharged as it had been obtained using misleading information. The funeral had been set for October 18, which was a Saturday but M had received no request for the funeral not to take place and A was a trustee, not the executor. Under Nigerian law, in the absence of an executor, burial arrangements fell to the deceased's relatives.

Held, granting the application, that the injunction should be discharged. If full disclosure had been made to the judge, it was unlikely that it would have been granted on a without notice application. As the correct date for the funeral had not been given, the judge had been prevented from having the matter listed for a hearing on notice. This would have allowed evidence about the lack of contact with M to be put in answer to A's claims that she was being unco-operative, and an admission that there was some doubt as to A's rights under Nigerian law would have shown that the case was not as clear cut as A had represented.

ABDULLAHI v. MUDASHIRU, [2003] EWHC 2836, [2004] W.T.L.R. 913, Lloyd, J., Ch D.

3967. Beneficiaries–Limitation periods–Claims against personal representatives–Earliest date for running of time

[Limitation Act 1980 s.21 (1) (b), s.21 (3), s.22 (a).]

The claimants (G) sought orders for the removal of their sister (M) as administratrix of the estate of their deceased father (L) and her replacement with an independent solicitor, a statement of inventory and account of the estate and an order directing the transfer back to the estate of land which M had assigned to herself and subsequently to her son, the third defendant. L had died intestate 12 and a half years before the commencement of the instant proceedings and M's administration of the estate had since been a continuous source of dispute. M submitted that when she assigned the land to herself she had then held it as a trustee and not as a personal representative. Therefore, a limitation period of six years applied under the Limitation Act 1980 s.21 (3) so that G's claim was time barred. Alternatively, M argued that if she remained a personal representative, G's claim was time barred by virtue of the 12 year limitation period contained in s.22 (a), which ran from the date of the deceased's death. If, however, by virtue of M's conversion of trust property to her own use, the case fell within s.21 (1) (b) and no limitation period applied, G's claim was barred by laches.

Held, giving judgment accordingly, that (1) G's claim fell within s.22 (a) of the Act. The earliest possible date of the commencement of the limitation period contained in s.22 (a) was the end of the executor's year. Consequently, G's claim was within the 12 year limitation period, *Ministry of Health v. Simpson* [1951] A.C. 251 applied and *Hornsey Local Board v. Monarch Investment Building Society* (1890) L.R. 24 Q.B.D. 1 distinguished. (2) The doctrine of laches was of no application to cases where statutory limitations applied, either expressly or by analogy, *Pauling's Settlement Trusts (No.1), Re* [1964] Ch. 303, [1963] C.L.Y. 3167 applied. (3) (Obiter) If s.22(a) did not apply to the claim, then s.21(1)(b) applied to the majority of the claim and the claim would not, therefore, be time barred.

GREEN v. GAUL; *sub nom.* LOFTUS (DECEASED), *Re*, [2005] EWHC 406, [2005] 1 W.L.R. 1890, Lawrence Collins, J., Ch D.

3968. Dispositions of property—Inter vivos gift—Presumption of undue influence rebutted by evidence

M applied to set aside a transfer of property made by his late father, F, to M's niece, N. M contended that the transfer had been made as a result of the undue influence of M's sister, S, N's mother. N had lived with her grandparents at times during her childhood and F had stated that he wanted to leave the house to her. However, in F's final will, drawn up a year before he died, F split his estate equally between M, S and N. In the last year of his life F was infirm and was cared for by S, as M was living abroad. Shortly before his death, F told S that he had made a mistake in his will and wanted to leave the house to N. With the help of S's husband, a former solicitor, F executed a transfer of the property for no consideration, but did not register it. A few days after F's death in July 2000, S registered the transfer. M brought the current application, arguing that F had placed trust and confidence in S, thereby giving rise to a presumption of undue influence.

Held, dismissing the application, that there was no undue influence and F had executed the transfer of his own free will. Although the circumstances surrounding the execution and registration of the transfer gave rise to a suspicion of undue influence this was not borne out by the evidence, *Royal Bank of Scotland Plc v. Etridge (No.2)* [2001] UKHL 44, [2002] 2 A.C. 773, [2001] C.L.Y. 4880 and *Papouis v. Gibson-West* [2004] EWHC 396, [2004] W.T.L.R. 485 applied. S had registered the transfer to give effect to F's wish, rather than as a means of securing an advantage for herself or N. Although F had placed trust and confidence in S in relation to day to day matters, he had not done so with respect to the transfer.

MICHAEL v. CANSICK, [2004] EWHC 1684, [2004] W.T.L.R. 961, Kevin Garnett Q.C., Ch D.

3969. Gifts—Real property—Purchase of lease by means of endowment mortgage—Meaning of "contrary or other intention" in s.35 Administration of Estates Act 1925

[Administration of Estates Act 1925 s.35.]

The claimant (R), the father and executor of the deceased (D), sought a declaration as to the true construction of a gift of property to the defendant (P), D's partner. D had purchased both the freehold reversion and the lease of a maisonette, the lease having been purchased with an endowment mortgage. Following D's death, R had used the proceeds of the endowment policy to discharge the mortgage. R contended that, in accordance with the Administration of Estates Act 1925 s.35, P took the property subject to the mortgage and took only the lease and not the reversion.

Held, granting a declaration in P's favour, that P had the right to take the lease free of the mortgage. By virtue of s.35 of the 1925 Act, devised property was normally to be used to discharge any mortgage debt. However, if written evidence was adduced to show that a testator had intended that the mortgage be repaid by another means, such as an insurance policy, that was sufficient to establish a "contrary or other intention" within the meaning of s.35. Endowment mortgages were generally entered into with the intention that the mortgage would be discharged upon death; any other interpretation undermined the purpose of particular arrangement and the court should recognise such arrangements, *Smith v. Clerical Medical and General Life Assurance Society* [1993] 1 F.L.R. 47, [1993] C.L.Y. 4137 considered. In the instant case, it was clear that D had intended the mortgage be discharged following his death by the monies from the endowment policy as he had increased the premiums to make up for the likely shortfall in the value of that policy. Although D had used an ambiguous term in his home made will by describing the property as his "apartment", all the evidence indicated that he had intended his property to be a gift to P and that meant both the lease and the freehold reversion, *Fleming's Will Trusts, Re* [1974] 1 W.L.R. 1552, [1974] C.L.Y. 4005 applied.

ROSS v. PERRIN-HUGHES; *sub nom*. ROSS (DECEASED), *Re*, [2004] EWHC 2559, [2005] W.T.L.R. 191, Leslie Kosmin Q.C., Ch D.

3970. Trusts–Undue influence–No evidentiary presumption of undue influence

The claimant (P) brought an action against the defendant (G), his sister. P claimed that G's inheritance from their aunt (B) of a flat and money in a bank account had been procured by undue influence. G had provided half of the purchase price for B's flat, the remainder having been raised by B herself. B and G entered into a deed of trust which provided that the proceeds of sale would go to G upon the sale of the property and in the event of B's death. Shortly afterwards, B altered her current bank account details so as to put it in the joint names of herself and G. Upon B's death, her will stated that her residuary estate should be left to G, P and another niece in equal shares. P maintained that the trust deed had been made under the undue influence of G and that the credit in the bank account had not accrued to G by right of survivorship.

Held, giving judgment for G in part, that G was entitled to the proceeds from the sale of the flat but not to the money in the bank account. No evidence had been adduced by P that raised any presumption of undue influence up to the making of the trust deed. The deed accurately reflected B's wishes and there was no evidence to suggest that B had been of unsound mind at the material time. G's name had been added to the bank account purely as a matter of convenience. There was evidence that G had made payments into the bank account but those sums were either small or were gifts from G to B; therefore B retained beneficial ownership of the money in the account.

PAPOUIS v. GIBSON-WEST; *sub nom*. BENNETT (FLORENCE LILIAN), IN THE ESTATE OF, [2004] EWHC 396, [2004] W.T.L.R. 485, Lewison, J., Ch D.

3971. Wills–Capacity–Dementia–Actual knowledge and understanding of contents

The appellant (H) appealed against a decision ([2004] EWHC 177) that a will made in 1994 by the testatrix (K) was valid. The 1994 will had revoked an earlier will under which H would have been entitled to share in K's substantial residuary estate. By the later will K left the residuary estate to the respondent (A). K suffered from dementia but it was in issue as to how much she was suffering at the time she executed the will. H submitted that K lacked testamentary capacity or, alternatively, that she did not know or approve of the will's contents. H submitted that, given that it was accepted that K was of doubtful capacity, the judge had erred in not requiring proof of actual understanding of the act of making a will, the nature and extent of the property being disposed of, and the beneficiaries, and that affirmative proof was needed of the knowledge that the dispositions made by the new will marked a significant change in financial terms to the dispositions made by the old will. H also argued that the judge had drawn the wrong inferences from the evidence. There was no suggestion of undue influence.

Held, dismissing the appeal, that the requirements for testamentary capacity and for knowledge and approval should not be conflated. The former required capacity to understand certain important matters relating to the will, *Banks v. Goodfellow* (1869-70) L.R. 5 Q.B. 549 applied. Given that K had given instructions for the making of the new will and that the evidence showed that she was well aware of the assets at her disposal, and the straightforward nature of the will, there was no requirement for any further explanation to be given to

K. It was for the court to determine in each case whether the requisite knowledge and approval had been proved. The will in the instant case was a straightforward one and there was no need to insist on evidence that K had the earlier dispositions in mind when she made the new will, *Kenward v. Adams* Times, November 29, 1975, [1975] C.L.Y. 3591 considered. The judge was justified on the evidence in holding that K did know and approve of the will's contents.

HOFF v. ATHERTON, [2004] EWCA Civ 1554, [2005] W.T.L.R. 99, Peter Gibson, L.J., CA (Civ Div).

3972. Wills–Class closing–Ambiguity–Australia

The Public Trustee brought a summons requesting clarification of the deceased's will. The will bequeathed an absolute gift of equal shares of the estate to the deceased's defendant grandchildren (B). A further clause provided that no "minor" beneficiary could take their share until they were 32 years old. It was submitted that this further clause was ambiguous and that it would allow vesting after the statutory perpetuity period had expired.

Held, giving judgment accordingly, that the gift to B was valid. The will had been badly drafted by the solicitor concerned and was to be treated as if it had been drafted by a layperson. Therefore, the word "minor" could be deleted. There was a presumption that the vesting of an interest occurred as early as possible, *Duffield v. Duffield* 4 E.R. 1334 considered. The clause deferred possession of the gift and not the vesting of the interest. This was a class gift and the age requirement was a condition subsequent to the obtaining of the vested interest. The statutory "wait and see" rules prevented the gift from failing at the expiry of the perpetuity period. In any event it was established law that if the second clause failed, the absolute gift would take effect, *Lassence v. Tierney* 41 E.R. 1379 considered.

PUBLIC TRUSTEE v. BENNETT (2004-05) 7 I.T.E.L.R. 392, Gzell, J., Sup Ct (NSW).

3973. Wills–Cy pres doctrine–Intention to benefit Christian organisations–Testator predeceased by executors and named beneficiaries–Canada

The Public Trustee sought directions as to the validity of B's will. The will provided for 20 per cent of B's estate to go to named beneficiaries and 80 per cent to Christian organisations that she had supported during her lifetime, subject to the proviso that if her beneficiaries predeceased her, their share of the 20 per cent would also be applied in favour of the Christian groups. All the beneficiaries, two of whom had been appointed as the executors under the will, predeceased B. B's heirs at law argued that the will was void for uncertainty and that since both executors had died, the property which was subject to their appointment lapsed into the residue of the estate.

Held, giving directions, that the will and evidence obtained from B's bank accounts disclosed a general and specific intention to make charitable gifts in favour of Christian missions and organisations. The will was therefore valid. As the bequests in question were of a charitable nature, the doctrine of lapse had no effect.

BRUCE'S ESTATE, *Re* (2004-05) 7 I.T.E.L.R. 280, Desroches, C.J.T.D., Sup Ct (PEI).

3974. Wills–Deeds of variation–Error in amount of nil rate band for inheritance tax–Intentions at time of execution of deed

The applicant (M) applied for rectification of a deed of variation of the will of her late husband. By the will, the whole estate passed to M with a gift over to the couple's two children. Subsequently, a deed of variation was executed so as to set up a discretionary trust and utilise the testator's nil rate band, thus avoiding excess liability to inheritance tax on the aggregated value of the two estates on M's death. The deed of variation was defective in that it added on the discretionary trust to an existing clause without varying the dispository effects of that clause and it created a trust fund of £200,000, which was the amount of the nil rate band at the date of execution of the deed of variation. However, the nil rate band at the date of the testator's death was £154,000, which left a sum of £46,000 liable to inheritance tax.

Held, granting the application, that the standard of proof required on a claim for rectification was "convincing proof", *Thomas Bates & Son Ltd v. Wyndham's (Lingerie) Ltd* [1981] 1 W.L.R. 505, [1981] C.L.Y. 1584 applied. The question was whether M had intended to save the maximum amount of inheritance tax by reference to the nil rate band in effect as at her husband's death, in which case it was not necessary to specify the exact sum, or whether she had intended to settle £200,000 on trust in the mistaken belief that this was the amount of the nil rate band, in which case rectification could not be justified. On the evidence, M's intention had been to create a discretionary trust of an amount equal to the nil rate band at the death of her husband. The will was rectified to substitute a form of words giving effect to a discretionary trust consisting of the amount of the nil rate band applicable to an estate at the relevant time, rather than substituting a set figure of £154,000.

MARTIN v. NICHOLSON, [2004] EWHC 2135, [2005] W.T.L.R. 175, Peter Smith, J., Ch D.

3975. Wills—Gifts—Incorrect description applied to gift of real property—Not possible accurately to determine subject matter of gift—Failure for uncertainty—Australia

The claimants (B), who were the sons of the testator (T), sought a declaration that a testamentary gift of property was invalid. By his will, T had made a gift of his principal residence "and the granny flat attached thereto and the lots on which [his] said principal residence and the said granny flat stand..." to two grandsons. The dispute arose from the fact that the house and granny flat were not, and never had been, on separate lots but formed part of the same property. The defendant executor (R) subsequently obtained planning permission for the creation of two lots by subdividing the land on which the property stood. B argued that the gifts were invalid because it was not possible to determine from the will what portion of the existing lot each beneficiary was to receive.

Held, granting the application, that in the construction of a will the court was to give the words their ordinary meaning, having regard to any admissible evidence of surrounding circumstances, *Hodgson, Re* [1936] Ch. 203 applied. A gift would only be found void for uncertainty where the disposition was incapable of any clear meaning. Where the court concluded that the testator intended to pass something and was able to determine by the language used and extrinsic evidence what was referred to, then the gift was valid irrespective of whether the testator had given the subject matter an erroneous description, *Gifford, Re* [1944] Ch. 186 and *Lewis's Will Trusts, Re* [1985] 1 W.L.R. 102, [1985] C.L.Y. 3640 applied. It was, however, necessary that the language of the will was capable of being fairly interpreted as applying to that subject matter, *Mulder, Re* [1943] 2 All E.R. 150 applied. Where a testator had not merely applied a wrong description to an item but held the mistaken belief that it actually existed as he had described it, the gift was likely to fail as the court could not remake the gift on the basis of what the testator may have wanted had he understood the position correctly, *Tetsall, Re* [1961] 1 W.L.R. 938, [1961] C.L.Y. 9182 applied. In the instant case, it appeared that T believed either that the main house and granny flat stood on separate lots or that separate lots would be created before his death. However, there was no evidence that prior to T's death the land had been used or enjoyed as separate lots in relation to the house and granny flat and it was not possible to determine what portions of the land T intended to pass with each dwelling. Nor was there any evidence that the subdivision created by R represented what T had intended. The gifts therefore failed for uncertainty.

BAKRANICH v. ROBERTSON (2004-05) 7 I.T.E.L.R. 609, Master Newnes, Sup Ct (WA) (Sgl judge).

3976. Wills–Illegitimacy–Adopted child's entitlement to inherit

[Adoption of Children Act 1926 s.5(2); Adoption Act 1976 s.39; Family Law Reform Act 1987 s.1, s.19(1)(b); Human Rights Act 1998 Sch.1 Part II Art.1.]

The claimant illegitimate child (T), who was later adopted by his father (X), claimed that under the terms of his grandfather's will made in 1930 he was entitled to inherit X's share under the will as a "child" of X. At the date of X's death, X was entitled to a three fifths share in the income from his father's estate. Under the terms of X's will, X left his entire estate to T. Accordingly, T claimed that he was entitled to the three fifths share. The defendant executors (N) argued that as T was illegitimate he was not entitled to inherit as a child of X. N further argued that the law relating to adoption did not assist in the instant case as the will was made in 1930. N argued that the income from the disputed shares accrued to X's brother (R) whilst R was alive and thereafter the whole of the grandfather's estate passed to R's children. T refuted N's case but argued that even if N was correct, he could still claim as the Human Rights Act 1998 was in force when X died.

Held, giving judgment for the defendant, that the legislation removing discrimination on the grounds of illegitimacy or adoption was not retrospective and, on the facts, the 1998 Act could not apply. It was a well established principle that a gift to a child was a gift to a legitimate child unless it was possible to construe a contrary intention in the will, *Brinkley's Will Trusts, Re* [1968] Ch. 407, [1967] C.L.Y. 4095 applied. Under the Family Law Reform Act 1987 s.1 any reference to any relationship between two persons was, unless a contrary intention appeared, to be construed without regard to whether the father and mother were married, and pursuant to s.19(1)(b) dispositions by will were to be construed in accordance with that section. However, s.19(1)(b) only applied to wills made after 1988, the date when the Act came into force. The Adoption of Children Act 1926 s.5(2) excluded adopted children from benefiting from a disposition made under a will. Although the Adoption Act 1976 s.39 would have assisted T, the Act did not apply to instruments which existed before 1976. The 1998 Act was of no assistance to T. There was no breach of Sch.1 Part II Art.1 as the disputed share of his grandfather's will was never one of his possessions. The litigation was between private individuals and did not create any new private rights. Further, although the legislation relating to adoption and illegitimacy had been changed so that there could not be discrimination on either of those grounds, the legislation was not retrospective so was of no assistance in the instant case. Accordingly, the disputed share passed to R and following his death would be distributed equally between his children.

UPTON v. NATIONAL WESTMINSTER BANK PLC, [2004] EWHC 1962, [2004] W.T.L.R. 1339, Judge Behrens, Ch D.

3977. Wills–Interpretation–Use of extrinsic evidence–Partial intestacy created by death of beneficiary and discovery of money buried in garden–Australia

[Administration and Probate Act 1919 (Australia) Part 3A.]

The claimant (D) sought a determination of questions arising from the construction of the will of a testator (T). The will, which was written in Ukrainian, directed that, after the payment of funeral expenses, T's house was to be sold and the proceeds divided between seven named persons living in Ukraine, however one of these had predeceased T. The will identified a bank account in T's name from which the expenses were to be paid, after the deduction of AUD 1,500 to be paid to those arranging his funeral, with the balance then going to the Ukrainian Association. The will also left certain items of porcelain to his estranged daughter. A separate note found in T's papers also revealed that AUD 67,000 was buried in the garden of his home.

Held, giving directions, that the will was to be interpreted by reference to the facts known to T at the time he made it. Although extrinsic evidence could be admitted to explain what T had written, it could not be used to determine what he intended. As the will made no provision for the money found in the garden it fell into residue along with the seventh share to the beneficiary who predeceased T. The partial intestacy thus created falling to be dealt with under the Administration and Probate Act 1919 (Australia) Part 3A.

DOBRYDEN v. WAGNER; *sub nom.* TKACZUK (DECEASED), *Re* (2004-05) 7 I.T.E.L.R. 496, Duggan, J., Sup Ct (SAus) (Sgl judge).

3978. Wills–Life interests–Surrender of life interest in favour of remaindermen with vested interests–Application of class closing rules–Australia

The applicant trustees of a will sought directions as to whether they could transfer property left to the testatrix's son (B) for life to his children on B's surrender of his interest in the property. The testatrix had left her house and half the residue of her estate to B on a life interest with remainder to his children in equal shares. The principal issues to be determined were (1) whether the remainder passed immediately to B's children upon his surrender of his life interest, or whether they would not benefit until B's death; (2) whether the class closing rules would apply upon B's surrender of his life interest.

Held, giving judgment accordingly, that (1) the property would pass to B's children immediately upon the surrender of B's interest in it, *Harker's Will Trusts, Re* [1969] 1 W.L.R. 1124, [1969] C.L.Y. 3664, *Hartigan, Re* [1989] 2 Qd. R. 401 and *Collins v. Equity Trustees Executors & Agency Co Ltd* [1997] V.R. 166 applied. (2) As the remainder interests were vested, were not dependent upon the remaindermen surviving or reaching a specified age and there was no gift over, the closing of the class of beneficiaries as at the date of surrender was not contrary to the testatrix's intention. Conditions imposed upon the receipt of an interest such as surviving a life tenant or reaching a certain age suggested an intention to delay possession, however, and the courts should be cautious in allowing earlier possession in such cases, *Syme (Deceased), Re* [1980] V.R. 109 followed, *Flower's Settlement Trusts, Re* [1957] 1 W.L.R. 401, [1957] C.L.Y. 3277 and *Taylor, Re* [1957] 1 W.L.R. 1043, [1957] C.L.Y. 3690 distinguished.

BASSETT v. BASSETT [2005] W.T.L.R. 51, Windeyer, J., Sup Ct (NSW).

3979. Wills–Republication–Original handed to daughter–Copy of codicil found after death–Presumption codicil revoked by evidence of change of intention–British Columbia

The applicant (P) applied for probate of T's will. T had given the original to her daughter after executing it in 1987 but no copy was found following her death. However a photocopy of a codicil was discovered, which purportedly changed the 1987 by stipulating that the residue was to be held on trust for T's disabled son, who was to receive monthly payments, continuing an allowance T had begun paying him during her lifetime, as opposed to being divided equally between her four children and two others, one of whom had predeceased T, as provided for by the will. The codicil stated "Due to circumstances, I wish to make the following changes to my will which was dated May 13, 1987". There was evidence that T had ceased making the inter vivos payments to her son.

Held, allowing the application, that although the codicil confirmed the 1987 will it could not incorporate it because it was not a valid testamentary document. As the original of the will had been handed to the daughter but the original of the codicil had not been found, the presumption arose that the codicil had been revoked, an inference borne out by the evidence that T had ceased to make the payments to her son contemplated by the terms of the codicil.

TURNER, IN THE ESTATE OF [2004] W.T.L.R. 1467, Bauman, J., Sup Ct (BC).

3980. Wills–Validity–Intention to attest–Deceased's knowledge and approval of contents of will

[Wills Act 1837 s.9.]

The appellant (D) appealed against the decision ([2004] EWHC 1613, [2004] W.T.L.R. 895) revoking a grant of probate to her as the deceased's widow on the basis that the deceased's will had not been validly executed. The deceased had been a successful solicitor and businessman and left a substantial estate. The claimants (C) were the children of his first marriage. The deceased had divorced his first wife and married D. D was the sole beneficiary and executrix under the deceased's will and obtained a grant of probate. The will had been drafted by one of D's daughters, who had no legal qualifications or experience. She also drafted a reciprocal will for D. C sought revocation of the grant of probate alleging that the will had not been duly executed in accordance with the Wills Act 1837 s.9 because the witnesses did not intend to attest the signature of the deceased and the deceased did not know and approve the contents of the will, for which he had not given instructions and which did not give effect to the strong moral obligations which the deceased felt towards his mother and children. The judge held that the deceased signed the will in the presence of two attesting witnesses but that those witnesses did not intend to attest the deceased's signature, and that D failed to discharge the burden on her to prove the deceased's knowledge and approval of the will.

Held, allowing the appeal and dismissing the cross-appeal, that (1) the judge was right that the court had to be satisfied that the witness had signed the will with the intention of attesting the testator's signature or of attesting the will, *Beadle (Deceased), Re* [1974] 1 W.L.R. 417, [1974] C.L.Y. 4011 approved, *Benjamin (Deceased), Re* (1934) 150 LT 417 disapproved. (2) When the will contained the signatures of the deceased and the witness and an attestation clause the presumption of due execution would prevail for policy reasons unless there was the strongest evidence that the witness did not intend to attest that he saw the deceased sign. In the absence of the strongest evidence, the intention of the witness to attest was inferred from the presence of the testator's signature on the will (particularly where, as in the instant case, it was expressly stated that in witness of the will the testator had signed), the attestation clause and, underneath that clause, the signature of the witness. (3) The judge erred in reaching the factual conclusion that the witnesses did not intend to attest. In favour of the judge's conclusion that the will was not validly executed was the evidence of the two witnesses to the will, and only their evidence. One witness gave evidence that she did not intend to witness the deceased's signature in the will but that was a wholly unimpressive piece of evidence given her categoric evidence that she did not see the deceased sign nor his signature when the judge had found that the deceased did sign in her presence before she signed. The other witness gave no direct evidence of the lack of intention to attest, but insofar as the judge drew an inference from his not having seen the deceased sign or his signature similar reasoning applied to that evidence. It was impossible to conclude that the judge had the strong evidence needed to rebut the presumption of due execution. (4) The judge was right to conclude that the deceased did sign the will in the presence of the witnesses and the cross-appeal on that issue was dismissed. (5) The judge was entitled to decide that the circumstances were such as to excite the suspicion of the court, and accordingly to throw the burden onto D of establishing that the will was executed with the knowledge and approval of the deceased. (6) It was surprising that the deceased excluded the claimants from the will save only as default beneficiaries. The way in which, and the haste with which, the will was drafted and the mistakes in it were also surprising. However the judge's factual conclusion that the deceased did not know and approve of the contents was wrong. The court had to consider the inherent probabilities and in so doing it had to look at all the relevant evidence, including the evidence of what happened after the will was executed, *Fuller v. Strum* [2001] EWCA Civ 1879, [2002] 1 W.L.R. 1097, [2002] C.L.Y. 4338 applied. In the circumstances, in the absence of any clear or cogent evidence to the contrary, it was fanciful to conclude that the deceased did not know or approve of the contents of the will.

SHERRINGTON v. SHERRINGTON, [2005] EWCA Civ 326, [2005] 3 F.C.R. 538, Peter Gibson, L.J., CA (Civ Div).

3981. Books

Biggs, A.K.–Probate: Lawyers Costs and Fees. Paperback: £13.95. ISBN 0 7545 2797 2. Tolley Publishing.

Bowley, Gordon—Making A Will Self-Help Guide. Paperback: £9.99. ISBN 1 84528 030 X. How To Books.

Cousal, Helen; King, Lesley—Private Client: Wills, Trusts and Estate Planning. Paperback: £24.95. ISBN 0 905835 75 1. Paperback: £25.95. ISBN 1 905391 09 9. The College of Law.

Cummins—Wills and Trusts Probate Law. Hardback: £32.99. ISBN 0 13 081150 5. Pearson US Imports & PHIPEs.

Dew, Richard—Wills, Power of Attorney and Probate Guide. Paperback: £11.99. ISBN 1 905261 07 1. Lawpack Publishing Ltd.

Elmhirst, Paul—Wills and Probate. "Which?" Consumer Guides. Paperback: £11.99. ISBN 1 84490 018 5. Which? Books.

Garsia, Marlene—How to Write Your Will. Paperback: £8.99. ISBN 0 7494 4471 1. Kogan Page.

Grant, James—Writing Your Own Will. Paperback: £9.99. ISBN 1 900694 08 5. Easyway Guides.

Knight, J.—Wills, Probate and Inheritance Tax for Dummies. For Dummies S. Paperback: £12.99. ISBN 0 7645 7055 2. John Wiley and Sons Ltd.

Lowe, Jonquil—Giving and Inheriting: The "Which?" Guide to Giving and Inheriting. "Which?" Consumer Guides. Paperback: £11.99. ISBN 1 84490 016 9. Which? Books.

Mouawad, Joyce—Succession: The Law of Wills and Estates. Paperback: £15.95. ISBN 1 85836 506 6. Old Bailey Press.

Peters, Julie—Straightforward Guide to Probate and the Law. Paperback: £8.99. ISBN 1 903909 70 8. Straightforward Publishing.

Piggot, Mike Semple—Wills and Succession. Law in a Box S., No. 18. CD-ROM: £19.95. ISBN 1 904783 74 0. Semple Piggot Rochez (Legal Education Ltd).

Ray, Ralph; Hitchmough, Andrew; Wilson, Elizabeth—Tottel's Practical Inheritance Tax Planning. Paperback: £75.95. ISBN 1 84592 072 4. Tottel Publishing.

Ross, Sidney—Inheritance Act Claims: Law and Practice. Paperback: £75.00. ISBN 0 421 89310 9. Sweet & Maxwell.

Scott, David—Emerald Hole Lawyer Creating Wills. Paperback: £9.99. ISBN 1 903909 68 6. Straightforward Publishing.

Steven, Andrew; Wortley, Scott; Reid, Kenneth—Property Trusts and Succession. Paperback: £35.00. ISBN 1 84592 153 4. Tottel Publishing.

Strathern, Marilyn—Kinship, Law and the Unexpected: Relatives Are Always a Surprise. Hardback: £40.00. ISBN 0 521 84992 6. Paperback: £13.99. ISBN 0 521 61509 7. Cambridge University Press.

Talbot, Alison—Probate Kit. Looseleaf/ring bound: £14.99. ISBN 1 904053 25 4. Law Pack Publishing.

Wade, Peter—Practical Guide to Obtaining Probate. Emerald Home Lawyer S. Paperback: £9.99. ISBN 1 903909 62 7. Straightforward Publishing.

Waterworth, Michael; Bedworth, Georgia—Rossdale-Probate and the Administration of Estates: A Practical Guide. Hardback: £75.00. ISBN 1 903927 66 8. Legalease.

Which? Books—Giving and Inheriting: An Action Pack from Which? "Which?" Action Pack S. Paperback: £10.99. ISBN 0 85202 980 2. Which? Books.

TAX

3982. Advance corporation tax—Agreements to lease—Retained rent—Income—Interests in land

[Income and Corporation Taxes Act 1988 Sch.A, Sch.D; Landlord and Tenant (Covenants) Act 1995 s.3.]

The appellant (P) appealed against estimated assessments to corporation tax. P had originally been the property owning company within the C group. Some of P's properties were sold in April 1995 to P's parent company (X) and an agreement to lease of other properties was entered into in August 1995 in favour of X. A further agreement to lease of the same plus some additional properties was entered into in

August 1996. The agreements did not provide for the payment of rent. The rent was expressed to be payable when the underleases were granted. The agreements provided that the parties should obtain the consent of the superior landlord before the lease would be granted. If consent was not obtained by a specified date, the agreements would cease to have effect. Under a business sale agreement, P then sold all its assets to another group company (Y) and retained the next rent payment due from X. X then sold the shares of P out of the group by way of a share sale agreement. The purchaser intended to offset the retained rent payment by creating a deduction in P. The benefit of this tax saving was to be split between the C group in the form of the sale price of the shares in P and the purchaser in the form of the balance of the rent. The proposed tax avoidance scheme did not work. P argued that the retained rent payment was not in fact rent and was not taxable under the Income and Corporation Taxes Act 1988 Sch.A because, during the relevant accounting period, P had no interest in land. Furthermore, P argued that it was also not liable to tax under Case VI to Sch.D of the 1988 Act.

Held, allowing the appeal in part, that (1) although the consent provisions appeared to impose a condition precedent on the creation of subleases and thus the payment of rent, the parties had acted as if rent had been payable in respect of all the properties immediately on entering into the 1995 and 1996 agreements. P had not given much urgency to obtaining the consents and, in the event, only a small proportion of the required consents had been obtained. The actions of the parties demonstrated that they had created annual tenancies and had charged rent in breach of the covenant against subletting without consent. The preferred interpretation was that the agreements created a condition subsequent that consents to subletting be obtained. Thus, the agreements created an immediate obligation on X to pay rent. (2) The 1996 agreement properties were subject to the Landlord and Tenant (Covenants) Act 1995. Under s.3 of that Act, the benefit of the covenant to receive the retained rent payment passed to Y upon the sale of P's assets in 1996. The purported retention of the retained rent was therefore void, but effect could be given to the subsequent business sale agreement on the basis that Y would receive the rent and pay an equivalent amount to P. Thus, P's rights in this respect were not property rights, but were best understood as a contractual right to consideration for sale of the assets. Those rights were effective as against Y under the business sale agreement and as against X under the share sale agreement. (3) The retained rent payment was not taxable under Sch.A to the 1998 Act as there was no source. (4) Both the part, being rent from properties let pursuant to the 1995 agreement to which the 1995 Act did not apply, and the balance of the retained rent payment were of an income nature, *John Lewis Properties Plc v. Inland Revenue Commissioners* [2002] EWCA Civ 1869, [2003] Ch. 513, [2003] C.L.Y. 4173 considered. (5) The part was originally a Sch.A source. The business sale agreement had not changed the nature of that source. The nature of the source could not change because P no longer had an interest in land. As that source had ceased, the part was not taxable under Case VI of Sch.D. (6) The balance was not rent and, owing to the effects of the 1995 Act, had no legal connection to the land. The balance was in the nature of income that was ejusdem generis with Sch.A income and, not being taxable under any other schedule, was accordingly taxable under Case VI of Sch.D.

PROPERTY CO v. INSPECTOR OF TAXES [2005] S.T.C. (S.C.D.) 59, Stephen Oliver Q.C., Sp Comm.

3983. Advance corporation tax–Retirement relief–Company purchase of director's shares–Financed by issue of preference shares bought by that director

[Income and Corporation Taxes Act 1988 s.219, s.221 (4), s.223(1), s.228(2).]

The first appellant company (P) appealed against an assessment for advance corporation tax. The second appellant (S), a director of P, appealed against an assessment of tax due on franked income. S held ordinary shares in P along with one other director (W) and both their wives. S was due to retire and wished to sell his shares in the company. It was decided that P would buy the shares because W and his wife were unable to do so. P had insufficient funds to buy the shares and it was decided that it would issue 130,000 interest bearing preference shares with no voting rights. S and his family would then purchase these shares with the funds raised paying for P's purchase of the ordinary shares owned by S and his wife. It was S's case that, owing to time pressures, a single share certificate had been issued in his name. However, S maintained that, in reality, he had only acquired 30,000 of the preference shares for his own benefit. It was claimed that the other 100,000 were for the benefit of his daughter. Thus, P and S challenged the assessments and argued that the arrangement fell within the Income and Corporation Taxes Act 1988 s.219. As a result of the transfer of the shares to S's daughter, the overall shareholding held by S and his wife was said to have fallen from 49.6 to 23 per cent and the reduction comfortably exceeded that required by s.221 (4) of the 1988 Act. Moreover, it was claimed that S would also satisfy the requirements of s.223(1) as he held less than 30 per cent of each of the rights identified in s.228(2) and he had no entitlement to acquire more.

Held, dismissing the appeal, that the evidence was clear that S's intention was to give his daughter the proceeds from the redemption of the shares but not the actual shares themselves. Furthermore, he had not given his daughter a proportion of the interest he had received. S had retained ownership of the preference shares and thus his shareholding in P had only reduced from 49.6 per cent to 46 per cent. Consequently, the requirements of s.221 (4) had not met. Furthermore, the transaction offended s.223(1) as S still had a connection with the company.

PRESTON MEATS LTD v. HAMMOND (INSPECTOR OF TAXES) [2005] S.T.C. (S.C.D.) 90, Colin Bishopp, Sp Comm.

3984. **Advance corporation tax—Subsidiary companies—Compensation for breach of EC law**

The appellant Inland Revenue appealed against the decision in a test case in group litigation ([2004] EWHC 2387, [2004] S.T.C. 1178, [2004] C.L.Y. 3681) that certain compensation or restitution due in respect of the premature payment of advance corporation tax (ACT) should bear interest calculated on a compound basis. In *Metallgesellschaft Ltd v. Inland Revenue Commissioners (C397/98)* [2001] Ch. 620 the European Court of Justice held that it was contrary to the EC Treaty Art.43 for United Kingdom tax law to differentiate, in the treatment of ACT on dividends paid by a subsidiary company to its parent, between cases where both subsidiary and parent were resident in the UK for tax purposes and cases where the subsidiary was resident in the UK but the parent was resident in another Member State . The ECJ went on to hold that a UK subsidiary of a parent company resident in another Member State which had been required to pay, and had paid, an amount in respect of corporation tax earlier than would have been the case had its parent been resident in the UK was entitled to compensation for the timing disadvantage which it had suffered, and that the amount of that compensation was to be determined by the national court. The judge determined that in a case where an amount equal to ACT actually paid by the subsidiary company was later set off against a liability to corporation tax on taxable profits, compensation for the period between the date of premature payment and the date of set off ("the premature tax payment period") should be calculated on the basis of compound interest, and that the amount of compensation should bear simple interest for the period from the date when an amount equal to the advance corporation tax paid was set off against corporation tax on taxable profits ("the post utilisation period"). The Revenue appealed against the decision that compensation for the premature tax payment period should be calculated on the basis of compound interest. The Revenue submitted that properly understood the decision of the ECJ in *Metallgesellschaft* was that an award based on simple interest would meet the need to provide full compensation for the loss of the use of money and that the judge in awarding compound interest departed from the normal approach under English domestic law.

Held, dismissing the appeal, that (1) In the instant case where there was no principal sum outstanding at the time when the action was commenced, a claim for interest by way of restitution or compensation for loss of the use of money during a period over which the principal sum was outstanding would not be allowed under UK domestic law, *President of India v. La Pintada Compania Navigacion SA (The La Pintada)* [1985] A.C. 104, [1984] C.L.Y. 123 considered. So, as the judge held, the domestic rules in relation to interest were unlikely to be of much (if any) assistance. The task for the English court was to give the remedy which Community law required in circumstances where domestic law would not provide a remedy. The remedy to be given by the national court had to be a "full" remedy, in the sense that it had to be such as would restore the equality of treatment guaranteed by Art.43. A full remedy for the loss of the use of money over a specified period could be measured by reference to the interest "accrued" on the amount of the tax paid prematurely. But there was no true analogy with the award of interest on a domestic judgment. The task of the national court was to ascertain the amount which the Member State had to pay to the claimant in order to restore the claimant to the position that it would have been in if it had not been required to pay an amount of corporation tax prematurely. (2) There was no support for the proposition that the ECJ assumed in *Metallgesellschaft* that an award based on simple interest would meet the need to provide full compensation for the loss of the use of money which the claimant had been required to pay prematurely, *Marshall v. Southampton and South West Hampshire AHA (No.2) (C271/91)* [1994] Q.B. 126, [1994] C.L.Y. 4927 and *Corus UK Ltd v. Commission of the European Communities (T171/99)* [2002] 1 W.L.R. 970, [2001] C.L.Y. 2483 considered. (3) It was generally accepted that in commercial cases an award based on compound, rather than simple, interest was more likely to reflect economic reality and to provide full, rather than partial, recompense for the loss of the use of money. The Inland Revenue accepted that compensation was to be measured by interest accrued at a single conventional rate for all claimants, which was to be a borrower's rate, and the judge was right to conclude that full compensation for the loss of the use of money required that interest was compounded. That applied to unutilised ACT as well as to utilised ACT. The judge's order should be varied so as to make clear that the rate of interest adopted dictated both the principle that interest should be compounded and the periods (or rests) at which it should be compounded.

SEMPRA METALS LTD (FORMERLY METALLGESELLSCHAFT LTD) v. INLAND REVENUE COMMISSIONERS, [2005] EWCA Civ 389, [2006] Q.B. 37, Chadwick, L.J., CA (Civ Div).

3985. Allowances—Sex discrimination—Inland Revenue's power to make extra statutory allowance to widowers

[Taxes Management Act 1970 s.1; Interpretation Act 1978 s.6; Income and Corporation Taxes Act 1988 s.262; Human Rights Act 1998 s.3, s.6, Sch.1 Part I Art.14, Sch.1 Part II Art.1.]

The appellant widower (W) appealed against the decision ([2003] EWCA Civ 814, [2003] 1 W.L.R. 2683, [2003] C.L.Y. 4169]) that he was not entitled to a tax allowance equivalent to the widow's bereavement allowance (abolished in relation to deaths on or after April 6, 2000) to which he would have been entitled as a widow under the Income and Corporation Taxes Act 1988 s.262. After the death of his wife W had complained that United Kingdom tax law, which allowed an income tax reduction to widows but not to widowers, was unfairly discriminatory. After the coming into force of the Human Rights Act 1998 W made a claim to the Inland Revenue for an allowance under s.262 on the ground that having to pay tax was something which affected a citizen's peaceful enjoyment of his possessions within the meaning of Sch.1 Part II Art.1 and that Sch.1 Part I Art.14 therefore required that in matters of taxation there should be no discrimination on grounds of sex, and that therefore the refusal of an allowance was an unlawful act, or failure to act, by the

Revenue under s.6(1) of the 1998 Act. W submitted that (1) it was possible to read s.262 as including widowers; (2) the Inland Revenue had statutory power to make an allowance to widowers by way of extra statutory concession under the care and management powers contained in the Taxes Management Act 1970 s.1; (3) he had been treated unfairly by comparison with other widowers who had received payments from the government after petitioning the European Court of Human Rights. The Inland Revenue submitted that the application of s.6(1) was excluded by s.6(2) because they had no statutory power to make widowers an allowance and so could not have acted differently within the meaning of s.6(2)(a).

Held, dismissing the appeal, that (1) it was not possible to read "widow" in s.262 as including "widower" by application of the Interpretation Act 1978 s.6, since a contrary intention was abundantly clear from the provisions of the 1988 Act. That conclusion was not affected by s.3 of the 1998 Act, which required statutes to be interpreted against a background which included the Convention and an assumption that they were not intended to be incompatible with Convention rights, but did not permit the word "widow" to be interpreted as referring to the more general concept of a surviving spouse. (2) The Inland Revenue did not have power under s.1 of the 1970 Act to make an extra statutory allowance to all widowers. They could not exercise their s.1 powers to concede, by extra statutory concession, an allowance which Parliament could have granted but did not grant, and on grounds not of pragmatism in the collection of tax but of general equity between men and women. Therefore the legislation gave the Inland Revenue no power to act otherwise than to disallow claims for allowances by widowers and they were therefore protected by s.6(2)(a). If W had had a cause of action he would not have been entitled to damages because if Parliament had paid proper regard to Art.14, it would have abolished the allowance for widows (as it had later done) rather than extended it to widowers, *Van Raalte v. Netherlands* (1997) 24 E.H.R.R. 503, [1998] C.L.Y. 3076 considered. (3) The Inland Revenue were not acting irrationally or unfairly abusing their powers by not paying W an allowance since he was not entitled to pecuniary damages and the Inland Revenue was entitled to take that point against W.

R. (ON THE APPLICATION OF WILKINSON) v. INLAND REVENUE COMMISSIONERS; *sub nom.* WILKINSON v. INLAND REVENUE COMMISSIONERS, [2005] UKHL 30, [2005] 1 W.L.R. 1718, Lord Nicholls of Birkenhead, HL.

3986. Appeals–Special Commissioners–Incapacity of one commissioner before appeal disposed of

[Taxes Management Act 1970 s.45(3).]

The claimant (H) sought judicial review of a decision of the defendant special commissioners refusing his application for a rehearing de novo of certain tax appeals to the commissioners which were already in process when one of the commissioners died and giving directions to carry those appeals to their conclusion. H and other taxpayers had embarked on a series of transactions involving a company incorporated in Singapore and an insurance company with the object of avoiding the payment of capital gains tax on the sale of certain land. The effectiveness of the scheme had been challenged by the Inland Revenue on the basis that certain of the agreements involved in the scheme and certain provisions of those agreements were ineffective as being "shams". H had appealed against assessments to tax to the special commissioners. The appeal was heard by two commissioners in 1997. The commissioners dealt with the issue of whether the scheme agreements constituted shams as a preliminary issue and decided the issue in favour of the Revenue. H's appeal to the High Court by way of case stated was allowed, but that decision was reversed by the Court of Appeal, which remitted the case stated and the assessments to the special commissioners. One of the commissioners hearing the appeal had since died and H questioned whether the remitted appeal had to be reheard by reason of the Taxes Management Act 1970 s.45(3). The surviving special commissioner was joined by another commissioner to replace the commissioner who had died and they decided that they could continue to hear the appeal. H argued that if he did not consent under s.45(3), and he did not, the existing appeal proceedings would have to be discarded and fresh appeals commenced before new commissioners.

Held, refusing the application, that (1) the balance of authority led to the conclusion that the common law position was that the death or incapacity of a judge in the middle of a case, including a commissioner in the course of a tax appeal, did not mean that there was no jurisdiction for a second judge to take over the case in mid trial and complete it. It would be open to him, particularly under modern rules of evidence, so to order the trial that costs thrown away were minimised. In a case not involving witnesses, that would be relatively easy. However, in the majority of cases, and in particular where witnesses were involved, it would be necessary, as a matter of case management, to try the matter de novo, *Odhams Press Ltd v. Cook* [1940] 3 All E.R. 15 and *Inland Revenue Commissioners v. TW Law Ltd* [1950] 2 All E.R. 196 considered. (2) Section 45(3) was not to be construed as requiring the consent of the parties where, for any reason, one of two special commissioners dealing with an appeal under the 1970 Act was incapacitated before the appeal in question was finally disposed of, so as to enable that to happen by permitting the appeal to be continued in front of the remaining commissioner or by a reconstituted panel of commissioners. Appeals lay to the commissioners as a body in office at the relevant time. Section 45 was not intended to deal with the jurisdiction of commissioners to continue with appeals in circumstances of incapacity in mid case.

R. (ON THE APPLICATION OF HITCH) v. SPECIAL COMMISSIONERS; *sub nom.* R. (ON THE APPLICATION OF HITCH) v. OLIVER (SPECIAL COMMISSIONER OF INCOME TAX), [2005] EWHC 291, [2005] 1 W.L.R. 1651, Evans-Lombe, J., QBD (Admin).

3987. Building societies–Interest–Dividends

INCOME TAX (BUILDING SOCIETIES) (DIVIDENDS AND INTEREST) (AMENDMENT) REGULATIONS 2005, SI 2005 3474; made under the Income and Corporation Taxes Act 1988 s.477A. In force: January 9, 2006; £3.00.

These Regulations amend the Income Tax (Building Societies) (Dividends and Interest) Regulations 1990 (SI 1990 2331) so that payments by building societies of alternative finance return or profit share return in relation to certain alternative finance arrangements can be paid without deduction of tax.

3988. Capital allowances–Corporation tax–Capital expenditure on provision of plant–Expenditure incurred for purpose of trade

[Capital Allowances Act 1990 s.24(1).]

The appellant (the Revenue) appealed against a decision ([2002] EWCA Civ 1853, [2003] S.T.C. 66, [2003] C.L.Y. 4145) that the respondent taxpayer (B) was entitled to capital allowances under the Capital Allowances Act 1990 s.24(1) in respect of expenditure incurred under contracts with the Irish Gas Board for the purchase and lease back of a gas pipeline. B was a member of the Barclays group and carried on the trade of providing asset based finance. It had acquired a pipeline from the Board for £91 million and leased it back to the Board on finance lease terms. The purchase price was deposited by the Board on terms with an investment company. The deposit was partly used to discharge the liability for rent under the lease and partly for the benefit of the Board. The deposit eventually followed an essentially circular route back into the control of Barclays Bank, which had advanced the purchase price to B. It was plain that all the arrangements were organised as part of a coordinated scheme. The issue for determination was whether B was nevertheless entitled to capital allowances in consequence of having paid £91m for the gas pipeline.

Held, dismissing the appeal, that *MacNiven (Inspector of Taxes) v. Westmoreland Investments Ltd* [2001] UKHL 6, [2003] 1 A.C. 311, [2001] C.L.Y. 5199 showed the need to focus carefully on the particular statutory provision and to identify its requirements before one could decide whether circular payments or elements inserted for the purpose of tax avoidance should be disregarded or treated as irrelevant for the purposes of the statute. The instant case, like *MacNiven*, illustrated the need for a close analysis of what, on a purposive construction, the statute actually required. Section 24(1) required that a trader should have incurred capital expenditure on the provision of machinery or plant for the purposes of his trade. When the trade was finance leasing, that meant that the capital expenditure should have been incurred to acquire the machinery or plant for the purpose of leasing it in the course of the trade. In such a case, it was the lessor as owner who suffered the depreciation in the value of the plant and was therefore entitled to an allowance against the profits of his trade. Those statutory requirements were, in the case of a finance lease, concerned entirely with the acts and purposes of the lessor. The Act said nothing about what the lessee should do with the purchase price, how he should find the money to pay the rent or how he should use the plant. In the instant case, the requirements of s.24(1) were satisfied. The finding of the special commissioners that the transaction "had no commercial reality" depended entirely upon an examination of what happened to the purchase price after B paid it to the Board. However, these matters did not affect the reality of the expenditure by B and its acquisition of the pipeline for the purposes of its finance leasing trade. The circularity of payments were happenstances. None of those transactions, whether circular or not, were necessary elements in creating the entitlement to the capital allowances, *MacNiven* considered.

BARCLAYS MERCANTILE BUSINESS FINANCE LTD v. MAWSON (INSPECTOR OF TAXES); *sub nom.* ABC LTD v. M (INSPECTOR OF TAXES), [2004] UKHL 51, [2005] 1 A.C. 684, Lord Nicholls of Birkenhead, HL.

3989. Capital allowances–Energy conservation–Machinery

CAPITAL ALLOWANCES (ENERGY-SAVING PLANT AND MACHINERY) (AMENDMENT) ORDER 2005, SI 2005 2424; made under the Capital Allowances Act 2001 s.45A, s.45C. In force: September 22, 2005; £3.00.

This Order amends the Capital Allowances (Energy-saving Plant and Machinery) Order 2001 (SI 2001 2541) which implemented legislation so as to introduce a scheme for 100 per cent first-year allowances to encourage businesses to invest in energy-saving plant and machinery. This Order substitutes new definitions of the "Energy Technology Criteria List" and the "Energy Technology Product List"; and makes amendments concerning energy-saving components of plant or machinery to extend the range of such components which qualify for the 100 per cent first-year allowance.

3990. Capital allowances–Environmental protection–Plant and machinery

CAPITAL ALLOWANCES (ENVIRONMENTALLY BENEFICIAL PLANT AND MACHINERY) (AMENDMENT) ORDER 2005, SI 2005 2423; made under the Capital Allowances Act 2001 s.45H, s.45I. In force: September 22, 2005; £3.00.

This Order amends the Capital Allowances (Environmentally Beneficial Plant and Machinery) Order 2003 (SI 2003 2076) which implemented legislation so as to introduce a scheme for 100 per cent first-year allowances to encourage businesses to invest in environmentally beneficial plant and machinery. This Order substitutes new definitions of the "the Water Technology Criteria List" and the "the Water Technology Product List"; and adds to the list of technology classes specified in the 2003 Order. It also provides that no first-year allowance is available in the case of certain expenditure unless an appropriate certificate of environmental benefit is in force.

3991. Capital allowances–Trade marks–Exclusive licences granted–Right to use mark during licence period–New Zealand

[Income Tax Act 1994 (New Zealand) s.EG1.]

The appellant trustees (S) appealed against the dismissal of their claims for depreciation allowance in respect of a number of trade marks under the Income

Tax Act 1994 (New Zealand) s.EG1. S had been the owners of a number of trade marks. They granted exclusive licences over the trade marks for a period of seven years in return for an annual royalty. Subsequently, they unsuccessfully claimed depreciation allowance in respect of the trade marks under s.EG1 of the 1994 Act, on the basis that they were the owners of the right to use the trade marks during the seven year period. S argued that, notwithstanding the licensees' exclusive right to use the trade marks, they had remained the owners of the right to use the trade marks during the seven year period. They maintained that the licensees merely had a contractual right to the trade marks.

Held, dismissing the appeal, that the licensees' contractual right to the trade marks was as capable of being property as any other intangible right. A trade mark proprietor, who had granted a licensee the exclusive right to use a trade mark, could not be the owner of the right to use that trade mark during the licence period. Any breach by the licensor would not only result in damages but entitled the licensee to apply for an injunction to restrain the licensor. In the instant case, if a third party made unauthorised use of the trade marks, the licence entitled the licensees to call on the trustees to take necessary action. That was entirely consistent with the exclusive right to use granted to the licensee, and was inconsistent with the notion that the trustees had retained the right to use. Moreover, if the trade marks remained unregistered, then the remedy for unauthorised use by a third party was a passing off action by the licensees and not the trustees. The fact that the trustees were not the owners of the right to use the trade marks did not mean that the licensees were the owners of that right, and thus entitled to claim depreciation allowance in respect of their rights under the agreement. S's claim to a depreciation allowance was not improved by the circumstance that the licensees could not have made that claim. S's claim to depreciation allowance failed for the reason that for the seven year period S did not own any depreciable intangible property. The trade marks, of which they were the owners, were not depreciable intangible property. The right to use the trade marks was depreciable intangible property, but during the seven year period S did not own that right. That right belonged to the exclusive licensees.

SIMKIN'S TRUSTEES v. INLAND REVENUE COMMISSIONER OF NEW ZEALAND; *sub nom.* TRUSTEES IN THE CB SIMKIN TRUST v. INLAND REVENUE COMMISSIONER OF NEW ZEALAND, [2004] UKPC 55, [2005] S.T.C. 268, Lord Bingham of Cornhill, Privy Council (New Zealand).

3992. Capital gains tax—Annual exempt amount—2005-2006

CAPITAL GAINS TAX (ANNUAL EXEMPT AMOUNT) ORDER 2005, SI 2005 721; made under the Taxation of Chargeable Gains Act 1992 s.3. In force: March 16, 2005; £3.00.

This Order specifies £8,500 as the amount which, by virtue of the Taxation of Chargeable Gains Act 1992, is the exempt amount for the year 2005-06 unless Parliament otherwise determines. The 1992 Act provides that an individual is chargeable to capital gains tax for a year of assessment only on the amount by which his taxable amount for the year exceeds the exempt amount. It provides that an individual's taxable amount for a year of assessment is the amount of chargeable gains on which he is chargeable to capital gains tax after any available allowable losses have been deducted and any available capital gains tax taper relief has been applied.

3993. Capital gains tax—Freedom of establishment—Sale of major shareholding to foreign company—European Community

[EC Treaty Art.43, Art.56.]

D challenged the imposition of tax liability upon the capital gains that he made when he sold shares in Belgian companies to a French company. Under Belgian law, D would not be liable for tax on any capital gains that he accrued through selling the shares if they were assigned to a Belgian company, association, establishment or body. However, if they were sold to a foreign organisation tax was payable. The

Belgian Court sought a preliminary ruling as to whether Belgian law conformed with Community law.

Held, giving a preliminary ruling, that the Belgian law did constitute an interference with D's rights under the EC Treaty Art.43. The inequality of the tax position was likely to deter D from pursuing his activities in another Member State through a company. Such unequal treatment constituted a restriction on the freedom of establishment of Belgian nationals who held capital in a company established in another Member State, provided the holding was sufficient to influence decisions and to determine the company's activities. If the transferor had an insufficient holding, the inequality would nevertheless amount to a restriction on the free movement of capital in contravention of the EC Treaty Art.56.

DE BAECK v. BELGIUM (C268/03) [2004] 2 C.M.L.R. 57, Judge Timmermans (President), ECJ.

3994. Capital gains tax–Gilt edged securities–Exemptions

CAPITAL GAINS TAX (GILT-EDGED SECURITIES) ORDER 2005, SI 2005 276; made under the Taxation of Chargeable Gains Act 1992 Sch.9 para.1. In force: February 9, 2005; £3.00.

This Order specifies two further gilt-edged securities, disposals of which are exempt from tax on chargeable gains in accordance with the Taxation of Chargeable Gains Act 1992 s.115.

3995. Capital gains tax–Holdover relief–Gift of shares to company under foreign control–Connected persons exercising control over donee company

[Taxation of Chargeable Gains Act 1992 s.165, s.167(2).]

The appellant (F) appealed against amendments to his self assessment. F had undertaken a scheme to minimise his liability to capital gains tax by gifting the shares he held in a private company (B) to a UK resident company. F had set up an Isle of Man settlement, the trustees of which acquired a parent and subsidiary company off the shelf. F took out a bond with an Irish insurance company (IL) and assigned it to the subsidiary company under the settlement. IL then acquired an off the shelf UK company (C) within the bond and F made the gift of his shareholding in B to it, claiming holdover relief under the Taxation of Chargeable Gains Act 1992 s.165. The relief was refused under s.167(2) on the grounds that C was effectively controlled by IL and therefore not resident in the UK, and was connected with the person making the disposal.

Held, dismissing the appeal, that F and IL were acting together to exercise control of C and were therefore connected persons for the purposes of s.167(2). Although IL was the legal and beneficial owner of C within the bond, and C became the legal and beneficial owner of the shares in B, the bondholder had contractual rather than ownership rights representing the entire value of the B shares. By virtue of the scheme, F ceased to be owner of the B shares and instead became life tenant under the settlement which ultimately held contractual rights of equivalent value to the B shares. IL as the issuer of the bond had no real economic interest in the B shares. IL was essentially within the control of the bondholder in relation to the funds within the bond. On the evidence, F understood at the time of the gift of the shares that he could continue to act as if her were the majority shareholder and his actions before and after the disposal showed that he made all the decisions in relation to the shares. Despite a lack of direct communication between F and IL with regard to the disposal of the shares, the evidence showed that they were acting together and it followed that holdover relief did not apply.

FOULSER v. MacDOUGALL (INSPECTOR OF TAXES) [2005] S.T.C. (S.C.D.) 374, John F Avery Jones, Sp Comm.

3996. Capital gains tax–Loss relief–Absence of actual disposal–Requirement to establish deemed disposal

[Income and Corporation Taxes Act 1988 s.574; Taxation of Chargeable Gains Act 1992 s.24(2).]

The appellant taxpayer (M) appealed against the Inland Revenue's refusal of his claim for loss relief under the Income and Corporation Taxes Act 1988 s.574 in respect of shares in a company (X). In June 1994, M had acquired two shares in X which represented X's entire issued share capital at the time. M was appointed its sole director. On the same date, X's nominal share capital was increased from £100 to £250,000 in ordinary shares of £1 each. Shortly afterwards, X purchased all of the issued shares in another company (Y) for £225,000. The money was paid to Y's parent company on November 8, 1994. The Y shares were X's only asset; but on 1 December 1994, Y went into liquidation. When M completed his 1994 to 1995 tax return, he entered under the heading "chargeable assets disposed of" the disposal of 224,998 shares in X for nil proceeds on December 1, 1994 following their acquisition on November 8, 1994 for £224,998. M submitted a claim under s.574 to have the loss incurred in respect of the shares in X set off against his total income for 1994 to 1995. The Revenue refused, arguing that there had been no actual disposal of the shares in X because M had continued to own them. Nor had there been a deemed disposal because M had not made a claim under the Taxation of Chargeable Gains Act 1992 s.24(2). M contended that (1) a s.24(2) claim was not a condition precedent to his s.574 claim; (2) but if it were, he had made a s.24(2) claim when he filled in the "chargeable assets disposed of" section of his tax return; (3) the Revenue had accepted in earlier correspondence that he had made a s.24(2) claim and so was estopped from denying it now.

Held, dismissing the appeal, that (1) a claim under s.574 required an "allowable loss" and that would require either an actual disposal by sale or by gift, or a deemed disposal in order to crystallise the loss incurred. The only way of demonstrating a deemed disposal was by virtue of a claim under s.24(2) of the 1992 Act. Thus a claim under s.24(2) was a condition precedent to a claim for loss relief under s.574 of the 1988 Act where the claimant could not demonstrate an actual disposal; (2) there was nothing in M's tax return that amounted to a claim under s.24(2). Nowhere did he indicate that there had been a deemed rather than an actual disposal, or that the value of the asset had become negligible. It was necessary for the inspector to be satisfied that the value of the asset had become negligible, and so M should have directed him to it by pointing unambiguously to what was being claimed. (3) The special commissioners had no statutory authority to consider estoppel, *Williams (Inspector of Taxes) v. Grundy's Trustees* [1934] 1 K.B. 524 applied. Without statutory authority the tribunal could not extend its jurisdiction to matters falling outside its own competence and within that of the courts.

MARKS v. McNALLY (INSPECTOR OF TAXES) [2004] S.T.C. (S.C.D.) 503, John Clark, Sp Comm.

3997. Capital gains tax–Qualifying corporate bonds–Loan notes–Rights of conversion into further loan notes and shares

[Income and Corporation Taxes Act 1988 Sch.18 para.1(5); Taxation of Chargeable Gains Act 1992 s.77, s.115, s.117.]

The appellant taxpayer (T) appealed against a decision ([2004] EWHC 1607, [2005] S.T.C. 617) that certain loan notes issued by a company in the context of a tax avoidance scheme were not qualifying corporate bonds within the Taxation of Chargeable Gains Act 1992 s.117. T and other shareholders of a company (W Ltd), which they wished to sell for a substantial sum, had transferred their shares by way of gift to a company (C Ltd) which was owned in part by the trustees of a settlement of which T and the other shareholders were settlors. The trustees of the settlement subscribed for shares and loan notes issued by C Ltd. The loan notes issued to the trustees gave the holder a right to convert them into new loan notes, and the second loan notes conferred a right to convert into ordinary shares. The shares in C Ltd and the loan notes were then sold to the outside purchaser along with the shares in W

Ltd not owned by C Ltd. The effect of the scheme by which W Ltd was sold to the outside purchaser was to transfer the gains that would otherwise have accrued to T and the other individual shareholders on their disposal of the shares in W Ltd to C Ltd to the gain which was treated as having accrued to them (under s.77 of the 1992 Act) on the disposal by the trustees of the shares and loan notes issued by C Ltd. In particular, the effect was to transfer some 95 per cent of those gains to the gain on the loan notes, which would have been exempt from capital gains tax under s.115 of the 1992 Act if they were qualifying corporate bonds. The Revenue submitted that the right to convert the first loan notes into the second loan notes carried with it the right conferred in the second loan notes to convert the underlying loan into shares, that that prevented the debt on the first loan notes from representing a normal commercial loan for the purposes of s.117(1) read with the Income and Corporation Taxes Act 1988 Sch.18 para.1 (5), and that it was immaterial that the second loan notes would themselves be corporate bonds within s.117(2AA).

Held, dismissing the appeal, that (1) T's argument that there was no right to convert the first loan notes into shares and that, if there were, that right would not be a right carried by the first loan notes failed to give proper effect to the statutory language, which referred to a corporate bond, the debt on which represented a normal commercial loan. The loan note was the security but it was the underlying debt which had to represent a normal commercial loan. The loan in the instant case was not and never had been a normal commercial loan for the purposes of s.117(1) of the 1992 Act. The loan was made on terms that the debt could be converted into shares in the company. The right to convert the loan into shares, albeit by a series of steps all of which lay within the control of the lender, was an essential term of the bargain between lender and borrower. The whole object of the loan, in the context of the tax avoidance scheme, was to ensure that the value of the existing C Ltd shares was diluted by the prospect that further shares would or could be issued at or near to par in the future. That object could only be achieved by conferring on the holders of the first loan notes a right to require conversion of the loan into shares. It was immaterial that the right to conversion could not be exercised until some time in the future or that it might never be exercised. The relevant question was whether the underlying loan carried any right to conversion into shares and that loan remained the same notwithstanding that the first loan notes were replaced by the second loan notes. (2) The court rejected the submission that it should construe Sch.18 para.1 (5) of the 1988 Act in the context of that Schedule in an unmodified form and hold that it related only to a "direct" right to conversion into shares and then apply that meaning when construing para.1 (5) in its modified form after making the substitution required by s.117(1) of the 1992 Act.

WESTON v. GARNETT (INSPECTOR OF TAXES); *sub nom.* BUSINESSMAN v. INSPECTOR OF TAXES, [2005] EWCA Civ 742, [2005] S.T.C. 1134, Pill, L.J., CA (Civ Div).

3998. Capital gains tax–Reliefs–Qualifying loans–Treatment of loan to company

[Taxation of Chargeable Gains Act 1992 s.253(1).]

The appellant (R) appealed against the dismissal of his appeal ([2004] EWHC 1596, [2004] S.T.C. 1544, [2004] C.L.Y. 3700) against an estimated assessment of capital gains tax, it having been found that a loan granted to R's company was not a "qualifying loan" within the Taxation of Chargeable Gains Act 1992 s.253(1). R's company had purchased premises with the intention of developing them. In March 1993 the company's current account was overdrawn. R's bank agreed to grant the company a loan for just under the amount owing. The express purpose of the loan was to refinance the existing borrowings. The loan was secured by legal charges over two of R's properties. R sold one of the properties in May 2004, realising a chargeable gain for the purposes of the Act. R credited the proceeds of the sale to the loan account, thereby reducing the company's indebtedness on that account. R sought to set off the payment to the loan account against his liability for capital gains tax on the disposal of the property. The tax inspector rejected that claim for relief. The general commissioners dismissed R's appeal and found that the bank loan was not a qualifying loan as it had not been used wholly for the purposes of the company's trade due to the absence of any formal contracts and the confusion in the documentary records which made it difficult to disentangle R's affairs from those of the company. Their decision was upheld on appeal. R submitted that (1) the appeal court and the commissioners erred in law by looking at the purpose for which the money in the company's current account had been used rather than at the purpose for which the loan had been used. The money lent was used by the company wholly for the purposes of its trade, in paying off virtually all its overdraft and enabling it to continue to trade; (2) the commissioners were not entitled to conclude that those monies were not used "wholly" for the purposes of the trade carried on by the company.

Held, dismissing the appeal, that (1) where a company had been lent money for the purposes of certain activities and then rescheduled its borrowing, one could only determine whether the new borrowing represented a qualifying loan by assessing the purpose for which the original borrowing was incurred. If the money lent was used to repay an existing indebtedness, the new loan stood in the place of the existing indebtedness. The company already had a liability for the overdraft to the bank in March 1993 before it converted its overdraft into the loan. The loan could be said to have been used to enable the company to pay off its overdraft. However, the underlying financial reality was that the company had incurred the debt to the bank before March 1993 and the only significant thing that changed on that date was the basis upon which the debt would be repaid. Accordingly, liability to repay that sum was not incurred by the company in March 1993 for the purposes of s.253(1). The new loan was not used to serve the purposes of the trade at all. It had been used to repay the old loan and so create a new debt. (2) The question of whether any of the money was spent "wholly" on a qualifying purpose was ultimately a matter for the commissioners, who had been entitled to find that R had failed to establish his case. The reasoning of the commissioners appeared to apply to the whole of the monies expended on the premises. Given the absence of documentation, the unsatisfactory way in which the affairs of R and his company were confused and the inconsistent way in which R had put his case, the commissioners were not satisfied that any of the money spent by the company in relation to the premises had been expended for the purpose of furthering its own trade as opposed to conferring a gratuitous benefit on R. That was a finding of fact which could not be interfered with.

ROBSON v. MITCHELL (INSPECTOR OF TAXES), [2005] EWCA Civ 585, [2005] S.T.C. 893, Auld, L.J., CA (Civ Div).

3999. Capital gains tax–Retirement relief–Certain assets withdrawn from partnership–Disposal of remainder of partnership assets

[Taxation of Chargeable Gains Act 1992 s.163, s.164.]

The appellant (T) appealed against the Revenue's decision to refuse to allow him retirement relief from capital gains tax following the sale of certain building land. T and his wife (W) worked in partnership as arable and sheep farmers. Together they co owned 100 acres of land. T and W determined to withdraw the co owned land from the business partnership. The land was to be withdrawn in connection with the intention of T and W to each dispose of a proportion of their business assets to their three children. T subsequently inherited some land, which was then shared by way of deed of gift between himself, his wife and the three children. On March 10, 2000, approximately 60 per cent of this inherited land was sold for residential development. All five family members contributed their share of the proceeds to the assets of the business. On the same day, T and W each gave a 30 per cent interest in their assets of the partnership to the three children. Consequently, each family member held a 20 per cent stake in the assets of the partnership. T then claimed retirement relief on a capital gain which was refused by the Revenue. The Revenue argued that as the co owned land had been withdrawn from the assets of the partnership, T and W had only made a disposal that reduced their interests in some of those assets. Although it was accepted that the sale of the building land was an associated disposal within the Taxation of Chargeable Gains Act 1992 s.164, the Revenue argued that the withdrawal of the co owned land and the disposal of the assets to the children, having occurred simultaneously, did not amount to a material disposal for the purposes of s.163 of the Act.

Held, allowing the appeal, that the new five person partnership had continued to operate on the co owned land following the transfer of all the business assets to the partnership. Thus, the transfer of the share in all the assets of the partnership as they existed at March 10, 2001 was all that was required for there to have been a material disposal for the purposes of s.163 of the Act. As it was accepted that the sale of the building land was an associated disposal, T and W had satisfied the conditions for relief given in s.163.

TODD v. FAWCETT (INSPECTOR OF TAXES) [2005] S.T.C. (S.C.D.) 97, JD Demack, Sp Comm.

4000. **Capital gains tax—Retirement relief—Disposal of business on ill health retirement—Existence of permanent incapacity as to ability to perform "work of the kind" previously undertaken**

The appellant (P) appealed against an amendment to her self assessment tax return. P had run a newsagent business in partnership with her husband. The business was sold when P was aged below 50. P was suffering from depression as a consequence of her husband's diagnosis with cancer and his subsequent death. P claimed capital gains tax relief on the grounds of ill health retirement on the disposal of her 50 per cent share in the business. In her application, P described her duties as "hands on management" but the medical evidence showed that at the date of her retirement P was incapable of carrying on her usual work because of her ill health, although she was unlikely to remain permanently incapable in this regard. P argued that her duties and responsibilities in the business were not dependent on her usual day to day activities, so that the term "work of the kind" which she previously undertook in the Taxation of Chargeable Gains Act 1992 Sch.6 para.3(1)(a) included the managerial responsibilities of a partner. The Inland Revenue found that P did not meet the legal requirements for ill health retirement relief, in particular the requirement for permanent incapacity, and that her application had been based on duties as an assistant to her husband rather than as a partner in the business.

Held, dismissing the appeal, that on the medical evidence P was unlikely to remain permanently incapable of "work of the kind" that she had previously done in the newsagent business, namely that she would have been able to perform the duties of a partner at some time in the future. This finding applied equally to P's and the Inland Revenue's definitions of "work of the kind". Since the legal requirement of para.3(1)(b) had not been fulfilled, it followed that P did not qualify for ill health retirement relief from the capital gain and the amendment to her self assessment stood.

PALMER v. RICHARDSON (INSPECTOR OF TAXES) [2005] S.T.C. (S.C.D.) 418, Michael Tildesley, Sp Comm.

4001. **Capital gains tax—Roll over relief—Acquisition of shares—Return of value to taxpayer**

[Taxation of Chargeable Gains Act 1992 s.164G, s.164L(3), s.164L(9), s.286.]

The appellant taxpayer (W) appealed against capital gains tax assessments by the respondent Revenue. W had sold shares in two companies and most of the proceeds of nearly £2 million were chargeable with capital gains tax. After the sale W had acquired shares in two other companies (R and B), which he controlled and which were connected within the meaning of the Taxation of Chargeable Gains Act 1992 s.286. W invested £1.1 million in shares in B which was a qualifying company under s.164G for the purposes of roll over relief. W had also lent R £900,000 as loan capital, which was being repaid around the time that W purchased shares in B. W contended that he was entitled to defer payment of the tax because of roll over relief on reinvestment. The Revenue contended that some of R's repayments were "arrangements" made in connection with W's acquisition of shares in B and amounted, under s.164L, to the return of the value of his investment in B. Accordingly, the Inland Revenue argued, those investments were not eligible for rollover relief.

Held, dismissing the appeal, that, on the facts, R's repayments were part of the arrangements for W's acquisition of shares in B, for which they provided the funds. The combined effect of s.164L(3) and s.164L(9) was that an acquisition of shares in a company would be treated as being a return of the value of the individual's investment if the company or a connected company repaid any existing debt owed to the individual. Since R was a company connected to B, its repayments to W were a return of value. Therefore, W's investments in B could not be treated as acquisitions of eligible shares for the purposes of roll over relief.

WAKEFIELD v. INSPECTOR OF TAXES [2005] S.T.C. (S.C.D.) 439, Richard Barlow (Chairman), Sp Comm.

4002. Capital gains tax–Roll over relief–Taxpayer's accountants found to have been negligent–Propriety of general commissioners' approach to assessment

[Taxes Management Act 1970 s.36.]

The appellant (M) appealed by way of case stated against the decision of the general commissioners to uphold an assessment of capital gains tax pursuant to the Taxes Management Act 1970 s.36. The assessment had determined, inter alia, that computations supplied to the Revenue by M's former accountants had been negligent. In particular, roll over relief in respect of a farm and stables had been claimed in the sum of £332,500 whereas the correct figure was £57,500. M argued that it had not been open to the general commissioners to conclude that he had not incurred the claimed expense or that his accountants had been negligent.

Held, dismissing the appeal, that whilst the court could not say that it would have reached the same conclusion as the general commissioners, it had been open to them to reach the conclusion that they had reached. Moreover, there was no error of law in the finding of negligence on the part of M's former accountants. Since the sum claimed in respect of roll over relief was wrong, it necessarily followed that the accountants had not applied the proper degree of care to the computation of it. It had been open to the inspector initially to take those computations at face value without then making further enquiries.

McEWAN v. MARTIN (INSPECTOR OF TAXES), [2005] EWHC 714, [2005] S.T.C. 993, Park, J., Ch D.

4003. Capital gains tax–Sale of assets–Disposal of fishing vessel, licence and fishing quota

[Taxation of Chargeable Gains Act 1992 s.2(2), s.39, s.41.]

The appellant fisherman (F), who belonged to a partnership which owned and operated a fishing vessel, appealed against a decision by the respondent (the Revenue) in relation to their liability to capital gains tax (CGT). F argued that (1) the sale of the vessel, its licence and fishing quota constituted the disposal of a single indivisible asset; (2) there had been double taxation because they had not been allowed relief against profits of trade.

Held, dismissing the appeal, that (1) the sale of the vessel, licence and quota constituted the sale of three separate assets. When computing liability to CGT each element of a bundle of assets was to be considered separately, *Aberdeen Construction Group Ltd v. Inland Revenue Commissioners* [1978] A.C. 885, [1979] C.L.Y. 371 followed. (2) By virtue of the Taxation of Chargeable Gains Act 1992 s.2(2), losses could only be offset against chargeable gains and they could not be relieved against trade profits which were chargeable to income tax. The provisions in s.39 and s.41 of the Act concerning the computation of deductions did not operate to enable an individual to offset a capital gains loss on one asset against a gain on another transaction or against income.

FULLARTON v. INLAND REVENUE COMMISSIONERS [2004] S.T.C. (S.C.D.) 207, T Gordon Coutts Q.C., Sp Comm.

4004. Capital gains tax–Settlements–Effect of tax avoidance scheme

[Taxation of Chargeable Gains Act 1992 s.77.]

The appellant (the Revenue) appealed against a decision ([2003] EWCA Civ 1792, [2004] S.T.C. 170) that monies comprised in the trust funds of a settlement made by the respondent (T) and the income therefrom which was payable to T did not constitute "derived property" within the meaning of the Taxation of Chargeable Gains Act 1992 s.77(8). The effect of the decision below was that T was liable to pay capital gains tax (CGT) on a disposal of shares at the 25 per cent rate of income tax rather than the 40 per cent rate. T, one of a number of shareholders in a company (E) who were negotiating the sale of their shares to another company, had sought to take part in a tax avoidance scheme, known as a "flip-flop" scheme, with a view to reducing his liability to CGT. For the purposes of that scheme T created a settlement and transferred most of his shares in E to himself and his wife as trustees of the settlement. T then created a second settlement. The trustees of the first settlement borrowed cash on the security of the shares, which they transferred to the trustees of the second settlement. T and his wife were then cut out from being beneficiaries of the first settlement, and in the following tax year the first settlement disposed of the shares. Section 77(2) of the Act was an anti avoidance provision that provided that a settlor would be regarded as having an interest in a settlement in certain circumstances even if he did not in fact have an interest. It did so by bringing in not only property comprised in the settlement, but also "derived property". The Revenue contended that T was to be regarded, under s.77(2), as having an interest in the first settlement during the relevant year, on the basis that the monies comprised in the trust funds of the second settlement at the relevant time and the income therefrom which was payable to T constituted "derived property" within the meaning of s.77(8).

Held, allowing the appeal, that the words "proceeds of...that property" in s.77(8) included all proceeds derived from the property, irrespective of the nature of the process used to extract value from the property for transfer to another, whether by sale or mortgage or otherwise. In the instant case, in relation to the proceeds of the mortgage of the shares, the monies comprised in the trust funds of the second settlement at the relevant time and the income therefrom which was payable to T constituted "derived property" within the meaning of s.77(8). "Derived property" did not cease to be derived property merely because it had passed out of the relevant settlement. The trust funds of the second settlement consisted of the proceeds of a mortgage of the shares, and the income payable to T represented the income from the mortgage of the shares. The rate of CGT chargeable in respect of the gain which accrued on the disposal of the shares was T's highest marginal rate of income tax, which was 40 per cent, and not the lower settlement rate of 25 per cent.

WEST (INSPECTOR OF TAXES) v. TRENNERY; *sub nom.* TEE v. INSPECTOR OF TAXES; TRENNERY v. WEST (INSPECTOR OF TAXES), [2005] UKHL 5, [2005] 1 All E.R. 827, Lord Steyn, HL.

4005. Capital gains tax–Share sales–Computational provisions of s.106A Taxation of Chargeable Gains Act 1992

[Taxation of Chargeable Gains Act 1992 s.106A.]

The appellant inspector of taxes (D) appealed against a decision of the commissioners ([2005] S.T.C. (S.C.D.) 165) that the capital gains tax (CGT) avoidance scheme of the respondent (H) was effective. H had been a resident in the United Kingdom and was a substantial shareholder in a public company. H had wished to sell a large amount of shares, which would have resulted in substantial CGT liabilities. H aimed to take advantage of the UK's double taxation agreement with Mauritius: instead of disposing of a large amount of shares at a gain, he created a discretionary settlement and transferred 100,000 shares to the settlement's trustees in the UK. Those trustees then sold their shares on the open market. On the same day, they retired and were replaced by a trustee from Mauritius. The following day, the Mauritius trustee instructed stockbrokers in the UK to purchase on the open market such number of shares as could be acquired for an amount equal to the net proceeds from the sale on the day before of the 100,000 shares. This had the effect that CGT did not accrue as the shares had been purchased within 30 days of the shares that had been disposed of and were therefore matched with the shares sold under the Taxation of Chargeable Gains Act 1992 s.106A. The Revenue assessed H to CGT, under s.106A(5)(a) of the Act, on the gain that had accrued to the UK trustees immediately before they were replaced by the Mauritian trustee. H appealed and the commissioners declined to hold that s.106A(5)(a) of the Act had the indirect effect contended for by the Revenue. D argued that s.106A(5)(a) of the Act was a deeming provision, and when the settlement was changed from the UK to Mauritius, the assets comprised in the trust fund must be taken to have included the shares and a capital gain was deemed to have accrued to the UK trustees, which gain was assessable on H.

Held, dismissing the appeal, that s.106A of the Act was a computational provision and its purpose was to lay down rules as to how the chargeable gain or allowable loss on the disposal was to be computed. When the computation was made, the purpose of the section was fulfilled. If there was not a disposal of securities, the section did not apply. When there was a disposal, actual or deemed, of securities, which in the instant case were shares, the shares disposed of were matched with the shares acquired in accordance with the rules in s.106A. Once the shares had been matched, the gain or loss was computed accordingly. When the process was completed, the application of s.106A to that particular disposal was at an end. Section 106A of the Act did not operate additionally to cause the continuing settled property of the settlement to be treated for the purposes of different CGT provisions as consisting of assets different from those which actually were the continuing settled property. Even if s.106A of the Act could be regarded as a deeming provision, the deeming was solely for the purpose of computing the gain or loss on the disposal of the 100,000 shares. It would carry with it the normal consequences for subsequent computations on future disposals of shares of the same class by the trustees of the same settlement. The deeming would have no further consequences. The decision of the commissioners had been correct.

HICKS v. DAVIES (INSPECTOR OF TAXES); *sub nom.* DAVIES (INSPECTOR OF TAXES) v. HICKS, [2005] EWHC 847, [2005] S.T.C. 850, Park, J., Ch D.

4006. Capital gains tax–Taper relief–Notice of enquiry regarding amendment– Time for enquiry running from filing of amendment or of self assessment tax return

[Taxes Management Act 1970 s.9A, s.9ZA; Taxation of Chargeable Gains Act 1992 s.2A.]

The taxpayer (S) appealed against an amendment made by an inspector increasing the taper relief rate applicable to a capital gain she had made. In January 2001, S filed a self assessed tax return, noting a taper relief rate on a taxable capital gain of 85 per cent. The gain had come from one close company share bought for £1 before April 1998 and sold in May 1999 for over £1 million. Some discussions ensued between the parties, with Inland Revenue officers seeking clarification of the proposed amendment. In October 2001, S amended the rate to 25 per cent, significantly decreasing the tax payable. In June 2002, the inspector sent a notice of enquiry concerning the amendment. Following closure of the enquiry in September 2003, the inspector amended the rate to OS's originally filed 85 per cent. S argued that the inquiry was time barred, the inspector's amendment was incorrect and the Inland Revenue had endorsed her amendment.

Held, dismissing the appeal, that the inquiry was not time barred, the inspector's assessment was correct and the Inland Revenue had not endorsed the amendment. The notice of enquiry was clearly in time as it had been issued within a year of the date of the amendment, as required by the Taxes Management Act 1970 s.9A(2)(c). The inspector's taper relief rate of 85 per cent was correct because the holding period under the Taxation of Chargeable Gains Act 1992 s.2A(8) was two years, being the period from April 1998 to May 1999 plus one year under s.2A(8)(b). The full relief by way of indexing claimed by S for a long holding was of almost no value, because the 43 per cent of the original purchase price of £1 had disappeared when the figures were rounded. Section 2A of the 1992 Act did not retrospectively apply tapering before March 1988. Inland Revenue officers had not sought or agreed to OS's amendment, which was made unilaterally by her under s.9ZA of the 1970 Act, and in fact they did not have the power to do so. They had only sought clarification to understand the amendment and its consequences and had not issued any formal notice of enquiry under s.9A of the 1970 Act before the June 2002 notice.

O'SULLIVAN v. PHILIP (INSPECTOR OF TAXES) [2005] S.T.C. (S.C.D.) 51, David Williams, Sp Comm.

4007. Capital gains tax–Valuation–Unquoted company shares–Calculation of market value–Information available to hypothetical arm's length purchaser

The appellant taxpayer (M) sought the determination of a preliminary issue arising in his appeal against a decision relating to his liability to capital gains tax. The preliminary issue was the market value of M's 66 per cent shareholding in a private company (R), a dealer in imported consumer electronic goods which had been incorporated in 1972. The relevant date for the valuation was March 31, 1982. The audited accounts for the year ended March 1981 showed a turnover of almost £1.5 million, of which 10.7 per cent was net profit. The 1982 accounts showed turnover of over £1.8 million, of which only 2.9 per cent was net profit. At that time, R was facing difficulties as an importer because of fluctuations in the currency markets but was taking steps to ameliorate the situation. M contended that the actual figures from the 1982 accounts were irrelevant as they would not have been available to a prospective purchaser on the valuation date and that an average figure based on the 1981 accounts and figures for previous years should be used, giving a net profit of £148,190, multiplied by a price/earnings ratio of 11.

Held, determining the preliminary issue, that M's approach to the valuation was unrealistic. It was likely that a hypothetical arm's length purchaser would attempt to familiarise himself with all aspects of R's business right up to the date of the hypothetical sale. Although the audited accounts for the year ended 1982 would not have been available, the actual figures provided the best available guide as to what the hypothetical purchaser would have discovered. A willing purchaser would have taken at least a cautiously optimistic view of R's prospects, given the difficulties it was facing, but was likely to consider it as a sound business overall. A realistic net profit at the valuation date was £95,910, and the appropriate multiplier was 10. Consequently, R's market value at March 31, 1982 was £959,100 and the value of M's shareholding was £633,006.

MARKS v. SHERRED (INSPECTOR OF TAXES) [2004] S.T.C. (S.C.D.) 362, Colin Bishopp, Sp Comm.

4008. Car tax–Imports–Charge imposed on vehicles used on Finnish roads–Payment required prior to registration–European Community

[Council Directive 83/183 on tax exemptions applicable to permanent imports from a Member State of the personal property of individuals.]

The Finnish Supreme Administrative Court sought a preliminary ruling on the interpretation of Council Directive 83/183 Art.1. After moving to Finland from the Netherlands, L was required to pay a car tax prior to registering the vehicle for private use in Finland. L argued that the charge amounted to a consumption tax, prohibited by Art.1 (1) of the Directive. The tax charge was subject to a discount of FMK 80,000 as the vehicle was being imported on a transfer of residence from another Member State, leaving L to pay FMK 20,198.

Held, giving a ruling, that the tax was charged on the use of the car on Finnish roads, however short in duration, not on registration, so it did not amount to an import tax in terms of the exemption in Art.1 (1), *Weigel v. Finanzlandesdirektion fur Vorarlberg (C387/01)* [2004] 3 C.M.L.R. 42 followed. L could not rely on the EC Treaty to guarantee a tax neutral treatment of her change of residence. It was for the national court to determine whether the reduction granted to L was sufficient to ensure that she was not placed in a less favourable position than those permanently resident in Finland, and if so, whether the less favourable treatment was objectively justifiable by reasons not connected with L's residence, *D'Hoop v. Office National de l'Emploi (C224/98)* [2003] All E.R. (EC) 527, [2003] C.L.Y. 1445 followed.

LINDFORS (C365/02), *Re; sub nom.* LINDFORS v. FINLAND (C365/02) [2005] All E.R. (EC) 745, Judge Jann (President), ECJ.

4009. **Car tax–Imports–Discrimination–Charge imposed on first registration of second hand car imported into Austria–Surcharge to reflect VAT charge–European Community**

[EC Treaty Art.90; Council Directive 83/183 on tax exemptions applicable to permanent imports from a Member State of the personal property of individuals Art.1 (1).]

The Austrian Supreme Administrative Court sought a preliminary ruling as to whether a vehicle registration tax chargeable on first registration of cars imported from other Member States was compatible with EC law. W, a German national, was charged the tax when he became resident in Austria. The tax, which was based on the fair market value of the car, subject to a deduction for depreciation, was increased by a 20 per cent surcharge because it had not been included in the car's chargeable value for VAT purposes.

Held, giving a ruling, that the tax did not come within the exemption in Council Directive 83/183 Art.1 (1), as it was chargeable on first registration in Austria and not on importation. The charge based on fair market value, with a deduction for depreciation, was applied without distinction to both imported second hand vehicles and those bought in Austria and was therefore compatible with the EC Treaty Art.90, *Institut National d'Assurances Sociales pour Travailleurs Independants (INASTI) v. Hervein (C393/99)* [2002] E.C.R. I-2829, [2002] C.L.Y. 4225 followed. However, the 20 per cent surcharge was discriminatory as it was applied almost exclusively to imported second hand cars, thereby constituting an internal tax that was incompatible with Art.90, *Cooperativa Co-frutta Srl v. Amministrazione delle Finanze dello Stato (193/85)* [1987] E.C.R. 2085, [1987] C.L.Y. 1583 and *Commission of the European Communities v. Denmark (106/84)* [1986] E.C.R. 833, [1987] C.L.Y. 1659 followed.

WEIGEL v. FINANZLANDESDIREKTION FUR VORARLBERG (C387/01) [2004] 3 C.M.L.R. 42, Judge Skouris (President), ECJ.

4010. **Civil partnerships–Tax treatment**

TAX AND CIVIL PARTNERSHIP REGULATIONS 2005, SI 2005 3229; made under the Finance Act 2005 s.103. In force: in accordance with Reg.1; £4.50.

These Regulations amend the Finance Act 1984, the Inheritance Tax Act 1984, the Finance Act 1985, the Finance Act 1986, the Income and Corporation Taxes Act 1988, the Finance Act 1990, the Taxation of Chargeable Gains Act 1992, the Finance Act 1996, the Finance Act 2000, the Finance Act 2002, the Income Tax (Earnings and Pensions) Act 2003, the Finance Act 2003, the Finance Act 2004 and the Income Tax (Trading and Other Income) Act 2005. They make amendments to provide for civil partnerships. The Regulations provide the same or similar tax treatment for persons who are, have been or may in the future be civil partners of each other as is given to persons who are, have been or may in the future be married to each other. They also provide the same or similar tax treatment for the formation of a civil partnership as is given to marriage. For some legislation the tax consequences are determined in part by whether persons are not married to each other but are living together as husband or wife, whether persons are not married to each other or whether a person is not married. The Regulations provide that the same or similar tax consequences apply where persons are not civil partners of each other but are living together as if they were, where persons are not civil partners of each other or where a person is not a civil partner, as the case may be.

4011. Civil partnerships–Tax treatment

TAX AND CIVIL PARTNERSHIP (NO.2) REGULATIONS 2005, SI 2005 3230; made under the Finance Act 2005 s.103. In force: December 5, 2005; £3.00.

These Regulations amend the Stamp Duty (Exempt Instruments) Regulations 1987 (SI 1987 516), the Personal Equity Plan Regulations 1989 (SI 1989 469), the Income Tax (Building Societies) (Dividends and Interest) Regulations 1990 (SI 1990 2231), the Income Tax (Deposit-takers) (Interest Payments) Regulations 1990 (SI 1990 2232), the Retirement Benefits Schemes (Restriction on Discretion to Approve) (Small Self-administered Schemes) Regulations 1991 (SI 1991 1614), the Retirement Benefits Schemes (Restriction on Discretion to Approve) (Additional Voluntary Contributions) Regulations 1993 (SI 1993 3016), the Retirement Benefits Schemes (Information Powers) Regulations 1995 (SI 1995 3103), the Personal Pension Schemes (Tables of Rates of Annuities) Regulations 1996 (SI 1996 1311), the Individual Savings Account Regulations 1998 (SI 1998 1870), the Retirement Benefits Schemes (Sharing of Pensions on Divorce or Annulment) Regulations 2000 (SI 2000 1085), the Insurance Companies (Overseas Life Assurance Business) (Excluded Business) Regulations 2000 (SI 2000 2089), the Personal Pension Schemes (Conversion of Retirement Benefits Schemes) Regulations 2001 (SI 2001 118), the Personal Pension Schemes (Transfer Payments) Regulations 2001 (SI 2001 119), the Inheritance Tax (Delivery of Accounts) (Excepted Estates) Regulations 2004 (SI 2004 2543) and the Pension Protection Fund (Tax) (2005-06) Regulations 2005 (SI 2005 1907). These Regulations amend secondary tax legislation to provide for civil partnerships. They make amendments in relation to tax to ensure that civil partners are treated in the same way as spouses; surviving civil partners are treated in the same way as widows and widowers; transactions entered into in consideration of the formation of a civil partnership are treated in the same way as transactions entered into in consideration of marriage; the dissolution or annulment of a civil partnership is treated in the same way as a divorce or the annulment of a marriage; a former civil partner is treated in the same was as an ex-spouse; and civil partnership status is treated equally with marital status.

4012. Climate change levy–Combined heat and power stations

CLIMATE CHANGE LEVY (COMBINED HEAT AND POWER STATIONS) REGULATIONS 2005, SI 2005 1714; made under the Finance Act 2000 s.30, Sch.6 para.15, Sch.6 para.16, Sch.6 para.146, Sch.6 para.147, Sch.6 para.148, Sch.6 para.149. In force: July 22, 2005; £3.00.

These Regulations, which revoke the Climate Change Levy (Combined Heat and Power Stations) Prescribed Conditions and Efficiency Percentages Regulations 2001 (SI 2001 1140) and the Climate Change Levy (Combined Heat and Power Stations) Prescribed Conditions and Efficiency Percentages (Amendment) Regulations 2003 (SI 2003 861), relate to the reliefs from climate change levy that may apply in the case of electricity produced in certified combined heat and power stations.

4013. Climate change levy–Exemptions and reliefs

CLIMATE CHANGE LEVY (MISCELLANEOUS AMENDMENTS) REGULATIONS 2005, SI 2005 1716; made under the Finance Act 2000 s.30, Sch.6 para.20A, Sch.6 para.22, Sch.6 para.39, Sch.6 para.41, Sch.6 para.43, Sch.6 para.53, Sch.6 para.59, Sch.6 para.60, Sch.6 para.62, Sch.6 para.114, Sch.6 para.125, Sch.6 para.146, Sch.6 para.147, Sch.6 para.149A. In force: July 22, 2005; £3.00.

These Regulations amend the Climate Change Levy (Registration and Miscellaneous Provisions) Regulations 2001 (SI 2001 7) and the Climate Change Levy (General) Regulations 2001 (SI 2001 838) to amend the existing rules about administering exemptions and other reliefs from climate change levy (CCL).

4014. Climate change levy – Fuel uses and recycling processes

CLIMATE CHANGE LEVY (FUEL USE AND RECYCLING PROCESSES) REGULATIONS 2005, SI 2005 1715; made under the Finance Act 2000 s.30, Sch.6 para.18, Sch.6 para.18A, Sch.6 para.146, Sch.6 para.147. In force: July 22, 2005; £3.00.

Climate change levy is charged on supplies of electricity, gas and solid fuels that are not for domestic or charity use. Supplies for non-fuel use are exempt, as are supplies for fuel use in a prescribed recycling process. These Regulations, which revoke the Climate Change Levy (Use as Fuel) Regulations 2001 (SI 2001 1138) and the Climate Change Levy (Use as Fuel) (Amendment) Regulations 2003 (SI 2003 665), specify non-fuel uses, specify everything else as fuel use and prescribe the relevant recycling processes.

4015. Common agricultural policy – Single payment scheme – Reliefs

FINANCE ACT 1993, SECTION 86(2), (SINGLE PAYMENT SCHEME) ORDER 2005, SI 2005 409; made under the Finance Act 1993 s.86. In force: March 22, 2005; £3.00.

This Order amends the Taxation of Chargeable Gains Act 1992 which specifies classes of assets which are subject to either roll-over relief or relief in the case of depreciating assets, in respect of gains accruing on the disposal of those assets (or of the interest in them) when used for the purposes of a trade where certain conditions have been met. The Order introduces another class of assets to the list, namely payment entitlements under the single payment scheme, which will be subject to relief. The single payment scheme is a new system of support payments for farmers under the EU Common Agricultural Policy introduced by Council Regulation 1782/2003 ([2003] OJ L270/1) establishing common rules for direct support schemes under the common agricultural policy and establishing certain support schemes for farmers.

4016. Companies – Retirement of directors – Purchase of company's own shares for benefit of trade – Ex gratia payment to retired directors

The appellant taxpayers (H and W) appealed against amendments to their self assessment tax returns. H and W, a married couple, had since the late 1960s been the sole directors and shareholders of a company that traded as a motor car sales and repairs business. H and W's son (R) became an employee of the company in 1983 and in 2000 H and W started making plans to retire. H obtained planning permission for the company's premises to be redeveloped. R was appointed a director of the company and the board of directors took advice as to the best way to bring about H and W's retirement without selling the shares outside the family or selling the business, as was their wish. In March 2001 the sale of the premises was completed for £1,120,000. R was given one voting share in the company and the board agreed to purchase all H and W's shares out of the company's distributable profits. H and W resigned as directors. The following day, the board agreed to pay H and W £30,000 each as an ex gratia payment in recognition of their services to the company. In all, H and W were paid £1,087,000, which included repayment of a loan by H to the company. R continued running the business but its profits were greatly reduced as it no longer had its own premises and was reliant on shared use of smaller premises. The respondent Inland Revenue took the view that the monies paid for H and W's shares were taxable as company distributions since the purchase was not done wholly or mainly for the purpose of benefiting the company's trade as set out in the Income and Corporation Taxes Act 1988 s.219 and that the ex gratia payments were taxable as emoluments. H and W contended that (1) it was the purpose of the share purchase and not its effect that was relevant, and it had been done in order to enable the company to continue to trade; (2) the ex gratia payments were not emoluments as H and W had by that time retired as directors.

Held, dismissing the appeal, that (1) the words of s.219 of the Act made it clear that the exemption only applied where the share purchase was for the purpose of benefiting the trade and not the company. It was the subjective intention of the directors that mattered, but consequences that were inevitably and inextricably linked to the purchase had to be taken as having been in the minds of the directors at the time of the purchase, *Vodafone Cellular Ltd v. Shaw (Inspector of Taxes)* [1997] S.T.C. 734, [1997] C.L.Y. 1062 applied. In the instant case, it was clear from the series of events, including the fact that the option of selling the business had been rejected, that the purpose of the share purchase had been to bring about H and W's retirement in a way that was most beneficial to them. They were paid a sum that was virtually equivalent to the sale proceeds of the trade premises, which then left the trade without adequate premises on which to continue and deprived it of capital loan assets it had formerly enjoyed. None of these matters could be said to have benefited the trade; therefore the purchase did not come within s.219. (2) Although the ex gratia payments were made after H and W's retirement as directors, they had been made in return for H and W having acted as directors and were therefore properly to be regarded as emoluments under s.19 of the Act, *McBride v. Blackburn (Inspector of Taxes)* [2003] S.T.C. (S.C.D.) 139, [2003] C.L.Y. 4232 applied.

ALLUM v. MARSH (INSPECTOR OF TAXES) [2005] S.T.C. (S.C.D.) 191, Nuala Brice, Sp Comm.

4017. **Construction industry–Subcontractors–Construction industry scheme (CIS) certificate–Requirement to comply with conditions–Meaning of "minor and technical" in s.565(4) Income and CorporationTaxes Act 1988**

[Income and CorporationTaxes Act 1988 s.561, s.565.]

The appellant Inspector of Taxes appealed against a decision of the general commissioners allowing the appeal of the respondent company (T) against the inspector's refusal to issue T with a construction industry scheme (CIS) certificate under the Income and Corporation Taxes Act 1988 s.561. T was a contractor in the construction industry. T had applied for a CIS certificate. During the entirety of the relevant "qualifying period", T had not paid its PAYE liabilities on time once. There was, however, no outstanding tax and no action had been taken or demand made by the Revenue in relation to late payment. The inspector had refused to issue the certificate to T on the basis that the failures by T to comply with its obligations in respect of PAYE during the qualifying period were not "minor and technical" and gave reason to doubt future compliance under s.565(8) of the Act. T appealed to the commissioners under s.561 (9). The commissioners decided to allow the appeal on the grounds that the Revenue had failed to take any action and that there was no outstanding tax.

Held, dismissing the appeal, that the expression "minor and technical" was not itself a technical expression. The purpose which Parliament had in mind was to procure strict compliance with tax obligations by making such compliance the price of obtaining a certificate. Parliament also recognised that failures to achieve such strict compliance might be, in the context of the grant of such certificates, venial. Whether in a particular case the failure was to be so regarded was a decision which had been left ultimately to the commissioners to be found as a matter of fact and degree, *Hudson (Inspector of Taxes) v. JDC Services Ltd* [2004] EWHC 602, [2004] S.T.C. 834, [2004] C.L.Y. 3710 applied. The touchstone of "minor and technical" required the court on occasions to decide that a conclusion of the commissioners in a particular case was so wide of the mark as to justify the court in substituting its own view, *Shaw (Inspector of Taxes) v. Vicky Construction Ltd* [2002] EWHC 2659, [2002] S.T.C. 1544, [2003] C.L.Y. 4251 considered. In the instant case, if the inspector himself had decided that, having regard to the relationship which existed between T and its local PAYE collection office, the non compliance, although persistent, could be regarded as minor and technical in the context of the decision which he was charged with making, a decision to grant the certificate could not have been regarded as a breach of his statutory duty or Wednesbury unreasonable. If the grant of a certificate was a possible course open to the inspector, it followed that it was also a possible course for the commissioners on appeal. The facts of the case put it on a borderline on which more than one view might have been taken. The commissioners took a different view from that of the inspector. Although criticisms could be made of the way in which they expressed their final conclusions, it was clear that they had addressed themselves to the questions posed by s.565(4), and that the conclusions that they came to were not impossible conclusions for a reasonable body of commissioners to have reached.

TEMPLETON (INSPECTOR OF TAXES) v. TRANSFORM SHOP OFFICE & BAR FITTERS LTD, [2005] EWHC 1558, 77 T.C. 229, Hart, J., Ch D.

4018. Controlled foreign companies–Exemptions

CONTROLLED FOREIGN COMPANIES (EXCLUDED COUNTRIES) (AMENDMENT) REGULATIONS 2005, SI 2005 185; made under the Income and Corporation Taxes Act 1988 s.748. In force: March 31, 2005; £3.00.

These Regulations amend the Controlled Foreign Companies (Excluded Countries) Regulations 1998 (SI 1998 3081) to change the alternative test for a company's residence so that it must be both incorporated and liable to tax in that territory on its profits.

4019. Controlled foreign companies–Exemptions

CONTROLLED FOREIGN COMPANIES (EXCLUDED COUNTRIES) (AMENDMENT NO.2) REGULATIONS 2005, SI 2005 186; made under the Income and Corporation Taxes Act 1988 s.748. In force: March 31, 2005; £3.00.

These Regulations amend the Controlled Foreign Companies (Excluded Countries) Regulations 1998 (SI 1998 3081) by imposing an additional requirement in respect of all controlled foreign companies that they should not have been involved in a scheme or arrangements, the purpose, or one of the main purposes, of which is to obtain a reduction in UK tax. They also make transitional provision in respect of accounting periods which would, in the ordinary course of events, end after the date on which these Regulations come into force.

4020. Corporation tax–Bad debt relief–Debentures transferred from taxpayer to another company in same group–Replacement as party to loan relationship

[Finance Act 1996 s.81 (1), s.84, Sch.9 para.12.]

The appellant company (G) appealed against a finding by the Inland Revenue that transactions by which G's parent company (GK) was substituted as debtor under loans secured by debenture were subject to the Finance Act 1996 Sch.9 para.12. A loss of £11,335,533 had accrued to G on novations of its liabilities under the loans to GK, who assumed responsibility for them in place of G on consideration of G becoming indebted to GK in the sum of £53,342,890. G argued that GK did not replace G as a party to a loan relationship within the meaning of para.12, as the novations released G and extinguished its debts. The debts owed by GK were, therefore, new debts which arose from the novation agreements and did not give rise to loan relationships under s.81 (1) of the 1996 Act. The Inland Revenue argued that para.12 applied, with the result that the loss accruing on the novation of the debenture agreements fell to be disregarded.

Held, allowing the appeal, that GK did not replace G as a party to the prior loan relationship. The novations resulted in the extinguishment of G's liabilities under the debentures and the creation of new liabilities on the part of GK under the debenture trust deeds, *Collins v. Addies (Inspector of Taxes)* [1992] S.T.C. 746, [1993] C.L.Y. 2267 applied. The wording of s.81 (1) did not, however, require that the debt arise immediately or directly from the original loan transaction. Although the debts assumed by GK arose immediately from the deeds of novation, they also arose from the loans made to G under the original debentures. The words "directly or indirectly" in para.12(1) did not adequately cover circumstances where the loan relationship as well as the party was replaced. Since the novation gave rise to a new legal relationship, it followed that

GK had not replaced G as a party as was obliged to bring the £11,335,533 into account under s.84.

GREENE KING NO.1 LTD v. ADIE (INSPECTOR OF TAXES) [2005] S.T.C. (S.C.D.) 398, Theodore Wallace, Sp Comm.

4021. Corporation tax–Bonds–Funding bonds issued in respect of interest payments on outstanding loans from non UK resident companies–Application of foreign exchange legislation to funding bonds

[Income and Corporation Taxes Act 1988 s.582; Finance Act 1993.]

The appellant (F), a subsidiary company, appealed against an assessment to corporation tax. F had entered into a number of loan agreements to borrow money from other subsidiaries in the same group, which subsidiaries were non UK resident. The agreements provided for F to borrow an amount in foreign currency and pay interest in the foreign currency on any outstanding balance on a quarterly basis. F accrued a substantial liability for interest on the loans and issued funding bonds under the Income and Corporation Taxes Act 1988 s.582 to the subsidiary group companies in respect of the interest obligations. F argued that the effect of s.582 was to prevent the funding bonds from being capital assets and turned them instead into a payment of interest or income for tax purposes, thus removing them from the ambit of the foreign exchange legislation in the Finance Act 1993. The Inland Revenue argued that s.582 provided only that payment of interest on the original bond was deemed to take place at the time of the issue of the funding bond, which was treated as if it were a payment of money's worth at that time, and the funding bond did not change its legal character.

Held, dismissing the appeal, that s.582 provided that the issue of the funding bonds was to be treated as a payment on the date of issue of an amount of interest due on the original bonds, *Cross (Inspector of Taxes) v. London and Provincial Trust Ltd* [1938] 1 K.B. 792 considered. It also provided that the redemption of the funding bonds was not to be treated as a payment of interest. It did not deal with any events other than issue and redemption, therefore any gains or losses arising were dealt with by the chargeable gains and foreign exchange legislation. Moreover, s.582 dealt with funding bonds only in their capacity as a substitute for interest on the original bonds and did not regulate the tax position of the funding bonds in their capacity as separate securities. It followed that the foreign exchange legislation did apply to the funding bonds.

FINANCE LTD v. INSPECTOR OF TAXES [2005] S.T.C. (S.C.D.) 407, Dr Nuala Brice, Sp Comm.

4022. Corporation tax–Capital assets–Subtraction of depreciation in unsold trading stock–Application of Income and Corporation Taxes Act 1988 s.74(1)(f)

[Income and Corporation Taxes Act 1988 s.74(1)(f).]

The appellant Inland Revenue appealed against the decision of Special Commissioners ([2004] S.T.C. (S.C.D.) 253) to permit the respondent company (M) to subtract the depreciation in its unsold stock from its figures for profit in calculating its liability to corporation tax. In M's profit and loss account for the year to December 1996 the company's profit on ordinary activities before taxation was stated to be £50,097,000 after charging £41,823,939 in respect of depreciation on tangible fixed assets. M's balance sheet recorded that as at December 28, 1996, M held stock valued at £131,398,000. The notes to the accounts indicated that depreciation of £3,039,000 had been included in the stock valuation. In its tax computation for the accounting period ended December 31, 1996, M added back to the figure of profit before tax the depreciation in respect of tangible fixed assets but subtracted the amount in respect of depreciation in unsold trading stock. The Inland Revenue took the view that that subtraction ought not to have been allowed and made the assessment accordingly. The Special Commissioners allowed M's appeal. The issue was whether the deductions allowable under Income and Corporation Taxes Act 1988 s.74(1)(f) extended to a part of a depreciation in capital assets which was not charged as an expense but was included as a cost in the carrying figure for stock.

Held, allowing the appeal, that (1) for the purpose of computing M's profits, what was relevant was the cost, and not the value, of stock at the end of the year. The choice between the two criteria was to be determined in favour of the former in accordance with current accepted principles of commercial accountancy, *Inland Revenue Commissioner v. Secan Ltd* 74 T.C. 1 disapproved. (2) Current commercial accountancy principles established that there was no notional purchase of opening or sale of closing stock. Instead, the stock was merely carried forward. (3) Section 74 prohibited any deduction or allowance for depreciation of capital assets in the computation of the taxable profits for the year to be charged under Case 1 of Schedule D. The prohibition was general and overrode any established accountancy principle governing the treatment of depreciation. Established accountancy principles had an important role in computing tax profits for tax purposes. They did not, however, qualify the application of s.74. The profit and loss account of M charged the full depreciation as an expense in computing profits for the year. The subtraction of the amount in respect of depreciation in unsold trading stock and capitalisation of that sum as an item of cost in the figure for stock was an exercise which accorded with establishing accounting principles but did not alter the character of that sum as depreciation or disapply s.74(1)(f). M's deduction of that figure in computing the amount of its profits was contrary to s.74 and the Special Commissioners were wrong to hold otherwise, *Barclays Mercantile Business Finance Ltd v. Mawson (Inspector of Taxes)* [2004] UKHL 51, [2005] 1 A.C. 684, [2005] 1 C.L. 381 followed.

MARS UK LTD v. SMALL (INSPECTOR OF TAXES); WILLIAM GRANT & SONS DISTILLERS LTD v. INLAND REVENUE COMMISSIONERS; *sub nom.* SMALL (INSPECTOR OF TAXES) v. MARS UK LTD, [2005] EWHC 553, [2005] S.T.C. 958, Lightman, J., Ch D.

4023. Corporation tax–Chargeable gains–Derivative contracts

FINANCE ACT 2002, SCHEDULE 26 (PARTS 2 AND 9) (AMENDMENT NO.3) ORDER 2005, SI 2005 3440; made under the Finance Act 2002 Sch.26 para.13. In force: December 31, 2005; £3.00.

This Order amends the Finance Act 2002 which deals with the taxation of derivative contracts. It makes a drafting amendment to provide a definition of "embedded derivative contract"; extends the scope of the concept of excluded types of property; makes amendments to extend the concept of a hedging relationship to include a relationship between a relevant contract and a liability of the company; and extends the treatment of net gains and losses on terminal exercise of an option to cover cases where rights treated as comprised in the derivative are (to any extent) disposed of.

4024. Corporation tax–Chargeable gains–Derivative contracts

FINANCE ACT 2002, SCHEDULE 26, PARTS 2 AND 9 (AMENDMENT) ORDER 2005, SI 2005 646; made under the Finance Act 2002 Sch.26 para.13. In force: March 16, 2005 at 3 pm; £3.00.

This Order amends the Finance Act 2002 to restrict the cases of relevant contract whose underlying subject matter is of shares or rights of a unit holder under a unit trust scheme which are prevented from being derivative contracts. A transitional provision is introduced in relation to contracts which become derivative contracts in consequence of this Order. It introduces amendments which insert a new provision to clarify the tax treatment in relation to host contracts and embedded derivatives where the underlying subject matter is of shares or rights of a unit holder under a unit trust scheme.

4025. Corporation tax–Contracts–Derivative contracts

FINANCE ACT 2002, SCHEDULE 26, PARTS 2 AND 9 (AMENDMENT NO.2) ORDER 2005, SI 2005 2082; made under the Finance Act 2002 Sch.26 para.13; and the Finance Act 2005 Sch.4 para.52. In force: in accordance with Reg.1; £3.00.

This Order, which amends the Finance Act 2002, extends the types of relevant contracts which are treated as derivative contracts to contracts which are treated for accounting purposes as, or as forming part of, a financial asset or liability; extend the type of relevant contract which is excluded from being a derivative contract by virtue of its underlying subject matter; makes transitional provisions in relation to relevant contracts which are chargeable assets but are not derivative contracts; clarifies the tax treatment in relation to host contracts and embedded derivatives primarily where the underlying subject matter is shares or rights of a unit holder under a unit trust scheme; provides for the treatment of net gains and losses on the terminal exercise of an option comprised in a derivative contract and provides for the treatment of credits and debits on the terminal exercise of an equity option; provides for the treatment of an issuer of convertible debt securities which are treated for accounting purposes as equity instruments; and clarifies the treatment of a host contract which is not itself a loan relationship.

4026. Corporation tax–Deductions–Meaning of "potential emoluments" in s.43(11)(a) Finance Act 1989

[Finance Act 1989 s.43(11)(a).]

The appellant taxpayer company (D) appealed against a decision ([2004] EWCA Civ 22, [2004] S.T.C. 339) that certain payments which it had made to an employee benefit trust were "potential emoluments" within the meaning of the Finance Act 1989 s.43(11)(a). The trust had been established "with a view to encouraging and motivating employees", and the relevant deed conferred on the trustee a wide discretion over capital and income to pay money and other benefits to any of the named beneficiaries and a power to lend them money. On December 21, 1998, D and its associated companies paid a total of £2.75 million to the trustee. No payments were made to the beneficiaries before December 31, 1998, when D's accounting year ended, but during 1999, most of the money was allocated to employees, part in the form of emoluments and part in other forms. The Revenue argued that the money was a "potential emolument" within the meaning of s.43(11)(a), since, under the terms of the trust, it could have been used to pay emoluments. The funds were held by an intermediary, the trustee, "with a view to their becoming relevant emoluments", so that the rule of non deductibility applied until and insofar as the funds were applied in the payment of emoluments.

Held, dismissing the appeal, that the payments to the employee benefit trust were "potential emoluments" within the meaning of s.43(11)(a). In the ordinary use of language, the whole of the funds were potential emoluments; they could be used to pay emoluments. As the Court of Appeal had noted, the words "with a view to their becoming relevant emoluments" in s.43(11)(a) applied both to the purpose for which amounts were held by an intermediary and to the purpose for which they were "reserved in the account of an employer"; the words had to have a similar meaning in both contexts. While it was true that such a construction of s.43(11)(a) had the effect that unless the funds were at some point applied in the payment of relevant emoluments, they would never become deductible, any untoward consequences could be avoided by segregating the funds held on trust to pay emoluments from funds held to benefit employees in other ways. If D's case that the payments made by the trustee were not "potential emoluments" were correct, the purpose of s.43 would easily be frustrated; by setting up a trust such as the one in the instant case, the taxpayer could achieve immediate deductibility of payments into the trust and postpone indefinitely the liability of employees to tax on the emoluments for which, in part, the money was eventually applied.

DEXTRA ACCESSORIES LTD v. MacDONALD (INSPECTOR OF TAXES); *sub nom.* MacDONALD (INSPECTOR OF TAXES) v. DEXTRA ACCESSORIES LTD, [2005] UKHL 47, [2005] 4 All E.R. 107, Lord Nicholls of Birkenhead, HL.

4027. Corporation tax—Foreign income—Profits from foreign income chargeable to foreign taxes—Availability of credit for foreign tax against whole of UK tax on Case I profit

[Corporation Taxes Act 1988 s.790, s.797.]

The appellant (L) appealed against estimated assessments to corporation tax in respect of accounting periods for the calendar years 1990 to 1998. L, a life assurance company, received income from foreign investments in the form of dividends and interest, the bulk of which was received after the deduction of foreign withholding tax at source. Where a Double Taxation Convention existed between the United Kingdom and the relevant country, L claimed credit relief for double taxation against UK tax. Where there was no such Convention in force, L claimed unilateral relief under the Corporation Taxes Act 1988 s.790 for the full amount of the foreign tax deducted. The main issue to be determined was whether L was entitled to credit for foreign tax on the basis and in the amount claimed in its calculations for 1992 and 1993. L argued that credit was available for the full foreign withholding tax of 20 because corporation tax of more than 20 was charged on the profit. The Inland Revenue argued that the maximum credit available was 3.3, being the tax on 10 and the same proportion of the profit as the foreign income proportion of the total receipts.

Held, determining preliminary issues in favour of the appellant, that the fund charged to overseas tax had to be identified with a fund chargeable also to UK tax, *George Wimpey International Ltd v. Rolfe (Inspector of Taxes)* [1989] S.T.C. 609, [1989] C.L.Y. 528 considered. The issue was whether foreign tax was to be credited against any tax paid on income taxed under Case I, or whether a mini Case I computation had to be done in order to ascertain the part of the profit referable to the foreign income. There was insufficient evidential support for the Inland Revenue's interpretation of the wording of the treaty provision or of s.797, which wording could not be read as limiting the relief by requiring a profit calculated by reference to the foreign income only. Section 797 of the 1988 Act set the limit for credit as the rate of corporation tax on the item of income as reduced by charges. In the instant case, the relevant income or chargeable gain was the actual Case I profit, therefore under s.797 the credit should not exceed the average rate of corporation tax on that profit. Accordingly, the full amount of foreign tax was creditable against any corporation tax charged on the whole of the Case I profits.

LEGAL & GENERAL ASSURANCE SOCIETY LTD v. THOMAS (INSPECTOR OF TAXES) (NO.1) [2005] S.T.C. (S.C.D.) 350, John F Avery Jones, Sp Comm.

4028. Corporation tax—Free movement of capital—Freedom of establishment—Tax credits—European Community

[EC Treaty Art.56, Art.58, Art.58(1)(a), Art.58(3); Law on Corporation Tax Credits (Finland) Art.1(4).]

A Finnish court referred a complaint by M, a resident of Finland who was liable for income tax on dividends he received from a Swedish company, to the European Court of Justice (ECJ). M contended that Finnish regulations on corporation tax credits, specifically the Law on Corporation Tax Credits (Finland) Art.1(4) on the taxation of dividends, were incompatible with the right to freedom of establishment under the EC Treaty Art.56 and could not be justified by the Art.58 derogation. Under Finnish law, a shareholder in a domestic company was, in addition to the dividend, paid a tax credit in proportion to the corporation tax paid by the undertaking. This tax credit was offset against tax on the dividend. In effect this meant that the shareholder need pay no further tax on income derived from capital. However, since M's income came from the dividends of a foreign company he was not entitled to offset corporation tax paid in Sweden against his tax liability in Finland. The rationale behind this rule was the avoidance of double taxation. The ECJ was asked to give a preliminary ruling as to (1) whether Art.56 precluded a corporation tax credit system like Finland's, and (2) whether Art.58 ought to be interpreted as being without prejudice to Finland's right to apply the relevant domestic law, since in Finland it was a condition for obtaining a corporation tax credit that the company distributing the dividend had paid the corresponding tax or supplementary tax in Finland.

Held, giving a preliminary ruling, that Art.56 and Art.58 precluded national legislation denying entitlement to a tax credit to a person fully taxable in Finland in respect of dividends paid by limited companies established in another state. Although direct taxation fell within the competence of Member States, they were nevertheless obliged to exercise it in a manner consistent with EC law, *Wielockx v. Inspecteur der Directe Belastingen (C80/94)* [1996] 1 W.L.R. 84, [1995] C.L.Y. 2786 applied. In the instant case, the tax credit applied solely in favour of dividends paid by companies established in Finland, thus disadvantaging persons fully taxable and resident in Finland who received dividends from companies in other Member States. The restriction would therefore deter persons fully taxable in Finland from investing in other Member States and therefore constituted an obstacle to companies from other Member States wishing to invest in Finland, *Staatssecretaris van Financien v. Verkooijen (C35/98)* [2002] S.T.C. 654, [2002] C.L.Y. 4433 applied. It was therefore an unlawful restriction on the free movement of capital, contrary to Art.56. Article 58 was to be interpreted strictly and did not mean that any tax legislation making a distinction between taxpayers based on where they invested capital was automatically compatible with the EC Treaty. Article 58 was itself limited by Art.58(3), which provided that national provisions should not take the form of arbitrary discrimination or disguised restrictions on the free movement of capital.

PROCEEDINGS BROUGHT BY MANNINEN (C319/02); *sub nom.* MANNINEN v. FINLAND (C319/02); MANNINEN, *Re* (C319/02) [2005] Ch. 236, Judge Skouris (President), ECJ.

4029. Corporation tax – Friendly societies

FRIENDLY SOCIETIES (MODIFICATION OF THE CORPORATION TAX ACTS) REGULATIONS 2005, SI 2005 2014; made under the Income and Corporation Taxes Act 1988 s.463. In force: August 12, 2005; £3.50.

The Income and Corporation Taxes Act 1988 s.463 provides that the enactments relating to corporation tax apply to the life or endowment business carried on by friendly societies in the same way as they apply to long-term business of insurance companies, subject to such modifications and exceptions as may be prescribed by the Treasury. These Regulations, which amend the Taxes Act 1988; the Finance Act 1989; the Finance Act 1991; the Taxation of Chargeable Gains Act 1992; the Finance Act 1996; the Finance Act 1997; the Finance Act 1999; the Capital Allowances Act 2001; the Finance Act 2002; the Individual Savings Account (Insurance Companies) Regulations 1998 (SI 1998 1871); the Financial Services and Markets Act 2000 (Consequential Amendments) (Taxes) Order 2001 (SI 2001 3629); and revoke the Friendly Societies (Modification of the Corporation Tax Acts) Regulations 1997 (SI 1997 473); the Friendly Societies (Modification of the Corporation Tax Acts) (Amendment No.2) Regulations 1997 (SI 1997 2877); the Friendly Societies (Modification of the Corporation Tax Acts) (Amendment) Regulations 1999 (SI 1999 2636); the Friendly Societies (Modification of the Corporation Tax Acts) (Amendment) Regulations 2000 (SI 2000 2710), the Friendly Societies (Modification of the Corporation Tax Acts) (Amendment) Regulations 2001 (SI 2001 3975), the Friendly Societies (Modification of the Corporation Tax Acts) (Amendment) Regulations 2003 (SI 2003 23); the Friendly Societies (Modification of the Corporation Tax Acts) (Amendment) Regulations 2004 (SI 2004 822); and the Friendly Societies (Modification of the Corporation Tax Acts) (Amendment) Regulations 2005 (SI 2005 2005), consolidate the regulations making such modifications, for accounting periods beginning on or after January 1, 2005. The Regulations also modify the life assurance tax provisions applying for 2005 onwards to take into account a number of changes made by the Financial Services Authority (FSA) to their Handbook, and changes made by the Finance (No.2) Act 2005 to the life assurance tax provisions. One major change made by the FSA is that for 2005 onwards, directive friendly societies are governed by the FSA's Interim

Prudential Sourcebook (Insurers), whereas non-directive societies are governed by the Interim Prudential Sourcebook (Friendly Societies).

4030. Corporation tax–Friendly societies–Insurance business

FRIENDLY SOCIETIES (MODIFICATION OF THE CORPORATION TAX ACTS) (AMENDMENT) REGULATIONS 2005, SI 2005 2005; made under the Income and Corporation Taxes Act 1988 s.463. In force: August 11, 2005; £3.00.

The Income and Corporation Taxes Act 1988 provides that the enactments relating to corporation tax apply to the life or endowment business carried on by friendly societies in the same way as they apply to long-term business of insurance companies, subject to such modifications and exceptions as may be prescribed by the Treasury. These Regulations amend the Friendly Societies (Modification of the Corporation Tax Acts) Regulations 1997 (SI 1997 473) for accounting periods beginning and ending in 2004. For that year, directive friendly societies are governed by the Interim Prudential Sourcebook (Insurers). These Regulations make technical amendments to include references to that Sourcebook, and amend references to the Interim Prudential Sourcebook (Friendly Societies) so as to refer to non-directive friendly societies.

4031. Corporation tax–Hearings–Failure to attend–Ill health

[General Commissioners (Jurisdiction and Procedure) Regulations 1994 (SI 1994 1812) Reg.10.]

The appellant taxpayer companies (S) appealed against penalties summarily imposed by the respondent commissioners under the General Commissioners (Jurisdiction and Procedure) Regulations 1994 Reg.10. Estimated corporation tax assessments had been raised against each of the S companies for a number of years. Appeals were raised against those assessments supported by abbreviated accounts. The commissioners issued notices under Reg.10 requiring S to produce analyses of the expenses claimed. At the hearing, S's representative did not appear by reason of ill health. The commissioners imposed penalties for failure to comply with the notices.

Held, dismissing the appeal, that the commissioners had the power to determine proceedings in the absence of a party who failed to attend. The commissioners had not gone ahead with the appeals against assessment on the basis that S needed to be heard but they had proceeded with the penalty hearings. Any defect in that decision was cured by the fact that the instant appeal had been by way of rehearing. Even though small companies were permitted to file abbreviated accounts without particularising items such as administrative expenses it did not mean that a breakdown of such items could not later be required by the commissioners, *Slater Ltd v. Beacontree General Commissioners (No.1)* [2002] S.T.C. 246, [2002] C.L.Y. 4506 applied. The notices served were not unduly onerous and S had not made sufficient efforts to comply. There was no reason to depart from the penalties imposed by the commissioners which were modest.

SLATER LTD v. BEACONTREE GENERAL COMMISSIONERS (NO.2); *sub nom.* SLATER LTD v. INLAND REVENUE COMMISSIONERS; SALTER LTD v. INLAND REVENUE COMMISSIONERS; SLATER v. GENERAL COMMISSIONERS OF INCOME TAX FOR BEACONTREE (NO.2), [2002] EWHC 2676, [2004] S.T.C. 1342, Park, J., Ch D.

4032. Corporation tax–Payments–Instalments

CORPORATION TAX (INSTALMENT PAYMENTS) (AMENDMENT) REGULATIONS 2005, SI 2005 889; made under the Taxes Management Act 1970 s.59E; and the Income and Corporation Taxes Act 1988 s.826A. In force: April 13, 2005; £3.00.

These Regulations amend the Corporation Tax (Instalment Payments) Regulations 1998 (SI 1998 3175) which make provision for quarterly instalment payments of corporation tax by large companies. The Regulations have effect in relation to accounting periods of companies ending on or after July 1, 2005 and provide that corporation tax and the supplementary charge in relation to ring fence profits and adjusted ring fence profits (which arise from a company's oil extraction activities or from oil rights) are payable in up to three instalments rather than four.

4033. Corporation tax–Reliefs–Payment of compensation and pension contribution for benefit of director–No evidence of payment in period for which deduction claimed

[Income and Corporation Taxes Act 1998 s.592.]

The appellant taxpayer company (R) appealed against a decision of the respondent Inland Revenue refusing to allow tax relief for a £160,000 contribution to a director's pension fund and £30,000 compensation to that director for loss of office. The Inland Revenue argued that (1) R's evidence that the pension payment was noted in its 1995 trading account, its supporting evidence that an aggregate of £350,000 had been placed in short term accounts while it sought an appropriate investment and that £100,000 had been placed in R's retirement benefit scheme in 1996, was insufficient; (2) despite Inland Revenue requests, R had failed to produce evidence that the compensation payment had been made, and, in any case, tax relief for that sum was not available because the director had lost his managing directorship as a result of R selling part of its business, and the compensation had not, therefore, been made for the purposes of carrying on R's trade.

Held, dismissing the appeal, that (1) the Inland Revenue had, entirely reasonably, sought evidence independent of R's trading account. The payment to the retirement benefit scheme had not been made into an exempt approved scheme in the accounting year in which it was actually paid under the Income and Corporation Taxes Act 1998 s.592 and therefore did not qualify for relief. It was not sufficient to make a reserve for a future anticipated payment. (2) For reasons similar to those given in respect of the pension contribution, there was no evidence that the compensation payment had been made. Further, the compensation payment did not qualify for tax relief as it was clearly a gratuitous payment made on the cessation of a business, *Inland Revenue Commissioner v. Cosmotron Manufacturing Co Ltd* [1997] 1 W.L.R. 1288, [1997] C.L.Y. 1064 applied.

RELKOBROOK LTD v. MAPSTONE (INSPECTOR OF TAXES) [2005] S.T.C. (S.C.D.) 272, Colin Bishopp, Sp Comm.

4034. Corporation tax–Tax credits–Research expenditure–Compatibility with equal treatment provisions–European Community

[EC Treaty Art.49.]

A question was referred to the European Court of Justice for a preliminary ruling as to the compatibility of French tax laws on research expenditure with the principle of equal treatment. The domestic legislation granted tax credits to entities paying corporation tax for expenditure on research but only where such research was carried out within France. The domestic court referred the question of whether this provision was precluded by the EC Treaty Art.49. The French government contended that the provision was necessary to ensure effective fiscal supervision and promote research.

Held, giving a preliminary ruling, that Art.49 precluded a Member State from giving tax credits only for research carried out in that Member State. The provision was, on its face, incompatible with Art.49 as it limited cross border activity and therefore amounted to unequal treatment. The court had to consider, however, whether such unequal treatment was justified. The principle of safeguarding the coherence of a tax system could only apply where there was a direct link between the tax deductions and the benefit, *Bachmann v. Belgium (C204/90)* [1994] S.T.C. 855, [1992] C.L.Y. 4805 applied. In the instant case there was no such link between general corporation tax and tax credits for research. Although promotion of research was in the public interest, the provision did not support the overall aim of encouraging cooperation in research between Member States and was therefore directly contrary to community policy. The principle of effective fiscal supervision required measurable and clear tax provisions and could not be used to justify a provision that did not allow a taxpayer to take advantage of a benefit simply because the expenditure in question had taken place in another Member State. There was no reason why clear and measurable evidence of such expenditure could not be provided.

LABORATOIRES FOURNIER SA v. DIRECTION DES VERIFICATIONS NATIONALES ET INTERNATIONALES (C39/04) [2005] 2 C.M.L.R. 5, Judge Rosas (President), ECJ.

4035. Customs duty–Agricultural levies–Recovery of claims

RECOVERY OF DUTIES AND TAXES ETC. DUE IN OTHER MEMBER STATES (CORRESPONDING UK CLAIMS, PROCEDURE AND SUPPLEMENTARY) (AMENDMENT) REGULATIONS 2005, SI 2005 1709; made under the Finance Act 2002 Sch.39 para.3. In force: July 19, 2005; £3.00.

These Regulations amend the Recovery of Duties and Taxes Etc. Due in Other Member States (Corresponding UK Claims, Procedure and Supplementary) Regulations 2004 (SI 2004 674) which make provision in respect of mutual assistance and recovery as between Member States in relation to duties and taxes. The Regulations make it clear that taxes listed in Council Directive 76/308 ([1976] OJ L73/18) on mutual assistance for the recovery of claims resulting from operations forming part of the system of financing the European Agricultural Guidance and Guarantee Fund are included as foreign claims. It also makes provision for corresponding UK claims in relation to foreign claims of the additional 10 States which joined the EU on May 1, 2004.

4036. Deductions–Subcontractors–Certificate of exemption under s.565 Income and Corporation Taxes Act 1988

[Income and Corporation Taxes Act 1988 s.561(9), s.565; Human Rights Act 1998 s.3, Sch.1 Part II Art.1.]

The Revenue appealed by way of case stated against a decision of the General Commissioners allowing the appeal of the respondent (H) against a refusal to renew a certificate under the Income and Corporation Taxes Act 1988 s.565. H was a subcontractor in the construction industry. The Revenue refused to renew H's certificate because H did not satisfy the criteria under s.565(3) as it had made late payments of tax and national insurance liabilities. The commissioners accepted evidence from H that it had sought help from the Revenue in its payments of tax liabilities, it had not been informed that late payment could endanger its certificate, a large sum of money had been taken from the company account without authority and if a certificate were not granted it was likely to go out of business. The commissioners allowed the renewal of the certificate on the basis that a decision that could have led to H going out of business would be disproportionate and inequitable. The Revenue submitted that, under s.565(4) of the Act, a taxpayer was not entitled to a certificate if either the failures to pay tax on time were not minor or technical, or, even if they were minor and technical, they nonetheless gave rise to a doubt that the taxpayer would fulfil the conditions in the future. H submitted that not to grant a certificate would be a disproportionate result, therefore the Human Rights Act 1998 s.3 should be applied so as to read into s.565 words that would avoid such a disproportionate result.

Held, allowing the appeal, that in order to read into s.565 a notion of proportionality there had to be an interference with a right protected under Sch.1 of the 1998 Act. The court was prepared to assume that a subcontractor's right to receive payment in gross, to which a certificate entitled him, was a possession that was protected under Sch.1 Part II Art.1. That possession was interfered with by the Revenue in requiring deductions from payments to subcontractors. The scheme of deduction had been devised to ensure the payment of tax by subcontractors. There was a considerable measure of proportionality in the scheme: the default position was to make deductions from payments to subcontractors, however subcontractors could receive payments in gross by obtaining a s.565 certificate; the fact that a subcontractor did not comply with the conditions in s.565(3) because of non compliance with tax obligations did not of itself rule out a certificate by virtue of s.565(4); there was the inevitable imprecision of the phrase "minor and technical" in s.565(4); the question in s.565(4) was whether failures to comply with tax obligations were minor or technical in the Revenue's opinion; the function of the commissioners under s.561 (9) was not only to review the Revenue's decision but to substitute their own opinion if necessary, *Hudson (Inspector of Taxes) v. JDC Services Ltd* [2004] EWHC 602, [2004] S.T.C. 834, [2004] C.L.Y. 3710 followed; the refusal of a certificate of exemption was not final. Therefore the interference with the right to receive payment in gross was justifiably interfered with. Consequently no Convention right had been infringed and there was no occasion to resort to s.3 of the 1998 Act, *Shaw (Inspector of Taxes) v. Vicky Construction Ltd* [2002] EWHC 2659, [2002] S.T.C. 1544, [2003] C.L.Y. 4251 applied.

BARNES (INSPECTOR OF TAXES) v. HILTON MAIN CONSTRUCTION LTD, [2005] EWHC 1355, [2005] S.T.C. 1532, Lewison, J., Ch D.

4037. Direct taxes–Exemptions–Share transfers–Applicability of transfer tax exemption to share capital reorganisations–Jamaica

[TransferTax Act 1971 (Jamaica) s.3, Sch.1 para.4(2), Sch.1 para.6.]

C appealed against the Stamp Commissioner's decision that theTransferTax Act 1971 (Jamaica) para.4 and para.6(1) did not exempt C's transfer of shares in a company, J, to a third company, CB, from tax on the value of the consideration. On April 27, 1999 C had agreed to transfer all the issued ordinary share capital and the bulk of the preference shares in J to CB in consideration of a debenture issued by CB in the sum of £37.7 million. The terms of the agreement were that (1) the debenture would be neither secured nor transferable, and (2) the principal debt would be interest free and was to be repaid by banker's cheque on May 7, 1999. In fact the debenture was not redeemed until May 11 and on this date CB paid $19.9 million and JMD 700,344.814 million and C accepted these payments in full settlement. The share transfer was assessed to tax pursuant to s.3 of the 1971 Act. However, Sch.1 para.4(2) provided that a reorganisation of a company's share capital should not be regarded as a disposal of the original shares. C therefore argued that CB's issue of the debenture in exchange for the original shares held by C in J amounted to such a reorganisation and should be treated as though CB and J were the same company.

Held, dismissing the appeal, that had the transaction been confined solely to the events of April 27, 1999 and the agreement concluded on that date, then it would have been correctly categorised as a reorganisation of share capital as defined in the 1971 Act, namely a debenture issued in exchange for shares. However, to interpret the transaction and the exemption provided by para.6(1) in such a way that all that was required to obtain a tax exemption was the insertion of a formal step into the transaction for no purpose other than the avoidance of tax was not compatible with any rational system of taxation. This could not have been what was intended by Jamaica's legislature. The 1971 Act should be interpreted as being aimed at the transaction as a whole, since the relevant transaction consisted of both the issue and the redemption of the debenture, *WT Ramsay Ltd v. Inland Revenue Commissioners* [1982] A.C. 300, [1981] C.L.Y. 1385 applied and *MacNiven (Inspector of Taxes) v. Westmoreland Investments Ltd* [2001] UKHL 6, [2003] 1 A.C. 311, [2001] C.L.Y. 5199 distinguished. Taking this transaction as a whole, it could not properly be described as an exchange of shares for a debenture and it was therefore liable to transfer tax.

CARRERAS GROUP LTD v. STAMP COMMISSIONER; *sub nom.* STAMP COMMISSIONER v. CARRERAS GROUP LTD, [2004] UKPC 16, [2004] S.T.C. 1377, Lord Nicholls of Birkenhead, PC (Jam).

4038. Double taxation—Lease of substantial equipment—Requirement of permanent establishment—Australia

[Australia-Singapore DoubleTaxation Agreement Art.4(1), Art.4(3), Art.10(4).]
The appellant (M), an offshore marine construction and engineering contractor, appealed against a decision concerning the tax treatment of payments made under a lease of substantial equipment. M, an Australian company, leased barges on bare boat charters from a Singapore corporation (C) for use in Australian waters. M claimed the payments made to C as allowable deductions under the Australia-Singapore double taxation agreement (the Singapore agreement) and did not deduct withholding tax. It was agreed that the barges were "substantial equipment" for the purposes of Art.4(3)(b) of the Singapore agreement, which also provided that an enterprise was deemed to have a "permanent establishment" in a state if substantial equipment was being used in that state "by, for or under contract with the enterprise". Article 10(4) provided that withholding tax did not have to be deducted from the payments under the lease where the recipient had a permanent establishment in the state where the equipment was being used. It was found at first instance that Art.4(3) was governed by Art.4(1), which required a fixed place of business for the carrying on of the enterprise and that payments under a lease of substantial equipment should not be treated differently from payments under leases of any other equipment. On appeal, M argued, inter alia, that Art.4(3) was a deeming provision which operated to expand the notion of permanent establishment rather than being governed by it.
Held, allowing the appeal, that C had a permanent establishment in Australia as a result of Art.4(3) of the Singapore agreement, which expanded the operation of Art.4(1). The permanent establishment was deemed to arise because the barges were being used in Australia by either C or M under contract with C. Article 4(3) was to be given its natural meaning since there was no reason to construe it any other way, having regard to the historical background, context and purpose of the Singapore agreement. It was not anomalous to differentiate between leases of "substantial equipment" and those of ordinary equipment, especially where there was international disagreement concerning the tax treatment of rental payments on equipment leases. The provisions of Art.10(4) applied, with the result that the payments did not fall to be taxed by withholding as royalties but as part of the taxable income of C, less any allowable deductions. It followed that the payments made by M to C were allowable deductions to M in calculating its income for the relevant period
McDERMOTT INDUSTRIES (AUST) PTY LTD v. COMMISSIONER OF TAXATION 7 I.T.L. Rep. 800, Hill, J., Fed Ct (Aus) (Full Ct).

4039. Employment—Employer financed retirement benefit schemes—Provision of information

EMPLOYER-FINANCED RETIREMENT BENEFITS SCHEMES (PROVISION OF INFORMATION) REGULATIONS 2005, SI 2005 3453; made under the Finance Act 2004 s.251. In force: April 6, 2006; £3.00.
These Regulations set out the prescribed information that must be supplied to the Inland Revenue by those persons responsible for administering employer-financed retirement benefits schemes. They provide for interpretation; prescribe the person who must supply information to the Inland Revenue; prescribe the information that must be supplied in relation to the coming into operation of a scheme; and prescribe the information that must be supplied in relation to the provision of relevant benefits.

4040. Energy efficiency—Solid wall insulation

ENERGY-SAVING ITEMS REGULATIONS 2005, SI 2005 1114; made under the IncomeTax (Trading and Other Income) Act 2005 s.312. In force: April 7, 2005; £3.00.
The Income Tax (Trading and Other Income) Act 2005 rewrites income tax legislation relating to trading, property and investment income as part of the Tax Law Rewrite Project. It also provides a deduction for expenditure on certain

energy-saving items installed in let residential properties; states that cavity wall insulation and loft wall insulation are energy-saving items; and gives the Treasury a power to specify other descriptions of items as being of an energy-saving nature. These Regulations specify solid wall insulation as an item of an energy-saving nature.

4041. Enterprise Investment Scheme-Reliefs-Overseas subsidiaries operating as branch offices-Use of money raised by share issue for qualifying business activity

[Income and Corporation Taxes Act 1988 s.289(1) (b), s.289(1) (c), s.289(3).]

The appellant taxpayer (F) appealed against the respondent Inland Revenue's refusal to grant tax relief in respect of two share issues used to fund loans to its overseas subsidiaries. F provided financial market analysis in London. It had started up two wholly owned overseas subsidiaries, which, like F, made losses. The subsidiaries were effectively branch offices which had provided analyses of the New York and Singapore markets. They had also sought clients for the analyses provided by the London office, which did not charge the subsidiaries for that service. The subsidiaries' expenses were funded by loans from F, which had obtained the loan funds by issuing shares. The Inland Revenue refused to issue enterprise investment scheme certificates to the two investors on the basis that the purpose of the share issues was not for a qualifying business activity under the Income and Corporation Taxes Act 1988 s.289(1). The Inland Revenue argued that (1) "the purpose" in s.289(1) (b) meant a sole, not mixed, purpose, and that part of F's purpose was to loan money to the overseas subsidiaries; (2) the share money was not employed wholly in the United Kingdom because the subsidiaries did not carry on their qualifying trade in the UK.

Held, allowing the appeal, that (1) F was eligible for relief under s.289(1)(b) because the shares were issued in order to raise money for the purpose of a qualifying business activity. F required the subsidiaries' services in order to carry on its own trade, and making loans was the means by which it obtained those services. F did not have the separate purpose of saving the subsidiaries' businesses; it was merely indirectly paying for their analyses. The subsidiaries' local sales did not make any difference. The phrase "for the purpose of" meant "main" not "sole" purpose, *Carvill v. Inland Revenue Commissioners (Transfer Purpose)* [2000] S.T.C. (S.C.D.) 143, [2000] C.L.Y. 5021 considered, although in the circumstances it was not necessary to make a finding on that issue. (2) F was eligible for relief under s.289(1)(c) because it had employed the money wholly for the purpose of its own qualifying business activities, not for the purpose of the subsidiaries' business activities. The word "wholly" related to the purpose, not the whole of the money raised; that reasoning was supported by s.289(3).

4CAST LTD v. MITCHELL (INSPECTOR OF TAXES) [2005] S.T.C. (S.C.D.) 287, John F Avery Jones, Sp Comm.

4042. European Union-Recovery of tax-Accession

RECOVERY OF TAXES ETC DUE IN OTHER MEMBER STATES (AMENDMENT OF SECTION 134 OF THE FINANCE ACT 2002) REGULATIONS 2005, SI 2005 1479; made under the Finance Act 2002 s.134. In force: June 27, 2005; £3.00.

These Regulations amend the definition of the "Mutual Assistance Recovery Directive" in the Finance Act 2002 to insert the Act of Accession which amends the Directive on accession of the Czech Republic, the Republic of Estonia, the Republic of Cyprus, the Republic of Latvia, the Republic of Lithuania, the Republic of Hungary, the Republic of Malta, the Republic of Poland, the Republic of Slovenia and the Slovak Republic.

4043. Excise duty–Fuel–Rebates

EXCISE DUTIES (SURCHARGES OR REBATES) (HYDROCARBON OILS ETC.) ORDER 2005, SI 2005 1978; made under the Excise Duties (Surcharges or Rebates) Act 1979 s.1, s.2. In force: September 1, 2005; £3.00.

This Order adjusts the liabilities to excise duty (and, where applicable, the rights to rebate in respect of such duty) in respect of liquid fuels that are chargeable by virtue of the Hydrocarbon Oil Duties Act 1979.

4044. Excise duty–Fuel–Reliefs

EXCISE DUTIES (ROAD FUEL GAS) (RELIEFS) REGULATIONS 2005, SI 2005 1979; made under the Hydrocarbon Oil Duties Act 1979 s.20AA. In force: September 1, 2005; £3.00.

These Regulations provide for a partial relief from the excise duty charged on road fuel gas. The relief is allowed only in respect of road fuel gas that is charged with duty on or after that date. The result of the application of the relief (which is provided in the form of a remission of part of the duty that is chargeable) is that the amount a person is liable to pay in respect of excise duty on road fuel gas is reduced by the amounts specified in these Regulations.

4045. Excise duty–Relief–Registered remote markers

HYDROCARBON OIL (REGISTERED REMOTE MARKERS) REGULATIONS 2005, SI 2005 3472; made under the Customs and Excise Management Act 1979 s.100G, s.100H; and the Hydrocarbon Oil Duties Act 1979 s.20AA, s.24. In force: January 10, 2006; £3.00.

These Regulations which amend the Excise Goods (Holding, Movement, Warehousing and REDS) Regulations 1992 (SI 1992 3135), the Excise Duties (Deferred Payment) Regulations 1992 (SI 1992 3152), the Warehousekeepers and Owners of Warehoused Goods Regulations 1999 (SI 1999 1278) and the Excise Goods (Sales on Board Ships and Aircraft) Regulations 1999 (SI 1999 1565), implement further European Parliament and Council Directive 2003/96 ([2003] OJ L283/51) Art.14, restructuring the Community framework for the taxation of energy products and electricity. They provide the machinery, and prescribe the procedures to be followed, for the approval and registration of registered remote markers engaged in marking gas oil, kerosene, or light oil used as furnace fuel with approved fiscal markers as a condition of entitlement to relief from excise duty.

4046. Finance Act 1995 (c.4)–Appointed Day and Savings Order

FINANCE ACT 1995 (DENATURED ALCOHOL) (APPOINTED DAY AND SAVINGS) ORDER 2005, SI 2005 1523 (C.67); made under the Finance Act 1995 s.5. Commencement details: bringing into force various provisions of the 1995 Act on July 1, 2005; £3.00.

This Order appoints July 1, 2005 as the day that the Finance Act 1995 s.5 and Sch.2 come into force and the day that the related repeals in Part 1 of Sch.29 to that Act have effect. It also provides for any approval, authorization or licence granted in relation to methylated spirits to be treated as if it had been granted in relation to denatured alcohol.

4047. Finance Act 2003 (c.14)–Appointed Day Order–S.189 and s.190

FINANCE ACT 2003, SECTIONS 189 AND 190, (APPOINTED DAY) ORDER 2005, SI 2005 1713 (C.72); made under the Finance Act 2003 s.189, s.190. Commencement details: bringing into force various provisions of the 2003 Act on July 22, 2005; £3.00.

This Order appoints July 22, 2005 as the day on or after which the Finance Act 2003 s.189 and s.190 have effect in relation to supplies of climate change levy's taxable commodities.

4048. Finance Act 2004 (c.12)–Appointed Day Order–S.18

FINANCE ACT 2004, SECTION 18 (APPOINTED DAY) ORDER 2005, SI 2005 2356 (C.98); made under the Finance Act 2004 s.18. Commencement details: bringing into force various provisions of the 2004 Act on October 14, 2005; £3.00.

This Order provides that the Finance Act 2004 s.18 shall have effect in relation to the issue of vehicle licences or trade licences on or after October 14, 2005. Section 18 of the Finance Act 2004 amends the Vehicle and Excise Registration Act 1994 to provide that a prescribed fee is payable when a credit card payment is accepted in respect of the vehicle excise duty payable upon the issue of a licence.

4049. Finance Act 2004 (c.12)–Appointed Day Order–S.141

FINANCE ACT 2004, SECTION 141 (APPOINTED DAY) ORDER 2005, SI 2005 123 (C.6); made under the Finance Act 2004 s.141. Commencement details: bringing into force various provisions of the 2004 Act on April 1, 2004; £3.00.

This Order appoints April 1, 2004 as the appointed day for the purposes of the Finance Act 2004 s.141.

4050. Finance Act 2005 (c.7)

This Act grants certain duties, alters other duties, and amends the law relating to the National Debt and the Public Revenue, and makes further provision in connection with finance.

This Act received Royal Assent on April 7, 2005.

4051. Finance (No.2) Act 2005 (c.22)

This Act grants certain duties, alters other duties, and amends the law relating to the National Debt and the Public Revenue, and makes further provision in connection with finance.

This Act received Royal Assent on July 20, 2005.

4052. Finance (No.2) Act 2005 (c.22)–Appointed Day Order–S.6

FINANCE (NO.2) ACT 2005, SECTION 6, (APPOINTED DAY AND SAVINGS PROVISIONS) ORDER 2005, SI 2005 2010 (C.88); made under the Finance (No.2) Act 2005 s.6. Commencement details: bringing into force various provisions of the 2005 Act on August 1, 2005; £3.00.

This Order appoints August 1, 2005 as the day on or after which the Finance (No.2) Act 2005 s.6 has effect. That section provides that Sch.1 to the Act shall come into force, amending the Value Added Tax Act 1994 Sch.11A.

4053. Finance (No.2) Act 2005 (c.22)–Appointed Day Order–S.45

FINANCE (NO.2) ACT 2005, SECTION 45, (APPOINTED DAY) ORDER 2005, SI 2005 3337 (C.142); made under the Finance (No.2) Act 2005 s.45. Commencement details: bringing into force various provisions of the 2005 Act on January 1, 2006 and April 6, 2006; £3.00.

The Finance Act 1993 Sch.19 contains administrative machinery under which Lloyd's managing agents make returns of syndicates' profits and losses for tax purposes, and for assessment and collection of tax. The Finance (No.2) Act 2005 creates a power for the Commissioners for Her Majesty's Revenue and Customs to make regulations replacing (and up-dating) Sch.19 (which regulations are being made simultaneously with this Order) and repeals Sch.19, providing for s.45 to come into force as provided by Treasury Order.

4054. Foreign exchange–Gains and losses–Bringing into account

EXCHANGE GAINS AND LOSSES (BRINGING INTO ACCOUNT GAINS OR LOSSES) (AMENDMENT) REGULATIONS 2005, SI 2005 2013; made under the

Finance Act 1996 s.84A; and the Finance Act 2002 Sch.23 para.26, Sch.26 para.16. In force: August 11, 2005; £3.00.

These Regulations amend the Exchange Gains and Losses (Bringing into Account Gains or Losses) Regulations 2005 (SI 2002 1970) which provide how and when certain exchange gains and losses are brought into account for tax purposes. The amendment is required as a result of amendments made to the Loan Relationships and Derivative Contracts (Disregard and Bringing into Account of Profits and Losses) Regulations 2004 (SI 2004 3256).

4055. General Commissioners–Child trust funds–Appeals

GENERAL COMMISSIONERS (JURISDICTION AND PROCEDURE) (AMENDMENT) REGULATIONS 2005, SI 2005 340; made under the Taxes Management Act 1970 s.56B. In force: March 14, 2005; £3.00.

These Regulations amend the General Commissioners (Jurisdiction and Procedure) Regulations 1994 (SI 1994 1812) to include appeals under regulations made under the Child Trust Funds Act 2004 s.13 or appeals made under s.22 of that Act within the definition of "proceedings". They also provide that the decisions of the general commissioners in relation to appeals and other proceedings to them under the enactments relating to stamp duty land tax may be appealed by way of case stated.

4056. Group relief–EC law–Jurisdiction of High Court and special commissioners– Loss relief group litigation order

[Income and Corporation Taxes Act 1988 Part X Ch.IV; EC Treaty Art.43, Art.56.]

The appellant (the Revenue) appealed against a decision ([2004] EWCA Civ 680, [2005] 1 W.L.R. 52) that the issues raised in the loss relief group litigation should be heard in the High Court. After the decisions in *ICI Plc v. Colmer (Inspector of Taxes)* [1999] 1 W.L.R. 2035, [1999] C.L.Y. 4667 and *Metallgesellschaft Ltd v. Inland Revenue Commissioners (C397/98)* [2001] Ch. 620, [2001] C.L.Y. 5173 had indicated that United Kingdom legislation restricting fiscal reliefs or advantages to cases where the relevant companies were resident in the UK might be inconsistent with the EC Treaty, many multinational groups with English operations made claims against the Revenue on the basis that the provisions of the Income and Corporation Taxes Act 1988 Part X Ch.IV restricting group relief to companies resident or carrying on an economic activity in the UK were incompatible with the EC Treaty Art.43 (freedom of establishment) and Art.56 (abolition of restrictions on movements of capital and payments). The claims had been made the subject of a group litigation order. In many instances claimants had both appealed to the special commissioners and started proceedings in the High Court. The Revenue submitted that the principal claims for relief covered by the loss relief group litigation order were not properly justiciable in the High Court and that claims for group relief should be made to an inspector of taxes and appealed to the general or special commissioners who would be able to give effect to directly applicable provisions of Community law, just as much as the High Court.

Held, allowing the appeal (Lords Hope and Walker dissenting), that (1) the tax appeal commissioners had exclusive jurisdiction to decide certain types of disputes arising in the administration of the tax system. A tax assessment disallowing a claim for group relief could not be altered except in accordance with the express provisions of the tax legislation. The statutory code made its own provision for appeals to the appeal commissioners in the first instance. High Court proceedings which were in substance an appeal against an assessment would be an abuse of process, *Argosam Finance Co Ltd v. Oxby (Inspector of Taxes)* [1965] Ch. 390, [1964] C.L.Y. 1813, *Vandervell's Trusts (No.1), Re* [1971] A.C. 912, [1970] C.L.Y. 2324 and *Barraclough v. Brown* [1897] A.C. 615 applied. The High Court had jurisdiction to decide a question of fact or law which was a basis for an assessment where the taxpayer and the Revenue so agreed, provided the assessment had not become final and provided the question suitable for decision by the court was not so close to the question of the assessment itself that the court should decline to entertain it, *Glaxo Group Ltd v. Inland Revenue Commissioners* [1995] S.T.C. 1075, [1995] C.L.Y. 879 approved. However, the taxpayer and the Revenue were each entitled to insist that the statutory procedure for dealing with disputed assessments should be followed. (2) When deciding an appeal against a refusal by an inspector to allow group relief the appeal commissioners were obliged to give effect to all directly enforceable Community rights notwithstanding the terms of the 1988 Act. (3) The claimants fell into two broad classes: those who could still obtain group relief because they had already applied to the Revenue for it or were still in time to do so, and those who were out of time to apply or to appeal. In the first class, where a claimant company could obtain through the statutory procedures the very tax relief of whose non availability it was complaining, there was no justification for the company bypassing the statutory route, which would have to be adapted as necessary to accommodate claims of non resident companies, and instead going to the High Court and claiming damages or a restitutionary remedy based on the proposition that the company had been wrongly refused the tax relief to which it was entitled under Community law. (4) Although it might be more convenient for all the claims to be heard in the High Court it could not be said that requiring claimants to follow the statutory route made pursuit of their claims practically impossible or excessively difficult, *Metallgesellschaft* considered. (5) The existence of certain "satellite" claims dependant on the main claims but outside the jurisdiction of the appeal commissioners was not sufficiently weighty to displace the conclusion that the main claims should be stayed where the statutory route was still available. (6) Where it was too late to make a group relief claim or to appeal against a refusal of relief the taxpayer's remedy lay in pursuing proceedings claiming restitutionary and other relief in respect of the UK's failure to give proper effect to Community law. The appeal commissioners had no jurisdiction to hear such claims. Claims in that class should therefore proceed in the High Court after the Revenue and the commissioners had been invited to extend the time limits appropriately. If a claimant had claims in both classes that was unfortunate but inherent in the distinction between the two classes, *ICI Plc* considered.

AUTOLOGIC HOLDINGS PLC v. INLAND REVENUE COMMISSIONERS; *sub nom.* TEST CLAIMANTS IN LOSS RELIEF GROUP LITIGATION v. INLAND REVENUE COMMISSIONERS; LOSS RELIEF GROUP LITIGATION ORDER CLAIMANTS v. INLAND REVENUE COMMISSIONERS, [2005] UKHL 54, [2006] 1 A.C. 118, Lord Nicholls of Birkenhead, HL.

4057. Income–Savings–Information requirements

REPORTING OF SAVINGS INCOME INFORMATION (AMENDMENT) REGULATIONS 2005, SI 2005 1539; made under the Finance Act 2003 s.199. In force: in accordance with Reg.1 (2); £3.00.

These Regulations, which amend the Reporting of Savings Income Information Regulations 2003 (SI 2003 3297), implement part of Council Directive 2003/48 ([2003] OJ L157/38) on taxation of savings income in the form of interest payments. The Regulations are amended to implement the amendments made to Council Directive 2003/48 by reason of the accession of the Czech Republic, Estonia, Cyprus, Latvia, Lithuania, Hungary, Malta, Poland, Slovenia and Slovakia; implement the agreements or other arrangements made with dependent or associated territories of the Member States; and reflect the abolition of the Inland Revenue and the transfer of its functions to Her Majesty's Revenue and Customs.

4058. Income–Savings–Information requirements–Montserrat

MONTSERRAT REPORTING OF SAVINGS INCOME INFORMATION ORDER 2005, SI 2005 1466; made under the West Indies Act 1962 s.5, s.7. In force: in accordance with Art.1 (2); £3.00.

This Order in Council ensures that arrangements are in place in Montserrat as envisaged by Council Directive 2003/48 ([2003] OJ L57/38) Art.17(2)(ii) on taxation of savings income in the form of interest payments. The Order requires information to be reported to the Inland Revenue Department in Montserrat about savings income paid to, or secured for, an individual resident in a Member State in the course of a business or profession. The same is required in respect of some entities resident in Member States.

4059. Income tax–Accrued income scheme–Interest payable on loan notes

[Income and Corporation Taxes Act 1988 s.717(2)(a).]

The appellant company (C) appealed against a notice of determination in respect of tax payable on loan notes sold by it to an associated company (O). Six loan notes of £25 million each were issued to C by another associated company in September 1994. The notes were redeemable in December 1995. Interest was stated to be at a fixed rate of 7.4 per cent per annum but was payable on three separate occasions and in different amounts. In May 1995 the notes were assigned to O, which then transferred them to a bank. The respondent Inland Revenue took the view that the balance of the gain made by C, after payment of income tax under the accrued income scheme, was taxable as income under the Income and Corporation Taxes Act 1988 s.717. C contended that the notes came within the exemption under s.717(2)(a) as they carried interest at a rate which was the same throughout the period of the loan.

Held, dismissing the appeal, that on a proper construction of s.717(2)(a) the loan notes did not carry a fixed rate of interest. It was necessary to look at the natural meaning of the words of the section. The term "throughout" required a consideration of the interest rate applicable at each relevant moment within the period and not just the interest payable overall. The word "carried" referred to a meaning attributable to the notes' express terms. Therefore at any time each note carried the rights that a holder would then have as a holder of the note, which did not include the right to interest that had already been paid in accordance with the note's terms. After the first instalment of interest was paid in June 1995, the notes carried entitlements to interest in the sum of the two remaining interest payments, due in September and December 1995, but no longer carried entitlement to the interest that had been paid in the first instalment. By contrast, before the first instalment was paid the interest outstanding was much higher since it still included the sums due under all three instalments. It could therefore not be said that the notes carried interest at the same rate at every point throughout the period.

CADBURY SCHWEPPES PLC v. WILLIAMS (INSPECTOR OF TAXES) [2005] S.T.C. (S.C.D.) 151, AN Brice, Sp Comm.

4060. Income tax–Appeals–Accountant's authority to agree figures with Revenue on behalf of taxpayer–Binding effect of s.70 certificates

[Taxes Management Act 1970 s.70; General Commissioners (Jurisdiction and Procedure) Regulations 1994 (SI 1994 1812) Reg.16(5).]

A appealed against the dismissal of his appeal against the Revenue in an action to recover arrears of income tax and national insurance. Following an inquiry into A's tax affairs, he had appointed an accountant, M, to deal with his appeals. At a meeting with the Revenue, M provisionally agreed that A would pay the sum of £160,000 to settle his liability. The Revenue issued certificates under the Taxes Management Act 1970 s.70 certifying the amount of tax payable in respect of each of the years in question. The Revenue obtained a determination from the General Commissioners at a hearing which neither M nor A attended and brought county court proceedings after A failed to pay the tax. The court held that it was bound by the Revenue's s.70 certificates. On appeal, A argued that (1) there had been no proper determination before the Commissioners since there had been no hearing on the merits; (2) the court was not bound by the Revenue's s.70 certificates; (3) M had not had the authority to agree the figures on his behalf; (4) he had not been advised of his appeal rights in relation to the determination, contrary to the General Commissioners (Jurisdiction and Procedure) Regulations 1994 Reg.16(5).

Held, dismissing the appeal, that the district and High Court judges had been right to conclude that the county court had no appellate jurisdiction in respect of the General Commissioners' determinations, *Inland Revenue Commissioners v. Soul* 51 T.C. 86, [1979] C.L.Y. 1493 applied. The district judge was bound by the figures in the s.70 certificates and there was no basis for suggesting that the certificates were less than sufficient. There had been no serious procedural irregularity before the Commissioners because, on the facts, M did have A's authority to act on his behalf. The Commissioners' confirmation of the figures put forward by the Revenue was a "determination", which was not affected by either (i) the Commissioners' lack of deliberation on the issues, which was because neither party had asked them to do so; (ii) A's failure to oppose the determination; or (iii) M's lack of opposition to the determination being contrary to instructions, which again was not supported by the evidence. Further, a failure to advise A of his appeal rights might allow the Commissioners to review the determination but could not form a basis upon which to challenge the determination in the court proceedings.

McCULLOUGH (INSPECTOR OF TAXES) v. AHLUWALIA, [2004] EWCA Civ 889, [2004] S.T.C. 1295, Waller, L.J., CA.

4061. Income tax–Appeals–Effect of bankruptcy–Appeals against assessments settled by trustee in bankruptcy

[Taxes Management Act 1970 s.54.]

The commissioners were required to determine preliminary issues arising in connection with appeals by the taxpayer (X) against assessments to income tax and national insurance contributions. X had been made bankrupt and the trustee in bankruptcy had given permission for X to appoint an accountant to deal with his tax affairs and thereby to reopen appeals against income tax and national insurance contributions and to commence similar appeals in relation to other years. The trustee supplied information about X's financial affairs directly to the respondent Revenue and as a result the original assessments were discharged and the Revenue agreed to limit its claims in respect of the fresh appeals. The Revenue's claims were then settled by the trustee. When X was discharged from bankruptcy he sought to proceed with all of the appeals. The preliminary issues for determination were whether (1) X had a right to pursue his appeals; (2) the trustee in bankruptcy had settled the appeals by agreement within the meaning of the Taxes Management Act 1970 s.54.

Held, determining the preliminary issues in favour of the respondent, that (1) by operation of the law of bankruptcy, X no longer had any right to pursue his appeals. His estate had vested in the trustee in bankruptcy on the date of the trustee's appointment. Even though the trustee had given X permission to deal with his tax affairs that permission had effectively been withdrawn when the trustee paid the sums owed by X to settle the claims, *Heath v. Tang* [1993] 1 W.L.R. 1421, [1993] C.L.Y. 222 and *Hurren (A Bankrupt), Re* [1983] 1 W.L.R. 183, [1982] C.L.Y. 1613 applied. The Special Commissioners had no jurisdiction to reopen appeals settled by the trustee in bankruptcy unless requested to do so by the Bankruptcy Court. (2) The trustee in bankruptcy, acting on behalf of X, had settled the appeals by agreement within the meaning of s.54 of the Act. Accordingly, X's appeals were bound to fail.

AHAJOT (COUNT ARTSRUNIK) v. WALLER (INSPECTOR OF TAXES) [2005] B.P.I.R. 82, Nuala Brice, Sp Comm.

4062. Income tax–Assessment–Error or mistake–Relief for bad debts–Right to make claim after assessment settled by agreement

[Taxes Management Act 1970 s.29(3), s.33, s.54; Income and Corporation Taxes Act 1988 s.74(1)(j).]

The appellant taxpayer (T) appealed against the respondent Commissioners' refusal to allow his claim for relief under the Taxes Management

Act 1970 s.33 as a result of errors made by him in not claiming bad debt tax relief. From 1993, T, an accountant, had lodged various assessment appeals. In 1996, he claimed relief from bad debts in relation to the tax years 1989 to 1990 and 1994 to 1995. After further discussion on bad debts and a meeting in November 1996, the Inland Revenue wrote proposing a calculation based on all agreed information. T replied, agreeing with the contents of that letter, but later appealed. He argued that (1) he had been mistaken in not regarding outstanding fees from five clients as bad debts in the year they were invoiced, and claimed that he had received information in 1995 and 1996 making it clear that at least three of those debts would not be paid; (2) he had not entered into an agreement with the Inland Revenue under s.54 of the 1970 Act because he had not replied unequivocally to the inspector's request for a written agreement, the inspector's letter had contained a question mark against one calculation, and T was waiting for formal assessments which would allow an automatic right of appeal; (3) in any case, the case law did not prevent him from making a s.33 claim following a s.54 agreement.

Held, dismissing the appeal, that (1) the Income and Corporation Taxes Act 1988 s.74(1)(j) did not permit the use of hindsight, but required the taxpayer to make a judgment at the time of drawing up the profit and loss account. T had not provided any evidence that two debts were bad in their respective years and his evidence showed that the remaining debts became bad in 1995 and 1996. (2) A reasonable person would have concluded from the circumstances that T had agreed to the Inland Revenue's proposed assessments including the issue of bad debt relief, which resulted in a s.54 agreement. The bad debt issue had featured prominently in correspondence between the parties, it had been noted in some detail at the meeting, the inspector's letter was the outcome of that meeting, and the question mark was simply a helpful reminder. (3) The legal principle in *Cenlon Finance Co Ltd v. Ellwood (Inspector of Taxes)* [1962] A.C. 782, [1962] C.L.Y. 1491, namely that the Inland Revenue could not make a discovery assessment under s.29(3) of the 1970 Act subsequent to a s.54 agreement, should be extended to prohibit a taxpayer from making a s.33 claim following a s.54 agreement, *Cenlon* applied and *Eagerpath Ltd v. Edwards (Inspector of Taxes)* [2001] S.T.C. 26, [2001] C.L.Y. 5200 considered.

THOMPSON v. INLAND REVENUE COMMISSIONERS [2005] S.T.C. (S.C.D.) 320, Michael Tildesley, Sp Comm.

4063. Income tax – Benefits in kind – Payment of legal costs by company – Director and company both having interest in outcome of litigation

[Income and Corporation Taxes Act 1988 s.154.]

The appellant company director (C) appealed against his tax assessment. C was the managing director and majority shareholder of a company (X). In 1994 X was having problems with an employee (L) who was also a minority shareholder. Two actions were subsequently brought against L, one by X for the return of company property and one by C for the repayment of a personal loan to L. The litigation was settled by agreement. L was ordered to pay X and C's costs on their claims, and X to pay L's costs on her counterclaim, the net result of which was that X paid £6,773 to L. The tax inspector took the view that payment of the legal costs by X amounted to a benefit in kind for C taxable under the Income and Corporation Taxes Act 1988 s.154. C contended that it was not a benefit as he had given valuable consideration by lending his name to the litigation.

Held, dismissing the appeal, that C did receive a benefit by reason of his employment that was to his advantage. Although X also received a benefit in that it was able to get rid of a minority shareholder who might have brought further actions against it, the benefit to C was more than incidental. The legal services had not been provided in house; therefore the overall value of the benefit had to be calculated on the actual cost of bringing in legal services from outside, *Pepper (Inspector of Taxes) v. Hart* [1993] A.C. 593, [1993] C.L.Y. 459 applied. The value of the benefit to C had to be ascertained by a just and reasonable apportionment of the expenses which would have been incurred by him in the conduct of his personal action, less any amount made good. C had not given fair value by lending his name to the litigation since C was an integral part of X and it was clearly of benefit to both X and C that the litigation was conducted as it had been.

XI SOFTWARE LTD v. LAING (INSPECTOR OF TAXES); COLLINS v. LAING (INSPECTOR OF TAXES) [2005] S.T.C. (S.C.D.) 249, K Khan, Sp Comm.

4064. Income tax – Business expenses – Mortgage interest – Set off against trading income

[Income and Corporation Taxes Act 1988 s.21 (1).]

The appellants (K), a husband and wife, appealed against their assessments to income tax. The husband was involved in the business of renovating houses and selling them on at a profit. His business had run into financial difficulties and the couple moved out of their jointly owned private residence, rented that property out and took out a mortgage secured against the property to repay the business borrowing. The husband argued that he was entitled to claim relief on the full interest payments on the mortgage as a business expense because the house had become part of the trading stock of his property business. The wife appealed against the charge to tax of her half share of the rental receipts from the property for a period prior to her marriage.

Held, allowing the appeals in part, that the interest paid on the mortgage could not be allowed in full as a business expense because the property that was security for the mortgage had not been appropriated to the trading stock of the husband's business. The property had originally been purchased as a private house and there was no evidence of a change of intention that the house would be transferred to trading stock. The business of renting out property was not the same business as the husband's business of renovating and selling property. However, pursuant to the Income and Corporation Taxes Act 1988 s.21 (1) either the "person receiving" or the "person entitled" to rental payments could be charged to tax. The section did not specify that "persons entitled" should be charged to tax before "persons receiving". Further, there was no requirement for a "person entitled" to evidence in writing his or her surrender of that entitlement. In any event, there was clear evidence that the wife had surrendered her entitlement to the rents received on the house and the husband alone was liable for tax.

KINGS v. KING (INSPECTOR OF TAXES); KINGS v. BARKER (INSPECTOR OF TAXES) [2004] S.T.C. (S.C.D.) 186, Michael Tildesley, Sp Comm.

4065. Income tax – Car fuel benefits

INCOME TAX (CAR BENEFITS) (REDUCTION OF VALUE OF APPROPRIATE PERCENTAGE) (AMENDMENT) REGULATIONS 2005, SI 2005 2209; made under the Income Tax (Earnings and Pensions) Act 2003 s.170. In force: April 6, 2006; £3.00.

These Regulations amend the Income Tax (Car Benefits) (Reduction of Value of Appropriate Percentage) Regulations 2001 (SI 2001 1123) so that Reg.3 shall cease to have effect in respect of any car registered on or after January 1, 2006. This waiver will continue for cars registered before January 1, 2006. They also provide that the standard reduction for hybrid electric and petrol cars shall be increased to 3 per cent and remove the additional discount "B"; and provide that the standard reduction for gas-only and bi-fuel gas and petrol cars shall be increased to 2 per cent and remove additional discount "B".

4066. Income tax – Charitable donations – Declarations

DONATIONS TO CHARITY BY INDIVIDUALS (APPROPRIATE DECLARATIONS) (AMENDMENT) REGULATIONS 2005, SI 2005 2790; made under the Finance Act 1990 s.25; and the Finance Act 1999 s.132, s.133. In force: November 1, 2005; £3.00.

These Regulations amend the Donations to Charity by Individuals (Appropriate Declarations) Regulations 2000 (SI 2000 2074) to remove the requirement for charities to send donors a written record of their declaration where it has been made orally, provided that the charity keeps sufficient records of declarations which can be audited by HM Revenue and Customs.

4067. Income tax–Child care providers–Exemptions

SECTION 318C INCOME TAX (EARNINGS AND PENSIONS) ACT 2003 (AMENDMENT) REGULATIONS 2005, SI 2005 770; made under the Income Tax (Earnings and Pensions) Act 2003 s.318D. In force: April 6, 2005; £3.00.

These Regulations amend the Income Tax (Earnings and Pensions) Act 2003 (which provides for an exemption from income tax for employee benefits in respect of certain employer-provided or employer-contracted child care). They extend the categories of child care providers whose care is covered by the exemption, to include providers approved under the Tax Credits (Approval of Child Care Providers) Scheme 2005 (SI 2005 93); while where that extended meaning of provider applies, excluding care in a relative's home, provided by a relative of the child, where that person only provides care for children of relatives or for his or her own children.

4068. Income tax–Construction industry scheme

INCOME TAX (CONSTRUCTION INDUSTRY SCHEME) REGULATIONS 2005, SI 2005 2045; made under the Taxes Management Act 1970 s.98A, s.113; the Finance Act 2003 s.205; and the Finance Act 2004 s.60, s.62, s.63, s.65, s.66, s.68, s.69, s.70, s.71, s.73, s.75, Sch.11 para.2, Sch.11 para.3, Sch.11 para.4, Sch.11 para.6, Sch.11 para.7, Sch.11 para.8, Sch.11 para.10, Sch.11 para.11, Sch.11 para.12, Sch.11 para.15, Sch.11 para.16. In force: in accordance with Reg.1; £6.00.

These Regulations make provisions in relation to the construction industry scheme established by the Finance Act 2004. They revoke the Income Tax (Sub-contractors in the Construction Industry) Regulations 1993 (SI 1993 743), the Income Tax (Sub-contractors in the Construction Industry) (Amendment) Regulations 1995 (SI 1995 217), the Income Tax (Sub-contractors in the Construction Industry) (Amendment No.2) Regulations 1995 (SI 1995 448), the Income Tax (Sub-contractors in the Construction Industry) (Amendment) Regulations 1996 (SI 1996 981), the Income Tax (Sub-contractors in the Construction Industry) (Amendment) Regulations 1998 (SI 1998 2622), the Income Tax (Sub-contractors in the Construction Industry) (Amendment) Regulations 1999 (SI 1999 825), the Income Tax (Sub-contractors in the Construction Industry) (Amendment No.2) Regulations 1999 (SI 1999 2159), the Income Tax (Sub-contractors in the Construction Industry) (Amendment) Regulations 2000 (SI 2000 1151), the Income Tax (Sub-contractors in the Construction Industry) (Amendment No.2) Regulations 2000 (SI 2000 1880), the Income Tax (Sub-contractors in the Construction Industry and Employments) (Amendment) Regulations 2000 (SI 2000 2742), the Income Tax (Sub-contractors in the Construction Industry) (Amendment) Regulations 2001 (SI 2001 1531), the Income Tax (Sub-contractors in the Construction Industry) (Amendment) Regulations 2002 (SI 2002 2225), the Income Tax (Sub-contractors in the Construction Industry and Employments) (Amendment) Regulations 2003 (SI 2003 536) and the Income Tax (Sub-contractors in the Construction Industry) (Amendment) Regulations 2004 (SI 2004 1075).

4069. Income tax–Costs–Unreasonable conduct of Inland Revenue in defending appeals

[Special Commissioners (Jurisdiction and Procedure) Regulations 1994 (SI 1994 1811) Reg.21.]

The applicant taxpayer (C) applied for an order that the defendant Inland Revenue should pay his costs in respect of his appeals against various Schedule E assessments from 1983. C was resident in the United Kingdom. He was a director of and the major shareholder in a group of companies engaged in the business of reinsuring in the UK risks underwritten in the United States. He was employed to work outside the UK as an international business division executive by the parent company of the group (H), established in Bermuda, and employed to work in the UK as an executive insurance broker by another company within the group. C claimed tax relief on that part of his remuneration earned outside the UK. The Inland Revenue began carrying out investigations into C's earnings in 1983, resulting in a decision by the Inland Revenue Special Office in 1986 that H was not resident in the UK. Nevertheless, in 1988 the Inland Revenue began further investigations, concluding again in 1991 that H was non resident. Assessments were made by the Inland Revenue in the course of its investigations, all of which were appealed by C. In 2000 the appeals were transferred to the Special Commissioners, who held that H had not been set up for tax avoidance purposes. Further correspondence between the parties and further preliminary hearings took place in which the Inland Revenue raised, inter alia, issues as to the validity of C's employment contracts. Ultimately, in December 2003 the Inland Revenue informed C that it would no longer defend his outstanding appeals. C contended that the Inland Revenue had acted wholly unreasonably in pursuing matters as long as it did, and accordingly claimed his costs of the appeal.

Held, allowing the application, that R did act wholly unreasonably within the definition set out in the Special Commissioners (Jurisdiction and Procedure) Regulations 1994 Reg.21. Given the information that R knew and the decisions reached both by it and the Special Commissioners, it should have concluded much sooner that it had no basis on which to defend the appeals. R should have carried out a thorough review of the matter in at least 2000, following the first decision of the Special Commissioners. C was entitled to all of his costs and expenses, including those of the instant hearing.

CARVILL v. FROST (INSPECTOR OF TAXES) (NO.1) [2005] S.T.C. (S.C.D.) 208, Stephen Oliver Q.C., Sp Comm.

4070. Income tax–Disclosure–Documents relating to private expenditure–Right to respect for private and family life

[Taxes Management Act 1970 s.19A; European Convention on Human Rights 1950 Art.8.]

The appellant taxpayer (T) appealed against the issue of a notice by the respondent Inland Revenue requiring him to produce documents in relation to his tax return. The Inland Revenue had opened an inquiry into T's tax return and had asked him to supply documents relating to his income and expenditure. T did not provide all the documents requested and so the Inland Revenue issued a notice under the Taxes Management Act 1970 s.19A. T appealed against the notice on the ground that the requirement to provide details of his private expenditure violated his right to respect for his private life under the European Convention on Human Rights 1950 Art.8. By the time of the appeal, some agreement had been reached and T had supplied most of the information requested.

Held, giving judgment accordingly, that the Inland Revenue's request for the documents relating to T's private expenditure was arguably intrusive and unnecessary. The notice was reasonable in respect of documents relating to T's income and allowable deductions, but not beyond that. The appeal was stood over for further argument, so that the Inland Revenue were given the opportunity to carry out their enquiry on the basis of the documents so far supplied. If they proved insufficient, then the appeal could be restored and argued in full.

TAYLOR v. BRATHERTON (INSPECTOR OF TAXES) [2005] S.T.C. (S.C.D.) 230, Colin Bishopp, Sp Comm.

4071. Income tax–Employees–Treatment of compensation payable under consent order settling unfair dismissal claim

[Income and Corporation Taxes Act 1988 s.19, s.131(1), s.148, s.154; Employment Rights Act 1996 s.114, s.119.]

The appellant Revenue appealed against a decision ([2004] EWHC 898, [2004] S.T.C. 1022) that a payment made to an employee (C) under a consent order settling an unfair dismissal claim was not taxable as an emolument under the Income and Corporation Taxes Act 1988 s.19 or as a benefit in kind under s.154 of the 1988 Act but fell within the "sweeping up" provisions of s.148 of the 1988 Act and, not exceeding £30,000, was free from tax. C had been employed by the local authority and received a car allowance, which was withdrawn from a number of employees in circumstances which the employment tribunal held amounted to unfair dismissal. The local authority agreed in a consent order to reinstate C and to pay him a basic award under the Employment Rights Act 1996 s.119 together with remuneration lost in respect of the car allowance. The Revenue amended C's self assessment to include that payment of £5,060 as taxable, either as an emolument under s.19, or as a benefit received from his employer. The Revenue argued that (1) the payment of £5,060 was not a payment of compensation for unfair dismissal, as the employment tribunal had no jurisdiction to make such an order in addition to an order for reinstatement; instead, the payment was taxable as an emolument under s.19 by virtue of s.114 of the 1996 Act, which required C's employer to treat him in all respects as if he had not been dismissed; (2) the payment was taxable as a benefit pursuant to s.154; (3) the payment was not a payment in connection with or in consequence of the termination of C's employment for the purposes of s.148.

Held, dismissing the appeal, that (1) an order for reinstatement under s.114(1) of the 1996 Act was only a direction to the employer, and its effect was not to override the actual facts relating to a payment. The fact that the local authority, the employees and the tribunal had overlooked or ignored the fact that the tribunal had no jurisdiction to make a basic award under s.119 at the same time as making the order for reinstatement under s.114 did not alter the fact that the consent order was made on the basis that s.119 applied. There was nothing to suggest that the order was not a true bargain between the parties. The payment to the employee was not a gratuity. The payment was not an emolument within the extended meaning of s.131(1) of the 1988 Act because it was not a reward for services or an inducement to future performance, *Hochstrasser (Inspector of Taxes) v. Mayes* [1960] A.C. 376, [1959] C.L.Y. 1543 and *Shilton v. Wilmshurst (Inspector of Taxes)* [1991] 1 A.C. 684, [1991] C.L.Y. 2092 applied. The payment was to compensate C for the unfair dismissal, and as it was paid to settle his claim, it was irrelevant that objection might have been taken to the agreement evidenced by the consent order or to the consent order itself. (2) Section 154 was not aimed at receipts resulting from fair bargains, *Mairs (Inspector of Taxes) v. Haughey* [1992] S.T.C. 495 applied. A bargain thought by each side to be worthwhile was sufficient. Section 154 was not satisfied since it had not been shown that the payment was made other than pursuant to a genuine compromise of the proceedings without any intention to give a gratuity to the employee. Accordingly, the payment was not a benefit within s.154. (3) The payment fell within the sweeping up provisions of s.148 and since it did not exceed £30,000, it was free from tax.

WILSON (INSPECTOR OF TAXES) v. CLAYTON, [2004] EWCA Civ 1657, [2005] S.T.C. 157, Peter Gibson, L.J., CA (Civ Div).

4072. **Income tax-Exemptions-Diplomatic immunity-Availability to citizen of Philippines employed by Namibian High Commission in UK**

[Vienna Convention on Diplomatic Relations 1961 Art.10, Art.37(3), Art.39(1).]

The appellant (J), a citizen of the Philippines, appealed against the dismissal of her claim for repayment of income tax. J had paid income tax on her earnings as a cook employed by the Namibian High Commission in London. J sought a rebate in reliance on the exemption available to "members of the service staff of [a] mission" under the Vienna Convention on Diplomatic Relations 1961 Art.37(3). J argued that the words of the Convention should be given their natural meaning. The Revenue contended that J's employment had not been notified to the Foreign and Commonwealth Office, which was a prerequisite to the enjoyment of the exemption under the Convention.

Held, dismissing the appeal, that J was not entitled to the exemption provided by Art.37(3) of the Convention. When construing Art.37(3), it was necessary to have regard to whatever light was thrown on the Convention's object and purpose by Art.39(1) and Art.10. According to Art.39(1), a member of the service staff of a mission already in the territory of the receiving state could enjoy the diplomatic privileges and immunities to which she was entitled from the moment when her appointment was notified to the relevant secretary of state. Article 10 required the Foreign and Commonwealth Secretary to be notified of the appointment of persons resident in the UK as members of a mission entitled to diplomatic privileges and immunities. Consequently, it could be held that notification as member of a mission was required before a person already in the country could enjoy diplomatic immunities such as the exemption under Art.37(3), *R. v. Secretary of State for the Home Department, ex p. Bagga* [1991] 1 Q.B. 485, [1991] C.L.Y. 2062 applied. Cogent evidence had been submitted showing that no such notification had taken place, and therefore, J could not claim the exemption.

JIMENEZ v. INLAND REVENUE COMMISSIONERS [2004] S.T.C. (S.C.D.) 371, John Walters Q.C., Sp Comm.

4073. Income tax–Indexation

INCOME TAX (INDEXATION) ORDER 2005, SI 2005 716; made under the Income and Corporation Taxes Act 1988 s.1. In force: March 16, 2005; £3.00.

The Income and Corporation Taxes Act 1988 s.1 (6) provides that the Treasury shall by order made by statutory instrument before each year of assessment specify the amounts which by virtue of that section shall, unless Parliament otherwise determines, be treated as specified for the purposes of s.1 (2) (aa) (starting rate limit of charge to income tax), and s.1 (2) (b) (basic rate limit of charge to income tax) of the Act for the year of assessment 2005-06. These amounts were specified for the year 2004-05 by the Income Tax (Indexation) Order 2004 (SI 2004 772). The amounts in s.1 (2) (aa) (b) of the Act are increased by this Order in accordance with the percentage increase in the retail prices index for September 2004 over that for September 2003.

4074. Income tax–Indexation

INCOME TAX (INDEXATION) (NO.2) ORDER 2005, SI 2005 3327; made under the Income and Corporation Taxes Act 1988 s.257C. In force: December 5, 2005; £3.00.

The Income and Corporation Taxes Act 1988 s.257C (3) operates to provide that the Treasury shall by order made by statutory instrument before April 6, 2006 specify the amounts which by virtue of that section shall, unless Parliament otherwise determines, be treated as specified for the purposes of s.257 (personal allowances), s.257A (married couple's allowances for those born before April 6, 1935) and s.265 (blind person's allowance) of the Act for the year of assessment 2005-06. The relevant amounts were specified for the year 2005-6 by the Income Tax (Indexation) (No.2) Order 2004 (SI 2004 3161). The amounts in s.257 (2) (personal allowance: age 65-74) and s.257 (3) (personal allowance: age 75 and over) were subsequently increased by reference to the rise in earnings by the Finance Act 2005. For 2005-06, the amounts in s.257, s.257A and s.265 (1) of the Act are increased by this Order in accordance with the percentage increase in the retail prices index for September 2005 over that for September 2004.

4075. Income tax–Individual savings accounts

INDIVIDUAL SAVINGS ACCOUNT (AMENDMENT) REGULATIONS 2005, SI 2005 609; made under the Income and Corporation Taxes Act 1988 s.333; the Taxation of Chargeable Gains Act 1992 s.151; and the Finance Act 1998 s.75. In force: April 6, 2005; £3.00.

These Regulations, which amend the Individual Savings Account Regulations 1998 (SI 1998 1870), correct a technical drafting defect in the Individual Savings Account Regulations (Amendment No.2) Regulations 2004 (SI 2004 2996). Those Regulations applied the "5 per cent test," used to identify if investments are cash-like in form, in a modified form to investments held in an ISA insurance component on April 6, 2005, to determine whether those investments will be held in a stocks and shares component or cash component from that date. These Regulations clarify the interaction between Reg.4C(3) and Reg.7(15) of the main Regulations.

4076. Income tax–Information exchange–Agreements–Aruba

TAX INFORMATION EXCHANGE AGREEMENT (TAXES ON INCOME) (ARUBA) ORDER 2005, SI 2005 1458; made under the Income and Corporation Taxes Act 1988 s.815C. In force: June 7, 2005; £3.00.

This Order sets out the Tax Information Exchange Agreement between the UK and Aruba.

4077. Income tax–Information exchange–Agreements–Guernsey

TAX INFORMATION EXCHANGE AGREEMENT (TAXES ON INCOME) (GUERNSEY) ORDER 2005, SI 2005 1262; made under the Income and Corporation Taxes Act 1988 s.815C. In force: May 7, 2005; £3.00.

This Order sets out the Tax Information Exchange Agreement between the UK and Guernsey.

4078. Income tax–Information exchange–Agreements–Isle of Man

TAX INFORMATION EXCHANGE AGREEMENT (TAXES ON INCOME) (ISLE OF MAN) ORDER 2005, SI 2005 1263; made under the Income and Corporation Taxes Act 1988 s.815C. In force: May 7, 2005; £3.00.

This Order sets out the Tax Information Exchange Agreement between the UK and the Isle of Man.

4079. Income tax–Information exchange–Agreements–Jersey

TAX INFORMATION EXCHANGE AGREEMENT (TAXES ON INCOME) (JERSEY) ORDER 2005, SI 2005 1261; made under the Income and Corporation Taxes Act 1988 s.815C. In force: May 7, 2005; £3.00.

This Order sets out the Tax Information Exchange Agreement between the UK and Jersey.

4080. Income tax–Information exchange–Agreements–Montserrat

TAX INFORMATION EXCHANGE AGREEMENT (TAXES ON INCOME) (MONTSERRAT) ORDER 2005, SI 2005 1459; made under the Income and Corporation Taxes Act 1988 s.815C. In force: June 7, 2005; £3.00.

This Order sets out the Tax Information Exchange Agreement between the UK and Montserrat.

4081. Income tax–Information exchange–Agreements–Netherlands Antilles

TAX INFORMATION EXCHANGE AGREEMENT (TAXES ON INCOME) (NETHERLANDS ANTILLES) ORDER 2005, SI 2005 1460; made under the Income and Corporation Taxes Act 1988 s.815C. In force: June 7, 2005; £3.00.

This Order sets out the Tax Information Exchange Agreement between the UK and the Netherlands Antilles.

4082. Income tax–Information exchange–Agreements–Virgin Islands

TAX INFORMATION EXCHANGE AGREEMENT (TAXES ON INCOME) (VIRGIN ISLANDS) ORDER 2005, SI 2005 1457; made under the Income and Corporation Taxes Act 1988 s.815C. In force: June 7, 2005; £3.00.

This Order sets out the Tax Information Exchange Agreement between the UK and the Virgin Islands.

4083. Income tax-Investigations-Application for award of costs against Inland Revenue-Meaning of wholly unreasonable behaviour "in connection with" hearing

[Special Commissioners (Jurisdiction and Procedure) Regulations 1994 (SI 1994 1811) para.21 (1).]

The taxpayer (C) applied for costs against the Inland Revenue for acting wholly unreasonably in connection with an appeal hearing. The Inland Revenue had undertaken an investigation into C's affairs that lasted four years. It had sought to clarify his earnings as a contracting bricklayer, the amount his wife had inherited and the amount spent on renovations to his house. After closure notices were issued, C appealed. The appeal hearing was adjourned and the substantive issues resolved in C's favour. C argued under the Special Commissioners (Jurisdiction and Procedure) Regulations 1994 Para.21 (1) that the Inland Revenue had "acted wholly unreasonably in connection with" the appeal hearing by undertaking an excessively long investigation and making various errors in relation to an income and expenditure test and details of certain sums.

Held, refusing the application, that the Inland Revenue had not acted wholly unreasonably in connection with the hearing or at all. The phrase "in connection with the hearing" mirrored the limitation on the quantum of costs to costs "of, or incidental to, the hearing". Therefore, just as the preceding investigation costs were not awardable, so action or inaction during the investigation period would not normally be "connected with" the hearing. The provision was aimed at conduct which had caused the awardable hearing costs to be greater than they should have been, *Scott (t/a Farthings Steak House) v. McDonald (Inspector of Taxes)* [1996] S.T.C. (S.C.D.) 381, [1996] C.L.Y. 3328 distinguished. In any event, the Inland Revenue had not acted unreasonably, let alone "wholly" unreasonably, in the course of the investigation.

CONLON v. HEWITT (INSPECTOR OF TAXES) [2005] S.T.C. (S.C.D.) 46, BMF O'Brien, Sp Comm.

4084. Income tax-Loss relief-Transfer of relevant discounted securities-Applicability of Ramsay doctrine

[Finance Act 1996 Sch.13 para.2, Sch.13 para.2(2).]

The appellant taxpayer (C) appealed against an amendment to his tax return disallowing his claim for relief for a loss of £2.48 million. C had been the chief executive of a company (G) which was taken over in 2000. Prior to the takeover, C had taken tax advice with a view to offsetting the taxable income he would make on the exercise of his share options. C accordingly set up a company (S) and borrowed £3.9 million from a bank on the security, inter alia, of a lien over 375,000 loan notes to be issued by S. C subscribed £3.75 million for the loan notes, and on the day after the takeover, C transferred the loan notes to his wife. C claimed loss relief for the difference between the amount he had subscribed for the loan notes and their deemed market value on the transfer date, on the basis that he had suffered a "loss" within the meaning of the Finance Act 1996 Sch.13 para.2(2). The Revenue disallowed the claim on the ground that the establishment of S and the transfer of the loan notes were purely for the purpose of tax avoidance. C argued that a taxpayer's underlying purpose was irrelevant to his entitlement to loss relief under Sch.13 para.2.

Held, allowing the appeal, that the term "loss" within Sch.13 para.2(2) had a specific statutory meaning which left no room for consideration of the taxpayer's purpose in effecting the relevant transactions, *WT Ramsay Ltd v. Inland Revenue Commissioners* [1982] A.C. 300, [1981] C.L.Y. 1385 applied and *MacNiven (Inspector of Taxes) v. Westmoreland Investments Ltd* [2001] UKHL 6, [2003] 1 A.C. 311, [2001] C.L.Y. 5199, *Collector of Stamp Revenue v. Arrowtown Assets Ltd* 6 I.T.L. Rep. 454 and *Scottish Provident Institution v. Inland Revenue Commissioners* [2003] S.T.C. 1035, [2003] C.L.Y. 4185 considered. In other words, para.2 was sufficiently "closely articulated", according to Lord Millett's phrase in *Arrowtown*, or sufficiently "legal", according to Lord Hoffmann's phrase in *Westmoreland*, to be unaffected by C's purpose in effecting the transactions. The amount C had paid for the loan notes exceeded the amount he was deemed to have obtained on their transfer to his wife, and under the express words of para.2(2), he had sustained a loss for the purposes of Sch.13. Even if C's purpose were considered relevant, his appeal would succeed on the basis that he had the commercial purpose of investment, in addition to a tax purpose for setting up S and subscribing to the loan notes.

CAMPBELL v. INLAND REVENUE COMMISSIONERS [2004] S.T.C. (S.C.D.) 396, Theodore Wallace, Sp Comm.

4085. Income tax—Losses—Trading—Retrospective effect

[Income and Corporation Taxes Act 1988 s.380.]

The appellant (N) appealed against a closure notice issued by the respondent tax inspector after an inquiry relating to his self assessment income tax return for 1998-99. N contended that the notice should have taken account of trading losses in the next year because the "carrying back" of losses under the Income and Corporation Taxes Act 1988 s.380 had the effect of reducing retrospectively his taxable income for 1998-99 so that there was no taxable income at the date tax for 1998-99 would otherwise have been due.

Held, dismissing the appeal, that the effect of "carrying back" losses under s.380 was to allow an amount equal to the tax paid, if it had been paid, to be reclaimed when the claim to carry back the loss was made. The section did not retrospectively reduce the taxable income for the earlier period. The liability to pay tax on the due date was not expunged by a later claim for loss relief. The effect of a later claim was neither to reopen the earlier year nor to reduce the taxable amount for that year, *Musashi Autoparts Europe Ltd (formerly TAP Manufacturing Ltd) v. Customs and Excise Commissioners* [2003] EWCA Civ 1738, [2004] S.T.C. 220, [2004] C.L.Y. 4019 applied.

NORTON v. THOMPSON (INSPECTOR OF TAXES) [2004] S.T.C. (S.C.D.) 163, Adrian Shipwright, Sp Comm.

4086. Income tax—National insurance contributions—Position of IT specialist under IR35 legislation

[Finance Act 2000 Sch.12 para.1(1); Social Security Contributions (Intermediaries) Regulations 2000 (SI 2000 727) Reg.6.]

The appellant company (F) appealed against a determination of the special commissioner. X had provided specialist information technology services through F, his service company, and an agency (E), to an end company (Y). The special commissioner had concluded that if there had been a direct contract between X and Y during the period of engagement, it would have been a contract of service and therefore, pursuant to the IR35 legislation, F would have been required to account for national insurance contributions and income tax for the relevant period. F argued that the special commissioner had erred in his construction of "client" under the Finance Act 2000 Sch.12 para.1(1) and the Social Security Contributions (Intermediaries) Regulations 2000 Reg.6. The Revenue contended that the special commissioner had been right to identify the client as Y, had applied the correct test in determining whether the notional contract was one of service, and had been correct to find that it had been.

Held, dismissing the appeal, that it was clear that Y had required the services of an IT specialist, and it could not be said that X had performed those services for the purpose of E's business. Y was the only party with whom it could be said that X performed services for business purposes. The special commissioner had been entitled to find that X had been part and parcel of Y's organisation and that the relationship between Y and X was such that the notional contract between them had been one of service.

FUTURE ONLINE LTD v. FOULDS (INSPECTOR OF TAXES); *sub nom.* FUTURE ONLINE LTD v. FAULDS (INSPECTOR OF TAXES), [2004] EWHC 2597, [2005] S.T.C. 198, Sir Donald Rattee, Ch D.

4087. Income tax—Notices of enquiry—Notice requiring taxpayer to produce documents—Discrepancy between income figure supplied by employer and that included in tax return

[Taxes Management Act 1970 s.19A.]

The taxpayer (M) appealed against an Inland Revenue notice issued under the Taxes Management Act 1970 s.19A requiring him to produce certain particulars and documents to justify a discrepancy between the gross income noted on his return and that supplied by his employers. M's request for postponement, on the ground that he was leaving for a nine month job in Australia, had been refused. In a letter, M argued that his employers had provided the income figure. M did not appear before the commissioner.

Held, dismissing the appeal, that there was clearly good reason why the particulars and documents were required because there was a large discrepancy between the returned income and that figure supplied by M's employers. M's argument that his employers had supplied the figures was clearly insufficient. The fact that M was working abroad was an insufficient reason for a postponement as he could have sent written reasons for the discrepancy, or he could have been represented or conducted his appeal by video link.

MURPHY v. GOWERS (INSPECTOR OF TAXES) [2005] S.T.C. (S.C.D.) 44, John F Avery Jones, Sp Comm.

4088. Income tax—Notices of enquiry—Request for production of documents—Reasonableness

[Taxes Management Act 1970 s.9A, s.19A.]

The appellant taxpayer (G), the proprietor of a small guest house, appealed against the issue of a notice of enquiry by the respondent Inland Revenue under the Taxes Management Act 1970 s.19A. The s.19A notice had been issued four months after a s.9A notice. It did not include a copy of s.19A or a leaflet about the enquiry, nor did it explain what was meant by "producing" documents. G objected to the notice on the general grounds that (1) it asked for too much information at an initial stage of the enquiry, other information should have been sought, it had been served on G's accountant and not on G, and it was generally unclear how G should respond; (2) specifically, a number of items in the notice were unreasonable, namely (i) the fact that the hotel register, visitors' book and guest record cards should legally remain on the premises meant he could not produce them as requested, (ii) G did not have documentary evidence confirming all expenses, (iii) the request for all bank statements should be limited to those relating to his business, and (iv) it was unclear, even in light of a second explanatory letter from the Inland Revenue, what cash movement reconciliations used by the accountant in preparing the return were required, and in any case such information was privileged.

Held, dismissing the appeal, that (1) given the interval between the two notices, it was reasonable for the Inland Revenue to seek full information in the s.19A notice and not deal with it in further stages. Section 19A was not limited to documents that the taxpayer considered appropriate, *Accountant v. Inspector of Taxes* [2000] S.T.C. (S.C.D.) 522, [2001] C.L.Y. 5314 applied. It was G and not the accountant who was directed to produce documents. Some aspects of the appeal would have been avoided if, first, the notice had more clearly explained that the Inland Revenue was not seeking documents not in G's possession and, secondly, how production should take place. (2)(i) It had been agreed that production of the register, book and cards could take place on the premises; (ii) under s.19A(2)(a), G was entitled to reply simply that the documentary evidence and the assets register were not in his power or possession; (iii) the item should be limited to business bank statements, and (iv) the privilege point did not arise because it appeared that the reconciliation documents were the accountant's and were not in the "possession or power" of

G. The Inland Revenue's letter cured any arguable unreasonableness in relation to the reconciliations.

GUEST HOUSE PROPRIETOR v. KENDALL (INSPECTOR OF TAXES) [2005] S.T.C. (S.C.D.) 280, David Williams, Sp Comm.

4089. Income tax–Partnerships–Calculation of assessment–Allocation of profits to partners

The appellant (C), a firm of chartered accountants, appealed against partnership tax assessments made on the preceding year basis and the allocation of the assessments between the partners. C had formed a partnership, including a partner (D), in 1983 and D had left in 1990. The partners had agreed a profit adjustment for the year ended April 1990, resulting in an additional benefit to D of £6,327. This was effected by adjusting the profit shares so that D's additional profit share represented a percentage of the total amount, and the other partners received their profit shares of this total amount. The other partners then reduced their salaries in proportion to the profit shares, resulting in negative salaries. D argued in favour of a different method of adjustment, as the partners' method resulted in a tax liability to D on the additional £6,327.

Held, dismissing the appeal, that the partners' method of adjusting the profit sharing ratios was to be preferred. Although this resulted in the creation of negative salaries as part of the calculation, this was nothing more than a method of arriving at the allocation of profits. The assessments and allocation of profits to the partners was determined accordingly.

CHARTERED ACCOUNTANTS FIRM v. BRAISBY (INSPECTOR OF TAXES) [2005] S.T.C. (S.C.D.) 389, John F Avery Jones, Sp Comm.

4090. Income tax–Partnerships–Computation and adjustment of profits–Burden of proof on partners to show assessment wrong

[European Convention on Human Rights 1950 Art.8.]

The appellants (S), restaurant owners, appealed against tax assessed on computations of profits of a restaurant business operated by them in partnership. The partnership had operated three restaurants under a common brand until the partnership ended in 1999. Each partner then took over one restaurant as a separate business. Partnership tax returns had been made for the years 1993 to 1994, 1994 to 1995, 1995 to 1996 and 1996 to 1997. An income tax inspection had commenced in 1996 in relation to the partnership and had found that additional income had been generated but not declared in accounting periods ended in 1994, 1995 and 1996. The inspector had decided that, given the assumption of continuity, the burden lay on the partners to show that there had been some change. The inspector had added £120,000 for the accounting period ended August 1994, and since the preceding year basis applied to the business, which had commenced in 1993, and given that profits had increased annually, this produced a revised gross profit rate for this period of 70 per cent. This led to increases of £72,891, £116,180 and £116,180 for the tax years ended 1994, 1995 and 1996 respectively. A further sum of £120,000 was also added to sales for the year ended 1997. On appeal, S argued that the assessments were excessive and failed to take into account S's explanations for unexplained bankings during the relevant periods.

Held, allowing the appeal in part, that although the burden lay on S to show that the assessment was wrong on the balance of probabilities, the evidence was such that neither side had been able to show the true extent to which the partnership's accounts were deficient, even on the balance of probabilities. S was give some allowance for bankings for which proper records no longer existed, but they had been given full opportunity to demonstrate the errors in the assessments and had largely failed to prove any such errors. In the circumstances, the sum to be added in respect of additional sales for the partnership accounting years of 1994, 1995 and 1996 was set at £80,000 in place of the original assessment of £120,000, and the appropriate adjustments were made to the assessment of tax due in the years ended 1994, 1995 and

1996, *Jonas v. Bamford (Inspector of Taxes)* [1973] S.T.C. 519, [1974] C.L.Y. 1866 applied.

SHARIFEE (T/A CAFE FLUTIST) v. WOOD (INSPECTOR OF TAXES) [2004] S.T.C. (S.C.D.) 446, Malcolm Gammie Q.C., Sp Comm.

4091. Income tax—Previously owned property

CHARGE TO INCOME TAX BY REFERENCE TO ENJOYMENT OF PROPERTY PREVIOUSLY OWNED REGULATIONS 2005, SI 2005 724; made under the Finance Act 1986 s.104; and the Finance Act 2004 Sch.15 para.1, Sch.15 para.4, Sch.15 para.7, Sch.15 para.9, Sch.15 para.14, Sch.15 para.20. In force: April 6, 2005; £3.00.

These Regulations are made pursuant to the Finance Act 2004 Sch.15 which provides for an income tax charge in relation to the benefit enjoyed by taxpayers in certain circumstances from continuing to enjoy assets they formerly owned. They prescribe the valuation date; prescribe the rate of interest to be used to determine the monetary benefit of assets enjoyed; make provision for a five yearly rather than an annual valuation of land and chattels; provide for exemptions from the charge; and make provision for the avoidance of a double charge where an inheritance tax charge also arises.

4092. Income tax—Professional fees

INCOME TAX (PROFESSIONAL FEES) ORDER 2005, SI 2005 1091; made under the Income Tax (Earnings and Pensions) Act 2003 s.343. In force: April 6, 2005; £3.00.

The Income Tax (Earnings and Pensions) Act 2003 s.343 provides for a deduction from employment income for an amount paid in respect of a professional fee. Professional fee means a fee mentioned in the Table in subsection (2) of the section. Under subsections (3) and (4) the Board of Inland Revenue may by order add fees to the Table. This Order amends the fee payable for the entry or retention of a name in the register maintained by the General Teaching Council for Northern Ireland.

4093. Income tax—Reliefs—Interpretation of "payment in lieu of notice" as used in termination letter—Garden leave

[Income and Corporation Taxes Act 1988 s.148.]

The appellant taxpayer (R) appealed against a decision of the respondent Inland Revenue that she was not entitled to relief from income tax on a "payment in lieu of notice". R had been told by her employer in September 2001 that she was being made redundant that same day. She was given a letter stating that her employment was terminated immediately, that she would not have to attend the office during her three month contractual notice period, but that she should make herself available for work, and that she would be paid her normal salary in lieu of notice. She was required to immediately return company property such as mobile phones and security passes. In her self assessment tax return, R claimed relief from tax on the money she was paid from September to December 2001. M refused the application on the ground that R had still been employed until December and had been taking garden leave. On appeal, R contended that her employment had been terminated in September and that the payment had been in lieu of notice and had been paid in monthly instalments.

Held, dismissing the appeal, that on a correct interpretation of the termination letter R's employment had ended in December. The phrase "payment in lieu of notice" was capable of several different interpretations and should be given the one that an ordinary reasonable employee was most likely to take it as meaning, *Chapman v. Letheby & Christopher Ltd* [1981] I.R.L.R. 440, [1982] C.L.Y. 1115 applied. In the instant case, a reasonable employee in R's position would have read the letter as enforcing R's contract by giving her three months' notice but exercising the employer's discretion to require her to take garden leave, *Delaney v. Staples (t/a De Montfort Recruitment)* [1992] 1 A.C. 687,

[1992] C.L.Y. 2028 applied. She had thus continued to be employed until December 2001 and the pay she received between September and December 2001 was not a tax free termination payment within the meaning of the Income and Corporation Taxes Act 1988 s.148.

IBE v. McNALLY (INSPECTOR OF TAXES); *sub nom.* REDUNDANT EMPLOYEE v. McNALLY (INSPECTOR OF TAXES) [2005] S.T.C. (S.C.D.) 143, John F Avery Jones, Sp Comm.

4094. Income tax–Retirement benefit scheme–Indexation of earnings cap

RETIREMENT BENEFIT SCHEMES (INDEXATION OF EARNINGS CAP) ORDER 2005, SI 2005 720; made under the Income and Corporation Taxes Act 1988 s.590C. In force: March 16, 2005; £3.00.

The Income and Corporation Taxes Act 1988 provides that in arriving at an employee's final remuneration, any excess over the permitted maximum for the year of assessment in which the employee's participation in the scheme ceases shall be disregarded. The earnings cap is calculated in accordance with the Finance Act 1993. The Act provides that if the retail prices index for the September preceding the year of assessment is higher than it was for the previous September, the earnings cap is calculated by increasing the previous year's figure by the same percentage as the percentage increase in the retail prices index, and, if the amount is not a multiple of £600, rounding it up to the nearest amount which is a multiple of £600. The retail prices index is defined in as "the general index of retail prices (for all items) published by the Office for National Statistics". The retail prices index was 188.1 for September 2004, compared with 182.5 for September 2003. This represents an increase of 3.1 per cent. Since applying that percentage to the previous year's earnings cap would produce the figure of £105,162, which is not divisible by £600, the earnings cap is increased for the year 2005-06 to £105,600. The limit imposed by the earnings cap will be replaced, for the year 2006-07 and subsequent years, by the lifetime allowance and the annual allowance limits contained in the Finance Act 2004.

4095. Income tax–Retirement benefits scheme–Permitted maximum

RETIREMENT BENEFITS SCHEMES (INCREASE IN PERMITTED MAXIMUM IN TRANSITIONAL CASES) ORDER 2005, SI 2005 723; made under the Income and Corporation Taxes Act 1988 s.590. In force: April 6, 2005; £3.00.

This Order increases, from £100,000 to £105,600, the permitted maximum used as part of the calculation of benefits payable to a class of employees from a retirement benefit scheme approved under the Income and Corporation Taxes Act 1988. It applies in the case of a scheme which was approved by the Board of Inland Revenue before the coming into force of the Finance Act 1989. It also applies in the case of an employee who, before June 1, 1989 joined a scheme which was in existence before March 14, 1989 and which was approved on or after July 27, 1989. The permitted maximum referred to in this Order is different from that applying to most retirement benefit schemes.

4096. Income tax–Retirement relief–Meaning of "unused relief" in s.655(1)(b) Income and Corporation Taxes Act 1988

[Income and Corporation Taxes Act 1988 s.655(1).]

The appellant taxpayer (L) appealed against the decision ([2004] EWHC 1811, [2004] S.T.C. 1606) affirming that her unused retirement annuity relief carried forward from a previous tax year was reduced by contributions she made to her personal pension scheme in the current tax year. L had claimed tax relief in respect of premiums paid under retirement annuity contracts and contributions paid to her personal pension. It was common ground that the claim to tax relief and the calculation of the relief to which L was entitled turned on the construction and application of the transitional set off provisions in the Income and Corporation Taxes Act 1988 s.655(1). Relying on s.655(1)(b) and accepting the Revenue's approach to construction, the judge held that for the current tax year, L's "unused" tax relief in respect of the payment of premiums under retirement annuity contracts was to be calculated by aggregating any unused relief from previous years and then deducting the amount of contributions to her personal pension scheme for the current tax year. L argued that relief for retirement annuity premiums and for personal pension contributions had to be given separately and that each year's unused tax relief had to be accounted for and utilised separately, on a year by year basis.

Held, dismissing the appeal, that the Revenue was right on the issue of the construction of s.655(1). The issue turned on the amount of "unused relief" that L was entitled to carry forward from previous years. The natural and ordinary meaning of the language of s.655(1) was that the expression "the individual's unused relief for any year" in s.655(1)(b) included both unused retirement annuity relief carried forward from the previous years and the unused relief arising in the current year. The unused retirement annuity relief was reduced by the amount of personal pension contributions paid by the taxpayer in that year under the approved personal pensions arrangements. The balance left after deductions was the amount of relief that the taxpayer could carry forward to the next year, when the same calculation was made. The language and scheme of the legislation was consistent with the Revenue's construction.

LONSDALE v. BRAISBY (INSPECTOR OF TAXES), [2005] EWCA Civ 709, [2005] S.T.C. 1049, Mummery, L.J., CA (Civ Div).

4097. **Income tax—Royalties—Exemptions**

EXEMPTION FROM INCOME TAX FOR CERTAIN INTEREST AND ROYALTY PAYMENTS (AMENDMENT TO SECTION 97(1) OF THE FINANCE ACT 2004 AND SECTION 757(2) OF THE INCOME TAX (TRADING AND OTHER INCOME) ACT 2005) ORDER 2005, SI 2005 2899; made under the Finance Act 2004 s.97; and the Income Tax (Trading and Other Income) Act 2005 s.767. In force: November 8, 2005; £3.00.

This Order amends the references in the Finance Act 2004 s.97(1) and in the Income Tax (Trading and Other Income) Act 2005 s.757(2) to the Council Directive on a common system of taxation applicable to interest and royalty payments made between associated companies of different Member States following the adoption of two Council Directives which amend that Directive.

4098. **Income tax—Self assessment—Clear case of negligence—Discovery assessment and closure notice**

The appellant taxpayer (D) appealed against a discovery assessment made by the respondent inspector of taxes for 1996/97 and a closure notice amending D's self assessment for 1997/98. D was a sole trader providing bookkeeping services to associated businesses. She accepted that there had been negligence in keeping her firm's accounts. The issues were: was there a loss of tax in 1996/97 attributable to negligence which would justify the discovery assessment, and what were D's trading profits in each year for tax purposes?

Held, giving judgment accordingly, that the facts showed clearly that for both years of assessment there had been a loss of income tax attributable to the negligence of D or those acting on her behalf. As the burden of proving neglect had been discharged by the inspector, the burden moved to D to disprove the correctness of the discovery assessment and closure notice, *Jonas v. Bamford (Inspector of Taxes)* [1973] S.T.C. 519, [1974] C.L.Y. 1866 applied. However, it was not possible to reconstruct a profit and loss account from the materials available, and it would be necessary to adjourn the appeal to give the parties time to prepare further submissions. The court made an interim decision and imposed a penalty of £250 on D for non-compliance with an earlier direction.

DOSHI v. ANDREW (INSPECTOR OF TAXES) [2005] S.T.C. (S.C.D.) 427, John F Avery Jones, Sp Comm.

4099. Income tax–Self assessment–Enquiry ending in amendment of return– Enquiry procedure

[Taxes Management Act 1970 s.9A, s.114, Sch.1A para.6.]

The appellant taxpayer (S) appealed against the amendment of his self assessment return, and the appellant company (SL), of which S was the sole director, appealed against notices of decision that it was liable for national insurance contributions (NIC) and notices of determination that it was liable for PAYE. The Inland Revenue had opened an inquiry into S's self assessment tax return pursuant to the Taxes Management Act 1970 s.9A. Continued failure by S to produce information to support his claims for reliefs and deductions led to service of a closure notice and the amendment of his return. The notices of determination followed failures by SL to comply with requests for production of information. S contended that the amendment was incompetent since the inquiry was the subject of an appeal to the House of Lords at the time, and a letter warning of the Inland Revenue's intention to make inquiries had not conformed to Sch.1A para.6 to the Act. SL contended that the NIC notices were invalid since S was a non resident and that the PAYE notices were incompetent as they misstated S's name, and S's tax liability was the subject of pending court proceedings.

Held, allowing the appeals in part, that (1) none of S's grounds of appeal against the closure notice or inquiry procedure was well founded. There had been no appeal to the House of Lords pending at the time of the closure notice. Further, the Inland Revenue's letter did not have to conform to Sch.1A, nor did the inquiry have to be conducted under that provision. (2) SL's ground of appeal against the NIC decision notices was completely lacking in specification and had not been substantiated. However, the Inland Revenue had modified its calculations in relation to the second decision notice as a result of the belated provision of further information by SL, and the appeal would be allowed to that extent. (3) The mistake as to one of S's initials in the PAYE determination notices was immaterial and no one could have been misled by it. Consequently, s.114 of the Act applied, and the notices could not be quashed on the basis of that mistake. The contention based on the existence of other proceedings was unfounded in fact, but the determination notices would be modified in the light of minor calculation errors and the production of SL's accounts for the final year of assessment.

SIWEK v. INLAND REVENUE COMMISSIONERS (NOTICE OF DETERMINATION) [2004] S.T.C. (S.C.D.) 493, J Gordon Reid Q.C., Sp Comm.

4100. Income tax–Self assessment–Failure to keep adequate records– Disallowance of rent not paid

[Taxes Management Act 1970.]

The appellant taxpayer (M), who ran a beautician business from a room in a property previously owned by her father, appealed against closure notices for two tax years. The inspector had, inter alia, increased the sales figures for both years on account of unidentified deposits in M's bank accounts. He also disallowed rent which M had not paid.

Held, allowing the appeal in part, that M had failed to maintain sufficient business records as required by the Taxes Management Act 1970. Although the inspector now accepted that the deposits had been identified with sales declared by M, the rent had to be disallowed because there was no evidence of an agreement between M and her father and it was accepted that no rent had been paid. In the second year, the property had been transferred to M and therefore no expenditure on rent was incurred.

McEWAN v. O'DONOGHUE (INSPECTOR OF TAXES) [2005] S.T.C. (S.C.D.) 437, John F Avery Jones, Sp Comm.

4101. **Income tax–Settlements–Structure of husband and wife company–Dividends as income arising under "arrangement"–Outright gift exclusion**

[Income and Corporation Taxes Act 1988 s.660A, s.660G.]

The appellant taxpayer (J) appealed against a decision of the Special Commissioners ([2005] S.T.C. (S.C.D.) 9) to dismiss his appeal against assessments to income tax made by the respondent (G), a tax inspector. J owned a company which had two shares. His wife had acquired one of the shares for £1. J worked for the company as an employee with an expectation that he would only draw a modest salary and with the intention that profits would be paid out as dividends, with half going to his wife. The Revenue argued that the dividends paid to J's wife on her share in the company were income arising under a settlement of which J was the settlor and therefore they were to be treated as J's income for income tax purposes by virtue of the Income and Corporation Taxes Act 1988 s.660A(1). The Revenue submitted that the corporate structure was not taken out of the concept of settlement by the outright gift exclusion in s.660A(6) because it was not an outright gift.

Held, dismissing the appeal, that the dividends were income arising under an "arrangement" within the meaning of s.660G(1) and s.660A(6) did not apply. The arrangement included the intention that J would only draw a low salary and that dividends would be paid. The fact that these elements were not legally binding did not prevent them from being parts of the arrangement. J's wife had acquired one share so that she would be in a position to receive dividends which, when received, would come to her as bounty. The establishment of such a structure with the future intention of bounty was an arrangement because an arrangement included the reasons for the arrangement and was not limited to the specific immediate consequences when an arrangement was made. J was the settlor. All of the company's receipts which enabled it to have profits and pay dividends were attributable to him. It was an important feature that J had provided funds directly or indirectly for the purposes of the settlement by working for the company in return for a low salary. In respect of husband and wife companies, it would be far more difficult for the Revenue to establish that there was a settlement of which the husband was the settlor if he was paid the going rate, *Crossland (Inspector of Taxes) v. Hawkins* [1961] Ch. 537, [1961] C.L.Y. 4252 applied. Section 660A(6) was intended for straightforward cases where one spouse gave income yielding property to the other and ordinary investment income continued to arise. There was far more comprised in the instant arrangement than would be covered by the expression "an outright gift" and in fact there was no outright gift as J's wife had purchased her share.

JONES v. GARNETT (INSPECTOR OF TAXES), [2005] EWHC 849, [2005] S.T.C. 1667, Park, J., Ch D.

4102. **Income tax–Share option schemes–Duty of company to deduct income tax from payments made to employees for release of share options**

[Income and Corporation Taxes Act 1988 s.135; Finance Act 1998 s.67; Income Tax (Employment) Regulations 1993 (SI 1993 744).]

The appellant company (D) appealed against a determination that it should have deducted income tax from payments made to its employees in return for the release of their share options. D, an internet service provider, was wholly acquired by another company on April 30, 1998 and became dormant. At the beginning of April 1998 D had entered into release agreements with those of its employees who held options to acquire shares in D, under which payment for the release would be made on April 30. The respondent Inland Revenue took the view that D should have accounted to it for income tax payable on those payments on the basis that (1) the Income and Corporation Taxes Act 1988 s.135 applied as there were no complications relating to the payments; (2) alternatively, that amendments to the 1988 Act were being carried out during that period under the Finance Act 1998 s.67, which either applied or should have been taken by D to be likely to apply to the payments. D argued that the 1988 Act did not apply and that the amendments had not come into force at the time of the payments.

Held, allowing the appeal, that (1) the 1988 Act did not specifically apply the Income Tax (Employment) Regulations 1993 to these particular payments, *Inland Revenue Commissioners v. Herd* [1993] 1 W.L.R. 1090, [1993] C.L.Y. 2294 applied. (2) The amendments to the 1988 Act did not come into force until August 1998 and therefore did not apply to the payments as made in April 1998. Thus, D was under no obligation to make deductions for income tax. Any argument that D should have made deductions on the possibility of legislation coming into force was simply untenable, *Bowles v. Bank of England* [1913] 1 Ch. 57 applied.

DEMON INTERNET LTD v. YOUNG (INSPECTOR OF TAXES) [2005] S.T.C. (S.C.D.) 233, Malcolm Gammie Q.C., Sp Comm.

4103. Income tax—Share option schemes—Payment received for cancellation of share options—Determination of amount of tax payable

Following a decision ([2003] S.T.C. (S.C.D.) 439, [2004] C.L.Y. 3771) concerning the liability to income tax of the appellant taxpayer (B), the court was required to determine the amount of tax due because B had been unable to reach an agreement with the respondent tax inspector (S). Central to the dispute was a payment that B had received for the cancellation of share options which was taxable as income. B argued that the Revenue's claim for tax was without merit and that it had acted with impropriety.

Held, giving judgment for the respondent, that it was not appropriate to revisit the earlier decision, *Silk v. Fletcher (Inspector of Taxes)* [2000] S.T.C. (S.C.D.) 565, [2001] C.L.Y. 5299 considered. In any event, none of B's submissions affected the substantive decision in the case and there was no evidence to suggest that there had been any procedural defects or other impropriety.

BLUCK v. SALTON (INSPECTOR OF TAXES) (NO.2) [2004] S.T.C. (S.C.D.) 177, Malcolm Gammie Q.C., Sp Comm.

4104. Income tax—Sportspersons—Territoriality principle—Companies with no UK tax presence

[Income and Corporation Taxes Act 1988 s.555, s.556.]

The appellant taxpayer (T) appealed against a decision ([2004] EWHC 487, [2004] S.T.C. 610) that he could be assessed to income tax under the Income and Corporation Taxes Act 1988 s.556 in respect of payments to a company controlled by T with no UK presence in connection with his activities as a sportsman in the UK. T was an international tennis player ordinarily resident and domiciled outside the UK. He had set up a company which had no tax presence in the UK and had entered into endorsement contracts with two manufacturers of sports clothing and equipment, neither of which had been resident or had a tax presence in the UK. T had come to the UK for a limited number of days a year in order to play in tournaments such as Wimbledon and the company received payments from the manufacturers which derived at least in part from T's activities in playing in those tournaments. The special commissioners and High Court held that T was liable to tax on the payments made to the company by the manufacturers by virtue of s.555 and s.556 of the Act. T contended that he was not liable to tax on the payments made to the company by the manufacturers by virtue of s.556(5), which provided that s.556(2) did not apply to such payments in cases where the collection obligation on the payer imposed by s.555(2) did not arise. Section 555(2) did not apply to the manufacturers in the instant case because (i) they had no tax presence in the UK and (ii) the Act did not have extra territorial effect by reason of the territoriality principle inherent in UK legislation. The Revenue contended that s.556(5) was addressed not to the collection mechanism in respect of particular payments but to whether particular payments were subject to tax at all.

Held, allowing the appeal, that s.556(5) excluded from the reach of s.556 any case where the payer did not have a s.555(2) obligation. The 1988 Act was a consolidating statute, which did not alter the law as stated in its predecessor legislation. The judge was wrong to hold that the territoriality principle had to be disapplied in the case of s.555(2) since to do otherwise would disrupt the purpose of the legislation. The territoriality principle was of particular strength in relation not only to legislation imposing a charge to tax but also to legislation imposing a duty to collect or account for tax. The obligation imposed on the payer by s.555(2) was not only burdensome but penal. The judge recognised the difficulty of enforcement in the instant case but erred in holding that such difficulty did not mean that the obligation in s.555(2) did not apply to the manufacturers. Enforceability was relevant to the prior question of whether the statutory obligation was intended to apply extra territorially at all, *Clark (Inspector of Taxes) v. Oceanic Contractors Inc* [1983] 2 A.C. 130, [1985] C.L.Y. 1766 applied. Issues of enforceability and the imposition of penalties indicated that s.555(2) should not be given extra territorial effect. In respect of payments made by the manufacturers to the company, T was not to be treated for the purposes of the 1988 Act as the person to whom those payments had been made.

AGASSI v. ROBINSON (INSPECTOR OF TAXES); *sub nom.* SET v. ROBINSON (INSPECTOR OF TAXES), [2004] EWCA Civ 1518, [2005] 1 W.L.R. 1090, Buxton, L.J., CA (Civ Div).

4105. **Income tax–Tax planning–Production contract to acquire film–Meaning of "arrangement" in s.99 Income Tax Act 1976 (New Zealand)**

[Income Tax Act 1976 (New Zealand) s.99.]

The appellant taxpayer (P) appealed against the decision ([2003] 2 N.Z.L.R. 77) of the Court of Appeal of New Zealand that a tax deduction claimed by P had been properly disallowed under the provisions of the Income Tax Act 1976 (New Zealand) s.99. Section 99 was a general anti avoidance provision which entitled the commissioner to adjust a taxpayers assessable income in order to counteract a tax advantage which he had obtained by a tax avoidance scheme. P was a member of syndicates formed to finance the production of two feature films in New Zealand. High rate taxpayers had been induced to become members in part by the prospect of obtaining a depreciation allowance which would allow them to set off against their taxable income from other sources the whole of their investment in the film, and in part by the opportunity to fund the investment with moneys borrowed under a non recourse loan agreement thereby allowing them to increase the amount of their investment, and therefore of the amount available for deduction from their taxable income, without increasing their exposure to loss. The investors, including P, entered into a production contract under which they incurred a liability to pay to the production company an amount representing their own investment and the proceeds of a non recourse loan from a third party lender. In the case of both films, one of which was successful and one of which was never commercially released, the investors' money had been spent on production costs but the non recourse loan, having not been needed, had been returned to the lender immediately it was received. The respondent commissioner accepted P's claim to deduct the actual costs of production provided by the investors but disallowed the claim to deduct the amount of the non recourse loan. The commissioner argued that for the purpose of s.99 the scheme as a whole constituted the relevant arrangement, comprising the non recourse loan, the inflation of the costs of the film and the circular movement of the loan funds. He further argued that the arrangement had the purpose or effect of generating a claim to tax relief which was achieved by the contrivance or pretence that the production cost included the amount of the loan when in reality it did not.

Held, allowing the appeal (Lords Bingham and Scott dissenting on the issue of tax avoidance), that (1) the commissioner was entitled at his option to identify the whole or any part or parts of a single composite scheme as the "contract, agreement, plan or understanding" which constituted the "arrangement" for the purpose of s.99. (2) The "arrangement" which the commissioner had identified had the purpose or effect of reducing the investors' liability to tax and, whether or not they were parties to the arrangement or the relevant part or parts of it, they were affected by it. The "arrangement" did not require a consensus or meeting of minds; the taxpayer need not be a party to "the arrangement" and need not be privy to its details, *Inland Revenue Commissioner v. BNZ Investments Ltd* [2002] 1 N.Z.L.R. 450 considered. (3) The tax advantage which the investors obtained did not amount to tax avoidance within s.99. Investors in films were entitled to depreciate their full acquisition costs. That was so however much the film actually cost the production company to make and by whatever means the investors had obtained the funds to finance the acquisition, *Inland Revenue Commissioner v. Challenge Corp* [1987] A.C. 155, [1987] C.L.Y. 2036 considered. It was wrong to suggest that the purpose of the statutory depreciation regime, when invoked by persons who had incurred a liability to pay a capital sum to acquire a film, was not satisfied unless the disponer applied the proceeds in making the film. The fact that the investment was funded by a non recourse loan did not alter the fact that the investors had suffered the economic burden of paying the full amount required under the production contract to acquire the film. The investors were entitled to the corresponding depreciation allowance. (4) (Obiter) Had the necessary allegations been made and the necessary facts found, the commissioner might have been able successfully to challenge the scheme on the basis that the investors' obligation to make the payment which they incurred was to the extent of the nonrecourse loan not exclusively incurred as the consideration for the acquisition of the film. (5) (Per Lords Bingham and Scott) The right to depreciate the cost of producing a film and to deduct the depreciation from taxable income was a tax advantage and if the cost was met, or was purported to be met, by the proceeds of a non-recourse loan, the tax advantage claimed by the borrower was a tax advantage to which s.99 applied if the depreciation claim was not within the purpose of the statutory depreciation regime. If the cost of acquisition of a film was inflated for no commercial reason other than that of qualifying for a higher tax deduction than would otherwise be available the amount of the inflation could not be regarded as the sort of cost that the statutory regime was intended to assist or encourage. The non recourse loan was in fact nothing of the sort but was no more than a device to produce a higher capital sum to be depreciated and thereby a higher tax deduction.

PETERSON v. INLAND REVENUE COMMISSIONER, [2005] UKPC 5, [2005] S.T.C. 448, Lord Bingham of Cornhill, PC (NZ).

4106. Income tax—Tax returns—Claim for relief based on error or mistake

[Taxes Management Act 1970 s.33.]

The appellant taxpayer (C) appealed against the respondent Inland Revenue's refusal to grant relief under the Taxes Management Act 1970 s.33 for errors in his tax returns that had been caused by an oversight. The Inland Revenue had introduced self assessment and payments on account and offered the opportunity, by using form SA303, to apply to reduce such payments. In 1997, C wrote asking for that form, suggesting that the Inland Revenue had made tax computation errors in previous years. His subsequent tax returns claimed relief based on the actual cost of running his business car. On later discovering that he could have claimed more relief under a fixed rate per mile scheme, C argued that the six year time limit for 1995 to 1996 claims had started from 1997, as his letter was sufficient to amount to a claim for relief under s.33, and that he had simply overlooked making subsequent returns on the fixed profit basis. The Inland Revenue argued that C could not claim for increased relief for the 1995 to 1996 year because the scheme was not in effect before the 1996 to 1997 year and it was only available when a taxpayer changed cars, which was not C's situation.

Held, dismissing the appeal, that C's 1997 letter could not reasonably be considered to be notification of a claim falling within s.33. The term "error in the computations" pointed to an error of arithmetic, not the basis on which C was claiming motoring expenses relief. C had been unaware in 1997 that the alternative method of claiming expenses was available to him and had not promptly followed up his letter with adequate detail on the basis of his claim. C did not otherwise qualify for relief under s.33. He could not take advantage of the fixed mileage scheme, a concession from an otherwise statutory requirement, because it was not available in 1995 to 1996; because of his long dispute with the Inland Revenue, C had not paid income tax for 1995 to 1996; and although the claim could be amended, C should not have included claims for capital allowances in his s.33 claim. In effect, C's claim was for relief from his own or his agent's mistake. It followed that his claim in respect of the period 1995 to 1996 was out of time and in respect of the periods 1996 to 1997 onwards he had not brought himself within the qualifying conditions for s.33.

COOK v. WOOD (INSPECTOR OF TAXES) [2005] S.T.C. (S.C.D.) 267, Colin Bishopp, Sp Comm.

4107. Income tax–Tax returns–Electronic communications–Incentive payments

INCOME TAX (INCENTIVE PAYMENTS FOR VOLUNTARY ELECTRONIC COMMUNICATION OF PAYE RETURNS) (AMENDMENT) REGULATIONS 2005, SI 2005 826; made under the Finance Act 2000 s.143, Sch.38. In force: in accordance with Reg.1 (1); £3.00.

These Regulations amend the Income Tax (Incentive Payments for Voluntary Electronic Communications of PAYE Incentive Returns) Regulations 2003 (SI 2003 2495) by inserting a new definition of "the PAYE Regulations" and extending the concept of a person who is treated as paying PAYE income. They replace references to the Income Tax (Employments) Regulations 1993 (SI 1993 744) with references to the corresponding provisions of the Income Tax (Pay as You Earn) Regulations 2003 (SI 2003 2682); provide that an incentive is not payable where a small employer has been established, employs employees or makes payments of PAYE income for an impermissible purpose; and ensure that decisions cannot be the subject of more than one appeal and that notices of appeal must be in writing.

4108. Income tax–Tax returns–Notice of enquiry by tax inspector–Irrelevant objection by taxpayer's accountants

[Taxes Management Act 1970 s.19A.]

The appellant taxpayer (B) appealed against the issue of a notice by the respondent Inland Revenue requiring him to produce documents in relation to his tax return. An enquiry had been opened into B's tax return and he had been asked to supply documents relating to his income and expenditure. B's accountants (C) entered into correspondence with the Inland Revenue, during the course of which they refused to supply the documents on the ground that there was a "fundamental issue" in respect of the tax law system that had to be addressed before the documents would be supplied. C did not set out the fundamental issue, and eventually launched the current appeal on B's behalf. Neither C nor B attended the appeal hearing. The Inland Revenue maintained that the notice issued under the Taxes Management Act 1970 s.19A was reasonable and necessary for the enquiry and that the documents requested would be in B's possession or power.

Held, dismissing the appeal, that there was nothing to suggest that the notice was unreasonable nor that B would not be able to supply the documents requested. The argument put forward by C appeared to be about changing the law and bore no relation to the appeal. A copy of the decision would be sent to the Institute of Chartered Accountants in England and Wales to enable them to consider whether to investigate C's actions.

BALTRUSAITIS v. BYRNE (OFFICER OF THE BOARD) [2005] S.T.C. (S.C.D.) 188, John F Avery Jones, Sp Comm.

4109. Income Tax (Trading and Other Income) Act 2005 (c.5)

This Act restates, with minor changes, certain enactments relating to income tax on trading income, property income, savings and investment income and certain other income.

This Act received Royal Assent on March 24, 2005.

4110. Indirect taxes–Debts–Priority of mortgages–Mortgagees' obligation to pay Goods and Services Tax–Right to reimbursement–New Zealand

[Land Transfer Act 1952 (New Zealand) s.104; Goods and Services Tax 1985 (New Zealand) s.5(2), s.17(1)(b).]

E, the second mortgagee of a freehold property, appealed against a decision that B, the first mortgagee, was not obliged to pay goods and services tax (GST) on the sale of the property until its own debt and any subsequent encumbrances were paid. New Zealand law required that the sale of such property be treated as a supply made by the mortgagor, pursuant to the Goods and Services Tax 1985 (New Zealand) s.5(2). However, in the event of such a deemed supply the mortgagee was obliged to pay to the Commissioner the amount of tax charged on that supply pursuant to s.17(1)(b). B therefore accounted to the Commissioner for the GST due on the sale and then reimbursed itself out of the proceeds of sale, discharging its own debt. E then brought proceedings against B and the Commissioner, contending that B was not obliged to pay the GST until its debts and any subsequent encumbrances had been paid. E argued that s.17(1)(b) of the 1985 Act conflicted with the Land Transfer Act 1952 s.104, which stipulated that the proceeds of sale arising on a sale by a mortgagee would be applied firstly to expenses occasioned by the sale, secondly to what was owing to the mortgagee and thirdly to any subsequent registered mortgages or encumbrances in the order of their priority. The High Court interpreted s.17(1)(b) as meaning that the duty to pay the Commissioner was qualified by the words "if there is any money left over after paying off any charges on the property". However, the Court of Appeal disagreed, holding that the words should be given their natural meaning.

Held, dismissing the appeal, that (1) s.17(1)(b) meant that although a sale by a mortgagee was deemed to be a supply in the course of a taxable activity by the mortgagor, it was nevertheless the mortgagee who was obliged to pay the tax. (2) There was no conflict between s.104 of the 1952 Act and s.17(1)(b) of the 1985 Act since the latter did not purport to interfere with the order of priorities stipulated by s.104; (3) Section 17(1)(b) did not require the mortgagee to pay the GST out of the proceeds of sale or out of any particular fund, but merely stated that the mortgagee was required to pay it. (4) In requiring payment of GST the Crown did not seek to assert any priority in the distribution of the mortgagor's assets. (5) Clearly the payment of GST was "an expense occasioned by the sale" in accordance with s.104(a). Accordingly, B was entitled to deduct it from the proceeds of sale before payment of its own debt and was accountable to subsequent encumbrancers only for the balance.

EDGEWATER MOTEL LTD v. INLAND REVENUE COMMISSIONER, [2004] UKPC 44, [2004] S.T.C. 1382, Lord Nicholls of Birkenhead, PC (NZ).

4111. Individual savings accounts–Shares and securities

INDIVIDUAL SAVINGS ACCOUNT (AMENDMENT NO.2) REGULATIONS 2005, SI 2005 2561; made under the Income Tax (Trading and Other Income) Act 2005 s.694, s.695, s.696, s.701; and the Taxation of Chargeable Gains Act 1992 s.151. In force: October 6, 2005; £3.00.

These Regulations amend the Individual Savings Account Regulations 1998 (SI 1998 1870) to extend the annual subscription limits to April 5, 2010; to apply the "cash like test" to shares and securities; and to make small changes to the annual information returns required from account managers.

4112. Individual savings accounts—Shares and units—Qualifying investments

INDIVIDUAL SAVINGS ACCOUNT (AMENDMENT NO.3) REGULATIONS 2005, SI 2005 3350; made under the Taxation of Chargeable Gains Act 1992 s.151; and the Income Tax (Trading and Other Income) Act 2005 s.694, s.695, s.696, s.701. In force: December 27, 2005; £3.00.

These Regulations amend the Individual Savings Account Regulations 1998 (SI 1998 1870) to provide that shares or units in non-UCITS retail schemes (a new type of collective investment scheme recognised by the Financial Services Authority) are qualifying investments for ISA stocks and shares components, provided that the shares or units can be redeemed at least twice monthly; to allow deposit accounts with Credit Unions to be qualifying investments for cash components; to clarify the wording of the "5 per cent test" (which a number of investments must satisfy in order to qualify for stocks and shares components); and to allow Alternative Financial Arrangements (provided for in the Finance Act 2005 and which include Shari'a contracts) to be qualifying investments for cash components.

4113. Inheritance tax—Business property relief—Historic house run as business open to public—Part of interior closed to public—Extent to which relief applied

[Inheritance Tax Act 1984 s.104, s.110(b).]

The appellant (S), executor of the Eighth Marquess of Hertford, appealed against the respondent Inland Revenue's assessment of the percentage of the value of Ragley Hall that was eligible for business property relief under the Inheritance Tax Act 1984 s.104. Ragley Hall, together with its land, contents and the business of opening it to the public, had been transferred to S as a gift by his father within seven years of his death, subject to a provision that the living quarters be leased back to his father. The Inland Revenue assessed only 78 per cent of the value of the property as eligible for business property relief under s.104, this being the proportion of the interior open to the public, with the rest used for accommodation. S contended that the whole value should be eligible for relief as a net asset of the business within the meaning of s.110(b) of the Act. He argued that as there was no provision within the Act for apportionment and the property was mainly used for business purposes its entire value should be eligible for relief. Alternatively, S argued that the property was indivisible as the whole structure protected and supported the public areas, and the entire exterior could be viewed by the public.

Held, allowing the appeal, that 100 per cent of the value of the freehold was eligible for relief. In most cases, a building owned by one party would be a single asset. Here, the nature of the business and the part played in it by Ragley Hall led to the conclusion that it was indeed a single asset and the section leased to S's father was part of that asset. The whole building was, therefore, indispensable to the business being carried on and it followed that the whole value was eligible for relief.

SEYMOUR (NINTH MARQUESS OF HERTFORD) v. INLAND REVENUE COMMISSIONERS [2005] S.T.C. (S.C.D.) 177, Judith Powell, Sp Comm.

4114. Inheritance tax—Double charges—Relief

INHERITANCE TAX (DOUBLE CHARGES RELIEF) REGULATIONS 2005, SI 2005 3441; made under the Finance Act 1986 s.104. In force: January 4, 2006; £3.00.

The Finance Act 1986 confers power to make provision by regulations for avoiding double charges to inheritance tax with respect to transfers of value made, and other events occurring, on or after March 18, 1986. Those powers were exercised in the Inheritance Tax (Double Charges Relief) Regulations 1987 (SI 1987 1130) and in the Charge to Income Tax by Reference to Enjoyment of Property Previously Owned Regulations 2005 (SI 2005 724). Those powers are further exercised in these Regulations. The Regulations apply where an individual enters into arrangements under which there are transfers both of property and of a debt owed to the deceased; the debt is then written off; and, on the deceased's death on or after April 6, 2005, both the relevant property (or any property then representing the chargeable property) and the debt are chargeable to inheritance tax. Where these Regulations apply, two separate amounts must be calculated. The first amount is the inheritance tax chargeable on the deceased's death, but disregarding the value transferred represented by the relevant property (or by any property then representing that property). The second amount is the inheritance tax chargeable on the deceased's death, but disregarding the value transferred represented by the debt. The total inheritance tax chargeable is then reduced to the first amount or to the second amount.

4115. **Inheritance tax—Gifts—Inter vivos transfer of half share in property as joint tenants—Inclusion of entire property in value of estate immediately before death**

The appellant (M), an executor, appealed against a notice of determination issued by the Inland Revenue that the whole of a property was included in the value of the estate of the deceased (D) immediately before his death for Inheritance Tax purposes. D's niece (G) went to live with D under an informal arrangement which lasted from 1996 to D's death in 2001. In 1996, D drafted a will stating that if G was still living with him at his death, she could stay there for the remainder of her life. That will was not executed. D then extended the property to include extra rooms for G's use. In 2000, D transferred a half interest in the property to G as a joint tenant by way of gift and executed a will leaving his share in the property to her for avoidance of doubt. On D's death, Inheritance tax became payable on the gift. M argued that D's actions in making the draft will and his extension of the property indicated that he intended to make a gift to G of an interest in the property before the actual transfer in 2000, on the basis of proprietary estoppel on account of her care for him.

Held, dismissing the appeal, that there was no gift earlier than 2000. The evidence suggested that if D had made a promise to G to give her an interest in the property in return for her looking after him, he would have made that clear. When he did decide to make such a gift, he effected the 2000 transfer. The fact that he was considering leaving G a life interest when he made his draft will in 1996 indicated that he had not promised her any interest in the property in his lifetime. The arrangement they had at that time, was contractual rather than amounting to an interest in property. The transfer deed executed in 2000 clearly stated that D was "solely and beneficially interested in the property", which again indicated that he did not consider himself to be giving effect to any previous gift. Neither was the extension of the property any indication of a gift, as it was equally consistent with D retaining the entire ownership of the property.

MOGGS v. INLAND REVENUE COMMISSIONERS [2005] S.T.C. (S.C.D.) 394, John F Avery Jones, Sp Comm.

4116. **Inheritance tax—Indexation**

INHERITANCE TAX (INDEXATION) ORDER 2005, SI 2005 718; made under the Inheritance Tax Act 1984 s.8. In force: March 16, 2005; £3.00.

This Order substitutes a new table of rate bands and rates for the table which was substituted by the Inheritance Tax (Indexation) Order 2004 (SI 2004 771) in relation to chargeable transfers made in the year beginning April 6, 2004.

4117. **Inheritance tax—Interests in possession—Insolvent estate—Aggregating personal or free estate and interests in possession in settled property**

[Inheritance Tax Act 1984 s.5(1), s.5(3), s.49, s.49(1), s.222.]

The appellant trustees (T) appealed under the Inheritance Tax Act 1984 s.222 against a determination of the Inland Revenue that where a person died insolvent the excess of his liabilities over the assets in his estate could not be used to reduce the value of the assets comprised in settlements in which he was interested for the purpose of computing the amount chargeable to tax. The deceased had died with virtually no assets. His liabilities were considerable and there was a net deficiency in his estate of £44,671. The deceased was interested as tenant for life in certain assets or funds under each of three settlements. Under s.49 of the 1984 Act the value of the property comprised in the life interests fell to be treated as property to which he was beneficially entitled, and that value formed part of the sum in relation to which inheritance tax was calculated. T submitted inheritance tax returns in which they claimed to be able to deduct from the values of each settlement the amount of the deficiency in the deceased's personal or free estate. The Inland Revenue did not accept that deduction and issued a notice of determination accordingly. T submitted that, by virtue of s.5(3) of the 1984 Act, which provided that in "determining the value of a person's estate at any time his liabilities at that time shall be taken into account", they were entitled to deduct the deficiency of £44,671 in the deceased's personal estate from the values of the settled funds so as to arrive at a net sum in respect of which inheritance tax had to be calculated. The Inland Revenue submitted that only the assets in the free estate were answerable in law for the free estate's liabilities and that once those assets were exhausted there were no other assets answerable for those liabilities, and that since the trust assets were not available to pay the deceased's personal liabilities, those liabilities could not be offset against them for inheritance tax purposes.

Held, dismissing the appeal, that (1) the Inland Revenue was right that the net liabilities were not available to reduce the estate beyond the value of the free estate's assets that were liable to meet them. Section 49(1), which brought in the settled assets, did so by deeming the deceased to be beneficially entitled to "the property" in which his life interest subsisted. That had to mean the "net property" from which liabilities had been notionally deducted. That notion could be applied in s.5(1) so that the property of the deceased that was brought into the aggregation was his personal estate net of his liabilities. It was not necessary for s.5(3) to provide for a second time that the debts were to be deducted in arriving at the value of the deceased's property, or estate, and it did not have that effect. The personal estate comprised the property in it net of liabilities; once it was reduced to zero by those liabilities its value could not decline further, and any additional liabilities had nothing against which they could be offset. The zero sum was aggregated with the settled property (net of trust liabilities) which was brought in by s.49(1). (2) If that was wrong, the Revenue's argument was right that the effect of s.5(3) was that the liabilities were taken into account by offsetting them against assets out of which they could properly be met, but no further. In the instant case the liabilities could only be deducted from the assets which were liable to bear them, *Barnes (Deceased), Re* [1939] 1 K.B. 316 applied.

ST BARBE GREEN v. INLAND REVENUE COMMISSIONERS; *sub nom.* GREEN v. INLAND REVENUE COMMISSIONERS, [2005] EWHC 14, [2005] 1 W.L.R. 1772, Mann, J., Ch D.

4118. Inheritance tax–Joint accounts–Building society account transferred to deceased and her daughters–Gifts with reservation

[Inheritance Tax Act 1984 s.5(2); Finance Act 1986 s.102.]

The appellants (S), daughters of the deceased, appealed against notices of determination to inheritance tax issued by the respondent (the Revenue) in respect of the funds held in a building society account. The deceased had transferred the account from her sole name into that of her own and S some six years before her death. All subsequent payments into and out of the account had been made by the deceased, save for withdrawals by S made on the deceased's behalf in the years immediately prior to her death. The inheritance tax return stated that the account had passed by survivorship and one third of the balance was returned as the deceased's share. The Revenue maintained that (1) the whole balance of the account was taxable under the Inheritance Tax Act 1984 s.5(2); (2) in the alternative, there had been a gift with reservation under the Finance Act 1986 s.102. S argued that there had been a tenancy in common of the account.

Held, dismissing the appeal, that (1) the deceased had had the power to deal with the account as she thought fit but S had had no such general power.

There was no evidence that S had had ownership of separate shares and therefore there had been no tenancy in common. Further, the argument that there had been a tenancy in common was inconsistent with the tax return which stated that one third of the balance passed beneficially by survivorship. Therefore s.5(2) of the 1984 Act applied, *Figgis, Re* [1969] 1 Ch. 123, [1968] C.L.Y. 4065 applied. (2) The account had been held beneficially as joint tenants. The gift was a gift of a chose in action consisting of the whole account, not two thirds of the initial balance. Possession and enjoyment of the account had not been assumed by S before the deceased's death because the deceased had still been entitled to a share. The account had not been enjoyed to the entire exclusion of the deceased as all benefits from the account were enjoyed by the deceased. Accordingly, there had been a gift with reservation.

SILLARS v. INLAND REVENUE COMMISSIONERS [2004] S.T.C. (S.C.D.) 180, John F Avery Jones, Sp Comm.

4119. Inheritance tax–Life insurance–Power to assign or nominate beneficiaries– Proceeds forming part of estate

[Inheritance Tax Act 1984 s.5.]

K appealed against a decision that a life insurance policy in the name of her deceased brother, L, was chargeable to inheritance tax. L had worked in the US since 1995 and his employer had taken out a life policy on his behalf. L was entitled to name beneficiaries of the policy, and he chose to name K and his other sister, R. L had the power to change the nominated beneficiary or assign the policy at any time, and if no beneficiary was nominated the proceeds of the policy would pass into his estate. The Revenue decided that L had been beneficially entitled to the proceeds of the policy pursuant to the Inheritance Tax Act 1984 s.5, so that the proceeds were liable to inheritance tax. On appeal, K argued that the policy was a direct benefit payable to the next of kin, and did not form part of L's estate.

Held, dismissing the appeal, that the proceeds of the policy were taxable under s.5. The ability to change beneficiaries at will meant that L had a general power to dispose of the policy's proceeds. It was not solely payable to L's next of kin, but could be paid to a charity or left to form part of his estate. It therefore came within the definition of property in s.5(2) and was thus part of L's estate for inheritance tax purposes.

KEMPE v. INLAND REVENUE COMMISSIONERS [2004] S.T.C. (S.C.D.) 467, Nuala Brice, Sp Comm.

4120. Inheritance tax–Title to land–Disputed ownership of family home–Validity of title

The appellant taxpayer (T) appealed against a notice of determination issued by the Inland Revenue regarding the inheritance tax payable following his sister's death. T's mother had bequeathed the family home to his sister and the title was duly transferred to her in 1972. When the sister died in 2002 and the Revenue calculated the inheritance tax payable on her estate, T contended that his sister had not been the owner of the whole of the family home because she had not signed any document accepting title to the property.

Held, dismissing the appeal, that T's sister was the owner of the whole of the family home immediately before her death. At her death she was the heritable proprietrix of the property. Her title was valid and unimpeachable. No attempt had ever been made to set it aside. Accordingly, the property in its entirety formed part of her estate for the purposes of inheritance tax.

THOMSON v. INLAND REVENUE COMMISSIONERS [2004] S.T.C. (S.C.D.) 520, J Gordon Reid Q.C., Sp Comm.

4121. Inheritance tax–Works of art–Exemption from inheritance tax conditional on allowing public access by appointment–Justice of varying undertaking to allow open public access

[Inheritance Tax Act 1984 s.35A; Finance Act 1998; Human Rights Act 1998 Sch.1 Part I Art.8, Part II Art.1.]

The appellant (X), owner of X Grade 1 listed house, appealed against X variation of his undertaking to allow public access to works of art in the house upon conditions of exemption from inheritance tax. X had given an undertaking in 1996 to lend the art to public galleries and to allow prearranged viewings in return for the exemption, but had opted to pay the tax on the house itself in order to avoid having to grant public access to it. On the introduction of the Finance Act 1998, open public access was required to works of art. In 2003 the Inland Revenue proposed X variation to X's undertaking to allow public access without appointment, which the Inheritance Tax Act 1984 s.35A permitted them to do if it was just and reasonable in the circumstances. X argued that the variation was not just and reasonable as he had X legitimate expectation regarding his obligations under the undertaking as long as he abided by its terms, and the 1998 Act did not alter that position. Further, X argued that there were issues concerning security risks to his home and chattels in allowing open public access and the attendant costs of taking appropriate security measures. Moreover, X argued that the proposed variation interfered with his rights under the Human Rights Act 1998 Sch.1 Part I Art.8 and Part II Art.1.

Held, allowing the appeal, that in X's particular circumstances it was not reasonable to vary the undertaking. However, there was no legitimate expectation because the variation had been proposed in accordance with the Inland Revenue's statutory duty, *R. v. Inland Revenue Commissioners, ex p. Unilever Plc* [1996] S.T.C. 681, [1995] C.L.Y. 895 and *R. v. North and East Devon HA, ex p. Coughlan* [2001] Q.B. 213, [1999] C.L.Y. 2643 distinguished. There was X public interest consideration in that the proposals would expose X to greater security risks, which weighed against the "just and reasonable" factor. It was also unreasonable to make X open his house for access to the works of art without pre appointment where he had paid inheritance tax on it to avoid that very situation. In terms of the human rights issues, Sch.1 Part II Art.1 was not invoked because X's property rights arising under the undertakings were not "possessions" in the sense of legal rights. Neither was there any breach of Art.8, as any interference in X's private life was interference by the public, not by X public authority. In the circumstances, the disadvantages that the proposed variation would impose on X outweighed the need to achieve greater public access to the works of art.

APPLICATION TO VARY THE UNDERTAKINGS OF A, *Re* [2005] S.T.C. (S.C.D.) 103, Stephen Oliver Q.C., Sp Comm.

4122. Insurance companies–Corporation tax–Apportionment

INSURANCE COMPANIES (CORPORATION TAX ACTS) (AMENDMENT) ORDER 2005, SI 2005 3465; made under the Income and Corporation Taxes Act 1988 s.431A. In force: January 6, 2006; £3.00.

This Order amends the Income and Corporation Taxes Act 1988, the Finance Act 1989, the Finance Act 1996, the Finance Act 2003 and the Finance (No.2) Act 2005. It makes amendments relating to companies carrying on life assurance business, primarily to amend the apportionment rules to ensure that income and gains of such a company's inherited estate are not attributed to any category of business where the income and gains would be exempt from tax.

4123. Landfill tax–Exemptions

LANDFILL TAX (SITE RESTORATION, QUARRIES AND PET CEMETERIES) ORDER 2005, SI 2005 725; made under the Finance Act 1996 s.46. In force: April 6, 2005; £3.00.

This Order makes amendments to certain sections of the Finance Act 1996 relating to exemptions. These amendments are required following the amendment to s.66 of the Act which added to the categories of landfill site land

TAX

in relation to which a permit under regulations under the Pollution Prevention and Control Act 1999 s.2 or under regulations under the Environment (Northern Ireland) Order 2002 (SI 2002 3153 (NI.7)) Art.4 is in force. It also makes amendments so that a landfill site operator whose site is covered by a permit has the same entitlement to the exemption from landfill tax for restoring a landfill site with qualifying material as is available to an operator whose site is covered by a licence or a resolution; so that a landfill site covered by a permit authorising only the disposal of qualifying material is a qualifying landfill site for the purposes of the exemption from landfill tax for filling quarries as is a site covered by a licence or a resolution; and so that the exemption from landfill tax for the disposal of the remains of dead domestic pets at pet cemeteries applies to a landfill site covered by a permit in the same way as it applies to a site covered by a licence or resolution.

4124. Landfill tax–Site operators–Benefits

LANDFILL TAX (AMENDMENT) REGULATIONS 2005, SI 2005 759; made under the Finance Act 1996 s.51, s.53, s.62. In force: in accordance with Reg.1 (2); £3.00.

These Regulations amend the Landfill Tax Regulations 1996 (SI 1996 1527) so that a landfill site operator whose site is covered by a permit and who is directed by a relevant authority to remove waste from his site to another site is entitled to a credit in the same way as an operator whose site is covered by a licence or resolution; a landfill site operator whose site is covered by a permit has the same entitlement to temporarily dispose of qualifying material tax free for site restoration purposes as an operator whose site is covered by a licence or resolution; the maximum amount as a percentage of his annual landfill tax liability that a landfill site operator may claim as credit in the scheme whereby operators are entitled to credit based on the contributions they give to approved bodies with objects concerned with the environment is reduced.

4125. Loan agreements–Derivative contracts–Profits and losses–Bringing into account

LOAN RELATIONSHIPS AND DERIVATIVE CONTRACTS (DISREGARD AND BRINGING INTO ACCOUNT OF PROFITS AND LOSSES) (AMENDMENT) REGULATIONS 2005, SI 2005 2012; made under the Finance Act 1996 s.84A, s.85B; and the Finance Act 2002 Sch.26 para.16, Sch.26 para.17C. In force: August 11, 2005; £3.00.

These Regulations amend the Loan Relationships and Derivative Contracts (Disregard and Bringing into Account of Profits and Losses) Regulations 2004 (SI 2004 3256) which allow certain profits and losses from loan relationships and derivative contracts to be left out of account, to be brought into account in a different way or to be brought into account at a later date. The Regulations clarify the order of priority for matching the loan relationship or derivative contract with shares, ships or aircraft; exclude certain relationships deemed to be loan relationships; and insert a new provision to explain how the value of an obligation under a derivative contract is calculated to enable the limit of matching to be determined. They clarify the extent to which an asset is matched; extend the time limit for making an election; make amendments so that fair value movements as a result of a change of accounting basis are disregarded in determining a company's profit or loss; provide how fair value profits and losses are to be brought into account in relation to expenditure which is depreciated over a period; and exclude certain amounts in relation to convertible securities and loan relationships with embedded derivatives from amounts recognised in determining a company's profit or loss.

4126. Loan agreements–Derivative contracts–Profits and losses–Bringing into account

LOAN RELATIONSHIPS AND DERIVATIVE CONTRACTS (DISREGARD AND BRINGING INTO ACCOUNT OF PROFITS AND LOSSES) (AMENDMENT NO.2)

REGULATIONS 2005, SI 2005 3374; made under the Finance Act 1996 s.84A, s.85B, Sch.9 para.19B; the Finance Act 2002 Sch.26 para.16, Sch.26 para.17C; and the Finance Act 2005 Sch.4 para.52. In force: December 29, 2005; £3.00.

These Regulations amend the Loan Relationships and Derivative Contracts (Disregard and Bringing into Account of Profits and Losses) Regulations 2004 (SI 2004 3256) which allow certain profits and losses from loan relationships and derivative contracts to be left out of account, to be brought into account in a different way or to be brought into account at a later date.

4127. National insurance contributions–Agency workers–Freelance worker providing services through company–Employment status

[Social Security Contributions (Intermediaries) Regulations 2000 (SI 2000 727) Reg.6(1).]

The appellant taxpayer company (N) appealed against a decision of the respondent Inland Revenue classifying the freelance work undertaken by its sole director and owner (R) for another company as that of an employee. N had entered into a series of seven consecutive six month contracts with an agency (RM) for R to provide freelance computer services to another company (NP). The contract required R to give priority to the NP work. NP provided training and equipment, although R used his own computer and mobile phone. He was paid on a daily rate, but without the usual additional employee benefits. R led a team of NP employees, had some involvement in NP's personnel issues and was required to report to an NP manager. R worked exclusively for NP and generally at NP's office. When his contract was terminated, his work was taken over by NP employees. The Inland Revenue sent a notice determining that the Social Security Contributions (Intermediaries) Regulations 2000 Reg.6(1) applied. R argued that (1) the notice was invalid because, while being named in the notice, NP had not received a copy; (2) he was not an employee of NP.

Held, dismissing the appeal, that (1) The Inland Revenue's notice was valid because, although NP might have had to pay national insurance contributions, it was legally in the same position whether or not the 2000 Regulations applied, as it would have continued to pay RM the same amount. (2) Applying the IR35 hypothetical contract, R would clearly have been an employee. The important factors were that he had managerial responsibility for a team of NP employees, he reported regularly to an NP manager, he was carrying out continuous support and maintenance work rather than a specific assignment, he was paid a daily rate and could not earn more by working longer hours, he had no other clients, and the arrangement was terminable on four weeks' notice. Some factors pointed away from employment, such as the absence of the usual fringe benefits, even though he had a holiday entitlement, and payment against invoices and work sheets. Some factors were not relevant, such as the provision of equipment and the lack of control over how he did his work. While it was important to R, IR35 did not seem to pay attention to the risk of not being able to renew the contract, but assumed a hypothetical contract for each six monthly contract. The fact that there was a continuous series of six monthly contracts unrelated to any particular assignment made the employment case stronger. (Obiter) The court would have preferred a much more detailed description of the type of work R performed, particularly from NP's point of view.

NETHERLANE LTD v. YORK [2005] S.T.C. (S.C.D.) 305, John F Avery Jones, Sp Comm.

4128. National insurance contributions–Contractors–Services provided through intermediary

[Social Security Contributions (Intermediaries) Regulations 2000 (SI 2000 727) Reg.6(1)(c).]

The appellant company (X) appealed against two decisions that it was liable to pay national insurance contributions on payments for services provided to two defence companies (M and B) by its director and shareholder (Y). Y was an experienced software engineer specialising in defence work. X had contracted with an agent (C) to find end users of its services. C had entered into contracts with M and B under which Y was to be provided as a contractor to work on particular projects. Y had to work at their premises but could take time off when he wanted. He had bought his own reference material and spent some time at home each week keeping up with developments. His work had been overseen by a manager, but he had not needed instruction or control. There was a contractual possibility that he could be substituted. He had not been entitled to employee benefits and had been dependent on payment by C to X. X disputed the Inland Revenue's contention that, if the arrangements had taken the form of contracts between Y and each of M and B, Y would have been regarded as an employee under the Social Security Contributions (Intermediaries) Regulations 2000 Reg.6(1)(c).

Held, allowing the appeals, that if the arrangements between Y and each of M and B had taken the form of contracts, they would have been contracts for the provision of services and not contracts of employment. Y had not hired helpers, provided his own equipment, assumed any great financial risk or had much opportunity to profit from sound management in the performance of his task. However, those factors were not sufficiently important to determine whether the hypothetical contract in the instant case would be a contract for services or a contract of service, since the secret nature of Y's work precluded him from carrying on his profession in the entrepreneurial way which might otherwise be available. It was more significant in the instant case that neither M nor B had been obliged to keep Y in work during his engagements, Y had not been obliged to perform a particular amount of work, Y had not needed permission to take time off, Y could have been substituted, although the situation was very unlikely to have arisen, and Y had not been entitled to employee benefits, *Market Investigations Ltd v. Minister of Social Security* [1969] 2 Q.B. 173, [1969] C.L.Y. 2337 and *Montgomery v. Johnson Underwood Ltd* [2001] EWCA Civ 318, [2001] I.C.R. 819, [2001] C.L.Y. 2264 applied, *Synaptek Ltd v. Young (Inspector of Taxes)* [2003] EWHC 645, [2003] S.T.C. 543, [2003] C.L.Y. 4030 and *Ready Mixed Concrete (South East) Ltd v. Minister of Pensions and National Insurance* [1968] 2 Q.B. 497, [1968] C.L.Y. 2550 considered.

ANSELL COMPUTER SERVICES LTD v. RICHARDSON (INSPECTOR OF TAXES) [2004] S.T.C. (S.C.D.) 472, Graham Aaronson Q.C., Sp Comm.

4129. **Overpayments–Mistake of law–Taxpayer's entitlement to restitutionary remedy**

[Limitation Act 1980 s.5, s.32; EC Treaty.]

The Inland Revenue appealed against a decision ([2003] EWHC 1779, [2003] 4 All E.R. 645, [2003] C.L.Y. 4142) that the claims of the respondent (D) were not statute barred. The European Court of Justice in *Metallgesellschaft Ltd v. Inland Revenue Commissioners (C397/98)* [2001] E.C.R. I-1727 held that it was contrary to the EC Treaty provisions on freedom of establishment for United Kingdom law to deny the right to make a group income election where the parent company was resident in a Member State other than the UK. The ECJ further held that the claimants were entitled to compensation for the premature payment of advance corporation tax (ACT) later set off against liability for mainstream corporation tax. Further claims based on *Metallgesellschaft* were brought forward as test cases pursuant to a group litigation order. In the instant case, D sought compensation in respect of various payments of ACT made prematurely by it. D's primary claim was restitutionary; alternatively, it claimed damages for breach of statutory duty by the Revenue in failing to ensure that the relevant statutory regime complied with Community law. In its defence, the Revenue pleaded that the claim in relation to payments of ACT made in 1993, 1995 and 1996 was statute barred since the limitation period for breach of statutory duty and in restitution was six years. The judge held that D made the payments of ACT under a mistake of law, that English law recognised a claim in restitution to recover money paid under a mistake of law, that such a claim was available where the money was paid to the Revenue in discharge of what was mistakenly thought to be a liability for taxes, and that D had only discovered its mistake when the ECJ gave judgment in *Metallgesellschaft*. The Revenue argued that (1) the judge had been wrong to conclude, on the basis of *Woolwich Building Society (formerly Woolwich Equitable Building Society) v. Inland Revenue Commissioners* [1993] A.C. 70, [1992] C.L.Y. 2508 and *Kleinwort Benson Ltd v. Lincoln City Council* [1999] 2 A.C. 349, [1998] C.L.Y. 2297, that English law recognised a cause of action for mistake of law in relation to an overpayment of tax; (2) the judge should have held that the claims in relation to the payments in question were not brought until the schedule to the particulars of claim was amended to include details of the payments.

Held, allowing the appeal in part (Buxton, L.J. dissenting on the second issue), that (1) a claimant who made a payment to the Revenue under a mistake of law was not entitled to a restitutionary remedy in respect of that payment otherwise than under the *Woolwich* principle (where the demand was unlawful) or under the relevant statutory regime (where the demand was lawful), *Woolwich* and *Kleinwort Benson* considered. D had plainly made a mistake of law in believing that the ACT was payable when on the true state of the law it was not. Thus the payments were made pursuant to an unlawful demand. The appropriate cause of action was under *Woolwich* and the limitation period under *Woolwich* was six years under the Limitation Act 1980 s.5. D could not rely on a restitutionary claim under *Kleinwort Benson* or on s.32 of the 1980 Act, and its claim in respect of the 1993 payment was statute barred. (2) The judge had been right that the claims in respect of all three payments in question were brought when the claim form was issued, since it pleaded claims in respect of all payments of ACT made by D and the amendments to include particulars of the payments did not add new claims. Therefore the claims in respect of the 1995 and 1996 payments were not statute barred, *Metallgesellschaft* considered.

DEUTSCHE MORGAN GRENFELL GROUP PLC v. INLAND REVENUE COMMISSIONERS; *sub nom.* INLAND REVENUE COMMISSIONERS v. DEUTSCHE MORGAN GRENFELL GROUP PLC, [2005] EWCA Civ 78, [2006] 2 W.L.R. 103, Buxton, L.J., CA (Civ Div).

4130. Penalties–Notices–Mistakes–Effect on validity of notices

[Taxes Management Act 1970 s.19A, s.114.]

The appellant taxpayer (X) appealed against the Inland Revenue's imposition of daily penalties for his failure to comply with notices under the Taxes Management Act 1970 s.19A. X had submitted tax returns for two successive years based on estimates. The Inland Revenue issued two s.19A notices requiring details of the actual figures and, in relation to the second year, completion of a self assessment tax return. X did not comply. Two penalty notices each charged a daily penalty of £340 for an initial period and two further penalty notices each charged a daily penalty of £510 for a subsequent period. The £340 penalty notice for the first year gave the wrong date for the s.19A notice to which it related. Both £340 notices stated a total penalty of £340 in bold but elsewhere specified a penalty of £340 per day, and both stated that they were for failure to produce documents specified in s.19A notices. None of the penalty notices stated the tax year to which it related, and none had a copy of the relevant s.19A notice attached. X contended that the errors in the penalty notices rendered them invalid and incapable of being saved by s.114 of the Act, and that the sums charged were excessive.

Held, allowing the appeal in part, that the £340 penalty notice for the first year was completely misleading in referring to the date of another s.19A notice relating to a different year. It could not be regarded as conforming or according in substance with the intent of the Act and could not therefore be saved by s.114. The £340 penalty notices were also bad for stating two different figures for the penalty and for failing, despite reference to the relevant s.19A notice, to accurately specify what X had failed to do for which the penalty was being imposed. Both errors were gross errors which could not be saved by s.114, *Fleming (Inspector of Taxes) v. London Produce Co* [1968] 1 W.L.R. 1013, [1968] C.L.Y. 1857 applied. It would have been helpful but it was not necessary for the penalty notices to specify the relevant tax year or attach a copy of the relevant s.19A notice. In view of that conclusion, there was nothing wrong with the £510 notices. However, their amounts were excessive, representing 41 and 25 per cent respectively of X's tax liability for the two years, and should be halved.

AUSTIN v. PRICE (INSPECTOR OF TAXES) [2004] S.T.C. (S.C.D.) 487, John F Avery Jones (Chairman), Sp Comm.

4131. Pension schemes–Appeals

TAXES MANAGEMENT ACT 1970 (MODIFICATIONS TO SCHEDULE 3 FOR PENSION SCHEME APPEALS) ORDER 2005, SI 2005 3457; made under the Finance Act 2004 s.156, s.159, s.253, s.269, s.271. In force: April 6, 2006; £3.00.

This Order makes modifications to the Taxes Management Act 1970 Sch.3 in respect of appeals by scheme administrators under those provisions of the Finance Act 2004 Ch.2 or Ch.7 of Pt 4; which confer a right of appeal to the General Commissioners.

4132. Personal equity plans–Investments–Shares and securities

PERSONAL EQUITY PLAN (AMENDMENT) REGULATIONS 2005, SI 2005 2562; made under the Income Tax (Trading and Other Income) Act 2005 s.694, s.695, s.696, s.701; and the Taxation of Chargeable Gains Act 1992 s.151. In force: October 6, 2005; £3.00.

These Regulations amend the Personal Equity Plan Regulations 1989 (SI 1989 469) to apply the "cash like test" to shares and securities and to make a small change to the annual information returns required from account managers.

4133. Personal equity plans–Shares and units–Qualifying investments

PERSONAL EQUITY PLAN (AMENDMENT NO.2) REGULATIONS 2005, SI 2005 3348; made under the Taxation of Chargeable Gains Act 1992 s.151; and the Income Tax (Trading and Other Income) Act 2005 s.694, s.695, s.696, s.701. In force: December 27, 2005; GP3.00.

These Regulations amend the Personal Equity Plan Regulations 1989 (SI 1989 469) to provide that shares or units in non-UCITS retail schemes (a new type of collective investment scheme recognised by the Financial Services Authority) are qualifying investments for Personal Equity Plans (PEPs), provided that the shares or units can be redeemed at least twice monthly; and to clarify the wording of the "5 per cent test" (which a number of investments must satisfy in order to qualify for PEPs).

4134. Reliefs–Foreign investment–Acquisition of shares in capital company–Relief denied where company established in another Member State–Free movement of capital–European Community

[EC Treaty Art.56(1), Art.58(1)(c); Income Tax Law (Luxembourg) Art.129(c).]

The Luxembourg court sought a preliminary ruling on the interpretation of the EC Treaty Art.56(1) and Art.58(1)(a). The Income Tax Law (Luxembourg) Art.129(c) provided for tax relief on the acquisition of shares in fully taxable resident capital companies. Under the Double Taxation Convention agreed between Belgium and Luxembourg, dividends paid by a company having its seat in one contracting State in favour of a resident of the other contracting State were taxable in the latter State. However, the State in which the company declaring the dividends had its seat could tax the dividends up to the value of 15 per cent of the gross amount of the dividends paid. Taxpayers resident in Luxembourg (W) claimed income tax relief under Art.129(c) in relation to their subscription for shares in the capital of a Belgian company. The Luxembourg Administrative Court overturned the tax authorities refusal to grant the requested relief on the ground that Art.129(c) of the national tax law was incompatible with those provisions of the EC Treaty which covered the free movement of capital. The tax authorities appealed and the European Court of Justice was asked to rule as to whether Art.56(1) and Art.58(1)(a) of the EC Treaty precluded national laws which denied the availability of tax relief to natural persons for the acquisition of shares representing cash contributions in capital companies established in another Member State.

Held, giving a preliminary ruling, that a legislative provision such as Art.129(c) of the national tax law had the effect of discouraging nationals of the Member State concerned from investing their capital in companies which had their seat in another Member State. Moreover, such a provision also had a restrictive effect in relation to companies established in other Member States as it constituted an obstacle to the raising of capital in Luxembourg since it made the acquisition of shares in companies whose seat was in another Member State less attractive than the acquisition of shares in Luxembourg companies. The denial of relief in such circumstances could not be objectively justified on the ground of safeguarding the cohesion of the tax system. There was no direct link between the tax advantage in question and an offsetting fiscal levy, *Staatssecretaris van Financien v. Verkooijen (C35/98)* [2002] S.T.C. 654, [2002] C.L.Y. 4433 and *Bachmann v. Belgium (C204/90)* [1994] S.T.C. 855, [1992] C.L.Y. 4805 considered. The tax advantage was not offset by the taxation of dividends paid by the company as there was no guarantee that any dividend would be paid and, even if they were paid, the amount of the advantage would significantly exceed any benefit which might result from any subsequent taxation of that dividend. Moreover, the inability to take advantage of the Double Taxation Convention could not be regarded as disadvantageous to persons investing in companies established in Luxembourg as the foregoing by that Member State of part of the tax on dividends provided no benefit to the taxpayer concerned. Hence, Art.129(c) of the national tax law infringed Art.56 of the EC Treaty.

MINISTRE DES FINANCES v. WEIDERT (C242/03) [2005] S.T.C. 1241, Judge Jann (President), ECJ.

4135. **Reliefs–Small or medium-sized enterprises–Research and development**

RESEARCH AND DEVELOPMENT TAX RELIEF (DEFINITION OF "SMALL OR MEDIUM-SIZED ENTERPRISE") ORDER 2005, SI 2005 3376; made under the Finance Act 2000 Sch.20 para.2; and the Finance Act 2002 Sch.12 para.2. In force: in accordance with Art.1; £3.00.

This Order amends the definitions of a "small or medium-sized enterprise" for the purposes of tax relief for expenditure in respect of research and development by such enterprises under the Finance Act 2000 and for large companies and small and medium-sized enterprises under the Finance Act 2002.

4136. **Self assessment–Notices of enquiry–Requirement for tax inspector not other officer to conduct enquiries–Scope of enquiry**

[Inland Revenue Regulation Act 1890 s.39; Taxes Management Act 1970 s.8, s.9A.]

The appellant taxpayer (B) appealed against the issue of a notice of enquiry by the respondent Inland Revenue under the Taxes Management Act 1970 s.9A and applied for a closure notice. B's tax advisor (S) had filed B's 2002 self assessment return noting that the accompanying accounts, working sheets and schedules were integral to the return. Various Inland Revenue employees sought further information on aspects relating to loan interest relief and business goodwill. A s.9A enquiry notice was issued, followed by a s.19A notice. S replied, suggesting that the respective officers had been working from computerised information and did not have the accompanying papers. B argued that (1) the initial Inland Revenue employee (D), who qualified at a grade below that of inspector, was not an "officer of the Board" as defined in the Inland Revenue Regulation Act 1890 s.39; (2) contrary to the Inland Revenue Enquiry Manual, the Inland Revenue had made piecemeal enquiries, moving from one aspect to another; (3) his "return" under s.8 of the 1970 Act was the complete paper version, not the Revenue's transcribed electronic record; (4) actions begun by an inspector could not be continued by another employee who was not an inspector.

Held, dismissing the appeal, that (1) D was an "officer" for the purposes of s.9A because s.39 of the 1890 Act referred only to an "Officer of Inland Revenue", not to inspectors or employees, and Parliament could not have intended the inconvenience of only inspectors being permitted to issue s.9A notices in relation to self assessment returns. Thus, there was no formal statutory requirement that all enquiries be issued by inspectors as such. (2) The scope of a s.9A enquiry could not be questioned because any distinction between "full" and "aspect" enquiries was a matter of administrative practice only, not a matter of law. Any remedy against the Revenue's possible failure to follow its Manual should be pursued elsewhere. (3) Because an enquiry notice could be issued on a purely random basis, it did not matter if the Inland Revenue based its decision on a computer record or a paper return. Whether there was a remedy against the Inland Revenue's failure to use information in its possession was a separate question, outside the tribunal's jurisdiction. (4) No proceedings had been commenced or administrative acts undertaken by any inspectors. (Obiter) It was desirable for the Revenue's practice and software to be changed to ensure that the computer record disclosed the existence of additional documents filed with a return.

BENSOOR v. DEVINE (INSPECTOR OF TAXES) [2005] S.T.C. (S.C.D.) 297, John Clark, Sp Comm.

4137. Shipping–Tonnage tax companies–Training commitment

TONNAGE TAX (TRAINING REQUIREMENT) (AMENDMENT) REGULATIONS 2005, SI 2005 2295; made under the Finance Act 2000 Sch.22 para.29, Sch.22 para.31, Sch.22 para.36. In force: October 1, 2005; £3.00.

These Regulations further amend the Tonnage Tax (Training Requirement) Regulations 2000 (SI 2000 2129) by increasing the amount of the payments in lieu of training. In respect of a relevant four month period falling on or after October 1, 2005 the figure by which the number of months is to be multiplied is increased from £608 to £621. In the case of a higher rate payment where there has been a failure to meet the training requirement, the basic rate to be used in the calculation is increased from £553 to £565.

4138. Special Commissioners–Appeals–Taxpayer seeking to challenge s.19A notice in further appeal

[Taxes Management Act 1970 s.19A, s.97(1).]

The appellant taxpayer (M) appealed against a Special Commissioner's dismissal of his appeal. The Inland Revenue had served a notice upon M under the Taxes Management Act 1970 s.19A requiring him to produce profit and loss accounts and balance sheets for a certain period. M objected as he claimed he did not have sufficient records to enable him to produce the documents sought. The Inland Revenue then served penalty notices under s.97(1) of the Act. M's appeal against the s.19A notice had been dismissed by the Special Commissioner. M argued that it was unlawful and incorrect to require him to produce the documents as he did not have the necessary figures available and that such requirement infringed his human rights.

Held, dismissing the appeal, that it was no longer open to M when challenging the penalty notices to object to the contents of the s.19A notice. M had challenged that notice before the Special Commissioner and s.19A provided that a Special Commissioner's determination was final and conclusive. It was not open to M to challenge the penalty notices by seeking to impugn the notice from which the penalties arose. There was nothing unlawful or incorrect about the penalty notices and there was no question of M's human rights having been infringed.

MURAT v. INLAND REVENUE COMMISSIONERS; *sub nom.* MURAT v. ORNOCH (INSPECTOR OF TAXES); R. (ON THE APPLICATION OF MURAT) v.

INLAND REVENUE COMMISSIONERS, [2004] EWHC 3123, [2005] S.T.C. 184, Moses, J., QBD (Admin).

4139. Special Commissioners—Child trust funds—Appeals

SPECIAL COMMISSIONERS (JURISDICTION AND PROCEDURE) (AMENDMENT) REGULATIONS 2005, SI 2005 341; made under the Taxes Management Act 1970 s.56B. In force: March 14, 2005; £3.00.

These Regulations amend the Special Commissioners (Jurisdiction and Procedure) Regulations 1994 (SI 1994 1811) to include appeals under regulations made under the Child Trust Funds Act 2004 s.13 or appeals made under s.22 of that Act within the definition of "proceedings".

4140. Special Commissioners—Hearings—Costs—Failure to explain assessment—Meaning of "wholly unreasonable" behaviour

[Income and Corporation Taxes Act 1988 s.19(1), s.154; Special Commissioners (Jurisdiction and Procedure) Regulations 1994 (SI 1994 1811) Reg.21 (1).]

The applicant taxpayers (C and X), whose appeal against a decision of the respondent Revenue had been partly allowed, sought the costs of that hearing. The Revenue had considered that payments made by C's company X for legal services were taxable as either emoluments or benefits in kind. Accordingly, they would be chargeable against, respectively, either X under the Income and Corporation Taxes Act 1988 s.19(1) or C under s.154. The Revenue issued a decision notice requiring a sum for Class 1 national insurance contributions. C and X appealed, and seven days before the hearing the Revenue indicated that it was not pursuing the emoluments argument under s.19(1), and consequently there would be no Class 1 NIC charge on X. The appeal was, therefore, allowed on that ground, but was subsequently dismissed on the other arguments. C contended that the Revenue, in failing to explain the basis of the NIC liability and then abandoning the emoluments argument just before the hearing, had acted wholly unreasonably and was liable for costs.

Held, refusing the application, that for costs to be awarded under the Special Commissioners (Jurisdiction and Procedure) Regulations 1994 Reg.21 (1) against any party to proceedings, that party had to have acted "wholly unreasonably", and that was a very exacting standard. The Revenue could, without being wholly unreasonable, raise alternative grounds for pursuing a taxpayer for unpaid tax and then withdraw those grounds after being convinced by the taxpayer's arguments that they were without merit. The Revenue accepted that it could have explained its thinking more clearly, but that lack of effort was not wholly unreasonable.

XI SOFTWARE LTD v. LAING (INSPECTOR OF TAXES) (COSTS); *sub nom.* COLLINS v. LAING (INSPECTOR OF TAXES) (COSTS) [2005] S.T.C. (S.C.D.) 453, K Khan, Sp Comm.

4141. Stamp duties—Stamp duty land tax

STAMP DUTY LAND TAX (CONSEQUENTIAL AMENDMENT OF ENACTMENTS) REGULATIONS 2005, SI 2005 82; made under the Finance Act 2003 s.123. In force: February 11, 2005; £3.00.

These Regulations amend the National Health Service and Community Care Act 1990 and the Finance Act 1994 to make amendments consequent upon the introduction of stamp duty land tax. In this respect they replace provision made in respect of the treatment of NHS trusts by the Stamp Duty Land Tax (Consequential Amendment of Enactments) Regulations 2003 (SI 2003 2687). They also make provision for the disclosure of information to the Commissioner of Valuation for Northern Ireland.

4142. Stamp duties–Stamp duty reserve tax–Exemptions

STAMP DUTY AND STAMP DUTY RESERVE TAX (EXTENSION OF EXCEPTIONS RELATING TO RECOGNISED EXCHANGES) REGULATIONS 2005, SI 2005 1990; made under the Finance (No.2) Act 2005 s.50. In force: August 11, 2005; £3.00.

These Regulations extend the stamp duty and stamp duty reserve tax exemptions for sales of stock to intermediaries and for repurchase and stock lending to the multilateral trading facilities known as the Alternative Investment Market, OFEX and POSIT, operated by Investment Technology Ltd. They provide for the extended application of the Finance Act 1986 s.80A, s.80C, s.88A and s.89AA.

4143. Stamp duty land tax–Electronic communications

STAMP DUTY LAND TAX (ELECTRONIC COMMUNICATIONS) REGULATIONS 2005, SI 2005 844; made under the Finance Act 1999 s.132, s.133. In force: April 11, 2005; £3.00.

These Regulations provide for the electronic delivery of certain types of information to or by the Commissioner of Inland Revenue.

4144. Stamp duty land tax–Interest rates

TAXES (INTEREST RATE) (AMENDMENT) REGULATIONS 2005, SI 2005 2462; made under the Finance Act 1989 s.178. In force: September 26, 2005; £3.00.

These Regulations amend the Taxes (Interest Rate) Regulations 1989 (SI 1989 1297) to add provisions about interest rates in connection with stamp duty land tax, chargeable under the Finance Act 2003 Part 4.

4145. Stamp duty land tax–Prescribed persons–Exemptions

FINANCE ACT 2003, SECTION 66 (PRESCRIBED PERSONS) ORDER 2005, SI 2005 83; made under the Finance Act 2003 s.66. In force: February 11, 2005; £3.00.

This Order prescribes NHS foundation trusts for the purposes of the exemptions from stamp duty land tax conferred by the Finance Act 2003 s.66.

4146. Stamp duty land tax–Prescribed persons–Exemptions

FINANCE ACT 2003, SECTION 66 (PRESCRIBED TRANSACTIONS) ORDER 2005, SI 2005 645; made under the Finance Act 2003 s.66. In force: April 1, 2005; £3.00.

This Order exempts, from the charge to stamp duty land tax, land transactions which are effected under the Energy Act 2004 s.38 if either the purchaser or the vendor is a public body within the meaning of the Finance Act 2003 s.66.

4147. Tax–General insurance reserves

GENERAL INSURANCE RESERVES (TAX) (AMENDMENT) REGULATIONS 2005, SI 2005 3289; made under the Finance Act 2000 s.107. In force: December 21, 2005; £3.00.

These Regulations amends the General Insurance Reserves (Tax) Regulations 2001 (SI 2001 1757) which contain the main rules on computation of the amount of reserves under the Finance Act 2000. The Regulations specify rules to determine which currencies are to be used in calculations required under those Regulations.

4148. Tax credits–Child care providers–Approval

TAX CREDITS (APPROVAL OF CHILD CARE PROVIDERS) SCHEME 2005, SI 2005 93; made under the Tax Credits Act 2002 s.12, s.65. In force: April 6, 2005; £3.00.

This Scheme, which revokes with savings the Tax Credit (Approval of Home Child Care Providers) Scheme 2003 (SI 2003 463), provides for the approval of child care providers for the purposes of the Tax Credits Act 2002 s.12(5). It provides for the approval body to operate a system for the determination of applications for approval; for the approval body to provide information to the Commissioners of Inland Revenue in order to enable them to discharge their functions relating to working tax credit; for the period of validity of an approval; for the right to appeal against the refusal or withdrawal of approval; and for the charging of fees by the approval body.

4149. Tax credits–Child tax credit–Transitional provisions

TAX CREDITS ACT 2002 (TRANSITIONAL PROVISIONS) ORDER 2005, SI 2005 773; made under the Tax Credits Act 2002 s.62. In force: March 17, 2005; £3.00.

This Order makes transitional provisions in connection with the commencement of the abolition of the amounts referred to in the Tax Credits Act 2002 s.1 (3) (d) which comes into force on December 31, 2006 by virtue of the Tax Credits 2002 (Commencement No.4, Transitional and Savings) Order 2003 (SI 2003 962). The Regulations provide that a specified person is treated as making a claim, or a joint claim if he is a member of a married or unmarried couple or a polygamous unit, for a child tax credit on a specified date; define "specified person"; specify the period of the award as the period beginning with the later of on the the specified date and the date on which the Board notify the Department for Work and Pensions of an award of child tax credit, on which date the child premia will cease to be paid, and ending at the end of the tax year in which that date falls; and make provision in relation to existing recipients of the child premia to avoid duplication of payments.

4150. Tax credits–Child tax credit–Transitional provisions

TAX CREDITS ACT 2002 (TRANSITIONAL PROVISIONS) (NO.2) ORDER 2005, SI 2005 776; made under the Tax Credits Act 2002 s.62. In force: March 17, 2005; £3.00.

This Order makes transitional provisions in connection with the commencement of the abolition of the amounts referred to in the Tax Credits Act 2002 s.1 (3) (d) (the child premia in respect of income support or income based jobseekers allowance) which comes into force on December 31, 2006 by virtue of the Tax Credits 2002 (Commencement No.4 Transitional and Savings) Order 2003 (SI 2003 962). It makes provision in relation to existing recipients of the child premia to avoid duplication of payments.

4151. Tax credits–Civil partnerships

TAX CREDITS NOTIFICATION OF CHANGES OF CIRCUMSTANCES (CIVIL PARTNERSHIP) (TRANSITIONAL PROVISIONS) ORDER 2005, SI 2005 828; made under the Civil Partnership Act 2004 s.259. In force: April 8, 2005; £3.00.

This Order is made in consequence to the amendments to be made to the Tax Credits Act 2002 by the Civil Partnership Act 2004. It provides that where two people of the same sex are treated as a couple a change of circumstances is treated as having occurred for the purposes of s.6. Consequently, if one or both of those people have claimed a tax credit, Regulations made under the Tax Credits Act 2002 s.6 may require notification to be given of this change of circumstances.

4152. Tax credits–Employment and training–Provision of information

TAX CREDITS (PROVISION OF INFORMATION) (FUNCTION RELATING TO EMPLOYMENT AND TRAINING) REGULATIONS 2005, SI 2005 66; made under the Tax Credits Act 2002 s.65, s.67, Sch.5 para.5. In force: February 8, 2005; £3.00.

The Tax Credits Act 2002 enables information relating to tax credits, child benefit or guardian's allowance to be provided by the Board of Inland Revenue to the Secretary of State or the Department for Employment and Learning in Northern Ireland for the purposes of such functions relating to employment and training as may be prescribed. These Regulations prescribe the function relating to employment and training.

4153. Tax credits–Up rating

TAX CREDITS UP-RATING REGULATIONS 2005, SI 2005 681; made under the Tax Credits Act 2002 s.7, s.9, s.11, s.13, s.65. In force: April 6, 2005; £3.00.

These Regulations amend the Child Tax Credit Regulations 2002 (SI 2002 2007) by increasing the maximum rate of the elements of a child tax credit; the Working Tax Credit (Entitlement and Maximum Rate) Regulations 2002 (SI 2002 2005) by substituting a new Table prescribing the maximum rates for the elements of working tax credit other than the child care element; and by increasing the first income thresholds for those entitled to working tax credit and child tax credit of the Tax Credits (Income Thresholds and Determination of Rates) Regulations 2002 (SI 2002 2008).

4154. Tax credits–Working tax credit–Childcare

WORKING TAX CREDIT (ENTITLEMENT AND MAXIMUM RATE) (AMENDMENT) REGULATIONS 2005, SI 2005 769; made under the Tax Credits Act 2002 s.12, s.65. In force: April 6, 2005; £3.00.

These Regulations amend the Working Tax Credit (Entitlement and Maximum Rate) Regulations 2002 (SI 2002 2005) in respect of the child care element of Working Tax Credit. They extend the definition of child care for the purposes of the child care element of the Working Tax Credit to include care provided in accordance with the Tax Credits (Approval of Child Care Providers) Scheme 2005 (SI 2005 93); while where that extended definition of child care applies, excluding care in a relative's home, provided by a relative of the child, where that person only provides care for children of relatives or for his or her own children.

4155. Tax Credits Act 2002 (c.21)–Commencement No.4, Transitional Provisions and Savings Amendment Order

TAX CREDITS ACT 2002 (COMMENCEMENT NO.4, TRANSITIONAL PROVISIONS AND SAVINGS) (AMENDMENT) ORDER 2005, SI 2005 1106 (C.45); made under the Tax Credits Act 2002 s.61. Commencement details: bringing into force various provisions of the 2002 Act on April 5, 2005; £3.00.

This Order amends the Tax Credits Act 2002 (Commencement No.4, Transitional Provisions and Savings) Order 2003 (SI 2003 962) which provided for the abolition of the amounts referred to in the Tax Credits Act 2002 s.1(3)(d) (the child premia in respect of income support or income based jobseeker's allowance) on April 6, 2005. This Order amends that date to December 31, 2006.

4156. Tax planning–Company management–Common law test of central management and control

[Taxation of Chargeable Gains Act 1992 s.13, s.165; Finance Act 1994 s.249; UK/Netherlands Double Tax Convention Art.4.]

The appellant husband and wife (W) appealed against the dismissal of their appeal against an assessment to capital gains tax (CGT). W owned most of the shares in a successful company which they wished to sell. As part of a scheme to avoid CGT on part of the gain referable to a sale of the company, W gifted their shares to a new holding company and held over the gain under the Taxation of

Chargeable Gains Act 1992 s.165. W and a trust established by them owned 51 per cent of the shares in the new holding company and 49 per cent were owned by a British Virgin Islands company (CIL). CIL sold its 49 per cent holding to a Dutch subsidiary (Eulalia), which then sold those shares to the outside purchaser when the business was disposed of. W's advisers thought that no gain would arise on the disposal of the shares by CIL to Eulalia since it was a disposal between the members of a non resident group. The Inland Revenue assessed W to capital gains tax on the basis that, although CIL was resident outside the United Kingdom, Eulalia was resident in the UK, with the result that CIL's gain was attributable to W who were liable to capital gains tax under s.13 of the 1992 Act. The Special Commissioners dismissed W's appeal.

Held, allowing the appeal, that (1) on a proper application of the law to the facts, the only tenable conclusion for the Special Commissioners to have reached was that under the common law of corporate residence Eulalia was resident in the Netherlands. (2) There was no realistic difference between CIL and Eulalia in respect of whether they were resident in the UK at the time. Both companies were established or acquired abroad in order to implement particular parts of the wider tax saving scheme. Both were managed in the offices of overseas financial organisations. The Inland Revenue asserted that CIL was resident outside the UK and could not credibly assert that Eulalia was not. (3) The legal formalities such as the meetings approving the transaction and the signing of the documents were carried out by Eulalia abroad. It was possible for a company to be centrally controlled and managed in one jurisdiction and to carry out the legal formalities of a transaction in a different jurisdiction, but there was no evidence in the instant case that central management and control was in the first jurisdiction and not in the second. (4) Before mid July 1996 when Eulalia came into the scheme as a participant it could only have been resident in the Netherlands, and it was incumbent on the Inland Revenue to produce some evidence to show that there had then been a change of residence but it produced none. The purchase of Eulalia's shares by CIL did not of itself entail a change of residence. Further, CIL was itself resident out of the UK. (5) CIL and Eulalia's participation in the scheme was in itself no indication that they had become UK resident. Companies established in overseas jurisdictions to carry out some element in a wider scheme or business structure did not fail to be resident in their own jurisdictions merely because they were part of the scheme, *Untelrab Ltd v. McGregor* [1996] STC (SCD) 1 considered. (6) The burden on the appeal to the Special Commissioners was on W to show that Eulalia was not resident in the UK but in the Netherlands. W showed that Eulalia was incorporated in the Netherlands and was resident there until acquired by CIL, that CIL was non resident and that Eulalia was managed by a Dutch company in Amsterdam. In the circumstances the burden passed to the Inland Revenue to produce material to show that Eulalia was actually resident in the UK by showing where the management was situated. (7) The acts of management and control of Eulalia consisting of making board resolutions and signing documents took place in the Netherlands and that was where the company was resident. On the evidence Eulalia was not merely going through the motions of passing resolutions and signing documents but took effective decisions itself, even if it was guided and influenced by decisions taken by W and by the accountants who devised the scheme. (8) If Eulalia was not resident in the Netherlands under the common law test, it was resident there by virtue of the provisions of the Finance Act 1994 s.249 and because it was regarded as resident in the Netherlands by the Netherlands tax authorities and its place of effective management was situated there for the purposes of the UK/Netherlands Double Tax Convention Art.4.

WOOD v. HOLDEN (INSPECTOR OF TAXES); *sub nom.* R v. HOLDEN (INSPECTOR OF TAXES), [2005] EWHC 547, [2005] S.T.C. 789, Park, J., Ch D.

4157. Tax planning–Confidentiality orders–Anonymity of tax payer in court proceedings–New Zealand

[Bill of Rights Act 1990 (New Zealand) s.14.]

The appellant taxpayers (M) appealed against the discharge of confidentiality orders made in connection with taxation litigation. M was part of a group of taxpayers involved in a scheme which the Inland Revenue of New Zealand considered to be a tax avoidance scheme. The taxpayers filed challenges in the Taxation Review Authority and the Revenue designated M's challenges as test cases. The test cases were transferred to the High Court and confidentiality orders were made in favour of M. Those orders were later discharged on the application of the Revenue as the judge concluded that M had failed to provide evidence to counterbalance the principle of open justice. M argued that (1) the judge had been wrong to take the view that tax cases were subject to ordinary principles of open justice; (2) they had been subject to unacceptable unfairness as those taxpayers whose cases had not been transferred to the High Court, and whose behaviour had been identical, retained the benefit of anonymity in the Taxation Review Authority proceedings.

Held, dismissing the appeal, that (1) tax cases were subject to the ordinary principles of open justice. Taxpayer information might properly be treated as confidential but such matters had to be assessed in the context of open justice principles. Open justice considerations were reinforced by the Bill of Rights Act 1990 (New Zealand) s.14. Whilst each case had to be addressed on its merits, the drift of cases was increasingly towards open justice and against confidentiality, *Erris Promotions Ltd v. Inland Revenue Commissioner* 6 I.T.L. Rep. 364 considered. Tax cases in the High Court were dealt with in the same way as ordinary litigation. It was not the case therefore that all tax disputes heard in the High Court ought presumptively to be subject to confidentiality. (2) Given the legitimate public interest in full reporting of the instant litigation, the fact that other litigants had secured anonymity through procedural accident was not decisive.

MUIR v. INLAND REVENUE COMMISSIONER 7 I.T.L. Rep. 324, McGrath, J., CA (NZ).

4158. Tax planning–Corporation tax–Cross option tax avoidance scheme–Composite transactions

[Finance Act 1994 s.147, s.150A(1).]

The Inland Revenue appealed against a decision ([2003] S.T.C. 1035, [2003] C.L.Y. 4185) that a loss was allowable for corporation tax purposes under a "cross option" tax avoidance scheme entered into between a bank and the respondent (S). The bank had devised the scheme to take advantage of a prospective legislative change to the system for taxing gains on options to buy or sell bonds and gilts. Under the proposed change, all returns on such options would be treated as income, and losses made on disposals would be allowable as income losses. The scheme devised by the bank involved S granting the bank an option to buy short dated gilts, at a price below their market price, in return for a correspondingly large premium which would not be taxable under the old regime. After the new regime came into force, the bank would exercise the option, causing S to sell the gilts at well below market price thereby suffering an allowable loss. To avoid the risk of a rise or fall in interest rates during the currency of the option, the scheme provided for the bank's option to be matched by an option to buy the same amount of gilts granted by the bank to S. Premium and option price had been calculated to ensure that movements of money between the bank and S added up to the same amount, less the bank's fee. S claimed that the exercise of the options had given rise to an overall loss. However, the Revenue had assessed S to corporation tax on the basis that the loss was not allowable. The Revenue submitted that S could not treat the loss as an income loss because the bank's option was part of a larger self cancelling scheme; the bank did not have an "entitlement" to gilts for the purposes of the Finance Act 1994 s.150A(1); and there was no qualifying contract within s.147 of the Act. S relied upon the special commissioners' finding of fact that there was an outside, but commercially real, possibility that the options would not be exercised so as to cancel each other out, and that therefore the Revenue could not treat them as a single transaction.

Held, allowing the appeal, that the language of a taxing statute would often have to be given a wide practical meaning, which required the court to have regard to the whole of a series of transactions which were intended to have a commercial unity, *WT Ramsay Ltd v. Inland Revenue Commissioners* [1982] A.C. 300, [1981] C.L.Y. 1385 applied. Any uncertainty as to whether the cross options would not both be exercised arose from the fact that the parties had chosen to fix the strike price for S's option at a level which gave rise to an outside chance that the option would not be exercised. Thus the contingency upon which S relied for saying that there was no composite transaction was a part of that composite transaction, chosen not for any commercial reason but solely to enable S to claim that there was no composite transaction. It was true that it created a real commercial risk, but the odds were favourable enough to make it a risk which the parties were willing to accept in the interests of the scheme. It would destroy the value of the *Ramsay* principle if the effect of composite transactions had to be disregarded simply because the parties had deliberately included a commercially irrelevant contingency, creating an acceptable risk that the scheme might not work as planned. The composite effect of such a scheme should be considered as it was intended to operate and without regard to the possibility that, contrary to the intention and expectations of the parties, it might not work as planned. The special commissioners had erred in law in concluding that their finding that there was a realistic possibility of the options not being exercised simultaneously meant, without more, that the scheme could not be regarded as a single composite transaction. It was a single composite transaction and created no entitlement to gilts; there was therefore no qualifying contract within s.147 of the Act and no income loss.

SCOTTISH PROVIDENT INSTITUTION v. INLAND REVENUE COMMISSIONERS; *sub nom.* INLAND REVENUE COMMISSIONERS v. SCOTTISH PROVIDENT INSTITUTION, [2004] UKHL 52, [2004] 1 W.L.R. 3172, Lord Nicholls of Birkenhead, HL.

4159. Tax planning–Input tax–Deferred payments–Goods and services tax–New Zealand

[Goods and Services Tax Act 1985 (New Zealand) s.76.]

The appellant taxpayer (C), a New Zealand company registered for goods and services tax (GST) on an invoice basis, appealed against a decision of the respondent Commissioner to disallow its claim for GST tax credits. C had purchased plots of land from 114 companies, all of which had the same sole director. The companies had all issued invoices to C for the land but in each case payment had been deferred for between 10 and 20 years. The companies were registered to pay GST only when payment had been received. C claimed credit for GST on the companies' invoices. The Commissioner disallowed C's claim on the ground that it amounted to tax avoidance within the definition of the Goods and Services Tax Act 1985 (New Zealand) s.76. His decision was upheld on appeal to the Taxation Review Authority (the authority), which found that the scheme had been intended to defeat the intent and application of the Act. In the instant appeal, C argued that (1) the scheme had followed the letter of the Act and therefore could not be said to be contrary to it; (2) there was no evidence of a tax advantage to C and the authority had been wrong to find a subjective intention to avoid tax.

Held, dismissing the appeal, that (1) the Commissioner's decision had been correct. Section 76 of the Act was by its nature intended to have effect even where the Act as a whole had been complied with in order to defeat schemes that sought out loopholes or found ways of circumventing the rules, *Inland Revenue Commissioner v. BNZ Investments Ltd* [2002] 1 N.Z.L.R. 450 and *Inland Revenue Commissioner v. Auckland Harbour Board* [2001] UKPC 1, [2001] S.T.C. 130, [2001] C.L.Y. 5275 considered. It was therefore irrelevant that the scheme did not contravene any other part of the Act. (2) There was no requirement in s.76 that a tax advantage be proved. The authority had erred in holding that there needed to be evidence of subjective intention. The test was an objective one, which had been made out in the instant case since the scheme offended against the fundamental purpose of the Act, namely that a balance be achieved between a taxpayer's input and output tax and that there be no great delay between input and output relating to a particular supply in the context of accounting for GST.

CH'ELLE PROPERTIES (NZ) LTD v. INLAND REVENUE COMMISSIONER 7 I.T.L. Rep. 33, Rodney Hansen, J., HC (NZ).

4160. Tax planning–Stamp duty land tax–Avoidance schemes–Information

TAX AVOIDANCE SCHEMES (INFORMATION) (AMENDMENT) REGULATIONS 2005, SI 2005 1869; made under the Finance Act 2004 s.308, s.309, s.310, s.318. In force: August 1, 2005; £3.00.

These Regulations, which amend the Tax Avoidance Schemes (Information) Regulations 2004 (SI 2004 1864), prescribe the information which is to be given to HM Revenue and Customs under the Finance Act 2004 Part 7 in respect of stamp duty land tax.

4161. Tax planning–Stamp duty land tax–Avoidance schemes–Prescribed arrangements

STAMP DUTY LAND TAX AVOIDANCE SCHEMES (PRESCRIBED DESCRIPTIONS OF ARRANGEMENTS) REGULATIONS 2005, SI 2005 1868; made under the Finance Act 2004 s.306, s.318. In force: August 1, 2005; £3.00.

These Regulations prescribe arrangements which enable or might be expected to enable any person to obtain a tax advantage in relation to stamp duty land tax, and which a promoter is required to notify to the Inland Revenue.

4162. Taxation administration–Administrative machinery–Lloyd's underwriters

LLOYD'S UNDERWRITERS (TAX) REGULATIONS 2005, SI 2005 3338; made under the Finance Act 1993 s.182, s.184; the Finance Act 1994 s.229, s.230; the Finance Act 1999 s.132, s.133; and the Finance Act (No.2) Act 2005 s.45. In force: December 27, 2005; £3.00.

These Regulations amend the Finance Act 1993, the Lloyd's Underwriters (Tax) Regulations 1995 (SI 1995 351), the Income and Corporation Taxes (Electronic Communications) Regulations 2003 (SI 2003 282) and the Income Tax (Trading and Other Income) Act 2005. They provide administrative machinery for Lloyd's managing agents to make returns of syndicates' profits and losses for tax purposes, and for assessment and collection of tax.

4163. Taxation administration–Documents

ORDERS FOR THE DELIVERY OF DOCUMENTS (PROCEDURE) (AMENDMENT) REGULATIONS 2005, SI 2005 1131; made under the Taxes Management Act 1970 Sch.1AA para.2. In force: April 18, 2005; £3.00.

These Regulations amend the Orders for the Delivery of Documents (Procedure) Regulations 2000 (SI 2000 2875) in consequence of the transfer of the functions of the Board of Inland Revenue to Her Majesty's Revenue and Customs by the Commissioners for Revenue and Customs Act 2005.

4164. Taxation administration–Fixed penalty offences–Failure to comply with notice to produce documents–Infringement of taxpayer's human rights by imposition of criminal charge

[Taxes Management Act 1970 s.97AA (1) (a); Human Rights Act 1998 Sch.1 Part I Art.6.]

The appellant taxpayer (S) appealed against a penalty imposed by the respondent Inland Revenue in the sum of £50 under the Taxes Management Act 1970 s.97AA (1) (a) for failing to comply with a s.19A notice of enquiry. S had not appealed against the s.19A notice and the Inland Revenue had deducted the penalty from a payment to S. There was no suggestion of criminal evasion or errors by S. S argued that his rights under the Human Rights Act 1998 Sch.1 Part.I Art.6 had been breached because (1) the fixed penalty and the threat of a further daily penalty of £150 involved criminal charges; (2) he had been unable to obtain Criminal Defence Service funding for legal representation and the Inland Revenue had unreasonably delayed its response to his complaints; (3) the fixed penalty infringed S's right to silence and not to incriminate himself; (4) the penalty should not have been deducted before his appeal.

Held, dismissing the appeal, that (1) the imposition of the fixed penalty did not amount to a criminal charge under Art.6(1) because the domestic classification of the penalty was civil, the offence was regulatory and did not impute dishonesty and the penalty was in no sense severe, *Engel v. Netherlands (A/22)* (1979-80) 1 E.H.R.R. 647 applied. That classification was not affected by the future possibility of a daily penalty, which was not severe enough to make it criminal under Art.6. (2) The non availability of funding for representation and the Inland Revenue's delay in responding were not within the tribunal's jurisdiction. (3) The fixed penalty did not conflict with S's right to silence because there was no evidence that prosecutions or penalties involving criminal proceedings under Art.6(1) were contemplated, *Funke v. France (A/256-A)* [1993] 1 C.M.L.R. 897, [1994] C.L.Y. 2431 applied. Even if the fixed penalty had conflicted with S's right to silence, no remedy was available in the appeal. (4) While the deduction of the penalty was not within the tribunal's jurisdiction, S could have applied for a postponement and there was no suggestion of self incrimination as the purpose of the enquiry was merely to assess S's tax liability, *Murat v. Inland Revenue Commissioners* [2004] EWHC 3123, [2005] S.T.C. 184, [2005] 5 C.L. 544 considered.

SHARKEY v. DE CROSS (INSPECTOR OF TAXES); *sub nom.* SHARKEY v. DE CROOS (INSPECTOR OF TAXES) [2005] S.T.C. (S.C.D.) 336, Theodore Wallace, Sp Comm.

4165. Taxation administration—Search and seizure—Legal professional privilege—Examination of documents and emails obtained in tax fraud investigation—Australia

[Income Tax Assessment Act (Australia) s.263(1).]

J appealed against a decision reviewing the exercise of the Australian Tax Office's powers of search and seizure under the Income Tax Assessment Act (Australia) s.263(1). Acting in pursuit of those powers, ATO officers had raided two offices belonging to J in the course of a tax fraud investigation. During the search, large quantities of documents and emails were copied, computer files were searched and J's staff were refused access to the premises. J contended that ATO had copied material subject to legal professional privilege and that the search had been conducted in an illegal manner.

Held, allowing the appeal, that privilege was not infringed where privileged documents were taken and later returned unread and it could be permitted for such documents to be examined before a decision was made to copy them. However, s.263(1) did not permit the wholesale removal of documents from J's premises without consent. Documents could be removed if there was a reasonable belief that they could be used in evidence, as long as they were returned promptly once eliminated for this purpose. It was not permitted to copy large numbers of emails without first examining them and they should either be returned to J or destroyed, *Reynolds v. Commissioner of Police of the Metropolis* [1985] Q.B. 881, [1984] C.L.Y. 2533 applied.

JMA ACCOUNTING PTY LTD v. CARMODY (COMMISSIONER OF TAXATION) 7 I.T.L. Rep. 274, Spender, J., Fed Ct (Aus) (Full Ct).

4166. Taxation administration—Stamp duty land tax

STAMP DUTY LAND TAX (ADMINISTRATION) (AMENDMENT) REGULATIONS 2005, SI 2005 1132; made under the Finance Act 2003 s.113, Sch.13 para.32, Sch.13 para.36, Sch.13 para.37. In force: April 18, 2005; £3.00.

These Regulations amend the Stamp Duty Land Tax (Administration) Regulations 2003 (SI 2003 2837) in consequence of the transfer of the functions of the Board of Inland Revenue to the Commissioners for Her Majesty's Revenue and Customs by the Commissioners for Revenue and Customs Act 2005.

4167. Tonnage tax—Elections—Extended period

TONNAGE TAX (FURTHER OPPORTUNITY FOR ELECTION) ORDER 2005, SI 2005 1449; made under the Finance Act 2000 Sch.22 para.11. In force: July 1, 2005; £3.00.

This Order provides a further opportunity for the making of tonnage tax elections under the Finance Act 2000 Sch.22. It provides a further period during which tonnage tax elections may be made and adapts Sch.22 where a tonnage tax election is made by virtue of Art.2 of this Order.

4168. Tonnage tax—Ships—Disapplication

TONNAGE TAX (EXCEPTION OF FINANCIAL YEAR 2005) ORDER 2005, SI 2005 1480; made under the Finance Act 2000 Sch.22 para.22B. In force: July 1, 2005; £3.00.

This Order disapplies the Finance Act 2000 Sch.22 para.22A for the financial year 2005 which would otherwise have effect from June 30, 2005. The Finance Act 2005 introduced (to comply with European Community guidelines on State aid to maritime transport) a general requirement that ships entering the Tonnage Tax regime in future should be Community-flagged. The Finance Act 2000 Sch.22 para.22B(2) gives the Treasury power to disapply that rule on a year-by-year basis (subject to certain conditions for the financial year 2006 onwards). This Order accordingly disapplies that rule for financial year 2005.

4169. Working tax credit—Payment by employers

TAX CREDIT (PAYMENT BY EMPLOYERS, ETC.) (AMENDMENT) REGULATIONS 2005, SI 2005 2200; made under the Tax Credits Act 2000 s.24, s.25, s.65, s.67. In force: August 29, 2005; £3.00.

These Regulations amend the Working Tax Credit (Payment by Employers) Regulations 2002 (SI 2002 2172) and the Tax Credits (Payments by the Board) Regulations 2002 (SI 2002 2173) so that from November 7, 2005, all new claimants of working tax credit, and from April 1, 2006, all existing claimants of working tax credit, will be paid directly by the Commissioners for Her Majesty's Revenue and Customs rather than via employers. They also contain amendments to terminology in consequence of the transfer of the function of the Board of Inland Revenue to Her Majesty's Revenue and Customs by the Commissioners for Revenue and Customs Act 2005.

4170. Books

Anstey, Sharon; McKie, Simon—Tolley's Estate Planning. Paperback: £95.95. ISBN 0 7545 2862 6. Tolley Publishing.

Blazek, Jody—IRS Form 1023: Tax Preparation Guide for Nonprofits. Paperback: £22.95. ISBN 0 471 71525 5. John Wiley & Sons Inc.

Brennan, Philip—Tax Acts. Paperback: £56.66. ISBN 1 84592 141 0. Tottel Publishing.

Buckley, Michael—Buckley Capital Tax Acts. Paperback: £53.33. ISBN 1 84592 096 1. Tottel Publishing.

Burrows, Rita; Gravestock, Peter; Homer, Arnold—Tolley's Taxwise II. Paperback: £55.00. ISBN 0 7545 2877 4. Tolley Publishing.

Burrows, Rita; Homer, Arnold—Tolley'sTaxwise I (Revised Ed). Paperback: £61.00. ISBN 0 7545 2876 6. Tolley Publishing.

Campbell, Dennis—International Taxation of Low-Tax Transactions-Low-Tax Jurisdictions-Volume I. Paperback: £12.44. ISBN 1 4116 5028 X. Lulu Press Incorporated.

Campbell, Dennis—International Taxation of Low-Tax Transactions-High-Tax Jurisdictions-Volume I. Paperback: £44.33. ISBN 1 4116 5024 7. Lulu Press Incorporated.

Campbell, Dennis—International Taxation of Low-Tax Transactions-Low-Tax Jurisdictions-Volume II. Paperback: £44.82. ISBN 1 4116 5027 1. Lulu Press Incorporated.

Cannon, Patrick—Tolley's StampTaxes. Paperback: £99.00. ISBN 0 7545 2888 X. Tolley Publishing.

Chamberlain, Emma; Whitehouse, Chris—Pre-Owned Assets and Tax Planning Strategies: Capital Tax Planning in the New Era. Paperback: £129.00. ISBN 0 421 91730 X. Sweet & Maxwell.

Chidell, Ray; Sampson, Alison—Tolley's Tax Checklists. Looseleaf/ring bound: £79.00. ISBN 0 7545 0823 4. LexisNexis UK.

Chiltern's Orange Tax Guide. Paperback: £62.00. ISBN 1 4057 0742 9. Tolley Publishing.

Chiltern's Yellow Tax Guide. Paperback: £92.95. ISBN 1 4057 0743 7. Tolley Publishing.

Clarke, Giles—Offshore Tax Planning. Paperback: £120.00. ISBN 1 4057 0755 0. Tolley Publishing.

Collison, David; Tiley, John—Tiley and Collison's UK Tax Guide. Paperback: £99.00. ISBN 1 4057 0753 4. Tolley Publishing.

Douglas, Jane—Property Transactions: Stamp Duty Land Tax. Hardback: £79.00. ISBN 0 421 90310 4. Sweet & Maxwell.

Ferrier, Ian; Hutton, Matthew—Tolley's UK Taxation of Trusts. Paperback: £82.95. ISBN 0 7545 2891 X. Tolley Publishing.

Flint, Andrew; Walton, Kevin—Tolley's Capital GainsTax: Budget Edition and Main Annual. Paperback: £94.95. ISBN 0 7545 2858 8. Tolley Publishing.

Furchtgott-Roth, Diana—Tough Act to Follow?: The Real Reason Why the Telecommunications Act of 1996 Was a Failure. Hardback: £19.95. ISBN 0 8447 4235 X. The AEI Press.

Garrison, John C.—New Income Tax Scandal. Paperback: £14.00. ISBN 1 4134 9544 3. Xlibris Corporation.

Golding, Jon—Tolley's InheritanceTax. Paperback: £74.99. ISBN 0 7545 2865 0. Tolley Publishing.

Gormley, Laurence W.—EU Taxation Law. Hardback: £75.00. ISBN 1 904501 55 9. Richmond Law & Tax.

Hickey, Julian—Understanding Private Client Taxation. Paperback: £49.95. ISBN 1 85328 926 4. Law Society Publications.

Hoffman, Richard—Tax Planning and Compliance for Tax-Exempt Organizations. Paperback: £36.50. ISBN 0 471 67990 9. John Wiley & Sons Inc.

Hopkins, Bruce R.—Law of Tax-Exempt Organizations. Paperback: £50.50. ISBN 0 471 67988 7. John Wiley & Sons Inc.

Hutton, Matthew—Stamp Duty Land Tax. Paperback: £65.00. ISBN 1 84592 122 4. Tottel Publishing.

Hyatt, Thomas K.; Hopkins, Bruce R.—Law of Tax-Exempt Healthcare Organizations. Paperback: £44.50. ISBN 0 471 67987 9. John Wiley & Sons Inc.

Jacksack, Susan M.; Gada, Paul N.—CCH ToolkitTax Guide. CCH Business Owner's Toolkit S. Paperback: £15.50. ISBN 0 8080 1113 8. CCH Inc.

James, Malcolm—UK Tax System: An Introduction. Paperback: £39.95. ISBN 1 904905 22 6. Spiramus Press.

Lawley, Duard—Common SenseTax Reform. Paperback: £8.99. ISBN 1 4208 8312 7. AuthorHouse.

Lenehan, Orla—Taxation in the Republic of Ireland. Paperback: £66.66. ISBN 1 84592 143 7. Tottel Publishing.

Maas, Robert—Tottel's Taxation of Employments. Paperback: £74.95. ISBN 1 84592 014 7. Tottel Publishing.

Maas, Robert–Tottel's Property Taxes. Paperback: £75.95. ISBN 1 84592 198 4. Tottel Publishing.
Matthews, Jan; Eastaway, Nigel–Tottel's Self-Assessment. Paperback: £78.99. ISBN1 84592 005 8. Paperback: £78.99. ISBN1 84592 180 1. Tottel Publishing.
Matthews, Jan; Eastway, Nigel; Vallat, Richard–Corporation Tax Self-Assessment. Paperback: £78.95. ISBN 1 84592 035 X. Tottel Publishing.
McCutcheon, Barry D.; Hallam, Murray–McCutcheon on Inheritance Tax. Hardback: £195.00. ISBN 0 421 85860 5. Sweet & Maxwell.
Moore, Alan–Tax Magic. Hardback: £52.00. ISBN 1 905320 00 0. Alan Moore.
Nicholson, Dawn–Tottel's Tax Savers Guide. Paperback: £9.95. ISBN1 84592 219 0. Tottel Publishing.
Nock, Reg–Understanding Stamp Duty Land Tax. Paperback: £44.95. ISBN 1 85328 982 5. Law Society Publications.
O'Grady, Eileen; Cave, R–Practitioners Tax Handbook: Trusts, Wills, Probate and Tax Planning. Paperback: £75.00. ISBN 0 421 89400 8. Sweet & Maxwell.
Orange Tax Handbook. Paperback: £75.00. ISBN 1 4057 0740 2. Paperback: £99.95. ISBN 1 4057 0931 6. Tolley Publishing.
Pinfold, Louise; Walton, Kevin; Smailes, David–Tolley's Income Tax Workbook. Paperback: £27.95. ISBN 0 7545 2885 5. Tolley Publishing.
Pinfold, Louise; Walton, Kevin; Smailes, David–Tolley's Income Tax: Main Annual. Paperback: £85.95. ISBN 0 7545 2864 2. Tolley Publishing.
Pinfold, Louise; Walton, Kevin; Smailes, David–Tolley's Income Tax: Budget Edition and Main Annual. Paperback: £96.95. ISBN 0 7545 2863 4. Tolley Publishing.
Revenue Law, Principles and Practice. Paperback: £62.95. ISBN 1 84592 196 8. Tottel Publishing.
Rohatgi, Roy–Basic International Taxation: V. 2. Practice. Hardback: £95.00. ISBN 1 904501 35 4. Richmond Law & Tax Ltd.
Roth, Dik; Boelens, Rutgerd; Zwarteveen, Margreet–Liquid Relations: Contested Water Rights and Legal Complexity. Hardback: £46.95. ISBN 0 8135 3674 X. Paperback: £21.95. ISBN 0 8135 3675 8. Rutgers University Press.
Rowell, David; Wilson, Richard; Arthur, Stephen–Practical Lawyer Inheritance Tax Planning Guide. Paperback: £60.00. ISBN 1 903927 67 6. Legalease.
Smailes, David; Wareham, Robert–Tolley's Tax Data: Budget Edition. Paperback: £42.00. ISBN 0 7545 2868 5. Tolley Publishing.
Smailes, David; Wareham, Robert–Tolley's Tax Data: Finance Act Edition. Paperback: £42.00. ISBN 0 7545 2869 3. Tolley Publishing.
Snape, John; Souza, Jeremy De–Environmental Taxation Law: Policy, Contexts and Practice. Hardback: £75.00. ISBN 0 7546 2304 1. Ashgate.
Southern, David–Taxation of Banks and Banking. Paperback: £85.00. ISBN 0 7545 2227 X. Tolley Publishing.
Tax Annuals Set. Paperback: £243.95. ISBN 1 4057 0427 6. Paperback: £299.00. ISBN 1 4057 0923 5. Tolley Publishing.
Tax Indemnities and Warranties. Paperback: £85.00. ISBN 1 84592 127 5. Tottel Publishing.
Tax Office Directory. Spiral/comb bound: £31.00. ISBN 0 7545 2871 5. Spiral/comb bound: £33.95. ISBN 0 7545 2872 3. Tolley Publishing.
Thurston, John–Estate Planning for the Middle Income Client. Paperback: £49.95. ISBN 1 84592 009 0. Tottel Publishing.
Tiley, John–Revenue Law. Paperback: £45.00. ISBN 1 84113 536 4. Hart Publishing.
Tolley's Income Tax (Trading and Other Income) Act Handbook. Paperback: £39.95. ISBN 0 7545 2932 0. Tolley Publishing.
Tolley's Tax Computations. Paperback: £74.95. ISBN 0 7545 2867 7. Tolley Publishing.
Tolley's Tax Planning. Paperback: £208.95. ISBN 0 7545 2873 1. Tolley Publishing.
Tookey, Michael–Revenue Law. Paperback: £15.95. ISBN 1 85836 608 9. Old Bailey Press.
Tottel's Property Taxes. Paperback: £74.95. ISBN 1 84592 055 4. Tottel Publishing.
Tottel's Taper Relief. Paperback: £74.95. ISBN 1 84592 124 0. Tottel Publishing.
Walton, Kevin; Antczak, Gina–Tolley's Corporation Tax Workbook. Paperback: £27.95. ISBN 0 7545 2884 7. Tolley Publishing.

Walton, Kevin; Antczak, Gina—Tolley's Corporation Tax: Main Annual. Paperback: £85.95. ISBN 0 7545 2861 8. Tolley Publishing.

Walton, Kevin; Antczak, Gina—Tolley's Corporation Tax: Budget Edition and Main Annual. Paperback: £97.95. ISBN 0 7545 2860 X. Tolley Publishing.

Walton, Kevin; Dolton, Alan—Tolley's Tax Cases. Paperback: £86.95. ISBN 0 7545 2886 3. Tolley Publishing.

Walton, Kevin; Flint, Andrew—Tolley's Capital Gains Tax Workbook. Paperback: £27.95. ISBN 0 7545 2883 9. Tolley Publishing.

Walton, Kevin; Flint, Andrew—Tolley's Capital Gains Tax: Main Annual. Paperback: £82.95. ISBN 0 7545 2859 6. Tolley Publishing.

Wareham, Robert; Antczak, Gina—Whillans's Tax Tables. Paperback: £29.50. ISBN 1 4057 0750 X. Tolley Publishing.

Wareham, Robert; Antczak, Gina—Whillans's Tax Tables: Budget Edition. Paperback: £29.50. ISBN 1 4057 0741 0. Tolley Publishing.

Whitehouse, Chris; Chamberlain, Emma—Taxation Aspects of the Family Home. Paperback: £85.00. ISBN 0 7545 2800 6. Tolley Publishing.

Whiteman, Peter; Gammie, Malcolm; Herbert, Mark; Sherry, Michael—Whiteman on Capital Gains Tax: Supplement 15. Paperback: £135.00. ISBN 0 421 91570 6. Sweet & Maxwell.

Whiteman, Peter; Goy, David; Sandison, Francis; Sherry, Michael—Whiteman on Income Tax. Hardback: £155.00. ISBN 0 421 89020 7. Sweet & Maxwell.

Whiteman, Peter; Goy, David; Sandison, Francis; Sherry, Michael—Whiteman on Income Tax: Supplement 16. Paperback: £165.00. ISBN 0 421 91750 4. Sweet & Maxwell.

Williams, Hugh; King, Brian—How to Avoid Inheritance Tax. Paperback: £9.99. ISBN 1 905261 09 8. Lawpack Publishing Ltd.

Wilson, Martin—Tottel's Capital Allowances: Transactions and Planning. Paperback: £82.95. ISBN 1 84592 190 9. Tottel Publishing.

Wolff, Florian; Voelker, Dietmar; Bott, Kristofer—German Tax and Business Law Guide. Paperback: £165.00. ISBN 0 421 91330 4. Sweet & Maxwell.

Yellow and Orange Tax Handbooks. Paperback: £200.00. ISBN 1 4057 0933 2. Tolley Publishing.

Yellow Tax Handbook. Paperback: £120.00. ISBN 1 4057 0924 3. Paperback: £81.00. ISBN 1 4057 0744 5. Tolley Publishing.

TELECOMMUNICATIONS

4171. Broadcasting—Foreign satellite services

FOREIGN SATELLITE SERVICE PROSCRIPTION ORDER 2005, SI 2005 220; made under the Broadcasting Act 1990 s.177. In force: February 21, 2005; £3.00.

The Broadcasting Act 1990 gives the Secretary of State power to make orders proscribing foreign satellite services in any case where the Office of Communications consider the quality of such a service to be unacceptable and have notified to her details of that service and their reasons for considering that such an order should be made. They cannot consider the quality of a service to be unacceptable unless they are satisfied that it repeatedly includes in its programmes matter which offends against good taste or decency or is likely to encourage or incite crime or to lead to disorder or to be offensive to public feeling. This Order proscribes the service known as "Extasi TV" (sometimes seen spelt "Exstasi TV").

4172. Broadcasting—Television licences—Fees

COMMUNICATIONS (TELEVISION LICENSING) (AMENDMENT) REGULATIONS 2005, SI 2005 606; made under the Communications Act 2003 s.365, s.402. In force: April 1, 2005; £3.00.

These Regulations amend the provisions prescribing the fees payable for TV licences in the Communications (Television Licensing) Regulations 2004 (SI 2004 692) to increase the fee for a basic black and white only TV licence; the issue fee and subsequent instalments for the premium instalment licence; to the instalments payable for the budget instalment licence and the easy entrance licence; the provisions relating to the interim TV licence; the provisions relating to TV licence fees for hotels, hospitality areas and mobile units are amended to reflect the rise in the fees payable for basic black and white only and colour TV licences.

4173. Broadcasting—Wireless telegraphy—Licence fees

WIRELESS TELEGRAPHY (LICENCE CHARGES) REGULATIONS 2005, SI 2005 1378; made under the Wireless Telegraphy Act 1998 s.1, s.2; and the Communications Act 2003 s.403. In force: June 13, 2005; £6.00.

These Regulations revoke the Wireless Telegraphy (Licence Charges) Regulations 2002 (SI 2002 1700), the Wireless Telegraphy (Licence Charges) (Amendment) Regulations 2003 (SI 2003 2983) and the Wireless Telegraphy (Licence Charges) (Amendment) (Channel Islands and Isle of Man) Regulations 2003 (SI 2003 2984). The Regulations provide for fees to be paid to the Office of Communications in respect of wireless telegraphy licences granted under the Wireless Telegraphy Act 1949 s.1.

4174. Communications—Premium rate services—Maximum penalty

COMMUNICATIONS ACT 2003 (MAXIMUM PENALTY AND DISCLOSURE OF INFORMATION) ORDER 2005, SI 2005 3469; made under the Communications Act 2003 s.123 s.393. In force: December 30, 2005; £3.00.

This Order, which amends the Communications Act 2003, makes provision connected with the regulation of premium rate services pursuant to the Communications Act 2003. It raises the maximum penalty that the Office of Communications can impose under s.96 of the Act, in respect of breaches of the code regulating the provision and content of premium rate services, from £100,000 to £250,000.

4175. Electronic communications—Guernsey—Consequential modifications

COMMUNICATIONS (BAILIWICK OF GUERNSEY) (AMENDMENT) ORDER 2005, SI 2005 856; made under the Communications Act 2003 s.402, s.411. In force: March 31, 2005; £3.00.

This Order amends the Communications (Bailiwick of Guernsey) Order 2003 (SI 2003 3195) which extended, in part the Communications Act 2003 to the Bailiwick of Guernsey. In particular this Order amends the 2003 Order so as to extend specified sections to take account of consequential modifications.

4176. Electronic communications—OFCOM—Jersey

COMMUNICATIONS (JERSEY) (AMENDMENT) ORDER 2005, SI 2005 855; made under the Communications Act 2003 s.402, s.411. In force: March 31, 2005; £3.00.

This Order amends the Communications (Jersey) Order 2003 (SI 2003 3195) which extended, in part the Communications Act 2003 to the Bailiwick of Jersey. In particular this Order amends the 2003 Order so as to extend specified sections to take account of consequential modifications.

4177. Electronic communications—Vehicles—Automotive short range radar equipment—Exemptions

WIRELESS TELEGRAPHY (AUTOMOTIVE SHORT RANGE RADAR) (EXEMPTION) REGULATIONS 2005, SI 2005 353; made under the Wireless Telegraphy Act 1949 s.1. In force: March 17, 2005; £3.00.

These Regulations exempt the establishment or installation of automotive short range radar equipment in a vehicle and the use of automotive short range radar equipment so established or installed from the requirement to be licensed. The equipment must operate within the frequency band between 77 gigahertz and

81 gigahertz, meet the mean power density requirements and not cause undue interference to other users of the frequency band. The Regulations also implement the Commission Decision 2004/545 ([2004] OJ L241/66) on the harmonisation of radio spectrum in the 79 GHz range for the use of automotive short-range radar equipment in the Community.

4178. Electronic communications–Vehicles–Automotive short range radar equipment–Exemptions

WIRELESS TELEGRAPHY (AUTOMOTIVE SHORT RANGE RADAR) (EXEMPTION) (NO.2) REGULATIONS 2005, SI 2005 1585; made under the Wireless Telegraphy Act 1949 s.1. In force: July 1, 2005; £3.00.

These Regulations exempt the establishment or installation of automotive short range radar equipment in a vehicle and the use of automotive short range radar equipment so established or installed from the requirement to be licensed under the Wireless Telegraphy Act 1949.

4179. Equipment–Seizure–Goods not bearing type approval stamp required by national law–Right to judicial protection–European Community

[Council Directive 99/5 on radio equipment and telecommunications terminal equipment and the mutual recognition of their conformity.]

The Italian court referred to the European Court of Justice the question whether Council Directive 99/5 precluded national legislation whereby an importer could not bring court proceedings to challenge a measure adopted by the public authorities under which goods sold to a retailer had been seized. The reference was made in the context of S's appeal against an administrative penalty imposed for an infringement of domestic law in connection with the production of radio-controlled scale model aeroplanes which did not bear the type approval stamp required by Italian law. S was the producer of the units, which had been seized from V, a retailer operating in the model making sector, who had also been fined. The authorities refused to return the models on the ground that S had no standing to challenge the seizure order, which had been addressed to V.

Held, giving a preliminary ruling, that (1) in principle, it was for national law to determine an individual's standing and legal interest in bringing proceedings but Community law required that national law did not undermine the right to effective judicial protection. The principle of effective judicial protection of the rights conferred on individuals by the Community legal order did not, in circumstances such as the present, preclude domestic legislation under which an importer was not allowed to bring court proceedings to challenge a measure adopted by the public authorities where there was a legal remedy available to the importer which ensured respect for the rights conferred on him by Community law.

SAFALERO SRL v. PREFETTO DI GENOVA (C13/01) [2003] Info. T.L.R. 431, Judge Puissochet (President), ECJ.

4180. Licences–Discrimination–Fees charged for granting of licences–European Community

[Council Directive 97/13 on a common framework for general authorisations and individual licences in the field of telecommunications services Art.(2).]

The Austrian court stayed an appeal by the applicant telecommunications company (C) against the grant of additional band frequency to another telecommunications company (M), whose major shareholder was the state and sought a preliminary ruling from the European Court of Justice as to the compatibility of the national legislation with Community law. The national law provided that such extra frequency could be allocated to a public undertaking in a dominant market position without the imposition of an additional fee, which C contended was discriminatory under Council Directive 97/13 Art.9(2).

Held, giving a preliminary ruling, that the prohibition on discrimination laid down in Parliament and Council Directive 97/13 did not preclude national legislation under which additional frequencies in the band reserved for the DCS 1800 standard could be allocated to existing holders of a licence to provide digital mobile telecommunications services according to the GSM 900 standard without the imposition of a separate fee, even though the operator which had been granted a licence to provide services according to the DCS 1800 standard had had to pay a fee. However, this applied only if the fee charged to the existing operators for their GSM 900 licence, including the subsequent allocation without additional payment of additional frequencies in the frequency band reserved for the DCS 1800 standard, appeared to be equivalent in economic terms to the fee imposed on the operator which held the DCS 1800 licence.

CONNECT AUSTRIA GESELLSCHAFT FUR TELEKOMMUNIKATION GmbH v. TELEKOM-CONTROL-KOMMISSION (C462/99) [2005] 5 C.M.L.R. 6, Judge Edward (President), ECJ.

4181. OFCOM–Membership

OFFICE OF COMMUNICATIONS (MEMBERSHIP) ORDER 2005, SI 2005 2718; made under the Office of Communications Act 2002 s.1. In force: October 26, 2005; £3.00.

This Order amends the Office of Communications Act 2002 to increase the maximum membership of the Office of Communications from nine to ten.

4182. Radio–Radio frequency identification equipment–Licensing–Exemptions

WIRELESS TELEGRAPHY (RADIO FREQUENCY IDENTIFICATION EQUIPMENT) (EXEMPTION) REGULATIONS 2005, SI 2005 3471; made under the Wireless Telegraphy Act 1949 s.1. In force: January 31, 2006; £3.00.

These Regulations exempt the establishment or installation of radio frequency identification equipment and the use of radio frequency identification equipment so established or installed from the requirement to be licensed under the Wireless Telegraphy Act 1949 s.1 (1).

4183. Telecommunications networks–Fees–Entitlement to require financial payments from licence holders–European Community

[Council Directive 97/13 on a common framework for general authorisations and individual licences in the field of telecommunications services.]

The Italian court referred to the European Court of Justice the questions of whether Member States were entitled under Council Directive 97/13 to require undertakings such as the applicants (AI), who were companies holding licences to operate public telecommunications networks, to make financial payments other than and in addition to those allowed by the Directive. AI had brought actions against the respondents (M) in respect of an interministerial decree imposing on undertakings which held licences a charge calculated on the basis of a percentage of their turnover. AI contended that, by introducing the contested charge, the national law was in effect re establishing the royalty that was applicable in Italy when telecommunications services were subject to a monopoly, and was therefore in breach of Community law. M argued that the contested charge was merely a contribution towards the costs incurred in bringing about the liberalisation of the telecommunications sector and, moreover, applied for only a limited period.

Held, giving a preliminary ruling, that (1) Council Directive 97/13 was one of the measures adopted for the complete liberalisation of telecommunications services and infrastructures and, to that end, established a common framework for general authorisations intended to make a significant contribution to the entry of new operators to the market. That framework set out, *inter alia*, the nature and scope of financial payments which Member States might impose on undertakings in the field of telecommunications services which were required to be based on objective, non discriminatory and transparent criteria. (2) The contested charge was calculated on the basis of the turnover of undertakings which held individual licences and thereby introduced a financial obstacle to the liberalisation process. Accordingly, such a charge was contrary to the objectives sought by the Community legislature and went beyond the common framework established by the Directive.

ALBACOM SpA v. MINISTERO DEL TESORO, DEL BILANCIO E DELLA PROGRAMMAZIONE ECONOMICA (C292/01) [2003] Info. T.L.R. 446, Wathelet (President), ECJ.

4184. Telecommunications networks–Interconnection–Meaning of "interconnection" under Council Directive 97/33

[Telecommunications (Interconnection) Regulations 1997 (SI 1997 2931) Reg.6(6); Council Directive 97/33 on interconnection in telecommunications with regard to ensuring universal service and interoperability through application of the principles of open network provision.]

B appealed against a direction that it should provide V, a mobile telephone operator, with radio base station backhaul circuits on wholesale terms. V relied on such circuits to connect its telephone masts to telephone exchanges, which were in turn connected to B's and other operators' networks. B contended that the direction was ultra vires on the ground that the parties' dispute was not a "dispute concerned with interconnection" for the purposes of the Telecommunications (Interconnection) Regulations 1997 Reg.6(6). The issue was whether B's supply of the circuits amounted to interconnection for the purposes of Council Directive 97/33 and the Regulations.

Held, allowing the appeal, that the concept of "interconnection" under the Directive was limited to the connection of public telecommunications networks for the purpose of achieving "end to end" interoperability, allowing the end user of one network to communicate with the end user of another. The essential function of radio base station backhaul circuits was to allow V to complete its own network, rather than to ensure interoperability between networks. Any contribution which the circuits made to interoperability had to be regarded as too remote, and it was irrelevant that the supply involved transmission over B's network. Consequently, B's supply of the circuits did not constitute "interconnection" within the meaning of the Directive and Reg.6(6) of the Regulations, and the direction had no legal effect.

BRITISH TELECOMMUNICATIONS PLC v. OFFICE OF COMMUNICATIONS (FORMERLY DIRECTOR GENERAL OF TELECOMMUNICATIONS), [2004] CAT 8, [2004] Comp. A.R. 574, Sir Christopher Bellamy (President), CAT.

4185. Telecommunications networks–Rights of way–Implementation of Commission Directive 90/388–European Community

[Commission Directive 90/388 on Competition in the Markets for Telecommunication Services Art.4d; Commission Directive 96/19 amending Directive 90/388 with regard to the implementation of full competition in telecommunications markets.]

The European Commission commenced proceedings against the defendant Member State (L) seeking a declaration that, by failing to ensure in practice the effective transposition into domestic law of Commission Directive 90/388 Art.4d, L had failed to fulfil its Community obligations. Article 4d, as amended by Commission Directive 96/19, provided that Member States should not discriminate between the providers of public telecommunications networks with regard to the granting of rights of way for the provision of such networks. The Commission argued that where the granting of additional rights of way to providers was not possible due to non economic reasons in the public interest, which could cause a Member State to impose conditions on the establishment or operation of telecommunications networks, the Member States should ensure access to existing facilities which had been established under rights of way.

Held, granting the declaration, that (1) in relation to the transposition of a Directive into the legal order of a Member State, it was essential that the national law effectively ensured that the Directive was applied fully, that the legal position under national law was sufficiently precise and clear and that individuals were made fully aware of their rights, *Commission of the European Communities v. Greece (C365/93)* [1995] E.C.R. I-499, [1995] C.L.Y. 1897 considered. (2) The question whether a Member State had failed to fulfil its obligations had to be determined by reference to the situation as it was at the end of the period laid down in the reasoned opinion provided by the Commission. Therefore, the court was not entitled to take account of changes introduced by subsequent legislation in considering the merits of the Commission's action and it was clear that the domestic law in force at the relevant time did not meet the requirements of Art.4d.

COMMISSION OF THE EUROPEAN COMMUNITIES v. LUXEMBOURG (C97/01) [2003] Info. T.L.R. 420, Judge Puissochet (President), ECJ.

4186. Telecommunications systems–Personal data–Netherlands–Transposition of Directive 97/66 Art. 6 and Art.9–European Community

[Council Directive 97/66 concerning the processing of personal data and the protection of privacy in the telecommunications sector Art.6, Art.9; Law Governing the Telecommunications Sector (Netherlands) 1998 s.11 (5) (1), s.11 (5) (3).]

The European Commission sought a declaration that the Netherlands had failed to correctly transpose Council Directive 97/66 Art.6 and Art.9 into national law. The Commission argued that (1) the Law Governing the Telecommunications Sector (Netherlands) 1998 s.11 (5) (1) derogated from the principle set out in Art.6(1) of the Directive insofar as the general administrative measure envisaged should have included an exhaustive list of information; (2) although s.11 (5) (3) of the national law referred to implementing provisions, the Netherlands government had failed to communicate them to the Commission; (3) Article 9(a) of the Directive had not been transposed into national law.

Held, granting the application, that (1) the Netherlands government had failed to adopt all the provisions necessary for the transposition of Art.6(1) of the Directive. (2) At the expiry of the period laid down in the reasoned opinion, the implementing provisions at issue had not been communicated to the Commission. Moreover, the failure to adopt those provisions by that date could not be reasonably relied on to justify that infringement. (3) No Netherlands provisions transposed Art.9(a) of the Directive.

COMMISSION OF THE EUROPEAN COMMUNITIES v. NETHERLANDS (C350/02) [2004] Info. T.L.R. 229, Judge Jann (President), ECJ.

4187. Books

Bolter, Walter G.–Telecommunication Policy for the 90s. Hardback: £62.50. ISBN 1 56324 918 9. M.E. Sharpe.

Campbell, Dennis–International Telecommunications Law-Volume I. Paperback: £45.99. ISBN 1 4116 5812 4. Lulu Press Incorporated.

Dettore, Mike; Kalyvas, James R.; Sullivan, Kirk N.–Negotiating Telecommunications Agreements Line by Line. Line by Line S. Paperback: £99.95. ISBN 1 59622 112 7. Aspatore Books.

Scherer, Joachim–Baker and Mckenzie: Telecommunications Law in Europe. Hardback: £170.00. ISBN 1 84592 078 3. Tottel Publishing.

Valcke, Peggy; Queck, Robert; Lievens, Eva–EU Communications Law: Significant Market Power in the Mobile Sector. Hardback: £49.95. ISBN 1 84542 416 6. Edward Elgar.

Winning Legal Strategies for Telecom Companies: Top Lawyers on Telecommunications Regulations and Creating Legal Game Plans. Inside the Minds S. Paperback: £37.95. ISBN 1 58762 012 X. Aspatore Books.

TORTS

4188. Breach of contract–Intention–Inducing breach of employment contracts– Requisite intention for tort of interfering with contractual relations

The appellant company (M) appealed against the dismissal of its action against the respondent (D), for damages for inducing two directors of M to breach their contracts of employment. M was a property development company. Two directors of M had formed companies to exploit opportunities available to M. When M discovered the existence of the companies, it dismissed the two directors and sued them. M also sued D, who had provided the finance to enable the directors to appropriate the opportunity which belonged to M. It was common ground that D's acts had amounted to interference with the directors' contracts of employment. D's case was that he had only agreed to fund the project after having received assurances from the directors that there was no conflict of interest with regard to their employment by M because M had considered and rejected the site. The judge dismissed the claim against D on the grounds that D had accepted and relied on the assurance that there was no conflict of interest with M, that D had been entitled to rely on the assurance, and that those features prevented the inference being drawn that D must have known that the directors were acting in breach of their duties as employees. Therefore M had failed to establish that D intended to procure a breach of or interfere with the performance of the employment contracts. M submitted that for the tort of interfering with a subsisting contract, once the requisite knowledge was established, the element of intention merely required that the acts of interference with a contractual relationship were voluntary or deliberate, rather than involuntary or accidental, and that the requisite intention could be inferred where the breach of contract necessarily resulted from achieving the object with which the defendant acted.

Held, dismissing the appeal, that the requisite intention for the purposes of the tort of interference with contractual relations was a specific subjective intention, *Douglas v. Hello! Ltd (No.6)* [2005] EWCA Civ 595, [2005] 2 F.C.R. 487 applied. There were good policy reasons for confining the ambit of the tort in that way. In the instant case, D knew that the two were executive directors of M and that his funding of the site would prevent M from developing the site itself, but he did not consider that there was any conflict of interest because of the assurance that he had been given, and no specific intention to cause harm had therefore been shown. The tort of interference with contractual rights was not satisfied by showing that the defendant was reckless as to whether his conduct interfered with the claimant's contractual rights or not. Specific intention to cause harm had to be shown in the case of direct as well as indirect interference. The principle that a person was presumed to intend the reasonable consequences of his acts did not apply to the question whether the defendant had the intention necessary for the purposes of the tort of interference with contractual relations. A defendant to a claim based on the tort of interference with contractual relations was not prevented from relying on a mistake he made on the law to explain why he took the action he did.

MAINSTREAM PROPERTIES LTD v. YOUNG, [2005] EWCA Civ 861, [2005] I.R.L.R. 964, Sedley, L.J., CA (Civ Div).

4189. Economic torts–Conversion–Invalidly appointed receivers–Unlawful interference with contractual relations

The appellant receivers (R) and solicitors (P) appealed against the judgment given in favour of the claimants (C) in the sum of £1,854,000. C were civil engineering contractors. C were undercapitalised and underfunded and heavily dependent on receiving payments under contracts with their main customer. The customer suspended C from its list of approved contractors and withheld payment for work done. C owed a substantial sum to their specialist subcontractor (S). S agreed to refinance C with a loan of £1.1 million and took an assignment of the bank's security. The refinancing did not go ahead but S appointed R on the advice of P on the basis that the bank's security was security for the pre existing indebtedness of C to S. R took control of C's business but the main customer terminated its contracts with C and C went into liquidation. R eventually settled the dispute with C's customer for £400,000. C commenced proceedings against R, S and P claiming that R's appointment was invalid. The judge held that R's appointment was invalid and that P's advice was negligent, but that C's liquidation was inevitable. C sought as damages the difference between the value of the business when R were appointed and the actual realisations made by R. The judge held that (in addition to trespass and conversion in relation to C's land and chattels) the tort of interference with contractual relations was made out and awarded damages including £1,820,000 for the value of contract debtors, stock and work in progress. The damages were reduced by £300,000 as the costs of a notional liquidation and the judge held that the liquidators actual costs and expenses over and above that figure were recoverable as damages and directed an inquiry. R and P submitted that (1) the invalidly appointed receivers did not commit the tort of wrongful interference with contractual relations because the tort required deliberate interference with a contract with a view to bringing about its breach; (2) the judge should have held that the liquidators' remuneration and expenses were only claimable as against R to the extent that they were caused by the tortious acts of the receivers, were not too remote, and were not part of the preparation by the liquidators for the litigation. C submitted that if there was no wrongful interference with contractual relations R committed a tort in the nature of conversion of C's contractual rights.

Held, allowing the appeal and dismissing the cross appeal (Mance, L.J. dissenting on the issue of wrongful interference with contractual relations), that (1) the tort of wrongful interference with contractual relations did not extend to the interference by a third party with the right of a party to a contract to perform the contract and manage his contractual rights as he chose when that interference was not directed at procuring an actionable wrong such as a breach of contract nor at hindering or impeding the performance of the contract. In the instant case R would have liked to perform the contracts and to do so in the name and on behalf of C, but C's customer was not willing to let that happen. The essence of the tort was that the alleged tortfeasor sought to procure an actionable wrong. The fact that the tort had been extended to include prevention of the due performance of a primary obligation even though no secondary obligation to make monetary compensation came into existence did not justify a further extension of the tort to circumstances where the alleged tortfeasor was not intending to prevent the performance of any primary obligation of the contract, *Torquay Hotel Co Ltd v. Cousins* [1969] 2 Ch. 106, [1969] C.L.Y. 3574 and *Merkur Island Shipping Corp v. Laughton Shaw and Lewis (The Hoegh Anapa)* [1983] 2 A.C. 570, [1983] C.L.Y. 3794 considered. It would be a significant extension which could not be justified to bring within the tort a case where the interference was not directed at hindering performance of the contractual obligations, but went only to who as between R and C should be managing the contractual rights. Further the case finally upheld by the judge could not be treated as one of valuation as at the date of R's purported appointment which was the basis of C's claim. (2) The judge did not err in principle in directing an inquiry as to what costs of the liquidators could be recovered over and above the £300,000 on the basis that they had been caused by the receivership. (3) As a matter of English law there could be no conversion of a chose in action. Convenient though it would be for English law to recognise a tort, in the case of invalidly appointed receivers, where the receivers wrongfully took control of a business, it was not open to the court to invent such a tort. The judge was right to reject the claim based on conversion of contractual rights.

OBG LTD v. ALLAN; *sub nom.* OBG LTD v. ALLEN, [2005] EWCA Civ 106, [2005] Q.B. 762, Peter Gibson, L.J., CA (Civ Div).

4190. **Economic torts–Unlawful means conspiracy–Cause of action in conspiracy against foreign company involved in "carousel" or "missing trader" frauds**

[Value Added Tax Act 1994.]

The claimant commissioners brought proceedings to recover VAT lost in "carousel" or "missing trader" frauds, alleging conspiracy by the defendant (T) to cheat the Revenue by unlawful means, and a preliminary issue was tried as to whether the commissioners had a cause of action in conspiracy against T. T was a Spanish company which had two English bank accounts but was not a taxable person in the United Kingdom. The commissioners claimed that T had been involved in a series of "carousel" or "missing trader" frauds in relation to the sale of mobile phones from Spain to the UK. The "unlawful means" said to have been adopted within the conspiracy was the common law offence of cheating the Revenue. T denied the conspiracy and denied that the commissioners' allegations were capable of constituting a cause of action for the purposes of the tort of conspiracy. T argued that (1) the conspiracy claim was an attempt to circumvent the statutory scheme under the Value Added Tax Act 1994 for recovering overpaid or wrongly paid VAT which could not be operated against T because it was a foreign company and not a taxable person in the UK; (2) the facts relied on by the commissioners did not and could not amount to "unlawful means" so as to found an unlawful means conspiracy; (3) an action in conspiracy did not lie where there had been no harm to or interference with the other party's trade or business.

Held, determining the preliminary issues, that (1) the agreed facts showed that the transactions had no economic purpose other than to cheat Customs and Excise. T was a Spanish company and was not subject to UK VAT because it was not a taxable person under the 1994 Act. It had monies in its UK bank accounts that had been used in the bogus transactions. As that money was not recoverable under the 1994 Act in any event, the contention that the 1994 Act was the only proper vehicle for obtaining recovery of payments made wrongly was itself wrong. The conspiracy alleged was not a way of circumventing the statutory scheme. It stood alone as a possible method of recovery against T, as a company registered outside the UK. (2) The notion of "unlawfulness" in unlawful means conspiracy was not limited to civil wrongdoing, breaches of contract and breaches of fiduciary duty which might themselves give rise to compensation. The unlawful means in the instant case was the commission of the common law offence of cheating the Revenue. Cheating included any form of fraudulent conduct which resulted in diverting money from the Revenue and, whatever the position on crime generally, fraud was always "unlawful means" for the purposes of the tort of conspiracy. A claim in the tort of conspiracy could be used to bring to account a party such as T, a Spanish company, against whom Customs and Excise would otherwise have no direct redress. Customs and Excise would have a cause of action against other parties to the alleged conspiracy on the basis at least that the payments were made by Customs and Excise as a result of fraudulent misrepresentation. (3) The tort of conspiracy to use unlawful means was not limited to cases in which the claimant was injured in its trade or business, *Kuwait Oil Tanker Co SAK v. Al-Bader (No.3)* [2000] 2 All E.R. (Comm) 271, [2000] C.L.Y. 5106 applied.

CUSTOMS AND EXCISE COMMISSIONERS v. TOTAL NETWORK SL, [2005] EWHC 1, [2005] S.T.C. 637, Hodge, J., QBD.

4191. Harassment–Injunctions–Standard of proof

[Protection from Harassment Act 1997 s.3; Crime and Disorder Act 1998 s.1; European Convention on Human Rights 1950.]

The appellant sisters (LH and JH) appealed against a decision to grant an injunction under the Protection from Harassment Act 1997 s.3 restraining them from harassing the respondent (J). LH lived near J. The judge had stated that there had been a considerable amount of bad blood between two separate camps. He found five allegations, which primarily concerned abusive and threatening behaviour on the part of LH and JH towards J, proven. LH and JH argued that the judge had erred by applying the civil, rather than the criminal, standard of proof to the allegations made against them, and that an application for an injunction under s.3 of the 1997 Act was akin to an application for an anti-social behaviour order under the Crime and Disorder Act 1998 s.1, in respect of which the criminal standard applied. JH also argued that there was an insufficient link between the two incidents in which she had been involved to amount to a "course of conduct". She maintained that the two incidents, between which there had been a gap of over eight months, were spontaneous and unplanned, and that the judge had erred by referring to her family connection with LH.

Held, dismissing the appeals, that (1) a key difference between an injunction under the 1997 Act and an order under the 1998 Act was that the former was a private remedy sought by an individual, whereas the latter was sought by an authority. Whereas the 1997 Act was directed to giving protection from harassment, the 1998 Act was aimed at the "prevention of crime and disorder". It was plain that the criminal standard of proof was ill adapted to the degree of flexibility that was required to be applied in civil proceedings for the grant of an injunction, *Thomas v. News Group Newspapers Ltd* [2001] EWCA Civ 1233, [2002] E.M.L.R. 4, [2001] C.L.Y. 4418, *Cream Holdings Ltd v. Banerjee* [2004] UKHL 44, [2004] 3 W.L.R. 918, [2005] 1 C.L. 192 and *S (A Child) (Identification: Restrictions on Publication), Re* [2004] UKHL 47, [2004] 3 W.L.R. 1129, [2005] 1 C.L. 206 applied. The submission that the criminal standard should be applied paid insufficient regard to the fact that the rights of the claimant under the European Convention on Human Rights 1950 were engaged, and focused unduly on the rights of the defendant. In the circumstances, the civil standard of proof should be applied to proceedings under s.3 of the 1997 Act. In applying that standard, the courts should follow the approach set out in *H (Minors) (Sexual Abuse: Standard of Proof), Re* [1996] A.C. 563, [1996] C.L.Y. 632, *H (Minors)* applied and *U (A Child) (Serious Injury: Standard of Proof), Re* [2004] EWCA Civ 567, [2004] 3 W.L.R. 753, [2004] 7 C.L. 176 considered. (2) The words "course of conduct" were ordinary English words; it was for the tribunal of fact to evaluate the incidents, bearing in mind that there had to be "at least two occasions" and that there had to be a link between the two to reflect the meaning of "course". The fact that the two incidents in which JH had been involved were spontaneous and unplanned did not preclude a finding that they were part of a course of conduct; conduct could be spontaneous and unplanned and at the same time highly repetitive. Further, it had been the family solidarity which had led JH to be involved at all and which had given rise to the apprehension that she might continue to behave in the same way in the future. Moreover, the threatening language that JH had used spoke for itself; if a person threatened something and later did something similar, it would be natural for the tribunal of fact to find a link. The judge's finding in respect of JH could not therefore be faulted.

HIPGRAVE v. JONES; *sub nom.* JONES v. HIPGRAVE, [2004] EWHC 2901, [2005] 2 F.L.R. 174, Tugendhat, J., QBD.

4192. **Malicious prosecution–Prosecutors powers and duties–Duties at time of decision to charge**

[Police and Criminal Evidence Act 1984 s.37; Value Added Tax Act 1994 s.72(8).]

The appellant (C) appealed against the judge's decision to dismiss his claims against the respondent commissioners for wrongful arrest, false imprisonment and malicious prosecution. The commissioners had suspected that a company (T) was involved in a VAT fraud relating to the sale of mobile phones; that C was involved in the business of T and that he, along with T's sole director (S), was involved in the fraud. C and S were arrested and charged with an offence under the Value Added Tax Act 1994 s.72(8). C was held in custody for seven days. Several months later, counsel for the commissioners advised that there was insufficient evidence against C and two weeks after giving her advice the case against C was discontinued. C, who had claimed to have been an independent selling agent unaware of T's VAT dealings, argued that the judge had been wrong to dismiss his claims.

Held, dismissing the appeal, that (1) the judge's findings on C's claim for wrongful arrest could not be impugned. Although the judge did not expressly find that there had been a reasonable basis for the commissioners' officers to suspect that C was knowingly involved in the fraud, it was implicit that he did so find. Given that C was believed to be selling for T, it had been entirely reasonable for those officers to suspect that he had known what was going on. (2) As to the claim for false imprisonment, the judge's finding concerning the lawfulness of C's continued detention could be criticised to the extent that he had not applied his mind directly to the relevant statutory provision, namely the Police and Criminal Evidence Act 1984 s.37. However, that omission did not vitiate the judge's decision: there was every reason to conclude that C's continued detention had been lawful. (3) As to C's claim for malicious prosecution and the issue of whether the commissioners had had reasonable and probable cause to prosecute, consideration had to be given to the elements of the offence with which the suspect was to be charged. There had to be prima facie admissible evidence of each element of the offence. Although anything plainly inadmissible should be left out of the account, it was not necessary or appropriate, at the time of charging, to consider the possibility that evidence might be excluded at the trial after full legal argument or in the exercise of the judge's discretion. Nor was it necessary to test the full strength of the defence. In the instant case, there had to be prima facie evidence that C had done some act or acts with the intention of enabling or assisting T to evade its VAT liabilities on consignments of mobile phones; while the evidence of guilty knowledge on C's part was not strong, there was circumstantial evidence showing that he had known that T was involved in VAT fraud. Accordingly, the commissioners' officers had had reasonable and probable cause to charge C. As to the question of malice, C's challenge to the judge's findings on that issue was hopeless.

COUDRAT v. REVENUE AND CUSTOMS COMMISSIONERS, [2005] EWCA Civ 616, [2005] S.T.C. 1006, Mummery, L.J., CA (Civ Div).

4193. **Misfeasance in public office–Prison officers–Interference with privileged correspondence with solicitor–Requirement to show proof of damage– Exemplary damages**

[Prison Rules 1999 (SI 1999 728) r.39.]

W, a serving prisoner, appealed against the refusal of his claim for damages for misfeasance in public office against the Home Office and named prison officers. W had claimed that various prison officers had unlawfully opened privileged correspondence addressed to him in breach of the Prison Rules 1999 r.39, which had prejudiced his chances of success in various legal proceedings, and that his sense of pride and dignity had been injured. The judge had decided that misfeasance in public office was not actionable per se, and that although three prison officers in separate incidents had acted in bad faith, W had not sustained any loss to justify an award of damages. W submitted that the tort of misfeasance in public office was actionable without proof of damage and that he was entitled to an award of exemplary damages.

Held, allowing the appeal, that there were two types of misfeasance in public office. The first was where the claimant had suffered a quantifiable loss as a result of a public officer's wrongful and malicious act which had exposed the claimant to economic or material injury and where it was unnecessary to prove a violation of a free standing right, *Three Rivers DC v. Bank of England (No.3)* [2003] 2 A.C. 1, [2000] C.L.Y. 270 applied. The second was where the wrongful act interfered with a right which needed no proof of loss as in the instant case. W's constitutional right to an unimpeded free flow of communications with his solicitor about contemplated legal proceedings was fundamentally important and this had been maliciously infringed by the three prison officers which justified an action of misfeasance in public office without proof of special damage, *R. v. Secretary of State for the Home Department, ex p.*

Leech (No.2) [1994] Q.B. 198, [1994] C.L.Y. 3849 and *Ashby v. White* (1703) 2 Ld. Raym. 938 applied, *Three Rivers* considered. W was entitled to at least nominal damages against each of the three prison officers, *Owners of the Steamship Mediana v. Owners of the Lightship Comet* [1900] A.C. 113 applied. However, it was for the trial judge to determine the claim for exemplary damages and there was no reason why the level of any damages awarded should be as high as the guidance provided by *Thompson v. Commissioner of Police of the Metropolis* [1998] Q.B. 498, [1997] C.L.Y. 1765, *Thompson* distinguished.

WATKINS v. SECRETARY OF STATE FOR THE HOME DEPARTMENT, [2004] EWCA Civ 966, [2005] Q.B. 883, Brooke, L.J., CA.

4194. **Occupiers liability–Duty of care–Liability for personal injuries suffered in diving accident–Hidden underwater object–Occupier's knowledge of danger**

[Occupier's Liability Act 1984 s.1 (3), s.1 (4).]

The appellant (R) appealed against a decision ([2003] EWHC 1029) that the respondent company (A) was not liable for the severe injuries he had suffered as a result of diving into a disused gravel pit. The injuries were sustained as a result of R doing a running dive into shallow water and hitting his head on a fibre glass container which was lying on the bottom with silt covering its surface. A was a licensee who was permitted by licence to make use of the water. The activities that A was licensed to carry out on the water had nothing to do with R's entry into the water. R was not a visitor of A's and had ignored a prohibition notice on swimming. R submitted that the trial judge should have found that the requirements of the Occupier's Liability Act 1984 s.1 (3) were met so that there was a duty of care owed by A to him. R also argued that A had failed to exercise reasonable care so that there was a breach of s.1 (4).

Held, dismissing the appeal, that R had failed on the evidence to establish the threshold requirement for the existence of a duty of care in s.1 (3) (a). The evidence clearly established that A was not aware of the existence of the fibre glass container and R was unable to establish that A had reasonable grounds to believe that the obstruction existed, *Tomlinson v. Congleton BC* [2003] UKHL 47, [2004] 1 A.C. 46, [2003] C.L.Y. 4360 considered.

RHIND v. ASTBURY WATER PARK LTD, [2004] EWCA Civ 756, *The Independent*, June 25, 2004, Judge, L.J., CA.

4195. **Occupiers liability–Duty of care–Snowboarding accident on artificially created slope–Extent of duty to maintain safe standard of snow coverage**

[Occupiers' Liability Act 1957.]

The claimant (M) brought an action for damages for personal injury against the defendant (S), operators of an indoor skiing venue, following an accident during a snowboarding lesson. M had been practising turns shortly before the end of her two hour lesson when she fell sustaining bilateral wrist fractures. Damages had been agreed. M claimed that S had been negligent or in breach of its duty under the Occupiers' Liability Act 1957 in that S had caused or committed there to be an insufficient covering of snow thereby exposing ice. S gave evidence as to the procedure for maintaining the piste, which involved grooming it three times a day using tractors and snow plough blowers to redistribute the snow. There were also a number of ski patrols situated at the bottom and half way up the slope to monitor the condition of the snow. They would take necessary remedial action either manually or by cordoning off the area. M's teacher gave evidence that she could not remember the actual conditions, but that she would have moved the class had she considered the conditions dangerous. In fact, she had never found conditions too dangerous and had never moved a class.

Held, giving judgment for S, that the evidence of the conditions of the slope was not sufficient to establish a breach of S's duty under the 1957 Act. Snowboarding was not a risk free activity nor was it reasonably practical to produce and maintain a piste in pristine condition throughout the day. To impose such a duty would be to impose too high a standard. Icy patches were an inherent risk with skiing or snowboarding. There was evidence of significant icy patches at the top of the slope, but only some icy patches where M had her accident. The conditions were not such as to have represented a breach of the duty of care and although there might at times be patches of ice forming in the snow, that did not constitute a failure to take reasonable care.

MOORES v. SNOW DOME LTD, July 20, 2004, Judge McKenna, CC (Birmingham). [*Ex rel.* Davies Arnold Cooper Solicitors, 6-7 Bouverie Street, London].

4196. Occupiers liability – Duty of care – Tripping accident on woodland trail – Extent of duty owed to visitors to nature reserve

[Occupiers' Liability Act 1957.]

The claimant (M) brought an action against the defendant nature reserve owner (R) for damages for personal injury arising from a tripping accident which had occurred on a nature reserve owned and managed by R. M had taken his dogs for a walk on the reserve which was open to the public. The area was remote woodland and the path which M used was a trail cut through the woodland. The trail had a number of small sapling stumps present which had been left behind after the path had been cleared by R some two years previously. M claimed that whilst walking on the trail, he had tripped on one such stump and that had caused him to fall face first onto another stump, alleged to have been three inches high. In the fall, M claimed to have impaled his eye on the stump. M claimed that he was a visitor to R's property under the Occupiers' Liability Act 1957 and R was in breach of its duty of care for allowing small sapling stumps to be present on the trail. In particular, M alleged that such stumps were a danger because they gave rise to a reasonably foreseeable risk of a penetrating injury to any visitor who fell onto them.

Held, granting judgment for the defendant, that M had failed to prove that the accident had occurred in the manner he had alleged. Even had M been able to satisfy the court that he had tripped on a stump and then fallen onto another stump, the claim would still have failed, *Darby v. National Trust for Places of Historic Interest or Natural Beauty* [2001] EWCA Civ 189, [2001] 3 L.G.L.R. 29, [2001] C.L.Y. 4504, *Jolley v. Sutton LBC* [2000] 1 W.L.R. 1082, [2000] C.L.Y. 4239 and *Tomlinson v. Congleton BC* [2003] UKHL 47, [2004] 1 A.C. 46, [2003] C.L.Y. 4360 considered. Stumps such as these were commonplace in woodlands and on woodland trails and the presence of such a stump on the footpath was not a breach of duty under the Act considering the nature of the area in question, the type of visitor who could be expected in such a place, the small number of visitors who walked in this part of the reserve and the absence of any previous accident or complaint. The accident as alleged by M was not reasonably foreseeable. Even if it was reasonably foreseeable that a visitor might suffer a serious penetrating injury by falling on such a stump, the risk of that was very small and to impose liability on the occupier would be to hold that R and other occupiers of such places are under a duty to remove from woodland trails or other such locations, not only all protruding stumps, but also all sharp pieces of bracken, sticks and other materials resulting from path clearing and subsequent maintenance work which might conceivably cause some penetrating injury. That would go far beyond the duty to take such care as in all the circumstances was reasonable to see that visitors were reasonably safe in walking such trails or the purposes for which they were there: unreasonable or disproportionate responses were not required.

MILLS-DAVIES v. RSPB; *sub nom.* MILLS-DAVIES v. ROYAL SOCIETY FOR THE PROTECTION OF BIRDS, May 21, 2004, Judge Jones, QBD. [*Ex rel.* Lyons Davidson Solicitors, Victoria House, 51 Victoria Street, Bristol].

4197. Tort types – Removal – British citizens displaced from British Indian Ocean Territory – Tort of unlawful exile

[Crown Proceedings Act 1947; Limitation Act 1980 s.28(1).]

The applicants (C), former inhabitants of the Chagos Islands and their descendants, applied for leave to appeal against a decision ([2003] EWHC

2222) to strike out the entirety of their claims against the British Government (UK) for damages to compensate them for their enforced removal or exclusion from their homeland in the 1960s and 1970s. A compensation payment of £650,000 had been made by the UK to a total of 595 displaced families in the late 1970s. One of the last deportees (V) had brought an action in 1975 claiming damages for intimidation, deprivation of liberty and assault. A settlement was reached in 1982 which was designed to settle the claims of all the islanders in return for payment of £4,000,000 into a trust fund. Upon receipt of a share of this sum, 1,344 islanders signed quittance forms. The causes of action which C wished to resurrect were misfeasance in public office, unlawful exile and deceit. C contended that the state could be institutionally liable.

Held, refusing the application, that (1) those islanders who had signed quittance forms bindingly compromised the claims which they now sought to pursue, *R. (on the application of Bancoult) v. Secretary of State for the Foreign and Commonwealth Office* [2001] Q.B. 1067, [2000] C.L.Y. 96 considered. (2) The state had no tortious liability at common law. The Crown Proceedings Act 1947 only served to make the Crown vicariously liable for the torts of its servants. Thus, the claim for unlawful exile had to fail. Moreover, in the absence of evidence demonstrating that officers of state knew that the depopulation scheme was illegal, the claim for misfeasance in public office was not viable, *Three Rivers DC v. Bank of England (No.3)* [2003] 2 A.C. 1, [2000] C.L.Y. 270 considered. (3) C founded their claim in deceit on the allegation that the UK had made false representations to third parties such as the United Nations, the UK Parliament and the Government of Mauritius with the intention that those bodies should be dissuaded from intervening in the situation. It was possible that, in certain exceptional circumstances, for instance where a defendant, by the very making of the deceitful statement or for some other reason, had assumed liability to a claimant, a cause of action in deceit could exist. (4) The claim that the Constitution of Mauritius had applied to Chagos Islands and that it had been justiciably violated by the enforced removals was an arguable point. (5) It was conceivable that a court might be prepared to hold that, by its conduct, the UK had rendered it inequitable for it take a limitation point. It was also possible that C might have succeeded in arguing that time was prevented from running by virtue of the fact that they were "under a disability" within the meaning of the Limitation Act 1980 s.28(1). However, given the events of 1975 to 1983, from the initiation of V's action to the setting up of the trust fund, there was no possibility of showing that the unconscionability or disability, if proved, survived beyond 1983. Thus, any viable claim would inevitably have been defeated on grounds of limitation.

CHAGOS ISLANDERS v. ATTORNEY GENERAL, [2004] EWCA Civ 997, *The Times*, September 21, 2004, Dame Elizabeth Butler-Sloss (President), CA (Civ Div).

4198. Unlawful interference–Contractual rights–Necessary ingredients of actionable interference with contractual rights–Supply of beverages to tied public houses

The appellant (B), a wholesale supplier of beverages, appealed against an order giving summary judgment for the respondent (U), the owner of tenanted public houses, and granting an indefinite injunction restraining B from knowingly selling or promoting the supply of tied products to U's tenants. B had supplied one of U's tenants (T) with tied products on a number of occasions during a three or four month period. Those supplies had been made in response to unsolicited telephone orders placed by T. U sought to enforce its terms of trading with its tenants by circulating to wholesale suppliers, including B, lists identifying those of its public houses which were subject to a tie. B had instructed its telesales operators to ask publicans placing orders whether the pub was tied. If the answer was yes then no supply would be made. No cross check was made against the lists supplied by U, B taking the view that to do so would be uncommercial. B had supplied T in reliance on his assertion that his pub was not tied. B argued that the judge had erred in holding that it had had sufficient knowledge of the terms of the contract between T and U and that it had intended that T should breach those terms such that its supplies to T amounted to an actionable interference with that contract; rejecting its assertion that it would be commercially disastrous for it to be required to check each order against U's lists; and finding there was a sufficiently strong probability that it would commit further acts of tortious interference with U's contracts with its tenants to justify the grant of indefinite injunctions in respect of all the public houses included in U's lists.

Held, allowing the appeal, that (1) for there to have been an actionable interference with contractual rights, the breach of contract complained of had to have been brought about by some act of a third party which was in itself unlawful. That act need not necessarily have taken the form of persuasion or procurement or inducement of the contract breaker. An actionable interference in its primary form would be made out where direct persuasion or procurement or inducement was applied by the third party to the contract breaker, with knowledge of the contract and the intention of bringing about its breach. Where the contract breaker was a willing party to the breach, without any persuasion by the third party, but the third party, with knowledge of the contract in question, had dealings with the contract breaker which the third party knew to be inconsistent with the contract, that would amount to an unlawful act and he would have committed an actionable interference, *DC Thomson & Co Ltd v. Deakin* [1952] Ch. 646, [1952] C.L.Y. 3396 applied. Where, as in the instant case, the contract breaker was a willing party to the breach, it was for the claimant to show that the third party knew that his dealing with the contract breaker was inconsistent with that contract, *British Industrial Plastics Ltd v. Ferguson* [1940] 1 All E.R. 479 applied. B had not had the requisite knowledge and intention. This was not a "blind eye" case where the defendant had chosen not to search for what he knew was there to be found, *Emerald Construction Co v. Lowthian* [1966] 1 W.L.R. 691, [1966] C.L.Y. 12214 distinguished. Nor was it a case where, once read, the information supplied was likely to be retained in the memory. The lists supplied by U were not static, pubs being sold out of the estate from time to time, nor did they provide details of the nature of the obligations imposed by the ties to which individual tenants were subject. Thus, knowledge of the content of the lists was no more than knowledge that a tenant had been subject to some form of tie at the date the lists were compiled and did not equate with knowledge of a tie at the time orders were placed. The fact that B had instructed its telesales staff to ask whether the pub was tied was indicative of an intention by B not to interfere with U's terms of trading with its tenants. (2) Whether the judge had been justified in granting indefinite injunctions depended on whether U had established that, in circumstances where B did not know that the supply it agreed to make would be in breach of a tie, B would act wrongfully in making the supply without doing all that it could to protect U from the foreseeable possibility that the person placing the order would lie when asked whether or not the pub was subject to a tie. To impose an obligation for B to do more than ask potential customers whether they were subject to a tie, it would be necessary to be satisfied that the risk of receiving a dishonest answer was such that no honest supplier would think that reliance could be placed on a negative reply. But then, it would be necessary to ask what more the honest supplier had to do. These were not questions suitable for determination on an application for summary judgment.

UNIQUE PUB PROPERTIES LTD v. BEER BARRELS & MINERALS (WALES) LTD, [2004] EWCA Civ 586, [2005] 1 All E.R. (Comm) 181, Brooke, LJ, CA.

4199. Vicarious liability—Harassment—Employee's harassment of another in breach of s.1 Protection from Harassment Act 1997—Employer's liability

[Protection from Harassment Act 1997 s.1, s.3.]

The appellant (M) appealed against a decision striking out his claim against the respondent NHS trust for damages for breach of the statutory duty set out in the Protection from Harassment Act 1997 s.1 and entering judgment for the trust. M had been employed by the trust and alleged that his manager had harassed, bullied and intimidated him while acting in the course of her employment. The judge below had found that s.3 of the Act did not create a statutory tort for which an employer could be vicariously liable. M submitted that (1) the authorities strongly suggested that an employer might be vicariously liable for breach of a statutory duty imposed only on his employee; (2) there was no good reason why vicarious liability should not apply to breaches of the 1997 Act; (3) a company could be a "person" capable of harassment of "another" within the meaning of s.1 of the Act; (4) the fact that an employer could not be held criminally liable for an employee's breach of the duty under s.1 did not mean that the employer could not be civilly vicariously liable for the same conduct under s.3.

Held, allowing the appeal (Scott Baker, L.J. dissenting in part), that (1) vicarious liability was not restricted to common law claims. An employer could be vicariously liable for breach of a statutory duty imposed only on its employee, so long as it was fair and just to impose vicarious liability and so long as there was a close connection between the employee's offending conduct and the nature of his employment, *Harrison v. National Coal Board* [1951] A.C. 639, *Nicol v. National Coal Board* [1952] 102 L.J. 357 and *Darling Island Stevedoring Co v. Long* (1957) 31 A.L.J. 208, [1958] C.L.Y. 2280 considered, *Lister v. Hesley Hall Ltd* [2002] UKHL 22, [2001] 1 A.C. 215, *Dubai Aluminium Co Ltd v. Salaam* [2002] UKHL 48, [2003] 2 A.C. 366, [2003] C.L.Y. 3046 and *Bernard v. Attorney-General of Jamaica* [2004] UKPC 47, (2004) 148 S.J.L.B. 1281 applied. (2) An employer could be vicariously liable under s.3 of the Act for harassment, in breach of s.1 of the Act, committed by one of its employees in the course of his employment, *Thomas v. News Group Newspapers Ltd* [2001] EWCA Civ 1233, [2002] E.M.L.R. 4, [2001] C.L.Y. 4418 considered. (3) There was no reason why a corporate employer should not have the same vicarious responsibility as a non corporate employer for his employee's breaches of statutory duty. A company could be a "person" capable of harassing "another" within the meaning of the Act, *DPP v. Dziurzynski* [2002] EWHC 1380, (2002) 166 J.P. 545 considered. (4) There was a wealth of authority to support the view that an employer could be vicariously liable in civil proceedings for his employee's criminal conduct, even if the employer could not be held criminally liable for that conduct. (5) (Per Scott Baker, L.J.) An employer could not be civilly vicariously liable under s.3 of the Act for harassment committed by an employee in the course of his employment. Parliament could not have intended to extend so considerably by a side route an employer's liability at common law. Harassment was of a personal nature and was usually inflicted on one individual by another. Applying a purposive interpretation to the Act, there was nothing to suggest that vicarious liability should attach to the perpetrator's employer for acts of harassment committed in the workplace.

MAJROWSKI v. GUY'S AND ST THOMAS'S NHS TRUST, [2005] EWCA Civ 251, [2005] Q.B. 848, Auld, L.J., CA (Civ Div).

4200. Vicarious liability – Police officers – Liability of employer for unlawful off duty shooting – Jamaica

The appellant (B) appealed against a decision of the Court of Appeal of Jamaica that the Attorney General was not vicariously liable for the unlawful shooting of B by a police officer. B had been using a public telephone when an off duty officer announced "police" and demanded the phone. When B refused the officer shot him. The Attorney General denied that the officer was acting in the course of his employment or for his employer's benefit. B submitted that the contrary was true as a police officer was duty bound to preserve the peace on behalf of his employer at all times, that he had asserted his authority as a police officer and it did not matter whether he had done so in furtherance of his duty as a police officer. Furthermore, the officer had shot B using a revolver that his employer had given him and which he was permitted to carry when off duty, and the officer had subsequently arrested B and charged him with an offence, thereby asserting that at the time of the offence he was acting in the execution of his duty as a police officer.

Held, allowing the appeal, that an employer could be vicariously liable notwithstanding that the employee was acting exclusively for his or her own benefit. It was necessary to consider whether the unlawful shooting was so closely connected with the officer's employment that it would be fair and just to hold the Attorney General vicariously liable, *Lister v. Hesley Hall Ltd* [2001] UKHL 22, [2002] 1 A.C. 215, [2001] C.L.Y. 5359 applied and *Dubai Aluminium Co Ltd v. Salaam* [2002] UKHL 48, [2003] 2 A.C. 366, [2003] C.L.Y. 3046 applied. It was of prime importance that the shooting followed immediately upon the announcement by the officer that he was a policeman, which was probably calculated to create the impression that he was acting on police business. The subsequent arrest of B showed that the officer considered that B had interfered with the execution of his duties as a police officer. Moreover, the creation of the risk inherent in giving the officer a revolver for use at home reinforced the conclusion that vicarious liability was established.

BERNARD v. ATTORNEY GENERAL OF JAMAICA, [2004] UKPC 47, [2005] I.R.L.R. 398, Lord Bingham of Cornhill, PC (Jam).

4201. Books

Bermingham, Vera—Tort. Paperback: £6.50. ISBN 0 421 89070 3. Paperback: £6.50. ISBN 0 421 89070 3. Sweet & Maxwell.

Cameron, Gordon—Delict. Book (details unknown): £12.50. ISBN 0 414 01585 1. W.Green & Son.

Collins, Matthew—Law of Defamation and the Internet. Hardback: £125.00. ISBN 0 19 928182 3. Oxford University Press.

Cooke, John—Law of Tort. Foundation Studies in Law S. Paperback: £27.99. ISBN 1 4058 1229 X. Longman.

Cracknell, D.G.—Obligations: The Law of Tort. Paperback: £15.95. ISBN 1 85836 606 2. Old Bailey Press.

Harpwood, Vivenne—Modern Tort Law. Paperback: £24.95. ISBN 1 85941 976 3. Cavendish Publishing Ltd.

Howarth, David—Tort Law. Paperback: £28.00. ISBN 1 84113 572 0. Hart Publishing.

Koziol, Helmut; Steininger, Barbara—European Tort Law. Tort & Insurance Law. Paperback: £98.50. ISBN 3 211 24479 4. Springer-Verlag Vienna.

Madden, M.Stuart—Exploring Tort Law. Hardback: £45.00. ISBN 0 521 85136 X. Paperback: £19.99. ISBN 0 521 61680 8. Cambridge University Press.

Martin-Casals, Miquel—Children in Tort Law: Pt. 1. Children As Tortfeasors. Tort & Insurance Law, V. 17. Paperback: £65.50. ISBN 3 211 24480 8. Springer-Verlag Vienna.

Piggot, Mike Semple—Tort Law. Law in a Box S., No. 2. CD-ROM: £19.95. ISBN 1 904783 58 9. Semple Piggot Rochez (Legal Education Ltd).

Principles of European Tort Law: Text and Commentary. Paperback: £23.00. ISBN 3 211 23084 X. Springer-Verlag Vienna.

Quinn, Frances; Elliott, Catherine—Tort Law. Paperback: £19.99. ISBN 1 4058 0711 3. Longman.

Samuel, Geoffrey—Cases and Materials on Torts. Cases & Materials S. Paperback: £24.00. ISBN 1 84641 016 9. Law Matters Publishing.

Tort Lawcards. Lawcards S. Looseleaf/ring bound: £6.95. ISBN 1 84568 015 4. Cavendish Publishing Ltd.

Tugendhat, Michael; Christie, Iain—Law of Privacy and the Media: Main Work and Second Cumulative Supplement. Paperback: £195.00. ISBN 0 19 928344 3. Oxford University Press.

Tugendhat, Michael; Christie, Iain—Law of Privacy and the Media: Second Cumulative Supplement. Paperback: £55.00. ISBN 0 19 928343 5. Oxford University Press.

Turner, Chris—Tort Law. Key Facts S. Paperback: £5.99. ISBN 0 340 88948 9. Hodder & Stoughton Ltd.

Wadlow, Christopher—Law of Passing-off: Unfair Competition by Misrepresentation. Paperback: £65.00. ISBN 0 421 91960 4. Sweet & Maxwell.

Wagner, Gerhard—Tort Law and Liability Insurance. Tort & Insurance Law, V.16. Paperback: £60.00. ISBN 3 211 24482 4. Springer-Verlag Vienna.

TRANSPORT

4202. Airports-Guided transport systems

TRANSPORT (GUIDED SYSTEMS) (ENGLAND) (AMENDMENT) ORDER 2005, SI 2005 2290; made under the Transport and Works Act 1992 s.26. In force: September 12, 2005; £3.00.

This Order amends the Transport (Guided Systems) Order 1992 (SI 1992 2044) by removing a guided transport system at Gatwick Airport (which has been closed down), amending the description of a guided transport system at Stansted Airport to include its extension to satellite 2, substituting a new guided transport system and amending the description of the termini at Birmingham International Airport, and revising the reference to Birmingham International railway station and Birmingham International Airport to reflect the significant developments that have taken place at the location of both termini.

4203. Bus services-Fares-Travel concessions

TRAVEL CONCESSIONS (EXTENSION OF ENTITLEMENT) (ENGLAND) ORDER 2005, SI 2005 3224; made under the Greater London Authority Act 1999 s.242; and the Transport Act 2000 s.147, s.160. In force: Art.3: April 1, 2006; remainder: December 30, 2005; £3.00.

This Order amends Transport Act 2000 so that, outside Greater London, persons to whom a statutory travel concession permit has been issued by a travel concession authority are entitled to be provided with free bus travel between places in the authority's area. It also amends the Greater London Authority Act 1999 so that if, immediately before January 1 in a financial year, arrangements are not in place whereby London residents who are disabled or 60 years of age or over are eligible to have free bus travel, a "free travel scheme" shall have effect from April 1 in the next following financial year.

4204. Carriage of goods-Dangerous goods-Transportable pressure equipment

CARRIAGE OF DANGEROUS GOODS AND USE OF TRANSPORTABLE PRESSURE EQUIPMENT (AMENDMENT) REGULATIONS 2005, SI 2005 1732; made under the Health and Safety at Work etc Act 1974 s.15, s.43, s.80, s.82, Sch.3 para.1, Sch.3 para.2, Sch.3 para.3, Sch.3 para.4, Sch.3 para.6, Sch.3 para.15, Sch.3 para.16, Sch.3 para.20. In force: July 22, 2005; £4.00.

These Regulations amend the Order of Secretary of State (No.9) Relating to Compressed Acetylene Contained in a Porous Substance 1919 (SI 1919 809), the Chemicals (Hazard Information and Packaging for Supply) Regulations 2002 (SI 2002 1689), the Carriage of Dangerous Goods and use of Transportable Pressure Equipment Regulations 2004 (SI 2004 568) and the Health and Safety (Fees) Regulations 2005 (SI 2005 676). The Regulations implement Commission Directive 2004/89 ([2004] OJ L293/14) adapting for the fifth time to technical progress Council Directive 96/49 on the approximation of the laws of the Member States with regard to the transport of dangerous goods by rail; Commission Directive 2004/110 ([2004] OJ L365/24) adapting for the sixth time to technical progress Council Directive 96/49 on the approximation of the laws of the Member States with regard to the transport of dangerous goods by rail; and Commission Directive 2004/111 ([2004] OJ L365/25) adapting for the fifth time to technical progress Council Directive 94/55 on the approximation of the laws of the Member States with regard to the transport of dangerous goods by road. The Regulations provide alternative requirements for the carriage of dangerous goods in bulk; make provision for security relating to identification requirements for carriers and their personnel and site security plans for high consequence dangerous goods; make provision relating to non-compliance in relation to radioactive materials; clarify when dangerous goods may be carried in multiple element gas containers; and reinstate a provision relating to the fire-resistance of orange-coloured plates for carriage within Great Britain.

4205. Carriage of goods–Motor vehicles–Type approval–Fees

INTERNATIONAL TRANSPORT OF GOODS UNDER COVER OF TIR CARNETS (FEES) (AMENDMENT) REGULATIONS 2005, SI 2005 2457; made under the Finance Act 1973 s.56. In force: September 30, 2005; £3.00.

These Regulations amend the International Transport of Goods under Cover of TIR Carnets (Fees) Regulations 1988 (SI 1988 371) which prescribe the fees payable in connection with the approval of a road vehicle design-type, and with the issue of a certificate of approval for a road vehicle, in pursuance of Annex 3 to the Customs Convention on the International Transport of Goods under Cover of TIR Carnets of November 14, 1975. "TIR" is the acronym for "Transports Internationaux Routiers". The Regulations make amendments to prescribed fees.

4206. Channel Tunnel–International cooperation

CHANNEL TUNNEL (INTERNATIONAL ARRANGEMENTS) ORDER 2005, SI 2005 3207; made under the Channel Tunnel Act 1987 s.11. In force: December 19, 2005; £3.00.

This Order brings into effect a binational regulation signed on October 25, 2005 on behalf of the Governments of the United Kingdom of Great Britain and Northern Ireland and the French Republic by the Intergovernmental Commission. The purpose of that Regulation is to implement Council Directive 91/440 ([1991] OJ L237/25) on the development of the Community's railways, Council Directive 95/18 ([1995] OJ L143/70) on the licensing of railway undertakings and European Parliament and Council Directive 2001/14 ([2001] OJ L75/26) on the allocation of railway infrastructure capacity and the levying of charges for the use of railway infrastructure and safety certification.

4207. Disability Discrimination Act 1995 (c.50)–Commencement No.11 Order

DISABILITY DISCRIMINATION ACT 1995 (COMMENCEMENT NO.11) ORDER 2005, SI 2005 1122 (C.50); made under the Disability Discrimination Act 1995 s.70. Commencement details: bringing into force various provisions of the 1995 Act on April 6, 2005; £3.00.

This Order provides for the coming into force of the Disability Discrimination Act 1995 s.49, to the extent that it relates to provisions in the Act about the carriage of guide dogs and assistance dogs in taxis and private hire vehicles, and the granting of accessibility certificates and approval certificates in respect of public service vehicles. Section 49 makes it an offence for a person, with intent to deceive, to forge, alter, use, lend or allow another person to use a relevant document; and makes it an offence to knowingly make a false statement in order to obtain certain relevant documents.

4208. Heavy goods vehicles–Licensing–Fees

GOODS VEHICLES (LICENSING OF OPERATORS) (FEES) (AMENDMENT) (REGULATIONS) 2005, SI 2005 2345; made under the Goods Vehicles (Licensing of Operators) Act 1995 s.45, s.57. In force: September 30, 2005; £3.00.

These Regulations increase the fees which are payable under the Goods Vehicles (Licensing of Operators) (Fees) Regulations 1995 (SI 1995 3000).

4209. International carriage by rail–Convention–Ratification

RAILWAYS (CONVENTION ON INTERNATIONAL CARRIAGE BY RAIL) REGULATIONS 2005, SI 2005 2092; made under the Railways and Transport

Safety Act 2003 s.103, Sch.6 para.2, Sch.6 para.3, Sch.6 para.4, Sch.6 para.7, Sch.6 para.8, Sch.6 para.9. In force: in accordance with Reg.1; £3.00.

These Regulations, which revoke the International Transport Conventions Act 1983 (Certification of Commencement of Convention) Order 1985 (SI 1985 612), the International Transport Conventions Act 1983 (Amendment) Order 1992 (SI 1992 237) and the International Transport Conventions Act 1983 (Amendment) Order 1994 (SI 1994 1907), amend the Damages (Scotland) Act 1976, the Civil Jurisdiction and Judgments Act 1982, the International Transport Conventions Act1983, the Damages (Scotland) Act1993, the Contracts (Rights of Third Parties) Act1999, the Pressure Systems Safety Regulations 2000 (SI 2000 128) and the Chemicals (Hazard Information and Packaging for Supply) Regulations 2002 (SI 2002 1689). The Regulations provide that the 1999 Protocol to the Convention concerning International Carriage by Rail 1980 shall have the force of law following its ratification by, and entry into force for, the UK.

4210. International carriage by road–Dangerous goods–Fees

INTERNATIONAL CARRIAGE OF DANGEROUS GOODS BY ROAD (FEES) (AMENDMENT) REGULATIONS 2005, SI 2005 2456; made under the Finance Act 1973 s.56. In force: September 30, 2005; £3.00.

These Regulations amend the International Carriage of Dangerous Goods by Road (Fees) Regulations 1988 (SI 1988 370) which prescribe the fees payable in connection with the issue of special certificates of approval for vehicles used to carry dangerous goods, in pursuance of the European Agreement concerning the International Carriage of Dangerous Goods by Road. An ADR certificate is a special certificate of approval as defined in the 1988 Regulations "ADR" is the acronym for "Accord European Relatif au Transports International des Marchandises Dangereuses par Route". The Regulations increase the fees prescribed by the 1988 Regulations where an ADR certificate is applied for.

4211. Light rail–Merseyside

MERSEYTRAM (LIVERPOOL CITY CENTRE TO KIRKBY) ORDER 2005, SI 2005 120; made under the Transport and Works Act 1992 s.1, s.3, s.5, Sch.1 para.1, Sch.1 para.2, Sch.1 para.3, Sch.1 para.4, Sch.1 para.7, Sch.1 para.8, Sch.1 para.9, Sch.1 para.10, Sch.1 para.11, Sch.1 para.12, Sch.1 para.13, Sch.1 para.15, Sch.1 para.16, Sch.1 para.17. In force: February 11, 2005; £10.50.

This Order, which amends the Compulsory Purchase Act 1965 and the Land Compensation Act 1973, authorises the Merseyside Passenger Transport Executive (known as Merseytravel) to construct and operate a tram system between King's Dock in the City of Liverpool and Kirkby in the Metropolitan Borough of Knowsley and, for that purpose, compulsorily or by agreement to acquire land and rights in land and to use land. It contains a number of protective provisions for the benefit of affected undertakings.

4212. Light rail–West Midlands

MIDLAND METRO (BIRMINGHAM CITY CENTRE EXTENSION, ETC.) ORDER 2005, SI 2005 1794; made under the Transport and Works Act 1992 s.1, s.5, Sch.1 para.1, Sch.1 para.2, Sch.1 para.3, Sch.1 para.4, Sch.1 para.5, Sch.1 para.6, Sch.1 para.7, Sch.1 para.8, Sch.1 para.9, Sch.1 para.10, Sch.1 para.11, Sch.1 para.12, Sch.1 para.13, Sch.1 para.15, Sch.1 para.16, Sch.1 para.17. In force: July 22, 2005; £7.50.

This Order authorises West Midlands Passenger Transport Executive to construct an extension to the Midland Metro light rail system from a junction with the existing Metro line 1 near the existing St Paul's Metro stop in the City of Birmingham to a terminus at Hagley Road, Edgbaston, and, for that purpose, compulsorily to acquire land and rights in land. It contains a number of protective provisions for the benefit of affected undertakings.

4213. Light rail—West Midlands

MIDLAND METRO (WEDNESBURY TO BRIERLEY HILL AND MISCELLANEOUS AMENDMENTS) ORDER 2005, SI 2005 927; made under the Transport and Works Act 1992 s.1, s.5, Sch.1 para.1, Sch.1 para.2, Sch.1 para.3, Sch.1 para.4, Sch.1 para.5, Sch.1 para.6, Sch.1 para.7, Sch.1 para.8, Sch.1 para.9, Sch.1 para.10, Sch.1 para.11, Sch.1 para.12, Sch.1 para.13, Sch.1 para.15, Sch.1 para.17. In force: March 22, 2005; £7.50.

This Order, which modifies the Tramways Act 1870 and the application of the Road Traffic Regulation Act 1984, authorises West Midlands Passenger Transport Executive to construct an extension to the Midland Metro light rail system from a junction with the existing Metro line 1 in Wednesbury in the Metropolitan Borough of Sandwell to Brierley Hill town centre in the Metropolitan Borough of Dudley and, for that purpose, compulsorily to acquire land and rights in land. It makes certain ancillary provisions in relation to the existing Metro line 1 and contains a number of protective provisions for the benefit of affected undertakings.

4214. Local authorities—Parking provisions—London

TRANSPORT FOR LONDON (CONSEQUENTIAL PROVISIONS) ORDER 2005, SI 2005 56; made under the Greater London Authority Act 1999 s.405, s.406, s.420. In force: February 14, 2005; £3.00.

This Order modifies provisions of the London Local Authorities Act 1995 and the London Local Authorities Act 2000 relating to parking so as to apply them to Transport for London as well as to London borough councils.

4215. Motor vehicles—Construction and use

ROAD VEHICLES (CONSTRUCTION AND USE) (AMENDMENT) (NO.3) REGULATIONS 2005, SI 2005 2987; made under the Road Traffic Act 1988 s.41. In force: December 12, 2005; £3.00.

The Road Vehicles (Construction and Use) Regulations 1986 (SI 1986 1078) include provisions which prescribe construction requirements for minibuses and coaches. These Regulations make amendments so that compliance with European Parliament and Council Directive 2001/85 ([2001] OJ L42/1) relating to special provisions for vehicles used for the carriage of passengers comprising more than eight seats in addition to the driver's seat, and amending Directives 70/156 and 97/27 is offered as an alternative, as the Directive provides that Member States shall not refuse or prohibit sale or entry into service of a vehicle, or of bodywork intended to be part of the vehicle which may be type approved separately, if the requirements of the Directive and its Annexes are met. The Regulations provide that the requirements of the 1986 Regulations may alternatively be met by a vehicle satisfying such of the Annexes of Directive 2001/85 as apply to it.

4216. Motor vehicles—Construction and use

ROAD VEHICLES (CONSTRUCTION AND USE) (AMENDMENT) (NO.4) REGULATIONS 2005, SI 2005 3165; made under the Road Traffic Act 1988 s.41. In force: December 12, 2005; £3.00.

These Regulations amend the Road Vehicles (Construction and Use) Regulations 1986 (SI 1986 1078) so that the definition of "Community Directive, followed by a number", also includes Directives adopted by the European Parliament and the Council of the European Parliament. The Regulations also implement European Parliament and Council Directive 2003/97 ([2003] OJ L25/1) relating to the type-approval of devices for indirect vision and of vehicles equipped with these devices, amending Directive 70/156 and repealing Directive 71/127.

4217. Motor vehicles-Construction and use

ROAD VEHICLES (CONSTRUCTION AND USE) (AMENDMENT) (NO.5) REGULATIONS 2005, SI 2005 3170; made under the Road Traffic Act 1988 s.41. In force: December 12, 2005; £3.00.

These Regulations amend the Road Vehicles (Construction and Use) Regulations 1986 (SI 1986 1078) to make it clear that it is compliant with the limit values set out in Council Directive 88/77 ([1988] OJ L36/33) relating to the measures to be taken against the emission of gaseous pollutants from diesel engines for use in vehicles. They also allow the continued use of speed limiters set at a maximum speed of 100 kilometres per hour, when fitted to passenger carrying vehicles that were either first used before January 1, 2005 and with a maximum gross weight exceeding 10 tonnes; or first used before October 1, 2001 and with a maximum gross weight exceeding 7.5 tonnes but not exceeding 10 tonnes.

4218. Motor vehicles-Construction and use-Emissions

ROAD VEHICLES (CONSTRUCTION AND USE) (AMENDMENT) REGULATIONS 2005, SI 2005 1641; made under the Road Traffic Act 1988 s.41. In force: August 1, 2005; £3.00.

These Regulations amend the Road Vehicles (Construction and Use) Regulations 1986 (SI 1986 1078) to modify the definition of "the emissions publication" so as to refer to the most recent edition of the publication entitled "In Service Exhaust Emission Standards for Road Vehicles". The publication contains in-use emissions limits that petrol-engined cars and light vans are required to meet at MoT and Roadside emissions tests. The publication updates new models of petrol-engined passenger cars and light commercial vehicles, which have come onto the market since the last amending Regulations came into effect on August 1, 2004, and also revises a small amount of data on existing models.

4219. Motor vehicles-Construction and use-Emissions

ROAD VEHICLES (CONSTRUCTION AND USE) (AMENDMENT) (NO.2) REGULATIONS 2005, SI 2005 2560; made under the Road Traffic Act 1988 s.41. In force: October 21, 2005; £3.00.

These Regulations amend the Road Vehicles (Construction and Use) Regulations 1986 (SI 1986 1078) which govern the construction, equipment, maintenance and use of road vehicles. They make amendments to permit the fitting of a bell, gong, siren or two-tone horn to a motor vehicle under the lawful control of the Commissioners for Her Majesty's Revenue and Customs and used for the purposes of the investigation of serious crime; or owned or operated by the Secretary of State for Defence and used for the purpose of activity which either prevents or decreases exposure to radiation arising from a radiation accident or emergency, or is connected with an event which could lead to such an accident or emergency.

4220. Motor vehicles-Driving instruction-Driving tests

MOTOR CARS (DRIVING INSTRUCTION) REGULATIONS 2005, SI 2005 1902; made under the Road Traffic Act 1988 s.123, s.125, s.125A, s.125B, s.127, s.129, s.132, s.133B, s.134, s.135. In force: Reg.10: January 1, 2007; Reg.11: January 1, 2007; remainder: August 10, 2005; £12.00.

These Regulations, which amend the Motor Cars (Driving Instruction) (Amendment) Regulations 1991 (SI 1991 1129), revoke the Motor Cars (Driving Instruction) Regulations 1989 (SI 1989 2057), the Motor Cars (Driving Instruction) (Amendment) Regulations 1990 (SI 1990 1113), the Motor Cars (Driving Instruction) (Amendment) Regulations 1992 (SI 1992 1621), the Motor Cars (Driving Instruction) (Amendment) Regulations 1994 (SI 1994 554), the Motor Cars (Driving Instruction) (Amendment) Regulations 1995 (SI 1995 1218), the Motor Cars (Driving Instruction) (Amendment) Regulations 1996 (SI 1996 1983), the Motor Cars (Driving Instruction) (Amendment) Regulations 1997 (SI

1997 650), the Motor Cars (Driving Instruction) (Amendment) Regulations 1998 (SI 1998 2247), the Motor Cars (Driving Instruction) (Amendment) Regulations 2000 (SI 2000 1805), the Motor Cars (Driving Instruction) (Amendment) Regulations 2002 (SI 2002 2640), the Motor Cars (Driving Instruction) (Amendment) Regulations 2003 (SI 2003 3027), the Motor Cars (Driving Instruction) (Amendment) Regulations 2004 (SI 2004 2871) and the Motor Cars (Driving Instruction) (Amendment) (No.2) Regulations 2004 (SI 2004 3159). The amendments made are as follows: candidates for parts of the examination are required to produce the evidence of identity and entitlement to drive to the examiner before undertaking each part of the examination; a candidate for the test of driving technique (part of the driving ability and fitness test) must satisfy the examiner of his ability to carry out vehicle safety checks; the examiner of instructional ability and fitness test has the discretion to play two of three specified roles to conduct the test, one of which is a role as a qualified driver undertaking driver development training; motor cars provided by candidates for the purpose of a driving ability and fitness test, the instructional ability and fitness test and the test of continued ability and fitness to give instruction must have a seat belt, head restraint and (where appropriate) an additional rear view mirror available for use by the examiner; fees for the driving ability and fitness test and the instructional ability and fitness test are increased; and the fee for a licence is increased.

4221. Motor vehicles – Driving instruction – Driving tests – Hazard perception tests

MOTOR CARS (DRIVING INSTRUCTION) (AMENDMENT) REGULATIONS 2005, SI 2005 2716; made under the Road Traffic Act 1988 s.132, s.134. In force: November 1, 2005; £3.00.

These Regulations amend the Motor Cars (Driving Instruction) Regulations 2005 (SI 2005 1902) so as to require that during the practical instructional ability and fitness test, the car provided for the test must be fitted with "L" plates only while the examiner is playing the role of a novice or partly trained pupil or pupil who is at about driving test standard. There is no longer any requirement for "L" plates when the examiner is playing the role of a qualified driver undertaking driver development training. The Regulations concern the type of hazard perception tests that the Registrar can take into account for the purpose of enabling him to decide whether or not to retain the name of an approved driving instructor on the register under the Road Traffic Act 1988. They also make amendments so that the Registrar can take only take into account hazard perception tests equivalent to the tests specified in those Regulations where such tests are conducted by any person for the Secretary of State.

4222. Motor vehicles – Driving licences

MOTOR VEHICLES (DRIVING LICENCES) (AMENDMENT) (NO.2) REGULATIONS 2005, SI 2005 2717; made under the Road Traffic Act 1988 s.89, s.105. In force: November 1, 2005; £3.00.

These Regulations amend the Motor Vehicles (Driving Licences) Regulations 1999 (SI 1999 2864) so as to broaden the categories of vehicle in which a disabled driver may supervise a provisional licence holder to include not only cars, but also other categories and sub-categories of vehicles. They also broaden the categories of vehicle in respect of which any person supervising a provisional licence holder must hold a full licence for a minimum three year period; broaden the definition of "working day" to include Saturday; concern the arrangements for taking tests, both theory and practical, in respect of motor bicycles and large vehicles that are arranged by instructors on behalf of applicants; reduce the period of time that must elapse between the date the instructor supplies an applicant's details to the examiner and the test day itself to one clear working day; and reduce the period of notice required for a cancellation without loss of a fee from 10 to 3 clear working days.

4223. Motor vehicles–Driving licences–Fees

MOTOR VEHICLES (DRIVING LICENCES) (AMENDMENT) REGULATIONS 2005, SI 2005 1975; made under the Road Traffic Act 1988 s.89, s.105. In force: August 10, 2005; £3.00.

These Regulations increase some of the fees payable under the Motor Vehicle (Driving Licences) Regulations 1999 (SI 1999 2864). They amend the fees payable upon application for a practical or a unitary driving test where the test is to be conducted on or after the coming into force of these Regulations but before April 1, 2006 and then on or after April 1, 2006. They also amend the fees payable upon application for a theory test and increase the fee payable to the Secretary of State by persons authorised to conduct theory tests.

4224. Motor vehicles–EC type approval

MOTOR VEHICLES (EC TYPE APPROVAL) (AMENDMENT) REGULATIONS 2005, SI 2005 2454; made under the European Communities Act 1972 s.2. In force: October 19, 2005; £3.00.

These Regulations amend the Motor Vehicles (EC Type Approval) Regulations 1998 (SI 1998 2051) so that the definition of "the Framework Directive" encompasses the amendments made to Council Directive 70/156 ([1970] OJ L42/1) relating to the type approval of motor vehicles and their trailers by Commission Directive 2004/104 ([2004] OJ L337/13) adapting to technical progress Council Directive 72/245 relating to the radio interference (electromagnetic compatibility) of vehicles and amending Directive 70/156 on the approximation of the laws of the Member States relating to the type-approval of motor vehicles and their trailers.

4225. Motor vehicles–Police powers

ROAD TRAFFIC ACT 1988 (RETENTION AND DISPOSAL OF SEIZED MOTOR VEHICLES) REGULATIONS 2005, SI 2005 1606; made under the Road Traffic Act 1988 s.165B. In force: July 6, 2005; £3.00.

Under the Road Traffic Act 1988 the police have certain powers to seize and remove motor vehicles. These Regulations provide for the retention, safe keeping and disposal by the police or persons authorised by them, of vehicles seized under those powers.

4226. Motor vehicles–Registration–Vehicle identity checks–Fees

ROAD VEHICLES (REGISTRATION AND LICENSING) (AMENDMENT) REGULATIONS 2005, SI 2005 2344; made under the Vehicle Excise and Registration Act 1994 s.22, s.22A. In force: September 30, 2005; £3.00.

These Regulations, which amend the Road Vehicles (Registration and Licensing) Regulations 2002 (SI 2002 2742), increase the fee for a Vehicle Identity Check, or for a further Vehicle Identity Check on appeal, by 2.86 per cent from £35 to £36.

4227. Motor vehicles–Registration and licensing–Disclosure of information

ROAD VEHICLES (REGISTRATION AND LICENSING) (AMENDMENT) (NO.2) REGULATIONS 2005, SI 2005 2713; made under the Vehicle Excise and Registration Act 1994 s.22ZA. In force: October 31, 2005; £3.00.

These Regulations, which amend the Road Vehicles (Registration and Licensing) Regulations 2002 (SI 2002 2742), provide that information relating to the payment of the mobility supplement of the war pension and the higher rate mobility component of disability living allowance, and to the suspension of an entitlement to receive the latter, is prescribed for the purposes of the Vehicle Excise and Registration Act 1994 s.22ZA. Information so prescribed may be disclosed by the Secretary of State or, in relation to social security functions in Northern Ireland, by the relevant Northern Ireland department to another Secretary of State in order to verify entitlement to an exemption from vehicle excise duty by virtue of the keeper or user of a vehicle being entitled to receive such a benefit.

4228. Motor vehicles–Road safety–Lighting

ROAD VEHICLES LIGHTING (AMENDMENT) REGULATIONS 2005, SI 2005 2559; made under the Road Traffic Act 1988 s.41. In force: October 21, 2005; £3.00.

These Regulations amend the Road Vehicles Lighting Regulations 1989 (SI 1989 1796) which contain provisions for the construction, maintenance and use of lighting systems on vehicles. They make changes to the definition of "Emergency vehicle"; provide a definition of "abnormal load escort vehicle"; remove the requirement that an emergency vehicle shall be a motor vehicle thereby permitting non-motor emergency vehicles to use blue flashing lights; delete references to the now defunct "Naval Emergency Monitoring Organisation" and "Royal Air Force Armament Support Unit"; amend the definition of "Emergency vehicle" to include a vehicle under the lawful control of the Commissioners for Her Majesty's Revenue and Customs and used for the purposes of the investigation of serious crime; make changes with respect to pedal cycle lights; permit pedal cycles or trailers drawn by, or a sidecar attached to, a pedal cycle to be fitted with front and rear position lamps which flash; exempt obligatory front and rear position lamps which flash and are fitted to a pedal cycle or a trailer drawn by, or a sidecar attached to, a pedal cycle from marking requirements; and require the flash rate for any rear position lamp fitted to a pedal cycle or trailer drawn by a sidecar attached to a pedal cycle to be between 60 and 240 flashes per minute.

4229. Motor vehicles–Road safety–Testing–Exemptions

ROAD VEHICLES LIGHTING (AMENDMENT) (NO.2) REGULATIONS 2005, SI 2005 3169; made under the Road Traffic Act 1988 s.41. In force: December 12, 2005; £3.00.

These Regulations amend the Road Vehicles Lighting Regulations 1989 (SI 1989 1796) to add a new exemption. A vehicle used by a vehicle examiner will be exempt from the requirements in Part 2 (governing the fitting of lamps, reflectors, rear markings and devices) and Part 3 (governing the maintenance and use of lamps, reflectors, rear markings and devices), where the intended purpose is to submit that vehicle for an examination at a vehicle testing station in order to make sure that the examination carried out there is in accordance with the required testing standards. The exemption also allows the vehicle to be driven away from the vehicle testing station after the completion of the examination. In order to fall within the exemption two requirements must be met. Firstly, the vehicle must be being used by a vehicle examiner who has been authorised in writing by the Secretary of State for these purposes. Secondly, the vehicle examiner using the vehicle must reasonably believe that any defects in the vehicle do not give rise to a danger of injury to any person while it is being used for the purpose specified in the exemption.

4230. Motor vehicles–Seat belts–Exemptions

MOTOR VEHICLES (WEARING OF SEAT BELTS) (AMENDMENT) REGULATIONS 2005, SI 2005 27; made under the Road Traffic Act 1988 s.14. In force: March 1, 2005; £3.00.

These Regulations amend the Motor Vehicles (Wearing of Seat Belts) Regulations 1993 (SI 1993 176) by substituting for the delivery drivers' exemption an exemption for the driver of, or a passenger in, a goods vehicle while on a journey which does not exceed 50 metres and is undertaken for the purpose of delivery or collection; and replacing the reference to the Motor Vehicles (Driving Licences) Regulations 1987 (SI 1987 1378) Reg.9 with a reference to the Motor Vehicles (Driving Licences) Regulations (SI 1999 2864) Reg.17 which has superseded it and defines "qualified driver" differently.

4231. Motor vehicles–Testing–Fees

GOODS VEHICLES (PLATING AND TESTING) (AMENDMENT) REGULATIONS 2005, SI 2005 2343; made under the Road Traffic Act 1988 s.49, s.51. In force: September 30, 2005; £3.00.

These Regulations amend the Goods Vehicles (Plating and Testing) Regulations 1988 (SI 1988 1478) to make extensive amendments to the fees prescribed by the 1988 Regulations. The Regulations change the fee payable on an application for a first examination or periodical test; and change the fee payable on an application for a re-test or further re-test carried out within 14 days after the vehicle was submitted for its first examination, periodic test or previous re-test.

4232. Motor vehicles–Testing–Fees

MOTOR VEHICLES (TESTS) (AMENDMENT) REGULATIONS 2005, SI 2005 1832; made under the Road Traffic Act 1988 s.45, s.46. In force: August 1, 2005; £3.00.

These Regulations amend the Motor Vehicles (Tests) Regulations 1981 (SI 1981 1694) which make provision for certain motor vehicles to be examined by persons authorised by the Secretary of State and for test certificates to be issued for vehicles that are found to meet certain requirements. The Regulations prescribe the fees payable for examinations of vehicles pursuant to applications made.

4233. Motor vehicles–Testing–Fees

MOTOR VEHICLES (TESTS) (AMENDMENT) (NO.2) REGULATIONS 2005, SI 2005 2341; made under the Road Traffic Act 1988 s.45, s.46. In force: September 30, 2005; £3.00.

These Regulations amend the Motor Vehicles (Tests) Regulations 1981 (SI 1981 1694) which make provision for certain motor vehicles to be examined by persons authorised by the Secretary of State and for test certificates to be issued for vehicles that are found to meet certain requirements. The Regulations prescribe the fees payable for examinations of vehicles.

4234. Motor vehicles–Transport services–Disability discrimination

DISABILITY DISCRIMINATION (TRANSPORT VEHICLES) REGULATIONS 2005, SI 2005 3190; made under the Disability Discrimination Act 1995 s.21, s.21ZA. In force: December 4, 2006; £3.00.

These Regulations provide for certain provisions in the Disability Discrimination Act 1995 Part 3 to apply to the providers of certain transport services.

4235. Motor vehicles–Vehicle excise duty–Credit card payments–Prescribed fees

ROAD VEHICLES (PAYMENT OF DUTY BY CREDIT CARD) (PRESCRIBED FEE) REGULATIONS 2005, SI 2005 2460; made under the Vehicle Excise and Registration Act 1994 s.19C, s.57. In force: October 14, 2005; £3.00.

These Regulations prescribe the fee which is payable under the Vehicle Excise and Registration Act 1994 upon the acceptance of a credit card payment in respect of the vehicle excise duty payable upon each vehicle licence or trade licence for which application is made. The fee is £2.50 and such amount has been approved by the Treasury. The Regulations also prescribe the meaning of "credit card".

4236. Motor vehicles–Vehicle registration plates–Suppliers–Registration

VEHICLES CRIME (REGISTRATION OF REGISTRATION PLATE SUPPLIERS) (ENGLAND AND WALES) (AMENDMENT) REGULATIONS 2005, SI 2005 2981; made under the Vehicles (Crime) Act 2001 s.17, s.24, s.25, s.41. In force: December 1, 2005; £3.00.

These Regulations amend the Vehicles Crime (Registration of Registration Plate Suppliers) (England and Wales) Regulations 2002 (SI 2002 2977). They define the expressions "fixed", "registration certificate" and "registration document" and exempt from being considered as the selling of registration plates the transfer of possession of a registration plate by virtue of a sale or transfer of the vehicle to which it is fixed where the plate has not been fixed to that vehicle by or on behalf of the seller thereof; provide that there is no requirement to obtain information regarding the connection of a purchaser to a vehicle or to verify the name and address where the registration plate is fixed to a vehicle which is sold or transferred; provide that registered persons no longer have to retain records relating to payment methods; require registered suppliers of registration plates to record particulars or numbers unique to the purchaser of a registration plate from documents used to verify that person's name and address and provide for the recording of reference numbers from registration documents or certificates; provide that in the absence of a photocard driving licence the name and address of the purchaser are to be verified by one or more specified documents which meet specified requirements and make additions to the list of documents which may be used for such purpose; and make some corrections and additions to the list of documents which may be used to establish a connection with the registration mark or vehicle.

4237. Parking–Special parking areas–Stockton-on-Tees

ROAD TRAFFIC (PERMITTED PARKING AREA AND SPECIAL PARKING AREA) (BOROUGH OF STOCKTON-ON-TEES) ORDER 2005, SI 2005 2155; made under the Road Traffic Act 1991 Sch.3 para.1, Sch.3 para.2, Sch.3 para.3. In force: September 5, 2005; £3.00.

This Order applies to the whole of the borough of Stockton-on-Tees except the roads specified in art.3. The Order designates the borough of Stockton-on-Tees, other than the excepted roads, as both a permitted parking area and a special parking area in accordance with the Road Traffic Act 1991. It also applies with modifications various provisions of that Act to the designated area and modifies the Road Traffic Regulation Act 1984 in relation to the designated area.

4238. Parking–Special parking areas–Woking

ROAD TRAFFIC (PERMITTED PARKING AREA AND SPECIAL PARKING AREA) (COUNTY OF SURREY) (BOROUGH OF WOKING) ORDER 2005, SI 2005 1645; made under the Road Traffic Act 1991 Sch.3 para.1, Sch.3 para.2, Sch.3 para.3. In force: July 25, 2005; £3.00.

This Order designates the borough of Woking, other than the excepted roads, as both a permitted parking area and a special parking area in accordance with the Road Traffic Act 1991. It also applies with modifications various provisions of Part II of that Act to the designated area and modifies the Road Traffic Regulation Act 1984 in relation to the designated area.

4239. Passenger vehicles–Accessibility requirements–Disabled persons

PUBLIC SERVICE VEHICLES ACCESSIBILITY (AMENDMENT) REGULATIONS 2005, SI 2005 2988; made under the Disability Discrimination Act 1995 s.40, s.41. In force: December 12, 2005; £3.00.

The Public Service Vehicles Accessibility Regulations 2000 (SI 2000 1970) prescribe wheelchair accessibility requirements and general accessibility requirements for single-deck and double-deck buses and coaches. These Regulations make amendments so that compliance with European Parliament and Council Directive 2001/85 ([2001] OJ L42/1) relating to special provisions for vehicles used for the carriage of passengers comprising more than eight seats in addition to the driver's seat, and amending Directives 70/156 and 97/27 is offered as an alternative, as the Directive provides that Member States shall not refuse or prohibit sale or entry into service of a vehicle, or of bodywork intended to be part of the vehicle which may be type approved separately, if the requirements of the Directive and its Annexes are met. The Regulations provide that the requirements of the 2000 Regulations specified may alternatively be met by a vehicle satisfying both the requirements of such of the Annexes as apply to it and the requirements of Annex VII to the Directive.

4240. Passenger vehicles–Buses–Community bus permit–Fees

COMMUNITY BUS (AMENDMENT) REGULATIONS 2005, SI 2005 2353; made under the Public Passenger Vehicles Act 1981 s.52, s.60. In force: September 30, 2005; £3.00.

These Regulations amend the Community Bus Regulations 1986 (SI 1986 1245) to increase the fee for a community bus permit granted under the Transport Act 1985 s.22 from £44 to £50 (an increase of 13.6 per cent).

4241. Passenger vehicles–Buses–Permits–Fees

MINIBUS AND OTHER SECTION 19 PERMIT BUSES (AMENDMENT) REGULATIONS 2005, SI 2005 2354; made under the Public Passenger Vehicles Act 1981 s.52, s.60. In force: September 30, 2005; £3.00.

These Regulations, which amend the Minibus and Other Section 19 Permit Buses Regulations 1987 (SI 1987 1230), increase the fee for a permit granted under the Transport Act 1985 s.19 in respect of the use of a large bus from £17 to £19 (an increase of 11.8 per cent) and in respect of the use of a small bus from £9 to £10 (an increase of 11.1 per cent).

4242. Passenger vehicles–Certificates and type approvals–Fees

PUBLIC SERVICE VEHICLES (CONDITIONS OF FITNESS, EQUIPMENT, USE AND CERTIFICATION) (AMENDMENT) (NO.2) REGULATIONS 2005, SI 2005 2342; made under the Public Passenger Vehicles Act 1981 s.10, s.52, s.60. In force: September 30, 2005; £3.00.

These Regulations, which amend the Public Service Vehicles (Conditions of Fitness, Equipment, Use and Certification) Regulations 1981 (SI 1981 257), prescribe the fees payable for inspections of public service vehicles, prescribe the fees payable for vehicle type approval, prescribe the fee payable for a certificate of conformity and prescribe the fee payable for the issue of a duplicate certificate.

4243. Passenger vehicles–Goods vehicles–Digital tachographs

PASSENGER AND GOODS VEHICLES (RECORDING EQUIPMENT) REGULATIONS 2005, SI 2005 1904; made under the European Communities Act 1972 s.2. In force: August 5, 2005; £3.00.

These Regulations amend the Transport Act 1968 and the Road Traffic (Foreign Vehicles) Act 1972 to take account of the new, digital tachograph, provided for by Council Regulation 2135/98 ([1998] OJ L274/1), which amended Regulation 3821/85 on recording equipment in road transport. They also make changes to the enforcement regime, which applies to both analogue tachographs and digital tachographs.

4244. Passenger vehicles–Goods vehicles–Tachographs–Fees

PASSENGER AND GOODS VEHICLES (RECORDING EQUIPMENT) (APPROVAL OF FITTERS AND WORKSHOPS) (FEES) (AMENDMENT) REGULATIONS 2005, SI 2005 2458; made under the Finance Act 1973 s.56. In force: September 30, 2005; £3.00.

These Regulations amend the Passenger and Goods Vehicles (Recording Equipment) (Approval of Fitters and Workshops) (Fees) Regulations 1986 (SI 1986 2128) so as to increase the fees for the approval of fitters or workshops for the installation or repair of recording equipment (tachographs). The fee for the issue of an approval is increased by 13.1 per cent from £275 to £311 and for the renewal of an approval by 13.4 per cent from £112 to £127.

4245. Passenger vehicles–Goods vehicles–Tachographs–Fees

PASSENGER AND GOODS VEHICLES (RECORDING EQUIPMENT) (TACHOGRAPH CARD FEES) REGULATIONS 2005, SI 2005 1140; made under the European Communities Act 1972 s.2. In force: June 1, 2005; £3.00.

These Regulations provide for the issuing of driver cards, company cards, workshop cards and control cards for use with digital tachographs, which are tachographs complying with Council Regulation 3821/85 ([1985] OJ L370/8) on recording equipment in road transport, and for the replacement of cards which expire, are damaged, malfunction, are lost, or are stolen. They provide for the payment of specified fees in respect of driver cards, which are held by drivers of vehicles required to be fitted with digital tachographs by the Community Recording Equipment Regulation, and company cards, which are held by the operators of such vehicles.

4246. Passenger vehicles–Local services–Registration–Fees

PUBLIC SERVICE VEHICLES (REGISTRATION OF LOCAL SERVICES) (AMENDMENT) (ENGLAND AND WALES) REGULATIONS 2005, SI 2005 2355; made under the Public Passenger Vehicles Act 1981 s.52, s.60. In force: September 30, 2005; £3.00.

These Regulations, which amend the Public Service Vehicles (Registration of Local Services) Regulations 1986 (SI 1986 1671), increase the fee for the registration of, or the variation of the registration of, a local bus service. The fee for a local bus service other than a community bus service is increased from £45 to £51 (an increase of 13.3 per cent).

4247. Passenger vehicles–Public hire vehicles–Conditions of fitness

PUBLIC SERVICE VEHICLES (CONDITIONS OF FITNESS, EQUIPMENT, USE AND CERTIFICATION) (AMENDMENT) (NO.3) REGULATIONS 2005, SI 2005 2986; made under the Public Passenger Vehicles Act 1981 s.6, s.60; and the Road Traffic Act 1988 s.41. In force: December 12, 2005; £3.00.

The Public Passenger Vehicles Act 1981 requires that a vehicle adapted to carry more than eight passengers and used as a Public Service Vehicle shall not be used on a road unless a certificate has been issued indicating that prescribed conditions of initial fitness have been fulfilled. These prescribed conditions may be found in the Public Service Vehicles (Conditions of Fitness, Equipment, Use and Certification) Regulations 1981 (SI 1981 257). It is necessary that the 1981 Regulations are modified so that requirements of European Parliament and Council Directive 2001/85 ([2001] OJ L42/1) relating to special provisions for vehicles used for the carriage of passengers comprising more than eight seats in addition to the driver's seat, and amending Directives 70/156 and 97/27 are offered as an alternative, as the Directive provides that Member States shall not refuse or prohibit sale or entry into service of a bus or coach, or of bodywork intended to be part of the bus or coach which may be type approved separately, if the requirements of the Directive and its Annexes are met. These Regulations provide that the requirements in the 1981 Regulations may alternatively be met by a vehicle satisfying such of the Annexes of the Directive as apply to it.

4248. Passenger vehicles–Public hire vehicles–Conditions of fitness

PUBLIC SERVICE VEHICLES (CONDITIONS OF FITNESS, EQUIPMENT, USE AND CERTIFICATION) (AMENDMENT) (NO.4) REGULATIONS 2005, SI 2005 3128; made under the Road Traffic Act 1988 s.41. In force: December 13, 2005; £3.00.

These Regulations amend the Public Service Vehicles (Conditions of Fitness, Equipment, Use and Certification) Regulations 1981 (SI 1981 257) so that a steam-powered vehicle manufactured before January 1, 1955 is eligible to be issued with a certificate of initial fitness under the Public Passenger Vehicles Act 1981 s.6, even though it does not meet the requirements of reg.14 of the 1981 Regulations. Reg.14 requires that the exhaust pipe of a public service vehicle shall be fitted or shielded so that inflammable material is prevented from falling upon the pipe from another part of the vehicle and causing fire, and the outlet of the pipe shall be either at the rear, or on the offside and far enough to the rear, to prevent so far as practicable fumes from entering the vehicle.

4249. Public service vehicles–Conditions of fitness–Certificates–Fees

PUBLIC SERVICE VEHICLES (CONDITIONS OF FITNESS, EQUIPMENT, USE AND CERTIFICATION) (AMENDMENT) REGULATIONS 2005, SI 2005 1403; made under the Public Passenger Vehicles Act 1981 s.52, s.60. In force: July 1, 2005; £3.00.

These Regulations amend the Public Service Vehicles (Conditions of Fitness, Equipment, Use and Certification) Regulations 1981 (SI 1981 257) to provide that the fee payable for the issue of a certificate of initial fitness on the first application is £215 in every case, removing the separate fee for the examination of seat belts in public service vehicles.

4250. Public transport–Grant of leasehold interest–Rickmansworth Station–London

TRANSPORT FOR LONDON (RICKMANSWORTH STATION) ORDER 2005, SI 2005 2156; made under the Greater London Authority Act 1999 s.163. In force: August 30, 2005; £3.00.

The Greater London Authority Act 1999 prohibits Transport for London from granting a leasehold interest in operational land for a term of more than fifty years without the consent of the Secretary of State. Under that Act, Transport for London is required to ensure that none of its subsidiaries does anything which Transport for London has no power to do (including anything which Transport for London has no power to do because the consent of the Secretary of State has not been obtained). The land which is the subject of this Order comprises most of the station car park at Rickmansworth Station in Hertfordshire, which is operational land. The grant of a leasehold interest in that land for a term of more than fifty years therefore requires the consent of the Secretary of State. The land is currently vested in London Underground Ltd, a subsidiary of Transport for London, and the grant of the leasehold interest will be made by that company. By this Order the Secretary of State for Transport gives consent to Transport for London for the grant of a leasehold interest for a term of more than fifty years in the land which is the subject of the Order. A condition has been attached to the Secretary of State's consent to require Transport for London to secure that permanent car parking facilities are provided to replace the existing car park at Rickmansworth Station. This should be done within a reasonable period following any development of the land which is the subject of this Order.

4251. Public transport–Land disposal–Waterloo Station–London

TRANSPORT FOR LONDON (WATERLOO STATION) ORDER 2005, SI 2005 1866; made under the Greater London Authority Act 1999 s.163. In force: August 3, 2005; £3.00.

The Greater London Authority Act 1999 prohibits Transport for London from disposing of the freehold interest in any operational land without the consent of the Secretary of State. Under that Act, Transport for London is required to ensure that none of its subsidiaries does anything which Transport for London has no power to do (including anything which Transport for London has no power to do because the consent of the Secretary of State has not been obtained). The land at York Road, London SE1 which is the subject of this Order has been operational land. It includes the area once occupied by the former Bakerloo Line ticket hall at Waterloo Station. The 1999 Act s.163(3) provides that consent under s.163 is not required in respect of land which was formerly operational land if a period of at least five years has elapsed since the land was last operational land, but such a period has not yet elapsed in this case. Its disposal therefore requires the consent of the Secretary of State. The land is currently vested in London Underground Limited, a subsidiary of Transport for London, and the disposal shall be made by that company.

4252. Public transport–Operators licences–Fees

PUBLIC SERVICE VEHICLES (OPERATORS' LICENCES) (FEES) (AMENDMENT) REGULATIONS 2005, SI 2005 2346; made under the Public Passenger Vehicles Act 1981 s.52, s.60. In force: September 30, 2005; £3.00.

These Regulations increase the fees which are payable under the Public Service Vehicles (Operators' Licences) (Fees) Regulations 1995 (SI 1995 2909).

4253. Railways–Accessibility–Disabled persons–Exemptions

RAIL VEHICLE ACCESSIBILITY (HEATHROW EXPRESS CLASS 360/2) EXEMPTION ORDER 2005, SI 2005 86; made under the Disability Discrimination Act 1995 s.47. In force: March 1, 2005; £3.00.

This Order authorises the use for carriage of specified rail vehicles forming the fleet of Class 360/2 Heathrow Express electric multiple-units even though they do not conform with one requirement of the Rail Vehicle Accessibility Regulations 1998 (SI 1998 2456) because the carpets in the vestibule do not contrast sufficiently with the carpets in the adjacent passenger saloon.

4254. Railways–Accessibility–Disabled persons–Exemptions

RAIL VEHICLE ACCESSIBILITY (HEATHROW EXPRESS CLASS 360/2) EXEMPTION (AMENDMENT) ORDER 2005, SI 2005 1404; made under the Disability Discrimination Act 1995 s.47. In force: June 27, 2005; £3.00.

This Order amends the Rail Vehicle Accessibility (Heathrow Express Class 360/2) Exemption Order 2005 (SI 2005 86) which authorises the use of specified rail vehicles even though they do not conform with the Rail Vehicle Accessibility Regulations 1998 (SI 1998 2456). The Order authorises the use of additional vehicles in the Class 360/2 fleet of electric multiple-units because the carpets in the vestibule do not contrast sufficiently with the carpets in the adjacent passenger saloon.

4255. Railways–Accessibility–Disabled persons–Exemptions

RAIL VEHICLE ACCESSIBILITY (VIRGIN WEST COAST CLASS 390) EXEMPTION ORDER 2005, SI 2005 329; made under the Disability Discrimination Act 1995 s.47. In force: March 28, 2005; £3.00.

This Order, which revokes the Rail Vehicle Accessibility (Virgin West Coast Class 390 Vehicles) Exemption Order 2002 (SI 2002 1699), authorises the use for carriage of specified rail vehicles which form the fleet of Class 390 electric multiple-units, even though they do not conform with certain provisions in the Rail Vehicle Accessibility Regulations 1998 (SI 1998 2456).

4256. Railways–Accidents–Investigation and reporting

RAILWAYS (ACCIDENT INVESTIGATION AND REPORTING) REGULATIONS 2005, SI 2005 1992; made under the Railways and Transport Safety Act 2003 s.2, s.6, s.7, s.9, s.11, s.13. In force: in accordance with Reg.1 (2); £4.00.

These Regulations implement provisions of European Parliament and Council Directive 2004/49 ([2004] OJ L164/44) on the safety of the Community's railways and amending Council Directive 2001/14 on the allocation of railway infrastructure capacity and the levying of charges for the use of railway infrastructure and safety certification, in so far as those articles have not already been implemented by the Railways and Transport Safety Act 2003 Part 1, which establishes the Rail Accident Investigation Branch, being a permanent body given power to investigate railway accidents and incidents.

4257. Railways—Accidents—Investigation and reporting

RAILWAYS (ACCIDENT INVESTIGATION AND REPORTING) (AMENDMENT) REGULATIONS 2005, SI 2005 3261; made under the Railways and Transport Safety Act 2003 s.11, s.13. In force: January 11, 2006; £3.00.

These Regulations amend the Railways (Accident Investigation and Reporting) Regulations 2005 (SI 2005 1992) to insert a definition of "working days" to describe the time within which accidents or incidents must be reported. They also insert the word "reasonably" before "determine" providing for the time within which a safety authority may require a person to consider or act upon a recommendation of the Rail Accident Investigation Branch and to provide it with certain information.

4258. Railways—Compulsory purchase—East Midlands Parkway Station

EAST MIDLANDS PARKWAY STATION (LAND ACQUISITION) ORDER 2005, SI 2005 8; made under the Transport and Works Act 1992 s.1, s.5, Sch.1 para.3, Sch.1 para.4, Sch.1 para.5, Sch.1 para.7, Sch.1 para.11, Sch.1 para.15. In force: January 28, 2005; £3.00.

This Order confers powers on Midland Main Line Ltd for the compulsory acquisition of land and rights over land, and for temporary use of land, in the Parish of Ratcliffe on Soar, in the Borough of Rushcliffe, Nottinghamshire, in connection with the provision of the proposed East Midlands Parkway Station. The Order does not authorise the construction of the station, parking facilities or any other development.

4259. Railways—Construction—Telford Railfreight, Donnington

TELFORD RAILFREIGHT TERMINAL (DONNINGTON) ORDER 2005, SI 2005 1163; made under the Transport and Works Act 1992 s.1, s.5, Sch.1 para.1, Sch.1 para.2, Sch.1 para.3, Sch.1 para.4, Sch.1 para.5, Sch.1 para.7, Sch.1 para.8, Sch.1 para.10, Sch.1 para.11, Sch.1 para.15, Sch.1 para.16, Sch.1 para.17. In force: May 4, 2005; £6.00.

This Order, which amends the Compulsory Purchase Act 1965 and the Land Compensation Act 1973, provides for the construction of a railway and other works, and the acquisition of land and rights, in connection with the Telford Railfreight (Donnington) scheme in the borough of Telford and Wrekin.

4260. Railways—Croydon Tramlink and Docklands Light Railway—Reserved services

TRANSPORT FOR LONDON (RESERVED SERVICES) (CROYDON TRAMLINK AND DOCKLANDS LIGHT RAILWAY) EXCEPTION ORDER 2005, SI 2005 763; made under the Greater London Authority Act 1999 s.207. In force: April 11, 2005; £3.00.

This Order excepts all agreements in respect of Croydon Tramlink and Docklands Light Railway, under which station or train operating functions are provided by a person other than Transport for London or its subsidiaries, from the requirement that the Secretary of State's consent be obtained before they are entered into or carried out. The Docklands Light Railway is now defined as including the City Airport and Woolwich Arsenal Extensions in addition to the railways previously listed in the Transport for London (Reserved Services) (Croydon Tramlink and Docklands Light Railway) Exception Order 2000 (SI 2000 1143) which is revoked by this Order.

4261. Railways—East Somerset—Safety provisions

EAST SOMERSET RAILWAY ORDER 2005, SI 2005 3143; made under the Transport and Works Act 1992 s.1, s.5, Sch.1 para.1, Sch.1 para.8, Sch.1 para.15, Sch.1 para.17. In force: December 1, 2005; £3.00.

This Order relates to the portions of the East Somerset Railway at Cranmore near Shepton Mallet in Somerset which at the date of this Order are owned by BRB

(Residuary) Ltd. The Order authorises the Owner to transfer the portions of the railway to East Somerset Railway Company Ltd together with certain statutory and other rights and liabilities. The Order also makes provision for the safety of works and equipment.

4262. Railways–Heritage property

RAILWAY HERITAGE SCHEME ORDER 2005, SI 2005 2905; made under the Railway Heritage Act 1996 s.2. In force: November 21, 2005; £3.00.

This Order, which revokes the Railway Heritage Scheme Order 1997 (SI 1997 39), gives effect to the Railway Heritage Scheme. The Scheme set out in the 1997 Order provided for the continued establishment of the Railway Heritage Committee, the duration and termination of membership of the Committee, proceedings of the Committee, establishment, membership, functions and proceedings of sub-committees, matters of administrative and secretarial assistance and expenses, and records of the Committee. That Order also enabled the Committee to set quorums for its meetings and those of sub-committees, and enabled the Committee to appoint a deputy chairman. These provisions have been largely re-enacted in the Scheme set out in this Order with references to the British Railways Board replaced by references to the Secretary of State. The sole substantive difference between the two Schemes is that there is no equivalent in this Scheme to the requirement for the approval of the British Railways Board to be obtained in relation to the membership and termination of membership of sub-committees.

4263. Railways–High Barnet Substation

TRANSPORT FOR LONDON (HIGH BARNET SUBSTATION) ORDER 2005, SI 2005 3232; made under the Greater London Authority Act 1999 s.163. In force: January 5, 2006; £3.00.

The Greater London Authority Act 1999 prohibits Transport for London from disposing of any freehold interest in operational land without the consent of the Secretary of State. Under that Act, Transport for London is required to ensure that none of its subsidiaries does anything which Transport for London has no power to do (including anything which Transport for London has no power to do because the consent of the Secretary of State has not been obtained). The land at Ivere Drive, Barnet, London EN5, which is the subject of this Order has been operational land. It comprises of the area formerly occupied by an electricity substation used in connection with the provision of railway services. The Act provides that consent is not required in respect of land which was formerly operational land if a period of at least five years has elapsed since the land was last operational land, but such a period has not yet elapsed in this case. Its disposal therefore requires the consent of the Secretary of State. The land is currently vested in London Underground Ltd, a subsidiary of Transport for London, and the disposal of the land will be made by that company. By this Order the Secretary of State for Transport gives consent to Transport for London for the disposal of the land which is the subject of the Order.

4264. Railways–Infrastructure–Access and management

RAILWAYS INFRASTRUCTURE (ACCESS AND MANAGEMENT) REGULATIONS 2005, SI 2005 3049; made under the European Communities Act 1972 s.2. In force: November 28, 2005; £5.50.

These Regulations, which revoke with saving the Railways Regulations 1998 (SI 1998 1340), implement Council Directive 91/440 ([1991] OJ L237/25) on the development of the Community's railways and European Parliament and Council Directive 2001/14 ([2001] OJ L75/29) on the allocation of railway infrastructure capacity and the levying of charges for the use of railway infrastructure and safety certification. The Regulations amend the Parliamentary Commissioner Act 1967, the House of Commons Disqualification Act 1975, the Northern Ireland Assembly Disqualification Act 1975, the Railways Act 1993, the Channel Tunnel Rail Link Act

1996, the Greater London Authority Act 1999, the Railways and Transport Safety Act 2003 and the Scottish Parliament (Disqualification) Order 2003 (SI 2003 409). The Regulations grant access and transit rights to international groupings and freight operators to the entire rail network in Great Britain, including access to terminals and ports linked to the rail network; grant all applicants certain rights of access to, and the supply of, the services listed; impose certain separation requirements between the bodies responsible for management of the railway infrastructure and railway undertakings; and set out the structure for the charging of fees for the use of railway infrastructure, and the charging principles.

4265. Railways−Light railways−Capacity enhancement−Docklands Light Railway

DOCKLANDS LIGHT RAILWAY (CAPACITY ENHANCEMENT) ORDER 2005, SI 2005 3105; made under the Transport and Works Act 1992 s.1, s.3, s.5, Sch.1 para.1, Sch.1 para.2, Sch.1 para.3, Sch.1 para.4, Sch.1 para.7, Sch.1 para.8, Sch.1 para.10, Sch.1 para.11, Sch.1 para.15, Sch.1 para.16, Sch.1 para.17. In force: November 25, 2005; £9.00.

This Order authorises Docklands Light Railway Ltd to construct and maintain works to increase capacity upon the Docklands Light Railway between Tower Gateway Station, Poplar Station and Lewisham Station and for those purposes compulsorily or by agreement to acquire land and rights in land.

4266. Railways−Passengers−Exemptions

RAILWAYS (RAIL PASSENGERS' COUNCIL AND RAIL PASSENGERS' COMMITTEES) (EXEMPTIONS) (AMENDMENT) ORDER 2005, SI 2005 1737; made under the Railways Act 1993 s.77. In force: July 23, 2005; £3.00.

This Order amends the Railways (Rail Passengers' Council and Rail Passengers' Committees) (Exemptions) Order 2003 (SI 2003 1695) so as to remove references to the Rail Passengers' Committees in anticipation of their abolition.

4267. Railways−Penalty fares

RAILWAYS (PENALTY FARES) (AMENDMENT) REGULATIONS 2005, SI 2005 1095; made under the Railways Act 1993 s.130. In force: May 3, 2005; £3.00.

These Regulations, which amend the Railways (Penalty Fares) Regulations 1994 (SI 1994 576), set the amount which can be charged as a penalty fare. The amount of any penalty fare which may be charged to a person present in or leaving a compulsory ticket area (other than a person leaving a train) shall be raised to £20, and the amount of any penalty fare which may be charged to a person in other circumstances shall be either £20 or twice the amount of the full single fare applicable in the case, whichever is the greater. They also provide that where proceedings are brought against a person for specified types of offence in respect of a failure to produce a ticket or other authority to travel when required to do so, that person shall cease to be liable for any penalty fare which he has been charged in respect of that failure and for the repayment of the penalty fare if it has already been paid.

4268. Railways−Provision of railway facilities−Exemptions

RAILWAYS (PROVISION ETC. OF RAILWAY FACILITIES) (EXEMPTIONS) ORDER 2005, SI 2005 2628; made under the Railways Act 1993 s.16B. In force: October 15, 2005; £3.00.

This Order exempts certain operators and railway facilities from provisions of the Railways Act 1993 which empower the Office of Rail Regulation to direct the owner or operator of a railway facility to provide new railway facilities or to improve or develop an existing railway facility.

4269. Railways–Train operating companies–Determination of turnover

RAILWAYS ACT 1993 (DETERMINATION OF TURNOVER) ORDER 2005, SI 2005 2185; made under the Railways Act 1993 s.55, s.57A. In force: August 3, 2005; £3.00.

This Order makes provision for the determination of the turnover of a relevant operator for the purposes of the Railways Act 1993.

4270. Railways–Undertakings–Licensing

RAILWAY (LICENSING OF RAILWAY UNDERTAKINGS) REGULATIONS 2005, SI 2005 3050; made under the European Communities Act 1992 s.2. In force: November 28, 2005; £4.50.

These Regulations, which revoke the Railways (Amendment) Regulations 1998 (SI 1998 1519), amend the Railway Fires Act 1905, the Insolvency Act 1986, the Town and Country Planning (Control of Advertising) Regulations 1992 (SI 1992 666), the Railways Act 1993, the London Underground (East London Line Extension) (No.2) Order 2001 (SI 2001 3682), the Enterprise Act 2002, the Docklands Light Railway (Silvertown and London City Airport Extension) Order 2002 (SI 2002 1066), the Civil Contingencies Act 2004, the Docklands Light Railway (Woolwich Arsenal Extension) Order 2004 (SI 2004 757), the British Transport Police (Police Services Agreement) Order 2004 (SI 2004 1522), the Railways Act 2005, the Central Rating List (Wales) Regulations 2005 (SI 2005 422 (W.40)) and the Central Rating List (England) Regulations 2005 (SI 2005 551). They implement Council Directive 95/18 ([1995] OJ L143/70) on the licensing of railway undertakings. The Regulations makes the provision of train services without having a European licence criminal offence; appoints the Office of Rail Regulation as the body to issue European licences; and provide that applicants for such licences must satisfy requirements as to good repute, professional competence, financial fitness and insurance cover for civil liabilities.

4271. Railways–Woodside Park Substation

TRANSPORT FOR LONDON (WOODSIDE PARK SUBSTATION) ORDER 2005, SI 2005 3231; made under the Greater London Authority Act 1999 s.163. In force: January 5, 2006; £3.00.

The Greater London Authority Act 1999 prohibits Transport for London from disposing of any freehold interest in operational land without the consent of the Secretary of State. Under that Act, Transport for London is required to ensure that none of its subsidiaries does anything which Transport for London has no power to do (including anything which Transport for London has no power to do because the consent of the Secretary of State has not been obtained). The land at Woodside Park, Woodside Grange Road, London N12 which is the subject of this Order has been operational land as defined in the 1999 Act. It comprises of the area formerly occupied by an electricity substation used in connection with the provision of railway services. The Act provides that consent is not required in respect of land which was formerly operational land if a period of at least five years has elapsed since the land was last operational land, but such a period has not yet elapsed in this case. Its disposal therefore requires the consent of the Secretary of State. The land is currently vested in London Underground Ltd, a subsidiary of Transport for London, and the disposal of the land will be made by that company. By this Order the Secretary of State for Transport gives consent to Transport for London for the disposal of the land which is the subject of the Order.

4272. Railways Act 2005 (c.14)

This Act amends the law relating to the provision and regulation of railway services.

This Act received Royal Assent on April 7, 2005.

4273. Railways Act 2005 (c.14)–Commencement No.1 Order

RAILWAYS ACT 2005 (COMMENCEMENT NO. 1) ORDER 2005, SI 2005 1444 (C.64); made under the Railways Act 2005 s.60. Commencement details: bringing into force various provisions of the 2005 Act on June 8, 2005 and June 26, 2005; £3.00.

This Order brings into force provisions of the Railways Act 2005.

4274. Railways Act 2005 (c.14)–Commencement No.2 Order

RAILWAYS ACT 2005 (COMMENCEMENT NO.2) ORDER 2005, SI 2005 1909 (C.82); made under the Railways Act 2005 s.60. Commencement details: bringing into force various provisions of the 2005 Act on July 24, 2005; £3.00.

This Order brings into force provisions of the Railways Act 2005 which transfer railway licensing functions from the Strategic Rail Authority to the Office of Rail Regulation; provide power for the Secretary of State to make transfer schemes at the end of franchise agreements; relate to the Rail Passengers' Council and Rail Passengers' Committees; and enable the Secretary of State and the National Assembly for Wales to secure the provision of substitute bus services where railway services are temporarily disrupted or discontinued.

4275. Railways Act 2005 (c.14)–Commencement No.3 Order

RAILWAYS ACT 2005 (COMMENCEMENT NO.3) ORDER 2005, SI 2005 2252 (C.94); made under the Railways Act 2005 s.60. Commencement details: bringing into force various provisions of the 2005 Act on August 21, 2005; £3.00.

This Order brings into force the Railways Act 2005 s.5 which enables the Scottish Ministers to prepare a strategy for carrying out their functions in relation to railways and railway services, and to revise that strategy from time to time.

4276. Railways Act 2005 (c.14)–Commencement No.4 Order

RAILWAYS ACT 2005 (COMMENCEMENT NO.4) ORDER 2005, SI 2005 2812 (C.117); made under the Railways Act 2005 s.60. Commencement details: bringing into force various provisions of the 2005 Act on October 16, 2005 and November 21, 2005; £3.00.

This Order brings into force provisions of the Railways Act 2005 which provide power for the Scottish Ministers to provide financial assistance for railway purposes; provide that the Scottish Ministers must notify the Secretary of State when they make or modify schemes for the provision of financial assistance in respect of rail freight; transfer the role of the Strategic Rail Authority as franchising authority in relation to railway passenger services to the Scottish Ministers; and provide power for the Scottish Ministers to make penalty fare regulations.

4277. Railways Act 2005 (c.14)–Transitional Provisions and Savings

RAILWAYS ACT 2005 (TRANSITIONAL PROVISIONS AND SAVINGS) ORDER 2005, SI 2005 1738; made under the Railways Act 2005 s.60. In force: July 24, 2005; £3.00.

This Order makes transitional provisions and savings in connection with the bringing into force of the Railways Act 2005 s.21(1) and the repeal of the Railways Act 1993 s.43(4) and 47(6) pursuant to Sch.13 of the 2005 Act.

4278. Railways and Transport Safety Act 2003 (c.20)–Commencement No.5 Order

RAILWAYS AND TRANSPORT SAFETY ACT 2003 (COMMENCEMENT NO.5) ORDER 2005, SI 2005 1991 (C.84); made under the Railways and Transport Safety Act 2003 s.120. Commencement details: bringing into force various provisions of the 2003 Act on October 17, 2005; £3.00.

This Order brings into force the Railways and Transport Safety Act 2003 ss.1-14.

4279. Road transport–Working time

ROAD TRANSPORT (WORKING TIME) REGULATIONS 2005, SI 2005 639; made under the European Communities Act1972 s.2. In force: April 4, 2005; £3.00.

These Regulations implement provisions of Council Directive 2002/15 ([2002] OJ L80/35) concerning the organisation of the working time of persons performing mobile road transport activities. The Regulations prescribe the maximum weekly working time and maximum average weekly working time of mobile workers who, in the course of their work, drive or travel in goods or passenger vehicles which are covered by the Community Drivers' Hours and they prescribe the reference periods over which such time is to be calculated .

4280. Tachographs–Heavy goods vehicles–Failure to use recording equipment– Meaning of "withdrawal" of tachograph record sheet

[Transport Act 1968 s.97(1)(a)(iii); Council Regulation 3821/85; Council Regulation 3821/85 Art.13, Art.15(2).]

The appellant (V) appealed by way of case stated from a decision of the magistrates' court to acquit the respondent (J) of two offences under the Transport Act 1968 s.97(1)(a)(iii) of using a vehicle in which the recording equipment was not used as provided by Council Regulation 3821/85, in that unauthorised withdrawal of the tachograph record sheet had been made before the end of the working period by the driver contrary to Art.15(2)] of the Regulation. J had been driving the goods vehicles on the two occasions and the magistrates had found that on both occasions the tachograph in the vehicle had been interfered with, resulting in a false reading, and that it had been J, as the driver, who had interfered with it. J's evidence was that, while travelling, he had opened the tachograph cover because the speedometer was not working properly and he thought that that action might unjam the speedometer. The result of J's actions in opening the tachograph on each of the two occasions was that the styli of the tachograph were no longer in contact with the chart in the tachograph on which would normally have been recorded the speed, the distance travelled and whether the vehicle was stationary or in motion. The magistrates found that the tachograph record sheet had not been removed from within the equipment and that there had therefore been no "withdrawal" of the record sheet for the purposes of the legislation. V submitted that (1) J's action in opening the tachograph so as to lift the record sheet from the styli amounted to a "withdrawal" of the record sheet on a purposive construction of the Regulation; (2) whatever the correct construction of the word "withdrawal", there had in the instant case been a failure to use the recording equipment as provided by Art.13 of the Regulation contrary to s.97(1)(a)(iii).

Held, allowing the appeal, that (1) on a broad purposive approach to the construction of the word "withdrawn" in the second part of Art.15(2), any action that lifted the record sheet from the styli before the end of the daily working period could be regarded as falling within that word. Such an action would withdraw the record sheet from such part of the mechanism so as to prevent its proper functioning and would amount to a withdrawal of the record sheet. The sheet would not have to be totally removed from the tachograph for there to be a withdrawal. The magistrates had erred and the case was remitted with a direction to convict. (2) As a matter of principle what had happened in the instant case could also have founded a charge under s.97(1)(a)(iii) by reference to Art.13, because that article required a driver to ensure the correct functioning and proper use of the recording equipment. Therefore if a driver interfered with the equipment with the result that it did not function properly, then, whatever his motive, he committed an offence under s.97(1)(a)(iii) unless he could rely on one of the specific defences set out in the 1968 Act. Prosecuting authorities should consider relying in appropriate cases on the terms of Art.13 and the first part of Art.15(2).

VEHICLE AND OPERATOR SERVICES AGENCY v. JONES, [2005] EWHC 2278, (2005) 169 J.P. 611, Keene, L.J., QBD (Admin Ct).

4281. Tractors–EC type approval

TRACTOR ETC (EC TYPE-APPROVAL) REGULATIONS 2005, SI 2005 390; made under the European Communities Act 1972 s.2. In force: July 1, 2005; £3.00.

These Regulations, which amend the Road Traffic Act 1988, implement European Parliament and Council Directive 2003/37 ([2003] OJ L171/1) on type approval of agricultural or forestry tractors, their trailers and interchangeable towed machinery, together with their systems, components and separate technical units and repealing Directive 74/150. They provide Decisions about granting EC type approval must be made in accordance with Council Directive 2003/37; the UK type-approval authority, who is the Secretary of State, can refuse to grant EC type approval if it considers there is a risk to road safety, the environment or the health and safety at work of any person; and the holder of an EC type approval certificate shall issue a certificate of conformity of production in respect of each individual vehicle subsequently manufactured or assembled.

4282. Transport Act 2000 (c.38)–Commencement No.11 Order

TRANSPORT ACT 2000 (COMMENCEMENT NO.11) ORDER 2005, SI 2005 2862 (C.121); made under the Transport Act 2000 s.275. Commencement details: bringing into force various provisions of the 2000 Act on October 15, 2005; £3.00.

This Order brings into force provisions of the Transport Act 2000 which provide for the insertion into the Railways Act 1993 of provisions permitting the Office of Rail Regulation to direct certain persons to improve or develop existing railway facilities or create new ones.

4283. Transport policy–Compulsory acquisition of land–Busways–Greater Manchester

GREATER MANCHESTER (LEIGH BUSWAY) ORDER 2005, SI 2005 1918; made under the Transport and Works Act 1992 s.1, s.5, Sch.1 para.1, Sch.1 para.2, Sch.1 para.3, Sch.1 para.4, Sch.1 para.6, Sch.1 para.7, Sch.1 para.8, Sch.1 para.9, Sch.1 para.10, Sch.1 para.11, Sch.1 para.12, Sch.1 para.15, Sch.1 para.16, Sch.1 para.17. In force: August 3, 2005; £6.50.

This Order authorises Greater Manchester Passenger Transport Executive to construct works and compulsorily to acquire land and rights in land for the purpose of a guided busway between Leigh and Newearth Road in Greater Manchester and includes powers for the operation and regulation of the guided busway and for traffic regulation and improvements on connecting roads.

4284. Transport policy–Quality contracts schemes–Commencement

TRANSPORT ACT 2000 (COMMENCEMENT OF QUALITY CONTRACTS SCHEMES) (ENGLAND) ORDER 2005, SI 2005 75; made under the Transport Act 2000 s.127. In force: March 1, 2005; £3.00.

This Order varies the application of the Transport Act 2000 s.127 (2) (b) in so far as it applies to England. It requires a quality contracts scheme to specify the date that it comes into operation. This date must not be earlier than 21 months after the date that the quality contracts scheme is made. Where the area of the scheme is wholly in England, this Order reduces the minimum period between the date of making the scheme and the date that the scheme comes into operation to six months.

4285. Tunnels–Construction–River Tyne

RIVER TYNE (TUNNELS) ORDER 2005, SI 2005 2222; made under the Transport and Works Act 1992 s.3, s.5, Sch.1 para.1, Sch.1 para.2, Sch.1 para.3, Sch.1 para.4, Sch.1 para.5, Sch.1 para.7, Sch.1 para.8, Sch.1 para.9, Sch.1 para.10, Sch.1 para.11, Sch.1 para.12, Sch.1 para.13, Sch.1 para.15, Sch.1 para.16, Sch.1 para.17;

and the Transport and Works (Descriptions of Works Interfering with Navigation) Order 1992 (SI 1992 3230). In force: August 26, 2005; £7.50.

This Order amends the Tyne Tunnel Act 1946, the Compulsory Purchase Act 1965, the Land Compensation Act 1973 and the Tyne and Wear Act 1976. It authorises the Tyne and Wear Passenger Transport Authority to construct, operate and maintain a tunnel for vehicles beneath the River Tyne and, for that purpose, compulsorily or by agreement to acquire land and rights in land and to use land. It also provides for the new tunnel and the existing vehicular and pedestrian and cycle tunnels under the River Tyne to be operated as a single undertaking and makes arrangements for the levying of tolls on those who use the new and existing tunnels in vehicles.

4286. Tunnels—Selly Oak New Road—Birmingham

BIRMINGHAM CITY COUNCIL (SELLY OAK NEW ROAD TUNNEL) SCHEME 2004 CONFIRMATION INSTRUMENT 2005, SI 2005 3173; made under the Highways Act 1980 s.106. In force: in accordance with Art.1; £3.00.

The Secretary of State has modified this Scheme as follows: Plan number TCS/2555/162 Rev A, which excludes the reception pit and light well, and is marked "The Birmingham City Council (Selly Oak New Road Tunnel) Scheme 2004" has been substituted for Plan number TCS/2555/162 of the same title.

4287. Vehicles—Abandoned vehicles—Disposal and removal—Wales

REMOVAL AND DISPOSAL OF VEHICLES (AMENDMENT) (WALES) REGULATIONS 2005, SI 2005 3252 (W.245); made under the Refuse Disposal (Amenity) Act 1978 s.3, s.4; and the Road Traffic Regulation Act 1984 s.99, s.101. In force: November 25, 2005; £3.00.

The Removal and Disposal of Vehicles Regulations 1986 (SI 1986 183) provide for the removal and disposal of vehicles. These Regulations amend the 1986 Regulations in relation to Wales (save for those parts of the Severn Crossings which are in Wales) so as to reduce the period of notice prescribed by the 1986 Regulations in two cases: where an authority proposes to remove a vehicle which appears to the authority to be abandoned and in their opinion is in such a condition that it ought to be destroyed, the notice period is reduced from 7 days to 24 hours from when a notice is affixed to the vehicle; and where an authority has removed a vehicle (but it is not in such a condition that it ought to be destroyed) and has located the owner, the period during which the owner is required to remove the vehicle from the custody of the authority is reduced from 21 days to 7 days from when the relevant notice is served on him. The authority may dispose of the vehicle after the expiry of that period, provided that there is no licence in force for that vehicle.

4288. Books

British Standards Institution—BS 8408:2005 Road Traffic Signs. Testing and Performance of Microprismatic Retroreflective Sheeting Materials. Specification. Hardback: £140.00. ISBN 0 580 45924 1. British Standards Institution.

Carr, Kenneth; Musters, Patrick—Road Traffic Offences Handbook. Paperback: £44.95. ISBN 1 85328 918 3. Law Society Publications.

Child, Peter—Notes for Company Drivers. Paperback: £7.99. ISBN 0 9540910 4 3. Benbow Publications.

Sampson, Fraser—Roads Policing: V. 3. Blackstone's Police Manuals. Paperback: £14.50. ISBN 0 19 928521 7. Oxford University Press.

Viegas, Jose Manuel—Interurban Road Charging for Trucks in Europe research in Transportation & Economics Vol 11 (Rtec). Hardback: £59.99. ISBN 0 7623 1142 8. Elsevier Science.

Wallis, Peter; McCormac, Kevin; Swift, Kathryn—Wilkinson's Road Traffic Offences: 2nd Supplement. Paperback: £58.00. ISBN 0 421 88100 3. Sweet & Maxwell.

Yelton, Michael—Trams and Buses and the Law: The Legal Background to the Operation of Trams, Trolleybuses and Buses Before Deregulation: a Guide for Historians and Enthusiasts. Paperback: £15.00. ISBN 1 874422 51 6. Adam Gordon.

TRUSTS

4289. Administration of estates—Limitations—Inter vivos gifts removed from deceased's estate by donor—Australia

[Limitation Act 1980 s.21, s.22.]

J appealed against a decision that she was not entitled to claim three pictures from the estate of her late adoptive father, S, on the basis of a constructive trust. J's adoptive mother, C, collected art works, including those of her husband, S. On C's death in 1976, her estate passed to her executors and trustees for J's benefit. J asserted, however, that three paintings removed by S from the former matrimonial home in 1977 were included in C's estate. J also contended that the balance of probabilities showed that S had donated the paintings to C absolutely and that the trust based nature of her claim precluded a limitation defence.

Held, dismissing the appeal, that the judge below had failed to consider the totality of the evidence in establishing whether S had dealt with the paintings prior to the grant of probate in a manner that constituted him a constructive trustee or executor de son tort. However, as there were no grounds to disapply the Limitation Act 1980 s.21 or s.22, J's claim could not succeed.

NOLAN v. NOLAN [2004] W.T.L.R. 1261, Ormiston, J., CA (Vic).

4290. Beddoe applications—Prospective costs orders—Applicant both trustee and executor—Appropriateness of Beddoe order—Hong Kong

The applicant bank (H) sought a prospective costs order from the estate of the deceased (F) in respect of an action brought by F's mother (T). F's will had been drawn up by H, which acted as the executor and trustee of the will. H was also the trustee of a discretionary trust which was the sole beneficiary of F's will. Without the bequest from F's will, the trust would have no substantial assets. T was unhappy with the will and sought disclosure by H of the trustee memorandum accompanying the will. The bank refused to disclose the memorandum and T subsequently sought an order for letters of administration in respect of the will. H contended that, since there was no beneficiary to resist T's application, it was entitled to a prospective costs order from the estate.

Held, refusing the application, that H was appearing as executor and trustee of the will and a trustee had a duty to remain neutral. However, in the instant case, H was also laying claim to the settlement. Where a trustee was claiming the settlement and had also drafted the will, it was unlikely that the trustee would be awarded any costs if the claim was unsuccessful, *Alsop Wilkinson v. Neary* [1996] 1 W.L.R. 1220, [1995] C.L.Y. 2213 applied. However, if H was to make an application for a prospective costs order in its capacity as trustee of the discretionary trust and the will was found to be invalid, the court could consider other options such as exercising the power of appointment as there would be no assets in the trust.

HSBC INTERNATIONAL TRUSTEE LTD v. TAM MEI KAM (2004-05) 7 I.T.E.L.R. 382, Hon Lam, J., CFI (HK).

4291. Beneficial interests—Deeds—Invasion of free volition—Actual and presumed undue influence—Forcefulness of personality

[Employment Rights Act 1996 s.230.]

The appellant (N) appealed against a decision that he had procured the resignation of the respondent (M) from a family trust by undue influence. M was the aged aunt of N. The family trust concerned a farm that had been left to M and her sister on the death of their parents. M's sister gave her interest in the property to her sons, N and J. The property was later vested in M, N and J on trust for sale to hold the net proceeds of sale as to half for M and one quarter each for N and J. The trustees granted a yearly agricultural tenancy of the property to N at a rent of £1 per annum fixed for five years. M assigned her beneficial interest to her son (S). S was to act as de facto trustee in her place. When N's rent free period expired S began to ask for rent. A dispute then arose between S and N. N demanded that M attend meetings of the trustees but she refused. A compromise was negotiated under which N and J would buy out S's interest and M would retire as trustee. However, S decided not to sell his interest in the property. N visited M, during which he told her that she would have to resign as a trustee if she refused to discuss farm matters with him or he would have to take her to court. M who disliked any form of confrontation and was frightened by the prospect of court, signed a deed of resignation from the trust. N submitted that (1) the judge was wrong to take account of M's vulnerability and in doing so he had elided actual and presumed undue influence; (2) it was necessary for M to establish that her signatures had been procured by overt acts of improper pressure or coercion and the judge had neither found that nor had there been evidence to support any such finding.

Held, dismissing the appeal, that (1) actual undue influence was something that had to be done to twist the mind of a donor whereas in cases of presumed undue influence it was more a case of what had not been done, namely ensuring that independent advice was available to the donor. The judge had not elided the two types of cases. Accordingly, there was no error in the judge's approach as the vulnerability of one party should feature in the analysis, likewise the forcefulness of the personality of the other. (2) In cases of undue influence the critical question was whether the persuasion or the advice had invaded the free volition of the donor to accept or reject the persuasion or advice or withstand the influence. The donor might be led but she must not be driven and her will must be of her own volition, *Allcard v. Skinner* (1887) L.R. 36 Ch. D. 145 and *Royal Bank of Scotland Plc v. Etridge (No.2)* [2001] UKHL 44, [2002] 2 A.C. 773, [2001] C.L.Y. 4880 considered. On the basis of the evidence it was clear that M's consent should not be treated as an expression of her free will. (3) The instant case was one where the court, as a court of conscience, should intervene to protect people from being forced, tricked or misled in any way by others into parting with their property.

DREW v. DANIEL; *sub nom.* DANIEL v. DREW, [2005] EWCA Civ 507, [2005] 2 F.C.R. 365, Ward, L.J., CA (Civ Div).

4292. **Beneficial interests – Tenancies in common – Incorporation of implied term for defeasible interests into agreement – New Zealand**

The appellant (X) appealed against a decision that the respondent (L) was entitled to a half share in the net proceeds of sale of a property. X and L, who were in an unmarried relationship, had purchased the property as a family home. Before the purchase was completed, they signed a written agreement setting out the financial arrangements agreed between them. Following the breakdown of their relationship, X sought an order for the sale of the property and orders in connection with the proceeds of sale that would have excluded L from any share. Recitals to the agreement provided that X and L would be registered as tenants in common in equal shares and that the purchase was to be funded solely by X. The operative part of the agreement provided that X would join in a lease for life of the property to X and L for their joint lives and that X would establish a family trust under which the property was to be transferred subject to loan back procedures and under which X, L and their children were principal beneficiaries. The agreement also provided that the arrangements were in satisfaction of all property claims that either party might have against the other. The intended lease for joint lives and the family trust were never completed so that the property was not transferred to the trust. X contended that although L had acquired a beneficial half share in the property, that share was subject to defeasance in the event that the parties' intentions expressed in the agreement were not fully carried out. The frustration of those intentions terminated L's beneficial interest and transferred it to X.

Held, dismissing the appeal, that private trusts could create beneficial interests subject to defeasance on the occurrence or non occurrence of specified events; however, defeasance conditions in such trusts were invariably express conditions. The defeasance condition for which X contended would have to have been an implied condition since there was no express provision in the agreement to the effect that L would forfeit her share if the lease and trust arrangements were not completed. The test for the implication into the agreement of the condition for the defeasance of L's beneficial half share would be that L, having been asked at the time the agreement was signed whether the implication of the condition corresponded with her intention, would have answered that it did. That would have led to L suggesting a number of variations to the agreement before assenting to the suggested implied term. It would be impossible for X to succeed in establishing a resulting trust in his favour through an implied condition for the defeasance of L's beneficial interest being read into the agreement. Once purchased, the property was to be held by X and L as tenants in common in equal shares, at law and beneficially. L was to establish a family trust for the benefit of the two of them, and the property, subject to a lease to them for their joint lives, was to be transferred to that trust. In return for the interests that L received under the agreement, she had agreed to give up all domestic property claims against X that she might otherwise have enjoyed. The breakdown of the parties' relationship had frustrated their intentions regarding the joint lease and the transfer to the family trust. However, that was no reason to put into reverse those parts of the agreement that had been implemented.

POTTER v. POTTER, [2004] UKPC 41, [2004] W.T.L.R. 1331, Lord Hoffmann, PC (NZ).

4293. Beneficiaries–Disclosure–Trust documents–Exercise of fundamental and inherent jurisdiction of court–Jersey

The appellant beneficiary of a trust appealed against a judgment ordering him to list all the documents in his possession requested in connection with a claim by another beneficiary (J) relating to the administration of the trust. J had complained that he had been unfairly treated by the trustees acting under C's control. C objected to disclosing certain documents because they had been prepared in relation to another trust of which he was the settlor.

Held, dismissing the appeal, that right to disclosure of trust documents came within the fundamental and inherent jurisdiction of the court to supervise the administration of trusts. As such, the need for a lis between the parties did not have the same significance as in ordinary litigation. The exercise of the jurisdiction merely required that the documents sought were relevant and in either the possession or under the control of the person against whom the order was sought. Therefore C was required to list all documents in his possession and give reasons for their non disclosure, *Schmidt v. Rosewood Trust Ltd* [2003] UKPC 26, [2003] 2 A.C. 709, [2003] C.L.Y. 4485 followed.

BROERE v. MOURANT & CO (TRUSTEES) LTD [2004] W.T.L.R. 1417, Richard Southwell Q.C., CA (Jer).

4294. Breach of trust–Dishonest assistance–Loan monies advanced to non party on directors' instructions–Fiduciary duty–Degree of knowledge required for accessory liability–Australia

The appellant (Y) appealed against orders dismissing its claim and ordering payment of a mortgage debt. Y, as mortgagor, had entered into a mortgage in favour of the respondent (M) to secure an advance of $520,000 to Y and others, including Y's directors (F). The mortgage, which was secured on land which may have been trust property, was subject to an extremely high rate of interest. F asked M to advance the loan monies to another company (V), which was not a party to the mortgage and with whom Y had common directors. M complied through her representative (R), and F were subsequently accused of breach of their fiduciary duty as directors in that they had diverted the funds to V. Y brought a claim against M based on accessory liability, alleging dishonest assistance. In the absence of any evidence that M or R were aware of any fraudulent intention on the part of F, it fell to be decided whether M's state of knowledge at the relevant time was such as to put her on enquiry, and what standard of knowledge was required to substantiate an accusation of dishonest assistance.

Held, dismissing the appeal, that in order to establish accessory liability it had to be shown that a person knew of facts which would indicate fraud or breach of trust to the reasonable man, or that he had deliberately avoided conducting enquiries in case he was to learn of such fraud, *Hospital Products v. United States Surgical Corp* 156 C.L.R. 41 and *Consul Development Pty Ltd v. DPC Estates Pty Ltd* 132 C.L.R. 373 applied. It was not necessary that the fiduciary's fraudulent scheme be fully known or understood in detail; it was sufficient to satisfy the test if such facts as were known would indicate to a reasonable person a general understanding that there had been a fraud, or a breach of trust or fiduciary duty. On the facts of the instant case, M and R's state of knowledge fell short of the standard required to satisfy the test. In the circumstances, it was highly unlikely that R would have engaged in activity which he knew or ought to have known was dishonest in order to benefit F, whom he had known only a short time, even weighed against the chance to gain a very high rate of interest, when to do so may have risked a large sum of money for which he was responsible.

YESHIVA PROPERTIES NO1 PTY LTD v. MARSHALL (2004-05) 7 I.T.E.L.R. 577, Mason (President), CA (NSW).

4295. Children—Trust funds

CHILD TRUST FUNDS (AMENDMENT) REGULATIONS 2005, SI 2005 383; made under the Child Trust Funds Act 2004 s.10, s.28. In force: April 6, 2005; £3.00.

These Regulations amend the Child Trust Funds Regulations 2004 (SI 2004 1450) which provide for the setting up of a Child Trust Fund accounts. The Regulations provide for a further government contribution of £250, under the Child Trust Fund Act 2004, for children in families receiving income support or jobseekers allowance who will not move from those benefits to Child Tax Credit until after April 5, 2005.

4296. Children—Trust funds—Appeals

CHILD TRUST FUNDS (NON-TAX APPEALS) REGULATIONS 2005, SI 2005 191; made under the Child Trust Funds Act 2004 s.23, s.24, s.28. In force: February 25, 2005; £3.00.

These Regulations amend the Taxes Management Act 1970, the Social Security Act 1998 and the Social Security (Northern Ireland) Order 1998 (SI 1998 1506 (NI.10)). They make provision for appeals against decisions of the Inland Revenue in respect of child trust funds, under the Child Trust Funds Act 2004. These appeals are to appeal tribunals within the Appeals Service, with a further right of appeal on a point of law to the Social Security Commissioners.

4297. Children—Trust funds—Credit unions

CHILD TRUST FUNDS (AMENDMENT NO.2) REGULATIONS 2005, SI 2005 909; made under the Child Trust Funds Act 2004 s.3, s.15, s.28. In force: April 6, 2005; £3.00.

These Regulations amend the Child Trust Funds Regulations 2004 (SI 2004 1450) to allow Credit Unions to act as a provider of child trust funds provided they are authorised persons under the Financial Services and Markets Act 2000.

4298. Cohabitants–Coownership–Declaration of trust as to proceeds of sale– Implied waiver of right to claim reimbursement of shared expenses

W, the survivor of a cohabiting couple, appealed against a decision ([2003] EWHC 3030) that G, his late partner's mother, was entitled to 20 per cent of the proceeds of sale of the couple's former shared home. Under an agreement and declaration of trust W and S agreed to share the expenses and outgoings equally but with W being entitled to 80 per cent of the proceeds of sale. Following S's death intestate, W sought a declaration of his entitlement to the proceeds of sale or an account of shared expenses and mortgage payments between the parties. At first instance, the judge held that W had impliedly waived his right to reimbursement of the shared expenses, but W contended that it was unfair to do so as waiver had not been pleaded and none of the requirements for waiver had been established.

Held, dismissing the appeal, that the domestic nature of the agreement was such that S could be taken to have understood that W would not enforce his right to reimbursement against her in respect of expenditure he met out of his own bank account. The clause on shared expenses was included in the agreement primarily to allow both W and S to obtain mortgage interest relief. W had never asked S to contribute to the expenses and an estoppel was pleaded at first instance based on a request to S not to work outside the home and this had the same effect as the implied waiver relied on by the judge at first instance.

WADE v. GRIMWOOD, [2004] EWCA Civ 999, [2004] W.T.L.R. 1195, Ward, L.J., CA (Civ Div).

4299. Constructive trusts–Breach of fiduciary relationship–Funds diverted from family business–Tracing–Canada

[Business Corporations Act 1985 (Ontario).]

C appealed against a decision that he held shares in a business as constructive trustee for his brother, M. He also appealed against punitive damages imposed for breach of fiduciary duty and against tracing orders made under the Business Corporations Act 1985 (Ontario). C also contended that the judge below had erred by allowing remedies under the Act as the alleged breaches predated its coming into force. C and M had succeeded to their father's scrap metal business but they subsequently fell out. M successfully claimed that C had diverted funds from the business into S, a company he controlled, which gave rise to the constructive trust. M also succeeded in a claim against E, the solicitor who had acted for the family business but his claim against the company's accountant failed. M cross appealed against that decision.

Held, dismissing the appeal and the cross appeal, that the business dealings of M and C gave rise to a fiduciary relationship that C had breached by procuring M's consent to transfer money from the family business to S. However, this breach by C did not allow M to claim a breach by the accountant. Although C's course of conduct predated the 1985 Act, M still qualified for protection because C's actions continued until after it entered into force and constituted the form of oppression that the Act was intended to rectify. E had failed to act in accordance with the fiduciary duty he owed to M by not explaining the nature of the documents M was required to sign or by ensuring that he was properly informed or obtained independent legal advice. M was entitled to be put back into the position he had been in before C's breach, which had motivated his own self interest so that he was properly liable to pay punitive damages, *Norberg v. Wynrib* [1992] 2 S.C.R. 226 applied. The tracing orders did not constitute a separate remedy but allowed M to trace the property to which he was beneficially entitled under the constructive trust, *Hodgkinson v. Simms* [1994] 3 S.C.R. 377 applied.

WAXMAN v. WAXMAN (2004-05) 7 I.T.E.L.R. 162, Doherty, J.A., CA (Ont).

4300. Constructive trusts–Resulting trusts–Lack of evidence as to contributions– Correct approach–Australia

The claimant (D) sought to prevent registration of a notice of severance of a joint tenancy issued by his defendant brother (R). D, R and their brother (J) had initially leased a house using money bequeathed to them in a will. They had each entered a ballot for the property upon the understanding that if any of them were successful they would lease the land as joint tenants and use the property as a holiday home. J won the ballot and the three brothers ultimately purchased the land as joint tenants. D paid the purchase price and both he and J made other financial contributions. R was the only sibling to exclusively occupy the property at any time. D contended that the intention had been that he, J and R would hold the property as trustees for themselves and their three other siblings and that they had reached an agreement that the tenancy would not be severed.

Held, giving judgment for D, that in circumstances where a resulting trust arose and a constructive trust could be imposed and the application of each led to different results, then a constructive trust would be imposed when the court believed that division of the beneficial interests in accordance with the legal interests would be unconscionable, *Muschinski v. Dodds* 160 C.L.R. 583 applied. When assessing the size of each party's beneficial interest the court should aim for fairness in distribution. There was no requirement to pursue complex factual investigations. The court should consider each party's respective contributions and divide the beneficial interest fairly between the parties in accordance with their financial and other contributions, *Baumgartner v. Baumgartner* 164 C.L.R. 137 applied. In the instant case, it had not been proved that an agreement had been reached as contended by D and there was insufficient evidence to make a precise calculation of each party's contribution. There was no reason to depart from the principle that R was entitled to a beneficial interest of one third. On the evidence adduced, J was entitled to a 10 per cent interest and it was not unconscionable for D to have an interest in the remainder.

ANSON v. ANSON (2004-05) 7 I.T.E.L.R. 318, Campbell, J., Sup Ct (NSW).

4301. Constructive trusts–Undue influence–Council house bought under right to buy–Son agreeing to pay mortgage in return for net sale proceeds

The claimant (J) sought to set aside a 1989 trust deed entered into by her and the defendant (DH), her son, who had purchased the council property of which J was tenant when she exercised her right to buy. The deed provided that DH was liable for the mortgage repayments, J could only sell with DH's consent and he was then entitled to the net sale proceeds. A caution against dealing with the property was lodged at the Land Registry and when J subsequently sought to sell the property DH refused to remove the caution. J contended that she had been induced to enter into the transaction because of D's undue influence and D asserted that the claim was barred under the doctrine of laches or on limitation grounds.

Held, allowing the claim, that the transaction reflected in the deed was totally in D's favour and he had failed to rebut the presumption of undue influence. The full extent of the trust deed only became apparent to J in 1998 and she had commenced the claim in 2002, although individual memories had faded over time, the laches argument could not succeed as the facts could still be ascertained and D had not shown that he had suffered any prejudice. The evidence showed that D had a dominant position in the transaction. Further, he had not shown that J had executed the deed on the basis of independent legal advice, with the result that the trust deed would be set aside and the parties' interests in the property would be held on a constructive trust by J on the basis of 60 per cent to J and 40 per cent to D, subject to his share standing the cost of discharging the mortgage prior to sale, *Royal Bank of Scotland Plc v. Etridge (No.2)* [2001] UKHL 44, [2002] 2 A.C. 773, [2001] C.L.Y. 4880 and *Popowski v. Popowski* [2004] EWHC 668, [2004] 2 P. & C.R. DG10 considered.

HUMPHREYS v. HUMPHREYS, [2004] EWHC 2201, [2005] 1 F.C.R. 712, Rimer, J., Ch D. [*Ex rel.* ,].

4302. Deeds–Rectification–Evidence of mistake–Failure to give effect to settlor's intention–Adverse tax consequences–Jersey

The applicant trustee sought rectification of a trust governed by the law of Jersey. The trust deed had been drawn up in 1996 by Dutch lawyers instructed by the settlor and provided that the trustees were obliged to pay trust income to the principal beneficiary, who was also the settlor. The trust also contained a power of appointment in favour of any of the beneficiaries at the principal beneficiary's discretion. On the evidence, the settlor's intention had been that the trustees pay the income of the trust to the principal beneficiary and that the power of appointment be exercisable with the prior written consent of the protector and not in her favour. Rectification was required in order to avoid the adverse tax consequences of the trust as drafted.

Held, granting the application, that on the evidence it was clear that the settlor's intention had been to make the power of appointment subject to the protector's written consent and not exercisable in her own favour, but only in favour of other beneficiaries. The settlor had given instructions that the trust should contain a life interest, of which she would be the life tenant and would have a right to income during her life. It was noted that, at the time the trust deed was prepared, the Dutch lawyers had been inexperienced in trusts of this type and had not appreciated the technical implications of a life interest trust. In the circumstances, the trustees was awarded their costs out of the trust fund and it was a matter for them to decide whether to pursue recovery of those costs from the professional advisers who had been at fault.

PEACH AND DOLPHIN TRUST (1988), *Re* (2004-05) 7 I.T.E.L.R. 570, Deputy Bailiff Birt, Royal Ct (Jer).

4303. Disclosure–Trust documents–Application by named beneficiaries–Exercise of inherent supervisory jurisdiction–Jersey

The appellant trustees of two Jersey trusts appealed against a decision of the Royal Court allowing an application by the respondents, certain named beneficiaries, for the disclosure of trust documents. The beneficiaries were resident in Saudi Arabia and some of them had entered into a Disengagement Agreement, the terms of which provided that they had divested themselves of their interests in the trusts in return for property in Saudi Arabia. The agreement was subsequently declared void by a Saudi court and the named beneficiaries sought disclosure in Jersey as it appeared that the trust property was being dissipated.

Held, dismissing the appeal, that the inherent supervisory jurisdiction of the Royal Court had been correctly exercised in the instant case. The respondents had at one time all been beneficiaries of the trusts. Furthermore, the finding that the Disengagement Agreement was void meant that they reverted to being beneficiaries until at least the underlying claims in the case were determined. Disclosure would also allow settlement of the family dispute which lay at the heart of the proceedings. Finally, there was no opposition to the application by the other beneficiaries and the objection was based on matters of expediency, as opposed to principle, *Schmidt v. Rosewood Trust Ltd* [2003] UKPC 26, [2003] 2 A.C. 709, [2003] C.L.Y. 4485 applied.

ALHAMRANI v. RUSSA MANAGEMENT LTD; *sub nom.* INTERNINE TRUST AND INTERTRADERS TRUST, *Re* (2004-05) 7 I.T.E.L.R. 308, Beloff, J.A., CA (Jer).

4304. Discretionary powers–Appointments–Wrong legal advice–Capital gains tax–Unintended consequences

[Taxation of Chargeable Gains Act 1992 s.71.]

The claimant trustees (T) claimed that a 2001 appointment under the trusts of a 1971 settlement made by the father of the second defendant (H) was not valid. By the combined effect of the 2001 appointment and an assignment made days later by H, certain valuable chattels in a historic house and a reversionary lease of its estate that together formed the subject of the appointment were held on the trusts of a 1987 settlement made by H. Overlooked was (i) the deemed disposal arising under the Taxation of Chargeable Gains Act 1992 s.71 which meant that hold over relief was not available; (ii) a problem of reserved benefit in that the assignment of H's contingent interest was a gift of excluded property and not a transfer of value and, although it could be a potentially exempt transfer, the consequences were expensive or very inconvenient. T submitted (1) that the 2001 appointment was not effective on the principle under *Hastings-Bass (Deceased), Re* [1975] Ch. 25, [1974] C.L.Y. 993 whereby the exercise of a discretionary power such as an appointment was void or voidable if the trustees failed to take into account matters that they should have considered, and if they had done so they would not have made the appointment; (2) alternatively, that it was ineffective because it was made or consented to under a fundamental misapprehension.

Held, giving judgment for T, that (1) where trustees were not under a duty to act, the relevant test was whether, if they had not misunderstood the effect that their actual exercise of the discretionary power would have had, they would have acted differently, *Hastings-Bass* applied. That was correct both on the authority of that case and of the subsequent line of cases, and also on principle. Only where the beneficiary could require the trustees to act should it be enough to show that they "might" have acted differently, *Stannard v. Fisons Pension Trust Ltd* [1992] I.R.L.R. 27, [1992] C.L.Y. 3332 and *Kerr v. British Leyland (Staff) Trustees Ltd* [2001] W.T.L.R. 1071, [2002] C.L.Y. 3366 considered. Where trustees acted under an obligation, the beneficiaries could require them to start again on the correct basis, but if they acted voluntarily so that they could not be so compelled, then the more demanding test of "would" have acted differently was justified. The court had no doubt that fiscal consequences might be relevant considerations that trustees should take into account and that a material difference between intended and actual consequences might be sufficient to bring the *Hastings-Bass* principle into play. T were bound to take them into account because the power of appointment was exercisable for the beneficiaries, and whether and how far one particular appointment, or another, or doing nothing, would be for that benefit would be very much affected by its fiscal treatment. On the evidence, the appointment by T was vitiated by their failure because of wrong legal advice to take into account its true consequences as regards capital gains tax, which, with those pertaining to inheritance tax, they were under a duty to consider, and did consider. If they had had the correct advice they would not have made the 2001 appointment. The effect of the exercise of their discretion was different from that which they intended, they failed to take into account things that they should have considered, and they would not have acted as they did had they known the correct position regarding capital gains tax. Accordingly the court applied the *Hastings-Bass* principle in the form of a reformulated version of the test in *Mettoy Pension Trustees Ltd v. Evans* [1990] 1 W.L.R. 1587, [1991] C.L.Y. 2726. Neither H nor his father would have consented to the appointment nor made the assignment. The 2001 appointment was set aside and declared to be of no effect. (2) There was an equitable jurisdiction to set aside a voluntary disposition for mistake where it was as to the effect of the disposition, but a mistake as to its consequences might not be enough, including a mistake as to fiscal consequences, *Gibbon v. Mitchell* [1990] 1 W.L.R. 1304, [1991] C.L.Y. 1724 and *Mettoy* considered.

SIEFF v. FOX; *sub nom.* BEDFORD ESTATES, *Re*, [2005] EWHC 1312, [2005] 1 W.L.R. 3811, Lloyd, L.J., Ch D.

4305. Discretionary trusts–Appointments–Setting aside deed of appointment with unintended inheritance tax consequences

[Inheritance Tax Act 1984 s.106.]

The claimant trustees (T) sought to set aside part of a deed of appointment on the footing that they failed to appreciate, consider and take into account the fact that that appointment generated very considerable inheritance tax liabilities. The first claimant (B) was the chairman of, and a substantial shareholder in, a successful company. He settled some of his shareholding on his son by creating an accumulation and maintenance settlement under which his son was to take an interest in possession in capital and income when he attained the age of 18, but until he reached the age of 35 that interest was liable to be divested by an appointment by the trustees (if they chose to make one) in favour of a "wider class" of beneficiaries. Very soon after the son acquired his interest in possession B became concerned at the size of the dividends the company was likely to declare and the amount of income his son would receive. B discussed with solicitors how his son's access to income could be restricted. The appointment of the assets on new discretionary trusts was suggested. It was in the minds of all parties that any appointment of assets was to be done in such a way as not to attract a charge to inheritance tax so far as possible. The solicitors drafted a deed of appointment under which the company shares, much the larger part of the assets, would be transferred to discretionary trusts for the benefit of the wider class including the son and B's step children, and the other assets consisting of quoted shares and cash would be retained on accumulation and maintenance trusts until the son's 25th birthday. The deed gave rise to a chargeable transfer and corresponding charge to inheritance tax in relation to the appointment into the discretionary trusts because business property relief was not available in respect of the company shares as the son had not then held the shares for two years after acquiring his interest in possession as required by the Inheritance Tax Act 1984 s.106. T submitted, relying on the principle in *Hastings-Bass (Deceased), Re* [1975] Ch. 25, [1974] C.L.Y. 993, that they did not appreciate that the deed of appointment would have the inheritance tax consequences it did and that, had they known, they would not have executed it and that it should be set aside so far as it appointed on the discretionary trusts.

Held, granting declaration in favour of claimants, that (1) The solicitors negligently failed to give full consideration to the tax consequences of the appointment and T did not think that a charge to tax would arise in respect of the deed of appointment in relation to the discretionary trusts. T executed the deed of appointment in circumstances in which they were seriously mistaken as to the tax consequences of what they were doing and they would not have executed it had they appreciated those consequences, at least so far as the discretionary trusts were concerned. Trustees had to consider the fiscal consequences of their acts, and a failure to do so was capable of leading to the application of the *Hastings-Bass* principle if it was clear that they would not have acted as they did if they had appreciated the true fiscal position, and in the instant case the principle led to the deed of appointment being declared invalid, *Abacus Trust Co (Isle of Man) Ltd v. National Society for the Prevention of Cruelty to Children* [2001] S.T.C. 1344 and *Hastings-Bass* applied. (2) If there was an additional requirement of a breach of duty or default on the part of the trustee or on the part of its advisers or agents before the principle in *Hastings-Bass* could be invoked, that requirement was satisfied in the instant case because both T and the solicitors were in breach of duty when they considered the deed of appointment, *Abacus Trust Co (Isle of Man) Ltd v. Barr* [2003] EWHC 114, [2003] 2 W.L.R. 1362 considered. (3) A mistake by trustees could invalidate merely part, as opposed to the whole, of their act, *Mettoy Pension Trustees Ltd v. Evans* [1990] 1 W.L.R. 1587, [1991] C.L.Y. 2726 and *BESTrustees v. Stuart* [2001] O.P.L.R. 341, [2003] C.L.Y. 3380 considered. The part of the appointment dealing with the other assets could stand and only the part appointing the company shares on discretionary trusts was declared invalid.

BURRELL v. BURRELL, [2005] EWHC 245, [2005] S.T.C. 569, Mann, J., Ch D.

4306. **Discretionary trusts–Protector's fiduciary powers of appointment–Challenge by late settlor's business partner–Inherent jurisdiction of court–Isle of Man**

P, the protector of a Manx resident trust, sought a declaration as to the validity of the appointment of two trustees. P's late brother, M, had purchased two houses for his extended family, including P and his parents. These were subsequently transferred to two Panamanian companies, whose entire share capital was held by the Manx trust. P had the power to appoint trustees, although she was prevented from appointing herself. At the time of M's death, the properties were security for a mortgage granted to S, M's former business partner. P, concerned that S wanted to remove her as protector of the trust, appointed a Jersey trust company and one of its directors as two new trustees of the Manx trust. S challenged the validity of those appointments by way of a cross petition, along with an order for P's removal as protector.

Held, allowing the application and refusing the cross petition, that P had appointed the new trustees to protect the interests of the beneficiaries of the Manx settlement and S had not impugned their suitability or independence. The appointment had been made in the exercise of P's fiduciary duty and the fact that she could not appoint herself as a trustee precluded the application of the rule against self dealing. The inherent power to remove a protector was not justified on the facts of the instant case, as it was the trustees and not P who could execute trusts of the settlement and the trustees could apply for P's removal if she acted improperly in the future.

PAPADIMITRIOU, PETITIONER [2004] W.T.L.R. 1141, Deemster Cain, HC (IoM).

4307. Fiduciary duty–Breach of trust–Solicitor liable to account for profits made after retainer terminated–Tax shelter business of former client–Canada

The appellant (C) appealed against a ruling that (S), a partner in a solicitor's firm, had not breached a terminated retainer and had not misused confidential information. C, which operated a number of tax shelter businesses, was advised by S that a change in the law meant the businesses could no longer be operated. C ended its contractual retainer with S but S continued to act when C required. The revenue authorities subsequently advised S that there was a possibility that a tax ruling could allow the businesses to continue, albeit under a different compliance regime. Despite this, S continued to advise C that he could not get round the rules. At the same time S had entered into an agreement with an employee of C (D) to obtain a tax ruling to enable them to set up a tax shelter business and in time they obtained the necessary ruling and subsequently went on to make substantial profits. C sought a ruling that S should account for those profits and that D had dishonestly assisted S.

Held, allowing the appeal in part, that S had a fiduciary duty to disclose his conflict of interest to C and this duty continued after the retainer was terminated. The fact that the tax ruling was initially only a distant possibility that gradually improved did not reduce S's duty, *Clark Boyce v. Mouat* [1994] 1 A.C. 428, [1993] C.L.Y. 3750 applied. Therefore, S was liable to account for the profits he had made in breach of duty. As the breach related to the creation of a business, the risks taken and the skill and resources S had used were to be taken into account and the profits arising from this aspect could not be claimed by C, *Boardman v. Phipps* [1967] 2 A.C. 46, [1966] C.L.Y. 11052 applied. There was insufficient evidence that D was aware of S's breach and therefore he was not a constructive trustee on the basis of knowing assistance in the breach, *Air Canada v. M&L Travel Ltd* [1993] 3 S.C.R. 787 and *Citadel General Insurance Co v. Lloyd's Bank Canada* [1997] 3 S.C.R. 805 applied.

CANADA INC v. STROTHER (2004-05) 7 I.T.E.L.R. 748, Newbury, J.A., CA (BC).

4308. Interests in possession–Inheritance tax–Close company in occupation of property comprising part of trust fund–Will unable to imply tenancy

[Inheritance Tax Act 1984 s.49(1).]

The appellants (O), the personal representatives of the deceased (J), appealed against a determination of the respondent commissioners that J's estate included premises belonging to the estate of her late husband (T). O were also the trustees of T's will. T owned a contractor's yard and premises, together with 75 per cent of the shareholding in a plant hire company. His three children owned five per cent each and J owned the remaining 10 per cent. After T's death, the will was varied so as to provide that the company was not required to pay to the estate any rent in respect of its use of the yard. T's shares passed to his son and the yard passed to O on a life interest for J with remainder to the three children. The yard was treated for inheritance tax purposes as having been transferred to J, and after J's death, the Inland Revenue made a determination that it was included in J's estate for tax purposes. However, O argued that the company had an interest in possession and that J's interest amounted to no more than her 10 per cent shareholding. The company denied the estate's claim for profits after J's death and maintained that it enjoyed an implied tenancy.

Held, allowing O's appeal, that J did not have an interest in possession in the yard at the time of her death. The company had the right to occupy the yard free of rent during J's lifetime by virtue of the varied will; accordingly only a 10 per cent share of the yard was deemed to be included in J's estate. On J's death, the yard ceased to be "settled property" and O was obliged to divide it up between the three children. The clause providing that the company was not required to pay rent for the yard was not an administrative provision but a dispositive provision in that it conferred rights of occupancy on the company and correspondingly abated J's life interest. O had no discretion to require the company to vacate the yard, as this would have conflicted with the direction to O not demand payment of rent. The company's right to occupy the yard was therefore an interest in possession under the Inheritance Tax Act 1984 s.49(1). The existence of a tenancy was not implied. The company's right to occupy was merely equitable and arose solely from the will, *Pearson v. Inland Revenue Commissioners* [1981] A.C. 753, [1980] C.L.Y. 228 applied.

OAKLEY v. INLAND REVENUE COMMISSIONERS [2005] S.T.C. (S.C.D.) 343, Stephen Oliver Q.C., Sp Comm.

4309. Public trustee—Fees

PUBLIC TRUSTEE (FEES) (AMENDMENT) ORDER 2005, SI 2005 351; made under the Public Trustee Act 1906 s.9. In force: April 1, 2005; £3.00.

This Order, which amends the Public Trustee (Fees) Order 1999 (SI 1999 855), sets out where executorship fees and annual administration fees have been increased. In addition, for the purposes of calculating the administration fee, this Order provides that the estate or trust will be valued as at September 30, 2004 (provided that the Public Trustee was acting on that date), instead of September 30, 2002.

4310. Purpose trusts—Validity—Estoppel by res judicata—Court not bound by earlier decision as to existence of trust—Canada

The court was asked to determine whether an arrangement constituted a purpose trust which could not be saved as a charitable trust. This issue arose in Phase II of the proceedings, the court having found in Phase I that the original "Quebec trust'" was in fact a trust, but the purpose trust point had not been argued. E claimed that the matter was *res judicata* and that in any event the trust was not a purpose trust as there were specified beneficiaries.

Held, giving judgment for C, that (1) the three conditions necessary to raise an estoppel by *res judicata* were not present since the prior decision had not been a final decision over the parties and the subject matter. The court was not being asked to withdraw from the bare finding previously agreed by the parties that there was a trust, but to build on the earlier decision by determining whether it was a valid and enforceable trust under the applicable law. It was open to the court to consider the matter again if it was in the interests of justice to do so, *420093 BC Ltd v. Bank of Montreal* (1995) 128 D.L.R. (4th) 488 considered. (2) For there to be a valid trust there had to be a beneficiary or *cestui que* trust, corporate or human, in whose favour performance of the trust might be decreed. In the instant case, there were no named beneficiaries in the deed. Accordingly, the trust was a purpose trust which could not stand. As it was not charitable, it was void, *Denley's Trust Deed, Re* [1969] 1 Ch. 373, [1968] C.L.Y. 3586 distinguished. (3) There had to be enrichment, a corresponding deprivation and an absence of any juristic reason for the enrichment to establish a constructive trust and these elements were missing in the instant case, *Pettkus v. Becker* [1980] 2 S.C.R. 834 considered.

ERNST & YOUNG v. CENTRAL GUARANTY TRUST CO (NO.2) (2004-05) 7 I.T.E.L.R. 69, Wilson, J., QB (Alta).

4311. **Resulting trusts–Payment of funds towards purchase of property in sole name of one party during relationship–Evidence rebutting presumption**

V claimed from Y sums representing the repayment of a loan and the value of V's share in a property held on a resulting trust. V, a Hindu doctor, started a relationship with Y, a Muslim, in 1976. V, who was divorced with two children, was 12 years older than Y, who at that time was still a student. V supported Y with financial gifts, and in 1980 Y purchased an investment property in his sole name with the help of £10,000 from V. In 1984 Y married a Muslim woman with whom he had two children, but his relationship with V continued until the early 1990s. In 1988, V was attacked at home by burglars. Shortly afterwards she moved out, allowing Y and his family to live there rent free. Y purchased the property from V for £200,000 in 1994. He gave her half the money, with the remainder owed as a loan secured on his investment property. The relationship between V and Y broke down soon afterwards and V contended that Y's investment property was a joint venture, and that her payment of £10,000 therefore gave rise to a resulting trust in her favour. With respect to the other property, V sought repayment of the £10,000 loan. Y argued that the £10,000 was a loan that he had since repaid, and that he had also repaid all but £4,000 of the second loan. V contended that those sums had been by way of gift or investment by Y in failed joint ventures.

Held, refusing the application, that V was only entitled to repayment of the loans, which had all but been achieved, save for the remaining balance of £4,000. The evidence in favour of a presumption of resulting trust was weak, since V had previously made no moves to assert her alleged rights in the property or the rent proceeds, and the circumstances of their relationship at the time pointed towards the sum merely being a loan. Thus Y's evidence easily rebutted the presumption. In addition, Y's evidence in relation to the repayment of both of the loans was preferred.

VAJPEYI v. YUSAF; *sub nom.* VAJPEYI v. YIJSAF, [2003] EWHC 2339, [2004] W.T.L.R. 989, Peter Prescott Q.C., Ch D.

4312. **Settled land–Transfer–Compliance with provisions of Settled Land Act 1925**

[Law of Property Act 1925 s.63; Settled Land Act 1925 s.18(1)(b), s.104, s.110(1).]

The claimant (P) sought to set aside transactions by which she had surrendered her interest in a house to the defendant (F), her son, and by which she had later given up any claim to recover that interest. In divorce proceedings the house had been directed to be held in trust for P for her life and subject thereto in trust for F absolutely. That subjected the property to a settlement governed by the Settled Land Act 1925. The usual restrictions entered on the register when registered land became subject to a strict settlement were not entered on the register, and P was able to borrow money secured by a charge over the property. In 1997 that mortgage was redeemed and P executed a transfer of the property to F in consideration for £60,000, the property then being valued at about £245,000. F was registered as the proprietor and borrowed money secured on the property. In 2001 P and F agreed to a full and final settlement in respect of title to the property by which P was to receive certain payments from F. P submitted that the 1997 transfer was void for non compliance with the requirements of the Settled Land Act or should be set aside for undue influence, and that the 2001 agreement was an unconscionable bargain. F submitted he could rely on s.110(1) of the Settled Land Act.

Held, giving judgment for F, that (1) if the transfer was to be regarded as giving effect to a sale of the settled property purportedly made by P as tenant for life, it would be void for failure to comply with the restrictions imposed by the Settled Land Act, in particular s.18(1)(b), and F could not rely on s.110 in the circumstances. But P and F were the only beneficiaries under the settlement and their right to put an end to the settlement was unaffected by the Settled Land Act. Both intended to transfer the property to F absolutely thereby extinguishing P's life interest. The 1997 transfer executed as a deed was effective to implement that intention under the Law of Property Act 1925 s.63. The transfer was apt to carry the legal estate to F and, there being no restriction on the register, the Land Registry acted correctly in registering F as the proprietor. P had a life interest which she could assign or surrender as she wished and the transfer was effective to include that interest. That was not prohibited by s.104 of the Settled Land Act. The transfer was effective to vest the property in F free from the interest of P. (2) The undue influence claim failed. P failed to show that F had sufficient involvement in her affairs, and the financial consequences of the transaction were not as disadvantageous to her as she claimed. The burden of justifying the transaction did not shift to F but if it did he had discharged it. (3) In any event F had substantially performed his obligations under the 2001 agreement and it was not to be set aside as an unconscionable bargain. Therefore it operated to release any claim by P to an interest in the property.

HUGHES v. HUGHES, [2005] EWHC 469, [2005] 1 F.C.R. 679, Sir Francis Ferris, Ch D.

4313. Settlements–Sham transactions–Land settled on daughter–Subsequently transferred to offshore trust–Evasion of capital gains tax

[Insolvency Act 1986 s.423.]

The applicant trustee in bankruptcy (H) applied to set aside a settlement of land as being either a sham or contrary to the Insolvency Act 1986 s.423. The bankrupt (N) had purchased agricultural land in 1986. He subsequently settled part of the land on his young daughter. Shortly afterwards, the respondents (S) were appointed as new, offshore trustees. The land was then sold at a large profit to a builder for development. When, despite loans from the trustees, N was unable to pay the capital gains tax on the land's sale, he was adjudicated bankrupt on a petition presented by the Inland Revenue. H contended that the settlement should be set aside as it was either (1) a sham to mislead the Inland Revenue; (2) or a transaction entered into at an undervalue in order to defraud a potential creditor, the Inland Revenue, contrary to s.423.

Held, granting the application, that (1) the settlement was not a sham, but it was contrary to s.423. A settlement could only be a sham if both the settlor and the trustees intended it to not be effective but to make a third party or a court believe that it was, *Snook v. London and West Riding Investments Ltd* [1967] 2 Q.B. 786, [1967] C.L.Y. 1836 followed. When N made the settlement for his daughter, although he intended to have an influence on the trustees' administrative decisions, he did not intend to retain beneficial ownership of the settled property. So the trust was not created to give a false impression. Nor did the trustees intend to participate in any sham. Although their loans to N were all breaches of trust, that did not imply that the trustees were complicit in a fraudulent design. (2) A settlement would be contrary to s.423 if it were for the purpose of prejudicing the interests of a person who might at some time make a claim against the settlor, *Inland Revenue Commissioners v. Hashmi* [2002] EWCA Civ 981, [2002] B.C.C. 943, [2003] C.L.Y. 4484 considered. Although there were two legitimate purposes behind N's settlement, a third was to evade tax by pretending that there was little difference between the value of the settled land and the cost to him in 1986. That purpose was to prejudice the interests of the Inland Revenue by inducing them to make a wrong assessment of capital gains tax.

HILL v. SPREAD TRUSTEE CO LTD; *sub nom.* NURKOWSKI, *Re*, [2005] EWHC 336, [2005] B.P.I.R. 842, Judge Weeks Q.C., Ch D.

4314. Trust funds—Beddoe applications—Use of corporate and trust assets to fund defence of US in rem proceedings against beneficiary—Isle of Man

[Criminal Justice Act 1991 (Isle of Man) s.7.]

B and G, directors of two British Virgin Island companies who were also trustees of a Manx settlement, sought permission to use trust funds to defend in rem proceedings brought by the US Department of Justice against P, a co director and beneficiary. P was the subject of fraud proceedings in the US, arising from his involvement in the management of a US company and B and G had been restrained from removing P's assets from the jurisdiction by an order made under the Criminal Justice Act 1991 (Isle of Man) s.7, subsequently varied to allow P's legal representatives to charge for fees and disbursements. B and G argued that the Manx bank accounts named in the US proceedings, for which default judgment had been granted to the US government, were corporate assets so that there was no requirement for them to seek a *Beddoe* order in the Manx court. The Attorney General contended that the funds should be subject to a constructive trust, given the nature of the dispute involving P in the US.

Held, ordering that the matter be determined by a Deemster who had not been involved in the proceedings to date, that corporate ownership of the bank accounts did not affect the coexisting interest in them of B and G as trustees, who therefore had to act in keeping with the trust's interests in mind. Given the involvement of the trust in the bank accounts a *Beddoe* style application should be made that would allow B and G to make full disclosure and enable the Attorney General to be fully involved in the proceedings, *Alsop Wilkinson v. Neary* [1996] 1 W.L.R. 1220, [1995] C.L.Y. 2213 distinguished.

POYIADJIS, *Re* [2004] W.T.L.R. 1169, Deemster Kerruish, HC (IoM).

4315. Trustees—Power of protector to remove trustees—Abuse of process by trustees—Guernsey

V appealed against an interim order in proceedings relating to trusts of which she was protector. The three trusts were established on behalf of V's family, with G as trustee. According to the trust deeds, V had the power to appoint and remove trustees. In September 2000 V wrote to G stating that she wished to appoint new trustees in G's place. G was unwilling to resign and V wrote another letter removing G. She also sought a declaration as to the validity of that removal and an order to transfer trust assets to C, the new trustee. G later sought directions as to V's removal as protector. The applications were heard together and both the court and G took the view that G had been properly removed, with only indemnities and payment of G's fees outstanding. However, in subsequent correspondence between the parties, G took the stance that it was still trustee and could choose whether to resign. The matter came back before the court on further occasions, and protracted arguments arose as to fees, indemnities and the preparation of trust accounts. G also sought to resurrect its original application for V's removal as protector. In October 2001 the matter came before a different judge, who dismissed V's application for a declaration that G had been removed as trustee in October 2000 and ordered V to pay costs.

Held, allowing the appeal, that the order of October 2001 was set aside and replaced by an order declaring that G had been properly removed as trustee in October 2000 and that the matter should be set down for a hearing on the issue of fees and indemnities payable to G. It was clear that G was deliberately prolonging matters and its application and insistence on indemnities and fees exceeded the clear terms of the trust deeds. The costs of the appeal and the hearing below were ordered to be paid by G on an indemnity basis.

VIRANI v. GUERNSEY INTERNATIONAL TRUSTEES LTD (NO.1) [2004] W.T.L.R. 1007, Elizabeth Gloster Q.C., CA (Gue).

4316. **Trustees–Removal from office–Calculation of remuneration–Solicitors and accountants fees–Guernsey**

Following a decision of the Guernsey Court of Appeal ([2004] W.T.L.R. 1007), the quantum of G's remuneration, fees and legal costs fell to be determined by the Royal Court. G was removed as trustee on October 10, 2000 by V in her role as protector of three family trusts. V had sought a declaration to that effect, and soon afterwards G brought its own application for V to be removed as protector. G ultimately transferred the trust assets to new trustees in January 2003. G asserted that it was entitled to be paid its fees and legal costs incurred in the litigation. However, V contended that remuneration had been agreed between the parties on the basis of £1,000 per annum for each trust and for each of the six family companies forming part of the trust assets.

Held, giving judgment, that G was entitled to remuneration only for legitimate expenditure up to October 10. Remuneration was to be on the basis agreed with V, and G was entitled to the fees paid to its solicitors for the period up until its removal as it had been legitimately taking advice as to the administration of the trusts. However, G's application to remove V as protector was a contentious matter that had been wrongly brought as G had already been removed as trustee before the application was made. No legal fees were awarded for that application and the accounts prepared to date were not proper trust accounts with the result that no accountant's fees could be claimed for their preparation.

VIRANI v. GUERNSEY INTERNATIONAL TRUSTEES LTD (NO.2) [2004] W.T.L.R. 1035, Patrick Talbot Q.C., Royal Ct (Gue).

4317. **Trustees liability–Fraud on a power–Distribution procured by widow in breach of will trust–New Zealand**

The appellant (LS) appealed against a decision dismissing her claim for breach of trust by the trustees of the estate of her late father (W). W had settled his residuary estate in trust, with net annual income payable to his wife (E) until her death, then in equal shares to his daughters, (P) and LS. As there was no substitution in favour of their issue, if P or LS predeceased E, all the income was payable to the survivor. P died in 1995 and E obtained a distribution of NZD 250,000 out of the capital of W's estate from the trustees, which she loaned to P's will trust, the beneficiaries of which were her two children. The debt was subsequently forgiven, and LS argued that it had been made in breach of the trustees' powers and that they had exercised their discretion for improper purposes, namely to remedy a perceived inequality under the will and to benefit persons who were not objects of the discretion conferred by the will. The trustees cross appealed against a finding that they had wrongly apportioned monies received by W's estate from a dividend distribution made by one of his companies that went into voluntary liquidation after his death, with the result that capital was paid to E as income.

Held, allowing the appeal and dismissing the cross appeal, that the distribution was a fraud on the power because it represented a deliberate scheme to subvert the terms of W's will. Therefore, the trustees were liable in both their personal capacities and as trustees to repay the sum, with interest, from the date of payment until its restoration, subject to agreement on repayment by P's trust. On the cross appeal, LS's pleadings had put in issue the source and ultimate destination of the dividend distribution in the court below and the trustees were now attempting to reopen the matter on appeal. LS had succeeded on her claim at first instance, based on the evidence before the court, and the decision reached would not be interfered with on appeal.

WONG LIU SHEUNG v. BURT [2005] W.T.L.R. 291, Anderson (President), CA (NZ).

4318. Trustees powers and duties—Powers of appointment—Agreement between trustees reached on telephone—Intention to exercise power of appointment—New Zealand

The applicant (K), one of two trustees of trusts forming part of the deceased's estate, applied to the court for determinations as to whether the trustees had validly exercised their discretion to appoint capital before the date of distribution and whether a court appointed expert should be appointed. The beneficiaries were the six children of the deceased and the trust fund was to be distributed to "any one or more of the children to the exclusion of the others and in such shares and proportions and in such manner as the trustees in their absolute discretion think fit." In default of such exercise of discretion by the trustees, the property was to be divided between the children in equal shares. The trustees were unable to agree how the funds should be distributed and no written agreement had been signed by the date of distribution, although the trustees had reached a verbal agreement during the course of a telephone conversation prior to the distribution date.

Held, granting the application, that (1) in the circumstances an inference could be drawn that the parties did not intend any agreement to be binding until a formal document was signed. The principal asset of the trust was land of substantial value and the possible appointment of capital to two beneficiaries to the exclusion of the other four, which was what was being contemplated, was a momentous decision. Moreover, normal trust practice supported the drawing of such an inference, *Carruthers v. Whitaker* [1975] 2 N.Z.L.R. 667 and *Concorde Enterprises v. Anthony Motors (Hutt) Ltd* [1981] 2 N.Z.L.R. 385, [1983] C.L.Y. 428 considered. (2) A court appointed expert should be appointed. Trustees existed for the benefit of those entitled under the relevant trust deed and they were subject to a supervisory jurisdiction of the court. The expert's role would be to report upon the proposals formulated by trustees in order to resolve the extended period of impasse which had arisen between them in the instant case.

KAIN v. HUTTON (NO.1) (2004-05) 7 I.T.E.L.R. 1, Panckhurst, J., HC (NZ).

4319. Trustees powers and duties—Resignation—Continuing locus standi to seek declaration after giving notice of intention to resign—Australia

The claimant (C) sought declarations that it could bring an action for the transfer of leases although it had given notice of its intention to resign as trustee. The defendant (F), which had resigned as trustee prior to C's appointment, applied for C's claim to be struck out on the ground that C's resignation meant that it lacked the standing to seek the declarations. C was trustee of two agricultural land projects. The investment deeds, which were concluded for tax planning purposes, granted leases to C, subject to the pre existing rights of farmers to occupy the land. C then granted sub leases to land managers, who were to manage the land as a managed investment scheme. However, C resigned as trustee, as provided for in the trust deed, after disagreeing with the managers over their decision to withdraw from a relief concession granted by the Australian Securities and Investment Commission. C subsequently gave notice that it wanted to revoke its resignation so that it could challenge the managers' decision to surrender certain leases which had been approved by F, notwithstanding the fact that F had retired as trustee prior to C's appointment. C contended that the managers were acting in pursuit of their own interests in surrendering the leases and by failing to continue with the relief concession.

Held, refusing to strike out the application, that C's ability to withdraw its resignation was governed by equitable principles which meant that the situation was not analogous to an employment situation. Termination of a trust relationship could only be carried out if permitted by the trust deed, by statute, or with the permission of the court, and even then some continuing liability remained. The deed allowed C to give three months' notice of its intention to resign so that the appointment did not end immediately and the manager then had a further 90 days in which to appoint a new trustee, when all C's obligations ceased. C therefore had standing to seek the declarations.

CUSTODIAL LTD v. CARDINAL FINANCIAL SERVICES LTD (2004-05) 7 I.T.E.L.R. 512, Atkinson, J., Sup CT (Qld).

4320. Trustees powers and duties—Tenancies in common—Right to occupy property held on trust—Breach of trust in selling property subject to trust

O sought declarations in respect of a property held on trust, damages for breach of trust and an order for sale. The property had been owned by O's mother, K, and H, her long term partner, as tenants in common. By her will, K left the property to O and his sister, S, equally, on condition that H was allowed to live in it for as long as he wanted. K had executed a severance of the joint tenancy but no restriction on dealing was entered on the register. K died in 1998. Shortly afterwards, H sold the property and brought a less expensive one.

Held, granting the application in part, that the property was held in trust and H should account to O and S for the difference in price between the original property and the new one, but it was not appropriate to order that the new property be sold. K's intention as to H's continued occupancy gave rise to a trust in H's favour and the property was held as to one half by O and H for O, and as to the other half by O and H for H. The trust passed into the new property, but H was in breach of trust by selling the old property and was liable to account for the difference in price. There would be no order for sale, however, as this would thwart the purpose of the trust by leaving H homeless.

OLSZANECKI v. HILLOCKS, [2002] EWHC 1997, [2004] W.T.L.R. 975, David Oliver Q.C., Ch D.

4321. Books

Cracknell, D G—Equity and Trusts. Paperback: £11.95. ISBN 1 85836 589 9. Old Bailey Press.

Edwards, Richard; Stockwell, Nigel—Trusts and Equity. Foundation Studies in Law S. Paperback: £29.99. ISBN 1 4058 1227 3. Longman.

Estates and Trusts: Leading Lawyers on the Best Strategies for the Planning. Inside the Minds S. Paperback: £37.95. ISBN 1 59622 081 3. Aspatore Books, US.

Haley, Michael; Mcmurty, Lara; Davern, Raymond; Price, Jeffrey W.; Shipwright, A.J.—Equity and Trusts. Textbook S. Paperback: £24.95. ISBN 0 421 59920 0. Sweet & Maxwell.

Halliwell, Margaret; De Than, Claire—Equity and Trusts. Paperback: £15.95. ISBN 1 85836 598 8. Old Bailey Press.

Hayton, David J.; Mitchell, Charles—Hayton and Marshall: Commentary and Cases on the Law of Trusts and Equitable Remedies. Paperback: £32.95. ISBN 0 421 90190 X. Sweet & Maxwell.

Hudson, Alastair—Equity and Trusts. Paperback: £29.95. ISBN 1 85941 977 1. Cavendish Publishing Ltd.

Jennings, Simon—Tolley's Planning and Administration of Offshore and Onshore Trusts. Looseleaf/ring bound: £245.00. ISBN 0 7545 0794 7. LexisNexis UK.

Moffat, Graham; Bean, Gerard; Dewar, John; Milner, Marina—Trusts Law: Text and Materials. Law in Context S. Paperback: £35.00. ISBN 0 521 67466 2. Cambridge University Press.

Mowbray, John; Tucker, Lynton; Le Poidevin, Nicholas; Simpson, Edwin—Lewin on Trusts. Hardback: £285.00. ISBN 0 421 87420 1. Sweet & Maxwell.

Paisley, Roderick—Trusts. Greens Practice Library. Hardback: £80.00. ISBN 0 414 01476 6. W. Green & Son.

Piggot, Mike Semple—Equity and Trusts. Law in a Box S., No. 6. CD-ROM: £19.95. ISBN 1 904783 62 7. CD-ROM: £19.95. ISBN 1 904783 62 7. Semple Piggot Rochez (Legal Education Ltd).

Ramjohn, Mohammed—Unlocking Trusts. Paperback: £18.99. ISBN 0 340 88694 3. Hodder Arnold H&S.

Smith, Lionel Percy; Mattei, Ugo; Smith, Lionel–Commercial Trusts in European Private Law. Common Core of European Private Law S. Hardback: £85.00. ISBN 0 521 84919 5. Cambridge University Press.

Steele, Gill–Trust Practitioner's Handbook. Paperback: £49.95. ISBN 1 85328 945 0. Law Society Publications.

Todd, Paul; Wilson, Sarah–Textbook on Trusts. Paperback: £25.99. ISBN 0 19 927632 3. Oxford University Press.

Trusts Lawcards. Lawcards S. Looseleaf/ring bound: £6.95. ISBN 1 84568 029 4. Cavendish Publishing Ltd.

Watt, Gary–Todd and Watt's Cases and Materials on Equity and Trusts. Paperback: £28.99. ISBN 0 19 927982 9. Oxford University Press.

Whitehouse, Christopher; Rothenberg, David–Trust Drafting and Precedents. Looseleaf / ring bound: £195.00. ISBN 0 7545 1624 5. LexisNexis UK.

Wylie, John; Keogan, Aileen; Mee, John–Law and Taxation of Trusts. Looseleaf/ring bound: £213.33. ISBN 1 84592 202 6. Tottel Publishing.

UTILITIES

4322. Electricity supply industry–Licences–Exemption

ELECTRICITY (EXEMPTION FROM THE REQUIREMENT FOR A GENERATION LICENCE) (ENGLAND AND WALES) ORDER 2005, SI 2005 2242; made under the Electricity Act 1989 s.5. In force: September 1, 2005; £3.00.

This Order grants an exemption from the requirements of the Electricity Act 1989 s.4(1) (which prohibits the generation of electricity without a licence or exemption) to Barrow Offshore Wind Limited in respect of the plant known as Barrow Offshore Wind Farm.

4323. Electricity supply industry–Licences–Exemptions

ELECTRICITY (CLASS EXEMPTIONS FROM THE REQUIREMENT FOR A LICENCE) (AMENDMENT) ORDER 2005, SI 2005 488; made under the Electricity Act 1989 s.5. In force: April 1, 2005; £3.00.

This Order extends to Scotland the class exemption in the Electricity (Class Exemptions from the Requirement for a Licence) Order 2001 (SI 2001 3270) for generators not exceeding 100 megawatts.

4324. Electricity supply industry–Renewable energy–Renewables obligation

RENEWABLES OBLIGATION ORDER 2005, SI 2005 926; made under the Electricity Act 1989 s.32, s.32A, s.32B, s.32C. In force: April 1, 2005; £5.50.

This Order, which revokes with savings the Renewables Obligation Order 2002 (SI 2002 914) and the Renewables Obligation (Amendment) Order 2004 (SI 2004 924), imposes an obligation on all electricity suppliers, which are licensed under the Electricity Act 1989 and which supply electricity in England and Wales, to supply to customers in Great Britain specified amounts of electricity generated by using renewable sources. The provisions of this Order are similar to the 2002 Order; however new provisions have been added relating to the recognition of NIROCs and the allocation of ROCs in respect of electricity generated in Great Britain but supplied to customers in Northern Ireland. The new provisions of the Order also introduce a surcharge on late payments received by the Authority and a procedure known as mutualisation.

4325. Electricity supply industry—Standards of performance—Compensation

ELECTRICITY (STANDARDS OF PERFORMANCE) REGULATIONS 2005, SI 2005 1019; made under the Electricity Act 1989 s.39, s.39A, s.39B, s.42A, s.60. In force: April 1, 2005; £4.50.

These Regulations, which revoke with saving the Electricity (Standards of Performance) Regulations 2001 (SI 2001 3265), introduce a number of changes in the standards of performance arrangements that have been consulted on by the Office of the Gas and Electricity Markets as part of the Electricity Distribution Price Control Review. They prescribe the sum which suppliers or electricity distributors must pay to a customer by way of compensation for failure to meet specified standards of performance in respect of the services to be provided by such suppliers or distributors. The sum payable differs between domestic and non-domestic customers, and between standards.

4326. Electricity supply industry—Uniform prices

ELECTRICITY ACT 1989 (UNIFORM PRICES IN THE NORTH OF SCOTLAND) ORDER 2005, SI 2005 490; made under the Electricity Act 1989 s.7B. In force: April 1, 2005; £3.00.

This Order ensures that holders of electricity transmission, distribution and supply licences cannot charge prices which take into account the geographical location of any domestic premises within a designated area of the north of Scotland.

4327. Gas supply industry—Exemptions

GAS ACT 1986 (EXEMPTION) ORDER 2005, SI 2005 16; made under the Gas Act 1986 s.6A. In force: February 1, 2005; £3.00.

The Gas Act 1986 provides for the granting by order of exemptions from the prohibition on conveying gas through pipes to any premises, or to a pipe-line system operated by a licensed gas transporter or the prohibition, on supplying to premises gas which has been conveyed to those premises through pipes. This Order grants an exemption to a person in respect of the conveyance of gas from an LNG import facility to a pipe-line system operated by a licensed gas transporter.

4328. Gas supply industry—Exemptions

GAS ACT 1986 (EXEMPTION) (NO.2) ORDER 2005, SI 2005 280; made under the Gas Act 1986 s.6A. In force: May 1, 2005; £3.00.

The Gas Act 1986 provides for the granting by order of exemptions from the prohibition contained in the 1986 Act s.5(1)(c) on arranging with a licensed gas transporter for gas to be introduced into, conveyed by means of or taken out of a pipe-line system operated by that transporter. This Order exempts any gas transporter who operates the National Transmission System (NTS) or a regional distribution network (DN) in relation to arrangements with another such transporter for gas to be taken out of the NTS or introduced into or taken out of a DN at certain connection points.

4329. Gas supply industry—Standards of performance—Compensation

GAS (STANDARDS OF PERFORMANCE) REGULATIONS 2005, SI 2005 1135; made under the Gas Act 1986 s.33A, s.33AA, s.33AB, s.33D, s.47. In force: April 1, 2005; £4.00.

These Regulations, which re-enact most of the provisions of the Gas (Standards of Performance) Regulations 2002 (SI 2002 475) and the Gas (Standards of Performance) (Amendment) Regulations 2002 (SI 2002 741), prescribe the sum which gas suppliers or gas transporters must pay to a customer by way of compensation for failure to meet specified standards of performance in respect of the services to be provided by such suppliers or distributors. The sum payable differs between domestic and non-domestic customers, and between standards. The main changes are: introducing new connection guaranteed standards of performance relating to the provision of quotations, challenging the accuracy of quotations, responding to land enquiries, specifying dates for commencement and substantial completion of work, substantially completing the connection on the specified date; and the introduction of a new schedule setting out a more comprehensive practice and procedure for determining standards of performance disputes.

4330. Gas supply industry–Standards of performance–Compensation

GAS (STANDARDS OF PERFORMANCE) (AMENDMENT) REGULATIONS 2005, SI 2005 1136; made under the Gas Act 1986 s.33A, s.33AA, s.33AB, s.33D, s.47. In force: March 21, 2005; £3.00.

These Regulations amend the Gas (Standards of Performance) Regulations 2005 (SI 2005 1135) to change the date they come into force from April 1, 2005 to May 1, 2005 so as to ensure that their coming into force coincides with the introduction of a new standard special licence condition governing standards of performance.

4331. Sewers and drains–Damage–Compensation claim for damage caused by mining subsidence–Actual or constructive knowledge–Limitation period

[Coal Mining Subsidence Act 1991 s.3.]

The claimant (S) brought a claim for compensation for damage to sewers which had been caused by mining subsidence. A preliminary issue was raised as to whether S had knowledge of the damage more than six years before giving notice of the claim to the defendant (C), thus falling foul of the limitation provisions. Under the Coal Mining Subsidence Act 1991 s.3, S was required to have knowledge that damage had occurred and its general nature and was deemed to have knowledge of any damage that could reasonably have been discovered through facts which it could itself ascertain, or those it could ascertain with the assistance of an expert if it was reasonable to consult an expert. S submitted that it had acted reasonably, that the state of its knowledge at the relevant time should not have obliged it to carry out any investigations into possible further damage beyond those it had already carried out, and that C would still have been liable whenever the damage was caused. C argued that S should have been aware of the damage earlier and should be deemed to have had constructive knowledge, since it was aware that mining was taking place in the area and that other sewers had been affected.

Held, giving judgment for C, that S had obtained the requisite knowledge of damage six years before the claim was founded and therefore it was time barred. It was necessary to consider whether S had taken the steps a reasonable sewer undertaker would have taken in the circumstances and the Sewer Rehabilitation Manual should be used to assess the reasonableness of S's actions, as it was objective. The change in the legislation did not remove S's obligations to undertake such reasonable investigations. It was for C to show that S could reasonably have discovered the damage, and upon it doing so it was for S to prove that it could not reasonably have acquired the requisite knowledge. Whilst it was reasonable for investigations to be made on the basis of complaints from the public regarding flooding, it was not reasonable to expect S to carry out its own survey to predict likely areas of damage unless there were reasonable grounds for believing that damage was likely to have occurred at a particular site. Although there was no basis for departing from the general rule that the successful party should receive its costs, as the tribunal had found for S on the important issue of whether it should have carried out a survey of the mines to predict where damage may occur, it was appropriate in the instant case that C be awarded only half its costs.

SEVERN TRENT WATER LTD v. COAL AUTHORITY [2005] R.V.R. 21, George Bartlett Q.C. (President), Lands Tr.

4332. Water supply—Access—Water fitting requirements

WATER SUPPLY LICENCE (PRESCRIBED WATER FITTINGS REQUIREMENTS) REGULATIONS 2005, SI 2005 3077; made under the Water Industry Act 1991 s.66A. In force: December 1, 2005; £3.00.

The Water Industry Act 1991 requires water undertakers to grant licensed water suppliers access to their supply systems under certain conditions in order to supply water to eligible premises of customers. One such condition relates to water fittings. A water undertaker is not required to grant access if there is a contravention of prescribed statutory requirements in relation to the water fittings used or to be used in connection with the supply of water to the premises to be supplied by the licensed water supplier or the use of water in those premises. These Regulations prescribe those statutory requirements as being certain requirements in the Water Supply (Water Fittings) Regulations 1999 (SI 1999 1148).

4333. Water supply—Drought

SOUTHERN WATER SERVICES LIMITED (WEIR WOOD RESERVOIR) (DROUGHT) ORDER 2005, SI 2005 2088; made under the Water Resources Act 1991 s.73, s.74, Sch.8 para.2. In force: July 27, 2005; £3.00.

This Order, which is made on the application of Southern Water Services Ltd makes provision to meet a threatened serious deficiency of water supply in the area to the north of the South Downs from near Petersfield in the west, to Steyning in the east, and Horsham and Crawley to the north, by reason of an exceptional shortage of rain.

4334. Water supply—Drought

SOUTHERN WATER SERVICES LIMITED (WEIR WOOD RESERVOIR) (DROUGHT) (NO.2) ORDER 2005, SI 2005 2141; made under the Water Resources Act 1991 s.73, s.74, Sch.8 para.2. In force: July 29, 2005; £3.00.

This Order, which is made on the application of Southern Water Services Ltd, makes provision to meet a threatened serious deficiency of water supply in the area to the north of the South Downs from near Petersfield in the west, to Steyning in the east, and Horsham and Crawley to the north, by reason of an exceptional shortage of rain. The Order revokes and replaces the Southern Water Services Limited (Weir Wood Reservoir) (Drought) Order 2005 (SI 2005 2088).

4335. Water supply—Fluoridation—Consultation requirements

WATER FLUORIDATION (CONSULTATION) (ENGLAND) REGULATIONS 2005, SI 2005 921; made under the Water Industry Act 1991 s.89, s.213, s.219. In force: April 1, 2005; £3.00.

These Regulations elaborate on the consultation requirements provided for in the Water Industry Act 1991 s.89, where a Strategic Health Authority propose to enter into, vary, maintain or terminate arrangements with a water undertaker to increase the fluoride content of water supplied by the undertaker. The Regulations provide for the Authority's proposal to be advertised within the area to which the arrangements relate, and set out the details to be included in any advertisement; prescribe the circumstances in which consultation is required in respect of a proposal to vary or maintain fluoridation arrangements; and specify the criteria by which the Authority are to determine whether, in the light of representations made to them, they should proceed with the proposal.

4336. Water supply—Fluoridation—Indemnities

WATER SUPPLY (FLUORIDATION INDEMNITIES) (ENGLAND) REGULATIONS 2005, SI 2005 920; made under the Water Industry Act 1991 s.90, s.213. In force: April 1, 2005; £3.00.

These Regulations, which apply to England only, set out the form and terms of the indemnity which the Secretary of State, with the consent of the Treasury, may agree with a water undertaker or a water supplier in respect of liabilities that may arise where water supplies are fluoridated at the request of a health authority.

4337. Water supply–License applications

WATER SUPPLY LICENCE (APPLICATION) REGULATIONS 2005, SI 2005 1638; made under the Water Industry Act 1991 s.17F, s.213, s.219. In force: Reg.1: July 11, 2005; Reg.2: July 11, 2005; Reg.3: July 11, 2005; remainder: August 1, 2005; £3.00.

The Water Industry Act 1991, as amended by the Water Act 2003, requires water undertakers to grant licensed water suppliers access to their supply systems under certain conditions and for certain purposes. These Regulations govern the procedure for granting water supply licences.

4338. Water supply–New customers

WATER SUPPLY LICENCE (NEW CUSTOMER EXCEPTION) REGULATIONS 2005, SI 2005 3076; made under the Water Industry Act 1991 s.17D, s.213. In force: December 1, 2005; £3.00.

The Water Industry Act 1991 requires water undertakers to grant licensed water suppliers access to their supply systems under certain conditions in order to supply water to eligible premises of customers. A number of requirements must be satisfied in relation to each of the premises supplied by a licensed water supplier. One such is that, at the time when the licensed water supplier first enters into an undertaking with a customer to give a supply of water to any premises, the total quantity of water estimated to be supplied to the premises annually pursuant to the undertaking is not less than 50 megalitres. These Regulations provide for the circumstances in which a licensed water supplier is not, for the purposes of the threshold requirement, to be treated as entering into an undertaking with a new customer to give a supply of water to any premises. In these circumstances, a new customer can be supplied by the licensed water supplier without the need to assess the volume to be supplied to the customer's premises.

4339. Water supply–Supply system prohibitions–Exceptions

WATER SUPPLY (EXCEPTIONS FROM SUPPLY SYSTEM PROHIBITIONS) REGULATIONS 2005, SI 2005 3075; made under the Water Industry Act 1991 s.66I, s.66J. In force: December 1, 2005; £3.00.

The Water Industry Act 1991 requires water undertakers to grant licensed water suppliers access to their supply systems under certain conditions and for certain purposes. A retail licence permits a licensed water supplier to use a water undertaker's supply system to supply water to eligible premises of customers. A combined licence additionally permits a licensed water supplier to introduce water into a water undertaker's supply system in order to supply that water to eligible premises of customers. Section 66I of the Act prohibits the use of a water undertaker's supply system for the purpose of supplying water to any premises of a customer. This prohibition does not apply if the supply is made by the water undertaker, by a licensed water supplier in pursuance of its licence or in such further circumstances as the Secretary of State or National Assembly for Wales may specify in regulations. Section 66J of the Act prohibits the introduction of water into a water undertaker's supply system (other than by the undertaker itself). This prohibition does not apply if the water is introduced by a licensed water supplier in pursuance of its licence, by another water undertaker under an agreement for a supply of water in bulk or in such further circumstances as the Secretary of State or Assembly may specify in regulations. It is a criminal offence to breach the prohibitions in s.66I or s.66J of the Act. These Regulations, which amend the Water Industry Act 1991, specify further circumstances in which the prohibitions in s.66I and s.66J of the Act do not apply.

VAT

4340. Assessment–Output tax–Validity of protective assessment–When assessment "made" for purposes of Value Added Tax Act 1994 s.73

[Value Added Tax Act 1994 s.73, s.73(9).]

The appellant taxpayer (C) appealed against a decision ([2003] EWHC 2541, [2004] S.T.C. 690) that a "protective" assessment made in respect of its liability to pay VAT had been validly made. Departing from standard internal procedure, but under directions from a line manager, a customs officer (G) had made the assessment on the normal assessment form, checked and signed it, and had then notified C of the assessment by letter. The usual procedure would have involved entering the signed form in the computerised ledger and generating an official notification form and updated ledger entry. G's letter advised that the assessment would be enforced if the forthcoming decision of the European Court of Justice in *Customs and Excise Commissioners v. Primback Ltd (C34/99)* [2001] 1 W.L.R. 1693, [2001] C.L.Y. 5555 was made in Customs' favour. Assessments were also made six months later in respect of the same accounting periods, following the realisation that C had some liability for VAT regardless of the decision in *Primback*. Those assessments were made using standard internal procedure and the sums involved were paid by C. Following the decision in *Primback* in 2001, Customs updated C's ledger with the 1999 assessment figures and demanded payment of the total amount with interest. C contended that the 1999 assessment was invalid because (1) there was no power within the Value Added Tax Act 1994 s.73 to make "protective assessments" which were by their nature speculative and conditional. Such assessments did not create an immediately enforceable debt; (2) G had never made a decision to assess C's liability as he had not made a cognitive decision to assess, but had merely followed instructions, which was not the exercise of his "best judgment" within the meaning of s.73; (3) an assessment was not "made" until the computerised checking and generation of the notification form had been completed; (4) the 1999 assessment had been superseded by the later assessments.

Held, dismissing the appeal, that (1) a "protective" assessment, having been made to protect Customs' position, was an assessment and, as such, when notified did create a debt under s.73(9) of the Act. The fact that enforcement was contingent on a future event did not alter the fact that an assessment had been made. (2) If, on an objective analysis, G had made an assessment, it was irrelevant to consider whether he had decided to do what he did, *Don Pasquale v. Customs and Excise Commissioners* [1990] 1 W.L.R. 1108, [1991] C.L.Y. 3632 considered. The fact that G had acted as he did on instructions from a colleague did not lead to the conclusion that he did not exercise his own best judgment. (3) The making of an assessment was an internal matter for Customs, in respect of which there was no prescribed statutory procedure, and it was not possible to arrive at a formula that would determine in every case whether or not an assessment had been made. Each case should be determined on its facts. In the instant case the assessment had been made when it was checked and signed by G, the computerisation process being a delegable ministerial function, *Burford v. Durkin (Inspector of Taxes)* [1991] S.T.C. 7, [1991] C.L.Y. 2081 applied. (4) The later assessments were an alternative to the 1999 assessment and did not supersede it, *University Court of the University of Glasgow v. Customs and Excise Commissioners* [2003] S.T.C. 495, [2003] C.L.Y. 5945 applied.

COURTS PLC v. CUSTOMS AND EXCISE COMMISSIONERS, [2004] EWCA Civ 1527, [2005] S.T.C. 27, Pill, L.J., CA (Civ Div).

4341. Bad debt relief–Conditional sale agreements–Charge for exempt supply of credit–Apportionment

[Value Added Tax Act 1994 s.36; Value Added Tax Regulations 1995 (SI 1995 2518) Reg.170.]

The appellant company (W) appealed against a VAT assessment. W provided finance for the purchase of motor cars by individuals on credit terms, usually in the form of conditional sale agreements under which W sold the car to the customer in return for a promise of instalment payments computed by reference to the aggregate of the cash price of the car, including VAT, and a charge for credit (the supply of which attracted no VAT). That aggregate was divided into equal instalments to be paid, usually monthly, over the whole contractual period, typically of up to three years. There was no express apportionment of each instalment due under the conditional sale agreements as between the part going towards the cash price and the part going towards the overall cost of credit. W accounted to Customs for VAT when the car was supplied to the customer but did not receive the VAT in full from the customer until the agreement had been duly performed. If there was a default by the customer, bad debt relief was available only in respect of the bad debt arising out of the sale of the goods, not in respect of any shortfall in payment for the supply of credit which did not attract VAT, and so in the process of writing off a bad debt it was to W's advantage, so far as VAT was concerned, to minimise that part of the instalment payments made before the default which was attributed to payment for the goods and to maximise the part which was attributed to payment for credit. W claimed to be entitled to use a method of apportionment which approximated to the actuarial method and was called "the rule of 78" or "the sum of the digits" method and which assumed that the cost of credit was spread in the ratio which the number of instalments remaining to be paid bore to the total number of instalments. Customs assessed W to VAT on the basis that the correct method of apportionment under the Value Added Tax Act 1994 s.36 and the Value Added Tax Regulations 1995 Reg.170 was on a time basis but that by extra statutory concession a straight line basis could be applied. The VAT and duties tribunal dismissed W's appeal against that assessment. W submitted that Community law gave primacy to the method of apportionment expressed or implied in the parties' own arrangements and that inconsistent provisions of United Kingdom law had to be disapplied.

Held, dismissing the appeal, that (1) the tribunal had treated the parties' contractual arrangements as of central importance but they were not relevant unless Community law gave primacy to them or the provisions of UK law denying them primacy were to be disapplied as ultra vires or irrational or inconsistent with Community law. (2) Nothing in Community law required that the parties' own arrangements as to apportionment had to oust domestic legislation, if there was any, on the same issue or had to be taken into account by that legislation, *Commission of the European Communities v. Germany (C427/98)* [2003] S.T.C. 301 considered. (3) In the light of s.36(6)(b) and the breadth of s.36(5)(f) of the 1994 Act, it was impossible to hold that Reg.170 was outside the respondent commissioners' rule making powers. Nor, given the need for simple and comprehensible rules, could the time basis of apportionment and Reg.170 be considered irrational under domestic law or so offensive as to be intolerable to Community law. (4) Therefore the contractual arrangements between the parties as to apportionment, if there were any, were overridden by the time apportionment prescribed by Reg.170. (5) If Reg.170 was not irrational, then W could not argue that the straight line basis offered by concession, which was more favourable to it, was irrational. (6) Even if an agreement between the parties could oust the domestic legislation, the parties' arrangements in the instant case did not include an agreement on any form of apportionment. (7) The accounting treatment used in W's accounts was not determinative, *Customs and Excise Commissioners v. General Motors Acceptance Corp (UK) Plc* [2004] EWHC 192, [2004] S.T.C. 577 considered. In any event, principles of commercial accountancy had to yield to requirements of tax law where they were in conflict. (8) The argument that, where the parties had not agreed on apportionment, it was necessary to find a "subjective value" failed because, were it relevant, the subjective value that would be relevant would be that ascribed respectively to credit and to goods by the car buyer as the recipient of the goods and services, and there was no evidence as to whether or how that was done.

ABBEY NATIONAL PLC v. CUSTOMS AND EXCISE COMMISSIONERS, [2005] EWHC 1187, [2006] S.T.C. 1, Lindsay, J., Ch D.

4342. Company cars–Employee benefits–Fuel

VALUE ADDED TAX (CONSIDERATION FOR FUEL PROVIDED FOR PRIVATE USE) ORDER 2005, SI 2005 722; made under the Value Added Tax Act 1994 s.57. In force: May 1, 2005; £3.00.

This Order, which amends the Value Added Tax Act 1994, increases the flat rate values used for calculating VAT in relation to engine type and size if road fuel of a business is used for private motoring by an average of 9.4 per cent for diesel vehicles and 5.8 per cent for those using other fuels.

4343. Compulsory purchase–Compensation–Reasonable cost of equivalent reinstatement–Sheldon doctrine–Exclusion of VAT from compensation

[Land Compensation Act 1961 s.5.]

The appellants (S) appealed against the decision of the Lands Tribunal that, in assessing the compensation to be paid on a compulsory purchase, on the basis of the reasonable cost of reinstatement of certain buildings, VAT on the reinstatement cost was to be left out of account where Customs by a Sheldon ruling had indicated that they would not seek to recover that VAT. The respondent secretary of state had served notices to treat for the acquisition of land on which a sports hall and other buildings had been built. Planning permission had been granted to build a replacement sports hall and other buildings elsewhere and the acquiring authority had agreed that compensation would be assessed pursuant to the Land Compensation Act 1961 s.5 on the reasonable cost of equivalent reinstatement. Customs had originally advised that input tax on the building works was deductible. Customs subsequently took the view that input tax on the construction costs should not have been deducted and issued an assessment accordingly. Customs withdrew that assessment on the basis that their original advice had been a misdirection, and confirmed under the Sheldon doctrine that they would not be pursuing the VAT recovered on the construction works. S claimed by way of compensation not only the cost of reconstructing the sports hall but also the VAT. On the basis that it was clear that the input tax in respect of the sports hall would not be recovered by Customs but that there might be doubt in relation to the other buildings, an indemnity was offered by the acquiring authority for a period of 10 years with respect to any repayment to Customs of any VAT reclaimed by them on the costs of equivalent reinstatement of the buildings other than the sports hall. S submitted that it was entitled to receive the VAT as part of the compensation because, despite Customs' Sheldon ruling, it was not "clear beyond peradventure", as required by *Stoke on Trent City Council v. Wood Mitchell & Co Ltd* [1980] 1 W.L.R. 254, [1979] C.L.Y. 301, that the VAT might not have to be returned in future.

Held, dismissing the appeal, that it was for S to establish the reasonable cost of reinstatement of the sports hall and other buildings. At present all that S could demonstrate as the reasonable cost of reinstatement was that which had been paid, which did not include the VAT. S suggested that it was possible that the VAT would one day be payable because Customs might go back on their assurance, or circumstances might arise in which the indemnity offered by the compensating authority would have to be called on. The proof of such a contingency was no different from any other contingency that a claimant might have to establish to prove his loss. If the establishment of a very small risk that VAT would have to be paid entitled S to 100 per cent of the VAT, the overwhelming likelihood was that S would be over compensated. The correct approach was to see whether S had established, on the balance of probabilities, that there was a risk that the VAT might have to be repaid. If S established the existence of that risk on the balance of probabilities then the court or the Lands Tribunal would have to evaluate that risk. The Lands Tribunal was correct to hold that, in the light of the assurances received, S had not established the existence of the risk. The tribunal was thus right not to evaluate the same. S had failed to establish the existence of any risk so far as the sports hall was concerned. The Lands Tribunal had not erred in law in relying on the Sheldon ruling. Any risk in relation to the other buildings was eliminated by the offer of an indemnity, *Stoke on Trent* distinguished.

SCOUT ASSOCIATION TRUST CORP v. SECRETARY OF STATE FOR THE ENVIRONMENT; *sub nom.* SCOUTS ASSOCIATION TRUST CORP v. SECRETARY OF STATE FOR THE ENVIRONMENT, [2005] EWCA Civ 980, [2005] S.T.C. 1808, Waller, L.J., CA (Civ Div).

4344. Exempt supplies–Airlines–Operator engaged on internal and international flights–Scope of Sixth Council Directive 77/388 Art.15 exemption–European Community

[Sixth Council Directive 77/388 on a common system for VAT Art.15.]

The Danish Western Regional Court sought a preliminary ruling on the interpretation of the Sixth Council Directive 77/388 Art.15. C, which operated both internal and international flights, challenged a finding that its internal operations were not exempt from VAT and sought an order for the repayment of VAT incurred in making those services. As C's fleet of aircraft carried out both internal and international flights, including flights commencing and terminating abroad, the national court sought an interpretation of the meaning of the phrase "operating for reward chiefly on international routes" in Art.15(6).

Held, giving a preliminary ruling, that the exemptions set out in Art.15 included fuel and provisions to aircraft defined in Art.15(6) and could apply to domestic flights where the airline was mainly engaged on international operations. However, to come within the exemption, internal flight business had to be a considerably smaller part of the operation than the airline's international activities and it was for the national court to assess the extent of both the internal and international operations in the context of Art.15(6).

CIMBER AIR A/S v. SKATTEMINISTERIET (C382/02) [2005] S.T.C. 547, Judge Timmermans (President), ECJ.

4345. Exempt supplies–Apportionment–Holding company engaged in mineral exploration and exploitation–Dealing in shares and making loans to group members–European Community

[Council Directive 77/388 on a common system for VAT Art.2, Art.4, Art.13B, Art.19.]

A preliminary ruling was sought on the interpretation of the Sixth Council Directive 77/388 Art.2, Art.4(2), Art.13B(d) and Art.19(2) as a result of questions that arose in the course of a challenge by E to VAT assessments. E, a holding company, was mainly engaged in mineral exploration and exploitation but it also dealt in shares and made loans to its subsidiaries. The Portuguese authorities determined that E had wrongly deducted as input tax all the VAT it had incurred, whereas an apportionment should have been made to reflect the exempt nature of some of its financial transactions. In the reference to the ECJ, the national court asked (1) whether E's financial transactions were "economic activities" under Art.4(2) that were exempt from VAT under Art.13B(d) as being incidental to its main activities, pursuant to Art.19(2), and (2) whether such activities were taxable under the Directive where payments to E exceeded its share of the transactions concerned, as set out in the contractual relationship between E and its subsidiaries.

Held, giving a ruling, that (1) the purchase and sale of shares were not "economic activities" under Art.4(2) as the resulting dividends and proceeds were not a proper exchange for services performed; therefore they were not included in the calculation of VAT under Art.19, *Cibo Participations SA v. Directeur Regional des Impots du Nord Pas de Calais (C16/00)* [2002] S.T.C. 460,

[2002] C.L.Y. 4746 and *Wellcome Trust Ltd v. Customs and Excise Commissioners (C155/94)* [1996] All E.R. (EC) 589, [1996] C.L.Y. 5893 followed. Interest payments from E's subsidiaries or from bank and treasury deposits were exempt from VAT under Art.13B(d). However, the nature of an "incidental transaction" in Art.19(2) could not be determined solely by reference to the income generated. In E's case, mineral prospecting, although its main activity, might generate little income, with the result that the inclusion of its financial transactions could lead to distortion, *Regie Dauphinoise-Cabinet A Forest Sarl v. Ministre du Budget (C306/94)* [1996] S.T.C. 1176 applied, and (2) a transaction carried out by E in excess of its contractual obligations to its subsidiaries for which it received payment was a supply of services for consideration for the purposes of Art.2(1).

EMPRESA DE DESENVOLVIMENTO MINEIRO SGPS SA (EDM) v. FAZENDA PUBLICA (C77/01) [2005] S.T.C. 65, Judge Jann (President), ECJ.

4346. **Exempt supplies—Charities—Children's holiday camps providing spiritual instruction**

[Value Added Tax Act 1994 Sch.9 Group 7 Item 9.]

E, a charity, appealed against a decision by the Commissioners that supplies relating to the provision of spiritual holiday camps for children which were staffed by unpaid volunteers were not exempt. The compulsory camp programme included recreational activities as well as a daily camp service and group bible studies. The purpose of the camps was to promote the Gospel with a view to teaching children about the Christian faith in a natural context. E contended that its supplies were "welfare services" provided by a charity otherwise than for profit and were thus exempt under the Value Added Tax Act 1994 Sch.9 Group 7 Item 9. The Commissioners held that since in previous years the camps had made a surplus the supplies were made for profit and the lack of a formal structure meant that the camps did not constitute a "course of instruction" not designed primarily for recreational purposes as required by Item 9.

Held, allowing the appeal, that (1) notwithstanding that there was no evidence as to E's intention with regard to the disposition of surpluses, since E was a registered charity it could be inferred that any profit made could only be applied to its charitable purposes. E had no policy to achieve profit and the charges it made did not give rise to an increasing surplus, *Customs and Excise Commissioners v. Bell Concord Educational Trust Ltd* [1990] 1 Q.B. 1040, [1990] C.L.Y. 4616 applied and *League of Friends of Poole General Hospital v. Customs and Excise Commissioners* (Unreported, 1993) distinguished; (2) when viewed objectively the camps provided a course of spiritual instruction which contained incidental elements of recreation. It was not necessary for the instruction to have a particular structure as long as the objective nature of the camp was primarily to provide spiritual instruction courses, *Customs and Excise Commissioners v. Redrow Group Plc* [1999] 1 W.L.R. 408, [1999] C.L.Y. 4994 and *Customs and Excise Commissioners v. Plantiflor Ltd* [2002] UKHL 33, [2002] 1 W.L.R. 2287, [2002] C.L.Y. 4785 applied. The fact that some younger children for whom much less explicit spiritual content was provided might regard the camps as primarily recreational was irrelevant since these children had no independent freedom of action and could not therefore distort competition in the sphere of holiday provision.

EVANGELICAL MOVEMENT OF WALES v. CUSTOMS AND EXCISE COMMISSIONERS [2004] B.V.C. 2165, John Walters Q.C. (Chairman), VAT and Duties Tribunal (London).

4347. **Exempt supplies—Equitable interests—Agreement to develop land—Sale to third party—Proceeds split between developer and land owner**

[Value Added Tax Act 1994 Sch.9 Group 1.]

L appealed against assessments to VAT imposed on the basis that the proceeds of a sale of property were standard rated supplies of construction services. L, a property developer, entered into an agreement with the landowner, B, under which

L was to redevelop certain properties. Subject to the grant of planning permission and listed building consent, L received a licence to occupy the land and carry out the work. L could then either purchase the properties from B for a specified sum, with completion deferred for 12 months, or if sold to a third party during that time, L was to receive a proportion of the sale price with B taking the remainder. Those sales were subject to L's approval and L contended that it obtained an equitable interest under the agreement with consideration for the sale to a third party being for the release of L's interest, which was exempt from VAT under the Value Added Tax Act 1994 Sch.9 Group 1.

Held, allowing the appeal, that the agreement gave L an equitable interest in the land and the consideration for the release was a "grant" for the purposes of Sch.9 Group 1 Note 1, even though L was liable to pay B part of the proceeds of sale. L's interest in the land only became valuable when it had carried out development at its own expense. In the instant case, the consideration was attributed to the release of the equitable interest as it was most closely connected with that supply, as opposed to the supply of land, *Naturally Yours Cosmetics Ltd v. Customs and Excise Commissioners (C230/87)* [1988] S.T.C. 879, [1989] C.L.Y. 1683 applied.

LATCHMERE PROPERTIES LTD v. CUSTOMS AND EXCISE COMMISSIONERS; *sub nom.* CUSTOMS AND EXCISE COMMISSIONERS v. LATCHMERE PROPERTIES LTD [2004] B.V.C. 2132, Theodore Wallace (Chairman), V&DTr.

4348. **Exempt supplies–Gambling–Gaming machines operated outside licensed public casinos–Application of exemption in Art.13B(f) of Sixth VAT Directive–European Community**

[EU Directive 77/388 on the harmonization of the laws of the Member States relating to turnover taxes -Common system of value added tax: uniform basis of assessment Art.13B(f).]

The German Bundesfinanzhof referred to the European Court of Justice questions regarding the interpretation of the Sixth VAT Directive Art.13B(f). The taxpayer (L) operated gaming and entertainment machines in restaurants and amusement arcades owned by him in Germany and disputed the national tax authority's ruling that the income from the machines did not qualify for the exemption in Art.13B(f), since it did not arise from a licensed public casino. The questions referred were whether (1) Germany was precluded from making the organisation of gambling subject to VAT if it was exempt when organised by a licensed public casino; (2) gambling machines and their operators outside casinos were comparable with those in casinos for the purposes of the exemption.

Held, giving a preliminary ruling, that (1) the effect of the Sixth VAT Directive was essentially to preclude domestic law which exempted all gambling machines from VAT when used in licensed public casinos, but not when the same activities were carried out by other traders. Although Member States were entitled to set conditions affecting the exemption, they were bound to respect the principle of fiscal neutrality, which meant that similar goods and supplies that were in competition with each other could not be treated differently for VAT purposes, *Adam v. Administration de l'Enregistrement et des Domaines (C267/99)* [2001] E.C.R. I-7467, [2003] C.L.Y. 4597 and *Commission of the European Communities v. Germany (C109/02)* [2003] E.C.R. I-12691 applied. (2) The identity of the provider of services and the legal means by which they carried out their activities was irrelevant in assessing whether the services supplied were comparable, *Fischer v. Finanzamt Donaueschingen (C283/95)* [1998] All E.R. (EC) 567, [1998] C.L.Y. 4911 applied. It followed that Member States were not entitled to set conditions which depended upon the identity of the gaming operator. The provisions of Art.13B(f) were accordingly incompatible with national legislation and had direct effect.

FINANZAMT GLADBECK v. LINNEWEBER (C453/02); FINANZAMT HERNE-WEST v. AKRITIDIS (C462/02) [2005] 1 C.M.L.R. 53, Judge Timmermans (President), ECJ.

4349. Exempt supplies—Health care—General care and domestic assistance provided by private company—European Community

[Sixth Council Directive 77/388 on a common system for VAT Art.13A(1); Turnover Tax Act (Germany).]

A preliminary ruling was sought as to the correct interpretation of the exemption in the Sixth Council Directive 77/388 Art.13A(1). A had challenged F's decision that it was liable to pay turnover tax at a reduced amount. A, a private company, provided an out patient care service to people in need of physical care or assistance. A objected to F's assessment on the ground that it should be exempt under the Turnover Tax Act (Germany) as it was providing medical services. The lower domestic courts dismissed A's action and when A appealed, questions were referred to the Court of Justice as to whether: (1) the exemption in Art.13A(1) applied only to individuals, not companies; (2) the exemption applied only to care of a therapeutic care nature and did not include general care or domestic assistance, and (3) such care or assistance was closely linked to welfare in Art.13(A)(1)(g).

Held, giving a ruling, that (1) the Art.13A(1) exemption had to be seen in the context of the common system of VAT, and the nature of the organisation or person providing the service was not a qualification for the exemption; (2) the definition of medical care in Art.13A(1)(c) only included services involved in diagnosing or treating diseases and disorders, *D v. W (C384/98)* [2002] S.T.C. 1200, [2000] C.L.Y. 5295 applied. Thus non therapeutic services of a general care or domestic nature did not come within Art.13A(1)(c), and (3) however, such services were a form of social assistance under Art.13A(1)(g). It was for the national court to determine whether A came within the exemption and also whether domestic legislation was compatible with the Directive.

AMBULANTER PFLEGEDIENST KUGLER GmbH v. FINANZAMT FUR KORPERSCHAFTEN I IN BERLIN (C141/00) [2004] 3 C.M.L.R. 54, Judge Macken (President), ECJ.

4350. Exempt supplies—Insurance agents—Services provided for insurance company by management consultants—Status under Sixth VAT Directive—European Community

[Council Directive 77/388 on a common system of value added tax Art.13B(a); Council Directive 77/92 on measures to facilitate the effective exercise of freedom of establishment and freedom to provide services in respect of the activities of insurance agents and brokers Art.2(1)(b).]

The Dutch court sought a preliminary ruling from the ECJ on whether services provided by management consultants (C) to a life assurance company (U) were "related services performed by...insurance agents" pursuant to the Sixth VAT Directive 77/388 Art.13B(a) and thus VAT exempt. On an appeal brought by the Dutch secretary of state the court found that the "back office" activities carried out by C, which included accepting applications for insurance, issuing policies and managing claims, could not be exempt as insurance transactions under Art.13B(a) because U alone bore the risks inherent in performing insurance activities and the insurance contracts were underwritten in the name of U, not C. The defendant accountancy company, of which C was part, contended that C's activities were identical to those of the "agent" outlined in Council Directive 77/92 Art.2(1)(b) in that it had a relationship with both the insurer and the insured and had the power to render U liable to the insured parties and beneficiaries.

Held, giving a preliminary ruling, that whether a company was an insurance agent depended upon the nature of its activities and not just upon its power to render an insurer liable to the insured. Part of C's activities included setting and paying commission for insurance agents, maintaining contact with them and supplying them with information. Such activities were not those of an insurance agent. Furthermore, C did not undertake essential aspects of an insurance agent's work, such as finding prospects and introducing them to the insurer. Accordingly, C's activities constituted a division of U's activities and were not

services performed by an insurance agent. The "back office" activities, therefore, did not fall within the VAT exemption under Art.13B (a).
STAATSSECRETARIS VAN FINANCIEN v. ARTHUR ANDERSEN & CO ACCOUNTANTS CS (C472/03) [2005] S.T.C. 508, Judge Jann (President), ECJ.

4351. **Exempt supplies–Interpretation of EC law–Letting of immovable property– Licence to occupy–European Community**

[Council Directive 77/388 on a common system of value added tax Art.13B (b).]
The Belgian court sought a preliminary ruling on the interpretation of the Sixth VAT Directive 77/388 Art.13B (b). A Belgian company (T) entered into contracts with three associated companies whereby each of those companies was permitted to carry on its activities in a property owned by T. Under the contracts, an annual rent was calculated by reference to the area occupied by each of the associated companies. T sought to deduct VAT on refurbishment work carried out at the property. The European Court of Justice was required to rule as to whether Art.13B (b) was to be interpreted so that transactions by which a company, via a number of contracts, simultaneously granted associated companies a licence to occupy a single property in return for a payment determined essentially on the basis of the area occupied constituted the "letting of immovable property".
Held, giving a preliminary ruling, that Art.13B (b) had to be interpreted as meaning that the transactions, where the contracts had as their essential object the passively making available of premises in return for payment related to the effluxion of time, constituted the "letting of immovable property" and not the provision of a service capable of being categorised differently. The actual period of the letting was not of itself the decisive factor in determining whether a contract was one for the letting of immovable property and it was not essential that the period of the letting was fixed at the time that the contract was concluded, *Blasi v. Finanzamt Munchen I (C346/95)* [1998] All E.R. (EC) 211, [1998] C.L.Y. 4897 considered. It was necessary to take account of the reality of the contractual relations. A payment which took into account factors other than the period of occupation could still be a "letting of immovable property", particularly where the other factors were clearly accessory. Article 13B (b) did not define "letting" and so the provision had to be interpreted in the light of the context in which it was used and the objectives and scheme of the Directive, with particular account taken of the underlying purpose of the exemption, *Stichting Goed Wonen v. Staatssecretaris van Financien (C326/99)* [2003] S.T.C. 1137, [2002] C.L.Y. 4786 considered.
BELGIUM v. TEMCO EUROPE SA (C284/03) [2005] S.T.C. 1451, Judge Jann (President), ECJ (1st Chamber).

4352. **Exempt supplies–Legal representation–Foreign company instructing Australian solicitors for court proceedings–Lack of presence in country– Australia**

[Goods and Services Tax Act 2000 (Australia) s.38-190(1).]
F, an unsuccessful litigant, challenged the decision of MI's solicitors to submit bills including goods and services tax, GST. F had failed in its application for substantive relief against MI, a US resident company, and its partner in MR, a joint venture company. Under the Goods and Services Tax Act 2000 (Australia) s.38-190(1) GST was not chargeable on supplies unconnected to goods or real property made to non residents that were not present in Australia when the services were supplied. The question arose as to whether the presence of two of MI's directors and a senior employee in Australia for the purposes of defending F's application meant that MI was present for the purposes of s.38-190(1).
Held, giving judgment for F, that MI had not been present in Australia when the legal services were performed. Neither the directors' presence nor the instruction of Australian solicitors, who were acting in the ordinary course of

their business, to represent MI was sufficient to establish a presence in Australia.

FIDUCIARY LTD v. MORNINGSTAR RESEARCH PTY LTD 7 I.T.L. Rep. 159, Gzell, J., Sup Ct (NSW).

4353. Exempt supplies–Medical certificates–Provision of information for employers and insurers

[Sixth Council Directive 77/388 on a common system for VAT Art.13A(1)(c).]

A, a medical practitioner, appealed against a decision of the Commissioners that services provided by A including paternity testing, issuing medical certificates, assessing insurance claims and the preparation of medical reports in relation to personal injury and clinical negligence claims were exempt under UK legislation implementing the Sixth Council Directive 77/388 Art. 13A1(c). Following a preliminary ruling by the ECJ in *D'Ambrumenil v. Customs and Excise Commissioners (C307/01)* [2004] Q.B. 1179, [2004] 6 C.L. 484 the tribunal sought to apply the ECJ's decision.

Held, allowing the appeal, that where the principle purpose of the preparation of a medical certificate was the protection of the health of the person concerned, the provision of such certificates was exempt from VAT. Thus the provision of medical certificates certifying fitness for travel was exempt where the giving of the certificate was intended principally to protect the health of the person concerned. Medical testing involving the taking of bodily samples to test for the presence of diseases or viruses such as the HIV virus which were carried out in order to inform a decision by a third party such as a prospective employer or insurer was not exempt from VAT, *D'Ambrumenil* applied.

D'AMBRUMENIL v. CUSTOMS AND EXCISE COMMISSIONERS [2004] V. & D.R. 134, Stephen Oliver (Chairman), VAT and Duties Tribunal (London).

4354. Exempt supplies–Medical treatment–Fixed fee dialysis treatment outsourced by NHS trust–Single composite supply

[Value Added Tax Act 1994 Sch.9 Group 7; Sixth Council Directive 77/388 on a common system for VAT Art.13A(1)(b).]

G appealed against a decision that the provision of fixed fee dialysis services to an NHS trust was exempt from VAT. G supplied the services on a per patient basis at its own facilities, with treatment carried out by qualified nurses under the supervision of a doctor. The price was determined by a contract stated to be exclusive of VAT, but Customs found that G was making a composite supply under the exemption in the Value Added Tax Act 1994 Sch.9 Group 7.

Held, dismissing the appeal, that each patient's treatment formed a single composite supply carried out by G for a flat rate fee, paid for by the NHS trust on a contracted out basis under the private finance initiative, *Card Protection Plan Ltd v. Customs and Excise Commissioners (C349/96)* [1999] 2 A.C. 601, [1999] C.L.Y. 4972 applied. Payment by the NHS trust for treatment did not alter the fact that it was provided by G in its own hospital premises for the purposes of the Sixth Council Directive 77/388 Art.13A(1)(b), with the supply of those services coming within Sch.9 Group 7 Item 1(d) as the treatment was carried out by medically qualified personnel.

GAMBRO HOSPAL LTD v. CUSTOMS AND EXCISE COMMISSIONERS; *sub nom.* GAMBRO HOSPITAL LTD v. CUSTOMS AND EXCISE COMMISSIONERS [2004] B.V.C. 2191, Richard Barlow (Chairman), V&DTr.

4355. Exempt supplies–Medical treatment–Supplies of laundry and disposal of clinical and non clinical waste not related to provision of health and medical care

[Sixth Council Directive 77/388 on a common system for VAT Art.13A(1)(b).]

U appealed against a Customs ruling that supplies of laundry to its hospital and the disposal of clinical and non clinical waste emanating from the premises were standard rated supplies. U, a charitable company, contended that the supplies should be exempt from VAT under the Sixth Council Directive 77/388 Art.13A(1)(b).

Held, dismissing the appeal, that the supplies were standard rated as they were used by U to provide medical services to all the patients in its hospital and were not related so closely to the provision of health and medical care that they qualified for exemption under Art.13A(1)(b), *Card Protection Plan Ltd v. Customs and Excise Commissioners (C349/96)* [1999] 2 A.C. 601, [1999] C.L.Y. 4972 and *D'Ambrumenil v. Customs and Excise Commissioners (C307/01)* [2004] Q.B. 1179, [2004] 6 C.L. 484 applied and *Commission of the European Communities v. France (C76/99)* [2001] E.C.R. I-249, [2001] C.L.Y. 5560 considered.

ULSTER INDEPENDENT CLINIC LTD v. CUSTOMS AND EXCISE COMMISSIONERS [2004] V. & D.R. 32, Stephen Oliver Q.C. (Chairman), VAT and Duties Tribunal (Belfast).

4356. Exempt supplies–Not for profit organisations–Management and administration of entity on essentially voluntary basis–Remunerated managing directors

[Value Added Tax Act 1994 Sch.9 Group 13; Sixth Council Directive 77/388 on a common system for VAT Art.13A.]

The appellant taxpayer (B) appealed against a decision that it was not entitled to exemption from VAT provided by the Sixth VAT Directive 77/388 Art.13A(1)(n) and the Value Added Tax Act 1994 Sch.9 Group 13. B was an orchestra which, organisationally and structurally, operated as a company. The musicians were all employed by the company, as were a number of administrative staff. B's board essentially equated to the board of a commercial company. B took the principal strategic decisions and supervised the activities of those who carried out the general administration. Most of the members of the board participated on a voluntary basis. One of the members was the managing director (M), who was remunerated. The tribunal found that B's activities were within the rationale of the cultural exemption under Art.13A(1)(n). However it held that M had a financial interest in B, and that his significant role on the board and in the running of B meant that B was not managed on an essentially voluntary basis. The issue was whether the fact that M was remunerated, against the background of all the other board members (apart from one) not being remunerated, had the effect that B was not managed and administered on an essentially voluntary basis for the purposes of Art.13A(2)(a) of the Directive. B submitted that the relevant exemption had to be construed in the light of the underlying basis of the exemption, which was to ensure that the body in question had no commercial purpose, and therefore the test was whether the remuneration of M gave B a commercial character. B further submitted that an employee who was being paid no more than a reasonable remuneration for his job did not have a "financial interest in the results of" the company in question, and the presence of one or more paid persons at the key decision making level did not necessarily mean that the management was not "essentially voluntary".

Held, dismissing the appeal, that (1) the test was not whether the remuneration of M gave B a commercial character as argued by B. That would mean a wholly remunerated board could be essentially voluntary and therefore satisfy the condition in Art.13A(2)(a). There was no authority for such a construction. However the mere payment of remuneration to a person did not give him a financial interest in the activities of the entity concerned or an interest in its results for the purposes of Art.13A(2)(a). The condition in the second indent of Art.13A(2)(a) posed two hurdles, which an entity had to overcome if it was to qualify for VAT exemption. The first was that no person with an interest in the results of the activities should participate in the management or administration of the entity, other than on an occasional or peripheral basis. If such a person did participate then the condition would not be fulfilled and the exemption would not be available. The second was that the management had to be essentially voluntary. That involved assessing the extent to which the relevant individuals were rewarded for their management activities, and an overall assessment as to whether that meant that the management was essentially voluntary. (2) The tribunal found that remuneration by itself constituted a financial interest in B's activities, and since that was a material part of its reasoning, it followed that the tribunal had erred. It failed to apply the correct test. The tribunal should have considered whether M had a direct or indirect financial interest in the results of the activities of B. If he did not have such an interest, it should then have gone on to consider separately whether the management of B was "essentially voluntary". The answer to that question did not necessarily lie in the simple fact that M had received remuneration. It depended on looking at how and by whom the management was conducted and placing his participation in that context. On the evidence, the position of B was that its board contained a number of volunteers and one significant person who was a full time employee, namely M. M was not paid any identifiable separate sum in respect of his board membership but his job as a whole involved his carrying out managerial functions as a board member at a high level, *Zoological Society of London v. Customs and Excise Commissioners (C267/00)* [2002] Q.B. 1252, [2002] C.L.Y. 4758 applied. The board was an active board that took the key decisions, and M was at all board meetings and contributed to a significant extent in the decision making process. His contribution at board level could not be ignored in assessing the voluntary quality of the board. It was apparent that when the tribunal held that M's role was "significant", it meant significant in the sense that it was real, substantial, wide ranging and constant. It was not the sort of participation that one could ignore in the same way that one could ignore occasional contributions. The fact that M was paid to make significant contributions meant that he was not a volunteer; and it also meant that overall the managerial body was not "essentially voluntary" for the purposes of Art.13A(2)(a). It followed that the tribunal had reached the right decision albeit via the wrong line of reasoning.

BOURNEMOUTH SYMPHONY ORCHESTRA v. CUSTOMS AND EXCISE COMMISSIONERS, [2005] EWHC 1566, [2005] S.T.C. 1406, Mann, J., Ch D.

4357. Exempt supplies—Real property—Lease back of properties by agent—Collection of rent from undertenants—Virtual assignments

[Value Added Tax Act 1994 Sch.10 para.8(1); Sixth Council Directive 77/388 on a common system for VAT Art.13B(b); .]

The appellant bank (B) appealed against two decisions of the commissioners relating to B's liability for VAT. B owned a large number of properties, both leasehold and freehold, some of which it still occupied and some of which were empty. It entered into an agreement with a company (M) under which the properties were transferred to M, but those which B still wished to occupy were leased back to B. M provided property management services under the agreement, which included acting as B's agent in negotiations with landlords and tenants and collecting rents. Some of the properties held on short leases required the consent of the landlord before assignment. In order to avoid the problem of consent not being granted or not being obtainable in time, B and M entered into virtual assignments in respect of those properties, under which B passed to M all the economic benefits and burdens of the leases in return for a principal fee equivalent to the rent B would have paid had there been a proper assignment. The commissioners took the view that the leaseback to B by M was a supply of property management services and that the rents from underleases collected by M belonged to B and were paid by B to M as consideration for its property management services. B contended that (1) the leaseback was a supply of immovable property and therefore exempt from VAT in accordance with the Sixth Council Directive 77/388 Art.13B(b); (2) the rents from the underleases accrued to M and therefore M was deemed to be the person granting the underleases under the Value Added Tax Act 1994 Sch.10 para.8(1), with the effect that M made an exempt supply to the undertenants.

Held, allowing the appeal in part, that (1) the leaseback was not an exempt supply. Under European Community law the term 'leasing or letting of immovable property', whilst broader in definition than in some national laws, had to have the basic ingredients of being a contract in which the owner of property transferred rights in that property for an agreed period for remuneration that reflected that period. A functional approach was necessary, but the main requirement was that the characteristics of a lease should be dominant. The virtual assignments did not pass to M any right to occupy the property or to take profits from any underletting, as such rights could not be passed without the consent of the head landlord. Those rights thus remained with B, and any provision in the virtual assignments purportedly granting those rights back to B were meaningless. The assignments, therefore, did not have any of the basic ingredients of a lease. The virtual assignments were simply personal agreements between B and M which set out how certain rights between them were to be exercised. The principal fee paid by B to M was a mixture of rents due to be passed on to B's landlords by M and fees for supply of property management services. (2) The word "accrue" had to be given its natural meaning and not a legalistic interpretation. Looking at it in that way, the rents for the underleases did accrue to M. They did not constitute payment for property management services, as they were intended to form part of the agreement's economic benefit to M. M was therefore to be treated as the person making the exempt supply of the underleases to the undertenants in accordance with the 1994 Act.

ABBEY NATIONAL PLC v. CUSTOMS AND EXCISE COMMISSIONERS [2004] B.V.C. 2367, Nuala Brice (Chairman), VAT and Duties Tribunal (London).

4358. **Exempt supplies–Sports and leisure facilities–Criteria for determining a non profit making organisation within Art.13(A)(1)(m) Sixth Directive 77/388**

[Value Added Tax Act 1994 Sch.9 Group 10 Item 3; Council Directive 77/388 on a common system of value added tax.]

The appellant taxpayer (D) appealed against a decision ([2004] EWHC 1761, [2004] S.T.C. 1563) dismissing its appeal against assessments to VAT on its supply of sporting facilities. D, a company operating proprietary golf and country clubs, was a wholly owned subsidiary of a company (L), which in turn was a wholly owned subsidiary of a holding company (M). S and his wife owned M, of which he was the sole director. He was also the director of L and the sole director of D. The principal activity of the group was the acquisition, development and operation of leisure complexes. D's memorandum of association precluded the distribution of any profits of the company and provided that surplus funds should be utilised for improvement of the sports facilities for the benefit of individuals using them. D appealed when it was assessed for VAT in respect of its supply of sporting facilities, arguing that the supplies were exempt under the Value Added Tax Act 1994 Sch.9 Group 10 Item 3. Notwithstanding that it had accepted that D's aim was to provide improved sporting facilities and that it was not S's primary intention to extract profits from D, the VAT and duties tribunal upheld the assessments on the basis that D was a profit making organisation for the relevant period. On appeal the judge had upheld the decision of the tribunal. D submitted that the judge had erred (1) in concluding that an organisation which did not have the aim of distributing profits and did not in fact do so might nevertheless not be a non profit making body for the purposes of the Sixth VAT Directive 77/388 Art.13A(1)(m). Furthermore, "profit" meaning "financial advantage for the organisation's members" described in *Kennemer Golf & Country Club v. Staatssecretaris van Financien (C174/00)* [2002] Q.B. 1252, [2002] C.L.Y. 4756 was limited to the distribution of surplus and did not extend to funds accumulated and retained within the organisation; (2) the test of whether an organisation had the aim of being non profit making was a subjective one and the question of D's intention was to be answered by reference to the intentions of its controller, S.

Held, dismissing the appeal, that (1) D was an integral part of the commercial operation of the M group and of S. D had made substantial surpluses stemming from its free use of the group's facilities and had built up substantial reserves. This was a clear financial advantage to the group and to S himself. *Kennemer* was not authority for the proposition that an organisation which had no power to make distributions of profits to its members was necessarily a "non profit making organisation" for the purposes of Art.13A(1)(m), *Kennemer* considered. The financial advantages which might accrue to an organisation's members were not limited to the distribution of surplus funds to members. Furthermore, whether or not an organisation was non profit making for the purposes of Art.13A(1)(m) depended on the aim which it pursued. (2) S's intentions in respect of D were relevant matters to take into account as part of the general context but they could not be conclusive in determining D's aim in making the supplies in question. When all the surrounding circumstances were taken into account, it was apparent that D's aim in making the supplies was to further the commercial aims of the group as a whole and, thereby, of S. Accordingly, D was not a non profit making organisation within Art.13A(1)(m) and the supplies of sporting facilities made by D were not exempt supplies for VAT purposes.

MESSENGER LEISURE DEVELOPMENTS LTD v. CUSTOMS AND EXCISE COMMISSIONERS; *sub nom.* MESSENGER LEISURE DEVELOPMENTS LTD v. REVENUE AND CUSTOMS COMMISSIONERS, [2005] EWCA Civ 648, [2005] S.T.C.1078, Lord Phillips of Worth Matravers, M.R., CA (Civ Div).

4359. Gambling–Gaming machines

VALUE ADDED TAX (BETTING, GAMING AND LOTTERIES) ORDER 2005, SI 2005 3328; made under the Value Added Tax Act 1994 s.31, s.96. In force: December 6, 2005; £3.00.

This Order amends the Value Added Tax Act 1994 which exempts from VAT supplies of betting, gaming and lotteries, subject to certain exceptions. One of these exceptions is the provision of a gaming machine. This Order extends the definition of gaming machine to all machines that are designed or adapted for gambling, subject to some limited exceptions.

4360. Input tax–Amendment

VALUE ADDED TAX (AMENDMENT) REGULATIONS 2005, SI 2005 762; made under the Value Added Tax Act 1994 s.26. In force: in accordance with Reg.1; £3.00.

These Regulations amend the Value Added Tax Regulations 1995 (SI 1995 2518) so as to restrict the degree of rounding up of the recoverable percentage of residual input tax in the case of larger businesses; to provide that approvals given or directions made by the Commissioners must be in writing; to provide for a use based method of attribution of input tax where neither the approved or directed method nor any of the 1995 Regulations specifies a method of attribution; and provides that, where a method makes partial provision for the attribution of any input tax, only such part as is not covered by the method shall be attributed on the basis of use.

4361. Input tax–Benefits in kind–Entertainment–Assessment of employee incentive scheme

[Value Added Tax (Input Tax) Order 1992 (SI 1992 3222) Art.5.]

The appellant car manufacturer (P), which ran an incentive scheme for the sales staff of dealers selling its cars, appealed against the commissioners' alternative assessments of the scheme's rewards. Under the scheme, the most successful sales staff were invited with their partners to a dinner dance followed by overnight hotel accommodation. The commissioners' preferred assessment was that the incentive was a business entertainment within the meaning of the Value Added Tax (Input Tax) Order 1992 Art.5, and so P could not recover the input tax it had incurred when it procured the supplies from third parties. P contended that the incentive was not entertainment because the participating staff had provided consideration by maximising car sales and the event was provided by virtue of a contractual obligation, ie: the staff who fulfilled the conditions of the scheme were entitled to attend with their guest. The commissioners' alternative assessment was that if the incentive had been for consideration, then P could recover the input tax it had incurred but it had to account for output tax on the value of the supplies it made.

Held, allowing the appeal in part, that (1) under Art.5, a taxable person would only be using goods and services for "business entertainment" if they were provided free, *Celtic Football & Athletic Co Ltd v. Customs and Excise Commissioners* [1983] S.T.C. 470 applied. In the instant case, the sales staff provided consideration because there was a clear link between the reward and the level of car sales, and the reward was offered by reason of an obligation, *Customs and Excise Commissioners v. Kilroy Television Co Ltd* [1997] S.T.C. 901, [1997] C.L.Y. 5004 considered. Furthermore, since the sales staff had provided consideration for the supply of the right to attend the event, it followed that the consideration extended to the supply of a ticket for their partners as well, *Peugeot Motor Co Plc v. Customs and Excise Commissioners (Employee Incentive Scheme)* [2000] S.T.I. 1554 applied. (2) The supplies to the successful sales staff were taxable supplies for a non monetary consideration and so P had to account for output tax on their value, although it would be able to offset the input tax it had incurred.

PEUGEOT CITROEN AUTOMOBILES LTD v. CUSTOMS AND EXCISE COMMISSIONERS [2004] V. & D.R. 157, Colin Bishopp (Chairman), VAT and Duties Tribunal (Manchester).

4362. **Input tax—Company cars, private use of company car for VAT purposes**

[Value Added Tax (Input Tax) Order 1992 (SI 1992 3222) Art.7(2G).]

The claimant (Customs) appealed against a decision of the VAT and duties tribunal that the defendant (R) had been entitled to deduct from input tax the VAT which had been incurred in the purchase of a business vehicle. R and his wife ran a hotel business and had intended to purchase the vehicle for business use. Leading up to the purchase R had consulted and taken advice from his accountant and obtained literature from Customs as to whether he would be able to deduct the VAT payable on the vehicle from input tax. R also contacted motor insurance brokers to ascertain if he could insure the vehicle for business purposes only. He had been informed that he would be able to insure the car for business use, but that any insurance policy would also have included cover for personal use. R's intention had always been that the use of the vehicle would only have been for business purposes. In light of the advice he had received he purchased the vehicle and took out business motor insurance, which had the attached private use cover. Customs rejected his claim for a reduction of input tax. The tribunal, allowing R's appeal, accepted that the vehicle had been available for private use, but held that R's intention had been that the vehicle would not have been available for private use, which had been unchallenged by Customs. It found that the insurance cover for private use, and the fact that the vehicle was being parked overnight in close proximity to R's residential accommodation to the rear of the hotel, had been relevant matters to be taken into consideration. However, the tribunal found that, given that R had made proper enquiries before purchasing the vehicle, the evidence had established that he had not intended from the outset to use the vehicle for private purposes. Customs argued that the tribunal had misdirected itself in law since it should have considered whether, notwithstanding its unchallenged finding that R had always intended the vehicle to have been used for business purposes only, R had taken effective steps to exclude private use.

Held, allowing the appeal, that the very limited circumstances in which a taxable person might have been able to recover input tax paid on business vehicles had been addressed in *Customs and Excise Commissioners v. Upton (t/ a Fagomatic)* [2002] EWCA Civ 520, [2002] S.T.C. 640, [2002] C.L.Y. 4766. There had been no doubt, in light of *Upton*, that the test was restrictive, so that although R had entered into the purchase of the vehicle in good faith and had taken appropriate advice, it had been clear that the tribunal had applied the wrong test, *Upton* applied. The effect of the Value Added Tax (Input Tax) Order 1992 art.7(2G) was that whatever the taxable person's intentions may have been, if he had not taken effective steps to exclude private use by physical or legal restrictions, any intention he may have held would have been nugatory. In the instant case, notwithstanding R's enquiries, his intentions not to have used the vehicle for private purposes had been defeated by his failure to take effective steps to have excluded that use.

ROBBINS v. CUSTOMS AND EXCISE COMMISSIONERS; *sub nom.* CUSTOMS AND EXCISE COMMISSIONERS v. ROBBINS, [2004] EWHC 3373, [2005] S.T.C. 1103, Lloyd, J., Ch D.

4363. **Input tax–Deduction–Costs incurred in making share issue and obtaining stock exchange listing–European Community**

[Sixth Council Directive 77/388 on a common system for VAT Art.2(1), Art.17, Art.13B(d)(5).]

The appellant company (K) appealed against a decision of the Linz District Tax Office (L) refusing to allow the deduction of input tax paid by K on supplies associated with a share issue and its admission to the Frankfurt Stock Exchange. The supplies included the cost of advertising, agency and legal fees and other forms of technical advice which enabled K to increase its capital by way of the share issue and stock exchange listing. L asserted that the refusal was correct because share issues were exempt from VAT under the Sixth Council Directive 77/388 Art.13B(d)(5). On appeal, the Austrian Independent Tax Tribunal sought a preliminary ruling to determine whether the supplies had been made for consideration for the purposes of Art.2(1), and if not, whether K had a right of deduction under Art.17, on the basis that the supplies were used by K in making taxable transactions.

Held, giving a preliminary ruling, that (1) issuing shares for the purposes of raising capital did not amount to the provision of a service for consideration under Art.2(1), *KapHag Renditefonds 35 Spreecenter Berlin-Hellersdorf 3 Tranche GbR v. Finanzamt Charlottenburg (C442/01)* [2003] E.C.R. I-6851 followed. (2) The right of deduction claimed by K was integral to the VAT system and had to be capable of being exercised in relation to inputs made by taxable persons acquiring goods or services which formed part of an output transaction that carried the right to deduct, *Rompelman v. Minister van Financien (268/83)* [1985] E.C.R. 655, [1985] C.L.Y. 1499, *Belgium v. Ghent Coal Terminal NV (C37/95)* [1998] All E.R. (EC) 223, [1998] C.L.Y. 4918, *Gabalfrisa SL v. Agencia Estatal de Administracion Tributaria (AEAT) (C147/98)* [2002] S.T.C. 535, [2002] C.L.Y. 4737 and *Abbey National Plc v. Customs and Excise Commissioners (C408/98)* [2001] 1 W.L.R. 769, [2001] C.L.Y. 5586 followed. As K had carried out the share issue to increase its capital as a way of benefiting its general trading activities, the supplies were part of its business overheads and were directly and immediately linked to its economic activities. Accordingly, Art.17(1) and Art.17(2) meant that K was entitled to deduct the expenses it incurred in making the share issue and obtaining the listing. The right of deduction would be restricted in the case of mixed supplies, as Art.17(5) only allowed the deduction of input tax that was attributable to taxable transactions, *Abbey National* and *Cibo Participations SA v. Directeur Regional des Impots du Nord Pas de Calais (C16/00)* [2002] S.T.C. 460, [2002] C.L.Y. 4746 followed.

KRETZTECHNIK AG v. FINANZAMT LINZ (C465/03) [2005] 1 W.L.R. 3755, Judge Jann (President), ECJ.

4364. **Input tax–Deductions–Civil law partnership–Sole object to set up limited company–No output transactions other than transfer of assets–Such transfer deemed not to be a supply–Entitlement to input tax deductions–European Community**

[Council Directive 77/388 on the harmonisation of the laws of the Member States relating to turnover taxes Art.5(8), Art.6(5), Art.17(2).]

The German Federal Finance Court sought a preliminary ruling on the interpretation of Council Directive 77/388 Art.17(2). A civil law partnership (FG) had been created with the sole object of setting up a company limited by shares (FA). Under German law, FG's assets, rights and obligations, if not transferred automatically, could only be transferred to FA by way of a separate legal transaction. Hence, FA was established by notarial act and FG transferred all its previously acquired assets to FA at their book value. In performing its sole object, FG effected no output transactions other than the transfer of its assets to FA. FG treated that transfer as the non taxable transfer of a business under the German VAT legislation (UStG). However, the authorities refused to allow FG input tax deductions on the VAT incurred on its input transactions on the ground that FG was not a "trader" since the only output transaction which it had intended to effect was the transfer of the business to FA and such a transfer was deemed not to be a taxable supply under the UStG. On appeal, the Finance Court found that FG was an undertaking and, as such, was entitled to deduct input tax even though it never intended to use the input services procured in order to effect the taxable transaction itself. The tax authorities appealed and the German court sought a ruling as to whether a partnership created for the sole purpose of establishing a capital company was entitled to deduct VAT paid by it where that partnership's only transaction had been to transfer all of its assets to the company once it had been established and where, because the Member State has exercised the options provided for in Art.5(8) and Art.6(5) of the Directive, such a transfer was deemed not to have been a supply of goods or services.

Held, giving a preliminary ruling, that (1) in order for a person to exercise the right to deduct given in Art.17(2), he had to be a "taxable person" within the meaning of the Directive and the goods or services in question had to have been used for the purposes of his taxable transactions. In this respect, a person who acquired goods for the purposes of an economic activity within the meaning of Art.4 did so as a taxable person even where the goods were not used immediately for such activities, *Lennartz v. Finanzamt Munchen III (C97/90)* [1995] S.T.C. 514, [1995] C.L.Y. 5057 and *Rompelman v. Minister van Financien (268/83)* [1985] E.C.R. 655, [1985] C.L.Y. 1499 followed. Moreover, the status of a taxable person was to be assessed solely on the basis of the criteria set out in Art.4. Accordingly, the scope of Art.4 could not be altered by the fact that a Member State had exercised the option provided for in Art.5(8). Thus, a partnership such as FG had to be regarded as a taxable person within the meaning of the Directive. (2) As FG's only output transaction was the transfer of its assets and as Germany had exercised the option under Art.5(8) and Art.6(5), FG had effected no taxable transaction within the meaning of Art.17(2). However, in order to ensure the neutrality of taxation, it had to be held that, where a Member State had exercised the option provided for in Art.5(8) and Art.6(5) and, according to those provisions, the recipient was to be treated as the successor to the transferor, a civil law partnership, as the transferor, had to be entitled to take account of the taxable transactions of the recipient so as to be entitled to deduct VAT paid on the input services which had been procured for the purposes of the recipient's taxable services.

FINANZAMT OFFENBACH AM MAIN-LAND v. FAXWORLD VORGRUNDUNGSGESELLSCHAFT PETER HUNNINGHAUSEN & WOLFGANG KLEIN GBR (C137/02) [2005] S.T.C. 1192, Judge Jann (President), ECJ.

4365. **Input tax—Deductions—Date of receipt of invoice for services supplied in previous tax year—European Community**

[Sixth Council Directive 77/388 on a common system for VAT Art.17, Art.18.]

A preliminary ruling was sought as to the right to deduct input tax under the Sixth Council Directive 77/388 Art.17 and Art.18 where a supply of services was made in one tax year, but the invoice was not received until the next tax year. T had sought to deduct input tax in the 1999 tax year for services supplied in that year, but where the invoice was only received in 2000. The tax authorities contended that the relevant time for deduction was when the invoice was received, and therefore the deduction could only be claimed for the 2000 tax year. T appealed, arguing that VAT was payable as soon as the service was received.

Held, giving a ruling, that the relevant date was the time when the invoice was received. Under Art.17(2)(a) the right to deduct arose when the services were supplied, but according to Art.18(2) the right could not be exercised until the invoice for the services had been received. The German version of the Directive was ambiguous, but the French and English versions made it clear that both conditions, delivery of service and receipt of invoice, had to be fulfilled before a deduction could be claimed, *Lennartz v. Finanzamt Munchen III (C97/ 90)* [1995] S.T.C. 514, [1995] C.L.Y. 5057 and *Metropol Treuhand Wirtschaftstreuhand GmbH v. Finanzlandesdirektion fur Steiermark (C409/99)* [2004] B.T.C. 5364, [2004] 9 C.L. 507 followed. This interpretation was in accordance with the principles of neutrality and proportionality since it ensured that deductions would only be claimed in the year of payment.

TERRA BAUBEDARF-HANDEL GmbH v. FINANZAMT OSTERHOLZ-SCHARMBECK (C152/02) [2005] S.T.C. 525, Judge Jann (President), ECJ.

4366. Input tax–Deductions–Derogation from Sixth VAT Directive–Motor vehicles not solely for business use–Limit on right to deduct–Legality of retrospective authorisation–European Community

[Council Directive 77/388 on a common system for VAT Art.6, Art.17, Art.27(1); Council Decision 2000/186 authorising Germany to apply measures derogating from articles 6 and 17 of the Sixth Directive 77/388 Art.2, Art.3.]

The German Federal Finance Court sought a preliminary ruling on the validity of Council Decision 2000/186 Art.2 and Art.3. The Decision purported to retrospectively authorise Germany's introduction of a measure derogating from the Sixth VAT Directive 77/388 Art.6 and Art.17, whereby the input tax on vehicles purchased after a specified date and used by a taxable person for both business and private use would be deductible at the rate of 50 per cent. A German taxpayer (S) claimed all of the VAT charged on his purchase, after the specified date, of a car which he allocated to his business and used as to 70 per cent for that purpose. S maintained that the German measure infringed Community law and that he should be entitled to rely on the more favourable rules in Art.17 of the Directive. The questions referred to the European Court of Justice included (1) whether Art.3 of the Decision, under which the authorisation was to have retroactive effect, was invalid; (2) whether Art.2 of the Decision infringed the substantive requirements of Art.27 of the Directive.

Held, giving a preliminary ruling, that (1) Community measures could only be given retroactive effect in exceptional cases, where the purpose to be achieved so demanded and the legitimate expectations of those concerned were duly respected. The requirement of legal certainty was to be observed all the more strictly in relation to rules which were liable to entail financial consequences. There was no suggestion in the Decision's preamble of any need for it to have retroactive effect. The German measure had not been authorised by the Council on the date on which it was to take effect and taxpayers had been entitled to believe that all input VAT paid on passenger cars remained deductible pursuant to the Directive. By permitting the retroactive application of the measure, Art.3 of the Decision infringed the principle of the protection of legitimate expectations and had to be regarded as invalid. (2) The imposition of a flat rate limit on the right to deduct constituted a necessary and proportionate means of preventing tax evasion and avoidance while making verification more straightforward and simplifying the system for charging VAT, *Ampafrance SA v. Directeur des Services Fiscaux de Maine-et-Loire (C177/99)* [2000] E.C.R. I-7013, [2003] C.L.Y. 4546 distinguished. Thus, Art.2 of the Decision met the substantive requirements of Art.27(1) of the Directive and was not invalid.

FINANZAMT SULINGEN v. SUDHOLZ (C17/01) [2005] S.T.C. 747, Judge Jann (President), ECJ.

4367. Input tax–Deductions–Time limits–Transitional provisions–Principle of effectiveness

[Value Added Tax Act 1994 s.80; Value Added Tax Regulations 1995 (SI 1995 2518) Reg.29(1A).]

The appellant company (C) appealed against the dismissal by the respondent commissioners of its claim to a payment in respect of underclaimed input tax relating to expenditure on staff entertaining. C had claimed sums by way of voluntary disclosure in June 2003 in respect of expenditure on staff entertainment which it had failed to deduct when accounting for VAT in periods from 1973 to 1997. The commissioners rejected the claim on the ground that it had been made outside the three year time limit for making a claim contained in the Value Added Tax Regulations 1995 Reg.29(1A). C appealed arguing that Reg.29(1A) should have included an adequate transitional provision and that the claim would have been in time if the commissioners had operated a transitional regime equivalent to that operated in relation to claims for repayment of overpaid tax under the Value Added Tax Act 1994 s.80. The VAT and duties tribunal held that C had not shown that it had suffered any disadvantage from the introduction of the Reg.29(1A) time limit without a transitional provision because there was no evidence that the amendments introduced to Reg.29 prevented C making any claim that it would otherwise have made. Customs submitted that C had to show that it would have made a claim if transitional provisions had in fact been introduced.

Held, dismissing the appeal, that (1) in the absence of a transitional period in the legislation, the most that a taxpayer could expect would be a reasonable time within which to make a claim under Reg.29. There was no reason why as a matter of Community law the taxpayer should be entitled to see replicated the scheme which the commissioners adopted in relation to s.80. The sole question was the duration of the reasonable period from August 2002, when the Community law requirement that there should be a transitional period was first recognised by the commissioners, during which a Reg.29 claim not subject to the new time limit could be made. C's claim made in June 2003 was made after the expiry of a period which would have been reasonable, *Marks & Spencer Plc v. Customs and Excise Commissioners (C62/00)* [2003] Q.B. 866, [2002] C.L.Y. 4775 and *Grundig Italiana SpA v. Ministero delle Finanze (C255/00)* [2003] All E.R. (EC) 176, [2003] C.L.Y. 1454 considered, *Fleming (t/a Bodycraft) v. Customs and Excise Commissioners* [2005] EWHC 232, [2005] S.T.C. 707, [2005] 7 C.L. 494 followed. (2) A requirement that C should need to prove that he would have made a claim if proper transitional provisions had been included was incompatible with the Community law principle of effectiveness. As a matter of Community law taxpayers in the position of C had, prior to the introduction of Reg.29(1A), a right to reclaim input tax. That right had been curtailed. Community law required those rights to be protected for a transitional period. If those rights were not properly protected during a transitional period by national laws, then Community law disapplied the national law to the extent necessary to preserve those rights. It would make it excessively difficult for a taxpayer to exercise his Community law rights if he had to prove that he would have exercised his right had a transitional period been included. However, if it was shown that a taxpayer could not have made a claim in the transitional period, his Community law rights were not infringed by the absence of the period and his claim would fail.

CONDE NAST PUBLICATIONS LTD v. CUSTOMS AND EXCISE COMMISSIONERS, [2005] EWHC 1167, [2005] S.T.C. 1327, Warren, J., Ch D.

4368. **Input tax–Fraud–Circular transactions involving "missing traders"–Preliminary reference to ECJ**

[EC Treaty Art.28; Sixth Council Directive 77/388 on a common system for VAT Art.2(1), Art.4, Art.5(1).]

B, a computer component dealer, appealed against a decision by the VAT and Duties Tribunal ([2003] V&DR 210) to uphold the Commissioners' refusal to repay VAT charged on B's purchases which had been sold on to zero rated traders. The Commissioners contended that the transactions were part of a carousel arrangement which began with a sale by a non UK EU supplier to a UK company, C. C, the "missing trader", would fail to account for the output tax on its sales and sold the goods to other UK companies at below market value thus enabling the other participants to sell at a profit. The circular transaction would end with a zero rated sale to a non UK EU recipient. B was not knowingly a party to the fraud but a number of its transactions involved such "missing traders" in the chain of supply. B contended that since the purchases and supplies it made actually took place it could not be asserted that they did not amount to supplies or the conduct of "economic activities" for VAT purposes on the basis that there was a fraudulent trader in the supply chain. Furthermore, the Tribunal's approach was capable of having a deterrent effect on trade contrary to the EC Treaty Art.28 and offended the principle of legal certainty.

Held, making a preliminary reference to the ECJ, that in order to resolve the issue it was necessary to refer to the ECJ questions relating to whether, in respect of the disputed transactions by B, (1) B was a "taxable person acting as such" within the Sixth Council Directive 77/388 Art.2(1); (2) B was carrying on an "economic activity" within Art.4 of the Directive; (3) the acquisitions by B were a "supply of goods" to B pursuant to Art.5(1) of the Directive; (4) the sales by B were a "supply of goods" by B within Art.5(1) of the Directive, and (4) any Community law principles had been breached.

BOND HOUSE SYSTEMS LTD v. CUSTOMS AND EXCISE COMMISSIONERS [2004] V. & D.R. 125, Jacob, J., Ch D.

4369. Input tax–Invoices–Proof of payment not sufficient–Late filing of EC sales list–Penalties

[Value Added Tax Regulations 1995 (1995 2518) Reg.29.]

The appellant taxpayer (M) appealed against two decisions of the respondent commissioners in relation to his VAT liability. M had claimed input tax for supplies for which he did not have VAT invoices, and the commissioners had refused his claim. M was required to provide a European Community sales list by November 11, 2002. The list was not received by the commissioners until February 3, 2003 and they imposed daily penalties for the default. M contended that (1) he had proof of payment for the supplies claimed, which ought to have been sufficient; (2) he had posted the list in the middle of November and it should have been received by the commissioners by November 30.

Held, allowing the appeal in part, that (1) proof of payment was not sufficient. In accordance with the Value Added Tax Regulations 1995 Reg.29, input tax could only be claimed by possession of a VAT invoice. (2) Although M had not shown a good reason for his default, on the evidence it was more likely than not that he had posted the list before November 30, therefore it would be deemed to have been received by that date. The penalty was accordingly reduced to reflect that finding.

MAGUIRE (T/A SKIAN MHOR) v. CUSTOMS AND EXCISE COMMISSIONERS [2004] V. & D.R. 288, T Gordon Coutts Q.C. (Chairman), VAT and Duties Tribunal (London).

4370. Input tax–Person supplied

VALUE ADDED TAX (INPUT TAX) (PERSON SUPPLIED) ORDER 2005, SI 2005 3291; made under the Value Added Tax Act 1994 s.24. In force: January 1, 2006; £3.00.

This Order revokes the Value Added Tax (Input Tax) (Person Supplied) Order 1991 (SI 1991 2306).

4371. Input tax–Publications–Fund raising–Recoverability of input tax

[Value Added Tax Act 1994 s.5(2)(a), Sch.4 para.5(1).]

The appellant charitable society appealed against a decision ([2004] B.V.C. 2317) that it could not recover input tax on the supply of fundraising services in connection with its newsletter. The respondent commissioners cross appealed against a decision that the newsletter was a deemed supply under the Value Added Tax Act 1994 Sch.4 para.5(1) so that the society could recover all input tax on the supply to it of goods and services used exclusively in the production and distribution of the newsletter. The newsletter was provided by the society to its committed donors, which were found by means of fundraising activities. The commissioners had disallowed input tax as they were of the view that the provision of the newsletter to the committed donors was not a supply because it was not made for consideration. On appeal, the tribunal concluded that the supply of the newspaper was not for consideration so was not a supply within s.5(2)(a) of the 1994 Act but was a deemed supply under Sch.4 para.5(1) of the 1994 Act, so that the society could recover all the tax on the supply to it of the goods and services used exclusively in the production and distribution of the newsletter but could not recover the tax on the supply of the fundraising activities. The society accepted the tribunal's findings but contended that the fundraising related to the raising of money for the general purposes of the society and therefore input tax fell to be dealt with in the same way as input tax on supplies to the society of its overheads in general, namely as residual input tax. The commissioners contended that the society was only entitled to credit on such supplies as residual input tax, meaning that there should be an apportionment of the supplies to taxable uses so as to give rise to a partial right to deduct the input tax in question.

Held, allowing the appeal and dismissing the cross appeal, that (1) the tribunal had failed to determine, because it had not been asked to do so, whether the donations received through the activities of the fundraising services were unrestricted and could be used for any purpose of the society, and assuming that they were, the extent to which the monies so raised were in fact used, by funding the society's general overheads, towards the society's taxable supplies. Accordingly, the matter was remitted to the tribunal, *Kretztechnik AG v. Finanzamt Linz (C465/03)* [2005] S.T.C. 1118 considered. (2) The tribunal had correctly decided that the society could recover all of the input tax on the supplies to it of goods and services used exclusively in the production and distribution of the newsletter, *Customs and Excise Commissioners v. West Herts College* [2001] S.T.C. 1245, [2001] C.L.Y. 5576 followed. There was nothing odd in treating as a supply, to its fullest extent, a disposal of goods made other than for consideration, even where the original input tax had been restricted.

CHURCH OF ENGLAND CHILDREN'S SOCIETY v. CUSTOMS AND EXCISE COMMISSIONERS; *sub nom.* CHURCH OF ENGLAND CHILDREN'S SOCIETY v. REVENUE AND CUSTOMS COMMISSIONERS, [2005] EWHC 1692, [2005] S.T.C. 1644, Blackburne, J., Ch D.

4372. **Input tax–Recovery of tax–Car provided to company employee for business use**

[Value Added Tax (Input Tax) Order 1992 (SI 1992 3222) Art.7.]

Customs appealed against a decision of the VAT and duties tribunal ([2004] V. & D.R. 166) allowing the appeal of the respondent company (E) against Customs' decision that it was not entitled to recover input tax incurred on the acquisition of a car. E had passed a board resolution ratifying its purchase of a car. It was minuted that the car was for business use only, for the use of one particular employee (P) and that any private use would be a breach of P's terms of employment. The car was purchased and was normally kept in a port near E's office and within 50 yards of P's home. The keys were kept in the office. The car insurance cover note applied to use for social and domestic purposes and for business purposes. E had been informed by its particular insurer that it was not possible to insure the car solely for business purposes. Customs refused E's claim to recover input tax incurred on acquiring the car on the basis that the Value Added Tax (Input Tax) Order 1992 Art.7(1) applied to the acquisition and the purchase did not fall within any of the exceptions in Art.7(2) and Art.7(2A) to Art.7(2G). E's appeal to the tribunal was allowed as, on the evidence, there was no intention that the car was to be made available for P's private use. Customs submitted that the tribunal's decision was perverse given that the car was suitable for private use, that the insurance cover note permitted it to be driven by others, that the physical circumstances meant that there was no physical bar preventing P or other insured drivers from using it for private purposes and that a "kitchen table resolution" did not represent an effective practical restraint on private use of the car. E argued that the tribunal's decision was one that it was plainly entitled to reach on the facts it found.

Held, dismissing the appeal, that the tribunal had not erred. The physical circumstances of where the car was kept did not mean that, as a matter of law, E had intended to make it available for P's private use. The tribunal had found that the board resolution was genuine and had properly taken it into account when determining the VAT effects of E's acquisition of the car. The facts of the instant case could be distinguished from those in *Customs and Excise Commissioners v. Upton (t/a Fagomatic)* [2002] EWCA Civ 520, [2002] S.T.C. 640, [2002] C.L.Y. 4766, *Upton* distinguished. Where an employer provided a car on terms that an employee should use it for business purposes and not for private purposes, provided those contractual terms were genuine in all aspects, "the relevant condition" in Art.7(2)(a)(iii) of the Order was satisfied and, assuming all other requirements for input tax recovery had been fulfilled, the employer was entitled to recover the input tax included in the price of the car. Such a contractual stipulation between a family company and a director who was a member of the family could equally satisfy the relevant condition.

ELM MILK LTD v. CUSTOMS AND EXCISE COMMISSIONERS; *sub nom.* CUSTOMS AND EXCISE COMMISSIONERS v. ELM MILK LTD, [2005] EWHC 366, [2005] S.T.C. 776, Park, J., Ch D.

4373. **Input tax—Repayments—Adjudication of claims—Limits of entitlement to repayments and interest**

[Value Added Tax Act 1994 s.78, s.79, Sch.11 para.1 (1); Sixth Council Directive 77/388 on a common system of VAT.]

In an action for judicial review, the claimant trader (U) sought declarations that its right to repayment of input tax arose on the date of submission of its claim to input tax, and that Customs was liable to pay interest on the sum in question from that date to the date of payment. U traded in a variety of high value, readily moveable, zero rated goods of the type which had frequently been the subject of missing trader intra Community fraud. Customs had therefore conducted lengthy investigations into U's claims for repayment of input tax and sought verification that they were genuine. U had complained that the periods taken to reach decisions on its claims to recover input tax in respect of seven months in 2003 were disproportionate and claimed that interest was due from the accrual of the right to input tax, which U argued was the date of submission of its claims, until the date of actual payment. The issues for determination were (1) whether Customs was under a duty to act proportionately in respect of repayment claims; (2) whether a right to deduct input tax arose when the claim was made; (3) whether U was entitled to interest for the period between claiming repayment of input tax and the making of payment.

Held, refusing the application, that (1) Customs was under a duty to conduct a reasonable and proportionate investigation into the validity of claims for a refund and repayment, *R. (on the application of Deluni Mobile Ltd) v. Customs and Excise Commissioners* [2004] EWHC 1030 applied. Customs was entitled to take a reasonable time to investigate claims prior to authorising deductions and repayments, and what was a reasonable time within which to complete an investigation depended on the particular facts, *R. v. Customs and Excise Commissioners, ex p. Strangewood* [1987] S.T.C. 502, [1987] C.L.Y. 3832 applied. The postponement of repayment of input tax pending the outcome of the investigation was compatible with the Sixth VAT Directive 77/388. The Community law principle of proportionality required that a balance was maintained between the conflicting interests of Customs in the protection of VAT revenues and the need of the taxable person for early repayment to finance the continued conduct of his business, together with the requirement that there was effective judicial control over the actions of Customs at the instance of the taxable person. (2) There was no duty on Customs to repay input tax until the claim had been agreed or upheld. There was a critical distinction between an unadjudicated claim to input tax and an admitted or established claim, and the protection from derogation under the Directive afforded to admitted or established claims did not extend to claims which were neither admitted nor adjudicated upon, *Capital One Developments Ltd v. Customs and Excise Commissioners* [2002] EWHC 197, [2002] S.T.C. 479, [2002] C.L.Y. 449 and *Garage Molenheide BVBA v. Belgium (C286/94)* [1998] All E.R. (EC) 61, [1998] C.L.Y. 4931 applied. (3) Customs had no power to pay interest under the Value Added Tax Act 1994 Sch.11 para.1 (1) when there was a delay between submission of the claim and repayment. The power to award interest was strictly limited in s.78 and s.79 of the 1994 Act. Community law did not oblige Member States to pay interest on repayments of input tax from the date of the making of the claim to repayment.

R. (ON THE APPLICATION OF UK TRADECORP LTD) v. CUSTOMS AND EXCISE COMMISSIONERS, [2004] EWHC 2515, [2005] S.T.C. 138, Lightman, J., QBD (Admin).

4374. Input tax–Repayments–Interest rates

[Supreme Court Act 1981 s.35A; Value Added Tax Act 1994 s.78, s.79, Sch.11 para.1 (1).]

The claimant company (E) sought judicial review of a decision of the respondent commissioners concerning the rate of interest that Customs had offered E in respect of the repayment of input tax credits. E had been dissatisfied with the decision of Customs to set off the credits for input tax to which it was entitled against an alleged liability of E to Customs. Accordingly E sought permission to apply for judicial review. Meanwhile Customs repaid E the principal amount owing and offered to pay E interest at the rates prescribed under the Value Added Tax Act 1994 s.78. E maintained that Customs was liable to pay a repayment supplement of five per cent under s.79 of the 1994 Act and interest at eight per cent under the Supreme Court Act 1981 s.35A. The question of whether E was entitled to a repayment supplement was due to be heard before the VAT and duties tribunal. In the instant application E argued that it was entitled to interest at eight per cent because the original judicial review proceedings were for the recovery of a debt but the debt was paid in full before judgment was given and therefore s.35A of the 1981 Act applied. Further or alternatively, E argued that it was entitled to such a rate of interest under Community law and under Sch.11 to the 1994 Act.

Held, giving judgment accordingly, that in the instant case, s.35A(1) of the 1981 Act was inapplicable as no judgment for any sum by way of principal had been or could now be given. However, there was no reason why E could not rely on s.35A(3) as that did not require that the proceedings were current as to principal money. It was sufficient that there were current proceedings for interest. The discretion conferred on the court by s.35A(3) of the 1981 Act to fix a rate of interest was unfettered. However, assuming that s.35A did apply in the instant case, it was both convenient and just to fix the appropriate rate or rates as those that would have been from time to time applicable under s.78 of the 1994 Act. There could only be a Community law obligation and interest rate if the domestic provisions were so materially out of step with prevailing commercial rates that they were unjust. In the instant case, it could not be said that the rates under s.78 of the 1994 Act were unjust. There was nothing in Sch.11 para.1 (1) of the 1994 Act that conferred an obligation on Customs to pay interest. Accordingly, E's claim to interest at eight per cent failed.

R. (ON THE APPLICATION OF ELITE MOBILE PLC) v. CUSTOMS AND EXCISE COMMISSIONERS, [2004] EWHC 2923, [2005] S.T.C. 275, Lindsay, J., QBD (Admin).

4375. Input tax–Repayments–Partnerships–Lease of business premises held by nominee company–Recovery of input tax on rent payments

[Law of Property Act 1925 s.34(2); Value Added Tax Act 1994 s.24(1).]

The appellant solicitors' firm (L) appealed against a finding of the respondent commissioners that it was not entitled to recover as input tax under the Value Added Tax Act 1994 s.24(1) VAT paid on the rent for its premises. In 1988 L, a partnership of over 20 partners, negotiated a lease for offices. Rather than take out the lease in the name of four partners only, as required under the Law of Property Act 1925 s.34(2), L set up a company (C) with a share capital of £2. The lease was conveyed to C. L covenanted to act as guarantor, to ensure that C fulfilled its obligations under the lease and to take over as tenant if C could no longer do so. C was entitled under the lease to allow L to occupy the premises. The rent was paid directly by L and all correspondence and invoices from the landlord were directed to L. L reclaimed as input tax the VAT it paid on the rent. The commissioners took the view that the supply of the lease was made by the landlord to C not to L, therefore L was not entitled to recover the VAT. L contended that the true relationship was between L and the landlord and that the inclusion of C was no more than a device designed to avoid the more risky arrangement of four partners holding the lease on behalf of all the others. The supply of the lease was effectively to L and L made use of it for its business purposes.

Held, allowing the appeal, that L was entitled to recover the VAT as input tax. The commercial reality of the arrangement was that the premises were let to L for its business purposes and that L was liable for all the outgoings. The arrangement was unique to this particular situation. The landlord would not have entered into the lease but for the covenants given by L, which went beyond those of a normal guarantor and could only have been given by L. C was a company with no capital or commercial value, and would not have entered into the lease without L's backing. No third party guarantor would have been prepared to take the role of L in the lease. L would not have allowed C to take the lease without the assurance that L could occupy the premises as if it were the tenant. It was necessary to look at the arrangement from the point of view of what was being received by L. L made all the payments of rent and VAT as part of its obligations under the lease and in return was able to occupy the premises. It therefore met the two fold test entitling it to recover the VAT, *Customs and Excise Commissioners v. Redrow Group Plc* [1999] 1 W.L.R. 408, [1999] C.L.Y. 4994 applied.

LESTER ALDRIDGE (A FIRM) v. CUSTOMS AND EXCISE COMMISSIONERS [2004] V. & D.R. 292, A Edward Sadler (Chairman), VAT and Duties Tribunal (London).

4376. **Input tax – Repayments – Repayment supplement – Effect on appellant's right to interest and applicable rate**

[Value Added Tax Act 1994 s.78, s.79, s.84(8).]

T appealed against the Commissioners' refusal to pay interest on a repayment of input tax. T's repayment claim was challenged by the Commissioners and T appealed. However, the Commissioners' refusal to repay the total amount claimed was withdrawn before the hearing of T's appeal and the Commissioners' agreed to a repayment supplement under the Value Added Tax Act 1994 s.79 but refused to pay further interest under s.84(8). The Commissioners contended that (1) s.84(8) did not apply since there had been no finding by the tribunal, and (2) since a s.79 supplement precluded s.78 interest, any s.78 interest paid should be offset against any s.79 supplement and the Tribunal should deduct the s.79 supplement percentage from the rate of interest which it would otherwise order under s.84(8).

Held, allowing the appeal, that (1) if the Commissioners' contention was correct it would mean that they could avoid an award of interest by withdrawing their decision at any time prior to the tribunal's decision. Parliament could not have intended such a result nor could it have intended that an appellant's right to claim interest under s.84(8) could be precluded by payment at a late stage following an appeal. Accordingly, s.84(8) overrode any perceived prohibition in s.78 which was purely directed at interest in cases of official error, *Bank Austria Trade Services Gesellschaft mbH v. Customs and Excise Commissioners* [2001] S.T.I. 528 followed, and (2) the provision for interest was mandatory but the rate was discretionary. Consideration had to be given to each case and the fact that T had borrowed the disputed input tax at a high rate was a factor relevant to the court's consideration as was the fact that T had received a supplement. It would not be proper to select an initial rate and deduct the rate of the supplement since s.84(8) referred to an annual rate whereas the s.79 supplement was a fixed percentage.

UK TRADECORP LTD v. CUSTOMS AND EXCISE COMMISSIONERS (NO.1) [2004] V. & D.R. 195, Theodore Wallace (Chairman), VAT and Duties Tribunal (London).

4377. Input tax—Repayments, effect of time limits under Reg.29(1A) of Value Added Tax Regulations 1995

[Value Added Tax Regulations 1995 (SI 1995 2518) Reg.29(1A).]

The appellant car dealer (F) appealed against a decision of the VAT and duties tribunal ([2004] V. & D.R. 172) affirming the respondent commissioners' refusal to repay input tax on three cars purchased by F in 1989 and 1990. F had purchased a batch of 13 cars but did not receive VAT invoices in respect of them. Not holding a VAT invoice, in 1993 F had made voluntary disclosure claiming repayment of input tax paid on 10 of the cars and the commissioners paid the claim after investigation. In 2000 F had made a repayment claim in respect of the other three cars. The commissioners had refused the claim, relying on the three year time limit for making repayment claims introduced in 1997 by amendment of the Value Added Tax Regulations 1995 Reg.29(1A). The tribunal had held that the commissioners could not rely on the three year cap because F had an accrued right to deduct input tax which could not be taken away. However, the tribunal had gone on to dismiss F's appeal on the ground that if the matter had been sent back to the commissioners they would inevitably have rejected the claim in the exercise of their discretion. On appeal, the commissioners were the effective appellants, seeking to overturn the tribunal's decision that they could not rely on the three year cap in Reg.29(1A).

Held, dismissing the appeal, that (1) notwithstanding that a person might have acquired established rights under Community law, Member States could regulate the procedure for the recovery of those rights, such as claims for the repayment of input tax not due, by the imposition of time limits for the commencement of those claims. However, the principle of effectiveness required that, where appropriate, national legislation should include transitional provisions to guard against persons with acquired rights being denied those rights as a result of the retrospective effect of any time limit imposed, *Marks & Spencer Plc v. Customs and Excise Commissioners (C62/00)* [2003] Q.B. 866, [2002] C.L.Y. 4775 applied. (2) Regulation 29(1A) was imposed without transitional provisions and thus to the extent that it might prevent individuals with accrued rights from recovering tax not due because, for instance, at the moment the time limit took effect they had an accrued claim but the period of the limit had already expired, those individuals would be entitled to require the taxing authority to repay the tax notwithstanding that their claims would otherwise be barred by limitation. (3) However, breach of a principle of Community law, such as the principle of effectiveness, did not have the effect of striking down the offending legislation, *Local Authorities Mutual Investment Trust v. Customs and Excise Commissioners* [2003] EWHC 2766, [2004] S.T.C. 246 applied. (4) Even in the case of individuals whose claims had accrued before the time limits were imposed, and who might therefore be in a position to require the national court to disapply the time limits to their claims if brought within a reasonable time after the imposition of the limits, their privileged position by comparison with those whose rights only accrued after the imposition of the time limits did not continue indefinitely thereafter. If they allowed too long a period to go by before making a claim, the national court might properly conclude that the principle of finality or legal certainty required it to refuse to disapply the limitation provisions, *Grundig Italiana SpA v. Ministero delle Finanze (C255/00)* [2003] All E.R. (EC) 176, [2003] C.L.Y. 1454 applied. (5) In the instant case, F's claim for repayment of input tax in relation to the three cars in question had been capable of being made by him since 1990 and he only put it forward three years and five months after the coming into force of Reg.29(1A), of which he must be taken to have had notice. In the circumstances the tribunal had been wrong, and the commissioners had been justified in refusing F's claim for repayment.

FLEMING (T/A BODYCRAFT) v. CUSTOMS AND EXCISE COMMISSIONERS; *sub nom.* FLEMING (T/A BODYCRAFT) v. REVENUE AND CUSTOMS COMMISSIONERS, [2005] EWHC 232, [2005] S.T.C. 707, Evans-Lombe, J., Ch D.

4378. Input tax–Road fuel–Reimbursement

VALUE ADDED TAX (INPUT TAX) (REIMBURSEMENT BY EMPLOYERS OF EMPLOYEES' BUSINESS USE OF ROAD FUEL) REGULATIONS 2005, SI 2005 3290; made under the Value Added Tax Act 1994 s.24. In force: January 1, 2006; £3.00.

These Regulations make provision in relation to the recovery of input tax by a taxable person (employer) in circumstances where road fuel is delivered to and paid for by his employee (acting in his employer's name and on his behalf) for use either in whole or in part for the purposes of his employer's business. They specify that the road fuel must be delivered to and paid for by an employee acting in his employer's name and on his behalf for use by him in whole or in part for the purposes of his employer's business in circumstances where there is an agreed reimbursement method in place.

4379. Input tax–Supply of services–VAT on legal fees indemnified under insurance policy–Criteria for "supply" within s.24(1)(a) Value Added Tax Act 1994

[Road Traffic Act 1988 s.148(7); Value Added Tax Act 1994 s.24(1).]

The appellant commissioners appealed against a decision of the VAT and duties tribunal ([2005] S.T.I. 122) that the respondent company (J) could reclaim as input tax a payment made of VAT on legal fees arising from the costs incurred by J's employee (D) in defending a criminal charge. D had been involved in a road traffic accident whilst driving for personal use a company car provided to him by J under his contract of employment. The car was insured under a business motor insurance policy paid for by J which indemnified D for his legal fees. Consequently, when a criminal prosecution was brought against D, the insurer paid the fees of D's defence lawyers. J had then paid the VAT on those fees and attempted to reclaim that payment as input tax to offset against its own liability to VAT. The tribunal had concluded that the insurance policy had been purchased for the purpose of J's business within the Value Added Tax Act 1994 s.24(1) and that the VAT on the legal fees was thus recoverable. The commissioners submitted that the tribunal had erred in considering the question of the purpose of the purchase of the policy as relevant to the recoverability of input tax on lawyers' services. The issues for the court were to whom the legal services had been supplied and, if to J, whether that supply had been for the purpose of the business. The commissioners submitted that the legal services had not been provided to J; they had been provided either to D or to the insurer, and therefore J could not reclaim the VAT as input tax.

Held, allowing the appeal, that (1) the tribunal had erred in its approach to considering whether the payment of VAT on D's legal fees satisfied s.24 of the 1994 Act. In particular, it had erred in failing to determine to whom the legal services had been provided. Although J may have derived a benefit from the services that the lawyers had supplied, it had not chosen, instructed or paid the lawyers and had obtained no contractual rights in relation to D's defence. It could not be said that the lawyers had carried out work at J's request, nor was there any evidence that J was under any liability to pay the lawyers' fees, *Customs and Excise Commissioners v. Redrow Group Plc* [1999] 1 W.L.R. 408, [1999] C.L.Y. 4994 distinguished. In addition, it was clear from the Road Traffic Act 1988 s.148(7) that although J was the policyholder, there was no privity of contract and D was in a position directly to demand indemnification from the insurer in all respects as if he himself had a contractual right to receive it. It could not be said that the supply of legal services was to J. (2) The tribunal had also erred in its approach to determining, for the purpose of s.24(1) of the 1994 Act, whether the legal services were provided for the purpose of J's business. As the legal services had not been provided to J, there was no need to conclude whether the services had been provided for the purpose of its business.

JEANCHARM LTD (T/A BEAVER INTERNATIONAL) v. CUSTOMS AND EXCISE COMMISSIONERS; *sub nom.* JEANCHARM LTD (T/A BEAVER INTERNATIONAL) v. REVENUE AND CUSTOMS COMMISSIONERS; REVENUE AND CUSTOMS COMMISSIONERS v. JEANCHARM LTD (T/A BEAVER INTERNATIONAL), [2005] EWHC 839, [2005] S.T.C. 918, Lindsay, J., Ch D.

4380. Input tax–Trading–Cessation of business whilst lease continuing–Meaning of "economic activity" in Sixth VAT Directive–European Community

[Sixth VAT Directive 77/388 on the harmonization of the laws of the Member States relating to turnover taxes -Common system of value added tax: uniform basis of assessment Art.4.]

The Danish court sought a preliminary ruling from the ECJ on what constituted "economic activity" for the purposes of the Sixth VAT Directive 77/388 Art.4. The appellant taxpayer (F) appealed against the Danish government's request for repayment of VAT refunds received between 1993 and 1998. In 1988 F, trading as a limited partnership, entered into a ten year lease on restaurant premises. In 1993 the restaurant closed but the lease could not be terminated early. Despite not having any input tax to declare F continued to reclaim input tax in respect of the costs incurred by the premises. The Danish government submitted that F could not be regarded as a taxable person for the purposes of Art.4 of the Directive because F had not been engaged in economic activity.

Held, giving a preliminary ruling, that under Art.4(1) a taxable person was somebody involved in economic activity, which may consist of a single act or a number of consecutive acts. Economic activity included preparatory acts and deductions could be made even if the economic activity did not subsequently take place, *Rompelman v. Minister van Financien (268/83)* [1985] E.C.R. 655, [1985] C.L.Y. 1499 applied. Where expenses were incurred in the winding up of a business these were part of the economic activity within Art.4 and therefore could be deducted, *Abbey National Plc v. Customs and Excise Commissioners (C408/98)* [2001] 1 W.L.R. 769, [2001] C.L.Y. 5586 applied. This approach could be justified because the VAT system was designed to create neutrality of taxation on economic activity where the activities were subject to VAT. A person remained a taxable person after they ceased an economic activity if they continued to pay for premises owing to an obligation imposed by the lease. Therefore where the taxpayer could establish a direct and immediate link between the economic activities and the payments made they were entitled to deduct the VAT, *Midland Bank Plc v. Customs and Excise Commissioners (C98/98)* [2000] 1 W.L.R. 2080, [2000] C.L.Y. 5302 applied. Such deductions were therefore permissible provided there was no fraud or abuse, which was for the national courts to determine *Kefalas v. Greece (C367/96)* [1998] E.C.R. I-2843, [1999] C.L.Y. 645 applied.

I/S FINI H v. SKATTEMINISTERIET (C32/03) [2005] S.T.C. 903, Judge Rosas (President), ECJ.

4381. Input tax–Zero rating–Repayments–Conversion of non residential parts of building–Creation of additional dwellings

[Value Added Tax Act 1994 s.35, Sch.8 group 5 note 9.]

The appellant Customs appealed against a decision ([2004] EWHC 2358, [2004] S.T.C. 1662) that the respondent (J) was, pursuant to the Value Added Tax Act 1994 s.35, entitled to a refund of VAT paid on supplies of building materials and services used in the conversion of a building into a residence. J had acquired for conversion into a family home a building which had been used as a school. Prior to the conversion, the building had been split into residential and non-residential parts. After the conversion, the new building contained four dwellings comprising a mansion and three staff flats. J had claimed a refund of the VAT incurred in the conversion of the building to residential use. The issue for determination was whether, for the purposes of Sch.8 Group 5 Note 9 of the 1994 Act and in order for the refund under s.35 to operate, additional dwellings arising out of a conversion had to be created in the non-residential part of the building alone, or could be created in the building as a whole. Customs contended that a relevant conversion for the purposes of Sch.8 Group 5 Note 9 had to be a conversion of the non-residential part of the building and that the additional dwellings had to result entirely from conversion of the non-residential part of the building.

Held, dismissing the appeal, that for the purposes of Sch.8 group 5 note 9, the result of the conversion of the non residential part of a building which already contained a residential part had to be the creation of an additional dwelling or dwellings, *Blom-Cooper v. Customs and Excise Commissioners* [2003] EWCA Civ 493, [2003] S.T.C. 669, [2003] C.L.Y. 4570 considered. The dwellings had to be additional to what was already in existence and could, therefore, be found in the converted building as a whole. Accordingly, Sch.8 group 5 note 9 had to be construed so that the result of the conversion was to create in the building as a whole an additional dwelling or dwellings. It was simply a matter of counting the number of dwellings in the building before the conversion and again once the conversion was completed. If there were more dwellings on the second count, Sch.8 Group 5 Note 9 would be satisfied. J had created three staff flats in addition to a mansion for himself. If that exceeded the number of dwellings in the building before its conversion, then J was entitled to his refund. Notwithstanding the need to construe s.35 strictly, that interpretation of Note 9 did not take too broad a view of the purpose which that section was to meet.

JACOBS v. CUSTOMS AND EXCISE COMMISSIONERS; *sub nom.* CUSTOMS AND EXCISE COMMISSIONERS v. JACOBS; REVENUE AND CUSTOMS COMMISSIONERS v. JACOBS, [2005] EWCA Civ 930, [2005] S.T.C. 1518, Ward, L.J., CA (Civ Div).

4382. **Motor vehicles–Leasing–Car leased from German undertaking–Used by business established in Austria–Deemed own consumption subject to VAT in Austria–European Community**

[Council Directive 77/388 on a common system for VAT Art.6(1), Art.6(2)(a), Art.9; Turnover Taxes Act 1994 (Austria) para.1(1)(2)(d).]

The Austrian Administrative Court sought a preliminary ruling on the interpretation of the Sixth VAT Directive 77/388. An Austrian company (C) had leased a car from a German undertaking and used it in Austria for the purposes of its business. VAT was paid by the lessor in Germany and passed on to C in the leasing charge. C obtained a refund of the German input tax. However, the Austrian authorities included the leasing charge in C's taxable turnover pursuant to the Turnover Taxes Act 1994 (Austria), under which supplies of goods or services connected with the leasing of cars were deemed not to be for business purposes and, under para.1(1)(2)(d), "own consumption" subject to VAT was deemed to have occurred to the extent that a trader incurred expenditure relating to supplies abroad which, had they been effected within the national territory, would not have entitled the trader to deduction of input tax. The provision only applied to the extent that the trader was entitled abroad to a refund of the foreign input tax. The European Court of Justice was asked to rule on whether para.1(1)(2)(d) of the Act was compatible with the Directive.

Held, giving a preliminary ruling, that (1) the leasing of vehicles was a supply of services within the meaning of Art.6(1) of the Directive. The place of taxation was deemed under Art.9 to be the place where the supplier had established his business or had a fixed establishment and not where the hired goods were used, *Berkholz v. Finanzamt Hamburg Mitte-Altstadt (168/84)* [1985] E.C.R. 2251, [1986] C.L.Y. 1495 and *Hamann v. Finanzamt Hamburg-Eimsbuttel (51/88)* [1991] S.T.C. 193, [1991] C.L.Y. 3660 followed. Thus, the German authorities' taxation of the transaction and the refund to C of the input tax passed on in the leasing charge complied with Community law. (2) Paragraph 1(1)(2)(d) of the Act did not comply with Art.6(2)(a) of the Directive, which was designed to prevent the non taxation of business goods used for private purposes. The assumption in para.1 (1) (2) (d) that the lessee was entitled to a refund of foreign tax only properly arose where the service was used for business purposes. Such a service could not at the same time be treated as use for purposes other than those of a business within Art.6(2)(a). Further, to tax a supply of services in another Member State when it had already lawfully been subject to VAT in the State of the supplier gave rise to double taxation contrary to the principle of fiscal neutrality. The fact that the liability fell on different parties did nothing to change the fact that one and the same economic transaction had been taxed twice. Accordingly, para.1 (1) (2) (d) of the Act was not compatible with the Directive.

COOKIES WORLD VERTRIEBSGESELLSCHAFT MBH IL v. FINANZLANDESDIREKTION FUR TIROL (C155/01) [2004] S.T.C. 1386, Judge Wathelet (President), ECJ.

4383. **Not for profit organisations–Commercial activities–Nurseries–Activities in course or furtherance of business**

[Value Added Tax Act 1994 Sch.8 Group 5 Item 2 Note 6.]

Customs appealed against a tribunal decision that the use by the respondent (S), a registered charity, of premises for the purpose of running a day nursery was use otherwise than in the course or furtherance of a business within the meaning of the Value Added Tax Act 1994 Sch.8 Group 5 Item 2 Note 6, with the consequence that construction works were zero rated for VAT purposes. Customs contended that the tribunal had wrongly treated a business activity and a charitable purpose as mutually exclusive, that it had wrongly applied *Yarburgh Childrens Trust v. Customs and Excise Commissioners* [2002] S.T.C. 207, [2002] C.L.Y. 4811, and that and the only reasonable conclusion open to it was that S was acting in the furtherance of a business. Customs argued that the correct test was not to conclude what was S's paramount concern in establishing and maintaining the nursery but rather to consider the intrinsic nature of the nursery, which was no different from that of commercial nurseries which were subject to VAT.

Held, dismissing the appeal, that the tribunal had not proceeded on the basis that business activity and charitable activity were mutually exclusive. It had used the word "charitable" in the colloquial sense of gift or concession in favour of a disadvantaged group, to be contrasted with business, namely operations directed to earning profits. There was no distinction to be drawn with the decision in *Yarburgh, Yarburgh* followed. The presence or absence of the pursuit of profits was not necessarily determinative of the issue, although an activity carried out purely for pleasure or social enjoyment was not a business for VAT purposes. Nor was the payment of fees the decisive factor, *Institute of Chartered Accountants in England and Wales v. Customs and Excise Commissioners* [1999] 1 W.L.R. 701, [1999] C.L.Y. 4990 applied. The test was whether the activity was a serious undertaking earnestly pursued with reasonable continuity; was substantial in amount; was conducted regularly on sound and recognised business principles; and was predominantly concerned with making taxable supplies to consumers for a consideration, *Customs and Excise Commissioners v. Lord Fisher* [1981] 2 All E.R. 147, [1981] C.L.Y. 2849 applied. S was not predominantly concerned with the making of taxable supplies for a consideration. Of particular relevance were the fact that the admissions policy was weighted in favour of disadvantaged children; the fact that the fees charged were lower than those charged by commercial nurseries even though S paid higher salaries to attract and retain better qualified staff; and the fact that the costs were pitched at levels designed only to cover the costs of the nursery after grants and donations.

CUSTOMS AND EXCISE COMMISSIONERS v. ST PAUL'S COMMUNITY PROJECT LTD; *sub nom.* ST PAUL'S COMMUNITY PROJECT LTD v. CUSTOMS AND EXCISE COMMISSIONERS, [2004] EWHC 2490, [2005] S.T.C. 95, Evans-Lombe, J., Ch D.

4384. Option to tax–Business tenancies–Non retrospective prior approval–Compatibility with Sixth Council Directive 77/388 Art.13C–European Community

[Sixth Council Directive 77/388 on a common system forVAT Art.13B, Art.13C.]

The Luxembourg Court of Appeal sought a preliminary ruling as to whether it was compatible with the Sixth Council Directive 77/388 Art.13C to make the right to opt for taxation on the leasing or letting of real property subject to obtaining prior non retrospective approval. V constructed an office building, which it let to tenants from January 1993. It then submitted a declaration of the option to tax in June 1993. Approval was granted with effect from July 1, 1993 but V was then refused permission to deduct a proportion of the input tax on the ground that the first six months of the letting was exempt from VAT because it pre dated approval of the option to tax.

Held, giving a preliminary ruling, that the right to deduct under Art.13C was a derogation from the general rule exempting leasing transactions in Art.13B (b) and was subject to the exercise of the right of option. Member States had a wide discretion in respect of the option, which included the requirement to obtain prior approval, *Belgocodex SA v. Belgium (C381/97)* [2000] S.T.C. 351, [2000] C.L.Y. 5305 followed. In the instant case, the need for prior non retrospective approval was intended to ensure that the right was fully exercised and the lack of retroactivity was not disproportionate where it was used to encourage lessors to seek approval in advance.

LUXEMBOURG v.VERMIETUNGSGESELLSCHAFT OBJEKT KIRCHBERG SARL (C269/03) [2005] S.T.C. 1345, Judge Jann (President), ECJ.

4385. Output tax–Exempt supplies–Buyer of property carrying out construction works

[Value Added Tax Act 1994 Sch.9 Group 1 Item 1.]

The appellant commissioners appealed against a decision allowing an appeal by the respondent (L) against an assessment to output tax. L was a residential property developer and the assessment related to property that was owned by a company (B) and was the subject of an agreement between B and L. The VAT and duties tribunal found that the agreement gave L an interest in land and that the consideration received by L from purchasers related to exempt supplies of interests in land within the Value Added Tax Act 1994 Sch.9 Group 1 Item 1. The commissioners submitted that, given competing analyses of the supplies made under the transaction constituted by the agreement, it was necessary, in order to determine what was being supplied, to ascertain the essential features of the transaction, irrespective of any artificiality in the way that it might be presented by the documentation setting out its terms. The essential feature or dominant purpose of the agreement was that L should provide B with construction works. L submitted that, on a true understanding of the agreement, although L agreed to carry out works on the property, it did so on its own behalf and for its own benefit in that the value of what it did was reflected in the value of its interest in the property, which it acquired under the agreement.

Held, dismissing the appeal, that the essential question was whether, on a construction of the agreement, the supply to each purchaser was by B, with L having made a supply to B of its construction services in consideration of a share in the overall proceeds, or whether L and B each contributed to the supply to the purchaser on the basis that the overall unit sale proceeds were to be divided between them so as to reflect their respective interests in the supply. The agreement recited that it was L that was desirous of developing the property. The cost of the work and development was at L's risk and the division of the sale proceeds reflected much more a joint venture between the parties than a simple supply of construction services by L. The supplies made by L were made with a view to enhancing its share of the ultimate profits from the project and were not a mere provision by L of a supply of construction services.

LATCHMERE PROPERTIES LTD v. CUSTOMS AND EXCISE COMMISSIONERS; *sub nom.* CUSTOMS AND EXCISE COMMISSIONERS v. LATCHMERE PROPERTIES LTD, [2005] EWHC 133, [2005] S.T.C. 731, Blackburne, J., Ch D.

4386. Output tax—Overpayments

VALUE ADDED TAX (AMENDMENT) (NO.2) REGULATIONS 2005, SI 2005 2231; made under the Value Added Tax Act 1994 s.18, s.80, s.80A. In force: September 1, 2005; £3.00.

These Regulations make consequential amendments to the Value Added Tax Regulations 1995 (SI 1995 2518) arising from amendments made to the Value Added Tax Act 1994 by the Finance (No.2) Act 2005. They make amendments to reflect the changes from claims for recovery of overpaid VAT to claims for credit for, or repayment of, overstated or overpaid VAT; amend the definitions of "claims" and "reimbursement arrangements"; make amendments to reflect the change to claims for credit of output tax over-accounted for or assessed by the Commissioners as output tax that was not output tax due; make amendments to reflect the change to claims for credit of output tax over-accounted for or assessed; provide for notification to be given by the claimant to the Commissioners of any credit not reimbursed to consumers and for any amount paid (or repaid) to be repaid to the Commissioners within the respective time limits laid down; and make amendments to reflect the change to claims for credit of output tax over-accounted for or assessed by the Commissioners as output tax that was not output tax due.

4387. Output tax—Overpayments—No time limit for correcting simple duplication of output tax—Interest on overpaid tax

[Value Added Tax Act 1994 s.80, s.80(4).]

The claimant (BT) applied for judicial review of the decision of the defendant commissioners refusing to repay the balance of overpaid VAT and interest on the repayment. BT's business involved the supply of telecommunications services. An error in BT's accounting software had caused an overpayment of VAT. The error was that on termination of a customer's monthly payment plan account with a positive balance the accounting software posted a positive rather than a negative amount to an account which was reflected in BT's VAT output account. That had led to an overpayment of some £40 million over an 11 year period. After the error had been discovered BT had sought repayment under the Value Added Tax Act 1994 s.80. The commissioners repaid the VAT overpaid in the three years before the making of the claim relying on s.80(4), declined to apply their published concession that there was no time limit for correcting an error consisting of a simple duplication of output tax, and rejected BT's claim for interest on the repayment. BT submitted that (1) the concession exempted the overpayment from the operation of s.80(4); (2) BT was entitled to interest under EC law.

Held, refusing the applications, that (1) the meaning of "simple" in the concession was that the concession was only available if the overpayment was a duplication or doubling up of payment of output tax and nothing else. On the evidence the erroneous payment by BT had been calculated by reference to the amount being refunded, namely the balance on the customer's account on termination, and not to any taxable supply by BT to the customer. On the basis of the facts on which the application for judicial review had been argued, the application was dismissed. If BT wished to argue that the factual basis on which the application had been argued was wrong then it could make a fresh application to the commissioners to apply the concession. (2) Decisions of the European Court of Justice established that EC law protected and provided redress when charges or taxes had been improperly levied but did not support the proposition that a person had any right under EC law in respect of payments of charges or taxes voluntarily, but mistakenly, made. It was for national law to provide remedies in such a case and under English domestic law no interest was payable, *Metallgesellschaft Ltd v. Inland Revenue Commissioners (C397/98)* [2001] Ch. 620, [2001] C.L.Y. 5173 and *Dilexport Srl v. Amministrazione delle Finanze dello Stato (C343/96)* [2000] All E.R. (EC) 600, [1999] ECR I-579, [2000] C.L.Y. 2406 considered. (3) The commissioners were entitled to costs. Their costs of the application in respect of the concession should be paid by BT on an indemnity basis because that application had in effect been aborted by the failure of BT to put forward what it said was the correct factual basis for its case.

R. (ON THE APPLICATION OF BRITISH TELECOMMUNICATIONS PLC) v. REVENUE AND CUSTOMS COMMISSIONERS, [2005] EWHC 1043, [2005] S.T.C. 1148, Lightman, J., QBD (Admin).

4388. Partnership assets–Sale of land–Transaction involving supply of land by partnership

[Value Added Tax Act 1994 Sch.10 para.8(a).]

The appellant partnership (F) appealed against a decision ([2004] EWHC 152, [2004] S.T.C. 772) that it was liable to value added tax in respect of a transfer of land from F to another partnership. The land in question was a partnership asset. The registered owners were the husband (H) and wife (W), who were the partners in F. F had elected to waive exemption from VAT in respect of the land. The land was zoned for industrial development and was worth £250,000. F had transferred the land to another partnership (D) between H and his former wife. H and W had each paid £125,000 into F's bank account and on the same day executed a Land Registry Form TR1 for transfer of whole registered title. The transferee of the land was stated to be H and his former wife, and the consideration was stated to be £125,000. At the time of the transfer H and his former wife each drew £125,000 out of D's bank account. Box 12 on the second page of the TR1 contained an "Additional Provision" to the effect that the interest transferred by the transfer and the consideration of £125,000 was exclusively in respect of W's interest in the property and that no transfer or dealing had taken place as a result of the transfer in respect of H's interest. Box 11 of the TR1, which covered the case where there was more than one transferee, provided that H and his former wife were to hold the property on trust for themselves as tenants in common in equal shares. F did not pay VAT in respect of the transfer. The VAT and duties tribunal, and the judge on appeal, found that F had made a supply of land for £250,000 on which it was liable to VAT. F submitted that (1) the tribunal had misconstrued the TR1 which clearly indicated that the transfer was a transfer only by W, who was not a taxable person, of her beneficial share in the land for £125,000 and had ignored the evidence that the two payments of £125,000 to F on the same day were not consideration for the land, but injections of capital into F; (2) the tribunal had erred in law in not applying the Value Added Tax Act 1994 Sch.10 para.8(a); (3) the judge had erred in his conclusions about the effect of Box 11 and Box 12 of the TR1 and should have concluded that Box 11 was of no relevance in determining the subject matter of the transfer or the identity of the transferor.

Held, dismissing the appeal, that (1) there was no error of law in the tribunal's construction of the TR1. There were indications in the document itself, read as a whole, that, despite whatever H, W and their legal advisers thought would be the legal effect of the document, it took effect as a transfer of the whole of the land. The tribunal was entitled to rely on its findings about the acquisition and holding of the land by H and W as a partnership asset, about the true amount of consideration for the transfer, and about the destination of the consideration. Those findings clearly pointed to a transfer of the whole of the land as a partnership asset of F. The submissions that H and W had agreed between themselves to take the land out of the partnership assets, treat it as their separate property, transfer only W's beneficial half share and then pay contributions of capital amounting to £125,000 each into F's bank account on the same date as the transfer by the TR1 were all contrary to the facts found by the tribunal. (2) The Value Added Tax Act 1994 Sch.10 para.8(a) did not apply to the facts as found by the tribunal as there was no mismatch between the person making the grant and the person to whom the benefit of the consideration for the grant accrued. Once it was accepted that F had made the grant of the land it was impossible to resist the inference that F received the benefit of the consideration of £250,000 for that grant of a partnership asset, and para.8 did not apply. (3) F was right that the declaration of trust in Box 11 of the TR1 was irrelevant to the issue as to the nature of the supply and who made it. However, the judge's error on that point did not justify interference with the decision of the tribunal. The tribunal's findings of fact justified the conclusion it reached without the need to rely on the declaration of trust provisions affecting transferees in Box 11.

FENGATE DEVELOPMENTS v. CUSTOMS AND EXCISE COMMISSIONERS, [2004] EWCA Civ 1591, [2005] S.T.C. 191, Mummery, L.J., CA (Civ Div).

4389. Penalties–Payments–Late payment of VAT–Agreement to pay by instalments concluded with Customs–Failure to reveal liability to default surcharge

M appealed against two default surcharges for late payment of VAT. M had experienced cash flow problems after a rapid expansion in its business and had agreed with Customs that it should be allowed to make payments by instalments. When negotiating the agreements, M was not told that default surcharges would still apply. Letters confirming the agreements set out the default periods concerned and stated that future VAT returns and payments were to be rendered on time, and that acceptance of the terms did not prevent or cancel M's liability to surcharge or interest on late payments in the future. M contended that the liability to surcharge on the instalments had not been mentioned when the agreement was concluded.

Held, allowing the appeal, that M had not been warned about the liability to default surcharges on the instalment payments when it entered into the agreement. Customs could not rely on the letters as they showed that the agreements were restricted to the periods stated, with the liability to subsequent penalties only arising in the absence of future later payment agreements.

MHC (MICHAEL HAMMOND PARTNERSHIP) v. CUSTOMS AND EXCISE COMMISSIONERS [2004] V. & D.R. 1, Richard Barlow (Chairman), VAT and Duties Tribunal (Manchester).

4390. Registration–Supplies and acquisitions–Limits

VALUE ADDED TAX (INCREASE OF REGISTRATION LIMITS) ORDER 2005, SI 2005 727; made under the Value Added Tax Act 1994 Sch.1 para.15, Sch.3 para.9. In force: April 1, 2005; £3.00.

This Order increases the VAT registration limits for taxable supplies and for acquisitions from other Member States from £58,000 to £60,000. The Order also increases the limit for cancellation of registration in the case of taxable supplies from £56,000 to £58,000, and in the case of acquisitions from other Member States from £58,000 to £60,000.

4391. Repayments–Museums and galleries

VALUE ADDED TAX (REFUND OF TAX TO MUSEUMS AND GALLERIES) (AMENDMENT) ORDER 2005, SI 2005 1993; made under the Value Added Tax Act 1994 s.33A. In force: August 10, 2005; £3.00.

This Order amends the Value Added Tax (Refund of Tax to Museums and Galleries) Order 2001 (SI 2001 2879) which specifies the bodies that are entitled to claim a refund of the VAT incurred by them that is attributable to the provision of free admission to specified museums and galleries that they operate. The Order makes amendments to include additional bodies.

4392. **Supplies–Consideration–Provision of meals for employees below cost price–Application of goods or services for private use–European Community**

[Council Directive 77/388 on a common system of value added tax Art.2, Art.5(6), Art.6(2)(b), Art.11A(1)(a); Mervardesskattelagen (Sweden) Ch.2 para.2(2).]

The appellant employer (H) appealed against a decision by the Swedish tax authority (R) that the provision of meals to H's employees for less than the cost price was a provision of a service rather than a supply of goods and was taxable under the rules on applications for private purposes. H argued that the meal provision was a supply of goods and the rules on applications for private use did not apply because the employees paid a consideration, albeit less than it cost H to provide the meal. The Swedish Supreme Administrative Court found that R's decision on private use was in accordance with the Mervardesskattelagen (Sweden) Ch.2 para.2(2) and referred for a preliminary ruling the issue of whether that national provision was contrary to the Sixth VAT Directive 77/388 Art.2, Art.5(6) and Art.6(2)(b).

Held, giving a preliminary ruling, that when a taxpayer provided goods or services to its staff for a consideration less than the cost price of those goods or services, that transaction should not be treated as the application of goods or services for private use. Art.5(6) and Art.6(2)(b) only applied to transactions effected free of charge and treated them, for VAT purposes, as supplies effected for consideration. Under Art.11A(1)(a), the taxable amount was the consideration actually received by H, even though it was less than the cost price of the meals provided. The consideration was the subjective monetary value, not a value estimated according to objective criteria.

HOTEL SCANDIC GASABACK AB v. RIKSSKATTEVERKET (C412/03) [2005] S.T.C. 1311, Judge Jann (President), ECJ.

4393. **Supplies–Food sales–Airports–Treatment of cold take away food**

[Value Added Tax Act 1994 Sch.8 Group 1 Note (3).]

The appellant catering group (W) appealed against a decision of a VAT and duties tribunal refusing to order the repayment of standard rate VAT paid by W on retail sales of cold take away food made to air passengers and others in the departure area at various United Kingdom airports. The supplies in question were made by W's subsidiary (C) at outlets within the "air side" area of the departure lounge of public airports. W sought repayment on the basis that it had paid a standard rate of VAT when the supplies should have been zero rated as "cold food not sold on the premises". The respondent commissioners rejected the claim for repayment, stating that the relevant "premises" were the whole of the departure area and all supplies of cold food in the departure areas of airports were supplies for consumption on the premises and therefore standard rated. The tribunal held that C was making supplies in the course of catering and that the entirety of the departure areas should be regarded as the "premises" for the purposes of the Value Added Tax Act 1994 Sch.8 Group 1 Note (3). W contended that the "premises" was the place where a supplier had established his business.

Held, dismissing the appeal, that (1) provided that the tribunal had properly identified the meaning of the word "catering" for the purposes of the Act, the question as to whether the particular activity constituted catering was a question of fact. Furthermore, for the purpose of Note (3), the determination of the premises from which the catering services were provided was also a question of fact and degree. The tribunal correctly considered that the word "catering" was a word that had a popular meaning and had plainly understood what had been required to be determined, namely whether the supply by C was catering. The tribunal's ruling that the "premises" encompassed the whole of the departure lounge could not be faulted. Therefore, on the evidence that was put before the tribunal, the appeal was dismissed. (2) (Obiter) For understandable reasons, the tribunal had not considered passengers who bought items to consume on aircraft, or airport and airline staff who did not consume the items

within the concessionary area or the airside area of the departure lounge. There
was no catering on such supplies.

WHITBREAD GROUP PLC v. CUSTOMS AND EXCISE COMMISSIONERS,
[2005] EWHC 418, [2005] S.T.C. 539, Peter Smith, J., Ch D.

4394. Supplies–Insurance contracts–Goods supplied with insurance backed guarantees–Separate transactions

The appellant furniture retailer (C) appealed against a decision of the respondent
commissioners in respect of VAT payable on transactions to customers relating to a
"product guarantee". Customers buying goods from C were given a one year
manufacturer's warranty. C additionally offered to customers buying goods for
over £200 a "five year guarantee" which effectively extended the warranty for a
further four years. The guarantee was in the form of insurance provided by various
underwriters brokered through another company (R). The price of the insurance
was calculated at 19 per cent of the price of the goods, but C would give the
customer a 19 per cent discount on the price, so that the customer paid no extra
for the insurance. Initially C's staff used a form (Form B) that bore a stamp giving
brief details of the guarantee scheme but making no mention of R or of insurance. A
different form (Form C) was later used which set out clearer details explaining the
scheme and identifying R. A box could be ticked on Form C if a customer did not
wish to purchase the insurance. In all cases, information on customers and their
purchases would be sent to R once a week, and R would issue insurance
certificates directly to the customers and would handle claims. The
commissioners took the view that the supply of the goods and the "guarantee"
to customers amounted to one transaction for the purposes of VAT calculation,
so that VAT was payable on the full retail price of the goods. C argued that there
were two transactions by two different suppliers, whereby C provided the goods at
a discounted price and R provided insurance for which the customer paid
consideration equivalent to 19 per cent of the price of the goods.

Held, allowing the appeal in part, that there were two separate supplies in
relation to Form C transactions but not in relation to Form B transactions and the
VAT consequences for each were different. The transactions had to be
considered objectively, although it was possible to look behind them to
ascertain their true economic purpose, *Tesco Plc v. Customs and Excise
Commissioners* [2003] EWCA Civ 1367, [2003] S.T.C. 1561, [2004] C.L.Y. 4015
applied. In Form B transactions, insufficient information was given to the
customer to displace the natural inference that they were dealing with C alone.
Such a customer would be told that they were obtaining a "Courts Five Year
Guarantee" at no extra cost, even though what they actually received was a four
year insurance package from R. Transactions using Form B were effectively one
transaction between the customer and C and therefore VAT was payable on the
full price of the goods. In Form C transactions, by contrast, the customer would
be made aware that part of the purchase price was going towards an insurance
package provided by R as agent for the underwriters, and the customer had
the option to purchase only the goods without the insurance. The goods were
therefore supplied by C and the insurance by R and so each was separately liable
for the VAT on those supplies, *Card Protection Plan Ltd v. Customs and Excise
Commissioners (C349/96)* [1999] 2 A.C. 601, [1999] C.L.Y. 4972
distinguished.

COURTS PLC v. CUSTOMS AND EXCISE COMMISSIONERS [2005] B.V.C.
2003, John F Avery Jones (Chairman), VAT and Duties Tribunal (London).

4395. Supply of goods–Leasing–Fuel management agreement–VAT refund on purchases by lessee–European Community

[Sixth Council Directive 77/388 on a common system for VAT Art.2(1), Art.5.]
The German Court sought a preliminary ruling from the European Court of Justice
on the appropriate interpretation of the Sixth Council Directive 77/388 Art.2(1)
and Art.5. D was a Dutch car leasing company which additionally offered clients a
fuel management agreement, which enabled the client to purchase fuel and oil

products for the leased vehicle at D's expense. The client was supplied with a credit card which was registered in D's name and the client then paid monthly instalments to D based on expected use. At the end of the year the account was settled according to actual consumption. D paid VAT on all supplies, including fuel, to the Netherlands authorities and applied for a refund on the VAT charged by the German authorities submitting that D's client had incurred the VAT and not D.

Held, giving a preliminary ruling, that the effect of Art.5(1) of the Directive was that there was not a supply of fuel to the client by D where the client purchased fuel for the leased vehicle despite the fuel being purchased in D's name and at D's expense. Article 5(1) covered any transfer of tangible property from one party to another which allowed that party to assume the rights of the owner of the property, *Staatssecretaris van Financien v. Shipping and Forwarding Enterprise Safe BV (C320/88)* [1991] S.T.C. 627, [1990] C.L.Y. 2242 applied. At no time did D have the right to determine how the fuel would be used. The fuel management agreement was a financing agreement and not an agreement for the supply of fuel as D did not actually supply any fuel but simply provided credit to allow its purchase.

AUTO LEASE HOLLAND BV v. BUNDESAMT FUR FINANZEN (C185/01) [2005] S.T.C. 598, Judge Wathelet (President), ECJ.

4396. Supply of goods–Secondhand goods–Horses purchased for training and resale–European Community

[Council Directive 77/388 on the harmonisation of the laws of the Member States relating to turnover taxes Art.5, Art.26a, Art.26aA(d).]

A Swedish court referred to the European Court of Justice two questions on the interpretation of the Sixth VAT Directive 77/388, namely (1) whether live animals could be regarded as secondhand goods for the purposes of Art.26a and were therefore subject to VAT on the profit margin rather than the total price; (2) whether animals, specifically horses, which were purchased from private individuals rather than from breeders and trained and resold for a specific purpose as riding horses, could be classed as secondhand goods.

Held, giving a preliminary ruling, that (1) live animals could be classed as secondhand goods for the purposes of Art.26aA(d) since they were "tangible, moveable property" within the meaning of Art.5, *R. v. Customs and Excise Commissioners, ex p. Tattersalls Ltd (10/87)* [1988] S.T.C. 630, [1989] C.L.Y. 1677 considered. A horse bought from a private individual, not a breeder, which was resold after training for a specific purpose could be classed as secondhand goods for VAT purposes. Indeed, to charge tax on the basis of the total price of the sale of the horse would amount to double taxation, as part of that price would include a sum paid as input VAT by the private individual from whom the vendor had bought the horse, which neither the vendor nor that individual could deduct. The phrase "as it is or after repair" in the definition of secondhand goods in Art.26aA should not be given a restrictive interpretation and it was not relevant that the increase in value of the animal resulted from a biological process or from training rather than a "repair". Further, it was economically fair and in line with the intention of the Community legislature to tax only the economic value added at the final phase of the economical cycle when the animal was in the taxable dealer's possession, rather than the entire sale price.

FORVALTNINGS AB STENHOLMEN v. RIKSSKATTEVERKET (C320/02) [2004] All E.R. (EC) 870, Judge Jann (President), ECJ.

4397. Supply of goods–Supply of services–Provision of pharmaceutical services by doctors–Personally administered injections of drugs

[Value Added Tax Act 1994 Sch.8 Group 12 Item 1A(a); National Health Service (Pharmaceutical Services) Regulations 1992 (SI 1992 662) Reg.20.]

The appellant (Customs) appealed against a decision ([2002] EWCA Civ 1870, [2003] S.T.C. 169) that personally administered injections of drugs by doctors in practices registered for VAT were separate supplies of the goods injected and were zero rated. Neither the National Health Service nor Customs were prepared to refund or make an allowance for VAT paid on drugs administered under the National Health Service (Pharmaceutical Services) Regulations 1992 Reg.20, which permitted certain doctors to dispense drugs as well as administer them. Customs argued that when a doctor dispensed drugs under Reg.20 he supplied goods as if he were a pharmacist, but when he administered a drug personally he was supplying an exempt service.

Held, allowing the appeal, that (1) in determining whether there was a supply of goods or a supply of goods and services what mattered was "the essential features of the transaction", *Card Protection Plan Ltd v. Customs and Excise Commissioners (C349/96)* [1999] 2 A.C. 601, [1999] C.L.Y. 4972 applied. The Court of Appeal had been correct that the classification of the transaction was a question of law. The fact that a price for the supply in question could be separately identified, because prescriptions for personally administered drugs were written, was not determinative. The level of generality that corresponded with social and economic reality was to regard the transaction as the patient's visit to the doctor for treatment, and not to split it into smaller units. Accordingly, the correct classification was that there was a single supply of services. (2) (Obiter) In any event the Court of Appeal had been wrong to categorise the supply of goods as zero rated. It was impossible to see how the personal administration of a drug by a doctor to a patient, who happened to be entitled to a supply of drugs under Reg.20, could be described as a supply "in accordance with a requirement or authorisation under" Reg.20, within the Value Added Tax Act 1994 Sch.8 Group 12 Item 1A(a). The doctor had no need of any authorisation under Reg.20 to give a patient an injection. Therefore, if personally administered drugs were a supply of goods, they would be standard rated.

BEYNON v. CUSTOMS AND EXCISE COMMISSIONERS; *sub nom.* BENYON v. CUSTOMS AND EXCISE COMMISSIONERS, [2004] UKHL 53, [2005] 1 W.L.R. 86, Lord Nicholls of Birkenhead, HL.

4398. **Supply of goods—Supply of services—Retailer's scheme for percentage of purchase price to be paid to card handling company for exempt supply of card handling services**

[Value Added Tax Act 1994.]

The appellant commissioners appealed against a decision ([2004] EWHC 1540, [2004] S.T.C. 1132) that, where a customer agreed to purchase goods from a retailer by credit or debit card in the knowledge that a fee of 2.5 per cent of the total purchase price would go to an associated company for card handling services, the retailer was only liable for VAT on 97.5 per cent of the total purchase price. The respondent retailer (D) had introduced a system in its stores under which customers who paid by card signed a slip containing an agreement that 2.5 per cent of the value of the purchase was payable to an associated company for card handling services. Notices to that effect were displayed in D's stores. The card handling company was a subsidiary of D but was not of the same VAT group. D claimed that as a result it was chargeable to VAT on only 97.5 per cent of the purchase price of goods, since the balance of 2.5 per cent went to the card handling company as an exempt card handling fee. The commissioners submitted that (1) there had been no contract for a supply of card handling services between the customer and the card handling company which altered or affected the contract between D and the customer for the sale of the goods at the full purchase price; (2) even if there was a contract between the card handling company and the customer, the commercial reality was that the card handling company provided no services and the customer provided no consideration.

Held, allowing the appeal, that (1) under the European Directives and the Value Added Tax Act 1994 the critical question was whether there was a supply of goods or services for consideration, and that question was to be answered by giving an autonomous European meaning to the concepts involved. The contractual effect of the arrangements between the parties was a starting point in the analysis of the incidence of VAT. The notification to customers in D's shops and at the point of sale and the till slip which the customer signed did not create a separate contract between the customer and the card handling company. Contracts were not made by mere assertion. D merely informed the customer that 2.5 per cent was being paid to the card handling company or at most required the customer to contract with it to pay 2.5 per cent of the price to the card handling company. That conclusion was reinforced by the use of a single ticket price in the stores and on both the retailer's and customer's copies of the till slip and by the difficulty in identifying any consideration moving from the card handling company to the customer, since once the customer's card had been accepted at the till the transaction was complete as far as they were concerned. (2) Since there was only one contract between a customer and D, whereby at the most the customer agreed to pay 2.5 per cent of the total consideration to the card handling company, D was to be treated as having made a supply for a consideration consisting of 100 per cent of the total paid by the customer. For the purposes of European law the full ticket price was to be regarded as the price, whether or not such price was paid by card. Even if there were a separate contract between the customer and the card handling company, D should be regarded as stipulating for and obtaining consideration consisting both of the 97.5 per cent of the price paid to it directly and the 2.5 per cent paid at its insistence to the card handling company to cover the cost of services which D had required to be rendered to it by the card handling company.

DEBENHAMS RETAIL PLC v. CUSTOMS AND EXCISE COMMISSIONERS; *sub nom*. REVENUE AND CUSTOMS COMMISSIONERS v. DEBENHAMS RETAIL PLC, [2005] EWCA Civ 892, [2005] S.T.C. 1155, Mummery, L.J., CA (Civ Div).

4399. Supply of goods—Zero rating—Taxpayer claiming repayment of overpaid VAT on confectionery—Rights under EC law

[Value Added Tax Act 1994 s.30, s.80, Sch.8 Part II Group 1; Sixth Council Directive 77/388 on a common system for VAT Art.28.]

The appellant retailer (M) appealed against a decision ([2003] EWCA Civ 1448, [2004] S.T.C. 1) that it did not have a directly enforceable Community law right to recover overpaid VAT in respect of its chocolate covered teacakes. M, in accordance with guidance published by the respondent commissioners, had for many years accounted for VAT at the standard rate on the sales of its own brand of chocolate covered teacakes. In 1994, the commissioners admitted that M's teacakes should have been zero rated under the Value Added Tax Act 1994 s.30 and Sch.8 Part II Group 1. M claimed, under s.80 of the Act, the repayment of all VAT for which it had wrongly accounted. Relying on the defence in s.80(3), the commissioners refused to repay all of M's claim, finding that M had passed on the VAT burden to its customers, but accepted that it would repay 10 per cent of the claim. In the light of a ruling of the European Court of Justice ([2003] Q.B. 866, [2002] C.L.Y. 4775) in the instant case, M had argued before the Court of Appeal that it had a directly enforceable Community law right to recover the overpaid VAT. That argument was rejected.

Held, referring questions to the ECJ, that the Advocate General's opinion and the ECJ's judgment had created doubt as to the relevant principles of Community law. But for the Advocate General's opinion, and other comments made by the European Commission, the instant court would have concluded that M had no directly enforceable right under Community law. Accordingly, a second reference was made to the ECJ. The ECJ was to consider: firstly, whether M, under the Sixth VAT Directive 77/388 Art.28, had a directly enforceable right not to be required to account for VAT on its teacakes otherwise than in accordance with the zero rating provisions properly applicable under United Kingdom national law; secondly, if Art.28 did not give M a directly enforceable right, whether the UK was required by the principle of fiscal neutrality to avoid discrimination between different types of traders so as to give M a directly enforceable right to complain of the discrimination; thirdly, if so, whether Community law required or permitted the remedy granted by the national court to depend on proof of financial loss, and on the absence of unjust enrichment. The parties should agree the draft questions to be referred.

MARKS & SPENCER PLC v. CUSTOMS AND EXCISE COMMISSIONERS (NO.5); SUSSEX UNIVERSITY v. CUSTOMS AND EXCISE COMMISSIONERS, [2005] UKHL 53, [2005] S.T.C. 1254, Lord Nicholls of Birkenhead, HL.

4400. Supply of services—Construction contracts—Non monetary consideration for discharge of agreement to provide construction services—Leases

[Value Added Tax Regulations 1995 (SI 1995 2518) s.93(1)(a).]

The appellant company (C) appealed against VAT assessments made by the respondent commissioners. In 1995 Eastbourne College (E) decided to build three new blocks, and engaged quantity surveyors and architects for that purpose. In 1997 E set up C, which was registered for VAT, and another company (P), which was not VAT registered. Both companies were controlled by E. E granted to P a 15 year lease of the land to be developed, which P leased back to E on the same terms for 15 years less a day. In November 1997 C and P entered into a contract under which C was to provide construction services to P, based on the existing plans, to bring about completion of the blocks. C was to be paid for the costs to it of providing the services plus two per cent. C then became the employer of the professional team carrying out the construction work and paid various invoices, on which it claimed input tax. C raised two invoices for £50,000 each to P, only the first of which was paid, and showed both as outputs on its Value Added Tax returns. In April 1998, when only some of the construction work had been completed, C acquired P's lease of the land for £100,000 and P's business including all its assets and obligations for £1. In 1999 the commissioners made an assessment under the VAT Regulations 1995 s.93(1)(a) of £581,825 on the basis that the April 1998 transaction constituted payment to C for non monetary consideration. C argued that the consideration for the assignment of the lease had been the payment of £100,000 and it had nothing to do with the discharge of the construction contract. In any event, no money had been due to C at the time of the transaction, therefore s.93(1)(a) did not arise as there was no contractual debt.

Held, allowing the appeal in part, that s.93(1)(a) did apply but the amount assessed had been too high. The agreement between C and P did not include the costs of any work carried out prior to the agreement. Immediately before the April 1998 transaction, C had no right to be paid by P for any future work. The transaction had the effect of bringing the agreement of November 1997 to an end, thus discharging all obligations under that agreement. The value of the land under the lease was greater than £100,000, but the liabilities incurred by C under the 1997 agreement were substantial. The value of the lease under the 1998 transaction was thus the value of the liability discharged plus £100,000. There was therefore a direct link between the assignment of the lease and the discharge of the 1997 agreement, which meant that the lease was non monetary consideration. As the liability discharged was only the cost to C of the services performed by it for P plus two per cent, the assessment was too high and would need to be recalculated.

CROSS LEVELS DEVELOPMENTS LTD v. CUSTOMS AND EXCISE COMMISSIONERS [2004] V. & D.R. 248, Theodore Wallace (Chairman), V&DTr.

4401. Supply of services—Deductions—Reverse charge procedure—Tax liability of recipient of services—European Community

[Council Directive 77/388 on a common system of value added tax Art.18(1), Art.22(3).]

The German Court referred questions concerning the interpretation of the Sixth VAT Directive arising in an appeal by the appellant tax authority (F) against a decision concerning the liability of the respondent (B) to VAT. F had refused to permit B, who was domiciled in Germany, to deduct VAT on services supplied by a building contractor. F was of the opinion that the services had not been supplied by the company named on the invoice but has been carried out by another unknown company with the result that B was liable to VAT on the transactions.

The German court sought to determine whether in circumstances where the reverse charge procedure applied the taxable person who was the recipient of services had a right to make deductions if the invoice did not comply with the formalities laid down in Art.22(3) of the Directive.

Held, giving a preliminary ruling, that on a proper interpretation of Art.18(1), only Art.18(1)(d) applied to the reverse charge procedure. Therefore a taxable person who was liable as the recipient of services for the VAT relating thereto was not obliged to hold an invoice drawn up in accordance with Art.22(3) in order to be able to exercise his right to deduct. The taxpayer only had to fulfil the formalities laid down by the Member State concerned. As regards Art.18(1)(d), the imposition and extent of formalities to be complied with in order to be able to exercise the right to deduct should not exceed what was strictly necessary for the purposes of verifying the correct application of the reverse charge procedure concerned.

FINANZAMT GUMMERSBACH v. BOCKEMUHL (C90/02) [2005] S.T.C. 934, Judge Jann (President), ECJ.

4402. **Supply of services–Intermediaries–Power of Commission to make decisions–Place of supply–European Community**

[Council Directive 77/388 on the harmonisation of the laws of the Member States relating to turnover taxes Art.8, Art.9(1), Art.28.]

The Supreme Court of the Netherlands referred to the European Court of Justice two questions on the interpretation of the Sixth VAT Directive, namely (1) whether Art.28b(E)(3) of the Directive only referred to services by intermediaries where the recipient of the service was a taxable person within the meaning of the Directive or a non taxable legal person under Art.28a; (2) whether regard should be had to the place where the transaction was carried out, as if the transaction were a supply or service by a taxable person in accordance with Art.8. L, who was resident in the Netherlands, purchased yachts in France from a French vendor for another Dutch purchaser. No VAT was declared in either country and the national authorities subsequently charged VAT retroactively on the supplies of services.

Held, giving a preliminary ruling, that Art.28b(A) and Art.28b(B) of the Sixth VAT Directive regulated the place of supply in intra Community transactions as a derogation from Art.8. Article 28b(E) of the Directive was an exception to the provisions of Art.9(1). It had to be determined which provision applied on the facts of the case, *Dudda v. Finanzamt Bergish Gladbach (C327/94)* [1996] S.T.C. 1290 applied. In the instant case, the applicable provision was Art.28b(E)(3), which did not distinguish whether or not the recipients of services were subject to VAT. The purpose of Art.28b was to establish the location of the intermediary's activities, and this did not require the transaction to be subject to VAT.

STAATSSECRETARIS VAN FINANCIEN v. LIPJES (C68/03) [2004] S.T.C.1592, Judge Jann (President), ECJ.

4403. **Supply of services–Leases–Underleases–Supplies of agency and property management services–Exempt supply of leasing or letting of immovable property**

[Value Added Tax Act 1994 Sch.10 para.8; Sixth Council Directive 77/388 on a common system for VAT Art.13B.]

The appellant (X) appealed against a decision that the supply of the leasing or letting of immovable property by a third party (M) to X was a standard rated supply of agency and property management services. The commissioners cross appealed against a decision that rents, in respect of underleases granted by X to undertenants, had accrued to M for the purposes of the Value Added Tax Act 1994 Sch.10 para.8, with the result that M was to be treated as the person who had made the exempt supplies to the undertenants. X had held a number of freehold and leasehold properties. It sold some of them to M, which leased them back to X. By a virtual assignment, X assigned the economic benefit and burden of short leases to M as it was unable to assign those leases without the consent of the landlord. X remained in occupation and paid a fee to M similar to the rent that would have been payable under a formal leaseback. It was agreed that M would pay the rents due from X to the landlords. Before and after the assignment, X granted underleases of some of the properties to undertenants and, by the virtual assignment, assigned to M the right to receive their rents. X contended that the characteristics of a lease predominated in the rights and obligations assumed by the parties. The commissioners argued that the effect of the virtual assignment was to give neither a legal nor an equitable interest to M and as X had conferred no right to occupy on M, M could not have made a supply of letting of the property back to X.

Held, allowing the appeal and dismissing the cross appeal, that (1) "letting", as provided for in the Sixth Council Directive 77/388 Art.13B, could include a situation where no right of occupation was granted. Under the virtual assignment, M was entitled to have assigned to it the leases, the rights to all rents paid by underleases, the right to payment in respect of X's occupation, and the right to deal with the leases in all respects as if it was the legal owner. Those rights could be equated with a legal assignment for the purposes of the Directive. They represented the essential features of a letting as identified by the European authorities, *Maierhofer v. Finanzamt Augsburg-Land (C315/00)* [2003] S.T.C. 564, [2003] C.L.Y. 4532 and *Stichting Goed Wonen v. Staatssecretaris van Financien (C326/99)* [2003] S.T.C. 1137, [2002] C.L.Y. 4786 considered. The principal fee was paid pursuant to an agreement between X and M, under which X occupied the property pending the completion of the assignment to M, on which M could insist. The tribunal's conclusion that it was being paid in connection with the exempt supply to X by the landlord and as to the balance for agency and management services provided by the third party was wrong. The nature of the M's supply to X did not change on execution of the legal assignment by virtue of M then enjoying a right of occupation of the premises. In relying upon the principle of neutrality, the transaction that the parties had sought to create was a letting in accordance with the Directive. (2) The provisions of Sch.10 para.8 of the 1994 Act were clear and unambiguous and the tribunal had been correct in deciding that under the virtual assignment, the rents of the underleases accrued to M within the meaning of para.8 so that M was to be treated as the person who had made the exempt supplies to the undertenants and when the rents of the underleases had been paid to M they did not constitute consideration paid by X for standard rated supplies of agency and property management services.

ABBEY NATIONAL PLC v. CUSTOMS AND EXCISE COMMISSIONERS, [2005] EWHC 831, [2005] 3 E.G.L.R. 73, Hart, J., Ch D.

4404. Supply of services–Place of supply–Slot gaming machines–Offshore undertakings–Liability for VAT–European Community

[Sixth Council Directive 77/388 on a common system for VAT Art.6(1), Art.9.]

The appellant (C), a company with a Guernsey place of establishment, appealed against a VAT and duties tribunal decision that it was liable to VAT on gaming machine services supplied in the UK under the Sixth Council Directive 77/388 Art.9(2). C was formed following a reorganisation carried out by its parent company (R) as part of a tax avoidance scheme, under which C installed and operated gaming machines that were provided and serviced by another subsidiary (M) for use in premises owned by R but managed by C. As a result of this structure, C claimed that the place of supply of gaming services was Guernsey so that no VAT liability arose, but that C could claim the repayment of input tax on services provided to it by the other group members. The High Court stayed the appeal and sought a preliminary ruling on the correct interpretation of Art.9(2) in the context of a supply of entertainment made by a group of companies without a common place of establishment.

Held, giving a preliminary ruling, that the supply of gaming machines for use by the public was a supply of entertainment services for the purposes of Art.6(1). Article 9 sets out the rules for determining the place where services were supplied, with Art.9(1) setting out the general principle and Art.9(2) giving specific instances where a deemed supply took place; there was no priority accorded to Art.9(1) as the intention is that Art.9 will prevent either double taxation or non taxation, *Berkholz v. Finanzamt Hamburg Mitte-Altstadt (168/ 84)* [1985] E.C.R. 2251, [1986] C.L.Y. 1495 and *Maatschap MJM Linthorst v. Inspecteur der Belastingdienst/Ondernemingen Roermond (C167/95)* [1997] S.T.C. 1287, [1997] C.L.Y. 5020 followed. Under Art.9(2)(c) the provision of entertainment services was deemed to occur in the place where they were physically carried out.

RAL (CHANNEL ISLANDS) LTD v. CUSTOMS AND EXCISE COMMISSIONERS (C452/03) [2005] S.T.C. 1025, Judge Jann (President), ECJ.

4405. Supply of services–Telecommunications–Entitlement to charge VAT where supply made in Ireland

[Value Added Tax Act 1994 Sch.10A para.3; Sixth Council Directive 77/388 on a common system for VAT Art.3(1), Art.4(4), Art.9(1), Art.9(2)(e).]

The claimant Irish company (D) applied for judicial review, asserting that the United Kingdom was not entitled to charge VAT on the supply of telecommunications services by its fellow VAT group member in Ireland (T). D supplied phone cards for business purposes to independent distributors in the UK. The cards allowed the ultimate purchaser access to telecommunications services provided by T. The supply of phone cards within the Irish Republic attracted VAT as prepayment for telecommunications services, but when access was obtained to the services no VAT was payable. The converse applied in the UK, where VAT was chargeable on redemption of the card. As a result, D did not have to account for VAT on the supply of the cards in the UK and T did not have to account for VAT on the redemption of those cards because the service was provided in Ireland. The commissioners argued that (1) it was plain that the Sixth Council Directive 77/ 388 contemplated that the supply of telecommunication services fell within the scope of VAT and therefore the domestic provisions should be interpreted to ensure that VAT was charged. In particular, under the Value Added Tax Act 1994 Sch.10A para.3, "VAT due" meant due in the European Union or under the Directive and D had failed to account for any VAT in respect of its supply; (2) alternatively, as the companies supplying the card and the telecommunications services were in the same VAT group, they were the same "person" for the purposes of Sch.10A para.3(1) of the Act, which meant "taxable person"; therefore the cards were retail vouchers on which VAT was charged on the supply to an end user in the UK.

Held, granting the application, that (1) the essential dispute turned on the principle to be derived from the Sixth Council Directive as to the extent of the right conferred, or duty placed, on a Member State to construe its domestic legislation so as to avoid non taxation of a supply that was within the scope of the charge to VAT. Article 9(1) of the Directive made it clear that the supply of services by T was deemed to be in the place of its establishment from which the service was supplied, namely Ireland. There was nothing in the Directive empowering or requiring the UK to charge VAT in circumstances where, under Art.9(1) of the Directive, the place of supply was Ireland, and Sch.10A para.3(3) of the 1994 Act could not be construed as if T had failed to account for any VAT due under the Directive. Under the Directive, the UK had no right or obligation to impose a charge on a supplier from Ireland that did not fall within Art.9(2)(e), *Dudda v. Finanzamt Bergisch Gladbach (C327/94)* [1996] S.T.C. 1290 followed. Accordingly, the UK was not entitled to charge VAT on the supply of telecommunications services by T to redeemers of D's cards bought within the UK. (2) Under Art.4(4) of the Directive, legally independent persons could be treated as one taxable person when established in the Member State and closely bound by other links, but not when they were not established in the Member State. D and T were not eligible to be members of a VAT group in the UK. Even if they were seen as a single taxable person, the legislation only referred to persons, not taxable persons, and did not refer to a VAT group. No principle could be derived from the Directive requiring the UK to treat D and T as the same person within Art.3(1) of the Directive.

R. (ON THE APPLICATION OF IDT CARD SERVICES IRELAND LTD) v. CUSTOMS AND EXCISE COMMISSIONERS, [2004] EWHC 3188, [2005] S.T.C. 314, Moses, J., QBD (Admin).

4406. Supply of services–Tour operators–Package holidays–Affect on taxable amount where available discounts not achieved

[Value Added Tax Act 1994 Sch.6 para.4(1); Sixth Council Directive 77/388 on a common system for VAT Art 11A.3(a).]

S, a holiday company operating within the Tour Operators Margin Scheme (TOMS), appealed against the Commissioners' refusal to allow its claim for repayment of overpaid tax. S offered its customers discounts for early payments which were claimed by some but not all of S's customers. On the basis of two ECJ decisions S contended that the portion of its supplies which fell outside TOMS were subject to the ordinary rules for determining the taxable value of the supplies and those rules also provided the starting point for determining the taxable amount for the supplies which fell within the scheme. Accordingly, pursuant to the Value Added Tax Act 1994 Sch.6 para.4(1) and the Sixth Council Directive 77/388 Art 11A.3(a) the taxable amount was the discounted price whether or not this was achieved. The Commissioners rejected this argument stating that the taxable amount was the discounted price only where the discount was achieved.

Held, dismissing the appeal, that (1) where there were composite supplies comprising "in house" and "bought in" services it was necessary to determine what the overall price of the supply was by applying the rule in Art. 11A(a) ie: the taxable amount was the consideration actually received, *Madgett (t/a Howden Court Hotel) v. Customs and Excise Commissioners (C308/96)* [1998] S.T.C. 1189, [1999] C.L.Y. 5002, *Customs and Excise Commissioners v. First Choice Holidays Plc (C149/01)* [2003] All E.R. (EC) 705, [2003] C.L.Y. 4588 and *Naturally Yours Cosmetics Ltd v. Customs and Excise Commissioners (C230/87)* [1988] S.T.C. 879, [1989] C.L.Y. 1683 followed; (2) it was then necessary to divide the consideration between the two types of supply and apply the margin to those supplies which fell within TOMS ie: the "bought in" supplies. It was only here that special rules applied, thus (3) Art. 11A(a) applied to the stage of deciding the taxable amount in order to calculate the first stage in determining the value of the supplies, however (4) under the general scheme of VAT in both UK and Community law tax was payable by reference to actual consideration paid rather than by reference to the terms agreed by the parties. Accordingly although Sch.6 para.4(1) was ambiguous it had to be interpreted to mean that the discount had to be achieved in order to reduce the amount of consideration subject to tax.

SAGA HOLIDAYS LTD v. CUSTOMS AND EXCISE COMMISSIONERS [2004] B.V.C. 2200, Richard Barlow (Chairman), VAT and Duties Tribunal (London).

4407. Tax planning–Avoidance schemes–Designation

VALUE ADDED TAX (DISCLOSURE OF AVOIDANCE SCHEMES) (DESIGNATIONS) (AMENDMENT) ORDER 2005, SI 2005 1724; made under the Value Added Tax Act 1994 Sch.11A para.3, Sch.11A para.4. In force: August 1, 2005; £3.00.

This Order amends the Value Added Tax (Disclosure of Avoidance Schemes) (Designations) Order 2004 (SI 2004 1933) by designating two new tax avoidance schemes and by designating a new provision included in or associated with tax avoidance schemes.

4408. Tax planning–Avoidance schemes–Disclosure

VALUE ADDED TAX (DISCLOSURE OF AVOIDANCE SCHEMES) (AMENDMENT) REGULATIONS 2005, SI 2005 2009; made under the Value Added Tax Act 1994 Sch.11A para.6, Sch.11A para.13. In force: August 1, 2005; £3.00.

These Regulations amend the Value Added Tax (Disclosure of Avoidance Schemes) Regulations 2004 (SI 2004 1929) which prescribe the time within which information concerning VAT avoidance schemes which are notifiable under the Value Added Tax Act 1994 must be provided to the Commissioners for Her Majesty's Revenue and Customs. They make provision for the form and manner of notification and the information to be provided. These Regulations amend the

2004 Regulations by prescribing the time in which such information must be provided; and provide that a taxable person is only required to notify the Commissioners of any designated scheme allocated the reference number 9 or 10 by the Value Added Tax (Disclosure of Avoidance Schemes) (Designations) Order 2004 (SI 2004 1933), or any scheme that includes, or is associated with, a provision of a description falling within that Order, where the claimed tax advantage relates to a prescribed accounting period which begins on or after August 1, 2005, unless the taxable person is already under a duty to notify.

4409. Tax rates–Boilers–Reduced rate

VALUE ADDED TAX (REDUCED RATE) (NO.2) ORDER 2005, SI 2005 3329; made under the Value Added Tax Act 1994 s.29A, s.96. In force: January 1, 2006; £3.00.

This Order amends the Value Added Tax Act 1994 which contains the Groups of supplies of goods and services that are subject to the reduced rate of VAT of five per cent. The Order amends Group 2 (installation of energy-saving materials) and extends the reduced rate to supplies of the services of installing boilers fuelled solely by wood, straw or similar vegetal matter in certain buildings and to supplies of the boilers so installed.

4410. Tax rates–Heat pumps–Reduced rate

VALUE ADDED TAX (REDUCED RATE) ORDER 2005, SI 2005 726; made under the Value Added Tax Act 1994 s.29A, s.96. In force: April 7, 2005; £3.00.

This Order amends the Value Added Tax Act 1994 which contains the Groups of supplies of goods and services that are subject to the reduced rate of VAT of 5 per cent. The Order amends Group 2 (installation of energy-saving materials); extends the reduced rate to supplies of the services of installing air source heat pumps and micro combined heat and power units in certain buildings and to supplies of the air source heat pumps and micro combined heat and power units so installed. By virtue of items 1 and 2 of Group 2, the installation must be in residential accommodation or in a building intended for use solely for a relevant charitable purpose.

4411. Taxable persons–Local authorities–Implementation of Sixth Council Directive 77/388 Art.4.5

[Value Added Tax Act 1994 s.80, s.94; Council Directive 77/388 on a common system for VAT Art.4.5.]

The appellant (Customs) appealed against a decision ([2004] B.V.C. 2181) on preliminary issues in the respondent local authority's appeal against Customs' refusal to pay a claim made under the Value Added Tax Act 1994 s.80. At issue was the local authority's liability to pay VAT on payments received in respect of its provision of off street parking facilities. The local authority had believed that it was exempt from the charge to VAT by the operation of the Sixth VAT Directive 77/388 Art.4.5. The issue to be determined was whether the second paragraph of Art.4.5 had been properly implemented into United Kingdom law. Customs submitted that it was possible to construe the 1994 Act so that it was consistent with Art.4.5 by reading additional words into the definition of "business" in s.94 of the Act.

Held, allowing the appeal, that (1) to interpret "business" in the way suggested by Customs would be to undertake a task that was not possible. It was clear that the UK legislature had made a deliberate decision in its treatment of local authorities and the proposed emendation suggested an entirely new charging regime for them, *Marleasing SA v. La Comercial Internacional de Alimentacion SA (C106/89)* [1990] E.C.R. I-4135 considered. (2) In any event, Art.4.5 of the Directive was directly applicable as between the local authority and Customs to the effect that the inconsistent provisions of the Act were nullified. The first two paragraphs of Art.4.5 were unconditional and sufficiently precise to bind Customs. The limitation to Art.4.5 on the ground of distortion of competition was a conditional limitation that required an assessment that was not exempt from judicial review, *Ufficio Distrettuale delle Imposte Dirette di Fiorenzuola d'Arda v. Comune di Carpaneto Piacentino (231/87)* [1991] S.T.C. 205, [1991] C.L.Y. 3661 followed. The local authority could rely on Art.4.5 and it was for the tribunal to determine whether treatment of the local authority as a non taxable person in respect of its provision of parking facilities was liable to give rise to a serious distortion of competition and thus render the local authority liable to VAT.

ISLE OF WIGHT COUNCIL v. CUSTOMS AND EXCISE COMMISSIONERS; *sub nom.* CUSTOMS AND EXCISE COMMISSIONERS v. ISLE OF WIGHT COUNCIL, [2004] EWHC 2541, [2005] S.T.C. 257, Pumfrey, J., Ch D.

4412. Taxable persons–Open ended investment companies–Advice supplied by bank–Reference to ECJ–European Community

[Council Directive 77/388 on the common system of VAT Art.4, Art.13B(d)(5).]

In proceedings commenced by the claimant (B) relating to the chargeability of VAT in Belgium on its fees the court was required to make a preliminary ruling as to whether open ended investment companies were taxable persons for the purposes of the Sixth VAT Directive. B gave advice to a number of such companies established in Luxembourg. The companies were not subject to VAT in Luxembourg and B did not charge VAT on its services to them. The Belgian tax authorities decided that VAT was chargeable and issued a demand to B.

Held, giving a preliminary ruling, that the companies were taxable persons and therefore VAT was payable on services supplied by B to them. In its definition of services carried out by taxable persons, Art.4 included the "exploitation of tangible or intangible property for the purposes of obtaining income therefrom on a continuing basis". Although the "simple acquisition and sale of securities" did not come within the definition, "transactions carried out in the course of a business trading in securities" could come within it, in accordance with Art.13B(d)(5). The service provided by the companies came into the latter category since it involved putting together and overseeing securities' portfolios on behalf of investors; thus the companies were taxable persons within the definition of Art.4.

BANQUE BRUXELLES LAMBERT SA (BBL) v. BELGIUM (C8/03) [2004] S.T.C. 1643, Judge Jann (President), ECJ.

4413. Transfer of going concern–Overpayment by previous owner–Transferee precluded from obtaining repayment–Unjust enrichment

[Value Added Tax Act 1994 s.80.]

S, the owner of a non profit making club, appealed against the refusal to repay VAT paid in error on behalf of a previous owner. The payment was made by D, the representative of a VAT group, whose subsidiary had formerly owned the club. S acquired the club as a transfer of a going concern, but this did not include the VAT registration at the time of the payment by D.

Held, dismissing the appeal, that the right to a repayment in the instant case came under the Value Added Tax Act 1994 s.80(1), which restricted the right to the person who had made the overpayment and s.80(3) allowed a defence on the ground that repayment would lead to unjust enrichment. The restriction under s.80(3) would have precluded S's claim even if the VAT registration had been included in the transfer of the going concern.

SHENDISH MANOR LTD v. CUSTOMS AND EXCISE COMMISSIONERS [2004] V. & D.R. 64, Theodore Wallace (Chairman), V&DTr.

4414. Underdeclarations–Investigations–Civil penalty proceedings–Compliance with PACE Code C

[Police and Criminal Evidence Act 1984 s.60(1), s.67(9); Value Added Tax Act 1994 s.60; Human Rights Act 1998 Sch.1 Part I Art.6(3)(c).]

The appellant (K) appealed against a decision of the VAT and duties tribunal that he had exceeded the VAT registration threshold, that the consequent assessment to

VAT was made to the best judgment of the respondent commissioners and that the imposition of a civil evasion penalty was valid. K had operated a dry cleaning business. He was not registered for VAT. Following investigations and an interview under a VAT Notice 730 in respect of civil evasion penalty, the commissioners issued K with a notice of compulsory registration. As K did not submit a VAT return, the commissioners issued a penalty under the Value Added Tax Act 1994 s.60 and assessed the VAT due. The tribunal found that there had been deliberate suppression of sales by K and that the commissioners had used best judgment and discharged the burden on them of proving K's dishonesty. K submitted that (1) he had been incompetently represented before the tribunal by his accountant and the tribunal should have ensured that he was aware of his right under the Human Rights Act 1998 Sch.1 Part I Art.6(3)(c) to be legally represented; (2) the tribunal was wrong to have admitted or given weight to evidence emerging from the Notice 730 interview as it had been obtained unfairly because he should have been cautioned in accordance with the PACE codes of practice, Code Code C; (3) the tribunal had erred in relation to the burden and standard of proof applicable when considering an appeal against the imposition of a penalty under s.60 of the 1994 Act; (4) the tribunal had reached a conclusion that was irrational.

Held, dismissing the appeal, that (1) nothing occurred that should have alerted the tribunal to a need to interfere with the choice K had made as to his representation. The inept naming of the defence document as a "Statement of Case" was not something that should have alerted the tribunal and there was nothing in the point that the accountant's potential to be a witness of fact made it inappropriate for him to represent K. Further, there was nothing in the failure of the accountant to call K that should have alerted the tribunal to the fact that some flagrant mistake was being made in the representation of K such as to require the tribunal to take steps that K argued it should have taken. (2) Civil penalty proceedings did not involve an "offence" for the purposes of s.67(9). In the 1984 Act, "offence" meant an offence prosecuted in the criminal court. Although the Notice 730 in the instant case reserved the right to prosecute, K was informed at the interview that the matter was not being investigated with a view to prosecution, *R. v. Gill (Sewa Singh)* [2003] EWCA Crim 2256, [2004] 1 W.L.R. 469, [2003] C.L.Y. 744 distinguished. The officers conducting the interview were simply investigating whether K's VAT affairs were being conducted in accordance with the law and whether a civil penalty should be imposed. In any event, nothing in the 1984 Act required the VAT and duties tribunal, hearing an appeal against a s.60 civil penalty assessment, to exclude evidence on the ground of non compliance with PACE codes of practice, Code C. In the circumstances, there was no basis for suggesting that it was unfair of the tribunal to have admitted the evidence. (3) The tribunal had correctly identified that the burden of proving the matters set out in s.60(1)(a) and s.60(1)(b) lay on the commissioners. Further, it was clear that the tribunal had applied the correct standard of proof, namely the civil standard, and was satisfied that the evidence adduced by the commissioners was sufficiently strong to enable it to reach the conclusion that it did. (4) Whilst the methodology used in respect of the assessment was unsound in principle and there was a mistake in the calculation of the average price of a dry cleaning ticket issued by K's business, the mistake was not such as to justify the instant court altering the assessment. The mistake did not affect the tribunal's decision on the question of threshold and could not have affected its conclusion on K's dishonesty.

KHAN (T/A GREYHOUND DRY CLEANERS) v. CUSTOMS AND EXCISE COMMISSIONERS, [2005] EWHC 653, [2005] S.T.C. 1271, Hart, J., Ch D.

4415. **VAT–Zero rating–Clothes–Definition of 'young child' for zero rating of clothing–Clothing for 14 year olds**

[Value Added Tax Act 1994 Sch.8 Group 16 Item 1.]

The appellant company (H) appealed against a decision of the VAT and duties tribunal affirming the respondent commissioners' decision that certain children's clothing sold in H's stores did not qualify for zero rating under the Value Added Tax Act 1994 Sch.8 Group 16 Item 1. H produced and sold clothing for adults and children. The range of clothing sold was divided into two groups: for those aged 18 months to 13 plus and for those aged 16 to 24 years. When designing clothing for the first group, H designed items for an intended 10 year old with a height of 140 cm and then scaled the item up or down in size for the appropriate age. The upper size limit was suitable for a child 164 cm in height. H's shops contained size charts that indicated that 164cm was suitable for a child of 13 plus. Customs had produced a statement of practice that indicated that it regarded a young child as one up to their fourteenth birthday with the maximum heights being 161 cm for girls and 163 cm for boys. Customs ruled that clothing for children of 164 cm in height was not zero rated. The tribunal dismissed H's appeal and held that the statutory test was not dependent on shape but rather on whether the garment had been designed for young children and that the ordinary person would not regard a 14 year old as a 'young child'. H argued that the tribunal (1) had erred in law as it had treated the statement of practice as being the legal test when Parliament had actually intended to draw the line at puberty when the shape of children's bodies changed; and (2) had misconstrued the 'suitability test' since for the clothes not to qualify for zero rating they had to be suitable not just for persons of the minimum age of a child who could not properly be called a "young child" but also for a substantial class of older persons, and no reasonable tribunal could have reached the conclusion that the clothes were suitable for an older person.

Held, dismissing the appeal, that (1) the tribunal had not erred in law and had properly regarded the meaning of the words "young children" as a matter of fact for it to decide. The question was one of drawing the line at when someone ceased to be a child. The ordinary person would not describe a 14 year old as a young child. The distinction to be drawn between young children and older persons was one of age and not stage of development. (2) It was clear from the evidence that H regarded 164 cm as the size of clothing appropriate for children 14 years old. It was not unreasonable to conclude that H had designed 164 cm clothes as suitable for 14 year olds and not 'young children' within the meaning of the Act.

H&M HENNES LTD v. CUSTOMS AND EXCISE COMMISSIONERS; *sub nom.* H&M HENNES LTD v. REVENUE AND CUSTOMS COMMISSIONERS, [2005] EWHC 1383, [2005] S.T.C. 1749, Sir Donald Rattee, Ch D.

4416. VAT and duties tribunals – Litigants in person – Eligibility for legal aid – Extent of tribunal's duty to advise on eligibility

The appellant (Q) appealed against a ruling of the VAT and Duties Tribunal to uphold a decision of the Commissioners to recover penalties from him. The Commissioners' case was that two companies, of which Q was a director or managing officer, had engaged in dishonest conduct for the purpose of evading VAT. Q, who was personally liable for the imposed penalties, could not afford legal representation and believed he was not entitled to legal aid for a tribunal hearing. Q appeared as a litigant in person before the tribunal. He argued that he had been materially disadvantaged by having to represent himself at the hearing and that the tribunal's decision should be impugned because he had been compelled to appear without the benefit of legal representation.

Held, dismissing the appeal, that any omission on the part of the tribunal to raise with Q the possibility that he might have been eligible for legal aid was not an omission in the nature of an error of law about which Q was entitled to complain on appeal. The issue was whether the tribunal was under a positive duty at the hearing to raise with Q the possibility that he might be eligible for legal aid, and then to impose an adjournment on the parties so that the possibility might be explored. A court or tribunal hearing a substantive appeal was not automatically under a duty in every case of its own motion to raise with litigants in person the question whether he might be eligible for legal aid and, if it appeared he might be, to impose an adjournment so that he could seek it. If a litigant raised the matter himself, different considerations would arise. In the instant case, the matter had not been raised and, in any event, Q had been represented by his accountant at the directions and substantive hearings.

QAISAR v. CUSTOMS AND EXCISE COMMISSIONERS, [2004] EWHC 506, [2005] S.T.C. 119, Rimer, J., Ch D.

4417. **VAT groups—Vouchers—Sale of vouchers by parent company to subsidiary outside VAT group—Commercial reality**

The appellant company (K) appealed against a decision of the respondent commissioners in respect of VAT payable on gift vouchers. K was the parent company of a corporate group which included five high street retail companies. The companies also constituted a VAT group. K operated a scheme in which vouchers, known as Kingfisher Gift Vouchers in denominations of up to £25, would be sold to individual purchasers. The vouchers could then be redeemed for goods to the value of the voucher at any of the retail outlets in the group. In 2000 K decided to set up a new system to minimise VAT payable on the vouchers. A new company (F) was established, which was a wholly owned subsidiary of K but was not a member of the VAT group. K sold the vouchers to F at a discount of 18.52 per cent. F then sold the vouchers through the group retail outlets to individual purchasers at the face value of the voucher. The retail company received a 10 per cent commission on each voucher sold. Once the vouchers had been redeemed by a retail company in exchange for goods, K paid that company the full face value of the voucher less a redemption charge of 13.7 per cent. K paid VAT only on the consideration it received from F for the vouchers, which was the value of the vouchers less the 18.52 per cent discount. The commissioners took the view that VAT should be paid by K on the full face value since K was still effectively the seller of the vouchers to the purchasers. K argued that there was no direct link between it and the purchasers of the vouchers, as F acted entirely independently when it sold the vouchers and bore none of the risks in printing or storing them.

Held, dismissing the appeal, that K was liable to pay VAT on the full face value of the vouchers. A voucher was no more than a document which evidenced an obligation by someone to accept the voucher at its face value, and the consideration represented by the voucher was the sum actually received by the supplier of goods on the sale of the voucher, *Argos Distributors Ltd v. Customs and Excise Commissioners (C288/94)* [1997] Q.B. 499, [1996] C.L.Y. 5909 applied. However there were difficulties in applying these principles in the instant case since the seller of the vouchers and the supplier of the goods were not the same person and the sale of the vouchers was a two stage process. The contractual position between K and F was not conclusive, as it was open to the court to look beyond that arrangement if the evidence warranted it, *Ringside Refreshments v. Customs and Excise Commissioners* [2003] EWHC 3043, [2004] S.T.C. 426, [2004] C.L.Y. 4017 applied. The commercial reality of the situation was that F did not act independently. It was K who paid redemption money to the retail companies and also had the benefit of the interest that accrued between the date it received the money from F and the date that it paid the redemption. The scheme was designed and set up by K, not by F, and F always acted under the direction of K. F was effectively a group company only offering services to other companies within the group and not standing alone. The viewpoint of the purchaser was relevant when considering who made a supply for the purposes of VAT. In the instant case, the purchasers of the vouchers would have seen K as the supplier, since the vouchers were still called Kingfisher Gift Vouchers throughout and most of the point of sale publicity either mentioned F only in very small print or not at all.

KINGFISHER PLC v. CUSTOMS AND EXCISE COMMISSIONERS [2004] V. & D.R. 206, Nuala Brice (Chairman), VAT and Duties Tribunal (London).

4418. Zero rating–Confectionery–Breakfast confectionery product aimed at alternative breakfast market–Meaning of "biscuit"

[Value Added Tax Act 1994 Sch.8 Group 1 Item 1.]

U appealed against a decision by the Commissioners that U's confectionery breakfast product was not zero rated under the Value Added Tax Act 1994 Sch.8 Group 1 Item 1 since it was not a biscuit. The product was described as "crispy biscuit cereal bites" and contained a fruit flavoured cream filling. The product was targeted at the "alternative breakfast" market.

Held, allowing the appeal, that (1) the word "biscuit" had to be given its ordinary every day meaning and the tribunal was required to ask whether the man in the street would consider the product a biscuit. The tribunal was not required to determine the nature of the product if it was not a biscuit since it would simply fall into the residual standard rated class of confectionery, *Customs and Excise Commissioners v. Ferrero UK Ltd* [1997] S.T.C. 881, [1997] C.L.Y. 5047 followed, and (2) although biscuits were not commonly eaten for breakfast that was not the appropriate test since it depended on prejudice. The correct test was whether what one might eat for breakfast was a biscuit. It was clear that in the present day the term "biscuit" was applicable to a much wider range of products than that to which it was applied 40 years ago. Accordingly, the informed man on the street would conclude that the product was entitled to the name "biscuit" and thus the product should be regarded as a biscuit for VAT purposes.

UNITED BISCUITS (UK) LTD v. CUSTOMS AND EXCISE COMMISSIONERS [2004] V. & D.R. 201, Colin Bishopp (Chairman), VAT and Duties Tribunal (Manchester).

4419. Zero rating–Contracts for services–Supply of listing magazines as part of cable television contract

[Value Added Tax Act 1994 s.47; Council Directive 77/338 on a common system of VAT.]

The appellants (P and T) appealed against a decision ([2003] EWHC 3176, [2004] S.T.C. 517) that the supply by P of television listing magazines was part of a single supply of cable television services by regional subsidiaries of T. The respondent commissioners cross appealed. T had incorporated P as part of a scheme aimed at restoring a previous arrangement whereby it paid VAT in respect of the supply of cable television programmes and zero rated the magazines. As part of the scheme there was an agency agreement between P and the regional companies whereby P supplied the magazines and the regional companies were appointed as P's agents to create a contractual relationship between P and the customers in relation to the magazine. Existing customers were notified of the changes and there was an amended contract for new customers. P was not a member of T's group of companies for VAT purposes and customers could not decline the magazine. P and T argued that (1) in relation to the existing customers, by virtue of a partial novation the contract between the regional company and its customers remained in existence; (2) in relation to the new customers, the contract was between the customer on one side and the regional company and P on the other; (3) the judge had erred in treating as relevant the fact that a customer had to take the television services with the magazine as a package. The commissioners contended that the doctrine of ancillary supply in VAT law could apply where elements of a package were supplied by different suppliers; and under EC law the court should not follow domestic contract law, but should look to the economic reality of the situation which was that the contractual arrangements were artificial.

Held, allowing the appeal and dismissing the cross appeal, that (1) a novation could be partial. The issue was whether acceptance could be inferred from the customer's conduct. The less significant the change to the customer, the more readily acquiescence could be inferred by conduct. It was hardly a matter of concern to customers who supplied their magazines. As a general rule inertia did not create a contract, but continuing to pay the monthly bill could amount to acquiescence. The existing customers continued to pay for the cable service and the magazine thereby acquiescing in the new arrangements and becoming, by partial novation, contractually bound to P. (2) The contract for new customers provided that the magazine would be supplied by P, that payment for it would be due to P and that the regional company would collect payment from the customer as P's agent. That imposed a contractual relationship between P and the customer. The regional company was not acting in its own name and the Value Added Tax Act 1994 s.47 did not apply. (3) The expectation of the customer was relevant to the question of whether two contracts constituted, for VAT purposes, principal and ancillary contracts, but not to the question of whether there was more than one supplier, *Commission of the European Communities v. France (C404/99)* [2001] E.C.R. I-2667 considered and *Church Schools Foundation Ltd v. Customs and Excise Commissioners* [2001] EWCA Civ 1745, [2001] S.T.C. 1661, [2002] C.L.Y. 4790 distinguished. The judge was correct that there was nothing in *Card Protection Plan Ltd v. Customs and Excise Commissioners (C349/96)* [1999] 2 A.C. 601, [1999] C.L.Y. 4972 to justify the proposition that where there were two separate contracts, the supply made by P took the tax treatment applicable to the supply made by the regional company, *Card Protection Plan* considered. The economic reality of a transaction was antithetical to legal certainty and there were strong policy reasons against looking to the economic reality when determining the VAT position. The mere fact that a court sought to find the commercial reality of a transaction did not mean that it would seek to apply the economic reality of the transaction, which might have nothing to do with either the essential features of what the parties agreed or the legal structure of their transaction, *Muys en de Winter's Bouw-en Aannemingsbedrijf BV v. Staatssecretaris van Financien (C281/91)* [1997] S.T.C. 665, [1994] C.L.Y. 4959 considered. Economic reality also had to be distinguished from economic neutrality, which was a principle of VAT law. The concept of supply on VAT law turned on the Sixth VAT Directive 77/388 and not on the court's assessment of fairness.

TELEWEST COMMUNICATIONS PLC v. CUSTOMS AND EXCISE COMMISSIONERS, [2005] EWCA Civ 102, [2005] S.T.C. 481, Kennedy, L.J., CA (Civ Div).

4420. Zero rating–Interim payments–Amount of VAT assessment set off against input tax credits–Application for interim payment of VAT set off

[Value Added Tax Act 1994 s.81 (3), Sch.11 para.1; Civil Procedure Rules 1998 (SI 1998 3132) Part 25 r.25.1 (3), r.25.7; Council Directive 77/388 on a common system of VAT.]

The appellant taxpayer (T) appealed against the refusal to order an interim payment under the Civil Procedure Rules 1998 Part 25 r.25.7. The respondent commissioners cross appealed against the judge's decision to make no order for costs on T's application for an interim payment. T was assessed to VAT in the sum of £1.53 million in respect of mobile phones supplied to a Spanish company. The commissioners took the view that T had not supplied evidence that the goods had left the United Kingdom so as to fulfil the conditions for zero rating. The commissioners recouped part of the amount of the assessment by setting off £1.058 million of VAT input credits due to T pursuant to the Value Added Tax Act 1994 s.81 (3). T applied for judicial review of the commissioners' decision that the goods were not zero rated. The judge decided to refer questions on the interpretation of Sixth VAT Directive 77/388 Art.28c (A) to the European Court of Justice in order to determine the proper scope and interpretation of the conditions for zero rating. Because a decision on the reference would take some time, T applied pursuant to the Civil Procedure Rules 1998 Part 25 or the inherent jurisdiction for an interim payment of half of the VAT withheld by the commissioners in order to enable T to continue trading. The commissioners' position was that T's financial position was not such as to warrant an interim payment. The judge held that since the conditions in the 1998 Rules were not satisfied there could be no interim payment. T submitted that the judge was wrong to hold that there was no jurisdiction to grant interim relief under Part 25 since Part 25 r.25.1 (3) provided that the fact that a particular type of interim remedy was not listed in the rule did not affect any power the court might have to grant that remedy, and EC law required the national court to have the power to order interim relief in the instant case.

Held, dismissing the appeal and allowing the cross appeal, that (1) if there were no mechanism whereby a taxpayer in a position such as that of T could ever obtain an interim payment of the VAT withheld by the commissioners then that would involve an infringement of the principle of proportionality, *Garage Molenheide BVBA v. Belgium (C286/94)* [1998] All E.R. (EC) 61, [1998] C.L.Y. 4931 applied. (2) The commissioners had a discretion in the exercise of their care and management powers under Sch.11 para.1 to the 1994 Act to make interim payments in appropriate cases. That discretion was not to be exercised unreasonably or disproportionately. Thus, in refusing to make an interim payment, the commissioners must not go further than necessary to attain the objective of maintaining the common principles of VAT and, in particular, the effective recovery of VAT and the taxpayer's right to make authorised deductions from the amount of tax due. The exercise of the discretion was susceptible to judicial review. That was sufficient to meet the requirements of EC law. (3) The commissioners should make a clear statement of their policy on interim payments and publish the criteria by which they exercised the discretion to make interim payments. (4) T was not entitled to an interim payment under Part 25 r.25.7 because it did not satisfy the conditions specified in the rule. (5) The court had no inherent power to make an interim payment, *Moore v. Assignment Courier* [1977] 1 W.L.R. 638, [1977] C.L.Y. 2374 applied, *Capital One Developments Ltd v. Customs and Excise Commissioners* [2002] EWHC 197 doubted. (6) The reasons given by the judge did not justify a departure from the general rule that costs should follow the event. The commissioners were entitled to their costs of the application since they defeated the application for interim relief.

R. (ON THE APPLICATION OF TELEOS PLC) v. CUSTOMS AND EXCISE COMMISSIONERS (INTERIM RELIEF), [2005] EWCA Civ 200, [2005] 1 W.L.R. 3007, Ward, L.J., CA (Civ Div).

4421. **Zero rating—Student accommodation—Sleeper units hired as temporary student accommodation—Definition of caravans—Immovable property**

[Caravan Sites and Control of Development Act 1960 s.29(1); Value Added Tax Act 1994 Sch.8 Group 9 s.30; Sixth Council Directive on a common system for VAT Art.13B(b).]

The appellant university (K) appealed against a decision of the respondent commissioners that sleeping units it had installed on campus were not zero rated for VAT. K had hired 12 of the units during an academic year when it had a particularly high student intake. The units, each measuring 2.7 metres wide, were brought in by lorry and set up in a car park. Each unit stood on adjustable feet and some had fencing attached to discourage people from going underneath them. Ducting work was installed in the car park to supply electricity and other services. Each unit had a sleeping area with a bed, desk and chair, and a bathroom, but no kitchen or other cooking facilities. The commissioners took the view that the units were not caravans within the definition in the Value Added Tax Act 1994 Sch.8 Group 9 s.30 as they were not self contained living accommodation. K contended that (1) the units were equivalent to mobile homes and therefore counted as caravans for the purposes of the Act; (2) alternatively, the units were immovable property and therefore zero rated under the Sixth Council Directive Art.13B(b).

Held, dismissing the appeal, that (1) the word "caravan" was not defined in the Act. Some assistance could be gleaned from its use in the Caravan Sites and Control of Development Act 1960 s.29(1), on which the commissioners tended to rely, but other tests were also required. Such tests depended on the purpose behind zero rating of caravans, which was clearly intended to treat them as residential accommodation in the same way as houses. In order to be seen as such, a caravan would need to share the basic essentials of a house, which was to provide a place for shelter, sleeping, cooking and eating. The units did not provide all those basic essentials since they were not designed for cooking or eating, therefore they could not be described as self contained living accommodation capable of meeting the test for zero rating. (2) Immovable property had to have some substantial attachment to the ground requiring relatively major work to remove it, *Maierhofer v. Finanzamt Augsburg-Land (C315/00)* [2003] S.T.C. 564, [2003] C.L.Y. 4532 applied. The units in the instant case had only had slight attachment and had been removed after less than two hours' work. They were thus not immovable within the definition of the Directive.

UNIVERSITY OF KENT v. CUSTOMS AND EXCISE COMMISSIONERS [2004] B.V.C. 2215, John Clark (Chairman), VAT and Duties Tribunal (London).

4422. Books

Butler, Brian – Vat Acts. Paperback: £56.66. ISBN 1 84592 136 4. Tottel Publishing.

Dolton, Alan; Wareham, Robert – Tolley's Value Added Tax. Paperback: £121.00. ISBN 0 7545 2878 2. Paperback: £84.95. ISBN 0 7545 2879 0. Tolley Publishing.

Finn, Sean – VAT and Property Guide. Paperback: £39.95. ISBN 1 903927 61 7. Legalease.

Glaser, Maric – Tolley's VAT Business by Business Guide. Paperback: £69.95. ISBN 0 7545 2630 5. Tolley Publishing.

Homer, Arnold; Burrows, Rita; Lawrence, Nick – Tolley's Vatwise. Paperback: £55.00. ISBN 0 7545 2880 4. Tolley Publishing.

Potts, Julian – VAT in Property and Construction. Case in Point S. Paperback: £19.95. ISBN 1 84219 229 9. RICS.

Tolley's Value Added Tax and Tax Tutor. Book (details unknown): £184.21. ISBN 0 7545 2917 7. Tolley Publishing.

Tolley's Vat Planning 2004-5. Paperback: £98.95. ISBN 1 84592 015 5. Tottel Publishing.

Wareham, Robert – Tottel's Vat Planning. Paperback: £98.95. ISBN 1 84592 195 X. Tottel Publishing.

Wareham, Robert; Dolton, Alan – Tolley's VAT Cases. Paperback: £110.00. ISBN 0 7545 2889 8. Tolley Publishing.

WATER LAW

4423. Land drainage – Internal Drainage Boards – Broads and Norfolk Rivers

BROADS AND NORFOLK RIVERS INTERNAL DRAINAGE BOARDS ORDER 2005, SI 2005 429; made under the Land Drainage Act 1991 s.3, Sch.3 para.3. In force: in accordance with Art.1; £3.00.

This Order confirms a Scheme submitted by the Environment Agency for the abolition, on a date one month after the confirmation of this Order, of the Happisburgh to Winterton, the Lower Bure, Halvergate Fleet and Acle Marshes, the Middle Bure, the Muckfleet and South Flegg, the Repps, Martham and Thurne, the Smallburgh, the River Wensum, the Upper Bure, the Upper Yare and Tas, the Upper Nar, and the North Norfolk Internal Drainage Boards.

4424. Land drainage – Internal Drainage Boards – Isle of Axholme

ISLE OF AXHOLME INTERNAL DRAINAGE BOARD ORDER 2005, SI 2005 428; made under the Land Drainage Act 1991 s.3, Sch.3 para.3. In force: in accordance with Art.1; £3.00.

This Order confirms a Scheme submitted by the Environment Agency for the abolition, on a date one month after the confirmation of this Order, of the Adlingfleet and Whitgift Drainage Commissioners, the Althorpe, the Crowle Area, the South Axholme, the West Axholme and the West Butterwick Internal Drainage Boards.

4425. Land drainage—Internal Drainage Boards—Lower Severn

LOWER SEVERN INTERNAL DRAINAGE BOARD ORDER 2005, SI 2005 430; made under the Land Drainage Act 1991 s.3, Sch.3 para.3. In force: in accordance with Art.1; £3.00.

This Order confirms a Scheme submitted by the Environment Agency for the abolition, on a date one month after the confirmation of this Order, of the Lower Severn Internal Drainage Board, the North Gloucestershire Internal Drainage Board and the Longdon and Eldersfield Drainage Commissioners. A new "Lower Severn (2005) Internal Drainage Board" replaces these boards. The three former internal drainage districts are amalgamated to form the corresponding new internal drainage district.

4426. Land drainage—Internal Drainage Boards—North Somerset

NORTH SOMERSET INTERNAL DRAINAGE BOARD ORDER 2005, SI 2005 2725; made under the Land Drainage Act 1991 s.3, Sch.3 para.3. In force: in accordance with Art.1; £3.00.

This Order confirms (with modifications) a Scheme submitted by the Environment Agency for the abolition, on a date one month after the confirmation of this Order, of the North Somerset Internal Drainage Board and the Gordano Valley Internal Drainage Board.

4427. Land drainage—Internal Drainage Boards—Parrett

PARRETT INTERNAL DRAINAGE BOARD ORDER 2005, SI 2005 431; made under the Land Drainage Act 1991 s.3, Sch.3 para.3. In force: in accordance with Art.1; £3.00.

This Order confirms a Scheme submitted by the Environment Agency for the abolition, on a date one month after the confirmation of this Order, of the Aller, the Bridgwater and Pawlett, the Cannington and Wembdon, the Chedzoy Separate, the Curry Moor, the Dunster, the King Sedgemoor and Cary Valley, the Langport, the North Moor, the Othery, Middlezoy and Westonzoyland, the Stanmoor, the Stockland and the West Sedgemoor Internal Drainage Boards. These boards are replaced by a new "Parret Internal Drainage Board". The 13 former internal drainage districts are amalgamated to form the corresponding new internal drainage district.

4428. Land drainage—Internal Drainage Boards—Ramsey

RAMSEY INTERNAL DRAINAGE BOARD ORDER 2005, SI 2005 2477; made under the Land Drainage Act 1991 s.3. In force: in accordance with Art.1; £3.00.

This Order confirms a Scheme submitted by the Environment Agency for the abolition, on a date one month after the confirmation of this Order, of the Ramsey Second Internal Drainage Board and the Ramsey Fifth Internal Drainage Board.

4429. Land drainage—Internal Drainage Boards—River Deben

RIVER DEBEN INTERNAL DRAINAGE BOARD ORDER 2005, SI 2005 2512; made under the Land Drainage Act 1991 s.3. In force: in accordance with Art.1; £3.00.

This Order confirms a Scheme submitted by the Environment Agency for the abolition, on a date one month after the confirmation of this Order, of the River Deben (Upper) Internal Drainage Board and the River Deben (Lower) Internal Drainage Board.

4430. Water Act 2003 (c.37)–Commencement No.3 Order–England

WATER ACT 2003 (COMMENCEMENT NO.3) (ENGLAND) ORDER 2005, SI 2005 344 (C.12); made under the Water Act 2003 s.105. Commencement details: bringing into force various provisions of the 2003 Act on February 18, 2005; £3.00.

This Order brings into force certain provisions of the Water Act 2003 which provide for amendments to be made to the Water Act 2003; substitute the Water Industry Act 1991 s.89 which provides for consultations and introduces new powers to make regulations on the consultation process which relevant authorities will have to follow before requesting water undertakers to enter into arrangements or varying or terminating or maintaining them; and replace the Water Industry Act 1991 s.90 in relation to indemnities in respect of fluoridation.

4431. Water Act 2003 (c.37)–Commencement No.4, Transitional Provisions and Savings Order

WATER ACT 2003 (COMMENCEMENT NO.4, TRANSITIONAL PROVISIONS AND SAVINGS) ORDER 2005, SI 2005 968 (C.43); made under the Water Act 2003 s.104, s.105. Commencement details: bringing into force various provisions of the 2003 Act on April 1, 2005 and August 1, 2005; £3.00.

This Order, which partially revokes the Water Act 2003 (Commencement No.2, Transitional Provisions and Savings) Order 2004 (SI 2004 2528 (C.106)), brings into force certain provisions of the Water Act 2003.

4432. Water Act 2003 (c.37)–Commencement No.5, Transitional Provisions and Savings Order

WATER ACT 2003 (COMMENCEMENT NO.5, TRANSITIONAL PROVISIONS AND SAVINGS) ORDER 2005, SI 2005 2714 (C.109); made under the Water Act 2003 s.104, s.105. Commencement details: bringing into force various provisions of the 2003 Act on October 1, 2005, December 1, 2005 and April 1, 2006; £3.00.

This Order, which amends the Water Act 2003 (Commencement No.4, Transitional Provisions and Savings) Order 2005 (SI 2005 968 (C.43)), brings into force certain provisions of the Water Act 2003, and makes transitional provision and savings in respect of some of those provisions.

4433. Water charges–Vulnerable groups

WATER INDUSTRY (CHARGES) (VULNERABLE GROUPS) (AMENDMENT) REGULATIONS 2005, SI 2005 59; made under the Water Industry Act 1991 s.143A, s.213. In force: February 10, 2005; £3.00.

The Water Industry (Charges) (Vulnerable Groups) Regulations 1999 (SI 1999 3441) require water and sewerage undertakers' charges schemes to include special provision for assistance for certain groups of people on low incomes. The 1999 Regulations do not apply to any water or sewerage undertaker whose area is wholly or mainly in Wales. These Regulations amend the 1999 Regulations to expand the classes of people entitled to assistance.

4434. Water industry–Consumer Council for Water–Consequential and supplementary provisions

WATER ACT 2003 (CONSEQUENTIAL AND SUPPLEMENTARY PROVISIONS) REGULATIONS 2005, SI 2005 2035; made under the Water Act 2003 s.103. In force: in accordance with Reg.1; £4.00.

These Regulations amend the Water (Meters) Regulations 1988 (SI 1988 1048), the Director General of Water Services' Register (Inspection and Charges) Order 1989 (SI 1989 1154), the Water Supply and Sewerage Services (Customer Service Standards) Regulations 1989 (SI 1989 1159), the Food Safety Act 1990, the Urban Waste Water Treatment (England & Wales) Regulations 1994 (SI 1994 2841), the Public Interest Disclosure (Prescribed Persons) Order 1999 (SI 1999 1148), the Public Interest Disclosure (Prescribed Persons) Order 1999 (SI 1999 1549), the Water Industry (Charges) (Vulnerable Groups) Regulations 1999 (SI 1999

3441), the Water Industry (Prescribed Conditions) Regulations 1999 (SI 1999 3442), the Drinking Water (Undertakings) (England and Wales) Regulations 2000 (SI 2000 1297), the Water Supply (Water Quality) Regulations 2000 (SI 2000 3184), the Water Supply (Water Quality) Regulations 2001 (SI 2001 3911 (W.323)), the Water Environment (Water Framework Directive) (England and Wales) Regulations 2003 (SI 2003 3242), the Water Environment (Water Framework Directive) (Solway Tweed River Basin District) Regulations 2004 (SI 2004 99), the Water Mergers (Determination of Turnover) Regulations 2004 (SI 2004 3206) and the Water Industry (Prescribed Conditions) (Undertakers Wholly or Mainly in Wales) Regulations 2004 (SI 2004 701 (W.75)). The Water Industry Act 1991 establishes the Consumer Council for Water and abolishes the customer service committees. These Regulations make consequential amendments and supplementary provision to give effect to this.

4435. Water industry–Drought plans

DROUGHT PLAN REGULATIONS 2005, SI 2005 1905; made under the Water Industry Act 1991 s.37B, s.39B, s.213, s.219. In force: October 1, 2005; £3.00.

These Regulations, made together by the National Assembly for Wales in relation to undertakers whose area is wholly or mainly in Wales, and the Secretary of State in relation to all other undertakers, prescribe how water undertakers are to prepare and publish drought plans.

4436. Water industry–Licensed water suppliers–Penalties–Determination of turnover

WATER INDUSTRY (DETERMINATION OF TURNOVER FOR PENALTIES) ORDER 2005, SI 2005 477; made under the Water Industry Act 1991 s.22A. In force: April 1, 2005; £3.00.

The Water Industry Act 1991 provides that, in certain circumstances, the Water Services Regulation Authority (and until it is fully established, the Director General of Water Services), the National Assembly for Wales or the Secretary of State may impose a financial penalty for certain regulatory infringements. Financial penalties may be imposed on a company appointed as a relevant undertaker or a licensed water supplier and must be reasonable in all the circumstances of the case. Financial penalties must not exceed 10 per cent of the turnover of the company in question. This Order makes provision for the determination of the turnover of a company appointed as a relevant undertaker or a licensed water supplier for the purposes of financial penalties.

4437. Water supply–Licence holders–Market share

WATER SUPPLY LICENCE (MODIFICATION OF STANDARD CONDITIONS) ORDER 2005, SI 2005 2033; made under the Water Industry Act 1991 s.17J. In force: December 1, 2005; £3.00.

The Water Industry Act 1991 requires water undertakers to grant licensed water suppliers access to their supply systems under certain conditions and for certain purposes. A retail licence permits a licensed water supplier to use a water undertaker's supply system to supply water to eligible premises of customers. A combined licence additionally permits a licensed water supplier to introduce water into a water undertaker's supply system in order to supply that water to eligible premises of customers. The Act enables the Secretary of State, after consulting the National Assembly for Wales, to determine standard conditions in water supply licences. Once water supply licences have been granted, the Act permits standard licence conditions to be modified only in certain circumstances. The Act enables the Water Services Regulation Authority (and until it is fully established, the Director General of Water Services) to modify standard licence conditions if certain conditions are fulfilled. One such condition is that specified percentages of licence holders (by number or by market share) do not object to the modifications. Only certain holders of licences can object to certain modifications. Under the Act, these are known as "relevant licence holders". This Order specifies the relevant percentages and specifies how each relevant licence holder will be weighted for the purposes of measuring market share.

4438. Water supply–Water and sewerage undertakers–Threshold conditions

WATER AND SEWERAGE UNDERTAKERS (INSET APPOINTMENTS) REGULATIONS 2005, SI 2005 268; made under the Water Industry Act 1991 s.7, s.158. In force: April 1, 2005; £3.00.

The Water Industry Act 1991 permits the appointment of a company seeking to replace the existing water or sewerage undertaker for particular premises where the conditions prescribed in s.7(5) of the Act are satisfied. The Act prescribes two threshold conditions relating to the quantity of water supplied or likely to be supplied to the premises in any 12-month period. One threshold applies if the area of the relevant undertaker is wholly or mainly in Wales and another in all other cases. For all those other cases these Regulations amend the Act by lowering the threshold from 100 megalitres to 50 megalitres. As a consequence of this amendment, the Regulations also amend s.158(9)(b), which relates to powers to lay pipes in streets.

4439. Books

Weiss, Edith Brown; Chazournes, Laurence Boisson De; Bernasconi-Osterwalder, Nathalie–Fresh Water and International Economic Law. International Economic Law S. Hardback: £60.00. ISBN 0 19 927467 3. Hardback: £70.00. ISBN 0 19 927467 3. Oxford University Press.

NORTHERN IRELAND

ADMINISTRATION OF JUSTICE

4440. **County courts—Bad character and hearsay evidence—Applications procedure**

COUNTY COURT (AMENDMENT) RULES (NORTHERN IRELAND) 2005, SR 2005 143; made under the County Courts (Northern Ireland) Order 1980 (SI 1980 397 (NI.3)) Art.47; and the Criminal Justice (Evidence) (Northern Ireland) Order 2004 (SI 2004 1501 (NI.10)) Art.16, Art.35. In force: April 18, 2005; £3.00.

These Rules amend the County Court Rules (Northern Ireland) 1981 (SR 1981 225) to prescribe the procedure relating to applications to adduce evidence of bad character and notice of intention to adduce hearsay evidence. They also prescribe the procedure to be followed on an application to: adduce evidence of the bad character of persons other than the appellant or to cross examine a witness with a view to eliciting such evidence; oppose the admission of evidence of bad character of persons other than the appellant; adduce evidence of an appellant's bad character or to cross examine a witness with a view to eliciting such evidence; exclude evidence of an appellant's bad character.

4441. **Court security officers—Designation and employment**

COURT SECURITY OFFICERS (DESIGNATION AND EMPLOYMENT) REGULATIONS (NORTHERN IRELAND) 2005, SR 2005 326; made under the Justice (Northern Ireland) Act 2004 Sch.3 para.1. In force: July 25, 2005; £3.00.

The Justice (Northern Ireland) Act 2004 makes provision about court security officers. These Regulations prescribe training which must be completed; and conditions that must be satisfied, before a person may be designated or employed as a court security officer. They set out the content of the required training; and set out requirements about proof of identity, criminal record declarations and criminal record checks.

4442. **Employment tribunals—Fair employment tribunal—Procedure**

FAIR EMPLOYMENT TRIBUNAL (RULES OF PROCEDURE) REGULATIONS (NORTHERN IRELAND) 2005, SR 2005 151; made under the Fair Employment and Treatment (Northern Ireland) Order 1998 (SI 1998 3162 (NI.21)) Art.81, Art.82, Art.84, Art.84A, Art.84B, Art.85A, Art.85B. In force: April 3, 2005; £5.50.

These Regulations, which revoke the Fair Employment Tribunal (Rules of Procedure) Regulations (Northern Ireland) 2004 (SR 2004 164), make minor and drafting amendments and update statutory and other references.

4443. **Industrial tribunals—Constitution—Procedure**

INDUSTRIAL TRIBUNALS (CONSTITUTION AND RULES OF PROCEDURE) REGULATIONS (NORTHERN IRELAND) 2005, SR 2005 150; made under the Health and Safety at Work (Northern Ireland) Order 1978 (SI 1978 1039) (NI.9)) Art.26; and the Industrial Tribunals (Northern Ireland) Order 1996 (SI 1996 1921 (NI.18)) Art.3, Art.6, Art.9, Art.9A, Art.11, Art.12, Art.12A, Art.13, Art.14, Art.15, Art.15A, Art.21, Art.25. In force: April 3, 2005; £7.50.

These Regulations, which revoke the Tribunals (Northern Ireland) Order 1996 (SI 1996 1921), the Industrial Tribunals (Constitution and Rules of Procedure) Regulations (Northern Ireland) 2004 (SR 2004 165) and the Industrial Tribunals

(Constitution and Rules of Procedure) (Amendment) Regulations (Northern Ireland) 2004 (SR 2004 317), make minor and drafting amendments and update statutory and other references.

4444. Industrial tribunals–Members–Appointments

INDUSTRIAL TRIBUNALS (CONSTITUTION AND RULES OF PROCEDURE) (AMENDMENT) REGULATIONS (NORTHERN IRELAND) 2005, SR 2005 376; made under the Industrial Tribunals (Northern Ireland) Order 1996 (SI 1996 1921 (NI.18)) Art.3, Art.25. In force: August 31, 2005; £3.00.

These Regulations amend the Industrial Tribunals (Constitution and Rules of Procedure) Regulations (Northern Ireland) 2005 (SR 2005 150) so that the Lord Chancellor, rather than the Department for Employment and Learning, appoints full and part-time members to the panel of chairmen of industrial tribunals.

4445. Supreme Court–Civil partnerships–Enforcement of judgments

RULES OF THE SUPREME COURT (NORTHERN IRELAND) (AMENDMENT NO.5) 2005, SR 2005 449; made under the Judicature (Northern Ireland) Act 1978 s.55. In force: November 4, 2005; £3.00.

These Rules amend the Rules of the Supreme Court (Northern Ireland) 1980 (SR 1980 346) to assign to the Family Division all causes and matters in relation to dissolution or annulment of a civil partnership, legal separation of civil partners, a presumption of death order and related matters; proceedings under the Gender Recognition Act 2004; specified proceedings under the Civil Partnership Act 2004; and proceedings under Council Regulation 2201/2003 ([2003] OJ L338/1) concerning jurisdiction and the recognition and enforcement of judgments in matrimonial matters and matters of parental responsibility, so far as that Regulation relates to jurisdiction, recognition and enforcement in parental responsibility matters. They also provide for new forms.

ADMINISTRATIVE LAW

4446. Executive agencies–Regulation and Improvement Authority–Fees

REGULATION AND IMPROVEMENT AUTHORITY (FEES AND FREQUENCY OF INSPECTIONS) REGULATIONS (NORTHERN IRELAND) 2005, SR 2005 182; made under the Health and Personal Social Services (Quality, Improvement and Regulation) (Northern Ireland) Order 2003 (SI 2003 431 (NI.9)) Art.6, Art.13, Art.16, Art.17, Art.40, Art.48. In force: April 1, 2005; £3.00.

These Regulations prescribe the fees that are to be paid to the Health and Personal Social Services Regulation and Improvement Authority by establishments and agencies regulated from April 1, 2005. The fees are payable on an application for registration in respect of an establishment or agency; and on an application for the variation or removal of any condition for the time being in force in relation to the registration.

4447. Marriage–Registration–Fees

BIRTHS, DEATHS, MARRIAGES AND CIVIL PARTNERSHIPS (FEES) ORDER (NORTHERN IRELAND) 2005, SR 2005 478; made under the Births and Deaths Registration (Northern Ireland) Order 1976 (SI 1976 1041 (NI.14)) Art.47; the Marriage (Northern Ireland) Order 2003 (SI 2003 413 (NI.3)) Art.3, Art.19, Art.35, Art.36, Art.37; and the Civil Partnership Act 2004 s.157. In force: December 5, 2005; £3.00.

This Order, which revokes the Births, Deaths and Marriages (Fees) Order (Northern Ireland) 2003 (SR 2003 467), provides for the increase of various fees payable relating to the registration of births and deaths. It also provides for the increase of various fees payable under the Marriage (Northern Ireland) Order

2003 relating to giving notice for intended marriage, the solemnisation of civil marriage and providing marriage certificates. It also provides for the various new fees payable under the Civil Partnership Act 2004 relating to giving notice for intended civil partnership, the registration of civil partnership and providing civil partnership certificates.

4448. Ombudsmen–Salaries

SALARIES (ASSEMBLY OMBUDSMAN AND COMMISSIONER FOR COMPLAINTS) ORDER (NORTHERN IRELAND) 2005, SR 2005 36; made under the Ombudsman (Northern Ireland) Order 1996 (SI 1996 1298 (NI.7) Art.5; and the Commissioner for Complaints (Northern Ireland) Order 1996 (SI 1996 1297 (NI.8)) Art.4. In force: March 21, 2005; £3.00.

This Order, which revokes the Salaries (Assembly Ombudsman and Commissioner for Complaints) Order (Northern Ireland) 2003 (SR 2003 382), provides for an increase in the annual salaries payable to the Assembly Ombudsman for Northern Ireland and the Northern Ireland Commissioner for Complaints.

4449. Ombudsmen–Salaries

SALARIES (ASSEMBLY OMBUDSMAN AND COMMISSIONER FOR COMPLAINTS) (NO.2) ORDER (NORTHERN IRELAND) 2005, SR 2005 234; made under the Ombudsman (Northern Ireland) Order 1996 (SI 1996 1298 (NI.8)) Art.5; and the Commissioner for Complaints (Northern Ireland) Order 1996 (SI 1996 1297 (NI.7)) Art.4. In force: June 7, 2005; £3.00.

This Order, which revokes the Salaries (Assembly Ombudsman and Commissioner for Complaints) Order (Northern Ireland) 2005 (SR 2005 36), provides for an increase in the annual salaries payable to the Assembly Ombudsman for Northern Ireland and the Northern Ireland Commissioner for Complaints. This provision is made with retrospective effect from April 1, 2005.

4450. Public authorities–Accounts–Information–Designation of bodies

WHOLE OF GOVERNMENT ACCOUNTS (DESIGNATION OF BODIES) (NORTHERN IRELAND) ORDER 2005, SR 2005 327; made under the Government Resources and Accounts Act (Northern Ireland) 2001 s.15. In force: July 25, 2005; £3.00.

This Order designates bodies, for the financial year ending with March 31, 2005, for the purposes of the Government Resources and Accounts Act (Northern Ireland) 2001.

4451. Public processions–Forms

PUBLIC ORDER (PRESCRIBED FORMS) REGULATIONS (NORTHERN IRELAND) 2005, SI 2005 904; made under the Public Processions (Northern Ireland) Act 1998 s.6. In force: April 15, 2005; £3.00.

These Regulations prescribe the form for notice of a public procession as required by the Public Processions (Northern Ireland) Act 1998. They replace the form for notice of a public procession prescribed by the Public Order (Prescribed Forms) Regulations (Northern Ireland) 2004 (SI 2004 416) so that the organiser is required to specify the likely number of supporters.

4452. Public processions–Revised code of conduct

PUBLIC PROCESSIONS (NORTHERN IRELAND) ACT 1998 (CODE OF CONDUCT) ORDER 2005, SI 2005 901; made under the Public Processions (Northern Ireland) Act 1998 Sch.2 para.8. In force: April 15, 2005; £3.00.

This Order appoints April 15, 2005 as the date on which the revised Code of Conduct, which provides guidance to persons organising a public procession or protest meeting and regulates the conduct of persons organising, taking part in or supporting such a procession or organising or taking part in such a meeting, is to come into operation. The revised Code, which is issued by the Parades Commission for Northern Ireland, replaces the Code of Conduct which was brought into operation on July 31, 1999 by the Public Processions (Northern Ireland) Act 1998 (Code of Conduct) Order 1999 (SI 1999 2116), which is revoked by this Order.

4453. Public processions-Revised guidelines

PUBLIC PROCESSIONS (NORTHERN IRELAND) ACT 1998 (GUIDELINES) ORDER 2005, SI 2005 905; made under the Public Processions (Northern Ireland) Act 1998 Sch.2 para.8. In force: April 15, 2005; £3.00.

This Order, which revokes the Public Processions (Northern Ireland) Act 1998 (Guidelines) Order 1999 (SI 1999 2115), appoints April 15, 2005 as the date on which the revised guidelines relating to the exercise by the Parades Commission for Northern Ireland of certain functions under the Public Processions (Northern Ireland) Act 1998 (power to impose conditions on public processions and protest meetings) are to come into operation.

4454. Public processions-Revised procedural rules

PUBLIC PROCESSIONS (NORTHERN IRELAND) ACT 1998 (PROCEDURAL RULES) ORDER 2005, SI 2005 903; made under the Public Processions (Northern Ireland) Act 1998 Sch.2 para.8. In force: April 15, 2005; £3.00.

This Order, which revokes the Public Processions (Northern Ireland) Act 1998 (Procedural Rules) Order 1999 (SI 1999 2117) appoints April 15, 2005 as the date on which the revised procedural rules regulating and prescribing the practice and procedure to be followed by the Parades Commission for Northern Ireland in exercising the functions mentioned in the Public Processions (Northern Ireland) Act 1998 s.2(2) (power to mediate between parties to particular disputes concerning proposed public processions and to issue determinations in respect of particular proposed public processions and protest meetings), and by other persons or bodies in their dealings with the Commission in connection with the exercise of those functions, are to come into operation.

4455. Public Processions (Amendment) (Northern Ireland) Order 2005 (SI 2005 857 (NI.2))

This Order amends the Public Processions (Northern Ireland) Act 1998 to enable the Parades Commission to impose conditions on persons supporting a public procession; to enable the Commission to issue determinations in respect of protest meetings; to restate the powers of the Secretary of State to prohibit the holding of protest meetings; and to extend s.14 of that Act (breaking up processions) to cover protest meetings.

AGRICULTURE

4456. Agricultural policy-Direct support schemes-Cross compliance

COMMON AGRICULTURAL POLICY SINGLE PAYMENT AND SUPPORT SCHEMES REGULATIONS (NORTHERN IRELAND) 2005, SR 2005 256; made under the European Communities Act 1972 s.2. In force: May 12, 2005; £3.00.

These Regulations revoke the Sheep Annual Premium Regulations (Northern Ireland) 1992 (SR 1992 476), the Sheep Annual Premium (Amendment) Regulations (Northern Ireland) 1994 (SR 1994 404), the Sheep Annual Premium (Amendment) Regulations (Northern Ireland) 1995 (SR 1995 403), the Sheep Annual Premium (Amendment) Regulations (Northern Ireland) 1996 (SR 1996 497), the Deseasonalisation Premium (Protection of Payments) Regulations (Northern Ireland) 1996 (SR 1996 605), the Arable Area Payments Regulations (Northern Ireland) 1997 (SR 1997 477), the Sheep Annual Premium

(Amendment) Regulations (Northern Ireland) 1997 (SR 1997 485), the Deseasonalisation Premium (Protection of Payments) (Amendment) Regulations (Northern Ireland) 1997 (SR 1997 521), the Arable Area Payments (Amendment) Regulations (Northern Ireland) 1998 (SR 1998 308), the Sheep Annual Premium (Amendment) Regulations (Northern Ireland) 1998 (SR 1998 440), the Deseasonalisation Premium (Protection of Payments) (Amendment) Regulations (Northern Ireland) 1998 (SR 1998 447), the Deseasonalisation Premium (Protection of Payments) (Amendment) Regulations (Northern Ireland) 1999 (SR 1999 46) Sheep Annual Premium (Amendment) Regulations (Northern Ireland) 1999 (SR 2000 301) Arable Area Payments (Amendment) Regulations (Northern Ireland) 1999 (SR 1999 120), the Extensification Payment Regulations (Northern Ireland) 2001 (SR 2001 127), the Slaughter Premium Regulations (Northern Ireland) 2001 (SR 2001 199), the Sheep Annual Premium (Amendment) Regulations (Northern Ireland) 2001 (SR 2001 411), the Beef Special Premium Regulations (Northern Ireland) 2001 (SR 2001 363), the Beef Special Premium (Amendment) Regulations (Northern Ireland) 2002 (SR 2002 335), the Sheep Annual Premium (Amendment) Regulations (Northern Ireland) 2002 (SR 2002 368), the Sheep Annual Premium and Suckler Cow Premium Quotas Regulations 2003 (SI 2003 2261), the Slaughter Premium (Amendment) Regulations (Northern Ireland) 2003 (SR 2003 192), and the Sheep Annual Premium (Amendment) Regulations (Northern Ireland) 2003 (SR 2003 490). They make provision in Northern Ireland for the administration of Council Regulation 1782/2003 ([2003] OJ L270/1) establishing common rules for direct support schemes under the common agricultural policy and establishing certain support schemes for farmers, Commission Regulation 796/2004 ([2004] OJ L141/18) laying down detailed rules for the implementation of cross-compliance, modulation and the integrated administration and control system, and Commission Regulation 1973/2004 ([2004] OJ L345/1) in relation to establishing a new system of direct support schemes (including the Single Payment Scheme) under the Common Agricultural Policy which came into force on January 1, 2005.

4457. Agricultural policy–Direct support schemes–Cross compliance

COMMON AGRICULTURAL POLICY SINGLE PAYMENT AND SUPPORT SCHEMES (CROSS COMPLIANCE) REGULATIONS (NORTHERN IRELAND) 2005, SR 2005 6; made under the European Communities Act 1972 s.2. In force: January 10, 2005; £3.00.

These Regulations make provision for the administration and enforcement of Council Regulation 1782/2003 ([2003] OJ L270/1) establishing common rules for direct support schemes under the common agricultural policy and establishing certain support schemes for farmers and Commission Regulation 796/2004 ([2004] OJ L141/18) laying down detailed rules for the implementation of cross compliance, modulation and the integrated administration and control system provided for in Council Regulation 1782/2003, in relation to cross compliance under the new system of direct support schemes (including the Single Payment Scheme) under the Common Agricultural Policy (CAP) to come into force on January 1, 2005. The Regulations designate the Department of Agriculture and Rural Development as the competent national authority responsible for providing farmers with a list of the statutory management requirements and standards of good agricultural and environmental condition on his land; set out the standards of good agricultural and environmental condition which will apply in Northern Ireland; and provide that farmers with agri-environment commitments which directly and necessarily conflict with the standards will not be penalised for breaching the standards.

4458. Agricultural policy–Direct support schemes–Set aside

COMMON AGRICULTURAL POLICY SINGLE PAYMENT AND SUPPORT SCHEMES (SET-ASIDE) REGULATIONS (NORTHERN IRELAND) 2005, SR

2005 310; made under the European Communities Act 1972 s.2. In force: July 29, 2005; £3.00.

These Regulations make provision in Northern Ireland for the administration of Council Regulation 1782/2003 ([2003] OJ L270/1) establishing common rules for direct support schemes under the common agricultural policy and establishing certain support schemes for farmers, Commission Regulation 795/2004 ([2004] OJ L141/1) laying down detailed rules for the implementation of the single payment scheme provided for in Council Regulation 1782/2003 and Commission Regulation 1973/2004 ([2004] OJ L345/1) laying down detailed rules for the application of Council Regulation 1782/2003 in relation to the obligation to set aside land under the new Single Farm Payment Scheme for farmers.

4459. Agricultural policy–Wine

See AGRICULTURE. §103

4460. Agricultural produce–Marketing–Grants

INFORMATION AND COMMUNICATION TECHNOLOGY GRANT SCHEME (NORTHERN IRELAND) 2005, SR 2005 278; made under the Agriculture (Northern Ireland) Order 1993 (SI 1993 2665 (NI.10)) Art.26. In force: July 1, 2005; £3.00.

This Scheme provides for the payment of grants for carrying out proposals described in the Schedule for the organisation, promotion, encouragement, development, co-ordination or facilitation of the marketing of agricultural produce or anything derived from such produce.

4461. Agricultural produce–Milk–Quota arrangements

DAIRY PRODUCE QUOTAS REGULATIONS (NORTHERN IRELAND) 2005, SR 2005 70; made under the European Communities Act 1972 s.2. In force: March 31, 2005; £6.00.

These Regulations, which revoke the Dairy Produce Quotas Regulations (Northern Ireland) 2002 (SR 2002 88) and the Dairy Produce Quotas (Amendment) Regulations (Northern Ireland) 2004 (SR 2004 59), implement Council Regulation 1788/2003 ([2003] OJ L279/123) establishing a levy in the milk and milk products sector and Commission Regulation 595/2004 ([2004] OJ L94/22) laying down detailed rules for applying Council Regulation 1788/2003 establishing a levy in the milk and milk products sector.

4462. Animal products–Bone in beef–Placing on market–Restrictions

BOVINE PRODUCTS (RESTRICTION ON PLACING ON THE MARKET) REGULATIONS (NORTHERN IRELAND) 2005, SR 2005 439; made under the European Communities Act 1972 s.2. In force: November 7, 2005; £3.00.

These Regulations, which revoke the Fresh Meat (Beef Controls) Regulations (Northern Ireland) 1996 (SR 1996 404) and amend the By-Products (Identification) Regulations (Northern Ireland) 1999 (SR 1999 418), give effect to Commission Decision 2005/598 ([2005] OJ L204/22) Art.1 (1) prohibiting the placing on the market of products derived from bovine animals born or reared within the UK before August 1, 1996 for any purpose and exempting such animals from certain control and eradication measures laid down in Regulation 999/2001. The Regulations also apply with modifications certain provisions of the Food Safety (Northern Ireland) Order 1991 (SI 1991 762 (NI.7)) for the purposes of these Regulations; provide for the inspection and seizure of products that are suspected of having been placed on the market in contravention of these Regulations; create offences and penalties; and make provision for their enforcement.

4463. Animal products – Bone in beef – Placing on market – Restrictions

BOVINE PRODUCTS (RESTRICTION ON PLACING ON THE MARKET) (NO.2) REGULATIONS (NORTHERN IRELAND) 2005, SR 2005 515; made under the European Communities Act 1972 s.2. In force: January 1, 2006; £3.00.

These Regulations, which revoke the Bovine Products (Restriction on Placing on the Market) Regulations (Northern Ireland) 2005 (SR 2005 439), amend the Animal By-Products (Identification) Regulations (Northern Ireland) 1999 (SR 1999 418). They apply with modifications certain provisions of the Food Safety (Northern Ireland) Order 1991 (SI 1991 762 (NI.7)); provide for the inspection and seizure of products that are suspected of having been placed on the market in contravention of these Regulations; create offences and penalties; and make provision for their enforcement.

4464. Animal products – Diseases and disorders – TSE

TRANSMISSIBLE SPONGIFORM ENCEPHALOPATHY (AMENDMENT) REGULATIONS (NORTHERN IRELAND) 2005, SR 2005 25; made under the European Communities Act 1972 s.2. In force: March 1, 2005; £3.00.

These Regulations amend the Transmissible Spongiform Encephalopathy Regulations (Northern Ireland) 2002 (SR 2002 225) by correcting a technical defect in Reg.99 to make it clear that the penalties provided there under apply in the case of all offences under the 2002 Regulations.

4465. Animal products – Diseases and disorders – TSE

TRANSMISSIBLE SPONGIFORM ENCEPHALOPATHY (AMENDMENT NO.2) REGULATIONS (NORTHERN IRELAND) 2005, SR 2005 200; made under the European Communities Act 1972 s.2. In force: May 4, 2005; £3.00.

These Regulations amend the Transmissible Spongiform Encephalopathy Regulations (Northern Ireland) 2002 (SR 2002 225) to bring up to date the definition of "the Community Transitional Measures" to cover the amendment of European Parliament and Council Regulation /2001 ([2001] OJ L147/1) laying down rules for the prevention, control and eradication of certain transmissible spongiform encephalopathies by Commission Regulation 1494/2002 ([2002] OJ L225/3), Commission Regulation 1139/2003 ([2003] OJ L160/22), and Commission Regulation 1492/2004 ([2004] OJ L274/3). These Regulations also amend the definition of specified risk material to ensure that it now includes ileum on the list of tissues that have to be removed from older sheep and goats that have been slaughtered in a slaughterhouse or brought to a slaughterhouse following slaughter elsewhere.

4466. Animal products – Diseases and disorders – TSE

TRANSMISSIBLE SPONGIFORM ENCEPHALOPATHY (AMENDMENT NO.3) REGULATIONS (NORTHERN IRELAND) 2005, SR 2005 436; made under the European Communities Act 1972 s.2. In force: October 25, 2005; £3.00.

These Regulations, which amend the Transmissible Spongiform Encephalopathy Regulations (Northern Ireland) 2002 (SR 2002 225), give effect in part to Council Directive 95/53 ([1995] OJ L265/17) art.16a, fixing the principles governing the organization of official inspections in the field of animal nutrition. They also make provision for the enforcement of measures contained in European Parliament and Council Regulation 999/2001 ([2001] OJ L147/1) laying down rules for the prevention, control and eradication of certain transmissible spongiform encephalopathies.

4467. Animal products – Examination – Residues of veterinary medicinal products – Maximum residue limits

ANIMALS AND ANIMAL PRODUCTS (EXAMINATION FOR RESIDUES AND MAXIMUM RESIDUE LIMITS) (AMENDMENT) REGULATIONS (NORTHERN

IRELAND) 2005, SR 2005 451; made under the European Communities Act 1972 s.2. In force: November 14, 2005; £3.00.

These Regulations, which amend the Animals and Animal Products (Examination for Residues and Maximum Residue Limits) Regulations (Northern Ireland) 1998 (SR 1998 237), reflect EC law in the area of horse passports, namely, Commission Decision 2000/68 ([2000] OJ L23/72) amending Commission Decision 93/623 and establishing the identification of equidae for breeding and production, insofar as it calls for qualification of the prohibition in the 1998 Regulations against administration to food producing animals of veterinary medicinal products containing substances not listed in Annexes I, II or III to Council Regulation 2377/90 ([1990] OJ L224/1) laying down a Community procedure for the establishment of maximum residue limits of veterinary medicinal products in foodstuffs of animal origin.

4468. Animal products–Import and export controls

ANIMALS AND ANIMAL PRODUCTS (IMPORT AND EXPORT) (AMENDMENT) REGULATIONS (NORTHERN IRELAND) 2005, SR 2005 446; made under the European Communities Act 1972 s.2. In force: November 7, 2005; £4.00.

These Regulations, which amend the Animals and Animal Products (Import and Export) Regulations (Northern Ireland) 2005 (SR 2005 78), specify the compliance required under Community law for assembly centres handling sheep and goats which are permitted to be exported to other Member States.

4469. Animal products–Origin marking–Third country imports

PRODUCTS OF ANIMAL ORIGIN (THIRD COUNTRY IMPORTS) (AMENDMENT) REGULATIONS (NORTHERN IRELAND) 2005, SR 2005 554; made under the European Communities Act 1972 s.2. In force: December 9, 2005; £3.00.

These Regulations, which amend the Products of Animal Origin (Third Country Imports) Regulations (Northern Ireland) 2004 (SR 2004 464), implement Council Directive 97/78 ([1997] OJ L24/9) laying down the principles governing the organisation of veterinary checks on products entering the Community from third countries. They give effect to the restrictions on the importation of products derived from birds contained in Commission Decision 2005/760 ([2005] OJ L285/60) concerning certain protection measures in relation to highly pathogenic avian influenza in certain third countries for the import of captive birds.

4470. Animals–Diseases and disorders–Tuberculosis

TUBERCULOSIS CONTROL (AMENDMENT) ORDER (NORTHERN IRELAND) 2005, SR 2005 53; made under the Diseases of Animals (Northern Ireland) Order 1981 (SI 1981 1115 (NI.22)) Art.5, Art.10, Art.18, Art.19, Art.44, Art.46, Art.60, Sch.2 Part I para.4, Sch.2 Part II para.4. In force: March 28, 2005; £3.00.

This Order amends the Tuberculosis Control Order (Northern Ireland) 1 (SR 1 263) to correct an error therein.

4471. Animals–Feedingstuffs–Establishments–Fees

FEEDING STUFFS (ESTABLISHMENTS AND INTERMEDIARIES) (AMENDMENT) REGULATIONS (NORTHERN IRELAND) 2005, SR 2005 74; made under the European Communities Act 1972 s.2. In force: April 4, 2005; £3.00.

These Regulations amend the Feeding Stuffs (Establishments and Intermediaries) Regulations 1999 (SI 1999 1872) and implement Council Decision 98/728 ([1998] OJ L346/51) concerning a Community system of fees in the animal feed sector. They provide for the payment of fees and the reimbursement of the costs of laboratory analyses to the specified approval body by a person applying to that body for approval of an establishment; provide for the payment of fees and the reimbursement of the costs of laboratory analyses to the competent body by a person applying to it for approval as an "intermediary"; and specify the fees payable.

4472. Farmers–Weather aid scheme–Grants

AGRICULTURE (WEATHER AID 2002) SCHEME (NORTHERN IRELAND) 2005, SR 2005 468; made under the Agriculture (Temporary Assistance) Act (Northern Ireland) 1954 s.1, s.2. In force: October 28, 2005; £3.00.

This Scheme provides for payments to be made by the Department of Agriculture and Rural Development to producers in certain sectors of the agricultural industry who suffered financial losses whether resulting from reduced outputs or from increased production costs or both as a direct result of the abnormally adverse weather conditions in 2002.

4473. Farmers–Young farmers scheme–Grants

FINANCIAL ASSISTANCE FOR YOUNG FARMERS SCHEME ORDER (NORTHERN IRELAND) 2005, SR 2005 69; made under the Financial Assistance for Young Farmers (Northern Ireland) Order 2004 (SI 2004 3080 (NI.21)) Art.3. In force: April 4, 2005; £3.00.

The Scheme set out in the Schedule to this Order makes provision for grant towards expenditure incurred in servicing loans obtained by young persons for the purposes of, or in connection with, the implementation of a business plan relating to the establishment, expansion or carrying on of an agricultural business. A young person is defined, for the purposes of the Scheme, as a person under the age of 40 at the time he makes an application for grant under the Scheme.

4474. Farmers–Young farmers scheme–Grants

FINANCIAL ASSISTANCE FOR YOUNG FARMERS SCHEME (AMENDMENT) ORDER (NORTHERN IRELAND) 2005, SR 2005 540; made under the Financial Assistance for Young Farmers (Northern Ireland) Order 2004 (SI 2004 3080 (NI.21)) Art.3. In force: December 23, 2005; £3.00.

This Order extends the closing date for applications for a grant under the Financial Assistance for Young Farmers Scheme (Northern Ireland) 2005 (SR 2005 69) from April 3, 2008 to June 5, 2008.

4475. Food safety–Beef carcases–Classification

BEEF CARCASE (CLASSIFICATION) REGULATIONS (NORTHERN IRELAND) 2005, SR 2005 28; made under the European Communities Act 1972 s.2. In force: March 14, 2005; £3.00.

These Regulations, which revoke the Beef Carcase (Classification) Regulations (Northern Ireland) 1992 (SR 1992 1); the Beef Carcase (Classification) (Amendment) Regulations (Northern Ireland) 1994 (SR 1994 486); and the Beef Carcase (Classification) (Amendment) Regulations (Northern Ireland) 1998 (SR 1998 40), provide for the administration and enforcement of the Community system of classification of beef carcases as required by Commission Regulation 344/91 ([1991] OJ L141/15) laying down detailed rules for applying Council Regulation 1186/90 to extend the scope of the Community scale for the classification of carcases of adult bovine animals. The Regulations make provision for exemptions from the Community system; require every occupier of a regulated slaughterhouse to give the Department particulars of his business; authorise certain carcases to be identified using labels rather than marks; make provision for the granting of classification licences; require occupiers of regulated slaughterhouses to keep, retain and produce records; give the Livestock and Meat Commission for Northern Ireland power to carry out classification requirements for regulated carcases and make provision for its entering into agreements with the occupiers of regulated slaughterhouses for such a purpose; confer on authorised officers of the Department powers of entry and inspection for the purpose of ensuring compliance with the Community system and Regulations, and require that reasonable assistance be given to them at their request; create offences and penalties, and provide for defences.

4476. Genetically modified organisms – Feedingstuffs – Emergency controls

FEED (CORN GLUTEN FEED AND BREWERS GRAINS) (EMERGENCY CONTROL) REGULATIONS (NORTHERN IRELAND) 2005, SR 2005 233; made under the European Communities Act 1972 s.2. In force: May 3, 2005; £3.00.

These Regulations, which implement Commission Decision 2005/317 on emergency measures regarding the non-authorised genetically modified organism Bt 10 in maize products ([2005] OJ L101/14), amend the Genetically Modified Animal Feed Regulations (Northern Ireland) 2004 (SR 2004 386) to provide that where material which is condemned pursuant to those Regulations constitutes controlled products as defined in regulation 2(1) of these Regulations, the expenses reasonably incurred in connection with the destruction or disposal of those products shall be defrayed by the operator responsible for their first placing on the market of that material; to prohibit the first placing on the market of certain maize products originating from the US; make it an offence to breach that prohibition; apply with modifications certain provisions of the Agriculture Act 1970; apply with modifications certain provisions of the Feeding Stuffs (Sampling and Analysis) Regulations (Northern Ireland) 1 (SR 1 296); and provide for the inspection, seizure and detention of corn gluten feed or brewers grains illegally first placed on the market.

4477. Infectious disease control – Artificial insemination – Cattle – Imports

ARTIFICIAL INSEMINATION OF CATTLE (AMENDMENT) REGULATIONS (NORTHERN IRELAND) 2005, SR 2005 264; made under the Artificial Reproduction of Animals (Northern Ireland) Order 1975 (SI 1975 1834 (NI.17)) Art.5. In force: June 13, 2005; £3.00.

These Regulations, which amend the Artificial Insemination of Cattle Regulations (Northern Ireland) 1988 (SR 1988 339), implement Council Directive 2003/43 ([2003] OJ L143/23) amending Directive 88/407 laying down the animal health requirements applicable to intra-Community trade in and imports of semen of domestic animals of the bovine species which imposes additional testing requirements for donor bulls and for semen intended for intra-Community trade. The Regulations amend the definition of "the Directive"; prescribe the requirements for the acceptance by the holder of a storage centre licence of semen originating outside Northern Ireland; and update the licensing requirements for operators of quarantine storage depots.

4478. Infectious disease control – Import of potatoes – Egypt

POTATOES ORIGINATING IN EGYPT (AMENDMENT) REGULATIONS (NORTHERN IRELAND) 2005, SR 2005 460; made under the European Communities Act 1972 s.2. In force: November 14, 2005; £3.00.

These Regulations, which amend the Potatoes Originating in Egypt Regulations (Northern Ireland) 2004 (SR 2004 183) implement in Northern Ireland Commission Decision 2004/836 ([2004] OJ L360/30) amending Commission Decision 2004/4 authorising Member States temporarily to take emergency measures against the dissemination of Pseudomonas solanacearum (Smith) Smith (now referred to as Ralstonia solanacearum (Smith) Yabuuchi et al) as regards Egypt.

4479. Milk products—Reporting on prices

REPORTING OF PRICES OF MILK PRODUCTS REGULATIONS (NORTHERN IRELAND) 2005, SR 2005 286; made under the European Communities Act 1972 s.2. In force: July 1, 2005; £3.00.

These Regulations make provision for the implementation of Art.6 of Commission Regulation 562/2005 ([2005] OJ L95/11) laying down rules for the implementation of Council Regulation 1255/1999 as regards communications between the Member States and the Commission in the milk and milk products sector. They require milk processors to provide the Department with such information relating to the prices of certain milk products, as it may require by notice. Failure to comply with such a requirement is an offence punishable on summary conviction by a fine not exceeding level 5 on the standard scale.

4480. Organic farming—Animal housing—Grants

ORGANIC FARMING (CONVERSION OF ANIMAL HOUSING) (AMENDMENT) SCHEME (NORTHERN IRELAND) 2005, SR 2005 52; made under the Agriculture and Fisheries (Financial Assistance) (Northern Ireland) Order 1987 (SI 1987 166 (NI.1)) Art.16. In force: March 30, 2005; £3.00.

This Scheme amends the Organic Farming (Conversion of Animal Housing) Scheme (Northern Ireland) 2003 (SR 2003 472) by updating references to Community and UK legislation; replacing the references to the standards set out in the United Kingdom Register of Organic Food Standards (UKROFS) with references to the standards set out in the Compendium of UK Organic Standards May 2004 Edition; and providing that the closing date for claims for grant to be received by the Department of Agriculture and Rural Development under the principal Scheme shall be March 31, 2006 instead of March 31, 2005.

4481. Pesticides—Residue levels in crops, food and feedingstuffs

PESTICIDES (MAXIMUM RESIDUE LEVELS IN CROPS, FOOD AND FEEDING STUFFS) (AMENDMENT) REGULATIONS (NORTHERN IRELAND) 2005, SR 2005 51; made under the European Communities Act 1972 s.2. In force: April 11, 2005; £3.00.

These Regulations, which amend the provisions of the Pesticides (Maximum Residue Levels in Crops, Food and Feeding Stuffs) Regulations (Northern Ireland) 2002 (SR 2002 20), implement Commission Directive 2004/95 ([2004] OJ L301/42) amending Council Directive 90/642 as regards the maximum residue levels of bifenthrin and famoxadone fixed therein. They update the definition of "the Residues Directives" and substitute new maximum residue levels for residues of the pesticides Bifenthrin and Famoxadone.

4482. Pesticides—Residue levels in crops, food and feedingstuffs

PESTICIDES (MAXIMUM RESIDUE LEVELS IN CROPS, FOOD AND FEEDING STUFFS) (AMENDMENT NO.2) REGULATIONS (NORTHERN IRELAND) 2005, SR 2005 401; made under the European Communities Act 1972 s.2. In force: October 10, 2005; £3.50.

These Regulations amend the provisions of the Pesticides (Maximum Residue Levels in Crops, Food and Feeding Stuffs) Regulations (Northern Ireland) 2002 (SR 2002 20) and implement Commission Directive 2004/115 ([2004] OJ L374/64) amending Council Directive 90/642 as regards the maximum levels for certain pesticide residues fixed therein. They substitute new maximum residue levels for residues of the pesticides Azoxystrobin, Fenhexamid, Fenpropimorph, Iprovalicarb, Maneb Mancozeb Metiram Propineb Zineb, Metalaxyl, Metalaxyl-M, Methomyl thiodicarb, Myclobutanil and Penconazole.

4483. Plant varieties–Seeds–Fees

SEEDS (FEES) (AMENDMENT) REGULATIONS (NORTHERN IRELAND) 2005, SR 2005 40; made under the Seeds Act (Northern Ireland) 1965 s.1, s.2. In force: March 28, 2005; £3.00.

These Regulations amend the Seeds (Fees) (No.2) Regulations (Northern Ireland) 2002 (SR 2002 407) to correct the omission of the fees for official seeds labels and of triticale from the list of seed of the second generation.

4484. Plants–Plant health–Import inspections–Fees

PLANT HEALTH (IMPORT INSPECTION FEES) REGULATIONS (NORTHERN IRELAND) 2005, SR 2005 373; made under the European Communities Act 1972 s.2; and the Finance Act 1973 s.56. In force: September 1, 2005; £3.00.

These Regulations implement Article 13d of Council Directive 2000/29 ([2000] OJ L169/1), as last amended by Commission Directive 2005/15 ([2005] OJ L56/12), which requires Member States to charge fees to cover the costs occasioned by the documentary checks, identity checks and plant health checks of certain imports of plants, plant products and other objects from third countries provided for in Article 13a(1) of the Directive. The Regulations require importers to pay the fee specified in Schedule 1 for plant health checks which are carried out, except where reduced import inspection fees apply; specifies reduced fees which apply, whether or not an inspection is in fact carried out, in respect of plant health checks of certain cut flowers and fruits originating in the countries specified in that; require importers to pay the fee specified in Sch.3 for documentary checks and identity checks; require that different types of plants, plant products or other objects contained within the same consignment shall be treated as separate consignments and subject to separate fees; and require that importers must provide certain information concerning the consignment at least two days before it is landed in Northern Ireland.

4485. Plants–Plant health–Import inspections–Fees

PLANT HEALTH (IMPORT INSPECTION FEES) (WOOD AND BARK) REGULATIONS (NORTHERN IRELAND) 2005, SR 2005 380; made under the Finance Act 1973 s.56; and the European Communities Act 1972 s.2. In force: September 1, 2005; £3.00.

These Regulations implement Art.13d of Council Directive 2000/29 ([2000] OJ L169/1) which requires Member States to charge fees to cover the costs occasioned by the documentary checks, identity checks and plant health checks of imports of specified wood or isolated bark from third countries provided for in Art.13a(1) of the Directive.

4486. Plants–Plant health–Phytophthora ramorum

PLANT HEALTH (PHYTOPHTHORA RAMORUM) ORDER (NORTHERN IRELAND) 2005, SR 2005 23; made under the Plant Health Act (Northern Ireland) 1967 s.2, s.3, s.3B, s.4. In force: February 28, 2005; £3.00.

This Order, which revokes the Plant Health (Phytophthora ramorum) Order (Northern Ireland) 2003 (SR 2003 193), implements Commission Decision 2002/757 ([2002] OJ L252/37) on provisional emergency phytosanitary measures to prevent the introduction into and the spread within the Community of Phytophthora ramorum; Commission Decision 2004/426 ([2004] OJ L189/1) amending Decision 2002/757 on provisional emergency phytosanitary measures to prevent the introduction into and the spread within the Community of Phytophthora ramorum Werres, De Cock & Man in t Veld sp. nov; and Commission Decision 2004/278 ([2004] OJ L87/31) on the Community position on the amendment of the Appendices to Annex 4 to the Agreement between the European Community and the Swiss Confederation on trade in agricultural products. The Order prohibits the introduction and spread of the plant pest Phytophthora ramorum.

4487. Plants–Plant health–Phytophthora ramorum

PLANT HEALTH (PHYTOPHTHORA RAMORUM) (AMENDMENT) ORDER (NORTHERN IRELAND) 2005, SR 2005 265; made under the Plant Health Act (Northern Ireland) 1967 s.2, s.3, s.3B, s.4. In force: June 10, 2005; £3.00.

This Order removes drafting defects from the Plant Health (Phytophthora ramorum) Order (Northern Ireland) 2005 (SR 2005 23).

4488. Plants–Plant health–Phytophthora ramorum

PLANT HEALTH (WOOD AND BARK) (PHYTOPHTHORA RAMORUM) ORDER (NORTHERN IRELAND) 2005, SR 2005 252; made under the Plant Health Act (Northern Ireland) 1967 s.2, s.3, s.3A, s.3B, s.4. In force: May 30, 2005; £3.00.

This Order, which revokes the Plant Health (Wood and Bark) (Phytophthora ramorum) Order (Northern Ireland) 2003 (SR 2003 175), implements Commission Decision 2002/757 ([2002] OJ L252/37) on provisional emergency phytosanitary measures to prevent the introduction into and the spread within the Community of Phytophthora ramorum and Commission Decision 2004/278 ([2004] OJ L87/31) on the Community position on the amendment of the Appendices to Annex 4 to the Agreement between the European Community and the Swiss Confederation on trade in agricultural products. The Order prohibits the introduction into and spread within Northern Ireland of the pest Phytophthora ramorum; and places certain controls on the importation of susceptible wood from the US.

4489. Plants–Plant health–Protected zones

PLANT HEALTH (AMENDMENT) ORDER (NORTHERN IRELAND) 2005, SR 2005 204; made under the Plant Health Act (Northern Ireland) 1967 s.2, s.3, s.3A, s.3B, s.4. In force: April 29, 2005; £3.00.

This Order amends the Plant Health Order (Northern Ireland) 1993 (SR 1993 256) by removing certain townlands previously scheduled as safety zones to protect against spread of potato wart disease. The Order lifts restrictions on the growing of potatoes in the former safety zones.

4490. Plants–Plant protection products–Marketing

PLANT PROTECTION PRODUCTS REGULATIONS (NORTHERN IRELAND) 2005, SR 2005 526; made under the European Communities Act 1972 s.2. In force: January 26, 2006; £4.50.

These Regulations, which revoke the Plant Protection Products Regulations (Northern Ireland) 2004 (SR 2004 126) and the Plant Protection Products (Amendment) Regulations (Northern Ireland) 2004 (SR 2004 411), continue to implement Council Directive 91/414 ([1991] OJ L230/1) concerning the placing of plant protection products on the market; Commission Directive 2004/71 ([2004] OJ L127/104) amending Council Directive 91/414 to include Pseudomonas chlororaphis as active substance; Commission Directive 2004/99 ([2004] OJ L309/60) amending Council Directive 91/414 to include acetamiprid and thiacloprid as active substances; Commission Directive 2005/2 ([2005] OJ L20/15) amending Council Directive 91/414 to include Ampelomyces quisqualis and Gliocladium catenulatum as active substances; Commission Directive 2005/3 ([2005] OJ L20/19) amending Council Directive 91/414 to include imazosulfuron, laminarin, methoxyfenozide and s-metolachlor as active substances; Council Directive 2005/25 ([2005] OJ L90/1) amending Annex VI to Directive 91/414 as regards plant protection products containing micro-organisms; Commission Directive 2005/34 ([2005] OJ L125/5) amending Council Directive 91/414 to include etoxazole and tepraloxydim as active substances; Commission Directive 2005/58 ([2005] OJ L246/17) amending Council Directive 91/414 to include bifenazate and milbemectin as active substances; Commission Directive 2005/53 ([2005] OJ L241/51) amending Council Directive 91/414 to include chlorothalonil, chlorotoluron, cypermethrin, daminozide and thiophanate-methyl as active substances; Commission Directive 2005/54 ([2005] OJ L244/21) amending Council Directive 91/414 to include tribenuron as active substance; Commission Directive 2005/57 ([2005] OJ L246/14) amending Council Directive 91/414 to include MCPA and MCPB as active substances; and Commission Directive 2005/72 ([2005] OJ L279/63) amending Council Directive 91/414 to include chlorpyriphos, chlorpyriphos-methyl, mancozeb, maneb and metiram. The Regulations provide for the authorisation system in Northern Ireland under the operation of the Department of Agriculture and Rural Department; and impose a prohibition on the placing on the market and use of plant protection products unless they have been approved by the Department under the Regulations and are placed on the market and used in accordance with any conditions or requirements specified in their approval.

4491. Potatoes–Marketing–Inspection fees

MARKETING OF POTATOES (AMENDMENT) REGULATIONS (NORTHERN IRELAND) 2005, SR 2005 372; made under the Marketing of Potatoes Act (Northern Ireland) 1964 s.3, s.7, s.11. In force: September 1, 2005; £3.00.

These Regulations, which amend the Marketing of Potatoes Regulations (Northern Ireland) 1989 (SR 1989 221), revoke the Marketing of Potatoes (Amendment) Regulations (Northern Ireland) 2004 (SR 2004 208) and increase the fee payable for the inspection or examination of ware potatoes from £3.75 per tonne or part of a tonne to £3.90 per tonne or part of a tonne.

4492. Potatoes–Seed potatoes–Certification of crops–Fees

SEED POTATOES (CROP FEES) (AMENDMENT) REGULATIONS (NORTHERN IRELAND) 2005, SR 2005 156; made under the Seeds Act (Northern Ireland) 1965 s.1. In force: April 14, 2005; £3.00.

These Regulations, which amend the Seed Potatoes (Crop Fees) Regulations (Northern Ireland) 2004 (SR 2004 181), facilitate the reinstatement of charges for the certification and classification of Pre-basic Tissue Culture potatoes by introducing hourly rates, thus taking into account different methods of growing that do not lend themselves to charging per hectare or half hectare.

4493. Potatoes–Seed potatoes–Inspection fees

SEED POTATOES (TUBER AND LABEL FEES) (AMENDMENT) REGULATIONS (NORTHERN IRELAND) 2005, SR 2005 370; made under the Seeds Act (Northern Ireland) 1965 s.1. In force: September 1, 2005; £3.00.

These Regulations, which amend the Seed Potatoes (Tuber and Label Fees) Regulations (Northern Ireland) 1982 (SR 1982 236), revoke and replace the Seed Potatoes (Tuber and Label Fees) (Amendment) Regulations (Northern Ireland) 2004 (SR 2004 207). The Regulations increase the fee payable for the inspection of seed potatoes from £3.75 per tonne or part of a tonne to £3.90 per tonne or part of a tonne. The fee payable for the provision of official labels, whether or not the details have been printed thereon by the Department, has increased from £0.48 per 20 labels to £0.60 per 20 labels.

4494. Rural areas–Less favoured areas–Compensatory allowances

LESS FAVOURED AREA COMPENSATORY ALLOWANCES REGULATIONS (NORTHERN IRELAND) 2005, SR 2005 106; made under the European Communities Act 1972 s.2. In force: March 14, 2005; £3.00.

These Regulations, which amend the Farm Subsidies (Review of Decisions) Regulations (Northern Ireland) 2001 (SR 2001 391), implement Commission Regulation 817/2004 ([2004] OJ L153/30) laying down detailed rules for the application of Council Regulation 1257/1999. They also implement Measure 2 of the Northern Ireland Rural Development Programme. The Regulations define the conditions of eligibility for less favoured area compensatory allowance and the rates at which it is to be paid; provide for the exclusion of forage area in respect of claimants who held milk quota at March 31, 2004; confer powers of entry and inspection on persons authorised by the Department of Agriculture and Rural Development; and create offences of making false or misleading statements and of obstructing persons authorised by the Department.

4495. Waste management–Farm animals–Grants

FARM NUTRIENT MANAGEMENT SCHEME (NORTHERN IRELAND) 2005, SR 2005 5; made under the Agriculture and Fisheries (Financial Assistance) (Northern Ireland) Order 1987 (SI 1987 166 (NI.1)) Art.16. In force: January 16, 2005; £3.00.

These Regulations revoke the Farm Nutrient Management Scheme (Northern Ireland) 2004 (SR 2004 498). The Scheme allows the Department of Agriculture and Rural Development to pay grant for the provision, and replacement of facilities to collect and store farm animal waste and farm effluent and for the separation of rainwater from farm waste. The grant is available at a rate of 40 per cent on the first £85,000 of eligible expenditure incurred by an agricultural business for this purpose. The Scheme also allows for financial limits on the amount of grant payable and provides for the consideration of applications for grant during a given period to be suspended if those limits are breached. It also allows for applications for grant to be rejected once the financial resources available for the Scheme are exhausted. Before grant is paid, the expenditure to which it relates must be approved by the Department and there are restrictions on the approval of certain types of expenditure and further restrictions on the making of grant. The procedure for claiming grant is determined by the Department.

4496. Waste management–Farm animals–Grants

FARM NUTRIENT MANAGEMENT (AMENDMENT) SCHEME (NORTHERN IRELAND) 2005, SR 2005 407; made under the Agriculture and Fisheries (Financial Assistance) (Northern Ireland) Order 1987 (SI 1987 166 (NI.1)) Art.16. In force: September 29, 2005; £3.00.

This Scheme amends the Farm Nutrient Management Scheme (Northern Ireland) 2005 (SR 2005 5) and increases the rate of grant available from 40 per cent to 60 per cent on the first £85,000 of eligible expenditure incurred by an agricultural business for this purpose.

ANIMALS

4497. Animal health–Diseases and disorders–Infectious disease control–Preventive measures

AVIAN INFLUENZA (PREVENTIVE MEASURES) REGULATIONS (NORTHERN IRELAND) 2005, SR 2005 485; made under the European Communities Act 1972 s.2. In force: November 4, 2005; £3.00.

These Regulations give effect to Commission Decision 2005/734 ([2005] OJ L274/105) laying down biosecurity measures to reduce the risk of transmission of highly pathogenic avian influenza caused by Influenza virus A subtype H5N1 from birds living in the wild to poultry and other captive birds and providing for an early detection system in areas at particular risk. The Regulations require the Department to evaluate the risk of the transmission of avian influenza virus and to take appropriate measures to reduce that risk through the establishment of preventative zones and restricted premises.

4498. Animal health–Diseases and disorders–Infectious disease control–Zoos

AVIAN INFLUENZA (PREVENTIVE MEASURES IN ZOOS) REGULATIONS (NORTHERN IRELAND) 2005, SR 2005 486; made under the European Communities Act 1972 s.2. In force: November 4, 2005; £3.00.

These Regulations bring into force Commission Decision 2005/744 ([2005] OJ L279/75) laying down the requirements for the prevention of highly pathogenic avian influenza caused by influenza A virus of subtype H5N1 in susceptible birds kept in zoos in the Member States. They require the Department to evaluate the risk of the transmission of avian influenza virus to susceptible birds in zoos and to take appropriate measures to reduce such risk.

4499. Animal health–Infectious disease control–Laying flocks

SALMONELLA IN LAYING FLOCKS (SURVEY POWERS) REGULATIONS (NORTHERN IRELAND) 2005, SR 2005 132; made under the European Communities Act 1972 s.2. In force: April 18, 2005; £3.00.

These Regulations revoke the Salmonella in Laying Flocks (Survey Powers) Regulations (Northern Ireland) 2004 (SR 2004 525) to correct errors in the interpretation and offences provisions and make other minor drafting changes. The Regulations designate the Department for the purpose of selecting premises for sampling and give inspectors the powers required for selecting premises for sampling; provide powers for inspectors to enter premises for the purposes of the Commission Decision and for the purpose of enforcement of these Regulations; provide powers for inspectors to examine and retain records, take equipment and vehicles on to the premises, be accompanied by other persons, and request information, documentation and assistance, for the purpose of carrying out sampling; and prescribe offences and penalties.

4500. Feedingstuffs–Zootechnical products

FEEDINGSTUFFS (ZOOTECHNICAL PRODUCTS) (AMENDMENT) REGULATIONS (NORTHERN IRELAND) 2005, SR 2005 183; made under the European Communities Act 1972 s.2. In force: April 1, 2005; £3.00.

These Regulations amend the Feedingstuffs (Zootechnical Products) Regulations 1 (SI 1 1871) to provide for new fees payable for applications for the approval of, and subsequent official checks carried out at, premises manufacturing zootechnical additives, premixtures and/or feedingstuffs incorporating zootechnical additives or premixtures and premises exercising intermediary activities.

4501. Feedingstuffs–Zootechnical products

MEDICATED FEEDINGSTUFFS (AMENDMENT) REGULATIONS (NORTHERN IRELAND) 2005, SR 2005 184; made under the European Communities Act 1972 s.2. In force: April 1, 2005; £3.00.

These Regulations amend the Medicated Feedingstuffs Regulations 1998 (SI 1998 1046) to provide for new fees payable for applications in respect of the approval, or renewal of approval, of premises manufacturing authorised intermediate products; premises manufacturing medicated feedingstuffs incorporating medicated pre-mixes; and distributors of medicated feedingstuffs.

4502. Import controls–Cats and dogs–Rabies

RABIES (IMPORTATION OF DOGS, CATS AND OTHER MAMMALS) (AMENDMENT) ORDER (NORTHERN IRELAND) 2005, SR 2005 275; made under the Diseases of Animals (Northern Ireland) Order 1981 (SI 1981 1115 (NI.22)) Art.29, Art.60, Art.62, Sch.6 para.2. In force: June 20, 2005; £3.00.

This Order amends the Rabies (Importation of Dogs, Cats and Other Mammals) Order (Northern Ireland) 1977 (SR 1977 113) to extend exemptions from the requirement for a licence to import certain animals into Northern Ireland and to permit the free movement between England and Northern Ireland of any animal brought into England in accordance with the provisions of European Parliament and Council Regulation 998/2003 ([2003] OJ L146/1) on the animal health requirements applicable to the non-commercial movement of pet animals and amending Council Directive 92/65, and the Non-Commercial Movement of Pet Animals (England) Regulations 2004 (SI 2004 2362).

4503. Sheep and goats—Identification

SHEEP AND GOATS (RECORDS, IDENTIFICATION AND MOVEMENT) ORDER (NORTHERN IRELAND) 2005, SR 2005 535; made under the Diseases of Animals (Northern Ireland) Order 1981 (SI 1981 1115 (NI.22)) Art.5, Art.19, Art.44, Art.60. In force: December 1, 2005; £3.50.

This Order, which revokes the Identification and Movement of Sheep and Goats Order (Northern Ireland) 2004 (SR 2004 491), makes provision for the administration and enforcement of Council Regulation 21/2004 ([2004] OJ L5/8) establishing a system for the identification and registration of ovine and caprine animals and amending Regulation 1782/2003 and Directives 92/102 and 64/432. It deals with the notification of holdings, eartags and the identification of animals.

ARBITRATION

4504. Unfair arbitration agreements—Specified amounts

UNFAIR ARBITRATION AGREEMENTS (SPECIFIED AMOUNT) ORDER (NORTHERN IRELAND) 2005, SR 2005 219; made under the Arbitration Act 1996 s.91. In force: June 1, 2005; £3.00.

This Order, which revokes with saving the Unfair Arbitration Agreements (Specified Amount) Order (Northern Ireland) 1996 (SR 1996 598), specifies the amount of £5,000 for the purposes of the Arbitration Act 1996 s.91. However the new amount will only apply in relation to any arbitration agreement entered into after this Order comes into operation. The old amount will continue to apply in relation to any arbitration agreement entered into before that date.

CIVIL PROCEDURE

4505. Books

Expert Witness Directory of Ireland. Paperback: £55.00. ISBN 0 421 92120 X. Sweet & Maxwell.

COMPANY LAW

4506. Accounts—Directors remuneration—Reports

DIRECTORS' REMUNERATION REPORT REGULATIONS (NORTHERN IRELAND) 2005, SR 2005 56; made under the Companies (Northern Ireland) Order 1986 (SI 1986 1032 (NI.6)) Art.265. In force: March 30, 2005; £3.50.

The Companies (Northern Ireland) Order 1986 (SI 1986 1032 (NI.6)) requires a company to produce certain information concerning directors' remuneration by way of notes to the company's accounts. These Regulations, which amend the 1986 Order, exempt a quoted company from most of the requirements contained in Part I of Schedule 6 and instead require such a company to set out a large part of the information concerning directors' remuneration in the directors' remuneration report.

4507. Accounts—Directors reports—Financial reviews

COMPANIES (1986 ORDER) (OPERATING AND FINANCIAL REVIEW AND DIRECTORS' REPORT ETC.) REGULATIONS (NORTHERN IRELAND) 2005, SR

2005 61; made under the Companies (Northern Ireland) Order 1986 (SI 1986 1032 (NI.6)) Art.265. In force: March 31, 2005; £3.00.

These Regulations amend the Companies (Northern Ireland) Order 1986 (SI 1986 1032 (NI.6)) on accounts and audit in order to introduce a new requirement for directors of quoted companies to prepare operating and financial reviews for financial years; implement requirements relating to the directors' report in European Parliament and Council Directive 2003/51 ([2003] OJ L178/16) amending Council Directives 78/660, 83/349, 86/635 and 91/674 on the annual and consolidated accounts of certain types of companies, banks and other financial institutions and insurance undertakings.

4508. Accounts–Summary financial statements–Directors remuneration

COMPANIES (SUMMARY FINANCIAL STATEMENT) (AMENDMENT) REGULATIONS (NORTHERN IRELAND) 2005, SR 2005 57; made under the Companies (Northern Ireland) Order 1986 (SI 1986 1032 (NI.6)) Art.259. In force: March 30, 2005; £3.00.

These Regulations amend the Companies (Summary Financial Statement) Regulations (Northern Ireland) 1996 (SR 1996 179) following the introduction by the Directors' Remuneration Report Regulations (Northern Ireland) 2005 (SR 2005 56) of a requirement that certain companies should produce a directors' remuneration report. Certain of those companies which are permitted under the Companies (Northern Ireland) Order 1986 (SI 1986 1032 (NI.6)) to produce a Summary Financial Statement will fall within the category of companies required to produce a directors' remuneration report. The Regulations expand the disclosure required in a Summary Financial Statement to include either the whole or a summary of certain information concerning directors' remuneration contained in the notes to the accounts and in the directors' remuneration report.

4509. Companies (Audit, Investigations and Community Enterprise) (Northern Ireland) Order 2005 (SI 2005 1967 (NI.17))

This Order amends the law relating to company auditors and accounts, to the provision that may be made in respect of certain liabilities incurred by a company's directors, and to company investigations. It also makes provision for community interest companies.

4510. Company Directors Disqualification (Amendment) (Northern Ireland) Order 2005 (SI 2005 1454 (NI.9))

This Order, which amends the Company Directors Disqualification (Northern Ireland) Order 2002 (SI 2002 3150), empowers the High Court to disqualify a person for being a company director if a company of which he is a director commits a breach of competition law and the Court considers that his conduct as a director makes him unfit to be concerned in the management of a company.

4511. Company Directors Disqualification (Amendment) (Northern Ireland) Order 2005 (SI 2005 1454 (NI.9))–Commencement Order

COMPANY DIRECTORS DISQUALIFICATION (AMENDMENT) (2005 ORDER) (COMMENCEMENT) ORDER (NORTHERN IRELAND) 2005, SR 2005 514 (C.36); made under the Company Directors Disqualification (Amendment) (Northern Ireland) Order 2005 (SI 2005 1454 (NI.9)) Art.1. Commencement details: bringing into force various provisions of the 2005 Order on December 19, 2005; £3.00.

This Order brings the Company Directors Disqualification (Amendment) (Northern Ireland) Order 2005 (SI 2005 1454 (NI.9)) fully into operation. The 2005 Order amends the Company Directors Disqualification (Northern Ireland) Order 2002 (SI 2002 3150 (NI.4)) and empowers the High Court to disqualify a person from being a company director if a company of which he is a director commits a breach of competition law and the Court considers that his conduct as a director makes him unfit to be concerned in the management of a company.

4512. Register of companies–Contracts–Stamp duty

STAMP DUTY (CONSEQUENTIAL AMENDMENT OF ENACTMENTS) (NORTHERN IRELAND) REGULATIONS 2005, SI 2005 1634; made under the Finance Act 2003 Sch.20 para.7. In force: July 7, 2005; £3.00.

These Regulations make amendments to the Companies (Northern Ireland) Order 1986 (SI 1986 1032 (NI.6)) consequent upon the Finance Act 2003 Part 4 and the abolition of stamp duty, except on instruments relating to stock or marketable securities. They make amendments to remove the requirement to stamp the prescribed particulars of a contract which a company is required to deliver to the registrar of companies.

CONSTITUTIONAL LAW

4513. Constitutional Reform Act 2005 (c.4)–Commencement No.1 Order

CONSTITUTIONAL REFORM ACT 2005 (COMMENCEMENT NO.1) ORDER 2005, SI 2005 1431 (C.61); made under the Constitutional Reform Act 2005 s.148. Commencement details: bringing into force various provisions of the 2005 Act on June 15, 2005; £3.00.

This Order brings into force the Constitutional Reform Act 2005 s.123 (except to the extent that it inserts a new subsection 5A(6) into the Justice (Northern Ireland) Act 2002) and s.132.

4514. Constitutional Reform Act 2005 (c.4)–Commencement No.2 Order

CONSTITUTIONAL REFORM ACT 2005 (COMMENCEMENT NO.2) ORDER 2005, SI 2005 2284 (C.96); made under the Constitutional Reform Act 2005 s.148. Commencement details: bringing into force various provisions of the 2005 Act on August 31, 2005; £3.00.

This Order brings into force the Constitutional Reform Act 2005 s.15(2), Sch.5 para.122(4) and Sch.5 para.126(4).

4515. Northern Ireland Assembly–Powers during suspension

NORTHERN IRELAND ACT 2000 (MODIFICATION) (NO.2) ORDER 2005, SI 2005 2046; made under the Northern Ireland Act 2000 Sch.para.1. In force: July 22, 2005; £3.00.

While the Northern Ireland Act 2000 s.1 is in force, with the effect that the Northern Ireland Assembly is suspended, Sch. para.1 allows legislation by Order in Council for any matter for which the Assembly may legislate under the terms of the Northern Ireland Act 1998. This power to legislate by Order in Council is limited to the first six months of any period during which the 2000 Act s.1 is in force but may be extended by Order for a further period of up to six months at a time. The 2000 Act s.1 was brought into force again by the Northern Ireland Act (Suspension of Devolved Government) Order 2002 (SI 2002 2574) on October 15, 2002. The six month period beginning on October 15, 2002 has been extended by four further six month periods. This Order extends the period which would apart from this Order expire at the end of October 14, 2005 by a further six months until the end of April 14, 2006. The power to legislate by Order in Council will, however, lapse if the Assembly is restored before that date.

4516. **Northern Ireland Assembly–Suspension of devolved government–Modifications**

NORTHERN IRELAND ACT 2000 (MODIFICATION) ORDER 2005, SI 2005 868; made under the Northern Ireland Act 2000 Sch.para.1. In force: March 19, 2005; £3.00.

While the Northern Ireland Act 2000 s.1 is in force, with the effect that the Northern Ireland Assembly is suspended, Sch. para.1 allows legislation by Order in Council for any matter for which the Assembly may legislate under the terms of the Northern Ireland Act 1998. This power to legislate by Order in Council is limited to the first six months of any period during which the 2000 Act s.1 is in force but may be extended by Order for a further period of up to six months at a time. The 2000 Act s.1 was brought into force again by the Northern Ireland Act (Suspension of Devolved Government) Order 2002 (SI 2002 2574) on October 15, 2002. The six month period beginning on October 15, 2002 has been extended by four further six month periods. This Order extends the period which would apart from this Order expire at the end of April 14, 2005 by a further six months until the end of October 14, 2005. The power to legislate by Order in Council will, however, lapse if the Assembly is restored before that date.

4517. **Weapons–Decommissioning scheme–Amnesty period**

NORTHERN IRELAND ARMS DECOMMISSIONING ACT 1997 (AMNESTY PERIOD) ORDER 2005, SI 2005 418; made under the Northern Ireland Arms Decommissioning Act 1997 s.2. In force: February 25, 2005; £3.00.

Under the Northern Ireland Arms Decommissioning Act 1997 a decommissioning scheme must identify a period during which firearms, ammunition and explosives may be dealt with in accordance with the scheme. The 1997 Act was amended by the Northern Ireland Arms Decommissioning (Amendment) Act 2002. Under the 1997 Act, as amended, the day appointed by Order must be no more than twelve months after the date on which the Order was made and no later than February 27, 2003 or such later date as the Secretary of State may from time to time appoint. The Northern Ireland Arms Decommissioning Act 1997 (Amnesty Period) Order 2004 (SI 2004 464) appointed February 25, 2005 as the day before which the amnesty period identified in a decommissioning scheme must end. This Order appoints February 24, 2006 as the day before which the amnesty period identified in a decommissioning scheme must end.

CONSTRUCTION LAW

4518. **Building regulations–European standards–Testing**

BUILDING (AMENDMENT) REGULATIONS (NORTHERN IRELAND) 2005, SR 2005 295; made under the Building Regulations (Northern Ireland) Order 1979 (SI 1979 1709 (NI.16)) Art.3, Art.5, Sch.1 para.4, Sch.1 para.22. In force: October 3, 2005; £3.00.

These Regulations amend the Building Regulations (Northern Ireland) 2000 (SR 2000 389) to expand the definition of internal linings to include products and to extend the requirements relating to internal linings to include low rate of fire growth. These changes give recognition to testing to European standards.

4519. **Construction Industry Training Board–Levy on employers**

INDUSTRIAL TRAINING LEVY (CONSTRUCTION INDUSTRY) ORDER (NORTHERN IRELAND) 2005, SR 2005 294; made under the Industrial Training (Northern Ireland) Order 1984 (SI 1984 1159 (NI.9)) Art.23, Art.24. In force: August 31, 2005; £3.00.

This Order gives effect to proposals submitted by the Construction Industry Training Board to the Department for Employment and Learning for the imposition of a further levy upon employers in the construction industry for the purpose of raising money towards the expenses of the Board.

CONSUMER LAW

4520. Weights and measures–Equipment–British standards

WEIGHTS AND MEASURES (STANDARDS AMENDMENT) REGULATIONS (NORTHERN IRELAND) 2005, SR 2005 26; made under the Weights and Measures (Northern Ireland) Order 1981 (SI 1981 231 (NI.10)) Art.13. In force: March 1, 2005; £3.00.

These Regulations amend the Measuring Equipment (Liquid Fuel by Road Tanker) Regulations (Northern Ireland) 1984 (SR 1984 117), the Measuring Equipment (Measures of Length) Regulations (Northern Ireland) 1986 (SR 1986 308), the Weighing Equipment (Filling and Discontinuous Totalising Automatic Weighing Machines) Regulations (Northern Ireland) 1986 (SR 1986 311), the Capacity Serving Measures (Intoxicating Liquor) Regulations (Northern Ireland) 1993 (SR 1993 441), the Measuring Equipment (Capacity Measures) Regulations (Northern Ireland) 1998 (SR 1998 48), and the Measuring Equipment (Liquid Fuel and Lubricants) (Northern Ireland) Regulations 1998 (SR 1998 113). They amend references in the weights and measures Regulations to the standard EN 45001 which is replaced by a new standard, BS EN ISO/IEC 17025:2000 and make it clear in the case of each of the Regulations amended, an approved body is a body which has been accredited in relation to the specific product to which those Regulations apply.

4521. Weights and measures–Equipment–Fees

MEASURING INSTRUMENTS (EEC REQUIREMENTS) (VERIFICATION FEES) REGULATIONS (NORTHERN IRELAND) 2005, SR 2005 117; made under the Finance Act 1973 s.56. In force: April 18, 2005; £3.00.

These Regulations revoke with saving the Measuring Instruments (EEC Requirements) (Verification Fees) Regulations (Northern Ireland) 2003 (SR 2003 491) and prescribe the fees to be paid in respect of EC verification under the Measuring Instruments (EEC Requirements) Regulations 1988 and the Non-automatic Weighing Instruments Regulations 2000 and increase them by an average of 14 per cent.

4522. Weights and measures–Equipment–Filling instruments

WEIGHING EQUIPMENT (AUTOMATIC GRAVIMETRIC FILLING INSTRUMENTS) REGULATIONS (NORTHERN IRELAND) 2005, SR 2005 27; made under the Weights and Measures (Northern Ireland) Order 1981 (SI 1981 231 (NI.10)) Art.13. In force: March 1, 2005; £3.00.

These Regulations amend the Weighing Equipment (Filling and Discontinuous Totalising Automatic Weighing Machines) Regulations (Northern Ireland) 1986 (SR 1986 311) and implement, in Northern Ireland, International Recommendation OIML R 61 of the Organisation Internationale de Metrologie Legale relating to automatic gravimetric filling instruments, to the extent that the Recommendation applies to such instruments following the grant or renewal of a certificate of approval of a pattern by the Department under the Weights and Measures (Northern Ireland) Order 1981 (SI 1981 231 (NI.10)) Art.10.

4523. Weights and measures–Fit for use–Fees

WEIGHTS AND MEASURES (PASSING AS FIT FOR USE FOR TRADE AND ADJUSTMENT FEES) REGULATIONS (NORTHERN IRELAND) 2005, SR 2005

118; made under theWeights and Measures (Northern Ireland) Order 1981 (SI 1981 231 (NI.10)) Art.9, Art.43. In force: April 18, 2005; £3.00.

These Regulations revoke with saving theWeights and Measures (Passing as Fit for Use forTrade and Adjustment Fees) Regulations (Northern Ireland) 2003 (SR 2003 492) and prescribe the fees to be paid in having certain weighing or measuring equipment passed as fit for use for trade by inspectors of weights and measures and for the adjustment by them of weights and measures.

4524. Weights and measures–Measuring equipment–Testing

MEASURING EQUIPMENT (LIQUID FUEL AND LUBRICANTS) (AMENDMENT) REGULATIONS (NORTHERN IRELAND) 2005, SR 2005 472; made under the Weights and Measures (Northern Ireland) Order 1981 (SI 1981 231 (NI.10)) Art.9, Art.13. In force: December 5, 2005; £3.00.

These Regulations, which amend the Measuring Equipment (Liquid Fuel and Lubricants) Regulations (Northern Ireland) 1998 (SR 1998 113), prescribe the tests an inspector of weights and measures shall apply to measuring equipment with a view to passing it as fit for use for trade and stamping it.

4525. Weights and measures–Miscellaneous foods

WEIGHTS AND MEASURES (MISCELLANEOUS FOODS) (AMENDMENT) ORDER (NORTHERN IRELAND) 2005, SR 2005 516; made under the Weights and Measures (Northern Ireland) Order 1981 (SI 1981 231 (NI.10)) Art.19. In force: December 19, 2005; £3.00.

This Order amends the Weights and Measures (Miscellaneous Foods) Order (Northern Ireland) 1989 (SR 1989 69) which requires that certain foods are pre-packed only in the quantities prescribed. This Order gives effect to the judgment of the European Court of Justice in Case C-3/99 Cidrerie Ruwet SA v Cidre Stassen SA and HP Bulmer Ltd by exempting from that requirement imports into Northern Ireland (whether directly or indirectly through Great Britain) of pre-packed foods made up in a quantity which is not specified in Schedule 1 to the 1989 Order from a Member State of the European Community, or one of the other States in the European Economic Area, provided that it is lawful to sell such packages in that quantity in that other State.

CRIMINAL LAW

4526. Controlled drugs–Medical purposes

MISUSE OF DRUGS (AMENDMENT) (NO.2) REGULATIONS (NORTHERN IRELAND) 2005, SR 2005 360; made under the Misuse of Drugs Act 1971 s.7, s.10, s.22, s.31. In force: August 8, 2005; £3.00.

These Regulations amend the Misuse of Drugs Regulations (Northern Ireland) 2002 (SR 2002 1) to provides that the Misuse of Drugs Act 1971 s.5(1), which makes it unlawful for a person to have a controlled drug in his possession, will not apply to a fungus (of any kind) containing psilocin or an ester of psilocin (commonly known as magic mushrooms) in certain circumstances.

4527. Controlled drugs–Medical purposes

MISUSE OF DRUGS (DESIGNATION) (AMENDMENT) ORDER (NORTHERN IRELAND) 2005, SR 2005 359; made under the Misuse of Drugs Act 1971 s.7. In force: August 8, 2005; £3.00.

The Misuse of Drugs Act 1971 requires regulations to be made to allow the use for medical purposes of the drugs which are subject to control under the 1971 Act. This Order amends the Misuse of Drugs (Designation) Order (Northern Ireland) 2001 (SR 2001 431) by inserting into Part 1 of the Schedule to that Order a fungus of any kind which contains psilocin or an ester of psilocin (commonly known as magic mushrooms) and thereby designates such a fungus for the purposes of the 1971 Act.

4528. Drink driving offences–Rehabilitation orders–Experimental period–Termination of restrictions

COURSES FOR DRINK-DRIVE OFFENDERS (EXPERIMENTAL PERIOD) (TERMINATION OF RESTRICTIONS) ORDER (NORTHERN IRELAND) 2005, SR 2005 481; made under the Road Traffic (Offenders) (Northern Ireland) Order 1996 (SI 1996 1320 (NI.10)) Art.39. In force: December 31, 2005; £3.00.

The Road Traffic Offenders (Northern Ireland) Order 1996 Article 36, empowers a court to make an order requiring a person who has been convicted of a drink-drive offence to attend a rehabilitation course. Art.39(1) of that Order, as subsequently modified by order, restricts the exercise of this power to an experimental period terminating at the end of 2005, and during that period to the trial of certain offences in designated courts, unless those restrictions are removed by an order made under paragraph (2). This Order removes the restriction.

4529. Drugs–Controlled drugs–Supplementary prescribers

MISUSE OF DRUGS (AMENDMENT) REGULATIONS (NORTHERN IRELAND) 2005, SR 2005 119; made under the Misuse of Drugs Act 1971 s.7, s.10, s.22, s.31. In force: April 11, 2005; £3.00.

These Regulations amend the Misuse of Drugs Regulations (Northern Ireland) 2002 (SR 2002 1) to make provision for supplementary prescribers (a first level nurse, pharmacist or registered midwife who satisfies certain conditions); to insert a definition of "clinical management plan" and "supplementary prescriber"; and to provide that the term "prescription" includes a prescription issued by a supplementary prescriber for the medical treatment of a single individual.

4530. Firearms–Appeals and applications

FIREARMS (APPEALS AND APPLICATIONS) REGULATIONS (NORTHERN IRELAND) 2005, SR 2005 3; made under the Firearms (Northern Ireland) Order 2004 (SI 2004 702 (NI.3)) Art.2, Art.63, Art.74, Art.80. In force: February 1, 2005; £3.00.

These Regulations, which revoke the Firearms (Appeals and Applications) Regulations (Northern Ireland) 1990 (SR & O 1990 128), prescribe the procedure for making appeals to the Secretary of State regarding decisions of the Chief Constable made under the Firearms (Northern Ireland) Order 2004 (SI 2004 702 (NI.3)) and with applications to the Secretary of State for the removal of statutory prohibition on the holding of firearms and ammunition.

4531. Firearms (Amendment) (Northern Ireland) Order 2005 (SI 2005 1966 (NI.16))

This Order, which amends the Firearms (Northern Ireland) Order 2004 (SI 2004 702 (NI.3)), provides that air guns which use a self-contained gas cartridge system are prohibited. It amends the power to add to the list of prohibited weapons; and provides that carrying air guns or imitation firearms in a public place is an offence and adds it to the list of offences for which there is a power of summary arrest.

4532. Firearms (Northern Ireland) Order 2004 (SI 2004 702 (NI.3))–Commencement and Transitional Provisions Order

FIREARMS (NORTHERN IRELAND) ORDER 2004 (COMMENCEMENT AND TRANSITIONAL PROVISIONS) ORDER 2005, SR 2005 4 (C.1); made under the Firearms (Northern Ireland) Order 2004 (SI 2004 702 (NI.3)) Art.1, Art.80, Art.81.

In force: bringing into operation various provisions of the 2004 Order on February 1, 2005; £3.00.

This Order commences the provisions of the Firearms (Northern Ireland) Order 2004 (SI 2004 702 (NI.3)) in so far as they did not come into operation in accordance with the Order.

4533. Road traffic offences–Speed detection devices

ROAD TRAFFIC OFFENDERS (PRESCRIBED DEVICES) ORDER (NORTHERN IRELAND) 2005, SR 2005 263; made under the Road Traffic (Offenders) (Northern Ireland) Order 1996 (SI 1996 1320 (NI.10)) Art.23. In force: June 30, 2005; £3.00.

This Order prescribes a speed detection device for the purposes of the Road Traffic Offenders (Northern Ireland) Order 1996 Art.23 (speeding offences etc: admissibility of certain evidence). The device prescribed captures and records images of motor vehicles at two positions on the road and calculates the average speed of the vehicles between those positions.

4534. Terrorism–Terrorism Act 2000 Part VII–Continuation period

TERRORISM ACT 2000 (CONTINUANCE OF PART VII) ORDER 2005, SI 2005 350; made under the Terrorism Act 2000 s.112. In force: February 19, 2005; £3.00.

This Order continues in force for a further period of twelve months the provisions of the Terrorism Act 2000 Part VII (which extend to Northern Ireland only) with the exception of specified provisions.

4535. Unauthorised Encampments (Northern Ireland) Order 2005 (SI 2005 1961 (NI.11))

This Order makes provision for the removal by the police of trespassers on land in certain circumstances.

4536. Books

Walsh, Kathleen Moore; Hanly, Conor–Make That Grade Irish Criminal Law. Paperback: £14.99. ISBN 0 7171 3744 9. Gill & Macmillan.

CRIMINAL PROCEDURE

4537. Codes of practice–Criminal investigations

CRIMINAL PROCEDURE AND INVESTIGATIONS ACT 1996 (CODE OF PRACTICE) (NORTHERN IRELAND) ORDER 2005, SI 2005 2692; made under the Criminal Procedure and Investigations Act 1996 s.25. In force: July 15, 2005; £3.00.

This Order appoints July 15, 2005 as the day on which the revised code of practice prepared under the Criminal Procedure and Investigations Act 1996 s.23 and laid before each House of Parliament on May 25, 2005 is brought into operation in Northern Ireland. The code of practice, which contains provisions relating to the conduct of criminal investigations, applies in relation to suspected or alleged offences into which no criminal investigation has begun before the day on which the code comes into operation. The code brought into operation by this Order replaces the one brought into operation by the Criminal Procedure and Investigations Act 1996 (Code of Practice) (Northern Ireland) Order 1997 (SI 1997 3047) which is revoked.

4538. Court of Appeal–Prosecution appeals–Procedure

CRIMINAL APPEAL (PROSECUTION APPEALS) RULES (NORTHERN IRELAND) 2005, SR 2005 159; made under the Criminal Justice (Northern Ireland) Order 2004 (SI 2004 1500 (NI.9)) Art.32. In force: April 18, 2005; £3.00.

These Rules prescribe the procedures which apply in the Court of Appeal in relation to prosecution appeals under the Criminal Justice (Northern Ireland) Order 2004 (SI 2004 1500 (NI.9)) Art.17.

4539. Criminal appeals–Bad character evidence

CRIMINAL APPEAL (AMENDMENT) (NORTHERN IRELAND) RULES 2005, SR 2005 157; made under the Judicature (Northern Ireland) Act 1978 s.55; and the Criminal Justice (Evidence) (Northern Ireland) Order 2004 (SI 2004 1501 (NI.10)) Art.16, Art.35. In force: April 18, 2005; £3.00.

These Rules, which amend the Criminal Appeal (Northern Ireland) Rules 1968 (SR & O 1968 218), prescribe the procedure relating to applications to adduce bad character evidence; prescribe the procedure relating to the giving of notice of intention to adduce hearsay evidence; and take account of a number of amendments made to the Criminal Appeal (Northern Ireland) Act 1980 by the Courts Act 2003.

4540. Criminal Justice (Northern Ireland) Order 2005 (SI 2005 1965 (NI.15))

This Order amends the Prison Act (Northern Ireland) 1953, the Treatment of Offenders Act (Northern Ireland) 1968, the Magistrates' Courts (Northern Ireland) Order 1981 (SI 1981 1675 (NI.26)), the Police and Criminal Evidence (Northern Ireland) Order 1989 (SI 1989 1341 (NI.12)), the Road Traffic (Northern Ireland) Order 1995 (SI 1995 2994 (NI.18)), the Juries (Northern Ireland) Order 1996 (SI 1996 1141 (NI.6)), the Proceeds of Crime (Northern Ireland) Order 1996 (SI 1996 1299 (NI.9)), the Road Traffic Offenders (Northern Ireland) Order 1996 (SI 1996 1320 (NI.10)), the Employment Rights (Northern Ireland) Order 1996 (SI 1996 1919 (NI.16)), the Criminal Justice (Children) (Northern Ireland) Order 1998 (SI 1998 1504 (NI.9)), the Freedom of Information Act 2000, the Life Sentences (Northern Ireland) Order 2001 (SI 2001 2564 (NI.2)), the Justice (Northern Ireland) Act 2002, the Proceeds of Crime Act 2002, the Extradition Act 2003, the Access to Justice (Northern Ireland) Order 2003 (SI 2003 435 (NI.10)), the Prison (Amendment) (Northern Ireland) Order 2004 (SI 2004 704 (NI.5)) and the Anti-social Behaviour (Northern Ireland) Order 2004 (SI 2004 1988 (NI.12)). The Order makes miscellaneous amendments to criminal justice legislation, including amendments relating to anti-social behaviour orders, the administration of prisons and young offenders centres, the proceeds of crime and road traffic offences.

4541. Crown Court–Bad character and hearsay evidence–Applications procedure

CROWN COURT (AMENDMENT) RULES (NORTHERN IRELAND) 2005, SR 2005 80; made under the Judicature (Northern Ireland) Act 1978 s.52; and the Criminal Justice (Evidence) (Northern Ireland) Order 2004 (SI 2004 1501 (NI.10)) Art.16, Art.35. In force: April 18, 2005; £3.00.

These Rules amend the Crown Court Rules (Northern Ireland) Rules 1979 (SR 1979 90) to prescribe the procedure relating to applications to adduce evidence of bad character under the Criminal Justice (Evidence) (Northern Ireland) Order 2004 (SI 2004 1501 (NI.10)); and notice of intention to adduce hearsay evidence under that Order.

4542. Crown Court–Prosecution appeals–Procedure

CROWN COURT (PROSECUTION APPEALS) RULES (NORTHERN IRELAND) 2005, SR 2005 79; made under the Judicature (Northern Ireland) Act 1978 s.52;

and the Criminal Justice (Northern Ireland) Order 2004 (SI 2004 1500 (NI.9))
Art.32. In force: April 18, 2005; £3.00.

These Rules prescribe the procedures which apply in the Crown Court in relation
to prosecution appeals under the Criminal Justice (Northern Ireland) Order 2004
(SI 2004 1500 (NI.9)) Art.17. The 2004 Order provides for a prosecution right of
appeal to the Court of Appeal against rulings by a judge of the Crown Court, made
at any time (whether before or after the commencement of the trial) before the
judge starts his summing-up to the jury, that have the effect of terminating the
trial. The Rules make provision in relation to a request by the prosecution for an
adjournment to consider whether to appeal in respect of a ruling; prescribe the
manner in which such a request shall be made and the period for which the case
shall be adjourned; prescribe the manner in which the prosecution shall inform the
judge of its intention to appeal and provides for the making of an oral application for
leave to appeal; make provision for the procedure to be applied when determining
whether an appeal should be expedited; prescribe the manner in which documents
required to be served under these Rules may be served; and make transitional
provision in relation to the definition of a "public interest ruling".

4543. Forfeiture–Reciprocal enforcement

CRIMINAL JUSTICE (INTERNATIONAL CO-OPERATION) ACT 1990
(ENFORCEMENT OF OVERSEAS FORFEITURE ORDERS) (NORTHERN
IRELAND) ORDER 2005, SI 2005 3179; made under the Criminal Justice
(International Co-operation) Act 1990 s.9. In force: December 31, 2005; £4.00.

This Order makes provision in respect of the enforcement in Northern Ireland of
Orders made in designated countries for the forfeiture of anything in respect of
which an offence has been committed or which was used in connection with the
commission of such an offence. It revokes the Criminal Justice (International Co-
operation) Act 1990 (Enforcement of Overseas Forfeiture Orders) (Northern
Ireland) Order 1991 (SI 1991 1464), the Criminal Justice (International Co-
operation) Act 1990 (Enforcement of Overseas Forfeiture Orders)
(Amendment) Order 1992 (SI 1992 1721), the Criminal Justice (International Co-
operation) Act 1990 (Enforcement of Overseas Forfeiture Orders) (Amendment)
Order 1993 (SI 1993 1791), the Criminal Justice (International Co-operation) Act
1990 (Enforcement of Overseas Forfeiture Orders) (Amendment) (No.2) Order
1993 (SI 1993 3148), the Criminal Justice (International Co-operation) Act 1990
(Enforcement of Overseas Forfeiture Orders) (Amendment) Order 1994 (SI 1994
1640), the Criminal Justice (International Co-operation) Act 1990 (Enforcement of
Overseas Forfeiture Orders) (Amendment) Order 1996 (SI 1996 2878), the
Criminal Justice (International Co-operation) Act 1990 (Enforcement of
Overseas Forfeiture Orders) (Amendment) Order 1997 (SI 1997 1317), the
Criminal Justice (International Co-operation) Act 1990 (Enforcement of
Overseas Forfeiture Orders) (Amendment) (No.2) Order 1997 (SI 1997 2977),
the Criminal Justice (International Co-operation) Act 1990 (Enforcement of
Overseas Forfeiture Orders) (Amendment) Order 2001 (SI 2001 957), the
Criminal Justice (International Co-operation) Act 1990 (Enforcement of
Overseas Forfeiture Orders) (Amendment) Order 2002 (SI 2002 255) and the
Criminal Justice (International Co-operation) Act 1990 (Enforcement of
Overseas Forfeiture Orders) (Amendment) (No.2) Order 2002 (SI 2002 2845).

4544. Justice (Northern Ireland) Act 2002 (c.26)–Commencement No.8 Order

JUSTICE (NORTHERN IRELAND) ACT 2002 (COMMENCEMENT NO.8)
ORDER 2005, SR 2005 109 (C.9); made under the Justice (Northern Ireland)
Act 2002 s.87. In force: bringing into operation various provisions of the 2002
Act on April 1, 2005; £3.00.

This Order brings into force provisions of the Justice (Northern Ireland) Act
2002.

4545. Justice (Northern Ireland) Act 2002 (c.26)–Commencement No.9 and Transitional Provisions Order

JUSTICE (NORTHERN IRELAND) ACT 2002 (COMMENCEMENT NO.9 AND TRANSITIONAL PROVISIONS) ORDER 2005, SR 2005 281 (C.21); made under the Justice (Northern Ireland) Act 2002 s.87, s.89. In force: bringing into operation various provisions of the 2002 Act in accordance with Art.2, Art.3, Art.4 and Art.5; £3.00.

This Order brings into force provisions of the Justice (Northern Ireland) Act 2002 in relation to consents to prosecutions.

4546. Justice (Northern Ireland) Act 2002 (c.26)–Commencement No.10 Order

JUSTICE (NORTHERN IRELAND) ACT 2002 (COMMENCEMENT NO.10) ORDER 2005, SR 2005 391 (C.30); made under the Justice (Northern Ireland) Act 2002 s.87. In force: bringing into operation various provisions of the 2002 Act on August 30, 2005; £3.00.

This Order brings into force provisions of the Justice (Northern Ireland) Act 2002 specified in the Schedule.

4547. Justice (Northern Ireland) Act 2004 (c.4)–Commencement No.3 Order

JUSTICE (NORTHERN IRELAND) ACT 2004 (COMMENCEMENT NO.3) ORDER 2005, SR 2005 282 (C.22); made under the Justice (Northern Ireland) Act 2004 s.19. In force: bringing into operation various provisions of the 2004 Act in accordance with Art.2, Art.3, Art.4 and Art.5; £3.00.

This Order brings into force certain specified provisions of the Justice (Northern Ireland) Act 2004.

4548. Magistrates court–Bad character and hearsay evidence–Rules

MAGISTRATES' COURTS (AMENDMENT) RULES (NORTHERN IRELAND) 2005, SR 2005 162; made under the Magistrates' Courts (Northern Ireland) Order 1981 (SI 1981 1675 (NI.26)) Art.13; and the Criminal Justice (Evidence) (Northern Ireland) Order 2004 (SI 2004 1501 (NI.10)) Art.16, Art.35. In force: April 18, 2005; £3.00.

These Rules amend the Magistrates' Courts Rules (Northern Ireland) Rules 1984 (SR 1984 225) to prescribe the procedure relating to applications to adduce bad character evidence; and notice of intention to adduce hearsay evidence. They prescribe the procedure to be followed on an application to: adduce evidence of the bad character of persons other than the defendant or to cross examine a witness with a view to eliciting such evidence; oppose the admission of evidence of the bad character of persons other than the defendant; adduce evidence of a defendant's bad character or to cross examine a witness with a view to eliciting such evidence; exclude evidence of a defendant's bad character. The Rules provide that the defendant may waive service of any application or notice; and prescribe the procedure to be followed on an application to adduce hearsay evidence and oppose the admission of hearsay evidence.

4549. Serious offences–Retrials

CRIMINAL APPEAL (RETRIAL FOR SERIOUS OFFENCES) RULES (NORTHERN IRELAND) 2005, SR 2005 158; made under the Judicature (Northern Ireland) Act 1978 s.55; and the Criminal Justice Act 2003 s.93. In force: April 18, 2005; £3.00.

These Rules make provision for the procedure to be followed where an application is made under the Criminal Justice Act 2003 s.76 whereby a prosecutor may apply to the Court for a retrial, after an acquittal, where there is new and compelling evidence and it is in the interests of justice to do so.

4550. Serious offences–Retrials

CRIMINAL JUSTICE ACT 2003 (RETRIAL FOR SERIOUS OFFENCES) (NORTHERN IRELAND) ORDER 2005, SR 2005 203; made under the Criminal Justice Act 2003 s.97. In force: June 30, 2005; £3.00.

This Order provides the procedure for an application to the Court of Appeal in cases of retrial for serious offences.

4551. Supreme Court–Control orders–Applications procedure

RULES OF THE SUPREME COURT (NORTHERN IRELAND) (AMENDMENT NO.3) 2005, SR 2005 191; made under the Prevention of Terrorism Act 2005 Sch.para.3, Sch.para.4, Sch.para.5; and the Judicature (Northern Ireland) Act 1978 s.55. In force: in accordance with r.1; £3.00.

These Rules amend the Rules of the Supreme Court (Northern Ireland) 1980 (SR 1980 346) to prescribe the procedure relating to applications for control orders under the Prevention of Terrorism Act 2005.

4552. Supreme Court–Control orders–Applications procedure

RULES OF THE SUPREME COURT (NORTHERN IRELAND) (AMENDMENT NO.4) 2005, SR 2005 314; made under the Prevention of Terrorism Act 2005 Sch.para.3, Sch.para.4, Sch.para.5. In force: June 27, 2005; £3.00.

These Rules amend the Rules of the Supreme Court (Northern Ireland) 1980 (SR 1980 346) to prescribe the procedure relating to applications for control orders under the Prevention of Terrorism Act 2005.

4553. Supreme Court–Criminal evidence–Direct communication

RULES OF THE SUPREME COURT (NORTHERN IRELAND) (AMENDMENT NO.2) 2005, SR 2005 163; made under the Judicature (Northern Ireland) Act 1978 s.55. In force: April 18, 2005; £3.00.

These Rules amend the Rules of the Supreme Court (Northern Ireland) 1980 (SR 1980 346) so as to allow evidence of any particular fact to be given by live television link, telephone or any other method of direct communication. They also make amendments to include any postal address for the security in the description in the originating summons; and to reflect the requirement for notice to be sent in certain circumstances to prior mortgagees.

4554. Supreme Court–Statutory review and appeals–Applications procedure

RULES OF THE SUPREME COURT (NORTHERN IRELAND) (AMENDMENT) 2005, SR 2005 146; made under the Judicature (Northern Ireland) Act 1978 s.55; the Nationality, Immigration and Asylum Act 2002 s.103A; and the Asylum and Immigration (Treatment of Claimants, etc.) Act 2004 Sch.2 para.30. In force: April 18, 2005; £3.00.

These Rules amend the Rules of the Supreme Court (Northern Ireland) 1980 (SI 1980 346) to prescribe the procedure relating to applications for statutory review and appeals under the Nationality, Immigration and Asylum Act 2002 as amended by the Asylum and Immigration (Treatment of Claimants, etc.) Act 2004.

EDUCATION

4555. Boarding schools–School inspections

REGULATION AND IMPROVEMENT AUTHORITY (INSPECTION OF CHILDREN, RECORDS AND SCHOOLS) REGULATIONS (NORTHERN IRELAND) 2005, SR

2005 455; made under the Children (Northern Ireland) Order 1995 (SI 1995 755 (NI.2)) Art.176. In force: November 14, 2005; £3.00.

These Regulations, which revoke the Inspection of Premises, Children and Records (Children Accommodated in Schools) Regulations (Northern Ireland) 2000 (SR 2000 179), make provision for the inspection of schools, which provide accommodation for children.

4556. Colleges of Education (Northern Ireland) Order 2005 (SI 2005 1963 (NI.13))

This Order amends the Sex Discrimination (Northern Ireland) Order 1976 (SI 1976 1042 (NI.15)), the Education and Libraries (Northern Ireland) Order 1986 (SI 1986 594 (NI.3)), the Race Relations (Northern Ireland) Order 1997 (SI 1997 869 (NI.6)), the Special Educational Needs and Disability (Northern Ireland) Order 2005 (SI 2005 1117 (NI.6)) and the Freedom of Information Act 2000. The Order provides for the transfer of responsibility for the management of Stranmillis University College to a new governing body established by this Order and for the respective functions of the governing body and the Department for Employment and Learning in relation to the college; and contains amendments of other legislation in relation to the respective functions of the Department and the Department of Education in relation to colleges of education.

4557. Education and Libraries (Northern Ireland) Order 2003 (SI 2003 424 (NI.12))– Commencement No.2 Order

EDUCATION AND LIBRARIES (2003 ORDER) (COMMENCEMENT NO.2) ORDER (NORTHERN IRELAND) 2005, SR 2005 246 (C.19); made under the Education and Libraries (Northern Ireland) Order 2003 (SI 2003 424 (NI.12)) Art.1. In force: bringing into operation various provisions of the 2003 Order on April 29, 2005; £3.00.

This Order commences an amendment to the Education (Northern Ireland) Order 1998 (SI 1998 1759 (NI.13)) as provided by the consequential and supplementary amendments to the Education and Libraries (Northern Ireland) Order 2003 (SI 2003 424 (NI.12)), relating to the suspension of financial delegation in schools, provision for special schools and other miscellaneous financial provisions relating to schools.

4558. Education and Libraries (Northern Ireland) Order 2003 (SI 2003 424 (NI.12))– Commencement Order

EDUCATION AND LIBRARIES (2003 ORDER) (COMMENCEMENT) ORDER (NORTHERN IRELAND) 2005, SR 2005 133 (C.11); made under the Education and Libraries (Northern Ireland) Order 2003 (SI 2003 424 (NI.12)) Art.1. In force: bringing into operation various provisions of the 2003 Order on April 1, 2005; £3.00.

This Order brings into operation the provisions of the Education and Libraries (Northern Ireland) Order 2003 (SI 2003 424 (NI.12)) Part II, to introduce a Common Funding Scheme for the funding of grant-aided schools, other than a special school or a school established in a hospital.

4559. Education (Northern Ireland) Order 1998 (SI 1998 1759 (NI.13))– Commencement No.5 Order

EDUCATION (1998 ORDER) (COMMENCEMENT NO.5) ORDER (NORTHERN IRELAND) 2005, SR 2005 245 (C.18); made under the Education (Northern Ireland) Order 1998 (SI 1998 1759 (NI.13)) Art.1. In force: bringing into operation various provisions of the 1998 Order on April 29, 2005; £3.00.

This Order brings into force provisions of the Education (Northern Ireland) Order 1998 (SI 1998 1759 (NI.13)) which provide for the suspension, review, and appeal procedures relating to the withdrawal of financial delegation; which make provisions relating to the staff of controlled and maintained schools with delegated budgets; provide for the financing by boards of special schools, and provide for the preparation of financial statements for special schools managed by the board; provide for building and equipment grants for voluntary schools; and provide for miscellaneous financial provisions relating to schools.

4560. Educational institutions–Awards–Recognised bodies

EDUCATION (LISTED BODIES) (AMENDMENT) (NORTHERN IRELAND) ORDER 2005, SR 2005 379; made under the Education (Unrecognised Degrees) (Northern Ireland) Order 1988 (SI 1988 89 (NI.22)) Art.5. In force: August 30, 2005; £3.00.

This Order amends the Education (Listed Bodies) (Northern Ireland) Order 2004 (SR 2004 480) to add Kensington College of Business, London City College and the School of Technology and Management to the list of bodies providing courses in preparation for a degree.

4561. Grant maintained schools–School development plans

EDUCATION (SCHOOL DEVELOPMENT PLANS) REGULATIONS (NORTHERN IRELAND) 2005, SR 2005 303; made under the Education (Northern Ireland) Order 1998 (SI 1998 1759 (NI.13)) Art.13, Art.90. In force: September 1, 2005; £3.00.

These Regulations relate to the preparation and revision of school development plans in grant-aided schools.

4562. Higher education–Students–Approved plans–Fees

EDUCATION STUDENT FEES (APPROVED PLANS) REGULATIONS (NORTHERN IRELAND) 2005, SR 2005 367; made under the Higher Education (Northern Ireland) Order 2005 (SI 2005 1116 (NI.5)) Art.6, Art.7, Art.8, Art.9, Art.10, Art.14. In force: September 1, 2005; £3.00.

These Regulations prescribe for Northern Ireland various matters in relation to plans which a higher education institution must have approved by the Department for Employment and Learning before the institution is allowed to charge fees which exceed the basic amount. This amount is prescribed in the Student Fees (Amounts) Regulations Northern Ireland 2005 (SR 2005 290) at £1,200 and the circumstances in which it applies are set out in the Order.

4563. Higher education–Students–Fees

STUDENT FEES (AMOUNTS) REGULATIONS (NORTHERN IRELAND) 2005, SR 2005 290; made under the Higher Education (Northern Ireland) Order 2005 (SI 2005 1116 (NI.5)) Art.4, Art.14. In force: July 18, 2005; £3.00.

These Regulations are the first Regulations made under the Higher Education (Northern Ireland) Order 2005 (SI 2005 1116 (NI.5)) which enables the Department for Employment and Learning to impose a condition in relation to any grant made to the governing body of any higher education institution in Northern Ireland. This condition requires the governing body to secure that the fees payable for a qualifying course by a qualifying student do not exceed either the basic amount specified in these Regulations, or, where an institution has an approved plan in force, the amount specified in that plan which is not to exceed the higher amount specified in these Regulations. The Regulations prescribe the basic and higher amounts at £1,200 and £3,000 respectively. For an academic year of certain courses specified, lower basic and higher fee amounts of £600 and £1,500 respectively, apply instead.

4564. Higher education–Students–Grants

EDUCATION (STUDENT SUPPORT) REGULATIONS (NORTHERN IRELAND) 2005, SR 2005 340; made under the Education (Student Support) (Northern

Ireland) Order 1998 (SI 1998 1760 (NI.14)) Art.3, Art.8. In force: September 1, 2005; £7.50.

These Regulations, which revoke the Education (Grants for Disabled Postgraduate Students) Regulations (Northern Ireland) 2001 (SR 2001 285); the Education (Grants for Disabled Postgraduate Students) (Amendment) Regulations (Northern Ireland) 2002 (SR 2002 272); the Education (Student Support) Regulations (Northern Ireland) 2003 (SR 2003 298); the Education (Grants for Disabled Postgraduate Students) (Amendment) Regulations (Northern Ireland) 2003 (SR 2003 37); the Education (Student Support) (Amendment) Regulations (Northern Ireland) 2003 (SR 2003 339); the Education (Student Support) (Amendment) Regulations (Northern Ireland) 2004 (SR 2004 254); the Education (Grants for Disabled Postgraduate Students) (Amendment) Regulations (Northern Ireland) 2004 (SR 2004 323), the Education (Student Support) (Amendment) (No.2) Regulations (Northern Ireland) 2004 (SR 2004 517); the Education (Student Support) (Amendment) Regulations (Northern Ireland) 2005 (SR 2005 298); and the Education (Student Support) (Amendment) (No.2) Regulations (Northern Ireland) 2005 (SR 2005 323), provide for support for students taking designated higher education courses in respect of the academic year beginning on or after September 1, 2005.

4565. Higher education–Students–Grants

EDUCATION (STUDENT SUPPORT) (NO.2) REGULATIONS 2002 (AMENDMENT) REGULATIONS 2005, SI 2005 5; made under the Teaching and Higher Education Act 1998 s.22, s.42, s.43. In force: March 1, 2005; £3.00.

These Regulations amend the Education (Student Support) (No.2) Regulations 2002 (SI 2002 3200) which provide for support for students taking designated higher education courses. The Regulations provide that in the event of bankruptcies arising on or after March 1, 2005 in Northern Ireland, any debt arising from a student loan is protected from the effects of proceedings under the Insolvency (Northern Ireland) Order 1989 (SI 1989 2405 (NI.19)), irrespective of when that debt arose. Previously, only debt in respect of sums received by way of student loan after the commencement of bankruptcy proceedings were protected from the effects of such proceedings.

4566. Higher Education (Northern Ireland) Order 2005 (SI 2005 1116 (NI.5))

This Order, which amends the Education (Student Support) (Northern Ireland) Order 1998 (SI 1998 1760) and the Learning and Skills Act 2000, makes provision about fees payable by students in higher education and about grants and loans to students under the student support scheme.

4567. Landlord and tenant–Special educational needs–Alteration of premises

SPECIAL EDUCATIONAL NEEDS AND DISABILITY (EDUCATIONAL INSTITUTIONS) (ALTERATION OF LEASEHOLD PREMISES) REGULATIONS (NORTHERN IRELAND) 2005, SR 2005 371; made under the Special Educational Needs and Disability (Northern Ireland) Order 2005 (SI 2005 1117 (NI.6)) Art.32, Art.49, Sch.3 para.4, Sch.3 para.5. In force: September 1, 2005; £3.00.

These Regulations, which amend the Special Educational Needs and Disability (Northern Ireland) Order 2005 (SI 2005 1117 (NI.6)), contain provisions in respect of consents required under the terms of leases and sub-leases occupied by educational institutions whose governing bodies are subject to the duty of reasonable adjustment set out in art.30 of that Order. They set out circumstances for the purposes of where a lessor will be taken to have withheld his consent or to have reasonably or unreasonably withheld his consent to an application to make an alteration to premises made by or on behalf of the service provider; set out conditions for the purposes of art.32 of, and Sch.3 to, the Order, that it is reasonable for a lessor to attach to a grant of consent to an alteration of premises; and modify certain provisions of art.32 of, and Sch.3 to, the Order, that apply to a landlord who is the service provider's immediate landlord so that they apply to a landlord who is a service provider's superior landlord.

4568. Schools–Grammar schools–Charges

GRAMMAR SCHOOLS (CHARGES) (AMENDMENT) REGULATIONS (NORTHERN IRELAND) 2005, SR 2005 361; made under the Education Reform (Northern Ireland) Order 1989 (SI 1989 2406 (NI.20)) Art.132. In force: September 1, 2005; £3.00.

These Regulations amend the Grammar Schools (Charges) Regulations (Northern Ireland) 1992 (SR 1992 171) and revoke the Grammar Schools (Charges) (Amendment) Regulations (Northern Ireland) 2004 (SR 2004 313). In relation to a voluntary grammar school, the Board of Governors may charge only in respect of a pupil enrolled in the secondary department of the school for the purpose of meeting expenditure on the provision or alteration of school premises or on the provision of associated equipment. These Regulations increase the maximum amount which the Board of Governors may charge from £110 to £120.

4569. Special educational needs–Assessment and statements

EDUCATION (SPECIAL EDUCATIONAL NEEDS) REGULATIONS (NORTHERN IRELAND) 2005, SR 2005 384; made under the Education (Northern Ireland) Order 1996 (SI 1996 274 (NI.1)) Art.7A, Art.14, Art.16, Art.17, Art.18A, Art.19, Art.20, Art.20A, Art.23A, Art.28, Sch.1 para.2, Sch.1 para.3, Sch.2 para.2, Sch.2 para.4, Sch.2 para.8, Sch.2 para.9, Sch.2 para.10, Sch.2 para.11, Sch.2 para.13. In force: September 1, 2005; £4.50.

These Regulations, which revoke and replace with modifications the Education (Special Educational Needs) Regulations (Northern Ireland) 1997 (SR 1997 327) and the Education (Special Educational Needs) (Amendment) Regulations (Northern Ireland) 1998 (SR 1998 217), relate to the assessment of special educational needs and to statements of such needs under the Education (Northern Ireland) Order 1996 Part II.

4570. Special educational needs–Code of practice supplement–Appointed day

EDUCATION (SUPPLEMENT TO THE SPECIAL EDUCATIONAL NEEDS CODE OF PRACTICE) (APPOINTED DAY) (NORTHERN IRELAND) ORDER 2005, SR 2005 309; made under the Education (Northern Ireland) Order 1996 (SI 1996 274 (NI.1)) Art.5. In force: September 1, 2005; £3.00.

This Order appoints September 1, 2005 as the day on which the Supplement to the Code of Practice on the Identification and Assessment of Special Educational Needs (the Supplement) shall come into operation.

4571. Special educational needs–Disability tribunal–Claims and appeals

SPECIAL EDUCATIONAL NEEDS AND DISABILITY TRIBUNAL REGULATIONS (NORTHERN IRELAND) 2005, SR 2005 339; made under the Education (Northern Ireland) Order 1996 (SI 1996 274 (NI.1)) Art.22, Art.23, Art.28; and the Special Educational Needs and Disability (Northern Ireland) Order 2005 (SI 2005 1117 (NI.6)) Art.23, Art.49. In force: September 1, 2005; £4.50.

These Regulations, which revoke the Special Educational Needs Tribunal Regulations (Northern Ireland) 1997 (SR 1997 315) (with saving), make provision in relation to the establishment of and regulate the procedure of the Special Educational Needs and Disability Tribunal established by the Special Educational Needs and Disability (Northern Ireland) Order 2005 (SI 2005 1117 (NI.6)). The Regulations make provision for and regulate the procedures for both appeals, and claims in respect of disability discrimination in schools.

4572. Special Educational Needs and Disability Order (Northern Ireland) 2005 (SI 2005 1117 (NI.6))–Commencement No.1 Order

SPECIAL EDUCATIONAL NEEDS AND DISABILITY (2005 ORDER) (COMMENCEMENT NO.1) ORDER (NORTHERN IRELAND) 2005, SR 2005 336 (C.25); made under the Special Educational Needs and Disability Order (Northern Ireland) 2005 (SI 2005 1117 (NI.6)) Art.1. In force: bringing into operation various provisions of the 2005 Order on September 1, 2005; £3.00.

This Order provides for the coming into operation of the provisions of the Special Educational Needs and Disability (Northern Ireland) Order 2005 (SI 2005 1117 (NI.6)) specified in the Schedule. The provisions being brought into operation relate to special educational needs and disability discrimination in schools.

4573. Special Educational Needs and Disability Order (Northern Ireland) 2005 (SI 2005 1117 (NI.6))–Commencement No.2 Order

SPECIAL EDUCATIONAL NEEDS AND DISABILITY (2005 ORDER) (COMMENCEMENT NO.2) ORDER (NORTHERN IRELAND) 2005, SR 2005 337 (C.26); made under the Special Educational Needs and Disability Order (Northern Ireland) 2005 (SI 2005 1117 (NI.6)) Art.1. In force: bringing into operation various provisions of the 2005 Order on September 1, 2005; £3.00.

This Order provides for the coming into operation of provisions of the Special Educational Needs and Disability (Northern Ireland) Order 2005 (SI 2005 1117 (NI.6)) relating to disability discrimination in further and higher education.

4574. Special Educational Needs and Disability (Northern Ireland) Order 2005 (SI 2005 1117 (NI.6))

This Order amends the Education and Libraries (Northern Ireland) Order 1986 (SI 1986 593 (NI.3)), the Disability Discrimination Act 1995, the Education (Northern Ireland) Order 1996 (SI 1996 274 (NI.1)), the Equality (Disability, etc.) (Northern Ireland) Order 2000 (SI 2000 1110 (NI.2)) and the Justice (Northern Ireland) Act 2002. The Order makes amendments in relation to special educational needs; and makes further provision against discrimination, on grounds of disability, in schools and other educational institutions and by other educational and qualifications bodies.

4575. Students–Educational awards

STUDENTS AWARDS (AMENDMENT) REGULATIONS (NORTHERN IRELAND) 2005, SR 2005 466; made under the Education and Libraries (Northern Ireland) Order 1986 (SI 1986 594 (NI.3)) Art.50, Art.134. In force: November 20, 2005; £3.00.

These Regulations amend the Students Awards Regulations (Northern Ireland) 2003 (SR 2003 459) which ensure that students who began their courses before September 1, 1998, and certain other students, continue to receive students awards and payments under students awards until the end of their courses. They make amendments so that the new payment rates prescribed shall only apply in relation to an academic term which commences on or after September 1, 2005. Where an academic year starts before September 1, 2005, but ends after September 1, 2005, the old payment rates and the new payment rates shall be applied proportionally. The Regulations also create a new category of students who are eligible for students awards in respect of their attendance on courses; remove the lone parent grant; specify increases in the rates of fee awards in relation to courses at the University of Buckingham, the Guildhall School of Music and Heythrop College; and partially revoke the Students Awards (Amendment) Regulations (Northern Ireland) 2004.

4576. Students–Grants

EDUCATION (STUDENT SUPPORT) (2005 REGULATIONS) (AMENDMENT) REGULATIONS (NORTHERN IRELAND) 2005, SR 2005 445; made under the

Education (Student Support) (Northern Ireland) Order 1998 (SI 1998 1760 (NI.14)) Art.3, Art.8. In force: October 31, 2005; £3.00.

These Regulations amend the Education (Student Support) Regulations (Northern Ireland) 2005 (SR 2005 340) which provide for support for students taking designated higher education courses. The Regulations make amendments so that the maximum weekly amount of the childcare grant is increased; set out the circumstances in which income can be re-assessed so that it is no longer necessary for a drop in the parent's income to be as a result of an event beyond his control; and so that where there is a drop in the parent's income, it is the parent's income rather than the household income which may be re-assessed for the current financial year.

4577. Students–Grants–Eligibility

EDUCATION (STUDENT SUPPORT) (AMENDMENT) REGULATIONS (NORTHERN IRELAND) 2005, SR 2005 298; made under the Education (Student Support) (Northern Ireland) Order 1998 (SI 1998 1760 (NI.14)) Art.3, Art.8. In force: July 11, 2005; £3.00.

These Regulations amend the Education (Student Support) Regulations (Northern Ireland) 2003 (SR 2003 298) to exclude Regional Social Work Degree Trainees commencing Social Work Degree courses on or after September 1, 2005 from financial support.

4578. Students–Grants–Eligibility

EDUCATION (STUDENT SUPPORT) (AMENDMENT) (NO.2) REGULATIONS (NORTHERN IRELAND) 2005, SR 2005 323; made under the Education (Student Support) (Northern Ireland) Order 1998 (SI 1998 1760 (NI.14)) Art.3, Art.8. In force: July 25, 2005; £3.00.

These Regulations amend the Education (Student Support) Regulations (Northern Ireland) 2003 (SR 2003 298) which apply to the provision of support to students in relation to academic years beginning on or after September 1, 2003. The Regulations apply to the provision of support to students in relation to academic years beginning on or after September 1, 2004; create a new category of student eligible for bursaries, grants and loans for living costs; and insert a time limit for applying for grants or loans for living costs in the academic year beginning on or after September 1, 2004 for the new category of eligible student.

4579. Students–Loans

EDUCATION (STUDENT LOANS) (AMENDMENT) (NO.2) REGULATIONS (NORTHERN IRELAND) 2005, SR 2005 435; made under the Education (Student Loans) (Northern Ireland) Order 1990 (SI 1990 1506 (NI.11)) Art.3, Sch.2 para.1. In force: October 24, 2005; £3.00.

These Regulations amend the Education (Student Loans) Regulations (Northern Ireland) 1998 (SR 1998 58) by creating a new category of students who are eligible for loans under those Regulations. The 1998 Regulations govern mortgage style repayment loans. These loans are, for the most part, only available to those students who started their courses before August 1, 1998 or who are attending a further course immediately after having completed a course they commenced prior to August 1, 1998. They set out the time limit for applying for loans under the 1998 Regulations in respect of an academic year beginning on or after August 1, 2004 but before July 1, 2005. The Regulations also expand the scope of the definition of "eligible student" and amend the terms of loans taken out on or after August 31, 2005.

4580. Students–Loans–Mortgage style repayment loans

EDUCATION (STUDENT LOANS) (AMENDMENT) REGULATIONS (NORTHERN IRELAND) 2005, SR 2005 351; made under the Education

(Student Loans) (Northern Ireland) Order 1990 (SI 1990 1506 (NI.11)) Art.3, Sch.2 para.1. In force: August 1, 2005; £3.00.

These Regulations, which revoke the Education (Student loans) (Amendment) Regulations (Northern Ireland) 2004 (SR 2004 305), amend the Education (Student Loans) Regulations (Northern Ireland) 1998 (SR 1998 58), the Education (Student Loans) (Amendment) Regulations (Northern Ireland) 1998 (SR 1998 262), the Education (Student Loans) (Amendment) Regulations (Northern Ireland) 1999 (SR 1999 343), the Education (Student Loans) (Amendment) Regulations (Northern Ireland) 2000 (SR 2000 244), the Education (Student Loans) (Amendment) Regulations (Northern Ireland) 2001 (SR 2001 276) and the Education (Student Loans) (Amendment) Regulations (Northern Ireland) 2002 (SR 2002 241). The Regulations increase the maximum amounts that may be lent to students in relation to an academic year in line with inflation; enable persons who form civil partnerships and who are attending specified courses to be considered eligible for mortgage style repayment loans; and provide that the modifications do not take effect whilst the Civil Partnership Act 2004 s.1 is not in force.

ELECTORAL PROCESS

4581. Elections–European Parliament–Returning officers–Charges

PARLIAMENTARY ELECTIONS (RETURNING OFFICER'S CHARGES) (NORTHERN IRELAND) ORDER 2005, SI 2005 1160; made under the Representation of the People Act 1983 s.29. In force: April 11, 2005; £3.00.

This Order revokes and replaces the Parliamentary Elections (Returning Officer's Charges) (Northern Ireland) Order 1997 (SI 1997 774) which set limits used for the parliamentary election held on June 7, 2001. Under the Representation of the People Act 1983, the entitlement of a returning officer at a parliamentary election to recover his charges in respect of his expenses for or in connection with such an election depends upon: the expenses being of a kind specified in an order under that provision, the expenses being properly incurred, and the charges in respect of them being reasonable. The Order specifies the kinds of expenses incurred by a returning officer for or in connection with a parliamentary election in respect of which he is entitled to recover his charges, together (in the case of Part A) with the maximum recoverable amounts in respect of those charges. It also increases the maximum recoverable amounts from those that were specified in the 1997 Order.

4582. Electoral Registration (Northern Ireland) Act 2005 (c.1)

This Act makes provision about the registration of electors in Northern Ireland in cases where required information is not provided.

This Act received Royal Assent on February 24, 2005.

4583. Local elections–Change of date

ELECTORAL LAW ACT (NORTHERN IRELAND) 1962 (AMENDMENT) ORDER 2005, SI 2005 862; made under the Northern Ireland Act 1998 s.84. In force: March 23, 2005; £3.00.

This Order amends the Electoral Law Act (Northern Ireland) 1962 so as to change the date of local elections in Northern Ireland from the third Wednesday in May to the first Thursday in May. This will align the position in Northern Ireland with that in Great Britain.

4584. Local elections–Civil partnerships

LOCAL ELECTIONS (NORTHERN IRELAND) (AMENDMENT) ORDER 2005, SI 2005 1969; made under the Northern Ireland Act 1998 s.84. In force: December 5, 2005; £3.00.

This Order, which amends the Electoral Law Act (Northern Ireland) 1962 and the Local Elections (Northern Ireland) Order 1985 (SI 1985 454), makes amendments to the provisions relating to local elections in Northern Ireland which are consequential to the Civil Partnerships Act 2004. It gives civil partners the same status as a spouse in all matters connected with the conduct of local elections in Northern Ireland and amends the definition of "relative" to include civil partners.

4585. Local elections–Entry into polling stations–Control of persons

ELECTORAL LAW ACT (NORTHERN IRELAND) 1962 (AMENDMENT NO.2) ORDER 2005, SI 2005 863; made under the Northern Ireland Act 1998 s.84. In force: March 23, 2005; £3.00.

This Order amends the provisions of the Electoral Law Act (Northern Ireland) 1962 relating to the control of persons entering polling stations during local elections. It allows the presiding officer to admit members of the Electoral Commission and persons authorised by the Commission.

4586. Local elections–Expenses

ELECTORAL LAW ACT (NORTHERN IRELAND) 1962 (AMENDMENT NO.3) ORDER 2005, SI 2005 864; made under the Northern Ireland Act 1998 s.84. In force: March 23, 2005; £3.00.

This Order increases the maximum expenses that can be claimed by candidates at local elections in Northern Ireland by amending the current limits in the Electoral Law Act (Northern Ireland) 1962.

4587. Political parties–Donations–Excluded categories

POLITICAL PARTIES, ELECTIONS AND REFERENDUMS ACT 2000 (DISAPPLICATION OF PART IV FOR NORTHERN IRELAND PARTIES, ETC.) ORDER 2005, SI 2005 299; made under the Political Parties, Elections and Referendums Act 2000 s.70. In force: February 16, 2005; £3.00.

This Order disapplies provisions of the Political Parties, Elections and Referendums Act 2000, relating to the control of donations to registered parties, for the period of two years in relation to any party registered in the Northern Ireland register of political parties. It disapplies provisions for the period of two years in relation to every regulated donee who is either an individual ordinarily resident in Northern Ireland or a member association wholly or mainly consisting of members of a Northern Ireland party; and makes provision for registered parties, registered in the Northern Ireland register maintained by the Electoral Commission, to be excluded from the categories of permissible donors.

EMPLOYMENT

4588. Codes of practice–Disciplinary and grievance procedures

CODE OF PRACTICE (DISCIPLINARY AND GRIEVANCE PROCEDURES) (APPOINTED DAY) ORDER (NORTHERN IRELAND) 2005, SR 2005 152; made under the Industrial Relations (Northern Ireland) Order 1992 (SI 1992 807 (NI.5)) Art.90, Art.107. In force: April 3, 2005; £3.00.

This Order appoints April 3, 2005 as the day upon which the Code of Practice on Disciplinary and Grievance Procedures, issued by the Labour Relations Agency, shall come into effect.

4589. Disability discrimination–Codes of practice–Appointed day

DISABILITY DISCRIMINATION CODES OF PRACTICE (EMPLOYMENT AND OCCUPATION, AND TRADE ORGANISATIONS AND QUALIFICATIONS BODIES) (APPOINTED DAY) ORDER (NORTHERN IRELAND) 2005, SR 2005 293; made under the Disability Discrimination Act 1995 s.54A, s.67. In force: bringing into operation the 1995 Act Codes of Practice on June 13, 2005; £3.00.

This Order appoints June 13, 2005 as the date on which the Code of Practice for Trade Organisations and Qualifications Bodies and Code of Practice on Employment and Occupation shall come into effect.

4590. Employees rights–Increase of limits

EMPLOYMENT RIGHTS (INCREASE OF LIMITS) ORDER (NORTHERN IRELAND) 2005, SR 2005 12; made under the Employment Relations (Northern Ireland) Order 1999 (SI 1999 2790 (NI.9)) Art.33, Art.39. In force: February 6, 2005; £3.00.

This Order, which revokes the Employment Rights (Increase of Limits) Order (Northern Ireland) 2004 (SR 2004 64), increases the limits applying to certain awards of industrial tribunals, and other amounts payable under employment legislation, as specified in the Schedule to the Order.

4591. Employees rights–Information and consultation

INFORMATION AND CONSULTATION OF EMPLOYEES REGULATIONS (NORTHERN IRELAND) 2005, SR 2005 47; made under the Employment Relations Act 2004 s.43. In force: April 6, 2005; £5.00.

These Regulations, which amend the Employment Rights (Northern Ireland) Order 1996 (SI 1996 1919 (NI.16)) and the Industrial Tribunals (Northern Ireland) Order 1996 (SI 1996 1921 (NI.18)), implement Council Directive 2002/14 ([2002] OJ L80/29) establishing a general framework for improving information and consultation rights of employees in the European Community. The Regulations provide a method of calculating the number of employees in an undertaking, provide the employees of an undertaking with an entitlement to data to make the calculation and allow a complaint to be made to the Industrial Court that the employer has failed to provide such data or has supplied false or incomplete data.

4592. Employment agencies–Conduct

CONDUCT OF EMPLOYMENT AGENCIES AND EMPLOYMENT BUSINESSES REGULATIONS (NORTHERN IRELAND) 2005, SR 2005 395; made under the Employment (Miscellaneous Provisions) (Northern Ireland) Order 1981 (SI 1981 839 (NI.20)) Art.6, Art.7, Art.10. In force: Reg.26(7): December 25, 2005; Reg.32: December 25, 2005; remainder: September 25, 2005; £5.50.

These Regulations, which revoke the Conduct of Employment Agencies and Employment Businesses Regulations (Northern Ireland) 1982 (SR 1982 253), the Employment Agencies (Charging Fees to Workers) Regulations (Northern Ireland) 1982 (SR 1982 254) and the Employment Agencies (Charging Fees to Au Pairs) Regulations (Northern Ireland) 1982 (SR 1982 255), make provision to secure the proper conduct of employment agencies and employment businesses and to protect the interests of persons using their services.

4593. Employment Relations (Northern Ireland) Order 1999 (SI 1999 2790 (NI.9))–Commencement No.8 Order

EMPLOYMENT RELATIONS (1999 ORDER) (COMMENCEMENT NO.8) ORDER (NORTHERN IRELAND) 2005, SR 2005 394 (C.31); made under the Employment Relations (Northern Ireland) Order 1999 (SI 1999 2790 (NI.9)) Art.1. In force: bringing into operation various provisions of the 1999 Order on September 24, 2005; £3.00.

This Order brings into operation various provisions of the Employment Relations (Northern Ireland) Order 1999 (SI 1999 2790 (NI.9)).

4594. Employment Relations (Northern Ireland) Order 2004 (SI 2004 3078 (NI.19))–Commencement No.2 Order

EMPLOYMENT RELATIONS (2004 ORDER) (COMMENCEMENT NO.2 AND TRANSITIONAL PROVISIONS) ORDER (NORTHERN IRELAND) 2005, SR 2005 73 (C.6); made under the Employment Relations (Northern Ireland) Order 2004 (SI 2004 3078 (NI.19)) Art.1. Commencement details: bringing into force various provisions of the 2004 Order on March 13, 2005; £3.00.

This Order brings into operation on March 13, 2005, Art.17, Art.19, Art.28, Sch.1 para.15 and Sch.1 para.18 of the Employment Relations (Northern Ireland) Order 2004.

4595. Employment Relations (Northern Ireland) Order 2004 (SI 2004 3078 (NI.19))–Commencement No.3 and Transitional Provisions Order

EMPLOYMENT RELATIONS (2004 ORDER) (COMMENCEMENT NO.3 AND TRANSITIONAL PROVISIONS) ORDER (NORTHERN IRELAND) 2005, SR 2005 345 (C.27); made under the Employment Relations (Northern Ireland) Order 2004 (SI 2004 3078 (NI.19)) Art.1. In force: bringing into operation various provisions of the 2004 Order on July 24, 2005; £3.00.

This Order brings into operation the provisions of the Employment Relations (Northern Ireland) Order 2004 (SI 2004 3078 (NI.19)) listed in the Schedule to the Order.

4596. Employment (Miscellaneous Provisions) (Northern Ireland) Order 2005 (SI 2005 3424 (NI.20))

This Order amends the Employment (Miscellaneous Provisions) (Northern Ireland) Order 1981 (SI 1981 839 (NI.20)), the Industrial Relations (Northern Ireland) Order 1992 (SI 1992 807 (NI.5)), the Employment Rights (Northern Ireland) Order 1996 (SI 1996 1919 (NI.16)), and the Fair Employment and Treatment (Northern Ireland) Order 1998 (SI 1998 3162 (NI.21)). It provides for new enforcement powers in connection with the regulation of employment agencies and employment businesses and also amends the qualifications for certain appointments in relation to industrial tribunals and the Fair Employment Tribunal and provides for the enforcement of sums payable in pursuance of a decision of the Fair Employment Tribunal.

4597. Equal opportunities–Public bodies–Specification

FAIR EMPLOYMENT (SPECIFICATION OF PUBLIC AUTHORITIES) (AMENDMENT) ORDER (NORTHERN IRELAND) 2005, SR 2005 525; made under the Fair Employment and Treatment (Northern Ireland) Order 1998 (SI 1998 3162 (NI.21)) Art.50, Art.51. In force: January 1, 2006; £3.00.

This Order amends the Fair Employment (Specification of Public Authorities) Order (Northern Ireland) 2004 (SR 2004 494) which specifies a number of persons or bodies as public authorities for certain purposes under the Fair Employment and Treatment (Northern Ireland) Order 1998 (SI 1998 3162 (NI.21)) and provides for the persons who are to be treated for such purposes as the employees of some of those authorities. The Order adds bodies who are public authorities.

4598. Industrial tribunals–Equal pay

EQUAL PAY ACT 1970 (AMENDMENT) REGULATIONS (NORTHERN IRELAND) 2005, SR 2005 145; made under the European Communities Act 1972 s.2. In force: April 3, 2005; £3.00.

These Regulations amend the Equal Pay Act (Northern Ireland) 1970 which requires the industrial tribunal to follow a particular procedure when determining proceedings where there is a question as to whether the claimant and the comparator are doing work of equal value. The Regulations alter the procedure for such claims to allow the industrial tribunal to choose to determine the question of equal value itself or to appoint an independent expert to prepare a report on that question. In a case where there has already been a job evaluation study which has given different values to the work of the claimant and the comparator, the industrial tribunal must determine that the work is not of equal value unless it has reasonable grounds for suspecting that the study discriminated on the grounds of sex, or there are other reasons why it is not suitable to be relied upon.

4599. Sex discrimination – Equal treatment

EMPLOYMENT EQUALITY (SEX DISCRIMINATION) REGULATIONS (NORTHERN IRELAND) 2005, SR 2005 426; made under the European Communities Act 1972 s.2. In force: October 5, 2005; £3.50.

These Regulations, which amend the Equal Pay Act (Northern Ireland) 1970 and the Sex Discrimination (Northern Ireland) Order 1976 (SI 1976 276 (NI.2)), implement Council Directive 2002/73 ([2002] OJ L269/15) amending Council Directive 76/207 on the implementation of the principle of equal treatment for men and women as regards access to employment and working conditions. The Regulations make amendments which reflect the provisions of the Directive which deal with the definition of indirect discrimination, harassment, and genuine occupational requirements, and also necessitate amendments to the 1976 Order making it clear that discrimination on the grounds of pregnancy and maternity leave is unlawful sex discrimination.

4600. Books

Kelleher, Denis – Data Protection Law in Ireland. Hardback: £93.33. ISBN 1 84592 204 2. Tottel Publishing.

ENERGY

4601. Electricity – European requirements

ELECTRICITY ORDER 1992 (AMENDMENT) REGULATIONS (NORTHERN IRELAND) 2005, SR 2005 335; made under the European Communities Act 1972 s.2. In force: August 1, 2005; £3.00.

These Regulations inter alia amend the Electricity (Northern Ireland) Order 1992 (SI 1992 231 (NI.1)) to ensure that it conforms with the requirements of European Parliament and Council Directive 2003/54 ([2003] OJ L176/37) concerning common rules for the internal market in electricity. They also revoke and replace the Electricity Order 1992 (Amendment) Regulations (Northern Ireland) 1999 (SI 1999 250) and amend the Energy (Northern Ireland) Order 2003 (SI 2003 419 (NI.6)).

4602. Electricity supply industry – Determination of turnover for penalties

ELECTRICITY AND GAS (DETERMINATION OF TURNOVER FOR PENALTIES) ORDER (NORTHERN IRELAND) 2005, SR 2005 287; made under the Energy (Northern Ireland) Order 2003 (SI 2003 419 (NI.6)) Art.45. In force: July 20, 2005; £3.00.

The Energy (Northern Ireland) Order 2003 (SI 2003 419 (NI.6)) provides that where the Northern Ireland Authority for Energy Regulation is satisfied that a gas or electricity licence holder has contravened or is contravening any licence condition or certain requirements imposed on him by the Electricity (Northern Ireland) Order 1992 (SI 1992 231 (NI.1)), the Gas (Northern Ireland) Order 1996 (SI 1996 275 (NI.2)) or the 2003 Order; or an electricity licence holder who is a public electricity supplier is failing or has failed to achieve any standard of performance prescribed under the 1992 Order, the Authority may impose on the licence holder a penalty of such amount as is reasonable in all the circumstances of the case but not exceeding

10 per cent of the turnover of the licence holder. This Order makes provision for the determination of the turnover of the licence holder for those purposes.

4603. Energy efficiency-Grants

DOMESTIC ENERGY EFFICIENCY GRANTS (AMENDMENT NO.4) REGULATIONS (NORTHERN IRELAND) 2005, SR 2005 202; made under the Social Security (Northern Ireland) Order 1990 (SI 1990 1511 (NI.15)) Art.17. In force: April 25, 2005; £3.00.

The Domestic Energy Efficiency Grants Regulations (Northern Ireland) 2002 (SR 2002 56) enable the Department for Social Development to make or arrange for the making of grant for the improvement of energy efficiency in dwellings occupied by persons on low incomes with children, elderly persons on low incomes and persons in receipt of benefit relating to ill health or disability. These Regulations amend the 2002 Regulations to increase the grant limit for a Warm Homes Plus grant to £3,700.

ENVIRONMENT

4604. Consumer protection-Hazardous substances-Packaging and labelling

CHEMICALS (HAZARD INFORMATION AND PACKAGING FOR SUPPLY) (AMENDMENT) REGULATIONS (NORTHERN IRELAND) 2005, SR 2005 463; made under the European Communities Act 1972 s.2; and the Health and Safety at Work (Northern Ireland) Order 1978 (SI 1978 1039 (NI.9)) Art.17, Sch.3 para.1, Sch.3 para.2, Sch.3 para.14, Sch.3 para.15. In force: November 30, 2005; £3.00.

These Regulations amend the Chemicals (Hazard Information and Packaging for Supply) Regulations (Northern Ireland) 2002 (SR 2002 301). They introduce a new approved supply list thereby implementing in full Commission Directive 2004/73 ([2004] OJ L152/1) adapting to technical progress for the twenty-ninth time Council Directive 67/548 on the approximation of the laws, regulations and administrative provisions relating to the classification, packaging and labelling of dangerous substances.

4605. Environmental impact assessments-Water

WATER RESOURCES (ENVIRONMENTAL IMPACT ASSESSMENT) REGULATIONS (NORTHERN IRELAND) 2005, SR 2005 32; made under the European Communities Act 1972 s.2. In force: March 9, 2005; £3.00.

These Regulations provide (in relation to water management projects for agriculture in Northern Ireland), for the assessment of the effects of such projects on the environment in accordance with Council Directive 85/337 ([1985] OJ L175/40) on the assessment of the effects of certain public and private projects on the environment. The Regulations impose procedural requirements in relation to the consideration of applications or proposals for consent for a relevant project.

4606. Environmental protection-Countryside management-Grants

COUNTRYSIDE MANAGEMENT REGULATIONS (NORTHERN IRELAND) 2005, SR 2005 268; made under the European Communities Act 1972 s.2; and the Agriculture (Conservation Grants) (Northern Ireland) Order 1995 (SI 1995 3212 (NI.21)) Art.3. In force: June 1, 2005; £3.50.

These Regulations revoke the Countryside Management Regulations (Northern Ireland) 2001 (SR 2001 43). They supplement certain provisions of Council Regulation 1257/1999 ([1999] OJ L160/ 80) on support for rural development from the European Agricultural Guidance and Guarantee Fund (EAGGF); provide for payment of a grant in respect of an undertaking to follow the general environmental conditions set out in Sch.1; specify the requirements in relation to applications; specify restrictions on the acceptance of applications; make provision for beneficiaries under the Habitat Improvement Regulations (Northern Ireland) 1995 (SI 1995 134) to substitute for the unexpired period of an undertaking under any of those Regulations, an undertaking to which these Regulations apply; specify the maximum payment rate in respect of each activity which is the subject of an undertaking; permit the Department to refuse applications for grant in the event that the financial resources available for grant under the Regulations are insufficient; specify the conditions which apply where there is a change of occupation of the land to which an undertaking relates; impose an obligation on applicants to permit entry and inspection; and provide for the withholding and recovery of grant, recovery of interest and the imposition of penalties.

4607. Environmental protection–Genetically modified organisms–Transboundary movements

GENETICALLY MODIFIED ORGANISMS (TRANSBOUNDARY MOVEMENTS) REGULATIONS (NORTHERN IRELAND) 2005, SR 2005 209; made under the European Communities Act 1972 s.2. In force: May 31, 2005; £3.00.

These Regulations make provision for the enforcement of European Parliament and Council Regulation 1946/2003 ([2003] OJ L287/1) on transboundary movements of genetically modified organisms. They designate the Department as "Competent Authority" for Northern Ireland for the purpose of the Council Regulation; the Council Regulation provides that the Competent Authority is responsible for performing the administrative functions required by the Cartagena Protocol on Biosafety; make provision for the appointment of inspectors; provide powers of entry, including the power to carry out tests and inspections and to take samples; enable inspectors to require the provision of information; make it an offence to contravene specified Community provisions; to obstruct inspectors in the exercise of powers under these Regulations; and to give false information; and sets out a due diligence defence in respect of contravention of the specified Community provisions. They also make provision for offences committed due to the fault of another person.

4608. Environmental protection–Hazardous waste

HAZARDOUS WASTE (AMENDMENT) REGULATIONS (NORTHERN IRELAND) 2005, SR 2005 461; made under the Waste and Contaminated Land (Northern Ireland) Order 1997 (SI 1997 2778 (NI.19)) Art.30, Art.48, Art.77. In force: October 21, 2005; £3.00.

These Regulations amend the Hazardous Waste Regulations (Northern Ireland) 2005 (SR 2005 300).

4609. Environmental protection–Hazardous waste

LIST OF WASTES (AMENDMENT) REGULATIONS (NORTHERN IRELAND) 2005, SR 2005 462; made under the European Communities Act 1972 s.2. In force: November 14, 2005; £3.00.

These Regulations correct minor errors in the List of Wastes Regulations (Northern Ireland) 2005 (SR 2005 301).

4610. Environmental protection–Pollution control regime

POLLUTION PREVENTION AND CONTROL (AMENDMENT) AND CONNECTED PROVISIONS REGULATIONS (NORTHERN IRELAND) 2005, SR 2005 229; made under the Environment (Northern Ireland) Order 2002 (SI 2002 3153 (NI.7)) Art.4. In force: June 5, 2005; £3.00.

These Regulations amend the Industrial Pollution Control (Northern Ireland) Order 1997 (SI 1997 277 (NI.18)) and the Pollution Prevention and Control Regulations (Northern Ireland) 2003 (SR 2003 46). They remove the definitions of "organic compound" and "volatile organic compound" or "VOC"; delete the definition of "prescribed"; amend the criteria for determining a fit and proper person; and exclude certain activities carried out in installations or mobile plant used solely for research and development and testing of new products and processes.

4611. Environmental protection–Pollution control regime

POLLUTION PREVENTION AND CONTROL (AMENDMENT) AND CONNECTED PROVISIONS (NO.2) REGULATIONS (NORTHERN IRELAND) 2005, SR 2005 285; made under the Environment (Northern Ireland) Order 2002 (SI 2002 3153 (NI.7)) Art.4. In force: June 5, 2005; £3.00.

These Regulations, which revoke the Pollution Prevention and Control (Amendment) and Connected Provisions Regulations (Northern Ireland) 2005 (SR 2005 229), amend the Industrial Pollution Control (Northern Ireland) Order 1997 (SI 1997 2777 (NI.18)) and the Pollution Prevention and Control Regulations (Northern Ireland) 2003 (SR 2003 46). The Regulations remove the definitions of "organic compound" and "volatile organic compound" or "VOC"; delete the definition of "prescribed"; and exclude certain activities carried out in installations or mobile plant used solely for research and development and testing of new products and processes.

4612. Environmental protection–Pollution control regime

POLLUTION PREVENTION AND CONTROL (AMENDMENT) (NO.3) REGULATIONS (NORTHERN IRELAND) 2005, SR 2005 454; made under the Environment (Northern Ireland) Order 2002 (SI 2002 3153 (NI.7)) Art.4. In force: November 1, 2005; £3.00.

These Regulations amend the Pollution Prevention and Control Regulations (Northern Ireland) 2003 (SR 2003 46). They are made to take account of Volatile Organic Compounds in Paints, Varnishes and Vehicle Refinishing Products Regulations 2005 (SI 2005 2773) which implement European Parliament and Council Directive 2004/42 ([2004] OJ L143/87) on the limitation of emissions of volatile organic compounds due to the use of organic solvents in certain paints and varnishes and vehicle refinishing products and amending Directive 1/13. These Regulations delete from the scope of the 2003 Regulations one category of "vehicle refinishing".

4613. Environmental protection–Waste–Packaging

PRODUCER RESPONSIBILITY OBLIGATIONS (PACKAGING WASTE) (AMENDMENT) REGULATIONS (NORTHERN IRELAND) 2005, SR 2005 329; made under the Producer Responsibility Obligations (Northern Ireland) Order 1998 (SI 1998 1762 (NI.16)) Art.3. In force: August 8, 2005; £3.00.

These Regulations amend the Producer Responsibility Obligations (Packaging Waste) Regulations 1 (SI 1 115) which impose on producers obligations to recover and recycle packaging waste, and related obligations, in order to attain the targets in Council Directive 94/62 ([1994] OJ L365/10) on packaging and packaging waste. The Regulations allow reprocessors and exporters to apply for accreditation at any time throughout the year; remove the requirement to have applied for accreditation as a reprocessor or exporter by September 30th in the year preceding the year in which he is applying to be accredited; remove the requirement for the Department to have notified the applicant of its decision by November 30th, although the requirement to notify in writing remains; and make amendments so that where accreditation is granted in the proceeding year to that to which the application relates, from January 1st and in all other cases, from the date of the decision.

4614. Environmental protection–Water pollution–Nitrate vulnerable zones–Public participation

PROTECTION OF WATER AGAINST AGRICULTURAL NITRATE POLLUTION (AMENDMENT) REGULATIONS (NORTHERN IRELAND) 2005, SR 2005 306;

made under the European Communities Act 1972 s.2. In force: July 25, 2005; £3.00.

These Regulations, which amend the Protection of Water Against Agricultural Nitrate Pollution Regulations (Northern Ireland) 2003 (SR 2003 259) to require provision to be made for public participation in the preparation, review or revision of any action programme in Northern Ireland, implement European Parliament and Council Directive 2003/35 ([2003] OJ L156/17) on public participation in respect of the drawing up of certain plans and programmes relating to the environment.

4615. Genetically modified organisms–Deliberate release–Marketing

GENETICALLY MODIFIED ORGANISMS (DELIBERATE RELEASE) (AMENDMENT) REGULATIONS (NORTHERN IRELAND) 2005, SR 2005 272; made under the European Communities Act 1972 s.2. In force: June 30, 2005; £3.00.

These Regulations which amend the Genetically Modified Organisms (Deliberate Release) Regulations (Northern Ireland) 2003 (SR 2003 167), give effect in Northern Ireland to the consequential amendments made to European Parliament and Council Directive 2001/18 ([2001] OJ L106/1) on the deliberate release into the environment of genetically modified organisms by European Parliament and Council Regulation 1829/2003 ([2003] OJ L268/1) on genetically modified food and feed. They update references to relevant EC legislation; provide that, where products have been approved in accordance with legislative provisions other than those contained in the 2003 Regulations, those products are only exempt from the requirements of Art.5(1)(a) and Art.8(1)(a) of the Genetically Modified Organisms (Northern Ireland) Order 1991 if they have been marketed in accordance with any conditions or limitations imposed upon the consent that has been issued in relation to that product; provide for the marketing of genetically modified food and feed that has been authorised under the Food and Feed Regulation without the need for a marketing consent under Art.8(1)(a) of the Order, or an additional risk assessment under Art.5(1)(a) of the Order; provide that, until April 18, 2007, the placing on the market of traces of a genetically modified organism or a combination of genetically modified organisms in products intended for direct use as food or feed or for processing is exempt from the requirements; and clarify that the Department must not grant or refuse to consent to release genetically modified organisms before the end of the latest date on which the representations mentioned in Reg.20(f) of the 2003 Regulations can be made.

4616. Hazardous waste–Control regime

HAZARDOUS WASTE REGULATIONS (NORTHERN IRELAND) 2005, SR 2005 300; made under the Waste and Contaminated Land (Northern Ireland) Order 1997 (SI 1997 2778 (NI.19) Art.30, Art.48, Art.77. In force: July 16, 2005; £6.50.

These Regulations, which amend the Planning (Environmental Impact Assessment) Regulations (Northern Ireland) 1999 (SR 1999 73), the Waste and Contaminated Land (Northern Ireland) Order 1997 (SI 1997 2778 (NI.19)), the Packaging (Essential Requirements) Regulations 2003 (SI 2003 1941), the Producer Responsibility (Packaging Waste) Regulations (Northern Ireland) 1999 (SR 1999 115), Controlled Waste (Registration of Carriers and Seizure of Vehicles) Regulations (Northern Ireland) 1999 (SR 1999 362), the Environmental Protection (Disposal of Polychlorinated Biphenyls and Dangerous Substances) Regulations (Northern Ireland) 2000 (SR 2000 232), the Controlled Waste (Duty of Care) Regulations (Northern Ireland) 2002 (SR 2002 271), the Chemicals (Hazard Information and Packaging for Supply) Regulations (Northern Ireland) 2002 (SR 2002 301), the Pollution Prevention and Control Regulations (Northern Ireland) 2003 (SR 2003 46), the Waste Management Licensing Regulations (Northern Ireland) 2003 (SR 2003 493), the Landfill Regulations (Northern Ireland) 2003 (SR 2003 496), and the Landfill (Amendment) Regulations (Northern Ireland) 2004 (SR 2004 297) and revoke the SpecialWaste Regulations (Northern Ireland) 1998 (SR 1998 289) set out the regime for the control and tracking of the movement of hazardous waste for the purpose of implementing the HazardousWaste Directive (Directive 91/689/EC) in Northern Ireland.

4617. Hazardous waste—List of wastes

LIST OF WASTES REGULATIONS (NORTHERN IRELAND) 2005, SR 2005 301; made under the European Communities Act 1972 s.2. In force: July 16, 2005; £5.50.

These Regulations implement Commission Decision 2000/532 ([2000] OJ L226/3) replacing Decision 94/3 establishing a list of wastes and Council Decision 94/904 establishing a list of hazardous waste which adopted the List of Wastes.

4618. Industrial Pollution Control (Northern Ireland) Order 1997 (SI 1997 2777 (NI.18))—Commencement No.2 Order

INDUSTRIAL POLLUTION CONTROL (1997 ORDER) (COMMENCEMENT NO.2) ORDER (NORTHERN IRELAND) 2005, SR 2005 77 (C.7); made under the Industrial Pollution Control (Northern Ireland) Order 1997 (SI 1997 2777 (NI.18)) Art.1. In force: bringing into operation various provisions of the 1997 Order on April 3, 2005; £3.00.

This Order repeals the Alkali, etc Works Regulation Act 1906 in so far as it is not already repealed.

4619. Smoke control—Authorisation of fireplaces—Exemptions

SMOKE CONTROL AREAS (EXEMPTED FIREPLACES) (AMENDMENT) REGULATIONS (NORTHERN IRELAND) 2005, SR 2005 437; made under the Clean Air (Northern Ireland) Order 1981 (SI 1981 158 (NI.4)) Art.17. In force: October 30, 2005; £3.00.

The Smoke Control Areas (Exempted Fireplaces) Regulations (Northern Ireland) 1 (SR 1 289) prescribed those fireplaces exempted from the provisions of the Clean Air (Northern Ireland) Order 1981 Art.17. These Regulations further amend the 1 Regulations by prescribing additional classes of fireplaces in the Schedule which are exempted from the provisions of the Clean Air (Northern Ireland) Order 1981 Art.17.

4620. Waste—Shipment—Fees

TRANSFRONTIER SHIPMENT OF WASTE (FEES) REGULATIONS (NORTHERN IRELAND) 2005, SR 2005 90; made under the European Communities Act 1972 s.2. In force: April 6, 2005; £3.00.

These Regulations enable the Department to charge fees for the assessment and monitoring of Transfrontier Shipments of Waste and require fees to be paid for each notification of £450 and £25 for each shipment.

4621. Books

Ryall, Aine—Effective Judicial Protection and the Environmental Impact Assessment Directive in Ireland. Hardback: £45.00. ISBN 1 84113 500 3. Hart Publishing.

EQUITY

4622. Books

Reid, Madeleine–Equality Law in Ireland. Paperback: £93.33. ISBN 1845920651. Tottel Publishing.

FAMILY LAW

4623. Child support–Miscellaneous amendments

CHILD SUPPORT (MISCELLANEOUS AMENDMENTS) REGULATIONS (NORTHERN IRELAND) 2005, SR 2005 125; made under the Child Support (Northern Ireland) Order 1991 (SI 1991 2628 (NI.23)) Art.12, Art.19, Art.28B, Art.39, Art.47, Art.48, Sch.1 para.4, Sch.1 para.5, Sch.1 para.6, Sch.1 para.7, Sch.1 para.10, Sch.4B para.2, Sch.4B para.4; and the Child Support, Pensions and Social Security Act (Northern Ireland) 2000 s.28. In force: in accordance with Reg.1; £3.00.

These Regulations amend the Child Support (Maintenance Assessment Procedure) Regulations (Northern Ireland) 1992 (SR 1992 340), the Child Support (Maintenance Assessments and Special Cases) Regulations (Northern Ireland) 1992 (SR 1992 341), the Child Support (Maintenance Arrangements and Jurisdiction) Regulations (Northern Ireland) 1992 (SR 1992 466), the Child Support (Maintenance Calculation Procedure) Regulations (Northern Ireland) 2001 (SR 2001 17), the Child Support (Maintenance Calculations and Special Cases) Regulations (Northern Ireland) 2001 (SR 2001 18), the Child Support (Transitional Provisions) Regulations (Northern Ireland) 2001 (SR 2001 19) and the Child Support (Variations) Regulations (Northern Ireland) 2001 (SR 2001 20). They insert definitions of "family" and "partner"; make provision for the effective date of a decision, where a person with care has ceased to be the person with care in relation to a qualifying child in respect of whom the maintenance assessment was made, to be the date that person so ceased to be the person with care in relation to that child; make clarifying amendments; and provide for payments due and made under a maintenance order to be treated as child support maintenance where those payments have been made under that order after the date on which a maintenance calculation took effect and the maintenance order has ceased to have effect.

4624. Children–Care and accommodation–Miscellaneous amendments

CHILDREN ORDER (MISCELLANEOUS AMENDMENTS) REGULATIONS (NORTHERN IRELAND) 2005, SR 2005 186; made under the Children (Northern Ireland) Order (SI 1995 755 (NI.2)) Art.27, Art.28, Art.34B, Art.44, Art.45, Art.70, Art.73, Art.75, Art.89, Art.105, Art.183. In force: April 1, 2005; £3.00.

These Regulations amend the Representations Procedure (Children) Regulations (Northern Ireland) 1996 (SR 1996 451), the Arrangements for Placement of Children (General) Regulations (Northern Ireland) 1996 (SR 1996 453), the Review of Children's Cases Regulations (Northern Ireland) 1996 (SR 1996 461), the Placement of Children with Parents etc. Regulations (Northern Ireland) 1996 (SR 1996 463), the Refuges (Children's Homes and Foster Placements) Regulations (Northern Ireland) 1996 (SR 1996 480) and the Children (Secure Accommodation) Regulations (Northern Ireland) 1996 (SR 1996 487). The Regulations make miscellaneous amendments to Regulations which govern the placement, care and accommodation of children looked after by authorities in the exercise of their functions under the Children (Northern Ireland) Order 1995 (SI 1995 755 (NI.2)), and related matters.

4625. Children–Child protection–Care standards–Disqualification lists

PROTECTION OF CHILDREN AND VULNERABLE ADULTS (DEFINITIONS) REGULATIONS (NORTHERN IRELAND) 2005, SR 2005 105; made under the Protection of Children and Vulnerable Adults (Northern Ireland) Order 2003 (SI 2003 417 (NI.4)) Art.20, Art.48. In force: April 1, 2005; £3.00.

The Protection of Children and Vulnerable Adults (Northern Ireland) Order 2003, requires the Department to keep lists of persons considered unsuitable to work with children or vulnerable adults. These lists will be known as the Disqualification from Working with Children List and the Disqualification from Working with Vulnerable Adults List. These Regulations require childcare organisations and providers of care to vulnerable adults to refer individuals to the Department for inclusion in one or both Lists. These Regulations prohibit child care organisations from offering employment in a child care position to any individual who is included in the Disqualification from Working with Children List or the Department of Education's Disqualification from Working with Children List.

4626. Civil Partnership Act 2004 (c.33)–Commencement No.1 Order

CIVIL PARTNERSHIP ACT 2004 (COMMENCEMENT NO.1) (NORTHERN IRELAND) ORDER 2005, SI 2005 2399 (C.99); made under the Civil Partnership Act 2004 s.263. Commencement details: bringing into force various provisions of the 2004 Act on September 5, 2005; £3.00.

This Order brings into force the provisions of the Civil Partnership Act 2004 listed in Column 1 of the Schedule. These provisions of the Act are being commenced for the particular purpose or purposes specified in the corresponding entry in Column 2 of the Schedule. Where no particular purpose is specified, a provision is being commenced for all purposes. The purposes relate to the making of regulations, orders and rules of court under provisions of the Act and under provisions in existing legislation amended by the Act.

4627. Civil Partnership Act 2004 (c.33)–Commencement No.2 Order

CIVIL PARTNERSHIP ACT 2004 (COMMENCEMENT NO.2) (NORTHERN IRELAND) ORDER 2005, SI 2005 3058 (C.132); made under the Civil Partnership Act 2004 s.263. Commencement details: bringing into force various provisions of the 2004 Act on November 7, 2005; £3.00.

This Order brings into force provisions of the Civil Partnership Act 2004 for the purpose of the powers in these provisions to prescribe matters by regulations.

4628. Civil Partnership Act 2004 (c.33)–Commencement No.3 Order

CIVIL PARTNERSHIP ACT 2004 (COMMENCEMENT NO.3) (NORTHERN IRELAND) ORDER 2005, SI 2005 3255 (C.139); made under the Civil Partnership Act 2004 s.263. In force: bringing into operation various provisions of the 2004 Act on December 5, 2005; £3.00.

This Order brings into force provisions of the Civil Partnership Act 2004.

4629. Civil partnerships–Births, deaths and marriages–Registration

CIVIL PARTNERSHIP ACT 2004 (AMENDMENTS TO SUBORDINATE LEGISLATION) (NO.2) ORDER (NORTHERN IRELAND) 2005, SR 2005 532; made under the Civil Partnership Act 2004 s.259. In force: December 5, 2005; £3.00.

This Order makes amendments to the Registration (Births, Still-Births and Deaths) Regulations (Northern Ireland) 1973 (SR 1973 373), the Adopted Persons (Birth Records) Regulations (Northern Ireland) 1995 (SR 1995 484) and the Marriage Regulations (Northern Ireland) 2003 (SR 2003 468) relating to civil registration records.

4630. Civil partnerships–Consequential amendments

CIVIL PARTNERSHIP ACT 2004 (AMENDMENTS TO SUBORDINATE LEGISLATION) ORDER (NORTHERN IRELAND) 2005, SR 2005 520; made under the Civil Partnership Act 2004 s.259. In force: December 5, 2005; £3.00.

This Order amends the Cremation (Belfast) Regulations (Northern Ireland) 1961 (SR O 1961 61), the Intestate Succession (Interest) Order (Northern Ireland) 1985 (SR 1985 8), the Enduring Powers of Attorney Regulations (Northern Ireland) 1989 (SR 1989 64), the Adoption Agencies Regulations (Northern Ireland) 1989 (SR 1989 253), the Burial Grounds Regulations (Northern Ireland) 1992 (SR 1992 238), the Trade Union (Nominations) Regulations 1992 (SR 1992 239), the Definition of Independent Visitors (Children) Regulations (Northern Ireland) 1996 (SR 1996 434), the Representations Procedure (Children) Regulations (Northern Ireland) 1996 (SR 1996 451), the Placement of Children with Parents etc. Regulations (Northern Ireland) 1996 (SR 1996 463), the Registration of Clubs (Accounts) Regulations (Northern Ireland) 1997 (SR 1997 333), the Domestic Energy Efficiency Grants Regulations (Northern Ireland) 2002 (SR 2002 56), the Paternity and Adoption Leave Regulations (Northern Ireland) 2002 (SR 2002 377), the Statutory Paternity Pay and Statutory Adoption Pay (General) Regulations (Northern Ireland) 2002 (SR 2002 378), the Statutory Paternity Pay and Statutory Adoption Pay (Administration) Regulations (Northern Ireland) 2002 (SR 2002 379), the Flexible Working (Eligibility, Complaints and Remedies) Regulations (Northern Ireland) 2003 (SR 2003 174), the Paternity and Adoption Leave (Adoption from Overseas) Regulations (Northern Ireland) 2003 (SR 2003 222), the Statutory Paternity Pay (Adoption) and Statutory Adoption Pay (Adoption from Overseas) Regulations (Northern Ireland) 2003 (SR 2003 223), the Employment Equality (Sexual Orientation) Regulations (Northern Ireland) 2003 (SR 2003 497), the Housing Renewal Grants (Reduction of Grant) Regulations (Northern Ireland) 2004 (SR 2004 8), the Personal Social Services and Children' Services (Direct Payments) Regulations (Northern Ireland) 2004 (SR 2004 120) and the Limited Liability Partnerships Regulations (Northern Ireland) 2004 (SR 2004 307). It makes amendments consequential upon the Civil Partnership Act 2004.

4631. Civil partnerships–Consequential amendments

CIVIL PARTNERSHIP ACT 2004 (CONSEQUENTIAL AMENDMENTS) ORDER (NORTHERN IRELAND) 2005, SR 2005 479; made under the Civil Partnership Act 2004 s.254, s.259. In force: December 5, 2005; £3.00.

This Order amends the Health and Personal Social Services (Northern Ireland) Order 1972 (SI 1972 1265 (NI.14)), the Financial Provisions (Northern Ireland) Order 1976 (SI 1976 1212 (NI.21)), the Pneumoconiosos etc. (Workers' Compensation) (Northern Ireland) Order 1979 (SI 1979 925 (NI.9)), the Credit Unions (Northern Ireland) Order 1985 (SI 1985 1205 (NI.12)), the Insolvency (Northern Ireland) Order 1989 (SI 1989 2405 (NI.19)), the Children (Northern Ireland) Order (SI 1995 755 (NI.2)), and the Road Traffic (Northern Ireland) Order 1995 (SI 1995 2994 (NI 18)). It makes minor amendments to Northern Ireland legislation to take account of the Civil Partnership Act 2004.

4632. Civil partnerships–Forms and particulars

CIVIL PARTNERSHIP REGULATIONS (NORTHERN IRELAND) 2005, SR 2005 482; made under the Civil Partnership Act 2004 s.144, s.147, s.159. In force: December 5, 2005; £4.00.

These Regulations made under the Civil Partnership Act 2004 make provision for the various forms and particulars to be prescribed in connection with the preliminaries to, and the registering of civil partnerships. They also include procedures required for the approval of places by a local registration authority for civil partnership registration other than at the Registrar's Office. In particular they set out the form required for giving notice of a proposed civil partnership and the requirement for giving 14 days notice and the giving of notice in person; the particulars to be taken from each civil partnership notice and kept by the registrar; the form of civil partnership schedule; the parties who may apply for approval of a place for the registration of a civil partnership and the application procedures which those parties must follow for the different types of approval; the requirements for public notice of applications and third party objection procedure; the considerations to be taken into account by an authority in determining an application; the procedure for attaching standard conditions to a place approval and non-standard conditions to either place or temporary place approvals, the notification of decisions, and a restriction on successive applications; the duration of approvals and the procedure for renewal; the determination and charging of fees by an authority for the approval of places and renewal of approvals and in respect of the attendance by registrars at approved places; the grounds and procedures for revocation, suspension and variation of an approval; the procedures for review of any decision by an authority under these regulations; the grounds and procedures for appeal to the county court; the deeming of a person who takes over the interest in a place approval as the approval holder; the requirements for the keeping of registers of approved places; the duty on the Registrar General to issue supplementary guidance; the form of medical statement required where by reason of serious illness or disability a civil partnership registration is to take place at home or in hospital; the form of consents required for persons over 16 years of age but under 18 years of age and the particulars to be taken from each consent or court order; the provision for correcting errors and the form of the statutory declaration to be completed; the form of statement by a responsible authority where either party is detained in prison or hospital; the form of a certified copy of an entry in the civil partnership registration records in the custody of the registrar and the Registrar General; and the extract from the civil partnership registration records to be issued for certain statutory provisions and the list of these provisions.

4633. Civil partnerships–Housing benefit and child support–Consequential provisions

CIVIL PARTNERSHIP (PENSIONS, SOCIAL SECURITY AND CHILD SUPPORT) (CONSEQUENTIAL, ETC. PROVISIONS) ORDER (NORTHERN IRELAND) 2005, SR 2005 536; made under the Civil Partnership Act 2004 s.254, s.258, s.259. In force: December 5, 2005; £6.00.

This Order makes amendments to provisions of 54 pieces of subordinate legislation, and contains a transitional provision relating to housing benefit and a transitory provision for child support in relation to cases for which the provisions of the Child Support, Pensions and Social Security Act (Northern Ireland) 2000 are not yet in operation.

4634. Civil partnerships–Overseas relationships

CIVIL PARTNERSHIP (TREATMENT OF OVERSEAS RELATIONSHIPS) ORDER (NORTHERN IRELAND) 2005, SR 2005 531; made under the Civil Partnership Act 2004 s.215, s.259. In force: December 5, 2005; £3.00.

This Order makes provision relating to the treatment of overseas relationships treated as civil partnerships by virtue of the Civil Partnership Act 2004 which were registered in the country where they were entered into before the date on which the 2004 Act comes into force.

4635. Civil partnerships–Pension and benefit payments

CIVIL PARTNERSHIP (MISCELLANEOUS AND CONSEQUENTIAL PROVISIONS) ORDER (NORTHERN IRELAND) 2005, SR 2005 471; made under the Civil Partnership Act 2004 s.254, s.259. In force: in accordance with Art.1; £3.00.

This Order amends the Social Security Contributions and Benefits (Northern Ireland) Act 1992 and the Pensions (Northern Ireland) Order 1995 (SI 1995 3213 (NI.22)). It amends certain provisions of legislation relating to pensions and benefit payments, extending those provisions to cover civil partnerships.

4636. Civil partnerships–Pensions and benefit payments

CIVIL PARTNERSHIP (PENSIONS AND BENEFIT PAYMENTS) (CONSEQUENTIAL, ETC. PROVISIONS) ORDER (NORTHERN IRELAND) 2005, SR 2005 434; made under the Civil Partnership Act 2004 s.254, s.259. In force: in accordance with Art.1 (2) (3); £3.00.

This Order amends the Social Security Contributions and Benefits (Northern Ireland) Act 1992, the Pension Schemes (Northern Ireland) Act 1993, the Pensions (Northern Ireland) Order 1995 (SI 1995 3213 (NI.22)), the Welfare Reform and Pensions (Northern Ireland) Order 1999 (SI 1999 3147 (NI.11)) and the Pensions (Northern Ireland) Order 2005 (SI 2005 255 (NI.1)). It makes amendments relating to pensions and benefit payments, extending those provisions to civil partners and surviving civil partners.

4637. Civil partnerships–Recognition of overseas dissolutions, annulments and separations

See FAMILY LAW. §1608

4638. Civil partnerships–Relationships

CIVIL PARTNERSHIP ACT 2004 (RELATIONSHIPS ARISING THROUGH CIVIL PARTNERSHIP) ORDER (NORTHERN IRELAND) 2005, SR 2005 542; made under the Civil Partnership Act 2004 s.247, s.248. In force: December 5, 2005; £3.00.

This Order amends the Civil Partnership Act 2004 and applies s.246 to the provisions of certain existing subordinate legislation.

4639. County courts–Civil partnership proceedings–Designation

CIVIL PARTNERSHIP PROCEEDINGS COUNTY COURTS ORDER (NORTHERN IRELAND) 2005, SR 2005 499; made under the Civil Partnership Act 2004 s.188. In force: December 5, 2005; £3.00.

This Order designates the county courts sitting for the various county court divisions in Northern Ireland as civil partnership proceedings county courts in which civil partnership causes may be commenced and in which undefended civil partnership causes may be tried under the Civil Partnership Act 2004.

4640. Family proceedings–Civil partnerships

FAMILY PROCEEDINGS (AMENDMENT NO.2) RULES (NORTHERN IRELAND) 2005, SR 2005 497; made under the Family Law (Northern Ireland) Order 1993 (SI 1993 1576 (NI.6)) Art.12. In force: December 5, 2005; £10.50.

These Rules amend the Family Proceedings Rules (Northern Ireland) 1996 (SR 1996 322), which apply to proceedings in the High Court and county court in consequence of the Civil Partnership Act 2004, the Gender Recognition Act 2004, and the Law Reform (Miscellaneous Provisions) (Northern Ireland) Order 2005. They prescribe procedures for proceedings under the Civil Partnership Act.

4641. Family proceedings–High Court Master

FAMILY PROCEEDINGS (AMENDMENT) RULES (NORTHERN IRELAND) 2005, SR 2005 144; made under the Family Law (Northern Ireland) Order 1993 (SI 1993 1576 (NI.6)) Art.12. In force: April 18, 2005; £3.00.

These Rules amend the Family Proceedings Rules (Northern Ireland) 1996 (SR 1996 322) to amend the definition of Master so that in relation to proceedings in the High Court it means Master (High Court) rather than Master (Probate and Matrimonial); and to enable the court to hold a directions appointment by telephone or by using any other method of direct oral communication.

4642. Family proceedings–Stay of proceedings–Civil partnerships

FAMILY PROCEEDINGS (CIVIL PARTNERSHIP: STAYING OF PROCEEDINGS) RULES (NORTHERN IRELAND) 2005, SR 2005 498; made under the Family Law (Northern Ireland) Order 1993 (SI 1993 1576 (NI.6)) Art.12. In force: December 5, 2005; £3.00.

These Rules are made under the Family Law (Northern Ireland) Order 1993 (SI 1993 1576 NI.6)) as extended by the Civil Partnership Act 2004 s.231 which allows for provision to be made in relation to civil partnerships corresponding to the provision made in respect of marriages by the Matrimonial Causes (Northern Ireland) Order 1978 (SI 1978 1045 (NI.15)). That Order makes provision about the relationship between domestic proceedings for divorce, judicial separation, nullity of marriage and declarations as to the validity and subsistence of a marriage of the petitioner, and proceedings in another jurisdiction of a similar type, and provides for when those domestic proceedings shall or may be stayed. These Rules make similar provision about the relationship between domestic proceedings for an order of dissolution, separation or nullity of civil partnership or for a declaration as to the validity or subsistence of a civil partnership, and proceedings in another jurisdiction of a similar type.

4643. Financial provision–Dissolution–Civil partnerships

DISSOLUTION ETC. (PENSIONS) REGULATIONS (NORTHERN IRELAND) 2005, SR 2005 484; made under the Civil Partnership Act 2004 Sch.15 para.14, Sch.15 para.22, Sch.15 para.23, Sch.15 para.50, Sch.17 para.14. In force: December 5, 2005; £3.00.

These Regulations make provision relating to orders made under the Civil Partnership Act 2004, including those made after proceedings overseas, for ancillary relief in proceedings for dissolution, separation or nullity of civil partnership which relate to the pension rights of a party to the civil partnership. They provide in particular for: the valuation of pension rights by the court; notices of change of circumstances to be provided by the person responsible for the pension arrangement to the civil partner without pension rights, or by that civil partner to the person responsible for the pension arrangement; and the stay period during which pension sharing orders cannot take effect.

4644. Protection of Children and Vulnerable Adults (Northern Ireland) Order 2003 (SI 2003 417 (NI.4))–Commencement No.2 Order

PROTECTION OF CHILDREN AND VULNERABLE ADULTS (2003 ORDER) (COMMENCEMENT NO.2) ORDER (NORTHERN IRELAND) 2005, SR 2005 104 (C.8); made under the Protection of Children and Vulnerable Adults (Northern Ireland) Order 2003 (SI 2003 417 (NI.4)) Art.1. In force: bringing into operation various provisions of the 2003 Act on April 1, 2005; £3.00.

This Order brings into operation those Articles of the Protection of Children and Vulnerable Adults (Northern Ireland) Order 2003 which will place the Pre-Employment Consultancy Service Register on a statutory basis by the creation of two new lists: the Disqualification from Working with Children List and the Disqualification from Working with Vulnerable Adults List.

4645. Retirement pensions–Widowers–Civil partnerships

SOCIAL SECURITY (RETIREMENT PENSIONS AND GRADUATED RETIREMENT BENEFIT) (WIDOWERS AND CIVIL PARTNERSHIP) REGULATIONS (NORTHERN IRELAND) 2005, SR 2005 541; made under the Social Security Contributions and Benefits (Northern Ireland) Act 1992 s.62, s.171; the Social Security Administration (Northern Ireland) Act 1992 s.5, s.165; and the Pensions (Northern Ireland) Order 2005 (SI 2005 255 (NI.1)) Sch.9 para.22. In force: in accordance with Reg.1; £3.00.

These Regulations make provision relating to widowers, civil partners and surviving civil partners. They amend the Social Security (Graduated Retirement Benefit) (No.2) Regulations (Northern Ireland) 1978 (SR 1978 105), the Social

Security (Claims and Payments) Regulations (Northern Ireland) 1987 (SR 1987 465), the Social Security (Graduated Retirement Benefit) Regulations (Northern Ireland) 2005 (SR 2005 121), the Social Security (Claims and Payments) (Amendment) Regulations (Northern Ireland) 2005 (SR 2005 122) and the Social Security (Shared Additional Pension) (Miscellaneous Amendments) Regulations (Northern Ireland) 2005 (SR 2005 299).

4646. Books

Kilkelly, Ursula—Child Law. Hardback: £125.00. ISBN 1 85475 390 8. Butterworths Law (Ireland).

FINANCIAL REGULATION

4647. Administration orders—Insurers

FINANCIAL SERVICES AND MARKETS ACT 2000 (ADMINISTRATION ORDERS RELATING TO INSURERS) (NORTHERN IRELAND) ORDER 2005, SI 2005 1644; made under the Financial Services and Markets Act 2000 s.360, s.426, s.428. In force: October 1, 2005; £3.00.

This Order, which amends the Insolvency Rules (Northern Ireland) 1991 (SR 1991 364), applies, in relation to insurers, the Insolvency (Northern Ireland) Order 1989 (SI 1989 2405 (NI.19)) Part III with various modifications set out in the Schedule. It enables administration orders to be made in relation to such insurers. Article 4 provides that insolvency rules relating to mutual credit and set-off do not apply to sums due from an insurer to another party where, at the time the sums became due, an application for an administration order had been made in relation to the insurer.

FISHERIES

4648. Fishing—Byelaws—Angling controls

PUBLIC ANGLING ESTATE BYELAWS (NORTHERN IRELAND) 2005, SR 2005 267; made under the Fisheries Act (Northern Ireland) 1966 s.26. In force: July 4, 2005; £3.00.

These Byelaws revoke the Angling (Department of Agriculture Waters) Byelaws (Northern Ireland) 1989 (SR 1989 482), the Angling (Department of Agriculture Waters) Amendment Byelaws (Northern Ireland) 1992 (SR 1992 357), the Angling (Department of Agriculture Waters) Amendment Byelaws (Northern Ireland) 1994 (SR 1994 40), and the Angling (Department of Agriculture Waters) (Amendment No.2) Byelaws (Northern Ireland) 1994 (SR 1994 314), which provide for angling controls and restrictions on waters within the public angling estate of the Department of Culture, Arts and Leisure.

4649. Fishing—Close seasons for angling—Foyle and Carlingford

FOYLE AREA AND CARLINGFORD AREA (CLOSE SEASONS FOR ANGLING) (AMENDMENT) REGULATIONS 2005, SR 2005 400; made under the Foyle Fisheries Act 1952 s.13, s.28; and the Foyle Fisheries Act (Northern Ireland) 1952 s.13, s.27. In force: August 18, 2005; £3.00.

These Regulations, which revoke the Foyle Area and Carlingford Area (Close Seasons for Angling) (Amendment) Regulations 2004 (SR 2004 383), amend the Foyle Area and Carlingford Area (Close Seasons for Angling) Regulations 2001 (SR 2001 160) by bringing the beginning of the close season for salmon and trout in the River Strule and its tributaries upstream of its confluence with the River Owenkillew in line with the other rivers in the Foyle Area (except the

Rivers Foyle and Finn), prescribing a close season running from the October 21 to March 31 next following, both dates inclusive. These Regulations also prescribe a close season for Binevenagh Dam.

4650. Fishing–Conservation–Registration

REGISTRATION OF FISH BUYERS AND SELLERS AND DESIGNATION OF FISH AUCTION SITES REGULATIONS (NORTHERN IRELAND) 2005, SR 2005 419; made under the European Communities Act 1972 s.2. In force: September 30, 2005; £3.00.

These Regulations make provision for the administration and enforcement of Council Regulation 2371/2002 ([2002] OJ L358/59) Art.22 on the conservation and sustainable exploitation of fisheries resources under the Common Fisheries Policy and Council Regulation 2847/93 ([1993] OJ L261/1) Art.9 establishing a control system applicable to the common fisheries policy which impose requirements relating to the first marketing and purchasing of fish (first sale fish). The Regulations make provision for the registration by the Department of Agriculture and Rural Development of sellers of first sale fish, designation of fish auction sites and registration of buyers of first sale fish. They require registered fish sellers to maintain records of their sales of first sale fish and require buyers of first sale fish to maintain records of their purchases of first sale fish. The Regulations provide offences for the purposes of the enforcement of these registrations and designations.

4651. Fishing–Eels–Licence duties

EEL FISHING (LICENCE DUTIES) REGULATIONS (NORTHERN IRELAND) 2005, SR 2005 456; made under the Fisheries Act (Northern Ireland) 1966 s.15, s.19. In force: January 1, 2006; £3.00.

These Regulations, which revoke the Eel Fishing (Licence Duties) (No.2) Regulations (Northern Ireland) 2004 (SR 2004 499), amend the licence duties payable to the Fisheries Conservancy Board for Northern Ireland in respect of licences for the use of fishing engines for the taking of eels.

4652. Fishing–Fish health

FISH HEALTH (AMENDMENT) REGULATIONS (NORTHERN IRELAND) 2005, SR 2005 330; made under the European Communities Act 1972 s.2. In force: July 8, 2005; £3.00.

These Regulations amend the Fish Health Regulations (Northern Ireland) 1998 (SR 1988 310) which implement in respect of Northern Ireland, Council Directive 91/67 ([1991] OJ L46/1) concerning the animal health conditions governing the placing on the market of aquaculture animals and products and Council Directive 95/70 ([1995] OJ L332/33) introducing minimum community measures for the control of certain diseases affecting bivalve molluscs, to the extent that they are not implemented by other legislation. The Regulations prohibit the relaying within Northern Ireland of live molluscs, eggs and gametes from the Lough Foyle area as specified in the new Schedule 7 inserted into the 1998 Regulations.

4653. Fishing vessels–Carriage of nets and fishing gear

SHRIMP FISHING NETS ORDER (NORTHERN IRELAND) 2005, SR 2005 349; made under the Sea Fish (Conservation) Act 1967 s.3, s.15. In force: August 22, 2005; £3.00.

This Order regulates the carriage and use of any fishing nets with mesh size between 16 and 31 millimetres, measured in accordance with Commission Regulation 2108/1984 ([1984] OJ L194/22) laying down detailed rules for determining the mesh size of fishing nets. It sets out the national provisions called for by Council Regulation 850/98 ([1998] OJ L125/1) for the conservation of fishery resources through technical measures for the protection of juveniles of marine organisms, by specifying veil nets and sorting grids as the types of device required to be used.

4654. Fishing vessels–Control of satellite based vessel monitoring systems

SEA FISHING (ENFORCEMENT OF COMMUNITY SATELLITE MONITORING MEASURES) (NORTHERN IRELAND) ORDER 2005, SR 2005 452; made under the Fisheries Act 1981 s.30. In force: November 14, 2005; £3.00.

This Order which revokes Sea Fishing (Enforcement of Community Satellite Monitoring Measures) Order 2000 (SI 2000 181) provides for the enforcement of Commission Regulation 2244/2003 ([2003] OJ L333/17) laying down detailed provisions regarding satellite-based Vessel Monitoring Systems. The Order contains provisions relating to relevant Northern Ireland fishing boats, and British and Community fishing boats within the Northern Ireland zone and provisions relating to the installation of a satellite-tracking device; the switching off of a satellite-tracking device in port without prior notification; the information to be transmitted by the satellite-tracking device; the responsibilities relating to a satellite-tracking device and the technical failure or non-functioning of a satellite-tracking device. In addition the Order creates offences in respect of the contravention, by the person in charge of the relevant fishing boat (or the individuals otherwise specifically referred to), of the aforementioned provisions.

4655. Fishing vessels–Days at sea–Restrictions

SEA FISHING (RESTRICTION ON DAYS AT SEA) ORDER (NORTHERN IRELAND) 2005, SR 2005 350; made under the Fisheries Act 1981 s.30. In force: July 28, 2005; £3.50.

This Order, which amends the Sea Fishing (Enforcement of Community Control Measures) Order 2000 (SI 2000 51), provides for the administration and enforcement in Northern Ireland of provisions of Council Regulation 27/2005 ([2005] OJ L12/1) fixing for 2005 the fishing opportunities and associated conditions for certain fish stocks and groups of fish stocks, applicable in Community waters and, for Community vessels, in waters where catch limitations are required. Further, the Order provides for the enforcement in Northern Ireland of monitoring, inspection and surveillance provisions as set out in Council Regulation 423/2004 ([2004] OJ L270/70) establishing measures for the recovery of cod stocks.

4656. Shellfish–Emergency prohibitions–Amnesic shellfish poisoning–Scallops

See FOOD. §4672

4657. Shellfish–Emergency prohibitions–Diarrhetic shellfish poisoning–Scallops

See FOOD. §4673

FOOD

4658. Food composition–Specific nutritional purposes–Tryptophan

TRYPTOPHAN IN FOOD REGULATIONS (NORTHERN IRELAND) 2005, SR 2005 440; made under the Food Safety (Northern Ireland) Order 1991 (SI 1991 762 (NI.7)) Art.15, Art.25, Art.26, Art.47. In force: November 11, 2005; £3.00.

These Regulations, which revoke the Tryptophan in Food Regulations (Northern Ireland) 1990 (SR 1990 329), amend the Food for Particular Nutritional Uses (Addition of Substances for Specific Nutritional Purposes) Regulations (Northern Ireland) 2002 (SR 2002 264). The Regulations continue to prohibit the addition of tryptophan; add a new exception from the prohibitions in the Regulations in respect of laevorotatory tryptophan added to food supplements if certain conditions are met; insert a qualification to the existing exception in respect of laevorotatory tryptophan, its sodium, potassium, calcium or magnesium salts or its hydrochloride added to certain foods for particular nutritional use in that the added substance must comply with specified purity criteria; continue to provide for offences and a penalty; make provision as to enforcement; apply various provisions of the Food Safety (Northern Ireland) Order 1991 (SI 1991 762 (NI.7)) and include a presumption as regards food which contravenes the Regulations in certain circumstances.

4659. Food hygiene–Animal products–Poultrymeat

POULTRY MEAT, FARMED GAME BIRD MEAT AND RABBIT MEAT (HYGIENE AND INSPECTION) (AMENDMENT) REGULATIONS (NORTHERN IRELAND) 2005, SR 2005 35; made under the European Communities Act 1972 s.2. In force: March 14, 2005; £3.00.

These Regulations, which amend the Poultry Meat, Farmed Game Bird Meat and Rabbit Meat (Hygiene and Inspection) Regulations (Northern Ireland) 1995 (SR 1995 396) and the Products of Animal Origin (Import and Export) Regulations (Northern Ireland) 1998 (SR 1998 45), implement part of Council Directive 71/118 ([1971] OJ L55/23) on health problems affecting the production and placing on the market of fresh poultrymeat that prohibits poultrymeat from being placed on the market for human consumption if it has been treated with water retention agents or obtained under technologically similar conditions and likely as a result to present the same risk.

4660. Food hygiene–Licences

FOOD SAFETY (GENERAL FOOD HYGIENE) (AMENDMENT) REGULATIONS (NORTHERN IRELAND) 2005, SR 2005 408; made under the Food Safety (Northern Ireland) Order 1991 (SI 1991 762 (NI.7)) Art.18, Art.25, Art.47. In force: September 5, 2005; £3.00.

These Regulations amend the Food Safety (General Food Hygiene) Regulations (Northern Ireland) 1995 (SR 1995 360) to provide that a licence for a butcher's shop remains in operation for a year from the date of issue; and if a licence is granted to a person who has held a licence for not less than eight months and both licences relate to the same premises, the further licence becomes operative for a period of a year beginning on the expiry of the existing licence.

4661. Food hygiene–Official controls–Charges

FISHERY PRODUCTS (OFFICIAL CONTROLS CHARGES) REGULATIONS (NORTHERN IRELAND) 2005, SR 2005 524; made under the European Communities Act 1972 s.2. In force: January 1, 2006; £3.00.

These Regulations implement the provisions of Council Directive 85/73 ([1985] OJ L032/4) on the financing of veterinary inspections and controls that, following reforms to the Community regime on food hygiene that take effect on January 1, 2006, require fees to be collected for inspections of and controls on fishery products under European Parliament and Council Regulation 854/2004 ([2004] OJ L139/206) laying down specific rules for the organisation of official controls on products of animal origin intended for human consumption. The Regulations state what costs constitute the actual costs of exercising official controls for the purposes of the Regulations; provide the rates to calculate the sterling equivalent of any sums which are specified in Euros in the Regulations; prescribe how the length of an "account period" for the purposes of the Regulations is to be determined; provide that where a duty to pay charges under the Regulations is imposed on more than one person it may be enforced jointly or separately against such persons; require authorities to which charges are payable under the Regulations to calculate the charges, recalculate if an error is made and give notice of amounts due to those liable to pay; and provide for appeals against decisions of authorities imposing charges under the Regulations and lay down the requirements for the conduct and determination of such appeals.

4662. Food hygiene–Official controls–Charges

MEAT (OFFICIAL CONTROLS CHARGES) REGULATIONS (NORTHERN IRELAND) 2005, SR 2005 549; made under the European Communities Act 1972 s.2. In force: January 1, 2006; £3.00.

These Regulations revoke the Meat (Hygiene, Inspection and Examination for Residues) (Charges) Regulations (Northern Ireland) 1995 (SR 1995 431). They require the Agency to notify the operator of each slaughterhouse, game-handling establishment and cutting plant in which official controls have been exercised of the official controls charge that has arisen in relation to those officials controls; provide that any official controls charge so notified is payable by the operator to the Agency on demand; allow the Agency to refuse to exercise any further official controls at given premises where, despite a Court order requiring the operator of the premises to pay the official controls charge for which he is liable, he fails to comply with the order; require persons to supply the Agency on demand with such information as it may reasonably require for the purpose of calculating the official controls charge or notifying the operator of it, and to supply the Agency on demand with such evidence as it may reasonably require to verify that information; and provide that a person who in response to a demand for information or evidence knowingly or recklessly furnishes false or misleading information, or without reasonable excuse fails to comply within a reasonable time with a demand for information or evidence, is guilty of an offence.

4663. Food hygiene–Standards–Enforcement and execution

FOOD HYGIENE REGULATIONS (NORTHERN IRELAND) 2005, SR 2005 356; made under the European Communities Act 1972 s.2. In force: January 1, 2006; £5.00.

These Regulations, which amend the Eggs (Marketing Standards) Regulations (Northern Ireland) 1995 (SR 1995 382) and the Food Safety (Ships and Aircraft) Order (Northern Ireland) 2004 (SR 2004 99), revoke the Ice-Cream and Other Frozen Confections Regulations (Northern Ireland) 1968 (SR 1968 13), the Food Premises (Registration) Regulations (Northern Ireland) 1992 (SR 1992 167), the Eggs Products Regulations (Northern Ireland) 1993 (SR 1993 329), the Dairy Products (Hygiene) Regulations (Northern Ireland) 1995 (SR 1995 201), the Food Safety (General Food Hygiene) Regulations (Northern Ireland) 1995 (SR 1995 360), the Food Safety (Temperature Control) Regulations (Northern Ireland) 1995 (SR 1995 377), the Fresh Meat (Hygiene and Inspection) Regulations (Northern Ireland) 1997 (SR 1997 493), the Meat Products (Hygiene) Regulations (Northern Ireland) 1997 (SR 1997 494), the Minced Meat and Meat Preparations (Hygiene) Regulations (Northern Ireland) 1997 (SR 1997 495), the Wild Game Meat (Hygiene and Inspection) Regulations (Northern Ireland) 1997 (SR 1997 496), the Food Safety (Fishery Products and Live Shellfish) (Hygiene) Regulations (Northern Ireland) 1998 (SR 1998 207), the Gelatine (Intra-Community Trade) Regulations (Northern Ireland) 2001 (SR 2001 226) and the Collagen and Gelatine (Intra-Community Trade) Regulations (Northern Ireland) 2004 (SR 2004 7). They provide for the execution and enforcement there of: European Parliament and Council Regulation 852/2004 ([2004] OJ L139/1) on the hygiene of foodstuffs; European Parliament and Council Regulation 853/2004 ([2004] OJ L226/22) laying down specific hygiene rules for food of animal origin; and European Parliament and Council Regulation 854/2004 ([2004] OJ L155/206) laying down specific rules for the organisation of official controls on products of animal origin intended for human consumption. The Regulations create certain presumptions that, for the purposes thereof, specified food is intended for human consumption; provide that the Food Standards Agency is the competent authority for the purposes of the Community Regulations except where it has delegated competences as provided for in the Community Regulations; make provision for the enforcement and execution of these Regulations and of the Community Regulations; provide that where the commission of an offence thereunder is due to the act or default of some other person that other person is guilty of the offence; and provide that in proceedings for an offence thereunder it is a defence for the accused to prove that he took all reasonable precautions and exercised all due diligence to avoid the commission of the offence.

4664. Food labelling—Honey

HONEY (AMENDMENT) REGULATIONS (NORTHERN IRELAND) 2005, SR 2005 385; made under the Food Safety (Northern Ireland) Order 1991 (SI 1991 762 (NI.7)) Art.15, Art.16, Art.25, Art.47. In force: September 5, 2005; £3.00.

These Regulations correct errors in the Honey Regulations (Northern Ireland) 2003 (SR 2003 383), to ensure accurate transposition of Council Directive 2001/110 concerning honey ([2002] OJ L10/47).

4665. Food safety—Additives

MISCELLANEOUS FOOD ADDITIVES (AMENDMENT) REGULATIONS (NORTHERN IRELAND) 2005, SR 2005 19; made under the Food Safety (Northern Ireland) Order 1991 (SI 1991 762 (NI.7)) Art.15, Art.16, Art.25, Art.26, Art.47, Sch.1 para.1. In force: February 17, 2005; £3.00.

These Regulations amend the Miscellaneous Food Additives (Amendment) Regulations (Northern Ireland) 2004 (SR 2004 439) to correct a drafting error.

4666. Food safety—Additives

MISCELLANEOUS FOOD ADDITIVES (AMENDMENT NO.2) REGULATIONS (NORTHERN IRELAND) 2005, SR 2005 201; made under the Food Safety (Northern Ireland) Order 1991 (SI 1991 762 (NI.7)) Art.15, Art.16, Art.25, Art.26, Art.47, Sch.1 para.1. In force: May 28, 2005; £3.00.

These Regulations, which amend the Miscellaneous Food Additives Regulations (Northern Ireland) 1996 (SR 1996 50), implement European Parliament and Council Directive 2003/114 ([2003] OJ L24/58) amending Directive 95/2 on food additives other than colours and sweeteners. They make amendments by inserting a definition of flavouring; bringing up to date the definition of "Directive 95/2" to cover the amendment of that Directive by Directive 2003/114; substituting a new definition for the term "stabiliser" to include substances which increase the binding capacity of food; making an amendment to ensure that a flavouring which lawfully has in or on it a permitted miscellaneous additive can be used as an ingredient in a compound food; providing that where a permitted miscellaneous additive used in a flavouring performs a technological function in the final food in which that flavouring is an ingredient, it is to be regarded as an additive of the final food; prohibiting the use of additives in flavourings in quantities greater than the minimum necessary, or in circumstances where they would be a hazard to human health or misleading to the consumer, and making contravention an offence; and making transitional provision to allow the marketing of additives, flavourings or foods marketed or labelled before January 27, 2006, which are legal under existing rules.

4667. Food safety—Additives—Colours

COLOURS IN FOOD (AMENDMENT) REGULATIONS (NORTHERN IRELAND) 2005, SR 2005 75; made under the Food Safety (Northern Ireland) Order 1991 (SI 1991 762) Art.15, Art.16, Art.25, Art.26, Art.47, Sch.1 para.1. In force: April 1, 2005; £3.00.

These Regulations, which amend the Colours in Food Regulations (Northern Ireland) 1996 (SR 1996 49), implement Commission Directive 2004/47 ([2004] OJ L113/24) amending Directive 95/45 as regards mixed carotenes (E 160a (i)) and beta-carotene (E160a (ii)). The Regulations provide amended purity criteria for mixed carotenes E160a(i) and beta carotene E160a(ii); insert a transitional defence provision for products put on the market or labelled before April 1, 2005 which otherwise comply with the 1996 Regulation, allowing current stocks to be exhausted.

4668. Food safety–Additives–Sweeteners

SWEETENERS IN FOOD (AMENDMENT) REGULATIONS (NORTHERN IRELAND) 2005, SR 2005 18; made under the Food Safety (Northern Ireland) Order 1991 (SI 1991 762 (NI.7)) Art.15, Art.16, Art.25, Art.26, Art.47, Sch.1 para.1. In force: January 29, 2005; £3.00.

These Regulations, which amend the Sweeteners in Food Regulations (Northern Ireland) 1996 (SR 1996 48), implement European Parliament and Council Directive 2003/115 ([2004] OJ L24/65) amending Directive 94/35 on sweeteners for use in foodstuffs and Commission Directive 2004/46 ([2004] OJ L114/15) amending Directive 95/31 as regards E 955 sucralose and E 962 salt of aspartame-acesulfame. The Regulations bring up to date the definition of "Directive 94/35" so as to cover the amendment of that Directive by Directive 2003/115; bring up to date the definition of "Directive 95/31" so as to cover its amendment by Directive 2004/46; and substitute a new definition for the definition of the term "permitted sweetener" to reflect the fact that Sucralose and the Salt of aspartame-acesulfame are now permitted sweeteners.

4669. Food safety–Beef–Labelling–Enforcement of schemes

BEEF LABELLING (ENFORCEMENT) (AMENDMENT) REGULATIONS (NORTHERN IRELAND) 2005, SR 2005 450; made under the European Communities Act 1972 s.2. In force: November 14, 2005; £3.00.

These Regulations amend the Beef Labelling (Enforcement) Regulations (Northern Ireland) 2001 (SR 2001 271) to provide for an appeal to a magistrates' court if a person is aggrieved by a decision of an authorised officer to serve a notice pursuant to reg.5(2). On appeal against a notice the court may cancel the notice or affirm it with or without modifications.

4670. Food safety–Contaminants–Maximum levels

CONTAMINANTS IN FOOD REGULATIONS (NORTHERN IRELAND) 2005, SR 2005 538; made under the Food Safety (Northern Ireland) Order 1991 (SI 1991 762 (NI.7)) Art.15, Art.16, Art.25, Art.26, Art.32, Art.47. In force: January 1, 2006; £3.00.

These Regulations revoke the Contaminants in Food Regulations (Northern Ireland) 2004 (SR 2004 487) and the Contaminants in Food (Amendment) Regulations (Northern Ireland) 2005 (SR 2005 199). They make provision for the execution and enforcement of Commission Regulation 466/2001 ([2001] OJ L77/1) setting maximum levels for contaminants in foodstuffs. They implement Commission Directive 98/53 ([1998] OJ L201/93) laying down the sampling methods and the methods of analysis for the official control of the levels for certain contaminant in foodstuffs; Commission Directive 2001/22 ([2001] OJ L77/14) laying down the sampling methods and the methods of analysis for the official control of the levels of lead, cadmium, mercury and 3-MCPD in foodstuffs; Commission Directive 2002/26 ([2002] OJ L75/38) laying down the sampling methods and the methods of analysis for the official control of levels of ochratoxin A in foodstuffs; Commission Directive 2002/69 ([2002] OJ L209/5) laying down the sampling methods and the methods of analysis for the official control of dioxins and the determination of dioxin-like PCBs in foodstuffs; Commission Directive 2003/78 ([2003] OJ L203/40) laying down the sampling methods and the methods of analysis for the official control of the levels of patulin in foodstuffs; Commission Directive 2004/16 ([2004] OJ L42/16) laying down the sampling methods and the methods of analysis for the official control of the levels of tin in canned foods; and Commission Directive 2005/10 ([2005] OJ L34/15) laying down the sampling methods and the methods of analysis for the official control of the levels of benzo(a)pyrene in foodstuffs. The Regulations provide that it is an offence to place on the market certain foods if they contain contaminants of any kind specified in the Commission Regulation at levels exceeding those specified (subject to a derogation applicable to certain types of lettuce and spinach); to use food containing such contaminants at such levels as ingredients in the production of certain foods; to mix foods which do not comply with the maximum levels referred to above with foods which do comply; to mix foods to which the Commission Regulation relates and which are intended for direct consumption with foods to which the Commission Regulation relates and which are intended to be sorted or otherwise treated prior to consumption; or to detoxify by chemical treatment food not complying with the limits specified in the Commission Regulation. They also specify the enforcement authorities; and prescribe requirements in relation to the methods of sampling and the analysis of samples of foods subject to the Commission Regulation.

4671. Food safety–Contaminants–Maximum levels

CONTAMINANTS IN FOOD (AMENDMENT) REGULATIONS (NORTHERN IRELAND) 2005, SR 2005 199; made under the Food Safety (Northern Ireland) Order 1991 (SI 1991 762 (NI.7)) Art.15, Art.16, Art.25, Art.26, Art.47. In force: May 1, 2005; £3.00.

These Regulations, which amend the Contaminants in Food Regulations (Northern Ireland) 2004 (SR 2004 487), provide for the enforcement of the requirements of Commission Regulation 655/2004 ([2004] OJ L77/1) amending Regulation 466/2001 as regards nitrates in foods for infants and young children, and Commission Regulation 683/2004 ([2004] OJ L106/3) amending Regulation 466/2001 as regards aflatoxins and ochratoxin A in foods for infants and young children.

4672. Food safety–Emergency prohibitions–Amnesic shellfish poisoning–Scallops

FOOD PROTECTION (EMERGENCY PROHIBITIONS) (REVOCATION) ORDER (NORTHERN IRELAND) 2005, SR 2005 232; made under the Food and Environment Protection Act 1985 s.1, s.24. In force: May 3, 2005; £3.00.

This Order revokes the Food Protection (Emergency Prohibitions) Order (Northern Ireland) 2005 (SR 2005 205) which contains emergency prohibitions restricting various activities in order to prevent human consumption of scallops or food which is derived from scallops originating in waters in that part of ICES (International Council for the Exploration of the Sea) area VIIa which is within British Fishery limits and which is adjacent to Northern Ireland (off the East Coast).

4673. Food safety–Emergency prohibitions–Diarrhetic shellfish poisoning–Scallops

FOOD PROTECTION (EMERGENCY PROHIBITIONS) ORDER (NORTHERN IRELAND) 2005, SR 2005 205; made under the Food and Environment Protection Act 1985 s.1, s.24. In force: April 7, 2005; £3.00.

This Order contains emergency prohibitions restricting various activities in order to prevent human consumption of scallops or food which is derived from scallops originating in the designated area and which has been or may have been rendered unsuitable for human consumption in consequence of scallops having been affected by a toxin which causes diarrhetic shellfish poisoning in human beings. Fishing for or taking scallops and the movement of scallops out of the designated area is prohibited.

4674. Food safety–Genetically modified organisms–Traceability and labelling

GENETICALLY MODIFIED ORGANISMS (TRACEABILITY AND LABELLING) REGULATIONS (NORTHERN IRELAND) 2005, SR 2005 271; made under the European Communities Act 1972 s.2. In force: June 30, 2005; £3.00.

These Regulations make provision as respects Northern Ireland, for the execution and enforcement of European Parliament and Council Regulation 1830/2003 ([2003] OJ L286/1) concerning the traceability and labelling of genetically modified organisms and the traceability of food and feed products produced from genetically modified organisms and amending Directive 2001/18. The Regulations make provision for the appointment of inspectors; set out the powers of the inspectors including the power to carry out tests and inspections, to take samples, and to require the provision of information; make provision for district councils and the Department to obtain information; provide for the service by inspectors of notices dealing with incorrectly labelled products; make it an offence to contravene specified Community provisions, to obstruct inspectors in the exercise of powers under these Regulations, to fail to comply with any requirement of the inspectors and to give false information; make provision in respect of offences committed by third parties; and provide for offences committed by corporate bodies.

4675. Food safety—Hygiene and enforcement

FEED (HYGIENE AND ENFORCEMENT) REGULATIONS (NORTHERN IRELAND) 2005, SR 2005 546; made under the European Communities Act 1972 s.2. In force: January 1, 2006; £4.50.

These Regulations, which amend the Feeding Stuffs (Establishments and Intermediaries) Regulations 1999 (SI 1999 1872), the Feeding Stuffs (Enforcement) Regulations 1999 (SI 1999 2325), the Feeding Stuffs (Sampling and Analysis) (Amendment) Regulations (Northern Ireland) 2001 (SR 2001 209), the Feeding Stuffs (Amendment) Regulations (Northern Ireland) 2001 (SR 2001 428), the Feeding Stuffs (Amendment) Regulations (Northern Ireland) 2002 (SR 2002 263) and the Feeding Stuffs (Enforcement) (Amendment) Regulations (Northern Ireland) 2003 (SR 2003 287), revoke the Feeding Stuffs (Safety Requirements for Feed for Food-Producing Animals) Regulations (Northern Ireland) 2004 (SR 2004 506) and the Feeding Stuffs (Establishments and Intermediaries) (Amendment) Regulations (Northern Ireland) 2005 (SR 2005 74). They provide for the execution and enforcement of European Parliament and Council Regulation 178/2002 ([2002] OJ L31/1) laying down the general principles and requirements of food law, establishing the European Food Safety Authority and laying down procedures in matters of food safety; and of European Parliament and Council Regulation 183/2005 ([2005] OJ L25/1) laying down requirements for feed hygiene. They also make provisions as to administration generally, in particular so as to give effect to European Parliament and Council Regulation 882/2004 ([2004] OJ L191/1) on official controls performed to ensure the verification of compliance with feed and food law, animal health and animal welfare rules. The Regulations designate the competent authorities for the purposes of the various functions mentioned in Regulation 183/2005; identify those provisions of Regulation 183/2005 where failure to comply gives rise to an offence, and attach penalties to those offences; set out the requirements to be observed by anyone applying for an amendment to a registration or approval; provide for a right of appeal against decisions relating to registrations or approvals taken by the enforcement authority; and specify the fees payable by an applicant for approval or amendment to an approval.

4676. Food safety—Packaging—Plastics

MATERIALS AND ARTICLES IN CONTACT WITH FOOD REGULATIONS (NORTHERN IRELAND) 2005, SR 2005 210; made under the Food Safety (Northern Ireland) Order 1991 (SI 1991 762 (NI.7)) Art.15, Art.16, Art.25, Art.32, Art.47. In force: May 23, 2005; £3.00.

These Regulations revoke the Materials and Articles in Contact with Food Regulations (Northern Ireland) 1987 (SR 1987 432) and the Materials and Articles in Contact with Food (Amendment) Regulations (Northern Ireland) 1994 (SR 1994 174). They provide for the enforcement of European Parliament and Council Regulation 1935/2004 ([2004] OJ L338/4) on materials and articles intended to come into contact with food and repealing Directives 80/590 and 89/109. The Regulations control what substances may be used in the manufacture of regenerated cellulose film (RCF), which may vary according to whether or not it is coated with plastics; regulate what substances may be used to manufacture plastic coatings for RCF, and under what conditions; create a conditional derogation in respect of substances used as colorants or adhesives in the manufacture of non-plastic coated RCF; set up offences in relation to the sale, import or business use of non-compliant RCF; and create a conditional requirement for RCF, when marketed prior to the retail stage, to be accompanied by a declaration of legislative compliance.

4677. Food safety–Packaging–Plastics

PLASTIC MATERIALS AND ARTICLES IN CONTACT WITH FOOD (AMENDMENT) REGULATIONS (NORTHERN IRELAND) 2005, SR 2005 49; made under the Food Safety (Northern Ireland) Order 1991 (SI 1991 762 (NI.7)) Art.15, Art.16, Art.25, Art.26, Art.47. In force: March 18, 2005; £3.00.

These Regulations, which amend the Plastic Materials and Articles in Contact with Food Regulations (Northern Ireland) 1998 (SR 1998 264), implement Commission Directive 2004/19 ([2004] OJ L71/8) amending Commission Directive 2002/72 ([2004] OJ L220/18) relating to plastic materials and articles intended to come into contact with foodstuffs. The Regulations amend the definition of "additive" to maintain consistency with the Directive; remove references to lists of substances whose authorisations are now spent; extend to articles provisions of the 1998 Regulations that formerly only applied to materials; add a restriction on the use of additives in the manufacture of plastic materials and articles which relate to substances also used as food additives or flavourings; make provision for the procedure to be followed and the time limits to be observed by any person wishing to have an additive included in the Community list of authorised additives; amend the labelling requirements for plastic materials at the pre-retail stage so as to require additional information to be given; and provide a defence to breach the 1998 Regulations in respect of plastic materials or articles manufactured or imported into the European Community before March 1, 2006.

4678. Food safety–Smoke flavourings

SMOKE FLAVOURINGS REGULATIONS (NORTHERN IRELAND) 2005, SR 2005 76; made under the Food Safety (Northern Ireland) Order 1991 (SI 1991 762 (NI.7)) Art.15, Art.16, Art.25, Art.26, Art.47, Sch.1 para.1. In force: in accordance with Reg.1; £3.00.

These Regulations provide for the enforcement and execution of certain specified provisions of European Parliament and Council Regulation 2065/2003 ([2003] OJ L309/1) on smoke flavourings used or intended for use in or on foods. They formally designate the Food Standards Agency as the national competent authority to receive applications for the authorisation of new primary smoke condensates and primary tar fractions for use as such in or on foods, or in the production of derived smoke flavourings for use in or on foods; apply various provisions of the Food Safety (Northern Ireland) Order 1991 (SI 1991 762 (NI.7)) with some modifications in their application for the purposes of these Regulations; establish penalties for failing to comply with certain specified provisions of Regulation 2065/2003; and provide for district councils to enforce the provisions of these Regulations and Regulation 2065/2003.

4679. Imports–Emergency controls–Pistachios from Iran

FOOD (PISTACHIOS FROM IRAN) (EMERGENCY CONTROL) (AMENDMENT) REGULATIONS (NORTHERN IRELAND) 2005, SR 2005 30; made under the European Communities Act 1972 s.2. In force: February 9, 2005; £3.00.

These Regulations, which amend the Food (Pistachios from Iran) (Emergency Control) Regulations (Northern Ireland) 2003 (SR 2003 360), implement Commission Decision 2005/85 ([2005] OJ L30/12) imposing special conditions on the import of pistachios and certain products derived from pistachios originating in, or consigned from Iran. The new Decision provides that the health certificate required to accompany a consignment of "Iranian pistachios" shall be valid for import carried out no more than 4 months after the issue date of the health certificate; and provides that certain costs relating to the import controls on Iranian pistachios imposed by the Decision and the costs relating to official measures taken against non-compliant consignments of Iranian pistachios shall be borne by the person responsible for the consignment.

4680. Labelling—Food labelling

FOOD LABELLING (AMENDMENT) REGULATIONS (NORTHERN IRELAND) 2005, SR 2005 198; made under the Food Safety (Northern Ireland) Order 1991 (SI 1991 762 (NI.7)) Art.15, Art.16, Art.25, Art.26, Art.47. In force: May 20, 2006; £3.00.

These Regulations, which amend the Food Labelling Regulations (Northern Ireland) 1996 (SR 1996 383), implement Commission Directive 2004/77 ([2004] OJ L162/76) amending Directive 94/54 as regards the labelling of certain foods containing glycyrrhizinic acid and its ammonium salt. Glycyrrhizinic acid occurs naturally in the liquorice plant and its ammonium salt is manufactured from aqueous extracts of that plant. These Regulations require confectionery and drinks containing certain levels of that acid or salt to be labelled with the indication "contains liquorice" and for this to be coupled with a warning in certain cases. There are exemptions from these labelling requirements in the case of food which is not prepacked, food which is prepacked for direct sale, fancy confectionery products, small packages and certain indelibly marked glass bottles.

4681. Labelling—Food labelling—Allergenic ingredients

FOOD LABELLING (AMENDMENT NO.2) REGULATIONS (NORTHERN IRELAND) 2005, SR 2005 396; made under the Food Safety (Northern Ireland) Order 1991 (SI 1991 762 (NI.7)) Art.15, Art.16, Art.25, Art.47. In force: November 25, 2005; £3.00.

These Regulations amend the Food Labelling Regulations (Northern Ireland) 1996 (SR 1996 383) and implement Commission Directive 2005/26 ([2005] OJ L75/33) establishing a list of food ingredients or substances provisionally excluded from Annex IIIa of Directive 2000/13 of the European Parliament and of the Council. They confer an exemption until November 25, 2007 from the allergen labelling requirements in reg.34B of the 1996 Regulations in the case of certain ingredients originating from allergenic ingredients.

4682. Labelling—Food labelling—Allergenic ingredients

FOOD LABELLING (AMENDMENT NO.2) (AMENDMENT) REGULATIONS (NORTHERN IRELAND) 2005, SR 2005 475; made under the Food Safety (Northern Ireland) Order 1991 (SI 1991 762 (NI.7)) Art.15, Art.16, Art.25, Art.47. In force: November 25, 2005; £3.00.

These Regulations amend the Food Labelling (Amendment No.2) Regulations (Northern Ireland) 2005 which implement Commission Directive 2005/26 ([2005] OJ L75/33) establishing a list of food ingredients or substances provisionally excluded from Annex IIIa of Directive 2000/13. They confer an exemption until November 25, 2007 from the allergen labelling requirements in the Food Labelling Regulations (Northern Ireland) 1996 reg.34B in the case of certain ingredients originating from allergenic ingredients.

4683. Meat—Residues—Examinations—Charges

MEAT (EXAMINATIONS FOR RESIDUES) (CHARGES) REGULATIONS (NORTHERN IRELAND) 2005, SR 2005 556; made under the European Communities Act 1972 s.2. In force: January 1, 2006; £3.00.

These Regulations re-implement European Parliament and Council Directive 85/73 ([1985] OJ L32/14) on the financing of health inspections and controls of fresh meat and poultrymeat. They require the Department to make a charge relating to examinations for the presence of residues and provide for the level of charges (in Euros) to be levied. In addition, the Regulations determine who is liable to pay the charges and provide for their recovery.

GOVERNMENT ADMINISTRATION

4684. Civil service—Director of Public Prosecutions—UK nationality requirement for public service post—Vires of requirement

[European Communities (Employment in the Civil Service) Order 1991 (SI 1991 1221) Art.3; Civil Service (Northern Ireland) Order 1996 Art.4(2); EC Treaty Art.39(4); .]

The claimant solicitor (O) applied for judicial review of a decision by the defendant Northern Ireland government departments (R) that, as an Irish national, she was not eligible for a job that had been designated a "public service post". O had applied to the Director of Public Prosecutions, the second defendant, for a job as a legal assistant. In accordance with the Civil Service (Northern Ireland) Order 1996 Art.4(2), the first defendant Department of Finance and Personnel, which managed the Northern Ireland Civil Service, specified a UK nationality requirement for public service posts. O argued that (1) the nationality requirements were ultra vires; (2) having decided that a job was a public service post, the defendants maintained a discretion whether to restrict it to UK nationals.

Held, refusing the application, that (1) under the European Communities (Employment in the Civil Service) Order 1991 Art.3, an EU national could be employed in the Northern Ireland civil service as long as it was not in the public service. That restriction was allowed under the EC Treaty Art.39(4). The eligibility requirements added nothing to the existing law and were, therefore, intra vires. (2) Under the 1991 Order, once a Civil Service post had been correctly designated as public service, the decision maker had no discretion to disapply its restriction to UK nationals. In the instant case, R had considered the characteristics of the job and concluded that the post satisfied EC law criteria as a public service post. That decision was neither unreasonable, untenable nor unlawful.

O'CONNORS APPLICATION FOR JUDICIAL REVIEW, *Re* [2005] Eu. L.R. 719, Girvan, J, QBD (NI).

4685. Government bodies—Comptroller and Auditor General—Remuneration

SALARIES (COMPTROLLER AND AUDITOR GENERAL) ORDER (NORTHERN IRELAND) 2005, SR 2005 11; made under the Audit (Northern Ireland) Order 1987 (SI 1987 460 (NI.5)) Art.4. In force: March 7, 2005; £3.00.

This Order, which revokes the Salaries (Comptroller and Auditor General) Order (Northern Ireland) 2004 (SR 2004 20), provides for an increase in the annual salary payable to the Comptroller and Auditor General following recommendations made in the Report of the Review Body on Senior Salaries in 2004. The increase is made with effect from April 1, 2004.

4686. Government bodies—Comptroller and Auditor General—Remuneration

SALARIES (COMPTROLLER AND AUDITOR GENERAL) (NO.2) ORDER (NORTHERN IRELAND) 2005, SR 2005 489; made under the Audit (Northern Ireland) Order 1987 (SI 1987 460 (NI.5)) Art.4. In force: December 30, 2005; £3.00.

This Order, which revokes the Salaries (Comptroller and Auditor General) Order (Northern Ireland) 2005 (SR 2005 11), provides for an increase in the annual salary payable to the Comptroller and Auditor General following recommendations made in the Report of the Review Body on Senior Salaries in 2005 (Cm.6451). The increase is made with effect from April 1, 2005 under the Audit (Northern Ireland) Order 1987 (SI 1987 460) art.4(1).

HEALTH

4687. **Blood products–Collection and storage–Safety and quality**
See HEALTH. §1790

4688. **Dental services–Dental treatment–Maximum charges**
DENTAL CHARGES (AMENDMENT) REGULATIONS (NORTHERN IRELAND) 2005, SR 2005 72; made under the Health and Personal Social Services (Northern Ireland) Order 1972 (SI 1972 1265 (NI.14)) Art.98, Art.106, Sch.15. In force: April 1, 2005; £3.00.
These Regulations amend the Dental Charges Regulations (Northern Ireland) 1989 (SR 1989 111) and the Dental Charges (Amendment) Regulations (Northern Ireland) 2004 (SR 2004 93), to increase from £378 to £384 the maximum charge which a patient may be required to pay towards the cost of his treatment or appliance under general dental services or under a pilot scheme. The new charges shall apply only where the arrangements for treatment or supply of a dental appliance is made on or after April 1, 2005.

4689. **Dentistry–General dental services**
GENERAL DENTAL SERVICES (AMENDMENT) REGULATIONS (NORTHERN IRELAND) 2005, SR 2005 311; made under the Health and Personal Social Services (Northern Ireland) Order 1972 (SI 1972 1265 (NI.14)) Art.61, Art.106, Art.107. In force: July 18, 2005; £3.00.
These Regulations amend the Health and Personal Social Services General Dental Services Regulations (Northern Ireland) 1993 (SR 1993 326) which regulate the terms on which general dental services are provided under the Health and Personal Social Services (Northern Ireland) Order 1972. They insert a new provision into the terms of service banning the use of telephone services for the purposes of the provision of general dental services which make use of national rate numbers (starting with 087), premium rate numbers (starting with 090) or personal numbers (starting with 070); and make amendments so that Determination XI of the Statement of Dental Remuneration relates to the subject matter "Practice allowance".

4690. **Executive agencies–Independent health care–Quality of services**
INDEPENDENT HEALTH CARE REGULATIONS (NORTHERN IRELAND) 2005, SR 2005 174; made under the Health and Personal Social Services (Quality, Improvement and Regulation) (Northern Ireland) Order 2003 (SI 2003 431 (NI.9)) Art.2, Art.23, Art.25, Art.30, Art.31, Art.32, Art.48. In force: April 1, 2005; £4.00.
The Health and Personal Social Services (Quality, Improvement and Regulation) (Northern Ireland) Order 2003 (SI 2003 431 (NI.9)) establishes the Northern Ireland Health and Personal Social Services Regulation and Improvement Authority and provides for the registration and inspection of establishments and agencies, including independent health care establishments and agencies, by the Regulation and Improvement Authority. It also provides powers for regulations governing the conduct of establishments and agencies. These Regulations provide that "listed services" include treatment using the prescribed techniques and technology specified; modify definition of cosmetic surgery; defines the meaning of the term "independent clinic"; make provision about the fitness of the persons carrying on and managing an establishment or agency and require satisfactory information to be obtained in relation to the matters prescribed; and make provision about the conduct of establishments or agencies, in particular about the quality of the services to be provided in an establishment or agency, including matters relating to privacy, dignity and religious observance, the

staffing of the establishment or agency and the fitness of workers and about complaints and record keeping.

4691. Executive agencies–Regulation and Improvement Authority–Registration

REGULATION AND IMPROVEMENT AUTHORITY (REGISTRATION) REGULATIONS (NORTHERN IRELAND) 2005, SR 2005 99; made under the Health and Personal Social Services (Quality, Improvement and Regulation) (Northern Ireland) Order 2003 (SI 2003 431 (NI.9)) Art.12, Art.13, Art.15, Art.16, Art.17, Art.25, Art.48. In force: April 1, 2005; £3.50.

The Health and Personal Social Services (Quality, Improvement and Regulation) (Northern Ireland) Order 2003 (SI 2003 431 (NI.9)) establishes the Regulation and Improvement Authority and provides for the registration and inspection by the Regulation and Improvement Authority of establishments and agencies. These Regulations: specify the information and documents that are to be provided by an applicant for registration; require the responsible person to attend an interview; require the applicant to give notice of certain changes that take place, or details of staff engaged, after the application for registration is made and before it is determined; require the Regulation and Improvement Authority to keep a register in respect of each description of establishment or agency; specify the particulars that any certificate of registration is to contain; require a person who is registered in respect of an establishment or agency to return the certificate to the Regulation and Improvement Authority if the registration is cancelled; make provision in respect of an application by the registered person to apply for the variation or removal of a condition in relation to his registration; require the registered person to report the relevant circumstances to the Regulation and Improvement Authority if it appears that the establishment or agency is likely to cease to be financially viable; specify certain grounds on which the Regulation and Improvement Authority may cancel a person's registration; and provide for the registered person to apply for his registration to be cancelled.

4692. Health and Personal Social Services–Transfer of staff–Consultation requirements

REGULATION AND IMPROVEMENT AUTHORITY (CONSULTATION ON TRANSFER OF STAFF) REGULATIONS (NORTHERN IRELAND) 2005, SR 2005 43 (C.3); made under the Health and Personal Social Services (Quality, Improvement and Regulation) (Northern Ireland) Order 2003 (SI 2003 431 (NI.9)) Art.3, Art.48, Sch.1 para.16. In force: February 17, 2005; £3.00.

This Order prescribes the requirements about consultation to be complied with by the Health and Social Services Boards before the Department, by order, makes a scheme for the transfer of staff from Health and Social Services Boards to the Northern Ireland Health and Personal Social Services Regulation and Improvement Authority.

4693. Health services–Drugs and appliances–Fees

CHARGES FOR DRUGS AND APPLIANCES (AMENDMENT) REGULATIONS (NORTHERN IRELAND) 2005, SR 2005 97; made under the Health and Personal Social Services (Northern Ireland) Order 1972 (SI 1972 1265 (NI.14)) Art.98, Art.106, Sch.15. In force: April 1, 2005; £3.00.

These Regulations amend the Charges for Drugs and Appliances Regulations (Northern Ireland) 1997 (SR 1997 382) which provide for the making and recovery of charges for drugs and appliances supplied by doctors and chemists providing pharmaceutical services, and by hospitals and HSS trusts to out-patients. The Regulations increase specified charges for certain drugs and appliances.

4694. Health services–General medical services–Contracts

HEALTH AND PERSONAL SOCIAL SERVICES (GENERAL MEDICAL SERVICES CONTRACTS) (MISCELLANEOUS AMENDMENTS) REGULATIONS

(NORTHERN IRELAND) 2005, SR 2005 230; made under the Health and Personal Social Services (Northern Ireland) Order 1972 (SI 1972 1265 (NI.14)) Art.15C, Art.55B, Art.57A, Art.57B, Art.57E, Art.57F, Art.57G, Art.106, Art.107; and the Health and Personal Social Services (Northern Ireland) Order 1991 (SI 1991 194 (NI.1)) Art.8. In force: May 1, 2005; £3.00.

These Regulations amend the Health and Personal Social Services (General Medical Services Contracts) Regulations (Northern Ireland) 2004 (SR 2004 140), the Health and Personal Social Services (Primary Medical Services Performers Lists) Regulations (Northern Ireland) 2004 (SR 2004 149) and the General Medical Services Transitional and Consequential Provisions (No.2) (Northern Ireland) Order 2004 (SR 2004 156) relating to primary medical services. They widen the definition of general medical practitioner; restrict the categories of general medical practitioner who can act as the mandatory medical practitioner for the purposes of a general medical services contract; misapply the provisions relating to clinical reports in the case of out of hours services which are covered by the quality standards; and enable a contractor's list of patients which has been closed as a result of a determination by an assessment panel to re-open by agreement before the end of the closure period specified by that panel and, in certain circumstances, to re-close again during that period.

4695. Health services–Pharmaceutical services–Prescriptions–Repeat dispensing

PHARMACEUTICAL SERVICES AND CHARGES FOR DRUGS AND APPLIANCES (AMENDMENT) REGULATIONS (NORTHERN IRELAND) 2005, SR 2005 231; made under the Health and Personal Social Services (Northern Ireland) Order 1972 (SI 1972 1265 (NI.14)) Art.63, Art.64, Art.98, Art.106, Art.107, Sch.15; and the Health and Medicines (Northern Ireland) Order 1988 (SI 1988 2249 (NI.24)) Art.10. In force: May 1, 2005; £3.00.

These Regulations amend the Health and Medicines (Northern Ireland) Order 1988 (SR 1988 381) and the Charges for Drugs and Appliances Regulations (Northern Ireland) 1997 (SR 1997 382) to establish a scheme for repeat dispensing, which involves doctors issuing, and chemists dispensing in accordance with, repeatable prescriptions.

4696. Health services–Primary medical services–Prescription forms

GENERAL MEDICAL SERVICES TRANSITIONAL AND CONSEQUENTIAL PROVISIONS (NO.2) (AMENDMENT) ORDER (NORTHERN IRELAND) 2005, SR 2005 369; made under the Primary Medical Services (Northern Ireland) Order 2004 (SI 2004 311 (NI.2)) Art.5, Art.11. In force: August 25, 2005; £3.00.

This Order amends the General Medical Services Transitional and Consequential Provisions (No.2) (Northern Ireland) Order 2004 (SR 2004 156) to extend for a further year the period for which prescription forms (including repeatable prescription forms and batch issues when the appropriate regulations have been introduced) need not include the name of the contractor as required by various Regulations relating to primary medical services.

4697. Health services–Primary medical services–Supplementary prescribers

HEALTH AND PERSONAL SOCIAL SERVICES (PRIMARY MEDICAL SERVICES) (MISCELLANEOUS AMENDMENTS) REGULATIONS (NORTHERN IRELAND) 2005, SR 2005 368; made under the Health and Personal Social Services (Northern Ireland) Order 1972 (SI 1972 1265 (NI.14)) Art.57A, Art.57B, Art.57E, Art.57F, Art.57G, Art.106, Art.107; and the Health and Personal Social Services (Northern Ireland) Order 1991 (SI 1991 194 (NI.1)) Art.8. In force: August 25, 2005; £3.00.

These Regulations make various amendments to the Health and Personal Social Services (General Medical Services Contracts) Regulations (Northern Ireland) 2004 (SR 2004 140) and the Health and Personal Social Services (Primary Medical Services Performers Lists) Regulations (Northern Ireland) 2004 (SR

2004 149) which include: amending the definition of supplementary prescriber to include further health professionals; banning the use of telephone services for the purposes of general medical services contracts which make use of national rate numbers (starting with 087), premium rate numbers (starting with 090) or personal numbers (starting with 070); inserting provisions to enable the supply of medicines to patients by providers of out of hours services where certain conditions are met; extend the requirements for supply by instalments to diazepam; remove the restrictions preventing supplementary prescribers from prescribing controlled drugs or unlicensed medicines; and removing the provision relating to the Quality Information Preparation Scheme which ceased to exist on March 31, 2005.

4698. Health services–Travelling expenses–Remission of charges–Entitlement

TRAVELLING EXPENSES AND REMISSION OF CHARGES (AMENDMENT) REGULATIONS (NORTHERN IRELAND) 2005, SR 2005 107; made under the Health and Personal Social Services (Northern Ireland) Order 1972 (SI 1972 1265 (NI.14)) Art.45, Art.98, Art.106, Art.107, Sch.15 para.1, Sch.15 para.1B. In force: Reg.2: April 1, 2005; Reg.3: April 6, 2005; Reg.4: April 1, 2005; Reg.5: April 11, 2005; Reg.6: April 1, 2005; £3.00.

These Regulations amend the Travelling Expenses and Remission of Charges Regulations (Northern Ireland) 2004 (SR 2004 91) which provide for remission and payment of certain charges which would otherwise be payable under the Health and Personal Social Services (Northern Ireland) Order 1972 (SI 1972 1265 (NI.14)) and for the payment by the Department of travelling expenses incurred in attending a hospital. The Regulations make provisions for the insertion of several definitions; increase the income level at which recipients of tax credits are entitled to a full remission and payment of Health Service Travel Expenses and a remission of Health Service charges; and extend to five years the time period for which a notice of entitlement to remission of Health Service charges and the payment of Health Service Travel Expenses is valid where issued to a single person aged 65 or over, or to one of a couple where one partner is aged 60 or over and the other partner is aged 65 or over, where that person does not have certain types of income or a dependant child or young person in his household.

4699. Health services–Travelling expenses–Remission of charges–Entitlement

TRAVELLING EXPENSES AND REMISSION OF CHARGES (AMENDMENT NO.2) REGULATIONS (NORTHERN IRELAND) 2005, SR 2005 386; made under the Health and Personal Social Services (Northern Ireland) Order 1972 (SI 1972 1265 (NI.14)) Art.45, Art.98, Art.106, Art.107, Sch.15 para.1, Sch.15 para.1B. In force: September 1, 2005; £3.00.

These Regulations amend the Travelling Expenses and Remission of Charges Regulations (Northern Ireland) 2004 (SR 2004 91) which provide for remission and payment of certain charges which would otherwise be payable under the Health and Personal Social Services (Northern Ireland) Order 1972 (SI 1972 1265 (NI.14)) and for the payment by the Department of travelling expenses incurred in attending a hospital. They extend entitlement to payment in full of travel expenses and full remission of charges to a relevant child within the meaning of the Children (Northern Ireland) Order 1995 s.34B whom a responsible authority is supporting.

4700. Nursing agencies–Registration and inspection

NURSING AGENCIES REGULATIONS (NORTHERN IRELAND) 2005, SR 2005 175; made under the Health and Personal Social Services (Quality, Improvement and Regulation) (Northern Ireland) Order 2003 (SI 2003 431 (NI.9)) Art.2, Art.23, Art.25, Art.31, Art.32, Art.48. In force: April 1, 2005; £3.00.

These Regulations, which revoke the Nursing Agency (Northern Ireland) Regulations 1986 (SR 1986 338), apply in relation to nursing agencies in Northern Ireland only. The Health and Personal Social Services (Quality,

Improvement and Regulation) (Northern Ireland) Order 2003 (SI 2003 431 (NI.9)) establishes, in relation to Northern Ireland, the Health and Personal Social Services Regulation and Improvement Authority and provides for the registration and inspection of establishments and agencies, including nursing agencies, by the Regulation and Improvement Authority. It also provides powers to make regulations governing the conduct of establishments and agencies. The Regulations provide each agency must prepare a statement of purpose in relation to the matters; make provision about the fitness of the persons carrying on and managing an agency and require satisfactory information to be obtained in relation to the matters specified; prescribes the circumstances where a manager must be appointed in respect of the agency; make provision concerning the fitness of the manager; and impose general requirements in relation to the proper conduct of the agency, and the need for appropriate training.

4701. Opticians–Contact lenses–Specification

CONTACT LENS (SPECIFICATION) AND SIGHT TESTING (EXAMINATION AND PRESCRIPTION) (AMENDMENT) REGULATIONS (NORTHERN IRELAND) 2005, SR 2005 291; made under the Opticians Act 1989 s.25, s.26. In force: July 5, 2005; £3.00.

These Regulations, which amend the Sight Testing (Examination and Prescription) (No.2) Regulations (Northern Ireland) 1989 (SR 1989 281), set out the particulars which must be given to a patient by a medical practitioner when he issues a specification to a patient to whom he has fitted a contact lens.

4702. Opticians–Fees and payments

OPTICAL CHARGES AND PAYMENTS AND GENERAL OPHTHALMIC SERVICES (AMENDMENT) REGULATIONS (NORTHERN IRELAND) 2005, SR 2005 71; made under the Health and Personal Social Services (Northern Ireland) Order 1972 (SI 1972 1265 (NI.14)) Art.62, Art.98, Art.106, Art.107, Sch.15. In force: Reg.2: April 6, 2005; Reg.6: April 6, 2005; remainder: April 1, 2005; £3.00.

These Regulations amend the Optical Charges and Payments Regulations (Northern Ireland) 1997 (SR 1997 191) which provide for payments to be made, by means of a voucher system, in respect of costs incurred by certain categories of persons in connection with the supply, replacement and repair of optical appliances. The Regulations also amend the General Ophthalmic Services Regulations (Northern Ireland) 1986 (SR 1986 163) which provide for the arrangements under which ophthalmic medical practitioners and ophthalmic opticians provide General Ophthalmic Services. The Regulations increase the income level at which recipients of tax credits are entitled to health service optical vouchers; increase the redemption value of a voucher issued towards the cost of replacement of a single contact lens and to increase the maximum contribution by way of a voucher to the cost of repair of a frame; increase the value of vouchers issued towards the costs of the supply and replacement of glasses and contact lenses; increase the additional values for vouchers for prisms, tints, photochromic lenses and special categories of appliances; and increase the value of vouchers issued towards the cost of the repair and replacement of optical appliances.

4703. Opticians–Mobile services

GENERAL OPHTHALMIC SERVICES (AMENDMENT) REGULATIONS (NORTHERN IRELAND) 2005, SR 2005 292; made under the Health and Personal Social Services (Northern Ireland) Order 1972 (SI 1972 1265 (NI.14)) Art.62, Art.106, Art.107. In force: July 4, 2005; £3.00.

These Regulations amend the General Ophthalmic Services Regulations (Northern Ireland) 1986 (SR 1986 163) to make provision in relation to mobile services and for opticians to refer patients to a doctor within the hospital eye service and to so inform the patient's doctor and give that patient a statement to that effect. They also require the statement prepared by the Department of Health, Social Services and Public Safety to include allowances to be paid in respect of continuing education and training of ophthalmic medical practitioners and opticians.

4704. Pharmaceutical industry-Pharmaceutical Society of Northern Ireland-Members' registration fees

PHARMACEUTICAL SOCIETY OF NORTHERN IRELAND (GENERAL) (AMENDMENT) REGULATIONS (NORTHERN IRELAND) 2005, SR 2005 63; made under the Pharmacy (Northern Ireland) Order 1976 (SI 1976 1213 (NI.22)) Art.5. In force: June 1, 2005; £3.00.

These Regulations amend the Pharmaceutical Society of Northern Ireland (General) Regulations (Northern Ireland) 1994 (SR 1994 202) by increasing fees payable in respect of registration as a pharmaceutical chemist and as a student; restoration of a person's name to the register; and retention fees payable in respect of members of the Society.

4705. Books

Van Dokkum, Neil–Nursing Law for Irish Students. Paperback: £27.99. ISBN 0 7171 3837 2. Gill & Macmillan.

HEALTH AND SAFETY AT WORK

4706. Accidents-Disaster planning

CONTROL OF MAJOR ACCIDENT HAZARDS (AMENDMENT) REGULATIONS (NORTHERN IRELAND) 2005, SR 2005 305; made under the European Communities Act 1972 s.2; and the Health and Safety at Work (Northern Ireland) Order 1978 (SI 1978 1039 (NI.9)) Art.17, Art.40, Art.55, Sch.3 para.1, Sch.3 para.14, Sch.3 para.15, Sch.3 para.19. In force: July 25, 2005; £3.00.

These Regulations amend the Control of Major Accident Hazards Regulations (Northern Ireland) 2000 (SR 2000 93) so as to give effect to European Parliament and Council Directive 2003/105 ([2003] OJ L345/97) amending Council Directive 96/82 on the control of major-accident hazards involving dangerous substances. The Regulations provide for the sending of notifications by electronic means; modify the exclusions relating to mines, quarries, boreholes and waste land-fill sites; introduce a time limit for the preparation of a major accident prevention policy and modify time limits for notification, the submission of a safety report and the preparation of the on-site emergency plan; require the notification of certain modifications to the establishment; require notification when a safety report is revised or when a review of a report does not lead to revision; modify the requirement to consult persons working in the establishment on the preparation of the plan; require the Executive to consult the public when the off-site emergency plan is reviewed; require that schools, hospitals and other such establishments are supplied with safety information; and require specific training in planning for emergencies for all persons working in the establishment.

4707. Benefits-Industrial diseases-Disablement assessment-Occupational deafness

SOCIAL SECURITY (INDUSTRIAL INJURIES) (PRESCRIBED DISEASES) (AMENDMENT) REGULATIONS (NORTHERN IRELAND) 2005, SR 2005 37; made under the Social Security Contributions and Benefits (Northern Ireland) Act 1992 s.108, s.171; and the Social Security Administration (Northern Ireland) Act 1992 s.5. In force: March 14, 2005; £3.00.

These Regulations amend the Social Security (Industrial Injuries) (Prescribed Diseases) Regulations (Northern Ireland) 1986 (SR 1986 179) which prescribe diseases for which industrial injuries benefit is payable. They also amend the Social Security (1998 Order) (Commencement No.7 and Savings, Consequential and Transitional Provisions) Order (Northern Ireland) 1999 (SR 1999 310 (C.23)) and the Social Security (Industrial Injuries) (Prescribed Diseases) (Amendment) Regulations (Northern Ireland) 2000 (SR 2000 214). They make amendments in respect of concurrent employment in two or more occupations in relation to occupational deafness and delete, with consequential changes, obsolete exceptions which relate to claims in respect of occupational deafness made before October 3, 1984. The Regulations add osteoarthritis of the hip, Lyme disease and anaphylaxis to the list of prescribed diseases and adding to the description of allergic rhinitis and asthma. They also make changes to the description of the occupations in relation to which anthrax, ankylostomiasis and hepatitis are prescribed diseases.

4708. Construction industry–Work at height–Minimum requirements

WORK AT HEIGHT REGULATIONS (NORTHERN IRELAND) 2005, SR 2005 279; made under the Health and Safety at Work (Northern Ireland) Order 1978 Art.17, Art.55, Sch 3 para.1, Sch.3 para.8, Sch.3 para.10, Sch.3 para.13, Sch.3 para.14, Sch.3 para.15. In force: July 11, 2005; £3.50.

These Regulation, which amend the Shipbuilding and Ship-repairing Regulations (Northern Ireland) 1971 (SR and O 1971 372), the Docks Regulations (Northern Ireland) 1989 (SR 1989 320), the Loading and Unloading of Fishing Vessels Regulations (Northern Ireland) 1989 (SR 1989 321), the Workplace (Health, Safety and Welfare) Regulations (Northern Ireland) 1993 (SR 1993 37) and the Construction (Health, Safety and Welfare) Regulations (Northern Ireland) 1996 (SR 1996 510) impose health and safety requirements with respect to work at height, with certain exceptions including by instructors or leaders in recreational climbing and caving.

4709. Employers duties–Control of vibration

CONTROL OF VIBRATION AT WORK REGULATIONS (NORTHERN IRELAND) 2005, SR 2005 397; made under the Health and Safety at Work (Northern Ireland) Order 1978 (SI 1978 1039 (NI.9)) Art.17, Art.55, Sch.3 para.1, Sch.3 para.7, Sch.3 para.8, Sch.3 para.10, Sch.3 para.12, Sch.3 para.13, Sch.3 para.14, Sch.3 para.15, Sch.3 para.19. In force: October 3, 2005; £3.00.

These Regulations, which implement Council Directive 2002/44 ([2002] OJ L177/13) on the minimum health and safety requirements regarding the exposure of workers to the risks arising from physical agents (vibration), impose duties on employers to protect employees who may be exposed to risk from exposure to vibration at work, and other persons who might be affected by the work, whether they are at work or not. The Regulations also amend the Offshore Installations and Wells (Design and Construction etc.) Regulations (Northern Ireland) 1996 (SR 1996 228) and the Provision and Use of Work Equipment Regulations (Northern Ireland) 1 (SR 1 305).

4710. Employers duties–Divers

DIVING AT WORK REGULATIONS (NORTHERN IRELAND) 2005, SR 2005 45; made under the Health and Safety at Work (Northern Ireland) Order 1978 (SI 1978 1039 (NI.9)) Art.17, Art.55, Sch.3 para.1, Sch.3 para.3, Sch.3 para.4, Sch.3 para.5, Sch.3 para.13, Sch.3 para.14, Sch.3 para.15, Sch.3 para.20. In force: April 4, 2005; £3.00.

These Regulations, which revoke the Diving Operations at Work Regulations (Northern Ireland) 1994 (SR 1994 146), amend the Health and Safety (First-Aid) Regulations (Northern Ireland) 1982 (SR 1982 429), the Construction (Head Protection) Regulations (Northern Ireland) 1990 (SR 1990 424), the Offshore Installations (Safety Case) Regulations (Northern Ireland) 1993 (SR 1993 221), the Reporting of Injuries Diseases and Dangerous Occurrences Regulations (Northern Ireland) 1997 (SR 1997 455), the Confined Spaces

Regulations (Northern Ireland) 1 (SR 1 13), the Pressure Systems Safety Regulations (Northern Ireland) 2004 (SR 2004 222) and the Work in Compressed Air Regulations (Northern Ireland) 2004 (SR 2004 241). These Regulations impose requirements and prohibitions with respect to persons at work who "dive".

4711. Hazardous substances–Controls

CONTROL OF SUBSTANCES HAZARDOUS TO HEALTH (AMENDMENT) REGULATIONS (NORTHERN IRELAND) 2005, SR 2005 165; made under the Health and Safety at Work (Northern Ireland) Order 1978 (SI 1978 1039) (NI.9)) Art.2, Art.17, Art.55, Sch.3 para.1, Sch.3 para.7, Sch.3 para.8, Sch.3 para.10, Sch.3 para.13, Sch.3 para.14, Sch.3 para.15, Sch.3 para.19. In force: in accordance with Reg.1; £3.00.

These Regulations amend the Chemicals (Hazard Information and Packaging for Supply) Regulations (Northern Ireland) 2002 (SR 2002 301), the Control of Substances Hazardous to Health Regulations (Northern Ireland) 2003 (SR 2003 34) and the Control of Lead at Work Regulations (Northern Ireland) 2003 (SR 2003 35). They implement provisions of European Parliament and Council Directive 2003/53 ([2003] OJ L178/24) amending for the 26th time Council Directive 76/769 relating to restrictions on the marketing and use of certain dangerous substances and preparations (nonylphenol, nonylphenol ethoxylate and cement). They prohibit the supply and use of cement and cement-containing preparations containing when hydrated more than 0.0002 per cent soluble chromium VI of the dry weight of the cement except in certain fully automated and enclosed processes.

4712. Health and Safety Executive–Licences–Fees

HEALTH AND SAFETY (FEES) REGULATIONS (NORTHERN IRELAND) 2005, SR 2005 523; made under the European Communities Act 1972 s.2; and the Health and Safety at Work (Northern Ireland) Order 1978 (SI 1978 1039 (NI.9)) Art.40, Art.49, Art.55. In force: January 16, 2006; £3.00.

These Regulations, which revoke the Health and Safety (Fees) Regulations (Northern Ireland) 2004 (SR 2004 410), fix or determine the fees payable by an applicant to, in most cases, the Health and Safety Executive for Northern Ireland in respect of an application made for certain licences and approval of specified schemes.

HUMAN RIGHTS

4713. Gender recognition–Registers

GENDER RECOGNITION REGISTER (NORTHERN IRELAND) REGULATIONS 2005, SR 2005 187; made under the Gender Recognition Act 2004 s.10, Sch.3 para.23. In force: April 4, 2005; £3.00.

These Regulations make provision for entries to be made in the Gender Recognition Register and the marking of existing birth register entries once the Registrar General for Northern Ireland receives a copy of the full gender recognition certificate under the Gender Recognition Act 2004 s.10(1). The Regulations provide for an entry in the Gender Recognition Register to contain information that corresponds with the information recorded in the applicants existing birth record, apart from the new name and gender which will be obtained from the gender recognition certificate.

INFORMATION TECHNOLOGY

4714. Books

Kelleher, Denis; Muray, Karen–InformationTechnology Law in Ireland. Paperback: £80.00. ISBN 1 84592 111 9. Tottel Publishing.

INSOLVENCY

4715. Directors–Insolvent companies–Disqualification orders

INSOLVENT COMPANIES (DISQUALIFICATION OF UNFIT DIRECTORS) PROCEEDINGS (AMENDMENT) RULES (NORTHERN IRELAND) 2005, SR 2005 517; made under the Insolvency (Northern Ireland) Order 1989 (SI 1989 2405 (NI.19)) Art.359; and the Company Directors Disqualification (Northern Ireland) Order 2002 (SI 2002 3150 (NI.4)) Art.24. In force: December 19, 2005; £3.00.

These Rules amend the Insolvent Companies (Disqualification of Unfit Directors) Proceedings Rules (Northern Ireland) 2003 (SR 2003 358) which provide procedures for applications by the Department of Enterprise, Trade and Investment or the official receiver for the disqualification of directors by the High Court in Northern Ireland under Company Directors Disqualification (Northern Ireland) Order 2002 (SI 2002 3150 (NI.4)). The 2002 Order enables the Office of Fair Trading and certain specified regulators to make an application to the High Court for a competition disqualification order. The Court will be under an obligation to make a competition disqualification order where it is satisfied that the company has committed a breach of competition law, as defined in the 2002 Order, and where it considers that the conduct of the director in relation to that competition breach makes him unfit to be concerned in the management of a company. The amendments to the 2003 Rules provide for the procedures as set out in those Rules to apply to applications in Northern Ireland made by the Office of Fair Trading or a specified regulator under the 2002 Order.

4716. Financial Services Authority–Demands–Regulated activity debt

BANKRUPTCY (FINANCIAL SERVICES AND MARKETS ACT 2000) RULES (NORTHERN IRELAND) 2005, SR 2005 398; made under the Insolvency (Northern Ireland) Order 1989 (SI 1989 2405 (NI.9)) Art.359. In force: September 19, 2005; £3.00.

These Rules modify the Insolvency Rules (Northern Ireland) 1991 (SR 1991 364) in relation to a demand made by the Financial Services Authority to an individual that he establish to the Authority's satisfaction that he has a reasonable prospect of being able to pay a regulated activity debt when it falls due. The Rules make provision, amongst other things, as to the form and content of a demand, information to be given in a demand, requirements as to service and applications to set aside a demand.

4717. Insolvency (Northern Ireland) Order 2005 (SI 2005 1455 (NI.10))

This Order amends the Third Parties (Rights Against Insurers) Act (Northern Ireland) 1930; the Criminal Justice Act (Northern Ireland) 1945; the Transport Act (Northern Ireland) 1967; the Local Government Act (Northern Ireland) 1972; the Finance Act 1991; the Social Security (Consequential Provisions) (Northern Ireland) Act 1992; the Finance Act 1993; the Pension Schemes (Northern Ireland) Act 1993; the Finance Act 1994; the Finance Act 1996; the Financial Services and Markets Act 2000; the Finance Act 2001; the Solicitors (Northern Ireland) Order 1976 (SI 1976 583 (NI.12)); the Magistrates' Courts (Northern Ireland) Order 1981 (SI 1981 1675 (NI.26)); the Companies (Northern

Ireland) Order 1986 (SI 1986 1032 (NI.6)); the Companies (No.2) (Northern Ireland) Order 1990 (SI 1990 1504 (NI.10)); the Criminal Justice (Northern Ireland) Order 1994 (SI 1994 2795 (NI.15)); the Employment Rights (Northern Ireland) Order 1996 (SI 1996 1919 (NI.16)); the Construction Contracts (Northern Ireland) Order 1997 (SI 1997 274 (NI.1)); and the Company Directors Disqualification (Northern Ireland) Order 2002 (SI 2002 3150 (NI.4)). It empowers the High Court to disqualify a person for being a company director if a company of which he is a director commits a breach of competition law and the Court considers that his conduct as a director makes him unfit to be concerned in the management of a company.

INSURANCE

4718. Employer's liability—Compulsory insurance—Exemptions

EMPLOYER'S LIABILITY (COMPULSORY INSURANCE) (AMENDMENT) REGULATIONS (NORTHERN IRELAND) 2005, SR 2005 2; made under the Employer's Liability (Defective Equipment and Compulsory Insurance) (Northern Ireland) Order 1972 (SI 1972 963 (NI.6)) Art.7, Art.10. In force: February 28, 2005; £3.00.

These Regulations, which revoke the Employer's Liability (Compulsory Insurance) (Amendment) Regulations (Northern Ireland) 2004 (SR 2004 449), amend the Employer's Liability (Compulsory Insurance) Regulations (Northern Ireland) 1999 (SR 1999 448) which specify employers who are exempted from the requirements of the Employer's Liability (Defective Equipment and Compulsory Insurance) (Northern Ireland) Order 1972 (SI 1972 963 (NI.6)) to insure and maintain insurance against liability for personal injury suffered by their employees and arising out of and in the course of their employment. The specified employers are certain public bodies; the specified classes of employer include any employer to the extent that he is required to insure under a compulsory motor insurance scheme by virtue of the fact that his employees are carried on, or are alighting from or are entering into, a motor vehicle. The exemptions specified in the 1999 Regulations are additional to those contained in the 1972 Order. These Regulations add to the exemptions specified any employer which is a company that has only one employee and that employee also owns 50 per cent or more of the issued share capital in that company; and the Northern Ireland Legal Services Commission.

4719. Employer's liability—Compulsory insurance—Exemptions

EMPLOYER'S LIABILITY (COMPULSORY INSURANCE) (AMENDMENT NO.2) REGULATIONS (NORTHERN IRELAND) 2005, SR 2005 392; made under the Employer's Liability (Defective Equipment and Compulsory Insurance) (Northern Ireland) Order 1972 (SI 1972 963 (NI.6)) Art.7, Art.10. In force: September 26, 2005; £3.00.

These Regulations amend the Employer's Liability (Compulsory Insurance) Regulations (Northern Ireland) 1 (SR 1 448) which specify employers who are exempted from the requirements of the Employer's Liability (Defective Equipment and Compulsory Insurance) (Northern Ireland) Order 1972 (SI 1972 963 (NI.6)) to insure and maintain insurance against liability for personal injury suffered by their employees and arising out of and in the course of their employment. The specified employers are certain public bodies; the specified classes of employer include any employer to the extent that he is required to insure under a compulsory motor insurance scheme by virtue of the fact that his employees are carried on, or are alighting from or are entering into, a motor vehicle. The exemptions specified in the 1 Regulations are additional to those contained in the 1972 Order. These Regulations add to the exemptions the Northern Ireland Judicial Appointments Commission.

4720. Insurance companies–Winding up–Valuation rules

INSURERS (WINDING-UP) RULES (NORTHERN IRELAND) 2005, SR 2005 399; made under the Insolvency (Northern Ireland) Order 1989 (SI 1989 2405 (NI.19)) Art.359; and the Financial Services and Markets Act 2000 s.379. In force: September 19, 2005; £3.50.

These Rules supplement the Insolvency Rules (Northern Ireland) 1991 (SR1991 2405) in relation to the winding-up of insurers in Northern Ireland. They revoke, and re-make with modifications, the Insurance Companies (Winding-Up) Rules (Northern Ireland) 1992 (SR 1992 307). The Regulations provide for the valuation rules in relation to a company's general business policies; provide for the valuation rules in relation to a company's long-term business policies; introduce new requirements in relation to the valuation of unitised with-profits policies; specify that the interest rate or rates used to calculate the present value of future payments must be fair and reasonable; and change the basis of valuation from a modified net premium basis to a gross premium basis. They also make provision for the attribution of liabilities and assets to a company's long-term business in cases of doubt; require a liquidator to obtain actuarial advice before taking certain courses of action; allow the Department to require that assets of a company, representing its long-term business, be held by a trustee; oblige the liquidator to comply with certain requirements imposed on him by the Department in relation, for example, to refraining from making certain investments and to the provision of information and accounts; allow a liquidator to accept late payments of premiums and to compensate policy holders whose policies have lapsed; relate to the remuneration of a liquidator; and stipulate various notice requirements where a stop order has been made.

INTELLECTUAL PROPERTY

4721. Books

Clark, Robert; Smyth, Shane–Intellectual Property Law in Ireland. Hardback: £93.33. ISBN 1 84592 020 1. Tottel Publishing.

INTERNATIONAL TRADE

4722. Animal products–Import and export controls

ANIMALS AND ANIMAL PRODUCTS (IMPORT AND EXPORT) REGULATIONS (NORTHERN IRELAND) 2005, SR 2005 78; made under the European Communities Act 1972 s.2. In force: April 4, 2005; £6.00.

These Regulations amend the Diseases of Animals (Unlawful Importations) Order (Northern Ireland) 1963 (SR & O 1963 178), the Diseases of Animals (Importation of Poultry) Order (Northern Ireland) 1965 (SR & O 1965 175), the Diseases of Fish Act (Northern Ireland) 1967, the Sales, Markets and Lairs Order (Northern Ireland) 1975 (SR1975 294), the Rabies (Importation of Dogs, Cats and Other Mammals) Order (Northern Ireland) 1977 (SR1977 113) and the Importation of Animals Order (Northern Ireland) 1986 (SR1986 253). They revoke the Rabbits and Hares (Control of Importation) Order (Northern Ireland) 1967 (SR1967 294), the Risk of Infection (Oysters) Order (Northern Ireland) 1973 (SR1973 392), the Lobsters (Risk of Infection) Order (Northern Ireland) 1982 (SR1982 99), the Risk of Infection (Fish) Order (Northern Ireland) 1991 (SR1991 458) and the Animals and Animal Products (Import and Export) Regulations (Northern Ireland) 2004 (SR 2004 325). The Regulations implement Council Directive 90/425 ([1990] OJ L224/29) concerning veterinary and zootechnical checks applicable in intra-Community trade in certain live animals and products; and Council Directive 91/496 ([1991] OJ L268/56) laying down the principles governing the organization of veterinary checks on animals entering the Community from third countries and amending Directives 89/662, 90/425 and 90/675. The Regulations make it an offence to export, import or transport for intra-Community trade any animal or animal product to which Directive 90/425 applies except in accordance with that Directive. The Regulations makes provisions, which include: the procedure and requirements for the registration of dealers in animals and animal products; requirements and procedures for approval of centres and teams engaging in intra-Community trade in animals and animal products; and give to inspectors the powers of inspection and examination.

4723. Infectious disease control–Import of potatoes–Netherlands–Revocation

POTATOES ORIGINATING IN THE NETHERLANDS (NOTIFICATION) (REVOCATION) REGULATIONS (NORTHERN IRELAND) 2005, SR 2005 297; made under the European Communities Act 1972 s.2. In force: July 6, 2005; £3.00.

These Regulations revoke the Potatoes Originating in the Netherlands (Notification) Regulations (Northern Ireland) 1 (SR 1 1) which required a person intending to land in Northern Ireland potatoes grown in 1998 in the Netherlands to give to an inspector, at least two days prior notification of that intention and to provide a specified information about those potatoes, and provided plant health inspectors with powers to check compliance with and enforce the Regulations. They also prescribed a fee where a sample of seed potatoes was taken in exercise of those powers for the purpose of ascertaining whether the potatoes were infected with Pseudomonas solanacearum (Smith) Smith. These Regulations are now of no practical effect as potatoes originating in the Netherlands and grown in 1998 are no longer traded.

4724. Potatoes–Import controls–Notice–Netherlands

DUTCH POTATOES (NOTIFICATION) ORDER (NORTHERN IRELAND) 2005, SR 2005 296; made under the Plant Health Act (Northern Ireland) 1967 s.2, s.3, s.3B, s.4. In force: July 6, 2005; £3.00.

This Order places certain notification requirements upon persons importing potatoes from the Netherlands which have been grown during 2004 or later.

LANDLORD AND TENANT

4725. Rent–Registered rents–Increase

REGISTERED RENTS (INCREASE) ORDER (NORTHERN IRELAND) 2005, SR 2005 29; made under the Rent (Northern Ireland) Order 1978 (SI 1978 1050 (NI.20)) Art.33. In force: March 7, 2005; £3.00.

This Order increases the rents registered with the Northern Ireland Housing Executive under the Rent (Northern Ireland) Order 1978 (SI 1978 1050 (NI.20)) for the dwelling houses, which are let under regulated tenancies, by 3.1 per cent from March 7, 2005. Under the Rent Order a notice of increase of rent which gives effect to an increase made by virtue of this Order shall not take effect earlier than four weeks after the commencement of this Order; and not earlier than April 4, 2005. A landlord must give a tenant at least four weeks' notice of the increase.

4726. Books

Brennan, Gabriel–Landlord and Tenant Law. Law Society of Ireland Manuals S. Paperback: £39.99. ISBN 0 19 928025 8. Oxford University Press.
Wylie, John–Irish Landlord and Tenant Law Service. Looseleaf/ring bound: £283.71. ISBN 1 85475 313 4. Butterworths Law (Ireland).

LEGAL ADVICE AND FUNDING

4727. Access to Justice (Northern Ireland) Order 2003 (SI 2003 435 (NI.10))–Commencement No.3 Order

ACCESS TO JUSTICE (NORTHERN IRELAND) ORDER 2003 (COMMENCEMENT NO.3, TRANSITIONAL PROVISIONS AND SAVINGS) ORDER (NORTHERN IRELAND) 2005, SR 2005 111 (C.10); made under the Access to Justice (Northern Ireland) Order 2003 (SI 2003 435 (NI.10)) Art.1, Art.48. In force: bringing into operation various provisions of the 2003 Order on March 9, 2005; £3.00.

This Order brings into operation provisions of the Access to Justice (Northern Ireland) Order 2003 (SI 2003 435 (NI.10)) subject to the transitional provisions in Art.4 of this Order. The effect of the amendment is that the Legal Aid, Advice and Assistance (Northern Ireland) Order 1981 (SI 1981 228 (NI.8)) Art.37 is amended so as to replace the fair remuneration principle with the value for money test in respect of proceedings in the Crown Court.

4728. Access to Justice (Northern Ireland) Order 2003 (SI 2003 435 (NI.10))–Commencement No.4 Order

ACCESS TO JUSTICE (NORTHERN IRELAND) ORDER 2003 (COMMENCEMENT NO.4) ORDER (NORTHERN IRELAND) 2005, SR 2005 503 (C.35); made under the Access to Justice (Northern Ireland) Order 2003 (SI 2003 435 (NI.10)) Art.1. In force: bringing into operation various provisions of the 2003 Order on November 9, 2005; £3.00.

This Order brings into operation the Access to Justice (Northern Ireland) Order 2003 (SI 2003 435 (NI.10)) art.46(2).

4729. Criminal procedure–Costs–Crown Court

LEGAL AID FOR CROWN COURT PROCEEDINGS (COSTS) RULES (NORTHERN IRELAND) 2005, SR 2005 112; made under the Legal Aid, Advice and Assistance (Northern Ireland) Order 1981 (SI 1981 228 (NI.8)) Art.36. In force: April 4, 2005; £5.50.

These Rules prescribe the Crown Court remuneration for solicitors and counsel assigned under the Legal Aid, Advice and Assistance (Northern Ireland) Order 1981 (SI 1981 228 (NI.8)). They deal with the manner in which costs are to be determined and paid; and deal with the standard fees which shall be payable for most cases in the Crown Court.

4730. Criminal procedure–Costs–Discretionary rates

LEGAL AID IN CRIMINAL PROCEEDINGS (COSTS) (AMENDMENT NO.2) RULES (NORTHERN IRELAND) 2005, SR 2005 307; made under the Legal Aid, Advice and Assistance (Northern Ireland) Order 1981 (SI 1981 228 (NI.8)) Art.36. In force: July 1, 2005; £3.00.

These Rules amend the Legal Aid in Criminal Proceedings (Costs) Rules (Northern Ireland) 1992 (SR 1992 314) so as to alter the date after which certain work may be remunerated at discretionary instead of prescribed rates from June 30, 2005 to June 30, 2006.

4731. Criminal procedure–Crown Court proceedings–Determination of costs

LEGAL AID IN CRIMINAL PROCEEDINGS (COSTS) (AMENDMENT) RULES (NORTHERN IRELAND) 2005, SR 2005 113; made under the Legal Aid, Advice and Assistance (Northern Ireland) Order 1981 (SI 1981 228 (NI.8)) Art.36. In force: April 4, 2005; £3.00.

These Rules amend the Legal Aid in Criminal Proceedings (Costs) Rules (Northern Ireland) 1992 (SR 1992 314) to provide that those rules do not apply to the determination of costs in respect of Crown Court proceedings.

4732. Criminal procedure–Statement of means–Civil partnerships

LEGAL AID IN CRIMINAL CASES (STATEMENT OF MEANS) (AMENDMENT) RULES (NORTHERN IRELAND) 2005, SR 2005 500; made under the Legal Aid, Advice and Assistance (Northern Ireland) Order 1981 (SI 1981 228 (NI.8)) Art.36. In force: December 5, 2005; £3.00.

These Rules amend the Legal Aid in Criminal Cases (Statement of Means) Rules (Northern Ireland) 1999 (SR 1999 233) to insert a new marital status option of "Other" and to make reference to the legal status of civil partners, as created by the provisions of the Civil Partnership Act 2004, in the statement of means form which an applicant for free legal aid under the Legal Aid, Advice and Assistance (Northern Ireland) Order 1981 (SI 1981 288 (NI.8)) may be required to furnish.

4733. Legal advice–Assistance–Scale of contributions

LEGAL ADVICE AND ASSISTANCE (AMENDMENT) REGULATIONS (NORTHERN IRELAND) 2005, SR 2005 67; made under the Legal Aid, Advice and Assistance (Northern Ireland) Order 1981 (SI 1981 228 (NI.8)) Art.7, Art.22, Art.27. In force: April 11, 2005; £3.00.

These Regulations, which revoke the Advice and Assistance (Amendment) Regulations (Northern Ireland) 2004 (SR 2004 87), amend the Legal Advice and Assistance Regulations (Northern Ireland) 1981 (SI 1981 228 (NI.8)) so as to substitute a new scale of contributions payable for legal advice and assistance under the Legal Aid, Advice and Assistance (Northern Ireland) Order 1981 Art.7(2).

4734. Legal aid–Civil partnerships

LEGAL ADVICE AND ASSISTANCE (AMENDMENT NO.2) REGULATIONS (NORTHERN IRELAND) 2005, SR 2005 502; made under the Legal Aid, Advice and Assistance (Northern Ireland) Order 1981 (SI 1981 228 (NI.8)) Art.14, Art.22, Art.27. In force: December 5, 2005; £3.00.

These Regulations amend the Legal Advice and Assistance Regulations (Northern Ireland) 1981 (SR 1981 366) to insert references to the legal status of civil partners, as created by the provisions of the Civil Partnership Act 2004, to ensure an application for legal advice and assistance from any person who is in a civil partnership is determined in a manner consistent with the existing Regulations.

4735. Legal aid–Civil partnerships

LEGAL AID (ASSESSMENT OF RESOURCES) (AMENDMENT) REGULATIONS (NORTHERN IRELAND) 2005, SR 2005 501; made under the Legal Aid, Advice and Assistance (Northern Ireland) Order 1981 (SI 1981 228 (NI.8)) Art.14, Art.22, Art.27. In force: December 5, 2005; £3.00.

These Regulations amend the Legal Aid (Assessment of Resources) Regulations (Northern Ireland) 1981 (SR 1981 366) to insert references to the legal status of civil partners, as created by the provisions of the Civil Partnership Act 2004, to ensure an application for legal aid from any person who is in a civil partnership is determined in a manner consistent with the existing Regulations.

4736. Legal aid–Civil partnerships

LEGAL AID (GENERAL) (AMENDMENT) REGULATIONS (NORTHERN IRELAND) 2005, SR 2005 474; made under the Legal Advice and Assistance

Regulations (Northern Ireland) 1981 (SI 1981 228 (NI.8)) Art.22, Art.27. In force: December 5, 2005; £3.00.

These Regulations amend the Legal Aid (General) Regulations (Northern Ireland) 1965 (SR 1965 217) to insert references to the legal status of civil partners, as created by the provisions of the Civil Partnership Act 2004, to ensure an application for legal aid from any person who is in a civil partnership is determined in a manner consistent with the existing Regulations.

4737. Legal aid – Civil partnerships – Advice and assistance

LEGAL AID (COSTS OF SUCCESSFUL UNASSISTED PARTIES) (AMENDMENT) REGULATIONS (NORTHERN IRELAND) 2005, SR 2005 473; made under the Legal Aid, Advice and Assistance (Northern Ireland) Order 1981 (SI 1981 228 (NI.8)) Art.17. In force: December 5, 2005; £3.00.

These Regulations amend the Legal Aid (Costs of Successful Unassisted Parties) Regulations (Northern Ireland) 1965 (SR 1965 235) to insert references to the legal status of civil partners, as created by the provisions of the Civil Partnership Act 2004, to ensure an application for an order under the Legal Aid, Advice and Assistance (Northern Ireland) Order 1981 (SI 1981 228 (NI.8)) by any person who is in a civil partnership is determined in a manner consistent with the existing Regulations.

4738. Legal aid – Financial conditions – Calculation of disposable income – Limit increase

LEGAL ADVICE AND ASSISTANCE (FINANCIAL CONDITIONS) REGULATIONS (NORTHERN IRELAND) 2005, SR 2005 65; made under the Legal Aid, Advice and Assistance (Northern Ireland) Order 1981 (SI 1981 228 (NI.8)) Art.3, Art.7, Art.22, Art.27. In force: April 11, 2005; £3.00.

These Regulations, which revoked the Legal Advice and Assistance (Financial Conditions) Regulations (Northern Ireland) 2004 (SR 2004 88), amend the Legal Aid, Advice and Assistance (Northern Ireland) Order 1981 (SI 1981 228 (NI.8)) so as to increase the upper income limit to make legal advice and assistance available to those with disposable income of not more than £203 a week; and increase the lower income limit below which legal advice and assistance is available without payment of a contribution to £86 a week.

4739. Legal aid – Financial conditions – Calculation of disposable income – Limit increase

LEGAL AID (FINANCIAL CONDITIONS) REGULATIONS (NORTHERN IRELAND) 2005, SR 2005 66; made under the Legal Aid, Advice and Assistance (Northern Ireland) Order 1981 (SI 1981 228 (NI.8)) Art.9, Art.12, Art.22, Art.27. In force: April 11, 2005; £3.00.

These Regulations, which revoke the Legal Aid (Financial Conditions) Regulations (Northern Ireland) 2004 (SR 2004 87) (with saving), amend the Legal Aid, Advice and Assistance (Northern Ireland) Order 1981 (SI 1981 228 (NI.8)) so as to increase the upper income limit to make legal aid available to those with disposable incomes of not more than £8,681, or in connection with proceedings involving a personal injury £9,570; and increase the lower income limit below which legal aid is available without payment of a contribution to £2,931.

4740. Legal Aid (Northern Ireland) Order 2005 (SI 2005 3423 (NI.19))

This Order, which amends the Legal Advice and Assistance Regulations (Northern Ireland) 1981 (SI 1981 228 (NI.8)), and the Access to Justice (Northern Ireland) Order 2003 (SI 2003 435 (NI.10)), provides for the grant of legal aid in exceptional circumstances.

LEGAL PROFESSION

4741. Books

Bar Council of Ireland Directory, 2006. Book (details unknown): £25.00. ISBN 0 421 93170 1. Sweet & Maxwell.

Quinn, A.P.; Osborough, W.N.–Wigs and Guns: Irish Barristers and the Great War. Irish Legal History Society Series. Hardback: £40.00. ISBN 1 85182 935 0. Four Courts Press.

LEGISLATION

4742. Law Reform (Miscellaneous Provisions) (Northern Ireland) Order 2005 (SI 2005 1452 (NI.7))

This Order, which amends 18 statutory instruments and 21 acts, makes provision with respect to deeds and their execution. It clarifies the law in relation to escrows and abolishes the rule in Pigot's Case and the rule in Bain v. Fothergill; amends the law relating to family homes and domestic violence; abolishes a number of rules of common law relating to the property of married or engaged couples; and makes provision for the repeal of the Colonial Solicitors Act 1900 and the Trading Stamps Act (Northern Ireland) 1965. It also amends the Census Act (Northern Ireland) 1969 and the Damages Act 1996.

4743. Law Reform (Miscellaneous Provisions) (Northern Ireland) Order 2005 (SI 2005 1452 (NI.7))–Commencement and Transitional Saving Order

LAW REFORM (MISCELLANEOUS PROVISIONS) (2005 ORDER) (COMMENCEMENT AND TRANSITIONAL SAVING) ORDER (NORTHERN IRELAND), SR 2005 494 (C.34); made under the Law Reform (Miscellaneous Provisions) (Northern Ireland) Order 2005 (SI 2005 1452 (NI.7)) Art.1. In force: bringing into operation various provisions of the 2005 Order on November 15, 2005 and February 1, 2006; £3.00.

This Order brings into operation various provisions of the Law Reform (Miscellaneous Provisions) (Northern Ireland) Order 2005 (SI 2005 1452 (NI.7)).

LOCAL GOVERNMENT

4744. Grants–Central funds–Calculation of grant from Department of the Environment

LOCAL GOVERNMENT (GENERAL GRANT) (AMENDMENT) REGULATIONS (NORTHERN IRELAND) 2005, SR 2005 101; made under the Local Government (Miscellaneous Provisions) (Northern Ireland) Order 2002 (SI 2002 3149 (NI.3)) Art.4. In force: May 1, 2005; £3.00.

These Regulations amend the Local Government (General Grant) Regulations (Northern Ireland) 2003 to permit the Department to use data based on information available on March 31, 2005 and on March 31st in each successive year thereafter.

4745. Local Government (Northern Ireland) Order 2005 (SI 2005 1968 (NI.18))

This Order amends the Interpretation Act (Northern Ireland) 1954, the Local Government Act (Northern Ireland) 1972, the Superannuation (Northern Ireland) Order 1972 (SI 1972 1073 (NI.10)), the Local Government (Miscellaneous Provisions) (Northern Ireland) Order 1985 (SI 1985 1208

(NI.15)), the Audit (Northern Ireland) Order 1987 (SI 1987 460 (NI.5)), the Local Government (Miscellaneous Provisions) (Northern Ireland) Order 1992 (SI 1992 810 (NI.6)), the Litter (Northern Ireland) Order 1994 (SI 1994 1896 (NI.10)), the Local Government (Northern Ireland) Order 2002 (SI 2002 3149 (NI.3)) and the Audit and Accountability (Northern Ireland) Order 2003 (SI 2003 418 (NI.5)). The Order makes new provision for the audit of district council accounts, confers miscellaneous new powers on district councils and makes minor amendments to existing statutory provisions concerning such councils.

4746. Local Government (Northern Ireland) Order 2005 (SI 2005 1968 (NI.18))– Commencement No.1 Order

LOCAL GOVERNMENT (2005 ORDER) (COMMENCEMENT NO.1) ORDER (NORTHERN IRELAND) 2005, SR 2005 465 (C.33); made under the Local Government (Northern Ireland) Order 2005 (SI 2005 1968 (NI.18)) Art.1. In force: bringing into operation various provisions of the 2005 Order on November 1, 2005; £3.00.

This Order brings into operation provisions of the Local Government (Northern Ireland) Order 2005 (SI 2005 1968 (NI.18)) which provide for the Department, with the consent of the Comptroller and Auditor General for Northern Ireland, to designate a local government auditor as chief local government auditor; require the chief local government auditor to prepare and keep under review a code of audit practice; amend the Litter (Northern Ireland) Order 1994 (SI 1994 1896 (NI.10)); amend the Local Government (Miscellaneous Provisions) (Northern Ireland) Order 1985 (SI 1985 1208 (NI.15)); amend the Local Government (Northern Ireland) Act 1972; and the Superannuation (Northern Ireland) Order 1972.

PENOLOGY AND CRIMINOLOGY

4747. Prisoners–Release or discharge–Access to information–Civil partnerships

PRISONER RELEASE VICTIM INFORMATION (NORTHERN IRELAND) (AMENDMENT) SCHEME 2005, SR 2005 504; made under the Justice (Northern Ireland) Act 2002 s.68. In force: December 5, 2005; £3.00.

This Scheme makes alterations to the Prisoner Release Victim Information (Northern Ireland) Scheme 2003 (SR 2003 293). It amends the description of "close family member" so as to include a person who is a civil partner under the provisions of the Civil Partnership Act 2004; makes a minor drafting alteration; omits wording to clarify that information which may be made available under the Principal Scheme is, where reasonably practicable, to be provided before a decision is made on the temporary release of an offender. It also omits wording which relates to offenders with less than three months' imprisonment left to serve at the time the Principal Scheme came into force and which, by the passage of time, is no longer necessary.

4748. Prisons–Young offenders institutions–Amendments

PRISON AND YOUNG OFFENDERS CENTRE (AMENDMENT) RULES (NORTHERN IRELAND) 2005, SR 2005 153; made under the Prison Act (Northern Ireland) 1953 s.13. In force: in accordance with r.1; £3.00.

These Rules amend the Prison and Young Offenders Centre Rules (Northern Ireland) 1995 (SR 1995 8). They make amendments to the Rules which govern the circumstances and arrangements for the restriction of the association of a prisoner and which govern the circumstances and arrangements for the making of an order putting a prisoner under restraint. They insert a new prisoner complaints system, including provision in relation to the operation of the new Prisoner Ombudsman for Northern Ireland; make it possible for certain functions of a medical officer of a prison or a Young Offenders Centre to be carried out by a registered nurse; and remove references to the board of visitors.

4749. Probation Board for Northern Ireland–Victims–Access to information

PROBATION BOARD FOR NORTHERN IRELAND VICTIM INFORMATION SCHEME 2005, SR 2005 432; made under the Criminal Justice (Northern Ireland) Order 2005 (SI 2005 1965 (NI.15)) Art.25. In force: October 25, 2005; £3.00.

The purpose of this Scheme is to put in place a mechanism whereby if a crime results in the statutory supervision of an offender by the Probation Board for Northern Ireland, the victim of that crime should have access to information about the supervision of the offender.

PENSIONS

4750. Civil partnerships–Occupational pensions–Contracted out schemes–Entitlement

CIVIL PARTNERSHIP (CONTRACTED-OUT OCCUPATIONAL AND APPROPRIATE PERSONAL PENSION SCHEMES) (SURVIVING CIVIL PARTNERS) ORDER (NORTHERN IRELAND) 2005, SR 2005 433; made under the Civil Partnership Act 2004 s.255. In force: in accordance with Art.1 (2) (3); £3.00.

This Order amends the Personal and Occupational Pension Schemes (Abatement of Benefit) Regulations (Northern Ireland) 1987 (SR 1987 291), the Contracting-out (Protection of Pensions) Regulations (Northern Ireland) 1991 (SR 1991 39), the Pension Schemes (Northern Ireland) Act 1993, the Occupational Pension Schemes (Discharge of Protected Rights on Winding Up) Regulations (Northern Ireland) 1996 (SR 1996 94), the Protected Rights (Transfer Payment) Regulations (Northern Ireland) 1996 (SR 1996 509), the Contracting-out (Transfer and Transfer Payment) Regulations (Northern Ireland) 1996 (SR 1996 618), the Personal and Occupational Pension Schemes (Protected Rights) Regulations (Northern Ireland) 1997 (SR 1997 56), the Occupational Pension Schemes (Modification of Schemes) Regulations (Northern Ireland) 1997 (SR 1997 97), the Personal Pension Schemes (Appropriate Schemes) Regulations (Northern Ireland) 1997 (SR 1997 139) and the Occupational Pension Schemes (Discharge of Liability) Regulations (Northern Ireland) 1997 (SR 1997 159). The Regulations make provision for surviving civil partners to receive pensions under contracted-out occupational and appropriate personal pension schemes.

4751. Contribution notices–Restoration orders–Appropriate persons

PENSIONS REGULATOR (CONTRIBUTION NOTICES AND RESTORATION ORDERS) REGULATIONS (NORTHERN IRELAND) 2005, SR 2005 173; made under the Pensions (Northern Ireland) Order 2005 (SI 2005 255 (NI.1)) Art.34, Art.48, Art.287. In force: April 6, 2005; £3.00.

These Regulations make provision relating to the "moral hazard" provisions in the Pensions (Northern Ireland) Order 2005 (SI 2005 255 (NI.1)) Art.34 and Art.48. These Articles provide for two of the powers of the Pensions Regulator known as the "moral hazard" provisions, that is, the Regulator's power to issue contribution notices and to make restoration orders. They prescribe those schemes to which Art.34 and Art.48 of the Order do not apply. They also prescribe "appropriate persons" who may be involved in a transaction involving scheme assets which is at an undervalue.

4752. Occupational pension schemes–Audited accounts

OCCUPATIONAL PENSION SCHEMES (ADMINISTRATION AND AUDITED ACCOUNTS) (AMENDMENT) REGULATIONS (NORTHERN IRELAND) 2005, SR 2005 421; made under the Pension Schemes (Northern Ireland) Act 1993 s.107A, s.109, s.177; and the Pensions (Northern Ireland) Order 1995 (SI 1995

3213 (NI.22)) Art.41, Art.47, Art.49, Art.85, Art.86, Art.166. In force: in accordance with Reg.1; £3.00.

The Regulations, which amend the Occupational Pension Schemes (Requirement to obtain Audited Accounts and a Statement from the Auditor) Regulations (Northern Ireland) 1997 (SR 1997 40) and the Occupational Pension Schemes (Scheme Administration) Regulations (Northern Ireland) 1997 (SR 1997 94), partially revoke the Personal and Occupational Pension Schemes (Miscellaneous Amendments) Regulations (Northern Ireland) 1997 (SR 1997 160), the Personal and Occupational Pension Schemes (Miscellaneous Amendments) Regulations (Northern Ireland) 1 (SR 1 486), the Occupational Pension Schemes (Miscellaneous Amendments) Regulations (Northern Ireland) 2000 (SR 2000 69) and the Personal Pension Schemes (Payments by Employers) Regulations (Northern Ireland) 2000 (SR 2000 349). The Regulations amend the exemptions from the requirement to maintain audited accounts and introduces a "materiality" requirement in relation to the occasions where the auditor of a scheme is required to qualify a scheme's accounts; add a number of new definitions, amend the exemptions of schemes that are not required to appoint an auditor, and make consequential amendments; and make amendments to the list of schemes which are exempt from the requirement to appoint professional advisors, omit an obsolete regulation and make further amendments to the requirements to notify the Authority of the late payment of a contribution.

4753. Occupational pension schemes–Exemptions

OCCUPATIONAL PENSION SCHEMES (TRUST AND RETIREMENT BENEFITS EXEMPTION) REGULATIONS (NORTHERN IRELAND) 2005, SR 2005 412; made under the Pensions (Northern Ireland) Order 2005 (SI 2005 255 (NI.1)) Art.229, Art.232, Art.287. In force: September 22, 2005; £3.00.

These Regulations prescribe the description of schemes which are exempt from the requirement in the Pensions (Northern Ireland) Order 2005 (SI 2005 255 (NI.1)) that trustees or managers of an occupational pension scheme with its main administration in the UK must not accept a funding payment unless the scheme is established under irrevocable trust. They also prescribe the description of a scheme which is exempt from the requirement in the Order, that an occupational pension scheme with its main administration in the UK must be limited to retirement benefit-related activities.

4754. Occupational pension schemes–Indexation and disclosure of information

PERSONAL AND OCCUPATIONAL PENSION SCHEMES (INDEXATION AND DISCLOSURE OF INFORMATION) (MISCELLANEOUS AMENDMENTS) REGULATIONS (NORTHERN IRELAND) 2005, SR 2005 170; made under the Pension Schemes (Northern Ireland) Act 1993 s.8C, s.15, s.24, s.24A, s.109, s.164, s.177; the Pensions (Northern Ireland) Order 1995 (SI 1995 3213 (NI.22)) Art.51, Art.122, Art.166; and the Welfare Reform and Pensions (Northern Ireland) Order 1999 (SI 1999 3147 (NI.11)) Art.37, Art.73. In force: April 6, 2005; £3.00.

These Regulations amend the Occupational Pension Schemes (Indexation) Regulations (Northern Ireland) 1997 (SR 1997 8), the Personal and Occupational Pension Schemes (Protected Rights) Regulations (Northern Ireland) 1997 (SR 1997 56), the Occupational Pension Schemes (Disclosure of Information) Regulations (Northern Ireland) 1997 (SR 1997 98), the Occupational Pension Schemes (Discharge of Liability) Regulations (Northern Ireland) 1997 (SR 1997 159), the Personal and Occupational Pension Schemes (Miscellaneous Amendments) Regulations (Northern Ireland) 1997 (SR 1997 160), the Personal and Occupational Pension Schemes (Miscellaneous Amendments) Regulations (Northern Ireland) 1999 (SR 1999 486), the Pension Sharing (Pension Credit Benefit) Regulations (Northern Ireland) 2000 (SR 2000 146) and the Occupational and Personal Pension Schemes (Contracting-out) (Miscellaneous Amendments) Regulations (Northern Ireland) 2002 (SR 2002 109). The Regulations reflect amendments made by the Pensions (Northern

Ireland) Order 2005 (SI 2005 255 (NI.1)) to provisions that require increases in the rate of certain pensions. They also introduce requirements under the Occupational Pension Schemes (Disclosure of Information) Regulations (Northern Ireland) 1997 (SR 1997 98) for trustees of occupational pension schemes to provide information about the selection of annuities when benefits under a scheme become payable.

4755. Occupational pension schemes–Levies

OCCUPATIONAL PENSION SCHEMES (LEVIES) REGULATIONS (NORTHERN IRELAND) 2005, SR 2005 147; made under the Pensions (Northern Ireland) Order 2005 (SI 2005 255 (NI.1)) Art.103, Art.110, Art.157, Art.164, Art.171, Art.191, Art.287. In force: April 1, 2005; £3.00.

These Regulations impose the administration levy, the initial levy and the PPF Ombudsman levy provided for in the Pensions (Northern Ireland) Order 2005 (SI 2005 255 (NI.1)). The Regulations make provision for the imposition and payment of the administration levy and the PPF Ombudsman levy. They also make general provision as to how the amount of those levies is to be determined and the times at which they are to be paid and provides that no PPF Ombudsman levy is payable for the financial year ending with March 31, 2006. The Regulations make provision for the imposition and payment of the initial levy; provide that, while generally schemes that are only eligible schemes for part of the levy period are only liable for a proportionate part of the levy, there is no reduction in the initial levy if the scheme ceases to be eligible during the initial period; and make provision for the apportionment of levy payments between the levies where it is not apparent which levies a payment relates to, and enables apportionment to apply also where payments may relate to any pension protection levy or fraud compensation levy.

4756. Occupational pensions–Benefits–Revaluation percentages

OCCUPATIONAL PENSIONS (REVALUATION) ORDER (NORTHERN IRELAND) 2005, SR 2005 509; made under the Pension Schemes (Northern Ireland) Act 1993 Sch.3 para.2. In force: January 1, 2006; £3.00.

This Order specifies appropriate revaluation percentages. The percentages specified are relevant to the revaluation of benefits under occupational pension schemes, as required by the Pension Schemes (Northern Ireland) Act 1993.

4757. Occupational pensions–Civil partnerships

OCCUPATIONAL AND PERSONAL PENSION SCHEMES (CIVIL PARTNERSHIP) (MISCELLANEOUS AMENDMENTS) REGULATIONS (NORTHERN IRELAND) 2005, SR 2005 507; made under the Pension Schemes (Northern Ireland) Act 1993 s.8C, s.15, s.24. In force: December 5, 2005; £3.00.

These Regulations make consequential amendments to the Personal and Occupational Pension Schemes (Protected Rights) Regulations (Northern Ireland) 1997 (SR 1997 56) and the Occupational Pension Schemes (Discharge of Liability) Regulations (Northern Ireland) 1997 (SR 1997 159) to ensure that surviving civil partners are treated in the same way as widows and widowers.

4758. Occupational pensions–Contracted out schemes–Transfer of payments

PROTECTED RIGHTS (TRANSFER PAYMENT) (AMENDMENT) REGULATIONS (NORTHERN IRELAND) 2005, SR 2005 467; made under the Pension Schemes (Northern Ireland) Act 1993 s.24, s.177. In force: November 28, 2005; £3.00.

These Regulations amend the Protected Rights (Transfer Payment) Regulations (Northern Ireland) 1996 (SR 1996 509) and partly revoke the Stakeholder Pension Schemes Regulations (Northern Ireland) 2000 (SR 2000 262). The Regulations make amendments to include among the schemes that may give effect to a member's protected rights by making a transfer payment to an appropriate personal pension scheme or an occupational pension scheme, the money purchase part of a mixed benefit contracted-out scheme and a scheme which has ceased to be the money purchase part of a mixed benefit contracted-out scheme; and provide for transfer payments to be made to a money purchase contracted-out scheme or the money purchase part of a mixed benefit contracted-out scheme.

4759. Occupational pensions-Employer debt

OCCUPATIONAL PENSION SCHEMES (EMPLOYER DEBT) REGULATIONS (NORTHERN IRELAND) 2005, SR 2005 168; made under the Pensions (Northern Ireland) Order 1995 (SI 1995 3213 (NI.22)) Art.40, Art.49, Art.57, Art.60, Art.68, Art.75, Art.75A, Art.87, Art.115, Art.116, Art.122, Art.166. In force: April 6, 2005; £3.50.

These Regulations amend the Occupational Pension Schemes (Minimum Funding Requirement and Actuarial Valuations) Regulations (Northern Ireland) 1996 (SR 1996 570), the Occupational Pension Schemes (Investment) Regulations (Northern Ireland) 1996 (SR 1996 584) and the Occupational Pension Schemes (Winding Up) Regulations (Northern Ireland) 1996 (SR 1996 621). The Regulations are made as a consequence of provisions in the Pensions (Northern Ireland) Order 2005 (SI 2005 255 (NI.1)) and replace the Occupational Pension Schemes (Deficiency on Winding Up, etc.) Regulations (Northern Ireland) 1996 (SR 1996 585) where debts arise under the Pensions (Northern Ireland) Order 1995 (SI 1995 3213 (NI.22)) Art.75 in respect of certain occupational pension schemes which begin to wind up after April 6, 2005.

4760. Occupational pensions-Employer debt

OCCUPATIONAL PENSION SCHEMES (EMPLOYER DEBT, ETC.) (AMENDMENT) REGULATIONS (NORTHERN IRELAND) 2005, SR 2005 387; made under the Pensions (Northern Ireland) Order 1995 (SI 1995 3213 (NI.22)) Art.10, Art.56, Art.75, Art.75A, Art.87, Art.115, Art.116, Art.122, Art.166; and the Pensions (Northern Ireland) Order 2005 (SI 2005 255 (NI.1)) Art.2, Art.88, Art.119, Sch.1 para.2. In force: September 2, 2005; £3.00.

These Regulations amend the Occupational Pension Schemes (Minimum Funding Requirement and Actuarial Valuations) Regulations (Northern Ireland) 1996 (SR 1996 570), the Pension Protection Fund (Entry Rules) Regulations (Northern Ireland) 2005 (SR 2005 126), the Occupational Pension Schemes (Employer Debt) Regulations (Northern Ireland) 2005 (SR 2005 168), and the Pensions Regulator (Financial Support Directions, etc.) Regulations (Northern Ireland) 2005 (SR 2005 378).

4761. Occupational pensions-Equal treatment

OCCUPATIONAL PENSION SCHEMES (EQUAL TREATMENT) (AMENDMENT) REGULATIONS (NORTHERN IRELAND) 2005, SR 2005 377; made under the European Communities Act 1972 s.2; and the Pensions (Northern Ireland) Order 1995 (SI 1995 3213 (NI.22)) Art.63, Art.66, Art.166. In force: August 30, 2005; £3.00.

These Regulations amend the Equal Pay Act (Northern Ireland) 1970, the Pensions (Northern Ireland) Order 1995 (SI 1995 3213 (NI.22)) and the Occupational Pension Schemes (Equal Treatment) Regulations (Northern Ireland) 1995 (SR 1995 482). They amend the statutory provisions that require equal treatment of men and women in respect of occupational pension schemes. The amendments made by the Regulations reflect requirements of European Community law, as applied in a number of cases before the European Court of Justice and the domestic courts. The Regulations provide that the period within which a person can institute proceedings before an industrial tribunal is the same for both an equal treatment rule and an equality clause; modify the time limits that apply to proceedings about failure to comply with the equal treatment rule; and modify provisions of the Equal Pay Act 1970 that relate to armed forces.

4762. Occupational pensions–Fraud compensation payments

OCCUPATIONAL PENSION SCHEMES (FRAUD COMPENSATION PAYMENTS AND MISCELLANEOUS AMENDMENTS) REGULATIONS (NORTHERN IRELAND) 2005, SR 2005 381; made under the Pensions (Northern Ireland) Order 2005 (SI 2005 255 (NI.1)) Art.2, Art.165, Art.166, Art.168, Art.169, Art.172, Art.185, Art.188, Art.189, Art.280, Art.287; and the Welfare Reform and Pensions (Northern Ireland) Order 1 (SI 1 3147 (NI.11)) Sch.1 para.1. In force: September 1, 2005; £5.50.

These Regulations make provision in relation to the payment by the Board of the Pension Protection Fund of fraud compensation under the Pensions (Northern Ireland) Order 2005 Ch.4 of Part III. Fraud compensation is payable from September 1, 2005 where an employer in relation to an occupational pension scheme is insolvent, or unlikely to continue as a going concern, and the scheme has suffered a loss as a result of an act or omission which qualifies as a prescribed offence under reg.3 of these Regulations. They also amend the Pension Protection Fund (Reviewable Matters) Regulations (Northern Ireland) 2005 (SR 2005 127), the Pension Protection Fund (Provision of Information) Regulations (Northern Ireland) 2005 (SR 2005 129), and the Pension Protection Fund (Review and Reconsideration of Reviewable Matters) Regulations (Northern Ireland) 2005 (SR 2005 138).

4763. Occupational pensions–Guaranteed minimum pensions–Increase

GUARANTEED MINIMUM PENSIONS INCREASE ORDER (NORTHERN IRELAND) 2005, SR 2005 81; made under the Pension Schemes (Northern Ireland) Act 1993 s.105. In force: April 6, 2005; £3.00.

This Order specifies 3 per cent as the percentage by which that part of any guaranteed minimum pension attributable to earnings factors for the tax years 1988-1989 to 1996-1997 and payable by contracted-out, defined benefit occupational pension schemes is to be increased.

4764. Occupational pensions–Independent trustees

OCCUPATIONAL PENSION SCHEMES (INDEPENDENT TRUSTEE) REGULATIONS (NORTHERN IRELAND) 2005, SR 2005 169; made under the Pension Schemes (Northern Ireland) Act 1993 s.109, s.164, s.177; the Pensions (Northern Ireland) Order 1995 (SI 1995 3213 (NI.22)) Art.22, Art.23, Art.115, Art.122, Art.166; and the Pensions (Northern Ireland) Order 2005 (SI 2005 255 (NI.1)) Art.7, Art.88, Art.92, Art.287, Sch.1 para.2. In force: April 11, 2005; £3.00.

These Regulations, which revoke the Occupational Pension Schemes (Independent Trustee) Regulations (Northern Ireland) 1997 (SR 1997 99), amend the Personal and Occupational Pension Schemes (Miscellaneous Amendments No.2) Regulations (Northern Ireland) 1997 (SR 1997 544) and the Occupational Pension Schemes (Winding Up Notices and Reports, etc.) Regulations (Northern Ireland) 2002 (SR 2002 74). They make provision about the register of trustees and further provision about independent trustees.

4765. Occupational pensions–Internal controls

OCCUPATIONAL PENSION SCHEMES (INTERNAL CONTROLS) REGULATIONS (NORTHERN IRELAND) 2005, SR 2005 567; made under the European Communities Act 1972 s.2. In force: December 30, 2005; £3.00.

These Regulations amend the Pensions (Northern Ireland) Order 2005 (SI 2005 255 (NI.1)) to provide that the Pensions Regulator must issue a code of practice relating to the duty imposed by art.226A of that Order.

4766. Occupational pensions–Local government pension scheme–Membership

LOCAL GOVERNMENT PENSION SCHEME (AMENDMENT) REGULATIONS (NORTHERN IRELAND) 2005, SR 2005 206; made under the Superannuation

(Northern Ireland) Order 1972 (SI 1972 1073 (NI.10)) Art.9, Sch.3. In force: May 1, 2005; £3.00.

These Regulations amend the Local Government (Superannuation) (Milk Marketing Board for Northern Ireland) Regulations (Northern Ireland) 1997 (SR 1997 137) and the Local Government Pension Scheme Regulations (Northern Ireland) 2002 (SR 2002 352) which comprise the Local Government Pension Scheme. They provide for the Northern Ireland Local Government Officers' Superannuation Committee to make admission agreements to enable employees of non-Scheme employers to be members of the Scheme. The main changes are: to separate the requirements for "community" and "transferee" admission bodies into separate regulations; to extend the definition of transferee admission body, to include bodies (other than community admission bodies) that carry out a public service and have been approved by the Department for admission to the Scheme; and to require an indemnity or bond to be entered into by the transferee admission body where it is identified as being necessary following a risk assessment. They also make provision for the admission of community admission bodies and for the admission of transferee admission bodies.

4767. Occupational pensions—Local government pension scheme—Membership

LOCAL GOVERNMENT PENSION SCHEME (AMENDMENT NO.2) REGULATIONS (NORTHERN IRELAND) 2005, SR 2005 274; made under the Superannuation (Northern Ireland) Order 1972 (SI 1972 1073 (NI.10)) Art.9, Art.14, Sch.3. In force: June 1, 2005; £3.00.

These Regulations, which amend the Local Government Pension Scheme Regulations (Northern Ireland) 2002 (SR 2002 352), reduce the total membership required to become entitled to benefits from two years to three months; provide that where a member becomes entitled to a second ill-health pension and grant (unless by virtue of being in concurrent employments which cease simultaneously), the multiplier for that pension and grant will be his total membership without enhancement; removes provisions relating to re-employed pensioners' entitlement to elect for a single new pension and provides for when periods of former membership may be taken into account when calculating the total membership of a re-employed pensioner; provide that where a deferred member becomes an active member again and wants to elect to have his former membership aggregated with his current membership, he must give notice of his election within 12 months of the date he became an active member again or such longer period as his employer may allow and makes provision for when the unaggregated periods of membership should be taken into account; alters, from two years to three months, the amount of total membership required to determine the applicable calculation for surviving spouses long-term pension; and provide that employing authorities may increase an active member's total membership.

4768. Occupational pensions—Miscellaneous amendments

OCCUPATIONAL PENSION SCHEMES (MISCELLANEOUS AMENDMENTS) REGULATIONS (NORTHERN IRELAND) 2005, SR 2005 357; made under the Pensions (Northern Ireland) Order 2005 (SI 2005 255 (NI.1)) Art.2, Art.7, Art.64, Art.188, Art.189, Art.280, Art.287, Sch.6 para.23. In force: in accordance with Reg.1 (1); £5.50.

These Regulations amend the Pensions (Northern Ireland) Order 2005 (SI 2005 255 (NI.1)), the Pension Protection Fund (Multi-employer Schemes) (Modification) Regulations (Northern Ireland) 2005 (SR 2005 91), the Pension Protection Fund (Entry Rules) Regulations (Northern Ireland) 2005 (SR 2005 126), the Pension Protection Fund (Provision of Information) Regulations (Northern Ireland) 2005 (SR 2005 129), the Pension Protection Fund (Valuation) Regulations (Northern Ireland) 2005 (SR 2005 131), the Pension Protection Fund (Review and Reconsideration of Reviewable Matters) Regulations (Northern Ireland) 2005 (SR 2005 138), the Pension Protection Fund (Compensation) Regulations (Northern Ireland) 2005 (SR 2005 149), the Pensions Regulator (Notifiable Events) Regulations (Northern Ireland) 2005 (SR

2005 172), and the Pension Protection Fund and Pensions Regulator (Amendment) Regulations (Northern Ireland) 2005 (SR 2005 194). They provide that a civil partner will be entitled to receive a survivor's pension where the admissible rules of the scheme allow for such a payment to be made and for the amount of such compensation both where there are dependants of the civil partnership and where there are not; where a member has nominated a relevant partner to receive a survivor's pension under the admissible rules of the scheme, then a surviving spouse or civil partner shall not be entitled to compensation; and where a surviving spouse or civil partner is entitled to compensation and there is no nomination in place in favour of a relevant partner, then the relevant partner shall not be entitled to compensation.

4769. Occupational pensions–Notifiable events

PENSIONS REGULATOR (NOTIFIABLE EVENTS) REGULATIONS (NORTHERN IRELAND) 2005, SR 2005 172; made under the Pensions (Northern Ireland) Order 2005 (SI 2005 255 (NI.1)) Art.64, Art.287. In force: April 6, 2005; £3.00.

These Regulations prescribe those events the occurrence of which must be notified to the Regulator by an appropriate person by virtue of the Pensions (Northern Ireland) Order 2005 (SI 2005 255 (NI.1)). In relation to events in respect of certain occupational pension schemes the duty to notify the Regulator falls on the trustees or managers of the scheme; in relation to events in respect of employers in relation to eligible pension schemes, the duty falls on the employers.

4770. Occupational pensions–Pension protection

OCCUPATIONAL PENSION SCHEMES (MODIFICATION OF PENSION PROTECTION PROVISIONS) REGULATIONS (NORTHERN IRELAND) 2005, SR 2005 137; made under the Pensions (Northern Ireland) Order 2005 (SI 2005 255 (NI.1)) Art.151, Art.287. In force: April 6, 2005; £3.00.

These Regulations modify the Pensions (Northern Ireland) Order 2005 (SI 2005 255 (NI.1)) as it applies where any liability to provide pensions or other benefits to or in respect of any member or members under an occupational pension scheme that is an eligible scheme is discharged during an assessment period or on the day when that period will begin.

4771. Occupational pensions–Pension protection–Eligible schemes

PENSION PROTECTION FUND (ELIGIBLE SCHEMES) APPOINTED DAY ORDER (NORTHERN IRELAND) 2005, SR 2005 83; made under the Pensions (Northern Ireland) Order 2005 (SI 2005 255 (NI.1)) Art.110. In force: March 10, 2005; £3.00.

This Order appoints April 6, 2005 as the day on or after which an occupational pension scheme is not to be an eligible scheme if, immediately before that day, the scheme is being wound up.

4772. Occupational pensions–Personal pension schemes–General levy

OCCUPATIONAL AND PERSONAL PENSION SCHEMES (GENERAL LEVY) REGULATIONS (NORTHERN IRELAND) 2005, SR 2005 92; made under the Pension Schemes (Northern Ireland) Act 1993 s.164, s.170, s.177. In force: April 1, 2005; £3.00.

These Regulations, which revoke the Occupational and Personal Pension Schemes (Levy) Regulations (Northern Ireland) 1997 (SR 1997 142), the Occupational and Personal Pension Schemes (Levy) (Amendment) Regulations (Northern Ireland) 1999 (SR 1999 106) and the Occupational and Personal Pension Schemes (Levy) (Amendment) Regulations (Northern Ireland) 2000 (SR 2000 60), amend the Occupational and Personal Pension Schemes (Levy and Register) (Amendments) Regulations (Northern Ireland) 1998 (SR 1998 85), the Pension Sharing (Consequential and Miscellaneous Amendments) Regulations (Northern Ireland) 2000 (SR 2000 335) and the Occupational

Pension Schemes (Republic of Ireland Schemes Exemption) Regulations (Northern Ireland) 2000 (SR 2000 382). The Regulations make provision for the imposition and payment of a levy for the purpose of meeting the cost of the Pensions Ombudsman, the Regulatory Authority, and the scheme established under the Pensions Act 2004 s.106 for legal assistance in connection with proceedings before the Pensions Regulator Tribunal. They also make provision as to how the amount of the levy is to be determined, the times at which it is to be paid, and the circumstances in which it may be waived.

4773. Occupational pensions–Personal pension schemes–Payments

OCCUPATIONAL AND PERSONAL PENSION SCHEMES (PENSION LIBERATION) REGULATIONS (NORTHERN IRELAND) 2005, SR 2005 193; made under the Pensions (Northern Ireland) Order 2005 (SI 2005 255 (NI.1)) Art.15, Art.17, Art.287. In force: April 27, 2005; £3.00.

These Regulations make provision in relation to payments made into an occupational or personal pension scheme by reason of a restitution order made by the High Court under the Pensions (Northern Ireland) Order 2005 (SI 2005 255 (NI.1)) or of a repatriation order made by the Pensions Regulator. The Regulations amend references in the Pension Schemes (Northern Ireland) Act 1993 to "a transfer payment" and to "transfer credits" so that those terms apply appropriately to payments made to schemes under orders made under the 2005 Order. They modify the statutory discharges given to trustees or managers of schemes in the 1993 Act so that when an order under the 2005 Order is made, the trustees or managers shall have the benefit of those discharges if they have met the duty specified.

4774. Occupational pensions–Personal pensions–Registers

REGISTER OF OCCUPATIONAL AND PERSONAL PENSION SCHEMES REGULATIONS (NORTHERN IRELAND) 2005, SR 2005 93; made under the Pensions (Northern Ireland) Order 2005 (SI 2005 255 (NI.1)) Art.55, Art.56, Art.280, Art.287. In force: in accordance with Reg.1 (1); £3.00.

These Regulations, which amend the Occupational and Personal Pension Schemes (Penalties) Regulations (Northern Ireland) 2000 (SR 2000 107), the Pension Sharing (Consequential and Miscellaneous Amendments) Regulations (Northern Ireland) 2000 (SR 2000 335) and the Occupational Pension Schemes (Republic of Ireland Schemes Exemption) Regulations (Northern Ireland) 2000 (SR 2000 382), revoke the Register of Occupational and Personal Pension Schemes Regulations (Northern Ireland) 1997 (SR 1997 102), the Register of Occupational and Personal Pension Schemes (Amendment) Regulations (Northern Ireland) 1997 (SR 1997 544) and the Occupational and Personal Pension Schemes (Levy and Register) (Amendments) Regulations (Northern Ireland) 1998 (SR 1998 85). The Regulations make provision about the register of occupational and personal pension schemes; prescribe those pension schemes which are registrable; prescribe information which is "registrable information"; and provide that the Department shall provide an information service to be known as the Pension Tracing Service, which will help people to get back in touch with pension schemes of which they may be a member but with which they have lost contact. They also entitle the Department to be provided with information from the register, or to inspect the register, if it considers it necessary to carry on the Pension Tracing Service.

4775. Occupational pensions–Regulatory own funds

OCCUPATIONAL PENSION SCHEMES (REGULATORY OWN FUNDS) REGULATIONS (NORTHERN IRELAND) 2005, SR 2005 570; made under the European Communities Act 1972 s.2; and the Pensions (Northern Ireland) Order

2005 (SI 2005 255 (NI.1)) Art.55, Art.202, Art.211, Art.287. In force: December 30, 2005; £3.00.

These Regulations amend the Pensions (Northern Ireland) Order 2005 (SI 2005 255 (NI.1)) and the Occupational Pension Schemes (Scheme Funding) Regulations (Northern Ireland) 2005 (SR 2005 568). They implement European Parliament and Council Directive 2003/41 ([2003] OJ L235/10) Art.17, on the activities and supervision of institutions for occupational retirement provision and require that where an occupational pension scheme itself, rather than an employer, covers any liability for risks linked to death, disability or longevity, guarantees any investment performance, or guarantees to provide defined benefits, the scheme must have additional assets above its technical provisions, which are no less than the minimum required. They provide that the minimum additional assets required are 4 per cent of the scheme's technical provisions, plus 0.3 per cent of the amount by which the total amount which the scheme would be obliged to pay on the immediate death of all members of the scheme exceeds the technical provisions; provide that when an actuarial valuation is carried out the actuary must certify the calculation of the regulatory own funds requirement in the form set out in the Schedule to these Regulations; provides that, if the regulatory own funds requirement was not met as at the effective date of the actuarial valuation, the trustees or managers must take such steps as are necessary to ensure that the regulatory own funds requirement is met within two years after that date; provide that certification of the schedule of contributions must be in the form set out in the Schedule to these Regulations; provide that the statement of funding principles for the scheme must include the policy for securing that the regulatory own funds requirement is met; and provide that the annual report, accounts and actuarial valuation of an occupational pension scheme which is subject to the regulatory own funds requirement must state whether the regulatory own funds requirement applies to the scheme, and the date from which it applies.

4776. Occupational pensions–Winding up

OCCUPATIONAL PENSION SCHEMES (WINDING UP, ETC.) REGULATIONS (NORTHERN IRELAND) 2005, SR 2005 171; made under the Pension Schemes (Northern Ireland) Act 1993 s.5, s.21, s.93, s.97I, s.97L, s.109, s.178; the Pensions (Northern Ireland) Order 1995 (SI 1995 3213 (NI.22)) Art.49, Art.56, Art.57, Art.68, Art.73, Art.73A, Art.73B, Art.74, Art.76, Art.89, Art.115, Art.116, Art.121, Art.166; and the Welfare Reform and Pensions (Northern Ireland) Order1 (SI 13147 (NI.11)) Art.27, Art.73, Sch.5 para.8. In force: in accordance with Reg.1 (2); £4.50.

These Regulations amend the Occupational Pension Schemes (Contracting-out) Regulations (Northern Ireland) 1996 (SR 1996 493), the Occupational Pension Schemes (Minimum Funding Requirement and Actuarial Valuations) Regulations (Northern Ireland) 1996 (SR 1996 570), the Occupational Pension Schemes (Transfer Values) Regulations (Northern Ireland) 1996 (SR 1996 619), the Occupational Pension Schemes (Winding Up) Regulations (Northern Ireland) 1996 (SR 1996 621), the Occupational Pension Schemes (Payments to Employers) Regulations (Northern Ireland) 1997 (SR 1997 96), the Occupational Pension Schemes (Disclosure of Information) Regulations (Northern Ireland) 1997 (SR 1997 98), the Occupational Pension Schemes (Assignment, Forfeiture, Bankruptcy etc.) Regulations (Northern Ireland) 1997 (SR 1997 153), the Pension Sharing (Valuation) Regulations (Northern Ireland) 2000 (SR 2000 144), the Pension Sharing (Implementation and Discharge of Liability) Regulations (Northern Ireland) 2000 (SR 2000 145) and the Pension Sharing (Pension Credit Benefit) Regulations (Northern Ireland) 2000 (SR 2000 146). The Regulations are made as a consequence of provisions in the Pensions (Northern Ireland) Order 2005 (SI 2005 255 (NI.1)) and relate to the winding up of occupational pension schemes.

4777. Occupational pensions–Winding up–Multi employer schemes

OCCUPATIONAL PENSION SCHEMES (WINDING UP) (MODIFICATION FOR MULTI-EMPLOYER SCHEMES AND MISCELLANEOUS AMENDMENTS) REGULATIONS (NORTHERN IRELAND) 2005, SR 2005 363; made under the Pensions (Northern Ireland) Order 1995 (SI 1995 3213 (NI.22)) Art.56, Art.73, Art.73B, Art.115, Art.166. In force: August 31, 2005; £3.00.

These Regulations, which amend the Pensions (Northern Ireland) Order 1995 (SI 1995 3213 (NI.22)), the Occupational Pension Schemes (Minimum Funding Requirement and Actuarial Valuations) Regulations (Northern Ireland) 1996 (SR 1996 570) and the Occupational Pension Schemes (Winding up, etc.) Regulations (Northern Ireland) 2005 (SR 2005 171), modify the position where an occupational pension scheme that has more than one employer or has had more than one employer at any time since April 6, 2005 and whose rules do not provide for the partial winding up of the scheme if it is being wound up.

4778. Occupational pensions–Winding up–Transfer value

OCCUPATIONAL PENSION SCHEMES (WINDING UP, DEFICIENCY ON WINDING UP AND TRANSFER VALUES) (AMENDMENT) REGULATIONS (NORTHERN IRELAND) 2005, SR 2005 20; made under the Pension Schemes (Northern Ireland) Act 1993 s.109, s.177; and the Pensions (Northern Ireland) Order 1995 (SI 1995 3213 (NI.22)) Art.73, Art.75, Art.166. In force: February 15, 2005; £3.00.

These Regulations amend the Occupational Pension Schemes (Deficiency on Winding Up etc.) Regulations (Northern Ireland) 1996 (SR 1996 585), Occupational Pension Schemes (Transfer Values) Regulations (Northern Ireland) 1996 (SR 1996 619), Occupational Pension Schemes (Winding Up) Regulations (Northern Ireland) 1996 (SR 1996 621), and the Occupational Pension Schemes (Winding Up and Deficiency on Winding Up, etc.) (Amendment) Regulations (Northern Ireland) 2004 (SR 2004 60). The changes provide for the calculation of liabilities in the case of any occupational pension scheme. The Regulations also make amendments to require the scheme's liabilities to be calculated and valued on a basis which assumes that any accrued rights to a pension or other benefit under the scheme for members with more than two years of pensionable service, as well as any entitlement to the payment of a pension that has arisen under the scheme (including any increase in a pension), will be discharged by the purchase of annuities; and to require trustees who receive a request for a statement of entitlement to a guaranteed cash equivalent to inform the member, where the scheme is being wound up, that the value of the member's guaranteed cash equivalent may be affected by the scheme winding up, that a decision to take a guaranteed cash equivalent should be given careful consideration, and that the member should consider taking independent financial advice before deciding whether to take the guaranteed cash equivalent.

4779. Pension protection–Employers obligations

TRANSFER OF EMPLOYMENT (PENSION PROTECTION) REGULATIONS (NORTHERN IRELAND) 2005, SR 2005 94; made under the Pensions (Northern Ireland) Order 2005 (SI 2005 255 (NI.1) Art.235. In force: April 6, 2005; £3.00.

These Regulations concern the obligations of an employer under the Pensions (Northern Ireland) Order 2005 (SI 2005 255 NI.1)) Art.235 towards a person in relation to whom Art.234 of the Order applies.

4780. Pension protection–Overseas schemes–Transfer of payments

CONTRACTING-OUT, PROTECTED RIGHTS AND SAFEGUARDED RIGHTS (TRANSFER PAYMENT) (AMENDMENT) REGULATIONS (NORTHERN

IRELAND) 2005, SR 2005 85; made under the Pension Schemes (Northern Ireland) Act 1993 s.8C, s.16, s.24, s.64D, s.177. In force: April 6, 2005; £3.00.

These Regulations amend the Protected Rights (Transfer Payment) Regulations (Northern Ireland) 1996 (SR 1996 509) to insert a definition of "overseas arrangement" and remove the permanent emigration requirement in relation to transfer payments to overseas schemes or arrangements in respect of protected rights; amend the Contracting-out (Transfer and Transfer Payment) Regulations (Northern Ireland) 1996 (SR 1996 618) so that Reg.6 of those Regulations applies in respect of transfer payments made to an overseas arrangement and to remove the permanent emigration requirement in relation to transfer payments to overseas schemes or arrangements in respect of guaranteed minimum pensions and rights accrued after April 6, 1997 under a scheme contracted out by virtue of the Pension Schemes (Northern Ireland) Act 1993 s.5(2B); and amend the Pension Sharing (Pension Credit Benefit) Regulations (Northern Ireland) 2000 (SR 2000 146) to remove the permanent emigration requirement in relation to transfer payments to overseas schemes or arrangements in respect of safeguarded rights.

4781. Pension protection–Pensions regulator–Financial support directions

PENSIONS REGULATOR (FINANCIAL SUPPORT DIRECTIONS, ETC.) REGULATIONS (NORTHERN IRELAND) 2005, SR 2005 378; made under the Pensions (Northern Ireland) Order 2005 (SI 2005 255 (NI.1)) Art.2, Art.39, Art.40, Art.41, Art.280, Art.287. In force: September 1, 2005; £3.00.

These Regulations, which modify the Pensions (Northern Ireland) Order 2005 (SI 2005 255 (NI.1)), make further provision about the Regulator's power to issue financial support directions. They also, in relation to all the anti-avoidance provisions (that is, contribution notices, financial support directions and restoration orders) extend the meaning of employer to include former employers in specified circumstances and modify those provisions of the Order in their application to multi-employer schemes.

4782. Pension protection fund–Board of the Pension Protection Fund–Review and reconsideration

PENSION PROTECTION FUND (REVIEW AND RECONSIDERATION OF REVIEWABLE MATTERS) REGULATIONS (NORTHERN IRELAND) 2005, SR 2005 138; made under the Pensions (Northern Ireland) Order 2005 (SI 2005 255 (NI.1)) Art.189, Art.287. In force: April 6, 2005; £3.00.

These Regulations, which amend the Pensions Act 2004, provide for the review and reconsideration by the Board of the Pension Protection Fund of the reviewable matters specified in the Pensions (Northern Ireland) Order 2005 (SI 2005 255 (NI.1)) Sch.8.

4783. Pension protection fund–Compensation

PENSION PROTECTION FUND (COMPENSATION) REGULATIONS (NORTHERN IRELAND) 2005, SR 2005 149; made under the Pensions (Northern Ireland) Order 2005 (SI 2005 255 (NI.1)) Art.2, Art.287, Sch.6 para.4, Sch.6 para.6, Sch.6 para.9, Sch.6 para.13, Sch.6 para.16, Sch.6 para.18, Sch.6 para.20, Sch.6 para.23, Sch.6 para.24, Sch.6 para.25, Sch.6 para.26, Sch.6 para.28, Sch.6 para.31, Sch.6 para.33. In force: April 6, 2005; £3.50.

The Board of the Pension Protection Fund provides compensation for members of certain occupational pension schemes in the event of the insolvency of the scheme's sponsoring employer and where the pension scheme is under-funded at a certain level. These Regulations, which amend the Pensions (Northern Ireland) Order 2005 (SI 2005 255 (NI.1)), set out the conditions under which a person can receive early payment of compensation from the Board before he attains normal pension age. They prescribe the circumstances in which a widow or widower will not be entitled to receive periodic compensation following the death of their spouse; prescribes the circumstances in which a relevant partner or a surviving dependant will be entitled to receive periodic compensation following the death of his partner (in the case of a relevant partner) or his parent; prescribes the amount and duration of periodic compensation that can be paid to relevant partners who qualify for periodic compensation; prescribe the amount of periodic compensation that can be paid to surviving dependants who qualify for periodic compensation; prescribe the period during which periodic compensation can be paid to surviving dependants who qualify for periodic compensation; prescribe the effect of a change of circumstances in a case where periodic compensation is paid, and also provide for backdating of payments of periodic compensation in specific circumstances; and make modifications so that where compensation is paid by the Board in successive tranches, or the person entitled to the compensation has on a previous occasion become entitled to one or more lump sums from the scheme in question or from connected schemes, the restriction applies by aggregating the annual values of the former benefits or lump sums with the benefits payable in the latest tranche.

4784. Pension protection fund–Compensation–Provision of information

PENSION PROTECTION FUND (PROVISION OF INFORMATION) REGULATIONS (NORTHERN IRELAND) 2005, SR 2005 129; made under the Pensions (Northern Ireland) Order 2005 (SI 2005 255 (NI.1)) Art.2, Art.172, Art.185, Art.287. In force: April 6, 2005; £3.00.

These Regulations make provision relating to the information which the Board of the Pension Protection Fund, the members and beneficiaries of certain occupational pension schemes and the trustees or managers of such schemes are required to provide where compensation is, or may become, payable by the Board.

4785. Pension protection fund–Compensation cap

PENSION PROTECTION FUND (PENSION COMPENSATION CAP) ORDER (NORTHERN IRELAND) 2005, SR 2005 136; made under the Pensions (Northern Ireland) Order 2005 (SI 2005 255 (NI.1)) Sch.6 para.26. In force: April 6, 2005; £3.00.

This Order specifies the amount of the compensation cap for the purposes of the Pensions Act 2004. The compensation cap is an amount used by the Board of the Pension Protection Fund to determine the amount of compensation payable to a person who is under normal pension age on the assessment date and whose compensation is not derived from a pension payable on the grounds of ill health or a survivor's pension.

4786. Pension protection fund–Eligible schemes–Assessment of assets and liabilities

PENSION PROTECTION FUND (VALUATION) REGULATIONS (NORTHERN IRELAND) 2005, SR 2005 131; made under the Pensions (Northern Ireland) Order 2005 (SI 2005 255 (NI.1)) Art.2, Art.127, Art.129, Art.162, Art.172, Art.287. In force: April 6, 2005; £3.00.

These Regulations provide for the assessment of the assets and liabilities of eligible schemes in accordance with the Pensions (Northern Ireland) Order 2005 (SI 2005 255 (NI1)) Art.127 and Art.162.

4787. Pension protection fund–Eligible schemes–Entry rules

PENSION PROTECTION FUND (ENTRY RULES) REGULATIONS (NORTHERN IRELAND) 2005, SR 2005 126; made under the Pensions (Northern Ireland) Order 2005 (SI 2005 255 (NI.1)) Art.2, Art.104, Art.105, Art.106, Art.107, Art.110, Art.113, Art.114, Art.117, Art.118, Art.119, Art.122, Art.123, Art.130, Art.131, Art.132, Art.134, Art.135, Art.287. In force: in accordance with Reg.1 (1); £4.50.

These Regulations make provision relating to various requirements under the Pensions (Northern Ireland) Order 2005 (SI 2005 255 (NI.1)) Part III. They set out those schemes which are not "eligible schemes" for the purposes of Part III of the Order and therefore are not able to receive compensation from the Board of the Pension Protection Fund pursuant to the pension compensation provisions in that Part of the Order; provide that where, after the beginning of an assessment period in relation to an eligible scheme, the scheme ceases to be an eligible scheme in prescribed circumstances, the scheme shall, for the purposes of Part III of the Order, be treated as remaining an eligible scheme; make provision in respect of the period in which an insolvency practitioner is required to notify the Board of the occurrence of an insolvency event in relation to the employer in relation to an eligible scheme; and provide for certain events in relation to certain types of bodies (such as building societies, friendly societies and limited liability partnerships) to be classified as insolvency events. They also set out the circumstances in which insolvency proceedings in relation to the employer in relation to an eligible scheme are stayed or come to an end; set out the time limit for making applications; set out the circumstances which must exist before an insolvency practitioner in relation to an employer in relation to an eligible scheme or the Board is able to determine whether or not a scheme rescue has occurred or is not possible in relation to the scheme; and provide for the circumstances in which a transfer payment may be made during an assessment period in respect of a member's rights under an eligible scheme.

4788. Pension protection fund–Eligible schemes–Entry rules

PENSION PROTECTION FUND (ENTRY RULES) (AMENDMENT) REGULATIONS (NORTHERN IRELAND) 2005, SR 2005 364; made under the Pensions (Northern Ireland) Order 2005 (SI 2005 255 (NI.1)) Art.105, Art.109, Art.110, Art.113, Art.287. In force: August 24, 2005; £3.00.

These Regulations make various amendments to the Pension Protection Fund (Entry Rules) Regulations (Northern Ireland) 2005 (SR 2005 126) which include: inserting a definition; adding further insolvency events where a company or partnership in administration commences winding up or where a proposal for a voluntary arrangement is made; and to provide that where the employer is a trade union, in relation to which it is not possible for an insolvency event to occur, the trustees or managers of an eligible scheme must apply to the Board of the Pension Protection Fund for it to assume responsibility for that scheme under the 2005 Order where the condition in art.113(1)(a) of the Order is satisfied.

4789. Pension protection fund–Hybrid schemes

PENSION PROTECTION FUND (HYBRID SCHEMES) (MODIFICATION) REGULATIONS (NORTHERN IRELAND) 2005, SR 2005 84; made under the Pensions (Northern Ireland) Order 2005 (SI 2005 255 (NI.1)) Art.119, Art.280, Art.287. In force: April 6, 2005; £3.00.

These Regulations modify how the provisions of the Pensions (Northern Ireland) Order 2005 (SI 2005 255) operate in relation to hybrid schemes.

4790. Pension protection fund–Ill health pensions–Reviews

PENSION PROTECTION FUND (REVIEWABLE ILL HEALTH PENSIONS) REGULATIONS (NORTHERN IRELAND) 2005, SR 2005 130; made under the Pensions (Northern Ireland) Order 2005 (SI 2005 255 (NI.1)) Art.124, Art.125, Art.287, Sch.6 para.37. In force: April 6, 2005; £3.00.

These Regulations provide for the review of reviewable ill health pensions by the Board of the Pension Protection Fund, the procedure to be followed in relation to a review and the determination of compensation payable in respect of an ill health pension where the conditions set out in the Pensions (Northern Ireland) Order 2005 (SI 2005 255 (NI.1)) Art.125(3) are satisfied.

4791. Pension protection fund–Investigations–Maladministration

PENSION PROTECTION FUND (MALADMINISTRATION) REGULATIONS (NORTHERN IRELAND) 2005, SR 2005 128; made under the Pensions

(Northern Ireland) Order 2005 (SI 2005 255 (NI.1)) Art.190, Art.287. In force: April 6, 2005; £3.00.

These Regulations provide for the investigation by the Board of the Pension Protection Fund of allegations of maladministration.

4792. Pension protection fund—Levies consultation

PENSION PROTECTION FUND (PENSION PROTECTION LEVIES CONSULTATION) REGULATIONS (NORTHERN IRELAND) 2005, SR 2005 283; made under the Pensions (Northern Ireland) Order 2005 (SI 2005 255 (NI.1)) Art.159, Art.287. In force: June 20, 2005; £3.00.

These Regulations prescribe the manner and publication requirements for the consultation required under the Pensions (Northern Ireland) Order 2005 Art.159, which provides that the Board of the Pension Protection Fund must consult such persons as it considers appropriate before determining matters relating to the pension protection levies specified in Art.158(5) of the Order.

4793. Pension protection fund—Multi-employer schemes

PENSION PROTECTION FUND (MULTI-EMPLOYER SCHEMES) (MODIFICATION) REGULATIONS (NORTHERN IRELAND) 2005, SR 2005 91; made under the Pensions (Northern Ireland) Order 2005 (SI 2005 255 (NI.1)) Art.2, Art.280, Art.287. In force: in accordance with Reg.1 (1); £7.50.

These Regulations modify the provisions of the Pensions (Northern Ireland) Order 2005 (SI 2005 255 (NI.1)) as they apply in relation to multi-employer schemes.

4794. Pension protection fund—Ombudsman—Disclosure of information

PENSION PROTECTION FUND (PPF OMBUDSMAN) (AMENDMENT) ORDER (NORTHERN IRELAND) 2005, SR 2005 342; made under the Pensions (Northern Ireland) Order 2005 (SI 2005 255 (NI.1)) Art.191, Art.287. In force: July 21, 2005; £3.00.

This Order amends the Pension Protection Fund (PPF Ombudsman) Order (Northern Ireland) 2005 (SR 2005 135) which makes provision in respect of the Ombudsman for the Board of the Pension Protection Fund (PPF). It provides that the PPF Ombudsman may, during the course of his investigation of a reviewable matter referred to him by virtue of the Pensions (Northern Ireland) Order 2005 (SI 2005 255 (NI.1)) or of a complaint of maladministration referred to him by virtue of regulations made under the 2005 Order, disclose to specified persons information obtained during the course of the investigation.

4795. Pension protection fund—Ombudsman—Functions

PENSION PROTECTION FUND (PPF OMBUDSMAN) ORDER (NORTHERN IRELAND) 2005, SR 2005 135; made under the Pensions (Northern Ireland) Order 2005 (SI 2005 255 (NI.1)) Art.191, Art.287. In force: April 6, 2005; £3.00.

This Order makes provision in respect of the Pension Protection Fund (PPF) Ombudsman. It makes provision about the staff of the PPF Ombudsman; provides that the PPF Ombudsman may (with certain exceptions) delegate any functions to staff; provides that the PPF Ombudsman may require any person to provide information or furnish documents necessary to an investigation; and makes provision about restrictions on the disclosure of information held by the PPF Ombudsman.

4796. Pension protection fund—Ombudsman—Investigation of complaints

PENSION PROTECTION FUND (INVESTIGATION BY PPF OMBUDSMAN OF COMPLAINTS OF MALADMINISTRATION) REGULATIONS (NORTHERN

IRELAND) 2005, SR 2005 343; made under the Pensions (Northern Ireland) Order 2005 (SI 2005 255 (NI.1)) Art.193, Art.287. In force: July 21, 2005; £3.00.

These Regulations provide for matters to be referred to, and investigated and determined by, the Ombudsman for the Board of the Pension Protection Fund if they have been the subject of a complaint of maladministration about which there has either been an investigation and decision by both the Board of the Pension Protection Fund and a committee of the Board under the Pension Protection Fund (Maladministration) Regulations (Northern Ireland) 2005 (SR 2005 128) or such an investigation and decision by the Board and an application for an investigation and decision by such a committee without a decision having been given by the committee within the required time.

4797. Pension protection fund–Ombudsman–Reviewable matters

PENSION PROTECTION FUND (REFERENCE OF REVIEWABLE MATTERS TO THE PPF OMBUDSMAN) REGULATIONS (NORTHERN IRELAND) 2005, SR 2005 344; made under the Pensions (Northern Ireland) Order 2005 (SI 2005 255 (NI.1)) Art.192, Art.287. In force: July 21, 2005; £3.00.

These Regulations provide for a reviewable matter to be referred to, and investigated and determined by, the Ombudsman for the Board of the Pension Protection Fund following a reconsideration decision given by the Reconsideration Committee of the Board of the Pension Protection Fund under the Pension Protection Fund (Review and Reconsideration of Reviewable Matters) Regulations (Northern Ireland) 2005 (SR 2005 138).

4798. Pension protection fund–Pensions regulator

PENSION PROTECTION FUND AND PENSIONS REGULATOR (AMENDMENT) REGULATIONS (NORTHERN IRELAND) 2005, SR 2005 194; made under the Pensions (Northern Ireland) Order 2005 (SI 2005 255 (NI.1)) Art.2, Art.34, Art.48, Art.106, Art.110, Art.119, Art.123, Art.135, Art.189, Art.280, Art.287. In force: April 6, 2005; £3.00.

These Regulations amend the Pension Protection Fund (Multi-employer Schemes) (Modification) Regulations (Northern Ireland) 2005 (SR 2005 91), the Pension Protection Fund (Entry Rules) Regulations (Northern Ireland) 2005 (SR 2005 126), the Pension Protection Fund (Review and Reconsideration of Reviewable Matters) Regulations (Northern Ireland) 2005 (SR 2005 138) and the Pensions Regulator (Contribution Notices and Restoration Orders) Regulations (Northern Ireland) 2005 (SR 2005 173). They correct defective references; provide that schemes are not eligible schemes if they are neither tax approved nor relevant statutory schemes; make provision for where the Board of the Pension Protection Fund decides that the Reconsideration Committee should reconsider a reviewable matter; and provide that schemes are prescribed schemes if they have never been tax approved schemes or registered for tax purposes and are not relevant statutory schemes.

4799. Pension protection fund–Reviewable matters

PENSION PROTECTION FUND (REVIEWABLE MATTERS) REGULATIONS (NORTHERN IRELAND) 2005, SR 2005 127; made under the Pensions (Northern Ireland) Order 2005 (SI 2005 255 (NI.1)) Art.188, Art.280. In force: April 6, 2005; £3.00.

These Regulations amend the Pensions (Northern Ireland) Order 2005 (SI 2005 255 (NI.1)) to provide that the references to specified failures by the Board in Sch.8 to the Order are to be construed as references to failures by the Board to do the act or make a determination within the period prescribed in the Schedule to these Regulations; insert two further reviewable matters in respect of partially guaranteed schemes; and insert two further reviewable matters in respect of payments due under Art.150(2) of the Order and the issue of, or failure to issue, a valuation notice under the Pension Protection Fund (Entry Rules) Regulations (Northern Ireland) 2005 (SR 2005 126) Reg.2(5).

4800. Pension schemes–Categories

PENSION SCHEMES (CATEGORIES) REGULATIONS (NORTHERN IRELAND) 2005, SR 2005 413; made under the Pension Schemes (Northern Ireland) Act 1993 s.1, s.177; and the Welfare Reform and Pensions (Northern Ireland) Order 1 (SI 1 3147 (NI.11)) Art.9, Art.73. In force: in accordance with Reg.1 (1); £3.00.

These Regulations provide for certain pension schemes to fall within the definition of "occupational pension scheme" in the Pension Schemes (Northern Ireland) Act 1993. They also provide that certain stakeholder pension schemes which are occupational pension schemes are to be treated as personal pension schemes.

4801. Pension schemes–Freezing orders–Time limits

PENSIONS REGULATOR (FREEZING ORDERS AND CONSEQUENTIAL AMENDMENTS) REGULATIONS (NORTHERN IRELAND) 2005, SR 2005 114; made under the Pension Schemes (Northern Ireland) Act 1993 s.89A, s.95, s.177; and the Pensions (Northern Ireland) Order 2005 (SI 2005 255 (NI.1)) Art.19, Art.20, Art.26, Art.287. In force: April 6, 2005; £3.00.

These Regulations, which amend the Pension Schemes (Northern Ireland) Act 1993 and the Occupational Pension Schemes (Transfer Values) Regulations (Northern Ireland) 1996 (SR 1996 619), make provision relating to freezing orders. They prescribe the qualifications necessary for a person to be brought within the meaning of "the actuary"; make amendments to take account of the fact that it may be impossible to abide by the time limits; and extend the time limits where appropriate if a freezing order containing a relevant direction is or has been in effect. They also prescribe the period within which trustees or managers must give notice to the Pensions Regulator.

4802. Pensions Appeal Tribunals–Social security commissioners–Appeals

PENSIONS APPEAL TRIBUNALS (NORTHERN IRELAND) (AMENDMENT) RULES 2005, SR 2005 108; made under the Pensions Appeal Tribunals Act 1943 s.6, Sch.para.5, Sch.para.6. In force: April 6, 2005; £3.00.

These Rules amend the Pensions Appeal Tribunals (Northern Ireland) Rules 1981 (SR 1981 231) to provide for a new route of appeal from the Pensions Appeal Tribunal to the Social Security Commissioners, who for these purposes are to be known as Pensions Appeal Commissioners.

4803. Pensions Appeal Tribunals–Social security commissioners–Appeals procedure

PENSIONS APPEAL COMMISSIONERS (PROCEDURE) (NORTHERN IRELAND) REGULATIONS 2005, SI 2005 965; made under the Pensions Appeal Tribunals Act 1943 s.6, s.6C, s.6D, s.11A. In force: April 18, 2005; £3.00.

These Regulations prescribe the procedure of the Social Security Commissioners for Northern Ireland (to be known as Pensions Appeal Commissioners) in determining appeals and applications arising from decision of the Pensions Appeal Tribunal under the Pensions Appeal Tribunals Act 1943, as amended by the Armed Forces (Pension and Compensation) Act 2004.

4804. Pensions Compensation Board–Transitional adaptations and savings

PENSIONS (2005 ORDER) (PENSIONS COMPENSATION BOARD TRANSITIONAL ADAPTATIONS AND SAVINGS) ORDER (NORTHERN IRELAND) 2005, SR 2005 375; made under the Pensions (Northern Ireland) Order 2005 (SI 2005 255 (NI.1)) Art.287, Art.292. In force: September 1, 2005; £3.00.

This Order makes transitional adaptations and savings in connection with the dissolution of the Pensions Compensation Board.

4805. Pensions ombudsman – Disclosure of information – Specified persons

PENSIONS OMBUDSMAN (DISCLOSURE OF INFORMATION) (AMENDMENT OF SPECIFIED PERSONS) ORDER (NORTHERN IRELAND) 2005, SR 2005 442; made under the Pension Schemes (Northern Ireland) Act 1993 s.145. In force: November 1, 2005; £3.00.

This Order amends the Pension Schemes (Northern Ireland) Act 1993 by adding the body corporate which operates the Financial Ombudsman Service and any ombudsman of that service to the list of persons to whom the Pensions Ombudsman may disclose any information which he obtains for the purposes of an investigation, if he considers that the disclosure would enable or assist that person to discharge any of his functions.

4806. Pensions (Northern Ireland) Order 2005 (SI 2005 255 (NI.1))

This Order amends the Matrimonial Causes (Northern Ireland) Order 1978 (SI 1978 1045 (NI.15)), the Companies (Northern Ireland) Order 1986 (SI 1986 1032 (NI.6)), the Matrimonial and Family Proceedings (Northern Ireland) Order 1989 (SI 1989 677 (NI.4)), the Social Security Contributions and Benefits (Northern Ireland) Act 1992, the Social Security Administration (Northern Ireland) Act 1992, the Pension Schemes (Northern Ireland) Act 1993, the Pensions (Northern Ireland) Order 1995 (SI 1995 3213 (NI.22)), the Deregulation and Contracting Out (Northern Ireland) Order 1996 (SI 1996 1632 (NI.11)), the Employment Rights (Northern Ireland) Order 1996 (SI 1996 671 (NI.16)), the Bank of England Act 1998, the Social Security Contributions (Transfer of Functions, etc.) (Northern Ireland) Order 1999 (SI 1999 671), the Welfare Reform and Pensions (Northern Ireland) Order 1999 (SI 1999 3147 (NI.11)) and the Child Support, Pensions and Social Security Act (Northern Ireland) 2000. The Order, which is made only for purposes corresponding to the Pensions Act 2004, makes provision relating to pensions and financial planning for retirement, and for connected purposes.

4807. Pensions (Northern Ireland) Order 2005 (SI 2005 255 (NI.1)) – Commencement No.2 and Transitional Provisions Order

PENSIONS (2005 ORDER) (COMMENCEMENT NO.2 AND TRANSITIONAL PROVISIONS) ORDER (NORTHERN IRELAND) 2005, SR 2005 166 (C.12); made under the Pensions (Northern Ireland) Order 2005 (SI 2005 255 (NI.1)) Art.1, Art.287. In force: bringing into operation various provisions of the 2005 Order on March 25, 2005, April 1, 2005 and April 6, 2005; £3.00.

This Order, which amends the Pension Schemes (Northern Ireland) Act 1993, the Pensions (Northern Ireland) Order 1995 (SI 1995 3213 (NI.22)) and the Pensions (Northern Ireland) Order 2005 (SI 2005 255 (NI.1)), makes further provision for the coming into operation of the Pensions (Northern Ireland) Order 2005 (SI 2005 255 (NI.1)).

4808. Pensions (Northern Ireland) Order 2005 (SI 2005 255 (NI.1)) – Commencement No.3 Appointed Day and Amendment Order

PENSIONS (2005 ORDER) (COMMENCEMENT NO.3, APPOINTED DAY, TRANSITIONAL PROVISIONS AND AMENDMENT) ORDER (NORTHERN IRELAND) 2005, SR 2005 192 (C.14); made under the Pensions (Northern Ireland) Order 2005 (SI 2005 255 (NI.1)) Art.1, Art.86, Art.287. In force: bringing into operation various provisions of the 2005 Order on April 6, 2005; £3.00.

This Order, which amends the Pensions (2005 Order) (Commencement No.2 and Transitional Provisions) Order (Northern Ireland) 2005 (SI 2005 166 (C.12)), makes further provision for the coming into operation of the Pensions (Northern Ireland) Order 2005 (SI 2005 255 (NI.1)).

4809. **Pensions (Northern Ireland) Order 2005 (SI 2005 255 (NI.1))–Commencement No.4 Order**

PENSIONS (2005 ORDER) (COMMENCEMENT NO.4) ORDER (NORTHERN IRELAND), SR 2005 280 (C.80); made under the Pensions (Northern Ireland) Order 2005 (SI 2005 255 (NI.1)) Art.1. In force: bringing into operation various provisions of the 2005 Order on May 31, 2005; June 1, 2005 and June 20, 2005; £3.00.

This Order makes further provision for the coming into operation of the Pensions (Northern Ireland) Order 2005 on the following dates: May 31, 2005 for the purpose only of authorising the making of regulations relating to supplementary provisions about pension protection levies. The provision is brought fully into operation on June 1, 2005 for provisions relating to persons to be regarded as members or prospective members of occupational pension schemes and the times and circumstances at which they are treated as becoming, or ceasing to be, such a member; and June 20, 2005 for other provisions relating to Pension Protection Levies.

4810. **Pensions (Northern Ireland) Order 2005 (SI 2005 255 (NI.1))–Commencement No.5 and Appointed Day Order**

PENSIONS (2005 ORDER) (COMMENCEMENT NO.5 AND APPOINTED DAY) ORDER (NORTHERN IRELAND) 2005, SR 2005 321 (C.24); made under the Pensions (Northern Ireland) Order 2005 (SI 2005 255 (NI.1)) Art.1, Art.86, Art.287. In force: bringing into operation various provisions of the 2005 Order on June 30, 2005; July 1, 2005; September 1, 2005; September 22, 2005; and April 6, 2006; £3.00.

This Order makes further provision for the coming into operation of specified provisions of the Pensions (Northern Ireland) Order 2005 (SI 2005 255 (NI.1)).

4811. **Pensions (Northern Ireland) Order 2005 (SI 2005 255 (NI.1))–Commencement No.6 Order**

PENSIONS (2005 ORDER) (COMMENCEMENT NO.6) ORDER (NORTHERN IRELAND) 2005, SR 2005 411 (C.32); made under the Pensions (Northern Ireland) Order 2005 (SI 2005 255 (NI.1)) Art.1, Art.287. In force: bringing into operation various provisions of the 2005 Order on September 1, 2005, September 22, 2005, November 1, 2005 and November 14, 2005; £3.00.

This Order brings into force various provisions of the Pensions (Northern Ireland) Order 2005 (SI 2005 255 (NI.1)).

4812. **Pensions (Northern Ireland) Order 2005 (SI 2005 255 (NI.1))–Commencement No.7 Order**

PENSIONS (2005 ORDER) (COMMENCEMENT NO.7) ORDER (NORTHERN IRELAND) 2005, SR 2005 543 (C.37); made under the Pensions (Northern Ireland) Order 2005 (SI 2005 255 (NI.1)) Art.1. In force: bringing into operation various provisions of the 2005 Order in accordance with Art.2 and Art.3; £3.00.

This Order makes provision for the coming into operation of specified provisions of the Pensions (Northern Ireland) Order 2005 (SI 2005 255 (NI.1)).

4813. **Public services–Increase in rates**

PENSIONS INCREASE (REVIEW) ORDER (NORTHERN IRELAND) 2005, SR 2005 102; made under the Social Security Pensions (Northern Ireland) Order 1975 (SI 1975 1503 (NI.15)) Art.69. In force: April 11, 2005; £3.00.

Under the Social Security Pensions (Northern Ireland) Order 1975 (SI 1975 1503 (NI.15)), the Department of Finance and Personnel is required to provide by order for increases in the rates of public service pensions. This Order specifies the increases for pensions which became payable on or after April 12, 2004 and before April 11, 2005.

4814. Retirement pensions–Deferment

SOCIAL SECURITY (RETIREMENT PENSIONS ETC.) (TRANSITIONAL PROVISIONS) REGULATIONS (NORTHERN IRELAND) 2005, SR 2005 123; made under the Pensions (Northern Ireland) Order 2005 (SI 2005 255 (NI.1)) Sch.9 para.22. In force: April 6, 2005; £3.00.

These Regulations modify the provisions relating to the deferral of entitlement to retirement pension that are inserted in the Social Security Contributions and Benefits (Northern Ireland) Act 1992 Sch.5 by the Pensions (Northern Ireland) Order 2005 (SI 2005 255 (NI.1)). They also modify the new Sch.5A relating to the deferral of entitlement to shared additional pension.

4815. Stakeholder pensions–Transfer of scheme

STAKEHOLDER PENSION SCHEMES (AMENDMENT) REGULATIONS (NORTHERN IRELAND) 2005, SR 2005 110; made under the Welfare Reform and Pensions (Northern Ireland) Order 1 (SI 1 3147 (NI.11)) Art.3, Art.73. In force: April 6, 2005; £3.00.

These Regulations which amend the Stakeholder Pension Schemes Regulations (Northern Ireland) 2000 (SR 2000 262) and the Stakeholder Pension Schemes (Amendment No.2) Regulations (Northern Ireland) 2001 (SR 2001 119), revoke the Stakeholder Pension Schemes (Amendment) Regulations (Northern Ireland) 2002 (SR 2002 216). Amendments include the definition of "securities" to include shares in an investment trust, and the definition of the "dilution levy" is amended by reference to the Financial Services Authority Handbook; and members who withdraw an application for a transfer to a scheme of his choice must be given a month's notice before the trustees or manager of the scheme may transfer his rights to a scheme of their choice.

4816. State pension credit–Age related payments–Lump sum

AGE-RELATED PAYMENTS REGULATIONS (NORTHERN IRELAND) 2005, SR 2005 383; made under the Age-Related Payments (Northern Ireland) Order 2004 (SI 2004 1987 (NI.11)) Art.9. In force: September 1, 2005; £3.00.

These Regulations make provision for the payment of a one-off lump sum of £200 or £100 to households with occupants who have attained the age of 65 no later than the end of the week commencing Monday September 19, 2005 and who are not in receipt of the state pension credit guarantee credit and who are ordinarily resident in Northern Ireland on any day in that week. The Regulations also provide for the payment of £50 to households with occupants who have attained the age of 70 no later than the end of the week commencing Monday September 19, 2005 and who are in receipt of the state pension credit guarantee credit and ordinarily resident in Northern Ireland on any day in that week.

4817. Superannuation–Additional voluntary contributions–Health and Personal Social Services

HEALTH AND PERSONAL SOCIAL SERVICES (SUPERANNUATION) (ADDITIONAL VOLUNTARY CONTRIBUTIONS) (AMENDMENT) REGULATIONS (NORTHERN IRELAND) 2005, SR 2005 154; made under the Superannuation (Northern Ireland) Order 1972 (SI 1972 1073 (NI.10)) Art.12, Art.14, Sch.3. In force: May 9, 2005; £3.00.

These Regulations amend the Health and Personal Social Services (Superannuation) (Additional Voluntary Contributions) 1999 (SR 1999 294) which make provision for the payment of additional voluntary contributions by persons who are members of the Health and Personal Social Services (HPSS) Superannuation Scheme as constituted by the Health and Personal Social Services (Superannuation) Regulations (Northern Ireland) 1995 (SR 1995 95) or by their employers, in order to secure additional benefits financed by investment of those contributions. The Regulations clarify that "absence from work" means absence on ill-health and to provide that the member will be notified in writing of the Department's acceptance of an election; provide that an election shall be treated as not having ceased to have effect in circumstances where a contributor is in receipt of superannuation benefits under the Superannuation Scheme Regulations, or where he has left superannuable employment and he wishes to switch his AVC investments or future contributions to another authorised fund; and raise the limit for retirement pensions in cases where the member retires after the age of 60 and is entitled to a greater pension because of its postponement.

4818. Superannuation–Health and Personal Social Services

HEALTH AND PERSONAL SOCIAL SERVICES (SUPERANNUATION) (AMENDMENT) REGULATIONS (NORTHERN IRELAND) 2005, SR 2005 155; made under the Superannuation (Northern Ireland) Order 1972 (SI 1972 1073 (NI.10)) Art.12, Art.14, Sch.3. In force: May 9, 2005; £3.00.

These Regulations amend the Health and Personal Social Services (Superannuation) Regulations (Northern Ireland) 1995 (SR 1995 95) which provide for the superannuation of persons engaged in Health and Personal Social Services. The Regulations ensure that a member's contributions and benefits reflect the situation where that member is subject to an earnings cap following a break in superannuable employment; ensure that lump sums, which would otherwise be payable to persons whose right to the lumps sum has been forfeited because they have been convicted of the unlawful killing of the member, shall be payable to the personal representatives of the member; provide that both preserved benefits are paid and that a pension is not abated where a member returns to employment with an employing authority by virtue of a transfer of an undertaking to that authority; provide that periods of adoption and paternity leave count as superannuable service under the scheme; provide forfeiture of scheme benefits to persons other than a member where the beneficiary has been convicted of the unlawful killing of the member; and provide more choice for practitioners with mixed patterns of officer and practitioner service to have their benefits under the scheme calculated in the way most beneficial to them and in particular to enable them to have separate pensions in respect of periods of officer and practitioner service.

4819. Superannuation–Teachers

TEACHERS' SUPERANNUATION (AMENDMENT) REGULATIONS (NORTHERN IRELAND) 2005, SR 2005 181; made under the Superannuation (Northern Ireland) Order 1972 (SI 1972 1073 (NI.10)) Art.11, Art.14, Sch.3 para.1, Sch.3 para.13. In force: March 31, 2005; £3.00.

These Regulations, which amend the Teachers' Superannuation Regulations (Northern Ireland) 1998 (SR 1998 333), revoke the Teachers' Superannuation (Amendment) Regulations (Northern Ireland) 2003 (SR 2003 147). They retrospectively recognise the Department of Finance and Personnel's request that the scheme's accounts move from cash-based to resource-based accounting; provide that the closing balance in the teachers' superannuation account for the financial year ending on March 31, 2001 be an amount determined by the Government Actuary by reference to the value of the scheme assets specified; provides that increases paid under the Pensions Increases Act (Northern Ireland) 1971 are debited to the teachers' superannuation account; and ensure that the language used is consistent with modern actuarial methods.

4820. Superannuation–Teachers

TEACHERS' SUPERANNUATION (AMENDMENT) (NO.2) REGULATIONS (NORTHERN IRELAND) 2005, SR 2005 495; made under the Superannuation (Northern Ireland) Order 1972 (SI 1972 1073 (NI.10)) Art.11, Sch.3 para.1, Sch.3 para.3, Sch.3 para.4. In force: December 5, 2005; £3.00.

These Regulations amend the Teachers' (Compensation for Redundancy and Premature Retirement) Regulations (Northern Ireland) 1991 (SR 1991 132), the Teachers' Superannuation (Additional Voluntary Contributions) Regulations

(Northern Ireland) 1996 (SR 1996 260) and the Teachers' Superannuation Regulations (Northern Ireland) 1998 (SR 1998 333). Most of the amendments make provision following the creation of the status of civil partner by the Civil Partnership Act 2004.

PLANNING

4821. Planning agreements–Applications–Modification and discharge

PLANNING (MODIFICATION AND DISCHARGE OF PLANNING AGREEMENTS) REGULATIONS (NORTHERN IRELAND) 2005, SR 2005 353; made under the Planning (Northern Ireland) Order 1991 (SI 1991 1220 (NI.11)) Art.40A, Art.40B, Art.129. In force: August 31, 2005; £3.00.

The Planning (Northern Ireland) Order 1991 (SI 1991 1220 (NI.11)) enables a person against whom a planning agreement is enforceable to apply to the Department to have the application modified or discharged. It also provides for an appeal to the Planning Appeals Commission if such an application is refused or not determined. These Regulations make provision with respect to the form and content of such applications; the notification of and publicity for such applications; the determination of such applications; and appeals to the Planning Appeals Commission against the Department's determination on such applications.

4822. Planning permission–Applications–Fees

PLANNING (FEES) REGULATIONS (NORTHERN IRELAND) 2005, SR 2005 222; made under the Planning (Northern Ireland) Order 1991 (SI 1991 1220 (NI.11)) Art.127, Art.129. In force: May 18, 2005; £3.00.

These Regulations, which amend the Planning (Hazardous Substances) Regulations (Northern Ireland) 1993 (SR 1993 275), revoke the Planning (Fees) Regulations (Northern Ireland) 1995 (SR 1995 78) (with saving), the Planning (Fees) (Amendment) Regulations (Northern Ireland) 1996 (SR 1996 41), the Planning (Fees) (Amendment) Regulations (Northern Ireland) 1997 (SR 1997 104), the Planning (Fees) (Amendment) Regulations (Northern Ireland) 1998 (SR 1998 223), the Planning (Fees) (Amendment) Regulations (Northern Ireland) 2001 (SR 2001 225), the Planning (Fees) (Amendment) Regulations (Northern Ireland) 2003 (SR 2003 41), the Planning (Fees) (Amendment No.2) Regulations (Northern Ireland) 2003 (SR 2003 446) and the Planning (Fees) (Amendment) Regulations (Northern Ireland) 2004 (SR 2004 102). They reduce the required fee on submission of an application for listed building consent following a determination; provide for harmonisation of the fees which apply in designated areas for Listed Building Consent and Conservation Area Consent; provide for the payment of a fee in relation to an application for Hazardous Substances Consent; and provide for a simplified fees structure.

4823. Planning permission–Applications–Fees

PLANNING (FEES) (AMENDMENT) REGULATIONS (NORTHERN IRELAND) 2005, SR 2005 505; made under the Planning (Northern Ireland) Order 1991 (SI 1991 1220 (NI.11)) Art.127, Art.129. In force: December 9, 2005; £3.00.

These Regulations amend the Planning (Fees) Regulations (Northern Ireland) 2005 (SR 2005 222) which prescribe fees payable to the Department of the Environment in respect of applications made under the Planning (Northern Ireland) Order 1991 (SI 1991 1220 (NI.11)). The Regulations make amendments by applying the final condition to specified paragraphs; increase the fee for peat extraction from £150 to £1,500; and insert a maximum fee for Category 11 (A) and 11 (B).

4824. Planning permission–General development–Agricultural buildings and operations

PLANNING (GENERAL DEVELOPMENT) (AMENDMENT) ORDER (NORTHERN IRELAND) 2005, SR 2005 427; made under the Planning (Northern Ireland) Order 1991 (SI 1991 1220 (NI.11)) Art.13. In force: October 24, 2005; £3.00.

This Order amends the Planning (General Development) Order (Northern Ireland) 1993 (SR 1993 278) by substituting a new Part 6 Class A and Part 6 Class A2 for Part 6 Class A of Schedule 1. These classes describe development for which planning permission is granted for agricultural buildings and operations, subject to conditions. The new Part 6 Class A, which applies to development prior to January 1, 2008 increases the maximum size of: a building or excavation used or to be used for the storage of slurry or manure; or a building or structure used for both the accommodation of livestock and storage of slurry and manure, from 300 square metres to 600 square metres. The new Part 6 Class A2, which applies to development after December 31, 2007 reduces the maximum size permitted by the new Part 6 Class A from 600 square metres to 300 square metres.

4825. Planning policy–Hazardous substances

PLANNING (HAZARDOUS SUBSTANCES) (AMENDMENT) REGULATIONS (NORTHERN IRELAND) 2005, SR 2005 320; made under the Planning (Northern Ireland) Order 1991 (SI 1991 1220 (NI.11)) Art.81. In force: July 31, 2005; £3.00.

These Regulations amend the Planning (Hazardous Substances) Regulations (Northern Ireland) 1993 (SI 1993 275) to reflect the amended modifications of the enforcement provisions of the Planning (Northern Ireland) Order 1991 (SI 1991 1220).

4826. Planning (Amendment) (Northern Ireland) Order 2003 (SI 2003 430 (NI.8))–Commencement No.4 Order

PLANNING (AMENDMENT) (2003 ORDER) (COMMENCEMENT NO.4) ORDER (NORTHERN IRELAND) 2005, SR 2005 352 (C.28); made under the Planning (Amendment) (Northern Ireland) Order 2003 (SI 2003 430 (NI.8)) Art.1. In force: bringing into operation various provisions of the 2003 Order on August 31, 2005; £3.00.

This Order brings into operation on the Planning (Amendment) (Northern Ireland) Order 2003 (SI 2003 430 (NI.8)) art.23.

POLICE

4827. District Policing Partnerships (Northern Ireland) Order 2005 (SI 2005 861 (NI.4))

This Order makes provision about the membership of district policing partnerships in the period immediately following a local general election. It also amends the law on removal of members following conviction for a criminal offence and makes new provision about chairmen and vice-chairmen of district policing partnerships.

4828. Police officers–Continuance of office–Police Oversight Commissioner

POLICE (NORTHERN IRELAND) ACT 2000 (CONTINUANCE OF OFFICE OF COMMISSIONER) 2005, SR 2005 54; made under the Police (Northern Ireland) Act 2000 s.67. In force: May 30, 2005; £3.00.

This Order provides for the office of Police Oversight Commissioner to continue to exist until May 31, 2007.

4829. Police service–Disciplinary proceedings

POLICE SERVICE OF NORTHERN IRELAND (COMPLAINTS ETC.) (AMENDMENT) REGULATIONS 2005, SR 2005 341; made under the Police (Northern Ireland) Act 1998 s.25, s.26, s.64. In force: August 12, 2005; £3.00.

These Regulations amend the Royal Ulster Constabulary (Complaints etc.) Regulations 2000 (SR 2000 318) and the Royal Ulster Constabulary (Conduct) Regulations 2000 (SR 2000 315) in relation to the holding of disciplinary proceedings where the Police Ombudsman has directed the Chief Constable to bring such disciplinary proceedings. In addition provision is made to carry out amendments to the Royal Ulster Constabulary (Complaints etc.) Regulations 2001 (SR 2001 184) in line with comments made by the Joint Committee on Statutory Instruments in their 5th report.

4830. Police service–Police Service of Northern Ireland

POLICE SERVICE OF NORTHERN IRELAND REGULATIONS 2005, SR 2005 547; made under the Police (Northern Ireland) Act 1998 s.25. In force: January 13, 2006; £5.50.

These Regulations amend the Royal Ulster Constabulary (Unsatisfactory Performance) Regulations 2000 (SR 2000 316), the Police (Appointments) Regulations (Northern Ireland) 2003 (SR 2003 372), and the Police (Appointments) Regulations (Northern Ireland) 2004 (SR 2004 379), revoke the Royal Ulster Constabulary Regulations 1996 (SR 1996 473), the Royal Ulster Constabulary (Amendment) Regulations 1997 (SR 1997 362), the Royal Ulster Constabulary (Amendment) Regulations (SR 1999 412), the Police Service of Northern Ireland Regulations (SR 2000 95), the Police Service of Northern Ireland (Amendment) Regulations (SR 2003 184) and the Police Service of Northern Ireland (Amendment) Regulations 2004 (SR 2004 402).

4831. Police stations–Visitors–Reporting requirements–Conduct of interviews

LAY VISITORS' REPORTS ORDER 2005, SR 2005 420; made under the Police (Northern Ireland) Act 2000 s.73. In force: October 1, 2005; £3.00.

The Police (Northern Ireland) Act 2000 requires lay visitors to attend designated police stations and to report to the Northern Ireland Policing Board about the visit. It empowers the Secretary of State to require such reports to deal with such matters as he may specify. This Order requires the report to deal with the conduct of interviews with detainees.

RATES

4832. Rateable value–Determination of rateable value

RATES (REGIONAL RATES) ORDER (NORTHERN IRELAND) 2005, SR 2005 21; made under the Rates (Northern Ireland) Order 1977 (SI 1977 2157 (NI.28)) Art.7, Art.27. In force: April 1, 2005; £3.00.

This Order fixes the amounts of the regional rates for the year ending March 31, 2006. The Order fixes 27.27 pence in the pound as the amount of the regional rate in respect of those hereditaments (referred to as specified hereditaments) which are not dwelling-houses, private garages or private storage premises and 219.61 pence in the pound in respect of those hereditaments (referred to as unspecified hereditaments) which are. The Order also fixes 53.08 pence in the pound as the amount by which the normal regional rate is reduced in respect of unspecified hereditaments and hereditaments which, though not unspecified hereditaments, are used partly for the purposes of unspecified hereditaments.

REAL PROPERTY

4833. Lands tribunal–Salaries

LANDS TRIBUNAL (SALARIES) ORDER (NORTHERN IRELAND) 2005, SR 2005 269; made under the Administrative and Financial Provisions Act (Northern Ireland) 1962 s.18; and the Lands Tribunal and Compensation Act (Northern Ireland) 1964 s.2. In force: July 1, 2005; £3.00.

This Order, which revokes the Lands Tribunal (Salaries) Order (Northern Ireland) 2004 (SR 2004 194), provides for changes in the annual salaries payable to members of the Lands Tribunal for Northern Ireland following recommendations made in the Report of the Review Body on Senior Salaries in 2005. It increases, with effect from April 1, 2005, the annual salary of the President of the Lands Tribunal and all other members of the Tribunal.

4834. Books

Casey, Nuala; Brennan, Gabriel–Conveyancing. Law Society of Ireland Manuals S. Paperback: £49.99. ISBN 0 19 928028 2. Oxford University Press.
Wylie, John–Irish Conveyancing Law. Paperback: £110.00. ISBN 1 84592 086 4. Tottel Publishing.

ROAD TRAFFIC

4835. Health services charges

ROAD TRAFFIC (HEALTH SERVICES CHARGES) (AMENDMENT) REGULATIONS (NORTHERN IRELAND) 2005, SR 2005 60; made under the Health and Personal Social Services Act (Northern Ireland) 2001 s.25, s.37, s.57. In force: April 1, 2005; £3.00.

These Regulations amend the Road Traffic (Health Services Charges) Regulations (Northern Ireland) 2001 (SR 2001 125) which provide for a scheme for the recovery from insurers and certain other persons of charges in connection with the health services treatment of road traffic casualties. The Regulations increase the charges.

4836. Road safety–Traffic signs

TRAFFIC SIGNS (AMENDMENT NO.2) REGULATIONS (NORTHERN IRELAND) 2005, SR 2005 487; made under the Road Traffic Regulation (Northern Ireland) Order 1997 (SI 1997 276 (NI.2)) Art.28. In force: December 19, 2005; £3.00.

These Regulations amend the Traffic Signs Regulations (Northern Ireland) 1997 (SR 1997 386) to permit the display of the signs shown in the diagrams specified on a sign which is activated automatically by the speed of a vehicle approaching the equipment which controls the sign.

4837. Road works–Inspections–Fees

STREET WORKS (INSPECTION FEES) REGULATIONS (NORTHERN IRELAND) 2005, SR 2005 259; made under the Street Works (Northern Ireland) Order 1995 (SI 1995 3210 (NI.19)) Art.35. In force: July 1, 2005; £3.00.

These Regulations revoke the Street Works (Inspection Fees) Regulations (Northern Ireland) 2001 (SR 2001 409) to increase the fee prescribed for each chargeable inspection to £21.

4838. Traffic Management (Northern Ireland) Order 2005 (SI 2005 1964 (NI.14))

This Order, which amends the Chronically Sick and Disabled Persons (Northern Ireland) Act 1978, the Roads (Northern Ireland) Order 1993 (SI 1993 3160 (NI.15)), the Road Traffic Offenders (Northern Ireland) Order 1996 (SI 1996 1320 (NI.10)) and the Road Traffic Regulation (Northern Ireland) Order 1997 (SI 1997 276 (NI.2)), introduces a system of penalty charging for certain road traffic contraventions. It confers powers on the Department to immobilise or remove vehicles where a penalty charge is payable or recoverable from their owners. It also makes miscellaneous amendments, including amendments for the recognition of disabled persons' badges issued outside Northern Ireland.

4839. Trunk roads—Classification—M2

M2 IMPROVEMENTS (SANDYKNOWES TO GREENCASTLE) ORDER (NORTHERN IRELAND) 2005, SR 2005 255; made under the Roads (Northern Ireland) Order 1993 (SI 1993 3160 (NI.15)) Art.14, Art.15, Art.16. In force: July 11, 2005; £3.00.

This Order provides that 5350 metres of new carriageway specified and 20 metres of new bridge specified shall be special road subject to motorway traffic restrictions and be part of the M2 Motorway and Belfast-Antrim-Coleraine-Londonderry Trunk Road T7.

SENTENCING

4840. Prisoners—Release—Paramilitary organisations

NORTHERN IRELAND (SENTENCES) ACT 1998 (SPECIFIED ORGANISATIONS) ORDER 2005, SI 2005 2558; made under the Northern Ireland (Sentences) Act 1998 s.3. In force: September 14, 2005; £3.00.

Under the Northern Ireland (Sentences) Act 1998 the Secretary of State must specify an organisation if he believes that it is concerned in terrorism connected with the affairs of Northern Ireland, or in promoting or encouraging it, and that it has not established or is not maintaining a complete and unequivocal ceasefire. The Secretary of State is obliged to review the list of specified organisations from time to time. Following such a review the Secretary of State has decided that the Ulster Volunteer Force and the Red Hand Commando should be specified and that the Continuity IRA, the "Real" IRA, the Loyalist Volunteer Force, the Red Hand Defenders and the Orange Volunteers should continue to be specified. The effect of specifying an organisation is that a prisoner who is, or who would be likely to become, a supporter of such an organisation, is ineligible for release under the 1998 Act or, if released, is liable to recall to prison. The Order also revokes the Northern Ireland (Sentences) Act 1998 (Specified Organisations) Order 2004 (SI 2004 3009).

SOCIAL SECURITY

4841. Benefits—Child tax credit

SOCIAL SECURITY (TAX CREDITS) (AMENDMENT) REGULATIONS (NORTHERN IRELAND) 2005, SR 2005 393; made under the Social Security Contributions and Benefits (Northern Ireland) Act 1992 s.122, s.123, s.131, s.132, s.171; and the Jobseekers (Northern Ireland) Order 1995 (SI 1995 2705 (NI.15)) Art.6, Art.14, Art.15, Art.36. In force: September 8, 2005; £3.00.

These Regulations, which amend the Social Security (Working Tax Credit and Child Tax Credit Consequential Amendments) Regulations (Northern Ireland) 2003 (SR 2003 195), make provision in connection with the abolition of the special amounts and premia in income support and jobseeker's allowance for those with responsibility for children and young persons under the Tax Credits Act 2002 s.1. Such amounts and premia are replaced by child tax credit under that Act and the amendments ensure that, during the transitional period, no new awards of such amounts and premia are made, except to existing claimants who already have an amount in respect of a child or young person included in their applicable amount.

4842. Benefits—Claims and payments

SOCIAL SECURITY (CLAIMS AND PAYMENTS) (AMENDMENT NO.2) REGULATIONS (NORTHERN IRELAND) 2005, SR 2005 139; made under the Social Security Administration (Northern Ireland) Act 1992 s.5, s.165. In force: April 11, 2005; £3.00.

These Regulations, which amend the Social Security (Claims and Payments) Regulations (Northern Ireland) 1987 (SR 1987 465), the Social Security (Claims and Payments) (Amendment) Regulations (Northern Ireland) 1989 (SR 1989 40), the Social Security (Benefits for Widows and Widowers) (Consequential Amendments) Regulations (Northern Ireland) 2001 (SR 2001 108), the Social Security (Claims and Payments and Miscellaneous Amendments No.2) Regulations (Northern Ireland) 2002 (SR 2002 327) and the Social Security (Claims and Payments) (Amendment) Regulations (Northern Ireland) 2004 (SR 2004 85), provide an extended time for claiming bereavement benefit, or an increase in certain benefits in respect of an adult or child dependant, where death is difficult to establish; and omit an obsolete definition of "income support" and increase from £18.10 to £18.80 the amount allowed for personal expenses where a person is in accommodation for which part of his benefit is paid direct to the person to whom charges in respect of that accommodation are payable.

4843. Benefits—Claims and payments

SOCIAL SECURITY (CLAIMS AND PAYMENTS AND PAYMENTS ON ACCOUNT, OVERPAYMENTS AND RECOVERY) (AMENDMENT) REGULATIONS (NORTHERN IRELAND) 2005, SR 2005 14; made under the Social Security Administration (Northern Ireland) Act 1992 s.5, s.69, s.165. In force: May 2, 2005; £3.00.

These Regulations amend the Social Security (Claims and Payments) Regulations (Northern Ireland) 1987 (SR 1987 465) and the Social Security (Payments on account, Overpayments and Recovery) Regulations (Northern Ireland) 1988 (SR 1988 142). They enable a person to make a claim for graduated retirement benefit and retirement pension by telephone, unless the Department for Social Development directs that the claim must be made in writing; enable a person who has made such a claim to amend it by telephone; and provide for the date of a claim for graduated retirement benefit or retirement pension made by telephone. They also enable the Department to give notice, either orally or in writing, of the effect the Regulations would have in the event of an overpayment, to a person who makes a claim for graduated retirement benefit and retirement pension by telephone.

4844. Benefits—Entitlement—Reciprocal agreements

SOCIAL SECURITY (RECIPROCAL AGREEMENTS) ORDER (NORTHERN IRELAND) 2005, SR 2005 544; made under the Social Security Administration (Northern Ireland) Act 1992 s.155. In force: December 5, 2005; £3.00.

This Order provides for social security legislation to be modified, to reflect changes made to the benefit entitlement of spouses and civil partners by the and the Civil Partnership Act 2004, in relation to the Orders in Council and orders made by the Secretary of State listed which give effect to agreements made between the Governments of the UK and other countries providing for reciprocity in certain social security matters. It amends the Social Security Contributions and Benefits (Northern Ireland) Act 1992 and the Social Security Administration (Northern Ireland) Act 1992.

4845. Benefits–Miscellaneous amendments

SOCIAL SECURITY (MISCELLANEOUS AMENDMENTS) REGULATIONS (NORTHERN IRELAND) 2005, SR 2005 98; made under the Social Security Contributions and Benefits (Northern Ireland) Act 1992 s.122, s.132, s.132A, s.171; the State Pension Credit Act (Northern Ireland) 2002 s.15; and the Jobseekers (Northern Ireland) Order 1995 (SI 1995 2705 (NI.15)) Art.14, Art.36. In force: April 4, 2005; £3.00.

These Regulations amend the Income Support (General) Regulations (Northern Ireland) 1987 (SR 1987 459), the Housing Benefit (General) Regulations (Northern Ireland) 1987 (SR 1987 461), the Jobseeker's Allowance Regulations (Northern Ireland) 1996 (SR 1996 198) and the State Pension Credit Regulations (Northern Ireland) 2003 (SR 2003 28). The Regulations amend interpretation provisions in relation to the introduction of the Armed Forces and Reserve Forces Compensation Scheme; add certain payments made under the new scheme to the descriptions of income which are prescribed for the purposes of the State Pension Credit Act (Northern Ireland) 2002 s.15(1)(j); provide an income disregard for guaranteed income payments made under the new scheme; exclude from the full income disregard, payments of housing benefit received by claimants direct from an authority in respect of persons temporarily in their care; and remove outdated references to "earnings top-up" and "the Earnings Top-up Scheme".

4846. Benefits–Miscellaneous amendments

SOCIAL SECURITY (MISCELLANEOUS AMENDMENTS NO.2) REGULATIONS (NORTHERN IRELAND) 2005, SR 2005 424; made under the Social Security Contributions and Benefits (Northern Ireland) Act 1992 s.122, s.130, s.132, s.171; the State Pension Credit Act (Northern Ireland) 2002 s.15, s.19; and the Jobseekers (Northern Ireland) Order 1995 (SI 1995 2705 (NI.15)) Art.14, Art.15, Art.36. In force: in accordance with Reg.1; £3.00.

These Regulations amend the Income Support (General) Regulations (Northern Ireland) 1987 (SR 1987 459), the Housing Benefit (General) Regulations (Northern Ireland) 1987 (SR 1987 461), the Jobseeker's Allowance Regulations (Northern Ireland) 1996 (SR 1996 198) and the State Pension Credit Regulations (Northern Ireland) 2003 (SR 2003 28). The Regulations increase the lower capital limit of £3,000 to £6,000; remove some of the provisions that provide different capital limits in special circumstances and update references to capital limits in the regulations that deal with tariff income; provide that a person aged under 60, who opts not to take an occupational pension available to him under early release, is not treated as possessing the amount of any income or capital deferred; ensure that where money is paid to a third party on behalf of a claimant and is subsequently used by the third party to provide benefits in kind to the claimant, the money will not be disregarded; change references to adopters in the income and capital disregards of financial support in order to take account of the commencement of the Adoption and Children Act 2002; and change references to take account of the Carers and Direct Payments Act (Northern Ireland) 2002. The Regulations provide that a person aged 60 or over, who opts not to take an occupational pension available to him, shall be treated as possessing the amount of any income foregone from the date on which it could be expected to be acquired were an application to be made; and make it clear, in the case of a claimant aged 60 or over, that income which could be obtained from money purchase benefits under an occupational pension scheme is treated in the same way as such income under a personal pension scheme. They also insert a definition of "board and lodging accommodation".

4847. Benefits–Mortgage interest payments–Administration fees

SOCIAL SECURITY (CLAIMS AND PAYMENTS) (AMENDMENT NO.3) REGULATIONS (NORTHERN IRELAND) 2005, SR 2005 362; made under the

Social Security Administration (Northern Ireland) Act 1992 s.13A, s.165. In force: September 1, 2005; £3.00.

These Regulations, which revoke the Social Security (Claims and Payments) (Amendment) Regulations (Northern Ireland) 2004 (SR 2004 85), amend the Social Security (Claims and Payments) Regulations (Northern Ireland) 1987 (SR 1987 465) by reducing from £0.78 to £0.31 the fee which qualifying lenders pay for the purpose of defraying administrative expenses incurred by the Department for Social Development in making payments in respect of mortgage interest direct to those lenders.

4848. Benefits–Social fund–Maternity and funeral expenses

SOCIAL FUND MATERNITY AND FUNERAL EXPENSES (GENERAL) REGULATIONS (NORTHERN IRELAND) 2005, SR 2005 506; made under the Social Security Contributions and Benefits (Northern Ireland) Act 1992 s.134, s.171. In force: December 5, 2005; £3.00.

These Regulations amend the Social Fund (Maternity and Funeral Expenses) (General) (Amendment) Regulations (Northern Ireland) 1989 (SR 1989 71), the Social Fund (Miscellaneous Amendments) Regulations (Northern Ireland) 1990 (SR 1990 132), the Disability Living Allowance and Disability Working Allowance (Consequential Provisions) Regulations (Northern Ireland) 1992 (SR 1992 6), the Social Security (Social Fund and Claims and Payments) (Miscellaneous Amendments) Regulations (Northern Ireland) 1997 (SR 1997 155), the Social Security and Child Support (Tax Credits Consequential Amendments) Regulations (Northern Ireland) 1 (SR 1 385), the Social Fund (Winter Fuel Payment and Maternity and Funeral Expenses (General)) Regulations (Northern Ireland) 2000 (SR 2000 259), the Social Security (Capital Disregards and Recovery of Benefits Amendment) Regulations (Northern Ireland) 2001 (SR 2001 150), the Social Security (Capital Disregards Amendment No.2) Regulations (Northern Ireland) 2001 (SR 2001 157), the Social Fund (Miscellaneous Amendments) Regulations (Northern Ireland) 2002 (SR 2002 284), the State Pension Credit (Consequential, Transitional and Miscellaneous Provisions) Regulations (Northern Ireland) 2003 (SR 2003 191), the Social Security (Working Tax Credit and Child Tax Credit Consequential Amendments) Regulations (Northern Ireland) 2003 (SR 2003 195), the Social Security (Miscellaneous Amendments No.3) Regulations (Northern Ireland) 2004 (SR 2004 213) and the Social Security (Residential Care Homes, Nursing Homes and Independent Hospitals) Regulations (Northern Ireland) 2005 (SR 2005 458). They also revoke the Social Fund (Maternity and Funeral Expenses) (General) Regulations (Northern Ireland) 1987 (SR 1987 150), the Social Fund (Maternity and Funeral Expenses) (General) (Amendment) Regulations (Northern Ireland) 1988 (SR 1988 6), the Social Fund (Maternity and Funeral Expenses) (General) (Amendment No.2) Regulations (Northern Ireland) 1988 (SR 1988 22), the Social Fund (Maternity and Funeral Expenses) (General) (Amendment) Regulations (Northern Ireland) 1992 (SR 1992 394), the Social Fund (Maternity and Funeral Expenses) (General) (Amendment) Regulations (Northern Ireland) 1993 (SR 1993 99), the Social Fund (Maternity and Funeral Expenses) (General) (Amendment) Regulations (Northern Ireland) 1994 (SR 1994 68), the Social Fund (Maternity and Funeral Expenses) (General) (Amendment) Regulations (Northern Ireland) 1995 (SR 1995 190), the Social Fund (Maternity and Funeral Expenses) (General) (Amendment) Regulations (Northern Ireland) 1996 (SR 1996 423), the Social Fund (Maternity and Funeral Expenses) (General) (Amendment No. 2) Regulations (Northern Ireland) 1996 (SR 1996 571), the Social Fund (Maternity and Funeral Expenses) (General) (Amendment) Regulations (Northern Ireland) 1997 (SR 1997 472), the Social Fund (Maternity and Funeral Expenses) (General) (Amendment) Regulations (Northern Ireland) 1 (SR 1 499), the Social Fund (Maternity and Funeral Expenses) (General) (Amendment) Regulations (Northern Ireland) 2000 (SR 2000 49), the Social Fund (Maternity and Funeral Expenses) (General) (Amendment) Regulations (Northern Ireland) 2001 (SR 2001 318), the Social Fund (Maternity and Funeral Expenses) (General) (Amendment) Regulations

(Northern Ireland 2002 (SR 2002 14), the Social Fund (Maternity and Funeral Expenses) (General) (Amendment No.2) Regulations (Northern Ireland) 2002 (SR 2002 90), the Social Fund (Maternity and Funeral Expenses) (General) (Amendment) Regulations (Northern Ireland) 2003 (SR 2003 117), the Social Fund (Maternity and Funeral Expenses) (General) (Amendment No.2) Regulations (Northern Ireland) 2003 (SR 2003 264), the Social Fund (Maternity and Funeral Expenses) (General) (Amendment No.3) Regulations (Northern Ireland) 2003 (SR 2003 308) and the Social Fund (Maternity and Funeral Expenses) (General) (Amendment) Regulations (Northern Ireland) 2004 (SR 2004 408). The Regulations make provision for payments to be made out of the social fund to meet maternity expenses and funeral expenses.

4849. Benefits–Up rating

SOCIAL SECURITY BENEFITS UP-RATING ORDER (NORTHERN IRELAND) 2005, SR 2005 82; made under the Social Security Administration (Northern Ireland) Act 1992 s132, s.165. In force: in accordance with Art.1; £6.00.

This Order amends the National Insurance Act (Northern Ireland) 1966, the Social Security Contributions and Benefits (Northern Ireland) Act 1992, the Pension Schemes (Northern Ireland) Act 1993, the Social Security (Graduated Retirement Benefit) (No. 2) Regulations (Northern Ireland) 1978 (SR 1978 105), the Statutory Maternity Pay (General) Regulations (Northern Ireland) 1987 (SR 1987 30), the Income Support (General) Regulations (Northern Ireland) 1987 (SR 1987 459), the Income Support (Transitional) Regulations (Northern Ireland) 1987 (SR 1987 460), the Housing Benefit (General) Regulations (Northern Ireland) 1987 (SR 1987 461), the Social Security (Disability Living Allowance) Regulations (Northern Ireland) 1992 (SR 1992 32), the Social Security (Incapacity Benefit) Regulations (Northern Ireland) 1994 (SR 1994 461), the Social Security (Incapacity Benefit) (Transitional) Regulations (Northern Ireland) 1995 (SR 1995 35), the Jobseeker's Allowance Regulations (Northern Ireland) 1996 (SR 1996 198), the Statutory Paternity Pay and Statutory Adoption Pay (Weekly Rates) Regulations (Northern Ireland) 2002 (SR 2002 380), and the State Pension Credit Regulations (Northern Ireland) 2003 (SR 2003 28) and revokes the Social Security Benefits Up-rating Order (Northern Ireland) 2004 (SR 2004 82). The Order increases the rates and amounts of certain social security benefits and other sums.

4850. Benefits–Up rating

SOCIAL SECURITY BENEFITS UP-RATING REGULATIONS (NORTHERN IRELAND) 2005, SR 2005 96; made under the Social Security Contributions and Benefits (Northern Ireland) Act 1992 s.90, s.113, s.171; and the Social Security Administration (Northern Ireland) Act 1992 s.135, s.165. In force: April 11, 2005; £3.00.

The Regulations, which amend the Social Security Benefit (Dependency) Regulations (Northern Ireland) 1977 (SR 1977 74) and revoke the Social Security Benefits Up-rating Regulations (Northern Ireland) 2004 (SR 2004 83), provide that where a question has arisen about the effect of the Social Security Benefits Up-rating Order (Northern Ireland) 2005 on a benefit already in payment the altered rate will not apply until that question is determined. They also apply provisions of the Social Security Benefit (Persons Abroad) Regulations (Northern Ireland) 1978 (SR 1978 114) so as to restrict the application of the increases specified in the Up-rating Order in cases where the beneficiary lives abroad; raise from £165 to £170 and £21 to £22 the earnings limits for child dependency increases payable with a carer's allowance.

4851. Benefits–Work focused interviews

SOCIAL SECURITY (INCAPACITY BENEFIT WORK-FOCUSED INTERVIEWS) REGULATIONS (NORTHERN IRELAND) 2005, SR 2005 414; made under the

Social Security Administration (Northern Ireland) Act 1992 s.2A, s.2B, s.165. In force: October 3, 2005; £3.00.

These Regulations, which amend the Social Security (Work-focused Interviews) Regulations (Northern Ireland) 2003 (SR 2003 274), impose a requirement on certain persons who claim, or have claimed, incapacity benefit, income support on the grounds of incapacity, income support whilst they are appealing against a decision which embodies a determination that they are not incapable of work, or severe disablement allowance to take part in work-focused interviews.

4852. Benefits–Work focused interviews

SOCIAL SECURITY (WORK-FOCUSED INTERVIEWS AMENDMENT) REGULATIONS (NORTHERN IRELAND) 2005, SR 2005 443; made under the Social Security Administration (Northern Ireland) Act 1992 s.2A, s.165. In force: October 31, 2005; £3.00.

These Regulations amend the Social Security (Work-focused Interviews for Lone Parents) Regulations (Northern Ireland) 2001 (SR 2001 152), the Social Security (Work-focused Interviews) Regulations (Northern Ireland) 2001 (SR 2001 176), the Social Security Work-focused Interviews Regulations (Northern Ireland) 2003 (SR 2003 274) and the Social Security (Incapacity Benefit Work-focused Interviews) Regulations (Northern Ireland) 2005 (SR 2005 414). They require claimants taking part in most work-focused interviews to create and discuss an action plan for employment; make amendments so that a claimant in receipt of only Carer's Allowance or Bereavement Benefit is no longer required to take part in a work-focused interview; change the date on which a first work-focused interview is to take place for claimants of incapacity benefit, severe disablement allowance, income support on the grounds of incapacity and income support whilst appealing against a decision which embodies a determination that they are not incapable of work; and change the circumstances in which a claimant is classed as disabled. The Regulations also introduce a requirement for lone parents who have been in receipt of income support (other than income support on the grounds of incapacity or income support whilst appealing against a decision which embodies a determination that they are not incapable of work) for 12 months and who are responsible for a youngest child aged 14 to take part in a work-focused interview every 13 weeks; and make amendments so that for income support claimed whilst a person is appealing against a decision which embodies a determination that they are not incapable of work, the only relevant date is the date of that claim.

4853. Care–Children–Entitlement to benefits–Disapplication

CHILDREN (LEAVING CARE) SOCIAL SECURITY BENEFITS REGULATIONS (NORTHERN IRELAND) 2005, SR 2005 324; made under the Children (Leaving Care) Act (Northern Ireland) 2002 s.6. In force: September 1, 2005; £3.00.

These Regulations prescribe the categories of cases where the Children (Leaving Care) Act (Northern Ireland) 2002 s.6 does not apply.

4854. Child benefit–Guardians allowance–Weekly rates–Increase

CHILD BENEFIT AND GUARDIAN'S ALLOWANCE UP-RATING (NORTHERN IRELAND) ORDER 2005, SI 2005 683; made under the Social Security Administration (Northern Ireland) Act 1992 s.132, s.165. In force: April 11, 2005; £3.00.

This Order increases the weekly rate of guardian's allowance prescribed in the Social Security Contributions and Benefits (Northern Ireland) Act 1992 from £11.85 to £12.20. It also increases the weekly rates of child benefit prescribed in the Child Benefit and Social Security (Fixing and Adjustment of Rates) Regulations (Northern Ireland) 1976 (SR 1976 223) from £16.50 to £17.00 and from £11.05 to £11.40 respectively.

4855. Child trust funds-Appeals-Procedure

SOCIAL SECURITY COMMISSIONERS (PROCEDURE) (CHILD TRUST FUNDS) REGULATIONS (NORTHERN IRELAND) 2005, SR 2005 164; made under the Social Security Administration (Northern Ireland) Act 1992 s.22, s.165; and the Social Security (Northern Ireland) Order 1998 (SI 1998 1506 (NI.10)) Art.2, Art.15, Art.16, Art.28, Art.74, Sch.4. In force: April 18, 2005; £3.00.

These Regulations regulate the procedure of the Social Security Commissioners for Northern Ireland in determining appeals and applications arising from decisions of appeal tribunals in relation to child trust funds.

4856. Children-Trust funds-Appeals-Procedure

CHILD TRUST FUNDS (APPEALS) (NORTHERN IRELAND) REGULATIONS 2005, SI 2005 907; made under the Social Security (Northern Ireland) Order 1998 (SI 1998 1506 (NI.10)) Art.6, Art.8, Art.13, Art.15, Art.16, Art.28, Art.74, Sch.1 para.7, Sch.1 para.11, Sch.1 para.12, Sch.4 para.1, Sch.4 para.2, Sch.4 para.3, Sch.4 para.4, Sch.4 para.5, Sch.4 para.6. In force: March 25, 2005; £3.00.

These Regulations are made in consequence of the Child Trust Funds Act 2004 which provides that people who appeal may appeal to an appeal tribunal constituted under provisions in the Social Security Act 1998 as applied and modified by the Child Trust Funds (Non-tax Appeals) Regulations 2005 (SI 2005 191) made by the Treasury. These Regulations provide for the procedure for such child trust funds appeals. The procedure is almost the same as that prescribed for other appeals to such appeal tribunals.

4857. Civil partnerships-Categorisation of earners-Equal treatment

SOCIAL SECURITY (CATEGORISATION OF EARNERS) (AMENDMENT) (NORTHERN IRELAND) REGULATIONS 2005, SI 2005 3134; made under the Social Security Contributions and Benefits (Northern Ireland) Act 1992 s.2. In force: December 5, 2005; £3.00.

These Regulations amend the Social Security (Categorisation of Earners) Regulations (Northern Ireland) 1978 (SR 1978 401) to amend references to spouses so as to secure equality of treatment between civil partners and spouses in the application of the categorisation rules for the purposes of National Insurance Contributions.

4858. Civil partnerships-Consequential amendments

SOCIAL SECURITY (CIVIL PARTNERSHIP) (CONSEQUENTIAL AMENDMENTS) REGULATIONS (NORTHERN IRELAND) 2005, SR 2005 539; made under the Social Security Contributions and Benefits (Northern Ireland) Act 1992 s.48, s.113, s.122, s.130, s.131, s.132, s.171, Sch.5 para.2, Sch.5 para.3B, Sch.5 para.7B; the Social Security Administration (Northern Ireland) Act 1992 s.5, s.165; the Social Security (Northern Ireland) Order 1998 (SI 1998 1506 (NI.10)) Art.10, Art.11, Art.74; and the Child Support, Pensions and Social Security Act (Northern Ireland) 2000 Sch.7 para.10, Sch.7 para.20. In force: December 5, 2005; £3.00.

These Regulations amend the Social Security (Widow's Benefit and Retirement Pensions) Regulations (Northern Ireland) 1979 (SR 1979 243), the Social Security (General Benefit) Regulations (Northern Ireland) 1984 (SR 1984 92), the Income Support (General) Regulations (Northern Ireland) 1987 (SR 1987 459), the Housing Benefit (General) Regulations (Northern Ireland) 1987 (SR 1987 461), the Social Security (Claims and Payments) Regulations (Northern Ireland) 1987 (SR 1987 465), the Social Security and Child Support (Decisions and Appeals) Regulations (Northern Ireland) 1999 (SR 1999 162), the Housing Benefit (Decisions and Appeals) Regulations (Northern Ireland) 2001 (SR 2001 213), the Social Security, Child Support and Tax Credits (Miscellaneous Amendments) Regulations (Northern Ireland) 2005 (SR 2005 46) and the Social Security (Deferral of Retirement Pensions) Regulations (Northern Ireland) 2005 (SR 2005 120). They make minor amendments to a number of statutory rules relating to social security to reflect the new status of civil partnership. The amendments are consequential upon the Civil Partnership Act 2004.

4859. Contributions–Intermediaries–2005/06

SOCIAL SECURITY CONTRIBUTIONS (INTERMEDIARIES) (NORTHERN IRELAND) (AMENDMENT) REGULATIONS 2005, SI 2005 3132; made under the Social Security Contributions and Benefits (Northern Ireland) Act 1992 s.4A, s.121, s.171. In force: in accordance with Reg.1 (2)(3); £3.00.

These Regulations amend the Social Security Contributions (Intermediaries) (Northern Ireland) Regulations 2000 (SI 2000 728) as a result of the bringing into force of the Commissioners for Revenue and Customs Act 2005, the Pensions (Northern Ireland) Order 2005 (SI 2005 255 (NI.1)) and the Civil Partnership Act 2004. They make provision for the tax year 2005/06 in the case of a person to whom the 2000 Regulations would not apply but for an amendment coming into force during the tax year rather than at the beginning of a tax year.

4860. Food–Milk–Entitlement

WELFARE FOODS (AMENDMENT) REGULATIONS (NORTHERN IRELAND) 2005, SR 2005 190; made under the Social Security (Northern Ireland) Order 1988 (SI 1988 594 (NI.2)) Art.13; and the Social Security Contributions and Benefits (Northern Ireland) Act 1992 s.171. In force: April 6, 2005; £3.00.

These Regulations amend the Welfare Foods Regulations (Northern Ireland) 1988 (SR 1988 137) and the Welfare Foods (Amendment) Regulations (Northern Ireland) 2004 (SR 2004 161). They raise to £13,910 the figure for the income level that determines whether a person receiving Child Tax Credit but not Working Tax Credit and who meets other conditions is entitled to benefit under the Scheme. They also raise to £15,050 the figure for the maximum income level that determines whether a person entitled to tax credits and who meets other conditions is entitled to purchase dried milk at a reduced price under the Scheme.

4861. Food–Milk–Entitlement

WELFARE FOODS (AMENDMENT NO.2) REGULATIONS (NORTHERN IRELAND) 2005, SR 2005 519; made under the Social Security (Northern Ireland) Order 1988 (SI 1988 594 (NI.2)) Art.13; and the Social Security Contributions and Benefits (Northern Ireland) Act 1992 s.171. In force: November 28, 2005; £3.00.

These Regulations amend the Welfare Foods Regulations (Northern Ireland) 1988 (SR 1988 137) to change the definition of vitamins to ensure there is access to a suitable vitamin product for beneficiaries and deletes the definition of guaranteed credit. They also remove the entitlement to milk tokens under the Welfare Food Scheme for children not registered at a school as a direct result of their disability and to remove entitlement to low cost infant formula for these families with children under one year old who purchase it through clinics.

4862. Graduated retirement benefit–Deferment

SOCIAL SECURITY (GRADUATED RETIREMENT BENEFIT) REGULATIONS (NORTHERN IRELAND) 2005, SR 2005 121; made under the Social Security Contributions and Benefits (Northern Ireland) Act 1992 s.62, s.171. In force: April 6, 2005; £3.00.

These Regulations, which amend the National Insurance Act (Northern Ireland) 1966, the Social Security (Graduated Retirement Benefit) (No.2) Regulations (Northern Ireland) 1978 (SR 1978 105) and the Social Security (Abolition of Earnings Rule) (Consequential) Regulations (Northern Ireland) 1989 (SR 1989 373), make provision relating to the deferment of graduated retirement benefit arising from changes in the rules relating to the deferment of retirement pension made by the Pensions (Northern Ireland) Order 1995 (SI 1995 3213 (NI.22)) and the Pensions (Northern Ireland) Order 2005 (SR 2005 120).

4863. Housing benefit—Miscellaneous amendments

HOUSING BENEFIT (MISCELLANEOUS AMENDMENTS) REGULATIONS (NORTHERN IRELAND) 2005, SR 2005 148; made under the Social Security Contributions and Benefits (Northern Ireland) Act 1992 s.122, s.132, s.132A, s.171. In force: in accordance with Reg.1 (2) (3) (4); £3.00.

These Regulations make various amendments to the Housing Benefit (General) Regulations (Northern Ireland) 1987 (SR 1987 461).

4864. Housing benefit—Miscellaneous amendments

HOUSING BENEFIT (MISCELLANEOUS AMENDMENTS NO.2) REGULATIONS (NORTHERN IRELAND) 2005, SR 2005 185; made under the Social Security Contributions and Benefits (Northern Ireland) Act 1992 s.122, s.131, s.132, s.132A, s.133, s.171; and the Child Support, Pensions and Social Security Act (Northern Ireland) 2000 Sch.7 para.4, Sch.7 para.20. In force: Reg.2(6): April 3, 2005; remainder: April 4, 2005; £3.00.

These Regulations amend the Housing Benefit (General) Regulations (Northern Ireland) 1987 (SR 1987 461) to make provision which deals with the treatment of prisoners on temporary release; to provide that certain specified categories of retirement pension income will not be treated as notional income; to remove a provision excluding the award of an Enhanced Disability Premium in respect of a child whose capital exceeds a specified amount; and to provide for certain income from capital to be disregarded when calculating a claimant's income.

4865. Housing benefit—Miscellaneous amendments

HOUSING BENEFIT (MISCELLANEOUS AMENDMENTS NO.3) REGULATIONS (NORTHERN IRELAND) 2005, SR 2005 444; made under the Social Security Contributions and Benefits (Northern Ireland) Act 1992 s.122, s.129, s.131, s.132, s.132A, s.171; the Social Security Administration (Northern Ireland) Act 1992 s.5, s.165; and the Social Security (Northern Ireland) Order 1998 (SI 1998 1506 (NI.10)) Art.34, Art.74. In force: in accordance with Reg.1 (1); £3.00.

These Regulations amend the Housing Benefit (General) Regulations (Northern Ireland) 1987 (SR 1987 461) to remove provisions which provide for the reduction of a claimant's applicable amount where he or his partner is a long term patient; and to remove provisions which contain an equivalent provision which applies to claimants who have not reached the qualifying age for state pension credit. They make amendments which prevent non-dependent deductions being made where the non-dependent is a long term patient, by amending the definition of "patient" and the rule under which periods of time spent as a patient are calculated; and remove the requirement that arrears of working tax credit or child tax credit must be paid as a result of a change of circumstances in order to be disregarded in a claimant's assessment of capital.

4866. Housing benefit—Miscellaneous amendments

HOUSING BENEFIT (MISCELLANEOUS AMENDMENTS NO.4) REGULATIONS (NORTHERN IRELAND) 2005, SR 2005 493; made under the Social Security Contributions and Benefits (Northern Ireland) Act 1992 s.129, s.131, s.132, s.132A, s.133, s.171; the Social Security Administration (Northern Ireland) Act 1992 s.5, s.5A, s.165; the Social Security (Northern Ireland) Order 1998 (SI 1998 1506 (NI.10) Art.74; and the Child Support, Pensions and Social Security (Northern Ireland) Act 2000 Sch.7 para.1, Sch.7 para.13, Sch.7 para.14, Sch.7 para.15, Sch.7 para.20, Sch.7 para.23. In force: November 10, 2005; £3.00.

These Regulations amend the Housing Benefit (General) Regulations (Northern Ireland) (SR 1987 461) and the Housing Benefit (Decisions and Appeals) Regulations (Northern Ireland) 2001 (SR 2001 213). They provide that a person is considered to be disabled for the purpose of determining child care charge deductions if they cease to be registered as blind within the period that begins 28 weeks before the first Monday in September following their fifteenth birthday and ends on the day preceding the first Monday in September following the person's sixteenth birthday; that the tax rates to be used to determine the amount of tax and contributions that should be deducted to find the net amount of profit or earnings shall be the rate applicable to the assessment period; revoke rules linking a claim for housing benefit to certain social security benefits and introduce two new rules for determining the date of claim; align the time scales for providing information and backdating claims in the Housing Benefit Regulations with those used in other benefits and in the Decisions and Appeals Regulations; provide for the Northern Ireland Housing Executive to send an instrument for the first payment of a rent allowance to the claimant, made payable to the landlord, where it has superseded an earlier decision on the claim due to a change in the claimant's address; include lone parents in the list of those who have attained the qualifying age for state pension credit and who may be treated as severely disabled in the stipulated circumstances; extend the number of payments that should be fully disregarded in the calculation of income other than earnings; and amend the Decisions and Appeals Regulations to shorten the time before a relevant authority can terminate an award of housing benefit following the suspension of its payment.

4867. Housing benefit—Overpayments

HOUSING BENEFIT (GENERAL) (AMENDMENT NO.2) REGULATIONS (NORTHERN IRELAND) 2005, SR 2005 459; made under the Social Security Contributions and Benefits (Northern Ireland) Act 1992 s.122; and the Social Security Administration (Northern Ireland) Act 1992 s.73, s.165. In force: April 10, 2006; £3.00.

These Regulations amend the Housing Benefit (General) Regulations (Northern Ireland) 1987 (SR 1987 461) to change the meaning of "overpayment"; to insert an additional condition in the list of prescribed circumstances that must be satisfied for an overpayment not to be recovered from the person to whom it was paid; prescribe the person from whom recovery of an overpayment should be made in specified circumstances instead of the person to whom the payment was made; amends the terminology used in respect of an authority administering housing benefit; ensure a claimant's change of address is not treated as being a change of circumstances when calculating housing benefit payable in respect of the overpayment period; and to provide for recovery of overpaid housing benefit from benefits paid by Switzerland.

4868. Housing benefit—Tenancies—Rent free periods—Assistance scheme

HOUSING BENEFIT (GENERAL) (AMENDMENT) REGULATIONS (NORTHERN IRELAND) 2005, SR 2005 331; made under the Social Security Contributions and Benefits (Northern Ireland) Act 1992 s.122, s.132A, s.171. In force: August 1, 2005; £3.00.

These Regulations amend the Housing Benefit (General) Regulations (Northern Ireland) 1987 (SR 1987 461) which provide for a scheme whereby housing benefit is payable to persons who are liable to make certain payments in respect of a dwelling as their home. The Regulations make amendments to preserve the policy that housing benefit, for those whose tenancy has a rent and rate-free period, assists with the full rent only in the weeks in which the rent is actually paid; and to preserve the policy that housing benefit, for those whose tenancy has a rent and rate-free period, assists with the full rent only in the weeks in which the rent is actually due.

4869. Incapacity benefit—Allowances

SOCIAL SECURITY (INCAPACITY) (MISCELLANEOUS AMENDMENTS) REGULATIONS (NORTHERN IRELAND) 2005, SR 2005 415; made under the Social Security Contributions and Benefits (Northern Ireland) Act 1992 s.30E, s.167D, s.171, Sch.7 para.2. In force: October 1, 2005; £3.00.

These Regulations, which revoke the Social Security (Incapacity) (Miscellaneous Amendments) Regulations (Northern Ireland) 2004 (SR 2004

380), amend the Social Security (General Benefit) Regulations (Northern Ireland) 1984 (SR 1984 92), the Social Security (Incapacity Benefit) Regulations (Northern Ireland) 1994 (SR 1994 461) and the Social Security (Incapacity for Work) (General) Regulations (Northern Ireland) 1995 (SR 1995 41). They increase from £4,056 to £4,212 the amount which can be earned before disqualification for unemployability supplement; increase the earnings limit for councillor's allowance from £78 to £81; and increase from £78 to £81 the weekly limit for earnings from work which may be undertaken by a person without his being treated as capable of work.

4870. Incapacity benefit – Personal capability assessment – Incapacity for work

SOCIAL SECURITY (INCAPACITY FOR WORK) (GENERAL) (AMENDMENT) REGULATIONS (NORTHERN IRELAND) 2005, SR 2005 15; made under the Social Security Contributions and Benefits (Northern Ireland) Act 1992 s.167D, s.171. In force: February 10, 2005; £3.00.

These Regulations amend the Social Security (Incapacity for Work) (General) Regulations (Northern Ireland) 1995 (SR 1995 41) to set out the exceptional circumstances in which a person who is not incapable of work in accordance with the personal capability assessment is nevertheless to be treated as incapable of work. They also amend the Social Security (Incapacity for Work and Miscellaneous Amendments) Regulations (Northern Ireland) 1996 (SR 1996 601) and the Social Security (Incapacity for Work) (Miscellaneous Amendments) Regulations (Northern Ireland) 2000 (SI 2000 4).

4871. Industrial injuries – Compensation – Adjustments to lower rate of incapacity benefit

WORKMEN'S COMPENSATION (SUPPLEMENTATION) (AMENDMENT) REGULATIONS (NORTHERN IRELAND) 2005, SR 2005 142; made under the Social Security Contributions and Benefits (Northern Ireland) Act 1992 s.171, Sch.8 para.2; and the Social Security Administration (Northern Ireland) Act 1992 Sch.6 para.1. In force: April 13, 2005; £3.00.

These Regulations, which revoke the Workmen's Compensation (Supplementation) (Amendment) Regulations (Northern Ireland) 2004 (SR 2004 101), amend the Workmen's Compensation (Supplementation) Regulations (Northern Ireland) 1983 (SR 1983 101) by increasing the lower rates of lesser incapacity allowance consequential upon the increase in the maximum rate of that allowance made by the Social Security Benefits Up-rating Order (Northern Ireland) 2005 (SR 2005 96).

4872. Industrial injuries – Dependants – Permitted earnings limits

SOCIAL SECURITY (INDUSTRIAL INJURIES) (DEPENDENCY) (PERMITTED EARNINGS LIMITS) ORDER (NORTHERN IRELAND) 2005, SR 2005 95; made under the Social Security Contributions and Benefits (Northern Ireland) Act 1992 s.171, Sch.7 para.4. In force: April 13, 2005; £3.00.

Where a disablement pension with unemployability supplement is increased in respect of a child or children and the beneficiary is one of two persons who are spouses residing together or an unmarried couple, the Social Security Contributions and Benefits (Northern Ireland) Act 1992 provides that the increase shall not be payable in respect of the first child if the other person's earnings are £165 a week or more and in respect of a further child for each complete £21 by which the earnings exceed £165. This Order, which revokes the Social Security (Industrial Injuries) (Dependency) (Permitted Earnings Limits) Order (Northern Ireland) 2004 (SR 2004 84) and amends the Social Security Contributions and Benefits (Northern Ireland) Act 1992, substitutes the amount of £170 for the amount of £165 and the amount of £22 for the amount of £21.

4873. National insurance–Contributions

See SOCIAL SECURITY. §3890

4874. Nursing homes–Residential care homes–Independent hospitals–New regulatory system

SOCIAL SECURITY (RESIDENTIAL CARE HOMES, NURSING HOMES AND INDEPENDENT HOSPITALS) REGULATIONS (NORTHERN IRELAND) 2005, SR 2005 458; made under the Social Security Contributions and Benefits (Northern Ireland) Act 1992 s.67, s.72, s.122, s.129, s.131, s.132, s.132A, s.133, s.134, s.171; the Social Security Administration (Northern Ireland) Act 1992 s.1, s.5, s.165; the Social Security Fraud Act (Northern Ireland) 2001 s.6, s.7; the State Pension Credit Act (Northern Ireland) 2002 s.2, s.6, s.15, s.17, s.19; and the Jobseekers (Northern Ireland) Order 1995 (SI 1995 2705 (NI.15)) Art.6, Art.14, Art.22, Art.22B, Sch.1 para.1, Sch.1 para.8, Sch.1 para.8A, Sch.1 para.10, Sch.1 para.12. In force: November 14, 2005; £4.00.

These Regulations, which revoke the Income Support and Jobseeker's Allowance (Amounts for Persons in Residential Care and Nursing Homes) Regulations (Northern Ireland) 2001 (SR 2001 227), amend the Social Fund (Maternity and Funeral Expenses) (General) Regulations (Northern Ireland) 1987 (SR 1987 150), the Income Support (General) Regulations (Northern Ireland) 1987 (SR 1987 459), the Housing Benefit (General) Regulations (Northern Ireland) 1987 (SR 1987 461), the Social Security (Claims and Payments) Regulations (Northern Ireland) 1987 (SR 1987 465), the Social Fund (Cold Weather Payments) (General) Regulations (Northern Ireland) 1988 (SR 1988 368), the Social Security (Claims and Payments) (Amendment No.2) Regulations (Northern Ireland) 1989 (SR 1989 398), the Social Security (Miscellaneous Provisions) (Amendment) Regulations (Northern Ireland) 1991 (SR 1991 488), the Social Security (Attendance Allowance) Regulations (Northern Ireland) 1992 (SR 1992 20), the Social Security (Disability Living Allowance) Regulations (Northern Ireland) 1992 (SR 1992 32), the Social Security Benefits (Amendments Consequential Upon the Introduction of Community Care) Regulations (Northern Ireland) 1993 (SR 1993 149), the Jobseeker's Allowance Regulations (Northern Ireland) 1996 (SR 1996 198), the Social Fund Winter Fuel Payment Regulations (Northern Ireland) 2000 (SR 2000 91), the Social Security (Loss of Benefit) Regulations (Northern Ireland) 2002 (SR 2002 79), the Social Security (Amendment) (Residential Care and Nursing Homes) Regulations (Northern Ireland) 2002 (SR 2002 132), the State Pension Credit Regulations (Northern Ireland) 2003 (SR 2003 28) and the State Pension Credit (Consequential, Transitional and Miscellaneous Provisions) Regulations (Northern Ireland) 2003 (SR 2003 191). The Regulations make amendments to social security legislation that are consequential upon the introduction of a new regulatory system in Northern Ireland of "residential care homes", "nursing homes" and "independent hospitals" by the Health and Personal Social Services (Quality, Improvement and Regulation) (Northern Ireland) Order 2003 (SI 2003 431 (NI.9)).

4875. Pensions–Earnings factors–Calculation of additional pension

SOCIAL SECURITY REVALUATION OF EARNINGS FACTORS ORDER (NORTHERN IRELAND) 2005, SR 2005 33; made under the Social Security Administration (Northern Ireland) Act 1992 s.130, s.165. In force: April 6, 2005; £3.00.

This Order directs that the earnings factors relevant to the calculation of the additional pension in the rate of any long term benefit or of any guaranteed minimum pension, or to any other calculation required under the Pension Schemes Act 1993 Part III, are to be increased for the tax years specified in the Schedule to the Order by the percentage of their amount specified in that Schedule. The Order also provides for the rounding of fractional amounts for earnings factors relevant to the calculation of the additional pension in the rate of any long term benefit.

4876. Pensions–Shared additional pension

SOCIAL SECURITY (SHARED ADDITIONAL PENSION) (MISCELLANEOUS AMENDMENTS) REGULATIONS (NORTHERN IRELAND) 2005, SR 2005 299; made under the Social Security Contributions and Benefits (Northern Ireland) Act 1992 s.54, s.113, s.171, Sch.5A para.1, Sch.5A para.3, Sch.5A para.5; and the Social Security Administration (Northern Ireland) Act 1992 s.1, s.5, s.69, s.71, s.165. In force: in accordance with Reg.1 (1); £3.00.

These Regulations amend the Social Security Benefit (Persons Abroad) Regulations (Northern Ireland) 1978 (SR 1978 114), the Social Security (Overlapping Benefits) Regulations (Northern Ireland) 1979 (SR 1979 242), the Social Security (Widow's Benefit and Retirement Pensions) Regulations (Northern Ireland) 1979 (SR 1979 243), the Social Security (General Benefit) Regulations (Northern Ireland) 1984 (SR 1984 92), the Social Security (Claims and Payments) Regulations (Northern Ireland) 1987 (SR 1987 465), the Social Security (Payments on account, Overpayments and Recovery) Regulations (Northern Ireland) 1988 (SR 1988 142) and the Social Security (Deferral of Retirement Pensions) Regulations (Northern Ireland) 2005 (SR 2005 120). The Regulations make provision for claiming and paying Shared Additional Pension.

4877. Pensions–State pension credit–Assessed income

STATE PENSION CREDIT (AMENDMENT) REGULATIONS (NORTHERN IRELAND) 2005, SR 2005 513; made under the Social Security Contributions and Benefits (Northern Ireland) Act 1992 s.171; and the State Pension Credit Act (Northern Ireland) 2002 s.7, s.16, s.19. In force: December 18, 2005; £3.00.

These Regulations amend the State Pension Credit Regulations (Northern Ireland) 2003 (SR 2003 28) by removing the references to the claimant's retirement pension scheme or annuity contract. The effect of this is that where the arrangements under which the assessed amount is paid contain no provision for periodic increases in the amount payable, the claimant's assessed amount is deemed not to change during their assessed income period. They also remove the same references from the definition of "increased payment date"; and add financial assistance scheme payments to the descriptions of income listed as retirement pension income in the State Pension Credit Act (Northern Ireland) 2002.

4878. SERPS–State pension–Civil partnerships

SOCIAL SECURITY (INHERITED SERPS) (AMENDMENTS RELATING TO CIVIL PARTNERSHIP) REGULATIONS (NORTHERN IRELAND) 2005, SR 2005 496; made under the Welfare Reform and Pensions (Northern Ireland) Order 1 (SI 1 3147 (NI.11) Art.49, Art.73. In force: December 5, 2005; £3.00.

These Regulations amend the Social Security (Inherited SERPS) Regulations (Northern Ireland) 2001 (SR 2001 441) to extend the provisions of the Social Security (Inherited SERPS) Regulations (Northern Ireland) 2001 to surviving civil partners. They provide for the citation and commencement of the Regulations; make provision for a surviving civil partner, whose civil partner dies on or after December 5, 2005, to receive an increase in the rate of the additional pension under the State Earnings Related Pensions Scheme (SERPS) in the same way as a widower; and extend to surviving civil partners the provisions in the 2001 Regulations relating to the proportion of the additional pension used in the calculation of inheritable increments or a lump sum.

4879. SERPS–State pension–Deferment

SOCIAL SECURITY (INHERITED SERPS) (AMENDMENT) REGULATIONS (NORTHERN IRELAND) 2005, SR 2005 124; made under the Welfare Reform and Pensions (Northern Ireland) Order 1999 (SI 1999 3147 (NI.11)) Art.49, Art.73. In force: April 6, 2005; £3.00.

These Regulations amend the Social Security (Inherited SERPS) Regulations (Northern Ireland) 2001 (SR 2001 441) and make provision relating to changes to the regime for deferring entitlement to state pension made by the Pensions (Northern Ireland) Order 2005 (SI 2005 255).

4880. Social fund–Cold weather payments

SOCIAL FUND (COLD WEATHER PAYMENTS) (GENERAL) (AMENDMENT) REGULATIONS (NORTHERN IRELAND) 2005, SR 2005 447; made under the Social Security Contributions and Benefits (Northern Ireland) Act 1992 s.134, s.171. In force: November 1, 2005; £3.00.

These Regulations amend the Social Fund (Cold Weather Payments) (General) Regulations (Northern Ireland) 1988 (SR 1988 368) to omit a number of definitions for terms which are no longer used; amend the definition of "claimant" by adding references to "income-based jobseeker's allowance" and "state pension credit"; amend the definition of "postcode"; and add a definition of "state pension credit".

4881. Social security administration–Statutory maternity and sick pay–Production of documentation by employers

STATUTORY SICK PAY (GENERAL) AND STATUTORY MATERNITY PAY (GENERAL) (AMENDMENT) REGULATIONS (NORTHERN IRELAND) 2005, SR 2005 188; made under the Social Security Administration (Northern Ireland) Act 1992 s.107, s.122, s.124, s.165. In force: in accordance with Reg.1 (1); £3.00.

These Regulations, which revoke the Statutory Maternity Pay (General) and Statutory Sick Pay (General) (Amendment) Regulations (Northern Ireland) 2001 (SR 2001 36), amend the Statutory Sick Pay (General) Regulations (Northern Ireland) 1982 (SR 1982 263) and the Statutory Maternity Pay (General) Regulations (Northern Ireland) 1987 (SR 1987 30). The Regulations require employers to produce records relating to statutory sick pay to an authorised officer of the Inland Revenue within 30 days of a notice being issued to that effect; specify the types of documents that must be produced, where production must take place and that production does not affect any lien over the records; and make similar provision in relation to statutory maternity pay.

4882. State pension credit–Grants

INCOME-RELATED BENEFITS (AMENDMENT NO.2) REGULATIONS (NORTHERN IRELAND) 2005, SR 2005 550; made under the Social Security Contributions and Benefits (Northern Ireland) Act 1992 s.122, s.132, s.132A, s.134, s.171; the State Pension Credit Act (Northern Ireland) 2002 s.15, s.19; the Jobseekers (Northern Ireland) Order 1995 (SI 1995 2705 (NI.15)) Art.14, Art.36; and the Social Security (Recovery of Benefits) (Northern Ireland) Order (SI 1997 1183 (NI.12)) Sch.1 para.8. In force: December 12, 2005; £3.00.

These Regulations, which revoke the Income-related Benefits (Amendment) Regulations (Northern Ireland) 2005 (SR 2005 374), amend the Income Support (General) Regulations (Northern Ireland) 1987 (SR 1987 459), the Housing Benefit (General) Regulations (Northern Ireland) 1987 (SR 1987 461), the Jobseeker's Allowance Regulations (Northern Ireland) 1996 (SR 1996 198), the Social Security (Recovery of Benefits) Regulations (Northern Ireland) 1997 (SR 1997 429), the State Pension Credit Regulations (Northern Ireland) 2003 (SR 2003 28) and the Social Fund Maternity and Funeral Expenses (General) Regulations (Northern Ireland) 2005 (SR 2005 506). They make provision for grants paid by the London Bombings Relief Charitable Fund, and certain payments derived from these grants, to be disregarded when calculating that person's capital or income for the purpose of an award of benefit.

4883. State pension credit–Interim assistance grant

INCOME-RELATED BENEFITS (AMENDMENT) REGULATIONS (NORTHERN IRELAND) 2005, SR 2005 374; made under the Social Security Contributions and Benefits (Northern Ireland) Act 1992 s.122, s.132, s.171; the State Pension

Credit Act (Northern Ireland) 2002 s.15, s.19; and the Jobseekers (Northern Ireland) Order 1995 (SI 1995 2705 (NI.15)) Art.14, Art.36. In force: August 9, 2005; £3.00.

These Regulations amend the Income Support (General) Regulations (Northern Ireland) 1987 (SR 1987 459), the Housing Benefit (General) Regulations (Northern Ireland) 1987 (SR 1987 461) and the Jobseeker's Allowance Regulations (Northern Ireland) 1996 (SR 1996 198) so as to make provision for an interim assistance grant paid by the London Bombings Relief Charitable Fund to a person who was injured, or was a partner or close relative of someone killed, in or as a result of the terrorist attacks carried out in London on July 7, 2005, to be disregarded when calculating that person's capital for the purpose of an award of benefit where the grant is paid during the award. The disregard will last for the remainder of that award (or further awards if there is no break in-between). They also amend the State Pension Credit Regulations (Northern Ireland) 2003 (SR 2003 28) so as to provide for an interim assistance grant paid by that Fund to a person who was a partner or close relative of someone killed in, or as a result of, those attacks to be disregarded when calculating that person's income from capital for the purpose of an award of state pension credit where the grant is paid during the award. The disregard will last for the remainder of that award.

4884. State retirement pension–Claims

SOCIAL SECURITY (CLAIMS AND PAYMENTS) (AMENDMENT) REGULATIONS (NORTHERN IRELAND) 2005, SR 2005 122; made under the Social Security Administration (Northern Ireland) Act 1992 s.5, s.165. In force: in accordance with Reg.1 (1); £3.00.

These Regulations amend the Social Security (Claims and Payments) Regulations (Northern Ireland) 1987 (SR 1987 465) in respect of claims for retirement pension or graduated retirement benefit. They provide for claims for a Category A or Category B retirement pension or graduated retirement benefit to be made in advance of the date on which a period of deferment ends; provide that the time for claiming retirement pension or graduated retirement benefit for any day on which the claimant is entitled to the pension or benefit is the period of 12 months immediately following that day, instead of the period of 3 months beginning with that day; and make further provision for claims for a Category A or Category B retirement pension and graduated retirement benefit made on behalf of a person who has died.

4885. State retirement pension–Deferment

SOCIAL SECURITY (DEFERRAL OF RETIREMENT PENSIONS) REGULATIONS (NORTHERN IRELAND) 2005, SR 2005 120; made under the Social Security Contributions and Benefits (Northern Ireland) Act 1992 s.54, s.171, Sch.5 para.2, Sch.5 para.3, Sch.5 para.3B, Sch.5 para.7B. In force: April 6, 2005; £3.00.

These Regulations amend the Social Security (Widow's Benefit and Retirement Pensions) Regulations (Northern Ireland) 1979 (SR 1979 243), the Social Security (Miscellaneous Provisions) Regulations (Northern Ireland) 1989 (SR 1989 193) and the Social Security (Abolition of Earnings Rule) (Consequential) Regulations (Northern Ireland) 1989 (SR 1989 373), and make provision relating to changes to the regime for deferring entitlement to state pension made and brought forward by the Pensions (Northern Ireland) Order 2005 (SI 2005 255 (NI.1)), which provide, in particular, for an increased incremental rate for those deferring their state pension and for a choice between increments and a lump sum for those who have deferred their entitlement for 12 months or more.

4886. State retirement pension–Home responsibilities

SOCIAL SECURITY PENSIONS (HOME RESPONSIBILITIES) (AMENDMENT) REGULATIONS (NORTHERN IRELAND) 2005, SR 2005 16; made under the

Social Security Contributions and Benefits (Northern Ireland) Act 1992 s.121, s.171, Sch.3 para.5. In force: February 23, 2005; £3.00.

These Regulations amend the Social Security Pensions (Home Responsibilities) Regulations (Northern Ireland) 1994 (SI 1994 89) to provide that from the tax year 2004-2005 onwards where child benefit entitlement is transferred to a person in respect of a child in the first three months of a tax year and child benefit would have been payable to that person for the part of that year falling before that transfer but for the provisions of the Child Benefit (General) Regulations 2003 (SI 2003 493), that person shall be treated as if he were entitled to child benefit and as if child benefit had been payable to him for that part of that year, in order to be treated for the purpose of the 1994 Regulations as precluded from regular employment in that year due to responsibilities at home.

4887. State retirement pension–Low earnings threshold

SOCIAL SECURITY PENSIONS (LOW EARNINGS THRESHOLD) ORDER (NORTHERN IRELAND) 2005, SR 2005 34; made under the Social Security Administration (Northern Ireland) Act 1992 s.130A. In force: April 6, 2005; £3.00.

This Order directs that the low earnings threshold for the tax years following 2004-2005 shall be £12,100.

4888. Statutory maternity pay–Entitlement

STATUTORY MATERNITY PAY (GENERAL) (AMENDMENT NO.2) REGULATIONS (NORTHERN IRELAND) 2005, SR 2005 134; made under the Social Contributions and Benefits (Northern Ireland) Act 1992 s.160, s.167, s.171. In force: April 6, 2005; £3.00.

These Regulations amend the Statutory Maternity Pay (General) Regulations (Northern Ireland) 1987 (SR 1987 30) and the Statutory Maternity Pay (General) (Amendment) Regulations (Northern Ireland) 1996 (SI 1996 206) to include in normal weekly earnings for the purpose of calculating entitlement to statutory maternity pay any pay increase which applies to the whole or any part of the period between the beginning of the period when pay is calculated to determine entitlement to statutory maternity pay and the end of the period of statutory maternity leave. They also provide that where a woman who is entitled to statutory maternity pay in consequence of a pay increase referred to in Reg.21 (7) of the 1987 Regulations, the employer shall only make payments of statutory maternity pay in any week if, and to the extent that, her statutory maternity pay exceeds any maternity allowance received by her.

4889. Students–Income related benefits

SOCIAL SECURITY (STUDENTS AND INCOME-RELATED BENEFITS) (AMENDMENT) REGULATIONS (NORTHERN IRELAND) 2005, SR 2005 332; made under the Social Security Contributions and Benefits (Northern Ireland) Act 1992 s.122, s.132, s.171; and the Jobseekers (Northern Ireland) Order 1995 (SI 1995 2705 (NI.15)) Art.14, Art.36. In force: in accordance with Reg.1; £3.00.

These Regulations amend the Housing Benefit (General) Regulations (Northern Ireland) 1987 (SR 1987 461), the Income Support (General) Regulations (Northern Ireland) 1987 (SR 1987 459) and the Jobseeker's Allowance Regulations (Northern Ireland) 1996 (SR 1996 198) in so far as they relate to students and sums to be disregarded in the calculation of their entitlement to benefit. The Regulations increase the amounts of grant and loan income to be disregarded in respect of travel costs and the costs of books and equipment; and to take account of changes to the provision of support to students.

4890. Tax credits–Child support–Miscellaneous amendments

SOCIAL SECURITY, CHILD SUPPORT AND TAX CREDITS (MISCELLANEOUS AMENDMENTS) REGULATIONS (NORTHERN IRELAND) 2005, SR 2005 46; made under the Child Support (Northern Ireland) Order 1991 (SI 1991 2628

(NI.23)) Art.22; the Social Security Contributions and Benefits (Northern Ireland) Act 1992 s.122, s.123, s.171; the Social Security Administration (Northern Ireland) Act 1992 s.5, s.5A, s.69, s.72, s.165; the Social Security (Recovery of Benefits) (Northern Ireland) Order (SI 1997 1183 (NI.12)) Art.13; the Social Security (Northern Ireland) Order 1998 (SI 1998 1506) Art.7, Art.10, Art.11, Art.13, Art.15, Art.16, Art.17, Art.28, Art.74, Sch.4 para.1, Sch.4 para.3, Sch.4 para.4, Sch.4 para.6; and the Child Support, Pensions and Social Security Act (Northern Ireland) 2000 Sch.7 para.3, Sch.7 para.6, Sch.7 para.10, Sch.7 para.20. In force: March 18, 2005; £3.00.

These Regulations amend the Social Security (Industrial Injuries) (Prescribed Diseases) Regulations (Northern Ireland) 1986 (SR 1986 179), the Income Support (General) Regulations (Northern Ireland) 1987 (SI 1987 459), the Housing Benefit (General) Regulations (Northern Ireland) 1987 (SI 1987 461), the Social Security (Claims and Payments) Regulations (Northern Ireland) 1987 (SR 1987 465), the Social Security (Payments on account, Overpayments and Recovery) Regulations (Northern Ireland) 1988 (SR 1988 142), the Social Security (Persons from Abroad) (Miscellaneous Amendments) Regulations (Northern Ireland) 1996 (SR 1996 11), the Social Security and Child Support (Miscellaneous Amendments) Regulations (Northern Ireland) 2000 (SR 2000 215), the Social Security and Child Support (Miscellaneous Amendments) Regulations (Northern Ireland) 2002 (SR 2002 164), the Social Security and Child Support (Decisions and Appeals) (Miscellaneous Amendments) Regulations (Northern Ireland) 2002 (SR 2002 189), and the Social Security, Child Support and Tax Credits (Decisions and Appeals) (Amendment) Regulations (Northern Ireland) 2004 (SR 2004 516). They provide for the finality of a specified determination necessary to a benefit decision; make further provision in respect of specified benefit claims made to a relevant authority or designated office, the date of claim in relation to different benefits, claims for attendance allowance before existing awards expire, those appointed to act on behalf of a claimant and extinguishment of the right to payment of benefit; and provide for an interim payment where it is impractical to satisfy national insurance number requirements, the recovery of duplicate payments of benefit from payments of contribution-based jobseeker's allowance, the recovery of overpayments without prior revision or supersession of the original decision awarding benefit, clarification of the limitations on the right to deduct recoverable overpayments from prescribed benefits.

4891. Unfair dismissal – Continuity of employment

STATUTORY PATERNITY PAY AND STATUTORY ADOPTION PAY (GENERAL) (AMENDMENT) REGULATIONS (NORTHERN IRELAND) 2005, SR 2005 167; made under the Social Security Contributions and Benefits (Northern Ireland) Act 1992 s.167ZC, s.167ZL, s.171. In force: April 6, 2005; £3.00.

These Regulations amend the Statutory Paternity Pay and Statutory Adoption Pay (General) Regulations (Northern Ireland) 2002 (SR 2002 378) to provide for continuity of employment in respect of a dismissal where a person commences a statutory dispute resolution procedure and as a consequence is reinstated or re-engaged by their employer. The amendment has effect in relation to a reinstatement or re-engagement occurring on or after April 6, 2005.

4892. Unfair dismissal, continuity of employment

STATUTORY MATERNITY PAY (GENERAL) (AMENDMENT) REGULATIONS (NORTHERN IRELAND) 2005, SR 2005 62; made under the Social Security Contributions and Benefits (Northern Ireland) Act 1992 s.160, s.171. In force: April 6, 2005; £3.00.

These Regulations amend the Statutory Maternity Pay (General) Regulations (Northern Ireland) 1987 (SR 1987 30) to provide for continuity of employment in respect of a dismissal where a woman commences a statutory dispute resolution procedure and as a consequence of that procedure is reinstated or re-engaged by her employer. The amendment has effect in relation to a reinstatement or re-engagement of employment occurring on or after April 6, 2005.

SOCIAL WELFARE

4893. Care–Children–Local authorities duties

CHILDREN (LEAVING CARE) REGULATIONS (NORTHERN IRELAND) 2005, SR 2005 221; made under the Children (Northern Ireland) Order (SI 1995 755 (NI.2)) Art.34A, Art.34B, Art.34C, Art.34E, Art.34F, Art.35B, Art.35D. In force: September 1, 2005; £3.00.

These Regulations, which amend the Representations Procedure (Children) Regulations (Northern Ireland) 1996 (SR 1996 451), make provision about support for children and young people aged 16 and over who are, or have been, looked after by an authority. They prescribe further categories of children to whom authorities will, or as the case may be, will not, owe additional duties as provided for in the Children (Northern Ireland) Order 1995 (SI 1995 755 (NI.2)). The Regulations make provision about the assessment of needs, the preparation and review of pathway plans, and the keeping of records; make provision about assistance with education and training, and accommodation; and prescribes the functions of a personal adviser.

4894. Care proceedings–Care Tribunal

CARE TRIBUNAL REGULATIONS (NORTHERN IRELAND) 2005, SR 2005 178; made under the Health and Personal Social Services (Quality, Improvement and Regulation) (Northern Ireland) Order 2003 (SI 2003 431 (NI.9)) Art.44, Art.48, Sch.2 para.2. In force: April 1, 2005; £6.00.

These Regulations, which revoke the Social Care Tribunal Rules (Northern Ireland) 2003 (SR 2003 138), make provision about the proceedings of the Care Tribunal established by the Health and Personal Social Services (Quality, Improvement and Regulation) (Northern Ireland) Order 2003 (SI 2003 431 (NI.9)).

4895. Children (Leaving Care) Act (Northern Ireland) 2002 (c.11)–Commencement No.1 Order

CHILDREN LEAVING CARE (2002 ACT) (COMMENCEMENT NO.1) ORDER (NORTHERN IRELAND) 2005, SR 2005 189 (C.13); made under the Children (Leaving Care) Act (Northern Ireland) 2002 s.9. In force: bring into operation various provisions of the 2002 Act on April 25, 2005 and September 1, 2005; £3.00.

This Order brings into operation provisions of the Children (Leaving Care) Act (Northern Ireland) 2002 which amend the Children (Northern Ireland) Order (SI 1995 755 (NI.2)) as regards the arrangements to be made for the care and support of children who are, or have been looked after by Health and Social Services Trusts.

4896. Children (Leaving Care) Act (Northern Ireland) 2002 (c.11)–Commencement No.2 and Consequential Provisions Order

CHILDREN (LEAVING CARE) (2002 ACT) (COMMENCEMENT NO.2 AND CONSEQUENTIAL PROVISIONS) ORDER (NORTHERN IRELAND) 2005, SR 2005 319 (C.23); made under the Children (Leaving Care) Act (Northern Ireland) 2002 s.9. In force: bringing into operation various provisions of the 2002 Act on June 30, 2005 and September 1, 2005; £3.00.

This Order, which amends the Income Support (General) Regulations (Northern Ireland) 1987 (SR 1987 459), the Housing Benefit (General) Regulations (Northern Ireland) 1987 (SR 1987 461) and the Jobseeker's Allowance Regulations (Northern Ireland) 1996 (SR 1996 198), provides that the Children

(Leaving Care) Act (Northern Ireland) 2002 s.6 shall come into operation on June 30, 2005 for the purpose of making Regulations and on September 1, 2005 for all other purposes.

4897. Childrens welfare – Childrens homes – Registration and inspection

CHILDREN'S HOMES REGULATIONS (NORTHERN IRELAND) 2005, SR 2005 176; made under the Health and Personal Social Services (Quality, Improvement and Regulation) (Northern Ireland) Order 2003 (SI 2003 431 (NI.9)) Art.9, Art.23, Art.25, Art.30, Art.31, Art.32, Art.48. In force: April 1, 2005; £5.50.

The Health and Personal Social Services (Quality, Improvement and Regulation) (Northern Ireland) Order 2003 (SI 2003 431 (NI.9)) establishes, the Northern Ireland Health and Personal Social Services Regulation and Improvement Authority and provides for the registration and inspection of establishments and agencies, including children's homes, by the Regulation and Improvement Authority. It also provides powers for regulations governing the conduct of establishments and agencies. These new arrangements replace the regulatory system in relation to children's homes provided for by the Children (Northern Ireland) Order 1995 (SI 1995 755 (NI.2)), and these Regulations supersede the Children's Homes Regulations (Northern Ireland) 1996 (SR 1996 479). The Regulations, which amend the Health Services (Pilot Schemes: Miscellaneous Provisions and Consequential Amendments) Regulations (Northern Ireland) 1 (SR 1 100), exclude certain establishments from the definition of a children's home. These include establishments providing short-term overnight care, holidays, or other activities for less than 28 days a year in relation to any one child, and a wide range of establishments providing accommodation for those aged 16 or over, unless in either case, the establishment mainly accommodates children who are disabled. Further education colleges and establishments for young offenders are also excluded. The Regulations make provision about the persons carrying on and managing the home, and require satisfactory information to be available in relation to prescribed matters; make provision about the conduct of children's homes, in particular, as to welfare, health, education and religious observance, arrangements for contact and visitors, the management of behaviour, and the use of surveillance devices; and make provision about the suitability of premises, and the fire precautions to be taken.

4898. Health and Personal Social Services Act (Northern Ireland) 2001 (c.3) – Commencement No.7 Order

HEALTH AND PERSONAL SOCIAL SERVICES (2001 ACT) (COMMENCEMENT NO.7) ORDER (NORTHERN IRELAND) 2005, SR 2005 226 (C.15); made under the Health and Personal Social Services Act (Northern Ireland) 2001 s.57, s.61. In force: bringing into operation various provisions of the 2001 Act on April 26, 2005, June 1, 2005 and December 1, 2005; £3.00.

This Order brings into operation provisions of the Health and Personal Social Services Act (Northern Ireland) 2001 for the purpose of making regulations which will prescribe the registers maintained under legislation in England, Wales and Scotland which correspond to the provisions of the 2001 Act under which the register is maintained by the Northern Ireland Social Care Council; which provide for the protection of the title "social worker" by the creation of an offence, punishable by a fine of up to level 5 on the standard scale, for a person who is not registered as a social worker to use that title or hold himself out as a registered social worker with an intention to deceive; and enable the Department to make regulations to prohibit persons from working in certain categories of employment unless they are registered in an appropriate part of a relevant register.

4899. Health and Personal Social Services (Quality, Improvement and Regulation) (NI) Order 2003 (SI 2003 431 (NI.9))–Commencement No.3 Order

HEALTH AND PERSONAL SOCIAL SERVICES (QUALITY, IMPROVEMENT AND REGULATION) (2003 ORDER) (COMMENCEMENT NO.3 AND TRANSITIONAL PROVISIONS) ORDER (NORTHERN IRELAND) 2005, SR 2005 44 (C.4); made under the Health and Personal Social Services (Quality, Improvement and Regulation) (Northern Ireland) Order 2003 (SI 2003 431 (NI.9)) Art.1, Art.48. In force: bringing into operation various provisions of the 2003 Order on March 1, 2005 and April 1, 2005; £3.00.

This Order brings into operation various provisions of the Health and Personal Social Services (Quality, Improvement and Regulation) (Northern Ireland) Order 2003 (SI 2003 431 (NI.9)) relating to powers of the Regulation and Improvement Authority for regulation and registration of children's homes; independent clinics; independent hospitals; nursing homes; residential care homes; independent medical agencies and nursing agencies and right of appeal to, and provision for the Care Tribunal.

4900. Nursing homes–Registration and inspection

NURSING HOMES REGULATIONS (NORTHERN IRELAND) 2005, SR 2005 160; made under the Health and Personal Social Services (Quality, Improvement and Regulation) (Northern Ireland) Order 2003 (SI 2003 431 (NI.9)) Art.23, Art.25, Art.30, Art.31, Art.32, Art.48. In force: April 1, 2005; £4.00.

These Regulations are made under the Health and Personal Social Services (Quality, Improvement and Regulation) (Northern Ireland) Order 2003 (SI 2003 431 (NI.9)). The Order establishes the Northern Ireland Health and Personal Social Services Regulation and Improvement Authority and provides for the registration and inspection of establishments and agencies, including nursing homes, by the Regulation and Improvement Authority. It also provides powers for regulations governing the conduct of establishments and agencies. These new arrangements replace the regulatory system provided for in relation to nursing homes by the Registered Homes (Northern Ireland) Order 1992 (SI 1992 3204 (NI.20)). Under these Regulations, which revoke the Nursing Homes Regulations (Northern Ireland) 1993 (SR 1993 92) and the Nursing Homes (Amendment) Regulations (Northern Ireland) 1998 (SR 1998 140), each home must have a statement of purpose consisting of the matters set out in Sch.1, and supply a guide of the nursing home to each patient together with a statement giving information about fees payable. The Regulations make provision about the fitness of the persons carrying on and managing the nursing home, and require satisfactory information to be available in relation to certain specified matters; make provision about the conduct of nursing homes, in particular as to health and welfare of patients, and as to the facilities and services that are to be provided; make provision about the suitability of premises and fire precautions to be taken; and deal with miscellaneous matters including the giving of notices to the Regulation and Improvement Authority.

4901. Residential care–Assessment of resources–Qualifying income–Sums to be disregarded

HEALTH AND PERSONAL SOCIAL SERVICES (ASSESSMENT OF RESOURCES) (AMENDMENT) REGULATIONS (NORTHERN IRELAND) 2005, SR 2005 103; made under the Health and Personal Social Services (Northern Ireland) Order 1972 (SI 1972 1265 (NI.14)) Art.36, Art.99. In force: April 11, 2005; £3.00.

These Regulations, which amend the Health and Personal Social Services (Assessment of Resources) Regulations (Northern Ireland) 1993 (SR 1993 127), increase the capital limit set out in Reg.20 to £20,500; increase the capital limits set out in Reg.28(1) to £12,500 and £20,500; provide for an increase to £4.85 in the case of an individual or £7.20 for a couple of the amount of savings credit to be disregarded in calculating a resident's income; and provide a capital disregard for payments made under Art.4 or Art.5 of the Age-Related Payments (Northern Ireland) Order 2004 (SI 2004 1987 (NI.11)).

4902. Residential care–Residential care homes–Registration and inspection

RESIDENTIAL CARE HOMES REGULATIONS (NORTHERN IRELAND) 2005, SR 2005 161; made under the Health and Personal Social Services (Quality, Improvement and Regulation) (Northern Ireland) Order 2003 (SI 2003 431 (NI.9)) Art.23, Art.25, Art.30, Art.31, Art.32, Art.48. In force: April 1, 2005; £4.00.

The Health and Personal Social Services (Quality, Improvement and Regulation) (Northern Ireland) Order 2003 (SI 2003 431 (NI.9)) establishes the Northern Ireland Health and Personal Social Services Regulation and Improvement Authority and provides for the registration and inspection of establishments and agencies, including residential care homes, by the Regulation and Improvement Authority. It also provides powers for regulations governing the conduct of establishments and agencies. Under these Regulations, which revoke the Residential Care Homes Regulations (Northern Ireland) 1993 (SR 1993 91) and the Residential Care Homes (Amendment) Regulations (Northern Ireland) 1998 (SR 1998 139), each home must have a statement of purpose consisting of the matters specified, and supply a guide of the home to each resident together with a statement giving information about fees payable. They also make provision about the fitness of the persons carrying on and managing the home, and require satisfactory information to be available in relation to certain specified matters; make provision about the conduct of residential care homes, in particular as to the care, health, safety, welfare and protection of residents, and as to the facilities and services that are to be provided; and make provision about the suitability of premises and fire precautions to be taken.

4903. Social workers–Registration

REGISTRATION OF SOCIAL CARE WORKERS (RELEVANT REGISTERS) REGULATIONS (NORTHERN IRELAND) 2005, SR 2005 227; made under the Health and Personal Social Services Act (Northern Ireland) 2001 s.8, s.57. In force: June 1, 2005; £3.00.

These Regulations prescribe as relevant registers the registers maintained under provisions of the Care Standards Act 2000 and the Regulation of Care (Scotland) Act 2001 which appear to the Department of Health, Social Services and Public Safety to correspond to provisions of the 2001 Act.

TAX

4904. Budget (Northern Ireland) Order 2005 (SI 2005 860 (NI.3))

This Order authorises the issue out of the Consolidated Fund of Northern Ireland of certain sums for the service of the years ending March 31, 2005 and 2006 and appropriates those sums for specified purposes. The Order also authorises the use for the public service of certain resources for those years and revises the limits on the use of accruing resources in the year ending March 31, 2005.

4905. Budget (No.2) (Northern Ireland) Order 2005 (SI 2005 1962 (NI.12))

This Order authorises the issue out of the Consolidated Fund of Northern Ireland of a further sum for the services of the year ending March 31, 2006 and appropriates that sum for specified services in Northern Ireland. The Order also authorises the use for the public service of certain resources (including accruing resources) for the year ending March 31, 2006. In addition the Order authorises the use of excess amount of resources (including accruing resources) in respect of the year ending March 31, 2004. Finally the Order repeals the Budget Act (Northern Ireland) 2002 and the Budget (No.2) Act (Northern Ireland) 2002.

4906. Books

Smith, Kelly–Irish Tax Reports. Paperback: £56.66. ISBN 1 84592 201 8. Tottel Publishing.

Ward, John; Burke, Dara–Judge Irish Income Tax. Hardback: £86.66. ISBN 1 84592 146 1. Tottel Publishing.

TORTS

4907. Books

MacMahon, Bryan; Binchy, William–Casebook of Irish Law of Torts. Paperback: £80.00. ISBN 1 84592 031 7. Tottel Publishing.

Moore-Walsh, Kathleen–Make That Grade Irish Tort Law. Paperback: £14.99. ISBN 0 7171 4026 1. Gill & Macmillan.

TRANSPORT

4908. Heavy goods vehicles–Testing–Fees

GOODS VEHICLES (TESTING) (FEES) (AMENDMENT) REGULATIONS (NORTHERN IRELAND) 2005, SR 2005 406; made under the Road Traffic (Northern Ireland) Order 1995 (SI (1995 2994 (NI.18)) Art.65, Art.67, Art.110. In force: October 1, 2005; £3.00.

These Regulations amend the Goods Vehicles (Testing) Regulations (Northern Ireland) 2003 (SR 2003 304) by increasing specified fees relating to the testing of goods vehicles.

4909. Motor vehicles–Construction and use–Exhaust emissions

MOTOR VEHICLES (CONSTRUCTION AND USE) (AMENDMENT NO.3) REGULATIONS (NORTHERN IRELAND) 2005, SR 2005 402; made under the Road Traffic (Northern Ireland) Order 1995 (SI (1995 2994 (NI.18)) Art.55, Art.110. In force: October 1, 2005; £3.00.

These Regulations, which revoke the Motor Vehicles (Construction and Use) (Amendment No.4) Regulations (Northern Ireland) 2004 (SR 2004 356), amend the definition of "the emissions publication" in the Motor Vehicles (Construction and Use) Regulations (Northern Ireland) 1 (SR 1 454) so as to refer to the most recent edition of the publication entitled "In-Service Exhaust Emission Standards for Road Vehicles". The publication specifies, with respect to vehicles with spark ignition engines, the maximum permitted carbon monoxide content of exhaust emissions at idling speed and the limits for the ratio of air to petrol vapour entering the combustion chamber, in relation to each of the vehicle models named in the publication.

4910. Motor vehicles–Construction and use–Speed limitation devices

MOTOR VEHICLES (CONSTRUCTION AND USE) (AMENDMENT NO.2) REGULATIONS (NORTHERN IRELAND) 2005, SR 2005 249; made under the Road Traffic (Northern Ireland) Order 1995 (SI 1995 2994 (NI.18)) Art.55, Art.110. In force: June 20, 2005; £3.00.

These Regulations amend the Motor Vehicles (Construction and Use) Regulations (Northern Ireland) 1 (SR 1 454) in respect of the requirements for speed limiters on motor vehicles. They implement European Parliament and Directive 2002/85 ([2002] OJ L327/8) amending Council Directive 92/6 on the installation and use of speed limitation devices for certain categories of motor vehicles in the Community.

4911. Motor vehicles–Construction and use–Visual transmission

MOTOR VEHICLES (CONSTRUCTION AND USE) (AMENDMENT) REGULATIONS (NORTHERN IRELAND) 2005, SR 2005 22; made under the Road Traffic (Northern Ireland) Order 1995 (SI 1995 2994 (NI.18)) Art.55, Art.110. In force: April 22, 2005; £3.00.

These Regulations amend the Motor Vehicles (Construction and Use) Regulations (Northern Ireland) 1999 (SR 1999 454) in relation to the visual transmission requirements for light through windscreens and windows. They insert a new paragraph which expressly applies the requirements as to the visual transmission of windscreens and windows to any tint, film, other substance or material applied to a windscreen or window.

4912. Motor vehicles–Driving tests–Fees

MOTOR VEHICLES (DRIVING LICENCES) (AMENDMENT) (TEST FEES) REGULATIONS (NORTHERN IRELAND) 2005, SR 2005 403; made under the Road Traffic (Northern Ireland) Order 1981 (SI 1981 154 (NI.1)) Art.5, Art.218. In force: October 1, 2005; £3.00.

These Regulations amend the Motor Vehicles (Driving Licences) Regulations (Northern Ireland) 1996 (SR 1996 542) and revoke the Motor Vehicles (Driving Licences) (Amendment) (Test Fees) Regulations (Northern Ireland) 2003 (SR 2003 100) by increasing specified test fees.

4913. Motor vehicles–Road safety–Lighting

ROAD VEHICLES LIGHTING (AMENDMENT) REGULATIONS (NORTHERN IRELAND) 2005, SR 2005 1; made under the Road Traffic (Northern Ireland) Order 1995 (SI 1995 2994 (NI.18)) Art.55, Art.110. In force: March 31, 2005; £3.00.

These Regulations amend the Road Vehicles Lighting Regulations (Northern Ireland) 2000 (SR 2000 169) so as to specify different requirements for the alignment of dipped-beam headlamps for a vehicle having a maximum speed exceeding 25mph and a vehicle having a maximum speed not exceeding 25mph.

4914. Motor vehicles–Testing–Fees

MOTOR VEHICLE TESTING (AMENDMENT) (FEES) REGULATIONS (NORTHERN IRELAND) 2005, SR 2005 404; made under the Road Traffic (Northern Ireland) Order 1995 (SI 1995 2994 (NI.18)) Art.61(6), Art.62, Art.75(8), Art.81(8)(9), Art.110(2). In force: October 1, 2005; £3.00.

These Regulations amend the Motor Vehicle Testing Regulations (Northern Ireland) 2003 (SR 2003 303) by increasing most of the fees payable for examinations, re-examinations and appeals.

4915. Motor vehicles–Use of vehicles–Hearses

MOTOR VEHICLE TESTING (AMENDMENT) REGULATIONS (NORTHERN IRELAND) 2005, SR 2005 409; made under the Road Traffic (Northern Ireland) Order 1995 (SI 1995 2994 (NI.18)) Art.63, Art.110. In force: November 24, 2005; £3.00.

These Regulations amend the Motor Vehicle Testing Regulations (Northern Ireland) 2003 (SR 2003 303) to remove hearses from the use of vehicles to which the Road Traffic (Northern Ireland) Order 1995 (SI 1995 2994 (NI.18)) art.63(1) does not apply.

4916. Passenger vehicles–Goods vehicles–Tachographs

PASSENGER AND GOODS VEHICLES (RECORDING EQUIPMENT) (AMENDMENT) REGULATIONS (NORTHERN IRELAND) 2005, SR 2005 325;

made under the European Communities Act 1972 s.2. In force: July 25, 2005; £3.00.

These Regulations amend the Passenger and Goods Vehicles (Recording Equipment) Regulations (Northern Ireland) 1996 (SR 1996 145) so as to extend the current system for inspecting and checking recording equipment to include the work detailed in Council Regulation 2135/98 ([1998] OJ L274/1) amending Regulation 3821/85 on recording equipment in road transport and Directive 88/599 concerning the application of Regulations 3820/84 and 3821/85.

4917. Passenger vehicles–Goods vehicles–Tachographs

PASSENGER AND GOODS VEHICLES (RECORDING EQUIPMENT) (AMENDMENT NO.2) REGULATIONS (NORTHERN IRELAND) 2005, SR 2005 441; made under the European Communities Act 1972 s.2; and the Finance Act 1973 s.56. In force: October 31, 2005; £3.00.

These Regulations, which amend the Passenger and Goods Vehicles (Recording Equipment) Regulations (Northern Ireland) 1996 (SR 1996 145), provide for the issuing of driver cards, company cards and control cards for use with digital tachographs, which are tachographs complying with Annexes IB and II to the Council Regulation 3821/85 ([1985] OJ L370/8) on recording equipment in road transport, and for the replacement of cards which expire, are damaged, malfunction, are lost or are stolen. The Regulations also provide for the payment of specified fees in respect of driver cards, which are held by drivers of vehicles required to be fitted with digital tachographs by the Community Recording Equipment Regulation, and company cards, which are held by the operators of such vehicles.

4918. Passenger vehicles–Licensing–Fees

PUBLIC SERVICE VEHICLES (LICENCE FEES) (AMENDMENT) REGULATIONS (NORTHERN IRELAND) 2005, SR 2005 405; made under the Road Traffic (Northern Ireland) Order 1981 (SI 1981 154 (NI.1)) Art.61, Art.66, Art.218. In force: October 1, 2005; £3.00.

These Regulations amend the Public Service Vehicles Regulations (Northern Ireland) 1985 (SR 1985 123) by increasing specified fees relating to the initial application for a public service vehicle licence.

4919. Passenger vehicles–Public hire vehicles–Conditions of fitness

PUBLIC SERVICE VEHICLES (CONDITIONS OF FITNESS, EQUIPMENT AND USE) (AMENDMENT) REGULATIONS (NORTHERN IRELAND) 2005, SR 2005 270; made under the Road Traffic (Northern Ireland) Order 1981 (SI 1981 154 (NI.1)) Art.66, Art.218; and the Road Traffic (Northern Ireland) Order 1995 (SI 1995 2994 (NI.18)) Art.55, Art.110. In force: July 2, 2005; £3.00.

These Regulations amend the Public Service Vehicles (Conditions of Fitness, Equipment and Use) Regulations (Northern Ireland) 1995 (SI 1995 447) to require every vehicle licensed for public hire in the City of Belfast to have an effective means of communication between the passenger and the driver and where there is a sliding window fitted in the partition between the driver's seat and the passengers' compartment, the maximum width of the window opening shall not exceed 11.5 centimetres.

4920. Railways–Infrastructure–Access and management

RAILWAYS INFRASTRUCTURE (ACCESS, MANAGEMENT AND LICENSING OF RAILWAY UNDERTAKINGS) REGULATIONS (NORTHERN IRELAND) 2005, SR 2005 537; made under the European Communities Act 1972 s.2. In force: in accordance with Reg.1; £6.00.

These Regulations, which revoke the Railway Regulations (Northern Ireland) 2003 (SR 2003 53), implement Council Directive 91/44 ([1991] OJ L237/25) on the development of the Community's railways; Council Directive 95/18

([1995] OJ L143/70) on the licensing of railway undertakings; and Council Directive 2001/14 ([2001] OJ L75/26) on the allocation of railway infrastructure capacity and the levying of charges for the use of railway infrastructure. They grant access and transit rights to international groupings and freight operators to the Northern Ireland rail network; impose certain separation requirements between the bodies responsible for management of the railway infrastructure and railway undertakings; set out the structure for the charging of fees for use of railway infrastructure, and the charging principles; set out the framework and timetable for the process of allocating infrastructure capacity; allocate certain regulatory functions to the Department for Regional Development; and impose requirements for licensing of railway undertakings.

4921. Road transport–Passenger vehicles cabotage–Criminal offences

ROAD TRANSPORT (PASSENGER VEHICLES CABOTAGE) REGULATIONS (NORTHERN IRELAND) 2005, SR 2005 212; made under the European Communities Act 1972 s.2. In force: May 26, 2005; £3.00.

These Regulations, which amend the Transport Act (Northern Ireland) 1967 and the Road Traffic (Northern Ireland) Order 1981 (SI 1981 154 (NI.1)), implement Council Regulation 12/98 ([1998] OJ L4/10) laying down the conditions under which non-resident carriers may operate national road passenger transport services within a Member State. The Regulations make it a criminal offence to carry out a cabotage transport operation without a Community licence; fail without reasonable cause to produce the Community licence or a certified copy; use the vehicle in contravention of the requirement; and fail without reasonable cause to produce the control document. They also provide that the Department is the competent authority to communicate with the Commission; the Department shall be the competent authority to impose an administrative penalty; for police constables and examiners to be authorised inspecting officers; and for criminal offences in certain circumstances to be committed by a director, manager, secretary or similar officer of a body corporate.

4922. Road transport–Working time

ROAD TRANSPORT (WORKING TIME) REGULATIONS (NORTHERN IRELAND) 2005, SR 2005 241; made under the European Communities Act 1972 s.2. In force: June 16, 2005; £3.00.

These Regulations implement the provisions of Council Directive 2002/15 ([2002] OJ L80/35) on the organisation of the working time of persons performing mobile road transport activities. The Regulations prescribe the maximum weekly working time and maximum average weekly working time of mobile workers who, in the course of their work, drive or travel in goods or passenger vehicles covered by Council Regulation 3820/85 ([1985] OJ L370/1) on the harmonisation of certain social legislation relating to road transport and they prescribe the reference periods over which such time is to be calculated.

4923. Taxis–Motor Hackney Carriages–Belfast

MOTOR HACKNEY CARRIAGES (BELFAST) (AMENDMENT) BY-LAWS (NORTHERN IRELAND) 2005, SR 2005 248; made under the Road Traffic (Northern Ireland) Order 1981 (SI 1981 154 (NI.1)) Art.65. In force: June 18, 2005; £3.00.

These By-Laws amend the Motor Hackney Carriages (Belfast) By-Laws made by the Council of the County Borough of Belfast on June 5, 1951 by making provision for a new taxi stand at Mays Meadow.

4924. Taxis–Taxi stands–Dromore

TAXIS (DROMORE) BYE-LAWS (NORTHERN IRELAND) 2005, SR 2005 469; made under the Road Traffic (Northern Ireland) Order 1981 (SI 1981 154 (NI.1)) Art.65. In force: December 10, 2005; £3.00.

These Bye-Laws prescribe the exact location which may be used as stands or starting places for taxis in the town of Dromore, prescribe the maximum number of taxis which may use these stands or starting places and the hours available for use. The Bye-Laws also prohibit vehicles other than taxis from using the stands or starting places.

4925. Taxis–Taxi stands–Strabane

TAXIS (STRABANE) (AMENDMENT) BYE-LAWS (NORTHERN IRELAND) 2005, SR 2005 518; made under the Road Traffic (Northern Ireland) Order 1981 (SI 1981 154 (NI.1)) Art.65. In force: January 6, 2006; £3.00.

These Bye-laws, which revoke the Taxis (Strabane) (Amendment) Bye-Laws (Northern Ireland) 1996 (SR 1996 352), amend the Taxi (Strabane) Bye-Laws (Northern Ireland) 1988 by increasing, in the definition of "taxi", the number of seated passengers who can be carried from 6 to 8 in addition to the driver; prohibiting vehicles other than taxis from using the stands and starting places; and prescribing the new location of the taxi stand in Main Street, Strabane and increasing from 6 to 11 the number of taxis that may stand at that location.

UTILITIES

4926. Electricity supply industry–Grants

ELECTRICITY GRANTS (PRESCRIBED PURPOSE) REGULATIONS (NORTHERN IRELAND) 2005, SR 2005 177; made under the Energy (Northern Ireland) Order 2003 (SI 2003 419 (NI.6)) Art.61. In force: March 25, 2005; £3.00.

The Energy (Northern Ireland) Order 2003 (SI 2003 419 (NI.6)) enables the Department of Enterprise, Trade and Investment to make grants for certain energy purposes. It allows grants to be made to persons engaged in, or in commercial activities connected with the generation, transmission or supply of electricity. Grants cannot be made under Art.61 of the Order unless in the opinion of the Department the making of the grant is likely to achieve certain purposes and the amount is reasonable having regard to all the circumstances. These Regulations prescribe, as the purpose for which grant must be payable under Art.61 (1) (a) of the Order, the defraying of the cost of measures taken by the holders of electricity transmission or supply licences or exemptions to enable consumers to use electricity more efficiently and economically.

4927. Electricity supply industry–Renewable energy–Renewables obligation

RENEWABLES OBLIGATION ORDER (NORTHERN IRELAND) 2005, SR 2005 38; made under the Energy (Northern Ireland) Order 2003 (SI 2003 419 (NI.6)) Art.52, Art.53, Art.54, Art.55, Art.66. In force: April 1, 2005; £4.00.

This Order imposes an obligation on all electricity suppliers, who are licensed under the Electricity (Northern Ireland) Order 1992 (SI 1002 231 (NI.1)), to supply to customers in Northern Ireland specified amounts of electricity generated from renewable sources. As alternatives, in respect of all or part of an electricity supplier's renewables obligation, an electricity supplier is permitted to provide evidence that other licensed electricity suppliers have supplied electricity generated using renewable sources instead of it or to make a payment to the Northern Ireland Authority for Energy Regulation. Renewable sources include sources of energy such as wind, water, solar and biomass.

4928. Gas supply industry–Pipelines–Licences–Designation

GAS (DESIGNATION OF PIPELINES) ORDER (NORTHERN IRELAND) 2005, SR 2005 68; made under the Energy (Northern Ireland) Order 2003 (SI 2003 419 (NI.6)) Art.59. In force: March 19, 2005; £3.00.

This Order, which amends the Gas (Designation of Pipelines) Order (Northern Ireland) 2004 (SR 2004 404), designates part of the Scotland to Northern Ireland pipeline as a pipeline to which this power of modification applies.

WATER LAW

4929. Drainage (Amendment) (Northern Ireland) Order 2005 (SI 2005 1453 (NI.8))

This Order amends the Drainage (Northern Ireland) Order 1973 to allow the Department to dissolve, by order, certain drainage trusts and to make regulations authorising the Department to charge in respect of the exercise of its functions under that Order.

SCOTLAND

ADMINISTRATION OF JUSTICE

4930. Appeals—Competence—Appeals to Court of Session—Decree by default

[Sheriff Courts (Scotland) Act 1907 (c.51) s.29.]

Purported tenants of an agricultural holding sought declarator that they were joint tenants of the holding, that they had a right of access from a public road to the holding, and interdict preventing the proprietor of the land interfering with their peaceable possession. The pursuers averred that they were offered the tenancy in 1990 by a company who were the then proprietors (the fourth defenders). The subjects were thereafter disponed to the second defender, a further company, although title remained with the fourth defenders. Both were struck off the Register of Companies in 1995 and 1996. The fourth defenders were not restored, but the second defenders were restored in September 2001. Any rights of property in the subjects after the striking off vested at all material times in the Queen's and Lord Treasurer's Remembrancer (the third defender). The current proprietor of the land (the first defender) derived his title from the fourth defenders and convened the other defenders in the action. Summary decree was granted in the pursuers' favour in January 2001. The first and second defenders appealed to the sheriff principal who recalled the sheriff's interlocutor to the extent that it granted interdict. The Court of Session refused an appeal by the first and second defenders as incompetent in June 2001 and remitted the cause to the sheriff to proceed as accords, following which there were no further procedural steps on behalf of the second defender. Following further proceedings, a proof was fixed to deal with the pursuers' crave for interdict against the first defender in August 2002. The first defender appeared in person and sought to discharge the diet on the basis that his solicitor had withdrawn from acting due to illness and that no other firm had been willing to act for him at short notice. The sheriff refused to do so and further refused the first defender's request for leave to appeal. The first defender thereafter left court and interdict was granted in his absence. At an appeal against the interlocutor of August, the first defender submitted that the sheriff had exercised his discretion unreasonably in refusing to discharge the diet of proof and further sought to challenge an interlocutor refusing his motion to discharge the diet on August 21, 2002 to the same effect. The sheriff principal refused the appeal. The first defender appealed to the Court of Session and enrolled a motion seeking to allow a minute of amendment to his substantive defence in which he maintained that the offer of the lease was fabricated during the latter half of 1998 by persons unknown to him. He further sought to add averments that by disposition dated April 2003, the subjects were disponed to the second defender, which had changed its name, and that an application for first registration in the Land Register was in progression. The minute also called on the pursuers to give "fair specification" of the trade or business that was carried on from the subjects. The appellant argued that the sheriff on August 30, 2002, and the sheriff principal on December 16, 2002, had erred in granting summary decree, and in particular had erred in failing to recognise that he was entitled to challenge the relevancy and sufficiency of the respondents' averments and to put them to a proof of their averments. Issues of fact and law clearly arose, and the respondents had to prove that a valid agricultural tenancy was entered into in the informal manner contended and continued to subsist notwithstanding the averred dissolution of the lessor. The appellant accepted that he was rightly held to be in default but submitted that (1) in terms of the Sheriff Courts (Scotland) Act 1907 s.29 the appeal submitted to review the whole interlocutors in the cause and was available to, and could be insisted in, by all the parties to the cause; (2) his appeal was competent and the court, in any event, had a supereminent jurisdiction to entertain it in its discretion; (3) the minute of amendment should be allowed to enable him to raise the possibility that the offer of the lease was fabricated, and prove that the respondents had not entered into possession, had not carried on an agricultural trade or business, and had ceased to carry out agricultural operations on the land (although accepting that he had insufficient evidence to seek reduction of the offer document ope exceptionis); (4) he was entitled to put the respondents to proof of their averments if the appeal was to be decided on the basis of existing pleadings; (5) the true interest in the claim to vacant possession lay with the second defender, but he had title and interest by virtue of being convened as a defender and as owner of the land over which access was claimed; (6) the onus was on the respondents to establish that the lease was valid and that it continued despite the dissolution of the second defender; (7) his general denials were sufficient to make these issues to try.

Held, dismissing the appeal, that the appeal was incompetent where decree by default had been properly granted, and the summary decree interlocutors could not be opened while the decree by default remained unchallenged.

URQUHART v. SWEENEY 2005 S.L.T. 422, Lord Gill L.J.C., Lord Kirkwood, Lord McCluskey, 2 Div.

4931. Court of Session–Rules

ACT OF SEDERUNT (RULES OF THE COURT OF SESSION AMENDMENT NO.5) (MISCELLANEOUS) 2005, SSI 2005 193; made under the Court of Session Act 1988 s.5; and the Prevention of Terrorism Act 2005 Sch.para.4. In force: April 1, 2005; £3.00.

This Act of Sederunt makes amendments to the Rules of the Court of Session 1994 (SI 1994 1443) to make provision for certain appeals against penalties under the Finance Act 2003; to make amendments to Chapter 49 (family actions) in view of the Gender Recognition Act 2004; to omit Chapter 83 on applications for investigations pursuant to he Council of the European Communities; to insert a new Chapter 90 introducing procedure for applications to the court under the Freedom of Information Act of 2000 and Freedom of Information (Scotland) Act 2002. It also inserts a new Chapter 91 to introduce procedure for a reference by the Secretary of State under the Gender Recognition Act 2004.

4932. Court of Session–Rules

ACT OF SEDERUNT (RULES OF THE COURT OF SESSION AMENDMENT NO.7) (MISCELLANEOUS) 2005, SSI 2005 268; made under the Court of Session Act 1988 s.5. In force: June 7, 2005; £3.00.

This Act of Sederunt makes amendments to the Rules of the Court of Session 1994 (SI 1994 1443) consequent upon the Commissioners for Revenue and Customs Act 2005. It omits a rule allowing the court to reserve the question of expenses in applications under the Nationality, Immigration and Asylum Act 2002; corrects an error in the numbering of Chapter 70; makes provision requiring petitions for sequestration to contain averments about whether the proceedings are main or territorial proceedings; and inserts a rule into Chapter 74 of the Rules (administration procedure for companies) to provide for the fixing of a hearing in every case in which an interim order is made.

4933. Court of Session–Rules

ACT OF SEDERUNT (RULES OF THE COURT OF SESSION AMENDMENT NO.8) (MISCELLANEOUS) 2005, SSI 2005 521; made under the Court of Session Act 1988 s.5. In force: October 21, 2005; £3.00.

This Act of Sederunt, which amends the Rules of the Court of Session 1994 (SI 1994 1443), introduces new rules consequential upon the introduction of European Parliament and Council Regulation 805/2004 ([2004] OJ L143/15) creating a European Enforcement Order for uncontested claims. The new rules create a procedure for certifying certain judgments as European Enforcement Orders and enforcing European Enforcement Orders in Scotland; make a minor amendment to the Rules on preparing a case for a reference to the European Court of Justice; amend Part VI of Chapter 74 on the disqualification of company directors by inserting a reference to disqualification undertakings; amend the Rules on applications in civil recovery proceedings under the Proceeds of Crime Act 2002 consequent upon the amendment of that Act by the Serious and Organised Crime and Police Act 2005; introduce a new Chapter 92 into the Rules consequential upon the Inquiries Act 2005; and omit the guidance of the Court of Justice of the European Communities from Form 65.3 in the appendix to the Rules.

4934. Court of Session–Rules–Asylum and immigration

ACT OF SEDERUNT (RULES OF THE COURT OF SESSION AMENDMENT NO.6) (ASYLUM AND IMMIGRATION (TREATMENT OF CLAIMANTS, ETC.) ACT 2004) 2005, SSI 2005 198; made under the Court of Session Act 1988 s.5; and the Nationality, Immigration and Asylum Act 2002 s.103A. In force: April 4, 2005; £3.00.

This Act of Sederunt makes amendments to the Rules of the Court of Session 1994 (SI 1994 1443) to make provision consequent upon amendments to the Nationality, Immigration and Asylum Act 2002 by the Asylum and Immigration (Treatment of Claimants, etc.) Act 2004.

4935. Court of Session–Rules–Civil partnerships–Applications for separation or divorce

ACT OF SEDERUNT (RULES OF THE COURT OF SESSION AMENDMENT NO.9) (CIVIL PARTNERSHIP ACT 2004 ETC.) 2005, SSI 2005 632; made under the Court of Session Act 1988 s.5. In force: December 8, 2005; £9.00.

This Act of Sederunt makes amendments to the Rules of the Court of Session 1994 (SI 1994 1443) in order to make provision for applications under the Civil Partnership Act 2004 in relation to the dissolution or nullity of a civil partnership or the separation of civil partners. The amendments also make provision for a simplified procedure for divorce on the grounds of the issue of an interim gender recognition certificate.

4936. Court of Session–Rules–Enforcement of judgments

ACT OF SEDERUNT (RULES OF THE COURT OF SESSION AMENDMENT) (JURISDICTION, RECOGNITION AND ENFORCEMENT OF JUDGMENTS) 2005, SSI 2005 135; made under the Court of Session Act 1988 s.5. In force: March 2, 2005; £3.50.

This Act of Sederunt makes amendments to the Rules of the Court of Session 1994 (SI 1994 1443) in consequence of the Council Regulation 2201/2003 ([2003] OJ L338/1) concerning jurisdiction and the recognition and enforcement of judgments in matrimonial matters and matters of parental responsibility. It sets out a procedure for registration and enforcement of judgments under the Council Regulation; makes amendments so that any actions under the Hague Convention which are also under the Council Regulation are subject to new rules that are inserted into Chapter 70; make provision that actions under the Hague Convention, where the Council Regulation also applies, are intimated to a child who is the subject of the action, and gives the child an opportunity to give their views on the action to the court; inserts a new Chapter 88 into the Rules on civil cases involving parental responsibility that come under the Council Regulation; and makes provision that cases may be transferred between courts in different Member States if it is more appropriate that they be dealt with in that other Member State.

4937. Court of Session-Rules-Terrorism

ACT OF SEDERUNT (RULES OF THE COURT OF SESSION AMENDMENT NO.4) (PREVENTION OF TERRORISM ACT 2005) 2005, SSI 2005 153; made under the Court of Session Act 1988 s.5; and the Prevention of Terrorism Act 2005 Sch.para.4. In force: March 16, 2005; £3.00.

This Act of Sederunt makes amendments to the Rules of the Court of Session 1994 (SI 1994 1443) to make provision in respect of proceedings under the Prevention of Terrorism Act 2005.

4938. Court of Session-Shorthand writers-Fees

ACT OF SEDERUNT (RULES OF THE COURT OF SESSION AMENDMENT NO.3) (FEES OF SHORTHAND WRITERS) 2005, SSI 2005 148; made under the Court of Session Act 1988 s.5. In force: April 25, 2005; £3.00.

This Act of Sederunt, which amends the Rules of the Court of Session (SI 1994 1443), increases the fees payable to shorthand writers in the Court of Session by about 3.7 per cent.

4939. Court of Session-Solicitors-Fees

ACT OF SEDERUNT (RULES OF THE COURT OF SESSION AMENDMENT NO.2) (FEES OF SOLICITORS) 2005, SSI 2005 147; made under the Court of Session Act 1988 s.5. In force: April 25, 2005; £3.00.

This Act of Sederunt, which amends the Rules of the Court of Session (SI 1994 1443), amends the Table of Fees recoverable in respect of work carried out by solicitors in the Court of Session. The Act increases the fees which are recoverable by about 4.8 per cent; increases the fee recoverable for preparation of accounts of expenses; increases the limit on recovery of expenses paid to witnesses from £250 per day to £400 per day; and removes references to travelling time as a recoverable area of expense in Part VA of Chapter III (defended personal injuries actions commenced on or after April 1, 2003).

4940. Curator bonis-Discharge-Allegation of unwise investment-Application to "unwind" transaction

The petitioner (H) sought to be discharged as curator bonis to a ward (W) who had died in 2001 at the age of 87. W had suffered from Parkinson's and Alzheimer's disease and had lived in a nursing home from 1998 until his death. H applied to the Accountant of Court for discharge and objections were lodged by W's three sons (J). The Accountant of Court determined that a certificate of discharge should be issued but J appealed, arguing that they were unhappy with the way the sale of W's house had been conducted and that they had concerns about the investment of the proceeds given that H had not notified the financial adviser of W's age and state of health before making the investment. There had been a delay on H's part in obtaining investment advice and the money had lain in a Scottish Solicitors Deposit Account for approximately two years. In recognition of this, £600 had been taken from H's commission by the Accountant of Court. However, J sought to have the whole transaction unwound at H's expense. H argued that, while there had been a delay, it was not competent for the court to engage in the kind of unwinding exercise suggested.

Held, giving judgment accordingly, that when considering a petition to discharge a curator bonis the court may have regard to the conduct of the curator bonis, *Manners v. Strong's Judicial Factor* (1902) 4 F. (Ct. of Sess.) 829 applied. The curator was under a duty to exercise care, skill and diligence. However, in the instant case the difficulty lay in the lack of any proper focus in the pleadings relating to the amount of the alleged loss arising from H's failure in her duty and it was not appropriate for the court to unwind the estate in the manner sought by J. Opportunity was given for J to amend their answers and the case was ordered to be put out for discussion of further procedure.

HOPE, PETITIONER 2004 S.C.L.R. 943, Lord Bracadale, OH.

4941. Messengers at arms—Fees

ACT OF SEDERUNT (FEES OF MESSENGERS-AT-ARMS) 2005, SSI 2005 582; made under the Execution of Diligence (Scotland) Act 1926 s.6; and the Court of Session Act 1988 s.5. In force: January 1, 2006; £3.00.

This Act of Sederunt amends the Table of Fees in the Act of Sederunt (Fees of Messengers at Arms) (No.2) 2002 (SSI 2002 566), by increasing the fees payable to messengers at arms by 3.45 per cent.

4942. Messengers at arms and sheriff officers—Bonds of caution and policies of insurance

ACT OF SEDERUNT (MESSENGERS-AT-ARMS AND SHERIFF OFFICERS RULES AMENDMENT) (CAUTION AND INSURANCE) 2005, SSI 2005 199; made under the Debtors (Scotland) Act 1987 s.75. In force: April 14, 2005; £3.00.

This Act of Sederunt amends the provisions of the Act of Sederunt (Rules of Messengers-at-Arms and Sheriff Officers) 1991 (SI 1991 1397) which prescribe the persons from whom bonds of caution and policies of professional indemnity insurance are to be obtained by messengers-at-arms and sheriff officers.

4943. Parental responsibility—Jurisdiction and judgments

EUROPEAN COMMUNITIES (MATRIMONIAL AND PARENTAL RESPONSIBILITY JURISDICTION AND JUDGMENTS) (SCOTLAND) REGULATIONS 2005, SSI 2005 42; made under the European Communities Act 1972 Art.2. In force: March 1, 2005; £3.00.

These Regulations amend the Domicile and Matrimonial Proceedings Act 1973, the Child Abduction and Custody Act 1985, the Family Law Act 1986, the Children (Scotland) Act 1995, and revoke the European Communities (Matrimonial Jurisdiction and Judgments) (Scotland) Regulations 2001 (SSI 2001 36). The amendments make provisions operable in Scotland consistent with, and to clarify their relationship to, Council Regulation 2201/2003 ([2003] OJ L338/1) concerning jurisdiction and the recognition and enforcement of judgments in matrimonial matters and matters of parental responsibility.

4944. Registration Appeal Court—Appointments—Judges

ACT OF SEDERUNT (REGISTRATION APPEAL COURT) 2005, SSI 2005 59; made under the Representation of the People Act 1983 s.57. In force: February 7, 2005; £3.00.

This Act of Sederunt, which revokes the Act of Sederunt (Registration Appeal Court) 1997 (SI 1997 379), appoints three judges to hear registration appeals under the Registration of the People Act 1983 s.57.

4945. Registration Appeal Court—Appointments—Judges

ACT OF SEDERUNT (REGISTRATION APPEAL COURT) (NO.2) 2005, SSI 2005 382; made under the Representation of the People Act 1983 s.57. In force: August 1, 2005; £3.00.

This Act of Sederunt, which revokes the Act of Sederunt (Registration Appeal Court) 2005 (SSI 2005 59), appoints three judges to hear registration appeals under the Registration of the People Act 1983.

4946. Sheriff courts—Applications and appeals

ACT OF SEDERUNT (SUMMARY APPLICATIONS, STATUTORY APPLICATIONS AND APPEALS ETC. RULES) AMENDMENT (LAND REFORM (SCOTLAND) ACT 2003) 2005, SSI 2005 61; made under the Sheriff Courts (Scotland) Act 1971 s.32; and the Land Reform (Scotland) Act 2003 s.14, s.15, s.28. In force: February 9, 2005; £3.00.

This Act of Sederunt, which amends the Act of Sederunt (Summary Applications, Statutory Applications and Appeals etc. Rules) 1999 (SI 1999

929) sets out the procedure in the sheriff court where an owner of land wishes to appeal against a notice served by a local authority in the exercise of its duty to uphold access rights under the Land Reform (Scotland) Act 2003 and where an application is made for a declaration as to the existence and extent of access rights or rights of way.

4947. Sheriff courts–Bond of caution–Authorised persons

ACT OF SEDERUNT (ORDINARY CAUSE RULES) AMENDMENT (CAUTION AND SECURITY) 2005, SSI 2005 20; made under the Sheriff Courts (Scotland) Act 1971 s.32. In force: February 1, 2005; £3.00.

This Act of Sederunt amends the Sheriff Courts (Scotland) Act 1907 to provide that a bond of caution or other security may be given only by a person authorised in terms of the Financial Services and Markets Act 2000 s.31; and to require a bond of caution or other security document to state whether it is given by a person so authorised.

4948. Sheriff courts–Gender recognition certificates

ACT OF SEDERUNT (ORDINARY CAUSE RULES) AMENDMENT (GENDER RECOGNITION ACT 2004) 2005, SSI 2005 189; made under the Sheriff Courts (Scotland) Act 1971 s.32. In force: April 4, 2005; £3.00.

This Act of Sederunt amends the Sheriff Courts (Scotland) Act 1907 to insert a new rule which provides that the pursuer, in an application for divorce on the ground that an interim gender recognition certificate has been issued to either party to the marriage, must produce the interim gender recognition certificate (or a certified copy thereof) together with the initial writ. A second new rule is inserted which provides that an application for a corrected gender recognition certificate shall be made by minute in the process of the action in relation to which the gender recognition certificate was issued.

4949. Sheriff courts–Mental health–Care and treatment–Applications and appeals

ACT OF SEDERUNT (SUMMARY APPLICATIONS, STATUTORY APPLICATIONS AND APPEALS ETC. RULES) AMENDMENT (MENTAL HEALTH (CARE AND TREATMENT) (SCOTLAND) ACT 2003) 2005, SSI 2005 504; made under the Sheriff Courts (Scotland) Act 1971 s.32. In force: October 6, 2005; £3.00.

This Act of Sederunt amends the Act of Sederunt (Summary Applications, Statutory Applications and Appeals etc. Rules) 1999 (SI 1999 929) to make provision for miscellaneous procedure under the Mental Health (Care and Treatment) (Scotland) Act 2003. It inserts a new part which provides that applications for a removal order under s.293 and applications for the recall or variation of a removal order under s.295 of the Act shall be lodged with the sheriff clerk who will fix a date for a hearing; and where the sheriff principal remits an appeal to the Court of Session under s.320 of the Act, the process shall be transmitted to the Deputy Principal Clerk of Session within four days.

4950. Sheriff courts–Rules–Enforcement orders

ACT OF SEDERUNT (SHERIFF COURT EUROPEAN ENFORCEMENT ORDER RULES) 2005, SSI 2005 523; made under the Sheriff Courts (Scotland) Act 1971 s.32. In force: October 21, 2005; £3.00.

This Act of Sederunt makes rules of procedure in the sheriff court for applications for European Enforcement Order certificates for enforcement of judgments in other Member States of the European Community.

4951. Sheriff courts–Rules–Miscellaneous amendments

ACT OF SEDERUNT (ORDINARY CAUSE, SUMMARY APPLICATION, SUMMARY CAUSE AND SMALL CLAIM RULES) AMENDMENT

(MISCELLANEOUS) 2005, SSI 2005 648; made under the Sheriff Courts (Scotland) Act 1971 s.32. In force: January 2, 2006; £3.00.

This Act of Sederunt amends the Sheriff Courts (Scotland) Act 1907, the Act of Sederunt (Summary Applications, Statutory Applications and Appeals etc. Rules) 1999 (SI 1999 929), the Sederunt (Summary Cause Rules) 2002 (SSI 2002 132), and the Act of Sederunt (Small Claim Rules) 2002 (SSI 2002 133). It makes miscellaneous amendments to the rules of procedure in the sheriff court and amends the Ordinary Cause Rules, the Summary Applications, Statutory Applications and Appeals etc. Rules, the Summary Cause Rules and the Small Claim Rules.

4952. Sheriff courts–Sexual offences–Applications and appeals

ACT OF SEDERUNT (SUMMARY APPLICATIONS, STATUTORY APPLICATIONS AND APPEALS ETC. RULES) AMENDMENT (PROTECTION OF CHILDREN AND PREVENTION OF SEXUAL OFFENCES (SCOTLAND) ACT 2005) 2005, SSI 2005 473; made under the Sheriff Courts (Scotland) Act 1971 s.32. In force: October 7, 2005; £3.00.

This Act of Sederunt makes amendments to the Act of Sederunt (Summary Applications, Statutory Applications and Appeals etc. Rules) 1999 (SI 1999 929) consequential upon the Protection of Children and Prevention of Sexual Offences Act 2005.

4953. Sheriff courts–Sheriff officers–Fees

ACT OF SEDERUNT (FEES OF SHERIFF OFFICERS) 2005, SSI 2005 583; made under the Sheriff Courts (Scotland) Act 1907 s.40; and the Execution of Diligence (Scotland) Act 1926 s.6. In force: January 1, 2006; £3.00.

This Act of Sederunt amends the Table of Fees in the Act of Sederunt (Fees of Sheriff Officers) (No.2) 2002 (SSI 2002 567) by increasing the fees payable to sheriff officers by 3.45 per cent.

4954. Sheriff courts–Shorthand writers–Fees

ACT OF SEDERUNT (FEES OF SHORTHAND WRITERS IN THE SHERIFF COURT) (AMENDMENT) 2005, SSI 2005 150; made under the Sheriff Courts (Scotland) Act 1907 s.40. In force: April 25, 2005; £3.00.

This Act of Sederunt, which amends the Act of Sederunt (Fees of Witnesses and Shorthand Writers in the Sheriff Court) 1992 (SI 1992 1878) increases the fees payable to shorthand writers in the Sheriff Court by about 3.7 per cent.

4955. Sheriff courts–Solicitors and witnesses–Fees

ACT OF SEDERUNT (FEES OF SOLICITORS AND WITNESSES IN THE SHERIFF COURT) (AMENDMENT) 2005, SSI 2005 149; made under the Sheriff Courts (Scotland) Act 1907 s.40. In force: April 25, 2005; £3.00.

This Act of Sederunt makes amendments to the Table of Fees in the Schedule to the Act of Sederunt (Fees of Solicitors in the Sheriff Court) (Amendment and Further Provisions) 1993 (SI 1993 3080). It also amends the Act of Sederunt (Fees of Witnesses and Shorthand Writers in the Sheriff Court) 1992 (SI 1992 1878) in respect of payments made to witnesses.

4956. Books

Crozier, Paul–Criminal Advocacy. Paperback: £35.00. ISBN 0 414 01555 X. W.Green & Son.

Greens Sheriff Court Rules. Paperback: £36.00. ISBN 0 414 01620 3. W.Green & Son.

Kearney, Brian–Scottish Children's Hearing System in Action. Paperback: £25.00. ISBN 1 84592 056 2. Tottel Publishing.

Law Society Scotland Diploma Materials 2005, Civil Court Practice Student Manual 2005-2006. Book (details unknown): £15.00. ISBN 0 414 01637 8. W.Green & Son.
Law Society Scotland Diploma Materials 2005, Diploma Tutors Manual 2005-2006. Book (details unknown): £2.50. ISBN 0 414 01646 7. W.Green & Son.
Law Society Scotland Diploma Materials 2005, Public Administration Student Manual 2005-2006. Book (details unknown): £15.00. ISBN 0 414 01644 0. W.Green & Son.

ADMINISTRATIVE LAW

4957. Disability discrimination–Public authorities–Statutory duties

DISABILITY DISCRIMINATION (PUBLIC AUTHORITIES) (STATUTORY DUTIES) (SCOTLAND) REGULATIONS 2005, SSI 2005 565; made under the Disability Discrimination Act 1995 s.49D. In force: December 5, 2005; £3.00.

These Regulations impose duties on specified public authorities with the aim of assisting them to perform better their duties to promote equality of opportunity for disabled persons under the Disability Discrimination Act 1995.

4958. Judicial review–Competence–Jurisdiction of Court of Session–Decisions of procurator fiscal

[Human Rights Act 1998 (c.42) Sch.1 Part II Art.1; Act of Adjournal (Criminal Procedure Rules) 1996 (SI 1996 513) Sch.2 para.40.2.]

X, the owners of a factory which collapsed following an explosion, killing and injuring a number of people, sought judicial review of a decision by the Crown refusing their insurers access to the site and to items removed by the Crown. Access was denied on the basis that the site was being treated as a crime scene and that it was inappropriate for third parties to enter. The Crown submitted that the common law powers of the fiscal to investigate criminal offences could not be reviewed in this manner where the High Court alone had power over criminal matters. X submitted that judicial review was competent as the dispute concerned the fiscal's interference with their property rights and they could not go to the nobile officium as rights they sought to claim under the Human Rights Act 1998 could not be aired and such a procedure would not attract an award of damages. They further submitted that, in denying access, the fiscal had claimed wide powers of search where no reason had been given; the decision had been made without any time limit and not in relation to the circumstances of the case; the fiscal did not have an overall blanket common law power, without going to court; the fiscal's office and her public duty did not protect her from illegal acts; there were no greater or more extensive powers just because the subject matter was a sudden death; it was clear that the fiscal was not acting in her prosecution role but was only investigating sudden deaths, and where only sudden death was involved, X retained all civil rights; and under Sch.1 Part II Art.1 of the 1998 Act, any control by the fiscal had to be necessary in the general interest, and there had to be a fair balance of X's rights as against the public interest.

Held, dismissing the petition, that (1) the Outer House had jurisdiction to hear the petition where no process or proceedings had been initiated and there was no other ongoing litigation. (2) Any attempt by X to invite the nobile officium would fail as would any attempt to raise a devolution issue: the Act of Adjournal (Criminal Procedure Rules) 1996 Sch.2 para.40.2 did not allow any such minute without there being proceedings on indictment before the court, and this was purely a question of a right of property. (3) In the absence of any urgency to make payment to the claimants, priority to continue investigations had to be accorded to the fiscal, as the proper authority, who had to be allowed complete discretion and a proper timescale to do so, as the case involved a matter of public law, and the court could only take a different view if there were any suggestion of malice or an improper motive on the fiscal's part. (4) Given the importance of the role of the Crown, the complexity of the inquiry, and the short time scale involved, no Convention rights had been interfered with.

ICL PLASTICS LTD, PETITIONER; *sub nom.* ICL PLASTICS LTD v. SCOTTISH MINISTERS 2005 S.L.T. 675, Lord McEwan, OH.

4959. **Judicial review–Criminal injuries compensation–Refusal on basis of "same roof" rule**

[Human Rights Act 1998 (c.42) Sch.1 Part I Art.6, Art.14, Part II Art.1.]

S sought reduction of a decision of the Criminal Injuries Compensation Appeal Panel refusing her compensation in respect of sexual abuse inflicted by her father between 1968 and 1971, when she was aged between four and seven years old. She was refused compensation on the basis of the "same roof" rule in the Criminal Injuries Compensation Scheme 1996 para.7(b), which excluded claims involving family members living in the same household. S further sought declarator that para.7(b) was incompatible with the Human Rights Act 1998 Sch.1 Part I Art.6 and Sch.1 Part II Art.1, when taken with Sch.1 Part I Art.14.

Held, refusing the petition, that (1) the 1998 Act was not retrospective and a scheme which was valid when it was made could not be reduced and it made no difference when the decision on S's application was made. (2) Article 6 was not engaged: where any award was completely discretionary or ex gratia, no civil right in terms thereof was created, and because of the continuation of the "same roof" rule under para.7, the terms of Art.6 did not allow any court to create one. (3) S had no right personal to her under Sch.1 Part II Art.1 nor did she have any legitimate expectation. (4) Unless S could enjoy and exercise a Convention right, Art.14 was irrelevant.

S v. CRIMINAL INJURIES COMPENSATION BOARD 2004 S.L.T. 1173, Lord McEwan, OH.

4960. **Judicial review–Enforcement–Local authority's installation of wheelie bins– Interlocutor ordering removal–Change of circumstances**

[Roads (Scotland) Act 1984 (c.54); Environmental Protection Act 1990 (c.43) s.46; Act of Sederunt (Rules of the Court of Session 1994) 1994 (SI 1994 1443) Sch.2 r.15.2; Roads (Traffic Calming) (Scotland) Regulations 1994 (SI 1994 2488).]

A resident (M) lodged a note in terms of the Act of Sederunt (Rules of the Court of Session 1994) 1994 Sch.2 r.15.2 craving the court to order enforcement of an interlocutor (2001 S.C. 729, [2002] C.L.Y. 5802) under which the local authority (X) was required to remove wheelie bins and their associated structures from M's street within six weeks. M had sought judicial review of X's decision to install permanent wheelie bins in his street. X had purported to rely on the powers conferred by the Roads (Scotland) Act 1984 and the Roads (Traffic Calming) (Scotland) Regulations 1994 made thereunder. The bins were not dismantled or removed. X relied on a notice served on M in terms of the Environmental Protection Act 1990 s.46, following an environment and infrastructure committee meeting, which it averred constituted authority for the bins remaining on the street. M submitted that X's failure to remove the bins and associated structures was a deliberate attempt to flout the court order which still stood in his favour; the minutes of X's committee meeting did not record any decision or determination that the bins should be placed on his street on any different statutory basis from that which had already been found to have been ultra vires; and the order required the bins' removal, after which time it might be open to X to thereafter replace them by a different statutory power, but X could not leave them there and simply point to a different statutory justification for their remaining.

Held, refusing the prayer of the note, that (1) X had not disregarded or flouted the order of the court, nor had it been guilty of any abuse of process, and while it was unfortunate that the marking of a reclaiming motion and its subsequent abandonment had the result of delaying the effect of the interlocutor, both decisions were taken in good faith and on the advice of counsel. (2) X had completed the procedures necessary to enable it to continue to have the wheelie bins and associated structures complained of situated in M's street: the fact that the court had pronounced an interlocutor reducing its decision on one statutory basis did not preclude it from proceeding on another provided it was done without challenge and apparently in conformity with the necessary statutory requirements, which constituted a change of circumstances justifying the court in refusing to order the enforcement of the interlocutor.

McKELLER v. ABERDEEN CITY COUNCIL (NO.2); *sub nom.* McKELLAR v. ABERDEEN CITY COUNCIL (NO.2) 2005 S.C. 186, Lord Menzies, OH.

4961. Judicial review—Expulsion—Members—Clubs

W, three members of a golf club (B), sought judicial review of a decision of B's committee terminating their membership. The decision was taken following objections raised by W with the local planning authority in relation to an application, following an extraordinary general meeting of B, to relocate the site of the clubhouse following its destruction by fire. The committee found that the objections had violated a rule of the constitution relating to conduct which "appears to [the committee] to endanger the character, interests or good order of the Club, or who acts in breach of the ... decision of [the Club] in General meeting". B argued that the committee had been entitled to vote to suspend or expel W as the committee were entitled to take the view that W's conduct endangered the interests of B, and that they could have been said to have acted in breach of a decision of B in general meeting.

Held, reducing the decision, that the acts and conduct of W, in themselves, were entirely unobjectionable, that they only became the focus of objection from the committee because the proposal they had taken exception to had come from B, and that this was insufficient to render their conduct and acts susceptible to the committee's disciplinary jurisdiction.

WILES v. BOTHWELL CASTLE GOLF CLUB 2005 S.L.T. 785, Lord Glennie, OH.

4962. Judicial review—ICAS—Appeal committee—Unfairly prejudicial conduct

[Human Rights Act 1998 (c.42) Sch.1 Part I Art.6.]

H, a chartered accountant and member of ICAS, sought judicial review of a decision of ICAS's appeal committee on the basis that it had been vitiated by them having had prejudicial and irrelevant material before them. In 2003 and 2004, two complaints had been served on H, charging him with misconduct relating to the fraudulent activity of a company to which he had been appointed liquidator. The institute's investigating committee included its findings, a number of which were based on matters set out in the affidavit of another, in the summaries attached to each complaint, and in particular, concluded that the petitioner had acted dishonestly. Following a hearing, the institute's discipline committee found that there was insufficient evidence to conclude as a matter of fact that H had played any part in any criminal or fraudulent conspiracy to defraud creditors and that he could not be found to have acted dishonestly, although he had failed "to act or be seen to act, with the integrity, independence and objectivity required of him", and withdrew H's insolvency permit for a year. H appealed to the respondents, who were provided with a number of documents including the summaries and affidavits. H moved for the appeal hearing to be adjourned before a newly constituted tribunal which should not have sight of the summaries which were prejudicial to him by indicating guilt on his part which had not been borne out by the discipline committee's findings. The respondents refused the motion, distinguishing *Murphy v. General Teaching Council for Scotland* 1997 S.C. 172, [1997] C.L.Y. 6008 on the facts and circumstances of the case, quashed the discipline committee's decision and imposed a fine of £25,000 along with the immediate withdrawal of the petitioner's insolvency permit without limit of time. The respondents submitted that it was untenable and misguided for the petitioner to seek to argue that there had been no finding of a lack of integrity by the discipline committee; the primary consideration was the institute's reputation and the discipline committee had paid too much attention to the mitigation advanced by H; the discipline committee had made it clear that they refused to convict on the basis of unendorsed affidavits; and there was no authority to suggest that a body determining sentence should not know what charges were taken but not proved.

Held, quashing the decision, that (1) it was readily apparent that the discipline committee had not found H to have committed any acts of dishonesty and while he was convicted of two charges referring to him having failed to act with the required standards of integrity, such a finding was based on the Guide to Professional Ethics whereby it was possible for a member to breach a rule by failing to act with integrity and objectivity thus giving rise to the inference that he had in fact acted dishonestly or to breach it by failing to be seen to act with integrity and objectivity, which did not give rise to such an inference, which was the basis on which the committee's findings fell to be understood. Further, examination of the context of each charge, where the reference to integrity was made, was also indicative of the petitioner's breaches having been in the latter sense. (2) The summaries and affidavits contained prejudicial material and should not have been put before the respondents. It was a clear breach of the respondents' own rule that they took the material into consideration for any purpose, and they were obliged to invoke any procedure necessary to ensure compliance with the Human Rights Act 1998 Sch.1 Part I Art.6 which required the removal of any irrelevant prejudicial material; the fairness of the hearing afforded to H was immediately called into question on account of the loss of the requisite appearance of impartiality and where the institute had more than one legally qualified chairman available to them, it would not seem to have been difficult to set up a system whereby a chairman other than the one due to sit in an appeal considered all the papers before the discipline committee and sifted out any irrelevant material, especially that which might be considered prejudicial to an appellant; *Murphy* was relevant and lent support to the fact that the respondents had irrelevant prejudicial material before them which vitiated their decision, it made no difference that H was appealing only against sentence, his entitlement to natural justice and compliance with Art.6 applied to a hearing of that nature just as much as to one on the substantive merits of a case, *Murphy* considered.

HARRIS v. APPEAL COMMITTEE OF THE INSTITUTE OF CHARTERED ACCOUNTANTS OF SCOTLAND 2005 S.L.T. 487, Lady Smith, OH.

4963. **Judicial review–Interim relief–Prisoners rights–Specific performance–Competence**

[Crown Proceedings Act 1947 (c.44) s.21; Human Rights Act 1998 (c.42) Sch.1 Part I Art.6, Art.8; Prisons and Young Offenders Institutions (Scotland) Rules 1994 (SI 1994 1931) r.80(5).]

In a petition for judicial review of orders giving rise to his segregation contrary to the Human Rights Act 1998 Sch.1 Part I Art.6 and Art.8, R, a prisoner, moved for suspension ad interim of an order granted by S, the Scottish Ministers, under the Prisons and Young Offenders Institutions (Scotland) Rules 1994 r.80(5) which extended his initial period of segregation. The parties were agreed that the approach to interim suspension should be the same as that to interim interdict and S accepted that R could demonstrate a prima facie case but opposed the motion on the grounds of incompetence, et separatim the balance of convenience favoured refusal. R submitted that (1) the order could be competently granted where the Crown Proceedings Act 1947 s.21 did not refer to the remedy of suspension; (2) the purpose of an order for interim suspension was to preserve the status quo, as distinct from pronouncing an order for interdict or specific performance, and (3) the balance of convenience favoured granting the order where Art.8 was engaged, the authorisation for his detention in segregation might be renewed, full and adequate reasons had not been given for his detention, and the procedures smacked of arbitrary unfair decision making, contrary to the rule of law.

Held, refusing the motion, that the remedy of interim suspension was not so distinct from that which might be granted by way of interdict or specific performance as to escape the prohibition contained in s.21(1)(a) of the 1947 Act.

RALSTON v. SCOTTISH MINISTERS 2004 S.L.T. 1263, Lady Smith, OH.

4964. Judicial review−Interim relief−Specific performance−Interim orders sought against Crown−Competency

[Court of Session Act 1988 (c.36) s.45(b); Prisons (Scotland) Act 1989 (c.45); Human Rights Act 1998 (c.42) Sch.1 Part I Art.3, Art.8; Act of Sederunt (Rules of the Court of Session 1994) 1994 (SI 1994 1443) Sch.2 r.58.3(1).]

In petitions for judicial review of decisions to detain them in conditions allegedly violating the Human Rights Act 1998 Sch.1 Part I Art.3 and Sch.1 Part I Art.8, M, seven prisoners, sought an interim order ordaining S, the Scottish Ministers, to secure their confinement in conditions of detention where they did not, while sharing a cell, have to use a toilet facility in that cell and where they did not have to use a toilet facility other than a purpose built, fixed and flushing action toilet with a related supply of running water and wash basin. M also sought interim interdict prohibiting S from transferring them to conditions where they would have to share a cell when using a toilet facility in that cell, failing which, interim declarators in the same terms. M's complaints concerned the "slopping out" regime which, it was maintained, gave rise to increased risks to health, subjected them to inhuman and degrading treatment in terms of Art.3, or alternatively, involved an unjustified interference with their right to respect for their family life, contrary to Art.8. M submitted that (1) in the light of similar conditions averred and proved in *Napier v. Scottish Ministers* 2004 S.L.T. 555, [2004] 7 C.L. 581, they had averred a prima facie case of "serious ill treatment"; (2) the decision on the competency of the orders sought in *Beggs v. Scottish Ministers* 2004 S.L.T. 755, [2004] 8 C.L. 609, was wrong; (3) S had been given a statutory "jurisdiction" to incarcerate prisoners in terms of the Prisons (Scotland) Act 1989 which could be the subject of judicial review, or despite the terms of the Act of Sederunt (Rules of the Court of Session 1994) 1994 Sch.2 r.58.3(1), simply by a petition for the implement of statutory duty under the Court of Session Act 1988 s.45(b), and (4) the balance of convenience was in their favour.

Held, refusing the motion for interim orders in hoc statu, that (1) the principles of common law and the terms of r.58.3 required a petitioner to have exhausted any alternative ordinary or statutory remedies before invoking the supervisory jurisdiction but that had not been done ex facie of the petitions; (2) it was not immediately clear what bearing the supervisory jurisdiction of the court had on the matter complained of: persons remanded or convicted were ordered to be imprisoned under warrant of the court, not by S, and the keeping of prisoners generally in prisons of an inadequate type appeared to have little to with any decision or lack thereof on their part relative to an individual prisoner of a type which might be reviewed as part of the court's supervisory jurisdiction; (3) in an appropriate case, an interim declarator might be competent against the Crown but M had not made out a prima facie case which was so strong as to merit the summary granting of orders without affording S the opportunity to lodge written answers, and (4) while S attending to M's needs might not result in any major alteration to the status quo, it was clear that were the court to decide in their favour, the implications would be considerable since M did not appear to be in a materially different position from that in many other penal institutions, *Napier* and *Beggs* considered.

McKENZIE v. SCOTTISH MINISTERS 2004 S.L.T. 1236, Lord Carloway, OH.

4965. Judicial review−Licensing committees−Policy on irresponsible alcohol promotions−Lawfulness

[Licensing (Scotland) Act 1976 (c.66) s.17(1).]

M, public house licence holders, sought judicial review of a policy of X, a licensing board, which set a minimum price tariff at which alcohol should be sold. X indicated their intention to implement the new policy by October 19, 2004, after which time everyone applying for a regular or occasional extension of permitted hours would have an additional condition attached obliging the applicant to adhere to the policy. All on sale licence holders were requested to sign and return an undertaking that the minimum price tariff would apply during all of the hours the premises were open, with a threat of enforcement proceedings on failure to adhere. M sought declarator that the policy was unlawful and *ultra vires* of the Licensing (Scotland) Act 1976, and production and reduction thereof. X submitted that it was not unlawful for a licensing board to ask for an assurance from an applicant as to how he intended to operate the premises he sought to have licensed and to take that into account when deciding whether or not to grant a licence, nor was there anything unlawful in seeking undertakings from the holders of existing licences provided it was directed towards a licensing purpose.

Held, granting the petition, that (1) in endorsing and beginning to apply the policy, X had not complied with the legal principles applicable to the policies of licensing boards. (2) X could not refuse either the grant or renewal of a public house licence, or applications for regular extensions of permitted hours, solely on the basis that the applicant was unwilling to give an undertaking to sell alcohol in accordance with the minimum price tariff. A ground of refusal under s.17(1) of the Act had to be made out and X's declared intention to deem as "irresponsible" a licence holder who sold alcohol at prices below the minimum tariff indicated an intention to adopt a preconceived view which would be incompatible with their duty to follow an unbiased approach. (3) Even if a policy of a licensing authority had a legitimate purpose, it could not interfere with the terms of trade between a licence holder and his customer unless it had statutory authority to do so and the provisions of the Act did not give licensing boards the power to regulate, either directly or indirectly, the minimum prices below which alcohol might not be sold during permitted hours. (4) The provisions concerning the conditions a licensing board could attach to the grant of an occasional or regular extension of permitted hours might be thought to be wide enough to allow a licensing board to do what X intimated, but that statutory power had to be subject to some limitation and imposing the condition set out in the policy would go beyond regulating the licence holder's use of his licensed premises during the extension to permitted hours. (5) The effect of X's policy was not just to curb binge drinking but was intended to regulate the minimum prices at which alcohol could be sold at any time when on sales licence premises were open which interfered with and regulated the terms of trade between the licence holders of licensed premises and their customers and the fact that the policy might achieve a reduction in binge drinking and appeared to command wide support was insufficient to bring the endorsement and application of the policy within the scope of their statutory powers.

MITCHELLS & BUTLERS RETAIL LTD v. ABERDEEN CITY LICENSING BOARD 2005 S.L.T. 13, Lord Mackay of Drumadoon, OH.

4966. Judicial review—Natural justice—Expulsion from club—Compliance with club rules

C, a member of T, a golf club, sought declarator that decisions taken by T's council concerning his conduct, and by general meeting expelling him from the club, were unlawful and contrary to natural justice, and reduction thereof. C had instigated various proceedings against T since 1991. Following the publication of an article in a national newspaper in June 2001 which documented the proceedings and reported on C's recent damages action against T, a number of T's members requested the council to take action concerning C's breach of rule 22.1 of the rules of membership by conducting himself in a manner injurious to T. C accepted that he had not taken the opportunity which he had been afforded to respond to the members' complaint but submitted that (1) the decisions by the council did not make any "enquiry" as required by rule 22.1 and further, the members' letter of complaint did not give sufficient detail of the charges against him; (2) while the invalidity of T's council's decisions would render the members' decision invalid, it was in any event vitiated by a procedural impropriety by at least 21 members who had complained about his conduct also taking part in, and voting at, the general meeting. T inter alia disputed the competency of the petition in so far as it sought judicial review of the members' decision to expel him, submitting that the relationship between C and the other members was governed by the law of contract and as he would have a contractual remedy in the event of a breach, it was unnecessary and incompetent to invoke the court's supervisory jurisdiction.

Held, dismissing the petition, that (1) T's challenge to the competency of the judicial review proceedings had to be rejected. It was conceded that decisions taken by the council under rule 22 were susceptible to the court's supervisory jurisdiction on the basis that there was a tripartite relationship under which council members were entrusted by T's members as a whole with a decision making power in respect of any member whose conduct was in issue, and T's attempt to distinguish decisions by a general meeting under the same rule was not well founded where both were groups of members, whom the members as a whole had agreed inter se were to have authority to take a decision affecting such a member, thus both situations were capable of being characterised as involving a tripartite relationship; further, each of them involved the exercise of a limited power by a body on whom that power had been conferred, resulted in the taking of a decision with which the court could not interfere, provided the power was exercised lawfully within the limits by which it was circumscribed, and which was ex facie binding on the members unless set aside by the court. (2) C's submission that T's council had to carry out an inquiry before deciding to seek an explanation from the member whose conduct was in issue in terms of rule 22 appeared to be based on a misconstruction of the rules: if rule 22 was construed as requiring, at least in the context of a member being suspended or asked to resign, that the council should act only after inquiry, and that such inquiry should include giving notice to the member whose conduct was being inquired into, and afford him the opportunity of stating his case, it would make explicit the requirements of a fair hearing which would otherwise be held to be implicit. (3) C was informed of the terms of the complaint against him verbatim: the letter made tolerably clear the aspects of his conduct which had occasioned concern and had he genuinely required further specification in order to respond to the complaint, he could have requested it but, on the contrary, C had elected not to avail himself of that opportunity and could not now complain of not having had a fair opportunity to respond. (4) C's argument that it was unfair for the members who had signed the letter of complaint to take part in and vote at the general meeting was manifestly untenable where rule 22.2 required the council to call a general meeting of the club, sending a circular to "every" member and there was no reason why, as a matter of fairness, a signatory of the complaint should not take part in the general meeting at which the subject matter of the complaint was to be dealt, further, the implication of C's argument was that those who complained about his conduct ipso facto disqualified themselves and the reductio as absurdum was that, if all the other members complained about C's conduct, no one would be entitled to vote for his expulsion.

CROCKET v. TANTALLON GOLF CLUB 2005 S.L.T. 663, Lord Reed, OH.

4967. Judicial review–Natural justice–Suspension from golf club–Form of notice

The petitioner (P) sought judicial review of the decision of respondent (R) to suspend him from the club. P had been suspended after a charity golf event at which he did not comply with the required dress code, had not refrained from playing golf when asked to do so and had failed to ensure that his guests complied with the rules and general level of decorum required at the club. P argued that the procedures adopted by B breached the rules of natural justice and, in particular, that he had a right to know the nature and detail of the charges against him and to have the matter considered by an impartial body. R argued that there had been no breach of natural justice and that it should not be subject to the strict procedural rules applicable in court. In any event, R argued, it had given notice to P of the gist of the charges against him and had asked him for a response.

Held, granting the petition in part, that a golfing club could not be expected to conduct proceedings in the same way as a court but there was no recognised principle that the courts should refrain from exercising judicial review with regard to a sporting body, *McInnes v. Onslow Fane* [1978] 1 W.L.R. 1520, [1978] C.L.Y. 21 applied. R had failed to give P fair and adequate notice of the charges levelled against him. It was of particular concern that the behaviours complained of were never specified to P nor identified separately from those of the group he was with. P had not been notified that he was regarded as someone who had previously breached the rules of R. R's disciplinary council had the information before it relating to previous breaches of discipline by P and that information had influenced the decision to suspend P. A reasonable observer would have had real suspicions of partiality. Where a body, such as R's council, had prior knowledge of a member, they had to be particularly vigilant in avoiding the impression of partiality. In the instant case, they had not done so, *Murphy v. General Teaching Council for Scotland* 1997 S.C. 172, [1997] C.L.Y. 6008 and *R. v. Secretary of State for the Home Department, ex p. Doody* [1994] 1 A.C. 531, [1993] C.L.Y. 1213 applied. P's submission that the suspension of his membership had been determined in contravention of the rules of natural justice was well founded and he was entitled to refund of his membership fees.

IRVINE v. ROYAL BURGESS GOLFING SOCIETY OF EDINBURGH 2004 S.C.L.R. 386, Lady Smith, OH.

4968. Judicial review – Police Appeals Tribunal – Failure to give reasons

[Police Appeals Tribunals (Scotland) Rules 1996 (SI 1996 1644).]

C, a chief constable, sought reduction of a decision by the Police Appeals Tribunal (T) that the disposal by a misconduct hearing requiring a police constable to resign as an alternative to dismissal regarding five admitted counts of misconduct was unduly harsh and excessive. C submitted that T's decision was unsupported by adequate reasons and unreasonable having regard to the high standards of professional conduct required of police constables, and that the appeal should be heard de novo by a differently constituted tribunal. The police board conceded that no proper reasons were given, contrary to the requirements of the Police Appeals Tribunals (Scotland) Rules 1996, but that the court should not quash the decision but should order T to provide a statement of its reasons and consider the question of reasonableness thereafter; alternatively, if the decision were quashed, it was unnecessary for the appeal to be reheard, and T could simply issue a fresh decision.

Held, granting the petition, that T had not made a valid decision since that validity was conditional upon its compliance with the statutory requirement to give reasons, and the decision should be quashed, the consequence of which was that the appeal would have to be reheard by a freshly constituted tribunal so as to ensure that it was, and was perceived to be, impartial and free from preconceptions.

CHIEF CONSTABLE OF LOTHIAN AND BORDERS v. LOTHIAN AND BORDERS POLICE BOARD 2005 S.L.T. 315, Lord Reed, OH.

4969. Judicial review – Scottish Environment Protection Agency – Notice of variation of power station's authorisation

[Environmental Protection Act 1990 (c.43) s.10(2), s.11 (4); Pollution Prevention and Control (Scotland) Regulations 2000 (SI 2000 323) Sch.1 Part 1 s.1, s.5(1); Waste Incineration (Scotland) Regulations 2003 (SI 2003 170) Reg.3(2); Council Directive 75/442 Art.1 (a); Council Directive 2000/76 Art.3(5).]

P, operators of a power station burning coal and waste derived fuel, sought judicial review of a decision by E, an environment protection agency, to issue a notice of variation of the power station's authorisation under the Environmental Protection Act 1990 s.10(2) in 2003, requiring P to make an application under the Waste Incineration (Scotland) Regulations 2003 Reg.3(2). The waste derived fuel was produced from the sewage emanating from the public sewerage network operated by W, a water company. P and W submitted that the variation notice was based on an error of law, was ultra vires, and should be reduced since it proceeded on the basis that the power station fell within the ambit of Reg.3(2) of the 2003 Regulations when it was not a "waste incineration installation" since the activities carried on there did not include the incineration of waste: waste derived fuel was not "waste"as defined in theWaste Directive 75/442 Art.1 (a) nor was it waste as defined in the Pollution Prevention and Control (Scotland) Regulations 2000 Sch.1 Part 1 s.5(1). The Lord Ordinary refused to grant the declarator sought and P sought a further hearing in order to present arguments relating to the interpretation and application of the relevant domestic legislation. The hearing was conducted on the basis that waste derived fuel was "waste"as defined byArt.1 (a) of theWaste Directive and that the power station was a "co incineration plant" as defined by Council Directive 2000/76 Art.3(5). P submitted that the court should grant decree of declarator that the power station was not an existing waste incineration installation, and reduce the variation notice as issued by E notwithstanding the Lord Ordinary's decision that waste derived fuel was waste because the authorisation under which the power station operated was for the combustion of fuel not the incineration of waste, namely "any fuel", which was unqualified and could in principle include any substance which was burned.

Held, refusing the petition, that Reg.3(2) of the 2003 Regulations applied to the power station. (1) The authorisation of the power station was originally issued on April 30, 1993, at a time when the use of waste derived fuel was not envisaged, and when its use as a co fuel was proposed, P applied to E for a variation of the authorisation under s.11 (4) of the 1990 Act which was issued in December 1998 and amended the description of the authorised process and the conditions thereof. (2) The power station was "authorised as a waste incineration installation" from the time when the variation notice was issued in December 1998: a waste incineration installation was that part of an installation which included any activity falling within s.1 of Part 1 of Sch.1 to the 2000 Regulations which was carried out in a co incineration plant as defined in s.5(1), and an activity falling within s.1 (1) was undoubtedly authorised; the fact that the authorisation categorised the process carried on at the power station as a combustion process, rather than as a process of incineration, did not affect that conclusion where the description of the authorised process as a combustion process was consistent with the use of waste as a fuel in the course of that process, and it was apparent from the terms of the authorisation issued (as varied from December 1998) that such a use of waste was authorised, subject to conditions; in any event, the definition of a waste incineration installation in Reg.2(1) of the 2000 Regulations made it plain that such an installation did not need to have, or need to be eligible to have, a permit under s.5(1) of Sch.1. (3) The power station did not fall within the excluded category to which Reg.3(2) applied.

SCOTTISH POWER GENERATION LTD v. SCOTTISH ENVIRONMENT PROTECTION AGENCY (NO.2) 2005 S.L.T. 641, Lord Reed, OH.

4970. **Judicial review–Scottish Environment Protection Agency–Notice of variation of power station's authorisation–Meaning of "waste" in Art.1 (a) Council Directive 75/442**

[Pollution Prevention and Control (Scotland) Regulations 2000 (SI 2000 323) Sch.1 Part I s.5(1);Waste Incineration (Scotland) Regulations 2003 (SI 2003 170) Reg.3(2); Council Directive 75/442 on waste Art.1 (a).]

P, the operators of a power station burning coal and waste derived fuel, petitioned for judicial review of a decision by the Scottish Environment Protection Agency to issue a notice of variation of the power station's authorisation, and sought declarator that waste derived fuel was not waste as defined by theWaste Council Directive 75/442 Art.1 (a). The waste derived fuel was produced from the sewage emanating from the public sewerage network operated by a water company. P submitted that the notice was based on an error of law, was ultra vires and should be reduced as it proceeded on the basis that the power station fell within the ambit of theWaste Incineration (Scotland) Regulations 2003 Reg.3(2) when it was not a "waste incineration installation" since the activities carried on there did not include the co incineration of waste. P argued that waste derived fuel was not "waste" as defined in Art.1 (a) of the Directive nor was it waste as defined in the Pollution Prevention and Control (Scotland)

Regulations 2000 Sch.1 Part I s.5(1). P contended that the fuel was produced intentionally as a result of a complex industrial process and was designed for a particular purpose in response to a demand in the electricity generating market, its production was subject to a specification and to quality control and rejection procedures, its use replaced fossil fuels which would otherwise be burnt, in line with EC environmental policy, that which was produced was certain to be used as fuel at the power station, and the burning of it was strictly regulated.

Held, refusing to grant declarator that waste derived fuel was not waste as defined by Art.1(a) of the Directive and putting the case out by order, that (1) any material was capable of constituting "waste" within the meaning of Art.1(a) of the Directive in the event that it was discarded which, in that context, included in particular the use of waste as a means of generating electricity, the recycling of waste and the reclamation from it of substances which were intended for re use, and it followed that waste might be of economic value which its holder might be said to "discard" notwithstanding that it was put to some commercially valuable use. (2) There was no doubt that the sewage sludge received at the treatment centre was "waste" within the meaning of the Directive and while P maintained that the operation carried out at the centre was a complete recovery operation, the waste derived fuel could not be used under the same conditions of environmental protection as coal, or without any greater danger of harm to human health or the environment, thus as the processing of the sludge could not be regarded as a complete recovery operation, its status as "waste" was not altered within the meaning of the Directive.

SCOTTISH POWER GENERATION LTD v. SCOTTISH ENVIRONMENT PROTECTION AGENCY (NO.1) 2005 S.L.T. 98, Lord Reed, OH.

4971. Public authorities–Appointments–Specified authorities

PUBLIC APPOINTMENTS AND PUBLIC BODIES ETC. (SCOTLAND) ACT 2003 (AMENDMENT OF SPECIFIED AUTHORITIES) ORDER 2005, SSI 2005 540; made under the Public Appointments and Public Bodies etc. (Scotland) Act 2003 s.3. In force: October 26, 2005; £3.00.

This Order amends the list of specified authorities contained in the Public Appointments and Public Bodies etc. (Scotland) Act 2003.

4972. Public authorities–Appointments–Specified authorities

PUBLIC APPOINTMENTS AND PUBLIC BODIES ETC. (SCOTLAND) ACT 2003 (TREATMENT OF OFFICE OR BODY AS SPECIFIED AUTHORITY) ORDER 2005, SSI 2005 539; made under the Public Appointments and Public Bodies etc. (Scotland) Act 2003 s.3. In force: October 26, 2005; £3.00.

This Order provides that Bord na Gaidhlig, Scottish Further and Higher Education Funding Council, Scottish Local Authorities Remuneration Committee, Water Industry Commission and Scottish Charity Regulator shall, for the purposes of appointments to these bodies or offices, be treated as if they were specified authorities listed in the Public Appointments and Public Bodies etc. (Scotland) Act 2003.

AGENCY

4973. Commercial agents–Agreements–Termination–Compensation

[Commercial Agents (Council Directive) Regulations 1993 (SI 1993 3053) Reg.2, Reg.17, Sch.1 para.2, Sch.1 para.3, Sch.1 para.4.]

M, a sales agent for B, a company, raised an action seeking indemnity and compensation in terms of the Commercial Agents (Council Directive) Regulations 1993 Reg.17 following the termination of the agency agreement. The sheriff held that M's activities as a commercial agent were "secondary" in terms of Reg.2 of, and Sch.1 to, the 1993 Regulations and granted B decree of absolvitor. The sheriff considered that the concluding part of Sch.1 para.2 contained a substantive requirement that was only satisfied if "the commercial interests of the principal" was interpreted as meaning that "goodwill attached to the principal's product as a result of the efforts of the agent", and that on the evidence it was difficult to see where goodwill had accrued to B as a consequence of M's agency. M appealed, submitting that the sheriff had erred in his approach to Sch.1 para.2: read as a whole, it required no more than consideration of whether it was in B's commercial interests, in developing the market in question, to appoint a representative and it was going too far to look not only at "building up goodwill" but whether that enured to B's benefit subsequent to the termination of the agreement. Further, the fact that B manufactured goods constituted an indication, by virtue of Sch.1 para.3(a), that the arrangement fell within Sch.1 para.2, and was sufficient by itself to support the overall conclusion to that effect.

Held, dismissing the appeal, that the sheriff's fundamental interpretation of the schedule could not be criticised. It was appropriate to interpret the last part of Sch.1 para.2 as involving the creation of goodwill enuring to the principal in the agency agreement. Whilst the sheriff had approached the issue of the creation and existence of goodwill by examining the situation post termination of the agency agreement, that was because the arrangement between the parties had come to an end, and not because of any misdirection in law. Further and in any event, he was entitled to be fortified in his view by the relevant absence of the indicators in Sch.1 para.3 and Sch.1 para.4 pointing to the arrangement falling within Sch.1 para.2, and, in particular, the fact that the goods were not specifically identified with B in the market in question.

McADAM v. BOXPAK LTD 2005 S.L.T. (Sh Ct) 47, Sheriff Principal EF Bowen Q.C., Sh Ct.

AGRICULTURE

4974. Agricultural policy–Business development scheme–Variation

FARM BUSINESS DEVELOPMENT (SCOTLAND) VARIATION SCHEME 2005, SSI 2005 219; made under the Agriculture Act 1970 s.29. In force: June 1, 2005; £3.00.

This instrument amends the Farm Business Development (Scotland) Scheme 2001 which enables the payment of financial assistance for measures which are listed in the Schedule to the Scheme for that part of Scotland outwith the Highlands and Islands area. The total amount of financial assistance payable to one or more eligible person in respect of one eligible business is increased by £5,000 to £25,000, and in respect of an application for financial assistance in relation to a collaborative venture the total amount of financial assistance payable in respect of each eligible business is increased by £5,000 to £35,000.

4975. Agricultural policy–Direct support schemes

COMMON AGRICULTURAL POLICY SINGLE FARM PAYMENT AND SUPPORT SCHEMES (SCOTLAND) AMENDMENT REGULATIONS 2005, SSI 2005 257; made under the European Communities Act 1972 s.2. In force: May 16, 2005; £3.00.

These Regulations amend the Common Agricultural Policy Single Farm Payment and Support Schemes (Scotland) Regulations 2005 (SSI 2005 143) to update references to Community instruments to refer to Commission Regulation 394/2005 ([2005] OJ L63/17), Commission Regulation 118/2005 ([2005] OJ L24/15) and Commission Regulation 606/2005 ([2005] OJ L100/15). They Regulations authorise farmers to make use of the possibility introduced by Regulation 606/2005 to fix two different dates for the beginning of the ten month period for which parcels of eligible land have to be at the farmer's disposal to qualify for the Single Farm Payment Scheme.

4976. Agricultural policy–Direct support schemes

COMMON AGRICULTURAL POLICY SINGLE FARM PAYMENT AND SUPPORT SCHEMES (SCOTLAND) REGULATIONS 2005, SSI 2005 143; made under the European Communities Act 1972 s.2. In force: April 18, 2005; £6.00.

These Regulations amend the Sheep Annual Premium Regulations 1992 (SI 1992 2677), the Sheep Annual Premium (Amendment) Regulations 1994 (SI 1994 2741), the Sheep Annual Premium (Amendment) Regulations 1995 (SI 1995 2779), the Sheep Annual Premium (Amendment) Regulations 1996 (SI 1996 49), the Arable Area Payments Regulations 1996 (SI 1996 3142), the Sheep Annual Premium (Amendment) Regulations 1997 (SI 1997 2500), the Arable Area Payments (Amendment) Regulations 1997 (SI 1997 2969), the Arable Area Payments (Amendment) Regulations 1998 (SI 1998 3169), the Arable Area Payments (Amendment) Regulations 1999 (SI 1999 8), the Sheep Annual Premium (Amendment) Regulations 2001 (SI 2001 281), the Sheep Annual Premium and Suckler Cow Quotas Regulations 2003 (SI 2003 2261) and revoke the Common Agricultural Policy Support Schemes (Modulation) (Scotland) Amendment Regulations 2004 (SSI 2000 398), the Common Agricultural Policy Support Schemes (Modulation) (Scotland) Regulations 2000 (SSI 2000 429), the Suckler Cow Premium (Scotland) Regulations 2001 (SSI 2001 225), the Beef Special Premium (Scotland) Regulations 2001 (SSI 2001 445) and the Extensification Payment (Scotland) Regulations 2001 (SSI 2002 278). The Regulations make provision in Scotland for the administration of Council Regulation 1782/2003 ([2003] OJ L270/1), Commission Regulation 795/2004 ([2004] OJ L141/1) and Commission Regulation 796/2004 ([2004 OJ L141/18) in relation to establishing a new system of direct support schemes (including the Single Farm Payment Scheme) which came into force in January 2005 under the Common Agricultural Policy. They also make provision in Scotland for the administration of Commission Regulation 1973/2004 ([2004] OJ L345/1) and implement Chapter 16 of that Regulation in relation to the obligation to set aside land under the new Single Farm Payment Scheme. These provisions also implement part of Regulation 795/2004.

4977. Agricultural policy–Land management contracts–Menu scheme–Subsidies

LAND MANAGEMENT CONTRACTS (MENU SCHEME) (SCOTLAND) REGULATIONS 2005, SSI 2005 225; made under the European Communities Act 1972 s.2. In force: May 15, 2005; £6.00.

These Regulations, which amend the Agricultural Subsidies (Appeals) (Scotland) Regulations 2004 (SSI 2004 381), implement provisions of Council Regulation 1257/1999 ([1999] OJ L160/80) on support for rural development from the European Agricultural Guidance and Guarantee Fund. The Regulations provide for payment of aid to be made to any person who enters into an undertaking with the Scottish Ministers to carry out, or as the case may be to carry out and maintain, the activities relevant to at least one of the Menu Options set out in Sch.1 and to comply with the general environmental requirements set out in Sch.2 to the Regulations.

4978. Agricultural produce–Milk–Quota arrangements

DAIRY PRODUCE QUOTAS (SCOTLAND) REGULATIONS 2005, SSI 2005 91; made under the European Communities Act 1972 s.2; and the Finance Act 1973 s.56. In force: March 31, 2005; £6.00.

These Regulations, which amend the Milk Development Council Order 1995 (SI 1995 356), revoke and replace the Dairy Produce Quotas (Scotland) Regulations 2002 (SSI 2002 110), the Dairy Produce Quotas (Scotland) Amendment Regulations 2002 (SSI 2002 228) and the Dairy Produce Quotas (Scotland) Amendment Regulations 2004 (SSI 2004 118). The Regulations implement Council Regulation 1788/2003 ([2003] OJ L270/123) establishing a levy in the milk and milk products sector and Commission Regulation 595/2004 ([2004] OJ L94/22) laying down detailed rules for applying Council Regulation 1788/2003 establishing a levy in the milk and milk products sector. The new provisions included in these Regulations include: before approving a purchaser, the Scottish Ministers may oblige the purchaser to lodge such security as the Scottish Ministers may reasonably require; provisions relating to butterfat-adjusted deliveries and the liability of wholesale producers for levy on deliveries; a direct seller who does not provide a declaration of the sales made by that direct seller in a quota year by May 14 immediately following the end of that quota year and who is liable to pay levy in respect of such sales will pay levy at the full rate; and unless a wholesale producer has already paid levy, in certain circumstances the wholesale producer will be liable for the payment of levy to the Scottish Ministers where the purchaser of that wholesale producer has failed to do so.

4979. Agricultural produce–Seed potatoes–Fees

SEED POTATOES (FEES) (SCOTLAND) REGULATIONS 2005, SSI 2005 279; made under the Plant Varieties and Seeds Act 1964 s.16. In force: June 18, 2005; £3.00.

These Regulations which revoke the Seed Potatoes (Fees) (Scotland) Regulations 2004 (SSI 2004 250) prescribe the fees payable in respect of certain matters arising under the Seed Potatoes (Scotland) Regulations 2000.

4980. Animal products–Bone in beef–Placing on market–Restrictions

BOVINE PRODUCTS (RESTRICTION ON PLACING ON THE MARKET) (SCOTLAND) REGULATIONS 2005, SSI 2005 470; made under the European Communities Act 1972 s.2. In force: November 7, 2005; £3.00.

These Regulations, which amend the Animal By Products (Identification) Regulations 1995 (SI 1995 614), revoke the Fresh Meat (Beef Controls) (No.2) Regulations 1996 (SI 1996 2097), the Fresh Meat (Beef Controls) (No.2) (Amendment) Regulations 1996 (SI 1996 2522) and the Fresh Meat (Beef Controls) (No.2) Amendment (Scotland) Regulations 2000 (SSI 2000 449). They implement Commission Decision 2005/598 ([2005] OJ L204/22) prohibiting the placing on the market of products derived from bovine animals born or reared within the UK before August 1, 1996 for any purpose and exempting such animals from certain control and eradication measures laid down in Regulation 999/2001. They apply with modifications certain provisions of the Food Safety Act 1990 for the purposes of these Regulations; provide for the inspection and seizure of products that are suspected of having been placed on the market in contravention; create offences and penalties; and make provision for their enforcement including the appointment of authorised officers.

4981. Animal products–Bone in beef–Placing on market–Restrictions

BOVINE PRODUCTS (RESTRICTION ON PLACING ON THE MARKET) (SCOTLAND) (NO.2) REGULATIONS 2005, SSI 2005 586; made under the European Communities Act 1972 s.2. In force: January 1, 2006; £3.00.

These Regulations, which revoke the Bovine Products (Restriction on Placing on the Market) (Scotland) Regulations 2005 (SSI 2005 470), amend the Animal By Products (Identification) Regulations 1995 (SI 1995 614). The 2005 Regulations gave effect to Commission Decision 2005/598 ([2005] OJ L204/22) Art.1 (1), prohibiting the placing on the market of products derived from bovine animals born or reared within the UK before August 1, 1996 for any purpose and exempting such animals from certain control and eradication measures laid down in Regulation 999/2001. These Regulations apply with modifications certain provisions of the Food Safety Act 1990 for the purposes thereof; provide for the inspection and seizure of products that are suspected of having been placed on the market in contravention of reg.3; create offences and penalties; and make provision for their enforcement including the appointment of authorised officers.

4982. Animal products–Diseases and disorders–TSE

TSE (SCOTLAND) AMENDMENT REGULATIONS 2005, SSI 2005 173; made under the European Communities Act 1972 s.2. In force: May 1, 2005; £3.00.

These Regulations amend the TSE (Scotland) Regulations 2002 (SSI 2002 255) by bringing up to date the definition of "the Community Transitional Measures" in Reg.3(1) of that instrument so as to include amendments made to European Parliament and Council Regulation 999/2001 ([2001] OJ L147/1) laying down rules for the prevention, control and eradication of certain transmissible spongiform encephalopathies.

4983. Animal products–Diseases and disorders–TSE

TSE (SCOTLAND) AMENDMENT (NO.2) REGULATIONS 2005, SSI 2005 469; made under the European Communities Act 1972 s.2. In force: November 7, 2005; £3.00.

These Regulations amend the TSE (Scotland) Regulations 2002 (SI 2002 255) which give effect in Scotland to the enforcement and administration of European Parliament and Council Regulation 999/2001 ([2001] OJ L147/1) laying down rules for the prevention, control and eradication of certain transmissible spongiform encephalopathies. They implement the requirements contained in Regulation 999/2001 for TSE testing of bovine animals aged over 30 months slaughtered for human consumption.

4984. Animal products–Import and export controls

ANIMALS AND ANIMAL PRODUCTS (IMPORT AND EXPORT) (SCOTLAND) AMENDMENT REGULATIONS 2005, SSI 2005 278; made under the European Communities Act 1972 s.2. In force: July 1, 2005; £3.00.

These Regulations amend the Animals and Animal Products (Import and Export) (Scotland) Regulations 2000 (SSI 2000 216) to implement Council Directive 2003/50 ([2003] OJ L169/51) as regards the reinforcement of controls on movements of ovine and caprine animals.

4985. Animal products–Import and export controls

ANIMALS AND ANIMAL PRODUCTS (IMPORT AND EXPORT) (SCOTLAND) AMENDMENT (NO.2) REGULATIONS 2005, SSI 2005 502; made under the European Communities Act 1972 s.2; and the Finance Act 1973 s.56. In force: November 14, 2005; £3.00.

These Regulations amend the Animals and Animal Products (Import and Export) (Scotland) Regulations 2000 (SSI 2000 216) provide a statutory basis for the Poultry Health Scheme, which is implemented by the Scottish Ministers in order to ensure compliance with the rules set out in Council Directive 90/539 ([1990] OJ L303/6) on animal health conditions governing intra-Community trade in, and imports from third countries of, poultry and hatching eggs. The Regulations also make arrangements for the approval of laboratories to undertake Mycoplasma testing under the Poultry Health Scheme, including the details of the annual approval fee.

4986. Animal products–Origin marking–Third country imports

PRODUCTS OF ANIMAL ORIGIN (THIRD COUNTRY IMPORTS) (SCOTLAND) AMENDMENT (NO.2) REGULATIONS 2005, SSI 2005 645; made under the European Communities Act 1972 s.2. In force: December 16, 2005; £3.00.

These Regulations amend the Products of Animal Origin (Third Country Imports) (Scotland) Regulations 2002 (SSI 2002 445) which implement Council Directive 97/78 ([1997] OJ L24/9) laying down the principles governing the organisation of veterinary checks on products entering the Community from third countries. They give effect to the restriction on the importation of products derived from birds, other than poultry, contained in Commission Decision 2005/760 ([2005] OJ L285/60) concerning certain protection measures in relation to highly pathogenic avian influenza in certain third countries for the import of captive birds.

4987. Animals–Diseases and disorders–Tuberculosis

TUBERCULOSIS (SCOTLAND) ORDER 2005, SSI 2005 434; made under the Animal Health Act 1981 s.1, s.7, s.8, s.15, s.25, s.32, s.83, s.87, s.88. In force: September 23, 2005; £3.00.

This Order, which amends the Animal Health Orders (Divisional Veterinary Manager Amendment) Order 1995 (SI 1995 2922), revokes the Tuberculosis (Scotland) Order 1984 (SI 1984 2063) and the Tuberculosis (Scotland) Amendment Order 1990 (SI 1990 1908). The principal changes are: to introduce an obligation to apply a diagnostic test for tuberculosis to any animal moving from a holding in Scotland or to any animal which has arrived at a holding in Scotland from a holding in an area in Great Britain where there is a high incidence of bovine tuberculosis; to prohibit the movement of a bovine animal between the application of a diagnostic test for tuberculosis and the veterinary inspector being satisfied with the test; to clarify the power to impose movement restrictions on herds where an official tuberculin test has not been carried out by the due date; to introduce a duty to notify the isolation of the organism M. bovis when found in sample taken in a laboratory; and to remove the prescribed forms of Notice (previously Form A and Form B) previously set out in the Schedules to the 1984 Order.

4988. Animals–Feedingstuffs

FEEDING STUFFS (SCOTLAND) REGULATIONS 2005, SSI 2005 605; made under the Agriculture Act 1970 s.66, s.68, s.69, s.70, s.71, s.74, s.74A, s.79, s.84. In force: January 1, 2006; £13.50.

These Regulations, which amend the Feeding Stuffs (Sampling and Analysis) Regulations 1999 (SI 1999 1663), modify the Agriculture Act 1970 and revoke the Feeding Stuffs (Enforcement) Amendment (Scotland) Regulations 2001 (SI 2001 334), the Feeding Stuffs Amendment (Scotland) Regulations 2002 (SI 2002 285), the Feeding Stuffs (Scotland) Amendment Regulations 2003 (SI 2003 101), the Feeding Stuffs (Scotland) Amendment (No.2) Regulations 2003 (SI 2003 312), and the Feeding Stuffs (Scotland) Amendment (No.3) Regulations 2003 (SI 2003 474), to implement Commission Directive 2004/116 ([2004] OJ L379/81) amending the Annex to Council Directive 92/471 as regards the inclusion of Candida guillermondii, and also provide for the implementation, or as the case may be the continuing implementation, of 10 EC Directives and Decisions listed in the explanatory note.

4989. Animals–Feedingstuffs–Establishments–Fees

FEEDING STUFFS (ESTABLISHMENTS AND INTERMEDIARIES) AMENDMENT (SCOTLAND) REGULATIONS 2005, SSI 2005 116; made under the European Communities Act 1972 s.2. In force: April 1, 2005; £3.00.

These Regulations, which amend the Feeding Stuffs (Establishments and Intermediaries) Regulations 1999 (SI 1999 1872), implement Council Decision 98/728 ([1998] OJ L346/51) concerning a Community system of fees in the animal feed sector. They provide for the payment of fees and the reimbursement of the costs of laboratory analyses to the specified approval body by a person applying to that body for approval of an establishment; provide for the payment of fees and the reimbursement of the costs of laboratory analyses to the competent body by a person applying to it for approval as an "intermediary"; and specify the fees payable.

4990. Eggs–Marketing standards

EGGS (MARKETING STANDARDS) (ENFORCEMENT) (SCOTLAND) REGULATIONS 2005, SSI 2005 332; made under the European Communities

Act 1972 s.2; and the Food Safety Act 1990 s.6, s.16, s.17, s.19, s.26, s.48, Sch.1 para.5, Sch.1 para.7. In force: July 1, 2005; £3.00.

These Regulations revoke the Eggs (Marketing Standards) Regulations 1995 (SI 1995 1544), the Eggs (Marketing Standards) (Amendment) Regulations 1996 (SI 1996 1725), the Eggs (Marketing Standards) (Amendment) Regulations 1997 (SI 1997 1414) and the Eggs (Marketing Standards) (Amendment) Regulations 1998 (SI 1998 1665). They make provision for the enforcement and execution of certain specified Community provisions which relate to marketing standards for shell eggs and to the production and marketing of eggs for hatching and of farmyard poultry chicks.

4991. Farming—Organic farming—Aid payments

ORGANIC AID (SCOTLAND) AMENDMENT REGULATIONS 2005, SSI 2005 619; made under the European Communities Act 1972 s.2. In force: December 23, 2005; £3.00.

These Regulations amend the Organic Aid (Scotland) Regulations 2004 (SSI 2004 143) which make provision for the payment of aid to farmers who undertake to introduce organic farming methods and introduces new payments of aid to farmers: for capital items required to introduce organic farming methods; to use organic farming methods once aid for introducing such methods ceases; and to contribute to the cost of producing a conversion plan to apply for a conversion grant. The Regulations insert definitions of land formally in conversion and permanent pasture; amend the definitions of arable land, improved grassland, landlord, rough grazings, tenant and the Organic Standards Compendium; and insert an Electronic Communications Act 2000 provision enabling things done in writing in the principal Regulations to include a reference to an electronic communication.

4992. Food safety—Feedingstuffs—Zootechnical additives

FEEDING STUFFS (APPLICATION TO ZOOTECHNICAL ADDITIVES ETC.) (SCOTLAND) REGULATIONS 2005, SI 2005 3362 (S.11); made under the Agriculture Act 1970 s.66, s.68, s.69, s.70, s.71, s.74, s.74A, s.77, s.78, s.79, s.84. In force: January 3, 2006; £3.00.

These Regulations, which revoke the Feeding Stuffs (Establishments and Intermediaries) Regulations 1999 (SI 1999 1872), the Feeding Stuffs (Enforcement) Regulations 1999 (SI 1999 2325) and the Feeding Stuffs (Safety Requirements for Feed for Food-Producing Animals) Regulations 2004 (SI 2004 3254), make provision in relation to those zootechnical feed additives that fall within the categories of digestibility enhancers, gut flora stabilisers or substances which are intended to favourably affect the environment. They provide for the enforcement and execution of European Parliament and Council Regulation 1829/2003 ([2003] OJ L268/1) on genetically modified food and feed in so far as it applies to non-medicinal zootechnical additives; European Parliament and Council Regulation 1831/2003 ([2003] OJ L268/29) on additives for use in animal nutrition; European Parliament and Council Regulation 183/2005 ([2005] OJ L25/1) laying down requirements for feed hygiene; European Parliament and Council Regulation 178/2002 ([2002] OJ L31/1) laying down the general principles and requirements of food law, establishing the European Food Safety Authority and laying down procedures in matters of food safety; European Parliament and Council Regulation 882/2004 ([2004] OJ L191/1) on official controls performed to ensure the verification of compliance with feed and food law, animal health and animal welfare rules. They lay down procedures relating to secondary analysis of samples taken in connection with the enforcement of the Feed (Hygiene and Enforcement) (Scotland) Regulations 2005 (SSI 2005 608) by the laboratory of the Government Chemist.

4993. Food safety—Information requirements

OFFICIAL FEED AND FOOD CONTROLS (SCOTLAND) REGULATIONS 2005, SSI 2005 616; made under the European Communities Act 1972 s.2; and the Food Safety Act 1990 s.16, s.17, s.48. In force: January 1, 2006; £5.50.

These Regulations amend the General Food Regulations 2004 (SI 2004 3279) and the Feed (Hygiene and Enforcement) (Scotland) Regulations 2005 (SSI 2005 608) plus 44 other instruments. They also revoke the Imported Food (Scotland) Regulations 1985 (SI 1985 913), the Food Safety (Exports) Regulations 1991 (SI 1991 1476) and the Imported Food Regulations 1997 (SI 1997 2537). The Regulations impose prohibitions on the introduction of certain feed and food into Scotland in so far as non compliant with the European Parliament and Council Regulation 178/2002 ([2002] OJ L31/1) laying down the general principles and requirements of food law, establishing the European Food Safety Authority and laying down procedures in matters of food safety. The Regulations provide for the exchange and provision of information by competent authorities; and enable a competent authority to require a control body to provide information and make records available and provide that a person who fails to comply with a requirement to provide information or make records available, or in purported compliance with such a requirement furnishes false or misleading information, is guilty of an offence.

4994. Genetically modified organisms—Feedingstuffs—Emergency controls

FEED (CORN GLUTEN FEED AND BREWERS GRAINS) (EMERGENCY CONTROL) (SCOTLAND) REGULATIONS 2005, SSI 2005 246; made under the European Communities Act 1972 s.2. In force: May 6, 2005; £3.00.

These Regulations, which implement Commission Decision 2005/317 ([2005] OJ L101/14) on emergency measures regarding the non-authorised genetically modified organism Bt 10 in maize, amend the Genetically Modified Animal Feed (Scotland) Regulations 2004 (SSI 2004 433) to provide that where controlled products are condemned, the expenses incurred by the enforcement authority in connection with the destruction or disposal of those products shall be payable on demand by the operator responsible for their first placing on the market. The Regulations prohibit the first placing on the market of certain maize products originating from the US; make it an offence to breach that prohibition; apply with modifications certain provisions of the Agriculture Act 1970; apply with modifications certain provisions of the Feeding Stuffs (Sampling and Analysis) Regulations 1999 (SI 1999 1663) for the purposes of the Regulations; and provide for the inspection, seizure and detention of controlled products.

4995. Infectious disease control—Import of potatoes—Egypt

POTATOES ORIGINATING IN EGYPT (SCOTLAND) AMENDMENT REGULATIONS 2005, SSI 2005 39; made under the European Communities Act 1972 s.2. In force: February 28, 2005; £3.00.

These Regulations implement in Scotland, Commission Decision 2004/836 ([2004] OJ L360/30) amending Commission Decision 2004/4 authorising Member States temporarily to take emergency measures against the dissemination of Pseudomonas solanacearum (Smith) Smith (now referred to as Ralstonia solanacearum (Smith) Yabuuchi et al) as regards Egypt.

4996. Milk products—Reporting on prices

REPORTING OF PRICES OF MILK PRODUCTS (SCOTLAND) REGULATIONS 2005, SSI 2005 484; made under the European Communities Act 1972 s.2. In force: November 11, 2005; £3.00.

These Regulations make provision in Scotland for the implementation of Commission Regulation 562/2005 ([2005] OJ L95/11) Art.6 laying down rules for the implementation of Council Regulation 1255/1999 as regards communications between the Member States and the Commission in the milk and milk products sector. The Regulations require milk processors to provide such information relating to the prices of certain milk products as the Scottish Ministers may require by notice. Failure to comply with such a requirement is an offence punishable on summary conviction by a fine not exceeding level 5 on the standard scale.

4997. Pesticides–Residue levels in crops, food and feedingstuffs

PESTICIDES (MAXIMUM RESIDUE LEVELS IN CROPS, FOOD AND FEEDING STUFFS) (SCOTLAND) AMENDMENT REGULATIONS 2005, SSI 2005 109; made under the European Communities Act 1972 s.2. In force: March 25, 2005; £3.50.

These Regulations amend provisions of the Pesticides (Maximum Residue Levels in Crops, Food and Feeding Stuffs) (Scotland) Regulations 2000 (SSI 2000 22) and the Pesticides (Maximum Residue Levels in Crops, Food and Feeding Stuffs) (Scotland) Amendment (No.3) Regulations 2004 (SI 2004 399) to implement Commission Directive 2004/95 ([2004] OJ L301/42) amending Council Directive 90/642 as regards the maximum residue levels of bifenthrin and famoxadone fixed therein. The Regulations substitute new maximum residue levels for residue of the pesticides Bifenthrin and Famoxadone; and update the definition of "Residue Directives".

4998. Pesticides–Residue levels in crops, food and feedingstuffs

PESTICIDES (MAXIMUM RESIDUE LEVELS IN CROPS, FOOD AND FEEDING STUFFS) (SCOTLAND) AMENDMENT (NO.2) REGULATIONS 2005, SSI 2005 281; made under the European Communities Act 1972 s.2. In force: June 23, 2005; £3.50.

These Regulations which amend the Pesticides (Maximum Residue Levels in Crops, Food and Feeding Stuffs) (Scotland) Regulations 2000 (SSI 2000 22) and the Pesticides (Maximum Residue Levels in Crops, Food and Feeding Stuffs) (Scotland) Amendment Regulations 2005 (SSI 2005 109) implement Commission Directive 2004/115 ([2004] OJ L 374/64).

4999. Pesticides–Residue levels in crops, food and feedingstuffs

PESTICIDES (MAXIMUM RESIDUE LEVELS IN CROPS, FOOD AND FEEDING STUFFS) (SCOTLAND) REGULATIONS 2005, SSI 2005 599; made under the European Communities Act 1972 s.2. In force: December 22, 2005; £28.00.

These Regulations revoke the Pesticides (Maximum Residue Levels in Crops, Food and Feeding Stuffs) (Scotland) Regulations 2000 (SSI 2000 22), the Pesticides (Maximum Residue Levels in Crops, Food and Feeding Stuffs) (Scotland) Amendment Regulations 2001 (SSI 2001 84), the Pesticides (Maximum Residue Levels in Crops, Food and Feeding Stuffs) (Scotland) Amendment (No.2) Regulations 2001 (SSI 2001 221), the Pesticides (Maximum Residue Levels in Crops, Food and Feeding Stuffs) (Scotland) Amendment (No.3) Regulations 2001 (SSI 2001 435), the Pesticides (Maximum Residue Levels in Crops, Food and Feeding Stuffs) (Scotland) Amendment Regulations 2002 (SSI 2002 271), the Pesticides (Maximum Residue Levels in Crops, Food and Feeding Stuffs) (Scotland) Amendment (No.2) Regulations 2002 (SSI 2002 489), the Pesticides (Maximum Residue Levels in Crops, Food and Feeding Stuffs) (Scotland) Amendment Regulations 2003 (SSI 2003 118), the Pesticides (Maximum Residue Levels in Crops, Food and Feeding Stuffs) (Scotland) Amendment (No.2) Regulations 2003 (SSI 2003 445), the Pesticides (Maximum Residue Levels in Crops, Food and Feeding Stuffs) (Scotland) Amendment Regulations 2004 (SSI 2004 104),the Pesticides (Maximum Residue Levels in Crops, Food and Feeding Stuffs) (Scotland) Amendment (No.2) Regulations 2004 (SSI 2004 220), the Pesticides (Maximum Residue Levels in Crops, Food and Feeding Stuffs) (Scotland) Amendment (No.3) Regulations 2004 (SSI 2004 399), the Pesticides (Maximum Residue Levels in Crops, Food and Feeding Stuffs) (Scotland) Amendment Regulations 2005 (SSI 2005 109), and the Pesticides

(Maximum Residue Levels in Crops, Food and Feeding Stuffs) (Scotland) Amendment (No.2) Regulations 2005 (SSI 2005 281). They implement Council Directive 76/895 ([1976] OJ L340/26) relating to fruit and vegetables; Council Directive 86/362 ([1986] OJ L221/37); Council Directive 86/363 ([1986] OJ L221/43) as regards cereals and products of animal origin; Council Directive 90/642 ([1990] OJ L350/71) as regards certain products of plant origin (including fruit and vegetables), as amended; Commission Directive 2005/37 ([2000] OJ L141/10); Commission Directive 2005/46 ([2005] OJ L177/35); and Commission Directive 2005/48 ([2005] OJ L219/29). They specify new maximum residue levels on products of plant origin including cereals for the pesticides Carfentrazone-ethyl, Fenamidone, Isoxaflutole, Maleic Hydrazide, Mecoprop, Propyzamide, and Trifloxystrobin and create offences, specify penalties, provide defences and confer enforcement powers where maximum residue levels have been exceeded in respect of products put into circulation.

5000. Plant health–Licensing services–Fees

PLANT HEALTH FEES (SCOTLAND) AMENDMENT REGULATIONS 2005, SSI 2005 555; made under the European Communities Act 1972 s.2. In force: December 5, 2005; £3.00.

These Regulations increase certain fees in respect of licensing services chargeable under the Plant Health Fees (Scotland) Regulations 1996 (SSI 1996 1784).

5001. Plant varieties–Seeds–Cereal seeds–Marketing

CEREAL SEEDS (SCOTLAND) REGULATIONS 2005, SSI 2005 328; made under the Plant Varieties and Seeds Act 1964 s.16, s.36. In force: July 1, 2005; £9.00.

These Regulations, which amend the Seeds (Miscellaneous Amendments) Regulations 1997 (SI 1997 616), the Seeds (National Lists of Varieties) Regulations 2001 (SI 2001 3510), the Seeds (Fees) (Scotland) Regulations 2002 (SSI 2002 526), the Seeds (Miscellaneous Amendments) (No.2) (Scotland) Regulations 2002 (SSI 2002 564), revoke the Cereal Seeds Regulations 1993 (SI 1993 2005), the Cereal Seeds (Amendment) Regulations 1995 (SI 1995 1482), the Cereal Seeds (Amendment) Regulations 1999 (SI 1999 1860) and the Cereal Seeds (Amendment) (Scotland) Regulations 2000 (SSI 2000 248). The Regulations implement provisions of Council Directive 66/402 ([1966] OJ L125/2309) on the marketing of cereal seed; apply to the certification and marketing of cereal seed of the species specified; and include provisions which prohibit the marketing of cereal seed in Scotland unless it is seed of a listed variety which has been officially certified or Breeders Seed.

5002. Plants–Plant health–Imports–Restrictions

PLANT HEALTH (SCOTLAND) ORDER 2005, SSI 2005 613; made under the Plant Health Act 1967 s.2, s.3, s.4. In force: December 31, 2005; £19.50.

This Order revokes the Plant Health (Great Britain) Order 1993 (SI 1993 1320), the Plant Health (Great Britain) (Amendment) (Potatoes) Order 1993 (SI 1993 3213), the Plant Health (Great Britain) (Amendment) Order 1995 (SI 1995 1358), the Plant Health (Great Britain) (Amendment) (No.2) Order 1995 (SI 1995 2929), the Plant Health (Great Britain) (Amendment) Order 1996 (SI 1996 25), the Plant Health (Great Britain) (Amendment) (No.2) Order 1996 (SI 1996 1165), the Plant Health (Great Britain) (Amendment) (No.3) Order 1996 (SI 1996 3242), the Plant Health (Great Britain) (Amendment) Order 1997 (SI 1997 1145), the Plant Health (Great Britain) (Amendment) (No.2) Order 1997 (SI 1997 2907), the Plant Health (Great Britain) (Amendment) Order 1998 (SI 1998 349), the Plant Health (Great Britain) (Amendment) (No.2) Order 1998 (SI 1998 1121), the Plant Health (Great Britain) (Amendment) (No.3) Order 1998 (SI 1998 2245), the Plant Health (Amendment) (Scotland) Order 1999 (SSI 1999 22), the Plant Health (Scotland) Amendment (No.2) Order 1999 (SSI 1999 129), the Plant Health

(Great Britain) Amendment (Scotland) Order 2001 (SSI 2001 249), the Plant Health (Great Britain) (Amendment) (Scotland) Order 2002 (SSI 2002 164), the Plant Health (Great Britain) Amendment (Scotland) Order 2003 (SSI 2003 224) and the Plant Health (Great Britain) Amendment (Scotland) Order 2004 (SSI 2004 440). The Order also implements Council Directive 2002/89 ([2002] OJ L355/45) amending Directive 2000/29 on protective measures against the introduction into the Community of organisms harmful to plants or plant products and against their spread within the Community; Commission Directive 2004/103 ([2004] OJ L313/16) on identity and plant health checks of plants, plant products or other objects, listed in Part B of Annex V to Council Directive 2000/29, which may be carried out at a place other than the point of entry into the Community or at a place close by and specifying the conditions related to these checks; Commission Directive 2004/105 ([2004] OJ L319/9) determining the models of official phytosanitary certificates or phytosanitary certificates for re-export accompanying plants, plant products or other objects from third countries and listed in Council Directive 2000/29; Commission Directive 2005/16 ([2005] OJ L57/19) amending Annexes I to V to Council Directive 2000/29 on protective measures against the introduction into the Community of organisms harmful to plants or plant products and against their spread within the Community; Commission Directive 2005/17 ([2005] OJ L57/23) amending certain provisions of Directive 92/105 concerning plant passports; and Commission Decision 2005/260 ([2005] OJ L78/50) which comprises Decision 2/2005 of the Joint Committee on Agriculture set up by the Agreement between the European Community and the Swiss Confederation on trade in agricultural products concerning the amendments to the Appendices to Annex 4. It imposes restrictions and requirements on relevant material imported into Scotland from third countries, including material coming via another country in the European Community where the Scottish Ministers have agreed to inspect that material in Scotland.

5003. Plants–Plant protection products

PLANT PROTECTION PRODUCTS (SCOTLAND) REGULATIONS 2005, SSI 2005 331; made under the European Communities Act 1972 s.2. In force: July 1, 2005; £5.50.

These Regulations, which disapply the Farm and Garden Chemicals Regulations 1971 (SI 1971 729) and the Control of Pesticides Regulations 1986 (SI 1986 1510), revoke the Plant Protection Products (Scotland) Regulations 2003 (SSI 2003 579) and the Plant Protection Products (Scotland) Amendment Regulations 2004 (SSI 2004 368). The Regulations continue to implement in Scotland Council Directive 91/414 ([1991] OJ L230/1) concerning the placing of plant protection products on the market; continue to implement the Directives amending the 1991 Directive; and also implement Commission Directive 2004/99 ([1999] OJ L309/6) amending Council Directive 91/414 to include acetamiprid and thiacloprid as active substances, Council Directive 2005/25 ([2005] OJ L90/1) amending Annex VI to Directive 91/414 as regards plant protection products containing micro-organisms, Commission Directive 2005/2 ([1991] OJ L20/15) amending Council Directive 91/414 to include Ampelomyces quisqualis and Gliocladium catenulatum as active substances, Commission Directive 2005/3 ([2005] OJ L20/19) amending Council Directive 91/414 to include imazosulfuron, laminarin, methoxyfenozide and s-metolachlor as active substances and Commission Directive 2005/34 amending Council Directive 91/414 to include etoxazole and tepraloxydim as active substances.

5004. Plants–Plant varieties–Fodder plant seeds–Marketing

FODDER PLANT SEED (SCOTLAND) REGULATIONS 2005, SSI 2005 329; made under the Plant Varieties and Seeds Act 1964 s.16, s.36. In force: July 1, 2005; £9.00.

These Regulations, which amend the Seeds (Miscellaneous Amendments) Regulations 1997 (SI 1997 616), the Seeds (National Lists of Varieties)

Regulations 2001 (SI 2001 3510), the Seeds (Fees) (Scotland) Regulations 2002 (SSI 2002 526) and the Seeds (Miscellaneous Amendments) (No.2) (Scotland) Regulations 2002 (SSI 2002 564), revoke the Fodder Plant Seeds Regulations 1993 (SI 1999 2009), the Fodder Plant Seeds (Amendment) Regulations 1993 (SI 1993 2529), the Fodder Plant Seeds (Amendment) Regulations 1996 (SI 1996 1453), the Fodder Plant Seeds (Amendment) Regulations 1999 (SI 1999 1864), the Fodder Plant Seeds (Amendment) (Scotland) Regulations 2000 (SSI 2000 247) and the Fodder Plant Seeds Amendment (Scotland) Regulations 2004 (SSI 2004 380). The Regulations implement provisions of Council Directive 66/402 ([1966] OJ L125/2309) on the marketing of cereal seed; apply to the certification and marketing of fodder plant seed of the species specified; and include provisions which prohibit the marketing of fodder plant seed in Scotland unless it is Commercial Seed, seed of a listed variety which has been officially certified or Breeder's Seed.

5005. **Potatoes–Seed potatoes–Marketing**
SEED POTATOES (SCOTLAND) AMENDMENT REGULATIONS 2005, SSI 2005 280; made under the Plant Varieties and Seeds Act 1964 s.16, s.36. In force: June 17, 2005; £4.00.
These Regulations amend the Seed Potatoes (Scotland) Regulations 2000 (SSI 2000 201) to implement Council Directive 2002/56 ([2002] OJ L193/60) on the Marketing of Seed Potatoes.

5006. **Rural areas–Less Favoured Area Support Scheme**
LESS FAVOURED AREA SUPPORT SCHEME (SCOTLAND) AMENDMENT REGULATIONS 2005, SSI 2005 64; made under the European Communities Act 1972 s.2. In force: March 12, 2005; £3.00.
These Regulations, which amend the Less Favoured Area Support Scheme (Scotland) Regulations 2004 (SI 2004 70), make provision for the purposes of implementation of Commission Regulation 817/2004 ([2004] OJ L153/30) which lays down detailed rules for the application of Council Regulation 1257/1999 on support for rural development from the European Agricultural Guidance and Guarantee Fund.

5007. **Rural areas–Less Favoured Area Support Scheme**
LESS FAVOURED AREA SUPPORT SCHEME (SCOTLAND) AMENDMENT (NO.2) REGULATIONS 2005, SSI 2005 624; made under the European Communities Act 1972 s.2. In force: January 12, 2006; £3.00.
These Regulations amend the Less Favoured Area Support Scheme (Scotland) Regulations 2005 (SSI 2005 569) to correct an error in the table relating to the calculation of stocking density. The amendment corrects omissions from the 2005 Regulations in respect of the environmental legislation with which applicants to the Less Favoured Area Support Scheme must comply. The amendment corrects the omission of a table of payment rates for less disadvantaged land.

5008. **Rural areas–Less Favoured Area Support Scheme**
LESS FAVOURED AREA SUPPORT SCHEME (SCOTLAND) REGULATIONS 2005, SSI 2005 569; made under the European Communities Act 1972 s.2. In force: December 2, 2005; £4.50.
These Regulations revoke the Less Favoured Area Support Scheme (Scotland) Regulations 2004 (SSI 2004 70), the Common Agricultural Policy Single Payment and Support Schemes (Integrated Administration and Control System) Regulations 2005 (SSI 2005 218) and the Less Favoured Area Support Scheme (Scotland) Amendment Regulations 2005 (SSI 2005 64) (with savings). They make provision for the purposes of implementation of Council Regulation 1257/1999 ([1999] OJ L160/80) on support for rural development from the European Agricultural Guidance and Guarantee Fund (EAGGF) and

amending and repealing certain Regulations and Commission Regulation 817/ 2004 ([2004] OJ L153/30) laying down detailed rules for the application of Council Regulation 1257/1999 on support for rural development from the European Agricultural Guidance and Guarantee Fund (EAGGF). The Regulations apply to holdings in respect of which the Scottish Ministers are the competent authority under the Common Agricultural Policy Single Payment and Support Schemes (Integrated Administration and Control System) Regulations 2005 (SSI 2005 218).

5009. Rural areas-Stewardship-Payments

RURAL STEWARDSHIP SCHEME (SCOTLAND) AMENDMENT REGULATIONS 2005, SSI 2005 620; made under the Environment Act 1995 s.98. In force: December 23, 2005; £3.00.

These Regulations amend the Rural Stewardship Scheme (Scotland) Regulations 2001 (SSI 2001 300) which implemented Commission Regulation 1750/1999 ([1999] OJ L214/31) laying down detailed rules for the application of Council Regulation 1257/1999 on support for rural development from the European Agricultural Guidance and Guarantee Fund (EAGGF). The 2001 Regulations provide for payment of aid to be made to any person who enters into an undertaking with the Scottish Ministers to comply with the general environmental requirements set out in Schedule 1 and to carry out, or as the case may be, to carry out and maintain at least one of either the management activities set out in Schedule 2 or the capital activities set out in Schedule 3. The 2001 Regulations make provision for rates of payment for management and capital activities. The Regulations make amendments to insert definitions of the Crofters (Scotland) Act 1993 and the Agricultural Holdings (Scotland) Act 2003 and to update the reference to an EC Commission Regulations; to insert new definitions for five different categories of entrants into the Rural Stewardship Scheme who are eligible for one of the two sets of payments rates for management activities set out in Schedule 4; and to amend the definitions of landlord and tenant.

5010. Subsidies-Appeals

AGRICULTURAL SUBSIDIES (APPEALS) (SCOTLAND) AMENDMENT REGULATIONS 2005, SSI 2005 117; made under the European Communities Act 1972 s.2. In force: March 25, 2005; £3.00.

These Regulations amend the Organic Aid (Scotland) Regulations 2004 (SSI 2004 143) and the Agricultural Subsidies (Appeals) (Scotland) Regulations 2004 (SSI 2004 381). They make amendments to add to the list of decisions amenable to review and appeal certain decisions made under Council Regulation 1782/2003 ([2003] OJ L270/1) establishing common rules for direct support schemes under the common agricultural policy and establishing certain support schemes for farmers, Commission Regulation 2237/2003 ([2003] OJ L339/52) laying down detailed rules for the application of certain support schemes provided for in Title IV of Council Regulation 1782/2003 establishing common rules for direct support schemes under the common agricultural policy and establishing certain support schemes for farmers, Commission Regulation 795/2004 ([2004] OJ L141/1) laying down detailed rules for the implementation of the single payment scheme provided for in Council Regulation 1782/2003, Commission Regulation 796/2004 ([2004] OJ L141/18) laying down detailed rules for the implementation of cross-compliance, modulation and the integrated administration and control system provided for in Council Regulation 1782/2003 and other legislation implementing those Regulations. They update the reference to the Regulations which provide for the integrated administration and control system for subsidy payments under the Common Agricultural Policy in the UK.

5011. Books

Agnew, Crispin H.—Agricultural Law in Scotland. Hardback: £150.00. ISBN 1 84592 034 1. Tottel Publishing.

ANIMALS

5012. Animal health–Diseases and disorders–Preventive measures–Avian influenza

AVIAN INFLUENZA (PREVENTIVE MEASURES) (SCOTLAND) AMENDMENT REGULATIONS 2005, SSI 2005 646; made under the European Communities Act 1972 s.2. In force: December 16, 2005; £3.00.

These Regulations which amend the Avian Influenza (Preventive Measures) (Scotland) Regulations 2005 (SSI 2005 530) give effect to Commission Decision 2005/734 ([2005] OJ L274/105) laying down biosecurity measures to reduce the risk of transmission of highly pathogenic avian influenza caused by Influenza virus A subtype H5N1 from birds living in the wild to poultry and other captive birds and providing for an early detection system in areas at particular risk.

5013. Animal health–Diseases and disorders–Preventive measures–Avian influenza

AVIAN INFLUENZA (PREVENTIVE MEASURES) (SCOTLAND) REGULATIONS 2005, SSI 2005 530; made under the European Communities Act 1972 s.2. In force: October 28, 2005; £3.00.

These Regulations give effect to Commission Decision 2005/734 ([2005] OJ L274/105) laying down biosecurity measures to reduce the risk of transmission of highly pathogenic avian influenza caused by influenza A virus of subtype H5N1 from birds living in the wild to poultry and other captive birds and providing for an early detection system in areas at particular risk. These Regulations require the Scottish Ministers to evaluate the risk of the transmission of avian influenza virus and to take appropriate measures to reduce that risk; provide for the Scottish Ministers to declare avian influenza prevention zones or to serve notices on premises at risk and lists the measures which may be imposed in zones and premises; and prohibit the holding of poultry gatherings of birds anywhere in Scotland unless they are licensed by a veterinary inspector after a risk assessment.

5014. Animal health–Infectious disease control–Broiler flocks

SALMONELLA IN BROILER FLOCKS (SAMPLING POWERS) (SCOTLAND) REGULATIONS 2005, SSI 2005 496; made under the European Communities Act 1972 s.2. In force: November 14, 2005; £3.00.

These Regulations implement Commission Decision 2005/636 ([2005] OJ L228/14) concerning a financial contribution by the Community towards a baseline survey on the prevalence of Salmonella spp. in broiler flocks of Gallus gallus to be carried out in the Member States. The Regulations provide for selection of premises for sampling by the Scottish Ministers; provide powers for inspectors for the purposes of sampling to enter premises, to make inquiries, examine records, take samples and require assistance for the purpose of these Regulations; set out requirements for notices in writing; prescribe offences and penalties, including penalties for corporate bodies and provide for enforcement by the local authority except where the Scottish Ministers otherwise direct.

5015. Animal health–Infectious disease control–Poultry premises–Notification of information

AVIAN INFLUENZA (PREVENTIVE MEASURES) (DATE FOR IDENTIFICATION OF POULTRY PREMISES) (SCOTLAND) REGULATIONS 2005, SSI 2005 625; made under the European Communities Act 1972 s.2. In force: December 9, 2005; £3.00.

These Regulations partially implement Commission Decision 2005/734 ([2005] OJ L279/75) laying down biosecurity measures to reduce the risk of transmission of highly pathogenic avian influenza caused by Influenza virus A subtype H5N1 from birds living in the wild to poultry and other captive birds and providing for an early detection system in areas at particular risk. They specify the date by which a person who keeps 50 or more poultry on commercial poultry premises must notify information relating to those premises to the Scottish Ministers under the Avian Influenza (Preventive Measures) (Scotland) Regulations 2005 (SSI 2005 530).

5016. Animal health–Infectious disease control–Zoos–Avian influenza

AVIAN INFLUENZA (PREVENTIVE MEASURES IN ZOOS) (SCOTLAND) REGULATIONS 2005, SSI 2005 531; made under the European Communities Act 1972 s.2. In force: October 28, 2005 at 12 pm; £3.00.

These Regulations bring into force Commission Decision 2005/744 ([2005] OJ L279/25) laying down the requirements for the prevention of highly pathogenic avian influenza caused by influenza A virus of subtype H5N1 in susceptible birds kept in zoos in the Member States. They require the Scottish Ministers to evaluate the risk of the transmission of avian influenza virus to susceptible birds in zoos and to take appropriate measures to reduce such risk; provide for the Scottish Ministers to declare avian influenza prevention (zoos) zones or to serve notices of restrictions on premises; provide for the Scottish Ministers to require vaccination of susceptible birds in zoos if they think necessary; and deal with the powers of inspectors appointed by the Scottish Ministers and by local authorities, and with penalties and enforcement.

5017. Animal health–Infectious disease control–Zoos–Summary offences

AVIAN INFLUENZA (PREVENTIVE MEASURES IN ZOOS) (SCOTLAND) AMENDMENT REGULATIONS 2005, SSI 2005 647; made under the European Communities Act 1972 s.2. In force: January 23, 2006; £3.00.

These Regulations correct an error in the Avian Influenza (Preventive Measures in Zoos) (Scotland) Regulations 2005 (SI 2005 531) by reducing the maximum term of imprisonment, on summary conviction, for offences under the principal Regulations, from six months to three months.

5018. Diseases and disorders–Approved disinfectants

DISEASES OF ANIMALS (APPROVED DISINFECTANTS) AMENDMENT (NO.2) (SCOTLAND) ORDER 2005, SSI 2005 587; made under the Animal Health Act 1981 s.1, s.7, s.23. In force: November 21, 2005; £3.00.

This Order, which revokes the Diseases of Animals (Approved Disinfectants) Amendment (Scotland) Order 2004 (SSI 2004 537) and the Diseases of Animals (Approved Disinfectants) Amendment (Scotland) Order 2005 (SSI 2005 99), amend the Diseases of Animals (Approved Disinfectants) Order 1978 (SI 1978 32) and the Diseases of Animals (Approved Disinfectants) Amendment (Scotland) Order 2003 (SSI 2003 334). The Order lists disinfectants approved by the Scottish Ministers and lists disinfectants which, although no longer approved, may continue to be used as approved disinfectants until February 20, 2006.

5019. Diseases and disorders–Approved disinfectants

DISEASES OF ANIMALS (APPROVED DISINFECTANTS) AMENDMENT (SCOTLAND) ORDER 2005, SSI 2005 99; made under the Animal Health Act 1981 s.1, s.7, s.23. In force: March 2, 2005; £3.00.

This Order, which amends the Diseases of Animals (Approved Disinfectants) Order 1978 (SI 1978 32), provides an updated list of disinfectants approved by the Scottish Ministers. The Order is in identical terms to that substituted by the Diseases of Animals (Approved Disinfectants) Amendment (Scotland) Order 2004 (SSI 2004 537) except for corrections to the dilution rates for Action Iodophor Disinfectant, Biocid 15, Credence 200 and Fam 15.

5020. Horses–Passports

HORSE PASSPORTS (SCOTLAND) REGULATIONS 2005, SSI 2005 223; made under the European Communities Act 1972 s.2. In force: May 16, 2005; £3.00.

These Regulations, which revoke the Horse Passports Order 1997 (SI 1997 2789) (with saving) and the Horse Passports (Amendment) Order 1998 (SI 1998 2367), implement Council Directive 90/426 ([1990] OJ L224/42) on animal health conditions governing the movement and import from third countries of equidae, Council Directive 90/427 ([1990] OJ L224/55) on the zootechnical and genealogical conditions governing intra-Community trade in equidae, Commission Decision 92/353 ([1992] OJ L192/63) laying down the criteria for the approval or recognition of organisations and associations which maintain or establish stud books for registered equidae, Commission Decision 93/623 ([1993] OJ L298/45) establishing the identification document (passport) accompanying registered equidae and Commission Decision 2000/ 68 ([2000] OJ L23/72) amending Commission Decision 93/623 and establishing the identification of equidae for breeding and production. The Regulations specify which organisations are authorised to issue passports and give them powers and duties, make provision for applications for and issue of passports, specify the languages of passports and make provision for horses entering Scotland.

BANKING AND FINANCE

5021. Books

Crerar, Lorne D.–Law of Banking in Scotland. Paperback: £90.00. ISBN 1 84592 151 8. Tottel Publishing.

CHARITIES

5022. Charities and Trustee Investment (Scotland) Act 2005 (asp 10)

This Act of the Scottish Parliament makes provision about charities and other benevolent bodies; makes provision about fundraising in connection with charities and other benevolent bodies; and amends the law in relation to the investment powers of trustees.

This Act received Royal Assent on July 14, 2005.

5023. Religious groups–Recognised bodies–United Free Church of Scotland

CHARITIES (DESIGNATED RELIGIOUS BODIES) (SCOTLAND) ORDER 2005, SSI 2005 306; made under the Law Reform (Miscellaneous Provisions) (Scotland) Act 1990 s.3. In force: July 1, 2005; £3.00.

By this Order, the Scottish Ministers designate the United Free Church of Scotland as a recognised body as it appears to them to meet the criteria set out in the Law Reform (Miscellaneous Provisions) (Scotland) Act 1990 s.3.

CIVIL EVIDENCE

5024. Admissibility–Fatal accident inquiries–Privilege against self incrimination

[Fatal Accidents and Sudden Deaths Inquiry (Scotland) Act 1976 (c.14) s.5(2).]

S, the owner of a basement flat in which a fire occurred, resulting in the death of two of the tenants, appealed against his conviction of perjury and the subsequent imposition of 30 months' imprisonment after he lied when giving evidence at a fatal accident inquiry that there had been a working smoke detector in the hallway of the flat. S submitted that (1) the evidence given by him at the inquiry was rendered incompetent by the failure of the presiding sheriff to warn him that he could decline to answer on the ground that it could be self incriminatory, which was required in terms of the Fatal Accidents and Sudden Deaths Inquiry (Scotland) Act 1976 s.5(2), and thus it could not in law found a charge of perjury; (2) the sheriff had erred in both repelling an objection to the leading of the whole transcript of the inquiry proceedings which included evidence about a smoke detector in the flat's kitchen which was prejudicial to him, and in directing the jury that such evidence could be taken into account when it was irrelevant to the determination of the perjury charge; (3) a custodial sentence was inappropriate and excessive given the nature of the offence and his personal circumstances.

Held, dismissing the appeal, that (1) there was no irregularity or impropriety of any kind in the leading of S's evidence at the inquiry such as to render it incompetent. Before there could be a duty on the person conducting the inquiry to inform a witness that they were not compelled to answer a particular question, the answer would have to show the witness to have been guilty of a crime or offence and it had not been suggested that the non existence of functional smoke detectors, in the flat let in the circumstances in which the appellant's flat was let, constituted any offence. (2) As there was no proper basis on which counsel could have objected to the admission of evidence relating to what had been said at the inquiry, his failure to do so could not amount to a miscarriage of justice in those proceedings. (3) S's criticism of the sheriff's handling of the objection to lead the whole transcript of the inquiry proceedings in evidence, in particular that relating to the smoke detector in the flat's kitchen, and his subsequent directions to the jury, was without merit where evidence relating to the credibility of an accused in a criminal trial was plainly relevant evidence in that trial in so far as it was based upon conflicting statements. Further, the sheriff made it perfectly plain that the allegation of perjury, with which the jury was concerned, related only to the smoke detector in the flat's hallway. (4) The sentence imposed was not excessive. S had lied repeatedly during the inquiry that there was a smoke detector in the flat's hallway when he knew that evidence to be false, and while the presiding sheriff based his determination upon other evidence, that did not detract from the seriousness of S's perjury.

SINGH (HARPAL) v. HM ADVOCATE 2005 S.L.T. 478, Lord Cullen L.J.G., Lord Osborne, Lord Macfadyen, HCJ.

CIVIL PROCEDURE

5025. Arrestment–Warrants–Arrestment on the dependence–No justifying averments in writ

The appellant (R) appealed against decisions of the sheriff made in an action for damages raised by the respondent (K) against R for breach of contract. K sought damages for breach of contract from R and, in the crave for the initial writ, had craved a warrant for arrestment on the dependence. The sheriff had granted both a warrant to cite and a warrant for arrestment on the dependence. An arrestment was subsequently lodged in the hands of local council. R then moved the court to recall the warrant to arrest on the dependence and all arrestments used. That motion was refused as incompetent in relation to the recall of the warrant to arrest on the dependence and the recall of all arrestments was also refused. R appealed, arguing that the sheriff had erred in holding that (1) part of the motion was incompetent; (2) the warrant had been properly granted when there were no averments in the writ to justify it and the sheriff had been given information that was not in the writ; (3) the writ did not contain future or contingent claims; (4) K had established a specific need for the warrant for arrestment.

Held, dismissing the appeal, that (1) the sheriff had not erred in holding that recall of the warrant was incompetent. The procedure for preventing the use or effect of arrestment was well settled. (2) The procedure in applications for warrants for arrestment on the dependence did not mean that averments in support of the application were always necessary, *Advocate General for Scotland v. Taylor* 2004 S.C. 339, [2004] C.L.Y. 4956 followed. The grant of warrant should be a judicially considered act but that did not necessarily mean a hearing in a court before a judge. (3) The claim for damages had come into existence at the date of the breach and any contingent liabilities were minor. (4) The sheriff had been satisfied that the financial information demonstrated that there was a significant risk of R's insolvency and therefore K had established a specific need.

KELVIN HOMES LTD v. RITCHIE BROTHERS (PUBLIC WORKS CONTRACTORS) LTD 2004 S.C.L.R. 506, Sheriff Principal Iain Macphail Q.C., Sh Ct.

5026. Breach of undertaking–Scottish Ministers–Breach by prison services official

[Crown Proceedings Act 1947 (c.44) s.21 (1) (a).]

B, a prisoner in HM Prison Peterhead, presented a minute seeking an order that S, the Scottish Ministers, appear personally to answer for their breach of an undertaking given to the court in his proceedings for judicial review, and a finding that they were thus in contempt of court. B's petition had complained of a breach of his human rights by the interference with his privileged correspondence from his legal advisers and the Scottish Prisons Complaint Commissioner, and a failure by prison authorities to enforce a policy by which such interference could be avoided. When the petition came before the Lord Ordinary on September 5, 2003, S tendered an undertaking that any letters or packages sent to B by any of his legal advisers or by the commissioner would not be opened by any officer of the Scottish Prison Service. The Lord Ordinary pronounced a first order. At a hearing on December 16, 2004, S admitted a breach of the undertaking by a residential officer at Peterhead, who was unaware of the undertaking and who had opened a letter from the commissioner in B's presence, for which they apologised to the court, but denied contempt. S submitted that (1) in Scots law, proceedings against them fell to be regarded as proceedings against the Crown, thus by the Crown Proceedings Act 1947 s.21 (1) (a), the court had no jurisdiction to find them in contempt; (2) they were not a corporate body, and civil servants regularly took executive decisions in their name, that did not provide a foundation for vicarious liability; (3) there was no question of a deliberate attempt to flout the authority of the court and while the system for adherence to the terms of the undertaking that the prison governor had approved was unclear, it was a genuine effort.

Held, finding S in contempt of court and ordering the appearance of the Chief Executive of the Scottish Prison Service as representing S's alter ego and the Governor of HM Prison Peterhead as responsible for failing to take reasonable steps to ensure compliance with S's undertaking, so that it might be made in open court, that (1) s.21 of the 1947 Act did not make it incompetent to find S in contempt of court by reason of the breach of an undertaking to the court and the proceedings against them, whether on the petition or the minute, did not represent proceedings against the Crown. (2) A similar approach to that taken in *Hone v. Page* [1980] F.S.R. 500, [1981] C.L.Y. 2791, where the company, a servant or agent of which unknowingly did the act prohibited by a court order should be held to have committed a contempt of court as a result of failing in their duty to take all reasonable steps to ensure compliance by the relevant servants or agents, was valid in Scotland in determining whether S had been in contempt, *Hone* considered. (3) The undertaking given by S was breached by the action of a Scottish Prison Service official and whatever might be the precise legal relationship between them and civil servants at different levels within the Scottish administration, there was no doubt that it was implicit that S undertook that their civil servants would take adequate steps to ensure that the undertaking was being adhered to and in so far as there might have been any failure in that respect, they were responsible, it did not require the invocation of vicarious responsibility or agency. (4) S were in contempt of court: the history of repeated breaches of the minuter's right that letters from his legal advisers and the Scottish Prisons Complaint Commissioner should be free from interference had brought matters to such a pass that it proved necessary for an undertaking to be given to the court on S's behalf, it was abundantly obvious that close attention would have to be given to seeing that it was honoured, and the undertaking was simply not taken seriously enough.

BEGGS v. SCOTTISH MINISTERS (CONTEMPT OF COURT) 2005 S.C. 342, Lord Cullen L.P., Lord Macfadyen, Lady Cosgrove, 1 Div.

5027. **Capacity—Intervention—Intervention orders—Incapable adult—Codicil to will**

[Adults with Incapacity (Scotland) Act 2000 (asp 4) s.1 (2), s.53.]

T, the son of a woman aged 81 who was suffering from Alzheimer's disease and no longer able to sustain independent living, sought an intervention order under the Adults with Incapacity (Scotland) Act 2000 s.53 authorising his mother's solicitor to execute a codicil to her will. T's mother had executed her will in August 2001, when she had full capacity, which left her house to B, and the residue of her estate to the widow of another son. T's mother had further specified that T should be her principal beneficiary. Although T now had power to sell his mother's home, which lay empty, the wording of the testamentary provision meant that the net proceeds of the sale would fall into the residue of the estate to the benefit of his sister in law. The application was referred to the Office of the Public Guardian, which stated that the court should not interfere with the affairs of an adult unless it was satisfied that the intervention would benefit the adult, and suggested that intervention would not benefit the applicant in terms of s.1 (2) of the Act.

Held, granting the order, that (1) the court had to have clear information on which it could act and sufficient information had been given about the stated intentions of T's mother to satisfy the court that she would remedy the problem in the manner proposed if it was within her power to do so; refusal of the order would result in denial of justice to T and also in a positive injustice. (2) The Office of the Public Guardian had placed an unduly restrictive meaning on the word "benefit": although the intervention would not be to the direct benefit of T's mother, she had already authorised the selling of the house and potential investment of the proceeds in the power of attorney, and the money at least would be available to be used for her benefit in her remaining years whereas at present there were effectively no such assets.

T, APPLICANT 2005 S.L.T. (Sh Ct) 97, Sheriff JA Baird, Sh Ct.

5028. **Capacity—Intervention—Intervention orders—Incapable adult—Settlement of compensation claim**

[Adults with Incapacity (Scotland) Act 2000 (asp 4) s.53(5) (b).]

B, the son of a woman aged 85, sought an intervention order in terms of the Adults with Incapacity (Scotland) Act 2000 s.53(5) (b), authorising him to take certain steps to instruct solicitors to settle a compensation claim raised by his father, since deceased, who had developed lung disease through exposure to dust as a coal miner. His mother was no longer capable of taking decisions regarding her own financial affairs or giving instructions to settle the claim. All of the compensation received both directly by her, and on her succession to her late husband's estate would be used for her future care and the costs thereof.

Held, granting the order, that refusal of the proposed scheme in the particular circumstances would result in the denial of justice to B's mother, and the order was necessary and otherwise complied with the legislation.

B, APPLICANT 2005 S.L.T. (Sh Ct) 95, Sheriff JA Baird, Sh Ct (Glasgow).

5029. Civil appeals—Leave to appeal—Failure to obtain leave

[Act of Sederunt (Sheriff Court Ordinary Cause Rules 1993) 1993 (SI 1993 1956) r.2.1; Act of Sederunt (Rules of the Court of Session 1994) 1994 (SI 1994 1443) Sch.2 r.40.12.]

The appellant (W), who had brought a partly successful claim for damages against the respondent (T) in respect of an alleged breach of contract, appealed against the decision of the sheriff that he was liable to T for expenses, including those of the instant appeal. W had, without leave, appealed to the Court of Session where the matter was referred to a Lord Ordinary under the Act of Sederunt (Rules of the Court of Session 1994) 1994 Sch.2 r.40.12. The Lord Ordinary noted that the appeal was incompetent but, having regard to the fact that W maintained that the cause should be remitted to the sheriff principal, he directed that the appeal should proceed but on the basis that the issue of competency was brought before the Inner House. W moved the court to remit the cause to the sheriff principal with instruction to consider exercising the dispensing power contained in the Act of Sederunt (Sheriff Court Ordinary Cause Rules 1993) 1993 r.2.1, and to consider granting leave to appeal to the Court of Session. W accepted that his agents had laboured under the mistaken belief that, when the sheriff had dealt with expenses, there was a final judgment and accordingly, leave to appeal was not required.

Held, dismissing the appeal, that W was not entitled, as a matter of course, to have the case remitted. There had been a plain failure on W's part to apply for and obtain the leave without which the appeal was incompetent. W and his agents had clearly been of the mistaken view that leave to appeal had not been required as they believed that the sheriff's ruling on expenses was a final judgment.

WALKER v. TIDEWATER CYPRUS LTD 2004 S.C. 369, Lord Cullen L.P., Lord Marnoch, Lord Weir, 1 Div.

5030. Community charge—Enforcement—Arrestment of sum in building society account—Opportunity for debtor to demonstrate extent of liability to pay debt

The appellant debtor (S) appealed against the granting of a decree for payment of a sum arrested in a building society account by the respondent local authority in respect of outstanding community charge. The local authority had obtained summary warrants to enforce S's payment of community charge and later discovered that S had a building society account. The local authority arrested the money in that account and sought an order that the building society pay the money to it. The Sheriff held that S's defence was not soundly based in law as he had made no attempt to have the warrants or arrestment recalled. On appeal, S argued that he was not liable for the whole amount due to time spent in prison, bankrupt and on benefits.

Held, allowing the appeal in part, that S should have had the opportunity to prove that all or part of the money arrested was not owing to the local authority. As the arrestment was based upon a bond by a common debtor, there were defences available to the debtor relating to the creditor's rights as well as the validity of the arrestment, *Donaldson v. Ord* (1855) 17 D. 1053 considered. However, S could not challenge his liability under the summary warrant as it did not require that the person in respect of whom the warrant was sought be notified.

NORTH LANARKSHIRE COUNCIL v. SEXTON [2004] R.V.R. 301, Sheriff Principal JC McInnes Q.C., Sh Ct.

5031. Court rules—Personal injury claims—Proof—Proof before answer

[Act of Sederunt (Rules of the Court of Session 1994) 1994 (SI 1994 1443) Sch.2 para.43.6(5)(b).]

The defenders (S) to an action brought by the pursuer (H) for damages for personal injury sought a proof before answer. H had been injured when his foot was trapped between two steel mounds at work and in his pleadings he made reference to the relevant legislation concerning safety in the workplace. H made no reference in his pleadings to any failure of duty on the part of S. S raised a plea in law defence challenging the relevancy and specification of H's pleadings and accordingly sought a proof before answer so that the facts could be elicited.

Held, allowing a proof before answer, that (1) the pleadings raised questions of law which should properly be addressed and resolved after the facts had been elicited. It could not be said in advance of the leading of the evidence whether the facts averred were sufficient to support the legal conclusion which H required for success, *Moore v. Alexander Stephen & Sons Ltd* 1954 S.C. 331, [1954] C.L.Y. 4244 considered. The word "proof" in the Act of Sederunt (Rules of the Court of Session 1994) 1994 Sch.2 para.43.6(5)(b) included a proof before answer. (2) (Obiter) until there had been clarification of the appropriateness or otherwise of pleas in law in defences under the 1994 Rules affecting personal injury cases, defenders who continued to add pleas in law to their defences would have to seek a proof before answer unless the relevant pleas in law had been repelled by the court. Those defenders would also have to comply with the requirements of Sch.2 para.43.6(5)(b) and give notice of their grounds for seeking an order other than a proof or jury trial.

HAMILTON v. SEAMARK SYSTEMS LTD 2004 S.C. 543, Lady Paton, OH.

5032. Declaratory orders—Competence—Legal consequences

[Brussels Convention on Jurisdiction and Enforcement of Judgments in Civil and Commercial Matters 1968 Art.29.]

C, the director of a company, D, sought declarator that costs pronounced in a decree obtained against him in Delaware district court and a judgment for 11 million Canadian dollars awarded against him in Colorado were not enforceable by a merchant bank in Scotland, having been obtained through fraud on the court, and interdict against the merchant bank from taking any steps in Scotland and elsewhere to enforce them. Earlier proceedings brought by C before the English courts had been rejected. D had given an irrevocable undertaking to C and the court that they would not at any time seek to enforce or take steps entitling others to seek to enforce by action of decree conform in Scotland the orders and judgments previously obtained against C. The Lord Ordinary sustained D's pleas in law that in respect of this undertaking, the action was no longer necessary, and the court had no jurisdiction to entertain the proceedings and the action was incompetent. C reclaimed, contending that the Lord Ordinary had gone further than he was entitled to do. Initially, C argued that issues of jurisdiction had been dealt with at an earlier hearing before a different Lord Ordinary, O, who had allowed a proof before answer. However, he accepted that the conclusions for interdict had not then included the words "and elsewhere" and, further, that in light of *Turner v. Grovit (C159/02)* [2005] 1 A.C. 101, [2004] C.L.Y. 1393, interdicts, as now worded, could not competently be granted. C was granted leave to delete the words "and elsewhere" from the interdict conclusion. Thereafter, C maintained that it was not open to D to argue their jurisdiction plea in light of O's determination, which had been based on the pleadings as they now stood, and submitted that the point about the action being no longer necessary had been dealt with by the Extra Division when they refused D's motion to dismiss the proceedings in the light of the undertaking, D's plea and supporting averments added nothing, and while it was true that the undertaking rendered the conclusion for interdict (as amended) redundant, the declarators, if granted, might have some practical utility for C. They might be of assistance in seeking to have matters revisited in the English courts or to defend actions D might bring in other jurisdictions such as France, where C resided, and in obtaining finance in his business interests and improving his prospects.

Held, refusing the reclaiming motion, that (1) the declaratory conclusions had been emptied of content standing the fact that C accepted that there was no longer any basis for the court pronouncing the interdicts sought. The court should not pronounce declarators which were bare or academic, and to pronounce interlocutors simply for the practical benefits they might confer on those seeking them would go well beyond the court's proper function and had no support in authority, *Turner* considered. (2) The court had no jurisdiction to grant declarators which reviewed the judgments of foreign courts whose competency had not been attacked: fundamental principles of comity required courts not to embark on such exercises which were stoutly affirmed in the Brussels Convention 1968 Art.29.

CLARKE v. FENNOSCANDIA LTD (NO.3) 2005 S.L.T. 511, Lord Gill L.J.C., Lord Clarke, Lord Menzies, 2 Div.

5033. Defences–Loans–Decree in absence following failure to lodge notice of intention to defend–Reponing notes

The defender (J) appealed against the sheriff principal's decision to uphold the refusal of a reponing note denying liability for the repayment of a loan made to J by the pursuer (T). J's agents had failed to lodge a notice of intention to defend and a decree in absence had been pronounced against J. The reponing note explained the failure to lodge the notice and provided a defence to the action that, pursuant to an alleged specific agreement, the time for repayment of the loan monies had not yet arrived because the agreement was for repayment only when J "was able to do so". The sheriff had found that the alleged agreement as to the repayment date was ineffectual and unenforceable.

Held, allowing the appeal, that there had been an error of law. J had disclosed a stateable defence to T's action. A condition concerning the ability to repay was likely to be given legal effect, *Forbes v. Forbes* (1869) 8 M. 85 and *Forbes v. Johnstone* 1995 S.C. 220, [1995] C.L.Y. 6384 applied. The failure to enter appearance had been due to an unfortunate oversight caused by staff shortages and pressure of business within the offices of J's agents and therefore it was appropriate to exercise discretion in J's favour.

THOMPSON v. JARDINE 2004 S.C. 590, Lord Osborne, Lord Hamilton, Lord Johnston, Ex Div.

5034. Defences–Pleas–Time bar–Preliminary pleas

[Prescription and Limitation (Scotland) Act 1973 (c.52) s.17; Act of Sederunt (Sheriff Court Ordinary Cause Rules) 1993 (SI 1993 1956) r.2.1, r.22.]

H sought compensation from R, an insurance company, for losses sustained as a result of a road traffic accident in January 2001, allegedly caused by a party insured by R. The action was raised in March 2004 and R tabled a plea of time bar. At the options hearing, the sheriff repelled R's plea in law in terms of the Act of Sederunt (Sheriff Court Ordinary Cause Rules) 1993 r.22 on the basis that it was a preliminary plea in support of which no note had been lodged in process in terms of r.22.1 (1), and allowed a proof. R appealed, submitting that as the plea was to the merits of the action, which raised a substantive issue, no note under r.22 required to be lodged, which had support from a recent case in another sheriff court; alternatively, the court's dispensing power under r.2.1 should be exercised in their favour and the cause should be remitted to the sheriff either to fix a continued options hearing or a proof on the issue of time bar.

Held, allowing the appeal, that (1) a plea in law to the effect that an action was time barred under the Prescription and Limitation (Scotland) Act 1973 s.17 was a preliminary plea within the meaning of r.22.1 and in the absence of a note lodged under r.22.1 (1)(a) in support, the sheriff was obliged to repel R's plea in terms of r.22.1 (1)(3). (2) It would be appropriate to grant R relief in terms of r.2.1 where their solicitors' misinterpretation of r.22.1 was understandable, they would otherwise be deprived of the opportunity to advance what would be a complete answer to H's claim, they had made their position on time bar clear from the outset in their defences and it was not obvious what more could be said in support in a note under r.22.1. (3) The proper course would be to recall the sheriff's interlocutor and direct the sheriff clerk to fix a new date for an options hearing whereby the sheriff would be able to determine further procedure in the cause accordingly.

HUMPHREY v. ROYAL AND SUN ALLIANCE PLC 2005 S.L.T. (Sh Ct) 31, Sheriff Principal Sir SST Young Q.C., Sh Ct.

5035. Defences–Reponing note–Intention to defend stated–Failure to set out defence

[Human Rights Act 1998 (c.42) Sch.1 Part I Art.6(1); Mortgage Rights (Scotland) Act 2001 (asp 11) s.2; Act of Sederunt (Sheriff Court Ordinary Cause Rules) 1993 (SI 1993 1956) Sch.1 para.8.1 (1).]

The defender (G) challenged a decision of the sheriff refusing a reponing note lodged by G intimating his wish to defend an action brought by the pursuer (N), creditors in a standard security, by seeking an order in terms of the Mortgage Rights (Scotland) Act 2001 s.2. G acknowledged that the language of the Act of Sederunt (Sheriff Court Ordinary Cause Rules) 1993 Sch.1 para.8.1 (1) required that he set out his proposed defence, but submitted that the word "defence" could be interpreted loosely to mean fending off attack, and on that basis he was entitled to lodge a notice or minute of intention to defend. G also argued that the sheriff was bound to interpret Sch.1 para.8(1) in a way that was compatible with the Human Rights Act 1998 Sch.1 Part I Art.6(1), Art.8 and Art.13.

Held, giving judgment accordingly, that the reponing note did not contain a defence and was thus incompetent. Even if "defence" was interpreted in the wider sense, s.2 did not help G since its purpose was, at best, to delay attack. The order sought by G only suspended N's right to exercise its right of enforcement and did not offer a defence. G had not produced any evidence in support of his contention that Art.6(1), Art.8 or Art.13 applied in the instant case. The reponing note was accordingly refused.

NORTHERN ROCK PLC v. GOODWIN 2004 Hous. L.R. 88, Sheriff NC Stewart Q.C., Sh Ct (South Strathclyde, Dumfries and Galloway).

5036. Delay–Absolvitor–Inherent jurisdiction of sheriff

[Human Rights Act 1998 (c.42) Sch.1 Part I Art.6.]

W, a subcontractor, raised an action in October 1991 for payment of sums alleged to be due under a series of subcontracts. The action was sisted in March 1997 to allow W to consider amendment or possible settlement. No progress was made thereafter, and in May 2004, D learned that W's original solicitor no longer acted and another firm had been instructed. D, who stated that W's action was, and remained, irrelevant and lacking in specification, sought decree of absolvitor and decree of expenses on the grounds of W's inordinate and unexplained delay in pursuing the action, founding on *Newman Shopfitters Ltd v. MJ Gleeson Group Plc* 2003 S.L.T. (Sh Ct) 83, [2003] C.L.Y. 5291 as authority for the proposition that the sheriff court had an inherent jurisdiction to grant the remedy sought. W submitted that he had been badly let down by his solicitor, the remedy sought was not competent, and *Newman* ought not to be followed. In any event, it was distinguishable, as in this case there was an explanation for the delay. Further, the relevancy of the case would best be addressed at debate. In relation to the defenders' reliance on the Human Rights Act 1998, W argued that the obligations in Sch.1 Part I Art.6(1) were obligations of the state, and it was for the state to make the appropriate statutory provisions whereby they might be discharged.

Held, granting absolvitor, that (1) the sheriff court had an inherent jurisdiction to grant decree of absolvitor without proof of the facts on the basis of unexplained and inexcusable delay: such a delay might be inexcusable because no excuse was tendered, or because a reason was tendered which was not satisfactory. (2) The delay in this case was unarguably inordinate and W's solicitor's misconduct was not a satisfactory excuse. (3) D had suffered, and were likely to continue to suffer, serious prejudice as a result of the delay, *Newman* applied.

WILSON (T/A TW CONTRACTORS) v. DRAKE & SCULL SCOTLAND LTD; *sub nom.* WILSON (T/A TW CONTRACTORS) v. DRAKE & SKULL LTD 2005 S.L.T. (Sh Ct) 35, Sheriff D Convery.

5037. Delay—Court of Session—Inordinate delay by pursuer—Disposal

[Human Rights Act 1998 (c.42) s.6, s.8(1), Sch.1 Part I Art.6(1); Act of Sederunt (Rules of the Court of Session 1994) 1994 (SI 1994 1442) Sch.2 para.20.1.]

In an action by T against R, a firm of architects, alleging negligence in connection with designing and building a house, where the cause was sisted on T's unopposed motion in 1988, T enrolled a motion for recall. R moved the court to grant absolvitor either (1) in exercise of its inherent jurisdiction, which the court possessed notwithstanding the absence of specific provision enabling it to do so by the Act of Sederunt (Rules of the Court of Session 1994) 1994, having regard to the inordinate, unexplained and inexcusable delay on T's part in progressing the action subsequent to the sist pronounced in 1988, the serious prejudice to R by such delay, and the substantial risk to a fair consideration of the issues of fact caused by such delay, or (2) on the basis of the requirement in Sch.2 para.20.1 of the Rules, properly interpreted in the circumstances of the case, where the court was prohibited, in terms of the Human Rights Act 1998 s.6 from acting in a way which would be incompatible with their rights and the allowance of further procedure in the case would be a breach of their Art.6(1) right to have their civil rights and obligations determined at a fair and public hearing within a reasonable time by an independent and impartial tribunal. In terms of s.8(1) of the 1998 Act, the court had a discretion when choosing a remedy and once a breach was identified, the only way forward was to stop the proceedings, and the fact that parties were in control of the litigation did not remove the court's obligations.

Held, granting T's motion, that (1) there were competing arguments as to the reasonableness or otherwise of expecting a defender to enrol for recall of a sist to prevent deleterious delay and while the cases for and against were not determinative of the existence of a power which the court could exercise so as to dispose of an action against the will of a pursuer on the grounds of delay, the cases nevertheless lent support to the view that it was not a discretion the court already had and if it were to be contemplated, it was a discretion which ought to be fully considered and debated by the Rules Council. (2) In certain cases, the court had, by Act of Sederunt, made provision whereby the court was empowered to grant decree of dismissal or of default in circumstances where there had been delay and the fact that it had not so provided as a general rule, applicable in all types of action, was indicative of the court's intention not to confer the power sought given that it would have been a simple matter for such provision to have been made.

TONNER v. REIACH & HALL 2005 S.L.T. 936, Lady Smith, OH.

5038. Expenses—Assessment—Variation of contact order

[Act of Sederunt (Sheriff Court Ordinary Cause Rules) 1993 (SI 1993 1956) Sch.1 para.33; Act of Sederunt (Fees of Solicitors in the Sheriff Court) (Amendment and Further Provisions) 1993 (SI 1993 3080) Sch.1 Part I Chap.IV.]

An award of expenses was made in C's favour in respect of a minute by R to vary an order for contact. The auditor (X) disallowed C's account in total, on the grounds that it had wrongly been prepared on the basis that the proceedings initiated by R amounted to a new "family action". X substituted the prescribed fees under the Act of Sederunt (Fees of Solicitors in the Sheriff Court) (Amendment and Further Provisions) 1993 Sch.1 Part I Chap.IV. C lodged a note of objections, maintaining that, in terms of the Act of Sederunt (Sheriff Court Ordinary Cause Rules) 1993 Sch.1 para.33.1 (1) (h), R's application was an "application for, or in respect of, an order under section 11 of the Children (Scotland) Act 1995" and as such, a family action in its own right.

Held, sustaining the note to the extent of remitting the matter to X to tax the account of new to allow for work relating to further procedure appointed by the court, that it was not correct to treat R's application as amounting to the initiation of a new family action "in its own right". By virtue of Sch.1 para.33.65, the application was an action which required to be made within the original process which was already a "family action" for the purposes of the 1993 Rules, and X's view that C's account should be charged basically in the first instance in accordance with Sch.1 Part I Chap.IV of the scale of fees was correct, although it could include other matters where additional procedure in respect of the minute and answers had been appointed by the court.

COWAN v. RAMSAY 2005 S.L.T. (Sh Ct) 65, Sheriff KG Barr, Sh Ct (South Strathclyde, Dumfries and Galloway).

5039. Expenses–Breach of contract–Tender–Pursuer beating tender after minute of amendment

The defenders (B) reclaimed against the decision of a temporary judge that the pursuer (H) was entitled to full expenses from the date of diminution of value in respect of structural defects in a property sold by B to H. H had been awarded damages of £23,000 plus interest on the principal sum. Subsequently, the conclusion for interest was amended and interest was awarded from the date of diminution, taking the total sum to £39,000. B had lodged a minute of tender of £37,500 at the commencement of proof. The temporary judge held that H had beaten the tender and was entitled to full expenses. B argued that the judge had erred in her approach and that H had failed to beat the tender.

Held, granting the application, that in general a defender could not be expected to foresee alterations and amendments to a pursuer's claim. The question as to whether a tender had been beaten was to be determined at the date of the decision on the merits of the case and it should not be affected by subsequent amendments, *Orr v. Metcalfe* 1973 S.C. 57, [1973] C.L.Y. 3613 considered. In the instant case, the temporary judge had taken account of both the decision on the merits and the amendment. On the facts, it was just to award H expenses up to and including the second day of proof and H was liable to B for expenses incurred after that date.

HUGHES v. BARRATT URBAN CONSTRUCTION (SCOTLAND) LTD (EXPENSES) 2004 S.C. 445, Lord Kirkwood, Lord Macfadyen, Lord Brodie, Ex Div.

5040. Expenses–Modification–Action raised in Court of Session

[Act of Sederunt (Rules of the Court of Session 1994) 1994 (SI 1994 1443) Sch.2 Part 43.]

In B's action against E for damages for personal injuries brought under the revised rules, B moved for decree in terms of a minute of tender and acceptance, valuing her claim at £5,200, of which £4,500 was attributed to solatium. E asserted that expenses should be modified to the sheriff court scale without the sanction of counsel, submitting that the action was straightforward, when it was raised, B's counsel must have been aware, having regard to the medical report in their possession that the value of the claim would never exceed £5,000, and the new rules in the Court of Session were irrelevant as new rules introduced in the sheriff court in 1993 had not affected the position.

Held, granting B's motion and refusing E's motion, that (1) the award or settlement sum in this case was not trivial in relation to the expenses and the result of the case did not assist E; (2) in choosing the Court of Session, B had selected a procedure designed to encourage speedy and economic resolution of her claim and she could not justifiably be criticised for doing so rather than choosing to raise her action in the sheriff court, and (3) it did not necessarily follow that it was inappropriate for a straightforward claim which at the raising of the action was known to have a maximum value of £5,000 to be raised in the Court of Session, and it could be argued that the Act of Sederunt (Rules of the Court of Session 1994) 1994 Sch.2 Part 43 made such claims ideally suited to the new rules.

BENSON v. EDINBURGH CITY COUNCIL 2005 S.C. 24, Temporary Judge J Gordon Reid Q.C., OH.

5041. Expenses–Modification–Non complex case heard in Court of Session–Availability of jury trial

[Act of Sederunt (Rules of the Court of Session 1994) 1994 (SI 1994 1443) Sch.2 r.43; Act of Sederunt (Rules of the Court of Session Amendment No.2) (Personal Injuries Actions) 2002 (SI 2002 570).]

G enrolled for modification of its liability in expenses to that of the sheriff court ordinary scale without sanction for counsel in two separate claims for damages in personal injury actions brought by W and EG. The damages proceedings had been brought under Chap.43 of the Act of Sederunt (Rules of the Court of Session 1994) 1994 as substituted by the Act of Sederunt (Rules of the Court of Session Amendment No.2) (Personal Injuries Actions) 2002 and were settled by minute of tender and acceptance. W received £2,250 and EG £2,000. G argued that both cases were trivial and the litigation lacked complexity; counsel had not been required and W and EG should have pursued their actions in the sheriff court rather than the Court of Session.

Held, refusing the motion, that the discretion to modify expenses would be exercised in the interests of doing justice between the parties in cases where, without prejudice to the pursuer, the case could have proceeded in the sheriff court and its conduct in the Court of Session had been significantly more expensive, *McIntosh v. British Railways Board (No.1)* 1990 S.C. 338, [1990] C.L.Y. 5624 and *Coyle v. William Fairey Installations Ltd* 1991 S.C. 16, [1991] C.L.Y. 5001 considered. However, in the instant case, W and EG's counsel had made a genuine assessment at the outset that, in light of the new Rules, the cost of litigating in the Court of Session would be less. One of the objectives of the new procedure was to encourage settlement. It was difficult to envisage a situation where G would not have conceded liability, but if it had not done so, W and EG could have sought a jury trial, adding significantly to the costs. Leave to appeal was granted.

WILSON v. GLASGOW CITY COUNCIL; GOULD v. GLASGOW CITY COUNCIL 2004 S.L.T. 1189, Lady Smith, OH.

5042. Expenses–Taxation of account–Criticism of integrity of auditor–Competency of note of objections

[Act of Sederunt (Rules of the Court of Session 1994) (SI 1994 1443) Sch.2 para.42.4.]

G was found liable to R in certain expenses, and accounts thereof were remitted to the Auditor of Court to tax and report. Following a diet of taxation, to which G objected, the auditor issued a report. G lodged a note of objections under the Act of Sederunt (Rules of the Court of Session 1994) Sch.2 para.42.4 which attacked the auditor's integrity, criticised the auditor's failure to adjourn the diet of taxation, criticised members of the auditor's and court staff, and R's legal representatives, but did not contain any specification of the items in the account remitted to the auditor.

Held, repelling the note, that it was implicit in Sch.2 para.42.4 that it was designed to deal with objections to specific items in the auditor's report and the matters raised by G in his note could not competently be dealt with in the present proceedings, *Urquhart v. Ayrshire and Arran Health Board* 2000 S.L.T. 829, [2001] C.L.Y. 6245 approved.

GUPTA v. ROSS 2005 S.L.T. 548, Lord Osborne, Lord Hamilton, Lord Kingarth, Ex Div.

5043. Expenses–Third parties–Sheriff's award for time in proceedings as third party only

S, the second defenders in an action of damages, appealed against a sheriff's failure to award expenses in their favour against G, the first defenders, for the periods after C, the pursuer, adopted a case against them as second defenders in June 2001. S had been served with a third party notice by G in August 1996, from which time the latter were found liable in expenses, but the sheriff concluded that it would have been unjust to have found them liable beyond the period during which S were a third party because once C had joined them as second defenders, it would have made little difference what G did from that point on, and the main allegation of fault was directed against them.

Held, allowing the appeal, that (1) the general principle that responsibility for the expenses of a party who was brought into a case unnecessarily rested with a defender who brought them into the proceedings in the event of his being absolved was sound, and its application did not depend on the party being otherwise blameless in the litigation. (2) The sheriff's decision could not stand. There was no need for S to have been brought into the action as a separate party, the only justification for G's doing so was to protect themselves should it be established that S had failed in a contractual obligation which was an eventuality against which the former were protected by a contractual indemnity clause in any event, which the sheriff had failed to take into account as a material factor; and once G had brought S in as a separate party, it did not make a great deal of difference whether C adopted the case against them or not.

CONNELLY v. GA GROUP LTD (EXPENSES) 2005 S.L.T. (Sh Ct) 16, Sheriff Principal EF Bowen Q.C., Sh Ct.

5044.   Injunctions–Balance of convenience–Interim interdict–Broadcasting– Conflicting human rights

[Age of Legal Capacity (Scotland) Act 1991 (c.50) s.3, s.9; Human Rights Act 1998 (c.42) Sch.1 Part I Art.8, Art.10.]

X, a contributor to a documentary film commissioned by the BBC on the work of Glasgow sheriff court, raised an action against the corporation and the makers of the film seeking production and reduction of a "contributor's agreement" signed by X, by which she became a contributor to the film, or alternatively an order under the Age of Legal Capacity (Scotland) Act 1991 s.3, setting aside the agreement and any other agreement between the parties in terms of which the film makers filmed X, and for interdict and interim interdict against the BBC from broadcasting video film of X. X, aged 17 at the material time, was filmed initially attending the court to support her boyfriend, then latterly when she appeared from custody. X was dyslexic, her ability to read and write at the time of signing the agreement was extremely limited and she had received no legal advice before entering the agreement. X moved the court to grant interim interdict, submitting that (1) on April 10 or 11, 2003 when she had signed the agreement she had been intoxicated with alcohol and valium so that she lacked the capacity to contract or give consent due to the absence of reason and further that she had been offered incentives and had felt pressurised to participate; (2) on April 18, 2003 she had obtained the verbal agreement of the film makers to a veto over the use of footage of her; (3) in relation to filming on April 23, 2003 when X was in custody, she had only consented in the belief that she retained a right of veto and that she was unaware that she would be filmed in court; (4) since she lacked capacity to contract or give consent to be filmed as a result of intoxication L had breached the guidelines set down for filming by the sheriff principal of Glasgow and Strathkelvin, arguing that the contract entered into between the film makers and the Scottish Ministers, authorising the filming of the documentary, had created rights enforceable by way of jus quaesitum tertio; (5) if X had consented to being filmed, such consent was a prejudicial transaction in terms of s.3 of the 1991 Act; (6) broadcast of the documentary would infringe her rights under the Human Rights Act 1998 Sch.1 Part I Art.8, there was a real risk that she might come to serious self harm if it was broadcast and a very real risk existed that she would be subject to physical violence. The BBC submitted that (1) while X had had a bottle of tonic wine with her when she had signed the agreement she appeared to have been coherent and lucid, no incentives were offered and X had been a willing participant; (2) the film makers were always sensitive to the privileged position they occupied and were always at pains to comply with the sheriff principal's guidelines; (3) the film makers could not, would not and had not ceded any form of editorial control to X, as this would have been contrary to their contract with the BBC, but had indicated that they would have been happy to allow X to view footage in advance of broadcast and discuss any concerns; (4) the film makers had obtained X's consent to filming her before, during and after her court appearance in a conversation witnessed by a police officer; (5) neither the contract between the film makers and the Scottish Ministers, nor the sheriff principal's guidelines created a jus quaesitum tertio where the intention of the guidelines was to safeguard the administration of justice, not create rights attaching to third parties, and there was no intention on the part of the film makers and the Scottish Ministers to confer rights on third parties; (6) the various consents given by X did not have "legal effect" as envisaged by s.9 of the 1991 Act and, in any event, they did not constitute prejudicial transactions in terms of s.3; (7) they were entitled to broadcast the documentary material by virtue of their Art.10 rights.

Held, indicating preparedness to grant interim interdict against the BBC to restrain broadcast of those parts of the film relating to X, whether showing her directly or showing others referring to her thereby identifying her and disclosing information about her, pending resolution of issues relating to information contained in X's conclusion for interim interdict which might enable her to be identified if contained in an interlocutor, that (1) X had raised a question or questions to try and had a "real prospect of success", and while disputed facts at this stage were such that the court was unable to conclude, with any confidence, that X was more likely than not to succeed at proof, for reasons set out in the private opinion of the court, there was a significant risk of X suffering serious harm if the film were to be broadcast and an inability to satisfy the "more likely than not" test did not preclude the possibility of interim interdict to protect X. (2) X had engaged rights under Art.8 in relation to images of and information about her, and the balancing exercise both in respect of Art.8 and Art.10, and the balance of convenience test more generally, favoured X.

X v. BBC 2005 S.L.T. 796, Temporary Judge MG Thomson Q.C., OH.

5045. Injunctions—Trespass—Interdict—Airport roads

[Competition Act 1988 (c.41) s.18(1).]

P, the heritable proprietors of an international airport, sought interdict against W, the operators of an off site car park, from trespassing on the airport roads, and from driving buses and motor cars over such roads for the collection and dropping off of members of the public being conveyed to and from W's car parking facilities, without their express prior consent. At procedure roll, W averred that (1) P did not have the exclusive right to determine who entered upon the airport ground where the airport concourse was a public place to which members of the public had had recourse for more than 20 years, and a public right of way existed over the private roads owned by P which connected the main road to the concourse; (2) P were not entitled to use their ownership of the airport to exclude them in the manner and for the reasons sought as it would constitute an infringement of the Competition Act 1988 s.18(1) where it was essential for the effective operation of their business that they could access airport property.

Held, pronouncing interdict in the terms craved, that (1) it was not disputed that the main road was a public right of way but while the concourse was undoubtedly a place to which the public had resort, it was not one to which the public had an unrestricted right of access at all times, and such an averment was insufficient to entitle W to a proof before answer in the absence of sufficient supporting factual averments from which it could be inferred that the place was public in the sense in which that term was used in the law relating to public rights of way. (2) It was essential for a party claiming an infringement of s.18(1) to make a distinct averment in clear and precise terms of the relevant market, the definition of which was not something which should have to be inferred, but no such averment had been made by W where the only reference was to "car parking at the airport", and as abuse of dominant position could only take place within a defined market, it was impossible to say whether that abuse had been relevantly averred.

PIK FACILITIES LTD v. WATSON'S AYR PARK LTD 2005 S.L.T. 1041, Temporary Judge RF Macdonald Q.C., OH.

5046. Jurisdiction–Sheriff courts–Place where harmful event occurred–Damage to reputation–Personal jurisdiction

[Civil Jurisdiction and Judgments Act 1982 (c.27) Sch.8 para.2(c).]

C, a party litigant, raised an action in Glasgow sheriff court against D, the director of an organisation which employed him, alleging that he had made defamatory statements about C to third parties. D's address was unknown to C and neither the third parties nor the organisation were said to have any direct connection with Glasgow. Following debate, the sheriff sustained a plea of no jurisdiction and dismissed the action. C appealed, arguing that as he resided in Glasgow, that was where his reputation was damaged which thus fell to be regarded as the place where the "harmful event" occurred for the purposes of the Civil Jurisdiction and Judgments Act 1982 Sch.8 para.2(c).

Held, dismissing the appeal, that personal jurisdiction could not be created on the basis of a damaged reputation and there was no basis for holding that the "harmful event" occurred in Glasgow, *Shevill v. Presse Alliance SA* [1992] 2 W.L.R. 1, [1992] C.L.Y. 2790 and *Shevill v. Presse Alliance SA (C68/93)* [1995] 2 A.C. 18, [1995] C.L.Y. 3127 considered.

CAIRNS v. DOWNIE 2005 S.L.T. (Sh Ct) 14, Sheriff Principal EF Bowen Q.C., Sh Ct.

5047. Limitations–Personal injury claims–Failure of solicitor to raise action in time–Discretionary power to override time limit

[Prescription and Limitation (Scotland) Act 1973 (c.52) s.19A.]

The pursuers (K), the widow and daughters of a man who had died from carcinomatosis and pleural mesothelioma, sought damages from the defender (S), his former employer. The action had been raised in 1997, one month after the expiry of the three year limitation period. K had met with solicitors in 1996 but, following a mistake in the solicitors' office, their claim had not been actioned further. K argued that it would be equitable for the court to allow the action to be brought out of time under the Prescription and Limitation (Scotland) Act 1973 s.19A since it would cause S little prejudice and K would be unable to fund an action against the solicitors.

Held, giving judgment for S, that it would not be equitable to allow K to bring the action out of time under s.19A. The responsibility for it not having been raised in time rested entirely with the solicitors and K would have a remedy against them. If K were allowed to bring the action out of time S would be prejudiced by losing their statutory defence under s.17 of the Act.

KELLY v. STODDART SEKERS INTERNATIONAL PLC 2005 Rep. L.R. 12, Temporary Judge RF Macdonald Q.C., OH.

5048. Personal injury claims–Limitations–Action raised after expiry of limitation period–Discretionary power to override time limit

[Prescription and Limitation (Scotland) Act 1973 (c.52) s.17, s.19A.]

B, three former residents of a children's home, raised actions of damages against M, a religious order, for alleged physical abuse sustained in the 1960s and 1970s. The actions were raised in May 2000 and the basic triennium specified in the Prescription and Limitation (Scotland) Act 1973 s.17 had expired in each of the cases. M tabled pleas of time bar and the actions were appointed to the procedure roll. B sought to avail themselves of s.17(2)(b), arguing that they did not have knowledge of the relevant facts until the publication of newspaper articles about homes run by the defenders in 1997, at which time the limitation period began to run, and of the relief offered by s.19A. The Lord Ordinary rejected B's arguments under s.17(2)(b), holding that the limitation periods ran from the dates when each of B attained majority in accordance with s.17(3). M's pleas to the relevancy were sustained to the extent of excluding all reference to s.17(2)(b) from further consideration and a preliminary proof was allowed restricted to the pleas relating to time bar and the discretion under s.19A and the averments thereunder.

Held, dismissing the actions, that (1) all of B (i) suffered personal and psychological problems that would tend to inhibit them from raising court proceedings, both between the ages of 18 and 21, and subsequently, (ii) did not think that they would be believed if they made complaints about their treatment in the home, between the ages of 18 and 21, and for at least a substantial number of years thereafter, and (iii) did not consciously realise until 1997 that they could raise legal proceedings against M. (2) The length of time that had elapsed, namely 21 years between the date of the last of B's allegations and the raising of the present actions, was sufficient by itself to make it inequitable to allow B's actions to proceed where a major decline in the quality of justice was inevitable. (3) There was significant prejudice to M as a result of changes in the law since the statutory limitation periods had expired. (4) M were seriously prejudiced by the non availability of witnesses, the absence of documents, and the inability of such witnesses as had been traced to remember specific details of what happened at the home during the 1960s and 1970s. (5) Actual prejudice to M had been shown which was clear and serious, the existence of which was, by itself, sufficient reason for not allowing the actions to be brought under s.19A, notwithstanding the aforementioned reasons for B's failure to raise the actions timeously. (6) Additional prejudice would be caused to M by the scale of the litigation involved in the present cases where the expenses of defending such actions were substantial and likely to be disproportionately large by comparison with the value of the claims, although that factor was not conclusive by itself, while the unlikelihood of M being able to recover their expenses should they succeed in their defence, given that B were legally aided, would clearly be prejudicial. (7) Although there was a risk of prejudice both in the media publicity that occurred in 1997 and 1998, and in the form of the questionnaires used by B's solicitors to discover the nature of the allegations, neither were sufficient of themselves to lead to the refusal of an application under s.19A, but they were factors which could be taken into account. (8) The onus was on B to satisfy the court of any special circumstances and if they failed to do so, they had to lose their legal rights, which merely gave effect to the legislative policy, and that was the result which had to follow in the present case, and (9) While the gap of three years between the publication of the newspaper article and the service of the summonses clearly did not assist B by adding to the time that had already elapsed, such delay was understandable given the sheer volume of claims that had to be processed and the conduct of B's solicitors could not be regarded as a significant factor in deciding whether the court should exercise its discretion.

B v. MURRAY (NO.2) 2005 S.L.T. 982, Lord Drummond Young, OH.

5049. Personal injury claims–Limitations–Action raised after expiry of limitation period–Discretionary power to override time limit

[Prescription and Limitation (Scotland) Act 1973 (c.52) s.17, s.19A.]

T raised an action of damages against N for breach of their contractual obligation to withdraw sequestration proceedings against him. Sequestration was granted on January 19, 1997. A petition for recall was presented on February 11, 1999 and granted on March 9. T claimed that as a result of the sequestration he suffered loss of income and personal injuries in the form of stress, depression and anxiety. The action was signetted in November 2001. At procedure roll, N pled time bar respecting T's personal injuries claim in terms of the Prescription and Limitation (Scotland) Act 1973 s.17, and the pursuer invoked s 19A. The temporary judge concluded that it would not be equitable to allow the personal injuries element of T's case to proceed and allowed proof before answer. T reclaimed. N argued that esto the court did not reach the same conclusion as the temporary judge, any proof before answer should be restricted to the s.19A issue.

Held, allowing the reclaiming motion, that (1) the Lord Ordinary erred in taking the view that the fact that N had to face a timeously raised claim for damages for economic loss resulting from the same breach of contract was a neutral factor in considering whether equity favoured allowing the personal injuries action to proceed. (2) It was a point of considerable force that T had failed to pursue the claim with promptness when its availability was recognised and when it was realised that the triennium had expired, but N would have to deal with the economic loss claim on its merits regardless and it seemed likely that there would be a material degree of overlap between the evidence bearing on the former and that bearing on the personal injuries' claim. (3) It was inappropriate to reach a final conclusion on whether the court should exercise its discretion under s.19A in favour of T simply on the basis of the parties' respective pleadings, the more satisfactory course was to allow a proof before answer at large given the extent to which the facts bearing on time bar and those bearing on the merits of the claim were intermingled.

THOMSON v. NEWEY & EYRE LTD 2005 S.C. 373, Lord Marnoch, Lord Macfadyen, Lord Eassie, Ex Div.

5050. Pleadings–Court of Session–Relevancy and specification–Averments of loss–Statement of valuation of claim

[Administration of Justice Act 1982 (c.53) s.8.]

The pursuer (J) sought damages from the defender (M) for extensive injuries sustained in a road traffic accident which included a claim for necessary services in terms of the Administration of Justice (Scotland) Act 1982 s.8. J's pleadings stated only that her family provided necessary services and referred to a statement of valuation of claim which named two individuals. J sought a jury trial. M argued that J's pleadings were lacking in specification in relation to the services claim and a jury trial should not be allowed.

Held, giving judgment accordingly, that it was essential that the relatives for whom a claim was made and the sums due to them be specified in the pleadings. A statement of valuation of claim did not form part of the pleadings. It was not equivalent to a statement of claim and did not bind the parties as pleadings did. Any damages awarded under s.8 had to be accounted for to the relatives, who had to be properly identified. The naming of two relatives in the statement of valuation of claim merely indicated a person alleged to be providing the services in question at the time. In the instant case, J's pleadings were lacking in specification and gave no detail about either the services or the relatives. The cause was, therefore, unsuitable for jury trial.

JONES v. MK LESLIE LTD 2004 Rep. L.R. 136, Temporary Judge TG Coutts Q.C., OH.

5051. Pleadings–Solicitors–Relevancy and specification–"believed and averred"

B reclaimed against the dismissal of her action of damages for professional negligence against M, a firm of solicitors, in relation to a conveyancing transaction for the purchase of a house on the ground that it was irrelevant for want of specification for the necessary facts. B and her fiance had decided to purchase the property with the bulk of the purchase price having been contributed by B with her fiance contributing a small proportion and servicing a secured loan. The parties instructed M by means of a handwritten note that title to the property was to be taken in the proportions of four fifths to B and one fifth to her fiance with a side agreement providing that in the event of the parties' separation and the sale of the house, the sale proceeds would be divided according to those proportions, and B's fiance would remain responsible for the loan's repayment. The parties were married in 1998 and separated in 1999. B's primary case of fault was that M had failed in their duty to carry out her instructions as conveyed and was perilled on the proposition of fact that M were instructed to implement the handwritten note and the critical averments on which that case was based, namely "... it is believed and averred that [her fiance] instructed [the defenders] to implement the handwritten note of instructions". B's secondary case of fault was introduced as "[a] solicitor of ordinary skill acting with ordinary care would have sought specific instructions from the pursuer before departing from the written instructions given to him". B moved for leave to amend the sentence to insert "[h]aving received the handwritten note" at the beginning and substitute "arrangements set out in the handwritten note" for "written instructions given to him", thus basing the secondary case of fault on mere receipt of the note, which M had admitted. B submitted that the Lord Ordinary erred in holding that to make a relevant case, she had to make a categorical averment that M had been instructed to implement the handwritten note when it was sufficient to aver it as a matter of inference provided other primary facts capable of supporting that inference were averred. M submitted that (1) B's alternative secondary case should be refused because its basis on mere knowledge of the handwritten note was not followed through in her averments of loss where she sought recovery of £20,315.03, representing her acceptance of liability of the loan amount which she would not have had to repay had her instructions been acted upon, which was tied to the assertion that they had been instructed to implement the handwritten note; and (2) B had not averred that their alleged negligence had caused her any loss which, on a sound view of the law, she could not have avoided by appropriate legal action.

Held, allowing the reclaiming motion, that (1) any material fact might be pled by means of the formula "believed and averred" if there were also averments of primary fact which were capable of supporting the inference that the matter which was believed and averred was true. (2) It was sufficient for the relevancy of B's pleadings that the averred surrounding circumstances were capable of being able to support the averred inference that M had been instructed to implement the handwritten note. (3) The secondary case of fault, as B proposed to amend it, would be as well supported by averments of loss as the primary case of fault. (4) Whether B had relevantly averred that she had suffered loss caused by the alleged negligence on M's part should be reserved for decision after evidence had been led, B had set out in some detail the course which matters took after she and her husband separated and had done enough to entitle her to proof on her averments of loss.

BURNETT v. MENZIES DOUGAL WS 2005 S.L.T. 929, Lord Macfadyen, Lord Abernethy, Lord Kingarth, Ex Div.

5052. Possession claims—Possession of heritable property—Decree in absence—Reponing—Intention to defend stated—Failure to set out defence

[Mortgage Rights (Scotland) Act 2001 (asp 11) s.2.]

The pursuers (B), creditors in a standard security, sought to recover possession of the security subjects from the defender (S) following non payment of sums owed. Decree was granted in S's absence and S lodged a reponing note setting out her intention to defend the action by seeking an order in terms of the Mortgage Rights (Scotland) Act 2001 s.2. S argued that a minute under the 2001 Act amounted to a defence and the reponing note should, therefore, be granted.

Held, giving judgment accordingly, that S's actions in lodging a reponing note did nothing more than suspend the enforcement of the order to allow S more time to meet her obligations under the security. The reponing note did not in itself contain a valid defence and was accordingly refused, *Northern Rock Plc v. Goodwin* 2004 Hous. L.R. 88 applied.

BRADFORD & BINGLEY PLC v. SEMPLE 2004 Hous. L.R. 133, Sheriff I Dunbar, Sh Ct (Tayside, Central and Fife).

5053. Possession claims—Sheriff Courts—Possession of heritable property—Proper form of warrant

[Heritable Securities (Scotland) Act 1894 (c.44) s.5; Conveyancing and Feudal Reform (Scotland) Act 1970 (c.35) s.20; Mortgage Rights (Scotland) Act 2001 (asp 11) s.1 (1) (b); Act of Sederunt (Sheriff Court Ordinary Cause Rules) 1993 (SI 1993 1956) r.3.2 (3).]

The pursuer (C), a bank, raised an action seeking declarator that it was entitled to recover possession of subjects over which the defenders (H) had granted three standard securities, and were entitled to exercise all powers competent to a creditor. C also sought warrant for the ejection of H. C averred that H had not complied with calling up notices, a Form BB notice had been served together with a calling up notice in terms of the Mortgage Rights (Scotland) Act 2001, and that H had agreed to conditions in the securities that a warrant for summary ejection could competently proceed against them. When the writ was presented the sheriff clerk took the view that the appropriate warrant to cite was Form O2A on the basis that the Act of Sederunt (Sheriff Court Ordinary Cause Rules) 1993 r.3.2(3) applied. C maintained that the correct form was Form O1, the normal form of warrant. C argued that the action fell under the Conveyancing and Feudal Reform (Scotland) Act 1970 s.20 and not the Heritable Securities (Scotland) Act 1894 s.5, as the crave for ejection was based on the contractual consent contained in the standard security conditions and s.20 specifically preserved any remedy conferred by the contract to which the security related.

Held, giving judgment accordingly, that (1) the requisites of an application under s.5 of the 1894 Act were fulfilled, although in practical terms it was irrelevant whether the action proceeded under the 1894 Act or by virtue of the contractual security terms. (2) It was arguable that a debtor's default giving rise to a contractual right to eject was properly to be regarded as a contractual default requiring the court to provide the remedy on default. If that were the case, then it followed in any event that the application to the court for repossession was one to which s.1(1)(b) of the 2001 Act applied and therefore fell within r.3.2(3). Accordingly, a warrant to cite H had to be in Form O2A and would not be granted unless the initial writ contained averments that complied with r 3.2(3). (Obiter) To conclude that the requirements of s.5 had not been met where many lenders claimed to possess an "other remedy" deriving from the underlying documentation could lead to the avoidance of the notification requirements of the 2001 Act with the result that the opportunity to seek the remedies provided for may not be appreciated. Leave to appeal was granted.

CLYDESDALE BANK PLC v. HYLAND 2004 Hous. L.R. 116, Sheriff DS Williamson Q.C., Sh Ct (Tayside, Central and Fife).

5054. Proof-Liabilities-Proof or jury trial-Special cause-Road traffic accident-Involvement of Motor Insurers' Bureau

[Act of Sederunt (Rules of the Court of Session 1994) 1994 (SI 1994 1443) Sch.2 r.36.1.]

M, a pillion passenger on a motorbike, sought damages for injuries sustained in a road traffic accident from T, the driver of the bike, and C, the driver of the car with which the motorbike collided. T was uninsured and B, the Motor Insurers' Bureau, sisted themselves as party minuters, seeking a ruling on the applicability of the exception to their liability in a case where the injured person "knew or ought to have known" that the vehicle in which he was allowing himself to be carried was uninsured, contained in the Motor Insurers' Bureau (Compensation of Victims of Uninsured Drivers) Agreement 1998 cl.6(1)(e). B alleged fault on C's part and contributory negligence on M's part. M and B agreed that special cause existed such that the case should not go to jury trial, with which C disagreed. B further moved the court to order a divided proof in terms of the Act of Sederunt (Rules of the Court of Session 1994) 1994 Sch.2 r.36.1, ordaining that all questions except quantum be resolved first. M opposed the motion.

Held, allowing proof before answer and ordering proof on liability to be heard separately from, and prior to, proof on quantum, that (1) B's involvement in the proceedings made the action unsuitable for a jury trial. It would be impossible to avoid bringing up the question of insurance in the jury's presence, contrary to the current well established practice prohibiting mention or discussion of a party's indemnity insurance in the presence thereof. *White v. White* [2001] UKHL 9, [2001] 1 W.L.R. 481, [2001] C.L.Y. 3828 demonstrated not only that the proper construction and application of the concept of whether M "knew or ought to have known" that T was uninsured might not be easy to define, but also that a final definition might yet be awaited, rendering the question of B's exception from liability arising from cl.6(1)(e)(ii) unsafe to go to a jury; and there was the further combination of inter alia M's contributory negligence, the apportionment of liability between defenders, and the shifting of the onus of proof from M to B, and (2) it was appropriate to make an order in terms of r.36.1, *White* applied.

McFARLANE v. THAIN 2005 S.L.T. 221, Lady Paton, OH.

5055. Relief–Summonses–Dispensing power–Competency

[Act of Sederunt (Rules of the Court of Session 1994) 1994 (SI 1994 1443) Sch.2 r.2.1, r.13.13(6), r.43.3(2).]

B reclaimed against the refusal (2004 S.L.T. 774, [2004] 8 C.L. 544) of his motion to allow the summons in his personal injury action to be lodged late under the Act of Sederunt (Rules of the Court of Session 1994) 1994 Sch.2 r.2.1. B's solicitor, in ignorance of the new rules of court applicable to personal injuries actions, had failed to lodge the summons timeously for calling in terms of Sch.2 r.43.3 with the result that the instance had fallen in terms of Sch.2 r.43.3(2). The temporary judge refused the motion as incompetent, declining to follow *McDonald v. Kwok* 1999 S.L.T. 593, [1999] C.L.Y. 5665, and decided that esto B's action had been competent, he would have refused it in the exercise of his discretion. B adopted the reasoning in *McDonald*, and submitted that it was in the interests of justice that the dispensing power should be exercised and ignorance of the provisions of a rule normally fell within the ambit of the court's dispensing power under Sch.2 r.2.1.

Held, refusing the reclaiming motion, that *McDonald*, and the cases in which it had been followed, had been incorrectly decided, *McDonald* overruled. The terms of Sch.2 r.13.13(6) and Sch.2 r.43.3(2) were plain, and the meaning of the expression "the instance shall fall" was well understood. Where the summons had not called within the period specified by the rule, the automatic consequence was that the instance fell, and it was incompetent thereafter to apply to the court under Sch.2 r.2.1 to enable the summons to call, *McKidd v. Manson* (1882) 9 R. 790 applied.

BROGAN v. O'ROURKE LTD 2005 S.L.T. 29, Lord Hamilton, Lord Reed, Lord Weir, Ex Div.

5056. Summary applications–Time limits

[Act of Sederunt (Summary Applications, Statutory Applications and Appeals etc. Rules) 1999 (SI 1999 929) r.2.6.]

C, the tenant under an agricultural lease, made a summary application to the sheriff to have the award of M, an arbitrator, set aside. M had been appointed in an action of irritancy and removing raised by S, the landlords under the lease, in order to determine whether they had acquiesced in C's alleged breach of a residence condition in the lease. M's decision was intimated to C on May 2, 2002, and C's application was lodged on March 5, 2003. C advanced three reasons for the delay, namely the complexity of the issue of the competency of the summary application, for which counsel's opinion had been sought, the fact that S's action was continued on a number of occasions, which could almost be seen as approval of the delay, and the fact that he was resident in France. The sheriff found that the application was out of time in terms of the Act of Sederunt (Summary Applications, Statutory Applications and Appeals etc. Rules) 1999 r.2.6, and that special cause had not been shown for it to be heard. C appealed. He submitted that the sheriff had erred in taking into account prejudice to S, as this was prejudice that had already been suffered as a result of the application not having been lodged earlier, rather than prejudice which they would suffer if he allowed the application to be heard; by failing to take into account the prejudice C would suffer if the application was not heard; and in his weighing of the factors of respective prejudice that would arise from his hearing or not hearing the application.

Held, dismissing the appeal, that (1) the sheriff was entitled to conclude that far too much time had been allowed to elapse before the summary application was lodged for it to be allowed to proceed. (2) The sheriff had not erred in relation to the question of prejudice: the question was whether special cause had been made out and while the sheriff had been right to treat the prejudice claimed by S as a factor adverse to the establishing of special cause, the prejudice that if the application was not heard, C would lose the opportunity to bring M's decision under review, was self inflicted and formed an inevitable background to any application under r.2.6(3), and in this context C could not distance himself from his solicitor's delay.

CLARKE v. MacKENZIE 2005 S.C. 174, Lord Macfadyen, Lord Reed, Lord Drummond Young, Ex Div.

5057. Summary causes–Applications–Time limits

[Tenancy of Shops Act 1949 (c.25) s.1 (1).]

S made a summary cause application for renewal of a tenancy. S's agents had tendered a summary cause summons and partially completed form E200 in respect of court fees on December 16, 2004 to the sheriff clerk's office which was stamped "Lodged" and dated December 16, 2004. The agents were asked if a shortened period of notice was required, and if so, a solicitor would require to appear before the sheriff. The agents advised that they would be unable to arrange for appearance that day but it was likely someone would be able to do so the following day and took the summons away. On December 17 the agents returned the summons, a shortened period of notice of seven days was granted, and the summons was thereafter authenticated by the sheriff clerk's office changing the date stamped from "16" to "17" marking on it "fee paid". The sheriff concluded that the application had not been made timeously under the Tenancy of Shops Act 1949 s.1 (1) and dismissed it. Parties were agreed that if the application was made on December 16 it was timeous. S appealed, arguing that the application had been made on December 16. They had initiated proceedings by presenting the summons and tendering payment of the court dues. The actual date of payment was immaterial and completion of the "Fee Paid" part was a matter of housekeeping for the sheriff clerk. The sheriff clerk had altered the original form of date stamp which was irregular and could not be effective to alter the existing position that what was placed before the sheriff was a summons stamped as having been lodged on December 16.

Held, dismissing the appeal, that (1) in the context of s.1 (1), "apply" meant the presentation of a procedurally valid summons accompanied by the appropriate fee to the sheriff clerk together with a request, implicit or explicit, that that summons should be processed, which were all matters within the sole control of S and did not depend in any way on anything done by a sheriff clerk. (2) It could not be said that what happened on December 16, 2004 amounted to an "application", as S's agents failed to give any direction to the sheriff clerk that the summons should be processed. (3) The fact that a date stamp was imprinted on the summons on December 16, 2004 was of no significance, no steps were taken to institute any further procedure and the only application was made on December 17, 2004 which was out of time.

SUPERDRUG STORES PLC v. NETWORK RAIL INFRASTRUCTURE LTD 2005 S.L.T. (Sh Ct) 105, Sheriff Principal AL Stewart Q.C., Sh Ct.

5058. Summonses–Time limits–Relief–Dispensing power

[Administration of Justice (Scotland) Act 1972 (c.59) s.1; Act of Sederunt (Rules of the Court of Session 1994) 1994 (SI 1994 1443) Sch.2 r.2.1, r.43.3(2); Act of Sederunt (Rules of the Court of Session Amendment No. 2) (Personal Injuries Actions) 2002.]

R enrolled a motion invoking the court's dispensing power in terms of the Act of Sederunt (Rules of the Court of Session 1994) 1994 Sch.2 r.2.1 to allow his summons in his personal injury action against C to be called late. The summons was signeted on February 24, 2004. R's agent, who had focused his efforts in tracing C, had overlooked the new rules of court applicable to such actions by the Act of Sederunt (Rules of the Court of Session Amendment No. 2) (Personal Injuries Actions) 2002, and failed to lodge it timeously within three months and a day after the date of signeting, with the result that the instance had fallen in terms of Sch.2 r.43.3(2) of the 1994 Rules. R further enrolled a motion in terms of the Administration of Justice (Scotland) Act 1972 s.1 to ordain the agents in the sale of C's former residence to provide him with any information relating to C's current address.

Held, allowing the summons to be called late, that (1) it was competent to exercise the relieving power in terms of Sch.2 r.2.1 in the present circumstances, which was wholly consistent with the aim of the new rules, *Jackson v. McDougall* 2004 S.L.T. 770, [2004] 8 C.L. 545 and *McDonald v. Kwok* 1999 S.L.T. 593, [1999] C.L.Y. 5665 followed. (2) A motion under s.1 of the 1972 Act could only be made in a cause depending before the court, which commenced when the summons was served on the defender, or when the first order in a petition was granted, and as the summons had not yet been served on C, any application in terms of s.1 had to be by way of petition.

ROBERTS v. CHISHOLM 2004 S.L.T. 1171, Lady Paton, OH.

5059. Witnesses–Skilled persons–Certification

[Act of Sederunt (Rules of the Court of Session 1994) 1994 (SI 1994 1443) Sch.2 para.42.13.]

J, the pursuer in an action for reparation in respect of injuries sustained in a road accident, sought to have a doctor certified as an expert witness, whose charges would exceed the value of the claim which the parties had agreed to settle at £1,500. J had attended the doctor's clinic prior to the accident as part of a continuing investigation into neck pain and backache. J continued to visit the doctor after the accident, who recorded his findings and prepared a report at J's request which was produced when the initial writ was served on G. J's motion was granted by the sheriff. G appealed.

Held, allowing the appeal, that a skilled witness had to have been specifically employed to investigate, as provided by the Act of Sederunt (Rules of the Court of Session 1994) 1994 Sch.2 para.42.13, and it was not sufficient for a party to rely on a skilled person who had made investigations nor was it sufficient that the investigations were carried out prior to proof.

JONES v. GEORGE LESLIE LTD 2005 S.L.T. (Sh Ct) 113, Sheriff Principal EF Bowen Q.C., Sh Ct.

COMMERCIAL LAW

5060. Books

Cuisine, Douglas; Forte, Angelo–Scottish Cases and Materials in Commercial Law. Paperback: £35.00. ISBN 1 84592 148 8. Tottel Publishing.

Law Society Scotland Diploma Materials 2005, Civil Company and Commercial Student Manual 2005-2006. Book (details unknown): £15.00. ISBN 0 414 01638 6. W. Green & Son.

COMPETITION LAW

5061. Office of Fair Trading–Disclosure–Commercially confidential information

[Competition Act 1998 Chapter II; Competition Commission Appeal Tribunal Rules 2000 (SI 2000 261) r.17.]

The applicants (C) sought disclosure by the respondent Office of Fair Trading (OFT) of information connected to a witness statement made by OFT to the effect that the interveners (W) had not infringed the Competition Act 1998 Chapter II. C had made complaints to OFT about W's behaviour in the Scottish milk market, namely that W had engaged in anti competitive practices. OFT made a reference to the Competition Commission. The Commission found that W had engaged in conduct contrary to the public interest but it did not achieve the necessary majority for any action to be taken against W. OFT then began an investigation under the 1998 Act based on the Commission's findings but it failed to find sufficient evidence of infringement. C appealed against OFT's decision to close its file and the tribunal required OFT to file a witness statement explaining the reasons for its decision. OFT filed the statement but a section of it was redacted on grounds of commercial confidentiality. The tribunal ordered that the redacted part be disclosed to a confidentiality ring consisting of C's and W's advisers. C subsequently asked for disclosure of further material, including certain passages of the Commission's report in unredacted form and personal notes made by OFT staff in meetings on the basis that recovery and inspection of the material was both relevant and necessary to its appeal.

Held, refusing the application, that the starting point when considering C's request for recovery and inspection was the Competition Commission Appeal Tribunal Rules 2000 r.17 because the proceedings had begun prior to June 20, 2003. Pursuant to the 2000 Rules, the function of the tribunal in the instant hearing was not to consider the substance of OFT's decision on infringement but to decide whether it had materially erred in law in reaching it. It was necessary to balance C's interest in obtaining sufficient information upon which to base its appeal against the general interest in preventing disclosure that was unnecessarily burdensome on the litigation process and against W's interest in preserving business confidentiality, *Claymore Dairies Ltd v. Director General of Fair Trading (Disclosure: Confidentiality Ring)* [2003] CAT 12, [2004] Comp. A.R. 63, [2004] C.L.Y. 521 followed. Discovery would only be ordered by the tribunal where it was necessary, relevant and proportionate to do so, particularly where the information sought was commercially confidential. On the basis of the disclosure already made within the confidentiality ring, C had been able to advance a detailed case and, in the light of that, further disclosure was not justified. In any event, it would not be appropriate to order disclosure of personal notes made by OFT staff, which did not form part of OFT's documentation and which were not ordinarily disclosable.

CLAYMORE DAIRIES LTD v. OFFICE OF FAIR TRADING (DISCLOSURE: FURTHER INFORMATION), [2004] CAT 16, [2005] Comp. A.R. 1, Sir Christopher Bellamy (President), Competition Appeal Tribunal.

CONSTITUTIONAL LAW

5062. Devolution—Legislative competence

SCOTLAND ACT 1998 (MODIFICATIONS OF SCHEDULE 5) ORDER 2005, SI 2005 865 (S.3); made under the Scotland Act 1998 s.30. In force: March 23, 2005; £3.00.

This Order modifies the Scotland Act 1998 Sch.5 which defines what are reserved matters for the purposes of that Act. Accordingly it is concerned with matters which are outwith the legislative competence of the Scottish Parliament. It makes amendments which will will extend the legislative competence of the Scottish Parliament in relation to fire safety on construction sites and on premises that at July 1, 1999 were listed in the Fire Certificates (Special Premises) Regulations 1976 (SI 1976 2003).

5063. Devolution—Legislative competence

SCOTLAND ACT 1998 (MODIFICATIONS OF SCHEDULE 5) (NO.2) ORDER 2005, SI 2005 866 (S.4); made under the Scotland Act 1998 s.30. In force: March 23, 2005; £3.00.

This Order makes modifications to the Scotland Act 1998 Sch.5 which is concerned with matters which are outwith the legislative competence of the Scottish Parliament. The Order amends the definitions of "Place of detention", "person detained" and "Private telecommunication system" in the interpretation provisions in relation to the interception of communications.

5064. Devolution–Scottish Administration–Offices

SCOTTISH ADMINISTRATION (OFFICES) ORDER 2005, SI 2005 1467; made under the Scotland Act 1998 s.126. In force: in accordance with Art.1 (1); £3.00.

This Order, which amends the Scottish Administration (Offices) Order 1999 (SI 1999 1127), specifies Her Majesty's Chief Inspector of Fire and Rescue Authorities, Her Majesty's Inspector of Fire and Rescue Authorities and Assistant Inspector of Fire and Rescue Authorities as offices in the Scottish Administration which are not ministerial offices for the purposes of the Scotland Act 1998.

5065. Devolution–Scottish Ministers–Transfer of functions

SCOTLAND ACT 1998 (TRANSFER OF FUNCTIONS TO THE SCOTTISH MINISTERS, ETC.) ORDER 2005, SI 2005 849 (S.2); made under the Scotland Act 1998 s.63, s.113, s.124. In force: March 23, 2005; £3.00.

This Order, which amends the Road Traffic Regulation Act 1984 and the Roads (Scotland) Act 1984, provides for certain functions of a Minister of the Crown, so far as they are exercisable by that Minister in or as regards Scotland, to be exercisable by the Scottish Ministers instead of, or concurrently with, the Minister concerned. In relation to the Fire and Rescue Services Act 2004, this Order transfers to the Scottish Ministers functions in respect of Fire Authority pensions. In relation to the Electricity Act 1989, this Order transfers to the Scottish Ministers functions which relate to the principal objective and general duties of the Secretary of State in relation to consumers, the use of green certificates issued in Northern Ireland and consultation requirements. In relation to the Energy Act 2004, this Order transfers to the Scottish Ministers functions relating to consultation requirements in relation to functions exercisable under the Electricity Act 1989. In relation to the Food and Environment Protection Act 1985, the Food Safety Act 1990 and the Food Standards Act 1999, this Order transfers to the Scottish Ministers those functions, other than functions already devolved to the Scottish Ministers, relating to food safety and standards in respect of all substances considered food under European Parliament and Council Regulation 178/2002 ([2002] OJ L31/1) laying down the general principles and requirements of food law, establishing the European Food Safety Authority and laying down procedures in matters of food safety. In relation to the Road Traffic Regulation Act 1984, this Order transfers to the Scottish Ministers, subject to a requirement for the agreement of the Secretary of State, functions exercisable for purposes related to avoiding or reducing, or reducing the likelihood of, danger connected with terrorism. In relation to the Roads (Scotland) Act 1984, the Order transfers to the Scottish Ministers functions exercisable for purposes in connection with traffic calming which relate to avoiding or reducing, or reducing the likelihood of, danger connected with terrorism.

5066. Books

Laws of Scotland Consolidated Index. Hardback: £108.00. ISBN 1 4057 0906 5. Butterworths Law (Scotland).

CONSTRUCTION LAW

5067. Building regulations–Prescribed forms

BUILDING (FORMS) (SCOTLAND) REGULATIONS 2005, SSI 2005 172; made under the Building (Scotland) Act 2003 s.36. In force: May 1, 2005; £6.00.

These Regulations set out the forms prescribed for the purposes of the Building (Scotland) Act 2003 s.36 of the Act. They state that the forms prescribed are those set out in the Schedule to the Regulations. There is an index at the beginning of the Schedule which lists the 16 forms and their titles. The prescribed forms include those for building warrants and completion certificates as well as for various enforcement notices.

5068. Construction contracts–Adjudicators–Jurisdiction–Lapse on expiry of time limit

[Scheme for Construction Contracts (Scotland) Regulations 1998 (SI 1998 687) Sch.1 para.19.]

R, contractors under a construction contract, sought to enforce a decision by X, an adjudicator, to whom a dispute with D, the employers, had been referred. R posted a referral notice to X on September 18, 2003, which was collected from the post office on September 23. X requested R's consent to postpone his decision until at least October 23, which was confirmed by them on October 21. X wrote to the parties on October 23 informing them that he had made his decision and requesting payment of his fee. His decision was delivered to the parties on October 27. D pled that X's decision was ultra vires and should be reduced ope exceptionis because it was reached after the expiry of the 28 day time limit stipulated in the Scheme for Construction Contracts (Scotland) Regulations 1998 Sch.1 para.19 and as X had not previously sought R's consent to reaching his decision within 42 days, he was functus officio and his decision was rendered a nullity. The Lord Ordinary granted decree de plano, having found that on a proper view of the scheme, the provisions relating to the times in which X should reach his decision were directory rather than mandatory entailing nullity of any late decision, and delay by an adjudicator in producing his decision within those time limits did not bring the adjudication process to an end but enabled it to be continued with a fresh adjudicator, should either party so wish. D reclaimed. R submitted that (1) the court should be slow to apply the common law of arbitration to the interpretation of the statutory scheme. Schedule 1 para.19 did not expressly require that any extension to the 28 day period be made within that period and if the jurisdiction automatically expired, there would be no need for Sch.1 para.19(2). The true interpretation was that if the adjudicator failed to make his decision within the new time limit, he had at worst committed a procedural error but his jurisdiction nonetheless continued indefinitely until one of the parties invoked Sch.1 para.19(2). In any event, if the jurisdiction did not continue indefinitely in such a case, the delay in the present case was not material. (2) Alternatively, X's failure to reach a decision within the time limit in this case was not so serious as to render it a nullity where it was a technical failure rather than a fundamental error or impropriety.

Held, allowing the reclaiming motion (Lord Abernethy dissenting), that (1) the common law principles of arbitration did not give reliable guidance in the interpretation of the scheme. (2) On the face of it, X's decision was reached out of time and after a purported extension consented to out of time, but X did not nevertheless retain his jurisdiction where the true interpretation of Sch.1 para.19 was that it ceased on the expiry of that time limit if it had not already been extended. (3) R's alternative submission could not be accepted where it provided no hard and fast criterion by which a court could determine for how long after a time limit a failure to reach a decision could be considered to be merely technical, or in what circumstances the jurisdiction could be said to have come to an end. Per Lord Abernethy, that the provisions relating to the time in which the adjudicator should reach his decision under Sch.1 para.19(1)(a) of the scheme were directory rather than mandatory. Parliament's intention in providing for the right to refer disputes to adjudication was to introduce a speedy mechanism by which to settle disputes in construction contracts on an interim basis and while the aim of the scheme was clearly to reach a decision within a short time, it envisaged that the 28 days could be extended to 42 days if the referring party consented or even longer if all parties consented. Schedule 1 para.19(2) envisaged that an adjudicator might fail to reach his decision on time and also envisaged that the process would nevertheless be followed through, albeit with a new adjudicator, but it made little sense and would undermine Parliament's intention if that was the only way the adjudication could be achieved, it was plainly implicit that if a fresh notice was served and a new adjudicator was requested to act in terms of Sch.1 para.19(2)(a), the jurisdiction of the first adjudicator came to an end but it was also implicit that the latter retained jurisdiction to determine the dispute until that happened. Further, there did not have to be a time when a decision was so late that it amounted to a nullity, the scheme provided a mechanism in Sch.1 para.19(2) for dealing with situations where a decision was so delayed that one or other party to the dispute did not want to wait any longer, the practicalities of the situation were that it would usually not be in the interests of both parties to countenance serious delay and if it was, while it might be untidy, no harm was done by a continuation of the adjudicator's jurisdiction without limit of time.

RITCHIE BROTHERS (PWC) LTD v. DAVID PHILP (COMMERCIALS) LTD 2005 S.C. 384, Lord Gill L.J.C., Lord Abernethy, Lord Nimmo Smith, 2 Div.

5069. Construction contracts–Arbitration–Notices–Validity

S, employers under a construction contract, sought declarator that a notice of arbitration served by M, the contractors, was invalid and that the decision of an adjudicator was final and binding. In a parallel commercial action, M sought declarator that the notice was valid. By cl.67(2) of the governing ICE conditions of contract, any reference to arbitration was to be "conducted in accordance with ... the Scottish Arbitration Code". S submitted that the notice failed to comply with Art.1.3 thereof for lack of specification and further, that *Christiani & Nielsen Ltd v. Birmingham City Council* 52 Con. L.R. 56, [1997] C.L.Y. 923, in which it was held that a similarly worded provision did not apply to the act of referring but only to the subsequent conduct of the arbitration, was wrongly decided or was distinguishable.

Held, dismissing S's action and granting decree in M's action, that the wording in cl.67(2) should be construed as referring to the carrying on of the arbitration, rather than any prescribed procedure as to how it should be commenced: the dictionary definition of "conduct" was "to carry on a process"; if it had been intended by those who compiled the relevant conditions of contract that a notice of arbitration, designed to prevent the adjudicator's decision becoming final and binding, would not have such effect because of some failure in expression, that could and should have been made clear in cl.66(9)(a), which provided for the referral to arbitration, by inserting after the words "Notice of Arbitration", the words "being a Notice complying with the provisions of the Scottish Arbitration Code"; further support could be found in the fact that cl.67(2) also provided that any reference to arbitration be conducted in accordance with the ICE Appendix which contained a sample notice of arbitration, the validity of which was not dependent on compliance with Art.1 of the code, *Christiani* considered.

SCRABSTER HARBOUR TRUST v. MOWLEM PLC (T/A MOWLEM MARINE) 2005 S.L.T. 499, Lord Clarke, OH.

5070. Construction contracts–Contract terms–Provision for employers' determination in event of contractors' receivership

[Housing Grants, Construction and Regeneration Act 1996 (c.53) s.111.]

M, contractors, who were in receivership, raised an action for payment against W, their employers under a construction contract. The contract had been entered into in terms of the January 2000 version of the "Scottish Building Contract With Contractor's Design Section on Completion Edition" as issued by the Scottish Building Committee. W resisted payment on the basis that cl.27 of the contract allowed the employers to give notice determining the contract in the event of the contractors going into receivership, that such notice had been given, and the sum sued for by M had not so accrued. M argued that cl.27 effectively provided a scheme for withholding payment, W did not aver that any effective notice of intention to do so had been given by them in accordance with the Housing Grants, Construction and Regeneration Act 1996 s.111 and cl.27 had to be read so as to avoid conflict with s.111, or, if that was not possible, the relevant provisions thereof had to be struck down.

Held, dismissing the action, that s.111 did not have the effect of subverting the parties' contractual arrangements. Clause 27 was concerned with the situation where the contract was legitimately determined by the employer, which the legislative provisions were not intended to regulate.

MELVILLE DUNDAS LTD (IN RECEIVERSHIP) v. GEORGE WIMPEY UK LTD 2005 S.L.T. 24, Lord Clarke, OH.

5071. Construction contracts—Delay—Concurrent causes of loss

J brought a reclaiming motion against a decision (2004 S.L.T. 678, [2002] C.L.Y. 5404) that L's claim against it could proceed to proof. J, managing contractors of a building development, had employed L as contractors for part of the works. The works were completed 22 weeks late and L brought an action for damages for loss and expense, contending that J had caused the delay. The judge at first instance held that L could put its claim as a global claim, in which it could prove that a number of concurrent factors, all attributable to J, had caused certain losses, without having to show a direct causal link between each individual factor and loss. In its current motion, J argued that L's claim was not sufficiently robust to proceed to a proof before answer.

Held, refusing the reclaiming motion, that the judge below was right to allow the claim to proceed. It was open to L to make a global claim, provided it could prove that all the delaying and disruptive factors were attributable to J, *John Holland Construction & Engineering Pty Ltd v. Kvaerner RJ Brown Pty Ltd* 82 B.L.R. 81, [1997] C.L.Y. 932 applied. Should any of the factors be found not to be J's fault, the claim would fail. However, it was possible for L to make a hybrid global claim in which an area of the claim where fault was attributable to J could be treated as a global claim. Alternatively, where there were concurrent factors, only some of which were attributable to J, loss could be apportioned.

JOHN DOYLE CONSTRUCTION LTD v. LAING MANAGEMENT (SCOTLAND) LTD; *sub nom.* LAING MANAGEMENT (SCOTLAND) LTD v. JOHN DOYLE CONSTRUCTION LTD 2004 S.C. 713, Lord MacLean, Lord Johnston, Lord Drummond Young, Ex Div.

5072. Construction contracts—Payments—Consortium agreement—Right of retention prevalent over contractual obligation to pay

[Court of Session Act 1988 (c.36) s.47(2).]

Two companies, B and P, entered into a construction consortium agreement for the construction under a separate contract of a waste water treatment centre for a third company, W. The agreement provided under art.7.2.6g that B, as lead contractor, would pay any monies due to P within five days of receipt from W. P sought an order under the Court of Session Act 1988 s.47(2) ordaining B to make payment of £385,594.01 which had been withheld and declarator that B was not entitled to withhold payment. B accepted that the sum had been certified as due under the contract with W and that it had been withheld, but that no sum was currently due because (1) the scheme of the consortium agreement was such that only the net balance would be due to P, after offsetting any sum due to B in respect of P's defective performance of its project part. (2) The right of retention at common law applied to the parties' contract and B was entitled to withhold payment of any sum due until such time as it could be set off against the payment of compensation.

Held, refusing the motion, that (1) the scheme of the consortium agreement, by itself, was not sufficient to achieve the result that only a net balance was due under art.7.2.6g. (2) B had pled a relevant defence of retention. The breaches of contract averred were clearly substantial on the assumption they were made out and the inability to retain a sum which was approximately 28 per cent of the amount certified under the contract with W would clearly threaten the benefit B might reasonably expect to obtain from the parties' contract. (3) The decisive consideration was the integrity of the parties' contractual arrangements which required that the right of retention should prevail over any obligation to pay.

PURAC LTD v. BYZAK LTD 2005 S.L.T. 37, Lord Drummond Young, OH.

5073. Construction contracts–Taxation administration–Payment withheld pending exhibition of valid taxation administration–Competence

[Income Tax (Sub-contractors in the Construction Industry) Regulations 1993 (SI 1993 743) Reg.7F, Reg.33.]

H had entered into a subcontract with F to undertake construction work on a bridge. A settlement of H's claim was reached during arbitration after a dispute arose as to the amount to be paid under the contract following the completion of the works. The terms of the settlement provided that F would pay the pursuers £1.5 million together with VAT provided H produced a valid VAT invoice. F refused to make payment following receipt of an invoice in December 2003 on the basis that they were obliged to withhold payment until either a current "subcontractor's certificate" or a current "registration card", issued in terms of the Income Tax (Sub-contractors in the Construction Industry) Regulations 1993, had been exhibited, in accordance with Reg.7F and Reg.33. H held neither at the material time. H thereafter sought payment of the sum and interest together with VAT of £262,500. F paid the principal sums following receipt of a certificate, leaving the issue of H's claim for interest. F argued that the claim for interest could not run as the action was premature because it was raised before receipt of a certificate or registration card. H argued that the statutory provisions were freestanding and overlay, but did not affect or qualify, the subjacent contractual relationship. Alternatively, the sum sought was not affected by the legislation because it was not a payment under the construction contract but a payment made in terms of the compromise reached in the course of arbitration.

Held, dismissing the action, that (1) the sum which F agreed to pay to H was manifestly a sum payable under the construction contract. (2) The statutory provisions qualified contractual arrangements respecting payment of sums due under construction contracts between a contractor and a subcontractor by subjecting the subcontractor's contractual entitlement to the additional statutory requirement of his obtaining and exhibiting either a registration card or a subcontractor's tax certificate, the responsibility for which lay with H, and as the absence of the necessary documentation in December 2003 was attributable to them, F could not be said to have wrongfully withheld payment.

MT HOJGAARD A/S v. FORTH ESTUARY TRANSPORT AUTHORITY 2005 S.L.T. 187, Lord Eassie, OH.

CONSUMER LAW

5074. Enforcement orders–Defective goods–Interim orders

[Sale of Goods Act 1979 (c.54); Supply of Goods and Services Act 1982 (c.29) s.11C, s.11D; Enterprise Act 2002 (c.40) Part 8, s.211, s.217, s.218, s.222; Unfair Terms in Consumer Contracts Regulations 1999 (SI 1999 2083).]

O, the Office of Fair Trading, raised proceedings seeking a series of enforcement orders and interim enforcement orders against M, a double glazing company, and its directors under the Enterprise Act 2002 Part 8, preventing them from supplying defective goods. O averred that in fitting and installing the goods which it supplied to its customers, M regularly failed to exercise the requisite level of skill and care of a reasonably competent installer of windows, doors and conservatories. O further averred that M had a practice of regularly supplying goods in breach of the Supply of Goods and Services Act 1982 s.11D (2), s.11D (6) and s.11C (2), had committed a number of domestic and Community infringements under the 2002 Act, and by incorporating cl.7 in its "Quick Fit" contracts and cl.6 in its "QuickTrade" contracts, to the effect that any representation made before or at the time of signature to the contract not included in the printed form of the contract should be added in writing to the face of the contract and signed by the customer and first respondent, it had included and relied on an unfair provision in terms of the Unfair Terms in Consumer Contracts Regulations 1999. In relation to the directors it was averred that they had consented to or connived at conduct constituting infringements. The case called before the Outer House on O's motion for interim enforcement orders. M opposed the orders arguing that (1) the form of order under s.217 and s.218 of the 2002 Act should conform to the requirements of an interdict at common law: it had to be directed against a specific act that was alleged in contravention of the statute; and unless such orders were framed with the same precision as an interim interdict the person affected by the order would be uncertain what he had to do to avoid the penal consequences of breach of interdict; (2) the expression "likely to be granted" under s.218(1)(b) meant more likely than not, thus the court would have to reach the view that on a balance of probabilities an enforcement order would be granted; (3) Part 8 of the 2002 Act had no effect prior to the date when it came into force, consequently all complaints prior to that date ought to be disregarded; (4) their "Quick Trade" contract which used an independent contractor to carry out the installation work meant that the contract was between the customer and the independent contractor.

Held, granting interim enforcement orders, that (1) the function and purpose of s.217 and s.218, which were European in origin and designed to enforce European legislation, required that the principles governed by the Scots law of interdict should not apply to orders pronounced under these sections and it followed that such orders should be regarded as sui generis, accordingly the detailed rules of law relating to interim interdict did not apply to interim enforcement orders. (2) Section 218 involved a remedy that might have serious consequences for the person against whom it was used and the word "likely" under s.218(1)(b) meant that it should be more likely than not that an enforcement order would be granted. (3) Part 8 of the 2002 Act was intended to have retrospective effect and the conduct of a trader both before and after the date the provisions came into force was relevant to the question of whether an enforcement order should be granted. (4) On the basis of affidavits produced, it could be concluded that M's conduct involved and continued to involve repeated domestic infringements under s.211 of the 2002 Act where a substantial number of installations were found to be defective, the "Quick Fit" contract involved the supply of services in a substantial number of cases, and breaches of contract evidenced by documents produced by O, which included breaches of the Sale of Goods Act 1979 and the 1982 Act, were sufficiently extensive and serious to draw the inference that there was harm to the section of the public likely to buy M's products and services. (5) The customer's contract for fitting under the "Quick Trade" contract was with M and not the individual fitter. (6) The directors were accessories in terms of s.222 of the 2002 Act having consented to or connived in the conduct of M which constituted Community infringements. (7) The requirements of s.218 of the 2002 Act were satisfied where M's conduct in using cl.6 and cl.7 constituted a Community infringement, the use of the aforementioned in the contracts harming the collective interests of consumers. (8) The defects in M's products and services and the impact of the objectionable contractual terms was sufficiently serious to warrant action under Part 8.

OFFICE OF FAIR TRADING v. MB DESIGNS (SCOTLAND) LTD 2005 S.L.T. 691, Lord Drummond Young, OH (Outer House).

5075. **Hire purchase–Motor vehicles–Satisfactory quality–Right to rescind**

[Supply of Goods (Implied Terms) Act 1973 (c.13) s.10.]

L, the customer in a hire purchase transaction, sought to rescind from an agreement entered into with C, a finance company, in respect of a motor vehicle on the grounds that it was not of satisfactory quality as defined in the Supply of Goods (Implied Terms) Act 1973 s.10, and repayment of the deposit and two instalments (amounting to £9,658.42). The vehicle, a Range Rover with a purchase price of £51,550, was supplied by a dealer on March 9, 2001, and was rejected by L on March 30, 2001, although he continued to drive it until early June

2001, by which time it had been driven for nearly 6,000 miles. The sheriff found that the vehicle, as delivered, did have a number of defects but concluded that notwithstanding them, the vehicle was of satisfactory quality, as they were easy to rectify, were covered by the warranty and would not affect the durability, longevity or value of the vehicle. L appealed.

Held, allowing the appeal, that (1) the sheriff had misdirected herself in her approach to the issue of satisfactory quality. There was considerable room for doubt as to whether she had asked herself whether the vehicle, at that price, was of the standard that a reasonable person would have regarded as satisfactory, taking account of all relevant circumstances. (2) The vehicle had several defects at the time of delivery, only some of which were minor, and given that this was a very expensive car, sold as a high quality vehicle, an objective purchaser would not have expected to have had a vehicle with such defects delivered to him in implement of the agreement which he had entered into.

LAMARRA v. CAPITAL BANK PLC 2005 S.L.T. (Sh Ct) 21, Sheriff Principal JC McInnes Q.C., Sh Ct.

CONTRACTS

5076. Formation of contract—Offer and acceptance

U sought payment of £870 with interest and expenses from O after he parked on their property on numerous occasions although he was not the holder of a parking permit. A notice was displayed on U's property to the effect that persons parking without a permit would be liable to a fine of £30 per day. O accepted that if U were entitled to charge him £30 a day, the sum sued for was the total amount of charges for which he would be liable, but maintained that this charge was a penalty which U had no power to impose. The sheriff rejected that argument and granted decree as craved. O appealed by stated case. The sheriff principal considered the case stated by the sheriff was too broad and substituted two questions: (1) whether the sheriff erred in law by concluding that there was no distinction between a charge and a fine; (2) whether he erred in law by failing to state whether or not parking charges described as fines in an offer document would amount to a misrepresentation of the offeror's position.

Held, dismissing the appeal, that (1) it was clear that in the notice U were not purporting to assert any power to exact a monetary penalty after conviction of a criminal offence, or to impose a penalty of any kind, and the meaning of "fine" in this context was obviously "fee", which was one of the meanings given in standard dictionaries. (2) U's notice made it plain that their position was that anyone who parked on their property without a permit would have to pay them a fee of £30 per day on that account and O, by parking his vehicle on their property without a permit, made it plain that he accepted that position. (3) The issue raised in the second question would not be considered as it was not ventilated before the sheriff and, in any event, the description of the charge as a fine was accurate.

UNIVERSITY OF EDINBURGH v. ONIFADE 2005 S.L.T. (Sh Ct) 63, Sheriff Principal ID Macphail Q.C., Sh Ct.

5077. Formation of contract—Offer and acceptance—Exclusive distribution agreements

W, a Greek wine and spirit distributor, brought an action seeking specific implement of an exclusive distribution agreement allegedly concluded with D for distribution of D's product in Greece. The two companies had an existing distribution agreement and entered into negotiations for another contract to continue the relationship. Draft contracts were exchanged between X, an employee of W, and J, an employee of D, and by February 5, 2003, consensus in idem had been reached. J stated that final written copies of the contract would be sent to X for signature but they never arrived. D subsequently entered into an exclusive distribution agreement with another company and gave W formal notice of termination of the contract then in force. W argued that the draft contract became binding between the parties when consensus had been reached as there were no terms in the contract, or correspondence between the parties, to the effect that the contract would not come into force until signed. D argued that the contract had to be signed by both parties to become binding and that X, by never raising the point which he subsequently relied upon, namely that he believed a valid contract had formally been concluded, had accepted this to be the case. A argued that he had not raised this point as he was seeking to protect the relationship between the parties, further, W was reluctant to indulge in litigation.

Held, assoilzieing D, that (1) the evidence of the parties' conduct since February 5 was consistent with the position that their intentions were that there was to be no binding agreement between them until the document was formally executed. (2) X's explanations for not stating that he believed a binding agreement had already been formed did not provide a plausible explanation for a complete lack of reference to the existence thereof where he could have alluded to his belief in a measured way, which any commercial party might have done in the situation, without threatening legal proceedings.

WS KAROULIAS SA v. DRAMBUIE LIQUER CO LTD (NO.2) 2005 S.L.T. 813, Lord Clarke, OH.

5078. Interpretation–Indemnity clauses–Extension to third parties

D, the bareboat charterers of a semi submersible drilling rig, raised an action of damages against G, the managers of a tug/supply vessel, for losses allegedly sustained following a collision between the vessels. At the time of the collision neither party owned the rig or tug but were involved in operating them under charterparties with a third company (T), the defenders through agents for T. Clause 17.1.1 of the agreement regulating the pursuers' relationship with T provided that "for the purposes of the indemnities in favour of company [T]..."company" shall be deemed to include the company's other contractors at the worksite (who enter into or give a written undertaking to company that they are prepared to enter into a contract with a company incorporating similar contractual provisions)". The action came to a preliminary proof. The Lord Ordinary held that the tug owner's contention that they were protected by certain provisions of charterparties relevant to the delictual case brought by D was unsound. G reclaimed, arguing that cl.17.1.1 meant that any contractor with T who was offering indemnities to T to hold them harmless against their own actions, was entitled to the protection extended by the clause and could plead a hold harmless clause against D, notwithstanding their own fault. Further, in the context of the North Sea, there was a general practice whereby a "knock for knock" arrangement existed between all parties involved in a particular operation, even if this was not always capable of being achieved. This test was met by the fact that in G's agreement, indemnities were being offered to T, and the Lord Ordinary had taken too narrow a view of the word "similar".

Held, refusing the reclaiming motion, that G were not qualifying contractors within the bracketed part of cl.17.1.1. There was a large gap between the bilateral indemnities offered in G's agreement with T's agents and the multilateral indemnities contained in D's agreement with T, the terms of G's charter did not qualify, in the sense of "knock for knock", and D should not be regarded as having given up the right to sue in delict a party with whom they had no contractual relationship and who was not offering the same protection to T.

DIAMOND OFFSHORE DRILLING (UK) LTD v. GULF OFFSHORE NS LTD 2005 S.L.T. 589, Lord Cullen L.P., Lord Kirkwood, Lord Johnston, 1 Div.

CRIMINAL EVIDENCE

5079. Admissibility–Audio tape recordings–Interception of communications–Jury directions

[Interception of Communications Act 1985 (c.56) s.1, s.4(1).]

P, who had appeared alongside four coaccused, was convicted of being concerned in the importation of cannabis resin. At the trial, evidence was led of telephone calls between P and two Crown witnesses in the course of an undercover operation by Customs and Excise officers. The recordings had been made by a conventional tape recorder recording the sound heard in the ear piece of the telephone handset. P appealed against conviction on the grounds that (1) the recording of each conversation was in breach of the Interception of Communications Act 1985 s.1 and the trial judge had been wrong to allow it to be led in evidence; (2) the trial judge had misdirected the jury in that he failed to give adequate or proper directions on the application of the test of fairness in assessing the involvement of Customs and Excise in the commission of the offences: in particular he told them that the test was whether one of the officers had caused P to commit a crime that, but for his intervention, he would not otherwise have committed, whereas he should have gone further and directed the jury to consider questions of pressure, encouragement or inducement; (3) the charge had been unbalanced in that the trial judge had rehearsed in detail evidence relied upon by the Crown but had failed to properly or accurately rehearse the defence evidence.

Held, dismissing the appeal, that (1) for the 1985 Act to apply there had to be a communication in the course of transmission by electrical or other impulse within the meaning of s.4(1), and accessing of that electrical or other impulse which was in the course of communication, and as what was recorded was the spoken word with no attempt to access the electrical impulses transmitted by the public telecommunication system, the objection to the evidence had been rightly repelled. (2) having regard to the evidence given, particularly by P, who had not stated that he had been subjected to pressure, the directions in relation to fairness, including the test propounded by the trial judge, in the context of the charge read as a whole, did not constitute a misdirection and the issue of fairness was properly related to the evidence. (3) In the context of the evidence which had been given by P, and bearing in mind the limited extent to which the criticised evidence had been referred to and the fact that the entire defence case had been forcibly put to the jury in the closing speech on P's behalf, the trial judge had not failed to present the defence case fairly to the jury.

PORTER (THOMAS) v. HM ADVOCATE 2005 J.C. 141, Lord Kirkwood, Lord Penrose, Lord Wheatley, HCJ.

5080. Admissibility–Audio tape recordings–Police interviews

[Criminal Law (Consolidation) (Scotland) Act 1995 (c.39) s.50A(1)(a); Criminal Procedure (Scotland) Act 1995 (c.46) s.106.]

M appealed against conviction for racially aggravated harassment contrary to the Criminal Law (Consolidation) (Scotland) Act 1995 s.50A(1)(a), by making numerous telephone calls to the complainer at his home involving racial remarks and threats of violence. M was interviewed by police regarding the calls and the interview was recorded. Subsequently, the interview tape was passed to an expert who, having compared the interview tape with recordings made of the calls, provided a report inferring that M had made the calls. Neither the police nor M were aware at the time of the interview that the recording would be used for this purpose. M argued that (1) the evidence had been unfairly obtained: although he had been cautioned, he had not been warned that his recorded voice might be subjected to analysis and comparison with the recorded calls, thus he had not given informed consent to the use of the recorded interview and had been deprived of the opportunity not to speak at the interview; (2) new evidence had come to light: (i) a woman had submitted an affidavit stating that she had been present on an indeterminate date when abusive calls were made by her boyfriend, who had been the subject of a special defence of incrimination by the accused, and that the accused had not been present, and (ii) the incriminee had, first, submitted an affidavit stating that he had been responsible for abusive telephone calls to the complainer's number on an indeterminate date and that the accused had not been present on that occasion, and secondly, given a sample of his voice, expert opinion had been obtained that the caller was more likely to have been the incriminee. The new evidence passed the "reasonable explanation" test set out in the Criminal Procedure (Scotland) Act 1995 s.106 where the woman's evidence had not been led at the trial because her existence was not known until after the trial, and the incriminee's had not been led at trial as he could not be traced and M, following advice that a further adjournment of the trial, on grounds of the incriminee's unavailability, would be unlikely to succeed, had not raised the matter before the sheriff.

Held, dismissing the appeal, that (1) while it was not realistic to regard the normal caution as conveying a warning that the recording of the interview might be subjected to comparison with recordings of the calls, the caution was a proper procedural safeguard of the fairness of the interview and the recording of it was lawfully obtained. (2) The prosecuting authorities had legitimately obtained a sample of M's voice which could be regarded as objective evidence and it was not unfair to subject that material to expert analysis, weighing the interests of M against the public interest. (3) The new evidence did not pass the "reasonable explanation" test: the only attempts to trace the incriminee were informal attempts by M and there was no explanation as to why no more formal steps were taken to trace him and it was a tactical decision not to seek to adjourn the trial to attempt to trace him; and given that the woman had been the incriminee's girlfriend and had been present on one occasion when calls were made, some explanation was required of why her presence was not discovered in precognoscing the other parties present at the time and no explanation had been offered, further, her evidence was simply more evidence along the lines given by other witnesses and did not possess the requisite degree of significance to justify it being heard as additional evidence.

McINTYRE (COLIN McLEAN) v. HM ADVOCATE 2005 S.L.T. 757, Lord Cullen L.J.G., Lord Macfadyen, Lord Carloway, HCJ.

5081. Admissibility–Expert evidence–Opinion as to credibility of child complainer

[Criminal Procedure (Scotland) Act 1995 (c.46) s.275.]

X was charged on indictment with two charges of lewd, indecent and libidinous practices and behaviour against two girls. Applications by X under the Criminal Procedure (Scotland) Act 1995 s.275 had been granted. One of the applications, relating to the complainer in charge 1, narrated that she had given two statements to the police where she claimed to have been sexually abused, but that they differed in material respects. A consultant psychiatrist who had considered the statements along with the complainer's medical records concluded that the complainer had false memory syndrome secondary to significant mental illness which preceded her allegations of abuse, and it was more likely that the allegations of abuse were a symptom of the illness rather than a cause of it. The Crown sought to lead evidence from a consultant clinical psychologist who did not support the concept of false memory syndrome but rather supported that of the repression of memory as a method of dealing with traumatic memories. X objected on the basis that the evidence of the Crown's witness was plainly designed to bolster that of the complainer, which was an issue for the jury, further, that if the Crown sought to rebut the evidence of his witness, they should lead evidence of a suitably instructed psychiatrist and not that of a clinical psychologist.

Held, repelling the objection, that (1) the jury would need skilled assistance in order to understand the complainer's state of mind and reach a conclusion as to her credibility and reliability, and the evidence of the clinical psychologist met the conditions for the admissibility of expert evidence at common law. (2) The clinical psychologist's evidence as to the credibility and reliability of the complainer should not have been excluded on the ground that that was a collateral issue where only the complainer in each charge and X could testify as to whether the conduct alleged had taken place, and evidence tending to show whether or not the complainer was a reliable witness would be of great importance in resolving that issue. (3) Objection to the evidence on the basis of the general rule against oath helping was decisively trumped by the fundamental duty of the court to ensure that the trial was conducted with fairness, and it was essential for the Crown, prosecuting in the public interest, to be entitled to anticipate expert evidence and to demonstrate to the jury that there was another expert explanation and assessment of the complainer's state of mind which tended to indicate a different conclusion as to her veracity. (4) The clinical psychologist was appropriately qualified by training and experience to give the evidence proposed.

HM ADVOCATE v. A 2005 S.L.T. 975, Lord Macphail, HCJ.

5082. Admissibility—Hearsay evidence—Absent witness

[Criminal Procedure (Scotland) Act 1995 (c.46) s.259(2)(c).]

H was charged with housebreaking and reset. He was convicted and appealed, arguing that the sheriff had erred (1) in holding, before the trial began, that the requirements of the Criminal Procedure (Scotland) Act 1995 s.259(2)(c) for the admission of evidence of a missing witness in hearsay form had been satisfied; (2) in failing to desert the trial pro loco et tempore after a police officer had given evidence of a search which was substantially different from that given in a trial within a trial, and which the sheriff had ruled was inadmissible. The sheriff had rejected the suggestions made by H with a view to finding the witness, and while noting the willingness of the procurator fiscal depute to make further inquiries at her father's address, he took the view that as the accused had supplied the correct address of the latter only during the course of the hearing itself, it was not a relevant factor in considering whether there were other steps the Crown ought to have taken to find the witness. The Crown submitted that this approach and the sheriff's decision to direct the jury to ignore the officer's evidence were within the proper scope of his discretion.

Held, allowing the appeal, that (1) the sheriff had erred in holding, before the commencement of the trial, that without the suggested further steps being taken, it could be affirmed that all reasonable steps to find the witness had been taken and the sheriff should not have admitted the hearsay evidence at the stage that he did. (2) Given that, by the time the jury came to have to implement the direction to ignore the evidence of the search, they already had before them the difficult task of evaluating the untested hearsay evidence, it was asking too much to add to this the task of putting an obviously incriminating strand of evidence out of their minds, and it could not properly be said that fairness to the accused could be secured by directing the jury to ignore the evidence of the search.

HILL (BRIAN DAVID) v. HM ADVOCATE 2005 J.C. 259, Lord Macfadyen, Lord Nimmo Smith, Lord Brodie, HCJ.

5083. Admissibility—Hearsay evidence—Moorov doctrine not incompatible with right to fair trial

[Criminal Procedure (Scotland) Act 1995 (c.46) s.259; Human Rights Act 1998 (c.42) Sch.1 Part I Art.6.]

The appellant (J) appealed against his conviction of assault and robbery, in which he was alleged to have assaulted a 77 year old woman (E) in her own home and taken £95 in cash and four bank cards. He was also charged with assaulting and robbing a 71 year old woman (M) in her home the following day. E was unable to give evidence and hearsay evidence of her identification of J was led in terms of the Criminal Procedure (Scotland) Act 1995 s. 259. J attacked E's identification on the grounds that (1) there were differences between the description she gave to the police and his actual appearance; (2) E had only been 80 per cent certain of her photographic identification; and (3) less than

100 per cent sure at the identification parade and had also referred to a stand in at the parade who was unlike J in certain respects. J had been identified as the person using E's stolen bank card one hour after the robbery and the person responsible for robbing M. J did not dispute the evidence that he had robbed M and the Moorov doctrine was relied upon by the Crown to prove the charge of assaulting and robbing E. The trial judge directed the jury that they could not convict J of the offences against E unless they accepted the identification evidence and that the evidence of J's possession of E's bank cards raised the presumption that he had stolen them. On appeal J argued that the admission of hearsay evidence breached his right to a fair trial under the Human Rights Act 1998 Sch.1 Part I Art.6.

Held, dismissing the appeal, that taken as a whole, the case against J was not based on E's hearsay identification to a decisive degree and he had not been denied a fair trial as a result.

JOHNSTONE (GORDON) v. HM ADVOCATE 2004 S.C.C.R. 727, Lord Cullen L.J.G., Lord Kirkwood, Lord Emslie, HCJ.

5084. **Admissibility–Sexual behaviour–Legislative restriction on evidence of complainer's character–Compatibility with right to fair trial**

[Criminal Procedure (Scotland) Act 1995 s.274, s.275; Human Rights Act 1998 Sch.1 Part I Art.6.]

M was charged on indictment with indecent assault and rape and wished to lead evidence of the kind prohibited by the Criminal Procedure (Scotland) Act 1995 s. 274. M lodged a devolution minute arguing that s.274 and s.275 were incompatible with M's right to a fair trial and outwith the competence of the Scottish Parliament. M complained of the shortness of the time between indictment and submission of a notice under s.275 and that the application could be decided by a judge, other than the trial judge, in the abstract. M also argued that the fact that the crown was permitted to cross examine M and his witnesses without restriction and the fact that the defence was restricted by s.274 and would have to give advance notice created an inequality. The minute was refused and M appealed to the High Court.

Held, refusing the appeal, that (1) the aims of the legislation were legitimate and within the Scottish Parliament's discretion. (2) If s.274 had imposed an absolute prohibition then the Human Rights ACt 1998 Sch.1 Part I Art.6 would have been violated, however it did not and there were safeguards to protect the accused. (3) Under the conventional rules of evidence the court would normally exclude vague and general allegations so it was reasonable that the legislature minimise any prejudice to the complainer. (4) The 14 day notice period was not unfair, but the court was afforded a discretionary power if it was too short. (5) It was reasonable to deal with a s.275 application prior to trial, but the trial judge always had final say as far as the exclusion or admission of evidence was concerned. (6) There was nothing unfair in the fact that the Crown, in seeking to attack the complainer's character, would be required to show their hand -there was no human right to spring a surprise line of questioning on a complainer.

Observed: (1) that a prior co habitation between the accused and the complainer in a rape charge would not constitute engaging in sexual behaviour not forming part of the charge -such cohabitation would be outwith s.274. (2) The prohibition in s.274 did not extend to other offences which were not sexual but were dealt with at the same trial. (3) The problem was to reconcile the protection of the complainer with ensuring the accused's right to defend himself was not compromised, nor the fairness of the trial.

MOIR (MITCHELL JOHN) v. HM ADVOCATE; *sub nom.* MM v. HM ADVOCATE 2005 J.C. 102, Lord Gill L.J.C., Lord Osborne, Lord Johnston, HCJ.

5085. Admissibility—Sexual offences—Evidence from teachers as to child's propensity to lie

[Criminal Procedure (Scotland) Act 1995 (c.46) s.275.]

M, who had been charged on indictment with a number of offences including two charges of lewd, indecent and libidinous behaviour towards two children, one of whom was C, appealed against the court's refusal to admit certain evidence under the Criminal Procedure (Scotland) Act 1995 s.275, namely evidence from schoolteachers that C (1) had a tendency to relate events in a manner that showed him in the best light; (2) made up stories to an unusual degree; (3) told elaborate lies and could not be relied upon to tell the truth.

Held, dismissing the appeal, that M's application did not satisfy the requirements of s.275. The application was not concerned with specific occurrences or facts that the Crown relied upon to support its case, but rather, with general evidence as to C's credibility and reliability. This was not directly relevant to establishing M's guilt since it did not relate to C's credibility or reliability with regard to the particular behaviour with which M had been charged.

MacKAY (ALISDAIR JOHN) v. HM ADVOCATE 2005 J.C. 24, Lord Cullen L.J.G., Lord Macfadyen, Lady Cosgrove, HCJ.

5086. Admissibility—Surveillance—Invalid authorisation—Right to respect for private and family life

[Human Rights Act 1998 (c.42) Sch.1 Part I Art.8(1); Regulation of Investigatory Powers (Scotland) Act 2000 (asp 11) s.6.]

Two accused were charged on indictment with being concerned in the supply of cannabis resin and cannabis. At trial, the second accused raised as a devolution issue the admissibility of evidence obtained in the course of a surveillance operation conducted by police officers, which he submitted had been obtained in a manner which violated his rights under the Human Rights Act 1998 Sch.1 Part I Art.8(1) as the authorisation in respect thereof was invalid for want of adequate detail. The first accused contended that the evidence so obtained was likewise inadmissible against him. Following receipt of confidential information suggesting that the second accused was concerned in the supply of controlled drugs, authorisation of directed surveillance was granted under the Regulation of Investigatory Powers (Scotland) Act 2000 s.6. While under surveillance, the second accused was observed meeting the first accused in a street and taking a carrier bag from him, which was found to contain just under three kilograms of cannabis resin and approximately one kilogram of cannabis. The sheriff dismissed the devolution minute finding that what was done by the police at the time when the evidence was obtained did not require authorisation under the Act and it was therefore admissible, but held obiter that the authorisation was invalid and had it been required, the irregularity could not have been cured and the evidence would have been inadmissible. The accused appealed. The Crown accepted that the authorisation granted in respect of the directed surveillance of the second appellant was invalid for failing to adequately state the grounds on which it was necessary and proportionate to what was sought to be achieved, and failed to give a specific description of the directed surveillance that was authorised.

Held, dismissing the appeals, that (1) there was no logical basis for assuming that everything done under the invalid authorisation was, by virtue of that invalidity, an infringement of Art.8. (2) What was done did not amount to an infringement of the second appellant's rights under Art.8 as it did not involve the obtaining of private information about him or in any broader sense, nor did it involve any lack of respect for his private life where the bag had been handed to him in a public place, observable by anyone who happened to be in the vicinity.

GILCHRIST (KENNETH ALEXANDER) v. HM ADVOCATE; QUINN (DENNIS JAMES) v. HM ADVOCATE 2005 J.C. 34, Lord Cullen L.J.G., Lord Osborne, Lord Macfadyen, HCJ.

5087. Admissibility–Surveillance–Public interest

[Regulation of Investigatory Powers (Scotland) Act 2000 (c.23) s.5.]

The accused (C) and others objected to a decision made during the course of their trial for drug offences to admit evidence obtained during a police surveillance operation. The Crown sought to introduce evidence about the recovery of drugs from C's co accused (W) after he had been detained during the surveillance operation. Surveillance authorisation had been given with regard to C and it included a reference to the need to conduct surveillance on "individuals" who associated with C. It was accepted that at the time of his detention W was not the principal target of the authorised surveillance, but that he was a known associate of C. W argued that there had been no authorisation for the surveillance and a trial within a trial was held to determine the issue of admissibility.

Held, giving judgment for the Crown, that on a fair construction of the authorisation, it authorised the surveillance of associates of C. Even if the court had concluded that there had been an irregularity in obtaining the surveillance evidence, it would have excused it, since it was clear that the reporting officer genuinely believed it unnecessary to obtain specific authorisation to undertake surveillance of C's associates. Any irregularity would have been attributed to genuine error rather than deliberate defiance of the Regulation of Investigatory Powers (Scotland) Act 2000 s.5. If it had been necessary to balance the public interest against the interest of the accused, the court would have concluded that the balance fell in favour of the admissibility of the evidence.

HM ADVOCATE v. CAMPBELL (ROBERT); HM ADVOCATE v. WALLACE (JOHN) 2004 S.C.C.R. 529, Lord Hardie, HCJ.

5088. Admissibility–Telephone tapping–Written authorisation–Competence

[Human Rights Act 1998 (c.42) Sch.1 Part I Art.6, Art.8; Scotland Act 1998 (c.46) s.57(2); Regulation of Investigatory Powers Act 2000 (c.23) s.3(2)(b).]

Two accused were convicted of extortion. The first accused was further convicted of being concerned in the supply of cannabis resin. Both appealed on the basis that there was wrongly admitted at the trial evidence provided by the police of a telephone call said to have been made by the first accused to the home of a married couple in which the caller asked for money and threatened violence. This evidence provided essential corroboration of the case against the first accused and was also relevant to the second accused whose conviction depended on concert involving the first accused and another. The first accused submitted that the Crown had failed to prove that the installation of the recording device had been "authorised" under the Regulation of Investigatory Powers Act 2000 s.3(2)(b). The trial judge repelled this objection on the basis that any difficulty would be cured by the parol evidence of a police witness who had sought the authorisation, although he had little direct knowledge of the authorisation which had been issued, except becoming aware at some stage that it had been in writing. The second accused further submitted that the interception had involved a breach of the Human Rights Act 1998 Sch.1 Part I Art.8; accordingly the act of the Lord Advocate in leading the evidence was, in terms of the Scotland Act 1998 s.57(2), ultra vires; the evidence was central to the case; and the leading of it, and reliance on it, had rendered his trial unfair and had resulted in a miscarriage of justice.

Held, dismissing the appeals, that (1) production of the written authority was the "best" and prima facie, the only admissible evidence of granting the authority, and in failing to produce such authority, it followed that the appeals had to be decided on the basis that the Crown had failed to prove that authority under the 2000 Act was granted. (2) Not every breach of the law impacted on the admissibility of evidence at a criminal trial and the question was whether, on an application of the principles of *Lawrie (Jeanie) v. Muir* 1950 J.C. 19, a lack of authorisation under the 2000 Act could be excused. (3) The evidence was admissible in circumstances where the 2000 Act was not specifically directed at the protection of persons suspected of crime. The only evidence which emerged was of voice identification, which was far removed from the sort of "private information about a person" which the Act was fundamentally designed to protect. The uttering of threats of violence and an attempt at extortion could hardly be described as "private information". The police witness had clearly been acting in good faith and in the belief that authority under the Act had been granted. The phone tap had been authorised by the recipients of the call; and the interception fell within the "directed" rather than the "intrusive" category of "surveillance". (4) The human rights argument was unsound. The "act" of the Lord Advocate in attempting to lead evidence obtained in breach of Art.8 was perfectly proper; there was nothing so fundamental about a breach of Art.8 as to make it inappropriate to consider the effect of that breach in relation to Art.6 and the common law principle of "fairness" within the context of *Lawrie*. It was very questionable whether the second accused was in a position to claim a breach of Art.8 as he was not a party to the intercepted phone call or even mentioned in it. The evidence in question could not be regarded as constituting any meaningful interference with the first accused's private or family life, *Lawrie* applied.

HENDERSON (ALEXANDER) v. HM ADVOCATE; MARNOCH (DOUGLAS JOHN) v. HM ADVOCATE 2005 J.C. 301, Lord Marnoch, Lord Hamilton, Lord Weir, HCJ.

5089.   Corroboration–Identification–Sufficiency of evidence

[Wildlife and Countryside Act 1981 (c.69) s.1 (5) (a).]

G appealed against his conviction of disturbing an eagle at its nest in contravention of the Wildlife and Countryside Act 1981 s.1 (5) (a). G was identified by a witness, B, who had seen G in the vicinity of the nest and spoken to him. Evidence was also given by two of B's companions, who maintained they had seen someone at the nest, in the glen and talking to B. The two companions confirmed that the person they had seen had been carrying binoculars and a rucksack but could not identify G. G was found two days later in a nearby hostel with binoculars, a rucksack and a map of the area where the nest was located. G gave a false name to the police but bird watching paraphernalia was found at his London home. G lodged a submission of no case to answer, arguing that there had been insufficient evidence to corroborate B's identification, but was convicted. On appeal, G argued that the Sheriff had erred in repelling the submission.

Held, continuing the appeal (Lord Macfadyen dissenting), that the Sheriff had erred in repelling the submission of no case to answer. The question for the court was whether the material relied upon as corroboration actually provided the necessary support for or confirmation of the direct evidence and in the instant case the supporting evidence was apparently insufficient. At best, it demonstrated an interest in birdwatching. It was, however, impossible to decide whether G's conviction ought to be upheld until all the evidence in the case had been led.

Observed, per Lord Macfadyen, that it was not appropriate to assess separately the capability of each piece of evidence to support or confirm, but rather to ask whether the body of circumstantial evidence, taken as a whole, was capable of such support or confirmation.

GONSHAW v. BAMBER (NO.1) 2004 S.C.C.R. 482, Lord Osborne, Lord Macfadyen, Lord Abernethy, HCJ.

5090.   Corroboration–Identification–Sufficiency of evidence

P was charged with assaulting his former partner and his son, aged 10. During the trial the Crown was granted authority to use a screen during the son's testimony and that of P's stepdaughter, aged 16, who had witnessed events. The vulnerable witnesses gave evidence to the effect that the man they respectively knew as "Dad" and "Big B" was the perpetrator. Neither made a visual identification of P as the perpetrator in court, although he was identified as such in court by his former partner. P was convicted and appealed on the basis that his former partner's identification evidence was uncorroborated. The Crown did not oppose the appeal. The sheriff stated a case for the opinion of the High Court asking whether there was sufficient identification of P as the perpetrator, whether, in the foregoing circumstances, he was entitled to reject P's submission of no case to answer, and whether he was entitled to convict P.

Held, allowing the appeal and answering the questions in the negative, that (1) subject to certain statutory exceptions, no person could be convicted of a crime unless there was evidence of at least two witnesses implicating that person with the commission of the crime. (2) The burden of proof rested with the Crown throughout and the basic requirement to adduce corroborated evidence in support of the requisite identification was not absolved by the fact that the evidence touching on identification was not challenged by the defence. (3) No corroborated proof was adduced in circumstances where the necessary link in the chain of indirect identification was evidence that the man in the dock was the man answering the descriptive names given by the vulnerable witnesses. The link required to be spoken to by at least two witnesses, but only P's former partner did so, who was not in the relevant sense an independent witness, being the principle witness as to identification. (4) The circumstances that the person named by each vulnerable witness was P, and that the person whom the complaint was directed against was also so named did not advance proof of the assertion that the man named by these witnesses was the person appearing as the accused.

P v. WILLIAMS; *sub nom.* BP v. WILLIAMS 2005 S.L.T. 508, Lord Hamilton, Lady Paton, Lord Clarke, HCJ.

5091. Corroboration—Rape—Evidence of injury and distress

The appellant (G) appealed against his conviction of rape. At trial, the Crown relied upon the complainer's evidence that he had grabbed her and pulled her down to the floor before removing her clothing, biting her breast and forcing her legs apart. There was evidence of bruising to the complainer's breast and legs, possibly consistent with her legs being forced apart. She was also distressed after the incident. G maintained that the complainer had consented to intercourse and he appealed on the grounds that there was insufficient evidence of mens rea and the judge had failed to give clear directions on the matter.

Held, dismissing the appeal, that G's submissions depended on the case being treated as one of non forcible rape, but it was not a case of that type and the jury were entitled to treat the complainer's distress as corroboration of the use of force, and thereby, her lack of consent and G's knowledge of the lack of her consent.

GORDON (GRAHAM) v. HM ADVOCATE 2004 S.C.C.R. 641, Lord Cullen L.J.G., Lord Penrose, Lord Hamilton, HCJ.

5092. Corroboration—Sufficiency of evidence—Accused's behaviour before and after offence relied on as corroboration—No requirement for independent evidence

The appellant (C) appealed against his conviction for indecent assault. He had been a temporary lodger at a flat where the complainer (B), aged 15, and another girl were staying. C had made sexual overtures to both the girls and invited them to participate in sexual activity with him. B and C were alone together in a bedroom, following which B left the room in an obvious state of distress and C left the flat immediately after, leaving his personal possessions behind. Two boys witnessed B's exit from the room. B's evidence at C's trial was corroborated by the fact that one of the boys had been excluded from the room by C, by B's obvious distress and by C's precipitate departure.

Held, dismissing the appeal, that the circumstances were consistent with C's sexual conduct towards B having escalated to making physical advances of a sexual kind towards her in the privacy of the bedroom. The circumstances were such, in the courts view, that they supported or confirmed B's direct evidence and independent evidence was unnecessary. It was sufficient that there was corroborated evidence of an indecent assault. The fact that what had occurred was unwelcome to B was corroborated by the evidence of her distress, *Smith*

(Gregory Alexander) v. Lees 1997 J.C. 73, [1997] C.L.Y. 5761 distinguished and *Stirling v. McFadyen* 2000 S.C.C.R. 239, [2000] C.L.Y. 6005 considered.

CHAKAL v. BROWN; *sub nom.* CHAKAL v. GALLACHER 2004 S.C.C.R. 541, Lord MacLean, Lord Hamilton, Temporary Judge CGB Nicholson Q.C., HCJ.

5093. Fingerprints – Device approval

ELECTRONIC FINGERPRINTING ETC. DEVICE APPROVAL (SCOTLAND) ORDER 2005, SSI 2005 36; made under the Criminal Procedure (Scotland) Act 1995 s.18. In force: February 14, 2005; £3.00.

The Electronic Fingerprinting etc Device Approval (Scotland) Order 1997 (SI 1997 1939) approved the device known as the Digital Biometrics Incorporation (DBI) Tenprinter 1133S, with palmprint option, for the purpose of creating such records as are mentioned in the Criminal Procedure (Scotland) Act 1995. This Order approves the additional device known as the Smiths Heimann Biometric Device LS1 LITE U CE for the purpose of creating such records as are mentioned in the Criminal Procedure (Scotland) Act 1995 (records of a person's skin on an external part of the body).

5094. Murder – Medical evidence – Sufficiency

N was charged with the attempted murder of a baby by suffocation. At his trial, a submission of no case to answer was repelled and he was convicted. The baby had been left alone in N's care. According to N, the baby suddenly stopped breathing; he tried to revive him; and after about a minute he came round. The baby was taken to hospital where he was found to have a number of petechiae on his neck and forehead and some subconjunctival haemorrhages. The medical evidence was that this required a sudden rise in the pressure of the veins in the head, which could be caused by coughing, severe vomiting or by pressure on the neck or head. The consultant in charge of the case concluded that as the baby had not been coughing or vomiting either prior to or after his admission to hospital, there was no explanation for the petechiae and therefore they were non accidental injury, its source being suffocation. N argued that the combination of circumstances relied upon by the Crown was insufficient to found proof beyond reasonable doubt: the evidence did not establish an exhaustive exclusion of causes other than the conduct libelled. Further, the jury's verdict was one which no reasonable jury, properly directed, could have returned. There was no appropriate expert evidence to support the conviction, where the consultant had not approached matters in the way of a forensic pathologist, and another medical witness had said that it was not possible to determine the cause of petechiae on the basis of clinical examination alone.

Held, dismissing the appeal, that (1) the jury were entitled to hold that the effect of the Crown evidence was that any loss of breath suffered by the baby was due to his breathing having been restricted by N. There was positive evidence that none of the natural causes of petechiae had in fact occurred at any time during the evening and up to the time of the baby's admission to hospital, and while the jury had to consider N's account, they were entitled to consider its credibility and to reject it. (2) It was for the jury to decide whether and to what extent the consultant's analysis of what had happened was of material assistance. (3) It could not be said that the quality of the evidence was such that no reasonable jury could have convicted: in the light of the medical evidence, the jury were amply entitled to conclude that the conduct libelled was one of a number of possible causes of the petechiae and subconjunctival haemorrhages and while the evidence on which the Crown relied to exclude all other causes was not extensive, it did not raise merely suspicion or speculation that this conduct had occurred.

NOLAN (JAMES) v. HM ADVOCATE 2005 S.L.T. 474, Lord Cullen L.J.G., Lord Penrose, Lord Johnston, HCJ.

5095. Sufficiency of evidence–Corroboration–Possession of indecent photographs

[Civic Government (Scotland) Act 1982 (c.45) s.52(2), s.52A(1).]

H was charged with possessing indecent photographs or pseudo photographs of children contrary to the Civic Government (Scotland) Act 1982 s.52A(1). His computer was found to contain 2,203 pornographic images of females, three of which the police believed were girls under the age of 16. A consultant paediatrician gave evidence that in his view, two of the three pictures were of girls aged 14 years or younger. The sheriff upheld H's submission of no case to answer. The Crown appealed, arguing that the sheriff had erred in law in holding that they had led insufficient evidence that the children were under 16, and in acquitting H of the charge. H argued that the police evidence was not capable of corroborating the paediatrician's evidence and the Crown could not derive assistance in seeking corroboration from the titles affixed to the images.

Held, allowing the appeal, that (1) the essential fact which required to be proved was that the subject of an image was a child at any material time, not any particular age under 16. There was no requirement for the police to possess qualifications or experience which equipped them to determine the age of the girls when having regard to s.52(2) of the Act, which contemplated that a wide range of evidence might be available to demonstrate that a person was under the age of 16, as well as the fact that the legislation did not contain any requirement for the police to state what age they thought the girls were, and the observations in *R. v. Land (Michael)* [1999] Q.B. 65, [1997] C.L.Y. 1160, which concluded that the absence of expert evidence did not prevent the conclusion that a photo depicted the image of a child, *Land* followed. (2) No assistance as regards finding corroboration could be found from the titles affixed to the images.

GRIFFITHS v. HART 2005 J.C. 313, Lord Osborne, Lord Hamilton, Lord Emslie, HCJ.

5096. Vulnerable Witnesses (Scotland) Act 2004 (asp 3)–Commencement No.2, Saving and Transitional Provisions Order

VULNERABLE WITNESSES (SCOTLAND) ACT 2004 (COMMENCEMENT NO.2, SAVING AND TRANSITIONAL PROVISIONS) ORDER 2005, SSI 2005 590 (C.30); made under the Vulnerable Witnesses (Scotland) Act 2004 s.25. Commencement details: bringing into force various provisions of the 2004 Act on November 30, 2005; £3.00.

This Order brings into force for certain purposes the special measure of taking evidence by a commissioner as part of the first phase of the implementation of the Vulnerable Witnesses (Scotland) Act 2004.

5097. Vulnerable Witnesses (Scotland) Act 2004 (asp 3)–Commencement Order

VULNERABLE WITNESSES (SCOTLAND) ACT 2004 (COMMENCEMENT) ORDER 2005, SSI 2005 168 (C.7); made under the Vulnerable Witnesses (Scotland) Act 2004 s.25. Commencement details: bringing into force various provisions of the 2004 Act on April 1, 2005; £3.00.

This Order brings into force the first phase of the implementation of the Vulnerable Witnesses (Scotland) Act 2004.

CRIMINAL LAW

5098. Breach of the peace–Conviction of breach of the peace by threatening violence under deletion of disorderly conduct–Competency of conviction

[Criminal Procedure (Scotland) Act 1995 (c.46) Sch.5.]

The appellant (M) appealed against his conviction for breach of the peace. He was charged with the offence after shouting and swearing in the street and uttering threats of violence that placed the complainers in a state of fear and alarm. There were at least two other witnesses. M was convicted, under deletions, of breach of the peace by uttering threats of violence. On appeal to the High Court he argued that the deletions removed an essential element of the offence and that the verdict was incompetent and inconsistent with the case presented by the Crown.

Held, dismissing the appeal, that the verdict was competent. Breach of the peace required conduct that was genuinely alarming and disturbing in its context to any reasonable person and the Criminal Procedure (Scotland) Act 1995 Sch.5 distinguished two classes of cases, one of which did not include disorderly conduct, *Smith (Pamela) v. Donnelly* 2002 J.C. 65, [2001] C.L.Y. 6702 considered. It was for the jury to decide whether M's behaviour in a public place was likely to cause alarm and upset members of the public, even if that did not include the complainers themselves.

McGRAW (STEVEN MARTIN) v. HM ADVOCATE 2004 S.C.C.R. 637, Lord Penrose, Lord Osborne, Lady Smith, HCJ.

5099. Breach of the peace–Members of the Scottish Parliament–Freedom of expression–Proportionality

[Criminal Procedure (Scotland) Act 1995 (c.46) s.160; Human Rights Act 1998 (c.42) Sch.1 Part I Art.10, Art.11.]

Q, a Member of the Scottish Parliament, was charged with committing breach of the peace at a naval base. He had blocked the road leading to the base with a group of others and had refused to move when asked to do so by the police. Q was heard on a minute intimating that he intended to raise a devolution issue and contended that the proceedings against him were incompatible with the Human Rights Act 1998 Sch.1 Part I Art.10 and Art.11. The justice refused to find that a devolution issue existed. The case proceeded to trial, Q's submission of no case to answer was refused, he was convicted and fined £100. He appealed, submitting that in the context of a protest by an elected representative, interference by criminal sanction could be justified only if it was necessary in a democratic society. He further submitted that protest by action as well as by words was protected under Art.10, his protest had been peaceful, and the criminal proceedings against him were not proportionate to the legitimate aims listed in Art.10. The justice stated a case for the opinion of the High Court asking whether he had been correct in concluding that there was no devolution issue, whether he had been correct in repelling the submission of no case to answer in terms of the Criminal Procedure (Scotland) Act 1995 s.160 and whether, on the facts stated, he had been entitled to convict Q. The parties were agreed that the justice's determination on the existence of a devolution issue was in error.

Held, answering question one in the negative of consent and questions two and three in the affirmative, that (1) Q's conduct was clearly contrary to law and the actions taken against him were in pursuit of a legitimate aim and were proportionate, even on the basis that he was, and conceived himself to be, acting in a representative rather than in a personal capacity at the material time. (2) Where the democratic interest in freedom of expression by elected representatives could be met as readily by such a representative publicly demonstrating lawfully as unlawfully, there was no ground for holding that it was disproportionate to apply the law to him in the same way as to his fellow citizens.

QUINAN v. CARNEGIE; *sub nom.* QUINAN v. DONNELLY 2005 J.C. 279, Lord Hamilton, Lady Paton, Lord Clarke, HCJ.

5100. Breach of the peace–Running onto football pitch and waving flag during match

The appellant (X) appealed by way of case stated against a conviction of breaching the peace, for which he was charged on summary complaint in the sheriff court. X ran onto the pitch at Ibrox, waving a Union Jack flag, during a Rangers match against a European team. Rangers had just scored the first goal and the spectators were jubilant. At a pre match briefing the police had been instructed to arrest anyone who invaded the pitch. The sheriff repelled a plea of no case to answer and X was convicted after the sheriff found that X's behaviour could reasonably have been expected to incite others to behave in a disorderly manner and could have led to serious crowd control issues. On appeal, X argued that there was no basis for concluding that his behaviour was conducive to alarm or public disturbance, particularly since it had not been committed in an atmosphere of "tribal animosity".

Held, dismissing the appeal, that the sheriff was entitled to make the findings that she had. Given the charged atmosphere of a football crowd the risk of crowd trouble was an ever present threat. Although X had acted in front of a jubilant crowd, his actions created a serious risk that others would take the same action.

ALLISON v. HIGSON 2004 S.C.C.R. 720, Lord Gill L.J.C., Lord Hamilton, Lady Cosgrove, HCJ.

5101. Counterfeiting–False monetary instruments

FALSE MONETARY INSTRUMENTS (SCOTLAND) ORDER 2005, SSI 2005 321; made under the Criminal Law (Consolidation) (Scotland) Act 1995 s.46A. In force: July 1, 2005; £3.00.

The Criminal Law (Consolidation) (Scotland) Act 1995 makes it an offence for a person to counterfeit or falsify a specified monetary instrument or to have in his or her custody or control, equipment for making a specified monetary instrument. This Order specifies the monetary instruments to which the Act applies. The monetary instruments specified in the Order include (but are not limited to) those required to implement Art.2 of the EU Framework Decision of May 28, 2001 on combating fraud and counterfeiting of non-cash means of payment.

5102. Drink driving offences–Police powers and duties–Compatibility of random checks with right to respect for private and family life

[Road Traffic Act 1988 (c.52) s.5(1)(a), s.163; Human Rights Act 1998 (c.42) Sch.1 Part I Art.8.]

The appellant (M), a driver stopped by the police during a random check, appealed against his conviction for driving with excess alcohol contrary to the Road Traffic Act 1988 s.5(1)(a). M had smelt of alcohol when stopped and had been subjected to a breath test. M objected to the admissibility of the police officers' evidence on the grounds that the random check was incompatible with the Human Rights Act 1998 Sch.1 Part I Art.8 and that the officers had acted oppressively in the exercise of their powers within the meaning of s.163 of the 1988 Act.

Held, dismissing the appeal, that (1) the police checks constituted a systematic approach to the prevention and detection of criminal offences in general and were within the ambit of s.163. The random nature of the check in fact prevented it from being perceived as a "whim" or "caprice", *Stewart v. Crowe* 1999 S.L.T. 899, [1999] C.L.Y. 5870 followed; (2) s.163 represented a necessary and proportionate response by society in its attempt to prevent the commission of crime and did not amount to a breach of Art.8. Furthermore, s.163 was sufficiently clear and understandable to meet the test of "legality".

MILLER v. BELL 2004 S.C.C.R. 534, Lord Marnoch, Lady Cosgrove, Lord McEwan, HCJ.

5103. Emergency Workers (Scotland) Act 2005 (asp 2)–Commencement Order

EMERGENCY WORKERS (SCOTLAND) ACT 2005 (COMMENCEMENT) ORDER 2005, SSI 2005 229 (C.10); made under the Emergency Workers (Scotland) Act 2005 s.9. Commencement details: bringing into force various provisions of the 2005 Act on May 9, 2005; £3.00.

This Order brings into force the provisions of the Emergency Workers (Scotland) Act 2005 except s.9 which relates to short title and commencement. The Act creates new offences in relation to assaulting, obstructing or hindering someone who is providing emergency services, or someone who is assisting an emergency worker who is responding to emergency circumstances. The Act also creates similar offences in respect of health workers on hospital premises and persons assisting such workers.

5104. Intention–Hunting–Use of hounds to flush out fox–Intention to shoot fox–Pest control

[Protection of Wild Mammals (Scotland) Act 2002 s.1 (1), s.2 (1).]

The accused (X) was charged with a contravention of the Protection of Wild Mammals (Scotland) Act 2002 s.1 (1) by deliberately hunting a fox with 20 dogs. The evidence, which was not in dispute, was that X, a master of foxhounds, had been invited onto land for the purpose of killing foxes to protect the landowner's pheasants. X's stated intention was to use the hounds to "flush" out the foxes towards two persons with guns, who would then shoot the foxes. The hounds were controlled by X using a horn. X fox was flushed, but ran away from the guns and escaped.

Held, giving judgment for the accused, that although X was deliberately searching for a fox with dogs, he was doing so with the landowner's permission and with the intention of flushing foxes from cover for the purpose of shooting them so as to protect game birds and control the numbers of foxes as a pest species. The dogs were "under control" for the purposes of s.2(1) of the 2002 Act and there was evidence that they had responded to X's command. The fact that the fox had not in fact been shot did not mean that X had not taken effective action to shoot it within the meaning of the s.2(1) exception. The burden of proof was on the Crown to establish deliberate hunting of a wild mammal with dogs. In the instant case, X's purpose in being on the land fell within the excepted purposes under the Act and he was not guilty of an offence under s.1 (1). (Obiter) The purpose of the Act was to protect wild mammals from being hunted with dogs but to allow the humane dispatch of pest species by shooting. To this end, there was limited scope for the legitimate use of dogs, but that had to be accompanied by effective arrangements for shooting, and the use of "token guns" could not be adopted as a justification for the continuation of traditional foxhunting.

FRASER v. ADAMS 2005 S.C.C.R. 54, Sheriff TAK Drummond Q.C., Sh Ct (Lothian and Border).

5105. Offences–Sale of goods–Offensive weapons

CRIMINAL JUSTICE ACT 1988 (OFFENSIVE WEAPONS) (SCOTLAND) ORDER 2005, SSI 2005 483; made under the Criminal Justice Act 1988 s.141. In force: September 29, 2005; £3.00.

The Criminal Justice Act 1988 provides that any person who manufactures, sells or hires, or offers for sale or hire, exposes or has in his or her possession for the purpose of sale or hire, or lends or gives to any other person, a weapon to which that section applies shall be guilty of an offence and liable on summary conviction to imprisonment for a term not exceeding six months or a fine not exceeding level 5 on the standard scale or both. The import of any such weapon is prohibited by the 1988 Act. There are defences under s.141 of the 1988 in respect of weapons which are made available to a museum or gallery or used for cultural, artistic or educational purposes if lent or hired from a museum or gallery, and in respect of weapons used for the purposes of the Crown or of a visiting force as defined. This Order, which revokes the Criminal Justice Act 1988 (Offensive Weapons) Order 1988 (SI 1988 2019) and the Criminal Justice Act 1988 (Offensive Weapons) Amendment (Scotland) Order 2002 (SSI 2002 323), specifies the descriptions of weapons to which s.141 of the 1988 Act applies. Antique weapons, which are defined as weapons over 100 years old at the time of the alleged offence, are excluded. The Order also adds two new categories of weapon, the stealth knife and the straight, side handled or friction lock truncheon to the list of weapons previously specified.

5106. Prohibition of Female Genital Mutilation (Scotland) Act 2005 (asp 8)

This Act of the Scottish Parliament restates and amends the law relating to female genital mutilation and provides for extra-territorial effect.

This Act received Royal Assent on July 1, 2005.

5107. Racially aggravated offences–Findings of fact–Sufficiency of evidence

[Criminal Law (Consolidation) (Scotland) Act 1995 (c.39) s.50A(1)(b); Criminal Procedure (Scotland) Act 1995 (c.46) Sch.3 para.14(b).]

X was charged with inter alia acting in a racially aggravated manner which caused or intended to cause alarm or distress at a football match, contrary to the Criminal Law (Consolidation) (Scotland) Act 1995 s.50A(1)(b), by continually making abusive remarks towards two football players. The remarks were not heard by the players. The sheriff found inter alia that two spectators were upset and disgusted by the remarks and that X's conduct could reasonably be expected to have caused any observer to become alarmed or annoyed or to have provoked a disturbance. X was convicted and appealed by stated case. The Crown accepted that in a prosecution under s.50A(1)(b) the alarm or distress had to be that of the intended victim on which basis X's conviction could not be supported on the sheriff's findings in fact, but that the court should substitute a conviction for breach of the peace. Counsel were agreed that the appropriate question was whether, on the facts stated, the sheriff was entitled to convict.

Held, answering the question in the negative, that (1) the case had been unsatisfactorily drafted by the sheriff: he had rehearsed the evidence at length but had failed to state any questions for the court, but the court would ex proprio motu ask itself the question as agreed by counsel rather than return the case to the sheriff for revisal. (2) The sheriff had not found that the manner in which X acted was intended to cause alarm or distress to the complainers and a conclusion to that effect could not reasonably be inferred, particularly since he found X's remarks to have been inaudible on the field. (3) It was within the powers of the court to substitute the conviction: the Criminal Procedure (Scotland) Act 1995 Sch.3 para.14(b) would have made it competent for the sheriff to take that course had he been asked to do so and the proposed verdict was one that could have been returned at the trial if it had been sought by the Crown and the fact that it was not sought in this trial was irrelevant. (4) The court was entitled to dispose of the appeal by substituting such a verdict if the facts warranted it and the sheriff's findings provided an adequate basis for a conviction of breach of the peace.

ANDERSON v. GRIFFITHS 2005 J.C. 169, Lord Gill L.J.C., Lord Osborne, Lord Hamilton, HCJ.

5108. Racially aggravated offences–Racial harassment–Victims

[Criminal Law (Consolidation) (Scotland) Act 1995 (c.39) s.50A.]

M was charged with acting in a racially aggravated manner which caused or intended to cause alarm or distress at a football match, contrary to the Criminal Law (Consolidation) (Scotland) Act 1995 s.50A(1)(b), by shouting racial remarks at football players of African origin, and swearing. The sheriff found that M's remarks had alarmed or distressed a schoolboy who had been seated alongside. M was convicted and appealed by stated case. He did not attempt to deny that on the facts found his language had constituted racial abuse nor that the schoolboy was likely to have been alarmed or distressed by that abuse, but submitted that the provisions of s.50A(1)(b), properly construed, were aimed at racially aggravated conduct directed against a particular person where it caused actual distress to that person or was intended to do so. Accordingly, it was not relevant to aver in a charge libelling a contravention of s.50A(1)(b) that the victim of the racial abuse was a person other than the person towards whom it had been directed. The Crown submitted that the charge was relevant having regard to the reference to "a person" in s.50A(1)(b) in contrast to the use of the term "the person" in s.50A(2), and it was appropriate that anyone who had been caused alarm and distress by racially aggravated conduct on the part of an accused could be averred to be the victim thereof.

Held, quashing the conviction and substituting it for a conviction for breach of the peace that was racially aggravated, that (1) it was important to read s.50A(1) and s.50A(2) together and when the conduct of an accused caused or was intended to cause alarm and distress to a particular person, which was what s.50A(1) required before there could be a conviction, the characteristics of that conduct, which were required in terms of s.50A(2)(a), had to relate to the same person. (2) Only the footballers to whom the abuse was directed could be considered the complainers or victims in the charge and the schoolboy's involvement therein was thus outwith the scope of s.50A(1)(b) and the charge on which M was convicted was irrelevant. (3) The alternative phrase "intended to cause" in s.50A(1)(b) did not mean that the intended victim of the abuse need hear it so long as the evidence yielded the view that the accused intended to cause alarm or distress to the intended victim, thus s.50A(1)(a) should be construed as meaning either causing alarm or distress or attempting to do so, but not with it being necessary in the latter context that anything was achieved.

MARTIN v. BOTT 2005 S.L.T. 730, Lord Johnston, Lord Mackay of Drumadoon, Temporary Judge CGB Nicholson Q.C., HCJ.

5109. Road traffic offences—Identification of driver—Warnings

[Road Traffic Act 1988 (c.52) s.172.]

B appealed against his conviction for failing to provide information as to the driver of a car, kept by him, caught on camera travelling at 42 mph in a 30 mph zone. B pled not guilty at the local district court and submitted a motion of no case to answer at the close of the Crown case on the ground that the police officer who cautioned him in terms of the Road Traffic Act 1988 s.172 when B refused to provide information as to who was the driver at the time of the offence did not then warn him that such action was an offence. The motion was rejected by the justice. B averred that the justice had erred in rejecting the motion.

Held, dismissing the appeal, that (1) there was no qualification in s.172 itself to the effect that, before an offence was committed by failure to comply with the requirement, a warning or statement had to be made that failure to comply might amount to the commission of an offence. (2) The purpose of the explanation that failure to reply might amount to the commission of an offence in *Duncan v. MacGillivray* 1989 S.L.T. 48, [1988] C.L.Y. 4845 appeared simply to make it clear to the person addressed that a statutory requirement was being made in terms of the legislation and where a clear statutory requirement had already been made, any suggestion of a further legal requirement of an explanation would be in conflict with the legislation, *Duncan* considered.

BROWN v. FRAME 2005 J.C. 320, Lord Osborne, Lord Hamilton, Lord Emslie, HCJ.

5110. Shameless indecency—Verdict—Criminal appeals—Competence

[Criminal Procedure (Scotland) Act 1995 (c.46) s.118(2); Sex Offenders Act 1997 (c.51) s.1, s.2, Sch.1.]

S and P appealed against convictions for conducting themselves in a shamelessly indecent manner towards young girls in separate incidents, on the ground that, following the decision in *Webster v. Dominick* 2003 S.L.T. 975, [2003] C.L.Y. 5371, shameless indecency was not a nomen juris, the crime which was the subject of the charges was not known to the law of Scotland and nothing could be substituted for it. The Crown's primary position was that the offences in the single charge against S and two of the charges against P had been ones of lewd, indecent and libidinous practices, and it did not matter that an incorrect nomen juris had been made. Alternatively, if the convictions fell to be quashed, another conviction should be substituted by applying the Criminal Procedure (Scotland) Act 1995 s.118(2). The Crown accepted that in relation to charge 1 against P, the court could not substitute a verdict of guilty of lewd and libidinous practices as the complainer was 16, but submitted that the court could substitute one of indecent assault.

Held, dismissing S's appeal and allowing P's appeal, that (1) it was incorrect to simply treat certain convictions of shameless indecency as if they were convictions for lewd, indecent and libidinous practices where guilty verdicts had been returned on the charges as thus laid in accordance with the directions given, and although any future reference to shamelessness would be regarded as superfluous, the fact was that hitherto what was understood to have been the discrete crime of shameless indecency was charged as such for a number of years, and since it was a sexual offence within the Sex Offenders Act 1997 Sch.1, every person convicted of it became a sex offender subject to the notification requirements of s.1 and s.2 therein. (2) The High Court had power to substitute amended verdicts as proposed by the Crown except in relation to the first charge against P where deletion of the word "shamelessly" from the charges would leave words entirely descriptive of acts amounting to lewd, indecent and libidinous practices, the actus reus on the face of it would remain the same as would the mens rea, and there was no need to specify by any nomen juris the offence charged. (3) A verdict of indecent assault for P on charge 1 could not be substituted: the allegation in effect was that P had done something whether or not the complainer had consented; it was not part of the Crown case as charged that it required to prove lack of consent or that the acts were done with the mens rea necessary for that crime; the jury were not directed on this matter, and it followed that conviction on that charge had to be quashed. (4) Conviction in relation to the other charges against P relied on application of the *Moorov* doctrine in conjunction with the first charge, and it appeared that these could not be supported, *Webster* considered.

SNEDDON (GRAHAM) v. HM ADVOCATE; P v. HM ADVOCATE 2005 S.L.T. 651, Lord MacLean, Lord Kingarth, Lord Eassie, HCJ.

5111. Supply of drugs–Defences–Knowledge

[Misuse of Drugs Act 1971 (c.38) s.4(3)(b), s.28(2).]

Two accused (H and R) were charged on indictment with being concerned in the supply of ecstasy, contrary to the Misuse of Drugs Act 1971 s.4(3)(b). They were detained following a police surveillance operation in which they were seen collecting a carrier bag from two youths, which was later found to contain ecstasy tablets. H gave evidence that he thought the bag contained SIM cards. R told police that he thought it contained cigarettes. The trial judge, following *Salmon (Donald) v. HM Advocate* 1999 J.C. 67, [1999] C.L.Y. 5832, directed the jury that it was for the defence to prove on the balance of probabilities that the accused did not know or suspect or have reason to suspect that the bag contained controlled drugs. The Crown accepted that, in the light of *R. v. Lambert (Steven)* [2001] UKHL 37, [2002] 2 A.C. 545, [2001] C.L.Y. 3504, s.28(2) of the Act did not impose a legal burden of proof but only an evidential burden and that the trial judge had misdirected the jury, but submitted that there was no miscarriage of justice: the evidence was strongly incriminatory and the defence had not discharged the onus of displacing the inference that arose from it; H could see the top of the containers inside the bag and had not checked the contents; there was nothing to show that he had no reason to suspect drugs and there were no surrounding circumstances to support his statement that he expected SIM cards; it was difficult to see how R could have thought he was obtaining cigarettes in containers; there was conflict between the accused as to what the bag contained; and the court should proceed on the basis that the jury had rejected their evidence.

Held, allowing the appeals, that (1) the misdirection had given rise to a miscarriage of justice. (2) A clear distinction must to be drawn between the question of whether there was evidence which if believed, could support a defence under s.28, and the question of whether that evidence was such as to leave a reasonable doubt about the defence when it was considered in the light of the evidence as a whole. (3) As regards the first question, there was evidence on which each of the accused could rely in support of a defence under s.28: their evidence clearly implied that they neither suspected nor had reason to suspect that the bag contained controlled drugs; explicit evidence of this was not necessary, and whether that evidence was contradicted by other evidence was irrelevant from the point of view of raising a defence. (4) The second question would have been a matter for the jury had they been properly directed that they could not convict unless the Crown satisfied them beyond reasonable doubt that the defence under s.28 should be rejected, and it could not be answered in favour of the Crown, as the jury had been misdirected and as in any event, the court could not determine how they would have answered it, *Salmon* and *Lambert* considered.

HENVEY (STEVEN) v. HM ADVOCATE; REID (GEORGE) v. HM ADVOCATE 2005 S.L.T. 384, Lord Cullen L.J.G., Lord Kirkwood, Lord MacLean, Lord Osborne, Lord Hamilton, HCJ.

5112. Books

Brown, Alastair N.; Thomson, Lesley; Harris, Lorna—Proceeds of Crime. Greens Practice Library. Hardback: £110.00. ISBN 0 414 01445 6. W.Green & Son.

Connelly, Claire—Criminal Lawbasics. Paperback: £12.50. ISBN 0 414 01577 0. W.Green & Son.

Ferguson, Pamela; Sheldon, David—Scots Criminal Law. Paperback: £36.00. ISBN 1 84592 152 6. Tottel Publishing.

Gordon, Gerald H.; Christie, Michael G.A.—Criminal Law of Scotland: Vol 1 & V.2. Hardback: £20.00. ISBN 0 414 01572 X. W.Green & Son.

Gordon, Gerald H.; Christie, Michael G.A.—Criminal Law of Scotland: 1st Supplement. Hardback: £40.00. ISBN 0 414 01574 6. W.Green & Son.

Law Society Scotland Diploma Materials 2005, Criminal Court Practice Student Manual 2005-2006. Book (details unknown): £15.00. ISBN 0 414 01640 8. W.Green & Son.

CRIMINAL PROCEDURE

5113. Anti social behaviour—Amount of fixed penalties

ANTISOCIAL BEHAVIOUR (AMOUNT OF FIXED PENALTY) (SCOTLAND) ORDER 2005, SSI 2005 110; made under the Antisocial Behaviour etc. (Scotland) Act 2004 s.130. In force: April 1, 2005; £3.00.

This Order provides that the amount of the fixed penalty which is payable if a fixed penalty notice has been given for the commission of a fixed penalty offence in an area which has been prescribed by the Scottish Ministers by regulations under the Antisocial Behaviour etc. (Scotland) Act 2004 s.129(2) is £40.

5114. Anti social behaviour—Community reparation orders—Prescribed persons

COMMUNITY REPARATION ORDERS (REQUIREMENTS FOR CONSULTATION AND PRESCRIBED ACTIVITIES) (SCOTLAND) REGULATIONS 2005, SSI 2005 18; made under the Social Work (Scotland) Act 1968 s.27; the Criminal Procedure (Scotland) Act 1995 s.245K; and the Antisocial Behaviour etc. (Scotland) Act 2004 s.141. In force: February 10, 2005; £3.00.

These Regulations make provision in relation to offenders subject to Community Reparation Orders. Community Reparation Orders were introduced by the Antisocial Behaviour Etc. (Scotland) Act 2004 s.120. They list the persons or classes of person that a local authority is required to consult before making, revising or modifying provisions in a community justice scheme, prepared by the authority in terms of the Social Work (Scotland) Act 1968 s.27(2), that relate to individuals in the authority's area who are subject to a Community Reparation Order. They also list the activities that an individual who is subject to a Community Reparation Order may be required to undertake.

5115. Anti social behaviour–Fixed penalties–Offences–Additional information

ANTISOCIAL BEHAVIOUR (FIXED PENALTY NOTICE) (ADDITIONAL INFORMATION) (SCOTLAND) ORDER 2005, SSI 2005 130; made under the Antisocial Behaviour etc. (Scotland) Act 2004 s.130. In force: April 1, 2005; £3.00.

This Order prescribes the additional information that will be included on a fixed penalty notice given to a person if a constable has reason to believe that that person has committed a fixed penalty offence as defined by the Antisocial Behaviour etc. (Scotland) Act 2004 s.128(1). The 2004 Act provides that a fixed penalty notice shall include the specified information, and other such information as the Scottish Ministers prescribe.

5116. Anti social behaviour–Fixed penalties–Offences–Prescribed areas

ANTISOCIAL BEHAVIOUR (FIXED PENALTY OFFENCE) (PRESCRIBED AREA) (SCOTLAND) REGULATIONS 2005, SSI 2005 106; made under the Antisocial Behaviour etc. (Scotland) Act 2004 s.129. In force: April 1, 2005; £3.00.

These Regulations prescribe the Tayside combined police area as an area in which a person may be given a fixed penalty notice if a constable has reason to believe that the person has committed a fixed penalty offence as defined in the Antisocial Behaviour etc. (Scotland) Act 2004 s.128(1).

5117. Antisocial Behaviour etc. (Scotland) Act 2004 (asp 8)–Commencement and Savings Amendment Order

ANTISOCIAL BEHAVIOUR ETC. (SCOTLAND) (COMMENCEMENT AND SAVINGS) AMENDMENT ORDER 2005, SSI 2005 553 (C.27); made under the Antisocial Behaviour etc. (Scotland) Act 2004 s.141, s.145. Commencement details: bringing into force various provisions of the 2004 Act on November 9, 2005 and March 31, 2006; £3.00.

This Order amends the Antisocial Behaviour etc. (Scotland) (Commencement and Savings) Order 2004 (SSI 2004 420) so that the Antisocial Behaviour etc. (Scotland) Act 2004 Part 7 and Part 8 come into force on March 31, 2006. The Order also brings forward to November 9, 2005 the commencement of order and regulation making powers contained in the 2004 Act; and sets as March 31, 2006 the date for commencement of all remaining provisions of that Act.

5118. Assault–Basis of plea–Procedure for recording presentation of plea information

The appellants (M, H and X) appealed against sentences of 20 months' imprisonment imposed following their convictions of assault. M, H and X had pleaded guilty to charges of assault after a minor scuffle outside a public house during which the complainer had been brought to the ground and kicked, stamped and assaulted. There was video evidence of the incident. H and M brought their appeals on the basis that they had been involved only art and part in the attack but X submitted, despite the terms in which the plea was presented, that he had acted independently.

Held, allowing the appeals in part, that although M and H's sentences were not excessive, X's limited role was such that it distinguished him from the others. The difference between art and part guilt and X's independent involvement in the assault was, however, insignificant in the instant case and it was immaterial whether or not the issue raised in the appeal was resolved. In recognition of X's lesser role in the assault, his sentence was reduced to one of 12 months' imprisonment. (Obiter) It was essential for parties to ensure that when a plea was tendered, the terms on which it was tendered and the timing of tendering it be recorded either in a written communication to the Crown or by some agreed memorandum to set out what had been agreed. Without such communication, there was a risk of disadvantage to accused persons where the court could not be certain as to the basis on which they appeared before it.

MILLS (ARTHUR) v. HM ADVOCATE; HOPKINS (JOHN) v. HM ADVOCATE; McGUIRE (ROBERT) v. HM ADVOCATE 2005 S.C.C.R. 1, Lord Penrose, Lord Mackay of Drumadoon, HCJ.

5119. Bail conditions–Electronic monitoring requirements–Specified devices

BAIL CONDITIONS (SPECIFICATION OF DEVICES) AND RESTRICTION OF LIBERTY ORDER (SCOTLAND) AMENDMENT REGULATIONS 2005, SSI 2005 142; made under the Criminal Procedure (Scotland) Act 1995 s.24B, s.24D, s.245A, s.245C. In force: April 18, 2005; £3.00.

These Regulations, which amend the Restriction of Liberty Order (Scotland) Regulations 1998 (SI 1998 1802), make provision for the monitoring of certain groups of people by means of electronic or radio devices. The Regulations specify the methods by which compliance with movement restriction conditions, as defined in the Criminal Procedure (Scotland) Act 1995 may be monitored; specify the electronic and radio devices which may be used for monitoring the compliance of those on bail with movement restriction conditions; and amend the list of specified devices which may be used to monitor the compliance of offenders with the requirements of restriction of liberty orders.

5120. Childrens hearings–Supervision requirements–Movement restrictions

INTENSIVE SUPPORT AND MONITORING (SCOTLAND) AMENDMENT REGULATIONS 2005, SSI 2005 201; made under the Children (Scotland) Act 1995 s.17, s.31, s.70, s.103. In force: April 1, 2005; £3.00.

These Regulations amend provisions in the Intensive Support and Monitoring (Scotland) Regulations 2005 (SSI 2005 129) relating to the arrangements for monitoring compliance with a movement restriction condition contained in a supervision requirement. They set out the arrangements for monitoring compliance, under reference to the movement restriction care plan, details of which, together with those relating to the crisis response service, are now contained within Reg.4, rather than in the interpretation provisions of the principal Regulations.

5121. Childrens hearings–Supervision requirements–Movement restrictions

INTENSIVE SUPPORT AND MONITORING (SCOTLAND) REGULATIONS 2005, SSI 2005 129; made under the Children (Scotland) Act 1995 s.17, s.31, s.70, s.103. In force: April 1, 2005; £3.00.

These Regulations regulate the arrangements for monitoring compliance with a supervision requirement with a movement restriction condition, as defined within the Children (Scotland) Act 1995 s.70. They prescribe those local government areas to which the Regulations are to apply. As at April 1, 2005 these comprise the City of Edinburgh, Dundee City, East Dunbartonshire, Glasgow City, Highland, Moray and West Dunbartonshire. The Regulations detail the considerations for a children's hearing, in relation to which it must be satisfied, before imposing upon a child, within a supervision requirement, a movement restriction condition; set out the arrangements for monitoring compliance with a movement restriction condition, where such condition is imposed upon a child, within a supervision requirement, and designates persons in respect of the functions specified; prescribe the conditions which are to be imposed by the children's hearing, to the extent that it considers necessary, when imposing a movement restriction condition upon a child; set out what monitoring methods may be used; and make provision in relation to the variation of the designation of those persons who can monitor compliance with a movement restriction condition.

5122. Contempt of court—Right to fair and public hearing—Judges—Impartiality

[Human Rights Act 1998 (c.42) Sch.1 Part I Art.6.]

M, an advocate, petitioned the nobile officium in respect of a finding by Lord Hardie of contempt of court (2003 S.L.T. 1288). He was counsel in the case of T and had failed to appear when T's case called for trial. The court was advised that M was appearing at a first diet at Edinburgh sheriff court, and was also required to represent another accused (C) in a trial due to commence simultaneously at the High Court. The trial in T's case was continued to allow M to appear in C's case. At the continued hearing M confirmed that he would be available to conduct the trial, and explained that he had withdrawn from acting for C. The explanations tendered by M, including one that he had been informed that C's trial would not begin before 12 noon, made it clear that he had three concurrent commitments, one of which he believed would not require an appearance. Lord Hardie, having considered that M might be guilty of contempt of court by deliberately misleading the court by providing false information, fixed a hearing to enable him to obtain legal representation and thereafter answer the allegations. It was concluded that M had wilfully attempted to mislead the court by making statements that were careful and deliberate and deliberately misleading, going beyond recklessness, regarding C. M challenged the authority and competency of the procedures identified in *Wylie (James Williamson) v. HM Advocate* 1966 S.L.T. 149, [1966] C.L.Y. 13003 and *HM Advocate v. Airs* 1975 J.C. 64, [1975] C.L.Y. 3687 in the light of European jurisprudence, arguing that (1) the finding of contempt in respect of the events relating to C was made without sufficient inquiry; (2) any inquiry that was appropriate should have been carried out by remit to a different judge; (3) in terms of the Human Rights Act 1998 Sch.1 Part I Art.6, the conduct held to be contempt was criminal and he was therefore entitled to the benefit of the criminal provisions thereof protecting accused persons, and (4) accepting that contempt was not classified as criminal in Scots law, the scope for a dual approach in Scots law, distinguishing conduct amounting to contempt that was otherwise within the scope of general criminal law from conduct of an administrative or disciplinary character, was limited given the exposure to significant custodial penalties in all cases. The advocate depute submitted that the court should not adopt the course that European jurisprudence converted a matter regarded as sui generis by Scots law into a crime which would restrict the flexibility of the court to respond to problems as they arose, but should proceed by considering the penalty appropriate in the particular case where, within the common law concept of contempt of court, there were offences that ranged from the purely administrative to those that were clearly criminal in character.

Held, putting the case out by order to discuss the procedure to be adopted, that (1) that the finding of contempt had to be quashed. It was made solely in relation to C but it was plain from his opinion that Lord Hardie had formed a view at an early stage that M's explanations of his failure to appear in T's case on time were false. There were issues of fact to be determined at the hearing in relation to C where M stated that he had received information from a third party that the start time for the trial was noon and although his decision to act on such a basis might have been irresponsible and reckless, that would not have constituted contempt, and it was clear that an informed and objective observer would have expected M to have been afforded the opportunity to lead such evidence as was available to him to establish that the relevant information had been communicated to him, and to do so without the burden of a prior adverse opinion of his credibility having been formed by the judge adjudicating on the question of contempt. (2) The appropriate course was to remit the issue of M's disputed contempt to a member of the court to resolve, with the benefit of such evidence as could be placed before the court, and to report. It might be that the general observations in *Wylie* on procedural aspects of possible contempt would require in an appropriate case to be revisited in light of the incorporation of the Convention into Scots law and the consequential application of Convention jurisprudence, but this was not such a case. The incidence of contempt of court committed by legal representatives appearing for parties before the courts in this jurisdiction was rare and ordinarily, at least, it would not be necessary, in the interests of securing justice in the case being tried before the court, for any such issue of contempt to be addressed and resolved with particular urgency, in which regard, it was not typical of most forms of contempt and the observations in *Wylie* had no direct application; in any event, in so far as the observations approved a practice of the trial judge himself investigating and determining issues of contempt arising before him, they could not affect what was appropriate as further procedure in this case where it was plain that consideration afresh of the issue of contempt could not take place before Lord Hardie, *Wylie* and *Airs* considered.

MAYER (JOHN) v. HM ADVOCATE; *sub nom.* MAYER, PETITIONER 2005 J.C. 121, Lord Penrose, Lord Hamilton, Lord Abernethy, HCJ.

5123. Criminal appeals–Cross examination–Failure by Crown to cross examine– Clerk advising justice in private

[Human Rights Act 1998 (c.42) Sch.1 Part I Art.6(1).]

C had been charged on summary complaint with breach of the peace (charge 1) and wilfully and recklessly destroying or damaging property belonging to another (charge 3). C gave exculpatory evidence during her trial, and evidence was also led on her behalf from another witness. C was not cross examined by the prosecutor. The justice thereafter adjourned to consider her verdict and sought clarification from the deputy clerk of court as to the effect of the failure to cross examine. No question was raised by either party as to the advice tendered by the clerk. C was convicted and appealed by stated case on the basis that failure to cross examine evidence of an exculpatory nature inevitably resulted in an unfair trial; *Young (Andrew) v. Guild* 1985 J.C. 27, [1985] C.L.Y. 3853, in which failure to cross examine did not bar the prosecutor from seeking a conviction, ought to be reconsidered; and the Human Rights Act 1998 Sch.1 Part I Art.6(1) had been breached where the practice set out in *Clark (Christopher John) v. Kelly* [2003] UKPC D1, [2004] 1 A.C. 681, [2003] C.L.Y. 5167, relating to advice given by a clerk to a justice in private, had not been followed. The justice asked whether (1) she had been entitled to convict C of charge 1; (2) whether she had been entitled to convict C of charge 3; (3) whether the process had been tainted to the extent that C could not be said to have received a fair trial in terms of Art.6(1).

Held, dismissing the appeal, that (1) *Young* was not open to criticism: its views were in conformity with long standing practice and common sense, it was unlikely to lull defence agents into thinking it was unnecessary to lead further evidence, and the court would deal in an appropriate manner with the situation where failure to cross examine resulted in demonstrable prejudice to an accused. (2) Although the guidelines set forth in *Clark* had not been followed, that in itself did not breach C's Convention rights. The advice tendered by the clerk conformed with *Young*, thus no miscarriage of justice followed from that state of affairs, *Young* followed. (3) The observations by the High Court in *Clark* about the matters which should be raised in open court should now be regarded as superseded, *Clark* disapproved.

CHALMERS v. GRIFFITHS; *sub nom.* MacLEOD v. GRIFFITHS 2005 J.C. 158, Lord Gill L.J.C., Lord Osborne, Lord Hamilton, HCJ.

5124. Criminal appeals–Leave to appeal–Restricted terms–Appeal against restriction of grounds

[Criminal Procedure (Scotland) Act 1995 (c.46) s.107.]

The appellant (B), a prisoner, lodged a note of appeal against his conviction and sentence for murder. Leave to appeal was granted in restricted terms by letter which referred to Lord Bonomy as the first sift judge and stated that leave in respect of certain grounds had been refused. B thereafter applied for a review of the refusal of leave, ostensibly by the second sift under the Criminal Procedure (Scotland) Act 1995 s.107(4). Leave to appeal was again refused by letter, with the second sift judges stating that this was due to the reasons given by Lord Bonomy and that the grounds on which leave was refused were unstateable. B petitioned the nobile officium, inviting the court to quash the decision on the second sift and remit the matter for further consideration, maintaining that in the absence of adequate reasons for their decision, he could not know why the second sift judges rejected his submissions that various matters should be argued at the hearing of the appeal.

Held, granting the petition to the extent of setting aside the decision of the second sift judges, that the decision of the second sift judges was incompetent as it was not within the powers conferred by s.107(5) of the Act and followed from B's application under s.107(4) which was also incompetent. An appellant who obtained leave to appeal at the first or second sift, but was dissatisfied with the extent to which he might rely on his grounds of appeal, might apply to the court for leave in accordance with s.107(8), but it was not competent for an appellant who had obtained leave to appeal at the first sift where the first sift judge had specified only some of his grounds of appeal as arguable to apply for leave to appeal under s.107(4).

BEGGS, PETITIONER 2005 J.C. 174, Lord Cullen L.J.G., Lord Marnoch, Lord Macfadyen, HCJ.

5125. Criminal charges–Separation of charges–Risk of prejudice

[Sex Offenders Act 1997 (c.51) s.5(2).]

G was charged on an indictment libelling assault and attempted murder. The first charge narrated that he had entered a flat uninvited and assaulted the householder by punching and kicking him. The second charge narrated that he had broken into the house of a 70 year old woman and assaulted her by pushing her to the ground, removing part of her clothing, inserting an object into her private parts, repeatedly punching and kicking her, and stamping on her head. At a preliminary diet, G sought separation of the charges on the ground that there was a material risk of prejudice if they were tried together. The judge refused the motion, and after a trial, G was convicted of both charges. G appealed, arguing that (1) the refusal of his motion for separation of the charges constituted a miscarriage of justice, as the jury might have considered that if he used violence in the circumstances narrated in the first charge, it was more likely than not that he was the perpetrator of the more serious violence libelled in the second; (2) the judge had misdirected the jury by failing to direct them specifically on the averments in the second charge in relation to the assault on the complainer's private parts, in particular by failing to give a specific direction on mens rea to the effect that it was essential that the Crown should prove that the offence was committed for the purpose of sexual gratification, and to direct that the crucial facts in that element of the charge had to be proved by corroborated evidence. In any event, the trial judge should have directed the jury to consider whether G had committed a sexual assault. As it was, the trial judge had made the judgment that G had committed an indecent assault and so certified under the Sex Offenders Act 1997 s.5(2) after the jury had convicted him as libelled.

Held, dismissing the appeal, that (1) the decision whether to order separation of the charges was one for the discretion of the court and the rule to bring all charges under one indictment should only be departed from where there was a demonstrable risk that the accused would suffer prejudice, but the judge had applied the correct test and G had given no reason to think that he had, at trial, sustained prejudice of the kind apprehended at the preliminary hearing. (2) Indecent assault was not an independent sexual assault, but was essentially an assault aggravated by indecency in the manner of its commission, which was to be judged by an objective standard, and an assault might have the quality of indecency irrespective of the accused's intention or motive. (3) The question for the jury on this part of the indictment was whether the Crown had proved the relevant factual averments and the normal directions on mens rea were therefore sufficient. (4) Corroborative evidence in relation to the sexual assault was academic where G had agreed that there was a corroborated case against him on this part of the indictment. (5) Where the jury convicted on a libel that included a sexual element, the decision maker for the purposes of certification of a sexual offence was the trial judge, and his conclusion that the jury's conviction on the second charge without deletion implied the commission of an indecent assault was clearly correct.

GRAINGER (DARREN MICHAEL) v. HM ADVOCATE 2005 S.L.T. 364, Lord Gill, L.J.C., Lord Osborne, Lord MacKay of Drumadoon, HCJ.

5126. Criminal Justice (Scotland) Act 2003 (asp 7)–Commencement No.6 Order

CRIMINAL JUSTICE (SCOTLAND) ACT 2003 (COMMENCEMENT NO.6) ORDER 2005, SSI 2005 433 (C.21); made under the Criminal Justice (Scotland) Act 2003 s.89. Commencement details: bringing into force various provisions of the 2003 Act on October 4, 2005; £3.00.

This Order brings into force on the Criminal Justice (Scotland) Act 2003 s.2(a), s.7, s.8, s.9, s.10, s.41 and Sch.1 para.1 (3) (b).

5127. Declarations of incompatibility–Devolution issues–Criminal trials–Correct time to raise issue of compatibility

[Criminal Procedure (Scotland) Act1995 (c.46) s.274, s.275; Human Rights Act 1998 Sch.1 Part I Art.6(1); Sexual Offences (Procedure and Evidence) (Scotland) Act 2002 (asp 9) s.7, s.8; European Convention on Human Rights 1950.]

The petitioner (M) applied for special leave to appeal against a decision refusing to allow him to raise an issue as to the compatibility of Scottish legislative provisions with the European Convention on Human Rights 1950. M was awaiting trial on an indictment alleging a number of sexual offences. He sought to raise as a devolution issue the question whether the Criminal Procedure (Scotland) Act 1995 s.274 and s.275, as amended by the Sexual Offences (Procedure and Evidence) (Scotland) Act 2002 s.7 and s.8, were incompatible with his right to a fair trial under the Human Rights Act 1998 Sch.1 Part I Art.6(1). At first instance, the judge refused M's devolution minute. The appeal court refused M's subsequent appeal and his motion for leave to appeal to the Privy Council.

Held, dismissing the petition, that the issue that M sought to raise was best left to be considered after the trial. The proper course was for the Crown to be allowed to proceed to trial and for the issue of compatibility to be raised as a ground of appeal if a conviction followed and the issue remained relevant.

MOIR (MITCHELL JOHN) v. HM ADVOCATE (LEAVE TO APPEAL), [2004] UKPC D2, 2005 S.C. (P.C.) 1, Lord Bingham of Cornhill, Privy Council (Scotland).

5128. Delay–Devolution issues–Failure to afford priority after administrative error

[Human Rights Act 1998 (c.42) Sch.1 Part I Art.6(1).]

The appellant (C) was interviewed under caution in March 1998 and told in April 1999 that he would be prosecuted summarily. The case was called in August 1999; thereafter C lodged an appeal on a preliminary matter, which was refused in March 2002 and the case was remitted to the Sheriff. Following the consideration of and ultimate decision not to seek leave to appeal to the Privy Council, an administrative error resulted in no action being taken by the Sheriff in July 2002. The Procurator Fiscal noticed the error and in November 2002 wrote to the Sheriff seeking re enrollment. A diet was assigned for the calling of the case in April 2003. At that diet C lodged a devolution minute on the ground of unreasonable delay. R explained that the delay between July and November 2002 had been the result of time and resources spent on a high profile murder case, a change in Procurator Fiscal and the Procurator Fiscal depute's three month absence due to ill health. The minute was refused and C appealed to the High Court.

Held, allowing the appeal, that although there had been some explanation given for parts of the delay, the period taken as a whole could not be satisfactorily explained. No priority had been given to the case, as it should have been, upon its return to the Sheriff Court following the administrative error. If C had gone to trial in response to a diet which was to be fixed for April 23, 2003, his right to a fair and public hearing within a reasonable time, as protected by the Human Rights Act 1998 Sch.1 Part I Art.6(1) would have been breached. The complaint against C was accordingly dismissed.

CUNNINGHAM v. RALPH 2004 S.C.C.R. 549, Lord MacLean, Lord Hamilton, Temporary Judge CGB Nicholson Q.C., HCJ.

5129. Electronic monitoring requirements—Prescribed courts

REMOTE MONITORING REQUIREMENTS (PRESCRIBED COURTS) (SCOTLAND) REGULATIONS 2005, SSI 2005 141; made under the Criminal Procedure (Scotland) Act 1995 s.24B. In force: April 18, 2005; £3.00.

These Regulations prescribe that Glasgow, Stirling and Kilmarnock sheriff courts may impose a "remote monitoring requirement" as a condition of bail under the Criminal Procedure (Scotland) Act 1995 s.24A(1). This section provides that a person who has been refused bail may apply to the court for it to consider admitting him or her to bail subject to a movement restriction condition and a remote monitoring requirement. The Regulations also prescribe the High Court when hearing an appeal against a refusal of bail under this section; and prescribe certain courts which may impose remote monitoring requirements under s.24A(2) of the 1995 Act.

5130. Indictments—Formalities—Competence

[Criminal Procedure (Scotland) Act 1995 (c.46) s.64(4).]

C was charged on an indictment where the words "By Authority of Her Majesty's Advocate" were missing. The indictment was signed above the designation "Acting Procurator Fiscal". C made a plea to the competency of the indictment on the ground that it was a nullity for failure to comply with the provisions of the Criminal Procedure (Scotland) Act 1995 s.64(4). The sheriff repelled the submission. C appealed. The Crown argued that the ratio of *Christie (William) v. HM Advocate* 2004 J.C. 13, [2004] C.L.Y. 4658 applied and the indictment was competent.

Held, allowing the appeal, that the omission in the present case was more fundamental than that in *Christie*, and was fatal to the indictment as there was a complete failure to comply with s.64(4), *Christie* distinguished.

CRAWFORD (JAMES DAIR) v. HM ADVOCATE 2005 S.L.T. 1056, Lord Gill L.J.C., Lord Osborne, Lord Johnston, HCJ.

5131. Indictments—Service—Failure to serve indictment at domicile of citation on demolition of premises—Competence

[Misuse of Drugs Act 1971 (c.38) s.4(3)(b); Criminal Procedure (Scotland) Act 1995 (c.46) s.66; Act of Adjournal (Criminal Procedure Rules) 1996 (SI 1996 513) r.2.]

H was charged with a contravention of the Misuse of Drugs Act 1971 s.4(3)(b). He was liberated on bail, his domicile of citation having been specified as Flat 4/1, 2 Smeaton Street, Glasgow. Subsequently, the police tried to serve the copy indictment at this address but found that the flat had been demolished. On the procurator fiscal's instructions, the copy indictment was put through the letterbox of another flat which the police had been told was H's new address. At the first diet, the sheriff sustained H's plea that the indictment had not been competently served in terms of the Criminal Procedure (Scotland) Act 1995 s.66. The Crown appealed, arguing that service had been competently effected in terms of the Act of Adjournal (Criminal Procedure Rules) 1996 r.2.2(2)(d).

Held, refusing the bill of advocation, that (1) r.2.2(2)(d) did not enable the Crown to ignore the fact that a domicile of citation had been specified as a necessary prerequisite to granting bail to H, and (2) recourse to the general service provisions in r.2.3 did not advance the Crown's argument to any extent, and it followed that all the police officers could have done was affix the indictment to the site, as being the nearest place that could reasonably be regarded as equivalent to H's flat.

HM ADVOCATE v. HOLBEIN (JOHN) 2005 J.C. 178, Lord Cullen L.J.G., Lord Hamilton, Lord Sutherland, HCJ.

5132. Pleas—Change of plea—Assault to severe injury—Competence

R appealed against his conviction of assault to severe injury, permanent disfigurement and permanent impairment. R had pled guilty to the charge as libelled on the understanding, as accepted by the Crown, that he was guilty only on an art and part basis. His coaccused pled not guilty and was subsequently convicted on an amended indictment with the words "severe" and "permanent disfigurement and permanent impairment" deleted. R's solicitor then contacted the procurator fiscal, raising the possibility of an amendment to R's plea to reflect the verdict returned against the coaccused, which the procurator fiscal accepted by letter. At a subsequent hearing, the sheriff refused the motion for the accused to withdraw his guilty plea on the ground that it was incompetent. R submitted that (1) the letter bound the Crown in terms of which, the Crown had accepted the substance of the ground of the appeal and could not now oppose it; (2) the Crown, by amending the indictment during the trial, had accepted that the deleted averments could not be proved and thus, as the accused was only guilty art and part, he ought not to have been convicted in respect of those averments.

Held, dismissing the appeal, that (1) the letter sent by the procurator fiscal accepting the amendment was sent at a stage when the proceedings were no longer in the control of the Crown and thus was irrelevant. (2) A plea of guilty constituted a full admission of the libel and was not a conditional admission subject to reconsideration in the light of a subsequent decision of the court or a subsequent verdict in the trial of another party on the same charge, such a proposition being illogical as it would mean that if the coaccused had been acquitted, R would have been entitled to withdraw his plea in its entirety.

REEDIE (GRAHAM JOHN) v. HM ADVOCATE 2005 S.L.T. 742, Lord Gill L.J.C., Lord Penrose, Lord Macfadyen, HCJ.

5133. Right to fair trial—Delay—Three year delay between charge and appeal not unreasonable

[Human Rights Act 1998 (c.42) s.6(1), Sch.1 Part I Art.6.]

The appellant appealed against his conviction of being concerned in the supply of a controlled drug, claiming a breach of the Human Rights Act 1998 s.6(1). He had been charged on summary complaint in September 2000, convicted in March 2001 and sentenced to nine months' imprisonment. The appeal against conviction was brought in August 2001 and the papers were lodged, after delays, in February 2002. The hearing took place in September 2003 and the appeal was refused. The appellant was allowed time to lodge appropriate documents in respect of an appeal against sentence. The case was called in April 2004 and the appellant was granted leave to lodge his new appeal based on s.6(1) with regard to the delay between September 2000 and September 2003.

Held, dismissing the appeal, that in all the circumstances the period of delay could not be considered unreasonable. It was not such as to give rise to real concerns and was not incompatible with the right to a trial within a reasonable time under Sch.1 Part I Art.6 of the 1998 Act. The appellant had been at liberty throughout the three-year period and had been able to complete his university degree in that time.

McLARNON v. McLEOD; *sub nom.* McLARNON v. GRIFFITHS 2004 S.C.C.R. 397, Lord Hamilton, Lord Abernethy, Lord Philip, HCJ.

5134. Right to fair trial–Dock identification–Propriety of dock identification

[Criminal Procedure (Scotland) Act 1995 (c.46) s.92(1); Human Rights Act 1998 (c.42) Sch.1 Part I Art.6.]

The appellant (H) appealed against his conviction on charges of assault and robbery, asserting that the prosecution had infringed his rights under the Human Rights Act 1998 Sch.1 Part I Art.6(1) by relying on evidence from witnesses who identified him when he was sitting in the dock during his trial and that the prosecution had failed to disclose certain information to the defence. The first assault and robbery took place at a house and one victim identified H from police photographs but failed to pick him out on an identity parade. The second incident took place at a shop and again the victim identified H from police photographs. The victims identified H as the perpetrator in court and he was convicted. H submitted that the procedure of dock identification compelled the defendant to assist the Crown case against him contrary to his Art.6(1) right against self incrimination; that such evidence was so unfair and unreliable that it was incompatible with a fair trial under Art.6(1); and that the prosecution had infringed his rights under Art.6(1) by failing to disclose information about charges brought against the victims relating to drug dealing from the house where they were attacked.

Held, allowing the appeal, that (1) the quality of the witnesses' identification of H was not affected one way or the other by the fact that he was compelled to be present in court during his trial by virtue of the Criminal Procedure (Scotland) Act 1995 s.92(1). The requirement that the accused should usually be present throughout his trial was designed to promote his interests. Given the purpose of s.92(1), there was no basis for saying that the fact that a witness might identify the accused when he was present in court meant that his Art.6(1) right against self incrimination had been infringed. In the instant case, there was no suggestion that H had been asked to do anything to assist the Crown in proving the case against him, *Beattie (Jeffrey) v. Scott* 1990 J.C. 320, [1991] C.L.Y. 4568 considered. (2) Evidence derived from a witness identifying the accused in the dock was not, by its very nature, so unfair as to be incompatible with his Art.6(1) rights in all cases. Article 6 did not lay down that certain forms of evidence should be regarded as inadmissible. Questions of admissibility were left to the national legal systems. Article 6 guaranteed a fair trial and so, when the introduction of some form of evidence was said to have infringed the accused's Art.6 rights, the question was always whether admitting the evidence had resulted in the accused not having a fair trial in the circumstances of the particular case, considering such matters as his ability to challenge the evidence and any directions given by the judge to the jury. (3) A dock identification lacked the safeguards that were offered by an identification parade and the accused's position in the dock positively increased the risk of a wrong identification. In a case like the instant case, where a witness who had failed to pick out the accused at an identification parade was invited to try to identify him in court, the prosecutor was introducing into the trial a particular element of risk. Counsel for H had challenged the identification evidence and then cross examined the witnesses about it and the judge had directed the jury that the critical issue was the quality of the identification evidence. (4) In deciding whether H's trial was fair, the identification and non disclosure issues had to be considered together. (5) Information about the previous convictions of any witnesses to be led at the trial and information about any outstanding criminal charges they faced would be likely to be of material assistance to the proper preparation or presentation of the accused's defence. Under Art.6(1) the accused's agents and counsel were accordingly entitled to have that information disclosed so that they could prepare his defence. By failing to provide H with information about the outstanding charges against the victims, the Crown infringed his Art.6(1) right. (6) The failure to disclose information to the defence together with the reliance on the dock identifications were incompatible with

H's Art.6 right and taken together they resulted in an unfair trial. H's conviction was therefore quashed.

HOLLAND (JAMES) v. HM ADVOCATE, [2005] UKPC D1, 2005 S.C. (P.C.) 3, Lord Bingham of Cornhill, PC (Sc).

5135.   Right to fair trial–Judges–Temporary judges–Impartiality

[Law Reform (Miscellaneous Provisions) (Scotland) Act 1990 (c.40) s.35(3), Sch.4 para.6; Human Rights Act 1998 (c.42) Sch.1 Part I Art.6(1).]

K appeared before a temporary judge, a practising Queen's Counsel appointed under the Law Reform (Miscellaneous Provisions) (Scotland) Act 1990 s.35(3) for a three year period to act on such occasions as the Lord President might from time to time direct, on four charges of assault. K was sentenced to 10 years' imprisonment. K appealed against conviction and lodged a devolution issue that a temporary judge was not an independent and impartial tribunal in terms of the Human Rights Act 1998 Sch.1 Part I Art.6(1). K intimated that his appeal at the present stage would be restricted to his fourth ground of appeal relating to the impartiality of the temporary judge. K argued that the temporary judge lacked adequate security of tenure, that there should have been an automatic right to reappointment, that the independence and impartiality of the temporary judge was not secured by a proper legal framework, and that the absence of objective safeguards breached Art.6(1).

Held, dismissing the fourth ground of appeal and continuing the remaining grounds for determination by a court of three judges, that (1) the temporary judge had security of tenure at the material time and there was no need or justification for an automatic right of renewal of appointment where Sch.4 para.6 to the 1990 Act was designed to extend to a temporary judge, the status and immunities of a judge of the Court of Session or the High Court of Justiciary acting in that capacity, and the appointment was sufficient to carry the implication that it could not be terminated during its currency. (2) An informed observer had to be taken to be aware that appointments made by the Scottish Ministers were in practice on the recommendation of the Lord President, who was bound to act in a manner compatible with Convention rights, the latter's recommendations had always been followed by the Scottish Ministers, to which the Lord Advocate had never objected, and once the appointment had been made, the use of the temporary judge and allocation of cases to him was a matter for the Lord President. Thus a fair minded and informed observer, having regard to the circumstances said to give rise to a lack of independence and the information which could properly be regarded as being within his or her knowledge, particularly having regard both to the important role of the Lord President and minor role played by the Lord Advocate in relation to the appointment of the temporary judge, would conclude that he presented an appearance of independence and impartiality. (3) There was a satisfactory statutory framework in place to secure the independence and impartiality of the temporary judge in this case and there was no breach of Art.6(1).

KEARNEY (ARTHUR) v. HM ADVOCATE 2005 S.L.T. 74, Lord Kirkwood, Lord Hamilton, Lord Macfadyen, Lady Cosgrove, Lord Philip, HCJ.

5136.   Right to fair trial–Obligation of disclosure–Statements of Crown witness

[Scotland Act 1998 (c.46) s.57(2); European Convention on Human Rights 1950 Art.6(1).]

The appellant (S) appealed against his conviction for assault to severe injury, permanent disfigurement and permanent impairment. At the trial, a key witness for the Crown gave evidence that S had struck the victim with a hammer. The witness had not mentioned that fact in her statements to the police and had specifically stated that she had not seen a hammer being used. Although S was aware of the inconsistency, he was unable to cross-examine the witness as he had not been provided with copies of the statements. S's appeal was dismissed by the Appeal Court on the basis that it was for S to ask the Crown for the statements and, in the absence of any such request, there was no breach of duty on the part of the

Crown. S submitted that the act of the Lord Advocate in bringing proceedings, and seeking a conviction without having produced or disclosed the existence and contents of statements made to the police by a witness who was to corroborate the victim's account of the incident, was incompatible with his right to a fair trial under the European Convention on Human Rights 1950 Art.6(1).

Held, allowing the appeal, that (1) the statements had not been withheld on grounds of public interest. It was likely that the non disclosure of the statements was due to an error of judgment on the part of the prosecuting authorities. Whatever the reason, it had resulted in an inequality of arms at trial. The Crown had had in its possession statements that could have been used by S to undermine the witness's reliability and credibility. The statements were clearly likely to have been of material assistance given that the witness's evidence was an essential part of the Crown's case. It made no difference to the fairness of the trial that the Advocate Depute conducting the trial for the Crown was under the same disadvantage in not having access to the statements. The fact that the statements were not made available could not be attributed to any failure on the part of S. The duty of disclosure was on the Crown and it was a breach of that duty for the statements not to have been provided to S before the trial. S had been prejudiced because he had not been in a position to cross examine the witness when she changed her evidence about what she had said or not said to the police in interview. The unfairness to S had not been cured on appeal as the Appeal Court had erroneously assumed that the failure to produce the statements before trial was not due to any breach of duty on the part of the Crown and it had been for S to decide whether or not to ask for them. For those reasons, S's appeal under Art.6(1) succeeded, *McLeod (Alistair) v. HM Advocate (No.2)* 1998 J.C. 67, [1998] C.L.Y. 5607, *Edwards v. United Kingdom (A/247B)* (1993) 15 E.H.R.R. 417, [1993] C.L.Y. 2125 and *Rowe v. United Kingdom (28901/95)* (2000) 30 E.H.H.R. 1 considered. (2) By bringing the instant proceedings and seeking a conviction, the Lord Advocate had acted contrary to the Scotland Act 1998 s.57(2). On that basis the verdict was set aside and the conviction quashed as there had been a miscarriage of justice. The case was remitted to the High Court of Justiciary to consider whether authority should be granted to the Crown to bring a new prosecution. (3) (Obiter) the Crown Practice Statement on Disclosure, of November 2004, had changed the practice relating to the disclosure of Crown material in cases indicted in the High Court. The primary rule was that all witness statements, other than precognitions, in the possession of the Crown had to be disclosed. There was no duty on the defence to ask for them. There may be cases where a statement may need to be withheld or redacted in the public interest, but they were exceptions that the Crown would need to explain in the event of an application for disclosure by the defence.

SINCLAIR (ALVIN LEE) v. HM ADVOCATE, [2005] UKPC D2, 2005 S.C. (P.C.) 28, Lord Bingham of Cornhill, PC (Sc).

5137. **Right to fair trial–Sheriffs–Temporary sheriffs–Right to independent and impartial tribunal–Acquiescence**

[Human Rights Act 1998 (c.42) s.6(1), Sch.1 Part I Art.6(1); Scotland Act 1998 (c.46) s.57(2).]

X, three accused, were tried and sentenced before temporary sheriffs in respect of offences on separate summary complaints between 1999 and 2002. They sought suspension of their convictions in the light of *Starrs v. Ruxton* 2000 J.C. 208, [1999] C.L.Y. 5884, and lodged bills of suspension, some 23 to 29 months after their respective convictions. The Crown argued that X should be regarded as having acquiesced in challenging their convictions by reason of their delay in lodging the bills. X argued that (1) it was ultra vires of the procurator fiscals to proceed to prosecute before a temporary sheriff since it was incompatible with their rights under the Human Rights Act 1998 Sch.1 Part I Art.6(1); (2) there was a distinction between acquiescence and waiver and it was not possible to acquiesce in what was void; (3) the right of an accused to an independent and impartial tribunal was absolute and there was not even room for waiver; (4) *Lochridge v. Miller* 2002 S.L.T. 906, [2002] C.L.Y. 5493 had been wrongly decided, particularly given the observations in *HM Advocate v. R* [2002] UKPC D3, [2004] 1 A.C. 462, [2003] C.L.Y. 5410. The bills were heard before the High Court, which then remitted them to a court of five judges due to the uncertainty as to the possible effect of *HM Advocate v. R* on the availability in principle of acquiescence as a response to a challenge mounted against determinations made in respect of a conviction or sentence by a temporary sheriff.

Held, dismissing the appeal, that (1) the legal effect of X's convictions and sentences required to be considered in the light of the Scotland Act 1998 s.57(2), in conjunction with Art.6(1), as s.6(1) of the Human Rights Act had not been in force at the time of their convictions. (2) There was no question of the temporary sheriffs exceeding their jurisdiction in convicting or sentencing X as in their case, unlike that of the Lord Advocate, there was no statutory provision to the effect that they had no power to act in a way which was incompatible with X's Convention rights, they simply lacked the quality of independence and impartiality to which X were entitled. (3) Acquiescence was not incompatible with the right of an accused to an independent and impartial tribunal. (4) The bills were barred by acquiescence where, following *Starrs*, X knew that they had a well founded basis for challenging their convictions and sentences, it was likely that two of X had satisfied the penalties imposed, at least in part, without protest, there was ample time for the lodging of the bills prior to the Crown raising the question of waiver, and until the High Court sustained such a plea in August 2000, it was plainly arguable that a bill of suspension should not be refused on that ground, *Starrs* followed, *Lochridge* approved, *HM Advocate v. R* considered.

ROBERTSON v. FRAME; O'DALAIGH (AKA DALY) v. FRAME; RUDDY v. GRIFFITHS; *sub nom.* ROBERTSON v. HIGSON; RUDDY v. PROCURATOR FISCAL, PERTH 2005 J.C. 210, Lord Cullen L.J.G., Lord Hamilton, Lord Macfadyen, Lady Cosgrove, Lord Philip, HCJ.

5138. Rules—Community reparation orders

ACT OF ADJOURNAL (CRIMINAL PROCEDURE RULES AMENDMENT NO.2) (MISCELLANEOUS) 2005, SSI 2005 160; made under the Criminal Procedure (Scotland) Act 1995 s.305. In force: March 31, 2005; £3.00.

This Act of Adjournal amends the Criminal Procedure Rules 1996 (SI 1996 513) to make provisions consequent upon the Antisocial Behaviour etc. (Scotland) Act 2004, which makes a Community Reparation Order available as a sentence. It also makes provision that an incidental application by the prosecutor when the prosecutor's office is closed can be unsigned.

5139. Rules—Consequential amendments

ACT OF ADJOURNAL (CRIMINAL PROCEDURE RULES AMENDMENT) (CRIMINAL PROCEDURE (AMENDMENT) (SCOTLAND) ACT 2004) 2005, SSI 2005 44; made under the Criminal Procedure (Scotland) Act 1995 s.305. In force: February 1, 2005; £7.50.

This Act of Adjournal amends the Act of Adjournal (Criminal Procedure Rules) 1996 (SI 1996 513) to make provision consequential upon amendments to the Criminal Procedure (Scotland) Act 1995 by the Criminal Procedure (Amendment) (Scotland) Act 2004 and to make various other minor amendments.

5140. Rules—Mental health—Treatment orders

ACT OF ADJOURNAL (CRIMINAL PROCEDURE RULES AMENDMENT NO.4) (MENTAL HEALTH (CARE AND TREATMENT) (SCOTLAND) ACT 2003) 2005, SSI 2005 457; made under the Criminal Procedure (Scotland) Act 1995 s.305. In force: October 5, 2005; £3.00.

This Act of Adjournal amends the Criminal Procedure Rules 1996 (SI 1996 513) to make provision consequential upon amendments to the Criminal Procedure

(Scotland) Act 1995 by the Mental Health (Care and Treatment) (Scotland) Act 2003. It inserts new rules to set out procedure for a written application to the court for assessment orders or treatment orders under the 1995 Act. There are also provided rules of procedure for the court to make such orders ex proprio motu. A new rule is provided for procedure to allow the variation of an assessment order or review of a treatment order. New rule 7.6 sets out a procedure to allow an early diet to be fixed in certain circumstances where an interim compulsion order has been made by the court. Finally, rules provide for intimation on certain parties where the court changes the hospital specified in an assessment, treatment, interim compulsion, or compulsion order or hospital direction. It also inserts forms into the appendix for a written application for an assessment or treatment order, and forms of interlocutor where a hearing has been fixed that include a warrant to bring the accused person or offender to court.

5141. Rules–Sexual offences–Prevention orders

ACT OF ADJOURNAL (CRIMINAL PROCEDURE RULES AMENDMENT NO.5) (SEXUAL OFFENCES PREVENTION ORDERS) 2005, SSI 2005 472; made under the Criminal Procedure (Scotland) Act 1995 s.305. In force: October 7, 2005; £3.00.

This Act of Adjournal amends the Criminal Procedure Rules 1996 (SI 1996 513) to make provision consequential upon the application of provisions of the Sexual Offences Act 2003 to Scotland by the Protection of Children and Prevention of Sexual Offences Act 2005. In particular, new rules are inserted to provide a form of Sexual Offences Prevention Order and a procedure for applying for the variation, renewal or discharge of such an order.

5142. Rules–Vulnerable witnesses

ACT OF ADJOURNAL (CRIMINAL PROCEDURE RULES AMENDMENT NO.3) (VULNERABLE WITNESSES (SCOTLAND) ACT 2004) 2005, SSI 2005 188; made under the Criminal Procedure (Scotland) Act 1995 s.305. In force: April 1, 2005; £3.50.

This Act of Adjournal amends the Criminal Procedure Rules 1996 (SI 1996 513) to make provision consequential upon amendments to the Criminal Procedure (Scotland) Act 1995 by the Vulnerable Witnesses (Scotland) Act 2004. It inserts a new Rule to make provision for a notice by the prosecution of an intention to rely on a presumption as to identification by a witness prior to trial and a notice of intention to challenge that presumption by the accused; makes provision for lodging a child witness notice and reviewing the arrangements made for vulnerable witnesses to give evidence; and adds new forms.

5143. Rules–Vulnerable witnesses–Evidence on commission

ACT OF ADJOURNAL (CRIMINAL PROCEDURE RULES AMENDMENT NO.6) (VULNERABLE WITNESSES (SCOTLAND) ACT 2004) (EVIDENCE ON COMMISSION) 2005, SSI 2005 574; made under the Criminal Procedure (Scotland) Act 1995 s.305. In force: November 30, 2005; £3.00.

This Act of Adjournal amends the Criminal Procedure Rules 1996 (SI 1996 513) to make provision consequential upon amendments to the Criminal Procedure (Scotland) Act 1995 by the Vulnerable Witness (Scotland) Act 2004. It inserts new rules into the 1996 Rules on Evidence by Vulnerable Witnesses for taking evidence from a vulnerable witness by a commissioner. The new rules set out a procedure for the appointment of a commissioner and determination by the commissioner of the place and date for the commission to be held. The new rules also provide procedure for sealing and retaining copies of the video recording of the commission proceedings and for applications by the accused for leave to be present in the room during those proceedings. It also inserts a form of application for the accused to be present at a commission.

5144. Sexual offences—Notification requirements—Prescribed police stations

SEXUAL OFFENCES ACT 2003 (PRESCRIBED POLICE STATIONS) (SCOTLAND) AMENDMENT REGULATIONS 2005, SSI 2005 9; made under the Sexual Offences Act 2003 s.87. In force: February 18, 2005; £3.00.

These Regulations amend the Schedule to the Sexual Offences Act 2003 (Prescribed Police Stations) (Scotland) Regulations 2004 (SSI 2004 137). By virtue of the Sexual Offences Act 2003, relevant offenders must fulfil their notification requirements under that Act by attending any police station in their local police area which is prescribed for this purpose in regulations. The 2004 Regulations prescribed those police stations. These Regulations amend the principal regulations by removing the Divisional Police Headquarters located in Forfar from the list of prescribed police stations in the Tayside police area.

5145. Sexual offences—Notification requirements—Prescribed police stations

SEXUAL OFFENCES ACT 2003 (PRESCRIBED POLICE STATIONS) (SCOTLAND) AMENDMENT (NO.2) REGULATIONS 2005, SSI 2005 156; made under the Sexual Offences Act 2003 s.87. In force: May 12, 2005; £3.00.

These Regulations amend the Sexual Offences Act 2003 (Prescribed Police Stations) (Scotland) Regulations 2004 (SSI 2004 137) to remove the Craignure Police Station located in the Isle of Mull from the list of prescribed police station in the Strathclyde police area, and add Cambuslang Police Station in Glasgow, Tobermory Police Station in the Isle of Mull and Lamlash Police Station located in the Isle of Arran to the list of prescribed police stations for that police area.

5146. Sheriff courts—Vulnerable and intimidated witnesses

CRIMINAL PROCEDURE (AMENDMENT) (SCOTLAND) ACT 2004 (INCIDENTAL, SUPPLEMENTAL AND CONSEQUENTIAL PROVISIONS) ORDER 2005, SSI 2005 40; made under the Criminal Procedure (Amendment) (Scotland) Act 2004 s.26. In force: in accordance with Art.1; £3.00.

This Order makes amendments to the Criminal Procedure (Scotland) Act 1995 and the Vulnerable Witnesses (Scotland) Act 2004. The 2004 Act is amended to clarify that new s.81 (5) of the 1995 Act applies in relation to solemn cases in the sheriff court; to ensure that the provisions of s.92(2B) (b) and (2E) of the 1995 Act relating to the court appointing a solicitor to act for the accused in his absence do not apply where s.288E of the 1995 Act applies or where an order is made under s.288F(2) of that Act because in those circumstances s.288D of the 1995 Act makes provision relating to the appointment by the court of a solicitor to act for the accused; and to clarify that intimation of an application for a change of bail address may be sent to the local procurator fiscal and that this will satisfy the requirement to intimate to the Crown Agent. The 1995 Act is amended to clarify that a court at the first diet must deal with child witness notices and vulnerable witness applications that have been appointed to be dealt with at that diet.

5147. Summary procedure—Adjournment—Sheriff's competence to adjourn trial diet where case under appeal

[Criminal Procedure (Scotland) Act 1995 (c.46) s.174.]

M appealed to the High Court against an adjournment made by the Sheriff. M had been charged with road traffic offences on summary complaint and had lodged a devolution minute. The minute was refused by the Sheriff, leave to appeal under the Criminal Procedure (Scotland) Act 1995 s.174 was granted and the case was adjourned. The trial diet came before the Sheriff but was further adjourned on the basis that the appeal had not yet been heard. On appeal, M argued that the effect of s.174(2) was that only the High Court had power to make such an order.

Held, refusing the bill, that only the High Court had power to postpone a trial diet which was the subject of a s.174 appeal. However, what the Sheriff had done was to order an adjournment, which was an independent procedure from postponement. A diet was postponed when its date was altered in advance of the original date, but in the instant case the diet had called on its original date and been adjourned, *Reith v. Bates (Ross)* 1998 J.C. 224, [1998] C.L.Y. 5631 and *Vannet v. Milligan* 1998 S.L.T. 1018, [1998] C.L.Y. 5622 applied.

MITCHELL v. REITH 2004 S.C.C.R. 433, Lord Marnoch, Lord Hamilton, Temporary Judge Sir Gerald Gordon Q.C., HCJ.

5148. Summary procedure—Complaints—First page of complaint unsigned—Validity

[Criminal Procedure (Scotland) Act 1995 (c.46) s.138; Act of Adjournal (Criminal Procedure Rules) 1996 (SI 1996 513) Sch.2 para.16a.]

The procurator fiscal appealed against a decision that a complaint was invalid. M had been charged on summary complaint which took the form of two pages stapled together. The first page set out the charges and the second page was simply the procurator fiscal's signature and two blank *pro forma* forms. There was nothing on the second page to indicate that it was connected to the first. A competency hearing was held on the basis that the complaint had not been signed, as was required under the Criminal Procedure (Scotland) Act 1995 s.138 and the Act of Adjournal (Criminal Procedure Rules) 1996 Sch.2 para.16a. The Sheriff concluded that the complaint was not valid.

Held, dismissing the appeal, that (1) the signature of the procurator fiscal was an essential feature of a complaint. (2) There was nothing on the second page to indicate it formed part of the complaint. (3) There was no content in either page that related to content in the other and, accordingly, the complaint was not valid, *Milne v. Normand* 1994 S.L.T. 760, [1994] C.L.Y. 5601 distinguished.

McLEOD v. MILLAR; McLEOD v. TIERNEY 2004 S.C.C.R. 419, Lord Osborne, Lord Abernethy, Lord McCluskey, HCJ.

5149. Summary procedure—Defence's right of reply at trial—Defence not invited to speak after prosecution

[Road Traffic Act 1988 (c.52) s.2; Criminal Procedure (Scotland) Act 1995 (c.46) s.161.]

The appellant (W) brought a bill of suspension seeking the suspension of her convictions for assault and breach of the Road Traffic Act 1988 s.2 on the ground that her solicitor had been denied the right to speak last, as conferred by the Criminal Procedure (Scotland) Act 1995 s.161. M had been tried on summary complaint in the sheriff court where the prosecution was invited to speak after W's solicitor on the circumstance in which two prosecution witnesses had given statements to the media, although the prosecution was not expressly given the opportunity to reply to the solicitor's comments.

Held, dismissing the appeal, that the right conferred by s.161 was mandatory and not directory in nature and even in the case of a breach the proceedings were not automatically a nullity, *Drummond (Andrew Page) v. HM Advocate* 2003 S.L.T. 295, [2003] C.L.Y. 5431 and *HM Advocate v. Graham (Frederick)* 1985 S.L.T. 498, [1985] C.L.Y. 3912 considered. In the instant case there had been no oppression on the part of the sheriff and justice had been both done and seen to be done.

Observed: insofar as s.161 conferred a right, the proper approach was to determine whether the right had been denied to the accused.

WATSON v. GRIFFITHS 2004 S.C.C.R. 723, Lord Marnoch, Lord Philip, Temporary Judge CGB Nicholson Q.C., HCJ.

5150. Summary procedure—Jurisdiction—Trial of charge of failing to stop and report accident—Conditional offer offences

[Road Traffic Act 1988 (c.52) s.170(4), s.170(7); Road Traffic Offenders Act 1988 (c.53) s.10; Criminal Procedure (Scotland) Act 1995 (c.46) s.7(9).]

W appealed to the High Court against a decision that the district court had jurisdiction to try an offence under the Road Traffic Act 1988 s.170(4). W had been charged on summary complaint with failing to stop and report an accident in contravention of s.170(4). W argued that, pursuant to the Road Traffic Offenders Act 1988 s.10, a district court lacked jurisdiction to try any offence involving obligatory endorsement. The question for the court was whether a breach of s.170(4) was "an offence in respect of which a conditional offer may be sent" within the meaning of s.75 to s.77. If it was, then the district court had jurisdiction.

Held, allowing the appeal, that the intention of the legislation was to direct less serious traffic offences to the district court but an offence under s.170(4) was significantly more serious as it involved, *inter alia*, obligatory endorsement, and the district court did not have jurisdiction to try it. It was the intention of Parliament that, with regard to s.170 offences, only a breach of the less serious s.170(7) was to be a conditional offer offence. The case could not be remitted to the district court under the Criminal Procedure (Scotland) Act 1995 s.7(9) and then to the sheriff court, because s.7(9) was not applicable in cases where the charges were not punishable by imprisonment. There would also be difficulty in remitting a case to a court which had been held to have no jurisdiction. Further, s.7(9) did not expressly confer a right on the district court to remit to a lower court.

WILSON v. SHIELS; *sub nom.* WILSON v. STOTT 2004 J.C. 169, Lord Kirkwood, Lord Wheatley, Temporary Judge CGB Nicholson Q.C., HCJ.

5151. Trials—Judge's charge—Judge's failure to direct jury to approach identification evidence with care—Application of Moorov doctrine

B appealed against his convictions of assault with intent to rob and robbery. Both offences had been committed in the same area within a five-day period and the Crown sought to apply *Moorov (Samuel) v. HM Advocate* 1930 J.C. 68. In the first charge the complainer identified B at an identification parade and in court as the man who had punched him. In the second charge the complainer, a taxi driver, also identified B and refused to be shaken in his identification. B lodged a special defence incriminating another man, A, who, when called as a witness, admitted the second offence. A's blood was found on a syringe cap found in the taxi. On appeal, B argued that the Sheriff had (1) misdirected the jury in failing to direct them to regard the identification evidence with particular care; (2) undermined B's defence by suggesting that A's evidence lacked credibility; (3) erred in repelling the submission of no case to answer.

Held, allowing the appeal, that (1) the particular circumstances of each case governed the necessity and level of warning required and given by the trial judge to the jury with regard to the identification evidence. In the instant case, given that the identification evidence was crucial and strongly challenged, the Sheriff had failed to give the jury adequate direction and this constituted material misdirection. (2) The Sheriff had misdirected the jury with regard to A's credibility and the forensic evidence, resulting in a miscarriage of justice. (3) If it had been necessary to do so the Court would have concluded that the Crown's evidence had not been sufficient for conviction. There were numerous dissimilarities between the offences and the similarities were not sufficient to infer a pattern of criminal behaviour systematically pursued by B, *Moorov* distinguished and *Ogg (Peter Allan) v. HM Advocate* 1938 J.C. 152 considered.

BEATON (MICHAEL ANTHONY) v. HM ADVOCATE 2004 S.C.C.R. 467, Lord Kirkwood, Lord Hamilton, Lord Johnston, HCJ.

5152. Trials—Judges—Bias—Trial judge reading health and safety report before withholding part from defence—Risk of bias

[Health and Safety at Work etc. Act 1974 (c.37) s.3, s.33; Criminal Procedure (Scotland) Act 1995 (c.46) s.93.]

T, a public gas transporter charged with contraventions of the Health and Safety at Work etc. Act 1974 s.3 and s.33(1) in respect of an explosion resulting in fatalities, challenged decisions of Lord Carloway at a preliminary diet whereby he rejected submissions that he should not preside at T's trial or any pre trial proceedings relating thereto, and that a simultaneous transcription service using software such as LiveNote should be provided during the trial. T had presented a minute seeking recovery of a report by the Health and Safety Executive which followed an investigation of the circumstances of the explosion. The Crown opposed production. At the end of the discussion of the minute, Lord Carloway requested a copy of the report and in due course ordered the production of Pt.1, which contained general information on the nature and extent of the investigations and a summary of the conclusions of fact, but not Pt.2, which dealt with legal considerations, on the basis that it was a confidential communication to the procurator fiscal. T submitted that (1) while they did not seek to suggest procedural irregularity in Lord Carloway addressing the Crown's claim of confidentiality by looking at the report, they did not know to what extent his views about the evidence and their culpability might be coloured by his reading of the contents, which they could do nothing to counteract; (2) there was a danger that Lord Carloway might attach special significance to factors relied on by the Health and Safety Executive which were the subject of evidence, further, the Crown might place emphasis on such factors; (3) the context in which their application for the use of LiveNote at the trial had been made was that it had been suggested by a majority of the members of the court which had determined an earlier appeal as one of a number of procedural safeguards which would operate to protect their right to a fair trial, allowing the presiding judge and counsel to have an accurate and readily accessible record of the evidence led, which would be a significant aid in a potentially complex trial, and in the light of those judicial observations, they had a legitimate expectation that their application would be granted.

Held, dismissing the appeal, that (1) T had failed to demonstrate an objective basis for their fears of apparent bias on Lord Carloway's part. The mere fact that a judge required to determine whether certain evidence should not be disclosed to the defence was not sufficient to disqualify him from sitting as the trial judge. Part 2 of the report did not contain any statement of fact which was not also contained in Pt.1; thus T were not denied access to significant factual material available to the prosecution and the court, and were in a position to adduce evidence at trial, if they saw fit, to meet such factors bearing on culpability as might emerge from the report. Moreover, it would be plain to any fair minded and informed observer that the trial judge's approach to sentence, should that arise, would be based on evidence led at the trial and on any submissions made thereon, not on material which had come to his notice for another purpose prior thereto. (2) So far as concerned the making of a record under the Criminal Procedure (Scotland) Act 1995 s.93, it was open neither to Lord Carloway nor to the present court to direct that the record be made by means of LiveNote or any other equivalent service; further, on a fair reading of the appellate judges' observations, no ruling, binding on Lord Carloway or otherwise, was made that LiveNote should be the means of officially recording the trial proceedings, nor could any expectation of that mode of official record have legitimately been entertained.

TRANSCO PLC v. HM ADVOCATE (NO.3) 2005 J.C. 194, Lord Cullen L.J.G., Lord Osborne, Lord Hamilton, HCJ.

5153. Trials—Juries—Alleged prejudice of jurors—Miscarriage of justice

Two accused (G) were convicted of murder along with three other persons in 1992. Their cases were referred to the High Court by the Scottish Criminal Cases Review Commission in 2004, following an investigation into allegations of impropriety on the part of certain members of the jury. G alleged that a miscarriage of justice had arisen from the fact that during the trial, one of the jurors had viewed the locus while in the general area for reasons connected with his employment, then told other jurors about the visit, and that the brother of two co accused (X), who were convicted of culpable homicide, had formed intimate relationships with two female jurors, during the course of the trial. Under reference to *Aitken (William) v. Wood* 1921 J.C. 84, G submitted that the locus visit should be seen as meaning either that the juror had taken evidence outwith their presence or that he had acquired knowledge outwith the scope of the evidence given in court. Appeals against conviction on those grounds had previously been refused.

Held, dismissing the appeals, that (1) it could not be said that a juror's visit to the locus resulted in any miscarriage of justice where crimes were commonly committed in public places, it could hardly be objected to if a juror's journey for his own legitimate private purposes necessarily took him along the street in question and it was difficult to see that the position should be materially different merely because driving through the street constituted a diversion. Furthermore, the visit was made known to the trial judge who made it clear to the jury that they required to proceed only on the evidence led in the courtroom. (2) It did not follow from the fact that the trial judge would either have discharged the jurors or deserted the trial pro loco et tempore, had knowledge of the intimate relationships become known, that the convictions necessarily constituted a miscarriage of justice, as while it could be inferred that the female jurors could have been favourably inclined towards X, there was no basis for translating that possible partiality into a bias or prejudice against G, *Aitken* considered.

GRAY (WILLIAM) v. HM ADVOCATE; O'ROURKE (JAMES BERNARD) v. HM ADVOCATE 2005 J.C. 233, Lord Gill L.J.C., Lord Osborne, Lord Eassie, HCJ.

5154. **Trials–Jury directions–Judge's charge–Misdirection–Concert–Coaccused striking fatal blow**

[Criminal Procedure (Scotland) Act 1995 (c.46) s.119.]

The appellant (D) appealed against his conviction of murder. The victim had sustained a number of stab wounds after he was attacked by D and a coaccused in his home. It was accepted that the coaccused had struck the fatal blow, although the victim's wife, who had witnessed the incident, did not see a knife being used. D was thereafter convicted on the basis of concert and sentenced to life imprisonment with a punishment part of 12 years. D contended that (1) the judge had misdirected the jury on the law by omitting to charge them that they had to consider the evidence relating to each of the accused separately in respect of whether they had the mens rea for murder or culpable homicide; (2) the judge had misdirected the jury on concert when he stated that they had to be satisfied that D ought to have known or to have had the means of knowledge that his coaccused was going to use the knife before they could convict him of the consequences of a knife being used, implying that it was not necessary for D to have actual knowledge that his coaccused was using or was going to use the knife so long as he had the means of knowledge; (3) D's case was similar to *Peden (Marie) v. HM Advocate* 2003 S.L.T. 1047, [2003] C.L.Y. 5418, where the judge was held to have misdirected the jury in relation to concert when directing them that even if the appellant did not know that her coaccused had a knife, they could convict her if they considered that she ought to know that he did; it was also significant that the wife of the deceased in *Peden* had witnessed the incident but had not seen a knife being used. The Crown argued that *Peden* could be distinguished as there had been three blows by a knife and it had not been clear that the appellant had been involved in the attack from beginning to end; there was an irresistible inference in the instant case that D had seen his coaccused using the knife, even if not using it himself; even if there had been a misdirection, it had not resulted in a miscarriage of justice as there had been no room in this case for imputed knowledge.

Held, allowing the appeal, that (1) D could only have been convicted of murder if the jury were satisfied that it could be inferred from the evidence that D knew that his coaccused had a knife and was using it, and with that knowledge, had continued with the joint attack on the deceased. (2) The trial judge had misdirected the jury on concert, which had resulted in a miscarriage of justice where the inference that D had to have known that his coaccused was using a knife on the victim was not one, on the evidence, which the jury were entitled to draw. The possibility that the jury might have convicted on the basis of what D could have known, rather than what he actually knew, could not be excluded. The court granted authority to bring a new prosecution under the Criminal Procedure (Scotland) Act 1995 s.119, *Peden* considered.

DEMPSEY (STEPHEN) v. HM ADVOCATE 2005 J.C. 252, Lord Kirkwood, Lord Marnoch, Lord Penrose, HCJ.

5155. Trials–No case to answer–Miscarriage of justice

[Wildlife and Countryside Act 1981 (c.69) s.1 (5) (a); Criminal Procedure (Scotland) Act 1995 (c.46) s.106, s.175.]

G appealed against his conviction for intentionally disturbing a golden eagle whilst it was building a nest, or was in, on, or near a nest containing eggs or young, contrary to the Wildlife and Countryside Act 1981 s.1 (5) (a). His submission of no case to answer on the basis that there was insufficient evidence to identify him was rejected. G accepted that he was the person to whom a Crown witness had spoken near the nest but denied trying to get up to it. The question of whether the sheriff was entitled to repel G's submission was answered in the negative on June 25, 2004, thus leaving the remaining question for the present court of whether the sheriff was entitled to convict.

Held, allowing the appeal, that (1) the scope for a miscarriage of justice under the Criminal Procedure (Scotland) Act 1995 s.106 and s.175 might arise in a wide variety of circumstances but the question was not whether the circumstances constituted themselves a miscarriage of justice, but whether the conviction of the accused in those circumstances was a miscarriage. (2) Whether a miscarriage had occurred could only be determined by looking at a ruling in the context of the whole trial and in the present case it was plain that the effect of the sheriff's erroneous ruling was that he had wrongly deprived G of an acquittal on the charge and instead had placed him in the position that in order to give evidence in his own defence, he would have to supply the deficiency in the prosecution case. (3) There had been a miscarriage of justice where G's conviction was secured in circumstances in which he should have been acquitted immediately after the close of the prosecution evidence and should not have been required to consider giving evidence on his own behalf.

GONSHAW v. BAMBER (NO.2) 2004 S.L.T. 1270, Lord Cullen L.J.G., Lord Osborne, Lord Macfadyen, HCJ.

5156. Trials–Witness statements–Duty of disclosure–Miscarriage of justice

K was convicted of culpable homicide along with a coaccused. There was ample evidence that his coaccused had stabbed the deceased two or three times. The Crown case against K depended entirely on eyewitness testimony, and in particular that of the deceased's sister and her husband, who were the only eyewitnesses to an actual assault by K on the deceased. The case was referred to the court by the Scottish Criminal Cases Review Commission following an investigation into whether the Crown should have disclosed to the defence evidence that the position of the witnesses had considerably vacillated between that adopted before the trial and that adopted at the trial. K submitted that the Crown had been under a duty to disclose statements which had been made to the police by, among others, the deceased's sister, which gave different versions of the alleged assault, including one in which she said that K did not stab the deceased. The Crown conceded that these statements should have been disclosed, but argued that given the other eyewitness evidence, and the fact that the statement which differed the most was one made while under the influence of medication, there had been no miscarriage of justice.

Held, allowing the appeal and quashing the conviction, that there were material contradictions between the evidence of the deceased's sister and the statements she had made prior to the trial, and bearing in mind that the Crown relied on her evidence in court as being credible and reliable, disclosure of the latter would have been likely to have been of real importance to the defence, and the failure to do so had resulted in a miscarriage of justice.

KIDD (STEWART ANDERSON) v. HM ADVOCATE 2005 S.L.T. 375, Lord Kirkwood, Lady Cosgrove, Lord Philip, HCJ.

5157. Victim impact statements—Prescribed courts—Revocation

VICTIM STATEMENTS (PRESCRIBED COURTS) (SCOTLAND) REVOCATION ORDER 2005, SSI 2005 612; made under the Criminal Justice (Scotland) Act 2003 s.14. In force: November 30, 2005; £3.00.

This Order revokes the Victim Statements (Prescribed Courts) (Scotland) Order 2003 (SSI 2003 563) which prescribed the sheriff courts of Ayr, Edinburgh and Kilmarnock, and the High Court sitting at Edinburgh and Kilmarnock, for the purposes of the Criminal Justice (Scotland) Act 2003.

5158. Victim impact statements—Prescribed offences—Revocation

VICTIM STATEMENTS (PRESCRIBED OFFENCES) (SCOTLAND) REVOCATION ORDER 2005, SSI 2005 526; made under the Criminal Justice (Scotland) Act 2003 s.14. In force: November 25, 2005; £3.00.

This Order revokes the Victim Statements (Prescribed Offences) (Scotland) Order 2003 (SSI 2003 441), the Victim Statements (Prescribed Offences) (Scotland) Amendment Order 2003 (SSI 2003 519) and the Victim Statements (Prescribed Offences) (Scotland) Amendment (No.2) Order 2004 (SSI 2004 287). These Orders prescribe offences for the purposes of the Criminal Justice (Scotland) Act 2003.

5160. Warrants—Arrest warrants—Delay—Execution of warrant in order to serve sentence

W, who had received consistent concurrent sentences of five months' and two months' imprisonment following convictions convicted of racially aggravated breach of the peace and imprisonment for assault to severe injury, petitioned the nobile officium for suspension of a warrant for her apprehension dated September 10, 2003. W had appealed against sentence and had been granted interim liberation on June 26. Leave to appeal had been refused. On September 10, an appeal against that decision was refused and the warrant was issued. Nothing was done by police to execute the warrant from the time they received it, on September 22, 2003, until September 17, 2004, after which four unsuccessful visits were made to W's house. W argued that the authorities had failed to act with due diligence in the execution of the warrant and there were no special circumstances which would justify its execution after such undue delay. The Crown did not oppose the petition.

Held, granting suspension, that it would be oppressive to the accused if the authorities were now to execute the warrant 15 months after it was issued, *Beglan, Petitioner* 2002 S.L.T. 1175, [2002] C.L.Y. 5487 followed.

WAUGH (JEAN) v. HM ADVOCATE 2005 S.L.T. 451, Lord Gill L.J.C., Lord Marnoch, Lord Penrose, HCJ.

5161. Warrants—Intimate searches—Refusal to submit to internal search—Attempt to defeat ends of justice

The appellant (V) appealed against his conviction for attempting to defeat the ends of justice following his refusal to submit to an intimate search. V had been detained in a police station and a warrant had been obtained to take him to hospital to be examined by a doctor and a radiologist. The warrant was obtained on the basis that the police suspected V of having concealed controlled drugs internally. When he refused to co-operate with the examinations, V was arrested and not taken to hospital. V argued that his refusal to cooperate was not an offence because the terms of the warrant were such that his consent was not required. The respondent procurator fiscal argued that there had been no point in taking V to the hospital because the police were aware that no doctor would carry out the required examinations without V's consent.

Held, allowing the appeal, that V should have been taken to the hospital to put his lack of cooperation to the test. The doctors might have been satisfied with an X-ray, which would have been much less invasive than an intimate search, but as matters stood V had committed no crime by refusing to cooperate at the police station. His conviction was quashed accordingly.

VAUGHAN v. GRIFFITHS 2004 S.C.C.R. 537, Lord MacLean, Lady Cosgrove, Lord McEwan, HCJ.

5162. Warrants—Search warrants—Validity—Misuse of drugs

[Misuse of Drugs Act 1971 (c.38) s.23(3).]

L was charged with contraventions of the Misuse of Drugs Act 1971. L sought suspension of a search warrant relating to a flat on the basis that the application was erroneous. L averred that the police had general information about drugs being dealt by two females from the vicinity of the premises and attempts to identify the occupier of the premises had been unsuccessful. Prior to seeking the warrant, police officers had witnessed a woman coming from the block of flats, seen her acting suspiciously, arrested her, found drugs in her possession and had taken her to the police station where she had given her address as being elsewhere. L argued there was no direct evidence linking the woman with the flat. Furthermore, there was bad faith on the part of the police as, when they sought the warrant, they knew that the woman had given an address elsewhere and had given deliberately incomplete information to the justice of the peace.

Held, refusing the bill, that s.23(3) of the Act made it clear that a warrant might be granted if the justice was satisfied that there was a "reasonable ground for suspecting" the necessary circumstances as defined. The court had no hesitation in concluding that the information before the justice amply entitled her to grant the warrant, as the fact that the police had failed to inform the justice that the woman, when detained, had given an address elsewhere as her residence did not in any way undermine the significance of the information put before the justice nor demonstrate that there was any bad faith on the part of the police, and an averment by the police that the flat was "occupied" by the woman was not in any way inconsistent with residence elsewhere.

LAWSON v. HUTCHISON 2005 S.L.T. 872, Lord Osborne, Lord Philip,Temporary Judge CGB Nicholson QC, HCJ.

DAMAGES

5163. Loss of society—Children—Grief and sorrow—Averments of psychiatric injury—Relevancy to claim

[Damages (Scotland) Act 1976 (c.13) s.1 (4).]

The pursuers (R), the parents of a 15 year old girl killed in a road accident, sought damages from the defender (P), the driver of the vehicle. The deceased had been taken by air ambulance to hospital but had not regained consciousness and had died the next day. R argued that they had suffered distress and anxiety in contemplation of their daughter's suffering before she died. They claimed that both had been absent from work and had suffered bereavement reactions, stress, depression and adjustment disorders. R sought a jury trial. P argued that (1) reference to the deceased's suffering was irrelevant since she had not regained consciousness; (2) there was a difference between grief and sorrow caused by bereavement and other psychiatric disorders, which would be irrelevant to support a claim under the Damages (Scotland) Act 1976 s.1 (4) (b).

Held, giving judgment accordingly, that (1) s.1 (4) (a) did not apply in cases of sudden or instant death or where the deceased was unconscious and did not regain consciousness before death. (2) In a s.1 (4) (b) claim, the damages would only be for the grief and sorrow of a relative caused by the death of a loved one. This would cover a bereavement reaction, but not an illness or pathological condition from which a person suffered as the result of the death, therefore R's averments of psychiatric illness were irrelevant. There was a distinction between natural grief and psychiatric illness, and the latter could not be the subject of a claim under s.1 (4) (b) of the 1976 Act, *Gillies v. Lynch (No.1)*

2002 S.L.T. 1420, [2003] C.L.Y. 5439 not applied. R's arguments relating to loss of wages were relevant, but only for the purpose of demonstrating the extent of the grief and sorrow resulting from the death of their daughter.

ROSS v. PRYDE 2004 Rep. L.R.129,Temporary Judge RF Macdonald Q.C., OH.

5164. Loss of society–Jury trial–Complexity of medical evidence

[Damages (Scotland) Act 1976 (c.13) s.1 (4) (b).]

In an action for damages commenced by the pursuer (G) against the defenders (L) under the Damages (Scotland) Act 1976 s.1 (4) (b), L applied to amend their pleadings. G had averred that her daughter's death in a road traffic accident had caused her to develop certain psychiatric conditions. L wished to amend their pleadings so as to include G's pre existing chronic depressive disorder. L argued that the amendment they had introduced was complex and rendered the case unsuitable for a jury trial.

Held, granting the application, that whether complex issues of medical fact rendered a case unsuitable for jury trial was a matter of degree. One way of determining the issue was to consider if the trial judge would have difficulty directing the jury. In the instant case, it would be possible to give directions to a jury. The medical questions, although more complex than they were prior to the amendment, could not be considered so complex that the case be rendered unsuitable for trial by jury.

GILLIES v. LYNCH (NO.2) 2005 Rep. L.R. 9, Lord Macfadyen, OH.

5165. Loss of society–Relatives–Same sex partner of deceased and her son–Title to sue

[Damages (Scotland) Act 1976 (c.13) s.1 (4), Sch.1 para.1; Human Rights Act 1998 (c.42) s.3.]

The same sex partner of a woman who died in a road traffic accident on May 26, 1999 (the third pursuer), and her son (the fourth pursuer), X and Y respectively, sought damages from K under the Damages (Scotland) Act 1976 s.1 (4). The deceased and her daughter had cohabited with the pursuers. X and the deceased had exchanged vows and rings at a ceremony in 1994, had a joint tenancy, a joint bank account, and had nominated each other as next of kin. K contended that the definition of "relative" under Sch.1 to the Act showed that Parliament had deliberately intended to restrict the class of individuals to whom statutory claims were competent. X submitted that Sch.1 impliedly included same sex partners, failing that, Sch.1 para.1 (aa) was ambiguous and should be interpreted in the manner most favourable to the Convention to avoid discrimination. Further, a relevant case had been pled in respect of Y to the effect that the deceased had accepted him into her family, and for the purposes of para.1 (c), a "family" did not require to have two parents nor two heterosexual parents. The parties agreed that the Human Rights Act 1998 s.3 did not apply to the task of interpretation that required to be carried out with the relevant event having occurred prior to its coming into force.

Held, dismissing X's action and allowing proof before answer in Y's action, that (1) X did not qualify as a "relative" within the meaning of Sch.1 to the Act: X would have to have been able to demonstrate that she was living with the deceased before the accident as her husband which she could not do because she was of the female gender; the language plainly denoted a biological distinction between the deceased and cohabitee, and as it was a provision added by way of amendment in 1982 against a background of social recognition that a number of heterosexual couples were choosing to cohabit without being married, if Parliament had intended to extend claims to a person who had been in a same sex relationship with the deceased, it seemed unthinkable that the language used would have been chosen; (2) the provisions under consideration were in no way ambiguous, and (3) "family" in Sch.1 para.1 (c) was used in the context of circumstances where the deceased adult, prior to death, engaged in a loving and caring relationship with the child in question and undertook parental responsibilities: this could be fulfilled without the involvement of another adult in a heterosexual relationship, and an adult would not be disabled from so doing by reason of the fact that he or she cohabited in a same sex relationship.

TELFER v. KELLOCK 2004 S.L.T. 1290, Lady Smith, OH.

5166. Measure of damages–Loss of society–82 year old mother

[Damages (Scotland) Act 1976 (c.13) s.1 (4).]

C, the mother of a man who died aged 54 from mesothelioma as a result of exposure to asbestos while at work, sought damages of £20,000 for loss of society. C was aged 82 at the date of proof. The parties had had a good relationship: they had visited each other and kept in touch by telephone, the deceased had occasionally helped the pursuer with shopping and the garden, he had been supportive of her after the death of her second husband and her elder daughter, and prior to his diagnosis he had looked in on her once or twice a week. C was "shattered" when told of the deceased's diagnosis in the summer of 2001. She visited him often until the time of his death in September 2001, although there were times when the deceased, who was in great pain, felt unable to cope with seeing her, and she was with him when he died. C argued that the facts of the present case amounted to special circumstances and that all of the elements which the Damages (Scotland) Act 1976 s.1 (4) directed should be compensated were present.

Held, granting decree, that in the absence of more directly analogous material, taking as a guideline the £10,000 awarded to the 32 year old daughter of the deceased in *Murray's Executrix v. Greenock Dockyard Co Ltd* 2004 S.L.T. 1104, [2004] C.L.Y. 5075, £10,000 was a just figure for damages in all the circumstances, *Murray's Executrix* considered.

CRUICKSHANK v. FAIRFIELD ROWAN LTD 2005 S.L.T. 462, Lord Brodie, OH.

5167. Books

Bennett, Siggi A.–Personal Injury Damages in Scotland. Paperback: £60.00. ISBN 0 9534152 5 2. Barnstoneworth Press.

DELICT

5168. Breach of statutory duty–Workers–Duties owed to non employees– Member of public in loading bay

[Workplace (Health, Safety and Welfare) Regulations 1992 (SI 1992 3004) Reg.17.]

D, a customer at a shopping centre, raised an action of damages for injuries sustained when she was crushed against a wall of a loading bay area by an articulated lorry. D's only case of fault as against the second, or alternatively, the third defenders, as the party with control of the loading bay as a workplace, was their breach of duty under the Workplace (Health, Safety and Welfare) Regulations 1992 Reg.17. At debate, the Lord Ordinary dismissed the action in so far as directed against the second and third defenders on the basis that D had no title to sue. D reclaimed, submitting that the duties incumbent on the defenders were owed by them to a person who was present in the workplace, but who was not at work.

Held, refusing the reclaiming motion, that on a sound construction of the regulations in the relevant context, they afforded no protection to persons present in a workplace as visitors but not as workers.

DONALDSON v. HAYS DISTRIBUTION SERVICES LTD 2005 S.C. 523, Lord Cullen L.P., Lord Macfadyen, Lady Cosgrove, 1 Div.

5169. Occupiers liability–Local authority housing–Glass panel on front door– Reasonable foreseeability of breakage

[Occupiers' Liability (Scotland) Act 1960 (c.30) s.2(1).]

K sought damages from L, her local authority landlord, in respect of injuries sustained after her hand went through the window pane of her front door whilst she was trying to demonstrate problems with the door to two of L's workmen. The door shuddered when closed, the putty round the external face of the window was cracked, and the door rattled when it was windy. K reported the complaint to L, and a housing officer, B, attended the premises. K accepted that it was her hand movement which had caused the glass to break and that on a scale of 1 to 10, where 10 was slamming the door, she had used pressure at level three when demonstrating the problem to the workmen. K, relying on common law and the Occupiers' Liability (Scotland) Act 1960 s.2(1), argued that any reasonable system of inspection prior to leasing the property would have identified that the door was a major risk area where there was a reasonably foreseeable risk of glass breakage by accidental human impact within the terms of the British Standard Code of Good Practice for glazing for building BS6262:1982. K contended that it was L's duty to ensure that safety glass as specified in the British Standard flat safety glass for use in buildings BS6206:1981 was installed in the door, and that it was reasonably foreseeable that if such glass was not so installed, accidental contact with an ordinary glass plate could cause it to break into separate fragments. S, an independent health and safety consultant, gave evidence for K that the use of a single pane of glass in a front door of a dwellinghouse in the position in which it was situated was an obvious hazard as it was within an "impact zone" within which there was a real risk of accidental human contact. L submitted that (1) it was not reasonably foreseeable that K would push her hand against the glass panel thereby causing it to break; (2) although they accepted responsibility for maintenance as owners of the subjects, there had been a pre let inspection by K and B, they had responded to K's complaint, and had fulfilled all of their duties as owners or landlords; (3) without evidence as to building standards or alternative types of glass which could have been used, the court could not make any finding relevant to the matter although these were the averments on record which K had offered to prove; (4) there was insufficient evidence for the court to be satisfied about the term "impact zone"; (5) there was no evidence of any cause for the glass to break other than that K had put her hand on it; (6) if L were found liable, K should be found contributorily negligent. The parties agreed quantum of damages in the sum of £13,000 on a full liability basis.

Held, granting decree, that K's case on record was apt to cover the circumstances found in fact and L were in breach of their common law duty and statutory duty under the Act. There was little difficulty in accepting the evidence and concluding in fact that the use of a single pane of glass in the front door of a dwellinghouse was clearly a place where it was liable to break accidentally and that it was reasonably foreseeable that glass of that nature was liable to cause injury; accidental slamming could readily result in breakage as could hand pressure on another area of the door which might include a hand being placed partly on the glass panel. S's evidence that this was a reasonably foreseeable risk could be accepted and in those circumstances there was a duty on L to take reasonable care to guard against that particular danger by not using single pane plate glass in such a situation, but rather, as they did in September 2000, use an alternative such as perspex.

KERR v. EAST AYRSHIRE COUNCIL; *sub nom.* NIMMO v. EAST AYRSHIRE COUNCIL 2005 S.L.T. (Sh Ct) 67, Sheriff CG McKay, Sh Ct (North Strathclyde).

ECCLESIASTICAL LAW

5170. **Churches–Fundamental rights–Right of continued protest–Abandonment of essential principle**

F, the Free Church of Scotland (Continuing), raised an action seeking declarator that they were entitled to all the property and assets held by trustees for the body of Christians known as the Free Church of Scotland, and that C, the Free Church of Scotland (Residual), had no right or title to the property. Alternatively, F sought declarator that they were entitled to the property and assets in such proportion and upon such conditions as the court should determine. F submitted that C had abandoned the right of continued protest in 1995 by denying a dissenting minority the right to continue their protest against a decision not to proceed further against a professor who was the subject of an investigation into alleged sexual misconduct, and that by abandoning a fundamental principle of the Free Church, they had thus abandoned the constitution with the result that the pursuers were now the true Free Church of Scotland.

Held, dismissing the action, that (1) as the resolution of the dispute over the assets of the Free Church depended upon the alleged departure from a fundamental principle of the Free Church, the court had the limited jurisdiction outlined in *Mackay v. MacLeod* (Unreported, January 1952). (2) In searching for the fundamental principles to the Free Church, the court was neither restricted to the period around 1843 when the church came into existence, but could consider up until the date of debate, nor was it restricted to certain constitutional documents of the church such as those listed by C where it was necessary to examine all relevant and credible material expository of the essential fundamental principles thereof, nor was the court categorically excluded from considering the views and actings of individuals. (3) It had not been possible to identify a right of continued protest as a fundamental constitutional principle of the Free Church. The formation of the latter and activities of certain individuals, associations and others simply illustrated a determination to maintain and protect what were considered to be the substantive fundamental principles of the Free Church and protest was a means to that end, it was not in itself a fundamental constitutional principle. The preamble to the Act of 1951 did no more than set out the genesis of the Free Church, the problems which beset it and the members' determination to remain true to the fundamental principles, there was nothing therein, even when taken with surrounding circumstances and events, which could be construed as a fundamental constitutional principle of a right of continued protest, nor could other documents and materials referred to in the course of the debate properly be construed as referring to such a principle. (4) Protest was a flexible concept and a means of achieving an end and while there might well be circumstances in which an attempt to stifle a protest by a minority amounted to an aspect of departure from a fundamental tenet of the church, such a situation had not arisen in the present case. (5) As neither C nor F appeared to have departed from any fundamental tenet of the Free Church, neither had forfeited any entitlement to the assets and property held in trust but some or all of the pursuers might be in breach of promises or undertakings made on joining the Free Church and while matters still had to be ruled upon by the General Assembly, there were at least prima facie grounds of failure by F to comply with the discipline and government of the church in which circumstances, it would be inappropriate for the court to rule relevant and competent a possible apportionment of the property and assets between F and C, *Mackay* considered.

FREE CHURCH OF SCOTLAND v. GENERAL ASSEMBLY OF THE FREE CHURCH OF SCOTLAND 2005 S.C. 396, Lady Paton, OH.

EDUCATION

5171. Colleges-Board of governors-Elections-Edinburgh College of Art

EDINBURGH COLLEGE OF ART (SCOTLAND) ORDER OF COUNCIL 1995 (AMENDMENT) ORDER OF COUNCIL 2005, SSI 2005 313; made under the Further and Higher Education (Scotland) Act 1992 s.45, s.60. In force: July 1, 2005; £3.00.

This Order amends the Edinburgh College of Art (Scotland) Order of Council 1995 (SI 1995 471) which makes provision for the constitution, functions and powers of the Board of Governors of the Edinburgh College of Art, as governing body of that College, and the arrangements to be adopted by it in discharging its functions. The Edinburgh College of Art is an institution designated by the Scottish Ministers as eligible to receive support from the Scottish Higher Education Funding Council. The 1995 Order is amended to reflect the fact that all employees, whether full or part-time, should be eligible to vote and to stand for election to serve on the Board of Governors and the Academic Council of the College.

5172. Colleges-Board of governors-Elections-Glasgow School of Art

GLASGOW SCHOOL OF ART (SCOTLAND) AMENDMENT ORDER OF COUNCIL 2005, SSI 2005 525; made under the Further and Higher Education (Scotland) Act 1992 s.45, s.60. In force: November 28, 2005; £3.00.

This Order of Council amends the Glasgow School of Art (Scotland) Order of Council 1996 (SI 1996 120) which makes provision for the constitution, functions and powers of the Governors of The Glasgow School of Art, as governing body of the School, and the arrangements to be adopted by it in discharging its functions. The School is an institution designated by Scottish Ministers as eligible to receive support from the Scottish Higher Education Funding Council. The School is also a fundable body eligible to receive support from the Scottish Further and Higher Education Funding Council under the Further and Higher Education (Scotland) Act 2005. The School is a company incorporated under the Companies Acts and the powers and duties of the company are specified in the company's Memorandum and Articles of Association. The 1996 Order is amended to provide that all employees, whether full-time or part-time, shall be eligible to vote and to stand for election to serve as Governors of the School.

5173. Colleges-Establishment-Adam Smith College, Fife

ADAM SMITH COLLEGE, FIFE (ESTABLISHMENT) ORDER 2005, SSI 2005 298; made under the Further and Higher Education (Scotland) Act 1992 s.3. In force: August 1, 2005; £3.00.

This Order establishes The Adam Smith College, Fife. That college is under the control of a board of management in terms of the Further and Higher Education (Scotland) Act 1992. The Order therefore designates the name of the College as The Adam Smith College, Fife and establishes the body corporate to be known as "the Board of Management of The Adam Smith College, Fife".

5174. Education (Additional Support for Learning) (Scotland) Act 2004 (asp 4)– Commencement No.1 Order

EDUCATION (ADDITIONAL SUPPORT FOR LEARNING) (SCOTLAND) ACT 2004 (COMMENCEMENT NO.1) ORDER 2005, SSI 2005 154 (C.5); made under the Education (Additional Support for Learning) (Scotland) Act 2004 s.34, s.35. Commencement details: bringing into force various provisions of the 2004 Act on May 3, 2005; £3.00.

This Order brings into force the Education (Additional Support for Learning) (Scotland) Act 2004 s.17 and Sch.1. Section 17 creates the Additional Support Needs Tribunals for Scotland and introduces Schedule 1 which makes provision about the constitution, appointment to and procedures of the Tribunals, and other matters.

5175. **Education (Additional Support for Learning) (Scotland) Act 2004 (asp 4)–Commencement No.2 Order**

EDUCATION (ADDITIONAL SUPPORT FOR LEARNING) (SCOTLAND) ACT 2004 (COMMENCEMENT NO.2) ORDER 2005, SSI 2005 263 (C.13); made under the Education (Additional Support for Learning) (Scotland) Act 2004 s.34, s.35. Commencement details: bringing into force various provisions of the 2004 Act on May 18, 2005; £3.00.

This Order appoints May 18, 2005 as the date for the coming into force of certain provisions of the Education (Additional Support for Learning) (Scotland) Act 2004.

5176. **Education (Additional Support for Learning) (Scotland) Act 2004 (asp 4)–Commencement No.3 Order**

EDUCATION (ADDITIONAL SUPPORT FOR LEARNING) (SCOTLAND) ACT 2004 (COMMENCEMENT NO.3) ORDER 2005, SSI 2005 564 (C.28); made under the Education (Additional Support for Learning) (Scotland) Act 2004 s.34, s.35. Commencement details: bringing into force various provisions of the 2004 Act on November 14, 2005; £3.00.

This Order appoints the date for the coming into force of all remaining provisions of the Education (Additional Support for Learning) (Scotland) Act 2004 not already in force with certain exceptions.

5177. **Educational institutions–Educational awards–Recognised bodies**

EDUCATION (LISTED BODIES) (SCOTLAND) AMENDMENT ORDER 2005, SSI 2005 354; made under the Education Reform Act 1988 s.216. In force: June 17, 2005; £3.00.

The Education (Listed Bodies) (Scotland) Order 2004 (SSI 2004 539) lists the name of each body which is not a "recognised body" within the Education Reform Act 1988, but which appears to the Scottish Ministers either to provide any course which is in preparation for a degree to be granted by such a recognised body and is approved by or on behalf of that body; or to be a constituent college, school, hall or other institution of a university which is such a recognised body. Recognised bodies are universities, colleges or other bodies which are authorised by Royal Charter, or by or under Act of Parliament, to grant degrees and other bodies for the time being permitted by those bodies to act on their behalf in the granting of degrees. This Order the amends 2004 Order to add Kensington College of Business, London City College and the School of Technology and Management to the list of bodies providing courses in preparation for a degree.

5178. **Educational institutions–Educational awards–Recognised bodies**

EDUCATION (LISTED BODIES) (SCOTLAND) AMENDMENT (NO.2) ORDER 2005, SSI 2005 592; made under the Education Reform Act 1988 s.216. In force: December 1, 2005; £3.00.

This Order amends the Education (Listed Bodies) (Scotland) Order 2004 (SSI 2004 539) to remove Central School of Speech and Drama, Edge Hill College of Higher Education, Kent Institute of Art and Design, Laban Centre, London, Southampton Institute, the Surrey Institute of Art and Design University College and York St John College from the list of bodies appearing to the Scottish Ministers to be recognised bodies.

5179. Educational institutions–Recognised bodies

EDUCATION (RECOGNISED BODIES) AMENDMENT (SCOTLAND) ORDER 2005, SSI 2005 591; made under the Education Reform Act 1988 s.216. In force: December 2, 2005; £3.00.

This Order amends the Education (Recognised Bodies) Order 1999 (SI 1999 833) so as to update the list of bodies that appear to the Secretary of State to be recognised bodies.

5180. Educational policy–Children and young persons–Additional support needs

ADDITIONAL SUPPORT FOR LEARNING (CHANGES IN SCHOOL EDUCATION) (SCOTLAND) REGULATIONS 2005, SSI 2005 265; made under the Education (Additional Support for Learning) (Scotland) Act 2004 s.13. In force: November 14, 2005; £3.00.

These Regulations make provision for education authorities to take action in connection with changes which occur or are likely to occur in the school education of children and young persons who have additional support needs.

5181. Educational policy–Children and young persons–Coordinated support plans

ADDITIONAL SUPPORT FOR LEARNING (CO-ORDINATED SUPPORT PLAN) (SCOTLAND) AMENDMENT REGULATIONS 2005, SSI 2005 518; made under the Education (Additional Support for Learning) (Scotland) Act 2004 s.11, s.34. In force: November 14, 2005; £3.00.

These Regulations, which revoke the Additional Support for Learning (Co-ordinated Support Plan) (Scotland) Regulations 2005 (SSI 2005 266), prescribe the form and content of a co-ordinated support plan for a child or young person with additional support needs for the purposes of the Education (Additional Support for Learning) (Scotland) Act 2004. The Regulations also prescribe time limits and exceptions to such limits for the preparation and review of a plan, arrangements for keeping the plan, arrangements regarding the transfer of a plan to another education authority, arrangements for the disclosure without explicit consent of the plan to specified persons or in specified circumstances and arrangements for the discontinuance, retention and destruction of a plan.

5182. Educational policy–Children and young persons–Coordinated support plans

ADDITIONAL SUPPORT FOR LEARNING (CO-ORDINATED SUPPORT PLAN) (SCOTLAND) REGULATIONS 2005, SSI 2005 266; made under the Education (Additional Support for Learning) (Scotland) Act 2004 s.11, s.34. In force: November 14, 2005; £3.00.

These Regulations prescribe the form and content of a co-ordinated support plan for a child or young person with additional support needs for the purposes of the Education (Additional Support for Learning) (Scotland) Act 2004. The Regulations also prescribe time limits and exceptions to such limits for the preparation and review of a plan, arrangements for keeping the plan, arrangements regarding the transfer of a plan to another education authority, arrangements for the disclosure without explicit consent of the plan to specified persons or in specified circumstances and arrangements for the discontinuance, retention and destruction of a plan.

5183. Funding councils–Further and higher education–Dissolution

DISSOLUTION OF FUNDING COUNCILS (SCOTLAND) ORDER 2005, SSI 2005 437; made under the Further and Higher Education (Scotland) Act 2005 s.2. In force: October 3, 2005; £3.00.

This Order appoints October 3, 2005 for the dissolution of the Scottish Further Education Funding Council and the Scottish Higher Education Funding Council.

5184. Further and Higher Education (Scotland) Act 2005 (asp 6)

This Act makes provision establishing the Scottish Further and Higher Education Funding Council and provision as to its functions; makes provision as to support for further and higher education; and makes provision relating to bodies which provide further and higher education.

5185. Further and Higher Education (Scotland) Act 2005 (asp 6)–Commencement Order

FURTHER AND HIGHER EDUCATION (SCOTLAND) ACT 2005 (COMMENCEMENT) ORDER 2005, SSI 2005 419 (C.18); made under the Further and Higher Education (Scotland) Act 2005 s.36. Commencement details: bringing into force various provisions of the 2005 Act on September 8, 2005 and October 3, 2005; £3.00.

This Order brings into force on October 3, 2005 all the provisions of the Further and Higher Education (Scotland) Act 2005, with the exception of s.2 which comes into force on September 8, 2005.

5186. Further education–Higher education–Consequential modifications

FURTHER AND HIGHER EDUCATION (SCOTLAND) ACT 2005 (CONSEQUENTIAL MODIFICATIONS) ORDER 2005, SI 2005 2077 (S.8); made under the Scotland Act 1998 s.104, s.112, s.113. In force: October 3, 2005; £3.00.

This Order, which amends the Superannuation Act 1972, the House of Commons Disqualification Act 1975, the Sex Discrimination Act 1975 and the Race Relations Act 1976, makes provision in consequence of the Further and Higher Education (Scotland) Act 2005. That Act dissolves the existing Scottish Further Education Funding Council and Scottish Higher Education Funding Council and establishes the Scottish Further and Higher Education Funding Council. The new Council will have the duty to secure the provision of further and higher education and research and to make grants to institutions to achieve this. The Order amends four Acts of Parliament to insert references in these to the new Council, its members and, where appropriate, duties the new Council will be under. The provisions which apply to the new Council under this Order are in the same terms as those which applied to the former Councils.

5187. Further education corporations–Change of name–Falkirk College

FALKIRK COLLEGE OF FURTHER AND HIGHER EDUCATION (CHANGE OF NAME) ORDER 2005, SSI 2005 317; made under the Further and Higher Education (Scotland) Act 1992 s.3. In force: August 1, 2005; £3.00.

This Order changes the name of Falkirk College of Further and Higher Education to Forth Valley College of Further and Higher Education. That college is under the control of a board of management in terms of the Further and Higher Education (Scotland) Act 1992 and the Order therefore also changes the name of the board of management to reflect the new name of the college.

5188. Gaelic Language (Scotland) Act 2005 (asp 7)

This Act establishes a body having functions exercisable with a view to securing the status of the Gaelic language as an official language of Scotland commanding equal respect to the English language, including the functions of preparing a national Gaelic language plan, requires certain public authorities to prepare and publish Gaelic language plans in connection with the exercise of their functions and maintains and implement such plans, and issues guidance in relation to Gaelic education.

This Act received Royal Assent on June 1, 2005.

5189. Higher Education Act 2004 (c.8)–Commencement No.1 Order

HIGHER EDUCATION ACT 2004 (COMMENCEMENT NO.1) (SCOTLAND) ORDER 2005, SSI 2005 33 (C.3); made under the Higher Education Act 2004 s.52. Commencement details: bringing into force various provisions of the 2004 Act on January 31, 2005; £3.00.

This Order commences the Higher Education Act 2004 s.10(3) which makes provision for the Scottish Ministers to carry out, support or disseminate the results, and further the practical application of the results of research in the arts and humanities. It also makes provision for the Scottish Ministers, in relation to Scotland, to establish advisory bodies for the purposes of assisting them in matters connected with research in the arts and humanities and, if such a body is established, to appoint its members on terms which include payment of remuneration, allowances or pension benefits.

5190. Independent schools–Registration

REGISTRATION OF INDEPENDENT SCHOOLS (SCOTLAND) REGULATIONS 2005, SSI 2005 571; made under the Education (Scotland) Act 1980 s.98, s.98A. In force: December 31, 2005; £3.00.

The School Education (Ministerial Powers and Independent Schools) (Scotland) Act 2004 revises and amends the legislation governing independent schools within the Education (Scotland) Act 1980. These Regulations, which revoke the Registration of Independent Schools (Scotland) Regulations 1957 (SI 1957 1058) and the Registration of Independent Schools (Scotland) Amendment Regulations 1975 (SI 1975 1412), set out the information as to particulars which is to be provided to the Registrar of Independent Schools in relation to an application for registration of an independent school. They also require certain specified changes in those particulars to be notified to the Registrar. Provision is in addition made for the information as to particulars relating to a registered independent school to be notified to the Registrar within an Annual Return, in connection with the continuing registration of the school.

5191. Local education authorities–Additional support for learning–Appropriate agencies

ADDITIONAL SUPPORT FOR LEARNING (APPROPRIATE AGENCIES) (SCOTLAND) ORDER 2005, SSI 2005 325; made under the Education (Additional Support for Learning) (Scotland) Act 2004 s.23. In force: November 14, 2005; £3.00.

This Order specifies further appropriate agencies for the purposes of the Education (Additional Support for Learning) (Scotland) Act 2005. An education authority may request the help of those agencies in the exercise of any of its functions, as with other local authorities and Health Boards. The agencies specified by this Order are: the colleges of further education and higher education institutions set out in the Further and Higher Education (Scotland) Act 2005 Sch.2; the Scottish Agricultural College; and Careers Scotland.

5192. Local education authorities–Additional support for learning–Consequential modifications

EDUCATION (ADDITIONAL SUPPORT FOR LEARNING) (SCOTLAND) ACT 2004 (CONSEQUENTIAL MODIFICATIONS OF SUBORDINATE LEGISLATION) ORDER 2005, SSI 2005 517; made under the Education (Additional Support for Learning) (Scotland) Act 2004 s.32, s.34. In force: November 14, 2005; £3.00.

This Order amends the School Premises (General Requirements and Standards) (Scotland) Regulations 1967 (SI 1967 1199), the Jordanhill School Grant (Scotland) Regulations 1988 (SI 1988 328), the Education (Grants for Further Training of Teachers and Educational Psychologists Etc.) (Scotland) Regulations 1993 (SI 1993 974), the Education (Provision of Information as to Schools) (Scotland) Regulations 1993 (SI 1993 974), the Education (Provision of Information as to Schools) (Scotland) Regulations 1993 (SI 1993 1605), the

Adoption Agencies (Scotland) Regulations 1996 (SI 1996 3266), the Education (Lower Primary Class Sizes) (Scotland) Regulations 1999 (SI 1999 1080), the Education (Assisted Places) (Scotland) Regulations 2002 (SSI 2001 222), the St Mary's Music School (Aided Places) (Scotland) Regulations 2001 (SSI 2001 223), the Intercountry Adoption (Hague Convention) (Scotland) Regulations 2003 (SSI 2003 19) and the Pupils' Educational Records (Scotland) Regulations 2003 (SSI 2003 581). It makes consequential modifications to subordinate legislation.

5193. Local education authorities–Additional support for learning–Disabled persons

EDUCATION (ADDITIONAL SUPPORT FOR LEARNING) (SCOTLAND) ACT 2004 (CONSEQUENTIAL MODIFICATIONS) ORDER 2005, SI 2005 1791 (S.6); made under the Scotland Act 1998 s.104, s.112, s.113. In force: June 30, 2005; £3.00.

This Order makes provision in consequence of the Education (Additional Support for Learning) (Scotland) Act 2004. The Disability Discrimination Act 1995 s.28F requires education authorities in Scotland not to discriminate against a disabled pupil, or a disabled person who may be admitted to a school as a pupil, in carrying out their functions under the Acts listed in subsection (1)(b) of that section. The 2004 Act places new duties upon education authorities to make provision for additional support in connection with the school education of children and young persons having additional support needs. The Disability Discrimination Act 1995 is amended so that when education authorities carry out their functions under the 2004 Act the duty imposed by s.28F will apply.

5194. Local education authorities–Additional support for learning–Functions

ADDITIONAL SUPPORT FOR LEARNING (APPROPRIATE AGENCY REQUEST PERIOD AND EXCEPTIONS) (SCOTLAND) REGULATIONS 2005, SSI 2005 264; made under the Education (Additional Support for Learning) (Scotland) Act 2004 s.23. In force: November 14, 2005; £3.00.

These Regulations specify a period of ten weeks within which a request under the Education (Additional Support for Learning) (Scotland) Act 2004 for help by an education authority from an appropriate agency under that Act must be complied with. Such a request can only be made in relation to the exercise of the education authority's functions under that Act. The Regulations also provide for exceptions to that time limit, provided that for each exception the reasons for the delay and a new date must be supplied to the education authority.

5195. Local education authorities–Additional support for learning–Publication of information

ADDITIONAL SUPPORT FOR LEARNING (PUBLICATION OF INFORMATION) (SCOTLAND) REGULATIONS 2005, SSI 2005 267; made under the Education (Additional Support for Learning) (Scotland) Act 2004 s.26. In force: November 14, 2005; £3.00.

These Regulations amend the Education (Additional Support for Learning) (Scotland) Act 2004 to the extent of adding to the matters specified therein, in relation to which education authorities are required to publish information. They also provide for the timescale within which that information is to be published and set out details of the form and manner in which information is to be.

5196. Local education authorities–Additional support for learning–Transitional and savings provisions

EDUCATION (ADDITIONAL SUPPORT FOR LEARNING) (SCOTLAND) ACT 2004 (TRANSITIONAL AND SAVINGS PROVISIONS) ORDER 2005, SSI 2005

516; made under the Education (Additional Support for Learning) (Scotland) Act 2004 s.32, s.34. In force: November 14, 2005; £3.00.

This Order makes provision for transitional arrangements and savings to allow specified references and placing requests made under the Education (Scotland) Act 1980 to be determined under that Act notwithstanding the commencement of the Education (Additional Support for Learning) (Scotland) Act 2004. It amends the 1980 Act, the Education (Record of Needs) (Scotland) Regulations 1982 (SI 1982 1222) (with savings), the Education (Placing in Schools Etc. -Deemed Decisions) (Scotland) Regulations 1982 (SI 1982 1733) (with savings) and the Education (Appeal Committee Procedures) (Scotland) Regulations 1982 (SI 1982 1736) (with savings).

5197. Local education authorities–Young persons–Dispute resolution

ADDITIONAL SUPPORT FOR LEARNING DISPUTE RESOLUTION (SCOTLAND) REGULATIONS 2005, SSI 2005 501; made under the Education (Additional Support for Learning) (Scotland) Act 2004 s.16, s.34. In force: November 14, 2005; £3.00.

These Regulations make provision under the Education (Additional Support for Learning) (Scotland) Act 2004 s.16 for the resolution of certain disputes as specified in the Schedule to the Regulations between an education authority and a person belonging to the authority's area specified in subsection (1) of that section (a parent of a child or a young person or, where the young person lacks capacity, their parent).

5198. School Education (Ministerial Powers and Independent Schools) (Scotland) Act 2004 (asp 12)–Commencement No.1 Order

SCHOOL EDUCATION (MINISTERIAL POWERS AND INDEPENDENT SCHOOLS) (SCOTLAND) ACT 2004 (COMMENCEMENT NO.1) ORDER 2005, SSI 2005 10 (C.1); made under the School Education (Ministerial Powers and Independent Schools) (Scotland) Act 2004 s.9. Commencement details: bringing into force various provisions of the 2004 Act on January 31, 2005; £3.00.

This Order brings into force Part 1 of the School Education (Ministerial Powers and Independent Schools) (Scotland) Act 2004 together with certain minor and consequential amendments. Part 1 of the Act provides a new power for the Scottish Ministers to direct managers of grant-aided schools and education authorities to take specific action to secure improvement as identified after inspection by Her Majesty's Inspectorate of Education. It sets out the circumstances in which the Scottish Ministers are allowed to use this power, the procedure which requires to be followed, and the purpose and nature of the enforcement direction which may be given.

5199. School Education (Ministerial Powers and Independent Schools) (Scotland) Act 2004 (asp 12)–Commencement No.2 Order

SCHOOL EDUCATION (MINISTERIAL POWERS AND INDEPENDENT SCHOOLS) (SCOTLAND) ACT 2004 (COMMENCEMENT NO.2 AND TRANSITIONAL PROVISIONS) ORDER 2005, SSI 2005 570 (C.29); made under the School Education (Ministerial Powers and Independent Schools) (Scotland) Act 2004 s.9. Commencement details: bringing into force various provisions of the 2004 Act on December 31, 2005; £3.00.

This Order brings into force the remaining provisions of the School Education (Ministerial Powers and Independent Schools) (Scotland) Act 2004 which deal with independent schools.

5200. Schools–Aided places–St Mary's Music School

ST MARY'S MUSIC SCHOOL (AIDED PLACES) (SCOTLAND) AMENDMENT REGULATIONS 2005, SSI 2005 269; made under the Education (Scotland) Act 1980 s.73, s.74. In force: August 1, 2005; £3.00.

The Regulations amend the St Mary's Music School (Aided Places) (Scotland) Regulations 2001 (SSI 2001 223) to uprate the qualifying income levels for the remission of fees and charges and the making of grants under the aided places scheme.

5201. Schools–Assisted places–Grants–Qualifying income limits

EDUCATION (ASSISTED PLACES) (SCOTLAND) AMENDMENT REGULATIONS 2005, SSI 2005 270; made under the Education (Scotland) Act 1980 s.75A, s.75B. In force: August 1, 2005; £3.00.

These Regulations amend the Education (Assisted Places) (Scotland) Regulations 2001 (SSI 2001 222) to uprate the qualifying income levels for the remission of fees and charges and the making of grants under the assisted places scheme.

5202. Special educational needs–Additional Support Needs Tribunals for Scotland–Appointments

ADDITIONAL SUPPORT NEEDS TRIBUNALS FOR SCOTLAND (APPOINTMENT OF PRESIDENT, CONVENERS AND MEMBERS AND DISQUALIFICATION) REGULATIONS 2005, SSI 2005 155; made under the Education (Additional Support for Learning) (Scotland) Act 2004 Sch.1 para.2, Sch.1 para.3. In force: May 3, 2005; £3.00.

The Education (Additional Support for Learning) (Scotland) Act 2004 provides for the appointment of a President, a panel of individuals who are to serve as conveners and a panel of individuals who are to serve as members of the Additional Support Needs Tribunals for Scotland. These Regulations set out the requirements in relation to qualifications, training and experience for appointment as President, conveners and members.

5203. Special educational needs–Additional Support Needs Tribunals for Scotland–Practice and procedure

ADDITIONAL SUPPORT NEEDS TRIBUNALS FOR SCOTLAND (PRACTICE AND PROCEDURE) RULES 2005, SSI 2005 514; made under the Education (Additional Support for Learning) (Scotland) Act 2004 s.17, Sch.1. In force: November 14, 2005; £4.00.

These Rules prescribe the practice and procedure to be followed in proceedings before the Additional Support Needs Tribunals for Scotland.

5204. Special educational needs–Children and young persons–Placing requests and deemed decisions

ADDITIONAL SUPPORT FOR LEARNING (PLACING REQUESTS AND DEEMED DECISIONS) (SCOTLAND) REGULATIONS 2005, SSI 2005 515; made under the Education (Additional Support for Learning) (Scotland) Act 2004 s.22, s.34, Sch.2 para.4, Sch.2 para.6. In force: November 14, 2005; £3.00.

These Regulations make provision in relation to placing requests relating to children or young persons with additional support for learning needs provided for by the Education (Additional Support for Learning) (Scotland) Act 2004. They make provision for deeming decisions to have been taken by education authorities or appeal committees established under the Education (Scotland) Act 1980 where those bodies have not reached a decision in relation to a placing request on reference by the dates or within the periods prescribed in these Regulations. Such a deemed decision puts the person making the placing request or reference in a position to proceed to the next step in the appeal process under the Act by making a reference to an appeal committee, or by an appeal to the sheriff.

5205. Students—Graduate endowment—Grants

EDUCATION (GRADUATE ENDOWMENT, STUDENT FEES AND SUPPORT) (SCOTLAND) AMENDMENT REGULATIONS 2005, SSI 2005 341; made under the Education (Scotland) Act 1980 s.49, s.73, s.73B, s.74; the Education (Fees and Awards) Act 1983 s.1, s.2; and the Education (Graduate Endowment and Student Support) (Scotland) Act 2001 s.1. In force: July 2, 2005; £3.00.

These Regulations amend the Nursing and Midwifery Student Allowances (Scotland) Regulations 1992 (SI 1992 580), the Education Authority Bursaries (Scotland) Regulations 1995 (SI 1995 1739), the Education (Fees and Awards) (Scotland) Regulations 1997 (SI 1997 93), the Students' Allowances (Scotland) Regulations 1999 (SI 1999 1131), the Education (Student Loans) (Scotland) Regulations 2000 (SSI 2000 200), the Graduate Endowment (Scotland) Regulations 2001 (SSI 2001 280) and the Education Maintenance Allowances (Scotland) Regulations 2004 (SSI 2004 273) by creating a new category of student eligible for support and liable for the graduate endowment. That category comprises nationals of a Member State of the European Community other than the UK and the children of such nationals who are ordinarily resident in Scotland and who have been ordinarily resident in the UK and Islands for three years. In relation to the 1992 Regulations the ordinary residence in Scotland is not a requirement. They also amend the regulations so listed in so far as they presently provide as a qualification for ordinary residence for a requirement that residence should not be wholly or mainly for the purpose of receiving full time education to the effect that such requirement shall not apply to the newly created category of student.

5206. Students—Grants—Temporary protection—Eligibility

EDUCATION (STUDENT FEES AND SUPPORT) TEMPORARY PROTECTION (SCOTLAND) AMENDMENT REGULATIONS 2005, SSI 2005 217; made under the Education (Scotland) Act 1980 s.49, s.73, s.73B, s.74; and the Education (Fees and Awards) Act 1983 s.1, s.2. In force: May 7, 2005; £3.00.

These Regulations amend the Nursing and Midwifery Student Allowances (Scotland) Regulations 1992 (SI 1992 580), the Education Authority Bursaries (Scotland) Regulations 1995 (SI 1995 1739), the Education (Fees and Awards) (Scotland) Regulations 1997 (SI 1997 93), the Students' Allowances (Scotland) Regulations 1999 (SSI 1999 1131), the Education (Student Loans) (Scotland) Regulations 2000 (SSI 2000 200) and the Education Maintenance Allowances (Scotland) Regulations 2004 (SSI 2004 273). These Regulations are wholly concerned with the implementation of Council Directive 2001/55 ([2001] OJ L212/12) on minimum standards for giving temporary protection in the event of a mass influx of displaced persons and on measures promoting a balance of efforts between Member States in receiving such persons and bearing the consequences thereof and partly implement the requirements of the Directive. The Regulations introduce an eligible category of individuals for each academic year consisting of those who have been granted the status of temporary protection, who are under 18 years of age prior to the start of the current academic year and who meet residence conditions equivalent to those applying to UK nationals.

5207. Students—Loans—Information requirements

STUDENT LOANS (INFORMATION REQUESTS, MAXIMUM THRESHOLD, MAXIMUM REPAYMENT LEVELS AND HARDSHIP LOANS) (SCOTLAND) REGULATIONS 2005, SSI 2005 314; made under the Education (Scotland) Act 1980 s.73, s.73B, s.74. In force: June 30, 2005; £3.00.

These Regulations, which amend the Repayment of Student Loans (Scotland) Regulations 2000 (SSI 2000 110) and the Education (Student Loans) (Scotland) Regulations 2000 (SSI 2000 200), require the provision of information to the

Scottish Ministers by borrowers of student loans and the imposition of penalties upon failure to do so. They also increase the earnings threshold for repayment and remove all provisions on hardship loans.

5208. Students–Loans–Mortgage style repayment loans

EDUCATION (STUDENT LOANS) AMENDMENT (SCOTLAND) REGULATIONS 2005, SSI 2005 345; made under the Education (Student Loans) Act 1990 s.1, Sch.2 para.1. In force: August 1, 2005; £3.00.

These Regulations amend the Education (Student Loans) Regulations 1998 (SI 1998 211) governing loans made under the Education (Student Loans) Act 1990. These are mortgage style repayment loans made, for the most part, to students who began their courses before August 1, 1998. The Regulations increase the maximum amounts which may be lent to students in relation to an academic year in line with inflation.

5209. Superannuation–Teachers

TEACHERS' SUPERANNUATION (SCOTLAND) REGULATIONS 2005, SSI 2005 393; made under the Superannuation Act 1972 s.9, s.12, Sch.3. In force: In accordance with Reg.A1 (1); £13.50.

These Regulations, which amend the Teachers' (Superannuation and Compensation for Premature Retirement) (Scotland) Amendment Regulations 1993 (SI 1993 2513), revoke the Teachers' Superannuation (Scotland) Regulations 1992 (SI 1992 280), the Teachers' Superannuation (Scotland) Amendment Regulations 1994 (SI 1994 2699), the Teachers' Superannuation (Scotland) Amendment Regulations 1995 (SI 1995 1670), the Teachers' Superannuation (Scotland) Amendment Regulations 1997 (SI 1997 676), the Teachers' Superannuation (Scotland) Amendment Regulations 1998 (SI 1998 718), the Teachers' Superannuation (Scotland) Amendment Regulations 1999 (SI 1999 446), the Teachers' Superannuation (Scotland) Amendment Regulations 2000 (SSI 2000 366), the Teachers' Superannuation (Scotland) Amendment Regulations 2001 (SSI 2001 291), the Teachers' Superannuation (Scotland) Amendment Regulations 2002 (SSI 2002 288), the Teachers' Superannuation (Scotland) Amendment Regulations 2003 (SSI 2003 423) and the Teachers' Superannuation (Scotland) Amendment Regulations 2004 (SSI 2004 89) (with savings). In addition to minor and drafting alterations, these Regulations make specified changes of substance.

5210. Teachers–Employment–Requirements

REQUIREMENTS FOR TEACHERS (SCOTLAND) REGULATIONS 2005, SSI 2005 355; made under the Education (Scotland) Act 1980 s.2, s.73, s.74, s.90; and the Standards in Scotland's Schools etc. Act 2000 s.59. In force: September 30, 2005; £3.00.

These Regulations, which amend the Abolition of the Education (Scotland) Fund (Consequential Provisions) Regulations 1959 (SI 1959 476), the Teachers (Education, Training and Certification) (Scotland) Regulations 1965 (SI 1965 55), the Teachers (Education, Training and Registration) (Scotland) Regulations 1967 (SI 1967 1162), the Schools General (Scotland) Regulations 1975 (SI 1975 1135), the Jordanhill School Grant Regulations 1988 (SI 1988 328), the Self-Governing Schools (Application and Amendment of Regulations) (Scotland) Regulations 1994 (SI 1994 351), revoke the Schools (Scotland) Code 1956 (SI 1956 894), the Schools (Scotland) Code Amendment Regulations 1965 (SI1965 940), the Schools (Scotland) Code (Amendment No.1) Regulations 1968 (SI1968 1055), the Schools (Scotland) Code (Amendment No.1) Regulations 1971 (SI 1971 1079) and the Schools (Scotland) Code (Amendment No.1) Regulations 1972 (SI 1972 776). The Regulations concern the requirements to be met by education authorities in employing teachers in the course of discharging their duty under the Education (Scotland) Act 1980.

ELECTORAL PROCESS

5211. Elections–Boundaries–Parliamentary constituencies

PARLIAMENTARY CONSTITUENCIES (SCOTLAND) ORDER 2005, SI 2005 250 (S.1); made under the Parliamentary Constituencies Act 1986 s.4. In force: February 10, 2005; £3.50.

This Order, which revokes the Parliamentary Constituencies (Scotland) Order 1995 (SI 1995 1037), gives effect, without modifications, to the recommendations contained in the Fifth Periodic Report of the Boundary Commission for Scotland dated November 30, 2004. It sets out and describes the constituencies into which Scotland will be divided.

5212. Elections–Candidates–Expenses–Variation of limits

REPRESENTATION OF THE PEOPLE (VARIATION OF LIMITS OF CANDIDATES' LOCAL GOVERNMENT ELECTION EXPENSES) (SCOTLAND) ORDER 2005, SSI 2005 102; made under the Representation of the People Act 1983 s.76A. In force: April 1, 2005; £3.00.

This Order, which amends the Representation of the People Act 1983 and revokes the Representation of the People (Variation of Limits of Candidates' Local Government Election Expenses) (Scotland) Order 2003 (SSI 2003 76), increases the maximum amounts of candidates' election expenses at local government elections in Scotland.

EMPLOYMENT

5213. Contract of employment–Place of performance–Execution in England– Application in Scotland–Competence

[Employment Tribunals (Constitution and Rules of Procedure) (Scotland) Regulations 2001 (SI 2001 1170) Reg.11 (5) (b).]

P, employers, appealed to the Court of Session against a decision of an employment appeal tribunal upholding an employment tribunal's finding that the occasional delivery by F, an employee, of a lecture or address in Scotland was sufficient to bring him within the Employment Tribunals (Constitution and Rules of Procedure) (Scotland) Regulations 2001 Reg.11 (5) (b), thus rendering his application with the Central Office of the Employment Tribunals (Scotland) competent. The contract of employment was executed in England and provided for F's normal place of work as Newcastle. F sought to uphold the appeal tribunal's reasoning that any connection with Scotland was sufficient.

Held, allowing the appeal, that (1) the ordinary meaning of the words in Reg.11 (5) (b), leaving aside the matter of execution, was that the place of performance of the contract should be wholly or, at least, substantially in Scotland, which was clearly not the position in the present case. (2) While there was no jurisdictional distinction between an industrial tribunal sitting in Scotland and one sitting in England, that was not to say that in an age when the outcome of an application could be influenced by the choice of forum as between England and Scotland, it might not be desirable for there to be some meaningful connection between the forum and the subject matter of the application.

PRESCRIPTION PRICING AUTHORITY v. FERGUSON 2005 S.C.171, Lord Cullen L.P., Lord Marnoch, Lady Cosgrove, 1 Div.

5214. Employees–Unfair dismissal–Relevant period

[Employment Rights Act 1996 (c.18) s.108(1), s.210, s.211(1)(a).]

O applied to an employment tribunal claiming unfair dismissal. O's employers (P) argued that as she had commenced employment on April 8, 2002, she had not been continuously employed for one year as required by the Employment Rights Act 1996 s.108(1), where one week's written notice of termination of employment was delivered on March 27, 2003 and expired on April 3, 2003. The tribunal upheld this argument and O appealed to the Employment Appeal Tribunal which held the one week's notice expired on April 7, 2003 as O did not receive the letter until March 31, 2003, and thus her claim was admissible. P appealed, submitting, on the basis of *Dodds v. Walker* [1981] 1 W.L.R. 1027, [1981] C.L.Y. 1518, that the effect of s.211(1)(a) and s.210(2) was that a year commencing on April 8, 2002 did not end until April 8, 2003, by which date O was no longer employed by them.

Held, dismissing the appeal, that (1) as a matter of ordinary language and common understanding, the question of whether the period beginning with April 8, 2002 and ending with April 7, 2003 was a period of less than one year had to be answered in the negative: if the period of one year did not end until April 8, 2003, a year would comprise 366 days rather than 365. (2) *Dodds* could be distinguished as the corresponding date rule, which excludes from the computation the day on which the notice was given, contained therein, could not be applied if, by statute, the court was required, as in this case, to count the date on which the relevant event occurred as part of the relevant period, *Dodds* distinguished.

PACITTI JONES (A FIRM) v. O'BRIEN; *sub nom.* O'BRIEN v. PACITTI JONES (A FIRM) 2005 S.L.T. 793, Lord Hamilton, Lord Macfadyen, Lord Reed, Ex Div.

5215. Transfer of undertakings–Seafarers–Transfer of ferry business

[European Communities Act 1972 (c.68) s.2; Transfer of Undertakings (Protection of Employment) Regulations 1981 (SI 1981 1794) Reg.2(2); Council Directive 77/187 relating to the safeguarding of employees' rights in the event of transfers of undertakings Art.1(3), Art.7.]

The appellants (N), seafarers who had been employed on board a ferry service operated by the respondents (P), appealed against a decision that there had been a transfer of undertaking for the purposes of the Transfer of Undertakings (Protection of Employment) Regulations 1981 when the ferry service was taken over by another company (X). X did not use any of the ships which P had operated. N argued that (1) there had been no valid TUPE transfer, that they had been dismissed by way of redundancy and that they were therefore entitled to claim redundancy payments from P irrespective of whether they had been re employed by X; (2) Reg.2(2) of the 1981 Regulations was ultra vires by virtue of the European Communities Act 1972 s.2 because it purported to extend TUPE protection to seafarers employed in a ferry service, for whom protection was not required by Council Directive 77/187 Art.1(3).

Held, dismissing the appeal, that (1) on the facts, the tribunal had been entitled to find that there had been a TUPE transfer and that N had been employed in the undertaking or the parts transferred. An independent observer would have concluded that the ferry service had continued in basically the same way after the transfer. There was a retention of identity with the business being continued as a going concern. Accordingly, the undertaking had been transferred within the meaning of the 1981 Regulations. (2) Although it might be the case that regulations made under the 1972 Act could not broaden "the main thrust or effect" of the the 1977 Directive of TUPE protection to a group of workers who would otherwise be at risk of exclusion was not an abuse of the regulation making power. This was reinforced by the terms of Art.7 of the Directive and by *Castle View Services Ltd v. Howes* 2000 S.C. 419, [2000] C.L.Y. 6220, *Castle View* considered.

NUMAST v. P&O SCOTTISH FERRIES [2005] I.C.R. 1270, Bean, J., EAT.

5216. Unfair dismissal–Applications–Regional office of employment tribunals

[Employment Rights Act 1996 (c.18) s.111(2)(a); Employment Tribunals (Constitution and Rules of Procedure) (Scotland) Regulations 2001 (SI 2001 1170) Reg.2(1), Reg.8(1), Sch.1 para.23(3).]

M, whose employment with S was effectively terminated on May 31, 2002, faxed an application complaining of unfair dismissal to the Edinburgh office of the employment tribunals on August 31, 2002, namely the last day of the period during which a tribunal could consider a complaint by the Employment Rights Act 1996 s.111(2)(a). M's application thereafter was forwarded to the central office in Glasgow where it was date stamped on September 2, 2002. The employment tribunal concluded that as the Edinburgh office was not a regional office at which an originating application might be presented in terms of the Employment Tribunals (Constitution and Rules of Procedure) (Scotland) Regulations 2001 Sch.1 para.23(3), M's application had not been timeously presented. The Employment Appeal Tribunal dismissed M's appeal from the tribunal and he appealed to the Court of Session. M submitted that (1) both tribunals had reached the wrong conclusion on the construction of Sch.1 para.23(3) in the light of the definitions contained in Reg.2(1); it followed from the EAT's considerations that there was only one regional chairman in Scotland and that he was "appointed for the whole region" that the "area specified by the President" as the area of the regional chairman's responsibility in terms of Reg.8(1) had to be the whole of Scotland, but the EAT did not explain why that led to the conclusion that it was impossible to extend the definition of "Regional Office" to include the Edinburgh office; (2) the 2001 Regulations should be construed against the background of the earlier regulations.

Held, dismissing the appeal, that it was not possible to argue from the fact that there was a regional chairman for Scotland, validly appointed in terms of Reg.8(1), that Scotland had to be treated as a region for the purposes of the definition of "Regional Office of the Employment Tribunal" in Reg.2(1) where it was one thing for the President to specify an area in relation to the former and quite another to specify an area for which a regional office had been established. While the EAT went too far in saying that the phrase "or any Regional Office of the Employment Tribunals" should not be in the Scottish regulations and there was no reason of policy to support depriving Scottish applicants of the more relaxed regime for making applications, such an approach was irreconcilable with Reg.2(1) where the definition of "Regional Office of the Employment Tribunals" therein referred to a regional office which had been established "for an area specified by the President" and as such an area had not been specified for a regional office in Scotland, offices in sub areas within Scotland could not be brought within that definition.

MATHESON v. MAZARS SOLUTIONS LTD 2005 S.C. 420, Lord Macfadyen, Lady Cosgrove, Lord Cameron of Lochbroom, Ex Div.

5217. Unfair dismissal–Compensatory awards–Tribunal declining to award compensation for period from date of dismissal to date of hearing but awarding compensation of six months' future loss

[Employment Rights Act 1996 (c.18) s.123(1).]

B applied to an employment tribunal after he was summarily dismissed by D on January 18, 2001 on the ground of gross misconduct. D began an investigation into complaints against B on December 5, 2000, and on December 8, B was signed off with reactive depression. The hearing before the tribunal concluded on December 12, 2001 whereby it was determined that the dismissal had been unfair but that it would not be just and equitable to award B a compensatory award for the period from the date of dismissal to the date of the hearing, and instead he received an award representing six months' future loss. B appealed to the Employment Appeal Tribunal, arguing that the tribunal had erred in law by failing to award him a sum equivalent to four weeks' wages by way of notice entitlement and by failing to make a compensatory award for the period from the expiry of the notice period to the date of the hearing. The EAT increased the compensatory award by £15,050, having found that there was inconsistency in the tribunal's reasoning between the award of future loss and the award of only part of the period between the date of dismissal and the date of the hearing, and that it was impossible to determine why it had limited the period against a background of a finding that B had suffered from a reactive depressive illness and probably had done so from the date of his initial suspension, and certainly from the date of dismissal. D appealed, submitting that (1) B had no foundation in his notice of appeal for challenging the basis of the compensatory award on the ground of perversity, nor could he argue the notice pay point for the same reasons, and (2) the EAT had erred in saying that B's solicitor agreed that if the appeal succeeded, the award should be increased by £15,050 when he had conceded only that if the EAT were to hold B entitled to a compensatory award for wage loss during the period in question, the total amount for that period was correctly calculated at £15,050.

Held, allowing the appeal and remitting the case to the tribunal for reconsideration, that (1) the tribunal's decision to make no compensatory award for the period to the date of the hearing was not well founded, it was made without a proper basis of findings in fact and without proper and adequate reasons: there was no finding as to whether the dismissal was a cause of B's unfitness nor was there a satisfactory reason for the conclusion that there should be no compensatory award for the period from the dismissal to the hearing; (2) the EAT's decision to increase the award by £15,050 seemed to have proceeded on a misunderstanding since B's case before the tribunal raised the question of there being a pre-existing cause of his depression and sought to minimise the award on a just and equitable basis, A ought to have remitted the case to T to reconsider its decision on the compensatory award for the period January 18 to December 12, 2001 and explain its application of the Employment Rights Act 1996 s.123(1) with proper and intelligible reasons, and (3) the EAT was right in allowing B to raise the notice pay point since his entitlement to pay in lieu was obviously relevant to the calculation of the compensatory award and D could scarcely claim to have been at any significant disadvantage in having had to respond to the point, further, it could be inferred that no further reference was made to the point because the compensatory award exceeded the amount of the entitlement to pay in lieu.

BRUCE v. DIGNITY FUNERALS LTD; *sub nom.* DIGNITY FUNERALS LTD v. BRUCE 2005 S.C. 59, Lord Gill L.J.C., Lord MacLean, Lord Hardie, 2 Div.

5218. **Unfair dismissal–Misconduct–Reasonable grounds for belief of misconduct–Dismissal of teacher following injury to unruly pupil**

The appellant (P), a former teacher at the respondent school (O) for pupils with special educational needs, appealed against a decision of the Employment Appeal Tribunal (EAT) to allow O's appeal and accordingly to find that P had not been unfairly dismissed. P had been involved in a struggle with an unruly teenage pupil during which the pupil's elbow had been fractured. O commenced disciplinary proceedings, which the first instance tribunal found to be procedurally flawed, and P was subsequently summarily dismissed for gross misconduct. P submitted that the EAT applied the wrong test because O's genuine belief that P had been guilty of misconduct was not sufficient to make the dismissal fair.

Held, allowing the appeal, that the tribunal had misdirected itself in relation to the test to be applied to determine whether a dismissal for misconduct was fair. Although an employer might have a genuine belief that the misconduct had occurred, a dismissal was fair only if there were reasonable grounds in the mind of an employer on which to sustain that belief. The EAT had failed to consider whether, in the light of O's procedural irregularities, its decision could be said to be reasonable. An employer who dismissed an employee was not obliged to specify his reasons but if it did not specify reasons it was more difficult to justify the decision to dismiss. The decision of the EAT that O did not have reasonable grounds for its belief that P had been guilty of gross misconduct was warranted by the evidence and was based on the correct legal test, *British Home Stores Ltd v. Burchell* [1980] I.C.R. 303, [1980] C.L.Y. 1004 considered.

PORTER v. OAKBANK SCHOOL 2004 S.C. 603, Lord Gill L.J.C., Lord Kirkwood, Lord McCluskey, Ex Div.

5219. **Unfair dismissal—Right to respect for private and family life—Covert surveillance of employee's home—Compatibility of surveillance with right to privacy**

[Human Rights Act 1998 (c,42) Sch.1 Part I Art.8(1).]

The appellant (M) appealed against a finding that he had not been unfairly dismissed by the respondent company (S). M worked at a water treatment plant and lived in a nearby tied house. S suspected that M was falsifying his timesheets. S carried out covert surveillance upon M which included the filming of M coming and going from his house. Following a disciplinary procedure, M was dismissed. The tribunal concluded that there had been no breach of M's right under the Human Rights Act 1998 Sch.1 Part I Art.8(1) and that no evidence had been unlawfully, unreasonably or illegally obtained. M argued that (1) the tribunal had misdirected itself on the issue of Art.8(1), the matter not being one of privacy but a matter of respect for private and family life; (2) S should have restricted its surveillance to the workplace and workplace activities; (3) S's surveillance went far beyond that and as such was disproportionate.

Held, dismissing the appeal, that the tribunal had reached the conclusion it was entitled to reach upon the evidence. (1) At first sight, covert surveillance of a person's home unbeknown to him raised a presumption that the right to have one's private life respected was being invaded. If the issue stopped there Art.8(1) might have been engaged. However what mattered in the instant case was the question of proportionality. (2) S had considered how best to deal with the matter and had concluded that inserting cameras in the workplace would be impractical and ineffective. The aim of the surveillance was to see how many times M left the house to go to the plant. That bore on the accuracy or otherwise of M's timesheets. Thus it went to the heart of the investigation that S, as a public corporation, was bound to carry out to protect its assets. (3) Surveillance was not undertaken for external reasons. It went to the essence of the obligations and rights of S to protect its assets. As such it was not disproportionate, *Martin v. McGuiness* 2003 S.L.T. 1424, [2003] C.L.Y. 5271 applied.

McGOWAN v. SCOTTISH WATER [2005] I.R.L.R. 167, Lord Johnston, EAT (SC).

5220. **Wrongful dismissal—Damages—Bonus payments—Entitlement**

S, a former employee, raised an action for damages against T claiming wrongful dismissal. T conceded liability and the only contentious issues were the extent to which S's loss fell to be mitigated and his entitlement, or otherwise, to bonus payments. S had been managing director of T's technology division, in which capacity he had received bonus payments until February 2003, when he assumed the new role of director of business transformation. He was dismissed in October 2003. S submitted that, although there was no specific agreement regarding the nature and extent of his bonus entitlement in his new role, the court should make realistic assumptions and hold that his bonus entitlement would have continued. Further, a wrongfully dismissed employee was entitled to compensation for the loss of the chance to earn bonuses, even if he had no legal right to receive them. S accepted that income derived from fresh employment should be deducted from the damages awarded, but he disputed T's claim that he should have accepted a job offer from a company received four months after his dismissal, citing the commuting time involved, the substantial drop in remuneration and the fact that the job did not match his aspirations.

Held, allowing a further case management conference, that (1) the sums said to be payable by way of bonus entitlement did not form part of any compensation in respect of wrongful dismissal. The clause in S's contract which entitled him to receive bonus payments was discretionary. S had no track record in his new role: in the circumstances, his receipt of bonus payments in his new role was an unlikely prospect. Furthermore, at the time of his dismissal, there was no contractual obligation on the defenders to provide an annual bonus entitlement, *Clark v. BET Plc* [1997] I.R.L.R. 348, [1997] C.L.Y. 2207 distinguished. (2) There was nothing untoward in S's decision to refuse the job offer and it could not be said that he had failed to mitigate his loss.

STUART v. TELECOM SERVICES LTD 2005 S.L.T. (Sh Ct) 39, Sheriff CAL Scott, Sh Ct (Glasgow and Strathkelvin).

5221. Books

Craig, Victor; Walker, Steven J–Scottish Employment Law: An Introduction. Paperback: £25.00. ISBN 0 414 01623 8. W. Green & Son.

ENERGY

5222. Electricity industry–Applications for consent–Fees

ELECTRICITY (APPLICATIONS FOR CONSENT) AMENDMENT (SCOTLAND) REGULATIONS 2005, SSI 2005 295; made under the Electricity Act 1989 s.36, s.60, Sch.8 para.1. In force: July 1, 2005; £3.00.

These Regulations, which amend the Electricity (Applications for Consent) Regulations 1990 (SI 1990 455), increase the fees payable for consent applications in Scotland by substituting tables of new fees.

5223. Energy efficiency–Grants–Eligibility

HOME ENERGY EFFICIENCY SCHEME AMENDMENT (SCOTLAND) REGULATIONS 2005, SSI 2005 144; made under the Social Security Act 1990 s.15. In force: April 21, 2005; £3.00.

These Regulations amend the Home Energy Efficiency Scheme Regulations 1997 (SI 1997 790) which provide for the making of grants for the improvement of energy efficiency in dwellings occupied by persons on low income or elderly persons. They amend the financial limit in the 1997 Regulations in relation to increases in the income threshold for eligibility for grant for persons in receipt of child tax credit and working tax credit in line with increases to these payments effective from April 6, 2005.

ENVIRONMENT

5224. Air pollution–Air quality reviews

AIR QUALITY LIMIT VALUES (SCOTLAND) AMENDMENT REGULATIONS 2005, SSI 2005 300; made under the European Communities Act 1972 s.2. In force: June 25, 2005; £3.00.

These Regulations amend the Air Quality Limit Values (Scotland) Regulations 2003 (SSI 2003 428) so as to implement Art.2 of European Parliament and Council Directive 2003/35 ([2003] OJ L156/17) on public participation in respect of the drawing up of certain plans and programmes relating to the environment in respect of air quality plans and programmes, required by virtue of Art.8(3) of Council Directive 96/62 ([1996] OJ L296/55) on ambient air quality assessment and management.

5225. Conservation–Plant protection

WILDLIFE AND COUNTRYSIDE ACT 1981 (VARIATION OF SCHEDULE) (SCOTLAND) ORDER 2005, SSI 2005 308; made under the Wildlife and Countryside Act 1981 s.22. In force: June 30, 2005; £3.00.

This Order varies the Wildlife and Countryside Act 1981 by adding 13 species of plant to the list of species of plants which may not be planted or otherwise caused to grow in the wild.

5226. Environmental Assessment (Scotland) Act 2005 (asp 15)

This Act makes provision for the assessment of the environmental effects of certain plans and programmes, including plans and programmes to which European Parliament and Council Directive 2001/42/EC relates.

This Act received Royal Assent on December 14, 2005.

5227. Environmental protection–Financial assistance–Bio-energy Infrastructure Scheme

FINANCIAL ASSISTANCE FOR ENVIRONMENTAL PURPOSES (SCOTLAND) ORDER 2005, SSI 2005 324; made under the Environmental Protection Act 1990 s.153. In force: July 1, 2005; £3.00.

This Order varies the Environmental Protection Act 1990 so as to enable the Scottish Ministers to give financial assistance to, or for the purposes of, the Bio-energy Infrastructure Scheme for Scotland.

5228. Environmental protection–Pesticides–Possession

POSSESSION OF PESTICIDES (SCOTLAND) ORDER 2005, SSI 2005 66; made under the Wildlife and Countryside Act 1981 s.15A. In force: March 14, 2005; £3.00.

This Order prescribes types of ingredients of pesticides for the purposes of the Wildlife and Countryside Act 1981 s.15A. Possession of any pesticide containing a prescribed active ingredient is an offence.

5229. Environmental protection–Pollution control

POLLUTION PREVENTION AND CONTROL (SCOTLAND) AMENDMENT REGULATIONS 2005, SSI 2005 101; made under the Pollution Prevention and Control Act 1999 s.2. In force: April 1, 2005; £3.00.

These Regulations amend the Pollution Prevention and Control (Scotland) Regulations 2000 (SSI 2000 323) to, amongst other things, omit references to chromium, manganese, nickel and zinc in that provision and to qualify the application of that section to certain releases into the air; and to make provision for the incineration of animal waste with certain treatment capacities to be classified as Part A and B activities respectively.

5230. Environmental protection–Pollution control–Public participation

POLLUTION PREVENTION AND CONTROL (PUBLIC PARTICIPATION ETC.) (SCOTLAND) REGULATIONS 2005, SSI 2005 510; made under the Pollution Prevention and Control Act 1999 s.2. In force: November 16, 2005; £3.00.

These Regulations, which amend the Environmental Protection (Prescribed Processes and Substances) Regulations 1991 (SI 1991 472) and the Pollution Prevention and Control (Scotland) Regulations (SSI 2000 323), implement European Parliament and Council Directive 2003/35 ([2003] OJ L156/17) providing for public participation in respect of the drawing up of certain plans and programmes relating to the environment and amending Council Directives 85/337 and 96/61. The Regulations enable SEPA to grant a permit subject to the condition that the applicant obtains any relevant certificate of technical competence within 2 years, where satisfied that the person is a fit and proper person to carry out certain specified waste management activities; extend the application of that provision to mobile plant; extend the additional access to justice requirements in the Public Participation Directive to environmental non-governmental organisations; amend the definition of "vehicle coating" to exclude certain coating activities from the scope of that definition in certain circumstances; and require SEPA to include in the register the information resulting from the new public participation requirements.

5231. Environmental protection–Pollution control regime–Public participation–Designation

POLLUTION PREVENTION AND CONTROL (DESIGNATION OF PUBLIC PARTICIPATION DIRECTIVE) (SCOTLAND) ORDER 2005, SSI 2005 461; made under the Pollution Prevention and Control Act 1999 Sch.1 para.20. In force: October 5, 2005; £3.00.

This Order designates European Parliament and Council Directive 2003/35 ([2003] OJ L156/17) providing for public participation in respect of the drawing up of certain plans and programmes relating to the environment and amending with regard to public participation and access to justice Council Directives 85/337 and 96/61 as a relevant directive for the purposes of the Pollution Prevention and Control Act 1999. The purpose of the designation is to enable the powers in the Act to be used to transpose the Public Participation Directive.

5232. Environmental protection–Pollution control regime–Waste incineration installations

POLLUTION PREVENTION AND CONTROL (SCOTLAND) AMENDMENT (NO.2) REGULATIONS 2005, SSI 2005 340; made under the Pollution Prevention and Control Act 1999 s.2. In force: July 2, 2005; £3.00.

These Regulations amend the Pollution Prevention and Control (Scotland) Regulations 2000 (SSI 2000 323) to change the definition of "specified waste management activity" so as to include "the disposal of waste in a waste incineration installation". They provide that where a substantial change has resulted in the issue of a permit applicable to the part of the installation affected by the change, SEPA may on determination of an application for a permit for the remainder of the installation issue a consolidated permit for the whole installation; and extends provisions to mobile plants.

5233. Environmental protection–Waste–Packaging

PRODUCER RESPONSIBILITY OBLIGATIONS (PACKAGING WASTE) AMENDMENT (SCOTLAND) REGULATIONS 2005, SSI 2005 271; made under the Environment Act 1995 s.93, s.94. In force: May 19, 2005; £3.00.

These Regulations amend the Producer Responsibility Obligations (Packaging Waste) Regulations 1997 (SI 1997 648), which impose obligations on producers to recover and recycle packaging waste, and related obligations, to assist the UK in attaining the targets set out in Council Directive 94/62 ([1994] OJ L365/10) Art.6(1), on packaging and packaging waste. They make amendments to allow reprocessors and exporters to apply for, and SEPA to grant, accreditation at any time throughout the year.

5234. Environmental protection–Waste management

WASTE (SCOTLAND) REGULATIONS 2005, SSI 2005 22; made under the European Communities Act 1972 s.2; and the Pollution Prevention and Control Act 1999 s.2. In force: in accordance with Art.1 (1); £3.00.

These Regulations make miscellaneous changes to waste management legislation by amending the Environmental Protection Act 1990, the Controlled Waste (Registration of Carriers and Seizure of Vehicles) Regulations 1991 (SI 1991 1624), the Controlled Waste Regulations 1992 (SI 1992 588), the Waste Management Licensing Regulations 1994 (SI 1994 1056) and the Groundwater Regulations 1998 (SI 1998 2746).

5235. Environmental protection – Water pollution – Nitrate vulnerable zones

PROTECTION OF WATER AGAINST AGRICULTURAL NITRATE POLLUTION (SCOTLAND) AMENDMENT REGULATIONS 2005, SSI 2005 593; made under the European Communities Act 1972 s.2. In force: December 20, 2005; £3.00.

These Regulations amend the Protection of Water Against Agricultural Nitrate Pollution (Scotland) Regulations 1996 (SI 1996 1564) which gave effect to Council Directive 91/676 ([2005] OJ L375/1) concerning the protection of waters against pollution caused by nitrates from agricultural sources. The Regulations update the implementation of Art.5(1) (establishment of action programmes in respect of designated nitrate vulnerable zones) of the Directive and substitute the definition of "code of good agricultural practice" in the 1996 Regulations by reference to the Code of Good Practice for the Prevention of Environmental Pollution from Agricultural Activity, issued by the Scottish Ministers on March 11, 2005.

5236. Environmental protection – Water pollution – Nitrate vulnerable zones – Public participation

NITRATE (PUBLIC PARTICIPATION ETC.) (SCOTLAND) REGULATIONS 2005, SSI 2005 305; made under the European Communities Act 1972 s.2. In force: June 25, 2005; £3.00.

These Regulations amend the Protection of Water Against Agricultural Nitrate Pollution (Scotland) Regulations 1996 (SI 1996 1564) and the Designation of Nitrate Vulnerable Zones (Scotland) Regulations 2002 (SSI 2002 276). They give effect to the requirements of Art.2 of European Parliament and Council Directive 2003/35 ([2003] OJ L156/17) on public participation in respect of the drawing up of certain plans and programmes relating to the environment in respect of action programmes for nitrate vulnerable zones required by virtue of Art.5(1) of Council Directive 91/676 ([1996] OJ L375/1) concerning the protection of waters against pollution caused by nitrates from agricultural sources.

5237. Landfill allowances – Trading scheme

LANDFILL ALLOWANCES SCHEME (SCOTLAND) REGULATIONS 2005, SSI 2005 157; made under the Waste and Emissions Trading Act 2003 s.6, s.7, s.10, s.11, s.12, s.13, s.15, s.16, s.26, s.36. In force: in accordance with Reg.1 (2) (3); £3.50.

These Regulations implement Council Directive 99/31 ([1999] OJ L182/1) Art.5(1)(2) on the landfill of waste in Scotland. They make provision for implementing Ch.1 of Pt.1 of the Act including the landfill allowances scheme under that Part.

5238. Smoke control – Authorisation of fuel

SMOKE CONTROL AREAS (AUTHORISED FUELS) (SCOTLAND) AMENDMENT REGULATIONS 2005, SSI 2005 614; made under the Clean Air Act 1993 s.20, s.63. In force: January 1, 2006; £3.00.

These Regulations amend the Smoke Control Areas (Authorised Fuels) (Scotland) Regulations 2001 (SSI 2001 433) by making minor changes.

5239. Smoke control – Exempt fireplaces

SMOKE CONTROL AREAS (EXEMPT FIREPLACES) (SCOTLAND) ORDER 2005, SSI 2005 615; made under the Clean Air Act 1993 s.21. In force: January 1, 2006; £3.00.

This Order makes provision for exemption from the prohibition, under the Clean Air Act 1993 s.20, on the emission of smoke in smoke control areas. The Order exempts those fireplaces described in column 1 of the Schedule which comply with the conditions specified in column 2 from the prohibitions. The Order also amends the Smoke Control Areas (Exempted Fireplaces) (Scotland) Order 1999 (SSI 1999 58) to extend an existing class description of exempted fireplace and the conditions to be complied with in relation to it.

5240. Waste and Emissions Trading Act 2003 (c.33)–Commencement Order

WASTE AND EMISSIONS TRADING ACT 2003 (COMMENCEMENT) (SCOTLAND) ORDER 2005, SSI 2005 52 (C.4); made under the Waste and Emissions Trading Act 2003 s.40. Commencement details: bringing into force various provisions of the 2003 Act on February 3, 2005 and April 1, 2005; £3.00.

This Order brings the Waste and Emissions Trading Act 2003 s.4, s.5, s.9, s.10 and s.18 into force as regards Scotland only.

5241. Water Environment and Water Services (Scotland) Act 2003 (asp 3)–Commencement No.2 Order

WATER ENVIRONMENT AND WATER SERVICES (SCOTLAND) ACT 2003 (COMMENCEMENT NO.2) ORDER 2005, SSI 2005 235 (C.11); made under the Water Environment and Water Services (Scotland) Act 2003 s.38. Commencement details: bringing into force various provisions of the 2003 Act on June 1, 2005; £3.00.

This Order brings into force provisions of the Water Environment and Water Services (Scotland) Act 2003 which provide as follows: s.8 confers duties relating to the monitoring of the status of the water environment in each river basin district and the preparation of monitoring programmes on the Scottish Environment Protection Agency (SEPA); s.9 contains requirements relating to the setting of environmental objectives and programme of measures in the river basin management plan; s.10 requires SEPA to prepare and submit to the Scottish Ministers a river basin management plan for each river basin district, and sets out the matters which must be included in, and accompany, the plan; s.11 contains the publicity and consultation requirements relating to the river basin management plan; s.15 concerns the preparation of sub basin plans; and s.17 makes provision for the establishment of River Basin District Advisory Groups.

5242. Water policy–Controlled activities

WATER ENVIRONMENT (CONTROLLED ACTIVITIES) (SCOTLAND) REGULATIONS 2005, SSI 2005 348; made under the Water Environment and Water Services (Scotland) Act 2003 s.20, s.25, s.36, Sch.2. In force: in accordance with Reg.1; £7.50.

These Regulations are made under the Water Environment and Water Services (Scotland) Act 2003 which transposed European Parliament and Council Directive 2000/60 ([2000] OJ L327/1) establishing a framework for Community action in the field of water policy. These Regulations provide the mechanism by which most of the measures required under Art.11(3) of the Directive will be taken. They also make provision to meet the requirements of Art.23 of the Directive in respect of those measures.

5243. Water pollution–Codes of practice

WATER (PREVENTION OF POLLUTION) (CODE OF PRACTICE) (SCOTLAND) ORDER 2005, SSI 2005 63; made under the Control of Pollution Act 1974 s.51. In force: March 11, 2005; £3.00.

This Order, which revokes the Water (Prevention of Pollution) (Code of Practice) (Scotland) Order 1997 (SI 1997 1584) and the Water (Prevention of Pollution) (Code of Practice) (Scotland) Amendment Order 2001 (SSI 2001 175), approves the Code of Good Practice for the Prevention of Environmental Pollution from Agricultural Activity which is to be issued by the Scottish Ministers on March 11, 2005 insofar as it relates to pollution of water. This Code of Practice replaces the previous Code of Practice issued by the Secretary of State for Scotland on July 25, 1997 and supplemented by the Prevention of Environmental Pollution from Agricultural Activity, Nitrogen and Phosphorus Supplement. The Code gives practical guidance to persons engaged in agriculture with respect to activities that may cause water pollution and seeks to promote desirable practices by such persons in this field.

FAMILY LAW

5244. **Adoption–Freeing orders–Parents with learning disabilities unable to care for three children–No desire for contact–Consent unreasonably withheld**

A sought orders to free three brothers aged eight, seven and six for adoption. The parents, M and F, who both had learning difficulties, refused to consent to the adoption. They had an older first child who had been removed from them at five years of age and later freed for adoption. The three boys had lived with M and F since their birth; however, in 2000 they were placed in foster care. M and F received social work support throughout the period the children lived with them. In 1999, the children were placed on the child protection register as being at risk of emotional abuse and neglect. Numerous children's hearings took place which led to the children's removal to foster care. The main concerns raised were inadequate diet, poor hygiene, failure to respond to basic needs, poor stimulation, inability to set consistent and appropriate boundaries, aggression and violence within the family and a failure to secure the children's safety. Further, that despite the unprecedented level of social services' support, M and F had failed to make any real progress. M and F had had no contact with the children since 2002. A contended that consent was being unreasonably withheld and should be dispensed with as there was sufficient evidence that M and F had persistently failed to ensure that the children were adequately cared for.

Held, granting the petition, that the children should be freed for adoption. The parents had persistently failed to discharge their responsibility to safeguard and promote the health, development and welfare of their children. There was considerable evidence that they were unable to meet their children's basic needs despite a high level of support from social services. The parents were unreasonably withholding their consent to the adoption order. There was no evidence that their parenting skills had changed since 2000 or that they would co-operate with social services' advice. Further, there was no evidence that M and F had wanted contact with the children since 2002. Parental consent was dispensed with as no reasonable parent would withhold consent in the circumstances. Adoption was the only viable option for the children and it was in their interests for an order to be made.

ABERDEENSHIRE COUNCIL v. R; *sub nom.* ABERDEENSHIRE COUNCIL, PETITIONERS 2004 Fam. L.R. 93, Lady Smith, OH.

5245. **Adoption and Children Act 2002 (c.38)–Commencement No.1 Order**

ADOPTION AND CHILDREN ACT 2002 (COMMENCEMENT NO.1) (SCOTLAND) ORDER 2005, SSI 2005 643 (C.33); made under the Adoption and Children Act 2002 s.148. Commencement details: bringing into force various provisions of the 2002 Act on December 30, 2005; £3.00.

This Order brings into force specified provisions in the Adoption and Children Act 2002.

5246. **Breastfeeding etc. (Scotland) Act 2005 (asp 1)**

This Act of the Scottish Parliament makes it an offence to prevent or stop a child who is permitted to be in a public place or licensed premises from being fed milk in that place or on those premises; and makes provision in relation to the promotion of breastfeeding.

This Act received Royal Assent on January 18, 2005.

5247. Child abduction–Foreign judgments–Recognition and enforcement of foreign custody order–Change of circumstances

[European Convention on Recognition and Enforcement of Decisions concerning Custody of Children 1980 Art.9, Art.10(1)(a), Art.10(1)(b).]

The petitioner (F), the legal father of two children, sought their return to Malta. F and the mother (M) had married in Malta in 1993 and their child (S) had been born the same year. In 1998, another child (R) had been born. F was not R's natural father but R was registered as his legitimate child. M and F separated in 1998 and M removed herself and the children to Scotland in 2002. F petitioned the court to register and enforce a custody decision of the Maltese court and order M to deliver the two children to him in Malta. F maintained he did not know the whereabouts of M or the children. M opposed the petition, arguing that the European Convention on Recognition and Enforcement of Decisions concerning Custody of Children 1980 Art.9, Art.10(1)(a) and Art.10(1)(b) applied. Specifically, M argued that (1) she had not been served with any documents in the proceedings in Malta; (2) granting the petition would be contrary to the fundamental principles of Scottish law relating to the paramountcy of the welfare of the children; (3) circumstances had changed since the decree of the Maltese court. F argued that the exception to Art.9 applied because M had concealed her whereabouts, and that there had not been any change of circumstances sufficient to justify the application of Art.10(1)(b).

Held, dismissing the petition, that (1) on the evidence before the court, it could not be said that M had concealed her whereabouts, therefore Art.9 applied. (2) M had not satisfied the heavy burden on her to show that Art.10(1)(a) applied, so that the decision to assign care and custody to F could not be said to be manifestly incompatible with the welfare principle. (3) The change in circumstances, namely the long passage of time since the children had left Malta, meant that it would no longer be in accordance with the welfare of the children to return them to Malta. For the younger child, the time that had passed since the Maltese decision had been a very large part of his life and the older child had articulated a clear and apparently genuine wish to stay in Scotland. Both were settled and happy at school and with family. There was no reason for the court to exercise its residual discretion in favour of recognising the Maltese decision in the instant case, since to do so would be incompatible with the children's welfare.

S v. S 2004 Fam. L.R. 127, Lord Kingarth, OH.

5248. Child abduction–Habitual residence–Petition for return

[Hague Convention on the Civil Aspects of International Child Abduction 1980 Art.13.]

F, a father, petitioned for the return of S, his 12 year old son from his marriage to M, who had removed S from Ireland to Scotland. The family had resided continuously in Scotland until moving to Ireland in July 2002. On July 1, 2004, M and S visited Scotland, and she subsequently decided that she did not wish to return to Ireland. M argued that the move to Ireland was on a trial basis and that the Hague Convention on the Civil Aspects of International Child Abduction 1980 did not apply as S had not acquired habitual residence in Ireland, she had not lost her Scottish habitual residence and had not acquired Irish habitual residence. S further opposed the petition on the basis that he disliked his Irish school, had few friends there, disliked living in a rural area and was now reunited with friends in Scotland. F submitted that S had lost his Scottish habitual residence and had subsequently acquired Irish residence, having lived there for almost two years during which time he had attended school, F and M had jointly purchased property with the intention of renovating it, had opened a joint bank account and jointly registered for a telephone account. M had also obtained a Garda immigration card, had attended a course and had sought employment. F further argued that the approach to interpreting Art.13 of the Convention as set out in *W v. W* 2004 S.C. 63, [2003] C.L.Y. 5520 should be followed.

Held, refusing the petition, that (1) the habitual residence of a child whose parents were married was that of its parents, one of whom could not change the child's habitual residence without the agreement of the other, and given that there was clear evidence that M had lived an apparently regular family life in Ireland for a lengthy period and had jointly purchased property and applied for jobs which inferred a likelihood of an intention to continue beyond that time, she had acquired habitual residence in Ireland, thus the Convention applied and S had been wrongfully retained in Scotland. (2) It was not appropriate to follow the approach of *W v. W* where there was a weight of authority to the contrary effect. (3) Discretion refusing the order sought ought to be exercised, notwithstanding the terms of the Convention, there being exceptional circumstances, namely ample recording of articulate objection to the features of S's life in Ireland, albeit expressed in general terms, and S's ongoing education would be disrupted if the order was granted which would involve his removal from high school which he had attended for over half a term, and a return to primary school in Ireland, *W v. W* considered.

M, PETITIONER 2005 S.L.T. 2, Lady Smith, OH.

5249. Childminders–Registration–Cancellation–Failure to serve improvement notice

[Regulation of Care (Scotland) Act 2001 (asp 8) s.12(1)(b); Regulation of Care (Requirements as to Care Services) (Scotland) Regulations 2002 Reg.4(1)(a).]

H, a childminder, appealed against a decision of S, the Scottish Commission for the Regulation of Care, cancelling her registration on the basis that her service had been, or was being, carried out other than in accordance with relevant requirements contrary to the Regulation of Care (Scotland) Act 2001 s.12(1)(b). S had intimated their intention by a letter, which stated that despite having concerns regarding the safety and welfare of a child in her care, H had failed to disclose relevant information to the child protection unit, contrary to the Regulation of Care (Requirements as to Care Services) (Scotland) Regulations 2002 Reg.4(1)(a). It was a matter of concession that S had not served an improvement notice before giving notice under s.12(1). H argued that, having regard to s.12(1) and the whole scheme of the Act, the service provider required to be given an opportunity to improve before there could be a proposal to cancel. The importance of the notice was clearly recognised in s.12(1) and could not be regarded as directory rather than mandatory, furthermore the duty under Reg.4(1)(a) was purely general and did not talk about the manner in which the service was being provided or the particular acts of the service provider, and S's misinterpretation thereof amounted to an error in law going to the root of their decision.

Held, allowing the appeal, that (1) the wording of s.12(1) was clear in that improvement notices were fundamental to the scheme for the improvement of care services and could not be dispensed with even if the circumstances of a particular case suggested that no improvement was practically possible, and S's failure to follow the scheme of the Act they were purporting to apply represented an error in law going to the heart of the procedure which they followed, and entitled H to the remedy sought. (2) H's argument in relation to Reg.4 failed where it embraced individual service users, their particular requirements, and their future needs at the time the provision was being made. The bruises on a child might, depending on the proved circumstances, have given such cause for concern for the future safety of the child that someone under a duty to make provision for his welfare should have given specific details to the authorities. (3) The fact H succeeded on her first argument was sufficient to entitle her to succeed in her appeal without further procedure or inquiry.

HASTIE v. SCOTTISH COMMISSION FOR THE REGULATION OF CARE 2004 S.L.T. (Sh Ct) 131, Sheriff IC Simpson, Sh Ct (Tayside, Central and Fife).

5250. Children–Contact orders–Application by child for contact with half siblings–Competency

[Children (Scotland) Act 1995 (c.36) s.11; European Convention on Human Rights 1950; United Nations Convention on the Rights of the Child 1989.]

The pursuer (E), a 14 year old girl, raised an action seeking a contact order in respect of her half brother, aged 12, and half sister, aged 4, who resided with the defenders, E's mother and stepfather. E had lived with them as a family unit until she had been taken into foster care in 2002. The children's panel had determined that it was not in E's best interests to have contact with the defenders but it would be in her interests to have contact with her half siblings. The defenders argued that E appeared to be seeking a contact order under the Children (Scotland) Act 1995 s.11, which implied certain parental rights and responsibilities that could only be assumed if E was 16. E maintained that her starting point was the United Nations Convention on the Rights of the Child 1989 and the European Convention on Human Rights 1950.

Held, giving judgment accordingly, that the matter did not rest simply on a restrictive interpretation of s.11. Parliament was presumed to have legislated in conformity with the 1989 Convention and the 1950 Convention, *T, Petitioner* 1997 S.L.T. 724, [1996] C.L.Y. 6596 applied. Orders under s.11 could be made by the court of its own motion and where the court was considering such an order it simply had to consider the relevant material and decide what was conducive to the child's welfare, *White v. White* 2001 S.C. 689, [2001] C.L.Y. 6510 considered. In the instant case, it was possible for the court to make an order in E's favour or place parental responsibilities on the defenders to enable supervised contact to take place between E and her half siblings, *D v. H* 2004 S.L.T. (Sh Ct) 73, [2004] C.L.Y. 4744 distinguished. The defenders' plea in law was accordingly repelled. (Obiter) Since the defenders had conducted the debate entirely legalistically and their defences were merely skeletal, the next step was for the case to call in court as soon as possible to determine further procedure, which may be to fix an options hearing should the defenders wish to oppose the action or explore the possibility of a negotiated solution.

E v. E 2004 Fam. L.R. 115, Sheriff FR Crowe, Sh Ct (Tayside, Central and Fife).

5251. Children–Contact orders–Undefended action–Mother seeking to re enter process and lodge defences

[Act of Sederunt (Sheriff Court Ordinary Cause Rules) 1993 (SI 1993 1956) r.33.63, r.33.65.]

The appellant (M), a mother, appealed against a decision that she was not able to re enter the process after failing to appear at a peremptory diet. The respondent father (F) sought declarator of paternity of the two children, a residence order and an order for parental responsibilities and parental rights against M. M had lodged defences, but when she failed to attend the peremptory diet in October 2003 and an interlocutor was issued allowing the cause to proceed undefended. Six months later, M lodged a minute seeking to re enter the process, maintaining that she had not attended the diet because the parties had temporarily reconciled but had since separated again and she now required orders in connection with the children. The minute was refused on the basis that, as the interlocutor had not been appealed against, there was no authority for M to re enter the process. On appeal, M argued that if the minute was incompetent she was left with no means by which she could seek an order in relation to the children, and that there had been a change of circumstances since October 2003, in view of which there ought to be some way of allowing her a remedy.

Held, dismissing the appeal, that the court's primary concern had to be the welfare of the children and, with that in mind, there ought to be some means of drawing the court's attention to changed circumstances where these were relevant to the interests of the children. However, that did not necessarily mean restoring M to the position she had been in before she defaulted. M could make an application for an interim order as a person who was no longer a defender under the Act of Sederunt (Sheriff Court Ordinary Cause Rules) 1993 r.33.63, or wait for decree and lodge a minute in terms of r.33.65. In the instant case, M's minute did not make any specific assertions as to the best interests of the children, but merely sought to allow M back into the action as a defender. If, in his discretion, the sheriff considered that M had information relevant to the welfare of the children, it was not a prerequisite for the investigation of that information that M be allowed to re enter the process, *Black v. Black* 1995 G.W.D. 33-1713 considered. The difficulties in the instant case were largely attributable to the time that had elapsed, but this did not undermine the applicability of the general principles.

ROBB v. GILLAN 2004 Fam. L.R. 120, Sheriff Principal RA Dunlop Q.C., Sh Ct.

5252. **Children−Residence orders−Mother seeking permanent interdict to prevent father removing children−Risk of interference**

S, the Scottish mother of two children, born in 1994 and 1996, raised an action against Q, her former husband, on May 12, 2001, seeking an order interdicting him or anyone on his behalf from removing or attempting to remove their children from her care, and from molesting her. Interim interdict was granted on that date. Q was a French national, where he resided. The parties married in Scotland in June 1993, and were divorced in March 2001 in terms of a French tribunal, which further awarded custody of the children to Q. In December 1999, S removed the children to Scotland. The history of the legal proceedings in France and Scotland was largely undisputed. The current state of proceedings in France was that S held a decree in her favour providing that she should have sole parental authority over the children and that their place of residence be fixed as her home in Scotland. In Scotland, the children remained under the supervision of the children's hearing on the basis that they resided with S and had no contact with Q. S averred that Q and another man tried to force their way into her house to take the children. S further gave evidence of Q's membership of "Les Peres de Pontoise", a group which allegedly advocated "gangster methods", evidence of Q's admission that during January 2003 he had visited Scotland with a French film crew, who were preparing a documentary on the problems he had experienced in relation to his children,; and an alleged sighting of Q at the children's school in October 2003.

Held, assoilzieing Q, that (1) permanent interdict against molestation was a remedy that ought not to be granted lightly, *Cunningham v. Cunningham* 2001 Fam. L.R. 12, [2001] C.L.Y. 6519 followed. (2) On the basis of the evidence, taking into account the effect of the order that parental authority over the children was to be exclusively exercised by S, which was a significant change from the legal situation which prevailed before that, the court was not persuaded of a risk that Q would interfere in the S's care of the children, nor that there was sufficient basis for reasonable apprehension that Q would molest S in a manner which would warrant granting permanent interdict. S had not established on a balance of probabilities that Q intended to remove the children from her care on May 11, 2001, and the evidence relating to Q's membership of "Les Peres de Pontoise" did not assist where fathers such as Q was entitled to join together and protest about aspects of the administration of justice to which they objected.

S v. Q 2005 S.L.T. 53, Lord Mackay of Drumadoon, OH.

5253. **Childrens hearings−Childrens welfare−Grounds for referral−Member of same household as child in respect of whom offence committed**

[Children (Scotland) Act 1995 (c.36) s.52(2); Criminal Procedure (Scotland) Act 1995 (c.46) Sch.1.]

M appealed by stated case against a sheriff's decision finding grounds for referral to a children's hearing established in respect of her child K, who was born in January 2004. C, the reporter, had referred the case on the grounds that K was, or was likely to become, a member of the same household as M's child, D, who was born in July 1997, in respect of whom an offence under the Criminal Procedure (Scotland) Act 1995 Sch.1 had been committed in terms of the Children (Scotland) Act 1995 s.52(2)(d) and s.52(2)(e). The sheriff found that from D's birth until about June

28, 1998, he was normally cared for by M's parents, X. M lived with H (K's father), but a very strong bond then existed between M and X and she spent considerable time with them in their home and saw D every day. M and H looked after D overnight on June 27, 1998, and the following day he was admitted to hospital with injuries. The injuries were the result of an assault committed against D while he was in the care of M and H, or X. After treatment D was taken into care and subsequently adopted. Following K's birth, child protection measures were invoked and he was placed with carers. M and H saw K daily and X had supervised contact with him once a week. The sheriff asked (1) whether she was entitled to find that K was a member of the same household as D; (2) whether she was entitled to find the grounds for referral established. M conceded that the household of which D was a member included herself, but submitted that there was no proper basis for the sheriff's finding that she remained a member of that household.

Held, dismissing the appeal and answering both questions in the affirmative, that the sheriff was well entitled to find that K was likely to become a member of the same household as D. On the facts admitted or proved, the ties of affection and regular contact which held M and her parents together as a group when D was with them still continued and K would become a member of that same group of people who continued to be bound to each other, and who were already bound to K as they were to D, by ties of affection and regular contact.

CUNNINGHAM v. M 2005 S.L.T. (Sh Ct) 73, Sheriff Principal Iain Macphail Q.C., Sh Ct.

5254. Civil Partnership Act 2004 (c.33)–Commencement No.1 Order

CIVIL PARTNERSHIP ACT 2004 (COMMENCEMENT NO.1) (SCOTLAND) ORDER 2005, SSI 2005 428 (C.20); made under the Civil Partnership Act 2004 s.258, s.263. Commencement details: bringing into force various provisions of the 2004 Act on September 14, 2005; £3.00.

This Order brings into force provisions of the Civil Partnership Act 2004.

5255. Civil Partnership Act 2004 (c.33)–Commencement No.2 Order

CIVIL PARTNERSHIP ACT 2004 (COMMENCEMENT NO.2) (SCOTLAND) ORDER 2005, SSI 2005 604 (C.31); made under the Civil Partnership Act 2004 s.258, s.263. Commencement details: bringing into force various provisions of the 2004 Act on December 5, 2005; £3.00.

This Order brings into force the provisions of the Civil Partnership Act 2004 for Scotland in so far as they are not already in force.

5256. Civil partnerships–Births, still-births, deaths and marriages–Prescribed forms

REGISTRATION OF BIRTHS, STILL-BIRTHS, DEATHS AND MARRIAGES (PRESCRIPTION OF FORMS) (SCOTLAND) AMENDMENT REGULATIONS 2005, SSI 2005 595; made under the Registration of Births, Deaths and Marriages (Scotland) Act 1965 s.21, s.22, s.32, s.54. In force: December 5, 2005; £3.00.

These Regulations amend the Registration of Births, Still-Births, Deaths and Marriages (Prescription of Forms) (Scotland) Regulations 1997 (SI 1997 2348). A revised form of Certificate of Registration of Still-birth is substituted to enable more detail to be provided. Revised Death and Marriage register pages are substituted to reflect the changes brought about by the Civil Partnership Act 2004.

5257. Civil partnerships–Consequential amendments

CIVIL PARTNERSHIP ACT 2004 (CONSEQUENTIAL AMENDMENTS) (SCOTLAND) ORDER 2005, SSI 2005 623; made under the Civil Partnership Act 2004 s.259. In force: December 5, 2005; £3.00.

This Order makes provision consequential on the Civil Partnership Act 2004. It amends the Human Tissue Act 1961, the Conveyancing (Scotland) Act 1970, the

Marriage (Scotland) Act 1977, the Land Registration (Scotland) Act 1979, the Anatomy Act 1984, the Local Government Finance Act 1992, the Crofters (Scotland) Act 1993, the Mortgage Rights (Scotland) Act 2001 and the Land Reform (Scotland) Act 2003 to ensure that civil partners are given parity of treatment with spouses in areas of the law that are not contained within that Act.

5258. Civil partnerships–Consequential modifications

CIVIL PARTNERSHIP ACT 2004 (MODIFICATION OF SUBORDINATE LEGISLATION) ORDER 2005, SSI 2005 572; made under the Civil Partnership Act 2004 s.259. In force: December 5, 2005; £3.00.

This Order amends the Cremation (Scotland) Regulations 1935 (SR & O 1935 247), the Anatomy Regulations 1988 (SI 1988 44), the National Health Service (Charges to Overseas Visitors) (Scotland) Regulations 1989 (SI 1989 364), the Nursing and Midwifery Student Allowances (Scotland) Regulations 1992 (SI 1992 580), the Council Tax (Discounts) (Scotland) Regulations 1992 (SI 1992 1409), the Education Authority Bursaries (Scotland) Regulations 1995 (SI 1995 1739), the Education (Fees and Awards) (Scotland) Regulations 1997 (SI 1997 790), the Scotland Act 1998 (Transitory and Transitional Provisions) (Scottish Parliamentary Pension Scheme) Order 1999 (SI 1999 1082), the Students' Allowances (Scotland) Regulations 1999 (SI 1999 1131), the Scotland Act 1998 (Transitory and Transitional Provisions) (Publication and Interpretation etc. of Acts of the Scottish Parliament) Order 1999 (SI 1999 1379), the Education (Student Loans) (Scotland) Regulations 2000 (SSI 2000 200), the Graduate Endowment (Scotland) Regulations 2001 (SSI 2001 280), the Scottish Local Government Election Rules 2002 (SSI 2002 457), the Education Maintenance Allowances (Scotland) Regulations 2004 (SSI 2004 273) and the Council Tax (Discount for Unoccupied Dwellings) (Scotland) Regulations 2005 (SSI 2005 51). It makes modifications consequential to the Civil Partnership Act 2004 to ensure that civil partners are given parity of treatment and status as spouses in areas of law that are not contained within the 2004 Act.

5259. Civil partnerships–Jurisdiction and recognition of judgements

CIVIL PARTNERSHIP (JURISDICTION AND RECOGNITION OF JUDGMENTS) (SCOTLAND) REGULATIONS 2005, SSI 2005 629; made under the Civil Partnership Act 2004 s.219. In force: December 5, 2005; £3.00.

The Regulations apply to all civil partnerships including overseas relationships entitled to be treated as a civil partnership, by virtue of the Civil Partnership Act 2004. They allow for the recognition and non recognition of judgments issued before the coming into force of these Regulations and the 2004 Act; set out the criteria for accepting jurisdiction for dissolution, annulment or separation proceedings in respect of civil partners; set out the criteria for recognition and non recognition of a judgment; prevent the court from reviewing the jurisdiction of the court of the Member State that made the original judgment and also prevent a court from reviewing the substance of that judgment; ensure that a judgment is recognised notwithstanding that there might well have been a different outcome on the facts if the law of Scotland been applied to the judgment; and allow the court to sist proceedings for recognition of a judgment when there is an appeal outstanding against that judgment. The Regulations make provision for civil partnerships corresponding, as far as is possible in domestic law to the jurisdiction and recognition elements of Council Regulation 2201/2003 ([2003] OJ L338/1) for matrimonial matters as regards the law of Scotland.

5260. Civil partnerships–Marriage–Forms

MARRIAGE (PRESCRIPTION OF FORMS) (SCOTLAND) AMENDMENT REGULATIONS 2005, SSI 2005 596; made under the Marriage (Scotland) Act 1977 s.3, s.4, s.6, s.7. In force: December 5, 2005; £3.00.

These Regulations amend the Marriage (Prescription of Forms) (Scotland) Regulations 1997 (SI 1997 2349). Revised forms relating to the marriage notice (form M10 -regulation 3), the declaration to be made by parties to a marriage who are related by affinity (form DSR -regulation 4), the marriage schedule (regulation 5) and the certificate of no impediment (form M1 -regulation 6) are substituted to reflect changes brought about by the Civil Partnership Act 2004. In addition, the prescribed particulars to be entered in the marriage notice book for the purposes of the Marriage (Scotland) Act 1977 are amended to include a reference to civil partnership status.

5261. Civil partnerships–Overseas relationships

CIVIL PARTNERSHIP (OVERSEAS RELATIONSHIPS) (SCOTLAND) ORDER 2005, SSI 2005 573; made under the Civil Partnership Act 2004 s.259. In force: December 5, 2005; £3.00.

This Order makes provision relating to the treatment of overseas relationships treated as civil partnerships by virtue of the Civil Partnership Act 2004 which were registered in the country where they were entered into before the date on which the Act comes into force. It modifies the Act which determines when an overseas relationship formed before December 5, 2005 will be recognised as a civil partnership in order to ensure that a person cannot be recognised as being a party to more than one civil partnership or a civil partnership and a marriage at any one time.

5262. Civil partnerships–Recognition of dissolutions, annulments and separations

CIVIL PARTNERSHIP (SUPPLEMENTARY PROVISIONS RELATING TO THE RECOGNITION OF OVERSEAS DISSOLUTIONS, ANNULMENTS OR SEPARATIONS) (SCOTLAND) REGULATIONS 2005, SSI 2005 567; made under the Civil Partnership Act 2004 s.237. In force: December 5, 2005; £3.00.

These Regulations, which amend the Civil Partnership Act 2004, make supplemental provision for the recognition in Scotland of dissolutions and annulments of civil partnerships and the separation of civil partners obtained abroad.

5263. Civil partnerships–Registration–Prescription of forms

REGISTRATION OF CIVIL PARTNERSHIPS (PRESCRIPTION OF FORMS, PUBLICISATION AND ERRORS) (SCOTLAND) REGULATIONS 2005, SSI 2005 458; made under the Civil Partnership Act 2004 s.88, s.89, s.90, s.94, s.95, s.97, s.99, s.122, s.258. In force: December 5, 2005; £3.00.

These Regulations prescribe the forms and particulars which are required to be prescribed for Scotland under the Civil Partnership Act 2004. They prescribe the manner in which and means by which the names of intended civil partners and date on which the district registrar intends to register their partnership are to be publicised by the district registrar. They also prescribe the errors which a district registrar may, in addition to clerical errors, correct in an entry in the register of civil partnerships.

5264. Civil partnerships–Sheriff courts

ACT OF SEDERUNT (ORDINARY CAUSE RULES) AMENDMENT (CIVIL PARTNERSHIP ACT 2004) 2005, SSI 2005 638; made under the Sheriff Courts (Scotland) Act 1971 s.32; and the Civil Partnership Act 2004 s.117, s.226. In force: December 8, 2005; £12.50.

This Act of Sederunt, which amends the Sheriff Courts (Scotland) Act 1907 amends the rules of procedure in the sheriffs court to make provision in consequence of the Civil Partnership Act 2004.

5265. Civil partnerships – Step relationships

CIVIL PARTNERSHIP ACT 2004 (RELATIONSHIPS ARISING THROUGH CIVIL PARTNERSHIP) (SCOTLAND) ORDER 2005, SSI 2005 568; made under the Civil Partnership Act 2004 s.247. In force: December 5, 2005; £3.00.

This Order amends the Civil Partnership Act 2004 to insert references to specific provisions of the Damages (Scotland) Act 1976, the Agricultural Holdings (Scotland) Act 2003 and the Mental Health (Care and Treatment) (Scotland) Act 2003. This has the effect that references to "step" relationships in these provisions are read as including relationships arising through civil partnership.

5266. Divorce – Financial provision – Capital sum – Extensions of time

[Family Law (Scotland) Act 1985 (c.37) s.8(2), s.12(1)(b), s.14(2)(k).]

H, a husband, raised an action of divorce. W, his wife, sought payment of a capital sum for just under £62,000. The sheriff having heard evidence on the merits of the divorce, divorced the parties and allowed a period of 12 months for the granting of an order for a capital sum. Prior to the expiry of this period, W sought an extension, in order to allow the hearing on evidence to be completed. The sheriff refused the motion as incompetent. W appealed. H submitted that although the court had an inherent jurisdiction it could not be employed in this case. There was no uncertainty in the statutory provision and if the Family Law (Scotland) Act 1985 s.12(1)(b) had been intended to allow for an extension of the period specified, it would follow that a series of extensions could be applied for which would be inconsistent with the intention of the Act to achieve a resolution of financial matters on or soon after divorce. W argued that the extension of time which had been sought was competent in terms of s.14(2)(k).

Held, remitting the cause to the sheriff, that (1) this was an appropriate case in which to invoke the inherent jurisdiction of the court to enable the sheriff to do justice between the parties. On the assumption that W's claim had some merit, the events which had occurred would prevent her from obtaining a fair division of the net value of the matrimonial property and H would benefit to the extent that he would not have to comply with such an order and would retain matrimonial assets which he would otherwise have had to make over, where if the court had sat continuously from the start of the proof until its conclusion, the appeal would not have been necessary. (2) Extending the 12 month period could not properly be regarded as an ancillary order, in terms of s.14(2)(k), which was expedient to give effect to an order made under s.8(2), and it could not allow the court to override the clear terms of s.12(1)(b). (3) The sheriff was correct to hold that s.12(1)(b) required him to set a period within which the matters concerned required to be resolved and that that period could not be extended using the provisions of the Act.

LINDSAY v. LINDSAY 2005 S.L.T. (Sh Ct) 81, Sheriff Principal JC McInnes Q.C., Sh Ct.

5267. Divorce – Financial provision – Order for sale of matrimonial home as opposed to transfer to husband – Effect of increase in value of matrimonial home since relevant date

[Family Law (Scotland) Act 1985 (c.37) s.8, s.9(1)(a).]

The appellant (H), the husband, appealed against an order for payment of a capital sum to the respondent wife (W) and an order for sale of the former matrimonial home. W had raised an action of divorce against H, who sought a transfer of the title of the property into his name in exchange for £20,000. The relevant date was agreed to be August 11, 1998 and the value of the flat as at that date was £45,000. At the date of proof, the flat was worth £100,000. Decree of divorce was granted and H was ordered to pay W £14,570, representing half the value of H's pension at the relevant date and a sum to account for childcare. The flat was also ordered to be sold and the proceeds divided equally after certain deductions. On appeal, H argued, inter alia, that the sheriff should have followed *Wallis v. Wallis* 1993 S.C. (H.L.) 49, [1994] C.L.Y. 2186 and made an order to transfer the property to H to achieve an equal sharing of the net value of the property as at the relevant date; and that in taking the course recommended in *Jacques v. Jacques* 1997 S.C. (H.L.) 20, [1997] C.L.Y. 6053 he had exercised his discretion wrongly.

Held, dismissing the appeal, that the correct approach to making orders for financial provision was to value the matrimonial property as at the relevant date, then to decide upon the appropriate order to be made under the Family Law (Scotland) Act 1985 s.8. The approach to this decision was essentially a matter of discretion aimed at achieving a fair and practicable result in accordance with common sense. Section 9(1)(a) required the net value of the property to be shared fairly, which meant equally in the absence of special circumstances, *Jacques* considered. In the instant case, H and W were pro indiviso owners of the flat and as such any increase in value, under the current law, should benefit both parties. If H's approach were followed, he would gain an undeserved windfall of £18,000 and such a result would be so inequitable that no reasonable sheriff could conceivably make such an order, *Wallis* considered. Although the sheriff had begun by considering whether three were special circumstances justifying a transfer of property order as opposed to sale and division of the proceeds, he had examined all the relevant circumstances in the instant case and had been entitled to adapt the principle of equal division to take account of these and adjust the amount of the capital sum awarded to correct the imbalances between the parties.

McCASKILL v. McCASKILL 2004 Fam. L.R. 123, Sheriff Principal ID Macphail Q.C., Sh Ct.

5268. Family proceedings–Child witness notices–Forms

ACT OF SEDERUNT (CHILD CARE AND MAINTENANCE RULES) AMENDMENT (VULNERABLE WITNESSES (SCOTLAND) ACT 2004) 2005, SSI 2005 190; made under the Sheriff Courts (Scotland) Act 1971 s.32. In force: April 1, 2005; £3.00.

This Act of Sederunt amends the Act of Sederunt (Child Care and Maintenance Rules) 1997 (SI 1997 291 (S.19)) to provide for a form of child witness notice and for intimation of such notice by the party lodging the notice to all other parties to the proceedings and any safeguarder; to provide that a sheriff may, on receipt of a child witness notice, make an order authorising the use of special measures without holding a hearing; to provide for a form of application for review of arrangements for vulnerable witnesses and for intimation of such application by the applicant to all parties to the proceedings and any safeguarder; and to provide for a form of application for the admission of restricted evidence or the allowance of questioning.

5269. Fees–Births, deaths, marriages and divorce–Internet search sessions–Extension

BIRTHS, DEATHS, MARRIAGES AND DIVORCES (FEES) (SCOTLAND) AMENDMENT REGULATIONS 2005, SSI 2005 100; made under the Registration of Births, Deaths and Marriages (Scotland) Act 1965 s.28A, s.38, s.47, s.54. In force: April 1, 2005; £3.00.

These Regulations amend the Births, Deaths, Marriages and Divorces (Fees) (Scotland) Regulations 1998 (SI 1998 643) by extending the period during which an Internet search session may continue from 48 hours to 168 hours.

5270. Marriage–Forced marriages–Nullity–Jurisdiction

[Domicile and Matrimonial Proceedings Act 1973 (c.45) s.7(3A)(a), s.7(3B)(a); Council Regulation 1347/2000 on jurisdiction and the recognition and enforcement of judgments in matrimonial matters and in matters of parental responsibility for children of both spouses Art.2(1).]

S, a United Kingdom citizen, sought declarator of nullity of her marriage to an Indian national, in India on September 26, 2001, by reason of her lack of consent and the marriage having been entered into under duress. S averred that she had gone with her mother to India to visit relations and during the holiday her mother became determined that she should be married, contrary to her wishes. S's mother thereafter arranged for a marriage to take place between S and the groom, without S's knowledge. S's mother was in possession of her passport and travel documents and threatened to destroy them and leave her in India. S went through the marriage ceremony but refused to have sexual relations with the groom, left his house a week later and returned to Scotland on October 2, 2001, where she resumed her relationship with her boyfriend and began living with him, having no further contact with her husband. A summons was served personally on the husband on November 12, 2003 and on November 26 a three page typed document headed "written statement filed on behalf of the defender" was received by the court, unsigned, stating that the court had no jurisdiction, S had no cause to file the case, the marriage was not entered into under duress, decree of declarator should not be pronounced and the action should be dismissed. A minute for decree was lodged by S's agent on November 12, 2004 and the judge continued the cause by order for the court to contact the defender to ascertain if a defence to the action was to be lodged. No response was received and the case was continued to a further by order diet for submissions to be heard from S's agent on (1) jurisdiction; (2) whether the document headed "written statement" was a defence; (3) choice of law for duress; (4) sufficiency of evidence.

Held, granting declarator of nullity of marriage, that (1) the court had jurisdiction under the Domicile and Matrimonial Proceedings Act 1973 s.7(3A)(a), failing which, s.7(3B)(a), where S was domiciled in Scotland, and the fact that the marriage was celebrated in India did not affect the issue of jurisdiction as Council Regulation 1347/2000 was not restricted to cases where both parties could found jurisdiction under Art.2(1) and applied in a case such as the present where the respondent was not habitually resident or domiciled in, or a national of, a Member State. (2) Having considered the procedural history of the case, the court was satisfied that this was a case in which no defences had been lodged and that it should be allowed to proceed as an undefended action. (3) Declining to follow the obiter dictum of Lord Guthrie in *Di Rollo v. Di Rollo* 1959 S.C. 75, [1959] C.L.Y. 3556 that the question of consent should be decided by the lex loci celebrationis, the law governing the issue of consent to marriage was the law of the domicile of the party claiming lack of consent, *Di Rollo* considered. Capacity to marry was governed by the ante nuptial domicile of the party, and it appeared to accord with principle that consent should also be governed by the same law. (4) The threats of S's mother were of a serious nature and amounted to threats of immediate danger to S's liberty which caused her will to be overborne and vitiated her consent to marry.

SINGH v. SINGH; *sub nom.* KAUR v. SINGH 2005 S.L.T. 749, Temporary Judge RF Macdonald QC, OH.

5271. Marriage—Marriage ceremony—Nullity

S, a 21 year old Muslim woman, sought declarator of nullity of her marriage to H, her husband, a citizen of Pakistan. The parties were married in a civil ceremony on June 22, 1998 after being introduced by S's parents. It was agreed that the parties should undertake a civil ceremony as an extension to H's visa could be granted if he satisfied immigration authorities that he was married to S, but that they should not live together as husband and wife until undergoing a religious ceremony when S finished school. Extension of H's leave was subsequently granted until October 1999 on the basis of false information provided that the parties were living together. H received confirmation in February 2000 that he was entitled to remain indefinitely in the UK but later expressed reluctance to undertake a religious ceremony. S argued that the civil ceremony was simply an antecedent to a true marriage prescribed by the Muslim faith and that neither party had consented to being married by means of a registry office. At proof, the Lord Ordinary dismissed the action, having concluded that a civil marriage was not void merely because the parties to it did not regard it as having any religious significance and that on June 22, 1998, the parties had intended to be married for the purposes of civil law. S reclaimed.

Held, allowing the reclaiming motion, that (1) the true issue in the present case was whether, on the evidence that could be relied upon and the facts that could be deduced therefrom, the parties had exchanged matrimonial consent on June 22 given that they undeniably went through a regular ceremony of marriage, which individually they understood, and which they understood would be regarded as constituting marriage by Scots law for the purposes they had in mind. (2) It was clear that the Lord Ordinary, in applying the authorities to the facts he found, overlooked the essential requirement of a valid marriage that the parties exchange consent to become husband and wife, whereas the effect of the agreement to go through the registry office ceremony was expressly agreed, namely, that it would not result in the parties living together as husband and wife, for which a religious ceremony was essential. (3) An agreement that the parties would not become husband and wife in any real sense until some further condition was satisfied in the indefinite future was not a marriage, it might be considered a betrothal but what was material was that where parties had agreed that, notwithstanding the exchange of words of consent, the relationship that the language used would normally establish would not be established between them, the proceedings were sham, and should not be recognised. (4) It was open to the court to ensure that the prosecution authorities had relevant information if it appeared, as in this case, that the parties and their associates might have committed serious criminal offences and it was appropriate that the papers in the case be sent to the Lord Advocate.

H v. H 2005 S.L.T.1025, Lord Penrose, Lord Macfadyen, Lord Marnoch, Ex Div.

5272. Marriage–Registration–Fees

MARRIAGES AND CIVIL PARTNERSHIPS (FEES) (SCOTLAND) REGULATIONS 2005, SSI 2005 556; made under the Registration of Births, Deaths and Marriages (Scotland) Act 1965 s.37, s.38, s.54; the Marriage (Scotland) Act 1977 s.3; and the Civil Partnership Act 2004 s.88, s.95, s.122, s.134. In force: December 5, 2005; £3.00.

These Regulations amend the Births, Deaths, Marriages and Divorces (Fees) (Scotland) Regulations 1998 (SI 1998 643) to raise the fee for the submission of a marriage notice from £20 to £25. The Regulations also set fees for the submission of a notice of proposed civil partnership and for a civil partnership registration. They set fees for searches and the issuing of extracts of entries in the civil partnership register and the Register of Dissolutions of Civil Partnership.

5273. Protection of Children and Prevention of Sexual Offences (Scotland) Act 2005 (asp 9)

This Act of the Scottish Parliament makes it an offence to meet a child following certain preliminary contact, and makes other provision for the purposes of protecting children from harm of a sexual nature; and makes further provision about the prevention of sexual offences.

This Act received Royal Assent on July 12, 2005.

5274. Protection of Children and Prevention of Sexual Offences (Scotland) Act 2005 (asp 9)–Commencement and Savings Order

PROTECTION OF CHILDREN AND PREVENTION OF SEXUAL OFFENCES (SCOTLAND) ACT 2005 (COMMENCEMENT AND SAVINGS) ORDER, SSI 2005 480 (C.24); made under the Protection of Children and Prevention of Sexual Offences (Scotland) Act 2005 s.20. Commencement details: bringing into force various provisions of the 2005 Act on October 7, 2005; £3.00.

This Order brings into force all of the provisions of the Protection of Children and Prevention of Sexual Offences (Scotland) Act 2005, in so far as not already in force.

5275. Books

Bennett, Siggi A.–Divorce in the Sheriff Court. Hardback: £50.00. ISBN 0 9534152 6 0. Barnstoneworth Press.

Mair, Jane–Avizandum Statutes on Scots Family Law. Paperback: £15.95. ISBN 1 904968 04 X. Avizandum Publishing Ltd.

Norrie, Kenneth McK.–Children's Hearings in Scotland. Paperback: £45.00. ISBN 0 414 01587 8. W.Green & Son.

Plumtree, Alexandra–Getting It Right: Social Work Court Reports in Child Care Cases in Scotland. Paperback: £5.50. ISBN 1 903699 90 8. British Association for Adoption & Fostering.

Plumtree, Alexandra–Child Care Law: Scotland-A Summary of the Law in Scotland. Paperback: £6.95. ISBN 1 903699 74 6. British Association for Adoption & Fostering.

FINANCIAL REGULATION

5276. Books

Law Society Scotland Diploma Materials 2005, Financial Services Student Manual 2005-2006. Book (details unknown): £15.00. ISBN 0 414 01642 4. W.Green & Son.

FISHERIES

5277. Conservation–Salmon

CONSERVATION OF SALMON (ESK SALMON FISHERY DISTRICT) REGULATIONS 2005, SSI 2005 24; made under the Salmon Act 1986 s.10A. In force: February 16, 2005; £3.00.

These Regulations, which cease to have effect at midnight on February 15, 2010, make provision for the conservation of salmon. They prohibit fishing with a hook other than a single or double hook without barbs in the Esk salmon fishery district between February 16 and May 31, both dates inclusive, in each year; and require that any salmon caught by rod and line in the Esk salmon fishery district between February 16 and May 31, both dates inclusive, in each year be returned at once to the water from which it came with the least possible injury.

5278. Conservation–Salmon

CONSERVATION OF SALMON (RIVER ANNAN SALMON FISHERY DISTRICT) REGULATIONS 2005, SSI 2005 37; made under the Salmon Act 1986 s.10A. In force: February 25, 2005; £3.00.

These Regulations prohibit, in the River Annan salmon fishery district, the retention of salmon caught by rod and line. They shall cease to have effect at midnight on February 24, 2010.

5279. Conservation–Salmon–Annual closing time

ANNUAL CLOSE TIME (ESK SALMON FISHERY DISTRICT) ORDER 2005, SSI 2005 72; made under the Salmon Act 1986 s.6. In force: February 16, 2005; £3.00.

This Order, which ceases to have effect at midnight on February 15, 2010, prescribes the dates of the annual close time for the Esk Salmon Fishery District as September 1 to April 30, both dates inclusive, and thereby replaces the previous dates which were September 1 to February 15, both dates inclusive. This Order also prescribes September 1 to October 31, both dates inclusive, and February 16 to April 30, both dates inclusive, as the period within that annual close time during which fishing for salmon by rod and line is permitted.

5280. Fishing–Cetaceans–Monitoring

PREVENTION AND MONITORING OF CETACEAN BYCATCH (SCOTLAND) ORDER 2005, SSI 2005 330; made under the Fisheries Act 1981 s.30. In force: July 1, 2005; £3.00.

This Order makes provision for the enforcement of certain enforceable Community restrictions and other obligations relating to sea fishing by vessels in certain areas as set out in Council Regulation 812/2004 ([2004] OJ L150/12) which provides for Member States to monitor the bycatch of cetaceans by the implementation of an observer scheme. It also requires certain vessels to deploy acoustic devices in relation to certain gear whilst fishing. The Order creates offences in respect of the failure to allow an observer on board a fishing vessel or the obstruction of an observer from carrying out the functions of an observer.

5281. Fishing–Conservation–Prohibition of scallop dredging

REGULATION OF SCALLOP DREDGES (SCOTLAND) ORDER 2005, SSI 2005 371; made under the Sea Fish (Conservation) Act 1967 s.3, s.15. In force: July 21, 2005; £3.00.

This Order regulates the use and carriage of scallop dredges and applies to Scottish and relevant British fishing boats within the Scottish zone. It prohibits the use or carriage of scallop dredges which do not conform to certain technical specifications.

5282. Fishing–Enforcement of Community quotas

SEA FISHING (ENFORCEMENT OF COMMUNITY CONTROL MEASURES) (SCOTLAND) AMENDMENT ORDER 2005, SSI 2005 552; made under the Fisheries Act 1981 s.30. In force: December 1, 2005; £3.00.

This Order amends the Sea Fishing (Enforcement of Community Control Measures) (Scotland) Order 2000 (SSI 2000 7) and the Sea Fishing (Restriction on Days at Sea) (Scotland) Order 2005 (SSI 2005 90). The 2000 Order makes provision for the enforcement of restrictions and obligations contained in Council Regulation 1382/87 ([1987] OJ L132/11) establishing detailed rules concerning the inspection of fishing vessels. This Order updates the definition of the Council Regulation so that the application of certain measures to vessels equal to or greater than 10 metres are implemented; and amends the powers available to British sea-fishery officers so that the power to search the premises for documents and the power to require any person on the premises to do anything which appears to the British sea-fishery officer necessary for facilitating the search is not restricted to the purpose of ascertaining whether any person on the premises has committed an offence but can exercised for the purpose of ascertaining whether a relevant offence has been committed.

5283. Fishing–Enforcement of Community quotas

SEA FISHING (ENFORCEMENT OF COMMUNITY QUOTA AND THIRD COUNTRY FISHING MEASURES) (SCOTLAND) ORDER 2005, SSI 2005 311; made under the Fisheries Act 1981 s.30. In force: July 1, 2005; £3.50.

This Order, which revokes the Sea Fishing (Enforcement of Community Quota and Third Country Fishing Measures) (Scotland) Order 2004 (SSI 2004 209) (with saving), makes provision for the enforcement of certain enforceable Community restrictions and other obligations relating to sea fishing by Community vessels and third country vessels set out in Council Regulation 27/2005 ([2005] OJ L12/1) fixing for 2005 the fishing opportunities and associated conditions for certain fish stocks and groups of fish stocks, applicable in Community waters and, for Community vessels, in waters where catch limitations are required. The Council Regulation fixes total allowable catches and the quotas of Member States for 2005 and lays down certain conditions under which they may be fished. It also authorises fishing by vessels of Norway and the Faroe Islands for specified descriptions of fish in certain specified areas within the fishery limits of Member States in 2005 and imposes requirements concerning fishing quotas and authorised zones, methods of fishing, the holding of licences and observance of licence conditions, the keeping of logbooks, the making of reports and similar matters. The Order makes provision relating to the harbours in Scotland at which catches may be landed; makes provision for the Scottish Ministers to approve pelagic weighing systems for fisheries control purposes; and provides that where over 10 tonnes of herring, mackerel or horse mackerel is landed in Scotland buyers or holders of the fish must weigh the fish using a pelagic weighing system which is approved by the Scottish Ministers or which has been passed as fit for trade use in accordance with the Weighing Equipment (Beltweighers) Regulations 2001 (SI 2001 1208).

5284. Fishing—Fishing vessels—Breach of licence condition—Compatibility of condition with EC law

[Sea Fish (Conservation) Act 1967 (c.84); Human Rights Act 1998 (c.42) Sch.1 Part I Art.7; Council Regulation 2847/93 establishing a control system applicable to the common fisheries policy Art.38.]

The appellant (M), the master of a fishing vessel registered at Banff and licensed under the Sea Fish (Conservation) Act 1967, was charged with failing to comply with a condition attached to the vessel's licence, namely that he had failed to deposit a copy of the logsheet for the vessel prior to commencing the landing of sea fish. M lodged a devolution minute on the grounds that (1) the condition in question was insufficiently specific to establish an offence within the terms of the Human Rights Act 1998 Sch.1 Part I Art.7; (2) the imposition of the condition had no foundation in and was inconsistent with Community law, given that it imposed stricter requirements than those authorised by that law.

Held, dismissing the appeal, that (1) the wording of the condition was sufficiently clear to leave no real doubt as to its meaning and intent and there was no incompatibility with the requirement of certainty laid down by Art.7. (2) Council Regulation 2847/93 Art.38 permitted Member States to take supplementary measures which, so long as they complied with Community law and were consistent with the common fisheries policy, could impose stricter provisions designed to police and enforce that policy.

MATTHEW v. AITKEN; *sub nom.* MATTHEW v. PROCURATOR FISCAL, WICK 2004 S.C.C.R. 515, Lord Marnoch, Lord Hamilton, Temporary Judge Sir Gerald Gordon Q.C., HCJ.

5285. Fishing—Food safety—Prohibition of "fishing for and taking fish"—Competence

[Food and Environment Protection Act 1985 (c.48) s.1, s.22, Sch.1 para.1 (d); Food Protection (Emergency Prohibitions) (Amnesic Shellfish Poisoning) (East Coast) (No. 4) (Scotland) Order 2003 (SI 2003 393) Art.4.]

C was charged on summary complaint with a contravention of the Food Protection (Emergency Prohibitions) (Amnesic Shellfish Poisoning) (East Coast) (No 4) (Scotland) Order 2003 Art.4 and the Food and Environment Protection Act 1985 s.1 (1), s.1 (2) and s.1 (6). C tendered a plea to the competency, contending that the order was ultra vires because it purported to prohibit "fishing for or taking scallops" whereas the power conferred on the Scottish Ministers by the Act was to prohibit "fishing for and taking fish". At debate, the sheriff sustained the plea and dismissed the complaint, construing Sch.1 para.1 (d) to the Act as prohibiting the conjoined process of fishing for and taking fish, and finding it inappropriate to penalise for the taking of fish in isolation. The Crown appealed by bill of advocation.

Held, recalling the decision and remitting to the sheriff to proceed as accords, that (1) the different phrases used in the Act and the order were readily explained as a matter of syntax: to have used "or" instead of "and" in the context of an emergency order would not have permitted the prohibition of both fishing and taking, and the use of "or" was necessary in order to make it clear that the Scottish Ministers' powers were being exercised to the full extent permitted by Parliament. (2) The provisions in question were designed to protect the public from the risk of food poisoning and should accordingly be construed in the manner best calculated to afford effective protection and while construing the power as one prohibiting both fishing alone and taking alone rendered a person who took by accident vulnerable to a charge of contravening the prohibition, a defence was available under s.22 of the Act if he took all reasonable precautions and exercised all due diligence to avoid commission of the offence, which held a fair balance between the accidental offender and the public interest in avoiding the risk of food poisoning.

COLLEY v. POLAND 2005 S.L.T. 436, Lord Gill L.J.C., Lord Osborne, Lord Macfadyen, HCJ.

5286. Fishing–Prohibited methods of fishing–Firth of Clyde

SEA FISH (PROHIBITED METHODS OF FISHING) (FIRTH OF CLYDE) ORDER 2005, SSI 2005 67; made under the Sea Fish (Conservation) Act 1967 s.5, s.15, s.22. In force: February 14, 2005; £3.00.

This Order, which revokes the Sea Fish (Prohibited Methods of Fishing) (Firth of Clyde) Order 2004 (SSI 2004 55), prohibits all methods of fishing within certain areas of the Firth of Clyde. The prohibition does not apply to vessels fishing within the closed areas exclusively with scallop dredges, creels and trawls used for fishing for Norway lobsters.

5287. Fishing–Prohibition of fishing for cockles–Specified area

INSHORE FISHING (PROHIBITION OF FISHING FOR COCKLES) (SCOTLAND) AMENDMENT ORDER 2005, SSI 2005 140; made under the Inshore Fishing (Scotland) Act 1984 s.1. In force: March 9, 2005; £3.00.

This Order amends the Inshore Fishing (Prohibition of Fishing for Cockles) (Scotland) Order 1995 (SI 1995 1373) by substituting a new definition for "the specified area".

5288. Fishing–Salmon fishery district–Baits and lures–River Awe

RIVER AWE SALMON FISHERY DISTRICT (BAITS AND LURES) REVOCATION REGULATIONS 2005, SSI 2005 485; made under the Salmon and Freshwater Fisheries (Consolidation) (Scotland) Act 2003 s.33. In force: October 4, 2005; £3.00.

These Regulations revoke the River Awe Salmon Fishery District (Baits and Lures) Regulations 1991 (SI 1991 116 (S.9)).

5289. Fishing–Salmon fishery district–Designation–Argyll

ARGYLL SALMON FISHERY DISTRICT DESIGNATION ORDER 2005, SSI 2005 487; made under the Salmon and Freshwater Fisheries (Consolidation) (Scotland) Act 2003 s.34, s.35, Sch.1. In force: October 4, 2005; £3.00.

This Order designates the area described in the Schedule as a salmon fishery district to be known as the Argyll Salmon Fishery District and abolishes the existing Salmon Fishery Districts which are superseded by it. The Order makes provision for the annual close time and for the period within the annual close time during which fishing for and taking salmon by rod and line is permitted. The annual close time is from August 27 to February 10, both dates inclusive, in each year. Within the annual close time it is permitted to fish for and take salmon by rod and line in the period from August 27 to October 31, both dates inclusive, in each year.

5290. Fishing–Selling and buying–Control system

REGISTRATION OF FISH SELLERS AND BUYERS AND DESIGNATION OF AUCTION SITES (SCOTLAND) AMENDMENT REGULATIONS 2005, SSI 2005

438; made under the European Communities Act 1972 s.2. In force: October 1, 2005; £3.00.

These Regulations amend the Registration of Fish Sellers and Buyers and Designation of Auction Sites (Scotland) Regulations 2005 (SSI 2005 286) which provide for the implementation and enforcement of Council Regulation 2847/93 ([1993] OJ L261/1) Art.9 establishing a control system applicable to the common fisheries policy and Council Regulation 2371/2002 ([2002] OJ L358/59) Art.22 on the conservation and sustainable exploitation of fisheries resources under the Common Fisheries Policy. The Regulations make amendments to remove the offence of selling first sale fish from a fishing vessel to a buyer who is not a registered fish buyer. The Regulations also make amendments to lower the threshold for purchasing fish for private consumption from 50 kilogrammes to 25 kilogrammes.

5291. Fishing–Selling and buying–Control system

REGISTRATION OF FISH SELLERS AND BUYERS AND DESIGNATION OF AUCTION SITES (SCOTLAND) REGULATIONS 2005, SSI 2005 286; made under the European Communities Act 1972 s.2. In force: in accordance with Reg.1 (2); £3.00.

These Regulations provide for the implementation and enforcement of Council Regulation 2847/93 ([1993] OJ L261/1) Art.9 establishing a control system applicable to the common fisheries policy and Council Regulation 2371/2002 ([2002] OJ L358/59) Art.22 on the conservation and sustainable exploitation of fisheries resources under the Common Fisheries Policy. The Regulations make provision for the registration of fish sellers; provide that it is an offence for any person to sell first sale fish through a designated auction site if that person is not registered as a fish seller; make provision for the designation of auction sites; make provision for the registration of fish buyers and make provision for offences in relation to the purchase of fish by unregistered buyers. The Regulations also require registered fish buyers to maintain records of the purchase of first sale fish and make provision for offences in relation to record keeping.

5292. Fishing–Several fishery rights–Loch Crinan–Scallops

LOCH CRINAN SCALLOPS SEVERAL FISHERY ORDER 2005, SSI 2005 304; made under the Sea Fisheries (Shellfish) Act 1967 s.1, s.7. In force: June 25, 2005; £3.00.

This Order confers on Scallop Kings (1997) Ltd for a period of 12 years the right of several fishery for scallops in part of Loch Crinan described in the Schedule to the Order. It requires the harvesting of scallops under the right of several fishery to be carried out manually by divers; prohibits the permanent mooring of any boat or other floating structure within the limits of the area of the several fishery; specifies creels as implements of fishing the use of which is permitted within the fishery; prohibits the assignation or other transfer of the right of several fishery without the prior written consent of the Scottish Ministers; requires the limits of the fishery to be clearly marked and maintained; and provides that its effect will not prejudicially affect the rights of the Crown.

5293. Fishing vessels–Days at sea–Restrictions

SEA FISHING (RESTRICTION ON DAYS AT SEA) (SCOTLAND) ORDER 2005, SSI 2005 90; made under the Fisheries Act 1981 s.30. In force: March 1, 2005; £3.50.

This Order, which revokes the Sea Fishing (Restriction on Days at Sea) (Scotland) Order 2004 (SSI 2004 44) and the Sea Fishing (Restriction on Days at Sea) (Scotland) Amendment Order 2004 (SSI 2004 81), amends the Sea Fishing (Enforcement of Community Control Measures) (Scotland) Order 2000 (SSI 2000 7). It also provides for the enforcement of provisions in Council Regulation 27/2005 ([2005] OJ L12/1) fixing for 2005 the fishing opportunities and associated conditions for certain fish stocks and groups of fish stocks, applicable in Community waters and, for Community vessels, in waters where catch limitations are required. The Order contains provisions relating to the determination for certain fishing boats of the specified management periods; and the calculation of the number of days on which a vessel may be absent from port. It contains provisions relating to the deduction of days by the Scottish Ministers and the procedure to be followed in doing so.

5294. Salmon and Freshwater Fisheries (Consolidation) (Scotland) Act 2003 (asp 15)–Commencement Order

SALMON AND FRESHWATER FISHERIES (CONSOLIDATION) (SCOTLAND) ACT 2003 (COMMENCEMENT) ORDER 2005, SSI 2005 174 (C.8); made under the Salmon and Freshwater Fisheries (Consolidation) (Scotland) Act 2003 s.71. Commencement details: bringing into force various provisions of the 2003 Act on April 1, 2005; £3.00.

This Order appoints April 1, 2005 as the date for coming into force of provisions of the Salmon and Freshwater Fisheries (Consolidation) (Scotland) Act 2003.

5295. Shellfish–Emergency prohibitions–Amnesic shellfish poisoning

See FOOD. §5343, 5356, 5324, 5331, 5322, 5337, 5352, 5338, 5330, 5339, 5334, 5335, 5336, 5344, 5333, 5340, 5323, 5351, 5349, 5346, 5345, 5342, 5347, 5348, 5325, 5326, 5327, 5350, 5328, 5329, 5313, 5314, 5316, 5315, 5312, 5317, 5319, 5332

5296. Shellfish–Emergency prohibitions–Paralytic shellfish poisoning

See FOOD. §5357, 5360, 5359, 5361, 5358

FOOD

5297. Food composition–Food for particular nutritional uses–Specific nutritional purposes–Tryptophan

TRYPTOPHAN IN FOOD (SCOTLAND) REGULATIONS 2005, SSI 2005 479; made under the Food Safety Act 1990 s.6, s.16, s.26, s.48. In force: November 11, 2005; £3.00.

These Regulations, which revoke the Tryptophan in Food (Scotland) Regulations 1990 (SI 1990 1792), amend the Food for Particular Nutritional Uses (Addition of Substances for Specific Nutritional Purposes) (Scotland) Regulation 2002 (SSI 2002 397) and the Processed Cereal-based Foods and Baby Foods for Infants and Young Children (Scotland) Regulations 2004 (SSI 2004 8). The Regulations continue to prohibit the addition of tryptophan to food, and the sale, offer for sale and exposure for sale of food containing tryptophan, subject to exceptions. The main changes effected by these Regulations are: the addition of a new exception from the prohibitions in the Regulations in respect of laevorotatory tryptophan added to food supplements if certain conditions are met; the insertion of a qualification to the existing exception in respect of laevorotatory tryptophan, its sodium, potassium, calcium or magnesium salts or its hydrochloride added to certain foods for a particular nutritional use in that the added substance must comply with specified purity criteria. They also continue to provide for offences and a penalty; make provision as to enforcement; apply various provisions of the Food Safety Act 1990; and include a presumption as regards food which contravenes the Regulations in certain circumstances.

5298. Food composition—Food safety—Kava-kava

KAVA-KAVA IN FOOD REGULATIONS (NORTHERN IRELAND) 2005, SR 2005 288; made under the Food Safety (Northern Ireland) Order 1991 (SI 1991 762 (NI.7)) Art.15, Art.25, Art.26, Art.47. In force: July 11, 2005; £3.00.

These Regulations, which revoke the Kava-kava in Food Regulations (Northern Ireland) 2003 (SR 2003 10), prohibit the sale, possession for sale, offer, exposure or advertisement for sale of any food consisting of, or containing Kava-kava. These Regulations provide for an exception to the prohibition imposed above where the food is imported from an EEA State, if it originates from such a State but is in free circulation in Member States and is being, or is to be exported to an EEA State other than the UK.

5299. Food hygiene—Animal products—Poultry meat

POULTRY MEAT, FARMED GAME BIRD MEAT AND RABBIT MEAT (HYGIENE AND INSPECTION) AMENDMENT (SCOTLAND) REGULATIONS 2005, SSI 2005 81; made under the European Communities Act 1972 s.2. In force: March 17, 2005; £3.00.

These Regulations, which amend the Poultry Meat, Farmed Game Bird Meat and Rabbit Meat (Hygiene and Inspection) Regulations 1995 (SI 1995 540), implement Council Directive 71/118 ([1971] OJ L55/23) on health problems affecting the production and placing on the market of fresh poultry meat. They implement the provision which prohibits poultry meat from being placed on the market for human consumption if it has been treated with water retention agents or obtained under technologically similar conditions and is likely as a result to present the same risk.

5300. Food hygiene—Licences

FOOD SAFETY (GENERAL FOOD HYGIENE) AMENDMENT (SCOTLAND) REGULATIONS 2005, SSI 2005 435; made under the Food Safety Act 1990 s.16, s.19, s.26, s.48. In force: September 30, 2005; £3.00.

These Regulations amend the Food Safety (General Food Hygiene) Regulations 1995 (SI 1995 1763) which provide that a licence issued in relation to a butcher's shop remains in force for a period of one year. The 1995 Regulations also make provision for the commencement of that period in cases of renewal of licences of shorter duration. The Regulations provide that licences in force before the coming into force of these Regulations continue in force until December 31, 2005.

5301. Food hygiene—Official controls—Charges

FISHERY PRODUCTS (OFFICIAL CONTROLS CHARGES) (SCOTLAND) REGULATIONS 2005, SSI 2005 597; made under the European Communities Act 1972 s.2. In force: January 1, 2006; £3.00.

These Regulation implement the provisions of European Parliament and Council Directive 85/73 ([1985] OJ L032/4) on the financing of veterinary inspections and controls that, following reforms to the Community regime on food hygiene that take effect on January 1, 2006, require fees to be collected for inspections of and controls on fishery products under European Parliament and Council Regulation 854/2004 ([2004] OJ L139/206) laying down specific rules for the organisation of official controls on products of animal origin intended for human consumption. The Regulations state what costs constitute the actual costs of exercising official controls for the purposes of the Regulations; provide the conversion rate in order to calculate the Sterling equivalent of any sums which are specified in Euro in the Regulations; prescribe how the length of an "account period" for the purposes of the Regulations is to be determined; provide that where a duty is imposed under the Regulations on more than one person it may be enforced jointly or separately against such persons; require authorities to which charges are payable under the Regulations to calculate the charges, recalculate if an error is made, give notice of amounts due to those liable to pay and seek recovery of those charges; provide for an appeal to the sheriff against decisions of authorities imposing charges under the

Regulations and lay down the requirements for the conduct and determination of such appeals; and provide for the payment of charges by one food authority to another where charges are payable to more than one authority.

5302. Food hygiene–Official controls–Charges

MEAT (OFFICIAL CONTROLS CHARGES) (SCOTLAND) REGULATIONS 2005, SSI 2005 607; made under the European Communities Act 1972 s.2. In force: January 1, 2006; £3.00.

These Regulations, which amend the Food Standards Act 1999 (Transitional and Consequential Provisions and Savings) (Scotland) Regulations 2000 (SSI 2000 62), revoke the Meat (Hygiene and Inspection) (Charges) Amendment (Scotland) Regulations 2000 (SSI 2000 61) and the Meat (Hygiene and Inspection) (Charges) Amendment (Scotland) Regulations 2001 (SSI 2001 89). In the light of the modification to Council Directive 85/73 ([1985] OJ L032/4), these Regulations implement the provisions of that Directive that now require fees to be collected for inspections of and controls on meat of domestic ungulates, meat from poultry and lagomorphs, meat of farmed game and wild game meat under Regulation 854/2004 ([2004] OJ L155/206). The Regulations require the Food Standards Agency ("the Agency") to notify the operator of each slaughterhouse, game-handling establishment and cutting plant in which official controls have been exercised of the official controls charge that has arisen in relation to those officials controls; provide that any official controls charge so notified is payable by the operator to the Scottish Ministers on demand or to the Agency on their behalf; allow the Scottish Ministers to direct the Agency to refuse to exercise any further official controls at given premises where, despite a Court order requiring the operator of the premises to pay the official controls charge for which the operator is liable, that operator fails to comply with the order; and require persons to supply the Agency on demand with such information as it may reasonably require for the purpose of calculating the official controls charge or notifying the operator of it, and to supply the Agency on demand with such evidence as it may reasonably require to verify that information.

5303. Food hygiene–Products of animal origin

FOOD HYGIENE (SCOTLAND) REGULATIONS 2005, SSI 2005 505; made under the European Communities Act 1972 s.2. In force: January 1, 2006; £5.50.

These Regulations, which amend the Food Safety (Ships and Aircraft) (England and Scotland) Order 2003 (SI 2003 1895) and the Egg (Marketing Standards) (Enforcement) (Scotland) Regulations 2005 (SSI 2005 332), revoke the Ice-Cream (Scotland) Regulations 1948 (SI 1948 960), the Ungraded Eggs (Hygiene) (Scotland) Regulations 1990 (SI 1990 1336), the Food Premises (Registration) Regulations 1991 (SI 1991 2825), the Meat Hygiene Appeals Tribunal (Procedure) Regulations 1992 (SI 1992 2921), the Egg Products Regulations 1993 (SI 1993 1520), the Meat Products (Hygiene) Regulations 1994 (SI 1994 3082), the Fresh Meat (Hygiene and Inspection) Regulations 1995 (SI 1995 539), the Poultry Meat, Farmed Game Bird Meat and Rabbit Meat (Hygiene and Inspection) Regulations 1995 (SI 1995 540), the Dairy Products (Hygiene) (Scotland) Regulations 1995 (SI 1995 1372), the Food Safety (General Food Hygiene) Regulations 1995 (SI 1995 1763), the Wild Game Meat (Hygiene and Inspection) Regulations 1995 (SI 1995 2148), the Food Safety (Temperature Control) Regulations 1995 (SI 1995 2200), the Minced Meat and Meat Preparations (Hygiene) Regulations 1995 (SI 1995 3205), the Food Safety (Fishery Products and Live Shellfish) (Hygiene) Regulations 1998 (SI 1998 994), the Gelatine (Intra-Community Trade) (Scotland) Regulations 2001 (SSI 2001 169) and the Collagen and Gelatine (Intra-Community Trade) (Scotland) (No.2) Regulations 2003 (SSI 2003 568). They provide for the execution and enforcement there of: European Parliament and Council Regulation 852/2004 ([2004] OJ L139/1) on the hygiene of foodstuffs; European Parliament and Council Regulation 853/2004 ([2004] OJ L139/55) laying down specific hygiene rules for food of animal origin; and European

Parliament and Council Regulation 854/2004 ([2004] OJ L155/206) laying down specific rules for the organisation of official controls on products of animal origin intended for human consumption. The Regulations create certain presumptions that, for the purposes thereof, specified food is intended for human consumption; provide that the Food Standards Agency is the competent authority for the purposes of the Community Regulations and make provision for the Agency to delegate that function to, or enter into an arrangement concerning that function with, any other enforcement authority; make provision for the enforcement and execution of these Regulations and of the Community Regulations including the appointment of authorised officers; provide for specified enforcement measures to be available in respect of a food business operator; provide that where the commission of an offence under them is due to the act or default of some other person that other person is guilty of the offence; and provide that in proceedings for an offence under them it is a defence for the accused to prove that all reasonable precautions were taken and all due diligence exercised so as to avoid the commission of the offence. They also provide for the procurement and analysis of samples and provide powers of entry for authorised officers of an enforcement authority.

5304. Food labelling – Honey

HONEY (SCOTLAND) AMENDMENT REGULATIONS 2005, SSI 2005 307; made under the Food Safety Act 1990 s.16, s.17, s.26, s.48. In force: August 31, 2005; £3.00.

These Regulations amend the Honey (Scotland) Regulations 2003 (SSI 2003 569) to add a type of honey for which the description "honey" may be used in place of the reserved description, and correct a spelling error.

5305. Food safety – Additives

MISCELLANEOUS FOOD ADDITIVES AMENDMENT (SCOTLAND) REGULATIONS 2005, SSI 2005 214; made under the Food Safety Act 1990 s.16, s.17, s.26, s.48, Sch.1 para.1. In force: May 5, 2005; £3.00.

These Regulations, which amend the Miscellaneous Food Additives Regulations 1995 (SI 1995 3187), implement European Parliament and Council Directive 2003/114 ([2003] OJ L24/58) amending Directive 95/2 on food additives other than colours and sweeteners. The Regulations insert a definition of flavouring; bring up to date the definition of "Directive 95/2"; substitute a new definition for "stabiliser" to include substances which increase the binding capacity of food; ensure that a flavouring which lawfully has in or on it a permitted miscellaneous additive can be used as an ingredient in a compound food; and make other various amendments.

5306. Food safety – Additives – Colours

COLOURS IN FOOD AMENDMENT (SCOTLAND) REGULATIONS 2005, SSI 2005 94; made under the Food Safety Act 1990 s.16, s.17, s.26, s.48, Sch.1 para.1. In force: April 1, 2005; £3.00.

These Regulations, which implement Commission Directive 2004/47 ([2004] OJ L113/24) amending Directive 95/45 as regards mixed carotenes (E 160 a (i)) and beta-carotene (E 160 a (ii)), amend the Colours in Food Regulations 1995 (SI 1995 3124). The Regulations provide amended purity criteria for mixed carotenes E160 a (i) and beta carotene E160 a (ii); and provide that the new purity criteria will not apply to products which were put on the market or labelled before and which otherwise comply with the 1995 Regulations.

5307. Food safety – Bovine collagen – Human consumption

PRODUCTION OF BOVINE COLLAGEN INTENDED FOR HUMAN CONSUMPTION IN THE UNITED KINGDOM (SCOTLAND) REGULATIONS 2005, SSI 2005 218; made under the European Communities Act 1972 s.2; and the Food Safety Act 1990 s.6, s.16, s.19, s.26, s.48, s.49, Sch.1 para.3, Sch.1 para.5, Sch.1 para.6. In force: May 11, 2005; £3.00.

These Regulations amend the Bovines and Bovine Products (Trade) Regulations 1999 (SI 1999 1103) which give effect to Commission Decision 98/692 ([1998] OJ L328/28) amending Commission Decision 98/256 to provide for the export from the UK of deboned beef and beef products under the strict conditions of the Date-based Export Scheme and Commission Decision 98/564 ([1998] OJ L273/37) amending Council Decision 98/256 as regards certain emergency measures to protect against bovine spongiform encephalopathy. The Regulations amend the 1999 Regulations to lift the prohibition on the production of collagen derived from the hides and skins of bovine animals slaughtered in the UK and intended for human consumption in the UK; the prohibition on export of such collagen from Great Britain remains in force; and to make consequential amendments to enable use of such collagen in products for human consumption in the UK. The Regulations also impose requirements on the production of collagen derived from the hide and/or skin of a bovine animal slaughtered in the UK and intended for human consumption in the UK until January 1, 2006.

5308. Food safety–Contaminants

CONTAMINANTS IN FOOD (SCOTLAND) AMENDMENT REGULATIONS 2005, SSI 2005 277; made under the Food Safety Act 1990 s.16, s.17, s.26, s.48. In force: June 17, 2005; £3.00.

These Regulations amend the Contaminants in Food (Scotland) Regulations 2004 (SI 2004 525) to provide for the enforcement of Commission Regulation 655/2004 ([2004] OJ L104/48) and Commission Regulation 683/2004 ([2004 OJ L106/3).

5309. Food safety–Contaminants–Maximum levels

CONTAMINANTS IN FOOD (SCOTLAND) REGULATIONS 2005, SSI 2005 606; made under the Food Safety Act 1990 s.6, s.16, s.17, s.26, s.31, s.48. In force: January 1, 2006; £3.00.

These Regulations, which amend the Food Safety Act 1990 and the Food Safety (Sampling and Qualifications) Regulations 1990 (SI 1990 2463), revoke the Contaminants in Food (Scotland) Regulations 2004 (SSI 2004 525) and the Contaminants in Food (Scotland) Amendment Regulations 2005 (SSI 2005 277). They make provision for the execution and enforcement of Commission Regulation 466/2001 ([2001] OJ L77/1) setting maximum levels for contaminants in foodstuffs and implement Commission Directive 98/53 ([1998] OJ L201/93) laying down sampling and analysis methods for the official control of the levels for certain contaminants of foodstuffs; Commission Directive 2001/22 ([2001] OJ L77/14) laying down the sampling methods and the methods of analysis for the official control of the levels of lead, cadmium, mercury and 3-MCPD in foodstuffs; Commission Directive 2002/26 ([2002] OJ L75/38) laying down the sampling methods and the methods of analysis for the official control of levels of ochratoxin A in foodstuffs; Commission Directive 2002/69 ([2002] OJ L209/5) laying down the sampling methods and the methods of analysis for the official control of dioxins and the determination of dioxin-like PCBs in foodstuffs; Commission Directive 2003/78 ([2003] OJ L203/40) laying down the sampling methods and the methods of analysis for the official control of the levels of patulin in foodstuffs; Commission Directive 2004/16 ([2004] OJ L42/16) laying down the sampling methods and the methods of analysis for the official control of the levels of tin in canned foods; and Commission Directive 2005/10 ([2005] OJ L34/15) laying down the sampling methods and the methods of analysis for the official control of the levels of benzo(a)pyrene in foodstuffs. The Regulations provide that it is an offence to place on the market certain foods if they contain contaminants of any kind specified in the Commission Regulation at levels exceeding those specified (subject to a derogation applicable to certain types of lettuce and fresh spinach); use food containing such contaminants at such levels as ingredients in the production of certain foods; mix foods which do not comply with the maximum levels referred to above with foods which do; mix foods to which the Commission Regulation relates and which are intended for direct consumption with foods to which the Commission Regulation relates and which are intended to be sorted or otherwise treated prior to consumption; or detoxify by chemical treatment food not complying with the limits specified in the Commission Regulation.

5310. Food safety–Emergency controls–Chilli and chilli products

FOOD (CHILLI, CHILLI PRODUCTS, CURCUMA AND PALM OIL) (EMERGENCY CONTROL) (SCOTLAND) REGULATIONS 2005, SSI 2005 294; made under the European Communities Act 1972 s.2. In force: June 2, 2005; £3.00.

These Regulations, which revoke the Food (Chilli and Chilli Products) (Emergency Control) (Scotland) Regulations 2004 (SSI 2004 56), implement Commission Decision 2005/402 ([2005] OJ L135/34) on emergency measures regarding chilli, chilli products, curcuma and palm oil. The Regulations prohibit the importation of chilli, chilli products, curcuma and palm oil except where they are accompanied by an analytical report endorsed by a representative of the relevant competent authority, demonstrating that the product does not contain any of the prohibited substances Sudan I, Sudan II, Sudan III, Scarlet Red or Sudan IV; prohibit the placing on the market of chilli, chilli products, curcuma or palm oil which contain a prohibited substance; apply with modifications certain provisions of the Food Safety Act 1990 for the purposes of the Regulations and provide for sampling and analysis; provide for the destruction of chilli, chilli products, curcuma and palm oil which contravene the conditions of import or are illegally placed on the market; and make provision as to the payment of the cost of analysis, storage and destruction of products incurred by the local authority under the Regulations.

5311. Food safety–Emergency controls–Pistachios–Iran

FOOD (PISTACHIOS FROM IRAN) (EMERGENCY CONTROL) (SCOTLAND) AMENDMENT REGULATIONS 2005, SSI 2005 70; made under the European Communities Act 1972 s.2. In force: February 17, 2005; £3.00.

These Regulations, which amend the Food (Pistachios from Iran) (Emergency Control) (Scotland) Regulations 2003 (SSI 2003 414) and revoke the Food (Pistachios from Iran) (Emergency Control) (Amendment) Order 1997 (SSI 1997 3046), implement Commission Decision 2005/85 ([2005] OJ L30/12) imposing special conditions on the import of pistachios and certain products derived from pistachios originating in, or consigned from Iran.

5312. Food safety–Emergency prohibitions–Amnesic shellfish poisoning

FOOD PROTECTION (EMERGENCY PROHIBITIONS) (AMNESIC SHELLFISH POISONING) (EAST COAST) (SCOTLAND) ORDER 2005, SSI 2005 498; made under the Food and Environment Protection Act 1985 s.1, s.24. In force: October 6, 2005 at 4.45 pm; £3.00.

This Order contains emergency prohibitions restricting various activities in order to prevent human consumption of food rendered unsuitable for that purpose by virtue of shellfish having been affected by the toxin which causes amnesic shellfish poisoning in human beings. The Order designates an area of sea off the east coast of Scotland within which taking scallops is prohibited; and prohibits the movement of scallops out of that area.

5313. Food safety–Emergency prohibitions–Amnesic shellfish poisoning

FOOD PROTECTION (EMERGENCY PROHIBITIONS) (AMNESIC SHELLFISH POISONING) (WEST COAST) (NO.10) (SCOTLAND) ORDER 2005, SSI 2005 431; made under the Food and Environment Protection Act 1985 s.1, s.24. In force: September 2, 2005 at 4.30 pm; £3.00.

This Order contains emergency prohibitions restricting various activities in order to prevent human consumption of food rendered unsuitable for that purpose by virtue of shellfish having been affected by the toxin which causes amnesic shellfish poisoning in human beings. It designates areas of sea off the west coast of Scotland within which taking scallops is prohibited and prohibits the movement of scallops out of those areas.

5314. Food safety–Emergency prohibitions–Amnesic shellfish poisoning

FOOD PROTECTION (EMERGENCY PROHIBITIONS) (AMNESIC SHELLFISH POISONING) (WEST COAST) (NO.11) (SCOTLAND) ORDER 2005, SSI 2005 455; made under the Food and Environment Protection Act 1985 s.1, s.24. In force: September 15, 2005 at 4.30 pm; £3.00.

This Order contains emergency prohibitions restricting various activities in order to prevent human consumption of food rendered unsuitable for that purpose by virtue of shellfish having been affected by the toxin which causes amnesic shellfish poisoning in human beings. The Order designates areas of sea off the west coast of Scotland within which taking scallops is prohibited and prohibits the movement of scallops out of those areas.

5315. Food safety–Emergency prohibitions–Amnesic shellfish poisoning

FOOD PROTECTION (EMERGENCY PROHIBITIONS) (AMNESIC SHELLFISH POISONING) (WEST COAST) (NO.12) (SCOTLAND) ORDER 2005, SSI 2005 497; made under the Food and Environment Protection Act 1985 s.1, s.24. In force: October 6, 2005 at 4.45 pm; £3.00.

This Order contains emergency prohibitions restricting various activities in order to prevent human consumption of food rendered unsuitable for that purpose by virtue of shellfish having been affected by the toxin which causes amnesic shellfish poisoning in human beings. It designates areas of sea off the west coast of Scotland within which taking scallops is prohibited; and prohibits the movement of scallops out of those areas.

5316. Food safety–Emergency prohibitions–Amnesic shellfish poisoning

FOOD PROTECTION (EMERGENCY PROHIBITIONS) (AMNESIC SHELLFISH POISONING) (WEST COAST) (NO.13) (SCOTLAND) ORDER 2005, SSI 2005 520; made under the Food and Environment Protection Act 1985 s.1, s.24. In force: October 20, 2005 at 4.30 pm; £3.00.

This Order contains emergency prohibitions restricting various activities in order to prevent human consumption of food rendered unsuitable for that purpose by virtue of shellfish having been affected by the toxin which causes amnesic shellfish poisoning in human beings. It designates areas of sea off the west coast of Scotland within which taking scallops is prohibited; and prohibits the movement of scallops out of those areas.

5317. Food safety–Emergency prohibitions–Amnesic shellfish poisoning

FOOD PROTECTION (EMERGENCY PROHIBITIONS) (AMNESIC SHELLFISH POISONING) (WEST COAST) (NO.14) (SCOTLAND) ORDER 2005, SSI 2005 529; made under the Food and Environment Protection Act 1985 s.1, s.24. In force: October 27, 2005 at 4.45 pm; £3.00.

This Order contains emergency prohibitions restricting various activities in order to prevent human consumption of food rendered unsuitable for that purpose by virtue of shellfish having been affected by the toxin which causes amnesic shellfish poisoning in human beings. It designates areas of sea off the west coast of Scotland within which taking scallops is prohibited and prohibits the movement of scallops out of those areas.

5318. Food safety–Emergency prohibitions–Amnesic shellfish poisoning

FOOD PROTECTION (EMERGENCY PROHIBITIONS) (AMNESIC SHELLFISH POISONING) (WEST COAST) (NO.15) (SCOTLAND) ORDER 2005, SSI 2005

575; made under the Food and Environment Protection Act 1985 s.1, s.24. In force: November 10, 2005 at 4.30 pm; £3.00.

This Order contains emergency prohibitions restricting various activities in order to prevent human consumption of food rendered unsuitable for that purpose by virtue of shellfish having been affected by the toxin which causes amnesic shellfish poisoning in human beings. It designates areas of sea off the west coast of Scotland within which taking scallops is prohibited and prohibits the movement of scallops out of those areas.

5319. Food safety–Emergency prohibitions–Amnesic shellfish poisoning

FOOD PROTECTION (EMERGENCY PROHIBITIONS) (AMNESIC SHELLFISH POISONING) (WEST COAST) (NO.16) (SCOTLAND) ORDER 2005, SSI 2005 579; made under the Food and Environment Protection Act 1985 s.1, s.24. In force: November 11, 2005 at 4.30 pm; £3.00.

This Order contains emergency prohibitions restricting various activities in order to prevent human consumption of food rendered unsuitable for that purpose by virtue of shellfish having been affected by the toxin which causes amnesic shellfish poisoning in human beings. It designates areas of sea off the west coast of Scotland within which taking scallops is prohibited and prohibits the movement of scallops out of those areas.

5320. Food safety–Emergency prohibitions–Amnesic shellfish poisoning

FOOD PROTECTION (EMERGENCY PROHIBITIONS) (AMNESIC SHELLFISH POISONING) (WEST COAST) (NO.17) (SCOTLAND) ORDER 2005, SSI 2005 585; made under the Food and Environment Protection Act 1985 s.1, s.24. In force: November 18, 2005 at 4.30 pm; £3.00.

This Order contains emergency prohibitions restricting various activities in order to prevent human consumption of food rendered unsuitable for that purpose by virtue of shellfish having been affected by the toxin which causes amnesic shellfish poisoning in human beings. The Order designates areas of sea off the west coast of Scotland within which taking scallops is prohibited; and prohibits the movement of scallops out of those areas.

5321. Food safety–Emergency prohibitions–Amnesic shellfish poisoning

FOOD PROTECTION (EMERGENCY PROHIBITIONS) (AMNESIC SHELLFISH POISONING) (WEST COAST) (NO.18) (SCOTLAND) ORDER 2005, SSI 2005 626; made under the Food and Environment Protection Act 1985 s.1, s.24. In force: December 6, 2005 at 4.30 pm; £3.00.

This Order contains emergency prohibitions restricting various activities in order to prevent human consumption of food rendered unsuitable for that purpose by virtue of shellfish having been affected by the toxin which causes amnesic shellfish poisoning in human beings. It designates an area of sea off the west coast of Scotland within which taking scallops is prohibited; prohibits the movement of scallops out of that area; and imposes other restrictions in relation to the use of any scallops taken from that area.

5322. Food safety–Emergency prohibitions–Amnesic shellfish poisoning

FOOD PROTECTION (EMERGENCY PROHIBITIONS) (AMNESIC SHELLFISH POISONING) (WEST COAST) (NO.2) (SCOTLAND) ORDER 2005, SSI 2005 69; made under the Food and Environment Protection Act 1985 s.1, s.24. In force: February 11, 2005 at 4.30 pm; £3.00.

This Order contains emergency prohibitions restricting various activities in order to prevent human consumption of food rendered unsuitable for that purpose by virtue of shellfish having been affected by the toxin which causes amnesic shellfish poisoning in human beings. It designates an area within which taking scallops is prohibited; and prohibits the movement of scallops out of that area.

5323. Food safety—Emergency prohibitions—Amnesic shellfish poisoning

FOOD PROTECTION (EMERGENCY PROHIBITIONS) (AMNESIC SHELLFISH POISONING) (WEST COAST) (NO.3) (SCOTLAND) ORDER 2005, SSI 2005 208; made under the Food and Environment Protection Act 1985 s.1, s.24. In force: April 5, 2005 at 4.45 pm; £3.00.

This Order contains emergency prohibitions restricting various activities in order to prevent human consumption of food rendered unsuitable for that purpose by virtue of shellfish having been affected by the toxin which causes amnesic shellfish poisoning in human beings. It designates an area of sea off the west coast of Scotland within which taking scallops is prohibited; and prohibits the movement of scallops out of that area.

5324. Food safety—Emergency prohibitions—Amnesic shellfish poisoning

FOOD PROTECTION (EMERGENCY PROHIBITIONS) (AMNESIC SHELLFISH POISONING) (WEST COAST) (NO.4) (SCOTLAND) ORDER 2005, SSI 2005 260; made under the Food and Environment Protection Act 1985 s.1, s.24. In force: May 17, 2005 at 4.30 pm; £3.00.

This Order contains emergency prohibitions restricting various activities to prevent human consumption of food rendered unsuitable for that purpose by virtue of shellfish having been affected by the toxin which causes amnesic shellfish poisoning in human beings. It designates an area of sea off the west coast of Scotland within which taking scallops is prohibited; prohibits the movement of scallops out of that area; and imposes restrictions in relation to the use of any scallops taken from that area.

5325. Food safety—Emergency prohibitions—Amnesic shellfish poisoning

FOOD PROTECTION (EMERGENCY PROHIBITIONS) (AMNESIC SHELLFISH POISONING) (WEST COAST) (NO.5) (SCOTLAND) ORDER 2005, SSI 2005 379; made under the Food and Environment Protection Act 1985 s.1, s.24. In force: July 14, 2005 at 5 pm; £3.00.

This Order contains emergency prohibitions restricting various activities in order to prevent human consumption of food rendered unsuitable for that purpose by virtue of shellfish having been affected by the toxin which causes amnesic shellfish poisoning in human beings. It designates areas of sea off the west coast of Scotland within which taking scallops is prohibited and prohibits the movement of scallops out of those areas.

5326. Food safety—Emergency prohibitions—Amnesic shellfish poisoning

FOOD PROTECTION (EMERGENCY PROHIBITIONS) (AMNESIC SHELLFISH POISONING) (WEST COAST) (NO.6) (SCOTLAND) ORDER 2005, SSI 2005 384; made under the Food and Environment Protection Act 1985 s.1, s.24. In force: July 21, 2005 at 4.45 pm; £3.00.

This Order contains emergency prohibitions restricting various activities in order to prevent human consumption of food rendered unsuitable for that purpose by virtue of shellfish having been affected by the toxin which causes amnesic shellfish poisoning in human beings. The Order designates an area of sea off the west coast of Scotland within which taking scallops is prohibited and prohibits the movement of scallops out of that area.

5327. Food safety—Emergency prohibitions—Amnesic shellfish poisoning

FOOD PROTECTION (EMERGENCY PROHIBITIONS) (AMNESIC SHELLFISH POISONING) (WEST COAST) (NO.7) (SCOTLAND) ORDER 2005, SSI 2005 391; made under the Food and Environment Protection Act 1985 s.1, s.24. In force: July 29, 2005 at 12.30 pm; £3.00.

This Order contains emergency prohibitions restricting various activities in order to prevent human consumption of food rendered unsuitable for that purpose by virtue of shellfish having been affected by the toxin which causes amnesic shellfish poisoning in human beings. It designates areas of sea off the west coast of Scotland within which taking scallops is prohibited (articles 3 and 4 and the Schedule). It prohibits the movement of scallops out of those areas.

5328. Food safety–Emergency prohibitions–Amnesic shellfish poisoning

FOOD PROTECTION (EMERGENCY PROHIBITIONS) (AMNESIC SHELLFISH POISONING) (WEST COAST) (NO.8) (SCOTLAND) ORDER 2005, SSI 2005 410; made under the Food and Environment Protection Act 1985 s.1, s.24. In force: August 15, 2005 at 4.30 pm; £3.00.

This Order contains emergency prohibitions restricting various activities in order to prevent human consumption of food rendered unsuitable for that purpose by virtue of shellfish having been affected by the toxin which causes amnesic shellfish poisoning in human beings. The Order designates an area of sea off the west coast of Scotland within which taking scallops is prohibited; and prohibits the movement of scallops out of that area.

5329. Food safety–Emergency prohibitions–Amnesic shellfish poisoning

FOOD PROTECTION (EMERGENCY PROHIBITIONS) (AMNESIC SHELLFISH POISONING) (WEST COAST) (NO.9) (SCOTLAND) ORDER 2005, SSI 2005 421; made under the Food and Environment Protection Act 1985 s.1, s.24. In force: August 26, 2005 at 4.30 pm; £3.00.

This Order contains emergency prohibitions restricting various activities in order to prevent human consumption of food rendered unsuitable for that purpose by virtue of shellfish having been affected by the toxin which causes amnesic shellfish poisoning in human beings. The Order designates areas of sea off the west coast of Scotland within which taking scallops is prohibited and prohibits the movement of scallops out of those areas.

5330. Food safety–Emergency prohibitions–Amnesic shellfish poisoning

FOOD PROTECTION (EMERGENCY PROHIBITIONS) (AMNESIC SHELLFISH POISONING) (WEST COAST) (SCOTLAND) ORDER 2005, SSI 2005 34; made under the Food and Environment Protection Act 1985 1, 24. In force: January 21, 2005 at 3.30 pm; £3.00.

This Order contains emergency prohibitions restricting various activities in order to prevent human consumption of food rendered unsuitable for that purpose by virtue of shellfish having been affected by the toxin which causes amnesic shellfish poisoning in human beings. It designates areas within which taking scallops is prohibited; and prohibits the movement of scallops out of those areas.

5331. Food safety–Emergency prohibitions–Amnesic shellfish poisoning–Partial revocation

FOOD PROTECTION (EMERGENCY PROHIBITIONS) (AMNESIC SHELLFISH POISONING) (WEST COAST) (NOS.5 AND 9) (SCOTLAND) ORDERS 2004 PARTIAL REVOCATION ORDER 2005, SSI 2005 68; made under the Food and Environment Protection Act 1985 s.1, s.24. In force: February 11, 2005 at 4.30 pm; £3.00.

This Order is a partial revocation of the Food Protection (Emergency Prohibitions) (Amnesic Shellfish Poisoning) (West Coast) (No.5) (Scotland) Order 2004 (SSI 2004 323) and a partial revocation of the Food Protection (Emergency Prohibitions) (Amnesic Shellfish Poisoning) (West Coast) (No.9) (Scotland) Order 2004 (SSI 2004 359) which prohibited fishing for or taking scallops within the areas designated; movement of such scallops out of the designated areas; and landing, using in the preparation or processing for supply of food of, supplying and other specified activities in relation to, such scallops from the designated areas. The effect of this Order is to remove the prohibitions in respect of the areas of sea designated.

5332. Food safety–Emergency prohibitions–Amnesic shellfish poisoning–Partial revocation

FOOD PROTECTION (EMERGENCY PROHIBITIONS) (AMNESIC SHELLFISH POISONING) (WEST COAST) (NO.10) (SCOTLAND) PARTIAL REVOCATION ORDER 2005, SSI 2005 551; made under the Food and Environment Protection Act 1985 s.1, s.24. In force: November 8, 2005 at 4.30 pm; £3.00.

This Order partially revokes the Food Protection (Emergency Prohibitions) (Amnesic Shellfish Poisoning) (West Coast) (No.10) (Scotland) Order 2005 which prohibited fishing for or taking scallops within the areas designated; movement of such scallops out of the designated areas; and landing, using in the preparation or processing for supply of food of, supplying and other specified activities in relation to, such scallops from the designated areas. The effect of this Order is to remove the prohibitions in respect of the area of sea designated.

5333. Food safety–Emergency prohibitions–Amnesic shellfish poisoning–Partial revocation

FOOD PROTECTION (EMERGENCY PROHIBITIONS) (AMNESIC SHELLFISH POISONING) (WEST COAST) (NO.5) (SCOTLAND) ORDER 2004 PARTIAL REVOCATION ORDER 2005, SSI 2005 203; made under the Food and Environment Protection Act 1985 s.1, s.24. In force: April 1, 2005 at 4.30 pm; £3.00.

This Order is a partial revocation of the Food Protection (Emergency Prohibitions) (Amnesic Shellfish Poisoning) (West Coast) (No.5) (Scotland) Order 2004 (SSI 2004 323) which prohibited fishing for or taking scallops within the areas designated; movement of such scallops out of the designated areas; and landing, using in the preparation or processing for supply of food of, supplying and other specified activities in relation to, such scallops from the designated areas. The effect of this Order is to remove the prohibitions in respect of the area of sea designated.

5334. Food safety–Emergency prohibitions–Amnesic shellfish poisoning–Partial revocation

FOOD PROTECTION (EMERGENCY PROHIBITIONS) (AMNESIC SHELLFISH POISONING) (WEST COAST) (NO.7) (SCOTLAND) ORDER 2004 PARTIAL REVOCATION ORDER 2005, SSI 2005 89; made under the Food and Environment Protection Act 1985 s.1, s.24. In force: February 25, 2005 at 4.30 pm; £3.00.

This Order is a partial revocation of the Food Protection (Emergency Prohibitions) (Amnesic Shellfish Poisoning) (West Coast) (No.7) (Scotland) Order 2004 (SSI 2004 341) which prohibited fishing for or taking scallops within the areas designated; movement of such scallops out of the designated areas; and landing, using in the preparation or processing for supply of food of, supplying and other specified activities in relation to, such scallops from the designated areas. The effect of this Order is to remove the prohibitions in respect of the areas of sea designated.

5335. Food safety–Emergency prohibitions–Amnesic shellfish poisoning–Partial revocation

FOOD PROTECTION (EMERGENCY PROHIBITIONS) (AMNESIC SHELLFISH POISONING) (WEST COAST) (NO.7) (SCOTLAND) ORDER 2004 PARTIAL REVOCATION (NO.2) ORDER 2005, SSI 2005 177; made under the Food and Environment Protection Act 1985 s.1, s.24. In force: March 22, 2005 at 4.45 pm; £3.00.

This Order is a partial revocation of the Food Protection (Emergency Prohibitions) (Amnesic Shellfish Poisoning) (West Coast) (No.7) (Scotland) Order 2004 (SSI 2004 341) which prohibited fishing for or taking scallops within the areas designated in the Schedule to the principal Order; movement of such scallops out of the designated areas; and landing, using in the preparation or processing for supply of food of, supplying and other specified activities in relation to, such scallops from the designated areas. The effect of this Order is to remove the prohibitions in respect of the area of sea designated.

5336. Food safety–Emergency prohibitions–Amnesic shellfish poisoning–Partial revocation

FOOD PROTECTION (EMERGENCY PROHIBITIONS) (AMNESIC SHELLFISH POISONING) (WEST COAST) (NO.9) (SCOTLAND) ORDER 2004 PARTIAL REVOCATION ORDER 2005, SSI 2005 191; made under the Food and Environment Protection Act 1985 s.1, s.24. In force: March 24, 2005 at 4.45 pm; £3.00.

This Order revokes in part the Food Protection (Emergency Prohibitions) (Amnesic Shellfish Poisoning) (West Coast) (No.9) (Scotland) Order 2004 (SSI 2004 359) which prohibited fishing for or taking scallops within the areas designated; movement of such scallops out of the designated areas; and landing, using in the preparation or processing for supply of food of, supplying and other specified activities in relation to, such scallops from the designated areas. The effect of this Order is to remove the prohibitions in respect of the area of sea designated.

5337. Food safety–Emergency prohibitions–Amnesic shellfish poisoning–Partial revocation

FOOD PROTECTION (EMERGENCY PROHIBITIONS) (AMNESIC SHELLFISH POISONING) (WEST COAST) (NO.9) (SCOTLAND) ORDER 2004 PARTIAL REVOCATION (NO.2) ORDER 2005, SSI 2005 220; made under the Food and Environment Protection Act 1985 s.1, s.24. In force: April 19, 2005 at 4.30 pm; £3.00.

This Order is a partial revocation of the Food Protection (Emergency Prohibitions) (Amnesic Shellfish Poisoning) (West Coast) (No.9) (Scotland) Order 2004 (SSI 2004 359), which prohibited fishing for or taking scallops within the areas designated; movement of such scallops out of the designated areas; and landing, using in the preparation or processing for supply of food of, supplying and other specified activities in relation to, such scallops from the designated areas. The effect of this Order is to remove the prohibitions in respect of the areas of sea designated.

5338. Food safety–Emergency prohibitions–Amnesic shellfish poisoning–Revocation

FOOD PROTECTION (EMERGENCY PROHIBITIONS) (AMNESIC SHELLFISH POISONING) (ORKNEY) (NO.2) (SCOTLAND) ORDER 2004 REVOCATION ORDER 2005, SSI 2005 16; made under the Food and Environment Protection Act 1985 s.1. In force: January 17, 2005 at 4 pm; £3.00.

This Order revokes the Food Protection (Emergency Prohibitions) (Amnesic Shellfish Poisoning) (Orkney) (No.2) (Scotland) Order 2004 (SSI 2004 322) which prohibited fishing for or taking scallops within the area designated; movement of such scallops out of the designated area; and landing, using in the preparation or processing for supply of food, supplying and other specified activities in relation to certain scallops from the designated area. The effect of this Order is to remove the prohibitions in respect of the area of sea designated.

5339. Food safety–Emergency prohibitions–Amnesic shellfish poisoning–Revocation

FOOD PROTECTION (EMERGENCY PROHIBITIONS) (AMNESIC SHELLFISH POISONING) (ORKNEY) (NO.3) (SCOTLAND) ORDER 2004 REVOCATION ORDER 2005, SSI 2005 56; made under the Food and Environment Protection Act 1985 s.1. In force: February 3, 2005 at 4.30 pm; £3.00.

This Order revokes the Food Protection (Emergency Prohibitions) (Amnesic Shellfish Poisoning) (Orkney) (No.3) (Scotland) Order 2004 (SSI 2004 352) which prohibited fishing for or taking scallops within the area designated; movement of such scallops out of the designated area; and landing, using in the preparation or processing for supply of food, supplying and other specified activities in relation to certain scallops from the designated area. The effect of this Order is to remove the prohibitions in respect of the area of sea designated.

5340. Food safety—Emergency prohibitions—Amnesic shellfish poisoning—Revocation

FOOD PROTECTION (EMERGENCY PROHIBITIONS) (AMNESIC SHELLFISH POISONING) (WEST COAST) (NO.10) (SCOTLAND) ORDER 2004 REVOCATION ORDER 2005, SSI 2005 204; made under the Food and Environment Protection Act 1985 s.1. In force: April 1, 2005 at 4.30 pm; £3.00.

This Order revokes the Food Protection (Emergency Prohibitions) (Amnesic Shellfish Poisoning) (West Coast) (No.10) (Scotland) Order 2004 (SSI 2004 412) and the Food Protection (Emergency Prohibitions) (Amnesic Shellfish Poisoning) (West Coast) (No.10) (Scotland) Partial Revocation Order 2004 (SSI 2004 549) which prohibited fishing for or taking scallops within the areas designated; movement of such scallops out of the designated areas; and landing, using in the preparation or processing for supply of food, supplying and other specified activities in relation to, such scallops from the designated areas. The effect of this Order is to remove the prohibitions in respect of the areas of sea designated.

5341. Food safety—Emergency prohibitions—Amnesic shellfish poisoning—Revocation

FOOD PROTECTION (EMERGENCY PROHIBITIONS) (AMNESIC SHELLFISH POISONING) (WEST COAST) (NO.10) (SCOTLAND) REVOCATION ORDER 2005, SSI 2005 628; made under the Food and Environment Protection Act 1985 s.1. In force: December 7, 2005 at 2.30 pm; £3.00.

This Order revokes the Food Protection (Emergency Prohibitions) (Amnesic Shellfish Poisoning) (West Coast) (No.10) (Scotland) Order 2005 (SI 2005 431) which prohibited fishing for or taking scallops within the areas designated in the Schedule to that Order; movement of such scallops out of those areas; and landing, using in the preparation or processing for supply of food of, supplying and other specified activities in relation to, such scallops from the designated areas. The effect of this Order is to remove the prohibitions in respect of the areas of sea designated as Areas 2 8 in the Schedule to the principal Order. The Food Protection (Emergency Prohibitions) (Amnesic Shellfish Poisoning) (West Coast) (No.10) (Scotland) Partial Revocation Order 2005 (SI 2005 551) is also revoked.

5342. Food safety—Emergency prohibitions—Amnesic shellfish poisoning—Revocation

FOOD PROTECTION (EMERGENCY PROHIBITIONS) (AMNESIC SHELLFISH POISONING) (WEST COAST) (NO.11) (SCOTLAND) ORDER 2004 REVOCATION ORDER 2005, SSI 2005 228; made under the Food and Environment Protection Act 1985 s.1. In force: April 22, 2005 at 4.45 pm; £3.00.

This Order revokes the Food Protection (Emergency Prohibitions) (Amnesic Shellfish Poisoning) (West Coast) (No.11) (Scotland) Order 2004 (SSI 2004 418) which prohibited fishing for or taking scallops within the area designated; movement of such scallops out of the designated area; and landing, using in the preparation or processing for supply of food of, supplying and other specified activities in relation to, such scallops from the designated area. The effect of this Order is to remove the prohibitions in respect of the area of sea designated.

5343. Food safety–Emergency prohibitions–Amnesic shellfish poisoning– Revocation

FOOD PROTECTION (EMERGENCY PROHIBITIONS) (AMNESIC SHELLFISH POISONING) (WEST COAST) (NO.12) (SCOTLAND) ORDER 2004 REVOCATION ORDER 2005, SSI 2005 136; made under the Food and Environment Protection Act 1985 s.1. In force: March 2, 2005 at 4 pm; £3.00.

This Order revokes the Food Protection (Emergency Prohibitions) (Amnesic Shellfish Poisoning) (West Coast) (No.12) (Scotland) Order 2004 (SSI 2004 447) which prohibited fishing for or taking scallops within the area designated, movement of such scallops out of the designated area and landing, using in the preparation or processing for supply of food of, supplying and other specified activities in relation to, such scallops from the designated area. The effect of this Order is to remove the prohibitions in respect of the area of sea designated.

5344. Food safety–Emergency prohibitions–Amnesic shellfish poisoning– Revocation

FOOD PROTECTION (EMERGENCY PROHIBITIONS) (AMNESIC SHELLFISH POISONING) (WEST COAST) (NO.13) (SCOTLAND) ORDER 2004 REVOCATION ORDER 2005, SSI 2005 202; made under the Food and Environment Protection Act 1985 s.1. In force: April 1, 2005 at 4.30 pm; £3.00.

This Order revokes the Food Protection (Emergency Prohibitions) (Amnesic Shellfish Poisoning) (West Coast) (No.13) (Scotland) Order 2004 (SSI 2004 484), which prohibited fishing for or taking scallops within the areas designated; movement of such scallops out of the designated areas; and landing, using in the preparation or processing for supply of food of, supplying and other specified activities in relation to, such scallops from the designated areas. The effect of this Order is to remove the prohibitions in respect of the areas of sea designated.

5345. Food safety–Emergency prohibitions–Amnesic shellfish poisoning– Revocation

FOOD PROTECTION (EMERGENCY PROHIBITIONS) (AMNESIC SHELLFISH POISONING) (WEST COAST) (NO.2) (SCOTLAND) REVOCATION ORDER 2005, SSI 2005 227; made under the Food and Environment Protection Act 1985 s.1. In force: April 22, 2005 at 4.45 pm; £3.00.

This Order revokes the Food Protection (Emergency Prohibitions) (Amnesic Shellfish Poisoning) (West Coast) (No.2) (Scotland) Order 2005 (SSI 2005 69) which prohibited fishing for or taking scallops within the areas designated; movement of such scallops out of the designated areas; and landing, using in the preparation or processing for supply of food of, supplying and other specified activities in relation to, such scallops from the designated areas. The effect of this Order is to remove the prohibitions in respect of the areas of sea designated.

5346. Food safety–Emergency prohibitions–Amnesic shellfish poisoning– Revocation

FOOD PROTECTION (EMERGENCY PROHIBITIONS) (AMNESIC SHELLFISH POISONING) (WEST COAST) (NO.3) (SCOTLAND) ORDER 2004 REVOCATION ORDER 2005, SSI 2005 213; made under the Food and Environment Protection Act 1985 s.1. In force: April 11, 2005 at 4.45 pm; £3.00.

This Order revokes the Food Protection (Emergency Prohibitions) (Amnesic Shellfish Poisoning) (West Coast) (No.3) (Scotland) Order 2004 (SSI 2004 237) which prohibited fishing for or taking scallops within the area designated; movement of such scallops out of the designated area; and landing, using in the preparation or processing for supply of food of, supplying and other specified activities in relation to, such scallops from the designated area. The effect of this Order is to remove the prohibitions in respect of the area of sea designated.

5347. Food safety–Emergency prohibitions–Amnesic shellfish poisoning–Revocation

FOOD PROTECTION (EMERGENCY PROHIBITIONS) (AMNESIC SHELLFISH POISONING) (WEST COAST) (NO.3) (SCOTLAND) REVOCATION ORDER 2005, SSI 2005 272; made under the Food and Environment Protection Act 1985 s.1. In force: May 20, 2005 at 3.30 pm; £3.00.

This Order revokes the Food Protection (Emergency Prohibitions) (Amnesic Shellfish Poisoning) (West Coast) (No.3) (Scotland) Order 2005 (SSI 2005 208) which prohibited fishing for or taking scallops within the area designated; movement of such scallops out of the designated area; and landing, using in the preparation or processing for supply of food of, supplying and other specified activities in relation to, such scallops from the designated area. The effect of this Order is to remove the prohibitions in respect of the area of sea designated.

5348. Food safety–Emergency prohibitions–Amnesic shellfish poisoning–Revocation

FOOD PROTECTION (EMERGENCY PROHIBITIONS) (AMNESIC SHELLFISH POISONING) (WEST COAST) (NO.4) (SCOTLAND) REVOCATION ORDER 2005, SSI 2005 360; made under the Food and Environment Protection Act 1985 s.1. In force: June 24, 2005 at 3 pm; £3.00.

This Order revokes the Food Protection (Emergency Prohibitions) (Amnesic Shellfish Poisoning) (West Coast) (No.4) (Scotland) Order 2005 (SSI 2005 260) which prohibited fishing for or taking scallops within the area designated; movement of such scallops out of the designated area; and landing, using in the preparation or processing for supply of food of, supplying and other specified activities in relation to, such scallops from the designated area.

5349. Food safety–Emergency prohibitions–Amnesic shellfish poisoning–Revocation

FOOD PROTECTION (EMERGENCY PROHIBITIONS) (AMNESIC SHELLFISH POISONING) (WEST COAST) (NO.5) (SCOTLAND) ORDER 2004 REVOCATION ORDER 2005, SSI 2005 212; made under the Food and Environment Protection Act 1985 s.1. In force: April 11, 2005 at 4.45 pm; £3.00.

This Order revokes the Food Protection (Emergency Prohibitions) (Amnesic Shellfish Poisoning) (West Coast) (No.5) (Scotland) Order 2004 (SSI 2004 323) and the Food Protection (Emergency Prohibitions) (Amnesic Shellfish Poisoning) (West Coast) (No.5) (Scotland) Order 2004 Partial Revocation Order 2005 (SSI 2005 203). The 2004 Order prohibited fishing for or taking scallops within the areas designated; movement of such scallops out of the designated areas; and landing, using in the preparation or processing for supply of food of, supplying and other specified activities in relation to, such scallops from the designated areas. The effect of this Order is to remove the prohibitions in respect of the area designated.

5350. Food safety–Emergency prohibitions–Amnesic shellfish poisoning–Revocation

FOOD PROTECTION (EMERGENCY PROHIBITIONS) (AMNESIC SHELLFISH POISONING) (WEST COAST) (NO.5) (SCOTLAND) REVOCATION ORDER 2005, SSI 2005 406; made under the Food and Environment Protection Act 1985 s.1. In force: August 12, 2005 at 3.30 pm; £3.00.

This Order revokes the Food Protection (Emergency Prohibitions) (Amnesic Shellfish Poisoning) (West Coast) (No.5) (Scotland) Order 2005 (SSI 2005 379), which prohibited fishing for or taking scallops within the areas designated; movement of such scallops out of the designated areas; and landing, using in the preparation or processing for supply of food of, supplying and other specified activities in relation to, such scallops from the designated areas. The effect of this Order is to remove the prohibitions in respect of the areas of sea designated.

5351. **Food safety—Emergency prohibitions—Amnesic shellfish poisoning—Revocation**

FOOD PROTECTION (EMERGENCY PROHIBITIONS) (AMNESIC SHELLFISH POISONING) (WEST COAST) (NO.6) (SCOTLAND) ORDER 2004 REVOCATION ORDER 2005, SSI 2005 210; made under the Food and Environment Protection Act 1985 s.1. In force: April 6, 2005 at 4.45 pm; £3.00.

This Order revokes the Food Protection (Emergency Prohibitions) (Amnesic Shellfish Poisoning) (West Coast) (No.6) (Scotland) Order 2004 (SSI 2004 330) which prohibited fishing for or taking scallops within the area designated; movement of such scallops out of the designated area; and landing, using in the preparation or processing for supply of food of, supplying and other specified activities in relation to, such scallops from the designated area. The effect of this Order is to remove the prohibitions in respect of the area designated.

5352. **Food safety—Emergency prohibitions—Amnesic shellfish poisoning—Revocation**

FOOD PROTECTION (EMERGENCY PROHIBITIONS) (AMNESIC SHELLFISH POISONING) (WEST COAST) (NO.7) (SCOTLAND) ORDER 2004 REVOCATION ORDER 2005, SSI 2005 221; made under the Food and Environment Protection Act 1985 s.1. In force: April 19, 2005 at 4.30 pm; £3.00.

This Order revokes the Food Protection (Emergency Prohibitions) (Amnesic Shellfish Poisoning) (West Coast) (No.7) (Scotland) Order 2004 (SSI 2004 341) which prohibited fishing for or taking scallops within the areas designated; movement of such scallops out of the designated areas; and landing, using in the preparation or processing for supply of food of, supplying and other specified activities in relation to, such scallops from the designated areas. The effect of this Order is to remove the prohibitions in respect of the area of sea designated. The Order also revokes the Food Protection (Emergency Prohibitions) (Amnesic Shellfish Poisoning) (West Coast) (No.7) (Scotland) Partial Revocation Order 2004 (SSI 2004 553), the Food Protection (Emergency Prohibitions) (Amnesic Shellfish Poisoning) (West Coast) (No.7) (Scotland) Order 2004 Partial Revocation Order 2005 (SSI 2005 89) and the Food Protection (Emergency Prohibitions) (Amnesic Shellfish Poisoning) (West Coast) (No.7) (Scotland) Order 2004 Partial Revocation (No.2) Order 2005 (SSI 2005 177).

5353. **Food safety—Emergency prohibitions—Amnesic shellfish poisoning—Revocation**

FOOD PROTECTION (EMERGENCY PROHIBITIONS) (AMNESIC SHELLFISH POISONING) (WEST COAST) (NO.8) (SCOTLAND) ORDER 2004 REVOCATION ORDER, SSI 2005 273; made under the Food and Environment Protection Act 1985 s.1. In force: Msy 20, 2005; £3.00.

This Order revokes the Food Protection (Emergency Prohibitions) (Amnesic Shellfish Poisoning) (West Coast) (No.8) (Scotland) Order 2004 (SSI 2004 344) which prohibited fishing for or taking scallops within the area designated; movement of such scallops out of the designated area; and landing, using in the preparation or processing for supply of food of, supplying and other specified activities in relation to, such scallops from the designated area. The effect of this Order is to remove the prohibitions in respect of the area of sea designated.

5354. **Food safety—Emergency prohibitions—Amnesic shellfish poisoning—Revocation**

FOOD PROTECTION (EMERGENCY PROHIBITIONS) (AMNESIC SHELLFISH POISONING) (WEST COAST) (NO.9) (SCOTLAND) ORDER 2004 REVOCATION ORDER, SSI 2005 274; made under the Food and Environment Protection Act 1985 s.1. In force: May 20, 2005 at 3.30 pm; £3.00.

This Order revokes Food Protection (Emergency Prohibitions) (Amnesic Shellfish Poisoning) (West Coast) (No.9) (Scotland) Order 2004 (SSI 2004 359), the Food Protection (Emergency Prohibitions) (Amnesic Shellfish

Poisoning) (West Coast) (Nos.5 and 9) (Scotland) Orders 2004 Partial Revocation Order 2005 (SSI 2005 68), the Food Protection (Emergency Prohibitions) (Amnesic Shellfish Poisoning) (West Coast) (No.9) (Scotland) Order 2004 Partial Revocation Order 2005 (SSI 2005 191) and the Food Protection (Emergency Prohibitions) (Amnesic Shellfish Poisoning) (West Coast) (No.9) (Scotland) Order 2004 Partial Revocation (No.2) Order 2005 (SSI 2005 220). The Orders prohibited fishing for or taking scallops within the areas designated; movement of such scallops out of the designated areas; and landing, using in the preparation or processing for supply of food of, supplying and other specified activities in relation to, such scallops from the designated areas. The effect of this Order is to remove the prohibitions in respect of the area of sea designated.

5355. Food safety–Emergency prohibitions–Amnesic shellfish poisoning–Revocation

FOOD PROTECTION (EMERGENCY PROHIBITIONS) (AMNESIC SHELLFISH POISONING) (WEST COAST) (NO.9) (SCOTLAND) REVOCATION ORDER 2005, SSI 2005 627; made under the Food and Environment Protection Act 1985 s.1. In force: December 7, 2005 at 2.30 pm; £3.00.

This Order revokes the Food Protection (Emergency Prohibitions) (Amnesic Shellfish Poisoning) (West Coast) (No.9) (Scotland) Order 2005 (SSI 2005 421) which prohibited fishing for or taking scallops within the areas designated; movement of such scallops out of those areas; and landing, using in the preparation or processing for supply of food of, supplying and other specified activities in relation to, such scallops from the designated areas. The effect of this Order is to remove the prohibitions in respect of the areas of sea designated.

5356. Food safety–Emergency prohibitions–Amnesic shellfish poisoning–Revocation

FOOD PROTECTION (EMERGENCY PROHIBITIONS) (AMNESIC SHELLFISH POISONING) (WEST COAST) (SCOTLAND) REVOCATION ORDER 2005, SSI 2005 137; made under the Food and Environment Protection Act 1985 s.1. In force: March 4, 2005 at 4 pm; £3.00.

This Order revokes the Food Protection (Emergency Prohibitions) (Amnesic Shellfish Poisoning) (West Coast) (Scotland) Order 2005 (SSI 2005 34) which prohibited fishing for or taking scallops within the areas designated, movement of such scallops out of the designated areas, and landing, using in the preparation or processing for supply of food of, supplying and other specified activities in relation to, such scallops from the designated areas. The effect of this Order is to remove the prohibitions in respect of the areas of sea designated.

5357. Food safety–Emergency prohibitions–Paralytic shellfish poisoning

FOOD PROTECTION (EMERGENCY PROHIBITIONS) (PARALYTIC SHELLFISH POISONING) (EAST COAST) (SCOTLAND) ORDER 2005, SSI 2005 415; made under the Food and Environment Protection Act 1985 s.1, s.24. In force: August 19, 2005 at 4.30 pm; £3.00.

This Order contains emergency prohibitions restricting various activities in order to prevent human consumption of food rendered unsuitable for that purpose by virtue of shellfish having been affected by the toxin which causes paralytic shellfish poisoning in human beings. The Order designates an area of sea off the east coast of Scotland within which taking scallops is prohibited; and prohibits the movement of scallops out of that area.

5358. Food safety–Emergency prohibitions–Paralytic shellfish poisoning

FOOD PROTECTION (EMERGENCY PROHIBITIONS) (PARALYTIC SHELLFISH POISONING) (ORKNEY) (NO.2) (SCOTLAND) ORDER 2005, SSI 2005 548;

made under the Food and Environment Protection Act 1985 s.1, s.24. In force: November 4, 2005 at 4.30 pm; £3.00.

This Order, which forms part of Scots law only, contains emergency prohibitions restricting various activities in order to prevent human consumption of food rendered unsuitable for that purpose by virtue of shellfish having been affected by the toxin which causes paralytic shellfish poisoning in human beings. The Order designates an area of sea off the coast of Orkney within which taking scallops is prohibited and prohibits the movement of scallops out of that area.

5359.   Food safety–Emergency prohibitions–Paralytic shellfish poisoning

FOOD PROTECTION (EMERGENCY PROHIBITIONS) (PARALYTIC SHELLFISH POISONING) (ORKNEY) (SCOTLAND) ORDER 2005, SSI 2005 506; made under the Food and Environment Protection Act 1985 s.1, s.24. In force: October 10, 2005 at 5.15 pm; £3.00.

This Order contains emergency prohibitions restricting various activities in order to prevent human consumption of food rendered unsuitable for that purpose by virtue of shellfish having been affected by the toxin which causes paralytic shellfish poisoning in human beings. The Order designates areas of sea off the coast of Orkney within which taking scallops is prohibited and prohibits the movement of scallops out of those areas.

5360.   Food safety–Emergency prohibitions–Paralytic shellfish poisoning–Revocation

FOOD PROTECTION (EMERGENCY PROHIBITIONS) (PARALYTIC SHELLFISH POISONING) (EAST COAST) (SCOTLAND) REVOCATION ORDER 2005, SSI 2005 499; made under the Food and Environment Protection Act 1985 s.1. In force: October 6, 2005 at 4.45 pm; £3.00.

This Order revokes the Food Protection (Emergency Prohibitions) (Paralytic Shellfish Poisoning) (East Coast) (Scotland) Order 2005 (SSI 2005 415) which prohibited fishing for or taking scallops within the area designated; movement of such scallops out of the designated area; and landing, using in the preparation or processing for supply of food of, supplying and other specified activities in relation to, such scallops from the designated area. The effect of this Order is to remove the prohibitions in respect of the area of sea designated.

5361.   Food safety–Emergency prohibitions–Paralytic shellfish poisoning–Revocation

FOOD PROTECTION (EMERGENCY PROHIBITIONS) (PARALYTIC SHELLFISH POISONING) (ORKNEY) (SCOTLAND) REVOCATION ORDER 2005, SSI 2005 547; made under the Food and Environment Protection Act 1985 s.1. In force: November 4, 2005 at 4.30 pm; £3.00.

This Order revokes the Food Protection (Emergency Prohibitions) (Paralytic Shellfish Poisoning) (Orkney) (Scotland) Order 2005 (SSI 2005 506) which prohibited fishing for or taking scallops within the areas designated; movement of such scallops out of the designated areas; and landing, using in the preparation or processing for supply of food of, supplying and other specified activities in relation to, such scallops from the designated areas. The effect of this Order is to remove the prohibitions in respect of the areas of sea designated.

5362.   Food safety–Emergency prohibitions–Radioactivity in sheep–Partial revocation

FOOD PROTECTION (EMERGENCY PROHIBITIONS) (RADIOACTIVITY IN SHEEP) PARTIAL REVOCATION (SCOTLAND) ORDER 2005, SSI 2005 71; made under the Food and Environment Protection Act 1985 s.1, s.24. In force: February 17, 2005; £3.00.

The Food Protection (Emergency Prohibitions) (Radioactivity in Sheep) Order 1991 (SI 1991 20) contains emergency prohibitions restricting various activities in order to prevent human consumption of food which has been, or which may have been, rendered unsuitable for that purpose in consequence of the escape of radioactive substances from a nuclear reactor situated at Chernobyl in the Ukraine. This Order, which revokes in part the 1991 Order, reduces the area which is subject to restriction.

5363. Food safety—Hygiene and enforcement

FEED (HYGIENE AND ENFORCEMENT) (SCOTLAND) REGULATIONS 2005, SSI 2005 608; made under the European Communities Act 1972 s.2. In force: January 1, 2006; £4.50.

These Regulations, which amend the Food Standards Act 1999 (Transitional and Consequential Provisions and Savings) (Scotland) Regulations 2000 (SSI 2000 62) and the Feeding Stuffs (Amendment) Regulations 2003 (SSI 2003 1026), revoke the Feeding Stuffs (Establishments and Intermediaries) Regulations 1999 (SI 1999 1872), the Feeding Stuffs (Enforcement) Regulations 1999 (SI 1999 2325), the Feeding Stuffs (Sampling and Analysis) Amendment (Scotland) Regulations 2001 (SSI 2001 104), the Feeding Stuffs and the Feeding Stuffs (Enforcement) Amendment (Scotland) Regulations 2001 (SSI 2001 334), the Feeding Stuffs Amendment (Scotland) Regulations 2002 (SSI 2002 285), the Feeding Stuffs (Scotland) Amendment Regulations 2003 (SSI 2003 101), the Feeding Stuffs (Miscellaneous Amendments) (Scotland) Regulations 2003 (SSI 2003 277), the Feeding Stuffs (Safety Requirements for Feed for Food-Producing Animals) Regulations 2004 (SI 2004 3254) and the Feeding Stuffs (Establishments and Intermediaries) Amendment (Scotland) Regulations 2005 (SI 2005 116). The Regulations provide for the execution and enforcement of European Parliament and Council Regulation 183/2005 ([2005] OJ L35/1) laying down requirements for feed hygiene and European Parliament and Council Regulation 178/2002 ([2002] OJ L31/1) laying down the general principles and requirements of food law, establishing the European Food Safety Authority and laying down procedures in matters of food safety. The Regulations also give effect to European Parliament and Council Regulation 882/2004 ([2004] OJ L191/1) on official controls performed to ensure the verification of compliance with feed and food law, animal health and animal welfare rules in respect of official controls on feed hygiene and feed safety.

5364. Food safety—Packaging—Plastics

MATERIALS AND ARTICLES IN CONTACT WITH FOOD (SCOTLAND) REGULATIONS 2005, SSI 2005 243; made under the Food Safety Act 1990 s.6, s.16, s.17, s.26, s.31, s.48. In force: May 21, 2005; £3.00.

These Regulations, which amend the Food Safety (Export) Regulations 1991 (SI 1991 1476) and the Plastic Materials and Articles in Contact with Food Regulations 1998 (SI 1998 1376), revoke the Materials and Articles in Contact with Food Regulations 1987 (SI 1987 1523) and the Materials and Articles in Contact with Food (Amendment) Regulations 1994 (SI 1994 979). They provide for the enforcement of European Parliament and Council Regulation 1935/2004 ([2004] OJ L338/4) on materials and articles intended to come into contact with food and repealing Directives 80/590 and 89/109. The Regulations provide for designation of the competent authorities for the various purposes identified in the Community Regulation; re enact, without substantive amendments, the provisions of the 1987 Regulations relating to vinyl chloride; re enact provisions of the 1987 Regulations relating to regenerated cellulose film (RCF); control what substances may be used in the manufacture of RCF; regulate what substances may be used to manufacture plastic coatings for RCF; create offences in relation to the sale, import or business use of non-compliant RCF; and create a requirement for RCF, when marketed prior to the retail stage, to be accompanied by a declaration of legislative compliance.

5365. **Food safety-Packaging-Plastics**

PLASTIC MATERIALS AND ARTICLES IN CONTACT WITH FOOD AMENDMENT (SCOTLAND) REGULATIONS 2005, SSI 2005 92; made under the Food Safety Act 1990 s.16, s.17, s.26, s.48. In force: March 24, 2005; £3.00.

These Regulations, which amend the Plastic Materials and Articles in Contact with Food Regulations 1998 (SI 1998 1376), implement Commission Directive 2004/19 ([2004] OJ L71/8) amending Commission Directive 2002/72 ([2002] OJ L71/8) relating to plastic materials and articles intended to come into contact with foodstuffs. They substitute the definition of "additive" used in the Directive, for consistency; remove references to lists of substances whose authorisations are now spent; add a restriction on the use of additives in the manufacture of plastic materials and articles which relates to substances also used as food additives or flavourings; make provision for the procedure to be followed and the time limits to be observed by any person wishing to have an additive included in the Community list of authorised additives; and impose additional labelling requirements for plastic materials and articles at the pre-retail stage so as to make additional information available to users.

5366. **Food safety-Smoke flavourings**

SMOKE FLAVOURINGS (SCOTLAND) REGULATIONS 2005, SSI 2005 215; made under the Food Safety Act 1990 s.6, s.16, s.17, s.26, s.48, Sch.1 para.1. In force: in accordance with Reg.1; £3.00.

These Regulations provide for the enforcement and execution of certain specified provisions of European Parliament and Council Regulation 2065/2003 ([2003] OJ L309/1) on smoke flavourings used or intended for use in or on foods. They formally designate the Food Standards Agency as the national competent authority to receive applications for the authorisation of new primary smoke condensates and primary tar fractions for use as such in or on foods, or in the production of derived smoke flavourings for use in or on foods; and apply various provisions of the Food Safety Act 1990; establish penalties for failing to comply with certain specified provisions.

5367. **Labelling-Food labelling**

FOOD LABELLING AMENDMENT (SCOTLAND) REGULATIONS 2005, SSI 2005 222; made under the Food Safety Act 1990 s.16, s.17, s.26, s.48. In force: May 20, 2006; £3.00.

These Regulations, which amend the Food Labelling Regulations 1996 (SI 1996 1499), implement Commission Directive 2004/77 ([2004] OJ L162/76). The Regulations require confectionery and drinks containing certain levels of that acid or salt to be labelled with the indication "contains liquorice" and for this to be coupled with a warning in certain cases; provide exemptions from these labelling requirements in the case of food which is not prepacked, food which is prepacked for direct sale, fancy confectionery products, small packages and certain indelibly marked glass bottles; contain a transitional provision; and amend the definition of "Directive 94/54".

5368. **Labelling-Food labelling-Additives**

FOOD LABELLING (ADDED PHYTOSTEROLS OR PHYTOSTANOLS) (SCOTLAND) REGULATIONS 2005, SSI 2005 1; made under the Food Safety Act 1990 s.6, s.16, s.17, s.26, s.48. In force: February 1, 2005; £3.00.

These Regulations provide for the enforcement of Commission Regulation 608/2004 ([2004] OJ L97/44) concerning the labelling of foods and food ingredients with added phytosterols, phytosterol esters, phytostanols and/or phytostanol esters. The Commission Regulation requires such foods and food ingredients to be labelled with additional information, including the words "with added plant sterols/plant stanols". The Commission Regulation was made pursuant to European Parliament and Council Directive 2000/13 ([2000] OJ L109/29) on the approximation of the laws of the Member States relating to the labelling, presentation and advertising of foodstuffs. In consequence, the products covered by the Commission Regulation are foods and food ingredients which are to be delivered as such to the ultimate consumer or which are intended for supply to mass caterers. By virtue of the Directive, certain small packages and indelibly marked glass bottles are exempt from certain of the labelling requirements of the Commission Regulation. The Regulations create offences and prescribe a penalty; make provision as to the manner of labelling in the case of the required particulars; specify the enforcement authorities; provide a defence in relation to exports, in accordance with Council Directive 89/397 ([1989] OJ L186/23) on the official control of foodstuffs, as read with the ninth recital to that Directive; and apply various provisions of the Food Safety Act 1990.

5369. Labelling—Food labelling—Allergenic ingredients

FOOD LABELLING AMENDMENT (NO.2) (SCOTLAND) REGULATIONS 2005, SSI 2005 456; made under the Food Safety Act 1990 s.6, s.16, s.17, s.26, s.48. In force: November 25, 2005; £3.00.

These Regulations, which amend the Food Labelling Regulations 1996 (SI 1996 1499), implement in Scotland Commission Directive 2005/26 ([2005] OJ L75/33) establishing a list of food ingredients or substances provisionally excluded from Annex IIIa of Directive 2000/13 of the European Parliament and of the Council. The Regulations confer an exemption until November 25, 2007 from the allergen labelling requirements in the case of certain ingredients originating from allergenic ingredients; make some consequential amendments; and update the definition of "Directive 2000/13".

5370. Labelling—Food labelling—Allergenic ingredients

FOOD LABELLING AMENDMENT (NO.3) (SCOTLAND) REGULATIONS 2005, SSI 2005 542; made under the Food Safety Act 1990 s.6, s.16, s.17, s.26, s.48. In force: in accordance with Reg.1 (2); £3.00.

These Regulations, which amend the Food Labelling Regulations 1996 (SI 1996 1499) and revoke the Food Labelling Amendment (No.2) (Scotland) Regulations 2005 (SSI 2005 456), implement Commission Directive 2005/26 ([2005] OJ L75/33) establishing a list of food ingredients or substances provisionally excluded from Annex IIIa of Directive 2000/13 of the European Parliament and of the Council. The Regulations confer an exemption until November 25, 2007 from the allergen labelling requirements in the Food Labelling Regulations 1996 in the case of certain ingredients originating from allergenic ingredients; make some consequential amendments; and update the definition of "Directive 2000/13/EC".

GOVERNMENT ADMINISTRATION

5371. Budget (Scotland) (No.2) Act 2005 (asp 4)

This Act of the Scottish Parliament makes provision, for financial year 2005/06, for the use of resources by the Scottish Administration and certain bodies whose expenditure is payable out of the Scottish Consolidated Fund, authorising the payment of sums out of the Fund and for the maximum amounts of borrowing by certain statutory bodies; and makes provision, for financial year 2006/07, authorising the payment of sums out of the Fund on a temporary basis.

This Act received Royal Assent on March 17, 2005.

5372. Emergency Workers (Scotland) Act 2005 (asp 2)

This Act of the Scottish Parliament makes it an offence to assault or impede persons who are providing emergency services.

This Act received Royal Assent on February 1, 2005.

5373. National Archives of Scotland–Fees

ACT OF SEDERUNT (FEES IN THE NATIONAL ARCHIVES OF SCOTLAND) 2005, SSI 2005 77; made under the Public Records (Scotland) Act 1937 s.10. In force: March 1, 2005; £3.00.

This Act of Sederunt, which revokes the Act of Sederunt (Fees in the National Archives of Scotland) 2003 (SSI 2003 234), sets out the Table of Fees chargeable by the National Archives of Scotland. The inspection fee is being increased by £1 from £5 to £6. The other fees are unchanged although the form of the Table is the subject of minor amendment.

HEALTH

5374. Community health councils–Dissolution

DISSOLUTION OF LOCAL HEALTH COUNCILS (SCOTLAND) ORDER 2005, SSI 2005 122; made under the National Health Service Reform (Scotland) Act 2004 s.8. In force: April 1, 2005; £3.00.

This Order specifies April 1, 2005 as the date on which all local health councils established by virtue of the National Health Service (Scotland) Act 1978 s.7 are dissolved.

5375. Health boards–Medical services–Investigation of complaints

NATIONAL HEALTH SERVICE (SERVICE COMMITTEES AND TRIBUNAL) (SCOTLAND) AMENDMENT (NO.2) REGULATIONS 2005, SSI 2005 334; made under the National Health Service (Scotland) Act 1978 s.17P, s.25, s.26, s.27, s.105, s.106, s.108. In force: July 1, 2005; £3.00.

These Regulations amend the National Health Service (Service Committees and Tribunal) (Scotland) Regulations 1992 (SI 1992 434) which make provision as to the investigation of matters relating to services provided by doctors, dentists, pharmacists, ophthalmic medical practitioners and opticians under arrangements with Health Boards. They amend the definition of "optician" to mean an ophthalmic optician, as defined in the National Health Service (Scotland) Act 1978 s.108. The 1992 Regulations make provision about the manner in which an allegation ceases to be the subject of a complaint being investigated. These Regulations provide that an allegation remains the subject of a complaint being investigated until the conclusion of the conciliation process.

5376. Health boards–Membership and procedure

HEALTH BOARDS (MEMBERSHIP AND PROCEDURE) (SCOTLAND) AMENDMENT REGULATIONS 2005, SSI 2005 108; made under the National Health Service (Scotland) Act 1978 s.2, s.105, s.108, Sch.1 para.4, Sch.1 para.11. In force: April 1, 2005; £3.00.

These Regulations amend the Health Boards (Membership and Procedure) Regulations 2001 (SSI 2001 302) which make provision as to the membership and procedure of Health Boards established under the National Health Service (Scotland) Act 1978. They remove references to National Health Service trusts, their trustees and Chief Officers following the dissolution of all such bodies; make provision as to the procedure of Health Boards, their committees and sub-committees; and allow the chairperson or vice chairperson of a Health Board, committee or sub-committee to direct that a meeting may be conducted in any way in which each member is able to participate in the meeting although not present in a pre-determined place with the other members of the Board, committee or sub-committee.

5377. National Health Service—Common Services Agency—Members—Remuneration

COMMON SERVICES AGENCY (MEMBERSHIP AND PROCEDURE) AMENDMENT (SCOTLAND) REGULATIONS 2005, SSI 2005 550; made under the National Health Service (Scotland) Act 1978 s.10, s.105, s.108, Sch.5 para.3A, Sch.5 para.8. In force: December 1, 2005; £3.00.

These Regulations amend the Common Services Agency (Membership and Procedure) Regulations 1991 (SI 1991 564) which make provision with respect to the Common Services Agency for the Scottish Health Service. The 1991 Regulations provide that remuneration may be paid to those members of the Committee who are not officers of the Agency, a Health Board (which includes a Special Health Board) or of the Scottish Ministers. These Regulations prescribe the other members of the Committee (that is, the members other than the chairman) to whom such remuneration may be paid as being those members who are not members of the staff of a Health Board (including a Special Health Board) or of the Scottish Administration. Its primary effect is to enable remuneration to be paid to members of the Committee who are members of the staff of the Agency. They also remove references to National Health Services trusts and fund holding practices following the dissolution of all such trusts and practices.

5378. National Health Service—Dental services—Maximum charge

NATIONAL HEALTH SERVICE (DENTAL CHARGES) (SCOTLAND) AMENDMENT REGULATIONS 2005, SSI 2005 121; made under the National Health Service (Scotland) Act 1978 s.70, s.71, s.71A, s.105, s.108, Sch.11 para.3; and the National Health Service (Primary Care) Act 1997 s.20, s.39, s.40. In force: April 1, 2005; £3.00.

These Regulations amend the National Health Service (Dental Charges) (Scotland) Regulations 2003 (SSI 2003 158) which provide for the making and recovery of charges in respect of the supply of dental appliances under the NHS and in respect of the provision of dental treatment under general dental services or in accordance with pilot schemes. The Regulations increase the maximum charge in the aggregate which may be payable for all dental appliances supplied and other services provided in pursuance of any one contract or arrangement; and provide that the increased maximum charge applies only where the contract or arrangement leading to the supply of the appliances and provision of those services is made on or after April 1, 2005.

5379. National Health Service—Drugs and appliances—Fees

NATIONAL HEALTH SERVICE (CHARGES FOR DRUGS AND APPLIANCES) (SCOTLAND) AMENDMENT REGULATIONS 2005, SSI 2005 124; made under the National Health Service (Scotland) Act 1978 s.27, s.69, s.105, s.108. In force: April 1, 2005; £3.00.

These Regulations amend the National Health Service (Charges for Drugs and Appliances) (Scotland) Regulations 2001 (SSI 2001 430) which provide for the making and recovery of charges for drugs, medicines and appliances supplied by chemists providing pharmaceutical services, doctors providing services under a general medical services contract or Section 17C arrangements, or by Health Boards to out-patients. They increase the charges for drugs, medicines and appliances; the sum payable in respect of a pre-payment certificate; and other various charges.

5380. National Health Service—Drugs and appliances—Supply

NATIONAL HEALTH SERVICE (CHARGES FOR DRUGS AND APPLIANCES) (SCOTLAND) AMENDMENT (NO.3) REGULATIONS 2005, SSI 2005 617; made under the National Health Service (Scotland) Act 1978 s.27, s.69, s.105, s.108. In force: December 23, 2005; £3.00.

These Regulations amend the National Health Service (Charges for Drugs and Appliances) (Scotland) Regulations 2001 (SSI 2001 430) which provide for the making and recovery of charges for the supply of drugs, medicines and appliances under the National Health Service (Scotland) Act 1978. The amendments extend the 2001 Regulations to the supply of drugs, medicines and appliances by a chemist in terms of a Patient Group Direction issued by a Health Board in accordance with the Prescription Only Medicines (Human Use) Order 1997 (SSI 1997 1830) (exemption for persons conducting a retail pharmacy business who supply or administer prescription only medicines under a Patient Group Direction).

5381. National Health Service–General dental services–Practice expenses

NATIONAL HEALTH SERVICE (GENERAL DENTAL SERVICES) (SCOTLAND) AMENDMENT REGULATIONS 2005, SSI 2005 95; made under the National Health Service (Scotland) Act 1978 s.25, s.28A, s.105, s.108. In force: April 1, 2005; £3.00.

These Regulations amend the National Health Service (General Dental Services) (Scotland) Regulations 1996 (SI 1996 177) which make provision as to the arrangements with which dentists provide general dental services under the National Health Service in Scotland. The Regulations make amendments to add a new matter to the table of matters that are to be provided for in determinations and published in the Statement of Dental Remuneration.

5382. National Health Service–General medical services–Contracts

NATIONAL HEALTH SERVICE (GENERAL MEDICAL SERVICES CONTRACTS) (SCOTLAND) AMENDMENT REGULATIONS 2005, SSI 2005 337; made under the National Health Service (Scotland) Act 1978 s.17L, s.17N, s.105, s.106, s.108. In force: July 1, 2005; £3.00.

These Regulations amend the National Health Service (General Medical Services Contracts) (Scotland) Regulations 2004 (SSI 2004 116), which set out the framework for general medical services contracts under the National Health Service (Scotland) Act 1978 s.17J. In particular they make amendments to the conditions that must be met before a Health Board may enter into a general medical services contract with a medical practitioner, partnership or company limited by shares, and to the provision which a general medical services contract must include.

5383. National Health Service–Health boards–Scottish Health Council–Establishment

NHS QUALITY IMPROVEMENT SCOTLAND (ESTABLISHMENT OF THE SCOTTISH HEALTH COUNCIL) REGULATIONS 2005, SSI 2005 120; made under the National Health Service (Scotland) Act 1978 s.105, Sch.1 para.11. In force: April 1, 2005; £3.00.

These Regulations place a duty on NHS Quality Improvement Scotland to establish a committee to be known as the Scottish Health Council (SHC) and to delegate to the SHC the function of supporting, ensuring and monitoring the discharge of the duty under s.2B of the National Health Service (Scotland) Act 1978 (duty to encourage public involvement) and s.2D of the Act (duty to discharge functions in a manner that encourages equal opportunities and in particular the observance of the equal opportunity requirements) by Health Boards, Special Health Boards and the Common Services Agency for the Scottish Health Service.

5384. National Health Service–NHS Quality Improvement–Functions

NHS QUALITY IMPROVEMENT SCOTLAND (AMENDMENT) ORDER 2005, SSI 2005 115; made under the National Health Service (Scotland) Act 1978 s.2, s.105. In force: April 1, 2005; £3.00.

This Order, which amends the NHS Quality Improvement Scotland Order 2002 (SSI 2002 534), extends NHS Quality Improvement Scotland's functions of supporting ensuring and monitoring the quality of healthcare provided by the

National Health Service in Scotland to also cover health care secured by the National Health Service in Scotland.

5385. National Health Service—Occupational pensions—Compensation—Civil partnerships

NATIONAL HEALTH SERVICE (SUPERANNUATION SCHEME, INJURY BENEFITS, ADDITIONAL VOLUNTARY CONTRIBUTIONS AND COMPENSATION FOR PREMATURE RETIREMENT) (CIVIL PARTNERSHIP) (SCOTLAND) AMENDMENT REGULATIONS 2005, SSI 2005 544; made under the Superannuation Act 1972 s.10, s.12, s.24, Sch.3. In force: December 5, 2005; £3.00.

These Regulations amend the National Health Service Superannuation Scheme (Scotland) Regulations 1995 (SI 1995 365), the National Health Service Superannuation Scheme (Scotland) (Additional Voluntary Contributions) Regulations 1998 (SI 1998 1451), the National Health Service (Scotland) (Injury Benefits) Regulations 1998 (SI 1998 1594) and the National Health Service (Compensation for Premature Retirement) (Scotland) Regulations 2003 (SSI 2003 344). The amendments in these Regulations make provision following the introduction of the new status of civil partner by the Civil Partnership Act 2004.

5386. National Health Service—Opticians—Provision of ophthalmic services—Entitlement

NATIONAL HEALTH SERVICE (GENERAL OPHTHALMIC SERVICES) (SCOTLAND) AMENDMENT REGULATIONS 2005, SSI 2005 128; made under the National Health Service (Scotland) Act 1978 s.26, s.105, s.108. In force: April 6, 2005; £3.00.

These Regulations amend the National Health Service (General Ophthalmic Services) (Scotland) Regulations 1986 (SI 1986 965), which provide for arrangements under which ophthalmic medical practitioners and ophthalmic opticians provide general ophthalmic services under the NHS. They raise the relevant income level of a person or persons entitled to a free NHS sight test at the time an award of a tax credit is made under the Tax Credit Act 2002 s.14 from £14,600 to £15,050.

5387. National Health Service—Pharmaceutical services—Provision of medicinal products

NATIONAL HEALTH SERVICE (PHARMACEUTICAL SERVICES) (SCOTLAND) AMENDMENT (NO.2) REGULATIONS 2005, SSI 2005 618; made under the National Health Service (Scotland) Act 1978 s.27, s.105, s.108. In force: December 23, 2005; £3.00.

These Regulations amend the National Health Service (Pharmaceutical Services) (Scotland) Regulations 1995 (SI 1995 414) which regulate the provision of pharmaceutical services under the National Health Service (Scotland) Act 1978. These amendments make provision for pharmacists to supply certain drugs and appliances without a prescription form being presented where the drugs and appliances are supplied in accordance with the terms of a Patient Group Direction issued by a Health Board in accordance with the Prescription Only Medicines (Human Use) Order 1997 (SI 1997 1830).

5388. National Health Service—Primary medical services—Doctors—Performers lists

NATIONAL HEALTH SERVICE (SERVICE COMMITTEES AND TRIBUNAL) (SCOTLAND) AMENDMENT REGULATIONS 2005, SSI 2005 118; made under the National Health Service (Scotland) Act 1978 s.17P, s.25, s.26, s.27, s.105, s.106, s.108. In force: April 1, 2005; £3.00.

These Regulations amend the National Health Service (Service Committees and Tribunal) (Scotland) Regulations 1992 (SI 1992 434) which make provision as to the investigation of matters relating to services provided by doctors, dentists, pharmacists, ophthalmic medical practitioners and opticians under arrangements with Health Boards and primary care NHS trusts. They make amendments in relation to the investigation of matters relating to doctors so that arrangements are no longer made by Health Boards with medical practitioners included on a medical list for the provision by them of general medical services. Instead all doctors who perform primary medical services, pursuant to an arrangement made by them or under an arrangement made by another person with a Health Board, must be included in primary medical services performers lists.

5389. **National Health Service–Primary medical services–Performers lists**

NATIONAL HEALTH SERVICE (PRIMARY MEDICAL SERVICES PERFORMERS LISTS) (SCOTLAND) AMENDMENT REGULATIONS 2005, SSI 2005 333; made under the National Health Service (Scotland) Act 1978 s.17P, s.105, s.108. In force: July 1, 2005; £3.00.

These Regulations amend the National Health Service (Primary Medical Services Performers Lists) (Scotland) Regulations 2004 (SSI 2004 114), which provide for lists of medical practitioners who may perform primary medical services for which Health Boards are under a duty to provide or secure the provision of, to be kept by those Health Boards. They amend the definition of "general medical practitioner" in the 2004 Regulations so that references to one include all medical practitioners included on the General Practitioner Register or, until that Register comes into effect, who are suitably experienced or have an acquired right to practise as a general medical practitioner. The effect is to provide that all such medical practitioners may be included on a list and perform primary medical services for which a Health Board is under a duty to provide or secure the provision of. They also amend the definition of "GP Registrar" to clarify its meaning and to make the definition consistent with other definitions of GP Registrar in subordinate legislation on primary medical services.

5390. **National Health Service–Primary medical services–S.17C agreements**

NATIONAL HEALTH SERVICE (PRIMARY MEDICAL SERVICES SECTION 17C AGREEMENTS) (SCOTLAND) AMENDMENT REGULATIONS 2005, SSI 2005 336; made under the National Health Service (Scotland) Act 1978 s.17E, s.105, s.106, s.108. In force: July 1, 2005; £3.00.

These Regulations amend the National Health Service (Primary Medical Services Section 17C Agreements) (Scotland) Regulations 2004 (SSI 2004 116), which set out the framework for section 17C arrangements for the provision of primary medical services under the National Health Service (Scotland) Act 1978. The Regulations, inter alia, introduce a provision requiring a provider not to enter into arrangements for certain telephone services where they are to be used by patients contacting the practice; amend the provisions placing restrictions on prescribing by supplementary prescribes, to permit the prescribing and administration by them of controlled drugs and the prescribing by them of unlicensed medicines under section 17C arrangements; amend relating to the employment of GP Registrars, providing that the consent of the Scottish Ministers is no longer required for employing a GP Registrar; amend the provisions as to notice that must be given by a provider of services which is a company limited by shares to a Health Board, to make provision for notice to be given when a new director or secretary is appointed; and amend the provisions on disputes arising out of, or in connection with, the agreement that have been referred to the Scottish Ministers, to clarify the matter about which representations may be made to them before they reach a decision as to who should determine a dispute.

5391. National Health Service—Provision of pharmaceutical services—Supplementary prescribers

NATIONAL HEALTH SERVICE (PHARMACEUTICAL SERVICES) (SCOTLAND) AMENDMENT REGULATIONS 2005, SSI 2005 327; made under the National Health Service (Scotland) Act 1978 s.27, s.105, s.108. In force: July 1, 2005; £3.00.

These Regulations amend the National Health Service (Pharmaceutical Services) (Scotland) Regulations 1995 (SI 1995 414) which regulate the provision of pharmaceutical services under the National Health Service (Scotland) Act 1978. These Regulations amend the definition of "supplementary prescriber" to include additional categories of health care professional who may also prescribe as a supplementary prescriber. The additional categories of health care professional are persons who are registered in the parts of the register maintained under the Health Professions Order 2001 (SI 2001 254) for chiropodists and podiatrists, for physiotherapists or for diagnostic or therapeutic radiographers and against whose name in the register is recorded an annotation signifying that they are qualified to order drugs, medicines and appliances as a supplementary prescriber. The effect of the amendment is that the provision of pharmaceutical services in accordance with the 1995 Regulations will include the provision to persons of drugs, medicines and listed appliances ordered for them by those additional categories of health care professional.

5392. National Health Service—Road traffic accidents—Charges

ROAD TRAFFIC (NHS CHARGES) AMENDMENT (SCOTLAND) REGULATIONS 2005, SSI 2005 123; made under the Road Traffic (NHS Charges) Act 1999 s.3, s.16. In force: April 1, 2005; £3.00.

These Regulations amend the Road Traffic (NHS Charges) Regulations 1999 (SI 1999 785) which provide for a scheme for the recovery from insurers and other persons of charges in connection with the treatment of road traffic casualties by the National Health Service. They increase those charges in relation to incidents giving rise to treatment which occur on or after April 1, 2005.

5393. National Health Service—Supplementary prescribers—Drugs and appliances—Charges

NATIONAL HEALTH SERVICE (CHARGES FOR DRUGS AND APPLIANCES) (SCOTLAND) AMENDMENT (NO.2) REGULATIONS 2005, SSI 2005 326; made under the National Health Service (Scotland) Act 1978 s.27, s.69, s.105, s.108. In force: July 1, 2005; £3.00.

These Regulations amend the National Health Service (Charges for Drugs and Appliances) (Scotland) Regulations 2001 (SSI 2001 430) which provide for the making and recovery of charges for the supply of drugs, medicines and appliances under the National Health Service (Scotland) Act 1978. These Regulations amend the definition of "supplementary prescriber" to include additional categories of health care professional who may also prescribe as a supplementary prescriber. The additional categories of health care professional are persons who are registered in the parts of the register maintained under the Health Professions Order 2001 (SI 2001 254) for chiropodists and podiatrists, for physiotherapists or for diagnostic or therapeutic radiographers and against whose name in the register is recorded an annotation signifying that they are qualified to order drugs, medicines and appliances as a supplementary prescriber. The effect of the amendment is to make provision in the 2001 Regulations for the making and recovery of charges for the supply of drugs, medicines and appliances ordered by those additional categories of health care professional.

5394. National Health Service—Travelling expenses—Remission of charges

NATIONAL HEALTH SERVICE (TRAVELLING EXPENSES AND REMISSION OF CHARGES) (SCOTLAND) AMENDMENT REGULATIONS 2005, SSI 2005 3;

made under the National Health Service (Scotland) Act 1978 s.75A, s.105, s.108. In force: February 1, 2005; £3.00.

These Regulations amend the National Health Service (Travelling Expenses and Remission of Charges) (Scotland) (No.2) Regulations 2003 (SSI 2003 460) to insert a definition of "the State Pension Credit Regulations"; to increase the capital limit for entitlement under the principal Regulations for people living in care and maintains the calculation of entitlement in respect of people aged 60 and over; and provide that the earnings disregard set out in the 1987 Regulations should apply to a single person over 60 and to a couple where one or both of the partners is over 60.

5395. **National Health Service–Travelling expenses–Remission of charges**

NATIONAL HEALTH SERVICE (TRAVELLING EXPENSES AND REMISSION OF CHARGES) (SCOTLAND) AMENDMENT (NO.2) REGULATIONS 2005, SSI 2005 179; made under the National Health Service (Scotland) Act 1978 s.75A, s.105, s.108. In force: in accordance with Reg.1 (2) (3); £3.00.

These Regulations amend the National Health Service (Travelling Expenses and Remission of Charges) (Scotland) (No.2) Regulations 2003 (SSI 2003 460) to increase the amounts used as the basis for calculating entitlement to full remission and payment; and to extend to five years the validity of a notice of entitlement to remission of charges and the payment of hospital travel expenses issued to a single person aged 65 or over, or to one of a couple where one partner is aged 60 or over and the other partner is aged 65 or over, where that person does not have certain types of income or a dependant child or young person in their household. They also provide that a person issued with a five year notice of entitlement must notify the Scottish Ministers of any changes in the composition of their family or household during the life of the notice and enables the Scottish Ministers to withdraw or vary the notice if the person no longer fulfils the necessary criteria to be issued with that notice. The Regulations also increase the capital limits to be used in calculating entitlement to the payment of travel expenses and remission of charges for people permanently residing in certain types of accommodation.

5396. **National Health Service–Tribunals**

NATIONAL HEALTH SERVICE (TRIBUNAL) (SCOTLAND) AMENDMENT REGULATIONS 2005, SSI 2005 335; made under the National Health Service (Scotland) Act 1978 s.26, s.29, s.29A, s.32, s.105, s.108. In force: July 1, 2005; £3.00.

These Regulations amend the National Health Service (Tribunal) (Scotland) Regulations 2004 (SSI 2004 38) which make provision relating to the NHS Tribunal and representation to and procedures before it. The Regulations amend the definition of "optician" to mean an ophthalmic optician, as defined in the National Health Service (Scotland) Act 1978 s.108.

5397. **Opticians–Fees and payments**

NATIONAL HEALTH SERVICE (OPTICAL CHARGES AND PAYMENTS) (SCOTLAND) AMENDMENT REGULATIONS 2005, SSI 2005 119; made under the National Health Service (Scotland) Act 1978 s.26, s.70, s.73, s.74, s.105, s.108, Sch.11 para.2, Sch.11 para.2A. In force: Reg.2(3): April 6, 2005; remainder: April 1, 2005; £3.00.

These Regulations amend the National Health Service (Optical Charges and Payments) (Scotland) Regulations 1998 (SI 1998 642) which provide for payments to be made by means of a voucher system, in respect of costs incurred by certain categories of persons in connection with sight tests and the supply, replacement and repair of optical appliances. They amend the definition of "NHS sight test fee" to reflect the values of the two levels of fees for the National Health Service sight tests payable to ophthalmic medical practitioners and opticians. This fee is set at two levels depending on whether or not the sight test was carried out at the patient's home and the appropriate figure is used to calculate the value of assistance towards the cost of a sight test. The Regulations raise the relevant income level of a person or persons for the purpose of providing which persons, who are members of a family where one member is in receipt of certain tax credits, are eligible for a payment to meet or contribute towards the cost for the supply of an optical appliance; increase the redemption value of a voucher issued towards the cost of replacement of a single contact lens and to increase the maximum contribution by way of a voucher to the cost of repair of a frame; increase the value of vouchers towards the cost of the supply and replacement of optical appliances; and increase the additional values for vouchers for prisms, tints or photochromic lenses and special categories of appliances.

5398. Smoking, Health and Social Care (Scotland) Act 2005 (asp 13)

This Act of the Scottish Parliament prohibits smoking in certain wholly enclosed places; makes provision in relation to general dental services, general ophthalmic services, personal dental services and pharmaceutical care services; makes provision in relation to disqualification by the NHS Tribunal; enables the Scottish Ministers to establish a scheme for the making of payments to certain persons infected with hepatitis C as a result of NHS treatment; amends the Regulation of Care (Scotland) Act 2001 as respects what constitutes an independent health care service, the implementation of certain decisions by the Scottish Commission for the Regulation of Care or the Scottish Social Services Council and the provision of information to the Council; makes provision providing further time for applications to be made for registration of child care agencies and housing support services under the Regulation of Care (Scotland) Act 2001 and provides authorisation for the payment of certain grants to such services while not registered under that Act; amends the Adults with Incapacity (Scotland) Act 2000 as respects authorisation of medical treatment; enables the Scottish Ministers to form, participate in and provide assistance to companies for the purpose of providing facilities or services for persons exercising functions under the National Health Service (Scotland) Act 1978 or of making money available to the health service in Scotland; and amends the rules as to membership of and other matters relating to the Scottish Hospital Endowments Research Trust.

This Act received Royal Assent on August 5, 2005.

5399. Smoking, Health and Social Care (Scotland) Act 2005 (asp 13)– Commencement No.1 Order

SMOKING, HEALTH AND SOCIAL CARE (SCOTLAND) ACT 2005 (COMMENCEMENT NO.1) ORDER 2005, SSI 2005 492 (C.25); made under the Smoking, Health and Social Care (Scotland) Act 2005 s.43. Commencement details: bringing into force various provisions of the 2005 Act in accordance with Art.3; £3.00.

This Order, which amends the Public Finance and Accountability (Scotland) Act 2000, the Ethical Standards in Public Life etc. (Scotland) Act 2000 and the Freedom of Information (Scotland) Act 2002, brings into force specified provisions of the Smoking, Health and Social Care (Scotland) Act 2005.

5400. Smoking, Health and Social Care (Scotland) Act 2005 (asp 13)– Commencement No.2 Order

SMOKING, HEALTH AND SOCIAL CARE (SCOTLAND) ACT 2005 (COMMENCEMENT NO.2) ORDER 2005, SSI 2005 642 (C.32); made under the Smoking, Health and Social Care (Scotland) Act 2005 s.43. Commencement details: bringing into force various provisions of the 2005 Act on December 16, 2005; £3.00.

This Order appoints December 16, 2005 as the day for the coming into force of the Smoking, Health and Social Care (Scotland) Act 2005 s.4(6)(8)(9).

5401. Books

Mackie, Robert–New Public Management of Scotland: Local Government and the National Health Service. Paperback: £25.00. ISBN 0 414 01600 9. W. Green & Son.

HEALTH AND SAFETY AT WORK

5402. Accidents–Employers liabilities–Decorator suffering needle injury while working in local authority flat–Safe and reasonable inspection system

[Construction (Health, Safety and Welfare) Regulations 1996 (SI 1996 1592) Reg.5(2).]

The pursuer (M), a painter and decorator, sought damages from the defender local authority, his employer, after he was stabbed in the knee by a hypodermic syringe protruding from an electric fire while working in one of the local authority's flats. The flat had been abandoned and while the tenant was not a known drug user there was evidence that the local authority had knowledge of the problem of drugs paraphernalia within such properties. The flat had been inspected by a housing officer but no syringe had been seen. M maintained that the local authority had breached the Construction (Health, Safety and Welfare) Regulations 1996 Reg.5(2) and its common law duty to take reasonable care, arguing that (1) the flat was his workplace and as such gave rise to a breach under Reg.5(2); (2) the local authority had failed to prove that the presence of the syringe was not foreseeable. M argued that the whole system with regard to the risk posed by discarded needles was ineffective, since it relied on needles being found by chance.

Held, giving judgment accordingly, that (1) the 1996 Regulations did not apply as the redecoration work did not fall within the definition of construction work. (2) M had failed to establish a breach of the local authority's common law duty. The local authority's system of inspection was safe and reasonable in the circumstances and the flat had already been searched before tradesmen were admitted to commence work. On the evidence, the local authority had a reasonable and recognised system of inspection and had fulfilled its duty in this regard. As it appeared that the needle had been positioned deliberately between the bars of the fire, it was unlikely that it would have been found in the course of normal visual inspection of the room in any event. The local authority was accordingly assoilzied and M was liable to it for its expenses in the action.

MATTHEWS v. GLASGOW CITY COUNCIL 2004 Hous. L.R. 136, Sheriff CAL Scott, Sh Ct (Glasgow and Strathkelvin).

5403. Breach of statutory duty–Employers liabilities–Meaning of "falling a distance" in Reg.13(3)(b) Workplace (Health, Safety and Welfare) Regulations 1992

[Workplace (Health, Safety and Welfare) Regulations 1992 (SI 1992 3004) Reg.12(1), Reg.13(3)(b).]

The pursuer (C) sought damages from his employer (E) under the common law and under the Workplace (Health, Safety and Welfare) Regulations 1992. C had injured his knee after losing his footing in the mud whilst working on an embankment at a roundabout. He fell 20 feet to the bottom. C contended, amongst other things, that (1) the embankment was covered by Reg.12(1) of the Regulations; (2) the phrase "falling a distance" in Reg.13(3)(b) included a fall down an embankment.

Held, giving judgment for C in part, that (1) the embankment constituted a "workplace" within the meaning of Reg.12(1) but it did not constitute a "floor in a workplace." The embankment had not been constructed and therefore the words "shall be of a construction" in Reg.12(1) did not apply. (2) Regulation 13(3) was designed to cover falls from a height rather than falling to the ground and tumbling down an embankment. C's claim in respect of breach of statutory duty by E could not proceed but his common law action could be tried.

CAMPBELL v. EAST RENFREWSHIRE COUNCIL 2004 Rep. L.R. 89, Temporary Judge RF Macdonald Q.C., OH.

5404. Manual handling–Employers liabilities–Injury sustained when not using lifting equipment provided

[Manual Handling Operations Regulations 1992 (SI 1992 2793) Reg.4; Provision and Use of Work Equipment Regulations 1998 (SI 1998 2306) Reg.5.]

The pursuer (N), a maintenance engineer, raised an action for damages against the defenders (S), his employer, under the Provision and Use of Work Equipment Regulations 1998 Reg.5 and the Manual Handling Operations Regulations 1992 Reg.4 for injuries sustained in the course of his employment. N had been replacing a vacuum pump and he moved it by lifting it on a pallet because it had been difficult to position a fork lift truck. N maintained that the pallet was broken and that caused it to collapse, trapping his hand. N argued that the defect in the pallet caused his injury because there was no other way to move the pump than by manual handling and that S had failed to avoid that need. After a proof the court found that N had not proved that the pallet was broken prior to the incident.

Held, giving judgment for S, that since N had not shown that the pallet had been broken prior to the accident, his case under the 1998 Regulations could not succeed. Even if the pallet had been broken N's case would not have succeeded because there was no link between the broken pallet and N's injury. The duty on employers to avoid manual handling only arose where an employee needed to undertake a manual handling operation either as a result of specific instruction or where manual handling was the only way to carry out the required task. In the instant case, the only reason the pump had been moved manually was because N had chosen to do that. There had been no need for manual handling and therefore S could not be in breach of the 1992 Regulations.

NAPIER v. SCOTSMAN PUBLICATIONS LTD 2005 Rep. L.R. 2, Lady Smith, OH.

5405. Safe place of work–Safe plant and equipment–Sufficiency of instruction–Foreseeability

[Construction (Health, Safety and Welfare) Regulations 1996 (SI 1996 1592) Reg.5(2); Provision and Use of Work Equipment Regulations 1998 (SI 1998 2306) Reg.4(3).]

M, a roadman, sought damages from S, his employers, for injuries sustained when he tumbled down a bank while engaged in the construction of a passing place. The site at which M was working ran along the side of a hill and the passing place was constructed by placing material on the downhill side of the road, compacting it, and placing a layer on top. M was using a sit on roller to compact the second layer of tarmac when the roller started to tip over towards the bank. M pled breaches by the defenders at common law and under the Construction (Health, Safety and Welfare) Regulations 1996 and the Provision and Use of Work Equipment Regulations 1998. The temporary judge assoilzied S, having found M to have failed on all cases averred, and further found that esto S had been at fault, M would have been found to have been 75 per cent contributorily negligent. M reclaimed in respect of inter alia Reg.5(2) of the 1996 Regulations, arguing that the mere occurrence of the accident established a prima facie breach, which was conceded by S, and Reg.4(3) of the 1998 Regulations, on the basis that the fact of the accident demonstrated either that the place of work was unsafe or that the equipment was unsuitable for use at that place. S argued, under reference to Reg.5(2) of the 1996 Regulations, that although there was an undoubted risk if the machine was driven too close to the edge, it was not reasonably foreseeable that a trained operator would do so and in any event, the temporary judge had rejected all the suggested precautions as not reasonably practicable.

Held, allowing the reclaiming motion, that (1) M was entitled to succeed in his case under Reg.5(2) of the 1996 Regulations. The temporary judge made no explicit finding as to whether it was reasonably foreseeable that the known risk of the roller falling over if driven too close to the edge would materialise, and given the obviousness of the risk, it would be perverse to hold that it was not reasonably foreseeable. On the practicability of the precautions suggested, namely laying railway sleepers at the edge of the tarmac and making a wider verge beyond the edge of the tarmac, S had to fail in the absence of evidence as to cost or other disadvantages; and in the absence of any suggestion that M had deliberately or recklessly driven too close to the edge, as opposed to the circumstances of the accident indicating carelessness or inattention, there was a clear causal link between the proximity of the edge of the tarmac to the edge of the embankment and the mechanism of the accident. (2) S could not be held less than 50 per cent to blame for the accident.

McFARLANE v. SCOTTISH BORDERS COUNCIL 2005 S.L.T. 359, Lord Penrose, Lord Abernethy, Temporary Judge Sir David Edward Q.C., Ex Div.

5406. Work equipment–Duty of care–Safe plant and equipment

[Management of Health and Safety at Work Regulations 1992 (SI 1992 2051) Reg.16; Provision and Use of Work Equipment Regulations 1998 (SI 1998 2306) Reg.2, Reg.3(2), Reg.4, Reg.5, Reg.20.]

R, an offshore scaffolder, appealed against a sheriff's decision (2004 S.C.L.R. 672, [2005] 2 C.L. 532) assoilzieing S, his employers, in an action for damages for injuries sustained to his lower back in the course of his employment. R had been on board a semi submersible production platform and sustained injury when he was descending from an upper bunk in his cabin and the ladder gave way resulting in him falling approximately five feet onto the floor. R pled breaches by S of the Provision and Use of Work Equipment Regulations 1998 Reg.4, Reg.5 and Reg.20 but the sheriff found S not to have been liable on the basis that at the time when the accident took place, R was neither "at work" nor did the ladder and its metal retainers constitute "work equipment" within the meaning thereof. It was agreed that at the material time the platform was within the scope of the 1998 Regulations. R argued that (1) the Management of Health and Safety at Work Regulations 1992 Reg.16 applied to an employee in his position and had the effect that he was "at work" at all times when he was on an offshore installation, in territorial waters, either at a production site or in transit to a work site; (2) the use of a ladder to descend from a bunk, was, quite simply, an activity involving apparatus for use during a period when he was at work and on a straightforward interpretation of Reg.2(1) of the 1998 Regulations, constituted "work equipment"; (3) esto the court sustained his grounds of appeal thus far, the sheriff was bound to have found S in breach of Reg.4 and Reg.20 of the 1998 Regulations. S argued that Reg.16(2) of the 1992 Regulations restricted the extended definition of "at work" to the 1992 Regulations. S further contended that the ladder was not "work equipment" in relation to R because it was not being used to carry out work such as scaffolding, welding or other operations he might be required to carry out in the course of his work. S submitted that on the evidence, the sheriff was entitled to hold that the risk of injury was not reasonably foreseeable and that the ladder used on the platform was suitable, further, Reg.20 was irrelevant.

Held, dismissing the appeal, that (1) as at the date of R's accident, he was "at work" when he was on board the platform in the course of his employment with S. (2) Regulation 3(2) of the 1998 Regulations imposed obligations on the employer in respect of equipment provided for use or used by an employee at work and on the plain language of the regulation, in the context of the extended meaning of the expression "at work", the ladder and its associated support system was "work equipment". (3) So far as R's case was based on Reg.20, the risk relied upon arose from the misplacement of the ladder relative to its brackets, in a position of instability that, on the evidence, could not have been remedied by any means other than by moving it into the bracket provided for it and if the only solution to any risk thereby associated was to screw the ladder permanently in one position, the assembly at the time of the accident might never have been suitable, but, to the extent that it was unsuitable, it would not have been capable of being made suitable by stabilisation by clamping or otherwise. (4) The sheriff was not bound, on the evidence, to make a finding that the risk of injury associated with the improper placing of a ladder on the brackets provided, the state of balance being maintained for a period of time long enough to subsist when an employee such as R attempted to use the ladder to descend, was reasonably foreseeable, and in any event, the sheriff had a significant advantage over the court having seen the components of the ladder assembly, and his decision could not be said to have been plainly wrong such as would justify interference with his findings by the court.

ROBB v. M&I SALAMIS LTD 2005 S.L.T. 523, Lord Penrose, Lady Cosgrove, Lord Reed, Ex Div.

HERITABLE PROPERTY AND CONVEYANCING

5407. **Contract for sale of land–Conditions–Right to resile on non purification of suspensive condition–Timeous application**

The parties entered into a contract in which B offered to sell F their interest in the lease of a plot of ground. The contract was subject to suspensive conditions including provision for F to obtain detailed planning permission for change of use to and development of a private members' health and fitness club. The contract provided that either party would be entitled to resile at any time following December 31, 2001 if purification of the suspensive conditions had not taken place, further, with regard to the conditions, that "time was of the essence". F sought to resile from the missives on April 22, 2002 and renegotiate the financial terms of the contract, which included a reduction in the price from £684,000 to £500,000, after planning permission was initially refused then granted subject to conditions on March 20, 2002. B sought damages of £360,000 for breach of contract arguing that F had failed to resile within a reasonable time and the issue of whether or not F were entitled to resile was a matter for proof. B further argued that (1) it was necessary to look at the facts of the case and determine if an ultimatum issued by one of the parties was justified and decide whether the time limit selected entitling the seller to rescind was reasonable; (2) nothing had been done post December 31, 2001 to suggest that the agreement was at an end; (3) there was no authority to suggest that prejudice suffered needed to be material but they had incurred legal fees of £1,650 plus VAT between December 2001 and April 2002, and had abstained from seeking another purchaser; (4) F had merely contrived to use the situation to attempt to renegotiate the price.

Held, dismissing the action, that (1) it was not necessary to hold a proof before answer where the facts were straightforward, the material facts were in short compass, and it was agreed that each party was entitled to resile after December 31, 2001 as planning permission was not in place. (2) That *Rodger (Builders) Ltd v. Fawdry* 1950 S.C. 483, [1950] C.L.Y. 4871 could be distinguished in the context of a seller not being able to resile if the purchase price was not paid on the due date, *Rodger* distinguished. The phrase in the contract that "time was of the essence" had an obvious meaning and it was clear that B, when framing the offer, had deliberately chosen to make the grant or otherwise of planning permission an essential condition of the contract. (3) The crucial condition as to planning permission was left outstanding by the parties as at December 31 and either party could have resiled after that date. F were entitled to resile and had done so within a reasonable time, the instruction having been given just over a month after the grant of planning permission which was within the realms of a reasonable time in a business setting; and nothing was averred as to specific acts or omissions after December 31 which would have barred them from so doing.

BLUESTONE ESTATES LTD v. FITNESS FIRST CLUBS LTD 2004 S.L.T. (Sh Ct) 140, Sheriff FR Crowe, Sh Ct (Tayside, Central and Fife).

5408. Disposition of property—Rectification

[Law Reform (Miscellaneous Provisions) (Scotland) Act 1985 (c.73) s.8, s.9.]

B appealed against a sheriff's decision rectifying a disposition granted by W in J's favour by the substitution, for the inaccurate plan annexed to the disposition which excluded from the subjects conveyed part of the subjects which W and J had agreed should be sold to J, of an accurate plan. W had granted a disposition of an adjoining area of land to K, to which had been attached the same plan, so that land which should have been included in J's title was included in the land sold to K. K then sold that land to B. B accepted that J's disposition should be rectified in the way sought, but argued that the rectification should be with effect from a date no later than either his or K's date of entry, so as to preserve his priority of title to the disputed area over that of J. The sheriff held that B did not qualify for protection of his interests in terms of the Law Reform (Miscellaneous Provisions) (Scotland) Act 1985 s.9(2). B submitted that the sheriff had erred: the test under this provision of the Act was met where B had in good faith instructed a solicitor, S, to act for him, S had examined J's disposition in the course of examining title, B had concluded missives to purchase the disputed area, and had become heritable proprietor of it, and it was not necessary for him to have been aware of the plan's terms. Further, the sheriff's interlocutor bore to have granted a summary decree, although J's motion for a summary decree had been dropped, and J should have been found liable in the expenses occasioned by the motion for summary decree.

Held, dismissing the appeal, that (1) B had not established the requisite knowledge of the defectively expressed terms of J's disposition to found a case that he had acted in reliance on them, having failed to establish that he knew that the plan annexed to the disposition excluded the disputed area. (2) There was no basis, in any event, for a finding that B had acted in reliance on J's disposition and no basis for holding that B had acted any differently from the way in which he would have acted if J's disposition had correctly included the disputed area.

JONES v. WOOD 2005 S.L.T. 655, Lord Marnoch, Lord Macfadyen, Lord Clarke, Ex Div.

5409. Easements—Proprietary rights—Right of vehicular access—Extent of grant

J, the owner of land over which a servitude right of vehicular access from a public road had been granted in 1973, appealed against a sheriff's finding (2004 S.C.L.R. 135) that it included a right to park. M submitted, *inter alia*, that the physical features of the two tenements were such that it was plain that there had to be a right to turn in the vicinity of their property and a right to unload goods there, which J had conceded, and by the same process of reasoning, it would be unreasonable to deprive the dominant tenement of the right to park vehicles in the vicinity of its boundary and no distinction could be drawn between the right of a visitor to park a vehicle and the right of an occupier to do likewise. That ancillary right was necessary in order to render the right of access effective, which, in the context of the construction of an express grant, was the preferred test to that of whether it was necessary for the convenient and comfortable enjoyment of the property. Alternatively, over the years, the actings of the parties had enlarged the original right of access so as to include parking and M had acquired a servitude right to park by virtue of actings subsequent to 1973. J submitted that the law of Scotland did not recognise any "free standing" servitude of parking; a right to park could not, under the law of Scotland, be an incident of a servitude right of access; and neither had been created as an incident of a servitude right of access.

Held, dismissing the appeal (Lord Hamilton dissenting), that (1) while a grant of servitude had to be strictly construed, that principle on occasion had to yield to the competing principle that the grant of a right carried with it, by implication, what was necessary to its reasonable enjoyment; (2) in the circumstances of the present case, the right of access had to be construed as including the right to turn and the right to load and unload goods and passengers, and given the particular location of the dominant property, the length of the access route in question and the nature of the terrain traversed by that route, it would be unrealistic to draw a line between those implied rights and the entitlement of a visitor to park his vehicle for the duration of his visit, and having accepted that, there was no real distinction between that and a right on the part of the occupier to park for unlimited periods of time in connection with the reasonable use of his property, and (3) any purchaser of the servient tenement as at 1973 would readily have anticipated all of the foregoing rights as being necessary to the reasonable enjoyment of the dominant tenement.

MONCRIEFF v. JAMIESON 2005 S.C. 281, Lord Marnoch, Lord Hamilton, Lord Philip, Ex Div.

5410. Factors–Burdens of covenants–Recovery of factoring fees–Entitlement of former owner to act as factoring service

The claimant local authority sought payment of £150.19 from the respondent (B) in respect of factoring fees allegedly due under a burden contained in the land certificate for the property. The local authority had previously owned B's flat and still owned one flat in the building. The factoring service carried out by the local authority was not specified in the land certificate but information had been detailed in the form of a booklet distributed to all owners and occupiers. B denied liability for the sum claimed, arguing that the local authority had failed to provide the factoring services which they had outlined in their booklet, in particular failing to provide a proactive factoring service. B also argued that the local authority was not entitled, under the terms of the schedule of conditions, to fix the level of remuneration due to be paid to the factor. The local authority's predecessors had approved a level of charges for factoring services but it was not accepted that the local authority in the instant case was entitled to do so. The local authority argued that the booklet had been provided as a user friendly guide and was not intended to be a comprehensive set of rules, but rather had been written to avoid the impression that only reactive factoring would be carried out; in exceptional circumstances there would be proactive factoring.

Held, granting decree, that although the booklet could be considered a list of promises, aspirations or good intentions it was not contractually binding. The local authority held its position as factor as of right, and by entering into a contract with the local authority's predecessors, B had accepted that the superior would remain the factor notwithstanding that it no longer owned B's flat. It was reasonable to assume that if any potential purchaser of council property were not prepared to accept that the superior would be factor, the contract would not have been concluded. It was a matter of agreement that the local authority's predecessors had introduced the factoring service and had approved the level of charges. The instant local authority had derived its authority to determine factoring fees as statutory successors of that council.

WEST DUNBARTONSHIRE COUNCIL v. BARNES 2004 Hous. L.R. 64, Sheriff T Scott, Sh Ct (North Strathclyde).

5411. Land Reform (Scotland) Act 2003 (asp 2)–Commencement No.3 Order

LAND REFORM (SCOTLAND) ACT 2003 (COMMENCEMENT NO.3) ORDER 2005, SSI 2005 17 (C.2); made under the Land Reform (Scotland) Act 2003 s.100. Commencement details: bringing into force various provisions of the 2003 Act on February 9, 2005; £3.00.

This Order appoints February 9, 2005 as the date for the coming into force of the remaining provisions of the Land Reform (Scotland) Act 2003 Part 1. This will bring fully into force the provisions of the Act on access rights.

5412. Transfer of title–Writing–Disposition executed but not delivered– Competence

[Requirements of Writing (Scotland) Act 1995 (c.7).]

M, the heritable proprietor of subjects, sought to recover possession from A. A had funded the purchase of the subjects but the title was in M's name. M averred that the sum had been repaid, prior to which a disposition had been executed in A's favour but never delivered. M accepted that if the money had not been repaid, the disposition would be required to be delivered to A, but that as the exclusive purpose of taking title was to facilitate obtaining a visa for her Pakistani fiance, any agreement entered into would in any event be an illegal contract and unenforceable. A sought to have M ordained to implement the agreement by delivering the disposition. He averred that M's father had requested him to purchase the subjects in M's name to facilitate her fiance's acquisition of a visa, that no payment had been received by him and that M was simply holding the property on his behalf. The sheriff allowed a proof before answer. Before the sheriff principal it was argued that the contract by which the property had been purchased was a pactum illicitum and any obligation flowing therefrom was invalid and unenforceable. The sheriff principal concluded inter alia that for any agreement such as that contended for by A to be regarded as having been successfully completed, it required to be constituted in writing in terms of the Requirements of Writing (Scotland) Act 1995. A appealed. M argued that A's case had to fail because it was plainly and admittedly a pactum illicitum under which any obligations would not be enforced by the courts; where there were such averments, the case could be dealt with without proof; it did not matter that the fraudulent purpose was not carried out, it was the intention that mattered; and on such an arrangement not being enforced by the courts, the estate lay where it fell irrespective of any question of equity or putative agreement between the parties.

Held, allowing the appeal and remitting the case to the sheriff for a proof before answer with all pleas standing, that (1) the disposition, although not at this stage delivered, was capable of satisfying the formal statutory requirements of writing necessary to achieve the transfer of subjects as contended for by A, and (2) it was inappropriate to reach a conclusion on whether the contractual arrangements between the parties could properly be regarded on the basis of the pleadings alone as a pactum illicitum before inquiry into the whole facts and circumstances.

MALIK v. ALI 2004 S.L.T.1280, Lord Cullen L.P., Lady Cosgrove, Lord Wheatley, 1 Div.

5413. Books

Guthrie, Tom; Fletcher, Ian; Roxburgh, Roy–Scottish Property Law. Paperback: £36.00. ISBN 1 84592 057 0. Tottel Publishing.

Law Society Scotland Diploma Materials 2005, Conveyancing Student Manual 2005-2006. Book (details unknown): £15.00. ISBN 0 414 01639 4. W.Green & Son.

HOSPITALITY AND LEISURE

5414. Gambling–Licences–Fees

GAMING ACT (VARIATION OF FEES) (SCOTLAND) ORDER 2005, SSI 2005 319; made under the Gaming Act 1968 s.48, s.51. In force: July 4, 2005; £3.00.

This Order, which revokes the Gaming Act (Variation of Fees) (Scotland) Order 2003 (SSI 2003 403), increases the fees to be charged in relation to the grant, renewal and transfer of gaming licences in Scotland under the Gaming Act 1968.

HOUSING

5415. Anti social behaviour–Closure orders–Relevant test

[Antisocial Behaviour etc. (Scotland) Act 2004 (asp 8) s.30(2), s.40, s.143(1).]

M, the superintendent of a police force, sought a closure order in respect of premises occupied by W, the tenant. W had behaved in an anti social manner since he became tenant of the premises in January 2003, parties were held with loud music continuing into the early hours of the morning, windows were left open, people visited at all times of the day, cars came and went, often accompanied by the loud screeching of tyres, and there was a lot of shouting from the premises to people outside. This had resulted in many complaints to the police and the local authority which owned the property, while 60 people had attended a public meeting to complain about the respondent's behaviour and an elderly neighbour had suffered ill health. The only period of respite for the neighbours was between January and June 2004 when W was absent. No one lived with W and he was informed that homeless accommodation would be made available to him for a period of 28 days after which he would be entitled to make an application for a further tenancy.

Held, granting an order for three months, that (1) it was not necessary to engage on an analysis of the wording of the Antisocial Behaviour etc. (Scotland) Act 2004 s.30(2)(a) and s.30(2)(b) as defined by s.40 and s.143(1) where it seemed on any view that the conditions of those provisions that the respondent had engaged in anti social behaviour on the premises, and that the use of the premises was associated with the occurrence of relevant harm, were satisfied. (2) In deciding whether to make a closure order the court had to be satisfied that it was necessary to prevent the occurrence of relevant harm: it was a high test and on the facts of the present case, the test of necessity was well satisfied where the anti-social behaviour was of significant duration and burden to W's neighbours, and many attempts had been made by a number of agencies to try and resolve the matter to no avail.

McILRAVIE v. WALLACE; *sub nom.* SUPERINTENDENT OF FIFE CONSTABULARY'S APPLICATION, *Re* 2005 S.L.T. (Sh Ct) 2, Sheriff W Holligan, Sh Ct (Tayside).

5416. Anti social behaviour–Interim orders–Necessity

[Crime and Disorder Act 1998 (c.37) s.19.]

G, a housing association, sought an interim anti social behaviour order pursuant to the Crime and Disorder Act 1998 s.19 in respect of S following alleged anti social conduct. The motion came before the sheriff who continued consideration of it until a full hearing in May 2004. The sheriff determined that to grant the order at that stage would amount to acceptance of G's averments and that he was not prepared to do so in the light of detailed answers. G appealed, conceding that s.19(2A) gave the sheriff an overriding discretion, but argued that the sheriff had failed to consider whether the making of the order was necessary for the protection of relevant persons. The test of necessity was not high as set out in *Glasgow Housing Association v. O'Donnell* 2004 Hous. L.R. 78, and taking into account that it was still 13 weeks before the proof, an interim order could readily have been seen to be "necessary".

Held, dismissing the appeal, that while it could not be said that the sheriff had exercised his discretion on the matter to which he was directed in terms of the statute in that consideration ought to have been given to the "necessity" of making an anti social order, it was not appropriate for the present court to consider the motion afresh, this being a matter to be decided in the light of prevailing circumstances, *O'Donnell* considered.

GLASGOW HOUSING ASSOCIATION LTD v. SHARKEY 2005 S.L.T. (Sh Ct) 59, Sheriff Principal EF Bowen Q.C., Sh Ct.

5417. Anti social behaviour–Interim orders–Necessity of order

[Crime and Disorder Act 1998 (c.37) s.19(1), s.19(2A).]

The pursuers (G) applied for an interim anti social behaviour order pursuant to the Crime and Disorder Act 1998 alleging that the defender (O) and his wife had been guilty of anti social conduct towards a neighbouring couple (W). The conduct complained of was mainly concerned with the parking of O's car and the positioning of dustbins and had been the subject of unsuccessful action by the local authority, the police and the procurator fiscal. G argued that in deciding whether to grant an interim order under s.19(2A)(a) of the 1998 Act the court should accept its averments as being true, otherwise there could never be circumstances in which interim orders could be granted because the defenders could thwart the application by simply denying the allegations. Moreover, the terms of the order sought did not affect the parties' liberty. O argued that there was a genuine dispute between the parties and that G's application for an interim order was no more than an attempt to control O's actions.

Held, refusing the application, that (1) the starting point in applying the test under s.19(2A)(a) was to establish whether G had averred conduct which, if proved, satisfied the definition of anti social conduct in s.19(1)(a). Section 19(2A) gave the court a discretion as to whether or not to grant an interim anti social behaviour order, but that discretion was constrained by s.19(2A)(a). In the instant case, the behaviour complained of was such as to amount to anti social conduct if proved. (2) Under s.19(1)(b) it had to be established whether an order was necessary. In the instant case, O went further than merely denying the allegations made against them and indeed gave a contrasting account of events. On the material before the court, it was not necessary to grant an order at that stage. It was irrelevant that the proposed order did not involve a significant restriction of liberty, as that was not the test to be applied.

GLASGOW HOUSING ASSOCIATION v. O'DONNELL 2004 Hous. L.R. 78, Sheriff WH Holligan, Sh Ct (Glasgow and Strathkelvin).

5418. Grants–Assessment of contributions

HOUSING GRANTS (ASSESSMENT OF CONTRIBUTIONS) (SCOTLAND) AMENDMENT REGULATIONS 2005, SSI 2005 488; made under the Housing (Scotland) Act 1987 s.240A. In force: November 1, 2005; £3.00.

These Regulations amend the Housing Grants (Assessment of Contributions) (Scotland) Regulations 2003 (SSI 2003 461) which provide a means of assessment of an applicant's contribution to the cost of works for which improvement grants, repair grants and grants for a means of escape from fire for a house in multiple occupation may be given by a local authority. The amendments made by these Regulations apply the principal regulations where an application for costs of work to make a house suitable for the accommodation, welfare or employment of a disabled occupant is made on behalf of the disabled occupant. Where an application is made on behalf of a disabled occupant it is the total applicable income of the disabled occupant that is taken into account in the assessment of an applicant's contribution to the cost of works and not such income of the person who made the application on that disabled occupant's behalf.

5419. Housing associations–Scottish homes–Dissolution

SCOTTISH HOMES (DISSOLUTION) ORDER 2005, SSI 2005 609; made under the Housing (Scotland) Act 2001 s.87. In force: December 31, 2005; £3.00.

This Order specifies the date for the dissolution of Scottish Homes.

5420. Housing associations–Scottish homes–Transfer of property and liabilities

HOUSING (SCOTLAND) ACT 2001 (TRANSFER OF SCOTTISH HOMES PROPERTY AND LIABILITIES) ORDER 2005, SSI 2005 439; made under the Housing (Scotland) Act 2001 s.85, s.109. In force: October 1, 2005; £3.00.

This Order makes provision for the transfer of all remaining property, rights, interests and liabilities from Scottish Homes to the Scottish Ministers.

5421. Housing support grant–Aggregate amount and apportionment

HOUSING SUPPORT GRANT (SCOTLAND) ORDER 2005, SSI 2005 166; made under the Housing (Scotland) Act 1987 s.191, s.192. In force: April 1, 2005; £3.00.

This Order fixes for the year 2005-2006 the aggregate amount of the housing support grants payable to some local authorities under the Housing (Scotland) Act

1987 s.191. It prescribes the local authorities between whom the grant will be apportioned and provides the method of calculation.

5422. Local authorities – Housing support – Care services – Grants

HOUSING (SCOTLAND) ACT 2001 (PAYMENTS OUT OF GRANTS FOR HOUSING SUPPORT SERVICES) AMENDMENT ORDER 2005, SSI 2005 322; made under the Housing (Scotland) Act 2001 s.91. In force: July 1, 2005; £3.00.

This Order, which amends the Housing (Scotland) Act 2001 (Payments out of Grants for Housing Support Services) Order 2003 (SSI 2003 140), revokes the Housing (Scotland) Act 2001 (Payments out of Grants for Housing Support Services) Amendment (No.2) Order 2004 (SSI 2004 348). The Order reinstates the requirement for a provider of a housing support service which is a care service and is paid by a local authority out of grants provided by the Scottish Ministers under the Housing (Scotland) Act 2001, to be registered under the Regulation of Care (Scotland) Act 2001.

5423. Local authority housing – Right to buy – Exceptions – Occupation of house as condition of employment

[Housing (Scotland) Act 2001 (asp 10) Sch.1 para.1.]

M, the manager of a ferry service, applied to the Lands Tribunal for a finding that he had a right to purchase the house he occupied, which was supplied by his employers, H. M submitted that his contract of employment did not expressly state that residing in the house was for the better performance of his duties and that he could carry on his employment while residing elsewhere, although he accepted that it was a condition of his employment that he reside in the house. M received a 66.6 per cent reduction in rent as a consequence of his employment. H argued that (1) it was clear that the express requirement to live there was because of the job; (2) it was necessary to have a senior person resident to supervise and those duties would not be so well performed if he lived elsewhere; (3) the tribunal had to look at the system as it existed and not consider how it could be managed differently.

Held, refusing the application, that M did not have the right to purchase the house. H had established that, although residence was not absolutely necessary for the performance of M's job, the tenancy was not a Scottish secure one. M's presence was necessary for cash handling, security, reliability of the emergency system and efficiency of attendance to repairs and was accordingly "for the better performance of" his duties as an employee for the purposes of the Housing (Scotland) Act 2001 Sch.1 para.1. Furthermore the sizeable reduction in rent indicated the financial value to H of M's custodial duties.

McAUSLANE v. HIGHLAND COUNCIL 2004 Hous. L.R. 30, Lord McGhie, Lands Tr (Scot).

5424. Local authority housing – Right to buy – Notice of refusal – Reference to Lands Tribunal

[Housing (Scotland) Act 1987 (c.26) s.68(4).]

D applied to the Lands Tribunal for a finding under the Housing (Scotland) Act 1987 s.68(4) that he had a right to purchase the house he occupied after a notice of refusal had been issued by Q, the housing association. Q maintained that D was not a secure tenant and had no right to buy. Q later accepted that this ground was not well founded and maintained that D's application was being processed and there would be no need for a finding. D argued that there had been a delay in processing and asked the Tribunal to proceed.

Held, granting the application, that D had the right to buy his home. Whilst there was no reason to doubt that Q were dealing with matters in good faith, D was entitled to insist upon the application. D was also entitled to the expenses he had claimed, amounting to £70.50.

DONOHOE v. QUEENS CROSS HOUSING ASSOCIATION 2004 Hous. L.R. 42, JN Wright Q.C., Lands Tr (Scot).

5425. Local authority housing–Secure tenancies–Recovery of possession–Scottish secure tenancies

[Housing (Scotland) Act 1988 (c.43) s.12, s.16(1), Sch.5 Part II Ground 12; Housing (Scotland) Act 2001 (asp 10) s.14, s.41.]

P appealed against the granting of a decree for recovery of possession of the house she occupied and of rent arrears. G, a housing association, had raised proceedings under the Housing (Scotland) Act 1988 Sch.5 Part II Ground 12 to recover possession when P's arrears amounted to £1,131.25, which was more than three months' rent. The tenancy was an assured one within the meaning of s.12 of the 1988 Act but the tenancy agreement intimated that it could be terminated by G issuing a notice to quit, which it had done when the rent arrears stood at £966.63. Final decree was granted when the arrears amounted to £1,800. On appeal, P argued that (1) the order for recovery of possession was not competent because the tenancy had become a Scottish secure tenancy before grant of the final decree and G had failed to serve a notice under the Housing (Scotland) Act 2001 s.14; (2) it was not reasonable to grant the order since P had sought to make payments towards the arrears and had provided an explanation for them. Moreover, P was deaf and mute and consequently had difficulties in communicating instructions to solicitors. She had also been subject to domestic violence during the proceedings.

Held, dismissing the appeal, that (1) the tenancy had not become a Scottish secure tenancy and could only have become one if there had been an agreement under which it had become a tenancy as defined in s.41 of the 2001 Act. P's tenancy agreement had been terminated when G served a notice to quit and P's continued right to occupy was referable instead to the statutory assured tenancy granted to her under s.16(1) of the 1988 Act. (2) P had only made a few irregular rent payments during the course of the proceedings and her arrears had accumulated over a four-year period, ultimately reaching the sum of £3,647.54. Notwithstanding her personal circumstances, it could not be said that it was unreasonable to grant the order for possession.

GRAMPIAN HOUSING ASSOCIATION v. PYPER 2004 Hous. L.R. 22, Sheriff Principal Sir SST Young Q.C., Sh Ct.

5426. Multiple occupation–Licences–Objections–Failure to take objections into account

[Civic Government (Scotland) Act 1982 (c.45).]

The appellant (M) objected to a local licensing authority's grant of a multiple occupation licence to his neighbour (D), who had obtained the licence under the Civic Government (Scotland) Act 1982. M had raised concerns about safety and the suitability of D to hold such a licence, but his objections were repelled and a joint inspection team reported that the property was satisfactory. M argued that (1) the local authority had acted in a manner contrary to natural justice in reaching its decision and had exercised its discretion unreasonably; (2) his objections had been ignored and he had not been given an opportunity to challenge the joint inspection team's report. The local authority submitted that it was implicit in its reasons that the objections had been considered; the joint inspection team must have been satisfied that the necessary conditions had been met and this procedure was the only way that the local authority could deal with the high number of such applications.

]Held, allowing the appeal, that (1) the rules of natural justice precluded a licensing authority from taking a decision based either in whole or in part on facts within the knowledge of the authority without disclosure of those facts. The local authority in the instant case had erred in repelling M's objections at a stage before it knew whether they were well founded or not and in failing to afford M an opportunity to comment. (2) The local authority's regulatory committee was entitled, in the exercise of its discretion, to determine that D was a fit and proper person to hold a licence, although it was unfortunate its reasons did not state the basis on which such a decision had been reached. (3) The local authority's reasons for rejecting M's objections were, however, unreasonable in that it had failed to consider the merits of M's argument to the extent that it was based on safety grounds. The committee should have insisted on a report that dealt in a specific manner with the objections that had been raised and M should have been given the opportunity to comment on such a report before the committee reached its decision

MITCHELL v. EDINBURGH CITY COUNCIL 2004 Hous. L.R. 59, Sheriff RJD Scott, Sh Ct (Lothian and Border).

5427. Right to buy–Prescribed persons

RIGHT TO PURCHASE (PRESCRIBED PERSONS) (SCOTLAND) AMENDMENT ORDER 2005, SSI 2005 275; made under the Housing (Scotland) Act 1987 s.61. In force: June 24, 2005; £3.00.

This Order adds another person to the list of prescribed persons in the Right to Purchase (Prescribed Persons) (Scotland) Order 1993 (SI 1993 1625), namely a person that has become the employer of a former employee of a local authority managed school, where such an employee lives in a house provided by the local authority to enable that employee to better perform their duties and has transferred to the employment of that person and that person has become their landlord. An example of the effect of this order is that an employee, such as a janitor, can count the time spent in occupation of a house that they used to occupy as an employee of a local authority and now occupy under as an employee of a new person.

HUMAN RIGHTS

5428. Gender recognition–Disclosure of information

GENDER RECOGNITION (DISCLOSURE OF INFORMATION) (SCOTLAND) ORDER 2005, SSI 2005 125; made under the Gender Recognition Act 2004 s.22. In force: April 4, 2005; £3.00.

The Gender Recognition Act 2004 provides that it is an offence for a person who has acquired protected information in an official capacity to disclose the information to any other person. "Protected information" is defined as information relating to a person who has applied for a gender recognition certificate under the Act, and which concerns that application (or a subsequent application by them), or their gender prior to being granted a full gender recognition certificate. The Act sets out certain circumstances where disclosure of protected information does not constitute an offence (for example, where person to whom the information relates is not identifiable, or has agreed to the disclosure). This Order prescribes additional circumstances where the disclosure of protected information does not constitute an offence. These concern disclosure for the purpose of obtaining legal advice, religious purposes, disclosure for medical purposes, disclosure by or on behalf of a credit reference agency, and disclosure for purposes in relation to insolvency or bankruptcy.

5429. Gender recognition–Registers–Prescription of particulars

GENDER RECOGNITION (PRESCRIPTION OF PARTICULARS TO BE REGISTERED) (SCOTLAND) REGULATIONS 2005, SSI 2005 151; made under the Gender Recognition Act 2004 s.10, Sch.3 para.14. In force: April 4, 2005; £3.00.

These Regulations prescribe the particulars in relation to the person's birth and other matters which must be contained in an entry in the Gender Recognition Register maintained under the Gender Recognition Act 2004.

5430. Inhuman or degrading treatment or punishment–Standard of proof

[Human Rights Act 1998 (c.42) s.6, Sch.1 Part I Art.3; Scotland Act 1998 (c.46) s.57.]

In proceedings for judicial review brought by N, a prisoner, the Lord Ordinary found that S, the Scottish Ministers, had acted unlawfully in terms of the Human Rights Act 1998 s.6 and ultra vires in terms of the Scotland Act 1998 s.57, by acting in a manner incompatible with Sch.1 Part I Art.3 of the Human Rights Act 1998 and detaining N in conditions in which he was subjected to inhuman or degrading treatment. N was awarded damages. S reclaimed. The only issue debated was the appropriate standard of proof to be applied in civil domestic proceedings in determining whether or not there had been a breach of Art.3.

Held, granting declarator, that in civil proceedings in which a finding was sought that there had been an act or a failure to act by a public authority which was incompatible with Art.3, the appropriate standard of proof was proof on a balance of probabilities.

NAPIER v. SCOTTISH MINISTERS 2005 S.C. 307, Lord Cullen L.P., Lord Osborne, Lord Hamilton, 1 Div.

5431. Right to respect for private and family life–Extradition proceedings–Compatibility–Proportionality

[Extradition Act 1989 (c.33) s.8(1); Human Rights Act 1998 (c.42) Sch.1 Part I Art.3, Art.8; European Convention on Extradition Order 1990 (SI 1990 1507).]

W sought reduction of a decision of S, the Scottish Ministers, ordering his return to Estonia following his arrest under the Extradition Act 1989 s.8(1) for contraventions of the Estonian Penal Code, by organising the smuggling of narcotic drugs. A warrant was granted for his arrest in March 2001. He was later transferred to the state hospital where he was diagnosed as suffering from a severe adjustment disorder, which had arisen from his remand in prison, and was likely to deteriorate on his return. He was transferred back to prison in October 2002. His mental health problems ceased in December. W submitted that his extradition would constitute inhuman or degrading treatment contrary to the Human Rights Act 1998 Sch.1 Part I Art.3 having regard to the real risk of a seriously adverse effect on his health and well being, the dislocation to his family and private life, and the fact that he could be prosecuted in Scotland; was a disproportionate interference with his rights under Sch.1 Part I Art.8; and was a decision which no reasonable minister could have reached. The Lord Ordinary refused the petition. W reclaimed, submitting that the Lord Ordinary had erred in law (1) by applying the same approach to an extradition case as would apply to an immigration case and in affording S a wide margin of appreciation; (2) by finding that the extent of interference with his family and private life was the additional restriction of contract occasioned by his incarceration in Estonia as opposed to his detention in Scotland when a transfer to Estonia, the associated risk of deterioration in his mental condition, and undergoing a trial abroad constituted interference; (3) in his approach to proportionality by considering whether it was a proportionate interference with his family and private life to extradite him when he could be tried in Scotland for the same offence; (4) in failing to take account or give adequate weight to material considerations advanced by him in assessing the need for cooperation by the Estonian authorities; (5) by allowing states to enter into forum shopping to secure trial in the jurisdiction most likely to secure a conviction; (6) in failing to properly consider his submission that his challenge to the proportionality of extradition extended to situations in which the Lord Advocate renounced his right to prosecute in Scotland. At a fresh diet, a minute for the Lord Advocate was lodged explaining that no decision had been taken as to whether to prosecute the petitioner in Scotland.

Held, refusing the reclaiming motion, that (1) it was quite clear that the Lord Ordinary had in mind the risk of deterioration in W's mental condition which might follow extradition, it was difficult to understand why undergoing a trial in the context of incarceration should involve any greater interference with Art.8 than incarceration itself, and while the Lord Ordinary did not have the benefit of the availability of the House of Lords' decisions of *R. (on the application of*

Razgar) v. Secretary of State for the Home Department (No.2) [2004] UKHL 27, [2004] 2 A.C. 368, [2004] C.L.Y. 2029 and *R. (on the application of Ullah) v. Special Adjudicator* [2004] UKHL 26, [2004] 2 A.C. 323, [2004] C.L.Y. 2009, his approach was generally consistent therewith and if any criticism could be made, it was one which would operate to the respondents' benefit in that he did not recognise directly the existence of the high threshold which those cases had to overcome in relation to foreign aspects where it was alleged that there was an interference with Art.8 rights consequent upon removal from a country pursuant to an immigration or extradition decision. (2) No error of law could be detected in the Lord Ordinary's approach to either the interpretation of the provisions of the European Convention on Extradition Order 1990, the convention on extradition itself, or his assessment of the proportionality of the interference with W's Art.8 rights involved in extradition, and the mere possibility of W's prosecution in Scotland could not be seen as rendering his extradition unnecessary in a democratic society for the prevention of disorder or crime within the meaning of Art.8(2). (3) The fact the Lord Ordinary did not deal specifically with three considerations allegedly pertinent to the mounting of a prosecution against W in Scotland did not in any way vitiate his approach and the considerations could not be regarded as anything other than peripheral in any event. (4) The subject matter of the reclaimer's ground of appeal concerning the Lord Ordinary's equiparation of extradition and immigration cases became academic where his decision was expressed as a representation of his own view as opposed to an assessment of whether S's decision fell within the range open to them. (5) W's submission on forum shopping failed to take into account the nature and significance of the international obligations undertaken by the United Kingdom in relation to extradition, further, it was extravagant and without any foundation in fact. (6) The sixth ground of appeal was academic since there was no question of the Lord Advocate having renounced his right to prosecute W in Scotland, nor was there any other reason why such a prosecution, if it was at one time possible, could not now take place, *Razgar* and *Ullah* considered.

WRIGHT v. SCOTTISH MINISTERS (NO.2) 2005 S.C. 453, Lord Osborne, Lord Nimmo Smith, Lord Reed, Ex Div.

5432. Books

Finch, Valerie; Ashton, Christina—Human Rights and Scots Law. Paperback: £35.00. ISBN 0 414 01624 6. W. Green & Son.

Murdoch, Jim—Guide to Human Rights in Scotland. Paperback: £70.00. ISBN 1 84592 074 0. Tottel Publishing.

IMMIGRATION

5433. Asylum—Credibility

K, a Turkish national, reclaimed against the Lord Ordinary's refusal of his petition seeking judicial review of the refusal by the Immigration Appeal Tribunal of leave to appeal against the decision of an adjudicator refusing his appeal against the refusal, by the Home Secretary (S), of his claim for asylum. K submitted that the adjudicator had failed to give him a fair hearing, having failed to give him an opportunity to explain discrepancies between his statement of evidence form which mentioned no involvement with any political parties and evidence detailing daily involvement in the People's Democracy Party, and had failed to obtain a copy of a report referred to by a specialist in Middle Eastern affairs. S argued that (1) the discrepancy in K's evidence was clear and apparent, it was for him to decide whether or not to highlight it by seeking to address it and it was sufficient for K to know his credibility was in issue and that he was given the opportunity to address it; (2) the reasons given by the adjudicator left no substantial doubt as to whether she had erred in law.

Held, allowing the reclaiming motion and remitting the case for a rehearing before the asylum and immigration tribunal, that (1) the reasons supplied by the adjudicator for her decision were inadequate to the extent that there had been procedural unfairness, requiring that the decision be reduced, where her determination left the reader with no real idea of why and in what respects the expert evidence led by K was rejected and he was entitled to intelligible reasons for its rejection. (2) The adjudicator's failure to put her concerns regarding perceived contradictions or discrepancies of importance in K's evidence to him, meant that the hearing was conducted unfairly. (3) An adjudicator was not obliged to search for materials not placed before him even when it was referred to.

KOCA v. SECRETARY OF STATE FOR THE HOME DEPARTMENT 2005 S.C. 487, Lord Cullen L.P., Lord Macfadyen, Lord Clarke, IH (1 Div).

5434. Asylum–Credibility–Correct approach

B, a citizen of Pakistan, sought judicial review of a decision by the Immigration Appeal Tribunal refusing to grant her leave to appeal against the dismissal by X, an adjudicator, of her appeal against the decision to refuse her application for asylum. B claimed that she feared persecution from members of her family, that she was a victim of domestic violence, and that the authorities were either unable or unwilling to help her. X did not find B to be credible, citing various reasons including that she sought advice at an Asian centre before making her claim for asylum; that her allegations of hostility within the family were "impossible to reconcile" with the fact that the marriage was arranged within the family; that her claim that she was locked up and suffered a miscarriage was inconsistent with other evidence; and that her claim of being targeted was implausible as she came from the educated middle classes, where honour killings were not usually practised. The parties agreed that were B to be successful, the appropriate remedy would be to reduce the decisions of X and the IAT.

Held, reducing the decision and ordaining the Asylum and Immigration Tribunal to reconsider X's decision, that (1) the correct procedure under the relevant transitional provisions was to order the IAT to reconsider X's decision if the court thought that the appeal would have a real prospect of success or there was some other compelling reason why the appeal should be heard. (2) X's whole approach had been in error as he had not allowed himself the opportunity of looking at B's evidence as a whole and asking himself whether there was shown to be a real risk of persecution, and an appeal would have had a real prospect of success. (3) The examples given showed X had made findings as to B's credibility or as to the implausibility of her account on the basis of flawed reasoning and without there being identified any material on which such findings could properly be based.

BUTT v. SECRETARY OF STATE FOR THE HOME DEPARTMENT 2005 S.L.T. 865, Lord Glennie, OH.

5435. Asylum–Eligibility for assistance–Revocation

IMMIGRATION (ELIGIBILITY FOR ASSISTANCE) (SCOTLAND AND NORTHERN IRELAND) (REVOCATION) REGULATIONS 2005, SI 2005 2412; made under the Immigration and Asylum Act 1999 s.115, s.122, s.166. In force: in accordance with Reg.2; £3.00.

These Regulations, which revoke the Immigration (Eligibility for Assistance) (Scotland and Northern Ireland) Regulations 2000 (SI 2000 705), provide that the disapplication of s.115 (exclusion from benefits), and s.122(5) (support for children) of the Immigration and Asylum Act 1999 will come to an end.

5436. Asylum–Internal relocation–Persecution by Chinese authorities

L, a Chinese national, sought judicial review of a decision of X, an adjudicator, refusing his appeal against refusal of his application for asylum, and a decision of the Immigration Appeal Tribunal refusing him leave to appeal. L averred that he was a member of a Christian church in Jiangxi province, that he had been arrested and detained by the police as a result of his religious activities, and that an arrest warrant had been issued in relation to his escape from his last period of detention. X accepted that L was a member of the church, that a document produced by him was, on the balance of probabilities, a genuine wanted circular for him and his evidence about his arrests, but concluded that internal flight was an option where L's wife, who remained a church member, had moved to Fujian province, where their church practised openly, and that there would be no difficulty were L to be repatriated to that area. The Lord Ordinary dismissed the petition, and L reclaimed.

Held, allowing the reclaiming motion, that X's decision was vitiated by her failure to address the significance of persecution by officials of the state and the implications of the warrant: prima facie the fact of persecution by the state made it unlikely that internal flight was a safe option for L. The de facto tolerance of religious practice in certain provinces did not per se justify an assumption that an arrest warrant issued in one province would not be enforced in another; the question of the attitude of the authorities to the pursuing of the warrant was a readily discernible and obvious point of the type which X had responsibility to ascertain.

LIN v. SECRETARY OF STATE FOR THE HOME DEPARTMENT; *sub nom.* QUIN SHUE LIN (AKA CHEN RI LIN), PETITIONER 2005 S.L.T. 301, Lord Cullen L.P., Lord Reed, Lord Clarke, 1 Div.

5437. Asylum–Leave to appeal–Appropriate test

[Civil Procedure Rules 1998 (SI 1998 3132) Part 52 r.52.3(6); Immigration and Asylum Appeals (Procedure) Rules 2003 (SI 2003 652) r.18(4)(a).]

H, an Iranian national, applied for leave to appeal, following the refusal of leave to appeal by the Immigration Appeal Tribunal, against a decision of an immigration adjudicator refusing his appeal against a decision directing his removal.

Held, refusing the application, that the appropriate test to be adopted in considering whether leave to appeal should be granted was to consider whether the appeal would have a real prospect of success, as stated in the Immigration and Asylum Appeals (Procedure) Rules 2003 r.18(4)(a) on applications for permission to appeal to the IAT on a point of law, which was in line with the current terms of the Civil Procedure Rules 1998 Part 52 r.52.3(6) relating to permission to appeal, and consistent with *Campbell v. Dunoon & Cowal Housing Association Ltd (Leave to Appeal)* 1992 S.L.T. 1136, on an application for leave to appeal against a decision of the Employment Appeal Tribunal on a point of law, *Campbell* considered.

HOSEINI v. SECRETARY OF STATE FOR THE HOME DEPARTMENT 2005 S.L.T. 550, Lord Cullen L.P., Lady Paton, Lord Menzies, 1 Div.

5438. Asylum–Permission to appeal–Refusal–Relevant considerations

[Human Rights Act 1998 (c.42); Asylum Support Appeals (Procedure) Rules 2000 (SI 2000 541) r.18(2).]

M, an Iranian national, sought judicial review of a decision refusing to extend the time period in which to apply for leave to appeal against a decision dismissing his claim that his removal from the United Kingdom was in breach of the Human Rights Act 1998. M, who was legally represented throughout the proceedings, had sought leave two days after the end of the time period stipulated in the Asylum Support Appeals (Procedure) Rules 2000 r.18(2). M's legal representatives were advised by the Immigration Appeal Tribunal that submissions to extend time had to be made within seven days. However, M's legal representatives failed to do so and wrote to the IAT 21 days later, taking full responsibility for the delay. The IAT replied that the application was out of time and the reasons given for delay were inadequate. M argued that that decision was unreasonable. He contended that there had been a failure to make any provisional assessment of the substance of his application. Further, that insufficient regard had been given to the fact that the application was only two days late and that the delay was the fault of his legal representatives. M maintained that given that his claim had been based on a breach of his human rights, the degree of scrutiny required of his application was greater.

Held, allowing the application, that the decision was unreasonable. M's application for leave to appeal should have been heard. The decision not to extend the time limit because of inadequate reasons was perfunctory. The decision maker had failed to address the particular circumstances of M's application or consider the potential merits of the claim, which constituted an error of law, *R. v. Immigration Appeal Tribunal, ex p. Mehta (No.2)* [1976] Imm. A.R. 174 applied and *Wordie Property Co Ltd v. Secretary of State for Scotland* 1984 S.L.T. 345, [1984] C.L.Y. 4735 considered. It was not inevitable that the application would have been refused if proper consideration had been given. The decision was *Wednesbury* unreasonable. In the absence of material to justify the inference that the decision maker had addressed the merits and concluded that they were without substance, the minimal delay, compared with the consequences for M, amounted to special circumstances in which no reasonable decision maker could justify a refusal to extend the time limit, *R. (on the application of Ahsak) v. Secretary of State for the Home Department* [2002] EWHC 2182 distinguished.

MOHAMMADI v. ADVOCATE GENERAL FOR SCOTLAND; *sub nom*. MOHAMMADI v. SECRETARY OF STATE FOR THE HOME DEPARTMENT 2004 S.C.L.R. 612, Lord Hamilton, OH.

5439. **Asylum–Persecution–Refusal to undertake military service**

D, an Israeli citizen, applied for asylum on entering the United Kingdom in September 2001. His application was refused, and his appeal against that decision was refused by an adjudicator. D's appeal against the adjudicator's decision was refused by the Immigration Appeal Tribunal. D thereafter appealed against that decision to the Court of Session. D had undertaken the two years' compulsory military service required of Israeli citizens in 1992 and 1993 and had undertaken 50 days duty per year as a reservist until 2001. He submitted that he was likely to suffer persecution if returned to Israel for his refusal to undertake further military service. D had given evidence that while he would use arms if he believed in the cause, he objected to participating in the conflict between Israelis and Palestinians.

Held, allowing the appeal and remitting the case for a rehearing before the Asylum and Immigration Tribunal, that (1) the most helpful approach was to follow the order of issues identified by Potter, L.J. in *Krotov v. Secretary of State for the Home Department* [2004] EWCA Civ 69, [2004] 1 W.L.R. 1825, [2005] 3 C.L. 295, involving an examination of (a) whether the combatants were or might be required, on a sufficiently widespread basis, to act in breach of the basic rules of human conduct generally recognised by the international community, (b) whether they would be punished for refusing to do so, and (c) whether disapproval of such methods and fear of such punishment was the genuine reason for the refusal to serve in the conflict. (2) In the light of subsequent legal developments, the IAT's determination did not meet the test set out in *Singh (Daljit) v. Secretary of State for the Home Department* 2000 S.C. 219, [2000] C.L.Y. 6491, for adequacy and sufficiency of reasons. The IAT accepted that terrible atrocities were being committed in the current conflict, but had put the test higher than judicially recognised in *Krotov* and *Sepet v. Secretary of State for the Home Department* [2001] EWCA Civ 681, [2001] Imm. A.R. 452, [2001] C.L.Y. 3612, by requiring that the appellant demonstrate that he would be "compelled to act" in a way infringing internationally recognised standards. While the IAT had proceeded on the basis that the nature of the punishment for refusal to so act had to be such as to amount of itself to persecution or infringement of D's human rights, it was plain from *Krotov* that if condition (a) was satisfied, condition (b) required only that there be a punishment for refusal to act to constitute persecution; while preparedness in the past to undertake military service might be relevant to testing the sincerity of a later objection, the reasoning of the adjudicator and the tribunal did not make it clear that they were considering disapproval of the kind mentioned in *Krotov*, *Krotov*, *Singh* and *Sepet* applied.

DAVIDOV v. SECRETARY OF STATE FOR THE HOME DEPARTMENT 2005 S.C. 540, Lord Cullen L.P., Lord Hamilton, Lord Drummond Young, 1 Div.

5440. Asylum–Refusal–Female genital mutilation–Inhuman or degrading treatment or punishment

[Human Rights Act 1998 (c.42) Sch.1 Part I Art.3.]

J, a citizen of Sierra Leone, petitioned for judicial review of a decision refusing her leave to appeal against the dismissal by X, an adjudicator, of her appeal against the Home Secretary's decision to refuse her application for asylum. J claimed that she had a well founded fear of persecution in Sierra Leone and that the removal of herself and her daughters from the United Kingdom would breach the UK's obligations under the Human Rights Act 1998. X had not believed J's account of how she and her daughters had fled Sierra Leone after soldiers had broken into her house and abducted her husband, who, like her, was the leader of a Christian prayer group, and had rejected her claim that another main reason for fearing to return to Sierra Leone was that her daughters would be expected to undergo circumcision. J argued that X had failed to consider whether, notwithstanding that he disbelieved her, her daughters were members of a particular social group which was at a real and substantial risk of persecution because of the practice of female genital mutilation. Further, he had failed to consider whether her daughters would be subjected to inhuman and degrading treatment in terms of Sch.1 Part I Art.3 to the 1998 Act.

Held, dismissing the petition, that (1) on no conceivable view was the practice of female genital mutilation capable of being a reason for persecution. X had rejected J's evidence that she and her family were discriminated against because they were Christian and his findings made it clear that female genital mutilation was a lawful practice which was engaged in by almost all of Sierra Leone's ethnic groups. (2) There was no finding that there would be a real risk of her daughters being subjected to female genital mutilation against her wishes and therefore no evidence to establish that J's and her daughters' human rights would be infringed if J were returned.

JOHNSON v. SECRETARY OF STATE FOR THE HOME DEPARTMENT 2005 S.L.T. 393, Temporary Judge RF Macdonald Q.C., OH.

5441. Asylum–Refusal–Reasonableness

M, a Hutu and Rwandan national, sought judicial review of a decision by the Immigration Appeal Tribunal refusing to grant her leave to appeal against the dismissal by an adjudicator of her appeal against the decision to refuse her application for asylum. The grounds of appeal focused on the interpretation at the appeal hearing before the adjudicator where M submitted that the inconsistencies noted in her evidence were as a result of the wrong interpreter being used, the latter having been of Asian African origin and having spoken a different dialect.

Held, reducing the decision and remitting the case to the Asylum and Immigration Tribunal for such further procedure as it might consider appropriate, that (1) the argument based on the adjudicator's findings of implausibility was without merit where it was not contained in the grounds of appeal to the IAT, and such criticism could not be said to have been a readily discernible and obvious point which the latter ought to have considered regardless. (2) The IAT's decision to refuse M leave to appeal was unreasonable in the *Wednesbury* sense given the particular circumstances of the case. It was difficult to exclude the possibility that there might have been difficulties or errors in interpretation at various stages of M's application for asylum which might have resulted in misunderstandings or altered nuances with significant consequences in relation to views about her credibility. The IAT had expressly recorded a doubt or concern about possible issues relating to interpretation which constituted a compelling reason why M's appeal should be heard. While the IAT found comfort in the fact that M had been represented at the hearing, and that no substantive issue had been taken at the hearing with the interpretation or understanding of M's evidence, bearing in mind the importance to M of her application for asylum, and the possible serious consequences in the event of any misunderstanding or failure in communication, it was unreasonable to have relied on those factors as providing an adequate response to the concern about interpretation.

M v. SECRETARY OF STATE FOR THE HOME DEPARTMENT; *sub nom.* B, PETITIONER 2005 S.L.T. 721, Lady Paton, OH.

5442. Asylum–Refusal–Reasons

[Immigration and Asylum Appeals (Procedure) Rules 2000 (SI 2000 2333) r.18(6).]

W, a Sudanese national and her children applied for asylum. This was refused by the Home Secretary. Their appeal against this decision was refused by X, an adjudicator, and the Immigration Appeal Tribunal refused leave to appeal against that decision. W petitioned the court for judicial review. X concluded W was not credible. He found her evidence that her church had arranged for the payment of the air fares of herself and her two children to the United Kingdom was implausible. He noted her lack of an explanation of why the church would do so when questioned, and concluded that her refusal to disclose what other arrangements were made adversely affected her credibility. Further, X did not accept W's account of soldiers removing her husband and threatening that they would come back for her, concluding that if she had been of any interest to the soldiers they would have removed her also, and that it was unlikely they would have told W that they would come back for her as this would have encouraged her to leave. W argued that X had come to a subjective view of what was unlikely in her account and then found W incredible on the basis of this entirely subjective assessment, which was not legitimate. The Home Secretary argued that X had been entitled to have regard to the internal coherence of W's account and conclude that it did not make sense and in the context of the evidence given by her, X's approach and conclusion were entirely proper. The parties were agreed that were the court to find for W the correct procedure would be to reduce the determinations of both X and the IAT.

Held, reducing X's and the IAT's determinations, that (1) while the Immigration and Asylum Appeals (Procedure) Rules 2000 r.18(6) did not require the IAT to consider as a ground of appeal the point developed by W before the court, where W's grounds of appeal had not engaged the question as to whether X was entitled to come to the view that he had on her credibility, it was an obvious point with strong prospects of success. (2) X was entitled to approach W's account of how she was able to fly to the UK in the way that he had: the decision maker was entitled to draw on his common sense and his ability, as a practical and informed person, to identify what was or was not plausible and X had done no more than that. (3) The common sense, rationality, practical experience and general information to be imputed to a reasonable adjudicator were of only very limited use when it came to making judgments about the likely behaviour of the Sudanese security forces and X's reasoning could not be supported on this point.

WANI v. SECRETARY OF STATE FOR THE HOME DEPARTMENT 2005 S.L.T. 875, Lord Brodie, OH.

5443. Asylum seekers–Removal directions–Time limits–Application not determined within six months

[Immigration and Asylum Act 1999 (c.33) s.11 (2); Convention Determining the State Responsible for Examining Applications for Asylum Lodged in One of the EC Member States 1990 Art.11 (1).]

The petitioner (T), a Turkish national, sought judicial review of a decision of the secretary of state (S) to remove him from the United Kingdom and declarator that his transfer to Germany was ultra vires as the requirements of the Immigration and Asylum Act 1999 s.11 (2) had not been met. T had left Turkey for Germany with his family, where he claimed asylum, before travelling to the UK and claiming asylum. T stated at interview that he had not made any previous applications elsewhere. S contacted German authorities after finding a German receipt in T's possession. They confirmed that T had an outstanding asylum application. Following a request by S, Germany accepted responsibility for considering T's application. T and his family were accordingly detained with a view to their being transferred to Germany. T argued that (1) the certificate was *prima facie* invalid and affected his fundamental right not to be transferred against his wishes as Germany had not accepted responsibility to examine his application within the six-month period set out in the Dublin Convention 1990 Art.11 (1), and further, it was unreasonable for S to have issued the certificate as he could not properly have decided that Germany had accepted responsibility under the standing arrangements as it could not waive the time limit under the Convention; (2) even if a Member State, through no fault of its own, had no knowledge throughout the six month period that the facts of the case enabled it to request another Member State to accept a transfer, it was prevented from doing so when knowledge was subsequently acquired even if prompt action was taken at that point, and the same principle applied where an applicant had misled a Member State that there was no other Member State which could be asked to take responsibility.

Held, dismissing the petition, that (1) it was necessary to read into Art.11 (1) a qualification that the six month period would not run during any period that a Member State had been disabled from having knowledge that another Member State was responsible due to fraud or deceit on the part of the applicant. (2) The certificate was legal: the provisions of s.11 (2) of the Act did not mean that another Member State could only be said to have accepted responsibility "under standing arrangements" if all the provisions of the Convention had been complied with and there was no question of T advancing a case that it was not lawful under German domestic law for S's request to be acceded to. (3) T was not entitled to have S comply with the six month time limit for the same reasons given in *Ali v. Secretary of State for the Home Department* 2003 S.L.T. 674, [2003] C.L.Y. 5734, *Khairandish v. Secretary of State for the Home Department* 2003 S.L.T. 1358, [2004] 1 C.L. 467 and *Musaj v. Secretary of State for the Home Department* 2004 S.L.T. 623, [2004] 7 C.L. 583 for rejecting the proposition that T had a legitimate expectation that S would act only in accordance with the Convention. (4) It could not be said that it was not open to S to conclude that Germany had accepted responsibility under the Convention, and in any event T, by misleading S, was personally barred from founding on any failure to comply with the time limit, *Ali, Khairandish* and *Musaj* applied.

TEMEL v. SECRETARY OF STATE FOR THE HOME DEPARTMENT 2005 S.L.T. 204, Lady Smith, OH.

INSOLVENCY

5444. **Bankruptcy–Sequestration–Gratuitous alienation–Meaning of "assets" in s.34(4)(a) Bankruptcy (Scotland) Act 1985**

[Bankruptcy (Scotland) Act 1985 (c.66) s.34(4) (a).]

The appellant (W), the wife of a bankrupt, appealed against the decision of a sheriff that the value of pension policies held by her husband should not be considered as assets at the date of his sequestration. W's husband had gifted shares to her prior to the sequestration and the respondent (M), the trustee in bankruptcy, then sought a declaration that the gift of shares was a gratuitous alienation pursuant to the Bankruptcy (Scotland) Act 1985 s.34 and restoration of the shares to the bankrupt estate or payment of their value. W claimed a defence under s.34(4) (a) that immediately after the alienation her husband's assets had been greater than his liabilities because he would have been considered solvent if the total value of his pensions had been included. The sheriff held that none of the value of the pensions should be included. P appealed, arguing that the pensions value should have been included and that there was no definition of "assets" in the 1985 Act; since pension rights were treated as heritable incorporeal property they should therefore be described as an asset. M argued that the word "asset" had to be read as referring to liquid funds available to meet the claims of creditors. None of the money had been available to the creditors because W's husband had not elected to take a 25 per cent capital sum from the pension fund.

Held, dismissing the appeal, that the sheriff had been right to exclude the fund value of the pension policies, at least to the extent of 75 per cent. The general purpose of s.34(4) was to protect creditors and if a particular asset was beyond the reach of creditors it would be contrary to that purpose to allow it to be included in calculating the total assets. The 25 per cent proportion of the pension value would not have been included in calculation of assets at the time of the alienation of the shares as W's husband had not exercised his option to take 25 per cent of the capital pension funds, *Taylor v. Russo* 1977 S.L.T. (Sh. Ct.) 60, [1977] C.L.Y. 3218 distinguished.

McGRUTHER v. WALTON 2004 S.C.L.R. 319, Sheriff Principal RA Dunlop Q.C., Sh Ct.

5445. Bankruptcy–Sequestration–Gratuitous alienations–Reduction of dispositions

[Bankruptcy (Scotland) Act 1985 (c.66) s.34.]

X, the accountant in bankruptcy and permanent trustee on the estates of a debtor who was sequestrated on March 12, 1998, sought reduction of two dispositions dated August 6, 1992, but recorded on January 13, 1995, on the basis that they were gratuitous alienations at common law and challengeable under the Bankruptcy (Scotland) Act 1985 s.34. By the dispositions the debtor disponed first, in favour of himself and his wife (O), the whole subjects of which he was formerly heritable proprietor, and thereafter, to O, his one half pro indiviso share. At procedure roll, X claimed that the alienations became completely effectual on the date they were recorded. O resisted the claim on the basis that they became completely effectual when they were delivered to her agents on August 6, 1992 which was outwith the relevant five year period. At debate it was argued, in terms of s.34(4)(b), that looking at the overall effect of the transactions carried out, it could not be said without proof that the alienation was without adequate consideration.

Held, pronouncing decree de plano, that (1) s.34 was designed to enable the trustee to take certain steps in certain circumstances to return to the estate available for creditors that which had been alienated by the debtor prior to his sequestration and which, but for the alienation, would otherwise have been available by s.31. (2) The natural and reasonable interpretation was that, in relation to heritable property, mere delivery of a disposition would not, unless and until it was recorded, be a relevant alienation, in particular an alienation by which the property was transferred within the meaning of s.34(2)(a), or at any rate not one which could be said to be "completely effectual" where the contrary argument depended on reading the reference to the transfer of "property" in s.34(2)(a) in a non technical sense which would have the result that heritable property understood to have been alienated by the debtor completely effectually, by delivery of the disposition, would nevertheless, unless and until it was recorded, remain part of his whole estate capable of vesting in a trustee on sequestration. (3) In the circumstances, there was no proper basis for suggesting that the obligations undertaken were for adequate consideration.

ACCOUNTANT IN BANKRUPTCY v. ORR 2005 S.L.T. 1019, Lord Kingarth, OH.

5446. Bankruptcy–Sequestration–Reduction–Averments of fraud

[Bankruptcy (Scotland) Act 1985 (c.66) s.16, s.17.]

O, the lessors of commercial premises, presented a petition for sequestration of S, the director and shareholder of a company which had leased the premises, following his failure to make payment of rent allegedly owed for the quarter commencing on February 2, 2000. In terms of the lease, S had guaranteed payment to O of any sums due by the company. A charge for payment of £36,541.99 was served on July 17, 2002 and a sheriff awarded sequestration on September 12, 2002. S thereafter sought reduction of the sheriff's decision, a certificate of indebtedness to O, and the creditor's oath, contending that the award had been obtained by fraudulent means on O's part. S averred that O had waived any right to insist in payment of rent for that quarter after issuing a credit note cancelling the invoice on February 10, having conceded that no rent was due for that quarter by reason of their failure to allow timeous entry and to maintain the premises in a wind and watertight condition. S further averred that the company owed no rent at February 2, 2000 to which O had agreed, and that the rent actually due amounted to £3,313.80.

Held, dismissing the action, that (1) S had failed to aver a relevant and sufficiently specific case of fraud where specific averments were required to explain precisely how the fraud was said to have taken place, they had to indicate the person or persons responsible, and had to be sufficient to support the inference that those persons knew they were making false statements, or were reckless as to the accuracy of the statements made; (2) the existence of the credit note was made known to the sheriff in the course of the hearing the terms of which amounted to no more than a cancellation of the invoice of February 2, 2000, which was wholly consistent with the normal function of a credit note, and no necessary inference could be drawn that it had any greater significance: the terms of a fax sent by O's solicitor on September 11, 2002 clearly indicated that the writer did not consider that the credit note discharged or waived the underlying debt, and in those circumstances it was impossible to state that that belief was dishonest as it accorded with the normal function of a credit note and there were no averments to suggest that the belief was for some other reason dishonest; further, if that was true of the writer, it had to be equally true of the individuals responsible for the certificate of indebtedness and creditor's oath, at least in the absence of averments relating to their respective states of mind; (3) it could not be said that there was any dishonesty where sequestration was granted in the full knowledge of the existence of the credit note: the document said to render the representations false was itself before the court and it was for the sheriff to make what he would thereof; (4) S's action was competent notwithstanding that it involved a conclusion for reduction of an award of sequestration and there was provision in the Bankruptcy (Scotland) Act 1985 s.16 and s.17 for the recall of such an award, and (5) that an argument that there might have been a temporary waiver of liability was irrelevant as S had failed to give some indication of the terms of the waiver in his pleadings.

SMILLIE v. OLYMPIC HOUSE LTD 2004 S.L.T. 1244, Lord Drummond Young, OH.

5447. Bankruptcy–Sequestration–Trustee in bankruptcy–Title to sue–Heritable property–Land certificate

The defender (C) in eviction proceedings argued that the permanent trustee in bankruptcy (B) lacked the necessary title to sue as the name of C's predecessor, and not her own, appeared on the property's land certificate.

Held, giving judgment accordingly, that the particular identity of the trustee was unimportant. A permanent trustee had title to a debtor's heritable estate in Scotland and the title to sue was vested in the office of the permanent trustee, not in any individual. The first plea in law was accordingly repelled.

BLACKBURN v. COWIE 2004 Hous. L.R. 135, Sheriff CAL Scott, Sh Ct (Glasgow and Strathkelvin).

5448. Corporate insolvency–Winding up–Noter seeking order to sist in accordance with creditors' voluntary arrangement–Contingent creditor

[Insolvency Act 1986 (c.45) s.5(3)(a), s.147.]

M, the liquidator of X, an engineering company, sought an order to sist winding up proceedings in accordance with the terms of a creditors' voluntary arrangement (CVA). The application was initially brought under the Insolvency Act 1986 s.5(3)(a), but was subsequently allowed to be amended so as to proceed under s.147. M's application was opposed by S, who were mechanical and electrical subcontractors with whom X had entered into contract in 1990 to perform part of their work at an explosives handling jetty, and with whom they were now in arbitration. An order winding up X was granted in September 1991. M was appointed in 2001 and became the supervisor when the CVA was entered into later that month. Under the CVA, he was required to pay preferential creditors in full with funds to be made available, and then to apply for a sist; if granted, the directors would then conduct the arbitration. S sought protection of their rights as contingent creditors in respect of any future awards in arbitration. The Lord Ordinary granted the application and sisted the liquidation until the final decree in the arbitration (2003 S.C. 495). S reclaimed, submitting that the Lord Ordinary had failed to apply the settled judicial approach that a sist should not be granted unless the parties interested in it were given equivalent protection to what they had while the company was in liquidation, and had further proceeded on findings for which there was no reasonable basis.

Held, refusing the reclaiming motion, that (1) in the arbiter's exercise of his powers, he would be entitled in early course to require X to find security for S's legal or other costs and it was prima facie likely that, in the case of an insolvent corporate claimant, he would make such an order and the circumstance that, if the liquidation proceedings were not sisted and the arbitration were nonetheless to proceed, S would not require to seek security in that form did not entail that they were entitled to insist on the liquidator remaining in office or on the court requiring, as a condition of sisting the liquidation proceedings, that equivalent protection be afforded to them where the legitimate interests of other parties had also to be considered. (2) The Lord Ordinary's factual conclusions were warranted by the information before her, in particular that while a refusal of a sist would not necessarily have precluded X from advancing the arbitration, a grant was the only way in which such further procedure could be assured.

McGRUTHER v. JAMES SCOTT LTD; *sub nom.* McGRUTHER v. BLIN; McGRUTHER, NOTER 2004 S.C. 514, Lord Hamilton, Lord McCluskey, Lord Weir, Ex Div.

5449. Private examinations–Company directors–Self incrimination

[InsolvencyAct1986 (c.45) s.236(2); Human Rights Act1998 (c.42) Sch.1 Part I Art.6.]

The liquidator of a company presented a note to the Court of Session seeking to have four named individuals examined on oath in terms of the InsolvencyAct1986 s.236. He sought information in respect of certain disposals of heritable property by the company to another which he considered might constitute gratuitous alienations. One company director objected to answering related questions on the basis that he had a right not to incriminate himself. The examinee submitted that although the English position under *Bishopsgate Investment Management Ltd (In Provisional Liquidation) v. Maxwell* [1993] Ch. 1, [1992] C.L.Y. 2557 was that privilege against self incrimination had been abrogated under s.236, there were significant differences between English and Scots law in the context of corporate insolvency and the proper construction of s.236 in Scotland was that it did not abrogate against self incrimination.

Held, finding examinees to have to answer questions without any warning about self incrimination, that (1) examinees were not entitled to refuse to answer questions on the ground that the answers might incriminate them, *Bishopsgate* applied. (2) Section 236 applied in both jurisdictions and it would be inappropriate to construe it differently in Scotland which would result in examinees being in a different position from each other and create a bigger anomaly given that the statutory provision in question was the same. (3) The Human Rights Act 1998 Sch.1 Part I Art.6 did not engage s.236 in circumstances where an examination on oath was essentially investigative in nature and the presence of a judge provided greater protection than that of

those questioned in *R. v. Hertfordshire CC, ex p. Green Environmental Industries Ltd* [2000] 2 A.C. 412, [2000] C.L.Y. 2300, *Hertfordshire* considered.
LIQUIDATOR OF TAY SQUARE PROPERTIES LTD, NOTER 2005 S.L.T. 468, Lady Paton, OH.

INSURANCE

5450. Fire insurance–Breach of warranty–Misrepresentation of financial circumstances

The pursuers (O), who ran a lounge bar, nightclub and health club insured by the defenders (B), sought a declaration that B was bound to indemnify them for losses caused by fire. After B's had carried out investigations into the circumstances of the fire it declared the policy void. B argued that O had (1) breached a warranty by failing to keep all fire doors and shutters closed except during working hours; (2) materially misrepresented their financial circumstances on the policy form with regard to bankruptcy, the state of their finances with regard to the bank and cash handling. O argued that (1) although they had breached the warranty condition with regard to the fire doors that did not mean that B was entitled to refuse to indemnify them for the loss suffered as a result of the fire; (2) any misrepresentations about their financial position were not material to the risk of fire.
Held, granting a declaration in favour of B, that (1) O's non compliance with the risk protection condition relating to fire doors had increased the risk of fire damage and on construction of the warranty O were barred from making any claim in respect of damage resulting from the fire. (2) When determining whether O had truthfully answered the questions regarding bankruptcy regard had to be given to the interpretation of the question by a reasonable person. O's financial difficulties were clearly material. Where parties signed a contract and agreed that the information therein was material it did not matter if such statements would not otherwise be considered material. The fact that B had been entitled to act as it had, in handling the question of avoidance on the ground of O's non disclosure, did not mean that O were bound to accept, at that stage, the decision. However, the scope for challenging it in the instant action was limited. The contract had conferred the decision making power on B and for the court to substitute its decision for that of the contractually appointed decision maker would be wrong in principle.
O'CONNOR v. BULLIMORE UNDERWRITING AGENCY LTD (T/A LEISURE CONSORTIUM AT LLOYD'S) 2004 S.C.L.R. 346, Lord Macfadyen, OH.

INTELLECTUAL PROPERTY

5451. Copyright–Assignment–Action raised prior to execution–Personal right sufficient acquisition of title

[Copyright, Designs and Patents Act 1988 (c.48).]

T, a property development company, raised an action against D seeking to interdict them from developing a residential site on the basis that it would infringe their copyright in drawings for a semi detached house type. Copyright in the drawings originally belonged to W (formerly part of C, a partnership) who prepared them for the director of another development company, B. T averred that it was agreed between the parties that copyright in the drawings would pass to B, in support of which T produced correspondence sufficient to indicate a binding contract, and that on March 1, 2000, B executed an assignation of W's copyright in the drawings in their favour. The present action was raised on February 26, 2003 and T averred that on April 10, 2003, W executed an assignation in B's favour of copyright in all drawings for the house type and that esto the purported assignation of March 1 did not convey a valid title to copyright, the assignation of

April 10 simply completed their title, by accretion or ratification, to copyrights to which they were contractually entitled. D pled no title to sue, submitting that it was plain that only the owner of copyright had title to sue for infringement and at the time the action was raised, it rested in W, and T's claimed personal right to acquire it was not enough; even if the principle of accretion could be said to apply to moveable property and the purported assignation of April 10 could be said to have assigned W's right to B, T could only be said to have had a right to the copyright from that date; further, the purported assignation of April 10 could not have completed T's title in any event where it bore to be granted by the partnership of W described as "formerly C" but there was no link in the averments, nor any document produced, to indicate that W had assigned the copyright thereto.

Held, allowing proof before answer, that (1) T could not be said to have had full ownership of the relevant copyright at the time the action was raised by virtue of accretion; while there were indications in the authorities that the principles thereof could be applied to moveable property, there could be little doubt that the legal fiction of retrospective ownership would have no application to whether T could be said to have had legal title to sue D at the date the action was raised. (2) T could be said to have been substantially in possession of the right to bring the action, or to have had a substantial right to do so, requiring only formal completion. It was not disputed that they had, at the date of raising the action, a clear and unqualified personal right to demand an immediate assignation of the copyright from W, to which there was nothing in the averments to suggest that he would have done anything other than comply, nor were any authorities referred to in which it was held that a jus ad rem, or personal right to acquire title, was insufficient to enable proceedings to be raised. Further, if T could be said to have had at least sufficient title to raise the present proceedings, it would mean that the position in Scotland, in practice at least, was the same as the position of a so called equitable owner in England, and it would be unfortunate if the right to bring proceedings for infringement of copyright, the substantive law of which was common to both jurisdictions and governed by the Copyright, Designs and Patents Act 1988, was thought to be significantly different as between them. (3) T's rights had not already been completed by the document of April 10. It bore to be an assignation from the partnership of W which might have been the same in all but name to C but T had no averments that W himself assigned the relevant copyright to the partnership at any stage and in the absence of averment, it was not something the court could assume.

TAYPLAN LTD v. D&A CONTRACTS 2005 S.L.T. 195, Lord Kingarth, OH.

5452. Patents–European patents–Infringement–Revocation–Court bound to accept revocation

[Patents Act 1977 (c.37) s.77(4A); Human Rights Act 1998 (c.42) s.3; Convention on the Grant of European Patents 1973.]

I, a French company, raised an action against C, a Scottish company, seeking inter alia declarator that by manufacturing a pipeline C had infringed their European patent. C counterclaimed, seeking revocation of the patent as invalid by reason of lack of novelty and obviousness. C had notified the European Patent Office of their opposition to I's application for the patent but this was rejected and an appeal was pending. The Lord Ordinary granted declarator and interdict against C and repelled their counterclaim (2003 S.L.T. 1197). On February 17, 2004, a Board of Appeal of the European Patent Office annulled the decision of the Opposition Division and revoked the patent on the ground that it was obvious having regard to the prior art. I's request for a review was rejected as inadmissible and on May 26, 2004, they applied to the European Court of Human Rights in respect of proceedings before the board. C reclaimed against the Lord Ordinary's decision, maintaining that as a consequence of its revocation by the board, which the court had to recognise by the Patents Act 1977 s.77(4A), the patent fell to be regarded as void ab initio. I moved the court to sist the reclaiming motion pending the outcome of the decision of the European court, submitting that (1) the 1977 Act did not oblige the court either expressly or by necessary implication to grant the reclaiming motion; (2) the terms of s.77(4A) should be read down so as to be qualified by the words "unless to do so would be contrary to any Convention right", which could be done without cutting down the fundamental features of the Act, and in any event, the rule of interpretation in the Human Rights Act 1998 s.3 prevailed over the terms of the European Patent Convention, and (3) the protection sought was limited in scope and sisting the reclaiming motion would not affect the rights of third parties or the patents register, it would simply preserve the status quo in a private litigation between the parties.

Held, allowing the reclaiming motion, that (1) it was not possible to "read down" s.77(4A). An enactment in a contracting state which required its courts to apply a certain interpretative principle to the legislation of that state could not confer on those courts any right or discretion to ignore or reduce the effect which they would otherwise have to attribute to the decision of an international tribunal such as the Board of Appeal; (2) there was no logical or legal basis for the submission that the court could, on the one hand, accept the revocation within the United Kingdom and other designated states but, on the other hand, preserve as between the parties the liability which the Lord Ordinary found to have been established. The patent was a right of property created by the European Patent Convention and the effect of revocation thereunder was that, from the outset, I had no substantive right thereto and there was nothing in the Act which could justify preserving, as between the patentee and another party, some residual effect of a revoked European patent, and (3) even if the application to the European court were held to be both admissible and well founded, it would not, of itself, have any effect on the revocation of the patent where the court could not require the patent office to reinstate it and without overlooking the possible consequences of I's application, whether and with what effect, any measures might subsequently be introduced to enable the decision of the Board of Appeal to be reviewed, could not at this stage be more than a matter for speculation.

ITP SA v. COFLEXIP STENA OFFSHORE LTD 2005 S.C. 116, Lord Cullen L.P., Lord Macfadyen, Sir David Edward Q.C., IH.

5453. Plant breeders rights–Prior use exemption–Discontinuation

PLANT BREEDERS' RIGHTS (DISCONTINUATION OF PRIOR USE EXEMPTION) (SCOTLAND) ORDER 2005, SSI 2005 460; made under the Plant Varieties Act 1997 s.9. In force: November 4, 2005; £3.00.

This Order discontinues the prior use exemption in the Plant Varieties Act 1997 whereby in relation to varieties farm-saved prior to the 1997 Act coming into force a farmer is exempted from the liability under the 1997 Act to pay to the holder of plant variety rights a "sensibly lower" royalty than would otherwise be payable for the use of a protected variety of farm-saved seed.

INTERNATIONAL TRADE

5454. Animal products–Origin marking–Third country imports

PRODUCTS OF ANIMAL ORIGIN (THIRD COUNTRY IMPORTS) (SCOTLAND) AMENDMENT REGULATIONS 2005, SSI 2005 323; made under the European Communities Act 1972 s.2. In force: July 1, 2005; £3.00.

These Regulations amend the Products of Animal Origin (Third Country Imports) (Scotland) Regulations 2002 (SSI 2002 445) which implement Council Directive 97/78 ([1997] OJ L24/9) laying down the principles governing the organisation of veterinary checks on products entering the Community from third countries. These Regulations make provision for the administration and enforcement of European Parliament and Council Regulation 1774/2002 ([2002] OJ L273/1) laying down health rules concerning animal by-products not intended for human consumption laying down health rules concerning animal by-products not intended for human consumption, in relation to the disposal of unused on-board catering supplies. They provide for the approval of landfills for the disposal of unused on-board catering supplies. They also provide for the refusal to grant approvals, the grant of approvals subject to conditions, the amendment, suspension and revocation of approvals, and appeals against the foregoing. They make it an offence to fail to dispose of unused on-board catering supplies in landfill in accordance with the Regulations.

5455. Environmental protection—Genetically modified organisms—Transboundary movements

GENETICALLY MODIFIED ORGANISMS (TRANSBOUNDARY MOVEMENTS) (SCOTLAND) REGULATIONS 2005, SSI 2005 316; made under the European Communities Act 1972 s.2. In force: June 30, 2005; £3.00.

These Regulations make provision, for the execution and enforcement of European Parliament and Council Regulation 1946/2003 ([2003] OJ L287/1) on the transboundary movements of genetically modified organisms. The Council Regulation implements at Community level the procedures laid down in the Cartagena Protocol on Biosafety to the Convention on Biological Diversity which was signed by the Community and its Member States in 2000. In accordance with the Protocol, Community exporters are required to ensure that all requirements of the Advance Informed Agreement Procedure, as set out in the Protocol, are fulfilled. The Regulations designate the Scottish Ministers as "competent authority"; make provision for the appointment of inspectors; makes it an offence to contravene specified Community provisions; specify time limits for bringing prosecutions, and prescribe penalties.

5456. Infectious disease control—Import of potatoes—Netherlands

POTATOES ORIGINATING IN THE NETHERLANDS (NOTIFICATION) (SCOTLAND) ORDER 2005, SSI 2005 73; made under the Plant Health Act 1967 s.2, s.3, s.4. In force: March 14, 2005; £3.00.

This Order, which extends to Scotland only, places certain notification requirements upon persons who import potatoes which have been grown in the Kingdom of the Netherlands during 2004 or subsequently.

5457. Infectious disease control—Import of potatoes—Netherlands—Revocation

POTATOES ORIGINATING IN THE NETHERLANDS (SCOTLAND) REVOCATION REGULATIONS 2005, SSI 2005 74; made under the European Communities Act 1972 s.2. In force: March 14, 2005; £3.00.

These Regulations revoke the Potatoes Originating in The Netherlands Regulations 1997 (SI 1997 2441) and the Potatoes Originating in The Netherlands (Amendment) Regulations 1998 (SI 1998 3168) as they are no longer of practical effect.

5458. Plants—Plant health—Import inspections—Fees

PLANT HEALTH (IMPORT INSPECTION FEES) (SCOTLAND) REGULATIONS 2005, SSI 2005 216; made under the European Communities Act 1972 s.2; and the Finance Act 1973 s.56. In force: May 6, 2005; £3.00.

These Regulations implement Council Directive 2000/29 ([2000] OJ L169/1) Art.13d on protective measures against the introduction into the Community of organisms harmful to plants or plant products and against their spread within the Community which requires Member States to ensure the collection of fees to cover the costs occasioned by the documentary checks, identity checks and plant health checks of certain imports of plants, plant products and other objects from third countries provided for in Art.13a(1) of the Directive. Except where reduced import inspection fees apply, an importer is required to pay the fee specified in Sch.1 for plant health checks carried out in respect of each consignment of plants and plant products landed in Scotland from a third country. The Regulations specify reduced import inspection fees which apply, whether or not an inspection is in fact carried out, in respect of plant health checks of certain cut flowers and fruits originating in the countries specified; provide that an importer is required to pay the fee specified for documentary checks and identity checks; provide that different types of plants, plant products or other objects contained within the same consignment shall be treated as separate consignments and subject to separate fees; and that an importer must provide certain information concerning the consignment at least 48 hours before it is landed in Scotland.

LANDLORD AND TENANT

5459. Agricultural holdings–Leases

H, the tenant of a farm, appealed against a sheriff's interlocutor granting X, the heritable proprietors, decree of removing. The farm had originally been let to H's father in law and by way of an agreement entered into with X, his son, who was also H's husband, would be "taken into the lease". The agreement was recorded in a letter dated November 8, 1990. H's father in law died in May 1998, and her husband died shortly thereafter. H claimed that the interest in the subjects had passed to her husband and ultimately to her. She submitted that the agreement referred to in the letter provided for her late husband's substitution as sole tenant of the farm in place of his father, not the introduction of a joint tenancy, alternatively, if the letter properly construed had brought about the latter, it was a joint tenancy in the strict sense so that on her father in law's death, his interest accrued to her husband, leaving him as the sole tenant without the need for any transfer of interest.

Held, dismissing the appeal, that (1) the letter had to be determined objectively and the language used therein pointed unequivocally to the assumption of H's husband as an additional tenant in common with his father. (2) A joint tenancy only arose in the context of the interest being held by trustees or by an unincorporated association and there were no averments in the present case to bring the nature of the interest held by H's father in law and husband into either of those categories.

I & H BROWN (KIRKTON) LTD v. HUTTON 2005 S.L.T. 885, Lord Hamilton, Lord Macfadyen, Lord Reed, Ex Div.

5460. Agricultural holdings–Rent–Application for determination–Correct interpretation of s.13 Agricultural Holdings (Scotland) Act 1991

[Agricultural Holdings (Scotland) Act 1991 (c.55) s.13(1); Human Rights Act 1998 (c.42) s.3(1); Agricultural Holdings (Scotland) Act 2003 (asp 11) Sch.1 para.15.]

The landlord of a farm served a notice on the tenant on October 13, 2003 demanding arbitration as to the rent to be paid from December 4, 2004. The relevant procedures for variation of rent were governed at the material time by the Agricultural Holdings (Scotland) Act 1991 s.13(1), which provided that a landlord or the tenant of an agricultural holding could, whether the tenancy was created before or after the commencement of the Act, "by notice in writing served on the other party", demand a reference to arbitration of the question of what rent should be payable as from the next day after the date of the notice on which the tenancy could have been terminated by notice to quit. Section 13(1) was amended on November 27, 2003 by the Agricultural Holdings (Scotland) Act 2003 Sch.1 para.15, which provided that the landlord or tenant of an agricultural holding could have the question of rent payable determined by the Land Court "as from the next day after the date of the notice on which the tenancy could have been terminated by notice to quit (or notice of intention to quit) given on that date". On December 1, 2004 the landlord applied to the Land Court for an order determining the rent from December 4. Both parties agreed that the whole provisions of the section had no practical meaning as the first reference to "notice" in the original version had been deleted and the word "notice" when it first appeared in the second version had no ascertainable meaning, thus a rent could be fixed but it was impossible to say from what date it was to run.

Held, allowing the respondents to adjust their answers or submit a substitute set of answers, that the primary purpose of notice under the 1991 Act was to give notice of an intention to do something about rent, and in removing all reference to notice as if it was simply part of the machinery for arbitration, the draftsman had accidentally made the clause unworkable but meaning could be restored by acknowledging the obvious need for notice of intention to have a change of rent. (2) Section 13, as amended, required to be read in a way which allowed it to follow as closely as possible the intention of that section prior to amendment and this could be best reflected, except in relation to jurisdiction, by treating the Act as if the provision inserted by Sch.1 para.15 had been "following notice in writing served on the other party, have determined by the Land Court", and s.13(1) should thus be read as "(1) Subject to subsection (8) below, the landlord or the tenant of an agricultural holding may, whether the tenancy was created before or after the commencement of this Act, following notice in writing served on the other party, have determined by the Land Court the question what rent should be payable in respect of the holding as from the next day after the date of the notice on which the tenancy could have been terminated by notice to quit (or notice of intention to quit) given on that date". (3) The addition would restore the substantive structure of the section which was not intended to be changed, and the particular effect in the present case would be that the date from which the new rent would be payable would be determined by reference to the notice given on October 13, 2003, which would be December 4, 2004, although that date had not yet been agreed.

Observed (1) that the court had to strive to find a possible construction to remedy the matter where parties were agreed that a provision had no sensible meaning as it stood. (2) That the power expressly conferred on courts by the Human Rights Act 1998 s.3(1) was no wider than the power implicitly held by the court to do everything possible by way of construction to give effect to an Act of Parliament.

MORRISON-LOW v. PATERSON'S EXECUTORS 2005 S.L.T. (Land Ct) 2, Lord McGhie, A Macdonald, J Kinloch, Land Ct.

5461. Anti social behaviour–Landlord liability

ANTISOCIAL BEHAVIOUR NOTICE (LANDLORD LIABILITY) (SCOTLAND) REGULATIONS 2005, SSI 2005 562; made under the Antisocial Behaviour etc. (Scotland) Act 2004 s.78. In force: March 31, 2006; £3.00.

These Regulations prescribe the circumstances in which a landlord, who is subject to an antisocial behaviour notice under the Antisocial Behaviour etc. (Scotland) Act 2004 Pt 7, shall be liable for prescribed expenditure. The expenditure for which a landlord shall be liable is: payments made by local authorities to other parties for services connected with dealing with the relevant antisocial behaviour; and costs of the local authority which are directly connected to dealing with the relevant antisocial behaviour.

5462. Anti social behaviour–Management control orders–Recovery of expenditure

ANTISOCIAL BEHAVIOUR NOTICE (MANAGEMENT CONTROL ORDERS) (SCOTLAND) REGULATIONS 2005, SSI 2005 561; made under the Antisocial Behaviour etc. (Scotland) Act 2004 Sch.3 para.3. In force: March 31, 2006; £3.00.

These Regulations make provision for the expenditure which a local authority may incur when a management control order made by a sheriff in terms of the Antisocial Behaviour etc. (Scotland) Act 2004 s.74 is in place over a house. They provide that a local authority may recover expenditure from a landlord any time when expenditure exceeds income; introduce the Schedule to these regulations and require that any expenditure permitted in terms of the schedule must be considered necessary and reasonable; and specify the circumstances when the local authority can recover expenditure.

5463. Anti social behaviour–Notices–Advice and assistance

ANTISOCIAL BEHAVIOUR NOTICE (ADVICE AND ASSISTANCE) (SCOTLAND) REGULATIONS 2005, SSI 2005 563; made under the Antisocial Behaviour etc. (Scotland) Act 2004 s.80. In force: March 31, 2006; £3.00.

These Regulations require a local authority to give advice and assistance to a landlord upon whom it proposes to serve an antisocial behaviour notice under the Antisocial Behaviour etc. (Scotland) Act 2004 s.68. That advice and assistance will include general advice on such notices, relevant advice on the management of the antisocial behaviour at issue and advice on the consequences of not managing the antisocial behaviour.

5464. Anti social behaviour–Rent arrears–Appeals

PRIVATE LANDLORD REGISTRATION (APPEALS AGAINST DECISION AS TO RENT PAYABLE) (SCOTLAND) REGULATIONS 2005, SSI 2005 559; made under the Antisocial Behaviour etc. (Scotland) Act 2004 s.97. In force: March 31, 2006; £3.00.

These Regulations make provision in connection with appeals under the Antisocial Behaviour etc. (Scotland) Act 2004 s.97. Appeals under that section are against the decision of a local authority to serve a notice under s.94 in relation to the payment of rent, or a decision of a local authority not to revoke such a notice. They prescribe the matters which are to be included when notice is given by a landlord to a tenant under s.97(4); provide that if the landlord does not notify the tenant, the sheriff cannot order such payments to be made, in which case the liability for rent payments resumes from the date on which the sheriff grants the appeal; and make provision for the manner and timing of service of the notice upon the tenant.

5465. Anti social behaviour–Rent payable–Notices–Appeals

ANTISOCIAL BEHAVIOUR NOTICE (APPEALS AGAINST ORDER AS TO RENT PAYABLE) (SCOTLAND) REGULATIONS 2005, SSI 2005 560; made under the Antisocial Behaviour etc. (Scotland) Act 2004 s.72. In force: March 31, 2006; £3.00.

These Regulations make provision in connection with appeals under the Antisocial Behaviour etc. (Scotland) Act 2004 s.72. Appeals under that section are against the decision of a Sheriff to make a s.71 order in relation to the payment of rent following on from the service of an antisocial behaviour notice upon a landlord. They prescribe the matters which are to be included in a notice to a tenant of a house which is the subject of the notice; provide that if the landlord does not notify the tenant, the sheriff principal cannot require such payments to be made, in which case the liability for rent payments resumes from the date on which the sheriff principal grants the appeal; and make provision for the manner and timing of service of the notice upon the tenant.

5466. Leases–Extent–No written lease–Dispute as to extent of property included in lease

The pursuer (G), the heritable proprietor of a castle, its policies and home farm, sought declarator that a lease entered into between the defender (H) and the previous owners of the estate extended only to the area delineated in two plans of the house and garden. G also sought interdict preventing H from encroaching on her land and warrant for ejection. H had moved into the property on a verbal agreement and no written lease had been issued. G argued that H had illegally occupied buildings and ground which did not form part of the lease. H alleged that the lease had not been limited to the house and garden and that they had been given permission by the factor and another person who alleged to be the factor to occupy the outbuildings and land which they had been using.

Held, giving judgment accordingly, that G's evidence with regard to the extent of the lease was preferred. It was not accepted that the factor had failed to detail the subjects which the previous owners had offered to lease to H.

Moreover, H's approach in leading evidence as to what was not excluded, as opposed to what was included in the lease, was flawed. Declarator, interdict and summary ejection were accordingly granted. (Obiter) The evidence of the first defender as to the extent of the lease was irrelevant, given that he had not been a party to it nor present when it was negotiated.

GLOAG v. HAMILTON 2004 Hous. L.R. 91, Sheriff D Booker-Milburn, Sh Ct (Grampian, Highland and Islands).

5467. Leases–Interpretation–Repair covenants–Extent of obligation to repair–Maintenance of subjects

The pursuers (W), the proprietors of the landlords' interests under a lease entered into between a pension fund and the Secretary of State for the Environment, brought a claim against the defenders (S), successors to the secretary of state who had become the tenants under the lease, for a payment of £3,917, 709 on the grounds that S had failed to comply with the repair covenants in the lease. The lease specified an obligation to keep all internal and external parts in good condition and decorative order to the reasonable satisfaction of the landlords and to keep the premises in "the like good tenantable condition and repair" as they had been in when the lease began in 1977. S gave notice that they intended to quit and did so in November 2002. W intimated a draft final schedule of dilapidations. The lease terms permitted W to execute maintenance or repairs incumbent upon S and recover the costs from S. S had paid £650,000 towards the cost of the works and counterclaimed, seeking recovery of that sum from W on the grounds that W had failed to take account of the age of the premises in establishing what repairs were "needful and necessary".

Held, giving judgment accordingly, that S was required to carry out any works which a prudent owner would have carried out in order to maintain the premises so that they could be expected to last for their normal life. S's obligation was limited to such repair works as were "necessary and needful," which included those required to maintain the premises in the condition they would have been in had they been maintained by a reasonably minded owner, *Anstruther Gough Calthorpe v. McOscar* [1924] 1 K.B. 716 applied. However, in the instant case the lease required S to carry out works that went beyond the "repair" of individual parts of the premises. The fact that particular items were not in such a good state in 2002 as they were in 1977 did not automatically mean that S had failed to keep the premises in "the like good tenantable condition and repair". It followed that S was entitled to take account of the increasing age of the premises and on the facts had fulfilled its repair obligations under the lease. The action was put out for discussion as to further procedure.

WEST CASTLE PROPERTIES LTD v. SCOTTISH MINISTERS 2004 S.C.L.R. 899, Lord Mackay of Drumadoon, OH.

5468. Leases–Irritancy–Validity of notice

W, the tenants of a public house, concluded for reduction of a pre irritancy notice and an irritancy notice served by G, their landlords, and declarator that the lease remained in full force and effect. G served the notices, dated June 11, 2001 and June 29, 2001 respectively, as a result of W's non payment of rent due on May 10, 2001, which had occurred because the latter had been involved in a transfer of the assets of their pubs and bars division to another company, X. On May 27, X issued a cheque for the amount due in G's favour, which was cashed and credited to their account, but then returned by G as it had not been received from W. Further attempts by W to make payment were also returned. W asserted that (1) the pre irritancy notice did not comply with cl.sixth of the lease which required intimation of the actual intention of the landlord to irritate the lease whereas the notice of June 11 merely mentioned the landlords' entitlement to do so; (2) G were disabled from invoking the irritancy provisions in any event since the rent due had been paid by X's cheque of May 27, and even after the monies were returned to X, the rent did not thereby become unpaid; (3) alternatively, a cheque issued by them on June 12, which accorded with the practice that had been adopted by the parties regarding payment of rent, discharged the rent payment.

Held, granting decree of reduction of the notices and declarator that the lease remained in full force and effect, that (1) the notice of June 11 was effective notwithstanding its reference to entitlement rather than intention to irritate. The distinction was immaterial for present purposes, it was the entitlement to irritate that created the risk, the landlord's intention was an essentially subjective matter which might change during the period specified in the notice. (2) The cheque of May 27 was a valid payment of the rent due. At the time it was issued, X was acting as W's ad hoc agent for the purpose of effecting that payment; no assignation of the tenants' interest had been effected; the business transfer agreement between X and W specifically recognised that the obligation to pay the rent remained with the latter; and the payment was clearly intended to discharge W's obligation. (3) that the payment of rent was validly made by W's cheque of June 12, the failure to process it was not their responsibility and G were not entitled to enforce payment of the rent, or to enforce any remedies consequential upon non payment until they had given notice to W that the cheque had not been presented and given them a reasonable opportunity thereafter to make payment by some other means. (4) The pre irritancy notice was rendered ineffective by W having met the obligation giving rise thereto: the parties' agents had agreed on June 1 that X's cheque of May 27 should be returned and that W should be given a reasonable time thereafter to make payment; it was reasonable for W to wait until X's cheque had been returned before making payment themselves and since that was not clear until approximately June 11, issuing payment on June 12 was within a reasonable time of the parties' agreement, with the result that not only should the notice not have been sent, but the day after it was sent, W made a further valid payment of the rent. (5) The subsequent irritancy notice had to be held ineffective, but it was premature in any event: when it was sent on June 29, G had not given notice to W that their cheque of June 12 was not to be processed in the normal way, and esto that was incorrect, the onus was on them to establish that such notice had been given, which they had failed to discharge.

WHITBREAD GROUP PLC v. GOLDAPPLE LTD (NO.2) 2005 S.L.T. 281, Lord Drummond Young, OH.

5469. Leases–Occupation–Renunciation–Obligations under guarantee

The guarantors under a guarantee executed in favour of the landlords of an office building, which guaranteed the obligations owed by the tenants (K), sought declarator that the landlords had granted a lease of the subjects in favour of a company (C), evidenced by C's occupation thereof and the landlords' acceptance of rent from May 28 to November 27, 2002, that by so doing, the landlords had renounced the lease granted in favour of K, and that by virtue thereof, their obligations under the guarantee had been extinguished. The guarantors further sought an order ordaining the landlords to grant them a formal written discharge of their guarantee. In a separate, but parallel, action, the landlords sought declarator that the guarantors continued to be obliged to comply with their obligations under the guarantee, their acceptance of a lease of the subjects for a period commensurate with the residue of the duration of the lease on the same conditions as before, with effect from October 22, 2002, and payment of arrears due thereunder. After debate, the Lord Ordinary dismissed the guarantors' action and, subject only to determination of quantum, granted decree de plano in favour of the landlords. The guarantors reclaimed in both actions. In June 2002, K had gone into receivership. Shortly thereafter, its business had been sold to C, and, on October 14, the receivers wrote to the landlords' agents advising them that C were occupying the subjects "under a licence of occupation". They enclosed a cheque for rental payments from C for the period May 28 to November 27, 2002, but stated that they were not adopting the lease and were acting without personal responsibility. By letter dated October 21, the landlords' solicitors accepted the payment but called upon the receivers to formally adopt the lease. This was refused by email on October 22. In December 2002, the receivers sent another letter to the landlords' agents in the same terms, enclosing a cheque for rental payments for a further period. On January 10, 2003, the landlords wrote to the guarantors confirming that the guarantee would be enforced against them and called upon them to execute a new lease. The guarantors argued that (1) given the terms of the receivers' letter of October 14 and the landlords' acceptance of the accompanying cheque constituted knowledge of the existence of a lease between the landlords and C, and as two leases of the same subjects could not subsist at the same time, this put an end to the lease in favour of K and their guarantee; (2) since C were in legal occupation of the subjects, the landlords could not offer vacant possession and could not require the guarantors to accept a lease; (3) in an argument not before the Lord Ordinary, as the receivers had not invoked the "notwithstanding" clause in the lease by giving notice within 21 days of the receivership that they were adopting the lease, which would have obliged the landlords to allow them a six month period in which to attempt to dispose of K's interest in the lease, the receivers should be taken to have "refused to adopt" or "disclaimed" the lease in terms of cl.6 of the guarantee, with the effect that the landlords had three months within which to call on the guarantors to accept a new lease, which period had expired long before January 10, 2003.

Held, refusing the reclaiming motions, that (1) as the "notwithstanding" clause had not been invoked by the receivers, it did not come into operation and the parties' obligations under the contract remained otherwise entire. (2) The guarantors had failed to show that the circumstances relied on by them plainly implied that the landlords had renounced the lease in K's favour: even if, contrary to what was said in their letter on October 21, the landlords were aware of C's occupancy of the subjects, that did not yield the inference, far less the necessary inference, that they had renounced the lease where a tenant might allow another party to occupy the leased premises without necessarily creating any legal relationship between the licensee and the landlord; the receivers' letter of October 14 did not even purport to assert that the landlords had renounced the lease; the terms of the landlords' reply were wholly inconsistent with any inference of their renunciation of the lease; and this was not a case where acceptance of payment implied acceptance of any compromise or conditions on the basis of which payment was tendered.

KINGSTON COMMUNICATIONS (HULL) PLC v. STARGAS NOMINEES LTD; *sub nom.* STARGAS NOMINEES LTD v. KINGSTON COMMUNICATIONS (HULL) PLC 2005 S.C. 139, Lord Cullen L.P., Lord Marnoch, Temporary Judge Sir David Edward Q.C., 1 Div.

5470. Leases–Termination–Tenant remaining in occupation after notice of irritancy–Acceptance of rent after notice of irritancy–Waiver of right to terminate lease

The pursuers (W), landlords, sought declarator that the defenders (F) had incurred irritancy of a lease, the result of which was to void the lease, and sought removal of F from the subject property. W had issued a notice calling on F to make payment on an insurance premium and common charges. Failure to pay the charges would result in termination of the lease. The time period was extended and F made payment electronically a day after the deadline. W also accepted rent payments from F after that date. F maintained that W could not terminate the lease due to the invalidity of their notices, and that even if the notices were found to be valid, W had waived their right to insist on irritancy and terminate the lease by accepting the payments. F argued that W's conduct in accepting further rent payments was wholly inconsistent with the right to rely on an irritancy clause. W maintained that the matter in dispute turned upon an issue of fact, not law, and accordingly there should be an enquiry in the form of a proof before answer. W argued that F, while remaining in occupation incurred a liability to pay W a reasonable sum in respect of that occupation and that the right to serve a notice to quit under the irritancy clause existed "without prejudice to any other right of action or remedy available to the landlord".

Held, giving judgment accordingly, that the authorities indicated that waiver was always a matter of fact and circumstance, *Lousada & Co Ltd v. JE Lesser*

(Properties) Ltd 1990 S.C. 178, [1990] C.L.Y. 5365 and *Armia Ltd v. Daejan Developments Ltd* 1979 S.C. (H.L.) 56, [1979] C.L.Y. 3117 applied. However, acceptance of rent was "in all normal circumstances, an act so unequivocal that it must be taken to amount to a waiver of irritancy", *HMV Fields Properties Ltd v. Bracken Self Selection Fabrics Ltd* 1991 S.L.T. 31, [1991] C.L.Y. 5174 applied. The courts would be slow to dispense with the need for a proof unless the facts were agreed or irrefutable. An enquiry would be allowed where the leading evidence was based on relevant and specific averments. It was necessary to consider whether it could be inferred from F's averments that they were waiving their rights and whether W had then relied on a belief induced by F's conduct. In the instant case there ought to be an enquiry into whether and to what extent F had conducted their affairs on the basis that W had waived their rights under the irritancy notices, *James Howden & Co Ltd v. Taylor Woodrow Property Co Ltd* 1998 S.C. 853, [1998] C.L.Y. 5550 applied. A proof before answer was the appropriate course of action where the court had allowed an inquiry at large subject to the issue of relevant and specific averments.

WOLANSKI & CO TRUSTEES LTD v. FIRST QUENCH RETAILING LTD 2004 Hous. L.R. 110, Sheriff CAL Scott, Sh Ct (Glasgow and Strathkelvin).

5471. Local authorities–Private landlord registration–Housing categories

PRIVATE LANDLORD REGISTRATION (MODIFICATION) (SCOTLAND) ORDER 2005, SSI 2005 650; made under the Antisocial Behaviour etc. (Scotland) Act 2004 s.83. In force: January 1, 2006; £3.00.

This Order amends the Antisocial Behaviour etc. (Scotland) Act 2004, which in s.83 provides the registration of landlords for the purposes of Part 8 of the Act and lists categories of houses the use of which is to be disregarded for the purposes of registration. This Order adds additional categories to that list.

5472. Local authorities–Private landlord registration–Information and fees

PRIVATE LANDLORD REGISTRATION (INFORMATION AND FEES) (SCOTLAND) REGULATIONS 2005, SSI 2005 558; made under the Antisocial Behaviour (Scotland) Act 2004 s.83, s.87. In force: January 1, 2006; £3.00.

These Regulations prescribe the information that a person must provide and make provision for the fees that a person must pay in order to make a valid application for registration or for details of the person's registration to be amended.

5473. Public sector tenancies–Eviction–Warrant for ejection executed by change of locks

[Housing (Scotland) Act 1987 (c.26) s.48; Act of Sederunt (Summary Cause Rules, Sheriff Court) 1976 (SI 1976 476) r.19(1)(b).]

The appellant (D) sought to recall a decree for possession of the property in which he had been living. The respondent local authority had obtained the decree on March 15, 2002, with a warrant for ejection under the Housing (Scotland) Act 1987 s.48. On April 16, sheriff officers had attended to carry out the eviction and had found D's wife in the property. She had indicated that she was leaving, and had done so, leaving behind some furniture. The locks had then been changed. The housing department had subsequently relet the property to D's wife. D lodged a minute for recall at the end of May, maintaining that there had been no eviction, just a change of locks. The local authority maintained that the warrant had been properly executed because it had taken possession, the premises had been inventoried and keys handed in to the housing department.

Held, giving judgment accordingly, that the minute for recall had come too late. The tenancy had been terminated by the grant of decree and the changing of locks. The key handover to the housing department completed the execution of the warrant. Furthermore, the minute had been lodged six weeks after the execution of the warrant and in terms of the Act of Sederunt (Summary Cause Rules, Sheriff Court) 1976 r.19(1)(b) it should have been lodged no more than 14 days after execution of the charge. Having terminated the tenancy, the housing department was free to relet the property to whom it wished. It was irrelevant that it had in fact relet it to D's wife, and this did not support D's argument that there had been no eviction.

DEIGHAN v. EDINBURGH CITY COUNCIL 2004 Hous. L.R. 89, Sheriff JMS Horsburgh Q.C., Sh Ct (Lothian and Border).

5474. **Public sector tenancies—Housing benefit—Recovery of overpayment by deductions from benefit—Grounds for recovery of possession**

[Housing Benefit (General) Regulations 1987 (SI 1987 1971) Reg.101 (2) (c).]

The applicant local authority (A) sought to recover possession of a property tenanted by the respondent (M). A claimed that M was in arrears of rent to the extent of £129.50. M accepted that the amount owed was £129.50, but contended that what was owed was not rent but housing benefit, which was merely a debt and therefore could not found an action for recovery of possession. Accordingly, M maintained that A did not have a relevant or competent claim for repossession. Both parties agreed, regardless of its current nature, that the debt arose originally from an overpayment of housing benefit. A recovered the overpayment by deduction of a sum from the housing benefit M received and this in turn reduced the amount of benefit available to rebate M's ongoing rental obligations. M argued that the Housing Benefit (General) Regulations 1987 Reg.101 applied only to rent allowances and not rent rebates.

Held, continuing the case on a joint motion, that M, as claimant of the overpaid housing benefit, was the person to whom Reg. 101 (2) (c) of the 1987 Regulations applied. The local authority was accordingly entitled to deduct sums from M's housing benefit to recover the overpayment. The effect of the local authority's exercise of its statutory right of recovery against M's entitlement to housing benefit was that there was no longer enough of that benefit to meet M's contractual obligation to pay rent. Unless M made up the shortfall, the rent would fall into arrears and give rise to a ground of action for recovery of possession.

ABERDEEN CITY COUNCIL v. McCARTHY 2004 Hous. L.R. 53, Sheriff JK Tierney, Sh Ct (Grampian, Highland and Islands).

5475. **Public sector tenancies—Possession claims—Qualifying occupier as third party—Entitlement to apply for recall of decree**

[Housing (Scotland) Act 2001 (asp 10) s.15; Act of Sederunt (Summary Cause Rules) 2002 (SI 2000 132) r.24.1.]

The appellant local authority appealed against the recall of a decree by the sheriff in an action to recover possession of property tenanted by the respondent (K) and payment of rent arrears of £1,500. Notices had been served on K and his wife in terms of the Housing (Scotland) Act 2001. Decree was granted in K's absence and K's wife had lodged a minute of recall, which was refused. Thereafter K's son (WK) had lodged a minute of recall explaining that he had been unaware that he could appear as a third party and maintaining that he was a qualifying occupier who had not received notice of the proceedings because K was estranged from the family. Decree was recalled and on appeal the local authority argued that (1) WK was not a party in terms of the Act of Sederunt (Summary Cause Rules) 2002 r.24.1 and accordingly could not be a party to the action; (2) if it had been intended that any person who might have any interest in the case should be able to apply to have a decree recalled, the rule would have said so; (3) although a qualifying occupier could apply to become a party to the proceedings, WK had not entered the process in accordance with the 2002 Rules or the 2001 Act; (4) only a person against whom a decree had been granted could apply to have it recalled.

Held, allowing the appeal, that (1) on a proper construction of r.24.1 WK was not a third party and was not entitled to apply for recall of the decree. The rule appeared to apply only to pursuers, defenders and third parties who became parties to the action before its disposal. (2) WK would have had the right to apply to be sisted as a party under s.15 of the 2001 Act if he was a qualifying occupier, but he could no longer exercise that right once proceedings had been completed. (3) There was no good reason, either in s.15 or r.24.1, why the court should recall an otherwise competent decree granted against a party to the proceedings at the request of a person who claimed to be a qualifying occupant but had played no part in, nor been party to the proceedings prior to their completion, especially if the application was made long after decree was granted.

Observed, that assuming the local authority had made such enquiries as were necessary to establish, so far as reasonably practicable, whether there were any qualifying occupiers on whom a notice was required to be served, it was difficult to see how WK, if he was a qualifying occupier, could have exercised that right unless he became aware of the proceedings in some other way.

NORTH LANARKSHIRE COUNCIL v. KENMURE 2004 Hous. L.R. 50, Sheriff Principal JC McInnes Q.C., Sh Ct.

5476. Public sector tenancies–Possession claims–Rent arrears–Qualifying occupier sisted as party to the proceedings

[Housing (Scotland) Act 2001 (asp 10) s.14(4); Act of Sederunt (Summary Cause Rules) 2002 (SI 2002 132) r.24.1.]

The applicant local authority sought to recover possession of a property from the respondent tenant (P) following non payment of rent. Decree was granted and P subsequently lodged a minute of recall which was refused as incompetent. A qualifying occupier (M) sought to be sisted as a party to the proceedings and lodged a minute for recall, arguing that the proceedings were incompetent given that no notice complying with the Housing (Scotland) Act 2001 s.14(4) had been served on him and it would be unreasonable to grant decree in the local authority's favour. The local authority argued that (1) there was no statutory requirement to serve notice on qualifying tenants; (2) the decree granted was in foro and was a final judgment; only decrees in absence could be recalled; (3) only P could competently lodge a minute of recall; (4) the local authority's minute of recall had been unsuccessful and there could not, competently, be another. Even if M was a party who was, for the purposes of the Act of Sederunt (Summary Cause Rules) 2002 r.24.1, entitled to lodge minute for recall, he was also precluded by r.24.1 (2) from applying for recall more than once. The local authority also maintained that if M was sisted as a party, it would seek to amend the summons and include a crave for payment, jointly and severally with P, for the rent arrears.

Held, granting the application, that (1) there was no obstacle to M seeking to be sisted as a party. The words "a party" in r.24.1 should be interpreted to include a qualifying relative such as M. (2) If Parliament had made provision to enable qualifying relatives to be sisted in proceedings then it would be appropriate to read r.24.1 as entitling that relative to apply for recall of a decree granted in his or her absence, albeit that it may not have been a decree in absence as far as a party called as defender was concerned. (3) M's minute for recall was not incompetent. The rule did not stipulate that there would be no more than one minute for recall in an action, but that a party may apply for recall on one occasion only. M had not applied for recall previously and was entitled to do so.

Observed, that this decision might have undesirable consequences where, for example, there might be a number of qualifying relatives in any one case resulting in landlords facing a series of hearings covering more or less the same ground.

EDINBURGH CITY COUNCIL v. PORTER 2004 Hous. L.R. 46, Sheriff RJD Scott, Sh Ct (Lothian and Border).

5477. Repossession–Public sector tenancies–Tenant on low income and in ill health–Reasonableness of granting order

[Housing (Scotland) Act 2001 (asp 10) s.16.]

The applicant (X), a housing association, sought to recover possession of a house occupied by a single parent (F) and rent arrears amounting to £1,726.20.

Series of letters had been sent to F and an agreement had been reached in June 2002 that F would pay the full rent and a portion towards the arrears each month. However, after October 2002 no further payments were made. In February 2003 F attended X's offices and paid £600 towards the arrears, which then totalled £2,000. A notice of repossession was intimated to F in May 2003 but no response was given. In January 2004 F again attended X's offices and agreed a new schedule of arrears repayments but only £100 had been paid by February. F argued that in the circumstances it was not reasonable to evict her and account should be taken of both F's epilepsy and her 14 year old daughter's learning disability. She was under tremendous stress on a low income and trying to support her two teenage children. Further, F argued that there were outstanding housing benefit issues which were likely to affect her rent arrears balance.

Held, granting the application, that whilst F was clearly in a difficult position it was reasonable to grant the order, notwithstanding F's health, her daughter's health and F's low income. F had not acted reasonably in her dealings with X and could not be immune from the effects of the Housing (Scotland) Act 2001 s.16. F had failed to pay rent for considerable lengths of time, to communicate with or respond to X, to inform X of her difficulties and to make arrangements to make even minimal payments. A housing benefit reclaim of overpayment and credit of rent was deducted from F's arrears, resulting in an order for a reduced sum of £1,448.60. A decree for eviction was granted.

ANGUS HOUSING ASSOCIATION v. FRASER 2004 Hous. L.R. 83, Sheriff FR Crowe, Sh Ct (Tayside, Central and Fife).

5478. Tenants rights–Secure tenancies–Succession–Entitlement to succeed to secure tenancy on tenant's death

[Housing (Scotland) Act 1987 (c.26) s.52.]

The pursuer local authority sought to recover possession of heritable property following the death of a tenant. The defender (S), the tenant's son, sought a grant of the tenancy under the Housing (Scotland) Act 1987 s.52(1) and (2)(c). His application was refused on the basis that he was not entitled to succeed to the tenancy. The local authority maintained that the subject property was not and had not been S's main or only home during the 12 months preceding his mother's death.

Held, giving judgment accordingly, that S had not demonstrated on a balance of probabilities that he had a "real, tangible and substantial" connection to the property entitling him to succeed to the tenancy. There was the evidence from his mother's care workers that S was not there when they arrived but would come over from his own home later. There was also no evidence that S kept a room or stayed at the house for recognised periods, *Roxburgh DC v. Collins* 1991 S.L.T. (Sh Ct) 49, [1991] C.L.Y. 5195 considered. Decree was granted accordingly.

EAST LOTHIAN COUNCIL v. SKELDON 2004 Hous. L.R. 123, Sheriff BC Adair, Sh Ct (Lothian and Border).

5479. Tenants rights–Succession to secure tenancy–Qualified person

[Housing (Scotland) Act 2001 (asp 10) s.22, Sch.3 para.3.]

E, a local authority, sought to recover possession of property from J following the death of the tenant, her grandmother, in March 2004. The deceased had taken entry to the subjects under a secure tenancy in 1987 but had given notice to terminate her tenancy shortly before her death. J claimed to have moved into the property to look after the deceased in early January and had sought to take over the tenancy of the property after giving notice to terminate the tenancy of her own home. This was supported by her mother and sister although contrary to the evidence of other relatives and J's housing support worker who saw no signs of anyone living there other than the deceased. The deceased's housing support worker and doctor further stated that the deceased was very independent and would not have wanted J to live with her.

Held, granting decree, that the test of whether subjects constituted a person's "principal home" in terms of the Housing (Scotland) Act 2001 Sch.3 para.3 was whether the person concerned had a real, tangible and substantial connection with the house in question rather than any other place of residence which could not be established unless both physical signs of using or maintaining, and an intention to use a home, were present, and in the absence of such physical signs, J was not a qualified person in terms of s.22 of the Act.

EDINBURGH CITY COUNCIL v. JOHNSTON 2005 S.L.T. (Sh Ct) 100, Sheriff NMP Morrison QC, Sh Ct (Lothian and Border).

LEGAL ADVICE AND FUNDING

5480. Civil legal aid–Income limits for eligibility

CIVIL LEGAL AID (FINANCIAL CONDITIONS) (SCOTLAND) REGULATIONS 2005, SSI 2005 162; made under the Legal Aid (Scotland) Act 1986 s.36. In force: April 11, 2005; £3.00.

These Regulations increase certain of the financial limits of eligibility for civil legal aid under the Legal Aid (Scotland) Act 1986.

5481. Criminal procedure–Legal aid–Fees

CRIMINAL LEGAL AID (SCOTLAND) (FEES) AMENDMENT REGULATIONS 2005, SSI 2005 113; made under the Legal Aid (Scotland) Act 1986 s.33, s.36. In force: March 25, 2005; £4.50.

These Regulations amend the Criminal Legal Aid (Scotland) (Fees) Regulations 1989 (SI 1989 1491) so as to provide that where more than one letter is sent, each of which has a similar subject matter, the prescribed fee shall apply; and to provide that fees of Counsel will be determined by the Scottish Legal Aid Board, or after taxation by the Auditor of Court.

5482. Criminal procedure–Legal aid–Fees

CRIMINAL LEGAL AID (SCOTLAND) (FEES) AMENDMENT (NO.2) REGULATIONS 2005, SSI 2005 584; made under the Legal Aid (Scotland) Act 1986 s.33, s.36. In force: December 10, 2005; £3.00.

These Regulations amend the Criminal Legal Aid (Scotland) (Fees) Regulations 1989 (SI 1989 1491) so as to modify the method by which fees and outlays of Counsel are determined for work undertaken in connection with certain hearings under the Criminal Procedure (Scotland) Act 1995 s.76, confiscation hearings, appeals and for travel, accommodation and subsistence.

5483. Criminal procedure–Legal aid–Fixed payments

CRIMINAL LEGAL AID (FIXED PAYMENTS) (SCOTLAND) AMENDMENT REGULATIONS 2005, SSI 2005 93; made under the Legal Aid (Scotland) Act 1986 s.33, s.41A. In force: March 23, 2005; £3.00.

These Regulations amend the Criminal Legal Aid (Fixed Payments) (Scotland) Regulations 1999 (SI 1999 491) which make provision for fixed payments to be made from the Scottish Legal Aid Fund in respect of the professional services provided by a solicitor including certain prescribed outlays. They make amendments to provide for fixed payments to be made available to solicitors for their work in conducting adjourned trial diets in criminal summary proceedings where no evidence is led.

5484. Criminal procedure–Legal aid–Legal representative

CRIMINAL LEGAL AID (SCOTLAND) AMENDMENT REGULATIONS 2005, SSI 2005 450; made under the Legal Aid (Scotland) Act 1986 s.36. In force: October 5, 2005; £3.00.

These Regulations amend the Criminal Legal Aid (Scotland) Regulations 1996 (SI 1996 2555) to provide that the definition of "legal representative" is altered by the removal of reference to curator bonis, tutor and guardian, and by substituting reference to persons authorised to act on an adult's behalf under the Adults with Incapacity (Scotland) Act 2000 and on a patient's behalf under the Mental Health (Care and Treatment) (Scotland) Act 2003; and references to the Mental Health (Scotland) Act 1984 are replaced with references to the Mental Health (Care and Treatment) (Scotland) Act 2003. The Mental Health (Scotland) Act 1984 is replaced and repealed by the Mental Health (Care and Treatment) (Scotland) Act 2003.

5485. Legal advice–Assistance–Family proceedings

ADVICE AND ASSISTANCE (SCOTLAND) AMENDMENT REGULATIONS 2005, SSI 2005 111; made under the Legal Aid (Scotland) Act 1986 s.12. In force: April 11, 2005; £3.00.

These Regulations amend the Advice and Assistance (Scotland) Regulations 1996 (SI 1996 2447) to provide that a solicitor's right to prior payment of fees and outlays out of any property recovered or preserved for a client in respect of advice and assistance shall not apply to the first £4,531 recovered or preserved by virtue of certain family proceedings.

5486. Legal advice–Assistance–Income and capital limits

ADVICE AND ASSISTANCE (FINANCIAL CONDITIONS) (SCOTLAND) REGULATIONS 2005, SSI 2005 163; made under the Legal Aid (Scotland) Act 1986 s.11, s.36. In force: April 11, 2005; £3.00.

These Regulations, in relation to any case where an application for advice and assistance is made on or after April 11, 2005, increase the disposable income limit for eligibility for advice and assistance under the Legal Aid (Scotland) Act 1986 from £197 a week to £203 a week; increase the disposable capital limit for advice and assistance from £1,370 to £1,412; increase the weekly disposable income above which a person is required to pay a contribution from £83 to £86; and prescribe the scale of contributions to be paid where the weekly disposable income exceeds £86 but does not exceed £203. The Regulations also revoke the Advice and Assistance (Financial Conditions) (Scotland) Regulations 2004 (SSI 2004 141) except in relation to any case where an application for advice and assistance is made before April 11, 2005.

5487. Legal advice–Assistance–Mental incapacity

ADVICE AND ASSISTANCE (SCOTLAND) AMENDMENT (NO.3) REGULATIONS 2005, SSI 2005 339; made under the Legal Aid (Scotland) Act 1986 s.36. In force: July 1, 2005; £3.00.

These Regulations amend the Advice and Assistance (Scotland) Regulations 1996 (SI 1996 2447) so as to provide that the disposable income and disposable capital of incapable adults, as defined by the Adults with Incapacity (Scotland) Act 2000 s.1 (6), is taken into account by the Board in cases where advice and assistance applications relating to incapable adults are made.

5488. Legal advice–Assistance by way of representation–Mental health proceedings

ADVICE AND ASSISTANCE (ASSISTANCE BY WAY OF REPRESENTATION) (SCOTLAND) AMENDMENT (NO.2) REGULATIONS 2005, SSI 2005 482;

made under the Legal Aid (Scotland) Act 1986 s.9, s.36, s.37. In force: October 5, 2005; £3.00.

These Regulations amend the Advice and Assistance (Assistance by Way of Representation) (Scotland) Regulations 2003 (SSI 2003 179) so as to provide that assistance by way of representation under the Legal Aid (Scotland) Act 1986 is available for proceedings before the Mental Health Tribunal for Scotland, as established by the Mental Health (Care and Treatment) (Scotland) Act 2003; assistance by way of representation shall be available to persons without reference to s.8 and s.11 of the 1986 Act which relate to financial limits on the availability of advice and assistance and payment of contributions towards advice and assistance; and any grant of assistance by way of representation made before October 5, 2005 for proceedings under the Mental Health (Scotland) Act 1984 Part V shall continue until the case is disposed of as if these Regulations had not been made.

5489. Legal advice–Assistance by way of representation–Witnesses

ADVICE AND ASSISTANCE (ASSISTANCE BY WAY OF REPRESENTATION) (SCOTLAND) AMENDMENT REGULATIONS 2005, SSI 2005 165; made under the Legal Aid (Scotland) Act 1986 s.9. In force: in accordance with Reg.2; £3.00.

These Regulations amend the Advice and Assistance (Assistance by way of Representation) (Scotland) Regulations 2003 (SSI 2003 179) to provide that assistance by way of representation under the Legal Aid (Scotland) Act 1986 Part II is available for proceedings before the Asylum and Immigration Tribunal; and assistance by way of representation under Part II of the 1986 Act is available for persons who, as witnesses, are brought before the court in solemn criminal proceedings, having been apprehended for deliberately and obstructively failing to appear at any diet to which they have been cited. This assistance by way of representation shall be available without reference to s.8 and s.11 of the 1986 Act which relate to financial limits on the availability of advice and assistance and payment of contributions towards advice and assistance.

5490. Legal aid–Civil legal aid–Family proceedings

CIVIL LEGAL AID (SCOTLAND) AMENDMENT REGULATIONS 2005, SSI 2005 112; made under the Legal Aid (Scotland) Act 1986 s.36. In force: in accordance with Reg.2; £3.00.

These Regulations amend the Civil Legal Aid (Scotland) Regulations 2002 (SSI 2002 494) to provide that: where the Scottish Legal Aid Board is satisfied that an application to the Court of Session for review of a decision of the Asylum and Immigration Tribunal is initiated as a matter of special urgency, the Scottish Legal Aid Board may make legal aid available for the initiation of that application before an application for civil legal aid is made; and the requirement on the part of a person in receipt of civil legal aid to pay the amount of any net liability of the Scottish Legal Aid Fund shall not apply to the first £4,531 recovered or preserved by virtue of certain family proceedings.

5491. Legal aid–Civil legal aid–Fees

CIVIL LEGAL AID (SCOTLAND) (FEES) AMENDMENT REGULATIONS 2005, SSI 2005 449; made under the Legal Aid (Scotland) Act 1986 s.33, s.36. In force: October 5, 2005; £3.00.

These Regulations amend the Civil Legal Aid (Scotland) (Fees) Regulations 1989 (SI 1989 1490) as follows: the reference to the Mental Health (Scotland) Act 1984 is omitted and substituted with a reference to the Mental Health (Care and Treatment) (Scotland) Act 2003; and a savings provision is included so that solicitors' accounts for cases existing as at October 5, 2005 can continue to be paid in accordance with the regulatory regime existing immediately prior to the coming into force of these Regulations. The Mental Health (Scotland) Act 1984 is replaced and repealed by the Mental Health (Care and Treatment) (Scotland) Act 2003.

5492. Legal aid—Civil legal aid—Legal representative

CIVIL LEGAL AID (SCOTLAND) AMENDMENT (NO.2) REGULATIONS 2005, SSI 2005 448; made under the Legal Aid (Scotland) Act 1986 s.36. In force: October 5, 2005; £3.00.

These Regulations amend the Civil Legal Aid (Scotland) Regulations 2002 (SSI 2002 494) as follows: the definition of "legal representative" is extended to include persons authorised to act on a patient's behalf under the Mental Health (Care and Treatment) (Scotland) Act 2003; the reference to the Mental Health (Scotland) Act 1984 is removed where it makes provision as to the procedure for signing applications for civil legal aid where the applicant is unable to sign due to mental disorder and is substituted with a reference to the 2003 Act; and a reference to named persons, nominated and appointed in terms of the 2003 Act, is added which provides for the assessment of financial resources of persons who make applications for civil legal aid in a representative, fiduciary or official capacity. The Mental Health (Scotland) Act 1984 is replaced and repealed by the 2003 Act.

5493. Legal aid—Contempt of court—Proceedings

LEGAL AID IN CONTEMPT OF COURT PROCEEDINGS (SCOTLAND) AMENDMENT REGULATIONS 2005, SSI 2005 451; made under the Legal Aid (Scotland) Act 1986 s.36. In force: October 5, 2005; £3.00.

These Regulations amend the Legal Aid in Contempt of Court Proceedings (Scotland) Regulations 1992 (SI 1992 1227) as follows: the definition of "legal representative" is altered by the removal of the reference to curator bonis and guardian and substituting reference to persons authorised to act on an adult's behalf under the Adults with Incapacity (Scotland) Act 2000 and on a patient's behalf under the Mental Health (Care and Treatment) (Scotland) Act 2003; the reference to the Mental Health (Scotland) Act 1984 is removed where it makes provision as to the procedure for signing applications for legal aid where the applicant is unable to sign due to mental disorder and substituted with a reference to the Mental Health (Care and Treatment) (Scotland) Act 2003. The Mental Health (Scotland) Act 1984 is replaced and repealed by the Mental Health (Care and Treatment) (Scotland) Act 2003.

5494. Legal representation—Advice and assistance—Solicitors fees

ADVICE AND ASSISTANCE (SCOTLAND) AMENDMENT (NO.2) REGULATIONS 2005, SSI 2005 171; made under the Legal Aid (Scotland) Act 1986 s.33. In force: April 30, 2005; £3.00.

These Regulations amend the Advice and Assistance (Scotland) Regulations 1996 (SI 1996 2447) so as to provide for increased fees for solicitors for work done in civil matters where advice and assistance or assistance by way of representation has been given. An increase in fees for solicitors is further provided for advice and assistance given in respect of matters which are the subject of the Children (Scotland) Act 1995 Part II.

LEGAL METHODOLOGY

5495. Books

Scottish Law Directory: Fees Supplement 2005: The White Book. Paperback: £11.00. ISBN 1 4057 0377 6. Butterworths Law (Scotland).

LEGAL PROFESSION

5496. Solicitors–Scottish Solicitors Discipline Tribunal–Right to independent and impartial tribunal

[Solicitors (Scotland) Act 1980 (c.46) s.54; Human Rights Act 1998 (c.42) Sch.1 Part I Art.6(1).]

S, the Scottish Solicitors Discipline Tribunal, found R, a solicitor who had latterly practised on his own account, guilty of professional misconduct in respect of his repeated failures to reply to correspondence and other communications from the Law Society. After a hearing in R's absence in October 2002, S decided that his name should be struck off the roll. This followed a previous finding of professional misconduct in respect of analogous matters in November 2001, which had resulted in a fine of £5,000 and a decision to limit him to acting as a qualified assistant for three years. R's appeal to the Court of Session against S's decision was refused. R thereafter appealed by way of petition under the Solicitors (Scotland) Act 1980 s.54, submitting that: S was not an independent and impartial tribunal within the meaning of the Human Rights Act 1998 Sch.1 Part I Art.6(1); its solicitor members were appointed by the Lord President on the recommendation of the Law Society, who was the prosecuting authority, and lacked security of tenure; S had power to award payment of its own expenses in relation to a complaint, and a solicitor member might hope that his prospects would be enhanced if he became a member of S and gave decisions in favour of the Law Society; further, this was not capable of being remedied by the appeal procedure as the Lord President also decided which judges would hear the appeal; in addition, two of the tribunal members should have declined to sit as they had been members of the previous tribunal in November 2001; S had erred in refusing his request to adjourn the hearing fixed for October 2002 as he had wished to be heard in mitigation of sentence; and the sentence imposed was excessive where, *inter alia*, he had been prevented by the Law Society from taking up an offer of employment from a firm in May 2002, he had been sequestrated, his practice had been destroyed, and he was currently earning about £100 a week as a tennis coach.

Held, allowing the appeal in relation to sentence and substituting a direction that R limit to acting as a qualified solicitor with an employer approved by the Law Society for five years, that (1) the appointment procedure could not be regarded as detracting from the independence and impartiality of S. Solicitor members could not be said to lack the required degree of security of tenure in the context of the statutory provisions for the constitution of such tribunals, and in circumstances where they were appointed by the Lord President on the recommendation of the Law Society, they did not receive remuneration, and it was of significance that the Law Society did not have any power to terminate an appointment once it was made. (2) As a matter of general principle, in the event of an appeal, the Court of Session had full jurisdiction and provided the guarantees of Art.6(1), and the suggestion that the selection of appeal judges was influenced by the fact that the Lord President had appointed S's members was fanciful in the extreme. (3) R had at no stage sought to deny any professional misconduct and the fact that two solicitor members had been present at the hearing in November 2001 had not occasioned him any prejudice. The information about the previous finding was already in the public domain and, in any event, had to be disclosed to S in October 2002. (4) S had been fully justified in refusing to adjourn a hearing in October 2002 in circumstances where R had been given adequate notice, the application was received one day before the hearing, and other commitments on which R sought to found did not justify the request at such a late stage. (5) With some hesitation, the decision to strike R's name from the roll was excessive, taking into account the fact that there had been no complaint of professional misconduct when he had been a partner in two other firms, neither complaint involved dishonesty, and, in particular, the detrimental financial consequences of the Law Society's decision to defer consideration of the application to employ him until the disciplinary proceedings had been concluded.

ROBSON v. COUNCIL OF THE LAW SOCIETY OF SCOTLAND (NO.2) 2005 S.C. 125, Lord Kirkwood, Lord MacLean, Lord Osborne, Ex Div.

5497. Books

Law Society Scotland Diploma Materials 2005, Diploma Solutions 2005-2006. Book (details unknown): £6.50. ISBN 0 414 01645 9. W. Green & Son.

Law Society Scotland Diploma Materials 2005, Private Client Student Manual 2005-2006. Book (details unknown): £15.00. ISBN 0 414 01643 2. W. Green & Son.

Law Society Scotland Diploma Materials 2005, Professional Ethics Student Manual 2005-2006. Book (details unknown): £15.00. ISBN 0 414 01641 6. W. Green & Son.

LEGAL SYSTEMS

5498. Books

Laurie, Graeme T.; Gibson, Johanna—Generation Scotland: Legal and Ethical Aspects. Paperback: £5.00. ISBN 0 9549717 0 1. AHRC (Arts and Humanities Research Council) Research Centre for Studies in.

Macqueen, Hector; Hood, Parker; Wise, Morag; Dunlop, Laura; Wolffe, James; Young, Andrew; Johnston, David; Wolffe, Sarah P. L.—Gloag and Henderson: The Law of Scotland. Paperback: £49.00. ISBN 0 414 01634 3. W. Green & Son.

Mcgregor—Avizandum Statutes on Scots Law of Obligations. Paperback: £23.95. ISBN 1 904968 06 6. Avizandum Publishing Ltd.

Reid, Elspeth; Miller, David L. Carey—Mixed Legal System in Transition: T. B. Smith and the Progress of Scots Law. Edinburgh Studies in Law S. Hardback: £45.00. ISBN 0 7486 2335 3. Edinburgh University Press.

Scots Law Times. Hardback: £325.00. ISBN 0 414 01605 X. W. Green & Son.

Scottish Law Directory 2005. Hardback: £49.00. ISBN 1 4057 0376 8. Butterworths Law.

LICENSING

5499. Licences—Betting offices—Grounds for refusal—Competence

[Betting, Gaming and Lotteries Act 1963 (c.2) Sch.1 para.19(b)(ii).]

G, a licensing board, refused an application for a betting office licence on the grounds that, in terms of the Betting, Gaming and Lotteries Act 1963 Sch.1 para.19(b)(ii), it was inexpedient having regard to the demand for betting offices and the availability of such facilities in the area. The applicants, W, appealed to the sheriff who refused their appeal. W thereafter appealed to the Court of Session, arguing that the sheriff had erred in law by failing to hold that G had (1) exercised their discretion in an unreasonable manner where their statement of reasons failed to provide adequate reasons why they considered it would be inexpedient to grant the application; (2) acted contrary to natural justice where the transcript of proceedings disclosed that their vice convener had made numerous interventions and comments critical of both the application and its presentation on W's behalf, such as to create the suspicion that he was not acting impartially and was biased against the grant of the application.

Held, dismissing the appeal, that (1) the meaning of "inexpedient" in Sch.1 para.19(b)(ii) was simply that the grant would not be useful in the circumstances having regard to the factors mentioned. G, having concluded that the proposed facility was not needed for the purposes of meeting the demand existing for the time being in the light of the material before them and having given reasons as to why they were not persuaded by W's contention in relation to the claimed public benefit which would flow from increased competition and the standard of the proposed facilities, were entitled to refuse the application without identifying any particular deleterious consequence which might follow in the event it was granted. (2) It was evident that the focus of the legislation was upon the meeting of existing demand, rather than the simulation of new demand and G, having concluded that the granting of W's application would be inexpedient, were entitled to conclude that it would not be desirable in the public interest. (3) W's contention that the interventions and comments of G's vice convener contravened the rules of natural justice was based upon a misunderstanding of the meaning of the language used by him, from which no implication of bias or a closed mind could arise.

WILLIAM HILL ORGANISATION LTD v. GLASGOW CITY LICENSING BOARD 2005 S.C. 102, Lord Maclean, Lord Osborne, Lord Kingarth, Ex Div.

5500. Licences–Licensed premises–Suspension–Reasons

[Licensing (Scotland) Act 1976 (c.66) s.31.]

S, a public house licence holder, appealed against a sheriff's decision upholding a decision of the licensing board (N) to suspend his public house licence for one month for displaying items of a sectarian nature at the premises. The proceedings were initiated following N's receipt of a letter of complaint from the police. At N's hearing, it transpired that the items had been present for a number of years and had originally been expressly approved by the police, and despite N's promulgation of byelaws enabling the attachment of conditions to licences preventing such display, none had been attached to that of S. N concluded that S's actions amounted to misconduct, rendering him an unfit and improper person to be the holder of a licence, and that suspension thereof was in the public interest.

Held, allowing the appeal, that the sheriff had erred in law in holding that N had given "full and proper reasons" for its decision. There was real difficulty in ascertaining what precisely was thought to constitute "misconduct" on S's part; reference continued to be made to the terms of the letter of complaint despite the material departures therefrom in the course of the hearing. N's conclusion that S's actions amounted to misconduct in the absence of any ensuing public disorder and in the absence of any condition of his licence that he desist from so doing was not self evident. Further, while N was entitled to have regard to misconduct on the part of a licence holder in terms of the Licensing (Scotland) Act 1976 s.31 (3) (a), such a finding did not of itself mean that the requirements of s.31 (2) (a) had been satisfied.

SMITH v. NORTH LANARKSHIRE LICENSING BOARD 2005 S.L.T. 544, Lord Marnoch, Lord Macfadyen, Lord Clarke, Ex Div.

5501. Licences–Private hire vehicles–Applications for taxi licences–Refusal–Competence

[Civic Government (Scotland) Act 1982 (c.45) s.10(3), Sch.1 para.5(3).]

D, a company providing private car hire services, applied for taxi licences in respect of 71 vehicles. The application was refused on the ground that C, the licensing committee, which had determined that 507 was the number of taxi licences necessary to meet demand in the district following a survey in 2000, were satisfied that there was no significant unmet demand for taxis. D appealed to the sheriff, who allowed the appeal, and directed that the licences be granted, on the basis that demand should have been assessed in relation to the situation at the time when the application fell to be considered. X, an association of taxi licence holders, who had objected to the application, appealed to the Court of Session. They argued that the sheriff had erred in law where it was clear that C had looked at some material that postdated May 2000 but had not been persuaded by it, undue emphasis had been placed on the fact that C had not kept the matter under review since 2000, and had further erred by considering that C would have been obliged to grant the application where they still required to exercise their discretion under the

Civic Government (Scotland) Act 1982 Sch.1 para.5(3) and, as they might have viewed the fact that D was not on its waiting list as some "other good reason" for refusing the application, the sheriff should have remitted to them for reconsideration.

Held, dismissing the appeal, that (1) C had not informed themselves of the current demand for taxi services as they were bound to do. (2) Having regard to the restricted circumstances in which the power conferred by s.10(3) of the Act might be exercised, it could not have been the intention of Parliament to enable C to elevate the status of an informal waiting list, so that absence from it might constitute "other good reason" compelling them to refuse to grant a taxi licence.

DUNDEE TAXI CAB CO LTD v. DUNDEE CITY COUNCIL 2005 S.C. 503, Lady Cosgrove, Lord Drummond Young, Lord Cameron of Lochbroom, Ex Div.

5502. Licences–Private hire vehicles–Extensions of time

[Civic Government (Scotland) Act 1982 (c.45) s.3, s.10.]

C, a taxi licensing authority, sought an extension of the six month period under the Civic Government (Scotland) Act 1982 s.3(1) for reaching a final decision on four applications for taxi licences submitted by M. M opposed the extension. C maintained there was good reason to extend the statutory time period because they were awaiting receipt of a report by a firm of transport management consultants on whether there was any significant unmet demand for taxis. C had adopted a policy of limiting the number of taxi licences and a figure of 1,260 licences was considered sufficient in November 2002 following an earlier comprehensive survey of demand by independent consultants. M submitted that since the earlier survey C had done nothing to ascertain whether there was a significant unmet demand and had discouraged the lodging of applications for taxi licences, creating the false impression that there was no unmet demand. M argued further that C's inactivity meant that they could not satisfy the provisions of s.10(3) of the Act. M submitted that steps should have been taken in the autumn of 2003 to obtain a further survey rather than 10 months later; there was no continual assessment and C had brought the situation upon themselves as a result of their lack of action before May 2004. M contended that, had the survey been instructed earlier, there would have been no reason to wait for decisions to be made; C was the author of its own misfortune and there was no good reason to remedy that situation by granting an extension of time.

Held, granting the application, that (1) C had in place a system of keeping under review the question of demand and had employed a taxi licensing officer who was in daily contact with the taxi trade and the public and had conducted occasional stance surveys, and while there might have been some force in the submission that C had done nothing "proactively" since obtaining the earlier report if the consultant's survey had been initiated after M's applications were lodged, the process for the instruction of the survey had been ongoing for about five or six months and, further, there was no evidence to support the submission that a survey of demand should have been instructed in autumn 2003. (2) In seeking to achieve a balance between the right of M to have their applications determined speedily and the needs of C to have the information to enable them to reach informed decisions and so fulfil their statutory duties, it seemed that equity favoured C and there was good reason to extend the period. (3) It would be inappropriate to impose a shorter period than October 30, 2005 as to do so would compromise the democratic process and might deprive interested parties from a full discussion on the terms of the report.

EDINBURGH CITY COUNCIL v. 3MAXBLACK LLP 2005 S.L.T. (Sh Ct) 86, Sheriff KEC Mackie, Sh Ct (Lothian).

5503. Licences–Private hire vehicles–Refusal–Unmet demand–Competence

[Civic Government (Scotland) Act 1982 (c.45) s.10(3), s.20(2A).]

The appellant local authority appealed against a sheriff's decision allowing an appeal by D against the refusal to grant two taxi licences on the basis that they could not be refused if a segment of the population had a significantly inadequate number of taxis for their need. The licences were sought on the basis that D had bought two wheelchair accessible vehicles and was in a position to fulfil an unmet demand by the disabled section of the community. D submitted that the overall population included the disabled population and if there was significant unmet demand from the latter, it could not be said that there was no significant unmet demand in the area as a whole.

Held, allowing the appeal (Temporary Judge Sir David Edward Q.C. dissenting on the point of principle but not on the suggested course of disposal), that (1) the purpose of the Civic Government (Scotland) Act 1982 s.10(3) was to enable the licensing authority to restrict the number of licences to what was necessary to meet the "demand" in their area which could only be meaningfully assessed by reference to the overall demand in the area, and such a construction was further supported by the power in s.20(2A) to make regulations in relation to the carrying in taxis of disabled people. (2) The fact that there was no significant demand which was unmet did not mean that an application was automatically refused, a local authority still had to consider the application and in so doing, address whether there were circumstances which required the case to be looked at independently of their general policy on numbers in the sense in which the special needs of the disabled should, in the present case, have been taken into account.

DAVIES v. RENFREWSHIRE COUNCIL 2005 S.C. 315, Lord Marnoch, Lady Cosgrove, Temporary Judge Sir David Edward Q.C., Ex Div.

5504. Licences–Street trading–Councillors–Conflict of interest

C, a trader selling hot food from a van, appealed against a decision by F, a local authority's regulation subcommittee, to grant his application for a new licence but attach an exclusion zone of 100 metres from the annex to a school, thus preventing him from parking at and trading from a layby. One of the objections to C's application had come from the school's rector. C argued that F had acted contrary to natural justice where the same two councillors who sat in on school board meetings along with the rector had also sat on the subcommittee which had considered the rector's objection before making their decision on his application.

Held, remitting the case to F for reconsideration of their decision by a differently constituted committee, that (1) F's concern regarding road safety was that the habitual location of the van near a school in a bus layby would encourage children to congregate and they were entitled to draw inferences from the material before them on the basis of local knowledge and experience, further, their approach to the issue of litter raised legitimate concerns about the limitations on what C himself might be able to do to contain it. (2) It could be concluded that, by having a committee numbering six, two of whom included councillors who had sat in on school board meetings over the preceding months when the matter of the renewal of chip van licences and the creation of an exclusion zone had been raised and discussed, F had acted contrary to natural justice, and the request by one of the councillors that he be excluded was not only commendable but proved entirely correct. (3) The proper course at this point was not to modify F's decision and delete the reference to an exclusion zone where the procedural error was not of such magnitude that a differently constituted committee, excluding the two councillors, could not arrive at a proper decision.

CAMERON v. FIFE COUNCIL 2005 S.L.T. (Sh Ct) 115, Sheriff GJ Evans, Sh Ct (Tayside, Central and Fife).

5505. Licensing committees–Procedure–Voting–In public

[Licensing (Scotland) Act 1976 (c.66) s.5(7).]

C, the holders of an entertainment licence, sought judicial review of a decision of E, a licensing board, refusing an application to extend the permitted hours for the sale and supply of alcohol at a club. E had adjourned to deliberate its decision in private after hearing representations from C and the police. On returning to the meeting, a motion to refuse was seconded and put to E's members for a decision to be made. C contended that since there was no formal vote or show of hands, nor a unanimous oral response of "agreed", it was not plain how each member had voted, and an impression could be formed that a collective decision had been taken outwith C's presence, which contravened the Licensing (Scotland) Act 1976 s.5(7) and rendered the decision unlawful.

Held, refusing the petition, that (1) the only relevant issue under s.5(7) was whether the decision was taken in public, and on the evidence led, no decision was made in private where the procedure plainly involved a formal proposal duly seconded, an enquiry by the chairman as to whether that was agreed, an opportunity to demur, and a verbal indication of assent which the chairman and proposer took to be unanimous; (2) C appeared to have understood that ex facie a unanimous decision had been taken, and no complaint was made at the time that the decision was not intelligible or had not been properly taken, on the contrary, C implicitly treated the decision as valid in asking for a statement of reasons, and (3) E's concerns that certain individuals might still have harboured private reservations which, for whatever reason, they could not express, could not avail them in circumstances where members were given a chance to oppose the motion but chose not to take it.

CITY LEISURE (MUSSELBURGH) LTD v. EAST LOTHIAN LICENSING BOARD 2004 S.L.T. 1210, Lord Emslie, OH.

5506. Licensing (Scotland) Act 2005 (asp 16)

This Act of the Scottish Parliament makes provision for regulating the sale of alcohol, and for regulating licensed premises and other premises on which alcohol is sold.

This Act received Royal Assent on December 21, 2005.

5507. Off licences–Service stations–Off licence application–Reasonableness

[Licensing (Scotland) Act 1976 (c.66) s.17(1)(b).]

B, a filling station operator, applied for an off sale licence for premises comprising a filling station, shop and cafe. P, the licensing board, found that the premises in question were predominantly a filling station and, under the Licensing (Scotland) Act 1976 s.17(1)(b), they were "not suitable or convenient for the sale of alcoholic liquor" given that the weekly average value of fuel sales was significantly higher than non fuel sales, there was no pedestrian access to the local community to the premises, and the premises served traffic travelling along a major trunk road and the sale of non fuel items was ancillary and subsidiary to the petrol filling station use. The sheriff allowed B's appeal and granted the application. P appealed to the Court of Session.

Held, allowing the appeal, that (1) the sheriff's reasoning appeared to have been that the size of the turnover of the shop in non fuel sales was in itself so great that it could not be said that the shop should have been treated as merely ancillary to the filling station, but this did not take account of the relative magnitude of the fuel and non fuel sales, to which P evidently attached importance. (2) P were entitled to come to the conclusion which they did as they had to consider the relative significance of the use of the premises as a filling station and as a shop, against the background that the customers were very largely motorists drawn to the premises by the filling station.

BP EXPRESS SHOPPING LTD v. PERTH AND KINROSS LICENSING BOARD 2005 S.L.T. 862, Lord Cullen L.P., Lord Penrose, Temporary Judge Sir David Edward QC, 1 Div.

LOCAL GOVERNMENT

5508. Civil Contingencies Act 2004 (c.36)–Commencement Order

CIVIL CONTINGENCIES ACT 2004 (COMMENCEMENT) (SCOTLAND) ORDER 2005, SSI 2005 493 (C.26); made under the Civil Contingencies Act 2004 s.34. Commencement details: bringing into force various provisions of the 2004 Act on October 6, 2005, November 14, 2005 and May 15, 2006; £3.00.

This Order brings into force the remaining provisions of the Civil Contingencies Act 2004 Part 1.

5509. Council tax–Unoccupied dwellings–Discounts

COUNCIL TAX (DISCOUNT FOR UNOCCUPIED DWELLINGS) (SCOTLAND) REGULATIONS 2005, SSI 2005 51; made under the Local Government in Scotland Act 2003 s.33. In force: April 1, 2005; £3.00.

These Regulations make amendments to a provision in the Local Government Finance Act 1992 (the daily discount from council tax of twice the "appropriate percentage" for chargeable dwellings of which there is no resident) and make new provision in relation to council tax discounts for dwellings which have no resident. They provide that there shall be a discount of 50 per cent of the amount of council tax payable in respect of a chargeable dwelling where there is no resident of the dwelling; and give local authorities the power to modify the application of these Regulations within their areas in relation to certain classes of dwelling (i.e. empty dwellings and dwellings that are second homes) and in relation to different parts of their areas.

5510. Emergency powers–Contingency planning

CIVIL CONTINGENCIES ACT 2004 (CONTINGENCY PLANNING) (SCOTLAND) REGULATIONS 2005, SSI 2005 494; made under the Civil Contingencies Act 2004 s.2, s.4, s.6, s.12, s.15, s.17. In force: November 14, 2005; £4.00.

These Regulations relate to the extent of the duties imposed on certain bodies listed in the Civil Contingencies Act 2004 (duties to assess, and plan for emergencies and duties to provide advice and assistance to business) and the manner in which those duties are to be performed.

5511. Fire (Scotland) Act 2005 (asp 5)

This Act makes provision about fire and rescue authorities and joint fire and rescue boards; restates and amends the law in relation to fire services; makes provision in relation to the functions of such authorities and boards in connection with certain events and situations other than fires; makes provision for implementing in part Council Directives 89/391, 89/654, 91/383, 94/33, 98/24 and 1999/92; and makes other provision in relation to fire safety in certain non-domestic premises.

This Act received Royal Assent on April 1, 2005.

5512. Fire (Scotland) Act 2005 (asp 5)–Commencement No.1 Order

FIRE (SCOTLAND) ACT 2005 (COMMENCEMENT NO.1) ORDER 2005, SSI 2005 207 (C.9); made under the Fire (Scotland) Act 2005 s.88, s.90. Commencement details: bringing into force various provisions of the 2005 Act on April 6, 2005; £3.00.

This Order brings into force provisions of the Fire (Scotland) Act 2005 which enable orders or regulations to be made.

5513. Fire (Scotland) Act 2005 (asp 5)–Commencement No.2 Order

FIRE (SCOTLAND) ACT 2005 (COMMENCEMENT NO.2) ORDER 2005, SSI 2005 392 (C.17); made under the Fire (Scotland) Act 2005 s.88, s.90. Commencement details: bringing into force various provisions of the 2005 Act on August 2, 2005; £3.00.

This Order brings into force the following provisions of the Fire (Scotland) Act 2005, so far as they are not already in force: Pt 1, Pt 2, Pt 4 and Pt 5; and Sch.1, Sch.3 and Sch.4.

5514. Local authorities–Fire services–Additional functions

FIRE (ADDITIONAL FUNCTION) (SCOTLAND) ORDER 2005, SSI 2005 342; made under the Fire (Scotland) Act 2005 s.11. In force: in accordance with Art.1; £3.00.

This Order specifies those additional functions relating to emergencies which are to be conferred on the relevant authorities. In particular, it confers functions on relevant authorities in relation to chemical, biological, radiological or nuclear incidents, search and rescue, serious flooding, and serious transport incidents. Where a relevant authority has specialist resources available to it, including specialist trained personnel, that enable it to discharge its functions under this Order in relation to a particular type of emergency, the Order requires the authority to use those resources outwith its own area in response to a request for assistance from another authority where that type of emergency arises. The Order also stipulates what provision relevant authorities must make for the specified emergency situations.

5515. Local authorities–Fire services–Consequential modifications

FIRE (SCOTLAND) ACT 2005 (CONSEQUENTIAL MODIFICATIONS AND AMENDMENTS) ORDER 2005, SSI 2005 383; made under the Fire (Scotland) Act 2005 s.87, s.88. In force: in accordance with Art.1; £3.00.

This Order amends the Theatres Act 1968, the Gaming Act 1968, the Fire Precautions Act 1971, the Health and Safety at Work etc. Act 1974, the Local Government, Planning and Land Act 1980, the Zoo Licensing Act 1981, the Civic Government (Scotland) Act 1982, the Cinemas Act 1985, the Environment and Safety Information Act 1988, the National Health Service and Community Care Act 1990, the Capital Allowances Act 2001 and the Budget (Scotland) Act 2005. The Order makes amendments to and repeals provisions in primary legislation. These amendments and repeals are consequential for the purposes, or in consequence of, the Fire (Scotland) Act 2005.

5516. Local authorities–Fire services–Consequential modifications

FIRE (SCOTLAND) ACT 2005 (CONSEQUENTIAL MODIFICATIONS AND AMENDMENTS) (NO.2) ORDER 2005, SSI 2005 344; made under the Fire (Scotland) Act 2005 s.87, s.88. In force: in accordance with Art.1; £3.00.

This Order amends 31 SIs and 4 SSIs for the purposes of, or in consequence of, the Fire (Scotland) Act 2005. The effect of the subordinate legislation has not been altered; however, the terminology used in the subordinate legislation is updated.

5517. Local authorities–Fire services–Consequential modifications

FIRE (SCOTLAND) ACT 2005 (CONSEQUENTIAL PROVISIONS AND MODIFICATIONS) ORDER 2005, SI 2005 2060 (S.7); made under the Scotland Act 1998 s.104, s.112, s.113, s.114. In force: in accordance with Art.1 (2); £3.00.

This Order amends the Pensions (Increase) Act 1971, the Social Security (Employed Earners' Employments for Industrial Injuries Purposes) Regulations 1975 (SI 1975 465), the Income Support (General) Regulations 1987 (SI 1987 1967), the Housing Benefit (General) Regulations 1987 (SI 1987 1971), the Road Traffic Act 1988, the Council Tax Benefit (General) Regulations 1992 (SI 1992 1814), the Child Support (Maintenance Assessments and Special Cases)

Regulations 1992 (SI 1992 1815), the Vehicle Excise and Registration Act 1994, the Goods Vehicles (Licensing of Operators) Regulations 1995 (SI 1995 2869), the Jobseeker's Allowance Regulations 1996 (SI 1996 207), the Social Security Benefit (Computation of Earnings) Regulations 1996 (SI 1996 2745), the Local Government Pension Scheme (Scotland) Regulations 1998 (SI 1998 366), the Health and Safety (Enforcing Authority) Regulations 1998 (SI 1998 494), the Scotland Act 1998 (Concurrent Functions) Order 1999 (SI 1999 1592), the Child Support (Maintenance Calculations and Special Cases) Regulations 2000 (SI 2000 155), the State Pension Credit Regulations 2002 (SI 2002 1792), the Regulation of Investigatory Powers (Communications Data) Order 2003 (SI 2003 3172) and the Fire (Scotland) Act 2005. The Order inserts provisions into and makes modifications of the 2005 Act that enable relevant authorities to exercise their powers at sea, in the territorial sea not adjacent to Scotland and beyond the territorial sea of the UK, and to charge for those activities. It applies Part 3 of the 2005 Act (fire safety) to premises occupied by armed forces of the Crown, visiting forces or an international headquarters or defence organisation designated for the purposes of the International Headquarters and Defence Organisations Act 1964, and those which are situated within premises occupied solely for the purposes of the armed forces of the Crown but which are not themselves so occupied. In addition, it applies Part 3 to ships and hovercraft except in respect of normal ship-board activities of a ship's crew which are carried out solely by the crew under the direction of the master. It also provides that the definition of "relevant premises" includes these premises.

5518. Local authorities–Fire services–Firefighters–Pension scheme

FIREFIGHTERS' PENSION SCHEME AMENDMENT (SCOTLAND) ORDER 2005, SSI 2005 566; made under the Fire Services Act 1947 s.26; and the Superannuation Act 1972 s.12, s.16. In force: December 4, 2005; £4.00.

This Order amends the Firefighters' Pension Scheme, as set out in the Firemen's Pension Scheme Order 1992 (SI 1992 129), as it has effect in Scotland. Many of the amendments are consequential on the revocation of the Fire Services Act 1947 and its replacement by the Fire (Scotland) Act 2005. For example, references to fire authorities (unless retained for transitional purposes) are amended to references to fire and rescue authorities, and references to brigades are amended to references to fire and rescue services or, depending on the particular context, to fire and rescue authorities.

5519. Local authorities–Fire services–National framework

FIRE AND RESCUE SERVICES (FRAMEWORK) (SCOTLAND) ORDER 2005, SSI 2005 453; made under the Fire (Scotland) Act 2005 s.40. In force: October 6, 2005; £3.00.

The Fire (Scotland) Act 2005 requires the Scottish Ministers to prepare a document, which must set out priorities and objectives for relevant authorities in connection with the carrying out of their functions and may contain related guidance and such other matters relating to those authorities or those functions. Under the Act, relevant authorities must have regard to the document in carrying out their functions. The Act provides that the document has effect only when brought into effect by the Scottish Ministers by order. This Order gives effect on to the document prepared by the Scottish Ministers and entitled The Fire and Rescue Framework for Scotland 2005.

5520. Local authorities–Fire services–Premises

FIRE (SCOTLAND) ACT 2005 (RELEVANT PREMISES) REGULATIONS, SSI 2005 352; made under the Fire (Scotland) Act 2005 s.78. In force: June 15, 2005; £3.00.

These Regulations modify the definition of relevant premises in the Fire (Scotland) Act 2005 by deleting the reference to construction sites. The effect of this is that, subject to provisions, construction sites and premises which on

July 1, 1999 were of a description specified in the Fire Certificates (Special Premises) Regulations 1976 (SI 1976 2003) are relevant premises for the purposes of Part 3 of the 2005 Act.

5521. Local authorities–Members–Termination–Computation of time limits

[Local Government (Scotland) Act 1973 (c.65) s.34, s.35, s.231.]

F, a councillor, sought reduction of a decision by C, a local authority, that he was no longer a member thereof and that a vacancy was deemed to have occurred on December 19, 2004. F sought declarator that he remained a member of C, suspension ad interim of the decision that a vacancy existed, and interdict and interim interdict against C's chief executive from holding a by election for a new member. C relied on the Local Government (Scotland) Act 1973 s.35 as justification for cessation of F's membership by reason of his non attendance at council meetings for six consecutive months without approval. F had attended a relevant meeting on June 18, 2004 and thereafter on December 30, with some five meetings having been held in between, the first of which was on June 30 with the last on December 19. C submitted that the period of six months began on the date of the last meeting attended which was not an absurd construction of s.35 where there was power in elected members to requisition meetings, a power to approve non attendance, and was compatible with the English legislation; that F's signature and delivery of nomination papers for candidacy in the election on February 14, 2005 constituted resignation of his membership in terms of s.34 in any event; further, that F was barred from insisting upon the orders sought by mora, taciturnity and acquiescence where he presented a summary application in the sheriff court seeking an order against them under s.231 of the Act, interim orders for which were refused as incompetent on February 8, 2005 and the present petition was not presented until February 24, which was sufficient to act as a bar when taken with F's submission of nomination papers.

Held, granting the petition, that (1) F did not cease to be a member of C by virtue of s.35. The period of six consecutive months could not begin until the date of the first meeting which the member failed to attend with the end of the period of failure being identified by the date of the last meeting which F failed to attend before resuming attendance, thus the period of F's failure to attend began on June 30 and ended on December 19 and lasted less than a period of six consecutive months. (2) It would be going too far to construe the nomination papers as constituting a notice of resignation, which was required by s.34 as a matter of form. (3) C had not made out a plea of mora, taciturnity and acquiescence. There was no inevitable inconsistency between F's standing as a candidate in the by election with maintaining membership of C, at least until the election took place, and C could not reasonably infer from the fact that F had delivered nomination papers that he had given up the contention that he was still a councillor.

FOWLER v. FALKIRK COUNCIL 2005 S.L.T. 404, Lord Macfadyen, OH.

5522. Local authorities–Private landlord registration–Advice and assistance

PRIVATE LANDLORD REGISTRATION (ADVICE AND ASSISTANCE) (SCOTLAND) REGULATIONS 2005, SSI 2005 557; made under the Antisocial Behaviour etc. (Scotland) Act 2004 s.99. In force: March 31, 2006; £3.00.

These Regulations make provision for advice that the local authority must provide in connection with the registration of private landlords under the Antisocial Behaviour etc. (Scotland) Act 2004 Pt 8. They provide for general advice on good letting practice to be given by the local authority to every applicant for registration; require the local authority to provide more specific advice on action to take where it is minded to refuse or remove registration but it considers that there is action which the applicant or registered person could take which might lead the authority not to refuse or remove registration; and provide for the local authority to give advice and assistance to occupants where it takes action against the landlord. Where the action is the refusal or removal of registration, that advice is to be given to the occupants of all the landlord's houses that are subject to registration. Where the action is the service of a notice that no rent is payable under s.94 of the Act, the advice is to be given to the occupants of the house concerned.

5523. Local authorities, fire services–Charges

FIRE (CHARGING) (SCOTLAND) ORDER 2005, SSI 2005 343; made under the Fire (Scotland) Act 2005 s.16, s.88. In force: in accordance with Art.1 (1); £3.00.

The Fire (Scotland) Act 2005 provides that Scottish Ministers may, by order, authorise a relevant authority to charge a person of a specified description for any action of a specified description taken by the authority. This Order specifies the actions for which a relevant authority may make a charge and specify the description of the persons who may be subject to the charge.

5524. Local government finance–Housing revenue account–Contribution from general fund

HOUSING REVENUE ACCOUNT GENERAL FUND CONTRIBUTION LIMITS (SCOTLAND) ORDER 2005, SSI 2005 62; made under the Housing (Scotland) Act 1987 s.204. In force: March 15, 2005; £3.00.

This Order provides that local authorities may not include in their estimates for the year 2005/2006 any contribution from their general fund to their housing revenue account.

5525. Local government finance–Revenue support grant–Determination

LOCAL GOVERNMENT FINANCE (SCOTLAND) ORDER 2005, SSI 2005 19; made under the Local Government Finance Act 1992 Sch.12 para.1, Sch.12 para.9. In force: February 4, 2005; £3.00.

This Order, which amends the Local Government Finance (Scotland) Order 2004 (SSI 2004 14), determines the amount of the revenue support grant payable to each local authority in Scotland in respect of the financial year 2005-2006; determines the amount of non-domestic rate income to be distributed to each local authority in respect of that year; and redetermines the amount of the revenue support grant payable to each local authority in respect of the financial year 2004-2005.

MENTAL HEALTH

5526. Adults–Learning disabled persons–Consequential modifications

ADULTS WITH INCAPACITY (SCOTLAND) ACT 2000 (CONSEQUENTIAL MODIFICATIONS) (ENGLAND, WALES AND NORTHERN IRELAND) ORDER 2005, SI 2005 1790 (S.5); made under the Scotland Act 1998 s.104, s.112, s.113. In force: June 30, 2005; £3.00.

This Order makes provision where necessary in consequence of the Adults with Incapacity (Scotland) Act 2000. The 2000 Act amended the Child Support Act 1991 and the Social Security Administration Act 1992 including the definition under these Acts as regards Scotland of a mental health custodian. It also makes identical amendment to these Acts as regards England and Wales; and makes the same amendment to an equivalent Act, the Social Security Administration (Northern Ireland) Act 1992, as regards Northern Ireland.

5527. Court of Session–Mental health–Period for appeals

MENTAL HEALTH (PERIOD FOR APPEAL) REGULATIONS 2005, SSI 2005 416; made under the Mental Health (Care and Treatment) (Scotland) Act 2003 s.324, s.326. In force: October 5, 2005; £3.00.

The Mental Health (Care and Treatment) (Scotland) Act 2003 s.324(7) gives power to the Scottish Ministers to specify the period within which an appeal to the

Court of Session under s.322(2) of the Act is to be made. These Regulations specify that period as 21 days. The Act requires a decision of the Mental Health Tribunal for Scotland to be recorded in a document containing a full statement of the facts found and the reasons for the decision. The period of 21 days is linked in these Regulations either to the date on which the party is informed of the decision or, where the party has requested a copy of the document containing the facts found and reasons for the decision within 7 days of being informed of the decision, the date of receipt of that document.

5528. Court of Session–Mental health–Period for appeals

MENTAL HEALTH (PERIOD FOR APPEAL) (SCOTLAND) (NO.2) REGULATIONS 2005, SSI 2005 441; made under the Mental Health (Care and Treatment) (Scotland) Act 2003 s.324, s.326. In force: October 5, 2005; £3.00.

These Regulations, which revoke the Mental Health (Period for Appeal) Regulations 2005 (SSI 2005 416), specify the period within which an appeal to the Court of Session is to be made as 21 days. The Mental Health (Care and Treatment) (Scotland) Act 2003 requires a decision of the Mental Health Tribunal for Scotland to be recorded in a document containing a full statement of the facts found and the reasons for the decision. The period of 21 days is linked in these Regulations either to the date on which the party is informed of the decision or, where the party has requested a copy of the document containing the facts found and reasons for the decision within 7 days of being informed of the decision, the date of receipt of that document.

5529. Guardianship orders–Application–Medical certificates issued outwith time limit–Meaning of "shall" in Adults with Incapacity s.57(3) and s.57(4) (Scotland) Act 2000

[Adults with Incapacity (Scotland) Act 2000 (asp 4) s.3(1), s.57(3), s.57(4).]

The pursuer (S) lodged a summary application for a guardianship order under the Adults with Incapacity (Scotland) Act 2000. The medical certificates had been completed more than 30 days before the lodging of the application, contrary to s.57(3). S argued that the application should succeed notwithstanding the out of date medical certificates and a late mental health officer's report because there had been unavoidable delays.

Held, granting the application, that to refuse the application would offend against the purpose of the legislation and the fundamental principles set out in the Act. However, s.3(1) could not be interpreted as providing a sheriff with a dispensing power in relation to any failure to comply strictly with the procedures as set out in the Act. Nevertheless, the word "shall" in s.57(3) and s.57(4) was directory rather than mandatory.

STORK, PURSUER 2004 S.C.L.R. 513, Sheriff AD Vannet, Sh Ct (South Strathclyde, Dumfries and Galloway).

5530. Guardianship orders–Mental capacity–Appointment of welfare guardian

[Adults with Incapacity (Scotland) Act 2000 (asp 4) s.1(2), s.59(4).]

The pursuer, a local authority, made applications for a financial guardian and a welfare guardian for an adult (J) whose cognitive ability had been seriously damaged after an accident. J's wife (P) opposed the appointment of the chief social work officer as welfare guardian and sought the appointment herself. There was no opposition to the application for a financial guardian and no dispute that J did require such guardians. J lived in a hospital, but no longer required full time medical nursing care. P disagreed with the local authority's choice of accommodation for J. She argued that she was the best person to understand J's views and was accessible to him and aware of his needs. J and P had been happily married at the time of the accident and had shared the same outlook on life, and P maintained that J would have wanted her to be appointed. The local authority argued that P did not consult others with regard to J's best interests and the court should have regard to the Adults with Incapacity

(Scotland) Act 2000 s.59(4)(c), s.59(4)(d) and s.59(4)(e). The local authority also argued that, if P was to be appointed, the length of the appointment should be restricted to two years.

Held, giving judgment accordingly, that s.59 of the 2000 Act had to be read with s.1(2), which provided that there should not be intervention in the affairs of the mentally incapacitated adult unless the court was satisfied that such intervention would be of benefit. The best interests of the adult had to be borne in mind. The court ought also to have regard to the adult's views at the time he was able to express them. The contract of marriage between J and P and their common values were important. P was accordingly appointed as welfare guardian, but the appointment was restricted to a period of two years because J's accommodation requirements would need to be reassessed at that time. Although P had showed a good understanding of the need for impartiality when dealing with J's affairs, on the evidence there was a risk that she might struggle with the crucial decision of J's accommodation needs, therefore it was necessary to provide a safeguard for J and allow the local authority to make representations if necessary as to whether P should remain guardian at the end of the two year period.

NORTH AYRSHIRE COUNCIL v. JM 2004 S.C.L.R. 956, Sheriff Seith Ireland, Sh Ct (North Strathclyde).

5531. Health–Care and treatment–Code of practice–Discharge of functions

MENTAL HEALTH (CARE AND TREATMENT) (SCOTLAND) ACT 2003 (CODE OF PRACTICE) ORDER 2005, SSI 2005 417; made under the Mental Health (Care and Treatment) (Scotland) Act 2003 s.274. In force: October 5, 2005; £3.00.

This Order brings into force the code of practice issued under the Mental Health (Care and Treatment) (Scotland) Act 2003 which gives guidance to persons discharging functions under that Act. Any person discharging functions under that Act shall have regard (so far as they are applicable to the discharge of those functions by that person) to the provisions of the code.

5532. Health–Care and treatment–Consequential modifications

MENTAL HEALTH (CARE AND TREATMENT) (SCOTLAND) ACT 2003 (MODIFICATION OF SUBORDINATE LEGISLATION) ORDER 2005, SSI 2005 445; made under the Mental Health (Care and Treatment) (Scotland) Act 2003 s.330. In force: October 5, 2005; £3.00.

This Order makes modifications to 35 SIs and 15 SSIs which are consequential and supplemental to the Mental Health (Care and Treatment) (Scotland) Act 2003.

5533. Health–Care and treatment–Forms

MENTAL HEALTH (FORM OF DOCUMENTS) (SCOTLAND) REGULATIONS 2005, SSI 2005 444; made under the Mental Health (Care and Treatment) (Scotland) Act 2003 s.325. In force: October 5, 2005; £3.50.

The Regulations provide for the form of certain documents required or authorised under the Mental Health (Care and Treatment) (Scotland) Act 2003, the information to be set out in the forms and the circumstances in which those forms should be used.

5534. Health–Care and treatment–Modification of enactments

MENTAL HEALTH (CARE AND TREATMENT) (SCOTLAND) ACT 2003 (MODIFICATION OF ENACTMENTS) ORDER 2005, SSI 2005 465; made under the Mental Health (Care and Treatment) (Scotland) Act 2003 s.330. In force: September 27, 2005; £3.50.

This Order, which amends 34 UK Acts and 5 Acts of the Scottish Parliament, makes modification (including, where appropriate, repeals) to enactments having effect in Scotland. These modifications are consequential and supplemental to the Mental Health (Care and Treatment) (Scotland) Act 2003. The Order also makes modification to the 2003 Act to ensure that the purposes of the 2003 Act may be fully achieved and that full effect is given to the provisions of the Act.

5535. Health–Care and treatment–Nurses–Prescribed persons

MENTAL HEALTH (CLASS OF NURSE) (SCOTLAND) REGULATIONS 2005, SSI 2005 446; made under the Mental Health (Care and Treatment) (Scotland) Act 2003 s.299. In force: October 5, 2005; £3.00.

These Regulations prescribe the class of nurse who is empowered under the Mental Health (Care and Treatment) (Scotland) Act 2003 to detain a person already being treated in hospital. The class of nurse prescribed is a mental health or learning disabilities nurse registered in Sub-Part 1 of the Nurses' Part of the register kept in accordance with the Nursing and Midwifery Order 2001 (SI 2002 253).

5536. Health–Care and treatment–Nurses–Revocation

MENTAL HEALTH (CLASS OF NURSE) (SCOTLAND) REVOCATION ORDER 2005, SSI 2005 447; made under the Mental Health (Scotland) Act 1984 s.25. In force: in accordance with Art.1; £3.00.

This Order revokes the Mental Health (Class of Nurse) (Scotland) Order 1994 (SI 1994 1675) immediately before October 5, 2005. This avoids this Order being deemed to have effect on and after October 5, 2005 as if made under the Mental Health (Care and Treatment) (Scotland) Act 2003 s.299 by virtue of that Act.

5537. Health–Care and treatment–Transition of patients

MENTAL HEALTH (CARE AND TREATMENT) (SCOTLAND) ACT 2003 (TRANSITIONAL AND SAVINGS PROVISIONS) ORDER 2005, SSI 2005 452; made under the Mental Health (Care and Treatment) (Scotland) Act 2003 s.332. In force: October 5, 2005; £4.00.

This Order makes transitional and savings provisions in connection with the transition of patients to the regime created by the Mental Health (Care and Treatment) (Scotland) Act 2003.

5538. Health–Designated medical practitioners–Fees

MENTAL HEALTH (FEE PAYABLE TO DESIGNATED MEDICAL PRACTITIONERS) (SCOTLAND) REGULATIONS 2005, SSI 2005 175; made under the Mental Health (Care and Treatment) (Scotland) Act 2003 s.233. In force: October 5, 2005; £3.00.

These Regulations prescribe the fee payable to designated medical practitioners for discharge of their functions under the Mental Health (Care and Treatment) (Scotland) Act 2003 Pt.16.

5539. Health–Designated medical practitioners–Fees

MENTAL HEALTH (FEE PAYABLE TO DESIGNATED MEDICAL PRACTITIONERS) (SCOTLAND) (NO.2) REGULATIONS 2005, SSI 2005 412; made under the Mental Health (Care and Treatment) (Scotland) Act 2003 s.233. In force: October 5, 2005; £3.00.

These Regulations, which revoke the Mental Health (Fee Payable to Designated Medical Practitioners) (Scotland) Regulations 2005 (SI 2005 175), prescribe the fee payable to designated medical practitioners for discharge of their functions under the Mental Health (Care and Treatment) (Scotland) Act 2003 Pt.16. The Regulations set the fee at £141.56.

5540. Health–Mental Welfare Commission for Scotland–Authorised persons–Qualifications

MENTAL WELFARE COMMISSION FOR SCOTLAND (AUTHORISED PERSONS) REGULATIONS 2005, SSI 2005 205; made under the Mental Health (Care and Treatment) (Scotland) Act 2003 s.15. In force: October 5, 2005; £3.00.

The Mental Health (Care and Treatment) (Scotland) Act 2003 empowers a person authorised by the Mental Welfare Commission for Scotland to carry out in private a medical examination of a patient. It provides that an authorised person shall be a medical commissioner or a member of staff of the Commission who has such qualifications and experience and who has undertaken such training as may be prescribed by regulations. These Regulations prescribe the qualifications and experience required of those members of staff.

5541. Health–Mental Welfare Commission for Scotland–Provision of facilities–Prescribed persons

MENTAL WELFARE COMMISSION FOR SCOTLAND (PRESCRIBED PERSONS) REGULATIONS 2005, SSI 2005 176; made under the Mental Health (Care and Treatment) (Scotland) Act 2003 s.17. In force: October 5, 2005; £3.00.

The Mental Health (Care and Treatment) (Scotland) Act 2003 provides that specified persons shall provide to the Mental Welfare Commission for Scotland, or a person authorised by the Commission, all facilities necessary to enable the Commission, or the authorised person, to discharge their functions under the Act. The Scottish Ministers are empowered to prescribe persons who must provide the Commission, or an authorised person with such necessary facilities. These Regulations prescribe those additional persons as any persons who provide a Health Board, a Special Health Board or a local authority with services in connection with any of the functions of those bodies under the Act under contract or by arrangement.

5542. Medical commissioners–Mental Welfare Commission–Appointment

MENTAL WELFARE COMMISSION FOR SCOTLAND (APPOINTMENT OF MEDICAL COMMISSIONERS) REGULATIONS 2005, SSI 2005 261; made under the Mental Health (Care and Treatment) (Scotland) Act 2003 Sch.1 para.3. In force: October 5, 2005; £3.00.

The Mental Health (Care and Treatment) (Scotland) Act 2003 provides for the appointment of a minimum of three persons to serve as medical commissioners of the Mental Welfare Commission for Scotland. These Regulations list the qualifications and experience required of those persons.

5543. Medical examinations–Conflict of interest

MENTAL HEALTH (CONFLICT OF INTEREST) (SCOTLAND) REGULATIONS 2005, SSI 2005 262; made under the Mental Health (Care and Treatment) (Scotland) Act 2003 s.44, s.47, s.58. In force: October 5, 2005; £3.00.

These Regulations provide for the circumstances where there is, or is not, to be taken to be a conflict of interest, and where such a conflict of interest is permitted, in relation to certain medical examinations carried out under the Mental Health (Care and Treatment) (Scotland) Act 2003.

5544. Medical examinations–Conflict of interest

MENTAL HEALTH (CONFLICT OF INTEREST) (SCOTLAND) (NO.2) REGULATIONS 2005, SSI 2005 380; made under the Mental Health (Care and Treatment) (Scotland) Act 2003 s.44, s.47, s.58. In force: October 5, 2005; £3.00.

These Regulations replace and revoke the Mental Health (Conflict of Interest) (Scotland) Regulations 2005 (SSI 2005 262). The Regulations provide for the circumstances where there is, or is not, to be taken to be a conflict of interest, and where such a conflict of interest is permitted, in relation to certain medical examinations carried out under the Mental Health (Care and Treatment) (Scotland) Act 2003. They provide for the circumstances where there is to be taken to be a conflict of interest in relation to medical examinations to be carried out for the purpose of the granting of a short term detention certificate and an extension certificate; provide that specified circumstances are not to be taken to cause a conflict of interest where delay in carrying out the examination would involve a serious risk to health, safety or welfare of the patient or to the safety of others; provide for the circumstances where there is to be taken to be a conflict of interest in relation to medical examinations carried out in connection with an application for a compulsory treatment order; and provide that, notwithstanding a conflict in certain circumstances, the medical examinations may be carried out where delay would involve a serious risk to health, safety or welfare of the patient or to the safety of others.

5545. Medical treatment—Certificates

MENTAL HEALTH (CERTIFICATES FOR MEDICAL TREATMENT) (SCOTLAND) REGULATIONS 2005, SSI 2005 443; made under the Mental Health (Care and Treatment) (Scotland) Act 2003 s.245, s.246, s.325. In force: October 5, 2005; £3.00.

These Regulations prescribe the contents of the forms to be used for giving certificates in respect of the patient's consent to medical treatment and the patient's best interests with regard to giving that treatment.

5546. Medical treatment—Compulsion order—Part 9 care plans

MENTAL HEALTH (CONTENT AND AMENDMENT OF PART 9 CARE PLANS) (SCOTLAND) REGULATIONS 2005, SSI 2005 312; made under the Mental Health (Care and Treatment) (Scotland) Act 2003 s.137. In force: October 5, 2005; £3.00.

The Mental Health (Care and Treatment) (Scotland) Act 2003 provides that where a compulsion order has been made in respect of a patient, the patient's responsible medical officer shall, as soon as practicable after appointment, prepare a Part 9 care plan relating to the patient and include it in the patient's medical records. The Act requires the Part 9 care plan to record the medical treatment which it is proposed to give and which is being given to the patient while the patient is subject to the compulsory treatment order; and such other information relating to the care of the patient as may be prescribed. These Regulations prescribe this information and prescribe the circumstances in which the patient's responsible medical officer is required to amend the patient's Part 9 care plan.

5547. Medical treatment—Compulsory treatment order—Care plans

MENTAL HEALTH (CONTENT AND AMENDMENT OF CARE PLANS) (SCOTLAND) REGULATIONS 2005, SSI 2005 309; made under the Mental Health (Care and Treatment) (Scotland) Act 2003 s.76. In force: October 5, 2005; £3.00.

The Mental Health (Care and Treatment) (Scotland) Act 2003 provides that where a compulsory treatment order has been made in respect of a patient, the patient's responsible medical officer shall, as soon as possible after appointment, prepare a care plan relating to the patient and include it in the patient's medical records. It requires the care plan to set out (a) the medical treatment which it is proposed to give and which is being given to the patient while the patient is subject to the compulsory treatment order; and (b) such other information relating to the care of the patient as may be prescribed. These Regulations prescribe this other information and prescribe the circumstances in which the plan must be amended.

5548. Medical treatment–Consequential provisions

MENTAL HEALTH (CARE AND TREATMENT) (SCOTLAND) ACT 2003 (CONSEQUENTIAL PROVISIONS) ORDER 2005, SI 2005 2078 (S.9); made under the Scotland Act 1998 s.104, s.112, s.113. In force: in accordance with Art.1 (1) (2); £4.00.

This Order amends the Representation of the People Act 1983, the Mental Health Act 1983, the Mental Health (Hospital, Guardianship and Consent to Treatment) Regulations 1983 (SI 1983 893), the Mental Health (Scotland) Act 1984, the Insolvency Act 1986, the Mental Health (Northern Ireland) Order 1986 (SI 1986 595), the Income Support (General) Regulations 1987 (SI 1987 1967), the Housing Benefit (General) Regulations 1987 (SI 1987 1971), the Income and Corporation Taxes Act 1988, the Children Act 1989, the Insolvency (Northern Ireland) Order 1989 (SI 1989 2405), the National Health Service Trusts (Membership and Procedure) Regulations 1990 (SI 1990 2024), the Radioactive Substances (Hospitals) Exemption Order 1990 (SI 1990 2512), the Income Tax (Building Societies) (Dividends and Interest) Regulations 1990 (SI 1990 2231), the Income Tax (Deposit-Takers) (Interest Payments) Regulations 1990 (SI 1990 2232), the Savings Certificates Regulations 1991 (SI 1991 1031), the Savings Certificates (Children's Bonus Bonds) Regulations 1991 (SI 1991 1407), the Social Security (Attendance Allowance) Regulations 1991 (SI 1991 2740), the Social Security (Disability Living Allowance) Regulations 1991 (SI 1991 2890), the Social Security Contributions and Benefits Act 1992, the Council Tax Benefit (General) Regulations 1992 (SI 1992 1814), the Child Support (Maintenance Assessments and Special Cases) Regulations 1992 (SI 1992 1815), the Redundancy Payments (National Health Service) (Modification) Order 1993 (SI 1993 3167), the Jobseeker's Allowance Regulations 1996 (SI 1996 207), the Courts-Martial and Standing Civilian Courts (Army and Royal Air Force) (Additional Powers on Trial of Civilians) Regulations 1997 (SI 1997 579), the Individual Savings Account Regulations 1998 (SI 1998 1870), the Immigration and Asylum Act 1999, the Asylum Support Regulations 2000 (SI 2000 704), the Child Support (Maintenance Calculations and Special Cases) Regulations 2000 (SI 2001 155), the Nationality, Immigration and Asylum Act 2002, the State Pension Credit Regulations 2002 (SI 2002 1792), the Sexual Offences Act 2003, the Child Benefit (General) Regulations 2003 (SI 2003 493), the Guardian's Allowance (General) Regulations 2003 (SI 2003 495), the Community Care, Services for Carers and Children's Services (Direct Payments) (England) Regulations 2003 (SI 2003 762), the Communications (Television Licensing) Regulations 2004 (SI 2004 692) and the Community Care, Services for Carers and Children's Services (Direct Payments) (Wales) Regulations 2004 (SI 2004 1748). The Order makes provision consequential on the Mental Health (Care and Treatment) (Scotland) Act 2003, principally in respect of the law of England and Wales and Northern Ireland to provide for the reception of patients from Scotland and the removal of patients to Scotland. It provides that where patients are removed from Scotland to England and Wales they will become subject to the measure in England and Wales which most closely corresponds to the measure to which the patient was subject in Scotland. Where the patient is subject to a prison sentence the sentence will be treated as if it were imposed in a court in England and Wales.

5549. Medical treatment–Safeguards

MENTAL HEALTH (MEDICAL TREATMENT SUBJECT TO SAFEGUARDS) (SECTION 234) (SCOTLAND) REGULATIONS 2005, SSI 2005 291; made under the Mental Health (Care and Treatment) (Scotland) Act 2003 s.234. In force: October 5, 2005; £3.00.

These Regulations specify medical treatment which may be given to a patient under the Mental Health (Care and Treatment) (Scotland) Act 2003 only in accordance with the safeguards contained in s.235 or s.236 of that Act. The Regulations specify "deep brain stimulation" as such a medical treatment.

5550. Medical treatment—Safeguards

MENTAL HEALTH (MEDICAL TREATMENT SUBJECT TO SAFEGUARDS) (SECTION 237) (SCOTLAND) REGULATIONS 2005, SSI 2005 292; made under the Mental Health (Care and Treatment) (Scotland) Act 2003 s.237. In force: October 5, 2005; £3.00.

The Mental Health (Care and Treatment) (Scotland) Act 2003 requires that types of medical treatment mentioned in that section, or in regulations made under it, may be given to a patient only in accordance with the safeguards contained in s.238 or s.239 of that Act. The Regulations specify "transcranial magnetic stimulation" and "vagus nerve stimulation" as such medical treatments.

5551. Medical treatment—Safeguards

MENTAL HEALTH (SAFEGUARDS FOR CERTAIN INFORMAL PATIENTS) (SCOTLAND) REGULATIONS 2005, SSI 2005 401; made under the Mental Health (Care and Treatment) (Scotland) Act 2003 s.244. In force: October 5, 2005; £3.00.

These Regulations specify types of medical treatment which may be given to patients under the Mental Health (Care and Treatment) (Scotland) Act 2003, and provide that such treatment may only be given in accordance with certain safeguards. They prescribe the conditions which must be satisfied before medical treatment may be given to the patient; and list the types of medical treatment as electro-convulsive therapy, transcranial magnetic stimulation and vagus nerve.

5552. Medical treatment—Social circumstances report

MENTAL HEALTH (SOCIAL CIRCUMSTANCES REPORTS) (SCOTLAND) REGULATIONS 2005, SSI 2005 310; made under the Mental Health (Care and Treatment) (Scotland) Act 2003 s.231. In force: October 5, 2005; £3.00.

These Regulations prescribe the contents of a social circumstances report which is provided for in the Mental Health (Care and Treatment) (Scotland) Act 2003.

5553. Mental Health (Care and Treatment) (Scotland) Act 2003 (asp 13)— Commencement No.4 Amendment Order

MENTAL HEALTH (CARE AND TREATMENT) (SCOTLAND) ACT 2003 (COMMENCEMENT NO.4) AMENDMENT ORDER 2005, SSI 2005 375 (C.16); made under the Mental Health (Care and Treatment) (Scotland) Act 2003 s.333. Commencement details: bringing into force various provisions of the 2003 Act on October 5, 2005; £3.00.

This Order amends the Mental Health (Care and Treatment) (Scotland) Act 2003 (Commencement No.4) Order 2005 (SSI 2005 161) by extending those provisions of the Mental Health (Care and Treatment) (Scotland) Act 2003 which are excluded from commencement on October 5, 2005.

5554. Mental Health (Care and Treatment) (Scotland) Act 2003 (asp 13)— Commencement No.4 Amendment Order

MENTAL HEALTH (CARE AND TREATMENT) (SCOTLAND) ACT 2003 (COMMENCEMENT NO.4) AMENDMENT (NO.2) ORDER 2005, SSI 2005 459 (C.23); made under the Mental Health (Care and Treatment) (Scotland) Act 2003 s.333. In force: September 22, 2005; £3.00.

This Order amends the Mental Health (Care and Treatment) (Scotland) Act 2003 (Commencement No.4) Order 2005 (SSI 2005 161) to add a provision of the Mental Health (Care and Treatment) (Scotland) Act 2003 to the provisions of the Act which are excepted from commencing on October 5, 2005. It provides that s.101 (2) (b) of the Act should not commence on October 5, 2005.

5555. Mental Health (Care and Treatment) (Scotland) Act 2003 (asp 13)– Commencement No.4 Order

MENTAL HEALTH (CARE AND TREATMENT) (SCOTLAND) ACT 2003 (COMMENCEMENT NO.4) ORDER 2005, SSI 2005 161 (C.6); made under the Mental Health (Care and Treatment) (Scotland) Act 2003 s.333. Commencement details: bringing into force various provisions of the 2003 Act on March 21, 2005, October 5, 2005 and January 6, 2006; £3.00.

This Order appoints dates for the coming into force of the remaining provisions of the Mental Health (Care and Treatment) (Scotland) Act 2003.

5556. Mental hospitals–Withholding postal packets–Specified persons

MENTAL HEALTH (DEFINITION OF SPECIFIED PERSON: CORRESPONDENCE) (SCOTLAND) REGULATIONS 2005, SSI 2005 466; made under the Mental Health (Care and Treatment) (Scotland) Act 2003 s.281. In force: October 5, 2005; £3.00.

The Mental Health (Care and Treatment) (Scotland) Act 2003 s.271 provides that a postal packet sent to or by a specified person may in certain circumstances be withheld by the managers of the hospital. These Regulations specify those conditions.

5557. Mental hospitals–Withholding postal packets–Specified persons

MENTAL HEALTH (SPECIFIED PERSONS' CORRESPONDENCE) (SCOTLAND) REGULATIONS 2005, SSI 2005 408; made under the Mental Health (Care and Treatment) (Scotland) Act 2003 s.281, s.282, s.283. In force: October 5, 2005; £3.00.

These Regulations make provision with respect to the power under the Mental Health (Care and Treatment) (Scotland) Act 2003 for postal packets sent to or by detained patients to be withheld by hospital managers. The patients must be specified persons in terms of Regulations made under the 2003 Act. The Regulations add the Scottish Information Commissioner to the list of persons from whom postal packets sent by a specified person may not be withheld and whose postal packets sent to specified persons may not be withheld; oblige hospital managers who withhold a postal packet to take all reasonable steps to make the patient aware of the right to apply for a review of the decision to withhold the postal packet and to ensure that the patient can make use of independent advocacy services in connection with any such application; and provide for the intimation to the hospital managers of an application to the Mental Welfare Commission for Scotland to review the decision to withhold a postal packet.

5558. Mental patients–Cross border transfers

MENTAL HEALTH (CROSS-BORDER TRANSFER: PATIENTS SUBJECT TO DETENTION REQUIREMENT OR OTHERWISE IN HOSPITAL) (SCOTLAND) REGULATIONS 2005, SSI 2005 467; made under the Mental Health (Care and Treatment) (Scotland) Act 2003 s.290, s.326. In force: October 5, 2005; £4.00.

The Mental Health (Care and Treatment) (Scotland) Act 2003 provides for the transfer of patients subject to a detention requirement or otherwise in hospital from Scotland and for patients subject to corresponding measures in England, Wales, Northern Ireland, the Isle of Man or the Channel Islands to be received in Scotland. These Regulations make provision for those transfers to take place.

5559. Mental patients–Use of telephones

MENTAL HEALTH (USE OF TELEPHONES) (SCOTLAND) REGULATIONS 2005, SSI 2005 468; made under the Mental Health (Care and Treatment) (Scotland) Act 2003 s.284. In force: October 5, 2005; £3.00.

The Mental Health (Care and Treatment) (Scotland) Act 2003 s.284 provides for regulation of the use of telephones by such persons detained in a hospital as may be specified in Regulations. These Regulations specify the persons whose use of telephones may be regulated and the conditions of use.

5560. Mental Welfare Commission for Scotland–Functions–Procedure and delegation

MENTAL WELFARE COMMISSION FOR SCOTLAND (PROCEDURE AND DELEGATION OF FUNCTIONS) REGULATIONS 2005, SSI 2005 411; made under the Mental Health (Care and Treatment) (Scotland) Act 2003 Sch.1 para.8. In force: October 5, 2005; £3.00.

These Regulations make provision concerning the proceedings of, and the delegation of functions by, the Mental Welfare Commission for Scotland. In particular, they make provision for the appointment and composition of committees and sub committees for purposes determined by the Commission and its committees respectively and for the procedure of the Commission, its committees and sub committees, including the calling and chairing of meetings, the constitution of a quorum, the taking of decisions, including voting, the taking and approval of minutes and the suspension of a member from a meeting. Provision is also made for the delegation of functions of the Commission, but excluding certain excepted functions.

5561. Mental Welfare Commission for Scotland–Functions–Procedure and delegation

MENTAL WELFARE COMMISSION FOR SCOTLAND (PROCEDURE AND DELEGATION OF FUNCTIONS) (NO.2) REGULATIONS 2005, SSI 2005 442; made under the Mental Health (Care and Treatment) (Scotland) Act 2003 Sch.1 para.8. In force: October 5, 2005; £3.00.

These Regulations, which revoke the Mental Welfare Commission for Scotland (Procedure and Delegation of Functions) Regulations 2005 (SSI 2005 411), make provision concerning the proceedings of, and the delegation of functions by, the Mental Welfare Commission for Scotland.

5562. Mentally disordered offenders–Absconding

MENTAL HEALTH (ABSCONDING BY MENTALLY DISORDERED OFFENDERS) (SCOTLAND) REGULATIONS 2005, SSI 2005 463; made under the Mental Health (Care and Treatment) (Scotland) Act 2003 s.310. In force: October 5, 2005; £3.00.

The Mental Health (Care and Treatment) (Scotland) Act 2003 makes provision for taking into custody a patient who is subject to a relevant order or direction made under the criminal justice system and who breaches a relevant condition of that order or direction. These Regulations: prescribe the circumstances relating to individual orders or directions in which a patient is liable to be taken into custody; prescribes the persons who may take such patients into custody; prescribe the steps that may be taken with regard to a patient who has been taken into custody with reference to the particular order or direction to which the patient is subject; prescribe the circumstances in which a responsible medical officer must notify certain persons of a patient's unauthorised absence; prescribe the effect of unauthorised absence on the orders or directions to which the patient is subject; provide that the responsible medical officer of a patient subject to a compulsion order (without a restriction order) should notify the Mental Welfare Commission of that patient's unauthorised absence; provide that the responsible medical officer of a patient subject to a compulsion order and also subject to a restriction order, a hospital direction or a transfer for treatment direction should notify the Mental Welfare Commission and the Scottish Ministers of that patient's unauthorised absence; prescribe the effect of unauthorised absence on the orders or directions to which the patient is subject; provide for a review by the responsible medical officer where a patient who absconded was subject to a compulsion order, without a restriction order, and how this review fits with statutory reviews otherwise required under s.139 and s.140 of the 2003 Act; provide for a review by the responsible medical officer where a patient who absconded was subject to a compulsion order and a restriction order, a hospital direction or a transfer for treatment direction and how this review sits with statutory reviews otherwise required under s.182 or s.206 of the 2003 Act; provide for a review of certain other orders and when a patient's responsible medical officer may apply to the court for the order to which the patient is subject to be confirmed, or varied; and provide that a patient's responsible medical officer may revoke a certificate of suspension where a patient has absconded.

5563. Patients-Provision of information-Prescribed times

MENTAL HEALTH (PROVISION OF INFORMATION TO PATIENTS) (PRESCRIBED TIMES) (SCOTLAND) REGULATIONS 2005, SSI 2005 206; made under the Mental Health (Care and Treatment) (Scotland) Act 2003 s.260. In force: October 5, 2005; £3.00.

The Mental Health (Care and Treatment) (Scotland) Act 2003 requires the managers of a hospital, at each of the times specified, to take all reasonable steps to ensure that a patient is supplied with certain materials and is informed of the availability of independent advocacy services. The 2003 Act also applies to a patient who is detained in a hospital by virtue of the Act or the Criminal Procedure (Scotland) Act 1995 or, although not detained in a hospital, is subject to any of the certificates, orders, or directions specified. In addition to the times specified, the Scottish Ministers are empowered to prescribe the times when this should be done. These Regulations prescribe those other times.

5564. Removal orders-Representations

MENTAL HEALTH (REMOVAL ORDER) (SCOTLAND) REGULATIONS 2005, SSI 2005 381; made under the Mental Health (Care and Treatment) (Scotland) Act 2003 s.293. In force: October 5, 2005; £3.00.

These Regulations specify the persons, other than the person who is the subject of the application, who are to be afforded an opportunity by a sheriff to make representations and to lead or produce evidence before an application for a removal order under the Mental Health (Care and Treatment) (Scotland) Act 2003 is determined.

5565. Safety-Specified persons-Designation

MENTAL HEALTH (SAFETY AND SECURITY) (SCOTLAND) REGULATIONS 2005, SSI 2005 464; made under the Mental Health (Care and Treatment) (Scotland) Act 2003 s.286. In force: October 5, 2005; £3.00.

These Regulations authorise measures listed in the Mental Health (Care and Treatment) Act 2003 and provide for the designation of specified persons who are to be subject to the measures to protect the safety and security of themselves and others.

5566. Tribunals-Applications-Documents and reports

MENTAL HEALTH (COMPULSION ORDERS -DOCUMENTS AND REPORTS TO BE SUBMITTED TO THE TRIBUNAL) (SCOTLAND) REGULATIONS 2005, SSI 2005 365; made under the Mental Health (Care and Treatment) (Scotland) Act 2003 s.149, s.158, s.161, s.173. In force: October 5, 2005; £3.00.

The Mental Health (Care and Treatment) (Scotland) Act 2003 establishes the Mental Health Tribunal for Scotland "the Tribunal". These Regulations provide that particular documents must accompany certain types of application to the Tribunal and for reports that the Tribunal may itself require to be prepared and submitted to it in connection with certain applications or a particular determination.

5567. Tribunals–Applications–Documents and reports

MENTAL HEALTH (COMPULSORY TREATMENT ORDERS -DOCUMENTS AND REPORTS TO BE SUBMITTED TO THE TRIBUNAL) (SCOTLAND) REGULATIONS 2005, SSI 2005 366; made under the Mental Health (Care and Treatment) (Scotland) Act 2003 s.92, s.95, s.96, s.109. In force: October 5, 2005; £3.00.

The Mental Health (Care and Treatment) (Scotland) Act 2003 establishes the Mental Health Tribunal for Scotland. These Regulations provide that particular documents must accompany certain types of application to the Tribunal and for reports that the Tribunal may itself require to be prepared and submitted to it in connection with certain applications or references or a particular determination.

5568. Tribunals–Mental Health Tribunal–Practice and procedure

MENTAL HEALTH TRIBUNAL FOR SCOTLAND (PRACTICE AND PROCEDURE) RULES 2005, SSI 2005 420; made under the Mental Health (Care and Treatment) (Scotland) Act 2003 Sch.2 para.10. In force: October 5, 2005; £6.00.

These Rules prescribe the practice and procedure to be followed in proceedings before the Mental Health Tribunal for Scotland created under s.21 and Sch.2 to, the Mental Health (Care and Treatment) (Scotland) Act 2003. The Rules come into force on October 5, 2005.

5569. Tribunals–Mental Health Tribunal–Practice and procedure

MENTAL HEALTH TRIBUNAL FOR SCOTLAND (PRACTICE AND PROCEDURE) (NO.2) RULES 2005, SSI 2005 519; made under the Mental Health (Care and Treatment) (Scotland) Act 2003 s.21, s.326, Sch.2 para.10. In force: November 14, 2005; £6.50.

These Rules, which revoke the Mental Health Tribunal for Scotland (Practice and Procedure) Rules 2005 (SSI 2005 420), prescribe the practice and procedure to be followed in proceedings before the Mental Health Tribunal for Scotland created under the Mental Health (Care and Treatment) (Scotland) Act 2003.

5570. Books

McManus, J.J.; Thomson, Lindsay–Mental Health and Scots Law in Practice. Hardback: £60.00. ISBN 0 414 01475 8. W.Green & Son.

MOVEABLE PROPERTY

5571. Books

Miller, Carey; Irvine, David–Corporeal Moveables in Scots Law. Hardback: £135.00. ISBN 0 414 01400 6. W.Green & Son.

NEGLIGENCE

5572. Duty of care–Auditors–Absence of disclaimer–Extent of liability

[Companies Act 1985 (c.6) s.310.]

A bank brought an action of damages against a firm of accountants, alleging breach of a duty of care owed by the defenders to the pursuers in auditing the accounts of a company. The pursuers averred that to the defenders' knowledge the company, and a subsidiary of which the pursuers were also principal bankers, required a substantial overdraft facility from the pursuers in order to trade, the pursuers required to see monthly management accounts and relied on the annual audited accounts as supporting the accuracy of these statements, the pursuers had originally provided finance on the basis of a business plan prepared by the defenders and took a substantial equity stake in the company, and further, that the defenders were vicariously liable for a fraud committed by an employee, M, who had been seconded to act as the company's controller. The Lord Ordinary allowed proof before answer under exclusion of the case on vicarious liability. The defenders reclaimed and the pursuers cross appealed. The main issues were whether the pursuers had relevantly averred the existence of a duty of care on the defenders' part; the significance, if any, of the defenders' failure to issue a disclaimer of liability in respect of the audited accounts; whether the pursuers had pled a relevant claim for damages for losses sustained through their lending to the subsidiary company; and whether the pursuers had pled a relevant case of vicarious liability on the defenders' part for M's fraudulence.

Held, refusing the reclaiming motion, allowing the cross appeal and remitting the case to the Outer House for proof before answer on the whole record, that (1) the element of positive intention was not a sine qua non of the existence of a duty of care and the pursuers were entitled to inquiry on the averments made. (2) The absence of a disclaimer might be a relevant circumstance pointing to an assumption of responsibility in respect of the information or advice tendered, further the Companies Act 1985 s.310, which provided that a disclaimer made by an auditor was void, was irrelevant to this case where it applied to claims against the auditors by the company. (3) It could not be said, on any view, that the defenders' liability could not extend to the losses sustained by the pursuers in consequence of their lending to the subsidiary. (4) The Lord Ordinary ought not to have definitively concluded, without inquiry, that M's job title as financial controller of the company implied a responsibility subordinate only to the board thus rendering him in the company's pro hac vice employment; similarly, the Lord Ordinary was not entitled to conclude from the pleadings that even if M remained in the defenders' employment, the pursuers' pleadings were irrelevant in failing to disclose that his wrongdoing was so closely connected with his employment with the defenders that it was fair and just to hold them vicariously liable. (Per Lady Cosgrove) In a case such as this when all the facts were not known, when they and the legal principles turning on them were complex and the law, as here, was in a state of development, it could only be in a rare and exceptional case that the action could be disposed of on relevancy, of which this was not one.

ROYAL BANK OF SCOTLAND PLC v. BANNERMAN JOHNSTONE MacLAY 2005 S.C. 437, Lord Gill L.J.C., Lord Osborne, Lady Cosgrove, 2 Div.

5573. Duty of care–Fire services–Standard of care required of recruit

S, an instructor at the Scottish Fire Training School, sought damages from H, the employers of a fire services' recruit, for injuries sustained to his right leg during a football match. The football match was an organised tradition at the end of the 16 week training course. S averred that shortly after the match started, the recruit high tackled him, striking him with both feet in the middle of his right lower leg. S submitted that it was the recruit's duty to take all reasonable care, in the circumstances in which he found himself, for the safety of others. Parties were agreed that recklessness was not the test. S's position was that the level of care was that which was appropriate in the circumstances whereas H's primary position on liability was that what had occurred had been an unfortunate incident and that momentary carelessness, if proved, was not negligence in the circumstances. Further, H sought to distinguish *Lister v. Hesley Hall Ltd* [2001] UKHL 22, [2002] 1 A.C. 215, [2001] C.L.Y. 5359 on its facts on the question of their vicarious liability, stressing the informal nature of the match, and submitting that the present case failed the test that the act of the employee had to be committed in the course of the employer's business, so as to form part of it, and not merely coincidental in time with it. Damages were agreed at £6,000.

Held, assoilzieing H, that (1) S had established his material averments about the tackle. Very soon after the beginning of the match the ball was passed to S, who passed the ball forward and put his right foot on the ground; the recruit, who had started to run towards S before he passed the ball, was unable to stop himself from colliding with S and struck him with moderately severe force on the right lower leg with his booted foot; the recruit's leg was straight and the studs of his boot were showing and the court's finding that he struck S with one foot rather than two was not a significant modification of the latter's case. (2) The authorities demonstrated that the standard of care required of the recruit was that which was appropriate in all the circumstances and in determining liability, the circumstances were of crucial importance. (3) In a football match, any player when tackling an opponent might be guilty of an error of judgment and where that error caused injury to an opponent, the test of liability was whether the error was one that a reasonable player would not have made. (4) It was for S to show that the recruit had committed an error of judgment going beyond what might reasonably be regarded as excusable and in the absence of reliable, detailed, skilled and objective eyewitness evidence he had failed to discharge that burden, *Lister* considered.

SHARP v. HIGHLAND AND ISLANDS FIRE BOARD; *sub nom.* SHARP v. HIGHLANDS FIRE BOARD 2005 S.L.T. 855, Lord Macphail, OH.

5574. Duty of care – Local authorities powers and duties – Home help tripping on door sill – Relevancy

M, a home help, sought damages from N, her local authority employers, for injuries sustained when, on leaving a client's house, she tripped on the sill at the top of a flight of external steps and fell to the ground. M claimed against F in their capacity both as landlords and employers. She averred that F had installed a new door, frame and sill at the premises a few months prior to her accident, the latter of which was approximately three inches high and did not have a bevelled edge, and that the tenant had attended F's housing offices following installation to complain that the sill was too high and request the provision of a handrail for fear that he would fall. At procedure roll, F sought dismissal of the action as irrelevant, submitting that (1) there was not enough on record to establish that the physical characteristics of the locus, when taken together, constituted an "obvious danger"; (2) on the pleadings, there was no adequate basis on which the court could conclude that there was a duty incumbent on them to take the precautions desiderated where it was not clear why a reduction in height would qualify as an obvious precaution, nor was it clear what difference either a bevelled edge or handrail would have made; (3) the tenant's complaint was not enough to alert them to an obvious danger; (4) it was impossible to tell when the tenant's complaint had been made or to whom, which was important in order to assess the time available to them to take any steps since the precautions desiderated were structural alterations requiring time and an allocation of resources, to which an instantaneous response could not be expected.

Held, allowing proof before answer, that (1) M's pleadings had to be construed as a whole and they described not only several physical features at the locus arguably giving rise to a tripping hazard, but also a specific complaint made by the tenant that the door sill was too high and that he was frightened he would fall, which, if proved, were sufficient to attribute to N the necessary knowledge of a risk of injury, and the question would arise whether N had taken reasonable care for the safety of those using the house. (2) M had given clear notice of the content of the complaint, the person who made the complaint, the locus about which the complaint was made, and one precautionary measure which had been specifically requested, and it was sufficient for the purposes of a proof that M averred that the complaint was made "shortly after" installation of the new door and sill, while the accident occurred a "few months" thereafter, which provided M with a stateable case that N had a reasonable period in which to take precautionary measures.

MUIR v. NORTH AYRSHIRE COUNCIL 2005 S.L.T. 963, Lady Paton, OH.

5575. Duty of care—Medical treatment—Consultant psychiatrist—Duty to patient's father—Relevancy

F, a father, sought damages from a health board in respect of alleged negligence by Y, a consultant psychiatrist, in the treatment of his daughter X. X was admitted to a psychiatric unit for treatment following complaints of severe abdominal pains. F contended that X underwent recovered memory therapy, as a result of which she alleged that F and others had sexually abused her. X subsequently withdrew the allegations. F averred that Y had failed in his duty to act with reasonable care to avoid foreseeable harm to him resulting from his treatment of X: in particular, it was Y's duty to assess the likely veracity of any allegations of abuse resulting from the therapy, discuss any alleged abuse with the pursuer before encouraging X to speak to her siblings, and refrain from indicating, without proper assessment and investigation of the allegations, a belief to X's family members that they were probably true. F submitted that he was offering to prove that Y had stepped outside the treatment and management of X, that by encouraging X to confide in her relatives, he had voluntarily assumed a responsibility to them, that he was seeking to suggest that Y had fallen below the standards of an ordinary competent psychiatrist in the circumstances, and that monetary compensation for interference with rights and interests was recognised by law. Negligent representation damaging to a person's reputation could be made the subject of an action for negligence and solatium for distress could be claimed in an action of damages for personal injury.

Held, dismissing the action, that (1) there was nothing to suggest, at least with sufficient clarity to entitle F to a proof, that when Y allegedly told family members of his belief in the history of abuse that no longer formed part of his management and treatment of his patient, or part of the exercise of a perceived public duty to protect her from further harm, nor was there anything to clearly indicate circumstances in which it could be said that Y came at any stage into a special relationship with F such that he owed a duty to him as well as to X. (2) The appropriate means of redress where mere damage to reputation was caused by a statement or statements was an action of defamation and an action of damages based on a failure to fulfil a common law duty of care, without averment of any relevant consequential personal injury, was not a relevant head of loss. Further, insofar as F's averments of distress were designed to support a specific head of loss, they too were irrelevant in the absence of an identifiable psychiatric or psychological condition or illness.

FAIRLIE v. PERTH AND KINROSS HEALTHCARE NHS TRUST 2004 S.L.T. 1200, Lord Kingarth, OH.

5576. Duty of care—Occupiers liability—Unincorporated associations—Action brought against club by member

[Occupiers Liability (Scotland) Act 1960 (c.30) s.2(1).]

The pursuer (H), a member of a go karting club who had sustained serious injuries when a cart he was test driving collided with a wall on the circuit owned by the first defenders (W), appealed against the dismissal of his of his action against W and five named officials representing W. The court below had, in the alternative, allowed a proof before answer against the five persons as individuals and against the second defender regulatory body (R). H argued that he was entitled to name W as defenders pursuant to the Occupiers Liability (Scotland) Act 1960 and because W was liable for negligence on the part of its agents. R cross appealed, contending that it owed no duty to H as the incident had not occurred on a race day.

Held, dismissing the appeal and the cross appeal, that a club or other unincorporated association could be convened as defenders through the addition to its name of certain named individuals in a representative capacity. Where a claim against a club or association was based on delict or negligence there was no basis for the proposition that the liability of members would be other than personal with a claim for relief against whatever funds were held at the time in the name of the club or association. There was no place within the structure of an unincorporated association for the operation, as between the members themselves, of the principle of vicarious liability. The only delictual liabilities that could arise between members of an unincorporated body were those that arose directly from their personal actings as individuals. A recognition that all members of an unincorporated body were principals in a common enterprise was important when considering the effect of s.2(1) of the 1960 Act. Persons to whom duties were owed had to be persons other than the occupier. In the instant case, H was no less an occupier than any of his fellow members, *Prole v. Allen* [1950] 1 All E.R. 476 considered and *McCall v. Dumfries and Galloway Rugby Football Club* 1999 S.C.L.R. 977, [2000] C.L.Y. 5896 disapproved. The question of whether R owed a duty of care to H could not be determined without a hearing of the evidence.

HARRISON v. WEST OF SCOTLAND KART CLUB 2004 S.C. 615, Lord Cullen L.P., Lord Marnoch, Lady Cosgrove, 1 Div.

5577. Professional negligence–Surveyors–Valuation on behalf of lender financing property development–Duty of care in relation to developer

The pursuer (W), a property developer, brought a claim against the defenders (H), a firm of surveyors, for professional negligence. The development, which consisted of six flats, was built with the assistance of funding from a bank (D). D instructed H to provide a valuation of the residential development as forming the basis of a commercial loan. H's valuer (N) valued the resale price of the flats at £225,000 and the costs at £150,000. D made a secured loan of £114,000 to W, who later borrowed a further £30,000. N revalued the flats at £306,000 the same year. The flats were advertised for sale at a total price of £311,000 but failed to sell, whereupon D recalled its loan and reduced the asking price. W argued that H owed it a duty of care when carrying out the valuation and that, but for N's negligent over valuation, the flats would have sold in three months.

Held, granting a decree of absolvitor, that H had not owed a duty of care to W. W was an experienced businessman undertaking a commercial development for profit. He had employed other professionals, such as engineers and architects, and had approached a lender whose business was purely commercial. A commercial surveyor acting on behalf of a bank for loan purposes would not expect a property developer to be relying on that valuation for his sale price and marketing strategy, *Bank of Credit and Commerce International (Overseas) Ltd (In Liquidation) v. Price Waterhouse (No.2)* [1998] Lloyd's Rep. Bank. 85, [1998] C.L.Y. 3921 applied. Furthermore, there was no established practice of commercial lenders passing to potential borrowers valuation reports that the lenders themselves had commissioned. In all the circumstances, it had not been foreseeable that W would rely on N's valuation report, *Smith v. Eric S Bush (A Firm)* [1990] 1 A.C. 831, [1989] C.L.Y. 2566 applied. Even if negligence on the part of H had been established, the failure of the flats to sell could be attributed to factors other than price, such as the state of the property market at the relevant time or the way in which the flats had been advertised and marketed.

WILSON v. DM HALL & SONS [2005] P.N.L.R. 22, Lady Paton, OH.

NUISANCE

5578. Anti social behaviour–Noise pollution–Maximum levels

ANTISOCIAL BEHAVIOUR (NOISE CONTROL) (SCOTLAND) REGULATIONS 2005, SSI 2005 43; made under the Antisocial Behaviour etc. (Scotland) Act 2004 s.48, s.49, s.141. In force: February 28, 2005; £3.00.

These Regulations set down the maximum levels of noise which may be emitted at specified times of the day from property which is subject to the noise nuisance provisions in Part 5 of the Antisocial Behaviour etc. (Scotland) Act 2004. They also approve specified types of device for use in the measurement of noise emitted from relevant property, and contain provisions on the manner in which such devices are to be used and the testing of such devices.

PENOLOGY AND CRIMINOLOGY

5579. Management of Offenders etc. (Scotland) Act 2005 (asp 14)

This Act makes provision for the establishment of community justice authorities; makes further provision for the supervision and care of persons put on probation or released from prison etc.; amends the Prisoners and Criminal Proceedings (Scotland) Act 1993 Part 1, so as to make further provision as respects the release of prisoners on licence; makes further provision as respects the jurisdiction of the Scottish courts in proceedings for offences in relation to the notification requirements of the Sexual Offences Act 2003 Part 2; and makes provision about the recovery of compensation from offenders.

This Act received Royal Assent on December 9, 2005.

PENSIONS

5580. Local government–Paternity and adoption leave

LOCAL GOVERNMENT PENSION SCHEME (SCOTLAND) AMENDMENT REGULATIONS 2005, SSI 2005 293; made under the Superannuation Act 1972 s.7, s.12. In force: June 30, 2005; £4.00.

These Regulations make various amendments to the Local Government Pension Scheme (Scotland) Regulations 1998 (SI 1998 366) to take account of new entitlements to paternity and adoption leave provided for by the Employment Act 2002.

5581. Occupational pensions–Civil partnerships

LOCAL GOVERNMENT PENSIONS ETC. (CIVIL PARTNERSHIP) (SCOTLAND) AMENDMENT REGULATIONS 2005, SSI 2005 554; made under the Superannuation Act 1972 s.7, s.12, s.24. In force: December 5, 2005; £3.00.

These Regulations amend the Local Government (Discretionary Payments and Injury Benefits) (Scotland) Regulations 1998 (SI 1998 192), the Local Government Pension Scheme (Transitional Provisions) (Scotland) Regulations 1998 (SI 1998 364) and the Local Government Pension Scheme (Scotland) Regulations 1998 (SI 1998 366). The amendments provide survivor benefits for same sex partners of Local Government Pension Scheme members or eligible persons where the same sex partners have formed a civil partnership under the terms of the Civil Partnership Act 2004.

5582. Occupational pensions–Local government pension scheme

LOCAL GOVERNMENT PENSION SCHEME (SCOTLAND) AMENDMENT (NO.2) REGULATIONS 2005, SSI 2005 315; made under the Superannuation Act 1972 s.7. In force: June 30, 2005; £3.00.

These Regulations make amendments to the Local Government Pension Scheme (Scotland) Regulations 1998 (SI 1998 366) which are necessary as a result of the dissolution of Scottish Homes. They specify that the City of Edinburgh Council is the administering authority; and place an obligation on Scottish Ministers to make payments to that administering authority, should the actuary appointed by the administering authority determine that such payments are necessary to maintain the solvency of the fund.

5583. Occupational pensions–National Health Service–Compensation– Premature retirement

NATIONAL HEALTH SERVICE (SUPERANNUATION SCHEME, INJURY BENEFITS AND COMPENSATION FOR PREMATURE RETIREMENT) (SCOTLAND) AMENDMENT REGULATIONS 2005, SSI 2005 512; made under the Superannuation Act 1972 s.10, s.12, s.24, Sch.3. In force: November 21, 2005; £4.50.

These Regulations amend the National Health Service Superannuation Scheme (Scotland) Regulations 1995 (SI 1995 365), the National Health Service (Injury Benefits) (Scotland) Regulations 1998 (SI 1998 1594) and the National Health Service (Compensation for Premature Retirement) (Scotland) Regulations 2003 (SSI 2003 344) to take account of the introduction of the new contract for the provision of general medical services, which was introduced on April 1, 2004; and to remove references to National Health Service Trusts and Primary Care NHS Trusts. They also remove references to medical pilot schemes in NHS Scotland which have now ended; include new definitions and amend existing definitions relating to the types of medical services provided and the persons or bodies who provide them; and enable an employee of an out of hours provider that has retrospectively been approved as an employing authority under the terms of the Scheme to opt out of the Scheme during the retrospective period.

5584. Pensions Appeal Tribunals–Route of appeal

PENSIONS APPEAL TRIBUNALS (SCOTLAND) (AMENDMENT) RULES 2005, SSI 2005 152; made under the Pensions Appeal Tribunals Act 1943 Sch.para.5. In force: April 6, 2005; £3.00.

These Rules amend the Pensions Appeal Tribunals (Scotland) Rules 1981 (SI 1981 500) to provide for a new route of appeal from the Pensions Appeal Tribunal to the Social Security Commissioners, who for these purposes are to be known as Pensions Appeal Commissioners.

5585. Superannuation–Teachers–Civil partnerships

TEACHERS' SUPERANNUATION (SCOTLAND) AMENDMENT REGULATIONS 2005, SSI 2005 543; made under the Superannuation Act 1972 s.9, s.12, s.24, Sch.3. In force: December 5, 2005; £3.00.

These Regulations amend the Teachers' Superannuation (Additional Voluntary Contributions) (Scotland) Regulations 1995 (SI 1995 2814), the Teachers (Compensation for Premature Retirement and Redundancy) (Scotland) Regulations 1996 (SI 1996 2317) and the Teachers' Superannuation (Scotland) Regulations 2005 (SSI 2005 393). They make provision following the introduction of the new status of civil partner by the Civil Partnership Act 2004.

PERSONAL INJURY

5586. Measure of damages–Back and neck: whiplash injury: no previous condition

F, male, aged 28 at the date of proof, sustained whiplash injuries when his car collided with the rear of T's car. F suffered discomfort, was absent from work for five days and suffered pain in his neck and back which cleared up within six weeks. He was unable to attend the gym during this period and afterwards was unable to resume the training regime in which he had previously participated. As at the date of proof, he was still unable to resume his former regime without suffering back pain the following day. F could no longer enjoy a long lie in bed at the weekend without suffering 30 minutes of stiffness on rising. The medical evidence indicated that F's condition could take up to two years to resolve completely. The case fell within the description of a relatively moderate neck injury including minor soft tissue injuries in the JSB Guidelines and was close to the top end of awards in this category because of its continuation over an eight month period and future prognosis. Solatium: £1,700.

FAIRLEY v. THOMSON 2004 Rep. L.R. 142, Sheriff JD Allan, Sh Ct (Lothian and Border).

5587. Measure of damages—Back and spine: acceleration or exacerbation of pre-existing symptomatic condition

[Administration of Justice Act 1982 (c.53) s.8.]

The pursuer (P) claimed damages against the defenders (L) in respect of a severe spinal injury which left him confined to a wheelchair. Before the injury, P had had a job that involved considerable amounts of heavy lifting and had suffered bouts of back pain. He had attended two hospitals but neither could diagnose his condition. Shortly thereafter, P collapsed with an acute spinal lesion which resulted in cauda equina, a rare condition commonly producing double incontinence, loss of sexual function and loss of movement in the lower limbs. As a result of the injury, P suffered depression which had a significant chance of recurrence. His employment prospects were limited and declining in view of his disability, use of a wheelchair and the possible need for special facilities. In relation to past loss of earnings, account was taken of the recovery time from surgery and the unlikelihood that P would return to heavy lifting work with overtime, but a broad approach was taken in view of the fact that P had shown resilience and flexibility and might have achieved a supervisory or administrative job within six or nine months. Future loss earnings were arrived at by deducting from P's calculations a sum representing the likelihood of P finding work and continuing until he was 55. This was modestly reduced to reflect the possibility that P would not find work. While there was an agreed figure for accommodation costs based on the formula in *Roberts v. Johnstone* [1989] Q.B. 878, [1989] C.L.Y. 1202, a lower figure was substituted since there was no certainty that P would move house. Even if he did, he might move into rented accommodation, on which there was no evidence as to prices.

Held, assessing damages, that although P was unsuccessful in proving liability in negligence against L, consideration was given to what damages he would have been awarded had his claim succeeded. Solatium: £115,000. Past loss of earnings: £80,000. Future loss of earnings: £192,080. Award for services and care costs under the Administration of Justice Act 1982 s.8: £75,000. Adaptation costs: £9,650. Accommodation costs: £100,000.

PATTERSON v. LANARKSHIRE ACUTE HOSPITALS NHS TRUST 2004 S.C.L.R. 1062, Lord McCluskey, OH.

5588. Measure of damages—Back and spine: no previous condition

[Administration of Justice Act 1982 (c.53) s.8.]

B, a nurse, sought damages for personal injury she sustained whilst at work. B suffered mechanical back pain as a result of lifting boxes. Following the accident, B was confined to the house for several months. She suffered from severe pain and had to rely on her husband to perform household duties, such as vacuum cleaning, shopping, driving, lifting and cooking. B was unable to continue her leisure activities of dancing and hill walking. Her condition did not improve and she had to retire from work. B received treatment in the form of physiotherapy, traction and osteopathy. Further, she was prescribed analgesics by her GP. She was also seen by a consultant in pain management, who gave her steroid injections, and by a rheumatologist. B used a TENS machine for pain relief, although this had a negligible effect. Although the different forms of treatment relieved B's pain in the short term, it always returned. At the date of the hearing B continued to suffer from back pain. Y contended that B had been malingering and submitted video evidence which showed B performing a wide range of activities.

Held, assessing damages, that the evidence provided by B in respect of her back pain did not suggest that she was a malingerer. Solatium (agreed) £15,000; £49,349 for past loss of earnings; £79,690 for future loss of earnings. For loss of pension rights B was awarded £69,300; £6,000 for services under the

Administration of Justice Act 1982 s.8 and £750 for private osteopathic treatment.

BROWN v. YORKHILL NHS TRUST 2004 S.C.L.R. 660, Lord Abernethy, OH.

5589. Measure of damages – Back and spine: no previous condition

[Administration of Justice Act 1982 (c.53) s.8, s.9.]

The pursuer (D), a female aged 40, brought a claim for damages against the defender (G). D was working as a cook in a residential home owned by G when she slipped and fell on her back. Immediately after the fall D was unable to stand, was taken to hospital and prescribed painkillers which were only partly successful. Later diagnosis concluded that she had a soft tissue sprain of the right sacroiliac joint. D had difficulty lifting weights, could not lift her hands above her head and suffered continuous, but varied, pain. D had previously been active and enjoyed walking but after the injury she no longer went out of the house unaccompanied and could not go to the gym, readily use a bus or complete many household tasks. Marital relations were restricted. The prognosis was that, while there would continue to be some improvement and it was unlikely that there would be further deterioration, D would always have a "sensitive back". D returned to work, but after six months her condition deteriorated and she was dismissed. Thereafter, D received invalidity benefit.

Held, assessing damages, that D's claim was unsuccessful because the evidence did not support her claim that the injury occurred as a result of G's negligence. Nevertheless, the court considered what damages would have been awarded had D's claim succeeded. Solatium: £11,000, two thirds allocated to the past. Past loss of earnings: £9,633 per annum to date of proof, subject to deductions with interest at 4 per cent. Future loss of earnings: two further years' earnings plus £600 with a multiplier of 9. Award under Administration of Justice Act 1982 s.8 and s.9: £3,000 (past and future including interest).

COCHRANE v. GAUGHAN; *sub nom.* DALL v. GAUGHAN 2004 S.C.L.R. 1073, Lord Brodie, OH.

5590. Measure of damages – Foot

The pursuer (H), a 42 year old man, sought damages from the defender (D) for injuries suffered in the course of his employment. H, who had not been issued with steel toe capped boots, dropped a 25lb metal pole on his foot. He was taken to hospital, where it was established that he had suffered an undisplaced fracture of the fifth metatarsal bone of the left foot. The foot was plastered and H, unable to work for five weeks, suffered pain and required treatment. During this time he was cared for partly by his mother and his wife. Upon H's return to work, he had to wear loose footwear and initially found driving a lorry difficult. H made a full recovery and liability was admitted.

Held, assessing damages, that this was a modest claim and H was entitled to damages as follows: Solatium: £3,000. Services: £300 including interest.

HEATH v. DARBY GLASS LTD 2004 S.C.L.R. 1093, Sheriff M Croan, Sh Ct (North Strathclyde).

5591. Measure of damages – Hand

[Administration of Justice Act 1982 (c.53) s.8, s.9.]

D, female, aged 21 at the date of the accident, sought damages for personal injury for a serious injury to her dominant hand sustained at work. S had admitted liability, agreed damages and made an interim payment. However, D sought further damages in respect of medical treatment, past loss of earnings, future loss of earnings, travel expenses, and past and future services under the Administration of Justice Act 1982 s.8 and s.9. She suffered from burning and crushing. As a result, she experienced extreme pain. She was required to have several operations. Her hand was disfigured as most of her fingers had been amputated, leaving only her thumb. This caused her embarrassment and also hindered her ability to perform daily tasks to enable independent living. She suffered emotional problems in the form of aggression, depression, bad moods, self harm and dependency. D had worked on a production line in a factory and wanted to work. However, her ability to obtain work was limited as she had left school without any qualifications and had dyslexia.

Held, assessing damages, that sums under the heads claimed would be awarded. Solatium (agreed): £57,500. Past medical treatment: £3,947 (for prosthesis) and £1,600 (associated travel expenses). Future medical treatment: £120,000. Loss of earnings: £22,965. Future loss of earnings: £120,435. Additional travel expenses: £1,000 (past) and £1,000 (future). Past services: £20,000 (s.8) and £5,000 (s.9). Future services: £10,000 (s.8) and £5,000 (s.9).

DONNELLY v. FAS PRODUCTS LTD 2004 S.C.L.R. 678, Lord Brodie, OH.

5592. Measure of damages–Multiple injuries

W, a nursing assistant aged 34, sought damages from B for injuries sustained in a road traffic accident in 1997. W had been a pillion passenger on B's motorbike when it skidded and threw her on to the road. W suffered extensive injuries, some of which resulted in cognitive impairment. Her residual injuries included fatigue, poor short term memory, residual impairments in working memory, divided attention and verbal fluency. W returned to work in 2004 but claimed that the effects of the accident precluded her original intention to qualify as a nurse, with higher levels of earning.

Held, assessing damages, that (1) in all the circumstances £33,000 was appropriate for solatium, 50 per cent to the past. (2) In valuing W's loss of chance to qualify as a nurse, a two stage process should be followed (a) the qualification of her likely earnings (b) an assessment of the chance that she would have qualified. (3) The prospect of W qualifying was assessed at 25 per cent and appropriate award for the loss of that chance was £23,000.

WATT v. BRIDGES 2004 Rep. L.R. 96, Temporary Judge JG Reid Q.C., OH.

5593. Measure of damages–Respiratory organs: asbestos-related

[Damages (Scotland) Act 1976 (c.13) s.1 (4); Administration of Justice Act 1982 (c.53) s.8.]

R, male, aged 78 at the date of death, died as a result of mesothelioma caused by exposure to asbestos. R's widow sought damages from R's former employers, including solatium for R's suffering, for necessary services rendered to him and for loss of society. R had been a life long smoker and after diagnosis in 1998 had deteriorated significantly until his death in 1999. A few months before his death, R required morphine therapy and underwent mood changes, and his wife could no longer cope with him at home. His relationship with his son, daughter and grandchildren also suffered, although they had previously been close. The latter stages of mesothelioma were extremely distressing. R had to give up doing jobs around the house because of breathlessness and lost two stone in weight. By May 1999 he required the use of a wheelchair to go outside the house. R and his wife had been happily married for over 45 years at the time of his death. The medical evidence showed that, without mesothelioma, R's life expectancy would have been five years. The award for solatium reflected the loss of the years of life that R would probably have otherwise enjoyed, making an allowance for his general state of health. In reaching the award for loss of society, reliance was placed on *McLean v. William Denny & Bros Ltd* 2004 S.L.T. 422, *McLean* considered. Solatium: £47,500. Award for services under the Administration of Justice Act 1982 s.8: £5,000. Award for loss of society under the Damages (Scotland) Act 1976 s.1 (4) £28,000.

RYAN v. FAIRFIELD ROWAN LTD 2004 Rep. L.R. 138, Lord Drummond Young, OH.

5594. Measure of damages–Wrist

The pursuer (G), a female aged 65 who was right hand dominant, brought a claim for damages against the defender local authority when she fell whilst mounting a pavement, injuring her left wrist. G sustained a palmary displaced intra articular fracture of the left distal radius and spent six days in hospital. She had an operation to reduce the fracture and stabilise it with a plate and screws. G also underwent physiotherapy for eight or nine months but two and a half years later she was still suffering episodic sharp pains in her wrist and local tenderness. The wrist remained weak and she no longer drove, cycled or gardened. It was possible that further improvements could be made with an additional operation but G's medical history, age and decision not to go ahead precluded the possibility.

Held, assessing damages, that on the balance of probabilities G had failed to prove that her injuries resulted from the local authority's negligence. Nevertheless, the court considered what damages G would have been awarded had her claim succeeded. Solatium: £7,500 with a reduction of 25 per cent for contributory negligence.

GRANT v. HIGHLAND COUNCIL 2004 S.C.L.R. 1067, Sheriff D Booker-Milburn, Sh Ct (Grampian, Highland and Islands).

5595. Books

Sutherland, Lauren–Children in Personal Injury Litigation in Scotland. Paperback: £35.00. ISBN 0 414 01544 4. W.Green & Son.

PLANNING

5596. Compulsory purchase–Compensation–Development of site–Existing shop premises–Development value based on comparative evidence from same street

The applicant (M) sought compensation for the compulsory purchase of a single storey shop with land to the rear. M and the local planning authority (S) could not agree on the value of the property. They had agreed that the open market value of the property should be whichever was the greater of the existing use value or development value, with M arguing for a figure of £107,000 and S for £35,000. It was agreed that planning permission would be obtained for ground floor commercial premises and either residential or office use on two upper floors, but the parties could not agree on the method for calculating the development value. M contended that the comparative method should be used, whereas S asserted that a residual valuation method should be used and in any event the existing use valuation was the highest.

Held, giving judgment accordingly, that compensation of £72,901 was payable on the basis that existing use valuation produced a lower valuation. The development value gave a higher figure because the property would only be of interest to developers. As there was comparative evidence available from similar properties on the same street that method should be used rather than the residual method, but this would be acceptable in the absence of good comparative evidence. Once a reliable comparison had been identified other potentially reliably comparisons should then be examined to see if they cast any doubt on the valuation. The residual method depended on the reliability of the individual inputs to the calculation and minor differences in these inputs could significantly affect the outcome thus the comparative method was to be preferred.

McGEE v. SOUTH LANARKSHIRE COUNCIL [2005] R.V.R. 218, Lord McGhie, AR MacLeary, FRICS, Lands Tr (Scot).

5597. Lawful development certificates–Nursing homes–Right of use lost through abandonment–Relevant considerations

[Town and Country Planning (Scotland) Act 1997 (c.8) s.150.]

T, the owner of a site, applied to the local planning authority in 2002 under the Town and Country Planning (Scotland) Act 1997 s.150 for a certificate of lawful use or development as a nursing home. The site comprised a building which had previously been used as a maternity home, and latterly residential homes, until 1994. After T's acquisition of the site in October 1995, the building was left vacant and was demolished on the advice of the fire brigade in 1996. The planning authority refused the application and T appealed to an inquiry reporter. The reporter considered the relevant factors to have been the physical condition of the building, the period of non use of the property, whether there had been any other use in the intervening period and evidence regarding the owner's intentions, and concluded that the right to the use of the site as a nursing home had been lost through abandonment. T appealed to the Court of Session, submitting that the reporter had approached the facts without a proper understanding of the legal tests by which abandonment was to be judged and had left a material fact out of account, namely that the intention of the owner to reinstate the use of the site for a nursing home should have been considered first as the factor of prime importance.

Held, dismissing the appeal, that (1) the question of abandonment of an existing use was pre eminently one of fact; the reporter had correctly identified the factors by which the question was to be judged and his reasoning could not be faulted. (2) T's submission was based on a mistaken view of the law; the stated intention of the owner to resume the use in question was not, of itself, determinative, even where existence thereof was clearly proved; in any event, there was no evidence that T had ever evinced an unequivocal intention to reinstate the use of the site for a nursing home.

WILLIAM TRACEY LTD v. SCOTTISH MINISTERS 2005 S.L.T. 191, Lord Gill L.J.C., Lord Kirkwood, Lord Clarke, 2 Div.

5598. Planning applications–Local authorities powers and duties–Approval granted while appeal pending

L, investors in a retail development, sought reduction of a decision by N, a local authority, to issue outline planning permission for a mixed use development at a former steelworks site. L objected to the development on the basis that the retail element thereof was contrary to the National Planning Policy Guideline 8 and the structure plan. N's planning and environment committee resolved to grant planning permission subject to approval by the Scottish Ministers of the proposed first alteration to the structure plan. The ministers granted approval and L appealed to the Court of Session. While the appeal was pending before the Inner House, N resolved to issue permission. In response, L raised proceedings for judicial review and in July 2004, the Lord Ordinary declared the decision ultra vires, reduced it and interdicted N from issuing permission. The Lord Ordinary identified the issue as one of whether, in deciding an application without waiting for an appellate or other judicial determination, the outcome of which might materially affect the decision, N had acted in an unreasonable manner. An Extra Division of the Inner House unanimously rejected L's statutory appeal against the ministers' approval of the alteration to the structure plan and L informed N's head of legal services that they were pursuing the appeal to the House of Lords. After receiving advice from senior counsel that L's appeal to the House of Lords had no reasonable prospects of success, N decided to issue the planning permission. L sought to apply what was held by the Lord Ordinary to the appeal to the House of Lords and to the decision by N to issue planning permission, submitting that (1) the outcome of the appeal to the House of Lords on the alteration of the structure plan was a material consideration in any decision to issue planning permission for the development and only if N were able to be satisfied that the appeal was an abuse of process could they properly grant permission without awaiting the outcome; (2) if the former submission were incorrect, N's decision was vitiated by an erroneous understanding that the appeal to the House of Lords had no reasonable prospects of success.

Held, dismissing the petition, that (1) there was neither a general rule that a planning authority had to await the final outcome of an appeal or legal challenge that impacted materially on the decision it had to make nor was there a requirement by the authorities to hold that there was any such general rule where the issue was one of the reasonableness of the planning authority's decision in all the circumstances of the particular case which included, but were not confined to, the existence of the appeal or legal challenge and the possible outcomes thereof. (2) N had not acted unreasonably in accepting legal advice from senior counsel that the House of Lords' appeal had no reasonable prospects of success: a court exercising supervisory jurisdiction would rarely be in a position to conclude that a responsible senior counsel with considerable experience in planning law who had exercised his judgment in what was an imprecise art, amounted to a material error of law.

LAND SECURITIES GROUP PLC v. NORTH LANARKSHIRE COUNCIL 2005 S.L.T. 849, Lord Hodge, OH.

5599. Planning authorities–Compulsory purchase–Back to back agreement–Relevant considerations

[Town and Country Planning (Scotland) Act 1997 (c.8) s.189, s.191.]

S, owners and occupiers of part of a site, X, reclaimed against the refusal of their petition for judicial review seeking (a) declarator that decisions of the local authority, G, agreeing to the selection of B (also owners and occupiers of part of X) and entering into a back to back agreement with B for the use of compulsory purchase powers to achieve the redevelopment of X were ultra vires, et separatim unreasonable, (b) suspension of said decisions and suspension ad interim, and (c) reduction thereof. S submitted that when G decided to enter into the back to back agreement with B, they were not in a position to have proper regard to the purpose of securing the best use of the land, as required by the Town and Country Planning (Scotland) Act 1997 s.191 (1) read with s.191 (2) (a), nor did they have regard to the requirement under s.191 (3) that the land should not be disposed of otherwise than at the best price or on the best terms that could reasonably be obtained. G acknowledged that the criteria on the basis of which they had evaluated the competing proposals for development had not included the price or other terms on which the land would be acquired from them and that their general approach had proceeded on the assumption that full indemnification of their costs constituted the best price, which it was reasonable to assume where the value of individual properties would be approximately the same as the value of the site as a whole and to invite offers would merely set the market price which the Lands Tribunal would set in any event. Moreover, under s.191 (3) "best terms" were an alternative to the "best price" and by following the framework procedure, which was intended to identify, for the purposes of exercising a composite discretion, the preferred developer, having regard to the nature of the proposed development and the likely ability of the developer to carry the development through to completion, the requirements of s.189 of the Act and s.191 had been complied with.

Held, allowing the reclaiming motion, that (1) the planning authority had to make a judgment under s.191 (1) as to the aspects of disposal mentioned therein, according to what appeared to them to be expedient for the purposes mentioned in s.191 (2), and further, to obtain the best value they could for the land, consistently with the exercise of their power of disposal, in accordance with their obligation under s.191 (3). (2) G had given no consideration to whether reimbursement of their costs constituted the best value that could reasonably be obtained and it could not reasonably be assumed that the value fixed by the Lands Tribunal was equivalent to the best price reasonably obtainable, or that the value of an assembled site was equivalent to the combined values of the individual properties from which it had been assembled; nor could it reasonably be assumed that the true value of a site could be determined without a competitive marketing exercise, or that its development value could be accurately assessed before the terms of any planning permissions were known. Further, a planning authority had to give consideration to those matters in exercising their discretion to dispose of land under s.191 (1) and s.191 (2) but so far as appeared, G had proceeded throughout on an assumption that a back to back agreement on standard conditions with a single developer in respect of the entire site, in advance of receiving or determining applications for planning permission, was the most appropriate way of dealing with the site.

STANDARD COMMERCIAL PROPERTY SECURITIES LTD v. GLASGOW CITY COUNCIL 2005 S.L.T. 144, Lord Cullen L.P., Lord Kirkwood, Lord Reed, 1 Div.

POLICE

5600. Grants–Police authorities and joint police boards

POLICE GRANT (SCOTLAND) ORDER 2005, SSI 2005 107; made under the Police (Scotland) Act 1967 s.32. In force: April 1, 2005; £3.00.

This Order determines the aggregate amount of grants to be made under the Police (Scotland) Act 1967 s.32(1) out of money from the Scottish Consolidated Fund for police purposes to all police authorities and joint police boards for the financial year 2005-2006; and the amount of such grants to be made to each police authority or joint police board. The Order also sets out how and when the grant is payable.

5601. Occupational pensions–Part time employment–Police officers

POLICE PENSIONS (PART-TIME SERVICE) AMENDMENT (SCOTLAND) REGULATIONS 2005, SSI 2005 495; made under the Police Pensions Act 1976 s.1. In force: November 14, 2005; £3.00.

These Regulations amend the Police Pensions Regulations 1987 (SI 1987 257) and the Police Pensions (Purchase of Increased Benefits) Regulations 1987 (SI 1987 2215) as they apply in Scotland. The amendments make provision for part time police officers' pension benefits to be calculated as if they had been full-time officers, and then pro-rated for periods of part time service. This replaces the previous basis of calculation under which part time working counted as pensionable service on the basis of the actual hours served. This disadvantaged part time officers because under the Police Pension Scheme reckonable service is accrued at a faster rate after 20 reckonable years; therefore, it would have taken part time workers longer to reach the 20 reckonable years' threshold.

5602. Occupational pensions–Police–Amendments

POLICE PENSIONS AMENDMENT (SCOTLAND) REGULATIONS 2005, SSI 2005 200; made under the Police Pensions Act 1976 s.1. In force: May 3, 2005; £3.00.

These Regulations amend the Police Pensions Regulations 1987 (SI 1987 257) and the Police Pensions (Purchase of Increased Benefits) Regulations 1987 (SI 1987 2215). The Regulations apply in relation to an applicant to a police force who is assessed as being likely to be disproportionately expensive to the Police Pension Scheme by reason of a medical condition which will lead to his retirement. Such a person will be ineligible for early payment of an ordinary pension, for payment of an ill health pension on compulsory retirement, and for early payment of deferred pension because of permanent disablement. The Regulations provide that such a person will pay a correspondingly reduced rate of pension contributions; provide that the restrictions on eligibility for pension awards may also apply to a person who, having previously elected not to pay pension contributions, decides to cancel that election; and provide for the process whereby a person may be assessed as presenting a high risk of retirement on the grounds that he is permanently disabled such that the cost of providing benefits would be disproportionately high.

5603. Police officers–Deputy chief constables

CRIMINAL JUSTICE (SCOTLAND) ACT 2003 (AMENDMENT OF POLICE (SCOTLAND) ACT 1967) ORDER 2005, SSI 2005 361; made under the Criminal Justice (Scotland) Act 2003 s.84. In force: June 25, 2005; £3.00.

This Order amends the Police (Scotland) Act 1967 by inserting a new s.5ZA.

5604. Police officers–Pensions–Bullying–Permanent disability from performing ordinary duties

[Police Pensions Regulations 1987 (SI 1987 257).]

S, a police board, sought reduction of the decision of a medical referee certifying for the purposes of the Police Pensions Regulations 1987 that M, a police officer, was permanently disabled from performing the ordinary duties of a member of the police force due to phobic anxiety and that this condition was the result of an injury received in the execution of duty, namely bullying by a colleague and unwillingness to recognise her childcare needs. S argued that (1) the medical referee had erred in finding a number of matters to be established on the basis that they were "not disputed", where there had been little or no opportunity for the explicit challenge of assertions made by M at interview and all S's solicitor had meant in accepting that certain matters were not disputed was that they were not offering any further evidence beyond that already provided, not that they were departing from submissions made previously; (2) the medical referee had not acted with procedural fairness as M had been permitted to give her version of events without cross examination or challenge and no opportunity was given to S to adduce evidence to counter or respond to assertions made by M for the first time at the hearing; (3) the medical referee had failed to recognise that he had been presented with conflicting evidence and that questions of credibility and reliability arose, and had failed to adopt an appropriate procedure to allow credibility to be tested and conflicts between the evidence to be resolved; (4) the medical referee had found that there had been a persistent unwillingness to recognise M's childcare needs from the beginning of 1998 and a causal connection between bullying in 1995 and her condition in 2002, for which there was no basis in evidence. M argued that the petition was barred by mora, taciturnity and acquiescence.

Held, refusing the petition, that (1) the two principles of fairness germane to the proceedings were, first, that the person making the findings in exercise of an investigatory jurisdiction had to base their decision on evidence with some probative value, and secondly, they had to give fair consideration to any contentions or other relevant material submitted by the parties to the proceedings, and there had been no breach of these principles in the present case. (2) The medical referee had not acted unfairly in treating matters which were said to be "not disputed" as being accepted, where he had given the words their natural meaning. (3) It had not been unfair of the medical referee not to invite cross examination: there was no general obligation on a medical referee to allow cross examination, the fact that M's evidence was not subject to cross examination went to the weight of that material only, and no application had been made to cross examine. (4) The argument that the medical referee unfairly gave S no opportunity to counter assertions made by M for the first time at the hearing had to be rejected. The medical referee was addressed on S's behalf after M had been interviewed, and S's solicitor had an opportunity to make whatever submissions and representations he considered and had not sought the opportunity to adduce further evidence. (5) The medical referee had not failed to adopt an appropriate procedure to enable issues of credibility, reliability and alleged inconsistencies in the evidence to be addressed. He had stated that he was unable to identify any serious inconsistencies which was a conclusion on an issue of fact falling within his jurisdiction reflecting his assessment of matters germane to his decision and the court's jurisdiction was supervisory, not appellate. No argument to the effect that the medical referee had failed to have regard to material considerations had been presented, and the medical referee had not been invited to adopt a different procedure. (6) There had been evidence before the medical referee on which to base the findings criticised by S. S had not disputed M's description of how she was treated, and that there was a causal connection between the bullying experienced by her and her condition. The medical referee's conclusion that the bullying had affected M mentally, making her vulnerable to the development of psychiatric disorder, did not require to be the subject of evidence before him, as he had to draw an inference of the aetiology of M's condition in the light of medical knowledge and factual knowledge of her history, and in doing so the medical referee was entitled to apply his own medical knowledge so as to infer the causal connection between the bullying, of which there was evidence, and M's condition, which was not in dispute.

STRATHCLYDE JOINT POLICE BOARD v. McKINLAY 2005 S.L.T. 764, Lord Reed, OH.

5605. Police officers—Pensions—Permanent disability from performing ordinary duties

[Police Pensions Regulations 1987 (SI 1987 257).]

L, a police board, sought judicial review of the decision of R, a medical referee, certifying for the purposes of a claim under the Police Pensions Regulations 1987 that M, a police officer, was permanently disabled from performing the ordinary duties of a member of the police force by reason of a depressive illness as a result of an injury received in the execution of duty. M was initially certified as being unfit for work due to hypertension, situational anxiety and stress in 1999. He returned to work in 2000 but in June 2001 was again certified as being unfit for work for similar reasons. The following September, M intimated that he wished to retire on grounds of ill health. L referred M to a medical practitioner who considered him permanently disabled but not as a result of an injury received in the execution of duty. M appealed to R who he provided with written submissions focusing on his frustration at having been unable to continue with research he had undertaken in the 1990s and attend conferences, and complaining of senior officers' obstruction in connection with his desire to do so rather than work on other duties. R concluded that M had developed a depressive illness of moderate severity caused by the stress he faced at work which had built up from the early 1990s and which revolved around his perception that his abilities were not being recognised, and that there was a substantial causal connection between the circumstances to which he had been exposed when carrying out his duties as a police officer and his mental injury.

Held, granting the petition, that (1) there was a sense in which M's depression could be described as "brought about by stresses suffered actually through being at work" but a distinction could and should be drawn between stresses encountered while the officer was at work which arose out of the execution of his duties as a constable and those which were experienced while at work but which did not arise out of the execution of his duties, although they might be connected, and (2) applying the test in *R. (on the application of Stunt) v. Mallett* [2001] EWCA Civ 265, [2001] I.C.R. 989, [2001] C.L.Y. 4778, something external had to impact on the claimant while he was carrying out his duties but no event had been identified which caused M's perception that his abilities were not recognised nor had it been determined whether any such event arose in the course of the execution of his duty as a constable, *Stunt* applied.

LOTHIAN AND BORDERS POLICE BOARD v. MacDONALD 2004 S.L.T. 1295, Lord Reed, OH.

5606. Police powers—Motor vehicles—Retention and disposal

POLICE (RETENTION AND DISPOSAL OF MOTOR VEHICLES) (SCOTLAND) REGULATIONS 2005, SSI 2005 80; made under the Antisocial Behaviour etc. (Scotland) Act 2004 s.127. In force: March 17, 2005; £3.00.

Under the Antisocial Behaviour etc. (Scotland) Act 2004 s.126 (vehicles used in a manner causing alarm, distress or annoyance to members of the public) the police have certain powers to seize and remove motor vehicles. These Regulations provide for the retention, safe keeping and disposal by the police or persons authorised by the Chief Constable, of motor vehicles seized under those powers. Those authorised by the Chief Constable as well as constables themselves are referred to as the "retaining authority".

5607. Police powers and duties–Powers of arrest–Lawfulness of detention

[Police (Scotland) Act 1967 (c.77) s.17.]

B sought damages from the police for unlawful arrest and detention after she was arrested by police officers for driving without a licence, insurance or MOT certificate, and taken to a police station where she was detained for seven hours. At proof, the sheriff considered that the relevant issue was the state of the officers' knowledge at the time of the arrest, and that as they knew that B had committed the same offences about three weeks earlier, and that there were outstanding charges against her of a similar nature, they had been entitled in terms of the Police (Scotland) Act 1967 s.17 to arrest her in order to prevent the commission of such offences, even though they could not be punished by imprisonment. The sheriff principal took the same view and refused B's appeal. B appealed, submitting that the sheriff had misunderstood s.17, which was merely a general job description of a police officer and did not confer a power of arrest, and had erred in making assumptions as to the possible consequences of the offences on other road users where there was no finding that the police took those consequences into account in deciding to arrest nor that, if not arrested, she would have continued to commit the offences or was likely to have absconded, and, as the police knew her and where she lived and had seized her car, there was no likelihood of her continuing to commit the offences. In any event, the decision to arrest was unreasonable per se because the offences were trivial and there were other options available.

Held, dismissing the appeal, that the sheriff had committed no error of law in the decision he reached: he was entitled to find that the police had reasonable grounds to arrest B without warrant where she had not disputed her guilt at the locus and it was apparent that she was incorrigible in her commission of those offences. Moreover, in deciding whether the arrest was made on reasonable grounds, he was entitled to take into account the possible consequences of the offences which were not trivial as they could have had serious consequences if B had had an accident resulting in injury or loss of life or damage to property.

BECK v. CHIEF CONSTABLE OF STRATHCLYDE 2005 S.C. 149, Lord Gill L.J.C., Lord Penrose, Lord Weir, 2 Div.

5608. Serious Organised Crime and Police Act 2005 (c.15)–Commencement No.1 Order

SERIOUS ORGANISED CRIME AND POLICE ACT 2005 (COMMENCEMENT NO.1) (SCOTLAND) ORDER 2005, SSI 2005 358 (C.15); made under the Serious Organised Crime and Police Act 2005 s.178. Commencement details: bringing into force various provisions of the 2005 Act on July 1, 2005; £3.00.

This Order brings into force the Serious Organised Crime and Police Act 2005 s.96, s.156, s.164 and s.166(2) to the extent specified.

PRESCRIPTION

5609. Negative prescription–Construction contracts–Several defects becoming apparent at different times–Relevant date of knowledge

The pursuers (MF) brought an action against the defenders (M) to recover losses arising from a building contract. MF had entered into a contract with M whereby M would build a leisure centre, including a swimming pool, for MF. The build was completed in 1993 and the defects liability period ran until 1994. Two defects had been the bases of an action by MF in 2002 to recover damages from M. Those defects were conceded and rectified. Both defects had been manifest since 1994. In 1999, a third defect was noted when a hot water supply pipe failed after it had corroded externally. MF argued that (1) the third defect had not been apparent to its staff; (2) they would not have discovered it with reasonable diligence; (3) it was separate and distinct from the other two defects. M contended that (1) the state of knowledge of a corporate body did not depend on knowledge gained by one officer of a company but rather the state of knowledge of the whole company; (2) the manifestation of the third defect had been apparent from a period exceeding five years; (3) the running of the prescriptive period commenced when the first defect was discovered.

Held, giving judgment for MF in part, that (1) there were sufficient internal failures within MF's corporate organisation that it could not be said that first two defects would not have been found with reasonable diligence and those defects had prescribed. (2) The proper approach when determining the prescription period in a contract such as this was to examine each distinct defect separately, *Sinclair v. MacDougall Estates Ltd* 1994 S.L.T. 76, [1994] C.L.Y. 6161 applied. (3) The evidence demonstrated that MF were unaware of their having suffered loss as a result of the third defect more than five years before the action was raised and they could not have been aware of it with reasonable diligence.

MUSSELBURGH AND FISHERROW COOPERATIVE SOCIETY LTD v. MOWLEM SCOTLAND LTD 2004 S.C.L.R. 412, Lord Eassie, OH.

5610. Negative prescription – Personal injury – Plea of non valens agere cum effectu not applicable

A sought damages from M, a religious order, for injuries sustained whilst she was in their care at a residential home. A averred a series of assaults over a period of three years, ending in 1959 when she was aged 11. The action was raised in 2000. A conceded that the 20 year negative prescriptive period had *prima facie* begun in 1959 and had prescribed, but argued that her right of action had not been extinguished by virtue of the plea *non valens agere cum effectu*. A argued that she had been traumatised after leaving the home and could not make the claim effectual. Further, A argued that the plea was one which could be taken in actions of solatium. M sought dismissal on the ground that the events had prescribed and that A had presented no relevant averments to prevent prescription operating.

Held, pronouncing a decree of absolvitor, that (1) it was demonstrably arguable that the plea of *non valens agere cum effectu* had no application in actions of solatium and what was being sought was a novelty or extension of the plea. This was a proposition that had been judicially disapproved. (2) The legal disabilities of non age or unsoundness of mind were specifically excluded by statute as protection from the rules of prescription and it would be illogical to allow a lesser state of mental incapacity to allow application of the plea.

A v. MURRAY 2004 S.L.T. 1273, Temporary Judge TG Coutts Q.C., OH.

5611. Negative prescription – Short date from which time runs – Knowledge of pursuer

[Prescription and Limitation (Scotland) Act 1973 (c.52) s.6 (4) (a) (ii), s.11 (3).]

X raised an action of damages against W, a firm of solicitors, for losses allegedly suffered as a result of their failure to exercise the proper degree of care in providing him with professional services in connection with a series of property transactions in 1990 and 1991. X wanted to acquire a property for redevelopment for which he entered into a joint venture with another (B), the basis of which involved the property's subdivision into a number of flats. A company owned by X was to operate as the vehicle by which the joint venture acquired the property, part of which would be sold to a company owned by B which would in turn sell two of the flats to X and B. X averred that his interests were not properly protected when in December 1990, the loan funds borrowed by him and B jointly and severally were paid to the property vendors in part payment of the sums due by X's company, without receipt of the agreed contribution from B's company, and without the bank receiving an effective standard security over the whole subjects. The action was raised on October 26, 2001, although X admitted that he first became aware by March 1995 that the transactions had proved unprofitable. W pled prescription which was sustained by the Lord Ordinary and they were assoilzied. X reclaimed. X submitted that the Lord Ordinary was not entitled to conclude that he had failed to establish the facts required to enable him to benefit from the Prescription and Limitation (Scotland) Act 1973 s.11 (3) up to a point sufficiently late to avoid prescription and, in any event, that he was entitled to rely on s.6 (4) as W, in continuing to act for him and to provide legal advice, had induced X's error in believing that his interests were not in jeopardy.

Held, refusing the reclaiming motion, that (1) the Lord Ordinary had reached the correct conclusion on the application of s.11 (3). It was fatal to X's position that his case was based on the allegation that W had disbursed loan proceeds without instructions in the circumstances then pertaining which was an allegation of a clear breach of the terms on which he had engaged W and would have alerted a person of ordinary prudence to the need to make enquiries as to whether loss had been occasioned. (2) Standing the Lord Ordinary's finding that December 17, 1990 was the date on which relevant knowledge could have been obtained with reasonable diligence, s.6 (4) could not avail X. It was not suggested that he was in error in any relevant sense between December 1990 and March 1995 but without proof that error interrupted the running of prescription for a period sufficient to ensure that the aggregate term unaccounted for was less than the prescriptive period, he could not succeed.

ADAMS v. THORNTONS WS (NO.3) 2005 S.C. 30, Lord Marnoch, Lord Penrose, Temporary Judge Sir David Edward, Ex Div.

5612. Positive prescription–Possession claims–Occupation–A non domino disposition

[Titles to Land Consolidation (Scotland) Act 1868 (c.101) s.15; Prescription and Limitation (Scotland) Act 1973 (c.52) s.1.]

X sought reduction of an a non domino disposition in respect of part of heritable subjects, granted by Y and two others in favour of themselves in 1993, and docquets dated 1999 and 2000 by which the latter's share was conveyed to Y. The subjects had been conveyed to X's predecessors in 1944. Y maintained that the disposition was a valid foundation writ for the purposes of positive prescription in terms of s.1 (1) of the Prescription and Limitation (Scotland) Act 1973 s.1 (1) and they had possessed the subjects openly, peaceably and without judicial interruption from 1993 to 2003; the primary function of a disposition was executory not contractual; it was frequently the case that a person might be both disponer and disponee in a disposition of heritage; and, in conveyancing terms, the recording of the disposition equated to transfer.

Held, granting decree, that (1) the 1993 disposition was not a foundation writ for the purposes of positive prescription. (2) The transfer of property was essential for an effective conveyance of land and a person could not dispone a piece of land from himself to himself in exactly the same status or category as no transfer would have resulted. (3) Although the Titles to Land Consolidation (Scotland) Act 1868 s.15 removed the necessity to expede and record an instrument of sasine, it did not alter the underlying conveyancing theory which required transfer or delivery of the land by the disponer to the disponee. (4) The disposition was invalid ex facie for the purposes of s.1 (1A) of the 1973 Act, and thus s.1 (1) was excluded.

ABERDEEN COLLEGE BOARD OF MANAGEMENT v. YOUNGSON 2005 S.C. 335, Lord Menzies, OH.

RATES

5613. **Land valuation appeal court–Expenses–Unarguable appeals abandoned on counsel's advice at late stage–Award of expenses in favour of assessor**

The applicant (H), who represented 12 appellants (N) in appeals against decisions of the Valuation Appeals Committee, brought further appeals to the Lands Valuation Appeal Court in respect of the same 12 cases. The cases concerned the basis for the revaluation of hotels arising from the 2000 revaluation. The appeals were abandoned, on the advice of counsel, two days before the hearing. H had sought to appeal the decisions in the lower court without consulting counsel, who subsequently advised that the appeals were unarguable. The instant hearing was for the purpose of awarding expenses.

Held, awarding expenses in favour of the assessor, that the appeals should never have been brought. It was an abuse of process to bring unarguable appeals and at the very least the respondent could expect to have his expenses paid. In such circumstances, wasted costs against the representative personally could be considered. Where the advocate in the lower court was not legally qualified it was vital that he obtained counsel's advice on the merits of any appeal.

NORTH BRITISH TRUST HOTELS LTD v. ASSESSOR FOR THE HIGHLAND AND WESTERN ISLES AREA; *sub nom.* NORTH BRITISH TRUST HOTELS LTD v. HIGHLAND AND WESTERN ISLES AREA ASSESSOR 2005 S.L.T. 419, Lord Gill L.J.C., Lord Nimmo Smith, Lord Clarke, LVAC.

5614. **Non domestic rates**

NON-DOMESTIC RATES (LEVYING) (SCOTLAND) REGULATIONS 2005, SSI 2005 126; made under the Local Government etc. (Scotland) Act 1994 s.153. In force: April 1, 2005; £3.00.

These Regulations make provision as to the amount payable in certain circumstances as non domestic rates in respect of non domestic subjects in Scotland.

5615. **Non domestic rates–Rate for 2005/06**

NON-DOMESTIC RATE (SCOTLAND) ORDER 2005, SSI 2005 14; made under the Local Government (Scotland) Act 1975 s.7B, s.37. In force: April 1, 2005; £3.00.

This Order prescribes a rate of 46.1 pence in the pound as the non-domestic rate to be levied throughout Scotland in respect of the financial year 2005-2006. A rate of 48.8 pence in the pound was the figure prescribed as the non-domestic rate to be levied throughout Scotland by the Scottish Ministers for the financial year 2004-2005.

5616. **Non domestic rates–Rural areas**

NON-DOMESTIC RATING (RURAL AREAS AND RATEABLE VALUE LIMITS) (SCOTLAND) ORDER 2005, SSI 2005 103; made under the Local Government and Rating Act 1997 s.8, Sch.2 para.1, Sch.2 para.3, Sch.2 para.4. In force: April 1, 2005; £3.00.

The Local Government and Rating Act 1997 Sch.2 makes provision for mandatory relief from non-domestic rates for qualifying general stores, post offices and food stores. Provision is also made for discretionary relief for property used for purposes beneficial to the local community, in settlements of less than 3,000 people in areas of Scotland designated as rural areas by the Scottish Ministers. The Non Domestic Rating (Petrol Filling Stations, Public Houses and Hotels) (Scotland) Order 2003 (SSI 2003 188) prescribes conditions for the purposes of paragraph 3(2)(c)(ii) of Sch.2 which add petrol filling stations, public houses and hotels to the categories of lands and heritages that qualify for mandatory relief. This Order, which revokes the Non-Domestic Rating (Rural Areas and Rateable Value Limits) (Scotland) Order 1997 (SI 1997 2827), the Non-Domestic Rating (Rural Areas and Rateable Value Limits) (Scotland) Amendment Order 2000 (SSI 2000 57), the Non-Domestic Rating (Rural Areas and Rateable Value Limits) (Scotland) Amendment Order 2003 (SSI 2003 141) and the Non-Domestic Rating (Rural Areas and Rateable Value Limits) (Scotland) Amendment Order 2004 (SSI 2004 91), designates for the purposes of these provisions the local authority areas specified in column 1 of Sch.1 to the Order, under exclusion of the localities specified in column 2 of that Schedule.

5617. Non domestic rates–Rural rate relief–Maximum rateable values

NON-DOMESTIC RATING (FORMER AGRICULTURAL PREMISES) (SCOTLAND) ORDER 2005, SSI 2005 104; made under the Local Government and Rating Act 1997 Sch.2 para.3A. In force: April 1, 2005; £3.00.

The Local Government and Rating Act 1997 provides for mandatory rate relief on certain former agricultural premises. This Order, which revokes the Non-Domestic Rating (Former Agricultural Premises) (Scotland) Order 2003 (SSI 2003 142), provides that £7,000 is the maximum rateable value of lands and heritages that can be eligible for such relief.

5618. Non domestic rates–Subjects–Autoteller sites–Banks' rateable occupation

The Lands Tribunal stated a case at the instance of A, assessors, in relation to appeals referred to it by a bank and a building society, B, against entries in the rolls of five autoteller sites situated in retail stores on the basis that they were in rateable occupation of those who owned the machines. The tribunal had allowed B's appeals, finding that the subjects should not be treated as separate units of lands and heritages and should not be entered in the rolls because it was not possible to identify some degree of occupation by B which in a realistic way could be said to interfere with use of the whole premises for the retailer's purposes when it was clear that the machines were primarily for the benefit of the retailer in operating its store efficiently as a trading unit. A submitted that an area within larger subjects allocated for the positioning of a moveable item could constitute lands and heritages; the subjects were plainly in the possession of B who installed and operated them; B had exclusive occupation and use of the site for providing banking services; the occupation was of a permanent character; the retailer's rights to interfere with B's occupation and enjoyment of the subjects did not materially detract from their paramount occupation; and the exact legal nature of the agreement conferring that occupation was not conclusive.

Held, dismissing the appeals, that (1) the subjects should not have been entered in the rolls. The parties agreed that none of the machines was heritable by accession and each was a free standing piece of moveable property, thus all that A had entered in the roll were the areas of floor space on which the machines were placed, and an area of floor within larger subjects that was used as the site for an item of moveable property could only be entered in the roll as lands and heritages in separate rateable occupation if the ratepayer had a right of occupation of it. (2) The flaw in the appeals lay in the contention that the agreements conferred a right of occupation of the floor space upon B when neither had that effect where they both related to the supply, use and control of an item of moveable property that B supplied to the retailer for use as one of its retail attractions, neither agreement expressly or impliedly conferred any right of occupation of the site by B which, at most, had a right of access to the machine.

LANARKSHIRE VALUATION JOINT BOARD ASSESSOR v. CLYDESDALE BANK PLC; MARKS & SPENCER PLC v. LANARKSHIRE VALUATION JOINT BOARD ASSESSOR; MARKS & SPENCER PLC v. RENFREWSHIRE VALUATION JOINT BOARD ASSESSOR; *sub nom.* CLYDESDALE BANK PLC v. LANARKSHIRE VALUATION JOINT BOARD ASSESSOR 2005 S.L.T. 167, Lord Gill L.J.C., Lord Kingarth, Lord Clarke, LVAC.

5619. Non domestic rates—Valuation—Big box warehouses—Correct basis of assessment

The appellant ratepayer (B) appealed against the assessment of the rateable value of its leasehold subjects in the Abbotsinch Retail Park near Glasgow. The subjects consisted of a "big box" retail warehouse of 9,770 square metres with a garden centre and builder's yard. The assessor had based his assessment on the actual rent of the subjects, producing a rateable value of £1.44 million. B argued that the actual rent was not a reliable indicator of market rent since it had been a sitting tenant on the site which was then developed by its landlord (C) and it had effectively been offered inducements to surrender its old lease, sell C an adjoining piece of land and take up its current lease. B contended that the assessment should be by way of comparison with other big boxes, of which there were six in the Glasgow area of a comparable size. B argued for a rateable value of £965,000.

Held, allowing the appeal, that although the transaction between B and C had genuinely been at arm's length, the actual rent was not an open market one. The rent was part of a larger transaction involving payments by C to B for the transfer of a piece of additional land and the surrender of its existing lease, and although it was not possible to quantify the exact impact on the rent agreed, the payments certainly had an effect. Comparison with other big boxes was a more reliable indicator than comparison with smaller subjects on the same site, although only two other such developments in the Glasgow area were sufficiently similar. These both had a rateable value of £95 per square metre, but taking into account all the surrounding circumstances, an appropriate rate for the subjects under appeal would be £96. The rental rates for big boxes had increased substantially since the valuation date of 2000, and therefore, an annual growth rate of eight per cent would need to be factored into the assessment. Additionally, some reduction had to be made for the garden centre and builder's yard areas, which were not strictly part of the building. These calculations produced a rateable value of £975,000.

B&Q PLC v. RENFREWSHIRE VALUATION JOINT BOARD ASSESSOR [2004] R.A. 220, JN Wright Q.C., Lands Tr (Scot).

5620. Non domestic rates—Valuation—Factories—Rent

M, the owners of a purpose built factory, appealed to the valuation appeal committee following the revaluation of their premises in 2000. The committee had entered the factory in the valuation roll at a revised rateable value of £133,000. M appealed to the Lands Valuation Appeal Court, submitting that the committee had erred in law in finding the rent of £75,000 per annum, at which the subjects were let in December 1999, to have been irrelevant. The court allowed the appeal and remitted the case to the committee with a direction that it have a further hearing and make a fresh decision. The committee thereafter adhered to its previous decision and refused the appeal. M appealed.

Held, allowing the appeal and substituting a net annual value and rateable value of £75,000, that (1) the committee had to determine the rent at which the subjects might reasonably be expected to be let on the statutory terms at the valuation date and as M had led uncontradicted evidence that the rent struck in 1999 was a bona fide rent and that rental levels in the area had not changed materially between the valuation date and that date, the committee's failure to make findings to that effect could not be understood. (2) The committee had again failed to make any findings in fact on both the disadvantages of the location for subjects of its size or for the uses to which it lent itself, and on the comparison subjects relied on by the assessor, and had failed to explain how it interpreted the comparison evidence or what it had deduced from the assessor's list of rents. (3) Although the committee had given "careful and close consideration" to the actual rent of the subjects, it had given no weight to it, and the committee could not properly proceed in that way where the rent was primary evidence bearing directly on the statutory test and the assessor's comparison evidence included only four actual rents, only two of which were in the area and all of which were much smaller subjects. (4) The committee had thus acceded to the startling proposition that if the subjects had been let on the statutory hypotheses on the valuation date, they would have achieved a rent some 77 per cent greater than that actually achieved some 20 months later, which called for an explanation the committee had failed to provide. (5) The obvious conclusion was that however robust the assessor's level of rent was in the valuation of small to medium sized industrial units, it was unreliable in the valuation of subjects with special features such as those in the present case, which should have been clear to the committee from previous decisions of the court to which counsel had referred but which the committee appeared to have disregarded.

MAGELL LTD v. DUMFRIES AND GALLOWAY REGIONAL ASSESSOR (NO.2) 2005 S.L.T. 726, Lord Gill L.J.C., Lord Nimmo Smith, Lord Kingarth, LVAC.

5621. Non domestic rates–Valuation–Hydroelectric power station–Distribution via national grid–Aluminium manufacture

[Electricity Generators (Rateable Values) (Scotland) Order 2000 (SI 2000 86); Electricity Generators (Aluminium) (Rateable Values) (Scotland) Order 2000 (SI 2000 87).]

The ratepayer (AL) appealed against a calculation of the respondent assessor (H) that electricity generated at its hydro electric power station was not used "wholly or mainly for the manufacture of aluminium" and therefore the power station should be assessed at a higher rate under the Electricity Generators (Rateable Values) (Scotland) Order 2000 rather than a lower rate under the Electricity Generators (Aluminium) (Rateable Values) (Scotland) Order 2000. AL had operated two aluminium smelters, each supplied by electricity from a power station. After one smelter was closed, its associated power station and part of the national distribution grid were substantially modified to allow a priority supply of electricity to the other smelter 20 kilometres away, with excess electricity added to the national grid. The operating smelter took, on average, more than half of the station's electricity, with the distributor paying for the remaining electricity. By slightly reducing its originally planned capacity, AL was also able to sell the station's remaining electricity under the renewables obligation regime, worth twice what it gained from the sale of excess electricity.

Held, dismissing the appeal, that while the electricity might have been "in connection with", "for purposes ancillary to" or even "for" AL's economic benefit, it could not be said that such electricity was "wholly or mainly for the manufacture of aluminium". The existence of a priority facility did not affect that conclusion. All the electricity was for supply to the grid and that primary use was not displaced by the commercial and economic aspects of the supplied smelter. The tribunal was therefore not prepared to determine the matter by making a simple comparison between the amount exported by the power station and that imported by the smelter on the basis that the latter represented a different use in excess of the amount supplied to the grid. (Obiter) On the basis of the physical situation only, the power generated was not "for the manufacture of aluminium"; rather, there was a strong picture of supply to the distribution company. However, a dedicated connection might have met the definition. The renewables obligation situation also weakened AL's position, particularly when its value was considered.

ALCAN ALUMINIUM UK LTD v. HIGHLAND AND WESTERN ISLES VALUATION JOINT BOARD ASSESSOR [2005] R.A. 161, JN Wright Q.C., LandsTr (Scot).

5622. Non domestic rates–Valuation–Lands and heritages

VALUATION FOR RATING (DECAPITALISATION RATE) (SCOTLAND) REGULATIONS 2005, SSI 2005 41; made under the Valuation and Rating (Scotland) Act 1956 s.6. In force: March 1, 2005; £3.00.

These Regulation revoke the Valuation for Rating (Decapitalisation Rate) (Scotland) Regulations 1990 (SI 1990 505), the Valuation for Rating (Decapitalisation Rate) (Scotland) Regulations 1994 (SI 1994 3256) and the Valuation for Rating (Decapitalisation Rate) (Scotland) Amendment Regulations

2000 (SI 2000 56). They prescribe the decapitalisation rate to be applied when valuing lands and heritages in Scotland in accordance with the contractor's basis for the purposes of any valuation roll which comes into force on or after April 1, 2005. The decapitalisation rate prescribed is 3.33 per cent in the case of certain MoD property, church property, healthcare property and educational establishments and 5 per cent in any other case.

5623. **Non domestic rates – Valuation – Large shop premises – Referral of appeals to Lands Tribunal – Refusal**

[Valuation Appeal Committee (Procedure in Appeals under the Valuation Acts) (Scotland) Regulations 1995 (SI 1995 572) Reg.5.]

Three retailers in a city centre shopping centre who had appealed against the assessment of large shop premises applied to the valuation appeal committee to refer the appeals to the Lands Tribunal. The committee refused the applications. The retailers appealed to the tribunal against that decision on the grounds in the Valuation Appeal Committee (Procedure in Appeals under the Valuation Acts) (Scotland) Regulations 1995 Reg.5(1). The retailers proposed to argue that in the April 2000 revaluation the assessor erroneously valued the shops on a zoning basis in comparison with other smaller shops at the centre, rather than on an overall basis and under reference to comparisons with other large shops throughout Scotland. They submitted that (1) there were differing versions of the "overall" method sought by them and in relation to comparisons elsewhere in Scotland, the agreements behind the actual valuations would require to be explained; (2) there were complexities in relation to escalators, air conditioning, fitting out costs, turnover elements in some of the rents and the weighting to be given to inducements; (3) a substantial rise in rates had made zoning of large stores difficult and very large end allowances were required which would require to be explained carefully and the factual and opinion evidence was highly complex; (4) the law would be difficult to apply as to what relevantly required to be taken into account; (5) the decision in each appeal would be likely to be used as a precedent elsewhere in the locality; (6) there were distinguishing complexities in each appeal where the first retailer argued that their rent was two years after the tone date, the second retailer argued that although their store was let, its rent was not an open market rental, and the third retailer's store was substantially larger than the other two and was owner occupied.

Held, dismissing the appeals, that (1) none of the statutory grounds for referral were made out. (2) To bring a case under Reg.5(1)(a) or Reg.5(1)(b) required identification of an element or elements in the facts or the likely opinion evidence which was not straightforward and which, in the context of rating appeals, made the matter complex and no such element could be found in the present appeals. While the evidence might well be slightly more voluminous in these appeals than in some others the evidence on neither fact or opinion met the test of "complex or highly technical". (3) In relation to Reg.5(1)(c), the law applicable to these cases was neither uncertain nor difficult to apply where they were comparative principle valuations in which the basic issue appeared to be which other subjects within the same valuation category provided the better comparisons. (4) While the parties involved in the cases of two large shops opened more recently in the shopping centre would take an interest in the outcome of these appeals, that did not mean they raised a general issue which would give rise to a precedent under Reg.5(1)(d). The appeals involved the application of well established general principles to the particular circumstances and the question of methodology only arose once the primary issue as to best comparisons was resolved. (5) There was no reason to distinguish the third appellant's appeal because the shop was owner occupied and substantially larger, or the first and second appellants' appeals because of the particular circumstances relating to their leases.

NEXT PLC v. ASSESSOR FOR HIGHLAND AND WESTERN ISLES VALUATION JOINT BOARD 2005 S.L.T. (Lands Tr) 7, JN Wright Q.C., Lands Tr (Scot).

5624. **Non domestic rates–Valuation–Loss making super quarry–Assessment based on buildings, plant and machinery and royalties**

The appellant ratepayer (F) appealed against the entry in the valuation roll for a quarry at £1,500,000 net annual value. The assessment was based on the two separate elements of buildings, plant and machinery, which was assessed on the contractor's principle, and minerals, which were based on royalties. The quarry, which was operating at a loss, was termed a "super quarry", having an output in excess of 1 million tonnes. The assessor (H) contended that the figures used were appropriate with the royalties assessment based on a quarry in Somerset, which had the lowest royalties he could find.

Held, allowing the appeal, that a reduction was appropriate given the lack of profit so the net annual value would be reduced to £777,500. The economics of the loss making operation should be reflected in the royalties figure although the assessment was based on the quarry's potential and not F's profit. The assessment could not be a conventional application of the comparative principle due to the difficulties in directly comparing two quarries. Although any tenant would require a similar level of equipment for the agreed level of production, economic circumstances would be relevant to any negotiations with a tenant and thus an end allowance of 10 per cent on the buildings plant and machinery figure should be allowed. A reduction of 60 per cent on the royalty rate was justified due to the operating problems a tenant would face. The broad approach to the royalties' rate required H to take the lowest figure disclosed by other quarries and use it as a starting point.

FOSTER YEOMAN LTD v. HIGHLAND AND WESTERN ISLES VALUATION JOINT BOARD ASSESSOR [2005] R.A. 189, Lord McGhie, LandsTr (Scot).

5625. **Non domestic rates–Valuation–Shop unit over two floors in purpose built shopping centre–Basis of assessment**

The appellant ratepayer (W) appealed against the assessment of the rateable value of its two level shop unit in a purpose built shopping centre outside Glasgow. The centre, the only one of its kind in Scotland, had been designed to allow easy access by shoppers to both levels of the mall from car parking and bus and train stations. W's unit of 1,200 square metres was at one end of the main mall. The landlords in their overall planning for the centre had allowed only W and its main competitor to bid for it. The assessors had based their valuation on the rents of other units in the centre, which had been calculated on a zoned basis with reductions for units that were less advantageously sited. The assessors also made comparisons with city centre shopping centres in Scotland. They assessed the net annual rental value as £660,000, or £549 per square metre. W argued that the rateable value should reflect the actual rent and that a discount should be given for the fact that it had to operate over two levels, giving a value of £495,000 or £412 per square metre.

Held, allowing the appeal in part, that an appropriate net annual rental value was £556,500, or £463 per square metre. The actual rent was a factor to be taken into account but was not decisive. In the instant case, the actual rent was an arm's length rent but not an open market rent, given that the landlord had chosen to restrict letting of the unit to only two prospective tenants. The rents of other two level units in the centre were a better basis for assessment. The centre had been specifically designed to avoid the problems of two level sites experienced at other centres, and therefore, the fact that the unit was split over two levels was not in itself a difficulty worthy of discount. However, the unit had other disadvantages, such as the fact that its overall frontage was large compared with its depth and that it was situated close to a blank corridor. The zoning method was therefore not sufficient of itself to give an accurate value, and it was appropriate to make adjustments of 10 per cent for shape disadvantage and of five and 7.5 per cent respectively for location disadvantage in relation to the separate floors.

WH SMITH PLC v. GLASGOW ASSESSOR [2004] R.A. 197, JN Wright Q.C., LandsTr (Scot).

5626. Non domestic rates—Valuation—Stud farms

VALUATION (STUD FARMS) (SCOTLAND) ORDER 2005, SSI 2005 105; made under the Valuation and Rating (Scotland) Act 1956 s.7B; and the Local Government and Rating Act 1997 Sch.2 para.4. In force: April 1, 2005; £3.00.

The Valuation and Rating (Scotland) Act 1956 makes provision for the reduction of the rateable value of any lands and heritages the whole or any part of which consists of buildings which are used for the breeding and/or rearing of horses and occupied together with any agricultural land or agricultural building. This Order, which revokes the Valuation (Stud Farms) (Scotland) Order 2003 (SSI 2003 143), prescribes the amount for this purpose as £7,000.

5627. Non domestic rates—Valuation of utilities

NON-DOMESTIC RATING (VALUATION OF UTILITIES) (SCOTLAND) AMENDMENT ORDER 2005, SSI 2005 320; made under the Valuation and Rating (Scotland) Act 1956 s.6A. In force: July 1, 2005; £3.00.

This Order amends the Non-Domestic Rating (Valuation of Utilities) (Scotland) Order 2005 (SSI 2005 127) which put in place a new regime for the valuation of certain utilities whose values were previously prescribed in various orders made under the Local Government (Scotland) Act 1975 s.6. The Order specifies the lands and heritages to be valued within the gas industry, where these are occupied, or if unoccupied, owned, by Transco Plc. Where these lands and heritages would be treated as justifying separate entries in two or more valuation rolls, they are treated as justifying one entry in the valuation roll for West Dunbartonshire. This amendment is required as a consequence of the transfer of the gas distribution and storage network from Transco Plc to Scotland Gas Networks Ltd. The amendment provides that the lands and heritages where these are occupied, or if unoccupied, owned, by either Transco Plc or Scotland Gas Networks Ltd, as the case may be, will be treated as justifying one entry in the valuation roll, in respect of each company. The position is the same for Transco Plc and Scotland Gas Networks Ltd, so that these lands and heritages include those used for the purposes of production, treatment, transmission, distribution or storage of gas, during periods when such lands and heritages are occupied, or if unoccupied, owned, by those companies.

5628. Non domestic rates—Valuation of utilities

NON-DOMESTIC RATING (VALUATION OF UTILITIES) (SCOTLAND) ORDER 2005, SSI 2005 127; made under the Valuation and Rating (Scotland) Act 1956 s.6A; and the Local Government etc. (Scotland) Act 1994 s.27. In force: April 1, 2005; £3.00.

This Order puts in place a new regime for the valuation of certain utilities whose values were previously prescribed in various orders made under the Local Government (Scotland) Act 1975 s.6. This Order designates particular assessors to value the lands and heritages for each utility covered by the Order. It specifies the lands and heritages to be valued within each of the utilities and treated as a single entry in the valuation roll for the area specified; designates assessors to value the lands and heritages of each of the utilities specified; provides that a designated assessor shall have equivalent powers in relation to each valuation area in which there are lands and heritages to be valued in pursuance of the Order to those that assessor has in relation to the area of the joint board or valuation authority which appointed that assessor; and states that a valuation appeal committee constituted in relation to the area of the joint board or valuation authority which appointed the designated assessor may hear and determine appeals and complaints under the Valuation Acts in relation to assessments made by virtue of the Order.

5629. Non domestic rates-Valuation of utilities

NON-DOMESTIC RATING (VALUATION OF UTILITIES) (SCOTLAND) REVOCATION ORDER 2005, SSI 2005 178; made under the Local Government (Scotland) Act 1975 s.6. In force: April 1, 2005; £3.00.

This Order provides for the revocation of the BG Transco plc (Rateable Values) (Scotland) Order 2000 (SSI 2000 85), the Electricity Generators (Rateable Values) (Scotland) Order 2000 (SSI 2000 86), the Electricity Generators (Aluminium) (Rateable Values) (Scotland) Order 2000 (SSI 2000 87), the Electricity Lands (Rateable Values) (Scotland) Order 2000 (SSI 2000 88), the Railtrack plc (Rateable Values) (Scotland) Order 2000 (SSI 2000 91), the Electricity Lands and Water Undertakings (Rateable Values) (Scotland) Amendment Order 2000 (SSI 2000 284), the Docks and Harbours (Rateable Values) (Scotland) Order 2000 (SSI 2000 285), the Train Operating Companies (Rateable Values) (Scotland) (No.2) Order 2000 (SSI 2000 424), the Electricity Lands and Generators (Rateable Values) (Scotland) Variation Order 2002 (SSI 2002 158) and the Water Undertakings (Rateable Values) (Scotland) Order 2003 (SSI 2003 187). The revocations are made as part of a new regime for the valuation of the lands and heritages within these utilities, for the purposes of the valuation roll.

5630. Rateable value-Valuation appeal committee-Referral of appeal for determination-Refusal to refer

[Local Government (Scotland) Act 1966 (c.51) s.15; Valuation Appeal Committee (Procedure in Appeals under the Valuation Acts) (Scotland) Regulations 1995 (SI 1995 572) Reg.5, Reg.6(1).]

A public house chain appealed under the Valuation Appeal Committee (Procedure in Appeals under the Valuation Acts) (Scotland) Regulations 1995 Reg.6(1) against the refusal by a valuation appeal committee to refer its appeal to the tribunal under Reg.5(1). The matter for determination in the instant appeal was whether certain issues fell within the criteria set out in Reg.5.

Held, allowing the appeal, that (1) the nature of the evidence justified the description "complex and highly technical" within the meaning of Reg.5(1). (2) While evidence of different potential indices might raise quite difficult technical issues, the material would not fall to be regarded as "complex or highly technical" and the respondents were well able to deal with difficult technical questions. (3) The issue of the proper construction of the Local Government (Scotland) Act 1966 s.15 and its application to evidence of changing turnover was a basis for the contention that the law would be difficult to apply in terms of Reg.5(1)(c). (4) Clarification of an appropriate method of indexation and the application of s.15 thereto could not be resolved by looking only at the figures in the instant case and it was potentially an issue of sufficient importance to come under Reg.5(1)(d).

JD WETHERSPOON PLC v. ASSESSOR FOR HIGHLAND AND WESTERN ISLES VALUATION JOINT BOARD 2005 S.L.T. (LandsTr) 6, Lord McGhie, AR MacLeary, LandsTr (Scot).

REAL PROPERTY

5631. Agricultural land-Modification

LAND REFORM (SCOTLAND) ACT 2003 (MODIFICATION) ORDER 2005, SSI 2005 65; made under the Land Reform (Scotland) Act 2003 s.8. In force: February 9, 2005; £3.00.

This Order modifies the Land Reform (Scotland) Act 2003 by inserting a new provision which amends the definition of the expression "land on which crops are growing".

5632. Land registration–Fees

FEES IN THE REGISTERS OF SCOTLAND AMENDMENT ORDER 2005, SSI 2005 580; made under the Land Registers (Scotland) Act 1868 s.25. In force: November 28, 2005; £3.00.

This Order amends the Fees in the Registers of Scotland Order 1995 (SI 1995 1945) so as to increase certain fees for certain forms, provide a fee for the provision of a new service, namely the provision of information from the Land Register archive, and to provide standardised charges for extracts or copies of documents in place of the scheme of charges based upon the number of pages copied.

5633. Books

Greens Conveyancing Statutes. Paperback: £25.00. ISBN 0 414 01619 X. W. Green & Son.

REPARATION

5634. Personal injury–Negligence–Faulty equipment–Requirement to aver precise inspection intervals

M, a ground crew member, raised an action of damages against G, the operators and controllers of an aircraft, for injuries sustained to his head when a cargo door swung down suddenly whilst he was loading luggage. M maintained that, after the accident, he was advised by fellow crew that the door had been secured with a plastic strip for three weeks prior to the accident. M argued that G ought to have inspected the aircraft "sufficiently, regularly and thoroughly" in order to identify and repair the problem with the door. G argued that M's failure to define the interval and practicality of such inspections was fatal to his case.

Held, not dismissing the action, that it was not necessary in every case to aver the inspection interval. In certain cases it may have been obvious that failure to adopt certain measures inferred negligence, but in the instant case there was no authority to require dismissal of the action insofar as it was based on failure to specify particular inspection intervals.

MONTGOMERIE v. GLASGOW PRESTWICK INTERNATIONAL AIRPORT LTD 2004 Rep. L.R. 117, Temporary Judge JG Reid Q.C., OH.

ROAD TRAFFIC

5635. Bridges–Tolls–Skye Bridge

INVERGARRY-KYLE OF LOCHALSH TRUNK ROAD (A87) EXTENSION (SKYE BRIDGE CROSSING) TOLL ORDER (REVOCATION) ORDER 2005, SSI 2005 167; made under the New Roads and Street Works Act 1991 s.34. In force: May 2, 2005; £3.00.

This Order revokes the Invergarry-Kyle of Lochalsh Trunk Road (A87) Extension (Skye Bridge Crossing) Toll Order 1992 (SI 1992 1501) and the Invergarry-Kyle of Lochalsh Trunk Road (A87) Extension (Skye Bridge Crossing) Toll Order (Variation) Order 1999 (SSI 1999 196).

5636. Information requirements–Alternative routes

ROAD TRAFFIC (TEMPORARY RESTRICTIONS) PROCEDURE AMENDMENT (SCOTLAND) REGULATIONS 2005, SSI 2005 299; made under the Road Traffic Regulation Act 1984 s.16. In force: June 25, 2005; £3.00.

These Regulations amend the Road Traffic (Temporary Restrictions) Procedure Regulations 1992 (SI 1992 1215) to remove the requirement to show alternative routes and introduce an option either to show alternative routes or state where this information may be found.

5637. Motorways–Speed limits–M77

M77 (MALLETSHEUGH) (SPEED LIMIT) (SCOTLAND) REGULATIONS 2005, SSI 2005 655; made under the Road Traffic Regulation Act 1984 s.17. In force: in accordance with Reg.2; £3.00.

These Regulations impose a speed limit of 60mph on the special road authorised to be provided by the M77 Special Road (Floak to Malletsheugh) Special Road Scheme 1999.

5638. Parking–Charges–Holyrood Park

HOLYROOD PARK AMENDMENT REGULATIONS 2005, SSI 2005 15; made under the Parks Regulations (Amendment) Act 1926 s.2; and the Road Traffic Regulation Act 1984 s.62. In force: January 14, 2005; £3.00.

These Regulations, which amend the Holyrood Park Regulations 1971 (SI 1971 593), introduce a "pay and display" charging scheme for vehicle parking in the Broad Pavement car park to the south of the Palace of Holyroodhouse in Holyrood Park. The Regulations impose a general four-hour parking limit and a parking charge at the rate of £1 per hour or part thereof. There is no charge for the parking of motor cycles in the Park, nor for the parking of vehicles displaying a disabled person's badge. Nor is there any charge for parking vehicles in accordance with a parking permit issued by the Scottish Ministers. The Regulations provide for an excess charge of £30 in respect of vehicles parked in the Park for more than four hours and in respect of vehicles that do not display a valid parking ticket (unless no charge is payable as in the cases referred to above).

5639. Parking–Parking adjudicators–Appeals–South Lanarkshire

ROAD TRAFFIC (PARKING ADJUDICATORS) (SOUTH LANARKSHIRE COUNCIL) REGULATIONS 2005, SSI 2005 13; made under the Road Traffic Act 1991 s.73. In force: February 7, 2005; £3.00.

These Regulations prescribe the procedure to be followed in relation to appeals before parking adjudicators against decisions of the parking authority under a decriminalised parking regime in South Lanarkshire Council.

5640. Parking–Special parking areas–South Lanarkshire

ROAD TRAFFIC (PERMITTED PARKING AREA AND SPECIAL PARKING AREA) (SOUTH LANARKSHIRE COUNCIL) DESIGNATION ORDER 2005, SSI 2005 11; made under the Road Traffic Act 1991 Sch.3 para.1, Sch.3 para.2, Sch.3 para.3. In force: February 7, 2005; £3.00.

This Order extends to South Lanarkshire Council arrangements for enforcing parking controls already available in London and certain other areas in England and in Edinburgh, Glasgow, Perth and Kinross, Aberdeen and Dundee. It does so by designating South Lanarkshire local government area (with certain specified exceptions) as a permitted parking area and as a special parking area in accordance with the Road Traffic Act 1991. The Order applies to the designated area various provisions of the 1991 Act and modifies them where necessary. It also makes consequential modifications to certain provisions of the Road Traffic Regulation Act 1984 dealing with parking and related matters.

5641. Roads–Local authorities powers and duties–Construction and maintenance–Statutory entitlement to recover expenses incurred

[Roads (Scotland) Act 1970 (c.20) s.19(5); Roads (Scotland) Act 1984 (c.54) s.91, s.140, s.141.]

S, a property owner, engaged contractors to carry out substantial building works which resulted in the collapse of the property's rear wall. The wall also formed a retaining wall to the uphill slope of a street which was rendered unstable following its collapse. R, the roads authority, served a notice on the owner under the Roads (Scotland) Act 1984 s.91 (2) requiring her to carry out certain works to restore stability within 28 days. S failed to comply and R carried out the necessary works at an averred cost of £144,818.21, which they sought to recover. S sought dismissal, submitting that (1) s.91 and s.141 of the Act, as relied on by R, only conferred a limited power to recover expenses under the notice procedure route restricting entitlement to those circumstances set out in s.140(1)(e) or s.140(1)(f); (2) the literal meaning of s.140 was to be followed with the result that the cost of carrying out works required in terms of a s.91 (2) notice where the owner or occupier had failed to do so were not recoverable; (3) while there was provision for recovery in terms of the Roads (Scotland) Act 1970 s.19(5), the 1984 Act was not a consolidating statute, and in any event, work on retaining walls was not covered by the 1970 Act.

Held, allowing a proof restricted to quantum, that (1) the 1970 Act empowered the relevant roads authority, in some circumstances, to serve notices on owners and occupiers to carry out works and, in the event of their failing to do so, to carry out the works themselves, while the 1984 Act provided for many more occasions when a roads authority could do so, and the power to carry out the works in the event of default was to be found in s.141 (1), which covered all instances of notices having been served under the Act for works to be carried out within a specified period. (2) The fundamental flaw in S's approach was twofold in that it failed to account fully for the whole provisions of s.141, and failed to recognise that s.140 was concerned not with providing authority for the carrying out of works or the recovery of the cost of doing so but with the provision of a power of entry in certain cases and the recovery of costs that might be incurred only in respect of exercising that power. (3) The clear import of the wording used in s.141 (2) was that in every case where a roads authority had executed works in circumstances where an owner or occupier had failed to comply with a notice of the sort referred to in s.141 (1), the authority was entitled to seek to recover the expenses reasonably incurred by them in doing anything in relation to the land from the person required.

PERTH AND KINROSS COUNCIL v. SCOTT 2005 S.L.T. 89, Lady Smith, OH.

5642. Roads-Road user charging-Annual accounts

ROAD USER CHARGING SCHEMES (KEEPING OF ACCOUNTS AND RELEVANT EXPENSES) (SCOTLAND) REGULATIONS 2005, SSI 2005 654; made under the Transport (Scotland) Act 2001 s.81, Sch.1 para.1, Sch.1 para.4. In force: January 30, 2006; £3.00.

These Regulations provide for annual accounts to be kept in relation to charging schemes made under the Transport (Scotland) Act 2001. These accounts must be kept, prepared and published in accordance with proper accounting practices.

5643. Roads-Road user charging-Liability for charges

ROAD USER CHARGING (LIABILITY FOR CHARGES) (SCOTLAND) REGULATIONS 2005, SSI 2005 651; made under the Transport (Scotland) Act 2001 s.49, s.81. In force: January 30, 2006; £3.00.

These Regulations specify the persons liable for charges for road user charging schemes under the Transport (Scotland) Act 2001.

5644. Roads-Road user charging-Penalty charges

ROAD USER CHARGING (PENALTY CHARGES) (SCOTLAND) REGULATIONS 2005, SSI 2005 652; made under the Transport (Scotland) Act 2001 s.55, s.56, s.81. In force: January 30, 2006; £3.00.

These Regulations deal with the procedures relating to the imposition of penalty charges for road user charging schemes, under the Transport (Scotland) Act 2001. The Regulations cover requirements about the imposition of and liability for penalty charges, examination of and entry to vehicles, power of removal and disposal of vehicles, recovery of penalty charges in relation to removed vehicles, taking possession of vehicles and claims by registered keepers of vehicles after their disposal.

5645. Traffic wardens-Uniforms-South Lanarkshire

PARKING ATTENDANTS (WEARING OF UNIFORMS) (SOUTH LANARKSHIRE COUNCIL PARKING AREA) REGULATIONS 2005, SSI 2005 12; made under the Road Traffic Act 1984 s.63A. In force: February 7, 2005; £3.00.

These Regulations prescribe functions during the exercise of which, a parking attendant must wear such uniform as the Scottish Ministers may determine.

5646. Traffic wardens-Uniforms-South Lanarkshire

PARKING ATTENDANTS (WEARING OF UNIFORMS) (SOUTH LANARKSHIRE COUNCIL PARKING AREA) (NO.2) REGULATIONS 2005, SSI 2005 35; made under the Road Traffic Act 1984 s.63A.. In force: February 7, 2005; £3.00.

These Regulations revoke and replace the Parking Attendants (Wearing of Uniforms) (South Lanarkshire Council Parking Area) Regulations 2005 (SI 2005 12) which makes erroneous reference to the Dundee parking area. The Regulations prescribe functions during the exercise of which, a parking attendant must wear such uniform as the Scottish Ministers may determine.

SALE OF GOODS

5647. Breach of contract-Defective goods-Farming equipment-Right to return following repair

[Sale of Goods Act 1979 (c.54) s.35(2).]

R, a business carrying out farming, purchased and took delivery of equipment from L, a company, which proved to be defective. R accepted a replacement machine on loan and agreed to the defective machine being taken back to L's premises for inspection. The machine was thereafter repaired. R rejected the repaired machine on the basis that they had not been given any information by L as to the nature of the original defect, arguing that the contract was terminated as L was in breach of the contract of sale due to the condition of the goods, and sought repetition of the purchase price. Decree was granted in R's favour. L appealed to the sheriff principal who assoilzied them, finding in fact that the repaired machine was as good as it would have been had it left the factory as new and correctly assembled. It was not disputed that the equipment as delivered was disconform to contract but the only evidence as to whether the goods conformed to contract at the time of rejection came from L's fitter which was not challenged or contradicted. R appealed to the Court of Session.

Held, dismissing the appeal (Lord Marnoch dissenting), that R's challenge to the sheriff principal's approach on the factual issues had to fail where, if to succeed in the action, they required to demonstrate that the equipment, as at the time of rejection, was so defective as to render L in material breach of contract. The purported rejection and rescission came too late and R were obliged to accept the goods, subject to the protection afforded by the Sale of Goods Act 1979 s.35(2), where it was established that L had tendered a machine which was conform to contract at the time of rejection, albeit historically it had been so in breach, and so far as appeared, no contractually stipulated date for the performance of the obligation to deliver the goods conform to contract had come and passed, nor had an unreasonable time elapsed. (Per Lord Marnoch) (1) There was no underlying principle to support the thesis that the right of rejection or rescission would be lost if prior to the exercise of the right of rejection, a seller rendered goods which were said by then to conform to contract, and the thesis might be impracticable to operate where it gave rise to difficult questions of shifting onus of proof. (2) R, having acquired the right to reject the goods, could not have it taken away simply by the later renewed tendering of the goods in an allegedly repaired condition as a purported second tendering of the goods was quite simply "not performance within the meaning of the contract". (3) There was not even any performance in the present case as the goods, as tendered under contract, had been shown to be disconform to contract at the time of tendering and there was simply no provision for a second or later tendering of either the same or any other goods. (4) If, outwith the purview of the 1979 Act, L had an answer to R's claimed right of rejection, it had to be found within the domain of personal bar, but since that was not pled, either in its statutory form or at common law, and since the only argument advanced by L was unsound, his Lordship would have allowed the appeal.

J&H RITCHIE LTD v. LLOYD LTD 2005 S.C.155, Lord Marnoch, Lord Hamilton, Lord Philip, Ex Div.

SENTENCING

5648. Assault to severe injury—Undue leniency—Mitigation

B pled guilty to a charge that, while acting along with two others, he assaulted a man to his severe injury and to the danger of his life by punching and kicking him on the head, rendering him unconscious, and assaulted another man by repeatedly kicking and punching him on the head and stamping on his body. Earlier in the evening, B had been assaulted by the complainers in a nightclub. The sheriff, taking into account the fact that B, who had no previous convictions, had joined the army and his career would be cut short by a custodial sentence, imposed a sentence of 300 hours' community service and compensation orders of £500 and £100 respectively. The Lord Advocate appealed against sentence on the ground that it was unduly lenient.

Held, allowing the appeal and substituting three and a half years' imprisonment, that while bearing in mind B's previous good character and his plea of guilty, there was no provocation to which regard could properly be had, in law or more generally, in relation to the assaults and inadequate consideration had been given to the serious nature and consequences thereof, especially regarding the first complainer.

HM ADVOCATE v. BOOTH (RAYMOND GLENN) 2005 S.L.T. 337, Lord Cullen L.J.G, Lord Penrose, Lord Johnston, HCJ.

5649. Bail—Breach of order—Failure to appear for trial—No discount for guilty plea

The appellant (S) appealed against a total sentence of three and a half years' imprisonment imposed for offences of failing to appear for trial. S pleaded guilty to the charges of failure to appear, but after trial he was acquitted of the assault charges that were the subject of the original indictment. At sentencing, S was not given any discount for his pleas of guilty since the judge took the view that the pleas had been ones of convenience, designed to remove from the jury the knowledge that he had failed to attend for trial on two previous occasions. S was accordingly sentenced to consecutive imprisonment terms of 18 months and two years. On appeal, S argued that (1) the sentences were excessive in the light of his pleas, his personal circumstances and the circumstances of the offences; (2) the sentence was incompetent because it followed an adjournment in excess of four weeks without cause shown.

Held, allowing the appeal, that (1) the sentencing judge had misdirected himself, since an accused was entitled to tender a plea of guilty at any time. If the jury consequently heard nothing of the facts and circumstances, the accused should not be penalised for that. The pleas of guilty were not ones which deserved to attract a significant reduction in sentence. It was unlikely that the Crown would have used the mere fact that S had failed to appear for trial as evidence relevant to the proof of the substantive charges against him. The sentences were accordingly quashed and substituted by consecutive sentences of six months and one year. (2) Audio tape evidence showed that the adjournment before sentencing was to be more than four weeks because the judge was unavailable earlier. Having regard to that evidence, which was readily available, it was inappropriate for S to have framed his second ground of appeal, purporting to be based on a procedural irregularity, without a full investigation of the factual background having been carried out first.

SMITH (CRAIG CHARLES) v. HM ADVOCATE 2004 S.C.C.R. 521, Lord Penrose, Lord Mackay of Drumadoon, HCJ.

5650. Culpable homicide–Guilty pleas–Discount for early admission of guilt and consequent avoidance of trial

R appealed against a sentence of 12 years' imprisonment imposed on his conviction of culpable homicide. R was initially charged with murdering his three-month-old son by compressing the child's neck and placing his hand over his mouth and nose to stop him crying. R also admitted having used this method to quieten the child on other occasions. The Crown agreed to accept a plea of culpable homicide, which avoided the necessity for a trial and consequent distress to the family of the victim and other witnesses. The sentencing judge took the view that the case was a particularly serious one and that R's conduct had fallen little short of being wickedly reckless. He considered that any relevant mitigating factors had already been reflected in the acceptance of the culpable homicide plea and the sentence was intended to be at the top end of the scale for such an offence.

Held, allowing the appeal (Lord Philip dissenting), that the sentencing judge's report disclosed an error of approach to sentencing in that it had been unsound to treat the mitigating factors as having been reflected in the acceptance of the plea. R's plea, his evident remorse and the connected avoidance of distress to witnesses, as far as material, should have been taken into account in mitigation of the punishment that would have been appropriate had no such plea been tendered, *Du Plooy (Devonne) v. HM Advocate (No.1)* 2003 S.L.T. 1237, [2003] C.L.Y. 5404 considered. An appropriate base figure would be about 11 years, but this was a case in which a distinct and material reduction in sentence should be allowed to reflect R's plea and recognise the special significance of such a plea in sparing the distress of the victims' family and friends. A sentence of nine years' imprisonment was substituted accordingly. It was noted that failure to discount the sentence where a guilty plea had been tendered at an early stage would result in there being effectively no distinction in treatment between such a case and one where a person had denied responsibility throughout and been convicted of culpable homicide only after a trial.

RB v. HM ADVOCATE; *sub nom*. B v. HM ADVOCATE 2004 S.C.C.R. 443, Lord Hamilton, Lord Abernethy, Lord Philip, HCJ.

5651. Murder–Attempts–Prohibited firearms–Attempted murder of police officer–Undue leniency

M pled guilty to the attempted murder of a police officer by discharging a prohibited weapon at him. M had entered a police office, left to go to a nearby close and returned shortly thereafter with a double barrelled shotgun. M was sentenced to 10 years' detention with an extension period of five years. The Lord Advocate appealed against sentence on the ground it was unduly lenient, arguing that the trial judge failed to have sufficient regard to the fact that the offence was premeditated, it was committed using a firearm and in a police station, the victim was a police officer acting in the execution of his duty, there were no mitigating factors not mitigating explanation with regard to its commission, and M presented as a moderate to high risk of further offending.

Held, allowing the appeal and substituting life imprisonment, that the sentence was unduly lenient where it was difficult to conceive of a case of attempted murder more grave. It was undoubted fact that the offence was premeditated, the firearm was used against a police officer in the execution of his duty in a place designed to provide ready access by members of the public to the police service, and the assessment of risk presented by M was of great importance.

HM ADVOCATE v. MURRAY (PAUL FRANCIS) 2004 S.L.T. 1230, Lord Cullen L.J.G., Lord MacLean, Lord Osborne, HCJ.

5652. Murder – Life imprisonment – Punishment part of life sentence

[Human Rights Act 1998 (c.42) s.3(1), Sch.1 Part I Art.7; Scotland Act 1998 (c.46) s.101, Sch.6 para.13; Convention Rights (Compliance) (Scotland) Act 2001 (asp 7) Sch.1 Part 1 para.13.]

Four accused, F, M, N and C, were convicted of murder and sentenced to mandatory life sentences. They appealed against the orders by which the punishment parts of their sentences had been specified retrospectively under the Convention Rights (Compliance) (Scotland) Act 2001 Sch.1 Part 1 para.13. The High Court of Justiciary, following the ratio of *Stewart (William) v. HM Advocate (Sentencing)* 2002 S.L.T. 1307, [2002] C.L.Y. 6080, refused the grounds of appeal relating to lawfulness. The appellants brought their appeals before the Judicial Committee of the Privy Council under the Scotland Act 1998 Sch.6 para.13, which raised a devolution issue on whether the transitional provisions in Sch.1 Part 1 of the 2001 Act were within the legislative competence of the Scottish Parliament. The Judicial Committee accepted that the fixing of the punishment part in each case deprived the appellant of the review he had been led to expect but, having regard to s.101 of the Scotland Act 1998 and the Human Rights Act 1998 s.3(1), concluded that the legislation could be read in a way that was Convention compliant if the court, when fixing the punishment part, took into account events relating to reviews of the sentence by the parole board, which was incompatible with *Stewart*. The continued appeals on the punishment parts were remitted to a bench of five judges. Parties were agreed that *Stewart* should be overruled. The appellants submitted that the ratio of the Judicial Committee's decision was that it would be contrary to Sch.1 Part I Art.7 of the Human Rights Act 1998 for the provisions of the 2001 Act to result in an appellant serving longer in custody before his first, or next, review by the parole board and the only practical way to ensure that that guiding principle was observed was to set the date fixed for the relevant review in each case as a ceiling on the proper punishment part to be imposed. F's appeal was abandoned in the course of the hearing.

Held, allowing the appeals, that (1) *Stewart* and *McCreaddie (Derek Alexander) v. HM Advocate (Appeal against Sentence)* 2002 S.L.T. 1311, [2002] C.L.Y. 6079 would be overruled in the light of the Judicial Committee's decision, *Stewart* and *McCreaddie* overruled; (2) the Judicial Committee's decision established only that the proposed review in each case was a relevant, but not decisive, factor in the fixing of the punishment part and the weight to be given to it depended on the appellant's prospects of release at the relevant date, and (3) the logical starting point was to consider what punishment part would have been set in each case if it had been set at the date of sentence and decide whether it was of an appropriate length, and then look at subsequent events having a possible bearing on the appellant's prospects of release and decide what weight, if any, to give to them all in the circumstances by way of adjustment to the punishment part. For M, in all the circumstances, the punishment part of 14 years was excessive. Twelve years would have been appropriate, and taking into account subsequent events, a punishment part of 10 years would be substituted. For N, the punishment part of 14 years was appropriate, and proceeding on the basis that he would have had no realistic prospects of release at a first review date in August 2005, but making assumptions as favourable to him as could be made regarding his prospects of release, the punishment part would be reduced to 13 years. For C, the punishment part of 30 years was excessive, 20 years would have accurately reflected the gravity of the crime, and to reflect the likelihood of his early release, the punishment part should be moderated to 18 years.

FLYNN (PATRICK ANTHONY) v. HM ADVOCATE (NO.2); MEEK (PETER MITCHELL) v. HM ADVOCATE (NO.2); NICOL (JOHN GARY) v. HM ADVOCATE

(NO.2); McMURRAY (PETER) v. HM ADVOCATE (NO.2) 2005 J.C. 271, Lord Gill L.J.C., Lord MacLean, Lord Penrose, Lord Osborne, Lord Macfadyen, HCJ.

5653. Probation orders–Breach–Sentence length–Weight to attach to guilty plea

M, aged 20, pled guilty to charges of theft by shoplifting and dangerous driving for which the sheriff imposed one year's probation. M thereafter failed to attend three successive probation appointments resulting in the revocation of the order and the imposition of four months' detention. M appealed, arguing that the sheriff ought to have applied a discount in respect of the fact that he had pled guilty before the probation order was made.

Held, refusing the appeal, that once there had been a breach of probation, more had to be taken into account when assessing whether a discount was merited: it could not be said in absolute terms that the circumstances in which the original plea of guilty was tendered became irrelevant when a court had to reconsider the question of punishment after a breach of a probation order but the utilitarian value of the plea might be reduced or negated by the fact that, as a result of the breach of probation, a further diet was made necessary.

MacKIE v. STOTT; *sub nom.* MacKIE v. WARD 2005 J.C. 41, Lord Macfadyen, Lord Nimmo Smith, HCJ.

5654. Probation orders–Hearings–Competence

[Criminal Procedure (Scotland) Act 1995 (c.46) s.229(1), Sch.6.]

M was charged with breach of the peace. He pled guilty and a 12 month probation order was imposed, including a requirement that he attend the court for a probation progress hearing. At the progress hearing, M being absent, the sheriff fixed a further progress hearing despite a challenge by M's agent. The sheriff regarded the basis for fixing a progress hearing as the Criminal Procedure (Scotland) Act 1995 s.229(1)(a) and considered that it would be conducive to securing the good conduct of M, in the knowledge that he required to return to court when a progress report would be available. M lodged a bill of suspension, submitting that (1) s.229(1) did not provide authority for the fixing of a progress hearing once a probation order had been made and any additional requirement imposed should relate to the order itself but could not be one which involved further participation by the court; (2) the requirement inserted into the probation order referred only to the first progress hearing and provided no basis for a further hearing thereafter which would require amendment of the probation order which had not been done and could not competently have been done by the sheriff since in terms of Sch.6 to the Act such an amendment could only be made on application by the supervising officer.

Held, passing the bill, that s.229(1) did not provide authority for the fixing of a progress hearing and in the absence of express authority, a court was functus once it had finally disposed of a case by passing sentence and had no power to sit again in the same case.

McLAUGHLIN v. McQUAID; *sub nom.* McLAUGHLIN v. McQUADE 2005 S.L.T. 972, Lord Macfadyen, Lord Kinclaven, Temporary Judge CGB Nicholson Q.C., HCJ.

5655. Rape–Lewd practices–Offences against children entrusted to offender's care–Undue leniency

[Civic Government (Scotland) Act 1982 (c.45) s.52A; Criminal Procedure (Scotland) Act 1995 (c.46) s.210A.]

The Crown appealed against a sentence of five years' imprisonment imposed on T, aged 43, for two charges of lewd, indecent and libidinous practices, and one of rape, the offences having occurred over a four year period. T had handled and photographed the private parts of L, a friend of his daughters (aged between 6 and 10) and X, T's niece (aged between 13 months and 5 years) while the girls were sleeping in T's house and, on one occasion, T inserted his penis into the lower part of X's vagina to an extent of about 1cm, the medical opinion being that this could have been performed while X was asleep and without waking her. A concurrent sentence of three months' imprisonment, not the subject of appeal, was imposed for a further charge of possessing indecent photographs or pseudo photographs of children, contrary to the Civic Government (Scotland) Act 1982 s.52A. The sentencing judge took into account the very serious nature of the offences, the fact that they were committed against children entrusted to T's care, and the escalation in T's conduct from viewing pornography to contact offending against victims, but also noted that T, who was a first offender, had shown remorse and had pleaded guilty, that, according to a psychologist's report, he presented a low risk of reoffending, and that the charge of rape was of an unusual character. T emphasised the assistance he had given to the authorities and the fact that he had sought help after the investigation started, and submitted that the onus on the Crown to demonstrate that the sentence was unduly lenient posed a high test.

Held, allowing the appeal and substituting eight years' imprisonment with an extension period of five years, that (1) when all reasonable allowance was made for mitigatory factors, the gravity of T's offending was such that the sentence imposed was unduly lenient. (2) In the light of the reports on T, and in particular a further psychologist's report indicating that T was attracted to pre pubertal female children and posed a medium risk of reoffending against children with whom he was living, the appropriate type of sentence was an extended sentence under the Criminal Procedure (Scotland) Act 1995 s.210A.

HM ADVOCATE v. T; *sub nom*. HM ADVOCATE v. JT 2005 J.C. 86, Lord Cullen L.J.G., Lord Hamilton, Lady Cosgrove, HCJ.

5656. Restriction orders–Community service orders–Competence

M was charged with reset and possession of cannabis. The sheriff imposed a cumulo sentence of a three month restriction of liberty order and 150 hours' community service. M appealed, arguing that it was incompetent to impose both orders, which were discrete penalties.

Held, quashing the restriction of liberty order, that it was clear that Parliament had not contemplated the combination of these orders and the absence of any recognition in the legislation of the possibility of combining a restriction of liberty order with a community service order pointed to its incompetence.

MacAULEY v. HOUSTON 2005 S.L.T. 834, Lord Macfadyen, Lord Kinclaven, Temporary Judge CGB Nicholson Q.C., HCJ.

5657. Road traffic offences–Causing death by dangerous driving–Consumption of cannabis and previous convictions–Culpability–Undue leniency

The Lord Advocate appealed against M sentence of 18 months' imprisonment for causing death by dangerous driving and a concurrent sentence of six months for driving while disqualified on the ground that they were unduly lenient. M had been driving a car belonging to his brother in law (G) in an attempt to pinpoint a knocking sound that occurred when the car went round corners. G's car had been substantially modified and its controls and speed were enhanced. M had been smoking cannabis shortly before agreeing to go out in the car. After driving for two miles, M lost control driving out of a bend and the car skidded into a tree causing fatal injuries to G. It was accepted that M's driving had not been dangerous until he emerged from the bend and it appeared at that point he had swerved to enable G to hear the sound. It was not possible to determine whether cannabis consumption had impaired M's driving. At the time of the accident M was a disqualified driver and he had two previous convictions for possessing drugs. In his report, the trial judge stated that the jury could only have decided that M's driving had been dangerous because of his cannabis consumption. The Lord Advocate appealed against sentence, arguing that it had been unduly lenient and had failed to give proper weight to the circumstances.

Held, allowing the appeal, that M's driving had been dangerous independent of his cannabis consumption or lack of familiarity with the car. The sentence was

quashed and substituted for sentence of four years' imprisonment. The offence
was aggravated by M's drug consumption and previous convictions, and while it
was not possible to determine the effect of the cannabis, it would have slowed
his reactions and increased his culpability in deciding to drive a performance
enhanced car. Account was taken of the short distance over which the
dangerous driving took place and M's conduct since the accident.

Observed, that although not applicable in Scotland, English sentencing
guidelines gave useful examples of the significance of factors relevant to
aggravation or mitigation, such as the consumption of drugs and previous
convictions as indicators of higher culpability, *Attorney General's Reference
(No.152 of 2002), Re* [2003] EWCA Crim 996, [2003] 3 All E.R. 40, [2004]
C.L.Y. 3333 considered.

HM ADVOCATE v. MacPHERSON (THOMAS MacDONALD); *sub nom.* HM
ADVOCATE v. MacPHERSON (THOMAS DONALD) 2005 S.L.T. 397, Lord
Cullen L.J.G., Lord MacLean, Lord Osborne, HCJ.

5658. Road traffic offences—Driving while over the limit—Public informing police of erratic driving—Previous conviction—Maximum custodial sentence—Sentence length

The appellant (S) appealed against a maximum sentence of six months'
imprisonment, with two months' discount for a guilty plea to driving with an
alcohol level of 124mg per 100 ml of breath. S's car was seen to swerve across
the road by a member of the public who reported S to the police. S had been
convicted for drink driving seven years earlier.

Held, allowing the appeal, that the public appreciation of the danger created
by S and subsequent notification of the police could not be underestimated. S
had a previous conviction and the sheriff was correct to impose a custodial
sentence in the circumstances. However, it was not appropriate to begin the
custody period from the maximum, the previous conviction was seven years ago
and not of such materiality to justify taking the maximum sentence as the
appropriate starting place. In the circumstances, three months was appropriate
with a one month discount for the guilty plea.

SOHAL v. GALLACHER 2004 S.C.C.R. 577, Lord Penrose, Lord Hamilton, HCJ.

5659. Road traffic offences—Speeding—Fines—Accused unable to deliver licence which had already been submitted to DVLC for amendment—Sentence imposed greater than fixed penalty

B had been charged with driving at 56 mph in an area subject to a temporary limit
of 40 mph. He was issued with a fixed penalty notice which provided for a fixed
penalty of £60 and three penalty points. He sent a cheque for the amount but it was
returned as he was unable to deliver his licence, which had been sent to the DVLC
for amendment following a change of address. He was subsequently prosecuted.
He pled guilty by letter and explained the circumstances surrounding his attempt to
pay the fixed penalty. He was fined £100 and received three penalty points. B
appealed against the sentence.

Held, allowing the appeal and substituting a fine of £60 with three penalty
points, that where an offender had been offered a fixed penalty by notice and
could demonstrate that he had been prevented from implementing the terms of
the offer because he had delivered up his licence to the DVLC in order to meet
other obligations arising under the same statutory code, it would not be
consistent with a fair exercise of the discretionary power for the court to
penalise him beyond the terms of the fixed penalty notice.

BRYSON v. CURRIE; *sub nom.* BRYSON v. CAMERON 2005 J.C. 119, Lord
Penrose, Lord Mackay of Drumadoon, HCJ.

5660. Supply of drugs—Intimidation—Mitigation

S was charged with being concerned in the supply of heroin and cocaine. He had
been involved in supplying a network of dealers in the Aberdeen area, involving the

transportation of significant quantities of drugs there from Merseyside, which generated up to £11,000 per day in sales. S gave evidence that he had become involved as a result of intimidation by people with significant involvement in drug dealing. He had been attacked and struck on the arm with a meat cleaver and was then threatened with further attacks and threats were also directed towards his parents. The sentencing judge was provided with two reports on S by a clinical psychologist to the effect that he had limited intellectual capacity which could have rendered him susceptible to influence by others, particularly in combination with threats to his life and that of his family. Concurrent sentences of eight and a half years' imprisonment were imposed. S appealed against sentence, submitting that insufficient regard had been paid to his limited intellect which could make him more susceptible to influence than the average man, arguing that it appeared that the sentencing judge had, on grounds of policy, declined to regard the intimidation he had suffered as a mitigating factor. S founded on the intimidation in combination with his limited intellect and argued that there was no such policy, generally or specifically in drugs cases.

Held, allowing the appeal and substituting seven years' imprisonment, that (1) the innate susceptibility of an accused to pressure or intimidation which led to their offending was a relevant consideration. (2) While the court had some difficulty reconciling the psychologist's views of S's intellectual ability with the description given by the Crown of his role in running the Aberdeen operation, the sentencing judge had accepted that his offending had been brought about by intimidation, and standing the expert evidence of S's susceptibility, there had been a failure to take into account a relevant consideration which was of materiality.

STAFFORD v. HM ADVOCATE 2005 S.L.T. 836, Lord Cullen L.J.G., Lord Penrose, Lord Clarke, HCJ.

5661. Supply of drugs–Sentence length–Being concerned in supply of 350 ecstasy tablets in one day–No inference of substantial involvement

The appellant (F) appealed against a cumulo sentence of 11 years' imprisonment, which was imposed following his conviction of being concerned in the supply of cannabis resin between October 1 and November 2, 1999 and being concerned in the supply of ecstasy on one day. The cannabis charge related to the supply of 48kg of cannabis resin, and the ecstasy charge related to 350 tablets given in lieu of payment for a computer. F also admitted a number of previous convictions, including one in 1995 for being concerned in the supply of drugs which carried a sentence of six years' imprisonment.

Held, allowing the appeal, that (1) the trial judge was entitled to infer, having regard to the amount of cannabis, that the jury must have concluded that F had been concerned in drug dealing over the longer period to which the conviction related. (2) The judge had gone too far in drawing the inference that F had been substantially involved in dealing in ecstasy, given the short period of time involved. (3) In the instant case F's previous convictions formed the significant factor affecting the appropriate sentence. (4) Having regard to these arguments and the delay, a sentence of nine years' imprisonment was substituted.

FOLLEN (GARRY JOHN) v. HM ADVOCATE 2004 S.C.C.R. 647, Lord Cullen L.J.G., Lord Penrose, Lord Hamilton, HCJ.

SHIPPING

5662. Harbours–Empowerment–Caledonian MacBrayne Limited–Kennacraig

CALEDONIAN MACBRAYNE LIMITED (KENNACRAIG) HARBOUR EMPOWERMENT ORDER 2005, SSI 2005 353; made under the Harbours Act 1964 s.16. In force: June 15, 2005; £3.50.

This Order provides that Caledonian MacBrayne Ltd shall exercise jurisdiction as a harbour authority within the meaning of the Harbours Act 1964 s.57 and the powers of the harbour master shall be exercisable within the area the boundaries of which are described in Sch.1 to this Order and shown in red on the harbour map together with so much of the harbour premises as are not situated within that area. The Company may take such steps from time to time as it considers necessary or expedient for the improvement, maintenance and management of the harbour and the accommodation and facilities afforded therein or in connection therewith.

5663. Harbours–Revision–Caledonian MacBrayne–Oban Quay

CALEDONIAN MACBRAYNE (OBAN QUAY) HARBOUR REVISION ORDER 2005, SSI 2005 359; made under the Harbours Act 1964 s.14. In force: June 17, 2005; £3.00.

This Order authorises Caledonian MacBrayne to construct a new Roll on Roll off berthing facility at Oban, Argyll.

5664. Harbours–Revision–Constitution–Peterhead

PETERHEAD PORT AUTHORITY HARBOUR (CONSTITUTION) REVISION ORDER 2005, SSI 2005 491; made under the Harbours Act 1964 s.14. In force: October 5, 2005; £3.00.

This Order revokes the Peterhead Bay Harbour Trust and Transfer Order 1983 (SI 1983 316 (S.26)) (in part), the Peterhead Harbours Revision (Constitution) Order 2002 (SSI 2005 504) and the Peterhead Bay Authority (Constitution) Revision Order 2002 (SSI 2002 294) (in part). On January 1, 2006, this Order renames and constitutes the Peterhead Harbours Trustees (PHT) as the Peterhead Port Authority and provides for the trade assets and liabilities of the Peterhead Bay Authority (PBA) to be transferred on the previous day to the PHT and for the cessation of the separate corporate identity of the PBA.

5665. Harbours–Revision–Constitution–Scrabster

SCRABSTER HARBOUR REVISION (CONSTITUTION) ORDER 2005, SSI 2005 133; made under the Harbours Act 1964 s.14. In force: March 2, 2005; £3.00.

This Order alters the constitution of the Scrabster Harbour Trust in line with the recommendations of the Trust Ports Review published by the Department of the Environment, Transport and the Regions in January 2000 and endorsed by the Scottish Executive. The Order, which amends the Act for making and maintaining a Harbour at Scrabster Roads in the Bay of Thurso and County of Caithness, and Road thereto 1841 and the Scrabster Harbour Order Confirmation Act 1975, also extends the seaward limit of the harbour.

5666. Harbours–Revision–Constitution–Ullapool

ULLAPOOL HARBOUR REVISION (CONSTITUTION) ORDER 2005, SSI 2005 132; made under the Harbours Act 1964 s.14. In force: March 2, 2005; £3.00.

This Order reconstitutes the Ullapool Harbour Trustees as from December 1, 2005. It provides for the Trustees to consist of a body of eight Trustees with experience in relevant matters. Four Trustees will be elected by the Lochbroom voters and three Trustees will be appointed. The remaining Trustee will be the harbour master. The Order, which amends the Pier and Harbour Order Confirmation (No.4) Act 1911 and the Ullapool Harbour Order Confirmation Act 1984, includes other provisions with regard to the Trustees Constitution and repeals or revokes certain statutory provisions.

5667. Harbours–Revision–Constitution–Wick

WICK HARBOUR REVISION (CONSTITUTION) ORDER 2005, SSI 2005 276; made under the Harbours Act 1964 s.14. In force: May 24, 2005; £3.00.

This Order which amends the Pulteney Harbour Act 1879, the Wick & Pulteney Harbour Act 1899, the Wick & Pulteney Harbours Order Confirmation Act 1903, the Wick Harbour Order Confirmation Act 1914 and the Wick Harbour Order

Confirmation Act 1919 reconstitutes the Wick Harbour Trustees as from July 1, 2005. It provides for the renamed Wick Harbour Authority to consist of a body of seven members with experience in relevant matters, of which one member will be the harbour master.

5668. Harbours–Revision–Works–Inverness

INVERNESS HARBOUR REVISION (WORKS) ORDER 2005, SSI 2005 489; made under the Harbours Act 1964 s.14. In force: October 4, 2005; £3.00.

This Order authorises the Trustees of the Harbour of Inverness to carry out reclamation works, to construct a bund and protect with rock armour, construct a quay wall in Inverness and to continue and maintain the said quay wall and these works; and to carry out subsidiary works.

SOCIAL SECURITY

5669. Housing benefit–Overpayment of benefit–Recovery of overpayments by deduction from future payments–Landlord's right of appeal

[Housing Benefit (General) Regulations 1987 (SI 1987 1971) Reg 102; Child Support, Pensions and Social Security Act 2000 (c.19) Sch.7 para.6; Housing Benefit and Council Tax Benefit (Decisions and Appeals) Regulations 2001 (SI 2001 1002) Reg.3(1).]

The appellant (Q), a housing association, appealed against a decision of the appeal tribunal that it lacked jurisdiction to hear Q's appeal against a determination by the respondent local authority to recover overpaid housing benefit. The local authority had issued the determination against tenants of Q and sought to recover the overpayments by deducting sums from future housing benefit payments pursuant to the Housing Benefit (General) Regulations 1987 Reg.102. Q appealed to the appeal tribunal, who held that it had no jurisdiction to hear the appeal, then to the Social Security Commissioner, arguing that a right of appeal subsisted under the Child Support, Pensions and Social Security Act 2000 Sch.7 para. 6(1), para.(3) and para.(6), since a determination against a tenant was an indirect determination against a landlord. The local authority argued that (1) the right of appeal was only available to the person from whom the overpayment would be recovered and that a landlord could not claim to be the relevant person simply because the recovery method was against future payments of housing benefit; (2) the wording of the Housing Benefit and Council Tax Benefit (Decisions and Appeals) Regulations 2001 Reg.3(1) indicated that the "person affected" by the decision was the person from whom the local authority decided the overpayment was recoverable, which must be the same as the person the landlord decided to proceed against under Reg.102 of the 1987 Regulations.

Held, dismissing the appeal, that (1) the local authority's submissions were to be preferred. There was a clear distinction between a determination that there was a recoverable overpayment from a named person and the means by which that recovery was to be effected. Although the proposed means of recovery might affect future payments Q received from the local authority, that was not equivalent to a determination by the local authority that there had been a recoverable overpayment of housing benefit. The benefit still belonged to the tenant and the obligation to pay rent to Q also remained with the tenant. (2) It followed that Q had no right of appeal, being neither a claimant nor a person from whom an overpayment was recoverable within the terms of Reg.3(1) of the 2001 Regulations.

QUEEN'S CROSS HOUSING ASSOCIATION LTD v. GLASGOW CITY COUNCIL 2004 Hous. L.R. 125, Commissioner JD May Q.C., SS Comm.

5670. Income–Capital–Assessment

NATIONAL ASSISTANCE (ASSESSMENT OF RESOURCES) AMENDMENT (SCOTLAND) REGULATIONS 2005, SSI 2005 82; made under the National Assistance Act 1948 s.22. In force: April 11, 2005; £3.00.

These Regulations amend the National Assistance (Assessment of Resources) Regulations 1992 (SI 1992 2977) which concern the assessment of a person's liability to pay for accommodation provided under the Social Work (Scotland) Act 1968. They make amendments so that the capital limit set out in Reg.20 is increased from £19,000 to £19,500; the capital limits set in Reg.28(1) are increased from £11,750 and £19,000 to £12,000 and £19,500; and provides for an increase to the amount which should be disregarded from the calculation of income other than earnings from the financial assessment where a resident receives savings credit. They also amend the National Assistance (Assessment of Resources) Amendment (Scotland) Regulations 2004 (SSI 2004 103) which provided the previous capital limits.

5671. Income–Residential accommodation–Assessment of resources

NATIONAL ASSISTANCE (ASSESSMENT OF RESOURCES) AMENDMENT (NO.2) (SCOTLAND) REGULATIONS 2005, SSI 2005 522; made under the National Assistance Act 1948 s.22. In force: November 7, 2005; £3.00.

These Regulations amend the National Assistance (Assessment of Resources) Regulations 1992 (SI 1992 2977) which concern the assessment of a person's liability to pay for accommodation provided under the Social Work (Scotland) Act 1968. By virtue of the 1968 Act, accommodation provided under the 1968 Act or the Mental Health (Care and Treatment) (Scotland) Act 2003 s.25 shall be regarded as accommodation provided under the National Assistance Act 1948. The Regulations provide that any payments made under the Age Related Payments Act 2004 s.7 are to be disregarded as capital in the financial assessment of that person's resources.

5672. Residential accommodation–Sums for personal requirements

NATIONAL ASSISTANCE (SUMS FOR PERSONAL REQUIREMENTS) (SCOTLAND) REGULATIONS 2005, SSI 2005 84; made under the National Assistance Act 1948 s.22. In force: April 11, 2005; £3.00.

The National Assistance Act 1948 requires a local authority to assume in assessing a person's liability to pay for accommodation provided under the Social Work (Scotland) Act 1968 or the Mental Health (Scotland) Act 1984 s.7 that he or she will need for his or her personal requirements such sum per week as may be prescribed by regulations. These Regulations, which revoke the National Assistance (Sums for Personal Requirements) (Scotland) Regulations 2004 (SSI 2004 106), prescribe that that sum will be £18.80 per week.

SOCIAL WELFARE

5673. Adults–Learning disabled persons–Authorised establishments

ADULTS WITH INCAPACITY (MANAGEMENT OF RESIDENTS' FINANCES) (SCOTLAND) REGULATIONS 2005, SSI 2005 610; made under the Adults with Incapacity (Scotland) Act 2000 s.35. In force: December 2, 2005; £3.00.

These Regulations amend the Adults with Incapacity (Scotland) Act 2000 to restore private psychiatric hospitals to the list of authorised establishments in s.35(1) of the Act.

5674. Adults–Learning disabled persons–Countersignatures

ADULTS WITH INCAPACITY (COUNTERSIGNATORIES OF APPLICATIONS FOR AUTHORITY TO INTROMIT) (SCOTLAND) AMENDMENT REGULATIONS

2005, SSI 2005 631; made under the Adults with Incapacity (Scotland) Act 2000 s.26. In force: February 1, 2006; £3.00.

These Regulations amend the Adults with Incapacity (Countersignatories of Applications for Authority to Intromit) (Scotland) Regulations 2001 (SSI 2001 78) to include further classes of persons who may countersign an application made under the Adults with Incapacity (Scotland) Act 2000 s.26.

5675. Adults—Learning disabled persons—Welfare guardians

ADULTS WITH INCAPACITY (SUPERVISION OF WELFARE GUARDIANS ETC. BY LOCAL AUTHORITIES) (SCOTLAND) AMENDMENT REGULATIONS 2005, SSI 2005 630; made under the Adults with Incapacity (Scotland) Act 2000 s.10, s.86. In force: February 1, 2006; £3.00.

These Regulations amend the Adults with Incapacity (Supervision of Welfare Guardians etc. by Local Authorities) (Scotland) Regulations 2002 (SSI 2002 95) in respect of welfare guardians whose appointment is for at least a year. The intervals within which a local authority must arrange for visits, other than the initial visit, to an incapable adult and that adult's welfare guardian are extended from three to six months. Local authorities must continue to arrange to visit the welfare guardian, as well as the incapable adult, within three months of the guardian's appointment. The requirements on local authorities to arrange visits to welfare guardians do not apply where the Chief Social Work Officer is the welfare guardian.

5676. Capacity—Guardianship orders—Competence

[Human Rights Act 1998 (c.42) Sch.1 Part I Art.5, Art.6, Art.8; Adults with Incapacity (Scotland) Act 2000 (asp 4) s.1, s.57.]

P sought an order under the Adults with Incapacity (Scotland) Act 2000 s.57 appointing him as guardian with powers relating to the welfare, property and financial affairs of his mother, M, aged 77, who suffered from severe vascular dementia and was no longer capable of independent living or of managing her own affairs. The powers sought were to decide where she should live, to have access to confidential documents, and to consent to, or withhold consent to, medical treatment. M had been admitted to acute medical and rehabilitative care where her needs were assessed as being nursing home care. A safeguarder was appointed on June 22, 2004 and interim financial powers were granted in August 2004. A report by a mental health officer made it plain that he believed the proposed order would not benefit M having regard to the general principles of s.1 of the 2000 Act although it was accepted that the granting of financial powers were necessary. The report further stated that the order was not the least restrictive option; M had no desire to live elsewhere, so far as could be ascertained; P already had access to confidential documents; and M had stated that she did not wish P to be her guardian, although it was acknowledged that she easily became confused and it was accepted that he was a suitable person to be her guardian. An independent report agreed that P was suitable to be guardian and that financial powers were necessary, and further provided that it was impossible to ascertain M's views; while noting M's severely impaired capacity to make decisions, she was "compliant" with the care provided and to remaining where she was; and although recognising P's motivation, a selective approach should be taken towards incapable adults where the adult was incapable and "compliant", and welfare guardianship was not necessary to ensure health, care and welfare. P submitted that (1) there would be a legal vacuum if the order was not granted: there was no legal power authorising M's residence in her present placement; (2) he had been paying M's fees on the basis of her welfare voluntarily, but with no legal authority; (3) the continuation of such an informal arrangement was a breach of M's human rights under the Human Rights Act 1998 Sch.1 Part I Art.6; (4) the granting of the order with welfare powers was consistent with the principles of the Act and was supported by the primary care; (5) access to documents raised points under Sch.1 Part I Art.8 of the 1998 Act which ought to be regulated in order to prevent improper exercise; (6) medical treatment was being administered without actual consent.

Held, granting the order, that where an adult was compliant with the regime but was legally incapable of consenting to or disagreeing with it, that person was deprived of his or her liberty under Sch.1 Part I Art.5, and that step should not be taken without express statute governing it. In every case of the incapable but compliant adult, the least restrictive option was one which granted statutory powers of guardianship. This would benefit M and such benefit could not be achieved without intervention. No other procedure would be appropriate and it would not be acceptable for medical intervention to be dealt with ad hoc. There presently was a legal vacuum which would remain if the order sought was not granted.

MULDOON, APPLICANT 2005 S.L.T. (Sh Ct) 52, Sheriff JA Baird, Sh Ct (Glasgow and Strathkelvin).

5677. Care–Regulation of care–Deemed registration

REGULATION OF CARE (SCOTLAND) ACT 2001 (TRANSITIONAL PROVISIONS) ORDER 2005, SSI 2005 98; made under the Regulation of Care (Scotland) Act 2001 s.80. In force: April 1, 2005; £3.00.

Persons providing a school care accommodation service are deemed to have registered the service under the Regulation of Care (Scotland) Act 2001. This Order provides that deemed registration will cease in specified circumstances.

5678. Care–Regulation of care–Excepted services

REGULATION OF CARE (EXCEPTED SERVICES) (SCOTLAND) REGULATIONS 2002 PARTIAL REVOCATION REGULATIONS 2005, SSI 2005 96; made under the Regulation of Care (Scotland) Act 2001 s.2. In force: April 1, 2005; £3.00.

These Regulations partially revoke the Regulation of Care (Excepted Services) (Scotland) Regulations 2002 (SSI 2002 120) so that the school care accommodation services referred to now fall within the definition of "school care accommodation service".

5679. Care–Regulation of care–Fees

REGULATION OF CARE (FEES) (SCOTLAND) ORDER 2005, SSI 2005 97; made under the Regulation of Care (Scotland) Act 2001 s.24. In force: April 1, 2005; £3.00.

This Order, which revokes the Regulation of Care (Fees) (Scotland) Order 2004 (SSI 2004 93) prescribes the maximum fees which may be imposed by the Scottish Commission for the Regulation of Care in respect of applications for registration or for cancellation of registration of a care service, the annual continuation of any such registration, and applications for variation or removal of a condition of registration under the Regulation of Care (Scotland) Act 2001. It also prescribes the maximum fee for registration or for cancellation of registration of a limited registration service; the annual continuation of any such registration, and applications for variation or removal of a condition of registration.

5680. Care–Regulation of care–Prescribed registers

REGULATION OF CARE (PRESCRIBED REGISTERS) (SCOTLAND) ORDER 2005, SSI 2005 432; made under the Regulation of Care (Scotland) Act 2001 s.52. In force: September 28, 2005; £3.00.

The Regulation of Care (Scotland) Act 2001 provides that any person who, with intent to deceive, while not registered in any relevant register as a social worker, takes or uses the title of social worker, or purports in any other way to be a social worker shall be guilty of an offence and liable on summary conviction to a fine not exceeding Level 5 on the standard scale. It provides that a register is a "relevant register" if it is the register maintained by the Scottish Social Services Council or such register as may be prescribed, being a register maintained under a provision of the law of England and Wales or of Northern Ireland which appears to the Scottish Ministers to correspond to s.44(1) of the Act. These Regulations prescribe the following registers as relevant registers: the register maintained by the General Social Care Council under the Care Standards Act 2000 s.56(1); the register maintained by the Care Council for Wales or Cyngor Gofal Cymru under the Care Standards Act 2000; and the register maintained by the Northern Ireland Social Care Council under the Health and Personal Social Services Act (Northern Ireland) 2001 s.3(1).

5681. Care–Regulation of care–Social service workers–Registers

REGULATION OF CARE (SOCIAL SERVICE WORKERS) (SCOTLAND) AMENDMENT ORDER 2005, SSI 2005 611; made under the Regulation of Care (Scotland) Act 2001 s.44. In force: January 1, 2006; £3.00.

The Regulation of Care (Scotland) Act 2001 requires the Scottish Social Services Council to maintain a register of social workers, social service workers of any other description prescribed and persons participating in a course or employed in a position probationary to becoming either a social worker or social service worker of a qualified description. This Order amends the Regulation of Care (Social Service Workers) (Scotland) Order 2005 (SSI 2005 318) by inserting two additional descriptions of social service worker for this purpose, namely the manager of an adult day care service and the manager of a care home service for adults. These expressions are also defined.

5682. Care–Regulation of care–Social service workers–Registers

REGULATION OF CARE (SOCIAL SERVICE WORKERS) (SCOTLAND) ORDER 2005, SSI 2005 318; made under the Regulation of Care (Scotland) Act 2001 s.44. In force: July 1, 2005; £3.00.

The Regulation of Care (Scotland) Act 2001 requires the Scottish Social Services Council to maintain a register of social workers, social service workers of any other description prescribed and persons participating in a course or employed in a position probationary to becoming either a social worker or social service worker of a qualified description. This Order revokes the Regulation of Care (Social Service Workers) (Scotland) Order 2004 (SSI 2004 268) and prescribes a description of social service worker for the purposes of the Act. It re-enacts the reference to employees of the Scottish Commission for the Regulation of Care who are authorised persons within the meaning of s.25 and s.27 of the Act and also prescribes three additional descriptions of social service worker, namely residential child care workers who are managers of residential child care services, residential child care workers who are not managers of residential child care services but do supervise other residential child care workers and residential child care workers who are neither managers of residential child care services nor supervisors of other residential child care workers. The Order provides that chartered members of the British Psychological Society and those who are registered with or are a member of any of the other bodies listed are excluded from the prescribed descriptions of social service worker.

5683. Care homes–Registration–Cancellation

[Regulation of Care (Scotland) Act 2001 (asp 8) s.12(1)(b).]

Y, care home operators, appealed against a sheriff's decision refusing their appeal against a decision of S, the Scottish Commission for the Regulation of Care, to cancel their registration on the ground that the service provided by them was being carried on other than in accordance with relevant requirements, contrary to the Regulation of Care (Scotland) Act 2001 s.12(1)(b). Y had entered into an agreement with the owner of the care home in 2002 to manage the business. S intimated their decision to cancel registration some six months after serving Y with an improvement notice and listed, inter alia, a failure to demonstrate sufficient control over the premises to provide care service, a failure to demonstrate full compliance with the requirements of staffing notices, and a failure to implement a system for medications in compliance with best practice guidelines. T submitted that these grounds could not properly be considered by S when deciding whether to cancel the registration as they had been imposed by the registering authorities under earlier legislation which had not been carried forward and thus did not have effect.

Held, dismissing the appeal, that (1) the conditions attached to the registrations of the care home by the preceding authorities remained in force after the coming into effect of the Act; (2) the sheriff was entitled to reach the conclusion he did. The nature and number of shortcomings identified at the care home and the lack of action taken to address them over a prolonged period were indicative of a failure to make proper provision for the health and welfare of the service users and disclosed a very unsatisfactory state of affairs, potentially endangering those receiving care at the home, and (3) while there might have been some misunderstanding before the sheriff concerning the disposal of Y's summary application, it was not possible to believe that any conclusion should be reached other than that S's decision should be confirmed where this was not a marginal or borderline case and no useful purpose would be served by allowing a proof which would cause delay and expense and expose those being cared for at the home to continuing risk.

YASHI CARE LTD v. SCOTTISH COMMISSION FOR THE REGULATION OF CARE 2004 S.L.T. (Sh Ct) 134, Sheriff Principal JC McInnes Q.C., Sh. Ct.

5684. Community care–Direct payments–Eligibility

COMMUNITY CARE (DIRECT PAYMENTS) (SCOTLAND) AMENDMENT REGULATIONS 2005, SSI 2005 114; made under the Social Work (Scotland) Act 1968 s.12B, s.90. In force: April 1, 2005; £3.00.

These Regulations amend the Community Care (Direct Payments) (Scotland) Regulations 2003 (SSI 2003 243) to make all persons aged 65 or over who need care and attention arising out of infirmity or age eligible to receive direct payments subject to the other exclusions specified.

5685. Guardianship orders–Capacity–Adult with Prader Willi's syndrome seeking to restrict order–Competence

[Adults with Incapacity (Scotland) Act 2000 (asp 4) s.1 (3), s.57.]

E, a local authority, sought an order under the Adults with Incapacity (Scotland) Act 2000 s.57 appointing one of its office holders as guardian in relation to the personal welfare of Z, a woman aged 28, who suffered from Prader Willi's syndrome, a physiological condition, the effect of which was that she would go on eating as long as she could obtain food, and a mild degree of mental disability. The powers sought were namely (1) to decide where she should reside; (2) to allow access to her to all relevant professional staff; (3) to insist that she attend daily activities when required. E sought to place Z in a special residential home in England after arrangements for looking after her in her own flat in Edinburgh had broken down. Z did not oppose the order but submitted that power should be restricted to her own tenancy and in the Lothian area, except for the first three months of the order to enable E to implement a system of care in private accommodation with a team of supervisors. In June 2004, the sheriff granted the application, having concluded that Z's proposal was unworkable, and appointed E's director of social work as her guardian for a period of three years. Z appealed, arguing that the sheriff had erred in granting the power for that period when it should have been limited to six months. On the evidence, the sheriff was only entitled to find that such a power should be granted for the immediate future. The principle in s.1 (3) of the Act that any restriction should be "the least restrictive option" should be determined by the perspective of the adult in question in regard to her freedom rather than by the evidence of experts, and he had nowhere addressed the question of how long the power should last. Further, the power to insist she attended daily activities when required was unclear and should be deleted.

Held, dismissing the appeal, that (1) it was scarcely possible to find fault with the sheriff's decision to grant the power to decide where Z should reside for the whole three years of the guardianship order, because it was not argued to him that he should grant it for any lesser period and, in any event, such evidence as was led in the matter was much too sketchy to entitle an appellate court to conclude that he had erred. (2) On the evidence which the sheriff accepted, the arrangements for Z's domestic care had broken down and the only feasible option for the reasonably foreseeable future that was before the court was residence at the home in England; thus it was plainly within his discretion to confer on the guardian the power to decide where Z should reside in the unqualified terms sought in the application. (3) The third power was sufficiently intelligible when considered in the context of both parties' familiarity with the system at the residential home.

EDINBURGH CITY COUNCIL v. Z 2005 S.L.T. (Sh Ct) 7, Sheriff Principal ID Macphail Q.C., Sh Ct.

5686. Regulation of Care (Scotland) Act 2001 (asp 8)-Commencement No.6 Order

REGULATION OF CARE (SCOTLAND) ACT 2001 (COMMENCEMENT NO.6) ORDER 2005, SSI 2005 426 (C.19); made under the Regulation of Care (Scotland) Act 2001 s.81. Commencement details: bringing into force various provisions of the 2001 Act on September 1, 2005; £3.00.

This Order brings into force the Regulation of Care (Scotland) Act 2001 s.52(1)(a)(2).

SUCCESSION

5687. Intestacy-Confirmation to small estates

CONFIRMATION TO SMALL ESTATES (SCOTLAND) ORDER 2005, SSI 2005 251; made under the Confirmation to Small Estates (Scotland) Act 1979 s.1. In force: June 1, 2005; £3.00.

This Order increases from £25,000 to £30,000 the limit of value of a deceased person's estate at or below which confirmation of executors may be obtained by the simplified procedures prescribed by the Intestates Widows and Children (Scotland) Act 1875 (for small intestate estates) and by the Small Testate Estates (Scotland) Act 1876 (the small testate estates). The Confirmation to Small Estates (Scotland) Order 1999 (SI 1999 290) specifying the previous limit of £25,000 is revoked.

5688. Intestacy-Surviving spouses-Prior rights

PRIOR RIGHTS OF SURVIVING SPOUSE (SCOTLAND) ORDER 2005, SSI 2005 252; made under the Succession (Scotland) Act 1964 s.8, s.9. In force: June 1, 2005; £3.00.

This Order, which revokes the Prior Rights of Surviving Spouse (Scotland) Order 1999 (SI 1999 445), amends the Succession (Scotland) Act 1964 to increase the amounts prescribed in provisions relating to the rights of a surviving spouse when a person dies intestate.

5689. Books

Barr, Alan; Biggar, John; Dalgleish, Andrew-Drafting Wills in Scotland. Hardback: £140.00. ISBN 1 84592 040 6. Tottel Publishing.

Express Wills for Scotland CD-Rom. CD-ROM: £150.00. ISBN 0 414 01635 1. W.Green & Son.

Kessler, James; Thompson, Heather; Clark, Ian-Drafting Scottish Trusts and Will Trusts. Hardback: £130.00. ISBN 1 84592 149 6. Tottel Publishing.

Steven, Andrew J M; Wortley, Scott-Avizandum Statutes on Scots Property, Trusts and Succession Law. Paperback: £21.95. ISBN 1 904968 03 1. Avizandum Publishing Ltd.

TAX

5690. Budget—Use of resources

BUDGET (SCOTLAND) ACT 2004 AMENDMENT ORDER 2005, SSI 2005 164; made under the Budget (Scotland) Act 2004 s.7. In force: March 16, 2005; £3.00.

This Order amends the Budget (Scotland) Act 2004 which makes provision, for the financial year 2004/05, for the use of resources by the Scottish administration and certain bodies whose expenditure is payable out of the Scottish Consolidated Fund, for authorising the use of resources, and for limits on the borrowing of certain public bodies. The amendments made by this Order include: altering the overall cash authorisations in respect of the Scottish administration and the Forestry Commissioners; adding a type of accruing resource which may be used by the Scottish Executive Development Department; and altering the amount of borrowing in respect of Scottish Water.

5691. Corporation tax—Capital allowances—Plant—Inclusion of five a side football pitch as "plant and machinery"

[Capital Allowances Act 1990 (c.1) Sch.AA1 para.2.]

The appellant Inland Revenue appealed against a decision by the Special Commissioners ([2003] S.T.C. (S.C.D.) 115) allowing an appeal by the respondent (A) against an assessment of corporation tax. The Special Commissioners had concluded that the costs incurred in constructing five a side football pitches was expenditure on the provision of plant and machinery for capital allowance purposes pursuant to the Capital Allowances Act 1990 Sch.AA1 para.2. The pitches consisted of a playing surface of synthetic grass "carpet" laid in strips on top of a semi permeable terram on top of a loose stone drainage system. When the "carpet" wore out it could be replaced by specialist contractors. A claimed capital allowances for the excavation, infilling, drainage, terram and carpet for four accounting periods. A argued that they were entitled to allowances on the carpet, which was not fixed and not a structure, and on the expenditure on the excavation works and pitch build up. The Inland Revenue argued that the proper approach was to look at the whole expenditure on the pitch, and although there was no statutory definition of "plant" it was clear that plant did not include buildings and structures and the pitches were structures in much the same way a road constituted a structure. Further, the Inland Revenue argued that the Special Commissioner had been wrong to hold that the build up below the carpet amounted only to the alteration of land for the sole purpose of installing plant, namely the carpet, and that the pitch was ineligible for capital allowances as it could not properly be categorised as premises.

Held, dismissing the appeal, that the issue of whether the carpet could be regarded as a separate entity was a narrow one and, in the particular circumstances, the Special Commissioner had not erred in law in concluding that the relevant item was the carpet, which had a separate identity from the works beneath and was not fixed to those works, *Gray (Inspector of Taxes) v. Seymours Garden Centre (Horticulture)* [1995] S.T.C. 706, [1996] C.L.Y. 5563 considered. That being the case, the carpet could not be regarded as a "structure" in respect of which expenditure was excluded under Sch.AA1. Obiter, the terms "setting" and "plant" were not mutually exclusive and in deciding whether an item was plant or not it was important to consider the function it performed in the business, *Jarrold (Inspector of Taxes) v. John Good & Sons Ltd* [1963] 1 W.L.R. 214, [1963] C.L.Y. 1705 considered. The Special Commissioner was correct in holding that the pitch, or the carpet, could be regarded as both the setting and the means by which the business was carried on, *Shove (Inspector of Taxes) v. Lingfield Park 1991 Ltd* [2004] EWCA Civ 391, [2004] S.T.C. 805, [2004] C.L.Y. 3691 distinguished.

ANCHOR INTERNATIONAL LTD v. INLAND REVENUE COMMISSIONERS; *sub nom*. INLAND REVENUE COMMISSIONERS v. ANCHOR INTERNATIONAL LTD [2005] S.T.C. 411, Lord Kirkwood, Lord MacLean, Lord Osborne, Ex Div.

5692. Corporation tax–Capital assets–Depreciation in stock–Application of s.74(1)(f) Income and Corporation Taxes Act 1988

[Companies Act 1985 Sch.4 para.18; Income and Corporation Taxes Act 1988 s.74(1)(f); Finance Act 1998 s.42(1).]

C, the Commissioners of Inland Revenue, appealed against a decision of the Special Commissioners ([2004] S.T.C. (S.C.D.) 253) answering a question referred to them for determination in connection with W's tax return in W's favour. The Special Commissioners found that the adjustment required for the purposes of corporation tax by way of adding back depreciation to arrive at the amount of taxable profits was the amount of net depreciation and not the amount of gross depreciation. Since 1992, W had prepared its tax computations on the basis that the amount of depreciation to be added back to the accounting profits did not include that amount of the charge for depreciation represented by depreciation in stock. When the closing stock became the opening stock of the next year and was sold in the next year, the cost thereof was deducted from the profit and loss account and the amount of depreciation was added back in that year; if that opening stock was not sold in that year it was again added back in that year; and if that opening stock was not sold on that year it was again carried forward to the next year on the same basis. In 1995, the Revenue was prepared to accept that only the net depreciation need be added back for tax purposes so long as accurate records were kept of the amount of depreciation in stock but, in 2002, the Revenue informed the respondents that such computation was contrary to the rules of the Income and Corporation Taxes Act 1988 Sch D Case 1, with which s.74(1)(f) thereof required compliance, and that the amount of depreciation added back should include depreciation in stock. The respondents' tax computation for the year ending December 28, 2002 did not incorporate the change of practice and £9,567,271, representing the amount of depreciation in stock, had not been added back in the year in which it was incurred. It was agreed that W had computed their profits in accordance with generally accepted accounting practice (GAAP) and that whatever amount was included in the computation for depreciation had to be disallowed. C contended that the necessary adjustment for tax purposes required by s.74(1)(f) had not been made in W's tax computation, with the result that their taxable profits for the accounting period had been understated.

Held, allowing the appeal (Lord Reed dissenting), that (1) W's accounts for the year ending December 28, 2002 met the requirements of the first part of the Finance Act 1998 s.42(1) where the operating profit had been computed in accordance with GAAP notwithstanding that it was arrived at without bringing into account opening and closing stock, and notwithstanding the depreciation adjustments made in arriving at the net debit reflected in the operating profit, thus the question came to be whether W's computation for corporation tax purposes made the adjustment required by law for depreciation in computing profits for that purpose. (2) The authorities established that in computing the taxable profits of a trader, the latter had to make appropriate adjustments to reflect the opening and closing stock and work in progress held for the purposes of the trade, and while the court would yield full authority to accountants to determine the amounts to be taken to represent the tangible assets so held, it has adhered consistently to the view that it was for the court to say that in computing the full amount of the profits and gains arising in an accounting period, such an amount should be taken into account as a reflection of the cost incurred in acquiring or producing stock and work in progress, or, if lower, the net realisable value of those assets. (3) The taxpayer could not avoid the consequences of the rule by crediting the individual cost components to the expense accounts from which they were derived and so directly reducing the amount treated as expenses in the period, notwithstanding that those sums had been ascertained in accordance with GAAP where such a requirement was well established and could not be overthrown in the absence of clear justification in law. (4) The amount of depreciation that fell to be taken into account for closing stock in expressing the carrying amount was that apportioned out of gross depreciation provision for the period, if that was done there remained nothing in the name of depreciation in stock available to credit directly to the gross depreciation charge against revenue, thus the whole depreciation computed for the accounting period had to be added back in which was the amount that fell within s.74(1)(f) in respect of depreciation in accounts prepared under the Companies Act 1985 was the amount of depreciation that required to be written off in terms of para.18 of Sch.4 to the 1985 Act, whatever the application of that sum in or towards the indirect production costs of other assets, and in particular, stock. (5) While the observations in *Threlfall v. Jones (Inspector of Taxes)* [1994] Ch.107, on which W heavily relied anent the importance of developing accountancy principles, were wide and of general import, particularly where the greater the advances in accountancy theory and practice, the less the role of the court had to be in developing constraints on the application of contemporary accounting standards, s.42 of the 1998 Act expressed an obligation to compute taxable profits in accordance with current generally accepted accounting practice and the answer to the application of GAAP in the present case was that, properly understood in the light of the authorities, there was a rule of tax law that precluded the application of current United Kingdom GAAP in one respect, *Threlfall* considered.

REVENUE AND CUSTOMS COMMISSIONERS v. WILLIAM GRANT & SONS DISTILLERS LTD; *sub nom*. WILLIAM GRANT & SONS DISTILLERS LTD v. INLAND REVENUE COMMISSIONERS; INLAND REVENUE COMMISSIONERS v. WILLIAM GRANT & SONS DISTILLERS LTD [2006] S.T.C. 69, Lord Penrose, Lord Osborne, Lord Reed, Ex Div.

TRANSPORT

5693. Disabled persons–Mobility and Access Committee–Financial reporting

MOBILITY AND ACCESS COMMITTEE FOR SCOTLAND AMENDMENT REGULATIONS 2005, SSI 2005 589; made under the Transport (Scotland) Act 2001 s.72, s.81. In force: December 19, 2005; £3.00.

These Regulations make amendments to the Mobility and Access Committee for Scotland Regulations 2002 (SSI 2002 69) which established the Mobility and Access Committee for Scotland. They insert a definition of "financial year"; make amendments with the effect that the Committee is under a duty to prepare and publish, by no later than March 31 in each year, a proposed work programme for the next following financial year; and make amendments with the effect that the Committee is under a duty to prepare and submit to the Scottish Ministers by June 30 each year a report for the previous financial year.

5694. Local authorities powers and duties–Traffic orders

LOCAL AUTHORITIES' TRAFFIC ORDERS (PROCEDURE) (SCOTLAND) AMENDMENT REGULATIONS 2005, SSI 2005 338; made under the Road Traffic Regulation Act 1984 s.124, Sch.9 Part III. In force: July 1, 2005; £3.00.

These Regulations amend the Local Authorities' Traffic Orders (Procedure) (Scotland) Regulations 1999 (SI 1999 614) by introducing further paragraphs to allow authorities to apply to Scottish Ministers, on cause shown, for up to 4 six month extensions where the order cannot be made within the 2 year period specified.

5695. Motor vehicles–Removal storage and disposal–Prescribed charges

REMOVAL, STORAGE AND DISPOSAL OF VEHICLES (PRESCRIBED SUMS AND CHARGES ETC.) AMENDMENT (SCOTLAND) REGULATIONS 2005, SSI 2005 486; made under the Refuse Disposal (Amenity) Act 1978 s.4, s.5; and the Road Traffic Regulation Act 1984 s.101, s.102. In force: November 10, 2005; £3.00.

These Regulations, which amend the Removal, Storage and Disposal of Vehicles (Prescribed Sums and Charges etc.) Regulations 1989 (SI 1989 744), prescribe new sums and charges in respect of the removal, storage and disposal of vehicles by the police and local authorities.

5696. Partnerships–Regional transport–Establishment

REGIONAL TRANSPORT PARTNERSHIPS (ESTABLISHMENT, CONSTITUTION AND MEMBERSHIP) (SCOTLAND) ORDER 2005, SSI 2005 622; made under the Transport (Scotland) Act 2005 s.1, s.52. In force: December 1, 2005; £3.00.

The Transport (Scotland) Act 2005 s.1 (1) places the Scottish Ministers under a duty to, by order divide Scotland into regions for the purposes of Part 1 of that Act (Regional Transport) create, for each region, a body corporate to be known as the Transport Partnership; and provide as to the constitution and membership of each Transport Partnership. This Order provides for Transport Partnerships to be established.

5697. Passenger vehicles–Local services–Registration–Fees

PUBLIC SERVICE VEHICLES (REGISTRATION OF LOCAL SERVICES) (SCOTLAND) AMENDMENT REGULATIONS 2005, SSI 2005 346; made under the Public Passenger Vehicles Act 1981 s.52, s.60. In force: August 29, 2005; £3.00.

These Regulations amend the Public Service Vehicles (Registration of Local Services) (Scotland) Regulations 2001 (SSI 2001 219) to increase the fee for the registration of, or the variation of the registration of, a local bus service (other than a community bus service) from £45 to £51.

5698. Railways–Transfer of functions

TRANSFER OF RAIL FUNCTIONS TO THE SCOTTISH MINISTERS ORDER 2005, SSI 2005 598; made under the Transport (Scotland) Act 2005 s.13, s.52. In force: November 28, 2005; £3.00.

This Order provides for the transfer of functions of the Strathclyde Passenger Transport Authority and the Strathclyde Passenger Transport Executive relating to the provision and regulation of rail services conferred by the Transport Act 1968 and the Railways Act 1993 to the Scottish Ministers. The power to transfer these functions to the Scottish Ministers was brought within the competence of the Scottish Parliament by the Scotland Act 1998 (Modifications of Schedule 5) Order 2004 (SI 2004 3329). This Order also makes modifications of the enactments referred to above as a consequence of the transfer of the rail functions.

5699. Transport (Scotland) Act 2005 (asp 12)

This Act of the Scottish Parliament provides for the setting up and functions of new transport bodies and enables the Scottish Ministers to discharge certain transport functions; provides further for the control and co-ordination of road works and for the enforcement of the duties placed on those who carry them out; sets up national concessionary fares schemes; and makes other, miscellaneous modifications of the law relating to transport.

This Act received Royal Assent on August 5, 2005.

5700. Transport (Scotland) Act 2005 (asp 12)–Commencement No.1 Order

TRANSPORT (SCOTLAND) ACT 2005 (COMMENCEMENT NO.1) ORDER 2005, SSI 2005 454 (C.22); made under the Transport (Scotland) Act 2005 s.52, s.54. Commencement details: bringing into force various provisions of the 2005 Act on September 14, 2005, October 10, 2005 and April 3, 2006; £3.00.

This Order appoints various days for the coming into force of the provisions of the Transport (Scotland) Act 2005.

TRUSTS

5701. Baird Trust Reorganisation Act 2005 (asp 11)

This Act of the Scottish Parliament transfers the property, rights, interests and liabilities of the Baird Trust to a successor company limited by guarantee and dissolves the Baird Trust.

This Act received Royal Assent on July 19, 2005.

5702. Trust administration–Constitution–Restricted power to levy charges–Approval of scheme for variation

[Trusts (Scotland) Act 1921 (c.58) s.5; Law Reform (Miscellaneous Provisions) (Scotland) Act 1990 (c.40) s.9.]

X, the trustee of a public trust, the principal asset of which was a park, petitioned the court seeking authority to grant a lease or leases of a specified area thereof in terms of the Trusts (Scotland) Act 1921 s.5, and the approval of a scheme for the variation of the trust in terms of the Law Reform (Miscellaneous Provisions) (Scotland) Act 1990 s.9. The park consisted of walks, trees, outdoor pitches for team games and a pavilion, which had some changing rooms and accommodated a children's nursery. It was not disputed that the pavilion was in a dilapidated state and X averred that the cost of restoration alone would be £750,000, with the addition of upgrading bringing the cost to £1,610,000, when the trust funds were only £385,000. The provisions of the trust only entitled X to charge for the use of the facilities for "organised games" and it was averred that in modern conditions, there was a greater public demand for indoor recreational facilities. X proposed to rebuild the pavilion, extending it to provide a modern gymnasium, the income from which would be sufficient to finance both the capital cost and running costs. X then proposed to lease the pavilion for 30 years to an independent company, established to manage the leisure and recreation facilities. A local resident lodged answers in opposition, submitting that (1) the petition, so far as laid under s.5, was unnecessary since the trust deed expressly authorised the trustee to let cottages, which had in due course become the pavilion; (2) restoration of the pavilion was an option within the trust's resources which would be self financing and would retain the nursery; (3) there were serious doubts as to the financial soundness of the trustee's proposal as well as to the financial safeguards for the trust.

Held, granting the petition, that (1) the only relevant question was whether X had made out the preconditions of s.5 of the 1921 Act and s.9 of the 1990 Act. (2) X's case under s.5 had been convincingly made out where they did not already have a power to lease the pavilion and it could not be derived from that given in the original deed, in any event, even if the original power had any relevance to the proposal, it would not have covered any extended area on which X might develop. (3) An enhanced power to levy charges was plainly necessary for the survival of the trust and the requirements of s.9(1)(d)(iii) had been met where the presently restricted power prevented X from raising sufficient revenue to maintain the pavilion and from embarking on any scheme to restore it, let alone upgrade it.

INVERCLYDE COUNCIL v. DUNLOP 2005 S.L.T. 967, Lord Gill L.J.C., Lord Osborne, Lord Emslie, 2 Div.

5703. Books

Galbraith, H. Reynold–Scottish Trusts: A Drafting Guide. Audio CD: £69.00. ISBN 0 414 01599 1. W. Green & Son.

UNJUSTIFIED ENRICHMENT

5704. Recompense-Remedial works-Bridges-Other remedy available

[Roads (Scotland) Act 1984 (c.54).]

T, a utility company with statutory duties in relation to the provision and maintenance of gas pipelines, raised an action for recompense against G, a roads authority, in respect of works carried out on a bridge. The bridge carried two major gas pipelines. In 1987 a new road bridge was built and the old bridge which was the subject of the current action ceased to be used by motor vehicles. T averred that there had been concern about the bridge since the 1970s, structural engineering reports had been commissioned in 1979 and 1991 and there were serious concerns following a flood in 1994. A consultant was appointed in 1996 to produce a proposal for repair of the bridge and the works were carried out in 1998. Further remedial work was carried out in 2003 and 2004. G made a plea to the relevancy, arguing that they had not been enriched by T's actions as they could not have been compelled to carry out the works which T undertook as the authority could have chosen to stop up the bridge and remove it from their list of public roads. T argued that (1) they had averred the bridge was a road for the purposes of the Roads (Scotland) Act 1984, which required to be accepted in a debate on relevancy, so long as the bridge was a road under the 1984 Act G were under a statutory duty to maintain it and could be compelled to perform that duty, and as T had incurred expenditure on the repair works at a time when the bridge remained a road, the theoretical possibility that the authority could delist the bridge was neither here nor there; (2) there was no absolute requirement in an action for recompense that T should have pursued another remedy open to them; (3) while T required to plead special and strong circumstances, it was not incumbent on a pursuer to invoke the exception to the general rules that recompense was a subsidiary remedy expressly and to set out clearly the special and strong circumstances on which they founded. As special and strong circumstances T averred that they had been carrying out their statutory duty as the deterioration of the bridge was endangering the gas mains and did not want to incur the cost of diverting the mains to another route, and that they had acted to mitigate the risk to public safety.

Held, dismissing the action as irrelevant, that (1) the recent redefinition of the Scots law of unjustified enrichment had not superseded the old rules relating to the law of recompense such as the general rule that the remedy was not available where a pursuer had a legal remedy whether under common law or statute, but had chosen not to exercise it. (2) While it was possible that when challenged to maintain the bridge, G could have initiated the stopping up procedure which would have led to the delisting of the bridge, as a matter of relevancy it could not be said that so long as the bridge was a road, they could not be compelled to maintain it. (3) If a pursuer was to found on the exception to the general rule of the subsidiarity of recompense, it was incumbent on him to invoke the exception expressly and set out clearly the special and strong circumstances on which he founded. (4) T had not averred strong and special circumstances to take themselves out of the general rule that recompense could not be invoked if another legal remedy was available.

TRANSCO PLC v. GLASGOW CITY COUNCIL 2005 S.L.T. 958, Lord Hodge, OH.

UTILITIES

5705. Electricity generation-Non fossil fuel sources

ELECTRICITY FROM NON-FOSSIL FUEL SOURCES (SCOTLAND) SAVING ARRANGEMENTS ORDER 2005, SSI 2005 549; made under the Utilities Act 2000 s.67. In force: November 30, 2005; £3.00.

This Order revokes the Electricity from Non-Fossil Fuel Sources (Scotland) Saving Arrangements Order 2001 (SI 2001 3269) (with saving) and the

Electricity from Non Fossil Fuel Sources (Scotland) Saving Arrangements (Modification) Order 2002 (SSI 2002 93). This Order makes provision for the saving and modification of arrangements which have been made by supply successor companies in compliance with the Electricity Act 1989 s.32. It obliges supply successor companies in Scotland to ensure that a person nominated by them makes arrangements which replace arrangements which were made in the past by them in compliance the Electricity Act and relevant Orders and which secure the availability of a certain amount of generating capacity from non-fossil fuel generating stations.

5706. Electricity supply industry – Fossil fuel levy

FOSSIL FUEL LEVY (SCOTLAND) AMENDMENT REGULATIONS 2005, SSI 2005 641; made under the Electricity Act 1989 s.33, s.60. In force: April 1, 2006; £3.50.

These Regulations amend the Fossil Fuel Levy Regulations 1996 (SI 1996 293) to make adaptations following the introduction of the British Electricity Trading and Transmission Arrangements on April 1, 2005 and to make provision for payments out of levy to be made to a person nominated by the supply successor companies.

5707. Electricity supply industry – Licences – Exemption

ELECTRICITY (EXEMPTION FROM THE REQUIREMENT FOR A GENERATION LICENCE) (SCOTLAND) ORDER 2005, SI 2005 3041 (S.10); made under the Electricity Act 1989 s.5. In force: November 30, 2005; £3.00.

This Order grants an exemption from the requirements of the Electricity Act 1989 s.4(1) (which prohibits the generation of electricity without a licence or exemption) to Farr Windfarm Ltd in respect of the plant known as Farr Wind Farm and to Mid Hill Wind Ltd in respect of plant known as Mid Hill Wind Farm.

5708. Electricity supply industry – Renewable energy – Renewables obligation

RENEWABLES OBLIGATION (SCOTLAND) ORDER 2005, SSI 2005 185; made under the Electricity Act 1989 s.32, s.32A, s.32B, s.32C. In force: April 1, 2005; £6.00.

This Order, which revokes with savings the Renewables Obligation (Scotland) Order 2004 (SSI 2004 170), imposes an obligation on all electricity suppliers, which are licensed under the Electricity Act 1989 and which supply electricity in Scotland, to supply to customers in Great Britain specified amounts of electricity generated by using renewable sources.

5709. Water Services etc. (Scotland) Act 2005 (Commencement No.1 and Savings) Order 2005 (asp 3) – Commencement No.1 Order

WATER SERVICES ETC. (SCOTLAND) ACT 2005 (COMMENCEMENT NO.1 AND SAVINGS) ORDER 2005, SSI 2005 351 (C.14); made under the Water Services etc. (Scotland) Act 2005 s.34, s.37. Commencement details: bringing into force various provisions of the 2005 Act on June 20, 2005 and July 1, 2005; £3.00.

This Order appoints June 20, 2005 and July 1, 2005 for the coming into force of certain of the provisions of the Water Services etc. (Scotland) Act 2005.

5710. Water supply – Charges – Billing and collection

WATER SERVICES CHARGES (BILLING AND COLLECTION) (SCOTLAND) ORDER 2005, SSI 2005 54; made under the Water Industry (Scotland) Act 2002 s.37. In force: April 1, 2005; £3.00.

Responsibility for water and sewerage services in Scotland rests with Scottish Water, established under the Water Industry (Scotland) Act 2002. This Order provides, as regards the financial year 2005-06, for each local authority in Scotland to be responsible for demanding and recovering charges payable in respect of water supply and sewerage services provided by Scottish Water to dwellings in the area of the local authority (other than charges for a supply of water taken by meter). Provision is made for the local authorities to account to Scottish Water for sums collected, for the forms and procedures to be used or followed by the local authorities in demanding payment and for chargepayers to have a right of appeal to the relevant valuation appeal committee. This Order replaces the one previously in force in respect of the financial years 2002-03, 2003-04 and 2004-05, namely, the Water Services Charges (Billing and Collection) (Scotland) Order 2002 (SSI 2002 33). The value of F in respect of these years was determined. F is the minimum amount payable by Scottish Water to local authorities in respect of each dwelling for which the local authority provides billing and collection services.

5711. Water supply–Consequential provisions and modifications

WATER SERVICES ETC. (SCOTLAND) ACT 2005 (CONSEQUENTIAL PROVISIONS AND MODIFICATIONS) ORDER 2005, SI 2005 3172; made under the Scotland Act 1998 s.104, s.112, s.113. In force: November 11, 2005; £3.00.

This Order makes provisions and modifications in consequence of the Water Services etc. (Scotland) Act 2005. It amends the House of Commons Disqualification Act 1975, the Race Relations Act 1976, the Competition Act 1998, the Public Interest Disclosure (Prescribed Persons) Order 1999 (SI 1999 1549), the Utilities Act 2000 and the Enterprise Act 2002. The Order provides for a right of reference for Scottish Water, enabling it to require the Water Industry Commission (WIC) for Scotland to refer its determination of Scottish Water's charges under the Water Industry (Scotland) Act 2002 to the Competition Commission. The Order also provides for a right of reference to the Commission for water and sewerage services providers against the conditions of their licences granted under the 2005 Act, or against any modification of those conditions. The Order also modifies enactments as a consequence of the creation of the WIC in the 2005 Act, and to reflect the functions of the Commission in considering a reference under this Order.

5712. Water supply–Construction works–Abhainn Chro Bheinn

SCOTTISH WATER (ABHAINN CHRO BHEINN) WATER ORDER 2005, SSI 2005 513; made under the Water (Scotland) Act 1980 s.17, s.29, s.107. In force: October 21, 2005; £3.00.

This Order, which amends the Water (Scotland) Act 1980, revokes the Argyll County Council (Amhainn Chro Beinn, Kilchoan) Water Order 1955 (SI 1955 1229) on January 31, 2007. It provides that Scottish Water may for the purposes of the undertaking and by means of an intake (Work No.3), take water from the Abhainn Chro Bheinn in the area of the Highland Council.

5713. Water supply–Construction works–Allt Ach Na Braighe

SCOTTISH WATER (ALLT ACH NA BRAIGHE) WATER ORDER 2005, SSI 2005 577; made under the Water (Scotland) Act 1980 s.17, s.29, s.107. In force: November 11, 2005; £3.00.

This Order amends the Water (Scotland) Act 1980 and revokes the County of Ross and Cromarty (Allt Ach a'Braighe) Water Order 1968. It provides that Scottish Water may take water from the Allt Ach Na Braighe in the area of the Highland Council.

5714. Water supply–Construction works–Allt Beithe

SCOTTISH WATER (ALLT BEITHE) WATER ORDER 2005, SSI 2005 508; made under the Water (Scotland) Act 1980 s.17, s.29, s.107. In force: October 14, 2005; £3.00.

This Order, which revokes the Argyll County Council (Allt Beithe, Acharacle) Water Order 1959 (SI 1959 2004) with effect from January 31, 2007, amends theWater (Scotland) Act1980. It provides that ScottishWater may for the purposes of the undertaking and by means of an intake (Work No.2), take water from theAllt Beithe in the area of the Highland Council.

5715. **Water supply–Construction works–Allt nan Corp**

SCOTTISH WATER (ALLT NAN CORP) WATER ORDER 2005, SSI 2005 576; made under theWater (Scotland) Act1980 s.17, s.29, s.107. In force: November 11, 2005; £3.00.

This Order amends the Water (Scotland) Act 1980 and revokes the County Council of the County of Ross and Cromarty (Allt nan Corp) Water Order 1955. It provides that Scottish Water may for the purposes of the undertaking and by means of an intake (Works No.4), take water from the Allt nan Corp in the area of the Highland Council.

5716. **Water supply–Construction works–Loch a'Bhaid Luachraich**

SCOTTISH WATER (LOCH A'BHAID LUACHRAICH) WATER ORDER 2005, SSI 2005 509; made under the Water (Scotland) Act 1980 s.17, s.29, s.107. In force: October 14, 2005; £3.00.

This Order, which amends the Water (Scotland) Act 1980, revokes County of Ross and Cromarty (Allt Beitha, Aultbea) Water Order 1961, the County of Ross and Cromarty (Loch na Ba) Water Order 1961, and the Ross and Cromarty Water Board (Allt Loch a'Choire) Water Order 1972 with effect from April 1, 2006. It provides that, Scottish Water may, for the purposes of the undertaking and by means of an existing intake located at Ordnance Survey National Grid Reference NG 891 879 take water from Loch a'Bhaid Luachraich in the Highland Council area.

5717. **Water supply–Construction works–Loch Bealach na Gaoithe**

SCOTTISH WATER (LOCH BEALACH NA GAOITHE) WATER ORDER 2005, SSI 2005 578; made under the Water (Scotland) Act 1980 s.17, s.29, s.107. In force: November 11, 2005; £3.00.

This Order amends the Water (Scotland) Act 1980 and revokes the Inverness shire Water Board (Bealach na Gaoithe) Water Order 1969 (SI 1969 193). It provides that Scottish Water may take water from Loch Bealach na Gaoithe in the area of the Highland Council.

5718. **Water supply–Mill Loch**

SCOTTISH WATER (MILL LOCH) ORDER 2005, SSI 2005 649; made under the Water (Scotland) Act 1980 s.17, s.29, s.107. In force: December 23, 2005; £3.00.

This Order revokes the Argyll County Council (Mill Loch, Gigha) Water Order 1960 (SI 1960 1247).

5719. **Water supply–Sewerage–Charges–Reduction**

DOMESTIC WATER AND SEWERAGE CHARGES (REDUCTION) (SCOTLAND) REGULATIONS 2005, SSI 2005 53; made under the Water Industry (Scotland) Act 2002 s.40. In force: April 1, 2005; £3.00.

The Water Industry (Scotland) Act 2002 provides for the Scottish Ministers to make Regulations to reduce the amount of charges which would otherwise be payable by a person to a local authority in respect of services provided by Scottish Water. In accordance with this provision, these Regulations provide for such reductions in water and sewerage charges in Scotland from April 1, 2005 until March 31, 2006. The Regulations provide that only those persons who are liable to pay local authorities for the provision of water and sewerage services, by virtue of the Water Services Charges (Billing and Collection) (Scotland) Order 2005 (SSI 2005 54), are eligible for a reduction. They provide that a reduction is to be available to eligible persons where these persons are in receipt of council tax benefit and where the amount in charges that they are liable to pay in 2005-06 is in excess of

£255. It provides for the part of the charges in excess of £255 to be reduced in direct proportion to the council tax benefit received by virtue of the Social Security Contributions and Benefits Act 1992.

VAT

5720. Registration–Compulsory registration–Competence

[Value Added Tax Act 1994 (c.23) Sch.1 para.1 (1), Sch.1 para.5.]

The appellant (D) appealed against the dismissal of his appeal against a decision of the respondent commissioners to compulsorily register him for the purposes of VAT with effect from October 1996. D was a former racehorse trainer and insolvency practitioner.

Held, allowing the appeal, that the commissioners' attempt to effect a fresh registration of D with effect from October 1996 was incompetent and involved an error of law. Proceeding on the basis that D was registered under the original registration until the end of August 1996 and was a person who had been the maker of taxable supplies registered under the Value Added Tax Act 1994 until that time, the provisions of Sch.1 para.1 (1) to the Act could not begin to apply to him so as to create a prima facie liability for registration until September, but by Sch.1 para.5(3), a fresh registration could not take effect earlier than from November 1996. It was evident from the provisions of Sch.1 para.5 that Parliament had gone to considerable pains to establish a system of registration which involved a precise chronology and view of the various consequences of registration for the purposes of VAT, and it was important that that chronology was strictly adhered to.

DYER v. CUSTOMS AND EXCISE COMMISSIONERS [2005] S.T.C. 715, Lord Osborne, Lord Johnston, Temporary Judge Sir David Edward Q.C., Ex Div.

WATER LAW

5721. Drinking water–Protected areas

WATER ENVIRONMENT (DRINKING WATER PROTECTED AREAS) (SCOTLAND) ORDER 2005, SSI 2005 88; made under the Water Environment and Water Services (Scotland) Act 2003 s.6. In force: March 22, 2005; £3.00.

This Order identifies those bodies of water used for the abstraction of drinking water.

5722. Water Environment and Water Services (Scotland) Act 2003 (asp 3)–Commencement No.3 Order

WATER ENVIRONMENT AND WATER SERVICES (SCOTLAND) ACT 2003 (COMMENCEMENT NO.3) ORDER 2005, SSI 2005 256 (C.12); made under the Water Environment and Water Services (Scotland) Act 2003 s.38. Commencement details: bringing into force various provisions of the 2003 Act on May 20, 2005; £3.00.

This Order brings into force further provisions of the Water Environment and Water Services (Scotland) Act 2003 which give the Scottish Ministers the power by regulations to modify provisions for the purposes of giving effect to Community obligations, or exercising any related right including any derogation or right to make more onerous provision in respect of such obligations; and set out the matters to be included in a river basin management plan, and those matters to be included in revised plans.

5723. Water Services etc. (Scotland) Act 2005 (asp 3)

This Act establishes the Water Industry Commission for Scotland; creates offences in relation to the unauthorised use of the public water and sewerage systems; provides for licensing the provision of certain water and sewerage services; amends the system for fixing charges for services provided by Scottish Water; makes provision as to Scottish Water's functions; and makes provision in relation to coal mine water pollution.

This Act received Royal Assent on March 17, 2005.

WORDS AND PHRASES

The table below is a cumulative guide to words and phrases judicially considered in 2005:

(N) refers to a case in the Northern Ireland section.

(S) refers to a case in the Scottish section.

Law books

published during 2005

Aarons, Elaine–Tolley's Termination of Employment. Looseleaf/ring bound: £100.00. ISBN 0 7545 0824 2. LexisNexis UK.

Abadinsky, Howard–Probation and Parole: Theory and Practice. Hardback: £50.99. ISBN 0 13 118894 1. Prentice Hall.

Abbey, Robert; Richards, Mark–Practical Approach to Conveyancing. Paperback: £32.99. ISBN 0 19 928135 1. Paperback: £32.99. ISBN 0 19 928135 1. Oxford University Press.

ACCA Revision/Exam Kit: Paper 2.2-Corporate and Business Law. Paperback: £13.00. ISBN 1 84390 442 X. Financial Training Co Ltd.

Accounting Regulators. Paperback: £145.00. ISBN 1 904501 39 7. Richmond Law & Tax.

Adam Plainer, S J Berwin; Martin Pascoe, 3/4 South Square And Mike Jervis–Plainer: a Practical Guide to Buying and Selling Insolvent Businesses. Paperback: £85.00. ISBN 0 406 96297 9. Butterworths Law.

Adams, David–Banking and Capital Markets. Paperback: £24.95. ISBN 0 905835 77 8. Paperback: £25.95. ISBN 1 905391 01 3. The College of Law.

Adams, Trevor; Longshaw, Alex–Commercial Law and Practice. Paperback: £24.95. ISBN 0 905835 74 3. The College of Law.

Adams, Trevor; Longshaw, Alex–Commercial Law and Practice. Paperback: £25.95. ISBN 1 905391 03 X. The College of Law.

Adams, Trevor–Business and Company Legislation. College of Law LPC Guides S. Paperback: £25.95. ISBN 0 905835 92 1. The College of Law.

Adams, Trevor–Business Law and Practice. College of Law LPC Guides S. Paperback: £25.95. ISBN 0 905835 90 5. The College of Law.

Adamson, John E.–Law for Business. Hardback: £49.99. ISBN 0 538 44051 1. South Western College Publishing.

Addison, Neil–Civil Orders in the Criminal Courts. Paperback/CD-ROM: £49.95. ISBN 1 85328 936 1. Law Society Publications.

Addo, Michael K.–International Human Rights Law. The Library of Essays in International Law. Hardback: £130.00. ISBN 0 7546 2158 8. Ashgate.

Adler, Mark–Effective Legal Writing. Paperback: £24.95. ISBN 1 85328 985 X. Law Society Publications.

Advertising and Marketing Law: Leading Lawyers on Strategies for Structuring Agreements and Transactions, Handling IP Matters, and More. Inside the Minds S. Paperback: £49.95. ISBN 1 59622 194 1. Aspatore Books, US.

Aertsen, Ivo; Daems, Tom; Robert, Luc–Institutionalising Restorative Justice. Paperback: £27.50. ISBN 1 84392 158 8. Willan Publishing.

Agnew, Crispin H.–Agricultural Law in Scotland. Hardback: £150.00. ISBN 1 84592 034 1. Tottel Publishing.

Ahdar, Rex; Leigh, Ian–Religious Freedom in the Liberal State. Hardback: £50.00. ISBN 0 19 925362 5. Oxford University Press.

Ahuja, Ajay–Buy-to-let Bible. Paperback: £11.99. ISBN 1 904053 91 2. Law Pack Publishing.

Albert, Raymond; Skolnik, Louise–Social Welfare Programs: Narratives from Hard Times. Paperback: £21.00. ISBN 0 534 35918 3. Wadsworth.

Albi, Anneli–EU Enlargement and the Constitutions of Central and Eastern Europe. Cambridge Studies in European Law & Policy. Hardback: £45.00. ISBN 0 521 84541 6. Paperback: £19.99. ISBN 0 521 60736 1. Cambridge University Press.

Alder, John–Constitutional and Administrative Law. Palgrave Law Masters S. Paperback: £16.99. ISBN 1 4039 3392 8. Palgrave Macmillan.

Allen, Michael–Textbook on Criminal Law. Paperback: £22.99. ISBN 0 19 927918 7. Oxford University Press.

Allen, Robert–Crazy Laws and Lawsuits. Paperback: £6.99. ISBN 1 86105 843 8. Robson Books.

Allen, Tom–Property and the Human Rights Act 1998. Hardback: £25.00. ISBN 1 84113 203 9. Hart Publishing.

Almqvist, Jessica–Human Rights, Culture and the Rule of Law. Hardback: £35.00. ISBN 1 84113 506 2. Hart Publishing.

Alston, Philip; Robinson, Mary–Human Rights and Development: Towards Mutual Reinforcement. Paperback: £27.50. ISBN 0 19 928462 8. Paperback: £35.00. ISBN 0 19 928462 8. Oxford University Press.

Alston, Philip; Schutter, Olivier De–Monitoring Fundamental Rights in the EU: The Contribution of the Fundamental Rights Agency. Hardback: £40.00. ISBN 1 84113 534 8. Hart Publishing.

Alston, Philip–Labour Rights As Human Rights. Collected Courses of the Academy of European Law. Hardback: £50.00. ISBN 0 19 928105 X. Oxford University Press.

Alston, Philip–Non-State Actors and Human Rights. Collected Courses of the Academy of European Law. Hardback: £60.00. ISBN 0 19 927281, Paperback: £27.50. ISBN 0 19 927282 4. Oxford University Press. 6. Oxford University Press.

Alvarez, Jose E.–International Organisations As Law-makers. Oxford Monographs in International Law. Hardback: £65.00. ISBN 0 19 876562 2. Oxford University Press.

Anand, Sudhir; Peter, Fabienne; Sen, Amartya–Public Health, Ethics, and Equity. Paperback: £20.00. ISBN 0 19 927637 4. Oxford University Press.

Andenas, Mads; Ortino, Federico–WTO Law and Process. Paperback: £80.00. ISBN 0 903067 68 4. British Institute of International and Comparative.

Anderman, Steve–Intellectual Property Licensing and the New EU Competition Rules. Hardback: £95.00. ISBN 0 19 928214 5. Clarendon Press.

Anderson, Christian; Simonsen, Craig–Computer Aided Legal Research. Paperback: £26.99. ISBN 0 13 119774 6. Prentice Hall.

Anderson, Mark S.; Warner, Victor–A-Z Guide to Boilerplate and Commercial Clauses. Hardback: £99.00. ISBN 0 406 97733 X. Butterworths Law.

Anderson, Mark; Warner, Victor–A-Z Guide to Boilerplate and Commercial Clauses. Hardback: £99.00. ISBN 1 84592 093 7. Tottel Publishing.

Anderson, Matthew; Sarat, Austin–Studies in Law, Politics and Society. Studies in Law, Politics & Society. Hardback: £59.99. ISBN 0 7623 1189 4. JAI Press.

Anderson, Matthew; Sarat, Austin–Studies in Law, Politics and Society. Studies in Law, Politics & Society. Hardback: £70.49. ISBN 0 7623 1179 7. JAI Press.

Anderson, Ruth A.; McCall, Shelagh M.–Representing Sex Offenders. Paperback: £35.00. ISBN 0 414 01517 7. W.Green & Son.

Anderson, Terence J.; Schum, David A.; Twining, William–Analysis of Evidence. Paperback: £22.99. ISBN 0 521 67316 X. Cambridge University Press.

Anderson; Gardner–Criminal Law W/CD: 9th Ed. Book (details unknown)/CD-ROM: £53.93. ISBN 0 534 62456 1. Wadsworth.

Anglade, Lelia; Tackaberry, John–International Dispute Resolution: Vol 1. Materials. Hardback: £89.00. ISBN 0 421 88700 1. Sweet & Maxwell.

Anstey, Sharon; McKie, Simon—Tolley's Estate Planning. Paperback: £95.95. ISBN 0 7545 2862 6. Tolley Publishing.

Antitrust in the Global Era. Hardback: £50.00. ISBN 0 19 925574 1. Oxford University Press.

Appelbe, G.E.; Wingfield, Joy—Dale and Appelbe's Pharmacy Law and Ethics. Paperback: £34.95. ISBN 0 85369 604 7. Pharmaceutical Press.

Arlidge, Anthony; Parry, Jacques—Arlidge and Parry on Fraud, 1st Supplement. Paperback: £55.00. ISBN 0 421 92170 6. Sweet & Maxwell.

Arlidge, Anthony; Parry, Jacques—Arlidge and Parry on Fraud. Hardback: £149.00. ISBN 0 421 89210 2. Sweet & Maxwell.

Arnheim, Michael—Handbook of Human Rights Law: An Accessible Approach to the Issues and Principles. Paperback: £19.99. ISBN 0 7494 4480 0. Kogan Page.

Arrigo, Bruce—Criminal Behavior: A Systems Approach. Hardback: £45.99. ISBN 0 13 191521 5. Prentice Hall.

Arrowsmith, Peter; Golding, Jon—Tolley's National Insurance Contributions: Main Annual Plus Supplement. Paperback: £99.95. ISBN 0 7545 2866 9. Tolley Publishing.

Arrowsmith, Peter; Golding, Jon—Tolley's National Insurance Contributions: Main Annual. Paperback: £86.00. ISBN 0 7545 2765 4. Tolley Publishing.

Arrowsmith, Sue—Law of Public and Utilities Procurement. Hardback: £145.00. ISBN 0 421 75850 3. Sweet & Maxwell.

Article 19—Model Public Service Broadcasting Law: International Standards Theory. Paperback: £10.00. ISBN 1 902598 71 7. Article 19.

As-Sadr, Muhammad Baqir—Lessons in Islamic Jurisprudence. Paperback: £16.99. ISBN 1 85168 393 3. Oneworld Publications.

Asher, J.—Client Connection. Paperback: £25.99. ISBN 1 58852 123 0. ALM Publishing.

Ashiagbor, Diamond—European Employment Strategy: Labour Market Regulation and New Governance. Oxford Monographs on Labour Law. Hardback: £60.00. ISBN 0 19 927964 0. Oxford University Press.

Ashley, Colin—Preparing Ahead-Successful Management of Family Affairs in Later Life. Paperback: £9.99. ISBN 0 7552 0166 3. authorsonline.co.uk.

Ashworth, Allan—Contractual Procedures in the Construction Industry. Paperback: £29.99. ISBN 0 13 129827 5. Prentice Hall.

Ashworth, Andrew; Redmayne, Michael—Criminal Process. Paperback: £25.99. ISBN 0 19 927338 3. Oxford University Press.

Ashworth, Andrew—Sentencing and Criminal Justice. Law in Context S. Paperback: £21.99. ISBN 0 521 67405 0. Cambridge University Press.

Askey, Simon; McLeod, Ian—Studying Law. Palgrave Study Guides. Paperback: £11.99. ISBN 1 4039 9926 0. Palgrave Macmillan.

Askin, Kelly Dawn—Womens and International Human Rights Law: V. 4. Paperback: £92.99. ISBN 1 57105 306 9. Transnational Publishers, Inc.

Astor, Richard J.; Bennett, Emma. L.—Insurance Insolvency Law Sourcebook. Hardback: £85.00. ISBN 1 873994 96 6. Bartsky Publishing Ltd (Bartsky Medicine).

Atkinson, Duncan; Moloney, Tim—Blackstone's Guide to the Criminal Procedure Rules. Paperback: £29.95. ISBN 0 19 928904 2. Paperback: £29.95. ISBN 0 19 928904 2. Oxford University Press.

Auchie, Derek—Evidence Lawbasics. Paperback: £12.50. ISBN 0 414 01581 9. W.Green & Son.

Aust, Anthony—Handbook of International Law. Hardback: £55.00. ISBN 0 521 82349 8. Paperback: £24.99. ISBN 0 521 53034 2. Cambridge University Press.

Austin, Brice—Reserves, Electronic Reserves, and Copyright: The Past and the Future. Hardback: £28.50. ISBN 0 7890 2796 8. Paperback: £14.50. ISBN 0 7890 2797 6. Haworth Press, Inc.

Austin, Greg; Berry, Ken–New Grand Bargain for Peace: Towards a Reformation in International Security Law. Pamphlet/leaflet (stapled/folded): £4.95. ISBN 1 903558 61 1. Foreign Policy Centre.

Avgouleas, Emilios E.–Mechanics and Regulation of Market Abuse: A Legal and Economic Analysis. Hardback: £95.00. ISBN 0 19 924452 9. Oxford University Press.

Avgouleas, Emilios E.–Mechanics and Regulation of Market Abuse: A Legal and Economic Analysis. Hardback: £95.00. ISBN 0 19 924452 9. Oxford University Press.

Aziz, Miriam; Millns, Susan–Values in the Constitution of Europe. Hardback: £60.00. ISBN 0 7546 2439 0. Ashgate.

Backhouse, Constance; Backhouse, Nancy L.–Heiress Vs. the Establishment: Mrs. Campbell's Campaign for Legal Justice. Law & Society S. Paperback: £19.95. ISBN 0 7748 1053 X. University of British Columbia Press.

Bailey, David–Teaching Legal Skills. Hardback: £39.50. ISBN 1 85521 648 5. Paperback: £15.00. ISBN 1 85521 654 X. Ashgate.

Bailey, Suzanne; Barron, Chana–Constitutional Law. Printed material (details unknown): £52.00. ISBN 0 7668 4014 X. Delmar.

Bailey, S.H.; Jones, Brian; Mowbray, Alastair–Cases and Materials on Administrative Law. Paperback: £32.95. ISBN 0 421 90070 9. Sweet & Maxwell.

Bainbridge, David I.–Intellectual Property. Paperback: £36.99. ISBN 1 4058 0159 X. Longman.

Bainham, Andrew–International Survey of Family Law. Hardback: £65.00. ISBN 0 85308 983 3. Family Law.

Baker, Ellis; Lavers, Anthony–Expert Witness. Case in Point S. Paperback: £24.95. ISBN 1 84219 230 2. RICS.

Ballin, Ernst Hirsch; Senden, Linda–Co-actorship in the Development of European Law: The Quality of European Legislation and Its Implementation and Application in the National Legal Order. Hardback: £30.00. ISBN 90 6704 184 X. Asser Press.

Bamforth, Nicholas–Sex Rights: The Oxford Amnesty Lectures 2002. Paperback: £12.99. ISBN 0 19 280561 4. Oxford University Press.

Banking Regulators. Paperback: £195.00. ISBN 1 904501 36 2. Richmond Law & Tax.

Bankobeza, Gilbert M.–Ozone Protection: The International Legal Regime. Hardback: £50.00. ISBN 90 77596 08 9. Eleven International Publishing.

Bar Council of Ireland Directory, 2006. Book (details unknown): £25.00. ISBN 0 421 93170 1. Sweet & Maxwell.

Bar Directory. Hardback: £99.00. ISBN 0 421 92160 9. Sweet & Maxwell.

Bar, Christian Von–Principles of European Law: V. 1. Benevolent Intervention in Another's Affairs. European Civil Code S. Hardback: £70.00. ISBN 0 19 929601 4. Oxford University Press.

Barclay, Barry–Mana Tuturu: Maori Treasures and Intellectual Property Rights. Paperback: £18.50. ISBN 1 86940 350 9. Auckland University Press.

Barclay, L.–Small Business Employment Law for Dummies. For Dummies S. Paperback: £12.99. ISBN 0 7645 7052 8. John Wiley and Sons Ltd.

Barcroft, Charles; Stainforth, Paul–Finance Act Handbook. Paperback: £37.95. ISBN 1 4057 0776 3. Tolley Publishing.

Barendrecht, Maurits; Jansen, Chris; Loos, Marco; Pinna, Andrea; Cascao, Rui; Gulijk, Stephanie Van–Principles of European Law: V. 2. Service Contracts. European Civil Code S. Hardback: £160.00. ISBN 0 19 929600 6. Oxford University Press.

Barendt, Eric–Freedom of Speech. Hardback: £75.00. ISBN 0 19 924451 0. Oxford University Press.

Barker, K.–Licensing: The New Law. Paperback: £39.00. ISBN 0 85308 989 2. Jordans.

Barlow, R.F.D.; Wallington, R.A.; Meadway, Susannah L.; Waterworth, Michael; Sherrin, C.H.—Williams on Wills: Supplement. Paperback: £49.00. ISBN 1 4057 0897 2. Butterworths Law.

Barr, Alan; Biggar, John; Dalgleish, Andrew—Drafting Wills in Scotland. Hardback: £140.00. ISBN 1 84592 040 6. Tottel Publishing.

Barrett, Scott—Environment and Statecraft: The Strategy of Environmental Treaty-Making. Paperback: £12.99. ISBN 0 19 928609 4. Oxford University Press.

Barrie, Peter—Personal Injury Law: Liability, Compensation, Procedure. Paperback: £69.00. ISBN 0 19 927571 8. Oxford University Press.

Barth, S.C.—Hospitality Law: Managing Legal Issues in the Hospitality Industry. Hardback: £46.95. ISBN 0 471 46425 2. John Wiley & Sons Inc.

Bartlett, Peter—Blackstone's Guide to the Mental Capacity Act. Blackstone's Guide S. Paperback: £29.95. ISBN 0 19 928903 4. Paperback: £29.95. ISBN 0 19 928903 4. Oxford University Press.

Bassiouni, M.Cherif—Statute of the International Criminal Court and Related Instruments: Legislative History, 1994-2000. Hardback: £282.50. ISBN 1 57105 156 2. Transnational Publishers, Inc.

Baxter, Chloe; Brennan, Mark G.; Coldicott, Yvette; Moller, Maaike—Practical Guide to Medical Ethics and Law. Paperback: £19.95. ISBN 1 904627 31 5. PasTest.

Beale, Hugh—Chitty on Contracts, 2nd Supplement. Paperback: £79.00. ISBN 0 421 91230 8. Sweet & Maxwell.

Beale, Hugh—Chitty on Contracts. Paperback: £69.00. ISBN 0 421 88980 2. Sweet & Maxwell.

Bearman, Peri; Peters, Rudolph; Vogel, Frank E.—Islamic School of Law: Evolution, Devolution, and Progress. Hardback: £25.95. ISBN 0 674 01784 6. Harvard University Press.

Beatty, David M.—Ultimate Rule of Law. Paperback: £22.50. ISBN 0 19 928801 1. Oxford University Press.

Bebchuk, Lucian Arye—Corporate Law and Economic Analysis. Paperback: £27.00. ISBN 0 521 02283 5. Cambridge University Press.

Beckett, Julia; Koenig, Heidi O.—Public Administration and Law. ASPA Classics S. Hardback: £59.50. ISBN 0 7656 1542 8. Paperback: £19.95. ISBN 0 7656 1543 6. M.E. Sharpe.

Bedi, Shiv—Development of Human Rights Law by the Judges of the International Court of Justice. International Law S. Hardback: £65.00. ISBN 1 84113 576 3. Hart Publishing.

Beige Book, Forms of Contract, Rules for Dispute Review Boards. Forms of Contract S. Paperback: £20.00. ISBN 0 85295 495 6. Institution of Chemical Engineers.

Belitz, Hina; Crossley-Holland, Dominic—Penguin Guide to Employment Rights. Paperback (B format): £9.99. ISBN 0 14 102109 8. Penguin Books Ltd.

Bell, Andrew C—Nutshells-Employment Law. Paperback: £7.00. ISBN 0 421 92780 1. Sweet & Maxwell.

Bell, Cedric D.—Land: The Law of Real Property. Paperback: £15.95. ISBN 1 85836 602 X. Old Bailey Press.

Bell, John —Comparative Legal Cultures. International Library of Essays in Law & Legal Theory: Second Series -. Hardback: £120.00. ISBN 0 7546 2093 X. Dartmouth.

Bell, Stuart; McGillivray, Donald—Environmental Law. Paperback: £27.99. ISBN 0 19 926056 7. Paperback: £27.99. ISBN 0 19 926056 7. Oxford University Press.

Bellamy, Richard; Warleigh, Alex—Citizenship and Governance in the European Union. Continuum Collection S. Paperback: £16.99. ISBN 0 8264 7919 7. Continuum International Publishing Group-Academi.

Bellamy, Richard–Rule of Law and the Separation of Powers. International Library Essays in Law & Legal Theory (Second Series). Hardback: £120.00. ISBN 0 7546 2463 3. Ashgate.

Bellomo, Michael–LSAT Exam Cram. Paperback: £17.99. ISBN 0 7897 3414 1. Que.

Benacchio, Gian Antonio; Pasa, Barbara–Common Law For Europe. Hardback: £25.95. ISBN 963 7326 33 2. Central European University Press.

Bennett-Alexander, Dawn D.; Hartman, Laura Pincus–Employment Law for Business. Hardback: £104.99. ISBN 0 07 302895 9. Higher Education.

Bennett, Angela–Geneva Convention. Hardback: £20.00. ISBN 0 7509 4147 2. Sutton Publishing.

Bennett, Siggi A.–Divorce in the Sheriff Court. Hardback: £50.00. ISBN 0 9534152 6 0. Barnstoneworth Press.

Bennett, Siggi A.–Personal Injury Damages in Scotland. Paperback: £60.00. ISBN 0 9534152 5 2. Barnstoneworth Press.

Bennion, F.A.R.–Statutory Interpretation. Paperback: £55.00. ISBN 0 406 96648 6. Butterworths Law.

Benny, Richard; Jefferson, Michael; Sargeant, Malcolm–Employment Law. Blackstone's Law Q & A S. Paperback: £13.99. ISBN 0 19 929100 4. Oxford University Press.

Benson, Edward–Information and Consultation of Employees Regulations: A Special Bulletin. Paperback: £35.00. ISBN 0 85308 967 1. Jordans.

Beresford, Keith–Patenting Software Under the EPC. Hardback: £185.00. ISBN 0 421 90490 9. Sweet & Maxwell.

Bergstrom, Carl Fredrik–Comitology: Delegation of Powers in the European Union and the Committee System. Oxford Studies in European Law. Hardback: £50.00. ISBN 0 19 928001 0. Oxford University Press.

Berman, Greg–Good Courts: The Case for Problem-Solving Justice. Hardback: £16.99. ISBN 1 56584 973 6. The New Press.

Berman, Paul Schiff–The Globalization of International Law. International Library of Essays on Globalization & Law. Hardback: £125.00. ISBN 0 7546 2412 9. Ashgate.

Bermingham, Vera–Tort. Paperback: £6.50. ISBN 0 421 89070 3. Paperback: £6.50. ISBN 0 421 89070 3. Sweet & Maxwell.

Bernasconi-Osterwalder, Nathalie; Magraw, Daniel; Olivia, Maria Julia; Orellana, Marcus; Tuerk, Elisabeth–Environment and Trade: A Guide to WTO Jurisprudence. Hardback: £79.95. ISBN 1 84407 298 3. Earthscan Publications Ltd.

Bernstein, Jeffrey I.–Prentice Hall's Test Prep Guide to Accompany Police Field Operations. Paperback: £16.99. ISBN 0 13 170128 2. Prentice Hall.

Bertran, Luis De Carlos–Raising Capital in Europe: The Legal Framework Following the EU Prospectus Directive. Hardback: £95.00. ISBN 1 904501 49 4. Richmond Law & Tax.

Bettinger, Torsten; Willoughby, Tony; Abel, Sally–Domain Name Law and Practice: An International Handbook. Hardback: £165.00. ISBN 0 19 927825 3. Oxford University Press.

Beyleveld, Deryck; Townend, David; Rouille-Mirza, S.; Wright, J.–Data Protective Directive and Medical Research Across Europe. Hardback: £60.00. ISBN 0 7546 2367 X. Ashgate.

Bhala, Raj–Modern GATT Law. Hardback: £174.00. ISBN 0 421 79300 7. Sweet & Maxwell.

Bicks, Peter A.–Defending a Company in a Punitive Damages Case: A Comprehensive Approach to Defeating Punitive Damages in Light of Present-day Juror Attitudes. Winning Legal Strategies S. Paperback: £149.95. ISBN 1 59622 223 9. Aspatore Books,US.

Biddle, Dan–Adverse Impact and Test Validation: A Practitioners Guide to Valid and Defensible Employment Testing. Hardback: £39.95. ISBN 0 566 08654 9. Gower Publishing Limited.

Biggs, Ak–Lawyers Costs and Fees: Probate. Paperback: £13.95. ISBN 0 7545 2939 8. Tolley Publishing.

Biggs, A.K.–Probate: Lawyers Costs and Fees. Paperback: £13.95. ISBN 0 7545 2797 2. Tolley Publishing.

Biggs, Keith–Costs and Fees in Family Proceedings. Paperback: £14.95. ISBN 0 7545 2936 3. Tolley Publishing.

Biggs, Keith–Fees and Fixed Costs in Civil Actions. Paperback: £14.95. ISBN 1 84592 044 9. Tottel Publishing.

Biggs, Keith–Lawyers Costs and Fees: Fees and Fixed Costs in Civil Actions. Paperback: £14.95. ISBN 1 84592 216 6. Tottel Publishing.

Biggs, Kevin–Costs and Fees in Family Proceedings. Paperback: £14.95. ISBN 0 7545 2798 0. Tolley Publishing.

Bills Gaskell–Bills of Lading: Law and Practice. Hardback: £250.00. ISBN 1 84311 398 8. Informa Business Publishing.

Bird, Roger; Ward, Richard–Domestic Violence, Crime and Victims Act: A Practitioner's Guide. Paperback: £35.00. ISBN 0 85308 953 1. Jordans.

Bird, Roger–Ancillary Relief Handbook. Paperback: £49.50. ISBN 0 85308 970 1. Jordans.

Bird, Roger–Domestic Violence Law and Practice. Paperback: £45.00. ISBN 0 85308 974 4. Jordans.

Birkinshaw, Patrick–Birkinshaw: Government and Information-the Law Relating to Access, Disclosure and Their Regulation. Paperback: £70.00. ISBN 1 84592 088 0. Tottel Publishing.

Blackhall, J. Cameron–Planning Law and Practice. Paperback: £28.95. ISBN 1 85941 748 5. Cavendish Publishing Ltd.

Blackshaw, Ian S.; Seikmann, Robert C.R.–Sports Image Rights in Europe. Hardback: £65.00. ISBN 90 6704 195 5. Asser Press.

Blair, Roger D.; Cotter, Thomas F.–Intellectual Property: Economic and Legal Dimensions of Rights and Remedies. Hardback: £45.00. ISBN 0 521 83316 7. Paperback: £20.95. ISBN 0 521 54067 4. Cambridge University Press.

Blakeney, Michael; Kretschmer–Intellectual Property and Geographical Indicators: A Legal And Economic Analysis. Hardback: £65.00. ISBN 1 84376 950 6. Edward Elgar.

Blanck, Peter D.–Disability Rights. International Library of Essays on Rights. Hardback: £130.00. ISBN 0 7546 2452 8. Ashgate.

Blanco, E. Merino–Spanish Legislation System. Paperback: £22.95. ISBN 0 421 90230 2. Sweet & Maxwell.

Blanco, Luis Ortiz–Market Power in EC Antitrust Law. Hardback: £55.00. ISBN 1 84113 528 3. Hart Publishing.

Blanco, Luis Ortiz–Shipping Conferences Under EC Antitrust Law: Criticism of a Legal Paradox. Hardback: £125.00. ISBN 1 84113 527 5. Hart Publishing.

Blanke, Herm.-J.; Mangiameli, Stelio–Governing Europe Under a Constitution: The Hard Road from the European Treaties to a European Constitutional Treaty. Hardback: £34.50. ISBN 3 540 24042 X. Springer-Verlag Berlin and Heidelberg GmbH & Co. K.

Blazek, Jody–IRS Form 1023: Tax Preparation Guide for Nonprofits. Paperback: £22.95. ISBN 0 471 71525 5. John Wiley & Sons Inc.

Bloch, Selwyn; Brearley, Kate–Employment Covenants and Confidential Information: Law, Practice and Technique. Hardback: £90.00. ISBN 0 406 97731 3. Butterworths Law.

Blokker, Niels M.; Schrijver, N.J.–Netherlands Yearbook of International Law: V. 34. Netherlands Yearbook of International Law Series. Hardback: £70.00. ISBN 90 6704 188 2. Asser Press.

Bobrow, Jerry–Pass Key to the LSAT. Paperback: £5.99. ISBN 0 7641 2414 5. Barron's Educational Series.

Bogdandy, Armin von; Bast, Jurgen–Principles of European Constitutional Law. Hardback: £95.00. ISBN 1 84113 464 3. Hart Publishing.

Boisseleau, Francois; Roggenkamp, Martha–Regulation of Power Exchanges in Europe. Energy & Law S. Paperback: £64.00. ISBN 90 5095 317 4. Intersentia Publishers.

Bolt, Stephen–Rough Deal: A Plain English Guide to Drug Laws in NSW. Paperback: £16.50. ISBN 0 947205 92 6. Redfern Legal Centre Publishing.

Bolter, Walter G.–Telecommunication Policy for the 90s. Hardback: £62.50. ISBN 1 56324 918 9. M.E. Sharpe.

Bond, Tim; Sandhu, Amanpreet–Therapists in Court: Providing Evidence and Supporting Witnesses. Hardback: £60.00. ISBN 1 4129 1267 9. Paperback: £16.99. ISBN 1 4129 1268 7. Sage Publications Ltd.

Bond, Tina; Bridge, Jane; Black, Jill M.–LPC Family Law. Legal Practice Course Guides. Paperback: £26.99. ISBN 0 19 928484 9. Oxford University Press.

Bone–Employment Law Revision Guide. Paperback: £21.99. ISBN 1 84398 099 1. Chartered Institute of Personnel and Development.

Bone–Employment Law and Revision Guide Pack 2005. Paperback: £52.98. ISBN 1 84398 100 9. Chartered Institute of Personnel and Development.

Bonner, David; Hooker, Ian; White, Robin–Social Security Legislation: Vol 1. Non Means Tested Benefits, 2004/2005 Supplement (Supplement to Vols I, II, III and IV). Paperback: £42.00. ISBN 0 421 90560 3. Sweet & Maxwell.

Bonner, David; Hooker, Ian; White, Robin–Social Security Legislation: V. 1. Non Means Tested Benefits. Paperback: £77.00. ISBN 0 421 92030 0. Sweet & Maxwell.

Bonsignore, John J.; Katsh, Ethan; D'Errico, Peter; Pipkin, Ronald M.; Arons, Stephen; Rifkin, Janet–Before the Law: An Introduction to the Legal Process. Hardback: £23.95. ISBN 0 618 50345 5. Houghton Mifflin Co.

Bools, Lord and Aikens–Bills of Lading. Lloyd's Shipping Law Library. Hardback: £260.00. ISBN 1 84311 438 0. Informa Business Publishing.

Booth, Cherie; Squires, Daniel–Negligence Liability of Public Authorities. Hardback: £125.00. ISBN 0 19 926541 0. Oxford University Press.

Bossche, Peter van den–Law and Policy of the World Trade Organization: Text, Cases and Materials. Paperback: £45.00. ISBN 0 521 52981 6. Cambridge University Press.

Bothe, Michael; Rehbinder, Eckard–Climate Change Policy. Hardback: £50.00. ISBN 90 77596 05 4. Eleven International Publishing.

Bourgeois, Jacques–Trade Law Experienced: Pottering About in the GATT and WTO. Hardback: £125.00. ISBN 1 905017 03 0. Cameron May.

Bovis, Christopher–EC Public Procurement: Case Law and Regulation. Hardback: £135.00. ISBN 0 19 927792 3. Oxford University Press.

Bovis, Christopher–Public Procurement in the European Union. Hardback: £55.00. ISBN 1 4039 3607 2. Palgrave Macmillan.

Bowers, John; Honeyball, Simon–Textbook on Labour Law. Paperback: £23.99. ISBN 0 19 927063 5. Oxford University Press.

Bowers, John–A Practical Approach to Employment Law. Practical Approach S. Paperback: £39.95. ISBN 0 19 927374 X. Oxford University Press.

Bowers, L. Thomas; Langvardt, Arlen W; Mallor, Jane P; Barnes, A.James–Business Law: The Ethical, Global, and E-Commerce Environment. Hardback: £45.99. ISBN 0 07 110698 7. Higher Education.

Bowie, Vaughan; Fisher, Bonnie; Cooper, Cary–Workplace Violence: Issues, Trends, Strategies. Hardback: £27.50. ISBN 1 84392 134 0. Willan Publishing.

Bowley, Gordon–Making A Will Self-Help Guide. Paperback: £9.99. ISBN 1 84528 030 X. How To Books.

Bowrey, Kathy–Law and Internet Cultures. Paperback: £15.50. ISBN 0 521 60048 0. Cambridge University Press Network List.

Boyle, Fiona; Capps, Deveral; Plowden, Philip; Sandford, Clare–Practical Guide to Lawyering Skills. Paperback: £25.95. ISBN 1 85941 975 5. Cavendish Publishing Ltd.

BPP Professional Education–ACCA Paper 2.2 Corporate and Business Law (International): Passcards. Spiral/comb bound: £9.95. ISBN 0 7517 2165 4. BPP Professional Education.

BPP Professional Education–ACCA Paper 2.2 Corporate and Business Law (International): Practice and Revision Kit. Paperback: £12.95. ISBN 0 7517 2187 5. BPP Professional Education.

BPP Professional Education–ACCA Paper 2.2 Corporate and Business Law: I-Learn. CD-ROM: £34.95. ISBN 0 7517 2479 3. BPP Professional Education.

BPP Professional Education–ACCA Paper 2.2 Corporate and Business Law: I-Pass. CD-ROM: £24.95. ISBN 0 7517 2494 7. BPP Professional Education.

BPP Professional Education–ACCA Paper 2.2 Corporate and Business Law: Passcards. Spiral/comb bound: £9.95. ISBN 0 7517 2152 2. BPP Professional Education.

BPP Professional Education–ACCA Paper 2.2 Corporate and Business Law: Practice and Revision Kit. Paperback: £12.95. ISBN 0 7517 2174 3. BPP Professional Education.

BPP Professional Education–ACCA Paper 2.2 Corporate and Business Law: Study Text. Paperback: £24.95. ISBN 0 7517 2317 7. BPP Professional Education.

BPP Professional Education–CII CF1: UK Financial Services, Regulations and Ethics-I-Pass. CD-ROM: £24.95. ISBN 0 7517 2450 5. BPP Professional Education.

BPP Professional Education–CII CF1: UK Financial Services, Regulations and Ethics-Passcards. Spiral/comb bound: £10.95. ISBN 0 7517 2281 2. BPP Professional Education.

BPP Professional Education–CIMA C5 Business Law: I-Pass. CD-ROM: £24.95. ISBN 0 7517 2459 9. BPP Professional Education.

BPP Professional Education–CIMA C5 Business Law: Passcards. Spiral/comb bound: £9.95. ISBN 0 7517 1960 9. BPP Professional Education.

BPP Professional Education–CIMA C5 Business Law: Study Text. Paperback: £24.95. ISBN 0 7517 2289 8. BPP Professional Education.

BPP Professional Education–SII Unit 1: UK Financial Services, Regulations and Ethics-I-Pass. CD-ROM: £29.95. ISBN 0 7517 2445 9. BPP Professional Education.

BPP Professional Education–SII Unit 1: UK Financial Services, Regulations and Ethics-Passcard. Spiral/comb bound: £10.95. ISBN 0 7517 2277 4. BPP Professional Education.

BPP Professional Education–SII Unit 1: UK Financial Services, Regulations and Ethics-Text. Paperback: £32.95. ISBN 0 7517 2374 6. Paperback: £32.95. ISBN 0 7517 1950 1. BPP Professional Education.

Bracewell, Joyanne–Family Court Practice. Hardback: £199.00. ISBN 0 85308 980 9. Family Law.

Bradgate, Robert; White, Fidelma–LPC Commercial Law. Legal Practice Course Guides. Paperback: £26.99. ISBN 0 19 928492 X. Oxford University Press.

Brayne, Hugh; Carr, Helen–Law for Social Workers. Paperback: £24.99. ISBN 0 19 927551 3. Oxford University Press.

Breau, Susan–Humanitarian Intervention: The United Nations and Collective Responsibility. Hardback: £85.00. ISBN 1 905017 08 1. Cameron May.

Breen, P.J.–Consolidated Courts and Court Officers Acts. Consolidation S. Paperback: £85.00. ISBN 1 905536 00 3. Clarus Press Ltd.

Brennan, Bartley; Browne, Neil; Kubasek, Nancy K.–Legal Environment of Business: A Critical Thinking Approach. Hardback: £73.99. ISBN 0 13 149856 8. Prentice Hall.

Brennan, Blair, William; Jacob; Langstaff, Brian–Bullen and Leake and Jacob's Precedents of Pleadings, 1st Supplement. Paperback: £70.00. ISBN 0 421 90390 2. Sweet & Maxwell.

Brennan, Gabriel–Landlord and Tenant Law. Law Society of Ireland Manuals S. Paperback: £39.99. ISBN 0 19 928025 8. Oxford University Press.

Brennan, Gabriel–Landlord and Tenant Law. Law Society of Ireland Manuals S. Paperback: £39.99. ISBN 0 19 928025 8. Oxford University Press.

Brennan, Philip–Tax Acts. Paperback: £56.66. ISBN 1 84592 141 0. Tottel Publishing.

Brennan, Rosie–Immigration Advice At the Police Station. Paperback: £34.95. ISBN 1 85328 948 5. Law Society Publications.

Brhel, Martin–Courtroom Survival for Property Crime Cops. Paperback: £24.99. ISBN 0 13 113293 8. Prentice Hall.

Bridge, C.–Adoption: A Practical Guide. Paperback: £50.00. ISBN 0 85308 969 8. Family Law.

Briggs and Rees–Civil Jurisdiction and Judgments. Lloyd's Commercial Law Library. Hardback: £265.00. ISBN 1 84311 425 9. Informa Business Publishing.

Bright, Keith; Williams, Peter J.G.; Langton-Lockton, Sarah–Disability: Making Buildings Accessible-Special Report. Paperback: £99.00. ISBN 1 900648 48 2. Workplacelaw Network.

British Property Federation–BPF Consultancy Agreement. Paperback: £29.38. ISBN 1 900648 42 3. Workplacelaw Network.

British Standards Institution–BS 8408:2005 Road Traffic Signs. Testing and Performance of Microprismatic Retroreflective Sheeting Materials. Specification. Hardback: £140.00. ISBN 0 580 45924 1. British Standards Institution.

Britton, Alison–Healthcare Law and Ethics. Paperback: £25.00. ISBN 0 414 01526 6. W.Green & Son.

Britz, Marjie; Grennan, Sean–Organized Crime: A Worldwide Approach. Paperback: £37.99. ISBN 0 13 171094 X. Prentice Hall.

Broadhurst, Emily–Employment Law. Emerald Home Lawyer S. Paperback: £9.99. ISBN 1 903909 56 2. Straightforward Publishing.

Broadhurst, Emily–Family Law. Emerald Home Lawyer S. Paperback: £9.99. ISBN 1 903909 55 4. Straightforward Publishing.

Bronckers, Marco C. E. J.; Horlick, Gary N.–WTO Jurisprudence and Policy: Practitioners' Perspectives. Hardback: £125.00. ISBN 1 905017 06 5. Cameron May.

Broomfield, Steven–Consumer Law. Emerald Home Lawyer S. Paperback: £9.99. ISBN 1 903909 57 0. Straightforward Publishing.

Brough, Gordon H.–Private Limited Companies: Formation and Management. Paperback: £65.00. ISBN 0 414 01598 3. W.Green & Son.

Brown, Alastair N–Human Rights. Paperback: £12.50. ISBN 0 414 01614 9. W.Green & Son.

Brown, Alastair N.; Thomson, Lesley; Harris, Lorna–Proceeds of Crime. Greens Practice Library. Hardback: £110.00. ISBN 0 414 01445 6. W.Green & Son.

Brown, Michael–Butterworths Insurance Law Handbook. Paperback: £90.00. ISBN 1 4057 0617 1. Butterworths Law.

Brown, Rob; McKee, Heather; Treasaden, Ian; Puri, Basant–Mental Health Law. Paperback: £19.99. ISBN 0 340 88503 3. Hodder Arnold H&S.

Brown–Legal Terminology. Book (details unknown): £28.99. ISBN 1 4018 2012 3. Delmar.

Browne, Kevin; Catlow, Margaret–Civil Litigation. College of Law LPC Guides S. Paperback: £25.95. ISBN 0 905835 88 3. The College of Law.

Browne, Kevin; Pothecary, Judith–Welfare Benefits and Immigration Law. Paperback: £24.95. ISBN 0 905835 78 6. Paperback: £25.95. ISBN 1 905391 11 0. The College of Law.

Bryan, David–Guide to Consumer Law. Easyway Guides S. Paperback: £7.99. ISBN 1 900694 18 2. Easyway Guides.

Bryan, David–Straightforward Guide to Family Law. Paperback: £8.99. ISBN 1 903909 71 6. Straightforward Publishing.

Buck, Trevor; Bonner, David; Sainsbury, Roy–Making Social Security Law: The Role and Work of the Social Security and Child Support Commissioners. Hardback: £50.00. ISBN 0 7546 4381 6. Ashgate.

Buck, Trevor–Social Fund: Law and Practice. Paperback: £72.00. ISBN 0 421 88120 8. Sweet & Maxwell.

Buckley, Michael–Buckley Capital Tax Acts. Paperback: £53.33. ISBN 1 84592 096 1. Tottel Publishing.

Buckley, R.A.–Law of Negligence. Hardback: £195.00. ISBN 0 406 95941 2. Butterworths Law.

Burca, Grainne de; Witte, Bruno De–Social Rights in Europe. Hardback: £60.00. ISBN 0 19 928617 5. Oxford University Press.

Burca, Grainne de; Witte, Bruno De–Social Rights in Europe. Paperback: £27.50. ISBN 0 19 928799 6. Oxford University Press.

Burca, Grainne de–EU Law and the Welfare State: In Search of Solidarity. Collected Courses of the Academy of European Law. Hardback: £60.00. ISBN 0 19 928740 6. Paperback: £22.50. ISBN 0 19 928741 4. Oxford University Press.

Burchill, Richard–Democracy and International Law. Library of Essays in International Law. Hardback: £130.00. ISBN 0 7546 2422 6. Dartmouth.

Burn, Suzanne–Successful Use of Expert Witnesses in Civil Disputes. Paperback: £25.00. ISBN 0 7219 1450 0. Shaw & Sons.

Burnett, Justina–Getting Into Law. Getting Into Course Guides. Paperback: £11.99. ISBN 1 84455 067 2. Trotman.

Burnett, Rachel; Klinger, Paul–Drafting and Negotiating Computer Contracts. Hardback/CD-ROM: £190.75. ISBN 1 84592 024 4. Tottel Publishing.

Burney, Elizabeth–Making People Behave: The Creation and Enforcement of Anti-social Behaviour Policy. Hardback: £40.00. ISBN 1 84392 138 3. Paperback: £17.99. ISBN 1 84392 137 5. Willan Publishing.

Burrell, Robert; Coleman, Allison–Copyright Exceptions: The Digital Impact. Cambridge Studies in Intellectual Property Rights, No. 6. Hardback: £65.00. ISBN 0 521 84726 5. Cambridge University Press.

Burrows, Andrew–Remedies for Torts and Breach of Contract. Paperback: £33.99. ISBN 0 406 97726 7. LexisNexis UK.

Burrows, D.–Privilege and Confidentiality in Family Proceedings: A Special Bulletin. Paperback: £35.00. ISBN 0 85308 963 9. Family Law.

Burrows, Rita; Gravestock, Peter; Homer, Arnold–Tolley's Taxwise II. Paperback: £55.00. ISBN 0 7545 2877 4. Tolley Publishing.

Burrows, Rita; Homer, Arnold–Tolley's Taxwise I (Revised Ed). Paperback: £61.00. ISBN 0 7545 2876 6. Tolley Publishing.

Burton, Frances–Core Statutes on Family Law. Core Statutes S. Paperback: £10.00. ISBN 1 84641 009 6. Law Matters Publishing.

Burton, Frances–Family Law. Textbooks. Paperback: £24.00. ISBN 1 84641 017 7. Law Matters Publishing.

Busby, Nicole; Smith, Rhona K.M.–Core Statutes on EU Law. Core Statutes S. Paperback: £10.00. ISBN 1 84641 006 1. Law Matters Publishing.

Busby, Nicole–Employment Law Essentials. Paperback: £13.99. ISBN 1 84592 161 5. Tottel Publishing.

Business Law for Paralegals. Hardback: £42.00. ISBN 1 4018 3353 5. Delmar.

Business Lawcards. Lawcards S. Spiral/comb bound: £6.95. ISBN 1 84568 022 7. Cavendish Publishing Ltd.

Business Law. CIMA Exam Practice Kit S. Paperback: £14.95. ISBN 0 7506 6585 8. CIMA (Chartered Institute of Management Accountant.

Butler, Brian—Vat Acts. Paperback: £56.66. ISBN 1 84592 136 4. Tottel Publishing.

Butler, Sean C.—Guide to UK and EU Plant Variety Rights. Paperback: £45.00. ISBN 0 9550427 0 4. Transpose Technology Limited.

Butt, Paul—Commercial Property. Paperback: £24.95. ISBN 0 905835 80 8. Paperback: £25.95. ISBN 1 905391 04 8. The College of Law.

Butt, Paul—Property Law and Practice. Paperback: £25.95. ISBN 0 905835 89 1. The College of Law.

Butterworths Family Law Service: Pt. 129. Looseleaf/ring bound: £189.00. ISBN 1 4057 0279 6. Butterworths Law.

Butterworths Law Directory. Hardback: £69.00. ISBN 1 4057 0985 5. Butterworths Law.

Butterworths Medico-Legal Reports: V. 85. Hardback: £90.00. ISBN 1 4057 0770 4. Butterworths Law.

Butterworths Personal Injury Litigation Service: V. 74. Looseleaf/ring bound: £172.00. ISBN 1 4057 0653 8. Butterworths Law.

Cahill, Nessa—Enforcement of Company Law. Hardback: £110.00. ISBN 1 84592 105 4. Tottel Publishing.

Calabrese, Marianne; Calabrese, Susanne—So You Want to Be a Lawyer? Paperback: £12.95. ISBN 0 88391 136 1. Frederick Fell Publishers.

Caldwell, Zarrin—International Law: Justice Between Nations? Paperback: £4.95. ISBN 0 85233 008 1. Understanding Global Issues.

Callo, Kat—Making Sense of Leasehold Property. Paperback: £11.99. ISBN 1 904053 12 2. Law Pack Publishing.

Calvert, Clay; Pember, Don R.—Mass Media Law. Paperback: £68.99. ISBN 0 07 312685 3. McGraw Hill Higher Education.

Cambridge Yearbook of European Legal Studies: V. 7. Hardback: £85.00. ISBN 1 84113 561 5. Hart Publishing.

Cameron, Gordon—Delict. Book (details unknown): £12.50. ISBN 0 414 01585 1. W. Green & Son.

Campbell, Andrew; Gray, Joanna; Welch, Jane; Hamilton, Jenny; Mackay, Tom; MacNeil, Iain; Burling, Julian; Blair, Michael; Tebbatt, Philip—Butterworths Annotated Guide to the Financial Services and Markets Act 2000. Paperback: £225.00. ISBN 1 4057 0256 7. Butterworths Law.

Campbell, Christian—Legal Aspects of Doing Business in Europe-Volume III. Paperback: £52.32. ISBN 1 4116 5001 8. Lulu Press Incorporated.

Campbell, Dennis—International Agency and Distribution Law-Volume I. Paperback: £54.97. ISBN 1 4116 5019 0. Lulu Press Incorporated.

Campbell, Dennis—International Agency and Distribution Law-Volume II. Paperback: £54.82. ISBN 1 4116 5020 4. Lulu Press Incorporated.

Campbell, Dennis—International Agency and Distribution Law-Volume III. Paperback: £54.82. ISBN 1 4116 5021 2. Lulu Press Incorporated.

Campbell, Dennis—International Protection of Foreign Investment-Volume II. Paperback: £62.20. ISBN 1 4116 5025 5. Lulu Press Incorporated.

Campbell, Dennis—International Taxation of Low-Tax Transactions-High-Tax Jurisdictions-Volume I. Paperback: £44.33. ISBN 1 4116 5024 7. Lulu Press Incorporated.

Campbell, Dennis—International Taxation of Low-Tax Transactions-Low-Tax Jurisdictions-Volume I. Paperback: £12.44. ISBN 1 4116 5028 X. Lulu Press Incorporated.

Campbell, Dennis—International Taxation of Low-Tax Transactions-Low-Tax Jurisdictions-Volume II. Paperback: £44.82. ISBN 1 4116 5027 1. Lulu Press Incorporated.

Campbell, Dennis—International Telecommunications Law-Volume I. Paperback: £45.99. ISBN 1 4116 5812 4. Lulu Press Incorporated.

Campbell, Joseph Keim; O'Rourke, Michael; Shier, David—Law and Social Justice. Topics in Contemporary Philosophy S., V. 3. Hardback: £45.95. ISBN 0 262 03340 2. Bradford Book.

Cane, Peter; Tushnet, Mark–Oxford Handbook of Legal Studies. Paperback: £30.00. ISBN 0 19 924817 6. Oxford University Press.

Cann, Steven J.–Administrative Law. Hardback: £73.00. ISBN 1 4129 1396 9. Sage Publications Ltd.

Cannon, Patrick–Tolley's Stamp Taxes. Paperback: £99.00. ISBN 0 7545 2888 X. Tolley Publishing.

Cant, Christopher; Wood, Lana–Property Development Handbook: Transaction Structures. Paperback: £75.00. ISBN 1 903927 63 3. Legalease.

Cantor, N.L.–Making Medical Decisions for the Profoundly Mentally Disabled. Hardback: £22.95. ISBN 0 262 03331 3. The MIT Press.

Cappalli, Richard B.–Advanced Case Law Methods: A Practical Course. Hardback: £44.50. ISBN 1 57105 345 X. Transnational Publishers, Inc.

Card, Duncan Cornell; O'Conor, Mark–Information Technology Transactions: Legal and Commercial Strategies. Hardback: £99.00. ISBN 0 421 89540 3. Sweet & Maxwell.

Carey, Peter; Turle, Marcus–Freedom of Information Handbook. Paperback: £69.95. ISBN 1 85328 968 X. Law Society Publications.

Carey, P.; Verow, R.–Media and Entertainment Law. Paperback: £24.95. ISBN 0 905835 84 0. The College of Law.

Carmen, Del; Trulson, Darrel A.–Juvenile Justice Law. Hardback: £34.00. ISBN 0 534 52158 4. Wadsworth.

Carr, Helen; Cottle, Stephen; Baldwin, Timothy; King, Michael–Housing Act. Paperback: £35.00. ISBN 0 85308 952 3. Jordans.

Carr, Kenneth; Musters, Patrick–Road Traffic Offences Handbook. Paperback: £44.95. ISBN 1 85328 918 3. Law Society Publications.

Carroll, Stephen J; Hensler, Deborah R.; Gross, Jennifer; Sloss, Elizabeth M.; Schonlau, Matthias; Abrahamse, Allan F.; Ashwood, J.Scott–Asbestos Litigation. Paperback: £13.50. ISBN 0 8330 3078 7. RAND.

Carter, Robert–Matter Of Law: A Memoir Of Struggle In The Cause Of Equal Rights. Hardback: £16.99. ISBN 1 56584 830 6. The New Press.

Carvalho, Nuno Pires de–Trips Regime of Patent Rights. Hardback: £123.00. ISBN 90 411 2317 2. Kluwer Law and Taxation Publishers.

Casey, Denise–Business Law. Law Society of Ireland Manuals S. Paperback: £39.99. ISBN 0 19 928021 5. Paperback: £39.99. ISBN 0 19 928021 5. Oxford University Press.

Chalmers, James–Criminal Defences. Hardback: £135.00. ISBN 0 414 01521 5. W.Green & Son.

Chamberlain, Emma; Whitehouse, Chris–Pre-Owned Assets and Tax Planning Strategies: Capital Tax Planning in the New Era. Paperback: £129.00. ISBN 0 421 91730 X. Sweet & Maxwell.

Chambers, David; Butterfield, Roger–Alcohol & Entertainment Licensing: A Practical Guide. Paperback: £21.95. ISBN 0 7219 1690 2. Shaw & Sons.

Chamelin, Neil C.–Criminal Law for Police Officers. Hardback: £45.99. ISBN 0 13 118812 7. Prentice Hall.

Changes of Use of Buildings and Land: The Town and Country Planning (Use Classes) Order 1987. Paperback: £7.00. ISBN 0 11 753944 9. The Stationery Office Books.

Chappelle, Diane–Land Law. Foundation Studies in Law S. Paperback: £29.99. ISBN 1 4058 1223 0. Longman.

Charles Sampford; Fredrik Galtung–Measuring Corruption. Law Ethics & Governance. Hardback: £50.00. ISBN 0 7546 2405 6. Avebury Technical.

Cheeseman, Henry R.–Contemporary Business Law and E-Commerce Law. Hardback: £56.99. ISBN 0 13 149660 3. Prentice Hall.

Cheeseman, Henry R.–Essentials of Business Law. Paperback: £44.99. ISBN 0 13 144047 0. Prentice Hall.

Cheeseman, Henry R.–Student Study Guide. Paperback: £13.99. ISBN 0 13 144051 9. Prentice Hall.

Chen-Wishart, Mindy–Contract Law. Paperback: £24.99. ISBN 0 19 926814 2. Oxford University Press.

Cheyne, Ann–Legal Secretary's Guide. Paperback: £27.99. ISBN 0 19 926840 1. Oxford University Press.

Chidell, Ray; Sampson, Alison–Tolley's Tax Checklists. Looseleaf/ring bound: £79.00. ISBN 0 7545 0823 4. LexisNexis UK.

Child, Peter–Notes for Company Drivers. Paperback: £7.99. ISBN 0 9540910 4 3. Benbow Publications.

Childs, Penny–Criminal Law. Paperback: £6.50. ISBN 0 421 89010 X. Sweet & Maxwell.

Chiltern's Orange Tax Guide. Paperback: £62.00. ISBN 1 4057 0742 9. Tolley Publishing.

Chiltern's Yellow Tax Guide. Paperback: £92.95. ISBN 1 4057 0743 7. Tolley Publishing.

Choo, Andrew–Choo on Evidence. Paperback: £25.99. ISBN 0 19 876398 0. Oxford University Press.

Christou, Richard–Boilerplate: Practical Clauses. Paperback/CD-ROM: £129.00. ISBN 0 421 89890 9. Sweet & Maxwell.

Chuah, Jason–Law of International Trade. Paperback: £28.95. ISBN 0 421 90110 1. Sweet & Maxwell.

Cinar, Dilek–Diversity Justice and Democracy. Public Policy & Social Welfare S. Hardback: £27.50. ISBN 0 7546 4245 3. Ashgate.

Citizenship Foundation–Young Citizen's Passport: Your Guide to the Law in England and Wales. Paperback: £4.99. ISBN 0 340 91604 4. Hodder Murray.

Civil Procedure Handbook. Paperback: £34.95. ISBN 0 19 928514 4. Paperback: £34.95. ISBN 0 19 928514 4. Oxford University Press.

Clark, Ian–Legitimacy in International Society. Hardback: £30.00. ISBN 0 19 925842 2. Oxford University Press.

Clark, Robert; Smyth, Shane–Intellectual Property Law in Ireland. Hardback: £93.33. ISBN 1 84592 020 1. Tottel Publishing.

Clarke, Alison; Kohler, Paul–Property Law: Commentary and Materials. Law in Context S. Paperback: £34.99. ISBN 0 521 61489 9. Cambridge University Press.

Clarke, Giles–Offshore Tax Planning. Paperback: £120.00. ISBN 1 4057 0755 0. Tolley Publishing.

Clarke, Malcolm–Policies and Perceptions of Insurance Law in the Twenty First Century. Hardback: £60.00. ISBN 0 19 927330 8. Oxford University Press.

Clayton, Richard; Tomlinson, Hugh–Clayton Civ Act Against Police, 3rd Ed. Paperback: £46.00. ISBN 0 421 92260 5. Sweet & Maxwell.

Clements, Luke; Thomas, Philip A.–Human Rights Act: A Success Story? Paperback: £19.99. ISBN 1 4051 2375 3. Blackwell Publishing.

Clout, Imogen–Divorce: The Which? Guide to Divorce. Which? Consumer Guides. Paperback: £11.99. ISBN 1 84490 015 0. Which? Books.

Cobley, Cathy–Sex Offenders Law, Policy and Practice. Paperback: £60.00. ISBN 0 85308 979 5. Jordans.

Cohen, C. P.–Developing Rights of Indigenous Children. Hardback: £100.99. ISBN 1 57105 375 1. Transnational Publishers, Inc.

Cohen, Steve–Deportation Is Freedom!: The Orwellian World of Immigration Controls. Paperback: £14.95. ISBN 1 84310 294 3. Jessica Kingsley Publishers.

Cole, Alistair–Beyond Devolution and Decentralisation: Building Regional Capacity in Wales and Brittany. Devolution S. Hardback: £55.00. ISBN 0 7190 7092 9. Manchester University Press.

Coles, Joanne–Law of the European Union. Paperback: £15.95. ISBN 1 85836 604 6. Old Bailey Press.

Collins, Hugh; Ewing, K.D.; McColgan, Aileen–Labour Law: Text and Materials. Paperback: £28.00. ISBN 1 84113 362 0. Hart Publishing.

Collison, David; Tiley, John–Tiley and Collison's UK Tax Guide. Paperback: £99.00. ISBN 1 4057 0753 4. Tolley Publishing.

Commercial Lawcards. Lawcards S. Looseleaf/ring bound: £6.95. ISBN 1 84568 019 7. Cavendish Publishing Ltd.

Common Market Law Reports 04/2: V. 100. Hardback: £190.00. ISBN 0 421 91130 1. Sweet & Maxwell.

Common Market Law Reports: V. 101. Hardback: £190.00. ISBN 0 421 91150 6. Sweet & Maxwell.

Common Market Law Reports: V. 99. Hardback: £190.00. ISBN 0 421 91110 7. Sweet & Maxwell.

Common MLR Anti-Trust: Pt. 4. Hardback: £190.00. ISBN 0 421 91170 0. Sweet & Maxwell.

Common MLR Anti-Trust: Pt. 5. Hardback: £190.00. ISBN 0 421 91190 5. Sweet & Maxwell.

Company Law Handbook 2005. Paperback: £55.00. ISBN 1 84140 572 8. Croner CCH Group Ltd.

Company Lawcards. Lawcards S. Spiral/comb bound: £6.95. ISBN 1 84568 018 9. Cavendish Publishing Ltd.

Connelly, Claire–Criminal Lawbasics. Paperback: £12.50. ISBN 0 414 01577 0. W.Green & Son.

Connor, Paul; Pinfield, David; Taylor, Neil; Chapman, Julian–Blackstone's Police Investigator's Workbook. Blackstone's Police Manuals. Paperback: £35.00. ISBN 0 19 928919 0. Oxford University Press.

Connor, Paul–Blackstone's Police Investigators' Q&A. Paperback: £14.99. ISBN 0 19 928757 0. Oxford University Press.

Connor, Paul–Blackstone's Police Sergeants' Mock Examination Paper. Paperback: £14.99. ISBN 0 19 928831 3. Oxford University Press.

Conrad, Christian–Improving International Competition Order: An Institutional Approach. Hardback: £55.00. ISBN 1 4039 4790 2. Palgrave Macmillan.

Constitutional Lawcards. Lawcards S. Book: £6.95. ISBN 1 84568 028 6. Cavendish Publishing Ltd.

Constitutional Reform Act 2005: Explanatory Notes. Public General Acts-Elizabeth II, 2005, Chapter 4. Paperback: £7.50. ISBN 0 10 560405 4. The Stationery Office Books.

Contemporary Issues in Healthcare Law and Ethics. Paperback: £24.99. ISBN 0 7506 8832 7. Butterworth Heinemann.

Contract Lawcards. Lawcards S. Spiral/comb bound: £6.95. ISBN 1 84568 026 X. Cavendish Publishing Ltd.

Cook, Trevor–EU Intellectual Property Law. Hardback: £95.00. ISBN 1 904501 52 4. Richmond Law & Tax.

Cooke, Elizabeth–Modern Studies in Property Law: V.3. Hardback: £55.00. ISBN 1 84113 558 5. Hart Publishing.

Cooke, John–Law of Tort. Foundation Studies in Law S. Paperback: £27.99. ISBN 1 4058 1229 X. Longman.

Cooke, Jonathan–Step Accounting Guidelines: Guidelines for the Preparation of Trust and Estate Accounts in England and Wales. Paperback: £8.00. ISBN 0 9550262 0 2. Society of Trust and Estate Practitioners.

Cooper, Jonathan–European Human Rights Law Review, 2005: Vol 10. Hardback: £285.00. ISBN 0 421 93070 5. Sweet & Maxwell.

Corporate Administration. Professional Development S. Paperback: £29.95. ISBN 1 86072 318 7. ICSA Publishing Ltd (Institute of Chartered Secretaries & Administrators).

Cottier, Thomas; Pauwelyn, Joost; Burgi, Elisabeth–Human Rights and International Trade. International Economic Law S. Hardback: £60.00. ISBN 0 19 928582 9. Paperback: £30.00. ISBN 0 19 928583 7. Oxford University Press.

Cottier, Thomas–Intellectual Property Protection in WTO Law. Hardback: £125.00. ISBN 1 905017 11 1. Cameron May.

Cougias, Dorian J.–Compliance Book: From the Basics to Preparing for an Audit. Hardback: £24.99. ISBN 0 13 186720 2. Prentice Hall PTR.

Cousal, Helen; King, Lesley–Private Client: Wills, Trusts and Estate Planning. Paperback: £24.95. ISBN 0 905835 75 1. Paperback: £25.95. ISBN 1 905391 09 9. The College of Law.

Cowen, Gary; Driscoll, James; Target, Laurence–Commonhold: A Guide to the New Law. Paperback: £49.95. ISBN 1 85328 867 5. Law Society Publications.

Coyle-Shapiro, Jacqueline A.M.; Shore, Lynn M.; Taylor, M.Susan; Tetrick, Lois E.–Employment Relationship: Examining Psychological and Contextual Perspectives. Paperback: £24.99. ISBN 0 19 928683 3. Oxford University Press.

Coyle, Sean; Pavlakos, George–Jurisprudence or Legal Science? Hardback: £35.00. ISBN 1 84113 504 6. Hart Publishing.

CPS Charging Standards. Paperback: £15.95. ISBN 0 19 928513 6. Oxford University Press.

Cracknell, D G–English Legal System. Paperback: £11.95. ISBN 1 85836 588 0. Old Bailey Press.

Cracknell, D G–Equity and Trusts. Paperback: £11.95. ISBN 1 85836 589 9. Old Bailey Press.

Cracknell, D.G.–Constitutional and Administrative Law. Cracknell's Statutes S. Paperback: £11.95. ISBN 1 85836 584 8. Old Bailey Press.

Cracknell, D.G.–Contract, Tort and Remedies. Cracknell's Statutes S. Paperback: £11.95. ISBN 1 85836 583 X. Old Bailey Press.

Cracknell, D.G.–Criminal Law. Cracknell's Statutes S. Paperback: £11.95. ISBN 1 85836 586 4. Old Bailey Press.

Cracknell, D.G.–Employment Law. Cracknell's Statutes S. Paperback: £11.95. ISBN 1 85836 587 2. Old Bailey Press.

Cracknell, D.G.–European Union Legislation. Paperback: £11.95. ISBN 1 85836 590 2. Old Bailey Press.

Cracknell, D.G.–Land: The Law of Real Property. Cracknell's Statutes S. Paperback: £11.95. ISBN 1 85836 585 6. Old Bailey Press.

Cracknell, D.G.–Law of International Trade. Cracknell's Statutes S. Paperback: £11.95. ISBN 1 85836 582 1. Old Bailey Press.

Cracknell, D.G.–Obligations: Contract Law. Paperback: £15.95. ISBN 1 85836 605 4. Old Bailey Press.

Cracknell, D.G.–Obligations: The Law of Tort. Paperback: £15.95. ISBN 1 85836 606 2. Old Bailey Press.

Craig, Paul; Tomkins, Adam–Executive and Public Law: Power and Accountability in Comparative Perspective. Hardback: £50.00. ISBN 0 19 928559 4. Oxford University Press.

Craig, Victor; Walker, Steven J–Scottish Employment Law: An Introduction. Paperback: £25.00. ISBN 0 414 01623 8. W.Green & Son.

Cranston, Ross–How Law Works: The Machinery and Impact of Civil Justice. Hardback: £50.00. ISBN 0 19 929207 8. Oxford University Press.

Crawford, James R.–Creation of States in International Law. Hardback: £80.00. ISBN 0 19 826002 4. Oxford University Press.

Crawford, James; Lowe, Vaughan–British Year Book of International Law: V. 75. Hardback: £130.00. ISBN 0 19 928493 8. Oxford University Press.

Crerar, Lorne D.–Law of Banking in Scotland. Paperback: £90.00. ISBN 1 84592 151 8. Tottel Publishing.

Crews, Kenneth D.–Copyright Law for Librarians and Educators: Creative Strategies and Practical Solutions. Paperback: £32.95. ISBN 0 8389 0906 X. ALA Editions, US.

Criminal Law: Cases and Materials. Paperback: £34.95. ISBN 1 85941 935 6. Cavendish Publishing Ltd.

Criminal Lawcards. Lawcards S. Looseleaf/ring bound: £6.95. ISBN 1 84568 024 3. Cavendish Publishing Ltd.

Crozier, Paul—Criminal Advocacy. Paperback: £35.00. ISBN 0 414 01555 X. W.Green & Son.

Cryer, Robert; Bekou, Olympia—International Criminal Court. Library of Essays in International Law. Hardback: £135.00. ISBN 0 7546 2409 9. Ashgate.

Cryer, Robert—Prosecution of International Crimes: Integration and Selectivity in International Criminal Law. Cambridge Studies in International & Comparative Law. Hardback: £60.00. ISBN 0 521 82474 5. Cambridge University Press.

Cuisine, Douglas; Forte, Angelo—Scottish Cases and Materials in Commercial Law. Paperback: £35.00. ISBN 1 84592 148 8. Tottel Publishing.

Cullen, Deborah; Lane, Mary—Child Care Law: A Summary of the Law in England and Wales. Paperback: £7.95. ISBN 1 903699 73 8. British Association for Adoption & Fostering.

Cummins—Wills and Trusts Probate Law. Hardback: £32.99. ISBN 0 13 081150 5. Pearson US Imports & PHIPEs.

Current Law Case Citator 2002-2004. Hardback: £120.00. ISBN 0 421 91680 X. Sweet & Maxwell.

Current Law Statutes: V. 1. Hardback: £167.00. ISBN 0 421 91430 0. Sweet & Maxwell.

Current Law Statutes: V. 2. Hardback: £167.00. ISBN 0 421 91450 5. Sweet & Maxwell.

Current Law Statutes: V. 3. Hardback: £167.00. ISBN 0 421 91470 X. Sweet & Maxwell.

Current Law Statutes. Hardback: £455.00. ISBN 0 421 91980 9. Sweet & Maxwell.

Current Law Yearbook 2004 S/O Service. Hardback: £230.00. ISBN 0 421 91640 0. Sweet & Maxwell.

Current Law Yearbook 2004. Hardback: £365.00. ISBN 0 421 91720 2. Sweet & Maxwell.

Curtin, Deirdre; Kellerman, Alfred E.; Blockmans, Steven—EU Constitution: The Best Way Forward? Hardback: £70.00. ISBN 90 6704 200 5. Asser Press.

Curtin, D.M.; Nollkaemper, P.A.; Barnhoorn, L.A.N.M.—Netherlands Yearbook of International Law: V. 35. Hardback: £70.00. ISBN 90 6704 199 8. Asser Press.

Cushway, Barry—Employer's Handbook: An Essential Guide to Employment Law, Personnel Policies and Procedures. Hardback: £44.06. ISBN 0 7494 4350 2. Kogan Page.

Cuthbert, Mike—Nutshells-European Union Law. Paperback: £7.00. ISBN 0 421 92390 3. Sweet & Maxwell.

Cygan, Adam; Szyszczak, Erika—Szyszczak and Cygan: Understanding EU Law. Paperback: £12.95. ISBN 0 421 87860 6. Sweet & Maxwell.

D'Cruze, Shani; Walklate, Sandra; Pegg, Samantha; Croall, Hazel—Murder. Crime & Society S. Hardback: £40.00. ISBN 1 84392 170 7. Paperback: £17.99. ISBN 1 84392 169 3. Willan Publishing.

Dabbah, Maher; Lasok, Paul—Merger Control Worldwide. Hardback: £495.00. ISBN 0 521 85788 0. Cambridge University Press.

Dadamo, C.—French Law & Legal System. Book (details unknown): £26.95. ISBN 0 421 74090 6. Sweet & Maxwell.

Darbyshire, Penny—Darbyshire on the English Legal System. Paperback: £15.95. ISBN 0 421 90150 0. Sweet & Maxwell.

Data Protection Pocket Guide: BIP 0050:2004: Essential Facts At Your Fingertips. Paperback: £30.00. ISBN 0 580 44437 6. British Standards Institution.

Davies, Iwan; Davies, Iwan—Issues in International Commercial Law. Hardback: £65.00. ISBN 0 7546 2462 5. Ashgate.

Davis-White, Malcolm; Nicholson, Rosalin; Greenwood, Paul–Companies Court Practice and Procedure. Hardback: £94.95. ISBN 1 85328 950 7. Law Society Publications.

Davis, Mark–Bareboat Charters. Lloyd's Shipping Law Library. Hardback: £240.00. ISBN 1 84311 423 2. Informa Business Publishing.

Davison, James–JCT 2005 What's New? Hardback: £39.95. ISBN 1 84219 231 0. RICS.

Dawes, G.; Pianca, Andrew–Charity Accounts: A Practical Guide to the Charities SORP. Paperback: £60.00. ISBN 1 84661 001 X. Jordans.

Day, Frederick J.–Sports and Courts: An Introduction to Principles of Law and Legal Theory Using Cases from Professional Sports. Paperback: £10.41. ISBN 0 595 34315 5. iUniverse.com.

Deakin, Simon; Morris, Gillian S.–Labour Law. Paperback: £31.95. ISBN 1 84113 560 7. Hart Publishing.

Deakin, Simon; Wilkinson, Frank–Law of the Labour Market: Industrialisation, Employment, and Legal Evolution. Oxford Monographs on Labour Law. Hardback: £60.00. ISBN 0 19 815281 7. Oxford University Press.

Debroy, Bibek; Kaushik, P.D.–Reforming the Labour Market. Hardback: £34.99. ISBN 81 7188 441 5. Academic Foundation.

Delacroix, Sylvie–Legal Norms and Normativity: A Genealogical Enquiry. Hardback: £32.00. ISBN 1 84113 455 4. Hart Publishing.

Deleo–Guide to Understanding Constitution Law. Paperback: £23.99. ISBN 1 4018 5239 4. Delmar.

Delmas-Marty, Mireille; Spencer, J. R.–European Criminal Procedures. Cambridge Studies in International & Comparative Law, No. 25. Paperback: £40.00. ISBN 0 521 67848 X. Cambridge University Press.

Denicolo, Marie-Anne–Acquisitions and Group Structures-New Ed. Paperback: £24.95. ISBN 0 905835 81 6. The College of Law.

Denicolo, Marie-Anne–Acquisitions and Group Structures. Rev Ed. Paperback: £25.95. ISBN 1 905391 00 5. The College of Law.

Dennis, Ian–Law of Evidence. Paperback: £29.95. ISBN 0 421 88850 4. Sweet & Maxwell.

Deplege, Joanna–Organization of Global Negotiations: Constructing the Climate Change Regime. Hardback: £55.00. ISBN 1 84407 046 8. Earthscan.

Derbyshire, Wyn; Hardy, Stephen; Maffey, Stephen–Tupe-Law and Practice: An Overview. Paperback: £75.00. ISBN 1 904905 18 8. Spiramus Press.

Design and Build Contract Guide. Book (details unknown): £15.95. ISBN 0 418 82580 7. Sweet & Maxwell.

Design and Build Contract. Hardback: £26.95. ISBN 0 418 82570 X. Sweet & Maxwell.

Design and Build Sub-Contract Conditions. Book (details unknown): £26.95. ISBN 0 418 82600 5. Sweet & Maxwell.

Desmond, Helen; Jones, Emma; Antill, David–Employment Law. Textbook S. Paperback: £24.95. ISBN 0 421 82890 0. Sweet & Maxwell.

Dettore, Mike; Kalyvas, James R.; Sullivan, Kirk N.–Negotiating Telecommunications Agreements Line by Line. Line by Line S. Paperback: £99.95. ISBN 1 59622 112 7. Aspatore Books.

Dew, Richard–Wills, Power of Attorney and Probate Guide. Paperback: £11.99. ISBN 1 905261 07 1. Lawpack Publishing Ltd.

Dickie, John–Producers and Consumers in EU E-Commerce Law. Paperback: £25.00. ISBN 1 84113 454 6. Hart Publishing.

Diduck, Alison; Kaganas, Felicity–Family Law, Gender and the State. Paperback: £27.00. ISBN 1 84113 419 8. Hart Publishing.

DiGabriele, James–Forensic Accounting in Matrimonial Divorce. Hardback: £31.00. ISBN 1 930217 12 9. R T Edwards.

Dimitrov, Radoslav S.–Science and International Environmental Policy: Regimes and Nonregimes in Global Governance. Hardback: £47.00. ISBN 0

7425 3904 0. Paperback: £19.99. ISBN 0 7425 3905 9. Rowman & Littlefield Publishers.

Dimond, Bridgit C.—Legal Aspects of Health and Safety: British Journal of Nursing Monograph. Paperback: £22.50. ISBN 1 85642 282 8. Quay Books.

Dine, Janet—Company Law. Palgrave Law Masters S. Paperback: £14.99. ISBN 1 4039 2099 0. Palgrave Macmillan.

Dinstein, Yoram—War, Aggression and Self-defence. Paperback: £30.00. ISBN 0 521 61631 X. Cambridge University Press.

Dobson, Paul—Criminal Law. Paperback: £6.50. ISBN 0 421 89110 6. Sweet & Maxwell.

Dobson, Paul—Sale of Goods and Consumer Credit. Paperback: £28.00. ISBN 0 421 90130 6. Sweet & Maxwell.

Dodds, Malcolm—Family Law. Paperback: £15.95. ISBN 1 85836 600 3. Old Bailey Press.

Doherty, Michael—English and European Legal Systems. Paperback: £15.95. ISBN 1 85836 597 X. Old Bailey Press.

Doherty, Michael—Jurisprudence: The Philosophy of Law. Paperback: £15.95. ISBN 1 85836 601 1. Old Bailey Press.

Doig, Alan; Croall, Hazel—Fraud. Crime & Society S. Hardback: £40.00. ISBN 1 84392 173 1. Paperback: £17.99. ISBN 1 84392 172 3. Willan Publishing.

Dolton, Alan; Wareham, Robert—Tolley's Value Added Tax. Paperback: £121.00. ISBN 0 7545 2878 2. Paperback: £84.95. ISBN 0 7545 2879 0. Tolley Publishing.

Donovan, James M.; Anderson III, H. Edwin—Anthropology and Law. Anthropology &....S. Paperback: £13.50. ISBN 1 57181 424 8. Berghahn Books.

Doswald-Beck, Louise; Henckaerts, Jean-Marie—Customary International Humanitarian Law: V. 2. Hardback: £280.00. ISBN 0 521 83937 8. Cambridge University Press.

Douglas, Jane—Property Transactions: Stamp Duty Land Tax. Hardback: £79.00. ISBN 0 421 90310 4. Sweet & Maxwell.

Douzinas, Costas; Gearey, Adam—Critical Jurisprudence: A Textbook. Paperback: £22.00. ISBN 1 84113 452 X. Hart Publishing.

Dow, David; Lill, Jeff—Personal Injury and Clinical Negligence Litigation. Paperback: £24.95. ISBN 0 905835 83 2. Paperback: £25.95. ISBN 1 905391 08 0. The College of Law.

Downes, M.—Civil Partnerships. Paperback: £39.00. ISBN 0 85308 933 7. Jordans.

Doyle, Brian—Disability Discrimination. Paperback: £45.00. ISBN 0 85308 957 4. Jordans.

Doyle, Francis R.—Searching the Law. Paperback: £100.99. ISBN 1 57105 349 2. Transnational Publishers, Inc.

Doyle, L.; Keay, A.—Insolvency Legislation Handbook. Hardback: £75.00. ISBN 0 85308 961 2. Jordans.

Dresner, Steve; Kim, E. Kurt—Pipes: A Guide to Private Investment in Public Equity. Hardback: £45.00. ISBN 1 57660 194 3. Bloomberg Press.

Drexl, Josef; Kur, Annette—Intellectual Property and Private International Law: Heading for the Future. Paperback: £45.00. ISBN 1 84113 539 9. Hart Publishing.

Drobnig, Ulrich—Principles of European Law: V. 3. Personal Security Contracts. European Civil Code S. Hardback: £85.00. ISBN 0 19 929599 9. Oxford University Press.

Dromgoole, Sarah—International Trade Law. Paperback: £26.99. ISBN 0 273 61112 7. FT Prentice Hall.

Drummond, Susan G.—Mapping Marriage Law in Spanish Gitano Communities. Law and Society S. Hardback: £62.50. ISBN 0 7748 0925 6. University of British Columbia Press.

DS Smith Plc and Linpac Containers Ltd, A Report on the Completed Acquisition of Linpac Containers Ltd by DS Smith Plc. Paperback: £25.00. ISBN 0 11 702722 7. The Stationery Office Books.

Duckworth, Peter–Family Finance Toolkit. CD-ROM (software): £217.38. ISBN 0 85308 956 6. Family Law.

Duff, Andrew–Constitution for Europe. Hardback: £14.95. ISBN 1 903403 76 6. I.B. Paperback: £45.00. ISBN 1 903403 77 4. I.B. Tauris

Duff, Andrew–Struggle for Europe's Constitution. Paperback: £14.99. ISBN 1 903403 82 0. Federal Trust for Education & Research.

Duff, Anthony; Green, Stuart–Defining Crimes: The Special Part of the Criminal Law. Oxford Monographs on Criminal Law & Justice. Hardback: £50.00. ISBN 0 19 926922 X. Hardback: £50.00. ISBN 0 19 926922 X. Oxford University Press.

Duffield, Nancy; Sabine, Christa; Kempton, Jacqueline–Family Law and Practice. Paperback: £24.95. ISBN 0 905835 82 4. Paperback: £25.95. ISBN 1 905391 06 4. The College of Law.

Duffy, Helen–War on Terror and the Framework of International Law. Hardback: £55.00. ISBN 0 521 83850 9. Paperback: £27.00. ISBN 0 521 54735 0. Cambridge University Press.

Dukes, M.N.G.–Law and Ethics of the Pharmaceutical Industry. Hardback: £55.00. ISBN 0 444 51868 1. Elsevier.

Dutta, Ritwick; Yadav, Bhupender–Supreme Court on Forest Conservation. Paperback: £19.99. ISBN 81 7534 461 X. Universal Law Publishing Co Ltd.

Duxbury, Robert–Nutshells-Contract Law. Paperback: £7.00. ISBN 0 421 92410 1. Sweet & Maxwell.

Eady; Smith, A.T.H.–Arlidge, Eady and Smith on Contempt. Hardback: £302.40. ISBN 0 421 88340 5. Sweet & Maxwell.

Easton, Susan; Piper, Christine–Sentencing and Punishment: The Quest for Punishment. Paperback: £22.99. ISBN 0 19 927087 2. Oxford University Press.

Ebrahimi, Seyed–Mandatory Rules and Other Party Autonomy Limitations in International Contractual Obligations. Paperback: £27.99. ISBN 1 84401 297 2. Athena Press.

Edis, Anne–Mental Capacity Law and Practice. Paperback: £45.00. ISBN 1 903927 64 1. Legalease.

Edwards, Richard; Stockwell, Nigel–Trusts and Equity. Foundation Studies in Law S. Paperback: £29.99. ISBN 1 4058 1227 3. Longman.

Eeckhout, Piet; Tridimas, Takis–Yearbook of European Law: V. 23. Hardback: £130.00. ISBN 0 19 927469 X. Oxford University Press.

Eeckhout, Piet–Does Europe's Constitution Stop At the Water's Edge?: Law and Policy in the EU's External Relations. Walter Van Gerven Lectures S., No. 5. Paperback: £10.00. ISBN 90 76871 55 8. Europa Law Publishing, Netherlands.

Eeckhout, Piet–External Relations of the European Union: Legal and Constitutional Foundations. Oxford European Community Law Library. Paperback: £30.00. ISBN 0 19 928721 X. Oxford University Press.

Eicke, Tim; Grief, Nicholas–European Human Rights Reports: Vol 36. Hardback: £255.00. ISBN 0 421 88620 X. Sweet & Maxwell.

Eicke, Tim; Grief, Nicholas–European Human Rights Reports: Vol 37. Hardback: £255.00. ISBN 0 421 88640 4. Sweet & Maxwell.

Einhorn, Michael A.–Media, Technology and Copyright: Integrating Law and Economics. Paperback: £19.95. ISBN 1 84542 295 3. Edward Elgar.

Ekern, Yvonne; Hames, Joanne Banker–Introduction to Law. Paperback: £57.99. ISBN 0 13 118381 8. Prentice Hall.

Ekern, Yvonne; Hames, Joanne Banker–Legal Research, Analysis, and Writing: An Integrated Approach. Paperback: £53.99. ISBN 0 13 118888 7. Prentice Hall.

Elatar, Samir—Divorce: Its History Legislation and Modern Reality. Paperback: £6.95. ISBN 1 870582 42 X. Dar Al Taqwa.

Elgar Companion to Law and Economics. Hardback: £180.00. ISBN 1 84542 032 2. Edward Elgar.

Elkington—Skills for Lawyers. Paperback: £25.95. ISBN 0 905835 85 9. The College of Law.

Ellig, Jerry—Dynamic Competition and Public Policy: Technology, Innovation, and Antitrust Issues. Paperback: £23.99. ISBN 0 521 02181 2. Cambridge University Press.

Ellinger, E.P.; Lomnicka, Eva; Hooley, Richard—Ellinger's Modern Banking Law. Paperback: £36.99. ISBN 0 19 928119 X. Oxford University Press.

Elliot, Mark; Beatson, Jack; Matthews, Martin—Beatson, Matthews and Elliot's Administrative Law: Text and Materials. Paperback: £29.95. ISBN 0 19 926998 X. Oxford University Press.

Elliott, Catherine—Contract Law: AND Contract Law Generic Pin Card. Paperback: £22.99. ISBN 1 4058 1807 7. Longman.

Elliott, Catherine—English Legal System. Paperback: £23.99. ISBN 1 4058 1165 X. Longman.

Ellis, Evelyn—EU Anti-Discrimination Law. Oxford European Community Law Library. Hardback: £75.00. ISBN 0 19 926683 2. Oxford University Press.

Ellison, Robin; Jones, Grant—Dealing with Pensions: The Practical Impact of the Pensions Act 2004 on Mergers, Acquisitions and Insolvencies. Paperback: £95.00. ISBN 1 904905 06 4. Spiramus Press.

Ellison, Robin—Pension Trustee's Handbook. Hardback: £20.00. ISBN 1 85418 360 5. Thorogood.

Elliston, Sarah—Best Interests of the Child in Healthcare. Biomedical Law & Ethics Library S. Hardback: £49.00. ISBN 1 84472 043 8. UCL Press.

Elmhirst, Paul—Wills and Probate. Which? Consumer Guides. Paperback: £11.99. ISBN 1 84490 018 5. Which? Books.

Elmslie, Mark; Portman, Simon—Intellectual Property: The Lifeblood of Your Company. Hardback: £59.95. ISBN 1 84334 181 6. Paperback: £49.95. ISBN 1 84334 135 2. Chandos Publishing Oxford Ltd.

Elvin, David; Robinson, Jonathan—Environmental Assessment of Projects, Plans and Programmes: Law and Practice. Hardback: £80.00. ISBN 0 421 89330 3. Sweet & Maxwell.

Emberland, Marius—Human Rights of Companies: Exploring the Structure of ECHR Protection. Hardback: £50.00. ISBN 0 19 928983 2. Oxford University Press.

Emmerson, Ben; Ashworth, Andrew; Knowles, Julian—Human Rights and Criminal Justice. Hardback: £99.00. ISBN 0 421 87610 7. Sweet & Maxwell.

Employment Law Q and A's. Paperback: £19.95. ISBN 1 85524 693 7. Croner CCH Group Ltd.

Employment Lawcards. Lawcards S. Spiral/comb bound: £6.95. ISBN 1 84568 021 9. Cavendish Publishing Ltd.

Enalls, Simon—Social Security Benefits: A Practical Guide. Paperback: £49.95. ISBN 1 84592 197 6. Tottel Publishing.

Encyclopaedia of Forms and Precedents 22: Part 2 OB. Hardback: £201.00. ISBN 1 4057 0124 2. Butterworths Law.

Encyclopaedia of Forms and Precedents Consolidated Index. Paperback: £245.00. ISBN 1 4057 0826 3. Butterworths Law.

Encyclopaedia of Forms and Precedents Form Finder. Paperback: £245.00. ISBN 1 4057 0824 7. Butterworths Law.

Encyclopaedia of Forms and Precedents Volume 16 (2): V. 16. Hardback: £245.00. ISBN 1 4057 0128 5. Butterworths Law.

Encyclopaedia of Forms and Precedents: V 8. Pt 1. Hardback: £201.00. ISBN 0 406 97613 9. Butterworths Law.

Encyclopaedia of Forms and Precedents: Vol.35. Hardback: £201.00. ISBN 0 406 97478 0. Butterworths Law.

Engelman, Mark–Engelman's Developments in Intellectual Property Law. Paperback: £79.00. ISBN 1 84592 038 4. Tottel Publishing.

English Legal System Lawcard. Lawcards S. Looseleaf/ring bound: £6.95. ISBN 1 84568 040 5. Cavendish Publishing Ltd.

English, Jack; Card, Richard–Police Law. Paperback: £24.95. ISBN 0 19 928405 9. Oxford University Press.

Epstein, Adam–Entertainment Law. Hardback: £40.99. ISBN 0 13 114743 9. Prentice Hall.

Epstein, Lee–Courts and Judges. International Library of Essays in Law & Society S. Hardback: £115.00. ISBN 0 7546 2475 7. Ashgate.

Equal Opportunities Review Guide to Compensation in Discrimination Cases. Hardback: £95.00. ISBN 1 4057 1053 5. Butterworths Law.

Eric, Zyla–Punitive and Consequential Damages, Including Lost Profits, in a Construction Contract Dispute. Paperback: £9.12. ISBN 1 4116 4750 5. Lulu Press Incorporated.

Erman, Eva–Human Rights and Democracy. Hardback: £50.00. ISBN 0 7546 4486 3. Ashgate.

Esau, Alvin J.–Courts and the Colonies: The Litigation of Hutterite Church Disputes. Law and Society S. Paperback: £21.95. ISBN 0 7748 1117 X. University of British Columbia Press.

Essex, Nathan L.–Teacher's Pocket Guide to School Law. Paperback: £9.99. ISBN 0 205 45215 9. Allyn & Bacon.

Estates and Trusts: Leading Lawyers on the Best Strategies for the Planning. Inside the Minds S. Paperback: £37.95. ISBN 1 59622 081 3. Aspatore Books, US.

Estrin, Chere B.–Paralegal Career Guide. Paperback: £24.99. ISBN 0 13 118533 0. Prentice Hall.

Ethnographics of Law and Social Control. Sociology of Crime, Law & Deviance, V. 6. Hardback: £59.99. ISBN 0 7623 1128 2. JAI Press.

Etty, Thijs F.M.; Somsen, Han–Yearbook of European Environmental Law: V. 5. Hardback: £125.00. ISBN 0 19 927878 4. Hardback: £125.00. ISBN 0 19 927878 4. Oxford University Press.

EU Institutions' Register. Hardback: £130.00. ISBN 1 85743 330 0. Europa Publications.

European Competition Law Annual: What Is an Abuse of a Dominant Position? European Competition Law Annual. Hardback: £100.00. ISBN 1 84113 535 6. Hart Publishing.

European Union Lawcards. Lawcards S. Looseleaf/ring bound: £6.95. ISBN 1 84568 020 0. Cavendish Publishing Ltd.

Evans, Julie–Tottel's Purchase and Sale of a Private Company's Shares. Paperback: £72.95. ISBN 1 84592 177 1. Tottel Publishing.

Evans, Malcolm D.–International Law Documents. Blackstone's Statute Books. Paperback: £16.99. ISBN 0 19 928312 5. Oxford University Press.

Exall, Gordon–Periodical Payments-The New Law: A Special Bulletin. Paperback: £35.00. ISBN 0 85308 982 5. Jordans.

Expert Witness Directory of Ireland. Paperback: £55.00. ISBN 0 421 92120 X. Sweet & Maxwell.

Expert Witnesses Directory 2006 S/O Svce. Hardback: £150.00. ISBN 0 421 90810 6. Sweet & Maxwell.

Express Wills for Scotland CD-Rom. CD-ROM: £150.00. ISBN 0 414 01635 1. W. Green & Son.

Fagin, James A.–Criminal Justice. Hardback: £51.99. ISBN 0 205 45336 8. Allyn & Bacon.

Fairgrieve, Duncan–Product Liability in Comparative Perspective. Hardback: £50.00. ISBN 0 521 84723 0. Cambridge University Press.

Fairhurst, John–Law of the European Union. Foundation Studies in Law. Paperback: £27.99. ISBN 1 4058 1233 8. Longman.

Falkner, Gerda; Treib, Oliver; Hartlapp, Miriam; Leiber, Simone–Complying with Europe: EU Harmonisation and Soft Law in the Member States. Themes in European Governance S. Hardback: £45.00. ISBN 0 521 84994 2. Paperback: £19.99. ISBN 0 521 61513 5. Cambridge University Press.

Fallen: Confessions of a Disbarred Lawyer. Paperback: £14.98. ISBN 1 4116 0055 X. Lulu Press Incorporated.

Family Law-Issue 128. Paperback: £189.00. ISBN 1 4057 0278 8. Butterworths Law.

Family Lawcards. Lawcards S. Looseleaf/ring bound: £6.95. ISBN 1 84568 017 0. Cavendish Publishing Ltd.

Farmer, Lindsay–Criminal Law, Tradition and Legal Order: Crime and the Genius of Scots Law, 1747 to the Present. Paperback: £18.99. ISBN 0 521 02383 1. Cambridge University Press.

Faure, Michael; Skogh, Goran–Economic Analysis of Environmental Policy and Law: An Introduction. Paperback: £25.00. ISBN 1 84542 292 9. Edward Elgar.

Feeney, Michael–Taxation of Companies. Paperback: £86.66. ISBN 1 84592 130 5. Tottel Publishing.

Felstiner, Bill–Reorganization and Resistance: Legal Professions Confront a Changing World. Paperback: £35.00. ISBN 1 84113 246 2. Hart Publishing.

Ferdinandusse, W.N.–Direct Application of International Criminal Law in National Courts. Hardback: £55.00. ISBN 90 6704 207 2. Asser Press.

Ferguson, Pamela; Sheldon, David–Scots Criminal Law. Paperback: £36.00. ISBN 1 84592 152 6. Tottel Publishing.

Fergusson, Anne; D'Inverno, Isobel–Macroberts Commercial Property. Hardback: £65.00. ISBN 0 414 01618 1. W. Green & Son.

Ferraro, Eugene F.–Investigations in the Workplace. Hardback: £44.99. ISBN 0 8493 1648 0. Auerbach Publishers Inc.

Ferrera, Maurizio–Boundaries of Welfare: European Integration and the New Spatial Politics of Social Solidarity. Hardback: £50.00. ISBN 0 19 928466 0. Hardback: £50.00. ISBN 0 19 928466 0. Oxford University Press.

Ferrera, Maurizio–Boundaries of Welfare: European Integration and the New Spatial Politics of Social Solidarity. Paperback: £19.99. ISBN 0 19 928467 9. Paperback: £19.99. ISBN 0 19 928467 9. Oxford University Press.

Ferrier, Ian; Hutton, Matthew–Tolley's UK Taxation of Trusts. Paperback: £82.95. ISBN 0 7545 2891 X. Tolley Publishing.

Fersch, Ellsworth L–Thinking About the Insanity Defense: Answers to Frequently Asked Questions With Case Examples. Paperback: £11.20. ISBN 0 595 34412 7. iUniverse.com.

Fielding, Nigel–Police and Social Conflict. Contemporary Issues in Public Policy. Paperback: £22.00. ISBN 1 904385 23 0. The Glasshouse Press.

Financial Services Regulation in Europe. Hardback: £165.00. ISBN 1 904501 25 7. Richmond Law & Tax.

Financial Services: Investigations and Enforcement. Paperback: £120.00. ISBN 1 84592 205 0. Tottel Publishing.

Finch, Valerie; Ashton, Christina–Human Rights and Scots Law. Paperback: £35.00. ISBN 0 414 01624 6. W. Green & Son.

Findlay, Lorna; Wright, Stewart; George, Carolyn; Poynter, Richard–CPAG's Housing Benefit and Council Tax Benefit Legislation. Paperback: £71.00. ISBN 1 901698 82 3. CPAG.

Fine, Frank L.–EC Competition Law on Technology Licensing. Hardback: £125.00. ISBN 0 421 90320 1. Sweet & Maxwell.

Finkelstein, Claire–Hobbes on Law. Philosophers & Law. Hardback: £110.00. ISBN 0 7546 2178 2. Ashgate.

Finn, Sean–VAT and Property Guide. Paperback: £39.95. ISBN 1 903927 61 7. Legalease.

Fins, Alice–Opportunities in Paralegal Careers. Opportunities In... S. Paperback: £8.99. ISBN 0 07 143844 0. Higher Education.

Fiona Beveridge–Globalization and International Investment. International Library of Essays on Globalization & Law. Hardback: £125.00. ISBN 0 7546 2415 3. Ashgate.

Fitch–Introduction Law Paralegal. Hardback: £32.99. ISBN 0 13 863861 6. Pearson US Imports & PHIPEs.

Fitzgerald, Brian–Cyberlaw. International Library Essays in Law & Legal Theory (Second Series). Hardback: £250.00. ISBN 0 7546 2434 X. Ashgate.

Fitzpatrick, Brian–Police Officer's Guide to Going to Court. Paperback: £27.95. ISBN 0 19 928414 8. Oxford University Press.

FLBA–At a Glance: Essential Court Tables for Ancillary Relief. Paperback: £35.00. ISBN 1 85959 123 X. Class Publishing.

Flenley, William; Leech, Tom–Solicitors' Negligence. Paperback: £68.00. ISBN 1 84592 060 0. Tottel Publishing.

Fletcher, Ian; Roxburgh, Roy–Law and Practice of Receivership. Paperback: £115.00. ISBN 1 84592 199 2. Tottel Publishing.

Flint, Andrew; Walton, Kevin–Tolley's Capital Gains Tax: Budget Edition and Main Annual. Paperback: £94.95. ISBN 0 7545 2858 8. Tolley Publishing.

Flint, Michael–User's Guide to Copyright. Paperback: £72.00. ISBN 1 84592 068 6. Tottel Publishing.

Ford, John; Hughs, Mary; Ruebain, David–Education Law and Practice. Paperback: £45.00. ISBN 0 85308 951 5. Jordans.

Forde, Michael–Commercial Law Third Edition. Hardback: £79.33. ISBN 1 84592 203 4. Tottel Publishing.

Forlin, Gerard; Appleby, Michael–Corporate Liability: Work Related Deaths and Criminal Prosecutions. Paperback: £99.00. ISBN 1 84592 217 4. Tottel Publishing.

Forsyth, Christopher–Private International Law. Butterworths Common Law S. Hardback: £200.00. ISBN 0 406 96032 1. Butterworths Law.

Forsythe, David P.–Humanitarians: The International Committee of the Red Cross. Hardback: £45.00. ISBN 0 521 84828 8. Paperback: £17.99. ISBN 0 521 61281 0. Cambridge University Press.

Fortson, Rudi–Fortson Misuse of Drugs and Confiscation. Hardback: £95.00. ISBN 0 421 89230 7. Sweet & Maxwell.

Fosbrook, Deborah; Laing, Adrian C.–A-Z of Contract Clauses. Hardback: £195.00. ISBN 0 421 91250 2. Sweet & Maxwell.

Fosbrook, Deborah; Laing, Adrian C.–Media Contracts Handbook. Hardback: £185.00. ISBN 0 421 92020 3. Sweet & Maxwell.

Foskett, David–Law and Practice of Compromise: Litigation Library. Hardback: £180.00. ISBN 0 421 90300 7. Sweet & Maxwell.

Foster, Nigel–EC Legislation. Blackstone's Statute Book S. Paperback: £14.99. ISBN 0 19 928310 9. Oxford University Press.

Foster, Steve–Human Rights and Civil Liberties. Blackstone's Law Q & A S. Paperback: £13.99. ISBN 0 19 928656 6. Oxford University Press.

Fowler, John; Waterman, Chris–Digest of the Education Act 2005. Paperback: £15.00. ISBN 1 905314 01 9. National Foundation for Educational Research.

Framework Agreement Guide. Book (details unknown): £15.95. ISBN 0 418 82640 4. Sweet & Maxwell.

Framework Agreement Non-Binding. Book (details unknown): £18.95. ISBN 0 418 82650 1. Sweet & Maxwell.

Framework Agreement. Book (details unknown): £18.95. ISBN 0 418 82630 7. Sweet & Maxwell.

Francis, Andrew–Restrictive Covenants and Freehold Land. Hardback: £85.00. ISBN 0 85308 936 1. Jordans.

Fraser, Gary; Giles, Trefor; Crow, David; Form, Amanda–Mastering Policing Skills. Policing Skills S. Paperback: £19.00. ISBN 1 84641 012 6. Law Matters Publishing.

Fraud At The Elections: The Full Final and Definitive Judgment of Election Commissioner Richard Mawrey QC Handed Down on Monday 4th April 2005 in the Matters of Local Government Elections. Paperback: £5.00. ISBN 0 85124 708 3. Spokesman Books.

Freedland, Mark–Personal Employment Contract. Oxford Monographs on Labour Law. Paperback: £19.99. ISBN 0 19 929863 7. Oxford University Press.

Freeman, Michael–Child Welfare and the Law. Paperback: £26.95. ISBN 0 421 33990 X. Sweet & Maxwell.

French Civil Code. University of Texas At Austin Studies in Foreign & Transnational Law S. Hardback: £65.00. ISBN 1 84472 132 9. Paperback: £25.00. ISBN 1 84472 131 0. UCL Press.

French, Derek; Mayson, Stephen; Ryan, Christopher–Mayson, French and Ryan on Company Law. Paperback: £31.99. ISBN 0 19 928531 4. Paperback: £31.99. ISBN 0 19 928531 4. Oxford University Press.

French, Derek–Statutes on Company Law. Blackstone's Statute Books. Paperback: £16.99. ISBN 0 19 928311 7. Paperback: £16.99. ISBN 0 19 928311 7. Oxford University Press.

Friedman, Jack P.; Harris, Jack; Diskin, Barry–Real Estate Handbook. Hardback: £25.00. ISBN 0 7641 5777 9. Barron's Educational Series.

Fulbrook, Julian–Outdoor Pursuits and the Law. Hardback: £45.00. ISBN 0 7546 4235 6. Avebury Technical.

Fullerton, Karen; Macgregor, Megan–Legal Research Skills. Paperback: £22.00. ISBN 0 414 01589 4. W.Green & Son.

Furchtgott-Roth, Diana–Tough Act to Follow?: The Real Reason Why the Telecommunications Act of 1996 Was a Failure. Hardback: £19.95. ISBN 0 8447 4235 X. The AEI Press.

Furmston, Michael–Third Party Rights. Contract Law Library. Hardback: £125.00. ISBN 0 421 71650 9. Sweet & Maxwell.

Galbraith, H. Reynold–Scottish Trusts: A Drafting Guide. Audio CD: £69.00. ISBN 0 414 01599 1. W.Green & Son.

Galeotti, Anna Elisabetta–Toleration As Recognition. Paperback: £19.99. ISBN 0 521 61993 9. Cambridge University Press.

Gallagher, Peter; Low, Patrick; Stoler, Andrew L.–Managing the Challenges of WTO Participation: 45 Case Studies. Hardback: £60.00. ISBN 0 521 86014 8. Paperback: £29.99. ISBN 0 521 67754 8. Cambridge University Press.

Gallant, M. Michelle–Money Laundering and the Proceeds of Crime: Economic Crime and Civil Remedies. Hardback: £45.00. ISBN 1 84376 951 4. Edward Elgar.

Gamharter, Katharina–Access to Affordable Medicines: Developing Responses Under the Trips Agreement and EC Law. Europainstitut Wirtschaftsuniversitat Wien Publication S., V.25. Paperback: £40.00. ISBN 3 211 22670 2. Springer-Verlag Vienna.

Gane, Christopher–Sex Offences. Paperback: £40.00. ISBN 1 84592 058 9. Tottel Publishing.

Garbutt, John–Waste Management Law: A Practical Handbook. Hardback: £60.00. ISBN 0 421 89530 6. Sweet & Maxwell.

Garnett, Kevin; Davies, Gillian; Harbottle, Gwilym–Copinger and Skone James on Copyright. Hardback: £325.00. ISBN 0 421 87650 6. Sweet & Maxwell.

Garrard, John; Newell, James L.–Scandals in Past and Contemporary Politics. Hardback: £55.00. ISBN 0 7190 6551 8. Manchester University Press.

Garrison, John C.–New Income Tax Scandal. Paperback: £14.00. ISBN 1 4134 9544 3. Xlibris Corporation.

Garsia, Marlene–How to Write Your Will. Paperback: £8.99. ISBN 0 7494 4471 1. Kogan Page.

Gasoline Prices: Policies, Practices and Prospects. Hardback: £28.50. ISBN 1 59454 651 7. Nova Science Publishers, Inc.

Gaunt, Jonathan; Morgan, Paul–Gale on the Law of Easements. Paperback: £40.00. ISBN 0 421 89500 4. Sweet & Maxwell.

Gazzini, Tarcisio–Changing Rules on the Use of Force in International Law. Melland Schill Studies in International Law. Hardback: £60.00. ISBN 0 7190 7324 3. Manchester University Press.

Gearty, Conor A.–Principles of Human Rights Adjudication. Paperback: £17.99. ISBN 0 19 928722 8. Oxford University Press.

Genovese, Michael A.; Spitzer, Robert J.–Presidency and the Constitution: Constitutional Cases. Hardback: £40.00. ISBN 1 4039 6673 7. Paperback: £13.99. ISBN 1 4039 6674 5. Palgrave Macmillan.

Geoghegan, Thomas–Law in Shambles. Paperback: £7.00. ISBN 0 9728196 9 X. Prickly Paradigm Press.

Georgakopoulos, Nicholas L.–Principles and Methods of Law and Economics: Enhancing Normative Analysis. Hardback: £48.00. ISBN 0 521 82681 0. Paperback: £21.99. ISBN 0 521 53411 9. Cambridge University Press.

Geradin, Damien; Munoz, Rodolphe; Petit, Nicolas–Regulation Through Agencies in the EU: A New Paradigm of European Governance. Hardback: £85.00. ISBN 1 84542 267 8. Edward Elgar.

Geraint Howells; Stephen Weatherill–Consumer Protection Law. Hardback: £75.00. ISBN 0 7546 2331 9. Avebury Technical.

Gerven, Walter Van–European Union: A Polity of States and Peoples. Paperback: £24.00. ISBN 1 84113 529 1. Hart Publishing.

Ghose, K.–Beyond the Courtroom: A Lawyer's Guide to Campaigning. Paperback: £20.00. ISBN 1 903307 35 X. The Legal Action Group.

Ghosh, Rishab Aiyer–Code: Collaborative Ownership and the Digital Economy. Leonardo Book S. Hardback: £24.95. ISBN 0 262 07260 2. The MIT Press.

Gibbon, Kate Fitz–Who Owns the Past?: Cultural Policy, Cultural Property, and the Law. Hardback: £25.95. ISBN 0 8135 3687 1. Rutgers University Press.

Gilbar, Roy–Status of the Family in Law and Bioethics: The Genetic Context. Hardback: £55.00. ISBN 0 7546 4545 2. Ashgate.

Gill, Jon–Business Law for the Entrepreneur. Paperback: £19.95. ISBN 1 84549 014 2. Arima publishing.

Gilmore, Noel–Clearing the Air: The Battle Over the Smoking Ban. Paperback: £9.95. ISBN 0 9545335 6 9. Liberties Press.

Ginsburg, Tom; Kagan, Robert A.; Schultz, David A.–Institutions & Public Law: Comparative Approaches. Paperback: £19.30. ISBN 0 8204 7477 0. Peter Lang Publishing Inc,US.

Giubboni, Stefano–Social Rights and Market Freedom in the European Constitution: A Labour Law Perspective. Cambridge Studies in European Law & Policy. Hardback: £55.00. ISBN 0 521 84126 7. Cambridge University Press.

Glaser, Maric–Tolley's VAT Business by Business Guide. Paperback: £69.95. ISBN 0 7545 2630 5. Tolley Publishing.

Glasius, Marlies–International Criminal Court. Routledge Advances in International Relations & Global Politics, V. 39. Hardback: £55.00. ISBN 0 415 33395 4. Routledge,an imprint of Taylor & Francis Books Ltd.

Glazebrook, Peter–Statutes on Criminal Law. Blackstone's Statute Books. Paperback: £12.99. ISBN 0 19 928316 8. Paperback: £12.99. ISBN 0 19 928316 8. Oxford University Press.

Glenn, H.Patrick–On Common Laws. Hardback: £50.00. ISBN 0 19 928754 6. Oxford University Press.

Glover, Jeremy; Fenwick, Elliott–Building Contract Disputes: Materials and Cases Handbook. Paperback: £89.00. ISBN 0 421 87790 1. Sweet & Maxwell.

Goble, Dale D.; Scott, J. Michael; Davis, Frank W.–Endangered Species Act At Thirty: V. 1: Renewing the Conservation Promise. Hardback: £51.50. ISBN 1 59726 008 8. Paperback: £25.95. ISBN 1 59726 009 6. Island Press.

Goldenflame, Jake–Overcoming Sexual Terrorism: How to Protect Your Children from Sexual Predators. Hardback: £16.00. ISBN 0 595 67075 X. iUniverse.com.

Golding, Jon–Tolley's Inheritance Tax. Paperback: £74.99. ISBN 0 7545 2865 0. Tolley Publishing.

Goldrein, Iain; Aird, Richard; Grantham, Andrew–Commercial Litigation: Pre-Emptive Remedies: International Edition. Hardback: £199.00. ISBN 0 421 93360 7. Sweet & Maxwell.

Goldstein, Avery N.–Patent Law for English Scientists. Hardback: £44.99. ISBN 0 8247 2383 X. Marcel Dekker Inc.

Goldsworthy, Jeffrey–Interpreting Constitutions: A Comparative Study. Hardback: £50.00. ISBN 0 19 927413 4. Oxford University Press.

Goldthorpe, Liz; Monro, Pat–Child Law Handbook: Guide to Good Practice. Paperback: £39.95. ISBN 1 85328 712 1. Law Society Publications.

Good, Anthony–Anthropology and Expertise in the British Asylum Courts. Glasshouse S. Paperback: £50.00. ISBN 1 904385 55 9. The Glasshouse Press.

Gooddie, Howard–Buying Bargains At Property Auctions. Paperback: £11.99. ISBN 1 904053 89 0. Law Pack Publishing.

Goode, Roy M.–Principles of Corporate Insolvency Law. Hardback: £145.00. ISBN 0 421 90450 X. Paperback: £40.00. ISBN 0 421 93020 9. Sweet & Maxwell.

Gordley, James–Foundations of Private Law: Property, Tort, Contract, Unjust Enrichment. Hardback: £50.00. ISBN 0 19 929167 5. Oxford University Press.

Gordon, Gerald H.; Christie, Michael G.A.–Criminal Law of Scotland: 1st Supplement. Hardback: £40.00. ISBN 0 414 01574 6. W.Green & Son.

Gordon, Gerald H.; Christie, Michael G.A.–Criminal Law of Scotland: Vol 1 & V.2. Hardback: £20.00. ISBN 0 414 01572 X. W.Green & Son.

Gordon, Richard–Judicial Review: Law and Procedure. Hardback: £69.00. ISBN 0 421 89720 1. Sweet & Maxwell.

Gormley, Laurence W.–EU Taxation Law. Hardback: £75.00. ISBN 1 904501 55 9. Richmond Law & Tax.

Gosselin, Denise Kindshi–Heavy Hands: An Introduction to the Crimes of Family Violence. Paperback: £32.99. ISBN 0 13 118885 2. Prentice Hall.

Goudie, James; Walker, Paul; Himsworth, C.M.G.; Supperstone, Michael; Drewry, Gavin; Plender, Richard–Judicial Review. Hardback: £170.00. ISBN 0 406 97451 9. ButterworthsTolley.

Grant, James–Writing Your Own Will. Paperback: £9.99. ISBN 1 900694 08 5. Easyway Guides.

Gray, Kevin J.; Gray, Susan Francis–Land Law. Core Texts S. Paperback: £16.99. ISBN 0 19 928445 8. Paperback: £16.99. ISBN 0 19 928445 8. Oxford University Press.

Gray, Nichola; Brazil, Dominic–Blackstone's Guide to the Civil Partnerships Act 2004. Paperback: £34.95. ISBN 0 19 928570 5. Oxford University Press.

Greaney, Nicola; Morris, Fennella; Taylor, Beverley–Mental Capacity: A Guide to the New Law. Paperback: £39.95. ISBN 1 85328 903 5. Law Society Publications.

Greatonex, P.; Falkowski, D.–Anti-Social Behaviour Law. Hardback: £49.00. ISBN 1 84661 002 8. Jordans.

Green, David; Weber, Kris; Bradshaw, Michael; Russell, Charles–Employment Law Update: Special Report, Spring 2005. Paperback: £99.00. ISBN 1 900648 47 4. Workplacelaw Network.

Green, Scott–Sarbanes-Oxley: A Corporate Director's Compliance Guide. Hardback: £41.95. ISBN 0 471 73608 2. John Wiley & Sons Inc.

Green, Stuart P.–Lying, Cheating, and Stealing: A Moral Theory of White Collar Crime. Oxford Monographs on Criminal Law & Justice. Hardback: £40.00. ISBN 0 19 926858 4. Oxford University Press.

Greenberg, Bernard; Kunich, John Charles–Entomology and the Law: Flies As Forensic Indicators. Paperback: £27.00. ISBN 0 521 01957 5. Cambridge University Press.

Greenberg, Daniel; Goodman, Michael J–Craies on Legislation: A Practitioner's Guide to the Nature, Process, Effect and Interpretation of Legislation, 1st Supplement. Paperback: £40.00. ISBN 0 421 92740 2. Sweet & Maxwell.

Greenberg, Daniel; Goodman, Michael J–Craies on Legislation: A Practitioner's Guide to the Nature, Process, Effect and Interpretation of Legislation, Edition 8 Plus Supplement. Hardback: £235.00. ISBN 0 421 93780 7. Sweet & Maxwell.

Greenberg, Daniel; Milbrook, Alexandra–Stroud's Judicial Dictionary of Words and Phrases: 4th Supplement. Paperback: £70.00. ISBN 0 421 88970 5. Sweet & Maxwell.

Greenberg, Karen J.–Al Qaeda Now: Understanding Today's Terrorists. Hardback: £40.00. ISBN 0 521 85911 5. Paperback: £13.99. ISBN 0 521 67627 4. Cambridge University Press.

Greenfield, Steven; Osborn, Guy–Readings in Law and Popular Culture. Routledge Studies in Law, Society and Popular Culture S., V. 3. Hardback: £85.00. ISBN 0 415 37647 5. Routledge, an imprint of Taylor & Francis Books Ltd.

Greens Conveyancing Statutes. Paperback: £25.00. ISBN 0 414 01619 X. W. Green & Son.

Greens Sheriff Court Rules. Paperback: £36.00. ISBN 0 414 01620 3. W. Green & Son.

Greens Solicitors Professional Handbook. Paperback: £29.00. ISBN 0 414 01615 7. W. Green & Son.

Greenspan, Edward L.–Bernard Cohn Memorial Lectures in Criminal Law. Hardback: £32.00. ISBN 1 55221 102 9. Irwin Law Inc.

Greve, Michael S.–Harm-less Lawsuits?: What's Wrong with Consumer Class Actions. Paperback: £10.95. ISBN 0 8447 4215 5. The AEI Press.

Grier, Nicholas–Company Law. Paperback: £33.00. ISBN 0 414 01602 5. W. Green & Son.

Griffin, Stephen M.–Company Law Fundamental Principles. Paperback: £29.99. ISBN 0 582 78461 1. Longman.

Griffiths, Margaret–Commercial Law. Paperback: £15.95. ISBN 1 85836 592 9. Old Bailey Press.

Griffiths, Michael–Corporate Law. Professional Development S. Paperback: £27.50. ISBN 1 86072 316 0. ICSA Publishing Ltd (Institute of Chartered Secretaries & Administrators).

Grime, R.–Shipping Law. Paperback: £28.00. ISBN 0 421 60670 3. Sweet & Maxwell.

Grosz, Stephen; Beatson, Justice; Singh, Rabinder; Palmer, Stephanie; Hickman, T.–Grosz, Beatson and Duffy on Human Rights. Hardback: £115.00. ISBN 0 421 90250 7. Sweet & Maxwell.

Groves, Peter–Intellectual Property Practitioner. CPD in a Box S. CD-ROM: £29.50. ISBN 1 904783 56 2. Semple Piggot Rochez (Legal Education Ltd).

Groves, Rick; Sankey, Sian–Implementing New Powers for Private Sector Housing Renewal. Housing Market Renewal S. Paperback: £13.95. ISBN 1 85935 427 0. York Publishing Services-Joseph Rowntree Foundat.

Gruner, Richard S.–Corporate Criminal Liability and Prevention. Looseleaf release (unbound): £135.00. ISBN 1 58852 125 7. ALM Publishing.

Grzasko, Christina; Gribbin, Michael; Abel, Damian–Police Station Guide. Paperback: £75.00. ISBN 0 9549906 0 9. iLaw Publishing.

Gubby, Helen–English Legal Terminology: Legal Concepts in Language. Paperback: £17.95. ISBN 90 5454 499 6. Boom Juridische Uitgevers.

Guest, A.G.–Chalmers and Guest on Bills of Exchange. Hardback: £219.00. ISBN 0 421 87710 3. Sweet & Maxwell.

Guggenheim, Martin–What's Wrong with Children's Rights? Hardback: £18.95. ISBN 0 674 01721 8. Harvard University Press.

Gulshan, S.S.–Mercantile Law. Hardback: £37.50. ISBN 81 7446 368 2. Excel Books.

Gupta, Udayan–Entrepreneurial Lawyer: How Testa, Hurwitz, Thibeault Shaped a High-tech Culture. Hardback: £19.99. ISBN 1 896209 95 5. Bayeux Arts Incorporated.

Guthrie, Tom; Fletcher, Ian; Roxburgh, Roy–Scottish Property Law. Paperback: £36.00. ISBN 1 84592 057 0. Tottel Publishing.

Guthrie, Tom–Antisocial Behaviour Legislation. Paperback: £35.00. ISBN 0 414 01627 0. W. Green & Son.

Hague Conference Guide: Pt. 3. Preventative Measures. Paperback: £35.00. ISBN 0 85308 986 8. Jordans.

Hahn, Robert W.–Intellectual Property Rights in Frontier Industries: Software and Biotechnology. Paperback: £14.50. ISBN 0 8447 7191 0. The AEI Press.

Hale, Chris; Hayward, Keith; Wahidin, Azrini; Wincup, Emma–Criminology. Paperback: £25.99. ISBN 0 19 927036 8. Oxford University Press.

Haley, Michael; Mcmurty, Lara; Davern, Raymond; Price, Jeffrey W.; Shipwright, A.J.–Equity and Trusts. Textbook S. Paperback: £24.95. ISBN 0 421 59920 0. Sweet & Maxwell.

Hall, Daniel–Administrative Law: Bureaucracy in a Democracy. Paperback: £49.99. ISBN 0 13 118432 6. Prentice Hall.

Halliwell, Margaret; De Than, Claire–Equity and Trusts. Paperback: £15.95. ISBN 1 85836 598 8. Old Bailey Press.

Halsbury's Statutes Consolidated Index. Paperback: £170.00. ISBN 0 406 97194 3. Butterworths Law.

Halsbury's Statutes: Citator. Paperback: £187.00. ISBN 1 4057 0059 9. Butterworths Law.

Halsbury's Statutes: Consolidated Index. Hardback: £187.00. ISBN 1 4057 0454 3. Butterworths Law.

Halsbury's Statutes: Cumulative Supplement 2005. Hardback: £282.00. ISBN 1 4057 0064 5. Butterworths Law.

Halsbury's Statutes: Table of Cases 2005. Hardback: £187.00. ISBN 1 4057 0060 2. Butterworths Law.

Halsbury's Statutes: V. 42. Looseleaf/ring bound: £226.00. ISBN 1 4057 0955 3. Butterworths Law.

Halsbury's Statutory Instruments: Consolidated Index and Alphabetical List of Statutory Instruments. Paperback: £108.00. ISBN 1 4057 0206 0. Butterworths Law.

Halsbury's Statutory Instruments: EC Legislation Implementator. Paperback: £78.00. ISBN 1 4057 0112 9. Butterworths Law.

Halsey, Mark–Beyond Green Criminology. Advances in Criminology. Hardback: £55.00. ISBN 0 7546 2491 9. Ashgate.

Halstead, Peter–Human Rights. Paperback: £5.99. ISBN 0 340 88696 X. Hodder & Stoughton Ltd.

Halstead, Peter–Jurisprudence. Key Facts S. Paperback: £5.99. ISBN 0 340 88695 1. Hodder Arnold H&S.

Hamer, Andrew C.–ICSA Company Precedents and Forms. CD-ROM: £74.95. ISBN 1 86072 184 2. Paperback: £74.95. ISBN 1 86072 184 2. ICSA Publishing Ltd (Institute of Chartered Secretaries & Administrators).

Hamilton, J A–Avizandum Statutes on Scots Commercial and Consumer Law. Paperback: £23.95. ISBN 1 904968 05 8. Avizandum Publishing Ltd.

Hannibal, Martin; Mountford, Lisa–LPC Handbook on Criminal Litigation. Paperback: £29.99. ISBN 0 19 927606 4. Oxford University Press.

Hardy, Stephen T; Upex, Robert–Employment Law for Business Students. Hardback: £70.00. ISBN 1 4129 0021 2. Paperback: £22.00. ISBN 1 4129 0022 0. Sage Publications Ltd.

Hare–Documentary Credits: Law and Practice. Hardback: £195.00. ISBN 1 84311 428 3. Informa Business Publishing.

Harper, Mark; Baldwin, Camilla; Woelke, Andrea–Model Letters for Family Lawyers. Paperback: £60.00. ISBN 0 85308 977 9. Family Law.

Harpwood, Vivenne–Modern Tort Law. Paperback: £24.95. ISBN 1 85941 976 3. Cavendish Publishing Ltd.

Harries, Jill–Cicero and the Jurists. Hardback: £45.00. ISBN 0 7156 3432 1. Gerald Duckworth & Co. Ltd.

Harris, D.J.; Mowbray, A.R.–Cases and Materials on the European Convention on Human Rights. Paperback: £29.95. ISBN 0 406 97727 5. Butterworths Law.

Harrison, Rosemary Jane–Corporate Insolvency-Swift Question and Answer Guide to Corporate Insolvency Procedure: Corporate Insolvency. Maxims Global 21st United Kingdom Law Series. Paperback: £15.00. ISBN 0 9548628 1 3. Maxims Global.

Harvey on Industrial Relations and Employment Law: Pt. 176. Looseleaf/ring bound: £225.00. ISBN 1 4057 0585 X. Butterworths Law.

Harvey on Industrial Relations and Employment Law. Paperback: £202.00. ISBN 0 406 97278 8. Butterworths Tolley.

Harvey on Industrial Relations. Paperback: £203.00. ISBN 1 4057 0583 3. Butterworths Law.

Hassan, Abdullah Alwi Haji–Contracts in Islamic Law. Hardback: £37.50. ISBN 1 85043 929 X. I.B. Tauris.

Hassan, Daud–Protecting the Marine Environment from Land-Based Sources of Pollution. Hardback: £50.00. ISBN 0 7546 4601 7. Ashgate.

Hatton, Tim–New Fiduciary Standard: The 27 Prudent Investment Practices for Financial Advisers, Trustees, and Plan Sponsors. Hardback: £38.19. ISBN 1 57660 183 8. Bloomberg Press.

Hawke, Neil; Jones, Brian; Parpworth, Neil; Thompson, Katherine–Pollution Control: The Powers and Duties of Local Authorities. Paperback: £49.50. ISBN 0 7219 1590 6. Shaw & Sons.

Hayden, Tim; Wilmott, Clarke–Licensing for Conveyancers: A Practical Guide. Paperback: £44.95. ISBN 1 85328 966 3. Law Society Publications.

Hayes, Angela; Burnett, Calum–Practitioner's Guide to FSA Investigations and Enforcement. Paperback: £75.00. ISBN 1 898830 93 2. City and Financial Publishing.

Haynes, Andrew–Financial Services Law Guide. Paperback: £115.00. ISBN 1 84592 139 9. Tottel Publishing.

Haynes, Richard–Media Rights and Intellectual Property. Hardback: £45.00. ISBN 0 7486 2062 1. Edinburgh University Press.

Hayton, David J.; Mitchell, Charles–Hayton and Marshall: Commentary and Cases on the Law of Trusts and Equitable Remedies. Paperback: £32.95. ISBN 0 421 90190 X. Sweet & Maxwell.

Hayward, Ruth–Conflicts of Laws. Paperback: £29.95. ISBN 1 85941 972 0. Cavendish Publishing Ltd.

Hazell, Robert; Rawlings, Richard–Devolution, Lawmaking and the Constitution. Hardback: £35.00. ISBN 1 84540 037 2. Imprint Academic.

Head, J. W.–Future of the Global Economic Organizations: An Evaluation of Criticisms Leveled At the IMF, the Multilateral Development Banks, and the WTO. Hardback: £92.99. ISBN 1 57105 299 2. Transnational Publishers, Inc.

Health & Safety Executive–Giving Your Own Firework Display: How to Run and Fire It Safely. Paperback: £7.95. ISBN 0 7176 6162 8. Health and Safety Executive (HSE).

Health and Safety Training Toolkit: Annual Book. Paperback/CD-ROM: £155.00. ISBN 0 421 91560 9. Sweet & Maxwell.

Heath, Christopher; Petit, Laurence–Patent Enforcement Worldwide. Paperback: £50.00. ISBN 1 84113 538 0. Hart Publishing.

Heath, Christopher; Sanders, Anselm Kamperman–New Frontiers of Intellectual Property Law: IP and Cultural Heritage-Geographical Indications-Enforcement-Overprotection. Paperback: £45.00. ISBN 1 84113 571 2. Hart Publishing.

Heath, C.Antons–Intellectual Property Harmonisation with ASEAN and APEC. Hardback: £105.00. ISBN 90 411 2292 3. Kluwer Law International.

Hedley, Steve–Law of Electronic Commerce and the Internet in the UK and Ireland. Paperback: £35.00. ISBN 1 85941 973 9. Cavendish Publishing Ltd.

Heels, S.; Pema, A.–Anti-Social Behaviour Orders: A Special Bulletin. Paperback: £35.00. ISBN 1 84661 000 1. Jordans.

Heinze, Eric–Logic of Constitutional Rights. Applied Legal Phiosophy. Hardback: £55.00. ISBN 0 7546 2538 9. Ashgate.

Helen Watchirs–AIDS Audit: HIV and Human Rights. Hardback: £50.00. ISBN 0 7546 2421 8. AveburyTechnical.

Hellawell, Trevor–Environmental Law Handbook. Paperback: £44.95. ISBN 1 85328 978 7. Law Society Publications.

Henckaerts, Jean-Marie; Doswald-Beck, Louise–Customary International Humanitarian Law. Hardback: £300.00. ISBN 0 521 53925 0. Cambridge University Press.

Hennessy, Charles–Civil Procedure and Practice. Paperback: £34.00. ISBN 0 414 01611 4. W.Green & Son.

Herring, Jonathan–Criminal Law. Palgrave Law Masters S. Paperback: £16.99. ISBN 1 4039 3417 7. Palgrave Macmillan.

Hershman, David; McFarlane, Andrew–Hershman and McFarlane Children Act Handbook. Paperback: £30.00. ISBN 0 85308 992 2. Jordans.

Hertz, Ketilbjorn–Danish Arbitration Act. Paperback: £28.00. ISBN 87 574 1427 0. DJOF Publishing.

Hervey, Tamara; Kenner, Jeff–Economic and Social Rights Under the EU Charter of Fundamental Rights. Paperback: £24.00. ISBN 1 84113 563 1. Hart Publishing.

Hess; Harr–Careers in Crim Justice: 5th Ed. Book (details unknown)/CD-ROM: £21.37. ISBN 0 534 62620 3. Wadsworth.

Hesselink, Martijn; Rutgers, Jacobien W.; Diaz, Odavia Bueno; Scotton, Manola; Veldman, Murial–Principles of European Law: V. 4. Commercial Agency, Franchise, and Distribution Contracts. European Civil Code S. Hardback: £75.00. ISBN 0 19 929598 0. Oxford University Press.

Heward, Edmund–Lives of the Judges: Jessel, Cairns, Sowen and Bramwell. Hardback: £22.00. ISBN 1 902681 32 0. Barry Rose Law Publications.

Hewitson, Russell; Moss, Tom–Licensing Law Handbook: A Practical Guide to Liquor and Entertainment Licensing. Paperback: £49.95. ISBN 1 85328 954 X. Law Society Publications.

Hewitson, Russell–Conveyancers' Yearbook. Paperback: £23.50. ISBN 0 7219 1567 1. Shaw & Sons.

Hewitt, Ian–Joint Ventures. Hardback: £160.00. ISBN 0 421 85050 7. Sweet & Maxwell.

Hewitt, Lester L.–Patent Infringement Litigation: Step by Step from Dispute Through Trial for Executives, Witnesses, and In-house Counsel. Paperback: £99.95. ISBN 1 59622 195 X. Aspatore Books, US.

Hickey, Julian–Understanding Private Client Taxation. Paperback: £49.95. ISBN 1 85328 926 4. Law Society Publications.

Hill, Judith; Smith, Julian–Charities Act 2005: A Practitioner's Guide. Hardback: £50.00. ISBN 1 903927 48 X. Legalease.

Hill, R.–Practical Guide to Civil Litigation. Paperback: £45.00. ISBN 0 85308 990 6. Jordans.

Himma, Kenneth Einar; Bix, Brian–Law and Morality. International Library of Essays in Law & Legal Theory: Second Series. Hardback: £130.00. ISBN 0 7546 2577 X. Ashgate.

Hints on Advocacy. Paperback: £9.99. ISBN 81 7534 041 X. Universal Law Publishing Co Ltd.

Hirsch, Andrew von; Ashworth, Andrew–Proportionate Sentencing: Exploring the Principles. Oxford Monographs on Criminal Law & Justice. Hardback: £50.00. ISBN 0 19 927260 3. Oxford University Press.

Hirst, Richard–Criminal Law. Paperback: £15.95. ISBN 1 85836 594 5. Old Bailey Press.

Hodgart, Alan; Mayson, Stephen W.–Legal Business Guide to Law Firm Management. Paperback: £125.00. ISBN 1 903927 62 5. Legalease.

Hodges, Christopher–European Regulation of Consumer Product Safety. Hardback: £60.00. ISBN 0 19 928255 2. Oxford University Press.

Hodgkinson, Tristram; James, Mark–Expert Evidence: Law and Practice, Standing Order Service. Hardback: £170.00. ISBN 0 421 88930 6. Sweet & Maxwell.

Hoffman, Barbara T.–Art and Cultural Heritage: Law, Policy and Practice. Hardback: £45.00. ISBN 0 521 85764 3. Cambridge University Press.

Hoffman, David; Curzon, L.B.–Human Rights in the UK: AND Dictionary of Law (6th Revised Edition): An Introduction to the Human Rights Act 1998. Paperback: £29.99. ISBN 1 4058 3687 3. Longman.

Hoffman, Richard–Tax Planning and Compliance for Tax-Exempt Organizations. Paperback: £36.50. ISBN 0 471 67990 9. John Wiley & Sons Inc.

Hoffmann, Gretchen McCord–Copyright in Cyberspace 2: Questions and Answers for Librarians. Hardback: £52.95. ISBN 1 55570 517 0. Neal-Schuman Publishers.

Hofstotter, Bernhard–Non-Compliance of National Courts: Remedies in European Community Law and Beyond. Hardback: £40.00. ISBN 90 6704 205 6. Asser Press.

Hogan, Greer; Smith, Rhona K.M.–Core Statutes on Public Law and Human Rights. Core Statutes S. Paperback: £10.00. ISBN 1 84641 005 3. Law Matters Publishing.

Hogan, Greer–Constitutional and Administrative Law. Paperback: £6.50. ISBN 0 421 89090 8. Sweet & Maxwell.

Hogarth, Andrew; Awadalla, Katherine–Butterworths Personal Injury Litigation Service. Paperback: £31.50. ISBN 0 406 97588 4. Butterworths Law.

Holland, James; Burnett, Stuart–LPC Employment Law. Legal Practice Course Guides. Paperback: £26.99. ISBN 0 19 928485 7. Oxford University Press.

Hollington, Robin–Shareholders' Rights. Paperback: £45.00. ISBN 0 421 91940 X. Sweet & Maxwell.

Holm, Soren; Gunning, Jennifer–Ethics Law and Society:Volume 1. Hardback: £60.00. ISBN 0 7546 4583 5. Ashgate.

Holtam, John–Criminal Litigation. Paperback: £25.95. ISBN 0 905835 91 3. The College of Law.

Homer, Arnold; Burrows, Rita; Lawrence, Nick–Tolley's Vatwise. Paperback: £55.00. ISBN 0 7545 2880 4. Tolley Publishing.

Hopkins, Bruce R.–Law of Tax-Exempt Organizations. Paperback: £50.50. ISBN 0 471 67988 7. John Wiley & Sons Inc.

Hopton, Doug–Money Laundering: A Concise Guide for All Business. Hardback: £49.50. ISBN 0 566 08639 5. Gower Publishing Limited.

Hoskings-James, Yvette–Business Agreements Made Easy. Hardback: £11.99. ISBN 1 904053 84 X. Lawpack Publishing Ltd.

Hossain, Sara; Welchman, Lynn–Honour: Crimes, Paradigms, and Violence Against Women. Hardback: £60.00. ISBN 1 84277 626 6. Paperback: £19.95. ISBN 1 84277 627 4. Zed Books.

Hough, Alison–Employment Law. Paperback: £15.95. ISBN 1 85836 596 1. Old Bailey Press.

Houlgate, Laurence D.–Children's Rights, State Intervention, Custody and Divorce: Contradictions in Ethics and Family Law. Hardback: £69.95. ISBN 0 7734 6049 7. Edwin Mellen Press.

Howarth, David–Tort Law. Paperback: £28.00. ISBN 1 84113 572 0. Hart Publishing.

Howells, Geraint; Weatherill, Stephen–Consumer Protection Law. Paperback: £35.00. ISBN 0 7546 2338 6. Avebury Technical.

Hudson, Alastair–Equity and Trusts. Paperback: £29.95. ISBN 1 85941 977 1. Cavendish Publishing Ltd.

Human Rights and the Fight Against Terrorism, the Council of Europe Guidelines. Paperback: £7.00. ISBN 92 871 5694 8. Council of Europe.

Human Rights Lawcard. Lawcards S. Spiral/comb bound: £6.95. ISBN 1 84568 023 5. Cavendish Publishing Ltd.

Human Rights Reader. Hardback: £67.00. ISBN 0 415 95159 3. Routledge, an imprint of Taylor & Francis Books Ltd. Paperback (B format): £22.99. ISBN 0 415 95160 7. Routledge, an imprint of Taylor & Francis Books Ltd.

Humphreys, N.–Trade Union and Collective Employment Rights. Paperback: £50.00. ISBN 0 85308 960 4. Jordans.

Hunt, Dennis–Dismissal and Grievance Procedures: Framing and Operating Procedures to Meet Current Rules. Thorogood Professional Insights S. Paperback: £149.00. ISBN 1 85418 376 1. Thorogood.

Hunter, Rosemary; Keyes, Mary–Changing Law: Rights, Regulation, and Reconciliation. Law, Justice & Power S. Hardback: £55.00. ISBN 0 7546 2552 4. Ashgate.

Hurstfield, J.; Aston, J.; Ritchie, H; Mitchell, H–Qualifications Bodies and the Disability Discrimination Act. Paperback: £35.00. ISBN 1 85184 347 7. Institute for Employment Studies.

Husak, Doug; Marneffe, Peter de–Legalization of Drugs. For & Against S. Hardback: £25.00. ISBN 0 521 83786 3. Paperback: £10.99. ISBN 0 521 54686 9. Cambridge University Press.

Hutchinson, Allan C.–Evolution and the Common Law. Hardback: £45.00. ISBN 0 521 84968 3. Paperback: £19.99. ISBN 0 521 61491 0. Cambridge University Press.

Hutton, Glenn; Johnston, Dave; Sampson, Fraser–Evidence and Procedure: V. 2. Blackstone's Police Manuals. Paperback: £14.50. ISBN 0 19 928520 9. Paperback: £14.50. ISBN 0 19 928520 9. Oxford University Press.

Hutton, Matthew–Stamp Duty Land Tax. Paperback: £65.00. ISBN 1 84592 122 4. Tottel Publishing.

Hutton, Rosalie; Hutton, Glenn–Passing the National Admissions Test for Law (LNAT). Guides. Paperback: £12.00. ISBN 1 84641 001 0. Law Matters Publishing.

Hyatt, Thomas K.; Hopkins, Bruce R.–Law of Tax-Exempt Healthcare Organizations. Paperback: £44.50. ISBN 0 471 67987 9. John Wiley & Sons Inc.

I'anson Banks, Roderick–Lindley and Banks on Partnership, 1st Supplement. Paperback: £59.00. ISBN 0 421 91500 5. Sweet & Maxwell.

IChemE Contracts Working Party–Pink Book, Forms of Contract, Arbitration Rules. Paperback: £20.00. ISBN 0 85295 486 7. Institution of Chemical Engineers.

IChemE Contracts Working Party–White Book, Forms of Contract, Rules for Expert Determination. Paperback: £20.00. ISBN 0 85295 487 5. Institution of Chemical Engineers.

Identity of Constitutional Subject. Hardback: £50.00. ISBN 0 415 94973 4. Routledge, an imprint of Taylor & Francis Books Ltd.

IFI Claims–Patent Intelligence and Technology Report. Hardback: £283.00. ISBN 0 7817 6056 9. Lippincott Williams and Wilkins.

Illes, Judy–Neuroethics in the 21st Century: Defining the Issues in Theory, Practice and Policy. Hardback: £75.00. ISBN 0 19 856720 0. Oxford University Press.

Inns of Court School of Law–Advanced Civil Litigation (Professional Negligence) in Practice. Blackstone Bar Manual S. Paperback: £24.99. ISBN 0 19 928491 1. Oxford University Press.

Inns of Court School of Law–Advanced Criminal Litigation in Practice. Blackstone Bar Manual S. Paperback: £24.99. ISBN 0 19 928486 5. Oxford University Press.

Inns of Court School of Law–Advocacy. Blackstone Bar Manual S. Paperback: £26.99. ISBN 0 19 928147 5. Oxford University Press.

Inns of Court School of Law–Case Preparation. Blackstone Bar Manual S. Paperback: £26.99. ISBN 0 19 928148 3. Oxford University Press.

Inns of Court School of Law–Civil Litigation. Blackstone Bar Manual S. Paperback: £26.99. ISBN 0 19 928149 1. Paperback: £26.99. ISBN 0 19 928149 1. Oxford University Press.

Inns of Court School of Law–Company Law in Practice. Blackstone Bar Manual S. Paperback: £24.99. ISBN 0 19 928489 X. Oxford University Press.

Inns of Court School of Law–Conference Skills. Blackstone Bar Manual S. Paperback: £26.99. ISBN 0 19 928150 5. Oxford University Press.

Inns of Court School of Law–Employment Law in Practice. Blackstone Bar Manual S. Paperback: £24.99. ISBN 0 19 928488 1. Oxford University Press.

Inns of Court School of Law–Evidence. Blackstone Bar Manual S. Paperback: £26.99. ISBN 0 19 928153 X. Oxford University Press.

Inns of Court School of Law–Family Law in Practice. Blackstone Bar Manual S. Paperback: £24.99. ISBN 0 19 928490 3. Oxford University Press.

Inns of Court School of Law–Negotiation. Blackstone Bar Manual S. Paperback: £26.99. ISBN 0 19 928154 8. Oxford University Press.

Inns of Court School of Law–Opinion Writing. Blackstone Bar Manual S. Paperback: £26.99. ISBN 0 19 928155 6. Oxford University Press.

Inns of Court School of Law–Professional Conduct. Blackstone Bar Manual S. Paperback: £26.99. ISBN 0 19 928156 4. Oxford University Press.

Inns of Court School of Law–Remedies. Blackstone Bar Manual S. Paperback: £26.99. ISBN 0 19 928157 2. Paperback: £26.99. ISBN 0 19 928157 2. Oxford University Press.

Inns of Court School of Law–Test Yourself in Evidence, Civil Procedure, Criminal Procedure and Sentencing, 12th Rev. Ed.. Blackstone Bar Manual S. Paperback: £17.99. ISBN 0 19 927738 9. Oxford University Press.

Insurance Regulators. Paperback: £145.00. ISBN 1 904501 38 9. Richmond Law & Tax.

Intellectual Property and Entrepreneurship. Advances in the Study of Entrepreneurship, Innovation, & Economic Growth, V.; 15. Hardback: £63.50. ISBN 0 7623 1102 9. JAI Press.

Intellectual Property Lawcards. Lawcards S. Looseleaf/ring bound: £6.95. ISBN 1 84568 027 8. Cavendish Publishing Ltd.

International Trade and Business Law Review: V.4. Paperback: £41.00. ISBN 1 876905 23 9. Cavendish Publishing Ltd.

Ippolito, Richard A.–Economics for Lawyers. Hardback: £41.95. ISBN 0 691 12177 X. Princeton University Press.

Irish, Vivien–Intellectual Property Rights for Engineers. IEE Management of Technology S. Hardback: £26.00. ISBN 0 86341 490 7. Institution of Electrical Engineers.

Is It in Force? Paperback: £187.00. ISBN 1 4057 0061 0. Butterworths Law.

Jackman, Angela; Hay, Deborah; Wilkins, Pat–Practical Education Law. Paperback: £39.95. ISBN 1 85328 816 0. Law Society Publications.

Jacksack, Susan M.; Gada, Paul N.–CCH Toolkit Tax Guide. CCH Business Owner's Toolkit S. Paperback: £15.50. ISBN 0 8080 1113 8. CCH Inc.

Jackson, David–Enforcement of Maritime Claims. Hardback: £250.00. ISBN 1 84311 424 0. Informa Business Publishing.

Jackson, Emily–Medical Law: Text, Cases and Materials. Paperback: £29.99. ISBN 0 19 926127 X. Oxford University Press.

Jackson, Frank; Smith, Michael–Oxford Handbook of Contemporary Philosophy. Oxford Handbooks S. Hardback: £55.00. ISBN 0 19 924295 X. Oxford University Press.

Jacobs, Edward–Jacobs Child Support: The Legislationition. Paperback: £77.00. ISBN 0 421 91860 8. Sweet & Maxwell.

Jacobs, Susan–Case Studies in Criminal Procedure. Paperback: £24.99. ISBN 0 13 170044 8. Prentice Hall.

Jacobus–Real Estate Law. Hardback: £17.99. ISBN 0 324 20176 1. South Western College Publishing.

Jacobus–TX RE Broker and Law of Agency. Hardback: £14.99. ISBN 0 324 20020 X. South Western College Publishing.

Jaeger, Paul T.; Bowman, Cynthia Ann–Understanding Disability: Inclusion, Access, Diversity, and Civil Rights. Hardback: £28.99. ISBN 0 275 98226 2. Greenwood Publishing Group Inc.

Jaffe, Adam B.; Trajtenberg, Manuel–Patents, Citations and Innovations: A Window on the Knowledge Economy. Paperback/CD-ROM: £19.95. ISBN 0 262 60065 X. The MIT Press.

James, Frances–Straightforward Guide to the Process of Conveyancing. Paperback: £9.99. ISBN 1 903909 72 4. Straightforward Publishing.

James, Jennifer–Company Law Q&A. Q & A S. Paperback: £10.95. ISBN 1 85941 959 3. Cavendish Publishing Ltd.

James, Malcolm–UK Tax System: An Introduction. Paperback: £39.95. ISBN 1 904905 22 6. Spiramus Press.

James, Mark; Cook, Kate; Lee, Richard–Core Statutes on Criminal Law. Core Statutes S. Paperback: £10.00. ISBN 1 84641 008 8. Law Matters Publishing.

Jamieson, George–Family Agreements. Paperback: £35.00. ISBN 1 84592 004 X. Tottel Publishing.

Jarvis, Susan S.–Reducing Business Risk: Legal Reference Guide. Hardback: £39.99. ISBN 0 324 22231 9. South Western College Publishing.

Jason-Lloyd, Len–Drugs, Addiction and the Law: A Basic Guide. Hardback: £29.95. ISBN 1 85450 489 4. Elm Publications.

Jefferson, Michael; Richards, Paul; Elliott, Catherine; Stein, Stuart–Criminal Law: WITH Law of Contract (7th Revised Edition) AND English Legal System (6th Revised Edition) AND Law on the Web, a Guide for Students and Practitioners AND Contract Law Online Course. Paperback/Internet resource: £68.99. ISBN 1 4058 3725 X. Longman.

Jefferson, Michael–Criminal Law. Foundation Studies in Law S. Paperback: £27.99. ISBN 1 4058 1225 7. Longman.

Jenkins, Kirsty–Housing and Housing Benefit Law. Paperback: £37.95. ISBN 1 84592 003 1. Tottel Publishing.

Jennings, Marianne M.–Business Ethics. Paperback: £29.99. ISBN 0 324 31108 7. South Western College Publishing.

Jennings, Simon–Tolley's Planning and Administration of Offshore and Onshore Trusts. Looseleaf/ring bound: £245.00. ISBN 0 7545 0794 7. LexisNexis UK.

Jennings–Business Ethical Case Study and Selective Reading. Hardback: £29.99. ISBN 0 324 20489 2. South Western College Publishing.

Jeong, Ho-Won–Peacebuilding in Postconflict Societies: Strategy and Process. Paperback: £16.95. ISBN 1 58826 311 8. Lynne Rienner Publishers.

Jespersen, Jesper–Introduction to Macroeconomic Theory. Paperback: £31.00. ISBN 87 574 1345 2. DJOF Publishing.

Jessell, C.–Farms and Estates. Paperback: £49.50. ISBN 0 85308 984 1. Jordans.

John-Salakov, Andre–Journal of Civil and Criminal Justice Systems. Hardback: £25.99. ISBN 1 873156 79 0. Centre For Community Studies.

Johns, Robert–Using the Law in Social Work. Transforming Social Work Practice S. Paperback: £14.00. ISBN 1 84445 030 9. Learning Matters.

Johnson, Melanie; Lawson, Elizabeth; Field, Stephan; Adams, Lindsay; Lamb, John–Blackstone's Guide to the Domestic Violence, Crime and Victims Act. Blackstone's Guide S. Paperback: £29.95. ISBN 0 19 928189 0. Oxford University Press.

Johnston, William; Werlen, Thomas–Set-Off Law and Practice: An International Handbook. Hardback: £135.00. ISBN 0 19 929077 6. Oxford University Press.

Johnstone, Gerry; Van Ness, Daniel–Handbook of Restorative Justice. Hardback: £65.00. ISBN 1 84392 151 0. Paperback: £29.50. ISBN 1 84392 150 2. Willan Publishing.

Jones, Christopher; Woude, Van Der–EC Competition Law Handbook 2005/2006, Standing Order Service. Paperback: £172.00. ISBN 0 421 92660 0. Sweet & Maxwell.

Jones, Gareth–Goff and Jones: 1st Supplement: The Law of Restitution. Paperback: £55.00. ISBN 0 421 87390 6. Sweet & Maxwell.

Jones, K.V.Prichard; Adams, John N.–Franchising. Hardback: £135.00. ISBN 0 406 97734 8. Butterworths Law.

Jones, Michael A.; Morris, Anne E.–Statutes on Medical Law. Blackstone's Statute Books. Paperback: £18.99. ISBN 0 19 928315 X. Oxford University Press.

Jones, Richard–Mental Capacity Act Manual. Paperback: £35.00. ISBN 0 421 91820 9. Sweet & Maxwell.

Jones, Richard–Mental Health Act Manual: 1st Supplement. Paperback: £29.00. ISBN 0 421 91840 3. Sweet & Maxwell.

Jones, Roger–Incorporating a Business. Paperback: £59.95. ISBN 1 84592 109 7. Tottel Publishing.

Jordan, Andrew–Environmental Policy in the European Union: Actors, Institutions and Processes. Hardback: £80.00. ISBN 1 84407 157 X. Paperback: £22.95. ISBN 1 84407 158 8. Earthscan Publications Ltd.

Jordans–Civil Court Service 2005. Hardback/CD-ROM: £195.00. ISBN 0 85308 968 X. Jordans.

Jorgens, Konstantin J.; Boyd, Marcos Araujo; Sierra, Jose Luis Buendia; Keppenne, Jean-Paul; Beal, Kieron–EC Competition Procedure. Hardback: £215.00. ISBN 0 19 826889 0. Oxford University Press.

Joseph, David–Jurisdiction, Arbitration and Mediation Clauses. Hardback: £140.00. ISBN 0 421 90480 1. Sweet & Maxwell.

Joseph, Sarah; Schultz, Jenny; Castan, Melissa–International Covenant on Civil and Political Rights: Cases, Materials, and Commentary. Paperback: £40.00. ISBN 0 19 928541 1. Oxford University Press.

Junghans, C.–Intellectual Property Management: A Guide for Scientists, Engineers, Financiers, and Managers. Hardback: £34.95. ISBN 3 527 31286 2. Wiley-VCH.

Jurisprudence Lawcards. Lawcards S. Looseleaf/ring bound: £6.95. ISBN 1 84568 025 1. Cavendish Publishing Ltd.

Kaczmarek, Peggy; Levine, Elaine S.; Segal, Anne F.–Law and Mental Health Professionals: New Mexico. Hardback: £78.50. ISBN 1 59147 284 9. American Psychological Association.

Kaczorowska, Alina–Public International Law. Paperback: £15.95. ISBN 1 85836 607 0. Old Bailey Press.

Kane, Luan; Ashman, Linda–Sinclair: Warranties and Indemnities on Share and Asset Sales. Book (details unknown)/CD-ROM: £170.83. ISBN 0 421 86260 2. Sweet & Maxwell.

Kay, Dale; Baker, Janet–Solicitors' Accounts: A Practical Guide. Legal Practice Course Guides. Paperback: £26.99. ISBN 0 19 928137 8. Oxford University Press.

Kearney, Brian–Scottish Children's Hearing System in Action. Paperback: £25.00. ISBN 1 84592 056 2. Tottel Publishing.

Keenan, Denis–Business Law: AND Contract Law Generic Pin Card. Paperback: £32.99. ISBN 1 4058 1806 9. Longman.

Keenan, Denis–Company Law: AND Scottish Supplement. Paperback: £34.99. ISBN 1 4058 1160 9. Longman.

Keenan, Denis–Company Law. Paperback: £31.99. ISBN 1 4058 1158 7. Longman.

Keenan, Denis–Law for Business: AND Contract Law Generic Pin Card. Paperback/Internet resource: £33.99. ISBN 1 4058 2489 1. Longman.

Kelleher, Denis; Muray, Karen–Information Technology Law in Ireland. Paperback: £80.00. ISBN 1 84592 111 9. Tottel Publishing.

Kelleher, Denis; Murray, Karen–IT Law in the European Union. Hardback: £145.00. ISBN 0 421 83870 1. Sweet & Maxwell.

Kelleher, Denis–Data Protection Law in Ireland. Hardback: £93.33. ISBN 1 84592 204 2. Tottel Publishing.

Kelly, David; Holmes, Ann; Hayward, Ruth–Business Law. Paperback: £28.00. ISBN 1 85941 962 3. Cavendish Publishing Ltd.

Kelsen, Hans–General Theory of Law and State. Paperback: £31.50. ISBN 1 4128 0494 9. Transaction Publishers.

Kemp and Kemp: Personal Injury Law, Practice and Procedure. Looseleaf / ring bound: £175.00. ISBN 0 421 90510 7. Sweet & Maxwell.

Kendall, Christopher N.–Gay Male Pornography: An Issue of Sex Discrimination. Law & Society S. Paperback: £19.95. ISBN 0 7748 1077 7. John Wiley and Sons Ltd.

Kennedy, Helena–Just Law. Paperback: £8.99. ISBN 0 09 945833 0. Vintage.

Kennedy, T.P.; Cahill, Dermot; Power, Vincent–European Law. Law Society of Ireland Manuals S. Paperback: £39.99. ISBN 0 19 928023 1. Oxford University Press.

Kent, George; Twiss, Sumner B.; Kelsay, John; Coonan, Terry–Freedom from Want: The Human Right to Adequate Food. Advancing Human Rights S. Hardback: £31.25. ISBN 1 58901 055 8. Paperback: £16.95. ISBN 1 58901 056 6. Georgetown University Press.

Kenyon, Andrew–Defamation. Paperback: £40.00. ISBN 1 84472 021 7. UCL Press.

Keogh, Andrew; Craig, Brian–Criminal Contracting: A Compliance Guide. Paperback: £69.95. ISBN 1 85328 987 6. Law Society Publications.

Keogh, Andrew–Criminal Procedure Rules. Paperback: £29.95. ISBN 1 85328 919 1. Law Society Publications.

Keppel-Palmer, Marcus; Maughan, Caroline; Maughan, Mike; Webb, Julian; Boon, Andy–Lawyers' Skills. Blackstone Legal Practice Course Guide S. Paperback: £26.99. ISBN 0 19 928138 6. Oxford University Press.

Kessler, James; Thompson, Heather; Clark, Ian–Drafting Scottish Trusts and Will Trusts. Hardback: £130.00. ISBN 1 84592 149 6. Tottel Publishing.

Kibitlewski, Joseph L–A Comparison of a Citizen's Right to Silence Under American and English Political Systems. Criminology Studies S., No.23. Hardback: £64.95. ISBN 0 7734 6347 X. Edwin Mellen Press.

Kidner, Richard–Statutes on Employment Law. Blackstone's Statute Books. Paperback: £16.99. ISBN 0 19 928313 3. Oxford University Press.

Kilkelly, Ursula–Child Law. Hardback: £125.00. ISBN 1 85475 390 8. Butterworths Law (Ireland).

king-Devoreaux, Kelsee–Stunts Court = (Family/Children's Court-The Legal System). Hardback: £23.00. ISBN 1 4134 8047 0. Xlibris Corporation.

King, Harry–Knowing the Law in Spain: An Essential Guide for the British Property Owner, Resident or Long-term Visitor to Spain. Paperback: £12.99. ISBN 1 84528 059 8. How To Books.

King, Michael; Phillips, Ann–Charities Act 2005: A Guide to the New Law. Paperback: £39.95. ISBN 1 85328 913 2. Law Society Publications.

Klabbers, Jan–International Organizations. Library of Essays in International Law. Hardback: £125.00. ISBN 0 7546 2447 1. Ashgate.

Kleit, Andrew N.–Antitrust and Competition Policy. Business Economics S. Hardback: £160.00. ISBN 1 84376 319 2. Edward Elgar.

Klip, Andre; Sluiter, Goran–Annotated Leading Cases: V. 7. Paperback: £100.00. ISBN 90 5095 375 1. Intersentia Publishers.

Knell, Anne–Compact Employment Law Reference Book. Paperback: £26.00. ISBN 0 9535720 6 4. JEC Training Ltd.

Knight, J.–Wills, Probate and Inheritance Tax for Dummies. For Dummies S. Paperback: £12.99. ISBN 0 7645 7055 2. John Wiley and Sons Ltd.

Knight, William; Newman, Jane–Acquisition of Private Companies and Business Assets. Hardback: £144.94. ISBN 0 421 84000 5. Sweet & Maxwell.

Knowles, Roger–One Hundred and Fifty Contractual Problems and Their Solutions. Hardback: £49.50. ISBN 1 4051 2070 3. Blackwell Publishing.

Kok, Lex De; Bazelmans, Janneke–Emissions Trading. Hardback: £125.00. ISBN 1 904905 05 6. Spiramus Press.

Kolvin, Philip–Licensed Premises: Law and Practice Supplement. Paperback: £20.00. ISBN 1 84592 289 1. Tottel Publishing.

Kolvin, Philip–Licensed Premises: Law and Practice, with Updating Supplement. Hardback: £85.00. ISBN 1 84592 291 3. Tottel Publishing.

Korah, Valentine–Intellectual Property Rights and the EC Competition Rules. Hardback: £65.00. ISBN 1 84113 614 X. Hart Publishing.

Korn, Anthony; Sethi, Mohinderpal–Employment Tribunal Compensation. Paperback: £45.00. ISBN 0 19 928811 9. Oxford University Press.

Kostal, Rande W.–Jurisprudence of Power: Victorian Empire and the Rule of Law. Oxford Studies in Modern Legal History. Hardback: £50.00. ISBN 0 19 826076 8. Oxford University Press.

Koutrakos, Panos–EU International Relations Law. Paperback: £37.50. ISBN 1 84113 311 6. Hart Publishing.

Koziol, Helmut; Steininger, Barbara–European Tort Law. Tort & Insurance Law. Paperback: £98.50. ISBN 3 211 24479 4. Springer-Verlag Vienna.

Kranenborg, H.; Voermans, W.–Access to Information in the European Union: A Comparative Analysis of EC and Member State Legislation. Paperback: £25.00. ISBN 90 76871 46 9. Europa Law Publishing, Netherlands.

Kruse, Paul–Sarbanes-Oxley and Trademark Portfolio Management: Establishing Internal Controls for Compliance and Preventing Infringement. Hardback: £149.95. ISBN 1 59622 167 4. Aspatore Books.

Kumar, H.L.–Employer's Rights Under Labour Laws. Paperback: £11.50. ISBN 81 7534 445 8. Universal Law Publishing Co Ltd.

Kumar, H.L.–Transfer of Employees Under Labour Laws. Paperback: £9.99. ISBN 81 7534 462 8. Universal Law Publishing Co Ltd.

LaFollette, Hugh–Oxford Handbook of Practical Ethics. Oxford Handbooks in Philosophy S. Paperback: £27.50. ISBN 0 19 928423 7. Oxford University Press.

Laing, David; Mobley, Samantha; Gomez, Luis–Global Merger Control Manual. Spiral/comb bound/CD-ROM: £195.00. ISBN 1 905017 05 7. Cameron May.

Lamont, Camilla; Stacey, Myriam; Seifert, Anne–Lease Renewal. Case in Point S., No. 6. Paperback: £24.99. ISBN 1 84219 226 4. RICS.

Landman, Todd–Protecting Human Rights: A Comparative Study. Advancing Human Rights S. Paperback: £18.75. ISBN 1 58901 063 9. Paperback: £18.75. ISBN 1 58901 063 9. Georgetown University Press.

Lang, Beverley; Clarke, Gerard; Pannick, David–Administrative Court: Practice and Procedure. Hardback: £175.00. ISBN 0 421 90500 X. Sweet & Maxwell.

Langbein, John H.–Origins of Adversary Criminal Trial. Oxford Studies in Modern Legal History. Paperback: £15.99. ISBN 0 19 928723 6. Oxford University Press.

Langdon, John; Ortmeier, P.–Policing the Community: Introduction to Law Enforcement and Criminal Justice. Hardback: £28.99. ISBN 0 13 113777 8. Prentice Hall.

Langley, Aidan–Employee Reward Structures. CD-ROM: £95.00. ISBN 1 904905 08 0. Paperback: £95.00. ISBN 1 904905 04 8. Spiramus Press.

Langstaff, Brian; Buchan, Andrew; Latimer-Sayer, William–Personal Injury Schedules: Calculating Damages. Paperback: £82.00. ISBN 1 84592 053 8. Tottel Publishing.

Larsen, Flemming; Bredgaard, Thomas–Employment Policy from Different Angles. Paperback: £34.00. ISBN 87 574 1349 5. DJOF Publishing.

Larsen, P.B.–Aviation Law: Cases and Related Sources. Hardback: £68.99. ISBN 1 57105 340 9. Transnational Publishers, Inc.

Lattimer, Mark; Sands, Philippe–Justice for Crimes Against Humanity. Paperback: £25.00. ISBN 1 84113 568 2. Hart Publishing.

Laurie, Graeme T.; Gibson, Johanna–Generation Scotland: Legal and Ethical Aspects. Paperback: £5.00. ISBN 0 9549717 0 1. AHRC (Arts and Humanities Research Council) Research Centre for Studies in.

Lauterburg, Dominique–Core Statutes on Employment Law. Core Statutes S. Paperback: £10.00. ISBN 1 84641 007 X. Law Matters Publishing.

Law and Practice for Architects. Paperback: £19.99. ISBN 0 7506 5729 4. Architectural Press.

Law of Health and Safety At Work. Paperback: £47.50. ISBN 1 85524 689 9. Croner CCH Group Ltd.

Law Reports Set. Other printed material: £504.00. ISBN 1 4057 0623 6. Butterworths Law.

Law Society Scotland Diploma Materials 2005, Civil Company and Commercial Student Manual 2005-2006. Book (details unknown): £15.00. ISBN 0 414 01638 6. W.Green & Son.

Law Society Scotland Diploma Materials 2005, Civil Court Practice Student Manual 2005-2006. Book (details unknown): £15.00. ISBN 0 414 01637 8. W.Green & Son.

Law Society Scotland Diploma Materials 2005, Conveyancing Student Manual 2005-2006. Book (details unknown): £15.00. ISBN 0 414 01639 4. W.Green & Son.

Law Society Scotland Diploma Materials 2005, Criminal Court Practice Student Manual 2005-2006. Book (details unknown): £15.00. ISBN 0 414 01640 8. W.Green & Son.

Law Society Scotland Diploma Materials 2005, Diploma Solutions 2005-2006. Book (details unknown): £6.50. ISBN 0 414 01645 9. W.Green & Son.

Law Society Scotland Diploma Materials 2005, Diploma Tutors Manual 2005-2006. Book (details unknown): £2.50. ISBN 0 414 01646 7. W.Green & Son.

Law Society Scotland Diploma Materials 2005, Financial Services Student Manual 2005-2006. Book (details unknown): £15.00. ISBN 0 414 01642 4. W.Green & Son.

Law Society Scotland Diploma Materials 2005, Private Client Student Manual 2005-2006. Book (details unknown): £15.00. ISBN 0 414 01643 2. W.Green & Son.

Law Society Scotland Diploma Materials 2005, Professional Ethics Student Manual 2005-2006. Book (details unknown): £15.00. ISBN 0 414 01641 6. W.Green & Son.

Law Society Scotland Diploma Materials 2005, Public Administration Student Manual 2005-2006. Book (details unknown): £15.00. ISBN 0 414 01644 0. W.Green & Son.

Law Society–Directory of Solicitors and Barristers. Hardback: £94.95. ISBN 1 85328 963 9. Law Society Publications.

Law Society–Family Law Protocol. Paperback: £24.95. ISBN 1 85328 984 1. Law Society Publications.

Lawley, Duard–Common Sense Tax Reform. Paperback: £8.99. ISBN 1 4208 8312 7. AuthorHouse.

Laws of Scotland Consolidated Index. Hardback: £108.00. ISBN 1 4057 0906 5. Butterworths Law (Scotland).

Lawson, Richard; Glynn, Joanna; Gomez, David–Exclusion Clauses and Unfair Contract Terms. Hardback: £60.00. ISBN 0 421 89440 7. Sweet & Maxwell.

Lawson, Richard; Glynn, Joanna; Gomez, David–Fitness to Practise: Health Care Regulatory Law, Principle and Process. Hardback: £65.00. ISBN 0 421 90540 9. Sweet & Maxwell.

Leane, Geoff–International Law in the South Pacific: Policies and Practices. Hardback: £60.00. ISBN 0 7546 4419 7. Ashgate.

Lee, C.C.–Environmental Engineering Dictionary. Hardback: £89.00. ISBN 0 86587 848 X. Government Institutes Division, ABS Group Inc.

Lee, Maria–EU Environmental Law: Challenges, Change and Decision-making. Paperback: £30.00. ISBN 1 84113 410 4. Hart Publishing.

Lee, Robert; Stokes, Elen–Land Use and Liability. Hardback: £35.00. ISBN 1 84568 041 3. Cavendish Publishing Ltd.

Lee, R.S.–Giving Effect to the International Criminal Court: Methods and Techniques For Handling Issues of Criminal Law, Constitution and Sovereignty. Hardback: £100.99. ISBN 1 57105 155 4. Transnational Publishers, Inc.

Lee, Yong-Shik–Reclaiming Development in the World Trading System. Hardback: £35.00. ISBN 0 521 85296 X. Cambridge University Press.

Leech, Mark–Prisons Handbook: The Definitive 800-page Annual Guide to the Penal System of England and Wales. Paperback: £65.00. ISBN 0 9544829 2 1. MLA Press Ltd.

Legal Strategies for the Construction Industry: Leading Lawyers on Structuring Contracts, Handling Litigation, and Ensuring Successful Projects. Inside the Minds S. Paperback: £37.95. ISBN 1 59622 169 0. Aspatore Books,US.

Legh-Jones, Nicholas; Birds, John; Owen, David–Macgillivray on Insurance Law: 1st Supplement. Paperback: £80.00. ISBN 0 421 87730 8. Sweet & Maxwell.

Leigh, Karen–Guide to Law and the Family: A Comprehensive Guide to All Aspects of Family Law. Easyway Guides S. Paperback: £8.99. ISBN 1 900694 03 4. Straightforward Publishing.

Leigh, Karen–Straightforward Guide to Employment Law. Straightforward Guides S. Paperback: £7.99. ISBN 1 903909 67 8. Straightforward Publishing.

Lenehan, Orla–Taxation in the Republic of Ireland. Paperback: £66.66. ISBN 1 84592 143 7. Tottel Publishing.

Leo Zaibert–Punishment and Retribution. Law, Justice & Power. Hardback: £50.00. ISBN 0 7546 2389 0. Avebury Technical.

Letwin, Shirley Robin–On the History of the Idea of Law. Hardback: £48.00. ISBN 0 521 85423 7. Cambridge University Press.

Levy, Martyn–Leaseholders Handbook. Paperback: £8.99. ISBN 1 900694 28 X. Straightforward Publishing.

Lewis, David; Sargeant, Malcolm–Employment Law. Paperback: £28.99. ISBN 1 4058 0743 1. Longman.

Lewis, Tamara–Employment Law: An Adviser's Handbook. Paperback: £28.00. ISBN 1 903307 36 8. The Legal Action Group.

Lewison, Justice; Bignell, Janet–Lewinson's Drafting Business Leases. Paperback: £85.00. ISBN 0 421 90860 2. Sweet & Maxwell.

Lexis, Tolley's–Guide to Construction Contracts: Issue 16. Paperback: £66.00. ISBN 0 7545 2485 X. Tolley Publishing.

Leyland, Peter; Anthony, Gordon–Textbook on Administrative Law. Paperback: £24.99. ISBN 0 19 927937 3. Oxford University Press.

Liebling, Alison–Prisons and Their Moral Performance: A Study of Values, Quality, and Prison Life. Clarendon Studies in Criminology. Paperback: £19.99. ISBN 0 19 929148 9. Oxford University Press.

Lilley, Peter–Too Much of a Good Thing?: The Case for Controlled Immigration. Paperback: £7.50. ISBN 1 903219 95 7. Centre for Policy Studies.

Lindrup, Garth–Butterworths Competition Law Handbook. Paperback: £89.00. ISBN 1 4057 0002 5. Paperback: £99.00. ISBN 1 4057 1072 1. Butterworths Law.

Lipinski, Tomas A.–Librarian's Copyright Liability Handbook. Hardback: £52.95. ISBN 1 55570 532 4. Neal-Schuman Publishers Inc., U.S.

Lipton, Jacqueline–Information Law and Policy: Legal and Commercial Aspects of Valuable Information. Hardback: £45.00. ISBN 1 84113 332 9. Hart Publishing.

Lisman, John; Schoonderbeek, Carla–Introduction to EU Pharmaceutical Law. Paperback: £50.00. ISBN 1 904255 06 X. Brookwood Medical Publications.

Livens, Leslie–Livens's Share and Business Valuation Handbook. Paperback: £65.95. ISBN 1 84592 028 7. Tottel Publishing.

Livermore, Maree–Family Law Handbook. Paperback: £32.95. ISBN 0 947205 88 8. Redfern Legal Centre Publishing.

Lloyd, S.–Charities-The New Law: A Practical Guide to the Charities Act. Paperback: £39.00. ISBN 0 85308 971 X. Jordans.

Lockton, Deborah–Employment Law Q&A. Questions & Answers S. Paperback: £13.95. ISBN 1 85941 978 X. Cavendish Publishing Ltd.

Lolme, Jean Louis De–Constitution of England. Hardback: £13.95. ISBN 0 86597 464 0. Liberty Fund Inc.

Loose, Helen; Stalbow, Nick–Practical Lawyer Guide to Environmental Issues in Commercial Property Transactions. Paperback: £49.95. ISBN 1 903927 60 9. Legalease.

Lowe, David–Pocket Guide to LGV Drivers' Hours and Tachography Law: Including Working Time and Minimum Pay Rules. Paperback: £12.99. ISBN 0 7494 4568 8. Kogan Page.

Lowe, Jonquil–Giving and Inheriting: The Which? Guide to Giving and Inheriting. Which? Consumer Guides. Paperback: £11.99. ISBN 1 84490 016 9. Which? Books.

Lowry, John; Dignam, Alan–Company Law. Paperback: £16.99. ISBN 0 19 928446 6. Paperback: £16.99. ISBN 0 19 928446 6. Oxford University Press.

Lowry, John; Rawlings, Philip–Insurance Law: Doctrines and Principles. Paperback: £22.50. ISBN 1 84113 540 2. Hart Publishing.

Loyita Worley–Bial Handbook of Legal Information Management. Hardback: £70.00. ISBN 0 7546 4182 1. Ashgate.

Luba, Jan; Madge, Nic; McConnell, Derek–Defending Possession Proceedings. Paperback: £45.00. ISBN 1 903307 30 9. The Legal Action Group.

Luke, Thomas–Corporate Secretaryship. Professional Development S. Paperback: £27.50. ISBN 1 86072 317 9. ICSA Publishing Ltd (Institute of Chartered Secretaries & Administrators).

Maas, Robert–Tottel's Property Taxes. Paperback: £75.95. ISBN 1 84592 198 4. Tottel Publishing.

Maas, Robert–Tottel's Taxation of Employments. Paperback: £74.95. ISBN 1 84592 014 7. Tottel Publishing.

MacCormick, Neil–Rhetoric and The Rule of Law: A Theory of Legal Reasoning. Law, State & Practical Reason S. Hardback: £40.00. ISBN 0 19 826878 5. Oxford University Press.

MacDonald, Charles; Karia, Charles–Commercial Court and Arbitration Pleadings. Hardback: £135.00. ISBN 1 84592 036 8. Tottel Publishing.

Macdonald, Elizabeth–Macdonald: Exemption Clauses and Unfair Terms. Hardback: £160.00. ISBN 1 84592 067 8. Tottel Publishing.

MacFadyen–Court of Session Practice Main Work. Looseleaf/ring bound: £285.00. ISBN 1 84592 102 X. Tottel Publishing.

Macintosh, Kerry Lynn–Human Cloning and Legal Rights. Hardback: £40.00. ISBN 0 521 85328 1. Cambridge University Press.

Macintyre, Ewan–Business Law: AND Contract Law Generic Pin Card. Paperback: £34.99. ISBN 1 4058 1805 0. Longman.

Mackie, Robert–New Public Management of Scotland: Local Government and the National Health Service. Paperback: £25.00. ISBN 0 414 01600 9. W. Green & Son.

MacKinnon, Catharine A.–Women's Lives, Men's Laws. Hardback: £25.95. ISBN 0 674 01540 1. The Belknap Press.

MacLean, Iain; Maclean, Siobhan–Social Care and the Law: An NVQ Related Reference Guide for Direct Care Staff. Spiral/comb bound: £10.00. ISBN 1 903575 30 3. Kirwin Maclean Associates.

MacLean, Iain–Social Care and the Law. Spiral/comb bound: £10.00. ISBN 1 903575 34 6. Kirwin Maclean Associates.

Maclean, Mavis–Family Law and Family Values. Hardback: £40.00. ISBN 1 84113 547 X. Paperback: £22.00. ISBN 1 84113 548 8. Hart Publishing.

MacLean, Robert M.; Volpi, Bettina–EU Trade Barrier Regulation. Paperback: £95.00. ISBN 0 421 91920 5. Sweet & Maxwell.

MacMahon, Bryan; Binchy, William–Casebook of Irish Law of Torts. Paperback: £80.00. ISBN 1 84592 031 7. Tottel Publishing.

MacMillan, Fiona–New Directions in Copyright Law: Vol.1. New Directions in Copyright Law S. Hardback: £59.95. ISBN 1 84542 260 0. Edward Elgar.

MacNeil, Iain G.–Introduction to the Law on Financial Investment. Paperback: £35.00. ISBN 1 84113 478 3. Hart Publishing.

Macqueen, Hector; Hood, Parker; Wise, Morag; Dunlop, Laura; Wolffe, James; Young, Andrew; Johnston, David; Wolffe, Sarah P. L.–Gloag and Henderson: The Law of Scotland. Paperback: £49.00. ISBN 0 414 01634 3. W. Green & Son.

Macqueen, Hector; Waelde, Charlotte; Laurie, Graeme–Textbook on Intellectual Property. Paperback: £27.99. ISBN 0 19 926339 6. Oxford University Press.

Macrory, Richard–Reflections on 30 Years of EU Environmental Law: A High Level of Protection? Avosetta S., No. 7. Hardback: £85.00. ISBN 90 76871 50 7. Europa Law Publishing, Netherlands.

Madden, M.Stuart–Exploring Tort Law. Hardback: £45.00. ISBN 0 521 85136 X. Paperback: £19.99. ISBN 0 521 61680 8. Cambridge University Press.

Madge, Nic–Annotated Housing Statutes. Paperback: £55.00. ISBN 0 421 89430 X. Sweet & Maxwell.

Mair, Jane–Avizandum Statutes on Scots Family Law. Paperback: £15.95. ISBN 1 904968 04 X. Avizandum Publishing Ltd.

Majone, Giandomenico–Dilemmas of European Integration: The Ambiguities and Pitfalls of Integration by Stealth. Hardback: £40.00. ISBN 0 19 927430 4. Oxford University Press.

Major Project Sub-Contract Guide. Hardback: £15.95. ISBN 0 418 82810 5. Sweet & Maxwell.

Male, John; Jefferies, Tom–Rent Review. Case in Point S. Paperback: £24.95. ISBN 1 84219 225 6. RICS.

Malleson, Andrew–Whiplash and Other Useful Illnesses. Paperback: £17.95. ISBN 0 7735 2994 2. McGill-Queen's University Press.

Malleson, Kate–Legal System. Core Texts S. Paperback: £16.99. ISBN 0 19 928241 2. Paperback: £16.99. ISBN 0 19 928241 2. Oxford University Press.

Mallor, Jane P; Barnes, A.James; Bowers, L. Thomas; Langvardt, Arlen W–Business Law: The Ethical, Global, and E-Commerce Environment. Hardback: £108.99. ISBN 0 07 293399 2. Higher Education.

Malsch, Marijke; Smeenk, Wilma–Family Violence and Police Response in the EU: Policy and Practice in Europe. Advances in Criminology. Hardback: £50.00. ISBN 0 7546 2506 0. Ashgate.

Mambro, David Di–Butterworths Law of Limitation. Looseleaf/ring bound: £150.00. ISBN 0 406 92576 3. LexisNexis UK.

Mambro, Louise di; Bowles, Master; Leslie, Master–Civil Court Practice (the Green Book). Hardback/Audiobook on CD: £305.20. ISBN 1 4057 0402 0. Butterworths Law.

Mandaraka-Sheppard, Alexandra–Modern Admiralty Law. Paperback: £80.00. ISBN 1 85941 895 3. Cavendish Publishing Ltd.

Mandelstam, Michael–Community Care Practice and the Law. Paperback: £39.95. ISBN 1 84310 233 1. Jessica Kingsley Publishers.

Mantysaari, Petri–Comparative Corporate Governance: Shareholders As a Rule-maker. Paperback: £54.00. ISBN 3 540 25380 7. Springer-Verlag Berlin and Heidelberg GmbH & Co. K.

Maogoto, Jackson–Battling Terrorism: Legal Perspectives on the Use of Force and the War on Terror. Hardback: £55.00. ISBN 0 7546 4407 3. Ashgate.

Marciano, Alain; Josselin, Jean-Michel–Law and the State: A Political Economy Approach. New Horizons in Law & Economics S. Hardback: £90.00. ISBN 1 84376 800 3. Edward Elgar.

Markesinis, Basil S.; Unberath, Hannes; Johnston, Angus–German Law of Contract: A Comparative Treatise. Hardback: £140.00. ISBN 1 84113 471 6. Paperback: £55.00. ISBN 1 84113 472 4. Hart Publishing.

Markovits, D.–Adversary Lawyer. Hardback: £17.95. ISBN 0 691 12162 1. Princeton University Press.

Marmor, Andrei–Interpretation and Legal Theory. Paperback: £30.00. ISBN 1 84113 424 4. Hart Publishing.

Marquis, Louis–International Uniform Commercial Law: Towards a Progressive Consciousness. Applied Legal Phiosophy. Hardback: £55.00. ISBN 0 7546 2396 3. Ashgate.

Marsh–Juvenile Law. Hardback: £24.99. ISBN 1 4018 4019 1. Delmar.

Marshall, Anna-Maria–Confronting Sexual Harrassment. Hardback: £55.00. ISBN 0 7546 2520 6. Ashgate.

Marshall, David; McCarthy, Frances–APIL Personal Injury Law, Practice and Precedents. Hardback: £295.00. ISBN 0 85308 993 0. Jordans.

Marshall, James–Non-Contentious Intellectual Property. Hardback: £150.00. ISBN 0 421 83610 5. Sweet & Maxwell.

Marshall, Jane–Pensions Act 2004: Guide to the New Law. Paperback: £49.95. ISBN 1 85328 923 X. Law Society Publications.

Marshall, Jennifer–European Cross Border Insolvency. Hardback: £255.00. ISBN 0 421 88160 7. Sweet & Maxwell.

Marshall, Lee–Bootlegging: Romanticism and Copyright in the Music Industry. Hardback: £65.00. ISBN 0 7619 4490 7. Sage Publications Ltd.

Martin-Casals, Miquel–Children in Tort Law: Pt. 1. Children As Tortfeasors. Tort & Insurance Law, V. 17. Paperback: £65.50. ISBN 3 211 24480 8. Springer-Verlag Vienna.

Martin, Francisco Forrest; Schnably, Stephen J.; Wilson, Richard; Simon, Jonathan; Tushnet, Mark–International Human Rights and Humanitarian Law: Treaties, Cases, and Analysis. Hardback: £55.00. ISBN 0 521 85886 0. Cambridge University Press.

Martin, Jacqueline–Consumer Law. Key Facts S. Paperback: £5.99. ISBN 0 340 88758 3. Hodder & Stoughton Ltd.

Martin, Jacqueline–English Legal System. Paperback: £14.99. ISBN 0 340 89991 3. Hodder Arnold H&S.

Martin, Jacqueline–GCSE Law. Paperback: £14.99. ISBN 0 340 88939 X. Hodder Arnold H&S.

Martin, Jacqueline–Key Facts: The English Legal System. Key Facts. Paperback: £5.99. ISBN 0 340 91335 5. Hodder Arnold H&S.

Martin, Jill–Hanbury and Martin: Modern Equity. Paperback: £30.00. ISBN 0 421 79840 8. Sweet & Maxwell.

Maslen, Stuart–Commentaries on Arms Control Treaties Volume 1. Hardback: £100.00. ISBN 0 19 929679 0. Oxford University Press.

Maslen, Stuart–Commentaries on Arms Control Treaties: V. 1. Convention on the Prohibition of the Use, Stockpiling, Production, and Transfer of Anti-personnel Mines and on Their Destruction. Oxford Commentaries on International Law S. Paperback: £30.00. ISBN 0 19 928702 3. Oxford University Press.

Mason, Kenyon; Laurie, Graeme–Mason and McCall Smith's Law and Medical Ethics. Paperback: £21.99. ISBN 0 19 928239 0. Paperback: £21.99. ISBN 0 19 928239 0. Oxford University Press.

Matravers, Amanda–Women Sex Offenders. Hardback: £30.00. ISBN 1 84392 142 1. Willan Publishing.

Matthews, Jan; Eastaway, Nigel–Tottel's Self-Assessment. Paperback: £78.99. ISBN 1 84592 005 8. Paperback: £78.99. ISBN 1 84592 180 1. Tottel Publishing.

Matthews, Jan; Eastway, Nigel; Vallat, Richard–Corporation Tax Self-Assessment. Paperback: £78.95. ISBN 1 84592 035 X. Tottel Publishing.

Matthews, Paul; Malek, Hodge M.–Disclosure: 3rd Supplement. Paperback: £63.00. ISBN 0 421 87410 4. Sweet & Maxwell.

Matthews, Paul–Jervis on Coroners. Paperback: £49.00. ISBN 0 421 89480 6. Sweet & Maxwell.

Maughan, Caroline; Webb, Julian–Lawyering Skills and the Legal Process. Law in Context S. Paperback: £24.99. ISBN 0 521 61950 5. Cambridge University Press.

Mavroidis, Petros C.–Commentaries on the GATT/WTO Agreements: V. 1. General Agreement on Tariffs and Trade. Oxford Commentaries on International Law S. Hardback: £75.00. ISBN 0 19 927813 X. Oxford University Press.

Maxfield, T–Basics of Research Methods for Criminal Justice and Criminology. Paperback: £33.00. ISBN 0 534 61567 8. Wadsworth.

May, Christopher; Sell, Susan K.–Intellectual Property Rights: A Critical History. Hardback: £40.95. ISBN 1 58826 363 0. Lynne Rienner Publishers Inc, US.

May–White Book 2005. Paperback/CD-ROM: £393.13. ISBN 0 421 91240 5. Sweet & Maxwell.

May–White Service Book Volume 1 Civil Procedure. Hardback: £218.50. ISBN 0 421 91200 6. Sweet & Maxwell.

McAdams, Tony–Law, Business, and Society. Hardback: £96.99. ISBN 0 07 304810 0. Higher Education.

McAlhone, Christina; Stockdale, Michael–Evidence. Paperback: £6.50. ISBN 0 421 89130 0. Sweet & Maxwell.

McAlhone, Christina–Core Statutes on Evidence. Core Statutes S. Paperback: £10.00. ISBN 1 84641 014 2. Law Matters Publishing.

McCabe, Kimberly A.; Martin, Gregory M.; Schultz, David A.; DeJong, Christina–School Violence, the Media, and Criminal Justice Responses. Paperback: £11.60. ISBN 0 8204 6756 1. Peter Lang Publishing Inc, US.

McClean, J.D.–Morris: The Conflict of Laws. Paperback: £28.95. ISBN 0 421 89420 2. Sweet & Maxwell.

McConville, Mike; Mirsky, Chester L.–Jury Trials and Plea Bargaining: A True History. Hardback: £35.00. ISBN 1 84113 516 X. Hart Publishing.

McCord, James W.H.–Criminal Law and Procedure. Hardback: £52.00. ISBN 1 4018 6564 X. Delmar.

McCormack, Gerard–Registration of Company Charges. Paperback: £95.00. ISBN 0 85308 981 7. Jordans.

McCutcheon, Barry D.; Hallam, Murray–McCutcheon on Inheritance Tax. Hardback: £195.00. ISBN 0 421 85860 5. Sweet & Maxwell.

McDowell, Jacqui–Child Support Handbook. Paperback: £21.50. ISBN 1 901698 80 7. CPAG.

McFarlane, A.; Reardon, M.–Child Care and Adoption Law: A Practical Guide. Paperback: £40.00. ISBN 0 85308 972 8. Jordans.

McFayden, Norman–Offences Against Justice. Paperback: £40.00. ISBN 1 84592 052 X. Tottel Publishing.

McGee, Andrew–Mcgee: 1st Supplement: Limitation Periods. Paperback: £45.00. ISBN 0 421 87450 3. Sweet & Maxwell.

McGee, Andrew–Modern Law of Insurance. Hardback: £190.00. ISBN 0 406 97297 4. Butterworths Law.

McGhee, John–Snell's Equity: Supplement 1. Paperback: £50.00. ISBN 0 421 91670 2. Sweet & Maxwell.

McGiffen, Steven P.–European Union: A Critical Guide. Hardback: £14.99. ISBN 0 7453 2507 6. Paperback: £14.99. ISBN 0 7453 2506 8. Pluto Press Ltd.

McGourlay, Claire; Doak, Jonathon–Criminal Evidence in Context. Textbooks. Paperback: £23.00. ISBN 1 84641 004 5. Law Matters Publishing.

McGregor, Harvey–Mcgregor on Damages, 2nd Supplement. Paperback: £49.00. ISBN 0 421 90610 3. Sweet & Maxwell.

McGregor, Harvey–Mcgregor on Damages: Mainwork and Supplement. Hardback: £298.00. ISBN 0 421 86400 1. Sweet & Maxwell.

McGregor, Joan–Is It Rape?: On Acquaintance Rape and Taking Women's Consent Seriously. Live Questions in Ethics & Moral Philosophy S. Hardback: £55.00. ISBN 0 7546 5065 0. Paperback: £17.99. ISBN 0 7546 5066 9. Ashgate.

Mcgregor–Avizandum Statutes on Scots Law of Obligations. Paperback: £23.95. ISBN 1 904968 06 6. Avizandum Publishing Ltd.

McKendrick, Ewan–Contract Law: Text, Cases, and Materials. Paperback: £33.99. ISBN 0 19 927480 0. Oxford University Press.

McKendrick, Ewan–Contract Law. Palgrave Law Masters S. Paperback: £15.99. ISBN 1 4039 4869 0. Palgrave Macmillan.

McLean, Sheila A.M.–Genetics and Gene Therapy. The International Library of Medicine, Ethics & Law. Hardback: £120.00. ISBN 0 7546 2055 7. Ashgate.

McLean, Sheila A.M.–Medical Law. Hardback: £40.00. ISBN 1 85521 092 4. Ashgate.

McLean, Sheila–Assisted Dying. UCL S. Hardback: £49.00. ISBN 1 84472 055 1. Paperback: £25.00. ISBN 1 84472 054 3. UCL Press.

McLeod, Ian–Legal Method. Palgrave Law Masters S. Paperback: £14.99. ISBN 1 4039 4870 4. Palgrave Macmillan.

McLeod, Ian–Legal Theory. Palgrave Law Masters S. Paperback: £13.99. ISBN 1 4039 4871 2. Palgrave Macmillan.

McManus, J.J.; Thomson, Lindsay–Mental Health and Scots Law in Practice. Hardback: £60.00. ISBN 0 414 01475 8. W.Green & Son.

McMaster, Jodi–Interviewing and Investigating for Paralegals. Paperback: £41.99. ISBN 0 13 111891 9. Prentice Hall.

McQueen, Andrew–Saving the Family Home in Bankruptcy: A Bankruptcy Association Guide. Paperback: £14.95. ISBN 1 905069 03 0. Bankruptcy Association of Great Britain & Ireland.

McQueen, John–Bankruptcy Explained: The Bankruptcy Association's Practical Guide to UK Insolvency Laws. Paperback: £14.95. ISBN 1 905069 01 4. Bankruptcy Association of Great Britain & Ireland.

McTernan, Sean–Introduction to Media Law. Medialex Guidebook Series. Paperback: £25.00. ISBN 1 905394 00 4. MEDIALEX PUBLICATIONS.

McVicar, John–Libel: Linford Christie V. John McVicar. Hardback: £16.99. ISBN 1 903906 18 0. Artnik.

Mead, Larry; Sagar, David–CIMA Study Systems: Business Law. Looseleaf/ ring bound: £33.00. ISBN 0 7506 6707 9. CIMA (Chartered Institute of Management Accountant).

Meckled-Garcia, Saladin; Cali, Basak–Legalisation of Human Rights: Multidisciplinary Approaches. Hardback: £65.00. ISBN 0 415 36122 2. Paperback: £18.99. ISBN 0 415 36123 0. Routledge, an imprint of Taylor & Francis Books Ltd.

Medical Law. Paperback: £6.50. ISBN 0 421 89170 X. Sweet & Maxwell.

Meeson, Julie–Pocket Guide to the EU Directive: The Clinical Trial Directive 2001/20/EC. Hardback: £15.00. ISBN 0 9549345 1 2. Institute of Clinical Research.

Megarry; Wade–Megarry & Wade: the Law of Real Property. Hardback: £165.00. ISBN 0 421 84100 1. Sweet & Maxwell.

Mehigan, Simon; Saunders, John; Philips, Jeremy–Paterson's Licensing Acts 2006. Hardback: £234.00. ISBN 1 4057 0634 1. Butterworths Law.

Mehigan, Simon; Saunders, John; Phillips, Jeremy–Paterson's Licensing Acts 2005. Hardback: £225.00. ISBN 0 406 97987 1. Butterworths Law.

Meiners, Roger E.; Ringleb, Al H.–Legal Environment of Business. Hardback: £69.99. ISBN 0 324 31110 9. South Western College Publishing.

Mental Capacity: The New Law. Paperback: £40.00. ISBN 0 85308 976 0. Jordans.

Merkin, Robert–Arbitration Act. Hardback: £110.00. ISBN 1 84311 420 8. Informa Business Publishing.

Merrills, J.G.–International Dispute Settlement. Hardback: £65.00. ISBN 0 521 85250 1. Paperback: £33.00. ISBN 0 521 61782 0. Cambridge University Press.

Micklitz, Hans W.–Legal Politics and Court Activism in the European Union: Sunday Trading, Equal Treatment and Good Faith. Hardback: £60.00. ISBN 0 521 82516 4. Cambridge University Press.

Middleton, Kirsty–UK and EC Competition Documents. Blackstone's Statute Books. Paperback: £17.99. ISBN 0 19 928318 4. Paperback: £17.99. ISBN 0 19 928318 4. Oxford University Press.

Miles, George; Laidlaw, Pauline; Ollerenshaw, Zoe; Deneyer, Paulene; Smart, Elizabeth; Clout, Imogen; Firth, Clare; Cutts, Rachel–Foundations for the LPC. Blackstone Legal Practice Course Guide S. Paperback: £26.99. ISBN 0 19 928139 4. Oxford University Press.

Miller, Carey; Irvine, David–Corporeal Moveables in Scots Law. Hardback: £135.00. ISBN 0 414 01400 6. W.Green & Son.

Miller, William Ian–Eye for an Eye. Hardback: £16.99. ISBN 0 521 85680 9. Cambridge University Press.

Mills, Oliver–Biotechnological Inventions: Moral Restraints and Patent Law. Hardback: £55.00. ISBN 0 7546 2420 X. Avebury Technical.

Mills, Richard–Construction Adjudication. Case in Point S. Paperback: £24.95. ISBN 1 84219 235 3. RICS.

Mills, Stephen–Bills of Lading: A Guide to Good Practice. Paperback: £30.00. ISBN 0 9546537 1 8. North of England P&I Association.

Milman, David; Sealy, Len–Sealy and Milman's Annotated Guide to the Insolvency Legislation: Vol 2. Paperback: £60.00. ISBN 0 421 91620 6. Sweet & Maxwell.

Milman, David; Sealy, Len–Sealy and Milman: Vol 1: Annotated Guide to the Insolvency Legislation. Paperback: £95.00. ISBN 0 421 90470 4. Sweet & Maxwell.

Milman, David; Sealy, Len–Sealy and Milman: V. 1, 2: Annotated Guide to the Insolvency Legislation. Paperback: £68.00. ISBN 0 421 91740 7. Sweet & Maxwell.

Milman, David–Personal Insolvency Law, Regulation and Policy. Markets and the Law S. Hardback: £50.00. ISBN 0 7546 4302 6. Ashgate.

Milmo, Patrick; Rogers, W.V.H.; Parkes, Richard; Walker, Clive; Busuttil, Godwin–Gatley on Libel and Slander: 1st Supplement. Paperback: £49.00. ISBN 0 421 91270 7. Sweet & Maxwell.

Milner, Alan–Jersey Law Reports: Pt. 1. Paperback: £35.00. ISBN 1 902907 74 4. Law Reports International.

Mistelis, Loukas; Beale, Hugh; Marriott, Arthur; Lew, Julian D.M.; Davies, Paul; Cranston, Ross; Birks, Peter; Lowry, John–Dimensions in Commercial Law. Hardback: £60.00. ISBN 1 4057 1007 1. Butterworths Law.

Mitchell, Andrew–Challenges and Prospects for the WTO. Paperback: £85.00. ISBN 1 905017 04 9. Cameron May.

Mitchell, J.–Children Act Private Law Proceedings: A Handbook. Paperback: £40.00. ISBN 0 85308 997 3. Jordans.

Mitchell, Paul–Making of the Modern English Law of Defamation. Hardback: £40.00. ISBN 1 84113 304 3. Hart Publishing.

Moffat, Graham; Bean, Gerard; Dewar, John; Milner, Marina–Trusts Law: Text and Materials. Law in Context S. Paperback: £35.00. ISBN 0 521 67466 2. Cambridge University Press.

Moffatt, Jane–Employment Law. Law Society of Ireland Manuals S. Paperback: £39.99. ISBN 0 19 928022 3. Oxford University Press.

Montagu, Gerald; Weston, Mark–Legal Practice Companion. Companions. Paperback: £29.95. ISBN 1 84641 013 4. Law Matters Publishing.

Montgomery, Jonathan–Health Care Law. Paperback: £27.99. ISBN 0 19 927448 7. Oxford University Press.

Moore-Walsh, Kathleen–Make That Grade Irish Tort Law. Paperback: £14.99. ISBN 0 7171 4026 1. Gill & Macmillan.

Moore, Alan–Tax Magic. Hardback: £52.00. ISBN 1 905320 00 0. Alan Moore.

Moore, Matthew; Verry, John–Risk and Quality Management in Legal Practice. Paperback: £39.95. ISBN 1 85328 947 7. Law Society Publications.

Moore, Terence–Anthony and Berryman's Magistrates' Court Guide. Paperback: £54.00. ISBN 1 4057 0751 8. Butterworths Law.

Moore, Terry; Wilkinson, Tony–Youth Court Guide. Paperback: £52.00. ISBN 1 84592 138 0. Tottel Publishing.

Moore, Victor–A Practical Approach to Planning Law. Practical Approach S. Paperback: £29.95. ISBN 0 19 927279 4. Oxford University Press.

Moran, Alan; Luther, Peter–Core Statutes on Property Law. Core Statutes S. Paperback: £10.00. ISBN 1 84641 010 X. Law Matters Publishing.

Morgan, Richard; Burden, Kit–Morgan and Stedman on Computer Contracts. Book (details unknown): £186.36. ISBN 0 421 84200 8. Sweet & Maxwell.

Morley, Iain–Devil's Advocate. Paperback: £12.95. ISBN 0 421 91480 7. Sweet & Maxwell.

Morley, Nigel–Controlled Drugs in Primary Care: The Law, Probity and Good Practice. Paperback: £20.00. ISBN 0 9549560 0 1. Surelines Pharmaceutical Services Ltd.

Morrish, Peter; McLean, Ian; Katkhuda, Sam–Crown Court Index. Hardback: £95.00. ISBN 0 421 92420 9. Sweet & Maxwell.

Morrish, Peter; McLean, Ian–Crown Court Index. Hardback: £85.00. ISBN 0 421 88590 4. Sweet & Maxwell.

Morse, Geoffrey; Marshall, Enid A.; Morris, Richard; Crabb, Leticia–Charlesworth's Company Law. Paperback: £24.95. ISBN 0 421 88790 7. Sweet & Maxwell.

Moss, Gabriel; Fletcher, Ian F.; Snowden, Richard–Law of Receivers and Administrators of Companies. Hardback: £225.00. ISBN 0 421 91030 5. Sweet & Maxwell.

Mouawad, Joyce–Succession: The Law of Wills and Estates. Paperback: £15.95. ISBN 1 85836 506 6. Old Bailey Press.

Mowbray, John; Tucker, Lynton; Le Poidevin, Nicholas; Simpson, Edwin–Lewin on Trusts. Hardback: £285.00. ISBN 0 421 87420 1. Sweet & Maxwell.

Mullan, David–Administrative Law. Paperback: £25.00. ISBN 1 55221 009 X. The Federation Press.

Munday, R.J.C.–Evidence. Paperback: £16.99. ISBN 0 19 928510 1. Oxford University Press.

Munro, Jane; Convery, Jane–Constitutional Lawbasics. Paperback: £12.50. ISBN 0 414 01586 X. W. Green & Son.

Murdoch, Jim–Guide to Human Rights in Scotland. Paperback: £70.00. ISBN 1 84592 074 0. Tottel Publishing.

Murphy, James Bernard–Philosophy of Positive Law: Foundations of Jurisprudence. Hardback: £25.00. ISBN 0 300 10788 9. Yale University Press.

Murphy, Mark–Natural Law in Jurisprudence and Politics. Hardback: £45.00. ISBN 0 521 85930 1. Cambridge University Press.

Murphy, Peter; Stockdale, Eric–Blackstone's Criminal Practice. CD-ROM: £155.00. ISBN 0 19 928770 8. Oxford University Press.

Murphy, Peter; Stockdale, Eric–Blackstone's Criminal Practice. Hardback: £155.00. ISBN 0 19 928769 4. Hardback: £155.00. ISBN 0 19 928769 4. Oxford University Press.

Murphy, Peter–Murphy on Evidence. Paperback: £28.99. ISBN 0 19 928113 0. Oxford University Press.

Musgrove, Nigel–Licensing Handbook: A Guide to Obtaining a Licence and Running Licensed Premises. Fitzwarren Handbooks. Paperback: £11.95. ISBN 0 9545934 1 3. Fitzwarren Publishing.

Musker, David; Wilson, Nicholas; Wiseman, Imogen–ITMA/CIPA Design. Looseleaf/ring bound: £295.00. ISBN 0 421 87770 7. Sweet & Maxwell.

Mynors, Charles–Listed Buildings, Conservation Areas and Monuments. Hardback: £125.00. ISBN 0 421 75830 9. Sweet & Maxwell.

Nabulsi, Karma–Traditions of War: Occupation, Resistance, and the Law. Paperback: £18.99. ISBN 0 19 927947 0. Oxford University Press.

Narlikar, Amrita–World Trade Organization: A Very Short Introduction. Very Short Introduction S. Paperback: £6.99. ISBN 0 19 280608 4. Paperback: £6.99. ISBN 0 19 280608 4. Oxford University Press.

Natarajan, Mangai–Women Police. International Library of Criminology, Criminal Justice & Penology 2nd Series. Hardback: £125.00. ISBN 0 7546 2445 5. Ashgate.

Needham–Property Rights and Land Use Planning. Hardback: £75.00. ISBN 0 415 34373 9. Routledge, an imprint of Taylor & Francis Books Ltd. Paperback (B format): £25.00. ISBN 0 415 34374 7. Routledge, an imprint of Taylor & Francis Books Ltd.

Neier, Aryeh–Taking Liberties: Four Decades in the Struggle for Rights. Paperback: £14.99. ISBN 1 58648 291 2. PublicAffairs.

Nelson-Jones, Rodney–Butterworths Personal Injury Damages Statistics. Paperback: £35.00. ISBN 1 4057 1012 8. Butterworths Law.

Nelson, Douglas R.; Vandenbussche, Hylke–WTO and Anti-Dumping. Global Perspectives on the Global Trading System and the WTO S. Hardback: £295.00. ISBN 1 84376 602 7. Edward Elgar.

Nelson, Vincent; Robb, Adam–Law of Human Rights and Media. Hardback: £150.00. ISBN 0 421 78020 7. Sweet & Maxwell.

Nettlefold, Julian Henry–Trial by Deceit. Paperback: £15.00. ISBN 0 9526473 1 1. Family Practice Press.

Neustein, Amy; Lesher, Michael–From Madness to Mutiny: Why Mothers Are Running from the Family Courts and What Can Be Done About It. Hardback: £17.50. ISBN 1 58465 462 7. Northeastern University Press.

Newmark, Chris–Commercial Mediation: Mediators on Mediation. Hardback: £95.00. ISBN 0 406 97953 7. Butterworths Law.

Newmark, Chris–Mediators on Mediation: Leading Mediator Perspectives on the Practice of Commercial Mediation. Paperback: £95.00. ISBN 1 84592 081 3. Tottel Publishing.

Newton–Bankruptcy and Insolvency Taxation. Hardback: £97.50. ISBN 0 471 22808 7. John Wiley & Sons Inc.

Nicholson, Dawn–Tottel's Tax Savers Guide. Paperback: £9.95. ISBN 1 84592 219 0. Tottel Publishing.

Nielsen, Ruth; Treumer, Steen–New EU Public Procurement Directives. Paperback: £16.00. ISBN 87 574 1244 8. DJOF Publishing.

Nightingale, Paul–Lawyers Costs and Fees: Conveyancing Fees and Duties. Paperback: £17.95. ISBN 1 84592 070 8. Tottel Publishing.

Nock, Reg–Understanding Stamp Duty Land Tax. Paperback: £44.95. ISBN 1 85328 982 5. Law Society Publications.

Nolte, Georg–European and US Constitutionalism. Hardback: £50.00. ISBN 0 521 85401 6. Cambridge University Press.

Norrie, Kenneth McK.–Children's Hearings in Scotland. Paperback: £45.00. ISBN 0 414 01587 8. W. Green & Son.

O'Boyle, M.; Warbrick, Colin; Bates, Ed; Harris, D.J.–Law of the European Convention on Human Rights. Paperback: £28.95. ISBN 0 406 90594 0. LexisNexis UK.

O'Brien, David M.–Constitutional Law and Politics: V. 1. Paperback: £33.20. ISBN 0 393 92565 X. W.W. Norton & Company Ltd.

O'Brien, David M.–Constitutional Law and Politics: V. 2. Paperback: £34.60. ISBN 0 393 92566 8. W.W. Norton & Company Ltd.

O'Carroll, Maurice–Planning Law Enforcement. Paperback: £40.00. ISBN 1 84592 114 3. Tottel Publishing.

O'Connor, Bernard–Agriculture in WTO Law. Hardback: £85.00. ISBN 1 905017 12 X. Cameron May.

O'Day, Alan–Cyberterrorism. The International Library of Essays on Terrorism. Hardback: £100.00. ISBN 0 7546 2426 9. Ashgate.

O'Day, Alan–War on Terrorism. The International Library of Essays on Terrorism. Hardback: £100.00. ISBN 0 7546 2424 2. Ashgate.

O'Donnell, David–Professional Responsibility. Paperback: £40.00. ISBN 1 84592 054 6. Tottel Publishing.

O'Donoghue, Robert; Padilla, Jorge Atilano–Law and Economics of Article 82 EC. Hardback: £50.00. ISBN 1 84113 502 X. Hart Publishing.

O'Donovan, James–Lender Liability: English Edition. Hardback: £185.00. ISBN 0 421 88580 7. Sweet & Maxwell.

O'Grady, Eileen; Cave, R–Practitioners Tax Handbook: Trusts, Wills, Probate and Tax Planning. Paperback: £75.00. ISBN 0 421 89400 8. Sweet & Maxwell.

O'Hare, John; Browne, Kevin–O'Hare and Browne: Civil Litigation (Formerly O'Hare and Hill). Paperback: £59.00. ISBN 0 421 90690 1. Sweet & Maxwell.

O'Mara, John–Accounting for Partnerships: Law and Practice. Paperback: £63.33. ISBN 1 84592 144 5. Tottel Publishing.

O'Rourke, Raymond–European Food Law. Paperback: £95.00. ISBN 0 421 90290 6. Sweet & Maxwell.

Oditah, Fidelis–Legal Aspects of Receivables Financing. Hardback: £135.00. ISBN 0 421 57540 9. Sweet & Maxwell.

Ogletree, Charles J.–All Deliberate Speed: Reflections on the First Half-Century of Brown V. Board of Education. Paperback: £11.25. ISBN 0 393 32686 1. W W Norton & Co Ltd.

Ogowewo, Tunde–Jurisprudence of the Takeover Panel. Hardback: £40.00. ISBN 1 901362 77 9. Hart Publishing.

Oldham, Edwin W.–Freedom To Invent. Hardback: £23.00. ISBN 1 4134 5572 7. Paperback: £14.00. ISBN 1 4134 5571 9. Xlibris Corporation.

Oldham, Mika–Statutes on Family Law. Paperback: £16.99. ISBN 0 19 928321 4. Paperback: £16.99. ISBN 0 19 928321 4. Oxford University Press.

Orange Tax Handbook. Paperback: £75.00. ISBN 1 4057 0740 2. Paperback: £99.95. ISBN 1 4057 0931 6. Tolley Publishing.

Orebech, Peter; Bosselman, Fred; Bjarup, Jes; Callies, David; Chanock, Martin; Petersen, Hanne–Role of Customary Law in Sustainable Development. Cambridge Studies in Law & Society. Hardback: £60.00. ISBN 0 521 85925 5. Cambridge University Press.

Orlik, Deborah–Ethics: Top Ten Rules for Paralegals. Paperback: £19.99. ISBN 0 13 119321 X. Prentice Hall.

Ormerod, David–Criminal Law. Paperback: £28.95. ISBN 0 406 97730 5. LexisNexis UK.

Ormerod, David–Smith and Hogan Criminal Law: Cases and Materials. Paperback: £26.99. ISBN 0 406 97729 1. LexisNexis UK.

Osborne, Clarke–Practical Guide To E-commerce and Internet Law. Paperback: £39.95. ISBN 1 86072 310 1. ICSA Publishing Ltd (Institute of Chartered Secretaries & Administrators).

Osborne, Craig–Civil Litigation. Blackstone Legal Practice Course Guide S. Paperback: £26.99. ISBN 0 19 928140 8. Oxford University Press.

Osborough, W.N.; Brand, Paul; Costello, Kevin–Adventures of the Law. Hardback: £45.00. ISBN 1 85182 936 9. Four Courts Press.

Ottinger, Richard; Bradbrook, Adrian; Lyster, Rosemary–IUCN Academy of Environmental Law Research Studies. Hardback: £100.00. ISBN 0 521 84594 7. Cambridge University Press.

Owen, Tim; Tomlinson, Hugh; Knowles, Julian; Ryder, Matthew; Macdonald, Alison; Laddie, James; Bailin, Alex–Blackstone's Guide to the Serious Organised Crime and Police Act. Blackstone's Guide S. Paperback: £29.95. ISBN 0 19 928906 9. Paperback: £29.95. ISBN 0 19 928906 9. Oxford University Press.

Padfield, Nicola–Archbold: Magistrates' Courts Criminal Practice 2006. Hardback: £175.00. ISBN 0 421 90570 0. Sweet & Maxwell.

Paisley, Roderick–Trusts. Greens Practice Library. Hardback: £80.00. ISBN 0 414 01476 6. W. Green & Son.

Palladino, Joseph J.; Schmalleger, Frank–Criminal Law Today: An Introduction with Capstone Cases. Hardback: £53.99. ISBN 0 13 170287 4. Prentice Hall.

Palmer, Ann–Realizing the College Dream with Autism or Asperger Syndrome: A Parent's Guide to Student Success. Paperback: £13.99. ISBN 1 84310 801 1. Jessica Kingsley Publishers.

Palmer, Camilla; Wade, Joanna; Wood, Katie–Maternity and Parental Rights: A Parent's Guide to Rights At Work. Paperback: £27.00. ISBN 1 903307 40 6. The Legal Action Group.

Palmer, Ellie–Judicial Review, Socio-economic Rights and the Human Rights Act. Hardback: £30.00. ISBN 1 84113 372 8. Hart Publishing.

Palmer, Michael; Roberts, Simon–Dispute Processes: ADR and the Primary Forms of Decision Making. Law in Context S. Paperback: £19.99. ISBN 0 521 67601 0. Cambridge University Press.

Paper C5 Business Law. Paperback: £13.00. ISBN 1 84390 464 0. Financial Training Co Ltd.

Parisi, Francesco; Rowley, Charles K.–Origins of Law and Economics: Essays by the Founding Fathers. Locke Institute S. Hardback: £95.00. ISBN 1 84064 963 1. Edward Elgar.

Parkay, Forrest W.–Political and Legal Foundations for Becoming a Teacher. Paperback: £20.99. ISBN 0 205 42424 4. Allyn & Bacon.

Parker, Nigel–Music Business Infrastructure, Practice and Law. Paperback: £52.00. ISBN 0 421 89930 1. Sweet & Maxwell.

Parkinson, Michael G.; Parkinson, L.Marie–Law for Advertising, Broadcasting, Journalism, and Public Relations: A Comprehensive Text for Students and Practitioners. Paperback: £47.50. ISBN 0 8058 4975 0. Lawrence Erlbaum Associates, Inc.

Pasa, Barbara; Benacchio, Gian Antonio–Harmonization Of Civil And Commercial Law In Europe. Hardback: £28.95. ISBN 963 7326 35 9. Central European University Press.

Paterson, Alex K.–My Life At the Bar and Beyond. Hardback: £29.95. ISBN 0 7735 2988 8. McGill-Queen's University Press.

Paterson, A.A.; Ritchie, Bruce–Solicitors Practice, Conduct and Discipline. Paperback: £40.00. ISBN 0 414 01439 1.W.Green & Son.

Patrick, Hilary–Mental Health. Paperback: £45.00. ISBN 1 84592 062 7. Tottel Publishing.

Paul, Colin; Montagu, Gerald–Banking and Capital Markets Companion. Legal Practice Companions. Paperback: £29.95. ISBN 1 84641 015 0. Law Matters Publishing.

Paul, Ellen Frankel; Miller, Fred D.; Paul, Jeffrey–Personal Identity: V. 22. Social Philosophy & Policy S., No. 22. Paperback: £17.99. ISBN 0 521 61767 7. Cambridge University Press.

Pavlich, George–Governing Paradoxes of Restorative Justice. Criminology S. Paperback: £25.00. ISBN 1 904385 19 2.The Glasshouse Press.

Pearl, David–Care Standards Legislation Handbook. Paperback: £35.00. ISBN 0 85308 964 7. Jordans.

Peay, Jill–Seminal Issues in Mental Health Law. International Library Essays in Law & Legal Theory (Second Series). Hardback: £120.00. ISBN 0 7546 2419 6. Ashgate.

Pedley, Paul–Digital Copyright for Information Professionals: Single User Read Only. E-book: £24.95. ISBN 1 85604 559 5. Facet Publishing.

Pedley, Paul–Digital Copyright: Single User with Added Once Only Print Option. E-book: £34.95. ISBN 1 85604 573 0. E-book: £34.95. ISBN 1 85604 573 0. Facet Publishing.

Peeters, Carine; Potterie, Bruno Van Pottelsberghe De La–Economic and Management Perspectives on Intellectual Property Rights. Applied Econometrics Association S. Hardback: £55.00. ISBN 1 4039 4963 8. Palgrave Macmillan.

Pelton, Leroy H.–Frames of Justice: Implications for Social Policy. Hardback: £35.50. ISBN 0 7658 0296 1. Transaction Publishers.

Pember, Don R.–Mass Media Law. Paperback: £36.99. ISBN 0 07 110721 5. Higher Education.

Personal Injury Litigation-Issue 70. Looseleaf/ring bound: £162.00. ISBN 0 406 96373 8. Butterworths Law.

Perun, Halyna N.; Orr, Michael; Dimitriadis, Fannie–Guide to the Personal Health Information Protection Act 2004: A Practical Guide for Health Care Providers. Paperback: £32.00. ISBN 1 55221 100 2. Irwin Law Inc.

Pervasive and Core Topics. Paperback: £25.95. ISBN 0 905835 87 5. The College of Law.

Pestieau, Pierre–Welfare State in the European Union: Economic and Social Perspectives. Hardback: £45.00. ISBN 0 19 926101 6. Paperback: £20.00. ISBN 0 19 926102 4. Oxford University Press.

Peters, Julie–Straightforward Guide to Probate and the Law. Paperback: £8.99. ISBN 1 903909 70 8. Straightforward Publishing.

Pettit, Philip H.–Equity and the Law of Trusts. Paperback: £31.99. ISBN 0 19 928534 9. Paperback: £31.99. ISBN 0 19 928534 9. Oxford University Press.

Phelan, Margaret; Gillespie, James–Immigration Law Handbook. Paperback: £46.95. ISBN 0 19 928473 3. Oxford University Press.

Philips, Jeremy; Mehigan, Simon; Saunders, John–Patersons Licensing Acts. Paperback: £39.00. ISBN 1 4057 0799 2. Butterworths Law.

Phillips, Gillian; Scott, Karen–Employment Law. Paperback: £24.95. ISBN 0 905835 79 4. Paperback: £25.95. ISBN 1 905391 05 6. The College of Law.

Phillips, Jeremy; Simon, Ilanah–Trade Mark Use. Hardback: £65.00. ISBN 0 19 928033 9. Oxford University Press.

Phillips, Jeremy–Butterworths Intellectual Property Law Handbook. Paperback: £105.00. ISBN 1 4057 0898 0. Butterworths Law.

Phillips, Mark; Davis, Glen; Crystal, Michael–Butterworths Insolvency Law Handbook. Paperback: £74.00. ISBN 1 4057 0773 9. Butterworths Law.

Picarda, Hubert–Law and Practice Relating to Charities. Hardback: £245.00. ISBN 1 4057 0896 4. Butterworths Law.

Pickavance, Keith–Delay and Disruption in Construction Contracts. Hardback: £230.00. ISBN 1 84311 426 7. Informa Business Publishing.

Pierceson, Jason–Courts, Liberalism, and Rights. Hardback: £52.00. ISBN 1 59213 400 9. Temple University Press.

Piggot Semple, Mike–Conveyancing. Law in a Box S. CD-ROM: £19.95. ISBN 1 904783 84 8. Semple Piggot Rochez (Legal Education Ltd).

Piggot Semple, Mike–Immigration Law: CPD in a Box. CPD in a Box S. CD-ROM: £29.50. ISBN 1 904783 99 6. Semple Piggot Rochez (Legal Education Ltd).

Piggot Semple, Mike–UK Competition Law. Law in a Box S. CD-ROM: £19.95. ISBN 1 904783 83 X. Semple Piggot Rochez (Legal Education Ltd).

Piggot, Mike Semple–Advocacy. Law in a Box S., No. 15. CD-ROM: £19.95. ISBN 1 904783 71 6. Semple Piggot Rochez (Legal Education Ltd).

Piggot, Mike Semple–Civil Litigation. Law in a Box S., No. 13. CD-ROM: £19.95. ISBN 1 904783 69 4. Semple Piggot Rochez (Legal Education Ltd).

Piggot, Mike Semple–Commercial Law. Law in a Box S., No. 17. CD-ROM: £19.95. ISBN 1 904783 73 2. Semple Piggot Rochez (Legal Education Ltd).

Piggot, Mike Semple–Company Law. Law in a Box S., No. 12. CD-ROM: £19.95. ISBN 1 904783 68 6. Semple Piggot Rochez (Legal Education Ltd).

Piggot, Mike Semple–Constitutional and Administrative Law. Law in a Box S., No. 5. CD-ROM: £19.95. ISBN 1 904783 61 9. Semple Piggot Rochez (Legal Education Ltd).

Piggot, Mike Semple–Contract Law. Law in a Box S., No. 1. CD-ROM: £19.95. ISBN 1 904783 57 0. Semple Piggot Rochez (Legal Education Ltd).

Piggot, Mike Semple–Criminal Law. Law in a Box S., No. 4. CD-ROM: £19.95. ISBN 1 904783 60 0. Semple Piggot Rochez (Legal Education Ltd).

Piggot, Mike Semple–Criminal Litigation. Law in a Box S., No. 14. CD-ROM: £19.95. ISBN 1 904783 70 8. Semple Piggot Rochez (Legal Education Ltd).

Piggot, Mike Semple–Employment Law. Law in a Box S., No. 10. CD-ROM: £19.95. ISBN 1 904783 66 X. Semple Piggot Rochez (Legal Education Ltd).

Piggot, Mike Semple–English Legal System. Law in a Box S., No. 3. CD-ROM: £23.44. ISBN 1 904783 59 7. Semple Piggot Rochez (Legal Education Ltd).

Piggot, Mike Semple–Equity and Trusts. Law in a Box S., No. 6. CD-ROM: £19.95. ISBN 1 904783 62 7. CD-ROM: £19.95. ISBN 1 904783 62 7. Semple Piggot Rochez (Legal Education Ltd).

Piggot, Mike Semple–European Union Law. Law in a Box S., No. 9. CD-ROM: £19.95. ISBN 1 904783 65 1. Semple Piggot Rochez (Legal Education Ltd).

Piggot, Mike Semple–Evidence. Law in a Box S., No. 8. CD-ROM: £19.95. ISBN 1 904783 64 3. Semple Piggot Rochez (Legal Education Ltd).

Piggot, Mike Semple–Family Law. Law in a Box S., No. 16. CD-ROM: £19.95. ISBN 1 904783 72 4. Semple Piggot Rochez (Legal Education Ltd).

Piggot, Mike Semple–Intellectual Property Law. Law in a Box S., No. 11. CD-ROM: £19.95. ISBN 1 904783 67 8. Semple Piggot Rochez (Legal Education Ltd).

Piggot, Mike Semple–Land Law. Law in a Box S., No. 7. CD-ROM: £19.95. ISBN 1 904783 63 5. Semple Piggot Rochez (Legal Education Ltd).

Piggot, Mike Semple–Public and Administrative. Q&A in a Box S., No. 6. CD-ROM: £12.00. ISBN 1 904783 80 5. Semple Piggot Rochez (Legal Education Ltd).

Piggot, Mike Semple–Tort Law. Law in a Box S., No. 2. CD-ROM: £19.95. ISBN 1 904783 58 9. Semple Piggot Rochez (Legal Education Ltd).

Piggot, Mike Semple–Wills and Succession. Law in a Box S., No. 18. CD-ROM: £19.95. ISBN 1 904783 74 0. Semple Piggot Rochez (Legal Education Ltd).

Pinfield, David–Blackstone's Police Investigators' Mock Examination Paper. Paperback: £14.99. ISBN 0 19 928832 1. Oxford University Press.

Pinfold, Louise; Walton, Kevin; Smailes, David–Tolley's Income Tax Workbook. Paperback: £27.95. ISBN 0 7545 2885 5. Tolley Publishing.

Pinfold, Louise; Walton, Kevin; Smailes, David–Tolley's Income Tax: Budget Edition and Main Annual. Paperback: £96.95. ISBN 0 7545 2863 4. Tolley Publishing.

Pinfold, Louise; Walton, Kevin; Smailes, David–Tolley's Income Tax: Main Annual. Paperback: £85.95. ISBN 0 7545 2864 2. Tolley Publishing.

Planning for Town Centres: Planning Policy Statement Office of the Deputy Prime Minister 6. Paperback: £12.00. ISBN 0 11 753945 7. The Stationery Office Books.

Plowden, Philip–Criminal Litigation in Practice. Paperback: £25.99. ISBN 1 873298 82 X. Northumbria Law Press.

Plumtree, Alexandra–Child Care Law: Scotland-A Summary of the Law in Scotland. Paperback: £6.95. ISBN 1 903699 74 6. British Association for Adoption & Fostering.

Plumtree, Alexandra–Getting It Right: Social Work Court Reports in Child Care Cases in Scotland. Paperback: £5.50. ISBN 1 903699 90 8. British Association for Adoption & Fostering.

Pocket Guide to Legal Writing. Paperback: £10.99. ISBN 1 4018 6597 6. Delmar.

Pollard, Dave–Guide to the Pensions Act 2004. Paperback: £44.95. ISBN 0 7545 2730 1. Tolley Publishing.

Poole, Jill–Casebook on Contract Law. Paperback: £25.99. ISBN 0 19 927550 5. Paperback: £25.99. ISBN 0 19 927550 5. Oxford University Press.

Poole, Jill–Damages for Breach of Contract. Hardback: £146.00. ISBN 0 421 62640 2. Sweet & Maxwell.

Poore, Martin; Jenkins, Martin–Blackstone's Guide to the Pensions Act 2004. Paperback: £39.95. ISBN 0 19 928190 4. Oxford University Press.

Posner, Richard A.–Law Pragmatism and Democracy. Paperback: £10.99. ISBN 81 7534 458 X. Universal Law Publishing Co Ltd.

Posner, Richard A.–Law, Pragmatism and Democracy. Paperback: £11.95. ISBN 0 674 01849 4. Harvard University Press.

Potts, Julian–VAT in Property and Construction. Case in Point S. Paperback: £19.95. ISBN 1 84219 229 9. RICS.

Poudret, Jean Francois; Besson, Sebastien–Comparative Law of International Arbitration. Hardback: £185.00. ISBN 0 421 93210 4. Sweet & Maxwell.

Poulter, Mark; Holah, Allan–Gyngell and Poulter: A User's Guide to Trademarks. Paperback: £65.00. ISBN 1 84592 156 9. Tottel Publishing.

Powell, John; Stewart, Roger; Jackson–Jackson and Powell on Professional Negligence, 4th Supplement. Paperback: £49.00. ISBN 0 421 91460 2. Sweet & Maxwell.

Powell, Vincent–Legal Companion. A Think Book S. Hardback: £9.99. ISBN 1 86105 838 1. Robson Books.

Pozgar–Legal and Ethical Issues for Health P. Paperback: £31.99. ISBN 0 7637 2633 8. Jones and Bartlett Publishers International.

Practical Guide to Family Proceedings. Paperback: £45.00. ISBN 0 85308 978 7. Family Law.

Practitioner's Guide to Takeovers and Mergers in the European Union. Hardback: £130.00. ISBN 1 905121 06 7. City and Financial Publishing.

Prashad, B.K.–Encyclopaedic Survey of the Handicapped. Hardback: £125.00. ISBN 81 261 1967 5. Anmol Publications Pvt Ltd.

Price, Gail–Housing Law and Practice. Paperback: £25.95. ISBN 1 905391 07 2. The College of Law.

Prime Cost Building Contract. Paperback: £34.95. ISBN 0 418 82920 9. Sweet & Maxwell.

Principles of European Tort Law: Text and Commentary. Paperback: £23.00. ISBN 3 211 23084 X. Springer-Verlag Vienna.

Principles of Transnational Civil Procedure. Hardback: £30.00. ISBN 0 521 85501 2. Cambridge University Press.

Property Transactions: Planning and Environment. Paperback: £79.00. ISBN 0 421 91760 1. Sweet & Maxwell.

Provost, Rene–International Human Rights and Humanitarian Law. Cambridge Studies in International & Comparative Law, No. 22. Paperback: £24.99. ISBN 0 521 01928 1. Cambridge University Press.

Psychology and Law of Criminal Justice Processes. Hardback: £71.99. ISBN 1 59454 312 7. Nova Science Publishers, Inc.

Putman, William–Legal Research. Paperback: £26.99. ISBN 1 4018 7958 6. Delmar.

Que Development–Police Officer Exam Practice Questions. Exam Cram 2 S. Paperback/CD-ROM: £13.99. ISBN 0 7897 3273 4. Que.

Quinn, A.P.; Osborough, W.N.–Wigs and Guns: Irish Barristers and the Great War. Irish Legal History Society Series. Hardback: £40.00. ISBN 1 85182 935 0. Four Courts Press.

Quinn, Frances; Elliott, Catherine–Contract Law. Paperback: £19.99. ISBN 1 4058 0710 5. Longman.

Quinn, Frances; Elliott, Catherine–Criminal Law. Paperback: £21.99. ISBN 1 4058 3528 1. Longman.

Quinn, Frances; Elliott, Catherine–Tort Law. Paperback: £19.99. ISBN 1 4058 0711 3. Longman.

Quinn, Gerard; Flynn, Leo–EU Charter on Fundamental Rights. Hardback: £40.00. ISBN 0 19 924540 1. Oxford University Press.

Raby, Paul–Business Law in Practice. ICSA Diploma in Business Practice S. Hardback: £26.00. ISBN 1 86072 276 8. ICSA Publishing Ltd (Institute of Chartered Secretaries & Administrators).

Radcliffe, Jonathan–Patents World Law and Practice. Looseleaf/ring bound: £350.00. ISBN 0 421 78900 X. Sweet & Maxwell.

Radevsky, Anthony; Greenish, Damian–Hague on Leasehold Enfranchisement: 1st Supplement. Paperback: £48.00. ISBN 0 421 90680 4. Sweet & Maxwell.

Rajak, Harry–Company Liquidations. Hardback: £129.00. ISBN 0 421 92320 2. Sweet & Maxwell.

Rajamani, Lavanya–Differential Treatment in International Environmental Law. Oxford Monographs in International Law. Hardback: £60.00. ISBN 0 19 928070 3. Oxford University Press.

Ramage, Sally–Fraud and the Serious Fraud Office: Fraud Law: Book Two. Paperback: £13.90. ISBN 0 595 36121 8. iUniverse.com.

Ramjohn, Mohammed–Unlocking Trusts. Paperback: £18.99. ISBN 0 340 88694 3. Hodder Arnold H&S.

Ramraj, Victor V.; Hor, Michael; Roach, Kent–Global Anti-Terrorism Law and Policy. Hardback: £80.00. ISBN 0 521 85125 4. Cambridge University Press.

Ramsay, Iain D.C.–Consumer Law and Policy: Text and Materials on Regulating Consumer Markets. Paperback: £25.00. ISBN 1 84113 505 4. Hart Publishing.

Ramsey; Bakken–Public Policy and Crim Just. Book (details unknown): £13.00. ISBN 0 495 00804 4. Wadsworth.

Randall, Geoffrey–Housing Rights Guide. Paperback: £16.50. ISBN 1 903595 43 6. Shelter.

Rao, Palle Krishna–WTO: Text and Cases. Paperback: £17.50. ISBN 81 7446 430 1. Excel Books.

Ray, Ralph; Hitchmough, Andrew; Wilson, Elizabeth–Tottel's Practical Inheritance Tax Planning. Paperback: £75.95. ISBN 1 84592 072 4. Tottel Publishing.

Rayson, Jane; Mallender, Paul–Civil Partnership Act 2004: A Practical Guide. Paperback: £55.00. ISBN 0 521 61792 8. Cambridge University Press.

Reamer, Frederic G.–Heinous Crime: Cases, Causes and Consequences. Hardback: £42.00. ISBN 0 231 13188 7. Paperback: £16.00. ISBN 0 231 13189 5. Columbia University Press.

Reay, Rosamund–Evidence. Paperback: £15.95. ISBN 1 85836 599 6. Old Bailey Press.

Redgrave's Health and Safety Second Supplement. Paperback: £40.00. ISBN 0 406 97985 5. Butterworths Law.

Redgrave's Health and Safety: Third Supplement. Paperback: £44.00. ISBN 1 4057 0752 6. Butterworths Law.

Redman, John E.–Law of Landlord and Tenant: Issue 48. Looseleaf/ring bound: £145.00. ISBN 0 406 97248 6. Butterworths Law.

Reed, Chris–Internet Law: Text and Materials. Paperback: £19.99. ISBN 81 7534 474 1. Universal Law Publishing Co Ltd.

Reeves, Anthony–Give Me Your Money: A Straightforward Guide to Debt Collection. Paperback: £9.99. ISBN 1 903909 63 5. Straightforward Publishing.

Reichel, Philip–Handbook of Transnational Crime and Justice. Hardback: £29.99. ISBN 1 4129 2756 0. Sage Publications Ltd.

Reid, Elspeth; Miller, David L. Carey–Mixed Legal System in Transition: T. B. Smith and the Progress of Scots Law. Edinburgh Studies in Law S. Hardback: £45.00. ISBN 0 7486 2335 3. Edinburgh University Press.

Reid, Madeleine–Equality Law in Ireland. Paperback: £93.33. ISBN 1 84592 065 1. Tottel Publishing.

Reiff, Mark R.–Theory of Enforceability: Punishment, Compensation, and Law. Cambridge Studies in Philosophy & Law. Hardback: £45.00. ISBN 0 521 84669 2. Cambridge University Press.

Rennie, Robert–Land Tenure and Tenements Legislation. Paperback: £36.00. ISBN 0 414 01613 0. W. Green & Son.

Resolution Procedure Committee–Precedents for Separation and Pre-marital Agreements. Paperback: £66.00. ISBN 0 9526809 3 9. Solicitors Family Law Association.

Revenue Law, Principles and Practice. Paperback: £62.95. ISBN 1 84592 196 8. Tottel Publishing.

Reynolds, Amy L.; Barnett, Brooke–Communication and Law: Multidisciplinary Approaches to Research. Hardback: £73.50. ISBN 0 8058 4942 4. Lawrence Erlbaum Associates, Inc.

Reynolds, Francis M.B.–Bowstead and Reynolds on Agency. Hardback: £255.00. ISBN 0 421 85800 1. Sweet & Maxwell.

Reynolds, Kirk; Clark, Wayne–Renewal of Business Tenancies. Hardback: £274.00. ISBN 0 421 82980 X. Sweet & Maxwell.

Rhode, Deborah L.–Public Service and the Professions: Pro Bono in Principle and in Practice. Stanford Law & Politics. Hardback: £31.50. ISBN 0 8047 5106 4. Paperback: £12.95. ISBN 0 8047 5107 2. Stanford University Press.

Ribeiro, Robert–Commercial Contracts: Drafting Techniques and Precedents. Thorogood Professional Insights. Paperback: £169.00. ISBN 1 85418 271 4. Thorogood.

Ribeiro, Robert–Commercial Litigation: Damages and Other Remedies for Commercial Contract. Thorogood Professional Insights S. Hardback: £129.00. ISBN 1 85418 397 4. Thorogood.

Richards, Paul; Jefferson, Michael; Cooke, John; Stein, Stuart–Law of Contract: WITH Criminal Law (7th Revised Edition) AND Law of Tort (7th Revised Edition) AND Law on the Web, a Guide for Students and Practitioners. Paperback: £68.99. ISBN 1 4058 3642 3. Longman.

Richards, Paul–Law of Contract: AND Contract Law Generic Pin Card. Paperback/Internet resource: £28.99. ISBN 1 4058 1808 5. Longman.

Richards, Paul–Law of Contract: AND Onekey Blackboard Access Card. Foundation Studies in Law S. Paperback/Internet resource: £30.99. ISBN 1 4058 3209 6. Longman.

Richards, Paul–Law of Contract: AND Onekey Coursecompass Access Card. Paperback/Internet resource: £30.99. ISBN 1 4058 3210 X. Longman.

Richards, Paul–Law of Contract. Foundation Studies in Law S. Paperback: £27.99. ISBN 1 4058 1221 4. Longman.

Richardson, James; Thomas, David A–Archbold: Academic International CD: Criminal Pleading, Evidence and Practice. CD-ROM: £682.03. ISBN 0 421 88370 7. Sweet & Maxwell.

Richardson, James; Thomas, David A–Archbold: Criminal Pleading, Evidence and Practice 2006, Additional CD. CD-ROM: £85.00. ISBN 0 421 91080 1. Sweet & Maxwell.

Richardson, James; Thomas, David A–Archbold: Criminal Pleading, Evidence and Practice 2006, CD and Print Pack. Book (details unknown): £395.00. ISBN 0 421 90900 5. Sweet & Maxwell.

Richardson, James; Thomas, David A–Archbold: Criminal Pleading, Evidence and Practice 2006, Full Print - Supplements. Hardback: £310.00. ISBN 0 421 91040 2. Sweet & Maxwell.

Richardson, James; Thomas, David A–Archbold: Criminal Pleading, Evidence and Practice 2006, Network CD. CD-ROM: £190.00. ISBN 0 421 91100 X. Sweet & Maxwell.

Richardson, James; Thomas, David A–Archbold: Criminal Pleading, Evidence and Practice 2006, Network Licence. CD-ROM: £110.00. ISBN 0 421 91120 4. Sweet & Maxwell.

Richardson, James; Thomas, David A–Archbold: Criminal Pleading, Evidence and Practice 2006, Standalone CD. CD-ROM: £195.00. ISBN 0 421 90960 9. Sweet & Maxwell.

Richardson, James; Thomas, David A–Archbold: Criminal Pleading, Evidence and Practice 2006, Supplements Charged Separately. Hardback: £272.00. ISBN 0 421 91420 3. Sweet & Maxwell.

Richardson, James; Thomas, David A–Archbold: Criminal Pleading, Evidence and Practice 2006, Upgrade CD. CD-ROM: £85.00. ISBN 0 421 91060 7. Sweet & Maxwell.

Richardson, James; Thomas, David A.–Archbold: 3rd Supplement: Criminal Pleading, Evidence and Practice. Paperback: £35.00. ISBN 0 421 85510 X. Sweet & Maxwell.

Richardson, James; Thomas, David A.–Archbold: CD and Print Pack: Criminal Pleading, Evidence and Practice. Hardback/CD-ROM (software): £386.95. ISBN 0 421 88230 1. Sweet & Maxwell.

Richardson, James; Thomas, David A.–Archbold: Criminal Pleading, Evidence and Practice 2005. Paperback: £35.00. ISBN 0 421 88270 0. Sweet & Maxwell.

Richardson, James; Thomas, David A.–Archbold: Supplement 3: Criminal Pleading, Evidence and Practice 2005. Paperback: £35.00. ISBN 0 421 88290 5. Sweet & Maxwell.

Ricketson, Sam; Ginsburg, Jane–International Copyright and Neighbouring Rights: The Berne Convention and Beyond. Hardback: £225.00. ISBN 0 19 825946 8. Oxford University Press.

Riley, Leon; Turner, Chris; Donaldson, Angela; Huxley-Binns, Rebecca–Unlocking Legal Learning. Paperback: £18.99. ISBN 0 340 88761 3. Hodder Arnold H&S.

Ringleb; Meiners–Legal Environment of Business. Hardback: £69.99. ISBN 0 324 20485 X. South Western College Publishing.

Rittberger, Berthold–Building Europe's Parliament: Democratic Representation Beyond the Nation State. Hardback: £45.00. ISBN 0 19 927342 1. Oxford University Press.

Robb, Cairo A.R.–International Environmental Law Reports: Volume 4, Decisions of National Courts. International Environmental Law Reports S., 4. Paperback: £50.00. ISBN 0 521 65965 5. Cambridge University Press.

Roberson, Cliff; Birzer, Michael–Policing Today and Tomorrow. Paperback: £37.99. ISBN 0 13 119068 7. Prentice Hall.

Roberson, Cliff–Preventing Employees From Ruining Your Business. Paperback: £12.95. ISBN 1 59113 827 2. Booklocker.com.

Roberts, Catherine; Horan, Stephen–Financial Assistance for the Acquisition of Shares. Hardback: £115.00. ISBN 0 19 928569 1. Oxford University Press.

Roberts, David; Robson, Graham–Practical Approach to Housing Law. Paperback: £40.00. ISBN 1 85941 915 1. Cavendish Publishing Ltd.

Roberts, Julian–Law of Public Healthcare. Hardback: £75.00. ISBN 1 904501 54 0. Richmond Law & Tax.

Roberts, Mann–Essent of Bus Law and Legal Env-9th Rev Ed. Book (details unknown): £99.00. ISBN 0 324 30395 5. South Western College Publishing.

Roberts, Peter–Gas Sales and Transportation Agreements: Principles and Practice. Audio CD: £244.20. ISBN 0 421 88750 8. Hardback: £244.20. ISBN 0 421 88750 8. Sweet & Maxwell.

Rockwood, Richard M.–Focus Investor. Paperback: £14.00. ISBN 1 4134 7225 7. Xlibris Corporation.

Roe, Diana–Criminal Law. Paperback: £14.99. ISBN 0 340 90047 4. Hodder Arnold H&S.

Rogowski, Ralf–Company Law in Modern Europe. Hardback: £95.00. ISBN 1 85521 395 8. Ashgate.

Rohatgi, Roy–Basic International Taxation: V. 2. Practice. Hardback: £95.00. ISBN 1 904501 35 4. Richmond Law & Tax Ltd.

Rohsler, Carl–Gambling Act 2005: A Current Law Statute Guide. Paperback: £48.00. ISBN 0 421 92350 4. Sweet & Maxwell.

Ronaldson, Cheryl–Practitioner's Guide to the FSA Regulation of Lloyd's. Paperback: £75.00. ISBN 1 898830 87 8. City and Financial Publishing.

Rose, Francis–General Average: Law and Practice. Hardback: £160.00. ISBN 1 84311 418 6. Informa Business Publishing.

Rose, Francis–Statutes on Commercial and Consumer Law. Blackstone's Statute Books. Paperback: £18.99. ISBN 0 19 928319 2. Oxford University Press.

Rose, F.D.–Statutes on Contract, Tort and Restitution. Blackstone's Statute Books. Paperback: £14.99. ISBN 0 19 928320 6. Oxford University Press.

Rose, William; Sime, Stuart; French, Derek–Blackstone's Civil Practice. Hardback: £145.00. ISBN 0 19 927780 X. Oxford University Press.

Rosen, Gary–Right War?: The Conservative Debate on Iraq. Hardback: £35.00. ISBN 0 521 85681 7. Paperback: £12.99. ISBN 0 521 67318 6. Cambridge University Press.

Rosenfeld–Identity of Constitutional Subject. Paperback: £16.99. ISBN 0 415 94974 2. Routledge, an imprint of Taylor & Francis Books Ltd.

Rosenthal, Adam; Dray, Martin; Groves, Christopher–Barnsley's Land Options. Hardback: £160.00. ISBN 0 421 85610 6. Sweet & Maxwell.

Ross, Sidney–Inheritance Act Claims: Law and Practice. Paperback: £75.00. ISBN 0 421 89310 9. Sweet & Maxwell.

Rossi, Jim–Deregulation and the Incomplete Regulatory Contract. Hardback: £35.00. ISBN 0 521 83892 4. Cambridge University Press.

Roth, Dik; Boelens, Rutgerd; Zwarteveen, Margreet–Liquid Relations: Contested Water Rights and Legal Complexity. Hardback: £46.95. ISBN 0 8135 3674 X. Paperback: £21.95. ISBN 0 8135 3675 8. Rutgers University Press.

Rowe, Peter–Impact of Human Rights Law on Armed Forces. Hardback: £55.00. ISBN 0 521 85170 X. Cambridge University Press.

Rowell, David; Wilson, Richard; Arthur, Stephen–Practical Lawyer Inheritance Tax Planning Guide. Paperback: £60.00. ISBN 1 903927 67 6. Legalease.

Rowell, Oliver–Guide to Employment Law. Easyway Guides S. Paperback: £8.99. ISBN 1 900694 97 2. Easyway Guides.

Rowland, Mark; White, Robin–Social Security: Vol 3. Administration, Adjudication and the European Dimension: Legislation 2005. Paperback: £77.00. ISBN 0 421 92070 X. Sweet & Maxwell.

Rowley, C.K.–Law and Economics: V. 9. Law and Economics. Selected Works of Gordon Tullock S. Hardback: £13.95. ISBN 0 86597 528 0. Paperback: £8.95. ISBN 0 86597 539 6. Liberty Fund Inc.

Rozenberg, Joshua–Privacy and the Press. Paperback: £12.99. ISBN 0 19 928847 X. Oxford University Press.

Ruff, Anne–Contract Law. Paperback: £6.50. ISBN 0 421 89030 4. Sweet & Maxwell.

Russomanno, Joseph–Defending the First: Commentary on First Amendment Issues and Cases. LEA's Communication Series. Hardback: £52.95. ISBN 0 8058 4925 4. Lawrence Erlbaum Associates, Inc.

Ryall, Aine–Effective Judicial Protection and the Environmental Impact Assessment Directive in Ireland. Hardback: £45.00. ISBN 1 84113 500 3. Hart Publishing.

Ryder, Rodney D.–Internet Law and Policy. Hardback: £24.95. ISBN 0 19 566861 8. OUP India.

Sabalot, Deborah A.–Butterworths Financial Services Law Handbook. Paperback: £92.50. ISBN 1 4057 0777 1. Butterworths Law.

Sabri, Thaer–E-payments: Guide to Electronic Money and Online Payments. Paperback: £145.00. ISBN 1 84592 084 8. Tottel Publishing.

Sadler, Roger L.–Electronic Media Law. Paperback: £45.00. ISBN 1 4129 0588 5. Sage Publications Ltd.

Sahama–Criminal Justice: 7th Ed. Book (details unknown): £38.00. ISBN 0 534 64557 7. Wadsworth.

Salinger, Freddy–Factoring: The Law and Practice of Invoice Finance. Hardback: £135.00. ISBN 0 421 88320 0. Sweet & Maxwell.

Salvesen, Magda; Cousineau, Diane–Artists' Estates: Reputations in Trust. Hardback: £23.50. ISBN 0 8135 3604 9. Rutgers University Press.

Salvinder, Juss–Guide to the Asylum and Immigration (Treatment of Claimants, Etc) Act 2004. Paperback: £22.95. ISBN 1 85941 982 8. Cavendish Publishing Ltd.

Samaha–SG Criminal Justice 7e. Book (details unknown): £19.99. ISBN 0 495 00052 3. Wadsworth.

Sampford, Charles–Retrospectivity and the Rule of Law. Hardback: £60.00. ISBN 0 19 825298 6. Oxford University Press.

Sampson, Fraser; Hutton, Glenn; Johnston, David; Connor, Paul; Pinfield, Dave; Taylor, Neil; Chapman, Julian–Blackstone's Police Investigator's Manual and Workbook Pack. Blackstone's Police Manuals. Hardback: £65.00. ISBN 0 19 928760 0. Oxford University Press.

Sampson, Fraser; Hutton, Glenn; Johnston, David–Blackstone's Police Investigator's Manual. Blackstone's Police Manuals. Paperback: £35.00. ISBN 0 19 928759 7. Oxford University Press.

Sampson, Fraser; Hutton, Glenn; Johnston, David–Blackstone's Police Manuals. Paperback: £75.00. ISBN 0 19 928524 1. Paperback: £84.76; CD-ROM: £55.00. ISBN 0 19 928524 1; 0 19 928542 X. Oxford University Press.

Sampson, Fraser–Crime: V. 1. Blackstone's Police Manuals. Paperback: £14.50. ISBN 0 19 928519 5. Paperback: £14.50. ISBN 0 19 928519 5. Oxford University Press.

Sampson, Fraser–General Police Duties: V. 4. Blackstone's Police Manuals. Paperback: £14.50. ISBN 0 19 928522 5. Paperback: £14.50. ISBN 0 19 928522 5. Oxford University Press.

Sampson, Fraser–Roads Policing: V. 3. Blackstone's Police Manuals. Paperback: £14.50. ISBN 0 19 928521 7. Oxford University Press.

Samuel, Geoffrey–Cases and Materials on Torts. Cases & Materials S. Paperback: £24.00. ISBN 1 84641 016 9. Law Matters Publishing.

Samuel, Geoffrey–Understanding Contractual and Tortious Obligations. Understanding S. Paperback: £22.00. ISBN 1 84641 003 7. Law Matters Publishing.

Sandbrook, Claire–Enforcement of a Judgment. Paperback: £65.00. ISBN 0 421 87370 1. Sweet & Maxwell.

Sanders, Michael I.–Joint Ventures Involving Tax-Exempt Organizations. Paperback: £41.95. ISBN 0 471 67983 6. John Wiley & Sons Inc.

Sandon, Teresa–Lex 100: A Student Guide to the UK's Premier Law Firms 2005 / 06. Paperback: £9.99. ISBN 1 903927 53 6. Legalease.

Sands, Philippe; Galizzi, Paolo–Documents in European Community Environmental Law. Hardback: £120.00. ISBN 0 521 83303 5. Paperback: £60.00. ISBN 0 521 54061 5. Cambridge University Press.

Sarat, Austin–Capital Punishment: Vol.1,2: The Actors in the Process. International Library of Essays in Law & Society S. Hardback: £230.00. ISBN 0 7546 2503 6. Ashgate.

Sarat, Austin–Death Penalty: Vol.1,2: Influences and Outcomes. International Library of Criminology, Criminal Justice & Penology 2nd Series. Hardback: £250.00. ISBN 0 7546 2400 5. Ashgate.

Sarat, Austin–Law in the Liberal Arts. Paperback: £12.50. ISBN 0 8014 8905 9. Cornell University Press.

Sarat, Austin–Mercy on Trial: What It Means to Stop an Execution. Hardback: £18.95. ISBN 0 691 12140 0. Princeton University Press.

Sarat, Austin–Studies in Law, Politics and Society. Studies in Law, Politics & Society. Hardback: £59.99. ISBN 0 7623 1179 7. JAI Press.

Saunders, Joss–Mutual Obligations: NVCO's Guide to Contracts with Public Bodies. Paperback: £15.00. ISBN 0 7199 1537 6. NCVO Publications.

Saville; Justice Laws–Civil Court Service Autumn: Autumn Re-issue. Hardback: £97.50. ISBN 1 84661 005 2. Jordans.

Scamell, Ernest H.–Butterworths Property Law Handbook. Paperback: £70.00. ISBN 1 4057 0207 9. Butterworths Law.

Scanlan, Gary; McGee, Andrew; Williams, Christine–Law of Business Organisations. Textbooks. Paperback: £24.00. ISBN 1 84641 000 2. Law Matters Publishing.

Scherer, F.M.–Patents: Economics, Policy and Measurement. Hardback: £69.95. ISBN 1 84542 481 6. Edward Elgar.

Scherer, Joachim–Baker and Mckenzie: Telecommunications Law in Europe. Hardback: £170.00. ISBN 1 84592 078 3. Tottel Publishing.

Schlechtriem, Peter; Schwenzer, Ingeborg–Commentary on the UN Convention on the International Sale of Goods (CISG). Hardback: £165.00. ISBN 0 19 927518 1. Oxford University Press.

Schmidt, Patrick–Lawyers and Regulation: The Politics of the Administrative Process. Cambridge Studies in Law & Society. Hardback: £50.00. ISBN 0 521 84465 7. Cambridge University Press.

Schmidtz, David–Elements of Justice. Hardback: £40.00. ISBN 0 521 83164 4. Cambridge University Press.

Schnitzer, Simone–Understanding International Trade Law. Understanding S. Paperback: £20.00. ISBN 1 84641 002 9. Law Matters Publishing.

Schonlau, Justus–Drafting the EU Charter: Rights, Legitimacy and Process. Palgrave Studies in European Union Politics. Hardback: £45.00. ISBN 1 4039 9373 4. Palgrave Macmillan.

Schulenberg, Richard–Legal Aspects of the Music Industry. Hardback: £22.50. ISBN 0 8230 8364 0. Billboard Books.

Schwabach, Aaron–Internet and the Law: Technology, Society, and Compromises. Hardback: £69.50. ISBN 1 85109 731 7. ABC-CLIO.

Schwartz, David G.–Cutting the Wire: Gaming Prohibition and the Internet. Gambling Studies S. Hardback: £36.50. ISBN 0 87417 619 0. Paperback: £18.50. ISBN 0 87417 620 4. University of Nevada Press.

Scots Law Times. Hardback: £325.00. ISBN 0 414 01605 X. W.Green & Son.

Scott, Andrew; Hviid, Morten; Lyons, Bruce–Merger Control in the United Kingdom. Hardback: £145.00. ISBN 0 19 927688 9. Oxford University Press.

Scott, David–Emerald Hole Lawyer Creating Wills. Paperback: £9.99. ISBN 1 903909 68 6. Straightforward Publishing.

Scott, M.–Conveyancer's Fact Finder. Paperback: £14.99. ISBN 0 85308 965 5. Jordans.

Scott, Sionaidh Douglas–Law After Modernity. Legal Theory Today S. Hardback: £26.00. ISBN 1 84113 562 3. Hart Publishing.

Scottish Law Directory 2005. Hardback: £49.00. ISBN 1 4057 0376 8. Butterworths Law.

Scottish Law Directory: Fees Supplement 2005: The White Book. Paperback: £11.00. ISBN 1 4057 0377 6. Butterworths Law (Scotland).

Seal, Paul–Dissolving the Family Company. Paperback: £59.95. ISBN 1 84592 039 2. Tottel Publishing.

Searl, David–You and Your Property in Spain: Your Essential Guide to Property Ownership and Rental. Paperback: £12.99. ISBN 84 89954 46 1. Santana Books,Spain.

Seddon, Duran; Fitzpatrick, Pamela–Migration and Social Security Handbook. Paperback: £21.00. ISBN 1 901698 77 7. CPAG.

Segal, Leila–Education Law Update Year Book. Looseleaf/ring bound: £125.00. ISBN 0 9546874 7 7. Optimus Publishing.

Self, Roger–Tottel's Pension Fund Trustee Handbook. Paperback: £36.95. ISBN 1 84592 175 5. Tottel Publishing.

Semple, Piggot Mike–Jurisprudence. Law in a Box S. CD-ROM: £19.95. ISBN 1 904783 85 6. Semple Piggot Rochez (Legal Education Ltd).

Seres, Jonathan; Mitchell, Feargus–Pensions Risk and Strategy. Paperback: £59.00. ISBN 1 898830 75 4. City and Financial Publishing.

Shackleton, Stewart–Arbitration Law Reports and Review. Hardback: £295.00. ISBN 0 19 928645 0. Oxford University Press.

Shapiro, Hal–Fast Track: A Legal, Historical and Political Analysis. Hardback: £100.99. ISBN 1 57105 178 3. Transnational Publishers, Inc.

Sharland, John–Practical Approach to Local Government Law. Paperback: £39.95. ISBN 0 19 928347 8. Oxford University Press.

Sharpe–Genetic Testing: Care, Consent and Liability. Hardback: £48.95. ISBN 0 471 64987 2. John Wiley & Sons Inc.

Shaw, Edward–Dilapidations-Letters, Forms and Schedules. CD-ROM: £47.00. ISBN 1 84219 184 5. RICS.

Shay, Helen–Writer's Guide to Copyright and Law: Learn What Rights You Have As a Writer and How to Enjoy Them; What Obligations You Have, and How to Comply with Them. Paperback: £9.99. ISBN 1 85703 991 2. How To Books.

Sheard, Sally; Donaldson, Liam J.–Nation's Doctor: The Role of the Chief Medical Officer 1855-1998. Paperback: £40.00. ISBN 1 84619 001 0. Radcliffe Medical Press.

Shephard, Catherine–Public Companies and Equity Finance. Paperback: £24.95. ISBN 0 905835 73 5. Paperback: £25.95. ISBN 1 905391 10 2. The College of Law.

Shepperson, Tessa–Residential Lettings. Paperback: £11.99. ISBN 1 904053 90 4. Law Pack Publishing.

Sherriff, Gerald–Sherriff: Service Charges for Leasehold, Freehold and Commonhold. Paperback: £80.00. ISBN 1 84592 120 8. Tottel Publishing.

Sherwin, Richard K.–Popular Culture and Law. International Library of Essays in Law & Society S. Hardback: £115.00. ISBN 0 7546 2470 6. Ashgate.

Short Form of the Sub-Contract. Book (details unknown): £8.95. ISBN 0 418 82940 3. Sweet & Maxwell.

Shuttleworth, Colin; Julyan, Alan J.–Checklists for Solicitors. Paperback/Floppy disk: £55.00. ISBN 0 7520 0509 X. Sweet & Maxwell.

Siegan, Bernard H.–Economic Liberties and the Constitution. Hardback: £35.50. ISBN 0 7658 0572 3. Paperback: £21.50. ISBN 1 4128 0525 2. Transaction Publishers.

Silva, Niran De; Price, Richard–Knight's Complete Handbook for Polling Stations and the Count. Paperback: £29.95. ISBN 1 84592 208 5. Tottel Publishing.

Silverman, Frances–Conveyancing Handbook. Hardback: £79.95. ISBN 1 85328 928 0. Law Society Publications.

Sime, Stuart–Practical Approach to Civil Procedure. Paperback: £32.99. ISBN 0 19 928136 X. Paperback: £32.99. ISBN 0 19 928136 X. Oxford University Press.

Simester, Andrew; Hirsch, Andrew von–Incivilities: Regulating Offensive Behaviour. Hardback: £30.00. ISBN 1 84113 499 6. Hart Publishing.

Simester, Andrew–Appraising Strict Liability. Oxford Monographs on Criminal Law & Justice. Hardback: £50.00. ISBN 0 19 927851 2. Oxford University Press.

Simmons, David; Winfield, Helen–Paying for Care Handbook: A Guide to Services, Charges and Welfare Benefits for Adults in Need of Care in the Community or in Care Homes. Paperback: £18.50. ISBN 1 901698 81 5. CPAG.

Simply Legal: A Guide for Development Workers on the Legal Forms and Organisational Types for Community-based Organisations Across the Social Economy Sector. Paperback: £15.00. ISBN 0 9549677 0 4. Co-operatives UK.

Singleton, Susan–Commercial Agency Agreements Law and Practice: 2nd Ed. Floppy disk/Hardback: £116.32. ISBN 0 406 97955 3. Butterworths Law.

Singleton, Susan–Commercial Agency Agreements Law and Practice. Paperback: £116.32. ISBN 1 84592 099 6. Tottel Publishing.

Singleton, Susan–Freedom of Information Act. Thorogood Professional Insights S. Paperback: £169.00. ISBN 1 85418 347 8. Thorogood.

Singleton, Susan–Tolley's Business, the Internet and the Law. Looseleaf/ring bound: £78.00. ISBN 0 7545 1431 5. LexisNexis UK.

Skach, Cindy–Borrowing Constitutional Designs: Constitutional Law in Weimar Germany and the French Fifth Republic. Hardback: £18.95. ISBN 0 691 12345 4. Princeton University Press.

Skaine, Rosemarie–Female Genital Multilation: Legal, Cultural and Medical Issues. Paperback: £26.50. ISBN 0 7864 2167 3. McFarland & Company.

Slapper, Gary; Kelly, D.–English Legal System Q&A. Q & A S. Paperback: £11.95. ISBN 1 84568 001 4. Cavendish Publishing Ltd.

Slocombe, Melanie–Employment Law Guide. Paperback: £11.99. ISBN 1 904053 92 0. Law Pack Publishing.

Slocombe, Melanie–Employment Law Made Easy. Paperback: £11.99. ISBN 1 904053 88 2. Lawpack Publishing Ltd.

Slocombe, Melanie–Your Rights At Work Pocket Guide. Paperback: £3.99. ISBN 1 904053 83 1. Lawpack Publishing Ltd.

Slorach, J. Scott; Ellis, Jason G.–Business Law. Blackstone Legal Practice Course Guide S. Paperback: £26.99. ISBN 0 19 928141 6. Oxford University Press.

Slot, Piet Jan; Johnston, Angus—Introduction to Competition Law. Paperback: £22.00. ISBN 1 84113 445 7. Hart Publishing.

Smailes, David; Wareham, Robert—Tolley's Tax Data: Budget Edition. Paperback: £42.00. ISBN 0 7545 2868 5. Tolley Publishing.

Smailes, David; Wareham, Robert—Tolley's Tax Data: Finance Act Edition. Paperback: £42.00. ISBN 0 7545 2869 3. Tolley Publishing.

Smart, Huw; Watson, John—Blackstone's Police Q&As. Blackstone's Police Q & A S. Paperback: £46.00. ISBN 0 19 928529 2. Paperback: £46.00. ISBN 0 19 928529 2. Oxford University Press.

Smart, Huw; Watson, John—Crime. Paperback: £11.95. ISBN 0 19 928525 X. Paperback: £11.95. ISBN 0 19 928525 X. Oxford University Press.

Smart, Huw; Watson, John—Evidence and Procedure. Blackstone's Police Q&As. Paperback: £11.95. ISBN 0 19 928526 8. Oxford University Press.

Smart, Huw; Watson, John—General Police Duties. Blackstone's Police Q & A S. Paperback: £11.95. ISBN 0 19 928528 4. Paperback: £11.95. ISBN 0 19 928528 4. Oxford University Press.

Smart, Huw; Watson, John—Roads Policing. Blackstone's Police Q&As. Paperback: £11.95. ISBN 0 19 928527 6. Oxford University Press.

Smith & Williamson—Using Expert Witnesses. Paperback: £34.95. ISBN 1 85328 930 2. Law Society Publications.

Smith, Craig Alan—Failing Justice: Charles Evans Whittaker on the Supreme Court. Paperback: £29.95. ISBN 0 7864 2197 5. McFarland & Company.

Smith, Graham—Internet Law and Regulation. Hardback: £185.00. ISBN 0 421 90990 0. Sweet & Maxwell.

Smith, Huw Beverley; Ohly, Ansgar; Lucas-Schloetter, Agnes—Privacy, Property and Personality: Civil Law Perspectives on Commercial Appropriation. Cambridge Studies in Intellectual Property Rights. Hardback: £48.00. ISBN 0 521 82080 4. Cambridge University Press.

Smith, Kelly—Irish Tax Reports. Paperback: £56.66. ISBN 1 84592 201 8. Tottel Publishing.

Smith, Lionel Percy; Mattei, Ugo; Smith, Lionel—Commercial Trusts in European Private Law. Common Core of European Private Law S. Hardback: £85.00. ISBN 0 521 84919 5. Cambridge University Press.

Smith, Martin—Precedent Library for the General Practitioner. Paperback: £99.95. ISBN 1 85328 986 8. Law Society Publications.

Smith, Roger J.—Property Law. Longman Law S. Paperback: £31.99. ISBN 1 4058 0114 X. Longman.

Snape, John; Souza, Jeremy De—Environmental Taxation Law: Policy, Contexts and Practice. Hardback: £75.00. ISBN 0 7546 2304 1. Ashgate.

Sneath, David—Employment Tribunals. Paperback: £45.00. ISBN 0 85308 954 X. Jordans.

Sokol, Daniel; Bergson, Gillian; McKimm, Ashley—Medical Ethics and Law: Surviving on the Wards and Passing Exams. Paperback: £14.95. ISBN 0 9547657 1 0. Trauma Publishing.

Solomon, Nicola; Middleton, Simon—Personal Injury Practice and Procedure. Paperback: £72.00. ISBN 0 421 87550 X. Sweet & Maxwell.

Southern, David—Taxation of Banks and Banking. Paperback: £85.00. ISBN 0 7545 2227 X. Tolley Publishing.

Soyer, Baris—Warranties in Marine Insurance. Hardback: £85.00. ISBN 1 85941 943 7. Cavendish Publishing Ltd.

Speechley, Tom—Practical Guide to Acquisition Finance. Paperback: £125.00. ISBN 1 84592 017 1. Tottel Publishing.

Spencer, John; Spencer, Maureen—Human Rights Law. Paperback: £6.50. ISBN 0 421 89050 9. Sweet & Maxwell.

Spencer, Maureen; Spencer, John—Nutcases-Constitutional and Administrative Law. Paperback: £7.50. ISBN 0 421 92800 X. Sweet & Maxwell.

Sproston, Roger—Emerald Hole Lawyer Bankruptcy. Paperback: £9.99. ISBN 1 903909 69 4. Straightforward Publishing.

Sproston, Roger–Straightforward Guide to Housing Rights. Straightforward Guide to Housing Rights S. Paperback: £9.99. ISBN 1 903909 64 3. Straightforward Publishing.

Sproston, Roger–Straightforward Guide to Your Rights As a Private Tenant. Paperback: £8.99. ISBN 1 903909 59 7. Straightforward Publishing.

Squire, Nicholas; Healy, Kathleen; Broadbent, Joanna–Informing and Consulting Employees: The New Law. Paperback: £49.95. ISBN 0 19 928364 8. Paperback: £49.95. ISBN 0 19 928364 8. Oxford University Press.

Srebnick, Amy Gilman; Levy, Rene–Crime and Culture: An Historical Perspective. Advances in Criminology S. Hardback: £50.00. ISBN 0 7546 2383 1. Ashgate.

Stagg, Paul–Supplement: CPAG's Housing Benefit and Council Tax Benefit Legislation. Paperback: £20.00. ISBN 1 901698 70 X. CPAG.

Standard Building Contract with Approximate Quantities. Hardback: £26.95. ISBN 0 418 82950 0. Sweet & Maxwell.

Standard Building Contract with Quantities. Paperback: £26.95. ISBN 0 418 82320 0. Sweet & Maxwell.

Standard Building Contract Without Quantities. Paperback: £26.95. ISBN 0 418 82330 8. Sweet & Maxwell.

Stanley, Neil; Wolf, Susan–EC Environmental Law. Paperback: £30.00. ISBN 1 85941 947 X. Cavendish Publishing Ltd.

Stationery Office Books–BS 5839-6:2004: Fire Detection and Alarm Systems for Buildings. Code of Practice for the Design and Installation of Fire Detection and Alarm Systems in Dwellings. Paperback: £150.00. ISBN 0 580 44100 8. British Standards Institution.

Stationery Office Books–Building Act 1984: Amendments to Approved Document L1, Conservation of Fuel and Power in Dwellings: ODPM Circular Office of the Deputy Prime Minister 04/2005. Paperback: £6.00. ISBN 0 11 753947 3. The Stationery Office Books.

Stationery Office Books–Design Manual for Roads and Bridges. Vol.10: Environmental Design and Management. Section 3: Landscape Management. Part 3: The Establishment of an Herbaceous Plant Layer in Roadside Woodland. Paperback: £18.00. ISBN 0 11 552648 X. The Stationery Office Books.

Stationery Office Books–Design Manual for Roads and Bridges. Vol.4: Geotechnics and Drainage. Section 2: Drainage. Part 6: Combined Channel and Pipe System for Surface Water Drainage. Paperback: £15.00. ISBN 0 11 552647 1. The Stationery Office Books.

Stationery Office Books–Design Manual for Roads and Bridges. Vol.5: Assessment and Preparation of Road Schemes. Section 2: Preparation and Implementation. Part 4: Provision for Non-motorised Users. Paperback: £17.00. ISBN 0 11 552650 1. The Stationery Office Books.

Stationery Office Books–Design Manual for Roads and Bridges. Vol.5: Assessment and Preparation of Road Schemes. Section 2: Preparation and Implementation. Part 5: Non-motorised User Audits. Paperback: £18.00. ISBN 0 11 552649 8. The Stationery Office Books.

Stationery Office Books–Design Manual for Roads and Bridges. Vol.6: Road Geometry. Section 1: Links. Part 2: Cross-sections and Headrooms. Paperback: £20.00. ISBN 0 11 552652 8. The Stationery Office Books.

Stationery Office Books–Design Manual for Roads and Bridges. Vol.6: Road Geometry. Section 3: Highway Features. Part 5: The Geometric Design of Pedestrian, Cycle and Equestrian Routes. Paperback: £15.00. ISBN 0 11 552651 X. The Stationery Office Books.

Stationery Office Books–Design Manual for Roads and Bridges. Vol.8: Traffic Signs and Lighting. Section 2: Traffic Signs and Road Markings. Part 6: Traffic Signs to Retail Destinations and Exhibition Centres in England and Wales-Trunk Roads. Looseleaf/ring bound: £14.00. ISBN 0 11 552654 4. The Stationery Office Books.

Stationery Office Books—Drug Tariff: National Health Service, England and Wales. Paperback: £8.50. ISBN 0 11 782986 2. The Stationery Office Books.

Stationery Office Books—Feeding Stuffs (Sampling and Analysis) and the Feeding Stuffs (Enforcement) (Amendment) (England) (No.2) Regulations 2004. Paperback: £3.00. ISBN 0 11 049965 4. The Stationery Office Books.

Stationery Office Books—Well-maintained Highways, Code of Practice for Highway Maintenance Management. Paperback: £25.00. ISBN 0 11 552643 9. The Stationery Office Books.

Statsky—Essentials of Paralegalism 4e. Book (details unknown): £58.00. ISBN 1 4018 6193 8. Delmar.

Stauch, Marc; Tingle, John; Wheat, Kay—Text and Materials on Medical Law. Paperback: £33.00. ISBN 1 85941 934 8. Cavendish Publishing Ltd.

Steele, Gill—Trust Practitioner's Handbook. Paperback: £49.95. ISBN 1 85328 945 0. Law Society Publications.

Stefancic, Jean; Delgado, Richard—How Lawyers Lose Their Way: A Profession Fails Its Creative Minds. Hardback: £52.00. ISBN 0 8223 3454 2. Paperback: £12.95. ISBN 0 8223 3563 8. Duke University Press.

Stein, Alex—Foundations of Evidence Law. Hardback: £50.00. ISBN 0 19 825736 8. Oxford University Press.

Stephenson, Graham—Core Statutes on Contract, Tort and Restitution. Core Statutes S. Paperback: £10.00. ISBN 1 84641 011 8. Law Matters Publishing.

Steven, Andrew J M; Wortley, Scott—Avizandum Statutes on Scots Property, Trusts and Succession Law. Paperback: £21.95. ISBN 1 904968 03 1. Avizandum Publishing Ltd.

Steven, Andrew; Wortley, Scott; Reid, Kenneth—Property Trusts and Succession. Paperback: £35.00. ISBN 1 84592 153 4. Tottel Publishing.

Stewart, Andrew F.—Session Cases: Incorporating Issue 6. Hardback: £265.00. ISBN 0 414 01622 X. W. Green & Son.

Stewart, Moira—Landlord's Guide to Letting: How to Buy and Let Residential Property for Profit. Paperback: £9.99. ISBN 1 85703 750 2. How To Books.

Steyn, Johan—Democracy Through Law: Selected Speeches and Judgments. Collected Essays in Law S. Hardback: £60.00. ISBN 0 7546 2404 8. Ashgate.

Stokes, Simon—Digital Copyright: Law and Practice. Paperback: £35.00. ISBN 1 84113 514 3. Hart Publishing.

Stone, Marcus—Cross-Examination in Criminal Trials. Paperback: £39.00. ISBN 1 84592 103 8. Tottel Publishing.

Stone, Richard—Modern Law of Contract. Paperback: £25.95. ISBN 1 85941 882 1. Cavendish Publishing Ltd.

Stonefrost, Hilary—Duties and Liabilities of Insolvency Practitioners. Hardback: £99.00. ISBN 0 421 87430 9. Sweet & Maxwell.

Stookes, Paul—Practical Approach to Environmental Law. Practical Approach S. Paperback: £39.95. ISBN 0 19 927921 7. Paperback: £39.95. ISBN 0 19 927921 7. Oxford University Press.

Storm, Paul M.; Gerven, Dirk van—European Company: Volume 1. Law Practitioner S. Hardback: £85.00. ISBN 0 521 85974 3. Cambridge University Press.

Stranks, Jeremy W.—Health and Safety Law. Paperback: £29.99. ISBN 0 13 197646 X. Prentice Hall.

Stranks, Jeremy—Health and Safety Handbook: A Practical Guide to Health and Safety Law, Management Policies and Procedures. Hardback: £47.00. ISBN 0 7494 4392 8. Kogan Page.

Strathern, Marilyn—Kinship, Law and the Unexpected: Relatives Are Always a Surprise. Hardback: £40.00. ISBN 0 521 84992 6. Paperback: £13.99. ISBN 0 521 61509 7. Cambridge University Press.

Strong, S.I.—How to Write Law Essays and Exams. Paperback: £15.99. ISBN 0 19 928755 4. Oxford University Press.

Sub-Subcontract. Paperback: £8.95. ISBN 0 418 82390 1. Sweet & Maxwell.

Sullivan, Rory–Rethinking Voluntary Approaches in Environmental Policy. Hardback: £55.00. ISBN 1 84542 210 4. Edward Elgar.

Sullivan, Thomas F. P.–Environmental Law Handbook. State Environmental Law Handbook S. Hardback: £65.00. ISBN 0 86587 985 0. Government Institutes Division, ABS Group Inc.

Summers, Robert S.–Form and Function in a Legal System: A General Study. Hardback: £45.00. ISBN 0 521 85765 1. Cambridge University Press.

Summerskill, Michael Brynmor–Summerskill on Oil Rigs. Hardback: £195.00. ISBN 0 421 50820 5. Sweet & Maxwell.

Sussmuth, Rita; Weidenfeld, Werner–Managing Integration: The European Union's Responsibilities Towards Immigrants. Paperback: £14.99. ISBN 0 9742819 2 1. Migration Policy Institute.

Suter, Erich–Guide to Employment Statutes. Paperback: £1.00. ISBN 1 84398 137 8. Chartered Institute of Personnel and Development.

Sutherland, Lauren–Children in Personal Injury Litigation in Scotland. Paperback: £35.00. ISBN 0 414 01544 4. W.Green & Son.

Sweet, Robert–Commercial Leases: Tenants' Amendments. Paperback: £85.00. ISBN 0 421 89550 0. Sweet & Maxwell.

Swinson, Chris–International and UK Audit. Paperback: £79.95. ISBN 1 4057 0796 8. Butterworths Law.

Swinton, Ken; Paisley, Roderick–Property. Law Basics S. Paperback: £12.50. ISBN 0 414 01373 5. W.Green & Son.

Sykes, John–Intellectual Property in Designs. Hardback: £135.00. ISBN 0 406 97625 2. Butterworths Law.

Szego, G.–Financial Regulation. Hardback: £75.00. ISBN 0 470 01159 9. John Wiley and Sons Ltd.

Tackaberry, John; Anglade, Lelia; Bui, Victoria–International Dispute Resolution: Vol 2. International Dispute Resolution: Cases and Materials. Hardback: £89.00. ISBN 0 421 88720 6. Sweet & Maxwell.

Tadros, Victor–Criminal Responsibility. Oxford Monographs on Criminal Law & Justice. Hardback: £50.00. ISBN 0 19 926159 8. Oxford University Press.

Takeyama, Lisa N.; Gordon, Wendy J.; Liacos, Paul J.; Towse, Ruth–Developments in the Economics of Copyright: Research and Analysis. Hardback: £55.00. ISBN 1 84376 930 1. Edward Elgar.

Talbot, Alison–Probate Kit. Looseleaf/ring bound: £14.99. ISBN 1 904053 25 4. Law Pack Publishing.

Tams, Christian J.–Enforcing Obligations Erga Omnes in International Law. Cambridge Studies in International & Comparative Law, No. 43. Hardback: £55.00. ISBN 0 521 85667 1. Cambridge University Press.

Tan, Alan Khee-Jin–Vessel-source Marine Pollution: The Law and Politics of International Regulation. Cambridge Studies in International & Comparative Law, No. 45. Hardback: £50.00. ISBN 0 521 85342 7. Cambridge University Press.

Tax Annuals Set. Paperback: £243.95. ISBN 1 4057 0427 6. Paperback: £299.00. ISBN 1 4057 0923 5. Tolley Publishing.

Tax Indemnities and Warranties. Paperback: £85.00. ISBN 1 84592 127 5. Tottel Publishing.

Tax Office Directory. Spiral/comb bound: £31.00. ISBN 0 7545 2871 5. Spiral/comb bound: £33.95. ISBN 0 7545 2872 3. Tolley Publishing.

Taylor, Paul M.–Freedom of Religion: UN and European Human Rights Law and Practice. Paperback: £24.99. ISBN 0 521 67246 5. Cambridge University Press.

Taylor, William–Geography of Law: Landscape, Identity and Regulation. Onati International Series in Law & Society. Hardback: £35.00. ISBN 1 84113 556 9. Hart Publishing.

Tebbit, Mark–Philosophy of Law: An Introduction. Hardback: £65.00. ISBN 0 415 33440 3. Routledge,an imprint of Taylor & Francis Books Ltd.

Tebbit–Philosophy of Law Intro Ed2-2nd Ed. Paperback (B format): £15.99. ISBN 0 415 33441 1. Routledge,an imprint of Taylor & Francis Books Ltd.

Telling, A.E.; Duxbury, Robert–Telling and Duxbury's Planning Law and Procedure. Paperback: £26.99. ISBN 0 19 928804 6. Paperback: £26.99. ISBN 0 19 928804 6. Oxford University Press.

Tewksbury, Richard–Behind Bars: Readings on Prison Culture. Paperback: £29.99. ISBN 0 13 119072 5. Prentice Hall.

Thomas, E.W.–Judicial Process: Realism, Pragmatism, Practical Reasoning and Principles. Hardback: £50.00. ISBN 0 521 85566 7. Cambridge University Press.

Thomas, Meryl–Statutes on Property Law. Blackstone's Statute Books. Paperback: £14.99. ISBN 0 19 928317 6. Paperback: £14.99. ISBN 0 19 928317 6. Oxford University Press.

Thomas, Michael–Stamp Duty Land Tax. Paperback: £75.00. ISBN 0 521 60632 2. Cambridge University Press.

Thompson, Brian; Allen, Michael–Cases and Materials on Constitutional and Administrative Law. Paperback: £25.99. ISBN 0 19 927879 2. Oxford University Press.

Thorley, Simon; Miller, Richard; Burkill, Guy; Birss, Colin–Terrell on the Law of Patents. Hardback: £260.00. ISBN 0 421 88650 1. Sweet & Maxwell.

Thurston, John–Estate Planning for the Middle Income Client. Paperback: £49.95. ISBN 1 84592 009 0. Tottel Publishing.

Tierney, Stephen–Constitutional Law and National Pluralism. Paperback: £24.99. ISBN 0 19 929861 0. Oxford University Press.

Tiley, John–Revenue Law. Paperback: £45.00. ISBN 1 84113 536 4. Hart Publishing.

Tillotson, John–Text, Cases and Materials on European Union Law. Paperback: £30.95. ISBN 1 84568 012 X. Cavendish Publishing Ltd.

Times Law Reports Bound. Other printed material: £149.00. ISBN 1 4057 0888 3. Butterworths Law.

Timms, Judith–Children's Representation. Paperback: £60.00. ISBN 0 421 62630 5. Sweet & Maxwell.

Timothy, Patrick; Barker, Alison–Wontner's Guide to Land Registry Practice: Practitioner Series. Hardback: £75.00. ISBN 0 421 90040 7. Sweet & Maxwell.

Todd, Paul; Wilson, Sarah–Textbook on Trusts. Paperback: £25.99. ISBN 0 19 927632 3. Oxford University Press.

Todd, Paul–E-Commerce Law. Paperback: £27.00. ISBN 1 85941 942 9. Cavendish Publishing Ltd.

Tolley's Company Law Handbook. Paperback: £65.95. ISBN 0 7545 2747 6. Tolley Publishing.

Tolley's Employment Handbook. Paperback: £86.00. ISBN 0 7545 2881 2. Tolley Publishing.

Tolley's Guide to Construction Contracts Issue 17. Looseleaf/ring bound: £63.00. ISBN 0 7545 2852 9. Tolley Publishing.

Tolley's Guide to Construction Contracts: Pt. 19. Looseleaf/ring bound: £70.00. ISBN 0 7545 2854 5. Tolley Publishing.

Tolley's Income Tax (Trading and Other Income) Act Handbook. Paperback: £39.95. ISBN 0 7545 2932 0. Tolley Publishing.

Tolley's Tax Computations. Paperback: £74.95. ISBN 0 7545 2867 7. Tolley Publishing.

Tolley's Tax Planning. Paperback: £208.95. ISBN 0 7545 2873 1. Tolley Publishing.

Tolley's Value Added Tax and Tax Tutor. Book (details unknown): £184.21. ISBN 0 7545 2917 7. Tolley Publishing.

Tolley's Vat Planning 2004-5. Paperback: £98.95. ISBN 1 84592 015 5. Tottel Publishing.

Tomes, Jonathan P.—Sevicemember's Legal Guide. Paperback: £10.99. ISBN 0 8117 3232 0. Stackpole Books.

Tookey, Michael—Revenue Law. Paperback: £15.95. ISBN 1 85836 608 9. Old Bailey Press.

Tort Lawcards. Lawcards S. Looseleaf/ring bound: £6.95. ISBN 1 84568 015 4. Cavendish Publishing Ltd.

Tortell, Lisa—Monetary Remedies for Breach of Constitutional Rights: A Comparative Study. Human Rights S. Hardback: £45.00. ISBN 1 84113 511 9. Hart Publishing.

Toth, A.G.—Oxford Encyclopaedia of European Community Law: Law of the Internal Market Vol 2: The Law of the Internal Market. Hardback: £145.00. ISBN 0 19 825600 0. Clarendon Press.

Tottel's Property Taxes. Paperback: £74.95. ISBN 1 84592 055 4. Tottel Publishing.

Tottel's Taper Relief. Paperback: £74.95. ISBN 1 84592 124 0. Tottel Publishing.

Toulson, Roger; Phipps, Charles—Confidentiality. Hardback: £135.00. ISBN 0 421 87630 1. Sweet & Maxwell.

Trager, Robert; Russomanno, Joseph A; Ross, Susan Dente—Law of Journalism and Mass Communication. Paperback/Merchandise (details unknown): £46.99. ISBN 0 07 321344 6. McGraw Hill Higher Education.

Trechsel, Stefan; Summers, Sarah—Human Rights in Criminal Proceedings. Collected Courses of the Academy of European Law, No. XII/3. Hardback: £75.00. ISBN 0 19 829936 2. Oxford University Press.

Treitel, Guenter H.; Reynolds, Francis M.B.—Carver on Bills of Lading. Hardback: £263.00. ISBN 0 421 87700 6. Sweet & Maxwell.

Tremml, Bernd; Buecker, Bernard—Key Aspects of German Business Law: A Practical Manual. Hardback: £54.00. ISBN 3 540 28422 2. Springer-Verlag Berlin and Heidelberg GmbH & Co. K.

Tricker, Ray—Building Regulations in Brief. Paperback: £19.99. ISBN 0 7506 6703 6. Architectural Press.

Tridimas, Takis—European Court of Justice and the EU Constitutional Order: Essays in Judicial Protection. Paperback: £35.00. ISBN 1 84113 509 7. Hart Publishing.

Tritton, Guy—Intellectual Property in Europe. Hardback: £195.00. ISBN 0 421 90850 5. Sweet & Maxwell.

Trusts Lawcards. Lawcards S. Looseleaf/ring bound: £6.95. ISBN 1 84568 029 4. Cavendish Publishing Ltd.

Trybus, Martin—European Union Law and Defence Integration. Paperback: £35.00. ISBN 1 84113 440 6. Hart Publishing.

TSO—Building Regulations 2000: Conservation of Fuel and Power in Dwellings. Looseleaf/ring bound: £6.00. ISBN 0 11 753946 5. The Stationery Office Books.

Tucker, Katherine; George, Sarah—Discrimination Law for Employment Lawyers. Looseleaf/ring bound: £125.00. ISBN 0 421 87960 2. Sweet & Maxwell.

Tugendhat, Michael; Christie, Iain—Law of Privacy and the Media: Main Work and Second Cumulative Supplement. Paperback: £195.00. ISBN 0 19 928344 3. Oxford University Press.

Tugendhat, Michael; Christie, Iain—Law of Privacy and the Media: Second Cumulative Supplement. Paperback: £55.00. ISBN 0 19 928343 5. Oxford University Press.

Turle, Marcus—Freedom of Information Act Manual. Paperback: £79.00. ISBN 0 421 92240 0. Sweet & Maxwell.

Turner, Chris; Storey, Tony—Unlocking EU Law. Paperback: £18.99. ISBN 0 340 88759 1. Hodder Arnold H&S.

Turner, Chris—Contract Law. Key Facts S. Paperback: £5.99. ISBN 0 340 88949 7. Hodder & Stoughton Ltd.

Turner, Chris–Employment Law. Key Facts S. Paperback: £5.99. ISBN 0 340 88947 0. Hodder & Stoughton Ltd.

Turner, Chris–Tort Law. Key Facts S. Paperback: £5.99. ISBN 0 340 88948 9. Hodder & Stoughton Ltd.

Turner, Jonathan D.C.–Intellectual Property and EU Competition Law. Hardback: £95.00. ISBN 1 904501 45 1. Richmond Law & Tax.

Turner, Jonathan D.C.–Vertical Agreements and EU Competition Law. Hardback: £95.00. ISBN 1 904501 56 7. Richmond Law & Tax.

Tushnet, M.–Court Divided: The Rehnquist Court and the Future of Constitutional Law. Hardback: £19.99. ISBN 0 393 05868 9. W.W. Norton & Company Ltd.

Tweeddale, Andrew; Tweeddale, Keren–Arbitration of Commercial Disputes: International and English Law and Practice. Hardback: £180.00. ISBN 0 19 926540 2. Oxford University Press.

Uff, John–Construction Law. Paperback: £26.00. ISBN 0 421 90420 8. Sweet & Maxwell.

UK Financial Services, Regulations & Ethics. Paperback: £29.95. ISBN 0 7517 2193 X. BPP Business Education Ltd.

UK Ministry of Defence–Manual of the Law of Armed Conflict. Paperback: £30.00. ISBN 0 19 928728 7. Oxford University Press.

Ulph, Janet–Commercial Fraud: Civil Liability for Fraud, Human Rights, and Money Laundering. Hardback: £115.00. ISBN 0 19 826867 X. Oxford University Press.

Unjust Enrichment: Lawbasics. Paperback: £9.95. ISBN 0 414 01597 5. W.Green & Son.

Unlocking the English Legal System. Paperback: £18.99. ISBN 0 340 88693 5. Hodder Arnold H&S.

Valcke, Peggy; Queck, Robert; Lievens, Eva–EU Communications Law: Significant Market Power in the Mobile Sector. Hardback: £49.95. ISBN 1 84542 416 6. Edward Elgar.

Valverde, J.L.; Weissenberg, P.–Challenges of the New EU Pharmaceutical Legislation. Paperback: £60.00. ISBN 1 58603 521 5. IOS Press.

Van der Merwe, D.P.; Terblanche, S.S.; Naude, B.C.; Moodley, K.–Law of Evidence: Cases and Statutes. Paperback: £30.00. ISBN 0 7021 6725 8. Juta Legal and Academic Publishers.

Van Dokkum, Neil–Nursing Law for Irish Students. Paperback: £27.99. ISBN 0 7171 3837 2. Gill & Macmillan.

Vaver, David–Intellectual Property Rights: Major Writings. Hardback: £525.00. ISBN 0 415 33087 4. Routledge,an imprint of Taylor & Francis Books Ltd.

Ventura, John–Divorce for Dummies. For Dummies S. Paperback: £12.99. ISBN 0 7645 8417 0. Hungry Minds Inc,U.S.

Ventura, John–Law for Dummies. Paperback: £14.99. ISBN 0 7645 5830 7. Hungry Minds Inc.

Vermulst, Edwin–WTO Anti-Dumping Agreement: A Commentary. Oxford Commentaries on International Law S. Hardback: £75.00. ISBN 0 19 927707 9. Oxford University Press.

Viegas, Jose Manuel–Interurban Road Charging for Trucks in Europeresearch in Transportation & Economics Vol 11 (Rtec). Hardback: £59.99. ISBN 0 7623 1142 8. Elsevier Science.

Vince–Evidence Collection Field Guide. Spiral / comb bound: £13.99. ISBN 0 7637 4788 2. Jones and Bartlett Publishers International.

Vinter, Graham; Piarce, Gareth–Practical Project Finance. Hardback: £165.00. ISBN 0 421 90950 1. Sweet & Maxwell.

Vogler, Richard K.–World View of Criminal Justice: Hunger for Justice. International and Comparative Criminal Justice S. Hardback: £55.00. ISBN 0 7546 2467 6. Ashgate.

Voller, Paul–Charitable Incorporated Organisation. Hardback: £75.00. ISBN 1 903927 43 9. Legalease.

Vos, Esme de Guzman–Licensing and Distributing Software in Europe: A Country by Country Look At Structuring International Software Agreements To Fit Your Needs. Hardback: £219.95. ISBN 1 59622 007 4. Aspatore Books.

Vrins, Olivier; Schneider, Marius–Enforcement of Intellectual Property Rights Through Border Measures: Law and Practice in the EU. Hardback: £175.00. ISBN 0 19 928879 8. Oxford University Press.

Wade, Peter–Practical Guide to Obtaining Probate. Emerald Home Lawyer S. Paperback: £9.99. ISBN 1 903909 62 7. Straightforward Publishing.

Wade, Peter–Practical Guide to Residential Conveyancing. Emerald Home Lawyers S. Paperback: £9.99. ISBN 1 903909 60 0. Straightforward Publishing.

Wade, Peter–You and Your Legal Rights. Emerald Home Lawyers S. Paperback: £9.99. ISBN 1 903909 61 9. Straightforward Publishing.

Wadlow, Christopher–Law of Passing-off: Unfair Competition by Misrepresentation. Paperback: £65.00. ISBN 0 421 91960 4. Sweet & Maxwell.

Wagenaar, Willem Albert; Crombag, Hans–Popular Policeman and Other Cases: Psychological Perspectives on Legal Evidence. Hardback: £60.00. ISBN 90 5356 770 4. Amsterdam University Press.

Wagner, Andrea–How to Land Your First Paralegal Job. Paperback: £17.99. ISBN 0 13 118382 6. Prentice Hall.

Wagner, Gerhard–Tort Law and Liability Insurance. Tort & Insurance Law, V.16. Paperback: £60.00. ISBN 3 211 24482 4. Springer-Verlag Vienna.

Waite, John-Paul; Payne, Alan; Isted, Barry–Tottel's Employment Tribunal Handbook. Paperback: £45.00. ISBN 1 84592 006 6. Tottel Publishing.

Wallington, Peter; Lee, Robert G.–Statutes on Public Law and Human Rights. Blackstone's Statute Books. Paperback: £15.99. ISBN 0 19 928314 1. Paperback: £15.99. ISBN 0 19 928314 1. Oxford University Press.

Wallis, Peter; McCormac, Kevin; Swift, Kathryn–Wilkinson's Road Traffic Offences: 2nd Supplement. Paperback: £58.00. ISBN 0 421 88100 3. Sweet & Maxwell.

Walmsley, Keith–Butterworths Company Law Handbook. Paperback: £55.00. ISBN 1 4057 0774 7. Butterworths Law.

Walmsley, Keith–Butterworths Corporate Governance Handbook. Paperback: £69.00. ISBN 1 4057 1054 3. Butterworths Law.

Walsh, Elizabeth–Working in the Family Justice System. Paperback: £30.00. ISBN 0 85308 996 5. Jordans.

Walsh, Gavin–Worst Acts of Violence, Abortion, Law and Ethics in Humanity. Hardback: £18.99. ISBN 1 84401 437 1. Athena Press.

Walsh, Kathleen Moore; Hanly, Conor–Make That Grade Irish Criminal Law. Paperback: £14.99. ISBN 0 7171 3744 9. Gill & Macmillan.

Walston-Dunham, Beth–Medical Malpractice Law. Hardback: £29.99. ISBN 1 4018 5246 7. Delmar.

Walton, Christopher; Cooper, Roger; Wood, Simon E; Percy, R a–Charlesworth and Percy on Negligence, 4th Supplement. Paperback: £49.00. ISBN 0 421 90630 8. Sweet & Maxwell.

Walton, Kevin; Antczak, Gina–Tolley's Corporation Tax Workbook. Paperback: £27.95. ISBN 0 7545 2884 7. Tolley Publishing.

Walton, Kevin; Antczak, Gina–Tolley's Corporation Tax: Budget Edition and Main Annual. Paperback: £97.95. ISBN 0 7545 2860 X. Tolley Publishing.

Walton, Kevin; Antczak, Gina–Tolley's Corporation Tax: Main Annual. Paperback: £85.95. ISBN 0 7545 2861 8. Tolley Publishing.

Walton, Kevin; Dolton, Alan–Tolley's Tax Cases. Paperback: £86.95. ISBN 0 7545 2886 3. Tolley Publishing.

Walton, Kevin; Flint, Andrew–Tolley's Capital Gains Tax Workbook. Paperback: £27.95. ISBN 0 7545 2883 9. Tolley Publishing.

Walton, Kevin; Flint, Andrew–Tolley's Capital Gains Tax: Main Annual. Paperback: £82.95. ISBN 0 7545 2859 6. Tolley Publishing.

Ward, Adrian–Adults with Incapacity Legislation. Paperback: £38.00. ISBN 0 414 01580 0. W. Green & Son.

Ward, John; Burke, Dara–Judge Irish Income Tax. Hardback: £86.66. ISBN 1 84592 146 1. Tottel Publishing.

Wareham, Robert; Antczak, Gina–Whillans's Tax Tables: Budget Edition. Paperback: £29.50. ISBN 1 4057 0741 0. Tolley Publishing.

Wareham, Robert; Antczak, Gina–Whillans's Tax Tables. Paperback: £29.50. ISBN 1 4057 0750 X. Tolley Publishing.

Wareham, Robert; Dolton, Alan–Tolley's VAT Cases. Paperback: £110.00. ISBN 0 7545 2889 8. Tolley Publishing.

Wareham, Robert–Tottel's Vat Planning. Paperback: £98.95. ISBN 1 84592 195 X. Tottel Publishing.

Waring, Mike–Commercial Dispute Resolution. Paperback: £24.95. ISBN 0 905835 76 X. Paperback: £25.95. ISBN 1 905391 02 1. The College of Law.

Warne, David; Elliott, Nicholas–Banking Litigation. Hardback: £189.00. ISBN 0 421 88300 6. Sweet & Maxwell.

Warrell, David A.; Cox, Timothy M.; Firth, John D.; Benz, Edward J.–Oxford Textbook of Medicine. Paperback: £150.00. ISBN 0 19 856978 5. Oxford University Press.

Waterman, Chris; Fowler, John–Plain Guide to the Children Act 2004. Paperback: £20.00. ISBN 1 903880 76 9. National Foundation for Educational Research.

Waterworth, Michael; Bedworth, Georgia–Rossdale-Probate and the Administration of Estates: A Practical Guide. Hardback: £75.00. ISBN 1 903927 66 8. Legalease.

Watson, Philippa–EU Social and Employment Law. Hardback: £95.00. ISBN 1 904501 53 2. Richmond Law & Tax.

Watson, Robert; Watson, Louise–Business Accounting for Solicitors. Paperback: £48.00. ISBN 1 84592 206 9. Tottel Publishing.

Watt, Bob–UK Election Law: A Critical Examination. Glasshouse S. Hardback: £55.00. ISBN 1 85941 998 4. The Glasshouse Press. Paperback: £27.00. ISBN 1 85941 916 X. Cavendish Publishing Ltd.

Watt, Gary–Todd and Watt's Cases and Materials on Equity and Trusts. Paperback: £28.99. ISBN 0 19 927982 9. Oxford University Press.

Weatherill, Stephen–Cases and Materials on EU Law. Paperback: £28.99. ISBN 0 19 928223 4. Paperback: £28.99. ISBN 0 19 928223 4. Oxford University Press.

Weatherill, Stephen–EU Consumer Law and Policy. Elgar European Law S. Hardback: £59.95. ISBN 1 84376 963 8. Edward Elgar.

Webb, L. Dean; Underwood, Julie–School Law for Teachers: Concepts and Applications. Paperback: £23.99. ISBN 0 13 119242 6. Prentice Hall.

Webber, Gary; Dovar, Daniel–Residential Possession Proceedings. Paperback: £85.00. ISBN 0 421 91880 2. Sweet & Maxwell.

Wecht, Cyril H.–Forensic Science and the Law: Investigation Evidence in Criminal and Civil Cases. Hardback: £44.99. ISBN 0 8493 1970 6. CRC Press.

Weiler, Todd–International Law and Arbitration: Leading Cases from the ICSID, NAFTA, Bilateral Treaties and Customary International Law. Hardback: £125.00. ISBN 1 905017 07 3. Cameron May.

Weinreb, Lloyd L.–Legal Reason: The Use of Analogy in Legal Argument. Hardback: £30.00. ISBN 0 521 84967 5. Cambridge University Press.

Weiss, Edith Brown; Chazournes, Laurence Boisson De; Bernasconi-Osterwalder, Nathalie–Fresh Water and International Economic Law. International Economic Law S. Hardback: £70.00. ISBN 0 19 927467 3. Oxford University Press.

Weller, Marc–Rights of Minorities: A Commentary on the European Framework Convention for the Protection of National Minorities. Oxford Commentaries on International Law S. Hardback: £95.00. ISBN 0 19 927858 X. Oxford University Press.

Wellman, Christopher; Simmons, John—Is There a Duty to Obey the Law? For & Against S. Hardback: £30.00. ISBN 0 521 83097 4. Paperback: £12.99. ISBN 0 521 53784 3. Cambridge University Press.

Welsh, Tom; Greenwood, Walter; Banks, David—McNae's Essential Law for Journalists. Paperback: £16.99. ISBN 0 19 928418 0. Oxford University Press.

Westminster Media Forum—Intellectual Property and Rights Ownership. Paperback: £85.00. ISBN 1 905029 10 1. Westminster Forum Projects Ltd.

Wheeler, John—Essentials of the English Legal System. Frameworks S. Paperback: £19.99. ISBN 1 4058 1167 6. Longman.

Which? Books—Giving and Inheriting: An Action Pack from Which? Which? Action Pack S. Paperback: £10.99. ISBN 0 85202 980 2. Which? Books.

White, Jeremy; Obuoforibo, Belema—Tolley's Customs Duties Handbook. Paperback: £99.95. ISBN 1 4057 0754 2. Tolley Publishing.

White, Jeremy—Excise Duties Handbook. Paperback: £78.00. ISBN 0 7545 2887 1. Tolley Publishing.

Whitehouse, Chris; Chamberlain, Emma—Taxation Aspects of the Family Home. Paperback: £85.00. ISBN 0 7545 2800 6. Tolley Publishing.

Whitehouse, Christopher; Rothenberg, David—Trust Drafting and Precedents. Looseleaf/ring bound: £195.00. ISBN 0 7545 1624 5. LexisNexis UK.

Whiteman, Peter; Gammie, Malcolm; Herbert, Mark; Sherry, Michael—Whiteman on Capital Gains Tax: Supplement 15. Paperback: £135.00. ISBN 0 421 91570 6. Sweet & Maxwell.

Whiteman, Peter; Goy, David; Sandison, Francis; Sherry, Michael—Whiteman on Income Tax: Supplement 16. Paperback: £165.00. ISBN 0 421 91750 4. Sweet & Maxwell.

Whiteman, Peter; Goy, David; Sandison, Francis; Sherry, Michael—Whiteman on Income Tax. Hardback: £155.00. ISBN 0 421 89020 7. Sweet & Maxwell.

Wignall, Gordon; Napier, Michael—Conditional Fees: A Guide to Funding Litigation. Paperback: £39.95. ISBN 1 85328 992 2. Law Society Publications.

Wikeley, Nick; Williams, David—Social Security: V. 4. Tax Credits: Legislation 2005. Paperback: £77.00. ISBN 0 421 92090 4. Sweet & Maxwell.

Wilde, Robin de—Facts and Figures: Tables for the Calculation of Damages. Paperback: £41.00. ISBN 0 421 90530 1. Sweet & Maxwell.

Wilkie, Margaret; Malcolm, Rosalind; Luxton, Peter—Q & A: Equity and Trusts 2006-2007. Blackstone's Law Q & A S. Paperback: £13.99. ISBN 0 19 929099 7. Oxford University Press.

Williams, Andrew—EU Human Rights Policies: A Study in Irony. Oxford Studies in European Law. Paperback: £19.99. ISBN 0 19 929149 7. Oxford University Press.

Williams, Hugh; King, Brian—How to Avoid Inheritance Tax. Paperback: £9.99. ISBN 1 905261 09 8. Lawpack Publishing Ltd.

Williams; Brewer—Psychology and Law: An Empirical Perspective. Hardback: £45.00. ISBN 1 59385 122 7. Guilford Press.

Willis—Introduction to EU Competition Law. Hardback: £150.00. ISBN 1 84311 435 6. Informa Business Publishing.

Wilman, John—Brown: GCSE Law. Paperback: £13.95. ISBN 0 421 89790 2. Sweet & Maxwell.

Wilson, Caroline—Intellectual Property Law. Paperback: £6.50. ISBN 0 421 89150 5. Sweet & Maxwell.

Wilson, Catherine; Gillow, Elizabeth; Edwards, Gareth—Discrimination in Employment. Looseleaf release (unbound): £165.00. ISBN 1 903927 47 1. Legalease.

Wilson, Dean; Norris, Clive—Surveillance, Cime and Social Control. International Library of Criminology, Criminal Justice & Penology 2nd Series. Hardback: £120.00. ISBN 0 7546 2460 9. Ashgate.

Wilson, Martin—Tottel's Capital Allowances: Transactions and Planning. Paperback: £82.95. ISBN 1 84592 190 9. Tottel Publishing.

Wilson, Richard A.—Human Rights in the War on Terror. Hardback: £40.00. ISBN 0 521 85319 2. Paperback: £16.99. ISBN 0 521 61833 9. Cambridge University Press.

Winkler, Gunther—European Council. Paperback: £75.50. ISBN 3 211 27962 8. Springer-Verlag Vienna.

Winning Legal Strategies for Employment Law: What Every Company Should Know About Labor Law and Legal Compliance. Inside the Minds S. Paperback: £49.95. ISBN 1 58762 995 X. Aspatore Books.

Winning Legal Strategies for Telecom Companies: Top Lawyers on Telecommunications Regulations and Creating Legal Game Plans. Inside the Minds S. Paperback: £37.95. ISBN 1 58762 012 X. Aspatore Books.

Wintgens, Luc J.—Theory and Practice of Legislation: Essays in Legisprudence. Applied Legal Philosophy S. Hardback: £60.00. ISBN 0 7546 2461 7. Ashgate.

Witkey, J.—Equity Release: A Practioner's Guide. Paperback: £50.00. ISBN 0 85308 958 2. Jordans.

Woelke, Andrea—Civil Partnership: Law and Practice. Paperback: £49.95. ISBN 1 85328 973 6. Law Society Publications.

Wojciech Sadurski—Constitutional Theory. International Library Essays in Law & Legal Theory (Second Series). Hardback: £130.00. ISBN 0 7546 2363 7. Ashgate.

Wolcher, Louis—Beyond Transcendence in Law and Philosophy. Hardback: £60.00. ISBN 1 85941 988 7. Birkbeck Law Press.

Wolff, Florian; Voelker, Dietmar; Bott, Kristofer—German Tax and Business Law Guide. Paperback: £165.00. ISBN 0 421 91330 4. Sweet & Maxwell.

Womersley, Mark—Law and Practice of Corporate Governance. Looseleaf/ring bound: £245.00. ISBN 0 9550898 0 8. Vine Publications Ltd.

Wong, Carolyn—Lobbying for Inclusion: Rights Politics and the Making of Immigration Policy. Hardback: £32.95. ISBN 0 8047 5175 7. Stanford University Press.

Wood, Helen; Lush, Denzil; Bishop, David—Cohabitation: Law, Practice and Precedents. Hardback/CD-ROM (software): £75.00. ISBN 0 85308 962 0. Family Law.

Wood, Penny; Wikeley, Nick; Poynter, Richard; Bonner, David—Social Security: Vol 2. Income Related Benefits: Legislation 2005. Paperback: £77.00. ISBN 0 421 92050 5. Sweet & Maxwell.

Wood, Roderick J.; Cuming, Ronald C.C.; Walsh, Catherine—Personal Property Security Law. Paperback: £32.00. ISBN 1 55221 110 X. Irwin Law Inc.

Woodley, M.; Bone, Sheila—Osborn's Concise Law Dictionary. Paperback: £9.95. ISBN 0 421 90050 4. Sweet & Maxwell.

Woods, Michael; Jewell, Tim; Waite, Andrew—Environmental Law in Property Transactions. Paperback: £70.00. ISBN 0 406 97866 2. Butterworths Law.

Woolman, Stephen E; Lake, Jonathan—Woolman Contract. Paperback: £31.00. ISBN 0 414 01647 5. W. Green & Son.

Words and Phrases: 2005 Supplement. Paperback: £75.00. ISBN 1 4057 0775 5. Butterworths Law.

World Bank—Doing Business in 2006: Services for Business-Creating Jobs. Hardback: £21.50. ISBN 0 8213 5749 2. World Bank.

World Trade Organization—Dispute Settlement Reports: V. 4. Pages 1987-1818. World Trade Organization Dispute Settlement Reports. Hardback: £90.00. ISBN 0 521 85463 6. Cambridge University Press.

World Trade Organization–Dispute Settlement Reports: V. 5. Pages 1819-2070. World Trade Organization Dispute Settlement Reports. Hardback: £90.00. ISBN 0 521 85464 4. Cambridge University Press.

World Trade Organization–Dispute Settlement Reports: V. 6. Pages 2071-2578. World Trade Organization Dispute Settlement Reports. Hardback: £90.00. ISBN 0 521 85465 2. Cambridge University Press.

World Trade Organization–Dispute Settlement Reports: V. 6. World Trade Organization Dispute Settlement Reports. Hardback: £90.00. ISBN 0 521 85996 4. Cambridge University Press.

World Trade Organization–Dispute Settlement Reports: V. 7. Pages 2579-3042. World Trade Organization Dispute Settlement Reports. Hardback: £90.00. ISBN 0 521 85466 0. Cambridge University Press.

World Trade Organization–Dispute Settlement Reports: V. 7. World Trade Organization Dispute Settlement Reports. Hardback: £90.00. ISBN 0 521 85997 2. Cambridge University Press.

World Trade Organization–Dispute Settlement Reports: V. 8. Pages 3043-3594. World Trade Organization Dispute Settlement Reports. Hardback: £90.00. ISBN 0 521 85467 9. Cambridge University Press.

World Trade Organization–Dispute Settlement Reports: V. 8. World Trade Organization Dispute Settlement Reports. Hardback: £90.00. ISBN 0 521 85998 0. Cambridge University Press.

World Trade Organization–Dispute Settlement Reports: V. 9. World Trade Organization Dispute Settlement Reports. Hardback: £90.00. ISBN 0 521 85999 9. Cambridge University Press.

Worsdall, Anthea–Consumer Law for the Motor Trade. Paperback: £35.00. ISBN 1 84592 018 X. Tottel Publishing.

Wright, Alan–Organised Crime: Concepts, Cases, Controls. Hardback: £40.00. ISBN 1 84392 141 3. Paperback: £17.99. ISBN 1 84392 140 5. Willan Publishing.

Wroblesk; Hess–Police Operations 4e-4th Ed. Hardback: £39.00. ISBN 0 534 63222 X. Wadsworth.

Wylie, John; Keogan, Aileen; Mee, John–Law and Taxation of Trusts. Looseleaf/ring bound: £213.33. ISBN 1 84592 202 6. Tottel Publishing.

Wylie, John–Irish Conveyancing Law. Paperback: £110.00. ISBN 1 84592 086 4. Tottel Publishing.

Wylie, John–Irish Landlord and Tenant Law Service. Looseleaf/ring bound: £283.71. ISBN 1 85475 313 4. Butterworths Law (Ireland).

Wynn-Evans, Charles–Blackstone's Guide to the 2005 Transfer of Undertakings Regulations. Blackstone's Guide S. Paperback: £29.95. ISBN 0 19 928905 0. Oxford University Press.

Yaman Akdeniz–Internet Child Pornography and the Laws Response: National and International. Hardback: £50.00. ISBN 0 7546 2297 5. Ashgate.

Yellow and Orange Tax Handbooks. Paperback: £200.00. ISBN 1 4057 0933 2. Tolley Publishing.

Yellow Tax Handbook. Paperback: £120.00. ISBN 1 4057 0924 3. Paperback: £81.00. ISBN 1 4057 0744 5. Tolley Publishing.

Yelton, Michael–Trams and Buses and the Law: The Legal Background to the Operation of Trams, Trolleybuses and Buses Before Deregulation: a Guide for Historians and Enthusiasts. Paperback: £15.00. ISBN 1 874422 51 6. Adam Gordon.

You and the Law in Spain. Paperback: £19.95. ISBN 84 89954 41 0. Santana Books (Santana, Ediciones, S.L.).

Young, Kelly; Hubber, David–Shaw's Directory of Courts in the United Kingdom. Shaw's Directory of Courts in the United Kingdom. Paperback: £45.00. ISBN 0 7219 1632 5. Shaw & Sons.

Yule, Freya–Straightforward Guide to Competition Law of the United Kingdom. Paperback: £8.99. ISBN 1 903909 54 6. Straightforward Publishing.

Zaelke, Durwood; Kaniaru, Donald; Kruzikova, Eva–Making Law Work: Environmental Compliance and Sustainable Development. Paperback: £100.00. ISBN 1 905017 09 X. Cameron May.

Zakrzewski, Rafal–Remedies Reclassified. Hardback: £60.00. ISBN 0 19 927875 X. Oxford University Press.

Zalman, Marvin–Essentials of Criminal Procedure. Paperback: £32.99. ISBN 0 13 113601 1. Prentice Hall.

Zander, Michael–Police and Criminal Evidence Act, 1984. Paperback: £65.00. ISBN 0 421 90580 8. Sweet & Maxwell.

Zwaan, Jaap W.de; Jans, Jan H.; Nelissen, Frans A.; Blockmans, Steven–European Union, an Ongoing Process of Integration: Liber Amicorum Alfred E. Kellermann. Hardback: £55.00. ISBN 90 6704 187 4. Asser Press.

Zyla, Eric–Construction Contractor's Duty To Warn. Paperback: £7.53. ISBN 1 4116 4171 X. Lulu Press Incorporated.

INDEX 2005

asylum -*cont.*
  asylum seekers -*cont.*
    entitlement to support by making application for permission to appeal out of time, 05/2156
    extensions of time
      need to show real prospect of success, 05/2151
    fear of persecution
      country information evidence, 05/2188
    female genital mutilation
      inhuman or degrading treatment or punishment, 05/5440S
    fresh evidence submitted without notice of intention to rely on it, 05/2214
    grant of leave to remain
      special circumstances, 05/2149
    homosexuality
      relevance of discreet behaviour to avoid persecution in Bangladesh, 05/2164
    Immigration Appeal Tribunal
      jurisdiction of appeals, 05/2165
    immigration policy on disputed age
      credible medical evidence, 05/2145
    inhuman or degrading treatment or punishment
      appropriate approach to assessment of real risk of ill treatment, 05/2166
      sufficiency of state protection, 05/2167
    internal relocation
      IAT's entitlement to interfere with asylum adjudicator's findings of fact, 05/2217
      persecution by Chinese authorities, 05/5436S
    lawfulness of fast track scheme, 05/2155
    leave to appeal
      appropriate test, 05/5437S
    legality of pre entry clearance scheme operated by UK immigration officials at Prague Airport, 05/2162
    local authority assessment of age of applicant
      failure to pay regard to expert evidence, 05/2146
    obtaining leave by deception
      judicial review of sentence, 05/2171
    persecution
      adequacy of adjudicator's reasoning, 05/2173
      adjudicator failing to properly assess position in event of return, 05/2172
      claims of persecution due to homosexuality, 05/2140
      refusal to undertake military service, 05/5439S
    reasons for refusal, 05/5442S
    refugees
      internal relocation not required if unduly harsh or unreasonable, 05/2176
      refugee status of conscientious objectors, 05/2178
    refusal
      reasonableness, 05/5441S
    removal

asylum -*cont.*
  asylum seekers -*cont.*
    removal -*cont.*
      applicant relying on ill health of son and right to respect for private and family life, 05/2179
      effect of UK's failure to comply with procedural requirement, 05/2180
      reliance on Council Regulation 343/2003 Art.15, 05/2181
    removal directions
      application not determined within six months, 05/5443S
    support
      cash payments, 05/2185
    torture
      error of law in approach to medical evidence, 05/2187
      well founded fear of persecution in Albania, 05/2177
  immigration appeals
    appellants costs, 05/2712
Asylum and Immigration (Treatment of Claimants, etc.) Act 2004 (c.19)
  Commencement No.4 Order, 05/2141
  Commencement No.5 and Transitional Provisions, 05/2142
asylum policy
  judicial titles, 05/2143
asylum seekers
  accommodation
    reception conditions, 05/2144
  entry clearances
    refusal
      extent of right of respect for private and family life, 05/2195
  provision of accommodation, 05/2175
  response to enquiries, 05/2183
  support
    interim period, 05/2186
Audit Commission
  Auditor General for Wales
    functions, 05/61, 62
  transfer of assets, 05/63
auditors
  registered pension schemes, 05/2935
aviation
  air navigation
    carriage by air
      dangerous goods, 05/243
  airlines
    disability discrimination
      provision of wheelchairs for disabled passengers, 05/249
  publications, 05/254
aviation industry
  accidents
    investigations, 05/252
  flight delays and cancellations
    offences, 05/250
  insurance requirements, 05/253
bail
  prosecuting authorities, 05/836
bail conditions
  electronic monitoring requirements

best value -cont.
local authorities powers and duties
performance indicators and standards, 05/2774
police authorities
performance indicators, 05/3329
biofuels
labelling, 05/1342
birth
internet search sessions
extension, 05/5269S
blood products
collection and storage
safety, 05/1790, 1791
criminal offences
penalties, 05/1792
safety and quality, 05/1790, 1791
boarding schools
school inspections, 05/4555NI
Breastfeeding etc. (Scotland) Act 2005 (asp 1), 05/5246S
bridges
Erewash Canal, 05/3446
tolls
Severn Bridges, 05/3447
Skye Bridge, 05/5635S
broadcasting
copyright
licensing scheme
educational establishments, 05/2411
foreign satellite services, 05/4171
television licences
fees, 05/4172
budget
use of resources, 05/5690S
Budget (No.2) (Northern Ireland) Order 2005 (SI 2005 1962 (NI.12)), 05/4905NI
Budget (Northern Ireland) Order 2005 (SI 2005 860 (NI.3)), 05/4904NI
Budget (Scotland) (No.2) Act 2005 (asp 4), 05/5371S
building regulations
European standards
testing, 05/4518NI
prescribed forms, 05/5067S
building societies
income tax
interest, 05/3987
burials and cremation
fees
parochial fees, 05/994
Burma
financial sanctions
criminal offences, 05/2608
canals
compulsory acquisition of land
Ashby de la Zouch, 05/3244
capital allowances
energy conservation
machinery, 05/3989
environmental protection
plant and machinery, 05/3990
capital gains tax
annual exempt amount
2005-2006, 05/3992

capital gains tax -cont.
gilt edged securities
exemptions, 05/3994
care
care standards
social workers
registration, 05/4903NI
children
entitlement to benefits
disapplication, 05/4853NI
local authorities duties, 05/4893NI
regulation of care
deemed registration, 05/5677S
excepted services, 05/5678S
fees, 05/5679S
prescribed registers, 05/5680S
social service workers
registers, 05/5681S, 5682S
standards
adoption support agencies
registration, 05/3933
regulation, 05/3913
Care of Cathedrals (Amendment) Measure 2005 (No.2), 05/988
Care Standards Act 2000 (c.14)
Commencement No.21 Order
Wales, 05/3935
Carers (Equal Opportunities) Act 2004 (c.15)
Commencement Order
England, 05/3938
Wales, 05/3939
carriage by road
international carriage by road
dangerous goods
fees, 05/4210
road transport
working time, 05/4279, 4922NI
carriage of goods
motor vehicles
type approval
fees, 05/4205
Channel Tunnel
international cooperation, 05/4206
charitable accounts
accounts and audits, 05/281
charities
armed forces
transfer of assets
Royal Patriotic Fund Corporation, 05/280
charitable donations
declarations, 05/4066
charitable status
churches
pension scheme for church employees, 05/282
National Lottery
distributing bodies
New Opportunities Fund, 05/2766
grants
New Opportunities Fund, 05/1974
Millennium Commission
membership, 05/1975
transformational grants joint scheme
authorisation, 05/284
National Trust

childrens services
children and young people's plans
   publication and review, 05/3940
children and young persons
   list of services, 05/3941
   reviews, 05/3942
Church of England (Miscellaneous Provisions)
Measure 2005 (No.3), 05/989
churches
Churches Conservation Trust
   grants, 05/998
citizenship
British nationality
   English language, 05/2191
Civil Contingencies Act 2004 (c.36)
Commencement No.2 Order, 05/2775
Commencement No.3 Order, 05/2776
Commencement Order
   Scotland, 05/5508S
civil evidence
admissibility
   eyewitness evidence and magistrates' findings
     from linked criminal proceedings, 05/287
   fatal accident inquiries
     privilege against self incrimination, 05/
      5024S
   similar fact evidence
     potentially probative nature of evidence,
      05/302
   witness statements
     without prejudice communications, 05/289
burden of proof
   contract for sale of land
     master's erroneous reliance on burden of
      proof, 05/292
disclosable documents
   breach of right of defence to examine
     documents, 05/1435
disclosure
   litigation privilege
     misrepresentation relating to disclosure,
      05/293
disclosure and inspection
   litigation privilege
     applicability of "fraud exception", 05/294
expert evidence
   court's power to give permission for the
     instruction of experts, 05/296
legal professional privilege, inquiries
   scope of legal advice privilege, 05/299
negotiations
   admissibility of evidence of contract
     negotiations for purpose of construing
     contract, 05/288
oral evidence
   privilege
     disclosure of notes of evidence taken by
      solicitor at employment tribunal hearing,
      05/300
   witnesses abroad
     jurisdiction to hear oral evidence overseas,
      05/301
privilege against self incrimination
   evidence of public examination admitted at
     criminal trial

civil evidence -*cont.*
privilege against self incrimination -*cont.*
   evidence of public examination admitted at
     criminal trial -*cont.*
     compatibility with ECHR, 05/2092
publications, 05/304
video evidence
   witnesses
     fugitive seeking to give evidence by video
      conference link, 05/303
witness statements
   admissibility of fresh evidence, 05/290
Civil Partnership Act 2004 (c.33)
Commencement No.1 Order, 05/1591
   Northern Ireland, 05/4626NI
   Scotland, 05/5254S
Commencement No.2 Order, 05/1592
   Northern Ireland, 05/4627NI
   Scotland, 05/5255S
Commencement No.3 Order, 05/4628NI
civil partnerships
advice and assistance, 05/4737NI
approved premises, 05/65
armed forces
   Ulster Defence Regiment, 05/2932
births, deaths and marriages
   armed forces
     registration, 05/221
   registration, 05/4629NI
births, still-births, deaths and marriages
   prescribed forms, 05/5256S
categorisation of earners
   equal treatment, 05/3849, 4857NI
change of name
   enrolment of deeds, 05/1537
consequential amendments, 05/1593, 4630NI,
   4631NI, 4858NI, 5257S
consequential modifications, 05/5258S
consular services
   fees, 05/2596
county courts
   allocation of proceedings, 05/12
Court of Session
   applications for separation or divorce, 05/
     4935S
family proceedings, 05/1636, 4640NI
   consequential amendments, 05/1594
forms and particulars, 05/4632NI
housing benefit and child support
   consequential provisions, 05/4633NI
immigration control, 05/1595
jurisdiction of judgements, 05/1596, 5259S
legal aid, 05/4734NI, 4735NI, 4736NI
magistrates courts
   miscellaneous amendments, 05/1597
marriage
   forms, 05/5260S
marriages
   registration forms, 05/1598
Members of Parliament
   House of Commons
     beneficiaries, 05/1599
national insurance contributions, 05/3891
Naval Medical Compassionate Fund, 05/222
navy and marines

civil partnerships -cont.
  navy and marines -cont.
    property of deceased, 05/223
  occupational and personal pensions, 05/1600
  overseas relationships, 05/1602, 1603, 1604, 4634NI, 5261S
    consequential amendments, 05/1605
  pension and benefit payments, 05/4635NI
  pension schemes
    firefighters
      survivor benefits, 05/3035
  pensions, 05/1606
    consequential provisions, 05/4633NI
    judicial office holders, 05/2945
  pensions and benefit payments, 05/1607, 4636NI
  recognition of dissolutions, annulments and separations, 05/5262S
  recognition of judgements, 05/1596, 5259S
  recognition of overseas dissolutions, annulments and separations, 05/1608
  registration, 05/1609
    armed forces, 05/1610
    fees, 05/1611, 1612, 4447NI, 5272S
    forms, 05/1613
    prescription of forms, 05/5263S
  registration abroad, 05/1614
  relationships, 05/1615, 4638NI
  reporting of suspicious partnerships
    procedure, 05/1616
  reserve forces, 05/224
  same sex couples
    registration, 05/1593
  sheriff courts, 05/5264S
  social security
    pensions and child support, 05/1617
  step relationships, 05/5265S
  subordinate legislation
    consequential amendments
      Wales, 05/1618
  tax treatment, 05/4010, 4011
  vaccinations
    armed forces, 05/1942
civil procedure
  abuse of process
    automatic stay
      claim for damages for sexual abuse, 05/306
  addition of parties
    negligence action against private consultant
      liability of trust staff, 05/307
    third parties
      insurer's liability to insured under directors and officers liability insurance, 05/424
  adjournments
    bankruptcy petitions
      legal and evidential complexities, 05/308
  adjustment
    validity of expert's determination, 05/309
  admissions
    compromise
      binding effect of compromise, 05/311
    withdrawal
      entitlement to resile from admission leading to judgment, 05/312

civil procedure -cont.
  allocation of jurisdiction
    breach of exclusive jurisdiction clauses in certificate of insurance, 05/420
  amendments
    causes of action
      new claims arising out of same or substantially same facts, 05/313
    limitation periods
      claims brought almost six years after breach, 05/314
    substitution of parties, 05/315
  anti competitive practices
    lack of disclosed evidence
      claim having real prospects of success, 05/394
  anti social behaviour orders
    applications without notice, 05/316
    consultation
      effect of defendant's lack of involvement in decision making process, 05/318
    curfew requirements
      lawfulness of inclusion of curfew provision in anti social behaviour order, 05/319
  appeals
    extensions of time
      jurisdiction to vary time for filing appeal notice, 05/320
      no power to consider merits of case, 05/321
    Immigration Appeal Tribunal
      adjudicator's dismissal of claim as out of time, 05/322
    litigants in person
      adjudicator's duty to consider adjournment, 05/323
  applications without notice
    anti social behaviour injunctions, 05/324
  arrestment
    warrants
      arrestment on the dependence, 05/5025S
  bad character evidence
    applications procedure
      county courts, 05/4440NI
  breach of undertaking
    breach by prison services official, 05/5026S
  capacity
    intervention orders
      incapable adult, 05/5027S, 5028S
  case management
    costs capping orders, 05/327
    interim awards, 05/328
  causes of action
    defendants
      claimant paying costs of two defendants against which claims in negligence had failed, 05/359
  charging orders
    foreign currency judgment
      converting judgment debt into sterling prior to enforcement, 05/330
  civil appeals
    appeal withdrawn after compromise reached during adjournment, 05/334
    Court of Appeal

competition law -*cont.*
exclusive supply agreements -*cont.*
films, 05/579
leniency programmes
disclosure
documents pertaining to leniency application, 05/580
mergers
decision prohibiting merger adopted after withdrawal of notification
annulment of Commission Decision 2003/790, 05/582
dominant position
examination referred to Spanish competition authorities, 05/583
lawfulness of Commission's refusal to accept competency
time limits, 05/584
takeover bids
power of European Commission to make decisions, 05/585
Office of Fair trading
acquisitions
nature of guidance given, 05/587
administrative decision making
existence of appealable decision, 05/586
disclosure
commercially confidential information, 05/5061S
sports retailers
disclosure of sensitive information in commercial agreements to third parties, 05/588
pricing
application for interim relief on grounds of threat to commercial survival, 05/556
publications, 05/598
state aid
debt restructuring of failing company by State owned companies, 05/590
privatised industries
enforcement of tax and social security debts, 05/591
public service contracts
payments made to cover past and future losses, 05/592
shipbuilding
conditional authorisation of aid, 05/589
tax credits for investment in Basque country
no evidence of misuse of power in Commission investigation, 05/593
tax credits for investment in Basque county
no legitimate expectation of legality, 05/594
statements of objections
rights of defence, 05/595
telecommunications
tariffs
failure to comply with EC law, 05/596
unfair pricing
water supplies
sufficiency of interest, 05/597
veterinary medicinal products
fair trading, 05/581

compromise agreements
advice
description of persons, 05/1236
Comptroller and Auditor General for Wales
transfer of assets, 05/66
compulsory purchase
land acquisition
East Midlands Parkway Station, 05/4258
concurrent sentences
remand in custody
court directions, 05/3579
conditional fee agreements, 05/2700
confidential information
plastics industry
use by licensee of allegedly private information, 05/2416
confiscation orders
drug trafficking
decision to apply statutory presumption, 05/3749
conflict of laws
allocation of jurisdiction
action arising in Jamaica
forum conveniens, 05/604
anti suit injunctions
parallel proceedings to determine seat of arbitration, 05/600
arbitration clause in insurance contract
power of court second seised to consider application of arbitration exception, 05/599
banks
jurisdiction to order stay of proceedings, 05/601
construction of contract to determine jurisdiction
effect of service of suit clauses out of jurisdiction, 05/610
economic loss
loss incurred in another Member State, 05/603
family proceedings, 05/1645
indemnification agreement entered into by English and American companies
choice of law, 05/602
insurance claims
claim by charterer for vessel damage, 05/605
stay of proceedings, 05/606
internet libel
exercise of discretion in determining appropriate forum, 05/611
parallel proceedings
reference to without prejudice discussions to determine existence of dispute, 05/613
substantive or procedural law
measure of damages, 05/608
anti suit injunctions
exclusive English jurisdiction clause
permission to serve out of jurisdiction, 05/625
choice of forum
jurisdiction clauses, 05/614
choice of law

conflict of laws -*cont.*
  choice of law -*cont.*
    contracts
      no expressed choice of system of law, 05/616
    director's duties governed by law of place of incorporation
      speculative trading not outside authority of managing director, 05/615
  contracts
    choice of law
      characteristic performance, 05/617
  disputing the court's jurisdiction
    stay of proceedings
      application of Convention on the Contract for the International Carriage of Goods by Road, 05/618
  disputing the courts jurisdiction
    contractual and tortious claims arising from fraud
      court first seized, 05/607
  exclusive jurisdiction
    foreign proceedings
      scope of Art.16 of the Lugano Convention, 05/619
    jurisdiction clauses
      sale of shares in German company to English subsidiary, 05/620
  foreign judgments
    enforcement
      recovery of proceeds of fraud, 05/621
  jurisdiction
    contractual rights
      mail order, 05/623
  jurisdiction clauses
    anti suit injunctions
      stay of proceedings, 05/627
    application of clause to disputes with international element, 05/626
  publications, 05/629
  service out of jurisdiction
    pending actions
      stay of proceedings, 05/468
  shipping
    jurisdiction
      enforceability of limitation of liability fund, 05/624
  stay of proceedings
    forum shopping
      aircraft manufactured and repaired in United States with accident occurring in England, 05/622
conflict of laws, allocation of jurisdiction, service within jurisdiction on foreign principal's agent, 05/609
conflicts of laws
  service out of jurisdiction
    contract between beneficiary and issuing and confirming banks
      governing law of letter of credit, 05/628
conservation
  biocidal products, 05/1369
  countryside councils
    transfer of functions, 05/1357
  endangered species

conservation -*cont.*
  endangered species -*cont.*
    import and export controls
      criminal offences, 05/1358
    fishing
      prohibition of scallop dredging, 05/5281S
    plant protection, 05/5225S
    salmon
      annual closing time, 05/5279S
conservation areas
  listed buildings
    compilation of lists, 05/3259
Consolidated Fund Act 2005 (c.23), 05/2739
constitutional law
  Acts of Parliament
    Constitutionality
      correct procedure for amending entrenched provisions of Constitution, 05/630
  constitutional rights
    defence costs
      recoverability of defence costs from prosecution, 05/633
  constitutions
    letters patent
      power of Queen to issue letters patent, 05/634
  devolution
    Privy Council, 05/635
    Scottish Administration
      offices, 05/5064S
  National Assembly for Wales
    social services explanations, 05/3956
    transfer of functions, 05/87
  Northern Ireland Assembly
    legislatures, 05/4516NI
    powers during suspension, 05/4515NI
  parliamentary procedure
    validity of Parliament Act 1949
      consequent validity of Hunting Act 2004, 05/638
  political parties
    donations
      excluded categories, 05/4587NI
    registration
      prohibited words and expressions, 05/639
  publications, 05/640, 5066S
  Scottish Ministers
    transfer of functions, 05/5065S
  Scottish Parliament
    legislative competence, 05/5062S, 5063S
Constitutional Reform Act 2005 (c.4), 05/631
  Commencement No.1 Order, 05/4513NI
  Commencement No.2 Order, 05/4514NI
  Commencement No.3 Order, 05/14
  Transitional and Consequential Provisions Order, 05/632
construction
  fire precautions
    indemnities
      extent of principal contractors indemnity to sub sub contractor, 05/663
construction contracts
  adjudication
    jurisdiction

costs *-cont.*
 detailed assessment *-cont.*
  charging order against UK properties arising
   from foreign judgment
   setting transactions aside, 05/331
  expert witnesses
   power of court to make costs order against
    expert witness, 05/363
 fixed costs
  small claims track
   entitlement to fixed commencement costs
    of Part 20 claim, 05/364
 foreign lawyers
  arbitrator's award, 05/365
 indemnity costs
  declaration of freedom from restrictive
   covenants, 05/357
 intellectual property claims
  investigation into counterfeiting
   instruction of London solicitors, 05/372
 libel
  instruction of defamation specialist London
   based firm rather than local solicitors
   reasonableness of decision, 05/367
 no order for costs
  tribunal's discretion as to costs, 05/368
 patent proceedings
  apportionment of costs of first instance and
   appeal proceedings, 05/370
 proportionality
  conduct of litigants
   deduction of sum after assessment of
    costs, 05/371
 protective costs orders
  criteria applicable to protective costs order
   applications, 05/373
 security for costs
  foreign companies
   inability to pay costs, 05/465
 summary assessment
  entitlement to summary assessment following
   acceptance of Part 36 payment, 05/376
  requirement for disclosure of collective
   conditional fee agreement, 05/377
 very high costs cases
  Legal Services Commission's failure to send
   contract following notification, 05/856
costs orders
 fixed costs
  small claims track
   unreasonable conduct, 05/375
council tax
 alteration of lists
  Wales, 05/2778
 billing authorities
  civil partnerships, 05/2779
 civil procedure
  liability orders
   postal service of summonses, 05/387
 exempt classes of dwellings, 05/2780
 job-related dwellings
  discounts, 05/2781
 local authorities
  budget requirements
   maximum amounts, 05/2782

council tax *-cont.*
 unoccupied dwellings
  discounts, 05/5509S
 valuation bands
  Wales, 05/2783
 valuation lists
  Wales, 05/2784
council tax benefit
 subsidy to authorities, 05/3880
counterfeiting
 false monetary instruments, 05/5101S
**Countryside and Rights of Way Act 2000
(c.37)**
 Commencement No.6 Order
  Wales, 05/3392
 Commencement No.7 Order
  England, 05/3393
  Wales, 05/3394
 Commencement No.8 Order
  England, 05/3395
 Commencement No.9 Order
  England, 05/3396
 Commencement No.10 Order
  England, 05/3397
county courts
 care centres, 05/1632
 civil partnership proceedings
  designation, 05/18, 4639NI
 civil partnerships
  allocation of proceedings, 05/12
 fees, 05/389, 390
 patents
  jurisdiction, 05/19
Court of Appeal
 prosecution appeals
  procedure, 05/4538NI
 serious offences
  retrials, 05/931, 4549NI, 4550NI
Court of Protection
 enduring powers of attorney
  applications, 05/20
  prescribed forms, 05/21
 fees, 05/22
Court of Session
 mental health
  period for appeals, 05/5527S, 5528S
 rules
  asylum and immigration, 05/4934S
  civil partnerships
   applications for separation or divorce, 05/
    4935S
  enforcement of judgments, 05/4936S
  miscellaneous amendments, 05/4931S,
   4932S, 4933S
  terrorism, 05/4937S
 shorthand writers
  fees, 05/4938S
 solicitors
  fees, 05/4939S
court security officers
 designation, 05/23
 designation and employment, 05/4441NI
courts
 appeals
  adoption, 05/404

criminal evidence -*cont.*
identification
corroboration
sufficiency of evidence, 05/5089S
legal professional privilege
production order served on solicitors, 05/744
live video link
young offenders
special measures directions, 05/751
medical evidence
fresh evidence
shaken baby syndrome, 05/745
murder
medical evidence
sufficiency, 05/5094S
sudden infant death syndrome
conflicting expert evidence, 05/747
publications, 05/753
right to silence
adverse inferences
effect of accused's silence at trial, 05/748
sexual offences
legislative restriction on evidence of
complainer's character, 05/5084S
solemn procedure
citations, 05/750
sufficiency of evidence
corroboration
possession of indecent photographs, 05/
5095S
trials
judge's charge
judge's failure to direct jury to approach
identification evidence with care, 05/
5151S
video evidence
replaying recording of evidence in chief of
child witness at jury's request, 05/752
**Criminal Justice (Northern Ireland) Order
2005 (SI 205 1965 (NI.15)),** 05/4540NI
Criminal Justice (Scotland) Act 2003 (asp 7)
Commencement No.6 Order, 05/5126S
Criminal Justice Act 2003 (c.44)
Commencement No.7 Order, 05/862
Commencement No.8 and Transitional and
Saving Provisions Order, 05/863
Commencement No.9 Order, 05/864
Commencement No.10 and Saving Provisions
Order, 05/865
Commencement No.11 Order, 05/866
Supplementary Provisions Order, 05/867
**Criminal Justice and Court Services Act 2000
(c.43)**
Commencement No.14 Order, 05/868
Commencement No.15 Order, 05/869
criminal law
aggravated trespass
military bases
protests against war in Iraq, 05/754
aggravated vehicle taking
consistency of convictions for murder and
aggravated vehicle taking
meaning of "accident", 05/755
agricultural vehicles
operators licences

criminal law -*cont.*
agricultural vehicles -*cont.*
operators licences -*cont.*
error of fact by magistrates, 05/756
alternative verdicts
causing death by dangerous driving
Manslaughter by gross negligence, 05/757
breach of the peace
football matches, 05/5100S
Members of the Scottish Parliament
freedom of expression, 05/5099S
threats of violence, 05/5098S
buggery
criminal liability
honest belief victim over 16 years old, 05/
758
carriage by road
cabotage
offences, 05/4921NI
child abduction
criminal liability
mens rea of offence, 05/760
child sex offences
reporting restrictions, 05/815
communications offences
racism
grossly offensive telephone calls and
messages, 05/764
confessions
inconsistent statements
defence of duress, 05/765
conspiracy
knowledge
burden of proof, 05/767
money laundering
need to prove money represented proceeds
of crime, 05/768
counterfeiting
false monetary instruments, 05/5101S
Criminal Defence Service
funding, 05/2706
recovery of costs, 05/2707
culpable homicide
guilty pleas
discount for early admission of guilt and
consequent avoidance of trial, 05/
5650S
cultivation of cannabis
necessity
defence of medical necessity by
extraneous circumstances, 05/772
death penalty
murder
constitutionality of felony murder rule, 05/
773
defences
unprotected sexual intercourse
risk of contracting HIV, 05/766
disorderly behaviour
penalties
amount of penalty, 05/808
penalty notices
form of notice, 05/809
drink driving offences
breath tests

directors -*cont.*
  directors duties -*cont.*
    breach of fiduciary duty -*cont.*
      amendment to plead dishonest assistance, 05/522
  disqualification orders
    directors disqualification proceedings, 05/2306
  insolvent companies
    disqualification orders, 05/4715NI
directors powers and duties
  directors disqualification proceedings
    chairman's responsibility for "false and misleading" financial statements, 05/521
disability discrimination
  codes of practice
    appointed day, 05/4589NI
  educational institutions
    alteration of premises, 05/1006
  equal treatment
    code of practice
      appointed day, 05/1222
  prescribed forms
    questions and replies, 05/1225
  private clubs, 05/1226
  public authorities
    service providers, 05/2032
    statutory duties, 05/68, 4957S
  schools
    accessibility plans
      prescribed times, 05/1007
  service providers
    adjustment of premises, 05/1228
Disability Discrimination Act 1995 (c.50)
  Commencement No.11 Order, 05/4207
Disability Discrimination Act 2005 (c.13), 05/1230
  Commencement No.1 Order, 05/2033
  Commencement No.2 Order, 05/2034
disabled persons
  accessibility requirements
    public service vehicles, 05/4239
  adjustment of premises
    service providers, 05/1228
  council tax
    valuation bands
      Wales, 05/2783
  energy efficiency
    grants, 05/4603NI
  housing
    renewal grants
      forms, 05/1983
  railways
    accessibility
      exemptions, 05/4253, 4254, 4255
  special educational needs
    alteration of premises, 05/1006
  transport policy
    Mobility and Access Committee
      financial reporting, 05/5693S
disclosure and inspection
  court records
    relevant consideration when exercising discretion, 05/397

discrimination
  sex discrimination
    equal treatment, 05/1233, 4599NI
diseases and disorders
  anthrax, 05/1948
  approved disinfectants, 05/185, 5018S, 5019S
    fees, 05/186
    Wales, 05/187
  bovine animals
    compensation, 05/171
    market value, 05/172
  cattle
    tuberculosis, 05/4470NI, 4987S
    testing, 05/175
dispute resolution
  adjudicators
    jurisdiction
      power to investigate referrals on construction contracts, 05/648
  arbitration agreements
    scope of arbitration agreements
      forum for determining jurisdiction, 05/984
  compromise agreements, 05/1236
  mediation
    power of court to order attendance
      right to fair trial, 05/985
  publications, 05/986
District Policing Partnerships (Northern Ireland) Order 2005 (SI 2005 861 (NI.4)), 05/4827NI
divorce
  allocation of jurisdiction
    foreign proceedings
      appropriateness of Hemain or anti suit injunction, 05/1623
      husband issuing proceedings in France, 05/1622
  financial provision
    capital sum
      extensions of time, 05/5266S
    lump sum orders
      costs, 05/1626
    order for sale of matrimonial home
      value of matrimonial home, 05/5267S
  internet search sessions
    extension, 05/5269S
  petitions
    amendment relating to jurisdiction sought by wife, 05/1628
docks
  dockyard port
    Portsmouth, 05/3796
doctors
  general practice register, 05/1842
  misconduct
    serious professional misconduct
      proportionality of penalty, 05/1803
  professional conduct
    acquittal before criminal court
      lawfulness of later reference to GMC, 05/1804
    sexual relationship with psychiatric patient
      removal from register, 05/1805
    sexual relationship with vulnerable patient

employment -cont.
  unfair dismissal -cont.
    time limits
      reasonableness of decision to allow complaint outside time limit, 05/1336
    volunteers
      no contract of employment for voluntary worker, 05/1330
  vocational training
    pregnancy discrimination
      termination of bursary payments, 05/1337
  wages
    deduction as a result of industrial action
      jurisdictional findings of fact, 05/1338
    deductions
      local authority employee's contract transferred to private sector then back again, 05/1339
  wrongful dismissal
    compensation
      loss of opportunity to claim unfair dismissal, 05/1340
    damages
      entitlement to bonus payments, 05/5220S
Employment (Miscellaneous Provisions) (Northern Ireland) Order 2005 (SI 2005 3424 (NI.20)), 05/4596NI
Employment Appeal Tribunal
  costs
    sift procedure
      reasonableness of bringing or continuing appeal, 05/1243
Employment Relations (Northern Ireland) Order 1999 (SI 1999 2790 (NI.9))
  Commencement No.8 Order, 05/4593NI
Employment Relations (Northern Ireland) Order 2004 (SI 2004 3078 (NI.19))
  Commencement No.2 Order, 05/4594NI
  Commencement No.3 Order, 05/4595NI
Employment Relations Act 2004 (c.24)
  Commencement No.3 and Transitional Provisions Order, 05/1245
  Commencement No.4 and Transitional Provisions Order, 05/1246
employment tribunals
  costs
    unreasonable conduct of claim with no realistic prospect of success, 05/1220
  fair employment tribunal
    procedure, 05/4442NI
  judgments and orders
    review of strike out order, 05/1251
  procedure
    equal value claims, 05/1254
    state security, 05/1255
employments
  unfair dismissal
    compensatory awards, 05/5217S
enduring powers of attorney
  prescribed forms, 05/21, 30
    Welsh language, 05/31
energy
  biofuels
    labelling, 05/1342
  distribution of electricity, 05/1343

energy -cont.
  electricity
    European requirements, 05/4601NI
  electricity supply industry
    licences
      exemption, 05/4322, 5707S
  energy conservation
    grants, 05/3857
      eligibility, 05/5223S
  energy efficiency
    grants, 05/4603NI
  gas and electricity
    administration proceedings, 05/2316
  Nuclear Decommissioning Authority
    exempt activities, 05/1348
  public companies
    designation, 05/1352
  publications, 05/1354
  renewable energy
    renewable energy zones
      designation, 05/1353
Energy Act 2004 (c.20)
  Commencement No.4 Order, 05/1344
  Commencement No.5 Order, 05/1345
  Commencement No.6 Order, 05/1346
energy efficiency
  solid wall insulation, 05/4040
entry clearances
  applications
    fingerprints, 05/2197
  travel documents
    leave to enter and remain, 05/2202
environment
  air pollution
    air quality reviews, 05/5224S
      Wales, 05/1355
  commons
    public inquiries, 05/1356
  conservation
    habitats
      basis for grant of licence to relocate, 05/1359
  countryside access
    appeals
      Wales, 05/3373
    appeals procedures
      Wales, 05/3316
    maps, 05/3374
  emissions trading
    greenhouse gases, 05/1374, 1375
      national allocation plan, 05/1376
  energy consumption
    air conditioners
      labelling, 05/1347
  Environment Agency
    prosecutions
      definition of controlled waste, 05/1362
  environmental impact assessments
    development in national park, 05/1366
    land drainage
      improvement works, 05/1364
    rural areas, 05/1367
    water, 05/4605NI
  environmental protection
    Mediterranean Sea

food safety
additives, 05/1733, 4665NI, 4666NI, 5305S
  colours, 05/1734, 4667NI, 5306S
    Wales, 05/1735
  sweeteners, 05/4668NI
    Wales, 05/1736
  Wales, 05/1737, 1738
animal products
  hygiene and inspections
    poultry meat, 05/5299S
    poultrymeat, 05/4659NI
    slaughtering, 05/1722
  poultrymeat hygiene and inspections
    Wales, 05/1721
beef
  labelling schemes
    appeal to magistrates, 05/4669NI
beef carcases
  classification, 05/4475NI
bovine collagen
  human consumption, 05/1739, 5307S
    Wales, 05/1740
bovine products
  placing on market
    restrictions, 05/114, 115, 4462NI, 4463NI, 4980S, 4981S
    Wales, 05/116, 117
contaminants, 05/5308S
  maximum levels, 05/1741, 1742, 4670NI, 4671NI, 5309S
  Wales, 05/1743, 1744
emergency controls
  chilli and chilli products, 05/1745, 5310S
    Wales, 05/1746
  pistachios
    Iran, 05/1747, 5311S
  pistachios from Iran, 05/4679NI
    Wales, 05/1748
emergency prohibitions
  amnesic shellfish poisoning, 05/5312S, 5313S, 5314S, 5315S, 5316S, 5317S, 5318S, 5319S, 5320S, 5321S, 5322S, 5323S, 5324S, 5325S, 5326S, 5327S, 5328S, 5329S, 5330S, 5331S, 5332S, 5333S, 5334S, 5335S, 5336S, 5337S, 5338S, 5339S, 5340S, 5341S, 5342S, 5343S, 5344S, 5345S, 5346S, 5347S, 5348S, 5349S, 5350S, 5351S, 5352S, 5353S, 5354S, 5355S, 5356S
    scallops, 05/4672NI
  diarrhetic shellfish poisoning
    scallops, 05/4673NI
  paralytic shellfish poisoning, 05/5357S, 5358S, 5359S, 5360S, 5361S
  radioactivity in sheep, 05/5362S
feedingstuffs
  zootechnical additives, 05/4992S
food hygiene
  animal products
    Wales, 05/1723
genetically modified organisms
  traceability and labelling, 05/4674NI
    Wales, 05/1749
hygiene and enforcement, 05/137, 4675NI, 5363S

food safety -*cont.*
import controls, 05/1750
  Wales, 05/138
information requirements, 05/4993S
inspections and controls
  fees, 05/1751, 1752
packaging
  plastics, 05/1753, 1754, 4676NI, 4677NI, 5364S, 5365S
  Wales, 05/1755, 1756, 1757
scallops
  emergency prohibitions
    amnesic shellfish poisoning, 05/4672NI
    diarrhetic shellfish poisoning, 05/4673NI
smoke flavourings, 05/1758, 4678NI, 5366S
  Wales, 05/1759
foreign exchange
tax treatment
  gains and losses
    bringing into account, 05/4054
forfeiture
rights of re-entry
  prescribed sum and period
    Wales, 05/2658
fostering
private arrangements
  notification requirements, 05/1668
free movement of persons
residence
  child acquiring Irish citizenship on birth
    parent's right to reside with child in UK, 05/2207
freedom of association
freemasonry
  judicial membership
    foreseeability of disciplinary sanctions, 05/2039
freedom of movement of workers
public orders
  restriction of place of residence
    national of another Member State with terrorist links, 05/1462
friendly societies
accounts, 05/255, 276
insurance business
  corporation tax, 05/4030
funeral expenses
payments to civilians, 05/3069
Further and Higher Education (Scotland) Act 2005 (asp 6), 05/5184S
Commencement Order, 05/5185S
further education
colleges
  elections for board of governors
    Edinburgh College of Art, 05/5171S
  establishment
    Adam Smith College, Fife, 05/5173S
  Glasgow School of Art
    elections for governors, 05/5172S
  governance
    Central Sussex College, 05/1020
  transfer to higher education sector
    Leeds College of Music, 05/1005
consequential modifications, 05/5186S
further education corporations

grants
aided places scheme
St Mary's Music School, 05/5200S
assessment of contributions, 05/5418S
assisted places
incidental expenses, 05/1026
Wales, 05/1027
qualifying income limits, 05/1028, 5201S
Wales, 05/1029
churches
Churches Conservation Trust, 05/998
education
graduate endowment, 05/5205S
mandatory awards, 05/1030
energy conservation, 05/3857
eligibility, 05/5223S
energy efficiency, 05/4603NI
housing grants
assessment of contributions, 05/5418S
housing payments
non audit claims, 05/3870
housing renewal grants
forms, 05/1983
means test, 05/1984
Wales, 05/1985
housing support grant
aggregate amount and apportionment, 05/5421S
local government finance
central funds, 05/4744NI
revenue support grant
determination, 05/5525S
management of land
environmental stewardship scheme, 05/1368
National Lottery
Awards For All joint scheme
local community groups, 05/283
organic farming
animal housing, 05/4480NI
police grants, 05/5600S
students, 05/4575NI
eligibility, 05/1148, 4577NI, 4578NI
higher education, 05/1034, 1035, 4563NI, 4564NI, 4565NI
performing arts, 05/1031, 1032
temporary protection
eligibility, 05/5206S
ground rent
form of notice
Wales, 05/2659
harbours
empowerment
Caledonian MacBrayne Limited
Kennacraig, 05/5662S
revision
Caledonian MacBrayne
Oban Quay, 05/5663S
constitution
Cattewater, 05/3797
Peterhead, 05/5664S
Scrabster, 05/5665S
Ullapool, 05/5666S
Wick, 05/5667S
Great Yarmouth, 05/3798, 3799
pilotage

harbours -*cont.*
revision -*cont.*
pilotage -*cont.*
Langstone, 05/3800
works
Inverness, 05/5668S
hazardous substances
electrical equipment
restrictions of use, 05/1395
health and safety at work
controls, 05/1394, 4711NI
marketing and use
restrictions, 05/1394
packaging
labelling, 05/1360, 4604NI
health
advisory bodies
Commission on Human Medicines
establishment, 05/1788
medicinal products, 05/1789
members
terms of office, 05/1851
blood transfusion
Jehovah's Witnesses
opposition to treatment from patient and parents, 05/1793
care and treatment
consequential modifications, 05/5532S
forms, 05/5533S
nurses
prescribed persons, 05/5535S
revocation, 05/5536S
community health councils
terms of office
Wales, 05/1795
Council for Regulation of Health Care Professionals
appeals
right to appeal against acquittal in disciplinary proceedings, 05/1796
dentistry
General Dental Council
standards, 05/1797
doctors
alcohol abuse
GMC registration subject to conditions where impairment currently in remission, 05/1798
clinical negligence
referral of allegations of serious professional conduct to professional conduct committee, 05/1799
conduct amounting to serious professional misconduct, 05/1802
General Medical Council
medical assessors, 05/1800
professional conduct
court's jurisdiction to review professional conduct committee's finding of fact, 05/1801
embryology
genetic testing
HFEA's power to authorise tissue typing, 05/1809
executive agencies

health -*cont.*
  executive agencies -*cont.*
    quality of services, 05/4690NI
    Regulation and Improvement Authority
      fees, 05/4446NI
      registration, 05/4691NI
  general dental services
    agreements, 05/1876
    transitional provisions, 05/1877
  General Medical Council
    panels and investigation committee
      Registration Decisions Panel, 05/1813
    registration
      fees, 05/1841, 1845
      registration errors, 05/1847
  General Optical Council
    registration
      appeals, 05/1818
      training, 05/1820
  Health and Personal Social Services
    transfer of staff
      consultation requirements, 05/4692NI
  health boards
    funding
      mental health advice service, 05/1829
    primary medical services
      performers lists, 05/5389S
  health care
    disabled persons
      provision of disabled applicant with robotic
        arm, 05/1831
  Health Professions Council
    practice committees, 05/1834
  herbal medicinal products
    registration, 05/1856
  herbal medicines
    advisory committee
      establishment, 05/1855
  hospitals
    patients rights
      family proceedings concerning patient's
        best interest, 05/1837
  local health councils
    dissolution, 05/5374S
  medical devices
    consumer goods, 05/1921
  medical treatment
    application to reinsert feeding tube
      best interest test, 05/1850
    conditions for reimbursement of treatment in
      another Member State
      compatibility with EC law, 05/1849
    parental wishes
      right to withhold life prolonging medical
        treatment, 05/1848
    terminal illness
      best interests of child, 05/1794
    withdrawal of medical treatment
      lawfulness of guidance on withdrawal of
        artificial nutrition and hydration, 05/1812
  medicinal products
    provision of misleading information
      criminal offence, 05/1867
    supplementary prescribers, 05/1863
  medicines

health -*cont.*
  medicines -*cont.*
    homoeopathic medicinal products
      fees, 05/1857
    medicinal products
      human use, 05/1858
    medicinal products for human use
      advertising, 05/1859
  Mental Welfare Commission for Scotland
    authorised persons
      qualifications, 05/5540S
    provision of facilities
      prescribed persons, 05/5541S
  National Assembly for Wales
    inspections
      explanation of information, 05/1926
  National Health Service
    performers lists
      Wales, 05/1880
    primary medical services
      miscellaneous amendments, 05/1888,
        1889
  National Health Service Litigation Authority
    functions, 05/1936, 1937
  National Institute for Clinical Excellence
    consequential amendments, 05/1897
  National Institute for Health and Clinical
    Excellence
    constitution, 05/1898
    establishment, 05/1898
  National Patient Safety Agency
    additional functions, 05/1881
  NHS tribunal, 05/5396S
  opticians
    contact lenses
      specification, 05/1914, 4701NI
    professional conduct
      duty of disciplinary committee to give
        reasons within reasonable time, 05/1917
    transitional provisions, 05/1918
  patients
    provision of information
      prescribed times, 05/5563S
  personal dental services
    agreements, 05/1883
  pharmaceutical services
    provision of medicinal products, 05/5387S
  primary medical services
    doctors
      performers lists, 05/5388S
  professional conduct
    registration
      disciplinary sanctions for misconduct by
        eminent paediatrician, 05/1919
  public health
    tobacco products
      restrictions on advertising, 05/2740
  publications, 05/1943, 4705NI, 5401S
  Registration Appeals Panel
    appeals procedure, 05/1846
  social welfare
    childrens homes
      registration and inspection, 05/4897NI
    nursing agencies
      registration and inspection, 05/4700NI

health care -cont.
nursing and midwifery
election scheme, 05/1843
Postgraduate Medical Education and Training
Board
fees, 05/1808
Public Health Laboratory Service Board
accounts, 05/1832
supplementary prescribers
drugs and appliances
charges, 05/5393S
Health Protection Agency
consequential provisions, 05/1835
Health Protection Agency Act 2004 (c.17)
Commencement Order, 05/1836
health services
drugs and appliances
fees, 05/4693NI
general medical services
contracts, 05/4694NI
pharmaceutical services
prescriptions
repeat dispensing, 05/4695NI
primary medical services
prescription forms, 05/4696NI
supplementary prescribers, 05/4697NI
travelling expenses
remission of charges
entitlement, 05/4698NI, 4699NI
heavy goods vehicles
licensing
fees, 05/4208
testing
fees, 05/4908NI
heritable property
burdens of covenants
entitlement of former owner to act as
factoring service, 05/5410S
contract for sale of land
right to resile on non purification of
suspensive condition
timeous application, 05/5407S
easements
proprietary rights
right of vehicular access, 05/5409S
vehicular
acquisition by prescription or lost modern
grant notwithstanding illegal use, 05/
3404
possession claims
procedure
proper form of warrant, 05/5053S
publications, 05/5413S
sheriff courts
applications and appeals, 05/4946S
transfer of title
writing
disposition executed but not delivered, 05/
5412S
High Court
fees, 05/389
patents
jurisdiction, 05/19
higher education
awards

higher education -cont.
awards -cont.
recognised bodies, 05/4560NI
consequential modifications, 05/5186S
educational awards
recognised bodies, 05/1014, 1015, 5177S
Wales, 05/1016, 1017
fees
Wales, 05/1033
higher education corporations
dissolution
Kent Institute of Art and Design, 05/1038
Scottish Higher Education Funding Council
dissolution, 05/5183S
students
approved plans
fees, 05/4562NI
fees, 05/4563NI
grants, 05/1034, 1035, 4564NI, 4565NI,
4576NI
**Higher Education (Northern Ireland) Order
2005 (SI 2005 1116 (NI.5))**, 05/4566NI
Higher Education Act 2004 (c.8)
Commencement No.1 Order, 05/5189S
Commencement No.2 and Transitional Provision
Order
Wales, 05/1036
Commencement No.3 Order, 05/1037
highway control
local authorities
traffic orders, 05/5694S
road safety
traffic signs, 05/3482, 4836NI
strategic roads
designation, 05/3487
traffic wardens
uniforms
South Lanarkshire, 05/5645S, 5646S
highways
bus lane contraventions
approved local authorities, 05/3448
enforcement, 05/3449
penalty charges
approved devices, 05/3450
tribunals
bus lane adjudicators, 05/3451
congestion charges
payments
adjudicator's discretion to cancel penalty
charge, 05/3452
crime prevention
designated areas, 05/2902, 2903, 3453
liability for charges, 05/5643S
penalty charges, 05/5644S
annual accounting, 05/5642S
publications, 05/3516
road traffic regulation
speed limits
extent of statutory power to imposed
restricted road status, 05/3483
roads
local authorities powers and duties
construction and maintenance, 05/5641S
schools
special extinguishment and diversion orders

landlord and tenant -*cont.*
insurance policies -*cont.*
notice of cover
Wales, 05/2663
leaseholds
insurance policies
notice of cover, 05/2662
leases
agricultural holdings, 05/5459S
apportionment of rent
meaning of "qualifying tenant", 05/2666
assignment
clauses limiting liability on landlord's
covenants, 05/2665
dispute regarding extent of property included
in lease, 05/5466S
irritancy
validity of notice, 05/5468S
obligations under guarantee
renunciation, 05/5469S
repair covenants
extent of obligation to repair, 05/5467S
restrictive covenants
construction of user clause, 05/2668
surrender
need for unequivocal conduct, 05/2669
tenant's right to review yearly rent, 05/2667
waiver of right to terminate lease, 05/5470S
new business tenancies
correct approach to determining terms of
break clause, 05/2671
options
leases
interpretation of option agreement
concerning reassignment of lease, 05/
2672
possession claims
adjournment
power to order adjournment to enable
tenant to defeat claim, 05/2674
hearsay evidence
propriety of judge's approach to hearsay
and oral evidence, 05/298
possession orders
stay of execution
relevant considerations, 05/2675
private landlord registration
fees, 05/5472S
housing categories, 05/5471S
information, 05/5472S
local authorities
advice and assistance, 05/5522S
protected tenancies
joint tenancies
transitional provisions, 05/2676
possession claims
landlord relying on availability of alternative
accommodation owned by tenant, 05/
2677
public sector tenancies
housing benefit
grounds for recovery of possession, 05/
5474S
possession claims

landlord and tenant -*cont.*
public sector tenancies -*cont.*
possession claims -*cont.*
entitlement to apply for recall of decree, 05/
5475S
qualifying occupier sisted as party to the
proceedings, 05/5476S
warrant for eviction executed by change of
lock, 05/5473S
publications, 05/2695, 4726NI
rent reviews
calculation contrary to agreed assumptions of
landlord and tenant, 05/2678
delay
validity of rent review, 05/2679
expert
procedure for appointment of independent
chartered surveyor, 05/2680
rental value
failure to disregard potential for petrol
station despite restrictive covenant, 05/
2681
repair covenants
breach
value of reversionary interest, 05/2682
dilapidations
adequacy of repair as opposed to
replacement, 05/2684
implied repairing covenant under the Landlord
and Tenant Act 1985 s.11
measure of damages, 05/2683
repossession
public sector tenancies
tenant on low income and in ill health, 05/
5477S
rights of re-entry
prescribed sum and period
Wales, 05/2658
secure tenancies
notice requirements
Wales, 05/2686
possession claims
correct approach when grounds for
possession made out, 05/2687
right to buy, 05/2688
service charges
management fees included as part of service
charge
reasonableness, 05/2651
special educational needs
alteration of premises, 05/4567NI
subtenancies
consent
reasonableness of refusal and time taken to
reach decision, 05/2689
tenancies at will
termination
position of tenant, 05/2690
tenants rights
housing association granting tenancy to
appellant
appellant's rights as against local authority,
05/2691
secure tenancies
tenant's rights, 05/5478S

licensing -cont.
  betting offices -cont.
    licences -cont.
      grounds for refusal, 05/5499S
  certificates
    second appointed day, 05/2747
  football grounds
    seating, 05/3958
  gaming machines
    maximum prizes
      increase, 05/1964
  licence conditions
    local authorities powers and duties, 05/2752
  licences
    taxis
      extensions of time, 05/5502S
  licensed premises
    licences
      reasons for suspension, 05/5500S
    occasional licences
      abuse of process, 05/2756
  licensing authorities
    fees, 05/2759, 2760
    hearings, 05/2761, 2762
    premises, 05/2763, 2764
    registers
      information, 05/2765
  licensing committees
    procedure
      voting in public, 05/5505S
  personal licences, 05/2768
  premises licenses
    fees, 05/2748
  private hire vehicles
    refusal of application for taxi licences
      competence, 05/5501S
  prizes
    variation of monetary limits, 05/1967
  publications, 05/2769
  service stations
    off licence application
      reasonableness, 05/5507S
  street trading
    councillors
      conflict of interest, 05/5504S
  taxis
    refusal to grant taxi licence
      competence, 05/5503S
Licensing (Scotland) Act 2005 (asp 16), 05/5506S
Licensing Act 2003 (c.17)
  Commencement No.6 Order, 05/2757
  Commencement No.7 and Transitional Provisions Order, 05/2758
liciensing
  taxis
    local authorities powers and duties
      policy requiring information as to driving standard, 05/2754
limited liability partnerships
  administration orders, 05/2896
litigation
  tax
    confidentiality orders

litigation -cont.
  tax -cont.
    confidentiality orders -cont.
      anonymity of tax payers in court proceedings, 05/4157
loan agreements
  derivative contracts
    accounting periods, 05/1
    fair value accounting
      exchange gain and losses, 05/277
    profits and losses
      bringing into account, 05/4125, 4126
loans
  repayments
    student teachers, 05/1044
  students, 05/1149, 4579NI
    mortgage style repayment loans, 05/1150, 4580NI, 5208S
    repayments, 05/1151
local authorities
  adoption services, 05/1496
  adoption support services
    financial support, 05/1510
    Wales, 05/1501
  anti social behaviour notices
    advice to landlords, 05/5463S
    landlord liability, 05/5461S
  best value
    performance indicators and standards, 05/2774
  coats of arms
    Ystradgynlais Town Council
      Wales, 05/2795
  contracting out
    billing authorities
      business levy, 05/2797
  council tax limitations
    maximum amounts, 05/2782
  executives
    functions, 05/2798
  fire services
    additional functions, 05/5514S
    consequential modifications, 05/5515S, 5517S
    firefighters
      pension scheme, 05/5518S
    national framework, 05/5519S
    premises, 05/5520S
  foreign adoptions
    fees
      Wales, 05/1672
  functions
    hedgerow complaints, 05/2799
  housing
    grants
      assessment of contributions, 05/5418S
  housing support
    care services
      grants, 05/5422S
  housing support grant
    aggregate amount and apportionment, 05/5421S
  local development plans
    Wales, 05/3268
  parking provisions

negligence -*cont.*
  duty of care -*cont.*
    local authority housing
      mother's request for safety locks on windows, 05/2853
    local education authorities
      alleged delay in carrying out of background check, 05/2855
    medical treatment
      consultant psychiatrist's duty to patient's father, 05/5575S
    no direct contractual relationship
      pure economic loss, 05/2856
    proximity
      duty of care toward persons poisoned by drinking water, 05/2858
    reasonableness
      no liability between public authorities for care expenses of negligently injured third party, 05/2857
    schools
      pupil sexually abused by teacher, 05/2859
    ships
      passenger going overboard, 05/2860
    stress
      employee lack of support by employer, 05/2862
  employers liabilities
    damages for psychiatric injury arising from stress at work
      application of general principles to different factual situations, 05/2883
  fatal accidents claims
    liability of Motor Insurers Bureau, 05/2353
  faulty equipment
    requirement to aver precise inspection intervals, 05/5634S
  foreseeability
    wife exposed to asbestos from husband's clothing
      liability for mesothelioma caused by exposure, 05/2864
  investment funds
    measure of damages, 05/2863
  letters of intent
    FIDIC conditions of contract
      letter of intent constituting binding contract, 05/667
  limitations
    professional negligence claim against former solicitor, 05/2865
  local authorities
    establishing allegations of negligence at common law
      prospect of success, 05/2852
  local authorities powers and duties
    tripping accident on pedestrian crossing
      extent of statutory duty, 05/2888
  occupiers liability
    duty of care
      snow boarding accident on artificially created slope, 05/4195
  police officers
    involvement in fatal shooting

negligence -*cont.*
  police officers -*cont.*
    involvement in fatal shooting -*cont.*
      foreseeability of harm arising from subsequent criminal and disciplinary proceedings, 05/2884
  professional negligence
    limitation periods
      date of knowledge, 05/433
    surveyors
      duty of care in relation to developer, 05/5577S
  publications, 05/2892
  reversionary interests
    bailor's rights of recovery, 05/3239
  solicitors
    inadequate professional services
      compensation, 05/2729
  standard of care
    medical examinations
      failure to diagnose child's meningococcal infection, 05/2887
    tenant injured from fall into basement stairwell
      liability of landlord for tenant's injury, 05/2886
  vicarious liability
    control exercised over door stewards, 05/2889
    employers liabilities
      two separate employers vicariously liable for negligence of single employee, 05/2890
    GP indecently assaulting patients
      extent of statutory duty and common law duty of care, 05/2891
NHS trusts
  change of name
    Bedfordshire and Luton Community, 05/1899
    Hull and East Riding Community Health, 05/1900
    Kings Lynn and Wisbech Hospitals, 05/1901
  constitution
    Bedfordshire and Luton Community, 05/1899
    Hammersmith Hospitals, 05/1902
    Hull and East Riding Community Health, 05/1900
  dissolution
    North West Surrey Mental Health, 05/1903
    North West Surrey Surrey Oaklands, 05/1903
    Surrey Hampshire Borders, 05/1903
  establishment
    Surrey and Borders Partnership, 05/1903
  health boards
    membership and procedure, 05/5376S
  transfer of assets
    Cambridge University Hospitals, 05/1904
    Chelsea and Westminster Healthcare, 05/1905
    East Sussex County Healthcare, 05/1906
    Surrey and Borders Partnership, 05/1907
    Surrey Hampshire Borders, 05/1908
    University Hospital of North Staffordshire, 05/1909
    West Hertfordshire Hospitals, 05/1910
    West Suffolk Hospitals, 05/1911
  trust funds

occupational pensions -cont.
  winding up -cont.
    transfer value, 05/3001, 4778NI
OFCOM
  membership, 05/4181
offences
  international criminal law
    Myanmar, 05/2608
  sale of goods
    offensive weapons, 05/5105S
  sentencing
    electronic monitoring of offenders
      accreditation body, 05/3575
      police areas, 05/3576
      licence conditions, 05/3577
offensive weapons
  sale or supply
    criminal offence, 05/5105S
offshore installations
  safety case, 05/1958
  safety zones
    oil and gas industry, 05/1349, 1350, 1351
oil and gas industry
  offshore installations
    safety case, 05/1958
    safety zones, 05/1349, 1350, 1351
olympic games
  London, 05/3960
ombudsmen
  Assembly Ombudsman
    salaries, 05/4448NI, 4449NI
  Commissioner for Complaints
    salaries, 05/4448NI, 4449NI
  parliamentary commissioner
    investigations, 05/79
open ended investment companies
  annual general meetings, 05/1706
opticians
  contact lenses
    specification, 05/1914, 4701NI
  General Optical Council
    committee constitution, 05/1814
    contact lenses
      aftercare provision, 05/1815
      eye disorders, 05/1815
    functions, 05/1817
  ophthalmic services
    mobile services, 05/4703NI
  optical appliances
    vouchers, 05/1915, 4702NI, 5397S
      Wales, 05/1916
  patient referrals, 05/4703NI
  transitional provisions, 05/1918
organic farming
  animal housing
    grants, 05/4480NI
organised crime
  police
    designated sites, 05/3326
    powers of arrest, 05/3327
    serious offences, 05/3328
origin marking
  animal products
    third country imports, 05/126, 4469NI, 4986S, 5454S

origin marking -cont.
  animal products -cont.
    third country imports -cont.
      Wales, 05/127, 128
package holidays
  breach of contract
    hotel found to be dirty
      measure of damages, 05/1978
parental responsibility
  agreements, 05/1680
parking
  charges
    Holyrood Park, 05/5638S
  parking adjudicators
    appeals
      South Lanarkshire, 05/5639S
  special parking areas
    Barnsley, 05/3460
    Broxbourne, 05/3461
    Chiltern, 05/3462
    Coventry, 05/3463
    Doncaster, 05/3464
    Elmbridge, 05/3465
    Epsom and Ewell, 05/3466
    Hartlepool, 05/3467
    Havant, 05/3468
    Horsham, 05/3469
    Ipswich, 05/3470
    Leeds, 05/3471
    Mid Sussex, 05/3472
    New Forest, 05/3473
    Rotherham, 05/3474
    Sheffield, 05/3475
    South Lanarkshire, 05/5640S
    Spelthorne, 05/3476
    Stevenage, 05/3477
    Stockport, 05/3478
    Stockton-on-Tees, 05/4237
    Thurrock, 05/3479
    Torbay, 05/3480
    Welwyn Hatfield, 05/3481
    Woking, 05/4238
  traffic wardens
    uniforms
      South Lanarkshire, 05/5645S, 5646S
parks
  byelaws, 05/2809
  National Lottery
    joint scheme, 05/1976
Parliament
  occupational pensions, 05/2982
parliamentary ombudsman
  health protection agency, 05/80
  pension protection fund, 05/80
particulars of claim
  amendments
    same set of facts as those originally pleaded
      amendments amounting to new causes of action, 05/450
partnership
  partners
    solicitor holding himself out as partner in firm
      client's reliance on solicitor's representation, 05/2897
  partnership agreements

patents -*cont.*
infringement -*cont.*
limitation of inquiry as to damages, 05/2477
measure of damages, 05/2476
patent for paroxetine hydrochloride anhydrate
inventive step, 05/2478
inventive step
application of law of collation
validity of patent, 05/2480
challenge to primary finding of obviousness
strength of secondary evidence, 05/2481
diagonal cursor movement on remote control
lack of inventive step, 05/2482
information modelling amounting to
intellectual activity
lack of clarity, 05/2483
language translation by computer, 05/2484
joint inventors
identity of actual deviser
test for differentiating exclusive ownership
from joint ownership, 05/2486
miscellaneous amendments, 05/2487
opposition division
request to amend minutes of oral proceedings,
05/2488
revocation
patent based on prior art
lack of inventive step, 05/2489
software
technical function
patentability, 05/2492
technical function
invention containing excluded matter
patentability, 05/2490
software
invention containing excluded mater, 05/
2491
Patents Act 2004 (c.16)
Commencement No.3 and Transitional Provisions
Order, 05/2493
penology and criminology
life prisoners
disciplinary procedures
right to fair and public hearing, 05/2909
return to custody
measure of damages for delay, 05/2921
parole
reliance by board on prosecution for new
offence, 05/2907
parole board
lawfulness of special advocate procedure, 05/
2916
prison discipline
bias
deputy prison governor ruling on
lawfulness of search order, 05/2908
prison governors
obligations on adjudicating officers, 05/
2910
prisoners
health care, 05/2918
restrictions on correspondence with outside
NHS consultant
proportionality, 05/2913
prisoners rights

penology and criminology -*cont.*
prisoners rights -*cont.*
freedom of expression
right to work on autobiography prior to
intended publication, 05/2914
mental hospitals
secretary of state's duties, 05/2915
young offender institutions
opportunity to make representations before
making of segregation order, 05/2917
Probation Board for Northern Ireland
victims
access to information, 05/4749NI
publications, 05/2924
release on licence
return to custody
requirement for Parole Board to hold oral
hearing, 05/2920
young offender institutions
rules, 05/2922
young offenders
life prisoners
requirement of continuing review of
minimum term, 05/2923
pension protection
eligible schemes, 05/3008, 4771NI
assessment of assets and liabilities, 05/3009
employers obligations, 05/4779NI
overseas schemes
transfer of payments, 05/3019, 4780NI
pension protection fund
eligible schemes
assessment of assets and liabilities, 05/
4786NI
transfer of payments, 05/3010, 4789NI
pensions
age related payments
lump sum, 05/3061, 4816NI
appeals
Pensions Appeal Tribunal, 05/2925
armed forces, 05/2931
compensation
appeals, 05/2926
early departure payments scheme, 05/2930
Ulster Defence Regiment
civil partnerships, 05/2932
war pensions
appeals, 05/2933
Board of the Pension Protection Fund
appointment of members
procedure, 05/3004
limit on borrowing, 05/3016
review and reconsideration, 05/3005, 4782NI
civil partnerships, 05/1606
entitlement, 05/1607, 1617, 4636NI
claims and payments
electronic communications, 05/3824
contracted out schemes
civil partnerships
entitlement, 05/4750NI
transfer of payments, 05/2955, 4758NI
contribution notices
restoration orders
appropriate persons, 05/2937, 4751NI
early retirement

plants -*cont.*
  plant varieties -*cont.*
    cereal seeds -*cont.*
      Wales, 05/161
    fodder plant seeds
      marketing, 05/5004S
      Wales, 05/153
    genetically modified organisms
      beet seeds, 05/106
      cereal seeds, 05/107
      fodder plant seeds, 05/108
      vegetable seeds, 05/110
    seeds, 05/4483NI
      genetically modified food, 05/109
      registration, 05/155
    vegetable seeds
      Wales, 05/162
  protected species, 05/5225S
police
  continuance of office
    Police Oversight Commissioner, 05/4828NI
  criminal record certificates
    fees, 05/3323
  Crown Estate
    parks
      termination of employment and transfer, 05/2788
  disciplinary procedures
    suspension of police officer
      matters of public interest, 05/3334
  enhanced criminal record certificates
    indecent exposure allegations
      duty to disclose, 05/3324
  occupational pensions
    amendments, 05/5602S
    part time employment, 05/2983, 5601S
  organised crime
    designated areas, 05/3325
    designated sites, 05/3326
    powers of arrest, 05/3327
    serious offences, 05/3328
  police grants, 05/5600S
  police officers
    appointments, 05/3331
    disciplinary procedures
      application of principles of agency, 05/3333
    injury pensions
      date of assessment of degree of disablement, 05/3332
    pensions
      bullying, 05/5604S
      permanent disability from performing ordinary duties, 05/5605S
  police powers
    codes of practice, 05/3336
      revisions to Code C, 05/3337
    motor vehicles
      retention and disposal, 05/3338, 4225, 5606S
  police powers and duties
    anti social behaviour
      power to use force, 05/810
    crowd taking part in demonstration detained within police cordon

police -*cont.*
  police powers and duties -*cont.*
    crowd taking part in demonstration detained within police cordon -*cont.*
      lawfulness of detention, 05/3339
    demonstrations
      necessary contents of direction given under s.14 Public Order Act 1986, 05/3340
    duty of care
      victim of crime alleging existence of duties, 05/3342
    police enquiries
      abuse of process, 05/3343
    powers of arrest
      lawfulness of detention, 05/5607S
    removal of demonstrators by preventive actions short of arrest or detention, 05/3341
  police records
    recordable offences, 05/3344
  publications, 05/3348
  Royal Ulster Constabulary
    disciplinary proceedings, 05/4829NI
police authorities
  best value
    performance indicators, 05/3329
  lay justice members
    appointments
      selection panel, 05/3330
police officers
  applicants
    powers to test for controlled drugs, 05/3331
  deputy chief constables, 05/5603S
  promotion
    qualifying examinations, 05/3335
police service
  disciplinary proceedings, 05/4829NI
  Police Service of Northern Ireland, 05/4830NI
police stations
  visitors
    reporting requirements
      conduct of interviews, 05/4831NI
political parties
  donations
    excluded categories, 05/4587NI
pollution
  pollution control
    car fuel
      income tax, 05/4065
    volatile organic compounds
      solvent emissions, 05/1380
  pollution control regime, 05/4610NI, 4611NI, 4612NI, 5229S
  public participation, 05/1379, 5230S
    designation, 05/5231S
  waste incineration installations, 05/5232S
pollution control
  landfill sites
    Wales, 05/1407
    waste, 05/1407
      Wales, 05/1407
  offshore petroleum activities, 05/1378
  oil pollution
    shipping, 05/3803, 3804
  water pollution

roads -cont.
  motorways -cont.
    M27 -cont.
      speed limits, 05/3457
    M77
      speed limits, 05/5637S
    M275
      speed limits, 05/3457
    speed limits, 05/3456
  road safety
    lighting, 05/4228, 4913NI
    vehicles testing
      exemptions, 05/4229
  road user charging
    annual accounts, 05/5642S
    liability for charges, 05/5643S
    penalty charges, 05/5644S
  road works
    inspections
      fees, 05/4837NI
  special roads
    M2, 05/4839NI
  strategic roads
    designation, 05/3487
  trunk roads
    A1, 05/3490
    A2, 05/3491, 3492, 3493
    A7, 05/3494
    A11, 05/3495
    A21, 05/3496, 3497, 3498
    A30, 05/3499, 3500
    A40, 05/3501, 3502
    A66, 05/3503
    A120, 05/3504
    A419, 05/3505, 3506
    A428, 05/3507, 3508, 3509, 3510
    A470
      Wales, 05/3511
    A500, 05/3512
    A6514, 05/3513
    M40, 05/3514
robbery
  sentencing
    violent attack on elderly couple in own home
      undue leniency, 05/3731
  unlawful wounding
    night time knife attack on taxi driver
      offence committed during currency of
        suspended sentence, 05/3728
  violence
    robberies of small businesses
      undue leniency, 05/3729
rural areas
  countryside access
    appeals
      Wales, 05/3373
    appeals procedures
      Wales, 05/3316
    maps, 05/3374
  countryside management
    grants, 05/4606NI
  less favoured areas
    compensatory allowances, 05/4494NI
  rural rate relief, 05/5616S

safety at sea
  reporting requirements
    exemptions, 05/3807
  seamen
    medical fitness certificates, 05/3808
  small passenger ships
    bridge visibility, 05/3809
sale of goods
  breach of contract
    defective goods
      right to return following repair, 05/5647S
  delivery
    apparent authority
      liability of company, 05/3517
  publications, 05/3518
Salmon and Freshwater Fisheries (Consolidation) (Scotland) Act 2003 (asp 15)
  Commencement Order, 05/5294S
sanctions
  British overseas territories
    Democratic Republic of Congo
      restrictive measures, 05/2599
    Zimbabwe
      restrictive measures, 05/2601
  United Nations Measures
    Sudan
      overseas territories, 05/2616
satellites
  planning permission
    permitted development, 05/3301
scallops
  several fishery rights
    Loch Crinan, 05/5292S
school admissions
  admission arrangements
    appeals
      Wales, 05/1065
    primary schools
      Isles of Scilly, 05/1066
    variation, 05/1067
School Education (Ministerial Powers and Independent Schools) (Scotland) Act 2004 (asp 12)
  Commencement No.1 Order, 05/5198S
  Commencement No.2 Order, 05/5199S
school inspections
  boarding schools, 05/4555NI
schools
  admission arrangements
    appeals
      Wales, 05/1065
  aided places scheme
    St Mary's Music School, 05/5200S
  annual parents meetings
    exemptions
      Wales, 05/1080
  assisted places
    grants
      qualifying income limits, 05/5201S
  assisted places scheme
    incidental expenses, 05/1026
    Wales, 05/1027
  attendance targets, 05/1081
  children and young persons

schools -*cont.*
  children and young persons -*cont.*
    additional support needs, 05/5180S
    coordinated support plans, 05/5181S, 5182S
  day care
    registration
      Wales, 05/1573
  disability discrimination
    tribunal procedures
      claims and appeals, 05/4571NI
  disabled persons
    accessibility plans
      prescribed times, 05/1007
  finance, 05/1082
  grammar schools
    charges, 05/4568NI
  grant maintained schools
    school development plans, 05/4561NI
  independent schools
    registration, 05/5190S
    religious character designation, 05/1039, 1040, 1041
  information
    disabled access, 05/1083
  information and prospectuses, 05/1084
  inspections, 05/1085
  inspectors
    appointments, 05/1086, 1087, 1088
    removal, 05/1089
  maintained schools
    change of category, 05/1090
      Wales, 05/1091
    contracts
      code of practice, 05/1049
    councils
      Wales, 05/1050
    governing bodies
      Wales, 05/1051
    prescribed alteration
      Southwark London Borough Council, 05/1092
  national curriculum assessment arrangements
    Key Stage 3
      Wales, 05/1055, 1056
  national curriculum disapplication
    Key Stage 1
      Wales, 05/1057
  new maintained schools
    governing bodies and school management
      Wales, 05/1094
  performance
    information, 05/1095
    Key Stage 1, 05/1096
  primary schools
    admission arrangements
      coordination, 05/1066
    religious character designation, 05/1097, 1098, 1099, 1100, 1101, 1102, 1103, 1104, 1105, 1106, 1107, 1108, 1109, 1110, 1122
  prospectuses, 05/1084
  protection of staff and pupils
    special diversion orders
      Wales, 05/3488
    special extinguishment orders
      Wales, 05/3488

schools -*cont.*
  pupil referral units, 05/1111
  pupils
    information, 05/1112
      Wales, 05/1093
    performance information
      Key Stage 1, 05/1063
    performance targets, 05/1113, 1114
  pupils academic records
    disclosure and transfer, 05/1060
  religious character designation, 05/1115, 1116, 1117, 1118, 1119, 1120, 1121, 1123, 1124, 1125, 1126, 1127
  school governors
    allowances
      Wales, 05/1075
  school management
    school organisation proposals, 05/1076, 1077
    school session times
      Wanstead High School, 05/1128
  schools admissions
    variation of admission arrangements, 05/1067
  schools forums, 05/1132
  secondary education
    International General Certificate, 05/1135
  secondary schools
    governing bodies
      constitution, 05/1133
  standards
    development plans
      Wales, 05/1134
science
  publications, 05/3519
secondary education
  International General Certificate of Secondary Education
    Coventry City Council, 05/1135
    North West Federation of Schools, 05/1135
secondary schools
  governing bodies
    constitution, 05/1133
Secretaries of State
  transfer of functions
    Lord Chancellor, 05/1783, 1784
secure tenancies
  demotion orders
    notice requirements
      Wales, 05/2686
  right of first refusal, 05/2024
    Wales, 05/2025
security industry
  door supervisors, 05/2245
  immobilisation of vehicles, 05/2246, 2247, 2248, 2249
    duration of licences, 05/2250
  licences, 05/2251
    licensable activity, 05/2252
  licensed premises, 05/2249
  wheel clamping, 05/2246, 2247, 2248, 2253
    duration of licences, 05/2250
sentencing
  abuse of position of trust
    teachers
      defendant exposing himself to nine year old girl, 05/3520

shipping -*cont.*
 time charterparties -*cont.*
  time limits -*cont.*
   meaning of clause in Shelltime 4 form, 05/3816
 tonnage tax companies
  training commitment, 05/4137
 voyage charterparties
  demurrage
   construction of strike clause, 05/3817
 wrecks
  protection
   restricted area designation, 05/3818
ships
 tonnage tax
  exceptions, 05/4168
Smoking, Health and Social Care (Scotland) Act 2005 (asp 13), 05/5398S
 Commencement No.1 Order, 05/5399S
 Commencement No.2 Order, 05/5400S
social housing
 ombudsman
  Wales, 05/2026
social landlords
 qualifying lending institutions, 05/2028
 registration
  additional purposes or objects, 05/2028
social security
 benefits
  child tax credit, 05/3820, 4841NI
  civil partnerships, 05/1606, 4635NI
  claims and payments, 05/3821, 3822, 4842NI, 4843NI
   time limits, 05/3823
  electronic communications, 05/3824
  entitlement
   reciprocal agreements, 05/3825, 4844NI
  hospital in-patients, 05/3826
  miscellaneous amendments, 05/3831, 3832, 3864, 3867, 4845NI, 4846NI
  mortgage interest payments
   administration fees, 05/3833, 4847NI
  overpayments
   claimant's duty to disclose change in circumstances, 05/3834
  payment of pension and social security benefits
   objective justification for discriminatory provision, 05/3835
  re rating, 05/3890, 3897
  social fund
   maternity and funeral expenses, 05/3836, 4848NI
  up rating, 05/3837, 3838, 4849NI, 4850NI
  work focused interviews, 05/3839, 3840, 3841, 4851NI, 4852NI
 care homes
  regulation, 05/3913
 child benefit
  civil partnerships, 05/3925
  guardians allowance
   miscellaneous amendments, 05/3842
  weekly rates
   increase, 05/3844, 4854NI
 child support

social security -*cont.*
 child support -*cont.*
  appeals, 05/3846
  civil partnerships
   consequential provisions, 05/4633NI
 child trust finds
  appeals and applications
   procedure, 05/3916
 civil partnerships
  consequential amendments, 05/3850, 4858NI
 continuity of employment
  unfair dismissal, 05/1323, 4891NI, 4892NI
 contributions
  amounts to be disregarded, 05/3851
  calculation of earnings, 05/3852
  earnings limits, 05/3853
  employee training, 05/3894
  gender recognition, 05/3854
  intermediaries
   2005/06, 05/4859NI
  tax thresholds, 05/3853
 council tax benefit
  miscellaneous amendments, 05/3855
  water and sewerage charges
   reduction, 05/5719S
 earnings factors
  calculation of additional pension, 05/3898, 4875NI
 energy conservation
  grants, 05/3857
   eligibility, 05/5223S
 energy efficiency
  grants, 05/4603NI
 free movement of persons
  carers
   ancillary insurance benefits payable, 05/3859
 frontier workers
  unemployment benefits, 05/3860
 graduated retirement benefit
  claims, 05/3861
  deferment, 05/3862, 3863, 4862NI
 guardians allowance
  rates, 05/3843
  weekly rates
   increase, 05/3844, 4854NI
 housing benefit
  calculation of income other than earnings for housing benefit purposes, 05/3871
  civil partnerships
   consequential provisions, 05/4633NI
  council tax benefit
   offence of making false statement, 05/3869
  discretionary payments
   non audit claims, 05/3870
  miscellaneous amendments, 05/3865, 3866, 3868, 4863NI, 4864NI, 4865NI, 4866NI
  overpayment of benefit
   recovery of overpayment, 05/5669S
  overpayment of benefits
   extent of social security commissioner's powers on appeal, 05/3872
  overpayments, 05/4867NI

tax -cont.
  car tax -cont.
    imports -cont.
      charge imposed on vehicles used on Finnish roads, 05/4008
      surcharge to reflect VAT charge, 05/4009
  climate change levy
    combined heat and power stations, 05/4012
    fuel uses, 05/4014
    miscellaneous amendments, 05/4013
    recycling processes, 05/4014
  common agricultural policy
    single payment scheme
      reliefs, 05/4015
  companies
    retirement of directors
      purchase of company's own shares for benefit of trade, 05/4016
  construction industry
    subcontractors
      construction industry scheme (CIS) certificate, 05/4017
  controlled foreign companies
    exemptions, 05/4018, 4019
  corporation tax
    bad debt relief
      debentures transferred from taxpayer to another company in same group, 05/4020
    bonds
      funding bonds, 05/4021
    capital allowances
      inclusion of five a side football pitch as "plant and machinery", 05/5691S
    capital assets
      depreciation in stock, 05/5692S
      subtraction of depreciation in unsold trading stock, 05/4022
    chargeable gains
      derivative contracts, 05/4023, 4024
    deductions
      meaning of "potential emoluments" in s.43(11)(a) Finance Act 1989, 05/4026
    double taxation
      entitlement to credit for foreign tax, 05/4027
    free movement of capital
      freedom of establishment, 05/4028
    hearings
      failure to attend on grounds of ill health, 05/4031
    insurance companies
      apportionment, 05/4122
    overseas life insurance companies, 05/2360
    payments, 05/4032
    reliefs, 05/4033
    tax credits
      compatibility with equal treatment provisions, 05/4034
  Customs and Excise
    statistics of trade, 05/2622
  customs duty
    agricultural levies
      recovery of claims, 05/4035
  deductions

tax -cont.
  deductions -cont.
    subcontractors
      certificate of exemption under s.565 Income and Corporation Taxes Act 1988, 05/4036
  double taxation
    foreign investment
      acquisition of shares in capital company, 05/4134
    lease of substantial equipment
      permanent establishment in Australia, 05/4038
  employers tax relief
    restrictions, 05/2940
  energy saving items
    solid wall insulation, 05/4040
  Enterprise Investment Scheme
    reliefs
      use of money raised by share issue for qualifying business activity, 05/4041
  excise duty
    relief
      registered remote markers, 05/4045
  General Commissioners
    child trust funds
      appeals, 05/4055
  general insurance reserves, 05/4147
  group relief
    jurisdiction of High Court and special commissioners
      loss relief group litigation order, 05/4056
  income tax
    appeals
      accountant's authority to agree figures with Revenue on behalf of taxpayer, 05/4060
    child care providers
      exemptions, 05/4067
    partnerships
      method of allocation of profits to partners, 05/4089
    professional fees, 05/4092
    retail prices index, 05/4073, 4074
    share option schemes, 05/4102
    tax returns
      irrelevant objection by tax payers accountants, 05/3900
      notice of enquiry by tx inspector, 05/4108
  indirect taxes
    debts
      mortgagees' obligation to pay Goods and Services Tax, 05/4110
  individual savings accounts
    shares and units
      qualifying investments, 05/4112
  inheritance
    joint accounts, 05/4118
  inheritance tax
    business property relief
      extent to which relief applied, 05/4113
    double charges
      relief, 05/4114
    gifts
      proprietary estoppel, 05/4115

tax credits -*cont.*
  travelling expenses -*cont.*
    remission of charges -*cont.*
      entitlement, 05/4698NI
  welfare foods
    entitlement, 05/4860NI, 4861NI
  working tax credit
    childcare, 05/4154
    payment by employers, 05/4169
Tax Credits Act 2002 (c.21)
  Commencement No.4, Transitional Provisions and Savings Amendment Order, 05/4155
tax returns
  income tax
    electronic communications
      incentive payments, 05/4107
taxation
  fuel
    rates, 05/4342
  gains and losses
    tax treatment
      bringing into account, 05/4054
  stamp duties
    stamp duty reserve tax
      exemptions, 05/4142
taxation administration
  administrative machinery
    Lloyd's underwriters, 05/4162
taxis
  motor Hackney Carriages
    Belfast, 05/4923NI
  taxi stands
    Dromore, 05/4924NI
    Strabane, 05/4925NI
teachers
  conditions of employment, 05/1152, 1153, 1154, 1155
  employment
    requirements, 05/5210S
  General Teaching Council for Wales
    additional functions, 05/1156, 1157
  head teachers
    qualifications, 05/1158
      exemptions, 05/1159
      Wales, 05/1160
  induction periods, 05/1161
    Wales, 05/1162
  maintained schools
    staffing structure
      reviews, 05/1052
    staffing structure reviews
      Wales, 05/1053
  occupational pensions, 05/2994
  remuneration, 05/1152, 1153, 1154, 1155
  superannuation, 05/4819NI, 4820NI, 5209S
    civil partnerships, 05/5585S
  supply teachers
    General Teaching Council for Wales
      registration, 05/1163
  Teacher Training Agency
    additional functions, 05/1164
telecommunications
  broadcasting
    foreign satellite services, 05/4171
  equipment

telecommunications -*cont.*
  equipment -*cont.*
    seizure
      right to judicial protection, 05/4179
  licences
    discrimination
      fees charged for granting of licences, 05/4180
  OFCOM
    membership, 05/4181
  personal data
    Netherlands
      failure to correctly transpose Council Directive 97/66 Art.6 into national law, 05/4186
  publications, 05/4187
  radio frequency identification equipment
    licensing
      exemptions, 05/4182
  telecommunication networks
    fees
      entitlement to require financial payments from licence holders, 05/4183
  telecommunications networks
    meaning of "interconnection" under Council Directive 97/33, 05/4184
    rights of way
      implementation of EC law, 05/4185
  wireless telegraphy
    licences
      fees, 05/4173
tenancies
  housing benefit
    assistance scheme, 05/3877, 4868NI
terrorism
  proscribed organisations, 05/822
  Terrorism Act 2000 Part VII
    continuation period, 05/4534NI
  United Nations measures, 05/2618
    Lebanon, 05/2619
    Syria, 05/2619
textiles
  labelling, 05/689
tonnage tax
  elections
    extended period, 05/4167
  ships
    disapplication, 05/4168
torts
  breach of contracts
    requisite intention for tort of interfering with contractual relations, 05/4188
  breach of statutory duty
    workers
      duties owed to non employees, 05/5168S
  economic torts
    conversion
      unlawful interference with contractual relations, 05/4189
  harassment
    injunctions
      standard of proof, 05/4191
  malicious prosecution
    prosecutors powers and duties